The Bible Commentary

F. C. Cook, *Editor*

Abridged and Edited by

J. M. Fuller

EXODUS TO RUTH

BAKER BOOK HOUSE

Grand Rapids, Michigan 49506

Heritage Edition

Fourteen Volumes 0834-4

When ordering by ISBN (International Standard Book Number), numbers listed above should be preceded by 0-8010-.

Reprinted from the 1879 edition published by John Murray, London, under the title, *The Student's Commentary on the Holy Bible*

Reprinted 1983 by Baker Book House Company

ISBN : 0-8010-0836-0

Printed and bound in the United States of America

EXODUS.

INTRODUCTION.

1. The book of Exodus consists of two distinct portions. The first (cc. i.—xix.) gives a detailed account of the circumstances under which the deliverance of the Israelites was accomplished. The second (cc. xx.—xl.) describes the giving of the law, and the institutions which completed the organization of the people as "a kingdom of priests, and an holy nation," xix. 6.

The name Exodus, *i. e.* "the going forth," assigned to it by the Alexandrian Jews, applies rather to the former portion than to the whole book.

The narrative is closely connected with that of Genesis, and shews not only that it was written by the same author, but that it formed part of one general plan. Still it is a distinct section; the first events which it relates are separated from the last chapter in Genesis by a considerable interval, and it presents the people of Israel under totally different circumstances. Its termination is marked with equal distinctness, winding up with the completion of the Tabernacle.

The book is divided into many smaller sections; each of which has the marks which throughout the Pentateuch indicate a subdivision. They are of different lengths, and were probably written on separate parchments or papyri, the longest not exceeding the dimensions of contemporary documents in Egypt.

They were apparently thus arranged for the convenience of public reading.[1]

This general view of the structure of the book is what might have been expected.

2. Some of the most convincing evidences of the Mosaic authorship are supplied by the contents of this book.

One argument is drawn from the representation of the personal character and qualifications of Moses, a representation perfectly intelligible as proceeding from Moses himself.

What other men have seen in Moses is—the chief agent in the greatest work ever intrusted to man, an agent whose peculiar and unparalleled qualifications are admitted alike by those who accept and by those who deny the Divine interposition: what the writer himself sees in Moses is—a man whose only qualification is an involuntary and reluctant surrender to the will of God. The only rational account of the matter is, that we have Moses' own history of himself and of his work.

Another argument rests on external facts. The book of Exodus

---

[1] The narrative portion of the book (cc. i.—xix.) is composed of the following sections: An Introduction. i. 1-7. ; (*a*) i. 8. & ii. ; (*b*) iii. 1—vi. 1 ; (*c*) vi. 2-27 ; (*d*) vi. 28—xi. end ; (*e*) xii. 1-42 ; (*f*) xii. 43—xiii. 16 ; (*g*) xiii. 17—xiv. end ; (*h*) xv. ; (*i*) xvi.—xix.

could not have been written by any man who had not passed many years in Egypt, and who had not also a thorough knowledge, such as could only be acquired by personal observation, of the Sinaitic Peninsula.

We have no probable alternative but to admit that the narrative in its substance came from Moses, or from a contemporary; and we can have little hesitation as to our choice between these alternatives, when we consider that none of the contemporaries of Moses had equal opportunities of observation, and that none were likely to have received the education and training which would have enabled them to record the events.

3. A weighty argument is drawn from the accounts of the miracles, by which Moses was expressly bidden to attest his mission, and by which he was enabled to accomplish the deliverance of his people.

We have throughout the miracles the characteristics of local colouring, of adaptation to the circumstances of the Israelites, and of repeated announcements followed by repeated postponements, which enabled and indeed compelled the Israelites to complete that organization of their nation, without which their departure might have been, as it has been often represented, a mere disorderly flight.

There are some who fear to compromise the miraculous character of events by admitting any operation of natural causes to a share of them. Yet the inspired writer does not fail to record that it was by the east wind that the Lord brought the locusts (Exod. x. 13) and sent back the sea (xiv. 21), and by the mighty strong west wind (x. 19) took back the plague that he had sent. Nor is the miracle at all lessened, because the winds of heaven were made God's messengers and instruments in the doing it. The miracles in Egypt were supernatural in their greatness, in their concentration upon one period, in their coming and going according to the phases of the conflict between the tyrant and the captive race, in their measured gradation from weak to strong, as each weaker wonder failed to break the stubborn heart. King and people so regarded them; they were accustomed perhaps to frogs and lice and locusts; but to such plagues, so intense, so threatened, accomplished, and withdrawn, as it were so disciplined to a will, they were not accustomed; and they rightly saw them as miraculous and divinely sent. And further it will be noticed that the phenomena that are put to this use are such as mark the country where this great history is laid. No Jewish writer, who had lived in Palestine alone, could have imagined a narrative so Egyptian in its marks. All evidence tends to prove that the history was written by some one well conversant with Egypt; and we shall look in vain for any one, other than Moses himself, who possessed this qualification for writing under divine guidance the history of the emancipation of the Israelites.

The narrative which records them, remarkable as it is for artlessness and simplicity, is moreover not one which could have been concocted from documents of different ages, constructed on different principles, and full of internal discrepancies and contradictions. It is the production of one mind, written by one man, and by one who had alone witnessed all the events which it records, who alone was at that time likely to possess the knowledge or ability required to write the account.

4. The portion of the book, which follows the account of the departure from Egypt, has characteristics marked with equal distinctness, and bearing with no less force upon the question of authorship. These chapters also are pervaded by a peculiar tone, a local colouring, an atmosphere so to speak of the desert, which has made itself felt by all those who have explored the country.

Modern travellers point out the following coincidences between the narrative and their own experiences. Absence of water where no sources now exist, abundance of water where fountains are still found, and indications of a far more copious supply in former ages ; tracts, occupying the same time in the journey, in which food would not be found ; and in some districts a natural production similar to manna, most _abundant in rainy seasons (such as several notices shew the season of the Exodus to have been), but not sufficient for nourishment, nor fit for large consumption, without such modifications in character and quantity as are attributed in the narrative to a divine intervention. The late explorations of the Peninsula of Sinai have thrown much light upon the fact that the route taken by the Israelites was probably determined by conditions agreeing with incidental notices in the history ; and when we come to the chapters in which the central event in the history of Israel, the delivery of God's law, is recorded, we find localities and scenery which

travellers concur in declaring to be such as fully correspond to the exigencies of the narrative, and which in some accounts (remarkable at once for scientific accuracy and graphic power) are described in terms which shew they correspond, so far as mere outward accessories can correspond, to the grandeur of the manifestation.

5. A very valuable argument of the same evidential character is drawn from the account of the Tabernacle. In form, structure, and materials the tabernacle belongs altogether to the wilderness. The whole was a tent, not a fixed structure, such as would naturally have been set up, and in point of fact was very soon set up, in Palestine. The metals, bronze, silver and gold, were those which the Israelites knew, and doubtless brought with them from Egypt ; the names of many of the materials and implements which they used, and the furniture and accessories of the tabernacle, the dress and ornaments of the priests, are Egyptian ; and it is also certain that the arts required for the construction of the tabernacle, and for all its accessories, were precisely those for which the Egyptians had been remarkable for ages ; such as artizans who had lived under the influence of Egyptian civilization would naturally have learned.

Two separate accounts of the erection of the Tabernacle are given. In the first Moses relates the instructions which he received, in the second he describes the accomplishment of the work. Nothing would be less in accordance with the natural order of a history written at a later period than this double account. It is however fully accounted for by the obvious hypothesis that each part of the narrative was written at the time, and on the occasion, to which it immediately refers.

6. The Chronology of Exodus involves two questions, the duration of the sojourn of the Israelites in Egypt, and the date of their departure. So far as regards the direct statements in the Hebrew text, the answers to both questions are positive and unambiguous. Exodus xii. 40 gives 430 years for the sojourn, Genesis xv. 13 gives 400 years for the whole, or the greater portion, of the same period. Again, the first book of Kings, (vi. 1), fixes the Exodus at 480 years before the building of the Temple in the fourth year of Solomon's reign. This would settle the date within a few years, about 1490 B.C.; a date which appears on the whole to be reconcileable with the facts of history, and to rest on higher authority than any other which has been proposed.

THE SECOND BOOK OF MOSES,

CALLED

EXODUS.

CHAP. 1. NOW *a* these *are* the names of the children of Israel, which came into Egypt; every man and his household came with 2, 3 Jacob. Reuben, Simeon, Levi, and Judah, Issachar, Zebulun, 4, 5 and Benjamin, Dan, and Naphtali, Gad, and Asher. And all the souls that came out of the ¹loins of Jacob were *b* seventy souls: 6 for Joseph was in Egypt *already.* ¶ And *c* Joseph died, and all 7 his brethren, and all that generation. *d* And the children of Israel were fruitful, and increased abundantly, and multiplied, and waxed exceeding mighty; and the land was filled with them. 8 ¶ Now there *e* arose up a new king over Egypt, which knew not 9 Joseph. And he said unto his people, Behold, *f* the people of 10 the children of Israel *are* more and mightier than we: *g* come on, let us *h* deal wisely with them; lest they multiply, and it come to pass, that, when there falleth out any war, they join also unto our enemies, and fight against us, and *so* get them up out of the 11 land. Therefore they did set over them taskmasters *i* to afflict

¹ Heb. *thigh.*

a Gen. 46. 8,
ch. 6. 14.

b Gen. 46.
26, 27.
Deut. 10. 22.
c Gen. 50. 26.
d Gen. 46. 3.
Deut. 26. 5.
Acts 7. 17.
e Acts 7. 18.
f Ps. 105. 24.
g Ps. 10. 2.
& 83. 3, 4.
h Job 5. 13.
Ps. 105. 25.
Prov. 16. 25,
Acts 7. 19.
i Gen. 15. 13.
ch. 3. 7.
Deut. 26. 6.

I. 1. *Now*] Literally "And," indicating a close connection with the preceding narrative. This chapter in fact contains a fulfilment of the predictions recorded in Gen. xlvi. 3, and in Gen. xv. 13.

every man and his household] It may be inferred from various notices that the total number of dependents was considerable, a point of importance in its bearings upon the history of the Exodus (cp. Gen. xiii. 6, xiv. 14).

5. *seventy*] See Gen. xlvi. 27. The object of the writer in this introductory statement is to give a complete list of the heads of separate families at the time of their settlement in Egypt. See note on Num. xxvi. 5.

7. In no province does the population increase so rapidly as in that occupied by the Israelites. See note on Gen. xlvii. 6. At present it has more flocks and herds than any province in Egypt, and more fishermen, though many villages are deserted. Until the accession of the new king, the relations between the Egyptians and the Israelites were undoubtedly friendly. The expressions used in this verse imply the lapse of a considerable period after the death of Joseph.

the land was filled with them] i.e. the district allotted to them (Gen. xlv. 10).

8. The expressions in this verse are peculiar, and emphatic. "A new king" is a phrase not found elsewhere. It is understood by most commentators to imply that he did not succeed his predecessor in natural order of descent and inheritance. He "arose up over Egypt," occupying the land, as it would seem, on different terms from the

king whose place he took, either by usurpation or conquest. The fact that he knew not Joseph implies a complete separation from the traditions of Lower Egypt. At present the generality of Egyptian scholars identify this Pharaoh with Rameses II., but all the conditions of the narrative are fulfilled in the person of Amosis (or, Aahmes) I., the head of the 18th Dynasty. He was the descendant of the old Theban sovereigns, but his family was tributary to the Dynasty of the Shepherds, the Hyksos of Manetho; then ruling in the North of Egypt. Amosis married an Ethiopian princess, and in the third year of his reign captured Avaris, or Zoan, the capital of the Hyksos, and completed the expulsion of that race.

10. *any war*] The North Eastern frontier was infested by the neighbouring tribes, the Shasous of Egyptian monuments, and war was waged with Egypt by the confederated nations of Western Asia under the reigns of the successors of Amosis. These incursions were repulsed with extreme difficulty. In language, features, costume, and partly also in habits, the Israelites probably resembled those enemies of Egypt.

out of the land] The Pharaohs apprehended the loss of revenue and power, which would result from the withdrawal of a peaceful and industrious race.

11. *taskmasters*] The Egyptian "Chiefs of tributes." They were men of rank, superintendents of the public works, such as are often represented on Egyptian monuments, and carefully distinguished from the subordinate overseers. The Israelites were employed in forced labour, probably in de-

k ch. 2. 11.
Ps. 81. 6.
l Gen. 47. 11.

m ch. 2. 23.
& 3. 9.
Num. 20. 15.
n Ps. 81. 6.

o Prov. 16. 6.
p Dan. 3. 16,
18. & 6. 13.
Acts 5. 29.

q See Josh.
2. 4, &c.
r Prov. 11.
18.
Eccles. 8. 12.
Isai. 3. 10.
Heb. 6. 10.
s See 1 Sam.
2. 25.
2 Sam. 7.
11, 13, 27,
Ps. 127. 1.
t Acts 7. 19.
a ch. 6. 20.
1 Chr. 23. 13.
b Acts 7. 20.
Heb. 11. 23.

them with their *k* burdens. And they built for Pharaoh treasure 12 cities, Pithom *l* and Raamses. ¹ But the more they afflicted them, the more they multiplied and grew. And they were grieved 13 because of the children of Israel. And the Egyptians made the 14 children of Israel to serve with rigour : and they *m* made their lives bitter with hard bondage, *n* in morter, and in brick, and in all manner of service in the field : all their service, wherein they 15 made them serve, *was* with rigour. ¶ And the king of Egypt spake to the Hebrew midwives, of which the name of the one *was* 16 Shiphrah, and the name of the other Puah : and he said, When ye do the office of a midwife to the Hebrew women, and see *them* upon the stools ; if it *be* a son, then ye shall kill him : but if it *be* 17 a daughter, then she shall live. But the midwives *o* feared God, and did not *p* as the king of Egypt commanded them, but saved 18 the men children alive. And the king of Egypt called for the midwives, and said unto them, Why have ye done this thing, 19 and have saved the men children alive ? And *q* the midwives said unto Pharaoh, Because the Hebrew women *are* not as the Egyptian women ; for they *are* lively, and are delivered ere 20 the midwives come in unto them. *r* Therefore God dealt well with the midwives : and the people multiplied, and waxed very 21 mighty. And it came to pass, because the midwives feared God, 22 *s* that he made them houses. ¶ And Pharaoh charged all his people, saying, *t* Every son that is born ye shall cast into the river, and every daughter ye shall save alive.

CHAP. 2. AND there went *a* a man of the house of Levi, and took 2 *to wife* a daughter of Levi. And the woman conceived, and bare a son : and *b* when she saw him that he *was* a goodly *child*, she

¹ Heb. *And as they afflicted them, so they multiplied, &c.*

tachments, but they were not reduced to slavery, properly speaking, nor treated as captives of war. Amosis had special need of such labourers, as proved by the inscriptions.

treasure cities] "Magazines," depots of ammunition and provisions (1 Kings ix. 19 ; 2 Chron. viii. 4 and xxxii. 28).

Pithom and Raamses] Both cities were situate on the canal dug or enlarged in the 12th Dynasty. The former is known to have existed under the 18th Dynasty : both were in existence in the beginning of the reign of Rameses II., by whom they were fortified and enlarged. The name "Pithom" means "House or temple of Tum," the Sun God of Heliopolis (see xiii. 20). The name of Raamses, or Rameses, is generally assumed to have been derived from Rameses II., the Sesostris of the Greeks, but it was previously known as the name of the district. See Genesis xlv. 10 ; xlvii. 11.

14. The use of brick, at all times common in Egypt, was especially so under the 18th Dynasty. An exact representation of the whole process of brickmaking is given in a small temple at Thebes, erected by Tothmosis III., the fourth in descent from Amosis. Immense masses of brick are found at Belbeis, the modern capital of Sharkiya, *i.e.* Goshen, and in the adjoining district.

all manner of service in the field] Not

merely agricultural labour, but probably the digging of canals and processes of irrigation which are peculiarly onerous and unhealthy.

15. *Hebrew midwives*] Or "midwives of the Hebrew women." This measure at once attested the inefficacy of the former measures, and was the direct cause of the event which issued in the deliverance of Israel, viz. the exposure of Moses. The women bear Egyptian names, and were probably Egyptians.

16. *upon the stools*] Literally "two stones." The word denotes a peculiar seat, such as is represented on monuments of the 18th Dynasty, and is still used by Egyptian midwives.

21. *made them houses*] *i.e.* they married Hebrews and became mothers in Israel. The expression is proverbial. See marg. reff.

22. The extreme cruelty of the measure does not involve improbability. Hatred of strangers was always a characteristic of the Egyptians (see Gen. xliii. 32), and was likely to be stronger than ever after the expulsion of an alien race.

II. 1. *a man...a daughter of Levi*] Amram and Jochebed. See vi. 20.

2. *bare a son*] Not her firstborn ; Aaron and Miriam were older than Moses. The object of the writer is simply to narrate the

3 hid him three months. And when she could not longer hide him, she took for him an ark of bulrushes, and daubed it with slime and with pitch, and put the child therein: and she laid *it* in the 4 flags by the river's brink. *c*And his sister stood afar off, to wit 5 what would be done to him. And the *d*daughter of Pharaoh came down to wash *herself* at the river ; and her maidens walked along by the river's side ; and when she saw the ark among the 6 flags, she sent her maid to fetch it. And when she had opened *it*, she saw the child: and, behold, the babe wept. And she had compassion on him, and said, This *is one* of the Hebrews' children. 7 Then said his sister to Pharaoh's daughter, Shall I go and call to thee a nurse of the Hebrew women, that she may nurse the 8 child for thee? And Pharaoh's daughter said to her, Go. And 9 the maid went and called the child's mother. And Pharaoh's daughter said unto her, Take this child away, and nurse it for me, and I will give *thee* thy wages. And the woman took the 10 child, and nursed it. And the child grew, and she brought him unto Pharaoh's daughter, and he became *e*her son. And she

c ch. 15. 20.
Num. 26. 59.
d Acts 7. 21.

e Acts 7. 21.

events which led to the Exodus, and he omits to notice what had no direct bearing upon that object.

a goodly child] See marginal references. Probably Jochebed did not call in a midwife (i. 15), and she was of course cautious not to show herself to Egyptians. The hiding of the child is spoken of as an act of faith in Heb. xi. 23. It was done in the belief that God would watch over the child.

3. The ark was made of the papyrus which was commonly used by the Egyptians for light and swift boats. The species is no longer found in the Nile below Nubia. It is a strong rush, like the bamboo, about the thickness of a finger, three cornered, and attains the height of 10 to 15 feet. It is represented with great accuracy on the most ancient monuments of Egypt.

slime and pitch] The "slime" is probably the mud, of which bricks were usually made in Egypt, and which in this case was used to bind the stalks of the papyrus into a compact mass, and perhaps also to make the surface smooth for the infant. The pitch or bitumen, commonly used in Egypt, made the small vessel water-tight.

in the flags] This is another species of the papyrus, called tufi, or sufi (an exact equivalent of the Hebrew *suph*), which was less in size and height than the rush of which the ark was made.

5. The traditions which give a name to the daughter of Pharaoh are merely conjectural. Egyptian princesses held a very high and almost independent position under the ancient and middle empire, with a separate household and numerous officials. This was especially the case with the daughters of the first sovereigns of the 18th Dynasty.

Many facts concur in indicating that the residence of the daughter of Pharaoh and of the family of Moses, was at Zoan, Tanis, now San, the ancient Avaris (i. 8 note), on the

Tanitic branch of the river, near the sea, where crocodiles are never found, and which was probably the western boundary of the district occupied by the Israelites. The field of Zoan was always associated by the Hebrews with the marvels which preceded the Exodus. See Ps. lxxviii. 43.

to wash] It is not customary at present for women of rank to bathe in the river, but it was a common practice in ancient Egypt. The habits of the princess, as well as her character, must have been well known to the mother of Moses, and probably decided her choice of the place.

6. *She had compassion on him*] The Egyptians regarded such tenderness as a condition of acceptance on the day of reckoning. In the presence of the Lord of truth each spirit had to answer, "I have not afflicted any man, I have not made any man weep, I have not withheld milk from the mouths of sucklings" (' Funeral Ritual '). There was special ground for mentioning the feeling, since it led the princess to save and adopt the child in spite of her father's commands.

10. *he became her son*] See marg. ref. His training and education was, humanly speaking, all but indispensable to the efficient accomplishment of his work as the predestined leader and instructor of his countrymen. Moses probably passed the early years of his life in Lower Egypt, where the princess resided. There may however be substantial grounds for the tradition in Josephus that he was engaged in a campaign against the Ethiopians, thus shewing himself, as St. Stephen says, "mighty in word and deed."

Moses] The Egyptian origin of this word is generally admitted. The name itself is not uncommon in ancient documents. The exact meaning is "son," but the verbal root of the word signifies "produce," "draw forth." The whole sentence in Egyptian

called his name ¹Moses : and she said, Because I drew him out
11 of the water.   ¶And it came to pass in those days, ⁱwhen Moses
was grown, that he went out unto his brethren, and looked on
their ᵍburdens : and he spied an Egyptian smiting an Hebrew, one
12 of his brethren.   And he looked this way and that way, and when
he saw that *there was* no man, he ʰslew the Egyptian, and hid him
13 in the sand.   And ⁱwhen he went out the second day, behold, two
men of the Hebrews strove together : and he said to him that did
14 the wrong, Wherefore smitest thou thy fellow ?   And he said,
ᵏWho made thee ²a prince and a judge over us ? intendest thou
to kill me, as thou killedst the Egyptian ? And Moses feared, and
15 said, Surely this thing is known.   Now when Pharaoh heard
this thing, he sought to slay Moses.   But ˡMoses fled from the
face of Pharaoh, and dwelt in the land of Midian : and he sat
16 down by ᵐa well.   ⁿNow the ³priest of Midian had seven
daughters : ᵒand they came and drew *water*, and filled the
17 troughs to water their father's flock.   And the shepherds came
and drove them away : but Moses stood up and helped them, and
18 ᵖwatered their flock.   And when they came to ᵠReuel their
19 father, he said, How *is it that* ye are come so soon to day ? And
they said, An Egyptian delivered us out of the hand of the
shepherds, and also drew *water* enough for us, and watered the
20 flock.   And he said unto his daughters, And where *is* he ? Why

f Acts 7. 23, 24.
Heb. 11. 24.
g ch. 1. 11.

h Acts 7. 24.
i Acts 7. 26.

k Acts 7. 27, 28.

l Acts 7. 29.
Heb. 11. 27.

m Gen. 24.
11. & 29. 2.
n ch. 3. 1.
o 1 Sam. 9.
11.

p Gen. 29. 10.
q Num. 10.
29, called
also *Jethro,*
or, *Jether,*
ch. 3. 1, &c.

---

¹ That is, *Drawn out.*   ² Heb. *a man, a prince,*   ³ Or, *prince,* as Gen. 41. 45.
                                    Gen. 13. 8.

---

would exactly correspond to our Version.
She called his name Moses, *i.e.* "son," or
"brought forth," because she brought him
forth out of the water.

11. *went out unto his brethren*] At the end
of 40 years.   The Egyptian princess had
not concealed from him the fact of his belonging to the oppressed race, nor is it likely
that she had debarred him from intercourse
with his foster-mother and her family,
whether or not she became aware of the
true relationship.

an Egyptian] This man was probably one
of the overseers of the workmen, natives
under the chief superintendent (i. 11). They
were armed with long heavy scourges, made
of a tough pliant wood imported from
Syria.

12. The slaying of the Egyptian is not to
be justified, or attributed to a divine inspiration, but it is to be judged with reference
to the provocation, the impetuosity of Moses'
natural character, perhaps also to the habits
developed by his training at the court of
Pharaoh.   The act involved a complete
severance from the Egyptians, but, far from
expediting, it delayed for many years the
deliverance of the Irsraelites.   Forty years
of a very different training prepared Moses
for the execution of that appointed work.

13. *thy fellow*] **Thy neighbour:** the reproof was that of a legislator who established
moral obligations on a recognised principle.
Hence in the following verse the offender is
represented as feeling that the position
claimed by Moses was that of a Judge.   The

act could only have been made known by
the Hebrew on whose behalf Moses had
committed it.

15. No Egyptian king would have left
such an offence unpunished, but the position of Moses, as adopted son of a princess,
made it necessary even for a despotic sovereign to take unusual precautions.

the land of Midian] The Midianites occupied an extensive district from the eastern
coast of the Red Sea to the borders of
Moab.

16. *the Priest of Midian*] Reuel (*v.* 18).
His name, and the detailed notices in
ch. xviii., prove that he was a priest of the
one true God Who was known to the patriarchs especially under the name El.   The
great bulk of his tribe, certainly those who
lived farther north and more closely in contact with the Hamites of Canaan, were already plunged in idolatry.   The conduct of
the shepherds (*v.* 17) may indicate that his
person and office were lightly regarded by
the idolatrous tribes in his immediate neighbourhood.

18. *Reuel*] Or, as in Num. x. 29, Raguel.
The name means "friend of God."   It appears to have been not uncommon among
Hebrews and Edomites ; *e.g.* Gen. xxxvi. 4,
10.   If Reuel be identified with Jethro,
a point open to grave objection (see iii. 1),
then Reuel was his proper name, and Jether
or Jethro, which means "excellency," was
his official designation.

19. *An Egyptian*] They judged from his
costume, or language.

is it *that* ye have left the man? Call him, that he may *r* eat bread.
21 And Moses was content to dwell with the man : and he gave
22 Moses *s* Zipporah his daughter. And she bare *him* a son, and he
called his name, *¹t* Gershom: for he said, I have been *u* a stranger
23 in a strange land. ¶ And it came to pass *x* in process of time,
that the king of Egypt died : and the children of Israel *y* sighed
by reason of the bondage, and they cried, and *z* their cry came
24 up unto God by reason of the bondage. And God *a* heard their
groaning, and God *b* remembered his *c* covenant with Abraham,
25 with Isaac, and with Jacob. And God *d* looked upon the children
of Israel, and God *²e* had respect unto *them.*

CHAP. 3. NOW Moses kept the flock of Jethro his father in law,
a the priest of Midian : and he led the flock to the backside of the
2 desert, and came to *b* the mountain of God, *even* to Horeb. And

r Gen. 31.
54. & 43. 25.
s ch. 4. 25.
t ch. 18. 3.
u Acts 7. 29.
Heb. 11. 13.
x ch. 7. 7.
y Deut. 26. 7.
Ps. 12. 5.
z ch. 3. 9.
a ch. 6. 5.
b Ps. 105. 42.
c Gen. 15.14.
& 46. 4.
d ch. 4. 31.
e ch. 3. 7.
a ch. 2. 16.
b ch. 18. 5.
1 Kin. 19. 8.

¹ That is, *A stranger here.* 　　　　　　² Heb. *knew.*

---

21. Moses tells us nothing of what he may have learned from his father-in-law, but he must have found in him a man conversant with the traditions of the family of Abraham ; nor is there any improbability in the supposition that, as hereditary priest, Reuel may have had written documents concerning their common ancestors.

22. *Gershom*] The first syllable " Ger" is common to Hebrew and Egyptian, and means "sojourner." The second syllable "Shom" answers exactly to the Coptic " Shemmo," which means "a foreign or strange land."

23. *in process of time*] Nearly forty years (Acts vii. 30). This verse marks the beginning of another section. We now enter at once upon the history of the Exodus.

their cry came up unto God] This statement, taken in connection with the two following verses, proves that the Israelites retained their faith in the God of their Fathers. The divine name God, Elohim, is chosen because it was that which the Israelites must have used in their cry for help, that under which the covenant had been ratified with the Patriarchs (cp. Jas. v. 4).

24. *remembered*] This means that God was moved by their prayers to give effect to the covenant, of which an essential condition was the faith and contrition involved in the act of supplication. The whole history of Israel is foreshadowed in these words : God heard, remembered, looked upon, and knew them. It evidently indicates the beginning of a crisis marked by a personal intervention of God.

III. This chapter marks the commencement of the series of events which immediately preceded the Exodus. Hitherto the narrative has been studiously brief, stating only what was necessary to be known as preparatory to those events ; but from this point Moses dwells minutely on the details, and enables us to realize the circumstances of the catastrophe which in its immediate and remote consequences stands alone in the world's history

1. *Jethro his father-in-law*] Or "brother-in-law." The word in the Hebrew is a word signifying relative by marriage. When Moses arrived in Midian, Reuel was an elderly man (ii. 16) ; 40 years later (ii. 23 note), Reuel's son, Jethro, had probably succeeded him.

the backside] *i.e.* " to the west of the district." Among the Hebrews the East is before a man, the west behind him, the south and north on the right and left hand.

desert] Or **wilderness**, not a barren waste, but a district supplying pasturage. The district near Sherm, on the west of the gulf of Akabah, where Jethro may have resided, is described as barren and parched ; on the west and east are rocky tracts, but to the north-west lies the district of Sinai, where the pasturage is good and water abundant. The Bedouins drive their flocks thither from the lowlands at the approach of summer. From this it may be inferred that the events here recorded took place at that season.

to Horeb] More exactly, **towards Horeb.** Moses came to the mountain of God, *i.e.* Sinai, on his way towards Horeb, a name given to the northern part of the Sinaitic range. Moses calls Sinai "mountain of God" by anticipation, with reference to the manifestation of God. There is no authority for assuming that the spot was previously held sacred (see *v.* 5) ; but it has been lately shewn that the whole Peninsula was regarded by the Egyptians as specially consecrated to the gods from a very early time.

2. *the angel of the* LORD] See note on Gen. xii. 7. What Moses saw was the flame of fire in the bush ; what he recognized therein was an intimation of the Presence of God, Who maketh a flame of fire His angel. Cp. Ps. civ. 4. The words which Moses heard were those of God Himself, as all ancient and most modern divines have held, manifested in the Person of the Son.

of a bush] Literally **of the bush,** or "seneh," a word which ought perhaps to be retained as the proper name of a thorny

[c]the angel of the LORD appeared unto him in a flame of fire out
of the midst of a bush: and he looked, and, behold, the bush
3 burned with fire, and the bush *was* not consumed. And Moses
said, I will now turn aside, and see this [d]great sight, why the
4 bush is not burnt. And when the LORD saw that he turned aside
to see, God called [e]unto him out of the midst of the bush, and
5 said, Moses, Moses. And he said, Here *am* I. And he said,
Draw not nigh hither: [f]put off thy shoes from off thy feet, for the
6 place whereon thou standest *is* holy ground. Moreover he said,
[g]I *am* the God of thy father, the God of Abraham, the God of
Isaac, and the God of Jacob. And Moses hid his face; for [h]he
7 was afraid to look upon God. ¶ And the LORD said, [i]I have
surely seen the affliction of my people which *are* in Egypt, and
have heard their cry [k]by reason of their taskmasters; for [l]I know
8 their sorrows; and [m]I am come down to [n]deliver them out of
the hand of the Egyptians, and to bring them up out of that land
[o]unto a good land and a large, unto a land [p]flowing with milk and
honey; unto the place of [q]the Canaanites, and the Hittites, and
the Amorites, and the Perizzites, and the Hivites, and the Jebu-
9 sites. Now therefore, behold, [r]the cry of the children of Israel is
come unto me: and I have also seen [s]the oppression wherewith
10 the Egyptians oppress them. [t]Come now therefore, and I will
send thee unto Pharaoh, that thou mayest bring forth my people

[c] Isai. 63. 9. Acts 7. 30.
[d] Ps. 111. 2.
[e] Deut. 33. 16.
[f] ch. 19. 12. Josh. 5. 15. Acts 7. 33.
[g] Gen. 28. 13. Acts 7. 32.
[h] So 1 Kin. 19. 13. Isai. 6. 1, 5.
[i] ch. 2. 23. Neh. 9. 9. Ps. 106. 44. Acts 7. 34.
[k] ch. 1. 11.
[l] Gen. 18. 21.
[m] Gen. 11. 5. 7.
[n] ch. 6. 6, 8. & 12. 51.
[o] Deut. 1. 25. & 8. 7, 8, 9.
[p] ch. 13. 5.
[q] Gen. 15. 18.
[r] ch. 2. 23.
[s] ch. 1. 11.
[t] Ps. 105. 26. Mic. 6. 4.

---

shrub common in that district, a species of acacia.

4. *the* LORD *saw*] The interchange of the two divine names is to be observed; *Jehovah* saw, *God* called.

5. *put off thy shoes*] The reverence due to holy places thus rests on God's own command. The custom itself is well known from the observances of the Temple, it was almost universally adopted by the ancients, and is retained in the East.

holy ground] This passage is almost conclusive against the assumption that the place was previously a sanctuary. Moses knew nothing of its holiness after some 40 years spent on the Peninsula. It became holy by the Presence of God.

6. Our Saviour adduces this passage as a proof that the doctrine of the Resurrection was taught in the Old Testament (Matt. xxii. 32), and He calls this book the book of Moses (Mark xii. 26), two points to be borne in mind by readers of the Pentateuch.

7. *taskmasters*] Oppressors. A different word from that in i. 11.

I know] The expression implies personal feeling, tenderness, and compassion (cp. ii. 25. marg.).

8. The natural richness of Palestine, the variety and excellence of its productions, are attested by sacred (cp. Jer. xxxii. 22. Ez. xx. 6) and ancient writers, whose descriptions are strongly in contrast with those of later travellers. The expression "flowing with milk and honey" is used proverbially by Greek poets.

the Canaanites, &c.] This is the first passage in this book where the enumeration, so often repeated, of the nations then in possession of Palestine, is given. Moses was to learn at once the extent of the promise, and the greatness of the enterprise. In Egypt, the forces, situation, and character of these nations were then well known. Aahmes I. had invaded the south of Palestine in his pursuit of the Shasous; Tothmosis I. had traversed the whole land on his campaign in Syria and Mesopotamia; representations of Canaanites, and of the Cheta, identified by most Egyptologers with the Hittites, are common on monuments of the 18th and 19th Dynasties, and give a strong impression of their civilization, riches, and especially of their knowledge of the arts of war. In this passage, the more general designations come first—Canaanites probably includes all the races; the Hittites, who had great numbers of chariots (892 were taken from them by Tothmosis III. in one battle), occupied the plains; the Amorites were chiefly mountaineers, and, in Egyptian inscriptions, gave their name to the whole country; the name Perizzites probably denotes the dwellers in scattered villages, the half-nomad population; the Hivites, a comparatively unwarlike but influential people, held 4 cities in Palestine proper, but their main body dwelt in the north-western district, from Hermon to Hamath (see Josh. xi. 3, and Judg. iii. 3); the Jebusites at that time appear to have occupied Jerusalem and the adjoining district. Soon after their expulsion by Joshua, they seem to have recovered possession of part of Jerusalem, probably Mount Zion, and to have retained it until the time of David.

11 the children of Israel out of Egypt. ¶And Moses said unto God, ^uch. 6. 12.
^uWho *am* I, that I should go unto Pharaoh, and that I should bring ¹ Sam. 18.
12 forth the children of Israel out of Egypt? And he said, ^xCer-
tainly I will be with thee; and this *shall be* a token unto thee, that
I have sent thee: When thou hast brought forth the people out
13 of Egypt, ye shall serve God upon this mountain. And Moses
said unto God, Behold, *when* I come unto the children of Israel,
and shall say unto them, The God of your fathers hath sent me
unto you; and they shall say to me, What *is* his name? what
14 shall I say unto them? ¶ And God said unto Moses, I AM THAT
I AM: And he said, Thus shalt thou say unto the children of
15 Israel, ^yI AM hath sent me unto you. And God said moreover unto Moses, Thus shalt thou say unto the children of Israel,
The LORD God of your fathers, the God of Abraham, the God of
Isaac, and the God of Jacob, hath sent me unto you: this *is* ^zmy
16 name for ever, and this *is* my memorial unto all generations. Go,
and ^agather the elders of Israel together, and say unto them, The
LORD God of your fathers, the God of Abraham, of Isaac, and of
Jacob, appeared unto me, saying, ^bI have surely visited you,
17 and *seen* that which is done to you in Egypt: and I have said, ^cI
will bring you up out of the affliction of Egypt unto the land of
the Canaanites, and the Hittites, and the Amorites, and the
Perizzites, and the Hivites, and the Jebusites, unto a land flow-
18 ing with milk and honey. And ^dthey shall hearken to thy
voice: and ^ethou shalt come, thou and the elders of Israel, unto
the king of Egypt, and ye shall say unto him, The LORD God of
the Hebrews hath ^fmet with us: and now let us go, we beseech
thee, three days' journey into the wilderness, that we may sacri-
19 fice to the LORD our God. And I am sure that the king of Egypt

^u ch. 6. 12.
1 Sam. 18.
18.
Isai. 6. 5, 8.
Jer. 1. 6.
^x Gen. 31. 3.
Josh. 1. 5.
Rom. 3. 18.

^y ch. 6. 3.
John 8. 58.
2 Cor. 1. 20.
Heb. 13. 8.
Rev. 1. 4.
^z Ps. 135. 13.
Hos. 12. 5.
^a ch. 4. 29.

^b ch. 2. 25.
Luke 1. 68.
^c Gen. 15.
14, 16.
ver. 8.

^d ch. 4. 31.
^e ch. 5. 1, 3.

^f Num. 23.
3, 4, 15, 16.

---

11. *Who am I*] These words indicate humility (cp. Num. xii. 3), not fear. He feared
failure owing to incompetency, especially in
the power of expression.

12. *a token unto thee*] Or **the sign.** The
word means a declaration or promise of
God, which rests absolutely on His word,
and demands faith. The promise that God
would have the people serve Him in that
place was an assurance, if fully believed,
that all intervening obstacles would be removed by His power.

13. *What is his name*] The meaning of this
question is evidently: "By which name shall
I tell them the promise is confirmed?" Each
name of the Deity represented some aspect
or manifestation of His attributes (cp. Intro.
to Genesis, p. 8). What Moses needed was
not a new name, but direction to use that
name which would bear in itself a pledge of
accomplishment. Moses was familiar with
the Egyptian habit of choosing from the
names of the gods that which bore specially
upon the wants and circumstances of their
worshippers, and this may have suggested
the question which would be the first his
own people would expect him to answer.

14. *I am that I am*] That is, "I am what
I am." The words express absolute, and
therefore unchanging and eternal Being.
The name, which Moses was thus commissioned to use, was at once new and old; old

in its connection with previous revelations;
new in its full interpretation, and in its
bearing upon the covenant of which Moses
was the destined mediator.

15. *The LORD God, &c.*] Better, **Jehovah, God of your fathers, God of Abraham,
God of Isaac, and God of Jacob.** It corresponds exactly to the preceding verse, the
words **I am** and **Jehovah** being equivalent.
This name met all the requirements of
Moses, involving a twofold pledge of accomplishment; the pledges of ancient benefits
and of a new manifestation.

name...memorial] The name signifies that
by which God makes himself known, the
memorial that by which His people worship
Him.

18. *three days' journey*] *i.e.* A journey
which would occupy three days in going
and returning. This was a demand quite in
accordance with Egyptian customs. The
refusal of Pharaoh and the subsequent proceedings were revealed to Moses at once;
but it is important to observe that the first
request which Pharaoh rejected could have
been granted without any damage to Egypt,
or any risk of the Israelites passing the
strongly fortified frontier.

19. *no, not*] See the marginal rendering.
Others explain it to mean, Pharaoh will
not let the people go even when severely
smitten.

20 *g*will not let you go, ¹no, not by a mighty hand. And I will *h*stretch out my hand, and smite Egypt with *i*all my wonders which I will do in the midst thereof: and *k*after that he will let 21 you go. And I *l*will give this people favour in the sight of the Egyptians: and it shall come to pass, that, when ye go, ye shall 22 not go empty: *m*but every woman shall borrow of her neighbour, and of her that sojourneth in her house, jewels of silver, and jewels of gold, and raiment: and ye shall put *them* upon your sons, and upon your daughters; and *n*ye shall spoil ²the Egyptians.

CHAP. 4. AND Moses answered and said, But, behold, they will not believe me, nor hearken unto my voice: for they will say, 2 The LORD hath not appeared unto thee. And the LORD said unto him, What *is* that in thine hand? And he said, *a*A rod. 3 And he said, Cast it on the ground. And he cast it on the ground, and it became a serpent; and Moses fled from before it. 4 And the LORD said unto Moses, Put forth thine hand, and take it by the tail. And he put forth his hand, and caught it, and it 5 became a rod in his hand: that they may *b*believe that *c*the LORD God of their fathers, the God of Abraham, the God of 6 Isaac, and the God of Jacob, hath appeared unto thee. ¶And the LORD said furthermore unto him, Put now thine hand into thy bosom. And he put his hand into his bosom: and when he 7 took it out, behold, his hand *was* leprous *d*as snow. And he said, Put thine hand into thy bosom again. And he put his hand into his bosom again; and plucked it out of his bosom, 8 and, behold, *e*it was turned again as his *other* flesh. And it shall come to pass, if they will not believe thee, neither hearken to the voice of the first sign, that they will believe the voice of

¹ Or, *but by strong hand.*   ² Or, *Egypt.*

---

22. *shall borrow*] **shall ask.** The Egyptians had made the people serve " with rigour," and the Israelites when about to leave the country for ever were to ask or claim the jewels as a just, though very inadequate, remuneration for services which had made " their lives bitter." The Egyptians would doubtless have refused had not their feelings towards Moses (see xi. 3) and the people been changed, under God's influence, by calamities in which they recognized a divine interposition, which also they rightly attributed to the obstinacy of their own king (see x. 7). The Hebrew women were to make the demand, and were to make it of women, who would of course be specially moved to compliance by the loss of their children, the fear of a recurrence of calamity, perhaps also by a sense of the fitness of the request in connection with a religious festival.

jewels] Chiefly trinkets. These ornaments were actually applied to the purpose for which they were probably demanded, being employed in making the vessels of the sanctuary (cp. xxxv. 22).

sojourneth in her house] This indicates a degree of friendly and neighbourly intercourse, in accordance with several indirect notices, and was a natural result of long and peaceable sojourn in the district. The

Egyptians did not all necessarily share the feelings of their new king.

IV. With this chapter begins the series of miracles which resulted in the deliverance of Israel. The first miracle was wrought to remove the first obstacle, viz. the reluctance of Moses, conscious of his own weakness, and of the enormous power with which he would have to contend.

2. *a rod*] The word seems to denote the long staff which on Egyptian monuments is borne by men in positions of authority. It was usually made of acacia wood.

3. *a serpent*] This miracle had a meaning which Moses could not mistake. The serpent was probably the basilisk or Uræus, the Cobra. This was the symbol of royal and divine power on the diadem of every Pharaoh. The conversion of the rod was not merely a portent, it was a sign, at once a pledge and representation of victory over the king and gods of Egypt.

6. *leprous*] The instantaneous production and cure of the most malignant and subtle disease known to the Israelites was a sign of their danger if they resisted the command, and of their deliverance if they obeyed it. The infliction and cure were always regarded as special proofs of a divine intervention.

9 the latter sign. And it shall come to pass, if they will not believe also these two signs, neither hearken unto thy voice, that thou shalt take of the water of the river, and pour *it* upon the dry *land:* and *f* the water which thou takest out of the river
10 *1*shall become blood upon the dry *land*. ¶And Moses said unto the LORD, O my Lord, I *am* not *2*eloquent, neither *3*heretofore, nor since thou hast spoken unto thy servant: but *g*I *am* slow of
11 speech, and of a slow tongue. And the LORD said unto him, *h*Who hath made man's mouth? Or who maketh the dumb, or
12 deaf, or the seeing, or the blind? Have not I the LORD? Now therefore go, and I will be *i*with thy mouth, and teach thee
13 what thou shalt say. And he said, O my Lord, *k*send, I pray
14 thee, by the hand *of him whom* thou *4*wilt send. And the anger of the LORD was kindled against Moses, and he said, *Is* not Aaron the Levite thy brother? I know that he can speak well. And also, behold, *l*he cometh forth to meet thee: and when he
15 seeth thee, he will be glad in his heart. And *m*thou shalt speak unto him, and *n*put words in his mouth: and I will be with thy mouth, and with his mouth, and *o*will teach you what ye shall
16 do. And he shall be thy spokesman unto the people: and he shall be, *even* he shall be to thee instead of a mouth, and
17 *p*thou shalt be to him instead of God. And thou shalt take
18 *q*this rod in thine hand, wherewith thou shalt do signs. ¶And Moses went and returned to *5*Jethro his father in law, and said unto him, Let me go, I pray thee, and return unto my brethren which *are* in Egypt, and see whether they be yet alive. And
19 Jethro said to Moses, Go in peace. ¶And the LORD said unto Moses in Midian, Go, return into Egypt: for *r*all the men are
20 dead which sought thy life. And Moses took his wife and his sons, and set them upon an ass, and he returned to the land of

f ch. 7. 19.

g ch. 6. 12.
Jer. 1. 6.

h Ps. 91. 9.

i Isai. 50. 4.
Jer. 1. 9.
Matt. 10. 19.
k See Jonah
1. 3.

l ver. 27.
1 Sam. 10.
2, 3, 5.
m ch. 7. 1.
n Num. 22.
38.
Deut. 18. 18.
Isai. 51. 16.
Jer. 1. 9.
o Deut. 5. 31.
p ch. 7. 1.
& 18. 19.
q ver. 2.

r ch. 2. 15.
Matt. 2. 20.

---

1 Heb. *shall be and shall be.*
2 Heb. *a man of words.*
3 Heb. *since yesterday, nor since the third day.*
4 Or, *shouldest.*
5 Heb. *Jether.*

---

10. *eloquent*] See margin. The double expression "slow of speech (Ezek. iii. 5 marg.) and of a slow tongue" seems to imply a difficulty both in finding words and in giving them utterance, a very natural result of so long a period of a shepherd's life, passed in a foreign land.

since thou hast spoken] This expression seems to imply that some short time had intervened between this address and the first communication of the divine purpose to Moses.

12. Compare with this our Lord's promise to His Apostles; Matt. x. 19; Mark xiii. 11.

13. *And he said*] The reluctance of Moses is in accordance with the inner law of man's spiritual development, and specially with his own character; but under the circumstances it indicated a weakness of faith.

14. *anger*] The words of Moses (*v.* 13) indicated more than a consciousness of infirmity; somewhat of vehemence and stubbornness.

Aaron] This is the first mention of Aaron. The words "he can speak well," probably imply that Aaron had both the power and will to speak. Aaron is here called "the Levite," with reference, it may be, to the future consecration of this tribe.

he cometh forth] *i.e.* is on the eve of setting forth. Not that Aaron was already on the way, but that he had the intention of going to his brother, probably because the enemies of Moses were now dead. See *v.* 19.

15. *thou shalt speak*] Moses thus retains his position as "mediator;" the word comes to him first, he transmits it to his brother.

16. *instead of a mouth*] We may bear in mind Aaron's unbroken habitude of speaking Hebrew and his probable familiarity with Egyptian.

instead of God] The word "God" is used of persons who represent the Deity, as kings or judges, and it is understood in this sense here: "Thou shalt be to him a master."

20. *an ass*] Lit. "the ass," which according to Hebrew idiom means that he set them upon asses. This is the first notice of other sons besides Gershom.

the rod of God] The staff of Moses was consecrated by the miracle (*v.* 2) and became "the rod of God."

21 Egypt: and Moses took *the rod of God in his hand. And the LORD said unto Moses, When thou goest to return into Egypt, see that thou do all those *wonders before Pharaoh, which I have put in thine hand: but *u*I will harden his heart, that he 22 shall not let the people go. And thou shalt say unto Pharaoh, 23 Thus saith the LORD, *x*Israel *is* my son, *y*even my firstborn: and I say unto thee, Let my son go, that he may serve me: and if thou refuse to let him go, behold, *z*I will slay thy son, *even* thy 24 firstborn. ¶And it came to pass by the way in the inn, that the 25 LORD *a*met him, and sought to *b*kill him. Then Zipporah took *c*a sharp [1]stone, and cut off the foreskin of her son, and [2]cast *it* at his feet, and said, Surely a bloody husband *art* thou to me. 26 So he let him go: then she said, A bloody husband *thou art,* 27 because of the circumcision. ¶And the LORD said to Aaron, Go into the wilderness *d*to meet Moses. And he went, and met him 28 in *e*the mount of God, and kissed him. And Moses *f*told Aaron all the words of the LORD who had sent him, and all the *g*signs 29 which he had commanded him. ¶And Moses and Aaron *h*went and gathered together all the elders of the children of Israel: 30 *i*and Aaron spake all the words which the LORD had spoken unto 31 Moses, and did the signs in the sight of the people. And the people *k*believed: and when they heard that the LORD had *l*visited the children of Israel, and that he *m*had looked upon their affliction, then *n*they bowed their heads and worshipped. CHAP. 5. AND afterward Moses and Aaron went in, and told Pharaoh, Thus saith the LORD God of Israel, Let my people go,

[1] Or, *knife.* [2] Heb. *made it touch.*

---

21. *I will harden*] Calamities which do not subdue the heart harden it. In the case of Pharaoh the hardening was at once a righteous judgment, and a natural result of a long series of oppressions and cruelties.

22. *my firstborn*] The expression would be perfectly intelligible to Pharaoh, whose official designation was "son of Ra." In numberless inscriptions the Pharaohs are styled "own sons" or "beloved sons" of the deity. It is here applied for the first time to Israel; and as we learn from *v.* 23, emphatically in antithesis to Pharaoh's own firstborn.

24. *in the inn*] Or "resting place." See Gen. xlii. 27 note.

met him, and sought to kill him] Moses was attacked by a sudden and dangerous illness, which he knew was inflicted by God. The word "sought to kill" implies that the sickness, whatever might be its nature, was one which threatened death had it not been averted by a timely act. Zipporah believed that the illness of Moses was due to his having neglected the duty of an Israelite, and to his not having circumcised his son; the delay was probably owing to her own not unnatural repugnance to a rite, which though practised by the Egyptians, was not adopted generally in the East, even by the descendants of Abraham and Keturah. Moses appears to have been utterly prostrate and unable to perform the rite himself.

25. *sharp stone*] Not "knife," as in the margin. Zipporah used a piece of flint, in accordance with the usage of the patriarchs. The Egyptians never used bronze or steel in the preparation of mummies because stone was regarded as a purer and more sacred material than metal.

cast it at his feet] Showing at once her abhorrence of the rite, and her feeling that by it she had saved her husband's life. *a bloody husband*] Lit. "A husband of blood," or "bloods." The meaning is, the marriage bond between us is now sealed by blood. By performing the rite Zipporah had recovered her husband; his life was purchased for her by the blood of her child.

26. *So he let him go*] i.e. God withdrew His visitation from Moses.

Moses sent Zipporah and her children back to Jethro before he went to Egypt, xviii. 2. The journey would have been delayed had he waited for the healing of the child.

29. *all the elders*] The Israelites retained their own national organization; their affairs were administered by their own elders, who called a public assembly (*v.* 31) to hear the message brought by Moses and Aaron.

V. 1. *Pharaoh*] This king, probably Tothmosis II., the great grandson of Aahmes (i. 8), the original persecutor of the Israelites, must have been resident at this time in a city, probably Tanis (ii. 5), of Lower Egypt, situate on the Nile.

the LORD God] Jehovah God of Israel

2 that they may hold *a feast unto me in the wilderness. And   *a* ch. 10. 9.
  Pharaoh said, *b*Who *is* the LORD, that I should obey his voice *b* 2 Kin. 18.
  to let Israel go? I know not the LORD, *c*neither will I let 35.
3 Israel go. And they said, *d*The God of the Hebrews hath met Job 21. 15.
  with us: let us go, we pray thee, three days' journey into the *d* ch. 3. 18.
  desert, and sacrifice unto the LORD our God; lest he fall upon
4 us with pestilence, or with the sword. And the king of Egypt
  said unto them, Wherefore do ye, Moses and Aaron, let the
5 people from their works? get you unto your *e*burdens. And *e* ch. 1. 11.
  Pharaoh said, Behold, the people of the land now *are* *f*many, *f* ch. 1. 7, 9.
6 and ye make them rest from their burdens. ¶And Pharaoh
  commanded the same day the *g*taskmasters of the people, and *g* ch. 3. 7.
7 their officers, saying, Ye shall no more give the people straw to
  make brick, as heretofore: let them go and gather straw for
8 themselves. And the tale of the bricks, which they did make
  heretofore, ye shall lay upon them; ye shall not diminish *ought*
  thereof: for they *be* idle; therefore they cry, saying, Let us go
9 *and* sacrifice to our God. *1*Let there more work be laid upon the
  men, that they may labour therein; and let them not regard
10 vain words. ¶And the taskmasters of the people went out, and
  their officers, and they spake to the people, saying, Thus saith
11 Pharaoh, I will not give you straw. Go ye, get you straw
  where ye can find it: yet not ought of your work shall be
12 diminished. So the people were scattered abroad throughout
13 all the land of Egypt to gather stubble instead of straw. And
  the taskmasters hasted *them*, saying, Fulfil your works, *2your*
14 daily tasks, as when there was straw. And the officers of the
  children of Israel, which Pharaoh's taskmasters had set over
  them, were beaten, *and* demanded, Wherefore have ye not fulfilled your task in making brick both yesterday and to day, as
15 heretofore? ¶Then the officers of the children of Israel came
  and cried unto Pharaoh, saying, Wherefore dealest thou thus
16 with thy servants? There is no straw given unto thy servants,
  and they say to us, Make brick: and, behold, thy servants *are*
17 beaten; but the fault *is* in thine own people. But he said, Ye

1 Heb. *Let the work be*   2 Heb. *a matter of a day in*
 heavy upon the men.   *his day.*

---

demanded the services of His people. The
demand, according to the general views of
the heathens, was just and natural; the Israelites could not offer the necessary sacrifices in the presence of Egyptians.

2. *I know not the* LORD] Either Pharaoh
had not heard of Jehovah, or he did not
recognize Him as a God.

3. *three days' journey*] See iii. 18 note.

with pestilence, or with the sword] This
shews that the plague was well known to
the ancient Egyptians. The reference to
the sword is equally natural, since the Israelites occupied the eastern district, which
was frequently disturbed by the neighbouring Shasous.

4. *let*] *i.e.* hinder.

6. *their officers*] Or **scribes**. Hebrews able
to keep accounts in writing, appointed by the
Egyptian superintendents, and responsible
to them for the work; see *v.* 14. Subordinate officers are frequently represented on

Egyptian monuments, giving in written accounts to their immediate superiors.

7. Some of the most ancient buildings in
Egypt were constructed of bricks not
burned, but dried in the sun; they were
made of clay, or more commonly of mud,
mixed with straw chopped into small pieces.
An immense quantity of straw must have
been wanted for the works on which the
Israelites were engaged, and their labours
must have been more than doubled by this
requisition.

12. *stubble instead of straw*] Rather, for
the straw: *i.e.* to be prepared as straw.
This marks the season of the year, viz. early
spring, after the barley or wheat harvest,
towards the end of April. Their suffering
must have been severe: at that season the
pestilential sand-wind blows over Egypt
some 50 days, hence its name Chamsin. (cp.
Gen. xli. 6 note).

17. *Ye are idle*] The old Egyptian lan-

are idle, *ye are* idle : therefore ye say, Let us go *and* do sacrifice
18 to the LORD. Go therefore now, *and* work; for there shall no
straw be given you, yet shall ye deliver the tale of bricks.
19 And the officers of the children of Israel did see *that* they *were*
in *evil case*, after it was said, Ye shall not minish *ought* from
20 your bricks of your daily task. ¶ And they met Moses and
Aaron, who stood in the way, as they came forth from Pharaoh :

ʰ ch. 6. 9.

21 ʰand they said unto them, The LORD look upon you, and judge;
because ye have made our savour ¹to be abhorred in the eyes of
Pharaoh, and in the eyes of his servants, to put a sword in their
22 hand to slay us. ¶ And Moses returned unto the LORD, and
said, Lord, wherefore hast thou *so* evil entreated this people ?
23 Why *is* it *that* thou hast sent me ? For since I came to Pharaoh
to speak in thy name, he hath done evil to this people ; ²neither
hast thou delivered thy people at all.

CHAP. **6.** THEN the LORD said unto Moses, Now shalt thou see what
I will do to Pharaoh : for ᵃwith a strong hand shall he let them
go, and with a strong hand ᵇshall he drive them out of his land.
2 ¶ And God spake unto Moses, and said unto him, I *am* ³the LORD :
3 and I appeared unto Abraham, unto Isaac, and unto Jacob, by
the name of ᶜGod Almighty, but by my name ᵈ JEHOVAH was
4 I not known to them.   ᵉAnd I have also established my covenant with them, ᶠto give them the land of Canaan, the land of
5 their pilgrimage, wherein they were strangers. And ᵍI have also
heard the groaning of the children of Israel, whom the Egyptians keep in bondage ; and I have remembered my covenant.
6 Wherefore say unto the children of Israel, ʰI *am* the LORD, and
ⁱI will bring you out from under the burdens of the Egyptians,
and I will rid you out of their bondage, and I will ᵏredeem you
7 with a stretched out arm, and with great judgments : and I will
ˡtake you to me for a people, and ᵐI will be to you a God : and
ye shall know that I *am* the LORD your God, which bringeth you
8 out ⁿfrom under the burdens of the Egyptians. And I will bring
you in unto the land, concerning the which I did ⁴ºswear to give
it to Abraham, to Isaac, and to Jacob; and I will give it you

ᵃ ch. 3. 19.
ᵇ ch. 11. 1.
& 12. 31, 33,
39.
ᶜ Gen. 17. 1.
& reff.
ᵈ ch. 3. 14.
Ps. 68. 4.
& 83. 18.
John 8. 58.
Rev. 1. 4.
ᵉ Gen. 15. 18.
& 17. 4.
ᶠ Gen. 17. 8.
& 28. 4.
ᵍ ch. 2. 24.
ʰ ver. 2, 8.
ⁱ ch. 3. 17.
Deut. 26. 8.
Ps. 81. 6.
ᵏ ch. 15. 13.
Deut. 7. 8.
1 Chr. 17. 21.
Neh. 1. 10.
ˡ Deut. 4. 20.
& 14. 2.
& 26. 18.
2 Sam. 7. 24.
ᵐ ch. 29. 45.
Deut. 29. 13.
Rev. 21. 7.
ⁿ ch. 5. 4, 5.
Ps. 81. 6.
º Gen. 15. 18.
& reff.

¹ Heb. *to stink*, Gen. 34.
30. 1 Sam. 13. 4. & 27.
12. 2 Sam. 10. 6. 1 Chr.
19. 6.
² Heb. *delivering thou hast
not delivered.*
³ Or, *Jehovah.*
⁴ Heb. *lift up my hand.* See
Gen. 14. 22. Deut. 32.
40.

guage abounds in epithets which shew contempt for idleness. The charge was equally
offensive and ingenious ; one which would
be readily believed by Egyptians who knew
how much public and private labours were
impeded by festivals and other religious
ceremonies. Among the great sins which,
according to Egyptian belief, involved condemnation in the final judgment, idleness is
twice mentioned.

23. The earnestness of this remonstrance,
and even its approach to irreverence, are
quite in keeping with other notices of Moses'
naturally impetuous character. See iii. 13.

VI. 2, 3. There appears to have been an
interval of some months between the preceding events and this renewal of the promise to Moses. The oppression in the
mean time was not merely driving the
people to desperation, but preparing them

by severe labour, varied by hasty wanderings in search of stubble, for the exertions
and privations of the wilderness. Hence
the formal and solemn character of the announcements in the whole chapter.

2. *I am the* LORD, &c.] The meaning seems
to be this:—" I am Jehovah, and I appeared
to Abraham, Isaac, and Jacob as El Shaddai,
but as to my name Jehovah, I was not made
known to them." In other words, the full
import of that name was not disclosed to
them. See iii. 14.

3. *God Almighty*] Rather, "**El Shaddai**,"
it is better to keep this as a proper name.

6. *with a stretched out arm*] The figure is
common and quite intelligible ; it may have
struck Moses and the people the more
forcibly since they were familiar with the
hieroglyphic which represents might by two
outstretched arms.

9 for an heritage : I *am* the LORD.   And Moses spake so unto
the children of Israel : *p* but they hearkened not unto Moses for *p* ch. 5. 21.
10 ¹anguish of spirit, and for cruel bondage. ¶ And the LORD spake
11 unto Moses, saying, Go in, speak unto Pharaoh king of Egypt,
12 that he let the children of Israel go out of his land.   And Moses
spake before the LORD, saying, Behold, the children of Israel
have *q* not hearkened unto me; how then shall Pharaoh hear   *q* ver. 9.
13 me, *r* who *am* of uncircumcised lips?   And the LORD spake unto *r* ver. 30.
Moses and unto Aaron, and gave them a charge unto the chil-   ch. 4. 10.
dren of Israel, and unto Pharaoh king of Egypt, to bring the   Jer. 1. 6.
14 children of Israel out of the land of Egypt.   ¶ These *be* the
heads of their fathers' houses : *s* The sons of Reuben the first- *s* Gen. 46. 9.
born of Israel ; Hanoch, and Pallu, Hezron, and Carmi : these 1 Chr. 5. 3.
15 *be* the families of Reuben.   *t* And the sons of Simeon ; Jemuel, *t* Gen. 46. 10.
and Jamin, and Ohad, and Jachin, and Zohar, and Shaul the 1 Chr. 4. 24.
son of a Canaanitish woman : these *are* the families of Simeon. *u* Gen. 46. 11.
16 ¶ And these *are* the names of *u* the sons of Levi according to their 1 Chr. 6. 1,
generations ; Gershon, and Kohath, and Merari : and the years   *x* 1 Chr. 6.17.
17 of the life of Levi *were* an hundred thirty and seven years. *x* The *y* Num. 26.
sons of Gershon ; Libni, and Shimi, according to their families. 1 Chr. 6. 2,
18 And *y* the sons of Kohath ; Amram, and Izhar, and Hebron,   18.
and Uzziel : and the years of the life of Kohath *were* an hun-   *z* 1 Chr. 6.19.
19 dred thirty and three years.   And *z* the sons of Merari ; Mahali   *a* ch. 2. 1, 2.
and Mushi : these *are* the families of Levi according to their 1 Chr. 6.
20 generations.   And *a* Amram took him Jochebed his father's 37, 38.
sister to wife ; and she bare him Aaron and Moses : and the *c* Lev. 10. 4.
years of the life of Amram *were* an hundred and thirty and seven *d* Ruth 4.
21 years. And *b* the sons of Izhar ; Korah, and Nepheg, and Zithri. 19, 20.
22 And *c* the sons of Uzziel ; Mishael, and Elzaphan, and Zithri. Matt. 1. 4.
23 And Aaron took him Elisheba, daughter of *d* Amminadab, sister *e* Lev. 10. 1.
of Naashon, to wife ; and she bare him *e* Nadab, and Abihu, 1 Chr. 6. 3.

¹ Heb. *shortness*, or, *straitness*.

---

9. *they hearkened not*] The contrast between the reception of this communication and that recorded in iv. 31 is accounted for by the change of circumstances.
On the former occasion the people were
comparatively at ease, accustomed to their
lot, sufficiently afflicted to long for deliverance, and sufficiently free in spirit to hope
for it.

for anguish] See the margin ; out of
breath, as it were, after their cruel disappointment, they were quite absorbed by
their misery, unable and unwilling to attend
to any fresh communication.

11. *go out of his land*] Moses is now bidden
to demand not a permission for a three days'
journey (iii. 18 note), which might be within
the boundaries of Egypt, but for departure
from the land.

12. *uncircumcised lips*] An uncircumcised
ear is one that does not hear clearly ; an
uncircumcised heart one slow to receive and
understand warnings ; uncircumcised lips,
such as cannot speak fluently. The recurrence of the hesitation of Moses is natural ;
great as was the former trial this was far
more severe ; yet his words as ever imply fear
of failure, not of personal danger (see iii. 11).

13. *unto Moses and unto Aaron*] The final
and formal charge to the two brothers is
given, as might be expected, before the
plagues are denounced. With this verse
begins a new section of the history.

14. *These be the heads*] We have in the
following verses, not a complete genealogy,
but a summary account of the family of the
two brothers. Moses records for the satisfaction of Hebrew readers, to whom genealogical questions were always interesting,
the descent and position of the designated
leaders of the nation. See *vv.* 26, 27.

20. *Amram*] This can scarcely be the
same person who is mentioned in *v.* 18 ; but
his descendant and representative in the
generation immediately preceding that of
Moses. The intervening links are omitted,
as is the rule where they are not needed for
some special purpose, and do not bear upon
the history.

Jochebed] The name means "the glory of
Jehovah," one clear instance of the use of
the sacred name before the Exodus.

father's sister] This was within the prohibited degrees after the Law was given (Lev.
xviii. 12) but not previously.

j Num. 26.
11.

y Num. 25.
7, 11.
Josh. 24. 33.
h ver. 13.

i ch. 12. 17.
Num. 33. 1.
k ch. 5. 1, 3.
& 7. 10.
l ch. 32. 7.
& 33. 1.
Ps. 77. 20.
m ver. 2.
n ver. 11.
ch. 7. 2.
o ver. 12.
ch. 4. 10.
a ch. 4. 16.
Jer. 1. 10.
b ch. 4. 16.
c ch. 4. 15.
d ch. 4. 21.
c ch. 11. 9.
f ch. 4. 7.
g ch. 10. 1.
& 11. 9.
h ch. 6. 6.
i ver. 17.
ch. 8. 22.
& 14. 18.
Ps. 9. 16.
k ch. 3. 20.
l ver. 2.
m Deut. 20.
5. & 34. 7.
Acts 7. 23,
30.
n Isai. 7. 11.
John 2. 18.
& 6. 30.
o ch. 4. 2, 17.

24 Eleazar, and Ithamar. And the *j*sons of Korah; Assir, and Elkanah, and Abiasaph : these *are* the families of the Kor-25 hites. And Eleazar Aaron's son took him *one* of the daughters of Putiel to wife; and *y*she bare him Phinehas : these *are* the heads of the fathers of the Levites according to their families. 26 ¶These *are* that Aaron and Moses, *h*to whom the LORD said, Bring out the children of Israel from the land of Egypt according to 27 their *i*armies. These *are* they which *k*spake to Pharaoh king of Egypt, *l*to bring out the children of Israel from Egypt : these 28 *are* that Moses and Aaron. ¶And it came to pass on the day 29 *when* the LORD spake unto Moses in the land of Egypt, that the LORD spake unto Moses, saying, *m*I *am* the LORD, *n*speak thou 30 unto Pharaoh king of Egypt all that I say unto thee. And Moses said before the LORD, Behold, *o*I *am* of uncircumcised lips, and how shall Pharaoh hearken unto me ?

CHAP. 7. AND the LORD said unto Moses, See, I have made thee *a*a god to Pharaoh : And Aaron thy brother shall be *b*thy prophet. 2 Thou *c*shalt speak all that I command thee : and Aaron thy brother shall speak unto Pharaoh, that he send the children of 3 Israel out of his land. And *d*I will harden Pharaoh's heart, and *e*multiply my *f*signs and my wonders in the land of Egypt. 4 But Pharaoh shall not hearken unto you, *g*that I may lay my hand upon Egypt, and bring forth mine armies, *and* my people the children of Israel, out of the land of Egypt *h*by great judg-5 ments. And the Egyptians *i*shall know that I *am* the LORD, when I *k*stretch forth mine hand upon Egypt, and bring out the 6 children of Israel from among them. And Moses and Aaron 7 *l*did as the LORD commanded them, so did they. And Moses *was* *m*fourscore years old, and Aaron fourscore and three years old, 8 when they spake unto Pharaoh. ¶And the LORD spake unto 9 Moses and unto Aaron, saying, When Pharaoh shall speak unto you, saying, *n*Shew a miracle for you : then thou shalt say unto Aaron, *o*Take thy rod, and cast *it* before Pharaoh, *and* it shall

---

26, 27. This emphatic repetition shews the reason for inserting the genealogy. The names of Moses and Aaron are given twice and in a different order; in the 26th verse probably to mark Aaron as the elder in the genealogy, and in the 27th to denote the leadership of Moses.
28. This and the following verses belong to the next chapter. They mark distinctly the beginning of a subdivision of the narrative.
30. See ver. 12.
VII. With this chapter begins the series of miracles wrought in Egypt. They are progressive. The first miracle is wrought to accredit the mission of the brothers : it is simply credential, and unaccompanied by any infliction. Then come signs which shew that the powers of nature are subject to the will of Jehovah, each plague being attended with grave consequences to the Egyptians, yet not inflicting severe loss or suffering; then in rapid succession come ruinous and devastating plagues, murrain, boils, hail and lightning, locusts, darkness, and lastly, the death of the firstborn. Each of the inflictions has a demonstrable connection with Egyptian customs and phenomena; each is directly aimed at some Egyptian superstition; all are marvellous, not, for the most part, as reversing, but as developing forces inherent in nature, and directing them to a special end. The effects correspond with these characteristics; the first miracles are neglected; the following plagues first alarm, and then for a season, subdue, the king, who does not give way until his firstborn is struck. Even that blow leaves him capable of a last effort, which completes his ruin, and the deliverance of the Israelites.
1. *I have made thee a god*] Or "appointed thee." See marg. reff. Moses will stand in this peculiar relation to Pharaoh, that God will address him by a prophet, *i.e.* by one appointed to speak in His name. The passage is an important one as illustrating the primary and essential characteristic of a prophet, he is the declarer of God's will and purpose.
3. *wonders*] A word used only of portents wrought to prove a divine interposition; they were the credentials of God's messengers.
9. *thy rod*] Apparently the rod before described (iv. 2), which Moses on this occasion gives to Aaron as his representative.

10 become a serpent. And Moses and Aaron went in unto Pharaoh, and they did so *p* as the LORD had commanded : and Aaron cast
11 down his rod before Pharaoh, and before his servants, and it *q* became a serpent. Then Pharaoh also *r* called the wise men and *s* the sorcerers: now the magicians of Egypt, they also *t* did in
12 like manner with their enchantments. For they cast down every man his rod, and they became serpents : but Aaron's rod swal-
13 lowed up their rods. And he hardened Pharaoh's heart, that
14 he hearkened not unto them ; *u* as the LORD had said. ¶ And the LORD said unto Moses, *x* Pharaoh's heart *is* hardened, he re-
15 fuseth to let the people go. Get thee unto Pharaoh in the morning; lo, he goeth out unto the water; and thou shalt stand by the river's brink against he come; and *y* the rod which was
16 turned to a serpent shalt thou take in thine hand. And thou shalt say unto him, *z* The LORD God of the Hebrews hath sent me unto thee, saying, Let my people go, *a* that they may serve me in the wilderness : and, behold, hitherto thou wouldest not
17 hear. Thus saith the LORD, In this *b* thou shalt know that I *am* the LORD: behold, I will smite with the rod that *is* in mine hand upon the waters which *are* in the river, and *c* they shall be
18 turned *d* to blood. And the fish that *is* in the river shall die, and the river shall stink ; and the Egyptians shall *e* lothe to drink

p ver. 9.

q ch. 4. 3.
r Gen. 41. 8.
s 2 Tim. 3. 8.
t ver. 22.
ch. 8. 7, 18.

u ch. 4. 21.
ver. 4.
x ch. 8. 15.
& 10. 1, 20, 27.

y ch. 4. 2, 3.
ver. 10.

z ch. 3. 18.
a ch. 3. 12, 18.
& 5. 1, 3.
b ch. 5. 2.
ver. 5.
c ch. 4. 9.
d Rev. 16.
4, 6.
e ver. 24.

---

a serpent] A word different from that in iv. 3. Here a more general term, "Tannin," is employed, which in other passages includes all sea or river monsters, and is more specially applied to the crocodile as a symbol of Egypt. It occurs in the Egyptian ritual, nearly in the same form, "Tanem," as a synonym of the monster serpent which represents the principle of antagonism to light and life.

11. Three names for the magicians of Egypt are given in this verse. The "wise men" are men who know occult arts. The "sorcerers" are they who "mutter magic formulæ," especially when driving away crocodiles, snakes, asps, &c. It was natural that Pharaoh should have sent for such persons. The "magicians" are the "bearers of sacred words," scribes and interpreters of hieroglyphic writings. Books containing magic formulæ belonged exclusively to the king ; no one was permitted to consult them but the priests and wise men, who formed a council or college, and were called in by the Pharaoh on all occasions of difficulty. The names of the two principal magicians, Jannes and Jambres, who "withstood Moses," are preserved by St. Paul, 2 Tim. iii. 8. Both names are Egyptian.

enchantments] The original expression implies a deceptive appearance, an illusion, a juggler's trick, not an actual putting forth of magic power. Pharaoh may or may not have believed in a real transformation ; but in either case he would naturally consider that if the portent wrought by Aaron differed from that of the magicians, it was a difference of degree only, implying merely superiority in a common art. The miracle which followed (*v.* 12) was sufficient to con-

vince him had he been open to conviction. It was a miracle which shewed the truth and power of Jehovah in contrast with that of others.

13. *And he hardened*] Or **Pharaoh's heart was hardened.** See iv. 21.

15. *he goeth out unto the water*] The Nile was worshipped under various names and symbols ; at Memphis especially, as Hapi, *i.e.* Apis, the sacred bull, or living representation of Osiris, of whom the river was regarded as the embodiment or manifestation. If, as is probable, the king went to offer his devotions, the miracle would have peculiar force and suitableness. It was also the season of the yearly overflowing, about the middle of June ; and the daily rise of the water was accurately recorded, under the personal superintendence of the king. In early inscriptions the Nilometer is the symbol of stability and providential care.

17. *turned to blood*] This miracle would bear a certain resemblance to natural phenomena, and therefore be one which Pharaoh might see with amazement and dismay, yet without complete conviction. It is well known that before the rise the water of the Nile is green and unfit to drink. About the 25th of June it becomes clear, and then yellow, and gradually reddish like ochre ; an effect due to the presence of microscopic cryptogams and infusoria. The supernatural character of the visitation was attested by the suddenness of the change, by its immediate connection with the words and act of Moses, and by its effects. It killed the fishes, and made the water unfit for use, neither of which results follows the annual discoloration.

18. *shall lothe*] The water of the Nile has

_f_ ch. 8. 5, 6,
16.
& 9. 22.
& 10. 12, 21.
& 14. 21, 26.

_g_ ch. 17. 5.

_h_ Ps. 78. 44.
& 105. 29.

_i_ ver. 18.
_k_ ver. 11.

_l_ ver. 3.

_a_ ch. 3. 12,
18.
_b_ ch. 7. 14.
& 9. 2.
_c_ Rev. 16. 13.

_d_ Ps. 105. 30.

_e_ ch. 7. 19.

19 of the water of the river. ¶ And the LORD spake unto Moses, Say unto Aaron, Take thy rod, and _f_ stretch out thine hand upon the waters of Egypt, upon their streams, upon their rivers, and upon their ponds, and upon all their [1] pools of water, that they may become blood; and _that_ there may be blood throughout all the land of Egypt, both in _vessels of_ wood, and in _vessels of_
20 stone. And Moses and Aaron did so, as the LORD commanded; and he _g_ lifted up the rod, and smote the waters that _were_ in the river, in the sight of Pharaoh, and in the sight of his servants; and all the _h_ waters that _were_ in the river were turned to blood.
21 And the fish that _was_ in the river died; and the river stank, and the Egyptians _i_ could not drink of the water of the river; and
22 there was blood throughout all the land of Egypt. _k_ And the magicians of Egypt did so with their enchantments: And Pharaoh's heart was hardened, neither did he hearken unto them;
23 _l_ as the LORD had said. And Pharaoh turned and went into
24 his house, neither did he set his heart to this also. And all the Egyptians digged round about the river for water to drink; for
25 they could not drink of the water of the river. And seven days were fulfilled, after that the LORD had smitten the river.

CHAP. 8. AND the LORD spake unto Moses, Go unto Pharaoh, and say unto him, Thus saith the LORD, Let my people go, _a_ that
2 they may serve me. And if thou _b_ refuse to let _them_ go, behold,
3 I will smite all thy borders with _c_ frogs: and the river shall bring forth frogs abundantly, which shall go up and come into thine house, and into _d_ thy bedchamber, and upon thy bed, and into the house of thy servants, and upon thy people, and into
4 thine ovens, and into thy [2] kneadingtroughs: and the frogs shall come up both on thee, and upon thy people, and upon all thy
5 servants. ¶ And the LORD spake unto Moses, Say unto Aaron, _e_ Stretch forth thine hand with thy rod over the streams, over

[1] Heb. _gathering of their waters._   [2] Or, _dough._

always been regarded by the Egyptians as a blessing peculiar to their land. It is the only pure and wholesome water in their country, since the water in wells and cisterns is unwholesome, while rain water seldom falls, and fountains are extremely rare.

19. The _streams_ mean the natural branches of the Nile in Lower Egypt. The word _rivers_ should rather be _canals_; they were of great extent, running parallel to the Nile, and communicating with it by sluices, which were opened at the rise, and closed at the subsidence of the inundation. The word rendered _ponds_ refers either to natural fountains, or more probably to cisterns or tanks found in every town and village. The _pools_, lit. "gathering of waters," were the reservoirs, always large and some of enormous extent, containing sufficient water to irrigate the country in the dry season.

in vessels of wood] The Nile water is kept in vessels and is purified for use by filtering, and by certain ingredients such as the paste of almonds.

21. _the fish_, &c.] The Egyptians subsisted to a great extent on the fish of the Nile, though salt-water fish was regarded as impure. A

mortality among the fish was a plague much dreaded.

25. _seven days_] This marks the duration of the plague. The natural discoloration of the Nile water lasts generally much longer, about 20 days.

VIII. 2. _with frogs_] Some months appear to have elapsed between this and the former plague, if the frogs made their appearance at the usual time, that is in September. The special species mentioned here is of Egyptian origin. This plague was, like the preceding, in general accordance with natural phenomena, but marvellous both for its extent and intensity, and for its direct connection with the words and acts of God's messengers. It had also apparently, like the other plagues, a direct bearing upon Egyptian superstitions. There was a female deity with a frog's head, and the frog was connected with the most ancient forms of nature-worship in Egypt.

3. _into thine house_] This appears to have been peculiar to the plague, as such. It was specially the visitation which would be felt by the scrupulously clean Egyptians.

kneadingtroughs] Not "dough," as in the margin. See xii. 34.

the rivers, and over the ponds, and cause frogs to come up upon
6 the land of Egypt. And Aaron stretched out his hand over the
waters of Egypt; and *f* the frogs came up, and covered the land
7 of Egypt. *g* And the magicians did so with their enchantments,
8 and brought up frogs upon the land of Egypt. ¶ Then Pharaoh
called for Moses and Aaron, and said, *h* Intreat the LORD, that
he may take away the frogs from me, and from my people ; and
I will let the people go, that they may do sacrifice unto the
9 LORD. And Moses said unto Pharaoh, ¹Glory over me : ²when
shall I intreat for thee, and for thy servants, and for thy people,
³to destroy the frogs from thee and thy houses, *that* they may
10 remain in the river only ? And he said, ⁴To morrow. And he
said, *Be it* according to thy word : that thou mayest know that
11 ⁵there is none like unto the LORD our God. And the frogs shall
depart from thee, and from thy houses, and from thy servants,
12 and from thy people ; they shall remain in the river only. ¶ And
Moses and Aaron went out from Pharaoh : and Moses *k* cried
unto the LORD because of the frogs which he had brought
13 against Pharaoh. And the LORD did according to the word of
Moses ; and the frogs died out of the houses, out of the villages,
14 and out of the fields. And they gathered them together upon
15 heaps : and the land stank. But when Pharaoh saw that there
was *l* respite, *m* he hardened his heart, and hearkened not unto
16 them ; as the LORD had said. ¶ And the LORD said unto Moses,
Say unto Aaron, Stretch out thy rod, and smite the dust of the
land, that it may become lice throughout all the land of Egypt.
17 And they did so ; for Aaron stretched out his hand with his rod,
and smote the dust of the earth, and *n* it became lice in man,
and in beast ; all the dust of the land became lice throughout
18 all the land of Egypt. And *o* the magicians did so with their
enchantments to bring forth lice, but they *p* could not : so there
19 were lice upon man, and upon beast. Then the magicians said
unto Pharaoh, This *is* *q* the finger of God : and Pharaoh's *r* heart
was hardened, and he hearkened not unto them ; as the LORD

f Ps. 78. 45.
& 105. 30.
g ch. 7. 11.

h ch. 9. 28.
& 10. 17.
Num. 21. 7.
1 Kin. 13. 6.
Acts 8. 24.

i ch. 9. 14.
Deut. 33. 26.
2 Sam. 7. 22.
1 Chr. 17. 20.
Ps. 86. 8.
Isai. 46. 9.
Jer. 10. 6, 7.
k ver. 30.
ch. 9. 33.
& 10. 18.
& 32. 11.
Jam. 5. 16,
17, 18.
l Eccles. 8.
11.
m ch. 7. 14.

n Ps. 105. 31.
o ch. 7. 11.
p Luke 10.
18.
2 Tim. 3. 8,
9.
q 1 Sam. 6.
3, 9.
Ps. 8. 3.
Matt. 12. 28.
Luke 11. 20.
r ver. 15.

¹ Or, *Have* this *honour over
me, &c.*   ² Or, *against when.*
Heb. *to cut off.*   ⁴ Or, *against to-morrow.*

---

7. The magicians would seem to have
been able to increase the plague, but not to
remove it ; hence Pharaoh's application to
Moses, the first symptoms of yielding.
9. *Glory over me*] See the margin, "have
honour over me," *i.e.* have the honour,
or advantage over me, directing me when I
shall entreat God for thee and thy servants.
when] Or **by when**; *i.e.* for what exact
time. Pharaoh's answer in *v.* 10 refers to
this, **by to-morrow.** The shortness of the
time would, of course, be a test of the supernatural character of the transaction.
13. *villages*] Lit. inclosures, or courtyards.
16. It is observed by Hebrew commentators that the nine plagues are divided into
three groups : distinct warnings are given
of the first two plagues in each group ; the
third in each is inflicted without any previous notice ; viz. the third, *lice,* the sixth,
boils, the ninth, *darkness.*
the dust of the land] The two preceding
plagues fell upon the Nile. This fell on the

earth, which was worshipped in Egypt as
the father of the gods. An especial sacredness was attached to the black fertile soil of
the basin of the Nile, called Chemi, from
which the ancient name of Egypt is supposed to be derived.
lice] The Hebrew word occurs only in
connection with this plague. These insects
are generally identified with mosquitos, a
plague nowhere greater than in Egypt.
They are most troublesome towards October, *i.e.* soon after the plague of frogs, and
are dreaded not only for the pain and annoyance which they cause, but also because
they are said to penetrate into the body
through the nostrils and ears.
19. *the finger of God*] This expression is
thoroughly Egyptian ; it need not imply
that the magicians recognised Jehovah as
the God Who wrought the marvel. They
may possibly have referred it to a god hostile to their own protectors.

^s ch. 7. 15.

^t ver. 1.

^u ch. 9. 4,
6, 26.
& 10. 23.
& 11. 6, 7.
& 12. 13.

^x Ps. 78. 45.
& 105. 31.

^y Gen. 43.
32.
& 46. 34.
Deut. 7. 25,
26.
& 12. 31.
^z ch. 3. 18.
^a ch. 3. 12.

^b ver. 8.
ch. 9. 28.
1 Kin. 13. 6.

^c ver. 15.

^d ver. 12.

20 had said. ¶ And the LORD said unto Moses, ^sRise up early in the morning, and stand before Pharaoh; lo, he cometh forth to the water; and say unto him, Thus saith the LORD, ^tLet my 21 people go, that they may serve me. Else, if thou wilt not let my people go, behold, I will send ¹swarms *of flies* upon thee, and upon thy servants, and upon thy people, and into thy houses: and the houses of the Egyptians shall be full of 22 swarms *of flies*, and also the ground whereon they *are*. And ^uI will sever in that day the land of Goshen, in which my people dwell, that no swarms *of flies* shall be there; to the end thou mayest know that I *am* the LORD in the midst of the earth. 23 And I will put ²a division between my people and thy people: 24 ³to morrow shall this sign be. And the LORD did so; and ^xthere came a grievous swarm *of flies* into the house of Pharaoh, and *into* his servants' houses, and into all the land of Egypt: the land was ⁴corrupted by reason of the swarm *of flies*. 25 ¶ And Pharaoh called for Moses and for Aaron, and said, Go ye, 26 sacrifice to your God in the land. And Moses said, It is not meet so to do; for we shall sacrifice ^ythe abomination of the Egyptians to the LORD our God: lo, shall we sacrifice the abomination of the Egyptians before their eyes, and will they 27 not stone us? We will go ^zthree days' journey into the wilderness, and sacrifice to the LORD our God, as ^ahe shall command 28 us. And Pharaoh said, I will let you go, that ye may sacrifice to the LORD your God in the wilderness; only ye shall not go very 29 far away: ^bintreat for me. And Moses said, Behold, I go out from thee, and I will intreat the LORD that the swarms *of flies* may depart from Pharaoh, from his servants, and from his people, to morrow: but let not Pharaoh ^cdeal deceitfully any more in not letting the people go to sacrifice to the LORD. 30 ¶ And Moses went out from Pharaoh, and ^dintreated the LORD. 31 And the LORD did according to the word of Moses; and he removed the swarms *of flies* from Pharaoh, from his servants,

¹ Or, *a mixture of* noisome beasts, &c.   ² Heb. *a redemption.*   ³ Or, *by to morrow.*   ⁴ Or, *destroyed.*

20. *cometh forth to the water*] See vii. 15 note. It is not improbable that on this occasion Pharaoh went to the Nile with a procession in order to open the solemn festival, which was held 120 days after the first rise, at the end of October or early in November. At that time the inundation is abating and the first traces of vegetation are seen on the deposit of fresh soil. The plague now announced may be regarded as connected with the atmosphere, also an object of worship.

21. *swarms of flies*] Generally supposed to be the dog-fly, which at certain seasons is described as a far worse plague than mosquitos. Others however adopt the opinion that the insects were a species of beetle, which was reverenced by the Egyptians as a symbol of life, of reproductive or creative power. The sun-god, as creator, bore the name Chepera, and is represented in the form, or with the head, of a beetle.

22. *I will sever*, &c.] This severance constituted a specific difference between this and the preceding plagues. Pharaoh could

not of course attribute the exemption of Goshen from a scourge, which fell on the valley of the Nile, to an Egyptian deity, certainly not to Chepera (see the last note), a special object of worship in Lower Egypt.

25. *to your God*] Pharaoh now admits the existence and power of the God Whom he had professed not to know; but, as Moses is careful to record, he recognises Him only as the national Deity of the Israelites.

in the land] *i.e.* in Egypt, not beyond the frontier.

26. *the abomination*] *i.e.* an animal which the Egyptians held it sacrilegious to slay. The ox, bull, or cow, is meant. The cow was never sacrificed in Egypt, being sacred to Isis, and from a very early age the ox was worshipped throughout Egypt, and more especially at Heliopolis and Memphis under various designations, Apis, Mnevis, Amen-Ehe, as the symbol or manifestation of their greatest deities, Osiris, Atum, Ptah, and Isis.

27. *three days' journey*] See iii. 18 note.

32 and from his people; there remained not one. And Pharaoh ^ehardened his heart at this time also, neither would he let the people go.   e ver. 15.
ch. 4. 21.

CHAP. 9. THEN the LORD said unto Moses, ^aGo in unto Pharaoh, and tell him, Thus saith the LORD God of the Hebrews, Let my   a ch. 8. 1.
2 people go, that they may serve me. For if thou ^brefuse to let   b ch. 8. 2.
3 *them* go, and wilt hold them still, Behold, the ^chand of the   c ch. 7. 4.
LORD is upon thy cattle which *is* in the field, upon the horses, upon the asses, upon the camels, upon the oxen, and upon the
4 sheep: *there shall be* a very grievous murrain. And ^dthe LORD   d ch. 8. 22.
shall sever between the cattle of Israel and the cattle of Egypt: and there shall nothing die of all *that is* the children's of Israel.
5 And the LORD appointed a set time, saying, To morrow the
6 LORD shall do this thing in the land. And the LORD did that
thing on the morrow, and ^eall the cattle of Egypt died: but of   e Ps. 78. 50.
7 the cattle of the children of Israel died not one. And Pharaoh
sent, and, behold, there was not one of the cattle of the Israelites
dead. And ^fthe heart of Pharaoh was hardened, and he did not   f ch. 7. 14.
& 8. 32.
8 let the people go. ¶And the LORD said unto Moses and unto
Aaron, Take to you handfuls of ashes of the furnace, and let
Moses sprinkle it toward the heaven in the sight of Pharaoh.
9 And it shall become small dust in all the land of Egypt, and
shall be ^ga boil breaking forth *with* blains upon man, and upon   g Rev. 16. 2.
10 beast, throughout all the land of Egypt. And they took ashes
of the furnace, and stood before Pharaoh; and Moses sprinkled
it up toward heaven; and it became ^ha boil breaking forth *with*   h Deut. 28.
27.
11 blains upon man, and upon beast. And the ⁱmagicians could   i ch. 8. 18,
19.
not stand before Moses because of the boils; for the boil was
12 upon the magicians, and upon all the Egyptians. And the   2 Tim. 3. 9.
LORD hardened the heart of Pharaoh, and he hearkened not
13 unto them; ^kas the LORD had spoken unto Moses. ¶And the   k ch. 4. 21.
LORD said unto Moses, ^lRise up early in the morning, and stand   l ch. 8. 20.
before Pharaoh, and say unto him, Thus saith the LORD God of
14 the Hebrews, Let my people go, that they may serve me. For I

IX. 3. *a very grievous murrain*] Or " pestilence ;" but the word murrain, *i.e.* a great mortality, exactly expresses the meaning. This terrible visitation struck far more severely than the preceding, which had caused distress and suffering ; it attacked the resources of the nation.

the camels] These animals are only twice mentioned, here and Gen. xii. 16, in connection with Egypt. Though camels are never represented on the monuments, they were known to the Egyptians, and were probably used on the frontier.

6. *all the cattle*] *i.e.* which were left in the field ; cp. *vv.* 19—21.

7. *was hardened*] See iv. 21. Pharaoh probably attributed the exemption of the Israelites to natural causes. They were a pastoral race, well acquainted with all that appertained to the care of cattle ; and dwelling in a healthy district probably far more than the rest of Lower Egypt.

8. This marks a distinct advance and change in the character of the visitations. Hitherto the Egyptians had not been attacked directly in their persons. It is

the second plague which was not preceded by a demand and warning, probably on account of the peculiar hardness shewn by Pharaoh in reference to the murrain.

ashes of the furnace] The act was evidently symbolical : the ashes were to be sprinkled towards heaven, challenging, so to speak, the Egyptian deities. There may possibly be a reference to an Egyptian custom of scattering to the winds ashes of victims offered to Typhon.

9. *a boil*] Means probably a burning tumour or carbuncle breaking out in pustulous ulcers. The miracle consisting in the severity of the plague and its direct connection with the act of Moses.

11. This verse seems to imply that the magicians now formally gave way and confessed their defeat.

13—34. With the plague of hail begins the last series of plagues, which differ from the former both in their severity and their effects. Each produced a temporary, but real, change in Pharaoh's feelings.

14. *all my plagues*] This applies to all the plagues which follow ; the effect of each was

will at this time send all my plagues upon thine heart, and
m ch. 8. 10.   upon thy servants, and upon thy people; *m*that thou mayest
15 know that *there is* none like me in all the earth. For now I will
n ch. 3. 20.   *n*stretch out my hand, that I may smite thee and thy people
16 with pestilence; and thou shalt be cut off from the earth. And
o Rom. 9. 17.   in very deed for *o*this *cause* have I ¹raised thee up, for to shew
See ch. 14.   *in* thee my power; and that my name may be declared through-
17.
Prov. 16. 4.   17 out all the earth. As yet exaltest thou thyself against my
1 Pet. 2. 9.   18 people, that thou wilt not let them go? Behold, to morrow
about this time I will cause it to rain a very grievous hail, such
as hath not been in Egypt since the foundation thereof even
19 until now. Send therefore now, *and* gather thy cattle, and all
that thou hast in the field; *for upon* every man and beast which
shall be found in the field, and shall not be brought home, the
20 hail shall come down upon them, and they shall die. He
that feared the word of the LORD among the servants of Pha-
21 raoh made his servants and his cattle flee into the houses: and
p Rev. 16.   he that ²regarded not the word of the LORD left his servants
21.
q Josh. 10.   22 and his cattle in the field. ¶And the LORD said unto Moses,
11.   Stretch forth thine hand toward heaven, that there may be
Ps. 18. 13.
& 78. 47.   *p*hail in all the land of Egypt, upon man, and upon beast, and
& 105. 32.   upon every herb of the field, throughout the land of Egypt.
& 148. 8.
Isai. 30. 30.   23 And Moses stretched forth his rod toward heaven: and *q*the
Ezek. 38. 22.   LORD sent thunder and hail, and the fire ran along upon the
Rev. 8. 7.   ground; and the LORD rained hail upon the land of Egypt.
r Ps. 105. 33.
s ch. 8. 22.   24 So there was hail, and fire mingled with the hail, very grievous,
& 9. 4, 6. &   such as there was none like it in all the land of Egypt since it
10. 23. & 11.   25 became a nation. And the hail smote throughout all the land
7 & 12. 13.
Isai. 32. 18,   of Egypt all that *was* in the field, both man and beast; and the
19.   hail *r*smote every herb of the field, and brake every tree of the
t ch. 10. 16.   26 field. *s*Only in the land of Goshen, where the children of Israel
u 2 Chr. 12.
6.   27 *were*, was there no hail. ¶And Pharaoh sent, and called for Moses
Ps. 129. 4.   and Aaron, and said unto them, *t*I have sinned this time: *u*the
& 145. 17.
Lam. 1. 18.   28 LORD *is* righteous, and I and my people *are* wicked. *x*Intreat
Dan. 9. 14.   the LORD (for *it is* enough) that there be no *more* ³mighty thun-
x ch. 8. 8, 28.   derings and hail; and I will let you go, and ye shall stay no
& 10. 17.
Acts 8. 24.   29 longer. And Moses said unto him, As soon as I am gone out of
y 1 Kin. 8.   the city, I will *y*spread abroad my hands unto the LORD; *and*
22, 38.
Ps. 143. 6.   ¹ Heb. *made thee stand.*   ² Heb. *set not his heart*   ³ Heb. *voices of God,* Ps.
Isai. 1. 15.   *unto,* ch. 7, 23.   29. 3, 4.

foreseen and foretold. The words "at this
time" point to a rapid and continuous succession of blows. The plagues which precede appear to have been spread over a
considerable time; the first message of
Moses was delivered after the early harvest
of the year before, when the Israelites could
gather stubble, *i.e.* in May and April: the
second mission, when the plagues began,
was probably towards the end of June, and
they went on at intervals until the winter;
this plague was in February; see *v.* 31.
    15. *For now,* &c.] Better, **For now in-
deed, had I stretched forth my hand and
smitten thee and thy people with the pestilence, then hadst thou been cut off from
the earth.** The next verse gives the reason
why God had not thus inflicted a summary
punishment once for all.

    16. *have I raised thee up*] See the margin.
God kept Pharaoh "standing", *i.e.* permitted him to live and hold out until His
own purpose was accomplished.
    18. *a very grievous hail*] The miracle con-
sisted in the magnitude of the infliction and
in its immediate connection with the act of
Moses.
    19. In Egypt the cattle are sent to pas-
ture in the open country from January to
April, when the grass is abundant. They
are kept in stalls the rest of the year.
    20. *the word of the* LORD] This gives the
first indication that the warnings had a salutary effect upon the Egyptians.
    27. *the* LORD] Thus for the first time
Pharaoh explicitly recognizes Jehovah as
God (cp. v. 2).
    29. *the earth is the* LORD's] This declara-

the thunder shall cease, neither shall there be any more hail;
30 that thou mayest know how that the ²earth *is* the LORD's. But
as for thee and thy servants, *a*I know that ye will not yet fear
31 the LORD God. ¶And the flax and the barley was smitten:
32 *b*for the barley *was* in the ear, and the flax *was* bolled. But
the wheat and the rie were not smitten; for they *were* ¹not
33 grown up. ¶And Moses went out of the city from Pharaoh,
and *c*spread abroad his hands unto the LORD: and the thunders
and hail ceased, and the rain was not poured upon the earth.
34 And when Pharaoh saw that the rain and the hail and the thunders were ceased, he sinned yet more, and hardened his heart,
35 he and his servants. And *d*the heart of Pharaoh was hardened,
neither would he let the children of Israel go; as the LORD had
spoken ²by Moses.

CHAP. 10. AND the LORD said unto Moses, Go in unto Pharaoh:
*a*for I have hardened his heart, and the heart of his servants,
2 *b*that I might shew these my signs before him: and that *c*thou
mayest tell in the ears of thy son, and of thy son's son, what
things I have wrought in Egypt, and my signs which I have
done among them; that ye may know how that I *am* the LORD.
3 And Moses and Aaron came in unto Pharaoh, and said unto
him, Thus saith the LORD God of the Hebrews, How long wilt
thou refuse to *d*humble thyself before me? Let my people go, that
4 they may serve me. Else, if thou refuse to let my people go,
5 behold, to morrow will I bring the *e*locusts into thy coast: and
they shall cover the ³face of the earth, that one cannot be able to
see the earth: and *f*they shall eat the residue of that which is
escaped, which remaineth unto you from the hail, and shall eat
6 every tree which groweth for you out of the field: and they *g*shall
fill thy houses, and the houses of all thy servants, and the houses

z Ps. 24. 1.
1 Cor. 10.
26, 28.
a Isai. 26. 10.
b Ruth 1. 22.
& 2. 23.

c ver. 29.
ch. 8. 12.

d ch. 4. 21.

a ch. 4. 21.
& 7. 14.
b ch. 7. 4.
c Deut. 4. 9.
Ps. 44. 1.
& 71. 18.
& 78. 5, &c.
Joel 1. 3.
d 1 Kin. 21.
29.
2 Chr. 7. 14.
& 34. 27.
Job 42. 6.
Jer. 13. 18.
Jam. 4. 10.
e Prov. 30.
27.
Rev. 9. 3.
f ch. 9. 32.
Joel 1. 4.
& 2. 25.
g ch. 8. 3, 21.

¹ Heb. *hidden,* or, *dark.* ² Heb. *by the hand of Moses,* ch. 4. 13. ³ Heb. *eye,* ver. 15.

---

tion has a direct reference to Egyptian
superstition. Each God was held to have
special power within a given district; Pharaoh had learned that Jehovah was *a* God,
he was now to admit that His power extended over the whole earth. The unity
and universality of the Divine power,
though occasionally recognized in ancient
Egyptian documents, were overlaid at a very
early period by systems alternating between
Polytheism and Pantheism.

31. *the flax was bolled*] *i.e.* in blossom.
This marks the time. In the north of Egypt
the barley ripens and flax blossoms about
the middle of February, or at the latest
early in March, and both are gathered in
before April, when the wheat harvest begins. The cultivation of flax must have
been of great importance; linen was preferred to any material, and exclusively used
by the priests. It is frequently mentioned
on Egyptian monuments.

32. *rie*} Rather **spelt**, the common food
of the ancient Egyptians, now called *doora*
by the natives, and the only grain represented
on the sculptures: the name, however, occurs on the monuments very frequently in
combination with other species.

34, 35. *hardened*] Different words in the

Hebrew. In *v.* 34 the word means "made
heavy," *i.e.* obtuse, incapable of forming a
right judgment; in *v.* 35 it is stronger, and
implies a stubborn resolution.

X. 4. *the locusts*] The locust is less common in Egypt than in many eastern countries, yet it is well known, and dreaded as
the most terrible of scourges. They come
generally from the western deserts, but
sometimes from the east and the south-east.
No less than nine names are given to the
locust in the Bible, of which the word here
used is the most common; it signifies
"multitudinous," and whenever it occurs reference is made to its terrible devastations.

5. *the face*] Lit., cover "the eye of the
earth," alluding to the darkness which follows, when the whole atmosphere is filled
on all sides and to a great height by an innumerable quantity of these insects.

shall eat every tree] Not only the leaves,
but the branches and even the wood were attacked and devoured. The Egyptians were
passionately fond of trees.

6. *fill thy houses*] The terraces, courts,
and even the inner apartments are said to
be filled in a moment by a locust storm. Cp.
Joel ii. 9.

of all the Egyptians; which neither thy fathers, nor thy fathers'
fathers have seen, since the day that they were upon the earth
unto this day. And he turned himself and went out from Pharaoh.
7 ¶ And Pharaoh's servants said unto him, How long shall this man

h ch. 23. 33.
Josh. 23. 13.
1 Sam. 18.
21.
Eccles. 7.
26.
1 Cor. 7. 35.

be *h* a snare unto us? Let the men go, that they may serve the LORD
8 their God : knowest thou not yet that Egypt is destroyed ? And
Moses and Aaron were brought again unto Pharaoh : and he
said unto them, Go, serve the LORD your God : but ¹who *are*
9 they that shall go ? And Moses said, we will go with our young
and with our old, with our sons and with our daughters, with

i ch. 5. 1.

our flocks and with our herds will we go; for *i* we *must hold*
10 a feast unto the LORD. And he said unto them, Let the LORD
be so with you, as I will let you go, and your little ones : look *to*
11 *it ;* for evil *is* before you. Not so : go now ye *that are* men, and
serve the LORD ; for that ye did desire. And they were driven
12 out from Pharaoh's presence. ¶ And the LORD said unto Moses,

k ch. 7. 19.
l ver. 4. 5.

k Stretch out thine hand over the land of Egypt for the locusts, that
they may come up upon the land of Egypt, and *l* eat every herb
13 of the land, *even* all that the hail hath left. And Moses stretched
forth his rod over the land of Egypt, and the LORD brought an
east wind upon the land all that day, and all *that* night; *and*
14 when it was morning, the east wind brought the locusts. And

m Ps. 78. 46.
& 105. 34.
n Joel 2. 2.

m the locusts went up over all the land of Egypt, and rested in
all the coasts of Egypt : very grievous *were they; n* before them
there were no such locusts as they, neither after them shall be

o ver. 5.
p Ps. 105. 34.

15 such. For they *o* covered the face of the whole earth, so that the
land was darkened ; and they *p* did eat every herb of the land,
and all the fruit of the trees which the hail had left : and there
remained not any green thing in the trees, or in the herbs of the
16 field, through all the land of Egypt. ¶ Then Pharaoh ²called for

q ch. 9. 27.

Moses and Aaron in haste ; and he said, *q* I have sinned against
17 the LORD your God, and against you. Now therefore forgive, I

r ch. 9. 28.
1 Kin. 13. 6.

pray thee, my sin only this once, and *r* intreat the LORD your
18 God, that he may take away from me this death only. And he

s ch. 8. 30.

19 *s* went out from Pharaoh, and intreated the LORD. And the
LORD turned a mighty strong west wind, which took away the

t Joel 2. 20.

locusts, and ³cast them *t* into the Red sea ; there remained not

---

¹ Heb. *who, and who, &c.*　　　　² Heb. *hastened to call.*　　　　³ Heb. *fastened.*

---

7. For the first time the officers of Pharaoh intervene before the scourge is inflicted,
shewing at once their belief in the threat,
and their special terror of the infliction.
Pharaoh also for the first time takes measures to prevent the evil ; he does not indeed send for Moses and Aaron, but he per-
mits them to be brought into his presence.

let the men go] *i.e.* the men only, not all
the people. See *v.* 8.

9. *with our young,* &c.] The demand was
not contrary to Egyptian usage, as great
festivals were kept by the whole population.

10. *evil is before you*] *i.e.* "your intentions
are evil." Great as the possible infliction
might be, Pharaoh held it to be a less evil
than the loss of so large a population.

13. *an east wind*] See *v.* 4. Moses is careful to record the natural and usual cause of
the evil, portentous as it was both in

extent and in connexion with its denounce-
ment.

14. *went up*] At a distance the locusts
appear hanging, as it were, like a heavy
cloud over the land ; as they approach they
seem to rise, and they fill the atmosphere
overhead on their arrival.

over all the land] Travellers mention a
cloud of locusts extending over 500 miles,
and so compact while on the wing that it
completely hid the sun. This passage describes a swarm unprecedented in extent.

17. *this death only*] Pliny calls locusts a
pestilence brought on by divine wrath.
Pharaoh now recognizes the justice of his
servants' apprehensions, *v.* 7.

19. *west wind*] Literally "a sea wind,"
a wind blowing from the sea on the north-
west of Egypt.

Red sea] The Hebrew has the "Sea of
Suph": the exact meaning of which is dis-

20 one locust in all the coasts of Egypt. But the LORD ^uhardened
Pharaoh's heart, so that he would not let the children of Israel
21 go. ¶ And the LORD said unto Moses, ^xStretch out thine hand
toward heaven, that there may be darkness over the land of
22 Egypt, ¹even darkness which may be felt. And Moses stretched
forth his hand toward heaven; and there was a ^ythick darkness
23 in all the land of Egypt three days: they saw not one another,
neither rose any from his place for three days: ^zbut all the
24 children of Israel had light in their dwellings. ¶ And Pharaoh
called unto Moses, and ^asaid, Go ye, serve the LORD; only let
your flocks and your herds be stayed: let your ^blittle ones also go
25 with you. And Moses said, Thou must give ²us also sacrifices
and burnt offerings, that we may sacrifice unto the LORD our
26 God. Our cattle also shall go with us; there shall not an hoof be
left behind; for thereof must we take to serve the LORD our God;
and we know not with what we must serve the LORD, until we
27 come thither. But the LORD ^chardened Pharaoh's heart, and
28 he would not let them go. And Pharaoh said unto him, Get thee
from me, take heed to thyself, see my face no more; for in that
29 day thou seest my face thou shalt die. And Moses said, Thou
hast spoken well, ^dI will see thy face again no more.
CHAP. 11. AND the LORD said unto Moses, Yet will I bring one
plague more upon Pharaoh, and upon Egypt; afterwards he will
let you go hence: ^awhen he shall let you go, he shall surely
2 thrust you out hence altogether. Speak now in the ears of the
people, and let every man borrow of his neighbour, and every
woman of her neighbour, ^bjewels of silver, and jewels of gold.

^u ch. 4. 21.
& 11. 10.

^x ch. 9. 22.

^y Ps. 105. 28.

^z ch. 8. 22.

^a ver. 8.
^b ver. 10.

^c ver. 20.
ch. 4. 21.
& 14. 4, 8.

^d Heb. 11.
27.

^a ch. 12. 31,
33, 39.

^b ch. 3. 22.
& 12. 35.

¹ Heb. that one may feel darkness.　　　　² Heb. into our hands.

puted. Gesenius renders it "rush" or "sea-weed;" but it is probably an Egyptian word. A sea-weed resembling wood is thrown up abundantly on the shores of the Red Sea. The origin of the name "Red" Sea is uncertain: [naturalists have connected it with the presence of red infusoria, cp. vii. 17].

21. darkness] This infliction was specially calculated to affect the spirits of the Egyptians, whose chief object of worship was Ra, the Sun-god; and its suddenness and severity in connexion with the act of Moses mark it as a preternatural withdrawal of light. Yet it has an analogy in physical phenomena. After the vernal equinox the south-west wind from the desert blows some fifty days, not however continuously but at intervals, lasting generally some two or three days. It fills the atmosphere with dense masses of fine sand, bringing on a darkness far deeper than that of our worst fogs in winter. The consternation of Pharaoh proves that, familiar as he may have been with the phenomenon, no previous occurrence had prepared him for its intensity and duration, and that he recognized it as a supernatural visitation.

23. had light in their dwellings] The sand-storm, if such were the cause, may not have extended to the district of Goshen; but the expression clearly denotes a miraculous intervention, whether accomplished or not by natural agencies.

24. your flocks and your herds] Pharaoh still exacts what would of course be a complete security for their return: but the demand was wholly incompatible with the object assigned for the journey into the wilderness.

XI. 1. the LORD said] Or "the Lord had said." The first three verses of this chapter are parenthetical. Before Moses relates the last warning given to Pharaoh, he feels it right to recall to his readers' minds the revelation and command which had been previously given to him by the Lord.

when he shall let you go, &c.] When at last he lets you depart with children, flocks, herds, and all your possessions, he will compel you to depart in haste. Moses was already aware that the last plague would be followed by an immediate, departure, and, therefore, measures had probably been taken to prepare the Israelites for the journey. In fact on each occasion when Pharaoh relented for a season, immediate orders would of course be issued by Moses to the heads of the people, who were thus repeatedly brought into a state of more or less complete organization for the final movement.

2. every man] In iii. 22 women only were named; the command is more explicit when the time has come for its execution.

borrow] "ask." See iii. 22 note.

3 ^cAnd the LORD gave the people favour in the sight of the Egyptians. Moreover the man ^d Moses was very great in the land of
Egypt, in the sight of Pharaoh's servants, and in the sight of
4 the people. ¶ And Moses said, Thus saith the LORD, ^eAbout
5 midnight will I go out into the midst of Egypt: and ^fall the
firstborn in the land of Egypt shall die, from the firstborn of
Pharaoh that sitteth upon his throne, even unto the firstborn of
the maidservant that is behind the mill; and all the firstborn of
6 beasts. ^gAnd there shall be a great cry throughout all the land
of Egypt, such as there was none like it, nor shall be like it
7 any more. ^hBut against any of the children of Israel ⁱshall
not a dog move his tongue, against man or beast: that ye may
know how that the LORD doth put a difference between the Egypt-
8 ians and Israel. And ^kall these thy servants shall come down unto
me, and bow down themselves unto me, saying, Get thee out,
and all the people ¹that follow thee: and after that I will go
9 out. And he went out from Pharaoh in ²a great anger. ¶ And
the LORD said unto Moses, ^lPharaoh shall not hearken unto you;
10 that ^mmy wonders may be multiplied in the land of Egypt. And
Moses and Aaron did all these wonders before Pharaoh : ⁿand the
LORD hardened Pharaoh's heart, so that he would not let the
children of Israel go out of his land.

CHAP. 12. AND the LORD spake unto Moses and Aaron in the land
2 of Egypt, saying, ^aThis month shall be unto you the beginning
3 of months : it shall be the first month of the year to you. ¶ Speak
ye unto all the congregation of Israel, saying, In the tenth day
of this month they shall take to them every man a ³lamb, accord-

¹ Heb. that is at thy feet.   ² Heb. heat of anger.
So Judg. 4. 10. & 8. 5.   ³ Or, kid.
1 Kin. 20. 10. 2 Kin. 3. 9.

---

4. And Moses said] The following words
must be read in immediate connexion with
the last verse of the preceding chapter.

About midnight] This marks the hour, but
not the day, on which the visitation would
take place. There may have been, and probably was, an interval of some days, during
which preparations might be made both for
the celebration of the Passover, and the departure of the Israelites.

5. Two points are to be noticed : 1, The
extent of the visitation : the whole land
suffers in the persons of its firstborn, not
merely for the guilt of the sovereign, but for
the actual participation of the people in the
crime of infanticide (i. 22). 2, The limitation :
Pharaoh's command had been to slay all the
male children of the Israelites, one child
only in each Egyptian family was to die.
If Tothmosis II. was the Pharaoh, the visitation fell with special severity on his
family. He left no son, but was succeeded
by his widow.

the mill] This consisted of two circular
stones, one fixed in the ground, the other
turned by a handle. The work of grinding
was extremely laborious, and performed by
women of the lowest rank.

firstborn of beasts] This visitation has a
peculiar force in reference to the worship of
beasts, which was universal in Egypt; each
district having its own sacred animal,

adored as a manifestation or representative
of the local tutelary deity.

7. shall not a dog move his tongue] [A proverb expressive of freedom from alarm and
immunity from assault.]

XII. 1. This chapter was written some
time after the Exodus, probably when Moses
put together the portions of the book towards the end of his life. The statements
that these instructions were given in the
land of Egypt, and that they were given to
Moses and Aaron, are important : the one
marks the peculiar dignity of this ordinance, which was established before the
Sinaitic code ; the other marks the distinction between Moses and Aaron and all other
prophets. They alone were prophets of the
Law, i.e. no law was promulgated by any
other prophets.

2. This month] Abib (xiii. 4). It was called
by the later Hebrews Nisan, and corresponds nearly to our April. The Israelites
are directed to take Abib henceforth as the
beginning of the year ; the year previously
began with the month Tisri, when the harvest was gathered in ; see xxiii. 16. The injunction touching Abib or Nisan referred
only to religious rites; in other affairs
they retained the old arrangement, even in
the beginning of the Sabbatic year ; see
Levit. xxv. 9.

3. a lamb] The Hebrew word is general,

4 ing to the house of *their* fathers, a lamb for an house : and if the
household be too little for the lamb, let him and his neighbour
next unto his house take *it* according to the number of the souls ;
every man according to his eating shall make your count for the
5 lamb. Your lamb shall be *b*without blemish, a male [1]of the
first year : ye shall take *it* out from the sheep, or from the
6 goats : and ye shall keep it up until the *c*fourteenth day of the
same month : and the whole assembly of the congregation of
7 Israel shall kill it [2]in the evening. And they shall take of the
blood, and strike *it* on the two side posts and on the upper door
8 post of the houses, wherein they shall eat it. And they shall
eat the flesh in that night, roast with fire, and *d*unleavened
9 bread ; *and* with bitter *herbs* they shall eat it. Eat not of it raw,
nor sodden at all with water, but *e*roast *with* fire ; his head with

b Lev. 22.
19, 20, 21.
Mal. i. 8, 14.
Heb. 9. 14.
1 Pet. 1. 19.
c Lev. 23. 5.
Num. 9. 3.
& 28. 16.
Deut. 16.
1, 6.
d ch. 34. 25.
Num. 9. 11.
Deut. 16. 3.
1 Cor. 5. 8.
e Deut. 16. 7

[1] Heb. *son of a year*, Lev.
23. 12.

[2] Heb. *between the two
evenings*, ch. 16. 12.

---

meaning either a sheep or goat, male or female, and of any age ; the age and sex are
therefore specially defined in the following
verse. The direction to select the lamb on
the tenth day, the fourth day before it was
offered, was intended to secure due care in
the preparation for the great national festival. The custom certainly fell into desuetude at a later period, but probably not before the destruction of the Temple.

4. Tradition specifies ten as the least
number ; but the matter was probably left
altogether to the discretion of the heads of
families.

The last clause should be rendered :—
"each man according to his eating ye shall
count for the lamb."

5. *without blemish*] This is in accordance
with the general rule (marg. ref.) : although
in this case there is a special reason, since
the lamb was in place of the firstborn male
in each household. The restriction to the
first year is peculiar, and refers apparently
to the condition of perfect innocence in the
antitype, the Lamb of God.

6. *until the fourteenth day*] It should be
observed that the offering of our Lord on
the selfsame day is an important point in
determining the typical character of the
transaction. A remarkable passage in the
Talmud says : " It was a famous and old
opinion among the ancient Jews that the
day of the new year which was the beginning of the Israelites' deliverance out of
Egypt should in future time be the beginning of the redemption by the Messiah."

in the evening] The Hebrew has **between
the two evenings.** The meaning of the expression is disputed. The most probable
explanation is that it includes the time from
afternoon, or early eventide, until sunset.
This accords with the ancient custom of the
Hebrews, who slew the paschal lamb immediately after the offering of the daily sacrifice, which on the day of the Passover took
place a little earlier than usual, between
two and three p.m. This would allow about

two hours and a half for slaying and preparing all the lambs. It is clear that they
would not wait until sunset, at which time
the evening meal would take place. The
slaying of the lamb thus coincides exactly
with the death of our Saviour, at the ninth
hour of the day (Matt. xxvii. 46).

7. *the upper door post*] Or **lintel**, *v.* 23.
This direction was understood by the Hebrews to apply only to the first Passover :
it was certainly not adopted in Palestine.
The meaning of the sprinkling of blood is
hardly open to question. It was a representation of the offering of the life, substituted
for that of the firstborn in each house, as an
expiatory and vicarious sacrifice.

8. *in that night*] The night is thus clearly
distinguished from the evening when the
lamb was slain. It was slain before sunset,
on the 14th, and eaten after sunset, the beginning of the 15th.

with fire] Among various reasons given
for this injunction the most probable and
satisfactory seems to be the special sanctity
attached to fire from the first institution of
sacrifice (cp. Gen. iv. 4).

and unleavened bread] On account of the
hasty departure, allowing no time for the
process of leavening : but the meaning discerned by St. Paul, 1 Cor. v. 7, 8, and recognized by the Church in all ages, was assuredly implied, though not expressly declared in the original institution. Cp. our
Lord's words, Matt. xvi. 6, 12, as to the symbolism of leaven.

bitter herbs] The word occurs only here
and in Numbers ix. 11, in reference to herbs.
The symbolical reference to the previous
sufferings of the Israelites is generally admitted.

9. *raw*] i.e. "half-cooked."

sodden...with water] It was probably more
common to seethe than to roast meat; hence
the regrets expressed by the Israelites for
the seething pots of Egypt.

the purtenance thereof] or **its intestines.**
This verse directs that the lamb should be

f ch. 23. 18.
& 34. 25.

g Deut. 16. 5.
h ch. 11. 4, 5.
Amos 5. 17.

i Num. 33. 4.
k ch. 6. 2.
l ch. 13. 9.
m Lev. 23.
4, 5.
2 Kin. 23.
21.
n ver. 24, 43.
ch. 13. 10.
o ch. 13. 6, 7.
& 23. 15.
& 34. 18, 25.
Lev. 23. 5, 6.
Num. 28. 17.
Deut. 16.
3, 8.
1 Cor. 5. 7.

10 his legs, and with the purtenance thereof. *f*And ye shall let nothing of it remain until the morning; and that which remaineth 11 of it until the morning ye shall burn with fire. And thus shall ye eat it; *with* your loins girded,. your shoes on your feet, and your staff in your hand; and ye shall eat it in haste: *g*it *is* the LORD's 12 passover. ¶ For I *h*will pass through the land of Egypt this night, and will smite all the firstborn in the land of Egypt, both man and beast; and *i*against all the [1]gods of Egypt I will execute judg- 13 ment: *k*I am the LORD. And the blood shall be to you for a token upon the houses where ye *are:* and when I see the blood, I will pass over you, and the plague shall not be upon you [2]to destroy 14 *you*, when I smite the land of Egypt. ¶ And this day shall be unto you *l*for a memorial; and ye shall keep it a *m*feast to the LORD throughout your generations; ye shall keep it a feast *n*by an ordi- 15 nance for ever. *o*Seven days shall ye eat unleavened bread; even the first day ye shall put away leaven out of your houses: for whosoever eateth leavened bread from the first day until the

[1] Or, *princes*, ch. 21. 6. & 22. 28. Ps. 82. 1, 6. John 10. 34, 35.
[2] Heb. *for a destruction.*

roasted and placed on the table whole. No bone was to be broken (see *v.* 46, and marg. reff). The bowels were taken out, washed and then replaced. The Talmud prescribes the form of the oven of earthenware, in which the lamb was roasted, open above and below with a grating for the fire. Lambs and sheep are roasted whole in Persia, nearly in the same manner. This entire consumption of the lamb constitutes one marked difference between the Passover and all other sacrifices, in which either a part or the whole was burned, and thus offered directly to God. The whole substance of the sacrificed lamb was to enter into the substance of the people, the blood only excepted, which was sprinkled as a propitiatory and sacrificial offering. Another point of subordinate importance is noticed. The lamb was slain and the blood sprinkled by the head of each family: no separate priesthood as yet existed in Israel; its functions belonged from the beginning to the father of the family: when the priesthood was instituted the slaying of the lamb still devolved on the heads of families, though the blood was sprinkled on the altar by the priests; an act which essentially belonged to their office. The typical character of this part of the transaction is clear. Our Lord was offered and His blood shed as an expiatory and propitiatory sacrifice, but His whole Humanity is transfused spiritually and effectually into His Church, an effect which is at once symbolized and assured in Holy Communion, the Christian Passover.

10. This was afterwards a general law of sacrifices; at once preventing all possibility of profanity, and of superstitious abuse. The injunction is on both accounts justly applied by our Church to the Eucharist.

burn with fire] Not being consumed by

man, it was thus offered, like other sacrifices (*v.* 8), to God.

11. These instructions are understood by the Jews to apply only to the first Passover, when they belonged to the occasion. There is no trace of their observance at any later time. Each of the directions marks preparation for a journey; the long flowing robes are girded round the loins; shoes or sandals, not worn in the house or at meals, were fastened on the feet; and the traveller's staff was taken in hand.

the LORD's *passover*] The great and most significant name for the whole ordinance. The word Passover renders as nearly as possible the true meaning of the original, of which the primary sense is generally held to be " pass rapidly," like a bird with outstretched wings, but it undoubtedly includes the idea of sparing (*v.* 13). See Isaiah xxxi. 5, which combines the two great ideas involved in the word.

12. *I will pass through*] A word wholly distinct from that which means " pass over." The " passing through " was in judgment, the " passing over" in mercy.

against all the gods of Egypt] Cp. marg. ref. In smiting the firstborn of all living beings, man and beast, God smote the objects of Egyptian worship (cp. xii. 5).

14. *a memorial*] A commemorative and sacramental ordinance of perpetual obligation. As such it has ever been observed by the Hebrews. By the Christian it is spiritually observed; its full significance is recognized, and all that it foreshadowed is realized, in the Sacrament of Holy Communion.

15. *cut off*] The penalty inflicted on those who transgressed the command may be accounted for on the ground that it was an act of rebellion; but additional light is thrown upon it by the typical meaning assigned to leaven by our Lord, Matt. xvi. 6.

16 seventh day, [p]that soul shall be cut off from Israel. And in the first day there shall be [q]an holy convocation, and in the seventh day there shall be an holy convocation to you; no manner of work shall be done in them, save that which every [1]man must

17 eat, that only may be done of you. And ye shall observe the feast of unleavened bread; for [r]in this selfsame day have I brought your armies out of the land of Egypt: therefore shall ye observe this day in your generations by an ordinance for

18 ever. [s]In the first month, on the fourteenth day of the month at even, ye shall eat unleavened bread, until the one and twentieth

19 day of the month at even. [t]Seven days shall there be no leaven found in your houses: for whosoever eateth that which is leavened, [u]even that soul shall be cut off from the congregation of Israel,

20 whether he be a stranger, or born in the land. Ye shall eat nothing leavened; in all your habitations shall ye eat unleavened

21 bread. ¶Then Moses called for all the elders of Israel, and said unto them, [x]Draw out and take you a [2]lamb according to

22 your families, and kill the passover. [y]And ye shall take a bunch of hyssop, and dip it in the blood that is in the bason, and [z]strike the lintel and the two side posts with the blood that is in the bason; and none of you shall go out at the door of his

23 house until the morning. [a]For the LORD will pass through to smite the Egyptians; and when he seeth the blood upon the lintel, and on the two side posts, the LORD will pass over the door, and [b]will not suffer [c]the destroyer to come in unto your

24 houses to smite you. And ye shall observe this thing for an

25 ordinance to thee and to thy sons for ever. And it shall come to pass, when ye be come to the land which the LORD will give you, [d]according as he hath promised, that ye shall keep this

26 service. [e]And it shall come to pass, when your children shall say unto you, What mean ye by this service? That ye shall

27 say, [f]It is the sacrifice of the LORD's passover, who passed over the houses of the children of Israel in Egypt, when he smote

[1] Heb. soul.　　　　[2] Or, kid.

[p] Gen. 17. 14,
Num. 9. 13.
[q] Lev. 23. 7,
8.
Num. 28.
18, 25.

[r] ch. 13. 3.

[s] Lev. 23. 5.
Num. 28. 16.
[t] Ex. 23. 15.
& 34. 18.
Deut. 16. 3.
1 Cor. 5. 7, 8.
[u] Num. 9. 13.
[x] ver. 3.
Num. 9. 4.
Josh. 5. 10.
2 Kin. 23. 21.
Ezra 6. 20.
Matt. 26.
18, 19.
Mark 14.
12—16.
Luke 22.
7, &c.
[y] Heb. 11.
28.
[z] ver. 7.
[a] ver. 12, 13.
[b] Ezek. 9. 6.
Rev. 7. 3.
& 9. 4.
[c] 2 Sam. 24.
16.
1 Cor. 10. 10.
Heb. 11. 28.
[d] ch. 3. 8, 17.
[e] ch. 13. 8,
14.
Deut. 32. 7.
Josh. 4. 6.
Ps. 78. 6.
[f] ver. 11.

16. an holy convocation] An assembly called by proclamation for a religious solemnity. See Lev. xxiii. 2; Num. x. 2, 3. In the East the proclamation is made by the Muezzins from the minarets of the mosques.

save that, &c.] In this the observance of the festival differed from the Sabbath, when the preparation of food was prohibited. The same word for "work" is used here and in the 4th Commandment: it is very general, and includes all laborious occupation.

19. born in the land] A stranger or foreigner might be born in the land, but the word here used means "a native of the land," belonging to the country in virtue of descent, that descent being reckoned from Abraham, to whom Canaan was promised as a perpetual inheritance.

21. Draw out] i.e. draw the lamb from the fold and then take it to the house.

the passover] The word is here applied to the lamb; an important fact, marking the lamb as the sign and pledge of the exemption of the Israelites.

22. a bunch of hyssop] The species here designated does not appear to be the plant now bearing the name. It would seem to have been an aromatic plant, common in Palestine and near Mount Sinai, with a long straight stalk and leaves well adapted for the purpose of sprinkling.

bason] The rendering rests on good authority and gives a good sense: but the word means "threshold" in some other passages and in Egyptian, and is taken here in that sense by some Versions. If that rendering be correct it would imply that the lamb was slain on the threshold.

none...shall go out, &c.] There would be no safety outside the precincts protected by the blood of the lamb; a symbolism explained by the marg. reff.

27. It is the sacrifice of the LORD's passover] or This is the sacrifice of the Passover to Jehovah. The most formal and exact designation of the festival is thus given: but "the Passover" may mean either the act of God's mercy in sparing the Israelites, or the lamb which is offered in

g ch. 4. 31.
h Heb. 11.
28.
i ch. 11. 4.
k Num. 8. 17.
& 33. 4.
Ps. 78. 51.
& 135. 8.
& 136. 10.
l ch. 4. 23.
& 11. 5.
m ch. 11. 6.
Prov. 21. 13.
Amos 5. 17.
Jam. 2. 13.
n ch. 11. 1.
Ps. 105. 38.
o ch. 10. 9.
p ch. 10. 26.
q Gen. 27. 34.
r ch. 11. 8.
s. Gen. 20. 3.
t ch. 3. 22.
u ch. 3. 21.
x ch. 3. 22.
Ps. 105. 37.
y Num. 33.
3, 5.
z Gen. 47. 11.
a Gen. 12. 2.
& 46. 3.
ch. 38. 26.
Num. 1. 46.
& 11. 21.

the Egyptians, and delivered our houses. And the people *g*bowed
28 the head and worshipped. And the children of Israel went
away, and *h*did as the LORD had commanded Moses and Aaron,
29 so did they. ¶ *i*And it came to pass, that at midnight *k*the LORD
smote all the firstborn in the land of Egypt, *l*from the firstborn of
Pharaoh that sat on his throne unto the firstborn of the captive
30 that *was* in the ¹dungeon ; and all the firstborn of cattle. And
Pharaoh rose up in the night, he, and all his servants, and all
the Egyptians ; and there was a *m*great cry in Egypt ; for *there*
31 *was* not a house where *there was* not one dead. ¶ And *n*he called
for Moses and Aaron by night, and said, Rise up, *and* get you
forth from among my people, *o*both ye and the children of Israel ;
32 and go, serve the LORD, as ye have said. *p*Also take your flocks
and your herds, as ye have said, and be gone ; and *q*bless
33 me also. *r*And the Egyptians were urgent upon the people,
that they might send them out of the land in haste ; for they
34 said, *s*We *be* all dead *men*. And the people took their dough
before it was leavened, their ²kneadingtroughs being bound up
35 in their clothes upon their shoulders. And the children of Israel
did according to the word of Moses ; and they borrowed of the
36 Egyptians *t*jewels of silver, and jewels of gold, and raiment : *u*and
the LORD gave the people favour in the sight of the Egyptians,
so that they lent unto them *such things as they required*. And *x*they
37 spoiled the Egyptians. ¶ And *y*the children of Israel journeyed
from *z*Rameses to Succoth, about *a*six hundred thousand on foot

¹ Heb. *house of the pit.*   ² Or, *dough*, ch. 8. 3.

---

sacrifice : more probably the latter, as in
v. 21. This gives a clear sense to the expression "to Jehovah ; " the Passover-lamb
was a sacrifice offered to Jehovah by His
ordinance.

29. This plague is distinctly attributed
here and in *v.* 23 to the personal intervention of THE LORD ; but it is to be observed
that although the Lord Himself passed
through to smite the Egyptians, He employed the agency of "the destroyer"
(*v.* 23), in whom, in accordance with Heb.
xi. 28, all the Ancient Versions, and most
critics, recognize an Angel (cp. 2 Kings
xix. 35 ; 2 Sam. xxiv. 16).

32. *bless me also*] No words could shew
more strikingly the complete, though temporary, submission of Pharaoh.

34. *kneadingtroughs*] (Cp. marg. and
Deut. xxviii. 5). The troughs were probably small wooden bowls in which the cakes
when baked were preserved for use. The
Hebrews used their outer garment, or mantle, in the same way as the Bedouins at
present, who make a bag of the voluminous
folds of their burnous. See Ruth. iii. 15 ;
2 Kings iv. 39.

35. *borrowed*] "Asked of." See iii. 22
note.

36. *lent*] Or **gave**. The word in the Hebrew means simply "granted their request."
Whether the grant is made as a loan, or as
a gift, depends in every instance upon the
context. Here the word "spoiled" ought

to be regarded as conclusive that the grant
was a gift, a moderate remuneration for
long service, and a compensation for cruel
wrongs.

37. *Rameses*] See i. 11 note. Rameses
was evidently the place of general rendez-
vous, well adapted for that purpose as the
principal city of Goshen. The Israelites
were probably settled in considerable numbers in and about it. Pharaoh with his
army and court were at that time near the
frontier, and Rameses, where a large garrison was kept, was probably the place where
the last interview with Moses occurred.
The first part of the journey appears to
have followed the course of the ancient
canal. The site of Succoth cannot be exactly determined, but it lay about half-way
between Rameses and Etham (xiii. 20). The
name Succoth (*i.e.* "tents" or "booths" in
Hebrew), may have been given by the Israelites, but the same, or a similar word,
occurs in Egyptian in connection with the
district.

600,000] This includes all the males who
could march. The total number of the Israelites should therefore be calculated from
the males above twelve or fourteen, and
would therefore amount to somewhat more
than two millions. This is not an excessive
population for Goshen, nor does it exceed
a reasonable estimate of the increase of the
Israelites, including their numerous depen-
dants.

38 *that were* men, beside children. And ¹a mixed multitude went up also with them; and flocks, and herds, *even* very much cattle.
39 And they baked unleavened cakes of the dough which they brought forth out of Egypt, for it was not leavened; because *b*they were thrust out of Egypt, and could not tarry, neither had
40 they prepared for themselves any victual. ¶ Now the sojourning of the children of Israel, who dwelt in Egypt, *was* *c*four hundred
41 and thirty years. And it came to pass at the end of the four hundred and thirty years, even the selfsame day it came to pass, that all *d*the hosts of the LORD went out from the land of Egypt.
42 It *is* ²*e*a night to be much observed unto the LORD for bringing them out from the land of Egypt: this *is* that night of the LORD to be observed of all the children of Israel in their generations.
43 ¶ And the LORD said unto Moses and Aaron, This *is* *f*the ordi-
44 nance of the passover: There shall no stranger eat thereof: but every man's servant that is bought for money, when thou hast
45 *g*circumcised him, then shall he eat thereof. *h*A foreigner and
46 an hired servant shall not eat thereof. In one house shall it be eaten; thou shalt not carry forth ought of the flesh abroad out
47 of the house; *i*neither shall ye break a bone thereof. *k*All the
48 congregation of Israel shall ³keep it. And *l*when a stranger shall sojourn with thee, and will keep the passover to the LORD, let all his males be circumcised, and then let him come near and keep it; and he shall be as one that is born in the land: for no
49 uncircumcised person shall eat thereof. *m*One law shall be to him that is homeborn, and unto the stranger that sojourneth
50 among you. Thus did all the children of Israel; as the LORD
51 commanded Moses and Aaron, so did they. ¶ *n*And it came to pass the selfsame day, *that* the LORD did bring the children of Israel out of the land of Egypt *o*by their armies.

b ch. 6. 1.
& 11. 1.
ver. 33.
c Gen. 15. 13.
Acts 7. 6.
Gal. 3. 17.

d ch. 7. 4.

e See Deut. 16. 6.

f Num. 9. 14.

g Gen. 17. 12, 13.
h Lev. 22. 10.

i Num. 9. 12.
John 19. 33, 36.
k ver. 6.
Num. 9. 13.
l Num. 9. 14.

m Num. 9. 14.
& 15. 15, 16.
Gal. 3. 28.

n ver. 41.

o ch. 6. 26.

---

¹ Heb. *a great mixture.*
Num. 11. 4.　　² Heb. *a night of observations.*　　³ Heb. *do it.*

---

38. *a mixed multitude*] Probably remains of the old Semitic population, whether first brought into the district by the Hyksos or not is uncertain. As natural objects of suspicion and dislike to the Egyptians who had lately become masters of the country, they would be anxious to escape, the more especially after the calamities which preceded the Exodus.

very much cattle] This is an important fact, both as showing that the oppression of the Israelites had not extended to confiscation of their property, and as bearing upon the question of their maintenance in the Wilderness.

40. *who dwelt*] Read, **which they sojourned.** The obvious intention of Moses is to state the duration of the sojourn in Egypt.

43. *And the LORD said*] From this verse to xiii. 16 are instructions regarding the Passover. Such instructions were needed when the Israelites were joined by the "mixed multitude" of strangers; and they were probably given at Succoth, on the morning following the departure from Rameses.

no stranger] Lit. "son of a stranger." The

term is general; it includes all who were aliens from Israel, until they were incorporated into the nation by circumcision.

44. *servant*] The circumcision of the slave, thus enjoined formally on the first day that Israel became a nation, in accordance with the law given to Abraham, (see marg. ref.) made him a true member of the family, equally entitled to all religious privileges. In the household of a priest the slave was even permitted to eat the consecrated food: Lev. xxii. 11.

45. *A foreigner*] or **sojourner**: one who resides in a country, not having a permanent home, nor being attached to an Israelitish household.

46. *In one house*] i.e. "in one company." Each lamb was to be entirely consumed by the members of one company, whether they belonged to the same household or not.

break a bone] The typical significance of this injunction is recognized by St. John, (see marg. ref.) It is not easy to assign any other satisfactory reason for it. This victim alone was exempt from the general law by which the limbs were ordered to be separated from the body.

Chap. 13. AND the LORD spake unto Moses, saying, *a*Sanctify
2 unto me all the firstborn, whatsoever openeth the womb among
the children of Israel, both of man and of beast: it *is* mine.
3 ¶ And Moses said unto the people, *b*Remember this day, in which
ye came out from Egypt, out of the house of ¹bondage; for *c*by
strength of hand the LORD brought you out from this *place:*
4 *d*there shall no leavened bread be eaten. *e*This day came ye
5 out in the month Abib. And it shall be when the LORD shall
*f*bring thee into the land of the Canaanites, and the Hittites,
and the Amorites, and the Hivites, and the Jebusites, which he
*g*sware unto thy fathers to give thee, a land flowing with milk
and honey, *h*that thou shalt keep this service in this month.
6 *i*Seven days thou shalt eat unleavened bread, and in the seventh
7 day *shall be* a feast to the LORD. Unleavened bread shall be
eaten seven days; and there shall *k*no leavened bread be seen
with thee, neither shall there be leaven seen with thee in all thy
8 quarters. And thou shalt *l*shew thy son in that day, saying,
This is done because of that *which* the LORD did unto me when I
9 came forth out of Egypt. And it shall be for *m*a sign unto thee
upon thine hand, and for a memorial between thine eyes, that
the LORD's law may be in thy mouth: for with a strong hand
10 hath the LORD brought thee out of Egypt. *n*Thou shalt therefore
11 keep this ordinance in his season from year to year. ¶ And it
shall be when the LORD shall bring thee into the land of the Ca-
12 naanites, as he sware unto thee and to thy fathers, and shall
give it thee, *o*that thou shalt ²set apart unto the LORD all that
openeth the matrix, and every firstling that cometh of a beast
13 which thou hast; the males *shall be* the LORD's. And *p*every
firstling of an ass thou shalt redeem with a ³lamb; and if thou

¹ Heb. *servants.*   ² Heb. *cause to pass over.*   ³ Or, *kid.*

XIII. 2. *Sanctify unto me*] The command
is addressed to Moses. It was to declare
the will of God that all firstborn were to be
consecrated to Him, set apart from all other
creatures. The command is expressly based
upon the Passover. The firstborn exempt
from the destruction became in a new and
special sense the exclusive property of the
Lord : the firstborn of man as His ministers, the firstborn of cattle as victims. In
lieu of the firstborn of men the Levites were
devoted to the temple services.

4. *Abib*] April. Cp. xii. 2. It is uncertain
whether this name was ancient or given
then for the first time. It is found only in
the Pentateuch, six times as the name of the
first month, twice in the sense of young
wheat, hence its etymology, viz. the month
when the wheat began to ripen. The name
resembles the Egyptian Epiphi, and may
possibly have been derived from it.

5. *the Canaanites*] Five nations only are
named in this passage, whereas six are
named in iii. 8, and ten in the original promise to Abraham, Gen. xv. 19–21. The
first word Canaanite is generic, and includes
all the Hamite races of Palestine.

9. Hebrew writers have generally regarded this as a formal injunction to write
the precepts on slips of parchment, and to

fasten them on the wrists and forehead;
but other commentators are generally
agreed that it is to be understood metaphorically. The words appear to be put
into the mouths of the parents. They were
to keep all the facts of the Passover constantly in mind, and, referring to a custom
prevalent ages before Moses in Egypt, to
have them present as though they were inscribed on papyrus or parchment fastened
on the wrists, or on the face between the
eyes. If, as may be inferred from Deut.
vi. 7, 8, Moses adopted this custom, he
would take care to warn the people against
the Egyptian superstition of amulets. Modern Israelites generally allege this precept
as a justification for the use of phylacteries.

13. *an ass*] The ass could not be offered in
sacrifice, being an unclean animal :—possibly
the only unclean animal domesticated among
the Israelites at the time of the Exodus.
This principle was extended to every unclean beast ; see Num. xviii. 15.

thou shalt redeem] The lamb, or sheep, was
given to the priest for the service of the
Sanctuary.

firstborn of man] The price of redemption
was fixed at five shekels of the Sanctuary :
Num. iii. 47, where see note.

wilt not redeem it, then thou shalt break his neck: and all the
14 firstborn of man among thy children *q*shalt thou redeem. *r*And
it shall be when thy son asketh thee ¹in time to come, saying,
What *is* this? that thou shalt say unto him, *s*By strength of
hand the LORD brought us out from Egypt, from the house of
15 bondage: and it came to pass, when Pharaoh would hardly let
us go, that *t*the LORD slew all the firstborn in the land of Egypt,
both the firstborn of man, and the firstborn of beast: therefore
I sacrifice to the LORD all that openeth the matrix, being males;
16 but all the firstborn of my children I redeem. And it shall be
for *u*a token upon thine hand, and for frontlets between thine
eyes: for by strength of hand the LORD brought us forth out of
17 Egypt. ¶And it came to pass, when Pharaoh had let the people
go, that God led them not *through* the way of the land of the
Philistines, although that *was* near; for God said, Lest peradventure the people *x*repent when they see war, and *y*they return
18 to Egypt: but God *z*led the people about, *through* the way of the
wilderness of the Red sea: and the children of Israel went up
19 ²harnessed out of the land of Egypt. And Moses took the
bones of Joseph with him: for he had straitly sworn the children of Israel, saying, *a*God will surely visit you; and ye shall
20 carry up my bones away hence with you. And *b*they took
their journey from Succoth, and encamped in Etham, in the
21 edge of the wilderness. And *c*the LORD went before them by
day in a pillar of a cloud, to lead them the way; and by night
in a pillar of fire, to give them light; to go by day and night:
22 he took not away the pillar of the cloud by day, nor the pillar
of fire by night, *from* before the people.
CHAP. 14. AND the LORD spake unto Moses, saying, Speak unto
2 the children of Israel, *a*that they turn and encamp before *b*Pi-

¹ Heb. *to-morrow.*   ² Or, *by five in a rank.*

q Num. 3.
46, 47.
& 18. 15, 16.
r ch. 12. 26.
Deut. 6. 20.
Josh. 4. 6,
21.
s ver. 3.

t ch. 12. 29.

u ver. 9.
x ch. 14. 11,
12.
Num. 14.
1—4.
y Deut. 17.
16.
z ch. 14. 2.
Num. 33.
6, &c.
a Gen. 50.25.
Josh. 24. 32.
Acts 7. 16.
b Num. 33.6.
c ch. 14. 19,
24.
& 40. 38.
Num. 9. 15.
& 10. 34.
& 14. 14.
Deut. 1. 33.
Neh. 9. 12,
19.
Ps. 78. 14.
& 99. 7.
& 105. 39.
Isai. 4. 5.
1 Cor. 10. 1.
a ch. 13. 18.
b Num. 33. 7.

18. *harnessed*] More probably, "marshalled" or "in orderly array." There is not
the least indication that the Israelites had
been disarmed by the Egyptians, and as occupying a frontier district frequently assailed
by the nomads of the desert they would of
necessity be accustomed to the use of arms.
Cp. i. 10.

20. *Etham*] The house or "sanctuary of
Tum" (the Sun God worshipped specially by
that name in Lower Egypt), was in the immediate vicinity of Heliopolis, called by the
Egyptians the fortress of Zar, or Zalu (*i.e.*
of foreigners); the frontier city where the
Pharaohs of the 18th dynasty reviewed their
forces when about to enter upon a campaign
on Syria. The name Pithom (see i. 11) has
precisely the same meaning with Etham,
and may possibly be identified with it.

21. *pillar of cloud*] The Lord Himself did
for the Israelites by preternatural means
that which armies were obliged to do for
themselves by natural agents. The Persians
and Greeks used fire and smoke as signals
in their marches, and in a well-known papyrus, the commander of an Egyptian expedition is called "A flame in the darkness at
the head of his soldiers." By this sign then
of the pillar of cloud, the Lord showed Himself as their leader and general (xv. 3, 6).

XIV. 2. *That they turn*] *i.e.* away from
the wilderness, and go southwards, to the
west of the Bitter Lakes, which completely
separated them from the desert.

Pi-hahiroth] The place is generally identified with Ajrud, a fortress with a very
large well of good water, situate at the foot
of an elevation commanding the plain which
extends to Suez, at a distance of four leagues.
The journey from Etham might occupy two,
or even three days.

Migdol] A tower, or fort, the *Maktal* of
Egyptian monuments; it is probably to be
identified with Bir Suweis, about two miles
from Suez.

Baal-zephon] The name under which the
Phœnicians, who had a settlement in Lower
Egypt at a very ancient period, worshipped
their chief Deity. There can be no doubt it
was near Kolsum, or Suez. From the text
it is clear that the encampment of the Israelites extended over the plain from Pi-
hahiroth: their head-quarters being between
Bir Suweis and the sea opposite to Baal-
Zephon. At Ajrud the road branches off in
two directions, one leading to the wilderness
by a tract, now dry, but in the time of
Moses probably impassable (see next note);
the other leading to Suez, which was doubtless followed by the Israelites.

c Jer. 44. 1.

d Ps. 71. 11.

e ch. 4. 21.
& 7. 3.
f ch. 9. 16.
ver. 17, 18.
Rom. 9. 17,
22, 23.
g ch. 7. 5.
h Ps. 105. 25.

i ch. 15. 4.

k ver. 4.

l ch. 6. 1.
& 13. 9.
Num. 33. 3.
m ch. 15. 9.
Josh. 24. 6.

n Josh. 24. 7.
Neh. 9. 9.
Ps. 34. 17.
& 107. 6.
o Ps. 106. 7,
8.
p ch. 5. 21.
& 6. 9.

hahiroth, between cMigdol and the sea, over against Baal-3 zephon: before it shall ye encamp by the sea. For Pharaoh will say of the children of Israel, dThey *are* entangled in the 4 land, the wilderness hath shut them in. And eI will harden Pharaoh's heart, that he shall follow after them; and I fwill be honoured upon Pharaoh, and upon all his host; gthat the Egyptians may know that I *am* the LORD. And they did so. 5 ¶And it was told the king of Egypt that the people fled: and hthe heart of Pharaoh and of his servants was turned against the people, and they said, Why have we done this, that we 6 have let Israel go from serving us? And he made ready his 7 chariot, and took his people with him: and he took isix hundred chosen chariots, and all the chariots of Egypt, and captains over 8 every one of them. And the LORD khardened the heart of Pharaoh king of Egypt, and he pursued after the children of Israel: and lthe children of Israel went out with an high hand. 9 But the mEgyptians pursued after them, all the horses *and* chariots of Pharaoh, and his horsemen, and his army, and overtook them encamping by the sea, beside Pi-hahiroth, before Baal-10 zephon. ¶And when Pharaoh drew nigh, the children of Israel lifted up their eyes, and, behold, the Egyptians marched after them; and they were sore afraid: and the children of Israel 11 ncried out unto the LORD. oAnd they said unto Moses, Because *there were* no graves in Egypt, hast thou taken us away to die in the wilderness? Wherefore hast thou dealt thus with us, to carry 12 us forth out of Egypt? pIs not this the word that we did tell thee in Egypt, saying, Let us alone, that we may serve the Egyptians? For *it had been* better for us to serve the Egyptians,

---

3. *They are entangled,* &c.] The original intention of Moses was to go towards Palestine by the wilderness: when that purpose was changed by God's direction and they moved southwards, Pharaoh, on receiving information, was of course aware that they were completely shut in, since the waters of the Red Sea then extended to the Bitter Lakes. It is known that the Red Sea at some remote period extended considerably further towards the north than it does at present. In the time of Moses the water north of Kolsum joined the Bitter Lakes, though at present the constant accumulation of sand has covered the intervening space to the extent of 8000 to 10,000 yards.

5. *the people fled*] This was a natural inference from the change of direction, which indicated a determination to escape from Egypt. Up to the time when that information reached Pharaoh both he and his people understood that the Israelites would return after keeping a festival in the district adjoining Etham. From Etham the intelligence would be forwarded by the commander of the garrison to Rameses in less than a day, and the cavalry, a highly-disciplined force, would be ready for immediate departure.

7. *six hundred chosen chariots*] The Egyptian army comprised large numbers of chariots, each drawn by two horses, with two men, one bearing the shield and driving,

the other fully armed. The horses were thoroughbred, renowned for strength and spirit. Chariots are first represented on the monuments of the 18th dynasty. By "all the chariots of Egypt" we are to understand all that were stationed in Lower Egypt, most of them probably at Rameses and other frontier garrisons near the head-quarters of Pharaoh.

captains] The word (Shalishim, lit. third or thirtieth) may represent an Egyptian title. The king had about him a council of thirty, each of whom bore a title, Mapu, a "thirty man." The word occurs frequently in the books of Kings. David seems to have organized the Shalishim as a distinct corps (see 2 Sam. xxiii. 8 Heb.), retaining the old name, and adopting the Egyptian system.

9. *and his horsemen*] See *v.* 5.

11. *no graves in Egypt*] This bitter taunt was probably suggested by the vast extent of cemeteries in Egypt, which might not improperly be called the land of tombs.

12. *Let us alone*] This is a gross exaggeration, yet not without a semblance of truth: for although the Israelites welcomed the message of Moses at first, they gave way completely at the first serious trial. See the reference in margin. The whole passage foreshadows the conduct of the people in the wilderness.

13 than that we should die in the wilderness. And Moses said
unto the people, *q*Fear ye not, stand still, and see the salvation
of the LORD, which he will shew to you to day : ¹for the Egyptians whom ye have seen to day, ye shall see them again no more
14 for ever. *r*The LORD shall fight for you, and ye shall *s*hold your
15 peace. ¶And the LORD said unto Moses, Wherefore criest thou
unto me ? Speak unto the children of Israel, that they go for-
16 ward : but *t*lift thou up thy rod, and stretch out thine hand over
the sea, and divide it: and the children of Israel shall go on
17 dry *ground* through the midst of the sea. And I, behold, I will
*u*harden the hearts of the Egyptians, and they shall follow them:
and I will *x*get me honour upon Pharaoh, and upon all his host,
18 upon his chariots, and upon his horsemen. And the Egyptians
*y*shall know that I *am* the LORD, when I have gotten me honour
19 upon Pharaoh, upon his chariots, and upon his horsemen. ¶And
the angel of God, *z*which went before the camp of Israel, removed and went behind them ; and the pillar of the cloud went
20 from before their face, and stood behind them : and it came
between the camp of the Egyptians and the camp of Israel ; and
*a*it was a cloud and darkness *to them,* but it gave light by night
to these : so that the one came not near the other all the night.
21 And Moses *b*stretched out his hand over the sea ; and the
LORD caused the sea to go *back* by a strong east wind all that
night, and *c*made the sea dry *land,* and the waters were *d*divided.
22 And *e*the children of Israel went into the midst of the sea upon
the dry *ground :* and the waters *were f* a wall unto them on their
23 right hand, and on their left. ¶And the Egyptians pursued,
and went in after them to the midst of the sea, *even* all Pharaoh's
24 horses, his chariots, and his horsemen. And it came to pass,
that in the morning watch *g*the LORD looked unto the host of
the Egyptians through the pillar of fire and of the cloud, and
25 troubled the host of the Egyptians, and took off their chariot
wheels, ²that they drave them heavily : so that the Egyptians
said, Let us flee from the face of Israel ; for the LORD *h*fighteth
26 for them against the Egyptians. And the LORD said unto Moses,
*i*Stretch out thine hand over the sea, that the waters may come
again upon the Egyptians, upon their chariots, and upon their
27 horsemen. And Moses stretched forth his hand over the sea, and

q 2 Chr. 20.
15, 17.
Isai. 41. 10,
13, 14.

r ver. 25.
Deut. 1. 30.
Josh. 10.
14, 42.
2 Chr. 20. 29.
Neh. 4. 20.
Isai. 31. 4.
s Isai. 30. 15.
t ver. 21. 26.
u ver. 8.
ch. 7. 3.
x ver. 4.

y yer. 4.

z ch. 13. 21.
& 23. 20.
& 32. 34.
Num. 20. 16.
Isai. 63. 9.
a See Isai.
8. 14.
2 Cor. 4. 3.
b ver. 16.

c Ps. 66. 6.
d ch. 15. 8.
Josh. 3. 16.
& 4. 23.
Neh. 9. 11.
Ps. 74. 13.
& 106. 9.
& 114. 3.
e ver. 29.
Num. 33. 8.
Ps. 66. 6.
& 78. 13.
Isai. 63. 13.
1 Cor. 10. 1.
Heb. 11. 29.
f Hab. 3. 10.
g See Ps. 77.
17, &c.
h ver. 14.
i ver. 16.

¹ Or, *for whereas ye have
seen the Egyptians to
day, &c.*

² Or, *and made them to go
heavily.*

---

13. *for the Egyptians whom,* &c.] The true
sense is, ye shall never see the Egyptians
in the same way, under the same circumstances.

15. *Wherefore criest thou unto me ?*] Moses
does not speak of his intercession, and we only
know of it from this answer to his prayer.

19. *the angel of God*] Cp. marg. reff. and
see iii. 2.

21. *a strong east wind*] The agency by
which the object effected was natural (cp.
xv. 8 note) : and the conditions of the narrative are satisfied by the hypothesis, that the
passage took place near Suez.

the waters were divided] i.e. there was a
complete separation between the water of
the gulf and the water to the north of Kolsum.

22. *were a wall unto them*] Cp. Nahum
iii. 8. The waters served the purpose of an

intrenchment and wall ; the people could
not be attacked on either flank during the
transit ; to the north was the water covering
the whole district ; to the south was the Red
Sea.

24. *in the morning watch*] At sunrise, a
little before 6 A.M. in April.

troubled] By a sudden panic.

26. *that the waters may come*] A sudden
cessation of the wind, possibly coinciding
with a spring tide (it was full moon) would
immediately convert the low flat sand-banks
first into a quicksand, and then into a mass
of waters, in a time far less than would suffice for the escape of a single chariot, or
horseman loaded with heavy corslet.

27. *overthrew the Egyptians*] Better as in
the margin, **The Lord shook them off,**
hurled them from their chariots into the sea.

the sea *k*returned to his strength when the morning appeared; and the Egyptians fled against it; and the LORD *l*¹overthrew 28 the Egyptians in the midst of the sea. And *m*the waters returned, and *n*covered the chariots, and the horsemen, *and* all the host of Pharaoh that came into the sea after them; there re- 29 mained not so much as one of them. But *o*the children of Israel walked upon dry *land* in the midst of the sea; and the waters *were* a wall unto them on their right hand, and on their left. 30 ¶Thus the LORD *p*saved Israel that day out of the hand of the Egyptians; and Israel *q*saw the Egyptians dead upon the sea 31 shore. And Israel saw that great ²work which the LORD did upon the Egyptians: and the people feared the LORD, and *r*believed the LORD, and his servant Moses.

CHAP. 15. THEN sang *a*Moses and the children of Israel this song unto the LORD, and spake, saying,
  I will *b*sing unto the LORD, for he hath triumphed gloriously:
  The horse and his rider hath he thrown into the sea.
2* The LORD *is* my strength and *c*song,
  And he is become my salvation:
  He *is* my God, and I will prepare him *d*an habitation;
  My *e*father's God, and I *f*will exalt him.
3 The LORD *is* a man of *g*war:
  The LORD *is* his *h*name.
4 *i*Pharaoh's chariots and his host hath he cast into the sea:

1 Heb. *shook off*, Deut. 11. 4.   Neh. 9. 11.   Ps. 78. 53.   Heb. 11. 29.
² Heb. *hand*.

---

28. *not so much as one of them*] Escape would be impossible (*v.* 26). Pharaoh's destruction, independent of the distinct statement of the Psalmist, Ps. cxxxvi. 15, was in fact inevitable. The station of the king was in the vanguard : on every monument the Pharaoh is represented as the leader of the army. The death of the Pharaoh, and the entire loss of the chariotry and cavalry accounts for the undisturbed retreat of the Israelites through a district then subject to Egypt and easily accessible to their forces. If, as appears probable, Tothmosis II. was the Pharaoh, the first recorded expedition into the Peninsula took place 17 years after his death ; and 22 years elapsed before any measures were taken to recover the lost ascendancy of Egypt in Syria. So complete, so marvellous was the deliverance : thus the Israelites were "baptized unto Moses in the cloud and in the sea" (1 Cor. x. 2). When they left Baal-Zephon they were separated finally from the idolatry of Egypt : when they passed the Red Sea their independence of its power was sealed ; their life as a nation then began, a life inseparable henceforth from belief in Jehovah and His servant Moses, only to be merged in the higher life revealed by His Son.

XV. 1—18. With the deliverance of Israel is associated the development of the national poetry, which finds its first and perfect expression in this magnificent hymn. It was sung by Moses and the people, an expression which evidently points to him as the author. That it was written at the time is an assertion expressly made in the text, and it is supported by the strongest internal evidence. In every age this song gave the tone to the poetry of Israel ; especially at great critical epochs of deliverance : and in the book of Revelation (xv. 3) it is associated with the final triumph of the Church. The division of the song into three parts is distinctly marked : 1–5, 6–10, 11–18 : each begins with an ascription of praise to God ; each increases in length and varied imagery unto the triumphant close.

1. *He hath triumphed gloriously*] Lit. He is gloriously great.

the horse and his rider] The word "rider" may include horseman, but applies properly to the charioteer.

2. *The LORD is my strength and song*] My strength and song is Jah. See Ps. lxviii. 4. The name was chosen here by Moses to draw attention to the promise ratified by the name "I am."

I will prepare Him an habitation] I will glorify Him. Our Authorised Version is open to serious objection, as suggesting a thought (viz. of erecting a temple) which could hardly have been in the mind of Moses at that time, and unsuited to the occasion.

3. *a man of war*] Cp. Ps. xxiv. 8. The name has on this occasion a peculiar fitness : man had no part in the victory ; the battle was the Lord's.

the LORD is his name] " Jah is His name."
See *v.* 2.

4. *hath He cast*] " Hurled," as from a sling. See xiv. 27.

k His chosen captains also are drowned in the Red sea.
5 *l* The depths have covered them :
m They sank into the bottom as a stone.
6 *n* Thy right hand, O LORD, is become glorious in power :
Thy right hand, O LORD, hath dashed in pieces the enemy.
7 And in the greatness of thine *o* excellency thou hast overthrown them that rose up against thee :
Thou sentest forth thy wrath, *which* *p* consumed them *q* as
stubble.
8 And *r* with the blast of thy nostrils the waters were gathered
together,
s The floods stood upright as an heap,
And the depths were congealed in the heart of the sea.
9 *t* The enemy said, I will pursue, I will overtake, I will *u* divide
the spoil ;
My lust shall be satisfied upon them ;
I will draw my sword, my hand shall [1] destroy them.
10 Thou didst *x* blow with thy wind, *y* the sea covered them :
They sank as lead in the mighty waters.
11 *z* Who *is* like unto thee, O LORD, among the [2] gods ?
Who *is* like thee, *a* glorious in holiness, fearful *in* praises,
b doing wonders ?
12 Thou stretchedst out *c* thy right hand,
The earth swallowed them.
13 Thou in thy mercy hast *d* led forth the people *which* thou
hast redeemed :
Thou hast guided *them* in thy strength unto *e* thy holy habitation.
14 *f* The people shall hear, *and* be afraid :
g Sorrow shall take hold on the inhabitants of Palestina.

[1] Or, *repossess.*   [2] Or, *mighty ones ?*

k ch. 14. 7.
l ch. 14. 28.
m Neh. 9. 11.
n Ps. 118.
15, 16.
o Deut. 33.
26.
p Ps. 59. 13.
q Isai. 5. 24.
& 47. 14.
r ch. 14. 21.
2 Sam. 22.
16.
Job 4. 9.
2 Thess. 2. 8.
s Ps. 78. 13.
Hab. 3. 10.
t Judg. 5. 30.
u Gen. 49. 27.
Isai. 53. 12.
Luke 11. 22.
x ch. 14. 21.
Ps. 147. 18.
y ver. 5.
ch. 14. 28.
z 2 Sam. 7.
22.
1 Kin. 8. 23.
Ps. 71. 19.
Jer. 10. 6.
a Isai. 6. 3.
b Ps. 77. 14.
c ver. 6.
d Ps. 77. 15.
Is. 63. 12, 13.
Jer. 2. 6.
e Ps. 78. 54.
f Num. 14.
14.
Deut. 2. 25.
Josh. 2. 9.
g Ps. 48. 6.

his chosen captains] See xiv. 7 note.
5. *as a stone*] The warriors in chariots are always represented on the monuments with heavy coats of mail; the corslets of "chosen captains" consisted of plates of highly tempered bronze, with sleeves reaching nearly to the elbow, covering the whole body and the thighs nearly to the knee. The wearers must have sunk at once like a stone, or as we read in *v.* 10, like lumps of lead.
7. *thy wrath*] Lit. Thy burning, *i.e.* the fire of Thy wrath, a word chosen expressly with reference to the effect.
8. The blast of God's nostrils corresponds to the natural agency, the east wind (xiv. 21), which drove the waters back : on the north the waters rose high, overhanging the sands, but kept back by the strong wind : on the south they laid in massive rollers, kept down by the same agency in the deep bed of the Red Sea.
9. *The enemy said*] The abrupt, gasping utterances;—the haste, cupidity and ferocity of the Egyptians;—the confusion and disorder of their thoughts, belong to the highest order of poetry. They enable us to realize the feelings which induced Pharaoh and his host to pursue the Israelites over the treacherous sandbanks.

10. *Thou didst blow with thy wind*] Notice the solemn majesty of these few words, in immediate contrast with the tumult and confusion of the preceding verse. In xiv. 28, we read only, "the waters returned," here we are told that it was because the wind blew. A sudden change in the direction of the wind would bring back at once the masses of water heaped up on the north.
they sank as lead] See note on *v.* 5.
11. *among the gods*] Cp. Ps. lxxxvi. 8, Deut. xxxii. 16, 17. A Hebrew just leaving the land in which Polytheism attained its highest development, with gigantic statues and temples of incomparable grandeur, might well on such an occasion dwell upon this consummation of the long series of triumphs by which the "greatness beyond compare" of Jehovah was once for all established.
13. *thy holy habitation*] Either Palestine, regarded as the land of promise, sanctified by manifestations of God to the Patriarchs, and destined to be both the home of God's people, and the place where His glory and purposes were to be perfectly revealed : or Mount Moriah.
14. *the inhabitants of Palestina*] *i.e.* the country of the Philistines. They were the first who would expect an invasion, and the

h Gen. 36. 40.
i Deut. 2. 4.
k Num. 22. 3.
Hab. 3. 7.
l Josh. 5. 1.
m Deut. 2.
25.
Josh. 2. 9.
n 1 Sam. 25.
37.
o ch. 19. 5.
Ps. 74. 2.
Isai. 43. 1.
Jer. 31. 11.
Tit. 2. 14.
1 Pet. 2. 9.
p Ps. 44. 2.
q Ps. 78. 54.
r Ps. 10. 16.
& 29. 10.
& 146. 10.
Isai. 57. 15.
s ch. 14. 23.
Prov. 21. 31.
t ch. 14. 28.
u Judg. 4. 4.
1 Sam. 10. 5.
x Num. 26.
59.
y 1 Sam. 18.
6.
z Ps. 68. 11.
a 1 Sam. 18.
7.
b ver. 1.
c Gen. 16. 7.

15 *h*Then *i*the dukes of Edom shall be amazed;
*k*The mighty men of Moab, trembling shall take hold upon
     them;
*l*All the inhabitants of Canaan shall melt away.

16 *m*Fear and dread shall fall upon them;
By the greatness of thine arm they shall be *as* still *n*as a stone;
Till thy people pass over, O LORD, till the people pass over,
     o which thou hast purchased.

17 Thou shalt bring them in, and *p*plant them in the mountain
     of thine inheritance,
In the place, O LORD, *which* thou hast made for thee to
     dwell in,
In the *q*sanctuary, O LORD, *which* thy hands have es-
     tablished.

18   *r*The LORD shall reign for ever and ever.

19 For the *s*horse of Pharaoh went in with his chariots and with
     his horsemen into the sea, and *t*the LORD brought again the
     waters of the sea upon them; but the children of Israel went on

20 dry *land* in the midst of the sea. ¶ And Miriam *u*the prophetess,
     *x*the sister of Aaron, *y*took a timbrel in her hand; and all the

21 women went out after her *z*with timbrels and with dances. And
     Miriam *a*answered them,
     *b*Sing ye to the LORD, for he hath triumphed gloriously;
     The horse and his rider hath he thrown into the sea.

22 ¶ So Moses brought Israel from the Red sea, and they went out
     into the wilderness of *c*Shur; and they went three days in the

---

first whose district would have been invaded
but for the faintheartedness of the Israelites.
15. *the dukes of Edom*] See Gen. xxxvi. 15.
It denotes the chieftains, not the kings of
Edom.
the mighty men of Moab] The physical
strength and great stature of the Moabites are
noted in other passages : see Jer. xlviii. 29, 41.
Canaan] The name in this, as in many
passages of Genesis, designates the whole of
Palestine : and is used of course with reference to the promise to Abraham. It was
known to the Egyptians, and occurs frequently on the monuments as Pa-kanana,
which applies, if not to the whole of Palestine, yet to the northern district under Lebanon, which the Phœnicians occupied and
called Canaan.
17. *in the mountain of thine inheritance*]
See *v.* 13.
19. *For the horse*, &c.] This verse does not
belong to the hymn, but marks the transition from it to the narrative.
20. *And Miriam the prophetess*] The part
here assigned to Miriam and the women of
Israel is in accordance both with Egyptian
and Hebrew customs. The men are represented as singing the hymn in chorus, under
the guidance of Moses ; at each interval
Miriam and the women sang the refrain,
marking the time with the timbrel, and with
the measured rhythmical movements always
associated with solemn festivities. Compare
Judg. xi. 34, 2 Sam. vi. 5, and marg. reff.
The word used in this passage for the

timbrel is Egyptian, and judging from its
etymology and the figures which are joined
with it in the inscriptions, it was probably
the round instrument.
Miriam is called a prophetess, evidently
(Numbers xii. 2) because she and Aaron had
received divine communications. The word
is used here in its proper sense of uttering
words suggested by the Spirit of God. See
Genesis xx. 7. She is called the sister of
Aaron, most probably to indicate her special
position as co-ordinate, not with Moses the
leader of the nation, but with his chief aid
and instrument.
22. *So Moses*] Lit. **And Moses.** The history
of the journey from the Red Sea to Sinai
begins in fact with this verse, which would
more conveniently have been the commencement of another chapter.
from the Red sea] The station where Moses
and his people halted to celebrate their deliverance is generally admitted to be the
Ayoun Musa, *i.e.* the fountains of Moses.
It is the only green spot near the passage
over the Red Sea. There are several wells
there, which in the time of Moses were probably enclosed and kept with great care by
the Egyptians, for the use of the frequent
convoys to and from their ancient settlements
at Sarbut el Khadem and the Wady Mughara.
the wilderness of Shur] This name belongs
to the whole district between the north-
eastern frontier of Egypt and Palestine.
The word is undoubtedly Egyptian, and
is derived probably from the word Khar,

23 wilderness, and found no water. And when they came to ^dMarah,   ^d Num. 33. 8.
they could not drink of the waters of Marah, for they *were*
24 bitter: therefore the name of it was called ¹Marah. And the
people ^emurmured against Moses, saying, What shall we drink?   ^e ch. 16. 2.
25 And he ^fcried unto the LORD; and the LORD shewed him a tree,   ^f ch. 14. 10.
^g*which* when he had cast into the waters, the waters were made   ^g See 2 Kin.
sweet: there he ^hmade for them a statute and an ordinance,   ^h See Josh.
26 and there ⁱhe proved them, and said, ^kIf thou wilt diligently   24. 25.
hearken to the voice of the LORD thy God, and wilt do that   ⁱ ch. 16. 4.
which is right in his sight, and wilt give ear to his command-   Judg. 2. 22.
ments, and keep all his statutes, I will put none of these ^ldis-   Ps. 66. 10.
eases upon thee, which I have brought upon the Egyptians: for   ^k Deut. 7.
27 I *am* the LORD ^mthat healeth thee. ¶ⁿAnd they came to Elim,   12, 15.
where *were* twelve wells of water, and threescore and ten palm   27, 60.
trees: and they encamped there by the waters.   Ps. 41. 3, 4.

CHAP. 16. AND they took ^atheir journey from Elim, and all the   ⁿ Num. 33. 9.
congregation of the children of Israel came unto the wilderness   10, 11.
of ^bSin, which *is* between Elim and Sinai, on the fifteenth day   ^b Ezek. 30.
of the second month after their departing out of the land of   15.
2 Egypt. And the whole congregation of the children of Israel
3 ^cmurmured against Moses and Aaron in the wilderness: and the   ^c ch. 15. 24.
children of Israel said unto them, ^dWould to God we had died   Ps. 106. 25.
by the hand of the LORD in the land of Egypt, ^ewhen we sat by   1 Cor. 10. 10.
the flesh pots, *and* when we did eat bread to the full; for ye   ^e Num. 11.
have brought us forth into this wilderness, to kill this whole   4, 5.
4 assembly with hunger. ¶Then said the LORD unto Moses,
Behold, I will rain ^fbread from heaven for you; and the people   ^f Ps. 78. 24.
shall go out and gather ²a certain rate every day, that I may   John 6. 31.
5 ^gprove them, whether they will walk in my law, or no. And it   1 Cor. 10. 3.
shall come to pass, that on the sixth day they shall prepare *that*   ^g ch. 15. 25.

¹ That is, *Bitterness*, Ruth   ² Heb. *the portion of a day*
1. 20.   *in his day*, Prov. 30. 8.
     Matt. 6. 11.

---

which designated all the country between
Egypt and Syria proper.

three days] The distance between Ayoun
Musa and Huwara, the first spot where any
water is found on the route, is 33 geographical miles. The whole district is a tract
of sand, or rough gravel.

23. *Marah*] Now identified with the fount
of Huwara. The fountain rises from a large
mound, a whitish petrifaction, deposited by
the water, and is considered by the Arabians
to be the worst in the whole district.

25. *a tree*, &c.] The statement points to a
natural agency, but the result was manifestly
supernatural.

he made, &c.] The Lord then set before them the fundamental principle of im-
plicit trust, to be shown by obedience. The
healing of the water was a symbol of deliverance from physical and spiritual evils.

27. *Elim*] The valley of Gharandel, two
hours' journey south of Huwara.

twelve wells] Read **springs**; the Hebrew
denotes natural sources. These springs may
have been perennial when a richer vegetation clothed the adjacent heights.

XVI. 1. *the wilderness of Sin*] The desert
tract, called Debbet er Ramleh, extends

nearly across the peninsula from the Wady
Nasb in a south-easterly direction, between
the limestone district of Et Tih and the
granite of Sinai. The journey from the
station at Elim, or even from that on the
Red Sea, could be performed in a day: at
that time the route was kept in good condition by the Egyptians.

2. *murmured*] The want of food was first
felt after six weeks from the time of the
departure from Egypt, see *v.* 1: we have no
notice previously of any deficiency of bread.

3. *by the hand of the* LORD] This evidently
refers to the plagues, especially the last, in
Egypt: the death which befell the Egyptians appeared to the people preferable to
the sufferings of famine.

flesh pots, and...bread] These expressions
prove that the servile labours to which they
had been subjected did not involve privations: they were fed abundantly, either by
the officials of Pharaoh, or more probably
by the produce of their own fertile district.

4. *that I may prove them*] The trial consisted in the restriction to the supply of
their daily wants.

5. *it shall be twice as much*] They should
collect and prepare a double quantity.

h See ver. 22.
Lev. 25. 21.
i See ver.
12, 13.
& ch. 6. 7.
Num. 16.
28, 29, 30.
k See ver.10.
Isai. 35. 2.
& 40. 5.
John 11. 4,
40.
l Num. 16.
11.
m See 1
Sam. 8. 7.
Luke 10. 16.
Rom. 13. 2.
n Num. 16.
16.
o ver. 7.
ch. 13. 21.
1 Kin. 8.
10, 11.
p ver. 8.
q ver. 6.
r ver. 7.
s Num.·11.
31.
Ps. 78. 27.
& 105. 40.
t Num. 11. 9.
u Num. 11.7.
Deut. 8. 3.
Neh. 9. 15.
Ps. 78. 24.
x John 6.
31, 49, 58.
1 Cor. 10. 3.
y ver. 36.

which they bring in; and ᴴit shall be twice as much as they
6 gather daily. ¶ And Moses and Aaron said unto all the children
of Israel, ⁱAt even, then ye shall know that the LORD hath brought
7 you out from the land of Egypt: and in the morning, then ye
shall see ᵏthe glory of the LORD; for that he heareth your murmurings against the LORD: and ˡwhat are we, that ye murmur
8 against us? And Moses said, This shall be, when the LORD
shall give you in the evening flesh to eat, and in the morning
bread to the full; for that the LORD heareth your murmurings
which ye murmur against him: and what are we? Your mur-
9 murings are not against us, but ᵐagainst the LORD. And Moses
spake unto Aaron, Say unto all the congregation of the children
of Israel, ⁿCome near before the LORD: for he hath heard your
10 murmurings. And it came to pass, as Aaron spake unto the
whole congregation of the children of Israel, that they looked
toward the wilderness, and, behold, the glory of the LORD ᵒap-
11 peared in the cloud. And the LORD spake unto Moses, saying,
12 ᵖI have heard the murmurings of the children of Israel: speak
unto them, saying, ᑫAt even ye shall eat flesh, and ʳin the morning ye shall be filled with bread; and ye shall know that I am
13 the LORD your God. ¶And it came to pass, that at even ˢthe
quails came up, and covered the camp: and in the morning ᵗthe
14 dew lay round about the host. And when the dew that lay was
gone up, behold, upon the face of the wilderness there lay ᵘa small
15 round thing, as small as the hoar frost on the ground. And when
the children of Israel saw it, they said one to another, ¹It is
manna: for they wist not what it was. And Moses said unto
them, ˣThis is the bread which the LORD hath given you to eat.
16 This is the thing which the LORD hath commanded, Gather of it
every man according to his eating, ʸan omer ²for every man,
according to the number of your ³persons; take ye every man

¹ Or, What is this? or, It ² Heb. by the poll, or, ³ Heb. souls.
is a portion. head.

---

7. the glory of the LORD] the visible appearance described in v. 10.
10. appeared in the cloud] Or, "was seen
in a cloud." The definite article would imply that the cloud was the same which is
often mentioned in connection with the tabernacle. The people saw the cloud here
spoken of beyond the camp.
13. quails] This bird migrates in immense
numbers in spring from the south: it is nowhere more common than in the neighbourhood of the Red Sea. In this passage we
read of a single flight so dense that it covered the encampment. The miracle consisted in the precise time of the arrival and
its coincidence with the announcement.
15. It is manna] "Man" or "man-hut,"
i.e. white manna, was the name under which
the substance was known to the Egyptians,
and therefore to the Israelites. The manna
of the Peninsula of Sinai is the sweet juice
of the Tarfa, a species of tamarisk. It ex-
udes from the trunk and branches in hot
weather, and forms small round white
grains. In cold weather it preserves its
consistency, in hot weather it melts rapidly.
It is either gathered from the twigs of the

tamarisk, or from the fallen leaves underneath the tree. The colour is a greyish yellow. It begins to exude in May, and lasts
about six weeks. According to Ehrenberg
it is produced by the puncture of an insect.
It is abundant in rainy seasons, many years
it ceases altogether. The whole quantity
now produced in a single year does not exceed 600 or 700 pounds. It is found in the
district between the Wady Gharandel, i.e.
Elim, and Sinai, in the Wady Sheikh, and
in some other parts of the Peninsula. When
therefore the Israelites saw the "small
round thing," they said at once "this is
manna," but with an exclamation of surprise at finding it, not under the tamarisk
tree, but on the open plain, in such immense
quantities, under circumstances so unlike
what they could have expected: in fact they
did not know what it really was, only what
it resembled.
16. an omer] i.e. the tenth part of an
Ephah, see v. 36. The exact quantity cannot
be determined, since the measures varied at
different times. Josephus makes the omer
equal to six half-pints. The ephah was an
Egyptian measure, supposed to be about a

17 for *them* which *are* in his tents. And the children of Israel did
18 so, and gathered, some more, some less. And when they did
mete *it* with an omer, *he that gathered much had nothing over, *z* 2 Cor. 8. 15.
and he that gathered little had no lack; they gathered every
19 man according to his eating. And Moses said, Let no man leave
20 of it till the morning. Notwithstanding they hearkened not
unto Moses; but some of them left of it until the morning, and
it bred worms, and stank: and Moses was wroth with them.
21 And they gathered it every morning, every man according to
22 his eating: and when the sun waxed hot, it melted. ¶And it
came to pass, *that* on the sixth day they gathered twice as much
bread, two omers for one *man:* and all the rulers of the congre-
23 gation came and told Moses. And he said unto them, This *is*
that which the LORD hath said, To morrow *is* *a*the rest of the *a* Gen. 2. 3.
holy sabbath unto the LORD: bake *that* which ye will bake *to* ch. 20. 8.
day*, and seethe that ye will seethe; and that which remaineth & 35. 3.
24 over lay up for you to be kept until the morning. And they Lev. 23. 3.
laid it up till the morning, as Moses bade: and it did not *b*stink, *b* ver. 20.
25 neither was there any worm therein. And Moses said, Eat that
to day; for to day *is* a sabbath unto the LORD: to day ye shall
26 not find it in the field. *c*Six days ye shall gather it; but on the *c* ch. 20. 9.
seventh day, *which is* the sabbath, in it there shall be none.
27 And it came to pass, *that* there went out *some* of the people on
28 the seventh day for to gather, and they found none. And the *d* 2 Kin. 17.
LORD said unto Moses, How long *d*refuse ye to keep my com- 14.
29 mandments and my laws? See, for that the LORD hath given Ps. 78. 10,
22. & 106. 13.

bushel or one-third of a hin. The word
omer, in this sense, occurs in no other passage. It was probably not used at a later
period, belonging, like many other words,
to the time of Moses. It is found in old
Egyptian. See Lev. xix. 36.
17. *some more, some less*] It is evidently
implied that the people were in part at least
disobedient and failed in this first trial.
18. *had nothing over*] Whatever quantity
each person had gathered, when he measured
it in his tent, he found that he had just as
many omers as he needed for the consumption of his family.
20. *it bred worms*] This result was supernatural : no such tendency to rapid decom-
position is recorded of common manna.
21. *it melted*] This refers to the manna
which was not gathered.
22. *twice as much bread*] See *v.* 5.
From this passage and from *v.* 5 it is inferred that the seventh day was previously
known to the people as a day separate from
all others, and if so, it must have been
observed as an ancient and primeval institution.
23. *To-morrow,* &c.] Or, **To-morrow is a
rest, a Sabbath holy to Jehovah:** *i.e.* to-
morrow must be a day of rest, observed
strictly as a Sabbath, or festal rest, holy to
Jehovah.
bake, &c.] These directions shew that the
manna thus given differed essentially from
the natural product. Here and in Numbers
xi. 8 it is treated in a way which shews that it

had the property of corn, could be ground
in a mortar, baked and boiled. Ordinary
manna is used as honey, it cannot be
ground, and it melts when exposed to a moderate heat, forming a substance like barley
sugar, called "manna tabulata." In Persia
it is boiled with water and brought to the consistency of honey. The Arabs also boil the
leaves to which it adheres, and the manna
thus dissolved floats on the water as a glu-
tinous or oily substance. It is obvious that
these accounts are inapplicable to the manna
from heaven, which had the characteristics
and nutritive properties of bread.
25. *Eat that to day*] The practical observance of the Sabbath was thus formally instituted before the giving of the Law. The
people were to abstain from the ordinary
work of every-day life : they were not to
collect food, nor, as it would seem, even to
prepare it as on other days.
27. *there went out some of the people*] This
was an act of wilful disobedience. It is remarkable, being the first violation of the
express command, that it was not visited by
a signal chastisement: the rest and peace of
the "Holy Sabbath" were not disturbed by
a manifestation of wrath.
28. *How long*] The reference to *v.* 4 is obvious. The prohibition involved a trial of
faith, in which as usual the people were
found wanting. Every miracle formed
some part, so to speak, of an educational
process.
29. *abide ye every man in his place*] The

you the sabbath, therefore he giveth you on the sixth day the
bread of two days; abide ye every man in his place, let no man
30 go out of his place on the seventh day. So the people rested on
31 the seventh day. And the house of Israel called the name
thereof Manna: and *it was* like coriander seed, white; and the
32 taste of it *was* like wafers *made* with honey. ¶ And Moses said,
This *is* the thing which the LORD commandeth, Fill an omer of
it to be kept for your generations; that they may see the bread
wherewith I have fed you in the wilderness, when I brought
33 you forth from the land of Egypt. And Moses said unto
Aaron, *f* Take a pot, and put an omer full of manna therein,
and lay it up before the LORD, to be kept for your generations.
34 As the LORD commanded Moses, so Aaron laid it up *g* before the
35 Testimony, to be kept. And the children of Israel did eat
manna *h* forty years, *i* until they came to a land inhabited; they
did eat manna, until they came unto the borders of the land of
36 Canaan. Now an omer *is* the tenth *part* of an ephah.
CHAP. 17. AND *a* all the congregation of the children of Israel journeyed from the wilderness of Sin, after their journeys, according to the commandment of the LORD, and pitched in Rephidim:
2 and *there was* no water for the people to drink. *b* Wherefore
the people did chide with Moses, and said, Give us water that
we may drink. And Moses said unto them, Why chide ye with
3 me? Wherefore do ye *c* tempt the LORD? And the people
thirsted there for water; and the people *d* murmured against
Moses, and said, Wherefore *is* this *that* thou hast brought us up
out of Egypt, to kill us and our children and our cattle with

c Num. 11.
7, 8.

f Heb. 9. 4.
g ch. 25. 16.
& 40. 20.
Num. 17. 10.
Deut. 10. 5.
1 Kin. 8. 9.
h Num. 33.
38.
Deut. 8. 2.
Neh. 9. 20.
John 6. 31.
i Josh. 5. 12.
Neh. 9. 15.
a ch. 16. 1.
Num. 33.
12, 14.
b Num. 20.
3, 4.
c Deut. 6. 16.
Ps. 78. 18.
Isai. 7. 12.
Matt. 4. 7.
1 Cor. 10. 9.
d ch. 16. 2.

expression in Hebrew is peculiar and seems
almost to enjoin a position of complete repose; "in his place" is lit. under himself, as
the Oriental sits with his legs drawn up
under him. The prohibition must however
be understood with reference to its immediate object; they were not to go forth
from their place in order to gather manna,
which was on other days without the camp.
The spirit of the law is sacred rest. The
Lord gave them this Sabbath, as a blessing
and privilege. It was "made for man."
(Mark ii. 27.)

31. *Manna*] It was not indeed the common manna, as they then seem to have believed, but the properties which are noted
in this passage are common to it and the natural product: in size, form and colour it
resembled the seed of the white coriander, a
small round grain of a whitish or yellowish
grey.

33. *a pot*] The word here used occurs in
no other passage. It corresponds in form
and use to the Egyptian for a casket or vase
in which oblations were presented.

34. *the Testimony*] See marg. reff.

35. *did eat manna forty years*] This does
not necessarily imply that the Israelites
were fed exclusively on manna, or that the
supply was continuous during forty years:
but that whenever it might be needed, owing
to the total or partial failure of other food,
it was given until they entered the promised land. They had numerous flocks and

herds, which were not slaughtered (see
Numbers xi. 22), but which gave them milk,
cheese and of course a limited supply of
flesh: nor is there any reason to suppose
that during a considerable part of that time
they may not have cultivated some spots of
fertile ground in the wilderness. We may
assume, as in most cases of miracle, that the
supernatural supply was commensurate with
their actual necessity. The manna was not
withheld in fact until the Israelites had
passed the Jordan.

XVII. 1. *according to their journeys*]
The Israelites rested at two stations before
they reached Rephidim, viz. Dophkah and
Alush (Numbers xxxiii. 12–14). Dophkah
was in the Wady Sih, a day's journey from
the Wady Nasb. The wilderness of Sin
(xvi. 1) properly speaking ends here, the
sandstone ceases, and is replaced by the
porphyry and granite which belong to the
central formation of the Sinaitic group.
Alush may have been near the entrance to
the Wady Sheikh.

Rephidim] [Variously placed at Feiran at
the base of Mount Serbal, or at the pass of
El Watiyeh.]

2. *tempt the* LORD] It is a general characteristic of the Israelites that the miracles,
which met each need as it arose, failed to
produce a habit of faith: but the severity of
the trial, the faintness and anguish of thirst
in the burning desert, must not be overlooked in appreciating their conduct.

4 thirst? And Moses *cried unto the LORD, saying, What shall *e* ch. 14. 15.
5 I do unto this people? they be almost ready to *f*stone me. And *f* 1 Sam. 30.
the LORD said unto Moses, *g*Go on before the people, and take 6.
with thee of the elders of Israel; and thy rod; wherewith *h*thou John 8. 59.
6 smotest the river, take in thine hand, and go. *i*Behold, I will *g* Ezek. 2. 6.
stand before thee there upon the rock in Horeb; and thou shalt *h* ch. 7. 20.
smite the rock, and there shall come water out of it, that the *i* Num. 20.
people may drink. And Moses did so in the sight of the elders 10, 11.
7 of Israel. And he called the name of the place *k* 1Massah, and *k* Num. 20.
2Meribah, because of the chiding of the children of Israel, and & 114. 8.
because they tempted the LORD, saying, Is the LORD among us, 1 Cor. 10. 4.
8 or not? ¶ *l*Then came Amalek, and fought with Israel in 13.
9 Rephidim. And Moses said unto *m*Joshua, Choose us out men, *Ps.* 81. 7.
and go out, fight with Amalek: to morrow I will stand on the & 95. 8.
10 top of the hill with *n*the rod of God in mine hand. So Joshua *l* Gen. 36. 12.
did as Moses had said to him, and fought with Amalek: and Num. 24. 20.
11 Moses, Aaron, and Hur went up to the top of the hill. And it 1 Sam. 15. 2.
came to pass, when Moses *o*held up his hand, that Israel pre- *m* Called
12 vailed: and when he let down his hand, Amalek prevailed. But *Jesus,* Acts
Moses' hands *were* heavy; and they took a stone, and put *it* Heb. 4. 8.
under him, and he sat thereon; and Aaron and Hur stayed up *n* ch. 4. 20.
his hands, the one on the one side, and the other on the other *o* Jam. 5. 16.
side; and his hands were steady until the going down of the sun.
13 And Joshua discomfited Amalek and his people with the edge of
14 the sword. ¶ And the LORD said unto Moses, *p*Write this *for* a *p* ch. 34. 27.

¹ That is, *Tentation.*   ² That is, *Chiding,* or, *Strife.*

---

6. *the rock in Horeb*] [a rock situate, according to Arab tradition, in Wady Feiran. Horeb was a name given to the whole desert of Sinai and subsequently attached to the mountain. Palmer].

It is questioned whether the water thus supplied ceased with the immediate occasion; see 1 Cor. x. 4, the general meaning of which appears to be that their wants were ever supplied from Him, of Whom the rock was but a symbol, and Who accompanied them in all their wanderings.

7. *Massah...Meribah*] See margin. On the importance of this lesson see our Lord's words, Matt. iv. 7.

8. *Then came Amalek*] The attack occurred about two months after the Exodus, towards the end of May or early in June, when the Bedouins leave the lower plains in order to find pasture for their flocks on the cooler heights. The approach of the Israelites to Sinai would of course attract notice, and no cause of warfare is more common than a dispute for the right of pasturage. The Amalekites were at that time the most powerful race in the Peninsula; here they took their position as the chief of the heathens. They were also the first among the heathens who attacked God's people, and as such were marked out for punishment (see marg. reff.).

9. *Joshua*] This is the first mention of the great follower and successor of Moses. He died at the age of 110, some 65 years after this transaction. His original name

was Hosea, but Moses calls him by the full name, which was first given about forty years afterwards, as that by which he was to be known to succeeding generations. From this it may perhaps be inferred that this portion of Exodus was written, or revised, towards the end of the sojourn in the wilderness.

the rod of God] See iv. 20. The hill is supposed to be the height now called Feria on the north side of the plain Er Rahah; [or, Jebel Tahuneh over Feiran. Palmer].

10. *Hur*] Again mentioned with Aaron, in xxiv. 14. He was grandfather of Bezaleel, the great sculptor and artificer of the tabernacle, (xxxi. 2-5), and belonged to the tribe of Judah. (See 1 Chron. ii. 18-20.)

11. The act represents the efficacy of intercessory prayer—offered doubtless by Moses—a point of great moment to the Israelites at that time and to the Church in all ages.

12. *until the going down of the sun*] The length of this first great battle indicates the strength and obstinacy of the assailants. It was no mere raid of Bedouins, but a deliberate attack of the Amalekites, who had been probably thoroughly trained in warfare by their struggles with Egypt.

13. *with the edge of the sword*] This expression always denotes a great slaughter of the enemy.

14. *in a book*] **in the book,** *i.e.* the book which contained the history of God's dealings with His people. Moses was further

_q_ Num. 34.
20.
Deut. 25. 19.
1 Sam. 15.
3, 7.
& 30. 1, 17.
2 Sam. 8. 12.
Ezra 9. 14.
_a_ ch. 2. 16.
& 3. 1.
_b_ Ps. 44. 1.
& 77. 14, 15.
& 78. 4.
& 105. 5, 43.
& 106. 2, 8.
_c_ ch. 4. 26.
_d_ Acts 7. 29.
_e_ ch. 2. 22.

_f_ ch. 3. 1, 12.

_g_ Gen. 14. 17.
& 18. 2.
& 19. 1.
1 Kin. 2. 19.
_h_ Gen. 29. 13.
& 33. 4.

memorial in a book, and rehearse _it_ in the ears of Joshua : for _q_ I will utterly put out the remembrance of Amalek from under 15 heaven. And Moses built an altar, and called the name of it 16 ¹Jehovah-nissi : for he said, ²Because ³the LORD hath sworn _that_ the LORD _will have_ war with Amalek from generation to generation.

CHAP. 18. WHEN _a_ Jethro, the priest of Midian, Moses' father in law, heard of all that _b_ God had done for Moses, and for Israel his people, _and_ that the LORD had brought Israel out of Egypt ; 2 then Jethro, Moses' father in law, took Zipporah, Moses' wife, 3 _c_ after he had sent her back, and her _d_ two sons ; of which the _e_ name of the one _was_ ⁴Gershom ; for he said, I have been an 4 alien in a strange land : and the name of the other _was_ ⁵ Eliezer ; for the God of my father, _said he, was_ mine help, and delivered 5 me from the sword of Pharaoh : and Jethro, Moses' father in law, came with his sons and his wife unto Moses into the wilder-6 ness, where he encamped at _f_ the mount of God : and he said unto Moses, I thy father in law Jethro am come unto thee, and 7 thy wife, and her two sons with her. And Moses _g_ went out to meet his father in law, and did obeisance, and _h_ kissed him ; and they asked each other of _their_ ⁶ welfare ; and they came into the 8 tent. ¶ And Moses told his father in law all that the LORD had done unto Pharaoh and to the Egyptians for Israel's sake, _and_ all

¹ That is, _The_ LORD _my banner._ See Judg. 6. 24.
² Or, _Because the hand of_ Amalek _is against the_

throne of the LORD, therefore, &c.
³ Heb. _the hand upon the throne of the_ LORD.
⁴ That is, _A stranger there._

⁵ That is, _My God is an help._
⁶ Heb. _peace,_ Gen. 43. 27. 2 Sam. 11. 7.

---

instructed to impress the command specially on the mind of Joshua, as the leader to whom the first step towards its accomplishment would be entrusted on the conquest of Canaan. The work was not actually completed until the reign of Hezekiah, 1 Chron. iv. 43.

15. _Jehovah-nissi_] See the margin, "Jehovah my banner." As a proper name the Hebrew word is rightly preserved. The meaning is evidently that the name of Jehovah is the true banner under which victory is certain ; so to speak, the motto or inscription on the banners of the host. Inscriptions on the royal standard were well known. Each of the Pharaohs on his accession adopted one in addition to his official name.

16. _Because the_ LORD _hath sworn_] This rendering is incorrect. Our translators regard the expression as a solemn asseveration by the throne of God. To this however the objections are insuperable ; it has no parallel in Scriptural usage : God swears by Himself, not by His Throne. As the Hebrew text now stands the meaning is more satisfactorily given in the margin.

An alteration, slight in form, but considerable in meaning, has been proposed with much confidence, viz. "Nes," standard for "Kes," throne ; thus connecting the name of the altar with the sentence. Conjectural emendations are not to be adopted without necessity, and the obvious a priori probability of such a reading makes it im-

probable that one so far more difficult should have been substituted for it. One of the surest canons of criticism militates against its reception. The text as it stands was undoubtedly that which was alone known to the Targumists, the Samaritan, the Syriac, the Latin and the Arabic translators. The LXX. appear to have had a different reading, ἐν χειρὶ κρυφαίᾳ πολεμεῖ.

XVIII. The events recorded in this chapter could not have occupied many days, fifteen only elapsed between the arrival of the Israelites in the wilderness of Sin and their final arrival at Sinai, see xvi. 1, and xix. 1. This leaves however sufficient time for the interview and transactions between Moses and Jethro.

1. Jethro was in all probability the "brother in law" of Moses (iii. 1). On the parting from Zipporah, see iv. 26.

5. _the wilderness_] _i.e._, according to the view which seems on the whole most probable, the plain near the northern summit of Horeb, the mount of God. The valley which opens upon Er Rahah on the left of Horeb is called by the Arabs Wady Shueib, _i.e._ the vale of Hobab.

6. _and he said,_ &c.] Or, according to the Greek Version, "And it was told to Moses, saying, Lo, thy father in law Jether is come."

7. _asked each other of their welfare_] Addressed each other with the customary salutation, "Peace be unto you."

the travail that had [1]come upon them by the way, and how the
9 LORD [i]delivered them. And Jethro rejoiced for all the goodness
which the LORD had done to Israel, whom he had delivered out
10 of the hand of the Egyptians. And Jethro said, [k]Blessed be the
LORD, who hath delivered you out of the hand of the Egyptians,
and out of the hand of Pharaoh, who hath delivered the people
11 from under the hand of the Egyptians. Now I know that the
LORD is [l]greater than all gods: [m]for in the thing wherein they
12 dealt [n]proudly he was above them. And Jethro, Moses' father in
law, took a burnt offering and sacrifices for God : and Aaron
came, and all the elders of Israel, to eat bread with Moses' father
13 in law [o]before God. ¶ And it came to pass on the morrow, that
Moses sat to judge the people : and the people stood by Moses
14 from the morning unto the evening. And when Moses' father
in law saw all that he did to the people, he said, What is this
·thing that thou doest to the people? Why sittest thou thyself
alone, and all the people stand by thee from morning unto even?
15 And Moses said unto his father in law, Because [p]the people come
16 unto me to enquire of God : when they have [q]a matter, they
come unto me ; and I judge between [2]one and another, and I do
17 [r]make them know the statutes of God, and his laws. And
Moses' father in law said unto him, The thing that thou doest is
18 not good. [3]Thou wilt surely wear away, both thou and this
people that is with thee : for this thing is too heavy for thee ;
19 [s]thou art not able to perform it thyself alone. Hearken now
unto my voice, I will give thee counsel, and [t]God shall be with
thee : Be thou [u]for the people to God-ward, that thou mayest
20 [x]bring the causes unto God : and thou shalt [y]teach them ordinances and laws, and shalt shew them [z]the way wherein
21 they must walk, and [a]the works that they must do. Moreover
thou shalt provide out of all the people [b]able men, such as
[c]fear God, [d]men of truth, [e]hating covetousness ; and place

[i] Ps. 78. 42.
& 107. 2.
[k] Gen. 14. 20.
2 Sam. 18.
28.
Luke 1. 68.
[l] 2 Chr. 2. 5.
Ps. 95. 3.
& 97. 9.
[m] ch. 14. 27.
[n] 1 Sam. 2. 3.
Neh. 9. 10.
Job 40. 11.
Ps. 31. 23.
Luke 1. 51.
[o] Deut. 12. 7.
1 Chr. 29. 22.
1 Cor. 10. 18.
21, 31.
[p] Lev. 24. 12.
Num. 15. 34.
[q] ch. 24. 14.
2 Sam. 15. 3.
Acts 18. 15.
1 Cor. 6. 1.
[r] Lev. 24. 15.
Num. 15. 35.
[s] Num. 11.
14, 17.
Deut. 1. 9.
[t] ch. 3. 12.
[u] ch. 20. 19,
Deut. 5. 5.
[x] Num. 27. 3,
[y] Deut. 4. 1.
[z] Ps. 143. 8.
[a] Deut. 1. 18.
[b] ver. 25.
2 Chr. 19. 5
—10.
[c] Gen. 42. 18.
2 Sam. 23. 3.
[d] Ezek. 18. 8.
[e] Deut. 16.
19.

[1] Heb. found them, Gen.
44. 34. Num. 20. 14.
[2] Heb. a man and his
fellow.
[3] Heb. fading thou wilt
fade.

11. greater than all gods] See xv. 11. The
words simply indicate a conviction of the incomparable might and majesty of Jehovah.
for in...above them] i.e. the greatness of
Jehovah was shewn in those transactions
wherein the Egyptians had thought to deal
haughtily and cruelly against the Israelites.
Jethro refers especially to the destruction
of the Egyptian host in the Red Sea.
12. a burnt offering and sacrifices] This
verse clearly shows that Jethro was recognized as a priest of the true God, and is of
great importance in its bearings upon the
relation between the Israelites and their
congeners, and upon the state of religion
among the descendants of Abraham.
13. from the morning unto the evening] It
may be assumed as at least probable that
numerous cases of difficulty arose out of the
division of the spoil of the Amalekites (xvii.
13), and causes would have accumulated
during the journey from Elim.
15. to enquire of God] The decisions of
Moses were doubtless accepted by the people
as oracles. The internal prompting of the
Spirit was a sufficient guidance for him, and

a sufficient authority for the people.
18. Thou wilt surely wear away] From
decay and exhaustion.
19. counsel] Jethro draws the distinction
between the functions of the legislator and
the judge.
to God-ward] Lit. "before God," standing
between them and God, both as His minister or representative and also as the representative of the people, their agent, so to
speak, or deputy before God.
20. teach them] The Hebrew word is emphatic, and signifies "enlightenment." The
text gives four distinct points, (a) the "ordinances," or specific enactments, (b) "the
laws," or general regulations, (c) "the way,"
the general course of duty, (d) "the works,"
each specific act.
21. able men] The qualifications are remarkably complete, ability, piety, truthfulness, and unselfishness. From Deut. i. 13,
it appears that Moses left the selection of
the persons to the people, an example followed by the Apostles ; see Acts vi. 3.
rulers of thousands, &c.] The numbers
appear to be conventional, corresponding

such over them, *to be* rulers of thousands, *and* rulers of hun-
22 dreds, rulers of fifties, and rulers of tens : and let them judge
the people *f*at all seasons : *g*and it shall be, *that* every great
matter they shall bring unto thee, but every small matter they
shall judge : so shall it be easier for thyself, and *h*they shall
23 bear *the burden* with thee. If thou shalt do this thing, and God
command thee *so*, then thou shalt be *i*able to endure, and all
24 this people shall also go to *k*their place in peace. ¶ So Moses
hearkened to the voice of his father in law, and did all that he
25 had said. And *l*Moses chose able men out of all Israel, and
made them heads over the people, rulers of thousands, rulers of
26 hundreds, rulers of fifties, and rulers of tens. And they *m*judged
the people at all seasons : the *n*hard causes they brought unto
27 Moses, but every small matter they judged themselves. And
Moses let his father in law depart; and *o*he went his way into
his own land.

CHAP. 19. IN the third month, when the children of Israel were gone
forth out of the land of Egypt, the same day *a*came they *into*
2 the wilderness of Sinai. For they were departed from *b*Rephidim, and were come *to* the desert of Sinai, and had pitched in
the wilderness ; and there Israel camped before *c*the mount.
3 And *d*Moses went up unto God, and the LORD *e*called unto him
out of the mountain, saying, Thus shalt thou say to the house of
4 Jacob, and tell the children of Israel ; *f*Ye have seen what I did
unto the Egyptians, and *how g*I bare you on eagles' wings, and
5 brought you unto myself. Now *h*therefore, if ye will obey my
voice indeed, and keep my covenant, then *i*ye shall be a peculiar
treasure unto me above all people : for *k*all the earth *is* mine :
6 and ye shall be unto me a *l*kingdom of priests, and an *m*holy

Margin references

j ver. 26.
y ver. 26.
Lev. 24. 11.
Num. 27. 2.
Deut. 17. 8.
h Num. 11.
17.
i ver. 18.
k Deut. 30. 16.
l Deut. 1. 15.
Acts 6. 5.

m ver. 22.
n Job 29. 16.
o Num. 10.
29, 30.
a Num. 33.
15.
b ch. 17. 1, 8.
c ch. 3. 1, 12.
d ch. 20. 21.
Acts 7. 38.
e ch. 3. 4.
f Deut. 29. 2.
g Isai. 63. 9.
h Deut. 5. 2.
i Deut. 4. 20.
Ps. 135. 4.
Jer. 10. 16.
Mal. 3. 17.
Tit. 2. 14.
k ch. 9. 29.
Job 41. 11.
l Deut. 33.
2, 3, 4.
m Lev. 20.
24, 26.

---

nearly, but not exactly, to the military, or civil divisions of the people : the largest division 1000 is used as an equivalent of a gens under one head, Num. i. 16, x. 4 ; Josh. xxii. 14.

The word "rulers," sometimes rendered "princes," is general, including all ranks of officials placed in command. The same word is used regularly on Egyptian monuments of the time of Moses.

23. *to their place*] *i.e.* to Canaan, which is thus recognised by Jethro as the appointed and true home of Israel. Cp. Num. x. 29, 30.

24. *hearkened*] Nothing can be more characteristic of Moses, who combines on all occasions distrust of himself and singular openness to impressions, with the wisdom and sound judgment which chooses the best course when pointed out.

27. *into his own land*] Midian (ii. 15).

XIX. 1, 2. *the wilderness...the desert of Sinai*] If the mount from which the Law was delivered be the rock of Ras Safsafeh, then the spacious plain of Er Rahah would be the "desert" of Sinai (see *v.* 17).

3. *Moses went up unto God*] This seems to imply that the voice was heard by Moses as he was ascending the mount.

house of Jacob] This expression does not occur elsewhere in the Pentateuch. It has a peculiar fitness here, referring doubtless to the special promises made to the Patriarch.

4. *on eagles' wings*] Both in the Law (Deut. xxxii. 11) and in the Gospel (Matt. xxiii. 37), the Church is compared to fledgelings which the mother cherishes and protects under her wings : but in the Law that mother is an eagle, in the Gospel a hen ; thus shadowing forth the diversity of administration under each Covenant : the one of power, when God manifested when He brought His people out of Egypt with a mighty hand and an outstretched arm, and led them into the promised land ; the other of grace, when Christ came in humility and took the form of a servant and became obedient unto death, even the death of the Cross. Cp. also Rev. xii. 14.

5. *a peculiar treasure*] A costly possession acquired with exertion, and carefully guarded. The peculiar relation in which Israel stands, taken out of the heathen world and consecrated to God, as His slaves, subjects, and children, determines their privileges, and is the foundation of their duties. The same principle applies even in a stronger sense to the Church. See Acts xx. 28 ; 1 Cor. vi. 20 ; 1 Pet. ii. 9.

all the earth is mine] It was a point of great practical importance, to impress upon the Jews that their God was no mere national Deity. Cp. Deut. x. 14 ; Ps. xxiv. 1.

6. *a kingdom of priests*] Israel collectively is a royal and priestly race : a dynasty of

nation. These *are* the words which thou shalt speak unto the
7 children of Israel. ¶ And Moses came and called for the elders of
the people, and laid before their faces all these words which the
8 LORD commanded him. And [n]all the people answered together,
and said, All that the LORD hath spoken we will do. And
9 Moses returned the words of the people unto the LORD. And
the LORD said unto Moses, Lo, I come unto thee [o]in a thick
cloud, [p]that the people may hear when I speak with thee, and
[q]believe thee for ever. And Moses told the words of the people
10 unto the LORD. ¶ And the LORD said unto Moses, Go unto
the people, and [r]sanctify them to day and to morrow, and let
11 them [s]wash their clothes, and be ready against the third day: for
the third day the LORD [t]will come down in the sight of all the
12 people upon mount Sinai. And thou shalt set bounds unto the
people round about, saying, Take heed to yourselves, *that ye* go
not up into the mount, or touch the border of it: [u]whosoever
13 toucheth the mount shall be surely put to death: there shall not
an hand touch it, but he shall surely be stoned, or shot through;
whether *it be* beast or man, it shall not live: when the [1][x]trumpet
14 soundeth long, they shall come up to the mount. ¶ And Moses
went down from the mount unto the people, and [y]sanctified the
15 people; and they washed their clothes. And he said unto the
people, [z]Be ready against the third day: [a]come not at *your* wives.
16 ¶ And it came to pass on the third day in the morning, that
there were [b]thunders and lightnings, and a [c]thick cloud upon
the mount, and the [d]voice of the trumpet exceeding loud; so
17 that all the people that *was* in the camp [e]trembled. And
[f]Moses brought forth the people out of the camp to meet with
18 God; and they stood at the nether part of the mount. And
[g]mount Sinai was altogether on a smoke, because the LORD descended upon it [h]in fire: [i]and the smoke thereof ascended as
the smoke of a furnace, and [k]the whole mount quaked greatly.
19 And [l]when the voice of the trumpet sounded long, and waxed
louder and louder, [m]Moses spake, and [n]God answered him by a
20 voice. And the LORD came down upon mount Sinai, on the
top of the mount: and the LORD called Moses *up* to the top of
21 the mount; and Moses went up. And the LORD said unto
Moses, Go down, [2]charge the people, lest they break through
22 unto the LORD [o]to gaze, and many of them perish. And let the

[n] ch. 24. 3, 7. Deut. 5. 27.
[o] ver. 16. Deut. 4. 11. Ps. 18. 11. Matt. 17. 5.
[p] Deut. 4. 12, 36. John 12. 29.
[q] ch. 14. 31.
[r] Lev. 11. 44, 45.
[s] ver. 14. Gen. 35. 2. Lev. 15. 5.
[t] ver. 16, 18. ch. 34. 5. Deut. 33. 2.
[u] Heb. 12. 20.
[x] ver. 16, 19.
[y] ver. 10.
[z] ver. 11.
[a] 1 Sam. 21. 4, 5. Zech. 7. 3. 1 Cor. 7. 5.
[b] Ps. 77. 18. Heb. 12. 18. Rev. 4. 5.
[c] ver. 9. ch. 40. 34. 2 Chr. 5. 14.
[d] Rev. 1. 10.
[e] Heb. 12. 21.
[f] Deut. 4. 10.
[g] Deut. 4. 11. Judg. 5. 5. Isai. 6. 4. Hab. 3. 3.
[h] ch. 3. 2. & 24. 17. 2 Chr. 7. 1.
[i] Gen. 15. 17. Ps. 144. 5. Rev. 15. 8.
[k] Ps. 68. 8. Heb. 12. 26.
[l] ver. 13.
[m] Heb. 12. 21.
[n] Neh. 9. 13. Ps. 81. 7.
[o] See ch. 3. 5. 1 Sam. 6. 19.

[1] Or, *cornet*. [2] Heb. *contest*.

---

priests, each true member uniting in himself the attributes of a king and priest. Cp. 1 Pet. ii. 5. Rev. i. 6.

an holy nation] The holiness of Israel consisted in its special consecration to God: it was a sacred nation, sacred by adoption, by covenant, and by participation in all means of grace. Cp. Deut. vii. 6, xxvi. 19, xxviii. 9. 1 Cor. iii. 17. 1 Thess. v. 27.

8. *All that the* LORD, &c.] By this answer the people accepted the covenant. It was the preliminary condition of their complete admission into the state of a royal priesthood.

10. *sanctify them*] The injunction involves bodily purification and undoubtedly also spiritual preparation. Cp. Heb. x. 22. The washing of the clothes was an outward symbol well understood in all nations.

12. *set bounds unto the people*] The low line of alluvial mounds at the foot of the cliff of Ras Safsafeh exactly answers to the bounds which were to keep the people off from touching the mount: but the bounds here spoken of were to be set up by Moses.

13. *touch it*] Rather "touch him." The person who had touched the mount was not to be touched, since the contact would be pollution.

17. *out of the camp*] The encampment must have extended far and wide over the plain in front of the mountain. From one entrance of the plain to the other there is space for the whole host of the Israelites.

18. *a furnace*] The word in the original is Egyptian, and occurs only in the Pentateuch.

22. *the priests also*] Sacrifices had hitherto been offered by firstborn, or the heads of families. See Gen. xiv. 18 note.

p Lev. 10. 3.
q 2 Sam. 6.
7, 8.
r ver. 12.
Josh. 3. 4.

a Deut. 5. 22.
b Deut. 5. 6.
Ps. 81. 10.
Hos. 13. 4.
c ch. 13. 3.
d Deut. 6.
14.
2 Kin. 17.
35.
Jer. 25. 6.
e Lev. 26. 1.
Deut. 4. 16.
Ps. 97. 7.

priests also, which come near to the LORD, *p*sanctify themselves, 23 lest the LORD *q*break forth upon them. And Moses said unto the LORD, The people cannot come up to mount Sinai: for thou chargedst us, saying, *r*Set bounds about the mount, and sanctify 24 it. And the LORD said unto him, Away, get thee down, and thou shalt come up, thou, and Aaron with thee: but let not the priests and the people break through to come up unto the LORD, lest he 25 break forth upon them. So Moses went down unto the people, and spake unto them.

CHAP. 20. AND God spake *a*all these words, saying,

2 *b*I am the LORD thy God, which have brought thee out of the 3 land of Egypt, *c*out of the house of ¹bondage. *d*Thou shalt have no other gods before me.

4 *e*Thou shalt not make unto thee any graven image, or any

¹ Heb. *servants.*

XX. 1–17. The Hebrew name which is rendered in our Version THE TEN COMMANDMENTS occurs in xxxiv. 28; Deut. iv. 13, x. 4. It literally means *the Ten Words.* The Ten Commandments are also called the Law, even the Commandment (xxiv. 12), THE WORDS OF THE COVENANT (xxxiv. 28), THE TABLES OF THE COVENANT (Deut. ix. 9), THE COVENANT (Deut. iv. 13), THE TWO TABLES (Deut. ix. 10, 17), and, most frequently, THE TESTIMONY (*e.g.* xvi. 34, xxv. 16), or THE TWO TABLES OF THE TESTIMONY (*e.g.* xxxi. 18). In the New Testament they are called simply THE COMMANDMENTS (*e.g.* Matt. xix. 17). The name DECALOGUE is found first in Clement of Alexandria, and was commonly used by the Fathers who followed him.

We thus know that the Tables were two, and that the commandments were ten, in number. But the Scriptures do not, by any direct statements, enable us to determine with precision how the Ten Commandments are severally to be made out, nor how they are to be allotted to the Two Tables. On each of these points various opinions have been held (see *v.* 12).

Of the Words of Jehovah engraven on the Tables of Stone, we have two distinct statements, one in Exodus (xx. 1–17) and one in Deuteronomy (v. 7–21), apparently of equal authority, but differing principally from each other in the Fourth, the Fifth, and the Tenth Commandments.

It has been supposed that the original Commandments were all in the same terse and simple form of expression as appears (both in Exodus and Deuteronomy) in the First, Sixth, Seventh, Eighth, and Ninth, such as would be most suitable for recollection, and that the passages in each copy in which the most important variations are found were comments added when the Books were written.

The account of the delivery of them in chap. xix. and in *vv.* 18–21 of this chap. is in accordance with their importance as the recognized basis of the Covenant between Jehovah and His ancient people

(xxxiv. 27, 28; Deut. iv. 13; 1 K. viii. 21, &c.), and as the Divine testimony against the sinful tendencies in man for all ages. While it is here said that "God spake all these words," and in Deut. v. 4, that He "talked face to face," in the New Testament the giving of the Law is spoken of as having been through the ministration of Angels (Acts vii. 53; Gal. iii. 19; Heb. ii. 2). We can reconcile these contrasts of language by keeping in mind that God is a Spirit, and that He is essentially present in the agents who are performing His will.

2. *which have brought thee out of the land of Egypt, out of the house of bondage*] It has been asked, Why, on this occasion, was not THE LORD rather proclaimed as "the Creator of Heaven and Earth"? The answer is, Because the Ten Commandments were at this time addressed by Jehovah not merely to human creatures, but to the people whom He had redeemed, to those who had been in bondage, but were now free men (vi. 6, 7, xix. 5). The Commandments are expressed in absolute terms. They are not sanctioned by outward penalties, as if for slaves, but are addressed at once to the conscience, as for free men. The well-being of the nation called for the infliction of penalties, and therefore statutes were passed to punish offenders who blasphemed the name of Jehovah, who profaned the Sabbath, or who committed murder or adultery. (See Lev. xviii. 24–30 note.) But these penal statutes were not to be the ground of obedience for the true Israelite according to the Covenant. He was to know Jehovah as his Redeemer, and was to obey him as such (Cp. Rom. xiii. 5).

3. *before me*] Literally, *before my face.* The meaning is that no god should be worshipped in addition to Jehovah. Cp. *v.* 23. The polytheism which was the besetting sin of the Israelites did not in later times exclude Jehovah, but associated Him with false deities. [Cp. the original of 1 Sam. ii. 25].

4. *graven image*] Any sort of image is here intended.

likeness *of any thing* that *is* in heaven above, or that *is* in the
5 earth beneath, or that *is* in the water under the earth : *f* thou
shalt not bow down thyself to them, nor serve them : for I the
LORD thy God *am g* a jealous God, *h* visiting the iniquity of the
fathers upon the children unto the third and fourth *generation*
6 of them that hate me; and *i* shewing mercy unto thousands of
them that love me, and keep my commandments.
7 *k* Thou shalt not take the name of the LORD thy God in vain ;
for the LORD *l* will not hold him guiltless that taketh his name
in vain.
8, 9 *m* Remember the sabbath day, to keep it holy. *n* Six days shalt
10 thou labour, and do all thy work : but the *o* seventh day *is* the
sabbath of the LORD thy God : *in it* thou shalt not do any work,

f ch. 23. 24.
2 Kin. 17. 35.
Isai. 44. 15.
g ch. 34. 14.
Deut. 4. 24.
h ch. 34. 7.
i ch. 34. 7.
k ch. 23. 1.
l Mic. 6. 11.
m ch. 31. 13.
Lev. 19. 3.
n ch. 23. 12.
Lev. 23. 3.
Luke 13. 14.
o Gen. 2. 2.

As the First Commandment forbids the worship of any false god, seen or unseen, it is here forbidden to worship an image of any sort, whether the figure of a false deity (Josh. xxiii. 7) or one in any way symbolical of Jehovah (see xxxii. 4). The spiritual acts of worship were symbolized in the furniture and ritual of the Tabernacle and the Altar, and for this end the forms of living things might be employed as in the case of the Cherubim (see xxv. 18 note) : but the Presence of the invisible God was to be marked by no symbol of Himself, but by His words written on stones, preserved in the ark in the Holy of Holies and covered by the Mercy-seat. The ancient Persians and the earliest legislators of Rome also agreed in repudiating images of the Deity.

a jealous God] Deut. vi. 15 ; Josh. xxiv. 19 ; Is. xlii. 8, xlviii. 11 ; Nahum i. 2. This reason applies to the First, as well as to the Second Commandment. The truth expressed in it was declared more fully to Moses when the name of Jehovah was proclaimed to him after he had interceded for Israel on account of the golden calf (xxxiv. 6, 7 ; see note).

5. *visiting the iniquity of the fathers upon the children*] (Cp. xxxiv. 7 ; Jer. xxxii. 18). Sons and remote descendants inherit the consequences of their fathers' sins, in disease, poverty, captivity, with all the influences of bad example and evil communications. (See Lev. xxvi. 39 ; Lam. v. 7 sq.) The "inherited curse" seems to fall often most heavily on the least guilty persons ; but such suffering must always be free from the sting of conscience ; it is not like the visitation for sin on the individual by whom the sin has been committed. The suffering, or loss of advantages, entailed on the unoffending son, is a condition under which he has to carry on the struggle of life, and, like all other inevitable conditions imposed upon men, it cannot tend to his ultimate disadvantage, if he struggles well and perseveres to the end. The principle regulating the administration of justice by earthly tribunals (Deut. xxiv. 16), is carried out in spiritual matters by the Supreme Judge.

6. *unto thousands*] **unto the thousandth generation.** Jehovah's visitations of chastisement extend to the third and fourth generation, his visitations of mercy to the thousandth ; that is, for ever. That this is the true rendering seems to follow from Deut. vii. 9. Cp. 2 S. vii. 15, 16.

7. Our translators make the Third Commandment bear upon any profane and idle utterance of the name of God. Others give it the sense, *Thou shalt not swear falsely by the name of Jehovah thy God.* The Hebrew word which answers to *in vain* may be rendered either way. The two abuses of the sacred name seem to be distinguished in Lev. xix. 12 (see Matt. v. 33). Our Version is probably right in giving the rendering which is more inclusive. The caution that a breach of this Commandment incurs guilt in the eyes of Jehovah is especially appropriate, in consequence of the ease with which the temptation to take God's name "in vain" besets men in their common intercourse with each other.

8. *Remember the sabbath day*] There is no distinct evidence that the Sabbath, as a formal ordinance, was recognised before the time of Moses (cp. Neh. ix. 14, Ezek. xx. 10–12, Deut. *v.* 15). The word *remember* may either be used. in the sense of *keep in mind* what is here enjoined for the first time, or it may refer back to what is related in xvi. 22–26.

10. *the sabbath*, &c.] **a Sabbath to Jehovah thy God.** The proper meaning of *sabbath* is, *rest after labour.* Cp. xvi. 26.

thy stranger that is within thy gates] Not a *stranger*, as is an unknown person, but a *lodger*, or *sojourner.* In this place it denotes one who had come from another people to take up his permanent abode among the Israelites, and who might have been well known to his neighbours. That the word did not primarily refer to foreign domestic servants (though all such were included under it) is to be inferred from the term used for *gates*, signifying not the doors of a private dwelling, but the gates of a town or camp.

thou, nor thy son, nor thy daughter, thy manservant, nor thy maidservant, nor thy cattle, *p*nor thy stranger that *is* within thy 11 gates: for *q*in six days the LORD made heaven and earth, the sea, and all that in them *is*, and rested the seventh day: wherefore the LORD blessed the sabbath day, and hallowed it.

12 *r*Honour thy father and thy mother: that thy days may be long upon the land which the LORD thy God giveth thee.

13 *s*Thou shalt not kill.

14 *t*Thou shalt not commit adultery.

15 *u*Thou shalt not steal.

16 *w*Thou shalt not bear false witness against thy neighbour.

17 *x*Thou shalt not covet thy neighbour's house, *y*thou shalt not covet thy neighbour's wife, nor his manservant, nor his maidservant, nor his ox, nor his ass, nor any thing that *is* thy neighbour's.

18 ¶ And *z*all the people *a*saw the thunderings, and the lightnings, and the noise of the trumpet, and the mountain *b*smoking: and 19 when the people saw *it*, they removed, and stood afar off. And they said unto Moses, *c*Speak thou with us, and we will hear: 20 but *d*let not God speak with us, lest we die. And Moses said unto the people, *e*Fear not: *f*for God is come to prove you, and 21 *g*that his fear may be before your faces, that ye sin not. ¶ And the people stood afar off, and Moses drew near unto *h*the thick 22 darkness where God *was*. ¶ And the LORD said unto Moses, Thus thou shalt say unto the children of Israel, Ye have seen that I 23 have talked with you *i*from heaven. Ye shall not make *k*with me gods of silver, neither shall ye make unto you gods of gold.

---

12. *Honour thy father and thy mother*] According to our usage, the Fifth Commandment is placed as the first in the second table; and this is necessarily involved in the common division of the Commandments into our duty towards God and our duty towards men. But the more ancient, and probably the better, division allots five Commandments to each Table (cp. Rom. xiii. 9), proceeding on the distinction that the First Table relates to the duties which arise from our filial relations, the Second to those which arise from our fraternal relations. The connexion between the first four Commandments and the Fifth exists in the truth that all faith in God centres in the filial feeling. Our parents stand between us and God in a way in which no other beings can. On the maintenance of parental authority, see xxi. 15, 17; Deut. xxi. 18–21.

that thy days may be long upon the land] Filial respect is the ground of national permanence (cp. Jer. xxxv. 18, 19; Matt. xv. 4–6; Mark vii. 10, 11). The Divine words were addressed emphatically to Israel, but they set forth a universal principle of national life (Eph. vi. 2).

13, 14. Matthew v. 21–32 is the best comment on these two verses.

15. The right of property is sanctioned in the Eighth Commandment by an external rule: its deeper meaning is involved in the Tenth Commandment.

17. As the Sixth, Seventh, and Eighth Commandments forbid us to injure our neighbour in deed, the Ninth forbids us to injure him in word, and the Tenth, in thought. No human eye can see the coveting heart; it is witnessed only by him who possesses it and by Him to Whom all things are naked and open (Luke xii. 15–21). But it is the root of all sins of word or deed against our neighbour (Jam. i. 14, 15).

18-21. Cp. Deut. v. 22–31. Aaron (xix. 24) on this occasion accompanied Moses in drawing near to the thick darkness.

22—xxiii. 33. A series of laws which we may identify with what was written by Moses in the book called the BOOK OF THE COVENANT, and read by him in the audience of the people (xxiv. 7).

The document cannot be regarded as a strictly systematic whole. Portions of it were probably traditional rules handed down from the Patriarchs, and retained by the Israelites in Egypt.

22-26. Nothing could be more appropriate as the commencement of the Book of the Covenant than these regulations for public worship. The rules for the building of altars must have been old and accepted, and are not inconsistent with the directions for the construction of the Altar of the Court of the Tabernacle, xxvii. 1-8 (cp. Josh. xxii. 26-28).

24 An altar of earth thou shalt make unto me, and shalt sacrifice thereon thy burnt offerings, and thy peace offerings, *l* thy sheep, and thine oxen : in all *m* places where I record my name I will
25 come unto thee, and I will *n* bless thee. And *o* if thou wilt make me an altar of stone, thou shalt not [1] build it of hewn stone : for
26 if thou lift up thy tool upon it, thou hast polluted it. Neither shalt thou go up by steps unto mine altar, that thy nakedness be not discovered thereon.

CHAP. 21. NOW these *are* the judgments which thou shalt *a* set
2 before them. ¶ *b* If thou buy an Hebrew servant, six years he shall serve : and in the seventh he shall go out free for nothing.
3 If he came in [2] by himself, he shall go out by himself : if he were
4 married, then his wife shall go out with him. If his master have given him a wife, and she have born him sons or daughters; the wife and her children shall be her master's, and he shall go
5 out by himself. *c* And if the servant [3] shall plainly say, I love my master, my wife, and my children ; I will not go out free :
6 then his master shall bring him unto the *d* judges ; he shall also bring him to the door, or unto the door post ; and his master shall *e* bore his ear through with an aul ; and he shall serve him
7 for ever. ¶ And if a man *f* sell his daughter to be a maidservant,
8 she shall not go out *g* as the menservants do. If she [4] please not her master, who hath betrothed her to himself, then shall he let her be redeemed : to sell her unto a strange nation he shall have
9 no power, seeing he hath dealt deceitfully with her. And if he have betrothed her unto his son, he shall deal with her after the
10 manner of daughters. If he take him another *wife;* her food, her raiment, *h* and her duty of marriage, shall he not diminish.
11 And if he do not these three unto her, then shall she go out
12 free without money. ¶ *i* He that smiteth a man, so that he die,

l Lev. 1. 2.
m Deut. 12.5.
1 Kin. 8. 43.
2 Chr. 6. 6.
Ezra 6. 12.
Neh. 1. 9.
Ps. 74. 7.
Jer. 7. 10, 12.
n Gen. 12. 2.
Deut. 7. 13.
o Deut. 27. 5.
a ch. 24. 3, 4.
Deut. 4. 14.
b Deut.15.12.
Jer. 34. 14.

c Deut. 15. 16, 17.
d ch. 12. 12. & 22. 8, 28.
e Ps. 40. 6.
f Neh. 5. 5.
g ver. 2, 3.

h 1 Cor. 7. 5.
i Gen. 9. 6.
Lev. 24. 17.
Num. 35. 30, 31.
Matt. 26. 52.

[1] Heb. *build them* with *hewing.*
[2] Heb. *with his body.*
[3] Heb. *saying shall say.*
[4] Heb. *be evil in the eyes of, &c.*

XXI. 1. *judgments*] *i.e.* decisions of the Law.

2. A Hebrew might be sold as a bondman in consequence either of debt (Lev. xxv. 39) or of the commission of theft (xxii. 3). But his servitude could not be enforced for more than six full years. Cp. marg. reff.

3. If a married man became a bondman, his rights in regard to his wife were respected : but if a single bondman accepted at the hand of his master a bondwoman as his wife, the master did not lose his claim to the woman or her children, at the expiration of the husband's term of service. Such wives, it may be presumed, were always foreign slaves.

6. *for ever*] That is, most probably, till the next Jubilee, when every Hebrew was set free. See Lev. xxv. 40, 50. The custom of boring the ear as a mark of slavery appears to have been a common one in ancient times, observed in many nations.

6. *unto the judges*] Literally, *before the gods* (*elohim*). The word does not denote *judges* in a direct way, but it is to be understood as the name of God, in its ordinary plural form, God being the source of all

justice. The name in this connection always has the definite article prefixed. See marg. reff. Cp. Ps. lxxxii. 1, 6 ; John x. 34.

7. A man might, in accordance with existing custom, sell his daughter to another man with a view to her becoming an inferior wife, or concubine. In this case, she was not " to go out," like the bondman ; that is, she was not to be dismissed at the end of the sixth year. But women who were bound in any other way, would appear to have been under the same conditions as bondmen. See Deut. xv. 17.

11. *if he do not these three unto her*] The words express a choice of one of three things. The man was to give the woman, whom he had purchased from her father, her freedom, unless (i) he caused her to be redeemed by a Hebrew master (*v.* 8) ; or, (ii) gave her to his son, and treated her as a daughter (*v.* 9) ; or, (iii) in the event of his taking another wife (*v.* 10), unless he allowed her to retain her place and privileges. These rules (*vv.* 7-11) are to be regarded as mitigations of the then existing usages of concubinage.

12. The case of murder of a free man and

k Num. 35.
22.
Deut. 19. 4.
l 1 Sam. 24.
4, 10, 18.
m Num. 35.
11.
Deut. 19. 3.
Josh. 20. 2.
n Num. 15.
30.
Deut. 19. 11.
Heb. 10. 26.
o 1 Kin. 2.
28—34.
2 Kin. 11. 15.
p Deut. 24. 7.
q Gen. 37. 28.
r ch. 22. 4.
s Lev. 20. 9.
Prov. 20. 20.
Matt. 15. 4.
t 2 Sam. 3.
29.
u Lev. 25.
45, 46.
x ver. 30.
Deut. 22.
18, 19.
y Lev. 24. 20.
Deut. 19. 21.
Matt. 5. 38.

13 shall be surely put to death. And *k*if a man lie not in wait, but
God *l*deliver *him* into his hand; then *m*I will appoint thee a place
14 whither he shall flee. But if a man come *n*presumptuously upon
his neighbour, to slay him with guile; *o*thou shalt take him from
15 mine altar, that he may die. And he that smiteth his father,
16 or his mother, shall be surely put to death. ¶ And *p*he that
stealeth a man, and *q*selleth him, or if he be *r*found in his hand,
17 he shall surely be put to death. ¶ And *s*he that *1*curseth his
18 father, or his mother, shall surely be put to death. ¶ And if
men strive together, and one smite *2*another with a stone, or with
19 *his* fist, and he die not, but keepeth *his* bed: if he rise again, and
walk abroad *t*upon his staff, then shall he that smote *him* be
quit: only he shall pay *for* *3*the loss of his time, and shall cause
20 *him* to be thoroughly healed. And if a man smite his servant,
or his maid, with a rod, and he die under his hand; he shall be
21 surely *4*punished. Notwithstanding, if he continue a day or two,
22 he shall not be punished: for *u*he *is* his money. If men strive,
and hurt a woman with child, so that her fruit depart *from*
her, and yet no mischief follow: he shall be surely punished,
according as the woman's husband will lay upon him; and he
23 shall *x*pay as the judges *determine*. And if *any* mischief follow,
24 then thou shalt give life for life, *y*eye for eye, tooth for tooth,
25 hand for hand, foot for foot, burning for burning, wound for

---

1 Or, *revileth*.
2 Or, *his neighbour*.
3 Heb. *his ceasing*.
4 Heb. *avenged*, Gen. 4.
15, 24. Rom. 13. 4.

of a bondman. See *v.* 20 note. The law was
afterwards expressly declared to relate also
to foreigners, Lev. xxiv. 17, 21, 22; cp.
marg. reff.

13, 14. There was no place of safety for
the guilty murderer, not even the Altar of
Jehovah. Thus all superstitious notions connected with the right of sanctuary were excluded. Adonijah and Joab (1 K. i. 50, ii.
28) appear to have vainly trusted that the
vulgar feeling would protect them, if they
took hold of the horns of the Altar on which
atonement with blood was made (Lev. iv. 7).
But for one who killed a man "at unawares," that is, without intending to do it,
the Law afterwards appointed places of
refuge, Num. xxxv. 6–34; Deut. iv. 41–
43, xix. 2–10; Josh. xx. 2-9. It is very
probable that there was some provision answering to the cities of refuge, that may
have been based upon old usage, in the
camp in the Wilderness.

15, 16, 17. The following offences were
to be punished with death :—
Striking a parent, cp. Deut. xxvii. 16.
Cursing a parent, cp. marg. reff.
Kidnapping, whether with a view to retain the person stolen, or to sell him, cp.
marg. reff.

19. *quit*] *i.e.* if one man injured another
in a quarrel so as to oblige him to keep his
bed, he was free from the liability to a
criminal charge (such as might be based
upon *v.* 12) : but he was required to compensate the latter for the loss of his time,
and for the cost of his healing.

20, 21. The Jewish authorities appear to

be right in referring this law, like those in
vv. 26, 27, 32, to foreign slaves (see Lev.
xxv. 44–46). The protection here afforded
to the life of a slave may seem to us but a
slight one; but it is the very earliest trace
of such protection in legislation, and it
stands in strong and favourable contrast
with the old laws of Greece, Rome, and
other nations. If the slave survived the
castigation a day or two, the master did not
become amenable to the law, because the
loss of the slave was accounted, under the
circumstances, as a punishment.

22–25. The rule would seem to refer to a
case in which the wife of a man interfered in
a quarrel. This law, the *jus talionis*, is elsewhere repeated in substance, cp. marg. reff.
and Gen. ix. 6. It has its root in a simple
conception of justice, and is found in the
laws of many ancient nations. It serves in
this place as a maxim for the magistrate in
awarding the amount of compensation to be
paid for the infliction of personal injury.
The sum was to be as nearly as possible the
worth in money of the power lost by the
injured person.—Our Lord quotes *v.* 24 as
representing the form of the Law, in order
to illustrate the distinction between the
letter and the spirit (Matt. v. 38). The
tendency of the teaching of the Scribes and
Pharisees was to confound the obligations of
the conscience with the external requirements of the Law. The Law, in its place,
was still to be "holy and just and good,"
(Rom. vii. 12,) but its direct purpose was
to protect the community, not to guide the
heart of the believer, who was not to exact

26 wound, stripe for stripe. And if a man smite the eye of his
servant, or the eye of his maid, that it perish; he shall let him
27 go free for his eye's sake. And if he smite out his manservant's
tooth, or his maidservant's tooth; he shall let him go free for his
28 tooth's sake. ¶ If an ox gore a man or a woman, that they die :
then ᶻthe ox shall be surely stoned, and his flesh shall not be   ᶻ Gen. 9. 5.
29 eaten; but the owner of the ox *shall be* quit. But if the ox were
wont to push with his horn in time past, and it hath been testified
to his owner, and he hath not kept him in, but that he hath
killed a man or a woman; the ox shall be stoned, and his owner
30 also shall be put to death. If there be laid on him a sum of
money, then he shall give for ᵃthe ransom of his life whatsoever   ᵃ ver. 22.
31 is laid upon him. Whether he have gored a son, or have gored a   Num. 35. 31.
daughter, according to this judgment shall it be done unto him.
32 If the ox shall push a manservant or a maidservant; he shall
give unto their master ᵇthirty shekels of silver, and the ᶜox shall   ᵇ See Zech.
33 be stoned. ¶ And if a man shall open a pit, or if a man shall   11. 12, 13.
34 dig a pit, and not cover it, and an ox or an ass fall therein; the   Matt. 26. 15.
owner of the pit shall make *it* good, *and* give money unto the   Phil. 2. 7.
35 owner of them; and the dead *beast* shall be his. ¶ And if one   ᶜ ver. 28.
man's ox hurt another's, that he die; then they shall sell the
live ox, and divide the money of it; and the dead *ox* also they
36 shall divide. Or if it be known that the ox hath used to push in
time past, and his owner hath not kept him in; he shall surely
pay ox for ox; and the dead shall be his own.
CHAP. 22. IF a man shall steal an ox, or a ¹sheep, and kill it, or   ᵃ 2 Sam. 12.
sell it; he shall restore five oxen for an ox, and ᵃfour sheep for   6.
2 a sheep. If a thief be found ᵇbreaking up, and be smitten   See Prov.
3 that he die, *there shall* ᶜno blood *be shed* for him. If the sun   6. 31.
be risen upon him, *there shall be* blood *shed* for him; *for* he   Luke 19. 8.
should make full restitution; if he have nothing, then he shall   ᵇ Matt. 24.
4 be ᵈsold for his theft. If the theft be certainly ᵉfound in his   43.
hand alive, whether it be ox, or ass, or sheep; he shall ᶠrestore   ᶜ Num. 35.
5 double. ¶ If a man shall cause a field or vineyard to be eaten,   27.
                                                                      ᵈ ch. 21. 2.
¹ Or, *goat*.   ᵉ ch. 21. 16.
                                                                      ᶠ See ver. 1,
                                                                      7. Prov.6.31.

---

eye for eye, tooth for tooth, but to love his
enemies, and to forgive all injuries.
26, 27. Freedom was the proper equivalent for permanent injury.
28-32. The animal was slain as a tribute
to the sanctity of human life (Cp. marg. reff.
and Gen. iv. 11). It was stoned, and its flesh
was treated as carrion. Guilty negligence
on the part of its owner was reckoned a
capital offence, to be commuted for a fine.
In the case of a slave, the payment was
the standard price of a slave, thirty shekels
of silver. See Lev. xxv. 44-46, xxvii. 3, and
the marg. reff. for the New Test. application of this fact.
33, 34. The usual mode of protecting a
well in the East was probably then, as now,
by building round it a low circular wall.
35, 36. The dead ox in this case, as well
as in the preceding one, must have been
worth no more than the price of the hide,
as the flesh could not be eaten. See Lev.
xvii. 1-6.
XXII. 1. The theft of an ox appears to
have been regarded as a greater crime than

the theft of a sheep, because it shewed a
stronger purpose in wickedness to take the
larger and more powerful animal. It may
have been on similar moral ground that the
thief, when he had proved his persistency in
crime by adding to his theft the slaughter,
or sale, of the animal, was to restore four
times its value in the case of a sheep (cp.
mârg. reff.), and five times its value in the
case of an ox; but if the animal was still in
his possession alive (see *v.* 4) he had to make
only twofold restitution.
2-4. If a thief, in breaking into a dwelling in the night, was slain, the person who
slew him did not incur the guilt of blood;
but if the same occurred in daylight, the
slayer was guilty in accordance with xxi. 12.
The distinction may have been based on the
fact that in the light of day there was a fair
chance of identifying and apprehending the
thief.
5. *shall put in his beast, and shall feed*]
Rather, **shall let his beast go loose, and
it shall feed.**

and shall put in his beast, and shall feed in another man's field;
of the best of his own field, and of the best of his own vineyard,
6 shall he make restitution. ¶ If fire break out, and catch in
thorns, so that the stacks of corn, or the standing corn, or the
field, be consumed *therewith*; he that kindled the fire shall
7 surely make restitution. ¶ If a man shall deliver unto his neighbour money or stuff to keep, and it be stolen out of the man's
8 house; *g* if the thief be found, let him pay double. If the thief
be not found, then the master of the house shall be brought
unto the *h* judges, *to see* whether he have put his hand unto his
9 neighbour's goods. For all manner of trespass, *whether it be*
for ox, for ass, for sheep, for raiment, *or* for any manner of lost
thing, which *another* challengeth to be his, the *i* cause of both
parties shall come before the judges; *and* whom the judges shall
10 condemn, he shall pay double unto his neighbour. ¶ If a man
deliver unto his neighbour an ass, or an ox, or a sheep, or any
beast, to keep; and it die, or be hurt, or driven away, no man
11 seeing *it: then* shall an *k* oath of the LORD be between them both,
that he hath not put his hand unto his neighbour's goods; and
the owner of it shall accept *thereof*, and he shall not make *it*
12 good. And *l* if it be stolen from him, he shall make resti-
13 tution unto the owner thereof. If it be torn in pieces, *then* let
him bring it *for* witness, *and* he shall not make good that which
14 was torn. And if a man borrow *ought* of his neighbour, and it
be hurt, or die, the owner thereof *being* not with it, he shall surely
15 make *it* good. *But* if the owner thereof *be* with it, he shall not
make *it* good: if it *be* an hired *thing*, it came for his hire.
16 ¶ And *m* if a man entice a maid that is not betrothed, and lie
17 with her, he shall surely endow her to be his wife. If her father
utterly refuse to give her unto him, he shall ¹ pay money accord-
18 ing to the *n* dowry of virgins. ¶ *o* Thou shalt not suffer a witch
19 to live. ¶ *p* Whosoever lieth with a beast shall surely be put to
20 death. ¶ *q* He that sacrificeth unto *any* god, save unto the LORD
21 only, he shall be utterly destroyed. ¶ *r* Thou shalt neither vex a

¹ Heb. *weigh*, Gen. 23. 16.

g ver. 4.

h ch. 21. 6.
& ver. 28.

i Deut. 25. 1.
2 Chr. 19. 10.

k Heb. 6. 16.
l Gen. 31. 39.
m Deut. 22.
28, 29.
n 1 Sam. 18.
25.
o Lev. 19.
26, 31.
Deut. 18.
10. 11.
1 Sam. 28.
3, 9.
p Lev. 18. 23.
& 20. 15.
q Num. 25.
2, 7, 8.
Deut. 13. 1.
& 17. 2, 3, 5.
r ch. 23. 9.
Lev. 19. 33.
& 25. 35.
Deut. 10. 19.
Jer. 7. 6.
Zech. 7. 10.
Mal. 3. 5.

---

8. It would appear that if the master of
the house could clear himself of imputation,
the loss of the pledged article fell upon its
owner.

9. *all manner of trespass*] He who was accused, and he who had lost the stolen property, were both to appear before the
judges (xviii. 25, 26).

10–13. This law appears to relate chiefly
to herdsmen employed by the owners of
cattle. When an animal was stolen (*v.* 12),
it was presumed either that the herdsman
might have prevented it, or that he could
find the thief and bring him to justice
(see *v.* 4). When an animal was killed by
a wild beast, the keeper had to produce
the mangled carcase, not only in proof of
the fact, but to shew that he had, by his
vigilance and courage, deprived the wild
beast of its prey.

15. *it came for his hire*] The sum paid for
hiring was regarded as covering the risk of
accident.

16, 17. See marg. reff.

18. *Thou shalt not suffer a witch to live*]
See marg. reff. and Lev. xx. 27. The
witch is here named to represent the class.
This is the earliest denunciation of witchcraft in the Law. In every form of witchcraft there is an appeal to a power not
acting in subordination to the Divine Law.
From all such notions and tendencies true
worship is designed to deliver us. The
practice of witchcraft was therefore an act
of rebellion against Jehovah, and, as such,
was a capital crime. The passages bearing
on the subject in the Prophets, as well as
those in the Law, carry a lesson for all ages.
Isa. viii. 19, xix. 3, xliv. 25, xlvii. 12, 13;
Micah v. 12, &c.

20. This was probably an old formula,
the sense of which, on its ethical side, is
comprised in the First and Second Commandments.

shall be utterly destroyed] The Hebrew
word here used is *cherem* (*i.e.* devoted). See
Lev. xxvii. 28.

21. *a stranger*] See xx. 10 note.

stranger, nor oppress him : for ye were strangers in the land of
22 Egypt. *Ye shall not afflict any widow, or fatherless child.
23 If thou afflict them in any wise, and they *cry at all unto me, I
24 will surely *hear their cry ; and my *wrath shall wax hot, and I
   will kill you with the sword ; and *your wives shall be widows, and
25 your children fatherless. ¶*If thou lend money to any of my
   people that is poor by thee, thou shalt not be to him as an usurer,
26 neither shalt thou lay upon him usury. *If thou at all take thy
   neighbour's raiment to pledge, thou shalt deliver it unto him by
27 that the sun goeth down : for that is his covering only, it is his
   raiment for his skin : wherein shall he sleep ? And it shall come
   to pass, when he *crieth unto me, that I will hear ; for I am
28 *gracious. ¶*Thou shalt not revile the ¹gods, nor curse the
29 ruler of thy people. ¶Thou shalt not delay to offer ²*the first of
   thy ripe fruits, and of thy ³liquors : *the firstborn of thy sons
30 shalt thou give unto me. *Likewise shalt thou do with thine
   oxen, and with thy sheep : *seven days it shall be with his dam ;
31 on the eighth day thou shalt give it me. ¶And ye shall be *holy
   men unto me : *neither shall ye eat any flesh that is torn of
   beasts in the field ; ye shall cast it to the dogs.

CHAP. 23. THOU *shalt not *raise a false report : put not thine hand
2 with the wicked to be an *unrighteous witness. *Thou shalt
   not follow a multitude to do evil ; *neither shalt thou ⁵speak in
3 a cause to decline after many to wrest judgment : neither shalt
4 thou countenance a poor man in his cause. ¶*If thou meet
   thine enemy's ox or his ass going astray, thou shalt surely bring
5 it back to him again. *If thou see the ass of him that hateth
   thee lying under his burden, ⁶and wouldest forbear to help him,
6 thou shalt surely help with him. ¶*Thou shalt not wrest the

*Ps. 94. 6.	
Isai. 1. 17.	
Ezek. 22. 7.	
Zech. 7. 10.	
Jam. 1. 27.	
*Deut. 15.	
Luke 18. 7.	
*ver. 27.	
Job 34. 28.	
Jam. 5. 4.	
*Ps. 69. 24.	
*Ps. 109. 9.	
Lam. 5. 3.	
*Neh. 5. 7.	
*Job 22. 6.	
*ver. 23.	
*ch. 34. 6.	
2 Chr. 30. 9.	
*Eccles. 10. 20.	
Jude 8.	
*Prov. 3. 9.	
*ch. 13. 2.	
*Deut. 15. 19.	
*Lev. 22. 27.	
*ch. 19. 6.	
*Lev. 22. 8.	
Ezek. 4. 14.	
*ver. 7.	
*ch. 20. 16.	
Matt. 26.	
59, 60, 61.	
*Gen. 7. 1.	
Matt. 27. 24.	
*ver. 6. 7.	
Ps. 72. 2.	
*Deut. 22. 1.	
Matt. 5. 44.	
Rom. 12. 20.	
*Deut. 22. 4.	
*Deut. 27.	
19. Job 31.	
13, 21.	
Isai. 10. 1, 2.	
Mal. 3. 5.	

¹ Or, judges, ver. 8, 9. Ps. 82. 6.	⁴ Or, receive.	cease to leave thy business for him ; thou shalt
² Heb. thy fulness.	⁵ Heb. answer.	surely leave it to join
³ Heb. tear.	⁶ Or, wilt thou cease to help him ? or, and wouldest	with him.

---

22. afflict] A word including all cold and contemptuous treatment. See Deut. x. 18. Contrast the blessing, Deut. xiv. 29.

25. See notes on Lev. xxv. 35–43 ; cp. Deut. xxiii. 19.

26, 27. The law regarding pledges is expanded, Deut. xxiv. 6, 10–13.

28. the gods] Heb. elohim. See xxi. 6 note. Many take it as the name of God (as in Gen. i. 1), and this certainly seems best to represent the Hebrew, and to suit the context. curse the ruler, &c.] See Acts xxiii. 5.

29, 30. The offering of Firstfruits appears to have been a custom of primitive antiquity and was connected with the earliest acts of sacrifice. See Gen. iv. 3, 4. The references to it here and in xxiii. 19 had probably been handed down from patriarchal times. The specific law relating to the firstborn of living creatures was brought out in a strong light in connection with the deliverance from Egypt (xiii. 2, 12, 13) ; cp. xxii. 27 ; Deut. xxvi. 2–11 ; Neh. x. 35. the first of thy ripe fruits, and of thy liquors] See the margin. The rendering of our Bible is a paraphrase.

31. The sanctification of the nation was emphatically symbolized by strictness of diet as regards both the kind of animal, and the mode of slaughtering. See Lev. chs. xi. and xvii.

XXIII. 1–3. These four commands, addressed to the conscience, are illustrations of the Ninth Commandment, mainly in reference to the giving of evidence in legal causes. Cp. 1 Kings xxi. 10 ; Acts vi. 11.

2. This verse might be more strictly rendered, Thou shalt not follow the many to evil ; neither shalt thou bear witness in a cause so as to incline after the many to pervert justice.

3. countenance] Rather, **show partiality** to a man's cause because he is poor (cp. Lev. xix. 15).

4, 5. So far was the spirit of the Law from encouraging personal revenge that it would not allow a man to neglect an opportunity of saving his enemy from loss.

5. The sense appears to be :—If thou see the ass of thine enemy lying down under his burden, thou shalt forbear to pass by him ; thou shalt help him in loosening the girths of the ass.

6–9. Four precepts evidently addressed to those in authority as judges :—

(a) To do justice to the poor.—Comparing v. 6 with v. 3, it was the part of the judge

h ver. 1.	7 judgment of thy poor in his cause. *h* Keep thee far from a false
Luke 3. 14.	matter; *i* and the innocent and righteous slay thou not: for *k* I
Eph. 4. 25.	
i Deut. 27.	8 will not justify the wicked. And *l* thou shalt take no gift: for
25.	the gift blindeth ¹ the wise, and perverteth the words of the
Ps. 94. 21.	
Matt. 27. 4.	9 righteous. Also *m* thou shalt not oppress a stranger: for ye
k ch. 34. 7.	know the ² heart of a stranger, seeing ye were strangers in the
Rom. 1. 18.	
l Deut.16.19.	10 land of Egypt. ¶ And *n* six years thou shalt sow thy land, and
Ps. 26. 10.	11 shalt gather in the fruits thereof: but the seventh *year* thou shalt
Isai. 1. 23.	let it rest and lie still; that the poor of thy people may eat: and
Ezek. 22. 12.	
m Deut. 10.	what they leave the beasts of the field shall eat. In like manner
19. & 24. 14.	thou shalt deal with thy vineyard, *and* with thy ³ oliveyard.
n Lev. 25. 3.	
o ch. 20. 8. 9.	12 *o* Six days thou shalt do thy work, and on the seventh day thou
	shalt rest: that thine ox and thine ass may rest, and the son of
	13 thy handmaid, and the stranger, may be refreshed. ¶ And in all
p Ps. 39. 1.	*things* that I have said unto you *p* be circumspect: and *q* make no
1 Tim. 4. 16.	mention of the name of other gods, neither let it be heard out of
q Num. 32.	
38.	14 thy mouth. ¶ *r* Three times thou shalt keep a feast unto me in
Deut. 12. 3.	15 the year. *s* Thou shalt keep the feast of unleavened bread: (thou
r Lev. 23. 4.	shalt eat unleavened bread seven days, as I commanded thee, in
Deut. 16. 16.	
s Deut. 16. 4.	the time appointed of the month Abib; for in it thou camest
t ch. 34. 20.	16 out from Egypt: *t* and none shall appear before me empty:) *u* and
u ch. 34. 22.	the feast of harvest, the firstfruits of thy labours, which thou

¹ Heb. *the seeing.*   ² Heb. *soul.*   ³ Or, *olive trees.*

---

to defend the poor against the oppression of the rich, and the part of the witness to take care lest his feelings of natural pity should tempt him to falsify evidence.

(*b*) To be cautious of inflicting capital punishment on one whose guilt was not clearly proved.—A doubtful case was rather to be left to God Himself, Who would "not justify the wicked," nor suffer him to go unpunished though he might be acquitted by an earthly tribunal. ' *v.* 7.

(*c*) To take no bribe or present which might in any way pervert judgment (*v.* 8); cp. Num. xvi. 15; 1 S. xii. 3; Acts xxvi. 26.

(*d*) To vindicate the rights of the stranger (*v.* 9)—rather, the **foreigner.** (xx. 10 note.) This verse is a repetition of xxii. 21, but the precept is there addressed to the people at large, while it is here addressed to the judges in reference to their official duties. The caution was perpetually necessary. Cp. Ezek. xxii. 7; Mal. iii. 5. The word rendered *heart* is more strictly *soul*, and would be better represented here by **feelings.**

10–12. This is the first mention of the Sabbatical year; the law for it is given at length in Lev. xxv. 2. Both the Sabbatical year and the weekly Sabbath are here spoken of exclusively in their relation to the poor, as bearing testimony to the equality of the people in their Covenant with Jehovah. In the first of these institutions, the proprietor of the soil gave up his rights for the year to the whole community of living creatures, not excepting the beasts: in the latter, the master gave up his claim for the day to the services of his servants and cattle.

12. *may be refreshed*] Literally, *may take breath.*

13. Cp. Deut. iv. 9; Josh. xxii. 5; Eph. v. 15.

14–17. This is the first mention of the three great Yearly Festivals. The Feast of Unleavened Bread, in its connection with the Paschal Lamb, is spoken of in chs. xii., xiii. : but the two others are here first named. The whole three are spoken of as if they were familiarly known to the people. The points that are especially enjoined are that every male Israelite should attend them at the Sanctuary (cp. xxxiv. 23), and that he should take with him an offering for Jehovah, presenting himself before his King with his tribute in his hand. That this condition belonged to all the Feasts, though it is here stated only in regard to the Passover, cannot be doubted. See Deut. xvi. 16.

15, 16. On the Feast of Unleavened Bread, or the Passover, see xii. 1-20, 43-50, xiii. 3-16, xxxiv. 18-20; Lev. xxiii. 4-14. On the Feast of the Firstfruits of Harvest, called also the Feast of Weeks, and the Feast of Pentecost, see xxxiv. 22; Lev. xxiii. 15-21. On the Feast of Ingathering, called also the Feast of Tabernacles, see Lev. xxiii. 34-36, 39-43.

16. *in the end of the year*] Cp. xxxiv. 22. The year here spoken of must have been the civil or agrarian year, which began after harvest, when the ground was prepared for sowing. Cp. Lev. xxiii. 39; Deut. xvi. 13-15. The sacred year began in spring, with the month Abib, or Nisan. See xii. 2 note, and Lev. xxv. 9.

when thou hast gathered] Rather, **when thou gatherest in.**

hast sown in the field: and [x]the feast of ingathering, *which is* in
the end of the year, when thou hast gathered in thy labours out
17 of the field. [y]Three times in the year all thy males shall appear
18 before the Lord GOD. ¶ [z]Thou shalt not offer the blood of my
sacrifice with leavened bread; neither shall the fat of my [1]sacri-
19 fice remain until the morning. [a]The first of the firstfruits of
thy land thou shalt bring into the house of the LORD thy God.
20 ¶ [b]Thou shalt not seethe a kid in his mother's milk. ¶ [c]Behold, I
send an Angel before thee, to keep thee in the way, and to bring
21 thee into the place which I have prepared. Beware of him, and
obey his voice, [d]provoke him not; for he will [e]not pardon your
22 transgressions: for [f]my name *is* in him. But if thou shalt
indeed obey his voice, and do all that I speak; then [g]I will be
an enemy unto thine enemies, and [2]an adversary unto thine
23 adversaries. [h]For mine Angel shall go before thee, and [i]bring
thee in unto the Amorites, and the Hittites, and the Perizzites,
and the Canaanites, the Hivites, and the Jebusites: and I will
24 cut them off. Thou shalt not [k]bow down to their gods, nor
serve them, [l]nor do after their works: [m]but thou shalt utterly
25 overthrow them, and quite break down their images. And ye
shall [n]serve the LORD your God, and [o]he shall bless thy bread,
and thy water; and [p]I will take sickness away from the midst of
26 thee. [q]There shall nothing cast their young, nor be barren, in
27 thy land: the number of thy days I will [r]fulfil. I will send [s]my
fear before thee, and will [t]destroy all the people to whom thou

[x] Deut. 16. 13.
[y] ch. 34. 23.
[z] Lev. 2. 11.
[a] ch. 22. 29.
[b] ch. 34. 26. Deut. 14. 21.
[c] Num. 20. 16. Ps. 91. 11.
[d] Num. 14. 11. Ps. 78. 40, 56. Eph. 4. 30.
[e] ch. 32. 34. Num. 14. 35. Josh. 24. 20. Jer. 5. 7. 1 John 5. 16.
[f] Isai. 9. 6. Jer. 23. 6. John 10. 30, 38.
[g] Gen. 12. 3.
[h] ver. 20.
[i] Josh. 24. 8, 11.
[k] ch. 20. 5.
[l] Lev. 18. 3.
[m] ch. 34. 13.
[n] 1 Sam. 7. 3.
[o] Deut. 7. 13.
[p] ch. 15. 26.
[q] Job 21. 10.
[r] Gen. 25. 8. 1 Chr. 23. 1.
[s] Gen. 35. 5.
[t] Deut. 7. 23.

[1] Or, *feast*.
[2] Or, *I will afflict them that afflict thee.*

18. *the blood of my sacrifice*] It is generally considered that this must refer to the Paschal Lamb. See xii. 7, 11, 13, 22, 23, 27.

the fat of my sacrifice] Strictly, **the fat of my feast**; the *best part* of the feast, that is, the Paschal Lamb itself. Cp. xxxiv. 25.

19. *The first of the firstfruits of thy land*] The *best*, or *chief* of the Firstfruits, that is, the two wave loaves described Lev. xxiii. 17. As the preceding precept appears to refer to the Passover, so it is likely that this refers to Pentecost. They are called in Leviticus, "the firstfruits unto the LORD;" and it is reasonable that they should here be designated the *chief* of the Firstfruits. If, with some, we suppose the precept to relate to the offerings of Firstfruits in general, the command is a repetition of xxii. 29.

Thou shalt not seethe a kid in his mother's milk] This precept is repeated. See marg. reff. If we connect the first of the two preceding precepts with the Passover, and the second with Pentecost, it seems reasonable to connect this with the Feast of Tabernacles. The only explanation which accords with this connexion is one which refers to a superstitious custom connected with the harvest; in which a kid was seethed in its mother's milk to propitiate in some way the deities, and the milk was sprinkled on the fruit trees, fields and gardens, as a charm to improve the crops of the coming year. Others take it to be a prohibition of a custom of great antiquity among the Arabs, of preparing a gross sort of food by stewing a kid in milk, with the addition of certain ingredients of a stimulating nature: and others take it in connexion with the prohibitions to slaughter a cow and a calf, or a ewe and her lamb, on the same day (Lev. xxii. 28), or to take a bird along with her young in the nest (Deut. xxii. 6). It is thus understood as a protest against cruelty and outraging the order of nature.

20. *an Angel*] See iii. 2, 8; Josh. v. 13; Isai. lxiii. 9.

22. The rendering in the margin is better. Cf. Deut. xx. 4.

23. *I will cut them off*] The national existence of the Canaanites was indeed to be *utterly* destroyed, every trace of their idolatries was to be blotted out, no social intercourse was to be held with them while they served other gods, nor were alliances of any kind to be formed with them. (See Deut. vii.; xii. 1-4, 29-31.) But it is alike contrary to the spirit of the Divine Law, and to the facts bearing on the subject scattered in the history, to suppose that any obstacle was put in the way of well disposed individuals of the denounced nations who left their sins and were willing to join the service of Jehovah. The spiritual blessings of the Covenant were always open to those who sincerely and earnestly desired to possess them. See xx. 10; Lev. xix. 34, xxiv. 22.

27. *destroy*] Rather, **overthrow**. See *v.* 23.

shalt come, and I will make all thine enemies turn their [1]backs
28 unto thee. And [u]I will send hornets before thee, which shall
drive out the Hivite, the Canaanite, and the Hittite, from before
29 thee. [w]I will not drive them out from before thee in one year;
lest the land become desolate, and the beast of the field multiply
30 against thee. By little and little I will drive them out from
31 before thee, until thou be increased, and inherit the land. And
[x]I will set thy bounds from the Red sea even unto the sea of
the Philistines, and from the desert unto the river: for I will
[y]deliver the inhabitants of the land into your hand; and thou
32 shalt drive them out before thee. [z]Thou shalt make no cove-
33 nant with them, nor with their gods. They shall not dwell in
thy land, lest they make thee sin against me : for if thou serve
their gods, [a]it will surely be a snare unto thee.

CHAP. 24. AND he said unto Moses, Come up unto the LORD, thou,
and Aaron, [a]Nadab, and Abihu, [b]and seventy of the elders of
2 Israel; and worship ye afar of. And Moses [c]alone shall come
near the LORD : but they shall not come nigh; neither shall the
3 people go up with him. ¶ And Moses came and told the people
all the words of the LORD, and all the judgments : and all the
people answered with one voice, and said, [d]All the words which
4 the LORD hath said will we do. ¶ And Moses [e]wrote all the
words of the LORD, and rose up early in the morning, and
builded an altar under the hill, and twelve [f]pillars, according to
5 the twelve tribes of Israel. And he sent young men of the
children of Israel, which offered burnt offerings, and sacrificed
6 peace offerings of oxen unto the LORD. And Moses [g]took half
of the blood, and put it in basons; and half of the blood he
7 sprinkled on the altar. And he [h]took the book of the covenant,
and read in the audience of the people : and they said, [i]All that
8 the LORD hath said will we do, and be obedient. And Moses
took the blood, and sprinkled it on the people, and said, Behold

Marginal references (left column):

[u] Deut. 7. 20.
Josh. 24. 12.
[w] Deut. 7. 22.

[x] Gen. 15. 18.
& reff.
[y] Josh. 21.
44.
Judg. 1. 4.
[z] ch. 34. 12.
Deut. 7. 2.
[a] Josh. 23.
13.
Judg. 2. 3.
1 Sam. 18.
21.
Ps. 106. 36.
[a] ch. 28. 1.
Lev. 10. 1, 2.
[b] ch. 1. 5.
Num. 11. 16.
[c] ver. 13, 15.
[d] ver. 7.
Deut. 5. 27.
Gal. 3. 19.
[e] Deut. 31. 9.
[f] Gen. 28. 18.

[g] Heb. 9. 18.

[h] Heb. 9. 19.
[i] ver. 3.

---

[1] Heb. neck, Ps. 18. 40.

---

28. *hornets*] Cp. marg. reff. The word
is used figuratively for a cause of terror and
discouragement. Bees are spoken of in the
like sense, Deut. i. 44; Ps. cxviii. 12.
29. *beast of the field*] i.e. destructive animals.
31. In *v.* 23, the limits of the Land of
Canaan, strictly so called, are indicated; to
this, when the Israelites were about to take
possession of it, were added the regions of
Gilead and Bashan on the left side of the
Jordan (Num. xxxii. 33–42 ; Josh. xiii. 29–
32). These two portions made up the Holy
Land, of which the limits were recognized,
with inconsiderable variations, till the final
overthrow of the Jewish polity. But in
this verse the utmost extent of Hebrew dominion, as it existed in the time of David
and Solomon, is set forth. The kingdom
then reached to Eloth and Ezion-geber on
the Ælanitic Gulf of the Red Sea (1 K. ix.
26), and to Tiphsah on the "River," that is,
the River Euphrates (1 K. iv. 24), having
for its western boundary "the Sea of the
Philistines," that is, the Mediterranean, and
for its southern boundary "the desert," that

is, the wildernesses of Shur and Paran (cp.
Gen. xv. 18; Deut. i. 7, xi. 24; Josh. i. 4).
XXIV. 1, 2 are placed by some with
great probability between verses 8 and 9.
4. *twelve pillars*] As the altar was a symbol of the Presence of Jehovah, so these
twelve pillars represented the presence of
the Twelve Tribes with whom He was
making the Covenant.
5. *young men of the children of Israel*] See
xix. 22; xxviii. 1; Lev. i. 5.
burnt offerings...peace offerings] The Burnt
offerings (Lev. i.) figured the dedication of
the nation to Jehovah, and the Peace offerings (Lev. iii.) their communion with Jehovah and with each other.
6. *he sprinkled*] Rather, he cast. See
Lev. i. 5.
7. *the book of the covenant*] See xx. 22 note.
The people had to repeat their assent to the
Book of the Covenant before the blood was
thrown upon them. Cp. 2 K. xxiii. 2, 21 ;
2 Chron. xxxiv. 30.
8. The blood which sealed the Covenant
was the blood of Burnt offerings and Peace
offerings. The Sin offering (Lev. iv.) had

[k]the blood of the covenant, which the LORD hath made with you
9 concerning all these words. ¶ Then [l]went up Moses, and Aaron,
10 Nadab, and Abihu, and seventy of the elders of Israel: and
they [m]saw the God of Israel: and *there was* under his feet as it
were a paved work of a [n]sapphire stone, and as it were the [o]body
11 of heaven in *his* clearness. And upon the nobles of the children
of Israel he [p]laid not his hand: also [q]they saw God, and did
12 [r]eat and drink. ¶ And the LORD said unto Moses, [s]Come up to
me into the mount, and be there: and I will give thee [t]tables of
stone, and a law, and commandments which I have written;
13 that thou mayest teach them. And Moses rose up, and [u]his
minister Joshua: and Moses [w]went up into the mount of God.
14 And he said unto the elders, Tarry ye here for us, until we come
again unto you: and, behold, Aaron and Hur *are* with you: if
any man have any matters to do, let him come unto them.
15 And Moses went up into the mount, and [x]a cloud covered the
16 mount. And [y]the glory of the LORD abode upon mount Sinai,
and the cloud covered it six days: and the seventh day he called
17 unto Moses out of the midst of the cloud. And the sight of the
glory of the LORD *was* like [z]devouring fire on the top of the
18 mount in the eyes of the children of Israel. And Moses went
into the midst of the cloud, and gat him up into the mount: and
[a]Moses was in the mount forty days and forty nights.

[k] Heb. 9. 20.
1 Pet. 1. 2.
[l] ver. 1.
[m] John 1. 18.
1 Tim. 6. 16.
1 John 4. 12.
[n] Rev. 4. 3.
[o] Matt. 17. 2.
[p] ch. 19. 21.
[q] ver. 10.
[r] Gen. 31. 54.
ch. 18. 12.
1 Cor. 10. 18
[s] ver. 2, 15. ;
[t] ch. 31. 18.
& 32. 15, 16.
Deut. 5. 22.
[u] ch. 32. 17.
[w] ver. 2.

[x] ch. 19. 9.
Matt. 17. 5.
[y] ch. 16. 10.
Num. 14. 10.

[z] ch. 3. 2.
& 19. 18.
Deut. 4. 36.
Heb. 12. 18,
[a] ch. 34. 28.
Deut. 9. 9.

not yet been instituted. That more complicated view of human nature which gave
to the Sin offering its meaning, had yet
to be developed by the Law, which was
now only receiving its ratification. The
Covenant between Jehovah and His people
therefore took precedence of the operation
of the Law, by which came the knowledge
of sin. Rom. iii. 20.

upon the people] Either upon the elders or
those who stood foremost; or, upon the
twelve pillars representing the Twelve
Tribes, as the first half had been cast upon
the altar, which witnessed to the Presence of
Jehovah. The blood thus divided between
the two parties to the Covenant signified the
sacramental union between the Lord and
His people. Cf. Ps. 1. 5; Zech. ix. 11.

9. It would appear that Moses, Aaron
with his two sons, and seventy of the elders
(xix. 7) went a short distance up the mountain to eat the meal of the Covenant (cp.
Gen. xxxi. 43-47), which must have consisted of the flesh of the Peace offerings (*v.*
5). Joshua accompanied Moses as his servant (*v.* 13).

10. *And they saw the God of Israel*] As
they ate the sacrificial feast, the Presence of
Jehovah was manifested to them with special distinctness. In the act of solemn worship, they perceived that He was present
with them, as their Lord and their Deliverer.
It is idle to speculate on the mode of this revelation. That no visible form was presented to their bodily eyes, we are expressly
informed, Deut. iv. 12; see xxxiii. 20;
cp. Isa. vi. 1. The latter part of this verse
may be read: *under His feet, it was like a*

*work of bright sapphire stone, and like the
heaven itself in clearness.* On the sapphire,
see xxviii. 18; cp. Ezek. i. 26. The pure
blue of the heaven above them lent its influence to help the inner sense to realize the
vision which no mortal eye could behold.

11. *he laid not his hand*] *i.e.* He did not
smite them. It was believed that a mortal
could not survive the sight of God (xxxiii.
20; Gen. xxxii. 30; Judg. vi. 22; xiii.
22): but these rulers of Israel were permitted to eat and drink, while they were en-
joying in an extraordinary degree the sense
of the Divine Presence, and took no harm.

12. Many Jews understand the *tables of
stone* to denote the Ten Commandments;
a law, the Law written in the Pentateuch;
and the *commandments* (or *the commandment*),
the oral or traditional law which was in
after ages put into writing in the Mishna
and the Gemara. But it is more probable
that the Ten Commandments alone are
spoken of, and that the meaning is, *the
Tables of stone with the Law, even the Commandment.*

18. During this period of forty days, and
the second period when the Tables were renewed, Moses neither ate bread nor drank
water. Cp. marg. reff. Elijah in like manner fasted for forty days, when he visited
the same spot (1 K. xix. 8). The two
who met our Saviour on the Mount of
Transfiguration (Matt. xvii. 3), the one representing the Law, the other representing
the Prophets, thus shadowed forth in their
own experience the Fast of Forty days in
the wilderness of Judæa.

CHAP. 25. AND the LORD spake unto Moses, saying, Speak unto
a ch. 35. 5, 2 the children of Israel, that they ¹bring me an ²offering: *a* of every
21.
Ezra 3. 5.   man that giveth it willingly with his heart ye shall take my
& 7. 16.   3 offering. And this *is* the offering which ye shall take of them ;
Neh. 11. 2.   4 gold, and silver, and brass, and blue, and purple, and scarlet,
            5 and ³fine linen, and goats' *hair*, and rams' skins dyed red, and
b ch. 27. 20.   6 badgers' skins, and shittim wood, *b*oil for the light, *c*spices for
c ch. 30. 23.   7 anointing oil, and for *d*sweet incense, onyx stones, and stones to
d ch. 30. 34.   8 be set in the *c*ephod, and in the *f*breastplate. And let them
e ch. 28. 4, 6.
f ch. 28. 15.   ¹ Heb. *take for me.*   ² Or, *heave offering.*   ³ Or, *silk,* Gen. 41. 42.

XXV. XXVI. Jehovah had redeemed the Israelites from bondage. He had made a Covenant with them and had given them laws. He had promised, on condition of their obedience, to accept them as His own " peculiar treasure," as " a kingdom of priests and an holy nation " (xix. 5, 6). And now He was ready visibly to testify that He made his abode with them. He claimed to have a dwelling for Himself, which was to be in external form a tent of goats' hair (*v.* 4), to take its place among their own tents, and formed out of the same material (see xxvi. 7 note). The special mark of His Presence within the Tent was to be the Ark or chest containing the Ten Commandments on two tables of stone (xxxi. 18), symbolizing the divine Law of holiness, and covered by the Mercy seat, the type of reconciliation.— Moses was divinely taught regarding the construction and arrangement of every part of the Sanctuary. The directions which were given him are comprised in xxv. 1-xxxi. 11. The account of the performance of the work, expressed generally in the same terms, is given xxxv. 21-xl. 33.

1-9. Moses is commanded to invite the people to bring their gifts for the construction and service of the Sanctuary and for the dresses of the priests.

2. *an offering*] The word is used here in its general sense, being equivalent to *korban*, (cp. St. Mark vii. 11). On the marginal rendering " heave offering," see note on xxix. 27.

that giveth it willingly with his heart] The public service of Jehovah was to be instituted by freewill offerings, not by an enforced tax. Cp. 1 Chron. xxix. 3, 9, 14 ; Ezra ii. 68, 69 ; 2 Cor. viii. 11, 12, ix. 7. On the zeal with which the people responded to the call, see xxxv. 21-29, xxxvi. 5-7.

3. *gold, and silver, and brass*] The supply of these metals possessed by the Israelites at this time probably included what they had inherited from their forefathers, what they had obtained from the Egyptians (xii. 35), and what may have been found amongst the spoils of the Amalekites (xvii. 8-13). But with their abundant flocks and herds, it can hardly be doubted that they had carried on important traffic with the trading caravans that traversed the wilder-

ness, some of which, most likely, in the earliest times were furnished with silver, the gold of Ophir (or gold of Sheba, as it seems to have been indifferently called), and with the " brass" (the alloy of copper and tin, called bronze) of Phœnicia and Egypt. Cp. xxxviii. 24 note.

4. *blue, and purple, and scarlet*] *i.e.* the material dyed with these colours. The Jewish tradition has been very generally received that this material was wool. Cp. Heb. ix. 19 with Lev. xiv. 4, 49, &c. When spun and dyed by the women, it was delivered in the state of yarn ; and the weaving and embroidering was left to Aholiab and his assistants, xxxv. 25, 35. The " blue " and " purple " dye are usually thought to have been obtained from shell-fish, the " scarlet " from the cochineal insect of the holm-oak.

fine linen] The fine flax or the manufactured linen, for which Egypt was famous (Ezek. xxvii. 7), and which the Egyptians were in the habit of using for dresses of state (Gen. xli. 42). It was used as the groundwork of the figured curtains of the Tabernacle as well as of the embroidered hangings of the Tent and the Court. See xxxv. 35.

5. *rams' skins dyed red*] Skins tanned and coloured like the leather now known as red morocco.

badgers' skins] Rather, leather, probably of a sky-blue colour, formed from the skins of the *tachash* (a general name for marine animals), which was well adapted as a protection against the weather.

shittim wood] The word *shittim* is the plural form of *shittah*, which occurs as the name of the growing tree, Is. xli. 19. The tree is satisfactorily identified with the *Acacia seyal*, a gnarled and thorny tree, somewhat like a solitary hawthorn in its habit and manner of growth, but much larger. It flourishes in the driest situations, and is scattered more or less numerously over the Sinaitic Peninsula. It appears to be the only good wood produced in the wilderness. No other kind of wood was employed in the Tabernacle or its furniture. In the construction of the Temple cedar and fir took its place (1 K. v. 8, vi. 18 ; 2 Chron. ii. 8).

6, 7. See notes to chs. xxvii., xxviii., xxx.

8. *sanctuary*] *i.e.* a hallowed place. This

make me a *g*sanctuary; that *h*I may dwell among them.
9 *i*According to all that I shew thee, *after* the pattern of the
tabernacle, and the pattern of all the instruments thereof, even
10 so shall ye make *it*. ¶ *k*And they shall make an ark *of* shittim
wood : two cubits and a half *shall be* the length thereof, and a
cubit and a half the breadth thereof, and a cubit and a half the
11 height thereof. And thou shalt overlay it with pure gold, within
and without shalt thou overlay it, and shalt make upon it a
12 crown of gold round about. And thou shalt cast four rings of
gold for it, and put *them* in the four corners thereof ; and two
rings *shall be* in the one side of it, and two rings in the other side
13 of it. And thou shalt make staves *of* shittim wood, and overlay
14 them with gold. And thou shalt put the staves into the rings by
15 the sides of the ark, that the ark may be borne with them. *l*The
staves shall be in the rings of the ark : they shall not be taken
16 from it. And thou shalt put into the ark *m*the testimony which

g ch. 36. 1.
Lev. 4. 6.
& 10. 4.
& 21. 12.
Heb. 9. 1, 2.
h ch. 29. 45.
1 Kin. 6. 13.
2 Cor. 6. 16.
Heb. 3. 6.
Rev. 21. 3.
i ver. 40.
k ch. 37. 1.
Deut. 10. 3.
Heb. 9. 4.
l 1 Kin. 8. 8.
m ch. 16. 34.
& 31. 18.
Deut. 10. 2.
& 31. 36.
1 Kin. 8. 9.
2 Kin. 11. 12.
Heb. 9. 4.

is the most comprehensive of the words that
relate to the place dedicated to Jehovah. It
included the Tabernacle with its furniture,
its Tent, and its Court.

that I may dwell among them] The purpose
of the Sanctuary is here definitely declared
by the Lord Himself. It was to be the constant witness of His Presence amongst His
people. Cp. marg. reff.

9. *According to all that I shew thee*] The
Tabernacle and all that pertained to it were
to be in strict accordance with the ideas revealed by the Lord to Moses (cp. *v*. 40, xxvi.
30 ; Acts vii. 44 ; Heb. viii. 5). The word
here translated *pattern* is also used to denote
the plans for the Temple which were given
by David to Solomon (1 Chron. xxviii. 11,
12, 19) ; it is elsewhere rendered *form, likeness, similitude*, Deut. iv. 16, 17 ; Ezek. viii.
3, 10.

the tabernacle] The Hebrew word signifies
the " dwelling-place." It here denotes the
wooden structure, containing the Holy
Place and the most Holy Place, with the
tent which sheltered it. See xxvi. 1 note.

10-16 (cp. xxxvii. 1-5). The ARK is uni-
formly designated in Exodus the ARK OF
THE TESTIMONY. Elsewhere it is called THE
TESTIMONY, THE ARK OF THE COVENANT
(most frequently in Deuteronomy and the
other books of the Old Testament), THE
ARK OF THE LORD, THE ARK OF GOD, THE
ARK OF THE STRENGTH OF THE LORD, and
THE HOLY ARK.

The Ark of the Covenant was the central
point of the Sanctuary. It was designed
to contain the Testimony (*v*. 16, xl. 20 ;
Deut. xxxi. 26), that is, the Tables of the
Divine Law, the terms of the Covenant between Jehovah and His people : and it was
to support the Mercy seat with its Cherubim, from between which He was to hold
communion with them (*v*. 22). On this account, in these directions for the construction of the Sanctuary, it is named first of
all the parts. But on the other hand, in
the narrative of the work as it was actually

carried out, we find that it was not made
till after the Tabernacle (xxxvii. 1-9).
It was suitable that the receptacle should
be first provided to receive and shelter the
most sacred of the contents of the Sanctuary
as soon as it was completed. The order in
which the works were executed seems to be
given in xxxi. 7-10, and xxxv. 11-19. The
completion of the Ark is recorded in xxxvii.
1-5. On its history, see the concluding note
to ch. xl.

10. *an ark*] Taking the cubit at 18
inches (see Gen. vi. 15 note), the Ark of the
Covenant was a box 3ft. 9in. long, 2ft. 3in.
wide, and 2ft. 3in. deep.

11. *overlay it with pure gold*] Words descriptive of the common process of gilding.
The Egyptians in early times were acquainted with both the art of gilding and
that of covering a substance with thin plates
of gold.

a crown of gold] That is, an edging or
moulding of gold round the top of the Ark,
within which the cover or Mercy seat (*v*.
17) may have fitted (cp. xxxviii. 2). There
were golden mouldings, called by the same
name, to the Table of Shewbread (*v*. 24,
xxxvii. 11, 12), and to the Golden Altar
(xxx. 3, xxxvii. 26).

12. *four corners thereof*] Rather, **its four
bases**, or feet. It is not unlikely that there
were low blocks, or plinths, placed under
the corners to which the rings were attached
(see *v*. 26), and that it is to them that the
word is here applied. The Ark, when it
was carried, must thus have been raised
above the shoulders of the bearers.

15. *they shall not be taken from it*] This
direction was probably given in order that
the Ark might not be touched by the hand
(cp. 2 S. vi. 6).

16. *the testimony*] Literally, *something
spoken again and again*. The stone Tables
of the Ten Commandments are called the
Testimony, or, the Tables of the Testimony,
as the Ark which contained them is called
the Ark of the Testimony, and the Taber-

[n] ch. 37. 6. Rom. 3. 25. Heb. 9. 5.

17 I shall give thee. ¶ And [n]thou shalt make a mercy seat *of*
pure gold: two cubits and a half *shall be* the length thereof,
18 and a cubit and a half the breadth thereof. And thou shalt
make two cherubims *of* gold, *of* beaten work shalt thou make
19 them, in the two ends of the mercy seat. And make one
cherub on the one end, and the other cherub on the other end:
even [1]of the mercy seat shall ye make the cherubims on the two
20 ends thereof. And [o]the cherubims shall stretch forth *their* wings
on high, covering the mercy seat with their wings, and their
faces *shall look* one to another; toward the mercy seat shall the
21 faces of the cherubims be. [p]And thou shalt put the mercy seat
above upon the ark; and [q]in the ark thou shalt put the testimony
22 that I shall give thee. And [r]there I will meet with thee, and I
will commune with thee from above the mercy seat, from

[o] 1 Kin. 8. 7. 1 Chr. 28. 18. Heb. 9. 5.
[p] ch. 26. 34.
[q] ver. 16.
[r] ch. 29. 42, 43. & 30. 6, 36. Lev. 16. 2. Num. 17. 4.

[1] Or, *of the* matter *of the mercy seat.*

---

nacle in which the Ark was placed, the Tabernacle of the Testimony. Taking this in connexion with the prohibitory form of the Commandments, the name must have been understood as signifying the direct testimony of Jehovah against sin in man (Deut. xxxi. 26, 27).

The Ark of the Covenant has been most generally likened to the arks, or moveable shrines, which are represented on Egyptian monuments. The Egyptian arks were carried by poles on the shoulders, and some of them had on the cover two winged figures not unlike what we conceive the golden Cherubim to have been. Thus far the similarity is striking. But there were points of great dissimilarity. Between the winged figures on the Egyptian arks there was placed the material symbol of a deity, and the arks themselves were carried about in religious processions, so as to make a show in the eyes of the people. We know not what they contained. As regards the Ark of the Covenant, the absence of any symbol of God was one of its great characteristics. It was never carried in a ceremonial procession: when it was moved from one place to another, it was closely packed up, concealed from the eyes even of the Levites who bore it. When the Tabernacle was pitched, the Ark was never exhibited, but was kept in solemn darkness. Rest, it is evident, was its appointed [condition. It was occasionally moved out of its place in the Holy of Holies, but only so long as the nation was without a settled capital, and had something of the character of an army on the march. Not less was it distinguished from all other arks in the simple grandeur of its purpose: it was constructed to contain the plain text of the Ten Commandments written on stone in words that were intelligible to all.

17–22. *a mercy seat of pure gold*] (Cp. xxxvii. 6–9.) In external form, the Mercy seat was a plate of gold with the Cherubim standing on it, the whole beaten out of one solid piece of metal (xxxvii. 7); it was placed upon the Ark and so took the place of a cover. *Mercy* seat expresses well the distinct significance and recognized designation of the Hebrew name.

18–20. The Cherubim of the Mercy seat were human figures, each having two wings. They must have been of small size, proportioned to the area of the Mercy seat. Comparing the different references to form in this place, in 2 Sam. xxii. 11 (Ps. xviii. 10), in Ezek. chs. i. x. and in Rev. ch. iv., it would appear that the name *Cherub* was applied to various combinations of animal forms. Amongst the Egyptians, the Assyrians and the Greeks, as well as the Hebrews, the creatures by far most frequently introduced into these composite figures, were man, the ox, the lion, and the eagle, as being types of the most important and familiarly known classes of living material beings. Hence the Cherubim, described by Ezekiel, have been regarded as representing the whole creation engaged in the worship and service of God (cp. Rev. iv. 9–11, v. 13); and it would be in harmony with this view to suppose that the more strictly human shape of the Cherubim of the Mercy seat represented the highest form of created intelligence engaged in the devout contemplation of the divine Law of love and justice. (Cp. 1 Pet. i. 12.) It is worthy of notice that the golden Cherubim from between which Jehovah spoke (*v.* 22) to His people bore witness, by their place on the Mercy seat, to His redeeming mercy; while the Cherubim that took their stand at the gate of Eden, Gen. iii. 24, to keep the way to the tree of life, witnessed to His condemnation of sin in man.

18. *of beaten work*] *i.e.* elaborately wrought with the hammer.

19. *even of the mercy seat*] See margin. The sense appears to be that the Cherubim and the Mercy seat were to be wrought out of one mass of gold. (Cp. xxxvii. 7.)

21. *the testimony*] See *v.* 16 note. Cp. xl. 20.

[s]between the two cherubims which *are* upon the ark of the testimony, of all *things* which I will give thee in commandment unto
23 the children of Israel. ¶ [t]Thou shalt also make a table *of* shittim wood: two cubits *shall be* the length thereof, and a cubit the
24 breadth thereof, and a cubit and a half the height thereof. And thou shalt overlay it with pure gold, and make thereto a crown
25 of gold round about. And thou shalt make unto it a border of an hand breadth round about, and thou shalt make a golden
26 crown to the border thereof round about. And thou shalt make for it four rings of gold, and put the rings in the four corners
27 that *are* on the four feet thereof. Over against the border shall
28 the rings be for places of the staves to bear the table. And thou shalt make the staves *of* shittim wood, and overlay them with
29 gold, that the table may be borne with them. And thou shalt make [u]the dishes thereof, and spoons thereof, and covers thereof, and bowls thereof, [1]to cover withal: *of* pure gold shalt thou

[s] Num. 7. 89.
1 Sam. 4. 4.
2 Sam. 6. 2.
2 Kin. 19. 15.
Ps. 80. 1.
& 90. 1.
Isai. 37. 16.
[t] ch. 37. 10.
1 Kin. 7. 48.
2 Chr. 4. 8.
Heb. 9. 2.

[u] ch. 37. 16.
Num. 4. 7.

[1] Or, *to pour out withal.*

23–30. (Cp. xxxvii. 10–16.) The Table and the Candlestick figured on the Arch of Titus at Rome are those of the Maccabæan times, but made as nearly as possible after the ancient models reproduced under the direction of Solomon and Zerubbabel. The details and size of the figure, and the description of Josephus, appear to agree very nearly with the directions here given to Moses, and to illustrate them in several particulars. Josephus says that the Table was like the so-called Delphic tables, richly ornamented pieces of furniture in use amongst the Romans, which were sometimes, if not always, covered with gold or silver.

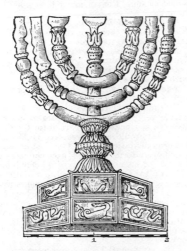

24. See *v.* 11 note. The moulding of the Table is still seen at the ends of the sculptured figure.

25. *a border*] Rather **a framing**, which reached from leg to leg so as to make the Table firm, as well as to adorn it with a second moulding of gold. Two fragments of such framing are still seen in the sculpture attached to the legs half-way down.

27. *Over against the border*] Rather, **Over against the framing;** that is, the rings were to be placed not upon the framing itself, but at the extremities of the legs answering to each corner of it.

29. *dishes*] deep vessels like *bowls*, similar to the large silver vessels (or *chargers*) which were filled with fine flour, and formed part of the offerings of the Princes of Israel (Num. vii. 13 sq.).

spoons] Rather, the small gold **cups** that

68   EXODUS. XXV.

w Lev. 24. 5, 6.
x 1 Kin.7.49.
Zech. 4. 2.
Heb. 9. 2.
Rev. 1. 12.
& 4. 5.

y ch. 27. 21.
& 30. 8.
Lev. 24. 3, 4.
2 Chr. 13. 11.

30 make them. And thou shalt set upon the table *w*shewbread
31 before me alway. ¶ *x*And thou shalt make a candlestick *of* pure
gold: *of* beaten work shall the candlestick be made : his shaft,
and his branches, his bowls, his knops, and his flowers, shall be
32 of the same. And six branches shall come out of the sides of it ;
three branches of the candlestick out of the one side, and three
33 branches of the candlestick out of the other side : three bowls
made like unto almonds, *with* a knop and a flower in one branch ;
and three bowls made like almonds in the other branch, *with*
a knop and a flower : so in the six branches that come out of the
34 candlestick. And in the candlestick *shall be* four bowls made
35 like unto almonds, *with* their knops and their flowers. And
there shall be a knop under two branches of the same, and a knop
under two branches of the same, and a knop under two branches
of the same, according to the six branches that proceed out of
36 the candlestick. Their knops and their branches shall be of the
37 same : all it *shall be* one beaten work *of* pure gold. And thou
shalt make the seven lamps thereof : and *y*they shall 1light the

1 Or, *cause to ascend.*

were filled with frankincense in the offerings of the Princes (Num. vii. 14), and represented on the Table in the sculpture.

covers...bowls] Or **flagons** and **chalices**,
such as were used for the rite of the Drink
offering, which appears to have regularly
accompanied every Meat offering (Lev.
xxiii. 18 ; Num. vi. 15, xxviii. 14, &c.).
The subject is important in its bearing upon
the meaning of the Shewbread : the corrected
rendering of the words tends to show that it
was a true Meat offering.

to cover withal] See the margin. The first
part of the verse might be better rendered :—
**And thou shalt make its bowls and its in-
cense-cups and its flagons and its chalices
for pouring out** *the Drink offerings.*

30. The Shewbread Table was placed in
the Holy Place on the north side (xxvi. 35).
Directions for preparing the Shewbread are
given in Lev. xxiv. 5-9. It consisted of
twelve large cakes of unleavened bread,
which were arranged on the Table in two
piles, with a golden cup of frankincense on
each pile. It was renewed every Sabbath
day. The stale loaves were given to the
priests, and the frankincense appears to
have been lighted on the Altar for a memorial. The Shewbread, with all the characteristics and significance of a great national
Meat offering, in which the twelve tribes
were represented by the twelve cakes, was
to stand before Jehovah *perpetually,* in
token that He was always graciously accepting the good works of His people, for
whom atonement had been made by the
victims offered on the Altar in the Court of
the Sanctuary. The Shewbread or bread
which is set forth would be more fairly rendered "Bread of the Presence." See notes
on Lev. xxiv. 5-9.

31–39. (Cp. xxxvii. 17–24.) *a candlestick of
pure gold*] A lamp-stand rather than a can-

dlestick. Its purpose was to support seven
oil-lamps. Its height appears to have been
about three feet, and its width two feet.
The original foot was lost or stolen when
the Candlestick was taken out of the Temple, and the pedestal in the sculpture was
added by some Roman artist to set off the
trophy.

*his shaft, and his branches, his bowls, his
knops, and his flowers*] Or, **its base, its stem,
its flower cups, its knobs, and its lilies.**

33. *three bowls made like unto almonds*]
Three cups of almond flowers. These appear to be the cups in immediate contact
with the knobs as shown in the sculpture.

a flower] A **lily** ; and this rendering well
agrees with the sculpture.

the candlestick] Here, and in the two following verses, the word appears to denote
the stem, as the essential part of the Candlestick. It would seem from *vv.* 33-35 that
the ornamentation of the Candlestick consisted of uniform members, each comprising
a series of an almond flower, a knob and a
lily ; that the stem comprised four of these
members ; that each pair of branches was
united to the stem at one of the knobs; and
that each branch comprised three members.
In comparing the description in the text
with the sculptured figure, allowance must
be made for some deviation in the sculptor's
copy.

37. *seven lamps*] These lamps were probably like those used by the Egyptian and
other nations, shallow covered vessels more
or less of an oval form, with a mouth at one
end from which the wick protruded. The
Candlestick was placed on the south side of
the Holy Place (xxvi. 35), with the line of
lamps parallel with the wall, or, according
to Josephus, somewhat obliquely. If the
wick-mouths of the lamps were turned outwards, they would give light over against

38 lamps thereof, that they may *give light over against ¹it. And
the tongs thereof, and the snuffdishes thereof, *shall be of* pure
39 gold. *Of* a talent of pure gold shall he make it, with all these
40 vessels. And ªlook that thou make *them* after their pattern,
²which was shewed thee in the mount.
CHAP. 26. MOREOVER ªthou shalt make the tabernacle *with* ten
curtains *of* fine twined linen, and blue, and purple, and scarlet:
2 *with* cherubims ³of cunning work shalt thou make them. The
length of one curtain *shall be* eight and twenty cubits, and the
breadth of one curtain four cubits : and every one of the curtains
3 shall have one measure. The five curtains shall be coupled
together one to another ; and *other* five curtains *shall be* coupled
4 one to another. And thou shalt make loops of blue upon the
edge of the one curtain from the selvedge in the coupling; and

z Num. 8. 2.

a ch. 26. 30.
Num. 8. 4.
1 Chr. 28.
11, 19.
Acts 7. 44.
Heb. 8. 5.
a ch. 36. 8.

¹ Heb. *the face of it.*
² Heb. *which thou wast
caused to see.*

³ Heb. *the work of a cunning workman,* or, *em-
broiderer.*

the Candlestick ; that is, towards the north
side [see Num. viii. 2].

Light was of necessity required in the
Tabernacle, and wherever light is used in
ceremonial observance, it may of course be
taken in a general way as a figure of the
Light of Truth ; but in the Sanctuary of
the covenanted people, it must plainly have
been understood as expressly significant
that the number of the lamps (seven) agreed
with the number of the Covenant. The
Covenant of Jehovah was essentially a Covenant of light.

37. *they shall light*] See margin and note
on Lev. i. 9.

38. *the tongs*] Used to trim and adjust the
wicks. (Cp. Is. vi. 6.)

the snuff-dishes] These were shallow vessels used to receive the burnt fragments of
wick removed by the tongs. The same Hebrew word is translated, in accordance with
its connection, *fire pans,* xxvii. 3, xxxviii. 3;
and *censers,* Numb. iv. 14, xvi. 6.

39. *a talent of pure gold*] about 94 lbs.

XXVI. 1-37. (Cp. xxxvi. 8-33.) The Tabernacle was to comprise three main parts,
the TABERNACLE (1-6), more strictly so-called,
its TENT (7-13), and its COVERING (*v.* 14)
(Cp. xxxv. 11, xxxix. 33, 34, xl. 19, 34;
Num. iii. 25, &c.). These parts are very
clearly distinguished in the Hebrew, but
they are confounded in many places of the
English Version [see *vv.* 7, 9, &c.]. The
TABERNACLE itself was to consist of curtains
of fine linen woven with coloured figures of
Cherubim, and a structure of boards which
was to contain the Holy Place and the Most
Holy Place; the TENT was to be a true tent
of goats' hair cloth to contain and shelter
the Tabernacle : the COVERING was to be of
red rams' skins and "tachash" skins (xxv. 5),
and was spread over the goats' hair tent as
an additional protection against the weather. On the external form of the Tabernacle and the arrangement of its parts, see
Cuts at the end of the chap.

1. *the tabernacle*] The *Mishkān, i.e.* the
dwelling-place ; the definite article regularly
accompanies the Hebrew word when the
Dwelling-place of Jehovah is denoted. But
in this place the word is not used in its full
sense as denoting the Dwelling-place of Jehovah : it denotes only the Tabernacle-cloth
(*v.* 6). The word is, in fact, employed with
three distinct ranges of meaning, (1) in its
strict sense, comprising the cloth of the
Tabernacle with its woodwork (xxvi. 1,
30, xxxvi. 13, xl. 18, &c.) ; (2) in a narrower
sense, for the Tabernacle-cloth only (xxvi.
1, 6, xxxv. 11, xxxix. 33, 34, &c.) ; (3) in a
wider sense, for the Tabernacle with its Tent
and Covering (xxvii. 19, xxxv. 18, &c.).

with ten curtains] Rather, of ten breadths.
Five of these breadths were united so as to
form what, in common usage, we should call
a large curtain (*v.* 3). The two curtains thus
formed were coupled together by the loops
and taches to make the entire tabernacle-
cloth (*v.* 6).

of cunning work] More properly, of the
work of the skilled weaver. The coloured
figures of Cherubim (see xxv. 4, 18) were to
be worked in the loom, as in the manufacture of tapestry and carpets (see *v.* 36
note). On the different kinds of workmen employed on the textile fabrics, see
xxxv. 35.

3. Each curtain formed of five breadths
(see *v.* 1), was 42 feet in length and 30 feet
in breadth, taking the cubit at 18 inches.

4. The meaning appears to be, *And thou
shalt make loops of blue on the edge of the
one breadth (which is) on the side (of the one
curtain) at the coupling ; and the same shalt
thou do in the edge of the outside breadth of
the other (curtain) at the coupling.* The
"coupling" is the uniting together of the
two curtains : ["selvedge" is the translation of a word signifying extremity or
end].

likewise shalt thou make in the uttermost edge of *another* cur-
5 tain, in the coupling of the second. Fifty loops shalt thou make
in the one curtain, and fifty loops shalt thou make in the edge
of the curtain that *is* in the coupling of the second ; that the
6 loops may take hold one of another. And thou shalt make fifty
taches of gold, and couple the curtains together with the taches :
7 and it shall be one tabernacle. ¶ And *b* thou shalt make curtains
of goats' hair to be a covering upon the tabernacle : eleven cur-
8 tains shalt thou make. The length of one curtain *shall be* thirty
cubits, and the breadth of one curtain four cubits : and the eleven
9 curtains *shall be all* of one measure. And thou shalt couple five
curtains by themselves, and six curtains by themselves, and shalt
10 double the sixth curtain in the forefront of the tabernacle. And
thou shalt make fifty loops on the edge of the one curtain *that is*
outmost in the coupling, and fifty loops in the edge of the curtain
11 which coupleth the second. And thou shalt make fifty taches of
brass, and put the taches into the loops, and couple the ¹tent
12 together, that it may be one. And the remnant that remaineth
of the curtains of the tent, the half curtain that remaineth, shall
13 hang over the backside of the tabernacle. And a cubit on the
one side, and a cubit on the other side ²of that which remaineth
in the length of the curtains of the tent, it shall hang over the
sides of the tabernacle on this side and on that side, to cover it.
14 And *c* thou shalt make a covering for the tent *of* rams' skins
15 dyed red, and a covering above *of* badgers' skins. ¶ And thou
shalt make boards for the tabernacle *of* shittim wood standing
16 up. Ten cubits *shall be* the length of a board, and a cubit and a
17 half *shall be* the breadth of one board. Two ³tenons *shall there*
be in one board, set in order one against another : thus shalt
18 thou make for all the boards of the tabernacle. And thou shalt
make the boards for the tabernacle, twenty boards on the south
19 side southward. And thou shalt make forty sockets of silver

b ch. 36. 14.

c ch. 36. 19.

---

¹ Or, *covering.*   ² Heb. *in the remainder,*   ³ Heb. *hands.*
                          or, *surplusage.*

---

5. The words "in the edge," &c. mean, *on the edge of the breadth that is at the coupling in the second (curtain).*
6. *taches of gold*] Each *tache,* or clasp, was to unite two opposite loops.
couple the curtains] *i.e.* couple the two outside breadths mentioned in *v.* 4.
7. *a covering upon the tabernacle*] **A Tent over the Tabernacle.** The Hebrew word here used, is the regular one for a tent of skins or cloth of any sort.
9. *tabernacle*] **Tent,** not tabernacle. The passage might be rendered, *thou shalt equally divide the sixth breadth at the front of the Tent.* In this way, half a breadth would overhang at the front and half at the back.
10. Or :—*And thou shalt make fifty loops on the edge of the outside breadth of the one (curtain) at the coupling, and fifty loops on the edge of the outside breadth of the other (curtain) at the coupling.*
11. In the Tent, clasps of bronze were used to unite the loops of the two curtains ; in the Tabernacle, clasps of gold, cp. *v.* 6 and *v.* 37.
couple the tent together] Not "covering," as in the margin. By "the tent" is here

meant the Tent-cloth alone.
13. The measure of the entire Tabernacle-cloth was about 60 ft. by 42 ; that of the Tent-cloth was about 67 ft. by 45. When the latter was placed over the former, it spread beyond it at the back and front about 3 ft. (the "half-curtain," *vv.* 9, 12) and at the sides 18 inches.
16. The board would therefore be about 15 ft. long, and 27 in. broad.
18. The entire length of the structure was about 45 ft. in the clear, and its width about 15 ft.
the south side southward] Or, **the south side on the right.** As the entrance of the Tabernacle was at its east end, the south side, to a person entering it, would be on the left hand : but we learn from Josephus that it was usual in speaking of the Temple to identify the south with the right hand and the north with the left hand, the entrance being regarded as the face of the structure and the west end as its back.
19. *sockets*] More literally, **bases,** or foundations. Each base weighed a talent, that is, about 94 lbs. (see xxxviii. 27), and

under the twenty boards; two sockets under one board for his
two tenons, and two sockets under another board for his two
20 tenons. And for the second side of the tabernacle on the north
21 side *there shall be* twenty boards: and their forty sockets *of* silver;
two sockets under one board, and two sockets under another
22 board. And for the sides of the tabernacle westward thou shalt
23 make six boards. And two boards shalt thou make for the
24 corners of the tabernacle in the two sides. And they shall be
¹coupled together beneath, and they shall be coupled together
above the head of it unto one ring: thus shall it be for them
25 both ; they shall be for the two corners. And they shall be eight
boards, and their sockets *of* silver, sixteen sockets; two sockets
26 under one board, and two sockets under another board. And
thou shalt make bars *of* shittim wood ; five for the boards of the
27 one side of the tabernacle, and five bars for the boards of the
other side of the tabernacle, and five bars for the boards of the
28 side of the tabernacle, for the two sides westward. And **the**
middle bar in the midst of the boards shall reach from end to
29 end. And thou shalt overlay the boards with gold, and make
their rings *of* gold *for* places for the bars : and thou shalt over-
30 lay the bars with gold. ¶And thou shalt rear up the tabernacle
ᵈaccording to the fashion thereof which was shewed thee in the
31 mount. ¶And ᵉthou shalt make a vail *of* blue, and purple, and
scarlet, and fine twined linen of cunning work : with cherubims
32 shall it be made: and thou shalt hang it upon four pillars of
shittim *wood* overlaid with gold: their hooks *shall be of* gold,
33 upon the four sockets of silver. And thou shalt hang up the vail
under the taches, that thou mayest bring in thither within the
vail ᶠthe ark of the testimony : and the vail shall divide unto you
34 between ᵍthe holy *place* and the most holy. And ʰthou shalt
put the mercy seat upon the ark of the testimony in the most
35 holy *place.* And ⁱthou shalt set the table without the vail, and
ᵏthe candlestick over against the table on the side of the tabernacle toward the south: and thou shalt put the table on the
36 north side. ¶And ˡthou shalt make an hanging for the door of
the tent, *of* blue, and purple, and scarlet, and fine twined linen,

ᵃ ch. 25. 9,
40 & 27. 8.
Acts 7. 44.
Heb. 8. 5.
ᶜ ch. 36. 35.
Lev. 16. 2.
2 Chr. 3. 14.
Matt. 27. 51.
Heb. 9. 3.
ᶠ ch. 40. 21.
ᵍ Lev. 16. 2.
Heb. 9. 2, 3.
ʰ ch. 25. 21.
& 40. 20.
Heb. 9. 5.
ⁱ ch. 40. 22.
Heb. 9. 2.
ᵏ ch. 40. 24.
ˡ ch. 36. 37.

¹ Heb. *twinned.*

must have been a massive block. The bases
formed a continuous foundation for the walls
of boards, presenting a succession of sockets or mortices (each base having a single
socket), into which the tenons were to fit.
They served not only for ornament but
also for the protection of the lower ends
of the boards from the decay which would
have resulted from contact with the
ground.

22. *the sides of the tabernacle westward*]
Rather, **the back of the Tabernacle towards the west.** See *v.* 18.

23. *in the two sides*] Rather, **at the back.**

24. The corner boards appear to have
been of such width, and so placed, as to
add 18 in. to the width of the structure,
making up with the six boards of full width
(*v.* 22) about 15 ft. in the clear (see *v.* 18).
The "ring" was so formed as to receive
two bars meeting "beneath" and "above"
at a right angle.

27. *for the two sides westward*] **For the
back towards the west.** Cp. *v.* 22.

28. *in the midst of the boards*] If we suppose the boards to have been of ordinary
thickness (*v.* 16), the bar was visible and
passed through an entire row of rings. In
any case, it served to hold the whole wall together.

31. *vail*] Literally *separation* (see xxxv.
12 note).

33. *taches*] Not the same as the *hooks* of
the preceding verse, but the clasps of the
tabernacle-cloth (see *v.* 6).

34, 35. See xxv. 10–16, 23, 31.

36. *the door of the tent*] **The entrance to
the Tent,** closed by the "hanging" or curtain (xxvii. 16).

wrought with needlework] **The work of the
embroiderer.** The entrance curtain of the
Tent and that of the Court (xxvii. 16) were
to be of the same materials, but embroidered with the needle, not wrought in

37 wrought with needlework. And thou shalt make for the
m ch. 36. 38.   hanging *m* five pillars *of* shittim *wood*, and overlay them with
gold, *and* their hooks *shall be of* gold: and thou shalt cast five
sockets of brass for them.

a ch. 38. 1.   **CHAP. 27.** AND thou shalt make *a* an altar *of* shittim wood, five
Ezek. 43. 13.   cubits long, and five cubits broad; the altar shall be foursquare:
2 and the height thereof *shall be* three cubits. And thou shalt make
the horns of it upon the four corners thereof: his horns shall be

---

figures in the loom (see *v*. 1, and xxxv. 35).

37. *five pillars*] These, it should be observed, belonged to the entrance of the Tent, not, in their architectural relation, to the entrance of the Tabernacle.

sockets of brass] Their bases (see *v*. 19) were of bronze (like the taches of the tent-cloth, *v*. 11), not of silver, to mark the inferiority of the Tent to the Tabernacle.

We are indebted to Mr. Fergusson for what may be regarded as a satisfactory reconstruction of the Sanctuary in all its main particulars. He holds that what sheltered the *Mishkān* was actually a Tent of ordinary form, such as common sense and practical experience would suggest as best suited for the purpose.

According to this view the five pillars at the entrance of the Tent (xxvi. 37) were graduated as they would naturally be at the entrance of any large tent of the best form, the tallest one being in the middle to support one end of a ridge-pole.

Such a ridge-pole, which must have been sixty feet in length, would have required support, and this might have been afforded by a plain pole in the middle of the structure. Over this framing of wood-work the Tent-cloth of goats' hair was strained with its cords and tent-pins in the usual way. (See cut.)

Above the Tent-cloth of goats' hair was spread the covering of red rams' skins.

The five pillars, to reach across the front of the Tent, must have stood five cubits (about 7½ ft.) apart. Their heads were united by **connecting rods** ("fillets" xxvii. 10) overlaid with gold (xxxvi. 38). The spaces at the sides and back may have been wholly or in part covered in for the use of the officiating priests, like the small apartments which in after times skirted three sides of the Temple. It was probably here that those portions of the sacrifices were eaten which were not to be carried out of the sacred precincts (Lev. vi. 16,

26). We may also infer that priests lodged in them. Cp. viii. 33; 1 S. iii. 2, 3.

XXVII. **1–8.** (Cp. xxxviii. 1–7.) The great Altar which stood in the Court immediately in front of the Tabernacle was commonly called the ALTAR OF BURNT-OFFERING, because on it were burnt the whole Burnt-offerings, and all those parts of the other animal sacrifices which were offered to the Lord. It was also called the BRAZEN ALTAR, because it was covered with bronze, in distinction from the Golden Altar or Altar of Incense (xxxix. 38, 39, xl. 5, 6).

2. *his horns shall be of the same*] These horns were projections pointing upwards in

3 of the same : and *b*thou shalt overlay it with brass. And thou
shalt make his pans to receive his ashes, and his shovels, and his
basons, and his fleshhooks, and his firepans : all the vessels
4 thereof thou shalt make *of* brass. And thou shalt make for it a
grate of network *of* brass; and upon the net shalt thou make
5 four brasen rings in the four corners thereof. And thou shalt
put it under the compass of the altar beneath, that the net may
6 be even to the midst of the altar. And thou shalt make staves
for the altar, staves *of* shittim wood, and overlay them with
7 brass. And the staves shall be put into the rings, and the staves
8 shall be upon the two sides of the altar, to bear it. Hollow with

b See Num.
16. 38.

the form either of a small obelisk, or of
the horn of an ox. They were to be
actually parts of
the Altar, not
merely superad-
ded to it. On them
the blood of the
Sin-offering was
smeared (xxix. 12;
Lev. iv. 7, viii.
15, ix. 9, xvi. 18).
To take hold of
them appears to
have been re-
garded as an em-
phatic mode of
laying claim to
the supposed right
of Sanctuary (xxi.
14 note; 1 K. i.
50).

3. *pans*] Rather
pots as in xxxviii.
3; 1 K. vii. 45. On
the use to which
these pots were
put in disposing of
the ashes of the
Altar, see Lev. i.
16.

basons] Vessels
used for receiving
the blood of the
victims and cast-
ing it upon the
Altar (see xxiv. 6,
Lev. i. 5, &c.).

fleshhooks] These
were for adjusting
the pieces of the
victims upon the
Altar (cf. 1 S. ii.
13).

firepans] The
same word is ren-
dered *snuffdishes*,
xxv. 38, xxxvii. 23:
censers, Lev. x. 1,
xvi. 12; Num. iv.
14, xvi. 6, &c.
These utensils ap-
pear to have been shallow metal vessels
which were employed merely to carry

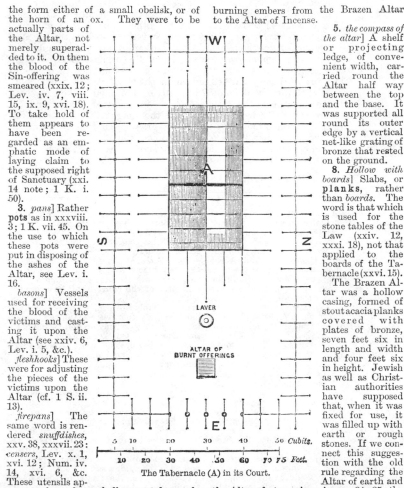

The Tabernacle (A) in its Court.

burning embers from the Brazen Altar
to the Altar of Incense.

5. *the compass of
the altar*] A shelf
or projecting
ledge, of conve-
nient width, car-
ried round the
Altar half way
between the top
and the base. It
was supported all
round its outer
edge by a vertical
net-like grating of
bronze that rested
on the ground.

8. *Hollow with
boards*] Slabs, or
planks, rather
than *boards*. The
word is that which
is used for the
stone tables of the
Law (xxiv. 12,
xxxi. 18), not that
applied to the
boards of the Ta-
bernacle (xxvi.15).

The Brazen Al-
tar was a hollow
casing, formed of
stout acacia planks
covered with
plates of bronze,
seven feet six in
length and width
and four feet six
in height. Jewish
as well as Christ-
ian authorities
have supposed
that, when it was
fixed for use, it
was filled up with
earth or rough
stones. If we con-
nect this sugges-
tion with the old
rule regarding the
Altar of earth and
the Altar of stone given in xx. 24, 25, the
woodwork might in fact be regarded merely

c ch. 25. 40.
& 26. 30.
d ch. 38. 9.

boards shalt thou make it: ^cas ¹it was shewed thee in the
9 mount, so shall they make it. ¶ And ^dthou shalt make the court
of the tabernacle: for the south side southward *there shall be*
hangings for the court *of* fine twined linen of an hundred cubits
10 long for one side: and the twenty pillars thereof and their
twenty sockets *shall be of* brass; the hooks of the pillars and
11 their fillets *shall be of* silver. And likewise for the north side in
length *there shall be* hangings of an hundred *cubits* long, and his
twenty pillars and their twenty sockets *of* brass; the hooks of
12 the pillars and their fillets *of* silver. And *for* the breadth of the
court on the west side *shall be* hangings of fifty cubits: their
13 pillars ten, and their sockets ten. And the breadth of the court
14 on the east side eastward *shall be* fifty cubits. The hangings of
one side *of the gate shall be* fifteen cubits: their pillars three, and
15 their sockets three. And on the other side *shall be* hangings
16 fifteen *cubits:* their pillars three, and their sockets three. And
for the gate of the court *shall be* an hanging of twenty cubits, *of*
blue, and purple, and scarlet, and fine twined linen, wrought
with needlework: *and* their pillars *shall be* four, and their sockets
17 four. All the pillars round about the court *shall be* filleted with
silver; their hooks *shall be of* silver, and their sockets *of* brass.
18 The length of the court *shall be* an hundred cubits, and the
breadth ²fifty every where, and the height five cubits *of* fine
19 twined linen, and their sockets *of* brass. All the vessels of the
tabernacle in all the service thereof, and all the pins thereof,
20 and all the pins of the court, *shall be of* brass. ¶ And ^ethou shalt
command the children of Israel, that they bring thee pure oil

e Lev. 24. 2.

---

¹ Heb. *he shewed.*　　　　　　　　² Heb. *fifty by fifty.*

---

as the case of the Altar on which the
victims were actually burned. The shelf
round the sides (*v.* 5) was required as a
stage for the priests to enable them to
carry on their work conveniently on the
top of the Altar. Hence it is said of Aaron
that he *came down* from the Altar (Lev. ix.
22). According to rabbinical tradition,
there was a slope of earth at the south
side banked up for the priest to ascend to
the stage (cp. Ex. xx. 26).

9-19. *The Court of the Tabernacle*]. (Cp.
xxxviii. 9-20) See Cut at the end of ch.
xxvi.

9. *the south side southward*] **The south
side on the right.** See xxvi. 18.

10. *sockets*] **Bases.** See xxvi. 19.

fillets] Rather, **Connecting rods**; curtain-
rods of silver connecting the heads of the
pillars. The hangings were attached to the
pillars by the silver hooks; but the length of
the space between the pillars would render
it most probable that they were also in some
way fastened to these rods.

13. *the east side eastward*] **On the front
side eastward.**

16. *an hanging*] An entrance curtain,
which, unlike the hangings at the sides and
back of the Court, could be drawn up, or
aside, at pleasure. The words are rightly
distinguished in our Bible in Num. iii. 26.

wrought with needlework] **The work of the
embroiderer.** See xxvi. 36, xxxv. 35. On
the materials, see xxv. 4.

17. *filleted with silver*] **Connected with
silver rods.** See *v.* 10.

19. *All the vessels,* &c.] **All the tools of
the tabernacle** *used* **in all its workmanship, and all its tent-pins, and all the
tent-pins of the court, shall be of bronze.**
—The working tools of the Sanctuary were
most probably such things as axes, knives,
hammers, &c. that were employed in making, repairing, setting up and taking down
the structure. Cp. Num. iii. 36.

the tabernacle] The word is here to be
taken as including both the *Mishkān* and
the Tent, as in Num. i. 51, 53, &c. (see
xxvi. 1 note).

the pins] Tent-pins.

20. *pure oil olive beaten*] The oil was to be
of the best kind. It is called *beaten*, because it was obtained by merely bruising
the olives in a mortar or mill, without the
application of heat. The finest oil is now
thus obtained from young fruit freshly gathered. The inferior kind is pressed from
unselected fruit, under stronger pressure,
and with the application of heat.

the lamp] *i.e.* the lamps of the Golden
Candlestick. (See xxv. 37.)

to burn] See the margin *to ascend up.* It

olive beaten for the light, to cause the lamp ¹to burn always.
21 In the tabernacle of the congregation ƒ without the vail, which
is before the testimony, ᵍAaron and his sons shall order it from
evening to morning before the LORD: ʰ*it shall be* a statute
for ever unto their generations on the behalf of the children of
Israel.
CHAP. 28. AND take thou unto thee ᵃAaron thy brother, and his
sons with him, from among the children of Israel, that he may
minister unto me in the priest's office, *even* Aaron, Nadab and
2 Abihu, Eleazar and Ithamar, Aaron's sons. And ᵇthou shalt
make holy garments for Aaron thy brother for glory and for
3 beauty. And ᶜthou shalt speak unto all *that are* wise hearted,
ᵈwhom I have filled with the spirit of wisdom, that they may
make Aaron's garments to consecrate him, that he may minister
4 unto me in the priest's office. And these *are* the garments
which they shall make; ᵉa breastplate, and ƒan ephod, and ᵍa
robe, and ʰa broidered coat, a mitre, and a girdle: and they
shall make holy garments for Aaron thy brother, and his sons,
5 that he may minister unto me in the priest's office. And they
shall take gold, and blue, and purple, and scarlet, and fine linen.

ƒ ch. 26. 31.
ᵍ ch. 30. 8.
1 Sam. 3. 3.
2 Chr. 13. 11.
ʰ ch. 28. 43.
& 29. 9, 28.
Lev. 3. 17.
Num. 18. 23.
& 19. 21.
1 Sam. 30.
25.
ᵃ Num. 18. 7.
Heb. 5. 1, 4.
ᵇ ch. 29. 5,
29 & 31. 10.
Lev. 8. 7, 30.
Num. 20.
26, 28.
ᶜ ch. 36. 1.
ᵈ ch. 31. 3.
& 35. 30, 31.
ᵉ ver. 15.
ƒ ver. 6.
ᵍ ver. 31.
ʰ ver. 39.

¹ Heb. *to ascend up.*

---

should be observed that the word does not
properly mean to burn in the sense of to
consume, but is the word regularly used to
express the action of fire upon what was
offered to Jehovah (see Lev. i. 9).
always] *i.e.* every night "from evening
till morning." Cp. xxx. 8.
21. *the tabernacle of the congregation*]
More literally, **the Tent of meeting.** This
is the first occurrence of this designation of
the Tabernacle, and the idea connected with
it is that of Jehovah meeting with either
Moses, or the priests, or (in a few cases)
with the people gathered into a congregation at the entrance of the Tent.
without the vail, which is before the testimony]
i.e. the Holy Place (see xxv. 16).
XXVIII. 1 – 43. (Cp. xxxix. 1 – 31.)
Moses is now commanded to commit all
that pertains to the Offerings made to the
Lord in the Sanctuary to the exclusive
charge of the members of a single family,
who were to hold their office from generation to generation. In the patriarchal
times, the external rites of worship had
generally been conducted by the head of the
tribe or family, in accordance with the principle involved in the dedication of the firstborn (xiii. 2; Num. iii. 12, 13). Moses,
as the divinely-appointed and acknowledged
leader of the nation, had, on a special occasion, appointed those who were to offer sacrifice, and had himself sprinkled the consecrating blood of the victims on the people
(xxiv. 5, 6, 8). On the completion of the
Tabernacle, after Aaron and his sons had
been called to the priesthood, he took chief
part in the daily service of the Sanctuary
(xl. 23-29, 31, 32) until the consecration of
the family of Aaron, on which occasion he
appears to have exercised the priest's office

for the last time (Lev. viii. 14–29; cp.
xxix. 10 – 26). The setting apart of the
whole tribe of Levi for the entire cycle of
religious services is mentioned Num. iii.
5-13, viii. 5-26, xviii. 1-32.
1. Nadab and Abihu, the two elder sons
of Aaron, had accompanied their father and
the seventy Elders when they went a part
of the way with Moses up the mountain
(xxiv. 1, 9). Soon after their consecration
they were destroyed for offering "strange
fire before the Lord" (Lev. x. 1, 2). Eleazar
and Ithamar are here mentioned for the
first time, except in the genealogy, vi. 23.
Eleazar succeeded his father in the High-
priesthood, and was himself succeeded by
his son Phinehas (Judg. xx. 28). But Eli,
the next High-priest named in the history,
was of the line of Ithamar. The representatives of both families held office at the
same time in the days of David. See 1 Chr.
xxiv. 1-3; 2 S. viii. 17.
3. *the spirit of wisdom*] See xxxi. 3 note.
What may be especially noticed in this
place is, that the spirit of wisdom given by
the Lord is spoken of as conferring practical
skill in the most general sense.
garments to consecrate him] A solemn recognition of the significance of an appointed
official dress. It expresses that the office is
not created or defined by the man himself
(Heb. v. 4), but that he is *invested* with it
according to prescribed institution. The
rite of anointing was essentially connected
with investiture in the holy garments (xxix.
29, 30; xl. 12-15).—The history of all nations shews the importance of these forms.
5. With the exception of the gold, the
materials were the same as those of the
Tabernacle-cloth, the vail of the Tabernacle
and the entrance-curtain of the Tent (xxvi.

6 *i* And they shall make the ephod *of* gold, *of* blue, and *of* purple,
7 *of* scarlet, and fine twined linen, with cunning work. It shall
have the two shoulderpieces thereof joined at the two edges
8 thereof; and *so* it shall be joined together. And the ¹curious
girdle of the ephod, which *is* upon it, shall be of the same,
according to the work thereof; *even of* gold, *of* blue, and purple,
9 and scarlet, and fine twined linen. And thou shalt take two
onyx stones, and grave on them the names of the children of
10 Israel: six of their names on one stone, and *the other* six names
11 of the rest on the other stone, according to their birth. With
the work of an engraver in stone, *like* the engravings of a signet,
shalt thou engrave the two stones with the names of the children
of Israel: thou shalt make them to be set in ouches of gold.
12 And thou shalt put the two stones upon the shoulders of the
ephod *for* stones of memorial unto the children of Israel: and

k ver. 29.
ch. 39. 7.
l See Josh.
4. 7.
Zech. 6. 14.
m ch. 39. 8.

k Aaron shall bear their names before the LORD upon his two
13 shoulders *l* for a memorial. And thou shalt make ouches *of*
14 gold; and two chains *of* pure gold at the ends; *of* wreathen
work shalt thou make them, and fasten the wreathen chains to
15 the ouches. ¶ And *m* thou shalt make the breastplate of judgment with cunning work; after the work of the ephod thou

¹ Or, *embroidered.*

1, 31, 36; xxv. 4). The gold was wrought
into thin flat wires which could either be
woven with the woollen and linen threads,
or worked with the needle. In regard to
the mixture of linen and woollen threads in
the High-priest's dress, see Lev. xix. 19.

6–12. *the ephod*] (xxxix. 2–7.) The Hebrew word has the same breadth of meaning
as our word *vestment.* The garment was
worn over the shoulders, and was the distinctive vestment of the High-priest, to
which "the breast-plate of judgment" was
attached (*vv.* 25–28).

cunning work] *Skilled* work, or work of
a *skilled* man (xxxv. 35).

7. Cp. xxxix. 4. The Ephod consisted of two principal pieces of cloth,
one for the back and the other for the
front, joined together by shoulder straps
(see *v.* 27 note). Below the arms, probably
just above the hips, the two pieces were
kept in place by a band attached to one of
the pieces. On the respect in which the
Ephod of the High-priest was held, see 1 S.
ii. 28, xiv. 3, xxi. 9, xxiii. 6–9, xxx. 7. But
an Ephod made of linen appears to have
been a recognised garment not only for the
common priests (1 S. xxii. 18), but also for
those who were even temporarily engaged
in the service of the Sanctuary (1 S. ii. 18;
2 S. vi. 14; 1 Chr. xv. 27).

8. *the curious girdle,* &c.] Rather :—*the
band for fastening it, which is upon it, shall
be of the same work, of one piece with it.* This
band being woven on to one of the pieces of
the Ephod, was passed round the body, and
fastened by buttons, or strings, or some
other suitable contrivance.

11. *like the engravings of a signet*] Cp.

vv. 21, 36. These words probably refer to a
peculiar way of shaping the letters, adapted
for engraving on a hard substance.—Seal
engraving on precious stones was practised
in Egypt from very remote times.

ouches of gold] Gold settings formed not
of solid pieces of metal, but of woven wire,
wreathed round the stones in what is called
cloisonnée work, a sort of filigree, often found
in Egyptian ornaments. These stones, as
well as those on the breastplate, were perhaps in the form of ovals, or rather
ellipses, like the cartouches, containing proper names, in hieroglyphic inscriptions.
The word *ouches* is used by Shakspeare,
Spenser, and some of their contemporaries
in the general sense of jewels.

12. *upon the shoulders*] i.e. upon the
shoulder-pieces of the ephod. See *v.* 7.

upon his two shoulders] Cp. Isa. ix. 6, xxii.
22. The High-priest had to represent the
Twelve Tribes in the Presence of Jehovah ;
and the burden of his office could not be so
aptly symbolized anywhere as on his shoulders, the parts of the body fittest for carrying
burdens.

13–30. Cp. xxxix. 8–21.

14. *two chains of pure gold shalt
thou make of wreathen work, twisted like
cords.*—They were more like cords of
twisted gold wire than chains in the ordinary
sense of the word. Such chains have been
found in Egyptian tombs.

15. *the breastplate of judgment*] The meaning of the Hebrew word rendered *breastplate,*
appears to be simply *ornament.* The term
breastplate relates merely to its place in the
dress.

shalt make it; *of* gold, *of* blue, and *of* purple, and *of* scarlet,
16 and *of* fine twined linen, shalt thou make it. Foursquare it
shall be *being* doubled; a span *shall be* the length thereof, and a
17 span *shall be* the breadth thereof. ⁿAnd thou shalt ¹set in it ⁿ ch. 39. 10,
settings of stones, *even* four rows of stones: *the first* row *shall be* &c.
a ²sardius, a topaz, and a carbuncle: *this shall be* the first row.
18 And the second row *shall be* an emerald, a sapphire, and a
19 diamond. And the third row a ligure, an agate, and an ame-
20 thyst. And the fourth row a beryl, and an onyx, and a jasper:
21 they shall be set in gold in their ³inclosings. And the stones
shall be with the names of the children of Israel, twelve, according to their names, *like* the engravings of a signet; every one
22 with his name shall they be according to the twelve tribes. And
thou shalt make upon the breastplate chains at the ends *of*
23 wreathen work *of* pure gold. And thou shalt make upon the
breastplate two rings of gold, and shalt put the two rings on
24 the two ends of the breastplate. And thou shalt put the two
wreathen *chains* of gold in the two rings *which are* on the ends
25 of the breastplate. And *the other* two ends of the two wreathen
chains thou shalt fasten in the two ouches, and put *them* on the
26 shoulderpieces of the ephod before it. And thou shalt make
two rings of gold, and thou shalt put them upon the two ends
of the breastplate in the border thereof, which *is* in the side of
27 the ephod inward. And two *other* rings of gold thou shalt make,
and shalt put them on the two sides of the ephod underneath,
toward the forepart thereof, over against the *other* coupling
28 thereof, above the curious girdle of the ephod. And they shall
bind the breastplate by the rings thereof unto the rings of the
ephod with a lace of blue, that *it* may be above the curious girdle
of the ephod, and that the breastplate be not loosed from the

¹ Heb. *fill in it fillings of stone.*   ² Or, *ruby.*   ³ Heb. *fillings.*

---

16. *doubled*] To give it stability, or to form what was used as a bag for the Urim and Thummim : the latter appears to be the more likely.

17. *settings*] Ouches of *cloisonnée* work, like those mentioned in *v.* 11.

a sardius] *i.e.* the red stone. The Sardian stone, or **sard**, was much used by the ancients for seals ; and it is perhaps the stone of all others the best for engraving.

topaz] Not the stone now called the topaz : it may have been the chrysolite, a stone of a greenish hue.

a carbuncle] More probably the **beryl**, which is a kind of emerald.

18. *an emerald*] Rather the garnet, which when cut with a convex face is termed the **carbuncle**.

a sapphire] Not the stone now called the sapphire ; the lapis-lazuli is most probably meant.

a diamond] There is no trace of evidence that the ancients ever acquired the skill to engrave on the diamond, or even that they were acquainted with the stone. The "diamond" here may possibly be some variety of chalcedony, or (perhaps) rock crystal.

19. *a ligure*] **Amber**, which came from Liguria.

20. *a beryl*] Supposed to be a brilliant yellow stone, identified with what is now known as the Spanish topaz.

a jasper] Probably the green jasper.

22. *chains,* &c.] See *v.* 14.

23. *on the two ends of the breastplate*] The extremities spoken of here, and in the next verse, must have been the upper corners of the square. The chains attached to them (*v.* 25) suspended the Breastplate from the ouches of the shoulder-pieces (*vv.* 9, 11, 12).

27. "And two rings of gold shalt thou make and put them on **the two shoulder-pieces of the Ephod, low down in the front of it, near the joining, above the band for fastening it.**" It would seem that the shoulder-pieces were continued down the front of the Ephod as far as the band (see *v.* 8) ; **the joining** appears to have been the meeting of the extremities of the shoulder-pieces with the band. These rings were attached to the shoulder-pieces just above this joining.

28. *the curious girdle of the ephod* **The band for fastening it** (see *v.* 8 note).

29 ephod. And Aaron shall bear the names of the children of
Israel in the breastplate of judgment upon his heart, when he

goeth in unto the holy *place*, *o*for a memorial before the LORD
30 continually. And *p*thou shalt put in the breastplate of judgment the Urim and the Thummim; and they shall be upon
Aaron's heart, when he goeth in before the LORD: and Aaron
shall bear the judgment of the children of Israel upon his heart
31 before the LORD continually. ¶ And *q*thou shalt make the robe
32 of the ephod all *of* blue. And there shall be an hole in the top
of it, in the midst thereof: it shall have a binding of woven work
round about the hole of it, as it were the hole of an habergeon,
33 that it be not rent. And *beneath* upon the [1]hem of it thou shalt
make pomegranates *of* blue, and *of* purple, and *of* scarlet,
round about the hem thereof; and bells of gold between them
34 round about: a golden bell and a pomegranate, a golden bell
and a pomegranate, upon the hem of the robe round about.
35 And it shall be upon Aaron to minister: and his sound shall be
heard when he goeth in unto the holy *place* before the LORD,

36 and when he cometh out, that he die not. ¶ And *r*thou shalt
make a plate *of* pure gold, and grave upon it, *like* the engravings

[1] Or, *skirts*.

---

29. See *v.* 12 ; the same names engraved
on the stones of the breastplate were worn
over the heart, the seat of the affections, as
well as of the intellect, to symbolize the relation of love and of personal interest which
the Lord requires to exist between the priest
and the people.
30. *the Urim and the Thummim*] *The
Light and the Truth*, or *perfection*.
From the way in which they are spoken
of here and in Lev. viii. 8, compared with
xxviii. 15-21, it would appear that the
Urim and the Thummim were some material things, previously existing and familiarly known, that they were separate from
the Breastplate itself, as well as from the
gems that were set upon it, and were kept
in the bag of the Breastplate (*v.* 16).
By means of them the Will of Jehovah,
especially in what related to the wars in
which His people were engaged, was made
known. They were formally delivered by
Moses to Aaron (Lev. viii. 8), and subsequently passed on to Eleazar (Num. xx. 28,
xxvii. 21). They were esteemed as the
crowning glory of the Tribe of Levi (Deut.
xxxiii. 8). There is no instance on record
of their being consulted after the time of
David.
The opinion has prevailed to a great extent that the Urim and the Thummim were
of Egyptian origin, and two small images of
precious stone, and that the Divine Will
was manifested through them by some
physical effect addressed to the eye or the
ear.
Others prefer the view that they were
some means for casting lots. Appeals to
lots were made under divine authority by
the chosen people on the most solemn occasions (Lev. xvi. 8 ; Num. xxvi. 55 ; Josh.

vii. 14-18, xiii. 6, xviii. 8 ; 1 S. xiv. 41, 42;
Acts i. 26), and it must have been a truth
commonly recognized by the people that
though " the lot was cast into the lap, the
whole disposing thereof was of the Lord "
(Prov. xvi. 33).
31-35. *the robe of the ephod*] (xxxix.
22-26.) A frock or robe of the simplest form,
woven without seam, wholly of blue. It was
put on by being drawn over the head. It
appears to have had no sleeves. It probably reached a little below the knees. It
must have been visible above and below the
Ephod, the variegated texture of which it
must have set off as a plain blue groundwork.
32. *an habergeon*] Corselets of linen, such
as appear to be here referred to, were well
known amongst the Egyptians.
35. *his sound*] Its sound, *i.e.* the sound of
the robe, that the people, who stood without, when they heard the sound of the bells
within the Tabernacle, might have a sensible proof that the High-priest was performing the sacred rite in their behalf, though
he was out of their sight.
that he die not] The bells also bore witness that the High-priest was, at the time
of his ministration, duly attired in the dress
of his office, and so was not incurring the
sentence of death (see also *v.* 43). An infraction of the laws for the service of the Sanctuary was not merely an act of disobedience ; it was a direct insult to the Presence
of Jehovah from His ordained minister,
and justly incurred a sentence of capital
punishment. Cp. xxx. 21 ; Lev. viii. 35,
x. 7.
36-43. Cp. xxxix. 27-31.
36. *HOLINESS TO THE LORD*] This
inscription testified in express words the

37 of a signet, HOLINESS TO THE LORD. And thou shalt put
it on a blue lace, that it may be upon the mitre; upon the fore-
38 front of the mitre it shall be. And it shall be upon Aaron's
forehead, that Aaron may *bear the iniquity of the holy things,
which the children of Israel shall hallow in all their holy gifts;
and it shall be always upon his forehead, that they may be
39 *accepted before the LORD. And thou shalt embroider the coat
of fine linen, and thou shalt make the mitre *of* fine linen, and
40 thou shalt make the girdle *of* needlework. "And for Aaron's
sons thou shalt make coats, and thou shalt make for them girdles,
and bonnets shalt thou make for them, for glory and for beauty.
41 And thou shalt put them upon Aaron thy brother, and his sons
with him; and shalt "anoint them, and 1ˣ consecrate them, and
sanctify them, that they may minister unto me in the priest's
42 office. And thou shalt make them ʸlinen breeches to cover
²their nakedness; from the loins even unto the thighs they shall
43 ³reach: and they shall be upon Aaron, and upon his sons, when
they come in unto the tabernacle of the congregation, or when
they come near ᶻunto the altar to minister in the holy *place;*
that they ᵃbear not iniquity, and die: ᵇ*it shall be* a statute for
ever unto him and his seed after him.

s Lev. 22. 9.
Num. 18. 1.
Isai. 53. 11.
Ezek. 4. 4,
5, 6.
John 1. 29.
Heb. 9. 28.
1 Pet. 2. 24.
t Lev. 1. 4.
& 22. 27.
Isai. 56. 7.
u ver. 4.
ch. 39. 27,
28, 29, 41.
w ch. 29. 7.
& 40. 15.
Lev. 10. 7.
x ch. 29. 9,
&c.
Lev. ch. 8.
Heb. 7. 28.
y ch. 39. 28.
Lev. 6. 10.
z ch. 20. 26.
a Lev. 20. 19,
20. & 22. 9.
Num. 9. 13.
b ch. 27. 21.
Lev. 17. 7.

¹ Heb. *fill their hand.*   ² Heb. *flesh of their naked-*
ness.   ³ Heb. *be.*

---

holiness with which the High-priest was invested in virtue of his sacred calling.
37. *a blue lace*] The plate was fastened
upon a blue band or fillet, so tied round the
mitre as to show the plate in front.
the mitre] A twisted band of linen (*v.* 39)
coiled into a cap, to which the name *mitre*,
in its original sense. closely answers, but
which, in modern usage, would rather be
called a *turban*.
38. *bear the iniquity of the holy things*]
The Hebrew expression "to bear iniquity"
is applied either to one who suffers the
penalty of sin (*v.* 43; Lev. v. 1, 17, xvii. 16,
xxvi. 41, &c.), or to one who takes away the
sin of others (Gen. l. 17; Lev. x. 17, xvi.
22; Num. xxx. 15; 1 S. xv. 25, &c.). In
several of these passages the verb is rightly
rendered to *forgive.*—The iniquity which is
spoken of in this place does not mean particular sins actually committed, but that
condition of alienation from God in every
earthly thing which makes reconciliation
and consecration needful. Cp. Num. xviii.
1. It belonged to the High-priest, as the
chief atoning mediator between Jehovah
and His people (see on *v.* 36), to atone for
the holy things that they might be "accepted before the Lord" (cp. Lev. viii. 15,
xvi. 20, 33, with the notes): but the common priests also, in their proper functions,
had to take their part in making atonement
(Lev. iv. 20, v. 10, x. 17, xxii. 16; Num.
xviii. 23, &c.).
39. *the coat of fine linen*] A long tunic, or
cassock. Josephus says that it was worn
next the skin, that it reached to the feet,
and that it had closely fitting sleeves. The

verb translated *embroider* appears rather to
mean **weave in diaper work.** The tissue
consisted of threads of one and the same
colour diapered in checkers, or in some small
figure.
the girdle of needlework] **The girdle of the
work of the embroiderer** (xxvi. 1, xxxv.
35). The word translated *girdle* is different from that so rendered in *v.* 8 (see note),
and is probably Egyptian. Josephus says
that it was wound several times round
the body, and that its ends ordinarily hung
down to the feet, but were thrown over the
shoulder when the priest was engaged in his
work.
40. *bonnets*] **Caps** of a simple construction
which seem to have been cup-shaped.
41-43. The dress of white linen was the
strictly sacerdotal dress common to the
whole body of priests (Ezek. xliv. 17, 18).
These were "for glory and for beauty" not
less than "the golden garments" (as they were
called by the Jews) which formed the High-
priest's dress of state (*v.* 2). The linen suit
which the High-priest put on when he went
into the Most Holy Place on the Day of
Atonement, appears to have been regarded
with peculiar respect (Cp. xxxi. 10; Lev.
xvi. 4, 23), though it is nowhere stated
that it was distinguished in its make or texture, except in having a girdle (*v.* 39) wholly
of white linen, instead of a variegated one.
The ancient Egyptian priests, like the Hebrew priests, wore nothing but white linen
garments in the performance of their duties.
43. *that they bear not iniquity and die*]
See *vv.* 35, 38 notes.

CHAP. 29. AND this *is* the thing that thou shalt do unto them to
hallow them, to minister unto me in the priest's office : *a* Take
2 one young bullock, and two rams without blemish, and *b* unleavened bread, and cakes unleavened tempered with oil, and
wafers unleavened anointed with oil : *of* wheaten flour shalt
3 thou make them. And thou shalt put them into one basket, and
bring them in the basket, with the bullock and the two rams.
4 And Aaron and his sons thou shalt bring unto the door of the
tabernacle of the congregation, *c* and shalt wash them with
5 water. *d* And thou shalt take the garments, and put upon Aaron
the coat, and the robe of the ephod, and the ephod, and the
breastplate, and gird him with *e* the curious girdle of the ephod :
6 *f* and thou shalt put the mitre upon his head, and put the holy
7 crown upon the mitre. Then shalt thou take the anointing
8 *g* oil, and pour *it* upon his head, and anoint him. ¶ And *h* thou
9 shalt bring his sons, and put coats upon them. And thou shalt
gird them with girdles, Aaron and his sons, and *i* put the bonnets
on them : and *i* the priest's office shall be theirs for a perpetual
10 statute : and thou shalt ² *k* consecrate Aaron and his sons. And
thou shalt cause a bullock to be brought before the tabernacle of the congregation : and *l* Aaron and his sons shall put
11 their hands upon the head of the bullock. And thou shalt kill
the bullock before the LORD, *by* the door of the tabernacle of the
12 congregation. And thou *m* shalt take of the blood of the bullock,
and put *it* upon *n* the horns of the altar with thy finger, and
13 pour all the blood beside the bottom of the altar. And *o* thou
shalt take all the fat that covereth the inwards, and ³ the caul
that is above the liver, and the two kidneys, and the fat that *is*
14 upon them, and burn *them* upon the altar. But *p* the flesh of the
bullock, and his skin, and his dung, shalt thou burn with fire
15 without the camp : it *is* a sin offering. ¶ *q* Thou shalt also take
one ram ; and Aaron and his sons shall *r* put their hands upon
16 the head of the ram. And thou shalt slay the ram, and thou
shalt take his blood, and sprinkle *it* round about upon the altar.
17 And thou shalt cut the ram in pieces, and wash the inwards of
him, and his legs, and put *them* unto his pieces, and ⁴ unto his head.
18 And thou shalt burn the whole ram upon the altar : it *is* a burnt
offering unto the LORD : it *is* a *s* sweet savour, an offering made
19 by fire unto the LORD. ¶ *t* And thou shalt take the other ram ;
and Aaron and his sons shall put their hands upon the head of the
20 ram. Then shalt thou kill the ram, and take of his blood, and put
it upon the tip of the right ear of Aaron, and upon the tip of the
right ear of his sons, and upon the thumb of their right hand, and
upon the great toe of their right foot, and sprinkle the blood upon
21 the altar round about. And thou shalt take of the blood that *is*
upon the altar, and of *u* the anointing oil, and sprinkle *it* upon
Aaron, and upon his garments, and upon his sons, and upon the
garments of his sons with him : and *w* he shall be hallowed, and
his garments, and his sons, and his sons' garments with him.
22 Also thou shalt take of the ram the fat and the rump, and the
fat that covereth the inwards, and the caul *above* the liver, and

a Lev. 8. 2.
b Lev. 2. 4.
& 6. 20, 21,
22.

c ch. 40. 12.
Lev. 8. 6.
Heb. 10. 22.
d ch. 28. 2.
Lev. 8. 7.
e ch. 28. 8.
f Lev. 8. 9.

g ch. 28. 41.
& 30. 25.
Lev. 8. 12.
& 10. 7.
& 21. 10.
Num. 35. 25.
h Lev. 8. 13.
i Num. 18. 7.
k ch. 28. 41.
Lev. 8. 22.
Heb. 7. 28.
l Lev. 1. 4.
& 8. 14.
m Lev. 8. 15.
n ch. 27. 2.
& 30. 2.
o Lev. 3. 3.

p Lev. 4. 11,
12, 21.
Heb. 13. 11.
q Lev. 8. 18.
r Lev. 1. 4—
9.

s Gen. 8. 21.
t ver. 3.
Lev. 8. 22.

u ch. 30. 25,
31.
Lev. 8. 30.
w ver. 1.
Heb. 9. 22.

---

¹ Heb. *bind.*
² Heb. *fill the hand of.*
³ It seemeth by anatomy
and the Hebrew doctors to be *the midriff.*
⁴ Or, *upon.*

XXIX. 1–37. THE CONSECRATION OF THE
PRIESTS. See notes to Lev. viii. ix.

4. *door of the tabernacle*] **Entrance of the
Tent.** See Lev. viii. 3.

the two kidneys, and the fat that is upon them, and the right
23 shoulder; for it is a ram of consecration: *and one loaf of
bread, and one cake of oiled bread, and one wafer out of the
24 basket of the unleavened bread that is before the LORD: and
thou shalt put all in the hands of Aaron, and in the hands of his
sons; and shalt ¹ʸwave them for a wave offering before the
25 LORD. ²And thou shalt receive them of their hands, and burn
them upon the altar for a burnt offering, for a sweet savour before the LORD: it is an offering made by fire unto the LORD.
26 And thou shalt take ªthe breast of the ram of Aaron's consecration, and wave it for a wave offering before the LORD: and ᵇit
27 shall be thy part. And thou shalt sanctify ᶜthe breast of the
wave offering, and the shoulder of the heave offering, which is
waved, and which is heaved up, of the ram of the consecration,
even of that which is for Aaron, and of that which is for his sons:
28 and it shall be Aaron's and his sons' ᵈby a statute for ever from
the children of Israel: for it is an heave offering: and ᵉit shall
be an heave offering from the children of Israel of the sacrifice
of their peace offerings, even their heave offering unto the LORD.
29 ¶And the holy garments of Aaron ᶠshall be his sons' after him,
30 ᵍto be anointed therein, and to be consecrated in them. And
²ʰthat son that is priest in his stead shall put them on ⁱseven
days, when he cometh into the tabernacle of the congregation to
31 minister in the holy place. ¶And thou shalt take the ram of
the consecration, and ᵏseethe his flesh in the holy place.
32 And Aaron and his sons shall eat the flesh of the ram, and the
ˡbread that is in the basket, by the door of the tabernacle of the
33 congregation. And ᵐthey shall eat those things wherewith the
atonement was made, to consecrate and to sanctify them: ⁿbut a
34 stranger shall not eat thereof, because they are holy. And if
ought of the flesh of the consecrations, or of the bread, remain
unto the morning, then ᵒthou shalt burn the remainder with fire:
35 it shall not be eaten, because it is holy. ¶And thus shalt thou
do unto Aaron, and to his sons, according to all things which I
have commanded thee: ᵖseven days shalt thou consecrate them.
36 And thou shalt ᑫoffer every day a bullock for a sin offering
for atonement: and thou shalt cleanse the altar, when thou hast
made an atonement for it, ʳand thou shalt anoint it, to sanctify
37 it. Seven days thou shalt make an atonement for the altar, and
sanctify it; ˢand it shall be an altar most holy: ᵗwhatsoever
38 toucheth the altar shall be holy. ¶Now this is that which thou
shalt offer upon the altar; ᵘtwo lambs of the first year ʷday by
39 day continually. The one lamb thou shalt offer ˣin the morning;
40 and the other lamb thou shalt offer at even: and with the one
lamb a tenth deal of flour mingled with the fourth part of an hin

¹ Or, shake to and fro.   ² Heb. he of his sons.

x Lev. 8. 26.

y Lev. 7. 30.
z Lev. 8. 28.

a Lev. 8. 29.
b Ps. 99. 6.
c Lev. 7. 31, 34.
Num. 18. 11, 18.
Deut. 18. 3.
d Lev. 10. 15.
e Lev. 7. 34.

f Num. 20. 26. 28.
g Num. 18. 8. & 35. 25.
h Num. 20. 28.
i Lev. 8. 35. & 9. 1, 8.
k Lev. 8. 31.
l Matt. 12. 4.
m Lev. 10. 14, 15, 17.
n Lev. 22. 10.
o Lev. 8. 32.
p Ex. 40. 12.
Lev. 8. 33, 34, 35.
q Heb. 10. 11.
r ch. 30. 26, 28, 29.
& 40. 10.
s ch. 40. 10.
t ch. 30. 29.
Matt. 23. 19.
u Num. 28. 3.
1 Chr. 16. 40.
2 Chr. 2. 4.
& 13. 11.
& 31. 3.
Ezra 3. 3.
w See Dan. 9. 27.
& 12. 11.
x 2 Kin. 16. 15.
Ezek. 46. 13, 14, 15.

---

27. The waving was the more solemn process of the two: it was a movement several
times repeated, while heaving was simply a
lifting up once.
33. a stranger] **One of another family,**
i.e. in this case, one not of the family of
Aaron.
38–46. The continual Burnt-offering] The
primary purpose of the national Altar is
here set forth. The victim slain every
morning and every evening was an acknowledgment that the life of the people belonged
to Jehovah; the offering of meal was an acknowledgment that all their works rightly
done were His due (see Lev. ii.); while
the incense symbolized their daily prayers.
39. at even] See xii. 6.
40. a tenth deal] i.e. the tenth part of
an Ephah; it is sometimes called an
Omer (xvi. 36; see Lev. xxiii. 13). The
Ephah seems to have been rather less than
four gallons and a half (see Lev. xix.

of beaten oil; and the fourth part of an hin of wine *for* a drink
41 offering. And the other lamb thou shalt *ᵛ*offer at even, and
shalt do thereto according to the meat offering of the morning, and according to the drink offering thereof, for a sweet
42 savour, an offering made by fire unto the LORD. *This shall be*
*ᶻ*a continual burnt offering throughout your generations *at* the
door of the tabernacle of the congregation before the LORD:
43 *ᵃ*where I will meet you, to speak there unto thee. And there I
will meet with the children of Israel, and *¹the tabernacle ᵇ*shall
44 be sanctified by my glory. And I will sanctify the tabernacle of
the congregation, and the altar: I will *ᶜ*sanctify also both Aaron
45 and his sons, to minister to me in the priest's office. And *ᵈ*I will
46 dwell among the children of Israel, and will be their God. And
they shall know that *ᵉ*I *am* the LORD their God, that brought
them forth out of the land of Egypt, that I may dwell among
them: I *am* the LORD their God.

CHAP. 30. AND thou shalt make *ᵃ*an altar *ᵇ*to burn incense upon:
2 *of* shittim wood shalt thou make it. A cubit *shall be* the length
thereof, and a cubit the breadth thereof; foursquare shall it be:
and two cubits *shall be* the height thereof: the horns thereof
3 *shall be* of the same. And thou shalt overlay it with pure gold,
the *²*top thereof, and the *³*sides thereof round about, and the
horns thereof; and thou shalt make unto it a crown of gold
4 round about. And two golden rings shalt thou make to it under
the crown of it, by the two *⁴*corners thereof, upon the two sides
of it shalt thou make *it;* and they shall be for places for the
5 staves to bear it withal. And thou shalt make the staves *of*
6 shittim wood, and overlay them with gold. And thou shalt put
it before the vail that *is* by the ark of the testimony, before the

Side references (left margin):
ʸ 1 Kin. 18.
29, 36.
2 Kin. 16. 15.
Ezra 9. 4, 5.
Ps. 141. 2.
Dan. 9. 21.
ᶻ ver. 38.
ch. 30. 8.
Num. 28. 6.
Dan. 8. 11,
12, 13.
ᵃ ch. 25. 22.
& 30. 6, 36.
Num. 17. 4.
ᵇ ch. 40. 34.
1 Kin. 8. 11.
2 Chr. 5. 14.
& 7. 1, 2, 3.
Ezek. 43. 5.
Hag. 2. 7, 9.
Mal. 3., 1.
ᶜ Lev. 21. 15.
& 22. 9, 16.
ᵈ Ex. 25. 8.
Lev. 26. 12.
Zech. 2. 10.
John 14.
17, 23.
2 Cor. 6. 16.
Rev. 21. 3.
ᵉ ch. 20. 2.
ᵃ ch. 37. 25.
& 40. 5.
ᵇ See ver. 7,
8, 10.
Lev. 4. 7, 18.

---

¹ Or, Israel.   ² Heb. *roof.*   ³ Heb. *walls.*   ⁴ Heb. *ribs.*

---

36 note) ; and the tenth deal of flour may
have weighed about 3 lbs. 2 oz.

an hin] The word appears to be Egyptian.
The measure was one-sixth of an ephah.
The quarter of a hin was therefore about a
pint and a half. See Lev. xix. 36 note.

beaten oil] See xxvii. 20.

wine for a drink offering] The earliest
mention of the Drink-offering is found in
connection with Jacob's setting up the stone
at Bethel (Gen. xxxv. 14). But it is here
first associated with the rites of the Altar.
The Law of the Drink-offering is stated
Num. xv. 5 sq. Nothing whatever is expressly said in the Old Testament regarding
the mode in which the wine was treated:
but it would seem probable, from the prohibition that it should not be poured upon
the Altar of Incense (xxx. 9), that it used to
be poured on the Altar of Burnt-offering.

42. *at the door of the tabernacle*] At the
entrance of the Tent.

43. *the (tabernacle) shall be sanctified*]
The word *tabernacle* is certainly not the right
one to be here supplied. What is probably
meant is the spot in which Jehovah promises to meet with the assembly of His
people. The verse may be rendered, **And
in that place will I meet with the children of Israel, and it shall be sanctified**
with my glory. See also the margin.

44, 45. The purpose of the formal consecration of the Sanctuary and of the priests
who served in it was, that the whole nation
which Jehovah had set free from its bondage in Egypt might be consecrated in its
daily life, and dwell continually in His presence as "a kingdom of priests and an holy
nation." (xix. 6.)

46. Cp. Gen. xvii. 7.

XXX. 1–10. (xxxvii. 25-28, xl. 26, 27.) *The*
Altar of Incense was to be a casing of boards
of shittim wood (xxv. 5), 18 inches square
and three feet in height (taking the cubit as
18 inches), entirely covered with plates of
gold. Four "horns" were to project upwards at the corners like those of the Altar
of Burnt-offering (xxvii. 2). A *crown* or
moulding of gold was to run round the top.
On each of two opposite sides there was to
be a gold ring through which the staves
were to be put when it was moved from
place to place.

4. *by the two corners thereof*] Not *corners.*
See margin. The sense appears to be: *And*
two gold rings shalt thou make for it under its
moulding; on its two sides shalt thou make
them (*i.e.* one ring on each side).

6. The place for the Altar of Incense was
outside the vail, opposite to the Ark of the

c mercy seat that *is* over the testimony, where I will meet with
7 thee. And Aaron shall burn thereon [1d] sweet incense every
morning : when c he dresseth the lamps, he shall burn incense
8 upon it. And when Aaron [23] lighteth the lamps [4] at even, he
shall burn incense upon it, a perpetual incense before the LORD
9 throughout your generations. Ye shall offer no f strange incense
thereon, nor burnt sacrifice, nor meat offering ; neither shall ye
10 pour drink offering thereon. And g Aaron shall make an atonement upon the horns of it once in a year with the blood of the
sin offering of atonements : once in the year shall he make
atonement upon it throughout your generations : it *is* most holy
11 unto the LORD. ¶ And the LORD spake unto Moses, saying,
12 h When thou takest the sum of the children of Israel after [5] their
number, then shall they give every man [i] a ransom for his soul
unto the LORD, when thou numberest them ; that there be no
13 k plague among them, when *thou* numberest them. l This they
shall give, every one that passeth among them that are numbered,
half a shekel after the shekel of the sanctuary : (m a shekel *is*
twenty gerahs :) n an half shekel *shall be* the offering of the LORD.
14 Every one that passeth among them that are numbered, from
twenty years old and above, shall give an offering unto the
15 LORD. The o rich shall not [6] give more, and the poor shall not
7 give less than half a shekel, when *they* give an offering unto the
16 LORD, to make an p atonement for your souls. And thou shalt
take the atonement money of the children of Israel, and q shalt

c ch. 25. 21,
22.
d ver. 34.
1 Sam. 2. 28.
1 Chr. 23. 13.
Luke 1. 9.
e ch. 27. 21.
f Lev. 10. 1.
g Lev. 16. 18.
& 23. 27.
h ch. 38. 25.
Num. 1. 2, 5.
& 26. 2.
2 Sam. 24. 2.
i See Num.
31. 50.
Job 33. 24.
& 36. 18.
Ps. 49. 7.
Matt. 20. 28.
1 Tim. 2. 6.
1 Pet. 1.
18, 19.
k 2 Sam. 24.
15.
l Matt. 17.
24.
m Lev. 27.
25.
Num. 3. 47.
Ezek. 45. 12.
n ch. 38. 26.
o Job 34. 19.
Prov. 22. 2.
Eph. 6. 9.
Col. 3. 25.
p ver. 12.
q ch. 38. 25.

1 Heb. *incense of spices.*
2 Or, *setteth up.*
3 Heb. *causeth to ascend.*

4 Heb. *between the two evens*, ch. 12. 6.
5 Heb. *them that are to be numbered.*

6 Heb. *multiply.*
7 Heb. *diminish.*

Covenant and between the Candlestick on the south side and the Shewbread Table on the north (xl. 22-24). It appears to have been regarded as having a more intimate connection with the Holy of Holies than the other things in the Holy Place ; and the mention of the Mercy-seat in this verse, if we associate with it the significance of incense as figuring the prayers of the Lord's people (Ps. cxli. 2 ; Rev. v. 8, viii. 3, 4), seems to furnish additional ground for an inference that the Incense Altar took precedence of the Table of Shewbread and the Candlestick.

7. *the lamps*] See xxv. 37.

7, 8. The offering of the Incense accompanied that of the morning and evening sacrifice. The two forms of offering symbolized the spirit of man reaching after communion with Jehovah, both in act and utterance. See Ps. cxli. 2.

9. By this regulation, the symbolism of the Altar of Incense was kept free from ambiguity. Atonement was made by means of the victim on the Brazen altar in the court outside ; the prayers of the reconciled worshippers had their type within the Tabernacle.

10. See marg. reff.

11-16. (xxxviii. 25-28.) *The Ransom of Souls.* On comparing these words with those of Num. i. 1-3, we may perhaps infer that the first passage relates to a mere

counting of the adult Israelites at the time when the money was taken from each, and that what the latter passage enjoins was a formal enrolment of them according to their genealogies and their order of military service.

a ransom for his soul] What the sincere worshipper thus paid was at once the fruit and the sign of his faith in the goodness of Jehovah, Who had redeemed him and brought him into the Covenant. Hence the payment is rightly called a *ransom* inasmuch as it involved a personal appropriation of the fact of his redemption. On the word *soul*, see Lev. xvii. 11.

that there be no plague] i.e. that they might not incur punishment for the neglect and contempt of spiritual privileges. Cp. xxviii. 35 ; 1 Cor. xi. 27-30 ; and the Exhortation in our Communion Service.

13. *half a shekel*] The probable weight of silver in the half-shekel would now be worth about 1s. 3½d. (Cp. Gen. xxiii. 16. See xxxviii. 24 note.) *Gerah* is, literally, a *bean*, probably the bean of the carob or locust-tree. It was used as the name of a small weight, as our word *grain* came into use from a grain of wheat.

15. Every Israelite stood in one and the same relation to Jehovah. See *vv.* 11, 12.

16. *tabernacle of the congregation*] Tent of meeting, here and in *vv.* 18, 20.

a memorial unto the children of Israel] The

appoint it for the service of the tabernacle of the congregation; that it may be *r* a memorial unto the children of Israel before the LORD, to make an atonement for your souls. ¶ And the LORD spake unto Moses, saying, *s* Thou shalt also make a laver *of* 18 brass, and his foot *also of* brass, to wash *withal:* and thou shalt *t* put it between the tabernacle of the congregation and the altar, 19 and thou shalt put water therein. For Aaron and his sons *u* shall 20 wash their hands and their feet thereat: when they go into the tabernacle of the congregation, they shall wash with water, that they die not; or when they come near to the altar to minister, 21 to burn offering made by fire unto the LORD : so they shall wash their hands and their feet, that they die not : and *w* it shall be a statute for ever to them, *even* to him and to his seed throughout 22 their generations. ¶ Moreover the LORD spake unto Moses, say-23 ing, Take thou also unto thee *x* principal spices, of pure *y* myrrh five hundred *shekels,* and of sweet cinnamon half so much, *even* two hundred and fifty *shekels,* and of sweet *z* calamus two hun-24 dred and fifty *shekels,* and of *a* cassia five hundred *shekels,* after the 25 shekel of the sanctuary, and of oil olive an *b* hin : and thou shalt make it an oil of holy ointment, an ointment compound after the 26 art of the [1] apothecary: it shall be *c* an holy anointing oil. *d* And

1 Or, *perfumer.*

---

silver used in the Tabernacle was a memorial to remind each man of his position before the Lord, as one of the covenanted people.

17-21. (xxxviii. 8.) The bronze for the "Laver of brass" and its foot was supplied from the bronze mirrors of the women who voluntarily gave up these articles of luxury. Bronze mirrors were much used by the ancient Egyptians. No hint is given as to the form of the Laver. The Brazen Sea and the ten Lavers that served the same purpose in the Temple of Solomon, were elaborately wrought in artistic designs and are minutely described (1 K. vii. 23-29).

19. *wash their hands and their feet*] On certain solemn occasions he was required to bathe his whole person (xxix. 4 ; Lev. xvi. 4). The Laver must also have furnished the water for washing those parts of the victims that needed cleansing (Lev. i. 9).

20. *that they die not*] See xxviii. 35 note.

22-33. Cp. xxxvii. 29.

23. *principal spices*] *i.e.* the best spices.

pure myrrh] Is a gum which comes from the stem of a low, thorny, ragged tree, that grows in Arabia Felix and Eastern Africa, called by botanists *Balsamodendron myrrha.* The word here rendered *pure,* is literally, *freely flowing,* an epithet which is explained by the fact that the best myrrh is said to exude spontaneously from the bark, while that of inferior quality oozes out in greater quantity from incisions made in the bark.

five hundred shekels] Probably rather more than 15¼ lbs. See xxxviii. 24.

cinnamon is obtained from a tree allied to the laurel that grows in Ceylon and other islands of the Indian Ocean, known in Botany as the *Cinnamomum zeylanicum.* It is the inner rind of the tree dried in the sun. It was imported from India in very early times by the people of Ophir, and brought with other spices from the south part of Arabia by the trading caravans that visited Egypt and Syria. The mention of these spices in Exodus may be taken as the earliest notice we have connected with commerce with the remote East.

two hundred and fifty shekels] about 7 lbs. 14 oz.

sweet calamus] The **fragrant cane** (or *rush*) was probably what is now known in India as the Lemon Grass.

24. *cassia* is the inner bark of an Indian tree (*Cinnamomum cassia*), which differs from that which produces cinnamon in the shape of its leaves and some other particulars. It was probably in ancient times, as it is at present, by far less costly than cinnamon, and it may have been on this account that it was used in double quantity.

an hin] Probably about six pints. See Lev. xix. 36.

25. *an oil of holy ointment*] Rather, **a holy anointing oil.**

after the art of the apothecary] According to Jewish tradition, the essences of the spices were first extracted, and then mixed with the oil. The preparation of the Anointing Oil, as well as of the Incense, was entrusted to Bezaleel (xxxvii. 29), and the care of preserving it to Eleazar the son of Aaron (Num. iv. 16). In a later age, it was prepared by the sons of the priests (1 Chr. ix. 30).

thou shalt anoint the tabernacle of the congregation therewith,
27 and the ark of the testimony, and the table and all his vessels,
28 and the candlestick and his vessels, and the altar of incense, and
  the altar of burnt offering with all his vessels, and the laver and
29 his foot. And thou shalt sanctify them, that they may be most
30 holy : *e*whatsoever toucheth them shall be holy. *f*And thou
  shalt anoint Aaron and his sons, and consecrate them, that *they*
31 may minister unto me in the priest's office. And thou shalt
  speak unto the children of Israel, saying, This shall be an holy
32 anointing oil unto me throughout your generations. Upon
  man's flesh shall it not be poured, neither shall ye make *any
  other* like it, after the composition of it : *g*it *is* holy, *and* it
33 shall be holy unto you. *h*Whosoever compoundeth *any* like it,
  or whosoever putteth *any* of it upon a stranger, *i*shall even be
34 cut off from his people. ¶And the LORD said unto Moses,
  *k*Take unto thee sweet spices, stacte, and onycha, and galbanum;
  these sweet spices with pure frankincense : of each shall there be
35 a like *weight :* and thou shalt make it a perfume, a confection
  *l*after the art of the apothecary, *1*tempèred together, pure *and*
36 holy : and thou shalt beat *some* of it very small, and put of it
  before the testimony in the tabernacle of the congregation,
  *m*where I will meet with thee : *n*it shall be unto you most holy.
37 And *as for* the perfume which thou shalt make, *o*ye shall not
  make to yourselves according to the composition thereof : it shall
38 be unto thee holy for the LORD. *p*Whosoever shall make like
  unto that, to smell thereto, shall even be cut off from his people.
CHAP. 31. AND the LORD spake unto Moses, saying, *a*See, I have
2 called by name Bezaleel the *b*son of Uri, the son of Hur, of the

e ch. 29. 37.
f ch. 29. 7,
&c.
Lev. 8. 12,
30.

g ver. 25, 37.

h ver. 38.

i Gen. 17. 14.
ch. 12. 15.
Lev. 7. 20,
21.
k ch. 25. 6.

l ver. 25.

m ch. 29. 42.
Lev. 16. 2.
n ver. 32.
ch. 29. 37.
Lev. 2. 3.
o ver. 32.
p ver. 33.

a ch. 35. 30.
& 36. 1.
b 1 Chr. 2.
20.

¹ Heb. *salted*, Lev. 2. 13.

---

32. *upon man's flesh*] *i.e.* on the persons
of those who were not priests who might
employ it for such anointing as was usual on
festive occasions (Ps. civ. 15 ; Prov. xxvii.
9 ; Matt. vi. 17, &c.).

33. *a stranger*] See xxix. 33.
cut off from his people] See xxxi. 14.

34–38. (xxxvii. 29.) The Incense, like the
Anointing Oil, consisted of four aromatic
ingredients.

stacte supposed to be either the gum of
the Storax-tree (*Styrax officinale*) found in
Syria and the neighbouring countries, or
the gum known as Benzoin, or Gum Benjamin, which is an important ingredient in
the incense now used in churches and mosks,
and is the produce of another storax-tree
(*Styrax benzoin*) that grows in Java and Su-
matra.

onycha, a perfume perhaps made from the
cap of the strombus, or wing-shell, which
abounds in the Red Sea.

galbanum, a gum of a yellowish brown
colour, in the form of either grains or
masses. It is imported from India, Persia,
and Africa ; but the plant from which it
comes is not yet certainly known.

pure frankincense] This was the most important of the aromatic gums. Like myrrh,
it was regarded by itself as a precious perfume (Cant. iii. 6 ; Matt. ii. 11), and it was
used unmixed with other substances in some

of the rites of the Law. The tree from
which it is obtained is not found in Arabia,
and it was most likely imported from India
by the Sabæans, like Cinnamon, Cassia,
and Calamus (see *v.* 23). The tree is
now known as the *Boswellia serrata*, or *B.
thurifera*, and grows abundantly in the
highlands of India. The frankincense of
commerce is a different substance, the
resin of the spruce and of some other kinds
of fir.

35. See *v.* 25.

tempered together] The four substances
were perhaps pounded and thoroughly
mixed together, and then fused into a mass.
This rendering is to be preferred to that in
the margin.

36. See *v.* 6.

37, 38. Cp. *vv.* 32, 33.

XXXI. 1–11. (xxxv. 30–35.) This solemn
call of Bezaleel and Aholiab is full of instruction. Their work was to be only that
of handicraftsmen. Still it was Jehovah
Himself Who called them by name to their
tasks, and the powers which they were now
called upon to exercise in their respective
crafts, were declared to have been given
them by the Holy Spirit. Thus is every
effort of skill, every sort of well-ordered labour, when directed to a right end, brought
into the very highest sphere of association.
There appears to be sufficient reason

[c] ch. 35. 31. 1 Kin. 7. 14.
[d] ch. 35. 34.
[e] ch. 28. 3. & 35. 10, 35. & 36. 1.
[f] ch. 36. 8.
[g] ch. 37. 1.
[h] ch. 37. 6.
[i] ch. 37. 10.
[k] ch. 37. 17.
[l] ch. 38. 1.
[m] ch. 38. 8.
[n] ch. 39. 1, 41. Num. 4. 5, 6, &c.
[o] ch. 30. 25, 31. & 37. 29.
[p] ch. 30. 34. & 37. 29.
[q] Lev. 19. 3, 30. & 26. 2. Ezek. 20. 12, 20. & 44. 24.
[r] ch. 20. 8. Deut. 5. 12. Ezek. 20. 12.
[s] ch. 35. 2.

3 tribe of Judah: and I have [c]filled him with the spirit of God, in
wisdom, and in understanding, and in knowledge, and in all
4 manner of workmanship, to devise cunning works, to work in
5 gold, and in silver, and in brass, and in cutting of stones, to set
them, and in carving of timber, to work in all manner of work-
6 manship. And I, behold, I have given with him [d]Aholiab, the
son of Ahisamach, of the tribe of Dan: and in the hearts of all
that are [e]wise hearted I have put wisdom, that they may make
7 all that I have commanded thee; [f]the tabernacle of the congregation, and [g]the ark of the testimony, and [h]the mercy seat that
8 *is* thereupon, and all the [1]furniture of the tabernacle, and [i]the
table and his furniture, and [k]the pure candlestick with all his
9 furniture, and the altar of incense, and [l]the altar of burnt offer-
10 ing with all his furniture, and [m]the laver and his foot, and [n]the
cloths of service, and the holy garments for Aaron the priest,
and the garments of his sons, to minister in the priest's office,
11 [o]and the anointing oil, and [p]sweet incense for the holy *place*:
according to all that I have commanded thee shall they do.
12, 13 ¶ And the LORD spake unto Moses, saying, Speak thou also
unto the children of Israel, saying, [q]Verily my sabbaths ye shall
keep: for it *is* a sign between me and you throughout your
generations; that *ye* may know that I *am* the LORD that doth
14 sanctify you. [r]Ye shall keep the sabbath therefore; for it *is*
holy unto you: every one that defileth it shall surely be put to
death: for [s]whosoever doeth *any* work therein, that soul shall

[1] Heb. *vessels.*

---

for identifying Hur, the grandfather of Bezaleel, with the Hur who assisted Aaron in supporting the hands of Moses during the battle with Amalek at Rephidim (xvii. 10), and who was associated with Aaron in the charge of the people while Moses was on the mountain (xxiv. 14). Josephus says that he was the husband of Miriam. It is thus probable that Bezaleel was related to Moses. He was the chief artificer in metal, stone, and wood; he had also to perform the apothecary's work in the composition of the Anointing Oil and the Incense (xxxvii. 29). He had precedence of all the artificers, but Aholiab appears to have had the entire charge of the textile work (xxxv. 35, xxxviii. 23).

3. *wisdom, understanding, knowledge*] Or, that "right judgment in all things" for which we specially pray on Whitsun-day; the perceptive faculty; and experience, a practical acquaintance with facts.

4. *to devise cunning works*] Rather, **to devise works of skill.** The Hebrew phrase is not the same as that rendered "cunning work" in respect to textile fabrics in xxvi. 1.

10. *and the cloths of service*] Rather, **And the garments of office**; that is, the distinguishing official garments of the High-priest. The three kinds of dress mentioned in this verse appear to be the only ones which were peculiar to the Sanctuary. They were: (1) The richly adorned state robes of the High-priest (see xxviii. 6–38, xxxix. 1 sq.). (2) The "holy garments" of white linen for the High-priest, worn on the most solemn occasion in the year (see xxviii. 39; Lev. xvi. 4. (3) The garments of white linen for all the priests, worn in their regular ministrations (see xxviii. 40, 41).

12–17. (xxxv. 2, 3.) *The Penal Law of the Sabbath.* In the Fourth Commandment the injunction to observe the Seventh Day is addressed to the conscience of the people (see xx. 8 note): in this place, the object is to declare an infraction of the Commandment to be a capital offence. The two passages stand in a relation to each other similar to that between Lev. xviii. xix. and Lev. xx. It seems likely that the penal edict was specially introduced as a caution in reference to the construction of the Tabernacle, lest the people, in their zeal to carry on the work, should be tempted to break the divine Law for the observance of the Day.

14. See Num. xv. 32–36. The distinction between the meaning of the two expressions, *to be cut off from the people*, and *to be put to death*, is here indicated. He who was cut off from the people had, by his offence, put himself out of the terms of the Covenant, and was an outlaw. On such, and on such alone, when the offence was one which affected the well-being of the nation, as it was in this case, death could be inflicted by the public authority.

15 be cut off from among his people. ¹Six days may work be done; but in the ᵘseventh *is* the sabbath of rest, ¹holy to the LORD : whosoever doeth *any* work in the sabbath day, he shall surely be
16 put to death. Wherefore the children of Israel shall keep the sabbath, to observe the sabbath throughout their generations,
17 *for* a perpetual covenant. It *is* ˣa sign between me and the children of Israel for ever : for ʸ*in* six days the LORD made heaven and earth, and on the seventh day he rested, and was refreshed.
18 ¶ And he gave unto Moses, when he had made an end of communing with him upon mount Sinai, ᶻtwo tables of testimony, tables of stone, written with the finger of God.
CHAP. 32. AND when the people saw that Moses ᵃdelayed to come down out of the mount, the people gathered themselves together unto Aaron, and said unto him, ᵇUp, make us gods, which shall ᶜgo before us ; for *as for* this Moses, the man that brought us up out of the land of Egypt, we wot not what is become of him.
2 And Aaron said unto them, Break off the ᵈgolden earrings, which *are* in the ears of your wives, of your sons, and of your
3 daughters, and bring *them* unto me. And all the people brake off the golden earrings which *were* in their ears, and brought
4 *them* unto Aaron. ᵉAnd he received *them* at their hand, and fashioned it with a graving tool, after he had made it a molten calf : and they said, These *be* thy gods, O Israel, which brought

¹ Heb. *holiness.*

t ch. 20. 9.
u Gen. 2. 2.
ch. 16. 23.
& 20. 10.

x ver. 13.
Ezek. 20.
12, 20.
y Gen. 1. 31.
& 2. 2.

z ch. 24. 12.
Deut. 4. 13.
2 Cor. 3. 3.
a ch. 24. 18.

b Acts 7. 40.
c ch. 13. 21.

d Judg. 8.
24, 25, 26, 27.

e ch. 20. 23.
Judg. 17. 3, 4.
1 Kin. 12. 28.
Neh. 9. 18.
Ps. 106. 19.
Isai. 46. 6.
Acts 7. 41.
Rom. 1. 23.

---

17. *was refreshed*] Literally, *he took breath.* Cp. xxiii. 12 ; 2 S. xvi. 14. The application of the word to the Creator, which occurs nowhere else, is remarkable.
18. *two tables of testimony*] See xxv. 16 ; xxxii. 15.
The Tables of stone which represented the Covenant between Jehovah and His people, and which, when covered with the Mercy-seat were to give the Sanctuary its significance, are now delivered to Moses in accordance with the promise in xxiv. 12.
The history of what relates to the construction of the Sanctuary is here interrupted, and is taken up again chap. xxxv. 1.
XXXII.-XXXIV. In all probability these three chapters originally formed a distinct composition. The main incidents recorded in them follow in the order of time, and are therefore in their proper place as regards historical sequence.
xxxii. 1-6. *The Golden Calf.* The people had, to a great extent, lost the patriarchal faith, and were but imperfectly instructed in the ·reality of a personal unseen God. Being disappointed at the long absence of Moses, they seem to have imagined that he had deluded them, and had probably been destroyed amidst the thunders of the mountain (xxiv. 15-18). They accordingly gave way to their superstitious fears and fell back upon that form of idolatry which was most familiar to them (see *v.* 4 note). The narrative of the circumstances is more briefly given by Moses at a later period in one of his addresses to the people (Deut. ix. 8-21, 25-29, x. 1-5, 8-11). It is worthy of

remark, that Josephus, in his very characteristic chapter on the giving of the Law, says nothing whatever of this act of apostacy, though he relates that Moses twice ascended the mountain.
1. *unto Aaron*] The chief authority during the absence of Moses was committed to Aaron and Hur (xxiv. 14).
make us gods] The substantive (*elohim*) is plural in form and may denote *gods.* But according to the Hebrew idiom, the meaning need not be plural, and hence the word is used as the common designation of the true God (Gen. i. 1, &c. See xxi. 6 note). It here denotes a god, and should be so rendered.
2. *Break off the golden earrings*] It has been very generally held from early times, that Aaron [did not willingly lend himself to the mad design of the multitude ; but that, overcome by their importunity, he asked them to give up such possessions as he knew they would not willingly part with, in the hope of putting a check on them. Assuming this to have been his purpose, he took a wrong measure of their fanaticism, for all the people made the sacrifice at once (*v.* 3). His weakness, in any case, was unpardonable and called for the intercession of Moses (Deut. ix. 20).
4. The sense approved by most modern critics is :—*and he received the gold at their hand and collected it in a bag and made it a molten calf.* The Israelites must have been familiar with the ox-worship of the Egyptians ; perhaps many of them had witnessed the rites of Mnevis at Heliopolis, almost

f Lev. 23. 2.
2 Kin. 10. 20.
2 Chr. 30. 5.
g 1 Cor. 10. 7.
h ver. 1.
ch. 33. 1.
Dan. 9. 24.
i Gen. 6. 11.
Deut. 4. 16.
Judg. 2. 19.
Hos. 9. 9.
k ch. 20. 3.
l 1 Kin. 12.
28.
m ch. 33. 3,
5. & 34. 9.
Deut. 31. 27.
2 Chr. 30. 8.
Isai. 48. 4.
Acts 7. 51.
n Deut. 9.
14, 19.
o ch. 22. 24.
p Num. 14.
12.
q Ps. 74. 1, 2.
& 106. 23.
r Num. 14.
13.
Deut. 32. 27.
s ver. 14.
t Gen. 22. 16.
Heb. 6. 13.
u Gen. 12. 7.
& reff.
w Deut. 32.
26.
1 Chr. 21. 15.
Ps. 106. 45.
Jer. 18. 8.

5 thee up out of the land of Egypt. And when Aaron saw *it*, he built an altar before it; and Aaron made *f* proclamation, and 6 said, To morrow *is* a feast to the LORD. And they rose up early on the morrow, and offered burnt offerings, and brought peace offerings; and the *g* people sat down to eat and to drink, and rose 7 up to play. ¶ And the LORD said unto Moses, *h* Go, get thee down; for thy people, which thou broughtest out of the land 8 of Egypt, *i* have corrupted *themselves*: they have turned aside quickly out of the way which *k* I commanded them: they have made them a molten calf, and have worshipped it, and have sacrificed thereunto, and said, *l* These *be* thy gods, O Israel, which 9 have brought thee up out of the land of Egypt. And the LORD said unto Moses, *m* I have seen this people, and, behold, it *is* a 10 stiffnecked people: now therefore *n* let me alone, that *o* my wrath may wax hot against them, and that I may consume them: and 11 *p* I will make of thee a great nation. ¶ *q* And Moses besought *l* the LORD his God, and said, LORD, why doth thy wrath wax hot against thy people, which thou hast brought forth out of the land of Egypt with great power, and with a mighty hand? 12 *r* Wherefore should the Egyptians speak, and say, For mischief did he bring them out, to slay them in the mountains, and to consume them from the face of the earth? Turn from thy fierce 13 wrath, and *s* repent of this evil against thy people. Remember Abraham, Isaac, and Israel, thy servants, to whom thou *t* swarest by thine own self, and saidst unto them, *u* I will multiply your seed as the stars of heaven, and all this land that I have spoken of will I give unto your seed, and they shall inherit *it* for ever. 14 And the LORD *w* repented of the evil which he thought to do unto

¹ Heb. *the face of the* LORD.

---

on the borders of the Land of Goshen, and they could not have been unacquainted with the more famous rites of Apis at Memphis. It is expressly said that they yielded to the idolatry of Egypt while they were in bondage (Josh. xxiv. 14; Ezek. xx. 8, xxiii. 3, 8); and this is in keeping with the earliest Jewish tradition (Philo). In the next verse, Aaron appears to speak of the calf as if it was a representative of Jehovah—"To-morrow is a feast to the LORD." The Israelites did not, it should be noted, worship a living Mnevis, or Apis, having a proper name, but only the golden type of the animal. The mystical notions connected with the ox by the Egyptian priests may have possessed their minds, and, when expressed in this modified and less gross manner, may have been applied to the LORD, Who had really delivered them out of the hand of the Egyptians. Their sin then lay, not in their adopting another god, but in their pretending to worship a visible symbol of Him Whom no symbol could represent. The close connection between the calves of Jeroboam and this calf is shewn by the repetition of the formula, "which brought thee up out of the land of Egypt" (1 Kings xii. 28).

These be thy gods] **This is thy god.** See *v.* 1 note.

7-35. The faithfulness of Moses in the office that had been entrusted to him was now to be put to the test. It was to be made manifest whether he loved his own glory better than he loved the brethren who were under his charge; whether he would prefer that he should himself become the founder of a "great nation," or that the LORD's promise should be fulfilled in the whole people of Israel. This may have been especially needful for Moses, in consequence of his natural disposition. See Num. xii. 3; and cp. iii. 11.—With this trial of Moses repeated in a very similar manner (Num. xiv. 11-23), may be compared the trial of Abraham (Gen. xxii.) and of our Saviour (Matt. iv. 8-10).

8. *These be thy gods...have brought*] **This is thy god, O Israel, who has brought—**

10. *let me alone*] But Moses did not let the LORD alone; he wrestled, as Jacob had done, until, like Jacob, he obtained the blessing (Gen. xxxii. 24-29).

14. This states a fact which was not revealed to Moses till after his second intercession when he had come down from the mountain and witnessed the sin of the people (*vv.* 30-34). He was then assured that the Lord's love to His ancient people would prevail. God is said, in the language of Scripture, to "repent," when His forgiving

15 his people. ¶And *Moses turned, and went down from the   *Deut. 9. 15.
mount, and the two tables of the testimony *were* in his hand :
the tables *were* written on both their sides; on the one side and
16 on the other *were* they written. And the *y* tables *were* the work   *y* ch. 31. 18.
of God, and the writing *was* the writing of God, graven upon the
17 tables. And when Joshua heard the noise of the people as they
shouted, he said unto Moses, *There is* a noise of war in the camp.
18 And he said, *It is* not the voice of *them that* shout for mastery,
neither *is it* the voice of *them that* cry for ¹being overcome : *but*
19 the noise of *them that* sing do I hear. And it came to pass, as
soon as he came nigh unto the camp, that *z* he saw the calf, and   *z* Deut. 9.
the dancing : and Moses' anger waxed hot, and he cast the tables   16, 17.
20 out of his hands, and brake them beneath the mount. *a* And he   *a* Deut. 9. 21.
took the calf which they had made, and burnt *it* in the fire, and
ground *it* to powder, and strawed *it* upon the water, and made
21 the children of Israel drink *of it*. ¶And Moses said unto Aaron,
b What did this people unto thee, that thou hast brought so great   *b* Gen. 20. 9.
22 a sin upon them ? And Aaron said, Let not the anger of my   & 26. 10.
lord wax hot : *c* thou knowest the people, that they *are* set on   *c* ch. 14. 11.
23 mischief. For they said unto me, *d* Make us gods, which shall go   & 15. 24.
before us : for *as for* this Moses, the man that brought us up out   & 16. 2, 20,
24 of the land of Egypt, we wot not what is become of him. And   28.
I said unto them, Whosoever hath any gold, let them break *it*   & 17. 2, 4.
off. So they gave *it* me : then I cast it into the fire, and there   *d* ver. 1.
25 *e* came out this calf. ¶And when Moses saw that the people   *e* ver. 4.
were *f* naked ; (for Aaron *g* had made them naked unto *their*   *f* ch. 33. 4, 5.
26 shame among ²their enemies :) then Moses stood in the gate of   *g* 2 Chr. 28.
the camp, and said, Who *is* on the LORD'S side ? *Let him come*   19.

¹ Heb. *weakness*.   ² Heb. *those that rose up against them*.

love is seen by man to blot out the letter of
His judgments against sin (2 Sam. xxiv. 16 ;
Joel ii. 13 ; Jonah iii. 10, &c.) ; or when the
sin of man seems to human sight to have
disappointed the purposes of grace (Gen.
vi. 6 ; 1 Sam. xv. 35, &c.). The awakened
conscience is said to "repent," when, having
felt its sin, it feels also the divine forgiveness : it is at this crisis that God, according to the language of Scripture, repents
towards the sinner. Thus the repentance
of God made known in and through the
One true Mediator reciprocates the repentance of the returning sinner, and reveals to
him atonement.

17, 18. Moses does not tell Joshua of the
divine communication that had been made
to him respecting the apostasy of the
people, but only corrects his impression by
calling his attention to the kind of noise
which they are making.

19. Though Moses had been prepared by
the revelation on the Mount, his righteous
indignation was stirred up beyond control
when the abomination was before his eyes.

20. See Deut. ix. 21. What is related in
this verse must have occupied some time
and may have followed the rebuke of
Aaron. The act was of course symbolical.
The idol was brought to nothing and the
people were made to swallow their own

sin (cp. Mic. vii. 13, 14).

22. Aaron's reference to the character of
the people, and his manner of stating what
he had done (*v.* 24), are very characteristic
of the deprecating language of a weak
mind.

23. *make us gods*] **Make us a god.**

25. *naked*] Rather **unruly**, or *licentious*.
shame among their enemies] Cp. Ps. xliv.
13 ; lxxix. 4 ; Deut. xxviii. 37.

26-29. The tribe of Levi, Moses' own
Tribe, now distinguished itself by immediately returning to its allegiance and obeying the call to fight on the side of Jehovah.
We need not doubt that the 3000 who were
slain were those who persisted in resisting
Moses. The spirit of the narrative forbids
us to conceive that the act of the Levites
was anything like an indiscriminate massacre. An amnesty had first been offered
to all in the words, "Who is on the LORD'S
side ? " Those who were forward to draw
the sword were directed not to spare their
closest relations or friends ; but this must
plainly have been with an understood
qualification as regards the conduct of those
who were to be slain. Had it not been so,
they who were on the LORD'S side would
have had to destroy each other. We need
not stumble at the bold, simple way in
which the statement is made.

h Num. 25. 5.
Deut. 33. 9.
i Num. 25.
11, 12, 13.
Deut. 13. 6.
1 Sam. 15.
18, 22.
Prov. 21. 3.
Zech. 13. 3.
Matt. 10. 37.
k 1 Sam. 12.
20, 23.
Luke 15. 18.
l 2 Sam. 16.
12.
Amos 5. 15.]
m Num. 25.
13.
n Deut. 9. 18.
o ch. 20. 23.
p Ps. 69. 28.
q Ps. 56. 8.
& 139. 16.
r Lev. 23. 30.
Ezek. 18. 4.
s ch. 33. 2.
Num. 20. 16.
t Deut. 32.
35.
Amos 3. 14.
Rom. 2. 5.
u 2 Sam. 12.
9.
Acts 7. 41.

a ch. 32. 7.

b Gen. 12. 7.
ch. 32. 13.
c ch. 32. 34.
& 34. 11.
d Deut. 7. 22.
Josh. 24. 11.

unto me. And all the sons of Levi gathered themselves together
27 unto him. And he said unto them, Thus saith the LORD God of
Israel, Put every man his sword by his side, *and* go in and out
from gate to gate throughout the camp, and ^hslay every man his
brother, and every man his companion, and every man his
28 neighbour. And the children of Levi did according to the word
of Moses : and there fell of the people that day about three
29 thousand men. ^{i 1}For Moses had said, ²Consecrate yourselves to
day to the LORD, even every man upon his son, and upon his
brother ; that he may bestow upon you a blessing this day.
30 ¶ And it came to pass on the morrow, that Moses said unto the
people, ^kYe have sinned a great sin : and now I will go up
unto the LORD ; ^lperadventure I shall ^mmake an atonement
31 for your sin. And Moses ⁿreturned unto the LORD, and said,
Oh, this people have sinned a great sin, and have ^omade them
32 gods of gold. Yet now, if thou wilt forgive their sin— ; and if
not, ^pblot me, I pray thee, ^qout of thy book which thou hast
33 written. And the LORD said unto Moses, ^rWhosoever hath sinned
34 against me, him will I blot out of my book. Therefore now
go, lead the people unto *the place* of which I have spoken unto
thee : ^sbehold, mine Angel shall go before thee : nevertheless ^tin
35 the day when I visit I will visit their sin upon them. ¶ And
the LORD plagued the people, because ^uthey made the calf, which
Aaron made.

CHAP. 33. AND the LORD said unto Moses, Depart, *and* go up hence,
thou ^aand the people which thou hast brought up out of the land
of Egypt, unto the land which I sware unto Abraham, to Isaac,
2 and to Jacob, saying, ^bUnto thy seed will I give it : ^cand I will
send an angel before thee ; ^dand I will drive out the Canaanite,

¹ Or, *And Moses said, Con-*   man hath been *against*   ² Heb. *Fill your hands.*
secrate yourselves to-day   his son, and against his
to the LORD, *because every*   brother, &c.

---

29. *Consecrate yourselves to day to the*
LORD, &c.] The margin contains the literal
rendering. Our version gives the most probable meaning of the Hebrew, as is supported by the best authority. The Levites
were to prove themselves in a special way
the servants of Jehovah, in anticipation of
their formal consecration as ministers of the
Sanctuary (cp. Deut. x. 8), by manifesting a
self-sacrificing zeal in carrying out the
divine command, even upon their nearest
relatives.
31. *returned unto the* LORD] *i.e.* he again
ascended the Mount.
gods of gold] a god of gold.
32. For a similar form of expression, in
which the conclusion is left to be supplied
by the mind of the reader, see Dan. iii. 15 ;
Luke xiii. 9, xix. 42; John vi. 62; Rom.
ix. 22.—For the same thought, see Rom. ix.
3. It is for such as Moses and St. Paul to
realize, and to dare to utter, their readiness
to be wholly sacrificed for the sake of those
whom God has entrusted to their love.
This expresses the perfected idea of the
whole Burnt-offering.
thy book] The figure is taken from the
enrolment of the names of citizens. This

is its first occurrence in the Scriptures. See
marg. reff. and Isa. iv. 3 ; Dan. xii. 1 ; Luke
x. 20; Phil. iv. 3 ; Rev. iii. 5, &c.
33, 34. Each offender was to suffer for
his own sin. Cp. xx. 5 ; Ezek. xviii. 4, 20.
Moses was not to be taken at his word.
He was to fulfil his appointed mission of
leading on the people towards the Land of
Promise.
34. *mine Angel shall go before thee*] See
marg. reff. and Gen. xii. 7.
in the day when I visit, &c.] Cp. Num.
xiv. 22–24. But though the LORD chastised the individuals, He did not take His
blessing from the nation.
XXXIII. **2, 3.** See iii. 8.
for I will not go up in the midst of thee]
The Covenant on which the original promise (xxiii. 20–23) was based had been
broken by the people. Jehovah now therefore declared that though His Angel should
go before Moses, He would withhold His
own favouring Presence. The nation should
be put on a level with other nations, to
lose its character as the people in special
covenant with Jehovah (see on *v.* 16). Thus
were the people forcibly warned that His
Presence could prove a blessing to them

the Amorite, and the Hittite, and the Perizzite, the Hivite, and
3 the Jebusite: ^eunto a land flowing with milk and honey: ^ffor
I will not go up in the midst of thee; for thou art a ^gstiffnecked
4 people: lest ^hI consume thee in the way. ¶And when the
people heard these evil tidings, ⁱthey mourned: ^kand no man
5 did put on him his ornaments. For the LORD had said unto
Moses, Say unto the children of Israel, ^lYe are a stiffnecked
people: I will come up ^minto the midst of thee in a moment, and
consume thee: therefore now put off thy ornaments from thee,
6 that I may ⁿknow what to do unto thee. And the children of
Israel stripped themselves of their ornaments by the mount Horeb.
7 ¶And Moses took the tabernacle, and pitched it without the
camp, afar off from the camp, ^oand called it the Tabernacle of
the congregation. And it came to pass, that every one which
^psought the LORD went out unto the tabernacle of the congrega-
8 tion, which was without the camp. And it came to pass, when
Moses went out unto the tabernacle, that all the people rose up,
and stood every man ^qat his tent door, and looked after Moses,
9 until he was gone into the tabernacle. ¶And it came to pass, as
Moses entered into the tabernacle, the cloudy pillar descended,
and stood at the door of the tabernacle, and the LORD ^rtalked
10 with Moses. And all the people saw the cloudy pillar stand at
the tabernacle door: and all the people rose up and ^sworshipped,
11 every man in his tent door. And ^tthe LORD spake unto Moses
face to face, as a man speaketh unto his friend. And he turned
again into the camp: but ^uhis servant Joshua, the son of Nun,
12 a young man, departed not out of the tabernacle. ¶And Moses
said unto the LORD, See, ^xthou sayest unto me, Bring up this
people: and thou hast not let me know whom thou wilt send
with me. Yet thou hast said, ^yI know thee by name, and thou
13 hast also found grace in my sight. Now therefore, I pray thee,
^zif I have found grace in thy sight, ^ashew me now thy way, that
I may know thee, that I may find grace in thy sight: and con-
14 sider that this nation is ^bthy people. And he said, ^cMy presence
15 shall go with thee, and I will give thee ^drest. And he said unto
him, ^eIf thy presence go not with me, carry us not up hence.
16 For wherein shall it be known here that I and thy people have

^e ch. 3. 8.
^f ver. 15, 17.
^g ch. 32. 9.
Deut. 9. 6,
13.
^h ch. 23. 21.
Num. 16.
21, 45.
ⁱ Num. 14.
1, 39.
^k 2 Sam. 19.
24.
1 Kin. 21. 27.
Isai. 32. 11.
^l ver. 3.
^m See Num.
16. 45, 46.
ⁿ Deut. 8. 2.
Ps. 139. 23.
^o ch. 29. 42,
43.
^p Deut. 4. 29.
2 Sam. 21. 1.
^q Num. 16.
27.
^r ch. 25. 22.
& 31. 18.
Ps. 99. 7.
^s ch. 4. 31.
^t Gen. 32. 30.
^u ch. 24. 13.
^x ch. 32. 34.
^y ver. 17.
Gen. 18. 19.
John 10. 3.
2 Tim. 2. 19.
^z ch. 34. 9.
^a Ps. 25. 4.
& 27. 11.
^b Deut. 9.
26, 29.
Joel. 2. 17.
^c ch. 13. 21.
Isai. 63. 9.
^d Josh.21.44.
Ps. 95. 11.
^e ver. 3.
ch. 34. 9.

only on condition of their keeping their
part of the covenant (v. 3). If they failed
in this, His presence would be to them "a
consuming fire" (Deut. iv. 24; cp. xxxii. 10).
5. I will come up, &c.] Better; If I were
to go up for one moment in the midst of
thee, I should consume thee.
that I may know, &c.] By that sign of
their repentance Jehovah would decide in
what way they were to be punished.
6. by the mount Horeb] From mount
Horeb onwards. They ceased to wear their
ornaments from the time they were at
Mount Horeb.
7. the tabernacle] The Tent. The only
word in the Old Testament which ought to
be rendered tabernacle (mishkān) does not
occur once in this narrative (xxvi. 1). What
is here meant is a tent appointed for this temporary purpose by Moses, possibly that in
which he was accustomed to dwell.
pitched it without the camp, afar off from
the camp] That the people might feel that

they had forfeited the Divine presence (see
xxv. 8). This tent was to be a place for
meeting with Jehovah, like the Tabernacle
which was about to be constructed.
The Tent of meeting (as it should be called,
see xxvii. 21 note, and note at end of Chap.
xl.) was placed "afar off from the camp,"
and the mediator and his faithful servant
Joshua were alone admitted to it (v. 11).
10. the tabernacle door] The entrance of
the Tent.
The people by their act of worship gave
another proof of their penitence.
11. face to face] See v. 20 note.
13. thy way] He desires not to be left in
uncertainty, but to be assured, by Jehovah's
mode of proceeding, of the reality of the
promises that had been made to him.
14. rest] This was the common expression
for the possession of the promised Land.
Deut. iii. 20; Josh. i. 13, 15; cp. Heb. iv. 8.
16. thou goest with us] It was this which
alone distinguished (rather than "sepa-

f Num. 14.
14.
g ch. 34. 10.
Deut. 4. 7.
2 Sam. 7. 23.
1 Kin. 8. 53.
h Gen. 19. 21.
Jam. 5. 16.
i ver. 12.
k ver. 20.
1 Tim. 6. 16.
l ch. 34. 5.
Jer. 31. 14.
m Rom. 9.
15, 16, 18.
n Rom. 4.
4, 16.
o Gen. 32. 30.
Deut. 5. 24.
Rev. 1. 16.
p Isai. 2. 21.
q Ps. 91. 1, 4.
r ver. 20.
John 1. 18.
a Deut. 10. 1.
b Deut. 10. 2.

c ch. 19. 20.
& 24. 12.
d ch. 19. 12.

e ch. 33. 19.
Num. 14. 17.
f Num. 14.
18.
2 Chr. 30. 9.
Neh. 9. 17.
Ps. 86. 15.
& 103. 8.

found grace in thy sight? *f* Is it not in that thou goest with us? So *g* shall we be separated, I and thy people, from all the people 17 that are upon the face of the earth. ¶ And the LORD said unto Moses, *h* I will do this thing also that thou hast spoken: for *i* thou hast found grace in my sight, and I know thee by name. 18, 19. And he said, I beseech thee, shew me *k* thy glory. And he said, *l* I will make all my goodness pass before thee, and I will proclaim the name of the LORD before thee; *m* and will be *n* gracious to whom I will be gracious, and will shew mercy on whom I 20 will shew mercy. And he said, Thou canst not see my face: 21 for *o* there shall no man see me, and live. And the LORD said, Behold, there is a place by me, and thou shalt stand upon a rock: 22 and it shall come to pass, while my glory passeth by, that I will put thee *p* in a clift of the rock, and will *q* cover thee with my 23 hand while I pass by: and I will take away mine hand, and thou shalt see my back parts: but my face shall *r* not be seen.

CHAP. 34. AND the LORD said unto Moses, *a* Hew thee two tables of stone like unto the first: *b* and I will write upon these tables the words that were in the first tables, which thou brakest. 2 And be ready in the morning, and come up in the morning unto mount Sinai, and present thyself there to me *c* in the top of the 3 mount. And no man shall *d* come up with thee, neither let any man be seen throughout all the mount; neither let the flocks 4 nor herds feed before that mount. ¶ And he hewed two tables of stone like unto the first; and Moses rose up early in the morning, and went up unto mount Sinai, as the LORD had com- 5 manded him, and took in his hand the two tables of stone. And the LORD descended in the cloud, and stood with him there, and 6 *e* proclaimed the name of the LORD. And the LORD passed by before him, and proclaimed, The LORD, The LORD *f* God, merciful

---

rated ") them from other nations, and which alone would render the Land of Promise a home to be desired. Cp. 2 Sam. vii. 23.

17. Cp. *v.* 13. His petition for the nation, and his own claims as a mediator, are now granted to the full.

18. *shew me thy glory*] The faithful servant of Jehovah, now assured by the success of his mediation, yearns, with the proper tendency of a devout spirit, for a more intimate communion with his Divine Master than he had yet enjoyed. He seeks for something surpassing all former revelations.

19. 20. But his request could not be granted in accordance with the conditions of human existence. The glory of the Almighty in its fulness is not to be revealed to the eye of man. Cp. Judg. vi. 22; Isai. vi. 5. A further revelation of the Divine goodness was however possible (see *vv.* 6, 7).

It was vouchsafed to St. Paul, as it had been to Moses, to have special "visions and revelations of the Lord" (2 Cor. xii. 1–4). But he had, also like Moses, to find the narrow reach of the intellect of man in the region of Godhead (1 Tim. vi. 16). However intimate may be our communion with the Holy One, we are still, as long as we are in the flesh, "to see through a glass darkly," waiting for the time when we shall

see, with no figure of speech, "face to face" (1 Cor. xiii. 12). Then we know "that we shall be like Him, for we shall see Him as He is" (1 John iii. 2).

19. *will be gracious*, &c.] Jehovah declares His own will to be the ground of the grace which He is going to shew the nation. St. Paul applies these words to the election of Jacob in order to overthrow the self-righteous boasting of the Jews (Rom. ix. 15).

20. Such passages as this, being clearly in accordance with what we know of the relation of spiritual existence to the human senses, shew how we are to interpret the expressions "face to face" (*v.* 11; Deut. xxxiv. 10), "mouth to mouth" (Num. xii. 8), and others of the like kind. See xxiv. 10; Isa. vi. 1; and cp. John xiv. 9.

XXXIV. 1. *Hew thee*] The former tables are called "the work of God;" cp. xxxii. 16. *the words*] See *v.* 28.

6, 7. This was the second revelation of the name of the God of Israel to Moses. The first revelation was of Jehovah as the self-existent One, Who purposed to deliver His people with a mighty hand (iii. 14); this was of the same Jehovah as a loving Saviour Who was now forgiving their sins. The two ideas that mark these revelations are found combined, apart from their historical development, in the Second Com-

and gracious, longsuffering, and abundant in *g*goodness and
7 *h*truth, *i*keeping mercy for thousands, *k*forgiving iniquity and
transgression and sin, and *l*that will by no means clear *the*
guilty; visiting the iniquity of the fathers upon the children,
and upon the children's children, unto the third and to the fourth
8 *generation.* And Moses made haste, and *m*bowed his head toward
9 the earth, and worshipped. And he said, If now I have found
grace in thy sight, O Lord, *n*let my Lord, I pray thee, go
among us; for *o*it *is* a stiffnecked people; and pardon our iniquity
10 and our sin, and take us for *p*thine inheritance. ¶ And he said,
Behold, *q*I make a covenant: before all thy people I will *r*do
marvels, such as have not been done in all the earth, nor in any
nation: and all the people among which thou *art* shall see the
work of the LORD: for it *is* *s*a terrible thing that I will do with
11 thee. *t*Observe thou that which I command thee this day: behold, *u*I drive out before thee the Amorite, and the Canaanite,
and the Hittite, and the Perizzite, and the Hivite, and the
12 Jebusite. *x*Take heed to thyself, lest thou make a covenant
with the inhabitants of the land whither thou goest, lest it be
13 for *y*a snare in the midst of thee: but ye shall *z*destroy their
14 altars, break their ¹images, and *a*cut down their groves: for
thou shalt worship *b*no other god: for the LORD, whose *c*name
15 *is* Jealous, *is* a *d*jealous God: *e*lest thou make a covenant with
the inhabitants of the land, and they *f*go a whoring after their
gods, and do sacrifice unto their gods, and *one* *g*call thee, and
16 thou *h*eat of his sacrifice; and thou take of *i*their daughters unto

¹ Heb. *statues.*

g Rom. 2. 4.
h Ps. 57. 10.
i ch. 20. 6.
k Ps. 103. 3.
Dan. 9. 9.
Eph. 4. 32.
1 John 1. 9.
l Josh.24.19.
m ch. 4. 31.
Nah. 1. 3.
n ch. 33. 15.
o ch. 33. 3.
p Deut. 32. 9.
q Deut. 5. 2.
& 29. 12, 14.
r Deut. 4. 32.
Ps. 77. 14.
s Ps. 145. 6.
Isai. 64. 3.
t Deut. 5. 32.
u ch. 33. 2.
x Deut. 7. 2.
y ch. 23. 33.
z Judg. 2. 2.
a Deut. 7. 5.
b ch. 20. 3, 5.
c So Isai. 9.
6. & 57. 15.
d ch. 20. 5.
e ver. 12.
f Judg. 2.17.
Jer. 3. 9.
Ezek. 6. 9.
g 1 Cor.10.27.
h Ps. 106. 28.
1 Cor. 8. 4.
i Deut. 7. 3.
Ezra 9. 2.

mandment, where the Divine unity is
shewn on its practical side, in its relation to
human obligations (cp. *v.* 14; xx. 4). Both in
the Commandment and in this passage, the
Divine Love is associated with the Divine
Justice ; but in the former there is a transposition to serve the proper purpose of the
Commandments, and the Justice stands
before the Love. This is strictly the legal
arrangement, brought out in the completed
system of the ceremonial Law, in which
the Sin-offering, in acknowledgment of the
sentence of Justice against sin, was offered
before the Burnt-offering and the Peace-
offering. But in this place the truth appears
in its essential order ; the retributive Justice of Jehovah is subordinated to, rather
it is made a part of, His forgiving LOVE
(see xxxii. 14 note). The visitation of God,
whatever form it may wear, is in all ages
the working out purposes of Love towards
His children. The diverse aspects of the
Divine nature, to separate which is the tendency of the unregenerate mind of man and
of all heathenism, are united in perfect harmony in the Lord Jehovah, of Whom the
saying is true in all its length and breadth,
"God is love" (1 Joh. iv. 8). It was the
sense of this, in the degree to which it was
now revealed to him, that caused Moses to
bow his head and worship (*v.* 8). But the
perfect revelation of the harmony was reserved for the fulness of time when "the
Lamb slain from the foundation of the

world" (Rev. xiii. 8) was made known to us
in the flesh as both our Saviour and our Judge.
9. This yearning struggle after assurance
is like the often-repeated utterance of the
heart, when it receives a blessing beyond
its hopes, "can this be real?"
10. *marvels*] Explained in the following
verse. Cp. 2 Sam. vii. 23; Ps. lxxvii. 14.
12-27. The precepts contained in these
verses are, for the most part, identical in
substance with some of those which follow
the Ten Commandments and are recorded
in "the Book of the Covenant" (xx.-xxiii.;
see xxiv. 7).
13. *cut down their groves*] This is the first
reference to what is commonly known as
grove-worship. The original word for *grove*
in this connection (*ashērāh*) is different
from that so rendered in Gen. xxi. 33.
Our translators supposed that what the
Law commands is the destruction of groves
dedicated to the worship of false deities (Judg.
vi. 25 ; 2 Kings xviii. 4); but inasmuch as the
worship of *ashērāh* is found associated with
that of Astarte, or *Ashtoreth* (Judg. ii. 13, x.
6 ; 1 S. vii. 4), it seems probable that while
Astarte was the personal name of the
goddess, the *ashērāh* was a symbol of her,
probably in some one of her characters,
wrought in wood in some conventional form.
15, 16. An expansion of *v.* 12. The unfaithfulness of the nation to its Covenant
with Jehovah is here for the first time
spoken of as a breach of the marriage

k Num. 25.
1, 2.
1 Kin. 11. 4.
l ch. 32. 8.
Lev. 19. 4.
m ch. 12. 15.
n ch. 13. 4.
o ch. 13. 2.
Ezek. 44. 30.
Luke 2. 23.
p ch. 13. 13.
Num. 18. 15.
q ch. 23. 15.
Deut. 16. 16.
1 Sam. 9. 7.
r ch. 20. 9.
s ch. 23. 16.
Deut. 16. 10.
t ch. 23. 14.
Deut. 16. 16.
u ch. 33. 2.
Lev. 18. 24.
Deut. 7. 1.
Ps. 78. 55.
& 80. 8.
x Deut. 12.
20. & 19. 8.
y See Gen.
35. 5.
2 Chr. 17. 10.
Prov. 16. 7.
Acts 18. 10.
z ch. 23. 18.
a ch. 23. 18.
b ch. 23. 19.
Deut. 26.
2, 10.
c ch. 23. 19.
Deut. 14. 21.
d ver. 10.
Deut. 4. 13.
& 31. 9.
e ch. 24. 18.
Deut. 9. 9.
f ver. 1.
ch. 31. 18.
Deut. 4. 13.
g ch. 32. 15.
h 2 Cor. 3. 7.

i ch. 24. 3.

thy sons, and their daughters *k*go a whoring after their gods,
17 and make thy sons go a whoring after their gods. *l*Thou shalt
18 make thee no molten gods. ¶The feast of *m*unleavened bread
shalt thou keep. Seven days thou shalt eat unleavened bread,
as I commanded thee, in the time of the month Abib: for in the
19 *n*month Abib thou camest out from Egypt. ¶*o*All that openeth
the matrix *is* mine; and every firstling among thy cattle, *whether*
20 ox or sheep, *that is male.* But *p*the firstling of an ass thou
shalt redeem with a ¹lamb: and if thou redeem *him* not, then
shalt thou break his neck. All the firstborn of thy sons thou
21 shalt redeem. And none shall appear before me *q*empty. ¶*r*Six
days thou shalt work, but on the seventh day thou shalt rest:
22 in earing time and in harvest thou shalt rest. ¶*s*And thou shalt
observe the feast of weeks, of the firstfruits of wheat harvest,
23 and the feast of ingathering at the ²year's end. *t*Thrice in
the year shall all your menchildren appear before the Lord GOD,
24 the God of Israel. For I will *u*cast out the nations before thee,
and *x*enlarge thy borders: *y*neither shall any man desire thy
land, when thou shalt go up to appear before the LORD thy God
25 thrice in the year. ¶*z*Thou shalt not offer the blood of my
sacrifice with leaven; *a*neither shall the sacrifice of the feast of
26 the passover be left unto the morning. ¶*b*The first of the firstfruits of thy land thou shalt bring unto the house of the LORD
thy God. ¶*c*Thou shalt not seethe a kid in his mother's milk.
27 ¶And the LORD said unto Moses, Write thou *d*these words:
for after the tenor of these words I have made a covenant with
28 thee and with Israel. *e*And he was there with the LORD forty
days and forty nights; he did neither eat bread, nor drink water.
And *f*he wrote upon the tables the words of the covenant, the
29 ten ³commandments. ¶And it came to pass, when Moses came
down from mount Sinai with the *g*two tables of testimony in
Moses' hand, when he came down from the mount, that Moses
wist not that *h*the skin of his face shone while he talked with
30 him. And when Aaron and all the children of Israel saw Moses,
behold, the skin of his face shone; and they were afraid to come
31 nigh him. And Moses called unto them; and Aaron and all the
rulers of the congregation returned unto him: and Moses talked
32 with them. And afterward all the children of Israel came nigh:
*i*and he gave them in commandment all that the LORD had

---

¹ Or, *kid.*   ² Heb. *revolution of the year.*   ³ Heb. *words.*

---

bond. The metaphor is, in any case, a
natural one, but it seems to gain point,
if we suppose it to convey an allusion to
the abominations connected with heathen
worship, such as are spoken of in Num.
xxv. 1-3.

21. See xx. 9, xxiii. 12. There is here
added to the Commandment a particular
caution respecting those times of year when
the land calls for most labour.—The old
verb *to ear* (*i.e.* to plough) is genuine
English.

24. *neither shall any man desire* &c.] Intended to encourage such as might fear the
consequences of obeying the Divine Law in
attending to their religious duties. Cp. Prov.
xvi. 7.

28. *he wrote*] *i.e.* Jehovah wrote (*v.* 1).

29. *the two tables of testimony*] Cp. xxxi.
18.

the skin of his face shone] Cp. Matt. xvii. 2.
The brightness of the Eternal Glory, though
Moses had witnessed it only in a modified
manner (xxxiii. 22, 23), was so reflected in
his face, that Aaron and the people were
stricken with awe, and feared to approach
him until he gave them words of encouragement.

The word translated *shine* is closely connected with a word translated *horn*; and
hence the Latin version and others have
rendered the verb *to be horned.* From this
rendering of the word has arisen the popular
representation of Moses with horns on his
forehead; *e.g.* in Michael Angelo's statue
at Rome.

33 spoken with him in mount Sinai. And *till* Moses had done
34 speaking with them, he put [k]a vail on his face. But [l]when
Moses went in before the LORD to speak with him, he took the
vail off, until he came out. And he came out, and spake unto
35 the children of Israel *that* which he was commanded. And the
children of Israel saw the face of Moses, that the skin of Moses'
face shone : and Moses put the vail upon his face again until he
went in to speak with him.

CHAP. 35. AND Moses gathered all the congregation of the children of Israel together, and said unto them, [a]"These *are* the
words which the LORD hath commanded, that *ye* should do them.
2 [b]Six days shall work be done, but on the seventh day there shall
be to you [1]an holy day, a sabbath of rest to the LORD : who-
3 soever doeth work therein shall be put to death. [c]Ye shall
kindle no fire throughout your habitations upon the sabbath day.
4 ¶And Moses spake unto all the congregation of the children of
Israel, saying, [d]This *is* the thing which the LORD commanded,
5 saying, Take ye from among you an offering unto the LORD :
[e]Whosoever *is* of a willing heart, let him bring it, an offering of
6 the LORD ; gold, and silver, and brass, and blue, and purple,
7 and scarlet, and fine linen, and goats' *hair*, and rams' skins
8 dyed red, and badgers' skins, and shittim wood, and oil for the
light, [f]and spices for anointing oil, and for the sweet incense,
9 and onyx stones, and stones to be set for the ephod, and for the
10 breastplate. And [g]every wise hearted among you shall come,
11 and make all that the LORD hath commanded ; [h]the tabernacle,
his tent, and his covering, his taches, and his boards, his bars,
12 his pillars, and his sockets, [i]the ark, and the staves thereof, *with*
13 the mercy seat, and the vail of the covering, the [k]table, and
14 his staves, and all his vessels, [l]and the shewbread, [m]the candlestick also for the light, and his furniture, and his lamps, with
15 the oil for the light, [n]and the incense altar, and his staves, [o]and
the anointing oil, and [p]the sweet incense, and the hanging
16 for the door at the entering in of the tabernacle, [q]the altar of
burnt offering, with his brasen grate, his staves, and all his
17 vessels, the laver and his foot, [r]the hangings of the court, his
pillars, and their sockets, and the hanging for the door of the
18 court, the pins of the tabernacle, and the pins of the court and

[k] 2 Cor. 3. 13.
[l] 2 Cor. 3. 16.

[a] ch. 34. 32.

[b] ch. 20. 9.
& 31. 14, 15.
Lev. 23. 3.
Num. 15.
32, &c.
Deut. 5. 12.
Luke 13. 14.
[c] ch. 16. 23.
[d] ch. 25. 1, 2.

[e] ch. 25. 2.

[f] ch. 25. 6.

[g] ch. 31. 6.
[h] ch. 26. 1,
2, &c.
[i] ch. 25. 10,
&c.
[k] ch. 25. 23.
[l] ch. 25. 30.
Lev. 24. 5, 6.
[m] ch. 25. 31,
&c.
[n] ch. 30. 1.
[o] ch. 30. 23.
[p] ch. 30. 34.
[q] ch. 27. 1.
[r] ch. 27. 9.

[1] Heb. *holiness*.

33—35. St. Paul refers to this passage as
shewing forth the glory of the Law, though
it was but a "ministration of condemnation," and was to be done away, in order to
enhance the glory of the Gospel, "the
ministration of the spirit," which is concealed by no vail from the eyes of believers, and is to last for ever (2 Cor. iii.
7-15).
33. *When* rather than *till* should be supplied. Moses did not wear the vail when
he was speaking to the people, but when
he was silent. See *v.* 35.
34. *Moses went in*] i.e. to the Tent of
meeting.
XXXV. The narrative of what relates
to the construction of the Sanctuary is now
resumed from xxxi. 18.
2. See xxxi. 12.

3. This prohibition is here first distinctly
expressed, but it is implied xvi. 23.
11. See xxvi. 1-37. It has been already
observed (xxv. 10) that in the instructions for making the Sanctuary, the Ark of
the Covenant, as the principal thing belonging to it, is mentioned first ; but in the
practical order of the work, as it is here
arranged, the Tabernacle with its Tent and
covering come first.
12. *the covering*] This is not the same as
the *covering* of *v.* 11, which denotes the
Covering of the Tent (see xxvi. 14) : the
word is used here for the entrance curtains
(see xxvi. 36, xxvii. 16).
18. The word *tabernacle* (*mishkān*) is here
used for the full name, **the Tabernacle of
the Tent of meeting.** It denotes the entire
structure.

*ch. 31. 10.
& 39. 1, 41.
Num. 4. 5,
6, &c.

t ver. 5, 22,
26, 29.
ch. 25. 2.
& 36. 2.
1 Chr. 28.
2, 9.
& 29. 9.
Ezra 7. 27.
2 Cor. 8. 12.
& 9. 7.
ᵘ 1 Chr. 29.
8.

w ch. 28. 3.
& 31. 6.
& 36. 1.
2 Kin. 23. 7.
Prov. 31.
19, 22, 24.
ˣ 1 Chr. 29.
6.
Ezra 2. 68.
ʸ ch. 30. 23.
ᶻ ver. 21.
1 Chr. 29. 9.

a ch. 31. 2,
&c.

b ch. 31. 6.
c ver. 31.
ch. 31. 3, 6.
1 Kin. 7. 14.
2 Chr. 2. 14.
Isai. 28. 26.

19 their cords, ˢthe cloths of service, to do service in the holy *place*,
the holy garments for Aaron the priest, and the garments of his
20 sons, to minister in the priest's office. ¶And all the congregation of the children of Israel departed from the presence of
21 Moses. And they came, every one ᵗwhose heart stirred him up,
and every one whom his spirit made willing, *and* they brought
the LORD's offering to the work of the tabernacle of the congregation, and for all his service, and for the holy garments.
22 And they came, both men and women, as many as were willing
hearted, *and* brought bracelets, and earrings, and rings, and
tablets, all jewels of gold: and every man that offered *offered* an
23 offering of gold unto the LORD. And ᵘevery man, with whom
was found blue, and purple, and scarlet, and fine linen, and
goats' *hair*, and red skins of rams, and badgers' skins, brought
24 *them*. Every one that did offer an offering of silver and brass
brought the LORD's offering: and every man, with whom was
found shittim wood for any work of the service, brought *it*.
25 And all the women that were ᵂwise hearted did spin with their
hands, and brought that which they had spun, *both* of blue, and
26 of purple, *and* of scarlet, and of fine linen. And all the women
27 whose heart stirred them up in wisdom spun goats' *hair*. And
ˣthe rulers brought onyx stones, and stones to be set, for the
28 ephod, and for the breastplate; and ʸspice, and oil for the light,
29 and for the anointing oil, and for the sweet incense. The
children of Israel brought a ᶻwilling offering unto the LORD,
every man and woman, whose heart made them willing to bring
for all manner of work, which the LORD had commanded to be
30 made by the hand of Moses. ¶And Moses said unto the children
of Israel, See, ᵃthe LORD hath called by name Bezaleel the son
31 of Uri, the son of Hur, of the tribe of Judah; and he hath filled
him with the spirit of God, in wisdom, in understanding, and in
32 knowledge, and in all manner of workmanship; and to devise
33 curious works, to work in gold, and in silver, and in brass, and
in the cutting of stones, to set *them*, and in carving of wood, to
34 make any manner of cunning work. And he hath put in his
heart that he may teach, *both* he, and ᵇAholiab, the son of
35 Ahisamach, of the tribe of Dan. Them hath he ᶜfilled with
wisdom of heart, to work all manner of work, of the engraver,
and of the cunning workman, and of the embroiderer, in blue,
and in purple, in scarlet, and in fine linen, and of the weaver,

---

19. *the cloths of service to do service in the
holy place*] Rather :—**the garments of office
to do service in the Sanctuary,** &c. See
xxxi. 10.

22. *bracelets*] Rather, **brooches.**

earrings] The Hebrew word signifies a
ring, either for the nose (see Gen. xxiv. 22)
or for the ear (xxxii. 2; Gen. xxxv. 4).
That ear-rings, not nose-rings, are here
meant is confirmed by what we know of
early Hebrew and Egyptian customs.

rings] Signet rings.

tablets] More probably, **armlets.** It is
most likely that all the articles mentioned
in this verse were of gold. The indulgence
of private luxury was thus given up for the
honour of the LORD. Cp. xxx. 18 note.

27. The precious stones (xxviii. 9) and
spices were contributed by the rulers,

who were more wealthy than the other
Israelites.

32-33. *curious works, cunning work*]
Works of skill. Cp. xxx. 4.

35. *the engraver*] **The artificer**, lit. *one
who cuts :* a general name for the workman,
to which was added the name of the material in which he worked ; thus the artificer
in wood, or carpenter ; the artificer in iron,
or smith, &c. *Vv.* 32, 33 and xxxi. 4, 5
enumerate the branches of work committed
to Bezaleel. What was under the charge of
Aholiab is here for the first time clearly
distinguished into the work of **the skilled
weaver,** that of the embroiderer, and that
of the weaver.

the cunning workman] **The skilled weaver,**
literally, *the reckoner.* He might have been
so called because he had nicely to count and

even of them that do any work, and of those that devise cunning work.

CHAP. 36. THEN wrought Bezaleel and Aholiab, and every [a]wise hearted man, in whom the LORD put wisdom and understanding to know how to work all manner of work for the service of the [b]sanctuary, according to all that the LORD had commanded.

2 ¶ And Moses called Bezaleel and Aholiab, and every wise hearted man, in whose heart the LORD had put wisdom, *even* every one [c]whose heart stirred him up to come unto the work to

3 do it: and they received of Moses all the offering, which the children of Israel [d]had brought for the work of the service of the sanctuary, to make it *withal*. And they brought yet unto

4 him free offerings every morning. And all the wise men, that wrought all the work of the sanctuary, came every man from

5 his work which they made; and they spake unto Moses, saying, [e]The people bring much more than enough for the service of the

6 work, which the LORD commanded to make. And Moses gave commandment, and they caused it to be proclaimed throughout the camp, saying, Let neither man nor woman make any more work for the offering of the sanctuary. So the people were

7 restrained from bringing. For the stuff they had was sufficient

8 for all the work to make it, and too much. ¶ [f]And every wise hearted man among them that wrought the work of the tabernacle made ten curtains *of* fine twined linen, and blue, and purple, and scarlet: *with* cherubims of cunning work made he

9 them. The length of one curtain *was* twenty and eight cubits, and the breadth of one curtain four cubits: the curtains *were* all

10 of one size. And he coupled the five curtains one unto another:

11 and *the other* five curtains he coupled one unto another. And he made loops of blue on the edge of one curtain from the selvedge in the coupling: likewise he made in the uttermost

12 side of *another* curtain, in the coupling of the second. [g]Fifty loops made he in one curtain, and fifty loops made he in the edge of the curtain which *was* in the coupling of the second: the

13 loops held one *curtain* to another. And he made fifty taches of gold, and coupled the curtains one unto another with the taches:

14 so it became one tabernacle. ¶ [h]And he made curtains *of* goats' *hair* for the tent over the tabernacle: eleven curtains he made

15 them. The length of one curtain *was* thirty cubits, and four cubits *was* the breadth of one curtain: the eleven curtains *were*

16 of one size. And he coupled five curtains by themselves, and

17 six curtains by themselves. And he made fifty loops upon the uttermost edge of the curtain in the coupling, and fifty loops made he upon the edge of the curtain which coupleth the second.

18 And he made fifty taches *of* brass to couple the tent together,

19 that it might be one. ¶ [i]And he made a covering for the tent *of* rams' skins dyed red, and a covering *of* badgers' skins above

Marginal references:
[a] ch. 28. 3. & 31. 6. & 35. 10, 35.
[b] ch. 25. 8.
[c] ch. 35. 21, 26. 1 Chr. 29. 5.
[d] ch. 35. 27.
[e] 2 Cor. 8. 2, 3.
[f] ch. 26. 1.
[g] ch. 26. 5.
[h] ch. 26. 7.
[i] ch. 26. 14.

---

calculate the threads in weaving figures after the manner of tapestry or carpet. His work was chiefly used in the curtains and vail of the Tabernacle, in the Ephod and the Breastplate (xxvi. 1, 31, xxviii. 6, 15, &c.).

the embroiderer] He worked with a needle, either shaping his design in stitches of coloured thread, or in pieces of coloured cloth sewn upon the groundwork. His work was employed in the **entrance curtains** of the Tent and the court, and in the girdle of the High-priest (xxvi. 36, xxvii. 16, xxviii.39).

the weaver] He appears to have worked in the loom in the ordinary way with materials of only a single colour. The tissues made by him were used for the Robe of the Ephod and its binding, and for the coats of the priests (xxviii. 32, xxxix. 22, 27).

These three classes of workers were men, while the spinners and dyers were women (*v.* 25).

XXXVI. See notes to ch. xxvi.

*ch. 26. 15. 20 *that.* ¶ *And he made boards for the tabernacle *of* shittim wood,
21 standing up. The length of a board *was* ten cubits, and the
22 breath of a board one cubit and a half. One board had two
  tenons, equally distant one from another : thus did he make
23 for all the boards of the tabernacle. And he made boards for
  the tabernacle ; twenty boards for the south side southward ;
24 and forty sockets of silver he made under the twenty boards :
  two sockets under one board for his two tenons, and two
25 sockets under another board for his two tenons. And for the
  other side of the tabernacle, *which is* toward the north corner,
26 he made twenty boards, and their forty sockets of silver ; two
  sockets under one board, and two sockets under another board.
27 And for the sides of the tabernacle westward he made six
28 boards. And two boards made he for the corners of the taber-
29 nacle in the two sides. And they were [1]coupled beneath, and
  coupled together at the head thereof, to one ring : thus he did
30 to both of them in both the corners. And there were eight
  boards ; and their sockets *were* sixteen sockets of silver, [2]under

l ch. 26. 26. 31 every board two sockets. ¶ And he made [l]bars of shittim wood ;
32 five for the boards of the one side of the tabernacle, and five
  bars for the boards of the other side of the tabernacle, and five
  bars for the boards of the tabernacle for the sides westward.
33 And he made the middle bar to shoot through the boards from
34 the one end to the other. And he overlaid the boards with gold,
  and made their rings *of* gold *to be* places for the bars, and over-

m ch. 26. 31. 35 laid the bars with gold. ¶ And he made [m]a vail *of* blue, and
  purple, and scarlet, and fine twined linen : *with* cherubims made
36 he it of cunning work. And he made thereunto four pillars *of*
  shittim *wood,* and overlaid them with gold : their hooks *were of*
37 gold ; and he cast for them four sockets of silver. ¶ And he

n ch. 26. 36. made an [n]hanging for the tabernacle door *of* blue, and purple,
38 and scarlet, and fine twined linen, [3]of needlework ; and the five
  pillars of it with their hooks : and he overlaid their chapiters and
  their fillets with gold : but their five sockets *were of* brass.

a ch. 25. 10. **CHAP. 37.** AND Bezaleel made [a]the ark *of* shittim wood : two cubits
  and a half *was* the length of it, and a cubit and a half the
2 breadth of it, and a cubit and a half the height of it : and he
  overlaid it with pure gold within and without, and made a
3 crown of gold to it round about. And he cast for it four rings
  of gold, *to be set* by the four corners of it ; even two rings upon
4 the one side of it,. and two rings upon the other side of it. And
  he made staves *of* shittim wood, and overlaid them with gold.
5 And he put the staves into the rings by the sides of the ark, to

b ch. 25. 17. 6 bear the ark. ¶ And he made the [b]mercy seat *of* pure gold : two
  cubits and a half *was* the length thereof, and one cubit and a half
7 the breadth thereof. And he made two cherubims *of* gold,
  beaten out of one piece made he them, on the two ends of the
8 mercy seat ; one cherub [4]on the end on this side, and another
  cherub [5]on the *other* end on that side : out of the mercy seat
9 made he the cherubims on the two ends thereof. And the cherubims spread out *their* wings on high, *and* covered with their
  wings over the mercy seat, with their faces one to another ; *even*
10 to the mercy seatward were the faces of the cherubims. ¶ And

---

[1] Heb. *twinned.*
[2] Heb. *two sockets, two
sockets under one board.*

[3] Heb. *the work of a needle-
worker,* or, *embroiderer.*

[4] Or, *out.of, &c.*
[5] Or, *out of, &c.*

XXXVII. See notes to ch. xxv.

he made *the table *of* shittim wood : two cubits *was* the length   *c* ch. 25. 23.
thereof, and a cubit the breadth thereof, and a cubit and a half
11 the height thereof: and he overlaid it with pure gold, and made
12 thereunto a crown of gold round about. Also he made thereunto
a border of an handbreadth round about; and made a crown of
13 gold for the border thereof round about. And he cast for it four
rings of gold, and put the rings upon the four corners that *were*
14 in the four feet thereof. Over against the border were the rings,
15 the places for the staves to bear the table. And he made the
staves *of* shittim wood, and overlaid them with gold, to bear the
16 table. And he made the vessels which *were* upon the table, his
*d*dishes, and his spoons, and his bowls, and his covers [1]to cover   *d* ch. 25. 29.
17 withal, *of* pure gold.   ¶And he made the *e*candlestick *of* pure   *e* ch. 25. 31.
gold: *of* beaten work made he the candlestick; his shaft, and
his branch, his bowls, his knops, and his flowers, were of the
18 same : and six branches going out of the sides thereof; three
branches of the candlestick out of the one side thereof, and three
19 branches of the candlestick out of the other side thereof: three
bowls made after the fashion of almonds in one branch, a knop
and a flower; and three bowls made like almonds in another
branch, a knop and a flower : so throughout the six branches
20 going out of the candlestick. And in the candlestick *were* four
21 bowls made like almonds, his knops, and his flowers: and a
knop under two branches of the same, and a knop under two
branches of the same, and a knop under two branches of the
22 same, according to the six branches going out of it. Their knops
and their branches were of the same: all of it *was* one beaten
23 work *of* pure gold. And he made his seven lamps, and his
24 snuffers, and his snuffdishes, *of* pure gold. *Of* a talent of pure
25 gold made he it, and all the vessels thereof.   ¶*f*And he made   *f* ch. 30. 1.
the incense altar *of* shittim wood : the length of it *was* a cubit,
and the breadth of it a cubit; *it was* foursquare; and two
cubits *was* the height of it; the horns thereof were of the same.
26 And he overlaid it with pure gold, *both* the top of it, and the
sides thereof round about, and the horns of it: also he made
27 unto it a crown of gold round about. And he made two rings of
gold for it under the crown thereof, by the two corners of it,
upon the two sides thereof, to be places for the staves to bear it
28 withal. And he made the staves *of* shittim wood, and overlaid
29 them with gold.   ¶And he made *g*the holy anointing oil, and   *g* ch. 30. 23,
the pure incense of sweet spices, according to the work of the   34.
apothecary.

CHAP. 38. AND *a*he made the altar of burnt offering *of* shittim   *a* ch. 27. 1.
wood : five cubits *was* the length thereof, and five cubits the
breadth thereof ; *it was* foursquare ; and three cubits the height
2 thereof. And he made the horns thereof on the four corners
of it ; the horns thereof were of the same : and he overlaid it
3 with brass. And he made all the vessels of the altar, the pots,
and the shovels, and the basons, *and* the fleshhooks, and the
4 firepans : all the vessels thereof made he *of* brass. And he made
for the altar a brasen grate of network under the compass there-
5 of beneath unto the midst of it. And he cast four rings for the
6 four ends of the grate of brass, *to be* places for the staves. And
he made the staves *of* shittim wood, and overlaid them with brass.

[1] Or, *to pour out withal.*

XXXVIII. 1-7: 9-20. See notes to ch. xxvii.

7 And he put the staves into the rings on the sides of the altar, to
8 bear it withal; he made the altar hollow with boards. ¶And he

b ch. 30. 18. made *b*the laver *of* brass, and the foot of it *of* brass, of the ¹look-
ingglasses of *the women* ²assembling, which assembled *at* the

c ch. 27. 9. 9 door of the tabernacle of the congregation. ¶ And he made *c*the
court: on the south side southward the hangings of the court
10 *were of* fine twined linen, an hundred cubits: their pillars *were*
twenty, and their brasen sockets twenty; the hooks of the pillars
11 and their fillets *were of* silver. And for the north side *the hangings were* an hundred cubits, their pillars *were* twenty, and their
sockets of brass twenty; the hooks of the pillars and their fillets
12 *of* silver. And for the west side *were* hangings of fifty cubits,
their pillars ten, and their sockets ten; the hooks of the pillars
13 and their fillets *of* silver. And for the east side eastward fifty
14 cubits. The hangings of the one side *of the gate were* fifteen
15 cubits; their pillars three, and their sockets three. And for the
other side of the court gate, on this hand and that hand, *were*
hangings of fifteen cubits; their pillars three, and their sockets
16 three. All the hangings of the court round about *were* of fine
17 twined linen. And the sockets for the pillars *were of* brass; the
hooks of the pillars and their fillets *of* silver; and the overlaying
of their chapiters *of* silver; and all the pillars of the court *were*
18 filleted with silver. And the hanging for the gate of the court
was needlework, *of* blue, and purple, and scarlet, and fine twined
linen: and twenty cubits *was* the length, and the height in the
breadth *was* five cubits, answerable to the hangings of the court.
19 And their pillars *were* four, and their sockets *of* brass four; their
hooks *of* silver, and the overlaying of their chapiters and their

d ch. 27. 19. 20 fillets *of* silver. And all the *d*pins of the tabernacle, and of the
21 court round about, *were of* brass. ¶This is the sum of the

e Num. 1.
50. 53.   tabernacle, *even* of *e*the tabernacle of testimony, as it was counted,
& 9. 15.   according to the commandment of Moses, *for* the service of the
& 10. 11.
& 17. 7, 8.   22 Levites, *f*by the hand of Ithamar, son to Aaron the priest. And
& 18. 2.   *g*Bezaleel the son of Uri, the son of Hur, of the tribe of Judah,
2 Chr. 24. 6.
Acts 7. 44.   23 made all that the LORD commanded Moses. And with him *was*
f Num. 4.   Aholiab, son of Ahisamach, of the tribe of Dan, an engraver,
28, 33.   and a cunning workman, and an embroiderer in blue, and in
g ch. 31. 2, 6.
h ch. 30. 13, 24 purple, and in scarlet, and fine linen. ¶All the gold that was
24.   occupied for the work in all the work of the holy *place*, even the
Lev. 5. 15.   gold of the offering, was twenty and nine talents, and seven
& 27. 3, 25.
Num. 3. 47.   hundred and thirty shekels, after *h*the shekel of the sanctuary.
& 18. 16.   ¹ Or, *brasen glasses*.   ² Heb. *assembling by troops*, as 1 Sam. 2. 22.

---

8. See marg. ref. The women who assembled **at the entrance of the Tent of meeting** were most probably devout women who
loved the public service of religion. The
giving up their mirrors for the use of the
Sanctuary was a fit sacrifice for such women
to make (cp. xxxv. 22 note).

21. *This is the sum,* &c.] "This is the
reckoning of the Tabernacle, **the Tabernacle of the Testimony as it was reckoned
up** according to the *commandment* of Moses,
by the service of the Levites, by the hand
of Ithamar," &c. The weight of the metals
was taken by the Levites, under the direction of Ithamar. The Tabernacle is called
the Tabernacle of the Testimony, or the de-
pository of the Testimony, *i.e.* the tables

of the Law (xxv. 16).

23. See xxxv. 35 note.

24. *of the holy place*] Rather, **of the Sanctuary.** The gold was employed not only in
the Holy Place, but in the Most Holy Place
and in the entrance to the Tent (xxxvi. 38).

the gold of the offering] **The gold of the
wave offering.**

talents...the shekel of the sanctuary] The
Shekel was the common standard of weight
and value with the Hebrews: and is probably to be estimated at 220 English grains
(just over half an ounce avoirdupois) and its
value in silver as 2s. 7d.—The Shekel of the
Sanctuary (or, *the Holy Shekel*) would seem
to denote no more than an *exact* Shekel,
"after the king's weight" (2 S. xiv. 26),

25 ¶ And the silver of them that were numbered of the congregation *was* an hundred talents, and a thousand seven hundred and threescore and fifteen shekels, after the shekel of the sanctuary:
26 *i* a bekah for ¹ every man, *that is,* half a shekel, after the shekel of the sanctuary, for every one that went to be numbered, from twenty years old and upward, for *k* six hundred thousand and
27 three thousand and five hundred and fifty *men.* And of the hundred talents of silver were cast *l* the sockets of the sanctuary, and the sockets of the vail; an hundred sockets of the hundred
28 talents, a talent for a socket. And of the thousand seven hundred seventy and five *shekels* he made hooks for the pillars, and
29 overlaid their chapiters, and filleted them. ¶ And the brass of the offering *was* seventy talents, and two thousand and four
30 hundred shekels. And therewith he made the sockets to the door of the tabernacle of the congregation, and the brasen altar,
31 and the brasen grate for it, and all the vessels of the altar, and the sockets of the court round about, and the sockets of the court gate, and all the pins of the tabernacle, and all the pins of the court round about.

CHAP. 39. AND of *a* the blue, and purple, and scarlet, they made *b* cloths of service, to do service in the holy *place,* and made the holy garments for Aaron; *c* as the LORD commanded Moses.
2 *d* And he made the ephod *of* gold, blue, and purple, and scarlet,
3 and fine twined linen. And they did beat the gold into thin plates, and cut *it into* wires, to work *it* in the blue, and in the purple, and in the scarlet, and in the fine linen, *with* cunning
4 work. They made shoulderpieces for it, to couple *it* together:
5 by the two edges was it coupled together. And the curious girdle of his ephod, that *was* upon it, *was* of the same, according to the work thereof; *of* gold, blue, and purple, and scarlet, and

i ch. 30. 13, 15.
k Num. 1. 46.
l ch. 26. 19, 21, 25, 32.

a ch. 35. 23.
b ch. 31. 10.
& 35. 19.
c ch. 28. 4.
d ch. 28. 6.

¹ Heb. *a poll.*

"current money with the merchant" (Gen. xxiii. 16).

In the reign of Joash, a collection similar to that here mentioned, apparently at the same rate of capitation, was made for the repairs of the Temple (2 Chr. xxiv. 9). The tax of later times, called *didrachma* (Matt. xvii. 27), was not, like this and that of Joash, a collection for a special occasion, but a yearly tax, for the support of the Temple, of a whole shekel.—See also xxx. 13.

The Talent contained 3000 shekels, as may be gathered from *vv.* 25, 26. According to the computation here adopted, the Hebrew Talent was 94¾ lbs. avoirdupois. The Greek (Æginetan) Talent, from which the LXX. and most succeeding versions have taken the name *talent*, was 82¼ lbs. The original Hebrew word *kikkär* would denote a circular mass, and nearly the same word, *kerker*, was in use amongst the Egyptians for a mass of metal cast in the form of a massive ring with its weight stamped upon it.

26. *a bekah*] Literally, *a half:* the words "half a shekel," &c. appear to be inserted only for emphasis, to enforce the accuracy to be observed in the payment. See xxx. 13.

—Respecting the capitation and the numbering of the people, see xxx. 12.

27. *sockets*] **Bases.** See marg. ref.

28. The hooks, chapiters, and fillets here spoken of belonged to the pillars of the Court. See xxvii. 10, 17.

24-29. According to the estimate of the shekel that has here been adopted, the weight of the metals mentioned in this chapter would be nearly as follows, in avoirdupois weight:—

Gold, 1 ton 4 cwt. 2 qrs. 13 lbs.
Silver 4 tons 4 cwt. 2 qrs. 20 lbs.
Bronze, 2 tons 19 cwt. 2 qrs. 11 lbs.

The value of the gold, if pure, in our money would be 175,075*l.* 13*s.*, and of the silver 38,034*l.* 15*s.* 10*d.* These quantities of the precious metals come quite within the limits of probability, if we consider the condition of the Israelites when they left Egypt (see xxv. 3 note), and the object for which the collection was made. Many have remarked that the quantities collected for the Tabernacle are insignificant when compared with the hoards of gold and silver collected in the East in recent, as well as in ancient, times.

XXXIX. See notes to ch. xxviii.

6 fine twined linen; as the Lord commanded Moses. ¶ *e* And they wrought onyx stones inclosed in ouches of gold, graven, as signets are graven, with the names of the children of Israel.
7 And he put them on the shoulders of the ephod, *that they should* be stones for a *f* memorial to the children of Israel; as the Lord
8 commanded Moses. ¶ *g* And he made the breastplate *of* cunning work, like the work of the ephod; *of* gold, blue, and purple, and
9 scarlet, and fine twined linen. It was foursquare; they made the breastplate double: a span *was* the length thereof, and a span
10 the breadth thereof, *being* doubled. *h* And they set in it four rows of stones: *the first* row *was* a ¹sardius, a topaz, and a car-
11 buncle: this *was* the first row. And the second row, an emerald,
12 a sapphire, and a diamond. And the third row, a ligure, an
13 agate, and an amethyst. And the fourth row, a beryl, an onyx, and a jasper: *they were* inclosed in ouches of gold in their inclosings.
14 And the stones *were* according to the names of the children of Israel, twelve, according to their names, *like* the engravings of a signet, every one with his name, according to the twelve tribes.
15 And they made upon the breastplate chains at the ends, *of*
16 wreathen work *of* pure gold. And they made two ouches *of* gold, and two gold rings; and put the two rings in the two ends
17 of the breastplate. And they put the two wreathen chains of
18 gold in the two rings on the ends of the breastplate. And the two ends of the two wreathen chains they fastened in the two ouches, and put them on the shoulderpieces of the ephod, before
19 it. And they made two rings of gold, and put *them* on the two ends of the breastplate, upon the border of it, which *was* on the
20 side of the ephod inward. And they made two *other* golden rings, and put them on the two sides of the ephod underneath, toward the forepart of it, over against the *other* coupling thereof, above
21 the curious girdle of the ephod. And they did bind the breastplate by his rings unto the rings of the ephod with a lace of blue, that it might be above the curious girdle of the ephod, and that the breastplate might not be loosed from the ephod; as the Lord
22 commanded Moses. ¶ *i* And he made the robe of the ephod *of*
23 woven work, all *of* blue. And *there was* an hole in the midst of the robe, as the hole of an habergeon, *with* a band round about
24 the hole, that it should not rend. And they made upon the hems of the robe pomegranates *of* blue, and purple, and scarlet,
25 *and* twined *linen*. And they made *k* bells *of* pure gold, and put the bells between the pomegranates upon the hem of the robe,
26 round about between the pomegranates; a bell and a pomegranate, a bell and a pomegranate, round about the hem of the
27 robe to minister *in;* as the Lord commanded Moses. ¶ *l* And they made coats *of* fine linen *of* woven work for Aaron, and
28 for his sons, *m* and a mitre *of* fine linen, and goodly bonnets *of*
29 fine linen, and *n* linen breeches *of* fine twined linen, *o* and a girdle *of* fine twined linen, and blue, and purple, and scarlet,
30 *of* needlework; as the Lord commanded Moses. ¶ *p* And they made the plate of the holy crown *of* pure gold, and wrote upon it a writing, *like to* the engravings of a signet, HOLINESS TO
31 THE LORD. And they tied unto it a lace of blue, to fasten *it* on high upon the mitre; as the Lord commanded Moses.
32 ¶ Thus was all the work of the tabernacle of the tent of the congregation finished: and the children of Israel did *q* according to

¹ Or, *ruby.*

33 all that the LORD commanded Moses, so did they. ¶ And they
brought the tabernacle unto Moses, the tent, and all his furniture, his taches, his boards, his bars, and his pillars, and his
34 sockets, and the covering of rams' skins dyed red, and the cover-
35 ing of badgers' skins, and the vail of the covering, the ark of
36 the testimony, and the staves thereof, and the mercy seat, the
37 table, *and* all the vessels thereof, and the shewbread, the pure
candlestick, *with* the lamps thereof, *even with* the lamps to be set
38 in order, and all the vessels thereof, and the oil for light, and
the golden altar, and the anointing oil, and [1] the sweet incense,
39 and the hanging for the tabernacle door, the brasen altar, and
his grate of brass, his staves, and all his vessels, the laver and
40 his foot, the hangings of the court, his pillars, and his sockets,
and the hanging for the court gate, his cords, and his pins, and
all the vessels of the service of the tabernacle, for the tent of the
41 congregation, the cloths of service to do service in the holy *place*,
and the holy garments for Aaron the priest, and his sons' gar-
42 ments, to minister in the priest's office. According to all that
the LORD commanded Moses, so the children of Israel [r] made all
43 the work. And Moses did look upon all the work, and, behold,
they had done it as the LORD had commanded, even so had they
done it: and Moses [s] blessed them.

CHAP. 40. AND the LORD spake unto Moses, saying, On the first
2 day of the [a] first month shalt thou set up [b] the tabernacle of the
3 tent of the congregation. And [c] thou shalt put therein the ark
4 of the testimony, and cover the ark with the vail. And [d] thou
shalt bring in the table, and [e] set in order [2] the things that are to
be set in order upon it; [f] and thou shalt bring in the candlestick,
5 and light the lamps thereof. [g] And thou shalt set the altar of
gold for the incense before the ark of the testimony, and put the
6 hanging of the door to the tabernacle. And thou shalt set the
altar of the burnt offering before the door of the tabernacle of
7 the tent of the congregation. And [h] thou shalt set the laver
between the tent of the congregation and the altar, and shalt
8 put water therein. And thou shalt set up the court round about,
9 and hang up the hanging at the court gate. And thou shalt take
the anointing oil, and [i] anoint the tabernacle, and all that *is*
therein, and shalt hallow it, and all the vessels thereof: and it
10 shall be holy. And thou shalt anoint the altar of the burnt
offering, and all his vessels, and sanctify the altar: and [k] it shall
11 be an altar [3] most holy. And thou shalt anoint the laver and
12 his foot, and sanctify it. [l] And thou shalt bring Aaron and his
sons unto the door of the tabernacle of the congregation, and
13 wash them with water. And thou shalt put upon Aaron the
holy garments, [m] and anoint him, and sanctify him; that he
14 may minister unto me in the priest's office. And thou shalt
15 bring his sons, and clothe them with coats: and thou shalt

[r] ch. 35. 10.

[s] Lev. 9. 22,
23.
Num. 6. 23.
Josh. 22. 6.
2 Sam. 6. 18.
1 Kin. 8. 14.
2 Chr. 30. 27.
[a] ch. 12. 2.
& 13. 4.
[b] ver. 17.
& ch. 26. 1,
30.
[c] ver. 21.
ch. 26. 33.
Num. 4. 5.
[d] ver. 22.
ch. 26. 35.
[e] ver. 23.
ch. 25. 30.
Lev. 24. 5, 6.
[f] ver. 24, 25.
[g] ver. 26.
[h] ver. 30.
ch. 30. 18.
[i] ch. 30. 26.
[k] ch. 29. 36,
37.
[l] Lev. 8. 1—
13.

[m] ch. 28. 41.

[1] Heb. *the incense of sweet*
spices.   [2] Heb. *the order thereof.*   [3] Heb. *holiness of holi-*
nesses.

XL. 2. See *v.* 17.
4. The directions given in Lev. xxiv. 5-9
are here presupposed, and must have been
issued before this chapter was written.
9-10. *most holy*] In *v.* 9 the Tabernacle
and its utensils are said to be rendered *holy*
by the anointing; the Altar and its utensils
are in *v.* 10 said to be *most holy*. The differ-

ence does not express a higher degree of
holiness: it is only used as a caution. The
position of the Altar exposed it to the
chance of being touched by the people when
they assembled in the Court, while they
were not permitted to enter the Tabernacle.
The Tabernacle itself, with all that belonged to it, is called *most holy* in xxx. 29.

anoint them, as thou didst anoint their father, that they may
minister unto me in the priest's office : for their anointing shall
n Num. 25.　surely be *n* an everlasting priesthood throughout their generations.
13.　　　　16 Thus did Moses : according to all that the LORD commanded
　　　　　17 him, so did he. ¶And it came to pass in the first month in the
o ver. 1.　　second year, on the first *day* of the month, *that* the *o* tabernacle
Num. 7. 1.　18 was reared up. And Moses reared up the tabernacle, and fas-
　　　　　tened his sockets, and set up the boards thereof, and put in the
　　　　　19 bars thereof, and reared up his pillars. And he spread abroad
　　　　　the tent over the tabernacle, and put the covering of the tent
　　　　　20 above upon it ; as the LORD commanded Moses. And he took
p ch. 25. 16.　and put *p* the testimony into the ark, and set the staves on the
　　　　　21 ark, and put the mercy seat above upon the ark : and he brought
q ch. 26. 33.　the ark into the tabernacle, and *q* set up the vail of the covering,
& 35. 12.　　and covered the ark of the testimony ; as the LORD commanded
r ch. 26. 35.　22 Moses. *r* And he put the table in the tent of the congregation,
　　　　　upon the side of the tabernacle northward, without the vail.
s ver. 4.　　23 *s* And he set the bread in order upon it before the LORD ; as the
t ch. 26. 35.　24 LORD had commanded Moses. *t* And he put the candlestick in
　　　　　the tent of the congregation, over against the table, on the side
u ver. 4.　　25 of the tabernacle southward. And *u* he lighted the lamps before
ch. 25. 37.　26 the LORD ; as the LORD commanded Moses. *x* And he put the
x ver. 5.
ch. 30. 6.　　27 golden altar in the tent of the congregation before the vail : *y* and
y ch. 30. 7.　　he burnt sweet incense thereon ; as the LORD commanded Moses.
z ver. 5.　　28 *z* And he set up the hanging *at* the door of the tabernacle.
ch. 26. 36.　29 *a* And he put the altar of burnt offering *by* the door of the taber-
a ver. 6.
b ch. 29. 38,　nacle of the tent of the congregation, and *b* offered upon it the
&c.　　　　burnt offering and the meat offering ; as the LORD commanded
c ver. 7.　　30 Moses. *c* And he set the laver between the tent of the congrega-
ch. 30. 18.　31 tion and the altar, and put water there, to wash *withal*. And

---

17. on the first day of the month] That is,
on the first of the month Nisan (xii. 2, xiii.
4), one year, wanting fourteen days, after
the departure of the Israelites from Egypt.
They had been nearly three months in
reaching the foot of Mount Sinai (xix. 1) ;
Moses had spent eighty days on the mountain (xxiv. 18, xxxiv. 28), and some time
must be allowed for what is related in chap.
xxiv., as well as for the interval between
the two periods which Moses spent on the
mountain (xxxiii. 1-23). The construction
of the Tabernacle and its furniture would
thus appear to have occupied something
less than half a year.

19. The Tent-cloth was spread over the
Tabernacle-cloth, and the covering of skins
was put over the Tent-cloth. See xxvi. 1 note.

20. the testimony] *i.e.* the Tables of stone
with the Ten Commandments engraved on
them (xxv. 16, xxxi. 18). Nothing else is
said to have been put into the Ark. These
were found there by themselves in the time
of Solomon (1 K. viii. 9 ; 2 Chr. v. 10).
The Pot of Manna was "laid up before
the testimony" (xvi. 34) ; Aaron's rod was
also placed "before the testimony" (Num.
xvii. 10) ; and the Book of the Law was
put at "the side of the Ark" (Deut. xxxi.
26). The expression "before the testi-

mony" appears to mean the space immediately in front of the Ark. Most interpreters
hold that the Pot of Manna and Aaron's
rod were at first placed between the Ark
and the Vail, and afterwards within the
Ark (Heb. ix. 4). It is very probable that
the pot and the rod had been put into the
Ark before it was taken by the Philistines,
but that they were not sent back with the
Ark and the tables. 1 Sam. iv. 11, vi. 11.

23-29. Moses performed these priestly
functions (xxviii. 1 note), before the holy
things with which they were performed
were anointed. The things had been made
expressly for the service of Jehovah, by His
command, and in this fact lay their essential sanctity, of which the anointing was
only the seal and symbol. Aaron and his
sons, on similar ground, having had the
divine call, took part in the service of the
Sanctuary as soon as the work was completed (*v.* 31). But Moses took part with
them, and most likely took the lead, until
they were consecrated and invested (Lev.
viii.) and publicly set apart for the office.

26. before the vail] That is, opposite to the
Ark, in the middle between the Table of
Shewbread on the North and the Candle-
stick on the South.

Moses and Aaron and his sons washed their hands and their feet
32 thereat: when they went into the tent of the congregation, and
when they came near unto the altar, they washed; ^das the LORD
33 commanded Moses. ^eAnd he reared up the court round about the
tabernacle and the altar, and set up the hanging of the court
34 gate. So Moses finished the work. ¶^fThen a cloud covered the
tent of the congregation, and the glory of the LORD filled the
35 tabernacle. And Moses ^gwas not able to enter into the tent of
the congregation, because the cloud abode thereon, and the
36 glory of the LORD filled the tabernacle. ^hAnd when the cloud
was taken up from over the tabernacle, the children of Israel
37 ¹went onward in all their journeys: but ⁱif the cloud were not
taken up, then they journeyed not till the day that it was taken
38 up. For ^kthe cloud of the LORD *was* upon the tabernacle by
day, and fire was on it by night, in the sight of all the house of
Israel, throughout all their journeys.

¹ Heb. *journeyed.*

Marginal references:
^d ch. 30. 19, 20.
^e ver. 8.
ch. 27. 9, 16.
^f ch. 29. 43.
Lev. 16. 2.
Num. 9. 15.
1 Kin. 8.
10, 11.
2 Chr. 5. 13.
& 7. 2.
Isai. 6. 4.
Hag. 2. 7, 9.
Rev. 15. 8.
^g Lev. 16. 2.
1 Kin. 8. 11.
2 Chr. 5. 14.
^h Num. 9.
17.
& 10. 11.
Neh. 9. 19.
ⁱ Num. 9. 19
—22.
^k ch. 13. 21.
Num. 9. 15.

34, 35. On the distinction between the Tent as the outer shelter and the Tabernacle as the *dwelling-place* of Jehovah, which is very clear in these verses, see xxvi. 1 note. The glory appeared as a light within and as a cloud on the outside.

35. Cp. the entrance of the High-priest into the Holy of Holies on the Day of Atonement, Lev. xvi. 2, 13. For special appearances of this glory in the Tabernacle, see Num. xiv. 10, xvi. 19, 42.

The Tabernacle, after it had accompanied the Israelites in their wanderings in the Wilderness, was most probably first set up in the Holy Land at Gilgal (Josh. iv. 19, v. 10, ix. 6, x. 6, 43). But before the death of Joshua, it was erected at Shiloh (Josh. xviii. 1, xix. 51). Here it remained as the national Sanctuary throughout the time of the Judges (Josh. xviii. 8, xxi. 2, xxii. 19; Judg. xviii. 31, xxi. 19; 1 S. i. 3, iv. 3). But its external construction was at this time somewhat changed, and *doors*, strictly so called, had taken the place of the entrance curtain (1 S. iii. 15): hence it seems to have been sometimes called *the temple* (1 S. i. 9, iii. 3), the name by which the structure of Solomon was afterwards commonly known. After the time of Eli it was removed to Nob in the canton of Benjamin, not far from Jerusalem (1 S. xxi. 1–9). From thence, in

the time of David, it was removed to Gibeon (1 Chr. xvi. 39, xxi. 29; 2 Chr. i. 3; 1 K. iii. 4, ix. 2). It was brought from Gibeon to Jerusalem by Solomon (1 K. viii. 4). After this, it disappears from the narrative of Scripture. When the Temple of Solomon was built, "the Tabernacle of the Tent" had entirely performed its work; it had protected the Ark of the Covenant during the migrations of the people until they were settled in the Land, and the promise was fulfilled, that the Lord would choose out a place for Himself in which His name should be preserved and His service should be maintained (Deut. xii. 14, 21, xiv. 24).

In accordance with its dignity as the most sacred object in the Sanctuary, the original Ark of the Covenant constructed by Moses was preserved and transferred from the Tabernacle to the Temple. The Golden Altar, the Candlestick and the Shewbread table were renewed by Solomon. They were subsequently renewed by Zerubbabel, and lastly by the Maccabees (see xxv. 23.) But the Ark was preserved in the Temple until Jerusalem was taken by the forces of Nebuchadnezzar (2 Chr. xxxv. 3; Jer. iii. 16). It was never replaced in the Second Temple. According to a rabbinical tradition, its site was marked by a block of stone.

LEVITICUS.

INTRODUCTION.

1. LEVITICUS, that is, the Levitical Book, is the name by which this portion of the law of Moses has always been called by the Hellenistic Jews and the Christian Church.

Leviticus is closely connected with Exodus at its commencement, and with Numbers at its conclusion; but differs from those books in its general exclusion of historical narrative. The only historical portions are the accounts of the Consecration of the priests, with the deaths of Nadab and Abihu (chs. viii.—x.), and of the punishment of the blasphemer (xxiv. 10—23). A large portion of it is occupied with instructions for the service of the Sanctuary.

2. The authorship of Leviticus is ascribed in the main to Moses.

The book has no pretension to systematic arrangement as a whole, nor does it appear to have been originally written all at one time.[1] There are præ-Mosaic fragments, together with passages probably written by Moses on previous occasions and inserted in the places they now occupy when the Pentateuch was put together; insertions

also occur of a later date which were written, or sanctioned, by the Prophets and holy men who, after the Captivity, arranged and edited the Scriptures of the Old Testament.

3. The instructions respecting the offerings for the Altar contained in Leviticus were recorded with a view to the guidance of those who were practically conversant with the service of the Tabernacle. They do not furnish a methodical statement for the information of those who are strangers to the subject. A short sketch of the ritual of the Altar, may therefore well form part of an Introduction to the study of this Book.

The whole sacrificial system of the Hebrew Law was intended for a people already brought into covenant with the living God, and every sacrifice was assumed to have a vital connexion with the spirit of the worshipper. A Hebrew sacrifice, like a Christian Sacrament, possessed the inward and spiritual grace, as well as the outward and visible sign;[2] and may have borne to each man a very different amount of meaning, according to the religious conditions of the mind. One may have come in devout obedience to the voice of the Law, with little more than

---

[1] The contents of Leviticus may be tabulated as follows :—(a) i–vii.; (b) viii.; (c) ix.; (d) x.; (e) xi.; (f) xii.; (g) xiii. xiv.; (h) xv.; (i) xvi.; (j) xvii.; (k) xviii. 1–18; (l) xviii. 19–30; (m) xix.; (n) xx.; (o) xxi.–xxii. 16; (p) xxii. 17–33; (q) xxiii.; (r) xxiv. 1–9; (s) xxiv. 10–23; (t) xxv.; (u) xxvi.; (v) xxvii.

[2] Ps. xl. 6; l. 8–14; Prov. xxi. 3; Is. i. 11–15; Jer. vii. 21–23; Hos. vi. 6; Mic. vi. 7, 8. Cp. 1 Sam. xv. 22; Matt. v. 23, 24.

a vague sense that his offering in some way expressed his own spiritual wants, and that the fact that he was permitted to offer it, was a sacramental pledge of God's good will and favour towards him. But to another, with clearer spiritual insight, the lessons conveyed in the symbols of the Altar must have all converged with more or less distinctness towards the Lamb slain from the foundation of the world,[3] Who was to come in the fulness of times that He might fulfil all righteousness,[4] and realize in the eyes of men the true Sin-offering, Burnt-offering, and Peace-offering.[5]

The general name for what was formally given up to the service of God was *korbān*,[6] which exactly answers to the English words, *offering* and *oblation*. Whatever offerings were brought to be sacrificed on the Altar, may be thus classed:—

Offerings for the Altar.

Animal.[7]	*Vegetable.*
1 Burnt-offerings,	1 Meat and Drink-offerings for the Altar in the Court.
2 Peace-offerings,	
3 Sin-offerings.	
	2 Incense and Meat-offerings for the Holy Place within the Tabernacle.

The offerings for the Altar were (1) public,[8] and (2) private sacrifices; the mode of conducting which was nearly the same. The

[3] Rev. xiii. 8.
[4] Matt. iii. 15.
[5] 2 Cor. v. 21; Eph. v. 2; Eph. ii. 13, 14; 1 Cor. v. 7; Joh. vi. 54.
[6] Cp. Mark vii. 11. See ii. 12; xxvii. 30; Num. xviii. 12, 26; Num. vii. 3; xxxi. 50.
[7] Besides these three classes there were the peculiar offerings connected with the Paschal Lamb (Ex. xii. 3), the Scape goat (xvi. 10), and the Red Heifer (Num. xix. 2).
[8] Ex. xxix. 38–44; Num. xxviii. xxix.

first three chapters of Leviticus relate entirely to private voluntary offerings.

The external distinction between the three classes of animal sacrifices may be thus broadly stated:— the Burnt-offering was wholly burnt upon the Altar; the Sin-offering was in part burnt on the Altar, and in part, either given to the priests or burnt outside the camp; and the Peace-offering was shared between the Altar, the priests and the sacrificer. This formal difference is immediately connected with the distinctive meaning of each kind of sacrifice. See pp. 229, 230.

Five animals are named in the Law as suitable for sacrifice, the ox, the sheep, the goat, the dove and the pigeon. It is worthy of notice that these were all offered by Abraham in the great sacrifice of the Covenant.[9]

Three conditions met in the sacrificial quadrupeds; (1) they were clean according to the Law; (2) they were commonly used as food; and, being domesticated, (3) they formed a part of the home wealth of the sacrificers.[1]

Every animal offered in sacrifice was to be perfect, without spot or blemish;[2] and might vary in age between not less than a week and three years.[3]

The man who offered a private sacrifice led with his own hands the victim into the Court of the Sanctuary, and formally presented it to the priest in front of the Tabernacle.[4] The sacrificer then

[9] Gen. xv. 9.
[1] The absence of one or more of these conditions explains the exclusion of many animals, and (among vegetable offerings) of many natural productions.
[2] xxii. 18–25 and reff.
[3] xxii. 27; Ex. xxii. 30; Gen. xv. 9.
[4] See note on i. 3. Cp. i. 4; xvi. 21.

laid, or rather pressed, his hand upon its head, and according to Jewish traditions, always uttered a prayer or confession of some sort while his hand rested on the head of the victim, except in the case of Peace-offerings. The regular place for slaughtering the animals for Burnt-offerings, Sin-offerings and Trespass-offerings, was the north side of the Altar.[5] Tradition tells us that before the sacrificer laid his hand upon the head of the victim, it was bound by a cord to one of the rings fixed for the purpose on the north side of the Altar, and that at the very instant when the words of the prayer, or confession, were ended, the fatal stroke was given. The Peace-offerings and the Paschal lambs, might, it would seem, be slain in any part of the Court.[6]

The mode of killing appears not to have differed from that of slaughtering animals for food. The throat was cut while a priest or assistant held a bowl under the neck to receive the blood.[7] The sacrificer, or his assistant, then flayed the victim and cut it into pieces,[8] probably while the priest was engaged in disposing of the blood.

In sacrificing the Burnt-offerings, the Peace-offerings and the Trespass-offerings,[9] the priests "sprinkled" or rather cast the blood about, so that the blood should be diffused over the sides of the Altar. In the Sin-offerings, the priest had to take some of the blood with his finger and put it upon the

horns of the Altar of Burnt-offering, and to pour out what remained at the bottom of the Altar, if the Sin-offering was for one of the common people, or for a ruler : if the Sin-offering was for the Congregation or for the High-priest, in addition to these two processes, the High-priest himself had to bring a portion of the blood into the Sanctuary, to sprinkle it with his finger seven times before the vail, and to put some of it upon the horns of the Altar of Incense.[1]

The great Altar of the Temple was furnished with two holes at its south-west corner through which the blood ran into a drain which conveyed it to the Cedron. There was probably some arrangement of this kind for taking the blood away from the Altar in the Wilderness.

When the blood was disposed of, the skin removed, and the animal cut into pieces, the sacrificer, or his assistant, washed the entrails and feet. In the case of a Burnt-offering, all the pieces were then taken to the Altar and salted. The priest next piled the pieces on the Altar, the hind limbs being probably put at the base of the pile, then the entrails and other viscera with the fat, then the fore limbs, with the head at the top.

The parts burnt upon the Altar of the Peace-offering, the Sin-offering and the Trespass-offering, were the same in each case ; and consisted of the fat, and the kidneys, and the caul above the liver.[2]

The parts of the victims which regularly fell to the priests were :—

Of the Burnt-offerings, only the hide, the whole of the flesh being consigned to the Altar : of the

---

[5] i. 11; vi. 25; vii. 2.
[6] Cp. i. 11 with iii. 2. See i. 5, &c. &c. ; Ex. xxxvii. 1 ; Cp. 2 Chron. xxx. 17.
[7] ix. 9, xvii. 3.
[8] i. 5, 6, &c.
[9] i. 5, 11; iii. 2, 8, 13; vii. 2.

[1] See notes to ch. iv.
[2] ix. 10. See note.

Peace-offerings, the breast and the right shoulder (or leg), which might be eaten by the priests and their families in any unpolluted place. The hide appears to have been retained by the sacrificer : of the Sin-offerings and the Trespass-offerings, the whole of the flesh (except the fat portions burnt on the Altar), and probably the hide. The flesh could only be eaten within the precinct of the Tabernacle. It was distinguished from the "holy" flesh of the Peace-offerings as being "most holy." [3]

Connected with the priests' breast and shoulder is the inquiry as to the two ceremonies called *waving* and *heaving*. The shoulder, which belonged to the officiating priest, was heaved, and the breast, which was for the common stock of the priests in general, was waved before the Lord. Each process appears to have been a solemn form of dedicating a thing to the use of the Sanctuary. The term strictly rendered Heave-offering appears to be used in as wide a sense as *korbān*, for offerings in general.[4] That rendered Wave-offering is not so broadly applied. The Rabbinists say that heaving was a moving up and down, waving a moving to and fro. But, as waving appears to have been the more solemn process of the two, it was probably, in accordance with its derivation,[5] a movement several times repeated, while heaving was simply a lifting up once.

Every Burnt-offering and Peace-offering was accompanied by a Meat-offering (rather Vegetable-offering, see ch. ii. with the notes) and a Drink-offering (Ex. xxix. 43). There is no mention of this in Leviticus. The quantities of flour, oil and wine were proportioned to the importance of the victims.

The whole of the Meat-offerings and Drink-offerings, with the exception of what was burnt, or poured, on the Altar, fell to the lot of the priests. See ii. 3.

The Sin-offering and the Trespass-offering were sacrificed without either Meat-offering or Drink-offering.

4. In the earliest record of sacrifice (Gen. iv. 3—5) the name given in common to the animal and vegetable offerings is *minchāh* (*i.e.* a gift), which the Law afterwards restricted to the vegetable-offerings (ii. 1 note).

The sacrifices of Noah after the flood consisted of Burnt-offerings of clean beasts and birds offered upon an altar.[6]

The Covenant sacrifice of Abraham[7] consisted of one of each of the five animals which the Law afterwards recognized as fit for sacrifice. But the cutting in twain of the four-footed victims appears to mark it as a peculiar rite belonging to a personal covenant, and to distinguish it from the classes of sacrifices ordained by the Law.

Among the different aspects under which the offering up of Isaac (Gen. xxii.) may be viewed, there is perhaps one which most directly connects it with the history

---

[3] vi. 25, 26. ; vii. 6.
[4] Ex. xxv. 2. See also Num. v. 9; Deut. xii. 6, &c.
[5] The Hebrew verb is applied to such actions as using a saw, or other tool, Ex. xx. 25 ; Josh. viii. 31 ; Isa. x. 15, xxx. 28, &c. For instances of waving, see xxiii. 11, 17.

[6] Gen. viii. 20, 21. Cp. the language used with that of i. 9, ii. 3, 9, 13, iii. 5, &c.
[7] Gen. xv. 9-17.

of sacrifice.—Abraham had still one great lesson to learn. He did not clearly perceive that Jehovah did not require his gifts. The Law had not yet been given which would have suggested this truth to him by the *single* victim appointed for the Burnt-offering and for the Sin-offering, and by the sparing handful of the Meat-offering. To correct and enlighten him, the Lord "tempted" him to offer up, as a Burnt-offering, his most cherished possession, the centre of his hopes. The offering, had it been completed, would have been an actual gift to Jehovah, not a ceremonial act of worship: it would have been not an outward and visible sign of an inward and spiritual grace, but a stern reality in itself. Isaac was not, as regards his father's purpose, in any proper sense a symbol or representative. Nor is there any hint that would justify us in making the voluntary submission of Isaac a significant part of the transaction. The act of the patriarch in giving up his own flesh and blood was an analogue rather than a type of the sacrifice of the Great High Priest who gave up Himself as a victim. In order to instruct Abraham that the service of the Altar fulfilled its purpose in being the expression of the spiritual condition of the worshipper, the Lord Himself provided a ram which was accepted instead of the beloved son. Abraham had already made the offering of himself in his ready faith and obedience; the acceptable means for expressing this fact was appointed in the "ram caught in a thicket by his horns."

Isaac and Jacob built altars:[8] and the sacrifices offered by Jacob

at Mizpah[9] appear to have been strictly Peace-offerings.

Sacrificial worship was familiarly known to the Israelites in Egypt: and the history of Jethro seems to show that it was common to the two great branches of the Semitic stock.[1]

We thus see that if we take the narrative of Scripture for our guide, the most ancient sacrifices were Burnt-offerings: and that the radical idea of sacrifice is to be sought in the Burnt-offering rather than in the Peace-offering, or in the Sin-offering. Assuming that the animal brought to the Altar represented the person of him who offered it, and noting that the flesh was spoken of not as destroyed by burning, but as sent up in the fire like incense towards heaven;[2]—the act of sacrifice intimated that the believer confessed the obligation of surrendering himself, body, soul and spirit, to the Lord of heaven and earth Who had been revealed to him. The truth expressed then in the whole Burnt-offering is the unqualified self-sacrifice of the person.

In the Peace-offerings of the patriarchal age, before the institution of a national priesthood, there is no reason to doubt that, as in the Peace-offerings of the Law, certain portions of the victim were burned upon the altar, and that the remainder of the flesh was eaten by the offerer and those who were associated with him by participation in the spirit of the sacrifice.

In the scriptural records there is no trace either of the Sin-offering, or of any special treatment of the

---

[8] Gen. xxvi. 25, xxxiii. 20, xxxv. 1, 7.

[9] Gen. xxxi. 54, xlvi. 1.
[1] See Ex. xviii. 12 note.
[2] See i. 9 note.

blood of victims, before the time of Moses. Not that we need imagine a single act of sacrifice to have been performed since the first transgression, without a consciousness of sin in the mind of the worshipper. Earnest devotion to a Holy God in a fallen creature must necessarily include a sense of sin and unworthiness. But the feeling which most prominently found its expression in the Burnt-offerings of Noah (for example), must have been rather, the sense of present deliverance, of thankfulness deeper than words, of complete self-surrender to the solemn bond now laid upon him in the Covenant.

The first instance of the blood of a sacrifice being noticed in any way occurs in the account of the institution of the Passover ;[3] the next is in connexion with the Burnt-offerings and Peace-offerings of the Covenant of Sinai.[4]

We are left in no doubt as to the sacrificial meaning of the blood. As the material vehicle of the life of the victim, it was the symbol of the life of the offerer. In contrast with the flesh and bones it expressed in a distinct manner the immaterial principle which survives death. This is distinctly assigned as the reason for its appointed use in the rites of atonement.[5]

The Sin-offering is to be regarded as a creation of the Law. It was the voice of the Law that awakened the distinct consciousness of sin in the individual mind.[6]

In the perfected sacrificial system, the three classes of offerings are to be regarded as representing distinct aspects of divine truth connected with man's relation to Jehovah. But it is important to observe that in no sacrifice was the idea of the Burnt-offering left out.[7]

The natural order of victims in the sacrificial service of the Law was, first the Sin-offering, then the Burnt-offering, and last the Peace-offering. This answers to the spiritual process through which the worshipper had to pass. He had transgressed the Law, and he needed the atonement signified by the Sin-offering : if his offering had been made in truth and sincerity, he could then offer himself to the Lord as an accepted person, as a sweet savour, in the Burnt-offering, and in virtue of this acceptance, he could enjoy communion with the Lord and with his brethren in the Peace-offering.

The main additions made to the ritual of sacrifice by the Levitical Law consisted in the establishment of one national Altar, the institution of the national Priesthood, and all those particulars that were peculiar to the Sin-offerings and the Trespass-offerings. In these particulars, which in spite of prophetic teaching must have been difficult and obscure to the Israelite, we can now clearly trace the forecast shadows of the spotless Saviour Who was to come, to stand for the sinful race as its head, to make the offering of Himself as both priest and victim, to perfect the work of redemption by Himself, and so to enter into the presence of God for us as a sweet savour.[8]

---

[3] Ex. xii. 7, 22. 23.
[4] Ex. xxiv. 4-8. See notes.
[5] See xvii. 11 note.
[6] Rom. iii. 20, vii. 7.

[7] See iii. 5 note ; Ex. xxix. 31-42.
[8] Heb. x. 19, 20, 21.

THE THIRD BOOK OF MOSES,

CALLED

LEVITICUS.

Chap. 1. AND the Lord ^acalled unto Moses, and spake unto him 2 ^bout of the tabernacle of the congregation, saying, Speak unto the children of Israel, and say unto them, ^cIf any man of you bring an offering unto the Lord, ye shall bring your offer- 3 ing of the cattle, *even* of the herd, and of the flock. ¶ If his offering *be* a burnt sacrifice of the herd, let him offer a male ^dwithout blemish : he shall offer it of his own voluntary will at the door of the tabernacle of the congregation before the Lord. 4 ^eAnd he shall put his hand upon the head of the burnt offering ; and it shall be ^faccepted for him ^gto make atonement for him. 5 And he shall kill the ^hbullock before the Lord : ⁱand the priests, Aaron's sons, shall bring the blood, ^kand sprinkle the blood round about upon the altar that *is by* the door of the tabernacle

a Ex. 19. 3.
b Ex. 40. 34.
c ch. 22. 18, 19.

d Ex. 12. 5.
ch. 22. 20.
e Ex. 29. 10.
f ch. 22. 21.
g Num.15.25.
Rom. 5. 11.
h Mic. 6. 6.
i 2 Chr. 35. 11.
Heb. 10. 11.
k ch. 3. 8.

I. 1. *the* Lord] In the Hebrew text of Leviticus, JEHOVAH is the name by which God is usually called. Where Elohim occurs, it is generally with a possessive pronoun, so as to designate Him as the God of the chosen people (ii. 13 ; xi. 45 ; xviii. 21 ; xix. 12, 14, 32, &c.).

the tabernacle of the congregation] Rather, **the Tent of meeting.** See Ex. xxvii. 21 note. When JEHOVAH was about to give His people the law of the Ten Commandments (Ex. xix. 3) He called to Moses from the top of Mount Sinai in thunders and lightnings and a thick cloud. When He was now about to give them the laws by which their formal acts of worship were to be regulated, He called to Moses out of the Tabernacle which had just been constructed at the foot of the mountain. (Ex. xxv. 22.)

2. *speak unto the children of Israel*] It is important to observe that these first instructions (i. 2–iii. 17) are addressed expressly to the individual who felt the need of sacrifice on his own account. They were not delivered through the priests, nor had the officiating priest any choice as to what he was to do. He was only to examine the victim to see that it was perfect (xxii. 17–24), and to perform other strictly prescribed duties (vi. 8–vii. 21). The act of offering was to be voluntary on the part of the worshipper, but the mode of doing it was in every point defined by the Law. The presenting of the victim at the entrance of the Tabernacle was in fact a symbol of the free will submitting itself to the Law of the Lord. Such acts of sacrifice are to be distinguished from the public offerings, and those ordained for individuals on special occasions (see iv. 2 note), which belonged to the religious education of the nation.

offering] Heb. *korbān:* the general name for what was formally given up to the ser-

vice of God (cp. Mark vii. 11), and exactly answering to the words *offering* and *oblation.*

3. *burnt*] Lit. that (offering) which ascends (as a flame).

a male without blemish] Males were required in most offerings, as the stronger sex which takes precedence of the other. But females were allowed in Peace-offerings (iii. 1, 6), and were expressly prescribed in the Sin-offerings of the common people (iv. 28, 32 ; v. 6).

at the door of the tabernacle of the congregation] Wherever these words occur they should be rendered, **at the entrance of the Tent of meeting.** The place denoted is that part of the court which was in front of the Tabernacle, in which stood the brazen Altar and the laver, and where alone sacrifices could be offered. See Cut to Ex. xxvi.

4. *And he shall put his hand upon the head of the burnt offering*] The usual ceremony. By it the sacrificer identified himself with his victim (iii. 2, 8 ; iv. 15 ; viii. 14 ; Rom. xii. 1).

to make atonement for him] This phrase belongs more especially to the Sin-offerings and the Trespass-offerings (cp. iv. 20, 26, 31, 35 ; v. 16, 18 ; vi. 7, &c.) It is not used in reference to the Peace-offerings, and but rarely in reference to the Burnt-offerings. It should be noticed that it is here introduced in close connection with the imposition of hands by the worshipper, not, as it is when it refers to the Sin-offering, with the special functions of the priest, iv. 26, 35 ; 2 Chr. xxix. 23.

5. *And he shall kill the bullock*] Tradition states that before the laying on of the hand, the victim was bound by a cord to a ring on the north side of the Altar; as the words of the prayer were ended, the throat was cut and the blood received into a bowl held by an assistant.

6 of the congregation. And he shall flay the burnt offering, and
7 cut it into his pieces. And the sons of Aaron the priest shall put

l Gen. 22. 9. 8 fire upon the altar, and *l*lay the wood in order upon the fire : and
the priests, Aaron's sons, shall lay the parts, the head, and the
fat, in order upon the wood that *is* on the fire which *is* upon the
9 altar : but his inwards and his legs shall he wash in water : and
the priest shall burn all on the altar, to be a burnt sacrifice, an

m Gen. 8. 21. 10 offering made by fire, of a *m*sweet savour unto the LORD.   ¶And
Ezek. 20.
28, 41.   if his offering be of the flocks, *namely*, of the sheep, or of the
2 Cor. 2. 15.   goats, for a burnt sacrifice ; he shall bring it a male *n*without
Eph. 5. 2. 11 blemish.   *o*And he shall kill it on the side of the altar northward
Phil. 4. 18.
n ver. 3.   before the LORD : and the priests, Aaron's sons, shall sprinkle
Deut. 15. 21. 12 his blood round about upon the altar.   And he shall cut it into
Mal. 1. 14.   his pieces, with his head and his fat : and the priest shall lay
o ver. 5.   them in order on the wood that *is* on the fire which *is* upon the
13 altar : but he shall wash the inwards and the legs with water :
and the priest shall bring *it* all, and burn *it* upon the altar : it *is*
a burnt sacrifice, an offering made by fire, of a sweet savour unto

p ch. 5. 7. 14 the LORD.   ¶And if the burnt sacrifice for his offering to the
& 12. 8.   LORD be of fowls, then he shall bring his offering of *p* turtledoves,
Luke 2. 24.

---

sprinkle the blood] Rather, **throw the
blood**, so as to make the liquid cover a considerable surface. [The Christian significance of this typical action is referred to in
Heb. xii. 24 ; 1 Pet. i. 2.]

by the door of the tabernacle] At the entrance of the Tent.

6. *And he shall flay*] The sacrificer, or his
assistant, had to skin and cut up the victim.
The hide was the perquisite of the officiating priest. (vii. 8.)

his pieces] That is, its proper pieces, the
parts into which it was usual for a sacrificed
animal to be divided.

7. *put fire upon the altar*] This must specifically refer to the first Burnt-offering on
the newly constructed Altar. The rule was
afterwards to be, "it shall never go out,"
(vi. 13.)

8. The parts of the victim were then
salted by the priest in conformity with the
rule, (ii. 13 ; Ezek. xliii. 24 ; Mark ix. 49),
and placed "in order" upon the wood, *i.e.*
in the same relation to each other that they
had in the living animal.

9. The parts which were washed were the
stomach, and bowels, and feet, divided from
the carcase at the knee-joint.

the priest shall burn] The verb here translated *burn*, is applied exclusively to the
burning of the incense, to the lights of the
Tabernacle, and to the offerings on the
Altar. The primary meaning of its root
seems to be *to exhale odour*. (See the margin
of xxiv. 2 ; Ex. xxx. 8). The word for
burning in a common way is quite different,
and is applied to the burning of those parts
of victims which were burned without the
camp (iv. 12, 21 ; Num. xix. 5, &c.). The
importance of the distinction is great in its
bearing on the meaning of the Burnt-offering. The substance of the victim was re-

garded not as something to be consumed,
but as an offering of a sweet-smelling savour
sent up in the flame to Jehovah.

10. *of the flocks*] These directions are more
brief than those for the bullock. The Burnt-
offering of the sheep must have been that
with which the people were most familiar
in the daily morning and evening service.
Ex. xxix. 38-42. Sheep were preferred for
sacrifice when they could be obtained, except
in some special Sin-offerings in which goats
were required (iv. 23, ix. 3, xvi. 5). The
lamb "without blemish " is a well-known
type of Christ. Heb. ix. 14 ; 1 Pet. i. 19.

11. *northward before the* LORD] That is,
on the north side of the Altar. See also
iv. 24, 29, 33, vii. 2. This was probably an
arrangement of some practical convenience.
On the west side of the Altar stood the
laver ; on the east side was the place of
ashes (see *v.* 16 note) ; and the south side,
where appears to have been the slope by
which the priests went up to the Altar,
must have been left clear for thoroughfare.

14. *of turtledoves, or of young pigeons*]
The offering of a bird was permitted to one
who was too poor to offer a quadruped.
(Cp. marg. reff.) But in certain rites of
purification birds were appointed for all,
whatever might be their circumstances. See
xv. 14, 29 ; Num. vi. 10. The limitation of
the age of the pigeons may be accounted
for by the natural habits of the birds. It
would seem that the species which are most
likely to have been the sacrificial dove and
pigeon are the common turtle and the blue-
rock pigeon, a bird like our stock-dove, and
considerably larger than the turtle. The
turtles come in the early part of April, but
as the season advances they wholly disappear. The pigeons, on the contrary, do not
leave the country ; and their nests, with

15 or of young pigeons. And the priest shall bring it unto the altar, and [1]wring off his head, and burn *it* on the altar; and the
16 blood thereof shall be wrung out at the side of the altar : and he shall pluck away his crop with [2]his feathers, and cast it *q* beside *q* ch. 6. 10.
17 the altar on the east part, by the place of the ashes: and he shall cleave it with the wings thereof, but *r* shall not divide *it* asunder : *r* Gen. 15. 10. and the priest shall burn it upon the altar, upon the wood that *is* upon the fire : *s* it *is* a burnt sacrifice, an offering made by fire, *s* ver. 9. 13. of a sweet savour unto the LORD.

CHAP. 2. AND when any will offer *a* a meat offering unto the LORD, *a* ch. 6. 14. his offering shall be *of* fine flour ; and he shall pour oil upon it, & 9. 17.
2 and put frankincense thereon: and he shall bring it to Aaron's Num. 15. 4. sons the priests: and he shall take thereout his handful of the flour thereof, and of the oil thereof, with all the frankincense thereof; and the priest shall burn *b* the memorial of it *b* See note upon the altar, *to be* an offering made by fire, of a sweet savour and Isai. 66. 3. 3 unto the LORD : and *c* the remnant of the meat offering *shall be* *c* ch. 7. 9. Aaron's and his sons' : *d* it *is* a thing most holy of the offerings of & 10. 12, 13. *d* Ex. 29. 37.

[1] Or, *pinch off the head with the nail.*   [2] Or, *the filth thereof.* Num. 18. 9.

---

young ones in them, may be easily found at any season of the year. Hence it would appear, that when turtledoves could not be obtained, nestling pigeons were accepted as a substitute.

16. *his crop with his feathers*] The weight of authority is in favour of the marginal rendering. It is most probable that the feathers were burnt with the body, and that the wings, mentioned in *v.* 17, were not mutilated.

the place of the ashes] The ashes were daily removed from the Altar (except on certain holy days) and thrown into a heap on its eastern side. When the heap became inconveniently large, it was removed in vessels appropriated to the purpose (see Ex. xxvii. 3) to a spot without the camp. (iv. 12, vi. 11.)

II. 1. *a meat offering*] Better translated bowl, cp. Num. vii. 13. in *v.* 4 **an oblation of a meat offering** (*korbān* [see i. 2] *minchah*). Minchah signifies literally *a gift;* and it appears to have been applied specially to what was given by an inferior to a superior (Gen. xxxii. 18-20, xliii. 11; Judg. iii. 15; 1 S. x. 27): but in the technical language of the Law, it regularly denoted the vegetable offerings as distinguished from the animal offerings. Our translators have rendered it *meat-offering,* applying the word *meat,* according to old usage, as a general term for food. Vegetable-offering or Meal-offering would be a more convenient rendering.

The meaning of the Minchah appears to be much more simple than that of the animal sacrifices. The Minchah, as a sacrifice, was something surrendered to God, which was of the greatest value to man as a means of living. It might thus seem to be merely eucharistic. But it should not be overlooked that the grain had been modified, and made useful, by man's own labour. Hence it has

been supposed that the Minchah expressed a confession that all our good works are wrought in God and are due to Him.

The order in which the kinds of offering are named agrees with their development in order of time. The Burnt-offering and the Minchah answer to the first two offerings on record (Gen. iv. 3, 4; Amos v. 22).

Three kinds of Minchah are here mentioned ; (1) *vv.* 1-3 ; (2) *vv.* 4-7 ; (3) *vv.* 14-16. Of each of them a small portion was burnt on the Altar "for a memorial," and the remainder was given to the priests. The offerings of flour belonged to the priests at large, but those of cakes and wafers to the officiating priests, vii. 9, 10. Instructions to the priests are given in vi. 14-23.

1. *fine flour*] finely bolted flour of wheat. It was probably always presented in a bowl, cp. Num. vii. 13.

oil] For the purpose of anointing and as food ; in both senses a symbol of divine grace. *frankincense*] See Ex. xxx. 34 note.

2. Better : "And he shall bring it to Aaron's sons, the priests; and the (officiating) **priest shall take from it,**" &c.

memorial] The regular name not only for the portion of the Minchah which was burnt on the Altar (*vv.* 9, 16, v. 12, vi. 15; Num. v. 26), but for the frankincense which was laid upon the Shewbread (xxiv. 7). It is the word which is applied to the prayers and alms of Cornelius, Acts x. 4.

3. *a thing most holy*] Literally, *a holy of holies.* All offerings were *holy,* including the portions of the Peace-offerings which were eaten by the laity ; but that was *most holy* of which every part was devoted either to the Altar, or to the use of the priests. Such were the Minchahs, the Shewbread, the incense, and the flesh of the Sin- and Trespass-offerings. Cp. the similar distinction between Places (Ex. xxvi. 33). The most

e Ex. 29. 2.

f ver. 2.
g Ex. 29. 18.
h ver. 3.

i ch. 6. 17.
See Matt.
16. 12.
Mark 8. 15.
Luke 12. 1.
1 Cor. 5. 8.
Gal. 5. 9.
k Ex. 22. 29.
ch. 23. 10, 11.
l Mark 9. 49.
Col. 4. 6.
m Num. 18.
19.
n Ezek. 43.
24.
o ch. 23. 10,
14.

4 the Lord made by fire. ¶ And if thou bring an oblation of a meat offering baken in the oven, *it shall be* unleavened cakes of fine flour mingled with oil, or unleavened wafers *e*anointed with oil.
5 And if thy oblation *be* a meat offering *baken* [1]in a pan, it shall be
6 *of* fine flour unleavened, mingled with oil. Thou shalt part it in
7 pieces, and pour oil thereon : it *is* a meat offering. And if thy oblation *be* a meat offering *baken* in the fryingpan, it shall be
8 made *of* fine flour with oil. And thou shalt bring the meat offering that is made of these things unto the Lord : and when it is presented unto the priest, he shall bring it unto the altar.
9 And the priest shall take from the meat offering *f*a memorial thereof, and shall burn *it* upon the altar : *it is* an *g*offering made
10 by fire, of a sweet savour unto the Lord. And *h*that which is left of the meat offering *shall be* Aaron's and his sons' : *it is* a
11 thing most holy of the offerings of the Lord made by fire. No meat offering, which ye shall bring unto the Lord, shall be made with *i*leaven : for ye shall burn no leaven, nor any honey,
12 in any offering of the Lord made by fire. *k*As for the oblation of the firstfruits, ye shall offer them unto the Lord : but they
13 shall not [2]be burnt on the altar for a sweet savour. And every oblation of thy meat offering *l*shalt thou season with salt ; neither shalt thou suffer *m*the salt of the covenant of thy God to be lacking from thy meat offering : *n*with all thine offerings
14 thou shalt offer salt. ¶ And if thou offer a meat offering of thy firstfruits unto the Lord, *o*thou shalt offer for the meat offering of thy firstfruits green ears of corn dried by the fire, *even* corn

[1] Or, *on a flat plate*, or, *slice*.   [2] Heb. *ascend*.

holy food was eaten in "the holy place," that is the precinct of the Tabernacle, probably in the priests' lodgings ; but the priests'portion of the Peace-offerings might be eaten by the priests and their families in any "clean place" (x. 12-14).

4–10. The four kinds of bread and the three cooking utensils which are mentioned in this section were probably such as were in common use in the daily life of the Israelites ; and there appears no reason to doubt that they were such as are still used in the East.   The variety of the offerings was most likely permitted to suit the different circumstances of the worshippers.

4. *oven*] This was probably a portable vessel of earthenware ; in shape a cone about 3 ft. 6 in. high, and 1 ft. 6 in. in diameter. Similar jars are now used for the same purpose by the Arabs. After the vessel has been thoroughly heated by a fire lighted in the inside, the cakes are placed within it, and the top is covered up until they are sufficiently baked. Meantime the outside of the vessel is turned to account. Dough rolled out very thin is spread over it, and a sort of wafer is produced considerably thinner than a Scotch oat-cake.

5. *a pan*] Rather, as in the margin, a flat plate. It was probably of earthenware, like the oven.

6. *part it in pieces*] Break, not cut. The Bedouins are in the habit of breaking up their cakes when warm and mixing the frag-

ments with butter when that luxury can be obtained.

7. *fryingpan*] Rather, pan, commonly used for boiling. It is possible that the cakes here spoken of were boiled in oil. The "pan" and the "frying pan" (*vv.* 5, 7) may have been the common cooking implements of the poorest of the people.

11, 12. *As for the oblation of the firstfruits*] Rather, As an oblation of firstfruits. The words refer to the leaven and honey mentioned in *v.* 11 which might be offered amongst the firstfruits and tithes (Deut. xxvi. 2, 12 ; cp. 2 Chr. xxxi. 5). Honey, being used to produce fermentation, and leaven (or, a small piece of fermented dough) were excluded because fermentation was an apt symbol of the working of corruption in the human heart.

13. *with all thine offerings thou shalt offer salt*] Not only every Minchah, but every animal offering was to be accompanied by salt. It was the one symbol which was never absent from the Altar of Burnt-offering, showing the imperishableness of the love of Jehovah for His people. In its unalterable nature, it is the contrary of leaven. The Arabs are said to retain in common use the expression, "a covenant of salt ;" and the respect they pay to bread and salt in their rites of hospitality is well known.

14. *green ears of corn*] Rather, "fresh ears of corn ;" that is, corn just ripe, freshly gathered. Parched corn, such as is

15 beaten out of *p*full ears. And *q*thou shalt put oil upon it, and
16 lay frankincense thereon: it *is* a meat offering. And the priest
shall burn *r*the memorial of it, *part* of the beaten corn thereof,
and *part* of the oil thereof, with all the frankincense thereof: *it
is* an offering made by fire unto the LORD.

CHAP. 3. AND if his oblation *be* a *a*sacrifice of peace offering, if he
offer *it* of the herd; whether *it be* a male or female, he shall
2 offer it *b*without blemish before the LORD. And *c*he shall lay
his hand upon the head of his offering, and kill it *at* the door of
the tabernacle of the congregation: and Aaron's sons the priests
3 shall sprinkle the blood upon the altar round about. And he
shall offer of the sacrifice of the peace offering an offering made
by fire unto the LORD; *d*the ¹fat that covereth the inwards, and
4 all the fat that *is* upon the inwards, and the two kidneys, and
the fat that *is* on them, which *is* by the flanks, and the ²caul
5 above the liver, with the kidneys, it shall he take away. And
Aaron's sons *e*shall burn it on the altar upon the burnt sacrifice,
which *is* upon the wood that *is* on the fire: *it is* an offering made
6 by fire, of a sweet savour unto the LORD. ¶ And if his offering
for a sacrifice of peace offering unto the LORD *be* of the flock;
7 male or female, *f*he shall offer it without blemish. If he offer
a lamb for his offering, then shall he offer it before the LORD.
8 And he shall lay his hand upon the head of his offering, and kill
it before the tabernacle of the congregation: and Aaron's sons
shall sprinkle the blood thereof round about upon the altar.
9 And he shall offer of the sacrifice of the peace offering an offering made by fire unto the LORD; the fat thereof, *and* the whole
rump, it shall he take off hard by the backbone; and the fat
that covereth the inwards, and all the fat that *is* upon the in-
10 wards, and the two kidneys, and the fat that *is* upon them,
which *is* by the flanks, and the caul above the liver, with the
11 kidneys, it shall he take away. And the priest shall burn it
upon the altar: *it is* *g*the food of the offering made by fire unto
12 the LORD. ¶ And if his offering *be* a goat, then *h*he shall offer it
13 before the LORD. And he shall lay his hand upon the head of it,
and kill it before the tabernacle of the congregation: and the
sons of Aaron shall sprinkle the blood thereof upon the altar

p 2 Kin. 4.
42.
q ver. 1.
r ver. 2.

a ch. 7. 11,
29.
& 22. 21.
b ch. 1. 3.
c Ex. 29. 10.
ch. 1. 4, 5.

d Ex. 29. 13,
22.
ch. 4. 8, 9.

e Ex. 29. 13.
ch. 6. 12.

f ver. 1, &c.

g See ch. 21.
6, 8, 17, 21,
22.
& 22. 25.
Ezek. 44. 7.
Mal. 1. 7, 12.
h ver. 1, 7,
&c.

¹ Or, *suet*.   ² Or, *midriff over the liver*, and *over the kidneys*.

---

here spoken of, is a common article of food
in Syria and Egypt, and was very generally
eaten in ancient times.

beaten out] Not rubbed out by the hands,
as described in Luke vi. 1, but bruised or
crushed so as to form groats.

III. 1. The Peace-offering (like the Burnt-
offering, i. 3, and the Minchah, ii. 1) is here
spoken of as if it was familiarly known before the giving of the Law. "Peace-offering"
seems preferable to "thank-offering," which
occurs in several places in the margin of our
Bible. "Thank-offering" appears to be the
right name for a subordinate class of Peace-
offering.

2. *kill it at the door*, &c.] See i. 3. Tradition says that the Peace-offerings might be
killed in any part of the Court.

3. "The fat that covereth the inwards"
refers to the caul or transparent membrane
which has upon it a network of fatty tissue:

"the fat upon the inwards" refers to the
small lumps of suet found upon the intestines of healthy animals.

4. *the caul above the liver*] Probably the membrane covering the upper part of the liver.

5. *upon the burnt sacrifice*] Upon the
ashes of the continual Burnt-offering (Ex.
xxix. 38), in accordance with vi. 12.

7. *a lamb*] **A sheep.** The word signifies a
full-grown sheep, in its prime.

8. See i. 4, 5 notes.

9. *the whole rump*] **The whole fat tail:**
i.e. the tail of the kind of sheep well known
in the East, and often weighing 15lbs. and
even as much as 50lbs. when the sheep has
been increased by artificial fattening.

11. *burn it*] See i. 9 note.

12. See i. 10 note. Birds were not accepted
as Peace-offerings, most probably because
they were, by themselves, insufficient to
make up a sacrificial meal.

14 round about. And he shall offer thereof his offering, *even* an offering made by fire unto the LORD; the fat that covereth the
15 inwards, and all the fat that *is* upon the inwards, and the two kidneys, and the fat that *is* upon them, which *is* by the flanks, and the caul above the liver, with the kidneys, it shall he take
16 away. And the priest shall burn them upon the altar: *it is* the food of the offering made by fire for a sweet savour: *i*all the fat
17 *is* the LORD'S. *It shall be* a *k*perpetual statute for your generations throughout all your dwellings, that ye eat neither *l*fat nor *m*blood.

CHAP. 4. AND the LORD spake unto Moses, saying, Speak unto the
2 children of Israel, saying, *a*If a soul shall sin through ignorance against any of the commandments of the LORD *concerning things* which ought not to be done, and shall do against any of them:
3 ¶*b*If the priest that is anointed do sin according to the sin of the people; then let him bring for his sin, which he hath sinned, *c*a

---

16. Rather, **as food of an offering made by fire for a sweet savour, shall all the fat be for Jehovah.** Our bodily taste and smell furnish figures of the satisfaction with which the LORD accepts the appointed symbols of the true worship of the heart. All that was sent up in the fire of the Altar, including the parts of the Sin-offering (iv. 31), as well as the Burnt-offering (i. 9, &c.), was accepted for "a sweet savour:" but the word *food* may here have a peculiar fitness in its application to the Peace-offering, which served for food also to the priests and the offerer, and so symbolized communion between the LORD, His ministers, and His worshippers.

the fat is the LORD'S] The significance of this appears to consist in the fact that its proper development in the animal is, in general, a mark of perfection.

17. *blood*] See xvii. 11 note.

throughout all your dwellings] The suet was neither to be eaten in sacrificial meals in the Sanctuary, nor in ordinary meals in private houses.

IV. 1, 2. *And the* LORD *spake...Israel*] This formula is the commencement of a distinct section of the Law.

2. *If a soul shall sin*] The Sin-offering was a new thing, instituted by the Law. The older kinds of sacrifice (ii. 1; iii. 1) when offered by individuals were purely voluntary: no special occasions were prescribed. But it was plainly commanded that he who was conscious that he had committed a sin should bring his Sin-offering. In the abridged rules for Sin-offerings in Numbers xv. 22-31, the kind of sin for which Sin-offerings were accepted is contrasted with that which cut off the perpetrator from among his people (cp. *v.* 22 with *v.* 30). The two classes are distinguished in the language of our Bible as sin through ignorance and presumptuous sin. The distinction is clearly recognized in Ps. xix. 12, 13 and Heb. x. 26. 27. It seems evident that the classification thus indicated refers immediately to the

relation of the conscience to God, not to outward practices, nor, immediately, to outward actions. The presumptuous sinner, literally he who sinned "with a high hand," might or might not have committed such a crime as to incur punishment from the civil law: it was enough that he had with deliberate purpose rebelled against God (see Prov. ii. 13-15), and *ipso facto* was "cut off from among his people" and alienated from the divine covenant (see vii. 20; Ex. xxxi. 14; cp. Matt. xii. 31; 1 Joh. v. 16). But the other kind of sin, that for which the Sin-offering was appointed, was of a more complicated nature. It appears to have included the entire range of "sins, negligences and ignorances" for which we are accustomed to ask forgiveness. Sin-offerings were required not only when the conscience accused the offender of having yielded to temptation, but sometimes for what were breaches of the Law committed strictly in ignorance (*vv.* 13, 23, 28, v. 17), and sometimes on account of ceremonial pollution. They are thus to be regarded as protests against everything which is opposed to the holiness and purity of the divine Law. They were, in short, to be offered by the worshipper as a relief to the conscience whenever he felt the need of atonement.

sin through ignorance] **Sin through error;** that is, through straying from the right way. See Ps. cxix. 67; Eccles. v. 6.

3. *the priest that is anointed*] *i.e.* the High-priest. (Cp. viii. 12, xxi. 10; Ex. xxix. 7). On the anointing of the other priests see note on viii. 13.

The graduation of the Sin-offerings is remarkable. It might seem that the distinction addressed itself more pointedly to each individual according to his rank and consequent responsibility (see *v.* 32).

according to the sin of the people] Rather, **to bring guilt on the people.** The whole nation is concerned in every transgression of its representative.

young bullock without blemish unto the LORD for a sin offering.
4 And he shall bring the bullock *d*unto the door of the tabernacle   *d* ch. 1. 3, 4.
of the congregation before the LORD; and shall lay his hand
upon the bullock's head, and kill the bullock before the LORD.
5 And the priest that is anointed *e*shall take of the bullock's blood,   *e* ch. 16. 14.
6 and bring it to the tabernacle of the congregation: and the   Num. 19. 4.
priest shall dip his finger in the blood, and sprinkle of the blood
seven times before the LORD, before the vail of the sanctuary.
7 And the priest shall *f*put *some* of the blood upon the horns of   *f* ch. 8. 15.
the altar of sweet incense before the LORD, which *is* in the taber-   & 9. 9.
nacle of the congregation; and shall pour *g*all the blood of the   & 16. 18.
bullock at the bottom of the altar of the burnt offering, which   *g* ch. 5. 9.
8 *is at* the door of the tabernacle of the congregation. And he
shall take off from it all the fat of the bullock for the sin offering; the fat that covereth the inwards, and all the fat that *is*
9 upon the inwards, and the two kidneys, and the fat that *is* upon
them, which *is* by the flanks, and the caul above the liver, with
10 the kidneys, it shall he take away, *h*as it was taken off from the   *h* ch. 3. 3, 4,
bullock of the sacrifice of peace offerings: and the priest shall   5.
11 burn them upon the altar of the burnt offering. *i*And the skin   *i* Ex. 29. 14.
of the bullock, and all his flesh, with his head, and with his legs,   Num. 19. 5.
12 and his inwards, and his dung, even the whole bullock shall he
carry forth [1]without the camp unto a clean place, *k*where the   *k* ch. 6. 11.
ashes are poured out, and *l*burn him on the wood with fire: *l* Heb. 13. 11.
13 [2]where the ashes are poured out shall he be burnt. ¶ And *m*if   *m* Num. 15.
the whole congregation of Israel sin through ignorance, *n*and   24.
the thing be hid from the eyes of the assembly, and they have   Josh. 7. 11.
done *somewhat against* any of the commandments of the LORD   *n* ch. 5. 2,
concerning things which should not be done, and are guilty;   3, 4, 17.
14 when the sin, which they have sinned against it, is known, then
the congregation shall offer a young bullock for the sin, and
15 bring him before the tabernacle of the congregation. And the
elders of the congregation *o*shall lay their hands upon the head   *o* ch. 1. 4.

---

[1] Heb. *to without the camp.*   [2] Heb. *at the pouring out of the ashes.*

---

5. The treatment of the blood was peculiar in the Sin-offerings. In the inferior
Sin-offerings it was smeared on the horns of
the Altar of Burnt-offering (*vv.* 25, 30, 34),
while in this offering for the High-priest,
and in that for the nation, the High-priest
himself sprinkled the blood seven times
within the Tabernacle and smeared it on
the horns of the Altar of Incense (*vv.* 6, 7,
17, 18). The different modes of sprinkling
appear to have marked successive degrees
of consecration in advancing from the Altar
of Burnt-offering to the Presence of Jehovah within the vail.

6. *before the vail of the sanctuary*] This is
generally understood to mean the floor of
the Holy Place in front of the vail.

7. *pour*] All the blood that was left after
the sprinkling and the smearing should be
disposed of in such a manner as to suit the
decorum of divine service. It had no sacrificial significance.

12. *a clean place where the ashes are poured
out*] See i. 16 note. It was a place free from im-
purities, not like those referred to in xiv. 40, 45.
The flesh, though it was burned in an ordi-

nary way, and not sent up in the fire of the
Altar (see i. 9 note), was not to be confounded
with carrion, but was associated with the
remains of the sacrifices.—The priests could
not eat the flesh of this victim or of that
offered for the sin of the congregation, as
they ate that of other Sin-offerings (vi. 26.
Cp. x. 17, 18), because they were in these
cases in the position of offerers. (xvi. 27;
Heb. xiii. 11.) The same rule was observed
in regard to the Meat-offering of the priests,
vi. 23. It was only of the Peace-offering
that the offerer himself could partake.

13. *congregation...assembly*] Each of the
Hebrew words signifies the people in a collected body. It does not appear that there
is any difference between them in the connexion in which they are here used.

14. *when the sin...is known*] Cp. 1 S. xiv.
31–35.

15. In this case the imposition of hands
is performed by the elders in behalf of the
nation. But in other respects the rites were
performed by the High-priest in the same
manner as in the Sin-offering for himself.

of the bullock before the LORD : and the bullock shall be killed
16 before the LORD. ^pAnd the priest that is anointed shall bring
17 of the bullock's blood to the tabernacle of the congregation : and
the priest shall dip his finger *in some* of the blood, and sprinkle
18 *it* seven times before the LORD, *even* before the vail. And he
shall put *some* of the blood upon the horns of the altar which *is*
before the LORD, that *is* in the tabernacle of the congregation,
and shall pour out all the blood at the bottom of the altar of the
burnt offering, which *is at* the door of the tabernacle of the con-
19 gregation. And he shall take all his fat from him, and burn *it*
20 upon the altar. And he shall do with the bullock as he did ^qwith
the bullock for a sin offering, so shall he do with this : ^rand the
priest shall make an atonement for them, and it shall be forgiven
21 them. And he shall carry forth the bullock without the camp, and
burn him as he burned the first bullock : it *is* a sin offering for
22 the congregation. When a ruler hath sinned, and ^sdone *somewhat*
through ignorance *against* any of the commandments of the
LORD his God *concerning things* which should not be done, and
23 is guilty; or ^tif his sin, wherein he hath sinned, come to his
knowledge; he shall bring his offering, a kid of the goats, a
24 male without blemish: and ^uhe shall lay his hand upon the
head of the goat, and kill it in the place where they kill the
25 burnt offering before the LORD : it *is* a sin offering. ^xAnd the
priest shall take of the blood of the sin offering with his finger,
and put *it* upon the horns of the altar of burnt offering, and
shall pour out his blood at the bottom of the altar of burnt
26 offering. And he shall burn all his fat upon the altar, as ^ythe
fat of the sacrifice of peace offerings : ^zand the priest shall make
an atonement for him as concerning his sin, and it shall be for-
27 given him. ¶And ^aif ¹any one of the ²common people sin
through ignorance, while he doeth *somewhat against* any of the
commandments of the LORD *concerning things* which ought not
28 to be done, and be guilty; or ^bif his sin, which he hath sinned,
come to his knowledge : then he shall bring his offering, a kid
of the goats, a female without blemish, for his sin which he hath
29 sinned. ^cAnd he shall lay his hand upon the head of the sin
offering, and slay the sin offering in the place of the burnt
30 offering. And the priest shall take of the blood thereof with his
finger, and put *it* upon the horns of the altar of burnt offering,
and shall pour out all the blood thereof at the bottom of the
31 altar. And ^dhe shall take away all the fat thereof, ^eas the fat
is taken away from off the sacrifice of peace offerings; and the
priest shall burn *it* upon the altar for a ^fsweet savour unto the
LORD; ^gand the priest shall make an atonement for him, and it

p ver. 5.
Heb. 9. 12,
13, 14.

q ver. 3.
r Num. 15.
25.
Dan. 9. 24.
Rom. 5. 11.
Heb. 2. 17.
& 10. 10,
11, 12.
1 John 1. 7.
& 2. 2.
s ver. 2, 13.
t ver. 14.

u ver. 4, &c.

x ver. 30.

y ch. 3. 5.
z ver. 20.
Num. 15. 28.

a ver. 2.
Num. 15. 27.

b ver. 23.

c ver. 4, 24.

d ch. 3, 14.
e ch. 3. 3.
f Ex. 29. 18.
ch. 1. 9.
g ver. 26.

¹ Heb. *any soul.*   ² Heb. *people of the land.*

---

18. *the altar...in the tabernacle*] *i.e.* the
Altar of Incense (cp. *vv.* 5–7).

22. *ruler*] Either the head of a tribe
(Num. i. 4–16), or the head of a division of a
tribe (Num. xxxiv. 18; cp. Josh. xxii. 30).

23. *or if his sin*] Rather, **And if** his sin.
come to his knowledge] *i.e.* when he had become conscious of his sin.
a kid of the goats] **A shaggy he-goat**, in
distinction from a smooth-haired he-goat.
It was the regular Sin-offering at the yearly
Festivals (xvi. 9, 15; Num. xxviii. 15,

22, 30), and at the consecration of the
priests (ix. 3); while the smooth-haired
goat appears to have been generally offered
for the other sacrifices (Ps. l. 9; Isa. i. 11).

24. See i. 11.

27. *the common people*] Literally, as in the
margin, "the people of the land." Cp. xx.
2, 4; 2 K. xi. 18. It was the ordinary designation of the people, as distinguished from
the priests and the rulers.

28. *a kid of the goats*] **A shaggy she-
goat.**

32 shall be forgiven him. And if he bring a lamb for a sin offering,
33 ʰ he shall bring it a female without blemish. And he shall lay   ʰ ver. 28.
his hand upon the head of the sin offering, and slay it for a sin
34 offering in the place where they kill the burnt offering. And
the priest shall take of the blood of the sin offering with his
finger, and put *it* upon the horns of the altar of burnt offering,
and shall pour out all the blood thereof at the bottom of the
35 altar: and he shall take away all the fat thereof, as the fat of
the lamb is taken away from the sacrifice of the peace offerings ;
and the priest shall burn them upon the altar, ⁱ according to the   ⁱ ch. 3. 5.
offerings made by fire unto the LORD : ᵏ and the priest shall make   ᵏ ver. 26. 31.
an atonement for his sin that he hath committed, and it shall be
forgiven him.

CHAP. 5. AND if a soul sin, ᵃ and hear the voice of swearing, and   ᵃ 1 Kin. 8.
is a witness, whether he hath seen or known *of it :* if he do not   31.
2 utter *it*, then he shall ᵇ bear his iniquity. Or ᶜ if a soul touch   Matt. 26. 63.
any unclean thing, whether *it be* a carcase of an unclean beast,   ch. 7. 18.
or a carcase of unclean cattle, or the carcase of unclean creeping   & 17. 16.
things, and *if* it be hidden from him ; he also shall be unclean,   & 19. 8.
3 and ᵈ guilty. Or if he touch ᵉ the uncleanness of man, what-   Num. 9. 13.
soever uncleanness *it be* that a man shall be defiled withal, and   ᶜ ch. 11. 24,
it be hid from him ; when he knoweth *of it*, then he shall be   Num. 19.
4 guilty. Or if a soul swear, pronouncing with *his* lips ᶠ to do evil,   11, 13, 16.
or ᵍ to do good, whatsoever *it be* that a man shall pronounce   ᵈ ver. 17.
with an oath, and it be hid from him; when he knoweth *of it*,   & 13, & 15.
5 then he shall be guilty in one of these. And it shall be, when   ᶠ See 1 Sam.
he shall be guilty in one of these *things*, that he shall ʰ confess   Acts 23. 12.
6 that he hath sinned in that *thing :* and he shall bring his tres-   ᵍ See Mark
pass offering unto the LORD for his sin which he hath sinned, a   ʰ ch. 16. 21.
female from the flock, a lamb or a kid of the goats, for a sin   & 26. 40.
offering ; and the priest shall make an atonement for him con-   Num. 5. 7.
7 cerning his sin. ¶ And ⁱ if ¹ he be not able to bring a lamb, then   12.
   ⁱ ch. 12. 8.
   & 14. 21.

¹ Heb. *his hand cannot reach to the sufficiency of a lamb.*

---

32. *a lamb*] **A sheep.** See iii. 7 note. Three
points are to be observed in regard to the
victims for Sin-offerings.—(*a*) The common
people had to offer a female, as the less valuable animal ; they might present either a
sheep or a goat to suit their convenience :
(*b*) the rulers had always to offer a male-
goat : (*c*) the goat was preferred to the
sheep, unlike the victim for a Peace-offering or a Burnt-offering.

The Sin-offerings were not accompanied
by Meat-offerings or Drink-offerings. See
Num. xv. 3–11.

V. 1–13. Special occasions are mentioned
on which Sin-offerings are to be made with
a particular confession of the offence for
which atonement is sought (*v.* 5).

1. *swearing*] **Adjuration.** The case appears to be that of one who has been put
upon his oath as a witness by a magistrate,
and fails to utter all he has seen and heard
(cp. marg. reff. and Prov. xxix. 24 ; Num.
v. 21).

2, 3. *hid from him*] Either through forgetfulness or indifference, so that purification had been neglected. In such a case
there had been a guilty negligence, and a

Sin-offering was required. On the essential connection between impurity and the
Sin-offering, see xii. 1.

4. *pronouncing*] **Idly speaking** (Ps. cvi.
33). The reference is to an oath to do
something uttered in recklessness or passion
and forgotten as soon as uttered.

6. *his trespass offering*] Rather, **as his
forfeit**, that is, whatever is due for his
offence. The term "Trespass-offering" is out
of place here, since it has become the current designation for a distinct kind of Sin-
offering mentioned in the next section (see
v. 14 note).

a lamb or a kid of the goats] **A sheep** (iv.
32) **or a shaggy she-goat** (iv. 23).

7–10. See i. 14–16, xii. 8. In the larger
offerings of the ox and the sheep, the fat
which was burnt upon the Altar represented,
like the Burnt-offering, the dedication of
the worshipper ; in this case, the same
meaning was conveyed by one of the birds
being treated as a distinct Burnt-offering.

7. *a lamb*] **One of the flock**, either a sheep
or a goat.

for his trespass, which he hath committed]
As his forfeit for the sin he hath committed.

<table>
<tr><td>

k ch. 1. 14.

l ch. 1.´15.

m ch. 4. 7,
18, 30, 34.

n ch. 1. 14.
o ch. 4. 26.

p Num. 5. 15.

q ch. 2. 2.
r ch. 4. 35.

s ch. 4. 26.

t ch. 2. 3.
u ch. 22. 14.

x Ezra 10. 19.
y Ex. 30. 13.
ch. 27. 25.
z ch. 6. 5.
& 22. 14.
& 27. 13,
15, 27, 31.
Num. 5. 7.
a ch. 4. 26.
b ch. 4. 2.
c ver. 15.
ch. 4. 2, 13,
22, 27.
Ps. 19. 12.
Luke 12. 48.
d ver. 1, 2.
e ver. 15.

</td><td>

he shall bring for his trespass, which he hath committed, two *k*turtledoves, or two young pigeons, unto the LORD; one for a 8 sin offering, and the other for a burnt offering. And he shall bring them unto the priest, who shall offer *that* which *is* for the sin offering first, and *l*wring off his head from his neck, but 9 shall not divide *it* asunder: and he shall sprinkle of the blood of the sin offering upon the side of the altar; and *m*the rest of the blood shall be wrung out at the bottom of the altar: it *is* a 10 sin offering. And he shall offer the second *for* a burnt offering, according to the ¹*n*manner: *o*and the priest shall make an atonement for him his sin which he hath sinned, and it shall be 11 forgiven him. ¶ But if he be not able to bring two turtledoves, or two young pigeons, then he that sinned shall bring for his offering the tenth part of an ephah of fine flour for a sin offer-12 ing; *p*he shall put no oil upon it, neither shall he put any frankincense thereon: for it *is* a sin offering. Then shall he bring it to the priest, and the priest shall take his handful of it, *q*even a memorial thereof, and burn *it* on the altar, *r*according to the offerings made by fire unto the LORD: it *is* a sin offering. 13 *s*And the priest shall make an atonement for him as touching his sin that he hath sinned in one of these, and it shall be forgiven him: and *t*the remnant shall be the priest's, as a meat offering. 14, 15 ¶ And the LORD spake unto Moses, saying, *u*If a soul commit a trespass, and sin through ignorance, in the holy things of the LORD; then *x*he shall bring for his trespass unto the LORD a ram without blemish out of the flocks, with thy estimation by shekels of silver, after *y*the shekel of the sanctuary, for a tres-16 pass offering: and he shall make amends for the harm that he hath done in the holy thing, and *z*shall add the fifth part thereto, and give it unto the priest: *a*and the priest shall make an atonement for him with the ram of the trespass offering, and it shall 17 be forgiven him. ¶ And if a *b*soul sin, and commit any of these things which are forbidden to be done by the commandments of the LORD; *c*though he wist *it* not, yet *is* he *d*guilty, and shall 18 bear his iniquity. *e*And he shall bring a ram without blemish

</td></tr>
</table>

¹ Or, *ordinance.*

---

11. *tenth part of an ephah*] *i.e.* "the tenth deal;" probably less than half a gallon. See xix. 36 note. This Sin-offering of meal was distinguished from the ordinary Minchah (ii. 1) by the absence of oil and frankincense.

14.–vi. 7. The Trespass-offerings as they are described in this section and in vii. 1–7, are clearly distinguished from the ordinary Sin-offerings in these particulars:—

(1) They were offered on account of offences which involved an injury to some person (it might be the LORD Himself) in respect to property. See *v.* 16, vi. 4, 5.

(2) They were always accompanied by a pecuniary fine equal to the value of the injury done, with the addition of one-fifth. Cp. Num. v. 5–8.

(3) The treatment of the blood was more simple. Cp. iv. 5.

(4) The victim was a ram, instead of a female sheep or goat.

(5) There was no such graduation of offerings to suit the rank or circumstances of the worshipper as is set forth in iv. 3, 32, &c.

15. *commit a trespass*] Rather, here and in vi. 2, **perpetrate a wrong.** The word is different from that rendered trespass elsewhere in these chapters.

throughignorance]**Through inadvertence.** See iv. 2 note.

in the holy things of the LORD] The reference is to a failure in the payment of firstfruits, tithes or fees of any kind connected with the public service of religion by which the Sanctuary suffered loss; cf. Num. v. 6–8.

shekel of the sanctuary] See Exod. xxxviii. 24 note.

17. *though he wist it not*] Ignorance of the Law, or even of the consequences of the act at the time it was committed, was not to excuse him from the obligation to offer the sacrifice.

out of the flock, with thy estimation, for a trespass offering, unto the priest: ⁱand the priest shall make an atonement for him concerning his ignorance wherein he erred and wist *it* not, 19 and it shall be forgiven him. It *is* a trespass offering: ᵍhe hath certainly trespassed against the LORD.

CHAP. 6. AND the LORD spake unto Moses, saying, If a soul 2 sin, and ᵃcommit a trespass against the LORD, and ᵇlie unto his neighbour in that ᶜwhich was delivered him to keep, or in ¹²fellowship, or in a thing taken away by violence, or hath ᵈde- 3 ceived his neighbour; or ᵉhave found that which was lost, and lieth concerning it, and ⁱsweareth falsely; in any of all these 4 that a man doeth, sinning therein: then it shall be, because he hath sinned, and is guilty, that he shall restore that which he took violently away, or the thing which he hath deceitfully gotten, or that which was delivered him to keep, or the lost 5 thing which he found, or all that about which he hath sworn falsely; he shall even ᵍrestore it in the principal, and shall add the fifth part more thereto, *and* give it unto him to whom it 6 appertaineth, ³⁴in the day of his trespass offering. And he shall bring his trespass offering unto the LORD, ʰa ram without blemish out of the flock, with thy estimation, for a trespass 7 offering, unto the priest: ⁱand the priest shall make an atone- ment for him before the LORD: and it shall be forgiven him for 8 anything of all that he hath done in trespassing therein. ¶And 9 the LORD spake unto Moses, saying, Command Aaron and his sons, saying, This *is* the law of the burnt offering: It *is* the burnt offering, ⁵because of the burning upon the altar all night unto the morning, and the fire of the altar shall be burning in it. 10 ᵏAnd the priest shall put on his linen garment, and his linen breeches shall he put upon his flesh, and take up the ashes which the fire hath consumed with the burnt offering on the 11 altar, and he shall put them ⁱbeside the altar. And ᵐhe shall put off his garments, and put on other garments, and carry forth 12 the ashes without the camp ⁿunto a clean place. And the fire upon the altar shall be burning in it; it shall not be put out: and the priest shall burn wood on it every morning, and lay the burnt offering in order upon it; and he shall burn thereon ᵒthe 13 fat of the peace offerings. The fire shall ever be burning upon 14 the altar; it shall never go out. ¶ᵖAnd this *is* the law of the meat offering: the sons of Aaron shall offer it before the LORD, 15 before the altar. And he shall take of it his handful, of the flour of the meat offering, and of the oil thereof, and all the frankincense which *is* upon the meat offering, and shall burn *it* upon the altar *for* a sweet savour, *even* the ᵍmemorial of it, unto

ⁱ ver. 16.

ᵍ Ezra 10. 2.

ᵃ Num. 5. 6.
ᵇ ch. 19. 11.
Acts 5. 4.
Col. 3. 9.
ᶜ Ex. 22. 7,
10.
ᵈ Prov. 24.
28.
& 26. 19.
ᵉ Deut. 22.
1, 2, 3.
ⁱ Ex. 22. 11.
ch. 19. 12.
Jer. 7. 9.
Zech. 5. 4.
ᵍ ch. 5. 16.
Num. 5. 7.
2 Sam. 12. 6.
Luke 19. 8.
ʰ ch. 5. 15.

ⁱ ch. 4. 26.

ᵏ Ex. 28. 39,
40, 41, 43.
ch. 16. 4.
Ezek. 44.
17, 18.
ⁱ ch. 1. 16.
ᵐ Ezek. 44.
19.
ⁿ ch. 4. 12.

ᵒ ch. 3. 3, 9,
14.

ᵖ ch. 2. 1.
Num. 15. 4.

ᵍ ch. 2. 2, 9.

---

¹ Or, *in dealing.*
² Heb. *putting of the hand.*
³ Or, *in the day of his being found guilty.*
⁴ Heb. *in the day of his trespass.*
⁵ Or, *for the burning.*

VI. 1. In the Hebrew Bible *vv.* 1-7 form part of Ch. v. It is evident that they ought to do so.

5. *in the day of his trespass offering*] The restitution was thus to be associated with the religious act by which the offender tes- tified his penitence.

9. Rather, "**This, the Burnt-offering, shall be upon the fire on the Altar** all night unto the morning." See Ex. xxix.

38-46, with the notes.

10. *Ashes...with the burnt-offering*] Rather, the ashes to which the fire hath consumed the Burnt-offering.

13. *The fire shall ever be burning*] This was a symbol of the never-ceasing worship which Jehovah required of His people. It was essentially connected with their acts of sacrifice.

14-18. See ii. 1-10; Ex. xxix. 40, 41.

r ch. 2. 3.
Ezek. 44. 29.
s ver. 26.
ch. 10. 12, 13.
Num. 18. 10.
t ch. 2. 11.
u Num. 18.
9, 10.
x Ex. 29. 37.
ver. 25.
ch. 2. 3.
& 7. 1.
y ver. 29.
Num. 18. 10.
z ch. 3. 17.
a Ex. 29. 37.
ch. 22. 3, 4,
5, 6, 7.
b Ex. 29. 2.
c Ex. 16. 36.
d ch. 4. 3.
e Ex. 29. 25.
f ch. 4. 2.
g ch. 1. 3, 5,
11. & 4. 24,
29, 33.
h ver. 17.
ch. 21. 22.
i ch. 10. 17,
18.
Num. 18.
9, 10.
Ezek. 44.
28, 29.
k ver. 16.
l Ex. 29. 37.
& 30. 29.
m ch. 11. 33.
& 15, 12.
n ver. 18.
Num. 18. 10.
o ver. 25.
p ch. 4. 7,
11, 12, 18, 21.
& 10. 18.
& 16. 27.
Heb. 13. 11.
a ch. 5, & 6.
1—7.
b ch. 6. 17,
25.
& 21. 22.
c ch. 1. 11.

16 the LORD. And *r*the remainder thereof shall Aaron and his sons eat: *s*with unleavened bread shall it be eaten in the holy place; in the court of the tabernacle of the congregation they 17 shall eat it. *t*It shall not be baken with leaven. *u*I have given it *unto them for* their portion of my offerings made by fire; *x*it *is* most holy, as *is* the sin offering, and as the trespass offering. 18 *y*All the males among the children of Aaron shall eat of it. *z*It *shall be* a statute for ever in your generations concerning the offerings of the LORD made by fire: *a*every one that toucheth 19 them shall be holy. ¶And the LORD spake unto Moses, saying, 20 *b*This *is* the offering of Aaron and of his sons, which they shall offer unto the LORD in the day when he is anointed; the tenth part of an *c*ephah of fine flour for a meat offering perpetual, 21 half of it in the morning, and half thereof at night. In a pan it shall be made with oil; *and when it is* baken, thou shalt bring it in: *and* the baken pieces of the meat offering shalt thou offer 22 *for* a sweet savour unto the LORD. And the priest of his sons *d*that is anointed in his stead shall offer it: *it is* a statute for 23 ever unto the LORD; *e*it shall be wholly burnt. For every meat offering for the priest shall be wholly burnt: it shall not be 24, 25 eaten. ¶And the LORD spake unto Moses, saying, Speak unto Aaron and to his sons, saying, *f*This *is* the law of the sin offering: *g*In the place where the burnt offering is killed shall the 26 sin offering be killed before the LORD: *h*it *is* most holy. *i*The priest that offereth it for sin shall eat it: *k*in the holy place shall it be eaten, in the court of the tabernacle of the congregation. 27 *l*Whatsoever shall touch the flesh thereof shall be holy: and when there is sprinkled of the blood thereof upon any garment, thou shalt wash that whereon it was sprinkled in the holy place. 28 But the earthen vessel wherein it is sodden *m*shall be broken: and if it be sodden in a brazen pot, it shall be both scoured, and 29 rinsed in water. *n*All the males among the priests shall eat 30 thereof: *o*it *is* most holy. *p*And no sin offering, whereof *any* of the blood is brought into the tabernacle of the congregation to reconcile *withal* in the holy *place*, shall be eaten: it shall be burnt in the fire.

CHAP. 7. LIKEWISE *a*this *is* the law of the trespass offering: *b*it *is* 2 most holy. *c*In the place where they kill the burnt offering shall

---

16. *with unleavened bread shall it be eaten*] This should be, **it** (the remainder) **shall be eaten unleavened.**

20. See iv. 3. Aaron's sons here spoken of (as in *v.* 22) must be the succession of High-priests who succeeded him. The day of this offering was probably the eighth day of the ceremony of consecration (viii. 35, ix. 1), when the High-priest appears to have entered upon the duties of his office.

a meat offering perpetual] Jewish tradition is in favour of these words implying that this Minchah was offered by the High-priest as a daily rite from the time of his consecration.

21. *In a pan*] See ii. 5 note.

22. *it shall be wholly burnt*] Literally, *it shall ascend in fire as a whole Burnt-offering.*

23. *not be eaten*] Cp. *v.* 30, iv. 12 note.

25. *the place where, &c.*] See i. 11.

it is most holy] See ii. 3. The key to the peculiar sanctity of the flesh of the Sin-offering, as set forth in *vv.* 26—30, must, it would seem, be found in the words of Moses to the priests (x. 17). The flesh of the victim, which represented the sinner for whom atonement was now made, was to be solemnly, and most exclusively, appropriated by those who were appointed to mediate between the sinner and the Lord. The far-reaching symbolism of the act met its perfect fulfilment in the One Mediator Who took our nature upon Himself. (Phil. ii. 7).

28. *the earthen vessel*] Unglazed pottery would absorb some of the juices of the meat: and a vessel made holy could not be put to any other purpose.

30. *to reconcile withal*] generally rendered "to make atonement for."

the holy place] The outer apartment of the Tabernacle. See x. 18 note.

they kill the trespass offering: and the blood thereof shall he
3 sprinkle round about upon the altar. And he shall offer of it ^dall d Ex. 29. 13.
the fat thereof; the rump, and the fat that covereth the inwards, ch. 3. 4, 9,
10, 14, 15, 16.
4 and the two kidneys, and the fat that is on them, which is by & 4. 8, 9.
the flanks, and the caul that is above the liver, with the kidneys,
5 it shall he take away: and the priest shall burn them upon the
altar for an offering made by fire unto the LORD: it is a trespass
6 offering. ^eEvery male among the priests shall eat thereof: it e ch. 6. 16,
7 shall be eaten in the holy place: ^fit is most holy. As the 17, 18.
Num. 18.
sin offering is, so is ^gthe trespass offering: there is one law for 9, 10.
them: the priest that maketh atonement therewith shall have f ch. 2. 3.
g ch. 6. 25,
8 it. And the priest that offereth any man's burnt offering, even 26.
the priest shall have to himself the skin of the burnt offering & 14. 13.
9 which he hath offered. And ^hall the meat offering that is baken h ch. 2. 3, 10.
in the oven, and all that is dressed in the fryingpan, and ¹in the Num. 18. 9.
Ezek. 44, 29.
10 pan, shall be the priest's that offereth it. And every meat offer-
ing, mingled with oil, and dry, shall all the sons of Aaron have,
11 one as much as another. ¶And ⁱthis is the law of the sacrifice of i ch. 3. 1.
12 peace offerings, which he shall offer unto the LORD. If he offer & 22. 18, 21.
it for a thanksgiving, then he shall offer with the sacrifice of
thanksgiving unleavened cakes mingled with oil, and unleavened
wafers ^kanointed with oil, and cakes mingled with oil, of fine k ch. 2. 4.
Num. 6. 15.
13 flour, fried. Besides the cakes, he shall offer for his offering
^lleavened bread with the sacrifice of thanksgiving of his peace l Amos 4. 5.
14 offerings. And of it he shall offer one out of the whole oblation
for an heave offering unto the LORD, ^mand it shall be the priest's m Num. 18.
8, 11, 19.
15 that sprinkleth the blood of the peace offerings. ⁿAnd the flesh n ch. 22, 30.
of the sacrifice of his peace offerings for thanksgiving shall
be eaten the same day that it is offered; he shall not leave any
16 of it until the morning. But ^oif the sacrifice of his offering be a o ch. 19. 6,
vow, or a voluntary offering, it shall be eaten the same day that 7, 8.
he offereth his sacrifice: and on the morrow also the remainder
17 of it shall be eaten: but the remainder of the flesh of the sacri-
18 fice on the third day shall be burnt with fire. And if any of the
flesh of the sacrifice of his peace offerings be eaten at all on the

¹ Or, on the flat plate, or, slice.

VII. 1-7. See v. 14 note. In v. 2 "sprinkle"
should rather be cast (i. 5). All the details
regarding the parts put on the Altar are
repeated for each kind of sacrifice, because
the matter was one of paramount importance.

8. the skin of the burnt offering] It is most
likely that the skins of the Sin-offering and
the Trespass-offering also fell to the lot of
the officiating priest.

9, 10. See marg. reff.

11, &c. See iii. 1-17. What is here added,
relates to the accompanying Minchah (ii. 1),
the classification of Peace-offerings into (1)
Thank-offerings, (2) Peace-offerings and (3)
Voluntary-offerings, and the conditions to
be observed by the worshipper in eating the
flesh.

12. for a thanksgiving] i.e., a Thank-offering for mercies received.

13. for his offering] The leavened bread
was a distinct offering.

14. out of the whole oblation] Rather, out

of each offering. That is, one loaf or cake
out of each kind of Meat-offering was to be
a heave-offering (v. 32) for the officiating
priest. According to Jewish tradition,
there were to be ten cakes of each kind of
bread in every Thank-offering. The other
cakes were returned to the sacrificer.

16. The Vow-offering appears to have
been a Peace-offering vowed upon a certain condition; the Voluntary-offering, one
offered as the simple tribute of a devout
heart rejoicing in peace with God and man
offered on no external occasion (cp. xxii. 17-
25).

18, 19. It was proper that the sacrificial
meat should not be polluted by any approach to putrefaction. But the exclusion
of a mean-spirited economy may further
have furnished the ground for the distinction between the Thank-offerings and the
others. The most liberal distribution of
the meat of the offering, particularly
amongst the poor who were invited to par-

third day, it shall not be accepted, neither shall it be p imputed unto him that offereth it : it shall be an q abomination, and the 19 soul that eateth of it shall bear his iniquity. And the flesh that toucheth any unclean *thing* shall not be eaten ; it shall be burnt with fire : and as for the flesh, all that be clean shall eat thereof. 20 But the soul that eateth *of* the flesh of the sacrifice of peace offerings, that *pertain* unto the LORD, r having his uncleanness upon him, even that soul s shall be cut off from his people. 21 Moreover the soul that shall touch any unclean *thing, as* t the uncleanness of man, or *any* u unclean beast, or any w abominable unclean *thing,* and eat of the flesh of the sacrifice of peace offerings, which *pertain* unto the LORD, even that soul x shall be cut 22 off from his people. ¶ And the LORD spake unto Moses, saying, 23 Speak unto the children of Israel, saying, y Ye shall eat no 24 manner of fat, of ox, or of sheep, or of goat. And the fat of the 1 beast that dieth of itself, and the fat of that which is torn with beasts, may be used in any other use : but ye shall in no wise eat 25 of it. For whosoever eateth the fat of the beast, of which men offer an offering made by fire unto the LORD, even the soul that 26 eateth *it* shall be cut off from his people. z Moreover ye shall eat no manner of blood, *whether it be* of fowl or of beast, in any of 27 your dwellings. Whatsoever soul *it be* that eateth any manner 28 of blood, even that soul shall be cut off from his people. ¶ And 29 the LORD spake unto Moses, saying, Speak unto the children of Israel, saying, a He that offereth the sacrifice of his peace offerings unto the LORD shall bring his oblation unto the LORD of 30 the sacrifice of his peace offerings. b His own hands shall bring the offerings of the LORD made by fire, the fat with the breast, it shall he bring, that c the breast may be waved *for* a wave 31 offering before the LORD. d And the priest shall burn the fat upon the altar : e but the breast shall be Aaron's and his sons'. 32 And f the right shoulder shall ye give unto the priest *for* an 33 heave offering of the sacrifices of your peace offerings. He among the sons of Aaron, that offereth the blood of the peace offerings, and the fat, shall have the right shoulder for *his* part. 34 For g the wave breast and the heave shoulder have I taken of the children of Israel from off the sacrifices of their peace offerings, and have given them unto Aaron the priest and unto his sons 35 by a statute for ever from among the children of Israel. This *is the portion* of the anointing of Aaron, and of the anointing of his sons, out of the offerings of the LORD made by fire, in the day *when* he presented them to minister unto the LORD in the priest's 36 office ; which the LORD commanded to be given them of the children of Israel, h in the day that he anointed them, *by* a

1 Heb. *carcase,* ch. 17. 15. Deut. 14. 21. Ezek. 4. 14. & 44. 31.

take, would plainly be becoming when the sacrifice was intended especially to express gratitude for mercies received.

21. *unclean beast*] That is, carrion of any kind. See ch. xi.

shall be cut off] See Ex. xxxi. 14 note.

23. This is emphatically addressed to the people. They were not to eat in their own meal what belonged to the Altar of Jehovah, nor what was the perquisite of the priests. See *vv.* 33–36.

24. Cp. xi. 39.

26. *no manner of blood*] See xvii. 10-15.

30–32. *wave-offering...heave-offering*] The latter appears to be used (like *korban,* i. 2) for offerings in general. *Waving* (a moving to and fro, repeated several times) or *heaving* (a lifting up once) the offering was a solemn form of dedicating a thing to the use of the Sanctuary.

35. *the portion of the anointing,* &c.] Rather, **the appointed share of Aaron and of his sons.**

37 statute for ever throughout their generations. ¶ This *is* the law
*i*of the burnt offering, *k*of the meat offering, *l*and of the sin
offering, *m*and of the trespass offering, *n*and of the consecrations,
38 and *o*of the sacrifice of the peace offerings; which the LORD
commanded Moses in mount Sinai, in the day that he commanded
the children of Israel *p*to offer their oblations unto the LORD, in
the wilderness of Sinai.

i ch. 6. 9.
k ch. 6. 14.
l ch. 6. 25.
m ver. 1.
n Ex. 29. 1.
ch. 6. 20.
o ver. 11.
p ch. 1. 2.

CHAP. 8. AND the LORD spake unto Moses, saying, *a*Take Aaron
2 and his sons with him, and *b*the garments, and *c*the anointing
oil, and a bullock for the sin offering, and two rams, and a
3 basket of unleavened bread; and gather thou all the congregation together unto the door of the tabernacle of the congregation.
4 And Moses did as the LORD commanded him; and the assembly
was gathered together unto the door of the tabernacle of the
5 congregation. ¶ And Moses said unto the congregation, *d*This *is*
6 the thing which the LORD commanded to be done. And Moses
brought Aaron and his sons, *e*and washed them with water.
7 *f*And he put upon him the *g*coat, and girded him with the girdle,
and clothed him with the robe, and put the ephod upon him, and
8 he girded him with the curious girdle of the ephod, and bound *it*
unto him therewith. And he put the breastplate upon him:
also he *h*put in the breastplate the Urim and the Thummim.
9 *i*And he put the mitre upon his head; also upon the mitre, *even*
upon his forefront, did he put the golden plate, the holy crown;
10 as the LORD *k*commanded Moses. ¶ *l*And Moses took the
anointing oil, and anointed the tabernacle and all that *was*

a Ex. 29. 1,
2, 3.
b Ex. 28. 2, 4.
c Ex. 30. 24,
25.

d Ex. 29. 4.

e Ex. 29. 4.
f Ex. 29. 5.
g Ex. 28. 4.

h Ex. 28. 30.
i Ex. 29. 6.

k Ex. 28. 37,
&c.
l Ex. 30. 26,
27, 28, 29.

---

37. *of the consecrations*] That is, of the
sacrifices which were to be offered in the
Consecration of the priests. See marg. reff.
38. *wilderness of Sinai*] Cp. Ex. xix. 1.
Chs. viii. ix. x. THE SERVICE OF THE
SANCTUARY INAUGURATED. This is the only
historical portion of the Book of Leviticus,
with the exception of xxiv. 10-23.
VIII. 2. *A bullock—two rams—a basket*]
cp. Ex. xxix. 1-3. This shews the coherence
of this part of Leviticus with the latter
part of Exodus. The basket of unleavened
bread used on this occasion appears to
have contained (1) cakes or loaves of the
ordinary unleavened bread; (2) cakes of
oiled bread, rather, **oil bread** (see ii. 1, 4);
and (3) oiled wafers (see ii. 4, 6). Rabbinical
tradition says that there were six cakes of
each sort.
3. *gather*, &c.] Rather, **gather all the
assembly together towards the entrance of
the Tent of meeting.** See iv. 13. The whole
body of the people were summoned on this
occasion, and the elders probably occupied the
first places. The elders are specially called
together in an unequivocal manner to receive
directions to provide the first sacrifices for
the nation to be offered by the newly consecrated priests (ix. 1), and the body of the
people afterwards assemble as they do here
(ix. 5).—The spot designated was the portion of the Court in front of the Tabernacle
(see i. 3 note). Towards this space the people
were commanded to assemble to witness the

great national ceremony of the Consecration
of the priesthood, the solemn setting apart
of one of their families, the members of
which were henceforth to stand as mediators between them and Jehovah in carrying
out the precepts of the ceremonial law.
Those who could do so, may have come into
the Court, and a great number of others
may have occupied the heights which overlooked the enclosure of the Court. As the
series of ceremonies was repeated every day
during a week (v. 33), it is natural to suppose that some of the people attended on
one day and some on another.
6. *washed them with water*] Moses caused
them to bathe entirely (cp. xvi. 4), not
merely to wash their hands and feet, as
they were to do in their daily ministrations.
See marg. ref. This bathing, which the
High-priest had also to go through on the
Day of Atonement, was symbolical of the
spiritual cleansing required of all (2 Cor.
vii. 1), but especially of those who had to
draw near to God to make reconciliation
for the sins of the people (Heb. vii. 26;
Matt. iii. 15).
7-9. See notes on Exod. xxviii.
9. *the holy crown*] The golden plate of
the mitre was so called as the distinctive
badge of the High-priest's consecration.
See xxi. 12.
10. Moses first anointed with the holy
oil (Ex. xxx. 25) the Tabernacle and all
therein, that is, the Ark of the Covenant,

m Ex. 29. 7.
& 30. 30.
ch. 21. 10, 12.
Ps. 133. 2.
n Ex. 29. 8, 9.
o Ex. 29. 10.
Ezek. 43. 19.
p ch. 4. 4.
q Ex. 29. 12,
36.
ch. 4. 7.
Ezek. 43. 20,
26.
Heb. 9. 22.
r Ex. 29. 13.
ch. 4. 8.
s Ex. 29. 14.
ch. 4. 11, 12.

11 therein, and sanctified them. And he sprinkled thereof upon the altar seven times, and anointed the altar and all his vessels, both 12 the laver and his foot, to sanctify them. And he *m*poured of the anointing oil upon Aaron's head, and anointed him, to sanctify 13 him. *n*And Moses brought Aaron's sons, and put coats upon them, and girded them with girdles, and ¹put bonnets upon 14 them; as the LORD commanded Moses. ¶ *o*And he brought the bullock for the sin offering: and Aaron and his sons *p*laid their 15 hands upon the head of the bullock for the sin offering. And he slew it; *q*and Moses took the blood, and put it upon the horns of the altar round about with his finger, and purified the altar, and poured the blood at the bottom of the altar, and sanctified 16 it, to make reconciliation upon it. *r*And he took all the fat that was upon the inwards, and the caul above the liver, and the two 17 kidneys, and their fat, and Moses burnt it upon the altar. But the bullock, and his hide, his flesh, and his dung, he burnt with fire without the camp; as the LORD *s*commanded Moses.

¹ Heb. bound.

the Table of Shewbread, the Candlestick and the Golden Altar, with all the articles that belonged to them.

11. *sprinkled...the altar seven times*] The Altar of Burnt-offering was distinguished by this sevenfold sprinkling with the holy oil. The number of the Covenant was thus brought into connection with those acts of sacrifice by which the Covenant between Jehovah and the worshipper was formally renewed and confirmed.

12. As investing the priest with official garments was a recognition before men of the official position of the person (see Ex. xxviii. 3 note), so the anointing him with oil was an acknowledgment that all fitness for his office, all the powers with which he would rightly fulfil its duties, must come from the Lord.

So, again, with the sanctification of the Holy things. Each of them was intended by divine wisdom to convey a spiritual meaning to the mind of man. They were means of grace to the devout worshipper. The oil poured upon them was a recognition of this fact, and at the same time it made them holy and set them apart from all profane and ordinary uses. On kindred grounds, though to express another idea, the Altar was to be sanctified also by blood. See v. 15 note.

13. *Aaron's sons*] The common priests. Nothing is said here, or in Ex. xxix. 7-9, of the anointing of the common priests, though it is expressly commanded in Ex. xxviii. 41, xl. 15, and is evidently implied as a fact in vii. 36, x. 7, Num. iii. 3. It would seem that the anointing of the common priests consisted in some rite common to them and the High-priest (Ex. xl. 15), and this was the sprinkling mentioned in v. 30. Cp. further x. 7 with xxi. 12.

14-36. Moses as the mediator of the Covenant of the Law (Gal. iii. 19, Heb. viii. 6) was called to perform the priestly functions, in consecrating those on whom henceforth those functions were to devolve, and in inaugurating the legal order of sacrifices. See Ex. xl. 23 note. The Sin-offering was now offered for the first time. The succession in which the sacrifices followed each other on this occasion, first the Sin-offering, then the Burnt-offering, and lastly the Peace-offering, has its ground in the meaning of each sacrifice, and became the established custom in later ages. The worshipper passed through a spiritual process. He had transgressed the Law, and he needed the atonement signified by the Sin-offering: if his offering had been made in truth and sincerity, he could then offer himself as an accepted person, as a sweet savour, in the Burnt-offering; and in consequence, he could enjoy communion with the Lord and with his brethren in the Peace-offering.

14-17. See marg. reff. The flesh of the Sin-offering could not be eaten by any but a legally consecrated priest (vi. 25 note). Moses therefore could not eat of it himself, though he was, for the occasion, performing the duties of a priest. Those whom he was consecrating could not eat it, not only because they were not yet duly installed, but because the sacrifice was offered on their behalf, and the body of the victim stood to them in the same relation as that of the regular Sin-offering afterwards stood to the High-priest.

15. *purified the altar...sanctified it, to make reconciliation upon it*] The Altar had been sanctified by the anointing oil (v. 11) like the priests who were to officiate at it; it was now, like them, sanctified by blood, in acknowledgment of the alienation of all nature, in itself, from God, and the need of a reconciliation to Him of all things by blood. Col. i. 20; Heb. ix. 21, 22. See xvii. 11; Ex. xxviii. 38.

18 ¶ᵗAnd he brought the ram for the burnt offering: and Aaron   ᵗ Ex. 29. 15.
19 and his sons laid their hands upon the head of the ram. And
he killed *it;* and Moses sprinkled the blood upon the altar
20 round about. And he cut the ram into pieces; and Moses burnt
21 the head, and the pieces, and the fat. And he washed the inwards and the legs in water; and Moses burnt the whole ram
upon the altar: it *was* a burnt sacrifice for a sweet savour, *and*
an offering made by fire unto the LORD; ᵘas the LORD com-   ᵘ Ex. 29. 18.
22 manded Moses. ¶And ᵂhe brought the other ram, the ram of   ᵂ Ex. 29. 19,
consecration: and Aaron and his sons laid their hands upon the   31.
23 head of the ram. And he slew *it;* and Moses took of the blood
of it, and put *it* upon the tip of Aaron's right ear, and upon the
thumb of his right hand, and upon the great toe of his right foot.
24 And he brought Aaron's sons, and Moses put of the blood upon
the tip of their right ear, and upon the thumbs of their right
hands, and upon the great toes of their right feet: and Moses
25 sprinkled the blood upon the altar round about. ˣAnd he took   ˣ Ex. 29. 22.
the fat, and the rump, and all the fat that *was* upon the inwards,
and the caul *above* the liver, and the two kidneys, and their fat,
26 and the right shoulder: ʸand out of the basket of unleavened   ʸ Ex. 29. 23.
bread, that *was* before the LORD, he took one unleavened cake,
and a cake of oiled bread, and one wafer, and put *them* on
27 the fat, and upon the right shoulder: and he put all ᶻupon   ᶻ Ex. 29. 24,
Aaron's hands, and upon his sons' hands, and waved them *for* a   &c.
28 wave offering before the LORD. ᵃAnd Moses took them from   ᵃ Ex. 29. 25.
off their hands, and burnt *them* on the altar upon the burnt
offering: they *were* consecrations for a sweet savour: it *is* an
29 offering made by fire unto the LORD. And Moses took the breast,
and waved it *for* a wave offering before the LORD: *for* of the
ram of consecration it was Moses' ᵇpart; as the LORD commanded   ᵇ Ex. 29. 26.

18–21. Atonement having been made,
Aaron and his sons were now permitted, by
the laying on of their hands, to make themselves one with the victim, which was to be
sent up to Jehovah as "a burnt sacrifice for
a sweet savour, an offering made by fire
unto the Lord." All was done strictly according to the ritual (i. 3–9), except that
Moses performed the duties of the priest.

22. *the ram of consecration*] The sacrifice
of this ram was by far the most peculiar
part of the whole ceremony. The words
may be literally rendered *the ram of the fillings,* and the name has been supposed to
have reference to the ceremony in which
Moses filled the hands of the priests; see
v. 27. The offering was in the highest sense
the sacrifice of completion or *fulfilling,* as
being the central point of the consecrating
rite. The final perfection of the creature is
Consecration to the LORD.

23, 24. Before **casting forth the blood
round the Altar** in the usual manner, Moses
took a portion of the blood and put some of
it on the right extremities of each of the
priests. This, being performed with the
blood of the Peace-offering, has been supposed to figure the readiness of the priest
who is at peace with Jehovah to hear with
the ear and obey the divine word, to perform
with the hand the sacred duties of his office,

and to walk with the feet in the way of
holiness.

25–28. In the rite of filling the hands of
the priests, Moses took the portions of the
victim which usually belonged to the Altar,
with the right shoulder (or leg); he placed
upon them one cake of each of the three
kinds of unleavened bread contained in the
basket (see *v.* 2 note), and then put the whole
first upon the hands of Aaron and in succession upon the hands of his sons: in each case,
according to Jewish tradition, he put his
own hands under the hands of the priest,
moving them backwards and forwards, so as
to wave the mass to and fro.

In this remarkable ceremony the gifts of
the people appear to have been made over
to the priests, as if in trust, for the service
of the Altar. The articles were presented
to Jehovah and solemnly waved in the
hands of the priests, but not by their own
act and deed. The mediator of the Law,
who was expressly commissioned on this
occasion, was the agent in the process.

25. *the rump*] See iii. 9 note.

29. The heave-shoulder was the ordinary
perquisite of the officiating priest, but the
wave-breast appears to have been awarded
to Moses as the servant of Jehovah now
especially appointed for the priestly service.

c Ex. 29. 21. & 30. 30. Num. 3. 3.	30 Moses. ¶ And *c*Moses took of the anointing oil, and of the blood which *was* upon the altar, and sprinkled *it* upon Aaron, *and* upon his garments, and upon his sons, and upon his sons' garments with him ; and sanctified Aaron, *and* his garments, and his sons, 31 and his sons' garments with him. ¶ And Moses said unto Aaron
d Ex. 29. 31. 32.	and to his sons, *d*Boil the flesh *at* the door of the tabernacle of the congregation : and there eat it with the bread that *is* in the basket of consecrations, as I commanded, saying, Aaron and his
e Ex. 29. 34.	32 sons shall eat it. *e*And that which remaineth of the flesh and of 33 the bread shall ye burn with fire. And ye shall not go out of the door of the tabernacle of the congregation *in* seven days,
f Ex. 29. 30, 35. Ezek. 43. 25, 26. *g* Heb. 7. 16. *h* Num. 3. 7. & 9. 19. Deut. 11. 1. 1 Kin. 2. 3.	until the days of your consecration be at an end : for *f* seven days 34 shall he consecrate you. *g*As he hath done this day, *so* the LORD hath commanded to do, to make an atonement for you. 35 Therefore shall ye abide *at* the door of the tabernacle of the congregation day and night seven days, and *h*keep the charge of the 36 LORD, that ye die not: for so I am commanded. So Aaron and his sons did all things which the LORD commanded by the hand of Moses.
a Ezek. 43. 27.	CHAP. 9. AND *a*it came to pass on the eighth day, *that* Moses called 2 Aaron and his sons, and the elders of Israel ; and he said unto
b Ex. 29. 1. ch. 4. 3. & 8. 14. *c* ch. 8. 18. *d* ch. 4. 23. Ezra 6. 17. & 10. 19.	Aaron, *b*Take thee a young calf for a sin offering, *c*and a ram for a burnt offering, without blemish, and offer *them* before the 3 LORD. And unto the children of Israel thou shalt speak, saying, *d*Take ye a kid of the goats for a sin offering ; and a calf and a lamb, *both* of the first year, without blemish, for a burnt offering ;
e ch. 2. 4. *f* ver. 6, 23. Ex. 29. 43.	4 also a bullock and a ram for peace offerings, to sacrifice before the LORD ; and *e*a meat offering mingled with oil : for *f* to day 5 the LORD will appear unto you. ¶ And they brought *that* which Moses commanded before the tabernacle of the congregation : and all the congregation drew near and stood before the LORD. 6 And Moses said, This *is* the thing which the LORD commanded
g ver. 23. Ex. 24. 16.	that ye should do : and *g*the glory of the LORD shall appear unto 7 you. ¶ And Moses said unto Aaron, Go unto the altar, and

---

30. The sprinkling was on their garments as well as their persons, because it belonged to them in reference to the office with which they had been formally invested by putting on the garments. (See Ex. xxviii. 3 note). The union of the two symbols of the atoning blood and the inspiring unction appears to be a fit conclusion of the entire rite.

33—36. The rites of Consecration were to last a whole week, and thus, like the longer of the annual festivals, were connected in an emphatic manner with the sabbatical number of the Covenant. During this period the priests were not to leave the Holy precinct for the sake of any worldly business ; and the whole series of ceremonies, including the sacrifice of the Ram of Consecration, was to be gone through on each day. Cp. marg. reff.

33. Rather, **ye shall not go away from the entrance of the Tent.** With this agree Cranmer, · the Geneva Bible, &c. The meaning is evidently that they were not to go out of the court, as is more clearly expressed in *v.* 35.

35. *that ye die not*] See Ex. xxviii. 35 note.

IX. **1-6.** *on the eighth day*] i.e., on the first day after the week of Consecration.

2. *a young calf*] **A bull calf,** which might have been what we should call a yearling ox.

3. *a kid of the goats*] **A shaggy he-goat.** See iv. 23 note.

6. *the glory of the* LORD] Cp. Ex. xvi. 7.

7. It is to be remarked that Aaron offers no Peace-offering for himself. It was enough that he should participate in the Peace-offerings of the Consecration (viii. 31), and in the two Peace-offerings about to be sacrificed for the people.

His Sin-offering was probably regarded not so much as a sacrifice for his own actual sins as a typical acknowledgment of his sinful nature and of his future duty to offer for his own sins and those of the people. See marg. reff. " The law maketh men High-priests which have infirmity ; but the word of the oath, which was since the law, maketh the Son, Who is consecrated (in the margin, *perfected*, see viii. 22 note) for evermore," Heb. vii. 28.

*h*offer thy sin offering, and thy burnt offering, and make an
atonement for thyself, and for the people: and *i*offer the offering
of the people, and make an atonement for them; as the LORD
8 commanded. Aaron therefore went unto the altar, and slew the
9 calf of the sin offering, which *was* for himself. *k*And the sons
of Aaron brought the blood unto him: and he dipped his finger
in the blood, and *l*put *it* upon the horns of the altar, and poured
10 out the blood at the bottom of the altar: *m*but the fat, and the
kidneys, and the caul above the liver of the sin offering, he
11 burnt upon the altar; *n*as the LORD commanded Moses. *o*And
the flesh and the hide he burnt with fire without the camp.
12 And he slew the burnt offering; and Aaron's sons presented
unto him the blood, *p*which he sprinkled round about upon the
13 altar. *q*And they presented the burnt offering unto him, with
the pieces thereof, and the head: and he burnt *them* upon the
14 altar. *r*And he did wash the inwards and the legs, and burnt
15 *them* upon the burnt offering on the altar. ¶ *s*And he brought
the people's offering, and took the goat, which *was* the sin offering for the people, and slew it, and offered it for sin, as the first.
16 And he brought the burnt offering, and offered it *t*according to
17 the [1]manner. And he brought *u*the meat offering, and [2]took an
handful thereof, and burnt *it* upon the altar, *x*beside the burnt
18 sacrifice of the morning. He slew also the bullock and the ram
for *y*a sacrifice of peace offerings, which *was* for the people: and
Aaron's sons presented unto him the blood, which he sprinkled
19 upon the altar round about, and the fat of the bullock and of
the ram, the rump, and that which covereth *the inwards*, and
20 the kidneys, and the caul *above* the liver: and they put the fat
21 upon the breasts, *z*and he burnt the fat upon the altar: and the
breasts and the right shoulder Aaron waved *a*for a wave offering
22 before the LORD; as Moses commanded. ¶ And Aaron lifted
up his hand toward the people, and *b*blessed them, and came
down from offering of the sin offering, and the burnt offering,
23 and peace offerings. And Moses and Aaron went into the

h ch. 4. 3.
1 Sam. 3. 14.
Heb. 5. 3.
& 7. 27.
& 9. 7.
i ch. 4. 16, 20.
Heb. 5. 1.
k ch. 8. 15.
l See ch. 4. 7.
m ch. 8. 16.
n ch. 4. 8.
o ch. 4. 11.
& 8. 17.

p ch. 1. 5.
& 8. 19.
q ch. 8. 20.
r ch. 8. 21.
s ver. 3.
Isai. 53. 10.
Heb. 2. 17.
& 5. 3.

t ch. 1. 3, 10.
u ver. 4.
ch. 2. 1, 2.
x Ex. 29. 38.

y ch. 3. 1,
&c.

z ch. 3. 5, 16.
a Ex. 29. 24.
ch. 7. 30.

b Num. 6. 23.
Deut. 21. 5.
Luke 24. 50.

[1] Or, *ordinance.*   [2] Heb. *filled his hand out of it.*

---

9. Aaron did not act according to the
ordinary Law (iv. 5, 6, 7, 16, 17, 18), but as
Moses had done in the Sin-offering of the
Consecration ceremony (viii. 15; cp. also
iv. 25, 30, 34). The probable reason of this
was that he had not yet been formally introduced as the High-priest into the Holy
Place of the Tabernacle.

brought the blood] They most likely held
the basons in which the blood was received
as it ran from the victim, and then handed
them to their father. See i. 5.

15-21. In this first complete series of
offerings made by the High-priest, the sacrifices take their appointed order; first, the
Sin-offering to make atonement; then the
Burnt-offering, to signify the surrender of the
body, soul and spirit to Jehovah in heaven;
and lastly the Peace-offering, to show forth
the communion vouchsafed to those who are
justified and sanctified. See viii. 14 note.

22. Aaron having completed the offerings,
before he came down from the stage surrounding the Altar on which the priests

used to stand to officiate (see Exod. xxvii.
8), turned toward the people, and blessed
them; probably using the form which became the established one for the priests
(Num. vi. 24-26), and which is still maintained in the synagogues.

23. Aaron, having now gone through the
cycle of priestly duties connected with the
Brazen Altar, accompanies Moses into the
Tent of Meeting. It was reasonable that
Moses, as the divinely appointed leader of
the nation, should induct Aaron into the
Tabernacle.

blessed the people] This joint blessing of
the mediator of the Law and the High-priest
was the solemn conclusion of the Consecration and Inauguration. (Cp. 2 Chr. vi.
3-11.) According to one tradition the form
used by Moses and Aaron resembled Ps. xc.
17. But another form is given in the Targum of Palestine, "May your offerings be
accepted, and may the Lord dwell among
you and forgive you your sins."

tabernacle of the congregation, and came out, and blessed the people : ᶜand the glory of the LORD appeared unto all the people. 24 And ᵈthere came a fire out from before the LORD, and consumed upon the altar the burnt offering and the fat : *which* when all the people saw, ᵉthey shouted, and fell on their faces. CHAP. 10. AND ᵃNadab and Abihu, the sons of Aaron, ᵇtook either of them his censer, and put fire therein, and put incense thereon, and offered ᶜstrange fire before the LORD, which he 2 commanded them not. And there ᵈwent out fire from the LORD, 3 and devoured them, and they died before the LORD. Then Moses said unto Aaron, This *is it* that the LORD spake, saying, I will be sanctified in them ᵉthat come nigh me, and before all the 4 people I will be ᶠglorified. ᵍAnd Aaron held his peace. And Moses called Mishael and Elzaphan, the sons of ʰUzziel the uncle of Aaron, and said unto them, Come near, ⁱcarry your 5 brethren from before the sanctuary out of the camp. So they went near, and carried them in their coats out of the camp ; as 6 Moses had said. And Moses said unto Aaron, and unto Eleazar

---

24. The very ancient Jewish tradition has been widely adopted that the sacred fire of the Altar originated in this divine act, and that it was afterwards preserved on the Altar of the Tabernacle until the dedication of the Temple, when fire again " came down from heaven." (2 Chr. vii. 1.) But according to the sacred narrative the Altar-fire had been lighted in a natural way before this occasion. (Cp. viii. 16, ix. 10, 13, &c. ; Ex. xl. 29.) It would therefore seem that the fire which " came out from before the Lord " manifested itself, according to the words of *v.* 24, not in kindling the fuel on the Altar, but in the sudden consuming of the victim. For the like testimony to the acceptance of a sacrifice, see Judg. xiii. 19, 20 ; 1 K. xviii. 38 ; 1 Chr. xxi. 26, and probably Gen. iv. 4. The phrase *to turn a sacrifice to ashes*, became equivalent to *accepting it* (Ps. xx. 3, see margin). The fire of the altar was maintained in accordance with vi. 13.

X. The events recorded in this chapter must have occurred immediately after the offering of the sacrifices of inauguration, in the evening of the same day. See *v.* 19.

1. *Nadab and Abihu*] The two elder sons of Aaron (Ex. vi. 23 ; Num. iii. 2), who were amongst those invited to accompany Moses when he was going up Mount Sinai, but who were " to worship afar off," and not " come near the Lord." Ex. xxiv. 1, 2.

censer] See Ex. xxv. 38 note.

strange fire] The point of their offence is evidently expressed in this term. This may very probably mean that the incense was lighted at an unauthorized time. And we may reasonably unite with this the supposition that they were intoxicated (cp. *v.* 9), as well as another conjecture, that they made their offering of incense an accompaniment to the exultation of the people on the manifestation of the glory of the Lord (ix. 24). As

they perished not within the Tabernacle, but in front of it, it seems likely that they may have been making an ostentatious and irreverent display of their ministration to accompany the shouts of the people on their way towards the Tabernacle. The offence for which they were immediately visited with outward punishment was thus a flagrant outrage on the solemn order of the divine service, while the cause of their offence may have been their guilty excess.

2. The fire which had just before sanctified the ministry of Aaron as well pleasing to God, now brought to destruction his two eldest sons because they did not sanctify Jehovah in their hearts, but dared to perform a self-willed act of worship ; just as the same Gospel is to one a savour of life unto life, and to another a savour of death unto death (2 Cor. ii. 16).

3. Rather, **I will sanctify myself in them** that **come near to me** (*i.e.* the priests), **and I will glorify myself before all the people.** The words used by Moses on this occasion are not found elsewhere in the Pentateuch. But the sense is implied in such passages as Exod. xix. 22, xxviii. 41, xxix. 1, 44. Aaron's silence (cp. Psalm xxxix. 9) on this occasion may be compared with his reasonable and natural expostulation with Moses when his surviving sons were rebuked for not having eaten the flesh of the Sin-offering (*v.* 19).

4. The first cousins of Aaron (Ex. vi. 22) are selected by Moses to convey the bodies of Nadab and Abihu out of the camp and bury them, probably because they were the nearest relations who were not priests. See Num. ix. 6.

5. *coats*] See Ex. xxviii. 39. Life had been extinguished as if by a flash of lightning, but neither the bodies nor the dresses were destroyed.

6, 7. Aaron and his two surviving sons are forbidden to show the accustomed signs of

and unto Ithamar, his sons, *k*Uncover not your heads, neither
rend your clothes; lest ye die, and lest *l*wrath come upon all
the people: but let your brethren, the whole house of Israel,
7 bewail the burning which the LORD hath kindled. *m*And ye
shall not go out from the door of the tabernacle of the congregation, lest ye die: *n*for the anointing oil of the LORD *is* upon
8 you. And they did according to the word of Moses. ¶And the
9 LORD spake unto Aaron, saying, *o*Do not drink wine nor strong
drink, thou, nor thy sons with thee, when ye go into the tabernacle of the congregation, lest ye die: *it shall be* a statute for
10 ever throughout your generations: and that ye may *p*put difference between holy and unholy, and between unclean and
11 clean; *q*and that ye may teach the children of Israel all the
statutes which the LORD hath spoken unto them by the hand of
12 Moses. ¶And Moses spake unto Aaron, and unto Eleazar and
unto Ithamar, his sons that were left, Take *r*the meat offering
that remaineth of the offerings of the LORD made by fire, and
13 eat it without leaven beside the altar: for *s*it *is* most holy: and
ye shall eat it in the holy place, because it *is* thy due, and thy
sons' due, of the sacrifices of the LORD made by fire: for *t*so I
14 am commanded. And *u*the wave breast and heave shoulder
shall ye eat in a clean place; thou, and thy sons, and thy
daughters with thee: for *they be* thy due, and thy sons' due,
which are given out of the sacrifices of peace offerings of the
15 children of Israel. *x*The heave shoulder and the wave breast
shall they bring with the offerings made by fire of the fat, to

k Ex. 33. 5.
& 21. 1, 10.
Num. 6. 6.
Deut. 33. 9.
Ezek. 24. 16.
l Num. 16.
22, 46.
Josh. 7. 1.
2 Sam. 24. 1.
m ch. 21. 12.
n Ex. 28. 41.
o Ezek. 44.
21.
Luke 1. 15.
1 Tim. 3. 3.
Tit. 1. 7.
p ch. 11. 47.
Jer. 15. 19.
Ezek. 22. 26.
& 44. 23.
q Deut. 24. 8.
Neh. 8. 2.
Jer. 18. 18.
Mal. 2. 7.
r Ex. 29. 2.
ch. 6. 16.
Num. 18. 9.
s ch. 21. 22.
t ch. 2. 3.
& 6. 16.
u Ex. 29. 24.
ch. 7. 31, 34.
Num. 18. 11.
x ch. 7. 29.

---

mourning, or to leave the Court of the
Tabernacle in order to attend the funeral,
because, from their office, they were especially concerned as consecrated priests in
outwardly maintaining the honour of Jehovah. They were to bear visible testimony
to the righteousness of the punishment of
Nadab and Abihu. The people, on the
other hand, as not formally standing so
near to Jehovah, were permitted to "bewail" as an acknowledgment that the nation
had a share in the sin of its priests. (Cp.
1 Cor. xii. 26.)

6. *Uncover not your heads*] Or, *set free—
let go loose.* It was a custom to let the hair
grow long and fall loosely over the head and
face (xiii. 45; 2 Sam. xv. 30, xix. 4); and
the substance of the command would thus
be that they should not let the hair go dishevelled.—Rending the clothes in front so
as to lay open the breast was one of the
commonest manifestations of grief (see Gen.
xxxvii. 29, xliv. 13; 2 S. i. 11; Job i. 20;
Joel ii. 13, &c.). The garments as well
as the persons of the priests were consecrated; this appears to be the reason of the
prohibition of these ordinary signs of mourning. Cp. xx. 10.

lest ye die] See Exod. xxviii. 35 note.

7. *the anointing oil...is upon you*] See viii.
12, 30. The holy oil, as the symbol of the
Holy Spirit, the Spirit of Life and immor-
tality and joy, was the sign of the priests
being brought near to Jehovah. It was
therefore by its meaning connected both

with the general law which forbade the
High-priest ever to put on signs of mourning on account of death (xxi. 10-12), and
with the special reason for the prohibition
on this occasion.

9—11. When the priest was on duty he
was to abstain from wine and strong drink,
lest he should commit excess (see *v.* 1), and
so become disqualified for carrying out the
precepts of the ceremonial Law.

9. *strong drink*] The Hebrew word is employed here to denote strong drinks of any
kind except wine made from the grape.

10. *unholy...unclean*] Common, as not
consecrated; and what would occasion defilement by being touched or eaten. Cp.
Acts x. 14.

11. That is, "that you may, by your
example in your ministrations, preserve the
minds of the Israelites from confusion in
regard to the distinctions made by the divine
Law."

12—15. The argument is, that as such meals
were appointed in honour of Jehovah Himself, they ought to be conducted with due
reverence and discretion.

12. *beside the altar*] What is called "the
holy place" in *vv.* 13, 17: it should be rather,
a holy place, any part of the Holy precinct, as
distinguished from a merely "clean place"
(*v.* 14), either within or without the court of
the Tabernacle.

14. *wave breast and heave shoulder*] See
vii. 30 note.

wave *it for* a wave offering before the LORD; and it shall be thine, and thy sons' with thee, by a statute for ever; as the
y ch. 9. 3, 15. 16 LORD hath commanded. ¶And Moses diligently sought *y*the goat of the sin offering, and, behold, it was burnt: and he was angry with Eleazar and Ithamar, the sons of Aaron *which were*
z ch. 6. 26, 29. 17 left *alive*, saying, *z*Wherefore have ye not eaten the sin offering in the holy place, seeing it *is* most holy, and *God* hath given it you to bear the iniquity of the congregation, to make atonement
a ch. 6. 30. 18 for them before the LORD? Behold, *a*the blood of it was not brought in within the holy *place:* ye should indeed have eaten
b ch. 6. 26. 19 it in the holy *place*, *b*as I commanded. And Aaron said unto
c ch. 9. 8, 12. Moses, Behold, *c*this day have they offered their sin offering and their burnt offering before the LORD; and such things have
d Jer. 6. 20. & 14. 12. Hos. 9. 4. Mal. 1. 10, 13. befallen me: and *if* I had eaten the sin offering to day, *d*should 20 it have been accepted in the sight of the LORD? And when Moses heard *that*, he was content.

a Deut. 14. 4. Acts 10. 12, 14. **CHAP. 11.** AND the LORD spake unto Moses and to Aaron, saying 2 unto them, Speak unto the children of Israel, saying, *a*These *are* the beasts which ye shall eat among all the beasts that *are* 3 on the earth. Whatsoever parteth the hoof, and is clovenfooted, *and* cheweth the cud, among the beasts, that shall ye eat. 4 Nevertheless these shall ye not eat of them that chew the cud, or of them that divide the hoof; *as* the camel, because he cheweth 5 the cud, but divideth not the hoof; he *is* unclean unto you. And the coney, because he cheweth the cud, but divideth not the

---

16. The Law on the point in question was clear. See ii. 3, iv. 5, 16 notes. But on this occasion, though the Sin-offering which had been offered by Aaron was for the people (ix. 15), its blood was not carried into the Tabernacle. The priests might therefore have too readily supposed that their eating the flesh, or burning it, was a matter of indifference. Hence Moses explains that the appropriation of the flesh by the priests is an essential part of the act of atonement (*v.* 17).

it was burnt] It was consumed by fire in an ordinary way, not in the fire of the Altar. See i. 9.

17. *to bear the iniquity*] See Ex. xxviii. 38 note.

18. "The holy *place*," as it is called in our version, within the Tabernacle (see Ex. xxvi. 33, xxviii. 29, &c.) into which the blood was carried, is regularly called in Hebrew, simply, "the Holy" (as the innermost chamber is called "the Holy of Holies"), the adjective being used substantively; while the precinct in which the flesh of the Sin-offering was eaten is generally called in full the Holy Place, the substantive being expressed (*v.* 13).

19. That is: "Behold this very day, in which we have done our part in sacrificing Sin-offerings and Burnt-offerings to the Lord, this great calamity has befallen me. Could it have been well-pleasing to the Lord if those who have been so humbled as I and my sons have been by the sin of our relations and the divine judgment, had

feasted on the most Holy flesh of the Sin-offering?"

XI. 1. Jehovah speaks to Moses and Aaron conjointly. (Cp. xiii. 1, xv. 1.) The High-priest, in regard to the legal purifications, is treated as co-ordinate with the legislator.

2. Rather, "These are the animals which ye may eat out of all the beasts;" that is, out of the larger creatures, the quadrupeds, as distinguished from birds and reptiles. See Gen. i. 24. Of quadrupeds, those only might be eaten which completely divided the hoof and chew the cud (*vv.* 3-8).

3. *parteth*, &c.] Rather, is clovenfooted and completely separates the hoofs.

4. *divideth not the hoof*] The toes of the camel are divided above, but they are united below in a sort of cushion or pad resting upon the hard bottom of the foot, which is "like the sole of a shoe." The Moslems eat the flesh of the camel, but it is said not to be wholesome.

5. *the coney*] The old English name for a rabbit. The animal meant is the Hyrax Syriacus. It bears some resemblance to the guinea-pig or the marmot, and in its general appearance and habits (Prov. xxx. 26, Ps. civ. 18), it might easily be taken for a rodent. But Cuvier discovered that it is, in its anatomy, a true pachyderm, allied to the rhinoceros and the tapir, inferior to them as it is in size.

he cheweth the cud] The Hyrax has the same habit as the hare, the rabbit, the guinea-pig, and some other rodents, of

6 hoof; he *is* unclean unto you. And the hare, because he cheweth
the cud, but divideth not the hoof; he *is* unclean unto you.
7 And the swine, though he divide the hoof, and be clovenfooted,
8 yet he cheweth not the cud; *b*he *is* unclean to you. Of their
flesh shall ye not eat, and their carcase shall ye not touch;
9 *c*they *are* unclean to you. ¶ *d*These shall ye eat of all that *are*
in the waters: whatsoever hath fins and scales in the waters,
10 in the seas, and in the rivers, them shall ye eat. And all that
have not fins and scales in the seas, and in the rivers, of all
that move in the waters, and of any living thing which *is* in
11 the waters, they *shall be* an *e*abomination unto you: they shall
be even an abomination unto you; ye shall not eat of their
12 flesh, but ye shall have their carcases in abomination. What-
13 soever hath no fins nor scales in the waters, that *shall be* an
abomination unto you. ¶ *f* And these *are they which* ye shall
have in abomination among the fowls; they shall not be eaten,
they *are* an abomination: the eagle, and the ossifrage, and the
14, 15 ospray, and the vulture, and the kite after his kind; every
16 raven after his kind; and the owl, and the night hawk, and the
17 cuckow, and the hawk after his kind, and the little owl, and the
18 cormorant, and the great owl, and the swan, and the pelican,
19 and the gier eagle, and the stork, the heron after her kind, and
20 the lapwing, and the bat. ¶ All fowls that creep, going upon *all*
21 four, *shall be* an abomination unto you. Yet these may ye eat
of every flying creeping thing that goeth upon *all* four, which

b Isai. 65. 4.
& 66. 3. 17.
c Isai. 52. 11.
See Matt.
15. 11, 20.
Mark 7, 2,
15, 18.
Acts 10. 14,
15.
& 15. 29.
Rom. 14.
14, 17.
1 Cor. 8. 8.
Col. 2. 16, 21.
Heb. 9. 10.
d Deut. 14. 9.
e ch. 7. 18.
Deut. 14. 3.
f Deut. 14.
12.

---

moving its jaws when it is at rest as if it
were masticating. The rodents were familiarly spoken of as ruminating animals, just
as the bat was reckoned amongst birds because it flies (see *v.* 19), and as whales and
their congeners are spoken of as fish, when
there is no occasion for scientific accuracy.

7. *he divide the hoof,* &c.] It is clovenfooted and completely, &c. See *v.* 3 note. Of
all the quadrupeds of which the Law forbids the flesh to be eaten, the pig seems to
have been regarded as the most unclean.
Cp. marg. reff. Several other nations have
agreed with the Hebrews in this respect:
the reason being that its flesh is unwholesome, especially in warm climates.

9. Any fish, either from salt water or
fresh, might be eaten if it had both scales
and fins, but no other creature that lives in
the waters. Shellfish of all kinds, whether
mollusks or crustaceans, and cetaceous animals, were therefore prohibited, as well as
fish which appear to have no scales, like the
eel; probably because they were considered
unwholesome, and (under certain circumstances) found to be so.

13–19. As far as they can be identified,
the birds here mentioned are such as live
upon animal food. They were those which
the Israelites might have been tempted to
eat, either from their being easy to obtain,
or from the example of other nations, and
which served as types of the entire range of
prohibited kinds.

13. *the eagle*] Rather, the great vulture,
which the Egyptians are known to have

ranked as the first amongst birds. Cp. 2 S.
i. 23; Ps. ciii. 5; Prov. xxiii. 5, &c.

The *ossifrage*, or bone-breaker, was the
lammer-geyer, and the *ospray* (a corruption
of *ossifrage*) the sea-eagle.

14. *the vulture*] Rather, the (black) kite
(Isai. xxxiv. 15): *the kite,* rather the red kite,
remarkable for its piercing sight (Job
xxviii. 7).

15. *every raven after his kind*] *i.e.* the
whole family of corvidæ.

16. *and the owl,* &c.] Rather, "and the
ostrich, and the owl, and the gull, and the
hawk," &c.

18. *the swan*] More probably the ibis,
the sacred bird of the Egyptians. *The gier
eagle* is most likely the Egyptian vulture,
a bird of unprepossessing appearance and
disgusting habits, but fostered by the
Egyptians as a useful scavenger.

19. *the heron...the lapwing*] Rather, the
great plover—the hoopoe, so called from its
peculiar cry.

20. Rather, "All creeping things which
have wings," &c. The word rendered creeping things may be regarded as coextensive
with our word *vermin.* It is derived from a
verb which signifies not only to creep, but to
teem, or bring forth abundantly (Gen. i. 21,
viii. 17; Exod. viii. 3; Ps. cv. 30), and so
easily came to denote creatures which are
apt to abound, to the annoyance of mankind.

21. *legs above their feet, to leap withal
upon the earth*] The families of the Salta-
toria, of which the common cricket, the
common grasshopper, and the migratory
locust, may be taken as types.

22 have legs above their feet, to leap withal upon the earth; *even*
g Matt. 3. 4. these of them ye may eat; *g*the locust after his kind, and the
Mark 1. 6. bald locust after his kind, and the beetle after his kind, and the
23 grasshopper after his kind. But all *other* flying creeping things,
24 which have four feet, *shall be* an abomination unto you. And
for these ye shall be unclean: whosoever toucheth the carcase
25 of them shall be unclean until the even. And whosoever beareth
h ch. 14. 8. *ought* of the carcase of them *h*shall wash his clothes, and be
& 15. 5. 26 unclean until the even. ¶ *The carcases* of every beast which
Num. 19.   divideth the hoof, and *is* not clovenfooted, nor cheweth the cud,
10. 22.
& 31. 24.   *are* unclean unto you: every one that toucheth them shall be
27 unclean. And whatsoever goeth upon his paws, among all
manner of beasts that go on *all* four, those *are* unclean unto
you: whoso toucheth their carcase shall be unclean until the
28 even. And he that beareth the carcase of them shall wash his
clothes, and be unclean until the even: they *are* unclean unto
29 you. ¶ These also *shall be* unclean unto you among the creep-
i Isai. 66. 17. ing things that creep upon the earth; the weasel, and *i*the
30 mouse, and the tortoise after his kind, and the ferret, and the
31 chameleon, and the lizard, and the snail and the mole. These
are unclean to you among all that creep: whosoever doth touch
32 them, when they be dead, shall be unclean until the even. And
upon whatsoever *any* of them, when they are dead, doth fall, it
shall be unclean ; whether *it be* any vessel of wood, or raiment,
or skin, or sack, whatsoever vessel *it be*, wherein *any* work is
k ch. 15. 12. done, *k*it must be put into water, and it shall be unclean until
33 the even; so it shall be cleansed. And every earthen vessel,
whereinto *any* of them falleth, whatsoever *is* in it shall be
l ch. 6. 28. 34 unclean ; and *l*ye shall break it. Of all meat which may be
& 15. 12.   eaten, *that* on which *such* water cometh shall be unclean: and all
drink that may be drunk in every *such* vessel shall be unclean.
35 And every *thing* whereupon *any part* of their carcase falleth
shall be unclean ; *whether it be* oven, or ranges for pots, they
shall be broken down: *for* they *are* unclean, and shall be unclean
36 unto you. Nevertheless a fountain or pit, [1]*wherein there is*
plenty of water, shall be clean: but that which toucheth their
37 carcase shall be unclean. And if *any part* of their carcase fall
38 upon any sowing seed which is to be sown, it *shall be* clean. But
if *any* water be put upon the seed, and *any part* of their carcase
39 fall thereon, it *shall be* unclean unto you. ¶ And if any beast,
of which ye may eat, die ; he that toucheth the carcase thereof
m ch. 17. 15. 40 shall be unclean until the even. And *m*he that eateth of the
& 22. 8.   carcase of it shall wash his clothes, and be unclean until the
Deut. 14. 21.
Ezek. 4. 14.
& 44. 31.   [1] Heb. *a gathering together of waters.*

---

22. In the uncertainty of identifying these four creatures, it has been suggested that some of the names may belong to locusts in an imperfect state of development. Most modern versions have taken a safer course than our translators, by retaining the Hebrew names.

24–28. *unclean*] If the due purification was omitted at the time, through negligence or forgetfulness, a Sin-offering was required. See v. 2.

29, 30. The identification of "the creeping things" here named is not always certain. They are most likely those which were occasionally eaten. For the *tortoise* read the great lizard, for the *ferret* the gecko (one of the lizard tribe), for the *chameleon* the frog or the Nile lizard : by the word rendered *snail* is probably meant another kind of lizard, and by the *mole* the chameleon.

33. *earthen vessel*] See marg. reff.

35. See ii. 4. The word rendered "ranges for pots" has been conjectured to mean either an excavated fireplace, fitted to receive a pair of ovens, or a support like a pair of andirons.

even: he also that beareth the carcase of it shall wash his
41 clothes, and be unclean until the even. ¶ And every creeping
thing that creepeth upon the earth *shall be* an abomination; it
42 shall not be eaten. Whatsoever goeth upon the belly, and
whatsoever goeth upon *all* four, or whatsoever [1]hath more feet
among all creeping things that creep upon the earth, them ye
43 shall not eat; for they *are* an abomination. *n* Ye shall not make
your [2]selves abominable with any creeping thing that creepeth,
neither shall ye make yourselves unclean with them, that ye
44 should be defiled thereby. For I *am* the LORD your God: ye
shall therefore sanctify yourselves, and *o* ye shall be holy; for I
am holy: neither shall ye defile yourselves with any manner of
45 creeping thing that creepeth upon the earth. *p* For I *am* the
LORD that bringeth you up out of the land of Egypt, to be your
46 God: *q* ye shall therefore be holy, for I *am* holy. This *is* the law
of the beasts, and of the fowl, and of every living creature that
moveth in the waters, and of every creature that creepeth upon
47 the earth: *r* to make a difference between the unclean and the
clean, and between the beast that may be eaten and the beast
that may not be eaten.

CHAP. 12. AND the LORD spake unto Moses, saying, Speak unto
2 the children of Israel, saying, If a *a* woman have conceived seed,
and born a man child: then *b* she shall be unclean seven days;
c according to the days of the separation for her infirmity shall
3 she be unclean. And in the *d* eighth day the flesh of his fore-
4 skin shall be circumcised. And she shall then continue in the
blood of her purifying three and thirty days; she shall touch no
hallowed thing, nor come into the sanctuary, until the days of
5 her purifying be fulfilled. But if she bear a maid child, then
she shall be unclean two weeks, as in her separation: and she

n ch. 20. 25.

o Ex. 19. 6.
ch. 19. 2.
& 20. 7, 26.
1 Thess. 4. 7.
1 Pet. 1. 15,
16.
p Ex. 6. 7.
q ver. 44.

r ch. 10. 10.

a ch. 15. 19.
b Luke 2. 22.
c ch. 15. 19.
d Gen. 17.
12.
Luke 1. 59.
& 2. 21.
John 7. 22,
23.

---

[1] Heb. *doth multiply feet.*   [2] Heb. *souls.*

---

42. *Whatsoever goeth upon the belly]* i.e. all
footless reptiles, and mollusks, snakes of all
kinds, snails, slugs, and worms. *Whatsoever
goeth upon all four;* i.e. "creeping things,"
or vermin; such as the weasel, the mouse
or the lizard. *Whatsoever hath more feet;*
i.e. all insects, except the locust family
(*v.* 22 note), myriapods, spiders, and cater-
pillars.

44–47. These verses set forth the spiritual
ground on which the distinction between
clean and unclean is based. Cp. marg. reff.
and x. 10, xx. 25, 26; 1 Peter i. 15, 16.
The basis of the obligation to maintain
the distinction was the call of the Hebrews
to be the peculiar people of Jehovah. It
was to be something in their daily life to
remind them of the Covenant which distinguished them from the nations of the world.
By Jesus Christ it was revealed (Matt. xv.
11) to the elect people that they were no
longer to be tied by the letter of the Law
in regard to their food, but were to be left
to the exercise of a regenerated judgment.
They were to learn that the kingdom of
God is not eating, or abstaining from,
meats and drinks; but righteousness, and
truth, and peace, and joy in the Holy

Ghost (Rom. xiv. 17. Cp. Acts x. 15;
1 Tim. iv. 4).

XII.—XV. CEREMONIAL PURIFICATIONS.
The Purifications of the Law fall under
three heads; (i) those for defilement arising
from secretions; (ii) those for the Leprosy;
(iii) those for pollution from corpses. The
first and second classes are described in
these chapters; the last, as relates to
human corpses, in Num. xix. 11, &c., and
as relates to the bodies of dead animals, in
xi. 24–28, 31–40.

XII. This chapter would more naturally
follow the fifteenth. See Note to xv. 1.

3. On circumcision, see Gen. xvii. 5 note.

4. The Levitical law ascribed impurity
exclusively to the Mother, in no degree to
the Child.

5. Some have thought that this doubling
of each of the two periods was intended to
remind the people of the fact that woman
represents the lower side of human nature,
and was the first to fall into temptation.
1 Tim. ii. 13–15; 1 Pet. iii. 7. The ancients
had a notion that the mother suffers for a
longer time after the birth of a girl than
after the birth of a boy. The period required for the restoration of her health in

shall continue in the blood of her purifying threescore and six
^e Luke 2. 22. 6 days. ¶ And ^ewhen the days of her purifying are fulfilled, for a
son, or for a daughter, she shall bring a lamb ¹of the first year
for a burnt offering, and a young pigeon, or a turtle dove, for a
sin offering, unto the door of the tabernacle of·the congregation,
7 unto the priest : who shall offer it before the LORD, and make
an atonement for her ; and she shall be cleansed from the issue
of her blood. This *is* the law for her that hath born a male or a
^f ch. 5. 7.   8 female. ^fAnd if ²she be not able to bring a lamb, then she shall
Luke 2. 24.   bring two turtles, or two young pigeons ; the one for the burnt
^g ch. 4. 26.   offering, and the other for a sin offering : ^gand the priest shall
make an atonement for her, and she shall be clean.
CHAP. 13. AND the LORD spake unto Moses and Aaron, saying,
^a Deut. 28.   2 When a man shall have in the skin of his flesh a ³rising, ^aa scab,
27.
Isai. 3. 17.   ¹ Heb. *a son of his year.*   ² Heb. *her hand find not*   ³ Or, *swelling.*
sufficiency of.

the one case was thirty days, and in the other, it was forty or forty-two days. This notion may have been connected with a general custom of observing the distinction as early as the time of Moses.

6—8. The sacrificial act expressed an acknowledgment of sin and a dedication of herself to Jehovah. See viii. 14.

6. *of the first year*] Literally, as in the margin, *a son of his year.* This expression is supposed to mean one less than a year old, while *the son of a year* is one that has just completed its first year.

8. *a lamb*] Rather, **one of the flock**; either a sheep or a goat ; it is not the same word as in *v.* 6.

two turtles, or two young pigeons] See on i. 14. The Virgin Mary availed herself of the liberty which the Law allowed to the poor, and offered the inferior Burnt-offering (Luke ii. 24).

XIII., XIV. THE LAWS RELATING TO LEPROSY. The Leprosy is the most terrible of all the disorders to which the body of man is subject. There is no disease in which hope of recovery is so nearly extinguished. From a commencement slight in appearance, with but little pain or inconvenience, often in its earlier stage insidiously disappearing and reappearing, it goes on in its strong but sluggish course, generally in defiance of the efforts of medical skill, until it reduces the patient to a mutilated cripple with dulled or obliterated senses, the voice turned to a croak, and with features of ghastly deformity. When it reaches some vital part it generally occasions what seem like the symptoms of a distinct disease (most often Dysentery), and so puts an end to the life of the sufferer.

It was an all but universal impression that the Leprosy, above all other diseases, came upon man as an irresistible stroke of superhuman power, either in the way of punishment for personal sin or of an affliction with some definite purpose. This natural suggestion was confirmed and realized upon several occasions in the history of

the Israelites. A stroke of Leprosy was the mark of the divine displeasure at the slow faith of Moses (Ex. iv. 6), at the contumacy of Miriam (Num. xii. 10), at the dishonesty of Gehazi (2 K. v. 27), and at the impious presumption of Uzziah (2 Chr. xxvi. 19, 20). One of the denunciations against Joab, on account of the death of Abner, was that his children should be lepers (2 S. iii. 29).

It is now considered by all the best authorities that the Hebrew word for the disease does not denote the disease which is more properly called the Leprosy (see xiii. 12), but that which is known to physicians as the Elephantiasis : the origin of which is ascribed to an animal poison generated in or received into the blood, and accumulated therein probably by a process analogous to fermentation. This poison primarily affects either the skin, or the nerves and nervous centres. In this way, two forms of Elephantiasis are distinguished, the *Tuberculated,* and the *Anæsthetic* or *Non-tuberculated,* of which the former is the more common.

Medical skill appears to have been more completely foiled by Elephantiasis than by any other malady. The Anæsthetic form alone seems to be in some degree amenable to remedies and regimen.

The question whether Elephantiasis is contagious or not, is the one of most peculiar interest in connection with the Levitical law. Many facts tend to prove that, as a rule, it was not ; but that under certain circumstances (*e.g.* when the ulcers are running) contagion might be developed.

2. *the skin of his flesh*] An expression found nowhere but in this chapter. It probably denotes the cuticle or scarf skin, as distinguished from the cutis or true skin.

rising—scab—bright spot] The Hebrew words are the technical names applied to the common external signs of incipient Elephantiasis.

like the plague of leprosy] **Like a stroke of Leprosy.**

or bright spot, and it be in the skin of his flesh *like* the plague of
leprosy; *b*then he shall be brought unto Aaron the priest, or
3 unto one of his sons the priests: and the priest shall look on the
plague in the skin of the flesh: and *when* the hair in the plague
is turned white, and the plague in sight *be* deeper than the skin
of his flesh, it *is* a plague of leprosy: and the priest shall look on
4 him, and pronounce him unclean. If the bright spot *be* white
in the skin of his flesh, and in sight *be* not deeper than the skin,
and the hair thereof be not turned white; then the priest shall
5 shut up *him that hath* the plague seven days: and the priest
shall look on him the seventh day: and, behold, *if* the plague in
his sight be at a stay, *and* the plague spread not in the skin;
6 then the priest shall shut him up seven days more: and the
priest shall look on him again the seventh day: and, behold, *if*
the plague *be* somewhat dark, *and* the plague spread not in the
skin, the priest shall pronounce him clean: it *is but* a scab:
7 and he *c*shall wash his clothes, and be clean. But if the scab
spread much abroad in the skin, after that he hath been seen of
the priest for his cleansing, he shall be seen of the priest again:
8 and *if* the priest see that, behold, the scab spreadeth in the skin,
then the priest shall pronounce him unclean: it *is* a leprosy.
9 ¶ When the plague of leprosy is in a man, then he shall be
10 brought unto the priest; *d*and the priest shall see *him:* and,
behold, *if* the rising *be* white in the skin, and it have turned the
11 hair white, and *there be* [1]quick raw flesh in the rising; it *is* an
old leprosy in the skin of his flesh, and the priest shall pronounce
him unclean, and shall not shut him up: for he *is* unclean.
12 And if a leprosy break out abroad in the skin, and the leprosy
cover all the skin of *him that hath* the plague from his head even
13 to his foot, wheresoever the priest looketh; then the priest shall

b Deut. 17. 8, 9. Luke 17. 14.

c ch. 11. 25. & 14. 8.

d Num. 12. 10, 12. 2 Kin. 5. 27. 2 Chr. 26. 20.

[1] Heb. *the quickening of living flesh.*

---

3. *the hair in the plague is turned white*]
The sparing growth of very fine whitish hair
on leprous spots in the place of the natural
hair, appears to have been always regarded
as a characteristic symptom.

*the plague in sight be deeper than the skin
of his flesh*] Rather, **The stroke appears to
be deeper than the scarf skin.** The 'bright
spot' changed to a brownish colour with a
metallic or oily lustre, and with a clearly-
defined edge. This symptom, along with
the whitish hair, at once decided the case to
be one of Leprosy.

5. *and the plague spread not*] Rather, **advance not**, so as to shew that the disease is
under the cuticle and assuming the symptoms of *v.* 3.

6. *somewhat dark*] Rather, **somewhat
dim :** that is, if the spot is dying away.

7. *seen of the priest for his cleansing*] The
purport of these words is doubtful. They
probably mean " seen by the priest and
pronounced clean," and refer to the visit of
the suspected leper to the priest at the end
of the second week. But some have taken
the words to mean " seen by the priest with
a view to be pronounced clean," and regard
the sentence of the priest as provisional,
holding good only till the symptoms may

appear to resume their progress. Cp. *v.* 35.

10. *if the rising be white*] Or, **If there be a
white rising.** The term very probably denotes the white Bulla or patch of Anæsthetic Elephantiasis when it has re-appeared.

quick raw flesh in the rising] The margin
gives the literal rendering. The symptom
here noted exhibits a more advanced stage
of the disease. The expression might denote an ulcer or open sore with " proud
flesh " appearing in it.

12–17. The disease here indicated appears
to be that now known as Lepra vulgaris,
the common White Leprosy, or Dry Tetter.
It first shews itself in reddish pimples, the
surface of which becomes white and scaly,
spreading in a circular form till they meet
each other and cover large patches of the
body. It scarcely affects the general health,
and for the most part disappears of itself,
though it often lasts for years.

*from his head even to his foot, wheresoever
the priest looketh*] The first appearance of
the Lepra vulgaris may take place in any
part of the body, especially however at the
larger joints of the limbs ; but the spots of
Elephantiasis are almost always first seen
on those parts which are habitually exposed, the face, ears and hands.

consider : and, behold, *if* the leprosy have covered all his flesh,
he shall pronounce *him* clean *that hath* the plague : it is all
14 turned white : he *is* clean. But when raw flesh appeareth in
15 him, he shall be unclean. And the priest shall see the raw flesh,
and pronounce him to be unclean : *for* the raw flesh *is* unclean :
16 it *is* a leprosy. Or if the raw flesh turn again, and be changed
17 unto white, he shall come unto the priest ; and the priest shall
see him : and, behold, *if* the plague be turned into white ; then
the priest shall pronounce *him* clean *that hath* the plague : he *is*
18 clean. ¶ The flesh also, in which, *even* in the skin thereof, was
e Ex. 9. 9.   19 a *e* boil, and is healed, and in the place of the boil there be a
white rising, or a bright spot, white, and somewhat reddish, and
20 it be shewed to the priest ; and if, when the priest seeth it,
behold, it *be* in sight lower than the skin, and the hair thereof be
turned white ; the priest shall pronounce him unclean : it *is* a
21 plague of leprosy broken out of the boil. But if the priest look
on it, and, behold, *there be* no white hairs therein, and *if* it *be*
not lower than the skin, but *be* somewhat dark ; then the priest
22 shall shut him up seven days : and if it spread much abroad in
the skin, then the priest shall pronounce him unclean : it *is* a
23 plague. But if the bright spot stay in his place, *and* spread not,
it *is* a burning boil ; and the priest shall pronounce him clean.
24 ¶ Or if there be *any* flesh, in the skin whereof *there is* [1] a hot
burning, and the quick *flesh* that burneth have a white bright
25 spot, somewhat reddish, or white ; then the priest shall look
upon it : and, behold, *if* the hair in the bright spot be turned
white, and it *be in* sight deeper than the skin ; it *is* a leprosy
broken out of the burning : wherefore the priest shall pronounce
26 him unclean : it *is* the plague of leprosy. But if the priest look
on it, and, behold, *there be* no white hair in the bright spot, and
it *be* no lower than the *other* skin, but *be* somewhat dark ; then
27 the priest shall shut him up seven days : and the priest shall look
upon him the seventh day : *and* if it be spread much abroad in
the skin, then the priest shall pronounce him unclean : it *is* the
28 plague of leprosy. And if the bright spot stay in his place, *and*
spread not in the skin, but it *be* somewhat dark ; it *is* a rising of
the burning, and the priest shall pronounce him clean : for it *is*
29 an inflammation of the burning. ¶ If a man or woman have a
30 plague upon the head or the beard ; then the priest shall see the
plague : and, behold, if it *be* in sight deeper than the skin ; *and*
there be in it a yellow thin hair ; then the priest shall pronounce
him unclean : it *is* a dry scall, *even* a leprosy upon the head or
31 beard. And if the priest look on the plague of the scall, and,

[1] Heb. *a burning of fire.*

---

14. *raw flesh*] See *v.* 10.
18. *boil*] Probably ulcer. In Job ii. 7,
and Deut. xxviii. 27, 35, it would seem
highly probable that the word expresses the
ulcers of Elephantiasis.
20, 21. *lower than the skin*] Rather, **reaching below the scarf skin.**
23. *a burning boil*] Rather, **the scar of
the ulcer ;** literally, *the burn of the ulcer.*
24. The sense of this verse is :—*Or if
there be flesh of which the skin has been
affected by severe inflammation, and the sore
of the inflammation has become a glossy spot,
somewhat reddish or white.*

28. *And if the glossy spot continues unchanged and makes no advance in the skin,
and is rather indistinct* (see on *v.* 6), *it is the
mark of the inflammation, and the priest shall
pronounce him clean, for it is the* (*mere*) *hurt
of inflammation.*
30. *scall*] As this is the name for another
disease not allied to the Leprosy, it would
have been better to retain the original word
(*nethek*). It is a true Elephantiasis, and is
recognised by modern writers under the
name of the Fox mange.
31. *there is no black hair in it*] More probably, **there is no yellow hair in it.**

behold, it *be* not in sight deeper than the skin, and *that there is*
no black hair in it; then the priest shall shut up *him that hath*
32 the plague of the scall seven days: and in the seventh day the
priest shall look on the plague: and, behold, *if* the scall spread
not, and there be in it no yellow hair, and the scall *be* not in sight
33 deeper than the skin; he shall be shaven, but the scall shall he
not shave; and the priest shall shut up *him that hath* the scall
34 seven days more: and in the seventh day the priest shall look
on the scall: and, behold, *if* the scall be not spread in the skin,
nor *be* in sight deeper than the skin; then the priest shall pronounce him clean: and he shall wash his clothes, and be clean.
35 But if the scall spread much in the skin after his cleansing; then
36 the priest shall look on him: and, behold, if the scall be spread
in the skin, the priest shall not seek for yellow hair; he *is*
37 unclean. But if the scall be in his sight at a stay, and *that*
there is black hair grown up therein; the scall is healed, he *is*
38 clean: and the priest shall pronounce him clean. ¶ If a man
also or a woman have in the skin of their flesh bright spots, *even*
39 white bright spots; then the priest shall look: and, behold, *if* the
bright spots in the skin of their flesh *be* darkish white; it *is*
40 a freckled spot *that* groweth in the skin; he *is* clean. And the
man whose ¹hair is fallen off his head, he *is* bald; *yet is* he clean.
41 And he that hath his hair fallen off from the part of his head
42 toward his face, he *is* forehead bald: *yet is* he clean. And if
there be in the bald head, or bald forehead, a white reddish sore;
it *is* a leprosy sprung up in his bald head, or his bald forehead.
43 Then the priest shall look upon it: and, behold, *if* the rising of
the sore *be* white reddish in his bald head, or in his bald fore-
44 head, as the leprosy appeareth in the skin of the flesh; he is a
leprous man, he *is* unclean: the priest shall pronounce him
45 utterly unclean; his plague *is* in his head. ¶ And the leper in
whom the plague *is*, his clothes shall be rent, and his head bare,
and he shall *f* put a covering upon his upper lip, and shall cry,
46 *g* Unclean, unclean. All the days wherein the plague *shall be* in
him he shall be defiled; he *is* unclean: he shall dwell alone;

f Ezek. 24.
17, 22.
Mic. 3. 7.
g Lam. 4. 15.

¹ Heb. *head is pilled.*

---

37. *be in his sight at a stay*] Or, **Does not
alter in appearance.**
39. *freckled spot*] If *v.* 12 refers to the
Lepra vulgaris, the Hebrew *bōhak* here
may denote some kind of Eczema, a skin
disease of a somewhat similar external
character.
Verses 38, 39 would seem more in their
natural place between *vv.* 17, 18.
42. *sore*] Rather, **stroke.** It is the same
word which elsewhere in this and the next
chapter is rendered plague.
45. The leper was to carry about with
him the usual signs of mourning for the
dead. Cp. x. 6 and marg. reff.
The leper was a living parable in the
world of the sin of which death was the
wages; not the less so because his suffering
might have been in no degree due to his
own personal deserts: he bore about with
him at once the deadly fruit and the symbol of the sin of his race. Ex. xx. 5. As
his body slowly perished, first the skin,

then the flesh, then the bone, fell to pieces
while yet the animal life survived; he was
a terrible picture of the gradual corruption
of the spirit wrought by sin.
his head bare] Rather, "his head neglected." See x. 6 note.
Unclean, unclean] Cp. marg. ref.
46. *dwell alone*] More properly, **dwell
apart**; that is, separated from the people.
Though thus excluded from general intercourse with society, it is not likely that
lepers ceased to be objects of sympathy and
kindness, such as they now are in those
Christian and Moslem countries in which
the Leprosy prevails. That they associated
together in the Holy Land, as they do at
present, is evident from 2 K. vii. 3; Luke
xvii. 12. It has been conjectured that a
habitation was provided for them outside
Jerusalem, on the hill Gareb (Bezetha),
which is mentioned only in Jer. xxxi. 39.
without the camp] Cp. marg. reff. A leper
polluted everything in the house which he

47 *h* without the camp *shall* his habitation *be*. ¶ The garment also that the plague of leprosy is in, *whether it be* a woollen garment,
48 or a linen garment; whether *it be* in the warp, or woof; of linen, or of woollen; whether in a skin, or in any ¹ thing made of skin;
49 and if the plague be greenish or reddish in the garment, or in the skin, either in the warp, or in the woof, or in any ² thing of skin; it *is* a plague of leprosy, and shall be shewed unto the
50 priest: and the priest shall look upon the plague, and shut up *it*
51 *that hath* the plague seven days: and he shall look on the plague on the seventh day: if the plague be spread in the garment, either in the warp, or in the woof, or in a skin, *or* in any work that is made of skin; the plague *is* ² a fretting leprosy; it *is*
52 unclean. He shall therefore burn that garment, whether warp or woof, in woollen or in linen, or anything of skin, wherein the plague is: for it *is* a fretting leprosy; it shall be burnt in the
53 fire. ¶ And if the priest shall look, and, behold, the plague be not spread in the garment, either in the warp, or in the woof, or
54 in anything of skin; then the priest shall command that they wash *the thing* wherein the plague *is*, and he shall shut it up
55 seven days more: and the priest shall look on the plague, after that it is washed: and, behold, *if* the plague have not changed his colour, and the plague be not spread; it *is* unclean; thou shalt burn it in the fire; it *is* fret inward, ³ *whether* it *be* bare
56 within or without. And if the priest look, and, behold, the plague *be* somewhat dark after the washing of it; then he shall rend it out of the garment, or out of the skin, or out of the warp,
57 or out of the woof: and if it appear still in the garment, either in the warp, or in the woof, or in any thing of skin; it *is* a spreading *plague:* thou shalt burn that wherein the plague *is*
58 with fire. And the garment, either warp, or woof, or whatsoever thing of skin it *be*, which thou shalt wash, if the plague be departed from them, then it shall be washed the second time, and
59 shall be clean. This *is* the law of the plague of leprosy in a garment of woollen or linen, either in the warp, or woof, or any thing of skins, to pronounce it clean, or to pronounce it unclean.

CHAP. 14. AND the LORD spake unto Moses, saying, This shall be
2 the law of the leper in the day of his cleansing: He *a* shall be

---

¹ Heb. *work of.*
² Heb. *vessel*, or, *instrument.*

³ Heb. whether *it be bald in the head thereof, or in the forehead thereof.*

---

entered. A separate space used to be provided for lepers in the Synagogues.

47. *The garment*] Rather, **The clothing,** referring to the ordinary dress of the Israelites in the wilderness; viz., a linen tunic with a fringe (Num. xv. 38) and a woollen cloak or blanket thrown on in colder weather.

47–49. Rather, *And the clothing in which there is a stroke of Leprosy, whether the stroke is in clothing of wool or in clothing of linen; or in yarn for warp or in yarn for woof, either for linen clothing or for woollen clothing; or in a skin of leather or in any article made of leather.*

51. *a fretting leprosy*] *i.e.* a malignant or corroding Leprosy. What was the nature of the Leprosy in clothing, which produced greenish or reddish spots, cannot be precisely determined. It was most likely destructive mildew, perhaps of more than one kind.

56. *somewhat dark*] Rather, **somewhat faint.** Cp. *v.* 6.

57, 58, 59. *either* in these verses, should be **or.** See *vv.* 47, 49.

It should be noticed that no religious or symbolical rite is prescribed for Leprosy in clothing. The priest had only to decide whether the process of decay was at work in the article presented to him and to pronounce accordingly. Compare the Leprosy in houses, xiv. 33–53.

XIV. 1. The Leper was excluded not only from the Sanctuary but from the camp. The ceremony of restoration which he had to undergo was therefore twofold. The first part, performed outside the camp,

3 brought unto the priest: and the priest shall go forth out of the camp; and the priest shall look, and, behold, *if* the plague of
4 leprosy be healed in the leper; then shall the priest command to take for him that is to be cleansed two [1]birds alive *and* clean,
5 and *b*cedar wood, and *c*scarlet, and *d*hyssop: and the priest shall command that one of the birds be killed in an earthen vessel over
6 running water: as for the living bird, he shall take it, and the cedar wood, and the scarlet, and the hyssop, and shall dip them and the living bird in the blood of the bird *that was* killed over
7 the running water: and he shall *e*sprinkle upon him that is to be cleansed from the leprosy *f*seven times, and shall pronounce him clean, and shall let the living bird loose [2]into the open field.
8 ¶And he that is to be cleansed *g*shall wash his clothes, and shave off all his hair, *h*and wash himself in water, that he may be clean: and after that he shall come into the camp, and
9 *i*shall tarry abroad out of his tent seven days. But it shall be on the seventh day, that he shall shave all his hair off his head and his beard and his eyebrows, even all his hair he shall shave off: and he shall wash his clothes, also he shall wash his flesh in
10 water, and he shall be clean. ¶And on the eighth day *k*he shall take two he lambs without blemish, and one ewe lamb [3]of the

b Num. 19. 6.
c Heb. 9. 19.
d Ps. 51. 7.

e Heb. 9. 13.
·*f* 2 Kin. 5. 10, 14.

g ch. 13. 6.
h ch. 11. 25.

i Num. 12. 15.

k Matt. 8. 4. Mark 1. 44. Luke 5. 14.

[1] Or, *sparrows.*   [2] Heb. *upon the face of the field.*   [3] Heb. *the daughter of her year.*

---

entitled him to come within and to mix with his brethren, 3–9. The second part, performed in the Court of the Tabernacle and separated from the first by an interval of seven days, restored him to all the privileges of the Covenant with Jehovah, 10–32.

4. These birds were provided by the priest for the man. They were not, like the offerings for the Altar, brought by the man himself (cp. *v.* 4 with *v.* 10), they were not presented nor brought near the Sanctuary, nor was any portion of them offered on the Altar.

cedar wood, and scarlet, and hyssop] These three substances were used as the common materials in rites of purification (cp. Ex. xii. 22; Num. xix. 8; Ps. li. 7; Heb. ix. 19): the *cedar*, or juniper, the resin or turpentine of which was a preservative against decay, and employed in medicines for Elephantiasis and other skin diseases: the *scarlet*, a "tongue," or band, of twice-dyed scarlet wool, with which the living bird, the hyssop, and the cedar wood were tied together when they were dipped into the blood and water: the colour expressing the rosiness associated with health and vital energy: and the *hyssop* (see Ex. xii. 22), probably the Caper plant, whose cleansing virtues as a medicine, and use in the treatment of ulcers and diseases of the skin allied to Leprosy, were known to the ancients. It has been conjectured that the scarlet band was used to tie the hyssop upon the cedar, so as to make a sort of brush, such as would be convenient for sprinkling.

5. *running water*] Literally, living water, *i.e.* water fresh from the spring (Gen. xxvi. 19; Num. xix. 17).

7. *seven times*] The seal of the Covenant, expressed in the number seven (cp. *v.* 9), was renewed in sprinkling him who, during his Leprosy, had lived as an outcast. The details of a restoration to health and freedom appear to be well expressed in the whole ceremony. Each of the birds represented the Leper. They were to be of a clean kind, because they stood for one of the chosen race. The death-like state of the Leper during his exclusion from the camp was expressed by killing one of the birds. The living bird was identified with the slain one by being dipped in his blood mixed with the spring water that figured the process of purification, while the cured Leper was identified with the rite by having the same water and blood sprinkled over him. The bird then liberated was a sign that the Leper left behind him all the symbols of the death disease and of the remedies associated with it, and was free to enjoy health and social freedom with his kind. Cp. Col. ii. 12.

9. The best of all types of the healing of the Spirit, was the healing of the Leper. In his formal cleansing, consecration, and atonement by sacrifice (see notes on xiv. 9–20), the ministers of the Sanctuary bore public witness that he was restored to the blessing of communion with his brethren and with Jehovah. Hence when the Son of God proved His divine mission by healing the lepers (Matt. xi. 5), He did not excuse them from going to the priest to "offer for the cleansing those things which Moses commanded" (Mark i. 44; Luke v. 14) "for a testimony to the people" (Matt. viii. 4).

10, 11. Two **young rams** from one to three years old (not lambs), a ewe lamb in

first year without blemish, and three tenth deals of fine flour *for*
11 *l*a meat offering, mingled with oil, and one log of oil. And the
priest that maketh *him* clean shall present the man that is to be
made clean, and those things, before the LORD, *at* the door of the
12 tabernacle of the congregation : and the priest shall take one he
lamb, and *m* offer him for a trespass offering, and the log of oil,
13 and *n* wave them *for* a wave offering before the LORD : and he
shall slay the lamb *o* in the place where he shall kill the sin
offering and the burnt offering, in the holy place : for *p* as the
sin offering *is* the priest's, *so is* the trespass offering : *q* it *is* most
14 holy : and the priest shall take *some* of the blood of the trespass
offering, and the priest shall put *it* *r* upon the tip of the right ear
of him that is to be cleansed, and upon the thumb of his right
15 hand, and upon the great toe of his right foot : and the priest
shall take *some* of the log of oil, and pour *it* into the palm of his
16 own left hand : and the priest shall dip his right finger in the
oil that *is* in his left hand, and shall sprinkle of the oil with his
17 finger seven times before the LORD : and of the rest of the oil
that *is* in his hand shall the priest put upon the tip of the right
ear of him that is to be cleansed, and upon the thumb of his
right hand, and upon the great toe of his right foot, upon the
18 blood of the trespass offering : and the remnant of the oil that
is in the priest's hand he shall pour upon the head of him that
is to be cleansed : *s* and the priest shall make an atonement
19 for him before the LORD. And the priest shall offer *t* the sin
offering, and make an atonement for him that is to be cleansed
from his uncleanness ; and afterward he shall kill the burnt
20 offering : and the priest shall offer the burnt offering and the
meat offering upon the altar : and the priest shall make an
21 atonement for him, and he shall be clean. ¶ And *u* if he *be*
poor, and *1* cannot get so much ; then he shall take one lamb *for*
a trespass offering *2* to be waved, to make an atonement for him,
and one tenth deal of fine flour mingled with oil for a meat
22 offering, and a log of oil ; *w* and two turtledoves, or two young
pigeons, such as he is able to get ; and the one shall be a sin
23 offering, and the other a burnt offering. *x* And he shall bring

l ch. 2. 1.
Num. 15.
4, 9.

m ch. 5. 2,
18.
& 6. 6, 7.
n Ex. 29. 24.
o Ex. 29. 11.
ch. 1. 5, 11.
& 4. 4, 24.
p ch. 7. 7.
q ch. 2. 3.
& 7. 6.
& 21. 22.
r Ex. 29. 20.
ch. 8. 23.

s ch. 4. 26.
t ch. 5. 1, 6.
& 12. 7.

u ch. 5. 7.
& 12. 8.

w ch. 12. 8.
& 15. 14, 15.

x ver. 10, 11.

---

1 Heb. *his hand reach not.*   2 Heb. *for a waving.*

---

her first year (see xii. 6), three tenth parts
of an ephah (something over ten pints and
a half) of fine flour mingled with oil, and a
log (about half a pint ; see xix. 35) of oil.
The priest presented both the man and his
offerings to Jehovah **at the entrance of the
Tent of meeting.** See i. 3.

12. This Trespass-offering, with its blood
and the oil, must be regarded as the main
feature in the ceremony : no alteration
being permitted even in the case of the poor
(*vv.* 21–23). There appears to be no other
case in which an entire victim was waved
(see vii. 30) before Jehovah. The Levites
are spoken of as "a wave offering," Num.
viii. 11–15 (see margin). The man in this
case, represented by his Trespass-offering,
was dedicated as a Wave-offering in like
manner.

13. *it is most holy*] See vi. 25 note.

14. In the same way, and with the same

significance as in viii. 23. It is said that a
portion of the blood was caught by the
priest in the palm of his hand as it ran from
the victim.

16. The sevenfold sprinkling of the oil
before the Sanctuary, in addition to the
waving of it, seems to have been intended
to consecrate it to represent the spiritual
gift consequent upon the Covenant, the
sealing of which had been figured by the
sacramental blood of the offering.

17, 19. *him that is to be cleansed*] **Of him
that has been cleansed.** The significance
of the act is similar to that in viii. 11, 15.

19, 20. The cleansed Leper was now in a
position to avail himself of the accustomed
law of sacrifice as one completely restored.
The ewe lamb was now offered in his behalf
as a Sin-offering, one of the young rams as
a Burnt-offering, and the fine flour mingled
with oil as a Meat-offering.

them on the eighth day for his cleansing unto the priest, unto the door of the tabernacle of the congregation, before the LORD.

24 *y*And the priest shall take the lamb of the trespass offering, and the log of oil, and the priest shall wave them *for* a wave offering
25 before the LORD: and he shall kill the lamb of the trespass offering, *z*and the priest shall take *some* of the blood of the trespass offering, and put *it* upon the tip of the right ear of him that is to be cleansed, and upon the thumb of his right hand, and
26 upon the great toe of his right foot: and the priest shall pour of
27 the oil into the palm of his own left hand: and the priest shall sprinkle with his right finger *some* of the oil that *is* in his left
28 hand seven times before the LORD: and the priest shall put of the oil that *is* in his hand upon the tip of the right ear of him that is to be cleansed, and upon the thumb of his right hand, and upon the great toe of his right foot, upon the place of the
29 blood of the trespass offering: and the rest of the oil that *is* in the priest's hand he shall put upon the head of him that is to be
30 cleansed, to make an atonement for him before the LORD. And he shall offer the one of *a*the turtledoves, or of the young
31 pigeons, such as he can get; *even* such as he is able to get, the one *for* a sin offering, and the other *for* a burnt offering, with the meat offering: and the priest shall make an atonement for him
32 that is to be cleansed before the LORD. This *is* the law *of him* in whom *is* the plague of leprosy, whose hand is not able to get
33 *b*that which pertaineth to his cleansing. ¶And the LORD spake
34 unto Moses and unto Aaron, saying, *c*When ye be come into the land of Canaan, which I give to you for a possession, and I put the
35 plague of leprosy in a house of the land of your possession; and he that owneth the house shall come and tell the priest, saying,
36 It seemeth to me *there is* as it were *d*a plague in the house: then the priest shall command that they ¹empty the house, before the priest go *into it* to see the plague, that all that *is* in the house be not made unclean: and afterward the priest shall go in to see
37 the house: and he shall look on the plague, and, behold, *if* the plague *be* in the walls of the house with hollow strakes, greenish
38 or reddish, which in sight *are* lower than the wall; then the priest shall go out of the house to the door of the house, and
39 shut up the house seven days: and the priest shall come again the seventh day, and shall look: and, behold, *if* the plague be
40 spread in the walls of the house; then the priest shall command that they take away the stones in which the plague *is*, and they
41 shall cast them into an unclean place without the city: and he shall cause the house to be scraped within round about, and they shall pour out the dust that they scrape off without the city into
42 an unclean place: and they shall take other stones, and put *them* in the place of those stones; and he shall take other morter, and

y ver. 12.

z ver. 14.

a ver. 22.
ch. 15. 15.

b ver. 10.
c Gen. 17. 8.
Num. 32. 22.
Deut. 7. 1.
& 32. 49.

d Ps. 91. 10.
Prov. 3. 33.
Zech. 5. 4.

¹ Or, *prepare.*

33–53. This section is separated from that on Leprosy in clothing (xiii. 47–59) with which it would seem to be naturally connected, and is placed last of all the laws concerning Leprosy, probably on account of its being wholly prospective. While the Israelites were in the Wilderness, the materials of their dwellings were of nearly the same nature as those of their clothing, and would be liable to the same sort of decay.

They were therefore included under the same law.

I put the plague] Jehovah here speaks as the Lord of all created things, determining their decay and destruction as well as their production. Cf. Isai. xlv. 6, 7; Jonah iv. 7; Matt. xxi. 20.

37. *hollow strakes*, &c.] Rather, **depressed spots of dark green or dark red, appearing beneath** (the surface of) **the wall.**

43 shall plaister the house. And if the plague come again, and break out in the house, after that he hath taken away the stones, and after he hath scraped the house, and after it is plaistered; 44 then the priest shall come and look, and, behold, *if* the plague be spread in the house, it *is* *e*a fretting leprosy in the house: it 45 *is* unclean. And he shall break down the house, the stones of it, and the timber thereof, and all the morter of the house; and he shall carry *them* forth out of the city into an unclean place. 46 Moreover he that goeth into the house all the while that it is 47 shut up shall be unclean until the even. And he that lieth in the house shall wash his clothes; and he that eateth in the house 48 shall wash his clothes. And if the priest ¹shall come in, and look *upon it*, and, behold, the plague hath not spread in the house, after the house was plaistered: then the priest shall 49 pronounce the house clean, because the plague is healed. And *f*he shall take to cleanse the house two birds, and cedar wood, 50 and scarlet, and hyssop: and he shall kill the one of the birds in 51 an earthen vessel over running water: and he shall take the cedar wood, and the hyssop, and the scarlet, and the living bird, and dip them in the blood of the slain bird, and in the running 52 water, and sprinkle the house seven times: and he shall cleanse the house with the blood of the bird, and with the running water, and with the living bird, and with the cedar wood, and with the 53 hyssop, and with the scarlet: but he shall let go the living bird out of the city into the open fields, and *g*make an atonement for 54 the house: and it shall be clean. ¶ This *is* the law for all manner 55 of plague of leprosy, and *h*scall, and for the *i*leprosy of a garment, 56 *k*and of a house, and *l*for a rising, and for a scab, and for a bright 57 spot: to *m*teach ²when *it is* unclean, and when *it is* clean: this *is* the law of leprosy.

CHAP. 15. AND the LORD spake unto Moses and to Aaron, saying, 2 Speak unto the children of Israel, and say unto them, *a*When any man hath a ³running issue out of his flesh, *because of* his 3 issue he *is* unclean. And this shall be his uncleanness in his issue: whether his flesh run with his issue, or his flesh be stopped 4 from his issue, it *is* his uncleanness. Every bed, whereon he lieth that hath the issue, is unclean: and every ⁴thing, whereon he 5 sitteth, shall be unclean. And whosoever toucheth his bed shall wash his clothes, *b*and bathe *himself* in water, and be unclean 6 until the even. And he that sitteth on *any* thing whereon he sat that hath the issue shall wash his clothes, and bathe *himself* in 7 water, and be unclean until the even. And he that toucheth the flesh of him that hath the issue shall wash his clothes, and bathe 8 *himself* in water, and be unclean until the even. And if he that hath the issue spit upon him that is clean; then he shall wash

e ch. 13. 51.
Zech. 5. 4.

f ver. 4.

g ver. 20.

h ch. 13. 30.
i ch. 13. 47.
k ver. 34.
l ch. 13. 2.
m Deut. 24. 8.
Ezek. 44. 23.
a ch. 22. 4.
Num. 5. 2.
2 Sam. 3. 29.
Matt. 9. 20.
Mark 5. 25.
Luke 8. 43.

b ch. 11. 25.
& 17. 15.

¹ Heb. *in coming in shall come in, &c.*   ² Heb. *in the day of the unclean, and in the day of the clean.*   ³ Or, *running of the reins.*   ⁴ Heb. *vessel.*

---

49. *cleanse the house*] Strictly, *purge the house from sin.* The same word is used in *v.* 52; and in *v.* 53 it is said, " and make an atonement for it." Such language is used figuratively when it is applied to things, not to persons. The Leprosy in houses, the Leprosy in clothing, and the terrible disease in the human body, were representative forms of decay which taught the lesson that all created things, in their own nature, are

passing away, and are only maintained for their destined uses during an appointed period, by the power of Jehovah.

XV. This chapter would seem to take its place more naturally before the twelfth, with the subject of which it is immediately connected. Cp. especially xii. 2 with xv. 19. It stands here between two chapters, with neither of which has it any close connection.

his clothes, and bathe *himself* in water, and be unclean until
9 the even. And what saddle soever he rideth upon that hath the
10 issue shall be unclean. And whosoever toucheth any thing that
was under him shall be unclean until the even: and he that
beareth *any of* those things shall wash his clothes, and bathe
11 *himself* in water, and be unclean until the even. And whomsoever he toucheth that hath the issue, and hath not rinsed his
hands in water, he shall wash his clothes, and bathe *himself* in
12 water, and be unclean until the even. And the ^cvessel of earth, | *c* ch. 6. 28.
that he toucheth which hath the issue, shall be broken: and | & 11. 32, 33.
13 every vessel of wood shall be rinsed in water. And when he that
hath an issue is cleansed of his issue; then ^dhe shall number to | *d* ver. 28.
himself seven days for his cleansing, and wash his clothes, and | ch. 14. 8.
14 bathe his flesh in running water, and shall be clean. And on
the eighth day he shall take to him ^etwo turtledoves, or two | *e* ch. 14. 22,
young pigeons, and come before the LORD unto the door of the | 23.
tabernacle of the congregation, and give them unto the priest:
15 and the priest shall offer them, ^fthe one *for* a sin offering, and | *f* ch. 14. 30,
the other *for* a burnt offering; ^gand the priest shall make an | 31.
16 atonement for him before the LORD for his issue. ¶And ^hif any | *g* ch. 14. 19,
man's seed of copulation go out from him, then he shall wash all | 31.
17 his flesh in water, and be unclean until the even. And every | *h* ch. 22. 4.
garment, and every skin, whereon is the seed of copulation, | Deut. 23. 10.
18 shall be washed with water, and be unclean until the even. The
woman also with whom man shall lie *with* seed of copulation,
they shall *both* bathe *themselves* in water, and ⁱbe unclean until | *i* 1 Sam. 21. 4.
19 the even. ¶And ^kif a woman have an issue, *and* her issue in her | *k* ch. 12. 2.
flesh be blood, she shall be ¹put apart seven days: and whosoever
20 toucheth her shall be unclean until the even. And every thing
that she lieth upon in her separation shall be unclean: every
21 thing also that she sitteth upon shall be unclean. And whosoever toucheth her bed shall wash his clothes, and bathe *himself*
22 in water, and be unclean until the even. And whosoever toucheth any thing that she sat upon shall wash his clothes, and
23 bathe *himself* in water, and be unclean until the even. And if
it *be* on *her* bed, or on anything whereon she sitteth, when he
24 toucheth it, he shall be unclean until the even. And ^lif any man | *l* See ch. 20.
lie with her at all, and her flowers be upon him, he shall be un- | 18.
clean seven days; and all the bed whereon he lieth shall be unclean.
25 ¶And if ^ma woman have an issue of her blood many days out | *m* Matt. 9.
of the time of her separation, or if it run beyond the time of her | 20.
separation; all the days of the issue of her uncleanness shall be | Mark 5. 25.
| Luke 8. 43.
26 as the days of her separation: she *shall be* unclean. Every bed
whereon she lieth all the days of her issue shall be unto her as
the bed of her separation: and whatsoever she sitteth upon
27 shall be unclean, as the uncleanness of her separation. And
whosoever toucheth those things shall be unclean, and shall wash
his clothes, and bathe *himself* in water, and be unclean until the
28 even. But ⁿif she be cleansed of her issue, then she shall num- | *n* ver. 13.

¹ Heb. *in her separation*.

---

13. The mere cessation of the issue does
not make him clean : he must wait seven
days, &c., preparatory to his offering sacrifice.

16–18. Most of the ancient religions
made a similar recognition of impurity and
of the need of purification.

17. *every garment*] Cp. Jude, *v.* 23.

24. This must refer to an unexpected occurrence. Intercourse during the acknowledged period was a heavy crime, and was
to be punished by "cutting off" (xviii. 19,
xx. 18; Ezek. xviii. 6).

ber to herself seven days, and after that she shall be clean.
29 And on the eighth day she shall take unto her two turtles, or
two young pigeons, and bring them unto the priest, to the door
30 of the tabernacle of the congregation. And the priest shall offer
the one *for* a sin offering, and the other *for* a burnt offering;
and the priest shall make an atonement for her before the LORD
31 for the issue of her uncleanness. ¶Thus shall ye *o*separate the
children of Israel from their uncleanness; that they die not in
their uncleanness, when they *p* defile my tabernacle that *is* among
32 them. ¶ *q*This *is* the law of him that hath an issue, *r*and *of him*
33 whose seed goeth from him, and is defiled therewith; *s*and of her
that is sick of her flowers, and of him that hath an issue, of the
man, *t*and of the woman, *u*and of him that lieth with her that is
unclean.

CHAP. 16. AND the LORD spake unto Moses after *a*the death of the
two sons of Aaron, when they offered before the LORD, and died;
2 and the LORD said unto Moses, Speak unto Aaron thy brother,
that he *b*come not at all times into the holy *place* within the vail
before the mercy seat, which *is* upon the ark; that he die not:
3 for *c*I will appear in the cloud upon the mercy seat. Thus shall
Aaron *d*come into the holy *place:* *e*with a young bullock for a
4 sin offering, and a ram for a burnt offering. He shall put on
*f*the holy linen coat, and he shall have the linen breeches upon
his flesh, and shall be girded with a linen girdle, and with the
linen mitre shall he be attired: these *are* holy garments; there-
5 fore *g*shall he wash his flesh in water, and *so* put them on. And
he shall take of *h*the congregation of the children of Israel two

o ch. 11. 47.
Deut. 24. 8.
Ezek. 44. 23.
p Num. 5. 3.
& 19. 13, 20.
Ezek. 5. 11.
& 23. 38.
q ver. 2.
r ver. 16.
s ver. 19.
t ver. 25.
u ver. 24.

a ch. 10. 1, 2.
b Ex. 30, 10.
ch. 23. 27.
Heb. 9. 7.
c Ex. 25, 22.
1 Kin. 8. 10.
d Heb. 9. 7.
e ch. 4. 3.
f Ex. 28. 39,
42, 43.
ch. 6. 10.
Ezek. 44.
17. 18.
g Ex. 30. 20.
ch. 8. 6, 7.
h See ch. 4.
14.
Num. 29.11.
2 Chr. 29. 21.
Ezra 6. 17.
Ezek. 45.
22, 23.

31–33. This solemn admonition is addressed to Moses and Aaron, see *v.* 1.

31. *my tabernacle*] Strictly, *my dwelling-
place* (*mishkān*), as in viii. 10, xvii. 4, xxvi.
11. The word rendered "tabernacle" elsewhere in Leviticus, is properly **Tent.** See
Ex. xxvi. 1 note.

XVI. 1–34. The Day of Atonement, or,
as it is in the Hebrew, the Day of Atonements, is called by the Rabbins the Day,
and by St. Luke (probably) "the Fast."
See Acts xxvii. 9. Cp. with this chap.
xxiii. 26–32.

1. The reference to the death of Nadab
and Abihu is a notice of the occasion on
which the instructions were given, well calculated to add point and emphasis to the
solemn admonition to the High priest in
the second verse. The death of his sons (x. 2),
for drawing nigh to Jehovah in an unauthorised manner, was to serve as a warning to
Aaron himself never to transgress in this
respect.

2. *the holy place within the vail*] See Ex.
xxvi. 33, 34; Heb. ix. 3.

the cloud] Cp. Ex. xvi. 10 note.

the mercy seat] See Ex. xxv. 17 note.

3. *holy place*] This name here denotes **the
Sanctuary,** the whole sacred enclosure, the
Court of the Tabernacle. The offerings were
for Aaron and his sons, supplied by himself.

4. The High priest when he changed his
dress on this day was required **to bathe**

himself. In his "golden garments" he had,
on this day, and for the previous week, to
offer the regular daily sacrifices, and to perform the other sacerdotal duties of the
Sanctuary, which were usually performed
by a common priest.—The dress of white
linen, which he now put on, appears to
have been like the ordinary dress of the
common priests, except in the substitution
of a linen mitre for the bonnet (or **cap**), and
of a plain linen girdle for the variegated
one (Ex. xxviii. 40–43 notes). In preparing to
enter the Holy of Holies, he attired himself
in spotless white as a token of the holiness
without which none, in a spiritual sense,
can enter the divine Presence. He thus became a more distinct foreshadow of the
greater High Priest (Heb. vii. 26, vi. 19,
20). This significance belonged to the High
priest only in his official capacity as mediator: in his own person he had infirmity,
and was required "to offer up sacrifice,
first for his own sins, and then for the
people's." Heb. vii. 27. See on ix. 7–14.
On the same ground it was that, although
as a mediator he had to enter the Most
Holy place, as sinful man he needed the
cloud of incense as a vail to come between
him and the holiness of Jehovah. See *v.* 13.

5. *take of the congregation*] i.e. they were
to be supplied at the public cost.

two kids of the goats] This should be, **two
shaggy he-goats** (iv. 23 note), of the same
colour, size, and value.

kids of the goats for a sin offering, and one ram for a burnt
6 offering. And Aaron shall offer his bullock of the sin offering,
which *is* for himself, and *i*make an atonement for himself, and
7 for his house. And he shall take the two goats, and present
them before the LORD *at* the door of the tabernacle of the con-
8 gregation. And Aaron shall cast lots upon the two goats; one
9 lot for the LORD, and the other lot for the ¹scapegoat. And
Aaron shall bring the goat upon which the LORD's lot ²fell, and
10 offer him *for* a sin offering. But the goat, on which the lot fell
to be the scapegoat, shall be presented alive before the LORD, to
make *k*an atonement with him, *and* to let him go for a scape-
11 goat into the wilderness. ¶And Aaron shall bring the bullock
of the sin offering, which *is* for himself, and shall make an
atonement for himself, and for his house, and shall kill the bul-
12 lock of the sin offering which *is* for himself: and he shall take
*l*a censer full of burning coals of fire from off the altar before the
LORD, and his hands full of *m*sweet incense beaten small, and
13 bring *it* within the vail: *n*and he shall put the incense upon the
fire before the LORD, that the cloud of the incense may cover the
14 *o*mercy seat that *is* upon the testimony, that he die not: and*p*he
shall take of the blood of the bullock, and *q*sprinkle *it* with his
finger upon the mercy seat eastward ; and before the mercy seat
shall he sprinkle of the blood with his finger seven times.

i ch. 9, 7.
Heb. 5. 2.
& 7. 27, 28.

k 1 John 2.
2.

l ch. 10. 1.
Num. 16.
18. 46.
Rev. 8. 5.
m Ex. 30. 34.
n Ex. 30. 1.
Num. 16. 7.
Rev. 8. 3, 4.
o Ex. 25, 21.
p ch. 4. 5.
Heb. 9. 13,
25. & 10. 4.
q ch. 4. 6.

¹ Heb. *Azazel*.　　　　² Heb. *went up*.

---

6. *shall offer*] Rather, **shall present**, as
in *vv.* 7, 10, &c. The word expresses the
formal act of placing the victims in front of
the entrance of the Tabernacle.

for himself, and for his house] *i.e.* for
himself as the High priest and all the common priests. Cp. ix. 7-14 note.

8. The two goats formed a single Sin-
offering, *v.* 5. To bring out the meaning of
the sacrifice it was necessary that the act of
a living being should be performed after
death. See *v.* 22 note. As this could not
possibly be visibly set forth with a single
victim, two were employed, as in the case
of the birds in the rite for the healed leper
(xiv. 4–6).

for the scapegoat] Rather, **for Azazel**. The
word occurs nowhere else in the Old Testament but in this chapter, and is probably derived from a root in use in Arabic,
but not in Hebrew, signifying *to remove*, or
to separate.

Azazel is the pre-Mosaic name of an evil
personal being placed in opposition to Jehovah. Each goat, having been presented to
Jehovah before the lots were cast, stood in
a sacrificial relation to Him. The casting
of lots was an appeal to the decision of Jehovah (cp. Josh. vii. 16, 17, xiv. 2 ; Prov.
xvi. 33 ; Acts i. 26, &c.) ; it was therefore
His act to choose one of the goats for His
service in the way of ordinary sacrifice, the
other for His service in carrying off the sins
to Azazel (see note on *v.* 22). By this expressive outward sign the sins were sent
back to the author of sin himself, "the entirely separate one," who was banished from
the realm of grace.

The goat itself did not lose the sacred
character with which it had been endued in
being presented before Jehovah. It was, as
much as the slain goat, a figure of Him Who
bore our griefs and carried our sorrows, on
Whom the Lord laid the iniquity of us all
(Is. liii. 4, 6), that we might become a sanctified Church to be presented unto Himself,
not having spot or wrinkle or any such
thing (Eph. v. 26, 27).

10. *on which the lot fell to be the scapegoat*]
Rather, **on which the lot 'for Azazel' fell**.

an atonement with him] The goat "for
Azazel" was to be considered as taking his
part along with the other goat in the great
symbol of atonement.

for a scapegoat into the wilderness] Rather,
"**to Azazel**, into the Wilderness."

11-25. It is important, in reference to
the meaning of the Day of Atonement, to
observe the order of the rites as they are
described in these verses.

12. *a censer*] See Ex. xxv. 38 note.

the altar before the LORD] *i.e.* the Altar of
Burnt-offering on which the fire was always
burning.

14. The High priest must have come out
from the Most Holy place to fetch the
blood, leaving the censer smoking within,
and then have entered again within the
vail. He sprinkled the blood seven times
upon the Mercy seat, **on its east side** (not
"eastward"), and then seven times upon
the floor in front of it. If the Mercy seat
may be regarded as an Altar, the holiest
one of the three, on this one occasion in the
year atonement was thus made for it, as for
the other Altars, with sacrificial blood.

r Heb. 2. 17.
& 5. 2.
& 9. 7. 28.
s ver. 2.
Heb. 6. 19.

t See Ex. 29.
36.
Ezek. 45. 18.
Heb. 9. 22.

u See Ex.
34. 3.
Luke 1. 10.

x Ex. 30. 10.
ch. 4. 7, 18.

y Ezek. 43.
20.
z ver. 16.
Ezek. 45. 20.

a Isai. 53. 6.

b Isai. 53.
11, 12.
John 1. 29.
Heb. 9. 28.
1 Pet. 2. 24.

15 ¶ ᵣThen shall he kill the goat of the sin offering, that *is* for the people, and bring his blood ˢwithin the vail, and do with that blood as he did with the blood of the bullock, and sprinkle it
16 upon the mercy seat, and before the mercy seat: and he shall ᵗmake an atonement for the holy *place*, because of the uncleanness of the children of Israel, and because of their transgressions in all their sins: and so shall he do for the tabernacle of the congregation, that ¹remaineth among them in the midst of their
17 uncleanness. ᵘAnd there shall be no man in the tabernacle of the congregation when he goeth in to make an atonement in the holy *place*, until he come out, and have made an atonement for himself, and for his household, and for all the congregation of
18 Israel. And he shall go out unto the altar that *is* before the LORD, and ˣmake an atonement for it; and shall take of the blood of the bullock, and of the blood of the goat, and put *it*
19 upon the horns of the altar round about. And he shall sprinkle of the blood upon it with his finger seven times, and cleanse it, and ʸhallow it from the uncleanness of the children of Israel.
20 ¶ And when he hath made an end of ᶻreconciling the holy *place*, and the tabernacle of the congregation, and the altar, he shall
21 bring the live goat: and Aaron shall lay both his hands upon the head of the live goat, and confess over him all the iniquities of the children of Israel, and all their transgressions in all their sins, ᵃputting them upon the head of the goat, and shall send
22 *him* away by the hand of ²a fit man into the wilderness: and the goat shall ᵇbear upon him all their iniquities unto a land ³not inhabited: and he shall let go the goat in the wilderness.

¹ Heb. *dwelleth*.   ² Heb. *a man of opportunity*.   ³ Heb. *of separation*.

---

15. Having completed the atonement in the Holy of Holies on behalf of the priests, the High priest had now to do the same thing on behalf of the people.

16. *the "holy place"*] Here the place within the vail, the Holy of Holies.

tabernacle of the congregation] **Tent of meeting.** Atonement was now to be made for the Tabernacle as a whole. The sense is very briefly expressed, but there seems to be no room to doubt that the High priest was to sprinkle the blood of each of the victims before the Altar of Incense, as he had done before the mercy seat within the vail; and also to touch with blood the horns of the Altar of Incense (Ex. xxx. 10).

that remaineth among them in the midst of their uncleanness] Cp. *v.* 19. The most sacred earthly things which came into contact with the nature of man needed from time to time to be cleansed and sanctified by the blood of the Sin-offerings which had been taken into the Presence of Jehovah. See Ex. xxviii. 38 note.

18. The order of the ceremony required that atonement should first be made for the Most Holy Place with the Mercy seat, then for the Holy Place with the Golden Altar, and then for the Altar in the Court. See *vv.* 20, 33. The horns of the Brazen altar were touched with the blood, as they were in the ordinary Sin-offerings. iv. 25, 30, 34.

of the blood of the bullock, and of the blood of the goat] Some of the blood of the two victims was mingled together in a basin.

21. *confess over him*] The form of confession used on this occasion in later times was:—"O Lord, Thy people, the house of Israel, have transgressed, they have rebelled, they have sinned before Thee. I beseech Thee now absolve their transgressions, their rebellion, and their sin that they have sinned against Thee, as it is written in the law of Moses Thy servant, that on this day he shall make atonement for you to cleanse you from all your sins, and ye shall be clean."

a fit man] Literally, *a timely man*, or *a man at hand*. Tradition says that the man was appointed for this work the year before.

22. *unto a land not inhabited*] **Unto a place cut off**, or (as in the margin) a place "of separation."

It is evident that the one signification of the ceremony of this goat was the complete removal of the sins which were confessed over him. No symbol could so plainly set forth the completeness of Jehovah's acceptance of the penitent, as a Sin-offering in which a life was given up for the Altar, and yet a living being survived to carry away all sin and uncleanness.

23 ¶ And Aaron shall come into the tabernacle of the congregation, ^cand shall put off the linen garments, which he put on when he 24 went into the holy *place*, and shall leave them there: and he shall wash his flesh with water in the holy place, and put on his garments, and come forth, ^dand offer his burnt offering, and the burnt offering of the people, and make an atonement for himself, 25 and for the people. And ^ethe fat of the sin offering shall he 26 burn upon the altar. ¶ And he that let go the goat for the scapegoat shall wash his clothes, ^f and bathe his flesh in water, 27 and afterward come into the camp. ^g And the bullock *for* the sin offering, and the goat *for* the sin offering, whose blood was brought in to make atonement in the holy *place*, shall *one* carry forth without the camp; and they shall burn in the fire their 28 skins, and their flesh, and their dung. And he that burneth them shall wash his clothes, and bathe his flesh in water, and after-29 ward he shall come into the camp. ¶ And *this* shall be a statute for ever unto you: *that* ^hin the seventh month, on the tenth *day* of the month, ye shall afflict your souls, and do no work at all, *whether it be* one of your own country, or a stranger that 30 sojourneth among you: for on that day shall *the priest* make an atonement for you, to ⁱcleanse you, *that* ye may be clean from 31 all your sins before the LORD. ^kIt *shall* be a sabbath of rest unto you, and ye shall afflict your souls, by a statute for ever. 32 ^lAnd the priest, whom he shall anoint, and whom he shall ¹ ^mconsecrate to minister in the priest's office in his father's stead, shall make the atonement, and ⁿshall put on the linen clothes, 33 *even* the holy garments: and ^ohe shall make an atonement for the holy sanctuary, and he shall make an atonement for the

¹ Heb. *fill his hand.*

c Ezek. 42. 14.
& 44. 19.

d ver. 3, &.

e ch. 4. 10.
f ch. 15. 5.

g ch. 4. 12, 21. & 6. 30.
Heb. 13. 11.

h Ex. 30. 10.
ch. 23. 27.
Num. 29. 7.
Isai. 58. 3.
Dan. 10. 3.
i Jer. 51, 2.
Jer. 33. 8.
Eph. 5. 26.
Heb. 9. 13, 14.
1 John 1. 7.
k ch. 23. 32.
l ch. 4. 3, 5.
m Ex. 29. 29.
Num. 20. 26,
28.
n ver. 4.
o ver. 6, 16,
17, 18, 24.

26–28. Both he who led away the goat, and he who burned the parts of the Sin-offerings had to purify themselves. They who went out of the camp during a religious solemnity incurred uncleanness; hence the need of purification.

27. *shall burn in the fire*] *i.e.*, **consume in the fire**, not burn sacrificially. See i. 9.

29. *seventh month, on the tenth day*] The month Ethanim or Tisri, as being the seventh in the Sacred year, has been called the Sabbatical month. On the first day was celebrated the Feast of Trumpets (xxiii. 24), the tenth day was the Day of Atonement, and on the fourteenth day the Feast of Tabernacles commenced (xxiii. 24 note, Ex. xxiii. 16).

afflict your souls] The old term for fasting; but its meaning evidently embraces, not only abstinence from food, but that penitence and humiliation which give scope and purpose to the outward act of fasting. The Day of Atonement was the only public fast commanded by the Law of Moses. See further directions in xxiii. 27–32. On fasts observed in later times, see Zech. viii. 19, and marg. reff.

a stranger that sojourneth among you] Rather, **the foreigner who dwelleth among you.** See Ex. xx. 10 note. The meaning is,

one of foreign blood, who dwelt with the Israelites, had abjured false gods, and had become familiarly known to his neighbours, *e.g.* the Kenites (Judg. iv. 11, &c.); the Gibeonites (Josh. ix.); and a considerable portion of the "mixed multitude" (cp. Ex. xii. 38, 48). As the foreigner had the blessing and protection of the Law he was bound to obey its statutes.

33, 34. A summary of what was done on the Day of Atonement.

The Day was intended as an occasion for expressing more completely than could be done in the ordinary sacrifices the spiritual truth of atonement, with a fuller acknowledgment of the sinfulness and weakness of man and of the corruptible nature of all earthly things, even of those most solemnly consecrated and devoted to the service of God. It belonged to its observances especially to set forth, by the entrance of the High priest into the Holy of Holies, that atonement could only be effected before the throne of Jehovah Himself (cp. Matt. ix. 6; Mark ii. 7-10; Heb. iv. 16, &c.); and, by the goat sent into the Wilderness, that the sins atoned for were not only forgiven, but carried wholly away. See *v.* 22 note. The rites were a solemn gathering up of all other rites of atonement, so as to make them point more expressively to the

tabernacle of the congregation, and for the altar, and he shall make an atonement for the priests, and for all the people of the

34 congregation. *p* And this shall be an everlasting statute unto you, to make an atonement for the children of Israel for all their sins *q* once a year. And he did as the LORD commanded Moses.

CHAP. **17.** AND the LORD spake unto Moses, saying, Speak unto
2 Aaron, and unto his sons, and unto all the children of Israel, and say unto them; This *is* the thing which the LORD hath com-
3 manded, saying, What man soever *there be* of the house of Israel, *a* that killeth an ox, or lamb, or goat, in the camp, or that
4 killeth *it* out of the camp, *b* and bringeth it not unto the door of the tabernacle of the congregation, to offer an offering unto the LORD before the tabernacle of the LORD; blood shall be *c* imputed unto that man; he hath shed blood; and that man *d* shall
5 be cut off from among his people: to the end that the children of Israel may bring their sacrifices, *e* which they offer in the open field, even that they may bring them unto the LORD, unto the door of the tabernacle of the congregation, unto the priest, and
6 offer them *for* peace offerings unto the LORD. And the priest *f* shall sprinkle the blood upon the altar of the LORD *at* the door of the tabernacle of the congregation, and *g* burn the fat for a
7 sweet savour unto the LORD. And they shall no more offer their sacrifices *h* unto devils, after whom they *i* have gone a whoring. This shall be a statute for ever unto them throughout
8 their generations. ¶ And thou shalt say unto them, Whatsoever man *there be* of the house of Israel, or of the strangers which

---

revelation to come of God's gracious purpose to man in sending His Son to be delivered for our offences, and to rise again for our justification ; to be our great High Priest for ever after the order of Melchisedec, and to enter for us within the vail (Rom. iv. 25; Heb. vi. 20). The Day of Atonement expanded the meaning of every Sin-offering, in the same way as the services for Good Friday and Ash Wednesday expand the meaning of our Litany days throughout the year, and Easter Day, that of our Sundays.

XVII. This chapter, in its immediate bearing on the daily life of the Israelites, stands as the first of four (xvii.-xx.) which set forth practical duties, directing the Israelites to walk, not in the way of the heathen, but according to the ordinances of Jehovah.

3–7. Every domesticated animal that was slain for food was a sort of Peace-offering (*v.* 5). This law could only be kept as long as the children of Israel dwelt in their camp in the Wilderness. The restriction was removed before they settled in the Holy Land, where their numbers and diffusion over the country would have rendered its strict observance impossible. See Deut. xii. 15, 16, 20–24.

4. *blood shall be imputed unto that man*] *i.e.* he has incurred guilt in shedding blood in an unlawful manner.

cut off] See Ex. xxxi. 14 note.

5. Rather, **May bring their beasts for** slaughter, which they (now) slaughter in the open field, even that they may bring them before Jehovah to the entrance of the Tent of meeting unto the priests, and slaughter them as Peace-offerings to Jehovah.

7. *devils*] The word in the original is the "shaggy goat" of iv. 23. But it is sometimes employed, as here, to denote an object of heathen worship or a demon dwelling in the deserts (2 Chr. xi. 15; Isai. xiii. 21, xxxiv. 14). The worship of the goat, accompanied by the foulest rites, prevailed in Lower Egypt ; and the Israelites may have been led into this snare while they dwelt in Egypt.

This law for the slaughtering of animals was not merely to exclude idolatry from the chosen nation. It had a more positive and permanent purpose. It bore witness to the sanctity of life ; it served to remind the people of the solemnity of the grant of the lives of all inferior creatures made to Noah (Gen. ix. 2, 3) ; it purged and directed towards Jehovah the feelings in respect to animal food which seem to be common to man's nature; and it connected a habit of thanksgiving with the maintenance of our human life by means of daily food. 1 Tim. iv. 3–5. Having acknowledged that the animal belonged to Jehovah the devout Hebrew received back its flesh as Jehovah's gift.

8. *the strangers which sojourn*] The foreigners who dwell. See xvi. 29 note.

sojourn among you, *k*that offereth a burnt offering or sacrifice, 9 and *l*bringeth it not unto the door of the tabernacle of the congregation, to offer it unto the LORD ; even that man shall be cut 10 off from among his people. ¶ *m*And whatsoever man *there be* of the house of Israel, or of the strangers that sojourn among you, that eateth any manner of blood ; *n*I will even set my face against that soul that eateth blood, and will cut him off from among his 11 people. *o*For the life of the flesh *is* in the blood : and I have given it to you upon the altar *p*to make an atonement for your souls : for *q*it *is* the blood *that* maketh an atonement for the soul. 12 Therefore I said unto the children of Israel, No soul of you shall eat blood, neither shall any stranger that sojourneth among you 13 eat blood. ¶ And whatsoever man *there be* of the children of Israel, or of the strangers that sojourn among you, [1]which *r*hunteth and catcheth any beast or fowl that may be eaten ; he shall even *s*pour out the blood thereof, and *t*cover it with dust. 14 *u*For *it is* the life of all flesh ; the blood of it *is* for the life thereof : therefore I said unto the children of Israel, Ye shall eat the blood of no manner of flesh : for the life of all flesh *is* 15 the blood thereof : whosoever eateth it shall be cut off. ¶ *x*And every soul that eateth [2]that which died *of itself*, or that which

k ch. 1. 2, 3.
l ver. 4.
m Gen. 9. 4.
ch. 3. 17.
Deut. 12. 16.
1 Sam. 14.
33.
Ezek. 44.
n ch. 20. 3.
Jer. 44, 11.
Ezek. 14. 8.
o ver. 14.
p Matt. 26.
28.
Rom. 3. 25.
Eph. 1. 7.
Col. 1. 14.
Heb. 13. 12.
1 Pet. 1. 2.
1 John 1. 7.
Rev. 1. 5.
q Heb. 9. 22.
r ch. 7. 26.
s Deut.12.24.
t Ezek. 24.7.
u ver. 11.12.
x Ex. 22. 31.
ch. 22. 8.
Deut. 14. 21.

[1] Heb. *that hunteth any hunting.*   [2] Heb. *a carcase.*

---

or sacrifice] *i.e.*, a slaughtered offering of any kind, generally a Peace-offering.

10-14. The prohibition to eat blood is repeated in seven places in the Pentateuch, but in this passage two distinct grounds are given for the prohibition : first, its own nature as the vital fluid; secondly, its consecration in sacrificial worship.

11. Rather, For the soul of the flesh is in the blood ; and I have ordained it for you upon the Altar, to make atonement for your souls ; for the blood it is which makes atonement by means of the soul. In the Old Testament there are three words relating to the constitution of man ; (*a*) "life" as opposed to death (Gen. i. 20; Deut. xxx. 15); (*b*) the "soul" as distinguished from the body ; the individual life either in man or beast, whether united to the body during life, or separated from the body after death (cp. Gen. ii. 7) ; (*c*) the "spirit" as opposed to the f sh (Rom. viii. 6), and as distinguished from the life of the flesh ; the highest element in man ; that which, in its true condition, holds communion with God. The soul has its abode in the blood as long as life lasts. In *v.* 14, the soul is identified with the blood, as it is in Genesis ix. 4 ; Deut. xii. 23. That the blood is rightly thus distinguished from all other constituents of the body is acknowledged by the highest authorities in physiology.

"It is the fountain of life (says Harvey), the first to live, and the last to die, and the primary seat of the animal soul ; it lives and is nourished of itself, and by no other part of the human body." John Hunter inferred that it is the seat of life, because all the parts of the frame are formed and nourished from it. "And if (says he) it has

not life previous to this operation, it must then acquire it in the act of forming: for we all give our assent to the existence of life in the parts when once formed." Milne Edwards observes that, "if an animal be bled till it falls into a state of syncope, and the further loss of blood is not prevented, all muscular motion quickly ceases, respiration is suspended, the heart pauses from its action, life is no longer manifested by any outward sign, and death soon becomes inevitable ; but if, in this state, the blood of another animal of the same species be injected into the veins of the one to all appearance dead, we see with amazement this inanimate body return to life, gaining accessions of vitality with each new quantity of blood that is introduced, by-and-bye beginning to breathe freely, moving with ease, and finally walking as it was wont to do, and recovering completely." More or less distinct traces of the recognition of blood as the vehicle of life are found in Greek and Roman writers. The knowledge of the ancients on the subject may indeed have been based on the mere observation that an animal loses its life when it loses its blood : but it may deepen our sense of the wisdom and significance of the Law of Moses to know that the fact which it sets forth so distinctly and consistently, and in such pregnant connection, is so clearly recognized by modern scientific research.

14. Rather, **For the soul of all flesh is its blood with its soul** (*i.e.* its blood and soul together): **therefore spake I to the children of Israel, Ye shall not eat the blood of any flesh, for the soul of all flesh is its blood, &c.**

was torn *with beasts, whether* it *be* one of your own country,
or a stranger, *ʸ*he shall both wash his clothes, *ᶻ*and bathe *himself*
in water, and be unclean until the even: then shall he be clean.
16 But if he wash *them* not, nor bathe his flesh; then *ᵃ*he shall bear
his iniquity.

CHAP. 18. AND the LORD spake unto Moses, saying, Speak unto
2 the children of Israel, and say unto them, *ᵃ*I am the LORD your
3 God. *ᵇ*After the doings of the land of Egypt, wherein ye dwelt,
shall ye not do: and *ᶜ*after the doings of the land of Canaan,
whither I bring you, shall ye not do: neither shall ye walk in
4 their ordinances. *ᵈ*Ye shall do my judgments, and keep mine
5 ordinances, to walk therein: I *am* the LORD your God. Ye
shall therefore keep my statutes, and my judgments: *ᵉ*which
6 if a man do, he shall live in them: *ᶠ*I *am* the LORD. ¶ None
of you shall approach to any that is ¹near of kin to him, to
7 uncover *their* nakedness: I *am* the LORD. *ᵍ*The nakedness of
thy father, or the nakedness of thy mother, shalt thou not uncover: she *is* thy mother; thou shalt not uncover her naked-
8 ness. *ʰ*The nakedness of thy father's wife shalt thou not un-
9 cover: it *is* thy father's nakedness. *ⁱ*The nakedness of thy
sister, the daughter of thy father, or daughter of thy mother,
whether she be born at home, or born abroad, *even* their naked-
10 ness thou shalt not uncover. The nakedness of thy son's daughter, or of thy daughter's daughter, *even* their nakedness thou
11 shalt not uncover: for their's *is* thine own nakedness. The
nakedness of thy father's wife's daughter, begotten of thy father,
12 she *is* thy sister, thou shalt not uncover her nakedness. *ᵏ*Thou
shalt not uncover the nakedness of thy father's sister: she *is* thy
13 father's near kinswoman. Thou shalt not uncover the nakedness of thy mother's sister: for she *is* thy mother's near kins-
14 woman. *ˡ*Thou shalt not uncover the nakedness of thy father's
brother, thou shalt not approach to his wife: she *is* thine aunt.
15 *ᵐ*Thou shalt not uncover the nakedness of thy daughter in law:
she *is* thy son's wife; thou shalt not uncover her nakedness.

ʸ ch. 11. 25.
ᶻ ch. 15. 5.
ᵃ ch. 5. 1.
Num. 19. 20.

ᵃ ver. 4.
Ex. 6. 7.
ch. 11. 44.
Ezek. 20. 5.
ᵇ Ezek. 20.
7, 8.
ᶜ Ex. 23. 24.
ch. 20. 23.
Deut. 12. 4.
ᵈ Deut. 4.
1, 2.
ᵉ Ezek. 20.
11, 13, 21.
Luke 10. 28.
Rom. 10. 5.
Gal. 3. 12.
ᶠ Ex. 6. 2,
6, 29.
Mal. 3. 6.
ᵍ ch. 20. 11.
ʰ Gen. 49. 4.
Deut. 22. 30.
Ezek. 22. 10.
Amos 2. 7.
1 Cor. 5. 1.
ⁱ ch. 20. 17.
2 Sam. 13.
12.
ᵏ ch. 20. 19.

ˡ ch. 20. 20.
ᵐ Gen. 38.
18, 26.
ch. 20. 12.
Ezek. 22. 11.

¹ Heb. *remainder of his flesh.*

---

15. This law appears to be grounded on the fact that the body of an animal killed by a wild beast, or which has died of itself, still retains a great portion of its blood. The importance ascribed to this law in later times may be seen in 1 S. xiv. 32–35; Ezek. iv. 14, xliv. 31, and still more in the Apostolic decision regarding "things strangled," which is pointedly connected with blood (Acts xv. 20).

XVIII. **2.** *I am the* LORD *your God*] The frequent repetition of this formula in these parts of the Law may be intended to keep the Israelites in mind of their Covenant with Jehovah in connection with the common affairs of life, in which they might be tempted to look at legal restrictions in a mere secular light.

3. See *vv.* 24 30 note.

5. If a man keeps the *statutes* (*i.e.* the ordinances of *v.* 4) and *judgments* of the Divine Law, he shall not be "cut off from his people" (cp. *v.* 29), he shall gain true life, the life which connects him with Jehovah through his obedience. See marg. reff.

and Luke x. 28; Rom. x. 5; Gal. iii. 12.

6. *near of kin*] See margin. The term was evidently used to denote those only who came within certain limits of consanguinity, together with those who by affinity were regarded in the same relationship.

to uncover their nakedness] *i.e.* to have intercourse. The immediate object of this law was to forbid incest.

7. *or*] It might be rendered *and*, or rather, **even**; that is, which belongs to both parents as being "one flesh" (Gen. ii. 24; cp. *vv.* 8, 14). These prohibitions are addressed to men.

8. Cp. the case of Reuben, Gen. xlix. 3, 4. See 1 Cor. v. 1.

9. *thy sister*] What was here spoken of was the distinguishing offence of the Egyptians.

12. *thy father's sister*] The instance of Amram and Jochebed (Ex. vi. 20) seems to shew that marriage with an aunt was not considered wrong by the Israelites when they were in Egypt.

16 ⁿThou shalt not uncover the nakedness of thy brother's wife: it
17 is thy brother's nakedness. ^oThou shalt not uncover the nakedness of a woman and her daughter, neither shalt thou take her
son's daughter, or her daughter's daughter, to uncover her naked-
18 ness ; for they are her near kinswomen: it is wickedness. Nei-
ther shalt thou take ¹a wife to her sister, ^pto vex her, to uncover
19 her nakedness, beside the other in her life time. ^qAlso thou
shalt not approach unto a woman to uncover her nakedness, as
20 long as she is put apart for her uncleanness. Moreover ^rthou
shalt not lie carnally with thy neighbour's wife, to defile thyself
21 with her. And thou shalt not let any of thy seed ^spass through
the fire to Molech, neither shalt thou ^uprofane the name of thy
22 God: I am the Lord. ^xThou shalt not lie with mankind, as
23 with womankind: it is abomination. ^yNeither shalt thou lie
with any beast to defile thyself therewith: neither shall any
woman stand before a beast to lie down thereto ; it is ^zcon-
24 fusion. ¶ ^aDefile not ye yourselves in any of these things: ^bfor
in all these the nations are defiled which I cast out before you :
25 and^c the land is defiled: therefore I do ^dvisit the iniquity
thereof upon it, and the land itself ^evomiteth out her inhabitants.
26 ^fYe shall therefore keep my statutes and my judgments, and
shall not commit any of these abominations ; neither any of your
27 own nation, nor any stranger that sojourneth among you: (for
all these abominations have the men of the land done, which were
28 before you, and the land is defiled ;) that ^gthe land spue not you
out also, when ye defile it, as it spued out the nations that were
29 before you. For whosoever shall commit any of these abominations, even the souls that commit them shall be cut off from
30 among their people. Therefore shall ye keep mine ordinance,
^hthat ye commit not any one of these abominable customs,
which were committed before you, and that ye ⁱdefile not yourselves therein : ^kI am the Lord your God.
Chap. 19. AND the Lord spake unto Moses, saying, Speak unto all
2 the congregation of the children of Israel, and say unto them,

ⁿ ch. 20. 21.
^o ch. 20. 14.
^p 1 Sam. 1.6.
^q ch. 20. 18.
Ezek. 18. 6.
^r ch. 20. 10.
Deut. 5. 18.
Prov. 6. 29.
Mal. 3. 5.
Matt. 5. 27.
^s 2 Kin. 16. 3.
Jer. 19. 5.
Ezek. 20. 31.
& 23. 37.
^u ch. 19. 12.
Ezek. 36. 20.
Mal. 1. 12.
^x ch. 20. 13.
Rom. 1. 27.
1 Cor. 6. 9.
1 Tim. 1. 10.
^y ch. 20. 15.
Ex. 22. 19.
^z ch. 20. 12.
^a ver. 30.
Mark 7. 21.
1 Cor. 3. 17.
^b ch. 20. 23.
Deut. 18. 12.
^c Num. 35.
34.
Jer. 2. 7.
Ezek. 36. 17.
^d Ps. 89. 32.
Isni. 26. 21.
Jer. 5. 9, 29.
Hos. 2. 13.
^e ver. 28.
^f ver. 5. 30.
^g ch. 20. 22.
Jer. 9. 19.
Ezek. 36. 13.
^h ch. 20. 23.
Deut. 18. 9.
ⁱ ver. 24.
^k ver. 2. 4.

¹ Or, one wife to another, Ex. 26. 3.

16. thy brother's wife] That is, if she had
children. See Deut. xxv. 5. The law here
expressed was broken by Antipas in his
connexion with Herodias (Matt. xiv. 3, 4).
18. to vex her] Literally, to bind or pack
together. The Jewish commentators illustrate this by the example of Leah and
Rachel (Gen. xxix. 30).
21. Molech] See on xx. 2-5.
24-30. The land designed and consecrated for His people by Jehovah (xxv.
23) is here impersonated, and represented
as vomiting forth its present inhabitants, in
consequence of their indulgence in the abominations that have been mentioned. The
iniquity of the Canaanites was now full.
See Gen. xv. 16 ; cp. Isaiah xxiv. 1-6. The
Israelites in this place, and throughout his
chapter, are exhorted to a pure and holy
life, on the ground that Jehovah, the Holy
One, is their God and that they are His
people. Cp. xix. 2. It is upon this high
sanction that they are peremptorily forbidden to defile themselves with the pollutions
of the heathen. The only punishment here

pronounced upon individual transgressors
is, that they shall "bear their iniquity"
and be "cut off from among their people."
We must understand this latter phrase as
expressing an ipso facto excommunication
or outlawry, the divine Law pronouncing
on the offender an immediate forfeiture of
the privileges which belonged to him as one
of the people in Covenant with Jehovah.
See Ex. xxxi. 14 note. The course which the
Law here takes seems to be first to appeal
to the conscience of the individual man on
the ground of his relation to Jehovah, and
then (ch. xx.) to enact such penalties as the
order of the state required, and as represented the collective conscience of the nation
put into operation.
XIX. 2. Ye shall be holy, &c.] These
words express the keynote to the whole
book of Leviticus, being addressed to the
whole nation. There does not appear to be
any systematic arrangement in the laws
which follow. They were intended as
guards to the sanctity of the elect people,
enforcing common duties by immediate ap-

a ch. 11. 44.
l Pet. 1. 16.
b Ex. 20. 12.
c Ex. 20. 8.
d Ex. 20. 4.
1 John 5. 21.
e Ex. 34. 17.
Deut. 27. 15.
f ch. 7. 16.
g ch. 23. 22.
Ruth 2. 15.
h Ex. 20. 15.
i ch. 6. 2.
Eph. 4. 25.
k Ex. 20. 7.
Matt. 5. 33.
Jas. 5. 12.
l ch. 18. 21.
m Mark 10. 19.
1 Thes. 4. 6.
n Deut. 24. 14, 15.
James 5. 4.
o Rom.14.13.
p Eccles.5.7.
1 Pet. 2. 17.
q Ex. 23. 2, 3.
Deut. 1. 17.
Prov. 24. 23.
James 2. 9.
r Ex. 23. 1.
Ps. 15. 3.
Prov. 11. 13.
Ezek. 22. 9.
s Ex. 23. 1.
1 Kin. 21. 13.
t 1 John 2.9.
u Luke 17. 3.
Gal. 6. 1.
2 Tim. 4. 2.
x Prov. 20, 22.
Rom. 12. 17.
Eph. 4. 31.
Jam. 5. 9.
y Matt. 5. 43.
Rom. 13. 9.
Gal. 5. 14.

3 *a*Ye shall be holy : for I the LORD your God *am* holy. *b*Ye shall fear every man his mother, and his father, and *c*keep my 4 sabbaths : I *am* the LORD your God. *d*Turn ye not unto idols, *e*nor make to yourselves molten gods : I *am* the LORD your God. 5 And *f*if ye offer a sacrifice of peace offerings unto the LORD, ye 6 shall offer it at your own will. It shall be eaten the same day ye offer it, and on the morrow : and if ought remain until the third 7 day, it shall be burnt in the fire. And if it be eaten at all on the 8 third day, it *is* abominable ; it shall not be accepted. Therefore *every one* that eateth it shall bear his iniquity, because he hath profaned the hallowed thing of the LORD : and that soul shall 9 be cut off from among his people. ¶ And *g*when ye reap the harvest of your land, thou shalt not wholly reap the corners of thy field, neither shalt thou gather the gleanings of thy 10 harvest. And thou shalt not glean thy vineyard, neither shalt thou gather *every* grape of thy vineyard ; thou shalt leave them 11 for the poor and stranger : I *am* the LORD your God. *h*Ye shall 12 not steal, neither deal falsely, *i*neither lie one to another. And ye shall not *k*swear by my name falsely, *l*neither shalt thou pro- 13 fane the name of thy God : I *am* the LORD. *m*Thou shalt not defraud thy neighbour, neither rob *him :* *n*the wages of him that is hired shall not abide with thee all night until the morn- 14 ing. Thou shalt not curse the deaf, *o*nor put a stumblingblock 15 before the blind, but shalt *p*fear thy God : I *am* the LORD. *q*Ye shall do no unrighteousness in judgment : thou shalt not respect the person of the poor, nor honour the person of the mighty : 16 *but* in righteousness shalt thou judge thy neighbour. *r*Thou shalt not go up and down *as* a talebearer among thy people : neither shalt thou *s*stand against the blood of thy neighbour : I 17 *am* the LORD. *t*Thou shalt not hate thy brother in thine heart : *u*thou shalt in any wise rebuke thy neighbour, *l*and not suffer 18 sin upon him. *x*Thou shalt not avenge, nor bear any grudge against the children of thy people, *y*but thou shalt love thy 19 neighbour as thyself : I *am* the LORD. Ye shall keep my

l Or, *that thou bear not sin for him :* See Rom. 1. 32. 1 Cor. 5. 2. 1 Tim. 5. 22. 2 John 11.

peal to the highest authority. Cp. xviii. 24-30 note.

3. Cp. Ex. xx. 8, 12, xxxi. 13, 14. The two laws repeated here are the only laws in the Decalogue which assume a positive shape, all the others being introduced by the for- mula, " Thou shalt not."—These express two great central points, the first belonging to natural law and the second to positive law, in the maintenance of the well-being of the social body of which Jehovah was the acknowledged king.

5. Rather, **ye shall offer it that you may be accepted.**

9, 10. See Deut. xxiv. 19-21. " Grape " signifies **fallen fruit** of any kind ; and "vineyard" **a fruit garden** of any kind. Cp. Deut. xxiii. 24.

The poor is the poor Israelite—*the stranger* is properly **the foreigner,** who could possess no land of his own in the land of Israel.

11-13. *v.* 11 forbids injuries perpetrated by craft ; *v.* 13, those perpetrated by vio- lence or power, the conversion of might

into right. In *v.* 13 " defraud " should ra- ther be, **oppress.**

14. The meaning appears to be, *Thou shalt not utter curses to the deaf because he cannot hear thee, neither shalt thou put a stumbling-block in the way of the blind be- cause he cannot see thee* (cp. Deut. xxvii. 18), *but thou shalt remember that though the weak and poor cannot resist, nor the deaf hear, nor the blind see, God is strong, and sees and hears all that thou doest.* Cp. Job xxix. 15.

16. *stand against the blood of thy neigh- bour*] Either, to put his life in danger by standing up as his accuser (cp. Matt. xxvi. 60) ; or, to stand by idly when thy neighbour's life is in danger.—Whichever interpretation we adopt, the clause prohibits that which might interfere with the course of justice.

17. *not suffer sin upon him*] Rather, **not bear sin on his account ;** that is, either by bearing secret ill-will (Ephes. iv. 26), or by encouraging him to sin in withholding due rebuke (Rom. i. 32).

statutes. ¶ Thou shalt not let thy cattle gender with a diverse kind: *thou shalt not sow thy field with mingled seed: "neither shall a garment mingled of linen and woollen come upon thee.
20 And whosoever lieth carnally with a woman, that *is* a bond-maid, [1][2]betrothed to an husband, and not at all redeemed, nor freedom given her; [3][4]she shall be scourged; they shall not be
21 put to death, because she was not free. And *b*he shall bring his trespass offering unto the LORD, unto the door of the tabernacle
22 of the congregation, *even* a ram for a trespass offering. And the priest shall make an atonement for him with the ram of the trespass offering before the LORD for his sin which he hath done: and the sin which he hath done shall be forgiven him.
23 ¶ And when ye shall come into the land, and shall have planted all manner of trees for food, then ye shall count the fruit thereof as uncircumcised: three years shall it be as uncircumcised unto
24 you: it shall not be eaten of. But in the fourth year all the
25 fruit thereof shall be [5]holy *c*to praise the LORD *withal*. And in the fifth year shall ye eat of the fruit thereof, that it may yield
26 unto you the increase thereof: I *am* the LORD your God. ¶ *d*Ye shall not eat *any thing* with the blood: *e*neither shall ye use
27 enchantment, nor observe times. *f* Ye shall not round the corners of your heads, neither shalt thou mar the corners of thy
28 beard. Ye shall not *g*make any cuttings in your flesh for the
29 dead, nor print any marks upon you: I *am* the LORD. *h*Do not

z Deut. 22.
9, 10.
a Deut. 22.
11.

b ch. 5. 15.

c Deut. 12.
17, 18.
Prov. 3. 9.
d ch. 17. 10.
Deut. 12. 23.
e Deut. 18.
10, 11, 14.
1 Sam. 15.
23.
2 Kin. 17. 17.
2 Chr. 33 6.
Mal. 3. 5.
f ch. 21. 5.
Isai. 15. 2.
Jer. 9. 26.
g ch. 21. 5.
Deut. 14. 1.
Jer. 16. 6.
& 48. 37.
h Deut. 23.
17.

[1] Or, *abused by any.*
[2] Heb. *reproached by,* or, *for man.*
[3] Or, *they.*
[4] Heb. *there shall be a scourging.*
[5] Heb. *holiness of praises to the LORD.*

---

19. *linen and woollen*] The original word is found only here and in Deut. xxii. 11, where it is rendered "of divers sorts." It may denote such tissues as linsey woolsey.

20. *betrothed to an husband*] Rather, **who has been betrothed to a man.** The reference appears to be to a bondwoman who has been betrothed to a fellow-servant by her master. Death was the punishment for unfaithfulness in a betrothed woman in other cases. Cp. Deut. xxii. 23, 24.

she shall be scourged] Or, **They shall be chastised** (see margin). The Trespass-offering was especially due from the man as having not only sinned with the woman, but inflicted an injury on the rights of the master.

23. *fruit...uncircumcised*] *i.e.* unfit for presentation to Jehovah. In regard to its spiritual lesson, this law may be compared with the dedication of the first-born of beasts to Jehovah (Ex. xiii. 12, xxxiv. 19). Its meaning in a moral point of view was plain, and tended to illustrate the spirit of the whole Law.

26-28. Certain heathen customs, several of them connected with magic, are here grouped together. The prohibition to eat anything *with the blood* may indeed refer to the eating of meat which had not been properly bled in slaughtering (vii. 26, xvii. 10, &c.): but it is not improbable that there may be a special reference to some sort of magical or idolatrous rites. Cp. Ezek. xxxiii. 25.

26. *observe times*] It is not clear whether the original word refers to the fancied distinction between lucky and unlucky days, to some mode of drawing omens from the clouds, or to the exercise of "the evil eye."

27. *round the corners of your heads*] This may allude to such a custom as that of the Arabs described by Herodotus. They used to shew honour to their deity Orotal by cutting the hair away from the temples in a circular form. Cp. marg. reff.

mar the corners of thy beard] It has been conjectured that this also relates to a custom which existed amongst the Arabs, but we are not informed that it had any idolatrous or magical association. As the same, or very similar customs, are mentioned in xxi. 5, and in Deut. xiv. 1, as well as here, it would appear that they may have been signs of mourning.

28. *cuttings in your flesh for the dead*] Cp. marg. reff. Amongst the excitable races of the East this custom appears to have been very common.

print any marks] Tattooing was probably practised in ancient Egypt, as it is now by the lower classes of the modern Egyptians, and was connected with superstitious notions. Any voluntary disfigurement of the person was in itself an outrage upon God's workmanship, and might well form the subject of a law.

[i] ver. 3. ch. 26. 2.
[k] Eccles. 5. 1.
[l] Ex. 22. 18. ch. 20. 6. Deut. 18. 10. 1 Chr. 10. 13. Isai. 8. 19. Acts 16. 16.
[m] Prov. 20. 29. 1 Tim. 5. 1.
[n] ver. 14.
[o] Ex. 22. 21.
[p] Ex. 12. 48.
[q] Deut. 10. 19.
[r] ver. 15.
[s] Deut. 25. 13, 15. Prov. 11. 1.
[t] ch. 18. 4. Deut. 4. 5. & 5. 1. & 6. 25.
[a] ch. 18. 2.
[b] Deut. 12. 31. 2 Kin. 17. 17. 2 Chr. 33. 6. Jer. 7. 31. Ezek. 20. 26, 31.
[c] ch. 17. 10.

[1]prostitute thy daughter, to cause her to be a whore; lest the
land fall to whoredom, and the land become full of wickedness.
30 [i]Ye shall keep my sabbaths, and [k]reverence my sanctuary: I *am*
31 the LORD. [l]Regard not them that have familiar spirits, neither
seek after wizards, to be defiled by them: I *am* the LORD your
32 God. [m]Thou shalt rise up before the hoary head, and honour
the face of the old man, and [n]fear thy God: I *am* the LORD.
33 And [o]if a stranger sojourn with thee in your land, ye shall not
34 [2]vex him. [p]*But* the stranger that dwelleth with you shall be
unto you as one born among you, and [q]thou shalt love him as
thyself; for ye were strangers in the land of Egypt: I *am* the
35 LORD your God. [r]Ye shall do no unrighteousness in judgment,
36 in meteyard, in weight, or in measure. [s]Just balances, just
[3]weights, a just ephah, and a just hin, shall ye have: I *am* the
LORD your God, which brought you out of the land of Egypt.
37 [t]Therefore shall ye observe all my statutes, and all my judgments,
and do them: I *am* the LORD.

CHAP. 20. AND the LORD spake unto Moses, saying, [a]Again, thou
2 shalt say to the children of Israel, [b]Whosoever *he be* of the children of Israel, or of the strangers that sojourn in Israel, that
giveth *any* of his seed unto Molech; he shall surely be put to
3 death: the people of the land shall stone him with stones. And
[c]I will set my face against that man, and will cut him off from
among his people; because he hath given of his seed unto Molech,

[1] Heb. *profane*. [2] Or, *oppress*. [3] Heb. *stones*.

---

31. The devotion of faith, which would manifest itself in obedience to the commandment to keep God's Sabbaths and to reverence His Sanctuary (*v.* 30), is the true preservative against the superstition which is forbidden in this verse. The people whose God was Jehovah were not to indulge those wayward feelings of their human nature which are gratified in magical arts and pretensions. Cp. Isa. viii. 19.

familiar spirits] Literally, *bottles*. This application of the word is supposed to have been suggested by the tricks of ventriloquists, within whose bodies (as vessels or bottles) it was fancied that spirits used to speak. In other cases the word is used for the familiar spirit which a man pretended to employ in order to consult, or to raise, the spirits of the dead. See 1 S. xxviii. 7, 8.

wizard] A word equivalent to *a knowing man*, or, *a cunning man*.

32. The outward respect due to old age is here immediately connected with the fear of God. Cp. marg. reff.

33, 34. *the stranger*] **The foreigner.** See xvi. 29 note; Ex. xxiii. 9.

35, 36. The ephah is here taken as the standard of dry measure, and the hin (see Ex. xxix. 40 note) as the standard of liquid measure. Of the two very different estimates of the capacities of these measures, the more probable is that the ephah did not hold quite four gallons and a half, and the hin not quite six pints. The log was a twelfth part of the hin (xiv. 10).

36. *I am the* LORD *your God*, &c.] A full stop should precede these words. They introduce the formal conclusion to the whole string of precepts in this chapter, which are all enforced upon the ground of the election of the nation by Jehovah Who had delivered them from the bondage of Egypt.

XX. The crimes which are condemned in chapters xviii., xix. on purely spiritual ground, have here special punishments allotted to them as offences against the well-being of the nation.

2–5. Molech, literally, *the King*, called also Moloch, Milcom, and Malcham, was known in later times as "the abomination of the Ammonites" (1 Kings xi. 5). He appears to have been the fire-god of the eastern nations; related to, and sometimes made identical with, Baal, the sun-god. The nature of the rite and of the impious custom called passing children through the fire to Molech is very doubtful. The practices appear to have been essentially connected with magical arts, probably also with unlawful lusts, and with some particular form of profane swearing. The rite in the time of Moses belonged to the region rather of magic than of definite idolatrous worship, and may have been practised as a lustral charm, or fire-baptism, for the children of incest and adultery.

2. *stone him with stones*] The commonest form of capital punishment. It was probably preferred as being the one in which the execution was the act of the whole congregation.

3. *defile my sanctuary*] *i.e.* pollute the people as identified with their Sanctuary.

4 to ^ddefile my sanctuary, and ^eto profane my holy name   And if
the people of the land do any ways hide their eyes from the man,
when he giveth of his seed unto Molech, and ^fkill him not:
5 then ^gI will set my face against that man, and ^hagainst his
family, and will cut him off, and all that ⁱgo a whoring after
him, to commit whoredom with Molech, from among their people.
6 And ^kthe soul that turneth after such as have familiar spirits,
and after wizards, to go a whoring after them, I will even set
my face against that soul, and will cut him off from among his
7 people. ¶ ^lSanctify yourselves therefore, and be ye holy: for I
8 am the Lord your God. ^mAnd ye shall keep my statutes, and
9 do them: ⁿI am the Lord which sanctify you. ^oFor every one
that curseth his father or his mother shall be surely put to
death: he hath cursed his father or his mother; ^phis blood shall
10 be upon him. And ^qthe man that committeth adultery with
another man's wife, even he that committeth adultery with his
neighbour's wife, the adulterer and the adulteress shall surely be
11 put to death. ^rAnd the man that lieth with his father's wife
hath uncovered his father's nakedness: both of them shall surely
12 be put to death; their blood shall be upon them. ^sAnd if a man
lie with his daughter in law, both of them shall surely be put to
death: ^tthey have wrought confusion; their blood shall be upon
13 them. ^uIf a man also lie with mankind, as he lieth with a
woman, both of them have committed an abomination: they
shall surely be put to death; their blood shall be upon them.
14 ^xAnd if a man take a wife and her mother, it is wickedness:
they shall be burnt with fire, both he and they; that there be
15 no wickedness among you. ^yAnd if a man lie with a beast, he
16 shall surely be put to death: and ye shall slay the beast. And
if a woman approach unto any beast, and lie down thereto,
thou shalt kill the woman, and the beast: they shall surely be
17 put to death; their blood shall be upon them. ^zAnd if a man
shall take his sister, his father's daughter, or his mother's
daughter, and see her nakedness, and she see his nakedness; it
is a wicked thing; and they shall be cut off in the sight of their
people: he hath uncovered his sister's nakedness; he shall bear
18 his iniquity. ^aAnd if a man shall lie with a woman having her
sickness, and shall uncover her nakedness; he hath ¹discovered
her fountain, and she hath uncovered the fountain of her blood:
and both of them shall be cut off from among their people.
19 ^bAnd thou shalt not uncover the nakedness of thy mother's
sister, nor of thy father's sister: ^cfor he uncovereth his near
20 kin: they shall bear their iniquity. ^dAnd if a man shall lie
with his uncle's wife, he hath uncovered his uncle's nakedness:
21 they shall bear their sin; they shall die childless. ^eAnd if a
man shall take his brother's wife, it is ²an unclean thing: he
hath uncovered his brother's nakedness; they shall be childless.
22 ¶ Ye shall therefore keep all my ^fstatutes, and all my judg-

¹ Heb. made naked.   ² Heb. a separation.

d Ezck. 5. 11.
& 23. 38, 39.
e ch. 18. 21.
f Deut. 17.
2, 3, 5.
g ch. 17. 10.
h Ex. 20. 5.
i ch. 17. 7.

k ch. 19. 31.

l ch. 11. 44.
& 19. 2.
1 Pet. 1. 16.
m ch. 19. 37.
n Ex. 31. 13.
ch. 21. 8.
Ezek. 37. 28.
o Ex. 21. 17.
Matt. 15. 4.
p ver. 11.
2 Sam. 1. 16.
q ch. 18. 20.
Deut. 22. 22.
John 8. 4.
r ch. 18. 8.
Deut. 27. 23.
s ch. 18. 15.
t ch. 18. 23.
u ch. 18. 22.
See Gen. 19.
5.
Judg. 19. 22.

x ch. 18. 17.
Deut. 27. 23.

y ch. 18. 23.
Deut. 27. 21.

z ch. 18. 9.
Deut. 27. 22.
See Gen. 20.
12.

a ch. 18. 19.

b ch. 18. 12.
c ch. 18. 6.
d ch. 18. 14.

e ch. 18. 16

f ch. 18. 26.
& 19. 37.

14. The burning under the sentence of
the Law took place after the death of the
criminal by stoning, or strangling. Josh.
vii. 25.

17. cut off, &c.] See Ex. xxxi. 14 note.
The more full expression here used probably
refers to some special form of public excommunication, accompanied, it may be,
by expulsion from the camp.

20. they shall die childless] Either the offspring should not be regarded as lawfully
theirs, nor be entitled to any hereditary
privileges, or they should have no blessing
in their children.

22-26. The ground is here again stated
on which all these laws of holiness should
be obeyed. See xviii. 24-30 note.

ments, and do them : that the land, whither I bring you to dwell

23 therein, *g*spue you not out. *h*And ye shall not walk in the manners of the nation, which I cast out before you : for they committed all these things, and *i*therefore I abhorred them. 24 But *k*I have said unto you, Ye shall inherit their land, and I will give it unto you to possess it, a land that floweth with milk and honey : I *am* the LORD your God, *l*which have separated 25 you from *other* people. ¶ *m*Ye shall therefore put difference between clean beasts and unclean, and between unclean fowls and clean : *n*and ye shall not make your souls abominable by beast, or by fowl, or by any manner of living thing that ¹creepeth on 26 the ground, which I have separated from you as unclean. ye shall be holy unto me : *o*for I the LORD *am* holy, and *p*have 27 severed you from *other* people, that ye should be mine. ¶ *q*A man also or woman that hath a familiar spirit, or that is a wizard, shall surely be put to death : they shall stone them with stones : *r*their blood *shall be* upon them.

CHAP. 21. AND the LORD said unto Moses, Speak unto the priests the sons of Aaron, and say unto them, *a*There shall none be 2 defiled for the dead among his people : but for his kin, that is near unto him, *that is*, for his mother, and for his father, and 3 for his son, and for his daughter, and for his brother, and for his sister a virgin, that is nigh unto him, which hath had no 4 husband ; for her may he be defiled. *But* ²he shall not defile himself, *being* a chief man among his people, to profane himself. 5 *b*They shall not make baldness upon their head, neither shall they shave off the corner of their beard, nor make any cuttings 6 in their flesh. They shall be holy unto their God, and *c*not profane the name of their God : for the offerings of the LORD made by fire, *and* *d*the bread of their God, they do offer : therefore 7 they shall be holy. ¶ *e*They shall not take a wife *that is* a whore, or profane ; neither shall they take a woman *f* put away from 8 her husband : for he *is* holy unto his God. Thou shalt sanctify

¹ Or, *moveth.*
² Or, *being an husband*   *among his people, he shall not defile himself* for his   wife, &c. See Ezek. 24. 16, 17.

---

24. Cp. marg. reff.

25, 26. The distinction between clean and unclean for the whole people, and not for any mere section of it, was one great typical mark of "the kingdom of priests, the holy nation." See xi. 42 note.

25. *any manner of living thing that creepeth*] Rather, **any creeping thing**; that is, any vermin. See xi. 20-23. The reference in this verse is to dead animals, not to the creatures when alive.

XXI. 4. The sense seems to be that, owing to his position in the nation, the priest is not to defile himself in any cases except those named in *vv.* 2-3. The LXX. appear to have followed a different reading of the text which would mean, *he shall not defile himself for a moment.* The explanation in the margin of our version is hardly in keeping with the prohibition to Ezekiel on a special occasion. See Ezek. xxiv. 16.

5. These prohibitions given to the people at large (cp. marg. reff.) had a special fitness for the Hebrew priests. They

were the instruments of the divine will for averting death, all their sacrifices were a type of the death of Christ, which swallowed up death in victory (1 Cor. xv. 54-57), and it would therefore have been unsuitable that they should have the same freedom as other people to become mourners.

6. The word here and in *v.* 8 rendered *bread*, is the same as is rendered *food* in iii. 11, 16, &c., and *meat* in xxii. 11. The reader of the English Bible should keep in view that *bread*, *meat*, and *food*, were nearly equivalent terms when our translation was made, and represent no distinctions that exist in the Hebrew.

7. *profane*] A woman who has been seduced, or one of illegitimate birth.—A somewhat stricter rule for the priests' marriages was revealed to the prophet in later times, Ezek. xliv. 22.

8. The people of Israel are now addressed. They are commanded to regard the priests, who perform for them the service of the Altar, as holy in respect of their office.

him therefore; for he offereth the bread of thy God: he shall be
holy unto thee: [g]for I the LORD, which sanctify you, *am* holy. [g] ch. 20. 7.
9 [h]And the daughter of any priest, if she profane herself by play- [h] Gen. 38. 24.
ing the whore, she profaneth her father: she shall be burnt
10 with fire. ¶ [i]And *he that is* the high priest among his brethren, [i] Ex. 29. 29. ch. 16. 32. Num. 35. 25.
upon whose head the anointing oil was poured, and [k]that is con-
secrated to put on the garments, [l]shall not uncover his head, [k] Ex. 28. 2. ch. 16. 32.
11 nor rend his clothes; neither shall he [m]go in to any dead body, [l] ch. 10. 6.
12 nor defile himself for his father, or for his mother; [n]neither [m] Num. 19. 14.
shall he go out of the sanctuary, nor profane the sanctuary of
his God; for [o]the crown of the anointing oil of his God *is* upon [n] ch. 10. 7.
13 him: I *am* the LORD. And [p]he shall take a wife in her vir- [o] Ex. 28. 36. ch. 8. 9, 12.
14 ginity. A widow, or a divorced woman, or profane, *or* an harlot, [p] ver. 7. Ezek. 44. 22.
these shall he not take: but he shall take a virgin of his own
15 people to wife. Neither shall he profane his seed among his
16 people: for [q]I the LORD do sanctify him. ¶ And the LORD [q] ver. 8.
17 spake unto Moses, saying, Speak unto Aaron, saying, Whosoever *he be* of thy seed in their generations that hath *any* blemish,
18 let him not [r]approach to offer the [1]bread of his God. For what- [r] ch. 10. 3. Num. 16. 5. Ps. 65. 4.
soever man *he be* that hath a blemish, he shall not approach: a
blind man, or a lame, or he that hath a flat nose, or any thing
19 [s]superfluous, or a man that is brokenfooted, or brokenhanded, [s] ch. 22. 23.
20 or crookbackt, or [2]a dwarf, or that hath a blemish in his eye, or
21 be scurvy, or scabbed, or [t]hath his stones broken; no man that [t] Deut. 23. 1.
hath a blemish of the seed of Aaron the priest shall come nigh
to [u]offer the offerings of the LORD made by fire: he hath a [u] ver. 6.
blemish; he shall not come nigh to offer the bread of his God.
22 He shall eat the bread of his God, *both* of the [x]most holy, and of [x] ch. 2. 3, 10. & 6. 17, 29. Num. 18. 9.
23 the [y]holy. Only he shall not go in unto the vail, nor come nigh
unto the altar, because he hath a blemish; that [z]he profane not [y] ch. 22. 10, 11, 12. Num. 18. 19.
24 my sanctuaries: for I the LORD do sanctify them. And Moses
told *it* unto Aaron, and to his sons, and unto all the children [z] ver. 12.
of Israel.

CHAP. 22. AND the LORD spake unto Moses, saying, Speak unto
2 Aaron and to his sons, that they [a]separate themselves from the [a] Num. 6. 3.
holy things of the children of Israel, and that they [b]profane not [b] ch. 18. 21.
my holy name *in those things* which they [c]hallow unto me: I [c] Ex. 28. 38. Num. 18. 32. Deut. 15. 19.

[1] Or, *food*, ch. 3. 11. [2] Or, *too slender*.

---

9. *burnt with fire*] See xx. 14 note.

10. It was the distinguishing mark of the anointing of the High priest, that the holy oil was poured on his head like a crown (cp. viii. 12).

uncover his head] Rather, **let his hair be dishevelled.** See on x. 6.

12. *go out of the sanctuary*] *i.e.* not for the purpose to which reference is here made. The words do not mean, as some have imagined, that his abode was confined to the Sanctuary.

15. *profane his seed*] *i.e.* by a marriage which was not in keeping with the holiness of his office.

16-24. He was not treated as an outcast, but enjoyed his privileges as a son of Aaron, except in regard to active duties.

20. *a dwarf*] One who is small and wasted, either short, as in the text, or slender, as in the margin. It is hardly likely that dwarfishness would be overlooked in this enumeration. So most critical authorities.

scurvy or scabbed] These words most probably include all affected with any skin disease.

22. See ii. 3, vi. 25 note.

23. *sanctuaries*] The Places peculiarly Holy, including the Most Holy Place, the Holy Place, and the Altar.

This law is of course to be regarded as one development of the great principle that all which is devoted to the service of God should be as perfect as possible of its kind.

XXII. **2.** "Speak...that they **so abstain from touching** the holy things (*i.e.* the sacrificial food of all kinds) of the children of Israel **which they consecrate unto me,** that they profane not my holy name." This law related to the daily life and the ordinary food of the priests.

3 *am* the LORD. Say unto them, Whosoever *he be* of all your seed among your generations, that goeth unto the holy things, which the children of Israel hallow unto the LORD, *d*having his uncleanness upon him, that soul shall be cut off from my presence: 4 I *am* the LORD. What man soever of the seed of Aaron *is* a leper, or hath *e*a ¹running issue; he shall not eat of the holy things, *f*until he be clean. And *g*whoso toucheth any thing *that is* unclean *by* the dead, or *h*a man whose seed goeth from him; 5 or *i*whosoever toucheth any creeping thing, whereby he may be made unclean, or *k*a man of whom he may take uncleanness, 6 whatsoever uncleanness he hath; the soul which hath touched any such shall be unclean until even, and shall not eat of the 7 holy things, unless he *l*wash his flesh with water. And when the sun is down, he shall be clean, and shall afterward eat of the 8 holy things; because *m*it *is* his food. *n*That which dieth of itself, or is torn *with beasts*, he shall not eat to defile himself 9 therewith: I *am* the LORD. They shall therefore keep mine ordinance, *o*lest they bear sin for it, and die therefore, if they 10 profane it: I the LORD do sanctify them. ¶*p*There shall no stranger eat *of* the holy thing: a sojourner of the priest, or an 11 hired servant, shall not eat *of* the holy thing. But if the priest buy *any* soul ²with his money, he shall eat of it, and he that is 12 born in his house: *q*they shall eat of his meat. If the priest's daughter also be *married* unto ³a stranger, she may not eat of 13 an offering of the holy things. But if the priest's daughter be a widow, or divorced, and have no child, and is *r*returned unto her father's house, *s*as in her youth, she shall eat of her father's 14 meat: but there shall no stranger eat thereof. *t*And if a man eat *of* the holy thing unwittingly, then he shall put the fifth *part* thereof unto it, and shall give *it* unto the priest with the holy 15 thing. And *u*they shall not profane the holy things of the 16 children of Israel, which they offer unto the LORD; or *x*suffer them *x*to bear the iniquity of trespass, when they eat their holy 17 things: for I the LORD do sanctify them. ¶And the LORD 18 spake unto Moses, saying, Speak unto Aaron, and to his sons, and unto all the children of Israel, and say unto them, *y*Whatsoever *he be* of the house of Israel, or of the strangers in Israel, that will offer his oblation for all his vows, and for all his freewill offerings, which they will offer unto the LORD for a burnt 19 offering; *z*ye shall offer at your own will a male without blemish,

---

¹ Heb. *running of the reins.*   ² Heb. *with the purchase of his money.*   ⁴ Or, *lade themselves with the iniquity of trespass in their eating.*
³ Heb. *a man a stranger.*

---

3. *cut off from my presence*] *i.e.* excluded from the Sanctuary. See xx. 17.
4. See xv. 13–16.
5. *creeping things*] *i.e.* dead vermin. Cp. xi. 29.
6. *the soul*] Rather, **the person.** Compare the use of the word *body* in the Prayer Book version of Ps. liii. 1, and in the compounds *somebody, nobody.*
8. The pollution in the priests would be an aggravated one, inasmuch as they would have to forego their sacred functions. Cp. Ezek. iv. 14, xliv. 31. The general prohibition occurs in xi. 39, xvii. 15; Ex. xxii. 31.
10. *stranger*] **One of another family.** See Ex. xxix. 33 note.

11. This shows how completely a purchased bondsman was incorporated into the household. See Ex. xxi. 2, 20, 21 notes.
12. *a stranger*] **One of another family.**
14. *unwittingly*] **Inadvertently,** or "through ignorance." Cp. iv. 2 note.
15, 16. These verses are rather difficult. Their meaning appears to be:—*The holy things of the children of Israel which are heaved before Jehovah* (see vii. 30) *shall not be profaned; and they shall incur a sin of trespass who eat of their holy things (so as to profane them).*
19. *Ye shall offer at your own will a male*] Rather, **That it may be accepted** (so *v.* 29) **for you it shall be a male.** See

20 of the beeves, of the sheep, or of the goats. *a But* whatsoever hath a blemish, *that* shall ye not offer: for it shall not be acceptable
21 for you. And *b* whosoever offereth a sacrifice of peace offerings unto the LORD *c* to accomplish *his* vow, or a freewill offering in beeves, or [1] sheep, it shall be perfect to be accepted; there shall
22 be no blemish therein. *d* Blind, or broken, or maimed, or having a wen, or scurvy, or scabbed, ye shall not offer these unto the LORD, nor make *e* an offering by fire of them upon the altar unto
23 the LORD. Either a bullock or a [2] lamb that hath anything *f* superfluous or lacking in his parts, that mayest thou offer *for* a free-
24 will offering; but for a vow it shall not be accepted. Ye shall not offer unto the LORD that which is bruised, or crushed, or broken, or cut; neither shall ye make *any offering thereof* in
25 your land. Neither *g* from a stranger's hand shall ye offer *h* the bread of your God of any of these; because their *i* corruption *is* in them, *and* blemishes *be* in them: they shall not be
26 accepted for you. ¶ And the LORD spake unto Moses, saying,
27 *k* When a bullock, or a sheep, or a goat, is brought forth, then it shall be seven days under the dam; and from the eighth day and thenceforth it shall be accepted for an offering made by
28 fire unto the LORD. And *whether it be* cow or [3] ewe, ye shall not
29 kill it *l* and her young both in one day. And when ye will *m* offer a sacrifice of thanksgiving unto the LORD, offer *it* at your
30 own will. On the same day it shall be eaten up; ye shall leave
31 *n* none of it until the morrow: I *am* the LORD. ¶ *o* Therefore shall ye keep my commandments, and do them: I *am* the LORD.
32 *p* Neither shall ye profane my holy name; but *q* I will be hallowed among the children of Israel: I *am* the LORD which
33 *r* hallow you, *s* that brought you out of the land of Egypt, to be your God: I *am* the LORD.

CHAP. 23. AND the LORD spake unto Moses, saying, Speak unto
2 the children of Israel, and say unto them, *Concerning a* the feasts of the LORD, which ye shall *b* proclaim *to be* holy convocations,

[1] Or, *goats*.　　　[2] Or, *kid*.　　　[3] Or, *she goat*.

a Deut. 17. 1.
Mal. 1. 8.
Eph. 5. 27.
Heb. 9. 14.
1 Pet. 1. 19.
b ch. 3. 1, 6.
c ch. 7. 16.
Num. 15. 3, 8.
Deut. 23. 21, 23.
Ps. 61. 8.
& 65. 1.
Eccles. 5. 4, 5.
d ver. 20.
Mal. 1. 8.
e ch. 1. 9, 13.
& 3. 3, 5.
f ch. 21. 18.

g Num. 15. 15, 16.
h ch. 21. 6, 17.
i Mal. 1. 14.
k Ex. 22. 30.

l Deut. 22. 6.
m ch. 7. 12.
Ps. 107. 22.
& 116. 17.
Amos 4. 5.
n ch. 7. 15.
o ch. 19. 37.
Num. 15. 40.
Deut. 4. 40.
p ch. 18. 21.
q ch. 10. 3.
Matt. 6. 9.
Luke 11. 2.
r ch. 20. 8.
s Ex. 6. 7.
Num. 15. 41.
a ver. 4. 37.
b Ex. 32. 5.
2 Kin. 10. 20.
Ps. 81. 3.

i. 3. It is the same phrase as in *vv.* 20, 21, 27.

22, 23. Cp. xxi. 19; Deut. xv. 21.

24. The literal meaning of the passage in italics is, **and this shall ye not do in your land**. It appears to have been understood by the Jews as a prohibition of the mutilation of animals.

25. *a stranger's hand*] The word here rendered *stranger*, is not the same as that in *vv.* 10, 18: it means literally, *the son of the unknown*, and probably refers to one dwelling in another land who desired to show respect to the God of Israel. See 1 Kings viii. 41.

27. No victim was to be offered in sacrifice until it was a week old. The meaning of this law appears to be that the animal should realise a distinct existence in becoming less dependent on its mother, and able to provide for its own wants.

28. A law intended to remind the Israelites of the sacredness of the relation between the parent and its offspring. Cp. Ex. xxiii. 19 note.

XXIII. 1. The specified times for public worship according to the Law were; (1) The daily Morning and Evening sacrifices, sometimes called "the continual Burnt-offering." (2) The weekly Sabbath. (3) The day of the New Moon. (4) The "set feasts" (Num. xxix. 39) or appointed times of annual observance, of which there were five, the Passover, the Day of Pentecost, the Feast of Trumpets, the Day of Atonement, and the Feast of Tabernacles. For each of these occasions special sacrifices were appointed (Num. xxviii., xxix.).

2. *the feasts*] Literally, **the appointed times**. So in *vv.* 4, 37, &c. This section (1–38) sets forth for practical guidance the relation in which **the appointed times** of the LORD, weekly as well as annual, stood to the ordinary occupations of the people.

holy convocations] of sabbatical rest for the whole people; they owed their name to gatherings for religious edification, which, in later times, were probably held in every town and village in the Holy Land. There were in the course of the year, be-

c Ex. 20. 9.
ch. 19. 3.
Deut. 5. 13.
Luke 13. 14.
d ver. 2, 37.
Ex. 23. 14.
e Num. 9. 2.
Deut. 16.
1—8.
Josh. 5. 10.

f Ex. 12. 16.
Num. 28. 18,
25.

g Ex. 23. 16.
& 34. 22, 26.
Num. 15. 2.
& 28. 26.
Deut. 16. 9.
Josh. 3. 15.
h Rom. 11.
16.
1 Cor. 15. 20.
James 1. 18.
Rev. 14. 4.
i Ex. 29. 24.
k ch. 2. 14,
15, 16.

3 *even* these *are* my feasts. *c* Six days shall work be done : but the seventh day *is* the sabbath of rest, an holy convocation ; ye shall do no work *therein :* it *is* the sabbath of the LORD in all your 4 dwellings. *d* These *are* the feasts of the LORD, *even* holy convo- 5 cations, which ye shall proclaim in their seasons. *e* In the four- teenth *day* of the first month at even *is* the LORD's passover. 6 And on the fifteenth day of the same month *is* the feast of unleavened bread unto the LORD : seven days ye must eat un- 7 leavened bread. *f* In the first day ye shall have an holy convo- 8 cation : ye shall do no servile work therein. But ye shall offer an offering made by fire unto the LORD seven days : in the seventh day *is* an holy convocation : ye shall do no servile work 9, 10 *therein.* ¶ And the LORD spake unto Moses, saying, Speak unto the children of Israel, and say unto them, *g* When ye be come into the land which I give unto you, and shall reap the harvest thereof, then ye shall bring a [1] sheaf of *h* the firstfruits of your 11 harvest unto the priest : and he shall *i* wave the sheaf before the LORD, to be accepted for you : on the morrow after the sabbath 12 the priest shall wave it. And ye shall offer that day when ye wave the sheaf an he lamb without blemish of the first year for 13 a burnt offering unto the LORD. *k* And the meat offering thereof *shall be* two tenth deals of fine flour mingled with oil, an offering

     [1] Or, *handful.*   [2] Heb. *omer.*

---

sides the weekly Sabbaths, seven days of Holy Convocation (Ex. xii. 16 ; Num. xxviii. 18, 25, 26, xxix. 1, 12, 35), with a distinction between them as regards strict- ness of observance (cp. *vv.* 3, 28 with *v.* 7).

3. The seventh day had been consecrated as **the Sabbath of Jehovah**, figuring His own rest ; it was the acknowledged sign of the Covenant between God and His people. See Ex. xx. 1-11 notes. As such it properly held its place at the head of the days of Holy Convocation.

4. The recurrence of the Sabbatical num- ber in the five annual days of Holy Convo- cation should be noticed.

5-8. In these verses, the Passover, or Paschal Supper, and the feast of Un- leavened Bread, are plainly spoken of as distinct feasts. See Ex. xii. 6, 15, 17 ; Num. xxviii. 16, 17.

5. See Exod. xii. 6. According to the Hebrew mode of reckoning, the 15th day of the month began on the evening of the 14th. The day of Holy Convocation with which the feast of Unleavened bread com- menced (*v.* 7) was the 15th, and that with which it terminated was the 21st. Cp. Num. xxviii. 16, 17.

6. *feast*] The three festivals (often called the Great Festivals), Passover, Pentecost and Tabernacles, to which the name *chag*, i.e. a *feast* or *rejoicing*, properly belongs (*vv.* 6, 34, 39, 41), were distinguished by the attendance of the male Israelites at the national Sanctuary (cp. Ex. xxiii. 17, xxxiv. 23 ; Deut. xvi. 16). In later times they were called by the rabbins "pilgrimage feasts." It is worthy of note that the Hebrew word is identical with the Arabic *haj*, the name

of the pilgrimage to Mecca, from which comes the well-known word for a pilgrim, *haji.*

7. *no servile work*] Literally, no work of labour, no work that belongs to one's worldly calling, such as labour in agricul- ture or handicraft. The preparation of food was permitted (Ex. xii. 16), a licence not granted on the weekly Sabbath, or on the Day of Atonement (*vv.* 28, 30 ; Ex. xx. 10, xxxv. 3).

8. The sacrifices here meant are named in Num. xxviii. 19-24.

9-22. These verses contain a distinct command regarding the religious services immediately connected with the grain har- vest, given by anticipation against the time when the people were to possess the Pro- mised Land.

10. *sheaf*] The original word, *ōmer*, means either a sheaf (Deut. xxiv. 19 ; Ruth ii. 7), or a measure (Ex. xvi. 16). Our version is probably right in this place. The offering which was waved (vii. 30) was most likely a small sheaf of barley, the grain which is first ripe. The first fruits of the wheat har- vest were offered seven weeks later in the loaves of Pentecost. See *vv.* 15-17. The two offerings thus figure the very com- mencement and the completion of the grain harvest ; cp. Ruth i. 22, ii. 23.

11. *on the morrow after the sabbath*] It is most probable that these words denote the 16th of Abib, the day after the first day of Holy Convocation (see *vv.* 5-8 note), and that this was called *the Sabbath of the Pass- over,* or, *the Sabbath of Unleavened bread.*

13. *two tenth deals*] Two omers, or tenth parts of an ephah, about a gallon and three

made by fire unto the LORD *for* a sweet savour: and the drink
14 offering thereof *shall be* of wine, the fourth *part* of an hin. And
ye shall eat neither bread, nor parched corn, nor green ears,
until the selfsame day that ye have brought an offering unto
your God: *it shall be* a statute for ever throughout your gene-
15 rations in all your dwellings. And [l]ye shall count unto you
from the morrow after the sabbath, from the day that ye
brought the sheaf of the wave offering; seven sabbaths shall be
16 complete: even unto the morrow after the seventh sabbath shall
ye number [m]fifty days; and ye shall offer [n]a new meat offering
17 unto the LORD. Ye shall bring out of your habitations two
wave loaves of two tenth deals: they shall be of fine flour; they
shall be baken with leaven: *they are* [o]the firstfruits unto the
18 LORD. And ye shall offer with the bread seven lambs without
blemish of the first year, and one young bullock, and two rams:
they shall be *for* a burnt offering unto the LORD, with their
meat offering, and their drink offerings, *even* an offering made
19 by fire, of sweet savour unto the LORD. Then ye shall sacrifice
[p]one kid of the goats for a sin offering, and two lambs of the
20 first year for a sacrifice of [q]peace offerings. And the priest shall
wave them with the bread of the firstfruits *for* a wave offering
before the LORD, with the two lambs: [r]they shall be holy to the
21 LORD for the priest. And ye shall proclaim on the selfsame
day, *that* it may be an holy convocation unto you: ye shall do
no servile work *therein*: *it shall be* a statute for ever in all your

[l] Ex. 34. 22. ch. 25. 8. Deut. 16. 9.
[m] Acts 2. 1.
[n] Num. 28. 26.
[o] Ex. 22. 29. Num. 15. 17—21. Deut. 26. 1.
[p] ch. 4. 23, 28. Num. 28. 30.
[q] ch. 3. 1.
[r] Num. 18. 12. Deut. 18. 4.

---

quarters. See xix. 36 note. The double quantity (contrast Ex. xxix. 40; Num. xv. 4, xxviii. 19-21), implying greater liberality, was appropriate in a harvest feast.

drink offering] This and *vv.* 18, 37 are the only places in the book of Leviticus in which Drink-offerings are mentioned. See Ex. xxix. 40 note.

14. *bread...parched corn...green ears*] These are the three forms in which grain was commonly eaten. The old name *Abib* signified "the month of green ears." See Josh. v. 11.

15. *the morrow after the sabbath*] See *v.* 11 note.

seven sabbaths] More properly, **seven weeks** (cp. Deut. xvi. 9). The word Sabbath, in the language of the New Testament as well as the Old, is used for *week* (xxv. 8; Matt. xxviii. 1; Luke xviii. 12, &c.).

16. The morrow after the seventh week was the fiftieth day after the conclusion of a week of weeks. The day is called in the Old Testament, "the feast of harvest" (Ex. xxiii. 16), "the feast of weeks," "the feast of the first fruits of wheat harvest" (Ex. xxxiv. 22; Deut. xvi. 10), and "the day of the first fruits" (Num. xxviii. 26). The word "Pentecost" used in the heading of this chapter in English Bibles is found only in the Apocrypha and the New Testament, Tobit ii. 1; 2 Macc. xii. 32; Acts ii. 1, xx. 16; 1 Cor. xvi. 8.

17. *habitations*] Not strictly houses, but places of abode in a general sense. It seems here to denote the land in which the Israelites were to dwell so as to express that the flour was to be of home growth. The two loaves were to be merely waved before Jehovah and then to become the property of the priests. No bread containing leaven could be offered on the Altar (ii. 11 note). The object of this offering seems to have been to present to the Lord the best produce of the earth in the actual condition in which it is most useful for the support of human life. It thus represented in the fittest manner the thanksgiving which was proper for the season. The loaves appear to be distinctively called "the first fruits **for Jehovah**," and references to them are found in Rom. xi. 16; 1 Cor. xv. 20, 23; James i. 18; Rev. xiv. 4, &c. As these loaves offered before Jehovah sanctified the harvest of the year, so has "Christ the first fruits" sanctified the Church, which, in its union with Him as the First fruits, becomes also the sanctifier of the world. See the services for Whitsuntide.

18. More properly, **seven sheep of a year old** (to be distinguished from the lamb in *v.* 12), and **a young bull** which might be from one to three years old. Cp. Num. xxviii. 26, 27.

19. Properly, **a shaggy he-goat** (iv. 23) and **two sheep of a year old.**

20. When living creatures were *waved* (vii. 30) before Jehovah, it is said that they were led to and fro before the Tabernacle according to an established form.

21. *the selfsame day*] The Feast of Weeks was distinguished from the two other great annual Feasts by its consisting, according to

22 dwellings throughout your generations. And *s*when ye reap the harvest of your land, thou shalt not make clean riddance of the corners of thy field when thou reapest, *t*neither shalt thou gather any gleaning of thy harvest: thou shalt leave them unto the 23 poor, and to the stranger: I *am* the LORD your God. ¶And 24 the LORD spake unto Moses, saying, Speak unto the children of Israel, saying, In the *u*seventh month, in the first *day* of the month, shall ye have a sabbath, *x*a memorial of blowing of 25 trumpets, an holy convocation. Ye shall do no servile work *therein:* but ye shall offer an offering made by fire unto the 26, 27 LORD. ¶And the LORD spake unto Moses, saying, *y*Also on the tenth *day* of this seventh month *there shall be* a day of atonement: it shall be an holy convocation unto you; and ye shall afflict your souls, and offer an offering made by fire unto the 28 LORD. And ye shall do no work in that same day: for it *is* a day of atonement, to make an atonement for you before the 29 LORD your God. For whatsoever soul *it be* that shall not be afflicted in that same day, *z*he shall *be* cut off from among his 30 people. And whatsoever soul *it be* that doeth any work in that same day, *a*the same soul will I destroy from among his people. 31 Ye shall do no manner of work: *it shall be* a statute for ever 32 throughout your generations in all your dwellings. It *shall be* unto you a sabbath of rest, and ye shall afflict your souls: in the ninth *day* of the month at even, from even unto even, shall ye 33 *1*celebrate your sabbath. ¶And the LORD spake unto Moses, 34 saying, Speak unto the children of Israel, saying, *b*The fifteenth day of this seventh month *shall be* the feast of tabernacles *for* 35 seven days unto the LORD. On the first day *shall be* an holy

1 Heb. *rest.*

---

the Law, of only a single day. But in later times it is said that during the following six days the Israelites used to bring their offerings to the Temple, and to give the week something of a festal character in the suspension of mourning for the dead.

22. The repetition of the Law (see marg. ref.) is appropriately connected with the thanksgiving for the completed grain harvest.

24. *a sabbath*] Here and in *v.* 39 a word which should rather be rendered **a sabbatical rest.**

blowing of trumpets] Here and in Num. xxix. 1, literally *shouting.* There is no mention of trumpets in the Hebrew text of the Law in connection with the day. There is however no reason to doubt the tradition that the day was distinguished by a general blowing of trumpets throughout the land, and that the kind of trumpet generally used for the purpose was the curved horn of an animal or a cornet of metal, such as was used at Sinai (Ex. xix. 16), and on the Day of Jubilee (xxv. 9). It must have differed in this respect from the ordinary festival of the New moon when the long straight trumpet of the temple alone was blown (Num. x. 2; Ex. xxv. 23, see cut).

seventh month] Called by the Jews in later times Tisri, but in the Old Testament Etha-

nim, 1 K. viii. 2. According to the uniform voice of tradition "the first day" of this month was the first day of the Civil year in use before the Exodus, and was observed as the festival of the New year. Some have viewed it as a commemoration of the Creation of the world (Job xxxviii. 7): others, as the anniversary of the giving of the Law.

27. *Also*] **Surely.** On the peculiar rites of the Day, the tenth of Tisri, that is from the evening of the ninth day of the month to that of the tenth (*r.* 32), see ch. xvi.

34. *seven days*] Like the Passover, the feast of Tabernacles commenced at the Full moon, on the fifteenth of the month, and lasted for seven days. The week of the feast was followed by an eighth day, forming strictly no part of it (*v.* 36, Num. xxix. 35; Neh. viii. 18), which was a day of Holy Convocation, and appears to have been generally distinguished by the word translated "solemn assembly" (Deut. xvi. 8; 2 Kings x. 20; Is. i. 13; Joel i. 14, ii. 15). From its derivation the word in the original appears strictly to denote a *closing festival*, and this rendering would apply with the most perfect fitness to the day after the week of the Feast of Tabernacles, as the conclusion of the series of yearly festivals.

36 convocation: ye shall do no servile work *therein*. Seven days
ye shall offer an offering made by fire unto the LORD: ^con the
eighth day shall be an holy convocation unto you; and ye shall
offer an offering made by fire unto the LORD: it *is* a ^{1 d}solemn
37 assembly; *and* ye shall do no servile work *therein*. ^eThese *are*
the feasts of the LORD, which ye shall proclaim *to be* holy convocations, to offer an offering made by fire unto the LORD, a
burnt offering, and a meat offering, a sacrifice, and drink offer-
38 ings, every thing upon his day: ^fbeside the sabbaths of the
LORD, and beside your gifts, and beside all your vows, and beside all your freewill offerings, which ye give unto the LORD.
39 Also in the fifteenth day of the seventh month, when ye have
^ggathered in the fruit of the land, ye shall keep a feast unto the
LORD seven days: on the first day *shall be* a sabbath, and on the
40 eighth day *shall be* a sabbath. And ^hye shall take you on the
first day the ²boughs of goodly trees, branches of palm trees, and
the boughs of thick trees, and willows of the brook; ⁱand ye
41 shall rejoice before the LORD your God seven days. ^kAnd ye
shall keep it a feast unto the LORD seven days in the year. *It*
shall be* a statute for ever in your generations: ye shall celebrate
42 it in the seventh month. ^lYe shall dwell in booths seven days;
43 all that are Israelites born shall dwell in booths: ^mthat your
generations may know that I made the children of Israel to
dwell in booths, when I brought them out of the land of Egypt:
44 I *am* the LORD your God. And Moses ⁿdeclared unto the
children of Israel the feasts of the LORD.

CHAP. 24. AND the LORD spake unto Moses, saying, ^aCommand
2 the children of Israel, that they bring unto thee pure oil olive

Marginal references:
c Num. 29.
35.
Neh. 8. 18.
John 7. 37.
d Deut. 16. 8.
2 Chr. 7. 9.
Neh. 8. 18.
Joel 1. 14.
& 2. 15.
e ver. 2, 4.
f Num. 29.
39.

g Ex. 23. 16.
Deut. 16. 13.

h Neh. 8. 15.

i Deut. 16.
14, 15.
k Num. 29.
12.
Neh. 8. 18.

l Neh. 8. 14,
15, 16.
m Deut. 31.
13.
Ps. 78. 5, 6.

n ver. 2.

a Ex. 27. 20,
21.

¹ Heb. day of *restraint*.　　　　² Heb. *fruit*.

---

36. *an offering made by fire*] See *v.* 8. The
succession of sacrifices prescribed in Num.
xxix. 12-38, which forms such a marked
feature in the Feast of Tabernacles, tends
to show the distinctness of the "solemn
assembly" from the festal week.

37, 38. The meaning appears to be; *these
are the yearly appointed times on which ye
shall hold holy convocations and offer to Jehovah sacrifices, in addition to the Sabbath
offerings* (Num. xxviii. 9, 10) *and to all your
voluntary offerings.* Cp. Num. xxix. 39.

39. *Also*] **Surely.** The mode in which
the Feast of Tabernacles is here reintro-
duced, after the mention of it in *vv.* 34-36,
may suggest that this passage originally
formed a distinct document.

the fruit of the land] *i.e.* the produce, including the grain, the olives, the vintage
and the fruits of all kinds. The time of
year so indicated would answer in the Holy
Land to the beginning of October. See
Ex. xxiii. 16 note.

40. *the boughs of goodly trees*] Or, the
fruit (see margin) of the citron trees. It is
said that every Israelite at the Feast of
Tabernacles carried in one hand a bundle of
branches and in the other a citron. The
branches seem to have comprised the
boughs of palm-trees, "thick trees" and
willows here named. See note to *v.* 42;
Neh. viii. 15, 16.

42. *booths*] According to Jewish tradition,
what were used at the Feast of Tabernacles
were strictly *tabernacula*, structures of
boards, with a covering of boughs.

The "booth" in which the Israelite kept
the Feast, and the "tent" which was his
ordinary abode in the wilderness, had this in
common—they were temporary places of
sojourn, they belonged to camp-life. The
seven days of abode in the booths of the
festival was thus a fair symbol of the forty
years of abode in tents in the Wilderness.
The Feast might well become the appointed
memorial of this period of their history for
the ages to come.

all that are Israelites born] The omission
of the foreigners in this command is remarkable. Perhaps the intention was that
on this joyous occasion they were to be
hospitably entertained as guests. Cp. Deut.
xvi. 14.

44. *feasts*] **Appointed times.** See *v.* 2
note.

XXIV. 1-9. The oil for the lamps of the
Tabernacle and the meal for the Shewbread
were to be offerings from the Congregation,
like the meal for the Pentecostal loaves,
(xxiii. 17). It appears that the responsibility
of keeping up the lights rested on the High-
priest, but the actual service might be performed, on ordinary occasions, by the common priests. Cp. marg. reff.

beaten for the light, [1]to cause the lamps to burn continually.
3 Without the vail of the testimony, in the tabernacle of the congregation, shall Aaron order it from the evening unto the morning before the LORD continually : *it shall be* a statute for ever in
4 your generations. He shall order the lamps upon [b]the pure
5 candlestick before the LORD continually. ¶ And thou shalt take
fine flour, and bake twelve [c]cakes thereof : two tenth deals shall
6 be in one cake. And thou shalt set them in two rows, six
7 on a row, [d]upon the pure table before the LORD. And thou
shalt put pure frankincense upon *each* row, that it may be on
the bread for a memorial, *even* an offering made by fire unto the
8 LORD. [e]Every sabbath he shall set it in order before the LORD
continually, *being taken* from the children of Israel by an ever-
9 lasting covenant. And [f]it shall be Aaron's and his sons' ; [g]and
they shall eat it in the holy place : for it *is* most holy unto him
of the offerings of the LORD made by fire by a perpetual statute.
10 ¶ And the son of an Israelitish woman, whose father *was* an
Egyptian, went out among the children of Israel : and this son
of the Israelitish *woman* and a man of Israel strove together in
11 the camp ; and the Israelitish woman's son [h]blasphemed the
name *of the* LORD, and [i]cursed. And they [k]brought him unto
Moses : (and his mother's name *was* Shelomith, the daughter of
12 Dibri, of the tribe of Dan :) and they [l]put him in ward, [2][m]that
13 the mind of the LORD might be shewed them. And the LORD
14 spake unto Moses, saying, Bring forth him that hath cursed
without the camp ; and let all that heard *him* [n]lay their hands
15 upon his head, and let all the congregation stone him. And
thou shalt speak unto the children of Israel, saying, Whosoever
16 curseth his God [o]shall bear his sin. And he that [p]blasphemeth
the name of the LORD, he shall surely be put to death, *and* all
the congregation shall certainly stone him : as well the stranger,

[b] Ex. 31. 8.
& 39. 37.
[c] Ex. 25. 30.
[d] 1 Kin. 7.
48.
2 Chr. 4. 19.
Heb. 9. 2.
[e] Num. 4. 7.
2 Chr. 2. 4.
[f] Mark 2. 26.
Luke 6. 4.
[g] Ex. 29. 33.
ch. 8. 31.
& 21. 22.
[h] ver. 16.
[i] Job 1. 5.
Isai. 8. 21.
[k] Ex. 18. 22.
[l] Num. 15.
34.
[m] Ex. 18. 15.
Num. 27. 5.
[n] Deut. 13. 9.
& 17. 7.
[o] ch. 5. 1.
& 20. 17.
Num. 9. 13.
[p] 1 Kin. 21.
10, 13.
Ps. 74. 10.
Matt. 12. 31.
Mark 3. 28.
Jam. 2. 7.

[1] Heb. *to cause to ascend.*
[2] Heb. *to expound unto them according to the mouth of the* LORD.

---

5. Each cake or loaf of unleavened bread
(ii. 11) was to contain about six pounds and
a quarter (see Ex. xxix. 40 note) of fine flour.
The material was the same, both in quality
and in quantity, with that of each one of
the wave-loaves of Pentecost (xxiii. 17).
In the service of the Temple the preparation and arrangement of the cakes was
committed to the Levites (1 Chr. ix. 32,
xxiii. 29 ; 2 Chr. xiii. 11).

6. *two rows, six on a row*] Rather, **two
piles, six in a pile.** On the Table, see Ex.
xxv. 23–30.

7. The frankincense as a memorial (like
the handful of the Meat-offering, ii. 2), was
most likely cast upon the Altar-fire as "an
offering made by fire unto the Lord," when
the bread was removed from the Table on
the Sabbath-day (*v.* 8 ; 1 S. xxi. 6). The
frankincense was put into small gold cups,
one of which was placed upon each pile of
bread. (See Ex. xxv. 23–30 note.)

8. *being taken from the children of Israel*]
Each cake represented the offering of a
Tribe.

9. See ii. 3 note. It could have been only
by a stretch of the law that Ahimelech

gave a portion of the Shewbread to David
and his men, on the ground that they were
free from ceremonial defilement. 1 Sam.
xxi. 4-6 ; Matt. xii. 4.

· The Shewbread was a true Meat-offering
(see Ex. xxv. 29). The peculiar form in
which it was offered, especially in its being
brought into the Tabernacle and in its consisting of twelve loaves, distinguish it as
an offering made on behalf of the nation.

12. The offender may already have been
pronounced guilty by the rulers (see Ex.
xviii. 21, 22), and the case was referred
to Moses in order that the punishment
might be awarded by the divine decree.
No law had as yet been enacted against
blasphemy except by implication. See Ex.
xxi. 17, xxii. 28.

14. *lay their hands upon his head*] As a
protest against the impiety of the criminal,
symbolically laying the guilt upon his
head. Cp. the washing of hands, Deut. xxi.
6 ; Matt. xxvii. 24.

let all the congregation stone him] See
xx. 2 note.

16. *stranger*] i.e. **foreigner.** See xvi. 29
note.

as he that is born in the land, when he blasphemeth the name
17 *of the* LORD, shall be put to death. ¶ "And he that ¹killeth
18 any man shall surely be put to death. "And he that killeth a
19 beast shall make it good; ²beast for beast. And if a man cause
a blemish in his neighbour; as ⁸he hath done, so shall it be done
20 to him; breach for breach, eye for eye, tooth for tooth: as he
hath caused a blemish in a man, so shall it be done to him *again.*
21 ᵗAnd he that killeth a beast, he shall restore it: "and he that
22 killeth a man, he shall be put to death. Ye shall have ˣone
manner of law, as well for the stranger, as for one of your own
23 country: for I *am* the LORD your God. ¶ And Moses spake
to the children of Israel, ʸthat they should bring forth him that
had cursed out of the camp, and stone him with stones. And
the children of Israel did as the LORD commanded Moses.

CHAP. 25. AND the LORD spake unto Moses in mount Sinai, saying,
2 Speak unto the children of Israel, and say unto them, When ye
come into the land which I give you, then shall the land ³keep
3 "a sabbath unto the LORD. Six years thou shalt sow thy field,
and six years thou shalt prune thy vineyard, and gather in the
4 fruit thereof; but in the seventh year shall be a sabbath of rest
unto the land, a sabbath for the LORD: thou shalt neither sow
5 thy field, nor prune thy vineyard. ᵇThat which groweth of its
own accord of thy harvest thou shalt not reap, neither gather
the grapes ⁴of thy vine undressed: *for* it is a year of rest unto
6 the land. And the sabbath of the land shall be meat for you;
for thee, and for thy servant, and for thy maid, and for thy hired
7 servant, and for thy stranger that sojourneth with thee, and for
thy cattle, and for the beast that *are* in thy land, shall all the
8 increase thereof be meat. ¶ And thou shalt number seven sab-

Marginal references:

q Ex. 21. 12.
Num. 35. 31.
Deut. 19. 11,
12.
r ver. 21.
s Ex. 21. 24.
Deut. 19. 21.
Matt. 5. 38.
& 7. 2.
t ver. 18.
Ex. 21. 33.
u ver. 17.
x Ex. 12. 49.
ch. 19. 34.
Num. 15. 16.
y ver. 14.

a Ex. 23. 10.
See ch. 26.
34, 35.
2 Chr. 36. 21.

b 2 Kin. 19.
29.

¹ Heb. *smiteth the life of a man.*
² Heb. *life for life.*
³ Heb. *rest.*
⁴ Heb *of thy separation.*

XXV. The Sabbatical year and the year
of Jubilee belong to that great Sabbatical
system which runs through the religious
observances of the Law, but rest upon
moral rather than upon formally religious
ground. It is not therefore without reason
that they are here set apart from the set
times which fell strictly within the sphere
of religious observances.

3. *vineyard*] Rather, **fruit-garden**. The
Hebrew word is a general one for a planta-
tion of fruit-trees.

4. *a sabbath of rest*] See xxiii. 3 note. The
express prohibition of sowing and reaping,
and of pruning and gathering, affords a presumption in favour of the Sabbatical year
beginning, like the year of Jubilee (*v.* 9),
in the first month of the Civil year (xxiii.
24), the seventh of the Sacred year, when
the land was cleared of the crops of the preceding year.

The great material advantage of the
institution must have been the increased
fertility of the soil from its lying fallow one
year out of seven, at a time when neither
the rotation of crops nor the art of manur-
ing were understood. It must also have
kept up a salutary habit of economy in the
storing of corn. Cp. Gen. xli. 48-56. Its

great spiritual lesson was that there was no
such thing as absolute ownership in the
land vested in any man, that the soil was
the property of Jehovah, that it was to be
held in trust for Him, and not to be abused
by overworking, but to be made the most of
for the good of every creature which dwelt
upon it.

5. *vine undressed*] That is, *unpruned;*
lit. *Nazarite vine,* the figure being taken
from the unshorn locks of the Nazarite.
(Num. vi. 5.)

6. *the sabbath of the land shall be meat for
you*] That is, the produce of the untilled
land (its "increase," *v.* 7) shall be food for
the whole of you in common, rich and poor
without distinction (Ex. xxiii. 11).

8-13. The Land was to be divided by lot
among the families of the Israelites when
the possession of it was obtained. Num.
xxvi. 52-56, xxxiii. 54, &c. At the end of
every seventh sabbatical cycle of years, in
the year of Jubilee, each field or estate
that might have been alienated was to be
restored to the family to which it had been
originally allotted.

8. *seven sabbaths of years*] **seven weeks of
years.**

baths of years unto thee, seven times seven years ; and the space
of the seven sabbaths of years shall be unto thee forty and nine
9 years. Then shalt thou cause the trumpet [1] of the jubile to sound
on the tenth *day* of the seventh month, *c*in the day of atonement
10 shall ye make the trumpet sound throughout all your land. And
ye shall hallow the fiftieth year, and *d*proclaim liberty throughout *all* the land unto all the inhabitants thereof : it shall be a
jubile unto you ; *e*and ye shall return every man unto his posses-
11 sion, and ye shall return every man unto his family. A jubile
shall that fiftieth year be unto you : *f*ye shall not sow, neither
reap that which groweth of itself in it, nor gather *the grapes* in it
12 of thy vine undressed. For it *is* the jubile ; it shall be holy
unto you : *g*ye shall eat the increase thereof out of the field.
13 *h*In the year of this jubile ye shall return every man unto his
14 possession. And if thou sell ought unto thy neighbour, or
buyest *ought* of thy neighbour's hand, *i*ye shall not oppress one
15 another : *k*according to the number of years after the jubile thou
shalt buy of thy neighbour, *and* according unto the number of
16 years of the fruits he shall sell unto thee : according to the multitude of years thou shalt increase the price thereof, and according to the fewness of years thou shalt diminish the price of it :
for *according* to the number *of the years* of the fruits doth he sell
17 unto thee. ¶*l*Ye shall not therefore oppress one another ; *m*but
18 thou shalt fear thy God : for I *am* the LORD your God. *n*Wherefore ye shall do my statutes, and keep my judgments, and do
19 them ; *o*and ye shall dwell in the land in safety. And the land
shall yield her fruit, and *p*ye shall eat your fill, and dwell
20 therein in safety. ¶And if ye shall say, *q*What shall we eat
the seventh year ? Behold, *r*we shall not sow, nor gather in our
21 increase : then I will *s*command my blessing upon you in the
22 sixth year, and it shall bring forth fruit for three years. *t*And
ye shall sow the eighth year, and eat *yet* of *u*old fruit until the
ninth year ; until her fruits come in ye shall eat *of* the old *store*.
23 ¶The land shall not be sold ² ³ for ever : for *x*the land *is* mine ;

[marginal references, left column:]
₁ ch. 23. 2₄.
₁ Isai. 61. 2.
& 63. 4.
Jer. 3₄. 8.
Luke 4. 19.
e ver. 13.
Num. 36. 4.
f ver. 5.

g ver. 6, 7.
h ver. 10.
ch. 27. 2₄.
Num. 36. 4.
i ver. 17.
ch. 19. 13.
Mic. 2. 2.
1 Cor. 6. 8.
k ch.27.18.23.
l ver. 14.
m ver. 43.
ch. 19. 14.
n ch. 19. 37.
o Ps. 4. 8.
Prov. 1. 33.
Jer. 23. 6.
p ch. 26. 5.
Ez. 3₄. 25.
q Matt. 6.
25, 31.
r ver. 4, 5.
s See Ex. 16.
29.
Deut. 28. 8.
t 2 Kin. 19.
29.
u Josh. 5.
11, 12.
x Deut. 32.
43.
2 Chr. 7. 20.
Ps. 85. 1.
Joel 2. 18.

 ¹ Heb. *loud of sound*.   ² Or, *to be quite cut off*.   ³ Heb. *for cutting off*.

---

9. *cause the trumpet of the jubile to sound*]
Rather, **cause the sound of the cornet to
go through** (the land). The word *jubile*
does not occur in this verse in the Hebrew.
The trumpet is the *shophār*, *i.e.* the cornet
(rendered "shawm" in the Prayer-Book
version of Ps. xcviii. 7), either the horn of
some animal or a tube of metal shaped like
one. As the sound of the cornet (see *v.* 10
note) was the signal of the descent of Jehovah when He came down upon Sinai to
take Israel into Covenant with Himself
(Ex. xix. 13, 16, 19, xx. 18), so the same
sound announced, at the close of the great
Day of Atonement, after the Evening sacrifice, the year which restored each Israelite
to the freedom and the blessings of the
Covenant.

10. *the fiftieth year*] The Jubilee probably
coincided with each seventh Sabbatical
year, and was called the fiftieth, as being
the last of a series of which the first was the
preceding Jubilee.

a jubile] Commonly spelt *jubilee*. The original word first occurs in Ex. xix. 13, where it
is rendered "trumpet," marg. "cornet." It
most probably denotes the sound of the
cornet, not the cornet itself, and is derived
from a root, signifying to flow abundantly,
which by a familiar metaphor might be
applied to sound.

14. *sell ought*] *i.e.*, any piece of ground.
oppress one another] Rather, **overreach
one another.** (Cp. 1 Sam. xii. 3, 4).

15, 16. *the number of years of the fruits*]
i.e. according to the number of harvests.
The average value of a yearly crop might
of course be estimated, and the Sabbatical years were to be deducted from the
series.

18, 19. *in safety*] *i.e.*, secure from famine,
(xxvi. 5 ; Deut. xii. 10).

23, 24. These verses express the principle
on which the law of Jubilee, as it regards
the land, was based. The land belonged to
Jehovah, and it was He Who allotted it
amongst the families of Israel for their use.
No estate could therefore be alienated in

24 for ye *are* ^y^strangers and sojourners with me. And in all the
land of your possession ye shall grant a redemption for the land.
25 ^z^If thy brother be waxen poor, and hath sold away *some* of his
possession, and if ^a^any of his kin come to redeem it, then shall
26 he redeem that which his brother sold. And if the man have none
27 to redeem it, and ^1^himself be able to redeem it; then ^b^let him
count the years of the sale thereof, and restore the overplus unto
the man to whom he sold it; that he may return unto his posses-
28 sion. But if he be not able to restore *it* to him, then that which
is sold shall remain in the hand of him that hath bought it until
the year of jubile: ^c^and in the jubile it shall go out, and he shall
29 return unto his possession. ¶And if a man sell a dwelling house
in a walled city, then he may redeem it within a whole year after
30 it is sold; *within* a full year may he redeem it. And if it be not
redeemed within the space of a full year, then the house that *is*
in the walled city shall be established for ever to him that
bought it throughout his generations: it shall not go out in the
31 jubile. But the houses of the villages which have no wall round
about them shall be counted as the fields of the country: ^2^they
32 may be redeemed, and they shall go out in the jubile. ¶Not-
withstanding ^d^the cities of the Levites, *and* the houses of the
cities of their possession, may the Levites redeem at any time.
33 And if ^3^a man purchase of the Levites, then the house that was
sold, and the city of his possession, ^e^shall go out in *the year of*
jubile: for the houses of the cities of the Levites *are* their pos-
34 session among the children of Israel. But ^f^the field of the,
suburbs of their cities may not be sold; for it *is* their perpetual
35 possession. ¶And if thy brother be waxen poor, and ^4^fallen in
decay with thee; then thou shalt ^5g^relieve him: *yea, though he*
36 *be* a stranger, or a sojourner; that he may live with thee. ^h^Take
thou no usury of him, or increase: but ^i^fear thy God; that thy
37 brother may live with thee. Thou shalt not give him thy money
38 upon usury, nor lend him thy victuals for increase. ^k^I *am* the
LORD your God, which brought you forth out of the land of

^y^ 1 Chr. 29.
15.
Ps. 39. 12.
& 119. 19.
1 Pet. 2. 11.
^z^ Ruth 2. 20.
& 4. 4, 6.
^a^ See Ruth
3. 2, 9, 12.
Jer. 32. 7.
^b^ ver. 50. 51,
52.

^c^ ver. 13.

^d^ See Num.
35. 2.
Josh. 21. 2,
&c.
^e^ ver. 28.
^f^ See Acts
4. 36, 37.
^g^ Deut. 15.
7, 8.
Ps. 37. 26.
Prov. 14. 31.
Luke 6. 35.
Acts 11. 29.
Rom. 12. 10.
1 John 3. 17.
^h^ Ex. 22. 25.
Deut. 23. 19.
Neh. 5. 7.
Ps. 15. 5.
Prov. 28. 8.
Ez. 18. 8.
^i^ ver. 17.
Neh. 5. 9.
^k^ ch. 22. 32,
33.

^1^ Heb. *his hand hath
attained and found suffi-
ciency,* ch. 5. 7.
^2^ Heb. *Redemption be-
longeth unto it.*
^3^ Or, *one of the Levites redeem* them.
^4^ Heb. *his hand faileth.*
^5^ Heb. *strengthen.*

perpetuity, by any human authority, from
the family to whose lot it might fall.

24. *grant a redemption for the land*] i.e.
grant power to recover the land to the
original holder who had parted with it.

25. *If thy brother be waxen poor*] The Israelites never parted with their land except
under the pressure of poverty. Cp. the
answer of Naboth, 1 K. xxi. 3.

28. *it shall go out*] i.e. it shall be set
free.

30. *not go out*] Because most of the
houses in cities were occupied by artificers
and traders whose wealth did not consist in
lands.

32, 33. Rather, **And concerning the
cities of the Levites, the houses in the
cities of their possession,** &c. **If one of
the Levites redeems a house in the city,**
&c. The meaning appears to be, if a Levite
redeemed a house which had been sold to a
person of a different tribe by another Levite,

it was to revert in the Jubilee to the latter
Levite as its original possessor. The pur-
chaser of a Levite's house was in fact only
in the condition of a tenant at will, while
the fields attached to the Levitical cities
could never be alienated, even for a time.

For the application of the law of Jubilee
to lands dedicated to the service of the
Sanctuary, see xxvii. 16-25.

35. Rather, **And if thy brother** (an
Israelite) **becomes poor and falls into
decay with thee, thou shalt assist him
and let him live with thee like a resident
foreigner.** He was not to be regarded as an
outcast, but was to be treated with the same
respect and consideration as a resident
foreigner who, like him, could possess no
land, but could accumulate property and live
in comfort as a free man. See xvi. 29 note.

37. *lend him thy victuals for increase*] i.e.
supply him with food for thy own profit.

38. Here, and in *vv.* 42, 55, is expressed

Egypt, to give you the land of Canaan, *and* to be your God.

39 ¶ And *l*if thy brother *that dwelleth* by thee be waxen poor, and be sold unto thee; thou shalt not *1*compel him to serve as a 40 bondservant: *but* as an hired servant, *and* as a sojourner, he shall be with thee, *and* shall serve thee unto the year of jubile: 41 and *then* shall he depart from thee, *both* he and his children *m*with him, and shall return unto his own family, and *n*unto 42 the possession of his fathers shall he return. For they *are* *o*my servants, which I brought forth out of the land of Egypt: they 43 shall not be sold *2*as bondmen. *p*Thou shalt not rule over him 44 *q*with rigour; but *r*shalt fear thy God. Both thy bondmen, and thy bondmaids, which thou shalt have, *shall be* of the heathen that are round about you; of them shall ye buy bondmen 45 and bondmaids. Moreover of *s*the children of the strangers that do sojourn among you, of them shall ye buy, and of their families that *are* with you, which they begat in your land: and they 46 shall be your possession. And *t*ye shall take them as an inheritance for your children after you, to inherit *them for* a possession; *3*they shall be your bondmen for ever: but over your brethren the children of Israel, *u*ye shall not rule one over an- 47 other with rigour. ¶ And if a sojourner or stranger *4*wax rich by thee, and *x*thy brother *that dwelleth* by him wax poor, and sell himself unto the stranger *or* sojourner by thee, or to the stock of 48 the stranger's family: after that he is sold he may be redeemed 49 again; one of his brethren may *y*redeem him: either his uncle, or his uncle's son, may redeem him, or *any* that is nigh of kin unto him of his family may redeem him; or if *z*he be able, he 50 may redeem himself. And he shall reckon with him that bought him from the year that he was sold to him unto the year of jubile: and the price of his sale shall be according unto the number of years, *a*according to the time of an hired servant shall 51 it be with him. If *there be* yet many years *behind*, according unto them he shall give again the price of his redemption out of the 52 money that he was bought for. And if there remain but few years unto the year of jubile, then he shall count with him, *and* according unto his years shall he give him again the price of his 53 redemption. *And* as a yearly hired servant shall he be with

Marginal references (left column):

l Ex. 21. 2.
Deut. 15. 12.
1 Kin. 9. 22.
2 Kin. 4. 1.
Neh. 5. 5.
Jer. 34. 14.
m Ex. 21. 3.
n ver. 28.
o ver. 55.
Rom. 6. 22.
1 Cor. 7. 23.
p Eph. 6. 9.
Col. 4. 1.
q ver. 46.
Ex. 1. 13.
r ver. 17.
Ex. 1. 17, 21.
Deut. 25. 18.
Mal. 3. 5.
s Isai. 56. 3, 6.
t Isai. 14. 2.

u ver. 43.

x ver. 25, 35.

y Neh. 5. 5.

z ver. 26.

a Job 7. 1.
Isai. 16. 14.
& 21. 16.

Footnotes:

1 Heb. *serve thyself with him with the service, &c.* ver. 46. Ex. 1. 14. Jer. 25. 14. & 27. 7. & 30. 8.

2 Heb. *with the sale of a bondman.*

3 Heb. *ye shall serve yourselves with them*, ver. 39.

4 Heb. *his hand obtain, &c.* ver. 26.

---

the principle which was to limit and modify the servitude of Hebrew servants.

39, 40. The law here appears harmoniously to supplement the earlier one in Ex. xxi. 1–6. It was another check applied periodically to the tyranny of the rich. Cp. Jer. xxxiv. 8–17.

43. *fear thy God*] Jehovah was the Lord and Master of His people. To treat a Hebrew as a slave was therefore to interfere with the rights of Jehovah. Cp. Rom. xiv. 4.

44–46. Property in foreign slaves is here distinctly permitted. It was a patriarchal custom (Gen. xvii. 12). Such slaves might be captives taken in war (Num. xxxi. 6 seq.; Deut. xx. 14), or those consigned to slavery for their crimes, or those purchased of foreign slave-dealers. The price of a slave is supposed to have varied from thirty to fifty shekels. See notes to xxvii. 3, 4; Ex. xxi. 32; Zech. xi. 12, 13; Matt. xxvi. 15. The object of Moses, not at once to do away with slavery, but to discourage and to mitigate it. The Law would not suffer it to be forgotten that the slave was a man, and protected him in every way that was possible at the time against the injustice or cruelty of his master. See notes on Ex. xxi.

46. *your bondmen for ever*] i.e. they were not necessarily to be released in the Sabbatical year nor at the Jubilee.

47–54. *a sojourner or stranger*] Rather, a **foreigner who has settled among you.** See notes to Lev. xvi. 29; Ex. xx. 10.

him: *and the other* shall not rule with rigour over him in thy
54 sight. And if he be not redeemed [1]in these *years*, then [b]he
shall go out in the year of jubile, *both* he, and his children with
55 him. For [c]unto me the children of Israel *are* servants; they
are my servants whom I brought forth out of the land of Egypt :
I *am* the LORD your God.

CHAP. 26. YE shall make you [a]no idols nor graven image, neither
rear you up a [2]standing image, neither shall ye set up *any*
[3 4]image of stone in your land, to bow down unto it: for I *am*
2 the LORD your God. [b]Ye shall keep my sabbaths, and reve-
3 rence my sanctuary : I *am* the LORD. ¶[c]If ye walk in my
4 statutes, and keep my commandments, and do them ; [d]then I
will give you rain in due season, [e]and the land shall yield her
5 increase, and the trees of the field shall yield their fruit. And
[f]your threshing shall reach unto the vintage, and the vintage
shall reach unto the sowing time : and [g]ye shall eat your bread
6 to the full, and [h]dwell in your land safely. And [i]I will give
peace in the land, and [k]ye shall lie down, and none shall make
you afraid: and I will [5]rid [l]evil beasts out of the land, neither
7 shall [m]the sword go through your land. And ye shall chase
8 your enemies, and they shall fall before you by the sword. And
[n]five of you shall chase an hundred, and an hundred of you

[b] ver. 41.
[c] ver. 42.
[a] Ex. 20. 4, 5.
Deut. 5. 8.
Ps. 97. 7.
[b] ch. 19. 30.
[c] Deut. 11.
13, 14, 15.
[d] Isai. 30. 23.
[e] Ps. 67. 6.
Zech. 8. 12.
[f] Amos 9. 13.
[g] ch. 25. 18.
[h] ch. 25. 19.
Ez. 34. 25.
[i] 1 Chr. 22. 9.
Ps. 29. 11.
Isai. 45. 7.
Hag. 2. 9.
[k] Ps. 3. 5.
Isai. 35. 9.
Jer. 30. 10.
Ez. 34. 25.
Hos. 2. 18.
Zeph. 3. 13.
[l] 2 Kin. 17.
25.
Ez. 5. 17.
[m] Ez. 14. 17.
[n] Josh. 23. 10.

[1] Or, *by these* means.
[2] Or, *pillar.*
[3] Or, *figured stone.*
[4] Heb. *a stone of picture.*
[5] Heb. *cause to cease.*

---

54. *in these years*] More properly, **by one
of these means.** The extreme period of
servitude in this case was six years, as
when the master was a Hebrew (Ex. xxi. 2).

Looking at the law of the Jubilee from a
simply practical point of view, its operation
must have tended to remedy those evils
which are always growing up in the ordinary conditions of human society. It prevented the permanent accumulation of land
in the hands of a few, and periodically
raised those whom fault or misfortune had
sunk into poverty to a position of com-
petency. It must also have tended to keep
alive family feeling, and helped to preserve
the family genealogies.

But in its more special character, as a law
given by Jehovah to His peculiar people, it
was a standing lesson to those who would
rightly regard it, on the terms upon which
the enjoyment of the Land of Promise had
been conferred upon them. All the land
belonged to Jehovah as its supreme Lord,
every Israelite as His vassal belonged to
Him. The voice of the Jubilee horns, twice
in every century, proclaimed the equitable
and beneficent social order appointed for
the people; they sounded that acceptable
year of Jehovah which was to bring comfort
to all that mourned, in which the slavery of
sin was to be abolished, and the true liberty
of God's children was to be proclaimed
(Luke ii. 25 ; Isai. lxi. 2 ; Luke iv. 19; Acts
iii. 21 ; Rom. viii. 19–23 ; 1 Pet. i. 3, 4).

XXVI. 1. *idols*] Literally, *things of nought.*
Heb. *eleelim.* There appears to have been a
play on the similarity in sound of this word
to *Elohim* (God). Cp. 1 Cor. viii. 4.

standing image] Either an upright statue,
or a pillar, such as an obelisk or a Celtic
menhir, set up for an idolatrous purpose
(cp. Ex. xxxiv. 13 note). The public worship of Jehovah required, first, the exclusion of all visible symbols of deity as well
as of all idolatrous objects, and next (*v.* 2),
the keeping holy the times and the Place
appointed by the Law for His formal service. The word Sabbaths must here include
the whole of the set times. See xxiii. 3 note.

3–45. As "the Book of the Covenant"
(Ex. xx. 22–xxiii. 33) concludes with promises and warnings (Ex. xxiii. 20–33), so
does this collection of laws contained in the
Book of Leviticus. But the former passage
relates to the conquest of the Land of Promise, this one to the subsequent history of
the nation. The longer similar passage in
Deuteronomy (xxvii.–xxx.) is marked by
broader and deeper promises and denunciations having immediate reference not only
to outward consequences, but to the spiritual
death incurred by transgressing the Divine
will.

4. *rain in due season*] The periodical rains,
on which the fertility of the Holy Land so
much depends, are here spoken of. There
are two wet seasons, called in Scripture the
former and the latter rain (Deut. xi. 14 ;
Jer. v. 24 ; Joel ii. 23 ; Hos. vi. 3 ; Jam.
v. 7). The former or Autumn rain falls in
heavy showers in November and December.
In March the latter or Spring rain comes
on, which is precarious in quantity and duration, and rarely lasts more than two days.

5. Cp. marg. reff. ; Joel ii. 19 ; Job xi. 18.

8. *five of you shall chase*] A proverbial

LEVITICUS. XXVI.

23.
p Neh. 9. 23.
Ps. 107. 38.
q ch. 25. 22.
r Josh.22.19.
Rev. 21. 3.
s ch. 20. 23.
t 2 Cor. 6. 16.
u Jer. 7. 23.
Ez. 11. 20.
w ch. 25. 38.
x Jer. 2. 20.
Ez. 34. 27.
y Lam.2. 17.
Mal. 2. 2.
z ver. 43.
2 Kin. 17. 15.
a Deut. 28.
65.
b Deut. 28.
22.
c 1 Sam. 2.
33.
d Jer. 5. 17.
Mic. 6. 15.
e ch. 17. 10.
f Judg. 2. 14.
Jer. 19. 7.
g Ps. 106. 41.
h Ps. 53. 5.
Prov. 28. 1.
i 1 Sam. 2. 5.
k Isai. 25. 11.
Ez. 7. 24.
l Deut. 28.
23.
m Ps. 127. 1.
Isai. 49. 4.
n Hag. 1. 10.
o 2Kin.17.25.
p 2Chr.15.5.
Lam. 1. 4.
Zech. 7. 14.
q Amos 4. 6.

shall put ten thousand to flight: and your enemies shall fall 9 before you by the sword. For I will *o*have respect unto you, and *p*make you fruitful, and multiply you, and establish my 10 covenant with you. And ye shall eat *q*old store, and bring 11 forth the old because of the new. *r*And I will set my tabernacle 12 among you: and my soul shall not *s*abhor you. *t*And I will walk among you, and *u*will be your God, and ye shall be my 13 people. *w*I am the LORD your God, which brought you forth out of the land of Egypt, that ye should not be their bondmen; *x*and I have broken the bands of your yoke, and made you go 14 upright. ¶ *y*But if ye will not hearken unto me, and will not do 15 all these commandments; and if ye shall *z*despise my statutes, or if your soul abhor my judgments, so that ye will not do all 16 my commandments, *but* that ye break my covenant: I also will do this unto you; I will even appoint ¹over you *a*terror, *b*consumption, and the burning ague, that shall *c*consume the eyes, and cause sorrow of heart: and *d*ye shall sow your seed in vain, 17 for your enemies shall eat it. And *e*I will set my face against you, and *f*ye shall be slain before your enemies: *g*they that hate you shall reign over you; and *h*ye shall flee when none pur- 18 sueth you. And if ye will not yet for all this hearken unto 19 me, then I will punish you *i*seven times more for your sins. And I will *k*break the pride of your power; and I *l*will make your 20 heaven as iron, and your earth as brass: and your *m*strength shall be spent in vain: for *n*your land shall not yield her increase, neither shall the trees of the land yield their fruits. 21 And if ye walk ²contrary unto me, and will not hearken unto me; I will bring seven times more plagues upon you according 22 to your sins. *o*I will also send wild beasts among you, which shall rob you of your children, and destroy your cattle, and make you few in number; and *p*your *high* ways shall be desolate. 23 And if ye *q*will not be reformed by me by these things, but will

¹ Heb. *upon you*.　　　　² Or, *at all adventures with me*, and so ver. 24.

---

mode of expression for superiority in warlike prowess (Deut. xxxii. 30; Isai. xxx. 17).

9. *establish my covenant*] All material blessings were to be regarded in the light of seals of the "everlasting covenant." Cp. Gen. xvii. 4–8; Neh. ix. 23.

10. *bring forth the old because of the new*] Rather, **clear away the old before the new**; that is, in order to make room for the latter. Cp. marg. ref.

16. THE FIRST WARNING for disobedience is disease. "Terror" (lit. trembling) is rendered *trouble* in Ps. lxxviii. 33; Isai. lxv. 23. It seems here to denote that terrible affliction, an anxious temperament, the mental state ever at war with Faith and Hope. This might well be placed at the head of the visitations on a backslider who had broken the Covenant with his God. Cp. Deut. xxxii. 25; Jer. xv. 8; Prov. xxviii. 1; Job xxiv. 17; Ps. xxiii. 4.

consumption, and the burning ague] Cp. marg. ref. The first of the words in the original comes from a root signifying *to waste away*; the latter (better, fever), from one signifying *to kindle a fire*. Consumption is

common in Egypt and some parts of Asia Minor, but it is more rare in Syria. Fevers of different kinds are the commonest of all diseases in Syria and all the neighbouring countries. The opposite promise to the threat is given in Ex. xv. 26, xxiii. 25.

18. *for all this*] *i.e.* for all the afflictions in *vv.* 16, 17.

seven times] The sabbatical number is here proverbially used to remind the people of the Covenant. Cp. Gen. iv. 15, 24; Ps. cxix. 164; Prov. xxiv. 16; Luke xvii. 4.

19, 20. THE SECOND WARNING is utter sterility of the soil. Cp. Deut. xi. 17, xxviii. 18; Ezek. xxxiii. 28, xxxvi. 34, 35.

21, 22. THE THIRD WARNING is the multiplication of destructive animals, &c. Cp. Deut. xxxii. 24; Ezek. v. 17, xiv. 15; Judg. v. 6, 7; Isai. xxxiii. 8.

23–26. THE FOURTH WARNING. Jehovah now places Himself as it were in a hostile position towards His people who "will not be reformed" (rather, brought unto God: Jer. ii. 30). He will avenge the outraged cause of His Covenant, by the sword, pestilence, famine, and captivity.

24 walk contrary unto me; *r*then will I also walk contrary unto
25 you, and will punish you yet seven times for your sins. And *s*I
will bring a sword upon you, that shall avenge the quarrel of
my covenant: and when ye are gathered together within your
cities, *t*I will send the pestilence among you; and ye shall be
26 delivered into the hand of the enemy. *u*And when I have
broken the staff of your bread, ten women shall bake your
bread in one oven, and they shall deliver *you* your bread again
27 by weight: and *x*ye shall eat, and not be satisfied. And *y*if ye
will not for all this hearken unto me, but walk contrary unto
28 me; then I will walk contrary unto you also *z*in fury; and I,
29 even I, will chastise you seven times for your sins. *a*And ye
shall eat the flesh of your sons, and the flesh of your daughters
30 shall ye eat. And *b*I will destroy your high places, and cut
down your images, and *c*cast your carcases upon the carcases of
31 your idols, and my soul shall *d*abhor you. *e*And I will make
your cities waste, and *f*bring your sanctuaries unto desolation,
32 and I will not smell the savour of your sweet odours. *g*And I
will bring the land into desolation: and your enemies which
33 dwell therein shall be *h*astonished at it. And *i*I will scatter you
among the heathen, and will draw out a sword after you: and
34 your land shall be desolate, and your cities waste. ¶ *k*Then
shall the land enjoy her sabbaths, as long as it lieth desolate,
and ye *be* in your enemies' land; *even* then shall the land rest,
35 and enjoy her sabbaths. As long as it lieth desolate it shall
rest; because it did not rest in your *l*sabbaths, when ye dwelt

r 2 Sam. 22.
27.
Ps. 18. 26.
s Ez. 5. 17.
& pass.
t Num. 14.
12.
Jer. 14. 12.
Amos 4. 10.
u Ps. 105. 16.

x Isai. 9. 20.
y ver. 21. 24.
z Isai. 59.18.
Jer. 21. 5.
Ez. 5. 13.
a Deut. 28.
53.
b Isai. 27. 9.
c 2 Kin. 23.
20.
d Ps. 78. 59.
e Neh. 2. 3.
f Lam. 1. 10.
g Jer. 9. 11.

h 1 Kin. 9. 8.
i Deut. 4. 27.
& 28. 64.
k 2 Chr. 36.
21.

l ch. 25. 2.

26. Omit "*and.*"—"To break the staff
of bread," was a proverbial expression for
cutting off the supply of bread, the staff of
life (Ps. cv. 16; Ezek. iv. 16, v. 16, xiv.
13, cp. Isai. iii. 1). The supply was to be so
reduced that one oven would suffice for
baking the bread made by ten women for
ten families, and when made it was to be
dealt out in sparing rations by weight. See
2 K. vi. 25; Jer. xiv. 18; Lam. iv. 9; Ezek.
v. 12; Hos. iv. 10; Mic. vi. 14; Hagg. i. 6.
27-33. THE FIFTH WARNING. For *v.* 29
see 2 K. vi. 28, 29; Jer. xix. 8, 9; Lam. ii.
20, iv. 10; Ezek. v. 10 : for *v.* 30 see 2 Chr.
xxxiv. 3; Ezek. vi. 4; Jer. xiv. 19 : for *v.*
31 see 2 K. xxv. 9; Ps. lxxiv. 6, 7 : for *vv.*
32, 33 see Deut. xxviii. 37; Ps. xliv. 11;
Jer. ix. 16, xviii. 16; Ezek. v. 1-17; Jer. iv.
7; Ezek. ix. 6, xii. 15; Zech. vii. 14.
30. *high places*] There is no doubt that
the word here denotes elevated spots dedicated to false worship (see Deut. xii. 2), and
especially, it would seem, to that of Baal
(Num. xxii. 41; Josh. xiii. 17). Such spots
were however employed and approved for
the worship of Jehovah, not only before
the building of the Temple, but afterwards
(Jud. vi. 25, 26, xiii. 16-23; 1 S. vii. 10, xvi.
5; 1 K. iii. 2, xviii. 30; 2 K. xii. 3; 1 Chr.
xxi. 26, &c.). The three altars built by Abraham at Shechem, between Bethel and Ai,
and at Mamre, appear to have been on
heights, and so was the Temple.
The high places in the Holy Land may
thus have been divided into those dedicated

to the worship of Jehovah, and those which
had been dedicated to idols. And it would
seem as if there was a constant struggle
going on. The high places polluted by idol
worship were of course to be wholly condemned. They were probably resorted to
only to gratify a degraded superstition.
See xix. 31, xx. 2-5. The others might
have been innocently used for prayer and
religious teaching. But the temptation
appears to have been too great for the
temper of the people. They offered sacrifice and burnt incense on them; and hence
thorough reformers of the national religion,
such as Hezekiah and Josiah, removed
the high places altogether (2 K. xviii. 4,
xxiii. 5).
your images] The original word is rendered in the margin of our Bible *sun images*
(2 Chr. xiv. 5; Isai. xvii. 8; Ezek. vi. 4,
&c.). Phœnician inscriptions prove that the
word was commonly applied to images of
Baal and Astarte, the god of the sun and
the goddess of the moon. This exactly explains 2 Chr. xxxiv. 4 sq.
idols] The Heb. word here literally
means things which could be rolled about,
such as a block of wood or a lump of dirt.
It was no doubt a name given in derision.
Cp. Isai. xl. 20, xliv. 19; 2 K. i. 2.
31. *sanctuaries*] The Holy Places in the
Tabernacle and the Temple (Ps. lxviii. 35.
Cp. Ps. lxxiv. 7).
I will not smell the savour, &c.] See i. 9.
35. More literally : **All the days of its**

m Ez. 21. 7.
n Job 15. 21.
Prov. 28. 1.
o Isai. 10. 4.
1 Sam. 14.
15, 16.
p Josh. 7. 12.
q Deut. 4. 27.
Neh. 1. 8.
Jer. 3. 25.
Ez. 4. 17.
Hos. 5. 15.
Zech. 10. 9.
r Num. 5. 7.
1 Kin. 8. 33.
Neh. 9. 2.
Prov. 28. 13.
Dan. 9. 3, 4.
Luke 15. 18.
1 John 1. 9.
s Ez. 44. 7.
t 1 Kin. 21.
29.
2 Chr. 12. 6.
u Ex. 2. 24.
Ps. 106. 45.
Ez. 16. 60.
x Ps. 136. 23.
y ver. 34, 35.

z ver. 15.

a Deut. 4. 31.
2 Kin. 13. 23.
Rom. 11. 2.
b Rom. 11.
28.
c ch. 22. 33.
d Ps. 98. 2.
Ez. 20. 9.
e ch. 27. 34.
Deut. 6. 1.
John 1. 17.
f ch. 25. 1.

36 upon it. ¶ And upon them that are left *alive* of you *m*I will send a faintness into their hearts in the lands of their enemies; and *n*the sound of a ¹shaken leaf shall chase them; and they shall flee, as fleeing from a sword; and they shall fall when 37 none pursueth. And *o*they shall fall one upon another, as it were before a sword, when none pursueth: and *p*ye shall have 38 no power to stand before your enemies. And ye shall perish among the heathen, and the land of your enemies shall eat you 39 up. And they that are left of you *q*shall pine away in their iniquity in your enemies' lands; and also in the iniquities of 40 their fathers shall they pine away with them. ¶ *r*If they shall confess their iniquity, and the iniquity of their fathers, with their trespass which they trespassed against me, and that also 41 they have walked contrary unto me; and *that* I also have walked contrary unto them, and have brought them into the land of their enemies; if then their *s*uncircumcised hearts be *t*humbled, 42 and they then accept of the punishment of their iniquity: then will I *u*remember my covenant with Jacob, and also my covenant with Isaac, and also my covenant with Abraham will I re-43 member; and I will *x*remember the land. ¶ *y*The land also shall be left of them, and shall enjoy her sabbaths, while she lieth desolate without them: and they shall accept of the punishment of their iniquity: because, even because they *z*despised my judgments, and because their soul abhorred my statutes. 44 And yet for all that, when they be in the land of their enemies, *a*I will not cast them away, neither will I abhor them, to destroy them utterly, and to break my covenant with them: for I *am* 45 the LORD their God. But I will *b*for their sakes remember the covenant of their ancestors, *c*whom I brought forth out of the land of Egypt *d*in the sight of the heathen, that I might be their 46 God: I *am* the LORD. ¶ *e*These *are* the statutes and judgments and laws, which the LORD made between him and the children of Israel *f*in mount Sinai by the hand of Moses.

¹ Heb. *driven.*

---

desolation shall it rest that time which it rested not in your Sabbaths while ye dwelt upon it. That is, the periods of rest of which the land had been deprived would be made up to it. Cp. 2 Chr. xxxvi. 20, 21.

38. *the land of your enemies shall eat you up*] Cp. Num. xiii. 32; Ezek. xxxvi. 13.

39. *iniquity*] The meaning here is, **in the punishment of their iniquity**, and, in the next clause, **in the punishment of the iniquity** (as in *vv.* 41, 43) **of their fathers.** In the next verse the same Heb. word is properly represented by "iniquity." Our translators have in several places put one of the English words in the text and the other in the margin (Gen. iv. 13, xix. 15; 2 K. vii. 9; Ps. lxix. 27, &c.). The language of Scripture does not make that trenchant division between *sin* and *punishment* which we are accustomed to do. Sin is its own punishment, having in itself, from its very commencement, the germ of death. "Sin, when it is finished, bringeth forth death" (Jam. i. 15; Rom. ii. 5, v. 12).

40. *trespass*] The Hebrew word signifies an injury inflicted on the rights of a person, as distinguished from a sin or iniquity regarded as an outrage of the Divine law. Every wrong act is of course both a sin and a trespass against God. In this place Jehovah takes the breach of the Covenant as a personal trespass.

41. *uncircumcised hearts*] The outward sign of the Covenant might be preserved, but the answering grace in the heart would be wanting (Acts vii. 51; Rom. ii. 28, 29; Jer. vi. 10, ix. 26; cp. Col. ii. 11).

accept of the punishment of their iniquity] Literally, *enjoy their iniquity.* The word here and in *v.* 43 rendered "accept" in this phrase, is the same as is rendered "enjoy" in the expression "the land shall enjoy her sabbaths" (*v.* 34). The antithesis in *v.* 43 is this: *The land shall enjoy her sabbaths*—*and they shall enjoy the punishment of their iniquity.* The meaning is, that the land being desolate shall have the blessing of rest, and they having repented shall have the blessing of chastisement. The feelings of a devout

CHAP. 27. AND the LORD spake unto Moses, saying, Speak unto 2 the children of Israel, and say unto them, ^aWhen a man shall make a singular vow, the persons *shall be* for the LORD by thy 3 estimation. And thy estimation shall be of the male from twenty years old even unto sixty years old, even thy estimation shall be fifty shekels of silver, ^bafter the shekel of the sanctuary.

^a Num. 6. 2. See Judg. 11. 30, 31, 39. 1 Sam. 1. 11, 28.

^b Ex. 30. 13.

4 And if it *be* a female, then thy estimation shall be thirty shekels, 5 And if *it be* from five years old even unto twenty years old, then thy estimation shall be of the male twenty shekels, and for the 6 female ten shekels. And if *it be* from a month old even unto five years old, then thy estimation shall be of the male five shekels of silver, and for the female thy estimation *shall be* three 7 shekels of silver. And if *it be* from sixty years old and above; if *it be* a male, then thy estimation shall be fifteen shekels, and for 8 the female ten shekels. But if he be poorer than thy estimation, then he shall present himself before the priest, and the priest shall value him; according to his ability that vowed shall 9 the priest value him. And if *it be* a beast, whereof men bring an offering unto the LORD, all that *any man* giveth of such unto 10 the LORD shall be holy. He shall not alter it, nor change it, a good for a bad, or a bad for a good: and if he shall at all change beast for beast, then it and the exchange thereof shall be holy. 11 And if *it be* any unclean beast, of which they do not offer a sacrifice unto the LORD, then he shall present the beast before 12 the priest: and the priest shall value it, whether it be good or 13 bad: ¹as thou valuest it, *who art* the priest, so shall it be. ^cBut if he will at all redeem it, then he shall add a fifth *part* thereof 14 unto thy estimation. ¶And when a man shall sanctify his house *to be* holy unto the LORD, then the priest shall estimate it, whether it be good or bad: as the priest shall estimate it, 15 so shall it stand. ^dAnd if he that sanctified it will redeem his house, then he shall add the fifth *part* of the money of thy esti-16 mation unto it, and it shall be his. And if a man shall sanctify

^c ver. 15, 19.

^d ver. 13.

¹ Heb. *according to thy estimation, O priest, &c.*

---

captive Israelite are beautifully expressed in Tobit xiii. 1-18.

XXVII. DUES. The position which this chapter holds after the formal conclusion, xxvi. 46, suggests that it is of a supplementary character. There seems, however, no reason to doubt its Mosaic origin.

2-3. Rather, **When a man makes a special vow which concerns thy valuation of persons to Jehovah,** &c. The expression "thy estimation" is addressed either to Moses or to the priest (*v.* 12): it denoted a legal valuation. The vow of a person was perhaps most frequently made in cases of illness or danger, under the impulse of religious feeling, either in the way of thankfulness for blessings received, or of supplication for something desired. A man might dedicate himself, his wife, his child, or his bondservant. This might have been an old custom; but the Law ordained that he who had taken such a vow should pay a sum of money to the Sanctuary, determined according to the age and sex of the person.

3-7. The relative values of the persons appear to be regulated according to an estimate of the probable value of their future work:—

	Male.	Female.
From a month to five years	5	3 shekels.
From five years to twenty	20	10 ,,
From forty years to sixty	50	30 ,,
Sixty years and more	15	10 ,,

As regards the shekel of the Sanctuary, see Ex. xxxviii. 24 note.

8. *if he be poorer than thy estimation*] **Too poor (to pay) thy valuation.** Cp. v. 7, 11.

14. *sanctify*] *i.e.* vow to devote. This law relates to houses in the country (xxv. 31), which were under the same general law as the land itself, with a right of redemption for the inheritor till the next Jubilee. See *vv.* 17-19. For houses in walled towns the right of redemption lasted for only one year, (xxv. 29).

16. *some part of a field of his possession*] Rather, **a part of the land of his inheritance.**

unto the LORD *some part* of a field of his possession, then thy estimation shall be according to the seed thereof : [1]an homer of 17 barley seed *shall be valued* at fifty shekels of silver. If he sanctify his field from the year of jubile, according to thy estimation 18 it shall stand. But if he sanctify his field after the jubile, then the priest shall *reckon* unto him the money according to the years that remain, even unto the year of the jubile, and it shall 19 be abated from thy estimation. *f*And if he that sanctified the field will in any wise redeem it, then he shall add the fifth *part* of the money of thy estimation unto it, and it shall be assured 20 to him. And if he will not redeem the field, or if he have sold the field to another man, it shall not be redeemed any more. 21 But the field, *g*when it goeth out in the jubile, shall be holy unto the LORD, as a field *h*devoted ; *i*the possession thereof shall 22 be the priest's. And if *a man* sanctify unto the LORD a field which he hath bought, which *is* not of the fields of *k*his pos- 23 session ; *l*then the priest shall reckon unto him the worth of thy estimation, *even* unto the year of the jubile : and he shall give thine estimation in that day, *as* a holy thing unto the LORD. 24 *m*In the year of the jubile the field shall return unto him of whom it was bought, *even* to him to whom the possession of the 25 land *did belong.* And all thy estimations shall be according to the shekel of the sanctuary : *n*twenty gerahs shall be the shekel. 26 ¶ Only the [2 o]firstling of the beasts, which should be the LORD's firstling, no man shall sanctify it ; whether *it be* ox, or sheep : it 27 *is* the LORD's. And if *it be* of an unclean beast, then he shall redeem *it* according to thine estimation, *p*and shall add a fifth *part* of it thereto : or if it be not redeemed, then it shall be sold 28 according to thy estimation. ¶ *q*Notwithstanding no devoted thing, that a man shall devote unto the LORD of all that he hath,

e ch. 25. 15, 16.
f ver. 13.

g ch. 25. 10, 28, 31.
h ver. 28.
i Num.18.14.
Ez. 44. 29.
k ch. 25. 10, 25.
l ver. 18.

m ch. 25. 28.

n Ex. 30. 13.
Num. 3. 47.
& 18. 16.
Ez. 45. 12.
o Ex. 13. 2, 12. & 22. 30.
Num. 18. 17.
Deut. 15. 19.
p ver. 11, 12, 13.
q ver. 21.

---

[1] Or, the land of *an homer, &c.*   [2] Heb. *firstborn, &c.*

---

the seed thereof] *i.e.* the quantity of seed required to sow it properly. Thus the value of about 5½ bushels (an homer) was about 6*l.* 9*s.* 2*d.* (50 shekels. See Ex. xxxviii. 24.)

21. *devoted*] See *v.* 28 note.

25. On the shekel and the gerah, see Ex. xxx. 13, xxxviii. 24 notes.

28. *devoted thing*] The primary meaning of the Heb. word (*chérem*) is something cut off, or shut up. Its specific meaning in the Law is, that which is cut off from common use and given up in some sense to Jehovah, without the right of recal or commutation. It is applied to a field wholly appropriated to the Sanctuary (*v.* 21), and to whatever was doomed to destruction (1 S. xv. 21 ; 1 K. xx. 42). Our translators have often rendered the word by "cursed," or "a curse," which in some places may convey the right sense, but it should be remembered that the terms are not identical in their compass of meaning (Deut. vii. 26 ; Josh. vi. 17, 18, vii. 1 ; Isai. xxxiv. 5, xliii. 28, &c. Cp. Gal. iii. 13).

of man and beast] This passage does not permit human sacrifices. Man is elsewhere clearly recognised as one of the creatures which were not to be offered in sacrifice (Ex. xiii. 13, xxxiv. 20 ; Num. xviii. 15).

Therefore the application of the word *chérem* to man is made exclusively in reference to one rightly doomed to death and, in that sense alone, given up to Jehovah. The man who, in a right spirit, either carries out a sentence of just doom on an offender, or who, with a single eye to duty, slays an enemy in battle, must regard himself as God's servant rendering up a life to the claim of the Divine justice (cp. Rom. xiii. 4). It was in this way that Israel was required to destroy the Canaanites at Hormah (Num. xxi. 2, 3 ; cp. Deut. xiii. 12-18), and that Samuel hewed Agag in pieces before the Lord (1 S. xv. 33). In all such instances, a moral obligation rests upon him whose office it is to take the life : he has to look upon the object of his stroke as under a ban to the Lord (cp. Deut. xx. 4 ; Gal. iii. 13). There can therefore be neither redemption nor commutation.

It is evident that the righteousness of this law is not involved in the sin of rash or foolish vows, such as Saul's (1 S. xiv. 24) or Jephthah's (Judg. xi. 30).

And it seems hardly needful to add that sacrifice, as it is represented both in the Law and in the usage of the Patriarchs, is something very different from consecration

both of man and beast, and of the field of his possession, shall be
sold or redeemed: every devoted thing *is* most holy unto the
29 LORD. *r*None devoted, which shall be devoted of men, shall be
30 redeemed; *but* shall surely be put to death. And *s*all the
tithe of the land, *whether* of the seed of the land, *or* of the fruit
31 of the tree, *is* the LORD'S: *it is* holy unto the LORD. *t*And if a
man will at all redeem *ought* of his tithes, he shall add thereto
32 the fifth *part* thereof. And concerning the tithe of the herd, or
of the flock, *even* of whatsoever *u*passeth under the rod, the
33 tenth shall be holy unto the LORD. He shall not search whether
it be good or bad, *x*neither shall he change it: and if he change
it at all, then both it and the change thereof shall be holy; it
34 shall not be redeemed. ¶ *y*These *are* the commandments, which
the LORD commanded Moses for the children of Israel in mount
Sinai.

r Num. 21.
2, 3.
s Gen. 28. 22.
Num. 18. 21,
24.
2 Chr. 31. 5,
6, 12.
Neh. 13. 12.
Mal. 3. 8.
t ver. 13.
u See Jer. 33.
13.
Ez. 20. 37.
x ver. 10.
y ch. 26. 46.

---

under a ban, though a thing to be sacrificed
might come under the designation of *chērem*
in its wider sense. The sacrifice was always
the offering up of the innocent life of a
creature chosen, approved, and without
spot or blemish.

32. *whatsoever passeth under the rod*] According to rabbinical tradition, the animals
to be tithed were enclosed in a pen, and as
they went out one by one at the opening,
every tenth animal was touched with a rod
dipped in vermilion. Cp. marg. reff.

For a more full explanation of what relates to tithes, see marg. reff. and Gen. xiv.
20 ; Deut. xiv. 22, 28.

NUMBERS.

INTRODUCTION.

THE title commonly given to this Book is evidently suggested by the two numberings of the people recorded in chapters i. and xxvi.

The book narrates the history of the Israelites during their sojourn in the wilderness from the completion of the law-giving at Sinai, Lev. xxvii. 34, to their mustering in the plains of Moab for actual entry into the Land of Promise.[1]

The incidents are generally given in their chronological order, except in the third part. The five chapters comprised in this part appear to deal with a long period, from which only isolated episodes are given; and of these the dates can only be conjectured.

Between the two dates " the first day of the second month of the second year after they were come out of Egypt" (i. 1), and the death of Aaron (xxxiii. 38), intervene no less than thirty-eight years and three months (cp. Deut. ii. 14), the long and dreary period of tarrying in the wilderness till the disobedient generation had wasted away.[2]

From the death of Aaron to the date given in the opening verses of Deuteronomy (i. 1–3), occurred a space of exactly six months, in which all the events narrated in the fourth part of the Book of Numbers, from xx. 1 to the end, would seem to have occurred, with the probable exception of the defeat of the king of Arad (xxi. 1–3).

As regards the authorship and date of composition, the notes of time, the tenor of the contents, no less than the direct assertions of the text itself, lead to the conclusion that Moses is properly spoken of as the writer of the Book of Numbers. It is in substance his work; though many portions of it were probably committed to writing many years before the whole was completed; and the concluding chapters were not written until towards the close of the fortieth year after the Exodus.

---

[1] Its contents may be divided into four parts : (a) i.—x. 10 ; (b) x. 11—xiv ; (c) xv. —xix. ; (d) xx.—xxxvi.

[2] On the history of these years, see notes on xx. 1, and xxxiii. 19.

THE FOURTH BOOK OF MOSES,

CALLED

NUMBERS.

a Ex. 19. 1.
ch. 10. 11, 12.
b Ex. 25. 22.

c Ex. 30. 12.
& 38. 26.
ch. 26. 2, 63,
64.
2 Sam. 24. 2.
1 Chr. 21. 2.

d ch. 2. 14,
he is called
Reuel.
e ch. 7. 2.
1 Chr. 27. 16.
f Ex. 18. 21,
25.

CHAP. 1. AND the LORD spake unto Moses *a*in the wilderness of Sinai, *b*in the tabernacle of the congregation, on the first *day* of the second month, in the second year after they were come out
2 of the land of Egypt, saying, *c*Take ye the sum of all the congregation of the children of Israel, after their families, by the house of their fathers, with the number of *their* names, every
3 male by their polls; from twenty years old and upward, all that are able to go forth to war in Israel: thou and Aaron shall
4 number them by their armies. And with you there shall be a man of every tribe; every one head of the house of his fathers.
5 ¶And these *are* the names of the men that shall stand with
6 you: of *the tribe of* Reuben; Elizur the son of Shedeur. Of
7 Simeon; Shelumiel the son of Zurishaddai. Of Judah; Nah-
8 shon the son of Amminadab. Of Issachar; Nethaneel the son
9, 10 of Zuar. Of Zebulun; Eliab the son of Helon. Of the children of Joseph: of Ephraim; Elishama the son of Ammihud: of
11 Manasseh; Gamaliel the son of Pedahzur. Of Benjamin; Abidan
12 the son of Gideoni. Of Dan; Ahiezer the son of Ammishaddai.
13, 14 Of Asher; Pagiel the son of Ocran. Of Gad; Eliasaph the
15, 16 son of *d*Deuel. Of Naphtali; Ahira the son of Enan. *e*These *were* the renowned of the congregation, princes of the tribes
17 of their fathers, *f*heads of thousands in Israel. ¶And Moses and Aaron took these men which are expressed by *their* names:
18 and they assembled all the congregation together on the first *day* of the second month, and they declared their pedigrees after their families, by the house of their fathers, according to the number of the names, from twenty years old and upward, by
19 their polls. As the LORD commanded Moses, so he numbered
20 them in the wilderness of Sinai. ¶And the children of Reuben, Israel's eldest son, by their generations, after their families, by

---

I. 1–4. A month had passed away since the setting up of the tabernacle (Ex. xl. 2, 17): and the Sinaitic legislation was now complete (cp. Lev. xxvii. 34).

A census ("sum") was commanded, to be based not upon any fresh registration of individuals, but upon that which had accompanied the previous collection of the offerings. Cp. Ex. xxx. 11, &c. ; xxxviii. 25–28. The offerings had been probably tendered by the people in groups, and if certificates of registration were furnished to such groups, the new census might be easily carried out by means of these documents, and got through (*v.* 18) in a single day. The present registration enrolled persons "after their families, by the house of their fathers ; " and was superintended not by the Levites (see Ex. xxxviii. 21 and note), but by (*v.* 4) an assessor for each tribe to act in the business with Moses and Aaron. The purpose now in view was not religious only. The census now taken would serve as

a basis for various civil and military arrangements.

5–16. The princes of the tribes, selected (*v.* 4) under divine direction, were for the most part the same persons as those chosen a few months previously at the counsel of Jethro (Ex. xviii. 21–26). Nahshon, prince of Judah, is mentioned in Ex. vi. 23, and Elishama, in 1 Chr. vii. 26, 27. The peers of men like these were no doubt entitled, amongst their fellows, to the epithet " renowned," *v.* 16.

20–46. The enrolment, being taken principally for military purposes (cp. *vv.* 3, 20), would naturally be arranged by hundreds, fifties, &c. (cf. 2 K. i. 9, 11, 13). In eleven tribes the number enrolled consists of complete hundreds. The difference, in this respect, observable in the case of the tribe of Gad here (*v.* 25), and of the tribe of Reuben at the later census (xxvi. 7), is probably to be accounted for by the pastoral, and consequently nomadic, habits of these tribes,

the house of their fathers, according to the number of the names,
by their polls, every male from twenty years old and upward,
21 all that were able to go forth to war; those that were numbered
of them, *even* of the tribe of Reuben, *were* forty and six thousand
22 and five hundred. ¶ Of the children of Simeon, by their generations, after their families, by the house of their fathers, those
that were numbered of them, according to the number of the
names, by their polls, every male from twenty years old and
23 upward, all that were able to go forth to war; those that were
numbered of them, *even* of the tribe of Simeon, *were* fifty and
24 nine thousand and three hundred. ¶ Of the children of Gad, by
their generations, after their families, by the house of their
fathers, according to the number of the names, from twenty
years old and upward, all that were able to go forth to war;
25 those that were numbered of them, *even* of the tribe of Gad, *were*
26 forty and five thousand six hundred and fifty. ¶ Of the children
of Judah, by their generations, after their families, by the house
of their fathers, according to the number of the names, from
twenty years old and upward, all that were able to go forth to
27 war; those that were numbered of them, *even* of the tribe of
Judah, *were* threescore and fourteen thousand and six hundred.
28 ¶ Of the children of Issachar, by their generations, after their
families, by the house of their fathers, according to the number
of the names, from twenty years old and upward, all that were
29 able to go forth to war; those that were numbered of them,
even of the tribe of Issachar, *were* fifty and four thousand and
30 four hundred. ¶ Of the children of Zebulun, by their generations, after their families, by the house of their fathers, according to the number of the names, from twenty years old and
31 upward, all that were able to go forth to war; those that were
numbered of them, *even* of the tribe of Zebulun, *were* fifty and
32 seven thousand and four hundred. ¶ Of the children of Joseph,
namely, of the children of Ephraim, by their generations, after
their families, by the house of their fathers, according to the
number of the names, from twenty years old and upward, all
33 that were able to go forth to war; those that were numbered of
them, *even* of the tribe of Ephraim, *were* forty thousand and five
34 hundred. ¶ Of the children of Manasseh, by their generations,
after their families, by the house of their fathers, according to
the number of the names, from twenty years old and upward, all
35 that were able to go forth to war; those that were numbered of
them, *even* of the tribe of Manasseh, *were* thirty and two thou-
36 sand and two hundred. ¶ Of the children of Benjamin, by their
generations, after their families, by the house of their fathers,
according to the number of the names, from twenty years old
37 and upward, all that were able to go forth to war; those that
were numbered of them, *even* of the tribe of Benjamin, *were*
38 thirty and five thousand and four hundred. ¶ Of the children of Dan, by their generations, after their families, by
the house of their fathers, according to the number of the
names, from twenty years old and upward, all that were able
39 to go forth to war; those that were numbered of them, *even* of
the tribe of Dan, *were* threescore and two thousand and seven

---

which rendered it difficult to bring all their
members together at once for a census. Judah already takes precedence of his brethren

in point of numbers (cp. Gen. xlix. 8 note),
and Ephraim of Manasseh (cp. Gen. xlviii.
19, 20).

40 hundred. ¶ Of the children of Asher, by their generations, after their families, by the house of their fathers, according to the number of the names, from twenty years old and upward, 41 all that were able to go forth to war; those that were numbered of them, *even* of the tribe of Asher, *were* forty and one thousand 42 and five hundred. ¶ Of the children of Naphtali, throughout their generations, after their families, by the house of their fathers, according to the number of the names, from twenty years old and upward, all that were able to go forth to war; 43 those that were numbered of them, *even* of the tribe of Naphtali, 44 *were* fifty and three thousand and four hundred. ¶ *g* These *are* those that were numbered, which Moses and Aaron numbered, and the princes of Israel, *being* twelve men: each one was for 45 the house of his fathers. So were all those that were numbered of the children of Israel, by the house of their fathers, from twenty years old and upward, all that were able to go forth to 46 war in Israel; even all they that were numbered were *h* six hundred thousand and three thousand and five hundred and fifty. 47 But *i* the Levites after the tribe of their fathers were not num- 48 bered among them. For the LORD had spoken unto Moses, say- 49 ing, *k* Only thou shalt not number the tribe of Levi, neither 50 take the sum of them among the children of Israel: *l* but thou shalt appoint the Levites over the tabernacle of testimony, and over all the vessels thereof, and over all things that *belong* to it : they shall bear the tabernacle, and all the vessels thereof; and they shall minister unto it, *m* and shall encamp round about 51 the tabernacle. *n* And when the tabernacle setteth forward, the Levites shall take it down : and when the tabernacle is to be pitched, the Levites shall set it up : *o* and the stranger that com- 52 eth nigh shall be put to death. And the children of Israel shall pitch their tents, *p* every man by his own camp, and every man 53 by his own standard, throughout their hosts. *q* But the Levites shall pitch round about the tabernacle of testimony, that there be no *r* wrath upon the congregation of the children of Israel : *s* and the Levites shall keep the charge of the tabernacle of testi- 54 mony. ¶ And the children of Israel did according to all that the LORD commanded Moses, so did they.

CHAP. 2. AND the LORD spake unto Moses and unto Aaron, saying, 2 *a* Every man of the children of Israel shall pitch by his own standard, with the ensign of their father's house: *1b* far off about the tabernacle of the congregation shall they pitch.

g ch. 26. 64.

h Ex. 38. 26.
See Exod.
12. 37.
ch. 2. 32.
& 26. 51.
i ch. 2. 33.
See ch. 3.
& 4.
& 26. 57.
1 Chr. 6.
& 21. 6.
k ch. 2. 33.
& 26. 62.
l Ex. 38. 21.
ch. 3. 7, 8.
& 4. 15, 25,
26. 27, 33.
m ch. 3. 23,
29, 35, 38.
n ch. 10. 17,
21.
o ch. 3. 10, 38.
& 18. 22.
p ch. 2. 2, 34.
q ver. 50.
r Lev. 10. 6.
ch. 8. 19.
& 16. 46.
& 18. 5.
1 Sam. 6. 19.
s ch. 3. 7, 8.
& 8. 24, 25,
26.
& 18. 3, 4, 5.
& 31. 30, 47.
1 Chr. 23. 32.
2 Chr. 13. 11.
a ch. 1. 52.
b Josh. 3. 4.

1 Heb. *over against*.

47-54. When a census of the tribe of Levi takes place. (iii. 15, xxvi. 62), *all* the males are counted from a month old and upward, and not, as in the other tribes, those only who were of age for service in the field.

48. *had spoken*] Render **spake**. The formal appointment is only now made, in reward for their zeal (Ex. xxxii. 26–29), though reference to their future office appears previously in Lev. xxv. 32 sqq., and they had already acted as assistants to the priests (cp. Ex. xxxviii. 21).

II. 2. *standard...ensign*] The "standard" marked the division, or camp (cf. *vv.* 9, 16, 24, 31); the "ensign" the family. There

would thus be four "standards" only, one for each "camp" of three tribes. The "standard" was probably a solid figure or emblem mounted on a pole, such as the Egyptians used. Tradition appropriates the four cherubic forms (Ezek. i. 5–12 ; Rev. iv. 7 sqq.), the lion, man, ox, and eagle, to the camps of Judah, Reuben, Ephraim, and Dan respectively ; and this, as to the first, has a certain support from Gen. xlix. 9 (cp. Rev. v. 5), and as to the third, from Deut. xxxiii. 17.

far off] See margin, over against; *i.e.* facing the tabernacle on every side. The distance was perhaps 2000 cubits or rather more than ¼ mile : cp. Josh. iii. 4.

3 ¶ And on the east side toward the rising of the sun shall they of the standard of the camp of Judah pitch throughout their armies: and ^cNahshon the son of Amminadab *shall be* captain of
4 the children of Judah. And his host, and those that were numbered of them, *were* threescore and fourteen thousand and six
5 hundred. And those that do pitch next unto him *shall be* the tribe of Issachar: and Nethaneel the son of Zuar *shall be* captain
6 of the children of Issachar. And his host, and those that were numbered thereof, *were* fifty and four thousand and four hun-
7 dred. *Then* the tribe of Zebulun: and Eliab the son of Helon
8 *shall be* captain of the children of Zebulun. And his host, and those that were numbered thereof, *were* fifty and seven thousand
9 and four hundred. All that were numbered in the camp of Judah *were* an hundred thousand and fourscore thousand and six thousand and four hundred, throughout their armies. ^dThese
10 shall first set forth. ¶ On the south side *shall be* the standard of the camp of Reuben according to their armies: and the captain
11 of the children of Reuben *shall be* Elizur the son of Shedeur. And his host, and those that were numbered thereof, *were* forty and
12 six thousand and five hundred. And those which pitch by him *shall be* the tribe of Simeon: and the captain of the children of
13 Simeon *shall be* Shelumiel the son of Zurishaddai. And his host, and those that were numbered of them, *were* fifty and nine thou-
14 sand and three hundred. Then the tribe of Gad: and the captain
15 of the sons of Gad *shall be* Eliasaph the son of ¹Reuel. And his host, and those that were numbered of them, *were* forty and five
16 thousand and six hundred and fifty. All that were numbered in the camp of Reuben *were* an hundred thousand and fifty and one thousand and four hundred and fifty, throughout their armies.
17 ^eAnd they shall set forth in the second rank. ¶^fThen the tabernacle of the congregation shall set forward with the camp of the Levites in the midst of the camp: as they encamp, so shall they
18 set forward, every man in his place by their standards. ¶ On the west side *shall be* the standard of the camp of Ephraim according to their armies: and the captain of the sons of Ephraim

¹ *Deuel,* ch. 1. 14. & 7. 42, 47, & 10. 20.

^c ch. 10. 14.
Ruth 4. 20.
1 Chr. 2. 10.
Matt. 1. 4.
Luke 3. 32, 33.

^d ch. 10. 14.

^e ch. 10. 18.
^f ch. 10. 17, 21.

14. *Reuel*] Doubtless an error of transcription for Deuel (i. 14).
3-32. The following plan shows the general arrangement of the camp, which would vary in different places according to local exigencies. The area of the camp might be about three square miles.

North.

DAN.   Asher.   Naphtali.

Benjamin.   Merarites.   JUDAH.

West.   Manasseh.   Gershonites. | Sanctuary. | Moses, Aaron, and Priests.   Issachar.   *East.*

EPHRAIM.   Kohathites.   Zebulon.

Gad.   Simeon.   REUBEN.

South.

19 *shall be* Elishama the son of Ammihud.   And his host, and those
that were numbered of them, *were* forty thousand and five hun-
20 dred.   And by him *shall be* the tribe of Manasseh : and the
captain of the children of Manasseh *shall be* Gamaliel the son of
21 Pedahzur.   And his host, and those that were numbered of them,
22 *were* thirty and two thousand and two hundred.   Then the tribe
of Benjamin :   and the captain of the sons of Benjamin *shall be*
23 Abidan the son of Gideoni.   And his host, and those that were
numbered of them, *were* thirty and five thousand and four hun-
24 dred.   All that were numbered of the camp of Ephraim *were* an
hundred thousand and eight thousand and an hundred, through-

g ch. 10. 22.   out their armies.   *g*And they shall go forward in the third rank.
25 ¶ The standard of the camp of Dan *shall be* on the north side by
their armies : and the captain of the children of Dan *shall be*
26 Ahiezer the son of Ammishaddai.   And his host, and those that
were numbered of them, *were* threescore and two thousand and
27 seven hundred.   And those that encamp by him *shall be* the
tribe of Asher : and the captain of the children of Asher *shall be*
28 Pagiel the son of Ocran.   And his host, and those that were
numbered of them, *were* forty and one thousand and five hun-
29 dred.   Then the tribe of Naphtali : and the captain of the
30 children of Naphtali *shall be* Ahira the son of Enan.   And his
host, and those that were numbered of them, *were* fifty and three
31 thousand and four hundred.   All they that were numbered in
the camp of Dan *were* an hundred thousand and fifty and seven

h ch. 10. 25.   thousand and six hundred.   *h*They shall go hindmost with their
32 standards.   ¶ These *are* those which were numbered of the chil-

i Ex. 38. 26.   dren of Israel by the house of their fathers : *i*all those that were
ch. 1. 46.   numbered of the camps throughout their hosts *were* six hundred
& 11. 21.
33 thousand and three thousand and five hundred and fifty.   But

k ch. 1. 47.   *k* the Levites were not numbered among the children of Israel ;
34 as the LORD commanded Moses.   And the children of Israel did

l ch. 24. 2,   according to all that the LORD commanded Moses : *l*so they
5, 6.   pitched by their standards, and so they set forward, every one
after their families, according to the house of their fathers.
CHAP. 3.   THESE also *are* the generations of Aaron and Moses in
2 the day *that* the LORD spake with Moses in mount Sinai.   And

a Ex. 6. 23.   these *are* the names of the sons of Aaron ; Nadab the *a*firstborn,
3 and Abihu, Eleazar, and Ithamar.   These *are* the names of the

b Ex. 28. 41.   sons of Aaron, *b*the priests which were anointed, [1]whom he con-
Lev. 8.
c Lev. 10. 1.   4 secrated to minister in the priest's office.   *c*And Nadab and Abihu
ch. 26. 61.
1 Chr. 24. 2.   [1] Heb. *whose hand he filled.*

32–34. Such was the ideal form of the
encampment in the wilderness : a form reproduced in the square court with which the
Temple was eventually surrounded, and in
the vision of the heavenly city as seen by
Ezekiel (xlviii. 20), and by St. John (Rev.
xxi. 16 ; cp. Rev. xx. 9).   Thus the camp of
God's earthly people was divinely ordered
so as to set forth the completeness of His
Church; and to illustrate by its whole arrangement, which was determined by the
Tabernacle in the centre, both the de-
pendance of all on God, and the access
which all enjoyed to God.
    III. 1. The " generations " (see Gen. ii.

4) now given, though entitled those of
Aaron and Moses (Aaron standing first as
the elder brother), are those of Aaron only.
The personal dignity of Moses, though it
gave him rank as at the head of his tribe,
was not hereditary.   He had, and desired
to have (xiv. 12 ; Ex. xxxii. 10), no successor in his office but the distant Prophet
like unto himself (Deut. xviii. 18).   Aaron
was the ancestor of a regular succession of
priests.
    3. *whom he consecrated*] i.e. whom Moses
consecrated, or literally as marg., whose
" hand he filled," by conferring their office
upon them (Lev. viii. 1 seq.).

died before the LORD, when they offered strange fire before the
LORD, in the wilderness of Sinai, and they had no children: and
Eleazar and Ithamar ministered in the priest's office in the sight
5 of Aaron their father. ¶ And the LORD spake unto Moses, say-
6 ing, *d* Bring the tribe of Levi near, and present them before
7 Aaron the priest, that they may minister unto him. And they
shall keep his charge, and the charge of the whole congregation
before the tabernacle of the congregation, to do *e* the service of
8 the tabernacle. And they shall keep all the instruments of the
tabernacle of the congregation, and the charge of the children of
9 Israel, to do the service of the tabernacle. And *f* thou shalt give
the Levites unto Aaron and to his sons : they *are* wholly given
10 unto him out of the children of Israel. And thou shalt appoint
Aaron and his sons, *g* and they shall wait on their priest's office :
h and the stranger that cometh nigh shall be put to death.
11, 12 ¶ And the LORD spake unto Moses, saying, And I, behold, *i* I
have taken the Levites from among the children of Israel instead
of all the firstborn that openeth the matrix among the children
13 of Israel : therefore the Levites shall be mine ; because *k* all the
firstborn *are* mine; *l for* on the day that I smote all the firstborn in the land of Egypt I hallowed unto me all the firstborn
in Israel, both man and beast : mine shall they be : I *am* the
14 LORD. ¶ And the LORD spake unto Moses in the wilderness of
15 Sinai, saying, Number the children of Levi after the house of
their fathers, by their families : *m* every male from a month old
16 and upward shalt thou number them. And Moses numbered
them according to the [1] word of the LORD, as he was commanded.
17 *n* And these were the sons of Levi by their names ; Gershon, and
18 Kohath, and Merari. And these *are* the names of the sons of
19 Gershon by their families ; *o* Libni, and Shimei. And the sons
of Kohath by their families ; *p* Amram, and Izehar, Hebron,
20 and Uzziel. *q* And the sons of Merari by their families ; Mahli,
and Mushi. These *are* the families of the Levites according to
21 the house of their fathers. ¶ Of Gershon *was* the family of the
Libnites, and the family of the Shimites : these *are* the families
22 of the Gershonites. Those that were numbered of them, according to the number of all the males, from a month old and
upward, *even* those that were numbered of them *were* seven thou-
23 sand and five hundred. *r* The families of the Gershonites shall
24 pitch behind the tabernacle westward. And the chief of the
house of the father of the Gershonites *shall be* Eliasaph the son of
25 Lael. And *s* the charge of the sons of Gershon in the tabernacle
of the congregation *shall be* *t* the tabernacle, and *u* the tent, *x* the
covering thereof, and *y* the hanging for the door of the tabernacle
26 of the congregation, and *z* the hangings of the court, and *a* the
curtain for the door of the court, which *is* by the tabernacle, and
by the altar round about, and *b* the cords of it for all the service
27 thereof. ¶ *c* And of Kohath *was* the family of the Amramites,
and the family of the Izeharites, and the family of the Hebronites,

[1] Heb. *mouth.*

d ch. 8. 6.
& 18. 2.

e See ch. 1.
50.
& 8. 11, 15,
24, 26.
f ch. 8. 19.
& 18. 6.

g ch. 18. 7.
h ver. 38.
ch. 1. 51.
& 16. 40.
i ver. 41.
ch. 8. 16.
& 18. 6.
k Ex. 13. 2.
Lev. 27. 26.
ch. 8. 16.
Luke 2. 23.
l Ex. 13. 12,
15.
ch. 8. 17.

m ver. 39.
ch. 26. 62.

n Gen. 46.
11.
ch. 6. 16.
ch. 26. 57.
1 Chr. 6. 1,
16.
& 23. 6.
o Ex. 6. 17.
p Ex. 6. 18
q Ex. 6. 19.

r ch. 1. 53.

s ch. 4. 24,
25, 26.
t Ex. 25. 9.
u Ex. 26. 1.
x Ex. 26. 7,
14.
y Ex. 26. 36.
z Ex. 27. 9.
a Ex. 27. 16.
b Ex. 35. 18.
c 1 Chr. 26.
23.

---

7. *keep his charge*] i.e. so assist him that
the obligations incumbent on him and on
the congregation may be fulfilled.

13. The concluding words are better expressed thus : " Mine shall they be, Mine,
the Lord's." On the subject of the firstborn
see notes on *vv.* 43-51.

26. *the cords...the service thereof*] i.e. of
the Tabernacle, not of the hangings of the
Court ; for these, with their cords and other
fittings, belonged to the charge of the Merarites (*vv.* 36, 37). The Tabernacle was
under the care of the Gershonites.

27-32. Of the Levites, the Kohathites,

and the family of the Uzzielites: these *are* the families of the
28 Kohathites. In the number of all the males, from a month
old and upward, *were* eight thousand and six hundred, keeping
d ch. 1. 53.   29 the charge of the sanctuary. *d*The families of the sons of Kohath
30 shall pitch on the side of the tabernacle southward. And the
chief of the house of the father of the families of the Kohathites
e ch. 4. 15.   31 shall be Elizaphan the son of Uzziel. And *e*their charge *shall*
f Ex. 25. 10.   be *f*the ark, and *g*the table, a d *h*the candlestick, and *i*the
g Ex. 25. 23.
h Ex. 25. 31.   altars, and the vessels of the sanctuary wherewith they minister,
i Ex. 27. 1.   32 and *k*the hanging, and all the service thereof. And Eleazar the
& 30. 1.
k Ex. 26. 32.   son of Aaron the priest *shall be* chief over the chief of the Levites, *and have* the oversight of them that keep the charge of the
33 sanctuary. ¶ Of Merari *was* the family of the Mahlites, and the
34 family of the Mushites: these *are* the families of Merari. And
those that were numbered of them, according to the number of
all the males, from a month old and upward, *were* six thousand
35 and two hundred. And the chief of the house of the father of
l ch. 1. 53.   the families of Merari *was* Zuriel the son of Abihail: *l these* shall
m ch. 4. 31,   36 pitch on the side of the tabernacle northward. And *1m under*
32.
the custody and charge of the sons of Merari *shall be* the boards
of the tabernacle, and the bars thereof, and the pillars thereof,
and the sockets thereof, and all the vessels thereof, and all that
37 serveth thereto, and the pillars of the court round about, and
n ch. 1. 53.   38 their sockets, and their pins, and their cords. ¶ *n*But those that
encamp before the tabernacle toward the east, *even* before the
tabernacle of · the congregation eastward, *shall be* Moses, and
o ch. 18. 5.   Aaron and his sons, *o*keeping the charge of the sanctuary *p*for
p ver. 7, 8.   the charge of the children of Israel; and *q*the stranger that
q ver. 10.
r See ch. 26.   39 cometh nigh shall be put to death. *r*All that were numbered of
62.
the Levites, which Moses and Aaron numbered at the commandment of the LORD, throughout their families, all the males from
40 a month old and upward, *were* twenty and two thousand. ¶ And
s ver. 15.   the LORD said unto Moses, *s*Number all the firstborn of the
males of the children of Israel from a month old and upward,
t ver. 12. 45.   41 and take the number of their names. *t*And thou shalt take the
Levites for me (I *am* the LORD) instead of all the firstborn
among the children of Israel; and the cattle of the Levites
instead of all the firstlings among the cattle of the children of
42 Israel. And Moses numbered, as the LORD commanded him, all
43 the firstborn among the children of Israel. And all the firstborn
males by the number of names, from a month old and upward,

1 Heb. *the office of the charge.*

---

the kinsmen of Moses and Aaron, and the
most numerous, ·have the most important
charge confided to them, viz. that of the Ark,
the Altars, and the more especially sacred
furniture generally.

39. *twenty and two thousand*] A number
on which the commutation with the Firstborn of the Twelve tribes depends (*vv.* 43–
46). The actual total of the male Levites
is 22,300 (cp. *vv.* 22, 28, 34): and the extra
300 are considered by some to represent
those who, being first-born themselves in
the tribe of Levi, could not be available to
redeem the first-born in other tribes. Others
consider the difference due to an error in the
Hebrew text.

The tribe of Levi is shown by this census
to have been by far the smallest of the
tribes.

43. This result, when compared with the
number of male adults (603, 550, cp. ii. 32),
is small, the usual proportion of first-born
sons to a total male population being about
one in four: and the explanation offered is
that the law of Ex. xiii. 1, 2, prescribed a
dedication of those only who should be firstborn *thenceforward*.

On the other hand, the number is very
large to be born amongst two millions of
persons in a single year; and it must be admitted, that some unusual causes must have
been concerned. Such, not to mention the

of those that were numbered of them, were twenty and two thousand two hundred and threescore and thirteen. ¶ And the LORD
44 spake unto Moses, saying, *Take the Levites instead of all the
45 firstborn among the children of Israel, and the cattle of the
Levites instead of their cattle; and the Levites shall be mine: I
46 *am* the LORD. And for those that are to be *redeemed of the
two hundred and threescore and thirteen of the firstborn of the
47 children of Israel, *which are more than the Levites; thou shalt
even take *five shekels apiece by the poll, after the shekel of the
sanctuary shalt thou take *them*: (*the shekel *is* twenty gerahs:)
48 and thou shalt give the money, wherewith the odd number of
49 them is to be redeemed, unto Aaron and to his sons. And Moses
took the redemption money of them that were over and above
50 them that were redeemed by the Levites: of the firstborn of the
children of Israel took he the money; *a thousand three hundred and threescore and five *shekels*, after the shekel of the
51 sanctuary: and Moses *gave the money of them that were
redeemed unto Aaron and to his sons, according to the word of
the LORD, as the LORD commanded Moses.

CHAP. 4. AND the LORD spake unto Moses and unto Aaron, say-
2 ing, Take the sum of the sons of Kohath from among the sons
3 of Levi, after their families, by the house of their fathers, *from
thirty years old and upward even until fifty years old, all that
enter into the host, to do the work in the tabernacle of the con-
4 gregation. *This *shall be* the service of the sons of Kohath in
the tabernacle of the congregation, *about *the most holy things:
5 and when the camp setteth forward, Aaron shall come, and his
sons, and they shall take down *the covering vail, and cover the
6 *ark of testimony with it: and shall put thereon the covering of
badgers' skins, and shall spread over *it* a cloth wholly of blue,
7 and shall put in *the staves thereof. And upon the *table of
shewbread they shall spread a cloth of blue, and put thereon
the dishes, and the spoons, and the bowls, and covers to ¹cover
8 withal: and the continual bread shall be thereon: and they
shall spread upon them a cloth of scarlet, and cover the same
with a covering of badgers' skins, and shall put in the staves
9 thereof. And they shall take a cloth of blue, and cover the

u ver. 12. 41.

x Ex. 13. 13.
ch. 18. 15.
y ver. 39. 43.
z Lev. 27. 6.
ch. 18. 16.
a Ex. 30. 13.
Lev. 27. 25.
ch. 18. 16.
Ez. 45. 12.

b ver. 46, 47.

c ver. 48.

a See ch. 8.
24.
1 Chr. 23. 3,
24, 27.
b ver. 15.
c ver. 19.

d Ex. 26. 31.
e Ex. 25. 10,
16.

f Ex. 25. 13.
g Ex. 25. 23,
29, 30.
Lev. 24. 6, 8.

¹ Or, *pour out withal.*

Divine Blessing, may be found in the sudden development of national energies which would immediately ensue on the Exodus. Before that event, the miserable estate of the people, and especially the inhuman order for the destruction of their first-born, would check very seriously the ratio of marriages and births; and this ratio would naturally, when the check was removed, exhibit a sudden and striking increase.

44–51. This redemption money (see marg. reff.) would perhaps be exacted from the parents of the *youngest* children of the 22,273 (*v.* 43). The cattle of the Levites was doubtless taken in the gross as an equivalent for the first-born cattle of the other tribes, which of course, no less than the first-born of men, belonged to the Lord; and in future would have to be redeemed (xviii. 15; Deut. xv. 19).

IV. 4. *about the most holy things*] Omit

"about." The sense is, "this is the charge of the sons of Kohath, the most holy things:" *i.e.* the Ark of the Covenant, the Table of Shewbread, the Candlestick, and the Golden Altar, together with the furniture pertaining thereto. It appears, from a comparison of *vv.* 16, 28, and 33, that the ministry of the Kohathites was superintended by Eleazar, the elder of the two surviving sons of Aaron; and that of the two other families by Ithamar.

6. *wholly of blue*] Cp. Ex. xxv. 4 note. The third and external covering of the Ark only was to be of this colour. The Table of Shewbread had (*v.* 8) an outer wrapping of scarlet; the Altar (*v.* 13) one of purple.

put in the staves] Probably, "put the staves in order." These were never taken out of the golden rings by which the Ark was to be borne (see Ex. xxv. 14, 15), but would need adjustment.

h Ex. 25. 31.
i Ex. 25. 37, 38.

k Ex. 30. 1, 3.

l ch. 7. 9.
& 10. 21.
Deut. 31. 9.
2 Sam. 6. 13.
1 Chr. 15. 2, 15.
m 2 Sam. 6. 6, 7.
1 Chr. 13. 9, 10.
n ch. 3. 31.
o Ex. 25. 6.
Lev. 24. 2.
p Ex. 30. 34.
q Ex. 29. 40.
r Ex. 30. 23.
s ver. 4.

t See Ex. 19. 21.
1 Sam. 6. 19.

u ver. 3.

x ch. 3. 25, 26.

[h]candlestick of the light, [i]and his lamps, and his tongs, and his snuffdishes, and all the oil vessels thereof, wherewith they 10 minister unto it: and they shall put it and all the vessels thereof within a covering of badgers' skins, and shall put *it* upon 11 a bar. And upon [k]the golden altar they shall spread a cloth of blue, and cover it with a covering of badgers' skins, and shall 12 put to the staves thereof: and they shall take all the instruments of ministry, wherewith they minister in the sanctuary, and put *them* in a cloth of blue, and cover them with a covering 13 of badgers' skins, and shall put *them* on a bar: and they shall take away the ashes from the altar, and spread a purple cloth 14 thereon: and they shall put upon it all the vessels thereof, wherewith they minister about it,· even the censers, the fleshhooks, and the shovels, and the [1]basons, all the vessels of the altar; and they shall spread upon it a covering of badgers' skins, 15 and put to the staves of it. And when Aaron and his sons have made an end of covering the sanctuary, and all the vessels of the sanctuary, as the camp is to set forward; after that, [l]the sons of Kohath shall come to bear *it*: [m]but they shall not touch *any* holy thing, lest they die. [n]These *things are* the burden of the 16 sons of Kohath in the tabernacle of the congregation. ¶And to the office of Eleazar the son of Aaron the priest *pertaineth* [o]the oil for the light, and the [p]sweet incense, and [q]the daily meat offering, and the [r]anointing oil, *and* the oversight of all the tabernacle, and of all that therein *is*, in the sanctuary, and in 17 the vessels thereof. ¶And the LORD spake unto Moses and 18 unto Aaron, saying, Cut ye not off the tribe of the families of 19 the Kohathites from among the Levites: but thus do unto them, that they may live, and not die, when they approach unto [s]the most holy things: Aaron and his sons shall go in, and appoint 20 them every one to his service and to his burden: [t]but they shall not go in to see when the holy things are covered, lest they 21, 22 die. ¶And the LORD spake unto Moses, saying, Take also the sum of the sons of Gershon, throughout the houses of their 23 fathers, by their families; [u]from thirty years old and upward until fifty years old shalt thou number them; all that enter in [2]to perform the service, to do the work in the tabernacle of the 24 congregation. This *is* the service of the families of the Ger- 25 shonites, to serve, and for [3]burdens: and [x]they shall bear the curtains of the tabernacle, and the tabernacle of the congregation, his covering, and the covering of the badgers' skins that *is* above upon it, and the hanging for the door of the tabernacle 26 of the congregation, and the hangings of the court, and the hanging for the door of the gate of the court, which *is* by the tabernacle and by the altar round about, and their cords, and all the instruments of their service, and all that is made for them: 27 so shall they serve. At the [4]appointment of Aaron and his sons shall be all the service of the sons of the Gershonites, in all their

---

[1] Or, *bowls.*   [3] Or, *carriage.*   [4] Heb. *mouth.*
[2] Heb. *to war the warfare.*

---

20. *to see when the holy things are covered*] Render: **to see the holy things for an instant.** The expression means literally "as a gulp," *i.e.* for the instant it takes to swallow.
23. *enter in to perform the service*] Lit. as

in marg. "to war the warfare," or, as the same phrase in part is rendered, v. 3, "enter into the host to do the work." The language is military. The service of God is a sacred warfare (viii. 24, 25 marg. reading).

burdens, and in all their service: and ye shall appoint unto
28 them in charge all their burdens. This *is* the service of the
families of the sons of Gershon in the tabernacle of the congregation: and their charge *shall be* under the hand of Ithamar
29 the son of Aaron the priest. ¶ As for the sons of Merari, thou
shalt number them after their families, by the house of their
30 fathers; *y*from thirty years old and upward even unto fifty years   *y* ver. 3.
old shalt thou number them, every one that entereth into the
¹service, to do the work of the tabernacle of the congregation.
31 And *ᶻ*this *is* the charge of their burden, according to all their   *ᶻ* ch. 3. 36,
service in the tabernacle of the congregation; *ᵃ*the boards of   37.
the tabernacle, and the bars thereof, and the pillars thereof, and   *ᵃ* Ex. 26. 15.
32 sockets thereof, and the pillars of the court round about, and
their sockets and their pins, and their cords, with all their
instruments, and with all their service: and by name ye shall
33 *ᵇ*reckon the instruments of the charge of their burden. This *is*   *ᵇ* Ex. 38. 21.
the service of the families of the sons of Merari, according to all
their service, in the tabernacle of the congregation, under the
34 hand of Ithamar the son of Aaron the priest. ¶ *ᶜ*And Moses and   *ᶜ* ver. 2.
Aaron and the chief of the congregation numbered the sons of
the Kohathites after their families, and after the house of their
35 fathers, from thirty years old and upward even unto fifty years
old, every one that entereth into the service, for the work in the
36 tabernacle of the congregation: and those that were numbered
of them by their families were two thousand seven hundred and
37 fifty. These *were* they that were numbered of the families of the
Kohathites, all that might do service in the tabernacle of the congregation, which Moses and Aaron did number according to the
38 commandment of the LORD by the hand of Moses. ¶ And those
that were numbered of the sons of Gershon, throughout their
39 families, and by the house of their fathers, from thirty years
old and upward even unto fifty years old, every one that entereth
into the service, for the work in the tabernacle of the congre-
40 gation, even those that were numbered of them, throughout their
families, by the house of their fathers, were two thousand and
41 six hundred and thirty. *ᵈ*These *are* they that were numbered   *ᵈ* ver. 22.
of the families of the sons of Gershon, óf all that might do service in the tabernacle of the congregation, whom Moses and
Aaron did number according to the commandment of the LORD.
42 ¶ And those that were numbered of the families of the sons of
Merari, throughout their families, by the house of their fathers,
43 from thirty years old and upward even unto fifty years old,
every one that entereth into the service, for the work in the taber-
44 nacle of the congregation, even those that were numbered of
them after their families, were three thousand and two hundred.
45 These *be* those that were numbered of the families of the sons of
Merari, whom Moses and Aaron numbered *ᵉ*according to the   *ᵉ* ver. 29.

¹ Heb. *warfare.*

28, 33. The Gershonites and Merarites
are superintended by Ithamar, Aaron's
younger son, who had already had the oversight of the Tabernacle in its construction
(Ex. xxxviii. 21). Thus readily do the permanent offices of the leaders of the Israelite
community spring out of the duties which,
under the emergencies of the first year of
the Exodus, they had been led, from time

to time, to undertake.

32. *by name ye shall reckon the instruments*] Or, assign them to their bearers
singly, and "by name." These "instruments" comprised the heavier parts of the
Tabernacle; and the order seems intended
to prevent individual Merarites choosing
their own burden, and so throwing more
than the proper share on others.

46 word of the LORD by the hand of Moses. ¶ All those that were
numbered of the Levites, whom Moses and Aaron and the chief
of Israel numbered, after their families, and after the house of
47 their fathers, *f* from thirty years old and upward even unto fifty
years old, every one that came to do the service of the ministry,
and the service of the burden in the tabernacle of the congre-
48 gation, even those that were numbered of them, were eight
49 thousand and five hundred and fourscore. According to the
commandment of the LORD they were numbered by the hand of
Moses, *g* every one according to his service, and according to his
burden: thus were they numbered of him, *h* as the LORD commanded Moses.

CHAP. 5. AND the LORD spake unto Moses, saying, Command the
2 children of Israel, that they put out of the camp every *a* leper,
and every one that hath an *b* issue, and whosoever is defiled by
3 the *c* dead: both male and female shall ye put out, without the
camp shall ye put them; that they defile not their camps, *d* in
4 the midst whereof I dwell. And the children of Israel did so,
and put them out without the camp: as the LORD spake unto
5 Moses, so did the children of Israel. ¶ And the LORD spake
6 unto Moses, saying, Speak unto the children of Israel, *e* When a
man or woman shall commit any sin that men commit, to do a
7 trespass against the LORD, and that person be guilty; *f* then they
shall confess their sin which they have done: and he shall recompense his trespass *g* with the principal thereof, and add unto it
the fifth *part* thereof, and give *it* unto *him* against whom he hath
8 trespassed. But if the man have no kinsman to recompense the
trespass unto, let the trespass be recompensed unto the LORD,
even to the priest; beside *h* the ram of the atonement, whereby an
9 atonement shall be made for him. And every [1]*i* offering of all
the holy things of the children of Israel, which they bring unto
10 the priest, shall be his. And every man's hallowed things shall
be his: whatsoever any man giveth the priest, it shall be *k* his.
11, 12 ¶ And the LORD spake unto Moses, saying, Speak unto the
children of Israel, and say unto them, If any man's wife go
13 aside, and commit a trespass against him, and a man *l* lie with her
carnally, and it be hid from the eyes of her husband, and be kept

[1] Or, *heave offering.*

Marginal references

f ver. 3, 23, 30.

g ver. 15, 24, 31.
h ver. 1. 21.

a Lev. 13. 3, 46.
& ch. 12. 14.
b Lev. 15. 2.
c Lev. 21. 1.
ch. 9. 6, 10.
& 19. 11, 13.
& 31. 19.
d Lev. 26. 11, 12.
2 Cor. 6. 16.
e Lev. 6. 2, 3.
f Lev. 5. 5.
& 26. 40.
Josh. 7. 19.
g Lev. 6. 5.

h Lev. 6. 6, 7.
& 7. 7.
i Ex. 29. 28.
Lev. 6. 17, 18, 26.
& 7. 6, 7, 9, 10, 14.
ch. 18. 8, 9, 19.
Deut. 18. 3, 4.
Ez. 44. 29, 30.
k Lev. 10. 13.
l Lev. 18. 20.

V. The general purpose of the directions
given in this and the next chapter is to
attest and to vindicate, by modes in harmony with the spirit of the theocratical law,
the sanctity of the people of God. Thus
the congregation of Israel was made to
typify the Church of God, within which, in
its perfection, nothing that offends can be
allowed to remain (cp. St. Matt. viii. 22;
Rev. xxi. 27).

1–4. Cp. marg. reff. The precepts of Lev.
xiii. and xv. are now first fully carried out.
They could hardly have been so earlier,
during the hurry and confusion which must
have attended the march out of Egypt, and
the encampments which next followed.

5–10. The Law of restitution: a passage
supplementary to Lev. v. 5, &c., vi. 5, &c.

7. *recompense his trespass*] *i.e.* make restitution to the person whom he has injured.

8. *whereby an atonement shall be made for*

him] Lit. "which shall clear him of guilt
as to it," *i.e.* as to the trespass.

10. *And every man's hallowed things shall
be his*] *i.e.* the priest's. The heave offerings
(*v.* 9) and dedicatory offerings (*e.g.* firstfruits) were to be the perquisite of the officiating priests.

11–31. The trial of jealousy. As the
crime of adultery is peculiarly defiling and
destructive of the very foundations of social
order, the whole subject is dealt with at a
length proportionate to its importance. The
process prescribed has lately been strikingly
illustrated from an Egyptian "Romance,"
which refers to the time of Rameses the
Great, and may therefore well serve to illustrate the manners and customs of the Mosaic
times. This mode of trial, like several other
ordinances, was adopted by Moses from
existing and probably very ancient and
widely spread institutions.

close, and she be defiled, and *there be* no witness against her,
14 neither she be taken *with the manner;* and the spirit of jealousy
come upon him, and he be jealous of his wife, and she be defiled:
or if the spirit of jealousy come upon him, and he be jealous of
15 his wife, and she be not defiled: then shall the man bring his
wife unto the priest, and he shall bring her offering for her, the
tenth *part* of an ephah of barley meal; he shall pour no oil upon
it, nor put frankincense thereon; for it *is* an offering of jealousy,
an offering of memorial, *ᵐ*bringing iniquity to remembrance.
16 And the priest shall bring her near, and set her before the
17 LORD: and the priest shall take holy water in an earthen vessel;
and of the dust that is in the floor of the tabernacle the priest
18 shall take, and put *it* into the water: and the priest shall set
the woman before the LORD, and uncover the woman's head, and
put the offering of memorial in her hands, which *is* the jealousy
offering: and the priest shall have in his hand the bitter water
19 that causeth the curse: and the priest shall charge her by an
oath, and say unto the woman, If no man have lain with thee,
and if thou hast not gone aside to uncleanness ¹²*with another*
instead of thy husband, be thou free from this bitter water that
20 causeth the curse: but if thou hast gone aside *to another* instead
of thy husband, and if thou be defiled, and some man have lain
21 with thee beside thine husband: then the priest shall *ⁿ*charge
the woman with an oath of cursing, and the priest shall say unto
the woman, *ᵒ*The LORD make thee a curse and an oath among
thy people, when the LORD doth make thy thigh to ³rot, and thy
22 belly to swell; and this water that causeth the curse *ᵖ*shall go
into thy bowels to make *thy* belly to swell, and *thy* thigh to
23 rot: *�q*And the woman shall say, Amen, amen. And the priest
shall write these curses in a book, and he shall blot *them* out
24 with the bitter water: and he shall cause the woman to drink
the bitter water that causeth the curse: and the water that
causeth the curse shall enter into her, *and become* bitter.
25 Then the priest shall take the jealousy offering out of the
woman's hand, and shall *ʳ*wave the offering before the LORD, and
26 offer it upon the altar: *ˢ*and the priest shall take an handful of
the offering, *even* the memorial thereof, and burn *it* upon the
altar, and afterward shall cause the woman to drink the water.
27 And when he hath made her to drink the water, then it shall come

ᵐ 1 Kin. 17. 18.
Ez. 29. 16.

ⁿ Josh. 6. 26. 1 Sam.14.24. Neh. 10. 29.
ᵒ Jer. 29. 22.

ᵖ Ps. 109.18.

q Deut. 27. 15.

ʳ Lev. 8. 27.
ˢ Lev. 2.2, 9.

---

¹ Or, being *in the power of thy husband*, Rom. 7. 2.

² Heb. *under thy husband.*
³ Heb. *fall.*

---

15. The offering was to be of the cheapest and coarsest kind, barley (cp. 2 K. vii. 1, 16, 18), representing the abased condition of the suspected woman. It was, like the sin-offering (Lev. v. 11), to be made without oil and frankincense, the symbols of grace and acceptableness. The woman herself stood with head uncovered (*v.* 18), in token of her shame.

17. *the dust that is in the floor of the tabernacle*] To set forth the fact that the water was indued with extraordinary power by Him Who dwelt in the Tabernacle. Dust is an emblem of a state of condemnation (Gen. iii. 14; Micah vii. 17).

19. *gone aside*, &c.] Literally, "gone astray from" **thy husband by uncleanness**; cp. Hos. iv. 12.

23. *blot them out with the bitter water*] In order to transfer the curses to the water. The action was symbolical. Travellers speak of the natives of Africa as still habitually seeking to obtain the full force of a written charm by drinking the water into which they have washed it.

24. *shall cause the woman to drink*] Thus was symbolised both her full acceptance of the hypothetical curse (cp. Ezek. iii. 1–3; Jer. xv. 16; Rev. x. 9), and its actual operation upon her if she should be guilty (cp. Ps. cix. 18).

26. *the memorial thereof*] See marg. ref. "Memorial" here is not the same as "memorial" in *v.* 15.

27. Of itself, the drink was not noxious; and could only produce the effects here deto pass, *that*, if she be defiled, and have done trespass against her husband, that the water that causeth the curse shall enter into her, *and become* bitter, and her belly shall swell, and her thigh shall rot: and the woman [t]shall be a curse among her 28 people. And if the woman be not defiled, but be clean; then 29 she shall be free, and shall conceive seed. ¶ This *is* the law of jealousies, when a wife goeth aside *to another* [u]instead of her 30 husband, and is defiled; or when the spirit of jealousy cometh upon him, and he be jealous over his wife, and shall set the woman before the LORD, and the priest shall execute upon her 31 all this law. Then shall the man be guiltless from iniquity, and this woman [x]shall bear her iniquity.

CHAP. **6.** AND the LORD spake unto Moses, saying, Speak unto the 2 children of Israel, and say unto them, When either man or woman shall [1a]separate *themselves* to vow a vow of a Nazarite, to 3 separate *themselves* unto the LORD: [b]he shall separate *himself* from wine and strong drink, and shall drink no vinegar of wine, or vinegar of strong drink, neither shall he drink any liquor of 4 grapes, nor eat moist grapes, or dried. All the days of his [2]separation shall he eat nothing that is made of the [3]vine tree, 5 from the kernels even to the husk. All the days of the vow of his separation there shall no [c]razor come upon his head: until the days be fulfilled, in the which he separateth *himself* unto the 6 LORD, he shall be holy, *and* shall let the locks of the hair of his head grow. All the days that he separateth *himself* unto the 7 LORD [d]he shall come at no dead body. [e]He shall not make himself unclean for his father, or for his mother, for his brother, or for his sister, when they die: because the [4]consecration of his

Marginal references:
[t] Deut. 28. 37.
Ps. 83. 9, 11.
Jer. 24. 9.
& 29. 18, 22.
& 42. 18.
Zech. 8. 13.
[u] ver. 19.

[x] Lev. 20. 17, 19, 20.

[a] Lev. 27. 2.
Judg. 13. 5.
Acts 21. 23.
Rom. 1. 1.
[b] Amos 2. 12.
Luke 1. 15.

[c] Judg. 13. 5.
& 16. 17.
1 Sam. 1. 11.

[d] Lev. 21. 11.
ch. 19. 11, 16.
[e] Lev. 21. 1, 2, 11.
ch. 9. 6.

[1] Or, *make* themselves *Nazarites.*
[2] Or, *Nazariteship.*
[3] Heb. *vine of the wine.*
[4] Heb. *separation.*

scribed by a special interposition of God. We do not read of any instance in which this ordeal was resorted to: a fact which may be explained either (with the Jews) as a proof of its efficacy, since the guilty could not be brought to face its terrors at all, and avoided them by confession; or more probably by the license of divorce tolerated by the law of Moses. Since a husband could put away his wife at pleasure, a jealous man would naturally prefer to take this course with a suspected wife rather than to call public attention to his own shame by having recourse to the trial of jealousy.

The trial by Red water, which bears a general resemblance to that here prescribed by Moses, is still in use amongst the tribes of Western Africa.

VI. 1–21. The law of the Nazarite is appropriately added to other enactments which concern the sanctity of the holy nation. That sanctity found its highest expression in the Nazarite vow, which was the voluntary adoption for a time of obligations to high and strict modes of self-dedication resembling, and indeed in some particulars exceeding, those under which the priests were placed. The present enactments do not institute a new kind of observance, but only regulate one already familiar to the Israelites (*v.* 2).

2. *a Nazarite*] Strictly, *Nazirite*. This term signifies "separated," *i.e.*, as the words following show, "unto God." It became a technical term at an early date; cp. Judg. xiii. 5, 7, xvi. 17.

3. *liquor of grapes*] *i.e.* a drink made of grape-skins macerated in water.

4. *from the kernels even to the husk*] A sour drink was made from the stones of unripe grapes; and cakes were also made of the husks (Hos. iii. 1). This interdict figures that separation from the general society of men to which the Nazarite for the time was consecrated.

5. Amongst the Jews the abundance of the hair was considered to betoken physical strength and perfection (cp. 2 S. xiv. 25, 26), and baldness was regarded as a grave blemish (cp. Lev. xxi. 20 note, xiii. 40 seq.; 2 K. ii. 23; Isai. iii. 24). Thus the free growth of the hair on the head of the Nazarite represented the dedication of the man with all his strength and powers to the service of God.

7. *the consecration of his God*] *i.e.* the unshorn locks: cp. Lev. xxv. 5 note, where the vine, left during the Sabbatical year untouched by the hand of man, either for pruning or for vintage, is called simply a "Nazarite."

The third rule of the Nazarite interdicted

8 God *is* upon his head. All the days of his separation he *is* holy
9 unto the LORD. And if any man die very suddenly by him, and
he hath defiled the head of his consecration ; then he shall
*f*shave his head in the day of his cleansing, on the seventh day   *f* Acts 18. 18.
10 shall he shave it. And *g*on the eighth day he shall bring two   & 21. 24.
turtles, or two young pigeons, to the priest, to the door of the   *g* Lev. 5. 7.
11 tabernacle of the congregation: and the priest shall offer the one   & 15. 14, 29.
for a sin offering, and the other for a burnt offering, and make
an atonement for him, for that he sinned by the dead, and shall
12 hallow his head that same day. And he shall consecrate unto
the LORD the days of his separation, and shall bring a lamb of
the first year *h*for a trespass offering : but the days that were   *h* Lev. 5. 6.
13 before shall [1]be lost, because his separation was defiled. ¶And
this *is* the law of the Nazarite, *i*when the days of his separation   *i* Acts 21. 26.
are fulfilled : he shall be brought unto the door of the tabernacle
14 of the congregation: and he shall offer his offering unto the
LORD, one he lamb of the first year without blemish *k*for   *k* Lev. 4. 2,
a sin offering, and one ram without blemish *l* for peace offerings,   27, 32.
15 and a basket of unleavened bread, *m*cakes of fine flour mingled   *l* Lev. 3. 6.
with oil, and wafers of unleavened bread *n*anointed with oil, and   *m* Lev. 2. 4.
16 their meat offering, and their *o*drink offering. And the priest   *n* Ex. 29. 2.
shall bring *them* before the LORD, and shall offer his sin offering,   *o* ch. 15. 5,
17 and his burnt offering: and he shall offer the ram *for* a sacrifice   7, 10.
of peace offerings unto the LORD, with the basket of unleavened
bread: the priest shall offer also his meat offering, and his drink
18 offering. *p*And the Nazarite shall shave the head of his sepa-   *p* Acts 21. 24.
ration *at* the door of the tabernacle of the congregation, and shall
take the hair of the head of his separation, and put *it* in the fire
19 which *is* under the sacrifice of the peace offerings. And the
priest shall take the *q*sodden shoulder of the ram, and one un-   *q* 1 Sam. 2.
leavened cake out of the basket, and one unleavened wafer,   15.
and *r*shall put *them* upon the hands of the Nazarite, after *the*   *r* Ex. 29. 23,
20 *hair of* his separation is shaven : and the priest shall wave them   24.

[1] Heb. *fall.*

him from contracting any ceremonial defilement even under circumstances which excused such defilement in others : cp. Lev.
xxi. 1–3.

9–12. Prescriptions to meet the case of a
sudden death taking place " by him " (*i.e.*
in his presence). The days of the dedication
of the Nazarite had to be recommenced.

13. *when the days of his separation are fulfilled*] Perpetual Nazariteship was probably
unknown in the days of Moses ; but the
examples of Samson, Samuel, and John the
Baptist, show that it was in later times
undertaken for life. Again, Moses does not
expressly require that limits should be assigned to the vow ; but a rule was afterwards imposed that no Nazarite vow should
be taken for less than thirty days. To permit the vow to be taken for very short
periods would diminish its solemnity and
estimation.

14, 15. The sin-offering (cp. marg. reff.),
though named second, was in practice
offered first, being intended to expiate in-

voluntary sins committed during the period
of separation. The burnt-offering (Lev. i.
10 sqq.) denoted the self-surrender on which
alone all acceptableness in the Nazarite before God must rest ; the peace-offerings (Lev.
iii. 12 sqq.) expressed thankfulness to God
by whose grace the vow had been fulfilled.
The offerings, both ordinary and additional,
required on the completion of the Nazarite
vow involved considerable expense, and it
was regarded as a pious work to provide
the poor with the means of making them
(cp. Acts xxi. 23 sqq. ; 1 Macc. iii. 49).

18. *shave the head*] As the Nazarite had
during his vow worn his hair unshorn in
honour of God, so when the time was complete it was natural that the hair, the symbol of his vow, should be cut off, and offered
to God at the sanctuary. The burning of
the hair "in the fire under the sacrifice of
the peace offering," represented the eucharistic communion with God obtained by
those who realised the ideal which the
Nazarite set forth (cp. marg. ref.).

for a wave offering before the LORD : *s*this *is* holy for the priest,
with the wave breast and heave shoulder: and after that the
21 Nazarite may drink wine. This *is* the law of the Nazarite who
hath vowed, *and of* his offering unto the LORD for his separation,
beside *that* that his hand shall get: according to the vow which
22 he vowed, so he must do after the law of his separation. ¶ And
23 the LORD spake unto Moses, saying, Speak unto Aaron and unto
his sons, saying, On this wise *t*ye shall bless the children of
Israel, saying unto them,

24　　The LORD bless thee, and *u*keep thee:
25　　The LORD *w*make his face shine upon thee, and *x*be gracious
　　　unto thee:
26　　*y*The LORD lift up his countenance upon thee, and *z*give thee
　　　peace.
27 *a*And they shall put my name upon the children of Israel; and
　　*b*I will bless them.

CHAP. 7. AND it came to pass on the day that Moses had fully *a*set
up the tabernacle, and had anointed it, and sanctified it, and all
the instruments thereof, both the altar and all the vessels thereof,
2 and had anointed them, and sanctified them ; that *b*the princes
of Israel, heads of the house of their fathers, who *were* the
princes of the tribes, ¹and were over them that were numbered,

¹ Heb. *who stood.*

* Ex. 29. 27, 23.

t Lev. 9. 22.
1 Chr. 23. 13.
u Ps. 121. 7.
John 17. 11.
w Ps. 31. 16.
Dan. 9. 17.
x Gen. 43. 29.
y Ps. 4. 6.
z John 14. 27.
2 Thes. 3. 16.
a Deut. 28. 10.
2 Chr. 7. 14.
Isai. 43. 7.
Dan. 9. 18.
b Ps. 115. 12.
a Ex. 40. 18.
Lev. 8. 10,11.
b ch. 1. 4.

20. *the priest shall wave them*] *i.e.* by placing his hands under those of the Nazarite : cp. Lev. vii. 30.

21. *beside that that his hand shall get*] The Nazarite, in addition to the offerings prescribed above, was to present free-will offerings according to his possessions or means.

22–27. The priestly blessing (cp. Ecclus. xxxvi. 17) is appointed as a solemn form to be used by the priests exclusively, and in this function their office as it were culminates (cp. Lev. ix. 22 note). God Himself provides a formula, through which from time to time, as His people by obedience place themselves in true and right relationship to Him, the authorised mediators may pronounce and communicate His special blessing to them. It was a Jewish tradition that this blessing was given at the close of the daily sacrifice.

The structure of the blessing is remarkable. It is rhythmical, consists of three distinct parts, and mounts by gradual stages to that peace which forms the last and most consummate gift which God can give His people.

From a Christian point of view, and comparing the counterpart benediction of 2 Cor. xiii. 14, it is impossible not to see shadowed forth the doctrine of the Holy Trinity (cp. Isai. vi. 3 ; Matt. xxviii. 19). And the three several sets of terms correspond fittingly to the office of the Three Persons in Their gracious work for the redemption of man.

24. *The* LORD *bless thee, and keep thee*] The second clause here, as in the other three verses, defines more closely the general tenor of the preceding one. The singular

number, which is observed throughout, indicates that the blessing is conferred on Israel *collectively.*

25. *make his face shine*] This is an enhancement of the preceding benediction. "The face of God" imports not merely God's good will in general, but His active and special regard. With the "face" or "eye of the Lord" accordingly is connected alike the judicial visitation of the wicked (Ps. xxxiv. 16), and His mercies to the righteous (Ps. iv. 6).

26. *lift up his countenance upon thee*] *i.e.* specially direct His thought and care towards thee : cp. 2 K. ix. 32, and similar phrases in Gen. xliii. 29, xliv. 21. Through such loving providence alone could the peace of God in which the blessing closes be given.

27. *put my name upon the children of Israel*] *i.e.* pronounce My Sacred Name over them in blessing them. God will give effect to the benediction pronounced by the priests.

VII. 1. *on the day that*] *i.e.* "at the time that," cp. Gen. ii. 4. The presentation of the gifts in fact occupied twelve days, as the sequel shows.

The enactments set forth in the chapters from Lev. x. to Num. vi. inclusive, were doubtless promulgated at various times between the consecration of the Tabernacle and the departure from Sinai, but are for convenience set out connectedly. The contents of the present chapter are accordingly placed after them. The order pursued throughout is justly noted as one which would naturally suggest itself to a narrator who was contemporary with the events.

3 offered: and they brought their offering before the LORD, six covered wagons, and twelve oxen; a wagon for two of the princes, and for each one an ox: and they brought them before
4, 5 the tabernacle. And the LORD spake unto Moses, saying, Take *it* of them, that they may be to do the service of the tabernacle of the congregation ; and thou shalt give them unto the Levites,
6 to every man according to his service. And Moses took the
7 wagons and the oxen, and gave them unto the Levites. Two wagons and four oxen *c*he gave unto the sons of Gershon,
8 according to their service: *d*and four wagons and eight oxen he gave unto the sons of Merari, according unto their service,
9 *e*under the hand of Ithamar the son of Aaron the priest. But unto the sons of Kohath he gave none: because *f*the service of the sanctuary belonging unto them *g*was *that* they should bear
10 upon their shoulders. ¶And the princes offered for *h*dedicating of the altar in the day that it was anointed, even the
11 princes offered their offering before the altar. And the LORD said unto Moses, They shall offer their offering, each prince on
12 his day, for the dedicating of the altar. ¶And he that offered his offering the first day was *i*Nahshon the son of Amminadab,
13 of the tribe of Judah: and his offering *was* one silver charger, the weight thereof *was* an hundred and thirty *shekels*, one silver bowl of seventy shekels, after *k*the shekel of the sanctuary; both of them *were* full of fine flour mingled with oil for a *l*meat offer-
14, 15 ing: one spoon of ten *shekels* of gold, full of *m*incense: *n*one young bullock, one ram, one lamb of the first year, for a burnt
16, 17 offering: one kid of the goats for a *o*sin offering: and for *p*a sacrifice of peace offerings, two oxen, five rams, five he goats, five lambs of the first year : this *was* the offering of Nahshon the
18 son of Amminadab. ¶On the second day Nethaneel the son of
19 Zuar, prince of Issachar, did offer: he offered *for* his offering one silver charger, the weight whereof *was* an hundred and thirty *shekels*, one silver bowl of seventy shekels, after the shekel of the sanctuary ; both of them full of fine flour mingled with oil for a
20, 21 meat offering: one spoon of gold of ten *shekels*, full of incense : one young bullock, one ram, one lamb of the first year, for a burnt
22, 23 offering: one kid of the goats for a sin offering: and for a sacrifice of peace offerings, two oxen, five rams, five he goats, five lambs of the first year : this *was* the offering of Nethaneel
24 the son of Zuar. ¶On the third day Eliab the son of Helon,
25 prince of the children of Zebulun, *did offer:* his offering *was* one silver charger, the weight whereof *was* an hundred and thirty *shekels*, one silver bowl of seventy shekels, after the she-kel of the sanctuary ; both of them full of fine flour mingled with
26 oil, for a meat offering : one golden spoon of ten *shekels*, full of
27 incense: one young bullock, one ram, one lamb of the first
28 year, for a burnt offering: one kid of the goats for a sin offering :

c ch. 4. 25.
d ch. 4. 31.
e ch. 4. 28, 33.
f ch. 4. 15.
g ch. 4. 6, 8, 10, 12, 14.
2 Sam. 6. 13.
h See Deut. 20. 5.
1 Kin. 8. 63.
2 Chr. 7. 5.
Ezra 6. 16.
Neh. 12. 27.
Ps. 30. title.
i ch. 2. 3.
k Ex. 30. 13.
l Lev. 2. 1.
m Ex. 30. 34.
n Lev. 1. 2.
o Lev. 4. 23*
p Lev. 3. 1.

---

3. *covered wagons*] Some prefer to render "litter (Isai. lxvi. 20) wagons :" *i.e.* litters which were not on wheels, but borne by two oxen, one in front and one behind. Such conveyances would probably be more convenient than wheeled wagons in the rough country to be traversed.

7-9. To the Gershonites, who had to transport the hangings and coverings of the Tabernacle, two wagons are assigned : to the Merarites, who had the charge of the

solid parts of the Tabernacle, four wagons. The furniture and vessels the Kohathites were to carry on their own shoulders. Cp. iii. 25, 26, 31, 36, 37.

12-83. The several princes make their offerings in the order assigned to the tribes (ch. ii). It was doubtless the tribes themselves which presented these gifts through their chiefs. The twelve offerings are strictly alike, and were offered on twelve separate days.

29 and for a sacrifice of peace offerings, two oxen, five rams, five he
   goats, five lambs of the first year : this *was* the offering of Eliab
30 the son of Helon.   ¶ On the fourth day Elizur the son of Shedeur,
31 prince of the children of Reuben, *did offer :* his offering *was* one
   silver charger of the weight of an hundred and thirty *shekels*,
   one silver bowl of seventy shekels, after the shekel of the sanctuary ; both of them full of fine flour mingled with oil for a
32 meat offering : one golden spoon of ten *shekels*, full of incense :
33 one young bullock, one ram, one lamb of the first year, for
34 a burnt offering : one kid of the goats for a sin offering :
35 and for a sacrifice of peace offerings, two oxen, five rams, five
   he goats, five lambs of the first year : this *was* the offering of
36 Elizur the son of Shedeur.   ¶ On the fifth day Shelumiel the son
37 of Zurishaddai, prince of the children of Simeon, *did offer :* his
   offering *was* one silver charger, the weight whereof *was* an
   hundred and thirty *shekels*, one silver bowl of seventy shekels,
   after the shekel of the sanctuary ; both of them full of fine flour
38 mingled with oil for a meat offering : one golden spoon of ten
39 *shekels*, full of incense : one young bullock, one ram, one lamb of
40 the first year, for a burnt offering : one kid of the goats for a sin
41 offering : and for a sacrifice of peace offerings, two oxen, five
   rams, five he goats, five lambs of the first year : this *was* the
42 offering of Shelumiel the son of Zurishaddai.   ¶ On the sixth
   day Eliasaph the son of Deuel, prince of the children of Gad,
43 *offered :* his offering *was* one silver charger of the weight of an
   hundred and thirty *shekels*, a silver bowl of seventy shekels,
   after the shekel of the sanctuary ; both of them full of fine flour
44 mingled with oil for a meat offering : one golden spoon of ten
45 *shekels*, full of incense : one young bullock, one ram, one lamb
46 of the first year, for a burnt offering : one kid of the goats for a
47 sin offering : and for a sacrifice of peace offerings, two oxen, five
   rams, five he goats, five lambs of the first year : this *was* the
48 offering of Eliasaph the son of Deuel.   ¶ On the seventh day
   Elishama the son of Ammihud, prince of the children of Ephraim,
49 *offered :* his offering *was* one silver charger, the weight whereof
   was an hundred and thirty *shekels*, one silver bowl of seventy
   shekels, after the shekel of the sanctuary ; both of them full of
50 fine flour mingled with oil for a meat offering : one golden spoon
51 of ten *shekels*, full of incense : one young bullock, one ram, one
52 lamb of the first year, for a burnt offering : one kid of the goats
53 for a sin offering : and for a sacrifice of peace offerings, two oxen,
   five rams, five he goats, five lambs of the first year : this *was*
54 the offering of Elishama the son of Ammihud.   On the eighth
   day *offered* Gamaliel the son of Pedahzur, prince of the children
55 of Manasseh : his offering *was* one silver charger of the weight
   of an hundred and thirty *shekels*, one silver bowl of seventy
   shekels, after the shekel of the sanctuary ; both of them full of
56 fine flour mingled with oil for a meat offering : one golden spoon
57 of ten *shekels*, full of incense : one young bullock, one ram, one
58 lamb of the first year, for a burnt offering : one kid of the goats
59 for a sin offering : and for a sacrifice of peace offerings, two
   oxen, five he goats, five lambs of the first year : this *was*
60 *was* the offering of Gamaliel the son of Pedahzur.   ¶ On the
   ninth day Abidan the son of Gideoni, prince of the children of
61 Benjamin, *offered :* his offering *was* one silver charger, the
   weight whereof *was* an hundred and thirty *shekels*, one silver
   bowl of seventy shekels, after the shekel of the sanctuary ;

both of them full of fine flour mingled with oil for a meat offering:
62, 63 one golden spoon of ten *shekels*, full of incense : one young
bullock, one ram, one lamb of the first year, for a burnt offering :
64, 65 one kid of the goats for a sin offering : and for a sacrifice of
peace offerings, two oxen, five rams, five he goats, five lambs
of the first year : this was the offering of Abidan the son of
66 Gideoni. ¶ On the tenth day Ahiezer the son of Ammishaddai,
67 prince of the children of Dan, *offered :* his offering *was* one silver
charger, the weight whereof *was* an hundred and thirty *shekels*,
one silver bowl of seventy shekels, after the shekel of the sanctuary; both of them full of fine flour mingled with oil for a meat
68, 69 offering : one golden spoon of ten *shekels*, full of incense : one
young bullock, one ram, one lamb of the first year, for a burnt
70, 71 offering : one kid of the goats for a sin offering : and for a
sacrifice of peace offerings, two oxen, five rams, five he goats,
five lambs of the first year : this *was* the offering of Ahiezer
72 the son of Ammishaddai. ¶ On the eleventh day Pagiel the son
73 of Ocran, prince of the children of Asher, *offered :* his offering
was one silver charger, the weight whereof *was* an hundred and
thirty *shekels*, one silver bowl of seventy shekels, after the
shekel of the sanctuary; both of them full of fine flour mingled
74 with oil for a meat offering : one golden spoon of ten *shekels*, full
75 of incense : one young bullock, one ram, one lamb of the first
76 year, for a burnt offering : one kid of the goats for a sin offer-
77 ing : and for a sacrifice of peace offerings, two oxen, five rams,
five he goats, five lambs of the first year : this *was* the offering
78 of Pagiel the son of Ocran. ¶ On the twelfth day Ahira the son
79 of Enan, prince of the children of Naphtali, *offered :* his offering
was one silver charger, the weight whereof *was* an hundred and
thirty *shekels*, one silver bowl of seventy shekels, after the shekel
of the sanctuary; both of them full of fine flour mingled with
80 oil for a meat offering : one golden spoon of ten *shekels*, full of
81 incense : one young bullock, one ram, one lamb of the first year,
82 for a burnt offering : one kid of the goats for a sin offering :
83 and for a sacrifice of peace offerings, two oxen, five rams, five
he goats, five lambs of the first year : this *was* the offering of
84 Ahira the son of Enan. ¶ This *was* the dedication of the altar,
in the day when it was anointed, by the princes of Israel : twelve
chargers of silver, twelve silver bowls, twelve spoons of gold :
85 each charger of silver *weighing* an hundred and thirty *shekels*,
each bowl seventy : all the silver vessels *weighed* two thousand
86 and four hundred *shekels*, after the shekel of the sanctuary : the
golden spoons *were* twelve, full of incense, *weighing* ten *shekels*
apiece, after the shekel of the sanctuary : all the gold of the
87 spoons *was* an hundred and twenty *shekels*. All the oxen for the
burnt offering *were* twelve bullocks, the rams twelve, the lambs
of the first year twelve, with their meat offering : and the kids
88 of the goats for sin offering twelve. And all the oxen for the
sacrifice of the peace offerings *were* twenty and four bullocks,
the rams sixty, the he goats sixty, the lambs of the first year
sixty. This *was* the dedication of the altar, after that it was
89 ᑫanointed. ¶ And when Moses was gone into the tabernacle of ᑫ ver. 1.

84–88. The aggregate worth, by weight,
of the whole of the offerings was about 438*l*.
But the real worth of such a sum, when
measured by the prices of clothing and food
at that time, must have been vastly greater.

89. *with him*] *i.e.* as marg. " with God,"
not (as some) with himself.
  he heard the voice of one speaking] Rather,
he heard the voice speaking, or **conversing.** The effect was as though Moses **was**

r ch. 12. 8.
Ex. 33. 9. 11.
s Ex. 25. 22.

the congregation *r*to speak with ¹him, then he heard ˢthe voice
of one speaking unto him from off the mercy seat that *was* upon
the ark of testimony, from between the two cherubims: and he
spake unto him.

CHAP. 8. AND the LORD spake unto Moses, saying, Speak unto

a Ex. 25. 37.
& 40. 25.

2 Aaron, and say unto him, When thou *a*lightest the lamps,
the seven lamps shall give light over against the candlestick.
3 And Aaron did so; he lighted the lamps thereof over against

b Ex. 25. 31.

4 the candlestick, as the LORD commanded Moses. *b*And this work
of the candlestick *was of* beaten gold, unto the shaft thereof,

c Ex. 25. 18.
d Ex. 25. 40.

unto the flowers thereof, *was* *c*beaten work: *d*according unto
the pattern which the LORD had shewed Moses, so he made the
5, 6 candlestick. ¶And the LORD spake unto Moses, saying, Take
the Levites from among the children of Israel, and cleanse
7 them. And thus shalt thou do unto them, to cleanse them:

e ch. 19. 9,
17, 18.
f Lev. 14. 8,
9.
g Lev. 2. 1.
h See Ex. 29.
4.
& 40. 12.
i Lev. 8. 3.

Sprinkle *e*water of purifying upon them, and ²ᶠlet them shave
all their flesh, and let them wash their clothes, and *so* make
8 themselves clean. Then let them take a young bullock with
*g*his meat offering, *even* fine flour mingled with oil, and another
9 young bullock shalt thou take for a sin offering. *h*And thou
shalt bring the Levites before the tabernacle of the congregation:
*i*and thou shalt gather the whole assembly of the children of
10 Israel together: and thou shalt bring the Levites before the

k Lev. 1. 4.

LORD: and the children of Israel *k*shall put their hands upon
11 the Levites: and Aaron shall ³offer the Levites before the LORD
for an ⁴offering of the children of Israel, that ⁵they may execute

l Ex. 29. 10.

12 the service of the LORD. *l*And the Levites shall lay their hands

¹ That is, *God.*
² Heb. *let them cause a razor to pass over, &c.*
³ Heb. *wave.*
⁴ Heb. *wave offering.*
⁵ Heb. *they may be to execute, &c.*

audibly addressed by another person: how
this effect was produced we are not told.

Thus was the promise of Ex. xxv. 20-22
fulfilled; and that as an immediate response
on the part of God to the cheerful readiness
with which the tribes had made their offerings, and supplied everything needful for
the Holy Place and its service. All being
now complete as God had appointed, and
the camp purified from defilements, God
meets Moses the mediator of the people,
not as before on the peak of Sinai far away,
but in the midst of them, in the dwelling-
place which He henceforth vouchsafed to
tenant.

VIII. 1-4. The actual lighting of the
lamps (cp. marg. reff.) was to be done to
set forth symbolically the peculiar Presence
which God had now (vii. 89) actually established amongst His people.

5-22. The Levites could only undertake
their duties (iii., iv.) after the formal exchange of the Levites for the first-born (iii.
44-51).

The distinction between the "consecration" of the priests (Lev. viii.) and the less
solemn "purification" (*v.* 21) of the Levites
is marked. These rites of purification are
similar to those incumbent on the priests of
Egypt.

7. *water of purifying*] Lit. "sin water:"

i.e. water to cleanse from sin; no doubt
taken from the laver of the Sanctuary,
which was used by the priests for purification before they went into the Tabernacle to
minister (cp. v. 17; Ex. xxx. 18 seq.).

The "sprinkling" of so large a body of
men could have been only general, but
tokens of individual purification are specified (cp. also Lev. xiv. 8).

8. The two bullocks were "to make an
atonement for the Levites," and therefore
are presented in their name. These offerings are similar to those prescribed in Lev.
viii. 14 sqq. at the consecration of the
priests, except that the burnt-offering was
on that occasion a ram. The larger victim
corresponds to the larger number of the
Levites.

10. *the children of Israel*] *i.e.* through the
heads of their tribes, who (vii. 2) no doubt
acted for their tribesmen. This act, the
distinguishing feature of the ceremony, represented the transfer to the Levites of the
sacred duties originally incumbent on the
whole people.

11. *Offer...offering*] Cp. the margin Aaron
pointed to the Levites, and then waved his
hands, indicating (cp. Lev. vii. 30 note) that
the offering was dedicated to God, and,
again, by grant from Him, withdrawn for
the use of the priests.

upon the heads of the bullocks: and thou shalt offer the one *for*
a sin offering, and the other *for* a burnt offering, unto the LORD,
13 to make an atonement for the Levites. And thou shalt set the
Levites before Aaron, and before his sons, and offer them *for* an
14 offering unto the LORD. Thus shalt thou separate the Levites
from among the children of Israel: and the Levites shall be
15 *m*mine. And after that shall the Levites go in to do the service
of the tabernacle of the congregation: and thou shalt cleanse
16 them, and *n*offer them *for* an offering. For they *are* wholly given
unto me from among the children of Israel; *o*instead of such as
open every womb, *even instead of* the firstborn of all the children
17 of Israel, have I taken them unto me. *p*For all the firstborn of
the children of Israel *are* mine, *both* man and beast: on the day
that I smote every firstborn in the land of Egypt I sanctified
18 them for myself. And I have taken the Levites for all the first-
19 born of the children of Israel. And *q*I have given the Levites
as [1]a gift to Aaron and to his sons from among the children of
Israel, to do the service of the children of Israel in the tabernacle of the congregation, and to make an atonement for the
children of Israel: *r*that there be no plague among the children
of Israel, when the children of Israel come nigh unto the sanc-
20 tuary. ¶And Moses, and Aaron, and all the congregation of
the children of Israel, did to the Levites according unto all that
the LORD commanded Moses concerning the Levites, so did the
21 children of Israel unto them. *s*And the Levites were purified,
and they washed their clothes; *t*and Aaron offered them *as* an
offering before the LORD; and Aaron made an atonement for
22 them to cleanse them. *u*And after that went the Levites in to
do their service in the tabernacle of the congregation before
Aaron, and before his sons: *x*as the LORD had commanded Moses
23 concerning the Levites, so did they unto them. ¶And the
24 LORD spake unto Moses, saying, This *is it* that *belongeth* unto the
Levites: *y*from twenty and five years old and upward they
shall go in [2]to wait upon the service of the tabernacle of the
25 congregation: and from the age of fifty years they shall [3]cease
26 waiting upon the service *thereof*, and shall serve no more: but
shall minister with their brethren in the tabernacle of the congregation, *z*to keep the charge, and shall do no service. Thus shalt
thou do unto the Levites touching their charge.
CHAP. 9. AND the LORD spake unto Moses in the wilderness of
Sinai, in the first month of the second year after they were come

m ch. 3. 45.
& 16. 9.

n ver. 11. 13.

o ch. 3. 12,
45.

p Ex. 13. 2,
12, 13, 15.
ch. 3. 13.
Luke 2. 23.

q ch. 3. 9.

r ch. 1. 53.
& 16. 46.
& 18. 5.
2 Chr. 26. 16.

s ver. 7.

t ver. 11, 12.

u ver. 15.

x ver. 5.

y See ch. 4. 3.
1 Chr. 23.
3, 24, 27.

z ch. 1. 53.

[1] Heb. *given.* [2] Heb. *to war the warfare* [3] Heb. *return from the war-*
of, &c. 1 Tim. 1. 18. *fare of the service.*

---

19. *make an atonement for the children of
Israel*] *i.e.* by performing those services
which were due from the children of Israel;
the omission of which by the children of
Israel would, but for the interposition of
the Levites, have called down "wrath"
from God, or (i. 53) *plague*. The institution
of the Levites was an extension of that
mediatorial system which the people themselves, terrified at the direct manifestations
to them of the Divine Presence, desired;
see Deut. v. 25. Further, it is suggested to
us here as an act of mercy on the part of
God; yet even the priests and Levites
themselves were not always sufficiently

heedful and reverent. Cp. xvii. 10; Lev.
x. 1 seq.; 2 Sam. vi. 6 seq.

21. *were purified*] Rather, **purified themselves**; as directed in *v.* 7.

24. *twenty and five years old and upward*]
The permanent limit as distinguished from
the temporary (iv. 3, 23, 30), though David
found it necessary to extend the period of the
Levites' service by causing it to commence
at 20 years of age (1 Chron. xxiii. 24-28).
This rule continued in force from the time
of David downwards (cp. on 2 Chron. xxxi.
17; Ezra iii. 8).

IX. 1-5. Passover at Sinai. This, as
being kept in the first month, was prior in

2 out of the land of Egypt, saying, Let the children of Israel also
3 keep *the passover at his appointed season. In the fourteenth
day of this month, [1]at even, ye shall keep it in his appointed
season: according to all the rites of it, and according to all the
4 ceremonies thereof, shall ye keep it. And Moses spake unto the
5 children of Israel, that they should keep the passover. And
*they kept the passover on the fourteenth day of the first month
at even in the wilderness of Sinai: according to all that the
6 LORD commanded Moses, so did the children of Israel. ¶ And
there were certain men, who were *defiled by the dead body of a
man, that they could not keep the passover on that day: *and
7 they came before Moses and before Aaron on that day: and
those men said unto him, We *are* defiled by the dead body of a
man: wherefore are we kept back, that we may not offer an
offering of the LORD in his appointed season among the children
8 of Israel? And Moses said unto them, Stand still, and *I will
9 hear what the LORD will command concerning you. And the
10 LORD spake unto Moses, saying, Speak unto the children of
Israel, saying, If any man of you or of your posterity shall be
unclean by reason of a dead body, or *be* in a journey afar off,
11 yet he shall keep the passover unto the LORD. *The fourteenth
day of the second month at even they shall keep it, *and* *eat it
12 with unleavened bread and bitter *herbs*. *They shall leave none
of it unto the morning, *nor break any bone of it: *according to
13 all the ordinances of the passover they shall keep it. But the
man that *is* clean, and is not in a journey, and forbeareth to
keep the passover, even the same soul *shall be cut off from
among his people: because he *brought not the offering of the
14 LORD in his appointed season, that man shall *bear his sin. And
if a stranger shall sojourn among you, and will keep the passover
unto the LORD; according to the ordinance of the passover, and
according to the manner thereof, so shall he do: *ye shall have
one ordinance, both for the stranger, and for him that was born
15 in the land. ¶ And *on the day that the tabernacle was reared
up the cloud covered the tabernacle, *namely*, the tent of the testi-

Margin references:
a Ex. 12. 1.
Lev. 23. 5.
ch. 28. 16.
Deut.16. 1, 2.

b Josh. 5. 10.

c ch. 5. 2.
& 19. 11, 16.
See John 18.
28.
d Ex. 18. 15,
19, 26.
ch. 27. 2.
e ch. 27. 5.

f 2 Chr. 30.
2, 15.
g Ex. 12. 8.
h Ex. 12. 10.
i Ex. 12. 46.
John 19. 36.
k Ex. 12. 43.

l Gen. 17.14.
Ex. 12. 15.
m ver. 7.
n ch. 5. 31.

o Ex. 12. 49.

p Ex. 40. 34.
Neh. 9. 12,19.
Ps. 78. 14.

[1] Heb. *between the two evenings*, Ex. 12. 6.

time to the numbering of ch. i. 1 seq., and
to the other events narrated in this book.
It is, however, recorded here as introductory to the ordinance of the supplementary Passover; the observance of which was one of
the last occurrences during the halt at
Sinai.

5. In some details, the present Passover
differed both from that kept at the Exodus
itself and from all subsequent Passovers.
For example, the direction of Ex. xii. 22
could not be carried out in the letter whilst
the people were dwelling in tents; and may
be regarded as superseded by Lev. xvii. 3–6
(cp. Deut. xvi. 5 seq.).

In other points, such as how many lambs
would be wanted, how the blood of the
Paschal victims could be sprinkled upon
the altar in the time specified, &c., the ad-
ministrators of the Law of Moses would
here, as elsewhere, have, from the nature
of the case, power to order what might be
requisite to carry the law into effect.

6. *certain men*] Probably Mishael and
Elizaphan, who buried their cousins, Nadab
and Abihu, within a week of this Passover
(Lev. x. 4, 5).

11. The later Jews speak of this as the
"little Passover." Coming, as it did, a
month after the proper Passover, it afforded
ample time for a man to purify himself
from legal defilement, as also to return from
any but a very distant journey. Cp. Hezekiah's act (2 Chron. xxx. 1–3).

12. *according to all the ordinances*] *i.e.*
those relating to the Passover-lamb, not
those concerning the feast; for the Little
Passover lasted, according to the Jews, only
one day; nor was it held to be needful that
at it leaven should be put away out of the
houses.

15. *the cloud*, &c.] The phenomenon first
appeared at the Exodus itself, Ex. xiii. 21,
22. The cloud did not cover the whole
structure, but the "tent of the testimony,"
i.e. the enclosure which contained the "Ark
of the testimony" (Ex. xxv. 16, 22), and the

mony: and 𝑞at even there was upon the tabernacle as it were
16 the appearance of fire, until the morning. So it was alway: the
cloud covered it *by day*, and the appearance of fire by night.
17 And when the cloud 𝑟was taken up from the tabernacle, then
after that the children of Israel journeyed: and in the place
where the cloud abode, there the children of Israel pitched their
18 tents. At the commandment of the LORD the children of Israel
journeyed, and at the commandment of the LORD they pitched:
𝑠as long as the cloud abode upon the tabernacle they rested in
19 their tents. And when the cloud ¹tarried long upon the tabernacle many days, then the children of Israel 𝑡kept the charge of
20 the LORD, and journeyed. And so it was, when the cloud
was a few days upon the tabernacle; according to the commandment of the LORD they abode in their tents, and according to
21 the commandment of the LORD they journeyed. And so it was,
when the cloud ²abode from even unto the morning, and *that* the
cloud was taken up in the morning, then they journeyed:
whether *it was* by day or by night that the cloud was taken up,
22 they journeyed. Or *whether it were* two days, or a month, or a
year, that the cloud tarried upon the tabernacle, remaining
thereon, the children of Israel 𝑢abode in their tents, and jour-
23 neyed not: but when it was taken up, they journeyed. At the
commandment of the LORD they rested in the tents, and at the
commandment of the LORD they journeyed: they 𝑤kept the
charge of the LORD, at the commandment of the LORD by the
hand of Moses.

CHAP. 10. AND the LORD spake unto Moses, saying, Make thee
2 two trumpets of silver; of a whole piece shalt thou make them:
that thou mayest use them for the 𝑎calling of the assembly, and
3 for the journeying of the camps. And when 𝑏they shall blow
with them, all the assembly shall assemble themselves to thee at
4 the door of the tabernacle of the congregation. And if they
blow *but* with one *trumpet*, then the princes, *which are* 𝑐heads
of the thousands of Israel, shall gather themselves unto thee.
5 When ye blow an alarm, then 𝑑the camps that lie on the east
6 parts shall go forward. When ye blow an alarm the second
time, then the camps that lie 𝑒on the south side shall take their
7 journey: they shall blow an alarm for their journeys. But when
the congregation is to be gathered together, 𝑓ye shall blow, but
8 ye shall not 𝑔sound an alarm. 𝘩And the sons of Aaron, the
priests, shall blow with the trumpets; and they shall be to you

¹ Heb. *prolonged.*   ² Heb. *was.*

Marginal references:
𝑞 Ex. 13. 21.
& 40. 38.

𝑟 Ex. 40. 36,
ch. 10. 11,33,
34.
Ps. 80. 1.

𝑠 1 Cor. 10. 1.

𝑡 ch. 1. 53.
& 3. 8.

𝑢 Ex. 40. 36,
37.

𝑤 ver. 19.

𝑎 Isai. 1. 13.
𝑏 Jer. 4. 5.
Joel 2. 15.

𝑐 Ex. 18. 21.
ch. 1. 16.
& 7. 2.
𝑑 ch. 2. 3

𝑒 ch. 2. 10.

𝑓 ver. 3.
𝑔 Joel 2. 1.
𝘩 ch. 31. 6.
Josh. 6. 4.
1 Chr. 15. 24.

Holy Place. The phenomenon is now again
described in connexion with the journeyings which are to be narrated in the sequel
of the book.

22. *a year*] Lit. " days," idiomatically a
year (Lev. xxv. 29), an expression equivalent to " a full period," though not necessarily the period of a year.

X. 2. The trumpet was a straight instrument, differing in this respect from the
curved horn or cornet; and is represented,
among the other spoils of the temple, on
the Arch of Titus. See Ex. xxv. 23 cut.
From Egyptian monuments it appears that
the Jewish trumpet was copied from that
used in the armies of the Pharaohs. The

cornet was at first a simple ram's horn (Josh.
vi. 4), and the metal instrument of later
times preserved the original shape.

5, 6. *blow an alarm*] *i.e.* a long continuous
peal. Cp. *v.* 7, *ye shall blow, but not sound
an alarm*: *i.e.* blow in short, sharp notes,
not in a continuous peal. A third and
a fourth alarm were probably blown as
signals.

8. *the sons of Aaron*] As the trumpets
were emblematic of the voice of God, the
priests only were to use them. At this time
there were only two " sons of Aaron; " but
in later times, when the number of priests
was greater, more trumpets were used; we
read of seven in the times of Joshua and

i ch. 31. 6.
Josh. 6. 5.
2 Chr. 13. 14.
k Judg. 2. 18.
& 4. 3.
1 Sam. 10.
18.
Ps. 106. 42.
l Gen. 8. 1.
Ps. 106. 4.
m ch. 29. 1.
Lev. 23. 24.
1 Chr. 15. 24.
2 Chr. 5. 12.
Ezra 3. 10.
Neh. 12. 35.
Ps. 81. 3.
n ver. 9.
o ch. 9. 17.
p Ex. 40. 36.
ch. 2. 9, 16.
q Ex. 19. 1.
ch. 1. 1.
& 9. 5.
r Gen. 21. 21.
ch. 12. 16.
Deut. 1. 1.
s ver. 5. 6.
ch. 2. 34.
t ch. 2. 3, 9.
u ch. 1. 7.
x ch. 1. 51.
y ch. 4. 24, 31.
& 7. 6.
z ch. 2. 10, 16.

a ch. 4. 4, 15.
& 7. 9.
b ch. 2. 18, 24.

c ch. 2. 25, 31.
Josh. 6. 9.

9 for an ordinance for ever throughout your generations. And *i*if ye go to war in your land against the enemy that *k*oppresseth you, then ye shall blow an alarm with the trumpets; and ye shall be *l*remembered before the LORD your God, and ye shall be saved 10 from your enemies. Also *m*in the day of your gladness, and in your solemn days, and in the beginnings of your months, ye shall blow with the trumpets over your burnt offerings, and over the sacrifices of your peace offerings; that they may be to you *n*for 11 a memorial before your God: I *am* the LORD your God. ¶ And it came to pass on the twentieth *day* of the second month, in the second year, that the cloud *o*was taken up from off the taber-12 nacle of the testimony. And the children of Israel took *p*their journeys out of the *q*wilderness of Sinai; and the cloud rested 13 in the *r*wilderness of Paran. And they first took their journey *s*according to the commandment of the LORD by the hand of 14 Moses. ¶ *t*In the first *place* went the standard of the camp of the children of Judah according to their armies: and over his 15 host *was* *u*Nahshon the son of Amminadab. And over the host of the tribe of the children of Issachar *was* Nethaneel the son of 16 Zuar. And over the host of the tribe of the children of Zebulun 17 *was* Eliab the son of Helon. And the *x*tabernacle was taken down; and the sons of Gershon and the sons of Merari set for-18 ward, *y*bearing the tabernacle. ¶ And *z*the standard of the camp of Reuben set forward according to their armies: and over his 19 host *was* Elizur the son of Shedeur. And over the host of the tribe of the children of Simeon *was* Shelumiel the son of Zuri-20 shaddai. And over the host of the tribe of the children of Gad 21 *was* Eliasaph the son of Deuel. And the Kohathites set forward, bearing the *a*sanctuary: and *1 the other* did set up the tabernacle 22 against they came. ¶ And *b*the standard of the camp of the children of Ephraim set forward according to their armies: and 23 over his host *was* Elishama the son of Ammihud. And over the host of the tribe of the children of Manasseh *was* Gamaliel the 24 son of Pedahzur. And over the host of the tribe of the children 25 of Benjamin *was* Abidan the son of Gideoni. ¶ And *c*the standard of the camp of the children of Dan set forward, *which was* the

<hr>

1 That is, *the Gershonites and the Merarites:* See ver. 17. ch. 1. 51.

<hr>

David (see marg. reff.); and of a hundred and twenty in that of Solomon (2 Chr. v. 12).

9. For examples of the employment of trumpets in war cp. marg. reff. and 2 Chr. xx. 28. By employment of them was signi-fied the dependence of God's people on His aid.

10. *in the day of your gladness*] Cp. xxix. 1; Lev. xxiii. 24; 2 Chr. xxix. 27; Ezra iii. 10; Neh. xii. 35, 41; Ps. lxxxi. 3.

11. At this point commences the second great division of the book, extending to the close of chapter xiv. The remaining verses of the present chapter narrate the actual break up of the camp at Sinai and the order of the march.

12. *the wilderness of Paran*] See Gen. xiv. 6 note. The wilderness is mentioned here by anticipation. The earliest halting-places, Kibroth-hattaavah and Hazeroth, were not

within its limits (xi. 35, xii. 16).

13. Rather, **And they journeyed** (or, set forth) **in the order of precedence according to** (*i.e.* established by) **the commandment of the Lord**, &c., and described in *vv.* 14–28.

14. *according to their armies*] Cp. i. 3. There were three tribal hosts in each camp; and each tribe had of course its subdivisions.

17. A more precise determination of the method of executing the order given in ii. 17. The appointed place of the Tabernacle, in the midst of the host, was represented during the march by the Ark, the holy vessels, &c. carried by the Kohathites. The actual structure of the Tabernacle was borne in advance by the Gershonites and Merar-ites, immediately behind the camp of Judah; so as to be set up ready against the arrival of the sacred utensils borne by the Kohath-ites. Cp. chs. ii., iv.

rereward of all the camps throughout their hosts : and over his
26 host *was* Ahiezer the son of Ammishaddai. And over the host of
the tribe of the children of Asher *was* Pagiel the son of Ocran.
27 And over the host of the tribe of the children of Naphtali *was*
28 Ahira the son of Enan. [1][*d*]Thus *were* the journeyings of the   *d* ch. 2. 34.
children of Israel according to their armies, when they set for-
29 ward. ¶And Moses said unto Hobab, the son of [*e*]Raguel the   *e* Ex. 2. 18.
Midianite, Moses' father in law, We are journeying unto the
place of which the LORD said, [*f*]I will give it you : come thou   *f* Gen. 12. 7.
with us, and [*g*]we will do thee good : for [*h*]the LORD hath spoken   *g* Judg. 1.16.
30 good concerning Israel. And he said unto him, I will not go ;   & 4. 11.
31 but I will depart to mine own land, and to my kindred. And he   *h* Gen. 32.12.
said, Leave us not, I pray thee ; forasmuch as thou knowest how   & 6. 7, 8.
we are to encamp in the wilderness, and thou mayest be to us
32 [*i*]instead of eyes. And it shall be, if thou go with us, yea, it   *i* Job 29. 15.
shall be, that [*k*]what goodness the LORD shall do unto us, the   *k* Judg. 1.16.
33 same will we do unto thee. ¶And they departed from [*l*]the   *l* See Ex. 3. 1.
mount of the LORD three days' journey : and the ark of the
covenant of the LORD [*m*]went before them in the three days'   *m* Deut.1. 33.
34 journey, to search out a resting place for them. And [*n*]the   Josh. 3. 3.
cloud of the LORD *was* upon them by day, when they went out   Ps. 132. 8.
35 of the camp. ¶And it came to pass, when the ark set forward,   Jer. 31. 2.
that Moses said,   Ez. 20. 6.
[*o*]Rise up, LORD, and let thine enemies be scattered ;   *n* Ex. 13. 21.
And let them that hate thee flee before thee.   Neh. 9. 12.
36 And when it rested, he said,   *o* Ps. 68. 1.
Return, O LORD, unto the [2]many thousands of Israel.   & 132. 8.

[1] Heb. *These*.   [2] Heb. *ten thousand thousands*.

---

29. *Hobab, the son of Raguel*] Or Reuel
(Exod. ii. 18). Reuel was probably not
identical with Jethro : and Hobab was the
brother-in-law, not the father-in-law, of
Moses ; the Hebrew word translated in
A. V. "father-in-law," signifying simply
any relation by marriage (Exod. iii. 1 note).
Hobab (Judges i. 16, iv. 11) eventually accompanied the Israelites and obtained a
settlement with them in the land of Canaan.
Hobab and Jethro may have been brethren
and sons of Reuel.
31. *thou mayest be to us instead of eyes*]
A proverbial expression still in use in the
East. Hobab would indicate the spots
where water, fuel, and pasture might be
found, or warn them of the dangers from
hurricanes, and point out localities infested
by robbers.
33. *three days' journey*] Probably a technical expression for such a distance as could
not be traversed in a single day, and therefore not without intervals of encampment
and due provision : cp. Gen. xxx. 36 ; Exod.
iii. 18, v. 3, viii. 27, xv. 22. The technical
use of the phrase "Sabbath-day's journey"
for another average distance, Acts i. 12, is
similar.
the ark of the covenant of the LORD *went
before them*] From *v.* 21 and ii. 17 it would
appear that the usual place of the Ark
during the march was in the midst of the

host. It was evidently an exceptional case
when, in Josh. iii. 3, 6, the Ark preceded the
people into the bed of the Jordan. Hence
the words "went before them" do not here
imply local precedence. The phrase, or its
equivalent, is used of a leader going out in
command of his troops, xxvii. 17 ; Deut.
xxxi. 3 ; 1 Sam. xviii. 16 ; 2 Chr. i. 10 ;
and similarly the Ark may well be said to
have gone at the head of the Israelites,
when it was borne solemnly in the midst of
them as the outward embodiment of the Presence Whose sovereign word was their law.
a resting place] Lit. "rest." It is commonly understood of each successive encampment ; or, in particular, of the first
encampment. Yet the term would hardly
be here employed, did it not carry with it a
higher meaning, pointing to the promised
rest of Canaan, for which the Israelites
were now in full march, and from the speedy
enjoyment of which no sentence of exclusion as yet debarred them. Cp. marg. reff.
35, 36. Each forward movement and
each rest of the Ark was made to bear a
sacramental character. The one betokened
the going forth of God against His enemies ;
the other, His gathering of His own people
to Himself : the one was the pledge of victory, the other the earnest of repose.
v. 36 may be translated : "Restore" (*i.e.*
to the land which their fathers sojourned in),

a Deut. 9. 22.
b Ps. 78. 21.
c Lev. 10. 2.
ch. 16. 35.
2 Kin. 1. 12.
Ps. 106. 18.
d Jam. 5. 16.
e As Ex. 12. 38.
f Ps. 78. 18. & 106. 14. 1 Cor. 10. 6.
g Ex. 16. 3.
h ch. 21. 5.
i Ex. 16. 14, 31.
k Gen. 2. 12.
l Ex. 16. 31.
m Ex. 16. 13, 14.
n Ps. 78. 21.
o Deut. 1. 12.
p Isai. 40. 11.
q Isai. 49. 23. 1 Thes. 2. 7. r Gen. 26. 3. & 50. 24. Ex. 13. 5. s Matt. 15. 33. Mark 8. 4.
t Ex. 18. 18.

CHAP. 11. AND *a when* the people [1]complained, [2]it displeased the LORD: and the LORD heard *it;* *b* and his anger was kindled; and the *c* fire of the LORD burnt among them, and consumed *them that*
2 *were* in the uttermost parts of the camp. And the people cried unto Moses; and when Moses *d* prayed unto the LORD, the fire
3 [3]was quenched. And he called the name of the place [4]Taberah:
4 because the fire of the LORD burnt among them. ¶ And the *e* mixt multitude that *was* among them [5]fell a lusting: and the children of Israel also [6]wept again, and said, *f* Who shall
5 give us flesh to eat? *g* We remember the fish, which we did eat in Egypt freely; the cucumbers, and the melons, and the
6 leeks, and the onions, and the garlick: but now *h* our soul *is* dried away: there *is* nothing at all, beside this manna, *before* our
7 eyes. And *i* the manna *was* as coriander seed, and the [7]colour
8 thereof as the colour of *k* bdellium. *And* the people went about, and gathered *it,* and ground *it* in mills, or beat *it* in a mortar, and baked *it* in pans, and made cakes of it: and *l* the taste of it
9 was as the taste of fresh oil. And *m* when the dew fell upon the
10 camp in the night, the manna fell upon it. ¶ Then Moses heard the people weep throughout their families, every man in the door of his tent: and *n* the anger of the LORD was kindled greatly:
11 Moses also was displeased. *o* And Moses said unto the LORD, Wherefore hast thou afflicted thy servant? And wherefore have I not found favour in thy sight, that thou layest the burden of all
12 this people upon me? Have I conceived all this people? Have I begotten them, that thou shouldest say unto me, *p* Carry them in thy bosom, as a *q* nursing father beareth the sucking child, unto
13 the land which thou *r* swarest unto their fathers? *s* Whence should I have flesh to give unto all this people? For they weep
14 unto me, saying, Give us flesh, that we may eat. *t* I am not able

1 Or, *were as it were com-plainers.*
2 Heb. *it was evil in the ears of, &c.*
3 Heb. *sunk.*
4 That is, *A burning,* Deut. 9. 22.
5 Heb. *lusted a lust.*
6 Heb. *returned and wept.*
7 Heb. *eye of it as the eye of.*

"O LORD, the ten thousands of the thousands of Israel." (Cp. Psalm lxxxv. 4, where the verb in the Hebrew is the same.)

XI. This and the following three chapters recount the successive rebellions of the Israelites after their departure from Sinai; culminating in that by which they brought upon themselves the sentence of personal exclusion from the Land of Promise.

1. See marginal rendering. They murmured against the privations of the march.
the fire of the LORD] Probably lightning; cp. Ps. lxxviii. 21.

in the uttermost parts] Rather, **in the end.** The fire did not reach far into the camp. It was quickly quenched at the intercession of Moses.

3. *Taberah*] *i.e.* "burning": not the name of a station, and accordingly not found in the list given in ch. xxxiii., but the name of the spot where the fire broke out. This incident might seem (cp. *v.* 34) to have occurred at the station called, from another still more terrible event which shortly followed, Kibroth-hattaavah.

4-35. Occurrences at Kibroth-hattaavah.

4. *the mixt multitude*] The word in the original resembles our "riff-raff," and denotes a mob of people scraped together. It refers here to the multitude of strangers (see Ex. xii. 38) who had followed the Israelites from Egypt.

5. The natural dainties of Egypt are set forth in this passage with the fullness and relish which bespeak personal experience.

6, 7. *there is nothing at all, &c.*] Lit. "Nought at all have we except that our eyes are unto this manna;" *i.e.* "Nought else have we to expect beside this manna." On the manna see Ex. xvi. 15 note; on bdellium see Gen. ii. 12 note.

10. The weeping was general; every family wept (cp. Zech. xii. 12), and in a manner public and unconcealed.

11-15. The complaint and remonstrance of Moses may be compared with that in 1 K. xix. 4 seq.; Jonah iv. 1-3, and contrasted with the language of Abraham (Gen. xviii. 23 seq.) The meekness of Moses (cp. xii. 3) sank under vexation into despair. His language shows us how imperfect and prone to degeneracy are the best saints on earth.

to bear all this people alone, because *it is* too heavy for me.
15 And if thou deal thus with me, "kill me, I pray thee, out of
hand, if I have found favour in thy sight; and let me not *see
16 my wretchedness. ¶And the LORD said unto Moses, Gather
unto me *ʸ*seventy men of the elders of Israel, whom thou
knowest to be the elders of the people, and *ᶻ*officers over them;
and bring them unto the tabernacle of the congregation, that
17 they may stand there with thee. And I will *ᵃ*come down and
talk with thee there: and *ᵇ*I will take of the spirit which *is* upon
thee, and will put *it* upon them; and they shall bear the burden
of the people with thee, that thou bear *it* not thyself alone.
18 And say thou unto the people, *ᶜ*Sanctify yourselves against
to morrow, and ye shall eat flesh: for ye have wept *ᵈ*in the ears
of the LORD, saying, Who shall give us flesh to eat: *ᵉ*for *it was*
well with us in Egypt? Therefore the LORD will give you flesh,
19 and ye shall eat. Ye shall not eat one day, nor two days,
20 nor five days, neither ten days, nor twenty days; *ᶠbut* even
a ¹whole month, until it come out at your nostrils, and it be
loathsome unto you: because that ye have despised the LORD
which *is* among you, and have wept before him, saying, *ᵍ*Why
21 came we forth out of Egypt? And Moses said, *ʰ*The people,
among whom I *am, are* six hundred thousand footmen; and thou
hast said, I will give them flesh, that they may eat a whole
22 month. *ⁱ*Shall the flocks and the herds be slain for them, to
suffice them? Or shall all the fish of the sea be gathered together
23 for them, to suffice them? And the LORD said unto Moses,
*ᵏ*Is the LORD's hand waxed short? Thou shalt see now whether
24 *ˡ*my word shall come to pass unto thee or not. ¶And Moses
went out, and told the people the words of the LORD, and
*ᵐ*gathered the seventy men of the elders of the people, and set
25 them round about the tabernacle. And the LORD *ⁿ*came down
in a cloud, and spake unto him, and took of the spirit that *was*
upon him, and gave *it* unto the seventy elders: and it came to
pass, *that,* *ᵒ*when the spirit rested upon them, *ᵖ*they prophesied,
26 and did not cease. But there remained two *of the* men in the
camp, the name of the one *was* Eldad, and the name of the other

¹ Heb. *month of days.*

Marginal references:
ᵘ See 1 Kin. 19. 4.
ˣ Jonah 4. 3.
ˣ Zeph. 3. 15.
ʸ See Ex. 24. 1, 9.
ᶻ Deut. 16. 18.
ᵃ ver. 25.
& 18. 21.
Ex. 19. 20.
ᵇ 1 Sam. 10. 6.
2 Kin. 2. 15.
ᶜ Ex. 19. 10.
ᵈ Ex. 16. 7.
ᵉ ver. 5.
Acts 7. 39.
ᶠ Ps. 78. 29.
& 106. 15.
ᵍ ch. 21. 5.
ʰ Gen. 12. 2.
Ex. 12. 37.
& 38. 26.
ch. 1. 46.
ⁱ See 2 Kin. 7. 2.
Matt. 15. 33.
Mark 8. 4.
John 6. 7, 9.
ᵏ Isai. 50. 2.
& 59. 1.
ˡ ch. 23. 19.
Ez. 12. 25.
& 24. 14.
ᵐ ver. 16.
ⁿ ver. 17.
ch. 12. 5.
ᵒ See 2 Kin. 2. 15.
ᵖ See 1 Sam. 10. 5, 6, 10.
& 19. 20, 21, 23.
Joel 2. 28.
Acts 2. 17, 18.
1 Cor. 14. 1, &c.

---

16. *seventy men of the elders of Israel*]
Seventy elders had also gone up with Moses
to the Lord in the mount (Ex. xxiv. 1, 9).
Seventy is accordingly the number of col-
leagues assigned to Moses to share his burden with him. To it, the Jews trace the
origin of the Sanhedrim. Subsequent notices (xvi. 25 ; Josh. vii. 6, viii. 10, 33, ix. 11,
xxiii. 2, xxiv. 1, 31) so connect the elders
with the government of Israel as to point
to the fact that the appointment now made
was not a merely temporary one, though
it would seem to have soon fallen into
desuetude. We find no traces of it in the
days of the Judges and the Kings.

elders of the people, and officers over them]
In English idiom, "elders and officers of the
people." Both elders and officers appear in
Egypt (Ex. iii. 16, v. 6 seq.): the former
had headed the nation in its efforts after
freedom ; the latter were the subordinate,
though unwilling, agents of Egyptian

tyranny. The two classes no doubt were
working together; and from those who belonged to either, perhaps from those who
were both elders and officers, the council of
Seventy was to be selected.

17. *I will take of the spirit which is upon
thee*] Render rather *separate from the spirit,*
&c. ; *i.e.* they shall have their portion in the
same divine gift which thou hast.

25. *they prophesied*] *i.e.* under the extraordinary impulse of the Holy Ghost they
uttered forth the praises of God, or declared
His Will. Cp. marg. reff.

and did not cease] Rather, **and added not,**
i.e. they prophesied at this time only and
not afterwards. The sign was granted on
the occasion of their appointment to accredit them in their office; it was not continued, because their proper function was to
be that of governing not prophesying.

26. *of them that were written*] *i.e.* enrolled
amongst the Seventy. The expression

Medad; and the spirit rested upon them; and they *were* of

q See 1 Sam.
20. 26.
Jer. 36. 5.

them that were written, but *q*went not out unto the tabernacle: 27 and they prophesied in the camp. And there ran a young man, and told Moses, and said, Eldad and Medad do prophesy in the 28 camp. And Joshua the son of Nun, the servant of Moses, *one*

r See Mark
9. 38.
Luke 9. 49.
John 3. 26.
s 1 Cor. 14. 5.

of his young men, answered and said, My lord Moses, *r*forbid 29 them. And Moses said unto him, Enviest thou for my sake? *s*Would God that all the LORD's people were prophets, *and* that 30 the LORD would put his spirit upon them! And Moses gat him 31 into the camp, he and the elders of Israel. ¶ And there went

t Ex. 16. 13.
Ps. 78. 26,
27, 28.
& 105. 46.

forth a *t*wind from the LORD, and brought quails from the sea, and let *them* fall by the camp, [1]as it were a day's journey on this side, and as it were a day's journey on the other side, round about the camp, and as it were two cubits *high* upon the face of 32 the earth. And the people stood up all that day, and all *that* night, and all the next day, and they gathered the quails: he

u Ex. 16. 36.
Ez. 45. 11.

that gathered least gathered ten *u*homers: and they spread *them* 33 all abroad for themselves round about the camp. And while the

x Ps. 78. 30,
31.

*x*flesh *was* yet between their teeth, ere it was chewed, the wrath of the LORD was kindled against the people, and the LORD smote 34 the people with a very great plague. And he called the name of that place [2]Kibroth-hattaavah: because there they buried

y ch. 33. 17.

35 the people that lusted. ¶*y And* the people journeyed from Kibroth-hattaavah unto Hazeroth; and [3]abode at Hazeroth.

CHAP. 12. AND Miriam and Aaron spake against Moses because of

a Ex. 2. 21.

the [4]Ethiopian woman whom he had married: for *a*he had

---

[1] Heb. *as it were the way of a day*.　　[2] That is, *The graves of lust*, Deut. 9. 22.　　[3] Heb. *they were in, &c.*　　[4] Or, *Cushite*.

---

points to a regular appointment duly recorded and permanent.

29. *Enviest thou for my sake?*] (Cp. Mark ix. 38 sqq.) The other members of the Seventy had been with Moses (cp. *vv.* 16, 24, 25) when the gift of prophecy was bestowed on them. They received "of the spirit that was upon him," and exercised their office visibly through and for him. Eldad and Medad prophesying in the camp seemed to Joshua to be acting independently, and so establishing a separate centre of authority.

31. The south-east wind, which blew from the neighbouring Elanitic gulf of the Red Sea, brought the quails (Ex. xvi. 13).

two cubits high] Better, "two cubits above the face of the ground:" *i.e.* the quails, wearied with their long flight, flew about breast high, and were easily secured by the people, who spread them all abroad for themselves (*v.* 32), in order to salt and dry them. The quail habitually flies with the wind, and low.

32. *ten homers*] About 55 bushels. Cp. Lev. xxvii. 16.

33. *ere it was chewed*] Better, **ere it was consumed.** See *vv.* 19, 20. The surfeit in which the people indulged, as described in *v.* 32, disposed them to sickness. God's wrath, visiting the gluttonous through their gluttony, aggravated natural consequences into a supernatural visitation.

34, 35. [Kibroth-hattaavah has been identified by Palmer with the extensive remains, graves, &c., at Erweis El Ebeirig, and Hazeroth ("enclosures") with Ain Hadherah.]

XII. 1-15. Miriam, as a prophetess (cp. Ex. xv. 20, 21) no less than as the sister of Moses and Aaron, took the first rank amongst the women of Israel: and Aaron may be regarded as the ecclesiastical head of the whole nation. But instead of being grateful for these high dignities they challenged the special vocation of Moses and the exclusive authority which God had assigned to him. Miriam was the instigator, from the fact that her name stands conspicuously first (*v.* 1), and that the punishment (*v.* 10) fell on her alone. She probably considered herself as supplanted, and that too by a foreigner. Aaron was misled this time by the urgency of his sister, as once before (Ex. xxxii.) by that of the people.

1. *the Ethiopian* (Heb. "Cushite," cp. Gen. ii. 13, x. 6) *woman whom he had married*] It is likely that Zipporah (Ex. ii. 21) was dead, and that Miriam in consequence expected to have greater influence than ever with Moses. Her disappointment at his second marriage would consequently be very great.

The marriage of Moses with a woman descended from Ham was not prohibited, so long as she was not of the stock of Canaan (cp. Ex. xxxiv. 11-16); but it would at any

2 [1]married an Ethiopian woman. And they said, Hath the LORD
indeed spoken only by Moses? [b]Hath he not spoken also by us?
3 And the LORD [c]heard *it*. (Now the man Moses *was* very meek,
4 above all the men which *were* upon the face of the earth.) [d]And
the LORD spake suddenly unto Moses, and unto Aaron, and
unto Miriam, Come out ye three unto the tabernacle of the con-
5 gregation. And they three came out. [e]And the LORD came
down in the pillar of the cloud, and stood *in* the door of the
tabernacle, and called Aaron and Miriam: and they both came
6 forth. And he said, Hear now my words: If there be a prophet
among you, *I* the LORD will make myself known unto him [f]in
7 a vision, *and* will speak unto him [g]in a dream. [h]My servant
8 Moses *is* not so, [i]who *is* faithful in all [k]mine house. With him
will I speak [l]mouth to mouth, even [m]apparently, and not in
dark speeches; and [n]the similitude of the LORD shall he behold:
wherefore then [o]were ye not afraid to speak against my servant
9 Moses? And the anger of the LORD was kindled against them;
10 and he departed. And the cloud departed from off the tabernacle; and, [p]behold, Miriam *became* [q]leprous, *white* as snow:
and Aaron looked upon Miriam, and, behold, *she was* leprous.
11 And Aaron said unto Moses, Alas, my lord, I beseech thee, [r]lay
not the sin upon us, wherein we have done foolishly, and
12 wherein we have sinned. Let her not be [s]as one dead, of whom
the flesh is half consumed when he cometh out of his mother's
13 womb. And Moses cried unto the LORD, saying, Heal her now,
14 O God, I beseech thee. And the LORD said unto Moses, [t]If her
father had but spit in her face, should she not be ashamed seven

[1] Heb. *taken*.

[b] Ex. 15. 20. Mic. 6. 4.
[c] Gen. 29. 33. ch. 11. 1. 2 Kin. 19. 4. Isai. 37. 4. Ez. 35. 12.
[d] Ps. 76. 9.
[e] ch. 11. 25.
[f] Gen. 15. 1. Job 33. 15. Ez. 1. 1. Dan. 8. 2. Luke 1. 11, 22. Acts 10. 11.
[g] Gen. 31. 10. 1 Kin. 3. 5. Matt. 1. 20.
[h] Ps. 105. 26.
[i] Heb. 3. 2, 5.
[k] 1Tim.3.15.
[l] Ex. 33. 11. Deut. 34. 10.
[m] 1Cor.13.12.
[n] Ex. 33. 19.
[o] 2 Pet. 2. 10. Jude 8.
[p] Deut. 24. 9.
[q] 2 Kin. 5.27. & 15. 5. 2 Chr. 26. 19, 20.
[r] 2 Sam. 19. 19. & 24. 10. Prov. 30. 32.
[s] Ps. 88. 4.
[t] See Heb. 12. 9.

---

time have been offensive to that intense nationality which characterized the Jews. The Christian Fathers note in the successive marriage of Moses with a Midianite and an Ethiopian a foreshadowing of the future extension to the Gentiles of God's Covenant and its promises (cp. Ps. xlv. 9 seq.; Cant. i. 4 seq.); and in the murmuring of Miriam and Aaron a type of the discontent of the Jews because of such extension: cp. St. Luke xv. 29, 30.

2. *Hath the* LORD, *&c.*] *i.e.* Is it merely, after all, by Moses that the LORD hath spoken?

3. *the man Moses was very meek*] In this and in other passages in which Moses no less unequivocally records his own faults (cp. xx. 12 seq.; Ex. iv. 24 seq.; Deut. i. 37), there is the simplicity of one who bare witness of himself, but not to himself (cp. Matt. xi. 28, 29). The words are inserted to explain how it was that Moses took no steps to vindicate himself, and why consequently the Lord so promptly intervened.

8. *mouth to mouth*] *i.e.* without the intervention of any third person or thing: cp. marg. reff.

even apparently] Moses received the word of God direct from Him and plainly, not through the medium of dream, vision, parable, dark saying, or such like; cp. marg. reff.

the similitude of the LORD *shall he behold*] But, "No man hath seen God at any time," says St. John (i. 18: cp. 1 Tim. vi. 16, and especially Ex. xxxiii. 20 seq.). It was not therefore the Beatific Vision, the unveiled essence of the Deity, which Moses saw on the one hand. Nor was it, on the other hand, a mere emblematic representation (as in Ezek. i. 26 seq., Dan. vii. 9), or an Angel sent as a messenger. It was the Deity Himself manifesting Himself so as to be cognizable to mortal eye. The special footing on which Moses stood as regards God is here laid down in detail, because it at once demonstrates that the supremacy of Moses rested on the distinct appointment of God, and also that Miriam in contravening that supremacy had incurred the penalty proper to sins against the theocracy.

12. *as one dead*] Leprosy was nothing short of a living death, a poisoning of the springs, a corrupting of all the humours, of life; a dissolution little by little of the whole body, so that one limb after another actually decayed and fell away. Cp. notes on Lev. xiii.

13. *Heal her now, O God, I beseech thee*] Others render these words: "Oh not so; heal her now, I beseech Thee."

14. *If her father, &c.*] *i.e.* If her earthly parent had treated her with contumely (cp. Deut. xxv. 9) she would feel for a time humiliated, how much more when God has visited her thus?

u Lev. 13, 46.
ch. 5. 2, 3.
x Deut. 24. 9.
2 Chr. 26.
20, 21.
y ch. 11. 35.
& 33. 18.

a ch. 32. 8.
Deut. 1. 22.

b ch. 12. 16.
& 32. 8.
Deut. 1. 19.
& 9. 23.

c ch. 34. 19.
1 Chr. 4. 15.
d ver. 30.
ch. 14. 6. 30.
Josh. 14. 6,
7, 13, 14.
Judg. 1. 12.
e ver. 16.

f ver. 8.
Ex. 17. 9.
ch. 14. 6, 30.
g ver. 21.
h Gen. 14. 10.
Judg. 1. 9,
19.

i Neh. 9. 25,
35.
Ez. 34. 14.
k Deut. 31.
6, 7, 23.

days? Let her be *u*shut out from the camp seven days, and after
15 that let her be received in *again*. *x*And Miriam was shut out
from the camp seven days: and the people journeyed not till
16 Miriam was brought in *again*. ¶And afterward the people
removed from *y*Hazeroth, and pitched in the wilderness of
Paran.

CHAP. 13. AND the LORD spake unto Moses, saying, *a*Send thou
2 men, that they may search the land of Canaan, which I give
unto the children of Israel: of every tribe of their fathers shall
3 ye send a man, every one a ruler among them. And Moses by
the commandment of the LORD sent them *b*from the wilderness
of Paran: all those men *were* heads of the children of Israel.
4 And these *were* their names: of the tribe of Reuben, Shammua
5 the son of Zaccur. Of the tribe of Simeon, Shaphat the son of
6 Hori. *c*Of the tribe of Judah, *d*Caleb the son of Jephunneh.
7, 8 Of the tribe of Issachar, Igal the son of Joseph. Of the tribe
9 of Ephraim, *e*Oshea the son of Nun. Of the tribe of Benjamin,
10 Palti the son of Raphu. Of the tribe of Zebulun, Gaddiel the
11 son of Sodi. Of the tribe of Joseph, *namely*, of the tribe of
12 Manasseh, Gaddi the son of Susi. Of the tribe of Dan, Ammiel
13 the son of Gemalli. Of the tribe of Asher, Sethur the son of
14 Michael. Of the tribe of Naphtali, Nahbi the son of Vophsi.
15, 16 Of the tribe of Gad, Geuel the son of Machi. These *are* the
names of the men which Moses sent to spy out the land. And
17 Moses called *f*Oshea the son of Nun Jehoshua. ¶And Moses
sent them to spy out the land of Canaan, and said unto them,
Get you up this *way* *g*southward, and go up into *h*the mountain:
18 and see the land, what it *is;* and the people that dwelleth
19 therein, whether they *be* strong or weak, few or many; and
what the land *is* that they dwell in, whether it be good or bad;
and what cities they *be* that they dwell in, whether in tents, or in
20 strong holds; and what the land *is*, whether it *be* *i*fat or lean,
whether there be wood therein, or not. And *k*be ye of good
courage, and bring of the fruit of the land. ¶Now the time

XIII. 1. *And the* LORD *spake*] The mission of the spies was first suggested by the
Israelites themselves. See Deut. i. 22.

2. *a ruler*] A comparison of the list with
that of i. 5 seq. shows that they were not
the princes of the tribes, but heads of houses
or families (*v.* 4).

Of the names here given those of Joshua
and Caleb alone are otherwise known to
us.

16. Oshea, Hoshea, or Hosea, the name
also of the last king of Israel and the first
minor prophet, means " deliverance " or
"salvation." To this Moses added (probably, on this occasion) a syllable containing the sacred name, Jehovah or Jah : thus
intimating that salvation was from God,
and by the hand of him who bore the title
of " God's salvation." Jehoshua was contracted (cp. Neh. viii. 17) into Jeshua.

17. *southward*] Rather, " by the Negeb,"
or south-country ; a well-defined tract of
territory forming the southernmost and
least fertile portion of the land of Canaan
and of the subsequent inheritance of Judah.
It extended northward from Kadesh to

within a few miles of Hebron, and from the
Dead Sea westward to the Mediterranean
(see especially Josh. xv. 21–32).

into the mountain] The hill-country of
southern and central Canaan, mostly within
the borders of Judah and Ephraim. It
commences a few miles south of Hebron,
and extending northward to the plain of
Jezreel, runs out eventually north-westward into the sea in the headland of
Carmel.

19. *in tents*] *i.e.* in open unwalled villages.

20. *the time...of the firstripe grapes*] The
first grapes ripen in Palestine in July and
August : the vintage is gathered in September and October. This indication of
date tallies with what we should have inferred from the previous narrative. For
the Israelitish host had quitted Sinai on the
20th day of the second month (x. 11), or
about the middle of May : since then they
had spent a month at Kibroth-hattaavah
and a week at Hazeroth, and had accomplished, in all, from 150 to 200 miles of
march : it therefore must have been at least

21 *was* the time of the firstripe grapes. So they went up, and
searched the land *l*from the wilderness of Zin unto *m*Rehob, as
22 men come to Hamath. And they ascended by the south, and
came unto Hebron ; where *n*Ahiman, Sheshai, and Talmai, *o*the
children of Anak, *were*. (Now *p*Hebron was built seven years
23 before *q*Zoan in Egypt.)   *r*And they came unto the *1*brook of
Eshcol, and cut down from thence a branch with one cluster of
grapes, and they bare it between two upon a staff; and *they*
24 *brought* of the pomegranates, and of the figs. The place was
called the *2*brook *3*Eshcol, because of the cluster of grapes which
25 the children of Israel cut down from thence. And they returned
26 from searching of the land after forty days. ¶And they went
and came to Moses, and to Aaron, and to all the congregation
of the children of Israel, *s*unto the wilderness of Paran, to
*t*Kadesh; and brought back word unto them, and unto all the
27 congregation, and shewed them the fruit of the land. And they
told him, and said, We came unto the land whither thou sentest
us, and surely it floweth with *u*milk and honey; *x*and this *is* the
28 fruit of it. Nevertheless *y*the people *be* strong that dwell in the
land, and the cities *are* walled, *and* very great: and moreover
29 we saw *z*the children of Anak there. *a*The Amalekites dwell in
the land of the south: and the Hittites, and the Jebusites, and
the Amorites, dwell in the mountains: and the Canaanites dwell
30 by the sea, and by the coast of Jordan. ¶And *b*Caleb stilled
the people before Moses, and said, Let us go up at once, and

l ch. 34. 3.
Josh. 15. 1.
m Josh. 19.
28.
n Josh. 11. 21,
22.
& 15. 13, 14.
Judg. 1. 10.
o ver. 33.
p Josh. 21.
11.
q Ps. 78. 12.
Isai. 19. 11.
& 30. 4.
r Deut. 1. 24,
25.

s ver. 3.
t ch. 20. 1. 16.
Deut. 1. 19.
Josh. 14. 6.

u Ex. 3. 8.
& 33. 3.
x Deut. 1. 25.
y Deut. 1. 28.
& 9. 1.
z ver. 33.
a Ex. 17. 8.
ch. 14. 43.
b See ch. 14,
6, 24.
Josh. 14. 7.

1 Or, *valley*, ch. 32. 9.
Judg. 16. 4.   *2* Or, *valley*.   *3* That is, *A cluster of*
grapes.

the beginning of July, and may have been
a month later, when the spies were des-
patched into the land of promise.
   21. The wilderness of Zin was the north-
eastern portion of the wilderness of Paran.
Rehob (*mod.* Khurbeh) was probably the
Beth-rehob of Judg. xviii. 28, near Dan-
Laish; and apparently to the north of it,
since it gave its name to a Syrian kingdom
(2 S. viii. 3). The southern approach to
Hamath from the plain of Cœle-Syria, lay
between those two ranges of Lebanon called
Libanus and Antilibanus. A low screen of
hills connects the northernmost points of
these two ranges; and through this screen
the Orontes bursts from the upper Cœle-
Syrian hollow into the open plain of Hamath.
   22. The progenitor of the Anakim was
Arba "the father of Anak" (Josh. xv. 13),
from whom the city of Hebron took its
name of Kirjath-Arba. Ahiman, Sheshai,
and Talmai were probably not individual
warriors, but names of three tribes of the
Anakim. Hence we find them still in existence half a century later, when Caleb,
who now brought tidings of them, became
their eventual destroyer (Josh. xv. 14).
   Now Hebron, &c.] This parenthesis explains that these two cities had a common
founder, and were built, or perhaps, at
least in the case of Zoan (Tanis, see Ex. i. 8,
ii. 5 notes) rebuilt, by the Hyksos, to which
nations, once the conquerors of Egypt, the

Anakim perhaps belonged. The Hyksos
fortified and garrisoned Zoan as a defence
of their Eastern frontier.
   23. The brook of Eshcol is by some
identified with the rich valley immediately
to the north of Hebron; [but by others
with Wady Hanein to the south of He-
bron]. The valley was, in all likelihood,
originally named after one of the three
chiefs who were confederate with Abraham
(Gen. xiv. 24); but, as often came to pass,
the Israelites, wittingly or unwittingly,
took up in a new and significant sense the
name which they found; and to them the
valley thus became the Valley of the Cluster. Bunches of grapes are found in Palestine of many pounds weight.
   25. *after forty days*] They had no doubt
in this time explored the whole land. It
was however with the southern part that
the Israelites expected to have to deal immediately: and accordingly it is that which
is particularly referred to in the following
verses, Hebron and its vicinity above all.
   26. Kadesh is usually identified with
Ain-el-Weibeh, which lies in the Arabah,
about ten miles north of the place in which
Mount Hor abuts on that valley, [or with
Ain-Gadis in Jebel Magrah].
   29. *The Amalekites*] See xiv. 25 note.
   the Canaanites] *i.e.* those of the Phœnician race: the word is here used in its narrow sense: cp. Gen. x. 15–18 note.

c ch. 32. 9.
Deut. 1. 28.
Josh. 14. 8.
d ch. 14. 36.
e Amos 2. 9.
f Deut. 1. 28.
g Isai. 40. 22.
h 1 Sam. 17. 42.
a ch. 11. 4.
b Ex. 16. 2.
ch. 16. 41.
Ps. 106. 25.
c See ver. 28, 29.
d Neh. 9. 17.
e See Deut. 17. 16.
Acts 7. 39.
f ch. 16. 4.
g ver. 24. 30, 38.
h ch. 13. 27.
Deut. 1. 25.
i Deut.10.15.
1 Kin. 10. 9.
Ps. 22. 8.
Isai. 62. 4.
k ch. 13. 27.
l Deut. 9. 7.
m Deut.7.18.
n ch. 24. 8.
o Gen. 48. 21.
Ex. 33. 16.
Deut. 20. 1.
Josh. 1. 5.
Judg. 1. 22.
2 Chr. 13. 12.
Ps. 46. 7, 11.
Isai. 41. 10.
Amos 5. 14.
Zech. 8. 23.
p Ex. 17. 4.
q Ex. 16. 10.
Lev. 9. 23.
ch. 16. 19, 42.
r Deut. 9. 7.
Ps. 95. 8.
Heb. 3. 8.
s Deut. 1. 32.
Ps. 78. 22.
& 106. 24.
John 12. 37.
Heb. 3. 18.
t Ex. 32. 10.
u Ex. 32. 12.
Ps. 106. 23.
Deut. 9. 26.
Ez. 20. 9, 14.

31 possess it; for we are well able to overcome it. ^cBut the men that went up with him said, We be not able to go up against 32 the people; for they *are* stronger than we. And they ^dbrought up an evil report of the land which they had searched unto the children of Israel, saying, The land, through which we have gone to search it, *is* a land that eateth up the inhabitants thereof; and ^eall the people that we saw in it *are* ¹men of a 33 great stature. And there we saw the giants, ^fthe sons of Anak, which come of the giants: and we were in our own sight ^gas grasshoppers, and so we were ^hin their sight.

CHAP. 14. AND all the congregation lifted up their voice, and cried; 2 and ^athe people wept that night. ^bAnd all the children of Israel murmured against Moses and against Aaron: and the whole congregation said unto them, Would God that we had died in the land of Egypt! or ^cwould God we had died in this wil-3 derness! And wherefore hath the LORD brought us unto this land, to fall by the sword, that our wives and our children should be a prey? Were it not better for us to return into Egypt? 4 And they said one to another, ^dLet us make a captain, and ^elet 5 us return into Egypt. ¶ Then ^fMoses and Aaron fell on their faces before all the assembly of the congregation of the children 6 of Israel. ^gAnd Joshua the son of Nun, and Caleb the son of Jephunneh, *which were* of them that searched the land, rent 7 their clothes: and they spake unto all the company of the children of Israel, saying, ^hThe land, which we passed through to 8 search it, *is* an exceeding good land. If the LORD ⁱdelight in us, then he will bring us into this land, and give it us; ^ka land 9 which floweth with milk and honey. Only ^lrebel not ye against the LORD, ^mneither fear ye the people of the land; for ⁿthey *are* bread for us: their ²defence is departed from them, ^oand the 10 LORD *is* with us: fear them not. ^pBut all the congregation bade stone them with stones. And ^qthe glory of the LORD appeared in the tabernacle of the congregation before all the 11 children of Israel. ¶ And the LORD said unto Moses, How long will this people ^rprovoke me? And how long will it be ere they ^sbelieve me, for all the signs which I have shewed among them? 12 I will smite them with the pestilence, and disinherit them, and ^twill make of thee a greater nation and mightier than they. 13 And ^uMoses said unto the LORD, Then the Egyptians shall hear *it*, (for thou broughtest up this people in thy might from

¹ Heb. *men of statures.*   ² Heb. *shadow,* Ps. 121. 5. Isai. 30. 2, 3. Jer. 48. 45.

---

32. *a land that eateth up,* &c.] *i.e.* it is a land which from its position is exposed to incessant attacks from one quarter and another, and so its occupants must be always armed and watchful.

XIV. 5. Already Caleb had endeavoured to still the people before Moses (xiii. 30); already Moses himself (Deut. i. 29 seq.) had endeavoured to recall the people to obedience. After the failure of these efforts Moses and Aaron cast themselves down in solemn prayer before God (cp. xvi. 22); and the appearance of the glory of the LORD in the "Tabernacle of the congregation" (v. 10) was the immediate answer.

9. *their defence*] Lit. " their shadow," *i.e.*

their shelter as from the scorching sun : an Oriental figure. Cp. marg. reff.

12. *and disinherit them*] By the proposed extinction of Israel the blessings of the Covenant would revert to their original donor.

13–17. The syntax of these verses is singularly broken. As did St. Paul when deeply moved, so Moses presses his arguments one on the other without pausing to ascertain the grammatical finish of his expressions. He speaks here as if in momentary apprehension of an outbreak of God's wrath, unless he could perhaps arrest it by crowding in every topic of deprecation and intercession that he could mention on the instant.

14 among them;) and they will tell *it* to the inhabitants of this
land: *for* they have heard that thou LORD *art* among this
people, that thou LORD art seen face to face, and *that* thy cloud
standeth over them, and *that* thou goest before them, by day
15 time in a pillar of a cloud, and in a pillar of fire by night. Now
if thou shalt kill *all* this people as one man, then the nations
16 which have heard the fame of thee will speak, saying, Because
the LORD was not *able to bring this people into the land which
he sware unto them, therefore he hath slain them in the wilder-
17 ness. And now, I beseech thee, let the power of my Lord be
18 great, according as thou hast spoken, saying, The LORD *is*
longsuffering, and of great mercy, forgiving iniquity and
transgression, and by no means clearing *the guilty*, *visiting
the iniquity of the fathers upon the children unto the third and
19 fourth *generation*. *Pardon, I beseech thee, the iniquity of this
people *according unto the greatness of thy mercy, and *as thou
20 hast forgiven this people, from Egypt even 1until now. And
21 the LORD said, I have pardoned *according to thy word: but *as
truly *as* I live, *all the earth shall be filled with the glory of the
22 LORD. *Because all those men which have seen my glory, and
my miracles, which I did in Egypt and in the wilderness, and
have tempted me now *these ten times, and have not hearkened
23 to my voice; *2surely they shall not see the land which I sware
unto their fathers, neither shall any of them that provoked me
24 see it: but my servant *Caleb, because he had another spirit
with him, and *hath followed me fully, him will I bring into
the land whereinto he went; and his seed shall possess it.
25 (Now the Amalekites and the Canaanites dwelt in the valley.)
To morrow turn you, *and get you into the wilderness by the
26 way of the Red sea. ¶ And the LORD spake unto Moses and
27 unto Aaron, saying, *How long *shall I bear with* this evil congregation, which murmur against me? *I have heard the murmurings of the children of Israel, which they murmur against
28 me. Say unto them, *As truly as* I live, saith the LORD, *as ye
29 have spoken in mine ears, so will I do to you: your carcases
shall fall in this wilderness; and *all thàt were numbered of

1 Or, *hitherto*.   2 Heb. *If they see the land*.

x Ex. 15. 14.
Josh. 2. 9, 10.
& 5. 1.
y Ex. 13. 21.
& 40. 38.
ch. 10. 34.
Neh. 9. 12.
Ps. 78. 14.
& 105. 39.
z Deut. 9. 28.
Josh. 7. 9.

a Ex. 34. 6,7.
Ps. 103. 8.
& 145. 8.
Jonah 4. 2.
b Ex. 20. 5.
& 34. 7.
c Ex. 34. 9.
d Ps. 106. 45.
e Ps. 78. 38.
f Ps. 106. 23.
Jam. 5. 16.
1 John 5.
14, 15, 16.
g Ps. 72. 19.
h Deut. 1. 35.
Ps. 95. 11.
& 106. 26.
Heb. 3. 17.
i Gen. 31. 7.
k ch. 32. 11.
Ez. 20. 15.
l Deut. 1. 36.
Josh. 14. 6.
m ch. 32. 12.
n Deut. 1. 40.
o ver. 11.
Ex. 16. 28.
Matt. 17. 17.
p Ex. 16. 12.
q ver. 23.
ch. 26. 65.
& 32. 11.
Deut. 1. 35.
Heb. 3. 17.
r See ver. 2.
s ch. 1. 45.
& 26. 64.

21-23. Render : **But as truly as I live,
and as all the earth shall be filled with
the glory of the LORD; (*v.* 22) all those
men, &c. ; (*v.* 23) shall not see, &c.**

22. *these ten times*] Ten is the number
which imports completeness. Cp. Gen. xxxi.
7. The sense is that the measure of their
provocation was now full : the day of grace
was at last over. Some however enumerate
ten several occasions on which the people
had tempted God since the Exodus.
Ps. xc:, which is entitled "a Prayer of
Moses," has been most appropriately regarded as a kind of dirge upon those sentenced thus awfully by God to waste away
in the wilderness.

24. *my servant Caleb*] Caleb only is mentioned here as also in xiii. 30 seq. Both
passages probably form part of the matter
introduced at a later period into the narrative of Moses, and either by Joshua or
under his superintendence. Hence the name
of Joshua is omitted, and his faithfulness to-

gether with its reward are taken for granted.
In *vv.* 30, 38, both names are mentioned together ; and these verses in all likelihood
belong to the same original composition
as *vv.* 6-10.

25. Render : **And now the Amalekites
and the Canaanites are dwelling** (or abiding) **in the valley: wherefore turn you,**
&c. (that so ye be not smitten before them).
The Amalekites were the nomad bands that
roved through the open pastures of the
plain (*v.* 45) : the Canaanites, a term here
taken in its wider sense, were the Amorites
of the neighbouring cities (cp. *v.* 45 with
Deut. i. 44), who probably lived in league
with the Amalekites.

To morrow] Not necessarily the next day,
but an idiom for "hereafter," "henceforward" (cp. marg. reading in Ex. xiii. 14 ;
Josh. iv. 6).

by the way of the Red sea] That is, apparently, by the eastern or Elanitic gulf.

you, according to your whole number, from twenty years old
30 and upward, which have murmured against me, doubtless ye
shall not come into the land, *concerning* which I [1]sware to make
you dwell therein, [t]save Caleb the son of Jephunneh, and
31 Joshua the son of Nun. [u]But your little ones, which ye said
should be a prey, them will I bring in, and they shall know the
32 land which [x]ye have despised. But *as for* you, [y]your carcases,
33 they shall fall in this wilderness. And your children shall
[2] [z]wander in the wilderness [a]forty years, and [b]bear your whore-
34 doms, until your carcases be wasted in the wilderness. [c]After
the number of the days in which ye searched the land, *even*
[d]forty days, each day for a year, shall ye bear your iniquities,
even forty years, [e]and ye shall know my [3]breach of promise.
35 [f]I the LORD have said, I will surely do it unto all [g]this evil
congregation, that are gathered together against me: in this
wilderness they shall be consumed, and there they shall die.
36 ¶ [h]And the men, which Moses sent to search the land, who
returned, and made all the congregation to murmur against him,
37 by bringing up a slander upon the land, even those men that
did bring up the evil report upon the land, [i]died by the plague
38 before the LORD. [k]But Joshua the son of Nun, and Caleb the
son of Jephunneh, *which were* of the men that went to search
39 the land, lived *still*. ¶ And Moses told these sayings unto all
40 the children of Israel: [l]and the people mourned greatly. And
they rose up early in the morning, and gat them up into the top
of the mountain, saying, Lo, [m]we *be here*, and will go up unto
the place which the LORD hath promised: for we have sinned.
41 And Moses said, Wherefore now do ye transgress [n]the com-
42 mandment of the LORD? But it shall not prosper. [o]Go not up,
for the LORD *is* not among you; that ye be not smitten before
43 your enemies. For the Amalekites and the Canaanites *are* there
before you, and ye shall fall by the sword: [p]because ye are
turned away from the LORD, therefore the LORD will not be
44 with you. ¶ [q]But they presumed to go up unto the hill top:
nevertheless the ark of the covenant of the LORD, and Moses,
45 departed not out of the camp. [r]Then the Amalekites came
down, and the Canaanites which dwelt in that hill, and smote
them, and discomfited them, *even* unto [s]Hormah.
CHAP. 15. AND the LORD spake unto Moses, saying, [a]Speak unto
2 the children of Israel, and say unto them, When ye be come into

[t] ver. 38. ch. 26. 65. & 32. 12. Deut. 1. 36, 38.
[u] Deut. 1. 39.
[x] Ps. 106. 24.
[y] 1 Cor. 10. 5. Heb. 3. 17.
[z] ch. 32. 13.
[a] See Deut. 2, 14.
[b] Ez. 23. 35.
[c] ch. 13. 25.
[d] Ps. 95. 10. Ez. 4. 6.
[e] See 1 Kin. 8. 56.
[f] ch. 23. 19.
[g] ver. 27. 29. ch. 26. 65. 1 Cor. 10. 5.
[h] ch. 13. 31.
[i] 1 Cor. 10. 10. Heb. 3. 17. Jude 5.
[k] ch. 26. 65. Josh. 14. 6.
[l] Ex. 33. 4.
[m] Deut. 1. 41.
[n] ver. 25. 2 Chr. 24. 20.
[o] Deut. 1. 42.
[p] 2 Chr. 15. 2.
[q] Deut. 1. 43.
[r] ver. 43. Deut. 1. 44.
[s] ch. 21. 3. Judg. 1. 17.
[a] ver. 18. Lev. 23. 10. Deut. 7. 1.

[1] Heb. *lifted up my hand*, Gen. 14. 22.
[2] Or, *feed*.
[3] Or, *altering of my purpose*.

33. *your whoredoms*] Their several rebellions had been so many acts of faithless departure from the Lord Who had taken them unto Himself. And as the children of the unchaste have generally to bear in their earthly careers much of the disgrace and the misery which forms the natural penalty of their parents' transgression; so here the children of the Israelites, although suffered to hope for an eventual entry into Canaan, were yet to endure, through many long years' wandering, the appropriate punishment of their fathers' wilfulness.

34. *my breach of promise*] In the original, a word, found elsewhere only in Job xxx. 10, and meaning "my withdrawal," "my turning away." See margin.

45. *unto Hormah*] Lit. "the Hormah:" *i.e.* "the banning," or "ban-place." Cp. xxi. 3; Josh. xii. 14. According to the view taken of Kadesh (see xiii. 26), Hormah is identified, through its earlier name, Zephath (Judg. i. 17), with es-Safâh on the south-eastern frontier of Canaan, by which the Israelites quitted the Arabah for the higher ground, [or with Sebaita, which lies further to the west, about 25 miles north of Ain Gadis].

XV. The contents of the next five chapters must apparently be referred to the long period of wandering to which (xiv. 33) the people were condemned.

2. To the Israelites of the younger generation is conveyed the hope that the nation

3 the land of your habitations, which I give unto you, and ^bwill *b* Lev. 1. 2, 3.
make an offering by fire unto the LORD, a burnt offering, or a
sacrifice ^cin ¹performing a vow, or in a freewill offering, or ^din *c* Lev. 7. 16.
your solemn feasts, to make a ^esweet savour unto the LORD, of & 22. 18, 21.
4 the herd, or of the flock: then ^fshall he that offereth his offer- ch. 28. 19.
ing unto the LORD bring ^ga meat offering of a tenth deal of flour & 29. 2, 8.
5 mingled ^hwith the fourth *part* of an hin of oil. ⁱAnd the fourth *e* Gen. 8. 21.
part of an hin of wine for a drink offering shalt thou prepare Ex: 29. 18.
6 with the burnt offering or sacrifice, for one lamb. ^kOr for a ram, *f* Lev. 2. 1.
thou shalt prepare *for* a meat offering two tenth deals of flour *g* Ex. 29. 40.
7 mingled with the third *part* of an hin of oil. And for a drink Lev. 23. 13.
offering thou shalt offer the third *part* of an hin of wine, *for* a *h* Lev. 14. 10.
8 sweet savour unto the LORD. And when thou preparest a *i* ch. 28. 7, 14.
bullock *for* a burnt offering, or *for* a sacrifice in performing a *k* ch. 28. 12.
9 vow, or ^lpeace offerings unto the LORD: then shall he bring *l* Lev. 7. 11.
^mwith a bullock a meat offering of three tenth deals of flour *m* ch. 28. 12,
10 mingled with half an hin of oil. And thou shalt bring for a 14.
drink offering half an hin of wine, *for* an offering made by fire,
11 of a sweet savour unto the LORD. ⁿThus shall it be done for *n* ch. 28.
12 one bullock, or for one ram, or for a lamb, or a kid. According
to the number that ye shall prepare, so shall ye do to every one
13 according to their number. All that are born of the country
shall do these things after this manner, in offering an offering
14 made by fire, of a sweet savour unto the LORD. And if a stranger
sojourn with you, or whosoever *be* among you in your generations, and will offer an offering made by fire, of a sweet savour
15 unto the LORD; as ye do, so he shall do. ^oOne ordinance *shall* *o* Ex. 12. 49.
be both for you of the congregation, and also for the stranger ch. 9. 14.
that sojourneth *with you*, an ordinance for ever in your genera- ver. 29.
16 tions: as ye *are*, so shall the stranger be before the LORD. One
law and one manner shall be for you, and for the stranger that
17 sojourneth with you. ¶ And the LORD spake unto Moses, saying,
18 ^pSpeak unto the children of Israel, and say unto them, When *p* ver. 2.
19 ye come into the land whither I bring you, then it shall be, that, Deut. 26. 1.
when ye eat of ^qthe bread of the land, ye shall offer up an heave *q* Josh. 5.
20 offering unto the LORD. ^rYe shall offer up a cake of the first of 11, 12.
your dough *for* an heave offering: as *ye do* ^sthe heave offering 2, 10.
21 of the threshingfloor, so shall ye heave it. Of the first of your Prov. 3. 9.
dough ye shall give unto the LORD an heave offering in your & 23. 10.
22 generations. ¶ And ^tif ye have erred, and not observed all these *t* Lev. 4. 2.

¹ Heb. *separating*, Lev. 27. 2.

---

should yet enter into the Land of Promise.
The ordinances that follow are more likely
to have been addressed to adults than to
children; and we may therefore assume
that at the date of their delivery the new
generation was growing up, and the period
of wandering drawing towards its close.
During that period the Meat-offerings and
Drink-offerings prescribed by the Law had
been probably intermitted by reason of the
scanty supply of corn and wine in the wilderness. The command therefore to provide such offerings was a pledge to Israel
that it should possess the land which was to
furnish the wherewithal for them.
4–12. The Meat-offering is treated in Lev.
ii. The Drink-offering (Ex. xxix. 40; Lev.

xxiii. 13), hitherto an ordinary accessory to
the former, is now prescribed for every
sacrifice.
18. The general principle which includes
the ordinance of this and the three verses
following is laid down in Ex. xxii. 29, xxiii.
19.
20, 21. *dough*] "Coarse meal" (Neh. x.
37; Ezek. xliv. 30).
22–31. The heavy punishments which
had already overtaken the people might naturally give rise to apprehensions for the
future, especially in view of the fact that on
the approaching entrance into Canaan the
complete observance of the Law in all its
details would become imperative on them.
To meet such apprehensions a distinction is

23 commandments, which the LORD hath spoken unto Moses, *even*
all that the LORD hath commanded you by the hand of Moses,
from the day that the LORD commanded *Moses*, and henceforward

u Lev. 4. 13.   24 among your generations; then it shall be, *u*if *ought* be committed by ignorance [1]without the knowledge of the congregation,
that all the congregation shall offer one young bullock for a

x ver. 8, 9,   burnt offering, for a sweet savour unto the LORD, *x*with his meat
10.   offering, and his drink offering, according to the [2]manner, and

y See Lev. 4.   25 *y*one kid of the goats for a sin offering.   *z*And the priest shall
23.   make an atonement for all the congregation of the children of
ch. 28. 15.   Israel, and it shall be forgiven them; for it *is* ignorance: and
Ezra 6. 17.   they shall bring their offering, a sacrifice made by fire unto the
& 8. 35.   LORD, and their sin offering before the LORD, for their ignor-
z Lev. 4. 20.   26 ance: and it shall be forgiven all the congregation of the
children of Israel, and the stranger that sojourneth among them;

a Lev. 4. 27,   27 seeing all the people *were* in ignorance.   ¶ And *a*if any soul sin
28.   through ignorance, then he shall bring a she goat of the first

b Lev. 4. 35.   28 year for a sin offering.   *b*And the priest shall make an atonement
for the soul that sinneth ignorantly, when he sinneth by igno-
rance before the LORD, to make an atonement for him; and it

c ver. 15.   29 shall be forgiven him.   *c*Ye shall have one law for him that
[3]sinneth through ignorance, *both for* him that is born among the
children of Israel, and for the stranger that sojourneth among

d Deut. 17.   30 them.   ¶ *d*But the soul that doeth *ought* [4]presumptuously,
12.   *whether he be* born in the land, or a stranger, the same re-
Ps. 19. 13.   proacheth the LORD : and that soul shall be cut off from among
Heb. 10. 26.   31 his people.   Because he hath *e*despised the word of the LORD,
2 Pet. 2. 10.   and hath broken his commandment, that soul shall utterly be
e 2 Sam. 12.   32 cut off; *f*his iniquity *shall be* upon him.   ¶ And while the
9.   children of Israel were in the wilderness, *g*they found a man that
Prov. 13. 13.   33 gathered sticks upon the sabbath day.   And they that found
f Lev. 5. 1.   him gathering sticks brought him unto Moses and Aaron, and
Ez. 18. 20.   34 unto all the congregation.   And they put him *h*in ward, because
g Ex. 31. 14,   35 it was not declared what should be done to him.   And the LORD
15.   said unto Moses, *i*The man shall be surely put to death: all the
& 35. 2, 3.   congregation shall *k*stone him with stones without the camp.
h Lev. 24.12.   36 And all the congregation brought him without the camp, and
stoned him with stones, and he died; as the LORD commanded
i Ex. 31. 14,   37, 38 Moses.   ¶ And the LORD spake unto Moses, saying, Speak
15.
k Lev. 24. 14.
1 Kin. 21. 13.
Acts 7. 58.

---

[1] Heb. *from the eyes.*   [3] Heb. *doth.*
[2] Or, *ordinance.*   [4] Heb. *with an high hand.*

---

emphatically drawn between sins of ignorance (Lev. iv. 13 sqq.) and those of presumption (*vv.* 30, 31).   The passage deals
separately with imperfections of obedience
which would be regarded as attaching to
the whole nation (*vv.* 22–26), and those of
individuals (*vv.* 27–30).

24. *without the knowledge of the congregation*] Lit. as marg.   The words point to an
error of omission which escaped notice at
the time : *i.e.* to an oversight.

30. *presumptuously*] The original (cp.
margin, and Ex. xiv. 8) imports something
done wilfully and openly ; in the case of a
sin against God it implies that the act is
committed ostentatiously and in bravado.

reproacheth the LORD] Rather, **revileth** or

blasphemeth the LORD : cp. Ezek. xx. 27.

32. Moses mentions here, as is his wont
(cp. Lev. xxiv. 10–16), the first open transgression and its punishment in order to
exemplify the laws which he is laying
down.   The offence of Sabbath-breaking
was one for which there could be no excuse.
This law at least might be observed even
in the wilderness.   Transgression of it was
therefore a presumptuous sin, and was
punished accordingly.

34. Death had indeed been assigned as
the penalty (Ex. xxxi. 14, xxxv. 2) ; but it
had not been determined how that death
was to be inflicted.

38. *that they put upon the fringe of the
borders a ribband of blue*] Render **that they**

unto the children of Israel, and bid *l*them that they make them *fringes* in the borders of their garments throughout their generations, and that they put upon the fringe of the borders a
39 ribband of blue: and it shall be unto you for a fringe, that ye may look upon it, and remember all the commandments of the LORD, and do them; and that ye *m*seek not after your own heart and your own eyes, after which ye use *n*to go a whoring:
40 that ye may remember, and do all my commandments, and be
41 *o*holy unto your God. I *am* the LORD your God, which brought you out of the land of Egypt, to be your God: I *am* the LORD your God.

CHAP. 16. NOW *a*Korah, the son of Izhar, the son of Kohath, the son of Levi, and Dathan and Abiram, the sons of Eliab, and On,
2 the son of Peleth, sons of Reuben, took *men:* and they rose up before Moses, with certain of the children of Israel, two hundred and fifty princes of the assembly, *b*famous in the congregation,
3 men of renown : and *c*they gathered themselves together against Moses and against Aaron, and said unto them, [1] *Ye take* too much upon you, seeing *d*all the congregation *are* holy, every one of them, *e*and the LORD *is* among them: wherefore then lift
4 ye up yourselves above the congregation of the LORD ? And
5 when Moses heard *it*, *f*he fell upon his face : and he spake unto Korah and unto all his company, saying, Even to morrow the LORD will shew who *are* his, and *who is g*holy ; and will cause *him* to come near unto him : even *him* whom he hath *h*chosen

[1] Heb. It is *much for you.*

l Deut. 22.12.
Matt. 23. 5.

m See Deut.
29. 19.
Job 31. 7.
Jer. 9. 14.
Ez. 6. 9.
n Ps. 73. 27.
& 106. 39.
Jam. 4. 4.
o Lev. 11.44,
45.
Rom. 12. 1.
Col. 1. 22.
1 Pet. 1. 15.
a Ex. 6. 21.
ch. 26. 9.
& 27. 3.
Jude 11.
b ch. 26. 9.
c Ps. 106. 16.
d Ex. 19. 6.
e Ex. 29. 45.
ch. 14. 14.
& 35. 34.
f ch. 14. 5.
& 20. 6.
g ver. 3.
Lev. 21. 6,7,
8, 12, 15.
h Ex. 28. 1.
ch. 17. 5.
1 Sam. 2. 28.
Ps. 105. 26.

add to the fringes of the borders (or corners) **a thread of blue** (cp. marg. reff.)
These fringes are considered to be of Egyptian origin. The ordinary outer Jewish garment was a quadrangular piece of cloth like a modern plaid, to the corners of which, in conformity with this command, a tassel was attached. Each tassel had a conspicuous thread of deep blue, this colour being doubtless symbolical of the heavenly origin of the commandments of which it was to serve as a memento. Tradition determined that the other threads should be white,—this colour being an emblem of purity (cp. Isai. i. 18). The arrangement of the threads and knots, to which the Jews attached the greatest importance, was so adjusted as to set forth symbolically the 613 precepts of which the Law was believed to consist. In our Lord's time the Pharisees enlarged their fringes (Matt. xxiii. 5) in order to obtain reputation for their piety. In later times however the Jews have worn the fringed garment (*tālīth*) of a smaller size and as an under dress. Its use is still retained, especially at morning prayer in the Synagogue.

XVI. The date of this rebellion cannot be determined, but *vv.* 13, 14 probably point to a period not much later than that of the rebellion at Kadesh.

1. Amram and Izhar were brothers (cp. Ex. vi. 18), and thus Korah, the "son," *i.e.* descendant of Izhar, was connected by distant cousinship with Moses and Aaron. Though being a Kohathite, he was of that division of the Levites which had the most honourable charge, yet as Elizaphan, who had been made "chief of the families of the Kohathites" (iii. 30), belonged to the youngest branch descended from Uzziel (iii. 27), Korah probably regarded himself as injured ; and therefore took the lead in this rebellion. Of the others, On is not again mentioned. He probably withdrew from the conspiracy. Dathan, Abiram, and On were Reubenites ; and were probably discontented because the birthright had been taken away from their ancestor (Gen. xlix. 3), and with it the primacy of their own tribe amongst the tribes of Israel. The Reubenites encamped near to the Kohathites (cp. ii. 25 and plan), and thus the two families were conveniently situated for taking counsel together. One pretext of the insurrection probably was to assert the rights of primogeniture,—on the part of the Reubenites against Moses, on the part of Korah against the appointment of Uzziel.

2. The "princes" appear to have belonged to the other tribes (cp. xxvii. 3).

3. *all the congregation are holy*] Cp. marg. ref. Korah's object was not to abolish the distinction between the Levites and the people, but to win priestly dignity for himself and his kinsmen (*v.* 10). This ultimate design is masked for the present in order to win support from the Reubenites by putting forward claims to spiritual equality on behalf of every Israelite.

i ch. 3. 10.
Lev. 10. 3.
& 21. 17, 18.
Ez. 40. 46.
& 44. 15.

k 1 Sam. 18.
23.
Isai. 7. 13.
l ch. 3. 41, 45.
& 8. 14.
Deut. 10. 8.

m Ex. 16. 8.
1 Cor. 3. 5.

n ver. 9.

o Ex. 2. 14.
Acts 7. 27,
35.
p Ex. 3. 8.
Lev. 20. 24.
q Gen. 4. 4,
5.
r 1 Sam. 12.
3.
Acts 20. 33.
2 Cor. 7. 2.
s ver. 6, 7.
t 1 Sam. 12.
3, 7.
u ver. 42.
Ex. 16. 7.
Lev. 9. 6.
ch. 14. 10.
x ver. 45.
See Gen. 19.
17, 22.
Jer. 51. 6.
Acts 2. 40.
Rev. 18. 4.
y ver. 45.
Ex. 32. 10.
& 33. 5.
z ver. 45.
ch. 14. 5.
a ch. 27. 16.
Job 12. 10.
Eccles. 12. 7.
Isai. 57. 16.
Zech. 12. 1.
Heb. 12. 9.

6 will he cause to *i*come near unto him. This do; Take you 7 censers, Korah, and all his company; and put fire therein, and put incense in them before the LORD to morrow: and it shall be *that* the man whom the LORD doth choose, he *shall be* holy: 8 ye take too much upon you, ye sons of Levi. And Moses said 9 unto Korah, Hear, I pray you, ye sons of Levi: *seemeth it but* *k*a small thing unto you, that the God of Israel hath *l*separated you from the congregation of Israel, to bring you near to himself to do the service of the tabernacle of the LORD, and to stand before 10 the congregation to minister unto them? And he hath brought thee near *to him*, and all thy brethren the sons of Levi with 11 thee: and seek ye the priesthood also? For which cause *both* thou and all thy company *are* gathered together against the LORD: *m*and what *is* Aaron, that ye murmur against him? 12 ¶ And Moses sent to call Dathan and Abiram, the sons of Eliab: 13 which said, We will not come up: *n*is it a small thing that thou hast brought us up out of a land that floweth with milk and honey, to kill us in the wilderness, except thou *o*make thyself 14 altogether a prince over us? Moreover thou hast not brought us into *p*a land that floweth with milk and honey, or given us inheritance of fields and vineyards: wilt thou ¹put out the eyes 15 of these men? We will not come up. ¶ And Moses was very wroth, and said unto the LORD, *q*Respect not thou their offering: *r*I have not taken one ass from them, neither have I hurt one of 16 them. And Moses said unto Korah, *s*Be thou and all thy company *t*before the LORD, thou, and they, and Aaron, to morrow: 17 and take every man his censer, and put incense in them, and bring ye before the LORD every man his censer, two hundred and fifty censers; thou also, and Aaron, each *of you* his censer. 18 And they took every man his censer, and put fire in them, and laid incense thereon, and stood in the door of the tabernacle of 19 the congregation with Moses and Aaron. And Korah gathered all the congregation against them unto the door of the tabernacle of the congregation: and *u*the glory of the LORD appeared 20 unto all the congregation. ¶ And the LORD spake unto Moses 21 and unto Aaron, saying, *x*Separate yourselves from among this 22 congregation, that I may *y*consume them in a moment. And they *z*fell upon their faces, and said, O God, *a*the God of the spirits of all flesh, shall one man sin, and wilt thou be wroth 23 with all the congregation? And the LORD spake unto Moses, 24 saying, Speak unto the congregation, saying, Get you up from

¹ Heb. *bore out.*

9. "Seemeth" is not in the original. Render: **Is it too little for you,** *i.e.* "is it less than your dignity demands?"

11. The words of Moses in his wrath are broken. The Aaronic priesthood was of divine appointment; and thus in rejecting it, the conspirators were really rebelling against God.

13. With perverse contempt for the promises, Dathan and Abiram designate Egypt by the terms appropriated elsewhere to the land of Canaan.

14. *wilt thou put out the eyes of these men?*] *i.e.* "blind them to the fact that you keep none of your promises;" "throw dust in their eyes."

24. The tent, *the tabernacle* of Korah, as a Kohathite, stood on the south side of the Tabernacle of the Lord; and those of Dathan and Abiram, as Reubenites, in the outer line of encampment on the same side. Yet though the tents of these three were thus contiguous, they did not share the same fate. Korah and his company who dared to intrude themselves on the priestly office were destroyed by fire from the Lord at the door of the Tabernacle of the Lord (*v.* 35); the Reubenites, who had reviled Moses for the failure of the promises about the pleasant land, were suddenly engulfed whilst standing at their own tent-doors in the barren wilderness (*vv.* 31-33).

25 about the tabernacle of Korah, Dathan, and Abiram. ¶And Moses rose up and went unto Dathan and Abiram; and the
26 elders of Israel followed him. And he spake unto the congregation, saying, *b*Depart, I pray you, from the tents of these wicked men, and touch nothing of their's, lest ye be consumed
27 in all their sins. So they gat up from the tabernacle of Korah, Dathan, and Abiram, on every side: and Dathan and Abiram came out, and stood in the door of their tents, and their wives,
28 and their sons, and their little children. And Moses said, *c*Hereby ye shall know that the LORD hath sent me to do all these works; for I have not done them *d*of mine own mind.
29 If these men die ¹the common death of all men, or if they be *e*visited after the visitation of all men; then the LORD hath not
30 sent me. But if the LORD ²make *f*a new thing, and the earth open her mouth, and swallow them up, with all that appertain unto them, and they *g*go down quick into the pit; then ye shall
31 understand that these men have provoked the LORD. ¶*h*And it came to pass, as he had made an end of speaking all these words, that the ground clave asunder that was under them:
32 and the earth opened her mouth, and swallowed them up, and their houses, and *i*all the men that appertained unto Korah, and
33 all their goods. They, and all that appertained to them, went down alive into the pit, and the earth closed upon them: and
34 they perished from among the congregation. And all Israel that were round about them fled at the cry of them: for they said,
35 Lest the earth swallow us up also. And there *k*came out a fire from the LORD, and consumed *l*the two hundred and fifty men
36 that offered incense. ¶And the LORD spake unto Moses, saying,
37 Speak unto Eleazar the son of Aaron the priest, that he take up the censers out of the burning, and scatter thou the fire yonder;
38 for *m*they are hallowed. The censers of these *n*sinners against their own souls, let them make them broad plates for a covering of the altar: for they offered them before the LORD, therefore they are hallowed: *o*and they shall be a sign unto the children
39 of Israel. And Eleazar the priest took the brasen censers, wherewith they that were burnt had offered; and they were
40 made broad plates for a covering of the altar: to be a memorial unto the children of Israel, *p*that no stranger, which is not of the seed of Aaron, come near to offer incense before the LORD; that he be not as Korah, and as his company: as the LORD said
41 to him by the hand of Moses. ¶But on the morrow *q*all the congregation of the children of Israel murmured against Moses and against Aaron, saying, Ye have killed the people of the LORD.
42 And it came to pass, when the congregation was gathered against Moses and against Aaron, that they looked toward the

b Gen. 19.12, 14.
Isai. 52. 11.
2 Cor. 6. 17.
Rev. 18. 4.

c Ex. 3. 12.
Deut. 18. 22.
Zech. 2. 9,
11. & 4. 9.
John 5. 36.
d ch. 24. 13.
Jer. 23. 16.
Ez. 13. 17.
John 5. 30.
& 6. 38.
e Ex. 20. 5.
& 32. 34.
Job 35. 15.
Isai. 10. 3.
Jer. 5. 9.
f Job 31. 3.
Isai. 28. 21.
g ver. 33.
Ps. 55. 15.
h ch. 26. 10.
& 27. 3.
Deut. 11. 6.
Ps. 106. 17.
i See ver.17.
& ch. 26. 11.
1 Chr. 6. 22,
37.
k Lev. 10. 2.
ch. 11. 1.
Ps. 106. 18.
l ver. 17.
m See Lev.
27. 28.
n Prov. 20. 2.
Hab. 2. 10.
o ch. 17. 10.
& 26. 10.
Ez. 14. 8.

p ch. 3. 10.
2 Chr. 26. 18.

q ch. 14. 2.
Ps. 106. 25.

---

¹ Heb. as every man dieth.　　　² Heb. create a creature, Isai. 45. 7.

---

27. stood in the door of their tents] Apparently in contumacious defiance.
32. all the men, &c.] Not his sons (see xxvi. 11), but all belonging to him who had associated themselves with him in this rebellion.
35. Cp. marg. reff. The fire came out from the Sanctuary or the Altar.
37. Aaron as High-priest and as one of those that offered incense (v. 17), could not be defiled by going among the dead.

The censers were not to be used again for censers, nor the coals on them for kindling the incense to be offered before the Lord. Yet neither of them could fittingly be employed for common purposes. The censers therefore were beaten into plates for the Altar; the coals were scattered at a distance.
38. these sinners against their own souls] That is, "against their own lives." By their sin they had brought destruction upon themselves.

r Ex. 40. 34.
s ver. 19.
ch. 20. 6.
t ver. 21. 24.
u ver. 22.
ch. 20. 6.

tabernacle of the congregation : and, behold, ʳthe cloud covered
43 it, and ˢ the glory of the LORD appeared.   And Moses and Aaron
44 came before the tabernacle of the congregation.   And the LORD
45 spake unto Moses, saying, ᵗGet you up from among this congregation, that I may consume them as in a moment.   And ᵘthey
46 fell upon their faces.   And Moses said unto Aaron, Take a
censer, and put fire therein from off the altar, and put on incense,
and go quickly unto the congregation, and make an atonement

x 5 Lev.10.6.
ch. 1. 53.
& 8. 19.
& 11. 33.
& 18. 5.
1 Chr. 27. 24.
Ps. 106. 29.

for them : ˣfor there is wrath gone out from the LORD ; the
47 plague is begun.   And Aaron took as Moses commanded, and ran
into the midst of the congregation ; and, behold, the plague was
begun among the people : and he put on incense, and made an
48 atonement for the people.   And he stood between the dead and
49 the living ; and the plague was stayed.   Now they that died in
the plague were fourteen thousand and seven hundred, beside
50 them that died about the matter of Korah.   And Aaron returned
unto Moses unto the door of the tabernacle of the congregation :
and the plague was stayed.

CHAP. 17. AND the LORD spake unto Moses, saying, Speak unto the
2 children of Israel, and take of every one of them a rod according
to the house of *their* fathers, of all their princes according to the
house of their fathers twelve rods : write thou every man's name
3 upon his rod.   And thou shalt write Aaron's name upon the rod
of Levi : for one rod *shall be* for the head of the house of their
4 fathers.   And thou shalt lay them up in the tabernacle of the

a Ex. 25. 22.
& 29. 42, 43.
& 30. 36.
b ch. 16. 5.
c ch. 16. 11.

congregation before the testimony, ᵃwhere I will meet with you.
5 And it shall come to pass, *that* the man's rod, ᵇwhom I shall
choose, shall blossom : and I will make to cease from me the
murmurings of the children of Israel, ᶜwhereby they murmur
6 against you.   ¶And Moses spake unto the children of Israel,
and every one of their princes gave him ¹a rod apiece, for each
prince one, according to their fathers' houses, *even* twelve rods :
7 and the rod of Aaron *was* among their rods.   And Moses laid up

d Ex. 38. 21.
ch. 18. 2.
Acts 7. 44.

8 the rods before the LORD in ᵈthe tabernacle of witness.   ¶And
it came to pass, that on the morrow Moses went into the taber-

¹ Heb. *a rod for one prince, a rod for one prince.*

---

45. *they fell upon their faces*] In intercession for the people ; cp. *v.* 22, xiv. 5.
46. *a censer*] Rather, **the censer.** *i.e.* that
of the High-priest which was used by him
on the Great Day of Atonement : cp. Lev.
xvi. 12 ; Heb. ix. 4.
46–48. A striking proof of the efficacy of
that very Aaronic priesthood which the
rebels had presumed to reject.   The incense
offering which had brought down destruction when presented by unauthorised hands,
now in the hand of the true priest is the
medium of instant salvation to the whole
people.   Aaron by his acceptable ministration and his personal self-devotion foreshadows emphatically in this transaction
the perfect mediation and sacrifice of Himself made by Christ.
XVII. **2.** Cp. Ezek. xxxvii. 16 sqq.
3. *thou shalt write Aaron's name upon the
rod of Levi*] The Levites had taken part in
the late outbreak.   It was therefore necessary to vindicate the supremacy of the

house of Aaron over them ; and accordingly
his name was written on the rod of Levi,
although being the son of Kohath, the
second son of Levi (Ex. vi. 16 seq.), he
would not be the natural head of the tribe.
4. *before the testimony*] See *v.* 10 note.
6. The whole number of rods was twelve
exclusive of Aaron's, as the Vulgate expressly states.
8. *yielded almonds*] "Ripened almonds,"
i.e. "brought forth ripe almonds." The
name almond in Hebrew denotes the
"waking-tree," the "waking-fruit ;" and
is applied to this tree, because it blossoms
early in the season.   It serves here, as in
Jer. i. 11, 12, to set forth the speed and
certainty with which, at God's will, His
purposes are accomplished.   So again the
blossoming and bearing of Aaron's rod,
naturally impotent when severed from the
parent tree, may signify the profitableness,
because of God's appointment and blessing,
of the various means of grace (*e.g.* the

nacle of witness; and, behold, the rod of Aaron for the house
of Levi was budded, and brought forth buds, and bloomed
9 blossoms, and yielded almonds. And Moses brought out all the
rods from before the LORD unto all the children of Israel: and
10 they looked, and took every man his rod. ¶And the LORD said
unto Moses, Bring *Aaron's rod again before the testimony, to
be kept *for a token against the ¹rebels; *and thou shalt quite
11 take away their murmurings from me, that they die not. And
12 Moses did *so:* as the LORD commanded him, so did he. ¶And
the children of Israel spake unto Moses, saying, Behold, we die,
13 we perish, we all perish. *Whosoever cometh any thing near
unto the tabernacle of the LORD shall die: shall we be consumed
with dying?

CHAP. 18. AND the LORD said unto Aaron, *Thou and thy sons
and thy father's house with thee shall *bear the iniquity of the
sanctuary: and thou and thy sons with thee shall bear the
2 iniquity of your priesthood. And thy brethren also of the tribe
of Levi, the tribe of thy father, bring thou with thee, that they
may be *joined unto thee, and *minister unto thee; but *thou
and thy sons with thee *shall minister* before the tabernacle of
3 witness. And they shall keep thy charge, and *the charge of all
the tabernacle: *only they shall not come nigh the vessels of the
4 sanctuary and the altar, *that neither they, nor ye also, die. And
they shall be joined unto thee, and keep the charge of the tabernacle of the congregation, for all the service of the tabernacle:
5 *and a stranger shall not come nigh unto you. And ye shall
keep *the charge of the sanctuary, and the charge of the altar:
*that there be no wrath any more upon the children of Israel.
6 And I, behold, I have *taken your brethren the Levites from
among the children of Israel: *to you *they are* given *as* a gift
for the LORD, to do the service of the tabernacle of the congrega-
7 tion. Therefore *thou and thy sons with thee shall keep your
priest's office for every thing of the altar, and *within the vail;

¹ Heb. *children of rebellion.*

e Heb. 9. 4.
f ch. 16. 38.
g ver. 5.

h ch. 1. 51,
53.
& 18. 4, 7.

a ch. 17. 13.
b Ex. 28. 38.

c See Gen.
29. 34.
d ch. 3. 6, 7.
e ch. 3. 10.
f ch. 3. 25,
31, 36.
g ch. 16. 40.
h ch. 4. 15.

i ch. 3. 10.
k Ex. 27. 21.
& 30. 7.
Lev. 24. 3.
ch. 8. 2.
l ch. 16. 46.
m ch. 3. 12,
45.
n ch. 3. 9.
& 8. 19.
o ver. 5.
ch. 3. 10.
p Heb. 9. 3,
6.

---

priesthood, the Sacraments), which of
themselves and apart from Him could have
no such efficacy. Cp. Isai. iv. 2, xi. 1, liii.
2; Jer. xxxiii. 5; Zech. vi. 12.

10. *the testimony*] *i.e.* the Two Tables of
the Law; cp. Ex. xxv. 16 note. No doubt the
rod lay in front of the Tables within the Ark.
In the days of Solomon (1 Kings viii. 9)
there was nothing in the ark save the Two
Tables. Aaron's rod was probably lost
when the Ark was taken by the Philistines.

12, 13. A new section should begin with
these verses. They are connected retrospec-
tively with ch. xvi.; and form the immediate introduction to ch. xviii. The people
were terror-stricken by the fate of the company of Korah and by the plague. Presumption passed by reaction into despair.
Was there any approach for them to the
Tabernacle of the Lord? Was there any
escape from death, except by keeping aloof
from His Presence? The answers are supplied by the ordinances which testified that
the God of judgment was still a God of
grace and of love.

XVIII. 1. *the iniquity of the sanctuary*]
i.e. the guilt of the offences which an erring
people would be continually committing
against the majesty of God, when brought
into contact, through the ordinances, with
the manifestations of His Presence. Cp.
marg. ref.

the iniquity of your priesthood] As the
priests themselves were but men, they were
strengthened to bear the iniquity of their
own unintentional offences, by being entrusted with the ceremonial means of
taking it away (cp. Lev. xvi.). The word
"bear" has, in the Old Testament, this
double sense of "enduring" and "removing;" but in the person of Christ, Who
atoned by His own endurance, the two are
in effect one.

4. *a stranger*] *i.e.* every one not a Levite.
So in *v.* 7, it denotes every one who was not
a priest: cp. iii. 10, xvi. 40.

6, 7. The Lord instructs here the priests
that the office which they fill, and the help
which they enjoy, are gifts from Him, and
are to be viewed as such.

and ye shall serve : I have given your priest's office *unto you as*
a service of gift : and the stranger that cometh nigh shall be put
8 to death. ¶And the LORD spake unto Aaron, Behold, *q*I also
have given thee the charge of mine heave offerings of all the
hallowed things of the children of Israel ; unto thee have I given
them *r*by reason of the anointing, and to thy sons, by an ordi-
9 nance for ever. This shall be thine of the most holy things,
reserved from the fire : every oblation of their's, every *s*meat
offering of their's, and every *t*sin offering of their's, and every
*u*trespass offering of their's, which they shall render unto me,
10 *shall be* most holy for thee and for thy sons. *x*In the most holy
place shalt thou eat it ; every male shall eat it : it shall be holy
11 unto thee. And this *is* thine ; *y*the heave offering of their gift,
with all the wave offerings of the children of Israel : I have given
them unto *z*thee, and to thy sons and to thy daughters with
thee, by a statute for ever : *a*every one that is clean in thy house
12 shall eat of it. *b*All the [1]best of the oil, and all the best of the
wine, and of the wheat, *c*the firstfruits of them which they shall
13 offer unto the LORD, them have I given thee. *And* whatsoever
is first ripe in the land, *d*which they shall bring unto the LORD,
shall be thine ; *e*every one that is clean in thine house shall eat
14, 15 *of* it. *f*Every thing devoted in Israel shall be thine. Every
thing that openeth *g*the matrix in all flesh, which they bring
unto the LORD, *whether it be* of men or beasts, shall be thine :
nevertheless *h*the firstborn of man shalt thou surely redeem,
16 and the firstling of unclean beasts shalt thou redeem. And
those that are to be redeemed from a month old shalt thou redeem, *i*according to thine estimation, for the money of five
shekels, after the shekel of the sanctuary, *k*which *is* twenty
17 gerahs. *l*But the firstling of a cow, or the firstling of a sheep,
or the firstling of a goat, thou shalt not redeem ; they *are* holy :
*m*thou shalt sprinkle their blood upon the altar, and shalt burn
their fat *for* an offering made by fire, for a sweet savour unto the
18 LORD. And the flesh of them shall be thine, as the *n*wave breast
19 and as the right shoulder are thine. *o*All the heave offerings of
the holy things, which the children of Israel offer unto the LORD,
have I given thee, and thy sons and thy daughters with thee,
by a statute for ever : *p*it *is* a covenant of salt for ever before
20 the LORD unto thee and to thy seed with thee. ¶And the LORD
spake unto Aaron, Thou shalt have no inheritance in their land,
neither shalt thou have any part among them : *q*I *am* thy part
21 and thine inheritance among the children of Israel. And, behold, *r*I have given the children of Levi all the tenth in Israel

[1] Heb. *fat*, ver. 29.

q Lev. 6. 16,
18. & 7. 6.
ch. 5. 9.
r Ex. 29. 29.
& 40. 13, 15.
s Lev. 2. 2, 3.
t Lev. 4. 22.
u Lev. 5. 1.
x Lev. 6. 16,
18, 26, 29.
& 7. 6.
y Ex. 29. 27.
Lev. 7. 30.
z Lev. 10. 14.
Deut. 18. 3.
a Lev. 22. 2.
b Ex. 23. 19.
Deut. 18. 4.
Neh. 10. 35.
c Ex. 22. 29.
d Ex. 23. 19.
& 34. 26.
Lev. 2. 14.
ch. 15. 19.
Deut. 26. 2.
e ver. 11.
f Lev. 27. 28.
g Ex. 13. 2.
Lev. 27. 26.
ch. 3. 13.
h Ex. 13. 13.
& 34. 20.
i Lev. 27. 2, 6.
ch. 3. 47.
k Ex. 30. 13.
Lev. 27. 25.
ch. 3. 47.
Ez. 45. 12.
l Deut. 15.
19.
m Lev. 3. 2,
5.
n Ex. 29. 26.
Lev. 7. 31.
o ver. 11.
p Lev. 2. 13.
2 Chr. 13. 5.
q Deut. 10. 9.
Josh. 13. 14,
33.
Ps. 16. 5.
Ez. 44. 28.
r Lev. 27. 30,
32.
ver. 24. 26.
Neh. 10. 37.
& 12. 44.
Heb. 7. 5.

---

8. *by reason of the anointing*] See Lev.
vii. 35.

10. *in the most holy place*] Rather, "among
the most holy things ; " as in iv. 4 : *i.e.* "As
the most holy of things shalt thou eat it."
Accordingly only the males of the priestly
families could eat of the things here specified.

15. *surely redeem...redeem*] A stronger expression is intentionally used in reference
to the redemption of the first-born of man
than in reference to that of unclean beasts.
For the rule as to the former admitted of

no exception : the owner of the latter, if
unwilling to redeem, might destroy the
beasts. Cp. marg. reff.

19. *a covenant of salt*] Cp. marg. ref.
Covenants were ordinarily cemented in the
East by the rites of hospitality ; of which
salt was the obvious token, entering as it
does into every article of diet. It indicates
perpetuity : cp. Lev. ii. 13 note.

20. *I am thy part and thine inheritance*]
Cp. marg. reff.

21. Abraham paid tithes to Melchizedek :
Jacob had promised the tithe of all where-

for an inheritance, for their service which they serve, even *the
22 service of the tabernacle of the congregation. *Neither must
the children of Israel henceforth come nigh the tabernacle of the
23 congregation, *lest they bear sin, ¹and die. *But the Levites
shall do the service of the tabernacle of the congregation, and
they shall bear their iniquity: it shall be a statute for ever
throughout your generations, that among the children of Israel
24 they have no inheritance. *But the tithes of the children of
Israel, which they offer as an heave offering unto the LORD, I
have given to the Levites to inherit : therefore I have said unto
them, *Among the children of Israel they shall have no inheri-
25, 26 tance. ¶ And the LORD spake unto Moses, saying, Thus speak
unto the Levites, and say unto them, When ye take of the
children of Israel the tithes which I have given you from them
for your inheritance, then ye shall offer up an heave offering of
27 it for the LORD, even *a tenth part of the tithe. *And this your
heave offering shall be reckoned unto you, as though it were the
corn of the threshingfloor, and as the fulness of the winepress.
28 Thus ye also shall offer an heave offering unto the LORD of all
your tithes, which ye receive of the children of Israel; and ye
shall give thereof the LORD's heave offering to Aaron the priest.
29 Out of all your gifts ye shall offer every heave offering of the
LORD, of all the ²best thereof, even the hallowed part thereof out
30 of it. Therefore thou shalt say unto them, When ye have heaved
the best thereof from it, *then it shall be counted unto the
Levites as the increase of the threshingfloor, and as the increase
31 of the winepress. And ye shall eat it in every place, ye and
your households : for it is *your reward for your service in the
32 tabernacle of the congregation. And ye shall *bear no sin by
reason of it, when ye have heaved from it the best of it : neither
shall ye *pollute the holy things of the children of Israel, lest
ye die.
CHAP. 19. AND the LORD spake unto Moses and unto Aaron, saying,

¹ Heb. to die.　　　² Heb. fat, ver. 12.

s ch. 3. 7, 8.
t ch. 1. 51.

u Lev. 22. 9.
x ch. 3. 7.

y ver. 21.

z ver. 20.
Deut. 14. 27,
29. & 18. 1.

a Neh. 10.
38.
b ver. 30.

c ver. 27.

d Matt. 10.
10.
Luke 10. 7.
1 Cor. 9. 13.
1 Tim. 5. 18.
e Lev. 19. 8.
& 22. 16.
f Lev. 22. 2,
15.

---

with God blessed him if he should return in
peace to his father's house. But now first
the Lord's tithes are assigned to the Levites
for their support (cp. Lev. xxvii. 30). The
payment of tithes to them is recognised in
Neh. x. 37,*xii. 44 ; Tobit i. 7.

23. *bear their iniquity*] The words probably refer to the iniquity of the people ;
who would, had they approached the Tabernacle have fallen, from their proneness
to transgress, into overt acts of offence.
Against such a result they were, through
the ministrations of the Levites, mercifully
protected. Cp. *v.* 1.

24. Here the tithes (and in *v.* 26 the
priestly tithes) are to be dedicated to their
purpose by the ceremony of heaving them
to the Lord. The tithes, being solemnly
set apart for sacred purposes, became virtually a heave-offering, like the gifts for the
Tabernacle (Ex. xxv. 2).

27. *reckoned unto you*] Or, **by you.** The
Levites were, of their tithes, to pay tithe to
the priests, just as other Israelites paid
tithe to the Levites.

29. *out of all your gifts*] The spirit of this
law would extend to all the revenues of the
Levites ; of the increase of their cattle, as
well as of their tithes, a tithe would be paid
by them for the Lord's service.

32. *neither shall ye pollute,* &c.] Rather,
**and by not polluting the holy things of
the children of Israel, ye shall not die.**

XIX. The principle that death and all
pertaining to it, as being the manifestation
and result of sin (Gen. ii. 17), are defiling,
and so lead to interruption of the living
relationship between God and His people,
is not now introduced for the first time, nor
is it at all peculiar to the Mosaic law. It
was, on the contrary, traditional amongst
the Israelites from the earliest times, it is
assumed in various enactments made already (cp. v. 2, ix. 6 seq. ; Lev. x. 1, 7, xi.
8, 11, 24, xxi. 1 seq.), and it is traceable in
various forms amongst many nations, both
ancient and modern. Moses adopted, here
as elsewhere, existing and ancient customs,
with significant additions, as helps in the
spiritual education of his people.

2 This *is* the ordinance of the law which the LORD hath commanded, saying, Speak unto the children of Israel, that they
bring thee a red heifer without spot, wherein *is* no blemish,
3 *ᵃand* upon which never came yoke: and ye shall give her unto
Eleazar the priest, that he may bring her *ᵇ*forth without the
4 camp, and *one* shall slay her before his face: and Eleazar the
priest shall take of her blood with his finger, and *ᶜ*sprinkle of
her blood directly before the tabernacle of the congregation
5 seven times: and *one* shall burn the heifer in his sight; *ᵈ*her
skin, and her flesh, and her blood, with her dung, shall he burn:
6 and the priest shall take *ᵉ*cedar wood, and hyssop, and scarlet,
7 and cast *it* into the midst of the burning of the heifer. *ᶠ*Then
the priest shall wash his clothes, and he shall bathe his flesh in
water, and afterward he shall come into the camp, and the priest
8 shall be unclean until the even. And he that burneth her shall
wash his clothes in water, and bathe his flesh in water, and shall
9 be unclean until the even. And a man *that is* clean shall gather
up *ᵍ*the ashes of the heifer, and lay *them* up without the camp in
a clean place, and it shall be kept for the congregation of the
children of Israel *ʰ*for a water of separation: it *is* a purification
10 for sin. And he that gathereth the ashes of the heifer shall
wash his clothes, and be unclean until the even: and it shall be
unto the children of Israel, and unto the stranger that sojourneth
11 among them, for a statute for ever. ¶*ⁱ*He that toucheth the
12 dead body of any ¹man shall be unclean seven days. *ᵏ*He shall
purify himself with it on the third day, and on the seventh
day he shall be clean: but if he purify not himself the third
13 day, then the seventh day he shall not be clean. Whosoever
toucheth the dead body of any man that is dead, and purifieth

¹ Heb. *soul of man.*

The ordinance was probably given at this
time because the plague which happened
(xvi. 46-50) about the matter of Korah had
spread the defilement of death so widely
through the camp as to seem to require
some special measures of purification, more
particularly as the deaths through it were
in an extraordinary manner the penalty of
sin.

2. *a red heifer*] Red, in order to shadow
forth man's earthly body, even as the name
Adam bears allusion to the red earth of
which man's body was fashioned.

without spot, wherein is no blemish] As
with sin-offerings generally (Lev. iv. 3).

upon which never came yoke] So here and
elsewhere (see marg. reff.), in the case of
female victims.

3. The work would necessarily require a
priest; yet as it rendered him unclean for
the day (*v.* 22), the High-priest was relieved
from performing it.

without the camp] The defilement was
viewed as transferred to the victim that
was to be offered for its removal. Under
these circumstances the victim, like the defiled persons themselves, would be removed
outside the camp. The particular pollution
to be remedied by this ordinance was the
indirect one resulting from contact with

tokens and manifestations of sin, not the
direct and personal one arising from actual
commission of sin. So too the sinless Antitype had to bear the reproach of associating
with sinners (Luke v. 30, xv. 2). And
as the red heifer was expelled from the precincts of the camp, so was the Saviour cut
off in no small measure during His Life
from the fellowship of the chief representatives of the Theocracy, and put to death
outside Jerusalem between two thieves.
Cp. Heb. xiii. 11, 12.

6. Cp. Lev. xiv. 4 note.

9. *water of separation*] In viii. 7, the water
of purification from sin is the "water of
purifying." So that which was to remedy
a state of legal separation is here called
"water of separation."

10. He that gathered the ashes became
equally unclean with the others. For the
defilement of the people, previously transferred to the heifer, was regarded as concentrated in the ashes.

11-22. One practical effect of attaching
defilement to a dead body, and to all that
touched it, &c., would be to insure early
burial, and to correct a practice not uncommon in the East, of leaving the dead to
be devoured by the wild beasts.

not himself, [l]defileth the tabernacle of the LORD; and that soul
shall be cut off from Israel: because [m]the water of separation
was not sprinkled upon him, he shall be unclean; [n]his unclean-
14 ness *is* yet upon him. This *is* the law, when a man dieth in a
tent: all that come into the tent, and all that *is* in the tent, shall
15 be unclean seven days. And every [o]open vessel, which hath no
16 covering bound upon it, *is* unclean. And [p]whosoever toucheth
one that is slain with a sword in the open fields, or a dead body,
or a bone of a man, or a grave, shall be unclean seven days.
17 ¶ And for an unclean *person* they shall take of the [1][q]ashes of
the burnt heifer of purification for sin, and [2]running water shall
18 be put thereto in a vessel: and a clean person shall take
[r]hyssop, and dip *it* in the water, and sprinkle *it* upon the tent,
and upon all the vessels, and upon the persons that were there,
and upon him that touched a bone, or one slain, or one dead, or
19 a grave: and the clean *person* shall sprinkle upon the unclean on the third day, and on the seventh day: [s]and on the
seventh day he shall purify himself, and wash his clothes, and
20 bathe himself in water, and shall be clean at even. But the man
that shall be unclean, and shall not purify himself, that soul
shall be cut off from among the congregation, because he hath
[t]defiled the sanctuary of the LORD: the water of separation hath
21 not been sprinkled upon him; he *is* unclean. And it shall be a
perpetual statute unto them, that he that sprinkleth the water
of separation shall wash his clothes; and he that toucheth the
22 water of separation shall be unclean until even. And [u]whatso-
ever the unclean *person* toucheth shall be unclean; and [x]the
soul that toucheth *it* shall be unclean until even.

CHAP. 20. THEN [a]came the children of Israel, *even* the whole
congregation, into the desert of Zin in the first month.: and

[1] Heb. *dust*.   [2] Heb. *living waters shall be given*, Gen. 26. 19.

[l] Lev. 15. 31.
[m] ch. 8. 7.
[n] ver. 9.
[n] Lev. 7. 20.
& 22. 3.

[o] Lev. 11. 32.
ch. 31. 20.
[p] ver. 11.

[q] ver. 9.

[r] Ps. 51. 7.

[s] Lev. 14. 9.

[t] ver. 13.

[u] Hag. 2. 13.
[x] Lev. 15. 5.

[a] ch. 33. 36.

XX. & XXI. narrate the journey of the
people from Kadesh round Mount Seir to
the heights of Pisgah, near the Jordan, and
the various incidents connected with that
journey (cp. xxxiii. 37–41). This formed the
third and last stage of the progress of Israel
from Sinai to Canaan, and took place in the
fortieth year of the Exodus.

The incidents are apparently not narrated
in a strictly chronological order (see xxi. 1).
The leading purpose of ch. xx. seems to be
to narrate the loss by the people of their
original leaders before their entrance into
the Land of Promise.

1. *even the whole congregation*] This emphatic expression (cp. xiii. 26, xiv. 1) points
to a re-assembling of the people for the purpose of at last resuming the advance to the
Promised Land. During the past 38 years
the "congregation" had been broken up.
No doubt round the Tabernacle there had
continued an organised camp consisting of
the Levites and others, which had been
moved from time to time up and down the
country (cp. xxxiii. 18–36). But the mass
of the people had been scattered over the
face of the wilderness of Paran, and led a
nomadic life as best suited the pasturage of
the cattle; trafficking in provisions with

surrounding tribes (cp. Deut. ii. 26-29 ; Ps.
lxxiv. 14) ; and availing themselves of the
resources of a district which were in ancient times vastly greater than they now
are.

These natural resources were supplemented, where needful, by miraculous aid.
The whole guidance of Israel through the
wilderness is constantly referred to God's
special and immediately superintending
care (Deut. viii. 4 seq., xxix. 5 ; Neh. ix.
21 ; Isai. lxiii. 11–14 ; Amos ii. 10, &c.).

Yet though God's extraordinary bounty
was vouchsafed to them, it is probable that
this period was, amongst the perishing
generation at all events, one of great religious declension, or even apostasy. To it
must no doubt be referred such passages as
Ezek. xx. 15 seq. ; Amos v. 25 seq. ; Hosea
ix. 10.

into the desert of Zin] The north-eastern
part of the wilderness of Paran [or, now
definitely fixed by Palmer as the south-
eastern corner of the desert of Et-Tih, between Akabah and the head of Wady
Garaiyeh]. The place of encampment was
no doubt adjacent to the spring of Kadesh.

in the first month] *i.e.* of the fortieth year
of the Exodus.

b Ex. 15. 20. ch. 26. 59. *c* Ex. 17. 1. *d* ch. 16. 19, 42. *e* Ex. 17. 2. ch. 14. 2. *f* ch. 11. 1, 33. & 14. 37. & 16. 32, 35, 49. *g* Ex. 17. 3. *h* ch. 14. 5. & 16. 4, 22, 45. *i* ch. 14. 10. *k* Ex. 17. 5. *l* Neh. 9. 15. Ps. 78. 15, 16. & 105. 41. & 114. 8. Isai. 43. 20. & 48. 21. *m* ch. 17. 10. *n* Ps. 106. 33. *o* Ex. 17. 6. Deut. 8. 15. 1 Cor. 10. 4. *p* ch. 27. 14. Deut. 1. 37. & 3. 26. & 32. 51. *q* Lev. 10. 3. Ez. 20. 41. & 36. 23. 1 Pet. 3. 15. *r* Deut. 33. 8. Ps. 95. 8. *s* Judg. 11. 16, 17.	the people abode in Kadesh; and *b*Miriam died there, and was 2 buried there. ¶ *c*And there was no water for the congregation: *d*and they gathered themselves together against Moses and 3 against Aaron. And the people *e*chode with Moses, and spake, saying, Would God that we had died *f*when our brethren died 4 before the LORD! And *g*why have ye brought up the congregation of the LORD into this wilderness, that we and our cattle 5 should die there? And wherefore have ye made us to come up out of Egypt, to bring us in unto this evil place? It *is* no place 6 of seed, or of figs, or of vines, or of pomegranates; neither *is* there any water to drink. ¶ And Moses and Aaron went from the presence of the assembly unto the door of the tabernacle of the congregation, and *h*they fell upon their faces: and *i*the 7 glory of the LORD appeared unto them. And the LORD spake 8 unto Moses, saying, *k*Take the rod, and gather thou the assembly together, thou, and Aaron thy brother, and speak ye unto the rock before their eyes; and it shall give forth his water, and *l*thou shalt bring forth to them water out of the rock: so thou 9 shalt give the congregation and their beasts drink. And Moses took the rod *m*from before the LORD, as he commanded 10 him. And Moses and Aaron gathered the congregation together before the rock, and he said unto them, *n*Hear now, ye rebels; 11 must we fetch you water out of this rock? And Moses lifted up his hand, and with his rod he smote the rock twice: and *o*the water came out abundantly, and the congregation drank, 12 and their beasts *also*. And the LORD spake unto Moses and Aaron, Because *p*ye believed me not, to *q*sanctify me in the eyes of the children of Israel, therefore ye shall not bring this con- 13 gregation into the land which I have given them. *r*This *is* the water of ¹Meribah; because the children of Israel strove with 14 the LORD, and he was sanctified in them. ¶ *s*And Moses sent ¹ That is, *Strife.* See Ex. 17. 7.

2–6. The language of the murmurers is noteworthy. It has the air of a traditional remonstrance handed down from the last generation. Cp. marg. reff.

8. *take the rod*] That with which the miracles in Egypt had been wrought (Ex. vii. 8 seq., 19 seq., viii. 5 seq., &c.), and which had been used on a similar occasion at Rephidim (Ex. xvii. 5 seq.). This rod, as the memorial of so many Divine interpositions, was naturally laid up in the Tabernacle, and is accordingly (*v.* 9) described now as taken by Moses "from before the Lord."

11, 12. The command (*v.* 8) was "Speak ye unto the rock." The act of smiting, and especially with two strokes, indicates violent irritation on the part of Moses; as does also his unseemly mode of addressing the people: "Hear now, ye rebels." The form too of the question, "must *we*, &c.," directs the people not, as ought to have been the case, to God as their deliverer, but to Moses and Aaron personally. In fact the faithful servant of God, worn out by the reiterated perversities of the people, breaks down; and in the actual discharge of his duty as God's representative before Israel, acts un-

worthily of the great function entrusted to him. Thus Moses did not "sanctify God in the eyes of the children of Israel." Aaron might have checked the intemperate words and acts of Moses, and did not. Hence God punishes both by withdrawing them from their work for Him, and handing over its accomplishment to another.

13. *the water of Meribah*] *i.e.* "Strife." The place is called "Meribah in Kadesh" (xxvii. 14), and "Meribah-Kadesh" (Deut. xxxii. 51), to distinguish it from the "Meribah" of Ex. xvii. 2 seq.

and he was sanctified in them] An allusion doubtless to the name "Kadesh" (holy), which though not now bestowed, acquired a new significance from the fact that God here vindicated His own sanctity, punishing Moses and Aaron who had trespassed against it.

14. Cp. marg. ref. It appears from comparing xx. 1 with xxxiii. 38, that the host must have remained in Kadesh some three or four months. No doubt time was required for re-organization. In order to gain the banks of Jordan by the shortest route they had to march nearly due east from Kadesh, and pass through the heart

messengers from Kadesh unto the king of Edom, [t]Thus saith thy brother Israel, Thou knowest all the travel that hath [1]be-
15 fallen us: [u]how our fathers went down into Egypt, [w]and we have dwelt in Egypt a long time; [x]and the Egyptians vexed us,
16 and our fathers: and [y]when we cried unto the LORD, he heard our voice, and [z]sent an angel, and hath brought us forth out of Egypt: and, behold, we *are* in Kadesh, a city in the uttermost
17 of thy border: [a]let us pass, I pray thee, through thy country: we will not pass through the fields, or through the vineyards, neither will we drink *of* the water of the wells: we will go by the king's *high* way, we will not turn to the right hand nor to
18 the left, until we have passed thy borders. And Edom said unto him, Thou shalt not pass by me, lest I come out against thee
19 with the sword. And the children of Israel said unto him, We will go by the high way: and if I and my cattle drink of thy water, [b]then I will pay for it: I will only, without *doing* any
20 thing *else*, go through on my feet. And he said, [c]Thou shalt not go through. And Edom came out against him with much
21 people, and with a strong hand. Thus Edom [d]refused to give Israel passage through his border: wherefore Israel [e]turned
22 away from him. ¶And the children of Israel, *even* the whole congregation, journeyed from [f]Kadesh, [g]and came unto mount
23 Hor. And the LORD spake unto Moses and Aaron in mount
24 Hor, by the coast of the land of Edom, saying, Aaron shall be [h]gathered unto his people: for he shall not enter into the land which I have given unto the children of Israel, because [i]ye re-
25 belled against my [2]word at the water of Meribah. [k]Take Aaron
26 and Eleazar his son, and bring them up unto mount Hor: and strip Aaron of his garments, and put them upon Eleazar his son: and Aaron shall be gathered *unto his people*, and shall die there.
27 And Moses did as the LORD commanded: and they went up
28 into mount Hor in the sight of all the congregation. [l]And Moses stripped Aaron of his garments, and put them upon Eleazar his son; and [m]Aaron died there in the top of the mount: and Moses and Eleazar came down from the mount.
29 And when all the congregation saw that Aaron was dead, they mourned for Aaron [n]thirty days, *even* all the house of Israel.
CHAP. 21. AND *when* [a]king Arad the Canaanite, which dwelt in the south, heard tell that Israel came [b]by the way of the spies;

[1] Heb. *found us*, Ex. 18. 8.   [2] Heb. *mouth*.

Marginal references:
[t] Deut. 2. 4. Obad. 10. 12.
[u] Gen. 46. 6. Acts 7. 15.
[w] Ex. 12. 40.
[x] Ex. 1. 11. Deut. 26. 6. Acts 7. 19.
[y] Ex. 2. 23. & 3. 7.
[z] Ex. 3. 2. & 14. 19. & 23. 20. & 33. 2.
[a] See ch. 21. 22.
Deut. 2. 27.
[b] Deut. 2. 6, 28.
[c] Judg. 11. 17.
[d] See Deut. 2. 27, 29.
[e] Deut. 2. 4. Judg. 11. 18.
[f] ch. 33. 37.
[g] ch. 21. 4.
[h] Gen. 25. 8. ch. 27. 13. & 31. 2.
[i] ver. 12.
[k] ch. 33. 38. Deut. 32. 50.
[l] Ex. 29. 29.
[m] ch. 33. 38. Deut. 10. 6. & 32. 50.
[n] So Deut. 34. 8.
[a] ch. 33. 40. See Judg. 1. 16.
[b] ch. 13. 21.

of the Edomitish mountains. These are lofty and precipitous, traversed by two or three narrow defiles. Hence the necessity of the request in v. 17.

thy brother] An appeal to the Edomites to remember and renew the old kindnesses of Jacob and Esau (Gen. xxxiii. 1-17).

It appears from Judg. xi. 17 that a similar request was addressed to the Moabites.

16. *an angel*] See Gen. xii. 7; Ex. iii. 2, and notes. The term is to be understood as importing generally the supernatural guidance under which Israel was.

20. The Israelites, without awaiting at Kadesh the return of their ambassadors, commenced their eastward march. At the tidings of their approach the Edomites mustered their forces to oppose them; and on crossing the Arabah they found their

ascent through the mountains barred. The notice of this is inserted here to complete the narrative; but in order of time it comes after the march described in v. 22.

22. *mount Hor*] The modern Jebel Harun, situated on the eastern side of the Arabah, and close to Petra. This striking mountain, rising on a dark red bare rock, to a height of near 5,000 feet above the Mediterranean, is remarkable far and near for its two summits, on one of which is still shown a small square building, crowned with a dome, called the Tomb of Aaron.

26. The priestly garments, wherewith Moses had invested Aaron (Lev. viii. 7-9), were put upon Eleazar by way of solemn transference of Aaron's office to him; cp. 1 Kings xix. 19.

XXI. 1. *king Arad the Canaanite*] Rather,

then he fought against Israel, and took *some* of them prisoners.

*Gen. 28. 20.
Judg. 11. 30.
d Lev. 27. 28.

2 *c*And Israel vowed a vow unto the LORD, and said, If thou wilt indeed deliver this people into my hand, then *d*I will utterly 3 destroy their cities. And the LORD hearkened to the voice of Israel, and delivered up the Canaanites; and they utterly destroyed them and their cities: and he called the name of the

e ch. 20. 22.
& 33. 41.
f Judg. 11.
18.
g Ps. 78. 19.
h Ex. 16, 3.
& 17. 3.
i ch. 11. 6.
k 1 Cor. 10. 9.
l Deut. 8. 15.
m Ps. 78. 34.
n ver. 5.
o Ex. 8. 8,
28.
1 Sam. 12.
19.
1 Kin. 13. 6.
Acts 8. 24.

4 place ¹Hormah. ¶And *e*they journeyed from mount Hor by the way of the Red sea, to *f*compass the land of Edom : and the soul of the people was much ²³discouraged because of the way. 5 And the people *g*spake against God, and against Moses, *h*Wherefore have ye brought us up out of Egypt to die in the wilderness? for *there is* no bread, neither *is there any* water; and *i*our soul 6 loatheth this light bread. And *k*the LORD sent *l*fiery serpents among the people, and they bit the people ; and much people of 7 Israel died. *m*Therefore the people came to Moses, and said, We have sinned, for *n*we have spoken against the LORD, and against thee ; *o*pray unto the LORD, that he take away the ser- 8 pents from us. And Moses prayed for the people. And the LORD said unto Moses, Make thee a fiery serpent, and set it

¹ That is, *Utter destruction*.   ² Or, *grieved*.   ³ Heb. *shortened*, Ex. 6. 9.

"**the Canaanite, the king of Arad.**" Arad stood on a small hill, now called Tel-Arad, 20 miles south of Hebron.

in the south] See xiii. 17, 22.

by the way of the spies] *i.e.* through the desert of Zin, the route which the spies sent out by Moses 38 years before had adopted (cp. xiii. 21).

he fought against Israel] This attack (cp. xx. 1 and note), can hardly have taken place after the death of Aaron. It was most probably made just when the camp broke up from Kadesh, and the ultimate direction of the march was not as yet pronounced. The order of the narrative in these chapters, as occasionally elsewhere in this book (cp. ix. 1, &c.), is not that of time, but of subject-matter; and the war against Arad is introduced here as the first of the series of victories gained under Moses, which the historian now takes in hand to narrate.

3. *he called the name of the place*] Render, **the name of the place was called.** The transitive verb here is, by a common Hebrew idiom, equivalent to an impersonal one.

Hormah] *i.e.* "Ban." See xiv. 45 and note. In Judges i. 17, we read that the men of Judah and Simeon "slew the Canaanites that inhabited Zephath, and utterly destroyed it;" and further, that "the name of the city was called Hormah." But it does not follow that the name "Hormah" was first bestowed in consequence of the destruction of the place in the time of the Judges, and that in Numbers its occurrence is a sign of a post-Mosaic date of composition. The text here informs us that this aggression of the king of Arad was repelled, and avenged by the capture and sack of his cities; and that the Israelites "banned" them (cp. Lev. xxvii.

28, 29). But it was not the plan of the Israelites in the time of Moses to remain in this district. They therefore marched away south-eastward; and no doubt for the time the Canaanites resumed possession, and restored the ancient name (Zephath). But Joshua again conquered the king of this district, and finally in the time of the early Judges the ban of Moses and his contemporaries was fully executed. We have therefore in the passage before us the history of the actual origin of the name "Hormah."

4. The direct route to Moab through the valleys of Edom being closed against them (xx. 20, 21), they were compelled to turn southward. Their course lay down the Arabah ; until, a few hours north of Akaba (Ezion-Geber) the Wady Ithm opened to them a gap in the hostile mountains, allowed them to turn to their left, and to march northwards towards Moab (Deut. ii. 3). They were thus for some days (see xxii. 1 note) in the Arabah, a mountain plain of loose sand, gravel, and detritus of granite, which though sprinkled with low shrubs, especially near the mouths of the wadys and the courses of the winter-torrents, furnishes extremely little food or water, and is often troubled by sand-storms from the shore of the gulf. Hence "the soul of the people was much discouraged because of the way."

5. *this light bread*] *i.e.* "this vile, contemptible bread."

6. *fiery serpents*] The epithet (Deut. viii. 15, Isai. xiv. 29, xxx. 6) denotes the inflammatory effect of their bite. The peninsula of Sinai, and not least, the Arabah, abounds in mottled snakes of large size, marked with fiery red spots and wavy stripes, which belong to the most poisonous species, as the formation of the teeth clearly show.

8. *make thee a fiery serpent*] *i.e.* a serpent resembling in appearance the reptiles which

upon a pole: and it shall come to pass, that every one that is
9 bitten, when he looketh upon it, shall live. And *p*Moses made
a serpent of brass, and put it upon a pole, and it came to pass,
that if a serpent had bitten any man, when he beheld the serpent
10 of brass, he lived. ¶And the children of Israel set forward,
11 and *q*pitched in Oboth. And they journeyed from Oboth,
and *r*pitched at ¹Ije-abarim, in the wilderness which *is* before
12 Moab, toward the sun-rising. *s*From thence they removed, and
13 pitched in the valley of Zared. From thence they removed,
and pitched on the other side of Arnon, which *is* in the wilderness that cometh out of the coasts of the Amorites: for *t*Arnon
14 *is* the border of Moab, between Moab and the Amorites. Wherefore it is said in the book of the wars of the LORD,

²What he did in the Red sea, and in the brooks of Arnon,
15   And at the stream of the brooks that goeth down to the
dwelling of Ar,
    *u*And ³lieth upon the border of Moab.

16 ¶And from thence *they went* *x*to Beer : that *is* the well whereof
the LORD spake unto Moses, Gather the people together, and I

p 2 Kin. 18.
4.
John 3. 14,
15.

q ch. 33. 43.
r ch. 33. 44.
s Deut. 2. 13.

t ch. 22. 36.
Judg. 11. 18.

u Deut. 2. 18,
29.

x Judg. 9. 21.

Or, *Heaps of Abarim.*   ² Or, *Vaheb in Suphah.*   ³ Heb. *leaneth.*

---

attacked the people. The resemblance was of
the essence of the symbolism (cp. 1 Sam. vi. 5).
As the brazen serpent represented the instrument of their chastisement, so the looking
unto it at God's word denoted acknowledgment of their sin, longing for deliverance
from its penalty, and faith in the means
appointed by God for healing. In the serpent of brass, harmless itself, but made in
the image of the creature that is accursed
above others (Gen. iii. 14), the Christian
Fathers rightly see a figure of Him
(John iii. 14, 15) Who though "holy, harmless, undefiled, separate from sinners"
(Heb. vii. 26), was yet "made sin" (2 Cor.
v. 21), and "made a curse for us" (Gal. iii.
13). And the eye of faith fixed on Him
beholds the manifestation at once of the
deserts of sin, of its punishment imminent
and deprecated, and of the method of its
remission devised by God Himself.

10, 11. The earlier stations in this part
of their journey were Zalmonah and Punon
(xxxiii. 41, 42). Oboth was north of Punon,
east of the northern part of Edom, and is
pretty certainly the same as the present
pilgrim halting-place el-Ahsa. Ije ("ruinous
heaps") of Abarim, or Iim of Abarim, was
so called to distinguish it from another Iim
in south-western Canaan (Josh. xv. 29).
Abarim denotes generally the whole upland
country on the east of the Jordan. The
Greek equivalent of the name is Peræa.

12. *the valley of Zared*] Rather, the **brook**
or watercourse of Zared "the willow." It
is probably the present Wady Ain Franjy.

13. The Arnon, now the Wady Môjeb,
an impetuous torrent, divided the territory
which remained to the Moabites from that
which the Amorites had wrested from them,
v. 26.

14. Of "the book of the wars of the LORD"
nothing is known except what may be
gathered from the passage before us. It
was apparently a collection of sacred odes
commemorative of that triumphant progress of God's people which this chapter
records. From it is taken the ensuing fragment of ancient poetry relating to the passage of the Arnon, and probably also the
Song of the Well, and the Ode on the Conquest of the Kingdom of Sihon (*vv.* 17, 18,
27–30).

what he did, &c.] The words which follow
to the end of the next verse are a reference
rather than a quotation. Contemporaries
who had "the Book" at hand, could supply
the context. We can only conjecture the
sense of the words; which in the original are
grammatically incomplete. The marg. is
adopted by many, and suggests a better
sense : supplying some such verb as "conquered," the words would run "He" (*i.e.*
the Lord) "conquered Vaheb in Suphah,"
and the brooks, &c." Suphah would thus
be the name of a district remarkable for
its reeds and water-flags in which Vaheb
was situated.

15. *to the dwelling of Ar*] Ar (cp. *v.* 28,
Isai. xv. 1) was on the bank of the Arnon,
lower down the stream than where the
Israelites crossed. Near the spot where the
upper Arnon receives the tributary Nahaliel (*v.* 19), there rises, in the midst of the
meadow-land between the two torrents, a
hill covered with the ruins of the ancient
city (Josh. xiii. 9, 16; cp. Deut. ii. 36).

16. Beer is probably the "Well," afterwards known as Beer-elim, the "well of
heroes" (Isai. xv. 8).

y Ex. 15. 1. Ps. 105. 2. & 106. 12.	17 will give them water. yThen Israel sang this song, ¹Spring up, O well; ²sing ye unto it :
	18 The princes digged the well, The nobles of the people digged it,
z Isai. 33. 22.	By *the direction of* ᶻthe lawgiver, with their staves.

19 ¶And from the wilderness *they went* to Mattanah : and from
20 Mattanah to Nahaliel : and from Nahaliel to Bamoth : and
from Bamoth *in* the valley, that *is* in the ³country of Moab, to

a ch. 23. 28.	21 the top of ⁴Pisgah, which looketh ᵃtoward ⁵Jeshimon. ¶And
b Deut. 2. 26, 27. Judg. 11. 19. c ch. 20. 17.	ᵇIsrael sent messengers unto Sihon king of the Amorites, saying, 22 ᶜLet me pass through thy land : we will not turn into the fields, or into the vineyards; we will not drink *of* the waters of the well : *but* we will go along by the king's *high* way, until we be
d Deut. 29. 7.	23 past thy borders. ᵈAnd Sihon would not suffer Israel to pass through his border : but Sihon gathered all his people together,
e Deut. 2. 32. Judg. 11. 20. f Deut. 2. 33. & 29. 7. Josh. 12. 1, 2. & 24. 8. Neh. 9. 22. Ps. 135. 10. & 136. 19. Amos 2. 9.	and went out against Israel into the wilderness : ᵉand he came to 24 Jahaz, and fought against Israel. And ᶠIsrael smote him with the edge of the sword, and possessed his land from Arnon unto Jabbok, even unto the children of Ammon : for the border of 25 the children of Ammon *was* strong. And Israel took all these cities : and Israel dwelt in all the cities of the Amorites, in 26 Heshbon, and in all the ⁶villages thereof. For Heshbon *was* the city of Sihon the king of the Amorites, who had fought against the former king of Moab, and taken all his land out

27 of his hand, even unto Arnon. Wherefore they that speak in
proverbs say,

Come into Heshbon,
Let the city of Sihon be built and prepared:

¹ Heb. *Ascend.*	³ Heb. *field.*	⁵ Or, *The wilderness.*
² Or, *answer.*	⁴ Or, *The hill.*	⁶ Heb. *daughters.*

17, 18. This song, recognised by all authorities as dating from the earliest times, and suggested apparently by the fact that God in this place gave the people water not from the rock, but by commanding Moses to cause a well to be dug, bespeaks the glad zeal, the joyful faith, and the hearty co-operation amongst all ranks, which possessed the people. In after time it may well have been the water-drawing song of the maidens of Israel.

18. *by the direction of the lawgiver*] Some render, **with the lawgiver's sceptre;** *i.e.* under the direction and with the authority of Moses; cp. Gen. xlix. 10, and note.

19. *Nahaliel*] *i.e.* "brook of God;" the modern Wady Enkheileh. The Israelites must have crossed the stream not much above Ar.

Bamoth] Otherwise Bamoth-baal, "the high places of Baal" (xxii. 41) : mentioned as near Dibon (Dhiban) in Josh. xiii. 17, and Isai. xv. 2. See xxxii. 34.

20. *in the country of Moab*] Rather, **in the field of Moab** : the upland pastures, or flat downs, intersected by the ravine of Wady Wâleh.

Pisgah, which looketh toward Jeshimon] Or, "toward the waste." See xxxiii. 47. Pisgah was a ridge of the Abarim moun-

tains, westward from Heshbon. From the summit the Israelites gained their first view of the wastes of the Dead Sea and of the valley of the Jordan : and Moses again ascended it, to view, before his death, the Land of Promise. The interest attaching to the spot, and the need of a convenient name for it, has led Christians often to designate it as "Nebo," rather than as "the mountain of, or near to, Nebo;" but the latter is the more correct : Nebo denoted the town (Isai. xv. 2; Jer. xlviii. 1, 22) on the western slope of the ridge.

24. Jabbok (now Wâdy Zerka : cp. Gen. xxxii. 22) runs eastward under Rabbah of the children of Ammon, thence westward, and reaches the Jordan, 45 miles north of the Arnon. It was between Rabbah and Gerasa that it formed the Ammonite boundary.

25. *Heshbon*] Now Heshbân, a ruined city, due east of the point where the Jordan enters the Dead Sea ; conspicuous from all parts of the high plateau on which it stands, but concealed, like the rest of the plateau, from the valley beneath.

27. *they that speak in proverbs*] The original word is almost equivalent to "the poets." The word supplies the title of the Book of Proverbs itself ; and is used of the

28   For there is ^ga fire gone out of Heshbon,   ^g Jer. 48. 45,
     A flame from the city of Sihon :   46.
     It hath consumed ^hAr of Moab,   ^h Deut. 2. 9,
     And the lords of the high places of Arnon.   18.
29   Woe to thee, Moab!   Isai. 15. 1.
     Thou art undone, O people of ⁱChemosh :   ⁱ Judg. 11.
     He hath given his sons that escaped,   24.
     And his daughters, into captivity   1 Kin. 11. 7,
     Unto Sihon king of the Amorites.   33.
30   We have shot at them ;   2 Kin. 23.
     Heshbon is perished even ^kunto Dibon,   13.
     And we have laid them waste even unto Nophah,   Jer. 48. 7,
     Which *reacheth* unto ^lMedeba.   13.
                                                                  ^k Jer. 48.18,
                                                                  22.
                                                                  ^l Isai. 15. 2.

31, 32 ¶ Thus Israel dwelt in the land of the Amorites. And Moses   ^m ch. 32. 1.
     sent to spy out ^mJaazer, and they took the villages thereof, and   Jer. 48. 32.
33   drove out the Amorites that *were* there. ⁿAnd they turned and   ⁿ Deut. 3. 1.
     went up by the way of Bashan : and Og the king of Bashan   & 29. 7.
     went out against them, he, and all his people, to the battle ^oat   ^o Josh.13.12.
34   Edrei. And the LORD said unto Moses, ^pFear him not: for I   ^p Deut. 3. 2.
     have delivered him into thy hand, and all his people, and his   ^q ver. 24.
     land ; and ^qthou shalt do to him as thou didst unto Sihon king   Ps. 135. 10.
                                                                  & 136. 20.
35   of the Amorites, which dwelt at Heshbon. ^rSo they smote him,   ^r Deut. 3. 3.
     and his sons, and all his people, until there was none left him
     alive : and they possessed his land.
CHAP. 22. AND ^athe children of Israel set forward, and pitched   ^a ch. 33. 48.

---

parable proper in Ezek. xvii. 2 ; of the
prophecies of Balaam in xxiii. 7-10, xxiv.
3-9, &c. ; and of a song of triumph over
Babylon in Isai. xiv. 4.
    29. *Chemosh*] The national God of the
Moabites (cp. marg. reff.). The name probably means " Vanquisher," or " Master."
The worship of Chemosh was introduced
into Israel by Solomon (1 K. xi. 7 ; 2 K.
xxiii. 13). It was no doubt to Chemosh
that Mesha, king of Moab, offered up his
son as a burnt-offering (2 K. iii. 26, 27).
    In the first six lines (*vv.* 27, 28) the poet
imagines for the Amorites a song of exultation for their victories over Moab, and for
the consequent glories of Heshbon, their
own capital. In the next lines (*v.* 29)
he himself joins in this strain ; which now
becomes one of half-real, half-ironical
compassion for the Moabites, whom their
idol Chemosh was unable to save. But in
the last lines (*v.* 30) a startling change
takes place ; the new and decisive triumph
of the poet's own countrymen is abruptly
introduced ; and the boastings of the
Amorites fade utterly away. Of the
towns Heshbon was the northernmost, and
therefore, to the advancing Israelites, the
last to be reached. Medeba, now Mâdeba,
was four miles south of Heshbon (cp. 1 Chr.
xix. 7, 15).
    32. *Jaazer*] To be identified probably
with the ruins Sîr or es-Sîr, ten miles north
of Heshbon. The occupation of it by the
Israelites virtually completed their conquest of the Amorite kingdom ; and pre-

pared the way for the pastoral settlements
in it which they not long after established
(xxxii. 35).
    33. In these apparently unimportant
words is contained the record of the Israelitish (xxxii. 39) occupation of Gilead north
of the Jabbok ; a territory which, though
peopled, like southern Gilead, by the Amorites (Deut. iii. 9 ; Josh. ii. 10, &c.), formed
part of the domain of Og king of Bashan,
who was himself of a different race (Deut.
iii. 2 ; Josh. xii. 5, xiii. 11). We are not
told whether they were led thither by express warrant of God, or whether their advance upon Bashan was provoked by Og
and his people.
    at Edrei] Now Edhra'âh, vulgarly Der'a ;
situate on a branch of the Jarmuk. This
river formed the boundary between Gilead
and Bashan.
    XXII. With this chapter begins the
fourth and last division of the Book, comprising fourteen chapters. In them are
narrated the events which befell Israel
whilst encamped in the plains of Moab,
and certain instructions and arrangements
are laid down by Moses with reference to
their actual entry upon the promised inheritance.
    1. *the plains*] Heb. *araboth ;* the word is
the plural of that which is used to denote
the whole depressed tract along the Jordan
and the Dead Sea, and onward, where it is
still called the Arabah (cp. xxi. 4 note), to
the Elanitic gulf.

2 in the plains of Moab on this side Jordan *by* Jericho. ¶And
b Balak the son of Zippor saw all that Israel had done to the
3 Amorites. And *c* Moab was sore afraid of the people, because
they *were* many : and Moab was distressed because of the chil-
4 dren of Israel. And Moab said unto *d* the elders of Midian,
Now shall this company lick up all *that are* round about us, as
the ox licketh up the grass of the field. And Balak the son of
5 Zippor *was* king of the Moabites at that time. *e* He sent messengers therefore unto Balaam the son of Beor to *f* Pethor, which
is by the river of the land of the children of his people, to call
him, saying, Behold, there is a people come out from Egypt :
behold, they cover the [1] face of the earth, and they abide over
6 against me : come now therefore, I pray thee, *g* curse me this
people ; for they *are* too mighty for me : peradventure I shall
prevail, *that* we may smite them, and *that* I may drive them out
of the land : for I wot that he whom thou blessest *is* blessed,
7 and he whom thou cursest is cursed. ¶And the elders of Moab
and the elders of Midian departed with *h* the rewards of divination in their hand ; and they came unto Balaam, and spake unto
8 him the words of Balak. And he said unto them, *i* Lodge here
this night, and I will bring you word again, as the LORD shall
speak unto me : and the princes of Moab abode with Balaam.
9 *k* And God came unto Balaam, and said, What men *are* these
10 with thee ? And Balaam said unto God, Balak the son of Zippor,
11 king of Moab, hath sent unto me, *saying*, Behold, *there is* a
people come out of Egypt, which covereth the face of the earth :

Marginal references:

b Judg. 11. 25.
c Ex. 15. 15.
d ch. 31. 8. Josh. 13. 21.
e Deut. 23. 4. Josh. 13. 22. & 24. 9. Neh. 13. 1, 2. Mic. 6. 5. 2 Pet. 2. 15. Jude 11. Rev. 2. 14.
f See ch. 23. 7.
Deut. 23. 4.
g ch. 23. 7.
h 1 Sam. 9. 7, 8.
i ver. 19.
k Gen. 20. 3. ver. 20.

[1] Heb. *eye.*

---

on this side Jordan by Jericho] Rather,
across the Jordan of Jericho, *i.e.* that part
of Jordan which skirted the territory of
Jericho. This form of expression indicates
the site of the camp in its relation to the
well-known city of Jericho. See Deut.
i. 1.

2. Balak the son of Zippor] The comparison of *v.* 4 with xxi. 26 suggests that
Balak was not the hereditary king but a
Midianite, and that a change of dynasty
had taken place. His father's name, Zippor,
"Bird," reminds us of those of other Midianites, *e.g.* Oreb, "Crow," Zeeb, "Wolf."
Possibly the Midianitish chieftains had
taken advantage of the weakness of the
Moabites after the Amoritish victories to
establish themselves as princes in the land.

5. Balaam the son of Beor was from the
first a worshipper in some sort of the true
God; and had learned some elements of pure
and true religion in his home in the far
East, the cradle of the ancestors of Israel.
But though prophesying, doubtless even
before the ambassadors of Balak came to
him, in the name of the true God, yet prophecy was still to him as before a mere
business, not a religion. The summons of
Balak proved to be a crisis in his career :
and he failed under the trial. When the
gold and honours of Balak seemed to be
finally lost, he became reckless and desperate ; and, as if in defiance, counselled

the evil stratagem by which he hoped to
compass indirectly that ruin of God's people
which he had been withheld from working
otherwise. He thus, like Judas and Ahithophel, set in motion a train of events
which involved his own destruction.

The name Balaam signifies "destroyer,"
or "glutton," and is in part identical with
"Bela, son of Beor," the first king of Edom
(Gen. xxxvi. 32). The name "Beor" ("to
burn up") is that of the father, or possibly
ancestor, of the prophet.

*Pethor, which is by the river of the land of
the children of his people*] Rather, **Pethor
which was . . . . . land.** Pethor (Pitru,
Assyrian) was on the river Sagura (mod.
Sajur) near its junction with the Euphrates.

7. *Rewards of divination*] Rightly interpreted in 2 Pet. ii. 15 as "the wages of unrighteousness."

8. Balaam must surely have known that
God's blessing was on the people with
whose marvellous march forth from Egypt
he was acquainted (Ex. xv. 14, xviii. 1;
Josh. ii. 9), and from whom he had himself
probably learned much (cp. the language of
xxiii. 12 with Gen. xiii. 6, and that of xxiv.
9 with Gen. xlix. 9). But his reply to the
messengers next *morning (v.* 13), betrays
the desire to venture to the utmost of that
which God would not forbid rather than to
carry out God's will in hearty sincerity.

come now, curse me them; peradventure [1]I shall be able to
12 overcome them, and drive them out. And God said unto Balaam, Thou shalt not go with them; thou shalt not curse the
13 people: for *l* they *are* blessed. And Balaam rose up in the morn-   *l* ch. 23. 20.
ing, and said unto the princes of Balak, Get you into your land: Rom. 11. 29.
14 for the LORD refuseth to give me leave to go with you. And
the princes of Moab rose up, and they went unto Balak, and
15 said, Balaam refuseth to come with us. And Balak sent yet
16 again princes, more, and more honourable than they. And they
came to Balaam, and said to him, Thus saith Balak the son of
Zippor, [2]Let nothing, I pray thee, hinder thee from coming
17 unto me: for I will promote thee unto very great honour, and I
will do whatsoever thou sayest unto me: *m* come therefore, I   *m* ver. 6.
18 pray thee, curse me this people. And Balaam answered and
said unto the servants of Balak, *n* If Balak would give me his   *n* ch. 24. 13.
house full of silver and gold, *o* I cannot go beyond the word of   *o* 1 Kin. 22.
19 the LORD my God, to do less or more. Now therefore, I pray   14.
you, *p* tarry ye also here this night, that I may know what the   2 Chr. 18. 13.
20 LORD will say unto me more. *q* And God came unto Balaam at   *q* ver. 9.
night, and said unto him, If the men come to call thee, rise up,
and go with them; but *r* yet the word which I shall say unto   *r* ver. 35.
21 thee, that shalt thou do. And Balaam rose up in the morning,   ch. 23. 12,
22 and saddled his ass, and went with the princes of Moab. ¶And   26.
God's anger was kindled because he went: *s* and the angel of the   *s* Ex. 4. 24.
LORD stood in the way for an adversary against him. Now he
was riding upon his ass, and his two servants *were* with him.
23 And *t* the ass saw the angel of the LORD standing in the way,   *t* See 2 Kin.
and his sword drawn in his hand: and the ass turned aside out   6. 17.
of the way, and went into the field: and Balaam smote the ass,   Dan. 10. 7.
24 to turn her into the way. But the angel of the LORD stood in a   Acts 22. 9.
path of the vineyards, a wall *being* on this side, and a wall on   2 Pet. 2. 16.
25 that side. And when the ass saw the angel of the LORD, she   Jude 11.
thrust herself unto the wall, and crushed Balaam's foot against
26 the wall: and he smote her again. And the angel of the LORD
went further, and stood in a narrow place, where *was* no way to
27 turn either to the right hand or to the left. And when the ass
saw the angel of the LORD, she fell down under Balaam: and
Balaam's anger was kindled, and he smote the ass with a staff.
28 And the *u* LORD opened the mouth of the ass, and she said unto   *u* 2 Pet. 2.
   16.

[1] Heb. *I shall prevail in
fighting against him.*

[2] Heb. *Be not thou letted
from, &c.*

---

15. Balak, like the ancient heathen world
generally, not only believed in the efficacy
of the curses and incantations of the soothsayers, but regarded their services as strictly
venal. Hence, when his first offer was declined, he infers at once that he had not bid
high enough.
19. *ye also*] *i.e.* as the other envoys before
you. Had Balaam possessed a sincere spirit
of obedience, he would have found in the
first instructions (*v.* 12) a final decision upon
the matter. His hypocritical importunity
with God when the fresh messengers came
from Balak demonstrates his aversion to
God's declared will.
22. *the angel*] *i.e.* the Angel that led the
Israelites through the wilderness (cp. xx. 16
and reff.), and subsequently appeared as the

Captain of the LORD's host to Joshua (Josh.
vi. 13). In desiring to curse Israel, Balaam
was fighting against Israel's Leader. The
presence of the Angel in his path was designed to open his eyes, blinded by sin, to
the real character of his course of conduct.
24. *in a path of the vineyards*] *i.e.* in a
path shut in by vineyard-walls on each side.
The progress from the road through the
open field (*v.* 23) to that walled in, and
thence to the strait place, where there was
no room to turn (*v.* 26), shews that Balaam
was approaching a city, no doubt that
which was the goal of his journey.
28. *And the* LORD *opened the mouth of the
ass*] The account was perhaps given by
Balaam to the Israelites after his capture
in the war against Midian. Cp. xxxi. 8.

Balaam, What have I done unto thee, that thou hast smitten
29 me these three times? And Balaam said unto the ass, Because
thou hast mocked me: I would there were a sword in mine
30 hand, *for now would I kill thee. *And the ass said unto
Balaam, *Am* not I thine ass, ¹upon which thou hast ridden
²ever since *I was* thine unto this day? Was I ever wont to do so
31 unto thee? And he said, Nay. ¶Then the LORD *opened the
eyes of Balaam, and he saw the angel of the LORD standing in
the way, and his sword drawn in his hand: and he *bowed down
32 his head, and ³fell flat on his face. And the angel of the LORD
said unto him, Wherefore hast thou smitten thine ass these three
times? Behold, I went out ⁴to withstand thee, because *thy* way
33 is *perverse before me: and the ass saw me, and turned from
me these three times: unless she had turned from me, surely
34 now also I had slain thee, and saved her alive. And Balaam
said unto the angel of the LORD, *I have sinned; for I knew not
that thou stoodest in the way against me: now therefore, if it
35 ⁵displease thee, I will get me back again. And the angel of the
LORD said unto Balaam, Go with the men: *but only the word
that I shall speak unto thee, that thou shalt speak. So Balaam
36 went with the princes of Balak. ¶And when Balak heard that
Balaam was come, *he went out to meet him unto a city of Moab,
*which *is* in the border of Arnon, which *is* in the utmost coast.
37 And Balak said unto Balaam, Did I not earnestly send unto thee
to call thee? Wherefore camest thou not unto me? Am I not
38 able indeed *to promote thee to honour? And Balaam said unto
Balak, Lo, I am come unto thee: have I now any power at all
to say any thing? *The word that God putteth in my mouth,
39 that shall I speak. And Balaam went with Balak, and they
40 came unto ⁶Kirjath-huzoth. And Balak offered oxen and sheep,
and sent to Balaam, and to the princes that *were* with him.
41 And it came to pass on the morrow, that Balak took Balaam,
and brought him up into the *high places of Baal, that thence
he might see the utmost *part* of the people.
CHAP. 23. AND Balaam said unto Balak, *Build me here seven

x Prov. 12. 10.
v 2 Pet. 2. 16.
z See Gen. 21. 19. 2 Kin. 6. 17. Luke 24. 16, 31.
a Ex. 34. 8.
b 2 Pet. 2. 14, 15.
c 1 Sam. 15. 24, 30. & 26. 21. 2 Sam. 12. 13. Job 34. 31, 32.
d ver. 20.
e Gen. 14. 17.
f ch. 21. 13.
g ver. 17. ch. 24. 11.
h ch. 23. 26. & 24. 13. 1 Kin. 22. 14. 2 Chr. 18. 13.
i Deut. 12. 2.
a ver. 29.

¹ Heb. *who hast ridden upon me.*
² Or, *ever since thou* wast, &c.
³ Or, *bowed himself.*
⁴ Heb. *to be an adversary unto thee.*
⁵ Heb. *be evil in thine eyes.*
⁶ Or, *A city of streets.*

That which is here recorded was apparently
perceived by him alone amongst human
witnesses. God may have brought it about
that sounds uttered by the creature after its
kind became to the prophet's intelligence as
though it addressed him in rational speech.
Indeed to an augur, priding himself on his
skill in interpreting the cries and movements of animals, no more startling warning could be given than one so real as this,
yet conveyed through the medium of his
own art.

32. *is perverse*] Rather, **is headlong.** Cp.
St. Peter's words (2 Pet. ii. 16), "the
madness of the prophet."

35. *Go with the men*] A command, not a
permission merely. Balaam, no longer a
faithful servant of God, was henceforth
overruled in all his acts so that he might
subserve the Divine purpose as an instrument.

26. *a city of Moab*] Or, **Ir-Moab**, probably the same with Ar-Moab (xxi. 15).
As Balaam in his journey would avoid the
districts occupied by the Israelites, he must
have approached this city from the east, by
the course of the Nahaliel; and in the name
Balû'a, still borne by one of the upper
branches of this stream, there is perhaps a
reminiscence of the name of the prophet.

39. *Kirjath-huzoth*] *i.e.* "city of streets,"
within Balak's dominions, south of the
Arnon, and identified either with the ruins
of Shihân, 4 miles west by south of the site
assigned to Ar or Ir, or with Kirjathaim
(Kureiyat).

41. *that thence he might see*] Rather, **and
thence he saw.**

XXIII. 1. Balaam, after the general custom of the heathen, prefaced his divinations
by sacrifice. In the number of the altars
regard was probably had to the number of

2 altars, and prepare me here seven oxen and seven rams. And
Balak did as Balaam had spoken; and Balak and Balaam
3 [b]offered on *every* altar a bullock and a ram. And Balaam said
unto Balak, [c]Stand by thy burnt offering, and I will go: peradventure the LORD will come [d]to meet me: and whatsoever he
sheweth me I will tell thee. And [1]he went to an high place.
4 [e]And God met Balaam: and he said unto him, I have prepared
seven altars, and I have offered upon *every* altar a bullock and a
5 ram. And the LORD [f]put a word in Balaam's mouth, and said,
6 Return unto Balak, and thus thou shalt speak. And he returned
unto him, and, lo, he stood by his burnt sacrifice, he, and all the
7 princes of Moab. And he [g]took up his parable, and said,

> Balak the king of Moab hath brought me from Aram,
> Out of the mountains of the east, *saying*,
> [h]Come, curse me Jacob,
> And come, [i]defy Israel.

8   [k]How shall I curse, whom God hath not cursed?
> Or how shall I defy, *whom* the LORD hath not defied?
9   For from the top of the rocks I see him,
> And from the hills I behold him:
> Lo, [l]the people shall dwell alone,
> And [m]shall not be reckoned among the nations.
10   [n]Who can count the dust of Jacob,
> And the number of the fourth *part* of Israel?
> Let [2]me die [o]the death of the righteous,
> And let my last end be like his!

[b] ver. 14.
[c] ver. 15.
[d] ch. 24. 1.

[e] ver. 16.

[f] ch. 22. 35.
ver. 16.
Deut. 18. 18.
Jer. 1. 9.

[g] ver. 18.
ch. 24. 3, 15,
23.
Job 27. 1.
Ps. 78. 2.
Ez. 17. 2.
Mic. 2. 4.
Hab. 2. 6.
[h] ch. 22. 6,
11, 17.
[i] 1 Sam. 17.
10.
[k] Isai. 47.12,
13.
[l] Deut. 33.
28.
[m] Ex. 33. 16.
Ezra 9. 2.
Eph. 2. 14.
[n] Gen. 13.16.
& 22. 17.
[o] Ps. 116. 15.

---

[1] Or, *he went solitary.*   [2] Heb. *my soul*, or, *my life.*

---

the then known planets. Yet Balaam evidently intended his sacrifice as an offering
to the true God.

3. Balaam apparently expected to mark
some phenomenon in the sky or in nature,
which he would be able, according to the
rules of his art, to interpret as a portent. It
was for such "auguries" (not as A. V.
"enchantments" *v.* 23) that he now departed to watch; contrast xxiv. 1.

an high place] Or, "A bare place on the
hill," as opposed to the high place with its
grove of trees.

4. *God met Balaam*] God served His own
purposes through the arts of Balaam, and
manifested His will through the agencies
employed to seek it, dealing thus with Balaam in an exceptional manner. To God's
own people auguries were forbidden (Lev.
xix. 26).

I have prepared seven altars] And therefore Balaam expected that God on His part
would do what was desired by the donor;
cp. xxii. 15 note.

7. *Aram*] Or, "highland." This term denotes the whole elevated region, from the
north-eastern frontier of Palestine to the
Euphrates and the Tigris. The country
between these streams was specially designated "Aram-naharaim," or "Aram of the
two rivers;" the Greeks called it Mesopotamia; and here, according to Deut. xxiii.
4, was Balaam's home. Cp. xxii. 5 note.

9. *For from the top of the rocks,* &c.] The
"for" indicates the constraint under which
Balaam felt himself. He had been met by
God in his own way; from the cliff he had
watched for the expected augury; and by
the light of this he here interprets, according to the rules of his art, the destiny of
Israel.

dwell alone] *i.e.* apart from others, undisturbed by their tumults, and therefore in
safety and just security. Cp. the same idea
in marg. ref.; Jer. xlix. 31; and Micah
vii. 14. This tranquillity was realized by
the Israelites so long as they clave to God
as their shelter and protection. But the inward "dwelling alone" was the indispensable condition of the outward "dwelling
alone," and so soon as the influence of the
heathen world affected Israel internally,
the external power of heathenism prevailed
also. Balaam himself, when he eventually
counselled tempting the people into sin,
acted upon the knowledge that God's blessing and Israel's prosperity depended essentially on faithfulness to God.

10. *the fourth part of Israel*] *i.e.* each
one of the four camps, into which the host
of Israel was divided (see ch. ii.), seemed to
swarm with innumerable multitudes. Possibly Balaam could only see one camp. Balaam bears testimony in this verse to the
fulfilment of the promises in Gen. xiii. 16,
xxviii. 14.

11 And Balak said unto Balaam, What hast thou done unto me?
p ch. 22. 11,
17. & 24. 10.
q ch. 22. 38.
*p*I took thee to curse mine enemies, and, behold, thou hast
12 blessed *them* altogether. And he answered and said, *q*Must I
not take heed to speak that which the LORD hath put in my
13 mouth? ¶ And Balak said unto him, Come, I pray thee, with
me unto another place, from whence thou mayest see them: thou
shalt see but the utmost part of them, and shalt not see them
14 all: and curse me them from thence. And he brought him into
r ver. 1, 2.
the field of Zophim, to the top of ¹Pisgah, *r*and built seven
15 altars, and offered a bullock and a ram on *every* altar. And he
said unto Balak, Stand here by thy burnt offering, while I meet
s ch. 22. 35.
ver. 5.
16 *the* LORD yonder. And the LORD met Balaam, and *s*put a word
in his mouth, and said, Go again unto Balak, and say thus.
17 And when he came to him, behold, he stood by his burnt offering, and the princes of Moab with him. And Balak said unto
18 him, What hath the LORD spoken? And he took up his parable,
and said,

t Judg. 3. 20.
*t*Rise up, Balak, and hear;
Hearken unto me, thou son of Zippor:
u 1 Sam. 15.
29.
Mal. 3. 6.
Rom. 11. 29.
Tit. 1. 2.
Jam. 1. 17.
19 *u*God *is* not a man, that he should lie;
Neither the son of man, that he should repent:
Hath he said, and shall he not do *it?*
Or hath he spoken, and shall he not make it good?
20 Behold, I have received *commandment* to bless:
x Gen. 12. 2.
& 22. 17.
Num. 22. 12.
And *x*he hath blessed; and I cannot reverse it.
21 *y*He hath not beheld iniquity in Jacob,
y Rom. 4. 7.
z Ex. 13. 21.
& 29. 45, 46.
& 33. 14.
Neither hath he seen perverseness in Israel:
*z*The LORD his God *is* with him,
*a*And the shout of a king *is* among them.
a Ps. 89. 15.
b ch. 24. 8.
c Deut. 33.
17.
Job 39. 10.
22 *b*God brought them out of Egypt;
He hath as it were *c*the strength of an unicorn.

¹ Or, *The hill.*

---

the righteous] *i.e.* the ancestors of Israel,
who "died in faith, not having received the
promises, but having seen them afar off"
(Heb. xi. 13). With their histories Balaam
was familiar, particularly with that of
Abraham, "the righteous man" whom God
had "raised up from the east (and) called to
His foot" (Isai. xli. 2).

let my last end be like his] Render rather·
"last estate," for the reference is not so
much to the act of death, as to all that followed upon it—to the future, in which the
name and influence of the deceased person
would be perpetuated.

13. Balak seems to hope that the prophet's words in *v.* 10 reflected the impression conveyed by the scene before him at
the moment of the augury; and so that the
sight of a mere few straggling Israelites in
the utmost part of the camp might induce
a different estimate of their resources and
prospects.

14. *the field of Zophim*] Or, "of watch-
ers." It lay upon the top of Pisgah, north
of the former station, and nearer to the Israelitish camp; the greater part of which
was, however, probably concealed from it

by an intervening spur of the hill. Beyond
the camp Balaam's eye would pass on to
the bed of the Jordan. It was perhaps a
lion coming up in his strength from the
swelling of that stream (cp. Jer. xlix. 19)
that furnished him with the augury he
awaited, and so dictated the final similitude
of his next parable.

20. *I have received commandment to bless*]
Literally, "I have received to bless." The
reason of his blessing lay in the augury
which he acknowledged, and in the Divine
overruling impulse which he could not resist, not in any " commandment " in
words.

21. "Iniquity" and "perverseness" are
found together again in the Hebrew of Pss.
x. 7, xc. 10, and elsewhere; and import
wickedness together with that tribulation
which is its proper result.

the shout] The word is used (Lev. xxiii.
24 note) to describe the sound of the silver
trumpets. The "shout of a king" will
therefore refer to the jubilant sounds by
which the Presence of the Lord as their
King amongst them was celebrated by Israel.

22. *an unicorn*] A wild bull, the now

23 Surely *there is* no enchantment [1]against Jacob,
Neither *is there* any divination against Israel:
According to this time it shall be said of Jacob and of Israel,
*d*What hath God wrought!
24 Behold, the people shall rise up *e*as a great lion,
And lift up himself as a young lion:
*f*He shall not lie down until he eat *of* the prey,
And drink the blood of the slain.

25 And Balak said unto Balaam, Neither curse them at all, nor
26 bless them at all. But Balaam answered and said unto Balak,
Told not I thee, saying, *g*All that the LORD speaketh, that
27 I must do? ¶And Balak said unto Balaam, *h*Come, I pray
thee, I will bring thee unto another place; peradventure it will
28 please God that thou mayest curse me them from thence. And
Balak brought Balaam unto the top of Peor, that looketh *i*toward
29 Jeshimon. And Balaam said unto Balak, *k*Build me here seven
altars, and prepare me here seven bullocks and seven rams.
30 And Balak did as Balaam had said, and offered a bullock and a
ram on *every* altar.

CHAP. 24. AND when Balaam saw that it pleased the LORD to
bless Israel, he went not, as at *a*other times, [2]to seek for en-
2 chantments, but he set his face toward the wilderness. And
Balaam lifted up his eyes, and he saw Israel *b*abiding *in his
tents* according to their tribes; and the *c*spirit of God came upon
3 him. *d*And he took up his parable, and said,

Balaam the son of Beor hath said,
And the man [3]whose eyes are open hath said:
4 He hath said, which heard the words of God,
Which saw the vision of the Almighty,
*e*Falling *into a trance*, but having his eyes open:
5 How goodly are thy tents, O Jacob,
And thy tabernacles, O Israel!

d Ps. 31. 19.
& 44. 1.
e Gen. 49. 9.
f Gen. 49. 27.

g ch. 22. 38.
ver. 12.
1 Kin. 22.
14.
h ver. 13.

i ch. 21. 20.

k ver. 1.

a ch. 23. 3,
15.
b ch. 2. 2,
&c.
c ch. 11. 25.
1 Sam. 10.
10.
& 19. 20. 23.
2 Chr. 15. 1.
d ch. 23. 7,
18.
e See 1 Sam.
19. 24.
Ez. 1. 28.
Dan. 8. 18.
& 10. 15, 16.
2 Cor. 12. 2,
3, 4.
Rev. 1. 10,
17.

[1] Or, *in*.
[2] Heb. *to the meeting of enchantments.*
[3] Heb. *who had his eyes shut*, but now opened.

extinct Aurochs, formidable for its size, strength, speed, and ferocity.]
23. *enchantment...divination*] More strictly "augury" and "soothsayer's token," or the omen that was superstitiously observed. "Soothsayer" is the term applied to Balaam in Josh. xiii. 22.
The verse intimates that the seer was at last, through the overruling of his own auguries, compelled to own what, had he not been blinded by avarice and ambition, he would have discerned before—that there was an indisputable interference of God on Israel's behalf, against which all arts and efforts of man must prove vain. The sense suggested by margin (*i.e.* that the soothsayer's art was not practised in Israel) would be strictly true (cp. *v.* 4 note).
according, &c.] Rather, in due time it shall be told to Jacob, &c. God will, through His own divinely appointed means (*e.g.* the Urim and Thummim), reveal to Israel, as occasion may require, His will and purposes.
28. The position of Peor northward from Pisgah, along the Abarim heights, is ap-

proximately determined by the extant notices of Beth-peor.
Jeshimon was the waste, in the great valley below, where stood Beth-jeshimoth, "the house of the wastes."
XXIV. 2. Balaam gazed over the camp of Israel that stretched before him, and allowed the spectacle to work its own influence upon him.
3. *whose eyes are open*] *i.e.* opened in inward vision, to discern things that were hidden from ordinary beholders.
4. The "falling" of which Balaam speaks was the condition under which the inward opening of his eyes took place. It indicates the force of the Divine inspiration overpowering the seer. The faithful prophets of the Lord do not appear to have been subject to these violent illapses (Dan. viii. 17; Rev. i. 17).
In Balaam and in Saul (1 Sam. xix. 24) the word of God could only prevail by first subduing the alien will, and overpowering the bodily energies which the will ordinarily directs.

6 As the valleys are they spread forth,
As gardens by the river's side,
[f]As the trees of lign aloes [g]which the LORD hath planted,
And as cedar trees beside the waters.
7 He shall pour the water out of his buckets,
And his seed *shall be* [h]in many waters,
And his king shall be higher than [i]Agag,
And his [k]kingdom shall be exalted.
8 [l]God brought him forth out of Egypt;
He hath as it were the strength of an unicorn:
He shall [m]eat up the nations his enemies, and shall [n]break their bones,
And [o]pierce *them* through with his arrows.
9 [p]He couched, he lay down as a lion,
And as a great lion: who shall stir him up?
[q]Blessed *is* he that blesseth thee,
And cursed *is* he that curseth thee.

10 ¶ And Balak's anger was kindled against Balaam, and he [r]smote
his hands together: and Balak said unto Balaam, [s]I called thee
to curse mine enemies, and, behold, thou hast altogether blessed
11 *them* these three times. Therefore now flee thou to thy place:
[t]I thought to promote thee unto great honour; but, lo, the LORD
12 hath kept thee back from honour. And Balaam said unto
Balak, Spake I not also to thy messengers which thou sentest
13 unto me, saying, [u]If Balak would give me his house full of
silver and gold, I cannot go beyond the commandment of the
LORD, to do *either* good or bad of mine own mind; *but* what the
14 LORD saith, that will I speak? And now, behold, I go unto my
people: come *therefore, and* [x]I will advertise thee what this
15 people shall do to thy people [y]in the latter days. [z]And he took
up his parable, and said,

Balaam the son of Beor hath said,
And the man whose eyes are open hath said:
16 He hath said, which heard the words of God,
And knew the knowledge of the most High,

Ps. 1. 3.
Jer. 17. 8.
[g] Ps. 104. 16.
[h] Jer. 51. 13.
Rev. 17. 1, 15.
[i] 1 Sam. 15. 9.
[k] 2 Sam. 5. 12.
1 Chr. 14. 2.
[l] ch. 23. 22.
[m] ch. 14. 9. & 23. 24.
[n] Ps. 2. 9.
Isai. 38. 13.
Jer. 50. 17.
[o] Ps. 45. 5.
Jer. 50. 9.
[p] Gen. 49. 9.
[q] Gen. 12. 3. & 27. 29.
[r] Ez. 21. 14, 17. & 22. 13.
[s] ch. 23. 11.
Deut. 23. 4, 5.
Josh. 24. 9.
Neh. 13. 2.
[t] ch. 22. 17, 37.
[u] ch. 22. 18.
[x] Mic. 6. 5.
Rev. 2. 14.
[y] Gen. 49. 1.
Dan. 2. 28. & 10. 14.
[z] ver. 3, 4.

---

6. *as gardens by the river's side*] Balaam's language reflects the famous artificial gardens along the banks of his own river, the Euphrates.

as the trees of lign aloes which the LORD *hath planted*] The latter words contain an apparent reference to Paradise (cp. Gen. ii. 8). The aloe, imported from China and the far distant east, furnished to the ancients one of the most fragrant and precious of spices; cp. Ps. xlv. 8; Prov. vii. 17.

as cedar trees beside the waters] i.e. as the noblest of trees branching forth in the fairest of situations: an image of majestic beauty, as that of the last verse was of rare fecundity.

7. Balaam's native soil was ordinarily irrigated by water fetched from the neighbouring Euphrates, and carried in buckets suspended from the two ends of a pole. Thus the metaphor would import that Israel should have his own exuberant and unfailing channels of blessing and plenty. Some take the word to be predictive of the future benefits which, through the means of Israel, were to accrue to the rest of the world.

Agag] The name, apparently hereditary (cp. 1 S. xv.) to the chieftains of Amalek, means "high." The words point to the Amalekite kingdom as highly prosperous and powerful at the time (cp. *v.* 20); but also to be far excelled by the future glories of Israel. The Amalekites never in fact recovered their crushing defeat by Saul (1 S. xv. 2 seq.), though they appear again as foes to Israel in the reign of David (1 S. xxvii. and xxx). The remnant of them was destroyed in the reign of Hezekiah (1 Chr. iv. 43).

14. *I will advertise thee*] *i.e.* "I will advise thee," words which refer to the ensuing prophecy.

16. *and knew the knowledge of the most High*] With the addition of these words, which point to the greater importance and the more distinctly predictive character of what follows, the introduction to this last parable is the same as the introduction to the preceding parable.

Which saw the vision of the Almighty,
Falling *into a trance*, but having his eyes open :

17   ^aI shall see him, but not now :   ^a Rev. 1. 7.
I shall behold him, but not nigh :
There shall come ^ba Star out of Jacob,   ^b Matt. 2. 2.
And ^ca Sceptre shall rise out of Israel,   Rev. 22. 16.
And shall ¹smite the corners of Moab,   ^c Gen. 49. 10.
And destroy all the children of Sheth.   Ps. 110. 2.

18   And ^dEdom shall be a possession,   ^d 2 Sam. 8.
Seir also shall be a possession for his enemies ;   14.
And Israel shall do valiantly.   Ps. 60. 8, 9, 12.

19   ^eOut of Jacob shall come he that shall have dominion,   ^e Gen. 49. 10.
And shall destroy him that remaineth of the city.

20 And when he looked on Amalek, he took up his parable, and said,

Amalek *was* ²the first of the nations ;
But his latter end ³*shall be* that he perish for ever.

---

¹ Or, *smite through the princes of Moab*, 2 Sam. 8. 2. Jer. 48. 45.   ² Or, *the first of the nations that warred against Israel*, Ex. 17. 8.   ³ Or, *shall be even to destruction*, Ex. 17. 14. 1 Sam. 15. 3, 8.

---

17. Render, **I see him, though he be not now : I behold him, though he be not nigh.** Balaam here describes what is actually before him in inward vision.

him] *i.e.* the prince, represented in the succeeding words by the Star and Sceptre. The star has amongst all nations served as a symbol of regal power and splendour : and the birth and future glory of great monarchs were believed by the ancients to be heralded by the appearance of stars or comets : cp. also Is. xiv. 12 ; Dan. viii. 10 ; Rev. i. 16, 20, ii. 1, ix. 1.

the corners of Moab] Literally, " the two sides of Moab," *i.e.* the length and breadth of the land : cp. Jer. xlviii. 45.

destroy all the children of Sheth] Rather, " overthrow the sons of tumult," *i.e.* the warriors of Moab, whose valour and fierceness is frequently referred to elsewhere (cp. Ex. xv. 15 ; Is. xv. 4, xvi. 6, &c.) Cp. Jer. xlviii. 45.

18. *Seir*] The older name of the mountain-land, south of Moab, and east of the Arabah, which the Edomites inhabited (Gen. xxxii. 3, xxxvi. 8, 9).

19. *destroy him that remaineth of the city*] *i.e.* shall destroy those of every city that had previously escaped. The phrase tersely describes a conqueror who first defeats his enemies in battle, and then hunts out the fugitives till he has cut off all of every place (cp. 1 K. xi. 16).

The victories of David were a partial accomplishment of the predictions (*vv.* 14, 18), but did not exhaust them.

It is apparent that Edom and Moab are named by Balaam, as they are also by the prophets (cp. *e.g.* Is. xi. 14), as representatives of the heathen nations (*v.* 8) who were hostile to the Theocracy. As Jacob therefore figures as a constant type of the kingdom of Messiah in the prophets, so do Edom and Moab of the enemies of that kingdom ; and in the threatened ruin of Edom and Moab is indicated the eventual destruction of all that resist the kingdom of God in its power.

The "Star" and "Sceptre" of the prophecy, like the "Sceptre" and "Lawgiver" of Gen. xlix. 10, point also naturally to a line of princes rather than to an individual ; or rather are emblems of the kingdom of Israel generally. Thus the victories of David and his successors, generation after generation, over Edom and Moab, are unquestionably recurring and progressive accomplishments of what Balaam foretold ; but in addition the prophecy reaches forward to some further and culminating accomplishment ; and that too in "the latter days " (*v.* 14), the ordinary prophetic designation for the time of the Messiah (cp. marg. reff.).

To a Christian the connection between the Star and Sceptre of Balaam and the Star of the king of the Jews, which the wise men saw (St. Matt. ii. 2), is self-evident.

20. *when he looked*] *i.e.* in spirit, as he saw the Star (*v.* 17).

Amalek was the first of the nations] Rather, **is** pre-eminent amongst the neighbouring nations : cp. the same expression in Amos vi. 1. Hence the force of the words (*v.* 7) " higher than Agag," *i.e.* than the king of this powerful nation (cp. xiv. 45 ; Ex. xvii. 8). This rank, due to the warlike prowess of the tribe, Balaam contrasts with its approaching downfall and extinction.

21 And he looked on the Kenites, and took up his parable, and
　　said,
　　　　Strong is thy dwellingplace,
　　　　And thou puttest thy nest in a rock.
22　　Nevertheless [1]the Kenite shall be wasted,
　　　　[2]Until Asshur shall carry thee away captive.

23 And he took up his parable, and said,

　　　　Alas, who shall live when God doeth this!

f Gen. 10. 4.　24　And ships *shall come* from the coast of *f* Chittim,
Dan. 11. 30.
g Gen. 10.　　　And shall afflict Asshur, and shall afflict *g* Eber,
21, 25.　　　　And he also shall perish for ever.

　　　　　[1] Heb. *Kain*, Gen. 15. 19.
　　　　　[2] Or, *how long* shall it be ere *Asshur carry thee away captive?*

---

21. *the Kenites*] First mentioned (Gen.
xv. 19) as one of the tribes whose territory
was promised to Abraham. In Judg. i. 16,
where we read of them as moving with the
children of Judah, to establish themselves
in the pastures south of Arad, Moses'
father-in-law is spoken of as a Kenite (cp.
Judg. iv. 11). It appears therefore, since
Moses' father-in-law was a prince or priest of
Midian (Ex. ii. 15 seq.), that the Kenites
must have been of Midianitish extraction,
and so descended from Abraham through
Keturah (Gen. xxv. 2).

But it seems unlikely that the Kenites of
Gen. xv. 19, who were to be dispossessed by
the descendants of Abraham, were identical
with those of whom Balaam speaks, and
who were, because of good offices rendered
at the time of the Exodus, always regarded
as kinsmen and friends by Israel (cp. 1 S.
xv. 6, xxvii. 10). Rather, is it probable that
the Kenites of Gen. xv. 19 were a Canaanitish people, who derived their name from
the city Kain, which fell eventually within
the borders of the tribe of Judah (Josh. xv.
22) ; and that the descendants of Hobab,
who appear in Judg. i. 16 as making war in
this very district, possessed themselves of
this city, and with it of the name Kenite
also. This they would seem to have already
done when Balaam uttered his prediction ;
and in the next verse it is, as the margin
correctly indicates, not of the Kenite, but
of Kain the city, that he speaks. Nor is it
surprising to find them in possession of their
new abode in the Promised Land, while the
Israelites were yet in their tents. It may
well be that this roving band of Midianites
had already entered Canaan, perhaps along
the shores of the Dead Sea, and by routes
impracticable for the huge host of Israel,
and had, as a kind of advanced guard, made
a beginning of the conquest of the country.
From 1 Chr. ii. 54, 55, we learn that the
Rechabites were a branch of the Kenites ;
and the name Salmaites, always given to
the Kenites in the Targums, connects them
with Salma, the son of Caleb, there mentioned. Jer. xxxv. shows how tenaciously,
for many centuries, they held fast the no-

madic habits of their race.

*Strong is thy dwellingplace, and thou
puttest thy nest in a rock*] Render, **Strong**
(or firm) **be thy dwelling-place, and put
thou thy nest in the rock** (or cliff). In the
Hebrew there is a play on the words *ken*,
"nest," and *Kain*, the name of the Kenites'
abode. This nest in the cliff might be the
city of Hazazon-tamar or Engedi, if that be
(as is likely) the "city of palm-trees," from
which they went up subsequently (Judg. i.
16). But there is another site, about ten
miles south of Engedi, to which Balaam's
words would be more appropriate, on the
summit of the cliff rising perpendicularly
from the level of the western shore of the
Dead Sea, where was afterwards built the
city of Masada, the scene of the closing tra-
gedy of the Jewish-Roman war. It is not
likely that such a natural fortress would
ever have been unoccupied, or even excluded from a place in the list of the cities
of Judah. Nor is there any site in the Holy
Land which a rude but warlike people
might more fittingly designate as either
Ken, the Nest, or Kain, the Possession.

22. Render, **For Kain shall surely not
be destroyed** (lit. "be for destruction ")
until Asshur, &c. The words are not, as
they appear in A. V., a prediction of evil to
the Kenites, but a promise, on the contrary,
of safety to be long continued to them (cp.
x. 32 ; Jer. xxxv. 19).

23. *when God doeth this*] The eventual
carrying away of the allies of Israel by Assyria presented itself to Balaam as the ruin
of all peace and safety upon earth. One
prediction was however yet wanting, and is
next given, viz. that the conquerors of the
Kenites should fare no better than the Kenites themselves.

24. *Chittim*] *i.e.* Cyprus, the nearest of the
western islands, the only one visible from
Palestine, and so the representative to Balaam and to Israel of all those unknown
western regions across the Mediterranean
Sea, from which were at length to come the
conquerors of the mighty empires of the
East. Cp. Isai. xxiii. 1, 12 ; Jer. ii. 10.

25 ¶ And Balaam rose up, and went and ^h returned to his place: and Balak also went his way.

CHAP. 25. AND Israel abode in ^a Shittim, and ^b the people began
2 to commit whoredom with the daughters of Moab. And ^c they called the people unto ^d the sacrifices of their gods : and the
3 people did eat, and ^e bowed down to their gods. And Israel joined himself unto Baal-peor : and ^f the anger of the LORD was
4 kindled against Israel. And the LORD said unto Moses, ^g Take all the heads of the people, and hang them up before the LORD against the sun, ^h that the fierce anger of the LORD may be
5 turned away from Israel. And Moses said unto ⁱ the judges of Israel, ^k Slay ye every one his men that were joined unto Baal-
6 peor. ¶ And, behold, one of the children of Israel came and brought unto his brethren a Midianitish woman in the sight of Moses, and in the sight of all the congregation of the children of Israel, ^l who were weeping before the door of the tabernacle of
7 the congregation. And ^m when Phinehas, ⁿ the son of Eleazar, the son of Aaron the priest, saw it, he rose up from among the
8 congregation, and took a javelin in his hand ; and he went after the man of Israel into the tent, and thrust both of them through, the man of Israel, and the woman through her belly. So ^o the
9 plague was stayed from the children of Israel. And ^p those that
10 died in the plague were twenty and four thousand. ¶ And the
11 LORD spake unto Moses, saying, ^q Phinehas, the son of Eleazar, the son of Aaron the priest, hath turned my wrath away from

^h See ch. 31. 8.
^a ch. 33. 49.
Josh. 2. 1.
Mic. 6. 5.
^b ch. 31. 16.
1 Cor. 10. 8.
^c Josh. 22. 17.
Ps. 106. 28.
Hos. 9. 10.
^d Ex. 34. 15.
16.
1 Cor. 10. 20.
^e Ex. 20. 5.
^f Ps. 106. 29.
^g Deut. 4. 3.
Josh. 22. 17.
^h ver. 11.
Deut. 13. 17.
ⁱ Ex. 18. 21, 25.
^k Ex. 32. 27.
Deut. 13. 6,
9, 13, 15.
^l Joel 2. 17.
^m Ps. 106. 30.
ⁿ Ex. 6. 25.
^o Ps. 106. 30.
^p Deut. 4. 3.
1 Cor. 10. 8.
^q Ps. 106. 30.

Eber] i.e. the descendants of Shem. Of these Asshur was one (cp. marg. ref.), and is here specified by name, since the Assyrians attained, in the empires of Babylon and Nineveh, to an extraordinary grandeur, and were destined to a most signal and irretrievable fall.

he also] i.e. the conqueror of Asshur and Eber who should come across the sea. It is not revealed whence the blow should come that should overthrow in its turn the power that prevailed over the great monarchies of the East.

25. returned to his own place] i.e. amongst the Midianites to plot by new means against the people of God, and to perish in his sin (xxxi. 8, 16 ; Rev. ii. 14).

XXV. The records of the neighbouring cities of the plain, and the circumstances of the origin of Moab (Gen. xix. 30 seq.) suggest that the people amongst whom Israel was now thrown were more than ordinarily licentious.

2. and they called] i.e. "the daughters of Moab called."

3. joined himself] i.e. by taking part in the sacrificial meals as described in the last verse. Cp. Ex. xxxiv. 15 ; 1 Cor. x. 18. The worship of Baal was attended with the grossest impurity, and indeed partly consisted in it (Hos. iv. 14, ix. 10).

Baal-peor] i.e. the Baal worshipped at Peor, the place mentioned in xxiii. 28 (cp. Baal-meon, xxxii. 38). [The identification of this god with Chemosh (xxi. 29) is now given up.]

4. take] i.e. assemble the chiefs of the

people to thee (cp. the phrase "took men," in xvi. 1). The offenders were to be first slain by the hands of "the judges of Israel" (v. 5), and afterwards hung up "against the sun" (i.e. publicly, openly ; cp. 2 Sam. xii. 12) as an aggravation of their punishment. This would be done by impaling the body or fastening it to a cross. Cp. Deut. xxi. 23 note, and 2 Sam. xxi. 9.

6. a Midianitish woman] Lit. "the Midianitish woman," the particular one by whom he had been enticed (cp. v. 15 and xxxi. 18). Her high rank proves that Zimri had not fallen in with her by mere chance, but had been deliberately singled out by the Midianites as one whom they must at any price lead astray.

weeping before the door of the tabernacle] The plague (v. 9) had already broken out among the people : and the more God-fearing had assembled at the door of the Tabernacle of God (cp. marg. ref.) to intercede for mercy, when Zimri committed the fresh and public outrage just described.

8. into the tent] The inner recess in the tent, fashioned archwise, and appropriated as the sleeping-chamber and women's apartment.

9. twenty and four thousand] St. Paul (1 Cor. x. 8) says "three and twenty thousand," following probably the Jewish tradition which deducted one thousand as the number slain by the hands of their brethren.

11. hath turned my wrath away] The signal example thus made of a leading offender by Phinehas was accepted by God as an expiation (lit. in v. 13 "covering ;"

the children of Israel, while he was zealous [1] for my sake among
them, that I consumed not the children of Israel in [r]my jealousy.

12 Wherefore say, [s]Behold, I give unto him my covenant of peace:
13 and he shall have it, and [t]his seed after him, *even* the covenant of
   [u]an everlasting priesthood ; because he was [x]zealous for his God,
14 and [y]made an atonement for the children of Israel. ¶ Now the
name of the Israelite that was slain, *even* that was slain with
the Midianitish woman, *was* Zimri, the son of Salu, a prince of a
15 [2]chief house among the Simeonites. And the name of the Midianitish woman that was slain *was* Cozbi, the daughter of [z]Zur ; he
16 *was* head over a people, *and* a chief house in Midian. ¶ And
17 the LORD spake unto Moses, saying, [a]Vex the Midianites, and
18 smite them : for they vex you with their [b]wiles, wherewith they
have beguiled you in the matter of Peor, and in the matter of
Cozbi, the daughter of a prince of Midian, their sister, which was
slain in the day of the plague for Peor's sake.

CHAP. 26. AND it came to pass after the plague, that the LORD
spake unto Moses and unto Eleazar the son of Aaron the priest,
2 saying, [a]Take the sum of all the congregation of the children of
Israel, [b]from twenty years old and upward, throughout their
3 fathers' house, all that are able to go to war in Israel. And Moses
and Eleazar the priest spake with them [c]in the plains of Moab by
4 Jordan *near* Jericho, saying, *Take the sum of the people*, from
twenty years old and upward ; as the LORD [d]commanded Moses
and the children of Israel, which went forth out of the land of
5 Egypt. ¶ [e]Reuben, the eldest son of Israel : the children of

[1] Heb. *with my zeal :* See 2 Cor. 11. 2.   [2] Heb. *house of a father*

Marginal references:

[r] Ex. 20. 5.
Deut. 32. 16, 21.
1 Kin. 14. 22.
Ps. 78. 58.
Ez. 16. 38.
Zeph. 1. 18.
& 3. 8.
[s] Mal. 2. 4, 5. & 3. 1.
[t] See 1 Chr. 6, 4, &c.
[u] Ex. 40. 15.
[x] Acts 22. 3.
Rom. 10. 2.
[y] Heb. 2. 17.
[z] ch. 31. 8.
Josh. 13. 21.
[a] ch. 31. 2.
[b] ch. 31. 16.
Rev. 2. 14.

[a] Ex. 30. 12.
& 38. 25.
ch. 1. 2.
[b] ch. 1. 3.
[c] ver. 63.
ch. 22. 1.
& 31. 12.
& 33. 48.
& 35. 1.
[d] ch. 1. 1.
[e] Gen. 46. 8.
Ex. 6. 14.
1 Chr. 5, 1.

---

see on the typical significance Lev. i. 4),
and the exterminating wrath which had
gone forth against the whole people was
arrested (Ps. cvi. 30).

The act of Phinehas must be regarded as
exceptional. It was an extraordinary deed
of vengeance, justified by the singular atro-
city of the crime which provoked it ; but it
does not confer the right to every man to
punish summarily any gross and flagrant
breach of Divine law committed in his
presence. Cp. the act of Mattathias (1
Macc. ii. 24–26).

The act was its own justification. Its
merit consisted in the evidence it gave that
the heart of Phinehas was right before God.
He was "zealous with God's zeal," and
abhorred the presumptuous wickedness of
Zimri, as God abhorred it. He therefore
risked his own life by dealing according to
their deserts with two influential and defiant
evil doers ; and his act, done in the face
of Moses and the people, and for them, was
accepted by God as a national atonement; and
rewarded by the people (cp. the leadership
assigned to him in xxxi. 6 ; Josh. xxii. 13).

12. *my covenant of peace*] Equivalent to
"the Covenant of My peace." God established with Phinehas in particular that Covenant which He had made generally with all
his people ; and among its blessings peace
is specially mentioned, because of the peace
between God and the congregation which
Phinehas had brought about. As an addi-

tional gift there is assigned to him and his
seed for ever the office of peace-making, the
legitimate function of the priesthood (cp.
Eph. ii. 14) ; and the Covenant was thus to
him a Covenant not only of peace but of life
(cp. marg. ref.). Phinehas became high-
priest after the death of his father Eleazar,
and the office, with a short interruption from
the days of Eli to those of David, when for
unknown reasons it was filled by the descendants of his uncle Ithamar, was perpetuated in his line ; nor indeed is it known
to have departed from that line again until
the typical priesthood of the sons of Aaron
was merged in the actual priesthood of the
Saviour of mankind.

XXVI. The mustering of the tribes described in this chapter was immediately
preparatory to the war against Midian, and
to the invasion of Canaan which shortly
followed. With a view also to an,equitable
allotment of the land to be conquered (cp.
v. 54) the numbers of the several tribes were
taken according to their families.

1. *after the plague*] These words serve to
show approximately the date at which the
census was taken, and intimate the reason
for the great decrease in numbers which was
found to have taken place in certain tribes.
Cp. Deut. iv. 3 and *v.* 5 note in this chapter.

5 seq. The tribes are mentioned in the
same order as in the earlier census (ch. i.),
except that Manasseh here precedes Ephraim; probably as being now the larger tribe.

Reuben; Hanoch, *of whom cometh* the family of the Hanochites:
6 of Pallu, the family of the Palluites: of Hezron, the family of
7 the Hezronites: of Carmi, the family of the Carmites. These
are the families of the Reubenites: and they that were numbered
of them were forty and three thousand and seven hundred and
8, 9 thirty. And the sons of Pallu; Eliab. And the sons of Eliab;
Nemuel, and Dathan, and Abiram. This *is that* Dathan and
Abiram, *which were* [f]famous in the congregation, who strove   [f] ch. 16. 1, 2.
against Moses and against Aaron in the company of Korah,
10 when they strove against the LORD: [g]and the earth opened her   [g] ch. 16. 32,
mouth, and swallowed them up together with Korah, when that   35.
company died, what time the fire devoured two hundred and
11 fifty men: [h]and they became a sign. Notwithstanding [i]the   [h] ch. 16. 38.
12 children of Korah died not.   ¶ The sons of Simeon after their   See 1 Cor.
families: of [k]Nemuel, the family of the Nemuelites: of Jamin,   10. 6.
the family of the Jaminites: of [l]Jachin, the family of the Jachin-   [i] Ex. 6. 24.
13 ites: of [m]Zerah, the family of the Zarhites: of Shaul, the   [k] Gen. 46.
14 family of the Shaulites. These *are* the families of the Simeonites,   10.
15 twenty and two thousand and two hundred.   ¶ The children of   Ex. 6. 15,
Gad after their families: of [n]Zephon, the family of the Zephon-   [l] 1 Chr. 4. 24,
ites: of Haggi, the family of the Haggites: of Shuni, the family   Jarib.
16 of the Shunites: of [1]Ozni, the family of the Oznites: of Eri, the   [m] Gen. 46.
17 family of the Erites: of [o]Arod, the family of the Arodites: of   [n] Gen. 46.16.
18 Areli, the family of the Arelites. These *are* the families of the   Ziphion.
children of Gad according to those that were numbered of them,   [o] Gen. 46.16,
19 forty thousand and five hundred.   ¶ [p]The sons of Judah *were* Er   Arodi.
20 and Onan: and Er and Onan died in the land of Canaan. And   [p] Gen. 38. 2,
&c.
& 46. 12.

[1] Or, *Ezbon*, Gen. 46. 16.

The following table shews the numbers of
the tribes at each census:

	At Sinai.	In the Plains of Moab.
Reuben	46,500	43,730
Simeon	59,300	22,200
Gad	45,650	40,500
Judah	74,600	76,500
Issachar	54,400	64,300
Zebulun	57,400	60,500
Ephraim	40,500	32,500
Manasseh	32,200	52,700
Benjamin	35,400	45,600
Dan	62,700	64,400
Asher	41,500	53,400
Naphtali	53,400	45,400
	603,550	601,730

Seven of the tribes, of which three are
tribes belonging to the camp of Judah, shew
an increase of numbers; and five, among
whom are the three belonging to the camp
of Reuben, shew a decrease. The greatest
increase of any one tribe is in Manasseh.
The most remarkable decrease is in Simeon,
which now shews less than half its former
strength. To this tribe Zimri, the chief offender in the recent transgression, belonged
(xxv. 14). Probably his tribesmen generally
had followed his example, and had accordingly suffered most severely in the plague.
In the parting blessing of Moses, uttered at

no great interval from this date, the tribe
of Simeon alone is omitted.

The families of all the tribes, excluding
the Levites, number fifty-seven. The ancestral heads after whom these families are
named correspond nearly with the grandchildren and great-grandchildren of Jacob,
enumerated in Gen. xlvi. 8 seq. Both lists
consist mainly of grandchildren of Jacob,
both contain also the same two grandchildren of Judah, and the same two grandchildren of Asher. The document in Genesis
should be regarded as a list, not of those
who went down in their own persons with
Jacob into Egypt, but of those whose
names were transmitted to their posterity
at the date of the Exodus as the heads of
Israelitish houses, and who may thus be
reckoned the early ancestors of the people.

10. *together with Korah*] i.e. they were
engulphed at the same time that Korah
perished; for Korah himself appears to
have died amongst the two hundred and
fifty incense offerers at the door of the
Tabernacle, not with Dathan and Abiram
(cp. xvi. 32 note).

11. *the children of Korah died not*] Cp. v.
58. Samuel the prophet was of this family,
and Heman, "the king's seer" (1 Chr. vi.
22, 33, xxv. 5). Several of the Psalms
appear from the titles to have been composed for the sons of Korah: cp. titles of
Pss. xlii., xliv., xlv., &c.

q 1 Chr. 2. 3.　　ᵠthe sons of Judah after their families were; of Shelah, the
family of the Shelanites: of Pharez, the family of the Pharzites:
21 of Zerah, the family of the Zarhites. And the sons of Pharez
were; of Hezron, the family of the Hezronites: of Hamul, the
22 family of the Hamulites. These *are* the families of Judah according to those that were numbered of them, threescore and sixteen

r Gen. 46.13.　23 thousand and five hundred. ¶ ʳ *Of* the sons of Issachar after their
1 Chr. 7. 1.　　families: *of* Tola, the family of the Tolaites: of ¹Pua, the family
24 of the Punites: of ²Jashub, the family of the Jashubites: of
25 Shimron, the family of the Shimronites. These *are* the families
of Issachar according to those that were numbered of them,

s Gen.46.14.　26 threescore and four thousand and three hundred. ¶ ˢ *Of* the
sons of Zebulun after their families: of Sered, the family of the
Sardites: of Elon, the family of the Elonites: of Jahleel, the family
27 of the Jahleelites. These *are* the families of the Zebulunites according to those that were numbered of them, threescore thousand

t Gen. 46. 20.　28 and five hundred. ¶ ᵗThe sons of Joseph after their families *were*
u Josh. 17. 1.　29 Manasseh and Ephraim. Of the sons of Manasseh: of ᵘMachir,
1 Chr. 7. 14,　the family of the Machirites: and Machir begat Gilead: of
15.　　　　　30 Gilead *come* the family of the Gileadites. These *are* the sons of
x Called,　　Gilead: of ˣJeezer, the family of the Jeezerites: of Helek, the
Abiezer,
Josh. 17. 2.　31 family of the Helekites: and *of* Asriel, the family of the Asriel-
Judg. 6. 11,　32 ites: and *of* Shechem, the family of the Shechemites: and *of*
24, 34.　　　Shemida, the family of the Shemidaites: and *of* Hepher, the
y ch. 27. 1.　33 family of the Hepherites. And ʸZelophehad the son of Hepher
& 36. 11.　　had no sons, but daughters: and the names of the daughters
of Zelophehad *were* Mahlah, and Noah, Hoglah, Milcah, and
34 Tirzah. These *are* the families of Manasseh, and those that
were numbered of them, fifty and two thousand and seven hun-
35 dred. ¶These *are* the sons of Ephraim after their families: of

z 1 Chr. 7.20,　Shuthelah, the family of the Shuthalhites: of ᶻBecher, the
Bered.　　family of the Bachrites: of Tahan, the family of the Tahanites.
36 And these *are* the sons of Shuthelah: of Eran, the family of the
37 Eranites. These *are* the families of the sons of Ephraim according to those that were numbered of them, thirty and two thousand and five hundred. These *are* the sons of Joseph after their

a Gen. 46.21.　38 families. ¶ᵃThe sons of Benjamin after their families: of Bela,
1 Chr. 7. 6.　　the family of the Belaites: of Ashbel, the family of the Ashbel-
b Gen. 46. 21,　39 ites: of ᵇAhiram, the family of the Ahiramites: of ᶜShupham,
Ehi.　　　the family of the Shuphamites: of Hupham, the family of the
1 Chr. 8. 1,　40 Huphamites. And the sons of Bela were ᵈArd and Naaman:
Aharah.　　*of Ard*, the family of the Ardites: *and* of Naaman, the family of
c Gen. 46. 21,　41 the Naamites. These *are* the sons of Benjamin after their
Muppim and
Huppim.　　families: and they that were numbered of them *were* forty
d 1 Chr. 8. 3,　42 and five thousand and six hundred. ¶ᵉThese *are* the sons of
Addar.　　Dan after their families: of ³Shuham, the family of the Shuham-
e Gen. 46. 23.　43 ites. These *are* the families of Dan after their families. All the
families of the Shuhamites, according to those that were num-
bered of them, *were* threescore and four thousand and four hun-
f Gen. 46. 17.　44 dred. ¶ᶠ*Of* the children of Asher after their families: of Jimna,
1 Chr. 7. 30.　the family of the Jimnites: of Jesui, the family of the Jesuites:
45 of Beriah, the family of the Beriites. Of the sons of Beriah: of
Heber, the family of the Heberites: of Malchiel, the family of the
46 Malchielites. And the name of the daughter of Asher *was* Sarah.
47 These *are* the families of the sons of Asher according to

¹ Or, *Phuvah*.　　　² Or, *Job*.　　　³ Or, *Hushim*.

those that were numbered of them; *who were* fifty and three
48 thousand and four hundred. ¶ [g] *Of* the sons of Naphtali after their
families: of Jahzeel, the family of the Jahzeelites: of Guni, the
49 family of the Gunites: of Jezer, the family of the Jezerites: of
50 [h] Shillem, the family of the Shillemites. These *are* the families
of Naphtali according to their families: and they that were
numbered of them *were* forty and five thousand and four hun-
51 dred. ¶ [i] These *were* the numbered of the children of Israel, six
hundred thousand and a thousand seven hundred and thirty.
52, 53 ¶ And the LORD spake unto Moses, saying, [k] Unto these the
land shall be divided for an inheritance according to the number
54 of names. [l] To many thou shalt [1] give the more inheritance, and
to few thou shalt [2] give the less inheritance: to every one shall
his inheritance be given according to those that were numbered
55 of him. Notwithstanding the land shall be [m] divided by lot:
according to the names of the tribes of their fathers they shall
56 inherit. According to the lot shall the possession thereof be
57 divided between many and few. ¶ [n] And these *are* they that
were numbered of the Levites after their families: of Gershon,
the family of the Gershonites: of Kohath, the family of the
58 Kohathites: of Merari, the family of the Merarites. These *are*
the families of the Levites: the family of the Libnites, the
family of the Hebronites, the family of the Mahlites, the family
of the Mushites, the family of the Korathites. And Kohath
59 begat Amram. And the name of Amram's wife *was* [o] Jochebed,
the daughter of Levi, whom *her mother* bare to Levi in Egypt:
and she bare unto Amram Aaron and Moses, and Miriam their
60 sister. [p] And unto Aaron was born Nadab, and Abihu, Eleazar,
61 and Ithamar. And [q] Nadab and Abihu died, when they offered
62 strange fire before the LORD. [r] And those that were numbered
of them were twenty and three thousand, all males from a month
old and upward: [s] for they were not numbered among the children of Israel, because there was [t] no inheritance given them
63 among the children of Israel. ¶ These *are* they that were numbered by Moses and Eleazar the priest, who numbered the children of Israel [u] in the plains of Moab by Jordan *near* Jericho.
64 But [x] among these there was not a man of them whom Moses and
Aaron the priest numbered, when they numbered the children of
65 Israel in the wilderness of Sinai. For the LORD had said of
them, They [y] shall surely die in the wilderness. And there was not
left a man of them, [z] save Caleb the son of Jephunneh, and Joshua
the son of Nun.

CHAP. 27. THEN came the daughters of [a] Zelophehad, the son
of Hepher, the son of Gilead, the son of Machir, the son of

[g] Gen. 46. 24. 1 Chr. 7. 13.
[h] 1 Chr. 7. 13, *Shallum.*
[i] See ch. 1. 46.
[k] Josh. 11. 23. & 14. 1.
[l] ch. 33. 54.
[m] ch. 33. 54. & 34. 13. Josh. 11. 23. & 14. 2.
[n] Gen. 46. 11. Ex. 6. 16, 17, 18, 19. 1 Chr. 6. 1, 16.
[o] Ex. 2. 1, 2. & 6. 20.
[p] ch. 3. 2.
[q] Lev. 10. 1, 2. ch. 3. 4. 1 Chr. 24. 2.
[r] See ch. 3. 39.
[s] ch. 1. 49.
[t] ch. 18. 20. Deut. 10. 9. Josh. 13. 14, 33. & 14. 3.
[u] ver. 3.
[x] ch. 1. Deut. 2. 14, 15.
[y] ch. 14. 28, 29. 1 Cor. 10. 5, 6.
[z] ch. 14. 30.
[a] ch. 26. 33. & 36. 1. 11. Josh. 17. 3.

[1] Heb. *multiply his inheritance.*
[2] Heb. *diminish his inheritance.*

---

51. This shews a decrease of 1820 from the number at Sinai; a decrease due to the recent plague.

56. *according to the lot,* &c.] This method was adopted not only in order to preclude jealousies and disputes, but also that the several tribes might regard the territories as determined for them by God Himself: cp. Prov. xvi. 33.

59. *whom her mother bare*] Literally, "whom she bare;" the subject is wanting, and the verb is in the feminine gender. The words "her mother" are merely conjectural. The text is probably imperfect.

62. The total number of male Levites, 23,000, shews an increase of 1,000 on the number at Sinai (iii. 39). It is doubtless to be taken as a round number; and, as before, includes the male children from a month old and upward, as well as the male adults.

64. It appears from Deut. ii. 14, 15 that the generation numbered at the former census had perished before the host crossed the brook Zered.

XXVII. **1.** Women in Israel had not, up

Manasseh, of the families of Manasseh the son of Joseph: and these *are* the names of his daughters; Mahlah, Noah, and Hog-2 lah, and Milcah, and Tirzah. And they stood before Moses, and before Eleazar the priest, and before the princes and all the congregation, *by* the door of the tabernacle of the congregation, 3 saying, Our father [b]died in the wilderness, and he was not in the company of them that gathered themselves together against the LORD [c]in the company of Korah; but died in his own sin, and 4 had no sons. Why should the name of our father be [1]done away from among his family, because he hath no son? [d]Give unto us *therefore* a possession among the brethren of our father. 5, 6 ¶ And Moses [e]brought their cause before the LORD. And the 7 LORD spake unto Moses, saying, The daughters of Zelophehad speak right: [f]thou shalt surely give them a possession of an inheritance among their father's brethren; and thou shalt cause 8 the inheritance of their father to pass unto them. And thou shalt speak unto the children of Israel, saying, If a man die, and have no son, then ye shall cause his inheritance to pass unto his 9 daughter. And if he have no daughter, then ye shall give his 10 inheritance unto his brethren. And if he have no brethren, then 11 ye shall give his inheritance unto his father's brethren. And if his father have no brethren, then ye shall give his inheritance unto his kinsman that is next to him of his family, and he shall possess it: and it shall be unto the children of Israel [g]a statute 12 of judgment, as the LORD commanded Moses. ¶ And the LORD said unto Moses, [h]Get thee up into this mount Abarim, and see the 13 land which I have given unto the children of Israel. And when thou hast seen it, thou also [i]shalt be gathered unto thy people, 14 as Aaron thy brother was gathered. For ye [k]rebelled against my commandment in the desert of Zin, in the strife of the congregation, to sanctify me at the water before their eyes: that *is* the [l]water of Meribah in Kadesh in the wilderness of Zin. 15, 16 And Moses spake unto the LORD, saying, Let the LORD, [m]the God of the spirits of all flesh, set a man over the congregation,

[b] ch. 14. 35. & 26. 64, 65.
[c] ch. 16. 1, 2.
[d] Josh. 17. 4.
[e] Ex. 18. 15, 19.
[f] ch. 36. 2.
[g] ch. 35. 29.
[h] ch. 33. 47. Deut. 3. 27. & 32. 49. & 34. 1.
[i] ch. 20, 24, 28. & 31. 2. Deut. 10. 6.
[k] ch. 20. 12. Deut. 1. 37. & 32. 51. Ps. 106. 32.
[l] Ex. 17. 7.
[m] ch. 16. 22. Heb. 12. 9.

[1] Heb. *diminished*.

---

to the present time, enjoyed any distinct right of inheritance. Yet a father, whether sons had been born to him or not, had the power, either before or at his death, to cause part of his estate to pass to a daughter; in which case her husband married into her family rather than she into his, and the children were regarded as of the family from which the estate had come. Thus Machir, ancestor of Zelophehad, although he had a son Gilead, left also, as is probable, an inheritance to his daughter, the wife of Hezron of the tribe of Judah, by reason of which their descendants, among whom was Jair, were reckoned as belonging to the tribe of Manasseh (xxxii. 41; 1 Chr. ii. 21 seq.).

2. *by the door of the tabernacle of the congregation*] The place of solemn assembly of the elders. The daughters of Zelophehad made their suit to the princes, the heads of tribes and of families, who were making the census under the superintendence of Moses and Eleazar.

3. *but died in his own sin*] *i.e.* perished under the general sentence of exclusion from the Land of Promise passed on all the older generation, but limited to that generation alone. By virtue of the declaration in xiv. 31 the daughters of Zelophehad claim that their father's sin should not be visited upon them.

4. *give unto us*] As representing our father; that so he, through us his representatives, may enjoy a like inheritance with his brethren.

12. *mount Abarim*] See xxi. 20 note.

16. *the God of the spirits of all flesh*] An acknowledgment that man, who is but flesh (cp. Gen. vi. 3), is of himself helpless; and "lives and moves and has his being" in God (Acts xvii. 28). The words are suitably employed here to introduce an entreaty that God would not leave the congregation without a guide and leader, and in xvi. 22 as a preface to an intercession that the whole people should not suffer for the sin of a few.

17 [n]which may go out before them, and which may go in before
them, and which may lead them out, and which may bring
them in; that the congregation of the LORD be not [o]as sheep
18 which have no shepherd. And the LORD said unto Moses,
Take thee Joshua the son of Nun, a man [p]in whom is the spirit,
19 and [q]lay thine hand upon him; and set him before Eleazar the
priest, and before all the congregation; and [r]give him a charge
20 in their sight. And [s]thou shalt put some of thine honour upon
him, that all the congregation of the children of Israel [t]may be
21 obedient. [u]And he shall stand before Eleazar the priest, who
shall ask counsel for him [x]after the judgment of Urim before the
LORD: [y]at his word shall they go out, and at his word they shall
come in, both he, and all the children of Israel with him, even all
22 the congregation. ¶And Moses did as the LORD commanded
him: and he took Joshua, and set him before Eleazar the priest,
23 and before all the congregation: and he laid his hands upon him,
[z]and gave him a charge, as the LORD commanded by the hand
of Moses.

CHAP. 28. AND the LORD spake unto Moses, saying, Command
2 the children of Israel, and say unto them, My offering, and [a]my
bread for my sacrifices made by fire, for [1]a sweet savour unto
3 me, shall ye observe to offer unto me in their due season. And
thou shalt say unto them, [b]This is the offering made by fire
which ye shall offer unto the LORD; two lambs of the first year
4 without spot [2]day by day, for a continual burnt offering. The
one lamb shalt thou offer in the morning, and the other lamb
5 shalt thou offer [3]at even; and [c]a tenth part of an ephah of flour
for a [d]meat offering, mingled with the fourth part of an [e]hin of
6 beaten oil. It is [f]a continual burnt offering, which was ordained

Reference column (right margin):
[n] Deut. 31.2.
1 Sam. 8. 20.
2 Chr. 1. 10.
[o] 1 Kin. 22.
17.
Zech. 10. 2.
Matt. 9. 36.
Mark 6. 34.
[p] Gen. 41.
38.
Judg. 3. 10.
& 11. 29.
1 Sam. 16.
13, 18.
[q] Deut. 34. 9.
[s] 1 Sam.10.6.
2 Kin. 2. 15.
[t] Josh. 1. 16,
17.
[u] See Josh.
9. 14.
Judg. 1. 1.
& 20. 18, 23.
1 Sam. 23. 9.
& 30. 7.
[x] Ex. 28. 30.
[y] Josh. 9. 14.
1 Sam. 22.
10, 13, 15.
[z] Deut. 3. 28.
& 31. 7.
[a] Lev. 3. 11.
& 21. 6, 8.
Mal. 1. 7, 12.
[b] Ex. 29. 38.
[c] Ex. 16. 36.
ch. 15. 4.
[d] Lev. 2. 1.
[e] Ex. 29. 40.
[f] Ex. 29. 42.
See Amos
5. 25.

[1] Heb. a savour of my rest.　　[2] Heb. in a day.　　[3] Heb. between the two
evenings, Ex. 12. 6.

---

18. in whom is the spirit] Cp. Gen. xli.
38. Joshua was endowed by God with the
requisite spiritual qualifications for the
office. Moses however was to lay his hands
upon him, both in order to confer formal
and public appointment, and also (cp. Deut.
xxxiv. 9) to confirm and strengthen the
spiritual gifts already bestowed. The previous reception of the inner grace did not
dispense with that of the outward sign; cp.
the case of Cornelius (Acts x. 44—48); and
St. Paul's Baptism after his miraculous conversion (Acts ix. 18).

20. of thine honour] i.e. of thy dignity
and authority (cp. xi. 17, 28). Joshua was
constituted forthwith vice-leader under
Moses, by way of introduction to his becoming chief after Moses' death.

21. and he shall stand before Eleazar the
priest, &c.] Joshua was thus to be inferior
to what Moses had been. For Moses had
enjoyed the privilege of unrestricted direct
intercourse with God: Joshua, like all
future rulers of Israel, was to ask counsel
mediately, through the High-priest and
those means of enquiring of God wherewith
the High-priest was entrusted. Such counsel
Joshua seems to have omitted to seek when
he concluded his hasty treaty with the

Gibeonites (Joshua ix. 3 seq.).
judgment of Urim] See Ex. xxviii. 30 note.
XXVIII. The daily offering had been
already commanded (Ex. xxix. 38), and no
doubt additional offerings had become customary on Festivals. But no such elaborate system as is here prescribed was or
could possibly have been observed in the
wilderness: cp. Deut. xii. 8, 9. The regulations of this and the next chapter therefore
point to the immediate prospect of that
settlement in Canaan which alone could
enable the Israelites to obey them. Cp. the
ordinances in ch. xv.

2. My offering, and my bread, &c.] Or,
my offering, even my bread, &c. Offering is here korban (cp. Lev. i. 2; Mark
vii. 11), a term in itself of quite general
import, but often especially applied, as
apparently in this instance, to the Meat-
offering which accompanied the sacrifices.
This Meat-offering connected itself, from its
very nature, with the life of the Israelites
in Canaan, not with their life in the wilderness; and it was annexed to the animal
sacrifices as a token that the people must
dedicate to God their property and the
fruits of their labour as well as their own
persons. See xv. 2 note and Lev. xxi. 6.

in mount Sinai for a sweet savour, a sacrifice made by fire unto
7 the LORD. And the drink offering thereof *shall be* the fourth

g Ex. 29. 42.

part of an hin for the one lamb : *g*in the holy *place* shalt thou
cause the strong wine to be poured unto the LORD *for* a drink
8 offering. And the other lamb shalt thou offer at even : as the
meat offering of the morning, and as the drink offering thereof,
thou shalt offer *it*, a sacrifice made by fire, of a sweet savour
9 unto the LORD. ¶ And on the sabbath day two lambs of the first
year without spot, and two tenth deals of flour *for* a meat offer-
10 ing, mingled with oil, and the drink offering thereof : *this is*

h Ez. 46. 4.
i ch. 10. 10.
1 Sam. 20. 5.
1 Chr. 23. 31.
2 Chr. 2. 4.
Ezra 3. 5.
Neh. 10. 33.
Isai. 1. 13.
Ez. 45. 17.
& 46. 6.
Hos. 2. 11.
Col. 2. 16.
k ch. 15. 4—
12.

*h*the burnt offering of every sabbath, beside the continual burnt
11 offering, and his drink offering. ¶ And *i*in the beginnings of
your months ye shall offer a burnt offering unto the LORD ; two
young bullocks, and one ram, seven lambs of the first year with-
12 out spot ; and *k*three tenth deals of flour *for* a meat offering,
mingled with oil, for one bullock ; and two tenth deals of flour
13 *for* a meat offering, mingled with oil, for one ram ; and a several
tenth deal of flour mingled with oil *for* a meat offering unto
one lamb ; *for* a burnt offering of a sweet savour, a sacrifice
14 made by fire unto the LORD. And their drink offerings shall be
half an hin of wine unto a bullock, and the third *part* of an hin
unto a ram, and a fourth *part* of an hin unto a lamb : this *is*
the burnt offering of every month throughout the months of the

l ver. 22.
ch. 15. 24.

15 year. And *l*one kid of the goats for a sin offering unto the
LORD shall be offered, beside the continual burnt offering, and

m Ex. 12. 6.
Lev. 23. 5.
ch. 9. 3.
Deut. 16. 1.
Ez. 45. 21.
n Lev. 23. 6.
o Ex. 12. 16.
Lev. 23. 7.

16 his drink offering. ¶ *m*And in the fourteenth day of the first
17 month *is* the passover of the LORD. *n*And in the fifteenth day
of this month *is* the feast : seven days shall unleavened bread
18 be eaten. In the *o*first day *shall be* an holy convocation ; ye
19 shall do no manner of servile work *therein :* but ye shall offer
a sacrifice made by fire *for* a burnt offering unto the LORD ;
two young bullocks, and one ram, and seven lambs of the first

p ver. 31.
Lev. 22. 20.
ch. 29. 8.
Deut. 15. 21.

20 year : *p*they shall be unto you without blemish : and their
meat offering *shall be of* flour mingled with oil : three tenth
deals shall ye offer for a bullock, and two tenth deals for a ram ;
21 a several tenth deal shalt thou offer for every lamb, through-

q ver. 15.

22 out the seven lambs : and *q*one goat *for* a sin offering, to make
23 an atonement for you. Ye shall offer these beside the burnt
offering in the morning, which *is* for a continual burnt offering.
24 After this manner ye shall offer daily, throughout the seven
days, the meat of the sacrifice made by fire, of a sweet savour

---

7. The original of the word "strong
wine" (*shechar*) is a term usually employed
to describe strong drink other than wine
(Lev. x. 9 note). The Israelites in the wilderness had, in their lack of wine, substituted *shechar* made from barley for it.
They had thus observed the spirit, though
not the letter of the ordinance. The Drink-
offering was either poured round the foot of
the Altar ; or on the Altar, and so upon the
flesh of the sacrifice by which the Altar was
covered (cp. Ex. xxx. 9).

9-10. The Sabbath-offering, not previously enjoined, consisted of two lambs,
properly accompanied, in addition to the
regular daily offering.

11-15. The New-moon offering is here also
commanded for the first time. The goat as

a Sin-offering, though mentioned last, would
seem in fact to have been offered first (cp.
the precedents in Ex. xxix. ; Lev. v., viii.,
ix., xiv., xvi.). The Sin-offering, which (xv.
22-26) had been contemplated in cases where
a sin had been committed ignorantly without the knowledge of the congregation, was
henceforth not to be offered merely at discretion, as circumstances might seem to
require, but to be regularly repeated, not
less frequently than once a month.

16-25. The Passover offering was the
same as that of the New moon, and was repeated on each of the seven days of the
Festival, thus marking the importance and
the solemnity of the occasion. The details
of the offering had not been previously prescribed.

unto the LORD: it shall be offered beside the continual burnt
25 offering, and his drink offering. And ^ron the seventh day ye
shall have an holy convocation; ye shall do no servile work.
26 ¶ Also ^sin the day of the firstfruits, when ye bring a new meat
offering unto the LORD, after your weeks *be out*, ye shall have
27 an holy convocation; ye shall do no servile work: but ye shall
offer the burnt offering for a sweet savour unto the LORD; ^ttwo
28 young bullocks, one ram, seven lambs of the first year; and
their meat offering of flour mingled with oil, three tenth deals
29 unto one bullock, two tenth deals unto one ram, a several tenth
30 deal unto one lamb, throughout the seven lambs; *and* one kid
31 of the goats, to make an atonement for you. Ye shall offer
them beside the continual burnt offering, and his meat offering,
(^uthey shall be unto you without blemish) and their drink
offerings.

CHAP. 29. AND in the seventh month, on the first *day* of the
month, ye shall have an holy convocation; ye shall do no servile
2 work: ^ait is a day of blowing the trumpets unto you. And ye
shall offer a burnt offering for a sweet savour unto the LORD;
one young bullock, one ram, *and* seven lambs of the first year
3 without blemish: and their meat offering *shall be of* flour mingled
with oil, three tenth deals for a bullock, *and* two tenth deals for
4 a ram, and one tenth deal for one lamb, throughout the seven
5 lambs: and one kid of the goats *for* a sin offering, to make an
6 atonement for you: beside ^bthe burnt offering of the month,
and his meat offering, and ^cthe daily burnt offering, and his
meat offering, and their drink offerings, ^daccording unto their
manner, for a sweet savour, a sacrifice made by fire unto the
7 LORD. ¶ And ^eye shall have on the tenth *day* of this seventh
month an holy convocation; and ye shall ^f afflict your souls: ye
8 shall not do any work *therein :* but ye shall offer a burnt offering unto the LORD *for* a sweet savour; one young bullock, one
ram, *and* seven lambs of the first year; ^gthey shall be unto you
9 without blemish: and their meat offering *shall be of* flour mingled
with oil, three tenth deals to a bullock, *and* two tenth deals to
10 one ram, a several tenth deal for one lamb, throughout the
11 seven lambs: one kid of the goats *for* a sin offering; beside ^hthe
sin offering of atonement, and the continual burnt offering, and
12 the meat offering of it, and their drink offerings. ¶ And ⁱon
the fifteenth day of the seventh month ye shall have an holy
convocation; ye shall do no servile work, and ye shall keep a
13 feast unto the LORD seven days: and ^kye shall offer a burnt
offering, a sacrifice made by fire, of a sweet savour unto the
LORD; thirteen young bullocks, two rams, *and* fourteen lambs
14 of the first year; they shall be without blemish: and their meat

r Ex. 12. 16.
& 13. 6.
Lev. 23. 8.
s Ex. 23. 16.
& 34. 22.
Lev. 23. 10,
15.
Deut. 16. 10.
Acts 2. 1.
t See Lev.
23. 18, 19.

u ver. 19.

a Lev. 23. 24.

b ch. 28. 11.
c ch. 28. 3.
d ch. 15. 11,
12.

e Lev. 16. 29.
& 23. 27.
f Ps. 35. 13.
Isai. 58. 5.

g ch. 28. 19.

h Lev. 16. 3,
5.

i Lev. 23. 34.
Deut. 16. 13.
Ez. 45. 25.

k Ezra 3. 4.

26-31. The Festival offering at the season
of firstfruits was to be offered on one day
only; and was the same with that of the
New moon and Passover. It nearly though
not entirely accords with the sacrificial
offering prescribed in Lev. xxiii. 18 seq.

XXIX. 1-6. The ordinance of the Feast
of Trumpets was to be observed on the
opening day of that month within which
the Great Day of the Atonement and the
Feast of Tabernacles fell (cp. Lev. xxiii. 23
seq.). The special offering for the day anticipated that of the Great Day of Atonement.

7-11. The offering on the Great Day of
Atonement was the same with that just
specified. The great ceremonies of the day
are described in Lev. xvi.

12-34. Feast of Tabernacles: cp. Lev.
xxiii. 33 seq. The offerings required at this
feast were the largest of all. It was especially one of thankfulness to God for the
gift of the fruits of the earth; and the
quantity and the nature of the offerings
(see *vv.* 7-11) were determined accordingly.

offering *shall be of* flour mingled with oil, three tenth deals unto
every bullock of the thirteen bullocks, two tenth deals to each
15 ram of the two rams, and a several tenth deal to each lamb of
16 the fourteen lambs : and one kid of the goats *for* a sin offering;
beside the continual burnt offering, his meat offering, and his
17 drink offering. And on the second day *ye shall offer* twelve
young bullocks, two rams, fourteen lambs of the first year with-
18 out spot : and their meat offering and their drink offerings for
the bullocks, for the rams, and for the lambs, *shall be* according

l ver. 3, 4, 9,
10.
ch. 15. 12.
& 28. 7, 14.

19 to their number, *l* after the manner : and one kid of the goats
for a sin offering; beside the continual burnt offering, and the
20 meat offering thereof, and their drink offerings. And on the
third day eleven bullocks, two rams, fourteen lambs of the first
21 year without blemish; and their meat offering and their drink
offerings for the bullocks, for the rams, and for the lambs, *shall*

m ver. 18.

22 *be* according to their number, *m* after the manner : and one goat
for a sin offering; beside the continual burnt offering, and his
23 meat offering, and his drink offering. And on the fourth day
ten bullocks, two rams, *and* fourteen lambs of the first year with-
24 out blemish : their meat offering and their drink offerings for
the bullocks, for the rams, and for the lambs, *shall be* according
25 to their number, after the manner : and one kid of the goats *for*
a sin offering; beside the continual burnt offering, his meat
26 offering, and his drink offering. And on the fifth day nine
bullocks, two rams, *and* fourteen lambs of the first year without
27 spot : and their meat offering and their drink offerings for the
bullocks, for the rams, and for the lambs, *shall be* according to
28 their number, after the manner : and one goat *for* a sin offering;
beside the continual burnt offering, and his meat offering, and
29 his drink offering. And on the sixth day eight bullocks, two
30 rams, *and* fourteen lambs of the first year without blemish : and
their meat offering and their drink offerings for the bullocks,
for the rams, and for the lambs, *shall be* according to their
31 number, after the manner : and one goat *for* a sin offering; beside the continual burnt offering, his meat offering, and his
32 drink offering. And on the seventh day seven bullocks, two
33 rams, *and* fourteen lambs of the first year without blemish : and
their meat offering and their drink offerings for the bullocks,
for the rams, and for the lambs, *shall be* according to their
34 number, after the manner : and one goat *for* a sin offering;
beside the continual burnt offering, his meat offering, and his

n Lev. 23. 36.

35 drink offering. On the eighth day ye shall have a *n* solemn
36 assembly : ye shall do no servile work *therein:* but ye shall
offer a burnt offering, a sacrifice made by fire, of a sweet savour
unto the LORD : one bullock, one ram, seven lambs of the first
37 year without blemish : their meat offering and their drink offer-

---

32. Stress is laid on the number seven, the holy symbolical Covenant number, by way of intimation that the mercies of the harvest accrued by virtue of God's Covenant. The diminishing number of bullocks sacrificed on the preceding days of the Feast (cp. *vv.* 13, 17, &c.), is adjusted simply to obtain the coincidence before us on the seventh day ; but some have thought that the gradual evanescence of the Law till the time of its absorption in the Gospel is here presignified in the Law itself.

35-38. The offerings prescribed for the closing day of the Feast of Tabernacles were the same with those appointed for the Feast of Trumpets and the Day of Atonement. The solemnities of the month thus terminated, as a whole, with the same sacrifices with which, three weeks before, they had been introduced ; and the Day of Atonement, even though succeeded by the rejoicings of the Feast of Tabernacles, thus left its impress on the whole month.

ings for the bullock, for the ram, and for the lambs, *shall be*
38 according to their number, after the manner: and one goat *for* a
sin offering; beside the continual burnt offering, and his meat
39 offering, and his drink offering. ¶These *things* ye shall ¹do
unto the LORD in your ⁰set feasts, beside your ᵖvows, and your
freewill offerings, for your burnt offerings, and for your meat
offerings, and for your drink offerings, and for your peace offer-
40 ings. And Moses told the children of Israel according to all that
the LORD commanded Moses.

CHAP. 30. AND Moses spake unto ᵃthe heads of the tribes concerning the children of Israel, saying, This *is* the thing which
2 the LORD hath commanded. ᵇIf a man vow a vow unto the
LORD, or ᶜswear an oath to bind his soul with a bond; he shall
not ²break his word, he shall ᵈdo according to all that proceed-
3 eth out of his mouth. If a woman also vow a vow unto the
LORD, and bind *herself* by a bond, *being* in her father's house in
4 her youth; and her father hear her vow, and her bond wherewith she hath bound her soul, and her father shall hold his
peace at her: then all her vows shall stand, and every bond
5 wherewith she hath bound her soul shall stand. But if her
father disallow her in the day that he heareth; not any of her
vows, or of her bonds wherewith she hath bound her soul, shall
stand: and the LORD shall forgive her, because her father dis-
6 allowed her. And if she had at all an husband, when ³she
vowed, or uttered ought out of her lips, wherewith she bound
7 her soul; and her husband heard *it*, and held his peace at her
in the day that he heard *it*: then her vows shall stand, and her
8 bonds wherewith she bound her soul shall stand. But if her
husband ᵉdisallowed her on the day that he heard *it*; then he
shall make her vow which she vowed, and that which she
uttered with her lips, wherewith she bound her soul, of none
9 effect: and the LORD shall forgive her. But every vow of a
widow, and of her that is divorced, wherewith they have bound

o Lev. 23. 2.
1 Chr. 23.31.
2 Chr. 31. 3.
Ezra 3. 5.
Neh. 10. 33.
Isai. 1. 14.
ᵖ Lev. 7. 11,
16. & 22. 21.
a ch. 1. 4, 16.
ᵇ Lev. 27. 2.
Deut. 23. 21.
Judg. 11. 30,
35.
Eccles. 5. 4.
c Lev. 5. 4.
Matt. 14. 9.
Acts 23. 14.
ᵈ Job 22. 27.
Ps. 22. 25.
Nah. 1. 15.

ᵉ Gen. 3. 16.

¹ Or, *offer*.
² Heb. *profane*, Ps. 55. 20.
³ Heb. *her vows were upon her*, Ps. 56. 12.

XXX. The regulations respecting vows
appropriately follow those given respecting
sacrifices, since a large proportion of vows
would always relate to the presentation
of such offerings. Rules had already been
given (Lev. xxvii.) for the estimation of
things vowed to God. It is probable that
this fresh legislation dealing specially with
vows made by persons in a state of tutelage,
was occasioned by some case of practical
difficulty that had recently arisen; and it is
addressed by Moses to "the heads of the
tribes" (v. 1), who would in their judicial
capacity have to determine questions on
these subjects.

There is no provision in the chapter for
annulling vows made by boys and young
men; from which it has been inferred that
the vows of males were in all cases and circumstances binding.

2. The "vow" was positive; the "bond"
negative or restrictive. By a vow a man
engaged to dedicate something to God, or
to accomplish some work for Him: by a
bond he debarred himself from some privilege or enjoyment. A vow involved an

obligation to do: a bond, an obligation to
forbear doing.

3. *being in her father's house in her youth*]
It was not ordinarily till her betrothal or
marriage, that the female passed (some suppose by purchase) from the power of her
father to that of her husband.

5. *the LORD shall forgive her*] *i.e.* shall re-
mit the obligation. (Cp. 2 K. v. 18.)

6. Rather, **And if she shall at all be an
husband's, and her vows shall be upon her,
or a rash utterance of her lips, wherewith she hath bound her soul**, &c. The
"at all" intimates that the case of a girl betrothed but not yet actually married is here
especially contemplated. After betrothal, a
woman continued to reside, till the period of
her marriage arrived, in her father's house;
but her property was from that time forward vested in her husband, and she was so
far regarded as personally his, that an act
of faithlessness to him was, like adultery,
punishable with death (Deut. xxii. 23, 24).
Hence his right to control her vows even
before he actually took her home as his
wife.

10 their souls, shall stand against her. And if she vowed in her husband's house, or bound her soul by a bond with an oath;
11 and her husband heard *it*, and held his peace at her, *and* disallowed her not: then all her vows shall stand, and every bond
12 wherewith she bound her soul shall stand. But if her husband hath utterly made them void on the day he heard *them; then* whatsoever proceeded out of her lips concerning her vows, or concerning the bond of her soul, shall not stand: her husband
13 hath made them void; and the LORD shall forgive her. Every vow, and every binding oath to afflict the soul, her husband may
14 establish it, or her husband may make it void. But if her husband altogether hold his peace at her from day to day; then he establisheth all her vows, or all her bonds, which *are* upon her: he confirmeth them, because he held his peace at her in the day
15 that he heard *them*. But if he shall any ways make them void after that he hath heard *them;* then he shall bear her iniquity.
16 These *are* the statutes, which the LORD commanded Moses, between a man and his wife, between the father and his daughter, *being yet* in her youth in her father's house.

^a ch. 25. 17.
^b ch. 27. 13.

CHAP. **31.** AND the LORD spake unto Moses, saying, ^aAvenge the
2 children of Israel of the Midianites: afterward shalt thou ^bbe
3 gathered unto thy people. And Moses spake unto the people, saying, Arm some of yourselves unto the war, and let them go
4 against the Midianites, and avenge the LORD of Midian. ¹Of every tribe a thousand, throughout all the tribes of Israel, shall
5 ye send to the war. So there were delivered out of the thousands of Israel, a thousand of *every* tribe, twelve thousand armed

^c ch. 10. 9.
^d Deut. 20. 13.
Judg. 21. 11.
1 Sam. 27. 9.
1 Kin. 11.15, 16.
^e See Judg. 6. 1, 2, 33.
^f Josh. 13. 21.

6 for war. And Moses sent them to the war, a thousand of *every* tribe, them and Phinehas the son of Eleazar the priest, to the war, with the holy instruments, and ^cthe trumpets to blow in
7 his hand. And they warred against the Midianites, as the LORD
8 commanded Moses; and ^dthey slew all the ^emales. And they slew the kings of Midian, beside the rest of them that were slain; namely, ^fEvi, and Rekem, and Zur, and Hur, and Reba,

---

¹ Heb. *A thousand of a tribe, a thousand of a tribe.*

XXXI. **2.** *the Midianites*] The Moabites are not included. It would thus seem that it was the Midianites, and they only, who deliberately set themselves to work the corruption of Israel.

3. *Avenge the* LORD *of Midian*] The war against the Midianites was no ordinary war. It was indeed less a war than the execution of a Divine sentence against a most guilty people.

Doubtless there were many amongst the Midianites who were personally guiltless as regards Israel. But the rulers deliberately adopted the counsel of Balaam against Israel, and their behests had been but too readily obeyed by their subjects. The sin therefore was national, and the retribution could be no less so.

But the commission of the Israelites in the text must not be conceived as a general license to slay. They had no discretion to kill or to spare. They were bidden to exterminate without mercy, and brought back to their task (*v.* 14) when they shewed signs of flinching from it. They had no alterna-

tive in this and similar matters except to fulfil the commands of God; an awful but doubtless salutary manifestation, as was afterwards the slaughter of the Canaanites, of God's wrath against sin; and a type of the future extermination of sin and sinners from His kingdom.

5. *were delivered*] Or, "were told off."

6. *Phinehas*] He was marked out as the fitting director of the expedition by his conduct (cp. xxv. 7-13) in the matter of Zimri and Cozbi.

with the holy instruments, and the trumpets] Or rather, "with the holy instruments, to wit, the trumpets," for the trumpets themselves seem to be the instruments intended.

8. *And they slew...were slain*, &c.] Render: **And the kings of Midian they put to death, beside those that fell in the battle; namely,** &c. From which it would seem that beside these five, put to death after the battle, there were other Midianitish kings who perished fighting. The five chieftains here mentioned were vassals of Sihon the Amorite (Josh. xiii. 21).

five kings of Midian: [o]Balaam also the son of Beor they slew
9 with the sword. And the children of Israel took *all* the women
of Midian captives, and their little ones, and took the spoil of all
10 their cattle, and all their flocks, and all their goods. And they
burnt all their cities wherein they dwelt, and all their goodly
11 castles, with fire. And [h]they took all the spoil, and all the prey,
12 *both* of men and of beasts. And they brought the captives, and
the prey, and the spoil, unto Moses, and Eleazar the priest, and
unto the congregation of the children of Israel, unto the camp
13 at the plains of Moab, which *are* by Jordan *near* Jericho. ¶And
Moses, and Eleazar the priest, and all the princes of the con-
14 gregation, went forth to meet them without the camp. And
Moses was wroth with the officers of the host, *with* the captains
over thousands, and captains over hundreds, which came from
15 the [1]battle. And Moses said unto them, Have ye saved [i]all the
16 women alive? Behold, [k]these caused the children of Israel,
through the [l]counsel of Balaam, to commit trespass against the
LORD in the matter of Peor, and [m]there was a plague among the
17 congregation of the LORD. Now therefore [n]kill every male
among the little ones, and kill every woman that hath known
18 man by lying with [2]him. But all the women children, that have
not known a man by lying with him, keep alive for yourselves.
19 And [o]do ye abide without the camp seven days: whosoever hath
killed any person, and [p]whosoever hath touched any slain,
purify *both* yourselves and your captives on the third day, and
20 on the seventh day. And purify all *your* raiment, and all [3]that
is made of skins, and all work of goats' *hair*, and all things
21 made of wood. ¶And Eleazar the priest said unto the men of
war which went to the battle, This *is* the ordinance of the law
22 which the LORD commanded Moses; only the gold, and the silver,
23 the brass, the iron, the tin, and the lead, every thing that may
abide the fire, ye shall make *it* go through the fire, and it shall be
clean: nevertheless it shall be purified [q]with the water of separation: and all that abideth not the fire ye shall make go through the
24 water. [r]And ye shall wash your clothes on the seventh day, and
ye shall be clean, and afterward ye shall come into the camp.
25, 26 ¶And the LORD spake unto Moses, saying, Take the sum of the
prey [4]that was taken, *both* of man and of beast, thou, and Eleazar
27 the priest, and the chief fathers of the congregation: and [s]divide
the prey into two parts; between them that took the war upon
them, who went out to battle, and between all the congregation:
28 and levy a tribute unto the LORD of the men of war which went
out to battle: [t]one soul of five hundred, *both* of the persons, and

[g] Josh. 13.
22.

[h] Deut. 20.
14.

[i] See Deut.
20. 14.
1 Sam. 15. 3.
[k] ch. 25. 2.
[l] ch. 24. 14.
2 Pet. 2. 15.
Rev. 2. 14.
[m] ch. 25. 9.
[n] Judg. 21.
11.

[o] ch. 5. 2.
[p] ch. 19. 11,
&c.

[q] ch. 19. 9,
17.

[r] Lev. 11. 25.

[s] Josh. 22. 8.
1 Sam. 30.
27.

[t] See ver. 30,
47.
& ch. 18. 26.

---

[1] Heb. *host of war*.
[2] Heb. *a male*.
[3] Heb. *instrument*, or, *vessel of skins*..
[4] Heb. *of the captivity*.

---

10. *goodly castles*] Rather, both here and
in Gen. xxv. 16, **hamlets.** The word is derived from a word (*tōr*) signifying "a row"
or "range" (cp. Ezek. xlvi. 23); and probably indicates those collections of rude dwellings, made of stones piled one on another
and covered with tent-cloths, which are
used by the Arabs to this day; and which
are frequently mentioned as *douars* in narratives of the French campaigns in Algeria.
These dwellings would be formed usually in
a circle. See the word "Hazeroth," in xi. 35.
11. The "prey" refers to the captives

and live-stock: the "spoil" to the ornaments and other effects.
16. *caused...to commit trespass*] More lit.,
"became to the children of Israel for a
cause (or, incitement) of treachery to the
Lord."
22. *brass*] Render **copper.** See Gen. iv. 22
note. The verse is curious as illustrating the
variety of metals in use at this early date
for domestic purposes. All these metals
were common in Egypt centuries before the
date of the Exodus.

29 of the beeves, and of the asses, and of the sheep: take *it* of their
half, and give *it* unto Eleazar the priest, *for* an heave offering
30 of the LORD. And of the children of Israel's half, thou shalt
take ^uone portion of fifty, of the persons, of the beeves, of the
asses, and of the ¹flocks, of all manner of beasts, and give them
unto the Levites, ^xwhich keep the charge of the tabernacle of
31 the LORD. And Moses and Eleazar the priest did as the LORD
32 commanded Moses. And the booty, *being* the rest of the prey
which the men of war had caught, was six hundred thousand and
33 seventy thousand and five thousand sheep, and threescore and
34 twelve thousand beeves, and threescore and one thousand asses,
35 and thirty and two thousand persons in all, of women that had
36 not known man by lying with him. And the half, *which was*
the portion of them that went out to war, was in number three
hundred thousand and seven and thirty thousand and five hun-
37 dred sheep: and the LORD's tribute of the sheep was six hundred
38 and threescore and fifteen. And the beeves *were* thirty and six
thousand; of which the LORD's tribute *was* threescore and
39 twelve. And the asses *were* thirty thousand and five hundred;
40 of which the LORD's tribute *was* threescore and one. And the
persons *were* sixteen thousand; of which the LORD's tribute *was*
41 thirty and two persons. And Moses gave the tribute, *which was*
the LORD's heave offering, unto Eleazar the priest, ^yas the LORD
42 commanded Moses. And of the children of Israel's half, which
43 Moses divided from the men that warred, (now the half *that*
pertained unto the congregation was three hundred thousand and
44 thirty thousand and seven thousand and five hundred sheep, and
45 thirty and six thousand beeves, and thirty thousand asses and
46, 47 five hundred, and sixteen thousand persons;) even ^zof the
children of Israel's half, Moses took one portion of fifty, *both* of
man and of beast, and gave them unto the Levites, which kept
the charge of the tabernacle of the LORD; as the LORD com-
48 manded Moses. ¶ And the officers which *were* over thousands of
the host, the captains of thousands, and captains of hundreds,
49 came near unto Moses: and they said unto Moses, Thy servants
have taken the sum of the men of war which *are* under our
50 ²charge, and there lacketh not one man of us. We have therefore
brought an oblation for the LORD, what every man hath ³gotten,
of jewels of gold, chains, and bracelets, rings, earrings, and

Margin notes:
^u See ver. 42—47.
^x ch. 3. 7, 8, 25, 31, 36. & 18. 3, 4.
^y See ch. 18. 8, 19.
^z ver. 30.

¹ Or, *goats.*   ² Heb. *hand.*   ³ Heb. *found.*

---

29. *an heave-offering*] Render simply **an offering**, and cp. xviii. 24. The verb from which the word here rendered "heave-offering" is derived, is rightly translated "levy" in *v.* 28.

32. Cp. *v.* 11, and render "And the prey" (*i.e.* the live prey) "in addition to the spoil which the men of war seized, &c." The "spoil" is described in *v.* 50.
The number of sheep, beeves, asses, and persons taken is given in this and following verses in round thousands. Hence the Lord's tribute (*vv.* 29, 37, 38, &c.), being the five-hundredth part of the half, comes out also in round numbers. The enormous amount both of live stock and of personal ornament was characteristic of the Midianites. When they invaded Israel in the days

of the Judges, their wealth was still of the same kind (Judg. vi. 5, viii. 24 seq.). The Bedouins, notwithstanding their wild nomadic life, retain their ancestral love of finery to the present day.

49. There is no mention of any resistance on the part of the Midianites. The Israelites saw in this and in the preservation of all those engaged, proofs that the Lord had been with them in the work, and hence the free-will oblation of *v.* 50.

50. The "chains" were "armlets" (2 Sam. i. 10). The "rings" were "finger-rings," or "seal-rings;" and the "tablets" were worn suspended from the neck (Ex. xxxv. 22).

to make an atonement for our souls before the LORD] Cp. Ex. xxx. 11-16. The atonement

tablets, ^ato make an atonement for our souls before the LORD.
51 And Moses and Eleazar the priest took the gold of them, *even* all
52 wrought jewels. And all the gold of the ¹offering that they
offered up to the LORD, of the captains of thousands, and of the
captains of hundreds, was sixteen thousand seven hundred and
53 fifty shekels. (*For* ^bthe men of war had taken spoil, every man
54 for himself.) And Moses and Eleazar the priest took the gold of
the captains of thousands and of hundreds, and brought it into
the tabernacle of the congregation, ^c*for* a memorial for the
children of Israel before the LORD.

CHAP. **32.** NOW the children of Reuben and the children of Gad
had a very great multitude of cattle: and when they saw the
land of ^aJazer, and the land of Gilead, that, behold, the place
2 *was* a place for cattle; the children of Gad and the children of
Reuben came and spake unto Moses, and to Eleazar the priest,
3 and unto the princes of the congregation, saying, Ataroth, and
Dibon, and Jazer, and ^bNimrah, and Heshbon, and Elealeh, and
4 ^cShebam, and Nebo, and ^dBeon, *even* the country ^ewhich the
LORD smote before the congregation of Israel, *is* a land for
5 cattle, and thy servants have cattle: wherefore, said they, if we
have found grace in thy sight, let this land be given unto thy
6 servants for a possession, *and* bring us not over Jordan. And
Moses said unto the children of Gad and to the children of
Reuben, Shall your brethren go to war, and shall ye sit here?
7 And wherefore ²discourage ye the heart of the children of Israel
from going over into the land which the LORD hath given them?
8 Thus did your fathers, ^fwhen I sent them from Kadesh-barnea
9 ^gto see the land. For ^hwhen they went up unto the valley of
Eshcol, and saw the land, they discouraged the heart of the
children of Israel, that they should not go into the land which
10 the LORD had given them. ⁱAnd the LORD's anger was kindled
11 the same time, and he sware, saying, Surely none of the men
that came up out of Egypt, ^kfrom twenty years old and upward,
shall see the land which I sware unto Abraham, unto Isaac, and
12 unto Jacob; because ^lthey have not ³wholly followed me: save
Caleb the son of Jephunneh the Kenezite, and Joshua the son of

¹ Heb. *heave offering.*   ² Heb. *break.*   ³ Heb. *fulfilled after me.*

Margin notes:

^a Ex. 30. 12, 16.

^b Deut. 20. 14.

^c Ex. 30. 16.

^a ch. 21. 32.
Josh. 13. 25.
2 Sam. 24. 5.

^b ver. 36,
Beth-nimrah.
^c ver. 38,
Shibmah.
^d ver. 38,
Baal-meon.
^e ch. 21. 24,
34.

^f ch. 13. 3,
26.
^g Deut. 1. 22.
^h ch. 13. 24,
31.
Deut. 1. 24,
28.
ⁱ ch. 14. 11,
21.
Deut. 1. 34.
^k ch. 14. 28,
29.
Deut. 1. 35.
^l ch. 14. 24,
30.

---

was not for any special offence committed
(which would have called for a sacrifice of
blood-shedding), but rather like the half-
shekel given at the census in Ex. *l. c.*, was
an acknowledgment of having received un-
deserved mercies. These, if unacknow-
ledged, would have entailed guilt on the
soul.

52. The value of the offering was about
20,000*l.*

53. This verse seems to imply that the
soldiers, as distinct from the officers (cp. *v.*
49), did not make any offering from their
plunder. Of course besides the gold there
would be much spoil of less precious materials; see *vv.* 20, 22.

XXXII. The record of the last war to
the east of the Jordan is followed by the assignment of the lands already conquered to
the tribes of Reuben and Gad and to certain families of the tribe of Manasseh.

1. *Jazer*] Cp. marg. ref. This district,
although included in the land of Gilead,
seems to have had especial attractions for
the Israelitish settlers. All travellers in
Gilead, the modern Belka, bear witness to
its richness as compared with the country to
the west of the Jordan. Its general character is that of an upland pasture, undulating
and thickly timbered. In the last respect
its northern portions excel its southern; but
for fertility of soil the southern province is
preferred by the Arabs, in whose lips it has
passed into a proverb: "Thou canst not
find a country like the Belka."

3. See *vv.* 34-38 notes.

8. *your fathers*] The generation of the
Exodus was now substantially extinct. Cp.
xxvi. 64, 65.

Kadesh-barnea] See xiii. 26.

12. *the Kenezite*] Kenaz (Gen. xxxvi. 11)
was the name of one of the "dukes of

m ch. 14. 24.
Deut. 1. 36.
Josh. 14. 8,
9.
n ch. 14. 33,
34, 35.
o ch. 26. 64,
65.
p Deut. 1. 34.
q Deut. 30.
17.
Josh. 22. 16,
18.
2 Chr. 7. 19.
& 15. 2.
r Josh. 4. 12,
13.

s Josh. 22. 4.

t ver. 33.
Josh. 12. 1.
& 13. 8.
u Deut.;3. 18.
Josh. 1. 14.
& 4. 12, 13.

x Deut. 3. 20.
Josh. 11. 23.
y Josh. 22. 4.
z Deut. 3. 12,
15, 16.
Josh. 1. 15.
& 13. 8, 32.
& 22. 4, 9.
a Gen. 4. 7.
& 44. 16.
Isai. 59. 12.
b ver. 16, 34,
&c.
c Josh. 1. 14.
d Josh. 4. 12.

e Josh. 1. 13.

f Deut. 3. 12
—17.
Josh. 12. 6.
g ch. 21. 24,
33, 35.

13 Nun : *m*for they have wholly followed the LORD. And the LORD'S anger was kindled against Israel, and he made them *n*wander in the wilderness forty years, until *o*all the generation, that had 14 done evil in the sight of the LORD, was consumed. And, behold, ye are risen up in your fathers' stead, an increase of sinful men, to augment yet the *p*fierce anger of the LORD toward Israel. 15 For if ye *q*turn away from after him, he will yet again leave them in the wilderness; and ye shall destroy all this people. 16 And they came near unto him, and said, We will build sheep-17 folds here for our cattle, and cities for our little ones: but *r*we ourselves will go ready armed before the children of Israel, until we have brought them unto their place : and our little ones shall dwell in the fenced cities because of the inhabitants of the land. 18 *s*We will not return unto our houses, until the children of Israel 19 have inherited every man his inheritance. For we will not inherit with them on yonder side Jordan, or forward; *t*because our inheritance is fallen to us on this side Jordan eastward. 20 And *u*Moses said unto them, If ye will do this thing, if ye will 21 go armed before the LORD to war, and will go all of you armed over Jordan before the LORD, until he hath driven out his 22 enemies from before him, and *x*the land be subdued before the LORD : then afterward *y*ye shall return, and be guiltless before the LORD, and before Israel; and *z*this land shall be your pos-23 session before the LORD. But if ye will not do so, behold, ye have sinned against the LORD : and be sure *a*your sin will find 24 you out. *b*Build you cities for your little ones, and folds for your sheep; and do that which hath proceeded out of your mouth. 25 And the children of Gad and the children of Reuben spake unto Moses, saying, Thy servants will do as my lord command-26 eth. *c*Our little ones, our wives, our flocks, and all our cattle, 27 shall be there in the cities of Gilead : *d*but thy servants will pass over, every man armed for war, before the LORD to battle, as my 28 lord saith. ¶ So *e*concerning them Moses commanded Eleazar the priest, and Joshua the son of Nun, and the chief fathers of the 29 tribes of the children of Israel : and Moses said unto them, If the children of Gad and the children of Reuben will pass with you over Jordan, every man armed to battle, before the LORD, and the land shall be subdued before you; then ye shall give them the 30 land of Gilead for a possession : but if they will not pass over with you armed, they shall have possessions among you in the land 31 of Canaan. And the children of Gad and the children of Reu-ben answered, saying, As the LORD hath said unto thy servants, 32 so will we do. We will pass over armed before the LORD into the land of Canaan, that the possession of our inheritance on this 33 side Jordan *may be* our's. ¶ And *f*Moses gave unto them, *even* to the children of Gad, and to the children of Reuben, and unto half the tribe of Manasseh the son of Joseph, *g*the kingdom of

---

Edom : " but Israel and Edom were of kin-dred origin, and the use of similar names by the two peoples is not surprising.

23. *be sure your sin will find you out*] Lit. " know ye your sin that it will find you out." Moses implies that their sin would eventually bring its own punishment along with it.

27. *before the* LORD] *i.e.* immediately in front of the sacred tokens of the Lord's Presence ; cp. x. 17 note.

33. *half the tribe of Manasseh*] That is, (cp. *v.* 39; Josh. xvii. 1) the families of Ma-chir. Moses, when assigning to the pastoral tribes the inheritance which they desired, appropriated to these Manassites specially the district they had already subdued, as a reward for their valour and exploits. Thus the whole of the conquered country was provisionally disposed of, and the forward-ness and valour of the Machirites rewarded. It seems clear from *v.* 39 and Josh. xvii. 1,

Sihon king of the Amorites, and the kingdom of Og king of
Bashan, the land, with the cities thereof in the coasts, *even* the
34 cities of the country round about.   And the children of Gad
35 built *h* Dibon, and Ataroth, and *i* Aroer, and Atroth, Shophan, and
36 *k* Jaazer, and Jogbehah, and *l* Beth-nimrah, and Beth-haran,
37 *m* fenced cities: and folds for sheep.   And the children of
38 Reuben *n* built Heshbon, and Elealeh, and Kirjathaim, and
o Nebo, and *p* Baal-meon, (*q* their names being changed,) and
Shibmah: and ¹gave other names unto the cities which they
39 builded.   And the children of *r* Machir the son of Manasseh
went to Gilead, and took it, and dispossessed the Amorite which
40 *was* in it.   And Moses *s* gave Gilead unto Machir the son of
41 Manasseh; and he dwelt therein.   And *t* Jair the son of Manasseh went and took the small towns thereof, and called them
42 *u* Havoth-jair.   And Nobah went and took Kenath, and the villages thereof, and called it Nobah, after his own name.

¹ Heb. *they called by names the names of the cities.*

h ch. 33. 45.
i Deut. 2. 36,
k ver. 1. 3,
Jazer.
l ver. 3,
Nimrah.
m ver. 24.
n ch. 21. 27.
o Isai. 46. 1.
p ch. 22. 41.
q See ver. 3.
Ex. 23. 13.
Josh. 23. 7.
r Gen. 50. 23.
s Deut. 3. 12,
13, 16.
Josh. 13. 31.
& 17. 1.
t Deut. 3. 14.
Josh. 13. 30.
1 Chr. 2. 21,
22, 23.
u Judg.10. 4.
1 Kin. 4. 13.

---

that the claims of the Machirites arose simply out of their exploits.

34-36. The cities here named fall into three
groups. On *Dibon*, cp. xxi. 19. The Moabite
stone was discovered here in 1868. This
city, occupied on the first acquisition of the
territory by the Gadites, and assigned by
Joshua to the Reubenites, was eventually
recaptured by the Moabites, in whose hands
it remained.   *Ataroth, i.e.* " crowns " (? At-
târûs) was seven miles north-west of Dibon.
Aroer (Arâir) lay between Dibon and the
Arnon.

Atroth, Shophan, was **Atroth-Shophan,**
i.e. Atroth, or Ataroth of Shophan, or " of
the burrow; " thus distinguished from the
Ataroth named in the verse preceding from
which it was probably not far distant.
These four cities may be styled the Dibon
settlement.

35. *Jaazer* (cp. *v.* 1) with the neighbouring *Jogbehah* (Jebeiha), seven miles to the
north-east, formed the second group.

36. The third Gadite settlement lay in
the valley of the Jordan, to the west of the
preceding. It comprised the cities of *Beth-
nimrah* (Nimrun) and *Beth-haran* (Beit-ha-
ran).

37, 38. The Reubenites established themselves more compactly than the Gadites.
Elealeh (el-'Al) a mile to the north-east;
Nebo (Nebbeh) probably three miles to the
south-west ; *Baal-meon* (Main) nearly two
miles to the south ; *Kirjathaim* (? Kureiyat) : and *Shibmah*, more properly Sibmah,
famous at a later period for its vines (cp.
Isai. xvi. 8), four miles east of Heshbon ;—
all clustered round the old Amoritish Capital. The Reubenites probably retained at
the partition all these cities with the exception of Heshbon, which, passing to the
Levites, were thenceforth reckoned as within the tribe of Gad.

Neither the Reubenites nor the Gadites
were "builders" in the sense of founders of
the cities of which they thus took posses-

sion. They probably fortified them, for the
first time or afresh, so as to render them
places of safety for their families during
the campaigns on the other side of the Jordan ; and provided them with all conveni-
ences for their flocks and herds.

39. *the children of Machir*] Machir, the
son of Manasseh, was long since dead :
even his sons had been brought up upon
Joseph's knees (Gen. l. 23). But the renown
acquired by his descendants raised his family almost to the dignity of a tribe ; and
the Machirites are in the next verse styled
Machir, just as the children of Judah or of
Ephraim are often spoken of as Judah or
Ephraim. So in Judg. v. 14 Machir is
coupled with Ephraim and Zebulun.

went] *i.e.* "had gone : " the statement is
preparatory to the ensuing record of the
grant to them of the land they had won.

Gilead] More strictly part of north Gilead ; which, though inhabited by the
Amorites, had belonged to the kingdom of
Og. Gilead was the district from which had
sprung the ancestress of the Machirites (cp.
1 Chron. vii. 14).

41. The exploits of Jair—he was the conqueror of Argob (Deut. iii. 14)—gave new
lustre to his name ; and the fame of the
family is attested by the history of Jair the
Israelitish judge, doubtless a descendant ;
perhaps also by the mention of Jairus (Luke
viii. 41), the ruler of the synagogue at the
neighbouring city of Capernaum.

Havoth-jair] That is, the villages, or rather groups of tents, or "kraals," of Jair.
Originally they were twenty-three in number (1 Chr. ii. 22): in the days of the younger
Jair, to whom they probably descended by
inheritance, they either had increased to
thirty, or were reckoned at that round
number (Judg. x. 4).

42. *Kenath*] Now Kenawât, an important
site near the southern extremity of the
tract el-Lejah, and on the western slopes of
the mountains of the Haurân. The name

CHAP. 33. THESE *are* the journeys of the children of Israel, which
went forth out of the land of Egypt with their armies under the
2 hand of Moses and Aaron. And Moses wrote their goings out according to their journeys by the commandment of the LORD : and
3 these *are* their journeys according to their goings out. ¶ And
they *a*departed from Rameses in *b*the first month, on the fifteenth day of the first month ; on the morrow after the passover
the children of Israel went out *c*with an high hand in the sight
4 of all the Egyptians. For the Egyptians buried all *their* firstborn, *d*which the LORD had smitten among them : *e*upon their
5 gods also the LORD executed judgments. *f*And the children of
6 Israel removed from Rameses, and pitched in Succoth. And
they departed from *g*Succoth, and pitched in Etham, which *is* in
7 the edge of the wilderness. And *h*they removed from Etham,
and turned again unto Pi-hahiroth, which *is* before Baal-zephon ;
8 and they pitched before Migdol. And they departed from before
Pi-hahiroth, and *i*passed through the midst of the sea into the
wilderness, and went three days' journey in the wilderness of
9 Etham, and pitched in Marah. And they removed from Marah,
and *k*came unto Elim : and in Elim *were* twelve fountains of
water, and threescore and ten palm trees ; and they pitched
10 there. And they removed from Elim, and encamped by the
11 Red sea. And they removed from the Red sea, and encamped in
12 the *l*wilderness of Sin. And they took their journey out of the
13 wilderness of Sin, and encamped in Dophkah. And they de-
14 parted from Dophkah, and encamped in Alush. And they
removed from Alush, and encamped at *m*Rephidim, where was
15 no water for the people to drink. And they departed from
16 Rephidim, and pitched in the *n*wilderness of Sinai. And they
removed from the desert of Sinai, and pitched *o*at ¹Kibroth-
17 hattaavah. And they departed from Kibroth-hattaavah, and
18 *p*encamped at Hazeroth. And they departed from Hazeroth,

a Ex. 12. 37.
b Ex. 12. 2.
& 13. 4.
c Ex. 14. 8.

d Ex. 12. 29.
e Ex. 12. 12.
& 18. 11.
Isai. 19. 1.
Rev. 12. 8.
f Ex. 12. 37.
g Ex. 13. 20.
h Ex. 14. 2, 9.

i Ex. 14. 22.
& 15. 22, 23.

k Ex. 15. 27.

l Ex. 16. 1.

m Ex. 17. 1.
& 19. 2.

n Ex. 16. 1.
& 19. 1, 2.
o ch. 11. 34.

p ch. 11. 35.

¹ That is, *The graves of lust.*

---

given to it by its conqueror, as in other
cases, fell ere long into disuse, and the old
name has held its ground to this day.

The notices, both Scriptural and traditional, of the conquest of north-eastern
Gilead and Bashan by the Machirites,
plainly intimate that it was effected by a
few chiefs of great military prowess, who
overran rapidly a far larger district than
they could colonize. The father of Jair,
however, Segub, was of the tribe of Judah
(cp. xxvii. 1, and note; 1 Chr. ii. 21, 22),
and it is likely that the Manassite leaders
induced many of the more adventurous of
this tribe, and some possibly of other tribes,
to join them in their enterprize against
Bashan (see Josh. xix. 34).

The Machirites did not exterminate the
whole population of this district (see Josh.
xiii. 15, &c). The conquest of the district
east of Jordan seems never to have been so
effectually accomplished as that on the other
side.

During the troublous times of the Judges
the eastern Manassites rendered good service to the nation; cp. Judg. v. 14. Gideon,
and probably Jephthah, were of this tribe,

and reflect in a later generation the warlike
and adventurous spirit which Jair and Nobah exhibited in the days of Moses.

XXXIII. 1-49. This list was written
out by Moses at God's command (*v.* 2),
doubtless as a memorial of His people throughout this long
and trying period.

3-6. For these places, see marg. reff.

8. *Pi-hahiroth*] Heb. "Hahiroth," but
perhaps only by an error of transcription.
The omitted "pi" is however only a common Egyptian prefix.

wilderness of Etham] *i.e.* that part of the
great wilderness of Shur which adjoined
Etham ; cp. Ex. xv. 22 note.

The list of stations up to that at Sinai
agrees with the narrative of Exodus except
that we have here mentioned (*v.* 10) an
encampment by the Red Sea, and two
others, Dophkah and Alush (*vv.* 12-14),
which are there omitted. On these places
see Ex. xvii. 1 note.

16, 17. See xi. 35 note.

18. *Rithmah*] The name of this station is
derived from *retem*, the broom-plant, the
"juniper" of the A. V. This must be the

19 and pitched in ^qRithmah. And they departed from Rithmah, q ch. 12. 16.
20 and pitched at Rimmon-parez. And they departed from Rim-
21 mon-parez, and pitched in Libnah. And they removed from
22 Libnah, and pitched at Rissah. And they journeyed from
23 Rissah, and pitched in Kehelathah. And they went from Kehe-
24 lathah, and pitched in mount Shapher. And they removed from
25 mount Shapher, and encamped in Haradah. And they re-
26 moved from Haradah, and pitched in Makheloth. And they re-
27 moved from Makheloth, and encamped at Tahath. And they
28 departed from Tahath, and pitched at Tarah. And they re-
29 moved from Tarah, and pitched in Mithcah. And they went
30 from Mithcah, and pitched in Hashmonah. And they departed
31 from Hashmonah, and ^rencamped at Moseroth. And they
32 departed from Moseroth, and pitched in Bene-jaakan. And they
removed from ^sBene-jaakan, and ^tencamped at Hor-hagidgad.
33 And they went from Hor-hagidgad, and pitched in Jotbathah.
34 And they removed from Jotbathah, and encamped at Ebronah.
35 And they departed from Ebronah, ^uand encamped at Ezion-
36 gaber. And they removed from Ezion-gaber, and pitched in the
37 ^wwilderness of Zin, which *is* Kadesh. And they removed from
^xKadesh, and pitched in mount Hor, in the edge of the land of
38 Edom. ¶And ^yAaron the priest went up into mount Hor at
the commandment of the LORD, and died there, in the fortieth
year after the children of Israel were come out of the land of
39 Egypt, in the first *day* of the fifth month. And Aaron *was* an
hundred and twenty and three years old when he died in mount
40 Hor. ¶And ^zking Arad the Canaanite, which dwelt in the
south in the land of Canaan, heard of the coming of the children
41 of Israel. ¶And they departed from mount ^a Hor, and pitched
42 in Zalmonah. And they departed from Zalmonah, and pitched
43 in Punon. And they departed from Punon, and ^bpitched in
44 Oboth. And ^cthey departed from Oboth, and pitched in ^{1d}Ije-
45 abarim, in the border of Moab. And they departed from Iim,

¹ Or, *Heaps of Abarim.*

Marginal notes:
r Deut. 10. 6.
s See Gen. 36. 27.
Deut. 10. 6.
1 Chr. 1. 42.
t Deut. 10. 7.
u Deut. 2. 8.
1 Kin. 9. 26.
& 22. 48.
w ch. 20. 1.
& 27. 14.
x ch. 20. 22, 23.
& 21. 4.
y ch. 20. 25, 28.
Deut. 10. 6.
& 32. 50.
z ch. 21. 1, &c.
a ch. 21. 4.
b ch. 21. 10.
c ch. 21. 11.
d ch. 21. 11.

---

same encampment as that which is said in
xiii. 26 to have been at Kadesh.

19. *Rimmon-parez*] Or rather **Rimmon-perez**, *i.e.* "Rimmon (*i.e.* the Pomegranate) of the Breach." It may have been here that the sedition of Korah occurred.

19–36. The stations named are those visited during the years of penal wandering. The determination of their positions is, in many cases, difficult, because during this period there was no definite line of march pursued. But it is probable that the Israelites during this period did not overstep the boundaries of the Wilderness of Paran (as defined in x. 12), except to pass along the adjoining valley of the Arabah ; while the Tabernacle and organized camp moved about from place to place amongst them (cp. xx. 1).

Rissah, Haradah, and *Tahath* are probably the same as Rasa, Aradeh, and Elthi of the Roman tables. The position of Hashmonah (Heshmon in Josh. xv. 27) in the Azazimeh mountains points out the road followed by the children of Israel to be that which skirts the south-western extremity of Jebel Magrah.

34. *Ebronah*] *i.e,* "passage." This station apparently lay on the shore of the Elanitic gulf, at a point where the ebb of the tide left a ford across. Hence the later Targum renders the word "fords."

35. *Ezion-gaber*] "Giant's backbone." The Wâdy Ghadhyân, a valley running eastward into the Arabah some miles north of the present head of the Elanitic gulf. A salt marsh which here overspreads a portion of the Arabah may be taken as indicating the limit to which the sea anciently reached ; and we may thus infer the existence here in former times of an extensive tidal haven, at the head of which the city of Ezion-geber stood. Here it was that from the time of Solomon onward the Jewish navy was constructed (1 Kings ix. 26, xxii. 49).

41–49. *Zalmonah* and *Punon* are stations on the Pilgrim's road ; and the general route is fairly ascertained by a comparison of these verses with xxi. 4, &c.

*ch. 32. 34.
Ez. 6. 14.
ᵍ ch. 21. 20.
Deut. 32. 49.
ʰ ch. 22. 1.

ⁱ ch. 25. 1.
Josh. 2. 1.

ᵏ Deut. 7. 1, 2.
& 9. 1.
Josh. 3. 17.
ˡ Ex. 23. 24, 33. & 34. 13.
Deut. 7. 2, 5.
& 12. 3.
Josh. 11. 12.
Judg. 2. 2.
ᵐ ch. 26. 53, 54, 55.

ⁿ Josh. 23. 13.
Judg. 2. 3.
Ps. 106. 34, 36.
See Ex. 23, 33.
Ez. 28. 24.
ᵃ Gen. 17. 8.
Deut. 1. 7.
Ps. 78. 55.
& 105. 11.
Ez. 47. 14.
ᵇ Josh. 15. 1.
See Ez. 47. 13, &c.
ᶜ Gen. 14. 3.
Josh. 15. 2.
ᵈ Josh. 15. 3.
ᵉ ch. 13. 26.
& 32. 8.

46 and pitched ᵉin Dibon-gad. And they removed from Dibon-
47 gad, and encamped in Almon ƒ-diblathaim. And they removed
from Almon-diblathaim, ᵍand pitched in the mountains of
48 Abarim, before Nebo. And they departed from the mountains
of Abarim, and ʰpitched in the plains of Moab by Jordan near
49 Jericho. And they pitched by Jordan, from Beth-jesimoth even
50 unto ¹ⁱAbel-shittim in the plains of Moab. ¶And the LORD
spake unto Moses in the plains of Moab by Jordan near Jericho,
51 saying, Speak unto the children of Israel, and say unto them,
52 ᵏWhen ye are passed over Jordan into the land of Canaan; ˡthen
ye shall drive out all the inhabitants of the land from before
you, and destroy all their pictures, and destroy all their molten
53 images, and quite pluck down all their high places: and ye shall
dispossess the inhabitants of the land, and dwell therein: for I
54 have given you the land to possess it. And ᵐye shall divide the
land by lot for an inheritance among your families: and to the
more ye shall ²give the more inheritance, and to the fewer ye
shall ³give the less inheritance: every man's inheritance shall be
in the place where his lot falleth; according to the tribes of your
55 fathers ye shall inherit. But if ye will not drive out the inhabitants of the land from before you; then it shall come to pass,
that those which ye let remain of them shall be ⁿpricks in your
eyes, and thorns in your sides, and shall vex you in the land
56 wherein ye dwell. Moreover it shall come to pass, that I shall
do unto you, as I thought to do unto them.

CHAP. 34. AND the LORD spake unto Moses, saying, Command the
2 children of Israel, and say unto them, When ye come into ᵃthe
land of Canaan; (this is the land that shall fall unto you for an
inheritance, even the land of Canaan with the coasts thereof:)
3 ¶Then ᵇyour south quarter shall be from the wilderness of Zin
along by the coast of Edom, and your south border shall be the
4 outmost coast of ᶜthe salt sea eastward: and your border shall
turn from the south ᵈto the ascent of Akrabbim, and pass on to
Zin: and the going forth thereof shall be from the south ᵉto

¹ Or, The plains of Shittim.   ² Heb. multiply his inheri-   ³ Heb. diminish his inheri-
                               tance.   tance.

50-56. The expulsion of the Canaanites and the destruction of their monuments of idolatry had been already enjoined (see marg. reff.); and v. 54 is substantially a repetition from Ex. xxvi. 53-55. But the solemn warning of vv. 55, 56 is new. A call for it had been furnished by their past transgressions in the matter of Baal-peor, and by their imperfect fulfilment, at the first, of Moses' orders in the Midianitish war.

XXXIV. 2. the land of Canaan] The name Canaan is here restricted to the territory west of the Jordan.

3-5. The southern boundary commenced at the Dead Sea. The broad and desolate valley by which the depressed bed of that sea is protected toward the south, is called the Ghôr. A deep narrow glen enters it at its south-west corner; it is called Wâdy-el-Fikreh, and is continued in the same south-western direction, under the name of Wady el-Marrah; a wady which loses itself among

the hills belonging to "the wilderness of Zin;" and Kadesh-barnea (see xiii. 26 note), which is "in the wilderness of Zin," will be, as the text implies, the southern-most point of the southern boundary. Thence, if Kadesh be identical with the present Ain el-Weibeh, westward to the river, or brook of Egypt, now Wady el-Arish, is a distance of about seventy miles. In this interval were Hazar-addar and Azmon; the former being perhaps the general name of a district of Hazerim, or nomad hamlets (see Deut. ii. 23), of which Addar was one: and Azmon, perhaps to be identified with Kesam, the modern Kasâimeh, a group of springs situate in the north of one of the gaps in the ridge, and a short distance west of Ain el-Kudeirât.

[Others consider the boundary line to have followed the Ghôr along the Arabah to the south of the Azazimeh mountains, thence to Gadis round the south-east of that mountain, and thence to Wady el-Arish.]

Kadesh-barnea, and shall go on to *f*Hazar-addar, and pass on to
5 Azmon : and the border shall fetch a compass from Azmon
*g*unto the river of Egypt, and the goings out of it shall be at the
6 sea. ¶And *as for* the western border, ye shall even have
the great sea for a border : this shall be your west border.
7 ¶And this shall be your north border : from the great sea ye
8 shall point out for you *h*mount Hor : from mount Hor ye shall
point out *your border* *i*unto the entrance of Hamath ; and the
9 goings forth of the border shall be to *k*Zedad : and the border
shall go on to Ziphron, and the goings out of it shall be at
10 *l*Hazar-enan : this shall be your north border. ¶And ye shall
11 point out your east border from Hazar-enan to Shepham : and
the coast shall go down from Shepham *m*to Riblah, on the east
side of Ain ; and the border shall descend, and shall reach unto
12 the *1*side of the sea *n*of Chinnereth eastward : and the border
shall go down to Jordan, and the goings out of it shall be at
*o*the salt sea : this shall be your land with the coasts thereof
13 round about. ¶And Moses commanded the children of Israel,
saying, *p*This *is* the land which ye shall inherit by lot, which the
LORD commanded to give unto the nine tribes, and to the half
14 tribe : *q*for the tribe of the children of Reuben according to the
house of their fathers, and the tribe of the children of Gad
according to the house of their fathers, have received *their*
15 *inheritance* ; and half the tribe of Manasseh have received
their inheritance : the two tribes and the half tribe have received
their inheritance on this side Jordan *near* Jericho eastward,
16 toward the sunrising. ¶And the LORD spake unto Moses,
17 saying, These *are* the names of the men which shall divide the
land unto you : *r*Eleazar the priest, and Joshua the son of Nun.
18 And ye shall take one *s*prince of every tribe, to divide the land
19 by inheritance. And the names of the men *are* these : of the
20 tribe of Judah, Caleb the son of Jephunneh. And of the tribe of

f See Josh.
15. 3, 4.

g Gen. 15.18.
Josh. 15. 4,
47.
1 Kin. 8. 65.
Isai. 27. 12.

h ch. 33. 37.
i ch. 13. 21.
2 Kin. 14.
25.
k Ezek. 47.
15.
l Ezek. 47.
17.

m 2 Kin. 23.
33.
Jer. 39. 5, 6.
n Deut. 3. 17.
Josh. 11. 2.
& 19. 35.
Matt. 14. 34.
Luke 5. 1.
o ver. 3.
p ver. 1.
Josh. 14. 1,
2.
q ch. 32. 33.
Josh. 14. 2,
3.

r Josh. 14. 1.
& 19. 51.
s ch. 1. 4, 16.

1 Heb. *shoulder.*

7—9. The northern border. On the
"mount Hor," cp. xx. 22 note. Here the
name denotes the whole western crest of
Mount Lebanon, eighty miles in length,
commencing east of Zidon, and terminating
with the point immediately above the entrance of Hamath (cp. xiii. 21). The extreme point in the northern border of the
land was the city of Zedad (Sadad), about
thirty miles east of the entrance of Hamath.
Hence the border turned back south-westward to Ziphron (Zifrân), about forty miles
north-east of Damascus. Hazar-enan may
be conjecturally identified with Ayûn ed-
Dara, a fountain situate in the very heart
of the great central chain of Antilibanus.

10—12. Shepham, the first point after
Hazar-enan, is unknown. The name Riblah is by some read Har-bel, *i.e.* "the
Mountain of Bel ;" the Har-baal-Hermon
of Judg. iii. 3. No more striking landmark
could be set forth than the summit of Hermon, the southernmost and by far the
loftiest peak of the whole Antilibanus
range, rising to a height of ten thousand
feet, and overtopping every other mountain

in the Holy Land. Ain, *i.e.* the fountain, is
understood to be the fountain of the Jordan ;
and it is in the plain at the south-western
foot of Hermon that the two most celebrated sources of that river, those of
Daphne and of Paneas, are situate.
The "sea of Chinnereth" is better known
by its later name of Gennesaret, which is
supposed to be only a corruption of Chinnereth. The border ran parallel to this sea,
along the line of hill about ten miles further
east.

16—29. Of the representatives now selected
through Moses beforehand, who were all
princes, *i.e.* heads of chief families, in their
respective tribes (see xiii. 2), Caleb alone,
of the tribe of Judah, is otherwise known
to us (see xiii. 4 seq.). The order in which
the tribes are named is peculiar to this passage. If they be taken in pairs, Judah and
Simeon, Benjamin and Dan, Manasseh and
Ephraim, Zebulun and Issachar, Asher and
Naphtali, the order of the pairs agrees with
the order in which the allotments in the
Holy Land, taken also in couples, followed
each other in the map from south to north.

21 the children of Simeon, Shemuel the son of Ammihud. Of the
22 tribe of Benjamin, Elidad the son of Chislon. And the prince of
23 the tribe of the children of Dan, Bukki the son of Jogli. The
prince of the children of Joseph, for the tribe of the children of
24 Manasseh, Hanniel the son of Ephod. And the prince of the
tribe of the children of Ephraim, Kemuel the son of Shiphtan.
25 And the prince of the tribe of the children of Zebulun, Elizaphan
26 the son of Parnach. And the prince of the tribe of the children
27 of Issachar, Paltiel the son of Azzan. And the prince of the
28 tribe of the children of Asher, Ahihud the son of Shelomi. And
the prince of the tribe of the children of Naphtali, Pedahel the
29 son of Ammihud. These *are they* whom the LORD commanded
to divide the inheritance unto the children of Israel in the land of
Canaan.

CHAP. 35. AND the LORD spake unto Moses in the plains of Moab
2 by Jordan *near* Jericho, saying, *a* Command the children of Israel,
that they give unto the Levites of the inheritance of their possession cities to dwell in; and ye shall give *also* unto the Levites
3 suburbs for the cities round about them. And the cities shall
they have to dwell in; and the suburbs of them shall be for
4 their cattle, and for their goods, and for all their beasts. And
the suburbs of the cities, which ye shall give unto the Levites,
shall reach from the wall of the city and outward a thousand
5 cubits round about. And ye shall measure from without the
city on the east side two thousand cubits, and on the south side
two thousand cubits, and on the west side two thousand cubits,
and on the north side two thousand cubits; and the city *shall be*
in the midst: this shall be to them the suburbs of the cities.
6 And among the cities which ye shall give unto the Levites *there
shall be* *b* six cities for refuge, which ye shall appoint for the
manslayer, that he may flee thither: and [1] to them ye shall add
7 forty and two cities. *So* all the cities which ye shall give to the
Levites shall be *c* forty and eight cities: them *shall ye give* with
8 their suburbs. And the cities which ye shall give *shall be* *d* of
the possession of the children of Israel: *e* from *them that have*
many ye shall give many; but from *them that have* few ye shall
give few: every one shall give of his cities unto the Levites
9 according to his inheritance which [2] he inheriteth. ¶ And the
10 LORD spake unto Moses, saying, Speak unto the children of

a Josh. 14. 3,
4.
& 21. 2.
See Ez.
45. 1, &c.
& 48. 8, &c.

b ver. 13.
Deut. 4. 41.
Josh. 20. 2,
7, 8.
& 21. 3, 13,
21, 27, 32, 36,
38.
c Josh. 21.
41.
d Josh. 21. 3.
e ch. 26. 54.

[1] Heb. *above them ye shall give.*   [2] Heb. *they inherit.*

XXXV. **2.** *suburbs*] Rather, "pasture-
grounds," required for their large cattle,
for their sheep and goats, and for all their
beasts whatsoever they might be (*v.* 3).
   5. *from without the city*] Omit "from."
The demarcation here intended would run
parallel to the wall of the city, outside
which it was made. To guard against any
restrictions of area, due to such causes as
the irregular forms of the cities or the physical obstacles of the ground, it was ordained
that the suburb should, alike on north,
south, east, and west, present, at a distance
of a thousand cubits (or, nearly one-third of
a mile) from the wall, a front not less than
two thousand cubits in length; and, by
joining the extremities of these measured
fronts according to the nature of the

ground, a sufficient space for the Levites
would be secured.
   6. The Levitical cities were in an especial
manner the Lord's; and therefore the places
of refuge, where the manslayer might remain under the protection of a special institution devised by Divine mercy, were appropriately selected from amongst them.
No doubt also the Priests and Levites
would be the fittest persons to administer
the law in the doubtful cases which would
be sure to occur: cp. *v.* 24 note.
   8. Nine cities were eventually given to
the Levites from the large joint inheritance
of Judah and Simeon; three were taken
from the territory of Naphtali, and the
other tribes gave each four apiece.

Israel, and say unto them, *f* When ye be come over Jordan into *f* Deut. 19.2.
11 the land of Canaan; then *g* ye shall appoint you cities to be Josh. 20. 2.
cities of refuge for you; that the slayer may flee thither, which *g* Ex. 21. 13.
12 killeth any person ¹at unawares. *h* And they shall be unto you *h* Deut. 19.6.
cities for refuge from the avenger; that the manslayer die not, Josh. 20. 3,
13 until he stand before the congregation in judgment. And of 5, 6.
these cities which ye shall give *i* six cities shall ye have for refuge. *i* ver. 6.
14 *k* Ye shall give three cities on this side Jordan, and three cities *k* Deut. 4. 41.
shall ye give in the land of Canaan, *which* shall be cities of Josh. 20. 8.
15 refuge. These six cities shall be a refuge, *both* for the children
of Israel, and *l* for the stranger, and for the sojourner among *l* ch. 15. 16.
them: that every one that killeth any person unawares may flee
16 thither. *m* And if he smite him with an instrument of iron, so *m* Ex. 21. 12,
that he die, he *is* a murderer: the murderer shall surely be put 14.
17 to death. And if he smite him ²with throwing a stone, where- Lev. 24. 17.
with he may die, and he die, he *is* a murderer: the murderer Deut. 19. 11,
18 shall surely be put to death. Or *if* he smite him with an hand 12.
weapon of wood, wherewith he may die, and he die, he *is* a
19 murderer: the murderer shall surely be put to death. *n* The *n* ver. 21, 24,
revenger of blood himself shall slay the murderer: when he 27.
20 meeteth him, he shall slay him. But *o* if he thrust him of hatred, Deut. 19. 6,
21 or hurl at him *p* by laying of wait, that he die; or in enmity Josh. 20.3,5.
smite him with his hand, that he die: he that smote *him* shall *o* Gen. 4. 8.
surely be put to death; *for* he *is* a murderer: the revenger of 2 Sam. 3. 27.
22 blood shall slay the murderer, when he meeteth him. But if & 20. 10.
he thrust him suddenly *q* without enmity, or have cast upon him 1 Kin. 2. 31,
23 any thing without laying of wait, or with any stone, wherewith 32.
a man may die, seeing *him* not, and cast *it* upon him, that he *p* Ex. 21. 14.
24 die, and *was* not his enemy, neither sought his harm: then *r* the Deut. 19. 11.
congregation shall judge between the slayer and the revenger of *q* Ex. 21.13.

r ver. 12.
Josh. 20. 6.

¹ Heb. *by error.*   ² Heb. *with a stone of the hand.*

---

12. *the avenger*] Heb. *goel*, a term of which the original import is uncertain. The very obscurity of its etymology testifies to the antiquity of the office which it denotes. That office rested on the principle of Gen. ix. 6, "whoso sheddeth man's blood, by man shall his blood be shed." The unwritten code of the East conceded to the nearest kinsman of a murdered man the right of avenging the blood that had been shed. Such rude justice necessarily involved grave evils. It gave no opportunity to the person charged with crime of establishing his innocence; it recognised no distinction between murder, manslaughter, and accidental homicide; it perpetuated family blood-feuds, the avenger of blood being liable to be treated in his turn as a murderer by the kinsman of the man whom he had slain. These grievances could not be removed as long as there was no central government, but they might be mitigated; and to do this was the object of the institution in the text (cp. Ex. xxi. 13).

Among the Arab tribes, who are under the control of no central authority, the practice of blood-revenge subsists in full force to the present day.

12. *the congregation*] *i.e.* local court, con-

sisting of the elders of the city (Josh. xx. 4).

16-25. The sense is: Inasmuch as to take another man's life by any means soever is murder, and exposes the murderer to the penalty of retaliation; so, if the deed be done in enmity, it is in truth very murder, and the murderer shall be slain; but if it be not done in enmity, then the congregation shall interpose to stay the avenger's hand.

19. *when he meeteth him*] Provided, of course, it were without a city of refuge.

24. The case of the innocent slayer is here contemplated. In a doubtful case there would necessarily have to be a judicial decision as to the guilt or innocence of the person who claimed the right of asylum.

25. The homicide was safe only within the walls of his city of refuge. He became a virtual exile from his home. The provisions here made serve to mark the gravity of the act of manslaughter, even when not premeditated; and the inconveniences attending on them fell, as is right and fair, upon him who committed the deed.

unto the death of the high priest] The atoning death of the Saviour cast its shadow before on the statute-book of the Law and

25 blood according to these judgments: and the congregation shall
deliver the slayer out of the hand of the revenger of blood, and the
congregation shall restore him to the city of his refuge, whither
s Josh. 20. 6.   he was fled: and *s*he shall abide in it unto the death of the high
t Ex. 29. 7.   26 priest, *t*which was anointed with the holy oil. But if the slayer
Lev. 4. 3.
& 21. 10.   shall at any time come without the border of the city of his
27 refuge, whither he was fled; and the revenger of blood find him
without the borders of the city of his refuge, and the revenger of
28 blood kill the slayer; ¹he shall not be guilty of blood: because
he should have remained in the city of his refuge until the death
of the high priest: but after the death of the high priest the
29 slayer shall return into the land of his possession. So these
u ch. 27. 11.   *things* shall be for *u*a statute of judgment unto you throughout
30 your generations in all your dwellings. ¶ Whoso killeth any
x Deut. 17. 6.   person, the murderer shall be put to death by the *x*mouth of wit-
& 19. 15.   nesses: but one witness shall not testify against any person *to*
Matt. 18. 16.
2 Cor. 13. 1.   31 *cause him* to die. Moreover ye shall take no satisfaction for the
Heb. 10. 28.   life of a murderer, which *is* ²guilty of death: but he shall be
32 surely put to death. And ye shall take no satisfaction for him
that is fled to the city of his refuge, that he should come again
33 to dwell in the land, until the death of the priest. So ye shall
y Ps. 106. 38.   not pollute the land wherein ye *are:* for blood *y*it defileth the
Mic. 4. 11.   land: and ³the land cannot be cleansed of the blood that is shed
z Gen. 9. 6.   34 therein, but *z*by the blood of him that shed it. *a*Defile not
a Lev. 18. 25.   therefore the land which ye shall inhabit, wherein I dwell: for
Deut. 21. 23.
b Ex. 29. 45,   *b*I the LORD dwell among the children of Israel.
46.   CHAP. 36. AND the chief fathers of the families of the *a*children of
a ch. 26. 29.   Gilead, the son of Machir, the son of Manasseh, of the families
of the sons of Joseph, came near, and spake before Moses, and
before the princes, the chief fathers of the children of Israel:
b ch. 26. 55.   2 and they said, *b*The LORD commanded my lord to give the land
& 33. 54.   for an inheritance by lot to the children of Israel: and *c*my
Josh. 17. 3.
c ch. 27. 1, 7.   lord was commanded by the LORD to give the inheritance of
Josh. 17. 3,   3 Zelophehad our brother unto his daughters. And if they be
4.   married to any of the sons of the *other* tribes of the children of

¹ Heb. *no blood* shall be *to*   ³ Heb. *there can be no ex-*
him, Ex. 22. 2.   *piation for the land.*
² Heb. *faulty to die.*

---

on the annals of Jewish history. The High-
priest, as the head and representative of
the whole chosen family of sacerdotal mediators, as exclusively entrusted with some of
the chief priestly functions, as alone privi-
leged to make yearly atonement within the
Holy of Holies, and to gain, from the mysterious Urim and Thummim, special revelations of the will of God, was, preeminently,
a type of Christ. And thus the death of
each successive High-priest presignified that
death of Christ by which the captives were
to be freed, and the remembrance of transgressions made to cease.

30. *by the mouth of witnesses*] *i.e.* two
witnesses, at the least (cp. marg. reff.).
The provisions of this and the following
verses protect the enactments of this chapter from abuse. The cities of refuge were
not intended to exempt a criminal from deserved punishment.

31. *no satisfaction*] Rather, **ransom** (see
Ex. xxi. 30). The permission to demand
pecuniary compensation for murders (expressly sanctioned by the Koran) undoubtedly mitigates, in practice, the system
of private retaliation ; but it does so by
sacrificing the principle named in *vv.* 12, 33.

34. *for I the* LORD *dwell,* &c.] An emphatic protest against all enactment or re-
laxation of laws by men for their own private convenience.

XXXVI. **1-13.** The daughters of Zelophehad had obtained an ordinance (xxviii.
6-11) which permitted the daughters of an
Israelite dying without male issue to inherit their father's property. The chiefs of
the Machirites, of whom Zelophehad had
been one, now obtain a supplemental enactment, directing that heiresses should **marry**
within their own tribe.

Israel, then shall their inheritance be taken from the inheritance of our fathers, and shall be put to the inheritance of the tribe [1]whereunto they are received: so shall it be taken from the lot
4 of our inheritance. And when [d]the jubile of the children of   *d* Lev. 25. 10. Israel shall be, then shall their inheritance be put unto the inheritance of the tribe whereunto they are received: so shall their inheritance be taken away from the inheritance of the
5 tribe of our fathers. ¶ And Moses commanded the children of Israel according to the word of the LORD, saying, The tribe of
6 the sons of Joseph [e]hath said well. This *is* the thing which the   *e* ch. 27. 7. LORD doth command concerning the daughters of Zelophehad, saying, Let them [2]marry to whom they think best; [f]only to the   *f* ver. 12.
7 family of the tribe of their father shall they marry. So shall not the inheritance of the children of Israel remove from tribe to tribe: for every one of the children of Israel shall [3][g]keep   *g* 1 Kin. 21.
8 himself to the inheritance of the tribe of his fathers. And [h]every   3. *h* 1 Chr. 23. daughter, that possesseth an inheritance in any tribe of the   22. children of Israel, shall be wife unto one of the family of the tribe of her father, that the children of Israel may enjoy every
9 man the inheritance of his fathers. Neither shall the inheritance remove from *one* tribe to another tribe; but every one of the tribes of the children of Israel shall keep himself to his own
10 inheritance. Even as the LORD commanded Moses, so did the
11 daughters of Zelophehad: [i]for Mahlah, Tirzah, and Hoglah,   *i* ch. 27. 1. and Milcah, and Noah, the daughters of Zelophehad, were mar-
12 ried unto their father's brothers' sons: *and* they were married [4]into the families of the sons of Manasseh the son of Joseph, and their inheritance remained in the tribe of the family of their
13 father. ¶ These *are* the commandments and the judgments, which the LORD commanded by the hand of Moses unto the children of Israel [k]in the plains of Moab by Jordan *near*   *k* ch. 26. 3. Jericho.   & 33. 50.

[1] Heb. *unto whom they shall be.*   [2] Heb. *be wives.*   [3] Heb. *cleave to the, &c.*   [4] Heb. *to some that were of the families.*

---

4. *be taken away*] *i.e.* be permanently taken away. The jubilee year, by not restoring the estate to the tribe to which it originally belonged, would in effect confirm the alienation.

11. *unto their father's brothers' sons*] Or more generally, "unto the sons of their kinsmen."

DEUTERONOMY.

INTRODUCTION.

THE ordinary name of the book is derived, through the LXX. and Vulgate from that sometimes employed by the Jews, "repetition of the law," and indicates correctly enough the character and contents of the book.[1]

The bulk of Deuteronomy consists of addresses spoken within the space of forty days, and beginning on the first day of the eleventh month in the fortieth year.

The speeches exhibit an unity of style and character which is strikingly consistent with such circumstances. They are pervaded by the same vein of thought, the same tone and tenor of feeling, the same peculiarities of conception and expression. They exhibit matter which is neither documentary nor traditional, but conveyed in the speaker's own words.

Their aim is strictly hortatory; their style earnest, heart-stirring, impressive, in passages sublime, but throughout rhetorical; they keep constantly in view the circumstances then present and the crisis to which the fortunes of Israel had at last been brought Moses had before him not the men to whom by God's command he delivered the law at Sinai, but the generation following which had grown up in the wilderness. Large portions of the law necessarily stood in abeyance during the years of wandering; and of his present hearers many must have been strangers to various prescribed observances and ordinances. Now however on their entry into settled homes in Canaan a thorough discharge of the various obligations laid on them by the Covenant would become imperative; and it is to this state of things that Moses addresses himself. He speaks to hearers neither wholly ignorant of the Law, nor yet fully versed in it. Much is assumed and taken for granted in his speeches; but in other matters he goes into detail, knowing that instruction in them was needed. Sometimes too opportunity is taken of promulgating regulations which are supplementary or auxiliary to those of the preceding books; some few modifications arising out of different or altered circumstances are now made; and the whole Mosaic system is completed by the addition of several enactments in chapters xii.–xxvi. of a social, civil, and

---

[1] The contents of Deuteronomy consist (1) of three addresses to the people delivered by Moses in the eleventh month of the fortieth year after the Exodus (chs. i.–xxx.); and (2) of certain final acts and words of Moses, viz. the solemn appointment of his successor (xxxi.), his Song (xxxii.), and Blessing (xxxiii.), which together with the account of his death (xxxiv.) form an appropriate conclusion to the book and to the whole Pentateuch. Part (2) was probably added to the rest by Joshua or some other duly authorized prophet or leader of the people, after the death of Moses.

political nature. These would have been wholly superfluous during the nomadic life of the desert; but now that the permanent organization of Israel as a nation was to be accomplished, they could not be longer deferred. Accordingly the legislator, at the command of God, completes his great work by supplying them. Thus he provides civil institutions for his people accredited by the same Divine sanctions as had been vouchsafed to their religious rites.

The preceding books displayed Moses principally in the capacity of legislator or annalist. Deuteronomy sets him before us in that of a prophet. And he not only warns and teaches with an authority and energy which the sublimest pages of the Four Greater Prophets cannot surpass, but he delivers some of the most notable and incontrovertible predictions to be found in the Old Testament. The prophecy in xviii. 18 had no doubt its partial verifications in successive ages, but its terms are satisfied in none of them. The prospect opened by it advances continually until it finds its rest in the Messiah, Who stands alone as the only complete counterpart of Moses, and as the greater than he. Chapters xxviii., xxxii. furnish other and no less manifest examples.

It is generally allowed that Deuteronomy must, in substance, have come from one hand. The book presents, the last four chapters excepted, an undeniable unity in style and treatment; it is cast, so to speak, in one mould; its literary characteristics are such that we cannot believe the composition of it to have been spread over any long period of time: and these facts are in full accord with the traditional view which ascribes the book to Moses.

Assertions as to the spuriousness[2] of Deuteronomy, though put forward very positively, appear when sifted to rest upon most insufficient arguments. The alleged anachronisms, discrepancies, and difficulties admit for the most part of easy and complete explanation; and no serious attempt has ever been made to meet the overwhelming presumption drawn from the unanimous and unwavering testimony of the ancient Jewish Church and nation that Moses is the author of this book.

Deuteronomy has in a singular manner the attestation of the Apostles and of our Lord. St. Paul, in Romans x. 8 and xv. 11 argues from it at some length, and expressly quotes it as written by Moses; St. Peter and St. Stephen (Acts iii. 22, vii. 37) refer to the promise of "a Prophet like unto" Moses, and regard it as given, as it professes to be, by Moses himself; our Lord, wielding "the sword of the Spirit which is the word of God" against the open assaults of Satan, thrice resorts to Deuteronomy for the texts with which He repels the tempter, St. Matt. iv. 4–10. To urge in reply that the inspiration of the Apostles, and

---

[2] The older scholars of Germany unhesitatingly affirmed that Deuteronomy was written long after the rest of the Pentateuch was extant in its present shape. The newer school sees no less certainly in Deuteronomy the primæval quarry out of which the writers concerned in the production of the preceding books drew their materials. Out of this conflict of opinions one inference may safely be drawn. The allegation so positively made that the very style of Deuteronomy betrays its late origin is arbitrary and baseless.

even the indwelling of the Spirit "without measure" in the Saviour, would not necessarily preserve them from mistakes on such subjects as the authorship of ancient writings, or to fortify such assertions by remarking that our Lord as the Son of Man was Himself ignorant of some things, is to overlook the important distinction between ignorance and error. To be conscious that much truth lies beyond the range of the intelligence is compatible with the perfection of the creature: but to be deceived by the fraud of others and to fall into error, is not so. To assert then that He Who is "the Truth" believed Deuteronomy to be the work of Moses and quoted it expressly as such, though it was in fact a forgery introduced into the world seven or eight centuries after the Exodus, is in effect, even though not in intention, to impeach the perfection and sinlessness of His nature, and seems thus to gainsay the first principles of Christianity.

THE FIFTH BOOK OF MOSES,

CALLED

DEUTERONOMY.

a Josh. 9. 1,
10.
& 22. 4. 7.

b Num. 13.
26.
ch. 9. 23.
c Num. 33.
38.
d Num. 21.
24, 33.

e Josh. 13.
12.
f Ex. 3. 1.
g See Ex. 19.
1.
Num. 10. 11.

CHAP. 1. THESE *be* the words which Moses spake unto all Israel *a*on this side Jordan in the wilderness, in the plain over against ¹the Red *sea*, between Paran, and Tophel, and Laban, and 2 Hazeroth, and Dizahab. (*There are* eleven days' *journey* from 3 Horeb by the way of mount Seir *b*unto Kadesh-barnea.) And it came to pass *c*in the fortieth year, in the eleventh month, on the first *day* of the month, *that* Moses spake unto the children of Israel, according unto all that the LORD had given him in 4 commandment unto them; *d*after he had slain Sihon the king of the Amorites, which dwelt in Heshbon, and Og the king of 5 Bashan, which dwelt at Astaroth *e*in Edrei: on this side Jordan, in the land of Moab, began Moses to declare this law, saying, 6 ¶ The LORD our God spake unto us *f* in Horeb, saying, Ye have 7 dwelt long *g*enough in this mount: turn you, and take your journey, and go to the mount of the Amorites, and unto ²all *the places* nigh thereunto, in the plain, in the hills, and in the vale, and in the south, and by the sea side, to the land of the Canaanites, and unto Lebanon, unto the great river, the river

¹ Or, *Zuph.*   ² Heb. *all his neighbours.*

I. 1, 2. These verses are prefixed as a connecting link between the contents of the preceding books and that of Deut. now to follow. The sense of the passage might be given thus : "The discourses of Moses to the people up to the eleventh month of the fortieth year" (cp. *v.* 3) "have now been recorded." The proper names which follow seem to belong to places where "words" of remarkable importance were spoken. They are by the Jewish commentators referred to the spots which witnessed the more special sins of the people, and the mention of them here is construed as a pregnant rebuke. The Book of Deut. is known amongst the Jews as "the book of reproofs."

on this side Jordan] Rather, **beyond Jordan** (as in iii. 20 and 25). The phrase was a standing designation for the district east of Jordan, and in times when Greek became commonly spoken in the country was exactly represented by the proper name Peræa.

in the wilderness, in the plain] The former term denotes the desert of Arabia generally ; the latter the sterile tract ('Arabah,' Num. xxi. 4 note) which stretches along the lower Jordan to the Dead Sea, and is continued thence to the Gulf of Akaba.

over against the Red sea] Render : **over against Suph.** "Sea" is not in the original text. "Suph" is either the pass *es Sufah* near Ain-el-Weibeh (Num. xiii. 26 note), or the name of the alluvial district (Num. xxi. 14 note).

Tophel is identified with Tufileh, the

Tafyle of Burckhardt, still a considerable place,—some little distance S.E. of the Dead Sea. Paran is probably "mount Paran" (xxxiii. 2) ; or a city of the same name near the mountain. Cp. Gen. xiv. 6.

Laban is generally identified with Libnah (Num. xxxiii. 20), and Hazeroth with Ain Hadherah (Num. xi. 34 note) ; but the position of Dizahab is uncertain.

2. For Kadesh see Num. xiii. 26 note ; and for Horeb see Ex. iii. 1.

4. *Astaroth*] On this place cp. Gen. xiv. 5 and note.

in Edrei] These words should, to render the sense clear, come next after "slain." The battle in which Sihon and Og were defeated took place at Edrei.

5. *in the land of Moab*] This district had formerly been occupied by the Moabites, and retained its name from them : but had been conquered by the Amorites. Cp. Num. xxi. 26, xxii. 4 notes.

declare] Render, **explain** the Law already declared.

6. The first and introductory address of Moses to the people is here commenced. It extends to iv. 40, and is continued by the *vv.* iv. 41–49. A summary of the address is given in the chapter-headings usually found in English Bibles.

7. *to the mount of the Amorites*] *i.e.* to the mountain district occupied by the Amorites, reaching into the Negeb, and part of the territory assigned to the tribe of Judah.

8 Euphrates. Behold, I have [1]set the land before you: go in and possess the land which the LORD sware unto your fathers, [h]Abraham, Isaac, and Jacob, to give unto them and to their
9 seed after them. ¶ And 'I spake unto you at that time, saying,
10 I am not able to bear you myself alone: the LORD your God hath multiplied you, and, behold, [k]ye are this day as the stars
11 of heaven for multitude. ([l]The LORD God of your fathers make you a thousand times so many more as ye are, and bless you,
12 [m]as he hath promised you!) [n]How can I myself alone bear
13 your cumbrance, and your burden, and your strife? [o] [2]Take you wise men, and understanding, and known among your
14 tribes, and I will make them rulers over you. And ye answered me, and said, The thing which thou hast spoken is good for us
15 to do. So I took the chief of your tribes, wise men, and known, [p]and [3]made them heads over you, captains over thousands, and captains over hundreds, and captains over fifties, and captains
16 over tens, and officers among your tribes. And I charged your judges at that time, saying, Hear the causes between your brethren, and [q]judge righteously between every man and his
17 [r]brother, and the stranger that is with him. [s]Ye shall not [4]respect persons in judgment; but ye shall hear the small as well as the great; ye shall not be afraid of the face of man; for [t]the judgment is God's: and the cause that is too hard for you,
18 [u]bring it unto me, and I will hear it. And I commanded you
19 at that time all the things which ye should do. ¶ And when we departed from Horeb, [x]we went through all that great and terrible wilderness, which ye saw by the way of the mountain of the Amorites, as the LORD our God commanded us; and [y]we
20 came to Kadesh-barnea. And I said unto you, Ye are come unto the mountain of the Amorites, which the LORD our God
21 doth give unto us. Behold, the LORD thy God hath set the land before thee: go up and possess it, as the LORD God of thy fathers hath said unto thee; [z]fear not, neither be discouraged.
22 And ye came near unto me every one of you, and said, We will send men before us, and they shall search us out the land,

[h] Gen. 12. 7.
& reff.
[i] Ex. 18. 18.
Num. 11. 14.
[k] Gen. 15. 5.
ch. 10. 22.
& 28. 62.
[l] 2 Sam. 24. 3.
[m] Gen. 15. 5.
& 22. 17.
& 26. 4.
Ex. 32. 13.
[n] 1 Kin. 3.
8, 9.
[o] See Ex. 18. 21.
Num. 11. 16, 17.
[p] Ex. 18. 25.

[q] ch. 16. 18.
John 7. 24.
[r] Lev. 24. 22.
[s] Lev. 19. 15.
ch. 16. 19.
1 Sam. 16. 7.
Prov. 24. 23.
James 2. 1.
[t] 2 Chr. 19. 6.
[u] Ex. 18. 22, 26.
[x] Num. 10. 12.
ch. 8. 15.
Jer. 2. 6.
[y] Num. 13. 26.

[z] Josh. 1. 9.

[1] Heb. given.
[2] Heb. Give.
[3] Heb. gave.
[4] Heb. acknowledge faces.

9-15. This appointment of the "captains" (cp. Ex. xviii. 21 seq.) must not be confounded with that of the elders in Num. xi. 16 seq. The former would number 78,600; the latter were seventy only.

A comparison between this passage and that in Exodus makes it obvious that Moses is only touching on certain parts of the whole history, without regard to order of time, but with a special purpose. This important arrangement for the good government of the people took place before they quitted Horeb to march direct to the Promised Land. This fact sets more clearly before us the perverseness and ingratitude of the people, to which the orator next passes; and shows, what he was anxious to impress, that the fault of the 40 years' delay rested only with themselves.

19. that great and terrible wilderness] Cp. viii. 15. This language is such as men would employ after having passed with toil and

suffering through the worst part of it, the southern half of the Arabah (see Num. xxi. 4 note); and more especially when they had but recently rested from their marches in the plain of Shittim, the largest and richest oasis in the whole district on the Eastern bank near the mouth of the Jordan.

22, 23. The plan of sending the spies originated with the people; and, as in itself a reasonable one, it approved itself to Moses; it was submitted to God, sanctioned by Him, and carried out under special Divine direction. The orator's purpose in this chapter is to bring before the people emphatically their own responsibilities and behaviour. It is therefore important to remind them, that the sending of the spies, which led immediately to their murmuring and rebellion, was their own suggestion.

The following verses to the end of the chapter give a condensed account, the fuller one

and bring us word again by what way we must go up, and into
23 what cities we shall come. And the saying pleased me well:
24 and *a* I took twelve men of you, one of a tribe: and *b* they turned
and went up into the mountain, and came unto the valley of
25 Eshcol, and searched it out. And they took of the fruit of the
land in their hands, and brought it down unto us, and brought
us word again, and said, *c* It is a good land which the LORD our
26 God doth give us. ¶ *d* Notwithstanding ye would not go up,
but rebelled against the commandment of the LORD your God:
27 and ye murmured in your tents, and said, Because the LORD
e hated us, he hath brought us forth out of the land of Egypt, to
28 deliver us into the hand of the Amorites, to destroy us. Whither
shall we go up? Our brethren have [1] discouraged our heart,
saying, *f* The people is greater and taller than we; the cities are
great and walled up to heaven; and moreover we have seen the
29 sons of the *g* Anakims there. Then I said unto you, Dread not,
30 neither be afraid of them. *h* The LORD your God which goeth
before you, he shall fight for you, according to all that he did
31 for you in Egypt before your eyes; and in the wilderness, where
thou hast seen how that the LORD thy God *i* bare thee, as a man
doth bear his son, in all the way that ye went, until ye came
32 into this place. Yet in this thing *k* ye did not believe the LORD
33 your God, *l* who went in the way before you, *m* to search you out
a place to pitch your tents in, in fire by night, to shew you by
34 what way ye should go, and in a cloud by day. ¶ And the LORD
heard the voice of your words, and was wroth, *n* and sware, say-
35 ing, *o* Surely there shall not one of these men of this evil generation see that good land, which I sware to give unto your
36 fathers, *p* save Caleb the son of Jephunneh; he shall see it,
and to him will I give the land that he hath trodden upon, and
to his children, because *q* he hath [2] wholly followed the LORD.
37 *r* Also the LORD was angry with me for your sakes, saying, Thou
38 also shalt not go in thither. *s* But Joshua the son of Nun,
t which standeth before thee, he shall go in thither: *u* encourage
39 him: for he shall cause Israel to inherit it. *x* Moreover your
little ones, which *y* ye said should be a prey, and your children,
which in that day *z* had no knowledge between good and evil,
they shall go in thither, and unto them will I give it, and they
40 shall possess it. *a* But as for you, turn you, and take your
41 journey into the wilderness by the way of the Red sea. ¶ Then
ye answered and said unto me, *b* We have sinned against the
LORD, we will go up and fight, according to all that the LORD
our God commanded us. And when ye had girded on every
man his weapons of war, ye were ready to go up into the hill.
42 And the LORD said unto me, Say unto them, *c* Go not up, neither
fight; for I am not among you; lest ye be smitten before your

---

[1] Heb. *melted*, Josh. 2. 11.　　　　　[2] Heb. *fulfilled* to go *after*.

---

being in Num. xiii. and xiv., of the occurrences which led to the banishment of the
people for forty years into the wilderness.

37. The sentence on Moses was not passed
when the people rebelled during their first
encampment at Kadesh, but some thirty-
seven years later, when they had re-assem-
bled in the same neighbourhood at Meribah
(see Num. xx. 13 note). He alludes to it here

as having happened not many months previously, bearing on the facts which were to
his purpose in pricking the conscience of the
people.

41. *ye were ready to go up into the hill*]
Rather, perhaps, "ye made light of going
up;" *i.e.* "ye were ready to attempt it as a
trifling undertaking." *V.* 43 shows the issue
of this spirit in action; cp. marg. reff.

43 enemies. So I spake unto you; and ye would not hear, but
rebelled against the commandment of the Lord, and [1][d]went   *d* Num. 14.
44 presumptuously up into the hill. And the Amorites, which   44, 45.
dwelt in that mountain, came out against you, and chased you,
45 [e]as bees do, and destroyed you in Seir, *even* unto Hormah. And   *e* Ps. 118. 12.
ye returned and wept before the Lord; but the Lord would
46 not hearken to your voice, nor give ear unto you. [f]So ye   *f* Num. 13.
abode in Kadesh many days, according to the days that ye   25.
                                                                     & 20. 1. 22.
abode *there*.   Judg. 11. 17.
Chap. 2. THEN we turned, and took our journey into the wilder-
ness by the way of the Red sea, [a]as the Lord spake unto   *a* Num. 14.
2 me: and we compassed mount Seir many days. And the Lord   25.
                                                                     ch. 1. 40.
3 spake unto me, saying, Ye have compassed this mountain [b]long   *b* See ver. 7,
4 enough: turn you northward. And command thou the people,   14.
saying, [c]Ye *are* to pass through the coast of your brethren the   *c* Num. 20.
                                                                     14—20.
children of Esau, which dwell in Seir; and they shall be afraid
5 of you: take ye good heed unto yourselves therefore: meddle
not with them; for I will not give you of their land, [2]no, not so
much as a foot breadth; [d]because I have given mount Seir   *d* Gen 36. 8.
6 unto Esau *for* a possession. Ye shall buy meat of them for   Josh. 24. 4.
money, that ye may eat; and ye shall also buy water of them
7 for money, that ye may drink. For the Lord thy God hath
blessed thee in all the works of thy hand: he knoweth thy
walking through this great wilderness: [e]these forty years the   *e* ch. 8. 2, 3,
Lord thy God *hath been* with thee; thou hast lacked nothing.   4.
8 ¶[f]And when we passed by from our brethren the children of   *f* Judg. 11.
Esau, which dwelt in Seir, through the way of the plain from   18.
[g]Elath, and from Ezion-gaber, we turned and passed by the way   *g* 1 Kin. 9.
9 of the wilderness of Moab. And the Lord said unto me, [3]Dis-   26.
                                                                     h Num. 21.
tress not the Moabites, neither contend with them in battle: for   28.
I will not give thee of their land *for* a possession; because I   *i* Gen. 19.
                                                                     36, 37.
10 have given [h]Ar unto [i]the children of Lot *for* a possession. [k]The   *k* Gen. 14. 5.
Emims dwelt therein in times past, a people great, and many,   *l* Num. 13.
11 and tall, as [l]the Anakims; which also were accounted giants,   22, 33.
                                                                     ch. 9. 2.
12 as the Anakims; but the Moabites call them Emims. [m]The   *m* Gen. 14. 6.
                                                                     & 36. 20.
[1] Heb. *ye were presump-*   [2] Heb. *even to the treading*   [3] Or, *Use no hostility*   ver. 22.
tuous, and went up.   *of the sole of the foot.*   *against Moab.*

---

44. *the Amorites*] In Num. xiv. 45, it is
"the Amalekites and the Canaanites" who
are said to have discomfited them. The
Amorites, as the most powerful nation of
Canaan, lend their name here, as in other
passages (*e.g. v.* 7) to the Canaanitish tribes
generally.

II. 1-3. *V.* 1 seems to refer in general
terms to the long years of wandering, the
details of which were not to Moses' present
purpose. The command of *vv.* 2 and 3 relates to their journey from Kadesh to Mount
Hor (Num. xx. 22; xxxiii. 37), and directs
their march round the south extremity of
Mount Seir, so as to "compass the land of
Edom" (Judg. xi. 18; Num. xxi. 4), and so
northwards towards the Arnon, *i.e.*, "by
the way of the wilderness of Moab," (*v.* 8).
This circuitous path was followed because
of the refusal of the Edomites to allow the
people to pass through their territory.

4. Cp. marg. ref. Though the Edomites

resisted the passage through the midst of
their land, they did not, and probably could
not, oppose the "passing through the
coast" or along their eastern frontier.

5. *I have given mount Seir to Esau*] Though
the descendants of Esau were conquered by
David (2 Sam. viii. 14), yet they were not
dispossessed of their land, and in the reign
of Jehoshaphat they regained their independence (2 Kings viii. 20-22).

8. Elath (Akaba) is at the northern extremity of the eastern arm of the Red Sea, and
gives to that arm the name of the Elanitic
Gulf. The name means "trees;" and is still
justified by the grove of palm-trees at Akaba.

9. The Moabites and the Ammonites (*v.*
19) being descended from Lot, the nephew
of Abraham (Gen. xix. 30-38), were, like
the Edomites, kinsmen of the Israelites.

10-12. For the Emims, Horims, and Anakims, see marg. reff. These verses are either
parenthetic or the insertion of a later hand.

Horims also dwelt in Seir beforetime; but the children of Esau [1]succeeded them, when they had destroyed them from before them, and dwelt in their [2]stead; as Israel did unto the land of 13 his possession, which the LORD gave unto them. Now rise up, *said I*, and get you over [n]the [3]brook Zered. And we went over 14 the brook Zered. And the space in which we came [o]from Kadesh-barnea, until we were come over the brook Zered, *was* thirty and eight years; [p]until all the generation of the men of war were wasted out from among the host, [q]as the LORD sware 15 unto them. For indeed the [r]hand of the LORD was against them, to destroy them from among the host, until they were consumed. 16 ¶ So it came to pass, when all the men of war were consumed 17 and dead from among the people, that the LORD spake unto me, 18 saying, Thou art to pass over through Ar, the coast of Moab, 19 this day: and *when* thou comest nigh over against the children of Ammon, distress them not, nor meddle with them: for I will not give thee of the land of the children of Ammon *any* posses- sion; because I have given it unto [s]the children of Lot *for* a 20 possession. (That also was accounted a land of giants: giants dwelt therein in old time; and the Ammonites call them [t]Zam- 21 zummims; [u]a people great, and many, and tall, as the Anakims; but the LORD destroyed them before them; and they suc- 22 ceeded them, and dwelt in their stead: as he did to the children of Esau, [x]which dwelt in Seir, when he destroyed [y]the Horims from before them; and they succeeded them, and dwelt in their 23 stead even unto this day: and [z]the Avims which dwelt in Hazerim, *even* unto [a]Azzah, [b]the Caphtorims, which came forth out of Caphtor, destroyed them, and dwelt in their stead.) 24 Rise ye up, take your journey, and [c]pass over the river Arnon: behold, I have given into thine hand Sihon the Amorite, king of Heshbon, and his land: [4]begin to possess *it*, and contend with 25 him in battle. [d]This day will I begin to put the dread of thee and the fear of thee upon the nations *that are* under the whole heaven, who shall hear report of thee, and shall tremble, and be 26 in anguish because of thee. ¶ And I sent messengers out of the wilderness of Kedemoth unto Sihon king of Heshbon[e] with words 27 of peace, saying, [f]Let me pass through thy land: I will go along by the high way, I will neither turn unto the right hand nor to 28 the left. Thou shalt sell me meat for money, that I may eat; and give me water for money, that I may drink: [g]only I will 29 pass through on my feet; ([h]as the children of Esau which dwell in Seir, and the Moabites which dwell in Ar, did unto me;) until I shall pass over Jordan into the land which the LORD our God

Marginal references:

[n] Num. 21. 12.
[o] Num. 13. 26.
[p] Num. 14. 33. & 26. 64.
[q] Num. 14. 35. ch. 1. 34, 35. Ez. 20. 15.
[r] Ps. 78. 33. & 106. 26.

[s] Gen. 19. 38.

[t] Gen. 14. 5, *Zuzims.*
[u] See ver. 10.

[x] Gen. 36. 8.
[y] Gen. 14. 6. & 36. 20—30. ver. 12.
[z] Josh. 13. 3.
[a] Jer. 25. 20.
[b] Gen. 10.14. Amos 9. 7.
[c] Num. 21. 13, 14. Judg. 11.18, 21.
[d] Ex. 15. 14, 15. ch. 11. 25. Josh. 2. 9.

[e] ch. 20. 10.
[f] Num. 21. 21, 22. Judg. 11.19.

[g] Num. 20. 19.
[h] See Num. 20. 18. ch. 23. 3, 4. Judg. 11. 17, 18.

---

[1] Heb. *inherited them.*
[2] Or, *room.*
[3] Or, *valley,* Num. 13. 23.
[4] Heb. *begin, possess.*

---

13. The words, "said I," are not in the Hebrew. The words "rise up, and get you over the brook Zered" (Num. xxi. 12 note) connect themselves with *v.* 9, and form the conclusion of what God said to Moses.

20–23. These verses, like *vv.* 10–12, are in all likelihood an addition made by a later reviser.

20. *Zamzummims*] A giant race usually identified with the Zuzims of Gen. xiv. 5.

23. *the Avims which dwelt in Hazerim, even unto Azzah*] Read **Gaza**, of which Azzah is the Hebrew form. " Hazerim "

is not strictly a proper name, but means " villages," or " enclosures," probably such as are still common in the East. The Avims are no doubt identical with the Avites of Josh. xiii. 3, and were doubtless a scattered remnant of a people conquered by the Caphtorim (Gen. x. 14 note) and living in their " enclosures " in the neighbourhood of Gerar. The word, which means " ruins," seems itself expressive of their fallen state.

26. *Kedemoth*] Lit. " Easternmost parts;" the name of a town afterwards assigned to

30 giveth us. [f]But Sihon king of Heshbon would not let us pass by him: for [k]the LORD thy God [l]hardened his spirit, and made his heart obstinate, that he might deliver him into thy hand, as
31 *appeareth* this day. And the LORD said unto me, Behold, I have begun to [m]give Sihon and his land before thee: begin to
32 possess, that thou mayest inherit his land. [n]Then Sihon came
33 out against us, he and all his people, to fight at Jahaz. And [o]the LORD our God delivered him before us; and [p]we smote him,
34 and his sons, and all his people. And we took all his cities at that time, and [q]utterly destroyed [1]the men, and the women, and
35 the little ones, of every city, we left none to remain: only the cattle we took for a prey unto ourselves, and the spoil of the
36 cities which we took. [r]From Aroer, which *is* by the brink of the river of Arnon, and *from* the city that *is* by the river, even unto Gilead, there was not one city too strong for us: [s]the LORD our
37 God delivered all unto us: only unto the land of the children of Ammon thou camest not, *nor* unto any place of the river [t]Jabbok, nor unto the cities in the mountains, nor unto [u]whatsoever the LORD our God forbad us.

CHAP. 3. THEN we turned, and went up the way to Bashan: and [a]Og the king of Bashan came out against us, he and all his
2 people, to battle [b]at Edrei. And the LORD said unto me, Fear him not: for I will deliver him, and all his people, and his land, into thy hand; and thou shalt do unto him as thou didst unto
3 [c]Sihon king of the Amorites, which dwelt at Heshbon. So the LORD our God delivered into our hands Og also, the king of Bashan, and all his people: [d]and we smote him until none was
4 left to him remaining. And we took all his cities at that time, there was not a city which we took not from them, threescore cities, [e]all the region of Argob, the kingdom of Og in Bashan.
5 All these cities *were* fenced with high walls, gates, and bars;

[f] Num. 21. 23.
[k] Josh. 11. 20.
[l] Ex. 4. 21.
[m] ch. 1. 8.
[n] Num. 21. 23.
[o] ch. 7. 2. & 20. 16.
[p] Num. 21. 24.
ch. 29. 7.
[q] Lev. 27. 28. ch. 7. 2, 26.
[r] ch. 3. 12. & 4. 48. Josh. 13. 9.
[s] Ps. 44. 3.
[t] Gen. 32. 22. Num. 21. 24. ch. 3. 16.
[u] ver. 5, 9, 19.
[a] Num. 21. 33, &c. ch. 29. 7.
[b] ch. 1. 4.
[c] Num. 21. 34.
[d] Num. 21. 35.
[e] 1 Kin. 4. 13.

[1] Heb. *every city of men, and women, and little ones.*

---

the Reubenites, and given out of that tribe to the Levites. Cp. Josh. xiii. 18; 1 Chr. vi. 79.

34. *utterly destroyed the men, and the women, and the little ones, of every city*] Render, **laid under ban** (cp. Lev. xxvii. 28 note) **every inhabited city, both women and children**: these last words being added by way of fuller explanation.

36. *Aroer, which is by the brink of the river of Arnon*] Aroer stood on the north bank of the river, and was assigned (Josh. xiii. 9, 16) to the tribe of Reuben, of which it formed the most southerly city. The valley of the Arnon is here deep, and the descent to it abrupt. In Roman times it was spanned by a viaduct the ruins of which still remain, and which was probably built on the lines of the original structure of Mesha (2 Kings iii. 5). Aroer here must not be confounded with "Aroer, which is before Rabbah" (Josh. xiii. 25). This latter place was "built," *i.e.* rebuilt, by the Gadites (Num. xxxii. 34); it belonged to that tribe, and was consequently far to the north of the Arnon. A third Aroer in the tribe of Judah is mentioned in 1 Sam. xxx. 28.

"The city that is by the river," literally,

"in the midst of the river" (cp. Josh. xiii. 9, 16) is Ar Moab (cp. Num. xxi. 15 note).

III. 4. *threescore cities*] Probably the cities of Jair in Bashan described in *v.* 14 as Bashan-havoth-jair.

all the region of Argob] The Hebrew word here rendered "region," means literally "rope" or "cable"; and though undoubtedly used elsewhere in a general topographical sense for portion or district (*e.g.* Josh. xvii. 5), has a special propriety in reference to Argob (mod. Lejah). The name Argob means "stone-heap," and is paraphrased by the Targums, Trachonitis (Luke iii. 1), or "the rough country;" titles designating the more striking features of the district. Its borders are compared to a rugged shore-line; hence its description in the text as "the girdle of the stony country," would seem peculiarly appropriate. [Others identify Argob with the east quarter of the Hauran.]

5. *gates, and bars*] Lit. "Double gates and a bar." The stone doors of Bashan, their height pointing to a race of great stature, and the numerous cities (deserted) exist to illustrate the statements of these verses.

6 beside unwalled towns a great many. And we utterly destroyed them, as we did unto Sihon king *f*of Heshbon, utterly destroying 7 the men, women, and children, of every city. But all the cattle, 8 and the spoil of the cities, we took for a prey to ourselves. And we took at that time out of the hand of the two kings of the Amorites the land that *was* on this side Jordan, from the river of 9 Arnon unto mount Hermon; (*which* *g*Hermon the Sidonians 10 call Sirion; and the Amorites call it *h*Shenir;) *i*all the cities of the plain, and all Gilead, and *k*all Bashan, unto Salchah and 11 Edrei, cities of the kingdom of Og in Bashan. *l*For only Og king of Bashan remained of the remnant of *m*giants; behold, his bedstead *was* a bedstead of iron; *is* it not in *n*Rabbath of the children of Ammon? Nine cubits *was* the length thereof, and 12 four cubits the breadth of it, after the cubit of a man. ¶ And this land, *which* we possessed at that time, *o*from Aroer, which *is* by the river Arnon, and half mount Gilead, and *p*the cities 13 thereof, gave I unto the Reubenites and to the Gadites. *q*And the rest of Gilead, and all Bashan, *being* the kingdom of Og, . gave I unto the half tribe of Manasseh; all the region of Argob, 14 with all Bashan, which was called the land of giants. *r*Jair the son of Manasseh took all the country of Argob *s*unto the coasts of Geshuri and Maachathi; and *t*called them after his 15 own name, Bashan-havoth-jair, unto this day. *u*And I gave 16 Gilead unto Machir. And unto the Reubenites *w*and unto the Gadites I gave from Gilead even unto the river Arnon half the

---

9. Hermon, the southern and culminating point of the range of Lebanon, was also the religious centre of primæval Syria. Its Baal sanctuaries not only existed but gave it a name before the Exodus. Hence the careful specification of the various names by which the mountain might easily have become known to Moses through the constant traffic which had gone on from the most ancient times between Sidon and Egypt.

10. *Salchah*] Cp. Josh. xii. 5; 1 Chr. v. 11, where it is named as belonging to the tribe of Gad. It lies seven hours' journey to the south-east of Bostra or Bozrah of Moab. As the eastern border city of the kingdom of Bashan it was no doubt strongly fortified.

Edrei] Cp. Num. xxi. 33 note.

11. *giants*] Or Rephaim : see marg. ref. note.

a bedstead of iron] The "iron" was probably the black basalt of the country, which not only contains a large proportion, about 20 per cent., of iron, but was actually called iron, and is still so regarded by the Arabians. Iron was indeed both known and used, principally for tools (see *e.g.* xix. 5 and cp. Gen. iv. 22 note), at the date in question by the Semitic people of Palestine and the adjoining countries; but bronze was the ordinary metal of which weapons, articles of furniture, &c., were made.

The word translated "bedstead" is derived from a root signifying "to unite" or "bind together," and so "to arch" or "cover with a vault." The word may then

certainly mean "bier," and perhaps does so in this passage. Modern travellers have discovered in the territories of Og sarcophagi as well as many other articles made of the black basalt of the country.

is it not in Rabbath of the children of Ammon ?] Probably after the defeat and death of Og at Edrei the remnant of his army fled into the territory of the friendly Ammonites, and carried with them the corpse of the giant king.

after the cubit of a man] *i.e.* after the usual and ordinary cubit, counted as men are wont to count. Taking 18 inches to the cubit, the bedstead or sarcophagus would thus be from thirteen to fourteen feet long.

14. These Geshurites held territory adjoining, if not included within, Bashan. They are not to be confounded with those mentioned in Josh. xiii. 2, who were neighbours of the Philistines (1 Sam. xvii. 8).

The exact position of Maachah like that of Geshur cannot be ascertained; but it was no doubt amongst the fastnesses which lay between Bashan and the kingdom of Damascus, and on the skirts of Mount Hermon.

unto this day] This expression, like our "until now," does not, as used in the Bible, necessarily imply that the time spoken of as elapsed is long. It may here denote the duration of the time then present of that which had been already some months accomplished.

16. The sense is that the Reubenites and Gadites were to possess the district from the Jabbok on the north to the Arnon on the south, including the middle part of the

valley, and the border even unto the river Jabbok, *which is the
17 border of the children of Ammon ; the plain also, and Jordan,
and the coast thereof, from *Chinnereth *even unto the sea of
the plain, *even the salt sea, ¹under Ashdoth-pisgah eastward.
18 ¶And I commanded you at that time, saying, The LORD your
God hath given you this land to possess it: *ye shall pass over
armed before your brethren the children of Israel, all that are
19 ²meet for the war. But your wives, and your little ones, and
your cattle, (for I know that ye have much cattle,) shall abide
20 in your cities which I have given you; until the LORD have
given rest unto your brethren, as well as unto you, and until they
also possess the land which the LORD your God hath given them
beyond Jordan: and then shall ye °return every man unto his
21 possession, which I have given you. ¶And ᵈI commanded
Joshua at that time, saying, Thine eyes have seen all that the
LORD your God hath done unto these two kings: so shall the
22 LORD do unto all the kingdoms whither thou passest. Ye shall
not fear them: for °the LORD your God he shall fight for you.
23, 24 ¶And ᶠI besought the LORD at that time, saying, O Lord
GOD, thou hast begun to shew thy servant ᵍthy greatness, and thy
mighty hand: for ʰwhat God is there in heaven or in earth, that
25 can do according to thy works, and according to thy might? I
pray thee, let me go over, and see ⁱthe good land that is beyond
26 Jordan, that goodly mountain, and Lebanon. But the LORD
ᵏwas wroth with me for your sakes, and would not hear me:
and the LORD said unto me, Let it suffice thee; speak no more
27 unto me of this matter. ˡGet thee up into the top of ³Pisgah,
and lift up thine eyes westward, and northward, and southward,
and eastward, and behold it with thine eyes: for thou shalt not
28 go over this Jordan. But ᵐcharge Joshua, and encourage him,
and strengthen him: for he shall go over before this people, and
he shall cause them to inherit the land which thou shalt see.
29 So we abode in ⁿthe valley over against Beth-peor.
CHAP. 4. NOW therefore hearken, O Israel, unto ᵃthe statutes and
unto the judgments, which I teach you, for to do them, that ye
may live, and go in and possess the land which the LORD God of

¹ Or, under the springs of   ² Heb. sons of power.   ³ Or, The hill.
Pisgah, or, the hill.

*Num. 21.
24.
Josh. 12. 2.
ʸ Num. 31.
11.
ᶻ Num. 34.
11.
ch. 4. 49.
ᵃ Gen. 14. 3.
ᵇ Num. 32.
20, &c.

ᶜ Josh. 22. 4.
ᵈ Num. 27.
18.

ᵉ Ex. 14. 14.
ch. 1. 30.
& 20. 4.
ᶠ See 2 Cor.
12. 8, 9.
ᵍ ch. 11. 2.
ʰ Ex. 15. 11.
2 Sam. 7. 22.
Ps. 71. 19.
ⁱ Ex. 3. 8.
ᵏ Num. 20.
12. & 27. 14.
ch. 1. 37.
& 31. 2.
Ps. 106. 32.
ˡ Num. 27.
12.
ᵐ Num. 27.
18, 23.
& 31. 3, 7.
ⁿ ch. 4. 46.
& 34. 6.
ᵃ Lev. 19.
37. & 20. 8.
ch. 5. 1.
& 8. 1.
Ez. 20. 11.
Rom. 10. 5.

valley of the Arnon, and the territory
("coast" or "border") thereto pertaining.
25. that goodly mountain] i.e. that mountainous district. The flat districts of the
East are generally scorched, destitute of
water, and therefore sterile: the hilly ones,
on the contrary, are of more tempered cli-
mate, and fertilised by the streams from
the high grounds. Cp. xi. 11.
The whole of this prayer of Moses is
very characteristic. The longing to witness
further manifestations of God's goodness
and glory, and the reluctance to leave un-
finished an undertaking which he had been
permitted to commence, are striking traits
in his character: cp. Ex. xxxii. 32 seq.,
xxxiii. 12, 18 seq.; Num. xiv. 12 seq.
26. the LORD was wroth with me for your
sakes] Here, as in i. 37 and iv. 21, the sin
of the people is stated to be the ground on
which Moses' prayer is denied. In xxxii.

51, and in Num. xxvii. 14 the transgression of Moses and Aaron themselves is
assigned as the cause of their punishment.
The reason why one side of the transaction
is put forward in this place, and the other
elsewhere, is evident. Here Moses is addressing the people, and mentions the
punishment of their leaders as a most impressive warning to them, whose principal
fault it was. In ch. xxxii. and Num. xxvii.,
God is addressing Moses, and visits on him,
as is fitting, not the sin of the people but
his own.
29. Beth-peor, i.e. the house of Peor, no
doubt derived its name from a temple of the
Moabite god Peor which was there situated.
It was no doubt near to Mount Peor (Num.
xxiii. 28), and also to the valley of the Jordan, perhaps in the Wady Heshban.
IV. The general entreaty contained in
this chapter is pointed by special mention

b ch. 12. 32.
Josh. 1. 7.
Prov. 30. 6.
Eccles. 12. 13.
Rev. 22. 18.
c Num. 25. 4, &c.
Josh. 22. 17
Ps. 106, 28.
d Job 28. 28.
Ps. 19. 7.
& 111. 10.
Prov. 1. 7.
e 2 Sam. 7. 23.
f Ps. 46. 1.
& 145. 18.
& 148. 14.
Isai. 55. 6.
g Prov. 4. 23.
h Prov. 3. 1, 3. & 4. 21.
i Gen. 18. 19.
ch. 6. 7.
& 11. 19.
Ps. 78. 5.
Eph. 6. 4.
k Ex. 19. 9, 16. & 20. 18.
Heb. 12. 18, 19.
l Ex. 19. 18.
ch. 5. 23.
m ch. 5. 4.
n ver. 33, 36.
o Ex. 20. 22.
1 Kin. 19. 12.
p ch. 9. 9.
q Ex. 34. 28.
r Ex. 24. 12.
& 31. 18.
s Ex. 21. 1.
& ch. 22.
& ch. 23.
t Josh. 23. 11.
u Isai. 40. 18.
x Ex. 32. 7.
y Ex. 20. 4.
ver. 23.
ch. 5, 8.
c Rom. 1. 23.

2 your fathers giveth you. *b*Ye shall not add unto the word which I command you, neither shall ye diminish *ought* from it, that ye may keep the commandments of the LORD your God which I 3 command you. Your eyes have seen what the LORD did because of *c*Baal-peor : for all the men that followed Baal-peor, 4 the LORD thy God hath destroyed them from among you. But ye that did cleave unto the LORD your God *are* alive every one 5 of you this day. ¶ Behold, I have taught you statutes and judgments, even as the LORD my God commanded me, that ye should 6 do so in the land whither ye go to possess it. Keep therefore and do them ; for this *is* *d*your wisdom and your understanding in the sight of the nations, which shall hear all these statutes, and say, Surely this great nation *is* a wise and understanding 7 people. For *e*what nation *is there* so great, who *hath* *f*God so nigh unto them, as the LORD our God *is* in all *things that* we call upon 8 him *for ?* And what nation *is there* so great, that hath statutes and judgments *so* righteous as all this law, which I set before you 9 this day ? Only take heed to thyself, and *g*keep thy soul diligently, *h*lest thou forget the things which thine eyes have seen, and lest they depart from thy heart all the days of thy life : but 10 *i*teach them thy sons, and thy sons' sons ; *specially* *k*the day that thou stoodest before the LORD thy God in Horeb, when the LORD said unto me, Gather me the people together, and I will make them hear my words, that they may learn to fear me all the days that they shall live upon the earth, and *that* they may 11 teach their children. And ye came near and stood under the mountain ; and the *l*mountain burned with fire unto the ¹midst 12 of heaven, with darkness, clouds, and thick darkness. *m*And the LORD spake unto you out of the midst of the fire : *n*ye heard the voice of the words, but saw no similitude ; *o*²only *ye heard* a 13 voice. *p*And he declared unto you his covenant, which he commanded you to perform, *even* *q*ten commandments ; and *r*he 14 wrote them upon two tables of stone. And *s*the LORD commanded me at that time to teach you statutes and judgments, that ye might do them in the land whither ye go over to possess 15 it. ¶ *t*Take ye therefore good heed unto yourselves ; for ye saw no manner of *u*similitude on the day *that* the LORD spake unto 16 you in Horeb out of the midst of the fire : lest ye *x*corrupt *yourselves*, and *y*make you a graven image, the similitude of any 17 figure, *z*the likeness of male or female, the likeness of any beast that *is* on the earth, the likeness of any winged fowl that flieth

¹ Heb. *heart.*   ² Heb. *save a voice.*

---

and enforcement of the fundamental principles of the whole Covenant (*vv.* 9-40), the spiritual nature of the Deity, His exclusive right to their allegiance, His abhorrence of idolatry in every form, His choice of them for His elect people. Cp. further Moses' third and last address, ch. xxvii.-xxx.

9-11. A full stop should end *v.* 9 ; and *v.* 10 begin, **At the time that thou stoodest**, &c. (11) **then ye came near**, &c. Moses, exhorting to heedful observance of the Law, strives to renew the impressions of that tremendous scene which attended its promulgation at Sinai.

12 seq. Hero-worship exhibited itself in the practice of setting up images of human form as household gods (Penates, cp. Gen. xxxi. 19, xxxv. 2), or as local and civic divinities : a practice forbidden by *v.* 16. Nature-worship in its baser shapes is seen in the Egyptian idolatry of animals and animal figures, and is condemned in *vv.* 17, 18 : whilst its less ignoble flight, the worship of the sun, moon, and stars, is forbidden in *v.* 19. The great legislator may be regarded as taking in the passage before us a complete and comprehensive survey of the various forms of idolatrous and corrupt worship practised by the surrounding Oriental nations, and as particularly and successively forbidding them every one.

18 in the air, the likeness of any thing that creepeth on the ground, the likeness of any fish that *is* in the waters beneath the earth:
19 and lest thou *a* lift up thine eyes unto heaven, and when thou seest the sun, and the moon, and the stars, *even* *b* all the host of heaven, shouldest be driven to *c* worship them, and serve them, which the LORD thy God hath [1] divided unto all nations under
20 the whole heaven. But the LORD hath taken you, and *d* brought you forth out of the iron furnace, *even* out of Egypt, *e* to be unto
21 him a people of inheritance, as *ye are* this day. Furthermore *f* the LORD was angry with me for your sakes, and sware that I should not go over Jordan, and that I should not go in unto that good land, which the LORD thy God giveth thee *for* an inheri-
22 tance: but *g* I must die in this land, *h* I must not go over Jordan: but ye shall go over, and possess *i* that good land.
23 Take heed unto yourselves, *k* lest ye forget the covenant of the LORD your God, which he made with you, *l* and make you a graven image, *or* the likeness of any *thing*, which the LORD
24 thy God hath forbidden thee. For *m* the LORD thy GOD *is*
25 a consuming fire, *even* *n* a jealous God. When thou shalt beget children, and children's children, and ye shall have remained long in the land, and *o* shall corrupt *yourselves*, and make a graven image, *or* the likeness of any *thing*, and *p* shall do evil in the sight of the LORD thy God, to provoke him to
26 anger: *q* I call heaven and earth to witness against you this day, that ye shall soon utterly perish from off the land whereunto ye go over Jordan to possess it; ye shall not pro-
27 long *your* days upon it, but shall utterly be destroyed. And the LORD *r* shall scatter you among the nations, and ye shall be left few in number among the heathen, whither the LORD shall
28 lead you. And *s* there ye shall serve gods, the work of men's hands, wood and stone, *t* which neither see, nor hear, nor eat,
29 nor smell. ¶ *u* But if from thence thou shalt seek the LORD thy God, thou shalt find *him*, if thou seek him with all thy heart
30 and with all thy soul. When thou art in tribulation, and all these things *z* are come upon thee, *x even* in the latter days, if thou *y* turn to the LORD thy God, and shalt be obedient unto his
31 voice; (for the LORD thy God *is z* a merciful God;) he will not forsake thee, neither destroy thee, nor forget the covenant of
32 thy fathers which he sware unto them. For *a* ask now of the days that are past, which were before thee, since the day that God created man upon the earth, and *ask b* from the one side of heaven unto the other, whether there hath been any *such thing*
33 as this great thing *is*, or hath been heard like it? *c* Did *ever* people hear the voice of God speaking out of the midst of the
34 fire, as thou hast heard, and live? Or hath God assayed to go *and* take him a nation from the midst of *another* nation, *d* by temptations, *e* by signs, and by wonders, and by war, and *f* by a mighty hand, and *g* by a stretched out arm, *h* and by great

[1] Or, *imparted*.   [2] Heb. *have found thee*, Ex. 18. 8. ch. 31. 17.

a ch. 17. 3.
Job 31. 26.
b Gen. 2. 4.
2 Kin. 17.
16. & 21. 3;
c Rom. 1.
25.
d 1 Kin. 8.
51.
Jer. 11. 4.
e Ex. 19. 5.
ch. 9. 29.
f Num. 20.
12.
g See 2 Pet.
1. 13, 14.
h ch. 3. 27.
i ch. 3. 25.
k ver. 9.
l ver. 16.
Ex. 20. 4.
m Ex. 24.
17.
Isai. 33. 14.
Heb. 12. 29.
n Ex. 20. 5.
ch. 6. 15.
Isai. 42. 8.
o ver. 16.
p 2 Kin. 17.
17, &c.
q ch. 30. 18.
Isai. 1. 2.
Mic. 6. 2.
r ch. 28. 62.
Neh. 1. 8.
s 1 Sam. 26.
19.
Jer. 16. 13.
t Ps. 115. 4.
Isai. 44. 9.
u Lev. 26.
39, 40.
ch. 30. 1.
2 Chr. 15. 4.
Neh. 1. 9.
Isai. 55. 6.
Jer. 29. 12.
x Gen. 49. 1.
Jer. 23. 20.
Hos. 3. 5.
y Joel 2. 12.
z 2 Chr. 30.
9.
Neh. 9. 31.
Ps. 116. 5.
Jonah 4. 2.
a Job 8. 8.
b Matt. 24.
31.
c Ex. 24. 11.
d ch. 7. 19.
e Ex. 7. 3.
f Ex. 13. 3.
g Ex. 6. 6.
h ch. 26. 8.

---

19. *divided*] *i.e.* "whose light God has distributed to the nations for their use and benefit, and which therefore being creatures ministering to man's convenience must not be worshipped as man's lords."

25–28. Cp. with these verses Lev. xxvi. 33–40, and ch. xxviii. 64 seq.

29–40. Unwilling, as it might seem, to close his discourse with words of terror, Moses makes a last appeal to them in these verses in a different strain.

34. *temptations*] Cp. vii. 18, 19, and xxix. 2, 3; not, *i.e.* the tribulations and persecutions undergone by the Israelites, but the plagues miraculously inflicted on the Egyptians.

terrors, according to all that the LORD your God did for you in
35 Egypt before your eyes? Unto thee it was shewed, that thou
mightest know that the LORD he *is* God; *i*there *is* none else
36 beside him. *k*Out of heaven he made thee to hear his voice, that
he might instruct thee: and upon earth he shewed thee his great
fire; and thou heardest his words out of the midst of the fire.
37 And because *l*he loved thy fathers, therefore he chose their seed
after them, and *m*brought thee out in his sight with his mighty
38 power out of Egypt; *n*to drive out nations from before thee
greater and mightier than thou *art*, to bring thee in, to give thee
39 their land *for* an inheritance, as *it is* this day. Know therefore this day, and consider *it* in thine heart, that *o*the LORD he *is*
God in heaven above, and upon the earth beneath: *there is* none
40 else. *p*Thou shalt keep therefore his statutes, and his commandments, which I command thee this day, *q*that it may go well
with thee, and with thy children after thee, and that thou mayest
prolong *thy* days upon the earth, which the LORD thy God giveth
41 thee, for ever. ¶Then Moses *r*severed three cities on this side
42 Jordan toward the sunrising; *s*that the slayer might flee thither,
which should kill his neighbour unawares, and hated him not in
times past; and that fleeing unto one of these cities he might
43 live: *namely*, *t*Bezer in the wilderness, in the plain country, of
the Reubenites; and Ramoth in Gilead, of the Gadites; and
44 Golan in Bashan, of the Manassites. ¶And this *is* the law
45 which Moses set before the children of Israel: these *are* the
testimonies, and the statutes, and the judgments, which Moses
spake unto the children of Israel, after they came forth out of
46 Egypt, on this side Jordan, *u*in the valley over against Beth-
peor, in the land of Sihon king of the Amorites, who dwelt at
Heshbon, whom Moses and the children of Israel *x*smote, after
47 they were come forth out of Egypt: and they possessed his land,
and the land *y*of Og king of Bashan, two kings of the Amorites,

i ch. 32. 39.
1 Sam. 2. 2.
Isai. 45. 5.
Mark 12. 29,
32.
k Ex. 19. 9.
& 24. 16.
Heb. 12. 18.
l ch. 10. 15.
m Ex. 13. 3.
n ch. 7. 1.
& 9. 1, 4, 5.

o ver. 35.
Josh. 2. 11.

p Lev. 22.31.

q ch. 5. 16.
& 6. 3, 18.
Eph. 6. 3.

r Num. 35.
6, 14.
s ch. 19. 4.

t Josh. 20. 8.

u ch. 3. 29.
x Num. 21.
24.
ch. 1. 4.
y Num. 21.
35.
ch. 3. 3, 4.

---

37. *he chose their seed after them*] Lit.
"*his* seed after *him*." Speaking of the love
of God to their fathers in general, Moses
has more especially in mind that one of
them who was called "the Friend of God"
(James ii. 23).

brought thee out in his sight] Lit. "by His
face:" *i.e.* by the might of His personal
Presence. Cp. Ex. xxxiii. 14, where God
promises "My Presence (lit. 'My face')
shall go with thee."

41-43. These verses are inserted between
two distinct and complete discourses for the
reason to which they themselves call attention ("*Then* Moses severed three cities,"
&c.); *i.e.* the fact narrated took place historically after Moses spoke the one discourse and before he delivered the other.
In thus severing the three cities of refuge
Moses carried out a previous command of
God (see marg. reff.); and so followed up
his exhortations to obedience by setting a
punctual example of it, as far as opportunity was given him.

43. *in the plain country*] Lit. "in the
land of the *Mishor*." The word means a
level tract of land; but when used (iii. 10;
Josh. xiii. 9, &c.) with the article, seems to
be the proper name for the smooth downs

of Moab, which reach from the Jordan eastward of Jericho far into the desert of Arabia,
and which form a striking contrast alike to
the rugged country west of the river, and to
the higher and remarkable districts belonging to Bashan northwards.

Bezer is, with little certainty, identified
with Bostra, or (1 Macc. v. 36) Bosor. Golan gave the name of Gaulonitis to a district
of some extent east of the sea of Galilee
and north of the Hieromax; but the exact
site of the city if uncertain.

44-49. These verses would be more properly assigned to the next chapter. They are
intended to serve as the announcement and
introduction of the address now to be commenced. *V.* 44 gives a kind of general title
to the whole of the weighty address, including in fact the central part and substance of the book, which now follows in
twenty-two chapters, divided into two
groups: (*a*) ch. v.-xi., (*b*) ch. xii.-xxvi.
The address was delivered when they had
already received the first fruits of those
promises (*v.* 46), the full fruition of which
was to be consequent on their fulfilment of
that Covenant now again about to be rehearsed to them in its leading features.

48 which *were* on this side Jordan toward the sunrising; *z*from
Aroer, which *is* by the bank of the river Arnon, even unto
49 mount Sion, which *is* *a*Hermon, and all the plain on this side
Jordan eastward, even unto the sea of the plain, under the
*b*springs of Pisgah.

CHAP. 5. AND Moses called all Israel, and said unto them, Hear,
O Israel, the statutes and judgments which I speak in your ears
this day, that ye may learn them, and ¹keep, and do them.
2, 3 *a*The LORD our God made a covenant with us in Horeb. The
LORD *b*made not this covenant with our fathers, but with us,
4 *even* us, who *are* all of us here alive this day. *c*The LORD talked
with you face to face in the mount out of the midst of the fire,
5 (*d*I stood between the LORD and you at that time, to shew you
the word of the LORD: for *e*ye were afraid by reason of the fire,
and went not up into the mount;) saying,
6 *f*I *am* the LORD thy God, which brought thee out of the land
7 of Egypt, from the house of ²bondage. *g*Thou shalt have none
other gods before me.
8 *h*Thou shalt not make thee *any* graven image, *or* any likeness
of any thing that *is* in heaven above, or that *is* in the earth
9 beneath, or that *is* in the waters beneath the earth : thou shalt
not bow down thyself unto them, nor serve them: for I the
LORD thy God *am* a jealous God, *i*visiting the iniquity of the
fathers upon the children unto the third and fourth *generation*
10 of them that hate me, *k*and shewing mercy unto thousands of
them that love me and keep my commandments.
11 *l*Thou shalt not take the name of the LORD thy God in vain :
for the LORD will not hold *him* guiltless that taketh his name
in vain.
12 *m*Keep the sabbath day to sanctify it, as the LORD thy God
13 hath commanded thee. *n*Six days thou shalt labour, and do all
14 thy work : but the seventh day *is* the *o*sabbath of the LORD thy
God : *in it* thou shalt not do any work, thou, nor thy son, nor
thy daughter, nor thy manservant, nor thy maidservant, nor
thine ox, nor thine ass, nor any of thy cattle, nor thy stranger
that *is* within thy gates; that thy manservant and thy maid-
15 servant may rest as well as thou. *p*And remember that thou
wast a servant in the land of Egypt, and *that* the LORD thy God
brought thee out thence *q*through a mighty hand and by a

z ch. 2. 36.
& 3. 12.

a ch. 3. 9.
Ps. 133. 3.

b ch. 3. 17.

a Ex. 19. 5.
ch. 4. 23.
b See Matt.
13. 17.
Heb. 8. 9.
c Ex. 19. 9.
ch. 34. 10.
d Ex. 20. 21.
Gal. 3. 19.
e Ex. 19. 16.
f Ex. 20. 2,
&c.
Lev. 26. 1.
ch. 6. 4.
Ps. 81. 10.
g Ex. 20. 3.
h Ex. 20. 4.

i Ex. 34. 7.

k Jer. 32. 18.
Dan. 9. 4.

l Ex. 20. 7.
Lev. 19. 12.
Matt. 5. 33.

m Ex. 20. 8.
n Ex. 23. 12.
& 35. 2.
Ez. 20. 12.
o Gen. 2. 2.
Ex. 16. 29.
Heb. 4. 4.

p ch. 15. 15.
& 16. 12.
& 24. 18. 22.
q ch. 4. 34.

¹ Heb. *keep to do them.*   ² Heb. *servants.*

---

48. Sion (see marg. ref. and note) must
not be confounded with Zion (cp. Ps. xlviii.
2).

V. 3. The "fathers" are, as in iv. 37,
the patriarchs, Abraham, Isaac, and Jacob.
With them God did indeed make a Covenant, but not the particular Covenant now
in question. The responsibilities of this
later Covenant, made at Sinai by the nation
as a nation, attached in their day and generation to those whom Moses was addressing.

6–21. Cp. Ex. xx. and notes.

Moses here adopts the Ten Words as a
ground from which he may proceed to reprove, warn, and exhort ; and repeats them,
with a certain measure of freedom and
adaptation (Mark x. 19) and
St. Paul (Eph. vi. 2, 3) deal similarly with
the same subject. Speaker and hearers re-

cognised, however, a statutory and authori-
tative form of the laws in question, which,
because it was familiar to both parties,
needed not to be reproduced with verbal
fidelity.

12–15. The exhortation to observe the
Sabbath and allow time of rest to servants
(cp. Ex. xxiii. 12) is pointed by reminding
the people that they too were formerly servants themselves. The bondage in Egypt
and the deliverance from it are not assigned
as grounds for the institution of the Sabbath, which is of far older date (see Gen.
ii. 3), but rather as suggesting motives for
the religious observance of that institution.
The Exodus was an entrance into rest from
the toils of the house of bondage, and is
thought actually to have occurred on the
Sabbath-day or "rest"-day.

stretched out arm: therefore the LORD thy God commanded thee to keep the sabbath day.

16 *r*Honour thy father and thy mother, as the LORD thy God hath commanded thee; *s*that thy days may be prolonged, and that it may go well with thee, in the land which the LORD thy God giveth thee.

17 *t*Thou shalt not kill.

18 *u*Neither shalt thou commit adultery.

19 *x*Neither shalt thou steal.

20 *y*Neither shalt thou bear false witness against thy neighbour.

21 *z*Neither shalt thou desire thy neighbour's wife, neither shalt thou covet thy neighbour's house, his field, or his manservant, or his maidservant, his ox, or his ass, or any *thing* that *is* thy neighbour's.

22 ¶These words the LORD spake unto all your assembly in the mount out of the midst of the fire, of the cloud, and of the thick darkness, with a great voice: and he added no more. And *a*he wrote them in two tables of stone, and delivered them unto me.

23 *b*And it came to pass, when ye heard the voice out of the midst of the darkness, (for the mountain did burn with fire,) that ye came near unto me, *even* all the heads of your tribes, and your

24 elders; and ye said, Behold, the LORD our God hath shewed us his glory and his greatness, and *c*we have heard his voice out of the midst of the fire: we have seen this day that God doth talk

25 with man, and he *d*liveth. Now therefore why should we die? For this great fire will consume us: *e*if we ¹hear the voice of the

26 LORD our God any more, then we shall die. *f*For who *is there* of all flesh, that hath heard the voice of the living God speaking

27 out of the midst of the fire, as we *have*, and lived? Go thou near, and hear all that the LORD our God shall say: and *g*speak thou unto us all that the LORD our God shall speak unto thee;

28 and we will hear *it*, and do *it*. ¶And the LORD heard the voice of your words, when ye spake unto me; and the LORD said unto me, I have heard the voice of the words of this people, which they have spoken unto thee: they *h*have well said all that they

29 have spoken. *i*O that there were such an heart in them, that they would fear me, and *k*keep all my commandments always,

¹ Heb. *add to hear.*

Marginal references: *r* Ex. 20. 12. Lev. 19. 3. ch. 27. 16. Eph. 6. 2, 3. Col. 3. 20. *s* ch. 4. 40. *t* Ex. 20. 13. Matt. 5. 21. *u* Ex. 20. 14. Luke 18. 20. Jam. 2. 11. *x* Ex. 20. 15. Rom. 13. 9. *y* Ex. 20. 16. *z* Ex. 20. 17. Mic. 2. 2. Hab. 2. 9. Luke 12. 15. Rom. 7. 7. & 13. 9. *a* Ex. 24. 12. & 31. 18. ch. 4. 13. *b* Ex. 20. 18. *c* Ex. 19. 19. *d* ch. 4. 33. Judg. 13. 22. *e* ch. 18. 16. *f* ch. 4. 33. *g* Ex. 20. 19. Heb. 12. 19. *h* ch. 18. 17. *i* ch. 32. 29. Ps. 81. 12. Isai. 48. 18. Matt. 23. 37. Luke 19. 42. *k* ch. 11. 1.

16. The blessing of general well-being here annexed to the keeping of the Fifth Commandment, is no real addition to the promise, but only an amplification of its expression.

21. The "field" is added to the list of objects specifically forbidden in the parallel passage (Ex. xx. 17). The addition seems very natural in one who was speaking with the partition of Canaan amongst his hearers directly in view.

22. *he added no more*] i.e. He spoke no more with the great voice directly to the people, but addressed all other communications to them through Moses. This unique and sublime phenomenon, followed up by the inscription of the Ten Words on the Two Tables by the finger of God, marks not only the holiness of God's Law in general, but the special eminence and per-

manent obligation of the Ten Words themselves as compared with the rest of the Mosaic enactments. The giving of the Two Tables did not take place until Moses had been on the Mount forty days and forty nights, as appears from the fuller account of ix. 9-12.

23-33. These verses contain a much fuller narrative of the events briefly described in Ex. xx. 18-21. Here it is important to call attention to the fact that it was on the entreaties of the people that Moses had taken on him to be the channel of communication between God and them. God approved (v. 28) the request of the people, because it shewed a feeling of their own unworthiness to enter into direct communion with God. The terrors of Sinai had done their work: they had awakened the consciousness of sin.

*l*that it might be well with them, and with their children for *l* ch. 4. 40.
30, 31 ever! Go say to them, Get you into your tents again. But
as for thee, stand thou here by me, *m*and I will speak unto thee *m* Gal. 3. 19.
all the commandments, and the statutes, and the judgments,
which thou shalt teach them, that they may do *them* in the land *n* ch. 17. 20.
32 which I give them to possess it. Ye shall observe to do there- Josh. 1. 7.
fore as the LORD your God hath commanded you: *n*ye shall not Prov. 4. 27.
33 turn aside to the right hand or to the left. Ye shall walk in *o*all Jer. 7. 23.
the ways which the LORD your God hath commanded you, that Luke 1. 6.
ye may live, *p*and *that it may be* well with you, and *that* ye may *p* ch. 4. 40.
prolong *your* days in the land which ye shall possess. *a* ch. 4. 1.
CHAP. 6. NOW these *are* *a*the commandments, the statutes, and the & 12. 1.
judgments, which the LORD your God commanded to teach you, *b* Ex. 20. 20.
that ye might do *them* in the land whither ye *1* go to possess it: Ps. 111. 10.
2 *b*that thou mightest fear the LORD thy God, to keep all his Eccles. 12.
statutes and his commandments, which I command thee, thou, *c* ch. 4. 40.
and thy son, and thy son's son, all the days of thy life; *c*and Prov. 3. 1.
3 that thy days may be prolonged. Hear therefore, O Israel, & 22. 17.
and observe to do *it;* that it may be well with thee, and that ye *e* Ex. 3. 8.
may increase mightily, *d*as the LORD God of thy fathers hath Mark 12. 29.
promised thee, in *e*the land that floweth with milk and honey. John 17. 3.
4, 5 ¶*f* Hear, O Israel : The LORD our God *is* one LORD : and *g*thou *g* ch. 10. 12.
shalt love the LORD thy God *h*with all thine heart, and with all *h* 2 Kin. 23.
6 thy soul, and with all thy might. And *i*these words, which I *i* ch. 11. 18.
7 command thee this day, shall be in thine heart: and *k*thou shalt Ps. 37. 31.
*2*teach them diligently unto thy children, and shalt talk of them Prov. 3. 3.
when thou sittest in thine house, and when thou walkest by the *k* ch. 4. 9.
8 way, and when thou liest down, and when thou risest up. *l*And Ps. 78. 4.
thou shalt bind them for a sign upon thine hand, and they shall *l* Ex. 13. 9.
9 be as frontlets between thine eyes. *m*And thou shalt write them ch. 11. 18.

1 Heb. *pass over.*　　　　*2* Heb. *whet,* or, *sharpen.*

VI. Moses proceeds to set forth more
particularly and to enforce the cardinal and
essential doctrines of the Decalogue, the nature and attributes of God, and the fitting
mode of honouring and worshipping Him.
Two objects are indicated (*vv.* 2, 3), the
glory of God and the welfare of man, as the
grand aims he has in view.

3. *in the land*] Better, **According as the
Lord the God of thy fathers promised thee
a land flowing with milk and honey.**

4. These words form the beginning of
what is termed the *Shema* ("Hear") in the
Jewish Services, and belong to the daily
Morning and Evening office. They may be
termed the Creed of the Jews.

This weighty text contains far more than
a mere declaration of the unity of God as
against polytheism ; or of the sole authority
of the Revelation He had made to Israel as
against other pretended manifestations of
His will and attributes. It asserts that the
Lord God of Israel is absolutely God, and
none other. He, and He alone, is Jehovah
the absolute, uncaused God; He Who had
by His election of them made Himself
known to Israel.

5. As there is but One God, and that God
Israel's God, so Israel must love God unre-

servedly and entirely. The "heart" is mentioned as the seat of the understanding ;
the "soul" as the centre of will and per-
sonality ; the "might" as representing the
outgoings and energies of all the vital powers.
The New Testament itself requires no
more than this total self-surrender of man's
being to his maker (Matt. xxii. 37). The
Gospel differs from the Law not so much in
replacing an external and carnal service of
God by an inward and spiritual one, as in
supplying new motives and peculiar assist-
ances for the attainment of that Divine
love which was from the first and all along
enjoined as "the first and great commandment."

8, 9. By adopting and regulating customary usages (*e.g.* Egyptian) Moses provides
at once a check on superstition and a means
of keeping the Divine Law in memory. On
the "frontlets," the "phylacteries" of the
New Test. (Matt. xxiii. 5), see Ex. xiii.
16 note. On *v.* 9 and xi. 20 is based the
Jewish usage of the *Mezuzah.* This word
denotes properly a door-post, as it is rendered here and in Ex. xii. 7, 22, xxi. 6
&c. Amongst the Jews however it is the
name given to the square piece of parchment, inscribed with *vv.* 4-9 and xi. 13-21,

10 upon the posts of thy house, and on thy gates. ¶And it shall be, when the LORD thy God shall have brought thee into the land which he sware unto thy fathers, to Abraham, to Isaac, and to Jacob, to give thee great and goodly cities, ⁿwhich thou

11 buildedst not, and houses full of all good *things*, which thou filledst not, and wells digged, which thou diggedst not, vineyards and olive trees, which thou plantedst not; ᵒwhen thou

12 shalt have eaten and be full; *then* beware lest thou forget the LORD, which brought thee forth out of the land of Egypt, from

13 the house of ¹bondage. Thou shalt ᵖfear the LORD thy God,

14 and serve him, and ᵠshalt swear by his name. Ye shall not ʳgo after other gods, ˢof the gods of the people which *are* round

15 about you; (for ᵗthe LORD thy God *is* a jealous God among you) ᵘlest the anger of the LORD thy God be kindled against thee,

16 and destroy thee from off the face of the earth. ¶ˣYe shall not

17 tempt the LORD your God, ʸas ye tempted *him* in Massah. Ye shall ᶻdiligently keep the commandments of the LORD your God, and his testimonies, and his statutes, which he hath commanded

18 thee. And thou ᵃshalt do *that which is* right and good in the sight of the LORD: that it may be well with thee, and that thou mayest go in and possess the good land which the LORD sware

19 unto thy fathers, ᵇto cast out all thine enemies from before

20 thee, as the LORD hath spoken. ¶*And* ᶜwhen thy son asketh thee ²in time to come, saying, What *mean* the testimonies, and the statutes, and the judgments, which the LORD our God

21 hath commanded you? Then thou shalt say unto thy son, We were Pharaoh's bondmen in Egypt; and the LORD brought us

22 out of Egypt ᵈwith a mighty hand: ᵉand the LORD shewed signs and wonders, great and ³sore, upon Egypt, upon Pharaoh,

23 and upon all his household, before our eyes: and he brought us out from thence, that he might bring us in, to give us the land

24 which he sware unto our fathers. And the LORD commanded us to do all these statutes, ᶠto fear the LORD our God, ᵍfor our good always, that ʰhe might preserve us alive, as *it is* at this

25 day. And ⁱit shall be our righteousness, if we observe to do all these commandments before the LORD our God, as he hath commanded us.

ⁿ Josh. 24. 13.
Ps. 105. 44.

ᵒ ch. 8. 10.

ᵖ ch. 10. 12, 20. & 13. 4.
Matt. 4. 10.
ᵠ Ps. 63. 11.
Isai. 45. 23.
Jer. 4. 2.
ʳ ch. 8. 19.
Jer. 25. 6.
ˢ ch. 13. 7.
ᵗ Ex. 20. 5.
ch. 4. 24.
ᵘ ch. 11. 17.
ˣ Luke 4. 12.
ʸ Ex. 17. 2.
Num. 20. 3, 4.
1 Cor. 10. 9.
ᶻ ch. 11. 13.
Ps. 119. 4.
ᵃ Ex. 15. 26.
ch. 12. 28.
& 13. 18.
ᵇ Num. 33. 52, 53.
ᶜ Ex. 13. 14.
ᵈ Ex. 3. 19.
& 13. 3.
ᵉ Ex. 7—12.
Ps. 135. 9.

ᶠ ver. 2.
ᵍ ch. 10. 13.
Job 35. 7.
Jer. 32. 39.
ʰ ch. 8. 1.
Ps. 41. 2.
Luke 10. 28.
ⁱ Lev. 18. 5.
ch. 24. 13.
Rom. 10. 3,5.

¹ Heb. *bondmen*, or, *servants.*

² Heb. *to morrow.*
³ Heb. *evil.*

which is rolled up in a small cylinder of wood or metal, and affixed to the right-hand post of every door in a Jewish house. The pious Jew touches the Mezuzah on each occasion of passing, or kisses his finger, and says in Hebrew Ps. cxxi. 8.

10—25. The Israelites were on the point of quitting a nomad life for a fixed and settled abode in the midst of other nations; they were exchanging a condition of comparative poverty for great and goodly cities, houses and vineyards. There was therefore before them a double danger; (1) a God-forgetting worldliness, and (2) a false tolerance of the idolatries practised by those about to become their neighbours. The former error Moses strives to guard against in the verses before us; the latter in vii. 1–11.

13. The command "to swear by His

Name" is not inconsistent with the Lord's injunction (Matt. v. 34), "Swear not at all." Moses refers to legal swearing, our Lord to swearing in common conversation. It is not the purpose of Moses to encourage the practice of taking oaths, but to forbid that when taken they should be taken in any other name than that of Israel's God. The oath involves an invocation of Deity, and so a solemn recognition of Him Whose Name is made use of in it. Hence it comes peculiarly within the scope of the commandment Moses is enforcing.

25. *it shall be our righteousness*] *i.e.* God will esteem us righteous and deal with us accordingly. Moses from the very beginning made the whole "righteousness of the Law" to depend entirely on a right state of the heart, in one word, on faith.

Chap. 7. WHEN the *a*LORD thy God shall bring thee into the land whither thou goest to possess it, and hath cast out many nations before thee, *b*the Hittites and the Girgashites, and the Amorites, and the Canaanites, and the Perizzites, and the Hivites, and the Jebusites, seven nations *c*greater and mightier than thou;
2 and when the LORD thy God shall *d*deliver them before thee; thou shalt smite them, *and* *e*utterly destroy them; *f*thou shalt make no covenant with them, nor shew mercy unto them:
3 *g*neither shalt thou make marriages with them; thy daughter thou shalt not give unto his son, nor his daughter shalt thou
4 take unto thy son. For they will turn away thy son from following me, that they may serve other gods: *h*so will the anger of the LORD be kindled against you, and destroy thee suddenly.
5 But thus shall ye deal with them; ye shall *i*destroy their altars, and break down their ¹images, and cut down their groves, and
6 burn their graven images with fire. *k*For thou *art* an holy people unto the LORD thy God: *l*the LORD thy God hath chosen thee to be a special people unto himself, above all people that
7 *are* upon the face of the earth. The LORD did not set his love upon you, nor choose you, because ye were more in number than
8 any people; for ye *were* *m*the fewest of all people: but *n*because the LORD loved you, and because he would keep *o*the oath which he had sworn unto your fathers, *p*hath the LORD brought you out with a mighty hand, and redeemed you out of the house of
9 bondmen, from the hand of Pharaoh king of Egypt. Know therefore that the LORD thy God, he *is* God, *q*the faithful God, *r*which keepeth covenant and mercy with them that love him
10 and keep his commandments to a thousand generations; and *s*repayeth them that hate him to their face, to destroy them: *t*he will not be slack to him that hateth him, he will repay him to
11 his face. Thou shalt therefore keep the commandments, and the statutes, and the judgments, which I command thee this
12 day, to do them. ¶*u*Wherefore it shall come to pass, ²if ye hearken to these judgments, and keep, and do them, that the LORD thy God shall keep unto thee *x*the covenant and the mercy
13 which he sware unto thy fathers: and he will *y*love thee, and bless thee, and multiply thee: *z*he will also bless the fruit of thy womb, and the fruit of thy land, thy corn, and thy wine, and thine oil, the increase of thy kine, and the flocks of thy sheep,
14 in the land which he sware unto thy fathers to give thee. Thou shalt be blessed above all people: *a*there shall not be male
15 or female barren among you, or among your cattle. And the LORD will take away from thee all sickness, and will put none

a ch. 31. 3.
Ps. 44. 2.
b Gen. 15.
19, &c.
Ex. 33. 2.
c ch. 4. 38.
& 9. 1.
d ver. 23.
ch. 23. 14.
e Lev. 27. 28,
29.
ch. 20. 16.
Josh. 6. 17.
f Ex. 23. 32.
Judg. 2. 2.
Josh. 2. 14.
g Josh. 23.
12.
1 Kin. 11. 2.
Ezra 9. 2.
h ch. 6. 15.
i Ex. 23. 24.
k Ex. 19. 6.
ch. 14. 2.
Ps. 50. 5.
Jer. 2. 3.
l Ex. 19. 5.
1 Pet. 2. 9.
m ch. 10. 22.
n ch. 10. 15.
o Ex. 32. 13.
Ps. 105. 8.
Luke 1. 55.
p Ex. 13. 3.
q Isai. 49. 7.
1 Cor. 1. 9.
r Ex. 20. 6.
Neh. 1. 5.
Dan. 9. 4.
s Isai. 59. 18.
Nah. 1. 2.
t ch. 32. 35.

u Lev. 26. 3.

x Ps. 105. 8.
Luke 1. 72.
y John 14.
21.
z ch. 28. 4.

a Ex. 23. 26.

---

¹ Heb. *statues,* or, *pillars.*　　　　　² Heb. *because.*

VII. 1–11. See vi. 10 note.

5. *their groves*] Render, **their idols of wood**: the reference is to the wooden trunk used as a representation of Ashtaroth; see *v.* 13 and Ex. xxxiv. 13 note.

7. *the fewest of all people*] God chose to Himself Israel, when as yet but a single family, or rather a single person, Abraham; though there were already numerous nations and powerful kingdoms in the earth. Increase (i. 10, x. 22) had taken place because of the very blessing of God spoken of in *v.* 8.

10. *repayeth them that hate him to their*

face] *i.e.* punishes His enemies in their own proper persons.

13. *flocks of thy sheep*] Render rather **the ewes of thy sheep.** The phrase is peculiar to Deuteronomy. The Hebrew word for ewes is the plural form of Ashtoreth the well-known name of the "goddess of the Zidonians" (1 K. xi. 5). This goddess, called by the classical writers Astarte, and identified with Venus, represented the fruitfulness of nature.

15. There seems to be here not so much a reference to the plagues inflicted miraculously by God on Egypt (cp. Ex. xv. 26),

b Ex. 9. 14.
ch. 28. 27.
c ver. 2.

d ch. 13. 8.
& 19. 13.
e Ex. 23. 33.
ch. 12. 30.
Ps. 106. 36.
f Num. 33.
53.
g ch. 31. 6.
h Ps. 105. 5.
i ch. 4. 34.
& 29. 3.

k Ex. 23. 28.

l Num. 11.
20.
Josh. 3. 10.
m ch. 10. 17.
Neh. 1. 5.
n Ex. 23. 59,
30.
o Josh. 10.
24, 25, 42.
p Ex. 17. 14.
ch. 9. 14.
q ch. 11. 25.
Josh. 1. 5.
r Ex. 32. 20.
ch. 12. 3.
1 Chr. 14. 12.
s Josh. 7. 1.
t Judg. 8.
27.
Zeph. 1. 3.
u ch. 17. 1.
x Lev. 27.
28.
ch 13. 17.
Josh. 6. 17.

a ch. 4. 1.
b ch. 1. 3.
Ps. 136. 16.
c Ex. 16. 4.
ch. 13. 3.
d 2 Chr. 32.
31.
e Ex. 16. 2.
f Ex. 16. 12.
g Matt. 4. 4.
Luke 4. 4.

of the [b]evil diseases of Egypt, which thou knowest, upon thee;
16 but will lay them upon all *them* that hate thee. And [c]thou
shalt consume all the people which the LORD thy God shall
deliver thee; [d]thine eye shall have no pity upon them: neither
shalt thou serve their gods; for that *will be* [e]a snare unto thee.
17 ¶ If thou shalt say in thine heart, These nations *are* more than I;
18 how can I [f]dispossess them? [g]Thou shalt not be afraid of them:
but shalt well [h]remember what the LORD thy God did unto
19 Pharaoh, and unto all Egypt; [i]the great temptations which
thine eyes saw, and the signs, and the wonders, and the mighty
hand, and the stretched out arm, whereby the LORD thy God
brought thee out: so shall the LORD thy God do unto all the
20 people of whom thou art afraid. [k]Moreover the LORD thy God
will send the hornet among them, until they that are left, and
21 hide themselves from thee, be destroyed. Thou shalt not be
affrighted at them: for the LORD thy God *is* [l]among you, [m]a
22 mighty God and terrible. [n]And the LORD thy God will [1]put
out those nations before thee by little and little: thou mayest
not consume them at once, lest the beasts of the field increase
23 upon thee. But the LORD thy God shall deliver them [2]unto
thee, and shall destroy them with a mighty destruction, until
24 they be destroyed. And [o]he shall deliver their kings into thine
hand, and thou shalt destroy their name [p]from under heaven:
[q]there shall no man be able to stand before thee, until thou have
25 destroyed them. The graven images of their gods [r]shall ye
burn with fire: thou [s]shalt not desire the silver or gold *that is*
on them, nor take *it* unto thee, lest thou be [t]snared therein: for
26 it *is* [u]an abomination to the LORD thy God. Neither shalt thou
bring an abomination into thine house, lest thou be a cursed
thing like it: *but* thou shalt utterly detest it, and thou shalt
utterly abhor it; [x]for it *is* a cursed thing.
CHAP. 8. ALL the commandments which I command thee this day
[a]shall ye observe to do, that ye may live, and multiply, and go
in and possess the land which the LORD sware unto your fathers.
2 And thou shalt remember all the way which the LORD thy God
[b]led thee these forty years in the wilderness, to humble thee, *and*
[c]to prove thee, [d]to know what *was* in thine heart, whether thou
3 wouldest keep his commandments, or no. And he humbled
thee, and [e]suffered thee to hunger, and [f]fed thee with manna,
which thou knewest not, neither did thy fathers know; that he
might make thee know that man doth [g]not live by bread only,

[1] Heb. *pluck off.*   [2] Heb. *before thy face,* ver. 2.

as to the terrible diseases with which, above
other countries, Egypt was infested. Cp.
xxviii. 27, 35. It is not without significance
that Egypt, which represents in Scripture
the world as contrasted with the Church,
should thus above other lands lie under the
power of disease and death.

25. *the silver or gold that is on them*] The
silver and gold with which the statues of
the gods were overlaid. St. Paul is probably
alluding to this command in Rom. ii. 22, and
his accusation of the Jew thus shows that
the prohibition of the text was very necessary.

lest thou be snared] As by the rich ephod
made by Gideon : cp. marg. ref.

VIII. **3.** *but by every* word *that proceedeth
out of the mouth of the* LORD] Lit. "every
outgoing of the mouth of the Lord." Cp.
xxix. 5, 6. The term "word" is inserted
by A. V. after the LXX., which is followed
by St. Matt. and St. Luke (see marg. reff.).
On the means of subsistence available to
the people during the wandering, see Num.
xx. 1 note. The lesson was taught, that it
is not nature which nourishes man, but God
the Creator by and through nature : and
generally that God is not tied to the particular channels ("bread only," *i.e.* the
ordinary means of earthly sustenance)
through which He is usually pleased to
work.

but by every *word* that proceedeth out of the mouth of the LORD
4 doth man live. [h]Thy raiment waxed not old upon thee, neither
5 did thy foot swell, these forty years. [i]Thou shalt also consider
in thine heart, that, as a man chasteneth his son, *so* the LORD
6 thy God chasteneth thee. Therefore thou shalt keep the commandments of the LORD thy God, [k]to walk in his ways, and to
7 fear him. For the LORD thy God bringeth thee into a good
land, [l]a land of brooks of water, of fountains and depths that
8 spring out of valleys and hills; a land of wheat, and barley, and
vines, and fig trees, and pomegranates; a land [1]of oil olive, and
9 honey; a land wherein thou shalt eat bread without scarceness,
thou shalt not lack any *thing* in it; a land [m]whose stones *are*
10 iron, and out of whose hills thou mayest dig brass. ¶ [n]When
thou hast eaten and art full, then thou shalt bless the LORD thy
11 God for the good land which he hath given thee. Beware that
thou forget not the LORD thy God, in not keeping his commandments, and his judgments, and his statutes, which I command
12 thee this day : [o]lest *when* thou hast eaten and art full, and hast
13 built goodly houses, and dwelt *therein;* and *when* thy herds and
thy flocks multiply, and thy silver and thy gold is multiplied,
14 and all that thou hast is multiplied; [p]then thine heart be lifted
up, and thou [q]forget the LORD thy God, which brought thee
15 forth out of the land of Egypt, from the house of bondage; who
[r]led thee through that great and terrible wilderness, [s]*wherein
were* fiery serpents, and scorpions, and drought, where *there was*
no water; [t]who brought thee forth water out of the rock of
16 flint; who fed thee in the wilderness with [u]manna, which thy
fathers knew not, that he might humble thee, and that he might
17 prove thee, [x]to do thee good at thy latter end; [y]and thou say in
thine heart, My power and the might of *mine* hand hath gotten
18 me this wealth. But thou shalt remember the LORD thy God :

[1] Heb. *of olive tree of oil.*

[h] ch. 29. 5.
Neh. 9. 21.
[i] 2 Sam. 7,
14.
Ps. 89. 32.
Prov. 3. 12.
Heb. 12. 5.
Rev. 3. 19.
[k] ch. 5. 33.
[l] ch. 11. 10.

[m] ch. 33. 25.
[n] ch. 6. 11.

[o] ch. 28. 47.
Prov. 30. 9.
Hos. 13. 6.

[p] 1 Cor. 4. 7.
[q] Ps. 106. 21.

[r] Isai. 63.
12, 13, 14.
Jer. 2. 6.
[s] Num. 21.
6.
Hos. 13. 5.
[t] Num. 20.
11.
Ps. 78. 15.
[u] ver. 3.
[x] Jer. 24. 5.
Heb. 12. 11.
[y] ch. 9. 4.
1 Cor. 4. 7.

---

4. They had clothes, it would seem, in
abundance (cp. Ex. xii. 34, 35) at the beginning of the forty years; and during
those years they had many sheep and oxen,
and so must have had much material for
clothing always at command. No doubt
also they carried on a traffic in these, as in
other commodities, with the Moabites and
the nomadic tribes of the desert. Such ordinary supplies must not be shut out of
consideration, even if they were on occasions supplemented by extraordinary providences of God, as was undoubtedly the case
with their food.

7-9. See Ex. iii. 8 note, and the contrast
expressed in xi. 10, 11, between Palestine
and Egypt.

The physical characteristics and advantages of a country like Palestine must have
been quite strange to Israel at the time
Moses was speaking : cp. iii. 25 note.
To have praised the fertility and excellence
of the Promised Land at an earlier period
would have increased the murmurings and
impatience of the people at being detained
in the wilderness : whereas now it encouraged them to encounter with more cheer-

fulness the opposition they would meet
from the inhabitants of Canaan.

8. *vines*] The abundance of wine in Syria
and Palestine is dwelt upon in the Egyptian
records of the campaigns of Thotmosis III.
In Egypt itself but little wine is produced.
The production of wine has in later times
gradually ceased in Palestine.

9. For *brass* read **copper** (Gen. iv. 22 note);
and compare the description of mining operations in Job xxviii. 1-11. Mining does not
seem to have been extensively carried on by
the Jews, though it certainly was by the
Canaanitish peoples displaced by them.
Traces of iron and copper works have been
discovered by modern travellers in Lebanon and many parts of the country; *e.g.* the
district of Argob (see iii. 4 notes) contains
iron-stone in abundance.

15. Render : "Who brought thee through
that great and terrible wilderness, the fiery
serpent and the scorpion, and the dry land
where are no waters." On the fiery serpents
see Num. xxi. 6 note.

16. *to do thee. good at thy latter end*]
This is presented as the result of God's
dealings.

- Prov. 10.
22.
Hos. 2. 8.
" ch. 7. 8.
b ch. 4. 26.
& 30. 18.

c Dan. 9. 11,
12.

a ch. 11. 31.
Josh. 3. 16.
b ch. 4. 38.
c ch. 1. 28.
d Num. 13.
22, 28, 32.

e ch. 31. 3.
Josh. 3. 11.
f ch. 4. 24.
Heb. 12. 29.
g ch. 7. 23.
h Ex. 23. 31.
ch. 7. 24.
i ch. 8. 17.
Rom. 11. 6,
20.
1 Cor. 4. 4.
k Gen. 15.
16.
Lev. 18. 24.
ch. 18. 12.
l Titus 3. 5.
m Gen. 12. 7.
& reff.

n ver. 13.
Ex. 32. 9.

o Ex. 14. 11.
Num. 11. 4.
& 20. 2.
ch. 31. 27.
p Ex. 32. 4.
Ps. 106. 19.
q Ex. 24. 12,
15.

r Ex. 24. 18.
& 34. 28.

s Ex. 31. 18.

t Ex. 19. 17.
& 20. 1.
ch. 4. 10.
& 10. 4.
& 18. 16.

²for *it is* he that giveth thee power to get wealth, *a*that he may establish his covenant which he sware unto thy fathers, as *it is* 19 this day. ¶ And it shall be, if thou do at all forget the LORD thy God, and walk after other gods, and serve them, and worship them, *b*I testify against you this day that ye shall surely 20 perish. As the nations which the LORD destroyeth before your face, *c*so shall ye perish; because ye would not be obedient unto the voice of the LORD your God.

CHAP. 9. HEAR, O Israel: Thou *art* to *a*pass over Jordan this day, to go in to possess nations *b*greater and mightier than thyself, 2 cities great and *c*fenced up to heaven, a people great and tall, *d*the children of the Anakims, whom thou knowest, and *of whom* thou hast heard *say*, Who can stand before the children of Anak!

3 Understand therefore this day, that the LORD thy God *is* he which *e*goeth over before thee; *as a* *f*consuming fire *g*he shall destroy them, and he shall bring them down before thy face: *h*so shalt thou drive them out, and destroy them quickly, as the 4 LORD hath said unto thee. ¶ *i*Speak not thou in thine heart, after that the LORD thy God hath cast them out from before thee, saying, For my righteousness the LORD hath brought me in to possess this land: but *k*for the wickedness of these nations 5 the LORD doth drive them out from before thee. *l*Not for thy righteousness, or for the uprightness of thine heart, dost thou go to possess their land: but for the wickedness of these nations the LORD thy God doth drive them out from before thee, and that he may perform *m*the word which the LORD sware unto 6 thy fathers, Abraham, Isaac, and Jacob. Understand therefore, that the LORD thy God giveth thee not this good land to possess it for thy righteousness; for thou *art* *n*a stiffnecked 7 people. ¶ Remember, *and* forget not, how thou provokedst the LORD thy God to wrath in the wilderness: *o*from the day that thou didst depart out of the land of Egypt, until ye came unto 8 this place, ye have been rebellious against the LORD. Also *p*in Horeb ye provoked the LORD to wrath, so that the LORD was 9 angry with you to have destroyed you. *q*When I was gone up into the mount to receive the tables of stone, *even* the tables of the covenant which the LORD made with you, then *r*I abode in the mount forty days and forty nights, I neither did eat bread 10 nor drink water: *s*and the LORD delivered unto me two tables of stone written with the finger of God; and on them *was written* according to all the words, which the LORD spake with you in the mount out of the midst of the fire *t*in the day of the 11 assembly. And it came to pass at the end of forty days and

---

IX. 1–29. The lesson of this chapter is exactly that of Eph. ii. 8, "By grace are ye saved through faith; and that not of yourselves; it is the gift of God: not of works, lest any man should boast."

In referring to their several rebellions Moses here, as elsewhere, has regard not so much to the order of time as to that of subject. (Cp. i. 9–15 note.) Such reasons as convenience and fitness to his argument sufficiently explain the variations observable when the statements of this chapter are minutely compared with those of Ex. xxxii.–xxxiv. In these variations we have simply such treatment of facts as is usual and warrantable between parties personally ac-

quainted with the matters.

3. *so shalt thou drive them out, and destroy them quickly*] This is not inconsistent with vii. 22, in which instant annihilation is not to be expected for the reasons assigned. Here Moses urges the people to trust in God's covenanted aid; since He would then make no delay in so destroying the nations attacked by them as to put them into enjoyment of the promises, and in doing so as fast as was for the well-being of Israel itself.

8. *Also in Horeb*] Rather, "even in Horeb." The time and circumstances made the apostasy at Horeb particularly inexcusable.

forty nights, *that* the LORD gave me the two tables of stone, *even*
12 the tables of the covenant. And the LORD said unto me, *u*Arise,   *u* Ex. 32. 7.
get thee down quickly from hence; for thy people which thou
hast brought forth out of Egypt have corrupted *themselves;* they
are *x*quickly turned aside out of the way which I commanded   *x* ch. 31. 29.
13 them; they have made them a molten image. ¶Furthermore   Judg. 2. 17.
*y*the LORD spake unto me, saying, I have seen this people, and,   *y* Ex. 32. 9.
14 behold, *z*it *is* a stiffnecked people: *a*let me alone, that I may   *z* ver. 6.
destroy them, and *b*blot out their name from under heaven: *c*and   ch. 10. 16.
I will make of thee a nation mightier and greater than they.   & 31. 27.
15 *d*So I turned and came down from the mount, and *e*the mount   2 Kin. 17. 14.
burned with fire: and the two tables of the covenant *were* in my   *a* Ex. 32. 10.
16 two hands. And *f*I looked, and, behold, ye had sinned against   *b* ch. 29. 20.
the LORD your God, *and* had made you a molten calf: ye had   & 109. 13.
turned aside quickly out of the way which the LORD had   *c* Num. 14.
17 commanded you. And I took the two tables, and cast them   12.
18 out of my two hands, and brake them before your eyes. And   *d* Ex. 32. 15.
I *g*fell down before the LORD, as at the first, forty days and   *e* Ex. 19. 18.
forty nights: I did neither eat bread, nor drink water, because   ch. 4. 11.
of all your sins which ye sinned, in doing wickedly in the sight   & 5. 23.
19 of the LORD, to provoke him to anger. *h*For I was afraid of   *f* Ex. 32. 19.
the anger and hot displeasure, wherewith the LORD was wroth   *g* Ex. 34. 28.
against you to destroy you. *i*But the LORD hearkened unto me   Ps. 106. 23.
20 at that time also. And the LORD was very angry with Aaron to   *h* Ex. 32. 10,
have destroyed him: and I prayed for Aaron also the same time.   11.
21 And *k*I took your sin, the calf which ye had made, and burnt   *i* Ex. 32. 14.
it with fire, and stamped it, *and* ground *it* very small, *even*   & 33. 17.
until it was as small as dust: and I cast the dust thereof into the   ch. 10. 10.
22 brook that descended out of the mount. And at *l*Taberah, and   Ps. 106. 23.
at *m*Massah, and at *n*Kibroth-hattaavah, ye provoked the LORD   *k* Ex. 32. 20.
23 to wrath. Likewise *o*when the LORD sent you from Kadesh-   Isai. 31. 7.
barnea, saying, Go up and possess the land which I have given
you; then ye rebelled against the commandment of the LORD   *l* Num. 11.
your God, and *p*ye believed him not, nor hearkened to his voice.   1, 3, 5.
24 *q*Ye have been rebellious against the LORD from the day that I   *m* Ex. 17. 7.
25 knew you. *r*Thus I fell down before the LORD forty days and   *n* Num. 11.
forty nights, as I fell down *at the first;* because the LORD had   4, 34.
26 said he would destroy you. *s*I prayed therefore unto the LORD,   *o* Num. 13.
and said, O Lord GOD, destroy not thy people and thine in-   3. & 14. 1.
heritance, which thou hast redeemed through thy greatness,   *p* Ps. 106.
   24, 25.
   q ch. 31. 27.
   r ver. 18.

   s Ex. 32. 11,
   &c.

---

18. *I fell down before the* LORD, *as at the*
first] Moses interceded for the people before
he came down from the mountain the first
time (Ex. xxxii. 11–13). This intercession is
only briefly alluded to in this verse. Afterwards he spent another forty days on the
mountain in fasting and prayer to obtain a
complete restitution of the Covenant (Ex.
xxxiv. 28). It is this second forty days, and
the intercession of Moses made therein (cp.
Ex. xxxiv. 9), that is more particularly
brought forward here and in *vv.* 25–29.

20. Israel could not even boast that its
heads and representatives continued faithful. Aaron had been already designated for
the High-priestly functions; but he fell
away with the rest of the people. It was due
therefore solely to the grace of God and the
intercession of Moses that Aaron himself

and his promised priesthood with him were
not cut off; just as at a later time, when
Aaron had actually to die for a new sin
Israel owed it still to the same causes that
Eleazar was substituted and the High-
priesthood perpetuated (cp. x. 6; Num. xx.
24–26).

22. See marg. ref. Taberah was the
name of a spot in or near the station of
Kibroth-hattaavah, and accordingly is not
named in the list of encampments given in
Num. xxxiii. 16. The separate mention of
the two is however here appropriate; for
each place and each name was a memorial
of an act of rebellion. The instances in
this and the next verse are not given in order
of occurrence. The speaker for his own
purposes advances from the slighter to the
more heinous proofs of guilt.

t Gen. 41. 57.
1 Sam. 14.
25.

u Ex. 32. 12.
Num. 14. 16.
x ch. 4. 20.
1 Kin. 8. 51.
Neh. 1. 10.
Ps. 95. 7.
a Ex. 34. 1,
2.
b Ex. 25. 10.
c Ex. 25. 16,
21.
d Ex. 25. 5,
10. & 37. 1.
e Ex. 34. 4.
f Ex. 34. 28.
y Ex. 20. 1.
h Ex. 19. 17.
ch. 9. 10.
& 18. 16.
i Ex. 34. 29.
k Ex. 40. 20.
l 1 Kin. 8. 9.
m Num. 33.
31.
n Num. 33.
30.
o Num. 20.
28. & 33. 38.
p Num. 33.
32, 33.
q Num. 3. 6.
r Num. 4. 15.
s ch. 18. 5.
t Lev. 9. 22.
Num. 6. 23.
ch. 21. 5.
u Num. 18.
20, 24.
ch. 18. 1, 2.
Ez. 44. 28.
x Ex. 34. 28.
ch. 9. 18.
y Ex. 32. 14.
& 33. 17.
ch. 9. 19.

which thou hast brought forth out of Egypt with a mighty 27 hand. Remember thy servants, Abraham, Isaac, and Jacob; look not unto the stubbornness of this people, nor to their wicked- 28 ness, nor to their sin : lest *t*the land whence thou broughtest us out say, *u*Because the Lord was not able to bring them into the land which he promised them, and because he hated them, he 29 hath brought them out to slay them in the wilderness. *x*Yet they *are* thy people and thine inheritance, which thou brought- est out by thy mighty power and by thy stretched out arm. CHAP. 10. AT that time the Lord said unto me, *a*Hew thee two tables of stone like unto the first, and come up unto me into the 2 mount, and *b*make thee an ark of wood. And I will write on the tables the words that were in the first tables which thou 3 brakest, and *c*thou shalt put them in the ark. And I made an ark *of* *d*shittim wood, and *e*hewed two tables of stone like unto the first, and went up into the mount, having the two tables in 4 mine hand. And *f*he wrote on the tables, according to the first writing, the ten [1]commandments, *g*which the Lord spake unto you in the mount out of the midst of the fire *h*in the day of the 5 assembly : and the Lord gave them unto me. And I turned myself and *i*came down from the mount, and *k*put the tables in the ark which I had made ; *l*and there they be, as the Lord 6 commanded me. ¶And the children of Israel took their journey from Beeroth *m*of the children of Jaakan to *n*Mosera: *o*there Aaron died, and there he was buried ; and Eleazar his son 7 ministered in the priest's office in his stead. *p*From thence they journeyed unto Gudgodah; and from Gudgodah to Jotbath, a 8 land of rivers of waters. ¶At that time *q*the Lord separated the tribe of Levi, *r*to bear the ark of the covenant of the Lord, *s*to stand before the Lord to minister unto him, and *t*to bless in 9 his name, unto this day. *u*Wherefore Levi hath no part nor in- heritance with his brethren ; the Lord *is* his inheritance, accord- 10 ing as the Lord thy God promised him. And *x*I stayed in the mount, according to the [2]first time, forty days and forty nights ; and *y*the Lord hearkened unto me at that time also, *and* the

[1] Heb. *words.*   [2] Or, *former days.*

X. 1–11. These verses are closely connected with the preceding chapter, and state very briefly the results of the intercession of Moses recorded in ix. 25–29. The people are reminded that all their blessings and privi- leges, forfeited by apostasy as soon as be- stowed, were only now their own by a new and most unmerited act of grace on the part of God, won from Him by the self-sacrific- ing mediation of Moses himself (*v.* 10).

1–5. The order for making the Ark and Tabernacle was evidently given before the apostasy of the people (Ex. xxv. seq.) ; but the tables were not put in the Ark until the completion and dedication of the Taber- nacle (Ex. xl.). But here as elsewhere (cp. ix. 1 note) Moses connects transactions closely related to each other and to his purpose without regard to the order of occurrence.

6. *there Aaron died*] *i.e.* whilst the people were encamped in Mosera or Moseroth. In xxxii. 50 as well as in Num. xx. 25 seq. Mount Hor is assigned as the place of

Aaron's death. It is plain then that Mo- serah was in the neighbourhood of Mount Hor. The appointment of Eleazar to mi- nister in place of Aaron, is referred to as a proof of the completeness and fulness of the reconciliation effected between God and the people by Moses. Though Aaron was sentenced to die in the wilderness for his sin at Meribah, yet God provided for the per- petuation of the High-priesthood, so that the people should not suffer. Cp. ix. 20 and note.

8. *At that time*] *i.e.* that of the encamp- ment at Sinai, as the words also import in *v.* 1. Throughout the passage the time of the important events at Sinai is kept in view ; it is reverted to as each incident is brought forward by Moses, alluded to suffi- ciently for his purpose, and dismissed.

Moses is evidently here speaking of the election by God of the tribe of Levi at large, priests and others also, for His own service.

11 LORD would not destroy thee. ^zAnd the LORD said unto me, Arise, ¹take *thy* journey before the people, that they may go in and possess the land, which I sware unto their fathers to give unto 12 them. ¶And now, Israel, ^awhat doth the LORD thy God require of thee, but ^bto fear the LORD thy God, ^cto walk in all his ways, and ^dto love him, and to serve the LORD thy God with all thy 13 heart and with all thy soul, to keep the commandments of the LORD, and his statutes, which I command thee this day ^efor thy 14 good? Behold, ^fthe heaven and the heaven of heavens *is* the 15 LORD's thy God, ^gthe earth *also*, with all that therein *is*. ^hOnly the LORD had a delight in thy fathers to love them, and he chose their seed after them, *even* you above all people, as *it is* this day. 16 Circumcise therefore ⁱ the foreskin of your heart, and be no more 17 ^kstiffnecked. For the LORD your God *is* ^lGod of gods, and ^mLord of lords, a great God, ⁿa mighty, and a terrible, which 18 ^oregardeth not persons, nor taketh reward: ^phe doth execute the judgment of the fatherless and widow, and loveth the 19 stranger, in giving him food and raiment. ^qLove ye therefore 20 the stranger : for ye were strangers in the land of Egypt. ^rThou shalt fear the LORD thy God ; him shalt thou serve, and to him 21 shalt thou ^scleave, ^tand swear by his name. ^uHe *is* thy praise, and he *is* thy God, ^xthat hath done for thee these great and 22 terrible things, which thine eyes have seen. Thy fathers went down into Egypt ^ywith threescore and ten persons ; and now the LORD thy God hath made thee ^z as the stars of heaven for multitude.

CHAP. 11. THEREFORE thou shalt ^alove the LORD thy God, and ^bkeep his charge, and his statutes, and his judgments, and his

¹ Heb. *go in journey.*

Right margin references:
z Ex. 32. 31.
& 33. 1.
a Mic. 6. 8.
b ch. 6. 13.
c ch. 5. 33.
d ch. 6. 5.
Matt. 22. 37.
e ch. 6. 24.
f 1 Kin. 8.27.
16. 16.
g Gen. 14.
19.
Ex. 19. 5.
Ps. 24. 1.
h ch. 4. 37.
i ch. 30. 6.
Jer. 4. 4.
Rom. 2. 28.
k ch. 9. 6, 13.
l Ps. 136. 2.
Dan. 2. 47.
m Rev. 17.
14.
n ch. 7. 21.
o Job 34. 19.
Acts 10. 34.
p Ps. 68. 5.
& 146. 9.
q Lev. 19. 33.
r Matt. 4. 10.
s ch. 11. 22.
t Ps. 63. 11.
u Ex. 15. 2.
x Ps. 106. 21.
y Ex. 1. 5.
z Gen. 15. 5.
a ch. 10. 12.
b Zech. 3. 7.

---

12. seq. After these emphatic warnings against self-righteousness the principal topic is resumed from ch. vi., and this division of the discourse is drawn to a conclusion in the next two chapters by a series of direct and positive exhortations to a careful fulfilment of the duties prescribed in the first two of the Ten "Words."

12. *what doth the* LORD *thy God require,* &c.] A noteworthy demand. God has in the Mosaic law positively commanded many th ngs. These however relate to external observances, which if need be can be enforced. But love and veneration cannot be enforced, even by God himself. They must be spontaneous. Hence, even under the law of ordinances where so much was peremptorily laid down, and omnipotence was ready to compel obedience, those sentiments, which are the spirit and life of the whole, have to be, as they here are, invited and solicited.

16. On Circumcision see Gen. xvii. 10. This verse points to the spiritual import of Circumcision. Man is by nature "very far gone from original righteousness," and in a state of enmity to God ; by Circumcision, as the sacrament of admission to the privileges of the chosen people, this opposition must be taken away ere man could enter into co-venant with God. It was through the flesh that man first sinned ; as it is also in the

flesh, its functions, lusts, &c., that man's rebellion against God chiefly manifests itself still. It was fitting therefore that the symbol which should denote the removal of this estrangement from God should be wrought in the body. Moses then fitly follows up the command "to circumcise the heart," with the warning "to be no more stiffnecked." His meaning is that they should lay aside that obduracy and perverseness towards God for which he had been reproving them, which had led them into so many transgressions of the Covenant and revolts from God, and which was especially the very contrary of that love and fear of God required by the first two of the Ten Commandments. The language associated with Circumcision in the Bible distinguishes the use made of this rite in the Jewish religion from that found amongst certain heathen nations. Circumcision was practised by some of them as a religious rite, designed (*e.g.*) to appease the deity of death supposed to delight in human suffering ; but not by any, the Egyptians probably excepted, at all in the Jewish sense and meaning.

The grounds on which Circumcision was imposed as essential by the Law are the same as those on which Baptism is required in the Gospel. The latter in the New Testament is strictly analogous to the former under the Old ; cp. Col. ii. 11, 12.

2 commandments, alway. And know ye this day: for *I speak*
not with your children which have not known, and which have
not seen *c*the chastisement of the LORD your God, *d*his greatness,
3 *e*his mighty hand, and his stretched out arm, *f*and his miracles,
and his acts, which he did in the midst of Egypt unto Pharaoh
4 the king of Egypt, and unto all his land; and what he did unto
the army of Egypt, unto their horses, and to their chariots;
*g*how he made the water of the Red sea to overflow them as they
pursued after you, and *how* the LORD hath destroyed them unto
5 this day; and what he did unto you in the wilderness, until ye
6 came into this place; and *h*what he did unto Dathan and Abiram,
the sons of Eliab, the son of Reuben: how the earth opened her
mouth, and swallowed them up, and their households, and their
tents, and all the ¹substance that ²*was* in their possession, in the
7 midst of all Israel: but *i*your eyes have seen all the great acts
8 of the LORD which he did. Therefore shall ye keep all the commandments which I command you this day, that ye may *k*be
strong, and go in and possess the land, whither ye go to possess
9 it; and *l*that ye may prolong *your* days in the land, *m*which
the LORD sware unto your fathers to give unto them and to their
10 seed, *n*a land that floweth with milk and honey. ¶ For the land,
whither thou goest in to possess it, *is* not as the land of Egypt,
from whence ye came out, *o*where thou sowedst thy seed, and
11 wateredst *it* with thy foot, as a garden of herbs: *p*but the land,
whither ye go to possess it, *is* a land of hills and valleys, *and*
12 drinketh water of the rain of heaven: a land which the LORD
thy God ³careth for: *q*the eyes of the LORD thy God *are* always
upon it, from the beginning of the year even unto the end of the

¹ Or, *living substance which*   ² Heb. was *at their feet.*   ³ Heb. *seeketh.*
followed them.

XI. 2. *And know,* &c.] Render : **And own
ye this day (for I have not to do with
your children which have not known
and which have not seen) the chastisement of the Lord, his greatness,** &c.
The "chastisement" consisted in the
many mighty acts, both of punishment and
mercy, through which God had guided them
from Egypt to the borders of the Promised
Land.

6. See margin. Literally, "every living
thing at their feet." The expression does
not mean their goods, which would be included in their "households and tents,"
but their followers (Num. xvi. 32).

10. Another motive for fidelity is added,
viz. the entire dependence of the Promised
Land upon God for its fertility. It was "a
land flowing with milk and honey;" yet
this its richness was not, as was that of
Egypt, the reward of human skill and labour, but was, on the contrary, the gift of
God simply and entirely; the effect of "the
former and the latter rains" sent by Him.
The spiritual significance of these and
many other such peculiarities of the Promised Land must not be overlooked.

Egypt and Canaan are distinguished in
this and the following verses, by certain of
their most remarkable physical traits. Canaan as a mountainous country (cp. iii. 25

note) was well watered, but by the rains of
heaven, on which it absolutely depended for
its crops. Artificial irrigation could do nothing to remedy this dependence. Hence
it was a land on which, so long as God's
people were faithful and consequently prosperous, "the eyes of God" would always
be : *i.e.* He would supply at each successive
season (cp. *vv.* 14, 15) the useful conditions
of productiveness. But Egypt, fit emblem
here as elsewhere of the world of nature in
distinction from the world of grace, though
of course deriving its all ultimately from
the Giver of all good things, yet directly and
immediately owed its riches and plenty to
human ingenuity and capital. It enjoyed
no rain worth speaking of, but drew its
water supply from the annual overflowing
of the Nile. This only lasts about a hundred days; but is rendered available for
agricultural purposes throughout the year
by an elaborate and costly system of tanks,
canals, forcing machines, &c. To these
mechanical appliances allusion is made in
v. 10. The inhabitants of Egypt probably
watered "with the foot" in two ways, viz.
by means of tread-wheels working sets of
pumps, and by means of artificial channels
connected with reservoirs, and opened,
turned, or closed by the feet. Both methods
are still in use in Egypt.

13 year. ¶And it shall come to pass, if ye shall hearken ʳdili-
gently unto my commandments which I command you this day,
ˢto love the Lord your God, and to serve him with all your heart
14 and with all your soul, that ᵗI will give you the rain of your
land in his due season, ᵘthe first rain and the latter rain, that
thou mayest gather in thy corn, and thy wine, and thine oil.
15 ˣAnd I will ¹send grass in thy fields for thy cattle, that thou
16 mayest ʸeat and be full. Take heed to yourselves, ᶻthat your
heart be not deceived, and ye turn aside, and ªserve other gods,
17 and worship them; and then ᵇthe Lord's wrath be kindled
against you, and he ᶜshut up the heaven, that there be no rain,
and that the land yield not her fruit; and lest ᵈye perish quickly
18 from off the good land which the Lord giveth you. ¶Therefore
ᵉshall ye lay up these my words in your heart and in your soul,
and ᶠbind them for a sign upon your hand, that they may be as
19 frontlets between your eyes. ᵍAnd ye shall teach them your
children, speaking of them when thou sittest in thine house, and
when thou walkest by the way, when thou liest down, and when
20 thou risest up. ʰAnd thou shalt write them upon the door posts of
21 thine house, and upon thy gates: that ⁱyour days may be multiplied, and the days of your children, in the land which the
Lord sware unto your fathers to give them, ᵏas the days of
22 heaven upon the earth. ¶For if ˡye shall diligently keep all
these commandments which I command you, to do them, to love
the Lord your God, to walk in all his ways, and ᵐto cleave
23 unto him; then will the Lord ⁿdrive out all these nations from
before you, and ye shall ᵒpossess greater nations and mightier
24 than yourselves. ᵖEvery place whereon the soles of your feet
shall tread shall be your's: ᵠfrom the wilderness and Lebanon,
from the river, the river Euphrates, even unto the uttermost
25 sea shall your coast be. ʳThere shall no man be able to stand
before you: for the Lord your God shall ˢlay the fear of you
and the dread of you upon all the land that ye shall tread upon,
26 ᵗas he hath said unto you. ¶ᵘBehold, I set before you this day
27 a blessing and a curse; ˣa blessing, if ye obey the commandments of the Lord your God, which I command you this day:
28 and a ʸcurse, if ye will not obey the commandments of the Lord
your God, but turn aside out of the way which I command you
this day, to go after other gods, which ye have not known.
29 And it shall come to pass, when the Lord thy God hath brought
thee in unto the land whither thou goest to possess it, that thou
shalt put ᶻthe blessing upon mount Gerizim, and the curse upon

¹ Heb. give.

ʳ ver. 22.
ch. 6. 17.
ˢ ch. 10. 12.
ᵗ Lev. 26. 4.
ch. 28. 12.
ᵘ Joel 2. 23.
Jam. 5. 7.
ˣ Ps. 104. 14.
ʸ ch. 6. 11.
Joel 2. 19.
ᶻ ch. 29. 18.
Job 31. 27.
ª ch. 8. 19.
& 30. 17.
ᵇ ch. 6. 15.
ᶜ 1 Kin. 8.
35.
2 Chr. 6. 26.
ᵈ ch. 4. 26.
& 30. 18.
Josh. 23. 13,
15, 16.
ᵉ ch. 6. 6.
& 32. 46.
ᶠ ch. 6. 8.
ᵍ ch. 4. 9, 10.
& 6. 7.
ʰ ch. 6. 9.
ⁱ ch. 4. 40.
Prov. 3. 2.
ᵏ Ps. 72. 5.
& 89. 29.
ˡ ver. 13.
ch. 6. 17.
ᵐ ch. 10. 20.
& 30. 20.
ⁿ ch. 4. 38.
& 9. 5.
ᵒ ch. 9. 1.
ᵖ Josh. 1. 3.
& 14. 9.
ᵠ Gen. 15.
18.
Ex. 23. 31.
Num. 34. 3.
ʳ ch. 7. 24.
ˢ ch. 2. 25.
ᵗ Ex. 23. 27.
ᵘ ch. 30. 1,
15, 19.
ˣ ch. 28. 2.
ʸ ch. 28. 15.
ᶻ ch. 27. 12.
Josh. 8. 33.

14. the first rain and the latter rain] The
former is the proper term for the autumn
rain, falling about the time of sowing, and
which may be named "the former," as occurring in the early part of the Hebrew
civil year, viz. in October and November.
The other word is applied to the spring
rain, which falls in March and April, because it fits the earth for the ingathering of
harvest. Between these two wet periods,
and except them, there was little or no rain
in Canaan.

21. The sense is: "Keep the covenant
faithfully, and so shall your own and your
children's days be multiplied as long as the

heaven covers the earth." The promise of
Canaan to Israel was thus a perpetual promise, but also a conditional one.

29. thou shalt put the blessing upon mount
Gerizim] Lit. thou shalt give, i.e. give utterance to it. On the ceremony see xxvii.
14 seq.

Mount Gerizim, barren like Ebal, was
probably selected as the hill of benediction
because it was the southernmost of the two,
the south being the region, according to Hebrew ideas, of light, and so of life and blessing. The situation of the mountains is
described more accurately in v. 30. The
words "by the way where the sun goeth

30 mount Ebal. *Are* they not on the other side Jordan, by the way
where the sun goeth down, in the land of the Canaanites, which
dwell in the champaign over against Gilgal, *a*beside the plains of
31 Moreh? *b*For ye shall pass over Jordan to go in to possess the
land which the LORD your God giveth you, and ye shall possess
32 it, and dwell therein. And ye shall observe *c*to do all the statutes and judgments which I set before you this day.

CHAP. 12. *a*THESE *are* the statutes and judgments, which ye shall
observe to do in the land, which the LORD God of thy fathers
giveth thee to possess it, *b*all the days that ye live upon the
2 earth. *c*Ye shall utterly destroy all the places, wherein the
nations which ye shall [1]possess served their gods, *d*upon the
high mountains, and upon the hills, and under every green tree:
3 and *e*ye shall [2]overthrow their altars, and break their pillars,
and burn their groves with fire; and ye shall hew down the
graven images of their gods, and destroy the names of them out
4 of that place. *f*Ye shall not do so unto the LORD your God.
5 But unto the place which the LORD your God shall *g*choose out
of all your tribes to put his name there, *even* unto his habitation

[1] Or, *inherit.*   [2] Heb. *break down.*

a Gen. 12. 6.
Judg. 7. 1.
b ch. 9. 1.
Josh. 1. 11.
c ch. 5. 32.
& 12. 32.
a ch. 6. 1.
b ch. 4. 10.
1 Kin. 8. 40.
c Ex. 34. 13.
ch. 7. 5.
d 2 Kin. 16.
4. & 17. 10,
11.
Jer. 3. 6.
e Num. 33.
52.
Judg. 2. 2.
f ver. 31.
g ver. 11.
ch. 26. 2.
Josh. 9. 27.
1 Kin. 8. 29.
2 Chr. 7. 12.
Ps. 78. 68.

---

down," should run, **beyond the road of the
west**; *i.e.* on the further side of the main
track which ran from Syria and Damascus
to Jerusalem and Egypt through the centre
of Palestine. This is called "the way of
the west" in contrast to the other main
route from Damascus to the south which
passed through the district east of Jordan.
The further specifications "Gilgal" and "the
plains (rather, **the oaks**, cp. Gen. xii. 6 note)
of Moreh," are added to define more particularly the section of Canaanites intended.
This Gilgal is perhaps to be found in Jiljilia, a large village about twelve miles
south of Gerizim.

XII. Moses now passes on to apply (xii.-
xxvi.) the leading principles of the Decalogue to the ecclesiastical, civil, and social
life of the people. Particulars will be noticed which are peculiar to the Law as given
in Deuteronomy; and even in laws repeated
from the earlier books various new circumstances and details are introduced. This is
but natural. The Sinaitic legislation was
nearly forty years old, and had been given
under conditions of time, place, and circumstance different and distinct from those now
present. Yet the Sinaitic system, far from
being set aside or in any way abrogated, is
on the contrary throughout presupposed
and assumed. Its existence and authority
are taken as the starting-point for what is
here prescribed, and an accurate acquaintance with it on the part of the people is
taken for granted.

3. *their groves*] Render **their idols of
wood**: and see vii. 5 note.

4. *i.e.* "The idolaters set up their altars
and images on any high hill, and under
every green tree at their pleasure, but *ye*
shall not do so; the Lord Himself shall determine the spot for your worship, and

there only shall ye seek Him." The religion of the Canaanites was human; its
modes of worship were of man's devising.
It fixed its holy places on the hills in the
vain thought of being nearer heaven, or in
deep groves where the silence and gloom
might overawe the worshipper. But such
superstitious appliances were not worthy of
the true religion. God had in it revealed
Himself to men, and manifested amongst
them His immediate Presence and power.
He would Himself assign the Sanctuary and
the ritual of His own service.

5. "To put his name there" means to
manifest to men His Divine Presence. The
Targumists rightly refer to the Shechinah; but the expression comprehends all
the various modes in which God vouchsafed
to reveal Himself and His attributes to men.

The purpose of the command of the text
is to secure the unity, and through unity
the purity of the worship of God. That
there should be one national centre for the
religion of the people was obviously essential to the great ends of the whole dispensation. Corruption began as soon as the precepts of the text were relaxed or neglected:
Cp. the case of Gideon, Judg. viii. 27; of
Micah, Judg. xviii.; of Jeroboam, 1 K. xii.
26 seq.

The words "the place which the LORD
shall choose to put His Name there" suggest
Jerusalem and Solomon's Temple to our
minds. But though spoken as they were
by a prophet, and interpreted as they are
by the Psalms (*e.g.* Ps. lxxviii. 67-69), they
have a proper application to the Temple,
yet they must not be referred exclusively to
it. The text does not import that God
would always from the first choose one and
the same locality "to put His Name there,"
but that there would always be a locality so

6 shall ye seek, and thither thou shalt come : and [h]thither ye shall
bring your burnt offerings, and your sacrifices, and your [i]tithes,
and heave offerings of your hand, and your vows, and your
freewill offerings, and the firstlings of your herds and of your
7 flocks : and [k]there ye shall eat before the LORD your God, and
[l]ye shall rejoice in all that ye put your hand unto, ye and your
8 households, wherein the LORD thy God hath blessed thee. ¶ Ye
shall not do after all *the things* that we do here this day, [m]every
9 man whatsoever *is* right in his own eyes. For ye are not as yet
come to the rest and to the inheritance, which the LORD your
10 God giveth you. But *when* [n]ye go over Jordan, and dwell in
the land which the LORD your God giveth you to inherit, and
when he giveth you rest from all your enemies round about, so
11 that ye dwell in safety; then there shall be [o]a place which the
LORD your God shall choose to cause his name to dwell there ;
thither shall ye bring all that I command you; your burnt
offerings, and your sacrifices, your tithes, and the heave offering of your hand, and all [1]your choice vows which ye vow unto
12 the LORD : and [p]ye shall rejoice before the LORD your God, ye,
and your sons, and your daughters, and your menservants,
and your maidservants, and the Levite that *is* within your
gates; forasmuch as [q]he hath no part nor inheritance with you.
13 [r]Take heed to thyself that thou offer not thy burnt offerings
14 in every place that thou seest : [s]but in the place which the LORD
shall choose in one of thy tribes, there thou shalt offer thy burnt
offerings, and there thou shalt do all that I command thee.
15 ¶ Notwithstanding [t]thou mayest kill and eat flesh in all thy

[h] Lev. 17. 3, 4.
[i] ver. 17.
ch. 14. 22.
& 15. 19.
[k] ch. 14. 26.
[l] ver. 12, 18.
Lev. 23. 40.
ch. 16. 11.
& 26. 11.
& 27. 7.
[m] Judg. 17.
6. & 21. 25.
[n] ch. 11. 31.

[o] ver. 5, 14,
18, 21, 26.
& ch. 14. 23.
& pass.
Josh. 18. 1.
1 Kin. 8. 29.
Ps. 78. 68.
[p] ver. 7.

[q] ch. 10. 9.
& 14. 29.
[r] Lev. 17. 4.
[s] ver. 11.

[t] ver. 21.

[1] Heb. *the choice of your vows.*

---

chosen by Him; and that thither the people
must bring their sacrifices, and not offer
them at their pleasure or convenience elsewhere. Neither does the text forbid the
offering of sacrifices to God at other places
than the one chosen by Him "to put His
Name there" on proper occasions and by
proper authority (cp. xxvii. 5, 6 ; Judg. vi.
24, xiii. 16 ; 1 Kings iii. 4, xviii. 31). The
text simply prohibits sacrifices at any other
locality than that which should be appointed or permitted by God for the purpose.

6. Some have objected that this command
cannot possibly have been ever carried out,
at all events until in later days the territory
which owned obedience to it was narrowed
to the little kingdom of Judah. But in
these and in other precepts Moses doubtless
takes much for granted. He is here, as
elsewhere, regulating and defining more
precisely institutions which had long been
in existence, as to many details of which
custom superseded the necessity of specific
enactment. No doubt the people well understood what Maimonides expressly tells
us in reference to the matter, namely, that
where immediate payment could not be
made, the debt to God was to be reserved
until the next great Feast, and then duly
discharged. The thing specially to be observed was that no kind of sacrifice was to
be offered except at the sacred spot fixed by
God for its acceptance.

7. An injunction that the feasts which
accompanied certain offerings (not specified)
were to be also held in the same place.

8. Moses points out that heretofore they
had not observed the prescribed order in
their worship, because during their migratory life in the wilderness it had been impossible to do so. During their wanderings
there were doubtless times when the Tabernacle was not set up for days together, and
when the daily sacrifice (Num. xxviii. 3),
together with many other ordinances, were
necessarily omitted (cp. Josh. v. 5). This
consideration must be carefully borne in
mind throughout Deuteronomy. It illustrates the necessity for a repetition of very
much of the Sinaitic legislation, and suggests
the reason why some parts are so urgently
reiterated and impressed, whilst others are
left unnoticed. Moses now warns the people
that as they were about to quit their unsettled mode of life, God's purpose of
choosing for Himself a place to set His
Name there would be executed, and the
whole of the sacred ritual would consequently become obligatory. The "rest and
safety" of Canaan is significantly laid down
(*vv.* 10, 11) as the indispensable condition
and basis for an entire fulfilment of the
Law : the perfection of righteousness coinciding thus with the cessation of wanderings, dangers, and toils.

15. Whilst a stringent injunction is laid

gates, whatsoever thy soul lusteth after, according to the bless-
u ver. 22.   ing of the LORD thy God which he hath given thee : *u*the unclean
x ch. 14. 5.   and the clean may eat thereof, *x*as of the roebuck, and as of the
& 15. 22.   16 hart. *y*Only ye shall not eat the blood; ye shall pour it upon
y Gen. 9. 4.
Lev. 7. 26.   17 the earth as water. Thou mayest not eat within thy gates the
& 17. 10.   tithe of thy corn, or of thy wine, or of thy oil, or the firstlings
ch. 15. 23.   of thy herds or of thy flock, nor any of thy vows which thou
                            vowest, nor thy freewill offerings, or heave offering of thine
z ver. 11, 12.   18 hand : *z*but thou must eat them before the LORD thy God in the
ch. 14. 23.   place which the LORD thy God shall choose, thou, and thy son,
                            and thy daughter, and thy manservant, and thy maidservant,
                            and the Levite that *is* within thy gates: and thou shalt rejoice
                            before the LORD thy God in all that thou puttest thine hands
a ch. 14. 27.   19 unto. *a*Take heed to thyself that thou forsake not the Levite
                         20 [1]as long as thou livest upon the earth. ¶ When the LORD thy
b Gen. 15. 18.   God shall enlarge thy border, *b*as he hath promised thee, and
& 28. 14.   thou shalt say, I will eat flesh, because thy soul longeth to eat
Ex. 34. 24.
ch. 11. 24.   flesh; thou mayest eat flesh, whatsoever thy soul lusteth after.
& 19. 8.   21 If the place which the LORD thy God hath chosen to put his
                            name there be too far from thee, then thou shalt kill of thy
                            herd and of thy flock, which the LORD hath given thee, as I
                            have commanded thee, and thou shalt eat in thy gates what-
c ver. 15.   22 soever thy soul lusteth after. *c*Even as the roebuck and the
                            hart is eaten, so thou shalt eat them : the unclean and the clean
d ver. 16.   23 shall eat *of* them alike. *d*Only [2]be sure that thou eat not the
e Gen. 9. 4.   blood : *e*for the blood *is* the life; and thou mayest not eat the
Lev. 17. 11.   24 life with the flesh. Thou shalt not eat it; thou shalt pour it
f ch. 4. 40.   25 upon the earth as water. Thou shalt not eat it; *f*that it may
Isai. 3. 10.   go well with thee, and with thy children after thee, *g*when thou
g Ex. 15. 26.
ch. 13. 18.   26 shalt do *that which is* right in the sight of the LORD. Only thy
1 Kin. 11.   *h*holy things which thou hast, and *i*thy vows, thou shalt take,
38.
h Num. 5. 9.   27 and go unto the place which the LORD shall choose: and *k*thou
& 18. 19.   shalt offer thy burnt offerings, the flesh and the blood, upon the
i 1 Sam. 1.   altar of the LORD thy God: and the blood of thy sacrifices shall
21, 22, 24.
k Lev. 1. 5,   be poured out upon the altar of the LORD thy God, and thou
9, 13.   28 shalt eat the flesh. Observe and hear all these words which I
& 17. 11.   command thee, *l*that it may go well with thee, and with thy
l ver. 25.   children after thee for ever, when thou doest *that which is* good
m Ex. 23. 23.   29 and right in the sight of the LORD thy God. ¶ When *m*the LORD
ch. 19. 1.   thy God shall cut off the nations from before thee, whither thou
Josh. 23. 4.   goest to possess them, and thou [3]succeedest them, and dwellest
n ch. 7. 16.   30 in their land; take heed to thyself *n*that thou be not snared [4]by
                            following them, after that they be destroyed from before thee;
o ver. 4.   and that thou enquire not after their gods, saying, How did
Lev. 18. 3,   31 these nations serve their gods? Even so will I do likewise. *o*Thou
26, 30.
2 Kin. 17.   [1] Heb. *all thy days.*   [3] Heb. *inheritest,* or, *pos-*   [4] Heb. *after them.*
15.   [2] Heb. *be strong.*   *sessest them.*

---

down that the old rule (cp. Lev. xvii. 3, &c.) must be adhered to as regards animals slain in sacrifice, yet permission is now given to slaughter at home what was necessary for the table. The ceremonial distinctions did not apply in such cases, any more than to "the roebuck" (or gazelle) "and hart," animals allowed for food but not for sacrifice.

21. *if the place,* &c.] Rather, " *Because,*

or *since,* the place will be too far from thee." The permission given in *vv.* 15, 16 is repeated, and the reason of it assigned.

30. This caution is based upon the notion generally entertained in the ancient heathen world, that each country had its own tutelary deities whom it would be perilous to neglect; cp. 1 K. xx. 23; 2 K. xvii. 26. Israel was to shun such superstitions as unworthy of the elect people of God.

shalt not do so unto the LORD thy God: for every [1]abomination to the LORD, which he hateth, have they done unto their gods; for [p]even their sons and their daughters they have burnt in the 32 fire to their gods. What thing soever I command you, observe to do it: [q]thou shalt not add thereto, nor diminish from it.

CHAP. 13. IF there arise among you a prophet, or a [a]dreamer of 2 dreams, [b]and giveth thee a sign or a wonder, and [c]the sign or the wonder come to pass, whereof he spake unto thee, saying, Let us go after other gods, which thou hast not known, and let 3 us serve them; thou shalt not hearken unto the words of that prophet, or that dreamer of dreams: for the LORD your God [d]proveth you, to know whether ye love the LORD your God with 4 all your heart and with all your soul. Ye shall [e]walk after the LORD your God, and fear him, and keep his commandments, and obey his voice, and ye shall serve him, and [f]cleave unto him. 5 And [g]that prophet, or that dreamer of dreams, shall be put to death; because he hath [2]spoken to turn you away from the LORD your God, which brought you out of the land of Egypt, and redeemed you out of the house of bondage, to thrust thee out of the way which the LORD thy God commanded thee to walk in. [h]So shalt thou put the evil away from the midst of 6 thee. ¶[i]If thy brother, the son of thy mother, or thy son, or thy daughter, or [k]the wife of thy bosom, or thy friend, [l]which is as thine own soul, entice thee secretly, saying, Let us go and serve other gods, which thou hast not known, thou, nor thy 7 fathers; namely, of the gods of the people which are round about you, nigh unto thee, or far off from thee, from the one end of the 8 earth even unto the other end of the earth; thou shalt [m]not consent unto him, nor hearken unto him; neither shall thine eye pity him, neither shalt thou spare, neither shalt thou conceal 9 him: but [n]thou shalt surely kill him; [o]thine hand shall be first upon him to put him to death, and afterwards the hand of all 10 the people. And thou shalt stone him with stones, that he die; because he hath sought to thrust thee away from the LORD thy God, which brought thee out of the land of Egypt, from the 11 house of [3]bondage. And [p]all Israel shall hear, and fear, and 12 shall do no more any such wickedness as this is among you. ¶[q]If

[p] Lev. 18. 21 & 20. 2.
ch. 18. 10.
Jer. 32. 35.
Ez. 23. 37.
[q] ch. 4. 2. & 13. 18.
Josh. 1. 7.
Prov. 30. 6.
Rev. 22. 18.
[a] Zech. 10. 2.
[b] Matt. 24. 24.
2 Thes. 2. 9.
[c] See ch. 18. 22.
Jer. 28. 9.
Matt. 7. 22.
[d] ch. 8. 2.
1 Cor. 11. 19.
2 Thes. 2. 11.
Rev. 13. 14.
[e] 2 Kin. 23. 3.
2 Chr. 34. 31.
[f] ch. 10. 20.
[g] ch. 18. 20.
Jer. 14. 15.
[h] 1 Cor. 5. 13.
[i] ch. 17. 2.
[k] See Gen. 16. 5.
ch. 28. 54.
Prov. 5, 20.
Mic. 7. 5.
[l] 1 Sam. 18. 1, 3.
& 20. 17.
[m] Prov. 1. 10.
[n] ch. 17. 5.
[o] ch. 17. 7.
[p] ch. 17. 13. & 19. 20.
[q] Josh. 22. 11, &c.
Judg. 20. 1,2.

[1] Heb. abomination of the.   [2] Heb. spoken revolt against the LORD.   [3] Heb. bondmen.

XIII. The admonition of the closing verse of the last chapter introduces a new series of warnings intended to serve as a further safeguard against violation of these duties. The true modes and forms of worship have been laid down : the next step is to legislate against the authors and abettors of false ones.

1. a prophet, or a dreamer of dreams] Cp. Num. xii. 6. The "prophet" received his revelations by vision or direct oral communication (Num. xxiv. 16; 2 Sam. vii. 4; 2 Cor. xii. 2); "the dreamer of dreams" through the medium of a dream (1 K. iii. 5; Matt. ii. 13).

2. The Lord had said, "Thou shalt have none other gods but Me." A prophet is here supposed who invites the people "to go after other gods." To such a one no credit is under any circumstances to be given, even

should he show signs and wonders to authenticate his doctrine. The standing rule of faith and practice had been laid down once for all ; that the people were to hold fast. The prophet who propounded another rule could only be an impostor.

A different case is considered in xviii. 18, &c.

5. The context and parallel passages (cp. xvii. 7 ; Lev. xx. 2) indicate that there was to be a regular judicial procedure, and that the manner of the execution was to be by stoning. In this the community was to take its part in order to show its horror at the crime, and to clear itself of complicity therein.

6. The omissions in this enumeration seem to imply that no one was bound to impeach father, mother, or husband.

12. City was to keep jealous watch over

thou shalt hear *say* in one of thy cities, which the LORD thy
13 God hath given thee to dwell there, saying, *Certain* men, ¹the
children of Belial, ʳare gone out from among you, and have
ˢwithdrawn the inhabitants of their city, saying, ᵗLet us go and
14 serve other gods, which ye have not known; then shalt thou
enquire, and make search, and ask diligently; and, behold, *if it
be* truth, *and* the thing certain, *that* such abomination is wrought
15 among you; thou shalt surely smite the inhabitants of that city
with the edge of the sword, ᵘdestroying it utterly, and all that
is therein, and the cattle thereof, with the edge of the sword.
16 And thou shalt gather all the spoil of it into the midst of the
street thereof, and shalt ˣburn with fire the city, and all the
spoil thereof every whit, for the LORD thy God: and it shall be
17 ʸan heap for ever; it shall not be built again. And ᶻthere shall
cleave nought of the ²cursed thing to thine hand: that the
LORD may ᵃturn from the fierceness of his anger, and shew thee
mercy, and have compassion upon thee, and multiply thee, ᵇas
18 he hath sworn unto thy fathers; when thou shalt hearken to
the voice of the LORD thy God, ᶜto keep all his commandments
which I command thee this day, to do *that which is* right in the
eyes of the LORD thy God.

CHAP. 14. YE *are* ᵃthe children of the LORD your God: ᵇye shall
not cut yourselves, nor make any baldness between your eyes for
2 the dead. ᶜFor thou *art* an holy people unto the LORD thy God,
and the LORD hath chosen thee to be a peculiar people unto
3 himself, above all the nations that *are* upon the earth. ¶ ᵈThou
4 shalt not eat any abominable thing. ᵉThese *are* the beasts
5 which ye shall eat: the ox, the sheep, and the goat, the hart,
and the roebuck, and the fallow deer, and the wild goat, and the
6 ³⁴pygarg, and the wild ox, and the chamois. And every beast
that parteth the hoof, and cleaveth the cleft into two claws, *and*
7 cheweth the cud among the beasts, that ye shall eat. Nevertheless these ye shall not eat of them that chew the cud, or of them
that divide the cloven hoof; *as* the camel, and the hare, and the
coney: for they chew the cud, but divide not the hoof; *therefore*
8 they *are* unclean unto you. And the swine, because it divideth

Marginal references (left):
ʳ 1 John 2. 19.
Jude 19.
ˢ 2 Kin. 17. 21.
ᵗ ver. 2. 6.

ᵘ Ex. 22. 20.
Lev. 27. 28.
Josh. 6. 17.

ˣ Josh. 6. 24.

ʸ Josh. 8. 28.
Isai. 17. 1.
& 25. 2.
Jer. 49. 2.
ᶻ ch. 7. 26.
Josh. 6. 18.
ᵃ Josh. 6. 26.
ᵇ Gen. 22. 17.
& 26. 4.
& 28. 14.
ᶜ ch. 12. 25, 28, 32.

ᵃ Rom. 8. 16. & 9. 8, 26.
Gal. 3. 26.
ᵇ Lev. 19. 28. & 21. 5.
Jer. 16. 6.
& 41. 5.
& 47. 5.
1 Thes. 4. 13.
ᶜ Lev. 20. 26.
ch. 7. 6.
& 26. 18, 19.
ᵈ Ez. 4. 14.
Acts 10. 13.
ᵉ Lev. 11. 2.

---

¹ Or, *naughty men:* See
  Judg. 19. 22. 1 Sam. 2.
  12. & 25. 17, 25. 1 Kin.
  21. 10, 13. 2 Cor. 6. 15.

² Or, *devoted.*
³ Or, *bison.*
⁴ Heb. *dishon.*

---

city, as man over man. The clause " which
the Lord thy God hath given thee to dwell
in " significantly reminds them that the real
ownership of their dwellings rested in the
Lord (cp. Lev. xxv. 23), and that they, the
mere tenants, must not allow His property
to become a centre of rebellion against His
just authority.

13. In xv. 9 and in Nah. i. 11 the word
Belial is rendered in our translation by the
adjective " wicked." The word means *worthlessness.*

16. *every whit, for the* LORD *thy God*]
Some prefer : " **as a whole offering to the
Lord thy God.**"

XIV. The whole life and walk of the
people were to be regulated by the principle
" ye are the children of the Lord your
God " (*v.* 1).

1. *make any baldness between your eyes*] *i.e.*
by shaving the forepart of the head and the
eyebrows. The practices named in this verse
were common amongst the heathen, and
seem to be forbidden, not only because such
wild excesses of grief (cp. 1 Kings xviii. 28)
would be inconsistent in those who as children of a heavenly Father had prospects
beyond this world, but also because these
usages themselves arose out of idolatrous
notions.

3-21. Cp. Lev. xi. The variations here,
whether omissions or additions, are probably to be explained by the time and circumstances of the speaker.

5. The " pygarg " is a species of gazelle,
and the " wild ox " and " chamois " are
swift kinds of antelope.

the hoof, yet cheweth not the cud, it *is* unclean unto you: ye shall not eat of their flesh, *f* nor touch their dead carcase.

9 ¶ *g* These ye shall eat of all that *are* in the waters: all that have 10 fins and scales shall ye eat: and whatsoever hath not fins and 11 scales ye may not eat: it *is* unclean unto you. ¶ *Of* all clean 12 birds ye shall eat. *h* But these *are they* of which ye shall not eat: 13 the eagle, and the ossifrage, and the ospray, and the glede, and 14 the kite, and the vulture after his kind, and every raven after 15 his kind, and the owl, and the night hawk, and the cuckow, and 16 the hawk after his kind, the little owl, and the great owl, and 17 the swan, and the pelican, and the gier eagle, and the cormorant, 18 and the stork, and the heron after her kind, and the lapwing, 19 and the bat. And *i* every creeping thing that flieth *is* unclean 20 unto you: *k* they shall not be eaten. *But of* all clean fowls ye 21 may eat. *l* Ye shall not eat *of* any thing that dieth of itself: thou shalt give it unto the stranger that *is* in thy gates, that he may eat it; or thou mayest sell it unto an alien: *m* for thou *art* an holy people unto the LORD thy God. *n* Thou shalt not 22 seethe a kid in his mother's milk. ¶ *o* Thou shalt truly tithe all the increase of thy seed, that the field bringeth forth year by 23 year. *p* And thou shalt eat before the LORD thy God, in the place which he shall choose to place his name there, the tithe of thy corn, of thy wine, and of thine oil, and *q* the firstlings of thy herds and of thy flocks; that thou mayest learn to fear the LORD 24 thy God always. And if the way be too long for thee, so that thou art not able to carry it; or *r* if the place be too far from thee, which the LORD thy God shall choose to set his name there, 25 when the LORD thy God hath blessed thee: then shalt thou turn *it* into money, and bind up the money in thine hand, and shalt 26 go unto the place which the LORD thy God shall choose: and thou shalt bestow that money for whatsoever thy soul lusteth after, for oxen, or for sheep, or for wine, or for strong drink, or for whatsoever thy soul *l* desireth: *s* and thou shalt eat there before the LORD thy God, and thou shalt rejoice, thou, and thine 27 household, and *t* the Levite that *is* within thy gates; thou shalt not forsake him; for *u* he hath no part nor inheritance with thee. 28 ¶ *x* At the end of three years thou shalt bring forth all the tithe of thine increase the same year, and shalt lay *it* up within thy

f Lev. 11. 26, 27.
g Lev. 11. 9.

h Lev. 11. 13.

i Lev. 11. 20.
k See Lev. 11. 21.
l Lev. 17. 15.
Ez. 4. 14.
m ver. 2.
n Ex. 23. 19.
& 34. 26.
o Lev. 27. 30.
ch. 12. 6, 17.
Neh. 10. 37.
p ch. 12. 5, 6, 7, 17, 18.
q ch. 15. 19, 20.

r ch. 12. 21.

s ch. 12. 7, 18. & 26. 11.
t ch. 12. 12, 18, 19.
u Num. 18. 20.
ch. 18. 1, 2.
x ch. 26. 12.
Amos 4. 4.

¹ Heb. *asketh of thee.*

---

21. The prohibition is repeated from Lev. xxii. 8. The directions as to the disposal of the carcase are peculiar to Deuteronomy, and their motive is clear. To have forbidden the people either themselves to eat that which had died, or to allow any others to do so, would have involved loss of property, and consequent temptation to an infraction of the command. The permissions now for the first time granted would have been useless in the wilderness. During the forty years' wandering there could be but little opportunity of selling such carcases; whilst non-Israelites living in the camp would in such a matter be bound by the same rules as the Israelites (Lev. xvii. 15, and xxiv. 22). Further, it would seem (cp. Lev. xvii. 15) that greater stringency is here given to the requirement of abstinence from that which had died of itself. Probably on this,

as on so many other points, allowance was made for the circumstances of the people. Flesh meat was no doubt often scarce in the desert. It would therefore have been a hardship to forbid entirely the use of that which had not been killed. Now however that the plenty of the Promised Land was before them, the modified toleration of this unholy food was withdrawn.

22. These words recall in general terms the command of the earlier legislation respecting tithes (cp. Lev. xxvii. 30; Num. xviii. 26), but refer more particularly to the second or Festival tithe, which was an exclusively vegetable one.

28, 29. Cp. marg. reff. The tithe thus directed in the third year to be dispensed in charity at home, was not paid in addition to that in other years bestowed on the sacred meals, but was substituted for it. The

29 gates : *y*and the Levite, (because *z*he hath no part nor inheritance with thee,) and the stranger, and the fatherless, and the widow, which *are* within thy gates, shall come, and shall eat and be satisfied; that *a*the LORD thy God may bless thee in all the work of thine hand which thou doest.

CHAP. 15. AT the end of *a*every seven years thou shalt make a re-
2 lease. And this *is* the manner of the release : Every ¹creditor that lendeth *ought* unto his neighbour shall release *it ;* he shall not exact *it* of his neighbour, or of his brother; because it is called
3 the LORD's release. *b*Of a foreigner thou mayest exact it *again:* but *that* which is thine with thy brother thine hand shall release;
4 ²save when there shall be no poor among you ; *c*for the LORD shall greatly bless thee in the land which the ˙LORD thy God
5 giveth thee *for* an inheritance to possess it : only *d*if thou carefully hearken unto the voice of the LORD thy God, to observe to
6 do all these commandments which I command thee this day. For the LORD thy God blesseth thee, as he promised thee : and *e*thou shalt lend unto many nations, but thou shalt not borrow; and *f*thou shalt reign over many nations, but they shall not reign
7 over thee. ¶If there be among you a poor man of one of thy brethren within any of thy gates in thy land which the LORD thy God giveth thee, *g*thou shalt not harden thine heart, nor shut
8 thine hand from thy poor brother : *h*but thou shalt open thine hand wide unto him, and shalt surely lend him sufficient for his
9 need, *in that* which he wanteth. Beware that there be not a ³thought in thy ⁴wicked heart, saying, The seventh year, the year of release, is at hand ; and thine *i*eye be evil against thy poor brother, and thou givest him nought ; and *k*he cry unto the
10 LORD against thee, and *l*it be sin unto thee. Thou shalt surely give him, and *m*thine heart shall not be grieved when thou givest unto him : because that *n*for this thing the LORD thy God shall bless thee in all thy works, and in all that thou puttest thine
11 hand unto. For *o*the poor shall never cease out of the land :

¹ Heb. *master of the lend-*   ² Or, *To the end that there*   ³ Heb. *word.*
ing of his hand.   *be no poor among you.*   ⁴ Heb. *Belial.*

---

three years would count from the Sabbatical year (see next chap.), in which year there would of course be neither payment of tithe nor celebration of the Feasts at the Sanctuary. In the third and sixth years of the septennial cycle the Feasts would be superseded by the private hospitality enjoined in these verses.

XV. 1–11. The Year of Release is no doubt identical with the Sabbatical Year of the earlier legislation (Ex. xxiii. 10 seq., and Lev. xxv. 2 seq.), the command of the older legislation being here amplified. The release was probably for the year, not total and final, and had reference only to loans lent because of poverty (cp. *vv.* 4, 7). Yet even so the law was found too stringent for the avarice of the people ; for it was one of those which the Rabbins "made of none effect by their traditions."

2. *because it is called the* LORD's *release*] Render, **because proclamation has been made of the Lord's release.** The verb is impersonal, and implies (cp. xxxi. 10) that "the solemnity of the year of release" has

been publicly announced.

3. The foreigner would not be bound by the restriction of the Sabbatical year, and therefore would have no claim to its special remissions and privileges. He could earn his usual income in the seventh as in other years, and therefore is not exonerated from liability to discharge a debt any more in the one than the others.

4. There is no inconsistency between this and *v.* 11. The meaning seems simply to be, "Thou must release the debt for the year, except when there be no poor person concerned, a contingency which may happen, for the Lord shall greatly bless thee." The general object of these precepts, as also of the year of Jubilee and the laws respecting inheritance, is to prevent the total ruin of a needy man, and his disappearance from the families of Israel by the sale of his patrimony.

9. Lit. : "Beware that there be not in thy heart a word which is worthlessness" (cp. xiii. 13 note).

therefore I command thee, saying, Thou shalt open thine hand wide unto thy brother, to thy poor, and to thy needy, in thy land.

12 ¶ And *p*if thy brother, an Hebrew man, or an Hebrew woman, be sold unto thee, and serve thee six years; then in the seventh

13 year thou shalt let him go free from thee. And when thou sendest him out free from thee, thou shalt not let him go away

14 empty: thou shalt furnish him liberally out of thy flock, and out of thy floor, and out of thy winepress: *of that* wherewith the LORD thy God hath *q*blessed thee thou shalt give unto him.

15 And *r*thou shalt remember that thou wast a bondman in the land of Egypt, and the LORD thy God redeemed thee: therefore

16 I command thee this thing to day. And it shall be, *s*if he say unto thee, I will not go away from thee; because he loveth thee

17 and thine house, because he is well with thee; then thou shalt take an aul, and thrust *it* through his ear unto the door, and he shall be thy servant for ever. And also unto thy maidservant

18 thou shalt do likewise. It shall not seem hard unto thee, when thou sendest him away free from thee; for he hath been worth *t*a double hired servant *to thee*, in serving thee six years: and the LORD thy God shall bless thee in all that thou doest.

19 ¶ *u*All the firstling males that come of thy herd and of thy flock thou shalt sanctify unto the LORD thy God: thou shalt do no work with the firstling of thy bullock, nor shear the firstling of

20 thy sheep. *x*Thou shalt eat *it* before the LORD thy God year by year in the place which the LORD shall choose, thou and thy

21 household. *y*And if there be *any* blemish therein, *as if it be* lame or blind, *or have* any ill blemish, thou shalt not sacrifice it

22 unto the LORD thy God. Thou shalt eat it within thy gates: *z*the unclean and the clean *person shall eat it* alike, as the roe-

23 buck, and as the hart. *a*Only thou shalt not eat the blood thereof; thou shalt pour it upon the ground as water.

CHAP. 16. OBSERVE the *a*month of Abib, and keep the passover unto the LORD thy God: for *b*in the month of Abib the LORD

p Ex. 21. 2.
Lev. 25. 39.
Jer. 34. 14.

q Prov. 10. 22.
r ch. 5. 15. & 16. 12.
s Ex. 21. 5, 6.

t See Isai. 16. 14. & 21. 16.
u Ex. 34. 19.
Lev. 27. 26.
Num. 3. 13.
x ch. 16. 11, 14.

y Lev. 22. 20.
ch. 17, 1.

z ch. 12. 15, 22.
a ch. 12. 16, 23.

a Ex. 12. 2, &c.
b Ex. 13. 4. & 34. 18.

---

14. *thou shalt furnish him liberally*] The verb in the Hebrew is remarkable. It means "thou shalt lay on his neck," "adorn his neck with thy gifts."

12-18. The commands here are repeated from Ex. xxi. 2-6, with amplifications relative to the maidservant (*v.* 12) and to the making (*vv.* 13 seq.) liberal provision for launching the freedman on an independent course of life. The release of the servant is connected with the Sabbatical principle though not with the Sabbatical year. It is noteworthy also that the prospect of a gift of this sort, the amount of which was left to the master's discretion, would be likely to encourage diligence and faithfulness during the years of servitude.

18. *he hath been worth a double hired servant to thee, in serving thee six years*] i.e. such a servant has earned twice as much as a common hired labourer would have done in the same time.

19-23. Cp. Ex. xiii. 11 seq. The directions of the preceding legislation (see Num. xviii. 15 seq.) are here assumed, with the injunction added, that the animals thus set apart to God (*v.* 19) were not to be used by

their owners for their earthly purposes. It is further allowed that firstborn animals which had a blemish should be regarded as exceptions, and instead of being given to God might be used as food (*vv.* 21, 22). The application of the firstborn of cattle is here directed as in xii. 6, 17 and xiv. 23: they are to be consumed in the sacred Feasts at the Sanctuary.

XVI. The cardinal point on which the whole of the prescriptions in this chapter turn, is evidently the same as has been so often insisted on in the previous chapters, viz. the concentration of the religious services of the people round one common Sanctuary. The prohibition against observing the great Feasts of Passover, Pentecost, and Tabernacle, the three annual epochs in the sacred year of the Jew, at home and in private, is reiterated in a variety of words no less than six times in the first sixteen verses of this chapter (2, 6, 7, 11, 15, 16). Hence it is easy to see why nothing is here said of the other holy days.

1-8. The Feast of Passover (Ex. xii. 1-27; Num. ix. 1-14; Lev. xxiii. 1-8). A re-enforcement of this ordinance was the more

c Ex. 12.-29, 42.
d Num. 28. 19.
e ch. 12. 5, 26.
f Ex. 12. 15, 19, 39.
& 13. 3, 6, 7.
& 34. 18.
g Ex. 13. 7.
h Ex. 12. 10.
& 34. 25.

i Ex. 12. 6.

k Ex. 12. 8, 9.
2 Chr. 35. 13.
l 2 Kin. 23. 23.
John 2. 13, 23. & 11. 55.
m Ex. 12. 16.
& 13. 6.
Lev. 23. 8.
n Ex. 23. 16.
& 34. 22.
Lev. 23. 15.
Num. 28. 26.
Acts 2. 1.
o ver. 17.
1 Cor. 16. 2.
p ch. 12. 7, 12, 18.
ver. 14.
q ch. 15. 15.

r Ex. 23. 16.
Lev. 23. 34.
Num. 29. 12.
s Neh. 8. 9, &c.

t Lev. 23. 39, 40.

2 thy God brought thee forth out of Egypt ^cby night. Thou shalt therefore sacrifice the passover unto the LORD thy God, of the flock and ^dthe herd, in the ^eplace which the LORD shall choose to 3 place his name there. ^fThou shalt eat no leavened bread with it; seven days shalt thou eat unleavened bread therewith, *even* the bread of affliction; for thou camest forth out of the land of Egypt in haste: that thou mayest remember the day when thou camest forth out of the land of Egypt all the days of thy life. 4 ^gAnd there shall be no leavened bread seen with thee in all thy coast seven days; ^hneither shall there *any thing* of the flesh, which thou sacrificedst the first day at even, remain all night 5 until the morning. ¶Thou mayest not ¹sacrifice the passover within any of thy gates, which the LORD thy God giveth thee: 6 but at the place which the LORD thy God shall choose to place his name in, there thou shalt sacrifice the passover ⁱat even, at the going down of the sun, at the season that thou camest forth 7 out of Egypt. And thou shalt ^kroast and eat *it* ^lin the place which the LORD thy God shall choose: and thou shalt turn in 8 the morning, and go unto thy tents. Six days thou shalt eat unleavened bread: and ^mon the seventh day *shall be* a ²solemn assembly to the LORD thy God: thou shalt do no work *therein.* 9 ¶ⁿSeven weeks shalt thou number unto thee: begin to number the seven weeks from *such time as* thou beginnest *to put* the 10 sickle to the corn. And thou shalt keep the feast of weeks unto the LORD thy God with ³a tribute of a freewill offering of thine hand, which thou shalt give *unto the LORD thy God,* ^oac-11 cording as the LORD thy God hath blessed thee: and ^pthou shalt rejoice before the LORD thy God, thou, and thy son, and thy daughter, and thy manservant, and thy maidservant, and the Levite that *is* within thy gates, and the stranger, and the fatherless, and the widow, that *are* among you, in the place which the 12 LORD thy God hath chosen to place his name there. ^qAnd thou shalt remember that thou wast a bondman in Egypt: and thou 13 shalt observe and do these statutes. ¶^rThou shalt observe the feast of tabernacles seven days, after that thou hast gathered 14 in thy ⁴corn and thy wine: and ^sthou shalt rejoice in thy feast, thou, and thy son, and thy daughter, and thy manservant, and thy maidservant, and the Levite, the stranger, and the fatherless, and the widow, that *are* within thy gates. ^tSeven days 15 shalt thou keep a solemn feast unto the LORD thy God in the

¹ Or, *kill.*
² Heb. *restraint,* Lev. 23, 36.
³ Or, *sufficiency.*
⁴ Heb. *floor, and thy winepress.*

---

necessary because its observance had clearly been intermitted for thirty-nine years (see Josh. vi. 10). One Passover only had been kept in the wilderness, that recorded in Num. ix., where see notes.

2. *sacrifice the passover*] *i.e.* offer the sacrifices proper to the Feast of the Passover, which lasted seven days. Cp. a similar use of the word in a general sense in John xviii. 28. In the latter part of *v.* 4 and in the following verses Moses passes, as the context again shows, into the narrower sense of the word Passover.

7. After the Paschal Supper in the courts or neighbourhood of the Sanctuary, they might disperse to their several "tents" or "dwellings" (1 K. viii. 66).

These would of course be within a short distance of the Sanctuary, because the other Paschal offerings were yet to be offered day by day for seven days, and the people would remain to share them; and especially to take part in the holy convocation on the first and seventh of the days.

9–12. Feast of Weeks; and *vv.* 13–17, Feast of Tabernacles. Nothing is here added to the rules given in Leviticus and Numbers except the clauses so often recurring in Deuteronomy and so characteristic of it, which restrict the public celebration of the Festivals to the Sanctuary, and enjoin that the enjoyments of them should be extended to the Levites, widows, orphans, &c.

place which the LORD shall choose : because the LORD thy God shall bless thee in all thine increase, and in all the works of
16 thine hands, therefore thou shalt surely rejoice. ¶ᵘThree times in a year shall all thy males appear before the LORD thy God in the place which he shall choose; in the feast of unleavened bread, and in the feast of weeks, and in the feast of tabernacles:
17 and ˣthey shall not appear before the LORD empty : every man shall give ¹as he is able, ᵛaccording to the blessing of the LORD
18 thy God which he hath given thee. ¶ᶻJudges and officers shalt thou make thee in all thy gates, which the LORD thy God giveth thee, throughout thy tribes: and they shall judge the people
19 with just judgment. ᵃThou shalt not wrest judgment; ᵇthou shalt not respect persons, ᶜneither take a gift: for a gift doth blind the eyes of the wise, and pervert the ²words of the right-
20 eous. ³That which is altogether just shalt thou follow, that thou mayest ᵈlive, and inherit the land which the LORD thy God
21 giveth thee. ¶ᵉThou shalt not plant thee a grove of any trees near unto the altar of the LORD thy God, which thou shalt make
22 thee. ᶠNeither shalt thou set thee up any ⁴image; which the LORD thy God hateth.

CHAP. 17. THOU ᵃshalt not sacrifice unto the LORD thy God any bullock, or ⁵sheep, wherein is blemish, or any evil-favouredness:
2 for that is an abomination unto the LORD thy God. ¶ᵇIf there be found among you, within any of thy gates which the LORD thy God giveth thee, man or woman, that hath wrought wicked-ness in the sight of the LORD thy God, ᶜin transgressing his
3 covenant, and hath gone and served other gods, and worshipped them, either ᵈthe sun, or moon, or any of the host of heaven,
4 ᵉwhich I have not commanded; ᶠand it be told thee, and thou hast heard of it, and enquired diligently, and, behold, it be true, and the thing certain, that such abomination is wrought in
5 Israel: then shalt thou bring forth that man or that woman, which have committed that wicked thing, unto thy gates, even that man or that woman, and ᵍshalt stone them with stones, till

ᵘ Ex. 23. 14, 17. & 34. 23.

ˣ Ex. 23. 15. & 34. 20.
ᵛ ver. 10.
ᶻ ch. 1. 16.
1 Chr. 23. 4.
& 26. 29.
2 Chr. 19. 5, 8.
ᵃ Ex. 23. 2.
Lev. 19. 15.
ᵇ ch. 1. 17.
Prov. 24. 23.
ᶜ Ex. 23. 8.
Prov. 17. 23.
Eccles. 7. 7.
ᵈ Ez. 18.5,9.
ᵉ Ex. 34. 13.
1 Kin. 14. 15.
2 Kin. 17.
16.
2 Chr. 33. 3.
ᶠ Lev. 26. 1.

ᵃ Mal. 1. 8, 13, 14.
ᵇ ch. 13. 6.
ᶜ Josh. 7. 11, 15.
Judg. 2. 20.
2 Kin. 18.12.
Hos. 8. 1.
ᵈ ch. 4. 19.
Job 31. 26.
ᵉ Jer. 7. 22, 23, 31.
ᶠ ch. 13. 12.
ᵍ Lev. 24. 14, 16.
ch. 13. 10.
Josh. 7. 25.

¹ Heb. according to the gift of his hand, 2 Cor. 8. 12. ² Or, matters. ³ Heb. Justice, justice. ⁴ Or, statue, or, pillar. ⁵ Or, goat.

18–22. These verses are closely connected in subject with the following chapter, and introduce certain directions for the ad-ministration of justice and the carrying on of the civil government of the people in Canaan. During the lifetime of Moses, he himself, specially inspired and guided by God, was sufficient, with the aid of the subordinate judges (cp. Ex. xviii. 13 seq.), for the duties in question. But now that Moses was to be withdrawn, and the people would soon be scattered up and down the land of Canaan, regular and per-manent provision must be made for civil and social order and good government.

21. a grove, &c.] Render, Thou shalt not plant for thee any tree as an idol : literally "as an Asherah," i.e. an image of Astarte or Ashtaroth, the Phœnician goddess (cp. vii. 5note,13). The word is rendered "grove" by A. V. also in vii. 5, xii. 3; Ex. xxxiv. 13; Judg. vi. 25, but cannot be maintained, for the word is connected with various verbs

which are quite inapplicable to a grove. The wooden idol in question was the stem of a tree, stripped of its boughs, set up-right in the ground, and rudely carved with emblems.

XVII. 1. This verse belongs in subject to the last chapter. It prohibits once more (cp. xv. 21) that form of insult to God which consists in offering to Him a blem-ished sacrifice.

any evil-favouredness] Render any evil thing. The reference is to the faults or maims enumerated in Lev. xxii. 22–24.

2–7. Cp. xiii. 1 seq. Here special refer-ence is made to the legal forms to be adopted, vv. 5–7. The sentence was to be carried into effect at "the gates" (cp. Gen. xix. 1 note) of the town in which the crime was committed; because, as "all the people" were to take a part, an open space would be requisite for the execution. Note the typi-cal and prophetical aspect of the injunc-tion; cp. Acts vii. 58; Heb. xiii. 12.

h Num. 35.
30.
ch. 19. 15.
Matt. 18. 16.
John 8. 17.
2 Cor. 13. 1.
1 Tim. 5. 19.
Heb. 10. 28.
i ch. 13. 9.
k ver. 12.
ch. 13. 5.
l 2 Chr. 19.
10.
Hag. 2. 11.
Mal. 2. 7.
m See Ex.
21. 13, 20.
Num. 35. 11,
16, 19.
ch. 19. 4.
n ch. 12. 5.
Ps. 122. 5.
o See Jer.18.
18.
p ch. 19. 17.
q Ez. 44. 24.
r Num. 15.
30.
Ezra 10. 8.
Hos. 4. 4.
s ch. 18. 5.
t ch. 13. 5.
u ch. 13. 11.
& 19. 20.
x 1 Sam. 8.
5, 19, 20.
y See 1 Sam.
9. 15.
1 Chr. 22.
10.
z Jer. 30. 21.
a 1 Kin. 4.
26.
Ps. 20. 7.
b Isai. 31. 1.
Ez. 17. 15.
c Ex. 13. 17.
Num. 14. 3,
4.

6 they die. ᵸAt the mouth of two witnesses, or three witnesses, shall he that is worthy of death be put to death; *but* at the
7 mouth of one witness he shall not be put to death. ⁱThe hands of the witnesses shall be first upon him to put him to death, and afterward the hands of all the people. So ᵏthou shalt put the
8 evil away from among you. ¶ ˡIf there arise a matter too hard for thee in judgment, ᵐbetween blood and blood, between plea and plea, and between stroke and stroke, *being* matters of controversy within thy gates : then shalt thou arise, ⁿand get thee
9 up into the place which the LORD thy God shall choose; and ᵒthou shalt come unto the priests the Levites, and ᵖunto the judge that shall be in those days, and enquire; ᑫand they shall
10 shew thee the sentence of judgment : and thou shalt do according to the sentence, which they of that place which the LORD shall choose shall shew thee; and thou shalt observe to do
11 according to all that they inform thee : according to the sentence of the law which they shall teach thee, and according to the judgment which they shall tell thee, thou shalt do : thou shalt not decline from the sentence which they shall shew thee, *to* the
12 right hand, nor *to* the left. And ʳthe man that will do presumptuously, ¹and will not hearken unto the priest ˢthat standeth to minister there before the LORD thy God, or unto the judge, even that man shall die : and ᵗthou shalt put away the
13 evil from Israel. ᵘAnd all the people shall hear, and fear, and
14 do no more presumptuously. ¶When thou art come unto the land which the LORD thy God giveth thee, and shalt possess it, and shalt dwell therein, and shalt say, ˣI will set a king over
15 me, like as all the nations that *are* about me ; thou shalt in any wise set *him* king over thee, ʸwhom the LORD thy God shall choose : one ᶻfrom among thy brethren shalt thou set king over thee : thou mayest not set a stranger over thee, which *is* not thy
16 brother. But he shall not multiply ᵃhorses to himself, nor cause the people ᵇto return to Egypt, to the end that he should multiply horses : forasmuch as ᶜthe LORD hath said unto you,

¹ Heb. *not to hearken.*

8–13. The cases in question are such as the inferior judges did not feel able to decide satisfactorily, and which accordingly they remitted to their superiors (cp. Ex. xviii. 23–27).

The Supreme Court (*v.* 9) is referred to in very general terms as sitting at the Sanctuary (*v.* 8). "The judge" would no doubt usually be a layman, and thus the court would contain both an ecclesiastical and a civil element. Jehoshaphat (2 Chr. xix. 4–11) organized his judicial system very closely upon the lines here laid down.

14. No encouragement is given to the desire, natural in an Oriental people, for monarchical government ; but neither is such desire blamed, as appears from the fact that conditions are immediately laid down upon which it may be satisfied. Cp. marg. reff.

15. The king, like the judges and officers (cp. xvi. 18), is to be chosen by the people ; but their choice is to be in accordance with the will of God, and to be made from

amongst "their brethren." Cp. 1 S. ix. 15, x. 24, xvi. 1 ; 1 K. xix. 16.

thou mayest not set a stranger over thee] The Jews extended this prohibition to all offices whatsoever (cp. Jer. xxx. 21); and naturally attached the greatest importance to it : whence the significance of the question proposed to our Lord, "Is it lawful to give tribute to Cæsar?" (Matt. xxii. 17). A Gentile head for the Jewish people, which it was a principal aim of the Law to keep peculiar and distinct from others, was an anomaly.

16. The horse was not anciently used in the East for purposes of agriculture or travelling, but ordinarily for war only. He appears constantly in Scripture as the symbol and embodiment of fleshly strength and the might of the creature (cp. Ps. xx. 7, xxxiii. 16, 17, cxlvii. 10; Job xxxix. 19 seq.), and is sometimes significantly spoken of simply as "the strong one" (cp. Jer. viii. 16). The spirit of the prohibition therefore is that the king of Israel must not, like other

17 ^d Ye shall henceforth return no more that way. Neither shall he multiply wives to himself, that ^ehis heart turn not away: neither shall he greatly multiply to himself silver and gold. 18 ^fAnd it shall be, when he sitteth upon the throne of his kingdom, that he shall write him a copy of this law in a book out of 19 ^gthat which is before the priests the Levites: and ^hit shall be with him, and he shall read therein all the days of his life: that he may learn to fear the LORD his God, to keep all the words 20 of this law and these statutes, to do them: that his heart be not lifted up above his brethren, and that he ⁱturn not aside from the commandment, to the right hand, or to the left: to the end that he may prolong his days in his kingdom, he, and his children, in the midst of Israel.

CHAP. 18. THE priests the Levites, and all the tribe of Levi, ^ashall have no part nor inheritance with Israel: they ^bshall eat the 2 offerings of the LORD made by fire, and his inheritance. Therefore shall they have no inheritance among their brethren: the 3 LORD is their inheritance, as he hath said unto them. ¶ And this shall be the priest's due from the people, from them that offer a sacrifice, whether it be ox or sheep; and ^cthey shall give unto the priest the shoulder, and the two cheeks, and the maw.

^d ch. 28. 68.
Hos. 11. 5.
See Jer. 42.
15.
^e See 1 Kin.
11. 3, 4.
^f 2 Kin. 11.
12.
^g ch. 31. 9,
26.
See 2 Kin.
22. 8.
^h Josh. 1. 8.
Ps. 119. 97.
ⁱ ch. 5. 32.
1 Kin. 15. 5.

^a Num. 18.
20.
& 26. 62.
ch. 10. 9.
^b Num. 18.
8, 9.
1 Cor. 9. 13.

^c Lev. 7. 30
—34.

---

earthly potentates, put his trust in costly and formidable preparations for war (cp. Hos. i. 7).

Egypt was the principal source whence the nations of western Asia drew their supplies of this animal (cp. Ex. xiv. 5 seq.; 1 K. x. 28, 29; 2 K. vii. 6); but intercourse, traffic, or alliance which would "cause the people to return to Egypt" would be to reverse that great and beneficent wonderwork of God which inaugurated the Mosaic Covenant, the deliverance from the bondage of Egypt; and to bring about of set purpose that which God threatened (xxviii. 68) as the sorest punishment for Israel's sin.

17. Multiplication of wives would lead to sensuality, and so to an apostasy no less fatal in effect than downright idolatry (cp. Ex. xxxiv. 16). This rule, like the others, abridges to the ruler of Israel liberties usually enjoyed without stint by the kings of the East. The restriction was in the days of Moses unprecedented; and demanded a higher standard in the king of Israel than was looked for amongst his equals in other nations.

neither shall he greatly multiply to himself silver and gold] In this third prohibition, as in the other two, excess is forbidden. Vast accumulation of treasure could hardly be effected without oppression; nor when effected fail to produce pride and a "trust in uncertain riches" (1 Tim. vi. 17).

18. It is in striking consistency with the dignity which everywhere throughout the Mosaic legislation surrounds the chosen people of God, that even if they will be "like as all the nations about" (v. 14), and be governed by a king, care should nevertheless be taken that he shall be no Oriental despot. He is to be of no royal caste, but "one from among thy brethren" (v. 15); he

is to bear himself as a kind of "primus inter pares," his heart "not being lifted up above his brethren" (v. 20); he is, like his subjects, to be bound by the fundamental laws and institutions of the nation, and obliged, as they were, to do his duty in his station of life with constant reference thereto. The spirit of the text is that of Matt. xxiii. 9.

a copy of this law] The whole Pentateuch, or at any rate the legal portion of the Pentateuch.

a book...before the priests the Levites] Cp. marg. ref.

XVIII. 1. Better, "there shall not be to the priests, the Levites, yea the whole tribe of Levi, any inheritance, &c."

and his inheritance] i.e. God's inheritance, that which in making a grant to His people of the Promised Land with its earthly blessings He had reserved for Himself; more particularly the sacrifices and the holy gifts, such as tithes and firstfruits. These were God's portion of the substance of Israel; and as the Levites were His portion of the persons of Israel, it was fitting that the Levites should be sustained from these. On the principle here laid down, cp. 1 Cor. ix. 13, 14.

3. For maw read stomach, which was regarded as one of the richest and choicest parts. As the animal slain may be considered to consist of three principal parts, head, feet, and body, a portion of each is by the regulation in question to be given to the priest, thus representing the consecration of the whole; or, as some ancient commentators think, the dedication of the words, acts, and appetites of the worshipper to God.

The text probably refers to Peace-offerings, and animals killed for the sacrificial meals held in connection with the Peace-offerings.

4 *d*The firstfruit *also* of thy corn, of thy wine, and of thine oil, and the first of the fleece of thy sheep, shalt thou give him.

5 For *e*the LORD thy God hath chosen him out of all thy tribes, *f*to stand to minister in the name of the LORD, him and his sons

6 for ever. ¶And if a Levite come from any of thy gates out of all Israel, where he *g*sojourned, and come with all the desire of

7 his mind *h*unto the place which the LORD shall choose; then he shall minister in the name of the LORD his God, *i*as all his brethren the Levites *do*, which stand there before the LORD.

8 They shall have like *k*portions to eat, beside [1] that which cometh

9 of the sale of his patrimony. ¶When thou art come into the land which the LORD thy God giveth thee, *l*thou shalt not learn

10 to do after the abominations of those nations. There shall not be found among you *any one* that maketh his son or his daughter *m*to pass through the fire, *n or* that useth divination, *or* an

11 observer of times, or an enchanter, or a witch, *o*or a charmer, or a consulter with familiar spirits, or a wizard, or a *p*necromancer.

12 For all that do these things *are* an abomination unto the LORD: and *q*because of these abominations the LORD thy God doth

13 drive them out from before thee. Thou shalt be [2]perfect with

14 the LORD thy God. For these nations, which thou shalt [3]possess, hearkened unto observers of times, and unto diviners: but as for thee, the LORD thy God hath not suffered thee so *to do*.

15 ¶*r*The LORD thy God will raise up unto thee a Prophet from the midst of thee, of thy brethren, like unto me; unto him ye

[1] Heb. *his sales by the fathers.*   [2] Or, *upright,* or, *sincere,*   [3] Or, *inherit.* Gen. 17. 1.

6–8. These verses presuppose that part of the Levites only will be in residence and officiating at the place of the Sanctuary, the others of course dwelling at their own homes in the Levitical cities, or "so-journing" elsewhere; cp. marg. reff. But if any Levite out of love for the service of the Sanctuary chose to resort to it when he might reside in his own home, he was to have his share in the maintenance which was provided for those ministering in the order of their course.

8. *beside that which cometh of the sale of his patrimony*] The Levites had indeed "no part nor inheritance with Israel," but they might individually possess property, and in fact often did so (cp. 1 K. ii. 26; Jer. xxxii. 7; Acts iv. 36). The Levite who desired to settle at the place of the Sanctuary would probably sell his patrimony when quitting his former home. The text directs that he should, notwithstanding any such private resources, duly enjoy his share of the per-quisites provided for the ministers at the sanctuary, and as he was "waiting at the altar" should be "partaker with the altar" (1 Cor. ix. 13).

10. *to pass through the fire*] *i.e.* to Moloch; cp. Levit. xx. 2 note.

that useth divination] Cp. Num. xxiii. 23 note.

observer of times...enchanter] Cp. Lev. xix. 26 note.

witch] Rather "sorcerer," cp. Ex. vii. 11 note.

11. *a charmer*] *i.e.* one who fascinates and subdues noxious animals or men, such as the famous serpent-charmers of the East (Ps. lviii. 4, 5).

a consulter with familiar spirits...a wizard] Cp. Lev. xix. 31 note.

necromancer] Lit. "one who interrogates the dead." The purpose of the text is obviously to group together all the known words belonging to the practices in question. Cp. 2 Chr. xxxiii. 6.

13. *perfect*] As in Gen. xvii. 1; Job i. 1; Matt. v. 48. The sense is that Israel was to keep the worship of the true God wholly uncontaminated by idolatrous pollutions.

15–19. The ancient Fathers of the Church and the generality of modern commentators have regarded our Lord as the Prophet promised in these verses. It is evident from the New Testament alone that the Messianic was the accredited interpretation amongst the Jews at the beginning of the Christian era (cp. marg. reff., and John iv. 25); nor can our Lord Himself, when He declares that Moses "wrote of Him" (John v. 45–47), be supposed to have any other words more directly in view than these, the only words in which Moses, speaking in his own person, gives any prediction of the kind. But the verses seem to have a further, no less evident if subsidiary, reference to a prophetical order which should stand from time to time, as Moses had done, between God and the people; which should make known God's will to the latter; which should by its

16 shall hearken; according to all that thou desiredst of the LORD thy God in Horeb *in the day of the assembly, saying, *Let me not hear again the voice of the LORD my God, neither let me see
17 this great fire any more, that I die not. And the LORD said unto me, "They have well *spoken that* which they have spoken.
18 *I will raise them up a Prophet from among their brethren, like unto thee, and *will put my words in his mouth; *and he
19 shall speak unto them all that I shall command him. *And it shall come to pass, *that* whosoever will not hearken unto my words which he shall speak in my name, I will require *it* of him.
20 But *the prophet, which shall presume to speak a word in my name, which I have not commanded him to speak, or *that shall speak in the name of other gods, even that prophet shall
21 die. And if thou say in thine heart, How shall we know the
22 word which the LORD hath not spoken? *When a prophet speaketh in the name of the LORD, *if the thing follow not, nor come to pass, that *is* the thing which the LORD hath not spoken, *but* the prophet hath spoken it *presumptuously : thou shalt not be afraid of him.

CHAP. 19. WHEN the LORD thy God *hath cut off the nations, whose land the LORD thy God giveth thee, and thou [1]succeedest
2 them, and dwellest in their cities, and in their houses; *thou shalt separate three cities for thee in the midst of thy land,
3 which the LORD thy God giveth thee to possess it. Thou shalt prepare thee a way, and divide the coasts of thy land, which the LORD thy God giveth thee to inherit, into three parts, that every
4 slayer may flee thither. And *this *is* the case of the slayer, which shall flee thither, that he may live : Whoso killeth his

*ch. 9. 10.
*Ex. 20. 19.
Heb. 12. 19.
*ch. 5. 28.
*ver. 15.
John 1. 45.
Acts 3. 22.
& 7. 37.
*Isai. 51. 16.
John 17. 8.
*John 4. 25.
& 8. 28.
& 12. 49. 50.
*Acts 3. 23.
*ch. 13. 5.
Jer. 14. 14.
Zech. 13. 3.
*ch. 13. 1.
Jer. 2. 8.
*Jer. 28. 9.
*See ch. 13. 2.
*ver. 20.
*ch. 12. 29.
*Ex. 21. 13.
Num. 35. 10, 14.
Josh. 20. 2.
*Num. 35. 15.
ch. 4. 42.

[1] Heb. *inheritest*, or, *possessest*.

---

presence render it unnecessary either that God should address the people directly, as at Sinai (*v.* 16; cp. v. 25 seq.), or that the people themselves in lack of counsel should resort to the superstitions of the heathen.

In fact, in the words before us, Moses gives promise both of a prophetic order, and of the Messiah in particular as its chief; of a line of prophets culminating in one eminent individual. And in proportion as we see in our Lord the characteristics of the Prophet most perfectly exhibited, so must we regard the promise of Moses as in Him most completely accomplished.

20. Cp. marg. reff.

21. *And if thou say in thine heart, How,* &c.] The passage evidently assumes such an occasion for consulting the prophet as was usual amongst the heathen, *e.g.* an impending battle or other such crisis (cp. 1 K. xxii. 11), in which his veracity would soon be put to the test. Failure of a prediction is set forth as a sure note of its being "presumptuous." But from xiii. 2 seq. we see that the fulfilment of a prediction would not decisively accredit him who uttered it : for the prophet or dreamer of dreams who endeavoured on the strength of miracles to seduce to idolatry was to be rejected and punished. Nothing therefore *contrary* to the revealed truth of God was to be ac-

cepted under any circumstances.

XIX. This and the next two chapters contain enactments designed to protect human life, and to impress its sanctity on Israel.

1–13. In these verses the directions respecting the preparation of the roads to the cities of refuge, the provision of additional cities in case of an extension of territory, and the intervention of the elders as representing the congregation, are peculiar to Deuteronomy and supplementary to the laws on the same subject given in the earlier books (cp. marg. ref.).

1, 2. The three cities of refuge for the district east of Jordan had been already named. Moses now directs that when the territory on the west of Jordan had been conquered, a like allotment of three other cities in it should be made. This was accordingly done; cp. Josh. xx. 1 seq.

3. *Thou shalt prepare thee a way*] It was the duty of the Senate to repair the roads that led to the cities of refuge annually, and remove every obstruction. No hillock was left, no river over which there was not a bridge ; and the road was at least two and thirty cubits broad. At cross-roads there were posts bearing the words *Refuge, Refuge*, to guide the fugitive in his flight. It seems as if in Isai. xl. 3 seq. the imagery were borrowed from the preparation of the ways to the cities of refuge.

5 neighbour ignorantly, whom he hated not [1]in time past; as when a man goeth into the wood with his neighbour to hew wood, and his hand fetcheth a stroke with the axe to cut down the tree, and the [2]head slippeth from the [3]helve, and [4]lighteth upon his neighbour, that he die; he shall flee unto one of those

^{d Num. 35. 12.}

6 cities, and live: [d]lest the avenger of the blood pursue the slayer, while his heart is hot, and overtake him, because the way is long, and [5]slay him; whereas he *was* not worthy of death, inas-
7 much as he hated him not [6]in time past. ¶Wherefore I command thee, saying, Thou shalt separate three cities for thee.

^{e Gen. 15. 18. ch. 12. 20.}

8 And if the LORD thy God [e]enlarge thy coast, as he hath sworn unto thy fathers, and give thee all the land which he promised
9 to give unto thy fathers; if thou shalt keep all these commandments to do them, which I command thee this day, to love the LORD thy God, and to walk ever in his ways; [f]then shalt thou

^{f Josh. 20. 7, 8.}

10 add three cities more for thee, beside these three: that innocent blood be not shed in thy land, which the LORD thy God giveth

^{g Ex. 21. 12. Num. 35. 16, 24. ch. 27. 24. Prov. 28. 17.}

11 thee *for* an inheritance, and *so* blood be upon thee. ¶But [g]if any man hate his neighbour, and lie in wait for him, and rise up against him, and smite him [7]mortally that he die, and fleeth
12 into one of these cities: then the elders of his city shall send and fetch him thence, and deliver him into the hand of the

<sup>h ch. 13. 8. & 25. 12.
i Num. 35. 33, 34. ch. 21. 9. 1 Kin. 2. 31.
k ch. 27. 17. Job 21. 2. Prov. 22. 28. Hos. 5. 10.
l Num. 35. 30. ch. 17. 6.
m Ps. 27. 12. & 35. 11.
n ch. 17. 9. & 21. 5.</sup>

13 avenger of blood, that he may die. [h]Thine eye shall not pity him, [i]but thou shalt put away *the guilt of* innocent blood from
14 Israel, that it may go well with thee. ¶[k]Thou shalt not remove thy neighbour's landmark, which they of old time have set in thine inheritance, which thou shalt inherit in the land that the
15 LORD thy God giveth thee to possess it. ¶[l]One witness shall not rise up against a man for any iniquity, or for any sin, in any sin that he sinneth: at the mouth of two witnesses, or at the
16 mouth of three witnesses, shall the matter be established. If a false witness [m]rise up against any man to testify against him
17 [8]*that which is* wrong; then both the men, between whom the controversy *is*, shall stand before the LORD, [n]before the priests
18 and the judges, which shall be in those days; and the judges shall make diligent inquisition: and, behold, *if* the witness *be* a false witness, *and* hath testified falsely against his brother;

<sup>o Prov. 19. 5, 9. Dan. 6. 24.
p ch. 13. 5. & 17. 7.</sup>

19 [o]then shall ye do unto him, as he had thought to have done unto his brother: so [p]shalt thou put the evil away from among

---

[1] Heb. *from yesterday the third day.*	[4] Heb. *findeth.*
[2] Heb. *iron.*	[5] Heb. *smite him in life.*
[3] Heb. *wood.*	[6] Heb. *from yesterday the third day.*
	[7] Heb. *in life.*
	[8] Or, *falling away.*

---

5. with the axe] Lit. "with the iron." Note the employment of iron for tools, and cp. iii. 11 note.

8, 9. Provision is here made for the anticipated enlargement of the borders of Israel to the utmost limits promised by God, from the river of Egypt to the Euphrates (Gen. xv. 18; Ex. xxiii. 31, and notes). This promise, owing to the sins of the people, did not receive its fulfilment till after David had conquered the Philistines, Syrians, &c.; and this but a transient one, for many of the conquered peoples regained independence on the dissolution of Solomon's empire.

14. As a man's life is to be held sacred, so are his means of livelihood; and in this connection a prohibition is inserted against re-

moving a neighbour's landmark : cp. marg. reff.

16. testify against him that which is wrong] Marg. more literally, "a falling away." The word is used (xiii. 5) to signify apostasy or revolt; here it is no doubt to be understood in the wider sense of any departure from the Law.

17. both the men, between whom the controversy is] Not the accused and the false witness, but the plaintiff and defendant (cp. Ex. xxiii. 1) who were summoned before the supreme court held, as provided in chap. xvii., at the Sanctuary. The judges acted as God's representative; to lie to them was to lie to Him.

19, 21. See marg. reff.

20 you. *q*And those which remain shall hear, and fear, and shall
21 henceforth commit no more any such evil among you. *r*And
thine eye shall not pity; but *s*life *shall go* for life, eye for eye,
tooth for tooth, hand for hand, foot for foot.

CHAP. 20. WHEN thou goest out to battle against thine enemies,
and seest *a*horses, and chariots, *and* a people more than thou, be
not afraid of them: for the LORD thy God *is* *b*with thee, which
2 brought thee up out of the land of Egypt. And it shall be,
when ye are come nigh unto the battle, that the priest shall
3 approach and speak unto the people, and shall say unto them,
Hear, O Israel, ye approach this day unto battle against your
enemies: let not your hearts ¹faint, fear not, and do not ²tremble,
4 neither be ye terrified because of them; for the LORD your God
is he that goeth with you, *c*to fight for you against your enemies,
5 to save you. ¶And the officers shall speak unto the people,
saying, What man *is there* that hath built a new house, and
hath not *d*dedicated it? Let him go and return to his house, lest
6 he die in the battle, and another man dedicate it. And what
man *is he* that hath planted a vineyard, and hath not *yet* ³eaten
of it? Let him *also* go and return unto his house, lest he die in
7 the battle, and another man eat of it. *e*And what man *is there*
that hath betrothed a wife, and hath not taken her? Let him go
and return unto his house, lest he die in the battle, and another
8 man take her. And the officers shall speak further unto the
people, and they shall say, *f*What man *is there that is* fearful
and fainthearted? Let him go and return unto his house, lest his
9 brethren's heart ⁴faint as well as his heart. And it shall be,
when the officers have made an end of speaking unto the people,
that they shall make captains of the armies ⁵to lead the people.
10 ¶When thou comest nigh unto a city to fight against it, *g*then
11 proclaim peace unto it. And it shall be, if it make thee answer
of peace, and open unto thee, then it shall be, *that* all the people
that is found therein shall be tributaries unto thee, and they
12 shall serve thee. And if it will make no peace with thee, but
13 will make war against thee, then thou shalt besiege it: and when
the LORD thy God hath delivered it into thine hands, *h*thou shalt
14 smite every male thereof with the edge of the sword: but the
women, and the little ones, and *i*the cattle, and all that is in the
city, *even* all the spoil thereof, shalt thou ⁶take unto thyself;

q ch. 17. 13.
& 21. 21.
r ver. 13.
s Ex. 21. 23.
Lev. 24. 20.
Matt. 5. 38.
a See Ps. 20.
7.
Isai. 31. 1.
b Num. 23.
21.
ch. 31. 6, 8.
2 Chr. 13.12.
& 32. 7, 8.

c ch. 1. 30.
& 3. 22.
Josh. 23. 10.

d See Neh.
12. 27.
Ps. 30, title.

e ch. 24. 5.

f Judg. 7. 3.

g 2 Sam. 20.
18, 20.

h Num. 31.
7.
i Josh. 8. 2.

¹ Heb. *be tender.*
² Heb. *make haste.*
³ Heb. *made it common:*

⁴ Heb. *melt.*

See Lev. 19. 23, 24. ch.
28. 30.

⁵ Heb. to be *in the head of
the people.*
⁶ Heb. *spoil.*

XX. 1. *horses, and chariots*] The most
formidable elements of an Oriental host,
which the Canaanites possessed in great
numbers; cp. Josh. xvii. 16; Judg. iv. 3; 1
S. xiii. 5. Israel could not match these
with corresponding forces (cp. xvii. 16 notes
and reff.), but, having the God of battles on
its side, was not to be dismayed by them;
the assumption being that the war had the
sanction of God, and was consequently just.

2. *the priest*] Not the High-priest, but
one appointed for the purpose, and called,
according to the Rabbins, "the Anointed of
the War:" hence perhaps the expression of
Jer. vi. 4, &c. "prepare ye" (lit. consecrate)
"war." Thus Phinehas went with the warriors to fight against Midian, (Num. xxxi.
6; cp. 1 S. iv. 4, 11; 2 Chr. xiii. 12).

5. *the officers*] See Ex. v. 6 note.
dedicated it] Cp. marg. reff. The expression is appropriate, because various ceremonies of a religious kind were customary
amongst the Jews on taking possession of a
new house. The immunity conferred in this
verse lasted, like that in *v.* 7 (cp. xxiv. 5),
for a year.

6. See marg. and reff. The fruit of newly-
planted trees was set apart from common
uses for four years.

9. The meaning is that the "officers"
should then subdivide the levies, and appoint leaders of the smaller divisions thus
constituted.

10-20. Directions intended to prevent
wanton destruction of life and property in
sieges.

k Josh. 22. 8.

and *k*thou shalt eat the spoil of thine enemies, which the LORD
15 thy God hath given thee. Thus shalt thou do unto all the cities
which are very far off from thee, which *are* not of the cities of

l Num. 21. 2,
3, 35.
& 33. 52.
ch. 7. 1. 2.
Josh. 11. 14.

16 these nations. But *l*of the cities of these people, which the
LORD thy God doth give thee *for* an inheritance, thou shalt save
17 alive nothing that breatheth: but thou shalt utterly destroy
them; *namely,* the Hittites, and the Amorites, the Canaanites,
and the Perizzites, the Hivites, and the Jebusites; as the LORD

m ch. 7. 4.
& 12. 30, 31.
& 18. 9.

18 thy. God hath commanded thee: that *m*they teach you not to do
after all their abominations, which they have done unto their

n Ex. 23. 33.

19 gods; so should ye *n*sin against the LORD your God. ¶ When
thou shalt besiege a city a long time, in making war against it
to take it, thou shalt not destroy the trees thereof by forcing an
axe against them: for thou mayest eat of them, and thou shalt
not cut them down (*1*for the tree of the field *is* man's *life*) *2*to
20 employ *them* in the siege: only the trees which thou knowest
that they *be* not trees for meat, thou shalt destroy and cut them
down; and thou shalt build bulwarks against the city that
maketh war with thee, until *3*it be subdued.

CHAP. 21. IF *one* be found slain in the land which the LORD thy
God giveth thee to possess it, lying in the field, *and* it be not
2 known who hath slain him: then thy elders and thy judges
shall come forth, and they shall measure unto the cities which
3 *are* round about him that is slain: and it shall be, *that* the city
which is next unto the slain man, even the elders of that city
shall take an heifer, which hath not been wrought with, *and*
4 which hath not drawn in the yoke; and the elders of that city
shall bring down the heifer unto a rough valley, which is neither
eared nor sown, and shall strike off the heifer's neck there in the

a ch. 10. 8.
1 Chr. 23. 13.
b ch. 17. 8, 9.

5 valley: and the priests the sons of Levi shall come near; for
*a*them the LORD thy God hath chosen to minister unto him, and
to bless in the name of the LORD; and *b*by their *4*word shall

c See Ps. 19.
12. & 26. 6.
Matt. 27. 24.

6 every controversy and every stroke be *tried:* and all the elders
of that city, *that are* next unto the slain *man,* *c*shall wash their
7 hands over the heifer that is beheaded in the valley: and they

1 Or, *for, O man, the tree*
of the field is *to be em-*
ployed in the siege.

2 Heb. *to go from before*
thee.

3 Heb. *it come down.*
4 Heb. *mouth.*

---

16. Forbearance, however, was not to be
shown towards the Canaanitish nations,
which were to be utterly exterminated (cp.
vii. 1-4). The command did not apply to
beasts as well as men (cp. Josh. xi. 11 and
14).

19. The parenthesis may be more literally
rendered "for man is a tree of the field,"
i.e. has his life from the tree of the field,
is supported in life by it (cp. xxiv. 6). The
Egyptians seem invariably to have cut
down the fruit-trees in war.

XXI. 2. The elders represented the citizens at large, the judges the magistracy:
priests (*v.* 5) from the nearest priestly
town, were likewise to be at hand. Thus all
classes would be represented at the purging
away of that blood-guiltiness which until
removed attached to the whole community.

3. The requirements as regards place and
victim are symbolical. The heifer represented the murderer, so far at least as to

die in his stead, since he himself could not
be found. As bearing his guilt the heifer
must therefore be one which was of full
growth and strength, and had not yet
been ceremonially profaned by human use.
The Christian commentators find here a
type of Christ and of His sacrifice for man:
but the heifer was not strictly a sacrifice or
Sin-offering. The transaction was rather
figurative, and was so ordered as to impress
the lesson of Gen. ix. 5.

4. *eared*] *i.e.* ploughed; cp. Gen. xlv. 6
note and reff. The word is derived from the
Latin, and is in frequent use by English
writers of the fifteenth and two following
centuries.

strike off the heifer's neck] Rather, "break
its neck" (cp. Ex. xiii. 13). The mode of
killing the victim distinguishes this lustra-
tion from the Sin-offering, in which there
would be of course shedding and sprinkling
of the blood.

shall answer and say, Our hands have not shed this blood,
8 neither have our eyes seen *it*. Be merciful, O LORD, unto thy
people Israel, whom thou hast redeemed, *d*and lay not innocent
blood ¹unto thy people of Israel's charge. And the blood shall
9 be forgiven them. So *e*shalt thou put away the *guilt of* innocent
blood from among you, when thou shalt do *that which is* right in
10 the sight of the LORD. ¶ When thou goest forth to war against
thine enemies, and the LORD thy God hath delivered them into
11 thine hands, and thou hast taken them captive, and seest among
the captives a beautiful woman, and hast a desire unto her, that
12 thou wouldest have her to thy wife; then thou shalt bring her
13 home to thine house; and she shall shave her head, and ²³pare
her nails; and she shall put the raiment of her captivity from
off her, and shall remain in thine house, and *f* bewail her father
and her mother a full month: and after that thou shalt go in
14 unto her, and be her husband, and she shall be thy wife. And
it shall be, if thou have no delight in her, then thou shalt let
her go whither she will; but thou shalt not sell her at all for
money, thou shalt not make merchandise of her, because thou
15 hast *g*humbled her. ¶ If a man have two wives, one beloved,
h and another hated, and they have born him children, *both* the
beloved and the hated; and *if* the firstborn son be her's that was
16 hated: then it shall be, *i*when he maketh his sons to inherit
that which he hath, *that* he may not make the son of the beloved
firstborn before the son of the hated, *which is indeed* the first-
17 born: but he shall acknowledge the son of the hated *for* the
firstborn, *k*by giving him a double portion of all ⁴that he hath:
for he *is* ¹the beginning of his strength; *m*the right of the first-
18 born *is* his. ¶ If a man have a stubborn and rebellious son, which
will not obey the voice of his father, or the voice of his mother,
and *that*, when they have chastened him, will not hearken unto
19 them: then shall his father and his mother lay hold on him, and
bring him out unto the elders of his city, and unto the gate of

d Jonah 1.
14.

e ch. 19. 13.

f See Ps. 45.
10.

g Gen. 34. 2.
ch. 22. 29.
Judg. 19. 24.
h Gen. 29.
33.
i 1 Chr. 5. 2.
& 26. 10.
2 Chr. 11. 19,
22.

k See 1 Chr.
5. 1.
l Gen. 49. 3.
m Gen. 25.
31, 33.

---

¹ Heb. *in the midst.*
² Or, *suffer to grow.*
³ Heb. *make,* or, *dress.*
⁴ Heb. *that is found with him.*

---

10 seq. The regulations which now follow in the rest of this and throughout the next chapter bring out the sanctity of various personal rights and relations fundamental to human life and society.

10–14. The war supposed here is one against the neighbouring nations after Israel had utterly destroyed the Canaanites (cp. vii. 3), and taken possession of their land.

12. The shaving the head (a customary sign of purification, Lev. xiv. 8; Num. viii. 7), and the putting away "the garment of her captivity," were designed to signify the translation of the woman from the state of a heathen and a slave to that of a wife amongst the Covenant-people. Consistency required that she should "pare" (dress, cp. 2 S. xix. 24), not "suffer to grow," her nails; and thus, so far as possible, lay aside everything belonging to her condition as an alien.

13. *bewail her father and her mother a full month*] This is prescribed from motives of humanity, that the woman might have time and leisure to detach her affections from

their natural ties, and prepare her mind for new ones.

14. *thou shalt not make merchandise of her*] Rather, **thou shalt not constrain her:** lit. "treat her with constraint," or "treat her as a slave."

15–17. Moses did not originate the rights of primogeniture (cp. Gen. xxv. 31), but recognized them, since he found them pre-existing in the general social system of the East. Paternal authority could set aside these rights on just grounds (Gen. xxvii. 33), but it is forbidden here to do so from mere partiality.

18–21. The formal accusation of parents against a child was to be received without inquiry, as being its own proof. Thus the just authority of the parents is recognized and effectually upheld (cp. Ex. xx. 12, xxi. 15, 17; Lev. xx. 9); but the extreme and irresponsible power of life and death, conceded by the law of Rome and other heathen nations, is withheld from the Israelite father. In this, as in the last law, provision is made against the abuses of a necessary authority.

20 his place; and they shall say unto the elders of his city, This
our son *is* stubborn and rebellious, he will not obey our voice;
21 *he is* a glutton, and a drunkard. And all the men of his city

n ch. 13. 5.
& 19. 19, 20.
& 22. 21, 24.
o ch. 13. 11.
p ch. 19. 6.
& 22. 26.
Acts 23. 29.
& 25. 11, 25.
& 26. 31.
q Josh. 8.
29.
& 10. 26, 27.
John 19. 31.
r Gal. 3. 13.
s Lev. 18. 25.
Num. 35. 34.
a Ex. 23. 4.

shall stone him with stones, that he die : *n*so shalt thou put evil
away from among you; *o*and all Israel shall hear, and fear.
22 ¶ And if a man have committed a sin *p*worthy of death, and he
23 be to be put to death, and thou hang him on a tree : *q*his body
shall not remain all night upon the tree, but thou shalt in any
wise bury him that day; (for *r*he that is hanged *is* ¹accursed of
God;) that *s*thy land be not defiled, which the LORD thy God
giveth thee *for* an inheritance.

CHAP. 22. THOU *a*shalt not see thy brother's ox or his sheep go
astray, and hide thyself from them : thou shalt in any case bring
2 them again unto thy brother. And if thy brother *be* not nigh
unto thee, or if thou know him not, then thou shalt bring it
unto thine own house, and it shall be with thee until thy brother
3 seek after it, and thou shalt restore it to him again. In like
manner shalt thou do with his ass; and so shalt thou do with his
raiment; and with all lost thing of thy brother's, which he hath
lost, and thou hast found, shalt thou do likewise : thou mayest

b Ex. 23. 5.

4 not hide thyself. *b*Thou shalt not see thy brother's ass or his
ox fall down by the way, and hide thyself from them : thou shalt
5 surely help him to lift *them* up again. ¶ The woman shall not
wear that which pertaineth unto a man, neither shall a man put
on a woman's garment : for all that do so *are* abomination unto
6 the LORD thy God. ¶ If a bird's nest chance to be before thee
in the way in any tree, or on the ground, *whether they be* young
ones, or eggs, and the dam sitting upon the young, or upon the

c Lev. 22. 28.

7 eggs, *c*thou shalt not take the dam with the young : *but* thou
shalt in any wise let the dam go, and take the young to thee;

d ch. 4. 40.

*d*that it may be well with thee, and *that* thou mayest prolong *thy*
8 days. ¶ When thou buildest a new house, then thou shalt make
a battlement for thy roof, that thou bring not blood upon thine

¹ Heb. *the curse of God :* See Num. 25. 4. 2 Sam. 21. 6.

---

22. There were four methods of execution
in use amongst the ancient Jews; stoning
(Ex. xvii. 4; Deut. xiii. 10, &c.), burning
(Lev. xx. 14; xxi. 9), the sword (Ex. xxxii.
27), and strangulation. The latter, though
not named in Scripture, is regarded by the
Rabbins as the most common, and the
proper one to be adopted when no other is
expressly enjoined by the Law. Suspension,
whether from cross, stake, or gallows, was
not used as a mode of taking life, but was
sometimes added after death as an enhancement of punishment. Pharaoh's chief baker
(Gen. xl. 19) was hanged after being put to
death by the sword; and similarly Joshua
appears (Jos. x. 26) to have dealt with the
five kings who made war against Gibeon.
Cp. also Num. xxv. 4.

23. *he that is hanged is accursed of God*]
i.e. "Bury him that is hanged out of
the way before evening : his hanging body
defiles the land; for God's curse rests
on it." The curse of God is probably
regarded as lying on the malefactor because, from the fact of his being hanged,
he must have been guilty of a peculiarly
atrocious breach of God's Covenant. Such

an offender could not remain on the face of
the earth without defiling it (cp. Lev. xviii.
25, 28; Num. xxxv. 34). Therefore after
the penalty of his crime had been inflicted,
and he had hung for a time as a public
example, the Holy Land was to be at once
and entirely delivered from his presence.
See Gal. iii. 13 for St. Paul's quotation of
this text and his application of it.

XXII. On the general character of the
contents of this chapter see xxi. 10 note.

5. *that which pertaineth unto a man*] *i.e.*
not only his dress but all that specially pertains distinctively to his sex; arms, domestic and other utensils, &c.

The distinction between the sexes is
natural and divinely established, and cannot
be neglected without indecorum and consequent danger to purity (cp. 1 Cor. xi. 3–15).

6–8. These precepts are designed to cultivate a spirit of humanity. Cp. xxv. 4;
Lev. xxii. 28; and 1 Cor. ix. 9, 10.

8. The roofs of houses in Palestine were
flat and used for various purposes. Cp.
Josh. ii. 6; 2 Sam. xi. 2; Acts x. 9, &c.
A battlement was almost a necessary protection. It was to be, according to the

9 house, if any man fall from thence. ¶ᵉThou shalt not sow thy
vineyard with divers seeds: lest the ¹fruit of thy seed which thou
10 hast sown, and the fruit of thy vineyard, be defiled. ᶠThou
11 shalt not plow with an ox and an ass together. ᵍThou shalt not
wear a garment of divers sorts, as of woollen and linen together.
12 ¶ Thou shalt make thee ʰfringes upon the four ²quarters of thy
13 vesture, wherewith thou coverest thyself. ¶ If any man take a
14 wife, and ⁱgo in unto her, and hate her, and give occasions of
speech against her, and bring up an evil name upon her, and
say, I took this woman, and when I came to her, I found her
15 not a maid : then shall the father of the damsel, and her mother,
take and bring forth the tokens of the damsel's virginity unto the
16 elders of the city in the gate: and the damsel's father shall say
unto the elders, I gave my daughter unto this man to wife, and
17 he hateth her ; and, lo, he hath given occasions of speech against
her, saying, I found not thy daughter a maid ; and yet these are
the tokens of my daughter's virginity. And they shall spread the
18 cloth before the elders of the city. And the elders of that city
19 shall take that man and chastise him; and they shall amerce him
in an hundred shekels of silver, and give them unto the father of
the damsel, because he hath brought up an evil name upon a
virgin of Israel: and she shall be his wife; he may not put her
20 away all his days. But if this thing be true, and the tokens of vir-
21 ginity be not found for the damsel: then they shall bring out
the damsel to the door of her father's house, and the men of her
city shall stone her with stones that she die : because she hath
ᵏwrought folly in Israel, to play the whore in her father's house:
22 ˡso shalt thou put evil away from among you. ¶ᵐIf a man be
found lying with a woman married to an husband, then they
shall both of them die, both the man that lay with the woman,
23 and the woman : so shalt thou put away evil from Israel. ¶ If
a damsel that is a virgin be ⁿbetrothed unto an husband, and a
24 man find her in the city, and lie with her ; then ye shall bring
them both out unto the gate of that city, and ye shall stone them
with stones that they die ; the damsel, because she cried not,
being in the city ; and the man, because he hath ᵒhumbled his
neighbour's wife: ᵖso thou shalt put away evil from among you.
25 ¶ But if a man find a betrothed damsel in the field, and the man
³force her, and lie with her: then the man only that lay with
26 her shall die : but unto the damsel thou shalt do nothing; there
is in the damsel no sin worthy of death : for as when a man
riseth against his neighbour, and slayeth him, even so is this
27 matter : for he found her in the field, and the betrothed damsel
28 cried, and there was none to save her. ¶ᵍIf a man find a damsel
that is a virgin, which is not betrothed, and lay hold on her, and
29 lie with her, and they be found ; then the man that lay with her

ᵉ Lev. 19. 19.

ᶠ See 2 Cor.
6. 14, 15, 16.
ᵍ Lev. 19. 19.

ʰ Num. 15.
38.
ⁱ Gen. 29.

Matt. 23. 5.
21.
Judg. 15. 1.

ᵏ Gen. 34. 7.
Judg. 20. 6,
10.
2 Sam. 13.
12, 13.
ˡ ch. 13. 5.
ᵐ Lev. 20.
10.
John 8. 5.
ⁿ Matt. 1. 18,
19.

ᵒ ch. 21. 14.
ᵖ ver. 21, 22.

ᵍ Ex. 22. 16,
17.

---

¹ Heb. fulness of thy seed.
² Heb. wings.

³ Or, take strong hold of
her, 2 Sam. 13. 14.

Rabbins, at least two cubits (about 3 ft.)
high.
9–11. Cp. marg. ref. The prohibition
of v. 10 was also dictated by humanity.
The ox and the ass being of such different
size and strength, it would be cruel to the
latter to yoke them together. These two
animals are named as being those ordinarily employed in agriculture ; cp. Isai.
xxxii. 20.

12. Cp. Num. xv. 38 and note.
19. The fine was to be paid to the father,
because the slander was against him principally as the head of the wife's family. If
the damsel were an orphan the fine reverted
to herself. The fact that the penalties attached to bearing false witness against a
wife are fixed and comparatively light indicates the low estimation and position of the
woman at that time.

r ver. 24.

s Lev. 18. 8.
& 20. 11.
ch. 27. 20.
1 Cor. 5. 1.
t See Ruth
3. 9.
Ez. 16. 8.

a Neh. 13. 1,
2.

b See ch. 2.
29.
c Num. 22.
5, 6.

d Ezra 9. 12.
e Gen. 25.
24, 25, 26.
Obad. 10. 12.
f Ex. 22. 21.
& 23. 9.
Lev. 19. 34.
ch. 10. 19.
g Lev. 15. 16.

h Lev. 15. 5.

shall give unto the damsel's father fifty *shekels* of silver, and she
shall be his wife; *r*because he hath humbled her, he may not
30 put her away all his days.   *s*A man shall not take his father's
wife, nor *t*discover his father's skirt.
CHAP. 23. HE that is wounded in the stones, or hath his privy
member cut off, shall not enter into the congregation of the
2 LORD.   A bastard shall not enter into the congregation of the
LORD ; even to his tenth generation shall he not enter into the
3 congregation of the LORD.   *a*An Ammonite or Moabite shall
not enter into the congregation of the LORD ; even to their tenth
generation shall they not enter into the congregation of the LORD
4 for ever : *b*because they met you not with bread and with water in
the way, when ye came forth out of Egypt; and *c*because they
hired against thee Balaam the son of Beor of Pethor of Mesopo-
5 tamia, to curse thee.   Nevertheless the LORD thy God would
not hearken unto Balaam ; but the LORD thy God turned the
curse into a blessing unto thee, because the LORD thy God loved
6 thee.   *d*Thou shalt not seek their peace nor their [1]prosperity all
7 thy days for ever.   Thou shalt not abhor an Edomite ; *e*for he *is*
thy brother: thou shalt not abhor an Egyptian ; because *f*thou
8 wast a stranger in his land.   The children that are begotten of
them shall enter into the congregation of the LORD in their third
9 generation.   ¶ When the host goeth forth against thine enemies,
10 then keep thee from every wicked thing.   *g*If there be among
you any man, that is not clean by reason ⸢of uncleanness that
chanceth him by night, then shall he go abroad out of the camp,
11 he shall not come within the camp : but it shall be, when evening [2]cometh on, *h*he shall wash *himself* with water : and when
12 the sun is down, he shall come into the camp *again*.   Thou shalt
have a place also without the camp, whither thou shalt go forth

---

[1] Heb. *good*.   [2] Heb. *turneth toward*.

XXIII. This chapter enjoins sanctity
and purity in the congregation of Israel as
a whole, and lays down certain rights and
duties of citizenship.

1. Cp. Lev. xxi. 17-24.   Such persons,
exhibiting a mutilation of that human
nature which was made in God's image,
were rejected from the Covenant entirely.
They could however be proselytes (cp. Acts
viii. 27).   The Old Test. itself foretells (Isai.
lvi. 3-5) the removal of this ban when under
the kingdom of Messiah the outward and
emblematic perfection and sanctity of Israel
should be fulfilled in their inner meaning
by the covenanted Presence and work of the
Holy Spirit in the Church.

2. *a bastard*] Probably, a child born of
incest or adultery.

even to his tenth generation] *i.e.* (see next
verse and Neh. xiii. 1), *for ever*.   Ten is the
number of perfection and completeness.

3-5. This law forbids only the naturali-
zation of those against whom it is directed.
It does not forbid their dwelling in the
land ; and seems to refer rather to the nations than to individuals.   It was not
understood at any rate to interdict marriage
with a Moabitess ; cp. Ruth i. 4, iv. 13.
Ruth however and her sister were doubtless
proselytes.

4. Cp. marg. ref.   The Moabites and the
Ammonites are to be regarded as clans of
the same stock rather than as two independent nations, and as acting together.   Cp.
2 Chr. xx. 1.

6. *i.e.* "thou shalt not invite them to be on
terms of amity with thee (cp. xx. 10 seq.),
nor make their welfare thy care" : cp. Ezra
ix. 12.   There is no injunction to hatred or
retaliation (cp. ii. 9, 19) ; but later history
contains frequent record of hostility between Israel and these nations.

7, 8. The Edomite, as descended from
Esau the twin brother of Jacob (cp. ii. 4),
and the Egyptian, as of that nation which
had for long shewn hospitality to Joseph and
his brethren, were not to be objects of
abhorrence.   The oppression of the Egyptians was perhaps regarded as the act of the
Pharaohs rather than the will of the people
(Ex. xi. 2, 3) ; and at any rate was not to
cancel the memory of preceding hospitality.

8. *in their third generation*] *i.e.* the great
grandchildren of the Edomite or Egyptian
alien : cp. the similar phrase in Ex. xx. 5.

9-14. The whole passage refers not to the
encampments of the nation whilst passing
from Egypt through the wilderness, but to
future warlike expeditions sent out from
Canaan.

13 abroad: and thou shalt have a paddle upon thy weapon; and it shall be, when thou [1]wilt ease thyself abroad, thou shalt dig therewith, and shalt turn back and cover that which cometh
14 from thee: for the LORD thy God [i]walketh in the midst of thy camp, to deliver thee, and to give up thine enemies before thee; therefore shall thy camp be holy: that he see no [2]unclean thing
15 in thee, and turn away from thee. ¶[k]Thou shalt not deliver unto his master the servant which is escaped from his master
16 unto thee: he shall dwell with thee, *even* among you, in that place which he shall choose in one of thy gates, where it [3]liketh
17 him best: [l]thou shalt not oppress him. ¶There shall be no [4]whore [m]of the daughters of Israel, nor [n]a sodomite of the sons
18 of Israel. Thou shalt not bring the hire of a whore, or the price of a dog, into the house of the LORD thy God for any vow: for even both these *are* abomination unto the LORD thy God.
19 ¶[o]Thou shalt not lend upon usury to thy brother; usury of money, usury of victuals, usury of anything that is lent upon
20 usury: [p]unto a stranger thou mayest lend upon usury; but unto thy brother thou shalt not lend upon usury: [q]that the LORD thy God may bless thee in all that thou settest thine hand
21 to in the land whither thou goest to possess it. ¶[r]When thou shalt vow a vow unto the LORD thy God, thou shalt not slack to
22 pay it: for the LORD thy God will surely require it of thee; and it would be sin in thee. But if thou shalt forbear to vow,
23 it shall be no sin in thee. [s]That which is gone out of thy lips thou shalt keep and perform; *even* a freewill offering, according as thou hast vowed unto the LORD thy God, which thou hast
24 promised with thy mouth. ¶When thou comest into thy neighbour's vineyard, then thou mayest eat grapes thy fill at thine
25 own pleasure; but thou shalt not put *any* in thy vessel. When thou comest into the standing corn of thy neighbour, [t]then thou mayest pluck the ears with thine hand; but thou shalt not move a sickle unto thy neighbour's standing corn.

CHAP. 24. WHEN a [a]man hath taken a wife, and married her, and it come to pass that she find no favour in his eyes, because he

Side references:
i Lev. 26. 12.
k 1 Sam. 30. 15.
l Ex. 22. 21.
m Lev. 19. 29.
See Prov. 2. 16.
n Gen. 19. 5.
2 Kin. 23. 7.
o Ex. 22. 25.
Lev. 25. 36, 37.
Neh. 5. 2, 7.
Ps. 15. 5.
Luke 6. 34, 35.
p See Lev. 19. 34.
& ch. 15. 3.
q ch. 15. 10.
r Num. 30. 2.
Eccles. 5. 4, 5.
s Num. 30. 2.
Ps. 66. 13, 14.
t Matt. 12. 1.
Mark 2. 23.
Luke 6. 1.
a Matt. 5. 31.
& 19. 7.
Mark 10. 4.

[1] Heb. *sittest down.*
[2] Heb. *nakedness of any thing.*
[3] Heb. *is good for him.*
[4] Or, *sodomitess.*

15, 16. The case in question is that of a slave who fled from a heathen master to the Holy Land. It is of course assumed that the refugee was not flying from justice, but only from the tyranny of his lord.

17. Cp. marg. ref. Prostitution was a common part of religious observances amongst idolatrous nations, especially in the worship of Ashtoreth or Astarte. Cp. Micah i. 7; Baruch vi. 43.

18. Another Gentile practice, connected with the one alluded to in the preceding verse, is here forbidden. The word "dog" is figurative (cp. Rev. xxii. 15), and equivalent to the "sodomite" of the verse preceding.

XXIV. In this and the next chapter certain particular rights and duties, domestic, social, and civil, are treated. The cases brought forward have often no definite connexion, and seem selected in order to illustrate the application of the great principles of the Law in certain important events and circumstances.

1–4. These four verses contain only one sentence, and should be rendered thus: If **a man hath taken a wife, &c., and given her a bill of divorcement;** and (*v.* 2) if she **has departed out of his house and become another man's wife;** and (*v.* 3) if the latter **husband hate her, then** (*v.* 4) her former **husband, &c.**

Moses neither institutes nor enjoins divorce. The exact spirit of the passage is given in our Lord's words to the Jews', "Moses because of the hardness of your hearts suffered you to put away your wives" (Matt. xix. 8). Not only does the original institution of marriage as recorded by Moses (Gen. ii. 24) set forth the perpetuity of the bond, but the verses before us plainly intimate that divorce, whilst tolerated for

hath found [1]some uncleanness in her: then let him write her a bill of [2]divorcement, and give *it* in her hand, and send her out of 2 his house. And when she is departed out of his house, she may 3 go and be another man's *wife*. And *if* the latter husband hate her, and write her a bill of divorcement, and giveth *it* in her hand, and sendeth her out of his house; or if the latter husband

Jer. 3. 1.

4 die, which took her *to be* his wife; [b]her former husband, which sent her away, may not take her again to be his wife, after that she is defiled; for that *is* abomination before the LORD: and thou shalt not cause the land to sin, which the LORD thy God

[c] ch. 20. 7.

5 giveth thee *for* an inheritance. ¶[c]When a man hath taken a new wife, he shall not go out to war, [3]neither shall he be charged with any business: *but* he shall be free at home one

[d] Prov. 5. 18.
[e] Ex. 21. 16.
[f] ch. 19. 19.
[g] Lev. 13. 2.
& 14. 2.
[h] See Luke 17. 32.
1 Cor. 10. 6.
[i] Num. 12. 10.
[k] Ex. 22. 26.
[l] Job 29. 11, 13.
& 31. 20.
2 Cor. 9. 13.
2 Tim. 1. 18.
[m] ch. 6. 25.
Ps. 106. 31.
& 112. 9.
Dan. 4. 27.
[n] Mal. 3. 5.
[o] Lev. 19. 13.
Jer. 22. 13.
James 5. 4.
[p] James 5. 4.
[q] 2 Kin. 14. 6.
2 Chr. 25. 4.
Jer. 31. 29, 30.
Ez. 18. 20.
[r] Ex. 22. 21, 22.
Prov. 22. 22.
Isai. 1. 23.
Jer. 5. 28.
& 22. 3.
Ez. 22. 29.
Zech. 7. 10.
Mal. 3. 5.
[s] Ex. 22. 26.

6 year, and shall [d]cheer up his wife which he hath taken. ¶No man shall take the nether or the upper millstone to pledge: for 7 he taketh *a man's* life to pledge. ¶[e]If a man be found stealing any of his brethren of the children of Israel, and maketh merchandise of him, or selleth him; then that thief shall die; [f]and 8 thou shalt put evil away from among you. ¶Take heed in [g]the plague of leprosy, that thou observe diligently, and do according to all that the priests the Levites shall teach you: as I com-9 manded them, *so* ye shall observe to do. [h]Remember what the LORD thy God did [i]unto Miriam by the way, after that ye were 10 come forth out of Egypt. ¶When thou dost [4]lend thy brother any thing, thou shalt not go into his house to fetch his pledge. 11 Thou shalt stand abroad, and the man to whom thou dost lend 12 shall bring out the pledge abroad unto thee. And if the man *be* 13 poor, thou shalt not sleep with his pledge: [k]in any case thou shalt deliver him the pledge again when the sun goeth down, that he may sleep in his own raiment, and [l]bless thee: and [m]it shall be righteousness unto thee before the LORD thy God. 14 ¶Thou shalt not [n]oppress an hired servant *that is* poor and needy, *whether he be* of thy brethren, or of thy strangers that *are* 15 in thy land within thy gates: at his day [o]thou shalt give *him* his hire, neither shall the sun go down upon it; for he *is* poor, and [5]setteth his heart upon it: [p]lest he cry against thee unto 16 the LORD, and it be sin unto thee. ¶[q]The fathers shall not be put to death for the children, neither shall the children be put to death for the fathers: every man shall be put to death for 17 his own sin. ¶[r]Thou shalt not pervert the judgment of the stranger, nor of the fatherless; [s]nor take a widow's raiment to

[1] Heb. *matter of nakedness.*
[2] Heb. *cutting off.*
[3] Heb. *not any thing shall*
pass upon him.
[4] Heb. *lend the loan of any thing to, &c.*
[5] Heb. *lifteth his soul unto it*, Ps. 25. 1. & 86. 4.

the time, contravenes the order of nature and of God. The divorced woman who marries again is "defiled" (*v.* 4), and is grouped in this particular with the adulteress (cp. Lev. xviii. 20). Our Lord then was speaking according to the spirit of the law of Moses when he declared, "Whoso marrieth her which is put away doth commit adultery" (Matt. xix. 9). He was speaking too not less according to the mind of the Prophets (cp. Mal. ii. 14-16). But Moses could not absolutely put an end to a practice which was traditional, and common to the Jews with other Oriental nations. His

aim is therefore to regulate and thus to mitigate an evil which he could not extirpate.

6. Cp. Ex. xxii. 25, 26.
7. Cp. xxi. 14, and Ex. xxi. 16.
10-13. Cp. Ex. xxii. 25-27.
13. *righteousness unto thee*] Cp. vi. 25 note.
16. A caution addressed to earthly judges. Amongst other Oriental nations the family of a criminal was commonly involved in his punishment (cp. Esth. ix. 13, 14). In Israel it was not to be so; cp. marg. reff.
17-22. Cp. marg. reff. The motive assigned for these various acts of consideration is one and the same (*vv.* 18, 22).

18 pledge: but ᵗthou shalt remember that thou wast a bondman in
Egypt, and the LORD thy God redeemed thee thence: therefore
19 I command thee to do this thing.   ¶ ᵘWhen thou cuttest down
thine harvest in thy field, and hast forgot a sheaf in the field,
thou shalt not go again to fetch it: it shall be for the stranger,
for the fatherless, and for the widow: that the LORD thy God
20 may ˣbless thee in all the work of thine hands.   When thou
beatest thine olive tree, ¹thou shalt not go over the boughs again:
it shall be for the stranger, for the fatherless, and for the widow.
21 When thou gatherest the grapes of thy vineyard, thou shalt not
glean it ²afterward: it shall be for the stranger, for the father-
22 less, and for the widow.   And ʸthou shalt remember that thou
wast a bondman in the land of Egypt: therefore I command
thee to do this thing.

CHAP. 25. IF there be a ᵃcontroversy between men, and they come
unto judgment, that the judges may judge them ; then they ᵇshall
2 justify the righteous, and condemn the wicked.   And it shall be,
if the wicked man be ᶜworthy to be beaten, that the judge shall
cause him to lie down, ᵈand to be beaten before his face, accord-
3 ing to his fault, by a certain number.   ᵉForty stripes he may
give him, and not exceed: lest, if he should exceed, and beat
him above these with many stripes, then thy brother should
4 ᶠseem vile unto thee.   ¶ ᵍThou shalt not muzzle the ox when he
5 ³treadeth out the corn.   ¶ ʰIf brethren dwell together, and one of
them die, and have no child, the wife of the dead shall not marry
without unto a stranger: her ⁴husband's brother shall go in
unto her, and take her to him to wife, and perform the duty of
6 an husband's brother unto her.   And it shall be, that the first-

Margin references:
ᵗ ver. 22.
ch. 16. 12.
ᵘ Lev. 19. 9,
10. & 23. 22.
ˣ ch. 15. 10.
Ps. 41. 1.
Prov. 19. 17.
ʸ ver. 18.
ᵃ ch. 19. 17.
Ez. 44. 24.
ᵇ See Prov
17. 15.
ᶜ Luke 12.
48.
ᵈ Matt. 10.
17.
ᵉ 2 Cor. 11.
24.
ᶠ Job 18. 3.
ᵍ Prov. 12.
10.
1 Cor. 9. 9.
1 Tim. 5. 18.
ʰ Matt. 22.
24.
Mark 12. 19.
Luke 20. 28.

¹ Heb. thou shalt not bough   ³ Heb. thresheth, Hos. 10.   ⁴ Or, next kinsman, Gen.
it after thee.   11.   38. 8. Ruth 1. 12, 13. &
² Heb. after thee.   3. 9.

XXV. 1, 2. Render: (1) **If there be a
controversy between men, and they come
to judgment, and the judges judge them,
and justify the righteous and condemn
the wicked** (cp. marg. ref. and Ex. xxiii. 7 ;
Prov. xvii. 15) ; (2) **then it shall be**, &c.
2. Scourging is named as a penalty in
Lev. xix. 20. The beating here spoken of
would be on the back with a rod or stick
(cp. Prov. х. 13, xix. 29, xxvi. 3).
3. The Jews to keep within the letter of
the law fixed 39 stripes as the maximum
(cp. marg. ref.). Forty signifies the full
measure of judgment (cp. Gen. vii. 12 ;
Num. xiv. 33, 34) ; but the son of Israel was
not to be lashed like a slave at the mercy of
another. The judge was always to be present to see that the Law in this particular
was not overpassed.
4. Cp. marg. reff. In other kinds of labour the oxen were usually muzzled. When
driven to and fro over the threshing-floor in
order to stamp out the grain from the chaff,
they were to be allowed to partake of the
fruits of their labours.
5–10. Law of levirate marriage. The law
on this subject is not peculiar to the Jews,
but is found (see Gen. xxxviii. 8) in all
essential respects the same amongst various

Oriental nations, ancient and modern. The
rules in these verses, like those upon divorce,
do but incorporate existing immemorial
usages, and introduce various wise and politic limitations and mitigations of them.
The root of the obligation here imposed
upon the brother of the deceased husband
lies in the primitive idea of childlessness
being a great calamity (cp. Gen. xvi. 4, and
note), and extinction of name and family
one of the greatest that could happen (cp.
ix. 14 ; Ps. cix. 12-15). To avert this the
ordinary rules as to inter-marriage are in
the case in question (cp. Lev. xviii. 16) set
aside. The obligation was onerous (cp. Ruth
iv. 6), and might be repugnant ; and it is
accordingly considerably reduced and restricted by Moses. The duty is recognized
as one of affection for the memory of the
deceased ; it is not one which could be
enforced at law. That it continued down
to the Christian era is apparent from the
question on this point put to Jesus by the
Sadducees (see marg. reff.).
5. no child] Lit. "no son." The existence of a daughter would clearly suffice.
The daughter would inherit the name and
property of the father; cp. Num. xxvii.
1-11.

t Gen. 38. 9.

k Ruth 4. 10.

l Ruth 4. 1, 2.

m Ruth 4. 6.

n Ruth 4. 7.

o Ruth 4. 11.

p ch. 19. 13.

q Prov. 11. 1.

r Ex. 20. 12.

s Prov. 11. 1.
1 Thes. 4. 6.

t Ex. 17. 8.

born which she beareth *i*shall succeed in the name of his brother 7 *which is* dead, that *k*his name be not put out of Israel. And if the man like not to take his *1*brother's wife, then let his brother's wife go up to the *1*gate unto the elders, and say, My husband's brother refuseth to raise up unto his brother a name in Israel, 8 he will not perform the duty of my husband's brother. Then the elders of his city shall call him, and speak unto him : and *if* 9 he stand *to it*, and say, *m*I like not to take her; then shall his brother's wife come unto him in the presence of the elders, and *n*loose his shoe from off his foot, and spit in his face, and shall answer and say, So shall it be done unto that man that will not 10 *o*build up his brother's house. And his name shall be called 11 in Israel, The house of him that hath his shoe loosed. ¶ When men strive together one with another, and the wife of the one draweth near for to deliver her husband out of the hand of him that smiteth him, and putteth forth her hand, and taketh him by 12 the secrets : then thou shalt cut off her hand, *p*thine eye shall 13 not pity *her.* ¶ *q*Thou shalt not have in thy bag *2*divers weights, 14 a great and a small. Thou shalt not have in thine house *3*divers 15 measures, a great and a small. *But* thou shalt have a perfect and just weight, a perfect and just measure shalt thou have: *r*that thy days may be lengthened in the land which the LORD 16 thy God giveth thee. For *s*all that do such things, *and* all that do unrighteously, *are* an abomination unto the LORD thy God. 17 ¶ *t*Remember what Amalek did unto thee by the way, when ye 18 were come forth out of Egypt; how he met thee by the way, and smote the hindmost of thee, *even* all *that were* feeble behind thee,

1 Or, *next kinsman's wife.*
2 Heb. *a stone and a stone.*
3 Heb. *an ephah and an ephah.*

---

9. *loose his shoe from off his foot*] In token of taking from the unwilling brother all right over the wife and property of the deceased. Planting the foot on a thing was an usual symbol of lordship and of taking possession (cp. Gen. xiii. 17; Josh. x. 24), and loosing the shoe and handing it to another in like manner signified a renunciation and transfer of right and title (cp. Ruth iv. 7, 8; Ps. lx. 8, and cviii. 9). The widow here is directed herself, as the party slighted and injured, to deprive her brother-law of his shoe, and *spit in his face* (cp. Num. xii. 14). The action was intended to aggravate the disgrace conceived to attach to the conduct of the man.

10. *The house,* &c.] Equivalent to "the house of the barefooted one." To go barefoot was a sign of the most abject condition; cp. 2 S. xv. 30.

12. This is the only mutilation prescribed by the Law of Moses, unless we except the retaliation prescribed as a punishment for the infliction on another of bodily injuries (Lev. xxiv. 19, 20). The act in question was probably not rare in the times and countries for which the Law of Moses was designed. It is of course to be understood that the act was wilful, and that the prescribed punishment would be inflicted according to the sentence of the judges.

13–19. Honesty in trade, as a duty to our neighbour, is emphatically enforced once more (cp. Lev. xix. 35, 36). It is noteworthy that St. John the Baptist puts the like duties in the forefront of his preaching (cp. Luke iii. 12 seq.); and that "the Prophets" (cp. Ezek. xlv. 10–12; Amos viii. 5; Mic. vi. 10, 11) and "the Psalms" (Prov. xvi. 11, xx. 10, 23), not less than "the Law," specially insist on them.

13. *divers weights*] *i.e.* stones of unequal weights, the lighter to sell with, the heavier to buy with. Stones were used by the Jews instead of brass or lead for their weights, as less liable to lose anything through rust or wear.

17–19. It was not after the spirit or mission of the Law to aim at overcoming inveterate opposition by love and by attempts at conversion (contrast Luke ix. 55, 56). The law taught God's hatred of sin and of rebellion against Him by enjoining the extinction of the obstinate sinner. The Amalekites were a kindred people (Gen. xxxvi. 15, 16); and living as they did in the peninsula of Sinai, they could not but have well known the mighty acts God had done for His people in Egypt and the Red Sea; yet they manifested from the first a persistent hostility to Israel (cp. Ex. xvii. 8, and note; Num. xiv. 45). They provoked therefore the sentence here pronounced, which was executed at last by Saul (1 S. xv. 3 seq.).

when thou *wast* faint and weary; and he *u*feared not God. 19 Therefore it shall be, *x*when the LORD thy God hath given thee rest from all thine enemies round about, in the land which the LORD thy God giveth thee *for* an inheritance to possess it, *that* thou shalt *y*blot out the remembrance of Amalek from under heaven; thou shalt not forget *it*.

CHAP. 26. AND it shall be, when thou *art* come in unto the land which the LORD thy God giveth thee *for* an inheritance, and 2 possessest it, and dwellest therein; *a*that thou shalt take of the first of all the fruit of the earth, which thou shalt bring of thy land that the LORD thy God giveth thee, and shalt put *it* in a basket, and shalt *b*go unto the place which the LORD thy God 3 shall choose to place his name there. And thou shalt go unto the priest that shall be in those days, and say unto him, I profess this day unto the LORD thy God, that I am come unto the country which the LORD sware unto our fathers for to give 4 us. And the priest shall take the basket out of thine hand, and 5 set it down before the altar of the LORD thy God. And thou shalt speak and say before the LORD thy God, *c*A Syrian *d*ready to perish *was* my father, and *e*he went down into Egypt, and sojourned there with a *f*few, and became there a nation, great, 6 mighty, and populous: and *g*the Egyptians evil entreated us, 7 and afflicted us, and laid upon us hard bondage: and *h*when we cried unto the LORD God of our fathers, the LORD heard our voice, and looked on our affliction, and our labour, and our 8 oppression: and *i*the LORD brought us forth out of Egypt with a mighty hand, and with an outstretched arm, and *k*with great 9 terribleness, and with signs, and with wonders: and he hath brought us into this place, and hath given us this land, *even l*a 10 land that floweth with milk and honey. And now, behold, I have brought the firstfruits of the land, which thou, O LORD, hast given me. And thou shalt set it before the LORD thy 11 God, and worship before the LORD thy God: and *m*thou shalt rejoice in every good *thing* which the LORD thy God hath given unto thee, and unto thine house, thou, and the Levite, and the 12 stranger that *is* among you. ¶ When thou hast made an end of

u Ps. 36. 1.
Prov. 16. 6.
Rom. 3. 18.
x 1 Sam. 15.
3.
y Ex. 17. 14.

a Ex. 23. 19,
& 34. 26.
Num. 18. 13.
ch. 16. 10.
Prov. 3. 9.
b ch. 12. 5.

c Hos. 12. 12.
d Gen. 43. 1,
2. & 45. 7. 11.
e Gen. 46. 1,
6.
Acts 7. 15.
f Gen. 46. 27.
ch. 10. 22.
g Ex. 1. 11,
14.
h Ex. 2. 23,
24, 25.
& 3. 9.
& 4. 31.
i Ex. 12. 37,
51.
& 13. 3, 14,
16.
ch. 5. 15.
k ch. 4. 34.
l Ex. 3. 8.
m ch. 12. 7,
12, 18.
& 16. 11.

XXVI. Two liturgical enactments having a clear and close reference to the whole of the preceding legislation, form a most appropriate and significant conclusion to it, viz. (1) the formal acknowledgment in deed and symbol of God's faithfulness, by presentment of a basket filled with firstfruits, and in word by recitation of the solemn formula prescribed in *v.* 3 and *vv.* 5–10; and (2) the solemn declaration and profession on the part of each Israelite on the occasion of the third tithe (*v.* 12).

2. On the subject of firstfruits see notes on Lev. xxiii. 9 seq. The firstfruits here in question are to be distinguished alike from those offered in acknowledgment of the blessings of harvest (cp. Ex. xxii. 29) at the Feasts of Passover and Pentecost, and also from the offerings prescribed in Num. xviii. 8 seq. The latter consisted of *preparations* from the produce of the earth, such as oil, flour, wine, &c.; whilst those here meant are the raw produce: the former were

national and public offerings, those of this chapter were private and personal. The whole of the firstfruits belonged to the officiating priest.

5. *A Syrian ready to perish was my father*] The reference is shown by the context to be to Jacob, as the ancestor in whom particularly the family of Abraham began to develop into a nation (cp. Isai. xliii. 22, 28, &c.). Jacob is called *a Syrian* (lit. Aramæan), not only because of his own long residence in Syria with Laban (Gen. xxix.-xxxi.), as our Lord was called a Nazarene because of his residence at Nazareth (Matt. ii. 23), but because he there married and had his children (cp. Hos. xii. 12); and might be said accordingly to belong to that more than to any other land.

12. See marg. ref. to Numbers and note. A strict fulfilment of the onerous and complicated tithe obligations was a leading part of the righteousness of the Pharisees : cp. Matt. xxiii. 23.

tithing all the *n*tithes of thine increase the third year, *which is* *o*the year of tithing, and hast given *it* unto the Levite, the stranger, the fatherless, and the widow, that they may eat 13 within thy gates, and be filled; then thou shalt say before the LORD thy God, I have brought away the hallowed things out of *mine* house, and also have given them unto the Levite, and unto the stranger, to the fatherless, and to the widow, according to all thy commandments which thou hast commanded me : I have not

transgressed thy commandments, *p*neither have I forgotten *them:* 14 *q*I have not eaten thereof in my mourning, neither have I taken away *ought* thereof for *any* unclean *use*, nor given *ought* thereof for the dead: *but* I have hearkened to the voice of the LORD my God, *and* have done according to all that thou hast commanded

15 me. *r* Look down from thy holy habitation, from heaven, and bless thy people Israel, and the land which thou hast given us, as thou swarest unto our fathers, a land that floweth with milk 16 and honey. ¶ This day the LORD thy God hath commanded thee to do these statutes and judgments: thou shalt therefore keep and do them with all thine heart, and with all thy soul.

17 Thou hast *s*avouched the LORD this day to be thy God, and to walk in his ways, and to keep his statutes, and his command-18 ments, and his judgments, and to hearken unto his voice: and

*t*the LORD hath avouched thee this day to be his peculiar people, as he hath promised thee, and that *thou* shouldest keep all his 19 commandments; and to make thee *u*high above all nations which he hath made, in praise, and in name, and in honour; and that thou mayest be *x*an holy people unto the LORD thy God, as he hath spoken.

CHAP. **27.** AND Moses with the elders of Israel commanded the people, saying, Keep all the commandments which I command 2 you this day. And it shall be on the day *a*when ye shall pass over Jordan unto the land which the LORD thy God giveth thee, that *b*thou shalt set thee up great stones, and plaister them with 3 plaister : and thou shalt write upon them all the words of this law, when thou art passed over, that thou mayest go in unto the

---

14. *I have not eaten thereof in my mourning*] When the Israelite would be unclean (cp. marg. reff.).

nor given ought thereof for the dead] The reference is not so much to the superstitious custom of placing food on or in tombs as to the funeral expenses, and more especially the usual feast for the mourners (cp. Jer. xvi. 7 ; Ez. xxiv. 17 ; Hos. ix. 4 ; Tob. iv. 17). The dedicated things were to be employed in glad and holy feasting, not therefore for funeral banquets ; for death and all associated with it was regarded as unclean.

16–19. A brief and earnest exhortation by way of conclusion to the second and longest discourse of the book.

17. *Thou hast avouched*] Lit. "made to say :" so also in the next verse. The sense is : "Thou hast given occasion to the Lord to say that He is thy God," *i.e.* by promising that He shall be so. Cp. Ex. xxiv. 7 ; Josh. xxiv. 14–25.

XXVII. Moses in a third discourse (xxvii.-xxx.), proceeds more specially to dwell on the sanctions of the Law. In these

chapters he sets before Israel in striking and elaborate detail the blessings which would ensue upon faithfulness to the Covenant, and the curses which disobedience would involve. The xxviith chapter introduces this portion of the book by enjoining the erection of a stone monument on which the Law should be inscribed as soon as the people took possession of the promised inheritance (*vv.* 1–10) ; and by next prescribing the liturgical form after which the blessings and cursings should be pronounced (*vv.* 11–26).

2. The stones here named are not those of which the altar (*v.* 5) was to be built, but are to serve as a separate monument witnessing to the fact that the people took possession of the land by virtue of the Law inscribed on them and with an acknowledgment of its obligations.

3. *all the words of this law*] *i.e.* all the laws revealed from God to the people by Moses, regarded by the Jews as 613 (cp. Num. xv. 38 note). The exhibition of laws in this manner on stones, pillars, or tables, was familiar to the ancients. The laws were

land which the LORD thy God giveth thee, a land that floweth
with milk and honey; as the LORD God of thy fathers hath
4 promised thee. Therefore it shall be when ye be gone over
Jordan, *that* ye shall set up these stones, which I command you
this day, *c*in mount Ebal, and thou shalt plaister them with
5 plaister. And there shalt thou build an altar unto the LORD
thy God, an altar of stones : *d*thou shalt not lift up *any* iron *tool*
6 upon them. Thou shalt build the altar of the LORD thy God of
whole stones : and thou shalt offer burnt offerings thereon unto
7 the LORD thy God : and thou shalt offer peace offerings, and
8 shalt eat there, and rejoice before the LORD thy God. And thou
shalt write upon the stones all the words of this law very plainly.
9 ¶ And Moses and the priests the Levites spake unto all Israel,
saying, Take heed, and hearken, O Israel; *e*this day thou art
10 become the people of the LORD thy God. Thou shalt therefore
obey the voice of the LORD thy God, and do his commandments
11 and his statutes, which I command thee this day. ¶ And Moses
12 charged the people the same day, saying, These shall stand
*f*upon mount Gerizim to bless the people, when ye are come
over Jordan ; Simeon, and Levi, and Judah, and Issachar, and
13 Joseph, and Benjamin : and *g*these shall stand upon mount Ebal
*1*to curse; Reuben, Gad, and Asher, and Zebulun, Dan, and
14 Naphtali. And *h*the Levites shall speak, and say unto all the
15 men of Israel with a loud voice, ¶ *i*Cursed *be* the man that

c ch. 11. 29.
Josh. 8. 30.

d Ex. 20. 25.
Josh. 8. 31.

e ch. 26. 18.

f ch. 11. 29.
Josh. 3. 33.
Judg. 9. 7.
g ch. 11. 29.
Josh. 8. 33.
h ch. 33. 10.
Josh. 8. 33.
Dan. 9. 11.
i Ex. 20. 4.
Lev. 19. 4.
ch. 4. 16, 23.
& 5. 8.
Isai. 44. 9.
Hos. 13. 2.

¹ Heb. *for a cursing.*

probably graven in the stone ["very plainly"
(*v.* 8) is by some rendered "scoop it out
well"], as are for the most part the Egyptian hieroglyphics, the "plaister" being
afterwards added to protect the inscription
from the weather.

4. *in mount Ebal*] Cp. marg. reff. The
Samaritan Pentateuch and Version read
here Gerizim instead of Ebal ; but the
original text was probably, as nearly all
modern authorities hold, altered in order to
lend a show of scriptural sanction to the
Samaritan temple on mount Gerizim.

The erection of the Altar, the offering
thereon Burnt offerings and Peace offerings
(*vv.* 6, 7), the publication of the Law in writing, form altogether a solemn renewal of
the Covenant on the entrance of the people
into the Promised Land, and recall the ceremonies observed on the original grant of the
Covenant at Sinai (cp. Ex. xxiv. 5). And
Ebal [the mount of "barrenness"], the
mount of cursing, was the fitting spot on
which to celebrate them. For the curses
were the penalties under which the children
of Israel bound themselves to keep the
Law. Suitably also was the same place
selected as that in which were to be set up
both the monumental stones containing the
Law, and the Altar at which the Covenant
was to be renewed. We must note too the
fact that *vv.* 15 sqq. set out verbatim the
curses only, the blessings being omitted.
The law because of man's sinfulness brings
on him first and chiefly a curse : cp. xxxi.
16, 17 ; Gal. iii. 10.

11-26. Cp. Josh. viii. 32-35. The solem-

nity was apparently designed only for the
single occasion on which it actually took
place.

12, 13. The tribes appointed to stand on
Gerizim to bless the people all sprang from
the two wives of Jacob, Leah and Rachel.
All the four tribes which sprang from the
handmaids Zilpah and Bilhah are located
on Ebal. But in order, as it would seem,
to effect an equal division, two tribes are
added to the latter from the descendants of
the wives, that of Reuben, probably because
he forfeited his primogeniture (Gen. xlix. 4);
and of Zebulun, apparently because he was
the youngest son of Leah.

The transaction presents itself as a solemn renewal of the covenant made by God
with Abraham and Isaac, but more especially with Jacob and his family. Accordingly the genealogical basis of the "twelve
patriarchs" (cp. Acts vii. 12 ; Rev. vii. 4
seq.), the sons of Jacob, is here assumed.
The tribes of Ephraim and Manasseh are
merged in the name of Joseph, their father ;
and Levi regains on this occasion his place
collaterally with the others. "The Levites" of *v.* 14 are no doubt "the priests
the Levites" (cp. Josh. viii. 33), in whom
the ministerial character attaching to the
tribe was more particularly manifested. It
is noteworthy that the group of tribes which
stood on Gerizim far exceeded the other in
numbers and in importance, thus perhaps
indicating that even by the Law the blessing should at length prevail.

15. The "Amen" attested the conviction
of the utterers that the sentences to which

maketh *any* graven or molten image, an abomination unto the LORD, the work of the hands of the craftsman, and putteth *it* in a secret *place.* *k*And all the people shall answer and say, Amen.
16 *l*Cursed *be* he that setteth light by his father or his mother.
17 And all the people shall say, Amen. *m*Cursed *be* he that removeth his neighbour's landmark. And all the people shall
18 say, Amen. *n*Cursed *be* he that maketh the blind to wander out
19 of the way. And all the people shall say, Amen. *o*Cursed *be* he that perverteth the judgment of the stranger, fatherless, and
20 widow. And all the people shall say, Amen. *p*Cursed *be* he that lieth with his father's wife ; because he uncovereth his
21 father's skirt. And all the people shall say, Amen. *q*Cursed *be* he that lieth with any manner of beast. And all the people
22 shall say, Amen. *r*Cursed *be* he that lieth with his sister, the daughter of his father, or the daughter of his mother. And
23 all the people shall say, Amen. *s*Cursed *be* he that lieth with his mother in law. And all the people shall say, Amen.
24 *t*Cursed *be* he that smiteth his neighbour secretly. And all the
25 people shall say, Amen. *u*Cursed *be* he that taketh reward to slay an innocent person. And all the people shall say, Amen.
26 *x*Cursed *be* he that confirmeth not *all* the words of this law to do them. And all the people shall say, Amen.

CHAP. **28.** AND it shall come to pass, *a*if thou shalt hearken diligently unto the voice of the LORD thy God, to observe *and* to do all his commandments which I command thee this day, that the LORD thy God *b*will set thee on high above all nations of the
2 earth : and all these blessings shall come on thee, and *c* overtake thee, if thou shalt hearken unto the voice of the LORD thy God.
3 *d* Blessed *shalt* thou *be* in the city, and blessed *shalt* thou *be* *e*in
4 the field. Blessed *shall be* *f*the fruit of thy body, and the fruit of thy ground, and the fruit of thy cattle, the increase of thy
5 kine, and the flocks of thy sheep. Blessed *shall* be thy basket
6 and thy ¹store. *g*Blessed *shalt* thou *be* when thou comest in,
7 and blessed *shalt* thou *be* when thou goest out. The LORD
h shall cause thine enemies that rise up against thee to be smitten before thy face : they shall come out against thee one way,
8 and flee before thee seven ways. The LORD shall *i* command the blessing upon thee in thy ²storehouses, and in all that thou *k*set-

¹ Or, *dough,* or, *kneadingtrough.*   ² Or, *barns,* Prov. 3. 10.

---

they responded were true, just, and certain ; so in Num. v. 22, and in our own Commination Office, which is modelled after this ordinance of Moses.

15–26. Twelve curses against transgressions of the Covenant. The first eleven are directed against special sins which are selected by way of example, the last comprehensively sums up in general terms and condemns all and every offence against God's Law. Cp. the marg. reff.

XXVIII. A comparison of this chapter with Ex. xxiii. 20–23 and Lev. xxvi. will shew how Moses here resumes and amplifies the promises and threats already set forth in the earlier records of the Law. The language rises in this chapter to the sublimest strains, especially in the latter part of it ; and the prophecies respecting the dispersion

and degradation of the Jewish nation in its later days are amongst the most remarkable in scripture. They are plain, precise, and circumstantial ; and the fulfilment of them has been literal, complete, and undeniable.

1–14. The Blessing. The six repetitions of the word "blessed" introduce the particular forms which the blessing would take in the various relations of life.

5. The "basket" or bag was a customary means in the East for carrying about whatever might be needed for personal uses (cp. xxvi. 2 ; John xiii. 29).

The "store" is rather the **kneading-trough** (Ex. viii. 3, xii. 34). The blessings here promised relate, it will be observed, to private and personal life : in *v.* 7 those which are of a more public and national character are brought forward.

test thine hand unto; and he shall bless thee in the land which
9 the LORD thy God giveth thee. *The LORD shall establish thee
an holy people unto himself, as he hath sworn unto thee, if thou
shalt keep the commandments of the LORD thy God, and walk
10 in his ways. And all people of the earth shall see that thou
art *called by the name of the LORD; and they shall be *afraid
11 of thee. And °the LORD shall make thee plenteous ¹in goods,
in the fruit of thy ²body, and in the fruit of thy cattle, and in
the fruit of thy ground, in the land which the LORD sware unto
12 thy fathers to give thee. The LORD shall open unto thee his
good treasure, the heaven ᵖto give the rain unto thy land in his
season, and ᑫto bless all the work of thine hand: and ʳthou
13 shalt lend unto many nations, and thou shalt not borrow. And
the LORD shall make thee ˢthe head, and not the tail; and thou
shalt be above only, and thou shalt not be beneath; if that thou
hearken unto the commandments of the LORD thy God, which
14 I command thee this day, to observe and to do *them:* ᵗand thou
shalt not go aside from any of the words which I command thee
this day, *to* the right hand, or *to* the left, to go after other gods
15 to serve them. ¶ But it shall come to pass, ᵘif thou wilt not
hearken unto the voice of the LORD thy God, to observe to do all
his commandments and his statutes which I command thee this
day; that all these curses shall come upon thee, and ˣovertake
16 thee: Cursed *shalt* thou *be* ʸin the city, and cursed *shalt* thou *be*
17 18, in the field. Cursed *shall be* thy basket and thy store. Cursed
shall be the fruit of thy body, and the fruit of thy land, the in-
19 crease of thy kine, and the flocks of thy sheep. Cursed *shalt*
thou *be* when thou comest in, and cursed *shalt* thou *be* when thou
20 goest out. The LORD shall send upon thee ᶻcursing, ᵃvexation,
and ᵇrebuke, in all that thou settest thine hand unto ³for to do,
until thou be destroyed, and until thou perish quickly; because
of the wickedness of thy doings, whereby thou hast forsaken me.
21 The LORD shall make ᶜthe pestilence cleave unto thee, until he
have consumed thee from off the land, whither thou goest to
22 possess it. ᵈThe LORD shall smite thee with a consumption,
and with a fever, and with an inflammation, and with an extreme burning, and with the ⁴sword, and with ᵉblasting, and
with mildew; and they shall pursue thee until thou perish.
23 And ᶠthy heaven that *is* over thy head shall be brass, and the
24 earth that *is* under thee *shall be* iron. The LORD shall make the
rain of thy land powder and dust: from heaven shall it come

Marginal references:

ᶦ Ex. 19. 5, 6.
ch. 7. 6.

ᵐ Num. 6, 27.
2 Chr. 7. 14.
Isai. 63. 19.
Dan. 9. 18.
ⁿ ch. 11. 25.
ᵒ ver. 4.
ch. 30. 9.
Prov. 10. 22.
ᵖ Lev. 26. 4.
ch. 11. 14.
ᑫ ch. 14. 29.
ʳ ch. 15. 6.
ˢ Isai. 9. 14, 15.
ᵗ ch. 5. 32.
& 11. 16.

ᵘ Lev. 26.14.
Lam. 2. 17.
Dan. 9. 11.
Mal. 2. 2.
ˣ ver. 2.
ʸ ver. 3, &c.

ᶻ Mal. 2. 2.
ᵃ 1 Sam. 14. 20.
Zech. 14. 13.
ᵇ Ps. 80. 16.
Isai. 30. 17.
& 51. 20.
& 66. 15.
ᶜ Lev. 26. 25.
Jer. 24. 10.
ᵈ Lev. 26.16.
ᵉ Amos 4. 9.

ᶠ Lev. 26. 19.

---

¹ Or, *for good.*
² Heb. *belly.*
³ Heb. *which thou wouldest do.*
⁴ Or, *drought.*

---

9. The oath with which God vouchsafed
to confirm His promises to the patriarchs
(cp. Gen. xxii. 16; Heb. vi. 13, 14) contained by implication these gifts of holiness
and eminence to Israel (cp. marg. reff.).

15–68. The curses correspond in form
and number (*vv.* 15-19) to the blessings (*vv.*
3-6), and the special modes in which these
threats should be executed are described in
five groups of denunciations (*vv.* 20-68).

20–26. First series of judgments. The
curse of God should rest on all they did, and
should issue in manifold forms of disease, in
famine, and in defeat in war.

20. *vexation*] Rather, **confusion**: the word
in the original is used (vii. 23; 1 S. xiv. 20)
for the panic and disorder with which the
curse of God smites His foes.

22. "Blasting" denotes (cp. Gen. xli. 23)
the result of the scorching east wind; "mildew" that of an untimely blight falling on
the green ear, withering it and marring its
produce.

24. When the heat is very great the atmosphere in Palestine is often filled with dust
and sand; the wind is a burning sirocco, and
the air comparable to the glowing heat at
the mouth of a furnace.

g ver. 7.
Lev. 26. 17.
ch. 32. 30.
Isai. 30. 17.

h Jer. 15. 4.
& 24. 9.
Ez. 23. 46.
i 1 Sam. 17.
44, 46.
Ps. 79. 2.
Jer. 7. 33.
k ver. 35.
l Ps. 78. 66.
m Jer. 4. 9.
n Job 5. 14.
Isai. 59. 10.
o Job 31. 10.
Jer. 8. 10.
p Job 31. 8.
Jer. 12. 13.
Amos 5. 11.
Mic. 6. 15.
Zeph. 1. 13.
q ch. 20. 6.

r Ps. 119. 82.

s ver. 51.
Lev. 26. 16.
Jer. 5. 17.
t ver. 67.
u ver. 27.

x 2 Kin. 17.
4, 6.
2 Chr. 33.
11.
y ch. 4. 28.
ver. 64.
Jer. 16. 13.
z 1 Kin. 9.
7, 8.
Jer. 24. 9.¹
Zech. 8. 13.
a Ps. 44. 14.
b Mic. 6. 15.
Hag. 1. 6.
c Joel 1. 4.

25 down upon thee, until thou be destroyed. *g*The LORD shall cause thee to be smitten before thine enemies: thou shalt go out one way against them, and flee seven ways before them: and 26 *h*shalt be ¹removed into all the kingdoms of the earth. And *i*thy carcase shall be meat unto all fowls of the air, and unto the beasts of the earth, and no man shall fray *them* away. 27 The LORD will smite thee with *k*the botch of Egypt, and with *l*the emerods, and with the scab, and with the itch, whereof 28 thou canst not be healed. The LORD shall smite thee with 29 madness, and blindness, and *m*astonishment of heart: and thou shalt *n*grope at noonday, as the blind gropeth in darkness, and thou shalt not prosper in thy ways: and thou shalt be only oppressed and spoiled evermore, and no man shall save *thee*. 30 *o*Thou shalt betroth a wife, and another man shall lie with her: *p*thou shalt build an house, and thou shalt not dwell therein: *q*thou shalt plant a vineyard, and shalt not ²gather the grapes 31 thereof. Thine ox *shall be* slain before thine eyes, and thou shalt not eat thereof: thine ass *shall be* violently taken away from before thy face, and ³shall not be restored to thee: thy sheep *shall be* given unto thine enemies, and thou shalt have 32 none to rescue *them*. Thy sons and thy daughters *shall be* given unto another people, and thine eyes shall look, and *r*fail *with longing* for them all the day long: and *there shall be* no might in 33 thine hand. *s*The fruit of thy land, and all thy labours, shall a nation which thou knowest not eat up; and thou shalt be only 34 oppressed and crushed alway: so that thou shalt be mad *t*for the 35 sight of thine eyes which thou shalt see. The LORD shall *u*smite thee in the knees, and in the legs, with a sore botch that cannot be healed, from the sole of thy foot unto the top of thy head. 36 The LORD shall *x*bring thee, and thy king which thou shalt set over thee, unto a nation which neither thou nor thy fathers have known; and *y*there shalt thou serve other gods, wood and stone. 37 And thou shalt become *z*an astonishment, a proverb, *a*and a byword, among all nations whither the LORD shall lead thee. 38 *b*Thou shalt carry much seed out into the field, and shalt gather 39 *but* little in; for *c*the locust shall consume it. Thou shalt plant vineyards, and dress *them*, but shalt neither drink *of* the wine, 40 nor gather *the grapes;* for the worms shall eat them. Thou shalt have olive trees throughout all thy coasts, but thou shalt not anoint *thyself* with the oil; for thine olive shall cast *his fruit*.

¹ Heb. *for a removing.*   *as common meat:* as ch.   ³ Heb. *shall not return to*
² Heb. *profane,* or, *use it*   20. 6.   *thee.*

---

25. *shalt be removed*] See margin. The threat differs from that in Lev. xxvi. 33, which refers to a dispersion of the people amongst the heathen. Here it is meant that they should be tossed to and fro at the will of others, driven from one country to another without any certain settlement.

27–37. Second series of judgments on the body, mind, and outward circumstances of the sinners.

27. The "botch" (rather "boil;" see Ex. ix. 9), the "emerods" or tumours (1 S. v. 6, 9), the "scab" and "itch" represent the various forms of the loathsome skin diseases which are common in Syria and Egypt.

28. Mental maladies shall be added to

those sore bodily plagues, and should (*vv.* 29–34) reduce the sufferers to powerlessness before their enemies and oppressors.

blindness] Most probably mental blindness; cp. Lam. iv. 14; Zeph. i. 17; 2 Cor. iii. 14 seq.

30–33. See marg. reff. for the fulfilment of these judgments.

38–48. Third series of judgments, affecting every kind of labour and enterprise until it had accomplished the total ruin of the nation, and its subjection to its enemies.

39. *worms*] *i.e.* the vine-weevil. Naturalists prescribed elaborate precautions against its ravages.

40. *cast, &c.*] Some prefer "shall be spoiled" or "plundered."

41 Thou shalt beget sons and daughters, but [1]thou shalt not enjoy
42 them ; for [d]they shall go into captivity. All thy trees and fruit
43 of thy land shall the locust [2]consume. The stranger that *is*
 within thee shall get up above thee very high; and thou shalt
44 come down very low. [e]He shall lend to thee, and thou shalt
 not lend to him : [f]he shall be the head, and thou shalt be the tail.
45 ¶ Moreover [g]all these curses shall come upon thee, and shall
 pursue thee, and overtake thee, till thou be destroyed; because
 thou hearkenedst not unto the voice of the LORD thy God, to
 keep his commandments and his statutes which he commanded
46 thee : and they shall be upon thee [h]for a sign and for a wonder,
47 and upon thy seed for ever. [i]Because thou servedst not the
 LORD thy God with joyfulness, and with gladness of heart, [k]for
48 the abundance of all *things ;* therefore shalt thou serve thine
 enemies which the LORD shall send against thee, in hunger, and
 in thirst, and in nakedness, and in want of all *things :* and he
 [l]shall put a yoke of iron upon thy neck, until he have destroyed
49 thee. [m]The LORD shall bring a nation against thee from far,
 from the end of the earth, [n]*as swift* as the eagle flieth ; a nation
50 whose tongue thou shalt not [3]understand ; a nation [4]of fierce
 countenance, [o]which shall not regard the person of the old, nor
51 shew favour to the young : and he shall [p]eat the fruit of thy
 cattle, and the fruit of thy land, until thou be destroyed : which
 also shall not leave thee *either* corn, wine, or oil, *or* the increase
 of thy kine, or flocks of thy sheep, until he have destroyed thee.
52 And he shall [q]besiege thee in all thy gates, until thy high and
 fenced walls come down, wherein thou trustedst, throughout all
 thy land : and he shall besiege thee in all thy gates throughout
53 all thy land, which the LORD thy God hath given thee. And
 [r]thou shalt eat the fruit of thine own [5]body, the flesh of thy
 sons and of thy daughters, which the LORD thy God hath given
 thee, in the siege, and in the straitness, wherewith thine enemies
54 shall distress thee : *so that* the man *that is* tender among you,
 and very delicate, [s]his eye shall be evil toward his brother, and
 toward [t]the wife of his bosom, and toward the remnant of his
55 children which he shall leave : so that he will not give to any of
 them of the flesh of his children whom he shall eat : because he
 hath nothing left him in the siege, and in the straitness, where-
56 with thine enemies shall distress thee in all thy gates. The
 tender and delicate woman among you, which would not adven-
 ture to set the sole of her foot upon the ground for delicateness
 and tenderness, [u]her eye shall be evil toward the husband of

[d] Lam. 1. 5.

[e] ver. 12.
[f] ver. 13.
Lam. 1. 5.
[g] ver. 15.

[h] Isai. 8. 18.
Ez. 14. 8.
[i] Neh. 9. 35,
36, 37.
[k] ch. 32. 15.

[l] Jer. 28. 14.
[m] Jer. 5. 15.
Luke 19. 43.
[n] Jer. 48. 40.
& 49. 22.
Lam. 4. 19.
Ez. 17. 3, 12.
Hos. 8. 1.
[o] 2 Chr. 36.
17.
Isai. 47. 6.
[p] ver. 33.
Isai. 1. 7.
& 62. 8.
[q] 2 Kin. 25.
1, 2, 4.

[r] Lev. 26. 29.
2 Kin. 6. 28,
29.
Jer. 19. 9.
Lam. 2. 20.
[s] ch. 15. 9.
[t] ch. 13. 6.

[u] ver. 54.

---

[1] Heb. *they shall not be
 thine.*
[2] Or, *possess.*
[3] Heb. *hear.*

[4] Heb. *strong of face,* Prov.
 7. 13. Eccles. 8. 1. Dan.
 8. 23.
[5] Heb. *belly.*

43, 44. Contrast *vv.* 12 and 13.
 46. *for ever*] Yet "the remnant" (Rom.
ix. 27, xi. 5) would by faith and obedience
become a holy seed.
 49-58. Fourth series of judgments, descriptive of the calamities and horrors which
should ensue when Israel should be subjugated by its foreign foes.
 49. The description (cp. marg. reffs.) applies undoubtedly to the Chaldeans, and in
a degree to other nations also whom God
raised up as ministers of vengeance upon

apostate Israel (*e.g.* the Medes). But it
only needs to read this part of the denunciation, and to compare it with the narrative of Josephus, to see that its full and
exact accomplishment took place in the
wars of Vespasian and Titus against the
Jews, as indeed the Jews themselves generally admit.
 49. *the eagle*] The Roman ensign ; cp.
Matt. xxiv. 28; and consult throughout this
passage the marg. reff.
 54. *evil*] *i.e.* grudging ; cp. xv. 9.

57 her bosom, and toward her son, and toward her daughter, and toward her [1] young one that cometh out [x] from between her feet, and toward her children which she shall bear: for she shall eat them for want of all *things* secretly in the siege and straitness, wherewith thine enemy shall distress thee in thy gates.
58 ¶ If thou wilt not observe to do all the words of this law that are written in this book, that thou mayest fear [y] this glorious and
59 fearful name, THE LORD THY GOD; then the LORD will make thy plagues [z] wonderful, and the plagues of thy seed, *even* great plagues, and of long continuance, and sore sicknesses, and
60 of long continuance. Moreover he will bring upon thee all [a] the diseases of Egypt, which thou wast afraid of; and they shall
61 cleave unto thee. Also every sickness, and every plague, which *is* not written in the book of this law, them will the LORD [2] bring
62 upon thee, until thou be destroyed. And ye [b] shall be left few in number, whereas ye were [c] as the stars of heaven for multitude; because thou wouldest not obey the voice of the LORD thy God.
63 And it shall come to pass, *that* as the LORD [d] rejoiced over you to do you good, and to multiply you; so the LORD [e] will rejoice over you to destroy you, and to bring you to nought; and ye shall be plucked from off the land whither thou goest to possess
64 it. And the LORD [f] shall scatter thee among all people, from the one end of the earth even unto the other; and [g] there thou shalt serve other gods, which neither thou nor thy fathers have
65 known, *even* wood and stone. And [h] among these nations shalt thou find no ease, neither shall the sole of thy foot have rest:
66 [i] but the LORD shall give thee there a trembling heart, and failing of eyes, and [k] sorrow of mind: and thy life shall hang in doubt before thee; and thou shalt fear day and night, and shalt have
67 none assurance of thy life: [l] in the morning thou shalt say, Would God it were even! And at even thou shalt say, Would God it were morning! For the fear of thine heart wherewith thou shalt fear, and [m] for the sight of thine eyes which thou shalt see.
68 And the LORD [n] shall bring thee into Egypt again with ships, by the way whereof I spake unto thee, [o] Thou shalt see it no more again: and there ye shall be sold unto your enemies for bondmen and bondwomen, and no man shall buy *you*.

Marginal references:
[x] Gen. 49. 10.
[y] Ex. 6. 3.
[z] Dan. 9. 12.
[a] ch. 7. 15.
[b] ch. 4. 27.
[c] ch. 10. 22. Neh. 9. 23.
[d] ch. 30. 9. Jer. 32. 41.
[e] Prov. 1. 26. Isai. 1. 24.
[f] Lev. 26. 33. ch. 4. 27. 28. Neh. 1. 8. Jer. 16. 13.
[g] ver. 36.
[h] Amos 9. 4.
[i] Lev. 26. 36.
[k] Lev. 26. 16.
[l] Job 7. 4.
[m] ver. 34.
[n] Jer. 43. 7. Hos. 8. 13. & 9. 3.
[o] ch. 17. 16.

[1] Heb. *after birth.*   [2] Heb. *cause to ascend.*

---

57. *young one*] The "afterbirth" (see margin). The Hebrew text in fact suggests an extremity of horror which the A. V. fails to exhibit. Cp. 2 K. vi. 29.

58-68. Fifth series of judgments. The uprooting of Israel from the Promised Land, and its dispersion amongst other nations. Examine the marg. reff.

58. *in this book*] i.e. in the book of the Law, or the Pentateuch in so far as it contains commands of God to Israel. Deuteronomy is included, but not exclusively intended. So *v.* 61; cp. xxvii. 3 and note, xxxi. 9.

66. *thy life shall hang in doubt before thee*] i.e. shall be hanging as it were on a thread, and that before thine own eyes. The Fathers regard this passage as suggesting in a secondary or mystical sense Christ hanging on the cross, as the life of the Jews who would not believe in Him.

68. This is the climax. As the Exodus from Egypt was as it were the birth of the nation into its Covenant relationship with God, so the return to the house of bondage is in like manner the death of it. The mode of conveyance, "in ships," is added to heighten the contrast. They crossed the sea from Egypt with a high hand, the waves being parted before them. They should go back again cooped up in slave-ships.

there ye shall be sold] Rather, "there shall ye offer yourselves, or be offered for sale." This denunciation was literally fulfilled on more than one occasion: most signally when many thousand Jews were sold into slavery and sent into Egypt by Titus; but also under Hadrian, when numbers were sold at Rachel's grave (Gen. xxxv. 19).

no man shall buy you] i.e. no one shall venture even to employ you as slaves, re-

Chap. 29. THESE *are* the words of the covenant, which the LORD commanded Moses to make with the children of Israel in the land of Moab, beside *a*the covenant which he made with them 2 in Horeb. ¶And Moses called unto all Israel, and said unto them, *b*Ye have seen all that the LORD did before your eyes in the land of Egypt unto Pharaoh, and unto all his servants, and 3 unto all his land; *c*the great temptations which thine eyes have 4 seen, the signs, and those great miracles: yet *d*the LORD hath not given you an heart to perceive, and eyes to see, and ears to 5 hear, unto this day. *e*And I have led you forty years in the wilderness: *f*your clothes are not waxen old upon you, and 6 thy shoe is not waxen old upon thy foot. *g*Ye have not eaten bread, neither have ye drunk wine or strong drink: that ye 7 might know that I *am* the LORD your God. And when ye came unto this place, *h*Sihon the king of Heshbon, and Og the king of Bashan, came out against us unto battle, and we smote 8 them: and we took their land, and *i*gave it for an inheritance unto the Reubenites, and to the Gadites, and to the half tribe of 9 Manasseh. *k*Keep therefore the words of this covenant, and do 10 them, that ye may *l*prosper in all that ye do. ¶Ye stand this day all of you before the LORD your God; your captains of your tribes, your elders, and your officers, *with* all the men of Israel, 11 your little ones, your wives, and thy stranger that *is* in thy camp, from *m*the hewer of thy wood unto the drawer of thy 12 water: that thou shouldest *l*enter into covenant with the LORD thy God, and *n*into his oath, which the LORD thy God maketh 13 with thee this day: that he may *o*establish thee to day for a people unto himself, and *that* he may be unto thee a God, *p*as he hath said unto thee, and *q*as he hath sworn unto thy fathers, to 14 Abraham, to Isaac, and to Jacob. ¶Neither with you only *r*do 15 I make this covenant and this oath; but with *him* that standeth here with us this day before the LORD our God, *s*and also with 16 *him* that *is* not here with us this day: (for ye know how we have dwelt in the land of Egypt; and how we came through 17 the nations which ye passed by; and ye have seen their abominations, and their *2*idols, wood and stone, silver and gold, which 18 *were* among them:) lest there should be among you man, or woman, or family, or tribe, *t*whose heart turneth away this day

a ch. 5. 2, 3.

b Ex. 19. 4.

c ch. 4. 34.
& 7. 19.
d See Isai.
6. 9, 10.
& 63. 17.
John 8. 43.
Acts 28. 26.
Eph. 4. 18.
2 Thes. 2.
11, 12.
e ch. 1. 3.
& 8. 2.
f ch. 8. 4.
g See Ex. 16.
12.
ch. 8. 3.
Ps. 78. 24.
h Num. 21.
23, 24, 33.
ch. 2. 32.
& 3. 1.
i Num. 32.
33.
ch. 3. 12, 13.
k ch. 4. 6.
Josh. 1. 7.
1 Kin. 2. 3.
l Josh. 1. 7.
m See Josh.
9. 21, 23, 27.
n Neh. 10.
29.
o ch. 28. 9.
p Ex. 6. 7.
q Gen. 17. 7.
r Jer. 31. 31,
32, 33.
Heb. 8. 7, 8.
s 1 Cor. 7. 14.

t ch. 11. 16.

---

1 Heb. *pass.*   2 Heb. *dungy gods.*

---

garding you as accursed of God, and to be shunned in everything.

XXIX. This and the following chapter contain the address of Moses to the people on the solemn renewal of the Covenant. Consult the marg. reff. for proof of historical statements or explanation of obscure words.

4. Ability to understand the things of God is the gift of God (cp. 1 Cor. ii. 13, 14); yet man is not guiltless if he lacks that ability. The people had it not because they had not felt their want of it, nor asked for it. Cp. 2 Cor. iii. 14, 15.

9. *that ye may prosper*] Literally, " that ye may act wisely." The connexion of the two ideas of wisdom in conduct and prosperity in circumstances is noteworthy.

11. The Covenant was national, and therefore embraced all the elements which make

up the nation. The "little ones" would of course be represented by their parents or guardians; the absent (*v.* 15) by those present; nor were the servants and proselytes to be excluded (cp. Acts ii. 39). The text is fairly alleged in justification of the Church's practice of admitting little ones into Covenant with God by Baptism, and accepting promises made on their behalf by sponsors.

15. *with him that is not here with us*] *i.e.* as the Jews explain, posterity; which throughout all generations was to be taken as bound by the act and deed of those present and living.

17. *idols*] See margin, "dungy gods;" *i.e.* clods or stocks which can be rolled about (cp. Lev. xxvi. 30).

18. The word here and in xxxii. 32 rendered "gall," is in Hos. x. 4 translated

from the LORD our God, to go *and* serve the gods of these nations;
u Acts 8. 23.
Heb. 12. 15.
u lest there should be among you a root that beareth [1][2] gall and
19 wormwood; and it come to pass, when he heareth the words of
this curse, that he bless himself in his heart, saying, I shall
w Num. 15.
39.
Eccles. 11. 9.
x Isai. 30. 1.
y Ez. 14. 7, 8.
z Ps. 74. 1.
a Ps. 79. 5.
Ez. 23. 25.
b ch. 9. 14.
c Matt. 24.
51.
have peace, though I walk *w* in the [3] imagination of mine
20 heart, *x* to add [4] drunkenness to thirst: *y* the LORD will not spare
him, but then *z* the anger of the LORD and *a* his jealousy shall
smoke against that man, and all the curses that are written in
this book shall lie upon him, and the LORD *b* shall blot out his
21 name from under heaven. And the LORD *c* shall separate him
unto evil out of all the tribes of Israel, according to all the
curses of the covenant that [5] are written in this book of the law:
22 So that the generation to come of your children that shall rise
up after you, and the stranger that shall come from a far land,
shall say, when they see the plagues of that land, and the sick-
23 nesses [6] which the LORD hath laid upon it; *and that* the whole
d Ps. 107. 34.
Jer. 17. 6.
e Jer. 20. 16.
land thereof *is* brimstone, *d* and salt, *and* burning, *that* it is not
sown, nor beareth, nor any grass groweth therein, *e* like the
overthrow of Sodom, and Gomorrah, Admah, and Zeboim, which
24 the LORD overthrew in his anger, and in his wrath: even all
f 1 Kin. 9.
8, 9.
Jer. 22. 8, 9.
nations shall say, *f* Wherefore hath the LORD done thus unto this
25 land? What *meaneth* the heat of this great anger? Then men
shall say, Because they have forsaken the covenant of the LORD
God of their fathers, which he made with them when he brought
26 them forth out of the land of Egypt: for they went and served
other gods, and worshipped them, gods whom they knew not,
27 and [7] *whom* he had not [8] given unto them: and the anger of the
g Dan. 9. 11,
13, 14.
LORD was kindled against this land, *g* to bring upon it all the

[1] Or, *a poisonful herb.*
[2] Heb. *rosh.*
[3] Or, *stubbornness,* Jer. 3.
17. & 7. 24.
[4] Heb. *the drunken to the thirsty.*
[5] Heb. *is written.*
[6] Heb. *wherewith the* LORD
hath made it sick.
[7] Or, *who had not given to them* any portion.
[8] Heb. *divided.*

"hemlock." It is the name of a plant of
intense bitterness, and of quick growth;
and is therefore repeatedly used in conjunction with "wormwood" (cp. Jer. ix. 15;
Lam. iii. 19; Amos vi. 12), to express
figuratively the nature and effects of sin
(cp. marg. reff.). The herb is probably
the poppy. Hence the "water" (*i.e.* juice)
"of gall" (Jer. viii. 14, xxiii. 15) would
be opium. This would explain its employment in the stupefying drink given
to criminals at the time of execution (cp.
Ps. lxix. 21; Matt. xxvii. 34), and the use
of the word as synonymous with poison
(cp. xxxii. 33; Job xx. 16).

wormwood is the plant "absinthium." It
is used to denote metaphorically the distress
and trouble which result from sin.

"The root that beareth gall and wormwood," means in this place any person lurking amongst them who is tainted with apostasy.

19. Cp. on the thought Jer. xxiii. 17.
The secret and presumptuous sinner is
meant who flatters himself that all is well
and will be well with him, since he follows
his own devices and prospers. Cp. Ps. lxxiii.
11 seq.

to add drunkenness to thirst] The sense is

probably: "Himself, drinking iniquity like
water, (Job xv. 16), he corrupts and destroys
others who are thirsting for it or prone to it."
The sense of the whole passage from *v.* 16
onward to *v.* 20 may be exhibited thus:
"Ye have seen the abominations of idolatry
amongst the heathen. Do you therefore
look diligently that there be no secret idolater amongst you; a root of bitterness to all
about him. Let there be no one, I say, who
when he hears the curses of the Law against
this sin, flatters himself, saying within himself, 'All will be well, for I walk unmolested in my own self-chosen path;' and
thus acting, not only takes his own fill of
sin, but destroys likewise every tempted
brother within his reach; for the LORD will
not spare him," &c.

23. The description is borrowed from the
local features of the Dead Sea and its
vicinity. The towns of the vale of Siddim
were fertile and well watered (cp. Gen. xiii.
10) until devastated by the wrath of God
(Gen. xix. 24, 25). The ruin of Israel and
its land should be of the like sort (cp. Lev.
xxvi. 31, 32; Ps. cvii. 34; Zeph. ii. 9). The
desolate state of Palestine at present, and
the traces of former fertility and prosperity,
are attested by every traveller.

28 curses that are written in this book: and the LORD [h]rooted them out of their land in anger, and in wrath, and in great indignation, and cast them into another land, as *it is* this day.

29 The secret *things belong* unto the LORD our God: but those *things which are* revealed *belong* unto us and to our children for ever, that *we* may do all the words of this law.

CHAP. 30. AND [a]it shall come to pass, when [b]all these things are come upon thee, the blessing and the curse, which I have set before thee, and [c]thou shalt call *them* to mind among all the

2 nations, whither the LORD thy God hath driven thee, and shalt [d]return unto the LORD thy God, and shalt obey his voice according to all that I command thee this day, thou and thy children,

3 with all thine heart, and with all thy soul; [e]that then the LORD thy God will turn thy captivity, and have compassion upon thee, and will return and [f] gather thee from all the nations, whither the

4 LORD thy God hath scattered thee. [g]If *any* of thine be driven out unto the outmost *parts* of heaven, from thence will the LORD

5 thy God gather thee, and from thence will he fetch thee: and the LORD thy God will bring thee into the land which thy fathers possessed, and thou shalt possess it; and he will do thee good,

6 and multiply thee above thy fathers. And [h]the LORD thy God will circumcise thine heart, and the heart of thy seed, to love the LORD thy God with all thine heart, and with all thy soul, that

7 thou mayest live. And the LORD thy God will put all these curses upon thine enemies, and on them that hate thee, which

8 persecuted thee. And thou shalt return and obey the voice of the LORD, and do all his commandments which I command thee

9 this day. [i]And the LORD thy God will make thee plenteous in every work of thine hand, in the fruit of thy body, and in the fruit of thy cattle, and in the fruit of thy land, for good: for the

Right margin references:
[h] 1 Kin. 14. 15.
2 Chr. 7. 20.
Ps. 52. 5.
Prov. 2, 22.

[a] Lev. 26. 40.
[b] ch. 28.

[c] ch. 4. 29.
1 Kin. 8. 47.

[d] Neh. 1. 9.
Isai. 55. 7.
Lam. 3. 40.
Joel 2. 12.
[e] Ps. 106. 45.
& 126. 1. 4.
Jer. 29. 14.
Lam. 3. 22, 32.
[f] Ps. 147. 2.
[g] ch. 28. 64.
Neh. 1. 9.

[h] ch. 10. 16.

[i] ch. 28. 11.

---

29. *the secret things belong unto the* LORD *our God*] This verse seems to be added as a solemn admonition on the part of Moses, in order to close the series of blessings and curses which he has delivered. The sense seems to be this : " The future, when and how these good and evil things will take effect, it lies with the Lord our God to determine ; it pertains not to man's sphere and duty. God's revealed will is that which we must carry out." The 17th of our Articles of Religion concludes with much the same sentiment.

XXX. The rejection of Israel and the desolation of the promised inheritance were not to be the end of God's dispensations. The closing words of the address therefore are words of comfort and promise. Cp. marg. ref. and iv. 29 seq. ; 1 K. viii. 46-50.

1–10. The chastisements of God would lead the nation to repent, and thereupon God would again bless them.

3. *will turn thy captivity*] Will change or put an end to thy state of captivity or distress (cp. Ps. xiv. 7, lxxxv. 2 ; Jer. xxx. 18). The rendering of the Greek version is significant ; " the Lord will heal thy sins."

The promises of this and the following verses had no doubt their partial fulfilment in the days of the Judges ; but the fact that various important features are re-

peated in Jer. xxxii. 37 seq., and in Ezek. xi. 19 seq., xxxiv. 13 seq., xxxvi. 24 seq., shews us that none of these was regarded as exhausting the promises. In full analogy with the scheme of prophecy we may add that the return from the Babylonian Captivity has not exhausted their depth. The New Testament takes up the strain (*e.g.* in Rom. xi.), and foretells the restoration of Israel to the covenanted mercies of God. True these mercies shall not be, as before, confined to that nation. The "turning again of the captivity" will be when Israel is converted to Him in Whom the Law was fulfilled, and Who died "not for that nation only," but also that he might "gather together in one the children of God that were scattered abroad" (John xi. 51, 52). Then shall there be "one fold and one shepherd" (John x. 16). But whether the general conversion of the Jews shall be accompanied with any *national* restoration, any recovery of their ancient prerogatives as the chosen people ; and further, whether there shall be any local replacement of them in the land of their fathers, may be regarded as of "the secret things" which belong unto God (xxix. 29); and so indeed our Lord Himself teaches us (Acts i. 6, 7).

6. *circumcise thine heart*] Cp. x. 16 note ; Jer. xxxii. 39 ; Ez. xi. 19.

LORD will again *rejoice over thee for good, as he rejoiced over
10 thy fathers : if thou shalt hearken unto the voice of the LORD
thy God, to keep his commandments and his statutes which are
written in this book of the law, *and* if thou turn unto the LORD
11 thy God with all thine heart, and with all thy soul.. ¶ For this
commandment which I command thee this day, *it is* not hidden
12 from thee, neither *is* it far off. *It is* not in heaven, that thou
shouldest say, Who shall go up for us to heaven, and bring it
13 unto us, that we may hear it, and do it ? Neither *is* it beyond
the sea, that thou shouldest say, Who shall go over the sea for us,
14 and bring it unto us, that we may hear it, and do it ? But the
word *is* very nigh unto thee, in thy mouth, and in thy heart, that
15 thou mayest do it. ¶ See, *I have set before thee this day life
16 and good, and death and evil ; in that I command thee this day
to love the LORD thy God, to walk in his ways, and to keep his
commandments and his statutes and his judgments, that thou
mayest live and multiply: and the LORD thy God shall bless
17 thee in the land whither thou goest to possess it. But if thine
heart turn away, so that thou wilt not hear, but shalt be drawn
18 away, and worship other gods, and serve them ; *I denounce
unto you this day, that ye shall surely perish, *and that* ye shall
not prolong *your* days upon the land, whither thou passest over
19 Jordan to go to possess it. *I call heaven and earth to record
this day against you, *that* *I have set before you life and death,
blessing and cursing: therefore choose life, that both thou and
20 thy seed may live : that thou mayest love the LORD thy God,
and that thou mayest obey his voice, and that thou mayest
cleave unto him : for he *is* thy *life, and the length of thy days:
that thou mayest dwell in the land which the LORD sware
unto thy fathers, to Abraham, to Isaac, and to Jacob, to give
them.

CHAP. **31.** AND Moses went and spake these words unto all Israel.
2 And he said unto them, I *am* an hundred and twenty years
old this day ; I can no more *go out and come in : also the

10-20. Ignorance of the requirements of
the law cannot be pleaded (*vv.* 10-14) ;
hence (*vv.* 15-20) life and death, good and
evil, are solemnly set before the people for
their own choice ; and an earnest exhortation to choose the better part concludes the
address.

11-14. "The righteousness which is of
faith " is really and truly described in these
words of the Law; and, under St. Paul's
guidance (see marg. reff.) we affirm was intended so to be. For the simplicity and
accessibility which Moses here attributes to
the Law of God neither is nor can be ex-
perimentally found in it except through the
medium of faith ; even though outwardly
and in the letter that Law be written out for
us so "that he may run that readeth," and
be set forth in its duties and its sanctions
as plainly as it was before the Jews by
Moses. The seeming ease of the commandment, and yet its real impossibility to the
natural man, form part of the qualifications of the Law to be our schoolmaster to
bring us unto Christ.

11. *not hidden from thee*] Rather, not too

hard for thee, as in xvii. 8.
neither is it far off] Cp. Luke xvii. 21.
13. The paraphrase of this verse in the
Jerusalem Targum is noteworthy, and
should be compared with St. Paul's rendering in Rom. x. 7 : "Neither is the law beyond the great sea, that thou shouldest say,
Oh that we had one like Jonah the prophet
who could descend into the depths of the
sea and bring it to us ! "
14. *in thy mouth, and in thy heart*] Cp.
vi. 6, xi. 18-20.
20. *that thou mayest love the* LORD] Cp.
vi. 5. Love stands first as the essential and
only source of obedience.
he is thy life] Or, "that " (*i.e.* "to love
the Lord ") "is thy life ; " *i.e.* the condition
of thy life and of its prolongation in the
Promised Land. Cp. iv. 40, xxxii. 47.
XXXI. **2.** *I am an hundred and twenty
years old*] The forty years of the wandering
had passed since Moses, then fourscore
years old, "spake unto Pharaoh " (Ex. vii.
7. Cp. xxxiv. 7).
I can no more go out and come in] Render
I shall not longer be able to go out and

LORD hath said unto me, ^cThou shalt not go over this Jordan.
3 The LORD thy God, ^dhe will go over before thee, and he will
destroy these nations from before thee, and thou shalt possess
them : and Joshua, he shall go over before thee, ^eas the LORD
4 hath said. ^fAnd the LORD shall do unto them ^gas he did to
Sihon and to Og, kings of the Amorites, and unto the land of
5 them, whom he destroyed. And ^hthe LORD shall give them up
before your face, that ye may do unto them according unto all
6 the commandments which I have commanded you. ⁱBe strong
and of a good courage, ^kfear not, nor be afraid of them : for the
LORD thy God, ^lhe it is that doth go with thee ; ^mhe will not
7 fail thee, nor forsake thee. ¶ And Moses called unto Joshua,
and said unto him in the sight of all Israel, ⁿBe strong and of a
good courage: for thou must go with this people unto the land
which the LORD hath sworn unto their fathers to give them ;
8 and thou shalt cause them to inherit it. And the LORD, ^ohe
it is that doth go before thee ; ^phe will be with thee, he will not
fail thee, neither forsake thee : fear not, neither be dismayed.
9 ¶ And Moses wrote this law, ^qand delivered it unto the priests
the sons of Levi, ^rwhich bare the ark of the covenant of the
10 LORD, and unto all the elders of Israel. And Moses commanded
them, saying, At the end of every seven years, in the solemnity
11 of the ^syear of release, ^tin the feast of tabernacles, when all
Israel is come to ^uappear before the LORD thy God in the
place which he shall choose, ^xthou shalt read this law before
12 all Israel in their hearing. ^yGather the people together, men,
and women, and children, and thy stranger that is within thy
gates, that they may hear, and that they may learn, and fear the
LORD your God, and observe to do all the words of this law :
13 and that their children, ^zwhich have not known any thing, ^amay
hear, and learn to fear the LORD your God, as long as ye live in
14 the land whither ye go over Jordan to possess it. ¶ And the
LORD said unto Moses, ^bBehold, thy days approach that thou
must die : call Joshua, and present yourselves in the tabernacle
of the congregation, that ^cI may give him a charge. And Moses
and Joshua went, and presented themselves in the tabernacle of
15 the congregation. And ^dthe LORD appeared in the tabernacle in

Marginal refs: ^c Num. 20. 12. & 27. 13. ch. 3. 27. ^d ch. 9. 3. ^e Num. 27. 21. ch. 3. 28. ^f ch. 3. 21. ^g Num. 21. 24, 33. ^h ch. 7. 2. ⁱ Josh. 10. 25. 1 Chr. 22. 13. ^k ch. 1. 29. & 7. 18. ^l ch. 20. 4. ^m Josh. 1. 5. Heb. 13. 5. ⁿ ver. 23. Josh. 1. 6. ^o Ex. 13. 21. & 33. 14. ch. 9. 3. ^p Josh. 1. 5. 1 Chr. 28. 20. ^q ver. 25. ch. 17. 18. ^r Num. 4. 15. Josh. 3. 3. 1 Chr. 15. 12, 15. ^s ch. 15. 1. ^t Lev. 23. 34. ^u ch. 16. 16. ^x Josh. 8. 34. 2 Kin. 23. 2. Neh. 8. 1. ^y ch. 4. 10. ^z ch. 11. 2. ^a Ps. 78. 6. ^b Num. 27. 13. ch. 34. 5. ^c ver. 23. ^d Ex. 33. 9.

---

come in: i.e. discharge my duties among
you. There is no inconsistency with xxxiv.
7. Moses here adverts to his own age as
likely to render him in future unequal to
the active discharge of his office as leader of
the people : the writer of the xxxivth chapter, one of Moses' contemporaries, remarks
of him that up to the close of life "his eye
was not dim, nor his natural force abated"
(v. 7); i.e. that he was to the last, in the
judgment of others, in full possession of
faculties and strength.

7, 8. Moses hands over to Joshua that
office as leader of the people, to which
he had already been designated (i. 38 ;
Num. xxvii. 23). He assigns also to the
Levitical priests and the elders, as the
ecclesiastical and civil heads of the nation,
the responsibility of teaching the law and
enforcing its observance (vv. 10-13). Both
these were symbolical acts, designed to
mark the responsibility of the parties con-

cerned after the death of Moses.
11. Cp. marg. reff. It is not to be supposed that the whole of the Pentateuch was
read, nor does the letter of the command
require that it should be so. This reading
could not be primarily designed for the information and instruction of the people,
since it only took place once in seven years ;
but was evidently a symbolical transaction,
intended, as were so many others, to impress
on the people the conditions on which they
held possession of their privileges and blessings.

14-23. The transaction recorded in these
verses may be regarded as the solemn inauguration of Joshua to the office to which he
had some time before (Num. xxvii. 22)
been called, and his recognition in it by
God, which were manifested by his being
summoned into the Tabernacle with Moses
whilst the Lord appeared in the pillar of
cloud (cp. Num. xi. 25, xii. 5).

a pillar of a cloud: and the pillar of the cloud stood over the door
16 of the tabernacle. ¶ And the LORD said unto Moses, Behold,
thou shalt ¹sleep with thy fathers; and this people will ᵉrise up,
and ᶠgo a whoring after the gods of the strangers of the land,
whither they go to be among them, and will ᵛforsake me, and
17 ʰbreak my covenant which I have made with them. Then my
anger shall be kindled against them in that day, and ⁱI will forsake them, and I will ᵏhide my face from them, and they shall
be devoured, and many evils and troubles shall ²befall them;
so that they will say in that day, ˡAre not these evils come upon
18 us, because our God is ᵐnot among us? And ⁿI will surely hide
my face in that day for all the evils which they shall have
19 wrought, in that they are turned unto other gods. Now therefore write ye this song for you, and teach it the children of
Israel: put it in their mouths, that this song may be ᵒa witness
20 for me against the children of Israel. For when I shall have
brought them into the land which I sware unto their fathers,
that floweth with milk and honey; and they shall have eaten
and filled themselves, ᵖand waxen fat; ᵠthen will they turn
unto other gods, and serve them, and provoke me, and break my
21 covenant. And it shall come to pass, ʳwhen many evils and
troubles are befallen them, that this song shall testify ³against
them as a witness; for it shall not be forgotten out of the
mouths of their seed: for ˢI know their imagination ᵗwhich
they ⁴go about, even now, before I have brought them into the
22 land which I sware. ¶ Moses therefore wrote this song the
23 same day, and taught it the children of Israel. ᵘAnd he gave
Joshua the son of Nun a charge, and said, ˣBe strong and of a
good courage: for thou shalt bring the children of Israel into
the land which I sware unto them, and I will be with thee.
24 ¶ And it came to pass, when Moses had made an end of ʸwriting
25 the words of this law in a book, until they were finished, that
Moses commanded the Levites, which bare the ark of the cove-
26 nant of the LORD, saying, Take this book of the law, ᶻand put

ᵉ Ex. 32. 6.
ᶠ Ex. 34. 15.
Judg. 2. 17.
ᵍ ch. 32. 15.
Judg. 2. 12.
& 10. 6, 13.
ʰ Judg. 2.
20.
ⁱ 2 Chr. 15.
2.
ᵏ ch. 32. 20.
Ps. 104. 29.
Isai. 8. 17.
& 64. 7.
Ez. 39. 23.
ˡ Judg. 6. 13.
ᵐ Num. 14.
42.
ⁿ ver. 17.
ᵒ ver. 26.

ᵖ ch. 32. 15.
Neh. 9. 25,
26.
Hos. 13. 6.
ᵠ ver. 16.
ʳ ver. 17.

ˢ Hos. 5. 3.
& 13. 5, 6.
ᵗ Amos 5. 25,
26.
ᵘ ver. 14.
ˣ ver. 7.
Josh. 1. 6.

ʸ ver. 9.

ᶻ See 2 Kin.
22. 8.

¹ Heb. lie down,   2 Sam.   ² Heb. find them, Neh. 9.   ³ Heb. before.
7. 12.   32.   ⁴ Heb. do.

---

16. The future apostasy of the people is
announced in the presence of Joshua that
the latter might be fully aware of the danger and strive in his day to avert it. This
he faithfully did (cp. Josh. xxiv. 31); but
we find him in his own last address to Israel
repeating (Josh. xxiii. 15, 16) the self-same
prediction and warning.

19. a witness for me against them] i.e. an
attestation from their own mouths at once
of God's benefits, their own duties, and their
deserts when they should fall away. Being
in verse it would be the more easily learned
and kept in memory. The use of songs for
such didactic purposes was not unknown to
the legislators of antiquity. Cp. also the
advice of St. Paul, "teaching and admonish-
ing one another in psalms and hymns and
spiritual songs" (Col. iii. 16).

23. he gave] i.e. the Lord gave.

24-29. Moses completes the writing out
of the book of the Law, and directs it to be
placed by the Ark of the Covenant.

24. The "book" here spoken of would
contain the whole Pentateuch up to this
verse, and be "the book of Moses," called
generally by the Jews "the Law" (cp. St.
Matt. xxii. 40; Gal. iv. 21).

25. the Levites, which bare the ark] i.e., as
in v. 9, "the priests the sons of Levi."
The non-priestly Levites could not so much
as enter the Sanctuary or touch the Ark (cp
Num. iv. 15). Though in the journeys
through the wilderness the Ark was borne
by the non-priestly Kohathites, yet on occasions of a more solemn and public character
it was carried by the priests themselves
(Josh. iii. 3 seq., iv. 9, 10, vi. 6, 12, viii. 33;
1 K. viii. 3).

26. put it in the side of the ark] Rather,
by the side of the ark. The two tables of
the Decalogue were in the Ark (1 K. viii.
9); the book of the Law was to be laid up
in the Holy of Holies close by the Ark of
the Covenant, probably in a chest. Cp.
2 K. xxii. 8.

it in the side of the ark of the covenant of the LORD your God, 27 that it may be there *for a witness against thee. *For I know thy rebellion, and thy *stiff neck: behold, while I am yet alive with you this day, ye have been rebellious against the LORD; 28 and how much more after my death? Gather unto me all the elders of your tribes, and your officers, that I may speak these words in their ears, *and call heaven and earth to record against 29 them. For I know that after my death ye will utterly *corrupt yourselves, and turn aside from the way which I have commanded you; and *evil will befall you *in the latter days; because ye will do evil in the sight of the LORD, to provoke him 30 to anger through the work of your hands. ¶ And Moses spake in the ears of all the congregation of Israel the words of this song, until they were ended.

CHAP. **32.** GIVE *ear, O ye heavens, and I will speak; And hear, O earth, the words of my mouth.
2 *My doctrine shall drop as the rain, My speech shall distil as the dew, *As the small rain upon the tender herb, And as the showers upon the grass:
3 Because I will publish the name of the LORD: *Ascribe ye greatness unto our God.
4 ¶ *He is *the Rock, *his work *is perfect:

a ver. 19.
b ch. 9. 24.
& 32. 20.
c Ex. 32. 9.
ch. 9. 6.

d ch. 30. 19.
& 32. 1.
e ch. 32. 5.
Judg. 2. 19.
Hos. 9. 9.
f ch. 28. 15.
g Gen. 49. 1.
ch. 4. 30.

a ch. 4. 26.
Ps. 50. 4.
Isai. 1. 2.
Jer. 2. 12.
b Isai. 55. 10.
1 Cor. 3. 6.
c Ps. 72. 6.
Mic. 5. 7.
d 1 Chr. 29.
11.
e 2 Sam. 22.
3. & 23. 3.
Ps. 18. 2, 31,
46.
Hab. 1. 12.
f 2 Sam. 22.
31.

---

27. *how much more after my death*] Hence *v.* 24 and the rest of the book (with the exception of the song, *v.* 19) must be regarded as a kind of appendix added after Moses' death by another hand; though the Blessing (xxxiii.) is of course to be regarded as a composition of Moses.

XXXII. **1–43.** Song of Moses. If *vv.* 1-3 be regarded as the introduction, and *v.* 43 as the conclusion, the main contents of the song may be grouped under three heads, viz. (1) *vv.* 4–18, the faithfulness of God, the faithlessness of Israel; (2) *vv.* 19–33, the chastisement and the need of its infliction by God; (3) *vv.* 34–42, God's compassion upon the low and humbled state of His people.

The Song differs signally in diction and idiom from the preceding chapters; just as a lyrical passage is conceived in modes of thought wholly unlike those which belong to narrative or exhortation, and is uttered in different phraseology.

There are, however, in the Song numerous coincidences both in thoughts and words with other parts of the Pentateuch, and especially with Deuteronomy; while the resemblances between it and Ps. xc. "A Prayer of Moses," have been rightly regarded as important.

The Song has reference to a state of things which did not ensue until long after the days of Moses. In this it resembles other parts of Deuteronomy and the Pentateuch which no less distinctly contemplate an apostasy (*e.g.* Deut. xxviii. 15; Lev. xxvi. 14), and describe it in general terms. If once we admit the possibility that Moses might foresee the future apostasy of Israel,

it is scarcely possible to conceive how such foresight could be turned to better account by him than by the writing of this Song. Exhibiting as it does God's preventing mercies, His people's faithlessness and ingratitude, God's consequent judgments, and the final and complete triumph of the Divine counsels of grace, it forms the summary of all later Old Testament prophecies, and gives as it were the framework upon which they are laid out. Here as elsewhere the Pentateuch presents itself as the foundation of the religious life of Israel in after times. The currency of the Song would be a standing protest against apostasy; a protest which might well check waverers, and warn the faithful that the revolt of others was neither unforeseen nor unprovided for by Him in Whom they trusted.

That this Ode must on every ground take the very first rank in Hebrew poetry is universally allowed.

1–3. Introduction.
1. Heaven and earth are here invoked, as elsewhere (see marg. reff.), in order to impress on the hearers the importance of what is to follow.

4. *He is the Rock, his work is perfect*] Rather, **the Rock, perfect is His work.** This epithet, repeated no less than five times in the Song (*vv.* 15, 18, 30, 31), represents those attributes of God which Moses is seeking to enforce, immutability and impregnable strength. Cp. the expression "the stone of Israel" in Gen. xlix. 24; and see 1 S. ii. 2; Ps. xviii. 2; Matt. xvi. 18; John i. 42. Zur, the original of "Rock," enters frequently into the composition of proper names of the Mosaic time, *e.g.* Num. i. 5, 6, 10, ii. 12, iii.

y Dan. 4. 37. Rev. 15. 3. *h* Jer. 10. 10. *i* Job 34. 10. Ps. 92. 15. *k* ch. 31. 29.	5	For *y*all his ways *are* judgment: *h*A God of truth and *i*without iniquity, Just and right *is* he. ¶ ¹*k*They have corrupted themselves, ²their spot *is* not *the* spot of his children:

l Matt. 17. 17.   *They are* a ¹perverse and crooked generation.

Luke 9. 41.   6   Do ye thus ᵐrequite the LORD,

Phil. 2. 15.   O foolish people and unwise?

m Ps. 116. 12.   *Is* not he ⁿthy father *that* hath °bought thee?

n Isai. 63. 16.   Hath he not ᵖmade thee, and established thee?

° Ps. 74. 2.

p Isai. 27. 11.   7   ¶ Remember the days of old,

& 44. 2.   Consider the years of ³many generations:

q Ex. 13. 14.   *q*Ask thy father, and he will shew thee;

Ps. 44. 1.   Thy elders, and they will tell thee.

r Zech. 9. 2.   When the Most High *r*divided to the nations their inheritance,

Acts 17. 26.   8   When he *s*separated the sons of Adam,

s Gen. 11. 8.   He set the bounds of the people

t Ex. 15. 16.   According to the number of the children of Israel.

1 Sam. 10. 1.   9   For *t*the LORD's portion *is* his people;

Ps. 78. 71.   Jacob *is* the ⁴lot of his inheritance.

u ch. 8. 15.

Jer. 2. 6.   10   He found him *u*in a desert land,

Hos. 13. 5.   And in the waste howling wilderness;

x Deut. 4. 36.   He ⁵led him about, he *x*instructed him,

y Ps. 17. 8.   He *y*kept him as the apple of his eye.

Prov. 7. 2.

Zech. 2. 8.   11   *z*As an eagle stirreth up her nest,

z Ex. 19. 4.   Fluttereth over her young,

ch. 1. 31.   Spreadeth abroad her wings, taketh them,

Isai. 31. 5.   Beareth them on her wings:

Hos. 11. 3.   12   *So* the LORD alone did lead him,

And *there was* no strange god with him.

---

¹ Heb. *he hath corrupted to himself.*
² Or, *that they are not his blot.*
³ Heb. *generation and generation.*
⁴ Heb. *cord.*
⁵ Or, *compassed him about.*

35, &c. Our translators have elsewhere rendered it according to the sense "everlasting strength" (Isai. xxvi. 4), "the Mighty One" (Isai. xxx. 29); in this chapter they have rightly adhered to the letter throughout.

5. Render, "It" (*i.e.* "the perverse and crooked generation") "hath corrupted itself before Him (cp. Isai. i. 4); they are not His children, but their blemish:" *i.e.* the generation of evil-doers cannot be styled God's children, but rather the shame and disgrace of God's children. The other side of the picture is thus brought forward with a brevity and abruptness which strikingly enforces the contrast.

6. *hath bought thee*] Rather perhaps, "hath acquired thee for His own," or "possessed thee:" cp. the expression "a peculiar people," marg. "a purchased people," in 1 Pet. ii. 9.

8. That is, whilst nations were being constituted under God's providence, and the bounds of their habitation determined under His government (cp. Acts xvii. 26), He had even then in view the interests of His elect, and reserved a fitting inheritance "according to the number of the children of Israel;"

i.e. proportionate to the wants of their population. Some texts of the Greek Version have "according to the number of the Angels of God;" following apparently not a different reading, but the Jewish notion that the nations of the earth are seventy in number (cp. Gen. x. 1 note), and that each has its own guardian Angel (cp. Ecclus. xvii. 17). This was possibly suggested by an apprehension that the literal rendering might prove invidious to the many Gentiles who would read the Greek version.

10—14. These verses set forth in figurative language the helpless and hopeless state of the nation when God took pity on it, and the love and care which He bestowed on it.

10. *in the waste howling wilderness*] Lit. "in a waste, the howling of a wilderness," *i.e.* a wilderness in which wild beasts howl. The word for "waste" is that used in Gen. i. 2, and there rendered "without form."

11. The "so," which the A. V. supplies in the next verse, should be inserted before "spreadeth," and omitted from *v.* 12. The sense is, "so He spread out His wings, took them up," &c.

12. *with him*] *i.e.* with God. The Lord

13	^aHe made him ride on the high places of the earth,	^a Isai. 58. 14.
	That he might eat the increase of the fields;	Ez. 36. 2.
	And he made him to suck ^bhoney out of the rock,	^b Job 29. 6.
	And oil out of the flinty rock;	Ps. 81. 16.
14	Butter of kine, and milk of sheep,	^c Ps. 81. 16.
	With fat of lambs,	^d Gen. 49.

13 ^aHe made him ride on the high places of the earth,
That he might eat the increase of the fields;
And he made him to suck ^bhoney out of the rock,
And oil out of the flinty rock;
14 Butter of kine, and milk of sheep,
With fat of lambs,
And rams of the breed of Bashan, and goats,
^cWith the fat of kidneys of wheat;
And thou didst drink the pure ^dblood of the grape.
15 ¶ But ^eJeshurun waxed fat, and ^fkicked:
^gThou art waxen fat, thou art grown thick, thou art covered
with fatness;
Then he ^hforsook God which ⁱmade him,
And lightly esteemed the ^kRock of his salvation.
16 ⁱThey provoked him to jealousy with strange gods,
With abominations provoked they him to anger.
17 ^mThey sacrificed unto devils, ¹not to God;
To gods whom they knew not,
To new gods that came newly up,
Whom your fathers feared not.
18 ⁿOf the Rock that begat thee thou art unmindful,
And hast ^oforgotten God that formed thee.
19 ¶ ^pAnd when the LORD saw it, he ²abhorred them,
^qBecause of the provoking of his sons, and of his daughters.
20 And he said, ^rI will hide my face from them,
I will see what their end shall be:
For they are a very froward generation,
^sChildren in whom is no faith.
21 ^tThey have moved me to jealousy with that which is not God;

Reference column:
^a Isai. 58. 14.
Ez. 36. 2.
^b Job 29. 6.
Ps. 81. 16.
^c Ps. 81. 16.
^d Gen. 49.
11.
^e ch. 33. 5.
^f 1 Sam. 2.
29.
^g ch. 31. 20.
Neh. 9. 25.
Ps. 17. 10.
Jer. 2. 7.
Hos. 13. 6.
^h ch. 31. 16.
Isai. 1. 4.
ⁱ ver. 6.
Isai. 51. 13.
^k 2 Sam. 22.
47.
Ps. 89. 26.
^l 1 Kin. 14.
22.
1 Cor. 10. 22.
^m Lev. 17. 7.
Ps. 106. 37.
1 Cor. 10. 20.
Rev. 9. 20.
ⁿ Isai. 17. 10.
^o Jer. 2. 32.
^p Judg. 2.
14.
^q Isai. 1. 2.
^r ch. 31. 17.
^s Isai. 30. 9.
Matt. 17. 17.
^t ver. 16.
Ps. 78. 58.

¹ Or, which were not God,
ver. 21.

² Or, despised, Lam. 2. 6.

---

alone delivered Israel; Israel therefore ought to have served none other but Him.

13. i.e. God gave Israel possession of those commanding positions which carry with them dominion over the whole land (cp. xxxiii. 29), and enabled him to draw the richest provision out of spots naturally unproductive.

14. breed of Bashan] Bashan was famous for its cattle. Cp. Ps. xxii. 12; Ezek. xxxix. 18.

fat of kidneys of wheat] i.e. the finest and most nutritious wheat. The fat of the kidneys was regarded as being the finest and tenderest, and was therefore specified as a part of the sacrificial animals which was to be offered to the Lord: cp. Ex. xxix. 13, &c.

the pure blood of the grape] Render, **the blood of the grape, even wine.** The Hebrew word seems (cp. Isai. xxvii. 2) a poetical term for wine.

15. Jeshurun] This word, found again only in xxxiii. 5, 26, and Isai. xliv. 2, is not a diminutive but an appellative (containing an allusion to the root, "to be righteous"); and describes not the character which belonged to Israel in fact, but that to which Israel was called. Cp. Num. xxiii. 21. The

prefixing of this epithet to the description of Israel's apostasy contained in the words next following is full of keen reproof.

16. They provoked him to jealousy] The language is borrowed from the matrimonial relationship, as in xxxi. 16.

17. devils] Render, **destroyers.** The application of the word to the false gods points to the trait so deeply graven in all heathen worship, that of regarding the deities as malignant, and needing to be propitiated by human sufferings.

not to God] Rather, "not God," i.e. which were not God; see margin and v. 21. Cp. xiii. 7, xxix. 25.

19. The anger of God at the apostasy of His people is stated in general terms in this verse; and the results of it are described, in words as of God Himself, in the next and following verses. These results consisted negatively in the withdrawal of God's favour (v. 20), and positively in the infliction of a righteous retribution.

daughters] The women had their full share in the sins of the people. Cp. Isai. iii. 16 seq., xxxii. 9 seq.; Jer. vii. 18, xliv. 15 seq.

20. I will see what their end shall be] Cp. the similar expression in Gen. xxxvii. 20.

21. God would mete out to them the same

" 1 Sam. 12.
21.
1 Kin. 16.
13, 26.
Ps. 31. 6.
Jer. 8. 19.
Acts 14. 15.
x Hos. 1. 10.
Rom. 10. 19.
y Jer. 15. 14.
& 17. 4.
Lam. 4. 11.
z Isai. 26.15.
a Ps. 7. 12,
13.
Ez. 5. 16.

b Lev. 26. 22.

c Lam. 1. 20
Ez. 7. 15.
2 Cor. 7. 5.

d Ez. 20. 13,
14, 23.

e Jer. 19. 4.
f Ps. 140. 8.

g Isai. 27.11.
Jer. 4. 22.
h ch. 5. 29.
& reff.
i Isai. 47. 7.
Lam. 1. 9.
k Lev. 26. 8.
l Ps. 41. 12.
Isai. 50. 1.

m 1 Sam. 2.
2.
n Jer. 40. 3.

They have provoked me to anger "with their vanities:
And *I will move them to jealousy with *those which are* not
    a people;
I will provoke them to anger with a foolish nation.

22 ¶ For *a fire is kindled in mine anger,
And ¹shall burn unto the lowest hell,
And ²shall consume the earth with her increase,
And set on fire the foundations of the mountains.

23 I will *heap mischiefs upon them;
"I will spend mine arrows upon them.

24 *They shall be* burnt with hunger, and devoured with ³burn-
    ing heat,
And with bitter destruction:
I will also send *the teeth of beasts upon them,
With the poison of serpents of the dust.

25 *The sword without,
And terror ⁴within, shall ⁵destroy
Both the young man and the virgin,
The suckling *also* with the man of gray hairs.

26 *I said, I would scatter them into corners,
I would make the remembrance of them to cease from among
    men:

27 Were it not that I feared the wrath of the enemy,
Lest their adversaries *should behave themselves strangely,
And lest they should *say, ⁶Our hand *is* high,
And the LORD hath not done all this.

28 For they *are* a nation void of counsel,
*Neither *is there any* understanding in them.

29 ¶*O that they were wise, *that* they understood this,
That they would consider their latter end!

30 How should *one chase a thousand,
And two put ten thousand to flight,
Except their Rock *had sold them,
And the LORD had shut them up?

31 For *their rock *is* not as our Rock,
*Even our enemies themselves *being* judges.

---

¹ Or, *hath burned.*
² Or, *hath consumed.*
³ Heb. *burning coals:* Hab.
  3. 5.
⁴ Heb. *from the chambers.*
⁵ Heb. *bereave.*
⁶ Or, *Our high hand, and
  not the* LORD, *hath done
  all this.*

---

measure as they had done to Him. Though chosen by the one God to be His own, they had preferred idols, which were no gods. So therefore would He prefer to His people that which was no people. As they had angered Him with their vanities, so would He provoke them by adopting in their stead those whom they counted as nothing. The terms, "not a people," and "a foolish nation," mean such a people as, not being God's, would not be accounted a people at all (cp. Eph. ii. 12; 1 Pet. ii. 10), and such a nation as is destitute of that which alone can make a really "wise and understanding people" (iv. 6), viz. the knowledge of the revealed word and will of God (cp. 1 Cor. i. 18-28).

24. *burning heat*] *i.e.* the fear of a pestilential disease. On the "four sore judgments," famine, plague, noisome beasts, the

sword, cp. Lev. xxvi. 22; Jer. xv. 2; Ezek. v. 17, xiv. 21.

26, 27. Rather, **I would utterly disperse them, &c., were it not that I apprehended the provocation of the enemy,** *i.e.* that I should be provoked to wrath when the enemy ascribed the overthrow of Israel to his own prowess and not to my judgments. Cp. ix. 28, 29; Ezek. xx. 9, 14, 22.

behave themselves strangely] Rather, **mistake it,** *i.e.* mistake the cause of Israel's ruin.

30. The defeat of Israel would be due to the fact that God, their strength, had abandoned them because of their apostasy.

31. *our enemies*] *i.e.* the enemies of Moses and the faithful Israelites; the heathen, more specially those with whom Israel was brought into collision, whom Israel was

32 For ^otheir vine ¹*is* of the vine of Sodom,
And of the fields of Gomorrah:
Their grapes *are* grapes of gall,
Their clusters *are* bitter:

33 Their wine *is* ^pthe poison of dragons,
And the cruel ^qvenom of asps.

34 *Is* not this ^rlaid up in store with me,
And sealed up among my treasures ?

35 ^sTo me *belongeth* vengeance, and recompence;
Their foot shall slide in *due* time:
For ^tthe day of their calamity *is* at hand,
And the things that shall come upon them make haste.

36 ¶ ^uFor the LORD shall judge his people,
^xAnd repent himself for his servants,
When he seeth that *their* ²power is gone,
And ^y*there is* none shut up, or left.

37 And he shall say, ^zWhere *are* their gods,
Their rock in whom they trusted,

38 Which did eat the fat of their sacrifices,
And drank the wine of their drink offerings ?
Let them rise up and help you,
And be ³your protection.

39 See now that ^aI, *even* I, *am* he, and ^b*there is* no god with me:
^cI kill, and I make alive;
I wound, and I heal:
Neither *is there any* that can deliver out of my hand.

40 ^dFor I lift up my hand to heaven,
And say, I live for ever.

41 ^eIf I whet my glittering sword,
And mine hand take hold on judgment;
^fI will render vengeance to mine enemies,
And will reward them that hate me.

42 I will make mine arrows ^gdrunk with blood,
And my sword shall devour flesh;
And that with the blood of the slain and of the captives,
From the beginning of ^hrevenges upon the enemy.

¹ Or, is worse *than the vine of Sodom, &c.*
² Heb. *hand.*
³ Heb. *an hiding for you.*

o Isai. 1. 10.
p Ps. 58. 4.
q Ps. 140. 3.
Rom. 3. 13.
r Job 14. 17.
Jer. 2. 22.
Hos. 13. 12.
Rom. 2. 5.
s Ps. 94. 1.
Rom. 12. 19.
Heb. 10. 30.
t 2 Pet. 2. 3.
u Ps. 135. 14.
x Judg. 2. 18.
Ps. 106. 45.
Jer. 31. 20.
Joel 2. 14.
y 1 Kin. 14. 10.
2 Kin. 9. 8.
z Judg. 10. 14.
Jer. 2. 28.
a Ps. 102. 27.
Isai. 41. 4.
b ch. 4. 35.
Isai. 45. 5.
c 1 Sam. 2. 6.
2 Kin. 5. 7.
Job 5. 18.
Ps. 68. 20.
Hos. 6. 1.
d Ex. 6. 8.
Num. 14. 30.
e Isai. 27. 1.
Ez. 21. 9, 10, 14.
f Isai. 1. 24.
Nah. 1. 2.
g Jer. 46. 10.
h Job 13. 24.
Jer. 30. 14.
Lam. 2. 5.

commissioned to "chase," but to whom, as a punishment for faithlessness, Israel was "sold," (*v.* 30). Moses leaves the decision, whether "their rock" (*i.e.* the false gods of the heathen to which the apostate Israelites had fallen away) or "our Rock" is superior, to be determined by the unbelievers themselves. For example, see Ex. xiv. 25; Num. xxiii. and xxiv.; Josh. ii. 9 seq.; 1 S. iv. 8 and v. 7 seq.; 1 K. xx. 28. That the heathen should thus be constrained to bear witness to the supremacy of Israel's God heightened the folly of Israel's apostasy.

32. *their vine*] *i.e.* the nature and character of Israel: cp. for similar expressions Ps. lxxx. 8, 14; Jer. ii. 21; Hos. x. 1.

Sodom...Gomorrah] Here, as elsewhere, and often in the prophets, emblems of utter depravity: cp. Isai. i. 10; Jer. xxiii. 14.

gall] Cp. xxix. 18 note.

35. Rather: "Vengeance is mine and re-

compence, at the time when their foot slideth.

36. *repent himself for*] Rather, **have compassion upon.** The verse declares that God's judgment of His people would issue at once in the punishment of the wicked, and in the comfort of the righteous.

none shut up, or left] A proverbial phrase (cp. 1 K. xiv. 10) meaning perhaps "married and single," or "guarded and forsaken," but signifying generally "all men of all sorts."

40–42. Render: **For I lift up my hand to heaven and say, As I live for ever, if I whet,** &c. On *v.* 40, in which God is described as swearing by Himself, cp. Isai. xlv. 23; Jer. xxii. 5; Heb. vi. 17. The lifting up of the hand was a gesture used in making oath (cp. Gen. xiv. 22; Rev. x. 5).

42. *from the beginning of revenges upon the enemy*] Render, (drunk with blood) **from the head** (*i.e.* the chief) **of the princes of the enemy.**

43   [i]Rejoice, O ye nations, *with* his people:
For he will [k]avenge the blood of his servants,
And [l]will render vengeance to his adversaries,
And [m]will be merciful unto his land, *and* to his people.

44 ¶ And Moses came and spake all the words of this song in the
45 ears of the people, he, and [2]Hoshea the son of Nun. And
Moses made an end of speaking all these words to all Israel:

46 and he said unto them, [n]Set your hearts unto all the words
which I testify among you this day, which ye shall command
47 your children to observe to do, all the words of this law. For it

is not a vain thing for you; [o]because it *is* your life: and through
this thing ye shall prolong *your* days in the land, whither ye go
48 over Jordan to possess it. ¶ [p]And the LORD spake unto Moses
49 that selfsame day, saying, Get thee up into this [q]mountain
Abarim, *unto* mount Nebo, which *is* in the land of Moab, that *is*
over against Jericho; and behold the land of Canaan, which I
50 give unto the children of Israel for a possession: and die in the
mount whither thou goest up, and be gathered unto thy people;

as [r]Aaron thy brother died in mount Hor, and was gathered
51 unto his people: because [s]ye trespassed against me among the
children of Israel at the waters of [3]Meribah-Kadesh, in the
wilderness of Zin; because ye [t]sanctified me not in the midst of
52 the children of Israel. [u]Yet thou shalt see the land before *thee;*
but thou shalt not go thither unto the land which I give the
children of Israel.

CHAP. 33. AND this *is* [a]the blessing, wherewith Moses [b]the man

---

[1] Or, *Praise his people, ye*
nations: or, *Sing ye.*

[2] Or, *Joshua.*
[3] Or, *Strife at Kadesh.*

---

43. *Rejoice, O ye nations, with His people*]
Some prefer the marginal rendering.
In this profound passage, there is shadowed forth the purpose of God to overrule
(1) the unbelief of the Jews to the bringing
in of the Gentiles; and (2) the mercy shewn
to the Gentiles to the eventual restoration
of the Jews (cp. Rom. xi. 25-36).
The Song closes as it began (*vv.* 1-3), with
an invitation to praise. It has reached,
through a long series of Divine interpositions, its grandest theme in this call to the
Gentiles, now heathen no more, to rejoice
over God's restored people, the Jews.
44-52. These verses were, no doubt,
added by the author of the supplement to
Deuteronomy. For the statements contained in them, consult the marg. reff.
XXXIII. The Blessing contains (1) an
Introduction, *vv.* 1-5; (2) the Benedictions
pronounced on the tribes individually, *vv.*
6-25; (3) a Conclusion, *vv.* 26-29.
It was no doubt spoken by Moses, probably on the same day and to the same
assembly as the Song (xxxii. 1-43), as soon
as he received the renewed notice of his
approaching decease (xxxii. 48), and just
before he ascended Mount Nebo. Like the
Blessing of Jacob (Gen. xlix.), to which it
has an intimate though independent correspondence throughout, it is the solemn farewell of the earthly head of the race. A comparison with Genesis (see the marg. reff.)

will shew how the blessings uttered by
Moses over the several tribes partly repeat,
partly enlarge and supplement, and sometimes modify or even reverse, the predictions of the dying Jacob.
This chapter, in striking contrast with
the last, is pervaded by a tone of happy
augury; and the total absence of warning
and reproof has been rightly noted as indicating that Moses is here speaking of the
ideal Israel, of the people of God as they
might and would have been but for their
perverseness, rather than foretelling what
would in fact be the fate and fortunes of
the twelve tribes. As the Song sets forth
the calamities with which God's justice will
visit Israel's fall, so does the Blessing describe the glory and greatness which would
from His mercy crown Israel's faithfulness.
The Song and the Blessing are therefore
correspondent, and mutually supplementary. The form into which the Blessing is
thrown exhibits the several tribes co-oper-
ating, each according to its peculiar characteristics and circumstances, for the accomplishment of the national mission.
1. The title "the man of God" in the
Old Testament is one who is favoured with
direct revelations, but not necessarily an
official prophet. The occurrence of the
title here is no doubt a token that the
Blessing was not, as was the Song, tran-
scribed by Moses himself. Cp. xxxi. 27.

2 of God blessed the children of Israel before his death. And he said,

c Ex. 19. 18.
Judg. 5. 4.
Hab. 3. 3.

  c The LORD came from Sinai,
And rose up from Seir unto them ;
He shined forth from mount Paran,
And he came with *d* ten thousands of saints :
From his right hand went ¹ a fiery law for them.

3 Yea, *e* he loved the people ;
f All his saints *are* in thy hand :
And they *g* sat down at thy feet ;
Every one shall *h* receive of thy words.

4 *i* Moses commanded us a law,
k Even the inheritance of the congregation of Jacob.

5 And he was *l* king in *m* Jeshurun,
When the heads of the people *and* the tribes of Israel were gathered together.

6 ¶ Let Reuben live, and not die ;
And let *not* his men be few.

7 ¶ And this *is the blessing* of Judah : and he said,

Hear, LORD, the voice of Judah,
And bring him unto his people :
n Let his hands be sufficient for him ;
And be thou *o* an help *to him* from his enemies.

8 ¶ And of Levi he said,
p Let thy Thummim and thy Urim *be* with thy holy one,

¹ Heb. *a fire of law.*

Marginal refs: c Ex. 19. 18. Judg. 5. 4. Hab. 3. 3. d See Ps. 68. 17. Dan. 7. 10. Acts 7. 53. Heb. 2. 2. Rev. 5. 11. e Ex. 19. 5. ch. 7. 7, 8. Ps. 47. 4. Hos. 11. 1. Mal. 1. 2. f ch. 7. 6. 1 Sam. 2. 9. Ps. 50. 5. g Luke 10. 39. Acts 22. 3. h Prov. 2. 1. i John 1. 17. & 7. 19. k Ps. 119. 111. l See Gen. 36. 31. Judg. 9. 2. & 17. 6. m ch. 32. 15. n Gen. 49. 8. o Ps. 146. 5. p Ex. 28. 30.

---

2. By "Seir" is to be understood the mountain-land of the Edomites, and by "mount Paran" the range which forms the northern boundary of the desert of Sinai (cp. Gen. xiv. 6 note). Thus the verse forms a poetical description of the vast arena upon which the glorious manifestation of the Lord in the giving of the Covenant took place.

with ten thousands of saints] Render, **from amidst ten thousands of holy ones :** lit. from myriads of holiness, *i.e.* holy Angels (cp. Zech. xiv. 5). God is represented as leaving heaven where He dwells amidst the host of the Angels (1 K. xxii. 19) and descending in majesty to earth (Mic. i. 3).

a fiery law] more lit. as in margin, with perhaps an allusion to the pillar of fire (Ex. xiii. 21). The word is much disputed.

3. *the people* are the twelve tribes, not the Gentiles ; and *his saints* refer to God's chosen people just before spoken of. Cp. vii. 18, 21 ; Ex. xix. 6 ; Dan. vii. 8-21.

5. *he was king*] *i.e.* not Moses but the Lord **became king.**

6. *let* not *his men be few*] Lit. "a number," *i.e.* "a small number," such as could be easily counted (cp. Gen. xxxiv. 30 note). While the verse promises that the tribe shall endure and prosper, yet it is so worded as to carry with it a warning. The Reubenites, occupied with their herds and flocks, appear, soon after the days of Joshua, to have lost their early energy, till in later

times its numbers, even when counted with the Gadites and the half of Manasseh, were fewer than that of the Reubenites alone at the census of Num. i. (Cp. 1 Chr. v. 18 with Num. i. 20.) No judge, prophet, or national hero arose out of this tribe.

The tribe of Simeon, which would according to the order of birth come next, is not here named. This omission is explained by reference to the words of Jacob concerning Simeon (Gen. xlix. 7). This tribe with Levi was to be "scattered in Israel." The fulfilment of this prediction was in the case of Levi so ordered as to carry with it honour and blessing ; but no such reversal of punishment was granted to Simeon. Rather had this latter tribe added new sins to those which Jacob denounced (cp. Num. xxvi. 5 note). Accordingly, though very numerous at the Exodus, it had surprisingly diminished before the death of Moses (cp. Num. i. 22, 23 with Num. xxvi. 12-14) ; and eventually it found territory adequate for its wants within the limits of another tribe, Judah. Cp. Josh. xix. 2-9.

7. *bring him unto his people*] Moses, taking up the promise of Jacob, prays that Judah, marching forth at the head of the tribes, might ever be brought back in safety and victory ; and intimates that God would grant help to accomplish this.

8. *thy holy one*] *i.e.* Levi, regarded as the representative of the whole priestly and

q Ex. 17. 7.
Num. 20. 13.
ch. 8. 2, 3.
Ps. 81. 7.
r Gen. 29. 32.
1 Chr. 17.
17.
Job 37. 24.
s Ex. 32. 26,
27, 28.
t See Jer. 18.
18.
Mal. 2. 5, 6.
u Lev. 10.11.
ch. 17. 9.
& 24. 8.
Ez. 44. 23,
24.
Mal. 2. 7.
x Ex. 30. 7,
8.
Num. 16. 40.
1 Sam. 2. 28.
y Lev. 1. 9.
Ps. 51, 19.
Ez. 43. 27.
z 2 Sam. 24.
23.
Ps. 20. 3.
Ez. 20. 40,
41.
a Gen. 49.25.
b Gen. 27.28.

c Gen. 49. 26.
d Hab. 3. 6.

e Ex. 3. 2.
Acts 7. 30,
35.
f Gen.49.26.

g 1 Chr. 5. 1.
h Num. 23.
22.
Ps. 2. 10.

^qWhom thou didst prove at Massah,
And with whom thou didst strive at the waters of Meribah;

9   Who said unto his father and to his mother, I have not ^rseen him;

^sNeither did he acknowledge his brethren, nor knew his own children:
For ^tthey have observed thy word, and kept thy covenant.

10   ^{1u}They shall teach Jacob thy judgments,
And Israel thy law:
^{2x}They shall put incense ³before thee,
^yAnd whole burnt sacrifice upon thine altar.

11   Bless, Lord, his substance,
And ^zaccept the work of his hands:
Smite through the loins of them that rise against him,
And of them that hate him, that they rise not again.

12 ¶ *And* of Benjamin he said,
The beloved of the Lord shall dwell in safety by him;
And the Lord shall cover him all the day long,
And he shall dwell between his shoulders.

13 ¶ And of Joseph he said,
^aBlessed of the Lord *be* his land,
For the precious things of heaven,
For ^bthe dew, and for the deep that coucheth beneath,

14   And for the precious fruits *brought forth* by the sun,
And for the precious things ⁴put forth by the ⁵moon,

15   And for the chief things of ^cthe ancient mountains,
And for the precious things ^dof the lasting hills,

16   And for the precious things of the earth and fulness thereof,
And *for* the good will of ^ehim that dwelt in the bush:
Let *the blessing* ^fcome upon the head of Joseph,
And upon the top of the head of him *that was* separated from his brethren.

17   His glory *is like* the ^gfirstling of his bullock,
And his horns *are like* ^hthe horns of ⁶unicorns:

¹ Or, *Let them teach, &c.*   ³ Heb. *at thy nose.*   ⁵ Heb. *moons.*
² Or, *let them put incense.*   ⁴ Heb. *thrust forth.*   ⁶ Heb. *an unicorn.*

Levitical stock which sprang from him. The contrast between the tone of this passage and that of Gen. xlix. 5-7 is remarkable. Though the prediction of Jacob respecting the dispersion of this tribe held good, yet it was so overruled as to issue in honour and reward. The recovery of God's favour is to be traced to the faithfulness with which Moses and Aaron, who came of this tribe, served God in their high offices; and to the zeal and constancy which conspicuous persons of the tribe (*e.g.* Phinehas, Num. xxv. 11 seq.), and the whole tribe itself (cp. Ex. xxxii. 26), manifested on critical occasions in supporting the leaders of the people. The same reasons led to Levi's being selected for the special service of God in the Sanctuary (ch. x. 8 seq., and Num. viii. 5 seq.); and for the office of instructing their brethren in the knowledge of the Law. The events at Massah and Meribah, the one occurring at the beginning, the other towards the end, of the forty years' wandering, serve

to represent the whole series of trials by which God proved and exercised the faith and obedience of this chosen tribe.

9. *Who said unto his father and to his mother*] Cp. Matt. x. 37; Luke xiv. 26.

11. *smite through the loins*] Rather, **smite the loins,** *i.e.* the seat of their strength.

12. *he shall dwell between his shoulders*] *i.e.* be supported by God as a son who is carried by his father (cp. i. 31). Benjamin was specially beloved of his father (Gen. xxxv. 18, xliv. 20); Moses now promises no less love to him from God Himself.

13–17. Comparing the words of Moses with those of Jacob, it will be seen that the patriarch dwells with emphasis on the severe conflicts which Joseph, *i.e.* Ephraim and Manasseh, would undergo (cp. Gen. xlix. 23, 24); while the lawgiver seems to look beyond, and to behold the two triumphant and established in their power.

17. Rather: "The first-born of his" (*i.e.* Joseph's) "bullock is his glory": the refer-

With them [i]he shall push the people together to the ends of the earth :
And [k]they *are* the ten thousands of Ephraim,
And they *are* the thousands of Manasseh.

18 ¶ And of Zebulun he said,
    [l]Rejoice, Zebulun, in thy going out;
    And, Issachar, in thy tents.
19   They shall [m]call the people unto the mountain ;
    There [n]they shall offer sacrifices of righteousness :
    For they shall suck *of* the abundance of the seas,
    And *of* treasures hid in the sand.

20 ¶ And of Gad he said,
    Blessed *be* he that [o]enlargeth Gad :
    He dwelleth as a lion,
    And teareth the arm with the crown of the head.
21   And [p]he provided the first part for himself,
    Because there, *in* a portion of the lawgiver, *was he* [1]seated ;
    And [q]he came with the heads of the people,
    He executed the justice of the LORD,
    And his judgments with Israel.

22 ¶ And of Dan he said,
    Dan *is* a lion's whelp :
    [r]He shall leap from Bashan.

23 ¶ And of Naphtali he said,
    O Naphtali, [s]satisfied with favour,

Marginal references:
[i] 1 Kin. 22. 11.
Ps. 44. 5.
[k] Gen. 48. 19.
[l] Gen. 49. 13, 14, 15.
[m] Isai. 2. 3.
[n] Ps. 4. 5.
[o] See Josh. 13. 10, &c.
[p] Num. 32. 16, 17, &c.
[q] Josh. 4. 12.
[r] Josh. 19. 47.
Judg. 18. 27.
[s] Gen. 49. 21.

[1] Heb. *cieled.*

ence being to Ephraim, who was raised by Jacob to the honours of the firstborn (Gen. xlviii. 20), and is here likened to the firstling of Joseph's oxen, *i.e.* of Joseph's offspring. The ox is a common emblem of power and strength.

18, 19. Zebulun possessed a commodious sea-shore and the fisheries of the Lake of Tiberias : and was therefore to thrive by commerce, and to rejoice in his " going out," *i.e.* in his mercantile enterprises. Issachar possessed a fertile inland district, and would therefore dwell at home and prosper in agriculture. Both tribes distinguished themselves in the contest with Jabin (cp. Judg. v. 14, 15, 18) : and of Zebulun it is particularly noted that it produced the officers and tacticians who led and marshalled the host which vanquished Sisera (see Judg. v. 14, and cp. 1 Chr. xii. 33).

19. *unto the mountain*] Cp. Ex. xv. 17.
sacrifices of righteousness] Sacrifices offered in a righteous spirit, and therefore well pleasing to God (cp. Ps. iv. 5, li. 19).
treasures hid in the sand] The riches of the seas in general. It is however noteworthy that the sand of these coasts was specially valuable in the manufacture of glass ; and glass was a precious thing in ancient times (cp. Job xxviii. 17). The murex from which the highly-prized purple

dye was extracted, was also found here. A typical reference to the conversion of the Gentiles is strongly suggested by Isai. lx. 5, 6, 16, and lxvi. 11, 12.

20. *i.e.* Blessed be God Who shall grant to Gad a spacious territory. Cp. the blessing of Shem (Gen. ix. 26).
with the crown] Rather, **yea, the crown.** The warlike character of this tribe is shewn by their leading the van in the long campaigns of Joshua (cp. Josh. iv. 12, 13, xxii. 1–4). Cp. also 1 Chr. v. 18–22, xii. 8 seq., and the acts of Jehu, the Gadite, in 2 K. ix. x.

21. The first fruits of the conquest made by Israel were assigned to Gad and Reuben by Moses, at their own request.
because...seated] Render, **because there was the leader's portion reserved,** *i.e.* there was reserved the fitting portion for Gad as a leader in war.
and he came, &c.] *i.e.* he joined the other leaders to fulfil the commands of God respecting the conquest of Canaan (cp. Num. xxxii. 17, 21, 32 ; Josh. i. 14). Moses regards the promise of the Gadites to do this as already redeemed.

22. Dan shall be like a lion which leaps forth from his covert in Bashan. Cp. Song of Solomon, iv. 8.

23. *satisfied with favour*] Cp. Gen. xlix. 21 and note.
the west and the south] *i.e.* taking the

And full with the blessing of the LORD:

See Josh. 19. 32, &c.

^tPossess thou the west and the south.

24 ¶ And of Asher he said,

u Gen. 49. 20.
x See Job 29. 6.
y ch. 8. 9.
z Ex. 15. 11.
Ps. 86. 8.

^u*Let* Asher *be* blessed with children;
Let him be acceptable to his brethren,
And let him ^xdip his foot in oil.

25 ¹Thy shoes *shall be* ^yiron and brass;
And as thy days, *so shall* thy strength *be.*

Jer. 10. 6.
a ch. 32. 15.
b Ps. 68. 4, 33, 34.
& 104. 3.
Hab. 3. 8.
c Ps. 90. 1.
d ch. 9. 3, 4.
e Num. 23. 9.
Jer. 23. 6.
& 33. 16.
f ch. 8. 7, 8.
g Gen. 27. 28.
ch. 11. 11.
h Ps. 144. 15.
i 2 Sam. 7. 23.
k Ps. 115. 9, 10, 11.
l 2 Sam. 22. 45.
Ps. 18. 44.
m ch. 32. 13.

26 ¶ *There is* ^znone like unto the God of ^aJeshurun,
^b*Who* rideth upon the heaven in thy help,
And in his excellency on the sky.

27 The eternal God *is thy* ^crefuge,
And underneath *are* the everlasting arms:
And ^dhe shall thrust out the enemy from before thee;
And shall say, Destroy *them.*

28 ^eIsrael then shall dwell in safety alone:
^fThe fountain of Jacob *shall be* upon a land of corn and wine;
Also his ^gheavens shall drop down dew.

29 ^hHappy *art* thou, O Israel:
ⁱWho *is* like unto thee, O people saved by the LORD,
^kThe shield of thy help, and who *is* the sword of thy excellency!
And thine enemies ^{l2}shall be found liars unto thee;
And ^mthou shalt tread upon their high places.

a Num. 27. 12.
& 33. 47.
ch. 32. 49.
b ch. 3. 27.
c Gen. 14. 14.

CHAP. **34.** AND Moses went up from the plains of Moab ^aunto the mountain of Nebo, to the top of ³Pisgah, that *is* over against Jericho. And the LORD ^bshewed him all the land of Gilead, 2 ^cunto Dan, and all Naphtali, and the land of Ephraim, and

¹ Or, Under *thy shoes* shall be *iron.*   ² Or, *shall be subdued.*   ³ Or, *The hill.*

---

words as referring not to geographical position but to national characteristics, "the sea and the sunny district." The possession of Naphtali included nearly the whole west coast of the Sea of Galilee, the Lake of Merom, the modern *Bahr el Huleh,* and the well-watered district near the springs of Jordan. It contained some of the grandest scenery and some of the most fertile land in Palestine. Josephus speaks of the shore of Gennesaret as "an earthly paradise;" and Porter describes it as "the garden of Palestine." The modern name for this district, "land of good tidings," is significant.

24. Rather, "Blessed above the sons" (*i.e.* of Jacob=most blessed amongst the sons of Jacob) "be Asher; let him be the favoured one of his brethren," *i.e.* the one favoured of God. The plenty with which this tribe should be blessed is described under the figure of dipping the foot in oil (cp. marg. ref.).

25. The strength and firmness of Asher is as if he were shod with iron and brass (cp. Rev. i. 15). The territory of this tribe probably contained iron and copper. Cp. marg. ref.

as thy days, so shall thy strength be] *i.e.*

"thy strength" (some prefer "thy rest") "shall be continued to thee as long as thou shalt live: thou shalt never know feebleness and decay."

26. Rather, **There is none like unto God, O Jeshurun**! See marg. ref. and note.

27. *thy refuge*] Rather, "dwellingplace." Cp. Ps. xc. 1, xci. 9.

28. *the fountain of Jacob shall be upon a land of corn and wine*] The A. V. does not preserve the symmetry of the clauses. Render, "Israel shall dwell in safety; alone shall the fountain of Jacob be" (cp. Ps. lxviii. 26; Isai. xlviii. 1); "in a land," &c.

29. *be found liars unto thee*] Perhaps rather, "cringe before thee." The verb means to shew a feigned or forced obedience: see marg. reff.

tread upon their high places] *i.e.* occupy the commanding positions in their land, and so have it in subjection.

XXXIV. **1.** *Dan*] This can hardly be the Dan (Dan-Laish) of Judg. xviii. 27 seq., which was not in Gilead. It is probably a town of this name which stood in the north of Peræa; perhaps the same as Dan-jaan, 2 S. xxiv. 6, and the Dan of Gen. xiv. 14.

3 Manasseh, and all the land of Judah, *d* unto the utmost sea, and
the south, and the plain of the valley of Jericho, *e* the city of
4 palm trees, unto Zoar. And the LORD said unto him, *f* This *is*
the land which I sware unto Abraham, unto Isaac, and unto
Jacob, saying, I will give it unto thy seed : *g* I have caused thee
to see *it* with thine eyes, but thou shalt not go over thither.
5 ¶ So Moses the servant of the LORD died there in the land of
6 Moab, according to the word of the LORD. And he buried him
in a valley in the land of Moab, over against Beth-peor : but *i* no
7 man knoweth of his sepulchre unto this day. *k* And Moses *was*
an hundred and twenty years old when he died : *l* his eye was
8 not dim, nor his ¹natural force ²abated. And the children
of Israel wept for Moses in the plains of Moab *m* thirty days :
so the days of weeping *and* mourning for Moses were ended.
9 ¶ And Joshua the son of Nun was full of the *n* spirit of wisdom ;
for *o* Moses had laid his hands upon him : and the children of
Israel hearkened unto him, and did as the LORD commanded
10 Moses. ¶ And there *p* arose not a prophet since in Israel like
11 unto Moses, *q* whom the LORD knew face to face, in all *r* the
signs and the wonders, which the LORD sent him to do in the
land of Egypt to Pharaoh, and to all his servants, and to all his
12 land, and in all that mighty hand, and in all the great terror
which Moses shewed in the sight of all Israel.

¹ Heb. *moisture.*   ² Heb. *fled.*

d ch. 11. 24.
e Judg. 1. 16.
2 Chr. 28.
15.
f Gen. 12. 7.
g ch. 3. 27.
& 32. 52.
h ch. 32. 50.
Josh. 1. 1.
i See Jude
9.
k ch. 31. 2.
l See Gen.
27. 1.
& 48. 10.
Josh. 14. 10,
11.
m See Gen.
50. 3, 10.
Num. 20. 29.
n Isai. 11. 2.
Dan. 6. 3.
o Num. 27.
18, 23.
p See chap.
18. 15, 18.
q Ex. 33. 11.
Num. 12. 6,
8.
ch. 5. 4.
r ch. 4. 34.
& 7. 19.

3. *unto Zoar*] Cp. Gen. xix. 22.

4. *I have caused thee to see it*] The sight
thus afforded to Moses, like that of "all
the kingdoms of the world in a moment of
time" (Luke iv. 5), was no doubt supernatural.

5. *according to the word of the* LORD] It
denotes that Moses died, not because his
vital powers were exhausted, but by the
sentence of God, and as a punishment for
his sin. Cp. xxxii. 51.

6. *no man knoweth of his sepulchre*] Hardly
lest the grave of Moses should become an
object of superstitious honour, for the Jews
were not prone to this particular form of
error. Bearing in mind the appearance of
Moses at the Transfiguration (Matt. xvii.
1-10), and what is said by St. Jude (*v.* 9),
we may conjecture that Moses after death
passed into the same state with Enoch and
Elijah ; and that his sepulchre could not be
found because he was shortly translated
from it.

9. *spirit of wisdom*] The practical wisdom
of the ruler is specially meant.

10. *there arose not a prophet since in
Israel*] Words like these can only have been
written some time, but not necessarily a
long time, after the death of Moses. They
refer more particularly to the wonders
wrought by the hand of Moses at the
Exodus and in the desert; and do but
re-echo the declaration of God Himself
(Num. xii. 6 seq). They may naturally
enough be attributed to one of Moses' successors, writing perhaps soon after the
settlement of the people in Canaan.

JOSHUA.

INTRODUCTION.

1. THIS book like several others of the historical books of Scripture derives its name from its contents. It takes up the history of the chosen people at the death of Moses, and continues it in a systematic and orderly narrative, through the leadership and government of his successor. It records almost exclusively the acts of Joshua in fulfilment of the commission laid upon him from God by the hand of Moses (cp. Deut. xxxi. 7, 8), and terminates with Joshua's death and burial.

The contents group themselves into two divisions of nearly equal length. The conquest of the land is described in twelve chapters, and then in twelve other chapters the subsequent partition of it together with Joshua's last acts and words.

The victories of Joshua described in the former of these portions were accompanied by repeated and stupendous interferences of God. This miraculous element has led some commentators to treat the book as altogether unhistorical. But it must not be forgotten that the miracles of the Book of Joshua do not stand alone. They grow as it were naturally out of the Divine interpositions on behalf of Israel in the days of Moses, and are but the close of a series of extraordinary providences begun in Egypt, and described in Exodus and the books following. No less do they stand intimately associated

with the future history and development of the Jewish Church and nation, and even with the wider and more remote issues of God's counsels as manifested, or to be manifested, in the Christian Church to the end of all things. Thus the conquest of Canaan by Joshua has other and vastly grander significances than its mere dimensions as a fact in history seem at first sight to suggest. It is not to be regarded simply as the invasion of a little district about as large as three average English counties by a tribe of nomads from the Arabian deserts. It was also the accomplishment by God of a purpose revealed of old ; it was an essential element in the plan ordained by Him for the preservation amongst men of His Law, Will, and Word ; it was designed to foreshadow in many important particulars His future dealings with mankind at large. But for the special help of God, the Israelites could not have effected the conquest at all, for they were hardly superior to the Canaanites in numbers, and were destitute of chariots and horses, and of all the more elaborate equipments for war, above all of the appliances requisite for reducing the cities (cp. Num. xiii. 28 ; Deut. i. 28, and ix. 1) in which Canaan abounded. God's promise was, however, pledged to their forefathers to give them this land; whatever then might be necessary to give effect to this promise it belonged to His faithfulness to accord; and the Book of Joshua consequently is an essential sequel to the Pentateuch as declaring the thorough fulfilment by God of the covenant made by Him through Moses with Israel, and thus as illustrating His inviolable faithfulness.[2]

But important as the theocratical and theological characteristics of the book are, both in themselves and as (so to say) vindicating the miraculous elements of the narrative, we must nevertheless not lose sight of the internal evidences of common and historical fact which it presents.

The invasion of Canaan by Joshua was evidently a carefully and skilfully conducted enterprise. An army marching upon Canaan from the south would find its path intercepted by range after range of heights, each, in the days of Moses and Joshua, bristling with towns and fortresses. The progress of such an army could be but slow, and at every step would be met by better organized resistance from an increasing number of enemies. When Israel, after forty years' expiation of the revolt at Kadesh, again arose at the command of God to resume the long deferred enterprise on Canaan, the host was conducted round the whole south-east corner of the land and directed upon its comparatively defenceless eastern flank above the Dead Sea. The whole of the strong military positions and fenced cities in the "south country" and the "hill country" of what was subsequently

the territory of Judah were thus taken in reverse and rendered comparatively useless. It is probable, too, that the southern Canaanites in particular were at this time greatly weakened by the invasions of Thotmes III., who had taken Gaza, apparently not many years previously, and no doubt had overrun the whole adjoining district (see note on xiii. 3). No less able were the measures adopted by Joshua to execute the plan thus judiciously laid down. The passage of the Jordan, by the special help of God, at a time of year when his enemies no doubt deemed the river to be an almost insurmountable obstacle to his advance (see on iii. 15): the seizing Gilgal, to serve as his foothold in the land : the capture and destruction of Jericho: the fall of Ai :—these events enabled him to throw the forces of Israel like a wedge through the very midst of the land almost to the western sea, and in its most vulnerable part, between the fastnesses of Judah on the south and the mountain district of Ephraim on the north. The Amorites on Joshua's left, cut off from the Hittites on his right by his whole army interposing between the two, were overpowered before Gibeon. The whole south was reduced into at least temporary subjection before the larger multitudes of the north could be mustered. These in their turn shared the fate of their brethren in the south ; Joshua broke their vast host to pieces on the shores of Lake Merom.

In these campaigns of Joshua it is impossible not to see the traces of strategical skill no less conspicuously than that presence of immediate and Divine suggestion and succour which the narrative asserts.

---

[2] These typical aspects and applications are well drawn out by Pearson " On the Creed," Art. ii.

2. The leading trait in the character of Joshua is courage—the courage of the warrior : this must have been already remarkable at the time of the Exodus (Ex. xvii. 9 seq.). Subsequently Joshua appears as in constant attendance on Moses (Ex. xxiv. 13 ; xxxii. 1 ; xxxiii. 11); he without doubt acquired on Sinai, and in the precincts of the Sanctuary, that unswerving faithfulness of service and unshaken confidence in God which marked his after career. He was naturally selected as one of the twelve "rulers" sent by Moses (Num. xiii. 2) to explore the land before the invasion of it was undertaken ; and the bold and truthful report brought back by him and Caleb (Num. xiv. 7–9), was no less characteristic than was his undaunted bearing before the incensed people (Num. xiv. 10). These qualities pointed him out as the fitting captain over the Lord's people, who should overthrow their enemies before them and put them in possession of the promised inheritance. Accordingly, at the express command of God, he was solemnly appointed to that office and duty by Moses before his death (Num. xxvii. 16–23; Deut. xxxi. 23).

Joshua was not a prophet (Ecclus. xlvi. 1; cp. Num. xxvii. 21), but a divinely inspired leader. After the great and peculiar work of his life was accomplished, he no longer held the same exclusive place at the head of Israel as before. In making the arrangements for settling the people in their homes, and establishing the theocracy on the lines laid down in the law of Moses, he acted in conjunction with Eleazar, the high-priest, and with the heads of the tribes (cp. xiv. 1; xvii. 4; xxi. 1). This was but natural. The armies had done their work and were dispersed, or were ready to disperse, to their several inheritances ; and the military authority of their general was consequently at an end. The latter years of his life were probably passed in retirement at Timnath-serah, whence he would seem to have emerged in extreme old age to meet the princes and the people in the great gathering at Shechem (xxiii., xxiv.), and to employ once more and finally his authority as the last survivor but one of a mighty generation, and as the hero of Israel's greatest triumphs, in order to engage his people more firmly and closely in their rightful allegiance to God.

The courage which was the leading feature in the character of Joshua was very distinctly and directly built upon faith (i. 5, 6). Joshua obeyed God's call unhesitatingly and to the end, but it was because he trusted wholly in the promise which accompanied it. Hence, along with his soldierly qualities, were found others seldom present in the same man. He combined justice as a magistrate with gentleness as a man (vii. 19); spirit as a ruler, with temper and discretion in dealing with the arrogant and exacting (xvii. 14 seq.); diligence and equity in disposing of the fruits of victory with a complete unselfishness as regarded himself (xix. 49–51). Perhaps conspicuous above all was his humility. From first to last his valour and his victories are referred to God as their giver. Of his own personal work in the achievements of his life there is in his last addresses scarcely one word.

3. The chronological dates presented in this book are few :—

a. Comparing iv. 19 and v. 6, if the date of the Exodus be assumed to be B.C. 1490, that of the invasion of Canaan will be B.C. 1450.

b. The duration of Joshua's wars with the Canaanites is spoken of loosely in xi. 18 as "a long time." The words of Caleb (xiv. 7 and 10: cp. Num. xiii. 17)—who was thirty-eight years old when he passed through the Red Sea, and seventy-eight when he passed through Jordan—help us to assign a period of seven years (in round numbers) for the campaigns of Joshua.

c. The duration of Joshua's rule, and consequently the number of years covered by the record of this book, is far more uncertain. He died when he was an hundred and ten (xxiv. 29). If (cp. Ex. xxxiii. 11) we suppose him to have been about the same age as Caleb, he will have been about seventy-eight years old when he invaded Canaan, and have been at the head of Israel not much less than thirty-two years altogether after the death of Moses, surviving about twenty-five years after his retirement to Timnath-serah (cp. xxiii. 1). Josephus, however, states that Joshua's rule after the death of Moses lasted for twenty-five years, and that he had previously been forty years associated with him. This would fix Joshua's age at the time of the Exodus at forty-five. On the whole, nothing more precise seems attainable now than this : that Joshua governed Israel from twenty-five to thirty years after the death of Moses, and that about the like number of years contains the events recorded in the book which bears his name.

4. No sufficient evidence exists to enable us with certainty to name the author. That he was one of " the elders that overlived Joshua" (xxiv. 31) is probable, for the book appears to have been written by one coeval with the events recorded, and, indeed, an eye-witness of them. The spirit of the narrative in the former or historical portion of the book, and the graphic yet spontaneous rendering of details, which it everywhere presents, bespeak one who saw what he describes. And the topographical information which abounds in the latter portion of the book is of such a nature, and is presented in such a form, as strongly to suggest the use of written, and apparently contemporary documents. Some parts of this information are minute and accurate (*e.g.* ch. xv.), other statements are far less definite and complete. No doubt some of these imperfections are due to disorder in the text, or to clauses having dropped out of it, but others are mainly due to the fact that the writer's knowledge was itself imperfect. These very anomalies of the writer's most valuable description of Palestine, inconvenient as they often are, seem thus to be attributable to the early date of his information. His documents were written whilst Israel was still a stranger in the land of his inheritance, and in parts of it still a foreign invader.

The hand of a writer contemporaneous with the events is indicated in several expressions, *e.g.* in v. 6, 7; vi. 25; x. 2, a notice which plainly borrows its terms from the state of things in Canaan at the time of the invasion; and in the record of ancient Canaanitish names of cities, though disused after the Israelites occu-

pied them, (xiv. 15 ; xv. 9, 15, 49 and 60.)[3]
The book cannot, in its present form at least, be ascribed to Joshua himself. The account of his death and that of Eleazar, with the few supplementary verses at the end of the book, might have been attached by another hand, as a conclusion to the historical work of Joshua, just as a like addition was made to the work of Moses. But there are up and down the book a number of historical notices, which point to a date clearly beyond the death of Joshua (cp. xv. 13–20 and Judg. i. 1–15 ; xv. 63, and Judg. i. 8 ; xv. 13–19 and Judg. xviii.).

For these reasons the opinion of the Rabbins and many moderns which names Joshua as himself the sole writer of this book, must apparently be abandoned. The evidence internal and external renders it likely that the book was composed partly from personal observation and inquiry, partly out of pre-existing and authentic documents, within a few years after the death of Joshua, and probably from materials furnished in part by Joshua himself.

5. The book of Joshua is a work complete in itself, with an organic unity and peculiar characteristics. This appears

(1) From the definiteness of the

[3] Passages occur which fix a *terminus ad quem*, later than which they cannot have been penned. Thus xvi. 10 (cp. 1 Kings ix. 16) must have been written before the beginning of the reign of Solomon. From xi. 8 and xix. 28, Sidon was the capital of Phœnicia ; but before the time of David, if not in or about B.C. 1208, the hegemony was transferred to Tyre. xv. 63 must belong to a time previous to the taking of Jerusalem and the destruction of the Jebusites by David (2 Sam. v. 6 seq.) ix. 27 implies that the site of the temple was not yet determined: cp. Deut. xvi. 5.

writer's purpose, and the thoroughness with which he executes it. He proposes to narrate the conquest of Canaan, and to present that conquest as a proof of God's fidelity to his Covenant. But the writer does not limit himself to the achievements of Joshua. Such additions to the main body of his story, which belongs to the lifetime and leadership of Joshua, as are contained in chs. xiii. and xv. are to be explained only by a reference to the writer's distinct and special aim.

(2) From the tokens of connexion and method apparent throughout. Not only does the first part, which records the wars (i.–xii.), evidently lead up to the second part (xiii.–xxiv.), which describes the partition of the territory when subdued, but the contents of each part taken singly are given in proper and chronological order, each transaction growing out of the one preceding.

(3) From the style and phraseology. These are marked by distinctive features, whether the book be compared with the Pentateuch or with the other and later historical books. The difference of style, words, and treatment in the historical chapters, as contrasted with the topographical chapters is only what might be expected from the diverse nature of the subjects, and from the self-evident fact that in much of the latter part of his task the author was working from pre-existing documents.

Certain discrepancies alleged to exist in the book do not seriously impair its unity and independence. The difficulties, *e.g.* in the account of the capture of Ai (ch. viii.) arise solely out of the numbers, and are far more probably due to a mistake in the numerals (see on viii. 3), which is by no means of infrequent occurrence, than to the presence in the narrative of two or three different versions of the events which the final editor omitted to harmonize.

The contradiction said to exist between some passages which speak of the land as completely subdued by Joshua, and of the Canaanites as utterly extirpated (xi. 16, 17, and 23; xii. 7, 8, &c.), and others which allude to "very much land," as still in possession of the native inhabitants (xiii. 1 seq.; xvii. 14 seq.; xxiii. 5, &c.), is to be explained partly by the theocratic view which the writer takes of his theme; a view which leads him to regard the conquest as complete when it was so *ex parte Dei*, and when all was done that was needed to enable the Israelites to realize fully the promises (cp. xxi. 43–45); partly also by the fact that territory was undoubtedly overrun by Joshua at the first onset, which was afterwards recovered by the Canaanites, and only again and finally wrested from them at a subsequent, sometimes a long subsequent, date. That the early campaigns of Joshua were in the nature of sudden raids, overpowering for the moment, but not effectually subduing the country, has probably much truth in it.

Thus then, the Book of Joshua, though based upon pre-existing materials of various kinds,[4] and sometimes incorporating them, appears to be a separate and complete work produced as a whole from one original hand. Its relation to the

Pentateuch is that of an independent treatise by a distinct author, who resumes a theme of which the first great and important portion had been finished by a predecessor. The Pentateuch is not to be looked upon as principally a historical work. It is the statute book of the Theocracy, and contains only such historical matter as illustrates the origin and import of God's Covenant with Israel. Joshua records how the temporal promises of that Covenant were accomplished; and describes how the basis was laid for the future development of the nation, under the special superintendence of God, by its settlement in Canaan. Thus regarded, this book is no more an appendage to the Pentateuch than the books of Judges and Samuel are an appendage to it. There is, assuredly, an intimate connexion amongst these writings throughout, a connexion which is expressly indicated by the connective conjunctions used in the beginning of each book (see note on i. 1). This is due to the fact that the several authors were moved to write by one and the same Spirit, and that their one purpose in successive ages was to record the dealings of God with their nation. Hence they have selected whatever declares or illustrates the divine call of Israel; God's methods in educating that people for its functions in His world; the preparations made through the chequered history of Israel for future issues bearing on the salvation of all mankind. We find at one time periods of considerable length, and events of great importance to secular history cursorily alluded to, whilst other occurrences, often of a biographical character, are dwelt upon with

---

[4] We have *e.g.* in x. 12 a citation from a poetical book (see note in loc.); whilst elsewhere the writer has before him documents of a geographical character.

anxious minuteness, because of their theocratic bearings. Accordingly the name "Earlier Prophets," given to this and the following books of Judges, Samuel, and Kings by the Jewish Church which has handed them down to us as canonical, is appropriate. They were written by inspired men, and treat their subject from the prophetical point of view.

The book of Joshua is repeatedly cited or referred to in the New Testament: cp. Acts vii. 45; Heb. iii. 5; iv. 8; xi. 30, 31; James ii. 25.

6. The land of Canaan was given as a free gift by God to the Israelites—they took possession of it because He bade them do so—and He no less bade them annihilate the Canaanitish nations without mercy.[5] The question then occurs in unbroken force, all palliative explanations being disallowed:—Is this merciless treatment of the Canaanites consistent with the attributes of the Deity, especially as those attributes are illustrated for us in the New Testament?

The destruction of the Canaanites is always presented in Scripture as a judgment of God sent on them because of their wickedness. They had not only fallen into total apostacy from God, but into forms of idolatry of the most degrading kind. Their false religion cannot be regarded as a mere error of judgment; cruelty the most atrocious, and unnatural crimes the most defiling were part and parcel of its observances.[6] Moreover they had proved themselves to be incor-

rigible. They had had not only the general warning of the Deluge, as had other nations of the earth, but the special one of the overthrow of Sodom and Gomorrah in the very midst of them. They had had also the example and instruction of Abraham and the patriarchs living for ages amongst them. Even after the miraculous providence of God had brought the Israelites out of Egypt and across the Jordan, and even when the sword was as it were hanging over their necks, it was but in one or two isolated cases that signs of repentance and recollection of God were manifested (cp. ii. 11; ix. 24). God had forborne for ages in vain (cp. Gen. xv. 16); in the days of Joshua the time for mercy had passed, and that of judgment had come. It is impossible to acknowledge God as the moral Governor of the earth, and not to admit that it may be right or even necessary for Him to remove such nations. The fact, therefore, that God is described as having not only permitted, but even enjoined and caused the extirpation of the Canaanitish nations, depraved as they were, is not inconsistent with His moral attributes. Men, as was long ago pointed out by Bishop Butler ('Anal.' ii. 3), have no right to either life or property, but what arises solely from the grant of God. When this grant is revoked they cease to have any right at all in either. And in the case before us the forfeiture decreed by God was merited, and the execution of it was therefore righteous.

God chose to inflict His righteous judgment by the hands of the Israelites, and expressly commissioned them to be His executioners. If it be objected that this is to re-

[5] Cp. Ex. xxiii. 32 seq.; xxxiv. 12 seq.; Num. xxxiii. 52 seq.; Deut. vii. 1 seq.; Josh. ix. 24.
[6] Cp. Lev. xviii. 21 seq.; Deut. xii. 30 seq.

present God as sanctioning cruelty, the answer is obvious:—it is no sanction of cruelty to direct a lawful sentence to be carried out by human agents (cp. Num. xxxi. 3). Nor would obedience to God's command in this matter make the Israelites brutal and bloodthirsty. The behaviour of the Israelites, on many occasions, proves that they shrank from a terrible duty of this sort when laid on them by God, and did it only so far as they were compelled to do it.[7]

The slaughter of the Canaanites served various important purposes besides the mere removal of them from the face of the earth. To make and keep the Jewish people as much as possible isolated, was a

---

[7] Cp. Num. xxxi. 13 seq. ; Josh. xvi. 10; xviii. 3 ; Judg. i. 28 and 35 ; 1 Sam. xv. 24).

marked and vital principle of the Old Testament dispensation. No more effectual means could have been adopted for inspiring God's people with an abhorrence for Canaanitish sins, to which they were not a little prone, than to make them the ministers of Divine vengeance for those sins.

They learnt by experiment that God would certainly root out those who fell away in apostacy from Him. They were warned also that if they fell into the sins of the Canaanites they would themselves be the victims of those same judgments of which they had been the reluctant executioners (cp. *e.g.* Deut. xxviii. 25). And the whole was so ordered as to exhibit a type, fearful no doubt yet salutary, of what must be the fate of the impenitent and obdurate in the upshot of God's righteous government.

THE BOOK

OF

JOSHUA.

a Ex. 24. 13.
Deut. 1. 38.
b Deut. 34. 5.
c Deut. 11. 24.
ch. 14. 9.
d Gen. 15. 18.
Ex. 23. 31.
Num. 34. 3
—12.
e Deut. 7. 24.
f Ex. 3. 12.
g Deut. 31. 8,
23.
ver. 9, 17.
ch. 3. 7.
& 6. 27.
Isai. 43. 2, 5.
h Deut. 31. 6,
8.
Heb. 13. 5.
i Deut. 31. 7,
23.
k Num. 27.
23.
Deut. 31. 7.
ch. 11. 15.
l Deut. 5. 32.
& 28. 14.

CHAP. 1. NOW after the death of Moses the servant of the LORD it came to pass, that the LORD spake unto Joshua the son of Nun, 2 Moses' *a*minister, saying, *b*Moses my servant is dead; now therefore arise, go over this Jordan, thou, and all this people, unto the land which I do give to them, *even* to the children of 3 Israel. *c*Every place that the sole of your foot shall tread upon, 4 that have I given unto you, as I said unto Moses. *d*From the wilderness and this Lebanon even unto the great river, the river Euphrates, all the land of the Hittites, and unto the great sea toward the going down of the sun, shall be your coast. 5 *e*There shall not any man be able to stand before thee all the days of thy life: *f*as I was with Moses, *so g*I will be with thee : 6 *h*I will not fail thee, nor forsake thee. *i*Be strong and of a good courage : for *1*unto this people shalt thou divide for an inheritance the land, which I sware unto their fathers to give them. 7 Only be thou strong and very courageous, that thou mayest observe to do according to all the law, *k*which Moses my servant commanded thee: *l*turn not from it *to* the right hand or *to* the

1 Or, *thou shalt cause this people to inherit the land, &c.*

I. Verses 1–9 of this chapter serve as an introduction to the history of the war, and pointedly call attention to the leading thought of the whole book,—that the invasion and subjugation of Canaan were undertaken by the Israelites at God's direct command and completed in His never-failing strength.

1. *Now, &c.*] Heb. : " and, &c." The statement following is thus connected with some previous one, which is assumed to be known to the reader. So Judges, Ruth, 1 Sam., &c., are by the same means linked on to the books preceding them. The connexion here is the closer, since the book of Deuteronomy concludes, and the book of Joshua opens, by referring to the death of Moses.

Moses, the servant of the LORD] On the epithet, see marg. ref. *b.*

Moses' minister] It is impossible altogether to pass by the typical application of this verse. Moses, representing the law, is dead ; Joshua, or, as that name is written in Greek, Jesus, is now bidden by God to do what Moses could not,—lead the people into the Promised Land. Joshua was "Moses' minister," just as Christ was " made under the Law ; " but it was Joshua, not Moses, who wrought out the accomplishment of the blessings which the Law promised. On the name Joshua, see Exod. xvii. 9 note, and Num. xiii. 16.

saying] No doubt directly, by an immediate revelation, but not as God spake to Moses, " mouth to mouth " (Num. xii. 8).

Though upon Joshua's appointment to be Moses' successor (Num. xxvii. 18 seq.), it had been directed that " counsel should be asked " for him through the medium of Eleazar "after the judgment of Urim," yet this was evidently a resource provided to meet cases of doubt and difficulty. Here there was no such case ; but the appointed leader, knowing well the purpose of God, needed to be stirred up to instant execution of it ; and the people too might require the encouragement of a renewed Divine command to set out at once upon the great enterprise before them (cp. *v.* 13).

4. Lebanon is spoken of as "this Lebanon," because visible from the neighbourhood in which Israel was encamped. (Cp. Deut. iii. 8, 9.) "The wilderness " of the text is the Desert of Arabia, which forms the southern, as Lebanon does the northern, limit of the Promised Land. The boundaries on the east and west are likewise indicated ; and the intervening territory is described generally as " all the land of the Hittites." The Hittites are properly the inhabitants of northern Canaan and Phœnicia (see Exod. iii. 8 note), but the name appears to be used here for the Canaanites in general, as in 1 Kings x. 29. On the boundaries of the Promised Land cp. Deut. xi. 24 ; Gen. xv. 18.

7. *prosper*] See margin. The literal rendering should be retained here since the notion of prosperity is separately introduced by a different word in *v.* 8.

[m] Deut. 17. 18, 19. [n] Ps. 1. 2.
8 left, that thou mayest [1]prosper whithersoever thou goest. [m]This
book of the law shall not depart out of thy mouth; but [n]thou
shalt meditate therein day and night, that thou mayest observe
to do according to all that is written therein: for then thou
shalt make thy way prosperous, and then thou shalt [2]have good
[o] Deut. 31. 7, 8, 23. Jer. 1. 8. [p] Ps. 27. 1.
9 success. [o]Have not I commanded thee? Be strong and of a
good courage; [p]be not afraid, neither be thou dismayed: for the
10 LORD thy God *is* with thee whithersoever thou goest. ¶ Then
11 Joshua commanded the officers of the people, saying, Pass through
the host, and command the people, saying, Prepare you victuals;
[q] ch. 3. 2. See Deut. 9. 1. & 11. 31.
for [q]within three days ye shall pass over this Jordan, to go in to
possess the land, which the LORD your God giveth you to possess
12 it. ¶ And to the Reubenites, and to the Gadites, and to half the
[r] Num. 32. 20—28. ch. 22. 2, 3, 4.
13 tribe of Manasseh, spake Joshua, saying, Remember [r]the word
which Moses the servant of the LORD commanded you, saying,
The LORD your God hath given you rest, and hath given you
14 this land. Your wives, your little ones, and your cattle, shall
remain in the land which Moses gave you on this side Jordan;
but ye shall pass before your brethren [3]armed, all the mighty
15 men of valour, and help them; until the LORD have given your
brethren rest, as *he hath given* you, and they also have possessed
[s] ch. 22. 4, &c.
the land which the LORD your God giveth them: [s]then ye shall
return unto the land of your possession, and enjoy it, which
Moses the LORD's servant gave you on this side Jordan toward
16 the sunrising. And they answered Joshua, saying, All that
thou commandest us we will do, and whithersoever thou sendest
17 us, we will go. According as we hearkened unto Moses in all
things, so will we hearken unto thee: only the LORD thy God
[t] ver. 5. 1 Sam. 20. 13. 1 Kin. 1. 37.
18 [t]be with thee, as he was with Moses. Whosoever *he be* that doth
rebel against thy commandment, and will not hearken unto thy
words in all that thou commandest him, he shall be put to death:
only be strong and of a good courage.
[a] Num. 25. 1.
CHAP. 2. AND Joshua the son of Nun [4]sent [a]out of Shittim two
men to spy secretly, saying, Go view the land, even Jericho.

[1] Or, *do wisely*, Deut. 29. 9.
[2] Or, *do wisely*, ver. 7.
[3] Heb. *marshalled by five:* as Ex. 13. 18.
[4] Or, *had sent.*

10. *officers*] The "scribes." (See Ex. v. 6 note, and Deut. xvi. 18.)

11. *Prepare you victuals*] The order was probably given with the knowledge that the manna would cease when the host crossed the Jordan (Ex. xvi. 35), and possibly because amidst their preparations there might not be opportunity to gather it in sufficient quantity. Nor does it appear that manna ever formed the whole and sole sustenance of the people. (Cp. Num. xx. 1 note.)

It is the view of the majority of commentators—Jewish and Christian, ancient and modern—that the "three days" here named are identical with those of iii. 2; and that the command of Joshua in the text was not in fact given until after the return of the spies. Here, as elsewhere in the Hebrew historical books and frequently in the Gospels, the order of time is superseded by the order of thought. For the purpose of the writer was not historical merely; it was, on the contrary, mainly religious and theoretical. Intending, then, to exhibit God as accomplishing His promises to the Covenant-people, he begins by informing us that God gave the word, and set Joshua and the host actually in motion to take possession of their inheritance. Having placed this leading fact in the forefront, he returns to mention in ch. ii. certain transactions closely relevant to the early stages of Joshua's conquests, but which had in fact happened before the camp was removed from the plains of Moab and immediately after the expiration of the thirty days' mourning for Moses. (Deut. xxxiv. 8.) The order of events was probably the following:—3rd Nisan, the spies are sent out (ii. 1); 6th, the spies return (ii. 23); 7th, the camp is removed from Shittim to the bank of Jordan (iii. 1), and the command (i. 11) is issued; 10th, the river is crossed (iv. 19).

14. *armed*] Rather, "arrayed" (see Ex. xiii. 18 note).

on this side Jordan] Cp. Deut. i. 1, note.

II. **1.** *an harlot's house*] In the face of the parallel passages (*e.g.* Lev. xxi. 7: Jer. v. 7)

And they went, and *b*came into an harlot's house, named *c*Rahab, *b* Heb. 11. 31.
2 and ¹lodged there. ¶ And *d*it was told the king of Jericho, saying, Jam. 2. 25.
Behold, there came men in hither to night of the children of *c* Matt. 1. 5.
3 Israel to search out the country. And the king of Jericho sent Prov. 21. 30.
unto Rahab, saying, Bring forth the men that are come to thee,
which are entered into thine house: for they be come to search
4 out all the country. ¶ *e*And the woman took the two men, and *e* See 2 Sam.
hid them, and said thus, There came men unto me, but I wist 17. 19, 20.
5 not whence they *were*: and it came to pass *about the time* of shut-
ting of the gate, when it was dark, that the men went out:
whither the men went, I wot not: pursue after them quickly;
6 for ye shall overtake them. But *f* she had brought them up to *f* See Ex. 1.
the roof of the house, and hid them with the stalks of flax, 17.
7 which she had laid in order upon the roof. And the men pur- 2 Sam. 17.
sued after them the way to Jordan unto the fords: and as soon 19.
as they which pursued after them were gone out, they shut the
8 gate. ¶ And before they were laid down, she came up unto
9 them upon the roof; and she said unto the men, I know that
the LORD hath given you the land, and that *g*your terror is fallen *g* Gen. 35. 5.
upon us, and that all the inhabitants of the land ²faint because Ex. 23. 27.
10 of you. For we have heard how the LORD *h*dried up the water & 11. 25.
of the Red sea for you, when ye came out of Egypt; and *i*what *h* Ex. 14. 21.
ye did unto the two kings of the Amorites, that *were* on the other ch. 4. 23.
11 side Jordan, Sihon and Og, whom ye utterly destroyed. And 24, 34, 35.
as soon as we had *k*heard *these things*, *l*our hearts did melt, 15.
neither ³did there remain any more courage in any man, because *l* ch. 5. 1.
& 7. 5.

¹ Heb. *lay.*   ² Heb. *melt*, Ex. 15. 15.   ³ Heb. *rose up.*   Isai. 13. 7.

the rendering advocated for obvious reasons *viz.* "the house of a woman, an innkeeper," cannot be maintained. Rahab must remain an example under the Law similar to that (Luke vii. 37) under the Gospel, of "a woman that was a sinner," yet, because of her faith, not only pardoned, but exalted to the highest honour. Rahab was admitted among the people of God; she inter-married into a chief family of a chief tribe, and found a place amongst the best remem-bered ancestors of King David and of Christ; thus receiving the temporal bless-ings of the Covenant in largest measure. The spies would of course betake them-selves to such a house in Jericho as they could visit without exciting suspicion; and the situation of Rahab's, upon the wall (*v.* 15), rendered it especially suitable. It appears from *v.* 4 that Rahab hid them before the King's messengers reached her house, and probably as soon as the spies had come to her house. It is therefore most likely that they met with Rahab out-side of Jericho (cp. Gen. xxxviii. 14), ascertained where in the city she dwelt, and that they might intrust themselves to her care. Rahab (*i.e.* "spacious," "wide." Cp. the name "Japheth" and Gen. ix. 27, note) is regarded by the Fathers as a type of the Christian Church, which was gathered out of converts from the whole vast circle of heathen nations.

4. *I wist not whence they were*] Rahab

acted as she did from a belief in God's de-clared word, and a conviction that resist-ance to His will would be both vain and wicked (*vv.* 9–11). Thus she manifested a faith both sound and practical, and is praised accordingly (Heb. xi. 31; James ii. 25). The falsehood to which she had recourse may be excused by the pressure of circumstances and by her own antecedents, but cannot be defended.

6. *stalks of flax*] Lit. "the carded fibres of the tree." The flax in Palestine grew to more than three feet in height, with a stalk as thick as a cane. It was probably with the flax stalks, recently cut (cp. Ex. ix. 31, note) and laid out on the house roof to dry, that Rahab hid the spies.

7. The sense is, that "they pursued along the way which leads to Jordan and across the fords;" probably those described in Judg. iii. 28.

11. *the LORD your God, he is God*] From the rumour of God's miraculous interpo-sitions Rahab believed, and makes the self-same confession to which Moses endeavours to bring Israel by rehearsing similar argu-ments (Deut. iv. 39). Rahab had only heard of what Israel had experienced. Her faith then was ready. It is noteworthy, too, that the same reports which work faith and con-version in the harlot, cause only terror and astonishment amongst her countrymen. (Cp. St. Luke viii. 37–39.)

n Deut. 4. 39.
n See 1 Sam.
20. 14, 15, 17.

o See 1 Tim.
5. 8.
p ver. 18.

q Judg. 1. 24.
Matt. 5. 7.
r Acts 9. 25.

s Ex. 20. 7.
t ver. 12.

u ch. 6. 23.

x Matt. 27.
25.

y Ex. 23. 31.
ch. 6. 2.
& 21. 44.

of you: for [m]the LORD your God, he *is* God in heaven above, 12 and in earth beneath. Now therefore, I pray you, [n]swear unto me by the LORD, since I have shewed you kindness, that ye will also shew kindness unto [o]my father's house, and [p]give me a true 13 token: and *that* ye will save alive my father, and my mother, and my brethren, and my sisters, and all that they have, and 14 deliver our lives from death. ¶ And the men answered her, Our life [1]for your's, if ye utter not this our business. And it shall be, when the LORD hath given us the land, that [q]we will deal 15 kindly and truly with thee. Then she [r]let them down by a cord through the window: for her house *was* upon the town wall, 16 and she dwelt upon the wall. And she said unto them, Get you to the mountain, lest the pursuers meet you; and hide yourselves there three days, until the pursuers be returned: and afterward 17 may ye go your way. ¶ And the men said unto her, We *will be* 18 [s]blameless of this thine oath which thou hast made us swear. [t]Behold, *when* we come into the land, thou shalt bind this line of scarlet thread in the window which thou didst let us down by: [u]and thou shalt [2]bring thy father, and thy mother, and thy 19 brethren, and all thy father's household, home unto thee. And it shall be, *that* whosoever shall go out of the doors of thy house into the street, his blood *shall be* upon his head, and we *will be* guiltless: and whosoever shall be with thee in the house, [x]his 20 blood *shall be* on our head, if *any* hand be upon him. And if thou utter this our business, then we will be quit of thine oath which 21 thou hast made us to swear. And she said, According unto your words, so *be* it. And she sent them away, and they de- 22 parted: and she bound the scarlet line in the window. And they went, and came unto the mountain, and abode there three days, until the pursuers were returned: and the pursuers sought 23 *them* throughout all the way, but found *them* not. So the two men returned, and descended from the mountain, and passed over, and came to Joshua the son of Nun, and told him all 24 *things* that befell them: and they said unto Joshua, Truly [y]the

[1] Heb. *instead of you to die.*　　　　　[2] Heb. *gather.*

---

12. *a true token*] Lit. "a sign" or "pledge of truth;" something to bind them to keep their promise faithfully. The "token" was the oath which the spies take (*v.* 14).

14. *Our life for yours*] See marg. This is (see *v.* 17) a form of oath, in which God is in effect invoked to punish them with death if they did not perform their promise to save Rahab's life. Cp. the more common form of oath, 1 Sam. i. 26, &c.

15. *upon the town wall*] The town wall probably formed the back wall of the house, and the window opened therefore into the country. (Cp. St. Paul's escape, 2 Cor. xi. 33).

18. The "line" or cord was spun of threads dyed with cochineal; *i.e.*, of a deep and bright scarlet colour. The colour would catch the eye at once, and supplied an obvious token by which the house of Rahab might be distinguished. The use of scarlet in the Levitical rites, especially in those

more closely connected with the idea of putting away of sin and its consequences (cp. *e.g.*, Lev. xiv. 4, 6, 51; Num. xix. 6), naturally led the Fathers, from St. Clement of Rome onwards, to see in this scarlet thread, no less than in the blood of the Passover (Ex. xii. 7, 13, &c.), an emblem of salvation by the Blood of Christ; a salvation common alike to Christ's messengers and to those whom they visit.

22. *unto the mountain*] Probably the mountains to the west and north of Jericho, called afterwards, from the belief that the forty days of our Lord's temptation were passed amongst them, the Quarantania. The spies avoided at the first the neighbourhood of the Jordan, where the pursuers sought them: and amidst the grottoes of the limestone rocks, which in later ages were the abode of numerous hermits, they could readily shelter themselves for three days.

LORD hath delivered into our hands all the land; for even all the inhabitants of the country do [1]faint because of us.
CHAP. **3.** AND Joshua rose early in the morning; and they re- *a* ch. 2. 1.
moved "from Shittim, and came to Jordan, he and all the children of Israel, and lodged there before they passed over.
2 And it came to pass *b*after three days, that the officers went *b* ch. 1. 10,
3 through the host; and they commanded the people, saying, 11.
*c*When ye see the ark of the covenant of the LORD your God, *c* See Num.
*d*and the priests the Levites bearing it, then ye shall remove from 10. 33.
d Deut. 31.
4 your place, and go after it. *e*Yet there shall be a space between 9, 25.
you and it, about two thousand cubits by measure : come not *e* Ex. 19. 12.
near unto it, that ye may know the way by which ye must go : *f* Ex. 19. 10.
5 for ye have not passed *this* way [2]heretofore. And Joshua said Num. 11. 18.
unto the people, *j*Sanctify yourselves : for to morrow the LORD ch. 7. 13.
1 Sam. 16. 5.
6 will do wonders among you. And Joshua spake unto the priests, Joel 2. 16.
saying, *g*Take up the ark of the covenant, and pass over before *g* Num. 4. 15.
the people. And they took up the ark of the covenant, and
7 went before the people. ¶And the LORD said unto Joshua, This
day will I begin to *h*magnify thee in the sight of all Israel, that *h* 1 Chr. 29.
they may know that, *i*as I was with Moses, *so* I will be with 25.
2 Chr. 1. 1.
8 thee. And thou shalt command *k*the priests that bear the ark of *i* ch. 1. 5.
the covenant, saying, When ye are come to the brink of the *k* ver. 3.
9 water of Jordan, *l*ye shall stand still in Jordan. And Joshua *l* ver. 17.
said unto the children of Israel, Come hither, and hear the words
10 of the LORD your God. And Joshua said, Hereby ye shall know *m* Deut. 5. 26.
that *m*the living God *is* among you, and *that* he will without fail 2 Kin. 19. 4.
*n*drive out from before you the Canaanites, and the Hittites, and Hos. 1. 10.
Matt. 16. 16.
the Hivites, and the Perizzites, and the Girgashites, and the 1 Thess. 1. 9.
11 Amorites, and the Jebusites. Behold, the ark of the covenant *n* Ex. 33. 2.
of *o*the Lord of all the earth passeth over before you into Jordan. Deut. 7. 1.
Ps. 44. 2.
12 Now therefore *p*take you twelve men out of the tribes of Israel, *o* ver. 13.
13 out of every tribe a man. And it shall come to pass, *q*as soon as Mic. 4. 13.
Zech. 4. 14.
p ch. 4. 2.
[1] Heb. *melt*, ver. 9.   [2] Heb. *since yesterday, and the third day.* *q* ver. 15, 16.

III. The contents of this and the next chapter, which record the miraculous passage of Israel over Jordan, are given in four sections :—(1) iii. 1–6, describing the preliminary directions ; (2) iii. 7–17, the commencement of the passage ; (3) iv. 1–14, the accomplishment of it ; (4) iv. 15–24, the conclusion of the passage and erection of a monument to commemorate it. A certain completeness and finish is given to each division of the narrative, and to effect this the writer more than once repeats himself, anticipates the actual order of events, and distributes into parts occurrences which in fact took place once for all.

1. "The acacia groves" (Ex. xxv. 5 note) of Shittim on both sides of Jordan line the upper terraces of the valley (cp. 2 K. vi. 4). They would be in this part at some six miles distance from the river itself.

2. These days (i. 11 note) were no doubt occupied in preparations of various kinds. The host consisted not of armed men only, but of women and children also ; and many arrangements would be necessary before they actually advanced into a hostile country.

4. The ark, which was since the making of the Covenant the special shrine and seat of God's Presence, went before to show the people that God, through its medium, was their leader. They were to follow at a distance that they might the better observe and mark how the miracle was accomplished. This they would do to the greatest advantage whilst coming down the heights, the ark going on before them into the ravine.

6. *they took up*] *i.e.* on the day following. The course of events is anticipated.

7. *This day will I begin to magnify thee*] One cause why the miracle now to be narrated was wrought is here suggested. As Moses was declared to be sent immediately from God with an extraordinary commission by the miracles which he worked, more especially that of dividing the Red Sea in two parts, so was Joshua both sent and accredited in a like manner. (Cp. i. 5, and iv. 14.) Other reasons are given in *v.* 10 and v. 1.

10. *the living God*] Cp. marg. ref. The gods of the heathen are "dead idols." On the names of the seven nations, see Gen. x. 16, &c., note.

the soles of the feet of the priests that bear the ark of the LORD,
 r the Lord of all the earth, shall rest in the waters of Jordan,
that the waters of Jordan shall be cut off *from* the waters that
come down from above; and they *s* shall stand upon an heap.
14 ¶And it came to pass, when the people removed from their tents,
to pass over Jordan, and the priests bearing the *t* ark of the
15 covenant before the people; and as they that bare the ark were
come unto Jordan, and *u* the feet of the priests that bare the ark
were dipped in the brim of the water, (for *x* Jordan overfloweth
16 all his banks *y* all the time of harvest,) that the waters which
came down from above stood *and* rose up upon an heap very far
from the city Adam, that *is* beside *z* Zaretan: and those that
came down *a* toward the sea of the plain, *even* *b* the salt sea,
failed, *and* were cut off: and the people passed over right
17 against Jericho. And the priests that bare the ark of the covenant of the LORD stood firm on dry ground in the midst of
Jordan, *c* and all the Israelites passed over on dry ground,
until all the people were passed clean over Jordan.

CHAP. 4. AND it came to pass, when all the people were clean
passed *a* over Jordan, that the LORD spake unto Joshua, saying,
2 *b* Take you twelve men out of the people, out of every tribe a
3 man, and command ye them, saying, Take you hence out of the
midst of Jordan, out of the place where *c* the priests' feet stood
firm, twelve stones, and ye shall carry them over with you, and
leave them in *d* the lodging place, where ye shall lodge this

Side notes:
r ver. 11.
s Ps. 78. 13.
t Acts 7. 45.
u ver. 13.
x 1 Chr. 12. 15.
Jer. 12. 5.
y ch. 4. 18.
z 1 Kin. 4. 12. & 7. 46.
a Deut. 3. 17.
b Gen. 14. 3.
Num. 34. 3.
c See Ex. 14. 29.
a Deut. 27. 2.
b ch. 3. 12.
c ch. 3. 13.
d ver. 19, 20.

---

15. *Jordan overfloweth all his banks*] Rather "is full up to all his banks," *i.e.* "brim-full." This remark strikingly illustrates the suddenness and completeness, not less than the greatness, of the marvel. The Jordan flows at the bottom of a deep valley, which descends to the water's edge on either side in two, occasionally in three, terraces. Within the lowest of these the stream, ordinarily less than 100 feet wide in this lower part of its course, is confined. The margin is overgrown with a jungle of tamarisks and willows, which in the spring is reached by the rising waters (cp. the figure in Jer. xlix. 19; l. 44); and the river, occasionally at least, fills the ravine which forms its proper bed to the brim. Its highest rise takes place about the time when Joshua had to cross it. By the middle of April the river cannot be forded; and, if passed at all, can only be so by swimming. This, however, was a hazardous feat (cp. 1 Chr. xii. 15); and though no doubt performed by the two spies, was utterly out of the power of the mixed multitude that followed Joshua. The mere fact that the whole vast host crossed the stream of Jordan at this season, is no small proof of the miracle here recorded. No human agency then known and available could have transported them speedily and safely from bank to bank.

16. The passage should run "rose up, an heap far away, by Adam, the city which is beside Zarthan." The city of Adam is not named elsewhere, and Zarthan (mentioned here and in marg.

reff.) has also disappeared. It is, however, probably connected with the modern *Kurn Sartabeh* (Horn of Sartabeh), the name given to a lofty and isolated hill some seventeen miles on the river above Jericho.

17. The miraculous passage to the Holy Land through Jordan is not less pregnant with typical meaning than that through the Red Sea (cp. 1 Cor. x. 1, 2). The solemn inauguration of Joshua to his office, and his miraculous attestation, by the same waters with which Jesus was baptized on entering on the public exercise of His ministry (cp. Matt. iii. 16, 17); the choice of twelve men, one from each tribe to be the bearers of the twelve stones, and the builders of the monument erected therewith (cp. 1 Cor. iii. 10; Rev. xxi. 14):—these were divinely ordered occurrences, not without a further bearing than their more immediate one upon Israel. Nor must in this point of view the name "Adam," the place whence flowed to the people the stream which cut them off from the promises, and the failure for the time under the rule of Joshua of the full and rapid flood which supplies the Dead Sea, be overlooked.

IV. 2. *Take you twelve men*] The order is given in the plural, because no doubt the tribes themselves were to choose their own representatives, the choice being approved by Joshua (*v.* 4). These twelve would be left with Joshua on the hither bank of the river, waiting to receive his orders after the rest of the people had made their way across (iii. 17; iv. 1).

4 night. Then Joshua called the twelve men, whom he had
prepared of the children of Israel, out of every tribe a man:
5 and Joshua said unto them, Pass over before the ark of the
LORD your God into the midst of Jordan, and take you up every
man of you a stone upon his shoulder, according unto the
6 number of the tribes of the children of Israel: that this may be
a sign among you, that *when your children ask *their fathers* [1]in
7 time to come, saying, What *mean* ye by these stones? Then ye
shall answer them, That *the waters of Jordan were cut off before
the ark of the covenant of the LORD; when it passed over Jordan,
the waters of Jordan were cut off: and these stones shall be for
8 *a memorial unto the children of Israel for ever. And the
children of Israel did so as Joshua commanded, and took up
twelve stones out of the midst of Jordan, as the LORD spake
unto Joshua, according to the number of the tribes of the
children of Israel, and carried them over with them unto the
9 place where they lodged, and laid them down there. And
Joshua set up twelve stones in the midst of Jordan, in the place
where the feet of the priests which bare the ark of the covenant
10 stood: and they are there unto this day. ¶For the priests which
bare the ark stood in the midst of Jordan, until every thing was
finished that the LORD commanded Joshua to speak unto the
people, according to all that Moses commanded Joshua: and the
11 people hasted and passed over. And it came to pass, when all
the people were clean passed over, that the ark of the LORD
12 passed over, and the priests, in the presence of the people. And
*the children of Reuben, and the children of Gad, and half
the tribe of Manasseh, passed over armed before the children of
13 Israel, as Moses spake unto them: about forty thousand [2]pre-
pared for war passed over before the LORD unto battle, to the
14 plains of Jericho. ¶On that day the LORD *magnified Joshua in
the sight of all Israel; and they feared him, as they feared
15 Moses, all the days of his life. And the LORD spake unto

e ver. 21.
Ex. 12. 26.
& 13. 14.
Deut. 6. 20.
Ps. 44. 1.
& 78. 3, 4, 5, 6.
f ch. 3. 13, 16.
g Ex. 12. 14.
Num. 16. 40.

h Num. 32.
20, 27, 28.

i ch. 3. 7.

---

[1] Heb. *to morrow.* [2] Or, *ready armed.*

---

8. *laid them down there*] *i.e.* in Gilgal (*v.*
20). Spoken of as the doers of this, because
it was done by the twelve who acted for
them.
9. Another set of stones is intended than
that before mentioned. The one set was
erected by the command of God at the spot
where they passed the night (*v.* 3); the
other by Joshua on the spot where the
priests' feet rested whilst they bore up the
ark during the passage of the people. This
spot was near, or perhaps on, the eastern
brink (cp. iii. 8). These stones would therefore mark the spot at which the people
crossed, as the others marked the place in
which they lodged the night after the
crossing; nor, as the stones would only be
reached by the water in flood time, and then
by the utmost edge of it, is there any reason
why they could not both be seen, and continue in their place as the writer asserts they
did up to the time when he wrote.
13. The plains of Jericho, consisting of
the higher terrace of the Jordan valley, are
almost seven miles broad. The mountains
of Judæa here recede somewhat from the

river, and leave a level and fertile space,
which, at the time of Joshua's invasion,
was principally occupied by a forest of
palms. Hence the name "city of palms,"
Deut. xxxiv. 3.
15. The passage of the priests to the
further bank had been already referred to,
v. 11; but the writer, in observance of his
general plan (cp. introductory remarks to
ch. iii.), re-introduces it here as the leading
feature in the concluding section of his account, and (as before) with mention of
God's special direction about it. The statement that on the removal of the ark the
waters of Jordan at once returned to their
former level (*v.* 18), heightens the impression which is especially inculcated throughout,—that the whole transaction was extraordinary and miraculous. The details and
incidents of the passage are no doubt open
to manifold discussion: but all such discussion will be futile unless it proceed throughout on the admission that we have here before us the record of a distinctly supernatural
interposition: cp. Introd. p. 1.

k Ex. 25. 16,
22.
16 Joshua, saying, Command the priests that bear *k*the ark of the
17 testimony, that they come up out of Jordan. Joshua therefore
commanded the priests, saying, Come ye up out of Jordan.
18 And it came to pass, when the priests that bare the ark of the
covenant of the LORD were come up out of the midst of Jordan,
and the soles of the priests' feet were [1]lifted up unto the dry

l ch. 3. 15.
    land, that the waters of Jordan returned unto their place, *l*and
19 [2]flowed over all his banks, as *they did* before. ¶And the people
came up out of Jordan on the tenth *day* of the first month, and

m ch. 5. 9.
n ver. 3.
20 encamped *m*in Gilgal, in the east border of Jericho. And *n*those
twelve stones, which they took out of Jordan, did Joshua pitch
21 in Gilgal. And he spake unto the children of Israel, saying,

o ver. 6.
    *o*When your children shall ask their fathers [3]in time to come,
22 saying, What *mean* these stones? Then ye shall let your

p ch. 3. 17.
children know, saying, *p*Israel came over this Jordan on dry
23 land. For the LORD your God dried up the waters of Jordan
from before you, until ye were passed over, as the LORD your

q Ex. 14. 21.
r 1 Kin. 8.
42, 43.
Ps. 106. 8.
s Ex. 15. 16.
1 Chr. 29. 12.
Ps. 89. 13.
t Ex. 14. 31.
Deut. 6. 2.
Jer. 10. 7.
God did to the Red sea, *q*which he dried up from before us,
24 until we were gone over: *r*that all the people of the earth might
know the hand of the LORD, that it *is* *s*mighty: that ye might
*t*fear the LORD your God [4]for ever.

CHAP. 5. AND it came to pass, when all the kings of the Amorites,
which *were* on the side of the Jordan westward, and all the kings of

a Num. 13.
29.
b Ex. 15. 14.
ch. 2. 9, 10.
Ps. 48. 6.
Ezek. 21, 7.
c 1 Kin. 10. 5.
d Ex. 4. 25.
the Canaanites, *a*which *were* by the sea, *b*heard that the LORD
had dried up the waters of Jordan from before the children of
Israel, until we were passed over, that their heart melted,
*c*neither was there spirit in them any more, because of the
2 children of Israel. ¶At that time the LORD said unto Joshua,
Make thee [5]*d*sharp knives, and circumcise again the children of
3 Israel the second time. And Joshua made him sharp knives,

---

[1] Heb. *plucked up.*   [3] Heb. *to morrow.*   [5] Or, *knives of flints.*
[2] Heb. *went.*   [4] Heb. *all days.*

---

19. Gilgal, mentioned here by anticipation (cp. v. 9), [the modern Jiljûlieh (Conder)], was on rising ground (cp. v. 3), and,
according to Josephus, nearly five miles from
the river, and consequently about two from
the city itself. The site of the camp was
no doubt fortified by Joshua, as it constituted for some time the abiding foothold in
Canaan, whence he sallied forth to subdue
the country. It was also the place of safety
where the ark, and no doubt also the
women, children, cattle, and other property
of the people were left. Hence the demo-
lition of Jericho and Ai, strong fortresses
in the neighbourhood of Gilgal, was no
doubt dictated by sound policy as well as by
religious obligations.

V. 1. The Amorites were the principal
of those nations which occupied the hill
country of Judæa (Gen. x. 16 note); the
Canaanites of those that dwelt on the coast
and low lands. These words are therefore
equivalent to "all the kings of the high-
landers, and all the kings of the low-
landers": *i.e.* the kings of all the tribes of
the country.

until we were passed over] The use of the
first person has been noted here, and in

verse 6 (cp. Acts xvi. 10), as suggesting the
hand of one who himself shared in what
he describes. But the text as read (though
not written) by the Jewish authorities here,
has the third person; as have some MSS.,
LXX., Vulg., &c.: and a change of person
like this in Hebrew, even if the text stand,
does not of itself warrant the inference.
(Cp. Ps. lxvi. 6.)

2. *Make thee sharp knives*] Render rather
as marg., and cp. marg. ref. and note.
Knives of flint or stone were in fact used
for circumcision, and retained for that and
other sacred purposes, even after iron had
become in common use. The rendering of
marg. is adopted by almost all ancient versions, by most commentators, and by the
Fathers generally, who naturally regarded
circumcision wrought by Joshua and by
means of knives of stone or rock, as symbolical of the true circumcision wrought by
Christ, Who is more than once spoken of as
the Rock (cp. 1 Cor. x. 4; Rom. ii. 29; Col.
ii. 11). See xxi. 42.

circumcise again, &c.] *i.e.* make that
which once was a circumcised people but is
not so now, once more a circumcised people.
(See *vv.* 4–7.)

and circumcised the children of Israel at [1]the hill of the fore-
4 skins. And this is the cause why Joshua did circumcise: *All
the people that came out of Egypt, *that were* males, *even* all the
men of war, died in the wilderness by the way, after they came
5 out of Egypt. Now all the people that came out were circumcised : but all the people *that were* born in the wilderness by the
way as they came forth out of Egypt, *them* they had not cir-
6 cumcised. For the children of Israel walked [f]forty years in the
wilderness, till all the people *that were* men of war, which came
out of Egypt, were consumed, because they obeyed not the voice
of the LORD : unto whom the LORD sware that [g]he would not
shew them the land, which the LORD sware unto their fathers
that he would give us, [h]a land that floweth with milk and honey.
7 And [i]their children, *whom* he raised up in their stead, them
Joshua circumcised: for they were uncircumcised, because they
8 had not circumcised them by the way. And it came to pass,
[2]when they had done circumcising all the people, that they

e Num. 14.
29.
& 26. 64, 65.
Deut. 2. 16.

f Num. 14.
33.
Deut. 1. 3. &
2. 7, 14.
Ps. 95. 10.
g Num.14.23.
Ps. 95. 11.
Heb. 3. 11.
h Ex. 3. 8.
i Num.14.31.
Deut. 1. 39.

[1] Or, *Gibeah-haaraloth.*   [2] Heb. *when the people had made
an end to be circumcised.*

---

3. *the hill of the foreskins*] *i.e.* the hill
where the foreskins, the emblem of all
worldly and carnal affections, were buried.
(Cp. Col. ii. 11-13 ; iii. 1-6.)
4-7. Of the whole nation those only were
already circumcised at the time of the passage of the Jordan who had been under
twenty years of age at the time of the murmuring and consequent rejection at Kadesh
(cp. marg. ref.). These would have been
circumcised before they left Egypt, and
there would still survive of them more than
a quarter of a million of thirty-eight years
old and upwards.
    The statements of these verses are of a
general kind. The "forty years" of *v.* 6 is
a round number, and the statement in the
latter part of *v.* 5 cannot be strictly accurate. For there must have been male children born in the wilderness during the first
year after the Exodus, and these must have
been circumcised before the celebration of
the Passover at Sinai in the first month of
the second year (cp. Num. ix. 1-5, and Ex. xii.
48). The statements of the verses are, however, sufficiently close to the facts for the
purpose in hand ; namely, to render a reason for the general circumcising which is
here recorded.
    The reason why circumcision was omitted
in the wilderness, was that the sentence of
Num. xiv. 28 seq. placed the whole nation
for the time under a ban ; and that the dis-
continuance of circumcision, and the consequent omission of the Passover, was a
consequence and a token of that ban. The
rejection was not, indeed, total, for the
children of the murmurers were to enter
into the rest ; nor final, for when the children had borne the punishment of the
fathers' sins for the appointed years, and
the murmurers were dead, then it was to be
removed, as now by Joshua. But for the
time the Covenant was abrogated, though

God's purpose to restore it was from the
first made known, and confirmed by the
visible marks of His favour which He still
vouchsafed to bestow during the wandering.
    The years of rejection were indeed ex-
hausted before the death of Moses (cp. Deut.
ii. 14) : but God would not call upon the
people to renew their engagement to Him
until He had first given them glorious
proof of His will and power to fulfil His
engagements to them. So He gave them
the first fruits of the promised inheritance—
the kingdoms of Sihon and Og ; and through
a miracle planted their feet on the very soil
that still remained to be conquered ; and
then recalled them to His Covenant. It is
to be noted, too, that they were just about
to go to war against foes mightier than
themselves. Their only hope of success
lay in the help of God. At such a crisis
the need of full communion with God would
be felt indeed ; and the blessing and strength
of it are accordingly granted.
    The revival of the two great ordinances
—circumcision and the Passover—after so
long an intermission could not but awaken
the zeal and invigorate the faith and
fortitude of the people. Both as seals and
as means of grace and God's good purpose
towards them then, the general circumcision of the people, followed up by the
solemn celebration of the Passover—the one
formally restoring the Covenant and reconciling them nationally to God, the other
ratifying and confirming all that circumcision intended—were at this juncture most
opportune.
    8. The circumcision must have taken
place on the day after the passage of Jordan, *i.e.* the 11th Nisan, and the Passover
was kept on the 14th of the same month.
For so long at least, they who had been
circumcised would be disabled from war (cp.
marg. ref.), though they would not neces-

k See Gen.
34. 25.
l Gen. 34. 14.
Ezek. 20. 7.
& 23. 3, 8.
m ch. 4. 19.
n Ex. 12. 6.
Num. 9. 5.

¹ Ex. 16. 35.

p Gen. 18. 2.
& 32. 24.
Ex. 23. 23.
Zech. 1. 8.
Acts. 1. 10.
q Num. 22.
23.
r Gen. 17. 3.
s Ex. 3. 5.
Acts 7. 33.

9 abode in their places in the camp, *k* till they were whole. And the LORD said unto Joshua, This day have I rolled away *l* the reproach of Egypt from off you. Wherefore the name of the
10 place is called ¹*m* Gilgal unto this day. ¶ And the children of Israel encamped in Gilgal, and kept the passover *n* on the four-
11 teenth day of the month at even in the plains of Jericho. And they did eat of the old corn of the land on the morrow after the pass-over, unleavened cakes, and parched *corn* in the selfsame day.
12 And *o* the manna ceased on the morrow after they had eaten of the old corn of the land; neither had the children of Israel manna any more; but they did eat of the fruit of the land of
13 Canaan that year. ¶ And it came to pass, when Joshua was by Jericho, that he lifted up his eyes and looked, and, behold, there stood *p* a man over against him *q* with his sword drawn in his hand: and Joshua went unto him, and said unto him, *Art* thou
14 for us, or for our adversaries? And he said, Nay; but *as* ²captain of the host of the LORD am I now come. And Joshua
15 *r* fell on his face to the earth, and did worship, and said unto him, What saith my lord unto his servant? And the captain of the LORD's host said unto Joshua, *s* Loose thy shoe from off thy foot; for the place whereon thou standest *is* holy. And Joshua

CHAP. 6. did so. (NOW Jericho ³ was straitly shut up because of
2 the children of Israel: none went out, and none came in.) And

---

¹ That is, *Rolling.*
² Or, *prince.* See Exod. 23. 20. Dan. 10. 13, 21.
& 12. 1. Rev. 12. 7. & 19. 11, 14.
³ Heb. *did shut up, and was shut up.*

---

sarily be debarred from keeping the feast. The submission of the people to the rite was a proof of faith, even though we remember that the panic of the Canaanites (*v.* 1) would render any immediate attack from them unlikely, and that there must have been a large number of "men of war" who would not need to be circumcised at all (see note on *v.* 4).

9. *the reproach of Egypt*] *i.e.* "reproach proceeding from Egypt." The expression probably refers to taunts actually uttered by the Egyptians against Israel, because of their long wanderings in the desert and failures to acquire a settlement in Canaan (cp. Ex. xxxii. 12; Num. xiv. 13-16; Deut. ix. 28 and xxxii. 27). These reproaches were now to end; for they had actually entered Canaan, and the restoration of the Covenant was a pledge from God to accomplish what was begun for them.

11. *old corn of the land*] Rather "**pro-duce of the land,**" the new corn just coming in at the time of the Passover. (So in *v.* 12.)

on the morrow after the passover] These words denote in Num. xxxiii. 3 the 15th Nisan, but must here apparently mean the 16th. For the Israelites could not lawfully eat of the new corn until the first fruits of it had been presented, and this was done on "the morrow after the Sabbath," *i.e.* the morrow after the first day of unleavened bread, which was to be observed as a Sab-bath, and is therefore so called. (Cp. Lev. xxiii. 7, 11, 14.)

The term Passover, which is sometimes used for the lamb slain on the evening of the 14th Nisan, sometimes for the paschal meal, sometimes for the whole eight days' festival, here means the first great day of the eight, the Sabbath of the first holy con-vocation.

13. *a man*] See notes on Gen. xii. 7; xviii. 2. The appearance was that of God manifested in the Person of His Word. Hence the command of *v.* 15. That the ap-pearance was not in a vision merely is clear from the fact that Joshua "went unto Him" and addressed Him.

14. *captain of the host of the LORD*] *i.e.* of the angelic host, the host of heaven (cp. 1 K. xxii. 19; 1 Sam. i. 3, &c.). The armed people of Israel are never called "the host of the Lord," though once spoken of in Ex. xii. 41 as "all the hosts of the Lord." The Divine Person intimates that He, the Prince (see marg. reff.) of the Angels, had come to lead Israel in the coming strife, and to over-throw by heavenly might the armies and the strongholds of God's and Israel's enemies. Accordingly, the capture of Jericho and the destruction of the Canaanites generally form a fit type of a grander and more com-plete conquest and excision of the powers of evil which yet waits accomplishment. (Cp. with this verse Matt. xxv. 31; 2 Thess. i. 7, 8.)

VI. 1. This verse is strictly parenthetical. It is inserted to explain the declaration com-menced *v.* 14, and interrupted by Joshua's question and obeisance *v.* 14, 15, but resumed in *v.* 2.

straitly shut up] See marg., *i.e.*, not only shut, but barred and bolted.

the LORD said unto Joshua, See, ^aI have given into thine hand   ^a ch. 2. 9, 24.
Jericho, and the ^bking thereof, *and* the mighty men of valour. ^b Deut. 7. 24.
3 And ye shall compass the city, all *ye* men of war, *and* go round
4 about the city once. Thus shalt thou do six days. And seven
priests shall bear before the ark seven ^ctrumpets of rams' horns: ^c See Judg.
and the seventh day ye shall compass the city seven times, and 7. 16, 22.
5 ^dthe priests shall blow with the trumpets. And it shall come to ^d Num. 10. 8.
pass, that when they make a long *blast* with the ram's horn, *and*
when ye hear the sound of the trumpet, all the people shall
shout with a great shout; and the wall of the city shall fall
down ¹flat, and the people shall ascend up every man straight
6 before him. ¶And Joshua the son of Nun called the priests,
and said unto them, Take up the ark of the covenant, and let
seven priests bear seven trumpets of rams' horns before the ark
7 of the LORD. And he said unto the people, Pass on, and
compass the city, and let him that is armed pass on before the
8 ark of the LORD. ¶And it came to pass, when Joshua had

¹ Heb. *under it.*

3-6. The command of the Lord as to the mode in which the fall of Jericho should be brought about is given in these verses in a condensed form. Further details (see *vv.* 8-10, 16, 17, &c.), were, no doubt, amongst the commands given to Joshua by the Angel.

4. *trumpets of rams' horns*] Render rather here and in verses 5, 6, 8, &c., "**trumpets of jubilee**" (cp. Lev. xxv. 10 note). The instrument is more correctly rendered "cornet" (see Lev. xxv. 9, note).

Various attempts have been made to explain the fall of Jericho by natural causes, as, *e.g.*, by the undermining of the walls, or by an earthquake, or by a sudden assault. But the narrative of this chapter does not afford the slightest warrant for any such explanations; indeed it is totally inconsistent with them. It must be taken as it stands; and so taken it intends, beyond all doubt, to narrate a miracle, or rather a series of miracles.

In the belief that a record is not necessarily unhistorical because it is miraculous, never perhaps was a miracle more needed than that which gave Jericho to Joshua. Its lofty walls and well-fenced gates made it simply impregnable to the Israelites—a nomad people, reared in the desert, destitute alike of the engines of war for assaulting a fortified town, and of skill and experience in the use of them if they had had them. Nothing but a direct interference of the Almighty could in a week's time give a city like Jericho, thoroughly on its guard and prepared (cp. ii. 9 seq. and vi. 1), to besiegers situated as were Joshua and the Israelites.

The fall of Jericho cogently taught the inhabitants of Canaan that the successes of Israel were not mere human triumphs of man against man, and that the God of Israel was not as "the gods of the countries." This lesson some of them at least learnt to their salvation, *e.g.*, Rahab and

the Gibeonites. Further, ensuing close upon the miraculous passage of Jordan, it was impressed on the people, prone ever to be led by the senses, that the same God Who had delivered their fathers out of Egypt and led them through the Red Sea, was with Joshua no less effectually than He had been with Moses.

And the details of the orders given by God to Joshua (*vv.* 3-5) illustrate this last point further. The trumpets employed were not the silver trumpets used for signalling the marshalling of the host and for other warlike purposes (cp. Num. x. 2), but the curved horns employed for ushering in the Jubilee and the Sabbatical Year (LXX., σάλπιγγες ἱεραί: cp. Lev. xxiii. 24 note). The trumpets were borne by priests, and were seven in number; the processions round Jericho were to be made on seven days, and seven times on the seventh day, thus laying a stress on the sacred number seven, which was an emblem more especially of the work of God. The Ark of God also, the seat of His special Presence, was carried round the city. All these particulars were calculated to set forth symbolically, and in a mode sure to arrest the attention of the people, the fact that their triumph was wholly due to the might of the Lord, and to that Covenant which made their cause His.

7. *he said*] The reading in the Hebrew text is "they said." Joshua no doubt issued his orders through the "officers of the people" (cp. i. 10).

him that is armed] *i.e.* the warriors generally, not a division only. "The rereward" (*v.* 9) was merely a detachment, and not a substantial portion of the host; and was told off, perhaps, from the tribe of Dan (cp. marg. ref.) to close the procession and guard the ark from behind. Thus the order would be, (1) the warriors, (2) the seven priests blowing the cornets, (3) the ark, (4) the rear-guard.

spoken unto the people, that the seven priests bearing the seven trumpets of rams' horns passed on before the LORD, and blew with the trumpets: and the ark of the covenant of the LORD
9 followed them. And the armed men went before the priests

e Num. 10. 25.

that blew with the trumpets, *e*and the ¹rereward came after the
10 ark, *the priests* going on, and blowing with the trumpets. And Joshua had commanded the people, saying, Ye shall not shout, nor ²make any noise with your voice, neither shall *any* word proceed out of your mouth, until the day I bid you shout; then
11 shall ye shout. So the ark of the LORD compassed the city, going about *it* once: and they came into the camp, and lodged

f Deut. 31. 25.

12 in the camp. ¶And Joshua rose early in the morning, *f*and the
13 priests took up the ark of the LORD. And seven priests bearing seven trumpets of rams' horns before the ark of the LORD went on continually, and blew with the trumpets: and the armed men went before them; but the rereward came after the ark of the LORD, *the priests* going on, and blowing with the trumpets.
14 And the second day they compassed the city once, and returned
15 into the camp: so they did six days. And it came to pass on the seventh day, that they rose early about the dawning of the day, and compassed the city after the same manner seven times:
16 only on that day they compassed the city seven times. And it came to pass at the seventh time, when the priests blew with the trumpets, Joshua said unto the people, Shout; for the LORD
17 hath given you the city. And the city shall be ³accursed, *even* it, and all that *are* therein, to the LORD: only Rahab the harlot shall live, she and all that *are* with her in the house, because

g ch. 2. 4.
h Deut. 7. 26.
& 13. 17.
ch. 7. 1, 11, 12.
i ch. 7, 25.
1 Kin. 18. 17, 18.
Jonah 1. 12.

18 *g*she hid the messengers that we sent. And ye, *h*in any wise keep *yourselves* from the accursed thing, lest ye make *yourselves* accursed, when ye take of the accursed thing, and make the
19 camp of Israel a curse, *i*and trouble it. But all the silver, and gold, and vessels of brass and iron, *are* ⁴consecrated unto the
20 LORD: they shall come into the treasury of the LORD. ¶So

k ver 5.
Heb. 11. 30.

the people shouted when *the priests* blew with the trumpets: and it came to pass, when the people heard the sound of the trumpet, and the people shouted with a great shout, that *k*the wall fell down ⁵flat, so that the people went up into the city, every man

l Deut. 7. 2.

21 straight before him, and they took the city. And they *l*utterly destroyed all that *was* in the city, both man and woman, young and old, and ox, and sheep, and ass, with the edge of the sword.
22 ¶But Joshua had said unto the two men that had spied out the country, Go into the harlot's house, and bring out thence the

---

¹ Heb. *gathering* host.
² Heb. *make your voice to be heard.*
³ Or, *devoted*, Mic. 4. 13.
⁴ Heb. *holiness.*
⁵ Heb. *under it.*

---

15. *on the seventh day*] Most probably a Sabbath day. The rising early would be necessary to give time for encompassing the city seven times. Jericho appears to have been a city of considerable size and population; and each passage of the large host round it could hardly have taken less than an hour and a half. Thus, with the necessary intervals of rest, the evening would be at hand when Joshua gave the signal to shout (*v.* 16); and the work of slaughter was probably commenced just as the hours of the Sabbath were passed.

17. *accursed*] Better as in marg., "devoted" (Lev. xxvii. 28 note). In other cases the inhabitants only of the towns were slain; their cattle and property became the booty of the victors. But Jericho, as the first Canaanitish city that was captured, was devoted by Israel as first-fruits to God, as a token that Israel received all the land from Him. Every living thing was put to death (Rahab and her household excepted) as a sacrifice to God, and the indestructible goods were (*v.* 19) brought into the treasury of the Sanctuary.

23 woman, and all that she hath, ^mas ye sware unto her. And the
young men that were spies went in, and brought out Rahab,
ⁿand her father, and her mother, and her brethren, and all that
she had; and they brought out all her ¹kindred, and left them
24 without the camp of Israel. And they burnt the city with fire,
and all that *was* therein : ^oonly the silver, and the gold, and the
vessels of brass and of iron, they put into the treasury of the
25 house of the LORD. And Joshua saved Rahab the harlot alive,
and her father's household, and all that she had; and ^pshe
dwelleth in Israel *even* unto this day; because she hid the
26 messengers, which Joshua sent to spy out Jericho. ¶And
Joshua adjured *them* at that time, saying, ^qCursed *be* the man
before the LORD, that riseth up and buildeth this city Jericho :
he shall lay the foundation thereof in his firstborn, and in his
27 youngest *son* shall he set up the gates of it. ¶^rSo the LORD
was with Joshua; and ^shis fame was *noised* throughout all the
country.

CHAP. 7. BUT the children of Israel committed a trespass in the
accursed thing : for ^a²Achan, the son of Carmi, the son of
³Zabdi, the son of Zerah, of the tribe of Judah, took of the
accursed thing : and the anger of the LORD was kindled against

^m ch. 2. 14.
Heb. 11. 31.

ⁿ ch. 2. 13.

^o ver. 19.

^p See Matt.
1. 5.

^q 1 Kin. 16.
34.

^r ch. 1. 5.
^s ch. 9. 1, 3.

^a ch. 22. 20.

---

¹ Heb. *families*.　　　² 1 Chr. 2. 7, *Achar*.　　　³ Or, *Zimri*, 1 Chr. 2. 6.

---

23. The part of the wall adjoining Rahab's
house had not fallen along with the rest.
Rahab and "all that she had," *i.e.*, the
persons belonging to her household, were
brought out and "left without the camp
of Israel." These words—literally "made
to rest outside the camp of Israel"—indicate that being still in their heathenism,
they were separated from the camp of the
Lord. This was only for a time. They
desired, and eventually obtained, admission
to the Covenant of the chosen people of
God (*v.* 25).

25. *even unto this day*] These words are
rightly noted as implying that the narrative
was written not long after the occurrences
which it records.

26. *adjured*] *i.e.* put an oath upon them ;
or, perhaps, actually caused them themselves to take an oath (cp. Matt. xxvi. 63).
The words of the oath have in the original
a rhythmical character which would tend to
keep them on the lips and in the memory of
the people.

buildeth this city] *i.e.* rebuilds the fortifications. Jericho was at once occupied by
the Benjamites (xviii. 21), and the natural
advantages of the situation were such that
it would not be likely to be left long desolate. Joshua speaks in the text as a
warrior. He lays a ban on the re-erection
of those lofty walls which had bidden defiance to God's host, and been by God's
signal interposition overthrown. Hiel, the
Bethelite, reckless of the prophecy recorded
in our text, began and completed the cir-
cumvallation of the city a second time (see
marg. ref.). Hiel did not found a new city
but only fortified an existing one.

he shall lay the foundation thereof in his

first-born] *i.e.*.when he begins this work his
eldest son shall die, when he completes it
his youngest shall die (see 1 K. xvi. 34
note).

This chapter read in the light of the New
Testament has indications of a further import and bearing than such as concerned
Joshua and the Jews. As Joshua, the
leader and captain of the Jewish theocracy,
is a type of Christ, so is Jericho to be
taken (with all Christian expositors) as a
type of the powers opposed to Christ and
His cause. The times which prepare for
the close of God's present dispensation are
signified in the days during which the people
obeyed and waited ; as the number of those
days, seven, the number of perfection, represents that "fullness of time," known only
to God, at which His dispensation will cul-
minate and close. Thus the circumstances
which lead up to the fall of Jericho are an
acted prophecy, as was that fall itself,
which sets forth the overthrow of all that
resists the kingdom of which Christ is the
head ; and particularly the day of judgment, in which that overthrow will be fully
and finally accomplished. St. Paul, in
describing that day, seems to borrow his
imagery from this chapter (see 1 Thess. iv.
16).

VII. 1. *committed a trespass*] (cp. Lev.
v. 15 note), "acted treacherously and committed a breach of faith." This suitably describes the sin of Achan, who had purloined
and hidden away that which had been dedicated to God by the ban (vi. 19).

The "trespass" was the act of one man,
yet is imputed to all Israel, who also
share in the penalty of it (*v.* 5). This is not
to be explained as though all the people

2 the children of Israel. ¶ And Joshua sent men from Jericho to Ai, which *is* beside Beth-aven, on the east side of Beth-el, and spake unto them, saying, Go up and view the country. And 3 the men went up and viewed Ai. And they returned to Joshua, and said unto him, Let not all the people go up; but let [1]about two or three thousand men go up and smite Ai; *and* make not 4 all the people to labour thither; for they *are but* few. So there

b Lev. 26. 17.
Deut. 28. 25.

went up thither of the people about three thousand men : *b*and 5 they fled before the men of Ai. And the men of Ai smote of them about thirty and six men : for they chased them *from* before the gate *even* unto Shebarim, and smote them [2]in the

c ch. 2. 9, 11.
Lev. 26. 36.
Ps. 22. 14.
d Gen. 37. 29,
34.
e 2 Sam. 1. 2.
& 13. 19.
Neh. 9. 1.
Job 2. 12.
f Ex. 5. 22.
2 Kin. 3. 10.

going down : wherefore *c*the hearts of the people melted, and 6 became as water. ¶ And Joshua *d*rent his clothes, and fell to the earth upon his face before the ark of the LORD until the eventide, he and the elders of Israel, and *e*put dust upon their 7 heads. And Joshua said, Alas, O Lord GOD, *f*wherefore hast thou at all brought this people over Jordan, to deliver us into the hand of the Amorites, to destroy us ? would to God we had 8 been content, and dwelt on the other side Jordan ! O Lord, what shall I say, when Israel turneth their [3]backs before their 9 enemies ! For the Canaanites and all the inhabitants of the

g Ps. 83. 4.
h See Ex. 32.
12.
Num. 14. 13.
i ver. 1.

land shall hear *of it*, and shall environ us round, and *g*cut off our name from the earth : and *h*what wilt thou do unto thy 10 great name ? ¶ And the LORD said unto Joshua, Get thee up ; 11 wherefore *i*liest thou thus upon thy face ? *i*Israel hath sinned, and they have also transgressed my covenant which I com-

k ch. 6. 17.
l See Acts 5.
1, 2.

manded them : *k*for they have even taken of the accursed thing, and have also stolen, and *l*dissembled also, and they have put *it*

[1] Heb. *about 2000 men, or about 3000 men.*   [2] Or, *in Morad.*   [3] Heb. *necks.*   [4] Heb. *fallest.*

---

participated in the covetousness which led to Achan's sin (*v.* 21). The nation as a nation was in Covenant with God, and is treated by Him not merely as a number of individuals living together for their own purposes under common institutions, but as a Divinely constituted organic whole. Hence the sin of Achan defiled the other members of the community as well as himself, and robbed the people collectively of holiness before God and acceptableness with Him. Israel had in the person of Achan broken the Covenant (*v.* 11); God therefore would no more drive out the Canaanites before them.

the accursed thing] Rather "in that which had been devoted or dedicated." Achan in diverting any of these devoted things to his own purposes, committed the sin of sacrilege, that of Ananias and Sapphira. (Acts v. 2, 3.)

Achan or *Achar*] (marg. ref.) the *n* and *r* being interchanged, perhaps for the sake of accommodating the name to the noun *achar*, "trouble" (*v.* 25). *Zabdi* is generally identified with the *Zimri* of 1 Chr. ii. 6. *Zerah* was twin brother of Pharez and son of Judah (Gen. xxxviii. 30). In this genealogy, as in others, several generations are omitted, most likely those which intervened between Zerah and Zabdi, and which covered the space between the migration of Jacob's

household to Egypt and the Exodus. (Num., 5, see note).

2. *Ai, Bethel*] See Gen. xii. 8 note. [Modern travellers place the former at Khan Haiy, in the neighbourhood of Deir Diwan.]

3. The total population of Ai was about twelve thousand (viii. 25). It could therefore hardly muster three thousand warriors.

5. *Shebarim*] Rather, perhaps, "the stone quarries." The smallness of the slaughter amongst the Israelites indicates that they fled early, probably without real conflict in battle.

6. On these signs of mourning, cp. marg. reff. and Lev. x. 6 ; Num. xx. 6 ; 1 Sam. iv. 12.

9. *what wilt thou do unto thy great name ?*] *i.e.* "after the Canaanites have cut off our name what will become of Thy Name ?" This bold expostulation, that of one wrestling in sore need with God in prayer, like the similar appeals of Moses in earlier emergencies (cp. marg. reff.), is based upon God's past promises and mercies. What would be said of God by the heathen if now He permitted Israel to be destroyed ?

10. God's answer is given directly, and in terms of reproof. Joshua must not lie helpless before God ; the cause of the calamity was to be discovered.

11. *also stolen, and dissembled also*] The anger of God and the heinousness of Israel's

12 even among their own stuff. ^mTherefore the children of Israel could not stand before their enemies, *but* turned *their* backs before their enemies, because ⁿthey were accursed: neither will I be with you any more, except ye destroy the accursed from
13 among you. Up, ^osanctify the people, and say, ^pSanctify yourselves against to morrow: for thus saith the LORD God of Israel, *There is* an accursed thing in the midst of thee, O Israel: thou canst not stand before thine enemies, until ye take away
14 the accursed thing from among you. In the morning therefore ye shall be brought according to your tribes: and it shall be, *that* the tribe which ^qthe LORD taketh shall come according to the families *thereof;* and the family which the LORD shall take shall come by households; and the household which the LORD shall
15 take shall come man by man. ^rAnd it shall be, *that* he that is taken with the accursed thing shall be burnt with fire, he and all that he hath: because he hath ^stransgressed the covenant of
16 the LORD, and because he ^thath wrought ¹folly in Israel. ¶ So Joshua rose up early in the morning, and brought Israel by
17 their tribes; and the tribe of Judah was taken: and he brought the family of Judah; and he took the family of the Zarhites:
18 and he brought the family of the Zarhites man by man; and Zabdi was taken: and he brought his household man by man;
and Achan, the son of Carmi, the son of Zabdi, the son of Zerah,
19 of the tribe of Judah, ^uwas taken. And Joshua said unto Achan, My son, ^xgive, I pray thee, glory to the LORD God of Israel, ^yand make confession unto him; and ^ztell me now what
20 thou hast done; hide *it* not from me. And Achan answered Joshua, and said, Indeed I have sinned against the LORD God
21 of Israel, and thus and thus have I done: when I saw among the spoils a goodly Babylonish garment, and two hundred

¹ Or, *wickedness.*

Marginal references:
^m See Num. 14. 45. Judg. 2. 14.
ⁿ Deut. 7. 26.
^o Ex. 19. 10.
^p ch. 3. 5.
^q Prov. 16. 33.
^r See 1 Sam. 14. 38, 39.
^s ver. 11.
^t Gen. 34. 7. Judg. 20. 6.
^u 1 Sam. 14. 42.
^x See 1 Sam. 6. 5. Jer. 13. 16. John 9. 24.
^y Num. 5. 6,7. 2 Chr. 30. 22. Ps. 51. 3. Dan. 9. 4.
^z 1 Sam. 14. 43.

sin are marked by the accumulation of clause upon clause. As a climax they had even appropriated to their own use the consecrated property purloined from God.
12. *accursed*] Cp. vi. 17, 18.
14. *the* LORD *taketh*] *i.e.* by lot. The Hebrew word for lot suggests that small stones, probably white and black ones, were used. These were probably drawn from a chest (cp. the expressions in xviii. 11, and xix. 1). The lot was regarded as directed in its result by God (marg. ref.); and hence was used on many important occasions by the Jews and by other nations in ancient times. *E.g.* (1.), for apportionment, as of Canaan among the Twelve Tribes (Num. xxvi. 55) ; of the Levitical cities (Josh. xxi. 4 seq.) ; of spoil or captives taken in war (Joel iii. 3). (2.) For detection of the guilty, as in the case of Achan, Jonathan (1 Sam. xiv. 42), and Jonah (Jon. i. 7). (3.) For determining the persons to undertake a dangerous or warlike enterprise (Judg. xx. 10). (4.) For making appointment to important functions (Lev. xvi. 8 seq. ; Acts i. 26); or for sharing the duties or privileges of an office amongst those concerned (1 Chr. xxiv. 31 ; Luke i. 9). The casting of lots before Haman (Esth. iii. 7) seems to have been with a view of de-

termining the lucky day for his undertaking against the Jews. One passage (Prov. xviii. 18) perhaps points also to the employment of the lot to decide litigation.
15. *burnt with fire*] *i.e.* after he had been put to death by stoning (*v.* 25; Lev. xx. 14).
19. *give glory to the* LORD] A form of solemn adjuration by which the person addressed was called upon before God to declare the truth. The phrase assumes that the glory of God is always promoted by manifestation of the truth (cp. marg. reff.).
21. *a goodly Babylonish garment*] Literally "a robe or cloak of Shinar," the plain in which Babylon was situated (Gen. x. 10). It was a long robe such as was worn by kings on state occasions (Jonah iii. 6), and by prophets (1 K. xix. 13 ; Zech. xiii. 4). The Assyrians were in early times famous for the manufacture of beautiful dyed and richly embroidered robes (cp. Ezek. xxiii. 15). That such a robe should be found in a Canaanitish city is natural enough. The productions of the far East found their way through Palestine both southward towards Egypt and westward through Tyre to the countries bordering on the Mediterranean. (Cp. Ezek. xxvii. 24 and the context.)

shekels of silver, and a ¹wedge of gold of fifty shekels weight,
then I coveted them, and took them; and, behold, they *are* hid
in the earth in the midst of my tent, and the silver under it.
22 So Joshua sent messengers, and they ran unto the tent; and,
23 behold, *it was* hid in his tent, and the silver under it. And they
took them out of the midst of the tent, and brought them unto
Joshua, and unto all the children of Israel, and ²laid them out
24 before the LORD. And Joshua, and all Israel with him, took
Achan the son of Zerah, and the silver, and the garment, and
the wedge of gold, and his sons, and his daughters, and his oxen,
and his asses, and his sheep, and his tent, and all that he had:
25 and they brought them unto ᵃthe valley of Achor. And Joshua
said, ᵇWhy hast thou troubled us? the LORD shall trouble thee
this day. ᶜAnd all Israel stoned him with stones, and burned
26 them with fire, after they had stoned them with stones. And
they ᵈraised over him a great heap of stones unto this day. So
ᵉthe LORD turned from the fierceness of his anger. Wherefore
the name of that place was called, ᶠThe valley of ³Achor, unto
this day.

CHAP. 8. AND the LORD said unto Joshua, ᵃFear not, neither be
thou dismayed: take all the people of war with thee, and arise,
go up to Ai: see, ᵇI have given into thy hand the king of Ai,
2 and his people, and his city, and his land: and thou shalt do to
Ai and her king as thou didst unto ᶜJericho and her king: only
ᵈthe spoil thereof, and the cattle thereof, shall ye take for a
prey unto yourselves: lay thee an ambush for the city behind it.
3 ¶So Joshua arose, and all the people of war, to go up against
Ai: and Joshua chose out thirty thousand mighty men of
4 valour, and sent them away by night. And he commanded them,

Margin: *a* ver. 26. ch. 15. 7. *b* ch. 6. 18. 1 Chr. 2. 7. Gal. 5. 12. *c* Deut. 17. 5. *d* Lam. 3. 53. *e* Deut. 13. 17. 2 Sam. 21. 14. *f* ver. 24. Isai. 65. 10. Hos. 2. 15. *a* Deut. 1. 21. & 7. 18. & 31. 8. ch. 1. 9. *b* ch. 6. 2. *c* ch. 6. 21. *d* Deut. 20. 14.

¹ Heb. *tongue.*   ² Heb. *poured.*   ³ That is, *Trouble.*

wedge of gold] *i.e.* some implement or ornament of gold shaped like a wedge or tongue. The name *lingula* was given by the Romans to a spoon and to an oblong dagger made in shape of a tongue. The weight of this "wedge" was fifty shekels, *i.e.* about twenty-five ounces (see Ex. xxxviii. 24 note). The silver was under the rest of the stolen property. The mantle would naturally be placed uppermost, and be used to cover up the others.

24. The sin had been national (*v.* 1 note), and accordingly the expiation of it was no less so. The whole nation, no doubt through its usual representatives, took part in executing the sentence. Achan had fallen by his own act under the ban (vi. 18), and consequently he and his were treated as were communities thus devoted (Deut. xiii. 15–17). It would appear too that Achan's family must have been accomplices in his sin; for the stolen spoil could hardly have been concealed in his tent without their being privy thereto.

26. *a great heap of stones*] As a memorial of Achan's sin and its punishment. (Cp. viii. 29 ; 2 Sam. xviii. 17.)

the valley of Achor] Cp. marg. reff. This valley formed part of the northern border of Judah (xv. 7); and must therefore have

lain amongst the ridges which cross the plain to the south of Jericho. But its exact site is uncertain. [Conder identifies it with Wady Kelt.]

VIII. **1.** God rouses Joshua from his dejection (vii. 6), and bids him march against Ai with the main body. Though Ai was but a small city (cp. *v.* 25 and vii. 3), yet the discouragement of the people rendered it inexpedient to send a second time a mere detachment against it; and the people of Ai had, as appears from *v.* 17, help from Bethel, and possibly from other places also. It was fitting too that all the people should witness with their own eyes the happy consequences of having faithfully put away the sin which had separated them from God.

3. *thirty thousand men*] Comparing *vv.* 3 and 12 ("five thousand men"), there is probably a mistake in the numbers of this verse, where an early copyist may have written the sign for 30,000 instead of that for 5,000.

sent them away by night] The selected 5,000 would accordingly post themselves in the main ravine between Ai and Bethel in the night and early morning. The neighbourhood in which Ai was situated is described as "a wild entanglement of hill and

saying, Behold, [e]ye shall lie in wait against the city, *even* behind   *e* Judg. 20.29.
5 the city: go not very far from the city, but be ye all ready: and
I, and all the people that *are* with me, will approach unto the
city: and it shall come to pass, when they come out against us,
6 as at the first, that [f]we will flee before them, (for they will come   *f* Judg .20.32.
out after us) till we have [1]drawn them from the city; for they
will say, They flee before us, as at the first: therefore we will flee
7 before them. Then ye shall rise up from the ambush, and seize
upon the city: for the LORD your God will deliver it into your
8 hand. And it shall be, when ye have taken the city, *that* ye shall
set the city on fire: according to the commandment of the LORD
9 shall ye do. [g]See, I have commanded you. Joshua therefore   *g* 2 Sam. 13. 28.
sent them forth: and they went to lie in ambush, and abode
between Beth-el and Ai, on the west side of Ai: but Joshua
10 lodged that night among the people. ¶ And Joshua rose up
early in the morning, and numbered the people, and went up,
11 he and the elders of Israel, before the people to Ai. [h]And all   *h* ver. 5.
the people, *even the people* of war that *were* with him, went up,
and drew nigh, and came before the city, and pitched on the
north side of Ai: now *there was* a valley between them and Ai.
12 And he took about five thousand men, and set them to lie in
ambush between Beth-el and Ai, on the west side [2]of the city.
13 And when they had set the people, *even* all the host that *was* on
the north of the city, and [3]their liers in wait on the west of
the city, Joshua went that night into the midst of the valley.
14 ¶ And it came to pass, when the king of Ai saw *it*, that they
hasted and rose up early, and the men of the city went out
against Israel to battle, he and all his people, at a time ap-
pointed, before the plain; but he [i]wist not that *there were* liers   *i* Jugd.20.34.
15 in ambush against him behind the city. And Joshua and all   Eccles. 9. 12.
Israel [k]made as if they were beaten before them, and fled by the   *k* Judg. 20.
16 way of the wilderness. And all the people that *were* in Ai were   36, &c.
called together to pursue after them: and they pursued after
17 Joshua, and were drawn away from the city. And there was
not a man left in Ai or Beth-el, that went not out after Israel:
18 and they left the city open, and pursued after Israel. And
the LORD said unto Joshua, Stretch out the spear that *is* in
thy hand toward Ai; for I will give it into thine hand. And

[1] Heb. *pulled.*   [2] Or, *of Ai.*   [3] Heb. *their lying in wait*, ver. 4.

---

valley;" and amidst its recesses the detachment could easily shelter itself from
observation until Joshua's other measures
were taken.

10. *numbered the people*] Rather, perhaps,
"mustered" or "arrayed" them for their
march. The distance from the camp at
Gilgal to Ai is about fifteen miles. In the
evening of the day after the despatch of the
5,000 liers in wait, Joshua and the host
might make their appearance in the neighbourhood of the city.

12. *he took*] Rather "had taken;" the
words refer to the ambuscade which Joshua
had detached during the previous night.

13. Joshua went down by night into the
valley where he would be seen at daylight
by the men of Ai, and was accompanied
no doubt by a picked body of troops. The
king of Ai, in the morning, would see

neither the ambush in his rear, nor the
whole of the great host of Israel amongst
the hills away to the north on his left; but
supposing, as it appears, that the Israelites
before him were a body detached as on the
former occasion to assail his city, he sallied
out promptly to attack them.

14. *at a time appointed*] Rather, "at the
place appointed," *i.e.* some spot suitable for
the drawing up of his men, which had been
assigned beforehand. This was "before the
plain," *i.e.* it was at the entrance of the
depressed tract of land which runs down to
the Jordan valley, up which lay the route
of the Israelites from Gilgal to Ai.

17. *or Bethel*] See *v.* 1 note.

18. No doubt Joshua had ascended the
heights, most likely those to the north of
the valley, so as to separate himself from
the flying Israelites on the lower ground,

Joshua stretched out the spear that *he had* in his hand toward
19 the city. And the ambush arose quickly out of their place, and
they ran as soon as he had stretched out his hand: and they
entered into the city, and took it, and hasted and set the city on
20 fire. And when the men of Ai looked behind them, they saw,
and, behold, the smoke of the city ascended up to heaven, and
they had no [1]power to flee this way or that way : and the people
21 that fled to the wilderness turned back upon the pursuers. And
when Joshua and all Israel saw that the ambush had taken the
city, and that the smoke of the city ascended, then they turned
22 again, and slew the men of Ai. And the other issued out of the
city against them ; so they were in the midst of Israel, some on
this side, and some on that side : and they smote them, so that
l Deut. 7. 2.   23 they *l*let none of them remain or escape. And the king of Ai
24 they took alive, and brought him to Joshua. And it came to
pass, when Israel had made an end of slaying all the inhabitants
of Ai in the field, in the wilderness wherein they chased them,
and when they were all fallen on the edge of the sword, until
they were consumed, that all the Israelites returned unto Ai,
25 and smote it with the edge of the sword. And *so* it was, *that* all
that fell that day, both of men and women, *were* twelve thou-
26 sand, *even* all the men of Ai. For Joshua drew not his hand
back, wherewith he stretched out the spear, until he had utterly
m Num. 31.   27 destroyed all the inhabitants of Ai. *m*Only the cattle and the
22, 26.   spoil of that city Israel took for a prey unto themselves, accord-
n ver. 2.   ing unto the word of the LORD which he *n*commanded Joshua.
o Deut. 13.   28 And Joshua burnt Ai, and made it *o*an heap for ever, *even* a
16.
p ch. 10. 26.   29 desolation unto this day. *p*And the king of Ai he hanged on a
Ps. 107. 40.   tree until eventide : *q*and as soon as the sun was down, Joshua
& 110. 5.   commanded that they should take his carcase down from the
q ch. 10. 27.
tree, and cast it at the entering of the gate of the city, and
r ch. 7. 26.   *r*raise thereon a great heap of stones, *that remaineth* unto this-
& 10. 27.
30 day. ¶ Then Joshua built an altar unto the LORD God of Israel,
s Deut. 27.   31 *s*in mount Ebal, as Moses the servant of the LORD commanded
4, 5.

[1] Heb. *hand.*

---

and to be visible to the men in ambush behind
the city. He now, at the command of God,
gives the appointed signal to the ambush.

29. Cp. Deut. xxi. 22, 23 notes.

30-35. The account of this solemnity is
very brief. An acquaintance with Deut.
xxvii. is evidently pre-supposed ; and the
three several acts of which the solemnity
consisted are only so far distinctly named
as is necessary to show that the commands
of Moses there given were fully carried out
by Joshua.

It is difficult to escape the conviction that
these verses are here out of their proper
and original place. The connection between
viii. 29, and ix. 1, is natural and obvious ;
and in ix. 3, the fraud of the Gibeonites is
represented as growing out of the alarm
caused by the fall of Jericho and Ai. It is,
moreover, extremely unlikely that a solemnity of this nature in the very centre of
the country should be undertaken by Joshua
whilst the whole surrounding district was
in the hands of the enemy ; or that, if undertaken, it would have been carried out un-

molested. "And the strangers that were
conversant among them" (*v.* 35), were present
at it. The distance from Gilgal in the Jordan
valley to Mount Ebal is fully thirty miles, unless—as is unlikely—another Gilgal (Deut.
xi. 29 note) be meant ; and so vast a host,
with its non-effective followers (*v.* 35), could
certainly not have accomplished a march
like this through a difficult country and a
hostile population in less than three days.
Moreover in ix. 6, x. 6, 15, 43, the Israelites are spoken of as still encamping at
Gilgal.

It is on the whole likely that, for these
and other reasons, this passage does not,
in our present Bible, stand in its proper
context ; and it has been conjectured that
the place from which these six verses have
been transferred is the end of chapter xi.
The "then" with which *v.* 30 opens in our
present text may well have served to introduce the account of the solemnity on Gerizim and Ebal at the end of the record of
Joshua's victories, to which indeed it forms
a suitable climax.

the children of Israel, as it is written in the *book of the law*   *t* Ex. 20. 25.
of Moses, an altar of whole stones, over which no man hath   Deut. 27. 5,6.
lift up *any* iron : and *u* they offered thereon burnt offerings   *u* Ex. 20. 24.
32 unto the LORD, and sacrificed peace offerings. And *x* he wrote   *x* Deut. 27. 2, 8.
there upon the stones a copy of the law of Moses, which he
33 wrote in the presence of the children of Israel. And all Israel,
and their elders, and officers, and their judges, stood on this
side the ark and on that side before the priests the Levites,
y which bare the ark of the covenant of the LORD, as well *z* the   *y* Deut. 31.
stranger, as he that was born among them ; half of them over   9, 29.
against mount Gerizim, and half of them over against mount   *z* Deut. 31. 12.
Ebal ; *a* as Moses the servant of the LORD had commanded before,   *a* Deut. 11.
34 that they should bless the people of Israel. And afterward   29. & 27. 12.
b he read all the words of the law, *c* the blessings and cursings,   *b* Neh. 8. 3.
35 according to all that is written in the book of the law. There   *c* Deut. 28. 2,
was not a word of all that Moses commanded, which Joshua   15, 45. & 29. 20, 21.
read not before all the congregation of Israel, *d* with the women,   & 30. 19.
and the little ones, and *e* the strangers that [1] were conversant   *d* Deut. 31.12. *e* ver. 33.
among them.
CHAP. 9. AND it came to pass, when all the kings which *were* on
this side Jordan, in the hills, and in the valleys, and in all the
coasts of *a* the great sea over against Lebanon, *b* the Hittite, and   *a* Num. 34. 6.
the Amorite, the Canaanite, the Perizzite, the Hivite, and the   *b* Ex. 3. 17. & 23. 23.
2 Jebusite, heard *thereof ;* that they *c* gathered themselves together,   *c* Ps. 83. 3, 5.
3 to fight with Joshua and with Israel, with one [2] accord. ¶ And   *d* ch. 10. 2.
when the inhabitants of *d* Gibeon *e* heard what Joshua had done   *e* ch. 6. 27.

[1] Heb. *walked.*   [2] Heb. *mouth.*

---

32. See note marg. ref.

34. *all the words of the law*] See Deut. xxxi. 11 seq. It would seem that Joshua, on the present occasion, must have read at least all the legislative portion of the Pentateuch before the people (cp. on Deut. xxvii. 3). The terms of this verse cannot be satisfactorily explained as importing only the blessings and curses of Deut. xxvii. and xxviii.

IX. 1, 2. The two verses serve as a general introduction to chapters ix., x., and xi. The Canaanites had recovered to some extent from their panic (*v.* 1), perhaps in consequence of the repulse of the Israelites before Ai. They resolved to make a league and to resist jointly the progress of the Israelites. The defection of Gibeon (*vv.* 3-27) determined the five kings of the Amorites, whose territories were nearest Gibeon, to take instant action against that city. Their forces were defeated by Joshua in the battle before Gibeon (x. 1 seq.). The other confederates subsequently gathered their armies together, xi. 1–5, and were defeated at the waters of Merom (xi. 6 seq.). The former of these two great battles gave Joshua possession of the southern half of Palestine west of Jordan ; the latter of the northern half.

1. *in the hills*] See Num. xiii. 17 note.

the valleys] Or "the vale" (the Shephelah, Deut. i. 7), which imports the lowland country between the mountains and the sea coast.

3. Gibeon was the head of the four towns (*v.* 17) occupied by the Hivites (xi. 19). The inhabitants were Amorites (2 Sam. xxi. 2) ; the name Amorites being used as a general name for the Canaanitish population (Deut. i. 44 note). The Hivites seem to have had a non-monarchical form of government (cp. *vv.* 3, 11), but their city was (x. 2) in size and importance equal to those cities which the kings of the country made their capitals. Gibeon signifies "pertaining to a hill," *i.e.* built on a hill (cp. Gibeah and Geba, towns in the same neighbourhood), and describes the site, which is on two of the rounded hills peculiar to this district. It is still known as *El-Jib*, and lies about five miles north of Jerusalem by the most direct route. It stands at the head of the pass of Beth-horon, through which lies the main route from Jerusalem and the lower Jordan valley to Joppa and the sea coast. Thus from its position, no less than from the number and valour of its people (x. 2), it was one of the most important cities of southern Canaan. Gibeon fell within the lot of Benjamin (xviii. 25), and was one of the cities assigned to the priests (xxi. 17). In later times it was famous as the scene of various events (2 Sam. ii. 12–17 ; xx. 4–13 ; 1 Kings ii. 28, 29, cp. with 1 Chr. xvi. 39). It was for a long time the spot where the Tabernacle of Moses, together with the Brazen Altar of burnt offering (1 Chr. xxi. 29) and other portions of the sacred furni-

4 unto Jericho and to Ai, they did work wilily, and went and
made as if they had been ambassadors, and took old sacks upon
5 their asses, and wine bottles, old, and rent, and bound up; and
old shoes and clouted upon their feet, and old garments upon
them; and all the bread of their provision was dry *and* mouldy.

f ch. 5. 10.   6 And they went to Joshua *f* unto the camp at Gilgal, and said
unto him, and to the men of Israel, We be come from a far
7 country: now therefore make ye a league with us. And the

g ch. 11. 19.   men of Israel said unto the *g* Hivites, Peradventure ye dwell
h Ex. 23. 32.   8 among us; and *h* how shall we make a league with you? And
Deut. 7. 2.
& 20. 16.   they said unto Joshua, *i* We *are* thy servants. And Joshua said
Judg. 2. 2.   9 unto them, Who *are* ye? and from whence come ye? And they
i Deut. 20.11.
2 Kin. 10. 5.   said unto him, *k* From a very far country thy servants are come
k Deut. 20.   because of the name of the LORD thy God: for we have *l* heard
15.   10 the fame of him, and all that he did in Egypt, and *m* all that he
l Ex. 15. 14.
Josh. 2. 10.   did to the two kings of the Amorites, that *were* beyond Jordan,
m Num. 21.   to Sihon king of Heshbon, and to Og king of Bashan, which
24, 33.   11 *was* at Ashtaroth. Wherefore our elders and all the inhabitants
of our country spake to us, saying, Take victuals ¹with you for
the journey, and go to meet them, and say unto them, We *are*
12 your servants: therefore now make ye a league with us. This
our bread we took hot *for* our provision out of our houses on
the day we came forth to go unto you; but now, behold, it is
13 dry, and it is mouldy: and these bottles of wine, which we
filled, *were* new; and, behold, they be rent: and these our garments and our shoes are become old by reason of the very long

n Num. 27.   14 journey. And ²the men took of their victuals, *n* and asked not
21.
Isai. 30. 1, 2.   15 *counsel* at the mouth of the LORD. And Joshua *o* made peace
See Judg.   with them, and made a league with them, to let them live: and
1. 1.
1 Sam. 22.   16 the princes of the congregation sware unto them. ¶ And it
10. & 30. 8.   came to pass at the end of three days after they had made a
2 Sam. 2. 1.   league with them, that they heard that they *were* their neigh-
o ch. 11. 19.
2 Sam. 21. 2.   17 bours, and *that* they dwelt among them. And the children of
Israel journeyed, and came unto their cities on the third day.
p ch. 18. 25,   Now their cities *were* *p* Gibeon, and Chephirah, and Beeroth, and
26, 23.

¹ Heb. *in your hand.*   ² Or, *they received the men by reason of their victuals.*

ture, were placed. It was the scene of the
magnificent ceremonial with which Solomon inaugurated his reign (1 K. iii.), but no
doubt lost much of its importance after the
Tabernacle and its accompaniments were
removed to the Temple of Solomon.
    4. *they did work wilily*] Lit. "they also,"
or "they too, did work, &c." The "also"
serves, apparently, to connect the stratagem of the Gibeonites with that employed
by the Israelites before Ai. It hints that
the Gibeonites resolved to meet craft with
craft.
    rent and bound up] *i.e.* the wine skins
were torn and roughly repaired by tying up
the edges of the rent. The more thorough
and careful way, hardly feasible in a hasty
journey, would have been to insert a patch.
    6. *camp at Gilgal*] Whilst Joshua was
engaged in more distant enterprises, the
women, children, and property of the
Israelites were left with a sufficient guard
at this place, where they had been estab-

lished immediately after crossing the Jordan (v. 9).
    7. Cp. marg. reff.
    14. The elders of Israel (*v.* 18), tasting
what was offered them by the Gibeonites,
pledged themselves according to the usage
of Eastern nations to peace and friendship
with them. They credited the story at
once, instead of seeking the direction of
God in the matter. The rendering of the
margin is not to be preferred to that of the
text.
    at the mouth of the LORD] *i.e.* by the Urim
and Thummim (Ex. xxviii. 30).
    17. Chephirah (*Kefir*) is situated eight or
nine miles west of Gibeon, and was an inhabited city in the days of Ezra and Nehemiah (Ezr. ii. 25; Neh. vii. 29).
    Beeroth (*Bireh*), about eight miles north
of Jerusalem, *i.e.* "city of
woods," is identified by Robinson with the
modern *Kuriet el Enab*, nine miles from
Jerusalem on the road to Jaffa [and by

18 Kirjath-jearim. And the children of Israel smote them not, *q* because the princes of the congregation had sworn unto them by the LORD God of Israel. And all the congregation mur- 19 mured against the princes. But all the princes said unto all the congregation, We have sworn unto them by the LORD God 20 of Israel: now therefore we may not touch them. This we will do to them; we will even let them live, lest *r* wrath be upon us, 21 because of the oath which we sware unto them. And the princes said unto them, Let them live; but let them be *s* hewers of wood and drawers of water unto all the congregation; as the princes 22 had *t* promised them. ¶ And Joshua called for them, and he spake unto them, saying, Wherefore have ye beguiled us, say- ing, *u* We *are* very far from you; when *x* ye dwell among us? 23 Now therefore ye *are* *y* cursed, and there shall [1] none of you be freed from being bondmen, and *z* hewers of wood and drawers of 24 water for the house of my God. And they answered Joshua, and said, Because it was certainly told thy servants, how that the LORD thy God *a* commanded his servant Moses to give you all the land, and to destroy all the inhabitants of the land from before you, therefore *b* we were sore afraid of our lives because 25 of you, and have done this thing. And now, behold, we *are* *c* in thine hand: as it seemeth good and right unto thee to do unto

q Ps. 15. 4.
Eccles. 5. 2.

r See 2 Sam.
21. 1, 2, 6.
Ezek. 17. 13,
15, 18, 19.
Zech. 5. 3, 4.
Mal. 3. 5.
s Deut. 29. 11.
t ver. 15.
u ver. 6, 9.
x ver. 16.
y Gen. 9. 25.
z ver. 21. 27.

a Ex. 23. 32.
Deut. 7. 1, 2.

b Ex. 15. 14.

c Gen. 16. 6.

[1] Heb. *not to be cut off from you.*

Conder with *Sôba*]. The town was num- bered amongst those belonging to Judah, and was in the northern boundary of that tribe. Beyond this city the six hundred Danites encamped on their famous expedi- tion to Laish (Judg. xviii. 12). Kirjath- jearim was also, and probably before the Israelitish conquests exclusively, called Baalah and Kirjath-baal (xv. 9, 60), names which seem to point to its early sanctity as a special seat of Baal-worship. To this place also the ark was brought from Beth- shemesh after it was sent back by the Philistines, and here it remained for twenty years (1 Sam. vi. 20, 21, vii. 2). It was fetched thence by David and deposited in the house of Obed-edom (2 Sam. vi. 2). Hence the allusion, Ps. cxxxii. 6, where David is said to have found the ark "in the fields of the wood."

21. Render "**they shall be** hewers of wood and drawers of water:" menial du- ties belonging to the lowest classes only (cp. marg. ref.). The curse of Noah (Gen. ix. 25) on the children of Ham was thus fulfilled to the letter in the case of these Hivites.

22. Were the Israelites bound to respect an oath thus procured by fraud? Were they right in doing so? Bp. Sanderson ("Works," vol. iv. pp. 269, 300, Oxf. edit.), determines these questions in the affirma- tive; and rightly, since the oath, though unlawfully taken, was not an oath taken to do an unlawful thing, *i.e.* a thing in itself unlawful. It was the carelessness of the Israelites themselves which betrayed them into this league. It was therefore their duty when they found themselves entrapped

into this unlawful covenant, to devise means by which they might respect both their own oath and God's purposes as inti- mated in His injunctions (Deut. vii. 2) against sparing the Canaanites. This was accomplished by granting their lives to the Gibeonites, but reducing them to a servile condition, which might be expected to dis- able them from influencing the Israelites to do wrong. It may be added, that had the Is- raelites broken their oath, taken solemnly in the Name of the Lord, they would have brought that Name into contempt amongst the heathen; and, whilst punishing perfidy in others, would have themselves, the Lord's people, incurred the reproach of perjury. The result showed that Joshua and the princes judged rightly in this matter. God gave to Israel a notable victory, crowned with special miracles, over the kings who were confederated against Gibeon, because of the treaty made with Israel (x. 4, 8, 13); and God punished as a national act of blood-guiltiness the slaughter of the Gibeon- ites by Saul, which was a distinct violation of the covenant here before us (cp. 2 Sam. xxi. 1). This sparing of the Gibeonites, as well as the previous sparing of Rahab and her household, must be borne in mind when the massacre of the Canaanites by Joshua and the Israelites is discussed.

24. It was mere fear which drove the Gibeonites to act as they did. They sought for union with God's people, not for its own sake, but to save their lives. Rahab's mo- tives were higher (ii. 9 seq.). Hence she was adopted into Israel; the Gibeonites re- mained for ever bondsmen of Israel.

26 us, do. And so did he unto them, and delivered them out of
the hand of the children of Israel, that they slew them not.

d ver. 21, 23.　27 And Joshua ¹made them that day ᵈhewers of wood and drawers
of water for the congregation, and for the altar of the LORD,

e Deut. 12. 5.　even unto this day, ᵉin the place which he should choose.

CHAP. 10. NOW it came to pass, when Adoni-zedec king of Jerusalem
had heard how Joshua had taken Ai, and had utterly destroyed

a ch. 6. 21.　it ; ᵃas he had done to Jericho and her king, so he had done to

b ch. 8. 22,　ᵇAi and her king; and ᶜhow the inhabitants of Gibeon had
26, 28.　2 made peace with Israel, and were among them ; that they

c ch. 9. 15.　ᵈfeared greatly, because Gibeon *was* a great city, as one of the

d Ex. 15. 14,　²royal cities, and because it *was* greater than Ai, and all the

15, 16.
Deut. 11. 25.　3 men thereof *were* mighty. Wherefore Adoni-zedec king of
Jerusalem sent unto Hoham king of Hebron, and unto Piram
king of Jarmuth, and unto Japhia king of Lachish, and unto
4 Debir king of Eglon, saying, Come up unto me, and help me,

e ver. 1.　that we may smite Gibeon : ᵉfor it hath made peace with Joshua

ch. 9. 15.　5 and with the children of Israel. Therefore the five kings of the
Amorites, the king of Jerusalem, the king of Hebron, the king

f ch. 9. 2.　of Jarmuth, the king of Lachish, the king of Eglon, ᶠgathered
themselves together, and went up, they and all their hosts, and
6 encamped before Gibeon, and made war against it. ¶ And the

g ch. 5. 10.　men of Gibeon sent unto Joshua ᵍto the camp to Gilgal, saying,
& 9. 6.　Slack not thy hand from thy servants ; come up to us quickly,
and save us, and help us : for all the kings of the Amorites that
7 dwell in the mountains are gathered together against us. So

h ch. 8. 1.　Joshua ascended from Gilgal, he, and ʰall the people of war
8 with him, and all the mighty men of valour. And the LORD

¹ Heb. *gave,* or, *delivered to be,*　　² Heb. *cities of the king-*
1 Chr. 9. 2. Ezra 8. 20.　　*dom.*

X. 1. *Adoni-zedec*] *i.e* "Lord of righteousness " (cp. Melchizedek, "King of
righteousness"); probably an official title
of the Jebusite kings.

Jerusalem] *i.e.* "foundation of peace,"
cp. Gen. xiv. 18. The city belonged to the
inheritance of Benjamin (xviii. 28), but was
on the very edge of the territory of Judah
(xv. 8). Hence it was the strong and warlike tribe of Judah which eventually captured the lower part of the city, most likely
in the days of Joshua's later conquests
(Judg. i. 8), and after the warlike strength
of the Jebusites had been weakened by the
defeat in the open field, recorded in this
chapter. The upper town, more especially
the fortified hill of Sion, remained in the
hands of the Jebusites, who accordingly
kept a footing in the place, along with the
men of Judah and Benjamin, even after the
conquest (xv. 63 ; Judg. i. 21); and would
seem, indeed, to have so far, and no doubt
gradually, regained possession of the whole,
that Jerusalem was spoken of in the days
of the Judges as a Jebusite city. David
finally stormed "the stronghold of Zion,"
and called it "the City of David" (2 Sam.
v. 6-9). It was, probably, only after this
conquest and the adoption by David of the
city as the religious and political metropolis

of the whole nation, that the name Jerusalem came into use (2 Sam. v. 5) in substitution for Jebus.

3. For Hebron, see Gen. xiii. 18. Jarmuth,
afterwards one of the cities of Judah (xv.
35), is probably identified with the modern
Yarmuk. Lachish was also a city of Judah
(xv. 39), and, like Jarmuth, occupied by
Jews after the captivity (Neh. xi. 30). It
was fortified by Rehoboam after the revolt
of the Ten Tribes (2 Chr. xi. 9), and seems
to have been regarded as one of the safest
places of refuge (2 Kings xiv. 19). Through
Lachish the idolatry of Israel was imported
into Judah (Micah i. 13), and of this sin the
capture of the city by Sennacherib was the
punishment (2 Kings xviii. 14-17 and xix.
8). Lachish is by most authorities identified with *Um Lakis,* lying some twenty
miles west of Eleutheropolis, on the road to
Gaza [and by Conder with *El Hesy*].
Eglon is the modern *Ajlân*.

6. The language reflects the urgency of
the crisis. Accordingly Joshua made a
forced march, accompanied only by his
soldiers (*v.* 7), and accomplished in a single
night the distance from Gilgal to Gibeon
(about fifteen miles in a direct line), which
on a former occasion had been a three days'
journey (ix. 17).

said unto Joshua, *Fear them not: for I have delivered them *i* ch. 11. 6.
into thine hand; *k*there shall not a man of them stand before $\begin{smallmatrix}\text{Judg. 4. 14.}\\ k \text{ ch. 1. 5.}\end{smallmatrix}$
9 thee. Joshua therefore came unto them suddenly, *and* went up
10 from Gilgal all night. And the LORD *l*discomfited them before *l* Judg. 4. 15.
Israel, and slew them with a great slaughter at Gibeon, and
chased them along the way that goeth up *m*to Beth-horon, and *m* ch. 16. 3, 5.
11 smote them to *n*Azekah, and unto Makkedah. And it came to *n* ch. 15. 25.
pass, as they fled from before Israel, *and* were in the going down
to Beth-horon, *o*that the LORD cast down great stones from *o* Ps. 18. 13,
heaven upon them unto Azekah, and they died: *they were* more $\begin{smallmatrix}\text{14. \& 77. 17.}\\ \text{Isai. 30. 30.}\end{smallmatrix}$
which died with hailstones than *they* whom the children of Israel Rev. 16. 21.

---

10. *Beth-horon*] The two places of this name, the upper and the lower Beth-horon (marg. ref.), are identified with the villages *Beit-ur el Foka* (the upper) and *Beit-ur et Tahta* (the lower) : *Beit-ur* being probably a corruption of Beth-horon. The name itself ("house of caves") points to the exceedingly rocky character of the district. Upper Beth-horon was between six and seven miles west of Gibeon; and "the way that goeth up to Beth-horon" must accordingly be the hilly road which leads from Gibeon to it. Between the two Beth-horons is a steep pass, "the going down to Beth-horon" (*v.* 11); and here the Amorites were crushed by the hailstones. The main road from Jerusalem and the Jordan valley to the sea-coast lay through the pass of Beth-horon ; and, accordingly, both the Beth-horons were secured by Solomon with strong fortifications (2 Chr. viii. 5). It was in this pass that Judas Maccabæus routed the Syrians under Seron (1 Macc. iii. 13 seq.), and here also, according to Jewish traditions, the destruction of the host of Sennacherib took place (2 K. xix. 35).

Azekah, which has not been as yet certainly identified, was in the hill country, between the mountains around Gibeon and the plain (see marg. ref.). It was fortified by Rehoboam (2 Chr. xi. 9) and besieged by the Babylonians (Jer. xxxiv. 7) shortly before the Captivity. It was an inhabited city after the return from the exile (Neh. xi. 30).

Makkedah] The exact site of this town is uncertain. It was situated in the plain between the mountains and the line of sea-coast which the Philistines held (xv. 41), and no great way north-east of Libnah (xii. 15, 16). [Warren (Conder) identifies it with the modern *el Mughâr*, a village on the south side of the valley of Torek.]

11. Cp. Ecclus. xlvi. 6. Frightful storms occasionally sweep over the hills of Judæa; but this was evidently a miraculous occurrence, like the hail which smote Egypt (Ex. ix. 24) and the tempest which fell on the Philistines at Ebenezer (1 Sam. vii. 10).

12-15. These four verses seem to be a fragment or extract taken from some other and independent source and inserted into the thread of the narrative after it had been completed, and inserted most probably by

another hand than that of the author of the Book of Joshua.

It is probable that verse 12 and the first half of verse 13 alone belong to the Book of Jasher and are poetical, and that the rest of this passage is prose.

The writer of this fragment seems to have understood the words of the ancient song literally, and believed that an astronomical miracle really took place, by which the motion of the heavenly bodies was for some hours suspended. (Cp. also Ecclus. xlvi. 4.) So likewise believed the older Jewish authorities generally, the Christian Fathers, and many commentators ancient and modern.

It must be allowed, indeed, that some of the objections which have been urged against this view on scientific grounds are easily answered. The interference, if such there were, with the earth's motion was not an act of blind power *ab extra* and nothing more. The Agent here concerned is omnipotent and omniscient, and could, of course, as well arrest the regular consequences of such a suspension of nature's ordinary working as He could suspend that working itself. It is, however, obvious, that any such stupendous phenomenon would affect the chronological calculations of all races of men over the whole earth and do so in a similarly striking and very intelligible manner. Yet no record of any such perturbation is anywhere to be found, and no marked and unquestionable reference is made to such a miracle by any of the subsequent writers in the Old or New Testament. For reasons like these, many commentators have explained the miracle as merely optical.

The various explanations show how strongly the difficulties which arise out of the passage have been felt. Accordingly stress has been laid by recent commentators on the admitted fact that the words out of which the difficulty springs are an extract from a poetical book. They must consequently, it is argued, be taken in a popular and poetical, and not in a literal sense. Joshua feared lest the sun should set before the people had fully "avenged themselves of their enemies." In his anxiety he prayed to God, and God hearkened to him. This is boldly and strikingly expressed in the

12 slew with the sword. ¶ Then spake Joshua to the LORD in the day when the LORD delivered up the Amorites before the children of Israel, and he said in the sight of Israel,

p Isai. 28. 21.
Hab. 3. 11.
q Judg. 12.
12.
r 2 Sam. 1.
18.

s See Isai.
38. 8.
t Deut. 1. 30.
ver. 42.
& ch. 23. 3.
u ver. 43.

p Sun, ¹stand thou still upon Gibeon; And thou, Moon, in the valley of *q* Ajalon.

13 ¶ And the sun stood still, and the moon stayed, until the people had avenged themselves upon their enemies. *r* Is not this written in the book of ²Jasher? So the sun stood still in the midst of 14 heaven, and hasted not to go down about a whole day. And there was *s* no day like that before it or after it, that the LORD hearkened unto the voice of a man: for *t* the LORD fought for 15 Israel. *u* And Joshua returned, and all Israel with him, unto 16 the camp to Gilgal. ¶ But these five kings fled, and hid them- 17 selves in a cave at Makkedah. And it was told Joshua, saying, 18 The five kings are found hid in a cave at Makkedah. And Joshua said, Roll great stones upon the mouth of the cave, and 19 set men by it for to keep them: and stay ye not, *but* pursue after your enemies, and ³ smite the hindmost of them; suffer them not to enter into their cities: for the LORD your God hath 20 delivered them into your hand. And it came to pass, when Joshua and the children of Israel had made an end of slaying them with a very great slaughter, till they were consumed, that 21 the rest *which* remained of them entered into fenced cities. And all the people returned to the camp to Joshua at Makkedah in

¹ Heb. *be silent.*   ² Or, *The upright?*   ³ Heb. *cut off the tail.*

words of the ancient book, which describes Joshua as praying that the day might be prolonged, or, in poetical diction, that the sun might be stayed, until the work was done. Similarly, Judg. v. 20 and Ps. xviii. 9-15 are passages which no one construes as describing actual occurrences : they set forth only internal, although most sincere and, in a spiritual sense, real and true convictions. This explanation is now adopted by theologians whose orthodoxy upon the plenary inspiration and authority of Holy Scripture is well known and undoubted.

12. *in the sight of Israel*] Literally, "before the eyes of Israel," *i.e.* in the sight or presence of Israel, so that the people were witnesses of his words. (Cp. Deut. xxxi. 7.)

Sun, stand thou still] Literally, as marg., "be silent" (cp. Lev. x. 3) ; or rather, perhaps, "tarry," as in 1 Sam. xiv. 9.

thou, moon] The words addressed to the moon as well as to the sun, indicate that both were visible as Joshua spoke. Below and before him, westward, was the valley of Ajalon ; behind him, eastward, were the hills around Gibeon. Some hours had passed, since in the early dawn he had fallen upon the host of the enemy, and the expression "in the midst of heaven" (*v.* 13) seems to import that it was now drawing towards mid-day, though the moon was still faintly visible in the west. If the time had been near sunset, Joshua would have seen the sun, not, as he did, eastward of him, but westward, sinking in the sea.

the valley of Ajalon] *i.e.* "the valley of the gazelles." This is the modern *Merj Ibn*

Omeir, described by Robinson, as a broad and beautiful valley running in a westerly direction from the mountains towards the great western plain. The ancient name is still preserved in *Yalo,* a village situated on the hill which skirts the south side of the valley.

13. *Book of Jasher*] *i.e.* as marg., "of the upright" or "righteous," a poetical appellation of the Covenant-people (cp. "Jeshurun" in Deut. xxxii. 15, and note ; and cp. Num. xxiii. 10 and 21 ; Ps. cxi. 1). This book was probably a collection of national odes celebrating the heroes of the theocracy and their achievements, and is referred to again (marg. ref.) as containing the dirge composed by David over Saul and Jonathan.

about a whole day] *i.e.* about twelve hours ; the average space between sunrise and sunset.

15. Joshua's return (cp. *v.* 43) to Gilgal was not until after he had, by the storm and capture of the principal cities of south Canaan, completed the conquest of which the victory at Gibeon was only the beginning.

This verse is evidently the close of the extract from an older work, which connected the rescue of Gibeon immediately with the return to Gilgal, and omitted the encampment at Makkedah (*v.* 21), and also the details given in *vv.* 28-42.

16. The thread of the narrative, broken by the four intermediate verses, 12-15, is now resumed from *v.* 11.

21. Joshua himself remained at Makkedah with the guards set before the cave.

peace: *none moved his tongue against any of the children of
22 Israel. ¶ Then said Joshua, Open the mouth of the cave, and
23 bring out those five kings unto me out of the cave. And they
did so, and brought forth those five kings unto him out of the
cave, the king of Jerusalem, the king of Hebron, the king of
24 Jarmuth, the king of Lachish, and the king of Eglon. And it
came to pass, when they brought out those kings unto Joshua,
that Joshua called for all the men of Israel, and said unto the
captains of the men of war which went with him, Come near,
y put your feet upon the necks of these kings. And they came
25 near, and put their feet upon the necks of them. And Joshua
said unto them, *z* Fear not, nor be dismayed, be strong and of
good courage: for *a* thus shall the LORD do to all your enemies
26 against whom ye fight. And afterward Joshua smote them, and
slew them, and hanged them on five trees: and they *b* were
27 hanging upon the trees until the evening. And it came to pass
at the time of the going down of the sun, *that* Joshua commanded,
and they *c* took them down off the trees, and cast them into the
cave wherein they had been hid, and laid great stones in the
28 cave's mouth, *which remain* until this very day. ¶And that day
Joshua took Makkedah, and smote it with the edge of the sword,
and the king thereof he utterly destroyed, them, and all the
souls that *were* therein ; he let none remain: and he did to the
29 king of Makkedah *d* as he did unto the king of Jericho. ¶ Then
Joshua passed from Makkedah, and all Israel with him, unto
30 Libnah, and fought against Libnah: and the LORD delivered
it also, and the king thereof, into the hand of Israel; and he
smote it with the edge of the sword, and all the souls that *were*
therein ; he let none remain in it; but did unto the king thereof
31 as he did unto the king of Jericho. ¶And Joshua passed from
Libnah, and all Israel with him, unto Lachish, and encamped
32 against it, and fought against it: and the LORD delivered
Lachish into the hand of Israel, which took it on the second
day, and smote it with the edge of the sword, and all the souls
that *were* therein, according to all that he had done to Libnah.
33 Then Horam king of Gezer came up to help Lachish; and
34 Joshua smote him and his people, until he had left him none remaining. ¶And from Lachish Joshua passed unto Eglon, and
all Israel with him; and they encamped against it, and fought
35 against it: and they took it on that day, and smote it with the
edge of the sword, and all the souls that *were* therein he utterly
destroyed that day, according to all that he had done to Lachish.
36 ¶And Joshua went up from Eglon, and all Israel with him, unto

x Ex. 11. 7.

y Ps. 107. 40.
& 110. 5.
& 149. 8, 9.
Isai. 26. 5.
Mal. 4. 3.
z Deut. 31.
6, 8.
ch. 1. 9.
a Deut. 3. 21.
& 7. 19.
b ch. 8. 29.
c Deut. 21.
23.
ch. 8. 29.

d ch. 6. 21.

The other warriors would not return from
the pursuit until the evening of the overthrow of the Amorites ; and the execution
of the kings and the capture of Makkedah
itself belong, no doubt, to the day following
(*vv.* 27, 28).

none moved his tongue] See marg. ref. and
note.

24. *put your feet upon the necks of these
kings*] A symbol of complete subjugation
(cp. marg. reff. and 1 Cor. xv. 25).

29. *Libnah*] The word means "white" or
"distinct," and undoubtedly points to some
natural feature of the spot, perhaps the
"Garde Blanche" of the Crusaders, a castle
which stood on or near the white cliffs which

bound the plain of Philistia to the east opposite to Ascalon. It was in the southern
part of the hill-country of Judah (xv. 42),
and was one of the cities afterwards assigned to the priests (xxi. 13).

33. Gezer lies on the southern border of
the tribe of Ephraim (xvi. 3). It was considerably to the northward of Joshua's present line of operations, and does not appear
to have been captured at this time. He
contented himself for the present with
repulsing the attack made upon him, slew
Horam (cp. xii. 12), inflicting a severe defeat upon his people, and then continued to
pursue his conquests over the confederated
kings and their allies in south Canaan.

e See ch.
14. 13.
& 15. 13.
Judg. 1. 10.

f See chap.
15. 15.
Judg. 1. 11.

g Deut. 20.
16, 17.
h Gen. 10.19.
i ch. 11. 16.

k ver. 14.

a ch. 10. 3.
b ch. 19. 15.
c Num. 34.
11.
d ch. 17. 11.
Judg. 1. 27.

37 *e*Hebron; and they fought against it: and they took it, and smote it with the edge of the sword, and the king thereof, and all the cities thereof, and all the souls that *were* therein; he left none remaining, according to all that he had done to Eglon; but 38 destroyed it utterly, and all the souls that *were* therein. ¶ And Joshua returned, and all Israel with him, to *f*Debir; and fought 39 against it: and he took it, and the king thereof, and all the cities thereof; and they smote them with the edge of the sword, and utterly destroyed all the souls that *were* therein; he left none remaining: as he had done to Hebron, so he did to Debir, and to the king thereof; as he had done also to Libnah, and to 40 her king. ¶So Joshua smote all the country of the hills, and of the south, and of the vale, and of the springs, and all their kings: he left none remaining, but utterly destroyed all that breathed, 41 as the LORD God of Israel *g*commanded. And Joshua smote them from Kadesh-barnea even unto *h*Gaza, *i*and all the country of 42 Goshen, even unto Gibeon. And all these kings and their land did Joshua take at one time, *k*because the LORD God of Israel 43 fought for Israel. And Joshua returned, and all Israel with him, unto the camp to Gilgal.

CHAP. 11. AND it came to pass, when Jabin king of Hazor had heard *those things*, that he *a*sent to Jobab king of Madon, and to 2 the king *b*of Shimron, and to the king of Achshaph, and to the kings that *were* on the north of the mountains, and of the plains south of *c*Chinneroth, and in the valley, and in the borders *d*of

---

37. *the king thereof*] No doubt the successor of the king slain at Makkedah (*v.* 23). *all the cities thereof*] *i.e.* the smaller towns dependent upon Hebron. The expression marks Hebron as the metropolis of other subject towns.

38. *Joshua returned*] The words mark a change in the direction of the march. Joshua from Hebron turned to the southwest, and attacked Debir or Kirjath-sepher and its dependencies (xv. 15).

40. See ix. 1. "The south" was the Negeb (Num. xiii. 17). Render "the springs" "slopes." The word here means the district of undulating ground between "the vale" (or *shephelah*) last named and "the hills."

41. *from Kadesh-barnea* (Num. xiii. 26) *unto Gaza*] This limits Joshua's conquests on the west, as the other line, "all the country of Goshen unto Gibeon," does on the east. Goshen (xv. 51) has not been identified. It was in the southern part of the territory of Judah, and is, of course, quite distinct from the Goshen of Gen. xlvi. 28.

42. *at one time*] *i.e.* in one campaign or expedition, which no doubt lasted some days, or perhaps weeks (cp. xi. 18).

XI. 1. *Jabin*] Probably the hereditary and official title of the kings of Hazor (see Judg. iv. 2). The word means literally "he shall understand," and is equivalent to "the wise" or "intelligent."

Hazor] This name, which means "enclosed" or "fortified," belonged also to two other towns in the south of Judah (cp. xv. 23, 25). The Hazor here in question, the head of the principalities of Northern Ca-

naan (*v.* 10) overlooked the lake of Merom, and was afterwards assigned to the tribe of Naphtali (xix. 36). It doubtless was one of the strongest fortresses in the north, both by nature and art. It is mentioned in Egyptian inscriptions of an early date. Its situation in the midst of a plain, though itself on a hill, rendered it peculiarly suitable as a stronghold for people whose main reliance was on horses and chariots (*v.* 4; Judg. iv. 3). Its position on the northern frontier led to its being fortified by Solomon (1 K. ix. 15). Its people were carried away captive, with those of the other cities of Naphtali, by Tiglath-Pileser (2 K. xv. 29). By the "plain of Nasor," where (1 Macc. xi. 67) Jonathan gained a victory over the Syrians, is doubtless to be understood "the plain of Asor" (*i.e.* Hazor). Hazor is conjecturally identified with the modern *Tell Kuraibeh*.

had heard those things] *i.e.* of the defeat of the southern Canaanites at Beth-horon and of the conquest of their country. The sites of Madon, Shimron, and of Achshaph, are unknown.

2. *on the north of the mountains*] Rather, "northwards in the mountains." The reference is to the mountain district of Galilee, called (xx. 7) "mount Naphtali."

on the plains south of Chinneroth] Literally "in the Arabah south of Chinneroth." The words describe the northern portion of the "Arabah" (see Deut. i. 1), or depressed tract, which extends along the Jordan from the lake of Gennesaret southwards.

Chinneroth] Identical with the later Gennesaret (see Num. xxxiv. 10). The lake

3 Dor on the west, *and* to the Canaanite on the east and on the west, and *to* the Amorite, and the Hittite, and the Perizzite, and the Jebusite in the mountains, *e* and *to* the Hivite under *f* Hermon
4 *g* in the land of Mizpeh. And they went out, they and all their hosts with them, much people, *h* even as the sand that *is* upon the sea shore in multitude, with horses and chariots very many.
5 And when all these kings were *1* met together, they came and pitched together at the waters of Merom, to fight against Israel.
6 ¶ And the LORD said unto Joshua, *i* Be not afraid because of them: for to morrow about this time will I deliver them up all slain before Israel: thou shalt *k* hough their horses, and burn
7 their chariots with fire. So Joshua came, and all the people of war with him, against them by the waters of Merom suddenly;
8 and they fell upon them. And the LORD delivered them into the hand of Israel, who smote them, and chased them unto *2* great Zidon, and unto *134* Misrephoth-maim, and unto the valley of Mizpeh eastward; and they smote them, until they

e Judg. 3. 3.
f ch. 13. 11.
g Gen. 31. 40.
h Gen. 22. 17.
& 32. 12.
Judg. 7. 12.
1 Sam. 13. 5.

i ch. 10. 8.

k 2 Sam. 8. 4.

l ch. 13. 6.

---

1 Heb. *assembled by appointment.*
2 Or, *Zidon-rabbah.*
3 Or, *Salt pits.*
4 Heb. *Burnings.*

---

derived its name from a town on its banks (cp. xix. 35).

in the valley] The northern part of the same flat district mentioned in ix. 1. This "valley" is the level plain adjacent to the sea and extending from Carmel southwards.

borders of Dor] Render "**highlands of Dor.**" Dor was a royal city, and gave its name to the district around it (cp. xii. 23; 1 K. iv. 11). Its importance was derived from its having an excellent and well-sheltered haven, and from the abundance among its rocks of the shell-fish which furnished the famous Tyrian purple. The site of Dor is identified by travellers as the modern *Tantura* or *Dandora*,—a name which is itself only a corruption of the ancient Dor. It lies near the foot of Carmel some six miles north of Cæsarea.

3. *Hermon*] See Deut. iii. 9 note.

the land of Mizpeh] or *Mizpah*, "the land of the watch-tower." The locality is probably identified as a plain stretching at the foot of Hermon south-westwards, from *Hasbeya*, towards the *Bahr el Huleh*. In a land abounding in striking points of view like Palestine, the name Mizpah was naturally, like "Belle Vue" amongst ourselves, bestowed on many places. The Mizpeh here mentioned must not be confounded with the Mizpeh of Gilead (xiii. 26, and Judg. xi. 29); nor with the Mizpeh of Judah (xv. 38); nor yet with that of Moab (1 Sam. xxii. 3).

5. *waters of Merom*] *i.e.* "the upper waters," the modern *Bahr el Huleh*, the lake Semechonitis, or Samochonitis of Josephus. This lake occupies the southern half of the *Ard el Huleh*, a depressed basin some fifteen miles long and three or four broad lying between the hills of Galilee on the west and the lower spurs of Hermon on the east. The size of the lake varies with the season, and the northern side of it ends in a large swamp. The shape of the lake is triangu-

lar, the point being at the south, where the Jordan, which enters it on the north, again quits it. There is a considerable space of table-land along the south-western shore, and here probably the troops of Jabin and his confederates were encamped, preparing to move southwards when Joshua and his army fell suddenly upon them.

6. *hough their horses*] *i.e.* cut the sinews of the hinder hoofs. This sinew once severed cannot be healed, and the horses would thus be irreparably lamed. This is the first appearance of horses in the wars with the Canaanites (Deut. xvii. 16 and note).

7. *suddenly*] As before, at Gibeon (x. 9), so now Joshua anticipates his enemies. Taken by surprise, and hemmed in between the mountains and the lake, the chariots and horses would have no time to deploy and no room to act effectively; and thus, in all probability, the unwieldy host of the Canaanites fell at once into hopeless confusion.

8. One portion of the defeated host fled north-westwards towards Zidon; the other north-eastwards up the *Ard el Huleh*.

Zidon, as the metropolis of various subject towns and territories, appears (xix. 28) to have been afterwards assigned to Asher, but was not, in fact, conquered by that tribe (Judg. i. 31). It is mentioned in Egyptian papyri of great antiquity, and by Homer, and was in the most ancient times the capital of Phœnicia. In later times it was eclipsed by Tyre (cp. 2 Sam. v. 11). The prophets frequently couple Tyre and Sidon together, as does also the New Test. (Is. xxiii. 2, 4, 12; Jer. xxvii. 3; xlvii. 4; Matt. xi. 22; xv. 21, &c.).

Both the site and signification of Misrephoth-maim are uncertain. Some have thought it identical with "Zarephath which belongeth to Zidon" (1 K. xvii. 9), the Sarepta of the New Test. The name is explained by

m ver. 6.

n Num. 33.
52.
Deut. 7. 2.
& 20. 16, 17.

o Ex. 34. 11,
12.
p Deut. 7. 2.
q ch. 1. 7.
r ch. 12. 8.
s ch. 10. 41.

t ch. 12. 7.

u Deut. 7. 24.
ch. 12. 7.
x ch. 9. 3, 7.
y Deut. 2. 30.
Judg. 14. 4.
1 Sam. 2. 25.
1 Kin. 12. 15.
Rom. 9. 18.
z Deut. 20.
16, 17.
a Deut. 1. 28.
ch. 15. 13.

9 left them none remaining. And Joshua did unto them ᵐas the LORD bade him : he houghed their horses, and burnt their 10 chariots with fire. ¶ And Joshua at that time turned back, and took Hazor, and smote the king thereof with the sword : for 11 Hazor beforetime was the head of all those kingdoms. And tney smote all the souls that *were* therein with the edge of the sword, utterly destroying *them :* there was not ¹any left to 12 breathe : and he burnt Hazor with fire. And all the cities of those kings, and all the kings of them, did Joshua take, and smote them with the edge of the sword, *and* he utterly destroyed 13 them, ⁿas Moses the servant of the LORD commanded. But *as for* the cities that stood still ²in their strength, Israel burned 14 none of them, save Hazor only ; *that* did Joshua burn. And all the spoil of these cities, and the cattle, the children of Israel took for a prey unto themselves ; but every man they smote with the edge of the sword, until they had destroyed them, neither 15 left they any to breathe. ᵒAs the LORD commanded Moses his servant, so ᵖdid Moses command Joshua, and �q so did Joshua : ³he left nothing undone of all that the LORD commanded Moses. 16 ¶ So Joshua took all that land, ʳthe hills, and all the south country, ˢand all the land of Goshen, and the valley, and the plain, and the mountain of Israel, and the valley of the same ; 17 *ᵗeven* from ⁴the mount Halak, that goeth up to Seir, even unto Baal-gad in the valley of Lebanon under mount Hermon : and ᵘall their kings he took, and smote them, and slew them. 18, 19 ⁵Joshua made war a long time with all those kings. There was not a city that made peace with the children of Israel, save ˣthe Hivites the inhabitants of Gibeon : all *other* they took in battle. 20 For ʸit was of the LORD to harden their hearts, that they should come against Israel in battle, that he might destroy them utterly, *and* that they might have no favour, but that he might 21 destroy them, ᶻas the LORD commanded Moses. ¶ And at that time came Joshua, and cut off ᵃthe Anakims from the mountains,

¹ Heb. *any breath.*
² Heb. *on their heap.*
³ Heb. *he removed nothing.*
⁴ Or, *the smooth mountain.*
⁵ Till 1445. ver. 23.

some (see marg.) as meaning hot-springs ; by others as salt-pits ; *i.e.* pits where the sea water was evaporated for the sake of its salt ; and again by others as " smelting factories near the waters." Some, tracing the word to quite another root, render it " heights of waters," or copious springs.

13. Render : " **But the cities standing each on its own hill** " (cp. Jer. xxx. 18). The meaning is simply that, with the exception of Hazor, Joshua did not burn the cities, but left them standing, each on its former site. This site is spoken of as a hill, because such was the ordinary site chosen for cities in Canaan (cp. Matt. v. 14).

17. *the mount Halak*] See marg. and ref. The name serves to mark the southern limit of Joshua's conquests. It suits equally well several of the ranges near the south border of Palestine, and it is uncertain which of them is the one here indicated.

Baal-gad (xii. 7 and xiii. 5) is probably Paneas, the Cæsarea Philippi of later times. The name means "troop or city of Baal,"

or a place where Baal was worshipped as the giver of " good luck." Cp. Is. lxv. 11. It was probably the same as *Baal-Hermon* (Judg. iii. 3 ; 1 Chr. v. 23 ; and see Deut. iii. 9).

18. *a long time*] At least five years ; according to others, seven years (see xiv. 10, and Introd. p. 4). This and the preceding chapter contain a very condensed account of the wars of Joshua, giving particulars about leading events only.

20. See marg. reff.

21. *at that time*] *i.e.* in course of the " long time " mentioned in *v.* 18.

the Anakims] See Num. xiii. 22. As it was the report of the spies respecting the Anakims which, above all, struck terror into the Israelites in the wilderness, and caused their faithless murmuring and revolt, so the sacred writer goes back here in his story to record pointedly the overthrow of this gigantic and formidable race. They had their chief settlements in the mountains around Hebron (x. 3) or Debir. See xv. 15. Anab was a city in the mountain district

from Hebron, from Debir, from Anab, and from all the mountains of Judah, and from all the mountains of Israel: Joshua
22 destroyed them utterly with their cities. There was none of the Anakims left in the land of the children of Israel: only in Gaza,
23 in *b*Gath, *c*and in Ashdod, there remained. ¶ So Joshua took the whole land, *d*according to all that the LORD said unto Moses; and Joshua gave it for an inheritance unto Israel *e*according to their divisions by their tribes. *f*And the land rested from war.
CHAP. 12. NOW these *are* the kings of the land, which the children of Israel smote, and possessed their land on the other side Jordan toward the rising of the sun, *a*from the river Arnon
2 *b*unto mount Hermon, and all the plain on the east: *c*Sihon king of the Amorites, who dwelt in Heshbon, *and* ruled from Aroer, which *is* upon the bank of the river Arnon, and from the middle of the river, and from half Gilead, even unto the river
3 Jabbok, *which is* the border of the children of Ammon; and *d*from the plain to the sea of Chinneroth on the east, and unto the sea of the plain, *even* the salt sea on the east, *e*the way to Beth-jeshimoth; and from ¹the south, under ² *f*Ashdoth-pisgah:
4 and *g*the coast of Og king of Bashan, *which was* of *h*the remnant
5 of the giants, *i*that dwelt at Ashtaroth and at Edrei, and reigned in *k*mount Hermon, *l*and in Salcah, and in all Bashan, *m*unto the border of the Geshurites and the Maachathites, and half Gilead,
6 the border of Sihon king of Heshbon. *n*Them did Moses the servant of the LORD and the children of Israel smite: and *o*Moses the servant of the LORD gave it *for* a possession unto the Reubenites, and the Gadites, and the half tribe of Manasseh.
7 ¶And these *are* the kings of the country *p*which Joshua and the children of Israel smote on this side Jordan on the west, from Baal-gad in the valley of Lebanon even unto the mount Halak, that goeth up to *q*Seir; which Joshua *r*gave unto the tribes of
8 Israel *for* a possession according to their divisions; *s*in the mountains, and in the valleys, and in the plains, and in the springs, and in the wilderness, and in the south country; *t*the Hittites, the Amorites, and the Canaanites, the Perizzites, the
9 Hivites, and the Jebusites: *u*the king of Jericho, one; *x*the king
10 of Ai, which *is* beside Beth-el, one; *y*the king of Jerusalem,
11 one; the king of Hebron, one; the king of Jarmuth, one;
12 the king of Lachish, one; the king of Eglon, one; *z*the king of

b 1 Sam. 17. 4.
c ch. 15. 46.
d Num. 34. 2, &c.
e Num. 26. 53.
ch. 14 to 19.
f ch. 14. 15. ver. 18.
a Num. 21. 24.
b Deut. 3. 8.
c Deut. 2. 33. & 3. 6.

d Deut. 3. 17.
e ch. 13. 20.
f Deut. 3. 17.
g Num. 21. 35.
Deut. 3. 4.
h Deut. 3. 11.
i Deut. 1. 4.
k Deut. 3. 8.
l Deut. 3. 10.
m Deut. 3. 14.
n Num. 21. 24, 33.
o Num. 32. 29, 33.

p ch. 11. 17.

q Gen. 14. 6.
r ch. 11. 23.
s ch. 10. 40.

t Ex. 3. 8.

u ch. 6. 2.
x ch. 8. 29.
y ch. 10. 23.

z ch. 10. 33.

¹ Or, *Teman.* ² Or, *The springs of Pisgah,* or, *The hill.*

---

of Judah, lying some distance south of Hebron. It still bears its ancient name.

22. *Gaza, Gath, Ashdod*] See xiii. 3 note.

23. These words import that Joshua had overcome all overt resistance. There were, however, many districts by no means thoroughly and finally subdued (xiii. 1-6).

XII. 1-6. Consult the notes to the passages referred to in the margin.

1. *all the plain on the east*] *i.e.* the Arabah or depressed tract along the east bank of Jordan, the modern El-Ghor (see Num. xxii. 1).

2. *from the middle of the river*] *i.e.* as appears from xiii. 9, 16, "from the city that is in the midst of the river;" vɪz., Ar Moab (see Deut. ii. 36).

3. *from the plain*] Render "over the

plain;" for the words describe not one of the boundaries of Sihon's kingdom, but part of the territory included in it, *i.e.* the eastern portion of the Ghor, between the Sea of Tiberias and the Dead Sea.

7-24. The names of the kings are given in the order of their actual encounter with Joshua. Those enumerated in *vv.* 10-18 either belonged to the league of the southern Canaanites (x. 1 seq.), the power of which was broken in the battle of Beth-horon, or were at any rate conquered in the campaign following that battle. Those mentioned in *vv.* 19-24 were in like manner connected with the northern confederates (xi. 1 seq.), who were defeated at the Waters of Merom.

a ch. 10. 38.
b ch. 10. 29.
c ch. 10. 28.
d ch. 8. 17.
Judg. 1. 22.
e 1 Kin. 4. 10.
f ch. 11. 10.
g ch. 11. 1.

h ch. 19. 37.

i ch. 11. 2.
k Isai. 9. 1.

a See ch.
14. 10.
& 23. 1.
b Judg. 3. 1.
c Joel 3. 4.
d 2 Sam. 3.
3. & 13. 37,
38.
e Jer. 2. 18.

13 Gezer, one; *a*the king of Debir, one; the king of Geder, one;
14, 15 the king of Hormah, one; the king of Arad, one; *b*the king of
16 Libnah, one; the king of Adullam, one; *c*the king of Mak-
17 kedah, one; *d*the king of Beth-el, one ; the king of Tappuah,
18 one; *e*the king of Hepher, one ; the king of Aphek, one ; the
19 king of ¹Lasharon, one ; the king of Madon, one; *f*the king of
20 Hazor, one ; the king of *g*Shimron-meron, one ; the king of
21 Achshaph, one; the king of Taanach, one; the king of Megiddo,
22 one; *h*the king of Kedesh, one; the king of Jokneam of Carmel,
23 one ; the king of Dor in the *i*coast of Dor, one ; the king of *k*the
24 nations of Gilgal, one ; the king of Tirzah, one : all the kings
thirty and one.

CHAP. 13. NOW Joshua *a*was old *and* stricken in years; and the
LORD said unto him, Thou art old *and* stricken in years, and
2 there remaineth yet very much land ²to be possessed. *b*This is
the land that yet remaineth : *c*all the borders of the Philistines,
3 and all *d*Geshuri, *e*from Sihor, which *is* before Egypt, even unto

¹ Or, *Sharon*, Isai. 33. 9.　　　　² Heb. *to possess it*, Deut.
31. 3.

13–20. The identification of several of
these places is still uncertain : the same
name (*e.g.* Aphek, *v.* 18) being applied to
various places in various parts of Palestine.
Geder, or Gedor (xv. 58), a city in the
mountain district in the south of the territory of Judah, is no doubt the modern
Jedur.

21. *Taanach*] A Levitical town (xxi. 25)
in the territory of Issachar, but assigned to
the Manassites (xvii. 11 ; cp. 1 Chr. vii. 29),
is identified with *Taanuk.* It was here that
Barak encountered the host of Sisera (Judg.
v. 19). Megiddo was near it, and is thought
to have been *el Lejjun* (the Roman Legion),
[or Mujedd'a (Conder)].

22. *Kedesh*] *i.e.* Kedesh Naphtali, a city
of refuge, a Levitical city, and the home of
Barak (Judg. iv. 6).

Jokneam] A Levitical city in the territory
of Zebulon (xix. 11) ; perhaps the modern
Kaimon. Tell *Kaimon* is a conspicuous and
important position, commanding the main
pass across the ridge of Carmel from Phœnicia to Egypt. This famous mountain
range (about fifteen miles long) no doubt received the name Carmel (the word means
"a fruitful field" as opposed to "wilderness") as descriptive of its character ; and
thus the name became an emblem of beauty
and luxuriance (Is. xxxv. 2 ; Cant. vii. 5,
&c.). Its highest part, about four miles from
Tell Kaimon, is nearly 1750 feet above the
sea. Its modern name, *Jebel Mar Elias,*
preserves still that association with the
great deeds of Elijah, from which Carmel
derives its chief Biblical interest. Mount
Carmel was probably, like Lebanon, from
very ancient Canaanitish times, regarded as
specially sacred ; and since the altar of the
Lord repaired by Elijah (1 K. xviii. 30)
was an old one which had been broken
down, Carmel was probably no less esteemed

by the Israelites also. In later times the
caves which abound towards the western
bluffs of the range have been frequented by
Christian, Jewish, and Mussulman anchor-
ites. The order of Carmelite or barefooted
friars took its rise from the convent founded
by St. Louis, which still crowns the western
headland.

23. *the king of the nations*] See Gen. xiv.
1 and note. It means king of certain mixed
and probably nomadic tribes, which regarded Gilgal (iv. 19) as their centre and
capital.

24. *Tirzah*] This place, the capital of
Jeroboam and his successors until the days
of Omri (1 K. xiv. 17, xv. 21, &c.), is identified by some with *Talluzah*, a town 3 m.
N.E. of Nablous, [by others with Teiasir].

XIII. Here commences the second portion of the book, the statements of which
were drawn from pre-existing documentary
records (cp. xviii. 9) ; the whole of the
history being introduced by a command of
God to Joshua to proceed to allot the land
amongst the tribes.

1. Joshua is bidden to allot the whole of
the Promised Land amongst the Twelve
Tribes in faith that God would perfect in
due time that expulsion of the Canaanites
which Joshua himself could not carry
further (see xi. 23).

2. This and *v.* 3 name the still unconquered districts in the southern half of the
land, *vv.* 4, 5, and 6 those in the north.

Geshuri] A district on the south of
Philistia, the inhabitants of which are again
named in 1 Sam. xxvii. 8 ; but are not to be
confounded with the land of the Geshurites
mentioned in *v.* 13, and in xii. 5.

3. Sihor is derived from a root signifying
"to be black," and is suitable enough as an
appellative of the Nile (Is. xxiii. 3). Here
it most probably stands for "the river of

the borders of Ekron northward, *which* is counted to the Canaanite: *f* five lords of the Philistines; the Gazathites, and the Ashdothites, the Eshkalonites, the Gittites, and the Ekronites;
4 also *g* the Avites: from the south, all the land of the Canaanites, and *1* Mearah that *is* beside the Sidonians, *h* unto Aphek, to the
5 borders of *i* the Amorites: and the land of the Giblites, and all Lebanon, toward the sunrising, *k* from Baal-gad under mount
6 Hermon unto the *l* entering into Hamath. All the inhabitants of the hill country from Lebanon unto *m* Misrephoth-maim, *and* all the Sidonians, them *n* will I drive out from before the children of Israel: only *o* divide thou it by lot unto the Israelites for an
7 inheritance, as I have commanded thee. Now therefore divide this land for an inheritance unto the nine tribes, and the half

f 1 Sam. 6.
4, 16.
g Deut. 2. 23.
h ch. 19. 30.
i See Judg.
1. 34.
k ch. 11. 17.
l Num. 13.21.

m ch. 11. 8.
n See ch.
23. 13.
Judg. 2. 21.
o ch. 14. 1.

¹ Or, *The cave.*

Egypt" (Num. xxxiv. 3 note), the modern *Wady el Arish.*

Ekron (*Akir*) lay on the northern boundary of Judah (xv. 11), and was actually conquered by the men of that tribe (Judg. i. 18), though assigned in the allotment of the land to Dan (xix. 43). It seems to have fallen again into the hands of the Philistines in the days of the Judges (1 Sam. v. 10), was reconquered by Samuel (cp. 1 Sam. vii. 14), but figures in subsequent times as a Philistine city only (cp. 1 Sam. xvii. 52; 2 K. i. 2, 16, &c.).

lords] The Hebrew word (*seren*) means "an axle," and is applied as a title peculiarly to the chiefs (cp. Judg. iii. 3 and marg. reff.) of the Philistines (Gen. x. 14).

Gaza was the most southern of the Philistine cities (cp. x. 41, xi. 22). It was allotted to the tribe of Judah (xv. 47), and was, with Askalon, taken by the warriors of that tribe (Judg. i. 18). Both cities were soon re-occupied by the Philistines, and subsequently are always mentioned as Philistine cities. Gaza lay on the direct route of the Egyptian armies in their invasions of Syria, by whom it was captured more than once. Special judgments are denounced against Gaza for the cruelty of its people towards the Jews in the time of their humiliation (Amos i. 6, 7; Zeph. ii. 4; Zech. ix. 5), and in the time of St. Jerome the ancient city was a ruin of which the foundations could hardly be traced, and the then existing town was built on another site. Gaza in later times an episcopal see, and is now a thriving place containing some 15,000 inhabitants, a larger population than that of Jerusalem.

Ashdod (*Esdud; Azotus*, Acts viii. 40) was, like Gaza, allotted to Judah (see xv. 46, 47), but was soon regained by the Philistines, and became a principal seat of their Dagon worship. Hither the ark of God was taken after its capture by the Philistines (1 Sam. v. 1 seq.). Its name (="fortress," "castle"), no less than its history (cp. 2 Chr. xxvi. 6; Is. xx. 1; Neh. iv. 7, &c.) indicates its importance as a stronghold; it withstood for twenty-nine years the longest siege on

record by the Egyptian king Psammetichus. Like Gaza, it was doomed by the Jewish prophets to desolation, and it was utterly destroyed by the Maccabees (1 Macc. x. 77-84, xi. 4). It was, however, rebuilt by the Romans, and figures in Christian times as an episcopal city.

Askelon (see Judg. i. 18), the birthplace of Herod the Great, figures as an important town and seaport in the history of the Crusades, and very massive ruins still attest the ancient strength and grandeur of the place. It is situated about midway between Gaza and Ashdod.

Gath seems to have been first taken by David (1 Chr. xviii. 1). It is not named again in the book of Joshua. It was the town of Goliath (1 Sam. xvii. 4), and is mentioned in David's elegy over Saul as a leading Philistine city (2 Sam. i. 20). It was the nearest of the Philistine cities to Jerusalem, but both the name and the city have perished; its site is conjecturally placed [by Conder] at Tell es Safi.

Avites] See Deut. ii. 23 note.

4. Read "on the south," and connect the words with the verse preceding. They indicate the southern limit of the still unconquered territory in this neighbourhood, as *v.* 3 gives the northern one.

Mearah] The "cave" (see marg.) has been referred to *Mugr Jezzin* ("cave of Jezzin"), between Tyre and Sidon, or to a district characterized by deep cave-like ravines near Sidon and Dan-Laish.

5. *Giblites*] The people of Gebal (*Jebail*, 22 m. N. of Beyrout). They were "stone-squarers" (1 K. v. 18) and (ship) "caulkers" (Ezek. xxvii. 9).

6. The A. V. would exhibit the sense more clearly if the words from the beginning of *v.* 2 to the words "the Sidonians" in this verse were placed in a parenthesis, and the order of the words before us changed thus: "I will drive them out." The "them" meaning the inhabitants of the "very much land to be possessed," spoken of in *v.* 1.

8 tribe of Manasseh, with whom the Reubenites and the Gadites
p Num. 32. have received their inheritance, *p*which Moses gave them, beyond
33.
Deut. 3. 13. Jordan eastward, *even* as Moses the servant of the LORD gave
ch. 22. 4. 9 them; from Aroer, that *is* upon the bank of the river Arnon,
q Num. 21. and the city that *is* in the midst of the river, *q*and all the plain
30.
r Num. 21. 10 of Medeba unto Dibon; and *r*all the cities of Sihon king of the
24, 25. Amorites, which reigned in Heshbon, unto the border of the
s ch. 12. 5. 11 children of Ammon; *s*and Gilead, and the border of the Geshurites and Maachathites, and all mount Hermon, and all Bashan
12 unto Salcah; all the kingdom of Og, in Bashan, which reigned
t Deut. 3. 11. in Ashtaroth and in Edrei, who remained of *t*the remnant of the
ch. 12. 4.
u Num. 21. 13 giants: *u*for these did Moses smite, and cast them out. Never-
24, 35. theless the children of Israel expelled *x*not the Geshurites, nor
x ver. 11. the Maachathites: but the Geshurites and the Maachathites
y Num. 18. 14 dwell among the Israelites until this day. *y*Only unto the tribe
20, 23, 24.
ch. 14. 3, 4. of Levi he gave none inheritance; the sacrifices of the LORD God
z ver. 33. of Israel made by fire *are* their inheritance, *z*as he said unto
15 them. ¶And Moses gave unto the tribe of the children of
16 Reuben *inheritance* according to their families. And their coast
a ch. 12. 2. was *a*from Aroer, that *is* on the bank of the river Arnon, *b*and
b Num.21.28. the city that *is* in the midst of the river, *c*and all the plain by
c Num.21.30. 17 Medeba; Heshbon, and all her cities that *are* in the plain;
d Num.21.23. 18 Dibon, and [1]Bamoth-baal, and Beth-baal-meon, *d*and Jahaza,
e Num.32.37. 19 and Kedemoth, and Mephaath, *e*and Kirjathaim, and *f*Sibmah,
f Num.32.38. 20 and Zareth-shahar in the mount of the valley, and Beth-peor,
g Deut. 3. 17. 21 and *g*[2]Ashdoth-pisgah, and Beth-jeshimoth, *h*and all the cities
h Deut. 3. 10. of the plain, and all the kingdom of Sihon king of the Amorites,
i Num. 21.24 which reigned in Heshbon, *i*whom Moses smote *k*with the
k Num. 31. 8. princes of Midian, Evi, and Rekem, and Zur, and Hur, and
Reba, *which were* dukes of Sihon, dwelling in the country.
l Num. 22. 5. 22 *l*Balaam also the son of Beor, the [3]soothsayer, did the children
of Israel slay with the sword among them that were slain by
23 them. And the border of the children of Reuben was Jordan,
and the border *thereof*. This *was* the inheritance of the children
of Reuben after their families, the cities and the villages thereof.

[1] Or, *The high places of Baal, and house of Baal-meon:* See Num. 32. 38.   [2] Or, *Springs of Pisgah,* or, *The hill.*   [3] Or, *diviner.*

8-33. The writer appends to the command of God (1-7) a statement that the other two tribes and a half had already had their inheritance marked out for them by Moses in the land east of Jordan. The boundaries of this territory as a whole are first set forth (8-14), and afterwards the portions assigned within it to the two tribes and a half are severally described (15-33).

14. See Deut. xviii. 1-5 and notes.

15-24. Inheritance of the tribe of Reuben. This territory was the most southerly of the trans-Jordanic possessions of Israel, and adjoined Moab, which lay only on the other side of the Arnon. Hence the Reubenites became in after times much intermixed with the Moabites, who in fact eventually acquired much of the land, and several, if not all, of the cities here named as belonging to Reuben. This acquisition was probably assisted by the fact that the territory north of Arnon had formerly belonged to the Moabites, from whom it was wrested by the Amorites (see Num. xxi. 26, &c. notes). It is not likely that the Amorite conquerors had completely extirpated the Moabite inhabitants. Hence, in the days when the Reubenites became engrossed in their pastoral pursuits, and probably not very long after the days of Joshua, the Moabites easily encroached on their inheritance, and in the end probably reoccupied nearly the whole of the ancient kingdom of Sihon (cp. Deut. xxxiii. 6 note).

17-21. See marg. reff. for some of these names. Heshbon, Kedemoth, and Mephaath became eventually Levitical cities.

21. *dukes of Sihon*] Rather "vassals of Sihon," probably those "dedicated" or "appointed" with a libation.

23. *Jordan &c.*] *i.e.* the Jordan and its territory (cp. similar expressions in Num. xxxiv.

24 ¶ And Moses gave *inheritance* unto the tribe of Gad, *even* unto
25 the children of Gad according to their families. [m]And their
coast was Jazer, and all the cities of Gilead, [n]and half the land
of the children of Ammon, unto Aroer, that *is* before [o]Rabbah;
26 and from Heshbon unto Ramath-mizpeh, and Betonim; and
27 from Mahanaim unto the border of Debir; and in the valley,
[p]Beth-aram, and Beth-nimrah, [q]and Succoth, and Zaphon, the
rest of the kingdom of Sihon king of Heshbon, Jordan and *his*
border, *even* unto the edge [r]of the sea of Chinnereth on the other
28 side Jordan eastward. This *is* the inheritance of the children
29 of Gad after their families, the cities, and their villages. ¶ And
Moses gave *inheritance* unto the half tribe of Manasseh: and
this was *the possession* of the half tribe of the children of Ma-
30 nasseh by their families. And their coast was from Mahanaim,
all Bashan, all the kingdom of Og king of Bashan, and [s]all the
31 towns of Jair, which *are* in Bashan, threescore cities: and half
Gilead, and [t]Ashtaroth, and Edrei, cities of the kingdom of Og
in Bashan, *were pertaining* unto the children of Machir the son
of Manasseh, *even* to the one half of the [u] children of Machir by
32 their families. ¶ These *are the countries* which Moses did distribute for inheritance in the plains of Moab, on the other side
33 Jordan, by Jericho, eastward. [x]But unto the tribe of Levi
Moses gave not *any* inheritance: the LORD God of Israel *was*
their inheritance, [y]as he said unto them.

CHAP. 14. AND these *are the countries* which the children of Israel
inherited in the land of Canaan, [a]which Eleazar the priest, and
Joshua the son of Nun, and the heads of the fathers of the tribes
of the children of Israel, distributed for inheritance to them.
2 [b]By lot *was* their inheritance, as the LORD commanded by the

[m] Num. 32. 35.
[n] Cp. Num. 21. 26, 28, 29, with Deut. 2. 19.
[o] Deut. 3. 11. 2 Sam. 11. 1.
[p] Num. 32. 36.
[q] Gen. 33. 17. 1 Kin. 7. 46.
[r] Num. 34. 11.
[s] Num. 32. 41. 1 Chr. 2. 23.
[t] ch. 12. 4.
[u] Num. 32. 39, 40.
[x] ver. 14. ch. 18. 7.
[y] Deut. 10. 9. & 18. 1, 2.
[a] Num. 34. 17, 18.
[b] Num. 26. 55. & 33. 54.

6; Deut. iii. 16). The portion of the tribe of Reuben at its northern extremity touched the Jordan; the main part of his inheritance lay on the east of the Dead Sea.

25. *all the cities of Gilead*] *i.e.* of Gilead in the narrower sense, included in the territory of Sihon, and distinct from Bashan (Deut. iii. 10).

half the land of the children of Ammon] *i.e.* that half of the Ammonite territory which had been conquered by the Amorites. This, after the overthrow of Sihon, the Israelites took for their own. The land which the Ammonites still held in the days of Moses, the Israelites were not permitted to attack.

Rabbah was a border fortress, the principal stronghold of the Ammonites (Num. xxi. 24), and the residence of their king. It was attacked and taken by Joab (2 Sam. xi. xii.; 1 Chr. xx. 1), but appears in later times again as an Ammonitish city (Jer. xlix. 3; Ezek. xxv. 5; Amos i. 13-15). In the third century B.C. it received from Ptolemy Philadelphus the name of Philadelphia, and was in later times the seat of a Christian bishop; but has now for many centuries been in ruins, remarkable for their grandeur and extent.

26. *the border of Debir*] Rather perhaps "the border of Lidbir," which is regarded as identical with the Lo-debar of 2 Sam. ix. 4, and xvii. 27, one of the towns from which provisions were brought to David at Mahanaim (Gen. xxxii. 2).

29–33. On the conquest of Bashan, see especially Num. xxxii. 33, &c. and notes.

XIV. **2.** *By lot*] We are not told in what manner the lot was cast. Perhaps two urns were employed, one containing a description of the several districts to be allotted, the other the names of the tribes; and the portion of each tribe would then be determined by a simultaneous drawing from the two urns. Or a drawing might be made by some appointed person, or by a delegate of each tribe from one urn containing the description of the ten inheritances. The lot only determined in a general way the position in the country of the particular tribe concerned, whether north or south, &c.; the dimensions of each territory being left to be adjusted subsequently, according to the numbers and wants of the tribe to be provided for. Since the predilections and habits of two tribes and a half were consulted in the apportionment to them of the trans-Jordanic territory (Num. xxxii. 1) there is no objection to the supposition that something of the same kind may have taken place, subject to the Divine approval, in the distribution of the lands to the nine and a

c ch. 13. 8, 32, 33.

3 hand of Moses, for the nine tribes, and *for* the half tribe. *c*For Moses had given the inheritance of two tribes and an half tribe' on the other side Jordan: but unto the Levites he gave none

d Gen. 48. 5.
1 Chr. 5. 1, 2.

4 inheritance among them. For *d* the children of Joseph were two tribes, Manasseh and Ephraim: therefore they gave no part unto the Levites in the land, save cities to dwell *in*, with their

e Num. 35. 2. ch. 21. 2.

5 suburbs for their cattle and for their substance. *e* As the LORD commanded Moses, so the children of Israel did, and they divided

f Num. 32. 12.
g Num. 14. 24, 30.
Deut. 1. 36. 38.
h Num. 13. 26.
i Num. 13. 6.
k Num. 13. 31, 32.
Deut. 1. 28.
l Num. 14. 24.
m ch. 1. 3.
n See Num. 13. 22.
o Num. 14, 30.

6 the land. ¶Then the children of Judah came unto Joshua in Gilgal: and Caleb the son of Jephunneh the *f* Kenezite said unto him, Thou knowest *g* the thing that the LORD said unto Moses the man of God concerning me and thee *h* in Kadesh-barnea.

7 Forty years old *was* I when Moses the servant of the LORD *i* sent me from Kadesh-barnea to espy out the land; and I

8 brought him word again as *it was* in mine heart. Nevertheless *k* my brethren that went up with me made the heart of the

9 people melt: but I wholly *l* followed the LORD my God. And Moses sware on that day, saying, *m* Surely the land *n* whereon thy feet have trodden shall be thine inheritance, and thy children's for ever, because thou hast wholly followed the LORD my

10 God. And now, behold, the LORD hath kept me alive, *o* as he said, these forty and five years, even since the LORD spake this word unto Moses, while *the children of* Israel [1] wandered in the wilderness: and now, lo, I *am* this day fourscore and five years

p See Deut. 34. 7.

11 old. *p* As yet I *am as* strong this day as *I was* in the day that Moses sent me: as my strength *was* then, even so *is* my strength

q Deut. 31. 2.
r Num. 13. 28, 33.
s Ps. 18. 32, 34. & 60. 12.
Rom. 8. 31.
t ch. 15. 14.
Judg. 1. 20.

12 now, for war, both *q* to go out, and to come in. Now therefore give me this mountain, whereof the LORD spake in that day; for thou heardest in that day how *r* the Anakims *were* there, and *that* the cities *were* great *and* fenced: *s* if so be the LORD *will be* with me. then *t* I shall be able to drive them out, as the LORD

[1] Heb. *walked.*

half other tribes; and the lot would thus be appealed to as finally deciding the matter and foreclosing jealousies and disputes.

It is apparent that the casting of the ten lots did not take place simultaneously. The tribe of Judah had precedence, whether by express appointment or because its lot "came up" first, does not appear. It was, as it seems, only after this tribe had settled upon its domains, that further lots were drawn for Ephraim and the half tribe of Manasseh. After this a pause, perhaps of some duration, appears to have occurred; the camp was moved from Gilgal to Shiloh; and the further casting of lots for the other seven tribes was proceeded with at the instigation of Joshua (see xviii. 10).

6. *the children of Judah*] No doubt, in particular, the kinsmen of Caleb, and perhaps other leading men of the tribe. These came before Joshua, with Caleb, in order to make it manifest that they supported his claim, to be secured in the possessions promised him by Moses before the general allotment should be made to the tribes (cp. marg. reff.).

9. *Moses sware*] *i.e.* God sware; and His promise, confirmed by an oath, was communicated, of course, through Moses.

10. *forty and five years*] The word of God to Moses was spoken after the return of the spies in the autumn of the second year after the Exodus (Num. xiii. 25); subsequently thirty-eight years elapsed before the people reached the Jordan (Num. xx. 1); after the passage of the Jordan seven more years had passed, when Caleb claimed Hebron, before the partition of the land amongst the nine tribes and a half. These seven years then correspond to the "long time" (xi. 18) during which Joshua was making war with the Canaanites. They are in the sequel of this verse added by Caleb to the years of wandering, since during them the people had no settled abodes.

12. The Anakims had in the course of Joshua's campaigns in the south been expelled from "this mountain," *i.e.* the mountain country round Hebron, but they had only withdrawn to the neighbouring cities of Philistia (xi. 22). Thence they had, as must be inferred from the text here, returned and reoccupied Hebron, probably when Joshua and the main force of the Israelites had marched northward to deal with

13 said. ¶ And Joshua ^ublessed him, ^xand gave unto Caleb the
14 son of Jephunneh Hebron for an inheritance. ^yHebron therefore became the inheritance of Caleb the son of Jephunneh the
Kenezite unto this day, because that he ^zwholly followed the
15 LORD God of Israel. And ^athe name of Hebron before *was*
Kirjath-arba; *which Arba was* a great man among the Anakims.
^bAnd the land had rest from war.

CHAP. 15. *THIS* then was the lot of the tribe of the children of
Judah by their families; ^a*even* to the border of Edom the ^bwil-
derness of Zin southward *was* the uttermost part of the south
2 coast. ¶ And their south border was from the shore of the salt
3 sea, from the ¹bay that looketh southward: and it went out to
the south side ^cto ²Maaleh-acrabbim, and passed along to Zin,
and ascended up on the south side unto Kadesh-barnea, and
passed along to Hezron, and went up to Adar, and fetched a
4 compass to Karkaa: *from thence* it passed ^dtoward Azmon, and
went out unto the river of Egypt; and the goings out of that
5 coast were at the sea: this shall be your south coast. ¶ And
the east border *was* the salt sea, *even* unto the end of Jordan.
And *their* border in the north quarter *was* from the bay of the
6 sea at the uttermost part of Jordan: and the border went up to
^eBeth-hogla, and passed along by the north of Beth-arabah;
and the border went up ^fto the stone of Bohan the son of
7 Reuben: and the border went up toward Debir from ^gthe valley
of Achor, and so northward, looking toward Gilgal, that *is* before
the going up to Adummim, which *is* on the south side of the
river: and the border passed toward the waters of En-shemesh,
8 and the goings out thereof were at ^hEn-rogel: and the border
went up ⁱby the valley of the son of Hinnom unto the south side

¹ Heb. *tongue.*   ² Or, *The going up to Acrabbim.*

^u ch. 22. 6.
^x ch. 10. 37.
1 Chr. 6. 55,
56.
^y ch. 21. 12.
^z ver. 8, 9.
^a Gen. 13. 18.
^b ch. 11. 23.

^a Num. 34. 3.
^b Num. 20. 1.

^c Num. 34. 4.

^d Num. 34. 5.

^e Gen. 50. 10.
^f ch. 18. 17.
^g ch. 7. 26.

^h 2 Sam. 17.
17.
1 Kin. 1. 9.
ⁱ ch. 18. 16.
2 Kin. 23. 10.
Jer. 19. 2, 6.

Jabin and his confederates. Caleb finally
drove out this formidable race and occupied
Hebron and its dependent towns and district permanently. See xv. 13 seq.

15. *a great man*] Literally the great man;
i.e. the renowned ancestor of the tribe,
regarded as the founder of its greatness
(xv. 13).

XV. The inheritance of the tribe of Judah is described first by its general boundaries on all four sides (*vv.* 1–12); then reference is again made, for the sake of completeness, to the special inheritance of Caleb
which lay within these boundaries (*vv.* 13–
20); and lastly a list of the towns is given
(*vv.* 21–63). Consult the marg. reff.

6. *the stone of Bohan*] This stone perhaps
commemorated some deed of valour belonging to the wars of Joshua (cp. 1 Sam. vii.
12). The stone was erected on the slope of
a hill (see marg. ref.), no doubt one of the
range which bounds the Jordan valley on
the west. But its exact site is wholly uncertain.

7. *the going up to Adummim*] Rather,
"the ascent or pass of Adummim" (cp.
v. 3, marg.), on the road from Jerusalem to
Jericho. Its name signifies "red" and is explained by Jerome as given because of the
frequent blood shed there by robbers. This

road is the scene of the parable of the Good
Samaritan. Possibly the name may be due
to some aboriginal tribe of "red men," who
held their ground in these fastnesses after
the invaders had driven them from the face
of the country elsewhere.

En-shemesh] *i.e.* "fountain of the sun;"
no doubt that now called "the Fountain of
the Apostles," about two miles from Jerusalem, and the only well on the road to
Jericho.

En-rogel] *i.e.* "fountain of the fullers"
near the walls of Jerusalem. It was here
that Jonathan and Ahimaaz concealed
themselves after the rebellion of Absalom,
in order to procure tidings for David, and
here Adonijah gave a feast to his adherents
preparatory to making an attempt on the
crown (cp. marg. reff.). It is probably the
modern "Fountain of the Virgin," the only
real spring near Jerusalem, from which the
Pool of Siloam is supplied. Others identify
it, less probably, with the "Well of Job,"
situated where the valleys of Kedron and Hinnom unite.

8. *the valley of the son of Hinnom*] This
valley begins on the west of Jerusalem at the
road to Joppa, and turning south-eastward
round the foot of Mount Zion joins the
deeper valley of Kedron on the south of the

<table>
<tr><td>

k ch. 18. 28.
Judg. 1. 21.
& 19. 10.
l ch. 18. 16.

m ch. 18. 15.

n 1 Chr. 13. 6.
o Judg. 18.
12.
p ch. 19. 43.
Judg. 14. 1.
q ch. 19. 43.

r ver. 47.
Num. 34. 6,
7.
s ch. 14. 13.

t ch. 14. 15.

u Judg. 1.
10, 20.
x Num.13.22.

</td><td>

of the <i>k</i> Jebusite; the same <i>is</i> Jerusalem: and the border went up to the top of the mountain that <i>lieth</i> before the valley of Hinnom westward, which <i>is</i> at the end <i>l</i> of the valley of the 9 giants northward: and the border was drawn from the top of the hill unto <i>m</i> the fountain of the water of Nephtoah, and went out to the cities of mount Ephron; and the border was drawn 10 <i>n</i> to Baalah, which <i>is</i> <i>o</i> Kirjath-jearim: and the border compassed from Baalah westward unto mount Seir, and passed along unto the side of mount Jearim, which <i>is</i> Chesalon, on the north side, and went down to Beth-shemesh, and passed on to <i>p</i> Tim-11 nah: and the border went out unto the side of <i>q</i> Ekron northward: and the border was drawn to Shicron, and passed along to mount Baalah, and went out unto Jabneel; and the goings 12 out of the border were at the sea. ¶ And the west border <i>was</i> <i>r</i> to the great sea, and the coast <i>thereof.</i> ¶ This <i>is</i> the coast of the children of Judah round about according to their families. 13 ¶ <i>s</i> And unto Caleb the son of Jephunneh he gave a part among the children of Judah, according to the commandment of the LORD to Joshua, <i>even</i> <i>t</i>1 the city of Arba the father of Anak, 14 which <i>city is</i> Hebron. And Caleb drove thence <i>u</i> the three sons of Anak, <i>x</i> Sheshai, and Ahiman, and Talmai, the children of

</td></tr>
</table>

¹ Or, Kirjath-arba.

city. It was in this ravine, more particularly at Tophet in the more wild and precipitous part of it towards the east, that the later kings of Judah offered the sacrifices of children to Moloch (2 Chr. xxviii. 3, xxxiii. 6, &c.). After these places had been defiled by Josiah, Tophet and the whole valley of Hinnom were held in abomination by the Jews, and the name of the latter was used to denote the place of eternal torment (Matt. v. 22). The Greek term Gehenna (γέεννα) is in fact formed from the Hebrew <i>gay-hinnom,</i> "valley of Hinnom." Hinnom is regarded either as the name of some ancient hero, or as an appellative (= "groaning" or "moaning"), bestowed on the spot because of the cries of the victims here offered to Moloch, and of the drums with which those cries were drowned.

the valley of the giants] Rather "the plain of Rephaim." This plain, named after an ancient and gigantic tribe of the land (Gen. xiv. 5), lies south-westward of Jerusalem, and is terminated by a slight rocky ridge forming the brow of the valley of Hinnom. The valley is fertile (Isa. xvii. 5) and broad, and has been on more than one occasion the camping ground for armies operating against Jerusalem (2 Sam. v. 18, 22, xxiii. 13).

9. Nephtoah is probably the modern <i>Ain Lifta,</i> two miles and a half north-westward of Jerusalem: and Mount Ephron is conjecturally connected with the city Ephrain (2 Chr. xiii. 19) or Ophrah (xviii. 23).

10. Mount Seir is not the well-known range of Edom. The name (= "shaggy mountain") is applicable to any rugged or well-wooded hill. Here it probably denotes the range which runs south-westward from Kirjath-jearim to the Wady Surar. Mount

Jearim, <i>i.e.</i> "woody mountain," is through its other name, Chesalon, identified with the modern <i>Kesla.</i>

Beth-shemesh] i.e. "house of the sun," called "Ir-shemesh" or "city of the sun" (xix. 41; cp. 1 K. iv. 9), a place assigned to Dan, and one of the cities which fell by lot to the Levites (xxi. 16). Beth-shemesh was the first place at which the ark rested after its return from the hands of the Philistines (1 Sam. vi. 12). It was the residence of one of Solomon's purveyors (1 K. iv. 9), and was the spot where at a later date Amaziah was defeated and slain by Jehoash (2 K. xiv. 11 seq.). It is no doubt the modern Ain Shems.

Timnah, called also Timnath, and Timnathah, belonged likewise to Dan, and is to be distinguished from other places of like name (Gen. xxxviii. 12; Josh. xxiv. 30). Timnah (= "portion") was evidently, like Gilgal, Ramah, Kirjath, and several other towns, of frequent use in Canaanitish topography.

11. <i>Jabneel</i>] The modern <i>Yebna,</i> about three miles from the coast and twelve miles south of Joppa. It is called Jabneh in 2 Chr. xxvi. 6, where Uzziah is recorded to have taken it from the Philistines and destroyed its fortifications. The town is repeatedly mentioned with its haven in the wars of the Maccabees (1 Macc. iv. 15; 2 Macc. xii. 8), and by Josephus under the name of Jamnia. It is described by Philo as a very populous town; and after the destruction of Jerusalem was for a long time the seat of the Sanhedrim, and was a famous school of Jewish learning. Its ruins, which are still considerable, stand on the brink of the <i>Wady Rubin.</i>

14. See marg. reff.

15 Anak. And ⱽhe went up thence to the inhabitants of Debir:
16 and the name of Debir before *was* Kirjath-sepher.   ᶻAnd Caleb
    said, He that smiteth Kirjath-sepher, and taketh it, to him will
17 I give Achsah my daughter to wife.   And ᵃOthniel the ᵇson of
    Kenaz, the brother of Caleb, took it: and he gave him Achsah
18 his daughter to wife.   ᶜAnd it came to pass, as she came *unto him*,
    that she moved him to ask of her father a field: and ᵈshe lighted
19 off *her* ass; and Caleb said unto her, What wouldest thou? Who
    answered, Give me a ᵉblessing; for thou hast given me a south
    land; give me also springs of water.   And he gave her the
20 upper springs, and the nether springs.   ¶This *is* the inheritance
    of the tribe of the children of Judah according to their families.
21 ¶And the uttermost cities of the tribe of the children of Judah
    toward the coast of Edom southward were Kabzeel, and Eder,
22, 23 and Jagur, and Kinah, and Dimonah, and Adadah, and
24 Kedesh, and Hazor, and Ithnan, Ziph, and Telem, and Bea-
25 loth, and Hazor, Hadattah, and Kerioth, *and* Hezron, which *is*

y ch. 10. 38.
Judg. 1. 11.
z Judg.1.12.
a Judg.1.13.
& 3. 9.
b Num.32.12.

c Judg.1.14.
d See Gen.
24. 64.
1 Sam.25.23.
e Gen. 33. 11.

---

15. The name Debir belonged to two
other places; viz., that named in *v.* 7, between Jerusalem and Jericho, and the Gadite town mentioned in xiii. 26. The Debir
here meant appears [and its site has been
conjecturally placed at Dhâherîyeh (Conder)] to have been situated in the mountain
district south of Hebron. It was one of the
towns afterwards assigned to the Levites.
Its other name (*v.* 49), *Kirjath-sannah, i.e.*
perhaps, "city of palm branches," or "city
of law, or sacred learning," no less than the
two given in the text, would indicate that
Debir was an ancient seat of Canaanitish
learning, for Debir probably is equivalent
to "oracle," and Kirjath-sepher means
"city of books." This plurality of names
marks the importance of the town, as the
inducement held out in *v.* 16, by Caleb, to
secure its capture (cp. 1 Sam. xvii. 25, xviii.
17), points to its strength.
17. Othniel was probably Caleb's younger
brother; the expression "son of Kenaz"
being only an equivalent for the "Kenezite" (xiv. 6).
18. *a field*] In Judg. i. 14, "the field,"
i.e. the well-known field asked by Achsah
and given by Caleb as a "blessing," *i.e.* as
a token of goodwill, which when the Book
of Judges was written had become historical. The "field" in question was doubtless
in the neighbourhood of Debir, and was
specially valuable because of its copious
springs. Achsah's dismounting was a sign
of reverence.
19. *a south land*] This term (*negeb*) which
is often equivalent to a proper name (*v.* 21),
importing the well-defined district which
formed the south of the Promised Land
(Num. xiii. 17 note), seems here used in its
more general sense (Ps. cxxvi. 4), for a dry
or barren land. The rendering of this
passage adopted by LXX., several Versions, and Commentators, &c., "thou hast
given me into a south land," *i.e.* "hast
given me in marriage into a south land," is

forced; the construction of the verb "to
give," with two accusatives, is natural and
common to many languages.
    springs of water] The Hebrew word is
found only here and in the parallel passage,
Judg. i. 15. Hence some take it as a proper name, "Gulloth-maim," which like
Beth-horon (xvi. 3, 5), was applied to two
distinct but adjoining places—distinguished
as "the upper" and "the lower." The
tract in question was no doubt a mountain
slope which had springs both on its higher
and lower ground; possibly the modern
Kurmul.
21–63. List of the towns of the tribe of
Judah. These are arranged in four divisions, according to the natural features of
the district; viz., those of the Negeb or
south country (21–32); of "the valley," or
"the plain" (*Shephelah*, 33–47); of "the
mountains" (48–60); and of "the wilderness" (61, 62). Many of the identifications
are still conjectural only.
21–32. The Negeb was for the most part
rocky and arid, and cannot have been at
any time very thickly peopled.
21. Kabzeel was the native place of Benaiah (2 Sam. xxiii. 20), who was famous as
a slayer of lions. The Negeb was a principal haunt of these beasts.
24. Telem may be the Telaim of 1 Sam.
xv. 4, where Saul mustered his army for the
expedition against the Amalekites. It is
possibly to be looked for at *El-Kuseir*, a
spot where the various routes towards different parts of the Negeb converge, and
which is occupied by the Arab tribe the
Dhullam, a word identical with Telem in its
consonants. Bealoth is probably the "Baalath-beer—Ramath of the south" (xix. 8),
and was one of the towns afterwards assigned to the Simeonites. It is identified
with the modern *Kurnub.*
25. *and Hezron which is Hazor*] In this
verse are the names of two towns only, not
of four. Two places bearing the common

26, 27 Hazor, Amam, and Shema, and Moladah, and Hazar-gaddah,
28 and Heshmon, and Beth-palet, and Hazar-shual, and Beer-
29, 30 sheba, and Bizjothjah, Baalah, and Iim, and Azem, and Elto-
/ 1 Sam. 27.   31 lad, and Chesil, and Hormah, and / Ziklag, and Madmannah,
6.   32 and Sansannah, and Lebaoth, and Shilhim, and Ain, and Rim-
           mon : all the cities *are* twenty and nine, with their villages :
ᵍ ch. 19. 41.   33, 34 ¶ *And* in the valley, ᵍ Eshtaol, and Zoreah, and Ashnah, and

topographical appellation, Hazor ("inclosure") are here mentioned and distinguished
as "Hazor Hadattah" and "Kerioth-Hez-
ron," otherwise termed Hazor, simply : the
former has been identified by some with *El-
Hudhera;* the latter is probably the modern
El-Kuryetein. Kerioth, prefixed to a name,
bespeaks military occupation, as Hazor
points to pastoral pursuits. The place
would therefore seem to be an ancient pastoral settlement which had been fortified by
the Anakims, and called accordingly Kerioth ; to which name the men of Judah,
after they had captured it, added that of
Hezron, in honour of one of their leading
ancestors (cp. Gen. xlvi. 12 ; Ruth iv. 18).
Kerioth was the home of Judas the traitor,
if the ordinary derivation of Iscariot (= *ish
K'rioth, i.e.* man of Kerioth) be accepted:
St. Matt. x. 4.
   26. Moladah is probably the modern
El-Milh, and like Hazar-shual (*Berrishaul*
near Gaza) (= "inclosure of foxes") occurs
(xix. 2, 3 ; 1 Chr. iv. 28), as a town belonging to Simeon, and (Neh. xi. 26, 27) as a
place occupied by Jews after the captivity.
   29-32. Baalah (xix. 3) is found in the
modern *Deir-el-Belah,* near Gaza. Iim, *i.e.*
"ruinous heaps" or "conical hills" (Num.
xxi. 11 note) is by some connected with
Azem ; and the compound name, *Ije Azem,*) is
traced in El-Aujeh, in the country of the
Azazimeh Arabs, in whose name the ancient Azem may perhaps be traced. Eltolad
is connected with *Wady-el-Thoula,* in the extreme south of the Negeb. Chesil appears
to be the town called Bethul (xix. 4), and
probably the Bethel (1 Sam. xxx. 27) situated
not far from Ziklag. The name Chesil (=
"fool") was most likely bestowed by way of
opprobrium (cp. the change of Bethel, house
of God, into Bethaven, house of vanity,
Hos. iv. 15). As Chesil signifies the group of
stars known as Orion (cp. Job xxxviii. 31 ;
Amos v. 8), probably it was the worship of
the heavenly bodies in particular that was
carried on here. Bethel may have been the
ancient name, and the spot was perhaps the
very one near Beer-sheba where Abraham
planted a tamarisk tree (Gen. xxi. 33). The
place is probably *El Khulasah,* the Elusa of
ecclesiastical writers, situated some fifteen
miles south-west of Beer-sheba. Jerome testifies to the fact, that the worship of Venus
as the morning star was practised there, and
Sozomen appears to be speaking of this
place, when he mentions a Bethel (Bηθελία)
in the territory of Gaza, populous and

famous for an ancient and splendid temple. The site of Ziklag is uncertain.
Madmannah and Sansannah correspond to
Beth-marcaboth (= "house of chariots")
and Hazar-susah (= "horse inclosure") in
xix. 5 (1 Chr. iv. 31). The latter names
point to two stations of passage on or near
the high road between Egypt and Palestine, and are represented by the modern
Minyay and *Wady-es-Suny,* on the caravan
route south of Gaza. Shilhim or Sharuhen,
(xix. 6), and Shaaraim (1 Chr. iv. 31) is traced
in *Khirbet-es-Seram,* near El Aujeh. Ain
and Rimmon were possibly originally two
towns, but in process of time became so
connected as to be treated as one name
(Neh. xi. 29). The place is probably the
present *Um-er-Rummamim, i.e.* "mother of
pomegranates," a place about ten miles
north of Beer-sheba.
   32. *twenty and nine*] The A. V. gives
thirty-four names. The difference is due
either to the confusion by an early copyist
of letters similar in form which were used
as numerals ; or to the separation in the
A. V. of names which in the original were
one (*e.g. v.* 25).
   33-47. "The valley" or the Shephelah,
is bounded on the south by the Negeb, on
the west by the Mediterranean, on the
north by the plain of Sharon, on the east
by "the mountains" (*v.* 48). It is a well-
defined district, of an undulating surface
and highly fertile character, thickly dotted,
even at the present time, with villages,
which are for the most part situated on the
different hills. The towns in this district,
like those in the Negeb, are classed in four
groups.
   33-36. First group of fourteen towns :
these belong to the north-eastern portion of
the Shephelah. Eshtaol and Zoreah were
afterwards assigned to the tribe of Dan, and
inhabited by Danites (Judg. xiii. 25, xviii.
2, 8, 11). The latter place was the home of
Samson (Judg. xiii. 2). It was one of the
cities fortified by Rehoboam (2 Chr. xi. 10),
and was re-occupied by the Jews after the
captivity (Neh. xi. 29). It is probably the
modern *Surah.* [Eshtaol has been identified with Eshua (Conder)]. Both places
were in later times partly peopled by Judahites from Kirjath-jearim ; perhaps after
the departure of the colony of Danites for
Dan-Laish. Zanoah is the present *Zanna,*
not far from Surah. Socoh is the modern
Shuweikah. Sharaim is perhaps to be sought
in the modern *Zakariya.* Gederah ("wall"

35 Zanoah, and En-gannim, Tappuah, and Enam, Jarmuth, and
36 Adullam, Socoh, and Azekah, and Sharaim, and Adithaim, and
Gederah, ¹and Gederothaim; fourteen cities with their villages:
37, 38 Zenan, and Hadashah, and Migdal-gad, and Dilean, and
39 ʰMizpeh, and Joktheel, Lachish, and Bozkath, and Eglon,   ʰ ch. 11. 3.
40, 41 and Cabbon, and Lahmam, and Kithlish, and Gederoth,
Beth-dagon, and Naamah, and Makkedah; sixteen cities with
42, 43 their villages: Libnah, and Ether, and Ashan, and Jiphtah,
44 and Ashnah, and Nezib, and Keilah, and Achzib, and Ma-
45 reshah; nine cities with their villages: Ekron, with her towns
46 and her villages: from Ekron even unto the sea, all that *lay*
47 ²near Ashdod, with their villages: Ashdod with her towns and
her villages, Gaza with her towns and her villages, unto ⁱthe   ⁱ ver. 4.
river of Egypt, and ᵏthe great sea, and the border *thereof*:   ᵏ Num. 34. 6.
48, 49 ¶ And in the mountains, Shamir, and Jattir, and Socoh, and
50 Dannah, and Kirjath-sannah, which *is* Debir, and Anab,
51 and Eshtemoh, and Anim, ˡand Goshen, and Holon, and   ˡ ch. 10. 41.
52 Giloh; eleven cities with their villages: Arab, and Dumah,   & 11. 16.
53 and Eshean, and ³Janum, and Beth-tappuah, and Aphekah,
54 and Humtah, and ᵐKirjath-arba, which *is* Hebron, and Zior;   ᵐ Gen. 13. 18.
55 nine cities with their villages: Maon, Carmel, and Ziph, and
56, 57 Juttah, and Jezreel, and Jokdeam, and Zanoah, Cain,
58 Gibeah, and Timnah; ten cities with their villages: Halhul,
59 Beth-zur, and Gedor, and Maarath, and Beth-anoth, and El-

¹ Or, *or*.   ² Heb. *by the place of*.   ³ Or, *Janus*.

---

or "fortress") was a name borne with various terminations by several places.

37–41. Second group of towns, containing
those in the middle portion of the Shephelah, and of which some only (x. 3, 10)
can be identified.

42–44. Third group; towns in the south
of the Shephelah. For Libnah see x.' 29.
Mareshah is believed to be near *Beit-jibrin*,
the ancient *Eleutheropolis*.

45–47. Fourth group: the towns of the
Philistine sea-coast: see xiii. 3.

48–60. This highland district extends
from the Negeb on the south to Jerusalem,
and is bounded by the Shephelah on the
west, and the "Wilderness" (*vv.* 61, 62) on
the east. The mountains, which are of limestone, rise to a height of near 3000 feet. At
present, the highlands of Judah present a
somewhat dreary and monotonous aspect.
The peaks are for the most part barren,
though crowned almost everywhere with the
ruins of ancient towns, and bearing on their
sides marks of former cultivation. Many of
the valleys, especially towards the south, are,
however, still very productive. The towns
here enumerated are given in six groups.

48–51. First group: towns on the south-
west. Dannah [is identified with *Idnah*
(Conder)]. Jattir (*Attir*), and Eshtemoh
(*Semua*) were priestly cities (xxi. 14; 1 Chr.
vi. 57), and the place to which David, after
routing the Amalekites, sent presents (1
Sam. xxx. 27, 28). Socoh is *Suweikeh*.

52–54. Second group of nine towns,
situated somewhat to the north of the last-

mentioned. Of these Dumah is perhaps the
ruined village *Ed Daumeh*, in the neighbourhood of Hebron; and Beth-tappuah, *i.e.*
"house of apples," *Teffuh*, a place which
has still a good number of inhabitants, is
conspicuous for its olive groves and vineyards, and bears on every side the traces of
industry and thrift.

55–57. Third group; lying eastward of
the towns named in the last two, and next
to "the wilderness."

55. The four towns retain their ancient
names with but little change. Maon (1 Sam.
xxiii. 24, xxv. 2), the home of Nabal, is to be
looked for in the conical hill, *Main*, the top
of which is covered with ruins. It lies
eight or nine miles south-east of Hebron.
Carmel (1 Sam. xxv. 2), the modern *Kurmul*, is a little to the north of *Main*. The
name belongs to more than one place (xii.
22). Ziph gave its name to "the wilderness" into which David fled from Saul (1
Sam. xxiii. 14).

58, 59. Fourth group. Towns north of
the last mentioned, of which Beth-zur and
Gedor are represented by *Beit-sur* and
Jedur.

After *v.* 59 follows in the Greek version a
fifth group of eleven towns, which appears
to have dropped in very ancient times out
of the Hebrew text, probably because some
transcriber passed unawares from the word
"villages" at the end of *v.* 59, to the same
word at the end of the missing passage. The
omitted group contains the towns of an important, well-known, and populous district

n ch. 9. 17.

o See Judg.
1. 8. 21.
2 Sam. 5. 6.
p Judg. 1.
21.

a Gen. 28. 19.
Judg. 1. 26.
b ch. 10. 10.
2 Chr. 8. 5.
c ch. 10. 33.
1 Kin. 9. 15.
d ch. 17. 14.

60 tekon; six cities with their villages: *n*Kirjath-baal, which *is* Kirjath-jearim, and Rabbah; two cities with their villages: 61, 62 in the wilderness, Beth-arabah, Middin, and Secacah, and Nibshan, and the city of Salt, and Engedi; six cities with their 63 villages. ¶ As for the Jebusites the inhabitants of Jerusalem, *o*the children of Judah could not drive them out: *p*but the Jebusites dwell with the children of Judah at Jerusalem unto this day.

CHAP. 16. AND the lot of the children of Joseph ¹fell from Jordan by Jericho, unto the water of Jericho on the east, to the wilderness that goeth up from Jericho throughout mount Beth-el, 2 and goeth out from Beth-el to *a*Luz, and passeth along unto the 3 borders of Archi to Ataroth, and goeth down westward to the coast of Japhleti, *b*unto the coast of Beth-horon the nether, and 4 to *c*Gezer: and the goings out thereof are at the sea. *d*So the children of Joseph, Manasseh and Ephraim, took their inhe-5 ritance. ¶ And the border of the children of Ephraim according to their families was *thus:* even the border of their inheritance

¹ Heb. *went forth* (*i.e.*, out of the urn).

---

lying immediately south of Jerusalem, and containing such towns as Tekoah (2 Sam. xiv. 2; Neh. iii. 5, 27; Amos i. 1); Bethlehem, the native town of David and of Christ (Gen. xxxv. 19); and Aetan, a Grecised form of Etam (2 Chr. xi. 6).

61, 62. This district, including the towns in "the wilderness," the scene of David's wanderings (1 Sam. xxiii. 24; Ps. lxiii. title), and of the preaching of the Baptist (Matt. iii. 1), and perhaps of our Lord's temptation (Matt. iv.), extended from the northern limit of Judah along the Dead Sea to the Negeb; it was bounded on the west by that part of "the mountains" or highlands of Judah, which adjoined Bethlehem and Maon. It abounds in limestone rocks, perforated by numerous caverns, and often of fantastic shapes. It is badly supplied with water, and hence is for the most part barren, though affording in many parts, now quite desolate, clear tokens of former cultivation. It contained only a thin population in the days of Joshua.

62. "The city of Salt" is not mentioned elsewhere, but was no doubt connected with "the valley of salt" (2 Sam. viii. 13). The name itself, and the mention of En-gedi (Gen. xiv. 7 note) suggest that its site must be looked for near the Dead Sea.

XVI. This and xvii. are closely connected, and assign the boundaries of "the children of Joseph," *i.e* of the kindred tribes of Ephraim and Manasseh. These two tribes, or more strictly speaking, the tribe of Ephraim and the half tribe of Manasseh, drew one lot only, no doubt, because it was all along intended that their inheritances should be adjacent. These chapters accordingly describe (1) the southern boundary of the whole territory of the children of Joseph (xvi. 1–4); (2) the limits of Ephraim in particular (xvi. 5–10) (3);

those of Manasseh (xvii. 1–13); and (4) the discontent of the descendants of Joseph with their inheritance is recorded, together with Joshua's answer to their complaints (xvii. 14–18).

The territory allotted to these two powerful tribes comprises the central and, in every way, the choicest part of Canaan west of the Jordan. The hills of this district, making up what is called (xx. 7) "Mount Ephraim," are less high and far less barren than those of Judah; the water supply is much larger; and the very rich and fertile plains of Sharon and Esdraelon are left between the rocky fastnesses of Benjamin on the south and the high lands of Galilee belonging to Issachar on the north.

1. *to the wilderness*] Strike out "to," for the word is in apposition to "lot." The wilderness is (xviii. 12) "the wilderness of Bethaven."

2. *of Archi*] Read "**of the Archite,**" also a designation of David's friend Hushai (2 Sam. xv. 32; xvi. 16, &c.). The word is derived from Erech (Gen. x. 10). But whether there was in the neighbourhood of Bethel a place bearing this Babylonian name, or whether a colony from the East had settled in this spot and brought the name with them, is unknown.

Ataroth] Called (*v.* 5 and xviii. 13) Ataroth-adar (= "crowns of fame or greatness") perhaps to distinguish it from two other places bearing the same name but situated on the other side of Jordan, in the territory of Gad (Num. xxxii. 34). It is identified with Atara, near the road from Jerusalem to Nablous.

3. *of Japhleti*] Rather "**of the Japhletite.**" All history of the name is lost.

5–8. From the abrupt manner in which the statements are introduced, as well as from their imperfect character, there is

on the east side was *Ataroth-addar, *unto Beth-horon the
6 upper; and the border went out toward the sea to *Michmethah
on the north side; and the border went about eastward unto
7 Taanath-shiloh, and passed by it on the east to Janohah; and
it went down from Janohah to Ataroth, *and to Naarath, and
8 came to Jericho, and went out at Jordan. The border went out
from Tappuah westward unto the *river Kanah; and the goings
out thereof were at the sea. This *is the inheritance of the tribe
9 of the children of Ephraim by their families. And *the separate
cities for the children of Ephraim *were* among the inheritance
of the children of Manasseh, all the cities with their villages.
10 *And they drave not out the Canaanites that dwelt in Gezer:
but the Canaanites dwell among the Ephraimites unto this day,
and serve under tribute.

CHAP. 17. THERE was also a lot for the tribe of Manasseh; for he
was the *firstborn of Joseph; *to wit,* for *Machir the firstborn
of Manasseh, the father of Gilead: because he was a man of
2 war, therefore he had *Gilead and Bashan. There was also *a lot*
for *the rest of the children of Manasseh by their families; *for
the children of *Abiezer, and for the children of Helek, *and for
the children of Asriel, and for the children of Shechem, *and for
the children of Hepher, and for the children of Shemida: these
were the male children of Manasseh the son of Joseph by their
3 families. ¶But *Zelophehad, the son of Hepher, the son of
Gilead, the son of Machir, the son of Manasseh, had no sons,
but daughters: and these *are* the names of his daughters,
4 Mahlah, and Noah, Hoglah, Milcah, and Tirzah. And they
came near before *Eleazar the priest, and before Joshua the son
of Nun, and before the princes, saying, *The LORD commanded
Moses to give us an inheritance among our brethren. Therefore
according to the commandment of the LORD he gave them an
5 inheritance among the brethren of their father. And there fell
ten portions to Manasseh, beside the land of Gilead and Bashan,
6 which *were* on the other side Jordan; because the daughters of
Manasseh had an inheritance among his sons: and the rest of
7 Manasseh's sons had the land of Gilead. ¶And the coast of
Manasseh was from Asher to *Michmethah, that *lieth* before

e ch. 18. 13.
f 2 Chr. 8. 5.
y ch. 17. 7.

h 1 Chr. 7.
28.
i ch. 17. 9.

k ch. 17. 9.

l Judg. 1. 29.
See 1 Kin.
9. 16.

a Gen. 41. 51.
& 46. 20.
b Gen. 50. 23.
c Deut. 3. 15.
d Num. 26.
29—32.
e 1 Chr. 7. 18.
f Num. 26. 31.
g Num. 26.
32.

h Num. 26.
33.
& 27. 1.
& 36. 2.

i ch. 14. 1.
k Num. 27.
6, 7.

l ch. 16. 6.

1 Num. 26. 30. *Jeezer.*

probability in the conjecture that some
words have, in these verses, fallen out of the
text. Few of the places are known for certain.
9. The verb "were," introduced by A.V.
in this verse should be omitted; and the
full stop after *v.* 8 replaced by a colon.
The purport of *v.* 9 is simply to add to the
inheritance of Ephraim, defined by the
preceding context, "the separate cities" or
more properly "single cities" which were
allotted to them in addition within the borders of Manasseh. The reasons for granting
these additional cities to the Ephraimites
can only be conjectured. Perhaps the territory assigned to this numerous tribe
proved on experiment to be too small; and
therefore some towns, which are named in
1 Chr. vii. 29, were given to them from the
kindred Manassites, the latter being recompensed (xvii. 11 note) at the expense of
Issachar and Asher.

XVII. 1. Manasseh, as the "first-born,"
was to receive not only the territory on the
east of Jordan won by the valour of the
Machirites, but also a portion with the other
tribes on the west of Jordan, the Holy Land
of Promise strictly so called. Thus, though
Ephraim took precedence of Manasseh, according to the prediction of Joseph (Gen.
xlviii. 20), yet Manasseh received "the
double portion" which was the peculiar
privilege of the first-born (Deut. xxi. 17).
2. *for the rest,* &c.] *i.e.* for those who
were not settled on the east of Jordan.
5. *ten portions*] *i.e.* five for the five
families descended from the male children
of Gilead, and five others for the five
daughters of Zelophehad, who represented
the sixth family, the Hepherites.
7. *Asher*] Not the tribe so called, but a
place somewhere towards the eastern end of
the boundary line here drawn: perhaps

Shechem; and the border went along on the right hand unto
8 the inhabitants of En-tappuah. *Now* Manasseh had the land of

m ch. 16. 8.
n ch. 16. 8.
o ch. 16. 9.

Tappuah : but *m* Tappuah on the border of Manasseh *belonged* to
9 the children of Ephraim; and the coast descended *n* unto the
¹river Kanah, southward of the river : *o* these cities of Ephraim
are among the cities of Manasseh : the coast of Manasseh also
was on the north side of the river, and the outgoings of it were
10 at the sea : southward *it was* Ephraim's, and northward *it was*
Manasseh's, and the sea is his border ; and they met together in

p 1 Chr. 7. 29.
q 1 Sam. 31.
10.
1 Kin. 4. 12.

11 Asher on the north, and in Issachar on the east. *p* And Manasseh
had in Issachar and in Asher *q* Beth-shean and her towns, and
Ibleam and her towns, and the inhabitants of Dor and her
towns, and the inhabitants of Endor and her towns, and the inhabitants of Taanach and her towns, and the inhabitants of

r Judg. 1.
27, 28.

12 Megiddo and her towns, *even* three countries. Yet *r* the children
of Manasseh could not drive out *the inhabitants of* those cities ;
13 but the Canaanites would dwell in that land. Yet it came to
pass, when the children of Israel were waxen strong, that they

s ch. 16. 10.
t ch. 16. 4.
u Gen. 48. 22.
x Gen. 48. 19.
Num. 26. 34,
37.

put the Canaanites to *s* tribute ; but did not utterly drive them
14 out. ¶ *t* And the children of Joseph spake unto Joshua, saying,
Why hast thou given me *but* *u* one lot and one portion to inherit,
seeing I am *x* a great people, forasmuch as the LORD hath blessed
15 me hitherto ? And Joshua answered them, If thou *be* a great

¹ Or, *brook of reeds.*

Teyasir, on the road from Sichem to Beth-shean.

9. *these cities*, &c.] The text is possibly corrupt. The intention seems to be to state that the cities lying south of the river, though within the limits of Manasseh, were in fact made over to Ephraim, and were amongst the "separate cities" (xvi. 9). On the contrary, the north bank of the river, both land and towns, belonged to Manasseh exclusively.

10. *southward*] *i.e.* of the river Kanah. Render, "they (*i.e.* the two kindred tribes of Ephraim and Manasseh, the northern border being treated here as common to the two) reached unto Asher." (See the map.) The northern border is only indicated in general terms, perhaps because the Israelites were not yet completely masters of this part of the country, and so had not precisely determined it.

11. Perhaps Beth-shean (in Issachar) and the other five towns (in Asher) were given to the Manassites in compensation for towns in the Manassite territory allotted to the Ephraimites. (See *v.* 9. Cp. xxi. 9.) To the wall of Beth-shean, or Bethshan (*Beisan*, about 5 miles west of the Jordan), the bodies of Saul and his sons were fastened by the Philistines after the battle on Mount Gilboa. After the exile it received the Greek name of Scythopolis, perhaps because it was principally tenanted by a rude and heathen population, styled in contempt Scythians. It was a border city of Galilee, and the chief town of the Decapolis. In Christian times it was the see of a bishop, who is

enumerated as present at Nicæa and other Councils of the Church.

Ibleam (Bileam, 1 Chr. vi. 70), perhaps *Jelameh*, was a Levitical town (xxi. 25 note). Near this place Ahaziah was mortally wounded by Jehu (2 K. ix. 27), and fled to Megiddo, which was no doubt not far distant.

three countries] Rather "the three hills." The district belonging to the last-mentioned three towns had a common name, derived no doubt from its natural features, and was called "the three hills." Cp. Decapolis, Tripolis, &c.

14. *seeing I am a great people*] The assertion can hardly have been warranted by facts, for at the census (Num. xxvi.) the two tribes of Manasseh and Ephraim together were not greatly more numerous than the single tribe of Judah ; and now that half the Manassites were provided for on the eastern side of Jordan, the remaining children of Joseph could hardly be stronger than the Danites or the Issacharites. The children of Joseph seem therefore to exhibit here that arrogant and jealous spirit which elsewhere characterises their conduct (Judg. viii. 1, xii. 1 ; 2 Sam. xix. 41 ; 2 Chr. xxviii. 7 &c.). A glance at the map shows that their complaint was in itself unreasonable. Their territory, which measured about 55 miles by 70, was at least as large in proportion to their numbers as that of any other tribe, and moreover comprehended some of the most fertile of the whole promised land.

15. Joshua was himself of the tribe of Ephraim, but far from supporting the de-

people, *then* get thee up to the wood *country*, and cut down for thyself there in the land of the Perizzites and of the ¹giants, if
16 mount Ephraim be too narrow for thee. And the children of Joseph said, The hill is not enough for us: and all the Canaanites that dwell in the land of the valley have *ᵛ*chariots of iron, *both ᵛ* Judg. 1.19 *they* who *are* of Beth-shean and her towns, and *they* who *are* ²of & 4. 3.
17 the valley of Jezreel. And Joshua spake unto the house of 1 Kin. 18. Joseph, *even* to Ephraim and to Manasseh, saying, Thou *art* a 2 Kin. 9. & great people, and hast great power: thou shalt not have one lot 10.
18 *only :* but the mountain shall be thine; for it *is* a wood, and thou shalt cut it down : and the outgoings of it shall be thine : for thou shalt drive out the Canaanites, *ᵃ*though they have iron *ᵃ* Deut. 20. 1. chariots, *and* though they *be* strong.

Chap. 18. AND the whole congregation of the children of Israel assembled together *ᵃ*at Shiloh, and *ᵇ*set up the tabernacle of the *ᵃ* Judg. 21. congregation there. And the land was subdued before them. 19.
2 ¶And there remained among the children of Israel seven tribes, *ᵇ* Judg. 18.
3 which had not yet received their inheritance. And Joshua said 1 Sam. 1. 24. unto the children of Israel, *ᶜ*How long *are* ye slack to go to & 4. 3, 4. possess the land, which the Lord God of your fathers hath given *ᶜ* Judg. 18. 9.

¹ Or, *Rephaims*, Gen. 14. 5. & 15. 20.

---

mands of his kinsmen he reproves them, and calls upon them to make good their great words by corresponding deeds of valour. He bids them clear the country of its woods and thus make room for ,settling their people. The "wood country" means probably the range which runs along the northern border of Manasseh, and which connects the mountains of Gilboa with Carmel. Mount Ephraim, (a name perhaps used by anticipation) called "the hill" (v. 16), and "the mountain of Israel" (xi. 16), is the eastern portion of the territory of Ephraim and Manasseh extending- towards the Jordan. This was a hilly, though by no means barren, district.

16. The possession by the Canaanites of chariots strengthened and tipped with iron, such as were used by the Egyptians (Ex. xiv. 7), is named here by the children of Joseph as a reason why they could not possess themselves of the plains. "The valley of Jezreel" is the broad low valley which sweeps from *Zerin* between the mountains of Gilboa and the range of little Hermon eastward down to the Jordan. It was most likely in this valley that the host of the Midianites was encamped, when attacked by Gideon (Judg. vii. 1, 8). The great plain of Jezreel, called the plain of Esdraelon (Esdrelom, Judith i., 8), extends from Carmel on the west to the hills of Gilboa, little Hermon, and Tabor on the east, a distance of full sixteen miles ; and its breadth between the rocky mass of southern Palestine and the bolder mountains of Galilee on the north, is about twelve miles. Its position as well as its open area make it the natural battle-field of Palestine.

17. *thou shalt not have one lot only*] i.e. by dispossessing the Canaanites, thou shalt

double the portion of land at thy disposal. The "but" with which A. V. begins *v.* 18 should be "**for.**"

XVIII. 1. After all overt resistance was overcome, the Tabernacle with its sacred contents was removed from its place of safety at Gilgal, in a corner of the land near the Jordan, to a central place, Shiloh, the modern *Seilun*, which is two or three miles east of the main road, and rather more than half way between Jerusalem and Nablous. Its choice as the national Sanctuary may indeed have been determined by Joshua, no doubt under Divine direction (Deut. xii. 11), because of its insignificance, in order to avoid local jealousies, as well as because of its position in the very centre of the whole land, and perhaps also because of its seclusion. Its very name (= "rest") was probably bestowed at this juncture when God had given the people rest from their enemies. The Tabernacle with its contents continued at Shiloh during the whole period of the Judges, until its capture by the Philistines. Shiloh (1 Sam. iv. 3, 4) seems to have fallen into desolation at an early date (Jer. vii. 12, xxvi. 6).

2. Two tribes and a half had already received their portions on the east of Jordan ; Judah, Ephraim, and the remaining half of Manasseh had also been provided for (xv.– xvii.). Thus there remained still seven tribes out of the twelve to be settled in their homes.

3. This backwardness probably arose from the indisposition of the people to abandon the nomad life in which they had been born and bred, and to settle in fixed abodes, and perhaps also from a dislike of the exterminating warfare incidental to a complete dispossessing of the Canaanites.

4 you? Give out from among you three men for *each* tribe: and
I will send them, and they shall rise, and go through the land,
and describe it according to the inheritance of them; and they
5 shall come *again* to me. And they shall divide it into seven

parts: *d* Judah shall abide in their coast on the south, and *e* the
6 house of Joseph shall abide in their coasts on the north. Ye
shall therefore describe the land *into* seven parts, and bring *the*

description hither to me, *f* that I may cast lots for you here be-
7 fore the LORD our God. *g* But the Levites have no part among
you; for the priesthood of the LORD *is* their inheritance: *h* and
Gad, and Reuben, and half the tribe of Manasseh, have received
their inheritance beyond Jordan on the east, which Moses the
8 servant of the LORD gave them. And the men arose and went
away: and Joshua charged them that went to describe the land,
saying, Go and walk through the land, and describe it, and
come again to me, that I may here cast lots for you before the
9 LORD in Shiloh. And the men went and passed through the
land, and described it by cities into seven parts in a book, and
10 came *again* to Joshua to the host at Shiloh. And Joshua cast
lots for them in Shiloh before the LORD: and there Joshua
divided the land unto the children of Israel according to their
11 divisions. ¶ And the lot of the tribe of the children of Benjamin came up according to their families: and the coast of their
lot came forth between the children of Judah and the children

12 of Joseph. *i* And their border on the north side was from
Jordan; and the border went up to the side of Jericho on the
north side, and went up through the mountains westward; and
the goings out thereof were at the wilderness of Beth-aven.
13 And the border went over from thence toward Luz, to the side of

Luz, *k* which *is* Beth-el, southward; and the border descended to
Ataroth-adar, near the hill that *lieth* on the south side *l* of the
14 nether Beth-horon. And the border was drawn *thence*, and compassed the corner of the sea southward, from the hill that *lieth*
before Beth-horon southward; and the goings out thereof were

at *m* Kirjath-baal, which *is* Kirjath-jearim, a city of the children
15 of Judah: this *was* the west quarter. And the south quarter
was from the end of Kirjath-jearim, and the border went out on

16 the west, and went out to *n* the well of waters of Nephtoah: and
the border came down to the end of the mountain that *lieth*

before *o* the valley of the son of Hinnom, *and* which *is* in the
valley of the giants on the north, and descended to the valley of
Hinnom, to the side of Jebusi on the south, and descended to

17 *p* En-rogel, and was drawn from the north, and went forth to
En-shemesh, and went forth toward Geliloth, which *is* over

against the going up of Adummim, and descended to *q* the stone
18 of Bohan the son of Reuben, and passed along toward the side

over against *r* 1 Arabah northward, and went down unto Arabah:

¹ Or, *The plain.*

---

4. *three men for each tribe*] *i.e.* twenty-
one*in all. Their duty would be to describe
the land, especially with reference to the
cities it contained (*v.* 9), that Joshua might
have the means of making a first apportionment amongst the tribes according to their
varying numbers.

10. *cast lots*] See xiv. 2 note.

11–28. See marg. reff. There are many
indications found in this and the next chap-

ter that the text is in great disorder, and
many of the places are still unknown.

14. *and compassed the corner*, &c.] Render
"**and turned on the west side southward.**" The meaning is, that at lower
Beth-horon the northern boundary-line of
Benjamin curved round and ran southward,
—Beth-horon being its extreme westerly
point.

19 and the border passed along to the side of Beth-hoglah north-ward: and the outgoings of the border were at the north [1] bay of the salt sea at the south end of Jordan: this *was* the south coast.
20 And Jordan was the border of it on the east side. ¶ This *was* the inheritance of the children of Benjamin, by the coasts thereof
21 round about, according to their families. ¶ Now the cities of the tribe of the children of Benjamin according to their families
22 were Jericho, and Beth-hoglah, and the valley of Keziz, and
23 Beth-arabah, and Zemaraim, and Beth-el, and Avim, and
24 Parah, and Ophrah, and Chephar-haammonai, and Ophni, and
25 Gaba; twelve cities with their villages: Gibeon, and Ramah,
26, 27 and Beeroth, and Mizpeh, and Chephirah, and Mozah, and
28 Rekem, and Irpeel, and Taralah, and Zelah, Eleph, and *Jebusi,   *ch. 15. 8.
which *is* Jerusalem, Gibeath, *and* Kirjath; fourteen cities with their villages. This *is* the inheritance of the children of Benjamin according to their families.

CHAP. 19. AND the second lot came forth to Simeon, *even* for the tribe of the children of Simeon according to their families: *a*and   *a* ver. 9.
their inheritance was within the inheritance of the children of
2 Judah. And *b*they had in their inheritance Beer-sheba, and   *b* 1 Chr. 4. 28.
3 Sheba, and Moladah, and Hazar-shual, and Balah, and Azem,   ch. 15. 26-32,
4, 5 and Eltolad, and Bethul, and Hormah, and Ziklag, and Beth-   42.
6 marcaboth, and Hazar-susah, and Beth-lebaoth, and Sharuhen;
7 thirteen cities and their villages: Ain, Remmon, and Ether, and
8 Ashan; four cities and their villages: and all the villages that *were* round about these cities to Baalath-beer, Ramath of the south. This *is* the inheritance of the tribe of the children of
9 Simeon according to their families. Out of the portion of the children of Judah *was* the inheritance of the children of Simeon:

[1] Heb. *tongue.*

---

21. The "Valley of Keziz," or *Emek-Keziz,* is perhaps the *Wady el Kaziz,* at no great distance east of Jerusalem.
22. Zemaraim, *i.e.* "two wooded hills," is supposed to be the ruins called *Es-Sumrah,* on the road from Jerusalem to Jericho.
23. Ophrah (xv. 9 note), to be distin-guished here and in 1 Sam. xiii. 17 from the Ophrah of Judg. vi. 11, is probably the Ephrain of 2 Chr. xiii. 19, and the Ephraim of John xi. 54. It is conjecturally identified with *Et-Taiyibeh,* on the road from Jerusalem to Bethel.
24. *Gaba*] This name, like Gibeah, Gibeon, &c. (ix. 3), indicates a town placed on a hill, and occurs repeatedly in various forms in the topography of Palestine. Gaba is the Gibeah of 1 Sam. xiii. 15, 16, xiv. 5, where the Hebrew has Geba, which is undoubtedly the correct reading throughout. The city was one of those assigned to the Levites (xxi. 17), and lay on the northern border of Judah. It is identified with the modern *Jeba,* lying on the side of a deep ravine op-posite to Michmash (*Mukhmas*). The famous "Gibeah of Saul," or "Gibeah of Benja-min" (the Gibeath of *v.* 28) lay at no great distance south-west of Geba, on the high road from Jerusalem to Bethel, and is pro-

bably to be looked for in the lofty and iso-lated *Tuleil-el-Ful.*
25. *Ramah*] *i.e.* "lofty;" probably the native town and abode of Samuel (1 Sam. i. 19, xxv. 1). Its exact site is uncertain.
26. *Mizpeh*] See xi. 3. Not the Mizpeh of xv. 38, but the place where Samuel judged the people and called them together for the election of a king (1 Sam. vii. 5-16, x. 17). In the Chaldæan times it was the residence of Gedaliah (2 K. xxv. 22: Jer. xl. 14). Its site is identified with *Neby Samwil,* about five miles north-west of Jerusalem.
XIX. 1-9. The inheritance of Simeon was taken out of the portion of Judah, which proved on experience to be larger than the numbers of that tribe required. The Simeonite territory is described by its towns, of which fourteen were in the Negeb, and four others (*v.* 7) partly in the Negeb and partly in "the valley." On the narrow confines here assigned to Simeon, and its insignificant position altogether amongst the Twelve Tribes, see Deut. xxxiii. 6 note.
6. *thirteen*] Fourteen names have been given. The error is probably due to the use of letters for numbers, which has led to many similar mistakes in other places (see xv. 32).

for the part of the children of Judah was too much for them:
*ver. 1.   ^ctherefore the children of Simeon had their inheritance within
10 the inheritance of them. ¶And the third lot came up for the
children of Zebulun according to their families: and the border
^d Gen. 49.   11 of their inheritance was unto Sarid: ^dand their border went up
13.   toward the sea, and Maralah, and reached to Dabbasheth, and
^e ch. 12. 22.   12 reached to the river that is ^ebefore Jokneam; and turned from
Sarid eastward toward the sunrising unto the border of Chisloth-
tabor, and then goeth out to Daberath, and goeth up to Japhia,
13 and from thence passeth on along on the east to Gittah-hepher,
to Ittah-kazin, and goeth out to Remmon-¹methoar to Neah;
14 and the border compasseth it on the north side to Hannathon:
15 and the outgoings thereof are in the valley of Jiphthah-el: and
Kattath, and Nahallal, and Shimron, and Idalah, and Beth-
16 lehem: twelve cities with their villages. This is the inheritance
of the children of Zebulun according to their families, these
17 cities with their villages. ¶And the fourth lot came out to
Issachar, for the children of Issachar according to their families.
18 And their border was toward Jezreel, and Chesulloth, and
19, 20 Shunem, and Haphraim, and Shihon, and Anaharath, and
21 Rabbith, and Kishion, and Abez, and Remeth, and En-gan-
22 nim, and En-haddah, and Beth-pazzez; and the coast reacheth to
Tabor, and Shahazimah, and Beth-shemesh; and the outgoings
of their border were at Jordan: sixteen cities with their villages.
23 This is the inheritance of the tribe of the children of Issachar
24 according to their families, the cities and their villages. ¶And
the fifth lot came out for the tribe of the children of Asher

¹ Or, which is drawn.

---

10. Sarid, not yet identified, was evidently a leading topographical point on the south frontier of Zebulun. The boundary passed westward until it touched the Kishon, near *Tell Kaimon* (xii. 22 note), and thence turned northward, leaving Carmel, which belonged to Asher, on its west. The territory of Zebulun accordingly would not anywhere reach to the Mediterranean, though its eastern side abutted on the sea of Galilee, and gave the tribe those "outgoings" attributed to it in the Blessing of Moses (Deut. xxxiii. 18). Daberath (*v.* 12) is probably *Deburieh*.

13. Gittah (or Gath)-hepher, the birthplace of the prophet Jonah (2 K. xiv. 25), is probably the modern village of *El-Meshhad*, where the tomb of the prophet is still shown, a short way from Nazareth, on the road to Tiberias.

Remmon-methoar to Neah] Read "**and goeth out to Remmon, which reacheth to Neah.**" (See margin.) Rimmon, a Levitical city (xxi. 35; 1 Chr. vi. 77) is probably the modern *Rummaneh*, in the plain of *El Buttauf*, about six miles north of Nazareth.

14. Hannathon, more properly Channathon, has been supposed by some to be the Cana of Galilee of the New Testament, and Jiphthah-el is probably the present *Jefat*; the *Jotapata* of Roman times, which was so long and valiantly defended by

Josephus against the legions of Vespasian. The "Valley" is the *Wady Abilin*; and Bethlehem (*v.* 15) is the present miserable village of *Beit-Lahm*.

15. *twelve cities*] Only five have been mentioned, and the names in the verses preceding are apparently not names of Zebulonite cities, but merely of points in or near the boundary line. It would therefore appear that seven names have disappeared from the text, and perhaps also the definition of the western frontier.

18. Jezreel and its famous and fertile plain are the choicest part of the inheritance of Issachar (xvii. 16).

Shunem] Here the Philistines pitched before the battle of Gilboa (1 Sam. xxviii. 4). The place is also known as the home of Abishag (1 K. i. 3), and in connection with Elisha (2 K. iv. 8, viii. 1). It is identified with *Solam* [or, Sulem], a small and poor village on the slope of Little Hermon.

21. *En-gannim*] *i.e.* "fountain of gardens;" also a Levitical city (xxi. 29), and called Anem (1 Chr. vi. 73), the modern *Jenin*, a place on the main road from Jerusalem to Nazareth, just where it enters the plain of Jezreel. Many of the places enumerated in these verses are not known. Tabor (*v.* 22) is perhaps not the famous mountain, but the town on it of the same name (1 Chr. vi. 77), given up to the Levites. Beth-shemesh (perhaps *Bessum*) is

25 according to their families. And their border was Helkath, and
26 Hali, and Beten, and Achshaph, and Alammelech, and Amad,
and Misheal ; and reacheth to Carmel westward, and to Shihor-
27 libnath ; and turneth toward the sunrising to Beth-dagon, and
reacheth to Zebulun, and to the valley of Jiphthah-el toward
the north side of Beth-emek, and Neiel, and goeth out to Cabul
28 on the left hand, and Hebron, and Rehob, and Hammon, and
29 Kanah, *even* unto great Zidon ; and *then* the coast turneth to   *f* ch. 11. 8.
Ramah, and to the strong city ¹Tyre ; and the coast˙turneth to   Judg. 1. 31.
Hosah ; and the outgoings thereof are at the sea from the coast
30 to *g*Achzib : Ummah also, and Aphek, and Rehob : twenty and   *g* Gen. 38. 5.
31 two cities with their villages. This *is* the inheritance of the   Judg. 1. 31.
tribe of the children of Asher according to their families, these   Mic. 1. 14.
32 cities with their villages. ¶ The sixth lot came out to the
children of Naphtali, *even* for the children of Naphtali according
33 to their families. And their coast was from Heleph, from Allon
to Zaanannim, and Adami, Nekeb, and Jabneel, unto Lakum ;
34 and the outgoings thereof were at Jordan : and *then* *h*the coast   *h* Deut. 33.
turneth westward to Aznoth-tabor, and goeth out from thence   23.
to Hukkok, and reacheth to Zebulun on the south side, and
reacheth to Asher on the west side, and to Judah upon Jordan
35 toward the sunrising. And the fenced cities *are* Ziddim, Zer,

¹ Heb. *Tzor*, 2 Sam. 5. 11.

---

not the same as Beth-shemesh of Judah
(xv. 10), nor of Naphtali (*v.* 38).
  25, 26. Helkath, a Levitical town (xxi. 31),
is probably *Yerka*, a village about seven or
eight miles north-west of Acre, in a Wady
of the same name. Alammelech was in the
Wady Melik, which joins the Kishon from
the north-east, not far from the sea.
  Shihor-libnath] *i.e.* "black-white." The
two words are now generally admitted to be
the name of a river, probably the modern
Nahr Zerka, or Blue River, which reaches
the sea about 8 miles south of Dor, and
whose name has a correspondence both to
black and white. Possibly we have in the
occurrence of the term Shihor here a trace
of the intercourse, which was close and continuous in ancient times, between Phœnicia
and Egypt (xiii. 3). Cabul (*v.* 27) still retains its ancient name ;—it lies between
four and five miles west of Jotapata and
about ten miles south-east of Acre.
  28–30. These verses refer to the northern
portion of the territory of Asher, on the
Phœnician frontier. Some names may
have dropped out of the text, the number
(*v.* 30) not tallying with the catalogue.
Ramah still retains its ancient name, and
lies about twelve miles south-east of Tyre.
Achzib is the modern *Zib*, on the coast,
eight or nine miles north of Acre.
  33. *from Allon to Zaanannim*] Render
"from the oak forest at Zaanannim."
From Judg. iv. 11 it appears that this oak
or oak-forest was near Kedesh.
  Adami, Nekeb] Render **"Adami of the
Pass."** Possibly the ancient *Deir el Ahmar*
("red cloister"), which derives its name

from the colour of the soil in the neighbourhood, as perhaps Adami did. The spot
lies about eight miles north-west of Baalbek.
  34. *Aznoth-tabor*] This place (="ears of
Tabor") was no doubt in the neighbourhood of Mount Tabor—probably on the
eastern slope ; and Hukkok on the western
slope.
  to Judah upon Jordan] *i.e.* to the "Havoth-jair" (Num. xxxii. 41), which were on
the opposite side of Jordan. Jair, from
whom these towns or villages were named,
traced his ancestry in the male line
through Hezron to Judah (Num. xxvii. 1) ;
and it is likely that he was assisted by
large numbers of his kinsmen of that tribe
in his rapid conquest of Bashan. Hence
the Havoth-jair were, in all likelihood,
largely colonised by Judahites, especially
perhaps that portion of them nearest the
Jordan. Thus that part of the river and
its valley adjacent to these settlements was
spoken of as "Judah upon Jordan," or
more literally "Judah of the Jordan" (cp.
Num. xxii. 1).
  35–38. The number of the fortified cities
of Naphtali is remarkable, though it does
not tally with the catalogue. It was no
doubt good policy to protect the northern
frontier by a belt of fortresses, as the south
was protected by the fenced cities of Judah.
Hammath, a Levitical city (cp. xxi. 32 ;
1 Chr. vi. 76), is not to be confounded with
the Hamath on the north-eastern frontier
of the land (Num. xiii. 21). The name
(from a root signifying "to be warm") probably indicates that hot springs existed
here ; and is perhaps rightly traced in

36 and Hammath, Rakkath, and Chinnereth, and Adamah, and
37 Ramah, and Hazor, and Kedesh, and Edrei, and En-hazor,
38 and Iron, and Migdal-el, Horem, and Beth-anath, and Beth-
39 shemesh; nineteen cities with their villages. This *is* the inheritance of the tribe of the children of Naphtali according to
40 their families, the cities and their villages. ¶*And* the seventh
lot came out for the tribe of the children of Dan according to
41 their families. And the coast of their inheritance was Zorah,

i Judg. 1. 35.

42 and Eshtaol, and Ir-shemesh, and *i*Shaalabbin, and Ajalon, and
43, 44 Jethlah, and Elon, and Thimnathah, and Ekron, and Eltekeh,
45 and Gibbethon, and Baalath, and Jehud, and Bene-berak, and
46 Gath-rimmon, and Me-jarkon, and Rakkon, with the border

k See Judg. 18.

47 ¹before ²Japho. And *k*the coast of the children of Dan went
out *too little* for them: therefore the children of Dan went up to
fight against Leshem, and took it, and smote it with the edge
of the sword, and possessed it, and dwelt therein, and called

l Judg. 18. 29.

48 Leshem, *l*Dan, after the name of Dan their father. This *is* the
inheritance of the tribe of the children of Dan according to their
49 families, these cities with their villages. ¶When they had
made an end of dividing the land for inheritance by their coasts,
the children of Israel gave an inheritance to Joshua the son of
50 Nun among them: according to the word of the Lord they gave

m ch. 24. 30.
n 1 Chr. 7. 24.
o Num. 34. 17.
ch. 14. 1.
p ch. 18. 1, 10.

him the city which he asked, *even* *m*Timnath-*n*serah in mount
51 Ephraim: and he built the city, and dwelt therein. ¶*o*These *are*
the inheritances, which Eleazar the priest, and Joshua the son of
Nun, and the heads of the fathers of the tribes of the children
of Israel, divided for an inheritance by lot *p*in Shiloh before the
Lord, at the door of the tabernacle of the congregation. So
they made an end of dividing the country.

a Ex. 21. 13.
Num. 35. 6, 11, 14.
Deut. 19. 2,9.

Chap. 20. THE Lord also spake unto Joshua, saying, Speak to
2 the children of Israel, saying, *a*Appoint out for you cities of

¹ Or, *over against.*   ² Or, *Joppa*, Jonah 1. 3. Acts 9. 36.

Ammaus, near Tiberias. Rakkath was,
according to the Rabbins, rebuilt by Herod
and called Tiberias. The name (= "bank,
shore") suits the site of Tiberias very well.
Migdal-el, perhaps the Magdala of Matt.
xv. 39, is now the miserable village of *El
Mejdel.*

46. Japho (the modern Jaffa, or Yafa),
elsewhere (see marg.) called Joppa, is often
mentioned in the history of the Maccabees
and was, as it still is, the leading port
of access to Jerusalem both for pilgrims
and for merchandise. It is a very ancient
town.

47. The words "too little" are an insertion of A. V. Render rather, "**the border
of the children of Dan was extended.**"
The Hebrew appears to mean "the children
of Dan enlarged their border because they
had not room enough."

The reason of this was that the Danites, a
numerous tribe (Num. xxvi. 5 note), found
themselves (Judg. i. 34, 35) cooped up
amongst the hills by the powerful and warlike Amorites. Hence the Danite expedition (see marg. ref.), which surprised the
Sidonian inhabitants of Leshem, an unwar-

like and peaceable race, exterminated them,
and annexed their city and territory to the
portion of Dan.

50. Nothing is said of any express command of God respecting the inheritance of
Joshua. But as such special portion appears
to have been promised to Caleb at the time
when he and Joshua alone out of the twelve
spies remained faithful (xiv. 6-9), it is probable that a like promise was made to
Joshua. The name of the place is also
written Timnath-heres (Judg. ii. 9), by a
transposition of the letters. The Rabbinical explanation that the name Timnath-
heres (*i.e.* "portion of the sun") was given
because a representation of the sun was
affixed to the tomb in memory of Joshua's
command to the sun to stand still, appears
to be an afterthought. The name Timnath-
serah (= "portion that remains") was perhaps conferred on the spot in consequence
of its being allotted to Joshua, the last
allotment made in the whole distribution of
his conquests. The site has been conjectured to be *Tibneh*, a village about five
miles north-west of Lydda [or, by Conder,
Kefr Hâres, nine miles south of Nablous].

3 refuge, whereof I spake unto you by the hand of Moses: that the
slayer that killeth *any* person unawares *and* unwittingly may
flee thither: and they shall be your refuge from the avenger of
4 blood. And when he that doth flee unto one of those cities shall
stand at the entering of *b*the gate of the city, and shall declare
his cause in the ears of the elders of that city, they shall take
him into the city unto them, and give him a place, that he may
5 dwell among them. *c*And if the avenger of blood pursue after
him, then they shall not deliver the slayer up into his hand;
because he smote his neighbour unwittingly, and hated him not
6 beforetime. And he shall dwell in that city, *d*until he stand
before the congregation for judgment, *and* until the death of the
high priest that shall be in those days : then shall the slayer
return, and come unto his own city, and unto his own house,
7 unto the city from whence he fled. ¶ And they [1]appointed
*e*Kedesh in Galilee in mount Naphtali, and *f*Shechem in mount
Ephraim, and *g*Kirjath-arba, which *is* Hebron, in *h*the moun-
8 tain of Judah. And on the other side Jordan by Jericho eastward, they assigned *i*Bezer in the wilderness upon the plain out
of the tribe of Reuben, and *k*Ramoth in Gilead out of the tribe
of Gad, and *l*Golan in Bashan out of the tribe of Manasseh.
9 *m*These were the cities appointed for all the children of Israel,
and for the stranger that sojourneth among them, that whosoever killeth *any* person at unawares might flee thither, and not
die by the hand of the avenger of blood, *n*until he stood before
the congregation.

CHAP 21. THEN came near the heads of the fathers of the Levites
unto *a*Eleazar the priest, and unto Joshua the son of Nun, and
unto the heads of the fathers of the tribes of the children of
2 Israel; and they spake unto them at *b*Shiloh in the land of
Canaan, saying, *c*The LORD commanded by the hand of Moses
to give us cities to dwell in, with the suburbs thereof for our
3 cattle. And the children of Israel gave unto the Levites out of
their inheritance, at the commandment of the LORD, these cities
4 and their suburbs. ¶ And the lot came out for the families of
the Kohathites: and *d*the children of Aaron the priest, *which
were* of the Levites, *e*had by lot out of the tribe of Judah, and
out of the tribe of Simeon, and out of the tribe of Benjamin,

b Ruth 4. 1, 2.

c Num. 35. 12.

d Num. 35. 12, 25.

e ch. 12. 22.
f Gen. 12. 6.
g ch. 14. 15.
h Luke 1. 39.
i Deut. 4. 43.
1 Chr. 6. 78.
k ch. 21. 38.
1 Kin. 22. 3.
l ch. 21. 27.
m Num. 35. 15.

n ver. 6.

a ch. 14. 1. & 17. 4.

b ch. 18. 1.

c Num. 35. 2.

d ver. 8, 19.

e See ch. 24. 33.

[1] Heb. *sanctified.*

XX. **4.** As soon as the manslayer presented himself at the city of refuge, the
elders of the city were to hold an inquiry,
and receive him provisionally into the city.
Afterwards, when the avenger of blood
should have tracked his victim to the city,
and appear to claim him, a more formal
and thorough investigation (*v.* 6) was to be
made. Consult the marginal references.

XXI. A list of the Levitical cities, varying in some particulars from that given in
this chapter, is also given in 1 Chr. vi. 54–81.

4. *thirteen cities*] This number is said to
be too great for the single family of Aaron.
But it appears (1 Chr. xxiv.) that the two
surviving sons of Aaron, Eleazar and Ithamar, had together 24 sons, the heads of the
priestly families. Since Aaron was 123
years old when he died (Num. xxxiii. 39),

his sons' grandchildren and great grandchildren were no doubt living in the closing
years of Joshua's course, and had to be provided with dwellings. They might altogether number several thousands. The "cities"
of Canaan were for the most part small; as
is manifest from the astonishing number of
them in proportion to the area of the land,
more particularly in the south, where the
portion of the priests was situated. The
priests or Levites would not occupy the
whole of the dwellings in any city, nor all
its "fields," nor necessarily and always all
its "villages" (cp. *v.* 12). Non-Levites, to
whom the cultivation of their land, and
other secular concerns, were entrusted, no
doubt resided in the Levitical cities or their
precincts. It appears, further, that several
of the cities here enumerated were only

f ver. 20, &c.

5 thirteen cities. And *f*the rest of the children of Kohath *had* by lot out of the families of the tribe of Ephraim, and out of the tribe of Dan, and out of the half tribe of Manasseh, ten cities.

g ver. 27, &c.

6 ¶And *g*the children of Gershon *had* by lot out of the families of the tribe of Issachar, and out of the tribe of Asher, and out of the tribe of Naphtali, and out of the half tribe of Manasseh in

h ver. 34, &c.

7 Bashan, thirteen cities. ¶*h*The children of Merari by their families *had* out of the tribe of Reuben, and out of the tribe of

i ver. 3.

8 Gad, and out of the tribe of Zebulun, twelve cities. ¶*i*And the children of Israel gave by lot unto the Levites these cities with their suburbs, *k*as the LORD commanded by the hand of

k Num. 35. 2.

9 Moses. ¶And they gave out of the tribe of the children of Judah, and out of the tribe of the children of Simeon, these

l ver. 4.

10 cities which are *here* [1]mentioned by name, *l*which the children of Aaron, *being* of the families of the Kohathites, *who were* of the

m 1 Chr. 6. 55.
n Gen. 13. 18.
o ch. 20. 7.
p ch. 14. 14.

11 children of Levi, had : for their's was the first lot. *m*And they gave them [2]the city of Arba the father of *n*Anak, which *city is* Hebron, *o*in the hill *country* of Judah, with the suburbs thereof

12 round about it. But *p*the fields of the city, and the villages thereof, gave they to Caleb the son of Jephunneh for his pos-

q 1 Chr. 6. 57, &c.
r ch. 15. 54.
s ch. 10. 2.
t ch. 15. 48.
u ch. 15. 50.
x 1 Chr. 6. 58, *Hilen.*
y ch. 15. 49.
z 1 Chr. 6. 59, *Ashan.*
a ch. 15. 55.
b ch. 15. 10.
c ch. 18. 25.
d ch. 18. 24, *Gaba.*
e 1 Chr. 6. 60, *Alemeth.*
f ver. 5.
1 Chr. 6. 66.
g ch. 20. 7.

13 session. Thus *q*they gave to the children of Aaron the priest

14 *r*Hebron with her suburbs, *to be* a city of refuge for the slayer; *s*and Libnah with her suburbs, and *t*Jattir with her suburbs,

15 *u*and Eshtemoa with her suburbs, and *x*Holon with her suburbs,

16 *y*and Debir with her suburbs, and *z*Ain with her suburbs, *a*and Juttah with her suburbs, *and* *b*Beth-shemesh with her suburbs;

17 nine cities out of those two tribes. And out of the tribe of Benjamin, *c*Gibeon with her suburbs, *d*Geba with her suburbs,

18 Anathoth with her suburbs, and *e*Almon with her suburbs; four

19 cities. All the cities of the children of Aaron, the priests, *were*

20 thirteen cities with their suburbs. ¶*f*And the families of the children of Kohath, the Levites which remained of the children of Kohath, even they had the cities of their lot out of the tribe

21 of Ephraim. For they gave them *g*Shechem with her suburbs in mount Ephraim, *to be* a city of refuge for the slayer; and

22 Gezer with her suburbs, and Kibzaim with her suburbs, and

23 Beth-horon with her suburbs; four cities. And out of the tribe of Dan, Eltekeh with her suburbs, Gibbethon with her suburbs,

24 Aijalon with her suburbs, Gath-rimmon with her suburbs; four

25 cities. And out of the half tribe of Manasseh, Tanach with her

26 suburbs, and Gath-rimmon with her suburbs; two cities. All the cities *were* ten with their suburbs for the families of the

[1] Heb. *called.*   [2] Or, *Kirjath-arba*, Gen. 23. 2.

---

wrested from the Canaanites at a later date.

5. The non-priestly Kohathites had been diminished by the destruction of Korah and his company (Num. xvi.). On comparing Num. xxvi. 57 seq. with Num. iii. 27 seq., two of the families of the Kohathites seem to have disappeared altogether. Hence it is not surprising that the rest of the Kohathites were sufficiently accommodated in ten cities.

9–19. The thirteen priestly cities (see marg. reff.) were all in the tribes of Judah, Simeon, and Benjamin. Thus, as Calvin remarks, God so overruled it that the priestly fami-

lies were placed *r* un 1 the spot which He had determined beforehand to choose as the site of His temple.

20–26. Of the cities of the non-priestly Kohathites, for Kibzaim we find Jokmeam in 1 Chr. vi. 68. This is perhaps another name for the same place, since both names may be derived from roots having a similar meaning ; and for Gath-rimmon in 1 Chr. vi. 70, Bileam is given, and probably correctly ; Gath-rimmon having apparently been repeated inadvertently from the preceding verse. Bileam is but another form of Ibleam (xvii. 11).

27 children of Kohath that remained. ¶ *h* And unto the children of   *h* ver. 6.
Gershon, of the families of the Levites, out of the *other* half
tribe of Manasseh *they gave* *i* Golan in Bashan with her suburbs,   *i* Deut. 4. 13.
to be a city of refuge for the slayer; and Beesh-terah with her
28 suburbs; two cities. And out of the tribe of Issachar, Kishon
29 with her suburbs, Dabareh with her suburbs, Jarmuth with her
30 suburbs, En-gannim with her suburbs; four cities. And out of
the tribe of Asher, Mishal with her suburbs, Abdon with her
31 suburbs, Helkath with her suburbs, and Rehob with her
32 suburbs; four cities. And out of the tribe of Naphtali,
k Kedesh in Galilee with her suburbs, *to be* a city of refuge for   *k* ch. 12. 22.
the slayer; and Hammoth-dor with her suburbs, and Kartan
33 with her suburbs; three cities. All the cities of the Gershonites according to their families *were* thirteen cities with their
34 suburbs. ¶ *l* And unto the families of the children of Merari, the   *l* ver. 7.
rest of the Levites, out of the tribe of Zebulun, Jokneam with   See 1 Chr. 6.
35 her suburbs, and Kartah with her suburbs, Dimnah with her   77.
36 suburbs, Nahalal with her suburbs; four cities. And out of
the tribe of Reuben, *m* Bezer with her suburbs, and Jahazah   *m* ch. 20. 8.
37 with her suburbs, Kedemoth with her suburbs, and Mephaath
38 with her suburbs; four cities. And out of the tribe of Gad,
n Ramoth in Gilead with her suburbs, *to be* a city of refuge for   *n* ch. 20. 8.
39 the slayer; and Mahanaim with her suburbs, Heshbon with her
40 suburbs, Jazer with her suburbs; four cities in all. So all the
cities for the children of Merari by their families, which were
remaining of the families of the Levites, were *by* their lot
41 twelve cities. ¶ *o* All the cities of the Levites within the pos-   *o* Num. 35. 7.
session of the children of Israel *were* forty and eight cities with
42 their suburbs. These cities were every one with their suburbs
43 round about them: thus *were* all these cities. ¶ And the LORD
gave unto Israel *p* all the land which he sware to give unto their   *p* Gen. 13. 15.
44 fathers; and they possessed it, and dwelt therein. *q* And the   *q* ch. 11. 23.
  & 22. 4.

27-33. Cp. xix. 18, &c. Of the cities of
the Gershonites, for Beesh-terah read
(**Beeshterah**.) The name is a contraction
of Beth-Ashterah (= "house of Ashterah")
and the city is undoubtedly the Ashtaroth
or Astaroth of Og (xii. 4; Deut. i. 4; 1 Chr.
vi. 71).
34-40. Merarite cities. Some of these
places are not found in the list of Zebulonite cities in xix. 10-16. The text is considered corrupt.
42. After this verse, the LXX. introduces
a passage (in part a repetition from xix.
49, 50), recording the grant of a special inheritance to Joshua, and also that he buried
at Timnath-serah the flint-knives with which
he had circumcised (v. 2 note) the people
after the passage of Jordan. The latter
statement, which has the authority of the
LXX. only, is a Jewish legend of early date.
43-45. There is no real inconsistency between the declarations of these verses and the
fact that the Israelites had not as yet possessed themselves of all the cities allotted to
the various tribes (Judg. i. 21-36),—nor did
at any time, subdue the whole extent of
country promised to them (Num. xxxiv.

1-12). God had fulfilled all His part of the
Covenant. It was no part of His purpose
that the native population should be annihilated suddenly (Deut. vii. 22); but they
were delivered into the hand of Israel, and
their complete dispossession could have been
effected at any time by that Divine aid
which was never wanting when sought. At
the time referred to in the text, the Canaanites were discouraged, broken in strength,
holding fast in isolated spots only up and
down the land in the very midst of the
tribes of God's people. The conquest of
Canaan was already *ex parte Dei* a perfect
work; just as in the New Testament the triumph of the individual Christian and of the
Christian Church in their warfare is often
spoken of as accomplished in view of the
Divine will that it should be so, and of
Divine grace that it may be so. It was therefore only the inertness and pusillanimity of
the Israelites which prevented the completion of the conquest when the allotment of
Canaan was made by Joshua; as it was
their subsequent backslidings which caused
God to turn the tide of victory against
them and even to cast them out of the land

r Deut. 7. 24.

• ch. 23. 14.

LORD gave them rest round about, according to all that he sware unto their fathers: and *r*there stood not a man of all their enemies before them; the LORD delivered all their enemies 45 into their hand.   *s*There failed not ought of any good thing which the LORD had spoken unto the house of Israel; all came to pass.

a Num. 32. 20.
Deut. 3. 18.
b ch.1.16,17.

CHAP. 22.   THEN Joshua called the Reubenites, and the Gadites, 2 and the half tribe of Manasseh, and said unto them, Ye have kept *a*all that Moses the servant of the LORD commanded you, 3 *b*and have obeyed my voice in all that I commanded you: ye have not left your brethren these many days unto this day, but have kept the charge of the commandment of the LORD your 4 God.   And now the LORD your God hath given rest unto your brethren, as he promised them: therefore now return ye, and get you unto your tents, *and* unto the land of your possession,

c Num.32.33.
Deut. 29. 8.
ch. 13. 8.
d Deut. 6. 6, 17.
& 11. 22.
e Deut. 10. 12.
f Gen. 47. 7.
Ex. 39. 43.
ch. 14. 13.
2 Sam. 6. 18.
Luke 24. 50.
g ch. 17. 5.

*c*which Moses the servant of the LORD gave you on the other 5 side Jordan.   But *d*take diligent heed to do the commandment and the law, which Moses the servant of the LORD charged you, *e*to love the LORD your God, and to walk in all his ways, and to keep his commandments, and to cleave unto him, and to 6 serve him with all your heart and with all your soul.   ¶ So Joshua *f*blessed them, and sent them away: and they went unto 7 their tents.   Now to the *one* half of the tribe of Manasseh Moses had given *possession* in Bashan: *g*but unto the *other* half thereof gave Joshua among their brethren on this side Jordan westward.   And when Joshua sent them away also unto their tents, 8 then he blessed them, and he spake unto them, saying, Return with much riches unto your tents, and with very much cattle, with silver, and with gold, and with brass, and with iron, and

h Num. 31. 27.
1 Sam. 30. 24.

with very much raiment: *h*divide the spoil of your enemies with 9 your brethren.   ¶And the children of Reuben and the children of Gad and the half tribe of Manasseh returned, and departed from the children of Israel out of Shiloh, which *is* in the land of

i Num. 32. 1, 26, 29.

Canaan, to go unto *i*the country of Gilead, to the land of their possession, whereof they were•possessed, according to the word 10 of the LORD by the hand of Moses.   And when they came unto the borders of Jordan, that *are* in the land of Canaan, the children of Reuben and the children of Gad and the half tribe of Manasseh built there an altar by Jordan, a great altar to see

promised to their forefathers and actually won in the campaigns of Joshua. See Introd., p. 6.

XXII. The events of this chap. are no doubt recorded in their proper historical order. The auxiliary forces of the trans-Jordanic tribes were not sent away immediately after the campaigns against the Canaanites were over. They set forth from Shiloh (*v*. 9), to which place the sanctuary had been removed (xviii. 1) after the conquest and the settlement of the children of Judah and of Joseph in their possessions, and after the appointment of the Levitical cities.

7, 8. The insertion of this explanation about the half tribe, and the repetition of Joshua's farewell, are examples of a marked characteristic of very ancient writers—and of Hebrew writers as much as any—that of

giving a completeness and finish to each section of their story. The Jewish historian scarcely ever quotes or reminds, but repeats so much as may be necessary to make his account of the transaction in hand fully intelligible by itself. (Cp. also xiii. 14 and 33, xiv. 3, xviii. 7.) It is quite possible, however, that the particulars peculiar to *v*. 8, may be due to some other narrative of the whole event than that to which *v*. 5 belongs, and may have been interwoven by a later reviser.

9. *Gilead*] Here used in the widest sense for the whole trans-Jordanic district.

10. The two tribes and a half erected this altar in order to keep alive their claim to have the same interest as the other tribes had in the Sanctuary of God, which was established on the west side of Jordan: and in order to forestall any assertion that the

11 to. ¶And the children of Israel [k]heard say, Behold, the children of Reuben and the children of Gad and the half tribe of Manasseh have built an altar over against the land of Canaan, in the borders of Jordan, at the passage of the children of Israel. [k] Deut. 13. 12, &c. Judg. 20. 12.

12 And when the children of Israel heard *of it*, [l]the whole congregation of the children of Israel gathered themselves together [l] Judg. 20. 1.

13 at Shiloh, to go up to war against them. And the children of Israel [m]sent unto the children of Reuben, and to the children of Gad, and to the half tribe of Manasseh, into the land of Gilead, [m] Deut. 13. 14. Judg. 20. 12.

14 [n]Phinehas the son of Eleazar the priest, and with him ten princes, of each [1]chief house a prince throughout all the tribes of Israel; and [o]each one *was* an head of the house of their [n] Ex. 6. 25. Num. 25. 7. [o] Num. 1. 4.

15 fathers among the thousands of Israel. And they came unto the children of Reuben, and to the children of Gad, and to the half tribe of Manasseh, unto the land of Gilead, and they spake

16 with them, saying, Thus saith the whole congregation of the LORD, What trespass *is* this that ye have committed against the God of Israel, to turn away this day from following the LORD, in that ye have builded you an altar, [p]that ye might rebel this day [p] See Lev. 17. 8, 9. Deut. 12. 13, 14.

17 against the LORD? *Is* the iniquity [q]of Peor too little for us, from which we are not cleansed until this day, although there [q] Num. 25.

18 was a plague in the congregation of the LORD, but that ye must turn away this day from following the LORD? and it will be, *seeing* ye rebel to day against the LORD, that to morrow [r]he will [r] Num. 16. 22. Deut. 4. 3.

19 be wroth with the whole congregation of Israel. Notwithstanding, if the land of your possession *be* unclean, *then* pass ye over unto the land of the possession of the LORD, [s]wherein the LORD'S tabernacle dwelleth, and take possession among us: but rebel not against the LORD, nor rebel against us, in building you an [s] ch. 18. 1.

20 altar beside the altar of the LORD our God. [t]Did not Achan the son of Zerah commit a trespass in the accursed thing, and wrath fell on all the congregation of Israel? and that man perished [t] ch. 7. 1, 5. [u] Deut. 10. 17. [x] 1 Kin. 8. 39.

21 not alone in his iniquity. ¶Then the children of Reuben and the children of Gad and the half tribe of Manasseh answered, Job 10. 7. & 23. 10.

22 and said unto the heads of the thousands of Israel, The LORD [u]God of gods, the LORD God of gods, he [x]knoweth, and Israel he shall know; if *it be* in rebellion, or if in transgression against Ps. 44. 21. & 139. 1, 2. Jer. 12. 3. 2 Cor. 11. 11, 31.

[1] Heb. *house of the father.*

Jordan itself was a natural barrier of exclusion between them and the Sanctuary, they built it on the west or Canaanitish bank of the Jordan and not on the east.

The word rendered "borders" is noteworthy; it means circuits, arrondissements.

12. *gathered themselves together*] The various tribes had already dispersed to their homes, and were now summoned together again.

17. *from which we are not cleansed until this day*] Phinehas, who had borne a conspicuous part in vindicating the cause of God against those who fell away to Baal-peor, means that terrible as the punishment had been, there were still those amongst them who hankered after Baal worship, and even practised it in secret. (Cp. Joshua's words, xxiv. 14–23.)

19. *unclean*] *i.e.* unholy because the

Sanctuary was not in it, but on the other side of Jordan.

22. The repeated invocation of God, and that by His three names (El, Elohim, Jehovah : cp. Ps. l. 1), marks the earnestness of the protestation. The conduct of the two tribes and a half has often been noted as exemplary. They had had a grave and capital crime most unexpectedly laid to their charge, of which they were entirely innocent. Yet there is no word of reproach or recrimination in their vindication of themselves. They are contented simply to repudiate the false accusation and to explain the real motives of conduct perhaps suggested to them by a precedent set by Moses (Ex. xvii. 15).

save us not this day] The words are a direct appeal to God, exactly equivalent in effect to our form "So help me God."

23 the LORD, (save us not this day,) that we have built us an altar to turn from following the LORD, or if to offer thereon burnt offering or meat offering, or if to offer peace offerings

v Deut. 18. 19. 1 Sam. 20. 16.

24 thereon, let the LORD himself *v*require *it;* and if we have not *rather* done it for fear of *this* thing, saying, ¹In time to come your children might speak unto our children, saying, What have

25 ye to do with the LORD God of Israel? For the LORD hath made Jordan a border between us and you, ye children of Reuben and children of Gad; ye have no part in the LORD : so shall your children make our children cease from fearing the

26 LORD. Therefore we said, Let us now prepare to build us an

27 altar, not for burnt offering, nor for sacrifice : but *that* it *may*

z Gen. 31. 48. ch. 24. 27. ver. 34. *a* Deut. 12. 5, 6, 11, 12, 17, 18, 26, 27.

be *z*a witness between us, and you, and our generations after us, that we might *a*do the service of the LORD before him with our burnt offerings, and with our sacrifices, and with our peace offerings; that your children may not say to our children in

28 time to come, Ye have no part in the LORD. Therefore said we, that it shall be, when they should *so* say to us or to our generations in time to come, that we may say *again*, Behold the pattern of the altar of the LORD, which our fathers made, not for burnt offerings, nor for sacrifices; but it *is* a witness between us

29 and you. God forbid that we should rebel against the LORD,

b Deut. 12. 13, 14.

and turn this day from following the LORD, *b*to build an altar for burnt offerings, for meat offerings, or for sacrifices, beside the altar of the LORD our God that *is* before his tabernacle.

30 ¶And when Phinehas the priest, and the princes of the congregation and heads of the thousands of Israel which *were* with him, heard the words that the children of Reuben and the children of Gad and the children of Manasseh spake, ²it pleased them.

31 And Phinehas the son of Eleazar the priest said unto the children of Reuben, and to the children of Gad, and to the children of

c Lev. 26. 11, 12. 2 Chr. 15. 2.

Manasseh, This day we perceive that the LORD *is* ᶜamong us, because ye have not committed this trespass against the LORD : ³now ye have delivered the children of Israel out of the hand of

32 the LORD. ¶And Phinehas the son of Eleazar the priest, and the princes, returned from the children of Reuben, and from the children of Gad, out of the land of Gilead, unto the land of Canaan, to the children of Israel, and brought them word again.

33 And the thing pleased the children of Israel; and the children

d 1 Chr. 29. 20. Neh. 8. 6. Dan. 2. 19. Luke 2. 28.

of Israel ᵈblessed God, and did not intend to go up against them in battle, to destroy the land wherein the children of Reuben

34 and Gad dwelt. ¶And the children of Reuben and the children of Gad called the altar ⁴*Ed :* for it *shall be* a witness between us that the LORD *is* God.

a ch. 21. 44. & 22. 4.

CHAP. 23. AND it came to pass a long time after that the LORD ᵃhad given rest unto Israel from all their enemies round about, that

¹ Heb. *To morrow.*
² Heb. *it was good in their eyes.*
³ Heb. *then.*
⁴ That is, A witness : So ch. 24. 27.

34. The word *Ed* is not found after "altar" in the text of most MSS., nor is it represented in the LXX. or Vulg. The passage should probably run, "the children of Reuben and the children of Gad named the altar, that (as they said) it might be, &c." The title placed on the altar was perhaps simply a witness between them that the Lord was God (Wordsworth).

XXIII. This and the next chapter contain the last addresses of Joshua. These addresses were no doubt amongst the closing acts of Joshua's life, but were evidently given on different occasions, and are of different character and scope. In the former Joshua briefly reminds the princes of the recent benefits of God towards them and their people, declares that God had fulfilled all

2 Joshua *b*waxed old, *and* [1]stricken in age. And Joshua *c*called
for all Israel, *and* for their elders, and for their heads, and for
their judges, and for their officers, and said unto them, I am
3 old *and* stricken in age : and ye have seen all that the LORD
your God hath done unto all these nations because of you ; for
4 the *d*LORD your God *is* he that hath fought for you. Behold,
*e*I have divided unto you by lot these nations that remain, to be
an inheritance for your tribes, from Jordan, with all the nations
5 that I have cut off, even unto the great sea [2]westward. And
the LORD your God, *f*he shall expel them from before you, and
drive them from out of your sight ; and ye shall possess their
6 land, *g*as the LORD your God hath promised unto you. *h*Be ye
therefore very courageous to keep and to do all that is written
in the book of the law of Moses, *i*that ye turn not aside there-
7 from *to* the right hand or *to* the left ; that ye *k*come not among
these nations, these that remain among you ; neither *l*make
mention of the name of their gods, nor cause to swear *by them*,
8 neither serve them, nor bow yourselves unto them : [3]but *m*cleave
9 unto the LORD your God, as ye have done unto this day. [4]*n*For
the LORD hath driven out from before you great nations and
strong : but *as for* you, *o*no man hath been able to stand before
10 you unto this day. *p*One man of you shall chase a thousand :
for the LORD your God, he *it is* that fighteth for you, *q*as he hath
11 promised you. ¶*r*Take good heed therefore unto [5]yourselves,
12 that ye love the LORD your God. Else if ye do in any wise *s*go
back, and cleave unto the remnant of these nations, *even* these
that remain among you, and shall *t*make marriages with them,
13 and go in unto them, and they to you : know for a certainty that
*u*the LORD your God will no more drive out *any of* these nations
from before you ; *x*but they shall be snares and traps unto you,
and scourges in your sides, and thorns in your eyes, until ye
perish from off this good land which the LORD your God hath
14 given you. ¶And, behold, this day *y*I *am* going the way of all
the earth : and ye know in all your hearts and in all your souls,
that *z*not one thing hath failed of all the good things which the
LORD your God spake concerning you ; all are come to pass unto
15 you, *and* not one thing hath failed thereof. *a*Therefore it shall
come to pass, *that* as all good things are come upon you, which
the LORD your God promised you ; so shall the LORD bring upon
you *b*all evil things, until he have destroyed you from off this
16 good land which the LORD your God hath given you. When ye
have transgressed the covenant of the LORD your God, which he
commanded you, and have gone and served other gods, and
bowed yourselves to them ; then shall the anger of the LORD be

b ch. 13. 1.
c Deut. 31.
23.
1 Chr. 28. 1.

d. Ex. 14. 14

e ch. 13. 2. 6.

f Ex. 23. 30.
ch. 13. 6.
g Num 33.
53.
h ch. 1. 7.
i Deut. 5. 32.
k Deut. 7. 2.
Prov. 4. 14.
Eph. 5. 11.
l Ex. 23. 13.
Ps. 16. 4.
Jer. 5. 7.
m Deut. 10.
20. & 11. 22.
n Deut. 11.
23.
o ch. 1. 5.
p Lev. 26. 8.
Judg. 3. 31.
& 15. 15.
2 Sam. 23. 8.
q Ex. 14. 14.
r ch. 22. 5.
s Heb. 10.
38, 39.
2 Pet. 2. 20,
21.
t Deut. 7. 3.
u Judg. 2. 3.
x Deut. 7. 16.
1 Kin. 11. 4.
y 1 Kin. 2. 2.
See Heb. 9.
27.
z ch. 21. 45.
Luke 21. 33.
a Deut. 28.
63.

b Lev. 26. 16.
Deut. 28. 15,
16, &c.

---

[1] Heb. *come into days*.
[2] Heb. *at the sunset*.
[3] Or, *For if ye will cleave,*
  &c.
[4] Or, *Then the LORD will*
  drive.
[5] Heb. *your souls.*

His promises, and exhorts to faithfulness on
their side to God that so His mercies may
not be withdrawn : in the latter he takes a
wider range, rehearses the gracious dealings
of God with the nation from its very origin,
and upon these as his grounds, he claims for
God their sincere and entire service. But
he grants them the option of withdrawing
from the Covenant if they so choose ; and
when they elect still to abide by it, it is solemnly renewed by the free consent of the
whole people. Joshua's reproofs and warnings are in sum and substance identical
with those with which Moses closed his
career (Deut. xxxi., &c.). Cp. throughout
the marg. reff.

2. all Israel, and for their elders] Omit
" and," which is not in the Hebrew. The
meaning is that Joshua summoned to him
all Israel as represented by its elders, &c.
(Deut. i. 15.) This gathering probably took
place at the Tabernacle at Shiloh.

kindled against you, and ye shall perish quickly from off the
good land which he hath given unto you.

a Gen. 35. 4.
b ch. 23. 2.
c 1 Sam. 10.
19.

CHAP. 24. AND Joshua gathered all the tribes of Israel to *a*Shechem, and *b*called for the elders of Israel, and for their heads, and
for their judges, and for their officers; and they *c*presented them-
2 selves before God. ¶ And Joshua said unto all the people, Thus

d Gen. 11.
26, 31.

saith the LORD God of Israel, *d*Your fathers dwelt on the other
side of the flood in old time, *even* Terah, the father of Abraham,

e Gen. 31. 19.
f Gen. 12. 1.
Acts. 7. 2, 3.
g Gen. 21. 2,
3.
h Gen. 25.
24, 25, 26.
i Gen. 36. 8.
k Gen. 46. 1,
6.
Acts 7. 15.
l Ex. 3. 10.
m Ex. 7 —12.
n Ex. 12. 37.
o Ex. 14. 2.
p Ex. 14. 9.
q Ex. 14. 10.
r Ex. 14. 20.
s Ex. 14. 27.
t Deut. 4. 34.
u ch. 5. 6.
x Num. 21.
21, 33.

3 and the father of Nachor: and *e*they served other gods. And *f*I
took your father Abraham from the other side of the flood, and
led him throughout all the land of Canaan, and multiplied his
4 seed, and *g*gave him Isaac. And I gave unto Isaac *h*Jacob and
Esau: and I gave unto *i*Esau mount Seir, to possess it; *k*but
5 Jacob and his children went down into Egypt. *l*I sent Moses also
and Aaron, and *m*I plagued Egypt, according to that which I did
6 among them: and afterward I brought you out. And I *n*brought
your fathers out of Egypt: and *o*ye came unto the sea; *p*and
the Egyptians pursued after your fathers with chariots and
7 horsemen unto the Red sea. And when they *q*cried unto the
LORD, *r*he put darkness between you and the Egyptians, *s*and
brought the sea upon them, and covered them; and *t*your eyes
have seen what I have done in Egypt: and ye dwelt in the wil-
8 derness *u*a long season. And I brought you into the land of
the Amorites, which dwelt on the other side Jordan; *x*and they
fought with you: and I gave them into your hand, that ye might
possess their land; and I destroyed them from before you.

y See Judg.
11. 25.
z Num. 22. 5.
a Deut. 23. 5.
b Num. 23.
11, 20.
c ch. 3. 14.
d ch. 6. 1.

9 Then *y*Balak the son of Zippor, king of Moab, arose and warred
against Israel, and *z*sent and called Balaam the son of Beor to
10 curse you: *a*but I would not hearken unto Balaam; *b*therefore
11 he blessed you still: so I delivered you out of his hand. And
*c*ye went over Jordan, and came unto Jericho: and *d*the men
of Jericho fought against you, the Amorites, and the Perizzites,
and the Canaanites, and the Hittites, and the Girgashites, the
Hivites, and the Jebusites; and I delivered them into your

e Ex. 23. 28.
Deut. 7. 20.

12 hand. And *e*I sent the hornet before you, which drave them
out from before you, *even* the two kings of the Amorites; but

f Ps. 44. 3, 6.
g Deut. 6. 10.

13 *f*not with thy sword, nor with thy bow. And I have given you a
land for which ye did not labour, and *g*cities which ye built not,
and ye dwell in them; of the vineyards and oliveyards which ye

h Deut. 10. 12.

14 planted not do ye eat. ¶ *h*Now therefore fear the LORD, and

---

XXIV. **1.** Shechem, situated between
those mountains, Ebal and Gerizim, which
had already been the scene of a solemn re-
hearsal of the Covenant soon after the first
entry of the people into the Promised Land
(viii. 30–35), was a fitting scene for the solemn renewal on the part of the people of
that Covenant with God which had been on
His part so signally and so fully kept. The
spot itself suggested the allusions to Abraham, Isaac, and Jacob, in Joshua's address; and its associations could not but give
peculiar force and moving effect to his appeals. This address was not made to the
rulers only but to the whole nation, not of
course to the tribes assembled in mass, but
to their representatives.

2. *the other side of the flood*] Better "on
the other side of the river," *i.e.* the Eu-

phrates. See marg. ref.

they served other gods] Possibly the
"images," or teraphim, which we find their
ancestor Laban calling "his gods" (see
marg. ref.); and of which it would seem that
there were, as Joshua spoke, some secret
devotees amongst the people (*vv.* 14, 25). It
is not stated that Abraham himself was an
idolater, though his fathers were. Jewish
tradition asserts that Abraham whilst in
Ur of the Chaldees was persecuted for his
abhorrence of idolatry, and hence was called
away by God from his native land. The
reference in the text to the original state of
those who were the forefathers of the nation, is made to show that they were no
better than others: God chose them not
for their excellences but of His own mere
motion.

serve him in ⁱsincerity and in truth: and ^kput away the gods
which your fathers served on the other side of the flood, and ^lin
15 Egypt; and serve ye the LORD. And if it seem evil unto you to
serve the LORD, ^mchoose you this day whom ye will serve;
whether ⁿthe gods which your fathers served that *were* on the
other side of the flood, or ^othe gods of the Amorites, in whose
land ye dwell: ^pbut as for me and my house, we will serve the
16 LORD. And the people answered and said, God forbid that we
17 should forsake the LORD, to serve other gods; for the LORD our
God, he *it is* that brought us up and our fathers out of the land
of Egypt, from the house of bondage, and which did those great
signs in our sight, and preserved us in all the way wherein we
18 went, and among all the people through whom we passed: and
the LORD drave out from before us all the people, even the Amorites which dwelt in the land: *therefore* will we also serve the
19 LORD; for he *is* our God. And Joshua said unto the people,
^qYe cannot serve the LORD: for he *is* an ^rholy God; he *is* ^sa
jealous God; ^the will not forgive your transgressions nor your
20 sins. ^uIf ye forsake the LORD, and serve strange gods, ^xthen
he will turn and do you hurt, and consume you, after that he
21 hath done you good. And the people said unto Joshua, Nay;
22 but we will serve the LORD. And Joshua said unto the people,
Ye *are* witnesses against yourselves that ^yye have chosen you
23 the LORD, to serve him. And they said, *We are* witnesses. Now
therefore ^zput away, *said he*, the strange gods which *are* among
24 you, and incline your heart unto the LORD God of Israel. And
the people said unto Joshua, the LORD our God will we serve,
25 and his voice will we obey. ¶ So Joshua ^amade a covenant with
the people that day, and set them a statute and an ordinance ^bin
26 Shechem. And Joshua ^cwrote these words in the book of the
law of God, and took ^da great stone, and ^eset it up there ^funder
27 an oak, that *was* by the sanctuary of the LORD. And Joshua
said unto all the people, Behold, this stone shall be ^ga witness
unto us; for ^hit hath heard all the words of the LORD which he
spake unto us: it shall be therefore a witness unto you, lest ye
28 deny your God. So ⁱJoshua let the people depart, every man
29 unto his inheritance. ¶ And it came to pass after these things,
that Joshua the son of Nun, the servant of the LORD, died, *being*
30 an hundred and ten years old. And they buried him in the
border of his inheritance in ^lTimnath-serah, which *is* in mount
31 Ephraim, on the north side of the hill of Gaash. ¶ And ^mIsrael
served the LORD all the days of Joshua, and all the days of the
elders that ¹overlived Joshua, and which had ⁿknown all the
32 works of the LORD, that he had done for Israel. ¶ And ^othe
bones of Joseph, which the children of Israel brought up out of

Marginal references:
ⁱ Gen. 17. 1.
Ps. 119. 1.
Eph. 6. 24.
^k Lev. 17. 7.
^l Ezek. 20. 7.
^m See Ruth 1. 15.
1 Kin. 18.21.
Ezek. 20. 39.
John 6. 67.
ⁿ ver. 14.
^o Ex. 23. 24.
^p Gen. 18.19.

^q Matt. 6. 24.
^r Lev. 19. 2.
Isai. 5. 16.
^s Ex. 20. 5.
^t Ex. 23. 21.
^u 1 Chr. 28. 9.
Ezra 8. 22.
Isai. 1. 28.
Jer. 17. 13.
^x Isai. 63. 10.
Acts 7. 42.
^y Ps.119.173.
^z Gen. 35. 2.
1 Sam. 7. 3.
^a See Exod. 15. 25.
^b ver. 26.
^c Deut.31.24.
^d See Judg. 9. 6.
^e See Gen. 28. 18.
^f Gen. 35. 4.
^g See Gen. 31. 48, 52.
ch. 22. 27.
^h Deut. 32. 1.
ⁱ Judg. 2. 6.
^k Judg. 2. 8.

^l ch. 19. 50.
Judg. 2. 9.
^m Judg. 2. 7.
ⁿ See Deut. 11. 2.
& 31. 13.
^o Gen. 50. 25.
Ex. 13. 19.

¹ Heb. pro*onged* their *days after Joshua.*

---

15. *choose*] Service of God in sincerity
and truth can only result from a free and
willing allegiance of the heart. This
accordingly is what Joshua invites, as
Moses had done before him (Deut. xxx.
15 seq.).

25. *made a covenant with the people*] i.e.
he solemnly ratified and renewed the Covenant of Sinai, as Moses had done before
him (Deut. xxix. 1). As no new or different

Covenant was made, no sacrifices were necessary.

26. Consult the marg. reff.
that was by the sanctuary of the LORD] i.e.
the spot where Abraham and Jacob had
sacrificed and worshipped, and which might
well be regarded by their posterity as a
holy place or sanctuary. Perhaps the very
altar of Abraham and Jacob was still remaining.

p Gen. 33.
19.

q Ex. 6. 25.
Judg. 20. 28.

Egypt, buried they in Shechem, in a parcel of ground *p* which Jacob bought of the sons of Hamor the father of Shechem for an hundred [1] pieces of silver: and it became the inheritance of the 33 children of Joseph. ¶ And Eleazar the son of Aaron died; and they buried him in a hill *that pertained to* *q* Phinehas his son, which was given him in mount Ephraim.

[1] Or, *lambs.*

---

33. [Eleazar's burial-place is placed by Conder not at Tibneh but in the village of 'Awertah.]

JUDGES.

INTRODUCTION.

THE Book of Judges, like the other Historical Books of the Old Testament, takes its name from the subject to which it chiefly relates, viz., the exploits of those JUDGES[1] who ruled Israel in the times between the death of Joshua and the rise of Samuel. The rule of the Judges (Ruth i. 1) in this limited sense was a distinct Dispensation, distinct from the leadership of Moses and Joshua, distinct from the more regular supremacy of Eli, the High-Priest, and from the Prophetic Dispensation inaugurated by Samuel (1 Sam. iii. 19–21 ; Acts iii. 24).

The book consists of three divisions. (1) The PREFACE, which extends to iii. 6 (incl.). (2) The MAIN NARRATIVE, iii. 7–xvi. 31. (3) THE APPENDIX, containing two detached narratives, (a) xvii. ; (b) xviii.–xxi. To these may be added the Book of Ruth, containing another detached narrative, which anciently was included under the title of JUDGES, to which book the first verse shows that it properly belongs.

(1) The general purpose of the Preface is to prepare the ground for the subsequent narrative ; to explain how it was that the heathen nations of Canaan were still so powerful, and the Israelites so destitute of Divine aid and protection against their enemies ; and to draw out the striking lessons of God's righteous judgment, which were afforded by the alternate servitudes and deliverances of the Israelites, according as they either forsook God to worship idols, or returned to Him in penitence, faith, and prayer. Throughout there is a reference to the threatenings and promises of the Books of Moses (ii. 15, 20, &c.), in order both to vindicate the power and faithfulness of Jehovah the God of Israel, and to hold out a warning to the future generations for whose instruction the Book was written. In the view which the writer was inspired to present to the Church, never was God's agency more busy in relation to the affairs of His people, than when, to a superficial observer, that agency had altogether ceased. On the other hand, the writer calls attention to the fact that those heroes, who wrought such wonderful deliverances for Israel, did it not by their own power, but were divinely commissioned, and divinely endowed with courage, strength, and victory. The writer of the Preface also directs the minds of the readers of his history to that vital doctrine, which it was one main object of the Old Testament Dispensation to keep alive in the world till the coming of Christ, viz., the Unity of God. All the calami-

---

[1] The Phœnician and Carthaginian *Suffete*, mentioned by Livy as corresponding in office to the Roman Consuls, is the same word as the Hebrew *Shophet*, Judge.

ties which he was about to narrate, were the fruit and consequence of idolatry. "Keep yourselves from idols," was the chief lesson which the history of the Judges was intended to inculcate.

The Preface consists of two very different portions; the recapitulation of events before, and up to, Joshua's death (i.–ii. 9), and the reflections on the history about to be related (ii. 10–iii. 6).

(2) The MAIN NARRATIVE contains, not consecutive annals of Israel as a united people, but a series of brilliant, striking, pictures, now of one portion of the tribes, now of another. Of some epochs minute details are given; other periods of eight or ten years, nay, even of twenty, forty, or eighty years, are disposed of in four or five words. Obviously in those histories in which we find graphic touches and accurate details, we have preserved to us narratives contemporary with the events narrated—the narratives, probably, of eye-witnesses and actors in the events themselves. The histories of Ehud, of Barak and Deborah, of Gideon, of Jephthah, and of Samson, are the product of times when the invasions of Moab, of Jabin, of Midian, of Ammon, and of the Philistines, were living realities in the minds of those who penned those histories. The compiler of the Book seems to have inserted bodily in his history the ancient narratives which were extant in his day. As the mind of the reader is led on by successive steps to the various exploits of the twelve Judges, and from them to Samuel, and from Samuel to David, and from David to David's son, it cannot fail to recognize the working of one Divine plan for

man's redemption, and to understand how Judges, and Prophets, and Kings were endowed with some portion of the gifts of the Holy Spirit, preparatory to the coming into the world of Him in Whom all the fulness of the Godhead should dwell bodily, and Who should save to the uttermost all that come to God by Him.

Some curious analogies have been noted between this, the heroic age of the Israelites, and the heroic ages of Greece and other Gentile countries. Here, as there, it is in the early settlement and taking possession of their new country, and in conflicts with the old races, that the virtues and prowess of the heroes are developed. Here, as there, there is oftentimes a strange mixture of virtue and vice, a blending of great and noble qualities, of most splendid deeds with cruelty and ignorance, licentiousness and barbarism. And yet, in comparing the sacred with the heathen heroes, we find in the former a faith in God and a religious purpose, of which Heathendom affords no trace. The exploits of the sacred heroes advanced the highest interests of mankind, and were made subservient to the overthrow of abominable and impure superstitions, and to the preserving a light of true religion in the world until the coming of Christ.

(3) The APPENDIX contains a record of certain events which happened " in the days when the judges ruled," but are not connected with any exploits of the Judges. Though placed at the end of the book, the two histories both manifestly belong chronologically to the beginning of it: the reason for

the place selected is perhaps that suggested in xvii. 1 note. Exact chronology forms no part of the plan of the book. The only guide to the chronology is to be found in the genealogies which span the period : and the evidence of these genealogies concurs in assigning an average of between seven and eight generations to the time from the entrance into Canaan to the commencement of David's reign, which would make up from 240 to 260 years. Deducting 30 years for Joshua, 30 for Samuel, and 40 for the reign of Saul (Acts xiii. 21), in all 100 years, we have from 140 to 160 years left for the events related in the Book of Judges. This is a short time, no doubt, but quite sufficient, when it is remembered that many of the *rests* and *servitudes* (iii. 8 note) therein related are not successive, but synchronize ; and that no great dependence can be placed on the recurring 80, 40, and 20 years, whenever they are not in harmony with historical probability.

The narratives which have the strongest appearance of synchronizing are those of the Moabite, Ammonite, and Amalekite servitude (iii. 12–30) which lasted *eighteen* years, and was closely connected with a Philistine invasion (iii. 31); of the Ammonite servitude which lasted *eighteen* years, and was also closely connected with a Philistine invasion (x. 7, 8) ; and of the Midianite and Amalekite servitude which lasted seven years (vi. 1), all three of which terminated in a complete expulsion and destruction of their enemies by the three leaders Ehud, Jephthah, and Gideon, heading respectively the Benjamites, the Manassites and the northern tribes, and the tribes be-

yond Jordan : the conduct of the Ephraimites as related in ch. viii. 1, xii. 1, being an additional very strong feature of resemblance in the two histories of Gideon and Jephthah. The 40 years of Philistine servitude mentioned in Judg. xiii. 1, seems to have embraced the last 20 years of Eli's judgeship, and the first 20 of Samuel's, and terminated with Samuel's victory at Eben-ezer : and, if so, Samson's judgeship of 20 years also coincided in part with Samuel's. The long *rests* of 40 and 80 years spoken of as following the victories of Othniel, Barak, and Ehud, may very probably have synchronized in whole or in part. It cannot however be denied that the chronology of this book is still a matter of uncertainty.

The time of the compilation of this Book, and the *final* arrangement of its component parts in their present form and in their present connexion in the series of the Historical Books of Scripture, may with most probability be assigned to the latter times of the Jewish monarchy, included in the same plan. (The Book of Ezra, it may be observed, by the way, is a continuation, not of Kings, but of Chronicles.) There is not the slightest allusion in the Book of Judges, to the Babylonish captivity. Only Judges iii. 5, 6, as regards the Canaanite races mentioned, and the context, may be compared with Ezra ix. 1, 2. The language of the Book of Judges points to the same conclusion. It is pure and good Hebrew, untainted with Chaldaisms or Persian forms. as are the later books.

The inference to which these and other such resemblances *tends*, is that the compilation of the

Book of Judges is of about the same age as that of the Books of Samuel and Kings, if not actually the work of the same hand. But no absolute certainty can be arrived at. The chief allusions to it in the New Testament are those in Heb. xi. 32 seq., and Acts xiii. 20. But there are frequent references to the histories contained in it in the Psalms and in the Prophets. See

Psalm lxxviii. 56, &c., lxxxiii. 9–11, cvi. 34–45, &c. ; Isaiah ix. 4, x. 26 ; Nehem. ix. 27, &c. See also 1 Sam. xii. 9–11 ; 2 Sam. xi. 21. Other Books to which it refers are Genesis, Exodus, Leviticus, Numbers, Deuteronomy, and Joshua. See marg. reff. to i. ii. 1–3, 6–10, 15, 20–23, iv. 11, vi. 8, 13, x. 11, xi. 13–26, xiii. 5, xvi. 17, xviii. 30, xix. 23, 24, xx. 26, 27, &c.

THE BOOK

OF

JUDGES.

CHAP. 1. NOW after the death of Joshua it came to pass, that the children of Israel *a* asked the LORD, saying, Who shall go up for 2 us against the Canaanites first, to fight against them? And the LORD said, *b* Judah shall go up: behold, I have delivered the 3 land into his hand. ¶ And Judah said unto Simeon his brother, Come up with me into my lot, that we may fight against the Canaanites; and *c* I likewise will go with thee into thy lot. So 4 Simeon went with him. And Judah went up; and the LORD delivered the Canaanites and the Perizzites into their hand: 5 and they slew of them in *d* Bezek ten thousand men. And they found Adoni-bezek in Bezek: and they fought against him, and 6 they slew the Canaanites and the Perizzites. But Adoni-bezek fled; and they pursued after him, and caught him, and 7 cut off his thumbs, and his great toes. And Adoni-bezek said, Threescore and ten kings, having [1] their thumbs and their great toes cut off, [2] gathered *their meat* under my table: *e* as I have done, so God hath requited me. And they brought him to 8 Jerusalem, and there he died. ¶ Now *f* the children of Judah had fought against Jerusalem, and had taken it, and smitten it

a Num. 27. 21. ch. 20. 18. *b* Gen. 49. 8.

c ver. 17.

d 1 Sam. 11. 8.

e Lev. 24. 19. 1 Sam.15.33. Jam. 2. 13. *f* See Josh. 15. 63.

---

[1] Heb. *the thumbs of their hands and of their feet.*   [2] Or, *gleaned.*

I. 1. *after the death of Joshua*] But from i. 1 to ii. 9 is a consecutive narrative, *ending* with the death of Joshua. Hence the events in this chapter and in ii. 1-6 are to be taken as belonging to the lifetime of Joshua. See ii. 11 note.

asked the LORD] The phrase is only found in *Judges* and *Samuel*. It was the privilege of the civil ruler, to apply to the High Priest to consult for him the Urim and Thummim (marg. ref.). (Cp. Josh. xiv. 1, xviii. 1, 10, xix. 51). Here it was not Phinehas, as Josephus concludes from placing these events after the death of Joshua, but Eleazar, through whom the children of Israel inquired " *Who*," (or, rather) " *which tribe of us shall go up?*"

2. *And the* LORD *said*] *i.e.* answered by Urim and Thummim. *The land* was the portion which fell to Judah by lot, not the whole land of Canaan (see iii. 11). The priority given to Judah is a plain indication of Divine direction. It points to the birth of our Lord of the tribe of Judah. Judah associated Simeon with him (*v.* 3) because their lots were intermingled (Josh. xix. 1).

4. *the Canaanites and the Perizzites*] See Gen. xii. 6, xiii. 7 notes. *Bezek* may be the name of a district. It has not yet been identified.

7. *threescore and ten kings*] We may infer from this number of conquered kings, that the intestine wars of the Canaanites were

among the causes which, under God's Providence, weakened their resistance to the Israelites. Adoni-Bezek's cruelty to the subject kings was the cause of his receiving (cp. marg. reff.) this chastisement. The loss of the thumb would unfit a man for handling sword or bow; the loss of the great toe would impede his speed.

8. Render " **and** *the children of Judah* **fought** *against Jerusalem,* **and took it, and smote it,**" &c. With regard to the capture of Jerusalem there is some obscurity. It is here said to have been taken, smitten with the edge of the sword, and burnt, by the children of Judah. In Josh. xii. 8, 10 the Jebusite and the king of Jerusalem are enumerated among Joshua's conquests, but without any distinct mention of the capture of the city; and in the marg. ref. we read that the Jebusites were not expelled from Jerusalem, but dwelt with the children of Judah (cp. i. 21). Further we learn from xix. 10-12 that Jerusalem was wholly a Jebusite city in the lifetime of Phinehas (xx. 28), and so it continued till the reign of David (2 Sam. v. 6-9). The conclusion is that Jerusalem was only taken once, viz. at the time here described, and that this was in the lifetime of Joshua; but that the children of Judah did not occupy it in sufficient force to prevent the return of the Jebusites, who gradually recovered complete possession.

9 with the edge of the sword, and set the city on fire. [g]And afterward the children of Judah went down to fight against the
Canaanites, that dwelt in the mountain, and in the south, and in
10 the [1]valley. And Judah went against the Canaanites that dwelt
in Hebron: (now the name of Hebron before *was* [h]Kirjath-
11 arba:) and they slew Sheshai, and Ahiman, and Talmai. [i]And
from thence he went against the inhabitants of Debir: and the
12 name of Debir before *was* Kirjath-sepher: ¶ [k]And Caleb said,
He that smiteth Kirjath-sepher, and taketh it, to him will I
13 give Achsah my daughter to wife. And Othniel the son of
Kenaz, [l]Caleb's younger brother, took it: and he gave him
14 Achsah his daughter to wife. [m]And it came to pass, when she
came *to him*, that she moved him to ask of her father a field:
and she lighted from off *her* ass; and Caleb said unto her, What
15 wilt thou? And she said unto him, [n]Give me a blessing: for
thou hast given me a south land; give me also springs of water.
And Caleb gave her the upper springs and the nether springs.
16 ¶ [o]And the children of the Kenite, Moses' father in law, went
up out [p]of the city of palm trees with the children of Judah into
the wilderness of Judah, which *lieth* in the south of [q]Arad; [r]and
17 they went and dwelt among the people. ¶ [s]And Judah went
with Simeon his brother, and they slew the Canaanites that
inhabited Zephath, and utterly destroyed it. And the name of
18 the city was called [t]Hormah. Also Judah took [u]Gaza with the
coast thereof, and Askelon with the coast thereof, and Ekron
19 with the coast thereof. And [x]the LORD was with Judah; and
[2]he drave out *the inhabitants of* the mountain; but could not
drive out the inhabitants of the valley, because they had
20 [y]chariots of iron. [z]And they gave Hebron unto Caleb, as Moses
21 said: and he expelled thence the three sons of Anak. ¶ [a]And
the children of Benjamin did not drive out the Jebusites that
inhabited Jerusalem; but the Jebusites dwell with the children
22 of Benjamin in Jerusalem unto this day. ¶ And the house of
Joseph, they also went up against Beth-el: [b]and the LORD *was*
23 with them. And the house of Joseph [c]sent to descry Beth-el.
24 (Now the name of the city before *was* [d]Luz.) And the spies

[g] Josh. 10. 36. & 11. 21. & 15. 13.
[h] Josh. 14. 15. & 15. 14.
[i] Josh. 15. 15.
[k] Josh. 15. 16, 17.
[l] ch. 3. 9.
[m] Josh. 15. 18, 19.
[n] Gen. 33. 11.
[o] ch. 4. 11. 1 Sam. 15. 6. 1 Chr. 2. 55. Jer. 35. 2.
[p] Deut. 34. 3.
[q] Num. 21. 1.
[r] Num. 10. 32.
[s] ver. 3.
[t] Josh. 19. 4.
[u] Josh. 11. 22.
[x] ver. 2.
[y] Josh. 17. 16. 18.
[z] Num. 14. 24.
[a] See Josh. 18. 28.
[b] ver. 19.
[c] Josh. 2. 1. & 7. 2.
[d] Gen. 28. 19.

[1] Or, *low country*. [2] Or, *he possessed the mountain*.

---

set the city on fire] A phrase found only at xx. 48; 2 K. viii. 12, and Ps. lxxiv. 7.

16. *the children of the Kenite*] See Num. xxiv. 21 note.

the city of palm trees] Jericho (see marg. ref.). The Rabbinical story is that Jericho, with 500 cubits square of land, was given to Hobab. The use of the phrase "city of palm trees" for "Jericho," is perhaps an indication of the influence of Joshua's curse (Josh. vi. 26). The very *name* of Jericho was blotted out. There are no palm trees at Jericho now, but Josephus mentions them repeatedly, as well as the balsam trees.

17. *Hormah*] See Num. xxi. 1 note. The destruction then vowed was now accomplished. This is another decisive indication that the events here related belong to Joshua's lifetime. This would be about six years after the vow.

18. It is remarkable that *Ashdod* is not here mentioned, as it is in Josh. xv. 46, 47, in conjunction with Gaza and Ekron; but that Askelon, which is not in the list of the cities of Judah at all, is named in its stead. (See Josh. xiii. 3 note.) It is a curious fact that when Rameses III. took Askelon it was occupied, not by Philistines, but apparently by Hebrews. Rameses began to reign B.C. 1269, and reigned 25 years. At any time between 1269 and 1244 such occupation of Askelon by Hebrews agrees with the Book of Judges.

21. This verse is nearly identical with Josh. xv. 63, except in the substitution of *Benjamin* for *Judah*. Probably the original reading *Judah* was altered in later times to *Benjamin*, because Jebus was within the border of Benjamin, and neither had the Benjamites expelled the Jebusites.

22. Bethel was within the borders of Benjamin, but was captured, as we here learn, by the house of Joseph, who probably retained it.

saw a man come forth out of the city, and they said unto him,
Shew us, we pray thee, the entrance into the city, and [e]we will
25 shew thee mercy. And when he shewed them the entrance into
the city, they smote the city with the edge of the sword; but
26 they let go the man and all his family. And the man went
into the land of the Hittites, and built a city, and called the
name thereof Luz: which is the name thereof unto this day.
27 ¶[f]Neither did Manasseh drive out *the inhabitants of* Beth-shean
and her towns, nor Taanach and her towns, nor the inhabitants
of Dor and her towns, nor the inhabitants of Ibleam and her
towns, nor the inhabitants of Megiddo and her towns: but the
28 Canaanites would dwell in that land. And it came to pass, when
Israel was strong, that they put the Canaanites to tribute, and
29 did not utterly drive them out. ¶[g]Neither did Ephraim drive
out the Canaanites that dwelt in Gezer; but the Canaanites
30 dwelt in Gezer among them. ¶Neither did Zebulun drive out
the inhabitants of Kitron, nor the [h]inhabitants of Nahalol; but
the Canaanites dwelt among them, and became tributaries.
31 ¶[i]Neither did Asher drive out the inhabitants of Accho, nor
the inhabitants of Zidon, nor of Ahlab, nor of Achzib, nor of
32 Helbah, nor of Aphik, nor of Rehob: but the Asherites [k]dwelt
among the Canaanites, the inhabitants of the land: for they did
33 not drive them out. ¶[l]Neither did Naphtali drive out the
inhabitants of Beth-shemesh, nor the inhabitants of Beth-anath ;
but he [m]dwelt among the Canaanites, the inhabitants of the
land: nevertheless the inhabitants of Beth-shemesh and of Beth-
34 anath [n]became tributaries unto them. ¶And the Amorites
forced the children of Dan into the mountain : for they would
35 not suffer them to come down to the valley : but the Amorites
would dwell in mount Heres [o]in Aijalon, and in Shaalbim : yet
the hand of the house of Joseph [1]prevailed, so that they became
36 tributaries. And the coast of the Amorites was [p]from [2]the going
up to Akrabbim, from the rock, and upward.
CHAP. 2. And an [3]angel of the LORD came up from Gilgal [a]to
Bochim, and said, I made you to go up out of Egypt, and have

[e] Josh. 2. 12, 14.

[f] Josh. 17. 11, 12, 13.

[g] Josh. 16. 10.
1 Kin. 9. 16.

[h] Josh. 19. 15.

[i] Josh. 19. 24—30.

[k] Ps. 106. 34, 35.

[l] Josh. 19. 38.

[m] ver. 32.

[n] ver. 30.

[o] Josh. 19. 42.

[p] Num. 34. 4.
Josh. 15. 3.

[a] ver. 5.

---

[1] Heb. *was heavy.* [2] Or, *Maaleh-akrabbim.* [3] Or, *messenger.*

---

26. The site of this new Luz is not known,
but "the land of the Hittites" was apparently in the north of Palestine, on the
borders of Syria (Gen. x. 15 note).
31. Cp. marg. ref. *Accho,* afterwards
called Ptolemais, now Akka or St. Jean
d'Acre, is named here for the first time.
32. It is an evidence of the power of the
Canaanite in this portion of the land that it
is not said (cp. *v.* 30) that the Canaanites
dwelt among the Asherites, but that the
Asherites (and *v.* 33, Naphtali) "dwelt
among the Canaanites ; " nor are the
Canaanites in Accho, Zidon, and the other
Asherite cities, said to have become tributaries.
34. The Amorites are usually found in
the mountain (Num. xiii. 29 ; Josh, x. 6).
Here they dwell in the valley, of which the
monuments of Rameses III. show them to
have been in possession when that monarch
invaded Syria. It was their great strength
in this district, and their forcible detention

of the territory of Dan, which led to the
expedition of the Danites (xviii.). The
house of Joseph lent their powerful aid in
subduing them, probably in the times of the
Judges.
36. *the going up to Akrabbim*] See marg.
and reff. ; properly "the ascent of scorpions," with which the whole region abounds.
the rock] **Petra,** the capital of Idumea, so
called from the mass of precipitous rock
which encloses the town, and out of which
many of its buildings are excavated. The
original word *Selah* is always used of the
rock at Kadesh-Barnea (Num. xx. 8–11),
near Petra (cp. Obad. 3). This leads us to
look for "the ascent of scorpions," here
coupled with *has-selah,* in the same neighbourhood.
II. 1. The *angel of the* LORD (not *an
angel*).] The phrase is used nearly sixty times
to designate the Angel of God's Presence.
See Gen. xii. 7 note. In all cases where
"the angel of the Lord" delivers a message,

Ex. 3. 6—8.
c Deut. 7. 2.
d Deut. 12. 3.
e ver. 20.

f Josh. 23. 13.
y ch. 3. 6.
h Ex. 23. 33.
& 34. 12.
Deut. 7. 16.

i Josh. 22. 6.
& 24. 28.
k Josh. 24. 31.
l Josh. 24. 20.
m Josh. 24.
30.
n Josh. 19.
50.
& 24. 30.
Timnath
serah.
o 1 Sam. 2.
12.
1 Chr. 28. 9.
Jer. 9. 3.
Gal. 4. 8.
2 Thess. 1. 8.
Tit. 1. 16.

brought you unto the land which I sware unto your fathers; 2 and ᵇI said, I will never break my covenant with you. And ᶜye shall make no league with the inhabitants of this land ; ᵈ ye shall throw down their altars : ᵉbut ye have not obeyed my voice : 3 why have ye done this ? Wherefore I also said, I will not drive them out from before you ; but they shall be ᶠas thorns in your 4 sides, and ᵍtheir gods shall be a ʰsnare unto you. And it came to pass, when the angel of the LORD spake these words unto all the children of Israel, that the people lifted up their 5 voice, and wept. And they called the name of that place 6 ¹Bochim : and they sacrificed there unto the LORD. ¶And when ⁱJoshua had let the people go, the children of Israel went 7 every man unto his inheritance to possess the land. ᵏAnd the people served the LORD all the days of Joshua, and all the days of the elders that ²outlived Joshua, who had seen all the great 8 works of the LORD, that he did for Israel. And ˡJoshua the son of Nun, the servant of the LORD, died, being an hundred and 9 ten years old. ᵐAnd they buried him in the border of his inheritance in ⁿTimnath-heres, in the mount of Ephraim, on the 10 north side of the hill Gaash. And also all that generation were gathered unto their fathers : and there arose another generation after them, which ᵒknew not the LORD, nor yet the works

¹ That is, *Weepers.*   ² Heb. *prolonged days after Joshua.*

he does it as if God Himself were speaking, without the intervening words " *Thus saith the Lord,*" which are used in the case of prophets. (Cp. vi. 8 ; Josh. xxiv. 2.)

When the host of Israel came up from Gilgal in the plain of Jericho, near the Jordan (Josh. iv. 19) to Shiloh and Shechem, in the hill country of Ephraim, the Angel who had been with them at Gilgal (Exod. xxiii. 20-23, xxxiii. 1-4 ; Josh. v. 10-15) accompanied them. The mention of Gilgal thus fixes the transaction to the period soon after the removal of the camp from Gilgal, and the events recorded in i. 1-36 (of which those related in *vv.* 1-29 took place before, and those in *vv.* 30-36, just after that removal). It also shews that it was the conduct of the Israelites, recorded in ch. i. as in Josh. xvi. xvii., which provoked this rebuke.

2. The two articles of the Covenant here specified (cp. marg. reff.) are those which the Israelites had at this time broken. The other important prohibition (Deut. vii. 3) is not specified by the Angel, and this is an indication that at the time the Angel spoke, intermarriages with the heathen spoken of (iii. 6) had not taken place ; and this again is another evidence of the early date of this occurrence.

3. " *Wherefore I also said* "] Rather because ye have done the things mentioned in *v.* 2, " I have now said (*i.e.* I now protest and declare) *that I will not drive them out from before you* " (cp. xix. 29). And it was the announcement of this resolution by the Angel that caused the people to weep.

The word thorns in this verse is supplied

by the A. V. from the similar passage in Joshua (see marg. ref.). Other Versions adopt a different reading of the original text, and prefer the sense "they shall be to you for adversaries " (cp. the last words of Num. xxxiii. 55).

5. *Bochim*] *i.e.* weepers. It was near Shechem, but the site is unknown. Cp. the names given to places for similar reasons in Gen. xxxv. 8, l. 11.

7. If Joshua was about 80 at the entrance into Canaan, 30 years would bring us to the close of his life. The " elders " would be all that were old enough to take part in the wars of Canaan (iii. 1, 2) ; and therefore, reckoning from the age of 20 to 70, a period of about 50 years may be assigned from the entrance into Canaan to the death of the elders, or 20 years after the death of Joshua.

the great works of the LORD] The overthrow of the Canaanitish nations.

8. *the servant of the* LORD] This is a title specially given to Moses (Deut. xxxiv. 5 ; Josh. i. 1). In later books, the phrase "the servant of God" is used (1 Chr. vi. 49 ; Neh. x. 29 ; Dan. ix. 11 ; Rev. xv. 3). It is applied to Joshua only here and in Josh. xxiv. 29. It is spoken of David (Ps. xviii., title), and generally of the prophets ; and, like the analogous phrase, "man of God," is transferred by St. Paul to the ministers of Christ under the New Testament (2 Tim. ii. 24 ; Jam. i. 1).

10. *all that generation*] *i.e.* the main body of those who were grown-up men at the time of the conquest of Canaan.

11 which he had done for Israel. ¶And the children of Israel did
12 evil in the sight of the LORD, and served Baalim: and they
 ᵖforsook the LORD God of their fathers, which brought them out   ᵖDeut.31.16.
 of the land of Egypt, and followed ᑫother gods, of the gods of   ᑫDeut.6.14.
 the people that *were* round about them, and ʳbowed themselves   ʳEx. 20. 5.
13 unto them, and provoked the LORD to anger. And they forsook
14 the LORD, ˢand served Baal and Ashtaroth. ¶ᵗAnd the anger   ˢch. 3. 7.
 of the LORD was hot against Israel, and he ᵘdelivered them into   ᵗch. 3. 8.
 the hands of spoilers that spoiled them, and ˣhe sold them into   ᵘ2 Kin. 17. 20.
 the hands of their enemies round about, so that they ʸcould not   ˣch. 3. 8.
15 any longer stand before their enemies. Whithersoever they   Ps. 44. 12. Isai. 50. 1.
 went out, the hand of the LORD was against them for evil, as   ʸLev.26.37.
 the LORD had said, and ᶻas the LORD had sworn unto them: and   Josh. 7. 12.
16 they were greatly distressed. ¶Nevertheless ᵃthe LORD raised   ᶻLev. 26. Deut. 28.
 up judges, which ¹delivered them out of the hand of those that   ᵃch. 3. 9.
17 spoiled them. And yet they would not hearken unto their   1Sam.12.11. Acts 13. 20.
 judges, but they ᵇwent a whoring after other gods, and bowed   ᵇEx. 34. 15.
 themselves unto them: they turned quickly out of the way   Lev. 17. 7.
 which their fathers walked in, obeying the commandments of
18 the LORD; *but* they did not so. And when the LORD raised
 them up judges, then ᶜthe LORD was with the judge, and   ᶜJosh. 1. 5.
 delivered them out of the hand of their enemies all the days of
 the judge: ᵈfor it repented the LORD because of their groanings   ᵈPs. 106. 34—45.
19 by reason of them that oppressed them and vexed them. And it
 came to pass, ᵉwhen the judge was dead, *that* they returned, and   ᵉch. 3. 12.
 ²corrupted *themselves* more than their fathers, in following other   & 4. 1, &c.
 gods to serve them, and to bow down unto them; ³they ceased
 not from their own doings, nor from their stubborn way.
20 ¶ᶠAnd the anger of the LORD was hot against Israel; and he   ᶠver. 14.
 said, Because that this people hath ᵍtransgressed my covenant   ᵍJosh. 23. 16.
 which I commanded their fathers, and have not hearkened unto

¹ Heb. *saved*.   ² Or, *were corrupt*.   ³ Heb. *they let nothing fall of their*.

---

11. *and the children of Israel*] Here begins
the narrative of what really did happen
"after the death of Joshua," but of which
ch. i. conveys no hint. Israel served the
Lord all the days of Joshua (i. 7). But
when Joshua was dead..."the children of
Israel did evil in the sight of the Lord,
and served Baalim, and forsook the God of
their fathers." And then follows. from
v. 14 to the end of the chapter, a summary
of the whole contents of the Book.
did evil in the sight of the LORD] Through
this Book and all the Historical Books,
this is the regular phrase for falling into
idolatry. It occurs seven times in Judges,
as descriptive of the seven apostasies of
Israel, which drew down upon them the
seven servitudes under (1) Chushan-Rishathaim, (2) Eglon, (3) Jabin, (4) Midian,
(5) the tyranny of Abimelech, (6) the Ammonites, (7) the Philistines. The recurrence
of the phrase marks the hand of one author
and of one book. For the opposite phrase,
see 1 K. xv. 5, 11, &c.
The plural of Baal, *Baalim*, refers to the
numerous images of Baal which they set up
and worshipped, as does the plural form,

Ashtaroth (*v.* 13), to those of the female
divinity, Astarte.
12. *provoked the* LORD *to anger*] A frequent expression in connexion with idolatry,
especially in Deut., in the Books of the
Kings, and in Jeremiah.
14, 15. Consult the marg. reff. The
phrase, *he sold them into the hands &c.*, is
first found in Deut. xxxii. 30.
16. *nevertheless* (rather "and") *the* LORD
raised up judges] This is the first introduction of the term JUDGE, which gives its
name to the Book (Introd. p. 67).
18. *it repented the* LORD] Rather, "the
Lord was moved with compassion," or
"was grieved," "*because* of their groanings." (Cp. xxi. 15.)
20. This verse is connected with *v.* 13.
The intermediate verses refer to much later
times; they have the appearance of being
the reflections of the compiler interspersed
with the original narrative. But *v.* 20
catches up the thread only to let it fall immediately. All that follows, down to the
end of iii. 7, seems to be another digression,
closing with words like those of ii. 13.
It does not appear how this message

<table>
<tr><td>^h Josh. 23.
13.
ⁱ ch. 3. 1, 4.
^k Deut. 8. 2,
16. & 13. 3.</td><td>21 my voice ; ^hI also will not henceforth drive out any from before
22 them of the nations which Joshua left when he died : ⁱthat
through them I may ^kprove Israel, whether they will keep the
way of the LORD to walk therein, as their fathers did keep it, or
23 not. Therefore the LORD ¹left those nations, without driving
them out hastily ; neither delivered he them into the hand of
Joshua.</td></tr>
</table>

^h Josh. 23.
13.
ⁱ ch. 3. 1, 4.
^k Deut. 8. 2,
16. & 13. 3.

21 my voice ; ^hI also will not henceforth drive out any from before
22 them of the nations which Joshua left when he died : ⁱthat
through them I may ^kprove Israel, whether they will keep the
way of the LORD to walk therein, as their fathers did keep *it*, or
23 not. Therefore the LORD ¹left those nations, without driving
them out hastily ; neither delivered he them into the hand of
Joshua.

^a ch. 2. 21,
22.

CHAP. **3**. NOW these *are* ^athe nations which the LORD left, to
prove Israel by them, *even* as many *of Israel* as had not known
2 all the wars of Canaan ; only that the generations of the children
of Israel might know, to teach them war, at the least such as

^b Josh 13.
2—6.

3 before knew nothing thereof; *namely,* ^bfive lords of the Philistines, and all the Canaanites, and the Sidonians, and the Hivites
that dwelt in mount Lebanon, from mount Baal-hermon unto

^c ch. 2. 22.

4 the entering in of Hamath. ^cAnd they were to prove Israel by
them, to know whether they would hearken unto the commandments of the LORD, which he commanded their fathers by the

^d Ps. 106.
35.

5 hand of Moses. ¶ ^dAnd the children of Israel dwelt among the
Canaanites, Hittites, and Amorites, and Perizzites, and Hivites,

^e Ex. 34. 16.
Deut. 7. 3.
^f ch. 2. 11.
^g ch. 2. 13.
^h Ex. 34. 13.
ch. 6. 25.
ⁱ ch. 2. 14.
^k Hab. 3. 7.

6 and Jebusites : and ^ethey took their daughters to be their wives,
and gave their daughters to their sons, and served their gods.
7 ^fAnd the children of Israel did evil in the sight of the LORD, and
forgat the LORD their God, ^gand served Baalim and ^hthe groves.
8 Therefore the anger of the LORD was hot against Israel, and he
ⁱsold them into the hand of ^kChushan-rishathaim king of ²Meso-
potamia : and the children of Israel served Chushan-rishathaim

¹ Or, *suffered*.   ² Heb. *Aram-naharaim*.

---

was given to Israel, whether by Angel, or
prophet, or Urim, nor indeed is it certain
whether any message was given. The words
may be understood as merely explaining
what passed through the Divine mind, and
expressing the thoughts which regulated the
Divine proceeding.

III. 1. *even as many of Israel*, &c.] These
words show that the writer has especially in
view the generation which came to man's
estate immediately after the close of the
wars with the Canaanites (Josh. xxiii. 1).
Cp. ii. 10.

3. *lords*] *Seranim,* a title used exclusively
of the princes of the five Philistine cities.
The title is probably of Phœnician origin.

Joshua appears to have smitten and subdued the Hivites as far north as Baal-Gad,
in the valley of Lebanon under Mount
Hermon (Josh. xi. 17, xii. 7), but no
further (Josh. xiii. 5). There was an un-
subdued Hivite population to the north of
Baal-hermon (probably Baal-Gad under
Hermon, since it is not synonymous with
Hermon ; see 1 Chr. v. 23), to the entering
in of Hamath : *i. e.* in the fertile valley of
Cœle-Syria. Hamath is always spoken of
as the extreme northern boundary of the
land of Canaan. It was the gate of approach
to Canaan from Babylon, and all the north
(Zech. ix. 2 ; Jer. xxxix. 5). It formed
part of the dominions of Solomon (2 Ch.r.
viii. 4), and of the future inheritance of

Israel, as described in vision by Ezekiel
(xlvii. 16).

6. See ii. 2 note.

7. *and the groves*] Lit. *Asheroth*, images of
Asherah [the goddess companion of Baal]:
see Deut. xvi. 21 note.

8. Here we hold again the thread of the
proper narrative, which seems as if it
ought to have run thus (i. 1) : Now, &c.
(iii. 8), therefore (or "and") &c.

served Chushan-Rishathaim] This is the
same phrase as in *v.* 14. From it is derived
the expression, "the times of servitude," as
distinguished from "the times of rest," in
speaking of the times of the Judges. Mesopotamia, or Aram-naharaim, was the seat
of Nimrod's kingdom, and Nimrod was the
son of Cush (Gen. x. 8-12). Rishathaim is
perhaps the name of a city, or a foreign
word altered to a Hebrew form. Nothing
is known from history, or the cuneiform
inscriptions, of the political condition of
Mesopotamia at this time, though Thotmes
I. and III. in the 18th Egyptian dynasty
are known to have invaded Mesopotamia.
It is, however, in accordance with such an
aggressive Aramean movement towards
Palestine, that as early as the time of
Abraham we find the kings of Shinar and
of Elam invading the south of Palestine.
There is also distinct evidence in the names
of the Edomitish kings (Gen. xxxvi. 32,
35, 37) of an Aramean dynasty in Edom

9 eight years. ¶ And when the children of Israel ¹cried unto the
LORD, the LORD ᵐraised up a ¹deliverer to the children of Israel,
who delivered them, *even* ⁿOthniel the son of Kenaz, Caleb's
10 younger brother. And °the Spirit of the LORD ²came upon him,
and he judged Israel, and went out to war: and the LORD
delivered Chushan-rishathaim king of ³Mesopotamia into his
11 hand; and his hand prevailed against Chushan-rishathaim. And
the land had rest forty years. And Othniel the son of Kenaz
12 died. ¶ᵖAnd the children of Israel did evil again in the sight
of the LORD: and the LORD strengthened ᵠEglon the king of
Moab against Israel, because they had done evil in the sight of
13 the LORD. And he gathered unto him the children of Ammon
and ʳAmalek, and went and smote Israel, and possessed ˢthe
14 city of palm trees. So the children of Israel ᵗserved Eglon the
15 king of Moab eighteen years. ¶ But when the children of Israel
ᵘcried unto the LORD, the LORD raised them up a deliverer,
Ehud the son of Gera, ⁴a Benjamite, a man ⁵lefthanded: and

l ver. 15.	
m ch. 2. 16.	
n ch. 1. 13.	
o See Num. 27. 18.	
1 Sam. 11. 6.	
2 Chr. 15. 1.	
p ch. 2. 19.	
q 1 Sam. 12, 9.	
r ch. 5. 14.	
s ch. 1. 16.	
t Deut. 28.48.	
u ver. 9.	
ch. 4. 3.	
& 6. 7.	
& 10. 10.	
1 Sam.12.10.	
Ps. 22. 5.	
& 106. 44.	
& 107. 13, 19.	

¹ Heb. *saviour*.	³ Heb. *Aram*.	⁵ Heb. *shut of his right hand*. ch. 20. 16.
² Heb. *was*.	⁴ Or, *the son of Gemini*.	

about the time of the early Judges. Cp., too, Job i. 17.

9. Othniel was already distinguished in Joshua's lifetime as a brave and successful leader. See Josh. xv. 16, 17.

10. *and the Spirit of the LORD came upon him*] The phrase occurs frequently in this Book and in the Books of Samuel and Kings. It marks the peculiar office of the Judges. They were saviours (*v.* 9 marg. Neh. ix. 27) called and directed by the Holy Spirit, Who endued them with extraordinary wisdom, courage, and strength for the work which lay before them (cp. vi. 34, xi. 29, xiii. 25, xiv. 6, 19), and were in this respect types of Christ the "Judge of Israel" (Mic. v. 1), in Whom "the Spirit of the Lord God" was "without measure" (Isai. xi. 2, lxi. 1; Matt. xii. 18-21; Joh. i. 32; Acts xiii. 2).

11. *the land* means here, as in i. 2, not the whole land of Canaan, but the part concerned, probably the land of the tribe of Judah. *Forty years*, here and elsewhere, is (like *fourscore years*, *v.* 30) a round number, perhaps equivalent to a generation.

12. The "strengthening" Eglon was the special work of God, and because Israel "had done evil," &c. Samuel's comment on the event is to the same effect (1 Sam. xii. 9).

13. The children of Ammon (Beni-Ammon), almost always so spoken of from their ancestor Ben-ammi (Gen. xix. 38), seem to be under the leadership of the king of Moab, as do also the Amalekites: this is perhaps the *strengthening* spoken of in *v.* 12. In ch. vi. the combination is Midianites, Amalekites, and children of the East, or Arab tribes. In the narrative of Jephthah's judgeship, the Ammonites alone are mentioned; but with a reference to the Moabites, and as if they were one people (xi. 24).

The Amalekites appear as the constant and bitter foes of the Israelites (Exod. xvii. 8 notes and reff.); and the naming a mountain in Ephraim, "*the mount of the Amalekites*" (xii. 15) is probably a memorial of this joint invasion of Moabites and Amalekites, and marks the scene either of their occupation, or of some signal victory over them.

The city of palm trees : *i.e.* Jericho (i. 16), having been utterly destroyed by Joshua, and not rebuilt till the time of Ahab (Josh. vi. 24-26 ; 1 K. xvi. 34), can only have existed at this time as an unwalled village, —like Jerusalem after its destruction by Nebuzaradan, till Nehemiah rebuilt its walls—and like its modern representative er-Riha, a village with a fortress for the Turkish garrison. This occupation of Jericho should be compared with the invasion in x. 9, where two out of the three tribes named, Benjamin and Ephraim, are the same as those here concerned, and where (x. 7) the Philistines are coupled with the Ammonites, just as here (*v.* 31) the Philistines are mentioned in near connexion with the Moabites. See Introd. p. 69.

15. *But when the children of Israel cried unto the LORD, the LORD raised them up a deliverer*] The very same words as are used at *v.* 9. See, too, ii. 16, 18, and Neh. ix. 27.

Ehud "the *Benjamite*" was of the family or house of Gera (2 Sam. xvi. 5), the son of Bela, Benjamin's first-born, born before Jacob's descent into Egypt (Gen. xlvi. 21), and then included among "the sons of Benjamin." The genealogy in 1 Chr. viii. 6 intimates that Ehud (apparently written Abihud in *v.* 3) became the head of a separate house.

left-handed] See marg. The phrase is thought to describe not so much a defect as

by him the children of Israel sent a present unto Eglon the king
16 of Moab. But Ehud made him a dagger which had two edges,
of a cubit length; and he did gird it under his raiment upon his
17 right thigh. And he brought the present unto Eglon king of
18 Moab: and Eglon was a very fat man. And when he had made
an end to offer the present, he sent away the people that bare
*Josh. 4. 20. 19 the present. But he himself turned again *from the [1]quarries
that were by Gilgal, and said, I have a secret errand unto thee,
O king: who said, Keep silence. And all that stood by him
20 went out from him. And Ehud came unto him; and he was
sitting in [2]a summer parlour, which he had for himself alone.
And Ehud said, I have a message from God unto thee. And he
21 arose out of his seat. And Ehud put forth his left hand, and
took the dagger from his right thigh, and thrust it into his belly:
22 and the haft also went in after the blade; and the fat closed
upon the blade, so that he could not draw the dagger out of his
23 belly; and [3]the dirt came out. Then Ehud went forth through
the porch, and shut the doors of the parlour upon him, and
24 locked them. When he was gone out, his servants came; and
when they saw that, behold, the doors of the parlour were
locked, they said, Surely he [4]covereth his feet in his summer
25 chamber. And they tarried till they were ashamed: and,
behold, he opened not the doors of the parlour; therefore they
took a key, and opened them: and, behold, their lord was fallen
26 down dead on the earth. And Ehud escaped while they tarried,
27 and passed beyond the quarries, and escaped unto Seirath. And

---

[1] Or, graven images.
[2] Heb. a parlour of cool-
ing: See Amos 3. 15.

[3] Or, it came out at the
fundament.

[4] Or, doeth his easement.
1 Sam. 24. 3.

---

the power to use left and right hands equally
well (cp. xx. 16; 1 Chr. xii. 2).
a present] i.e. tribute (2 Sam. viii. 2, 6;
1 K. iv. 21; Ps. lxxii. 10). The employment of Ehud for this purpose points him
out as a chief of some distinction. He
would be attended by a numerous suite
(v. 18). We may conclude that the destruction of the Benjamites (ch. xx.) had not
taken place at this time.
16. upon his right thigh] The proper side
for a left-handed man. It would give him
the appearance of being unarmed. The
narrative shows clearly that his action was
premeditated (v. 21).
19. Gilgal was in the immediate neighbourhood of Jericho (ii. 1), where doubtless
Eglon held his court at this time (v. 13).
quarries] Some take the original of this
word in its common meaning of carved
images or idols (see marg.).
20. Probably Ehud's first message (v. 19)
had been delivered to the attendants, and
by them carried to the king. Now Ehud is
admitted to the king's presence, into the
cool upper chamber.
I have a message from God unto thee] Ehud
believed himself to be accomplishing the
Divine mandate, and so his words were true
in a certain sense. But it was also a stratagem to cause the king to rise, that the

thrust might be sure. [The king rose at
once, in true Oriental respect for a Divine
message, or from fear (cp. Josh. ix. 24).]
22. The A.V. and margin give different
explanations of the last words of this
verse. Others explain it of a vestibule or
chamber, through which Ehud passed into
the porch where the entrance doors were:
He locked the doors, took the key with him,
and then retired through the midst of the
attendants below [or, more probably, through
the door which communicated directly with
the outside].
24. he covereth his feet] Cp. marg. reff.
The explanation of the phrase as "taking
sleep" suits both passages best.
25. a key] Literally "an opener." Probably a wooden instrument with which they
either lifted up the latch within, or drew
back the wooden bar or bolt. The chief
officer of Eglon's household probably had
a second key (cp. Isai. xxii. 15, 20-22,
xxxvii. 2).
26. Seirath] "The forest" or "weald,"
which evidently bordered on the cultivated
plain near Gilgal, and extended into "the
mountain or hill country of Ephraim."
Once there, he was safe from pursuit (cp. 1
Sam. xiii. 6), and quickly collected a strong
force of Ephraimites and probably the
bordering Benjamites.

it came to pass, when he was come, that *y*he blew a trumpet in
the *z*mountain of Ephraim, and the children of Israel went down
28 with him from the mount, and he before them. And he said
unto them, Follow after me: for *a*the LORD hath delivered your
enemies the Moabites into your hand. And they went down
after him, and took *b*the fords of Jordan toward Moab, and
29 suffered not a man to pass over. And they slew of Moab at
that time about ten thousand men, all ¹lusty, and all men of
30 valour; and there escaped not a man. So Moab was subdued
that day under the hand of Israel. And *c*the land had rest
31 fourscore years. ¶And after him was *d*Shamgar the son of
Anath, which slew of the Philistines six hundred men *e*with an
ox goad: *f*and he also delivered *g*Israel.
CHAP. 4. AND *a*the children of Israel again did evil in the sight of
2 the LORD, when Ehud was dead. And the LORD *b*sold them
into the hand of Jabin king of Canaan, that reigned in *c*Hazor;
the captain of whose host was *d*Sisera, which dwelt in *e*Ha-
3 rosheth of the Gentiles. And the children of Israel cried unto
the LORD: for he had nine hundred *f*chariots of iron; and
twenty years *g*he mightily oppressed the children of Israel.

¹ Heb *fat.*

y ch. 5. 14.
& 6. 34.
1 Sam. 13. 3.
z Josh.17.15.
a ch. 7. 9.
1 Sam.17.47.
b Josh. 2. 7.
ch. 12. 5.
c ver. 11.
d ch. 5. 6, 8.
1 Sam. 13.
19, 22.
e 1 Sam. 17.
47, 50.
f ch. 2. 16.
g ch. 4. 1, 3.
& 10. 7, 17.
1 Sam. 4. 1.
b ch. 2. 14.
c Josh. 11.
1, 10.
& 19. 36.
d 1 Sam.12.9.
Ps. 83. 9.
e ver. 13, 16.
f ch. 1. 19.
g ch. 5. 8.
Ps. 106. 42.

28. Ehud "went down" from the mountain of Ephraim into the Jordan valley beneath it, straight to the Jordan fords (Josh. ii. 7), so as to intercept all communication between the Moabites on the west side and their countrymen on the east.

30. *the land*] *i.e.* that portion of it which had suffered from the oppression of Moab, probably Benjamin and Ephraim chiefly (see *v.* 11).

In judging of the nature of Ehud's act there are many considerations which must greatly modify our judgment. Acts of violence or cunning, done in an age when human society applauded such acts, when the best men of the age thought them right, and when men were obliged to take the law into their own hands in self-defence, are very different from the same acts done in an age when the enlightened consciences of men generally condemn them, and when the law of the land and the law of nations give individuals adequate security. We can allow to Ehud faith and courage and patriotism, without being blind to those defective views of moral right which made him and his countrymen glory in an act which in the light of Christianity is a crime. It is remarkable that neither Ehud nor Jael are included in St. Paul's list in Heb. xi. 32.

31. From this verse and v. 6 we may gather that Shamgar was contemporary with Jael, and that he only procured a temporary and partial deliverance for Israel by his exploit. He may have been of the tribe of Judah.

an ox goad] An instrument of wood about eight feet long, armed with an iron spike or point at one end, with which to spur the ox at plough, and with an iron scraper at the other end with which to detach the earth from the ploughshare when it became encumbered with it. The fact of their deliverer having no better weapon enhances his faith, and the power of his Divine helper. At the same time it shows how low the men of Judah were brought at this time, being disarmed by their oppressors (v. 8), as was also the case later (1 Sam. xiii. 19).

IV. 2. See Josh. xi. 1 note. Since the events there narrated, Hazor must have been re-built, and have resumed its position as the metropolis of the northern Canaanites; the other cities must also have resumed their independence, and restored the fallen dynasties.

Harosheth [identified by Conder with El Harathîyeh, see *v.* 6] is marked by the addition *of the Gentiles*, as in *Galilee of the nations* (Gen. xiv. 1; Isai. ix. 1). The name *Harosheth* signifies *workmanship*, *cutting* and *carving*, whether in stone or wood (Ex. xxxi. 5), and hence might be applied to the place where such works are carried on. It has been conjectured that this being a great timber district, rich in cedars and fir-trees, and near Great Zidon (Josh. xi. 8), Jabin kept a large number of oppressed Israelites at work in hewing wood, and preparing it at Harosheth for transport to Zidon; and that these woodcutters, armed with axes and hatchets, formed the soldiers of Barak's army.

3. *oppressed*] The same word is used (Ex. iii. 9) of the oppression of Israel by the Egyptians. If they were put to task-work in hewing timber, their condition was very like that of their ancestors making bricks.

4 And Deborah, a prophetess, the wife of Lapidoth, she judged
ᵍ Gen. 35. 8. 5 Israel at that time. ʰ And she dwelt under the palm tree of
Deborah between Ramah and Beth-el in mount Ephraim : and
6 the children of Israel came up to her for judgment. And she
ⁱ Heb. 11. 32.
ᵏ Josh. 12.
22.
sent and called ⁱ Barak the son of Abinoam out ᵏ of Kedesh-
naphtali, and said unto him, Hath not the LORD God of Israel
commanded, *saying,* Go and draw toward mount Tabor, and
take with thee ten thousand men of the children of Naphtali
ˡ Ex. 14. 4.
ᵐ ch. 5. 21.
1 Kin. 18. 40.
Ps. 83. 9.
7 and of the children of Zebulun ? And ˡ I will draw unto thee to
the ᵐ river Kishon Sisera, the captain of Jabin's army, with his
chariots and his multitude; and I will deliver him into thine
8 hand. And Barak said unto her, If thou wilt go with me, then
I will go : but if thou wilt not go, with me, *then* I will not go.
9 And she said, I will surely go with thee : notwithstanding the
journey that thou takest shall not be for thine honour ; for the
ⁿ ch. 2. 14.
LORD shall ⁿ sell Sisera into the hand of a woman. And Debo-

---

4. *Deborah, a prophetess*] Her name, meaning *a bee,* is the same as that of Rebekah's
nurse (marg. ref.). The reason of her pre-
eminence is added. She was **"a woman,
a prophetess,"** like Miriam (Ex. xv. 20);
Huldah (2 K. xxii. 14), &c. In *vv.* 6, 9, 14,
we have examples of her prophetic powers,
and in ch. v. a noble specimen of prophetic
song. Though the other Judges are not called
prophets, yet they all seem to have had
direct communications from God, either of
knowledge, or power, or both (cp. iii. 10 note).
5. *she dwelt*] Rather, " **she sat,**" viz. to
judge the people (*v.* 10), but not in the usual
place, " the gate " (Ruth iv. 1, 2 ; Prov.
xxii. 22). It suited her character, and the
wild unsafe times better, that she should sit
under a palm-tree in the secure heights of
Mount Ephraim, between Ramah and
Bethel (xx. 33 note). This verse shows that
the Judges exercised the civil as well as
military functions of rulers (1 Sam. vii.
15–17).
6. The name *Barak* signifies *lightning,* an
appropriate name for a warrior. It is
found also as *Barca* or *Barcas,* among Punic
proper names. Cp. Mark iii. 17. On Kedesh-
Naphtali see marg. ref.
Deborah speaks of God as *Jehovah the
God of Israel,* because she speaks, as it were,
in the presence of the heathen enemies of
Israel, and to remind the Israelites, in the
day of their distress, that He was ready to
perform the mercy promised to their fathers,
and to remember His holy Covenant. This
title, too, would recall to their memories in
an instant all His past acts in Egypt, at
the Red Sea, in the wilderness, and in the
conquest of Canaan.
The object of " drawing (toward Mount
Tabor" rather, spreading out, cp. xx. 37) was
to effect a junction of the northern tribes
with the tribes of Ephraim and Benjamin,
who were separated from them by the plain
of Esdraelon, where Sisera's chariots would
naturally congregate and be most effective.
Mount Tabor rises from the plain of Es-

draelon, about 1,865 ft. above the sea, and
its broad top of nearly a mile in circumference afforded a strong position, out of reach
of Sisera's chariots. If El Harathiyeh be
Harosheth, Sisera must have marched from
the west. Harathiyeh is a height in the
range which separates Esdraelon from the
plains of Acre, under which the Kishon
breaks through in its course to the sea.
7. The brook or stream Kishon (Nahr
Mukutta), so called from its winding course,
caused by the dead level of the plain of
Esdraelon through which it flows, rises, in
respect to one of its sources or feeders, in
Mount Tabor, and flows nearly due west
through the plain, under Mount Carmel,
and into the Bay of Acre. In the early or
eastern part of its course, before it is re-
cruited by the springs on Carmel, it is
nothing but a torrent, often dry, but liable
to swell very suddenly and dangerously,
and to overflow its banks in early spring,
after rain or the melting of snow. The
ground on the banks of the Kishon near
Megiddo [Mujedd'a, see Josh. xii. 21 note]
becomes an impassable morass under the
same circumstances, and would be particularly dangerous to a large number of
chariots.
8. Barak, like Gideon (vi. 15, 36–40), and
Abraham (Gen. xv. 2, 3, xvii. 18), and
Moses (Ex. iv. 10, 13), and Peter (Matt.
xiv. 30, 31), exhibited some weakness of
faith at first. But this only makes his
example more profitable for our encouragement, though he himself suffered some loss
by his weakness (*v.* 9).
9. Mark the unhesitating faith and courage of Deborah, and the rebuke to Barak's
timidity, "the Lord shall sell Sisera into
the hand of a woman " (Jael, *v.* 22). For a
similar use of a weak instrument, that the
excellency of the power might be of God,
compare the history of Gideon and his 300,
David and his sling, Shamgar and his ox-
goad, Samson and the jawbone of the ass.
(See 1 Cor. i. 26–31.) Barak would pro-

10 rah arose, and went with Barak to Kedesh. And Barak called
°Zebulun and Naphtali to Kedesh; and he went up with ten
thousand men ᵖat his feet: and Deborah went up with him.
11 ¶ Now Heber �q the Kenite, *which was* of the children of
ʳHobab the father in law of Moses, had severed himself from
the Kenites, and pitched his tent unto the plain of Zaanaim,
12 ˢwhich *is* by Kedesh. ¶ And they shewed Sisera that Barak the
13 son of Abinoam was gone up to mount Tabor. And Sisera
¹gathered together all his chariots, *even* nine hundred chariots
of iron, and all the people that *were* with him, from Harosheth
14 of the Gentiles unto the river of Kishon. ¶ And Deborah said
unto Barak, Up; for this *is* the day in which the LORD hath
delivered Sisera into thine hand: ᵗis not the LORD gone out
before thee? So Barak went down from mount Tabor, and ten
15 thousand men after him. And ᵘthe LORD discomfited Sisera,
and all *his* chariots, and all *his* host, with the edge of the
sword before Barak; so that Sisera lighted down off *his* chariot,
16 and fled away on his feet. But Barak pursued after the chariots,
and after the host, unto Harosheth of the Gentiles: and all
the host of Sisera fell upon the edge of the sword; *and* there
17 was not ²a man left. ¶ Howbeit Sisera fled away on his feet to
the tent of Jael the wife of Heber the Kenite: for *there was*
peace between Jabin the king of Hazor and the house of Heber
18 the Kenite. And Jael went out to meet Sisera, and said unto
him, Turn in, my lord, turn in to me; fear not. And when
he had turned in unto her into the tent, she covered him with a
19 ³mantle. And he said unto her. Give me, I pray thee, a little
water to drink; for I am thirsty. And she opened ˣa bottle of
20 milk, and gave him drink, and covered him. Again he said
unto her, Stand in the door of the tent, and it shall be, when

° ch. 5. 18.
ᵖ See Ex. 11. 8.
1 Kin. 20. 10.
q ch. 1. 16.
ʳ Num. 10. 29.

ˢ ver. 6.

ᵗ Deut. 9. 3.
2 Sam. 5. 24.
Isai. 52. 12.
ᵘ Ps. 83. 9, 10.
See Josh. 10. 10.

ˣ ch. 5. 25.

¹ Heb. *gathered by cry*, or ² Heb. *unto one.* ³ Or, *rug*, or *blanket.*
proclamation.

bably think the *woman* must be Deborah.
The prophecy was only explained by its
fulfilment. Her presence as a prophetess
would give a divine sanction to Barak's attempt to raise the tribes of Zebulun and
Naphtali. To Barak himself it would be
a pledge of her truth and sincerity. She
probably commissioned some chief to raise
the tribes of Ephraim, Benjamin, and
Manasseh (v. 14, cp. Ps. lxxx. 2), while she
went with Barak and mustered Zebulun,
Naphtali, and Issachar.
10. Rather, "**and ten thousand men
went up** (to Tabor) **at his feet;**" *i.e.* as his
followers ("*after him,*" v. 14).
11. Read, "**Heber the Kenite had severed
himself from the Kenites which were of
the children of Hobab,**" &c., "**unto the
oak** (or *terebinth tree*) **in Zaanaim**" [or Bi-
tzaanaim, which Conder identifies with
Bessûm, twelve miles S.E. of Tabor, and
near Kedesh on the Sea of Galilee]. This
migration of Heber the Kenite, with a
portion of his tribe, from the south of
Judah to the north of Naphtali, perhaps
caused by Philistine oppression, had clearly
taken place recently. It is mentioned here
to account for the subsequent narrative,

but possibly also because the news of the
great muster of the Israelites at Kedesh had
been carried to Sisera by some of the tribe
(*v.* 12), whose tents we are here informed
were in the immediate neighbourhood of
Kedesh.
15. *lighted down off his chariot*] Probably his chariot stuck in the morass (note
on *v.* 7); or he might leave his chariot in
order to mislead his pursuers, and in hope
of gaining a place of safety while they were
following the track of the chariot-wheels
and the bulk of the host.
16. What with the overflowing of the
Kishon (v. 21), by which numbers were
drowned, and the panic which had seized
the defeated army, and made them an easy
prey to the sword of the pursuing Israelites,
Sisera's whole force was cut to pieces and
broken up.
17. Sisera went, not to Heber's tent, but
to Jael's, as more secure from pursuit.
Women occupied a separate tent. (Gen.
xviii. 6, 10, xxiv. 67.)
20. *Stand in the door*, &c.] The characteristic duplicity of the Oriental character,
both in Sisera and Jael, is very forcibly depicted in this narrative. It is only by the

any man doth come and enquire of thee, and say, Is there any
21 man here ? that thou shalt say, No. Then Jael Heber's wife
y ch. 5. 26. *v* took a nail of the tent, and ¹took an hammer in her hand, and
went softly unto him, and smote the nail into his temples, and
fastened it into the ground : for he was fast asleep and weary.
22 So he died. And, behold, as Barak pursued Sisera, Jael came
out to meet him, and said unto him, Come, and I will show
thee the man whom thou seekest. And when he came into her
tent, behold, Sisera lay dead, and the nail *was* in his temples.
z Ps. 18. 47. 23 ¶ So ²God subdued on that day Jabin the king of Canaan before
24 the children of Israel.. And the hand of the children of Canaan
²prospered, and prevailed against Jabin the king of Canaan,
until they had destroyed Jabin king of Canaan.

a Ps. 18. **CHAP. 5.** THEN *a* sang Deborah and Barak the son of Abinoam on
title. that day, saying,
b Ps. 18. 47. 2   Praise ye the LORD for the *b* avenging of Israel,
c 2 Chr. 17. *c* When the people willingly offered themselves.
16.
d Deut. 32. 3   *d* Hear, O ye kings ; give ear, O ye princes ;
1, 3. I, *even* I, will sing unto the LORD ;
Ps. 2. 10. I will sing *praise* to the LORD God of Israel.
e Deut. 33. 2. 4   ¶ LORD, *e* when thou wentest out of Seir,
When thou marchedst out of the field of Edom,
f 2 Sam.22.8. *f* The earth trembled, and the heavens dropped,
Isai. 64. 3. The clouds also dropped water.
g Deut. 4. 11.
Ps. 97. 5. 5   *g* The mountains ³melted from before the LORD,
h Ex. 19. 18. *Even* *h* that Sinai from before the LORD God of Israel.
i ch. 3. 31.
k ch. 4. 17. 6   ¶ In the days of *i* Shamgar the son of Anath,
l Lev. 26. 22. In the days of *k* Jael, *l* the highways were unoccupied,
Isai. 33. 8. And the ⁴travellers walked through ⁵byways.
Lam. 1. 4.

¹ Heb. *put*.   ³ Heb. *flowed*.   ⁵ Heb. *crooked ways*.
² Heb. *going went and was hard*.   ⁴ Heb. *walkers of paths*.

light of the Gospel that the law of truth is
fully revealed.
   21. If we can overlook the treachery and
violence which belonged to the morals of
the age and country, and bear in mind
Jael's ardent sympathies with the oppressed
people of God, her faith in the right of
Israel to possess the land in which they
were now slaves, her zeal for the glory of
Jehovah as against the gods of Canaan,
and the heroic courage and firmness with
which she executed her deadly purpose, we
shall be ready to yield to her the praise
which is her due. See iii. 30 note.
   24. See marg. The meaning is, that
Barak's great victory was the beginning of
a successful resistance to Jabin, by which
the Israelites recovered their independence,
and finally broke the Canaanite power. Accordingly we hear no more of Canaanite
domination in the Book of Judges.
   V. 1. Deborah, as " a prophetess," both
composed and sang this noble ode, which,
for poetic spirit and lyric fire, is not sur-
passed by any of the sacred songs in the
Bible. And, as Miriam took up the first
verse of the song of Moses (Ex. xv. 21),
and sang it as an antiphon, so Barak, with
the chorus of men, answered the song of

Deborah by singing *v.* 2, which is also
exactly suited for an antiphon, summing up
as it does the subject matter of the whole ode.
Cp. David's example (2 Sam. vi. 15).
   2. Render "**For the leading of the
leaders in Israel** (the princes), **for the willingness of the people** (to follow them)
bless ye the Lord." See Deut. xxxii. 42
note, and cp. *rv.* 9 and 13, where the *nobles*
and the *people* are again contrasted.
   4. Cp. Ps. lxviii. 7-9, and Habak. iii. 3-
16. The three passages relate to the same
events, and mutually explain each other.
The subject of them is the triumphant
march of Israel, with the LORD at their
head, to take possession of Canaan, and the
overthrow of Sihon, Og, and the Midianites.
This march commenced from Kadesh, in
the immediate neighbourhood of Seir, and
the victories which followed were an exact
parallel to the victory of Deborah and
Barak, accompanied as it had been with
the storm which made Kishon to overflow
his banks.
   6. Words descriptive of a state of weakness and fear, so that Israel could not frequent the highways. It is a graphic description of a country occupied by an
enemy.

7   *The inhabitants of* the villages ceased, they ceased in Israel,
    Until that I Deborah arose,
    That I arose *m* a mother in Israel.

8   They *n* chose new gods ;
    Then *was* war in the gates :
    o Was there a shield or spear seen
    Among forty thousand in Israel ?

9   My heart *is* toward the governors of Israel,
    That *p* offered themselves willingly among the people.
    Bless ye the LORD.

10   ¶ 1 *q* Speak, ye *r* that ride on white asses,
    s Ye that sit in judgment,
    And walk by the way.

11   *They that are delivered* from the noise of archers in the
    places of drawing water,
    There shall they rehearse the 2*t* righteous acts of the LORD,
    Even the righteous acts *toward the inhabitants* of his vil-
    lages in Israel :
    Then shall the people of the LORD go down to the gates.

12   ¶ *u* Awake, awake, Deborah :
    Awake, awake, utter a song :
    Arise, Barak, and *x* lead thy captivity captive, thou son of
    Abinoam.

13   Then he made him that remaineth *y* have dominion over the
    nobles among the people :
    The LORD made me have dominion over the mighty.

14   ¶ *z* Out of Ephraim *was there* a root of them *a* against
    Amalek ;
    After thee, Benjamin, among thy people ;
    Out of *b* Machir came down governors,

m Is. 40. 23.
n Deut. 32. 16.
o So 1 Sam. 13. 19, 22.

p ver. 2.

q Ps. 105. 2. & 145. 5.
r ch. 10. 4. & 12. 14.
s Ps. 107. 22.

t 1 Sam.12.7. Ps. 145. 7.

u Ps. 57. 8.

x Ps. 68. 18.

y Ps. 49. 14.

z ch. 3. 27.
a ch. 3. 13.

b Num. 32. 39, 40.

1 Or, *Meditate.*   2 Heb. *righteousnesses of the LORD.*

7. Render the word *villages* (here and in *v.* 11)*judgment, rule,* or *judges, rulers.* The sense is "**The princes** (or magistrates) ceased in Israel," *i.e.* there was no one to do justice in the gate, or defend men from their oppressors.

8. The "*war in the gates*" describes the hostile attacks of the Canaanites, which were the punishment of the idolatry of the Israelites (cp. marg. reff.), and the reduction of Israel to an unarmed and unresisting state under the Philistine dominion. See iii. 31 note.

9. *My heart, &c.*] In this deplorable weakness of Israel how noble was the conduct of the governors who volunteered to lead the people against their oppressors. Deborah's heart was filled with admiration as she thought of their patriotic devotion, and broke out into thanksgiving to Jehovah.

10. *ye that ride on white asses, &c.*] *i.e.* nobles or magistrates. Deborah appeals to the classes mentioned in *vv.* 6, 7, to bear witness to the happy change that had followed the overthrow of Jabin.
that sit in judgment] Rather "*that sit* on saddles," or *horse-cloths,*" a further description of those who ride on asses.

11. The sense of the A. V. is that, whereas formerly they could not go in safety to draw water from their wells, but were shot at by the archers of the enemy, now they were delivered from such tumults ; and standing round the wells in security rehearsed the righteous acts of the Lord in delivering them, and "**the righteous acts of His government in Israel.**" (See *v.* 7). *then shall the people of the LORD go down to the gates*] Israelites, who had hid themselves in caves and deserts, could return in security to the gates of their own cities for justice, or commerce, or to dwell there, now that the Canaanite was subdued.

12. Deborah incites Barak to carry off as his prey the captive Canaanites and their sheep and cattle (their "captivity").

13. This verse is otherwise rendered : "*then a remnant of the nobles came down ; the people of the LORD came down for me against the mighty.*" The following verses mention in detail who this "remnant" were.

14. Render "**Of Ephraim** (Deborah's own tribe) came down those whose root is in Mount Amalek (xii. 15); after thee (*O Ephraim) came* **Benjamin amongst thy**

And out of Zebulun they that [1]handle the pen of the writer.

15 And the princes of Issachar *were* with Deborah;

c ch. 4. 14. Even Issachar, and also *c*Barak :
He was sent on [2]foot into the valley.
[3]For the divisions of Reuben
There were great [4]thoughts of heart.

d Num. 32. 1. 16 Why abodest thou *d*among the sheepfolds,
To hear the bleatings of the flocks?
[5]For the divisions of Reuben *there were* great searchings of heart.

e See Josh. 17 *e*Gilead abode beyond Jordan :
13. 25, 31. And why did Dan remain in ships?
f Josh. 19. *f*Asher continued on the sea [6]shore,
29, 31. And abode in his [7]breaches.

g ch. 4. 10. 18 *g*Zebulun and Naphtali *were* a people *that* [8]jeoparded their lives
Unto the death in the high places of the field.

19 ¶The kings came *and* fought,
Then fought the kings of Canaan
In Taanach by the waters of Megiddo :

h Ps. 44. 12. *h*They took no gain of money.

i See Josh. 20 *i*They fought from heaven ;
10. 11.
Ps. 77. 17. *k*The stars in their [9]courses fought against Sisera.
k ch. 4. 15. 21 *l*The river of Kishon swept them away,
l ch. 4. 7. That ancient river, the river Kishon.
O my soul, thou hast trodden down strength.

22 Then were the horsehoofs broken

[1] Heb. *draw with the pen, &c.*	[4] Heb. *impressions.*	[7] Or, *creeks.*
[2] Heb. *his feet.*	[5] Or, *In.*	[8] Heb. *exposed to reproach.*
[3] Or, *In the divisions, &c.*	[6] Or, *port.*	[9] Heb. *paths.*

people ; **of Machir** (the west - Jordanic families of Manasseh. See Josh. xvii. 1-6) **there came down the chiefs, and of Zebulon they that handle the staff of the officer "** the military *scribe*, whose duty it was, like that of the Roman tribunes, to keep the muster roll, and superintend the recruiting of the army. (See 2 K. xxv. 19.)

15. *even Issachar,* &c.] *i.e.* "and, as well as Issachar, Barak also with the tribes of Zebulun and Naphtali, rushed down on foot from Mount Tabor into the valley to attack the iron chariots of Sisera."

For the divisions] Better : "among the brooks." Reuben ought to have followed in this catalogue of patriots, but with that abruptness for which this poem is so conspicuous, Deborah adverts to his absence instead.

16. *great searchings (thoughts, v.* 15) *of heart*] Deborah means to say that at first the Reubenites made magnanimous resolutions to help their brethren against Jabin. But they stayed at home, and let the opportunity slip.

17. The land of Gilead, on the east of Jordan, was divided between Gad and the half tribe of Manasseh, who are both comprehended here. Joppa was in the territory of Dan (Josh. xix. 46), and was in later times the sea-port for Jerusalem.

his breaches] Rather *havens ; i.e.* the creeks and bays and river-mouths by which their coast was broken. Josh. xix. 29.

18. In contrast with the selfishness of the tribes just named, Deborah reverts with enthusiasm to the heroic prowess of Zebulun and Naphtali.

19. The Canaanite hosts are now described, led to battle by their numerous kings. (Cp. Josh. xii. 21.)

they took no gain of money] *i.e.* either they got no booty, as they expected, or, they did not fight for plunder, but for life and victory (cp. iv. 16 and *v.* 30).

20. God fought on the side of Israel, and gave them the victory. Josephus relates that, just as the battle began, a violent tempest came on with a great downfall of rain, and a hailstorm, which, driving full in the faces of the Canaanites, so blinded and benumbed them with cold, that they could neither use their bows with effect nor even hold their swords.

21. The word translated *ancient* occurs only here. The phrase probably means that Kishon was celebrated from ancient times on account of the battles fought on its banks.

By the means of the [1]pransings, the pransings of their
   mighty ones.
23 ¶ Curse ye Meroz, said the angel of the LORD,
Curse ye bitterly the inhabitants thereof;
[m]Because they came not to the help [n]of the LORD,
   To the help of the LORD against the mighty.
24 ¶ Blessed above women shall [o]Jael
The wife of Heber the Kenite be,
[p]Blessed shall she be above women in the tent.
25 [q]He asked water, *and* she gave *him* milk;
She brought forth butter in a lordly dish.
26 [r]She put her hand to the nail,
And her right hand to the workmen's hammer;
And [2]with the hammer she smote Sisera, she smote off
   his head,
When she had pierced and stricken through his temples.
27 [3]At her feet he bowed, he fell, he lay down:
At her feet he bowed, he fell:
Where he bowed, there he fell down [4]dead.
28 ¶ The mother of Sisera looked out at a window,
And cried through the lattice,
Why is his chariot *so* long in coming?
Why tarry the wheels of his chariots?
29 Her wise ladies answered her,
Yea, she returned [5]answer to herself,
30 [s]Have they not sped? have they *not* divided the prey;
[6]To every man a damsel *or* two;
To Sisera a prey of divers colours,
A prey of divers colours of needlework,
Of divers colours of needlework on both sides, *meet* for
   the necks of *them that take* the spoil?
31 ¶ [t]So let all thine enemies perish, O LORD:
But *let* them that love him *be* [u]as the sun [x]when he
   goeth forth in his might.
And the land had rest forty years.

m ch. 21. 9.
Neh. 3. 5.
n 1 Sam. 17.
47. & 18. 17.
o ch. 4. 17.
p Luke 1. 28.
q ch. 4. 19.

r ch. 4. 21.

s Ex. 15. 9.

t Ps. 83. 9, 10.
u 2 Sam. 23, 4.
x Ps. 19. 5.

[1] Or, *tramplings*, or, *plungings.*
[2] Heb. *she hammered.*
[3] Heb. *Between.*
[4] Heb. *destroyed.*
[5] Heb. *her words.*
[6] Heb. *to the head of a man.*

---

22. Probably an allusion to the frantic efforts of the chariot-horses to disengage themselves from the morass (iv. 15 note). *mighty ones*] Applied to bulls (Ps. xxii. 12) and horses (Jer. viii. 16, xlvii. 3, l. 11); elsewhere, as probably here, to men.

23. The inhabitants of Meroz (a village 12 miles from Samaria) hung back, and gave no help in the day of battle, although it was Jehovah Who called them. Hence the curse pronounced by the Angel of the Lord.

24. The blessing here pronounced is in strong contrast with the curse of Meroz. Deborah speaks of Jael's deed by the light of her own age, which did not make manifest the evil of guile and bloodshed; the light in ours does.

25. *butter*] Rather *curdled milk*, probably a fermented and intoxicating drink. All

these marks of respect and friendship would lull Sisera into security.

26. Rather "she smote his head, and she struck and pierced through his temple."

28. The scene is changed to the palace of Sisera.

30. Render the latter part of the verse "a booty of dyed garments for Sisera, a booty of dyed garments *and* of party-coloured cloth, a dyed garment *and* two party-coloured clothes for the necks of the booty," the spoil or booty being either captive damsels, or captive cattle on whose necks these clothes are to be placed (either as ornament or as a burden; cp. viii. 21, 26). But possibly "the necks of the booty" may mean the backs or shoulders (of men or beasts) laden with booty.

31. A most striking conclusion, in which the spiritual truth which the whole narra-

a ch. 2. 19.
b Hab. 3. 7.

c 1 Sam. 13.6.
Heb. 11. 38.

d ch. 3. 13.
e Gen. 29. 1,
ch. 7. 12.
l Kin. 4. 30.
Job 1. 3.
f Lev. 26. 16.
Deut. 28. 30,
33, 51.
Mic. 6. 15.
g ch. 7. 12.

h ch. 3. 15.
Hos. 5. 15.

i Ps. 44. 2, 3.

k 2 Kin. 17.
35, 37, 38.
Jer. 10. 2.

CHAP. 6. *a*AND the children of Israel did evil in the sight of the LORD: and the LORD delivered them into the hand *b*of Midian 2 seven years. And the hand of Midian [1]prevailed against Israel: *and* because of the Midianites the children of Israel made them *c*the dens which *are* in the mountains, and caves, and strong 3 holds. And *so* it was, when Israel had sown, that the Midianites came up, and *d*the Amalekites, *e*and the children of the 4 east, even they came up against them; and they encamped against them, and *f*destroyed the increase of the earth, till thou come unto Gaza, and left no sustenance for Israel, neither 5 [2]sheep, nor ox, nor ass. For they came up with their cattle and their tents, and they came *g*as grasshoppers for multitude; *for* both they and their camels were without number: and they 6 entered into the land to destroy it. And Israel was greatly impoverished because of the Midianites; and the children of Israel 7 *h*cried unto the LORD. ¶And it came to pass, when the children 8 of Israel cried unto the LORD because of the Midianites, that the LORD sent [3]a prophet unto the children of Israel, which said unto them, Thus saith the LORD God of Israel, I brought you up from Egypt, and brought you forth out of the house of 9 bondage; and I delivered you out of the hand of the Egyptians, and out of the hand of all that oppressed you, and *i*drave them 10 out from before you, and gave you their land; and I said unto you, I *am* the LORD your God; *k*fear not the gods of the Amorites, in whose land ye dwell: but ye have not obeyed my voice. 11 ¶And there came an angel of the LORD, and sat under an oak

[1] Heb. *was strong.*　　　[2] Or, *goat.*　　　[3] Heb. *a man a prophet.*

---

tive is intended to convey, comes out. The enemies of the Lord will perish like the host of Sisera, and all their hopes will end, like those of Sisera's mother, in bitter disappointment and shame; but all that love our Lord Jesus Christ shall shine forth as the sun in the kingdom of their Father. Cp. Matt. xiii. 43; Dan. xii. 3.

VI. 1. *Midian*] See Gen. xxv. 2 note. They were remarkable not only for the vast number of their cattle (*v.* 5; Num. xxxi. 32-39), but also for their great wealth in gold and other metal ornaments, showing their connexion with a gold country. (Cp. Num. xxxi. 22, 50-54, with viii. 24-26.) At this time they were allies of the Amalekites and of the Arabian tribes called collectively "the children of the East" (*v.* 3). They seem to have extended their settlements to the east of Jordan, and to have belonged to the larger section of Arabs called Ishmaelites (viii. 24).

2. The word rendered *dens* is only found in this passage. It is best explained of ravines hollowed out by torrents, which the Israelites made into hiding-places.

4. Gaza indicates the extreme point south to which they spread their devastations, crossing the Jordan near Bethshan (Scythopolis), and entering by the valley of Jezreel, and sweeping along the whole of the maritime plain or Shephelah.

5. *grasshoppers*] Rather locusts (cp. Ex. x. 4-6, 14, 15; Joel i., ii.; Ps. lxxviii. 46).

8. *a prophet*] His name is not given. (Cp. 1 K. xiii.) This message is somewhat similar to that of the Angel, ii. 1-3. The reference to Ex. xx. 2 is plain, and supposes the people to whom the prophet addresses these words to be familiar with the facts recorded in that text.

10. A similar use of the name *Amorite,* instead of the more usual name *Canaanite,* occurs in Josh. xxiv. 15, 18. Perhaps a special reason may be found for the use of *Amorite,* if the prophet was addressing those who dwelt in the mountains, where the Amorites chiefly dwelt. The idolatries of the Amorites seem, too, to have been pre-eminently abominable (see 2 K. xxi. 11; 1 K. xxi. 26). It should be observed that the prophet's language, as it traces the misery of Israel to their sins, so also intimates the necessity of repentance and of breaking off their sins—specially the sin of idolatry—as preliminary to any deliverance. In exact accordance with this view, Gideon commences his work by throwing down the altar of Baal, and building up the altar of Jehovah (*vv.* 24, 25).

11. *an oak*] "The oak," indicating it as a well-known tree, still standing in the writer's days.

There was another Ophrah in Benjamin (Josh. xviii. 23). This Ophrah was in Manasseh, and was the village of Joash, the head, apparently, of the family of Abiezer, which was one of the families of Gilead,

which *wás* in Ophrah, that *pertained* unto Joash [1]the Abi-ezrite:
and his son [m]Gideon threshed wheat by the winepress, [1]to hide
12 *it* from the Midianites. And the [n]angel of the LORD appeared
unto him, and said unto him, The LORD *is* [o]with thee, thou
13 mighty man of valour. And Gideon said unto him, Oh my
LORD, if the LORD be with us, why then is all this befallen us?
and [p]where *be* all his miracles [q]which our fathers told us of,
saying, Did not the LORD bring us up from Egypt? but now
the LORD hath [r]forsaken us, and delivered us into the hands of
14 the Midianites. And the LORD looked upon him, and said, [s]Go
in this thy might, and thou shalt save Israel from the hand of
15 the Midianites: [t]have not I sent thee? And he said unto him,
Oh my LORD, wherewith shall I save Israel? behold, [u][2]my
family *is* poor in Manasseh, and I *am* the least in my father's
16 house. And the LORD said unto him, [x]Surely I will be with
17 thee, and thou shalt smite the Midianites as one man. And he
said unto him, If now I have found grace in thy sight, then
18 [y]shew me a sign that thou talkest with me. [z]Depart not hence,
I pray thee, until I come unto thee, and bring forth my [3]present,
and set *it* before thee. And he said, I will tarry until thou
19 come again. ¶ [a]And Gideon went in, and made ready [4]a kid,
and unleavened cakes of an ephah of flour: the flesh he put in
a basket, and he put the broth in a pot, and brought *it* out unto
20 him under the oak, and presented *it*. And the angel of God
said unto him, Take the flesh and the unleavened cakes, and
[b]lay *them* upon this rock, and [c]pour out the broth. And he did

[1] Heb. *to cause* it *to flee.*	*meanest:* Ex. 18. 21, 25.
[2] Heb. *my thousand* is *the*	Mic. 5. 2.

[3] Or, *meat offering.*
[4] Heb. *a kid of the goats.*

Margin references:
[1] Josh. 17. 2.
[m] Heb. 11. 32, called *Gedeon.*
[n] ch. 13. 3.
[o] Luke 1. 11.
[o] Josh. 1. 5.
[p] So Ps. 89. 49.
Isai. 59. 1.
[q] Ps. 44. 1.
[r] 2 Chr. 15. 2.
[s] 1 Sam. 12. 11.
Heb. 11. 32, 34.
[t] Josh. 1. 9. ch. 4. 6.
1 Sam. 9. 21.
[x] Ex. 3. 12. Josh. 1. 5.
[y] Ex. 4. 1—8. ver. 36. 37. Ps. 86. 17.
Isai. 7. 11.
[z] Gen. 18. 3, 5.
ch. 13. 15.
[a] Gen. 18. 6.
[b] ch. 13. 19.
[c] See 1 Kin. 18. 33, 34.

the son of Machir, the son of Manasseh (Num. xxvi. 30).

12. *thou mighty man of valour*] Known to God to be such, though as yet not known to be such either by himself or his countrymen (cp. Luke i. 28, 30).

13. The extreme bitterness of the national sufferings under the Midianite occupation breaks out in Gideon's language. The Angel's words, suitable to times of prosperity, seemed to be a mockery, when it was evident the Lord was not with them. (Cp. Deut. xxxi. 17.)

14. *the* LORD *looked upon him*] That gracious look conferred immediate strength (cp. Ephes. vi. 10; 2 Cor. xii. 9: John xx. 22; Acts iii. 6). The change of phrase from "the angel of the LORD" to "the LORD" is remarkable. When messages are delivered by the Angel of the Lord, the form of the message is as if God Himself were speaking (cp. ii. 1).

The sending implied a valid commission and sufficient powers. Cp. Exod. iii. 10; Isai. xliv. 26; Ezek. ii. 3; Zech. ii. 11; Mal. iii. 1; Luke x. 3; John xx. 21; and the term APOSTLE, as applied to our Lord (Heb. iii. 1) and to the Twelve.

15. Gideon now perceived that the Lord was speaking to him by His angel. He saw, however, no qualifications in himself, or in his family or tribe, for the office of

saviour to his people. He therefore desires some assurance that the message he had just received was indeed from God, and not a mere dream or delusion. He asks as a sign (*v.* 18) that his mysterious visitor should tarry under the oak till he should return to Him with his gifts and offerings.

17. *a sign*] If the Angel ate of Gideon's present it would be a conclusive proof of the reality of the vision. (Cp. John xxi. 9–13; Luke xxiv. 37–43; Acts x. 41.) It would also be a token of God's goodwill to Gideon. Cp. Gen. xviii. 3.

18. *my present*] My Minchah : the word used regularly, though not exclusively, for the meat and drink offering (Lev. ii. 1 note). Its double sense of an offering to God, and of a gift to man, suits the doubt in Gideon's mind as to who his visitor might be.

19. *unleavened cakes*] As being much more quickly baked (cp. Gen. xix. 3) [and as connected with the meat offering]. *An ephah*, containing 3 *measures*, was the quantity of flour commonly used at one baking (Gen. xviii. 6; Ex. xvi. 16).

presented it] A word especially, though not exclusively, proper for offerings to God. See Amos v. 25, where the same word is rendered *offered.*

20. *pour out the broth*] Libations were a very ancient form of offering (cp. Gen. xxxv. 14). The drink offerings of wine

21 so. Then the angel of the LORD put forth the end of the staff
that *was* in his hand, and touched the flesh and the unleavened
d Lev. 9. 24.
1 Kin. 18. 38.
2 Chr. 7. 1.
e ch. 13. 21.

f Gen. 16. 13.
& 32. 30.
Ex. 33. 20.
ch. 13. 22.
g Dan. 10.
19.
h ch. 8. 32.

i Ex. 34. 13.
Deut. 7. 5.
cakes; and *d*there rose up fire out of the rock, and consumed
the flesh and the unleavened cakes. Then the angel of the LORD
22 departed out of his sight. ¶ And when Gideon *e*perceived that
he *was* an angel of the LORD, Gideon said, Alas, O Lord GOD !
*f*for because I have seen an angel of the LORD face to face.
23 And the LORD said unto him, *g* Peace *be* unto thee; fear not:
24 thou shalt not die. Then Gideon built an altar there unto the
LORD, and called it ¹Jehovah-shalom : unto this day it *is* yet *h* in
25 Ophrah of the Abi-ezrites. ¶ And it came to pass the same
night, that the LORD said unto him, Take thy father's young
bullock, ²even the second bullock of seven years old, and throw
down the altar of Baal that thy father hath, and *i*cut down the
26 grove that *is* by it : and build an altar unto the LORD thy God
upon the top of this ³rock, ⁴in the ordered place, and take the
second bullock, and offer a burnt sacrifice with the wood of the
27 grove which thou shalt cut down. Then Gideon took ten men
of his servants, and did as the LORD had said unto him : and *so*
it was, because he feared his father's household, and the men of
the city, that he could not do *it* by day, that he did *it* by night.
28 ¶ And when the men of the city arose early in the morning, behold, the altar of Baal was cast down, and the grove was cut
down that *was* by it, and the second bullock was offered upon
29 the altar *that was* built. And they said one to another, Who
hath done this thing? And when they enquired and asked, they
30 said, Gideon the son of Joash hath done this thing. Then the
men of the city said unto Joash, Bring out thy son, that he may
die : because he hath cast down the altar of Baal, and because
31 he hath cut down the grove that *was* by it. And Joash said

¹ That is, *The LORD* send
　peace. Ex. 17. 15. Jer.
² Or, *and.*
33. 16.　Ezek. 48. 35.
³ Heb. *strong place.*
⁴ Or, *in an orderly manner.*

---

under the Levitical law were *poured* upon
the Altar (Ex. xxx. 9). The pouring of
the broth upon the rock was evidently of
the nature of a libation. It might also,
like the water poured by Elijah upon his
sacrifice, make the miracle of the fire that
consumed the sacrifice more apparent. (Cp.
1 K. xviii. 33.)
　22. *Alas, O Lord* GOD !] Cp. Josh. vii. 7.
　because I have seen an angel of the LORD]
Cp. marg. reff., in which the notion that it
was death for mortal man to see God appears clearly. The same notion prevailed
amongst the heathen.
　24. Gideon's naming the altar which he
built, in commemoration of the words of
peace spoken by the Angel, is very similar
to what we read of Abraham (Gen. xxii. 14),
and of Moses (Ex. xvii. 15, when he
named the altar *Jehovah-nissi*).
　25. *even*] Rather, as in the margin,
and. ' Two bullocks are spoken of. The
labour of both would be required for pulling
down and removing the altar of Baal, and
for bringing the materials for building the
Altar of Jehovah.
　the grove by it] Rather, " the idol upon

it," the Asherah, the wooden image of Astarte (iii. 7).
　26. *in the ordered place*] See marg. "**Build
an altar, &c., with the materials,**" "the
wood *laid in order* " (cp. Gen. xxii. 9), that,
viz., which he would find ready to hand in
the altar of Baal which he was to throw
down.
　the wood of the grove] "The (blocks of)
wood of the idol," *i.e.* the image of Astarte.
The command from God Himself to build
an Altar, and sacrifice upon it, is analogous
to Elijah's sacrifice (1 K. xviii.), and was
doubtless caused by the extraordinary circumstance of the defection of the Israelites
from the worship of the true God. Possibly, too, the Midianite invasion had made
the worship at Shiloh impossible at this
time.
　27. The mention of the "men of the
city " by the side of Gideon's "father's
household " suggests the probability of their
being a remnant of the Canaanite population, and the special patrons of Baal-worship.
　31. From the boldness of Joash in defending his son, it is likely that the majority of
the Abi-ezrites sided with him against "the

unto all that stood against him, Will ye plead for Baal? will ye save him? he that will plead for him, let him be put to death whilst *it is yet* morning : if he *be* a god, let him plead for him-
32 self, because *one* hath cast down his altar. Therefore on that day he called him [1][k]Jerubbaal, saying, Let Baal plead against
33 him, because he hath thrown down his altar. ¶ Then all [l]the Midianites and the Amalekites and the children of the east were gathered together, and went over, and pitched in [m]the valley of
34 Jezreel. But [n]the Spirit of the LORD [2]came upon Gideon, and he [o]blew a trumpet ; and Abi-ezer [3]was gathered after him.
35 And he sent messengers throughout all Manasseh ; who also was gathered after him : and he sent messengers unto Asher, and unto Zebulun, and unto Naphtali ; and they came up to
36 meet them. ¶ And Gideon said unto God, If thou wilt save
37 Israel by mine hand, as thou hast said, [p]Behold, I will put a fleece of wool in the floor ; *and* if the dew be on the fleece only, and *it be* dry upon all the earth *beside*, then shall I know that
38 thou wilt save Israel by mine hand, as thou hast said. And it was so : for he rose up early on the morrow, and thrust the fleece together, and wringed the dew out of the fleece, a bowl
39 full of water. And Gideon said unto God, [q]Let not thine anger be hot against me, and I will speak but this once : let me prove, I pray thee, but this once with the fleece ; let it now be dry only
40 upon the fleece, and upon all the ground let there be dew. And God did so that night : for it was dry upon the fleece only, and there was dew on all the ground.

CHAP. 7. THEN [a]Jerubbaal, who *is* Gideon, and all the people that *were* with him, rose up early, and pitched beside the well of Harod : so that the host of the Midianites were on the north

[k] 1 Sam. 12. 11.
[l] 2 Sam. 11. 21, Jerub-besheth ; that is, Let the shameful thing plead. See Jer. 11. 13.
[m] Hos. 9. 10. ver. 3.
[m] Josh. 17. 16.
[n] ch. 3. 10.
2 Chr. 12. 18.
2 Chr. 24. 20.
[o] Num. 10. 3. ch. 3. 27.
[p] See Ex. 4.
3, 4, 6, 7.
[q] Gen. 18. 32.

[a] ch. 6. 32.

[1] That is, *Let Baal plead*.   [2] Heb. *clothed*.   [3] Heb. *was called after him*.

---

men of the city," and already felt drawn towards Gideon as their national and religious leader (*v*. 34). Joash appears as the chief magistrate of Ophrah.

Will ye plead, &c.? will ye save?] The emphasis is upon *ye*, as much as to say, What business is it of yours?

32. *he called him*] *i.e.* "He was called" *Jerubbaal*, as being the person against whom it was popularly said that Baal might strive. See marg.

33. A fresh invasion, and the last, of Midianites, Amalekites, and Arabs (see *v*. 3). But the Israelites, instead of hiding in dens and caves, and tamely leaving all their substance as plunder to the invaders, now rally round their leader.

34. *the Spirit of the* LORD *came upon Gideon*] See marg. The word contains a striking thought. It is different from that used in the case of Othniel (iii. 10), Jephthah (xi. 29), and Samson (xiii. 25, xiv. 6, 19).

35. His own tribe, Manasseh, and the three northern tribes of Asher, Zebulon, and Naphtali hastened to join him. Issachar probably was unable to do so, because the Midianites were encamped in the heart of their country. Asher no longer "abode in his breaches," as in the time of Jabin

(v. 17), perhaps ashamed of their former backwardness, and stung by the rebuke of Deborah ; perhaps, too, from feeling the Midianite yoke much more galling than that of Jabin.

36. The caution of Gideon, desirous of being assured that he really had a promise from God, does not imply doubts as to God's faithfulness or power to fulfil His promise. Of such doubts there is not a trace in Gideon's character. He is a worthy example of faith (Heb. xi. 32).

37. The threshing-floors were and still are under the open air, and usually circular. The second sign (*v*. 40), would be more convincing than the former, because it is the nature of fleeces to attract and retain moisture.

VII. 1. *the well of Harod*] *i.e.* of trembling, evidently so called from the people who were *afraid* (*v*. 3). It is identified with great probability with *Ain Jalud*, a spacious pool at the foot of Gilboa ; [by Conder, with Ain el Jem'ain (the spring of the two troops)].

Moreh was, probably, the little Hermon, the Jebel ed-Duhy of the Arabs, which encloses the plain two or three miles north of Gilboa, which shuts it in on the south.

2 side of them, by the hill of Moreh, in the valley. And the
LORD said unto Gideon, The people that *are* with thee *are* too
many for me to give the Midianites into their hands, lest Israel
^*b*^vaunt themselves against me, saying, Mine own hand hath
3 saved me. Now therefore, go to, proclaim in the ears of the
people, saying, ^*c*^Whosoever *is* fearful and afraid, let him return
and depart early from mount Gilead. And there returned of
the people twenty and two thousand; and there remained ten
4 thousand. ¶And the LORD said unto Gideon, The people *are*
yet *too* many; bring them down unto the water, and I will try
them for thee there: and it shall be, *that* of whom I say unto
thee, This shall go with thee, the same shall go with thee; and
of whomsoever I say unto thee, this shall not go with thee, the
5 same shall not go. So he brought down the people unto the
water: and the LORD said unto Gideon, Every one that lappeth
of the water with his tongue, as a dog lappeth, him shalt thou
set by himself; likewise every one that boweth down upon his
6 knees to drink. And the number of them that lapped, *putting*
their hand to their mouth, were three hundred men: but all
the rest of the people bowed down upon their knees to drink
7 water. And the LORD said unto Gideon, ^*d*^By the three hundred
men that lapped will I save you, and deliver the Midianites
into thine hand: and let all the *other* people go every man unto
8 his place. So the people took victuals in their hand, and their
trumpets: and he sent all *the rest of* Israel every man unto his
tent, and retained those three hundred men: and the host of
9 Midian was beneath him in the valley. ¶And it came to pass
the same ^*e*^night, that the LORD said unto him, Arise, get thee
down unto the host; for I have delivered it into thine hand.
10 But if thou fear to go down, go thou with Phurah thy servant
11 down to the host: and thou shalt ^*f*^hear what they say; and
afterward shall thine hands be strengthened to go down unto
the host. Then went he down with Phurah his servant unto the
12 outside of the ^1^armed men that *were* in the host. And the
Midianites and the Amalekites and ^*g*^all the children of the east
lay along in the valley like grasshoppers for multitude; and
their camels *were* without number, as the sand by the sea
13 side for multitude. And when Gideon was come, behold, *there
was* a man that told a dream unto his fellow, and said, Behold,
I dreamed a dream, and, lo, a cake of barley bread tumbled into
the host of Midian, and came unto a tent, and smote it that it

b Deut. 8. 17.
Isai. 10. 13.
1 Cor. 1. 29.
2 Cor. 4. 7.
c Deut. 20. 8.

d 1 Sam. 14.
6.

e Gen. 46. 2.
3.

f ver. 13, 14,
15.
See Gen. 24.
14.
1 Sam. 14.
9, 10.
g ch. 6. 5, 33,
& 8, 10.

---

^1^ Or, *ranks by five*, Ex. 13. 18.

---

3. The proclamation was in accordance
with the Law (see marg. ref.). No mountain of the name of Gilead is known in this
locality, and it has been conjectured that
the right reading is Gilboa. Others think
that this may be a form of proclamation
customary in Manasseh.

4. *try*] The word used for refining metals
by separating the dross from the pure ore.
They who threw themselves on the ground
and drank freely were the more self-indul-
gent; while they who, remembering the
near presence of the enemy, slaked their
thirst with moderation, and without being
off their guard for an instant, were the true
soldiers of the army of God.

8. The sense is, "And they (the three
hundred) took the victuals and trumpets of
the people (*all the people* of v. 7) into their
hands," so that each of the three hundred
should have a trumpet and a pitcher.

11. *the armed men*] The word is rendered
harnessed in Ex. xiii. 18 (see note). The
most probable meaning of the word is *arrayed in divisions* or *ranks*.

13. *a cake of barley bread*] *i.e.* such a cake
as could hardly be eaten by men, it was so
vile: a term expressive of the contempt of
the Midianites for the people of Israel.

a tent] The *tent*, meaning, probably, the
tent of the king of Midian, or of the captain
of the host.

14 fell, and overturned it, that the tent lay along. And his fellow
answered and said, This *is* nothing else save the sword of Gideon
the son of Joash, a man of Israel: *for* into his hand hath God
15 delivered Midian, and all the host. ¶ And it was *so*, when
Gideon heard the telling of the dream, and [1]the interpretation
thereof, that he worshipped, and returned into the host of Israel,
and said, Arise; for the LORD hath delivered into. your hand
16 the host of Midian. And he divided the three hundred men *into*
three companies, and he put [2]a trumpet in every man's hand,
17 with empty pitchers, and [3]lamps within the pitchers. And he
said unto them, Look on me, and do likewise: and, behold,
when I come to the outside of the camp, it shall be *that*, as I do,
18 so shall ye do. When I blow with a trumpet, I and all that *are*
with me, then blow ye the trumpets also on every side of all the
19 camp, and say, *The sword* of the LORD, and of Gideon. ¶ So
Gideon, and the hundred men that *were* with him, came unto
the outside of the camp in the beginning of the middle watch;
and they had but newly set the watch: and they blew the
20 trumpets, and brake the pitchers that *were* in their hands. And
the three companies blew the trumpets, and brake the pitchers,
and held the lamps in their left hands, and the trumpets in their
right hands to blow *withal:* and they cried, The sword of the
21 LORD, and of Gideon. And they [h]stood every man in his place
round about the camp: [i]and all the host ran, and cried, and
22 fled. And the three hundred [k]blew the trumpets, and [l]the
LORD set [m]every man's sword against his fellow, even throughout all the host: and the host fled to Beth-shittah [4]in Zererath,
23 *and* to the [5]border of Abel-meholah, unto Tabbath. ¶ And the

[h] Ex. 14. 13.
14.
[i] 2 Kin. 7. 7.
[k] Josh. 6. 1.
See 2 Cor. 4.
7.
[l] Ps. 83. 9.
Isai. 9. 4.
[m] 1 Sam. 14.
20.
2 Chr. 20. 23.

[1] Heb. *the breaking thereof.*
[2] Heb. *trumpets in the hand.*
  of all of them.
[3] Or, *firebrands*, or, *torches.*
[4] Or, *toward.*
[5] Heb. *lip.*

---

14. *This is nothing else save the sword of Gideon*] The word rendered *tumbled* in *v.* 13, is rather descriptive of a sword **brandished** (cp. Gen. iii. 24). Hence the interpretation "the sword of Gideon." Hearing this dream and the interpretation would convince Gideon that he was indeed under the guidance of God, and so assure him of God's aid; and secondly, it would show him that a panic had already fallen upon the mind of the enemy.

16. Gideon himself took the command of one company, and sent the other two under their respective captains to different sides of the camp (*vv.* 18 and 21).

19. *the middle watch*] The old Jewish division of the night was three watches of four hours each. They are alluded to in Ex. xiv. 24; 1 Sam. xi. 11; Ps. lxiii. 6, xc. 4, cxix. 148, cxxx. 6; Lam. ii. 19. After the Jews fell under the power of the Romans, they used the Roman division of four watches of three hours each (Matt. xiv. 25; Mark xiii. 35). "The beginning" of the watch would be about eleven o'clock at night.

21. The effect to the Midianites would be, that they were surrounded by a mighty host. Their own camp being in darkness,

as soon as the confusion of flight began they would mistake friends for foes, and fleers for pursuers. When once fighting had begun by the first casual mistake, the clashing of swords and the shouts of the combatants in the camp, accompanied by the continuous blowing of Gideon's trumpets outside, would make it appear that the whole of the enemy was in the camp. Suspicion of treachery on the part of their allies would also be likely to arise in the minds of Midianites, Amalekites, and Arabs. Cp. a similar scene in marg. reff.

22. *Beth-shittah*—"House of the acacias," the same trees which gave their name to *Shittim* (Num. xxxiii. 49) in the plains of Moab, and which grew plentifully also in the peninsula of Sinai (Ex. xxv. 5)—perhaps *Shuttah*, in the valley of Jezreel; or it may be another name of Scythopolis, or Beth-shan (cp. 1 K. iv. 12). *Zererath* or *Zeredath*, near Succoth (viii. 5), the same as *Zeredah* in Ephraim, the birth-place of Jeroboam (1 K. xi. 26), and *Zartanah* (1 K. iv. 12). *Abel-meholah* (field of the dance), the birth-place of Elisha (1 K. xix. 16) is in the Jordan valley, 10 miles from Scythopolis, if. identified with Bethmaela: if the same as Abelmea, it lay between

men of Israel gathered themselves together out of Naphtali, and out of Asher, and out of all Manasseh, and pursued after 24 the Midianites. And Gideon sent messengers throughout all *n* mount Ephraim, saying, Come down against the Midianites, and take before them the waters unto Beth-barah and Jordan. Then all the men of Ephraim gathered themselves together, and 25 *o* took the waters unto *p* Beth-barah and Jordan. And they took *q* two princes of the Midianites, Oreb and Zeeb ; and they slew Oreb upon *r* the rock Oreb, and Zeeb they slew at the winepress of Zeeb, and pursued Midian, and brought the heads of Oreb and Zeeb to Gideon on the *s* other side Jordan.

CHAP. 8. AND *a* the men of Ephraim said unto him, [1] Why hast thou served us thus, that thou calledst us not, when thou wentest to fight with the Midianites ? And they did chide with him 2 [2] sharply. And he said unto them, What have I done now in comparison of you ? *Is* not the gleaning of the grapes of 3 Ephraim better than the vintage of Abi-ezer ? *b* God hath delivered into your hands the princes of Midian, Oreb and Zeeb : and what was I able to do in comparison of you ? Then their [3] anger was abated toward him, when he had said that. 4 ¶ And Gideon came to Jordan, *and* passed over, he, and the three hundred men that *were* with him, faint, yet pursuing 5 *them*. And he said unto the men of *d* Succoth, Give, I pray you, loaves of bread unto the people that follow me ; for they *be* faint, and I am pursuing after Zebah and Zalmunna, 6 kings of Midian. And the princes of Succoth said, *e* Are the hands of Zebah and Zalmunna now in thine hand, that *f* we 7 should give bread unto thine army ? And Gideon said, Therefore when the LORD hath delivered Zebah and Zalmunna into mine hand, *g* then I will [4] tear your flesh with the thorns of the 8 wilderness and with briers. And he went up thence *h* to Penuel, and spake unto them likewise : and the men of Penuel answered 9 him as the men of Succoth had answered *him*. And he spake

n ch. 3. 27.

o ch. 3. 28.
p John 1. 28.
q ch. 8. 3.
Ps. 83. 11.
r Isai. 10. 26.
s ch. 8. 4.
a Seech.12.1.
2 Sam. 19. 41.

b ch. 7. 24.
Phil. 2. 3.

c Prov. 15. 1.

d Gen. 33. 17.
Ps. 60. 6.

e See 1 Kin. 20. 11.
f See 1 Sam. 25. 11.

g ver. 16.
h Gen. 32. 30.
1 Kin. 12. 25.

[1] Heb. *What thing is this thou hast done unto us.*
[2] Heb. *strongly.*
[3] Heb. *spirit.*
[4] Heb. *thresh.*

Nablous and Scythopolis. [But see 1 K. xix. 16 note.] *Tabbath* was apparently lower down the Jordan valley, *i.e.* further south.
24. the *waters*] The streams which run from the mountain district of Ephraim into the Jordan in the district of Beth-shan, forming great pools and marshes, which the Midianites fleeing south would have to cross before they could reach the Jordan fords.
all *the men of Ephraim*] They had taken no previous part in the rising against Midian : nor had Gideon, of the smaller tribe of Manasseh, presumed before to summon his more powerful and arrogant brethren of the great tribe of Ephraim (see Josh. xvii. 14–18).
VIII. 1. The success of Gideon's enterprise mortified the pride of Ephraim, as the chief tribe, seeing that they had played a subordinate part. Cp. Judg. xii. 1.
2. A civil war with the great tribe of Ephraim would soon have turned Israel's victory into mourning. Gideon therefore

soothes their wounded pride by confessing that Ephraim had done more, though they had joined him so late in the day, than he had been able to effect in the whole campaign. The grape-gleaning of Ephraim was better than the whole vintage of Abi-ezer.
5. Succoth was in the tribe of Gad which was entirely trans-Jordanic (Josh. xiii. 27) ; and the ruins are at Sukkot, on the east of Jordan, a little south of Beth-shan.
Give, I pray you, &c.] Gideon might fairly expect so much aid from the trans-Jordanic tribes, and from so considerable a town as Succoth (*v.* 14).
6. The number of the followers of Zebah and Zalmunna was still so formidable, and Gideon's enterprise still so doubtful, that the men of Succoth (being on the same side of the Jordan) would not risk the vengeance of the Midianites by giving supplies to Gideon's men.
8. Succoth was in the valley or Ghor of the Jordan (*v.* 5), and Penuel apparently

also unto the men of Penuel, saying, When I ⁱcome again in
10 peace, ^kI will break down this tower. ¶ Now Zebah and Zalmunna *were* in Karkor, and their hosts with them, about fifteen
thousand *men*, all that were left of ^lall the hosts of the children
of the east: for there fell ¹an hundred and twenty thousand men
11 that drew sword. And Gideon went up by the way of them
that dwelt in tents on the east of ^mNobah and Jogbehah, and
12 smote the host: for the host was ⁿsecure. And when Zebah and
Zalmunna fled, he pursued after them, and ^otook the two kings
of Midian, Zebah and Zalmunna, and ²discomfited all the host.
13 ¶ And Gideon the son of Joash returned from battle before the
14 sun *was up*, and caught a young man of the men of Succoth,
and enquired of him: and he ³described unto him the princes
of Succoth, and the elders thereof, *even* threescore and seventeen
15 men. And he came unto the men of Succoth, and said, Behold
Zebah and Zalmunna, with whom ye did ^pupbraid me, saying,
Are the hands of Zebah and Zalmunna now in thine hand, that
16 we should give bread unto thy men *that are* weary? ^q And he
took the elders of the city, and thorns of the wilderness and
17 briers, and with them he ⁴taught the men of Succoth. ^rAnd he
beat down the tower of ^sPenuel, and slew the men of the city.
18 ¶ Then said he unto Zebah and Zalmunna, What manner of
men *were* they whom ye slew at ^tTabor? And they answered,
As thou *art*, so *were* they; each one ⁵resembled the children of
19 a king. And he said, They *were* my brethren, *even* the sons of
my mother: *as* the LORD liveth, if ye had saved them alive, I

Marginal references:
ⁱ 1 Kin. 22. 27.
^k ver. 17.
^l ch. 7. 12.
^m Num. 32. 35, 42.
ⁿ ch. 18. 27.
1 Thess. 5. 3.
^o Ps. 83. 11.
^p ver. 6.
^q ver. 7.
^r ver. 9.
^s 1 Kin. 12. 25.
^t ch. 4. 6.
Ps. 89. 12.

---

¹ Or, *an hundred and twenty thousand, every one drawing a sword*, ch. 20. 2, 15,
17, 25. 2 Kin. 3. 26.
² Heb. *terrified.*
³ Heb. *writ.*
⁴ Heb. *made to know.*
⁵ Heb. *according to the form, &c.*

---

in the mountain. No identification of Penuel has taken place. It was south of the brook Jabbok, and on Jacob's way to Succoth. Gideon, journeying in the opposite direction to Jacob, comes from Succoth to Penuel.

10. Zebah and Zalmunna seem to have fled nearly due east to Karkor, which was probably an enclosure of some kind (perhaps a walled sheepfold, cp. Num. xxxi. 32 note). Its site is unknown; but it was near *Nobah*, in the half-tribe of Manasseh in Gilead (Num. xxxii. 40), and *Jogbehah* was in the tribe of Gad (ib. 34, 35). Gideon, perhaps taking a circuit so as to come upon them from the east, fell suddenly upon them, apparently at night, surprised them, and smote them.

13. *before the sun was up*] The translation of the words is doubtful, because of the rarity of the word rendered "sun" (*Heres;* cp. ii. 9 note). Many suppose it to be the name of a mountain pass, and render it *from the ascent of Heres.*

14. The written (see marg.) list would enable Gideon to punish the guilty and spare the innocent people. Succoth was governed by a sanhedrim or council of *seventy elders* (cp. Num. xi. 16), with perhaps seven others of superior rank called *princes.*

16. *he taught*] Thought to be a false read-ing, for "he threshed," as in *v.* 7 marg.

17. *the men of the city*] Perhaps the rulers; who, it is likely, had possession of the tower or citadel, and so could tyrannize over the people. Gideon slew the great men, and beat down their towers, but did not injure the inhabitants.

18. *what manner of men*] Lit. "**Where are the men?**" The sense, *what manner of men*, is merely gathered from the tenor of the answer. Gideon doubtless knew that his brethren had been killed by Zebah and Zalmunna, and the desire of avenging their death was one motive for his impetuous pursuit and attack. His question was rather a taunt, a bitter reproach to his captives, preparing them for their fate. Zebah and Zalmunna, in their answer, did not give evidence against themselves. Their hope was by a flattering answer to soothe Gideon's wrath.

19. *the sons of my mother*] A much closer relation than that of brothers by the father only. (Cp. Gen. xliii. 29; Deut. xiii. 6; Ps. lxix. 8). This is the only hint preserved of the transaction. We cannot say exactly when the slaughter of Gideon's brethren on Mount Tabor took place, whether before the outbreak of the war (vi. 33), or in the retreat and flight of the Midianites (vii. 22).

20 would not slay you. And he said unto Jether his firstborn, Up, *and* slay them. But the youth drew not his sword: for he
21 feared, because he *was* yet a youth. Then Zebah and Zalmunna said, Rise thou, and fall upon us: for as the man *is, so is* his
^u Ps. 83. 11.   strength. And Gideon arose, and ^uslew Zebah and Zalmunna, and took away the ¹ornaments that *were* on their camels' necks.
22 ¶ Then the men of Israel said unto Gideon, Rule thou over us, both thou, and thy son, and thy son's son also: for thou hast
23 delivered us from the hand of Midian. And Gideon said unto them, I will not rule over you, neither shall my son rule over
^x 1 Sam. 8. 7. & 10. 19. & 12. 12.   24 you: ^xthe LORD shall rule over you. ¶ And Gideon said unto them, I would desire a request of you, that ye would give me every man the earrings of his prey. (For they had golden ear-
^y Gen. 25. 13. & 37. 25, 28.   25 rings, ^ybecause they *were* Ishmaelites.) And they answered, We will willingly give *them*. And they spread a garment, and did
26 cast therein every man the earrings of his prey. And the weight of the golden earrings that he requested was a thousand and seven hundred *shekels* of gold; beside ornaments, and ²collars, and purple raiment that *was* on the kings of Midian, and beside
27 the chains that *were* about their camels' necks. And Gideon
^z ch. 17. 5. ^a ch. 6. 24. ^b Ps. 106. 39. ^c Deut. 7. 16.   ^zmade an ephod thereof, and put it in his city, *even* ^ain Ophrah: and all Israel ^bwent thither a whoring after it: which thing
28 became ^ca snare unto Gideon, and to his house. ¶ Thus was Midian subdued before the children of Israel, so that they lifted
^d ch. 5. 31. & 1. 2.   up their heads no more. ^dAnd the country was in quietness
29 forty years in the days of Gideon. And Jerubbaal the son of
30 Joash went and dwelt in his own house. And Gideon had
^e ch. 9. 2, 5. ^f ch. 9. 1.   ^ethreescore and ten sons ³of his body begotten: for he had many
31 wives. ^fAnd his concubine that *was* in Shechem, she also bare
32 him a son, whose name he ⁴called Abimelech. And Gideon the

¹ Or, *ornaments like the moon.*   ² Or, *sweet jewels.*   ⁴ Heb. *set.*
                               ³ Heb. *going out of his thigh.*

20. It was Gideon's place to act the part of the "avenger of blood" (Num. xxxv. 12; Deut. xix. 6). The fierce manners of the age break out in the slaying of the captives (cp. 1 Sam. xv. 32, 33), and in Gideon's attempt to initiate his youthful son Jether in the stern work of slaying his country's enemies.

21. *the ornaments*] See marg. and cp. Isai. iii. 18. The custom of adorning the necks of their camels with gold chains and ornaments prevailed among the Arabs so late as the time of Mahomet.

24. In this desire for gold Gideon falls to the level of ordinary men, and we may see in it the first decline of his glory, leading to a sad tarnishing of the lustre of his bright name. The idolatrous honour paid to Gideon's ephod was probably a source of revenue to his house. Contrast the conduct of Abraham (Gen. xiv. 21–23), and of Elisha (2 K. v. 16, 26).

The *ear-ring* here mentioned is properly a *nose-ring* (cp. Gen. xxiv. 22 note). The custom of wearing nose-rings prevails in Eastern countries to the present day. The circumstance of Job's friends each contributing a nose-ring of gold (Job xlii. 11 note)

is a remarkable parallel to the incident in Gideon's history. Rings of gold were also used as money in Egypt, as appears on several early monuments, and by the Celts.

25. *they spread, &c.*] The LXX. reads "He spread his garment."

26. If the Ishmaelite nose-rings were half a shekel in weight, then 1,700 shekels weight of gold implied that 3,400 persons wearing gold rings had been slain. The "collars" were rather "ear-drops."

27. The ephod was that particular part of the High-Priest's dress which was necessary to be worn when he inquired of God by Urim and Thummim. It seems that Gideon being now the civil ruler, desired to have an ephod of his own, kept in his own city, to be worn by the priest whenever Gideon might summon him to inquire of the Lord for him. His relations with the tribe of Ephraim probably made him unwilling to resort to Shiloh. Cp. the act of Jeroboam (1 K. xii. 28).

31. Abimelech's mother was not reckoned among the wives, being, probably, one of the Canaanite population in Shechem (ix. 28): neither was Abimelech himself reck-

son of Joash died *g*in a good old age, and was buried in the
sepulchre of Joash his father, *h*in Ophrah of the Abi-ezrites.
33 ¶ And it came to pass, *i*as soon as Gideon was dead, that the
children of Israel turned again, and *k*went a whoring after
34 Baalim, *l*and made Baal-berith their god. And the children of
Israel *m*remembered not the LORD their God, who had delivered
them out of the hands of all their enemies on every side:
35 *n*neither shewed they kindness to the house of Jerubbaal,
namely, Gideon, according to all the goodness which he had
shewed unto Israel.

CHAP. 9. AND Abimelech the son of Jerubbaal went to Shechem
unto *a*his mother's brethren, and communed with them, and with
2 all the family of the house of his mother's father, saying, Speak,
I pray you, in the ears of all the men of Shechem, ¹Whether *is*
better for you, either that all the sons of Jerubbaal, *which are*
*b*threescore and ten persons, reign over you, or that one reign
over you? remember also that I *am* *c*your bone and your flesh.
3 And his mother's brethren spake of him in the ears of all the
men of Shechem all these words: and their hearts inclined ²to
4 follow Abimelech; for they said, He *is* our *d*brother. And they
gave him threescore and ten *pieces* of silver out of the house of
*e*Baal-berith, wherewith Abimelech hired *f*vain and light per-
5 sons, which followed him. And he went unto his father's house
*g*at Ophrah, and *h*slew his brethren the sons of Jerubbaal, *being*
threescore and ten persons, upon one stone: notwithstanding
yet Jotham the youngest son of Jerubbaal was left; for he hid
6 himself. And all the men of Shechem gathered together, and
all the house of Millo, and went, and made Abimelech king, ³by
7 the plain of the pillar that *was* in Shechem. ¶ And when they
told *it* to Jotham, he went and stood in the top of *i*mount
Gerizim, and lifted up his voice, and cried, and said unto them,

¹ Heb. *What* is *good?*
whether, &c.
² Heb. *after.*
³ Or, *by the oak of the*
pillar: See Josh. 24. 26.

g Gen. 25. 8.
Job 5. 26.
h ver. 27.
ch. 6. 24.
i ch. 2. 19
k ch. 2. 17.
l ch. 9. 4, 46.
m Ps. 78. 11,
42.
& 106. 13.
n ch. 9. 16.
Eccles. 9.
14, 15.

a ch. 8. 31.

b ch. 8. 30.
c Gen. 29.
14.

d Gen. 29.
15.
e ch. 8. 33.
f ch. 11. 3.
2 Chr. 13. 7.
Prov. 12. 11.
Acts 17. 5.
g ch. 6. 24.
h 2 Kin. 11.
1, 2.

i Deut. 11.
29.
Josh. 8. 33.
John 4. 20.

oned with the seventy other sons of Jerubbaal (ix. 24. Cp. xi. 1, 2).

33. *turned again*] Doubtless Gideon himself had no doubt prepared the way for this
apostasy by his unauthorised ephod. The
Law of Moses, with its strict unity of priesthood and Altar, was the divinely-appointed
and only effectual preservative from idolatry.

Baal-bereth] The god of covenants or
sworn treaties, corresponding to the Zeus
Orkius of the Greeks. The centre of this
fresh apostacy was at Shechem.

IX. 1. We are not told how soon after
the death of Gideon these events happened.
There must have been time for the apostacy
and establishment of Baal-worship, and for
the development of ill-will between Abimelech and his brethren.

2. *the men of Shechem*] Lit., "the masters."
Cp. Josh. xxiv. 11; 1 Sam. xxiii. 11, 12.

3. The Ephraimite pride revolted from
Abi-ezrite rulers, and inclined them to one
who was a Shechemite by birth. (Cp. the
same spirit in the time of David and
Rehoboam, 2 Sam. xx. 1; 1 K. xii. 16.)

5. Such wholesale slaughters have always
been common in Eastern monarchies, and

are among the fruits of polygamy.

6. Millo must have been a fortified place
close to, but separate from, Shechem, and
perhaps the same as the tower of Shechem
mentioned in *vv.* 46, 47. The building or
enlarging of the better-known Millo at Jerusalem was one of Solomon's great works
(1 K. ix. 15, 24). The population dwelling
in Millo though perhaps numerically small,
had great weight from possessing the stronghold. Their giving Abimelech the title of
king indicates the strong Canaanite influence
at Shechem. All the Canaanite chiefs were
called *kings*, but it was a title hitherto unknown in Israel. This title had not been
named by those Israelites who offered to make
Gideon their hereditary *ruler* (viii. 22, 23).

the plain of the pillar, &c.] Rather "*the oak*
of the garrison which is in Shechem." The oak
in question was probably called the "garrison oak," from a garrison being stationed
near it.

7. *the top of Mount Gerizim*] The ancient
Shechem was perhaps situated there. The
population of Shechem is supposed to have
been keeping some public festival outside
the city when Jotham addressed them,

Hearken unto me, ye men of Shechem, that God may hearken
8 unto you. [k]The trees went forth *on a time* to anoint a king
over them; and they said unto the olive tree, [l]Reign thou over
9 us. But the olive tree said unto them, Should I leave my fatness, [m]wherewith by me they honour God and man, and [1]go to
10 be promoted over the trees? And the trees said to the fig tree,
11 Come thou, *and* reign over us. But the fig tree said unto them,
Should I forsake my sweetness, and my good fruit, and go to be
12 promoted over the trees? Then said the trees unto the vine,
13 Come thou, *and* reign over us. And the vine said unto them,
Should I leave my wine, [n]which cheereth God and man, and go
14 to be promoted over the trees? Then said all the trees unto the
15 [2]bramble, Come thou, *and* reign over us. And the bramble said
unto the trees, If in truth ye anoint me king over you, *then*
come *and* put your trust in my [o]shadow: and if not, [p]let fire
come out of the bramble, and devour the [q]cedars of Lebanon.
16 Now therefore, if ye have done truly and sincerely, in that ye
have made Abimelech king, and if ye have dealt well with Jerubbaal and his house, and have done unto him [r]according to
17 the deserving of his hands; (for my father fought for you, and
[3]adventured his life far, and delivered you out of the hand of
18 Midian: [s]and ye are risen up against my father's house this
day, and have slain his sons, threescore and ten persons, upon
one stone, and have made Abimelech, the son of his maidservant, king over the men of Shechem, because he *is* your brother;)
19 if ye then have dealt truly and sincerely with Jerubbaal and with
his house this day, *then* [t]rejoice ye in Abimelech, and let him
20 also rejoice in you: but if not, [u]let fire come out from Abimelech, and devour the men of Shechem, and the house of Millo;
and let fire come out from the men of Shechem, and from the
21 house of Millo, and devour Abimelech. And Jotham ran away,
and fled, and went to [x]Beer, and dwelt there, for fear of Abime-
22 lech his brother. ¶ When Abimelech had reigned three years
23 over Israel, then [y]God sent an evil spirit between Abimelech
and the men of Shechem; and the men of Shechem [z]dealt
24 treacherously with Abimelech; [a]that the cruelty *done* to the
threescore and ten sons of Jerubbaal might come, and their

[k] See 2 Kin. 14. 9.
[l] ch. 8. 22, 23.
[m] Ps. 104. 15.
[n] Ps. 104. 15.
[o] Isai. 30. 2. Dan. 4. 12. Hos. 14. 7.
[p] ver. 20. Num. 21. 28. Ezek. 19. 14.
[q] 2 Kin. 14. 9. Ps. 104. 16.
[r] ch. 8. 35.
[s] ver. 5, 6.
[t] Isai. 8. 6. Phil. 3. 3.
[u] ver. 15, 56, 57.
[x] 2 Sam. 20. 14.
[y] 1 Sam. 16. 14. & 18. 9, 10. Isai. 19. 2, 14.
[z] Isai. 33. 1.
[a] 1 Kin. 2. 32. Esth. 9. 25. Ps. 7. 16. Matt. 23. 35, 36.

[1] Heb. *go up and down for* other *trees*.
[2] Or, *thistle*.
[3] Heb. *cast his life*.

8-20. This fable and that noted in the marg. ref. are the only two of the kind found in Scripture. Somewhat different are the parables of the O. T. 2 Sam. xii. 1-4, xiv. 5-11; 1 K. xx. 39, 40.

9. *honour God and man*] Alluding to the constant use of oil in the meat-offerings (Lev. ii. 1-16), and in the holy ointment (Ex. xxx. 24, 25). In like manner, the allusion in *v.* 13 is to the drink-offerings of wine. See Lev. xxiii. 13; Num. xv. 10.

14. *the bramble*] Said to be the Rhamnus Paliurus of Linnæus, otherwise called Spina-Christi, or Christ's Thorn, a shrub with sharp thorns. The application is obvious. The noble Gideon and his worthy sons had declined the proffered kingdom. The vile, base-born Abimelech had accepted it, and his act would turn out to the mutual ruin of himself and his subjects.

15. *if in truth*] *i.e.* consistently with truth, honour, and uprightness, as explained in the interpretation in *vv.* 16 and 19.

let fire come out, &c.] The propriety of the image is strictly preserved, for even the thorns of the worthless bramble might kindle a flame which would burn the stately cedars to the ground. See Ps. lviii. 9.

16-20. These verses contain the interpretation of the fable. In them Jotham points out the base ingratitude of the people in raising Abimelech upon the ruin of Gideon's house, and foretells the retribution which would fall upon both parties.

22. *had reigned*] Rather, **"had ruled."** It is not the phrase used in *v.* 6. It looks as if the Shechemites alone had made him *king*, and the rest of Israel had submitted to his *dominion*, without allowing his title of king.

blood be laid upon Abimelech their brother, which slew them;
and upon the men of Shechem, which [1]aided him in the killing
25 of his brethren. And the men of Shechem set liers in wait for
him in the top of the mountains, and they robbed all that came
26 along that way by them : and it was told Abimelech. And Gaal
the son of Ebed came with his brethren, and went over to
Shechem : and the men of Shechem put their confidence in him.
27 And they went out into the fields, and gathered their vineyards,
and trode *the grapes*, and made [2]merry, and went into *b*the house   *b* ver. 4.
of their god, and did eat and drink, and cursed Abimelech.
28 And Gaal the son of Ebed said, *c*Who *is* Abimelech, and who *is*   *c* 1 Sam. 25.
Shechem, that we should serve him ? *is* not *he* the son of Jerub-   10.
baal ? and Zebul his officer ? serve the men of *d*Hamor the   1 Kin. 12. 16.
29 father of Shechem : for why should we serve him ? And *e*would   *d* Gen. 34. 2, 6.
to God this people were under my hand! then would I remove   *e* 2 Sam. 15.
Abimelech. And he said to Abimelech, Increase thine army,   4.
30 and come out. ¶And when Zebul the ruler of the city heard
31 the words of Gaal the son of Ebed, his anger was [3]kindled. And
he sent messengers unto Abimelech [4]privily, saying, Behold,
Gaal the son of Ebed and his brethren be come to Shechem ;
32 and, behold, they fortify the city against thee. Now therefore
up by night, thou and the people that *is* with thee, and lie in
33 wait in the field : and it shall be, *that* in the morning, as soon as
the sun is up, thou shalt rise early, and set upon the city : and,
behold, *when* he and the people that *is* with him come out against
thee, then mayest thou do to them [5]as thou shalt find occasion.
34 ¶And Abimelech rose up, and all the people that *were* with him,
by night, and they laid wait against Shechem in four companies.
35 And Gaal the son of Ebed went out, and stood in the entering of
the gate of the city : and Abimelech rose up, and the people that
36 *were* with him, from lying in wait. And when Gaal saw the

[1] Heb. *strengthened his hands to kill.*
[2] Or, *songs:* See Isai. 16. 9, 10. Jer. 25. 30.
[3] Or, *hot.*
[4] Heb. *craftily,* or, *to Tormah.*
[5] Heb. *as thine hand shall find,* 1 Sam. 10. 7. & 25. 8. Eccles. 9. 10.

---

26. It does not appear who Gaal, son of
Ebed, was ; he may have been an officer
sent by Abimelech with a force to bring the
men of Shechem back to their allegiance,
but who tried to turn the rebellion to his
own account. He got into Shechem with
a band of men, " his brethren," unopposed by Zebul, Abimelech's officer, and
soon gained the confidence of the Shechemites.
27–29. Seditious and lawless acts (*vv.* 25,
26) now broke out into open rebellion. It
was at an idolatrous feast in the house of
Baal-berith, on occasion of the vintage,
and when they were excited with wine, that
the rebellion was matured. Those present
began to " curse Abimelech," to speak in-
sultingly of him, and to revile him (cp. Lev.
xx. 9 ; 2 Sam. xix. 21 ; Isai. viii. 21). Gaal,
the son of Ebed, who was watching the
opportunity, immediately incited them to
revolt from the dominion of Abimelech,
offering himself to be their captain ; adding
a message of defiance to Abimelech, ad-

dressed, probably, to Zebul, who was present but too weak to resent it on the spot.
27. *made merry*] The word translated
merry occurs only here and in Lev. xix. 24.
Its etymology gives the sense of *praises,*
thanksgivings; and its use in these two passages rather indicates that the fruits themselves which were brought to the House of
God with songs of praise, and eaten or
drunken with religious service, were so
called. The thank-offerings would be a
portion of the new wine of the vintage
which they had just gathered in.
28. Shechem is another designation of
Abimelech. Shechem means the son and
heir of Shechem, Abimelech's mother being
a Canaanite (*v.* 18).
31. *privily*] See marg. The word is probably the name of a place in *Tormah,* some
think the same as *Arumah* (*v.* 41). Zebul
was faithful to Abimelech, but dissembled
his sentiments, from being too weak to
oppose Gaal, till Abimelech came with his
army (*v.* 38).

people, he said to Zebul, Behold, there come people down from the top of the mountains. And Zebul said unto him, Thou seest 37 the shadow of the mountains as *if they were* men. And Gaal spake again and said, See there come people down by the [1]middle of the land, and another company come along by the plain of 38 [2]Meonenim. Then said Zebul unto him, Where *is* ·now thy

mouth, wherewith thou [f]saidst, Who *is* Abimelech, that we should serve him? *is* not this the people that thou hast despised? 39 go out, I pray now, and fight with them. And Gaal went out 40 before the men of Shechem, and fought with Abimelech. And Abimelech chased him, and he fled before him, and many were overthrown *and* wounded, *even* unto the entering of the gate. 41 And Abimelech dwelt at Arumah: and Zebul thrust out Gaal 42 and his brethren, that they should not dwell in Shechem. ¶ And it came to pass on the morrow, that the people went out into 43 the field; and they told Abimelech. And he took the people, and divided them into three companies, and laid wait in the field, and looked, and, behold, the people *were* come forth out of 44 the city; and he rose up against them, and smote them. And Abimelech, and the company that *was* with him, rushed forward, and stood in the entering of the gate of the city: and the two *other* companies ran upon all *the people* that *were* in the fields, 45 and slew them. And Abimelech fought against the city all that

g ver. 20. day; and [g]he took the city, and slew the people that *was* there-
h Deut. 29. 46 in, and [h]beat down the city, and sowed it with salt. ¶ And
23. when all the men of the tower of Shechem heard *that*, they
1 Kin. 12. 25. 47 entered into an hold of the house [i]of the god Berith. And it
2 Kin. 3. 25. was told Abimelech, that all the men of the tower of Shechem
i ch. 8. 33. 48 were gathered together. And Abimelech gat him up to mount

k Ps. 68. 14. [k]Zalmon, he and all the people that *were* with him; and Abime-lech took an axe in his hand, and cut down a bough from the trees, and took it, and laid *it* on his shoulder, and said unto the people that *were* with him, What ye have seen [3]me do, make 49 haste, *and* do as I *have done*. And all the people likewise cut down every man his bough, and followed Abimelech, and put *them* to the hold, and set the hold on fire upon them; so that all the men of the tower of Shechem died also, about a thousand

---

[1] Heb. *navel.*   [2] Or, *The regarders of times,*   [3] Heb. *I have done.*
Deut. 18. 14.

---

37. *the plain of Meonenim*] Translate " the oak of the soothsayers " (see marg.). Some well-known oak, so called, but which is not mentioned elsewhere.

42. After Gaal's expulsion, *the people went out into the field,* either to complete the vintage, or for some other agricultural operation. "They" (Zebul and his party) sent word of this to Abimelech.

44. This verse explains the purpose of both the present and the former division of Abimelech's forces into several companies, viz. that while some of the companies attacked the men of Shechem in the field, another company, starting from their ambush, might occupy the approach to the city gate, and so cut off their retreat.

45. *sowed it with salt*] Expressing by this

action his hatred, and his wish, that when utterly destroyed as a city, it might not even be a fruitful field. Salt is the emblem of barrenness (see marg. reff.).

46. *an hold of the house of the god Berith*] As combining the advantages of a *sanctuary* (cp. 1 K. ii. 28) and a fortress. The word rendered *hold* occurs elsewhere only in 1 Sam. xiii. 6, where it is rendered "*high-place.*" Its exact signification is uncertain.

48. *Zalmon*] A lofty and thickly-wooded hill, as the etymology of the name (*shady*) implies, in the immediate neighbourhood of Shechem: perhaps the same as Ebal. The setting fire to the hold, where the men of Shechem were all crowded together, with their wives and children, was the literal fulfilment of Jotham's curse in *v.* 20.

50 men and women. ¶ Then went Abimelech to Thebez, and en-
51 camped against Thebez, and took it. But there was a strong
tower within the city, and thither fled all the men and women,
and all they of the city, and shut *it* to them, and gat them up to
52 the top of the tower. And Abimelech came unto the tower, and
fought against it, and went hard unto the door of the tower to
53 burn it with fire. And a certain woman *l* cast a piece of a mill- *l* 2 Sam. 11.
54 stone upon Abimelech's head, and all to brake his scull. Then 21.
m he called hastily unto the young man his armourbearer, and *m* So 1 Sam.
said unto him, Draw thy sword, and slay me, that men say not 31. 4.
55 of me, A woman slew him. And his young man thrust him
through, and he died. And when the men of Israel saw that
Abimelech was dead, they departed every man unto his place.
56 ¶ *n* Thus God rendered the wickedness of Abimelech, which he *n* ver. 24.
57 did unto his father, in slaying his seventy brethren: and all the Job 31. 3.
evil of the men of Shechem did God render upon their heads: Ps. 94. 23.
and upon them came *o* the curse of Jotham the son of Jerubbaal. *o* ver. 20.
CHAP. 10. AND after Abimelech there *a* arose to *1 2* defend Israel *a* ch. 2. 16.
Tola the son of Puah, the son of Dodo, a man of Issachar;
2 and he dwelt in Shamir in mount Ephraim. And he judged
Israel twenty and three years, and died, and was buried in
3 Shamir. ¶ And after him arose Jair, a Gileadite, and judged
4 Israel twenty and two years. And he had thirty sons that
b rode on thirty ass colts, and they had thirty cities, *c* which *b* ch. 5. 10.
are called *3* Havoth-jair unto this day, which *are* in the land *c* Deut. 3. 14.
5, 6 of Gilead. And Jair died, and was buried in Camon. ¶ And *d* ch. 2. 11.
d the children of Israel did evil again in the sight of the LORD, & 3. 7. & 4.
and *e* served Baalim, and Ashtaroth, and *f* the gods of Syria, 1. & 6. 1.
and the gods of *v* Zidon, and the gods of Moab, and the gods *e* ch. 2. 13.
of the children of Ammon, and the gods of the Philistines, *f* ch. 2. 12.
7 and forsook the LORD, and served not him. And the anger of 33.
the LORD was hot against Israel, and he *h* sold them into the Ps. 106. 36.
h ch. 2. 14.

1 Or, *deliver.*   *2* Heb. *save.*   *3* Or, *the villages of Jair,* Num. 32. 41.   1 Sam. 12. 9.

---

50. The men of Thebez (modern Tubas)
had, doubtless, joined the Shechemites in
their rebellion against Abimelech.
52. *went hard unto the door,* &c.] *i.e.* went
close to the door. An act of manifest
danger, seeing the roof was covered with
persons who would be likely to throw down
missiles of all sorts on the heads of their
assailants. But the hatred of Abimelech,
and his thirst for revenge, made him despise
danger.
53. The phrase *all to* is now obsolete, and
means *quite, entirely,* as in Chaucer, Spenser,
and Milton.
X. 1. *defend*] The marginal reading "to
deliver," is far preferable. The word is the
same as in ii. 16, 18, iii. 9, 15, 31, &c., and is
the technical word applied to the judges. Cp.
Neh. ix. 27 (*saviours who saved them,* A.V.).
The term *there arose,* also marks Tola as
one of the Judges, properly so called, raised
by Divine Providence.
Tola and *Puah*] Both names of heads of
houses in the tribe of Issachar (1 Chr. vii.
1; Gen. xlvi. 13).
Shamir] Not the same as that mentioned
in Josh. xv. 48, which was in the hill country

of Judah. Issachar would seem from this
to have extended into the northern part of
mount Ephraim.
2. Jair the Gileadite was probably the
same person as is named in Num. xxxii. 41;
Deut. iii. 14, as having given the name of
Havoth-jair to certain villages in Bashan.
6. *the gods of Syria*] Or *Aram.* In the
times of the Judges the various tribes of
Aramites, or Syrians, were not compacted
into one state, nor were they till after the
time of Solomon. The national gods of
these various Aramean tribes were probably
the same; and their worship would be likely
to be introduced into the trans-Jordanic
tribes. It has been remarked that the
Hebrew words for "to divine," "to practise magic," "idolatrous priests," and other
like words, are of Syrian origin. The
Syriac ritual proved very attractive to
king Ahaz (2 K. xvi. 10-12). For the
national gods of the Zidonians, Moabites,
Ammonites, and Philistines, see 1 K. xi. 5,
7, 33; 1 Sam. v. 2-5.
7. The previous mention of the Philistines
as oppressors of Israel (iii. 31) seems to be
restricted to the south of Judah, when they

hands of the Philistines, and into the hands of the children of
8 Ammon. And that year they vexed and [1]oppressed the children
of Israel: eighteen years, all the children of Israel that *were* on
the other side Jordan in the land of the Amorites, which *is* in
9 Gilead. Moreover the children of Ammon passed over Jordan
to fight also against Judah, and against Benjamin, and against
10 the house of Ephraim; so that Israel was sore distressed. ¶ [i]And
the children of Israel cried unto the LORD, saying, We have
sinned against thee, both because we have forsaken our God,
11 and also served Baalim. And the LORD said unto the children
of Israel, *Did* not *I deliver you* [k]from the Egyptians, and [l]from
the Amorites, [m]from the children of Ammon, [n]and from the
12 Philistines? [o]The Zidonians also, [p]and the Amalekites, and
the Maonites, [q]did oppress you; and ye cried to me, and I
13 delivered you out of their hand. [r]Yet ye have forsaken me,
and served other gods: wherefore I will deliver you no more.
14 Go and [s]cry unto the gods which ye have chosen; let them
15 deliver you in the time of your tribulation. And the children
of Israel said unto the LORD, We have sinned: [t]do thou unto
us whatsoever [2]seemeth good unto thee; deliver us only, we
16 pray thee, this day. [u]And they put away the [3]strange gods
from among them, and served the LORD: and [x]his soul [4]was
17 grieved for the misery of Israel. ¶ Then the children of Ammon
were [5]gathered together, and encamped in Gilead. And the
children of Israel assembled themselves together, and encamped

i 1 Sam. 12.
10.
k Ex. 14. 30.
l Num. 21.
21, 24, 25.
m ch. 3. 12,
13.
n ch. 3. 31.
o ch. 5. 19.
p ch. 6. 33.
q Ps. 106.
42, 43.
r Deut. 32.
15.
Jer. 2. 13.
s Deut. 32.
37, 38.
2 Kin. 3. 13.
Jer. 2. 28.
t 1 Sam.3.18.
2 Sam. 15.
26.
u 2 Chr. 7.
14. & 15. 8.
Jer. 18. 7, 8.
x Ps. 106. 44,
45.
Isai. 63. 9.

[1] Heb. *crushed.*　　　　　[3] Heb. *gods of strangers.*　　　[4] Heb. *was shortened.*
[2] Heb. *is good in thine eyes.*　　　　　　　　　　　　　　　　　　[5] Heb. *cried together.*

---

co-operated with Moab. They appear to
have gradually increased in power till they
reached their height in the time of Saul.
In the present instance they were probably
in alliance with the Ammonites, holding
the western tribes in check, while the Ammonites subdued those on the east of Jordan.

8. *that year*] Perhaps the closing year of
the oppression, when the Ammonites passed
over the Jordan. For it was this crowning
oppression which brought the Israelites to
repentance (*vv.* 10, 15, 16), and so prepared
the way for the deliverance. Possibly in
the original narrative from which this portion of the Book of Judges is compiled,
"that year" was defined.

the land of the Amorites] Viz. of Sihon
king of the Amorites, Num. xxi. 21; Deut.
i. 4; Josh. xiii. 10; Ps. cxxxv. 11.

11. (See marg. reff.). The Israelites were
delivered from the *Egyptians* at the Exodus;
from the *Amorites* in the victories over
Sihon, and Og, and the five kings of the
Amorites (Josh. x. 5); from the *children of
Ammon* by Ehud; and from the *Philistines*, by the hand of Shamgar (cp. 1 Sam.
xii. 9).

12. *the Zidonians*] An allusion to the
time of Barak, when the Zidonians doubtless formed part of the great confederacy
of Canaanites under Jabin king of Hazor.
See Josh. xi. 8.

the Amalekites] In the time of Gideon
(marg. ref.).

the Maonites] Probably one of the tribes
of the "children of the East," who came
with the Midianites and Amalekites in the
time of Gideon, and may have been conspicuous for their hostility to Israel, and
for the greatness of their discomfiture,
though the record has not been preserved. The name is *Mehunims* in 2 Chr.
xxvi. 7.

17. The historian, having related the
preliminary incidents, now comes to the
final issue which forms the subject matter
of his narrative. On a certain occasion,
as on many previous ones, the Ammonites
were encamped in Gilead, with the intention of dispossessing the Israelites of the
whole country, or at least as far as the
river Jabbok (xi. 13), and of invading the
West-Jordanic tribes. The children of Israel
on the East of Jordan assembled together
to resist them, and pitched their camp
in Mizpeh. The narrative proceeds to detail what happened.

Mizpeh, as its name, "watch-tower" or
"look-out" indicates, was situated on a
height of Mount Gilead, and was, as
such, a strong post. It is almost always
written, "THE Mizpeh," or watch-tower.
Four or five places of the name occur in
Scripture.

18 in *Mizpeh. And the people *and* princes of Gilead said one to
another, What man *is he* that will begin to fight against the
children of Ammon? he shall *be head over all the inhabitants
of Gilead.
CHAP. 11. NOW *Jephthah the Gileadite was *a mighty man of
valour, and he *was* the son of ¹an harlot: and Gilead begat
2 Jephthah. And Gilead's wife bare him sons; and his wife's
sons grew up, and they thrust out Jephthah, and said unto him,
Thou shalt not inherit in our father's house; for thou *art* the son
3 of a strange woman. Then Jephthah fled ²from his brethren,
and dwelt in the land of Tob: and there were gathered *vain
4 men to Jephthah, and went out with him. ¶And it came to pass
⁵in process of time, that the children of Ammon made war
5 against Israel. And it was so, that when the children of Ammon
made war against Israel, the elders of Gilead went to fetch
6 Jephthah out of the land of Tob: and they said unto Jephthah, Come, and be our captain, that we may fight with the
7 children of Ammon. And Jephthah said unto the elders of
Gilead, *Did not ye hate me, and expel me out of my father's
house? and why are ye come unto me now when ye are in dis-
8 tress? *And the elders of Gilead said unto Jephthah, Therefore
we *turn again to thee now, that thou mayest go with us, and
fight against the children of Ammon, and be *our head over all
9 the inhabitants of Gilead. And Jephthah said unto the elders
of Gilead, If ye bring me home again to fight against the children of Ammon, and the LORD deliver them before me, shall I
10 be your head? And the elders of Gilead said unto Jephthah,
*The LORD *be witness between us, if we do not so according to
11 thy words. Then Jephthah went with the elders of Gilead, and
the people made him *head and captain over them: and Jeph-
12 thah uttered all his words *before the LORD in Mizpeh. ¶And

y Gen. 31. 49.
ch. 11. 11, 29.
x ch. 11. 8,
11.
a Heb. 11.
32, called
Jephthae.
b ch. 6. 12.
2 Kin. 5. 1.

c ch. 9. 4.
1 Sam. 22. 2.

d Gen. 26.
27.

e ch. 10. 18.
f Luke 17. 4.
g ch. 10. 18.

h Jer. 42. 5.

i ver. 8.
k ch. 10. 17.
& 20. 1.
1 Sam. 10.
17. & 11. 15.

¹ Heb. *a woman an harlot.*   ³ Heb. *after days.*   ⁴ Heb. *be the hearer between us.*
² Heb. *from the face.*

---

18. *and the people and princes,* &c.] The
inhabitants of Gilead appear as a separate
and independent community, electing their
own chief, without any reference to the
West-Jordanic tribes.
XI. **1.** The history of Jephthah appears
to be an independent history inserted by
the compiler of the Book of Judges. Verses
4 and 5 introduce the Ammonitish war
without any apparent reference to x.
17, 18.
A genealogy of Manasseh (1 Chr. vii. 14–
17) gives the families which sprang from
Gilead, and among them mention is made
of an *Aramitess* concubine as the mother of
one family. Jephthah, the son of Gilead
by a strange woman, fled, after his father's
death, to the land of Tob (*v.* 3), presumably
the land of his maternal ancestors (cp. ix.
1) and an *Aramean* settlement (2 Sam. x. 6,
8; 1 Macc. v. 13). It is difficult to conceive that Jephthah was literally the son of
Gilead, if Gilead was the son of Machir,
the son of Manasseh. Possibly *Gilead*
here denotes the heir of Gilead, the head
of the family, whose individual name has

not been preserved, nor the time when he
lived.
3. *the land of Tob*] To the north of Gilead,
toward Damascus. The readiness with
which Jephthah took to the freebooter's
life gives us a lively picture of the unsettled
times in which he lived.
7. This gives a wider signification to *vv.*
2, 3, and shows that Jephthah's *brethren*
include his fellow tribesmen.
9. Jephthah made his own aggrandisement
the condition of his delivering his country.
The circumstances of his birth and long
residence in a heathen land were little
favourable to the formation of the highest
type of character. Yet he has his record
among the faithful (Heb. xi. 32).
11. *Jephthah uttered all his words before
the LORD in Mizpeh*] This phrase designates
the presence of the Tabernacle, or the Ark,
or of the High Priest with Urim and
Thummim (xx. 26, xxi. 2; Josh. xviii. 8;
1 Sam. xxi. 7). The High Priest waited
upon Jephthah with the Ephod, and possibly the Ark, at his own house (see xx. 18
note). A trace of Jephthah's claim to unite

Jephthah sent messengers unto the king of the children of Ammon, saying, What hast thou to do with me, that thou art 13 come against me to fight in my land? And the king of the children of Ammon answered unto the messengers of Jephthah, [l]Because Israel took away my land, when they came up out of Egypt, from Arnon even unto [m]Jabbok, and unto Jordan: now 14 therefore restore those *lands* again peaceably. And Jephthah sent messengers again unto the king of the children of Ammon: 15 and said unto him, Thus saith Jephthah, [n]Israel took not away 16 the land of Moab, nor the land of the children of Ammon: but when Israel came up from Egypt, and [o]walked through the 17 wilderness unto the Red sea, and [p]came to Kadesh; then [q]Israel sent messengers unto the king of Edom, saying, Let me, I pray thee, pass through thy land: [r]but the king of Edom would not hearken *thereto*. And in like manner they sent unto the king of Moab: but he would not consent: and Israel [s]abode 18 in Kadesh. Then they went along through the wilderness, and [t]compassed the land of Edom, and the land of Moab, and [u]came by the east side of the land of Moab, [x]and pitched on the other side of Arnon, but came not within the border of Moab: for 19 Arnon *was* the border of Moab. And [y]Israel sent messengers unto Sihon king of the Amorites, the king of Heshbon; and Israel said unto him, [z]Let us pass, we pray thee, through thy 20 land into my place. [a]But Sihon trusted not Israel to pass through his coast: but Sihon gathered all his people together, 21 and pitched in Jahaz, and fought against Israel. And the LORD God of Israel delivered Sihon and all his people into the hand of Israel, and they [b]smote them: so Israel possessed all 22 the land of the Amorites, the inhabitants of that country. And they possessed [c]all the coasts of the Amorites, from Arnon even 23 unto Jabbok, and from the wilderness even unto Jordan. So now the LORD God of Israel hath dispossessed the Amorites from before his people Israel, and shouldest thou possess it? 24 Wilt not thou possess that which [d]Chemosh thy god giveth thee to possess? So whomsoever [e]the LORD our God shall drive out 25 from before us, them will we possess. And now *art* thou any thing better than [f]Balak the son of Zippor, king of Moab? did he ever strive against Israel, or did he ever fight against

Marginal references:
[l] Num. 21. 24, 25, 26.
[m] Gen. 32. 22.
[n] Deut. 2. 9, 19.
[o] Num. 14. 25.
Deut. 1. 40.
Josh. 5. 6.
[p] Num. 13.
26. & 20. 1.
Deut. 1. 46.
[q] Num. 20. 14.
[r] Num. 20. 18, 21.
[s] Num. 20. 1.
[t] Num. 21. 4.
Deut. 2. 1—8.
[u] Num. 21. 11.
[x] Num. 21. 13.
[y] Num. 21. 21.
Deut. 2. 26.
[z] Num. 21. 22.
[u] Num. 21. 23.
Deut. 2. 32.
[b] Num. 21. 24, 25.
[c] Deut. 2. 36.
[d] Num. 21. 29.
1 Kin. 11. 7.
Jer. 48. 7.
[e] Deut. 9. 4, 5. & 18. 12.
Josh. 3. 10.
[f] Num. 22. 2.
See Josh. 24. 9.

all Israel under his dominion is found in xii. 2, and breathes through his whole message to the king of the Ammonites. See *vv.* 12, 15, 23, 27.

13. *from Arnon even unto Jabbok,* &c.] The land bounded by the Arnon on the south, by the Jabbok on the north, by the Jordan on the west, and by the wilderness on the east was, of old, the kingdom of Sihon, but then the territory of Reuben and Gad.

15–28. Consult the marg. reff. If the Ark with the copy of the Law (Deut. xxxi. 26) was at Mizpeh, it would account for Jephthah's accurate knowledge of it; and this exact agreement of his message with Numbers and Deuteronomy would give additional force to the expression, *he uttered all his words before the* LORD (*r.* 11).

17. No mention is made of this embassy to Moab in the Pentateuch.

19. *into my place*] This expression implies

that the trans-Jordanic possessions of Israel were not included in the land of Canaan properly speaking.

21. The title *God of Israel* has a peculiar emphasis here, and in *v.* 23, in a narrative of transactions relating to the heathen and their gods.

24. Chemosh was the national god of the Moabites (see marg. reff.); and as the territory in question was Moabitish territory before the Amorites took it from "the people of Chemosh," this may account for the mention of Chemosh here rather than of Moloch, or Milcom, the god of the Ammonites. Possibly the king of the children of Ammon at this time may have been a Moabite.

25, 26. Jephthah advances another historical argument. Balak, the king of Moab, never disputed the possession of Sihon's kingdom with Israel.

26 them, while Israel dwelt in *Heshbon and her towns, and in
*Aroer and her towns, and in all the cities that *be* along by the
coasts of Arnon, three hundred years? why therefore did ye
27 not recover *them* within that time? Wherefore I have not
sinned against thee, but thou doest me wrong to war against
me: the LORD *the Judge *be judge this day between the chil-
28 dren of Israel and the children of Ammon. Howbeit the king
of the children of Ammon hearkened not unto the words of
29 Jephthah which he sent him. ¶ Then *the Spirit of the LORD
came upon ¹Jephthah, and he passed over Gilead, and Manasseh,
and passed over Mizpeh of Gilead, and from Mizpeh of Gilead
30 he passed over *unto* the children of Ammon. And Jephthah
*vowed a vow unto the LORD, and said, If thou shalt without
fail deliver the children of Ammon into mine hands, then it
31 shall be, that ²whatsoever cometh forth of the doors of my
house to meet me, when I return in peace from the children of
Ammon, *shall surely be the LORD'S, ³*and I will offer it up
32 for a burnt offering. ¶ So Jephthah passed over unto the children of Ammon to fight against them; and the LORD delivered
33 them into his hands. And he smote them from Aroer, even till
thou come to *Minnith, *even* twenty cities, and unto ⁴the plain
of the vineyards, with a very great slaughter. Thus the children of Ammon were subdued before the children of Israel.
34 ¶ And Jephthah came to *Mizpeh unto his house, and, behold,
*his daughter came out to meet him with timbrels and with
dances: and she *was his* only child; ⁵ ⁶ beside her he had neither

Right margin references:
*Num. 21. 25.
*Deut. 2. 36.
*Gen. 18. 25.
*Gen. 16. 5. & 31. 53. 1 Sam. 24.
12, 15.
*ch. 3. 10.
*Gen. 28. 20. 1 Sam. 1. 11.
*See Lev. 27. 2, 3, &c. 1 Sam. 1. 11, 28. & 2. 18.
*Ps. 66. 13.
*Ezek. 27. 17.
*ch. 10. 17. ver. 11.
*Ex. 15. 20. 1 Sam. 18. 6. Ps. 68. 25. Jer. 31. 4.

¹ Jephthah seems to have
been Judgeonly of North
east *Israel*.
² Heb. *that which cometh*

*forth, which shall come
forth.*
³ Or, *or I will offer it, &c.*

⁴ Or, *Abel*.
⁵ Or, *he had not of his own
either son or daughter.*
⁶ Heb. *of himself.*

---

29. *Then the Spirit of the* LORD, &c.] This
was the sanctification of Jephthah for his
office of Judge and saviour of God's people
Israel. Cp. vi. 34, xiii. 25. The declaration is one of the distinctive marks which
stamp this history as a divine history.
The geography is rather obscure, but the
sense seems to be that Jephthah first raised
all the inhabitants of Mount Gilead; then
he crossed the Jabbok into Manasseh, and
raised them; then he returned at the head
of his new forces to his own camp at Mizpeh
to join the troops he had left there; and
thence at the head of the whole army
marched against the Ammonites, who occupied the southern parts of Gilead.
31. The words of this verse prove con-
clusively that Jephthah intended his vow
to apply to human beings, not animals; for
only one of his household could be expected
to come forth from the door of his house to
meet him. They also preclude any other
meaning than that Jephthah contemplated
a human sacrifice. This need not, however,
surprise us, when we recollect his Syrian
birth and long residence in a Syrian city,
where such fierce rites were probably common. The Syrians and Phœnicians were
conspicuous among the ancient heathen nations for human sacrifices, and the transfer,

under such circumstances, to Jehovah of the
rites with which the false gods were honoured,
is just what one might expect. The circumstance of the Spirit of the Lord coming
on Jephthah (*v.* 29) is no difficulty; as it by
no means follows that because the Spirit of
God endued him with supernatural valour
and energy for vanquishing the Ammonites,
He therefore also endued him with spiritual
knowledge and wisdom. The Spirit of the
Lord came upon Gideon, but that did not
prevent his erring in the matter of the
ephod (viii. 27). Cp. 1 Cor. xii. 4-11;
Gal. ii. 11-14.
33. As in the conflicts with the Moabites,
Canaanites, and Midianites (iii., iv., vii.),
the battle was on Israelite territory, in self-
defence, not in aggressive warfare.
the plain of the vineyards] Rather, *Abel-
Ceramim* (cp. Abel-Meholah), identified
with an *Abel* situated amongst vineyards,
7 miles from Rabbah. *Minnith* is *Maanith*,
4 miles from Heshbon, on the road to Rabbah.
34. *his daughter came out to meet him*]
The precise phrase of his vow (*v.* 31). She
was his *only child*, a term of especial endear-
ment (see Jer. vi. 26; Zech. xii. 10). The
same word is used of Isaac (Gen. xxii. 2,
12, 16).

<table>
<tr><td>

*Gen. 37.
29, 34.

t Eccles. 5.
2—5.
u Num. 30. 2.
Ps. 15. 4.
x Num. 30. 2.
y 2 Sam. 18.
19, 31.

z ver. 31.
1 Sam. 1. 22,
24.
& 2. 18.

a See ch. 8.
1.

b Job 13. 14.
Ps. 119. 109.

</td></tr>
</table>

35 son nor daughter. And it came to pass, when he saw her, that he *rent his clothes, and said, Alas, my daughter! thou hast brought me very low, and thou art one of them that trouble me: for I ^thave opened my mouth unto the LORD, and ^uI can-
36 not go back. And she said unto him, My father, *if* thou hast opened thy mouth unto the LORD, ^xdo to me according to that which hath proceeded out of thy mouth; forasmuch as ^ythe LORD hath taken vengeance for thee of thine enemies, *even* of
37 the children of Ammon. And she said unto her father, Let this thing be done for me: let me alone two months, that I may ¹go up and down upon the mountains, and bewail my virginity, I
38 and my fellows. And he said, Go. And he sent her away *for* two months: and she went with her companions, and bewailed
39 her virginity upon the mountains. And it came to pass at the end of two months, that she returned unto her father, who ^zdid with her *according* to his vow which he had vowed: and she
40 knew no man. ¶And it was a ²custom in Israel, *that* the daughters of Israel went ³yearly ⁴to lament the daughter of Jephthah the Gileadite four days in a year.

CHAP. 12. AND ^athe men of Ephraim ⁵gathered themselves together, and went northward, and said unto Jephthah, Wherefore passedst thou over to fight against the children of Ammon, and didst not call us to go with thee? we will burn thine house upon
2 thee with fire. And Jephthah said unto them, I and my people were at great strife with the children of Ammon; and when I
3 called you, ye delivered me not out of their hands. And when I saw that ye delivered *me* not, I ^bput my life in my hands, and passed over against the children of Ammon, and the LORD delivered them into my hand: wherefore then are ye come up

¹ Heb. *go and go down.*　　³ Heb. *from year to year.*　　⁵ Heb. *were called.*
² Or, *ordinance.*　　　　　⁴ Or, *to talk with*, ch. 5. 11.

---

35. Jephthah was right in not being deterred from keeping his vow by the loss and sorrow to himself (cp. marg. reff.), just as Abraham was right in not withholding his son, his only son, from God, when commanded to offer him up as a burnt-offering. But Jephthah was wholly wrong in that conception of the character of God which led to his making the rash vow. And he would have done right not to slay his child, though the guilt of making and of breaking such a vow would have remained. Josephus well characterises the sacrifice as "neither sanctioned by the Mosaic law, nor acceptable to God."

36. The touching submission of Jephthah's daughter to an inevitable fate shows how deeply-rooted at that time was the heathen notion of the propriety of human sacrifice.

37. *bewail my virginity*] To become a wife and a mother was the end of existence to an Israelitish maiden. The premature death of Jephthah's daughter was about to frustrate this end.

40. There is no allusion extant elsewhere to this annual lamentation of the untimely fate of Jephthah's daughter. But the poetical turn of the narrative suggests that it may be taken from some ancient song (cp. the marginal note 4).

XII. 1. Cp. the similar complaint of the Ephraimites to Gideon (viii. 1), when a civil war was only avoided by Gideon's wise and patriotic moderation. The overbearing pride of Ephraim comes out in both occurrences (see also Josh. xvii. 14-18).

we will burn thine house upon thee with fire] Cp. the fierce threat of the Philistines to Samson's wife (xiv. 15), and the yet fiercer execution (xv. 6). Burning appears as a mode of capital punishment (Gen. xxxviii. 24; Josh. vii. 25), and as a mode of desperate warfare (i. 8, xx. 48; Josh. viii. 8, 19, &c.).

2. *when I called you*, &c.] This circumstance is not related in the main narrative. It is likely to have occurred when Jephthah was first chosen leader by the Gileadites, and when Ephraim would probably ignore his pretensions.

3. *I put my life in my hands*] Cp. 1 Sam. xix. 5; xxviii. 21. The phrase expresses the utmost possible risk, knowingly incurred.

4 unto me this day, to fight against me? ¶Then Jephthah
gathered together all the men of Gilead, and fought with
Ephraim: and the men of Gilead smote Ephraim, because they
said, Ye Gileadites ^care fugitives of Ephraim among the Eph-
5 raimites, *and* among the Manassites. And the Gileadites took
the ^dpassages of Jordan before the Ephraimites: and it was *so*,
that when those Ephraimites which were escaped said, Let me
go over; that the men of Gilead said unto him, *Art* thou an
6 Ephraimite? If he said, Nay; then said they unto him, Say
now ¹Shibboleth: and he said Sibboleth: for he could not frame
to pronounce *it* right. Then they took him, and slew him at the
passages of Jordan: and there fell at that time of the Ephraim-
7 ites forty and two thousand. ¶And Jephthah judged Israel six
years. Then died Jephthah the Gileadite, and was buried in
8 *one of* the cities of Gilead. ¶And after him ²Ibzan of Beth-
9 lehem judged Israel. And he had thirty sons, and thirty
daughters, *whom* he sent abroad, and took in thirty daughters
from abroad for his sons. And he judged Israel seven years.
10, 11 Then died Ibzan, and was buried at Beth-lehem. ¶And after
him ³Elon, a Zebulonite, judged Israel; and he judged Israel
12 ten years. And Elon the Zebulonite died, and was buried in
13 Aijalon in the country of Zebulun. ¶And after him ⁴Abdon
14 the son of Hillel, a Pirathonite, judged Israel. And he had
forty sons and thirty ⁵nephews, that ^erode on threescore and ten
15 ass colts: and he judged Israel eight years. And Abdon the son
of Hillel the Pirathonite died, and was buried in Pirathon in the
land of Ephraim, ^fin the mount of the Amalekites.

CHAP. **13.** AND the children of Israel ⁶^adid evil again in the sight
of the LORD; ⁷and the LORD delivered them ^binto the hand of

Marginal references:
e See 1 Sam. 25.
10.
Ps. 78. 9.
d Josh. 22.
11.
ch. 3. 28.
& 7. 24.

e ch. 5. 10.
& 10. 4.
f ch. 3. 13,
27. & 5. 14.

a ch. 2. 11.
& 3. 7.
& 4. 1.
& 6. 1.
& 10. 6.
b 1 Sam: ¦¦.
9.

¹ Which signifieth *a*
stream, or, *flood*, Ps. 69.
2, 15. Isai. 27. 12.

^{2, 3, 4} A civil Judge also in
North east *Israel*.
⁵ Heb. *sons' sons*.

⁶ Heb. *added to commit, &c*.
⁷ This seems a partial
captivity.

4. *because they said, &c.*] This passage is
extremely obscure. Render:—" *The men of*
Gilead smote Ephraim, for they (the Gileadites) *said,* **Ye are the fugitives of Ephraim.**
(Gilead lies between Ephraim and
Manasseh; and Gilead took the fords
of Jordan before Ephraim, and it came
to pass, when the fugitives of Ephraim
said Let me pass over, and the Gileadites
asked him, art thou an Ephraimite, and
he answered No, Then (the *Gileadites*) said
to him *say Shibboleth, &c.* So they (the
Gileadites) **slew them at the fords of Jor-**
dan"). All that is included in the parenthesis is explanatory of the brief statement
"They smote them, for they said, Ye are
the fugitives of Ephraim;" *i.e.* in spite of
denial they ascertained that they were the
fugitives of Ephraim, and so pitilessly
slaughtered them when they endeavoured to
return to their own country through Gilead.
This part of Gilead, where the fords were,
was clearly not in Manasseh, but in Gad. *Slew*
(*v.* 6) implies *slaughtering* in cold blood, not
killing in battle (see Jer. xxxix. 6). The
word in the original text is the proper word
for slaying animals for sacrifice.
6. *Shibboleth; and he said Sibboleth*] This
is a curious instance of dialectic difference

of pronunciation between the East and
West Jordanic tribes. It is an evidence of
the sound *sh* having passed into the Hebrew
from the East of Jordan, possibly from the
Arabians, with whom the sound is common.
forty-two thousand] The number includes
the slain in battle and those killed at the fords.
8. *Ibzan of Bethlehem*] Some have fancied
him the same as Boaz (Ruth ii. 1) of Beth-
lehem-Judah. Others, from the juxtaposition of Elon the Zebulonite (*v.* 11), understand Bethlehem in the tribe of Zebulon
(Josh. xix. 15).
11. *a Zebulonite*] The tribe of Zebulon
had shown its bravery, patriotism, and
prowess in the time of Barak (iv. 10, v. 18).
13. *a Pirathonite*] He was, therefore, an
Ephraimite (1 Chr. xxvii. 14). Its name
still lingers in *Feratah*, 6 miles west of
Shechem. The twenty-five years, apparently consecutive, occupied by the judgeship of Ibzan, Elon, and Abdon, seem to
have been very uneventful and prosperous,
since the only record of them, preserved in
the annals of their country, relates to the
flourishing families and peaceful magnificence of two of the number.
XIII. 1. The Philistines have been mentioned as oppressors of Israel in iii. 31, and

2 the Philistines forty years. ¶ And there was a certain man of

e Josh. 15. 33.
d ch. 2. 1.
Luke 1. 11, 13, 28, 31.
e ver. 14.
Num. 6. 2, 3.
Luke 1. 15.
f Num. 6. 5.
1 Sam. 1. 11.
g Num. 6. 2.
h See 1 Sam. 7. 13.
2 Sam. 8. 1.
1 Chr. 18. 1.
i Deut. 33. 1.
1 Sam. 2. 27.
& 9. 6.
1 Kin. 17. 24.
k Matt. 28. 3.
Luke 9. 29.
Acts 6. 15.
l ver. 17, 18.

^eZorah, of the family of the Danites, whose name was Manoah ;
3 and his wife was barren, and bare not. And the ^dangel of the
Lord appeared unto the woman, and said unto her, Behold now,
thou art barren, and bearest not: but thou shalt conceive, and
4 bear a son. Now therefore beware, I pray thee, and ^edrink not
5 wine nor strong drink, and eat not any unclean thing : for, lo,
thou shalt conceive, and bear a son ; and no ^frazor shall come
on his head : for the child shall be ^ga Nazarite unto God from
the womb: and he shall ^hbegin to deliver Israel out of the hand
6 of the Philistines. ¶ Then the woman came and told her husband, saying, ⁱA man of God came unto me, and his ^kcounte-
nance was like the countenance of an angel of God, very terrible :
but I ^lasked him not whence he was, neither told he me his
7 name : but he said unto me, Behold, thou shalt conceive, and
bear a son ; and now drink no wine nor strong drink, neither eat
any unclean thing : for the child shall be a Nazarite to God from
8 the womb to the day of his death. ¶ Then Manoah intreated the
Lord, and said, O my Lord, let the man of God which thou
didst send come again unto us, and teach us what we shall do
9 unto the child that shall be born. And God hearkened to the
voice of Manoah ; and the angel of God came again unto the
woman as she sat in the field : but Manoah her husband was not
10 with her. And the woman made haste, and ran, and shewed her
husband, and said unto him, Behold, the man hath appeared
11 unto me, that came unto me the other day. And Manoah arose,
and went after his wife, and came to the man, and said unto
12 him, Art thou the man that spakest unto the woman ? And he
said, I am. And Manoah said, Now let thy words come to pass.
¹How shall we order the child, and ^{2 3}how shall we do unto him ?
13 And the angel of the Lord said unto Manoah, Of all that I said
14 unto the woman let her beware. She may not eat of any thing

m ver. 4.

that cometh of the vine, ^mneither let her drink wine or strong

¹ Heb. What shall be the manner of the, &c.   ² Or, what shall he do ?   ³ Heb. what shall be his work ?

x. 7, 11; and the Israelite worship of the gods of the Philistines is spoken of in x. 6. But this is the first time that we have any detailed history in connection with the Philistines. They continued to be the pro- minent enemies of Israel till the time of David.

forty years] The Philistine dominion began before the birth of Samson (v. 5), and was in force during Samson's twenty years' judgeship (xiv. 4 ; xv. 20). The forty years are, therefore, about coincident with Sam- son's life.

2. *Zorah*] See marg. ref.

his wife was barren] To mark more dis- tinctly the high providential destiny of the child that was eventually born. Compare the similar circumstances of the birth of Isaac, Jacob, Samuel, and John the Baptist.

5. *a Nazarite*] See marg. ref. and note. The common Nazarite vow was for a limited time, like St. Paul's (Acts xviii. 18, xxi. 23–26). Others, like Samuel (1 Sam. i. 11), were Nazarites for life.

6. *a man of God*] The designation of a Prophet, of frequent use in the Books of Samuel and Kings (1 Sam. ii. 27, ix. 6, 7, 8, 10; 1 K. xii. 22, xiii. 1, 5, 6, 11), and applied to Timothy by St. Paul in the New Test. (1 Tim. vi. 11 ; 2 Tim. iii. 17).

his countenance] Rather, "his appear- ance," as the word is rendered in Dan. x. 18.

12. Translate, "**What shall be the manner** (or *ordering*) **of the child, and what shall be his work** (or *exploits*)." The original message of the Angel had given information on these two points : (1.) how the child was to be brought up, viz. as a Nazarite ; (2.) what he should do, viz. begin to deliver Israel. Manoah desires to have the in- formation repeated (cp. 1 Sam. xvii. 26, 27, 30). Accordingly, in v. 13 the Angel refers to, and enlarges upon, his former in- junctions.

14. Cp. Num. vi. 4. In both passages the vine is described by the somewhat un- usual though more accurate term, *vine of the wine*—the grape-bearing vine—to dis-

drink, nor eat any unclean *thing :* all that I commanded her let
15 her observe. ¶And Manoah said unto the angel of the LORD, I
pray thee, [n]let us detain thee, until we shall have made ready a
16 kid [1]for thee. And the angel of the LORD said unto Manoah,
Though thou detain me, I will not eat of thy bread : and if thou
wilt offer a burnt offering, thou must offer it unto the LORD.
17 For Manoah knew not that he *was* an angel of the LORD. And
Manoah said unto the angel of the LORD, What *is* thy name,
that when thy sayings come to pass we may do thee honour ?
18 And the angel of the LORD said unto him, [o]Why askest thou
19 thus after my name, seeing it *is* [2]secret ? So Manoah took a kid
with a meat offering, [p]and offered *it* upon a rock unto the LORD :
and *the angel* did wondrously ; and Manoah and his wife looked
20 on. For it came to pass, when the flame went up toward heaven
from off the altar, that the angel of the LORD ascended in the
flame of the altar. And Manoah and his wife looked on *it,* and
21 [q]fell on their faces to the ground. But the angel of the LORD
did no more appear to Manoah and to his wife. [r]Then Manoah
22 knew that he *was* an angel of the LORD. ¶And Manoah said
unto his wife, [s]We shall surely die, because we have seen God.
23 But his wife said unto him, If the LORD were pleased to kill us,
he would not have received a burnt offering and a meat offering
at our hands, neither would he have shewed us all these *things,*
nor would as at this time have told us *such things* as these.
24 ¶And the woman bare a son, and called his name [t]Samson :
25 and [u]the child grew, and the LORD blessed him. [x]And the
Spirit of the LORD began to move him at times in [3]the camp of
Dan [y]between Zorah and Esthaol.
CHAP. 14. AND Samson went down [a]to Timnath, and [b]saw a woman
2 in Timnath of the daughters of the Philistines. And he came
up, and told his father and his mother, and said, I have seen a
woman in Timnath of the daughters of the Philistines : now

[n] Gen. 18. 5

[o] Gen. 32. 29.

[p] ch. 6. 19, 20.

[q] Lev. 9. 24. Ezek. 1. 28. Matt. 17. 6.
[r] ch. 6. 22.
[s] Gen. 32. 30. ch. 6. 22.

[t] Heb. 11. 32.
[u] 1 Sam. 3. 19.
Luke 1. 80. & 2. 52.
[x] ch. 3. 10.
1 Sam. 11. 6. Matt. 4. 1.
[y] Josh. 15. 33. ch. 18. 11.
[a] Gen. 38. 13.
[b] Gen. 34. 2.

---

[1] Heb. *before thee.*   [2] Or, *wonderful,* Isa. 9. 6.   [3] Heb. *Mahaneh-dan,* as ch. 18. 12.

---

tinguish it from the wild cucumber vine
(2 K. iv. 39), or other plants to which the
name *vine* was applied.
15. The language of Manoah, like that
of Gideon (vi. 18), seems •to indicate some
suspicion that his visitor was more than
human. The word rendered *made ready,* is
also the proper word for *offering a sacrifice,*
and is so used by the Angel in the next
verse. By which it appears that the Angel
understood Manoah to speak of offering a
kid as a burnt-offering. Hence his caution, "thou must offer it unto the Lord."
(Cp. Rev. xix. 10, xxii. 8 ; Acts x. 25,
26.)
17. *do thee honour*] If applied to a man, it
would be by gifts, such for instance as Balak
promised to the prophet Balaam (Num.
xxii. 17), and such as were usually given
to seers (1 Sam. ix. 7, 8 ; 2 K. v. 5, 15) : if
to God, it would be by sacrifices (Isai. xliii.
23).
18. *secret*] Rather, "**wonderful**," as in
margin. In *v.* 19 the Angel "did wondrously," probably as the Angel that ap-

peared to Gideon had done, bringing fire
from the ock. See marg. reff. and notes.
24. *Samson*] The etymology is doubtful.
Perhaps it comes from a word signifying *to
minister,* in allusion to his Nazaritic consecration to the service of God.
25. *in the camp of Dan*] Rather "Mahaneh-Dan" (see marg.). The impulses
of the Spirit of the Lord perhaps took the
shape of burning indignation at the subjection of his brethren, and thoughts and plans
for their deliverance, but especially showed
themselves in feats of strength (xiv. 6, xv.
14, xvi. 30. Cp. Acts vii. 23–25).
XIV. **1.** *Timnath*] See Josh. xv. 10 and
note. It was below Zorah (xiii. 2), about
three miles S.W. of it.
2. *get her for me*] viz. by paying the requisite dowry (see marg. reff.) and gifts to
relations. Hence the frequent mention of
parents taking wives for their sons (Ex.
xxxiv. 16 ; Neh. x. 30), because the parents of
the bridegroom conducted the negotiation,
and paid the dower to the parents of the
bride.

c Gen. 21. 21.
& 34. 4.
d Gen.24.3,4.
e Gen. 34. 14.
Ex. 34. 16.
Deut. 7. 3.
f Josh.11. 20.
1 Kin. 12. 15.
2 Kin. 6. 33.
2 Chr. 10. 15.
g ch. 13. 1.
Deut. 28. 48.

h ch. 3. 10.
& 13. 25.
1 Sam. 11. 6.

i 1 Kin.10. 1.
Ezek. 17. 2.
Luke 14. 7.
k Gen. 29.27.
l Gen. 45. 22.
2 Kin. 5. 22.

3 therefore *c*get her for me to wife. Then his father and his mother said unto him, *Is there* never a woman among the daughters of *d*thy brethren, or among all my people, that thou goest to take a wife of the *e*uncircumcised Philistines? And Samson said

4 unto his father, Get her for me ; for [1]she pleaseth me well. But his father and his mother knew not that it *was f*of the LORD, that he sought an occasion against the Philistines : for at that

5 time *g*the Philistines had dominion over Israel. ¶ Then went Samson down, and his father and his mother, to Timnath, and came to the vineyards of Timnath : and, behold, a young lion

6 roared [2]against him. And *h*the Spirit of the LORD came mightily upon him, and he rent him as he would have rent a kid, and *he had* nothing in his hand : but he told not his father or his mother

7 what he had done. And he went down, and talked with the

8 woman ; and she pleased Samson well. And after a time he returned to take her, and he turned aside to see the carcase of the lion : and, behold, *there was* a swarm of bees and honey in

9 the carcase of the lion. And he took thereof in his hands, and went on eating, and came to his father and mother, and he gave them, and they did eat : but he told not them that he had taken

10 the honey out of the carcase of the lion. ¶ So his father went down unto the woman : and Samson made there a feast ; for so

11 used the young men to do. And it came to pass, when they saw him, that they brought thirty companions to be with him.

12 ¶ And Samson said unto them, I will now *i*put forth a riddle unto you : if ye can certainly declare it me *k*within the seven days of the feast, and find *it* out, then I will give you thirty [3]sheets and

13 thirty *l*change of garments : but if ye cannot declare *it* me, then shall ye give me thirty sheets and thirty change of garments. And they said unto him, Put forth thy riddle, that we may hear

14 it. And he said unto them,
Out of the eater came forth meat,
And out of the strong came forth sweetness.

---

[1] Heb. *she* is *right in mine eyes.* [2] Heb. *in meeting him.* [3] Or, *shirts.*

---

3. *the uncircumcised Philistines*] Cp. 1 Sam. xiv. 6, xvii. 26, xxxi. 4, for a similar use of the term as one of reproach. Also Acts xi. 3.

4. His father and mother very properly opposed Samson's marriage with a heathen woman, the daughter of the oppressors of his race. But they could not prevail, because it was the secret purpose of God by these means to "seek occasion" against the Philistines ; *i.e.* to make the misconduct of the father of Samson's wife, which He foresaw, the occasion of destruction to the Philistines. Cp. marg. reff. for similar statements.

8. The formal dowry and gifts having been given by Samson's father, an interval, varying according to the Oriental custom, from a few days to a full year, elapsed between the betrothal and the wedding, during which the bride lived with her friends. Then came the essential part of the marriage ceremony, viz. the removal of the bride from her father's house to that of the bridegroom or his father.

the carcase of the lion] The lion, slain by him a year or some months before, had now become a mere skeleton, fit for bees to swarm into. It was a universal notion among the ancients that bees were generated from the carcase of an ox.

10. *made a feast,* &c.] This was the wedding-feast, protracted in this instance seven days, in that of Tobias (Tob. viii. 19) fourteen days. It was an essential part of the marriage ceremony (Gen. xxix. 22 ; Esth. ii. 18 ; Matt. xxii. 2–4 ; Rev. xix. 7, 9).

11. *thirty companions*] These were "the children of the bride-chamber" (Matt. ix. 15; see *v.* 20). From the number of them it may be inferred that Samson's family was of some wealth and importance.

12. See marg. reff. Riddles formed one of the amusements of these protracted feasts.

sheets] Rather *linen shirts ;* the *garments* which follow are the outward garments worn by the Orientals.

14, 15. *three days...on the seventh day*] Proposed alterations, such as *six days...on*

15 And they could not in three days expound the riddle. And it
came to pass on the seventh day, that they said unto Samson's
wife, ^mEntice thy husband, that he may declare unto us the
riddle, ⁿlest we burn thee and thy father's house with fire : have
16 ye called us ¹to take that we have ? *is it* not *so ?* And Samson's
wife wept before him, and said, ^oThou dost but hate me, and
lovest me not : thou hast put forth a riddle unto the children of
my people, and hast not told *it* me. And he said unto her, Behold, I have not told *it* my father nor my mother, and shall I
17 tell *it* thee ? And she wept before him ²the seven days, while
their feast lasted : and it came to pass on the seventh day, that
he told her, because she lay sore upon him : and she told the
18 riddle to the children of her people. And the men of the city
said unto him on the seventh day before the sun went down,
What *is* sweeter than honey ?
And what *is* stronger than a lion ?
And he said unto them, If ye had not plowed with my heifer,
19 ye had not found out my riddle. ¶And ^pthe Spirit of the LORD
came upon him, and he went down to Ashkelon, and slew thirty
men of them, and took their ³spoil, and gave change of garments unto them which expounded the riddle. And his anger
20 was kindled, and he went up to his father's house. But Samson's
wife ^qwas *given* to his companion, whom he had used as ^rhis
friend.

CHAP. 15. BUT it came to pass within a while after, in the time of
wheat harvest, that Samson visited his wife with a kid ; and he
said, I will go in to my wife into the chamber. But her father
2 would not suffer him to go in. And her father said, I verily
thought that thou hadst utterly ^ahated her ; therefore I gave
her to thy companion : *is* not her younger sister fairer than she ?
3 ⁴take her, I pray thee, instead of her. ¶And Samson said concerning them, ⁵Now shall I be more blameless than the Philis-

m ch. 18. 5.
n ch. 15. 6.

c ch. 16. 15.

p ch. 3. 10.
& 13. 25.

q ch. 15. 2.
r John 3. 29.

a ch. 14. 20.

---

¹ Heb. *to possess us*, or, *to
impoverish us?*
² Or, the rest of *the seven*

days, &c.
³ Or, *apparel.*
⁴ Heb. *let her be thine.*

⁵ Or, *Now shall I be blame-
less from the Philistines,
though, &c.*

---

the *fourth day*, are unnecessary if it be
remembered that the narrator passes on
first to the seventh day (at *v.* 15), and then
goes back at *v.* 16 and beginning of *v.* 17
to what happened on the 4th, 5th, and 6th
days.

to take that we have] See marg. They
affirm, that they were only invited to the
wedding for the sake of plundering them by
means of this riddle, and if Samson's wife
was a party to plundering her own countrymen, she should suffer for it.

18. They try to give the answer in a way
to make it appear that they had guessed it.
Samson saw at once that she had betrayed
him. He lets them know in a speech,
which was of the nature of a riddle, that
he had discovered the treachery.

20. *his companion*] Perhaps one of those
mentioned in *v.* 11. The transaction denotes loose notions of the sanctity of marriage among the Philistines. It should be
noted carefully that the practical lesson
against ungodly marriages comes out most
strongly in this case and that the provi-

dential purpose which out of this evil
brought discomfiture to the Philistines, has
nothing to do with the right or wrong of
Samson's conduct.

XV. **1.** *visited his wife with a kid*] A
common present (see Gen. xxxviii. 17 ;
Luke xv. 29). From Samson's wife being
still in her father's house, it would seem
that she was only betrothed, not actually
married, to his companion.

2. *I gave her*] In marriage. Samson had
probably not heard of this before. Samson's father had paid the dowry for the
elder sister ; her father therefore offers her
sister in her room. The fear of Samson
probably also influenced him.

3. See marg. Before, when the Philistines injured him he was in covenant with
the Timnathites through his marriage and
by the rites of hospitality ; for which reason
he went off to Ashkelon to take his revenge
(xiv. 19). But now the Philistines themselves had broken this bond, and so he was
free to take his revenge on the spot.

4 tines, though I do them a displeasure. And Samson went and caught three hundred foxes, and took ¹firebrands, and turned tail to tail, and put a firebrand in the midst between two tails.
5 And when he had set the brands on fire, he let *them* go into the standing corn of the Philistines, and burnt up both the shocks,
6 and also the standing corn, with the vineyards *and* olives. Then the Philistines said, Who hath done this? And they answered, Samson, the son in law of the Timnite, because he had taken his

ᵇ ch. 14. 15.　wife, and given her to his companion. *ᵇ*And the Philistines
7 came up, and burnt her and her father with fire. ¶ And Samson said unto them, Though ye have done this, yet will I be avenged
8 of you, and after that I will cease. And he smote them hip and thigh with a great slaughter: and he went down and dwelt in
9 the top of the rock Etam. ¶ Then the Philistines went up, and

ᶜ ver. 19.　10 pitched in Judah, and spread themselves *ᶜ*in Lehi. And the men of Judah said, Why are ye come up against us? And they answered, To bind Samson are we come up, to do to him as he
11 hath done to us. Then three thousand men of Judah ²went to the top of the rock Etam, and said to Samson, Knowest thou not

ᵈ ch. 14. 4.　that the Philistines *are ᵈ*rulers over us? what *is* this *that* thou hast done unto us? And he said unto them, As they did unto
12 me, so have I done unto them. And they said unto him, We are come down to bind thee, that we may deliver thee into the hand of the Philistines. And Samson said unto them, Swear
13 unto me, that ye will not fall upon me yourselves. And they spake unto him, saying, No; but we will bind thee fast, and deliver thee into their hand: but surely we will not kill thee.

---

¹ Or, *torches.*　　　　　　² Heb. *went down.*

---

4. *foxes*] Rather, *jackals*, which are still very common in Palestine, especially about Joppa and Gaza. 1 Sam. xiii. 17 and Josh. xv. 28, xix. 3, are indications of the abundance of foxes or jackals giving names to places, especially in the country of the Philistines. It belongs to Samson's character, and agrees with the incident about the lion, that he should be an expert hunter. Ovid relates a very curious custom at Rome of letting loose foxes with lighted torches fastened to their tails in the circus at the Cerealia, in commemoration of the damage once done to the standing corn by a fox which a rustic had wrapped in hay and straw and set on fire, and which, running away, put the corn-fields in a blaze. This custom, which may have had a Phœnician origin, is a curious illustration of the narrative.

6. *burnt her and her father*] Out of revenge on Samson's nearest relations; or, as others think, as an act of justice in favour of Samson, and in hope of pacifying his anger. Burning was the punishment for adultery and kindred crimes among the Jews (Gen xxxviii. 24; Lev. xx. 14, xxi. 9). Samson's wife brought upon herself the very punishment which she sought to escape by betraying her husband (xiv. 15).

8. *hip and thigh*] A proverbial expression of doubtful origin, meaning all the *great* and

mighty, all the choice pieces like the thigh and shoulder.

in the top of the rock] Rather, "**the cleft of the rock.**" These **clefts** of the rock were the natural fortresses and hiding-places of the land. (Isai. ii. 21, lvii. 5. Cp. 1 Sam. xiii. 6 ; 1 K. xviii. 13.)

Etam] Not the same as the place in the territory of Simeon (1 Chr. iv. 32). Its situation is uncertain, but a site near Eleutheropolis (*Beth-jibrin*) is required; and there exist some extraordinary caverns in the soft limestone or chalky rock, fifteen or twenty feet deep, with perpendicular sides, opening into extensive excavations in the rock, about two hours from Eleutheropolis. [Conder conjectures it to be the same as Atab, a village 12 miles S.W. of Jerusalem, in the 'Arkûb or Ridge.]

9. *spread themselves*] An expression used of the Philistine mode of war (2 Sam. v. 18, 22), alluding to the compact way in which they came up the wadys, and then dispersed. Lehi is so called by anticipation (see *v.* 17).

11. The dispirited men of Judah were prepared to give up their champion, in order to conciliate their masters. This shows how hard was the task of the Judge, whose office it was to restore his countrymen to freedom and independence.

And they bound him with two new cords, and brought him up
14 from the rock. *And* when he came unto Lehi, the Philistines
shouted against him : and ^ethe Spirit of the LORD came mightily
upon him, and the cords that *were* upon his arms became as flax
that was burnt with fire, and his bands ¹loosed from off his
15 hands. And he found a ²new jawbone of an ass, and put forth
his hand, and took it, and ^fslew a thousand men therewith.
16 And Samson said,
   With the jawbone of an ass, ³heaps upon heaps,
   With the jaw of an ass have I slain a thousand men.
17 And it came to pass, when he had made an end of speaking,
that he cast away the jawbone out of his hand, and called that
18 place ⁴Ramath-lehi. ¶And he was sore athirst, and called on
the LORD, and said, ^gThou hast given this great deliverance into
the hand of thy servant : and now shall I die for thirst, and fall
19 into the hand of the uncircumcised ? But God clave an hollow
place that *was* in ⁵the jaw, and there came water thereout ; and
when he had drunk, ^hhis spirit came again, and he revived :
wherefore he called the name thereof ⁶En-hakkore, which *is* in
20 Lehi unto this day. ¶⁷And he judged Israel ⁱin the days of the
Philistines twenty years.

CHAP. 16. THEN went Samson to Gaza, and saw there ^san harlot,
2 and went in unto her. *And it was told* the Gazites, saying,
Samson is come hither. And they ^acompassed *him* in, and laid
wait for him all night in the gate of the city, and were ⁹quiet all
the night, saying, In the morning, when it is day, we shall kill
3 him. And Samson lay till midnight, and arose at midnight,
and took the doors of the gate of the city, and the two posts, and
went away with them, ¹bar and all, and put *them* upon his

Margin references:
- *e* ch. 3. 10. & 14. 6.
- *f* Lev. 26. 8. Josh. 23. 10. ch. 3. 31. 2 Sam. 23. 8—12.
- *g* Ps. 3. 7.
- *h* Gen. 45. 27.
- *6* Isai. 40. 29.
- *i* ch. 13. 1.
- *a* 1 Sam. 23. 26. Ps. 118. 10, 11, 12. Acts 9. 24.

---

¹ Heb. *were melted.*
² Heb. *moist.*
³ Heb. *an heap, two heaps.*
⁴ That is, *The lifting up of the jawbone,* or, *casting away of the jawbone.*
⁵ Or, *Lehi:*
⁶ That is, *The well of him that called,* or, *cried,* Ps. 34. 6.
⁷ He seems to have judged South west Israel dur-
ing twenty years of
their servitude of the
Philistines.
⁸ Heb. *a woman an harlot.*
⁹ Heb. *silent.*
¹ Heb. *with the bar.*

---

14. *the cords...became as flax,* &c.] *i.e.*
were as weak against his strength as half-
burnt flax which yields to the least pressure.

15. *slew a thousand men therewith*] Cp.
marg. reff. The Philistines, seized with a
panic at seeing Samson suddenly burst his
cords and rush at them, offered no resistance, but fell an easy prey to the blows of
their mighty foe. Some perhaps were
dashed down the cliffs in their flight.

16. There is a play upon the word, three
times repeated, which means both " an
ass " and also "a heap." The spirit of
riddle-making (xiv. 12, 18) is apparent in
this song of triumph (cp. v. 1 ; Ex. xv. 1 ;
1 Sam. xviii. 6, 7).

17. *Ramath-lehi*] Either the *height or hill*
of Lehi, or, *of the jaw-bone ;* or, as in margin,
the casting away of the jaw-bone, with allusion
to Samson casting it out of his hand, when
he had finished his war-song.

19. *an hollow place that was in the jaw*]
The right translation is, " **the hollow place**
which is in Lehi." The word translated

" hollow place," means *a mortar* (Prov.
xxvii. 22), and is here evidently a hollow or
basin among the cliffs of Lehi, which, from
its shape, was called "the mortar." A spring,
on the way from Socho to Eleutheropolis,
was commonly called Samson's spring in the
time of St. Jerome and writers in the 7th,
12th, and 14th centuries.

XVI. 1. *Gaza*] About 8 hours from
Eleutheropolis, and one of the chief strongholds of the Philistines.

3. Instead of forcing the doors open, he
tore the posts up, as it were, by the roots,
with the barred doors attached to them.
The word rendered " *went away with them,*"
means "to pluck up the tent-pins," and
hence " to remove." The present town of
Gaza (Ghuzzeh) is an open town, without
gates or walls, but the sites of the ancient
gates still remain visible. One of these, on
the south-east, is shown as the gate carried
off by Samson.

A partially-isolated hill, about half-an-
hour south-east of Gaza, and standing out
from the chain that runs up to Hebron,

shoulders, and carried them up to the top of an hill that *is*
4 before Hebron. ¶And it came to pass afterward, that he loved a
5 woman ¹in the valley of Sorek, whose name *was* Delilah. And
the lords of the Philistines came up unto her, and said unto her,
*b*Entice him, and see wherein his great strength *lieth*, and by
what *means* we may prevail against him, that we may bind him
to ²afflict him: and we will give thee every one of us eleven
6 hundred *pieces* of silver. ¶And Delilah said to Samson, Tell me,
I pray thee, wherein thy great strength *lieth*, and wherewith
7 thou mightest be bound to afflict thee. And Samson said unto
her, If thou bind me with seven ³ ⁴green withs that were never
8 dried, then shall I be weak, and be as ⁵another man. Then the
lords of the Philistines brought up to her seven green withs
9 which had not been dried, and she bound him with them. Now
there were men lying in wait, abiding with her in the chamber.
And she said unto him, The Philistines *be* upon thee, Samson.
And he brake the withs, as a thread of tow is broken when it
10 ⁶toucheth the fire. So his strength was not known. ¶And
Delilah said unto Samson, Behold, thou hast mocked me, and
told me lies: now tell me, I pray thee, wherewith thou mightest
11 be bound. And he said unto her, If they bind me fast with new
ropes ⁷that never were occupied, then shall I be weak, and be as
12 another man. Delilah therefore took new ropes, and bound him
therewith, and said unto him, The Philistines *be* upon thee,
Samson. And *there were* liers in wait abiding in the chamber.
13 And he brake them from off his arms like a thread. ¶And
Delilah said unto Samson, Hitherto thou hast mocked me, and
told me lies: tell me wherewith thou mightest be bound. And
he said unto her, If thou weavest the seven locks of my head
14 with the web. And she fastened *it* with the pin, and said unto
him, The Philistines *be* upon thee, Samson. And he awaked out
of his sleep, and went away with the pin of the beam, and with
15 the web. ¶And she said unto him, *c*How canst thou say, I
love thee, when thine heart *is* not with me? thou hast mocked
me these three times, and hast not told me wherein thy great
16 strength *lieth*. And it came to pass, when she pressed him
17 daily with her words, and urged him, *so* that his soul was
⁸vexed unto death; that he *d*told her all his heart, and said

b ch. 14. 15.
See Prov.
2. 16—19.
& 5. 3—11.
& 6. 24, 25,
26.
& 7. 21, 22,
23.

c ch. 14. 16.

d Mic. 7. 5.

---

¹ Or, *by the brook*.
² Or, *humble*.
³ Or, *new cords*.
⁴ Heb. *moist*.
⁵ Heb. *one*.
⁶ Heb. *smelleth*.
⁷ Heb. *wherewith work hath
not been done*.
⁸ Heb. *shortened*.

---

bears the name of "Samson's Mount." But
it may be doubted whether one of the hills
overlooking Hebron is not rather meant.

4. A village to the north of Eleutheropolis, called Caphar-Sorek, was still existing
in the time of Eusebius, near Zorah.

5. *and the lords of the Philistines*] See iii.
3 note.

his great strength lieth] Rather, "**wherein
his strength is great.**"

eleven hundred pieces of silver] The greatness of the bribe offered to Delilah, 5,500
shekels of silver, nearly two talents (Ex.
xxxviii. 24 note), shows the importance attached to Samson's capture.

11. *occupied*] The margin, "**wherewith
work hath not been done**," is better.

14. *and she fastened it with the pin*, &c.]
The meaning of the verses seems to be that
the seven long plaits, in which Samson's
hair was arranged, were to be woven as a
woof into the threads of a warp which stood
prepared on a loom in the chamber, which
loom Delilah fastened down with a pin, so
as to keep it firm and immoveable. But
Samson, when he awoke, tore up the pin
from its socket, and went away with the
loom and the pin fastened to his hair.

the beam] Rather, the "**loom**," or *frame*.
The beam is the wooden revolving cylinder,
on which the cloth is rolled as fast as it is
woven, the Hebrew word for which (1 Sam.
xvii. 7; 1 Chr. xi. 23, xx. 5) is quite different from that here used.

unto her, *There hath not come a razor upon mine head; for I
have been a Nazarite unto God from my mother's womb: if I be
shaven, then my strength will go from me, and I shall become
18 weak, and be like any *other* man. ¶ And when Delilah saw that
he had told her all his heart, she sent and called for the lords of
the Philistines, saying, Come up this once, for he hath shewed
me all his heart. Then the lords of the Philistines came up
19 unto her, and brought money in their hand. *And she made
him sleep upon her knees; and she called for a man, and she
caused him to shave off the seven locks of his head; and she
20 began to afflict him, and his strength went from him. And she
said, The Philistines *be* upon thee, Samson. And he awoke out
of his sleep, and said, I will go out as at other times before, and
shake myself. And he wist not that the LORD *was departed
21 from him. But the Philistines took him, and ¹put out his eyes,
and brought him down to Gaza, and bound him with fetters of
22 brass; and he did grind in the prison house. Howbeit the hair
23 of his head began to grow again ²after he was shaven. ¶ Then
the lords of the Philistines gathered them together for to offer
a great sacrifice unto Dagon their god, and to rejoice: for they
said, Our god hath delivered Samson our enemy into our hand.
24 And when the people saw him, they *praised their god: for they
said, Our god hath delivered into our hands our enemy, and the
25 destroyer of our country, ³which slew many of us. And it came
to pass, when their hearts were ⁴merry, that they said, Call for
Samson, that he may make us sport. And they called for
Samson out of the prison house; and he made ⁴them sport: and
26 they set him between the pillars. And Samson said unto the
lad that held him by the hand, Suffer me that I may feel the
pillars whereupon the house standeth, that I may lean upon
27 them. Now the house was full of men and women; and all the

* Num. 6. 5,
ch. 13. 5.

f Prov. 7. 26;
27.

g Num. 14.
9, 42, 43.
Josh. 7. 12.
1 Sam.16.14.
& 18. 12.
& 28. 15. 16.
2 Chr. 15. 2.

h Dan. 5. 4.

i ch. 9. 27.

¹ Heb. *bored out.*
² Or, *as when he was shaven.*
³ Heb. *and who multiplied our slain.*
⁴ Heb. *before them.*

20. The possession of his extraordinary strength is ascribed (*e.g.* xiii. 25) to the Presence of the Spirit of the Lord. Now the Lord, or the Spirit of the Lord, had departed from him, and so his strength had gone too. The practical lesson against the presumption of self-dependence, and the all-importance of a hearty dependence upon God's Holy Spirit, must not be overlooked.

21. *put out his eyes*] Thus effectually, as they thought, preventing any future mischief on his part, while they prolonged their own triumph and revenge. (Cp. Num. xvi. 14; 2 K. xxv. 7; Jer. xxxix. 7.)

They applied to the two feet fetters of brass (2 Sam. iii. 34; Jer. lii. 11), and made him "grind"—the special task of slaves and captives (Ex. xi. 5; Isai. xlvii. 2; Lam. v. 13).

23. Dagon was the national idol of the Philistines (1 Chr. x. 10), so called from Dag, a fish. The description of Dagon, in his temple at Ashdod (1 Sam. v. 4), exactly agrees with the representations of a fish-god on the walls of Khorsabad, on slabs at

Kouyunjik, and on sundry antique cylinders and gems. In these the figures vary. Some have a human form down to the waist, with that of a fish below the waist; others have a human head, arms, and legs, growing, as it were, out of a fish's body, and so arranged that the fish's head forms a kind of mitre to the man's head, while the body and fins form a kind of cloak, hanging down behind.

24. *Our God*, &c.] A portion of the Philistine triumphal song. Cp. ch. v., Ex. xv.

25. *that he may make us sport*] Rather, "that he may play for us," *i.e.* dance and make music. At an idolatrous feast, dancing was always accompanied with vocal and instrumental music.

26. More literally, "let me rest, and let me feel the pillars, that I may lean upon them." He feigned weariness with his dancing and singing, and asked to recover himself by leaning against the pillars. The flat roof, from the top of which, as well as under it, spectators could see what was being done on the stage in front, was mainly supported by two pillars. The lords and

k Deut. 22. 8.   lords of the Philistines *were* there; and *there were* upon the *k*roof
about three thousand men and women, that beheld while Samson
28 made sport. And Samson called unto the LORD, and said, O
l Jer. 15. 15.   Lord GOD, *l*remember me, I pray thee, and strengthen me, I
pray thee, only this once, O God, that I may be at once avenged
29 of the Philistines for my two eyes. And Samson took hold of
the two middle pillars upon which the house stood, and ¹on
which it was borne up, of the one with his right hand, and of
30 the other with his left. And Samson said, Let ²me die with the
Philistines. And he bowed himself with *all his* might: and the
house fell upon the lords, and upon all the people that *were*
therein. So the dead which he slew at his death were more than
31 *they* which he slew in his life. ¶Then his brethren and all the
house of his father came down, and took him, and brought *him*
m ch. 13. 25.   up, and *m*buried him between Zorah and Eshtaol in the burying
place of Manoah his father. And he judged Israel twenty
years.
CHAP. 17. AND there was a man of mount Ephraim, whose name
2 *was* Micah. And he said unto his mother, The eleven hundred
shekels of silver that were taken from thee, about which thou
cursedst, and spakest of also in mine ears, behold, the silver *is*
a Gen. 14. 19.   with me; I took it. And his mother said, *a*Blessed *be thou* of
Ruth 3. 10.   3 the LORD, my son. And when he had restored the eleven
hundred *shekels* of silver to his mother, his mother said, I had
wholly dedicated the silver unto the LORD from my hand for my
b See Exod.   son, to *b*make a graven image and a molten image: now there-
20. 4, 23.   4 fore I will restore it unto thee. Yet he restored the money unto
Lev. 19. 4.   his mother; and his mother *c*took two hundred *shekels* of silver,
c Isai. 46. 6.   and gave them to the founder, who made thereof a graven image
and a molten image: and they were in the house of Micah.
d ch. 8. 27.   5 And the man Micah had an house of gods, and made an *d*ephod,
e Gen. 31. 19,   and *e*teraphim, and ³consecrated one of his sons, who became
30.
Hos. 3. 4.
¹ Or, *he leaned on them.*   ² Heb. *my soul.*   ³ Heb. *filled the hand*, Ex.
29. 9. 1 Kin. 13. 33.

---

principal persons sat *under* the roof, while
the people, to the number of 3000, stood *on*
the flat roof. When the pillars were removed, the weight of 3000 people brought
the roof down with a fearful crash, and
those above fell together with the stones
and timbers upon those below, and a great
slaughter was the result, Samson himself
perishing under the ruins.
28. *at once avenged*] *i.e. with one final re-*
venge. These words do not breathe the
spirit of the Gospel, but they express a sentiment, natural to the age, knowledge, and
character of Samson.
31. "All the house of his father," in connection with "his brethren," must mean
the whole tribe of Dan, aiding his nearer
relations. The Danites, taking advantage
of the consternation of the Philistines, and
of the death of their lords and chief men,
went down in force to Gaza, and recovered the body of their great captain
and Judge, and buried him in his father's
sepulchre.

XVII. See Introduction, p. 68. The
only point of contact with the preceding
history of Samson is, that we are still concerned with the tribe of Dan. See xviii.
1, 2, note. Josephus combines in one narrative what we read here and in i. 34, and
places it, with the story in chapters xviii. -
xxi., immediately after the death of Joshua.
2. *thou cursedst*] or, *adjuredst me by* God.
Cp. Matt. xxvi. 63; Levit. v. 1.
3. Such a superstitious and unlawful
mode of worshipping Jehovah is quite of a
piece with viii. 27, xi. 31; 1 K. xii. 28, &c.
It argues but slight acquaintance with the
Ten Commandments, which, from the ignorance of reading and writing, were probably
not familiar to the Israelites in those unsettled times. The mother intimates that the
consecration of the silver was for the benefit
of her son and his house, not for her own
selfish advantage: and that she adheres to
her original design of consecrating this silver
for her son's benefit.
4. See viii. 27; Gen. xxxi. 19 notes.

6 his priest. ʲIn those days *there was* no king in Israel, ᵍ*but*
7 every man did *that which was* right in his own eyes. ¶ And
there was a young man out of ʰBeth-lehem-judah of the family
8 of Judah, who *was* a Levite, and he sojourned there. And the
man departed out of the city from Beth-lehem-judah to sojourn
where he could find *a place*: and he came to mount Ephraim to
9 the house of Micah, ¹as he journeyed. And Micah said unto
him, Whence comest thou? And he said unto him, I *am* a
Levite of Beth-lehem-judah, and I go to sojourn where I may
10 find *a place*. And Micah said unto him, Dwell with me, ⁱand be
unto me a ᵏfather and a priest, and I will give thee ten *shekels* of
silver by the year, and ²³a suit of apparel, and thy victuals. So
11 the Levite went in. And the Levite was content to dwell with
the man; and the young man was unto him as one of his sons.
12 And Micah ˡconsecrated the Levite; and the young man ᵐbe-
13 came his priest, and was in the house of Micah. Then said
Micah, Now know I that the LORD will do me good, seeing I
have a Levite to *my* priest.

CHAP. 18. IN ᵃthose days *there was* no king in Israel: and in those
days ᵇthe tribe of the Danites sought them an inheritance to
dwell in; for unto that day *all their* inheritance had not fallen
2 unto them among the tribes of Israel. And the children of Dan
sent of their family five men from their coasts, ⁴men of valour,
from ᶜZorah, and from Eshtaol, ᵈto spy out the land, and to
search it; and they said unto them, Go, search the land: who
when they came to mount Ephraim, to the ᵉhouse of Micah,
3 they lodged there. When they *were* by the house of Micah, they
knew the voice of the young man the Levite: and they turned
in thither, and said unto him, Who brought thee hither? and
4 what makest thou in this *place?* and what hast thou here? And
he said unto them, Thus and thus dealeth Micah with me, and
5 hath ʲhired me, and I am his priest. And they said unto
him, ᵍAsk counsel, we pray thee, ʰof God, that we may know
6 whether our way which we go shall be prosperous. And the
priest said unto them, ⁱGo in peace: before the LORD *is* your

¹ Heb. *in making his way.* ³ Heb. *an order of gar-* ⁴ Heb. *sons.*
² Or, *a double suit, &c.* *ments.*

Side notes: ʲch. 18. 1. & 19. 1. & 21. 25. Deut. 33. 5. ᵍDeut. 12. 8. ʰSee Josh. 19. 15. Ruth 1. 1. Mic. 5. 2. Matt. 2. 1. ⁱch. 18. 19. ᵏGen. 45. 8. Job 29. 16. ˡver. 5. ᵐch. 18, 30. ᵃch. 17. 6. & 21. 25. ᵇJosh. 19. 47. ᶜch. 13. 25. ᵈNum. 13. 17. Josh. 2. 1. ᵉch. 17. 1. ʲch. 17. 10. ᵍ1 Kin. 22. 5. Isai. 30. 1. Hos. 4. 12. ʰSeech.17.5. & ver. 14. ⁱ1 Kin. 22. 6.

6. *In those days,* &c.] This phrase, indicating distinctly that the writer lived after the establishment of the kingly government in Israel, is peculiar to the author of these last five chapters.

7. The Hebrew words for "*he sojourned there*" are, GER-SHOM, which words are used (xviii. 30) in the genealogy of this young Levite, whose name was "Jonathan, the son of Gershom." Hence some read here, "the son of Gershom."

8. Jonathan's state without a home gives us a vivid picture of what must have been the condition of many Levites.

10. *ten shekels*] About 25s. to 26s. (see Ex. xxxviii. 24).

13. This shows the ignorance as well as the superstition of the age (cp. 2 K. xviii. 22), and gives a picture of the lawlessness of the times. The incidental testimony to the Levitical priesthood is to be noted; but the idolatrous worship in the immediate neighbourhood of Shiloh is passing strange.

XVIII. 2. This identity of locality with the scene of Samson's birth and death indicates that both narratives are drawn from the same source, probably the annals of the tribe of Dan.

3. It does not follow that they had known him before, and recognized his voice, though it may be so. But the Hebrew equally bears the sense that they heard the voice of the Levite; and, attracted by it, went into the chapel (*v.* 18) where Jonathan was. They were probably just starting on their journey, but were still within the court or precincts of Micah's house. Micah had evidently not told them of his house of God, and his Levite. Their questions indicate surprise.

5. The sight of the ephod and teraphim suggested the notion of enquiring of God.

6. *before the* LORD, &c.] *i.e.* He looks favourably upon it. (Cp. Ezr. viii. 21, 22.)

7 way wherein ye go. ¶ Then the five men departed, and came to
k Josh. 19. 47, called *Leshem.* *k*Laish, and saw the people that *were* therein, *l*how they dwelt careless, after the manner of the Zidonians, quiet and secure :
l ver. 27, 28. and *there was* no ¹magistrate in the land, that might put *them* to shame in *any* thing; and they *were* far from the Zidonians, 8 and had no business with *any* man. And they came unto their
m ver. 2. brethren to *m*Zorah and Eshtaol : and their brethren said unto
n Num.13.30. Josh. 2. 23, 24. 9 them, What *say* ye ? And they said, *n*Arise, that we may go up against them : for we have seen the land, and, behold, it *is* very good : and *are* ye *o*still ? be not slothful to go, *and* to enter to
o 1 Kin. 22. 3. 10 possess the land. When ye go, ye shall come unto a people
p ver. 7, 27. *p*secure, and to a large land ; for God hath given it into your
q Deut. 8. 9. hands ; *q*a place where *there is* no want of any thing that *is* in 11 the earth. ¶ And there went from thence of the family of the Danites out of Zorah and out of Eshtaol, six hundred men *²*ap-12 pointed with weapons of war. And they went up, and pitched
r Josh. 15. 60. in *r*Kirjath-jearim, in Judah : wherefore they called that place
s ch. 13. 25. *s*Mahaneh-dan unto this day : behold, *it is* behind Kirjath-13 jearim. And they passed thence unto mount Ephraim, and
t ver. 2. *u* 1 Sam. 14. 28. 14 came unto *t*the house of Micah. *u*Then answered the five men that went to spy out the country of Laish, and said unto their
x ch. 17. 5. brethren, Do ye know that *x*there is in these houses an ephod, and teraphim, and a graven image, and a molten image ? now 15 therefore consider what ye have to do. And they turned thither-ward, and came to the house of the young man the Levite, *even*
y ver. 11. 16 unto the house of Micah, and ³saluted him. And the *y*six hun-dred men appointed with their weapons of war, which *were* of 17 the children of Dan, stood by the entering of the gate. And
z ver. 2, 14. *a* ch. 17. 4, 5. *z*the five men that went to spy out the land went up, *and* came in thither, *and* took *a*the graven image, and the ephod, and the teraphim, and the molten image : and the priest stood in the entering of the gate with the six hundred men *that were* ap-18 pointed with weapons of war. And these went into Micah's house, and fetched the carved image, the ephod, and the tera-
b Job 21. 5. & 29. 9. & 40. 4. phim, and the molten image. Then said the priest unto them, 19 What do ye ? And they said unto him, Hold thy peace, *b*lay
Prov. 30. 32. Mic. 7. 16. ¹ Heb. *possessor,* or, *heir of restraint.* ² Heb. *girded.* ³ Heb. *asked him of peace,* Gen. 43. 27. 1 Sam. 17. 22.

---

7. *Laish*] Afterwards called *Dan* (*v.* 29). The exact site has not been identified, but it was the northern extremity of Israel, near the sources of the Jordan, and about four miles from Panium, or Cæsarea-Philippi. It is thought to have stood where the village Tell-el-Kadi now stands.

after the manner of the Zidonians] The genius of the Zidonians being mechanical and commercial, not military, their colonists were apt to neglect fortifications and similar warlike precautions. In Solomon's time the Zidonians were especially skilful in hewing timber (1 K. v. 6 ; 1 Chr. xxii. 4), and it is highly probable, from their proximity to Lebanon, that such was the occupation of the men of Laish.

quiet and secure, &c.] This is a very obscure and difficult passage. Translate thus : " **Quiet and secure, and none of them do-**

ing any injury in the land, possessing **wealth,**" or *dominion.*

12. *Kirjath-jearim*] " City of forests," otherwise called " Kirjath-Baal " (marg. ref.), identified by Robinson with the modern *Kurit-el-Enab,* on the road from Jaffa to Jerusalem [and by Conder with Sôba].

14. *in these houses*] This agrees with what we saw at *vv.* 2 and 3 that the " house of God " and Jonathan's house were detached from Micah's. There were other houses besides (*v.* 22). The whole settle-ment was probably called Beth-Micah, contained in one court, and entered by one gate (*v.* 16).

17. The five went back to Micah's chapel (Micah's house, *v.* 18) and took the ephod, teraphim, &c., and brought them to the gate where the priest was talking to the six hundred men.

thine hand upon thy mouth, and go with us, ^cand be to us a   ^c ch. 17. 10.
father and a priest : *is it* better for thee to be a priest unto the
house of one man, or that thou be a priest unto a tribe and a
20 family in Israel ? And the priest's heart was glad, and he took
the ephod, and the teraphim, and the graven image, and went
21 in the midst of the people. So they turned and departed, and
put the little ones and the cattle and the carriage before them.
22 ¶ *And* when they were a good way from the house of Micah,
the men that *were* in the houses near to Micah's house were
23 gathered together, and overtook the children of Dan. And
they cried unto the children of Dan. And they turned their
faces, and said unto Micah, What aileth thee, ¹that thou comest
24 with such a company ? And he said, Ye have taken away my
gods which I made, and the priest, and ye are gone away : and
what have I more ? and what *is* this *that* ye say unto me, What
25 aileth thee ? And the children of Dan said unto him, Let not
thy voice be heard among us, lest ²angry fellows run upon thee,
26 and thou lose thy life, with the lives of thy household. And the
children of Dan went their way : and when Micah saw that they
were too strong for him, he turned and went back unto his house.
27 And they took *the things* which Micah had made, and the priest   ^d ver. 7, 10.
which he had, and ^dcame unto Laish, unto a people *that were*   Deut. 33. 22.
at quiet and secure : ^eand they smote them with the edge of the   ^e Josh.19.47.
28 sword, and burnt the city with fire. And *there was* no deliverer,   ^f ver. 7.
because it *was* ^ffar from Zidon, and they had no business with   ^g 2 Sam. 10.
any man ; and it was in the valley that *lieth* ^gby Beth-rehob.   6.
29 ¶And they built a city, and dwelt therein. And ^hthey called   ^h Josh. 19.
  - the name of the city ⁱDan, after the name of Dan their father,   47.
who was born unto Israel : howbeit the name of the city *was*   ⁱ Gen. 14. 14.
30 Laish at the first. And the children of Dan set up the graven   ch. 20. 1.
image : and Jonathan, the son of Gershom, the son of Manasseh,   1 Kin. 12.
he and his sons were priests to the tribe of Dan ^kuntil the day   29, 30.
31 of the captivity of the land. And they set them up Micah's   ^k ch. 13. 1.
graven image, which he made, ^lall the time that the house of   1 Sam. 4. 2,
God was in Shiloh.   3, 10, 11.
Ps. 78. 60.
^l Josh. 18. 1.
ch. 19. 18.

¹ Heb. *that thou art gathered together?*   ² Heb. *bitter of soul,* 2 Sam. 17. 8.

---

21. *and put the little ones,* &c., *before them*]
They expected a pursuit from Micah's
people, and arranged their order of march
accordingly.
the carriage] Rather, " *the valuables.*"
Some interpret it " the heavy baggage."
22. *were gathered together*] Literally, "were
called together." The men, who were all
Micah's workmen, were probably in the
fields with their master at the time of the
robbery. When the women saw what was
done they gave the alarm, and Micah called
the men together as quickly as possible,
and pursued the Danites and overtook
them.
27. *the things which Micah had made*]
Rather, from *v.* 24, "**the gods which Micah had made.**" See *v.* 31 ; Deut. xxvii.
15 ; Ex. xx. 4.
28. Rehob (as Dan afterwards) is mentioned as the northernmost point of the
land of Canaan (Num. xiii. 21), and its po-

sition is defined with reference to the entering in of Hamath.
a city] Rather, "**the** " *city.* They rebuilt
Laish, which they had burnt down (*v.* 29).
30. In the Hebrew text the name here
rendered MANASSEH is written M SH.
Without the N suspended over the line, the
word may be read MOSES, whose son was
Gershom (Ex. ii. 22), whose son or descendant
Jonathan clearly was. The Masoretes, probably grieved that a descendant of Moses
should have been implicated in idolatrous
worship, adopted this expedient for disguis-
ing the fact without absolutely falsifying
the text. The Vulgate has *Moses,* the Septuagint *Manasses.*
Verses 30, 31, seem to tell us that Jonathan's descendants were priests to the tribe
of Dan till the captivity (2 K. xv. 29, xvii.
6) ; and that the graven image was in
their custody till David's time, by whose

CHAP. 19. AND it came to pass in those days, *a*when *there was* no king in Israel, that there was a certain Levite sojourning on the side of mount Ephraim, who took to him [1]a concubine out of 2 *b*Beth-lehem-judah. And his concubine played the whore against him, and went away from him unto her father's house to Beth-lehem-judah, and was there [2][3]four whole months. 3 ¶ And her husband arose, and went after her, to speak [4]friendly unto her, *and* to bring her again, having his servant with him, and a couple of asses: and she brought him into her father's house: and when the father of the damsel saw him, he rejoiced 4 to meet him. And his father in law, the damsel's father, retained him ; and he abode with him three days : so they did eat 5 and drink, and lodge there. And it came to pass on the fourth day, when they arose early in the morning, that he rose up to depart : and the damsel's father said unto his son in law, [5]*c*Comfort thine heart with a morsel of bread, and afterward go your 6 way. And they sat down, and did eat and drink both of them together : for the damsel's father had said unto the man, Be content, I pray thee, and tarry all night, and let thine heart be 7 merry. And when the man rose up to depart, his father in law 8 urged him : therefore he lodged there again. And he arose early in the morning on the fifth day to depart : and the damsel's father said, Comfort thine heart, I pray thee. And they 9 tarried [6]until afternoon, and they did eat both of them. And when the man rose up to depart, he, and his concubine, and his servant, his father in law, the damsel's father, said unto him, Behold, now the day [7]draweth toward evening, I pray you tarry all night : behold, [8]the day groweth to an end, lodge here, that thine heart may be merry ; and to morrow get you early on your 10 way, that thou mayest go [9]home. But the man would not tarry that night, but he rose up and departed, and came [1]over against *d*Jebus, which *is* Jerusalem ; and *there were* with him two asses 11 saddled, his concubine also *was* with him. ¶ *And* when they *were* by Jebus, the day was far spent ; and the servant said unto his master, Come, I pray thee, and let us turn in into this city *e*of 12 the Jebusites, and lodge in it. And his master said unto him, We will not turn aside hither into the city of a stranger, that *is* 13 not of the children of Israel ; we will pass over *f*to Gibeah. And

[1] Heb. *a woman a concubine*, or, *a wife a concubine*.
[2] Or, *a year* and *four months*.
[3] Heb. *days four months*.
[4] Heb. *to her heart*, Gen. 34. 3.
[5] Heb. *strengthen*.
[6] Heb. *till the day declined*.
[7] Heb. *is weak*.
[8] Heb. it is *the pitching time of the day*.
[9] Heb. *to thy tent*.
[1] Heb. *to over against*.

order, perhaps, it was destroyed, though the idolatrous worship continued, or was revived, at Dan.

XIX. This history has no connexion whatever with the preceding. The note of time (xx. 28) shows that the date of it is in the lifetime of the first generation of settlers in Canaan.

1. *a concubine*] See marg. The name does not imply any moral reproach. A concubine was as much the man's wife as the woman so called, though she had not the same rights. See *vv*. 3, 4.

2. *played the whore against him*] Perhaps only meaning that she ran away from him,

and left him ; for she returned to her father's house.

9. This is a perfect picture of the manners of the time. It is probable that the father showed more than usual hospitality, in order to ensure the kind treatment of his daughter by her husband. These particulars are given to account for their journey running so far into the evening, which was the immediate cause of the horrible catastrophe which followed.

12. *city of a stranger*] This shows how completely, even in these early days, the Jebusite population had excluded both the tribes of Judah and Benjamin.

he said unto his servant, Come, and let us draw near to one of
14 these places to lodge all night, in Gibeah, or in *g*Ramah. And
they passed on and went their way; and the sun went down
upon them *when they were* by Gibeah, which *belongeth* to Benja-
15 min. And they turned aside thither, to go in *and* to lodge in
Gibeah: and when he went in, he sat him down in a street of
the city: for *there was* no man that *h*took them into his house to
16 lodging. ¶And, behold, there came an old man from *i*his work
out of the field at even, which *was* also of mount Ephraim; and
he sojourned in Gibeah: but the men of the place *were* Benja-
17 mites. And when he had lifted up his eyes, he saw a wayfaring
man in the street of the city: and the old man said, Whither
18 goest thou? and whence comest thou? And he said unto him,
We *are* passing from Beth-lehem-judah toward the side of
mount Ephraim; from thence *am* 1: and I went to Beth-lehem-
judah, but I *am now* going to *k*the house of the LORD; and
19 there *is* no man that *l*receiveth me to house. Yet there is both
straw and provender for our asses: and there is bread and wine
also for me, and for thy handmaid, and for the young man *which*
20 *is* with thy servants: *there is* no want of any thing. And the
old man said, *l*Peace be with thee; howsoever *let* all thy wants
21 *lie* upon me; *m*only lodge not in the street. *n*So he brought him
into his house, and gave provender unto the asses: *o*and they
22 washed their feet, and did eat and drink. ¶*Now* as they were
making their hearts merry, behold, *p*the men of the city, certain
*q*sons of Belial, beset the house round about, *and* beat at the
door, and spake to the master of the house, the old man, saying,
*r*Bring forth the man that came into thine house, that we may
23 know him. And *s*the man, the master of the house, went out
unto them, and said unto them, Nay, my brethren, *nay*, I pray
you, do not *so* wickedly; seeing that this man is come into mine
24 house, *t*do not this folly. *u*Behold, here *is* my daughter a
maiden, and his concubine; them I will bring out now, and
*x*humble ye them, and do with them what seemeth good unto
25 you: but unto this man do not ²so vile a thing. But the men
would not hearken to him: so the man took his concubine, and
brought her forth unto them; and they *y*knew her, and abused
her all the night until the morning: and when the day began to
26 spring, they let her go. Then came the woman in the dawning of the day, and fell down at the door of the man's house
27 where her lord *was*, till it was light. And her lord rose up in
the morning, and opened the doors of the house, and went out
to go his way: and, behold, the woman his concubine was fallen
down *at* the door of the house, and her hands *were* upon the
28 threshold. And he said unto her, Up, and let us be going. But

g Josh. 18. 25.

h Matt. 25. 43.
Heb. 13. 2.
i Ps. 104. 23.

k Josh. 18. 1.
ch. 18. 31.
& 20. 18.
1 Sam. 1. 3, 7.

i Gen. 43. 23.
ch. 6. 23.
m Gen. 19. 2.
n Gen. 24. 32.
o Gen. 18. 4.
John 13. 5.
p Gen. 19. 4.
ch. 20. 5.
Hos. 9. 9.
q Deut. 13. 13.
r Gen. 19. 5.
Rom. 1. 26.
s Gen. 19. 6.
t 2 Sam. 13.
12.
u Gen. 19. 8.
x Gen. 34. 2.
Deut. 21. 14.

y Gen. 4. 1.

---

¹ Heb. *gathereth*, ver. 15.   ² Heb. *the matter of this folly.*

---

14. *Gibeah, which belongeth to Benjamin*]
See Josh. xviii. 24 note.

15. *a street*] Probably the square or place
within the gates, where courts were held,
bargains made, and where the chief men
and strangers congregated.

16. *which was also of Mount Ephraim*] i.e.,
of the country of the Levite. This single
giver of hospitality was himself a stranger
and sojourner at Gibeah.

18. *the house of the* LORD] Probably at
Shiloh (marg. reff.). The Levite was pro-

bably one of those who ministered at the
Tabernacle. His two asses and servant
show him to have been in good circumstances, and he had a home of his own.

23. *this man is come into mine house*] He
appeals to the sacred rights of hospitality,
just as Lot did (Gen. xix. 8). Both cases
betray painfully the low place in the social
scale occupied by woman in the old world,
from which it is one of the glories of Christianity to have raised her.

ᶻ ch. 20. 5.

ᵃ ch. 20. 6.

ᵇ ch. 20. 7.
Prov. 13. 10.
ᵃ Deut. 13. 12.
Josh. 22. 12.
ch. 21. 5.
ᵇ ch. 18. 29.
1 Sam. 3. 20.
ᶜ ch. 10. 17.
& 11. 11.
ᵈ ch. 8. 10.

ᵉ ch. 19. 15.
ᶠ ch. 19. 22.

ᵍ ch. 19. 25, 26.
ʰ ch. 19. 29.

ⁱ Josh. 7. 15.

ᵏ ch. 19. 30.

ᶻnone answered. Then the man took her *up* upon an ass, and 29 the man rose up, and gat him unto his place. ¶And when he was come into his house, he took a knife, and laid hold on his concubine, and ᵃdivided her, *together* with her bones, into twelve 30 pieces, and sent her into all the coasts of Israel. And it was so, that all that saw it said, There was no such deed done nor seen from the day that the children of Israel came up out of the land of Egypt unto this day : consider of it, ᵇtake advice, and speak *your minds*.

CHAP. 20. THEN ᵃall the children of Israel went out, and the congregation was gathered together as one man, from ᵇDan even to Beer-sheba, with the land of Gilead, unto the LORD ᶜin 2 Mizpeh. And the chief of all the people, *even* of all the tribes of Israel, presented themselves in the assembly of the people of 3 God, four hundred thousand footmen ᵈthat drew sword. (Now the children of Benjamin heard that the children of Israel were gone up to Mizpeh.) ¶Then said the children of Israel, Tell *us*, 4 how was this wickedness? And ¹the Levite, the husband of the woman that was slain, answered and said, ᵉI came into Gibeah 5 that *belongeth* to Benjamin, I and my concubine, to lodge. ᶠAnd the men of Gibeah rose against me, and beset the house round about upon me by night, *and* thought to have slain me : ᵍand 6 my concubine have they ²forced, that she is dead. And ʰI took my concubine, and cut her in pieces, and sent her throughout all the country of the inheritance of Israel : for they ⁱhave com-7 mitted lewdness and folly in Israel. Behold, ye *are* all children 8 of Israel ; ᵏgive here your advice and counsel. ¶And all the people arose as one man, saying, We will not any *of* us go to 9 his tent, neither will we any *of* us turn into his house. But now this *shall be* the thing which we will do to Gibeah ; *we will* 10 *go up* by lot against it ; and we will take ten men of an hundred

---

¹ Heb. *the man the Levite.*   ² Heb. *humbled.*

---

29. *a knife*] Rather, " **the** " *knife*. The single household implement used, not like our knives at our meals, but for slaughtering and cutting up the animals into joints for eating (Gen. xxii. 6, 10 ; Prov. xxx. 14).

together with her bones, &c.] Rather, *into her bones*, or *bone by bone*, *into twelve pieces*. The *pieces* are synonymous with the *bones* (cp. Ezek. xxiv. 4, 5). There is something truly terrible in the stern ferocity of grief and indignation which dictated this desperate effort to arouse his countrymen to avenge his wrong. Cp. 1 Sam. xi. 7.

XX. 1. The *congregation* is the technical term for the whole community of the Israelitish people. Its occurrence here is an indication of the early date of these transactions.

from Dan to Beer-sheba] We cannot safely infer from this expression that the settlement of Dan, recorded in ch. xviii. had taken place at this time. It only proves that in the writer's time, from Dan to Beersheba was a proverbial expression for all Israel (cp. marg. ref.).

with the land of Gilead] Meaning all the trans-Jordanic tribes ; mentioned particularly, both to show that the whole congrega-

tion of the children of Israel, in its widest meaning, took part in the council, and also because of Jabesh-Gilead (xxi. 8, 10).

unto the LORD *in Mizpeh*] The phrase *unto the Lord*, implies the presence of the Tabernacle (xi. 11 note). Mizpeh in Benjamin (Josh. xviii. 26), from its connexion with Bethel and Ramah, is probably meant here. It is the same as that which appears as a place of nationa. assembly in 1 Sam. vii. 5, x. 17; 2 K. xxv. 23-25. It must have been near Shiloh and Gibeah, and in the north of Benjamin. The Benjamites were duly summoned with the other tribes; so that their absence was contumacious (*v.* 3).

2. *the chief*] Literally, "*the corner stones.*" (Cp. 1 Sam. xiv. 38.)

8. They bound themselves not to break up and disperse till they had punished the wickedness of Gibeah.

9. *by lot*] To determine who should go up first (*v.* 18). The shape of the ground probably made it impossible for the whole force to operate at once ; and the question of spoil would have something to do with the arrangement. (Cp. 1 Sam. xxx. 22-25.)

10. In order to make it possible for the

throughout all the tribes of Israel, and an hundred of a thousand, and a thousand out of ten thousand, to fetch victual for the people, that they may do, when they come to Gibeah of Benjamin, according to all the folly that they have wrought in
11 Israel. So all the men of Israel were gathered against the city,
12 ¹knit together as one man. ¶ ˡAnd the tribes of Israel sent men through all the tribe of Benjamin, saying, What wicked-
13 ness is this that is done among you? Now therefore deliver us the men, ᵐthe children of Belial, which are in Gibeah, that we may put them to death, and ⁿput away evil from Israel. But the children of Benjamin would not hearken to the voice of
14 their brethren the children of Israel: but the children of Benjamin gathered themselves together out of the cities unto Gibeah,
15 to go out to battle against the children of Israel. And the children of Benjamin were numbered at that time out of the cities twenty and six thousand men that drew sword, beside the inhabitants of Gibeah, which were numbered seven hundred
16 chosen men. Among all this people there were seven hundred chosen men ᵒlefthanded; every one could sling stones at an
17 hair breadth, and not miss. And the men of Israel, beside Benjamin, were numbered four hundred thousand men that drew
18 sword: all these were men of war. ¶ And the children of Israel arose, and ᵖwent up to the house of God, and �q asked counsel of God, and said, Which of us shall go up first to the battle against the children of Benjamin? And the LORD said, Judah
19 shall go up first. And the children of Israel rose up in the
20 morning, and encamped against Gibeah. And the men of Israel went out to battle against Benjamin; and the men of Israel put themselves in array to fight against them at Gibeah.
21 And ʳthe children of Benjamin came forth out of Gibeah, and destroyed down to the ground of the Israelites that day twenty
22 and two thousand men. ¶ And the people the men of Israel encouraged themselves, and set their battle again in array in the place where they put themselves in array the first day.
23 (ˢAnd the children of Israel went up and wept before the LORD

l Deut.13.14. Josh. 22. 13, 16.

m Deut. 13. 13. ch. 19. 22. *n* Deut. 17. 12.

o 1 Chr. 12. 2.

p ver. 23, 26. *q* Num.27.21. ch. 1. 1.

r Gen. 49. 27.

s ver. 26, 27.

¹ Heb. *fellows*.

---

force of Israel to keep the field, and do to the men of Gibeah what their wickedness deserved, every tenth man (forty thousand in all) was appointed to find provisions for the whole army.

15-17. Comparing the numbers here with those in Num. i. and xxvi., it is seen that in the case both of the Benjamites and the Israelites the numbers are diminished by about one-third, *i.e.* they appear as about two-thirds only of what they were at the last numbering in the plains of Moab. This diminution seems to indicate disturbed and harassing times. With this agrees the mention of the cities, as containing the whole Benjamite population. The inference is that the open country and unwalled villages were not safe, but that the Benjamites kept the Canaanites in subjection only by dwelling in fortified towns.

16. See iii. 15, and note. In the LXX. and Vulg. the seven hundred chosen men of

Gibeah are represented as the seven hundred left-handed slingers.

18. *went up to the house of God*] It should be "**to Bethel.**" At this time the Ark was at Bethel (cp. 1 Sam. x. 3), and not at Shiloh. It is not unlikely that though Shiloh was the chief residence of the Ark (Jer. vii. 12), yet the Tabernacle, being moveable, was, either at stated times, or as occasion required, moved to where the Judge resided, or the congregation assembled (cp. 1 Sam. vii. 16). On the present occasion the Ark may have been moved to Bethel for the convenience of proximity to the great national council at Mizpeh.

21. Gibeah, being on a hill, was difficult of access to an attacking army, and gave great advantage to the defenders, who fought from higher ground, and probably defended a narrow pass, while their companions on the walls could gall the assailants with their slingstones.

until even, and asked counsel of the LORD, saying, Shall I go up again to battle against the children of Benjamin my brother? 24 And the LORD said, Go up against him.) And the children of Israel came near against the children of Benjamin the second

t ver. 21. 25 day. And *t*Benjamin went forth against them out of Gibeah the second day, and destroyed down to the ground of the children of Israel again eighteen thousand men; all these drew the 26 sword. ¶ Then all the children of Israel, and all the people,

u ver. 18. *u*went up, and came unto the house of God, and wept, and sat there before the LORD, and fasted that day until even, and offered burnt offerings and peace offerings before the LORD.

x Josh. 18. 1.
1 Sam. 4. 3,
4.
y Josh. 24.
33.
z Deut. 10.
8. & 18. 5.

27 And the children of Israel enquired of the LORD, (for *x*the ark 28 of the covenant of God *was* there in those days, *y*and Phinehas, the son of Eleazar, the son of Aaron, *z*stood before it in those days,) saying, Shall I yet again go out to battle against the children of Benjamin my brother, or shall I cease? And the LORD said, Go up; for to morrow I will deliver them into thine hand.

a So Josh.
8. 4.

29, 30 ¶ And Israel *a*set liers in wait round about Gibeah. And the children of Israel went up against the children of Benjamin on the third day, and put themselves in array against Gibeah, as 31 at other times. And the children of Benjamin went out against the people, *and* were drawn away from the city; and they began *1*to smite of the people, *and* kill, as at other times, in the highways, of which one goeth up to *2*the house of God, and the 32 other to Gibeah in the field, about thirty men of Israel. And the children of Benjamin said, They *are* smitten down before us, as at the first. But the children of Israel said, Let us flee, and 33 draw them from the city unto the highways. And all the men of Israel rose up out of their place, and put themselves in array at Baal-tamar: and the liers in wait of Israel came forth out of 34 their places, *even* out of the meadows of Gibeah. And there came against Gibeah ten thousand chosen men out of all Israel,

b Josh. 8. 14.
Isai. 47. 11.

and the battle was sore: *b*but they knew not that evil *was* near 35 them. And the LORD smote Benjamin before Israel: and the children of Israel destroyed of the Benjamites that day twenty and five thousand and an hundred men: all these drew the 36 sword. ¶ So the children of Benjamin saw that they were

---

1 Heb. *to smite of the people wounded as at, &c.*   *2* Or, *Beth-el.*

---

26. *fasted until even*] The regular time for ending a fast among the Hebrews was sunset (cp. 1 Sam. xiv. 24 ; 2 Sam. i. 12). Such national fasts are called by the Rabbis *fasts of the congregation,* and were enjoined in times of great affliction. On the offerings, see Lev. i., iii.

28. *Phinehas, the son of Eleazar,* &c.] A most important chronological statement, which makes it probable that these events occurred within twenty years of the death of Joshua.

to-morrow] The two former answers only bade them go up against Benjamin ; now, for the first time, the promise is added, "To-morrow," &c. (cp. Josh. viii. 1).

29. The stratagem described is exactly that by which Joshua took Ai (marg. ref.).

31. *to the house of God*] "To Bethel," as in the margin.

On "Gibeah in the field," see Josh. xviii. 24 note.

33. Baal-tamar is only mentioned here. It took its name from some palm-tree that grew there ; perhaps the same as the "palm-tree of Deborah, between Ramah and Bethel" (iv. 5), the exact locality here indicated, since "the highway" (*v.* 31) along which the Israelites enticed the Benjamites to pursue them, leads straight to Ramah, which lay only a mile beyond the point where the two ways branch off.

the meadows of Gibeah] The word rendered *meadow* is only found here. According to its etymology, it ought to mean a *bare open place,* which is particularly unsuitable for an ambush. But by a change in the vowel-points, without any alteration in the letters, it becomes the common word for a *cavern.*

smitten : ^cfor the men of Israel gave place to the Benjamites, c Josh. 8. 15.
because they trusted unto the liers in wait which they had set
37 beside Gibeah. ^dAnd the liers in wait hasted, and rushed upon d Josh. 8. 19.
Gibeah; and the liers in wait ¹drew *themselves* along, and smote
38 all the city with the edge of the sword. Now there was an
appointed ²sign between the men of Israel ³and the liers in
wait, that they should make a great ⁴flame with smoke rise up
39 out of the city. And when the men of Israel retired in the
battle, Benjamin began ⁵to smite *and* kill of the men of Israel
about thirty persons: for they said, Surely they are smitten
40 down before us, as *in* the first battle. But when the flame
began to arise up out of the city with a pillar of smoke, the
Benjamites ^elooked behind them, and, behold, ⁶the flame of the e Josh. 8. 20.
41 city ascended up to heaven. And when the men of Israel turned
again, the men of Benjamin were amazed: for they saw that
42 evil ⁷was come upon them. Therefore they turned *their backs*
before the men of Israel unto the way of the wilderness; but
the battle overtook them; and them which *came* out of the cities
43 they destroyed in the midst of them. *Thus* they inclosed the
Benjamites round about, *and* chased them, and ^ftrode them f Jer. 51. 33.
down ⁸with ease ⁹over against Gibeah toward the sunrising.
44 And there fell of Benjamin eighteen thousand men; all these
45 *were* men of valour. And they turned and fled toward the wilderness unto the rock of Rimmon: and they gleaned of them in
the highways five thousand men; and pursued hard after them
46 unto Gidom, and slew two thousand men of them. So that all
which fell that day of Benjamin were twenty and five thousand
47 men that drew the sword; all these *were* men of valour. ^gBut g ch. 21. 13.
six hundred men turned and fled to the wilderness unto the
rock Rimmon, and abode in the rock Rimmon four months.
48 And the men of Israel turned again upon the children of Benjamin, and smote them with the edge of the sword, as well as the

¹ Or, *made a long* sound with the trumpet, Josh. 6. 5.	³ Heb. *with.*	tion.
² Or, *time.*	⁴ Heb. *elevation.*	⁷ Heb. *touched them.*
	⁵ Heb. *to smite the wounded.*	⁸ Or, *from Menuchah, &c.*
	⁶ Heb. *the whole consump-*	⁹ Heb. *unto over against.*

---

42. *the way of the wilderness*] *i.e.* the wilderness which extended from Jericho to the
hills of Bethel.

them which came out of the cities] These
must be the Benjamites (*v.* 15). Hence,
" *in the midst of them* " must mean *in their
own cities*, whither they severally fled for
refuge, but failed to find shelter (*v.* 48).
Anathoth, Alemath, Ramah, Ataroth,
Geba, Michmash, Ai, Bethel, Migron, &c.,
would probably be the cities meant, all
lying east and north of Gibeah.

43. The language and construction of
this verse is poetical; it seems to be an extract from a song, and to describe, in the
language of poetry, the same event which
the preceding verse described in that of
prose.

with ease] Or *rest* (Num. x. 33; Ps. xcv.
11). The expression is very obscure. The
margin takes it as the name of a place.

45. *Rimmon*] A village named *Rummon*,
situated on the summit of a conical chalky
hill, still exists, and forms a remarkable

object in the landscape, visible in all directions. It lies 15 miles north of Jerusalem.
It is a different place from Rimmon in the
south of Judah (Josh. xv. 32), and Remmon
in Zebulon (Josh. xix. 13). Gidom, mentioned nowhere else, was evidently close to
Rimmon.

46. In *v.* 35 the number given is 25,100.
Verses 44—46 give the details of the loss on
that day: 18,000, 5,000, and 2,000; in all
25,000. But as the Benjamites numbered
26,700 men (*v.* 15), and 600 escaped to the
rock of Rimmon, it is clear that 1,100 are
unaccounted for, partly from no account
being taken of those who fell in the battles
of the two first days, partly from the use of
round numbers, or from some other cause.
The numbers given both here and in *v.* 35 are
expressly restricted to those who fell on *that*
(the third) *day.*

48. They treated Benjamin as devoted to
utter destruction, as Jericho had been (Josh.
vi. 17, 21), and the whole tribe was all but
actually extirpated. We see in the punish-

men of *every* city, as the beast, and all that [1] came to hand : also they set on fire all the cities that [2] they came to.

a ch. 20. 1.

CHAP. 21. NOW *a*the men of Israel had sworn in Mizpeh, saying, There shall not any of us give his daughter unto Benjamin to

b ch. 20. 18, 26.

2 wife. And the people came *b*to the house of God, and abode there till even before God, and lifted up their voices, and wept
3 sore ; and said, O LORD God of Israel, why is this come to pass in Israel, that there should be to day one tribe lacking in Israel?
4 And it came to pass on the morrow, that the people rose early,

c 2 Sam. 24. 25.

and *c*built there an altar, and offered burnt offerings and peace
5 offerings. ¶ And the children of Israel said, Who *is there* among all the tribes of Israel that came not up with the congregation

d ch. 5. 23.

unto the LORD ? *d*For they had made a great oath concerning him that came not up to the LORD to Mizpeh, saying, He shall
6 surely be put to death. And the children of Israel repented them for Benjamin their brother, and said, There is one tribe
7 cut off from Israel this day. How shall we do for wives for them that remain, seeing we have sworn by the LORD that we
8 will not give them of our daughters to wives ? ¶ And they said, What one *is there* of the tribes of Israel that came not up to Mizpeh to the LORD ? And, behold, there came none to the

e 1Sam.11.1. & 31. 11.

9 camp from *e*Jabesh-gilead to the assembly. For the people were numbered, and, behold, *there were* none of the inhabitants of
10 Jabesh-gilead there. And the congregation sent thither twelve thousand men of the valiantest, and commanded them, saying,

f ver. 5. & ch. 5. 23. 1 Sam. 11. 7. *g* Num. 31. 17.

*f*Go and smite the inhabitants of Jabesh-gilead with the edge of
11 the sword, with the women and the children. And this *is* the thing that ye shall do, *g*Ye shall utterly destroy every male, and
12 every woman that [3]hath lain by man. And they found among the inhabitants of Jabesh-gilead four hundred [4]young virgins, that had known no man by lying with any male : and they

h Josh. 18. 1.

brought them unto the camp to *h*Shiloh, which *is* in the land of
13 Canaan. ¶ And the whole congregation sent *some* [5]to speak to

i ch. 20.47.

the children of Benjamin *i*that *were* in the rock Rimmon, and to
14 [6] call peaceably unto them. And Benjamin came again at that

[1] Heb. *was found.*	[3] Heb. *knoweth the lying*	[5] Heb. *and spake and called.*
[2] Heb. *were found.*	with *man.*	[6] Or, *proclaim peace,* Deut.
	[4] Heb. *young women virgins.*	20. 10.

ment inflicted the same ferocity which marked both the crime and the Levite's mode of requiring vengeance.

XXI. **2.** *to the house of God*] It should be, "**to Bethel.**" See xx. 18.

3. The repetition of the name of Israel is very striking in connexion with the title of Jehovah as *God of Israel.* It contains a very forcible pleading of the Covenant, and memorial of the promises. The very name "Israel" comprehended all the twelve tribes ; with one of them blotted out, the remnant would not be Israel.

4. It is not certain whether the brazen Altar was at Bethel at this time, or whether it may not have been elsewhere, *e.g.,* at Shiloh with the Tabernacle. Some, however, think that the Altar here mentioned was *additional* to the brazen Altar, in consequence of the unusual number of sacrifices

caused by the presence of the whole congregation (cp. 1 K. viii. 64 note).

8. *Jabesh-Gilead*] Is here mentioned for the first time. (See marg. reff.) The name of Jabesh survives only in the Wady Yabes (running down to the east bank of the Jordan), near the head of which are situated the ruins called Ed-Deir, which are identified with Jabesh-Gilead.

10. *And the congregation sent 12,000 men*] A thousand from each tribe ; they followed the precedent of Num. xxxi. 4.

11. *Ye shall utterly destroy*] More exactly, "**Ye shall devote to utter destruction,**" or *cherem* (Lev. xxvii. 28 note).

12. *to Shiloh*] Whither, as the usual place of meeting for the national assembly, the Israelites had moved from Bethel (a distance of about 10 miles), during the expedition of the 12,000 to Jabesh-Gilead.

time; and they gave them wives which they had saved alive of
the women of Jabesh-gilead : and yet so they sufficed them not.
15 And the people *k*repented them for Benjamin, because that the   *k* ver. 6.
16 LORD had made a breach in the tribes of Israel. ¶Then the
elders of the congregation said, How shall we do for wives for
them that remain, seeing the women are destroyed out of Ben-
17 jamin. And they said, *There must be* an inheritance for them
that be escaped of Benjamin, that a tribe be not destroyed out of
18 Israel. Howbeit we may not give them wives of our daughters:
*l*for the children of Israel have sworn, saying, Cursed *be* he that   *l* ver. 1.
19 giveth a wife to Benjamin. Then they said, Behold, *there is* a   ch. 11. 35.
feast of the LORD in Shiloh ¹yearly *in a place* which *is* on the
north side of Beth-el, ²on the east side ³of the highway that
goeth up from Beth-el to Shechem, and on the south of Lebonah.
20 Therefore they commanded the children of Benjamin, saying,
21 Go and lie in wait in the vineyards; and see, and, behold, if the
daughters of Shiloh come out *m*to dance in dances, then come ye   *m* See
out of the vineyards, and catch you every man his wife of the   Exod. 15. 20.
22 daughters of Shiloh, and go to the land of Benjamin. And it   ch. 11. 34.
shall be, when their fathers or their brethren come unto us to   1 Sam. 18. 6.
complain, that we will say unto them, ⁴Be favourable unto them   Jer. 31. 13.
for our sakes : because we reserved not to each man his wife in
the war : for ye did not give unto them at this time, *that* ye
23 should be guilty. And the children of Benjamin did so, and
took *them* wives, according to their number, of them that
danced, whom they caught : and they went and returned unto
their inheritance, and *n*repaired the cities, and dwelt in them.   *n* See ch.
24 And the children of Israel departed thence at that time, every   20. 48.
man to his tribe and to his family, and they went out from
25 thence every man to his inheritance. ¶*o*In those days *there was*   *o* ch. 17. 6.
no king in Israel: *p*every man did *that which was* right in his   & 18. 1.
own eyes.   & 19. 1.
     p Deut. 12. 8.
     ch. 17. 6.

¹ Heb. *from year to year.*   ³ Or, *on.*
² Or, *toward the sunrising.*   ⁴ Or, *gratify us in them.*

---

18. *for the children of Israel have sworn*]
See *v.* 1. Cp. Saul's rash oath (1 Sam. xiv.
24), and his breach of the oath made to the
Gideonites (2 Sam. xxi. 2). For the guilt
of a broken oath, see Ezek. xvii. 15-20 ; Ex.
xx. 7.
19. The Feast was probably the Passover,
or one of the three great Jewish Feasts. In
these unsettled times men went up to Shiloh
(Seilun) only once a year (1 Sam. i. 3) instead of thrice ; only the males kept the
Feasts, and therefore the virgins of Shiloh
would naturally be the only maidens present, and the public festival would be a
likely occasion for their festive dances. It
is, however, possible that some particular
feast peculiar to Shiloh is meant, like the
yearly sacrifice of David's family in Beth-
lehem (1 Sam. xx. 29).
22. *ye did not give*, &c.] *i.e.* they had not
broken the oath mentioned in *v.* 1, so as to

be guilty of taking the Lord's name in vain.
They did not give their daughters to Benjamin : the Benjamites had taken them
by force. Such casuistry as this condemns
the system of oaths, and illustrates the
wisdom of our Lord's precept (Matt. v.
33-37).
23. Cp. the very similar account of the
rape of the Sabine women by the Roman
youths at the festival of the Consualia, as
related by Livy.
25. The repetition of this characteristic
phrase (cp. xvii. 6, xviii. 1, xix. 1) is probably intended to impress upon us the idea
that these disorders arose from the want of
a sufficient authority to suppress them. The
preservation of such a story, of which the
Israelites must have been ashamed, is a
striking evidence of the Divine superintendence and direction as regards the Holy
Scriptures.

RUTH.

INTRODUCTION.

THE Book of Ruth is historically important as giving the lineage of David through the whole period of the rule of the Judges (i. 1), *i.e.* from Salmon who fought under Joshua, to "Jesse the Bethlehemite" (1 Sam. xvi. 1) ; and as illustrating the ancestry of "Jesus Christ, the son of David," who "was born in Bethlehem of Judea" (Matt. i. 1, ii. 1). The care with which this narrative was preserved through so many centuries before the birth of Christ is a striking evidence of the Providence of God, that "known unto God are all His works from the beginning of the world." The genealogy with which the Book closes (iv. 18), is also an important contribution to the chronology of Scripture history. We learn from it, with great distinctness, that Salmon, one of the conquering host of Joshua, was the grandfather of Obed, who was the grandfather of king David ; in other words, that four generations, or about 200 years, span the "days when the Judges ruled."

But the Book has another interest, from the charming view it gives us of the domestic life of pious Israelites even during the most troubled times. Had we only drawn our impressions from the records of violence and crime contained in the Book of Judges, we should have been ready to conclude that all the gentler virtues had fled from the land, while the children of Israel were alternately struggling for their lives and liberties with the tribes of Canaan, or yielding themselves to the seductions of Canaanite idolatry. But the Book of Ruth, lifting up the curtain which veiled the privacy of domestic life, discloses to us most beautiful views of piety, integrity, self-sacrificing affection, chastity, gentleness and charity, growing up amidst the rude scenes of war, discord, and strife.

The Book, from its contents, as anciently by its place in the Canon, belongs to the Book of Judges, and is a kind of appendix to it. In the present Hebrew Bible it is placed among the *Cethubim* or *Hagiographa*, in the group containing Song of Solomon, Ruth, Lamentations, Ecclesiastes, and Esther ; but in the Greek Septuagint and the Latin Vulgate it occupies the same place as in our English Bibles, which was its ancient place in the Hebrew Bible.

The language of the Book is generally pure Hebrew. But there are words of Chaldee form and origin,[1] and other expressions peculiar to the later Hebrew. The inference would be that the Book of Ruth was composed not before the later times of the Jewish monarchy ;

---

[1] *E.g.*, the originals of the verbs *go, abide fast* (ii. 8), *lay thee down, thou shalt do* (iii. 4), *put, get thee down* (iii. 3), *confirm* (iv. 7) ; the word translated twice *for them* but meaning *therefore* (i. 13), *Mara* (i. 20).

and this inference is somewhat strengthened by the way in which the writer speaks of the custom which prevailed *in former time* in Israel (iv. 7). Other expressions, which the Book has in common with the Books of Samuel and Kings, and a certain similarity of narrative, tend to place it upon about the same level of antiquity with those Books.[2]

The Books of the Old Testament, to the contents of which reference seems to be made in the Book of Ruth, are Judges, Leviticus, Deuteronomy, Genesis, 1 and 2 Samuel, and perhaps Job. Ruth is not quoted or referred to in the New Testament, except that the generations from Hezron to David in our Lord's genealogy seem to be taken from it.

No mystical or allegorical sense can be assigned to the history; but Ruth, the Moabitess, was undoubtedly one of the first fruits of the ingathering of Gentiles into the Church of Christ, and so an evidence of God's gracious purpose in Christ, "also to the Gentiles to grant repentance unto life;" and the important evangelical lesson is as plainly taught in her case, as in that of Cornelius, "that God is no respecter of persons, but in every nation he that feareth God, and worketh righteousness, is accepted of Him." The great doctrine of Divine Grace is also forcibly taught by the admission of Ruth, the Moabitess, among the ancestry of our Lord Jesus Christ.

---

[2] *E. g.*, originals of *Such a one* (iv. 1); *the Lord do so to me, and more also* (i. 17); *the beginning of barley harvest* (i. 22); *lifted up their voice and wept* (i. 9, 14); *blessed be he of the Lord* (ii. 20).

THE BOOK

OF

RUTH.

CHAP. 1. NOW it came to pass in the days when *a*the judges
¹ruled, that there was *b*a famine in the land. And a certain
man of *c*Beth-lehem-judah went to sojourn in the country of
2 Moab, he, and his wife, and his two sons. And the name of the
man *was* Elimelech, and the name of his wife Naomi, and the
name of his two sons Mahlon and Chilion, *d*Ephrathites of Beth-
lehem-judah. And they came *e*into the country of Moab, and
3 ²continued there. ¶And Elimelech Naomi's husband died; and
4 she was left, and her ' two sons. And they took them wives of
the women of Moab; the name of the one *was* Orpah, and the
name of the other Ruth: and they dwelled there about ten
5 years. And Mahlon and Chilion died also both of them; and
6 the woman was left of her two sons and her husband. ¶Then
she arose with her daughters in law, that she might return from
the country of Moab: for she had heard in the country of Moab
how that the LORD had *f*visited his people in *g*giving them
7 bread. Wherefore she went forth out of the place where she
was, and her two daughters in law with her; and they went on
8 the way to return unto the land of Judah. And Naomi said
unto her two daughters in law, *h*Go, return each to her mother's
house: *i*the LORD deal kindly with you, as ye have dealt with
9 *k*the dead, and with me. The LORD grant you that ye may find
*l*rest, each *of you* in the house of her husband. Then she
10 kissed them; and they lifted up their voice, and wept. And
they said unto her, Surely we will return with thee unto thy
11 people. ¶And Naomi said, Turn again, my daughters: why
will ye go with me? *are* there yet *any more* sons in my womb,

a Judg. 2. 16.
b See Gen.
12. 10.
2 Kin. 8. 1.
c Judg. 17. 8.

d See Gen.
35. 19.
e Judg. 3. 30.

f Ex. 4. 31.
g Ps. 132. 15.
Matt. 6. 11.

h See Josh.
24. 15.
i 2 Tim. 1.
16, 17, 18.
k ver. 5.
ch. 2. 20.
l ch. 3. 1.

---

¹ Heb. *judged*.   ² Heb. *were*.

I. 1. *in the days when the Judges ruled*]
"**Judged.**" This note of time, like that in
iv. 7, xviii. 1; Judg. xvii. 6, indicates that
this book was written after the rule of the
Judges had ceased. The genealogy (iv.
17-22) points to the time of David as the earliest when the book could have been written.

a famine] Caused probably by one of the
hostile invasions recorded in the Book of
Judges. Most of the Jewish commentators,
from the mention of Bethlehem, and the
resemblance of the names Boaz and Ibzan,
refer this history to the judge Ibzan (Judg.
xii. 8), but without probability.

the country of Moab] Here, and in *vv.*
2, 22, and iv. 3, literally "**the field**" or
"**fields.**" As the same word is elsewhere
used of the territory of Moab, of the Amalekites, of Edom, and of the Philistines, it
would seem to be a term pointedly used
with reference to a foreign country, not the
country of the speaker, or writer; and to
have been specially applied to Moab.

4. Marriages of Israelites with women of

Ammon or Moab are nowhere in the Law
expressly forbidden, as were marriages with
the women of Canaan (Deut. vii. 1-3). In the
days of Nehemiah the special law (Deut. xxiii.
3-6) was interpreted as forbidding them,
and as excluding the children of such marriages from the congregation of Israel (Neh.
xiii. 1-3). Probably the marriages of Mahlon and Chilion would be justified by
necessity, living as they were in a foreign
land. Ruth was the wife of the elder
brother, Mahlon (iv. 10).

8. The accompanying their mother-in-law
to the borders of their own land would probably be an act of Oriental courtesy.
Naomi with no less courtesy presses them
to return. The mention of the *mother's*
house, which the separation of the women's
house or tent from that of the men facilitates, is natural in her mouth, and has more
tenderness in it than *father's house* would
have had; it does not imply the death of
their fathers (ii. 11).

11-13. See marg. reff. and notes. The

m Gen. 38.
11.
Deut. 25. 5.

n Judg. 2.15.
Job 19. 21.
Ps. 32. 4.
o Prov. 17.
17.
& 18. 24.
p Judg. 11.
24.
q See Josh.
24. 15, 19.
2 Kin. 2. 2.
r 2 Kin. 2.
2, 4, 6.
s ch. 2. 11.
t 1 Sam. 3.
17. & 25. 22.
2 Sam. 19.
13.
2 Kin. 6. 31.
u Acts 21. 14.
x Matt.21.10.
y See Isai.
23. 7.
Lam. 2. 15.
z Job 1. 21.

a Ex. 9. 31,
32.
ch. 2. 23.
2 Sam. 21. 9.
a ch. 3. 2.
b ch. 4. 21.
c Lev. 19. 9.
Deut. 24. 19.

12 ^mthat they may be your husbands? Turn again, my daughters,
go *your way;* for I am too old to have an husband. If I should
say, I have hope, ¹*if* I should have an husband also to night,
13 and should also bear sons; would ye ²tarry for them till they
were grown? would ye stay for them from having husbands?
nay, my daughters; for ³it grieveth me much for your sakes
14 that ⁿthe hand of the LORD is gone out against me. And they
lifted up their voice, and wept again: and Orpah kissed her
15 mother in law; but Ruth ^oclave unto her. ¶And she said,
Behold, thy sister in law is gone back unto her people, and unto
16 ^pher gods: ^qreturn thou after thy sister in law. And Ruth
said, ^{4 r}Intreat me not to leave thee, *or* to return from following
after thee: for whither thou goest, I will go; and where thou
lodgest, I will lodge: ^sthy people *shall be* my people, and thy
17 God my God: where thou diest, will I die, and there will I be
buried: ^tthe LORD do so to me, and more also, *if ought* but
18 death part thee and me. ^uWhen she saw that she ⁵was sted-
fastly minded to go with her, then she left speaking unto her.
19 ¶So they two went until they came to Beth-lehem. And it
came to pass, when they were come to Beth-lehem, that ^xall the
city was moved about them, and they said, ^y*Is* this Naomi?
20 And she said unto them, Call me not ⁶Naomi, call me ⁷Mara:
21 for the Almighty hath dealt very bitterly with me. I went out
full, ^zand the LORD hath brought me home again empty: why
then call ye me Naomi, seeing the LORD hath testified against
22 me, and the Almighty hath afflicted me? ¶So Naomi returned,
and Ruth the Moabitess, her daughter in law, which
returned out of the country of Moab: and they came to Beth-
lehem ^ain the beginning of barley harvest.

CHAP. 2. AND Naomi had a ^akinsman of her husband's, a mighty
man of wealth, of the family of Elimelech; and his name *was*
2 ^{b a}Boaz. And Ruth the Moabitess said unto Naomi, Let me now
go to the field, and ^cglean ears of corn after *him* in whose sight
I shall find grace. And she said unto her, Go, my daughter.

---

¹ Or, if *I were with an husband.*
² Heb. *hope.*
³ Heb. *I have much bitterness.*
⁴ Or, *Be not against me.*
⁵ Heb. *strengthened herself.*
⁶ That is, *Pleasant.*
⁷ That is, *Bitter.*
⁸ Called *Booz,* Matt. 1. 5.

Levirate law probably existed among the
Moabites, and in Israel extended beyond
the *brother* in the strict sense, and applied
to the nearest relations, since Boaz was
only the kinsman of Elimelech (iii. 12).

14. The kiss at parting as well as at
meeting is the customary friendly and
respectful salutation in the East. The
difference between mere kindness of manner and self-sacrificing love is most vividly
depicted in the words and conduct of the
two women. Ruth's determination is sted-
fast to cast in her lot with the people of
the Lord (cp. marg. reff. and Matt. xv.
22–28).

19. *and they said*] *i.e. the women of Beth-
lehem said.* *They* in the Hebrew is feminine.

20. See marg. Similar allusions to the
meaning of names are seen in Gen. xxvii.
36; Jer. xx. 3.

the Almighty] Shaddai (see Gen. xvii. 1

note). The name ALMIGHTY is almost peculiar to the Pentateuch, and to the Book
of Job. It occurs twice in the Psalms, and
four times in the Prophets.

21. *the LORD hath testified against me*]
The phrase is very commonly applied to a
man who gives witness concerning (usually
against) another in a court of justice (Ex.
xx. 16; 2 Sam. i. 16; Isai. iii. 9). Naomi
in the bitterness of her spirit complains
that the Lord Himself was turned against
her, and was bringing her sins up for judgment.

II. 1. *a kinsman*] More literally *an acquaintance;* here (and in the feminine, iii. 2)
denoting the person with whom one is intimately acquainted, one's near *relation.* The
next kinsman of ii. 20, &c. *(goel),* is a wholly
different word.

Boaz] Commonly taken to mean, *strength
is in him* (cp. 1 K. vii. 21).

3 And she went, and came, and gleaned in the field after the
reapers: and her [1]hap was to light on a part of the field *belonging*
4 unto Boaz, who *was* of the kindred of Elimelech. ¶And, behold,
Boaz came from Beth-lehem, and said unto the reapers, [d]The
LORD *be* with you. And they answered him, The LORD bless
5 thee. Then said Boaz unto his servant that was set over the
6 reapers, Whose damsel *is* this? And the servant that was set
over the reapers answered and said, It *is* the Moabitish damsel
7 [e]that came back with Naomi out of the country of Moab: and
she said, I pray you, let me glean and gather after the reapers
among the sheaves: so she came, and hath continued even from
the morning until now, that she tarried a little in the house.
8 ¶Then said Boaz unto Ruth, Hearest thou not, my daughter?
Go not to glean in another field, neither go from hence, but
9 abide here fast by my maidens: *let* thine eyes *be* on the field
that they do reap, and go thou after them: have I not charged
the young men that they shall not touch thee? and when thou
art athirst, go unto the vessels, and drink of *that* which the
10 young men have drawn. Then she [f]fell on her face, and bowed
herself to the ground, and said unto him, Why have I found
grace in thine eyes, that thou shouldest take knowledge of me,
11 seeing I *am* a stranger? And Boaz answered and said unto her,
It hath fully been shewed me, [g]all that thou hast done unto thy
mother in law since the death of thine husband: and *how* thou
hast left thy father and thy mother, and the land of thy nativity,
and art come unto a people which thou knewest not heretofore.
12 [h]The LORD recompense thy work, and a full reward be given
thee of the LORD God of Israel, [i]under whose wings thou art
13 come to trust. Then she said, [2][k]Let me find favour in thy sight,
my lord; for that thou hast comforted me, and for that thou hast
spoken [3]friendly unto thine handmaid, [l]though I be not like
14 unto one of thine handmaidens. - And Boaz said unto her, At
mealtime come thou hither, and eat of the bread, and dip thy
morsel in the vinegar. And she sat beside the reapers: and he
reached her parched *corn*, and she did eat, and [m]was sufficed,
15 and left. ¶And when she was risen up to glean, Boaz com-

[d] Ps. 129. 7, 8.
Luke 1. 28.
2 Thess. 3.
16.

[e] ch. 1. 22.

[f] 1 Sam. 25. 23.

[g] ch. 1. 14, 16, 17.

[h] 1 Sam. 24. 19.
[i] ch. 1. 16.
Ps. 17. 8.
& 36. 7.
& 57. 1.
& 63. 7.
[k] Gen. 33.15.
1 Sam. 1. 18.
[l] 1 Sam. 25. 41.
[m] ver. 18.

[1] Heb. *hap happened.*
[2] Or, *I find favour.*

[3] Heb. *to the heart*, Gen.
34. 3. Judg. 19. 3.

---

7. *the house*] The shed or booth where
they took their meals, and were sheltered
from the sun in the heat of the day (see
Gen. xxxiii. 17).

8. The grammatical forms of the verbs
"go hence" and "abide," are peculiar and
Chaldaic. They are supposed to indicate
the dialect used at Bethlehem in the time
of Boaz.

9. *after them*] *i.e.* after my maidens. The
fields not being divided by hedges, but only
by *baulks*, it would be easy for her to pass off
Boaz's land without being aware of it, and
so find herself among strangers where Boaz
could not protect her.

10. *she fell on her face*] With Oriental
reverence (cp. Gen. xxxiii. 3, and marg.
ref.).

12. The similarity of expression here to
Gen. xv. 1, and in *v.* 11 to Gen. xii. 1,

makes it probable that Boaz had the case of
Abraham in his mind.

the LORD *God of Israel*] "Jehovah the
God of Israel." Cp. Josh. xiv. 14, where,
as here, the force of the addition, *the God of
Israel*, lies in the person spoken of being a
foreigner (see Judg. xi. 21 note).

14. To dip the morsel, or sop, whether it
were bread or meat, in the *dish* containing
the vinegar (cp. Matt. xxvi. 23; Mark xiv.
20: Ex. xxv. 29; Num. vii. 13) was, and
still is, the common custom in the East.

parched or "*roasted*" *corn*] The common
food of the country then (cp. 1 Sam. xvii. 17,
xxv. 18; 2 Sam. xvii. 28) and now.

and left] Or "reserved" (*v.* 18). Rather,
"had some over" (cp. Luke xv. 17). Verse
18 tells us that she took to her mother-in-law
what she had over.

manded his young men, saying, Let her glean even among the
16 sheaves, and ¹reproach her not : and let fall also *some* of the
handfuls of purpose for her, and leave *them*, that she may glean
17 *them*, and rebuke her not. So she gleaned in the field until even,
and beat out that she had gleaned : and it was about an ephah of
18 barley. And she took *it* up, and went into the city : and her
mother in law saw what she had gleaned : and she brought forth,

ⁿ ver. 14. and gave to her ⁿthat she had reserved after she was sufficed.
19 ¶ And her mother in law said unto her, Where hast thou gleaned
to day ? and where wroughtest thou ? blessed be he that did

ᵒ ver. 10. ᵒtake knowledge of thee. And she shewed her mother in law
Ps. 41. 1. with whom she had wrought, and said, The man's name with
20 whom I wrought to day *is* Boaz. And Naomi said unto her

ᵖ ch. 3. 10. daughter in law, ᵖBlessed *be* he of the LORD, who ᑫhath not left
2 Sam. 2. 5. off his kindness to the living and to the dead. And Naomi said
Job 29. 13.
ᑫ Prov. 17. unto her, The man *is* near of kin unto us, ʳ²one of our next
17. 21 kinsmen. And Ruth the Moabitess said, He said unto me also,
ʳ ch. 3. 9. Thou shalt keep fast by my young men, until they have ended
& 4. 6.
22 all my harvest. And Naomi said unto Ruth her daughter in
law, *It is* good, my daughter, that thou go out with his maidens,
23 that they ³meet thee not in any other field. So she kept fast by
the maidens of Boaz to glean unto the end of barley harvest and
of wheat harvest ; and dwelt with her mother in law.

CHAP. 3. THEN Naomi her mother in law said unto her, My
ᵃ 1 Cor. 7.36. daughter, ᵃshall I not seek ᵇrest for thee, that it may be well
1 Tim. 5. 8. 2 with thee ? And now *is* not Boaz of our kindred, ᶜwith whose
ᵇ ch. 1. 9. maidens thou wast ? Behold, he winnoweth barley to night in
ᶜ ch. 2. 8.
ᵈ 2 Sam. 14. 3 the threshingfloor. Wash thyself therefore, ᵈand anoint thee,
2. and put thy raiment upon thee, and get thee down to the floor :
but make not thyself known unto the man, until he shall have
4 done eating and drinking. And it shall be, when he lieth down,
that thou shalt mark the place where he shall lie, and thou shalt
go in, and ⁴uncover his feet, and lay thee down ; and he will
5 tell thee what thou shalt do. And she said unto her, All that
6 thou sayest unto me I will do. ¶ And she went down unto the
floor, and did according to all that her mother in law bade her.
ᵉ Judg. 19. 7 And when Boaz had eaten and drunk, and ᵉhis heart was merry,
6, 9, 22.
2 Sam.13.28.
Esth. 1. 10. ¹ Heb. *shame her not.* ³ Or, *fall upon thee.*
² Or, *one that hath right to redeem.* ⁴ Or, *lift up the clothes that are on his feet.*

---

17. *and beat out that she had gleaned*]
Viz. with a stick, as the word implies (cp.
Deut. xxiv. 20 ; Isai. xxvii. 12). This
method is still commonly practised. Ruth
gleaned enough to support herself and her
mother-in-law for five days (Ex. xvi. 16).

20. *Blessed be he of the* LORD, &c.] We
may gather from Naomi's allusion to the
dead that both her husband and son had
been faithful servants of Jehovah, the God
of Israel. His kindness to the dead consisted in raising up (as Naomi hoped) an heir
to perpetuate the name ; and, in general,
in His care for their widows.

one of our next kinsmen] The word here
is GOEL, the *redeemer*, who had the right (1)
of redeeming the inheritance of the person;
(2) of marrying the widow ; (3) of avenging
the death. (See Levit. xxv. 25-31, 47-55;

Deut. xxv. 5-10 ; xix. 1-13.) As these
rights belonged to the next of kin, GOEL
came to mean the nearest kinsman.

III. 2. *behold, he winnoweth barley*, &c.]
The simple manners of Boaz and his times
are here before us. This "mighty man of
wealth" assists personally in the winnow-
ing of his barley, which lies in a great heap
on the floor (*v.* 15), and sleeps in the open
threshing-floor to protect his grain from
depredation.

to-night] For the sake of the breeze which
springs up at sunset, and greatly facilitates
the cleansing of the corn tossed up across
the wind.

4. *uncover his feet*] Rather, " **the place of
his feet;** " the foot of his bed, as we should
say. So also *vv.* 7, 8.

he went to lie down at the end of the heap of corn: and she
8 came softly, and uncovered his feet, and laid her down.   And it
came to pass at midnight, that the man was afraid, and ¹turned
9 himself : and, behold, a woman lay at his feet.   And he said,
Who *art* thou ?   And she answered, I *am* Ruth thine handmaid :
*spread therefore thy skirt over thine handmaid; for thou *art*   *f* Ezek. 16. 8.
10 ²*g*a near kinsman.   And he said, *h* Blessed *be* thou of the LORD,   *v* ch. 2. 20.
my daughter : *for* thou hast shewed more kindness in the latter   & ver. 12.
end than *i* at the beginning, inasmuch as thou followedst not   *h* ch. 2. 20.
11 young men, whether poor or rich.   And now, my daughter, fear   *i* ch. 1. 8.
not ; I will do to thee all that thou requirest : for all the ³city of
12 my people doth know that thou *art* *k* a virtuous woman.   And   *k* Prov. 12. 4.
now it is true that I *am thy* *l* near kinsman : howbeit *m* there is a   *l* ver. 9.
13 kinsman nearer than I.   Tarry this night, and it shall be in the   *m* ch. 4. 1.
morning, *that* if he will *n* perform unto thee the part of a kins-   *n* Deut. 25. 5.
man, well ; let him do the kinsman's part : but if he will not do   ch. 4. 5.
the part of a kinsman to thee, then I will do the part of a kins-   Matt. 22. 24.
man to thee, *o as* the LORD liveth : lie down until the morning.   *o* Judg. 8. 19.
14 ¶ And she lay at his feet until the morning : and she rose up be-   Jer. 4. 2.
fore one could know another.   And he said, *p* Let it not be known   *p* Rom. 12.
15 that a woman came into the floor.   Also he said, Bring the ⁴vail   17.
that *thou hast* upon thee, and hold it.   And when she held it,   & 14. 16.
he measured six *measures* of barley, and laid *it* on her : and she   1 Cor. 10. 32.
16 went into the city.   And when she came to her mother in law,   2 Cor. 8. 21.
she said, Who *art* thou, my daughter ?   And she told her all   1 Thes. 5. 22.
17 that the man had done to her.   And she said, These six *measures*
of barley gave he me ; for he said to me, Go not empty unto thy
18 mother in law.   Then said she, *q* Sit still, my daughter, until   *q* Ps. 37. 3, 5.
thou know how the matter will fall : for the man will not be in
rest, until he have finished the thing this day.
CHAP. 4. THEN went Boaz up to the gate, and sat him down there :
and, behold, *a* the kinsman of whom Boaz spake came by ; unto   *a* ch. 3. 12.
whom he said, Ho, such a one ! turn aside, sit down here.   And
2 he turned aside, and sat down.   And he took ten men of *b* the   *b* 1 Kin.21.8.
elders of the city, and said, Sit ye down here.   And they sat   Prov. 31. 23.

¹ Or, *took hold on.*   ³ Heb. *gate.*
² Or, *one that hath right to redeem.*   ⁴ Or, *sheet,* or, *apron.*

8. *turned himself*] Rather, " **bent for-**
ward," so as to feel what it was which was
at his feet.⋅ The same word is translated
" took hold of," in Judg. xvi. 29.
9. *spread thy skirt, &c.*] The phrase indicates receiving and acknowledging her as a
wife.
10. *thou hast shewed more kindness, &c.*]
Lit., " **Thou hast made thy last kindness**
better than the first." Her last kindness
was her willingness to accept Boaz for her
husband, advanced in years as he was.
12, 13. By " kinsman," understand the
goel (ii. 20 note).
15. *the vail*] Quite a different word from
that rendered *vail,* in Gen. xxxviii. 14.   It
seems rather to mean a kind of loose **cloak,**
worn over the ordinary dress (see marg.).
six measures] i.e. six seahs, in all two
ephahs, twice as much as she gleaned (ii.
17), and a heavy load to carry ; for which
reason *he laid it on her,* probably placed it

on her head.   It is well known that women
can carry great weights when duly poised
on the head.
and she went into the city] The Hebrew
has " **he went,**" viz. Boaz, where accordingly we find him (iv. 1).
16. *who art thou, my daughter ?*] In the
dim twilight (*v.* 14) her mother was not sure
at first who the young woman was, who
sought admittance into the house.
IV. 1. The gate is the place of concourse, of business, and of justice in Oriental
cities (see Judg. xix. 15 note ; Gen. xxxiv.
20 ; Deut. xvi. 18).
Ho, such a one !] Indicating that the
name of the kinsman was either unknown
or purposely concealed (1 Sam. xxi. 2 ; 2 K.
vi. 8).
2. Every city was governed by elders
(see Deut. xix. 12 ; Judg. viii. 14).   For
the number *ten,* cp. Ex. xviii. 25.   Probably
the presence of, at least, ten elders was

3 down. And he said unto the kinsman, Naomi, that is come again out of the country of Moab, selleth a parcel of land, which 4 *was* our brother Elimelech's: and [1]I thought to advertise thee, saying, ^cBuy *it* ^dbefore the inhabitants, and before the elders of my people. If thou wilt redeem *it*, redeem *it :* but if thou wilt not redeem *it*, *then* tell me, that I may know : ^efor *there is* none to redeem *it* beside thee ; and I *am* after thee. And he 5 said, I will redeem *it*. Then said Boaz, What day thou buyest the field of the hand of Naomi, thou must buy *it* also of Ruth the Moabitess, the wife of the dead, ^fto raise up the name of 6 the dead upon his inheritance. ^gAnd the kinsman said, I cannot redeem *it* for myself, lest I mar mine own inheritance : redeem thou my right to thyself ; for I cannot redeem *it*. 7 ^hNow this *was the manner* in former time in Israel concerning redeeming and concerning changing, for to confirm all things ; a man plucked off his shoe, and gave *it* to his neighbour : and 8 this *was* a testimony in Israel. Therefore the kinsman said 9 unto Boaz, Buy *it* for thee. So he drew off his shoe. ¶ And Boaz said unto the elders, and *unto* all the people, Ye *are* witnesses this day, that I have bought all that *was* Elimelech's, and all that *was* Chilion's and Mahlon's, of the hand of Naomi. 10 Moreover Ruth the Moabitess, the wife of Mahlon, have I purchased to be my wife, to raise up the name of the dead upon his inheritance, ⁱthat the name of the dead be not cut off from among his brethren, and from the gate of his place : ye *are* wit- 11 nesses this day. And all the people that *were* in the gate, and

marginal references:
^c Jer. 32. 7.
^d Gen. 23.18.
^e Lev. 25. 25.
^f Gen. 38. 8.
Deut. 25. 5.
ch. 3. 13.
Matt. 22. 24.
^g ch. 3. 12.
^h Deut. 25. 7, 9.
ⁱ Deut. 25. 6.

---

[1] Heb. *I said I will reveal* in *thine ear.*

---

necessary to make a lawful public assembly, as among modern Jews *ten* are necessary to constitute a synagogue.

3. According to the law (Levit. xxv. 25–28), if any Israelite, through poverty, would sell his possession, the next of kin (the *goel*) had a right to redeem it by paying the value of the number of years remaining till the jubilee (see marg. ref.). This right Boaz advertises the *goel* of, so as to give him the option which the law secured to him of redeeming " our brother Elimelech's " land, *i.e.* our kinsman's, according to the common use of the term *brother*, for near relation (see Gen. xiii. 8, xxiv. 27 ; Lev. xxv. 25 ; Num. xxvii. 4 ; Judg. ix. 1).

4. See marg. ; a phrase explained by the act of removing the end of the turban, or the hair, in order to whisper in the ear (see 1 Sam. ix. 15 : 2 Sam. vii. 27).

5. Observe the action of the law of Levirate. Had there been no one interested but Naomi, she would have sold the land unclogged by any condition, the law of Levirate having no existence in her case. But there was a young widow upon whom the possession of the land would devolve at Naomi's death, and who already had a right of partnership in it, and the law of Levirate did apply in her case. It was, therefore, the duty of the *goel* to marry her and raise up seed to his brother, *i.e.* his kinsman. And he could not exercise his right of redeeming

the land, unless he was willing at the same time to fulfil his obligations to the deceased by marrying the widow. This he was unwilling to do.

6. *I mar mine own inheritance*] The meaning of these words is doubtful. Some explain them by saying that the *goel* had a wife and children already, and would not introduce strife into his family. Others think that there was a risk (which he would not incur) of the *goel's* own name being blotted out from his inheritance (*v.* 10). Others take the word translated *mar* in a sense of *wasting* or *spending*. If he had to find the purchase-money, and support Naomi and Ruth, his own fortune would be broken down, if, as is likely, he was a man of slender means. Boaz, being " a mighty man of wealth," could afford this.

redeem thou my right, &c.] Literally, *redeem my redemption*—perform that act of redemption which properly belongs to me, but which I cannot perform.

7. *in former time in Israel*] Showing that the custom was obsolete in the writer's days. The letter of the law (see marg. ref.) was not strictly followed. It was thought sufficient for the man to pull off his own shoe and give it to the man to whom he ceded his right, in the presence of the elders of his city.

11. See marg. There is something of a poetical turn in this speech of the elders,

the elders, said, *We are* witnesses. ^{k}The LORD make the woman ^{k} Ps. 127. 3. that is come into thine house like Rachel and like Leah, which $^{\& 128. 3.}$ two did ^{l}build the house of Israel: and ^{1}do thou worthily in ^{l} Deut. 25. 9.
12 ^{m}Ephratah, and ^{2}be famous in Beth-lehem: and let thy house ^{m} Gen. 35. be like the house of Pharez, ^{n}whom Tamar bare unto Judah, of $^{16, 19.}$ ^{o}the seed which the LORD shall give thee of this young woman. ^{n} Gen. 38.29. 1 Chr. 2. 4.
13 ¶ So Boaz ^{p}took Ruth, and she was his wife: and when he went $^{Matt. 1. 3.}$ in unto her, ^{q}the LORD gave her conception, and she bare a son. $^{o 1 Sam. 2.}$ 20.
14 And ^{r}the women said unto Naomi, Blessed *be* the LORD, which ^{p} ch. 3. 11. hath not ^{3}left thee this day without a ^{4}kinsman, that his name ^{q} Gen. 29.31. $^{\& 33. 5.}$
15 may be famous in Israel. And he shall be unto thee a restorer ^{r} Luke 1. 58. of *thy* life, and ^{5}a nourisher of ^{6}thine old age: for thy daughter $^{Rom. 12. 15.}$ in law, which loveth thee, which is ^{s}better to thee than seven ^{s} 1 Sam. 1. 8.
16 sons, hath born him. And Naomi took the child, and laid it in
17 her bosom, and became nurse unto it. ^{t}And the women her ^{t} Luke 1. 58, neighbours gave it a name, saying, There is a son born to $^{59.}$ Naomi; and they called his name Obed: he *is* the father of
18 Jesse, the father of David. ¶ Now these *are* the generations of
19 Pharez: ^{u}Pharez begat Hezron, and Hezron begat Ram, and ^{u} 1 Chr. 2.
20 Ram begat Amminadab, and Amminadab begat ^{x}Nahshon, and $^{4, \&c.}_{Matt. 1. 3.}$
21 Nahshon begat ^{y}^{7}Salmon, and Salmon begat Boaz, and Boaz ^{x} Num. 1. 7.
22 begat Obed, and Obed begat Jesse, and Jesse begat ^{z}David. ^{y} Matt. 1. 4. ^{z} 1 Chr. 2.15. Matt. 1. 6.

^{1} Or, *get thee riches,* or, $\quad$ ^{3} Heb. *caused to cease unto* $\quad$ ^{5} Heb. *to nourish,* Gen. 45.
power. $\qquad\qquad\qquad\qquad$ *thee.* $\qquad\qquad\qquad\qquad$ 11. Ps. 55. 22.
^{2} Heb. *proclaim thy name.* $\quad$ ^{4} Or, *redeemer.* $\qquad\qquad$ ^{6} Heb. *thy gray hairs.*
$\qquad\qquad\qquad\qquad\qquad\qquad\qquad\qquad\qquad\qquad\qquad\qquad$ ^{7} Or, *Salmah.*

---

and something prophetic in the blessing pronounced by them. It is unique and obscure. The Greek Version is unintelligible. Jerome seems to have had a slightly different reading, since he applies both clauses to Ruth. "May she be a pattern of virtue in Ephratah, and have a name famous in Bethlehem." The meaning of "be famous" seems to be, *Get thyself a name which shall be celebrated in Bethlehem,* as the head of a powerful and illustrious house: literally it is, *proclaim a name, i.e.* cause others to proclaim thy name, as in v. 14.

14. *without a kinsman*] *i.e.* Boaz, not the infant Obed.

17. *Obed*] *i.e. serving,* with allusion to the service of love and duty which he would render to his grandmother Naomi.

18. It is probable that there was a family-book for the house of Pharez, in which their genealogies were preserved, and important bits of history were recorded; and that the book of Ruth was compiled from it. (See Gen. ii. 4 note.)

21. *Salmon begat Boaz*] St. Matthew has preserved the additional interesting information that the mother of Boaz was Rahab (Josh. ii., vi.). It is possible that the circumstance that the mother of Boaz was a Canaanite may have made him less indisposed to marry Ruth the Moabitess. As regards the whole genealogy in *vv.* 18–22, it should be remarked that it occurs four times in Scripture, viz. here, 1 Chr. ii. 10–12; Matt. i. 3–6; and Luke iii. 32, 33, and is of considerable importance as being the genealogy of our Lord. One or two difficulties in it still remain unsolved.

The
Bible Commentary

F. C. Cook, *Editor*

Abridged and Edited by

J. M. Fuller

I SAMUEL TO ESTHER

BAKER BOOK HOUSE

Grand Rapids, Michigan 49506

Heritage Edition

Fourteen Volumes 0834-4

1. Genesis (Murphy)	0835-2	8. Minor Prophets (Pusey)	0842-5
2. Exodus to Esther (Cook)	0836-0	9. The Gospels	0843-3
3. Job	0837-9	10. Acts and Romans	0844-1
4. Psalms	0838-7	11. I Corinthians to Galatians	0846-8
5. Proverbs to Ezekiel (Cook)	0839-5	12. Ephesians to Philemon	0847-6
6. Isaiah	0840-9	13. Hebrews to Jude	0848-4
7. Daniel	0841-7	14. Revelation	0849-2

When ordering by ISBN (International Standard Book Number), numbers listed above should be preceded by 0-8010-.

Reprinted from the 1879 edition published by John Murray, London,
under the title, *The Student's Commentary on the Holy Bible*

Reprinted 1983 by Baker Book House Company

ISBN : 0-8010-0836-0

Printed and bound in the United States of America

SAMUEL.

INTRODUCTION.

THE double name of these Books, the FIRST AND SECOND BOOK OF SAMUEL,[1] as they are called in the printed Hebrew Bible, and the FIRST AND SECOND BOOK OF KINGS, as they are called in the Vulgate, well marks the two principal features which characterize them. They contain the record of the life and ministry of SAMUEL, the great Prophet and Judge of Israel, and they also contain the record of the rise of the KINGDOM of Israel. If again the Books of Samuel are taken as forming one history with the Books of Kings (the present line of division between 2 Sam. and 1 K. being an arbitrary one), then the division into four Books of Kings is a natural one. But if these Books are looked upon rather as an isolated history, then the name of Samuel is properly affixed to them, not only because he stands out as the great figure of that age, but because his administration of the affairs of Israel was the connecting link, the transitional passage, from the rule of the Judges to the reign of the Kings, distinct from each, but binding the two together.

The important place to be filled by Samuel in the ensuing history is seen at once in the opening chapters of the Book which bears his name. Further, the fact that Samuel's birth of her that had been barren is represented in Hannah's song as typical of the triumphs of the Church and of the Kingdom of Christ, is another indication of the very distinguished place assigned to Samuel in the economy of the Old Testament, borne out by the mention of him in such passages as Ps. xcix. 6; Jer. xv. 1; Acts iii. 24. Though, however, Samuel's personal greatness is thus apparent, it is no less clearly marked that his place is one not of *absolute* but of *relative* importance. When we view the history as a whole, the eye does not rest upon Samuel, and stop there, but is led on to the throne and person of David as typical of the Kingdom and Person of Christ. An incidental mark of this subordination may be seen in the fact that the Books of Samuel are really a continuation of the Book of Ruth; a Book which derived its significance from its containing a history of David's ancestors and genealogy. Clearly, therefore, in the mind of the sacred historian, the personal history of Samuel was only a link to connect DAVID with the Patriarchs, just as the subsequent history connects David himself with our Lord JESUS CHRIST.

But a still more remarkable and conclusive proof of the same subordination may be found in the circumstance, that it is only the closing years of Saul's reign of which any account whatever is given in

---

[1] In the Heb. MSS. the two make only one Book of Samuel.

this Book. For after having related a few facts connected with the beginning of Saul's reign, the historian passes over some 20 or 30 years (Acts xiii. 21) to relate an occurrence in the last quarter of Saul's reign, God's rejection of Saul from the kingdom, and His choice of "a man after His own heart" to be king in Saul's room (xiii. 13, 14).

The contents of the Books of Samuel consist mainly of three portions, (i.) the history of Samuel's life and judgeship from 1 Sam. i. to xii. inclusive; (ii.) the history of Saul's reign from xiii. 1 to xv. 35; (iii.) the history of David from xvi. 1 to the end of the second Book; this latter portion not being completed till 1 K. ii. 11.

The sources from which the narrative is derived, were probably (1), the Book of Jasher (2 Sam. i. 18); (2), David's Psalms (2 Sam. xxii., xxiii.); (3), the Chronicles of king David (1 Chr. xxvii. 24); (4), the Book of Samuel the Seer; (5), the Book of Nathan the Prophet; (6), the Book of Gad the Seer (1 Chr. xxix. 29, 2 Chr. ix. 29); (7), the national collection of genealogies.

Those sections which give full details of the sayings and doings of Samuel, are conjectured to be extracted from "the Book of Samuel the seer" (e.g. i.–xii.). Those sections which contain narratives in which Nathan bears a part (2 Sam. vii., xi., xii., 1 K. i. ii.) may be referred to the "Book of Nathan the seer." Such passages as 2 Sam. xxi., xxii. 5, xxiv., &c., are pretty certainly from the Book of Gad the Seer. We seem to see extracts from the Chronicles of the kingdom in such passages as 1 Sam. xiii. 1, and xi. 1–11, 15, xiv. 47–52, 2 Sam. ii. 8–11, iii. 1–5, v. 4–16, viii., xx.

23–26, xxi. 15–22, xxiii. 8–39; while the song of Hannah (1 Sam. ii. 1–10), the elegy on the death of Abner (2 Sam. iii. 33, 34), and the two Psalms (2 Sam. xxii., xxiii. 1–7), may, as well as the elegy on Saul and Jonathan, be taken from the Book of Jasher.

It is difficult to decide when the final arrangement of the Books of Samuel, in their present shape, was made. The series of historical books from Judges to the end of 2 Kings is formed on one plan, so that each book is a part of a connected whole. This would point to the time of Jeremiah the Prophet, as that when the whole historical series from Judges to Kings inclusive was woven into one work. In his use of the work of contemporary writers, the final compiler left out large portions of the materials before him.[2]

The chief quotations and resemblances from the Books of Samuel in the New Testament are[3] found in the writings of St. Luke and St.

<hr/>

[2] e.g. The whole of the beginning and middle of Saul's reign; the omission of the destruction of the Gibeonites (only incidentally referred to in chap. xxi.); the early history of Eli (who is mentioned quite suddenly in 1 Sam. i. 3); the transactions of Samuel's judgeship (of which only a few incidents are recorded); the details of David's wars with Moab and Edom; and many circumstances in the reign of David of which we have a full account in the Books of Chronicles.

[3] Matt. i. 6, xii. 3, 4; Mark ii. 25, 26; Luke i. 32, 33, 46, 47, 48, 68, vi. 3, 4; Acts ii. 30, iii. 24, vii. 46, xiii. 20–22; Rom. xi. 1, 2; 2 Cor. vi. 18; Heb. i. 5; Rev. xix. 9, xxi. 5, 7, xxii. 6. There is also a remarkable similarity in the phraseology of such passages as 1 Sam. i. 17, xx. 42, and Luke vii. 50, viii. 48; 1 Sam. ii. 1, and Luke i. 46, 47; 1 Sam. ii. 26, and Luke ii. 52; 1 Sam. xiv. 45; 2 Sam. xiv. 11, and Luke xxi. 18; Acts xxvii. 34; 1 Sam. xxv. 32, and Luke i. 68; 2 Sam. i. 16, and Acts xviii. 6; 2 Sam. xiv. 17, and Gal. iv. 14; 2 Sam. xvi. 10, and Matt. viii. 29; Luke viii. 28.

Paul. The title THE CHRIST ("the anointed"), given to the Lord Jesus (Matt. i. 16, ii. 4, xvi. 16; Luke ii. 26; John i. 20, 41, xx. 31; Acts ii. 30), is first found in 1 Sam. ii. 10; and the other designation of the Saviour as the SON OF DAVID (Matt. ix. 27, xv. 22, xxi. 9, 15, xxii. 42), is derived from 2 Sam. vii. 12--16.

In these books are passages which occur in duplicate elsewhere, chiefly in the Books of Chronicles and Psalms; and a careful comparison of these duplicate passages throws great light upon the manner in which the sacred historians used existing materials, incorporating them word for word, or slightly altering them for the sake of explanation, as seemed most expedient to them. It illustrates also the errors and fluctuations of scribes in transcribing MSS., especially in regard to proper names.

For these duplicate passages, and also on the chief quotations from other books in the Old Testament, consult the marginal references.

The style of the Books of Samuel is clear, simple, and forcible, and the Hebrew remarkably pure and

free from Chaldaisms. The chief difficulties are the geographical statements of 1 Sam. ix., x., the very difficult poem in 2 Sam. xxiii. 1–7, and the account of the mighty men which follows it, 8--39. There are also some manifest corruptions of the text;[4] but contradictions or disagreements of any kind in the statements of the Books of Samuel, as compared with each other, or with the Books of Chronicles, do not exist.

The time included in the history of these Books cannot be exactly defined, from the lack of any systematic chronology in them. But it may be estimated roughly at about 130 years, made up of the following subdivisions, the precise length of the first of which is a matter of conjecture :—

	Years.
The life of Samuel up to Saul's election to be king (1 Sam. viii. 1, 5), say	50
Saul's reign (Acts xiii. 21)	40
David's reign (2 Sam. v. 4)	40
	130

[4] e.g. 1 Sam. xiii. 1; 1 Sam. vi. 19; 2 Sam. xv. 7; 2 Sam. xxi. 8; 2 Sam. xxiii. 8; of the other mighty men in the same list; the names Ishbi-benob and Jaare-oregim, 2 Sam. xxi. 16, 19.

THE FIRST BOOK

OF

SAMUEL,

OTHERWISE CALLED, THE FIRST BOOK OF THE KINGS.

CHAP. 1. NOW there was a certain man of Ramathaim-zophim, of mount Ephraim, and his name *was* *a*Elkanah, the son of Jeroham, the son of Elihu, the son of Tohu, the son of Zuph, *b*an 2 Ephrathite : and he had two wives; the name of the one *was* Hannah, and the name of the other Peninnah : and Peninnah 3 had children, but Hannah had no children. ¶ And this man went up out of his city *c*1yearly *d*to worship and to sacrifice unto the LORD of hosts in *e*Shiloh. And the two sons of Eli, Hophni and 4 Phinehas, the priests of the LORD, *were* there. And when the time was that Elkanah *f*offered, he gave to Peninnah his wife, 5 and to all her sons and her daughters, portions : but unto Hannah he gave 2a worthy portion; for he loved Hannah :

1 Heb. *from year to year.*   2 Or, *a double portion.*

I. 1. Ramathaim-zophim may signify "the two hills (ix. 11–13) of the watchmen," so called from its being a post from which the watchmen looked out. But since *Zuph* is the name of the head of the family, it is more probable that *Zophim* means the *Zuphites,* the *sons of Zuph* (see *Zophai,* 1 Chr. vi. 26), from whom the land about Ramah was called "the land of Zuph," ix. 5. There is reason to believe that Elkanah —*an Ephrathite,* or inhabitant of Bethlehem (xvii. 12, Ruth i. 2) and of the territory of the tribe of Ephraim (1 K. xi. 26)—the father of Samuel, represents the fifth generation of settlers in Canaan, and therefore that Samuel was born about 130 years after the entrance into Canaan,—four complete generations, or 132 years,—and about forty years before David.

2. *he had two wives*] Cp. Gen. iv. 19. This was permitted by the law (Deut. xxi. 15), and sanctioned by the practice of Jacob (Gen. xxix.), Ashur (1 Chr. iv. 5), Shaharaim (1 Chr. viii. 8), David (1 Sam. xxv. 43), Joash (2 Chr. xxiv. 3), and others. *Hannah, i.e. Beauty* or *charm,* is the same as *Anna* (Luke ii. 36). *Peninnah, i.e.* a *Pearl,* is the same name in signification as *Margaret.*

The frequent recurrence of the mention of barrenness in those women who were afterwards famous through their progeny (as Sarah, Rebekah, Rachel) coupled with prophetic language of Hannah's song in the 2nd chapter, justifies us in seeking a mystical sense. Besides the apparent purpose of marking the children so born as raised up for special purposes by Divine Providence, the weakness and comparative barrenness of the Church of God, to be fol-

lowed at the set time by her glorious triumph and immense increase, is probably intended to be foreshadowed.

3. It is likely that during the unsettled times of the Judges (Judg. xxi. 25) the attendance of Israelites at the three Festivals (Ex. xxxiv. 23, Deut. xvi. 16) fell into desuetude or great irregularity, and this one feast (see marg. ref.), which may have coincided with the Feast of Pentecost or Tabernacles, may have been substituted for them.

the LORD *of Hosts*] This title of Jehovah which, with some variations, is found upwards of 260 times in the O. T., occurs here for the first time. The meaning of the word *hosts* is doubtless the same as that of *army* (Dan. iv. 35) and includes all the myriads of holy Angels who people the celestial spheres (1 K. xxii. 19). It is probably with reference to the idolatrous worship of the Host of Heaven that the title *the Lord of Hosts* was given to the true God, as asserting His universal supremacy (see Neh. ix. 6). In the N. T. the phrase only occurs once (Jam. v. 4).

and the two sons, &c.] It should be, "**and there the two sons of Eli, Hophni and Phinehas, were priests to the Lord,**" *i.e.* performed the functions of priests, in the old age of Eli (iv. 18), who is represented (*v.* 9) as sitting on a seat in the temple. The reading of the Greek Version "Eli was there, and his two sons, H. and Ph., priests of the LORD," is quite unnecessary, and indeed destroys the sense. The information here given concerning the sons of Eli is followed up in ii. 12, seq.

5. *a worthy portion*] Probably as in the margin. Naturally she would have had a single

6 *but the LORD had shut up her womb. And her adversary also
¹ʰprovoked her sore, for to make her fret, because the LORD had
7 shut up her womb. And *as* he did so year by year, ²³when she
went up to the house of the LORD, so she provoked her; there-
8 fore she wept, and did not eat. Then said Elkanah her husband
to her, Hannah, why weepest thou? and why eatest thou not? and
why is thy heart grieved? *am* not I ʲbetter to thee than ten sons?
9 ¶ So Hannah rose up after they had eaten in Shiloh, and after
they had drunk. Now Eli the priest sat upon a seat by a post
10 of ᵏthe temple of the LORD. ˡAnd she *was* ⁴in bitterness of
11 soul, and prayed unto the LORD, and wept sore. And she
ᵐvowed a vow, and said, O LORD of hosts, if thou wilt indeed
ⁿlook on the affliction of thine handmaid, and ᵒremember me,
and not forget thine handmaid, but wilt give unto thine hand-
maid ⁵a man child, then I will give him unto the LORD all the
days of his life, and ᵖthere shall no razor come upon his head.
12 ¶ And it came to pass, as she ⁶continued praying before the
13 LORD, that Eli marked her mouth. Now Hannah, she spake in
her heart; only her lips moved, but her voice was not heard:
14 therefore Eli thought she had been drunken. And Eli said unto
her, How long wilt thou be drunken? put away thy wine from
15 thee. And Hannah answered and said, No, my lord, I *am* a
woman ⁷of a sorrowful spirit: I have drunk neither wine nor
strong drink, but have �q poured out my soul before the LORD.
16 Count not thine handmaid for a daughter of ʳBelial: for out
of the abundance of my ⁸complaint and grief have I spoken
17 hitherto. Then Eli answered and said, ˢGo in peace·: and ᵗthe
God of Israel grant *thee* thy petition that thou hast asked of
18 him. And she said, ᵘLet thine handmaid find grace in thy
sight. So the woman ˣwent her way, and did eat, and her
19 countenance was no more *sad*. ¶ And they rose up in the
morning early, and worshipped before the LORD, and returned,

Gen. 30. 2.
ʰ Job 24. 21.

ʲ Ruth 4. 15.

ᵏ ch. 3. 3.
ˡ Job 7. 11.
& 10. 1.
ᵐ Gen.28.20,
ⁿ Gen. 29.32.
Ex. 4. 31.
2 Sam.16.12.
Ps. 25. 18.
ᵒ Gen. 8. 1.
& 30. 22.
ᵖ Num. 6. 5.
Judg. 13. 5.

q Ps. 62. 8.
& 142. 2.
ʳ Deut. 13.
13.
ˢ Judg.18.6.
Mark 5. 34.
Luke 7. 50.
& 8. 48.
ᵗ Ps. 20. 4, 5.
ᵘ Gen.33.15.
Ruth 2. 13.
ˣ Eccles.9.7.

---

¹ Heb. *angered her.*
² Or, *from the time that she, &c.*
³ Heb. *from her going up.*
⁴ Heb. *bitter of soul,* 2 Sam. 17. 8.
⁵ Heb. *seed of men.*
⁶ Heb. *multiplied to pray.*
⁷ Heb. *hard of spirit.*
⁸ Or, *meditation.*

---

portion of the sacrifice (cp. ix. 23), but because of his love to her he gave her a double portion, enough for two people (cp. Gen. xliii. 34).

7. *And as he did so,* &c.] It should rather be "**And so she did year by year, as often as she went up to the House of the Lord, so she provoked her.**" Though the verb is masculine, Peninnah must be the subject, because *as often as* SHE *went up* follows. The Vulgate has "*they* went up."

9. *after they had eaten,* &c.] Rather, "**after she had eaten and after she had drunk,**" which is obviously right. Hannah, in the bitterness of her spirit, could not enjoy her feast, and so, after eating and drinking a little, she arose and went to the temple, leaving her husband and Peninnah and her children at table, where she still found them on her return (*v.* 18).

upon a seat, &c.] Rather, "**upon the throne,**" the pontifical chair of state (iv. 13), which was probably set at the gate leading into the inner court of the Tabernacle.

the temple of the LORD] The application of the word *temple* to the Tabernacle is found only here, iii. 3, and Ps. v. 7 : and the use of this word here is thought by some an indication of the late date of the composition of this passage.

11. Vows are characteristic of this particular age of the Judges. (Cp. Judg. xi. 30, xxi. 5 ; 1 Sam. xiv. 24.) For the law of vows in the case of married women, see Num. xxx. 6-16 ; and for the nature of the vow, see marg. reff.

15. See *v.* 2 and note. She means that wine was not the cause of her present discomposure, but grief of heart.

18. A beautiful example of the composing influence of prayer. Hannah had cast her burden upon the Lord, and so her own spirit was relieved of its load. She now returned to the family feast, and ate her portion with a cheerful heart. (Acts ii. 46, 47.)

The word *sad* is not in the Hebrew text, but it fairly supplies the meaning intended.

_y_ Gen. 4. 1.
_z_ Gen. 30.
22.

_a_ ver. 3.

_b_ Luke 2. 22.
_c_ ver. 11. 28.
ch. 2. 11, 18.
& 3. 1.
_d_ Ex. 21. 6.
_e_ Num. 30. 7.
_f_ 2 Sam. 7.
25.
_g_ Deut. 12.
5, 6, 11.
_h_ Josh. 18. 1.

_i_ Luke 2. 22.
_k_ Gen. 42.
15.
2 Kin. 2. 2.
_l_ Matt. 7. 7.
_m_ ver. 11. 22.
_n_ Gen. 24.
26, 52.

_a_ Phil. 4. 6.
_b_ See Luke
1. 46. &c.
_c_ Ps. 92. 10.
& 112. 9.
_d_ Ps. 9. 14.
See Rev. 7.
10.
_e_ Ex. 15. 11.
Deut. 3. 24.
Ps. 86. 8.
_f_ Deut. 4. 35.
2 Sam. 22.
32.
_g_ Ps. 94. 4.
Mal. 3. 13.
Jude 15.

and came to their house to Ramah: and Elkanah _y_knew
20 Hannah his wife; · and _z_the LORD remembered her. Wherefore
it came to pass, [1]when the time was come about after Hannah
had conceived, that she bare a son, and called his name
[2]Samuel, _saying_, Because I have asked him of the LORD.
21 ¶ And the man Elkanah, and all his house, _a_went up to offer
22 unto the LORD the yearly sacrifice, and his vow. But Hannah
went not up ; for she said unto her husband, _I will not go up_
until the child be weaned, and _then_ I will _b_bring him, that he
23 may appear before the LORD, and there _c_abide _d_for ever. And
_e_Elkanah her husband said unto her, Do what seemeth thee
good ; tarry until thou have weaned him ; _f_only the LORD
establish his word. So the woman abode, and gave her son
24 suck until she weaned him. ¶ And when she had weaned him,
she _g_took him up with her, with three bullocks, and one ephah
of flour, and a bottle of wine, and brought him unto _h_the house
25 of the LORD in Shiloh : and the child was ˙young. And they
26 slew a bullock, and _i_brought the child to Eli. And she said, O
my lord, _k_as thy soul liveth, my lord, I _am_ the woman that
27 stood by thee here, praying unto the LORD. _l_For this child I
prayed ; and the LORD hath given me my petition which I asked
28 of him : _m_therefore also I have [3]lent him to the LORD ; as long
as he liveth [4]he shall be lent to the LORD. And he _n_worshipped
the LORD there.

CHAP. 2. AND Hannah _a_prayed, and said,
            _b_My heart rejoiceth in the LORD,
        _c_Mine horn is exalted in the LORD :
        My mouth is enlarged over mine enemies ;
        Because I _d_rejoice in thy salvation.
2   _e_ _There is_ none holy as the LORD ·
        For _there is_ _f_none beside thee :
        Neither _is there_ any rock like our God.
3   Talk no more so exceeding proudly ;
        _g_Let _not_ [5]arrogancy come out of your mouth :
        For the LORD _is_ a God of knowledge,
        And by him actions are weighed.

[1] Heb. _in revolution of days._
[2] That is, _Asked of God._
[3] Or, _returned him, whom I_

have obtained by petition,
to the LORD.
[4] Or, _he whom I have ob-_

tained by petition shall
be returned.
[5] Heb. _hard._

---

20. _Samuel_] _i.e._ _heard of God_, because
given in answer to prayer. The names
Ishmael and _Elishama_ have the same etymology.
22. _until the child be weaned_] Hebrew
mothers, as elsewhere in the East, usually
suckled their children till the age of two
complete years, sometimes till the age of
three.
26. _as thy soul liveth_] This oath is peculiar
to the Books of Samuel, in which it occurs
six times, and to the Books of Kings, in
which however it is found only once. See
note to _v._ 11.
II. 1. The song of Hannah is a prophetic
Psalm. It is poetry, and it is prophecy.
It takes its place by the side of the songs of
Miriam, Deborah, and the Virgin Mary, as
well as those of Moses, David, Hezekiah, and
other Psalmists and Prophets whose inspired

odes have been preserved in the Bible. The
peculiar feature which these songs have in
common is, that springing from, and in
their first conception relating to, incidents
in the lives of the individuals who composed
them, they branch out into magnificent descriptions of the Kingdom and glory of
Christ, and the triumphs of the Church, of
which those incidents were providentially
designed to be the types. The perception
of this is essential to the understanding of
Hannah's song. Cp. the marg. reff. throughout.
2. _any rock_, &c.] The term _rock_ as applied to God is first found in the song of
Moses (see Deut. xxxii. 4 note), where the
juxtaposition of _rock_ and _salvation_ in _v._ 15,
he lightly esteemed the rock of his salvation,
seems to indicate that Hannah was acquainted with the song of Moses.

4   *h*The bows of the mighty men *are* broken,
    And they that stumbled are girded with strength.
5   *i They that were* full have hired out themselves for bread;
    And *they that were* hungry ceased:
    So that *k*the barren hath born seven;
    And *l*she that hath many children is waxed feeble
6   *m*The LORD killeth, and maketh alive:
    He bringeth down to the grave, and bringeth up.
7   The LORD *n*maketh poor, and maketh rich:
    *o*He bringeth low, and lifteth up.
8   *p*He raiseth up the poor out of the dust,
    And lifteth up the beggar from the dunghill,
    *q*To set *them* among princes,
    And to make them inherit the throne of glory:
    For *r*the pillars of the earth *are* the LORD'S,
    And he hath set the world upon them.
9   *s*He will keep the feet of his saints,
    And the wicked shall be silent in darkness;
    For by *t*strength shall no man prevail.
10 The adversaries of the LORD shall be broken to pieces;
    *u*Out of heaven shall he thunder upon them:
    *x*The LORD shall judge the ends of the earth;
    And he shall give strength unto his king,
    And *y*exalt the horn of his anointed.
11 ¶ And Elkanah went to Ramah to his house. *z*And the child
12 did minister unto the LORD before Eli the priest. ¶ Now the
sons of Eli *were* *a*sons of Belial; *b*they knew not the LORD.
13 And the priest's custom with the people *was, that,* when any
man offered sacrifice, the priest's servant came, while the flesh
14 was in seething, with a fleshhook of three teeth in his hand; and
he struck *it* into the pan, or kettle, or caldron, or pot; all that
the fleshhook brought up the priest took for himself. So they
15 did in Shiloh unto all the Israelites that came thither. Also
before they *c*burnt the fat, the priest's servant came, and said to
the man that sacrificed, Give flesh to roast for the priest; for he
16 will not have sodden flesh of thee, but raw. And *if* any man

h Ps. 37. 15.

i Ps. 34. 10.
See ver. 36.
k Ps. 113. 9.
Gal. 4. 27.
l Isai. 54. 1.
Jer. 15. 9.
m Deut. 32. 39.
Job 5. 18.
Hos. 6. 1.
n Deut. 8.18.
o Ps. 75. 7.
p Ps. 113. 7, 8.
Dan. 4. 17.
Luke 1. 52.
q Job 36. 7.
r Job 38. 4.
Ps. 24. 2.
Heb. 1. 3.
s Ps. 91. 11.
& 121. 3.
t Zech. 4. 6.
2 Cor. 12. 9.
u ch. 7. 10.
Ps. 18. 13.
x Ps. 96. 13.

y Ps. 89. 24.

z ver. 18.
ch. 3. 1.

a Deut.13.13.
b Judg.2.10.
Jer. 22. 16.
Rom. 1. 28.

c Lev. 3. 3, 4, 5, 16.

---

5. See an instance in *v.* 36. See, too, in Ezek. xiii. 19, another example of hire paid in bread.
ceased] *i.e.* were at rest, did no work. The general sense is expressed by the translation of the Latin Version, "they were filled."
10. *he shall give strength,* &c.] This is a most remarkable passage, containing a clear and distinct prophecy of the Kingdom and glory of the Christ of God. (Cp. Luke i. 69, 70).
11. The word *minister* is used in three senses in Scripture: (1) of the service or ministration of both priests and Levites rendered unto the Lord (Ex. xxviii. 35, 43): (2) of the ministrations of the Levites as rendered to the priests, to aid them in Divine Service (Num. iii. 6): (3) of any service or ministration, especially one rendered to a man of God, as that of Joshua to Moses (Num. xi. 28). The application of it to Samuel as ministering to the Lord

before Eli the priest accords *most exactly* with Samuel's condition as a Levite.
12. *sons of Belial*] See marg. reff. note. The phrase is very frequent in the books of Samuel. In the N. T., St. Paul contrasts Christ and Belial, as if Belial were the name of an idol or the personification of evil (2 Cor. vi. 15). This probably led to the use of the term Belial in the A. V., instead of expressing its meaning, which is *mischief, wickedness.*
13. The Law of Moses defined exactly what was to be the priest's portion of every peace offering (Lev. vii. 31-35), as it also gave express directions about the burning of the fat (ib. 23-25, 31). It was therefore a gross act of disobedience and lawlessness on the part of Hophni and Phinehas to take more than the Law gave them. Incidental evidence is afforded by this passage to the existence of the Levitical Law at this time.

said unto him, Let them not fail to burn the fat [1] presently, and *then* take as *much* as thy soul desireth; then he would answer him, *Nay;* but thou shalt give *it me* now : and if not, I will 17 take *it* by force. Wherefore the sin of the young men was very

d Gen. 6. 11.
e Mal. 2. 8.
f ver. 11.
g Ex. 28. 6.
2 Sam. 6. 14.
h ch. 1. 3.
i Gen. 14. 19.

k ch. 1. 28.
l Gen. 21. 1.

m Gen. 21. 8.
ver. 26.
Luke 1. 80.
& 2. 40.
n See Ex.
38. 8.

o Num. 15. 30.

p Josh. 11. 20.
Prov. 15. 10.

great *d* before the LORD : for men *e* abhorred the offering of the 18 LORD. ¶ *f* But Samuel ministered before the LORD, *being* a 19 child, *g* girded with a linen ephod. Moreover his mother made him a little coat, and brought *it* to him from year to year, when she *h* came up with her husband to offer the yearly 20 sacrifice. And Eli *i* blessed Elkanah and his wife, and said, The LORD give thee seed of this woman for the [2] loan which is *k* lent to the LORD. And they went unto their own home. 21 And the LORD *l* visited Hannah, so that she conceived, and bare three sons and two daughters. And the child Samuel 22 *m* grew before the LORD. ¶ Now Eli was very old, and heard all that his sons did unto all Israel; and how they lay with *n* the women that [3] assembled *at* the door of the tabernacle of the 23 congregation. And he said, unto them, Why do ye such things ? for [4] I hear of your evil dealings by all this people. 24 Nay, my sons ; for *it is* no good report that I hear: ye make the 25 LORD's people [5] to transgress. If one man sin against another, the judge shall judge him : but if a man *o* sin against the LORD, who shall intreat for him ? Notwithstanding they hearkened not unto the voice of their father, *p* because the LORD would

[1] Heb. *as on the day.*
[2] Or, *petition which she asked, &c.*
[3] Heb. *assembled by troops.*
[4] Or, *I hear evil words of you.*
[5] Or, *to cry out.*

---

17. *the offering of the* LORD] *Minchah*, here in the general sense of *gift* or *offering* to God (cp. Mal. i. 10, 11, iii. 3). In its restricted sense, it is used of the meat offerings, the unbloody sacrifices, and is then coupled with bloody sacrifices, sacrifices of *slain* beasts. (See *v.* 29.)

18. *girded with a linen ephod*] This was the usual dress of the priests. It does not appear whether Levites wore an ephod properly. Possibly it was a mark of Samuel's special dedication to the Lord's service that he wore one. (See marg. ref.). The ephod was sometimes used as an idolatrous implement (Judg. viii. 27).

19. *a little coat*] The robe of the ephod was also one of the garments worn by the High Priest (see Ex. xxviii. 31 note). This pointed mention of the ephod and the robe as worn by the youthful Samuel, seems to point to an extraordinary and irregular priesthood to which he was called by God in an age when the provisions of the Levitical law were not yet in full operation, and in which there was no impropriety in the eyes of his contemporaries, seeing that nonconformity to the whole Law was the rule rather than the exception throughout the days of the Judges.

21. See marg. reff. The words *before the Lord* have special reference to his residence at the Tabernacle.

22. *women that assembled*] Or, "served." See marg. ref. and note. Probably such

service as consisted in doing certain work for the fabric of the Tabernacle as women are wont to do, spinning, knitting, embroidering, mending, washing, and such like.

25. The sense seems to be, If one man sin against another, the judge shall amerce him in the due penalty, and then he shall be free ; but if he sin against the Lord, who shall act the part of judge and arbiter for him? His guilt must remain to the great day of judgment.

because the LORD *would slay them*] There is a sense in which whatever comes to pass is the accomplishment of God's sovereign will and pleasure, and all the previous steps, even when they involve moral causes, by which this will and pleasure are brought about, are in this sense also brought about by God. How this truth, which reason and revelation alike acknowledge, consists with man's free will on the one hand ; or, when the evil deeds and punishment of a sinner are some of the previous steps, with God's infinite mercy and love on the other, is what cannot possibly be explained. We can only firmly believe both statements, (1) that God hath no pleasure in the death of him that dieth, and that He willeth not the death of a sinner, but rather that he should be converted and live ; (2) that the sins and the punishments of sin are accomplishments of God's eternal purpose (cp. marg. reff,, and Isai. vi. 9, 10 ; Mark iv.

26 slay them. ¶And the child Samuel *q*grew on, and was *r*in
27 favour both with the LORD, and also with men. ¶*s*And there
came a man of God unto Eli, and said unto him, Thus saith the
LORD, *t*Did I plainly appear unto the house of thy father, when
28 they were in Egypt in Pharaoh's house? And did I *u*choose
him out of all the tribes of Israel *to be* my priest, to offer upon
mine altar, to burn incense, to wear an ephod before me? and
*x*did I give unto the house of thy father all the offerings made
29 by fire of the children of Israel? Wherefore *y*kick ye at my
sacrifice and at mine offering, which I have commanded in *my*
*z*habitation; and honourest thy sons above me, to make yourselves fat with the chiefest of all the offerings of Israel my
30 people? Wherefore the LORD God of Israel saith, *a*I said indeed
that thy house, and the house of thy father, should walk before
me for ever: but now the LORD saith, *b*Be it far from me; for
them that honour me *c*I will honour, and *d*they that despise me
31 shall be lightly esteemed. Behold, *e*the days come, that I will
cut off thine arm, and the arm of thy father's house, that there
32 shall not be an old man in thine house. And thou shalt see *1*an
enemy *in my* habitation, in all *the wealth* which *God* shall give
Israel: and there shall not be *f*an old man in thine house for
33 ever. And the man of thine, *whom* I shall not cut off from

q ver. 21.
r Prov. 3. 4.
Luke 2. 52.
Acts 2. 47.
Rom. 14. 18.
s 1 Kin. 13.1.
t Ex. 4. 14.
u Ex. 28. 1.
Num. 16. 5.
& 18. 1.
x Lev. 7. 34,
35.
Num. 18.
8—19.
y Deut. 32.
15.
z Deut. 12.
5, 6.
a Ex. 29. 9.
b Jer. 18. 9.
c Ps. 18. 20.
& 91. 14.
d Mal. 2. 9.
e 1 Kin. 2. 27.
Ezek. 44. 10.
See ch. 4.
11, 18, 20.

f See Zech.
8. 4.
1 Sam. 22.18.

---

1 Or, *the affliction of the
tabernacle, for all the*   *wealth which God would
have given Israel.*

12; Rom. ix. 15). It may be explained
by saying that in the case of Hophni
and Phinehas God's *will* to slay them was
founded upon His foreknowledge of their
impenitence; while from another point of
view, in which God's *will* is the fixed point,
that impenitence may be viewed in its relation to that fixed point, and so dependent
upon it, and a necessary step to it.
  26. *And the child Samuel,* &c.] The account of our Lord's growth (Luke ii. 52)
is very similar; "And Jesus increased in
wisdom and stature, and in favour with
God and man." The literal version of the
passage before us is, "The child Samuel
advanced and grew and was good (or acceptable), both with the Lord, and also with men."
  27. *a man of God*] See Judg. xiii. 6 note.
The sudden appearance of the only prophet
of whom mention is made since Deborah,
without name, or any notice of his country,
is remarkable.
  28. *an ephod*] The High Priest's ephod,
in which was Urim and Thummim.
  did I give, &c.] The bountiful provision
made by God for His priests is mentioned
as the great aggravation of the covetousness
of Eli's sons (cp. 2 Sam. xii. 7-9).
  29. *Wherefore kick ye*] See marg. ref.
The well-fed beast becomes unmanageable
and refractory, and refuses the yoke, and
bursts the bonds (Jer. v. 5). So the priests,
instead of being grateful for the provision
made for them, in their pampered pride
became dissatisfied, wantonly broke the
laws of God which regulated their share of
the offerings, and gave themselves up to an

unbridled indulgence of their passions and
their covetousness.
  honourest thy sons above me] What restrained Eli from taking vigorous action
to vindicate God's honour, was his unwillingness to lose for his sons the lucrative
office of the priesthood. He was willing to
rebuke them, he was grieved at their mis-
deeds, but he was not willing to give up the
wealth and plenty which flowed into his
house from the offerings of Israel.
  30. *be it far from me*] The phrase so rendered is a favourite one in the Books of
Samuel, where it occurs ten or eleven times.
It is variously rendered in the A. V., *God
forbid,* and *Be it far from me, thee,* &c. Lit.,
Be it an abomination to me.
  31. *I will cut off thine arm,* &c.] A strong
phrase for breaking down the strength and
power, of which the arm is the instrument
in man (cp. Zech. xi. 17). See *v.* 33.
  32. The original text is rather obscure
and difficult of construction, but the A. V.
probably gives the sense of it. The marg.
gives another meaning.
  in all the wealth, &c.] The allusion is particularly to Solomon's reign, when Zadok
was made priest instead of Abiathar, 1 K.
ii. 26, 27. (See 1 K. iv. 20, seq.) The
enormous number of sacrifices then offered
must have been a great source of wealth to
the priests (1 K. viii. 63-66).
  33. The meaning is explained by *v.* 36.
Those who are not cut off in the flower of
their youth shall be worse off than those
who are, for they shall have to beg their
bread. (Cp. Jer. xxii. 10.)

g 1 Kin. 13.
3.
h ch. 4. 11.
i 1 Kin. 2. 35.
1 Chr. 29. 22.
Ezek. 44. 15.
k 2 Sam. 7.
11, 27.
1 Kin. 11. 38.
l Ps. 2. 2.
& 18. 50.
m 1 Kin. 2. 27.

a ch. 2. 11.
b Ps. 74. 9.
Amos 8. 11.
c Gen. 27. 1.
ch. 2. 22.
d Ex. 27. 21.
e ch. 1. 9.

f See Acts
19. 2.

mine altar, *shall be* to consume thine eyes, and to grieve thine heart: and all the increase of thine house shall die ¹in the 34 flower of their age. And this *shall be* ᵍa sign unto thee, that shall come upon thy two sons, Hophni and Phinehas; ʰin one 35 day they shall die both of them. And ⁱI will raise me up a faithful priest, *that* shall do according to *that* which *is* in mine heart and in my mind: and ᵏI will build him a sure house; and 36 he shall walk before ˡmine anointed for ever. ᵐAnd it shall come to pass, *that* every one that is left in thine house shall come *and* crouch to him for a piece of silver and a morsel of bread, and shall say, ²Put me, I pray thee, into ³one of the priests' offices, that I may eat a piece of bread.

CHAP. 3. AND ᵃthe child Samuel ministered unto the LORD before Eli. And ᵇthe word of the LORD was precious in those days; 2 *there was* no open vision. And it came to pass at that time, when Eli *was* laid down in his place, ᶜand his eyes began to wax 3 dim, *that* he could not see; and ere ᵈthe lamp of God went out ᵉin the temple of the LORD, where the ark of God *was*, and 4 Samuel was laid down *to sleep;* that the LORD called Samuel: 5 and he answered, Here *am* I. And he ran unto Eli, and said, Here *am* I; for thou calledst me. And he said, I called not; 6 lie down again. And he went and lay down. And the LORD called yet again, Samuel. And Samuel arose and went to Eli, and said, Here *am* I; for thou didst call me. And he answered, 7 I called not, my son; lie down iagain. ⁴Now Samuel ᶠdid not yet know the LORD, neither was the word of the LORD yet 8 revealed unto him. And the LORD called Samuel again the third time. And he arose and went to Eli, and said, Here *am* I; for thou didst call me. And Eli perceived that the LORD

---

¹ Heb. *men.*
² Heb. *Join.*
³ Or, *somewhat about the*

priesthood.
⁴ Or, *Thus* did *Samuel before he knew the* LORD,

and before the word of the LORD *was revealed unto him.*

---

thine eyes...thine heart] For a similar personification of the tribe or family, see Judg. i. 2-4.

35. Zadok is meant rather than Samuel. The High Priesthood continued in the direct descendants of Zadok as long as the monarchy lasted (see 1 Chr. vi. 8-15).

Mine anointed, in its first sense obviously means the kings of Israel and Judah (Ps. lxxxix. 20; Zech. iv. 14). But doubtless the use of the term MESSIAH (Χριστὸς) here and in *v.* 10, is significant, and points to the Lord's Christ, in Whom the royal and priestly offices are united (Zech. vi. 11-15 : see marg. reff.). In this connexion the substitution of the priesthood after the order of Melchisedec for the Levitical may be foreshadowed under *v.* 35 (see Heb. vii.).

36. *a piece*] The word is only found here; but is thought to be connected in etymology and in meaning with the *Gerah*, the smallest Hebrew coin, being the twentieth part of the shekel. The smallness of the sum asked for shows the poverty of the asker.

III. 1. See marg ref. note. Josephus says that Samuel's call to the prophetic office happened when he had just comp'eted his twelfth year (cp. Luke ii. 42).

was precious] (or *rare*) The song of Hannah, and the prophecy of the "man of God" (ii. 27 note), are the only instances of prophecy since Deborah. Samuel is mentioned as the first of the series of Prophets (Acts iii. 24).

no open vision] Better rendered, "**There was no vision promulgated or published.**" (Cp. 2 Chr. xxxi. 5.)

2. The passage should be rendered thus: —"And it came to pass at that time that Eli was sleeping in his place; and his eyes had begun to grow dim; he could not see. And the lamp of God was not yet gone out, and Samuel was sleeping in the temple of the Lord where the ark of God was; and the Lord called Samuel, &c." Eli's old age and dimness of sight is probably mentioned as the reason why Samuel thought Eli had called him. Being a blind and feeble old man, he was likely to do so if he wanted anything, either for himself, or for the service of the temple.

7. *did not yet know the* LORD] *i.e.* in His supernatural communication, as follows at the end of the verse. The text rendering of this verse is better than that of the margin.

9 had called the child. Therefore Eli said unto Samuel, Go, lie down: and it shall be, if he call thee, that thou shalt say, Speak, LORD; for thy servant heareth. So Samuel went and lay down
10 in his place. And the LORD came, and stood, and called as at other times, Samuel, Samuel. Then Samuel answered, Speak:
11 for thy servant heareth. ¶And the LORD said to Samuel, Behold I will do a thing in Israel, *g*at which both the ears of
12 every one that heareth it shall tingle. In that day I will perform against Eli *h*all *things* which I have spoken concerning
13 his house: ¹when I begin, I will also make an end. ²*i*For I have told him that I will *k*judge his house for ever for the iniquity which he knoweth; because *l*his sons made themselves
14 ³vile, and he ⁴ᵐrestrained them not. And therefore I have sworn unto the house of Eli, that the iniquity of Eli's house
15 ⁿshall not be purged with sacrifice nor offering for ever. ¶And Samuel lay until the morning, and opened the doors of the house of the LORD. And Samuel feared to show Eli the vision.
16 Then Eli called Samuel and said, Samuel, my son. And he
17 answered, Here *am* I. And he said, what *is* the thing that *the* LORD hath said unto thee? I pray thee hide *it* not from me ᵒGod do so to thee, and ⁵more also, if thou hide *any* ⁶thing from
18 me of all the things that he said unto thee. And Samuel told him ⁷every whit, and hid nothing from him. And he said, ᵖIt
19 *is* the LORD: let him do what seemeth him good. ¶And Samuel *q*grew, and *r*the LORD was with him, *s*and did let none
20 of his words fall to the ground. And all Israel from Dan even to Beer-sheba knew that Samuel *was* ⁵established *to be* a
21 prophet of the LORD. And the LORD appeared again in Shiloh: for the LORD revealed himself to Samuel in Shiloh by *u*the word

g 2 Kin. 21. 12.
Jer. 19. 3.
h ch. 2. 30—36.
i ch. 2. 29.
k Ezek. 7. 3.
& 18. 30.
l ch. 2. 12.
m ch. 2. 23.
n Num. 15. 30, 31.
Isai. 22. 14.

o Ruth 1. 17.

p Job 1. 21.
& 2. 10.
Ps. 39. 9.
Isai. 39. 8.
q ch. 2. 21.
r Gen. 39. 2, 21, 23.
s ch. 9. 6.
t Judg. 20. 1.
u ver. 1, 4.

Heb. *beginning and ending.*
¹²Or, *and I will tell him, &c.*
³ Or, *accursed.*
⁴ Heb. *frowned not upon them.*
⁵ Heb. *so add.*
⁶ Or, *word.*
⁷ Heb. *all the things, or, words.*
⁸ Or, *faithful.*

10. A Personal Presence, not a mere voice, or impression upon Samuel's mind, is here distinctly indicated. (Cp. Gen. xii. 7 note ; Rev. i. 1, xxii. 16.)
11. More accurately, "the which whosoever heareth both his ears shall tingle." This expressive phrase occurs again twice (marg. reff.) with reference to the destruction of Jerusalem by Nebuchadnezzar. It is remarkable that Jeremiah repeatedly compares the destruction of Jerusalem with the destruction of Shiloh (Jer. vii. 12, 14, xxvi. 6, 9. Cp. Ps. lxxviii. 60–64).
12. *when I begin*, &c.] Literally, as in the margin : meaning, I will go through with the performance from first to last.
13. *made themselves vile*] Rather, *have cursed themselves*, i.e. brought curses upon themselves.
he restrained them not] In the sense of punishing. He did not remove them from their office, which he ought to have done.
14. See marg. reff. The sin of the sons of Eli could not be purged by the appointed sacrifices of the Law. In blessed contrast with this declaration is the assurance of the N. T. (1 John i. 7 ; Acts xiii. 39).

15. *opened the doors*] We learn thus incidentally the nature of some of Samuel's duties. This duty was quite Levitical in its character. In the interval between Josh a and David, when the Tabernacle was stationary for the most part, it may have lost something of its *tent* character, and among other changes have had doors instead of the hanging
Samuel feared to show Eli the vision] Here was Samuel's first experience of the Prophet's cross : the having unwelcome truth to divulge to those he loved, honoured, and feared. Cp. the case of Jeremiah (Jer. xv. 10, xvii. 15·18, xx. 7–18).
18. *It is the* LORD, &c.] Compare the devout submission of Aaron (Lev. x. 3), and of Hezekiah (2 K. xx. 19). And, for the highest conceivable submission to the will of God, cp. Luke xxii. 42.
20. *from Dan*, &c.] See Judg. xx. 1 note.
21. The state described in *v.* 7 was henceforth reversed. Samuel now knew the Lord, and the Word of the Lord was revealed unto him.

4 of the LORD. AND the word of Samuel ¹²came to all Israel.
¶ Now Israel went out against the Philistines to battle, and

ª ch. 5. 1.
& 7. 12.

pitched beside ªEben-ezer: and the Philistines pitched in Aphek.
2 And the Philistines put themselves in array against Israel: and
when ³they joined battle, Israel was smitten before the Philistines:
and they slew of ⁴the army in the field about four thousand men.
3 ¶ And when the people were come into the camp, the elders of
Israel said, Wherefore hath the LORD smitten us to day before
the Philistines? Let us ⁵fetch the ark of the covenant of the
LORD out of Shiloh unto us, that, when it cometh among us, it
4 may save us out of the hand of our enemies. So the people sent
to Shiloh, that they might bring from thence the ark of the

ᵇ 2 Sam. 6. 2.
Ps. 80. 1.
& 99. 1.
ᶜ Ex. 25. 18.
Num. 7. 89.

covenant of the LORD of hosts, ᵇwhich dwelleth between ᶜthe
cherubims: and the two sons of Eli, Hophni and Phinehas, were
5 there with the ark of the covenant of God. ¶ And when the ark
of the covenant of the LORD came into the camp, all Israel
6 shouted with a great shout, so that the earth rang again. And
when the Philistines heard the noise of the shout, they said,
What meaneth the noise of this great shout in the camp of the
Hebrews? And they understood that the ark of the LORD was
7 come into the camp. And the Philistines were afraid, for they
said, God is come into the camp. And they said, Woe unto us!
8 for there hath not been such a thing ⁶heretofore. Woe unto
us! who shall deliver us out of the hands of these mighty Gods?
these are the Gods that smote the Egyptians with all the

ᵈ 1 Cor. 16.
13.

9 plagues in the wilderness. ᵈBe strong, and quit yourselves like
men, O ye Philistines, that ye be not servants unto the Hebrews,

ᵉ Judg. 13. 1.

ᵉas they have been to you: ⁷quit yourselves like men, and fight.

¹ Or, came to pass.	spread.	⁶ Heb. yesterday, or, the
² Heb. was.	⁴ Heb. the array.	third day.
³ Heb. the battle was	⁵ Heb. take unto us.	⁷ Heb. be men.

IV. 1. Some attach the opening words to
the close of ch. iii., as the complement of
what is there said, "The Lord revealed
himself to Samuel...in Shiloh, and the word
of Samuel went forth to all Israel." If
placed at the commencement of ch. iv.,
and in connexion with what follows, they
are to be understood in the sense that
Samuel called all Israel to battle against
the Philistines. (Cp. vii. 5.) But this is
not the natural interpretation of the words,
which seem clearly to belong to what went
before.

The mention of the Philistines connects
the narrative with Judg. xiii.-xvi. Since
the Philistine servitude lasted forty years
(Judg. xiii. 1), and seems to have terminated in the days of Samuel (vii. 13, 14)
in about the 20th year of his judgeship
(vii. 2); and since it had already begun
before the birth of Samson (Judg. xiii. 5),
and Samson judged Israel twenty years "in
the days of the Philistines" (Judg. xv. 20),
it seems to follow that the latter part of the
judgeship of Eli and the early part of that
of Samuel must have been coincident with
the life-time of Samson.

Eben-ezer] (or, the stone of help) The place
was afterwards so named by Samuel. See

marg. reff. Aphek, or the fortress, was
probably the same as the Aphek of Josh.
xii. 18. It would be towards the western
frontier of Judah, not very far from Mizpeh
of Benjamin, and near Shiloh (v. 4).

3. In the evening of the defeat of the
Israelites the elders held a council, and
resolved to send for the Ark, which is described in full, as implying that in virtue
of the Covenant God could not but give
them the victory (cp. Num. x. 35; Josh.
iii. 10).

4. the people sent] The expression is very
indicative of the political state so frequently
noted by the writer of the Book of Judges,
"In those days there was no king in
Israel."

6. of the Hebrews] This was the name by
which the Israelites were known to foreign
nations (cp. Ex. i. 15, ii. 6).

8. This is a remarkable testimony on the
part of the Philistines to the truth of the
events which are recorded in the Pentateuch. The Philistines would of course
hear of them, just as Balak and the people
of Jericho did (Num. xxii. 5; Josh. ii. 10).
with all the plagues, &c.] Rather, "with
every kind of plague," equivalent to with
utter destruction.

10 And the Philistines fought, and *f*Israel was smitten, and they
fled every man into his tent: and there was a very great
slaughter; for there fell of Israel thirty thousand footmen.
11 And *g*the ark of God was taken; and *h*the two sons of Eli,
12 Hophni and Phinehas, ¹were slain. ¶And there ran a man of
Benjamin out of the army, and ⁱcame to Shiloh the same day
13 with his clothes rent, and *k*with earth upon his head. And
when he came, lo, Eli sat upon *l*a seat by the wayside watching:
for his heart trembled for the ark of God. And when the man
14 came into the city, and told *it*, all the city cried out. And
when Eli heard the noise of the crying, he said, What *meaneth*
the noise of this tumult? And the man came in hastily, and
15 told Eli. Now Eli was ninety and eight years old; and *m*his
16 eyes ²were dim, that he could not see. And the man said unto
Eli, I *am* he that came out of the army, and I fled to day out of
17 the army. And he said, *n*What ³is there done, my son? And
the messenger answered and said, Israel is fled before the Philistines, and there hath been also a great slaughter among the
people, and thy two sons also, Hophni and Phinehas, are dead,
18 and the ark of God is taken. And it came to pass, when he
made mention of the ark of God, that he fell from off the seat
backward by the side of the gate, and his neck brake, and he
died: for he was an old man, and heavy. ⁴And he had judged
19 Israel forty years. ¶And his daughter in law, Phinehas' wife,
was with child, *near* ⁵to be delivered: and when she heard the
tidings that the ark of God was taken, and that her father in
law and her husband were dead, she bowed herself and tra-
20 vailed; for her pains ⁶came upon her. And about the time of
her death *o*the women that stood by her said unto her, Fear
not; for thou hast born a son. But she answered not, ⁷neither
21 did she regard *it*. And she named the child, ⁸*p*I-chabod, saying,
*q*The glory is departed from Israel: because the ark of God was
22 taken, and because of her father in law and her husband. And
she said, The glory is departed from Israel: for the ark of God
is taken.

f ver. 2.
Lev. 26. 17.
Deut. 28. 25.
Ps. 78. 9, 62.
g ch. 2. 32.
Ps. 78. 61.
h ch. 2. 34.
Ps. 78. 64.
i 2 Sam. 1. 2.
k Josh. 7. 6.
2 Sam.13.19.
Neh. 9. 1.
Job 2. 12.
l ch. 1. 9.

m 1 Kin. 14. 4.

n 2 Sam.1.4.

o Gen. 35. 17.
p ch. 14. 3.
q 2 Kin. 17. 23.
Ps. 26. 8.

¹ Heb. *died*.
² Heb. *stood*.
³ Heb. *is the thing*.
⁴ He seems to have been

a Judge to do justice
only, and that in South
west *Israel*.
⁵ Or, *to cry out*.
⁶ Heb. *were turned*.

⁷ Heb. *set not her heart*.
⁸ That is, *Where* is *the
glory?* or, There is *no
glory*.

---

12. Runners who were swift of foot, and
could go long distances were important and
well-known persons (cp. 2 Sam. xviii. 19–
31). There seem to have been always professional runners to act as messengers with
armies in the field (2 K. xi. 4, 6, 19, A. V.
guards).
earth upon his head] In token of bitter
grief. Cp. marg. reff.
15. *dim*] Rather, "set." The word is
quite different from that so rendered in
iii. 2. The phrase seems to express the
fixed state of the blind eye, which is not
affected by the light. Eli's blindness, while
it made him alive to sounds, prevented his
seeing the rent garments and dust-be-
sprinkled head of the messenger of bad
tidings.
18. A comparison of 2 Sam. xviii. 4, explains exactly the meaning of the *side of*

the gate, and Eli's position. His seat or
throne, without a back, stood with the side
against the jamb of the gate, leaving the
passage through the gate quite clear, but
placed so that every one passing through
the gate must pass in front of him.
forty years] This chronological note connects this Book with that of Judges. (Cp.
Judg. iii. 11, &c.) It is an interesting question, but one very difficult to answer, how
near to the death of Phinehas, the son of
Eleazar the High Priest, Eli's forty years of
judgeship bring us. It is probable that at
least one high priesthood intervened.
21. *is departed*] Properly, "Is gone into
captivity."
22. The lesson of the ruin brought upon
Churches by the covetousness and pro-
fligacy of their priests, which is here taught
us so forcibly, and which has been again and

CHAP. 5. AND the Philistines took the ark of God, and brought it
2 ^afrom Eben-ezer unto Ashdod. When the Philistines took the
ark of God, they brought it into the house of ^bDagon, and set
3 it by Dagon. And when they of Ashdod arose early on the
morrow, behold, Dagon *was* ^cfallen upon his face to the earth
before the ark of the LORD. And they took Dagon, and ^dset
4 him in his place again. And when they arose early on the
morrow morning, behold, Dagon *was* fallen upon his face to the
ground before the ark of the LORD; and ^ethe head of Dagon
and both the palms of his hands *were* cut off upon the threshold;
5 only ¹*the stump of* Dagon was left to him. Therefore neither
the priests of Dagon, nor any that come into Dagon's house,
6 ^ftread on the threshold of Dagon in Ashdod unto this day. ¶ But
^gthe hand of the LORD was heavy upon them of Ashdod, and he
^hdestroyed them, and smote them with ⁱemerods, *even* Ashdod
7 and the coasts thereof. And when the men of Ashdod saw that
it was so, they said, The ark of the God of Israel shall not abide
with us : for his hand is sore upon us, and upon Dagon our god.
8 They sent therefore and gathered all the lords of the Philistines
unto them, and said, What shall we do with the ark of the God
of Israel ? And they answered, Let the ark of the God of Israel
be carried about unto Gath. And they carried the ark of tho
9 God of Israel about *thither.* And it was *so,* that, after they had
carried it about, ^kthe hand of the LORD was against the city
^lwith a very great destruction : and ^mhe smote the men of the
city, both small and great, and they had emerods in their secret
10 parts. ¶ Therefore they sent the ark of God to Ekron. And it
came to pass, as the ark of God came to Ekron, that the Ekronites cried out, saying, They have brought about the ark of the
11 God of Israel to ²us, to slay us and our people. So they sent
and gathered together all the lords of the Philistines, and said,
Send away the ark of the God of Israel, and let it go again to his
own place, that it slay ³us not, and our people : for there was a
deadly destruction throughout all the city ; ⁿthe hand of God
12 was very heavy there. And the men that died not were smitten
with the emerods : and the cry of the city went up to heaven.

CHAP. 6. AND the ark of the LORD was in the country of the
2 Philistines seven months. And the Philistines ^acalled for the
priests and the diviners, saying, What shall we do to the ark of

Marginal references:

^a ch. 4. 1.
^b Judg. 16. 23.

^c Isai. 19. 1. & 46. 1, 2.
^d Isai. 46. 7.

^e Jer. 50. 2.
Ezek. 6. 4.
Micah 1. 7.

^f See Zeph. 1. 9.
^g ver. 7. 11.
Ex. 9. 3.
Acts 13. 11.
^h ch. 6. 5.
ⁱ Ps. 78. 66.

^k Deut. 2. 15.
ch. 7. 13.
& 12. 15.
^l ver. 11.
^m ver. 6.
Ps. 78. 66.

ⁿ ver. 6, 9.

^a Gen. 41. 8.
Matt. 2. 4.

---

¹ Or, *the fishy part.*   ³ Heb. *me not, and my.*
² Heb. *me, to slay me and my.*

---

again illustrated in Jews and Christians, is
too solemn and important to be overlooked.
When the glory of holiness departs from
what should be a holy community, the glory
of God's Presence has already departed,
and the outward tokens of His protection
may be expected to depart soon likewise.
(Cp. Ezek. x 18, xi. 23 ; Rev. ii. 5.) But
though particular churches may fall, our
Lord's promise will never fail the Catholic
Church (Matt. xxviii. 20).
V. 2. They brought it into the house of
Dagon (see marg. ref.) in order to enhance
the triumph of the gods of the Philistines
over the God of Israel. (Cp. xxxi. 9 Judg.
xvi. 23 ; Isai. xxxvii. 12.)
5. This custom still existed among the

worshippers of Dagon so late as the reign
of Josiah (see marg. ref.).
6. *emerods*] A corruption of *hemorrhoids.*
It is mentioned (Deut. xxviii. 27) among
the diseases with which God threatened to
punish the Israelites for disobedience.
8. The "lords" (see Judg. iii. 3) were very
unwilling to give up their triumph, and,
with the common heathen superstition,
imagined that some local bad luck was
against them at Ashdod. The result was to
bring the whole Philistine community under
the same calamity.
VI. 2. The word for *priest* here is the
same as that used for the priests of the true
God ; that for *diviners* is everywhere used of
idolatrous or superstitious divining. Three

3 the LORD? tell us wherewith we shall send it to his place. And
they said, If ye send away the ark of the God of Israel, send it
not [b]empty; but in any wise return him [c]a trespass offering:
then ye shall be healed, and it shall [d]be known to you why his
4 hand is not removed from you. Then said they, What *shall be*
the trespass offering which we shall return to him? They
answered, Five golden emerods, and five golden mice, [e]*according*
to the number of the lords of the Philistines: for one plague *was*
5 on [1]you all, and on your lords. Wherefore ye shall make images
of your emerods, and images of your mice that [f]mar the land; and
ye shall [g]give glory unto the God of Israel: peradventure he will
[h]lighten his hand from off you, and from off [i]your gods, and from
6 off your land. Wherefore then do ye harden your hearts, [k]as
the Egyptians and Pharaoh hardened their hearts? when he had
wrought [2]wonderfully among them, [l]did they not let [3]the people
7 go, and they departed? Now therefore make [m]a new cart, and
take two milch kine, [n]on which there hath come no yoke, and tie
8 the kine to the cart, and bring their calves home from them: and
take the ark of the LORD, and lay it upon the cart; and put
[o]the jewels of gold, which ye return him *for* a trespass offering,
in a coffer by the side thereof; and send it away, that it may
9 go. And see, if it goeth up by the way of his own coast to
[p]Beth-shemesh, *then* [4]he hath done us this great evil: but if
not, then [q]we shall know that *it is* not his hand *that* smote us;
10 it *was* a chance *that* happened to us. ¶ And the men did so;
and took two milch kine, and tied them to the cart, and shut up
11 their calves at home: and they laid the ark of the LORD upon
the cart, and the coffer with the mice of gold and the images of
12 their emerods. And the kine took the straight way to the way
of Beth-shemesh, *and* went along the highway, lowing as they
went, and turned not aside *to* the right hand or *to* the left;
and the lords of the Philistines went after them unto the

[b] Ex. 23. 15. Deut. 16. 16.
[c] Lev. 5. 15, 16.
[d] ver. 9.
[e] See ver. 17, 18. Josh. 13. 3. Judg. 3. 3.
[f] ch. 5. 6.
[g] Josh. 7. 19. Isai. 42. 12. Mal. 2. 2. John 9. 24.
[h] See ch. 5. 6, 11. Ps. 39. 10.
[i] ch. 5. 3, 4, 7.
[k] Ex. 7. 13.
[l] Ex. 12. 31.
[m] 2 Sam. 6. 3.
[n] Num. 19. 2.
[o] ver. 4, 5.
[p] Josh. 15. 10.
[q] ver. 3.

[1] Heb. *them.*
[2] Or, *reproachfully.*
[3] Heb. *them.*
[4] Or, *it.*

---

modes of divination are described (Ezek. xxi. 21, 22), by arrows, by teraphim, and by the entrails of beasts. (Cp. Ex. vii. 11; Dan. ii. 2).

3. *send it not empty*] See marg. reff. The heathen idea of appeasing the gods with gifts, and the scriptural idea of expressing penitence, allegiance, or love to God, by gifts and offerings to His glory and to the comfort of our fellow worshippers, coincide in the practical result.

4. It was a prevalent custom in heathen antiquity to make offerings to the gods expressive of the particular mercy received. Thus those saved from shipwreck offered pictures of the shipwreck, &c., and the custom still exists among Christians in certain countries.

The plague of the mice is analogous to that of the frogs in Egypt. The destructive power of field-mice was very great.

7. *a new cart ... kine on which there hath come no yoke*] This was so ordered in reverence to the Ark, and was a right and true feeling. See Mark xi. 2; Matt. xxvii. 60. For the supposed peculiar virtue of *new* things, see Judg. xvi. 7, 11.

9. Bethshemesh was the first Israelitish town they would come to, being on the border of Judah. (See marg. ref.)

12. *lowing as they went*] Milch kine had been chosen on purpose to make the sign more significant. Nature would obviously dispose the kine to go towards their calves; their going in an opposite direction was therefore plainly a Divine impulse overruling their natural inclination. And this is brought out more distinctly by the mention of their lowing, which was caused by their remembering their calves.

and the lords, &c.] This circumstance of the five satraps of the Philistines accompanying the Ark in person both made it impossible for the Israelites to practise any deceit (cp. Matt. xxvii. 63-66), and is also a striking testimony to the agitation caused among the Philistines by the plagues inflicted on them since the Ark had been in their country.

13 border of Beth-shemesh. And *they of* Beth-shemesh *were* reaping their wheat harvest in the valley : and they lifted up their
14 eyes, and saw the ark, and rejoiced to see *it*. And the cart came into the field of Joshua, a Beth-shemite, and stood there, where *there was* a great stone : and they clave the wood of the cart, and offered the kine a burnt offering unto the LORD.
15 And the Levites took down the ark of the LORD, and the coffer that *was* with it, wherein the jewels of gold *were*, and put *them* on the great stone : and the men of Beth-shemesh offered burnt offerings and sacrificed sacrifices the same day
16 unto the LORD. And when *the five lords of the Philistines
17 had seen *it*, they returned to Ekron the same day. ¶ *And these *are* the golden emerods which the Philistines returned *for* a trespass offering unto the LORD; for Ashdod one, for Gaza one, for Askelon one, for Gath one, for Ekron one ;
18 and the golden mice, *according to* the number of all the cities of the Philistines *belonging* to the five lords, *both* of fenced cities, and of country villages, even unto the ¹great *stone* of Abel, whereon they set down the ark of the LORD : *which stone remaineth* unto this day in the field of Joshua, the Beth-shemite.
19 ¶ And *he smote the men of Beth-shemesh, because they had looked into the ark of the LORD, even he smote of the people fifty thousand and threescore and ten men : and the people lamented, because the LORD had smitten *many* of the people
20 with a great slaughter. And the men of Beth-shemesh said, *Who is able to stand before this holy LORD God? and to
21 whom shall he go up from us ? And they sent messengers to the inhabitants of ˣKirjath-jearim, saying, The Philistines have

Side notes (left margin):
ʳ Josh. 13. 3.
ˢ ver. 4.
ᵗ See Ex. 13. 21.
Num. 4. 5.
2 Sam. 6. 7.
ᵘ 2 Sam. 6. 9.
Mal. 3. 2.
ˣ Josh. 18. 14.

¹ Or, *great stone.*

---

13. The whole population was in the field. The harvest work was suspended in an instant, and all the workmen ran to where the Ark was.

14. *a great stone*] (Cp. Gen. xxviii. 18 ; Judg. xiii. 19). This great stone was probably used as an altar on this occasion, and the kine stopping at it of their own accord was understood by the Bethshemites as an intimation that they were to offer sacrifices on it to the Lord God of Israel, Who had so wonderfully brought back the Ark from its captivity.

and they clave the wood of the cart, &c.] A similar expedient was resorted to by Araunah (2 Sam. xxiv. 22), and by Elisha (1 K. xix. 21).

15. The word *Levites* here probably means priests (Ex. iv. 14), sons of Levi, since Bethshemesh was one of the cities of the priests (Josh. xxi. 13-16). The burnt offering of the kine was not in any sense the offering of the men of Bethshemesh, but rather of the Philistine lords to whom the cart and the kine belonged. But the Bethshemites themselves, in token of their gratitude for such a signal mercy, now offered both burnt offerings and sacrifices, probably peace offerings, and doubtless feasted together with great joy and gladness (see 1 K. viii. 62–66 ; Ezr. vi. 16, 17). There is no-

thing whatever in the text to indicate that these sacrifices were offered otherwise than in the appointed way by the priests.

18. *the great stone of Abel*, &c.] Probably so called from the *lamentation* described in *v.* 19.

19. *fifty thousand and three score and ten*] Read *three score and ten*, omitting *fifty thousand*, which appears to have crept into the text from the margin. It is not improbable that in their festive rejoicing priests, Levites, and people may have fallen into intemperance, and hence into presumptuous irreverence (cp. Lev. x. 1, 9). God had just vindicated His own honour against the Philistines ; it must now be seen that He would be sanctified in them that come nigh Him (Lev. x. 3). It is obvious to observe how the doctrine of Atonement, and its necessity in the case of sinners, is taught in this and similar lessons as to the awful HOLINESS of God.

21. *Kirjath-jearim*] See Josh. ix. 17 note. It has been thought that there was a high place at Kirjath-jearim (the *hill*, ch. vii. 1), the remnant of its old heathen sanctity when it was called Kirjath-Baal, *the city of Baal* (see Josh. xviii. 14 ; 2 Sam. vi. 2); and that for this reason it was selected as a proper place to send the Ark to.

brought again the ark of the LORD : come ye down, *and* fetch
7 it up to you. AND the men of *ª*Kirjath-jearim came, and
fetched up the ark of the LORD, and brought it into the house
of *ᵇ*Abinadab in the hill, and sanctified Eleazar his son to keep
2 the ark of the LORD. ¶And it came to pass, while the ark
abode in Kirjath-jearim, that the time was long; for it was
twenty years : and all the house of Israel lamented after the
3 LORD. And Samuel spake unto all the house of Israel, saying,
If ye do *ᶜ*return unto the LORD with all your hearts, *then ᵈ*put
away the strange gods and *ᵉ*Ashtaroth from among you, and
*ᶠ*prepare your hearts unto the LORD, and *ᵍ*serve him only :
and he will deliver you out of the hand of the Philistines.
4 Then the children of Israel did put away *ʰ*Baalim and Ash-
5 taroth, and served the LORD only. ¶And Samuel said, *ⁱ*Gather
all Israel to Mizpeh, and I will pray for you unto the LORD.
6 And they gathered together to Mizpeh, *ᵏ*and drew water, and
poured *it* out before the LORD, and *ˡ*fasted on that day, and said
there, *ᵐ*we have sinned against the LORD. And Samuel judged
7 the children of Israel in Mizpeh. ¶And when the Philistines
heard that the children of Israel were gathered together to
Mizpeh, the lords of the Philistines went up against Israel.
And when the children of Israel heard *it*, they were afraid of
8 the Philistines. And the children of Israel said to Samuel,
*¹ⁿ*Cease not to cry unto the LORD our God for us, that he will

ª ch. 6. 21.
Ps. 132. 6.
ᵇ 2 Sam. 6. *⁛*.
ᶜ Deut. 30.
2—10.
1 Kin. 8. 48.
Isai. 55. 7.
Hos. 6. 1.
Joel 2. 12.
ᵈ Gen. 35. 2.
Josh. 24. 14,
23.
ᵉ Judg. 2. 13.
ᶠ 2 Chr. 30.
19.
Job 11. 13.
ᵍ Deut. 6. 13.
Matt. 4. 10.
ʰ Judg. 2. 11.
ⁱ Judg. 20. 1.
2 Kin. 25. 23.
ᵏ 2 Sam. 14.
14.
ˡ Neh. 9. 1.
Dan. 9. 3.
Joel 2. 12.
ᵐ Judg. 10.
10.
1 Kin. 8. 47.
Ps. 106. 6.
ⁿ Isai. 37. 4.

¹ Heb. *Be not silent from us from crying.* See Ps. 28. 1.

VII. 1. This verse belongs more properly
to ch. vi. Abinadab and his sons were
probably of the house of Levi. The catastrophe at Beth-shemesh must inevitably
have made the Israelites very careful to pay
due honour to the Ark in accordance with
the Law : but to give the care of the Ark to
those who were not of the house of Levi
would be a gross violation of the Law.

2. *and all the house of Israel lamented,* &c.]
The occupation of the country about Shiloh
by the Philistines (*v.* 3) was partly the
reason for the Ark being kept so long at
Kirjath-jearim. But another reason seems
to have been the fall of the Israelites into
idolatry, which made them neglect the Ark,
and brought upon them this Philistine servitude ; probably the last twenty years of
the Philistine oppression described in Judg.
xiii. 1, which is there expressly connected
with Israelite idolatry. Now, probably,
through the exhortations of Samuel, coupled
with the chastening of the Philistine yoke,
the Israelites repented and turned again to
the God of their fathers.

3-5. Cp. marg. reff. Twenty years of
Samuel's life had passed away since the last
mention of him (iv. 1). Now he appears in
the threefold character of Prophet, Judge,
and the acknowledged leader of the whole
people. His words were an answer to a
profession of repentance on the part of Israel, the practical proof of which would be
the putting away all their false gods. (Cp.
Judg. vi. 10 note.)

I will pray for you, &c.] So Moses prayed

for the people at Rephidim (Ex. xvii. 11,
12), and for Miriam (Num. xii. 13) ; so Elijah prayed at Carmel (1 K. xviii. 36, 42) ;
so Ezra prayed at the evening sacrifice
(Ezr. ix. 5); so the High Priest prayed for
the house of Israel on the Day of Atonement;
and so does our Lord Jesus Christ ever live
at God's right hand to make intercession
for us.

6. Two rites are brought together here
which belong especially to the Feast of Tabernacles and the Day of Atonement, respectively, viz. drawing and pouring out water,
and fasting. Hence some think that Samuel
chose the Feast of Tabernacles, and the fast
which preceded it, as the occasion for assembling the people. Others explain the pouring out water as the pouring out the heart
in penitence as it were water ; or, as a symbolical act expressing their ruin and help-
lessness (2 Sam. xiv. 14); or as typifying their
desire that their sins might be forgotten "as
waters that pass away" (Job xi. 16).

and Samuel judged] This seems to denote
the *commencement* of Samuel's Judgeship
civil and military, as having taken place at
Mizpeh on this occasion. As civil Judge he
did exactly what Moses did (Ex. xviii. 13-
16) ; as military Judge he did what Othniel,
Ehud, Barak, and Gideon had done before
him, organized and marshalled the people
for effectual resistance to their oppressors,
and led them out to victory.

7. This implies a united invasion by the
whole Philistine force. Hence the *terror*
of the Israelites. (Cp. Judg. xv. 11.)

9 save us out of the hand of the Philistines. And Samuel took
a sucking lamb, and offered *it for* a burnt offering wholly unto
o Ps. 99. 6. the LORD: and *o*Samuel cried unto the LORD for Israel; and
Jer. 15. 1. 10 the LORD ¹heard him. And as Samuel was offering up the
burnt offering, the Philistines drew near to battle against Israel:
p See Josh. *p*but the LORD thundered with a great thunder on that day
10. 10. upon the Philistines, and discomfited them; and they were
Judg. 4. 15.
2 Sam. 22. 11 smitten before Israel. And the men of Israel went out of
14, 15. Mizpeh, and pursued the Philistines, and smote them, until
q Gen. 28. 12 *they came* under Beth-car. Then Samuel *q*took a stone, and set
18.
& 31. 45. *it* between Mizpeh and Shen, and called the name of it ²Eben-
Josh. 4. 9. 13 ezer, saying, Hitherto hath the LORD helped us. *r*¶So the
r Judg. 13. 1. Philistines were subdued, and they *s*came no more into the
s ch. 13. 5. coast of Israel: and the hand of the LORD was against the
14 Philistines all the days of Samuel. And the cities which the
Philistines had taken from Israel were restored to Israel, from
Ekron even unto Gath; and the coasts thereof did Israel deliver
out of the hands of the Philistines. And there was peace be-
t ch. 12. 11. 15 tween Israel and the Amorites. ¶And Samuel *t*judged Israel
Judg. 2. 16. 16 all the days of his life. And he went from year to year ³in
circuit to Beth-el, and Gilgal, and Mizpeh, and judged Israel in
u ch. 8. 4. 17 all those places. And *u*his return *was* to Ramah; for there *was*
x Judg. 21. 4. his house; and there he judged Israel; and there he *x*built an
altar unto the LORD.

¹ Or, *answered.* ² That is, *The stone of help:* ³ Heb. *and he circuited.*
ch. 4. 1.

---

9. Samuel's preparation for intercessory
prayer, viz. the offering up an atoning sacrifice, is most significant (cp. Luke i. 9, 10).
The term here used for a *lamb* does not
occur in the Pentateuch; indeed it is only
found besides this place in Isai. lxv. 25.
The offering is in accordance with Levit.
xxii. 27.

the LORD *heard him*] Better as in marg.
The *answer* was not simply the granting the
asked-for deliverance, but the great thunder
(*v.* 10), which was "the voice of the Lord,"
the same voice with which the Lord answered Moses (Ex. xix. 19; Ps. xcix. 6).

11. *Beth-car*] This place is nowhere else
mentioned. It seems to have stood on a hill
overhanging the road from the Philistine
territory to Mizpeh, and close to Ebenezer,
iv. 1.

12. Shen was a *tooth-* or sharp-pointed
rock (see xiv. 4), nowhere else mentioned
and not identified.

13. *all the days of Samuel*] Not (as in *v.*
15), all the days of his *life*, but all the days
of his *government*, when as Judge he ruled
over Israel, before they asked for a king.

14. This shows the vigour and success of
Samuel's government. He seems not only
to have expelled the Philistines from the interior of the Israelitish country, but to have
attacked them in their own land, and taken
from them the cities, with the adjacent territory, which properly belonged to Israel,
but which the Philistines had taken possession of. In this war the Amorites, finding

the Philistines worse masters than the Israelites, made common cause with Samuel,
and assisted the Israelites in their wars
against the Philistines.

15. *Samuel judged Israel*, &c.] The repetition of the phrase in *vv.* 16, 17, in connexion with Samuel's circuit, is a proof that
it is his civil judgeship which is meant. The
military leadership of course belonged to
Saul, when he became king.

16. *Gilgal*] It is uncertain whether Gilgal
in the valley of the Jordan, or the modern
Jiljûlieh, the Gilgal of 2 K. ii. 1, iv. 38, be
meant; but far more probably the former
(see xi. 14 and note).

17. *and there he built an altar*] Whether
this altar was in connexion with the Tabernacle or not we have no means of deciding,
since we are in complete ignorance as to
where the Tabernacle was at this time, or
who was High Priest, or where he resided.
It is quite possible that Samuel may have
removed the Tabernacle from Shiloh to
some place near to Ramah; and indeed it
is in itself improbable that, brought up as
he was from infancy in the service of the
Tabernacle, he should have left it. At the
beginning of Solomon's reign we know it
was at Gibeon, close to Ramah (1 K. iii. 4;
2 Chr. i. 3–6). If the Tabernacle had been
at Shiloh at this time, it is likely that Shiloh
would have been one of the places at which
Samuel judged Israel. But Shiloh was probably waste, and perhaps unsafe on account
of the Philistines.

CHAP. 8. AND it came to pass, when Samuel was old, that he *made 2 his *sons judges over Israel. Now the name of his firstborn was Joel; and the name of his second, Abiah : *they were judges in* 3 Beer-sheba. And his sons *walked not in his ways, but turned aside *after lucre, and *took bribes, and perverted judgment. 4 Then all the elders of Israel gathered themselves together, and 5 came to Samuel unto Ramah, and said unto him, Behold, thou art old, and thy sons walk not in thy ways: now *make us a 6 king to judge us like all the nations. ¶ But the thing ¹displeased Samuel, when they said, Give us a king to judge us. 7 And Samuel prayed unto the LORD. And the LORD said unto Samuel, Hearken unto the voice of the people in all that they say unto thee : for *they have not rejected thee, but *they have 8 rejected me, that I should not reign over them. According to all the works which they have done since the day that I brought them up out of Egypt even unto this day, wherewith they have forsaken me, and served other gods, so do they also unto thee. 9 Now therefore ²hearken unto their voice : ³howbeit yet protest solemnly unto them, and *shew them the manner of the king 10 that shall reign over them. ¶ And Samuel told all the words of 11 the LORD unto the people that asked of him a king. And he said, *This will be the manner of the king that shall reign over you : *He will take your sons, and appoint *them for himself, for his chariots, and to be his horsemen ; and *some shall run before 12 his chariots. And he will appoint him captains over thousands, and captains over fifties ; and *will set them* to ear his ground, and to reap his harvest, and to make his instruments of war, 13 and instruments of his chariots. And he will take your daughters 14 *to be confectionaries, and to be cooks, and to be bakers. And *he will take your fields, and your vineyards, and your oliveyards, 15 *even the best of them*, and give *them* to his servants. And he will take the tenth of your seed, and of your vineyards, and 16 give to his ⁴officers, and to his servants. And he will take your menservants, and your maidservants, and your goodliest young 17 men, and your asses, and put *them* to his work. He will take 18 the tenth of your sheep: and ye shall be his servants. And ye

a Deut.16.18.
2 Chr. 19. 5.
b See Judg. 10. 4.
c Jer. 22. 15.
d Ex. 18. 21.
1 Tim. 3. 3.
e Deut.16.19.
Ps. 15. 5.
f ver. 19, 20.
Deut. 17. 14.

g See Ex. 16. 8.
h ch. 10. 19.
& 12. 17, 19.

ver. 11.

k See Deut. 17. 16, &c. ch. 10. 25.
l ch. 14. 52.

m 1 Kin. 21. 7.
See Ezek. 46. 18.

¹ Heb. *was evil in the eyes of Samuel.*
² Or, *obey.*
³ Or, *notwithstanding when thou hast solemnly protested against them, then*
thou shalt shew, &c.
⁴ Heb. *eunuchs,* Gen. 37. 36.

VIII. 1. This verse implies a long period, probably not less than twenty years, of which we have no account except what is contained in the brief notice in vii. 13-17. The general idea conveyed is of a time of peace and prosperity, analogous to that under other Judges.

2. The mention of Beer-sheba, on the extreme southern frontier of Judah, as the place where Samuel's sons judged Israel is remarkable. It was probably due to the recovery of territory from the usurpation of the Philistines (vii. 14).

6. See marg. which implies that the thing spoken of caused anger, indignation, or some revulsion of feeling (see Gen. xxi. 11, 12). The answer of the Lord (*v.* 7) shows that Samuel's personal feelings had been hurt. They were soothed by being reminded of the continued ingratitude of the people to God Himself, upon Whom, in fact, a greater slight was put by this very request for a king "like all the nations," than upon Samuel (cp. Matt. x. 24 ; John xv. 18, 20). For a comment on this transaction, see Hos. xiii. 9-11 ; Acts xiii. 21, 22.

12. This organization was as old as the time of Moses (Num. xxxi. 14 ; Deut. i. 15), and prevailed among the Philistines also (xxix. 2). The civil and military divisions were identical, and the civil officers were the same as the captains of thousands, hundreds, fifties, and tens, in time of war.

to ear his ground] Literally, "to plough his ploughing." *To ear* is an old English word, now obsolete, for *to plough.*

14-18. See illustrations in marg. reff.; 1 K. v. 13-18, xii. 4.

shall cry out in that day because of your king which ye shall have chosen you ; and the LORD "will not hear you in that day. 19 ¶ Nevertheless the people °refused to obey the voice of Samuel; 20 and they said, Nay; but we will have a king over us ; that we also may be ᵖlike all the nations ; and that our king may judge 21 us, and go out before us, and fight our battles. And Samuel heard all the words of the people, and he rehearsed them in the 22 ears of the LORD. And the LORD said to Samuel, ᑫHearken unto their voice, and make them a king. And Samuel said unto the men of Israel, Go ye every man unto his city.

CHAP. 9. NOW there was a man of Benjamin, whose name *was* ᵃKish, the son of Abiel, the son of Zeror, the son of Bechorath, 2 the son of Aphiah, ¹a Benjamite, a mighty man of ²power. And he had a son, whose name *was* Saul, a choice young man, and a goodly: and *there was* not among the children of Israel a good- 3 lier person than he : ᵇfrom his shoulders and upward *he was* higher than any of the people. And the asses of Kish Saul's father were lost. And Kish said to Saul his son, Take now one 4 of the servants with thee, and arise, go seek the asses. And he passed through mount Ephraim, and passed through the land of ᶜShalisha, but they found *them* not : then they passed through the land of Shalim, and *there they were* not: and he passed through 5 the land of the Benjamites, but they found *them* not. *And when* they were come to the land of Zuph, Saul said to his servant that *was* with him, Come, and let us return; lest my father leave 6 *caring* for the asses, and take thought for us. And he said unto him, Behold now, *there is* in this city ᵈa man of God, and *he is* an honourable man ; ᵉall that he saith cometh surely to pass : now let us go thither; peradventure he can shew us our way that we 7 should go. Then said Saul to his servant, But, behold, *if* we go, ᶠwhat shall we bring the man? for the bread ³is spent in our vessels, and *there is* not a present to bring to the man of God : 8 what ⁴have we ? And the servant answered Saul again, and said, Behold, ⁵I have here at hand the fourth part of a shekel of

¹ Or, *the son of a man of Jemini.*   ³ Heb. *is gone out of, &c.*   ⁵ Heb. *there is found in*
² Or, *substance.*   ⁴ Heb. *is with us.*   *my hand.*

---

20. *fight our battles*] It appears from xii. 12, that the warlike movements of Nahash had already begun to excite alarm.

22. A repetition for the third time (*vv.* 7, 9) of the expression of God's will in the matter, marks Samuel's great unwillingness to comply with the people's request. Besides the natural aversion which he felt to being thrust aside after so many years of faithful and laborious service, and the natural prejudice which he would feel at his age against a new form of government, he doubtless saw how much of the evil heart of unbelief there was in the desire to have a visible king for their leader, instead of trusting to the invisible Lord Who had hitherto led them. But God had His own purpose in setting up the kingdom which was to be typical of the kingdom of His only begotten Son. ⸜

IX. 1. The genealogy of Saul is here given as far as Aphiah (*Abiah*, 1 Chr. vii. 8), who was of the house of Becher the son of Benjamin (Gen. xlvi. 21). *Kish* (1 Chr. ix.

35-39) was the son of *Ner* the son of *Jehiel*, (or, *Abiel* here and xiv. 51), the first settler (*father*, 1 Chr. ix. 35) at Gibeon, or Gibeah of Saul, and who married *Maachah*, a daughter or granddaughter of Caleb. If so, it is obvious that the names of several generations are omitted between Kish and Abiel, and among them that from which the family of Matri (x. 21) was called.

4. The land of Shalisha was somewhere near Gilgal, *i.e.* Jiljûlieh. It is thought to derive its name from *three* (Shalosh) wadys which unite in the wady of Karawa. The situation of Shalim is not known : its etymology connects it more probably with the land of Shual (xiii. 17), apparently round Taiyibeh, which was about nine miles from Gibeah.

Zuph (*v.* 5), see i. 1 note.

7. Presents of bread or meat were as common as presents of money. (Cp. Ezek. xiii. 19 ; Hos. iii. 2.)

8. *the fourth part of a shekel*] In value about sixpence. Probably the shekel, like

silver: *that* will I give to the man of God, to tell us our way.
9 (Beforetime in Israel, when a man *g*went to enquire of God, *g* Gen. 25.22.
thus he spake, Come, and let us go to the seer: for *he that is* now
10 *called* a Prophet was beforetime called *h*a Seer.) Then said Saul *h* 1 Chr. 9. 2.
to his servant, ¹Well said; come, let us go. So they went unto & 26. 28.
11 the city where the man of God *was*. ¶ *And* as they went up ²the 2 Chr. 16. 7,
hill to the city, *i*they found young maidens going out to draw 10.
12 water, and said unto them, Is the seer here? And they an- *i* Gen. 24. 11.
swered them, and said, He is; behold, *he is* before you: make
haste now, for he came to day to the city; for *k*there *is* a ³sacri- *k* Gen. 31. 51.
13 fice of the people to day *l*in the high place: as soon as ye be ch. 16. 2.
come into the city, ye shall straightway find him, before he go *l* 1 Kin. 3. 2.
up to the high place to eat: for the people will not eat until he
come, because he doth bless the sacrifice; *and* afterward they
eat that be bidden. Now therefore get you up; for about ⁴this
14 time ye shall find him. And they went up into the city: *and*
when they were come into the city, behold, Samuel came out
15 against them, for to go up to the high place. ¶ *m*Now the LORD *m* ch. 15. 1.
had ⁵told Samuel in his ear a day before Saul came, saying, Acts 13. 21.
16 To morrow about this time I will send thee a man out of the
land of Benjamin, *n*and thou shalt anoint him *to be* captain over *n* ch. 10. 1.
my people Israel, that he may save my people out of the hand of
the Philistines: for I have *o*looked upon my people, because *o* Ex. 2. 25.
17 their cry is come unto me. And when Samuel saw Saul, the LORD & 3. 7, 9.
said unto him, *p*Behold the man whom I spake to thee of! this same *p* ch. 16. 12.
18 shall ⁶reign over my people. Then Saul drew near to Samuel Hos. 13. 11.
in the gate, and said, Tell me, I pray thee, where the seer's house
19 *is*. And Samuel answered Saul, and said, I *am* the seer: go up
before me unto the high place; for ye shall eat with me to day, and
to morrow I will let thee go, and will tell thee all that *is* in thine
20 heart. And as for *q*thine asses that were lost ⁷three days ago, *q* ver. 3.
set not thy mind on them; for they are found. And on whom
*r*is all the desire of Israel? *Is it* not on thee, and on all thy *r* ch. 8. 5, 19.
21 father's house? And Saul answered and said, *s*Am not I a Ben- & 12. 13.
jamite, of the *t*smallest of the tribes of Israel? and *u*my family *s* ch. 15. 17.
the least of all the families of the tribe of Benjamin? wherefore *t* Judg. 20.
46, 47, 48.
Ps. 68. 27.
u See Judg.
6. 15.

---

¹ Heb. *Thy word is good.* ⁴ Heb. *to day.* ⁶ Heb. *restrain in.*
² Heb. *in the ascent of the* ⁵ Heb. *revealed the ear of* ⁷ Heb. *to day three days.*
city. *Samuel.* See Ruth 4. 4
³ Or, *feast.* note.

---

our early English silver coins, was divided
into four quarters by a cross, and actually
subdivided, when required, into half and
quarter shekels.

9. This is manifestly a gloss inserted in
the older narrative by the later editor of the
sacred text, to explain the use of the term in
vv. 11, 18, 19. It is one among many instances
which prove how the very letter of the contemporary narratives was preserved by those
who in later times compiled the histories.
We cannot say exactly when the term *seer*
became obsolete. See marg. reff.

13. *before he go up*] By this phrase we see
that the high place was in the highest part
of the city. Like the "house of the god
Berith" (Judg. ix. 46), it was probably the
citadel of Ramah. There was connected
with the altar a room large enough for

thirty people to dine in (*v.* 22).

16. *that he may save my people out of the*
hand of the Philistines, &c.] These words
are not very easily reconcileable with vii.

13. It is possible that the aggressive
movements of the Philistines, after the long
cessation indicated by vii. 13, coupled with
Samuel's old age and consequent inability
to lead them to victory as before, were
among the chief causes which led to the cry
for a king. If this were so, the Philistine
oppression glanced at in this verse might in
a general survey be rather connected with
Saul's times than with Samuel's.

21. The tribe of Benjamin, originally the
smallest of all the tribes (Num. i. 36), if
Ephraim and Manasseh are reckoned as one
tribe, had been nearly annihilated by the
civil war recorded in Judg. xx. It had of

22 then speakest thou ¹so to me? ¶And Samuel took Saul and his servant, and brought them into the parlour, and made them sit in the chiefest place among them that were bidden, which *were* 23 about thirty persons. And Samuel said unto the cook, Bring the portion which I gave thee, of which I said unto thee, Set it by thee.

ˣ Lev. 7. 32, 33.
Ezek. 24. 4.

24 And the cook took up ˣthe shoulder, and *that* which *was* upon it, and set it before Saul. And *Samuel* said, Behold that which is ²left! set it before thee, *and* eat: for unto this time hath it been kept for thee since I said, I have invited the people. So Saul 25 did eat with Samuel that day. ¶And when they were come down from the high place into the city, *Samuel* communed

ʸ Deut. 22. 8.
2 Sam. 11. 2.
Acts 10. 9.

26 with Saul upon ʸthe top of the house. And they arose early: and it came to pass about the spring of the day, that Samuel called Saul to the top of the house, saying, Up, that I may send thee away. And Saul arose, and they went out both of them, he 27 and Samuel, abroad. *And* as they were going down to the end of the city, Samuel said to Saul, Bid the servant pass on before us, (and he passed on,) but stand thou still ³a while, that I may shew thee the word of God.

ᵃ ch. 9. 16.
& 16. 13.
2 Kin. 9. 3, 6.
ᵇ Ps. 2. 12.
ᶜ Acts 13. 21.
ᵈ Deut. 32. 9.
Ps. 78. 71.
ᵉ Gen. 35.
19, 20.
ᶠ Josh. 18.
28.

Chap. 10. THEN ᵃSamuel took a vial of oil, and poured *it* upon his head, ᵇand kissed him, and said, Is *it* not because ᶜthe LORD 2 hath anointed thee *to be* captain over ᵈhis inheritance? When thou art departed from me to day, then thou shalt find two men by ᵉRachel's sepulchre in the border of Benjamin ᶠat Zelzah; and they will say unto thee, The asses which thou wentest to seek are found: and, lo, thy father hath left ⁴the care of the asses, and sorroweth for you, saying, What shall I do for my 3 son? Then shalt thou go on forward from thence, and thou shalt come to the plain of Tabor, and there shall meet thee

ᵍ Gen. 28.22.
& 35. 1, 3, 7.

three men going up ᵍto God to Beth-el, one carrying three kids, and another carrying three loaves of bread, and another 4 carrying a bottle of wine: and they will ⁵salute thee, and give thee two *loaves* of bread; which thou shalt receive of their

---

¹ Heb. *according to this word?*   ³ Heb. *to day.*   ⁵ Heb. *ask thee of peace*
² Or, *reserved.*   ⁴ Heb. *the business.*   as Judg. 18. 15.

---

course not recovered from that terrible calamity in the time of Saul, and was doubtless literally much the smallest tribe at that time. Nothing could be more improbable, humanly speaking, than that this weak tribe should give a ruler to the mighty tribes of Joseph and Judah.

22. *the parlour*] The *hall* or *cell* attached to the chapel on the high place, in which the sacrificial feast was wont to be held. (Cp. 1 Chr. ix. 26.)

24. *the shoulder and its appurtenances*, would give the sense accurately. The right shoulder was the priest's portion in the Levitical sacrifices. Probably it was Samuel's own portion in this case, and he gave it to Saul as a mark of the highest honour.

26. *to the top of the house*] "**On the top.**" The bed on which Saul slept was on the top of the house. It is very common in the East to provide extra sleeping accommodation by placing a tent or awning on the house-top.

X. 1. *Is it not because*, &c.] Samuel

answers Saul's tacit or expressed wonder, by telling him why he did as he did. (Cp. ix. 21.)

2. How should Saul know that what Samuel said was the word of the Lord? Samuel gives him a sign, "Thou shalt find two men," &c. (Cp. Judg. vi. 36-40; Isai. vii. 11-14; John vi. 30; Mark xi. 2, xiv. 13, &c.)

Zelzah] A place absolutely unknown.

3. *The plain of Tabor*] It should be "**the oak or terebinth**" *of Tabor* (Judg. iv. 11 note). It has been ingeniously conjectured that *Tabor* is either a different form of *Deborah*, or a corruption of it, and that the *oak*, or *terebinth of Tabor*, is the same as *Allon-bachuth*, the oak under which Deborah was buried, and which lay *beneath Bethel* (Gen. xxxv. 8). The terebinth, where three men came upon Saul, must have been at some point previous to that where the road leading northwards from Jerusalem branches; when they reached that point they would go on with their offerings to Bethel, he would pursue his journey to Gibeah.

5 hands. After that thou shalt come to *h* the hill of God, *i* where
is the garrison of the Philistines: and it shall come to pass,
when thou art come thither to the city, that thou shalt meet a
company of prophets coming down *k* from the high place with a
psaltery, and a tabret, and a pipe, and a harp, before them;
6 *l* and they shall prophesy: and *m* the Spirit of the LORD will come
upon thee, and *n* thou shalt prophesy with them, and shalt be
7 turned into another man. And *l* let it be; when these *o* signs are
come unto thee, *2 that* thou do as occasion serve thee; for *p* God
8 *is* with thee. And thou shalt go down before me *q* to Gilgal;
and, behold, I will come down unto thee, to offer burnt offerings,
and to sacrifice sacrifices of peace offerings: *r* seven days shalt
thou tarry, till I come to thee, and shew thee what thou shalt
9 do.   ¶ And it was *so*, that when he had turned his *3* back to go
from Samuel, God *4* gave him another heart: and all those signs
10 came to pass that day. And *s* when they came thither to the hill,
behold, *t* a company of prophets met him; and *u* the Spirit of
11 God came upon him, and he prophesied among them. And it
came to pass, when all that knew him beforetime saw that, behold,
he prophesied among the prophets, then the people said, *5* one to
another, What *is* this *that* is come unto the son of Kish? *x Is*
12 Saul also among the prophets? And one *6* of the same place
answered and said, But *y* who *is* their father? Therefore it

h ver. 10.
t ch. 13. 3.

k ch. 9. 12.

l Ex. 15. 20, 21.
2 Kin. 3. 15.
1 Cor. 14. 1.
m Num. 11. 25.
ch. 16. 13.
n ver. 10.
ch. 19. 23, 24.
o Ex. 4. 8.
Luke 2. 12.
p Judg. 6. 12.
q ch. 11. 14, 15.
& 13. 4.
r ch. 13. 8.
s ver. 5.
t ch. 19. 20.
u ver. 6.
x ch. 19. 24.
Matt. 13. 54, 55.
John 7. 15.
Acts 4. 13.
y Isai. 54. 13.
John 6. 45.
& 7. 16.

1 Heb. *it shall come to pass,
that when these signs, &c.*
2 Heb. *do for thee as thine*
hand shall find, Judg. 9. 33.
3 Heb. *shoulder.*
4 Heb. *turned.*
5 Heb. *a man to his neigh*-
bour.
6 Heb. *from thence.*

---

5. *hill of God*] Rather, "**Gibeah**" *of God*,
and so in *v.* 10. Two things are clear; *one*
that Saul had got home when he got to
Gibeah of God, for there he found his
uncle, and no further journeying is so much
as hinted at, and the same word *Gibeah* describes his home at *v.* 26. The *other* that
there was a high place at Gibeah just above
the city, from which he met the company
of prophets *coming down*. Hence it is obvious to conclude that the name *Gibeah of
God* (which occurs nowhere else) was sometimes given to *Gibeah of Saul* on account of
the worship on its high place, or possibly,
that the name *Gibeah of God* described the
whole hill on a part of which the city Gibeah
stood.

where is the garrison of the Philistines] It
seems strange that Samuel should give this
description of Gibeah to Saul, who must
have been so well acquainted with it. Possibly they may be explanatory words inserted by the narrator with reference to
xiii. 2.

Musical instruments were the accompaniments of the prophetic song (1 Chr. xiii. 8,
xxv. 3). The *Psaltery* is a kind of lyre with
ten strings, in the shape of an earthen wine
bottle (*nebel*, whence νάβλα), which was
something like a sugar-loaf or a delta. The
tabret is a kind of drum or tambourine, or
timbrel, usually played by dancing women
(Ex. xv. 20: Judg. xi. 34. Cp. Jer. xxxi.
4). The pipe (*chalil*, literally the *bored* or
pierced instrument) is a kind of flute used on

occasions of joy and mirth (Isai. v. 12;
1 K. i. 40; Ps. lxviii. 25). The *harp*
(*cinnor*, whence the Greek κινύρα) was a
stringed instrument, and that played upon
by David (xvi. 16, xix. 9; Ps. xliii. 4,
lvii. 8).

6. *will come upon thee*] The word rendered *come*, means to *come* or *pass upon*, as
fire does when it breaks out and spreads
(Amos v. 6); hence it is frequently used
of the Spirit of God passing upon any one.
(See Judg. xiv. 19, xv. 14; below v. 10, xi.
6, xvi. 13.)

shalt be turned into another man] This
is a remarkable expression, and occurs
nowhere else. It describes the change in
point of mental power and energy which
would result from the influx of the Spirit of
the Lord (*v.* 9). In the case of Samson it
was a supernatural bodily strength; in the
case of Saul a capacity for ruling and leading the people of which before he was destitute, and which the Spirit wrought in him.
(Cp Acts i. 8; Isai. xi. 2-4.)

8. *seven days shalt thou tarry*, &c.] The
appointment here made is not to be confounded with that mentioned in marg. ref.

12. *But who is their father?*] This is a
very obscure phrase. If by *father* be intended the head or leader (cp. 1 Chr. xxv. 6;
2 K. ii. 12) of the prophets, the question
means: "What kind of leader can they have
to admit such a person as Saul into the
company?" Some Versions read *Who is his
father?* in the sense: "Who would have

13 became a proverb, *Is* Saul also among the prophets? And when he had made an end of prophesying, he came to the high place. 14 ¶ And Saul's uncle said unto him and to his servant, Whither went ye? And he said, To seek the asses: and when we saw 15 that *they were* no where, we came to Samuel. And Saul's uncle 16 said, Tell me, I pray thee, what Samuel said unto you. And Saul said unto his uncle, He told us plainly that the asses were found. But of the matter of the kingdom, whereof Samuel spake,

17 he told him not. ¶ And Samuel called the people together *unto 18 the Lord ^ato Mizpeh; and said unto the children of Israel, ^bThus saith the Lord God of Israel, I brought up Israel out of Egypt, and delivered you out of the hand of the Egyptians, and out of the hand of all kingdoms, *and* of them that oppressed 19 you : ^cand ye have this day rejected your God, who himself saved you out of all your adversities and your tribulations; and ye have said unto him, Nay, but set a king over us. Now therefore present yourselves before the Lord by your tribes, and by 20 your thousands. And when Samuel had ^dcaused all the tribes 21 of Israel to come near, the tribe of Benjamin was taken. When he had caused the tribe of Benjamin to come near by their families, the family of Matri was taken, and Saul the son of Kish was taken: and when they sought him, he could not be 22 found. Therefore they ^eenquired of the Lord further, if the man should yet come thither. And the Lord answered, Behold, 23 he hath hid himself among the stuff. And they ran and fetched him thence: and when he stood among the people, ^fhe was higher than any of the people from his shoulders and upwards. 24 And Samuel said to all the people, See ye him ^gwhom the Lord hath chosen, that *there is* none like him among all the people? 25 And all the people shouted, and said, ^h1God save the king. Then Samuel told the people ⁱthe manner of the kingdom, and wrote *it* in a book, and laid *it* up before the Lord. And Samuel sent 26 all the people away, every man to his house. ¶ And Saul also went home ^kto Gibeah ; and there went with him a band of 27 men, whose hearts God had touched. ^lBut the ^mchildren of Belial said, How shall this man save us? And ⁿthey despised him, ⁿand brought him no presents. But ²he held his peace.

¹ Heb. *Let the king live.*   ² Or, *he was as though he had been deaf.*

---

expected Kish to have a son among the prophets?" (Cp. Matt. xiii. 54, 55.)

14. From the order of the narrative, and the mention of Saul's servant, it looks as if Saul found his uncle at the high place. Perhaps some solemnity similar to that mentioned in ix. 19 was going on at this time, in which the prophets had been taking part.

19. For the use of "thousand" as equivalent to "family," see xxiii. 23 ; Judg. vi. 15 marg. In Num. i. 16 it may mean whole tribes.

20. *caused...to come near...was taken*] The Heb. phrases are exactly the same as in Josh. vii. 16, 17, where the A.V. renders the first has *brought.*

21. *the family of Matri*] This name occurs nowhere else among the families of Benjamin, or in the genealogy of Saul. (See ix. 1 note.)

22. *among the stuff*] Rather, " **the baggage.**" The assembly was like a camp, and

the baggage (impedimenta) of the whole congregation was probably collected in one place, where the waggons were arranged for protection.

25. *the manner of the kingdom*] i.e. the just prerogative of the kingdom, the law, or bill of rights, by which the king's power was limited as well as secured. It is not improbable that what Samuel wrote was simply a transcript of Deut. xvii. 14-20, which he *laid up before the Lord*, i.e. placed by the side of the Ark of the Covenant with the copy of the Law (see Deut. xxxi. 26). It would be ready for reference if either king or people violated the "law of the kingdom."

26. *a band of men*] Rather, " **the host,**" "men of valour." There seems to be an opposition intended between the *valiant men* and the *children of Belial* (v. 27 ; see marg. ref.

27. *presents*] The *minchah* was the token of homage and acknowledgment from the

Chap. 11. THEN ^aNahash the Ammonite came up, and encamped against ^bJabesh-gilead: and all the men of Jabesh said unto
2 Nahash, ^cMake a covenant with us, and we will serve thee. And Nahash the Ammonite answered them, On this *condition* will I make *a covenant* with you, that I may thrust out all your right
3 eyes, and lay it *for* ^da reproach upon all Israel. And the elders of Jabesh said unto him, ¹Give us seven days' respite, that we may send messengers unto all the coasts of Israel : and then, if *there be* no man to save us, we will come out to thee.
4 ¶ Then came the messengers ^eto Gibeah of Saul, and told the tidings in the ears of the people: and ^fall the people lifted up
5 their voices, and wept. And, behold, Saul came after the herd out of the field ; and Saul said, What *aileth* the people that they weep ? And they told him the tidings of the men of Jabesh.
6 ^gAnd the Spirit of God came upon Saul when he heard those
7 tidings, and his anger was kindled greatly. And he took a yoke of oxen, and ^hhewed them in pieces, and sent *them* throughout all the coasts of Israel by the hands of messengers, saying, ⁱWhosoever cometh not forth after Saul and after Samuel, so shall it be done unto his oxen. And the fear of the LORD fell on the
8 people, and they came out ²with one consent. And when he numbered them in ^kBezek, the children ^lof Israel were three hundred thousand, and the men of Judah thirty thousand.
9 ¶ And they said unto the messengers that came, Thus shall ye say unto the men of Jabesh-gilead, To morrow, by *that time* the sun be hot, ye shall have ³help. And the messengers came and
10 shewed *it* to the men of Jabesh; and they were glad. Therefore the men of Jabesh said, To morrow ^mwe will come out unto

Marginal references:
a 2 Sam. 10. 1.
b Judg. 21. 8.
c Gen. 26. 28.
Ex. 23. 32.
1 Kin. 20. 34.
Job 41. 4.
Ezek. 17. 13.
d Gen. 34. 14.
ch. 17. 26.

e ch. 10. 26.
& 15. 34.
2 Sam. 21. 6.
f Judg. 2. 4.
& 21. 2.

g Judg. 3. 10.
ch. 10. 10.
& 16. 13.
h Judg. 19.
29.
i Judg. 21.
5, 8, 10.

k Judg. 1. 5.
l 2 Sam. 24.
9.

m ver. 3.

¹ Heb. *Forbear us.*   ² Heb. *as one man*, Judg. 20. 1.   ³ Or, *deliverance.*

---

subject to the sovereign, and from the tributary nation to their suzerain. (See 2 Sam. viii. 2, 6; Judg. iii. 17, 18; 1 K. iv. 21 ; 2 K. xvii. 4, &c. ; Ps. lxxii. 10; Isai. xvi. 1.) Saul dissembled his resentment, and waited for the favourable tide which soon came with the invasion of Nahash.

XI. **1.** Nahash was king of the children of Ammon, as appears from xii. 12. He seems to have been connected with the family of David, since Abigail, David's sister, was "the daughter (perhaps *granddaughter*) of Nahash" (2 Sam. xvii. 25; 1 Chr. ii. 16, 17); and, perhaps, in consequence of this connexion, he and his family were very friendly to David (2 Sam. xvii. 27).

Jabesh-Gilead must have been re-peopled after its destruction (see marg. ref.). The Ammonites and Moabites resented the possession of Gilead by the Israelites (Judg. x. 6-18, xi.).

3. *the elders*] Observe the universal form of civil government among the Israelites, by elders (Judg. viii. 14, 16, &c.).

4. They came to Gibeah on account of the connexion between the Benjamites and the people of Jabesh (Judg. xxi.).

in the ears of the people] They did not even inquire for Saul, so little was he looked upon as king. Verse 5 shows how completely he was still in a private and humble station.

6. This time the Spirit of God came upon him, as upon the Judges before him, as a Spirit of supernatural energy and power.

7. Though not expressly stated, it is doubtless implied that he sent the portions by the messengers to the twelve tribes, after the analogy, and probably in imitation, of Judg. xix. 29. He made use of the revered name of Samuel to strengthen his own weak authority. Samuel accompanied Saul in the expedition (*v.* 12).

8. *he numbered them*] This was done to see who was absent (cp. Judg. xxi. 9).

Bezek has been conjectured to be the name of a district rather than of a town. Two villages retained the name in the time of Eusebius seventeen miles from Nablous, on the way to Beth-shean.

the children of Israel and the men of Judah] This looks like the language of later times, times perhaps subsequent to the establishment of the two kingdoms of Israel and Judah. Israel here (including Benjamin) is as ten to one compared with Judah. This is about the true proportion.

9. The distance from Bezek to Jabesh-Gilead would perhaps be about twenty miles.

10. *To-morrow*] Probably the last of the

you, and ye shall do with us all that seemeth good unto you.
11 And it was *so* on the morrow, that ⁿSaul put the people ^oin
three companies; and they came into the midst of the host in
the morning watch, and slew the Ammonites until the heat of
the day: and it came to pass, that they which remained were
12 scattered, so that two of them were not left together. ¶ And the
people said unto Samuel, ^pWho *is* he that said, Shall Saul reign
13 over us? ^qbring the men, that we may put them to death. And
Saul said, ^rThere shall not a man be put to death this day:
14 for to day ^sthe LORD hath wrought salvation in Israel. Then
said Samuel to the people, Come, and let us go ^tto Gilgal, and
15 renew the kingdom there. And all the people went to Gilgal;
and there they made Saul king ^ubefore the LORD in Gilgal; and
^xthere they sacrificed sacrifices of peace offerings before the
LORD; and there Saul and all the men of Israel rejoiced
greatly.

CHAP. 12. AND Samuel said unto all Israel, Behold, I have
hearkened unto ^ayour voice in all that ye said unto me, and
2 ^bhave made a king over you. And now, behold, the king
^cwalketh before you: ^dand I am old and grayheaded; and, be-
hold, my sons *are* with you: and I have walked before you
3 from my childhood unto this day. Behold, here I *am*: witness
against me before the LORD, and before ^ehis anointed: ^fwhose
ox have I taken? or whose ass have I taken? or whom have I
defrauded? whom have I oppressed? or of whose hand have I
received *any* ¹bribe ²to ^gblind mine eyes therewith? and I will
4 restore it you. And they said, Thou hast not defrauded us,
nor oppressed us, neither hast thou taken ought of any man's
5 hand. And he said unto them, The LORD *is* witness against
you, and his anointed *is* witness this day, ^hthat ye have not

Marginal references:
ⁿ See ch. 31.
11.
^o Judg.7. 16.

^p ch. 10. 27.
^q See Luke 19. 27.
^r 2 Sam. 19. 22.
^s Ex. 14. 13. ch. 19. 5.
^t ch. 10. 8.
^u ch. 10. 17.
^x ch. 10. 8.

^a ch. 8. 5, 19. 20.
^b ch. 10. 24.
^c Num. 27. 17.
ch. 8. 20.
^d ch. 8. 1.
^e ver. 5.
ch. 10. 1.
^f Num. 16. 15.
Acts 20. 33.
^g Deut. 16. 19.

^h John 18. 38.
Acts 23. 9.

¹ Heb. *ransom.*   ² Or, *that I should hide mine eyes at him.*

"seven days' respite" (*v.* 3). Their words
were spoken in guile, to throw the Ammonites off their guard.

11. The march from Bezek may have
begun the night before. This disposition
of the forces *in three companies* (imitating
Gideon's strategy, cp. marg. ref.) would not
have been made till the morning when they
were very near the Ammonitish forces.
"The morning watch" was the last of the
three watches, of four hours each, into
which the night was anciently divided by
the Hebrews. (See Judg. vii. 19 note.)
The time thus indicated would be between
two and six in the morning.

13. *There shall not a man,* &c.] An instance of great moderation, as well as good
policy, on the part of Saul. Cp. David's
conduct (marg. ref.).

14. *let us go to Gilgal*] *i.e.* to Gilgal by
Jericho, where was a famous sanctuary, in
the tribe of Benjamin.

15. *made Saul king*] The LXX. has
another reading, *and Samuel anointed Saul
king there.* The example of David, who,
besides his original anointing by Samuel
(xvi 12, 13), was twice anointed, first as
king of Judah (2 Sam. ii. 4), and again as

king over all Israel (do. v. 3), makes it probable that Saul was anointed a second time;
but this may be included in the word
"made king" (see xii. 3, 5).

XII. 2. *my sons are with you*] Possibly,
however, a tinge of mortified feeling at the
rejection of himself and his family, mixed
with a desire to recommend his sons to the
favour and goodwill of the nation, is at the
bottom of this mention of them.

3. *his anointed*] *i.e.* king Saul. The
title Messiah, χριστὸς, unctus, or anointed,
had been given to the High Priests (Lev.
iv. 3: cp. also ii. 10, 35); but this is the
earliest instance of an actual king of Israel
bearing the title of God's Christ, and thus
typifying the true Messiah or Christ of
God.

any bribe] Literally, a *ransom*, the fine
paid by a criminal in lieu of bonds or death
(Ex. xxi. 30), applied to the bribe paid to
an unjust judge to induce him to acquit the
guilty. (Cp. Am. v. 12.)

to blind, &c.] See marg. The phrase is
used of one who averts his eyes, as refusing
assistance, or as showing contempt, or, as
here, as winking at what is wrong.

found ought *in my hand. And they answered, *He is* witness.   *i* Ex. 22. *1.*
6 ¶And Samuel said unto the people, *k It is* the LORD that ¹advanced   *k* Mic. 6. 4.
Moses and Aaron, and that brought your fathers up out of the
7 land of Egypt. Now therefore stand still, that I may *l*reason   *l* Isai. 1. 18.
with you before the LORD of all the ²righteous acts of the LORD,   Mic. 6. 2.
8 which he did ³to you and to your fathers. *m*When Jacob was   *m* Gen. 46.
come into Egypt, and your fathers *n* cried unto the LORD, then   5, 6.
the LORD *o*sent Moses and Aaron, which brought forth your   *n* Ex. 2. 23,
9 fathers out of Egypt, and made them dwell in this place. And   *o* Ex. 3. 10
when they *p*forgat the LORD their God, *q*he sold them into   *p* Judg. 3. 7.
the hand of Sisera, captain of the host of Hazor, and into the   *q* Judg. 4. 2.
hand of *r* the Philistines, and into the hand of the king *s* of   *r* Judg. 10. 7.
10 Moab, and they fought against them. And they cried unto   & 13. 1.
the LORD, and said, *t*We have sinned, because we have for-   *s* Judg. 3. 12.
saken the LORD, *u*and have served Baalim and Ashtaroth :   *t* Judg. 10.
but now *x*deliver us out of the hand of our enemies, and we   10.
11 will serve thee. And the LORD sent *y*Jerubbaal, and Bedan,   *u* Judg. 2. 13.
and *z*Jephthah, and *a*Samuel, and delivered you out of the hand   *x* Judg. 10.
12 of your enemies on every side, and ye dwelled safe. And when   15, 16.
ye saw that *b*Nahash the king of the children of Ammon came   *y* Judg. 6.
against you, *c*ye said unto me, Nay ; but a king shall reign   *z* Judg. 11. 1.
13 over us : when *d*the LORD your God *was* your king. Now   *a* ch. 7. 13.
therefore *e*behold the king *f*whom ye have chosen, *and* whom   *b* ch. 11. 1.
ye have desired ! and, behold, *g*the LORD hath set a king over   *c* ch. 8. 5.
14 you. If ye will *h*fear the LORD, and serve him, and obey his   *d* Judg. 8. 23.
voice, and not rebel against the ⁴commandment of the LORD,   *e* ch. 10. 24.
then shall both ye and also the king that reigneth over you   *f* ch. 8. 5.
15 ⁵continue following the LORD your God : but if ye will *i*not   *g* Hos. 13. 11.
obey the voice of the LORD, but rebel against the commandment   *h* Josh. 24. 14.
of the LORD, then shall the hand of the LORD be against you,   *i* Lev. 26. 14,
16 *k*as *it was* against your fathers. Now therefore *l*stand and see   &c.
17 this great thing, which the LORD will do before your eyes. *Is it*   *k* ver. 9.
not *m*wheat harvest to day ? *n*I will call unto the LORD, and he   *l* Ex. 14. 13.
shall send thunder and rain ; that ye may perceive and see that   *n* ch. 7. 9, 10.

g Judg. 11. 1.
i ch. 7. 13.
& 9. 20.
i Lev. 26. 14,
Deut. 28. 15,
&c.
Josh. 24. 20.
m Prov. 26. 1.
Jam. 5. 16.

---

¹ Or, *made*.   ² Heb. *righteousnesses*, or,   ⁴ Heb. *mouth*.
³ Heb. *with*.   *benefits*, Judg. 5. 11.   ⁵ Heb. *be after*.

---

6. *advanced*] In the sense of *appointing*
them to their office. It is, literally, *made*
(see marg. ; 1 K. xii. 31 ; Heb. iii. 2).
Samuel's purpose is to impress the people
with the conviction that Jehovah was their
God, and the God of their fathers ; that to
Him they owed their national existence and
all their national blessings, and that faithfulness to Him, to the exclusion of all other
worship (*v.* 21) was the only safety of the
newly-established monarchy. Observe the
constant reference to the Exodus as the well-
known turning-point of their national life
(see iv. 8, vi. 6).

9. According to the present arrangement
of the Book of Judges, and the common
chronology, the oppression of Sisera must
have occurred about 200 years after the
entrance into Canaan. But Samuel here
places it as the first great servitude, before
that under Eglon king of Moab, or that
from which Shamgar delivered them. And
this is in accordance with the internal
evidence of the Book of Judges itself. It is

also the order of Judg. x. 11, except that
there the Ammonites (Judg. iii. 13) are
placed before the Philistines.

11. *Bedan*] No such name occurs among
the Judges who delivered Israel. Some
Versions and commentators read Barak, the
form of the letters of both words being in
Hebrew somewhat similar.

and Samuel] There is nothing improper
or out of place in Samuel mentioning his
own judgeship. It had supplied a remarkable instance of God's deliverance (vii. 12-
15) ; and, as it was the last as well as
one of the very greatest deliverances, it was
natural he should do so. The passage in
Heb. xi. 32 is quite as favourable to the
mention of Samuel here as to that of *Samson*, which some propose to read instead of
Samuel.

17. *wheat harvest*] Between May 15 and
June 15. Jerome's testimony (that of an
eye-witness) "I have never seen rain in the
end of June, or in July, in Judæa" is borne
out by modern travellers.

*o*your wickedness *is* great, which ye have done in the sight of
18 the LORD, in asking you a king. ¶ So Samuel called' unto the
LORD; and the LORD sent thunder and rain that day: and *p*all
19 the people greatly feared the LORD and Samuel. And all the
people said unto Samuel, *q*Pray for thy servants unto the LORD
thy God, that we die not: for we have added unto all our sins
20 *this* evil, to ask us a king. ¶ And Samuel said unto the people,
Fear not: ye have done all this wickedness: yet turn not aside
from following the LORD, but serve the LORD with all your
21 heart; and *r*turn ye not aside: *s*for *then should ye go* after vain
22 *things*, which cannot profit nor deliver; for they *are* vain. For *t*the
LORD will not forsake his people *u*for his great name's sake:
because *x*it hath pleased the LORD to make you his people.
23 Moreover as for me, God forbid that I should sin against the
LORD *1 y*in ceasing to pray for you: but *z*I will teach you the
24 *a*good and the right way: *b*only fear the LORD, and serve him
in truth with all your heart: for *c*consider *2*how *d*great *things* he
25 hath done for you. But if ye shall still do wickedly, *e*ye shall
be consumed, *f*both ye, and your king.

CHAP. **13.** SAUL *3*reigned one year; and when he had reigned two
2 years over Israel, Saul chose him three thousand *men* of Israel;
whereof two thousand were with Saul in Michmash and in mount
Beth-el, and a thousand were with Jonathan in *a*Gibeah of Benjamin: and the rest of the people he sent every man to his tent.
3 ¶ And Jonathan smote *b*the garrison of the Philistines that *was*
in *4*Geba, and the Philistines heard *of it.* And Saul blew the
trumpet throughout all the land, saying, Let the Hebrews hear.
4 And all Israel heard say *that* Saul had smitten a garrison of the
Philistines, and *that* Israel also *5*was had in abomination with
the Philistines. And the people were called together after Saul
5 to Gilgal. And the Philistines gathered themselves together to
fight with Israel, thirty thousand chariots, and six thousand

---

XIII. **1.** The text of this verse, omitted
by the LXX., is held to be corrupt, and
the numerals denoting Saul's age at his
accession as well as the duration of his
reign, are thought to be omitted or faulty.
Saul may have been about 30 at his accession, and have reigned some 32 years,
since we know that his grandson Mephibosheth was five years old at Saul's
death (2 Sam. iv. 4); and 32 added to the
seven and a half years between the death
of Saul and that of Ishbosheth, makes up
the 40 years assigned to Saul's dynasty in
Acts xiii. 21. Neither is there any clue to
the interval of time between the events recorded in the preceding chapter, and those
which follow in this and succeeding chapters. But the appearance of Jonathan as a
warrior (*v.* 2) compared with the mention of
Saul as "a young man" (ix. 2), implies an
interval of not less than ten or fifteen years,
perhaps more. The object of the historian
is to prepare the way for the history of
David's reign. He therefore passes at once
to that incident in Saul's reign, which led to

his rejection by God, as recorded in *vv.*
13, 14.
2. The state of things which preceded
the events described in this chapter seems
to have been a comparative peace between
Israel and the Philistines, since Saul had
only 3,000 men under arms. At the same
time Philistine garrisons continued to occupy the country of the Israelites in certain
strong places, whereof one was at Geba
(*Jeba*), in the immediate neighbourhood of
Gibeah (x. 5, xiii. 3), and exactly opposite
Michmash (*Mukhmas*), which was on the
northern edge of the great Wady Suweinit.
3. This was the first act in the war of
independence, and probably the first feat in
arms of the young hero Jonathan.
4. *to Gilgal*] The Wady Suweinit de-
bouches into the plain of the Jordan in
which Gilgal was situated. For the sanctity
of Gilgal, see above, xi. 14 note.
5. *thirty thousand chariots*] Probably a
copyist's mistake for *three hundred.* [Cp., for
a similar numerical variation, 1 Chr. xviii. 4
with 2 Sam. viii. 4.]

horsemen, and people as the sand which *is* on the sea shore in multitude : and they came up, and pitched in Michmash, east-
6 ward from Beth-aven. ¶ When the men of Israel saw that they were in a strait, (for the people were distressed,) then the people *c* did hide themselves in caves, and in thickets, and in rocks, and   *c* Judg. 6. 2.
7 in high places, and in pits. And *some of* the Hebrews went over Jordan to the land of Gad and Gilead. As for Saul, he *was* yet
8 in Gilgal, and all the people ¹ followed him trembling. *d* And   *d* ch. 10. 8. he tarried seven days, according to the set time that Samuel *had appointed :* but Samuel came not to Gilgal ; and the people were
9 scattered from him. And Saul said, Bring hither a burnt offering to me, and peace offerings. And he offered the burnt
10 offering. And it came to pass, that as soon as he had made an end of offering the burnt offering, behold, Samuel came ; and Saul went out to meet him, that he might ² salute him.
11 ¶ And Samuel said, What hast thou done ? And Saul said, Because I saw that the people were scattered from me, and *that* thou camest not within the days appointed, and *that* the Philistines gathered themselves together at Michmash ;
12 therefore said I, The Philistines will come down now upon me to Gilgal, and I have not ³ made supplication unto the LORD : I
13 forced myself therefore, and offered a burnt offering. And Samuel said to Saul, *e* Thou hast done foolishly : *f* thou hast not   *e* 2 Chr. 16. 9. kept the commandment of the LORD thy God, which he com-   *f* ch. 15. 11. manded thee : for now would the LORD have established thy
14 kingdom upon Israel for ever. *g* But now thy kingdom shall not   *g* ch. 15. 28. continue : *h* the LORD hath sought him a man after his own   *h* Ps. 89. 20. heart, and the LORD hath commanded him *to be* captain over   Acts 13. 22. his people, because thou hast not kept *that* which the LORD

¹ Heb. *trembled after him.*   ² Heb. *bless him.*   ³ Heb. *intreated the face.*

---

eastward from Bethaven] Or more simply "to the east of Bethaven," which (Josh. vii. 2) lay *on the east side of Bethel.* Bethaven [thought to be the same as Deir Diwân] lay between Bethel and Michmash, which had been evacuated by Saul.

6. *in thickets*] Literally, *among thorns.*

high places] Not the *high places* for worship, but holds or towers (Judg. ix. 46, 49); that particular kind of tower which was the work of the old Canaanite inhabitants, and which remained as ruins in the time of Saul.

7. The words *some of,* which are the emphatic words in the A.V., as distinguishing those who crossed the Jordan from those who hid themselves, are not in the Hebrew at all. *The Hebrews* seem to be distinguished from *the men of Israel* in *v.* 6. (Cp. xiv. 21.)

8. *had appointed*] This appointment has of course nothing whatever to do with that made years before (x. 8), the keeping of which is expressly mentioned at the natural time (xi. 15). But Samuel had again, on this later occasion, made an appointment at the end of seven days. It seems to have been as a trial of faith and obedience, under which, this time, Saul unhappily broke down.

9. There is a difference of opinion among commentators whether Saul himself offered

the sacrifices prepared for Samuel, thus entrenching upon the priest's office ; or whether he ordered the priests to sacrifice, as Solomon did. In the latter case his sin consisted in disobeying the word of God, Who had bidden him wait till Samuel came. And this is, on the whole, the more probable ; since Samuel's rebuke says nothing of any assumption of priesthood, such as we read in the case of Uzziah (2 Chr. xxvi. 18).

11. Saul had come from Michmash to Gilgal, expecting to gather the force of the whole nation around him. Instead of that, the people fled, leaving him in the exposed plain with only 600 men (*v.* 15). The Philistines occupied Michmash, and might at any moment pour down the valley upon Gilgal. Saul's situation was obviously one of extreme peril. A few hours' delay might prove fatal to him and his little army. Hence, he "forced" himself, &c.

13. *Thou hast done foolishly,* &c.] Motives of worldly expediency were not to be weighed against the express commandment of God. All the circumstances and all the dangers were as well known to God as they were to Saul, and God had bidden him wait till Samuel came. Here was exactly the same sin of wilful disobedience which broke out again, and was so severely reproved (xv. 17-23).

15 commanded thee. ¶ And Samuel arose, and gat him up from Gilgal unto Gibeah of Benjamin. And Saul numbered the people *that were* ¹present with him, ᶦabout six hundred men.

ch. 11. 2.

16 And Saul, and Jonathan his son, and the people *that were* present with them, abode in ²Gibeah of Benjamin: but the Philis-

17 tines encamped in Michmash. And the spoilers came out of the camp of the Philistines in three companies: one company turned unto the way *that leadeth* to ᵏOphrah, unto the land of

ᵏ Josh. 18. 23.

18 Shual: and another company turned the way *to* ᶦBeth-horon:

ᶦ Josh. 16. 3.
& 18. 13, 14.
ᵐ Neh. 11.
31.

and another company turned *to* the way of the border that looketh

19 to the valley of ᵐZeboim toward the wilderness. ¶ Now ⁿthere was no smith found throughout all the land of Israel: for the Philistines said, Lest the Hebrews make *them* swords or spears:

ⁿ See 2 Kin.
24. 14.
Jer. 24. 1.

20 but all the Israelites went down to the Philistines, to sharpen every man his share, and his coulter, and his axe, and his mat-

21 tock. Yet they had ³a file for the mattocks, and for the coulters, and for the forks, and for the axes, and ⁴to sharpen the goads.

ᵒ So Judg.
5. 8.

22 So it came to pass in the day of battle, that ᵒthere was neither sword nor spear found in the hand of any of the people that *were* with Saul and Jonathan: but with Saul and with Jonathan

ᵖ ch. 14. 1, 4.

23 his son was there found. ¶ ᵖAnd the ⁵garrison of the Philistines went out to the passage of Michmash.

Chap. 14. NOW ⁶it came to pass upon a day, that Jonathan the son of Saul said unto the young man that bare his armour,

---

¹ Heb. *found*.
² Heb. *Geba*, ver. 3.
³ Heb. *a file with mouths*.
⁴ Heb. *to set*.
⁵ Or, *standing camp*.
⁶ Or, *there was a day*.

---

15. *Samuel arose*] Saul could not return to his own station at Michmash, seeing it was occupied by the Philistines; so, perhaps by Samuel's advice (since, according to the text, he preceded him thither), he effected a junction with Jonathan at Gibeah. Some would read *Saul* instead of *Samuel*.

17. *the spoilers*] "The devastator:" the same word is used of the destroying Angel (Ex. xii. 23). The verse describes the system adopted by the Philistines by which for a time they subjugated the Israelites. From their central camp at Michmash they sent out three bands to kill and lay waste and destroy. One took a northerly direction towards Ophrah,—five miles east of Bethel, identified with *Ephrain* (2 Chr. xiii. 19) and the modern *Taiyibeh*,—and towards the land of Shual, possibly the same as Shalim (ix. 4); the second westward to Beth-horon; and the third eastward, by the unknown valley of Zeboim, toward the wilderness, *i.e.* the Jordan valley, towards Jericho.

19. *there was no smith*] This was the result of the fierce inroads described in the preceding verses, and the method adopted to make the Philistine conquests permanent.

20-21. The best rendering of the passage is perhaps as follows: "But all the Israelites went down to the Philistines to sharpen &c. (*v.* 21), whenever there was bluntness of edge to their shares and coulters and prong-forks and axes, and to point their goads."

Coulters and mattocks were cutting instruments of the type of the share.

22. This seems to be mentioned here, in anticipation of the narrative in the next chapter, to enhance the victory gained, through God's help (xiv. 23), by the comparatively unarmed Israelites over their enemies. What with occasional skirmishes with the Philistines, the necessity of using their arms for domestic purposes, accidental losses, and the ordinary wear and tear, coupled with the impossibility of renewing their arms from the want of smiths and forges, the people that were with Saul and Jonathan came to be very imperfectly armed. It has been observed, moreover, that the Benjamites were more famous for the use of the sling than for any other weapon (Judg. xx. 16), and this would be an additional cause of the paucity of swords and spears.

23. *the passage of Michmash*] The steep and precipitous path from Michmash to Geba, over the valley of Suweinit. The same term is used in Isai. x. 28, 29, where the march of the Assyrian army is described.

XIV. 1. *Now, &c.*] Rather "and," since this verse is in immediate dependence upon the preceding. When Jonathan saw the garrison come out again and again, in defiance "of the armies of the living God," at length "upon a day" he determined to attack them.

Come, and let us go over to the Philistines' garrison, that is on
2 the other side. But he told not his father. And Saul tarried in
the uttermost part of Gibeah under a pomegranate tree which is
in Migron: and the people that were with him were *about six *ch. 13. 15.
3 hundred men; and *Ahiah, the son of Ahitub, *I-chabod's *ch. 22. 9,
brother, the son of Phinehas, the son of Eli, the LORD's priest called Ahim-
in Shiloh, *wearing an ephod. And the people knew not that *ch. 4. 21.
4 Jonathan was gone. And between the passages, by which *ch. 2. 28.
Jonathan sought to go over *unto the Philistines' garrison, there *ch. 13. 23.
was a sharp rock on the one side, and a sharp rock on the other
side: and the name of the one was Bozez, and the name of the
5 other Seneh. The ¹forefront of the one was situate northward
over against Michmash, and the other southward over against
6 Gibeah. And Jonathan said to the young man that bare his
armour, Come, and let us go over unto the garrison of these uncircumcised: it may be that the LORD will work for us: for
there is no restraint to the LORD *to save by many or by few. *Judg. 7. 4,
7 And his armourbearer said unto him, Do all that is in thine 2 Chr. 14. 11.
heart: turn thee; behold, I am with thee according to thy heart.
8 Then said Jonathan, Behold, we will pass over unto these men,
9 and we will discover ourselves unto them. If they say thus
unto us, ²Tarry until we come to you; then we will stand still in
10 our place, and will not go up unto them. But if they say thus,
Come up unto us; then we will go up: for the LORD hath delivered them into our hand: and *this shall be a sign unto us. *See Gen.
11 ¶ And both of them discovered themselves unto the garrison of 24. 14.
the Philistines: and the Philistines said, Behold, the Hebrews Judg. 7. 11.
come forth out of the holes where they had hid themselves.

¹ Heb. tooth.   ² Heb. Be still.

2. under a pomegranate] Cp. xxii. 6; Judg.
iv. 5. Saul was at the northern extremity
of Gibeah, about an hour's march from
Geba, where Jonathan was.
  Migron, if the reading is correct, must be
a different place from the Migron of Isai.
x. 28.
  3. Whether *Ahiah* or *Ahijah* is the same
person as *Ahimelech the son of Ahitub* (see
marg. ref.), or whether Ahimelech was the
brother or son of Ahijah, and his successor
in the priesthood, it is impossible to say
certainly. Most probably *Ahijah* and
Ahimelech are variations of the same name ;
the latter element in each alone being different, *melech* (king) being substituted for
the divine name *Jah*. Cp. *Eliakim* and
Jehoiakim (2 K. xxiii. 34), *Eliab* and *Eliel*
(1 Chr. vi. 27, 34).
  This fragment of a genealogy is a very
valuable help to the chronology. The
grandson of Phinehas, the son of Eli, was
now High Priest ; and Samuel, who was
probably a few years older than Ahitub the
son of Phinehas, was now an old man. All
this indicates a period of about 50 years or
upwards from the taking of the Ark by the
Philistines.
  the LORD's priest in Shiloh] But as Eli was
so emphatically known and described in
chs. i.—iv., as God's Priest at Shiloh, and

as there is every reason to believe that
Shiloh was no longer the seat of the Ark in
Saul's time (see xxii. ; 1 Chr. xiii. 3-5), it is
better to refer these words to Eli, and not to
Ahijah, to whom the next words, *wearing
an ephod*, apply. (See ii. 28; Judg. i. 1
note.)
  4. [The southern cliff was called *Seneh*,
or "the acacia," and the same name still
applies to the modern valley, dotted by
acacias. The northern cliff was named
Bozez or "Shining." The valley runs nearly
due east, and the northern cliff is of ruddy
and tawny tint, crowned with gleaming
white chalk, and in the full glare of the sun
almost all the day. (Conder.)]
  6. It is remarkable that the epithet *uncircumcised*, used as a term of reproach, is
confined almost exclusively to the Philistines. (Cp. xvii. 26, 36; Judg. xiv. 3, xv.
18, &c.) This is probably an indication of
the long oppression of the Israelites by the
Philistines and of their frequent wars.
  10. Though it is not expressly said, as in
the case of Gideon (Judg. vi. 34), Othniel
(Judg. iii. 10), and others, that the Spirit
of the Lord came upon him, yet the whole
course of the narrative, especially vv. 13-
16, indicates an extraordinary divine interposition.

12 And the men of the garrison answered Jonathan and his armour-bearer, and said, Come up to us, and we will shew you a thing. And Jonathan said unto his armourbearer, Come up after me: 13 for the LORD hath delivered them into the hand of Israel. And Jonathan climbed up upon his hands and upon his feet, and his armourbearer after him: and they fell before Jonathan; and 14 his armourbearer slew after him. And that first slaughter, which Jonathan and his armourbearer made, was about twenty men, within as it were [1]an half acre of land, *which* a yoke of

h 2 Kin. 7. 7.
Job 18. 11.
i ch. 13. 17.

15 *oxen might plow.* ¶And *h*there was trembling in the host, in the field, and among all the people: the garrison, and *i*the spoilers, they also trembled, and the earth quaked: so it was

k Gen. 35. 5.

16 [2k]a very great trembling. And the watchmen of Saul in Gibeah of Benjamin looked; and, behold, the multitude melted away,

l ver. 20.

17 and they *l*went on beating down *one another.* Then said Saul unto the people that *were* with him, Number now, and see who is gone from us. And when they had numbered, behold, 18 Jonathan and his armourbearer *were* not *there.* And Saul said unto Ahiah, Bring hither the ark of God. For the ark of God 19 was at that time with the children of Israel. And it came to

m Num. 27. 21.

pass, while Saul *m*talked unto the priest, that the [3]noise that *was* in the host of the Philistines went on and increased: and 20 Saul said unto the priest, Withdraw thine hand. And Saul and all the people that *were* with him [4]assembled themselves, and

n Judg. 7. 22.
2 Chr. 20. 23.

they came to the battle: and, behold, *n*every man's sword was against his fellow, *and there was* a very great discomfiture. 21 Moreover the Hebrews *that* were with the Philistines before that time, which went up with them into the camp *from the country* round about, even they also *turned* to be with the Israelites that 22 *were* with Saul and Jonathan. Likewise all the men of Israel

o ch. 13. 6.

which *o*had hid themselves in mount Ephraim, *when* they heard that the Philistines fled, even they also followed hard after them

p Ex. 14. 30.
Ps. 44. 6, 7.
Hos. 1. 7.
q ch, 13. 5.
r Josh. 6. 26.

23 in the battle. *p*So the LORD saved Israel that day: and the 24 battle passed over *q*unto Beth-aven. ¶And the men of Israel were distressed that day: for Saul had *r*adjured the people,

[1] Or, *half a furrow of an acre of land,* Judg. 7. 21. [2] Heb. *a trembling of God.* [3] Or, *tumult.* [4] Heb. *were cried together.*

---

12. *we will show you a thing*] Said mockingly.

14. *within as it were an half acre,* &c.] The Hebrew s extremely obscure. Hence there is some probability that the true reading is preserved by the LXX. which translates the clause "*with darts and stones and flints of the field.*" Others take the words to mean "in about half the time that a yoke of oxen draw a furrow in the field."

15. *the earth quaked*] This naturally increased the panic to the utmost. Cp. vii. 10; Josh. x. 11; Ps. cxiv. 4.

16. *multitude*] The word is in *v.* 19 (margin) rendered *tumult.* It must have the same meaning here. The sentence is obscure and probably corrupt; perhaps it means, *and behold the tumult! and it went on* (increased) *melting away and beating down.*

18. For "the ark," some read "the ephod," owing to the improbability of the Ark being with Saul at this time, and from

the verb "Bring hither" being *never* applied to the Ark, but regularly to the ephod (xxiii. 9, xxx. 7). Moreover not the Ark, but the ephod with Urim and Thummim, was the proper instrument for inquiring of the Lord. If, however, the Hebrew text be correct, they must have brought the Ark into Saul's camp from Kirjath-jearim (vii.), possibly to be safe from the Philistines.

19. *Withdraw thine hand*] i.e. "Desist from what thou art about." Saul in his impatience to join the battle would not wait for the answer from God, which he had desired Ahijah to enquire for; just as later (*v.* 35) he would not wait to finish the altar which he had begun to build. Had he now waited he would doubtless have avoided the error into which he fell.

20. *assembled themselves*] See marg. Many Versions give the sense "shouted," which is far preferable, and only requires a different punctuation.

saying, Cursed *be* the man that eateth *any* food until evening,
that I may be avenged on mine enemies. So none of the people
25 tasted *any* food. *ˢAnd all *they of* the land came to a wood; and
26 there was *ᵗhoney upon the ground. And when the people were
come into the wood, behold, the honey dropped; but no man
27 put his hand to his mouth : for the people feared the oath. But
Jonathan heard not when his father charged the people with the
oath : wherefore he put forth the end of the rod that *was* in his
hand, and dipped it in an honeycomb, and put his hand to his
28 mouth ; and his eyes were enlightened. Then answered one of
the people, and said, Thy father straitly charged the people
with an oath, saying, Cursed *be* the man that eateth *any* food
29 this day. And the people were ¹faint. Then said Jonathan,
My father hath troubled the land : see, I pray you, how mine
eyes have been enlightened, because I tasted a little of this
30 honey. How much more, if haply the people had eaten freely
to day of the spoil of their enemies which they found ? for had
there not been now a much greater slaughter among the Philis-
31 tines ? ¶And they smote the Philistines that day from Mich-
32 mash to Aijalon : and the people were very faint. And the
people flew upon the spoil, and took sheep, and oxen, and
calves, and slew *them* on the ground : and the people did eat
33 *them* ᵘwith the blood. Then they told Saul, saying, Behold, the
people sin against the LORD, in that they eat with the blood.
And he said, Ye have ²transgressed : roll a great stone unto me
34 this day. And Saul said, Disperse yourselves among the people,
and say unto them, Bring me hither every man his ox, and
every man his sheep, and slay *them* here, and eat; and sin
not against the LORD in eating with the blood. And all the
people brought every man his ox ³with him that night, and slew
35 *them* there. And Saul ˣbuilt an altar unto the LORD : ⁴the same
36 was the first altar that he built unto the LORD. And Saul said,
Let us go down after the Philistines by night, and spoil them
until the morning light, and let us not leave a man of them.
And they said, Do whatsoever seemeth good unto thee. Then
37 said the priest, Let us draw near hither unto God. And Saul

ˢ Deut. 9. 28.
Matt. 3. 5.
ᵗ Ex. 3. 8.
Num. 13. 27.
Matt. 3. 4.

ᵘ Lev. 3. 17.
& 7. 26.
& 17. 10.
& 19. 26.
Deut. 12. 16,
23, 24.

ˣ ch. 7. 17.

¹ Or, *weary*, Judg. 4. 21.   ³ Heb. *in his hand*.   ⁴ Heb. *that altar he began*
² Or, *dealt treacherously*.   *to build unto the* LORD.

---

25. *all they of the land*] Lit., *all the land*,
probably meaning all those named in *vv.* 21,
22, who now flocked to the wood as a ren-
dezvous.
26. *the honey dropped*] Rather, " Behold
a stream of honey." The same thing may
be seen in Spain, where in woody and rocky
ground copious streams of honey are often
found.
27. *were enlightened*] *i.e.* he was refreshed,
when he was faint.
28. *And the people were faint*] Read, "are
faint," the words are part of the man's
complaint.
29. *hath troubled*] The same word as was
applied to Achan (Josh. vii. 25), and gave
its name to the valley of Achor. This additional reference to Joshua is remarkable
(cp. *v.* 24).
31. *Aijalon*] The modern Yalo. It lies
upon the side of a hill to the south of a fine

valley which opens from between the two
Bethhorons right down to the western
plain of the Philistines, exactly on the
route which the Philistines, when expelled
from the high country about Michmash and
Bethel, would take to regain their own
country. Aijalon would be 15 or 20 miles
from Michmash.
33. *sin against the* LORD] See marg. ref. *u*.
But the prohibition was older than the
Law of Moses (Gen. ix. 4). Cp. Acts xv.
20, 29.
35. *And Saul built*, &c.] *i.e.* of the great
stone which they had rolled to kill the oxen
and sheep upon, he began to build an altar
to Jehovah (see marg.) ; but he did not finish
it (cp. 1 Chr. xxvii. 24), in his haste to pursue the Philistines that night.
36. *Then said the priest*, &c.] Ahijah,
with equal courage and faithfulness, worthy
of his office as "the priest," when every

asked counsel of God, Shall I go down after the Philistines?

y ch. 28. 6.

z Josh. 7. 14.
ch. 10. 19.

a 2 Sam. 12.
5.

wilt thou deliver them into the hand of Israel? But *y*he
38 answered him not that day. And Saul said, *z*Draw ye near
hither, all the ¹chief of the people: and know and see wherein
39 this sin hath been this day. For, *a*as the LORD liveth, which
saveth Israel, though it be in Jonathan my son, he shall surely
die. But *there was* not a man among all the people *that*
40 answered him. Then said he unto all Israel, Be ye on one side,
and I and Jonathan my son will be on the other side. And the
41 people said unto Saul, Do what seemeth good unto thee. There-

b Prov. 16.
33.
Acts 1. 24.
c Josh. 7. 16.
ch. 10. 20.
d Josh. 7. 19.
e ver. 27.

fore Saul said unto the LORD God of Israel, ²*b*Give a perfect *lot*.
*c*And Saul and Jonathan were taken: but the people ³escaped.
42 And Saul said, Cast *lots* between me and Jonathan my son.
43 And Jonathan was taken. Then Saul said to Jonathan, *d*Tell
me what thou hast done. And Jonathan told him, and said, *e*I
did but taste a little honey with the end of the rod that *was* in

f Ruth 1. 17.
g ver. 39.

44 mine hand, *and*, lo, I must die. And Saul answered, *f*God do
45 so and more also: *g*for thou shalt surely die, Jonathan. And
the people said unto Saul, Shall Jonathan die, who hath wrought

h 2 Sam. 14.
11.
1 Kin. 1. 52.
Luke 21. 18.

this great salvation in Israel? God forbid: *h*as the LORD
liveth, there shall not one hair of his head fall to the ground;
for he hath wrought with God this day. So the people rescued
46 Jonathan, that he died not. Then Saul went up from following
the Philistines: and the Philistines went to their own place.
47 ¶ So Saul took the kingdom over Israel, and fought against all
his enemies on every side, against Moab, and against the

i ch. 11. 11.
k 2 Sam. 10.
6.

children of *i*Ammon, and against Edom, and against the kings
of *k*Zobah, and against the Philistines: and whithersoever he
48 turned himself, he vexed *them*. And he ⁴gathered an host, and

l ch. 15. 3, 7.
m ch. 31. 2.
1 Chr. 8. 33.

*l*smote the Amalekites, and delivered Israel out of the hands of
49 them that spoiled them. ¶Now *m*the sons of Saul were Jona-

¹ Heb. *corners*, Judg. 20. 2.   ³ Heb. *went forth*.
² Or, *Shew the innocent*.   ⁴ Or, *wrought mightily*.

---

one else yielded to Saul's humour, proposed
that they should draw near to God to enquire of Him. (Cp. 1 K. xxii. 7.)

37. *asked counsel*] The technical phrase
for enquiring of God by Urim and Thummim, and applied also to enquiry of other
oracles.

39. Saul's rashness becomes more and
more apparent. He now adds an additional
oath, to bring down yet further guilt in
"taking God's name in vain." The expressions in *vv.* 36, 40, indicate the fear in which
the people stood of Saul. None dared resist
his will.

41. *Give a perfect lot*] The phrase is obscure, but the meaning is probably as in
the margin.

47. Cp. 2 Sam. viii. 15. The preceding
narrative shows that before this time Saul
had been king in name only, since his country was occupied by the Philistines, and he
could only muster 600 men, and those but
half armed and pent up in a narrow stronghold. Now, however, on the expulsion of
the Philistines from his country, and the
return of the Israelites from their vassalage
and from their hiding places (*vv.* 21, 22),

Saul became king in deed as well as in
name, and acted the part of a king through
the rest of his reign in defending his people
against their enemies round about. A comprehensive list of these enemies, including
the Ammonite war which had already been
described (ch. xi.), and the Amalekite war
which follows in ch. xv., is given in *vv.* 47,
48. There is not the slightest indication from
the words whether this "taking the kingdom" occurred soon or many years after
Saul's anointing at Gilgal. Hence some
would place the clause 47-52 immediately
after ch. xi., or ch. xii., as a summary of
Saul's reign. The details of the reign, viz.
of the Philistine war in chs. xiii., xiv., of
the Amalekite war in ch. xv., and the other
events down to the end of ch. xxxi., preceded by the formulary, xiii. 1, would then
follow according to the common method of
Hebrew historical narrative.

Zobah] This was one of the petty Aramæan kingdoms flourishing at this time
(Ps. lx. title). It seems to have been situated between Damascus and the Euphrates.

49. This enumeration of Saul's children
and chief officers is according to the analogy

than, and Ishui, and Melchi-shua: and the names of his two
daughters *were these;* the name of the firstborn Merab, and the
50 name of the younger Michal : and the name of Saul's wife *was*
Ahinoam, the daughter of Ahimaaz : and the name of the
captain of his host *was* [1]Abner, the son of Ner, Saul's uncle.
51 *n* And Kish *was* the father of Saul ; and Ner the father of Abner *n* ch. 9. 1.
52 *was* the son of Abiel. And there was sore war against the
Philistines all the days of Saul : and when Saul saw any strong
man, or any valiant man, *o*he took him unto him. *o* ch. 8. 11.

Chap. 15. SAMUEL also said unto Saul, *a*The LORD sent me to *a* ch. 9. 16.
anoint thee *to be* king over his people, over Israel : now therefore hearken thou unto the voice of the words of the LORD.
2 Thus saith the LORD of hosts, I remember *that* which Amalek *b* Ex. 17. 8,
did to Israel, *b*how he laid *wait* for him in the way, when he 14.
3 came up from Egypt. Now go and smite Amalek, and *c*utterly Num. 24. 20.
destroy all that they have, and spare them not ; but slay both 18, 19.
man and woman, infant and suckling, ox and sheep, camel and *c* Josh. 6. 17.
4 ass. ¶And Saul gathered the people together, and numbered 21.
them in Telaim, two hundred thousand footmen, and ten Judg. 1. 16.
5 thousand men of Judah. And Saul came to a city of Amalek, *e* Gen. 18. 25.
6 and [2]laid wait in the valley. And Saul said unto *d*the Kenites, Rev. 18. 4.
*e*Go, depart, get you down from among the Amalekites, lest I *f* Ex. 18. 10.
destroy you with them : for *f*ye shewed kindness to all the 32.
children of Israel, when they came up out of Egypt. So the *g* ch. 14. 48.
7 Kenites departed from among the Amalekites. *g*And Saul & 25. 18.
smote the Amalekites from *h*Havilah *until* thou comest to *i* Gen. 16. 7.
8 *i*Shur, that *is* over against Egypt. And *k*he took Agag the 20. 34, 35.
king of the Amalekites alive, and *l*utterly destroyed all the *l* See ch.30.1.

d Num. 24.

& 4. 11.

Num. 10. 29,

h Gen. 2. 11.

k See 1 Kin.

---

[1] Heb. *Abiner.*   [2] Or, *fought.*

---

of the subsequent annals of David and
Solomon's reign. But the one here called
Ishui, is elsewhere (marg. reff.) called *Abinadab* ; and a fourth son, *Esh-baal* or *Ish-
bosheth,* is here omitted.
50. The only other *Ahimaaz* mentioned
in Scripture was the son of Zadok the priest.
The word *Ahi* (brother) is frequently found
in composition in names in the High Priest's
family, *e.g.* in Ahijah, Ahimelech. It is
not improbable that Ahimaaz may have
been of this family, as marriages between
the royal and priestly houses were not unusual (2 K. xi. 2 ; 2 Chr. xxii. 11), and perhaps it may have been owing to such a connexion that Ahijah was brought into prominence by Saul. If there be any truth in
the above supposition, it would be an indication that Saul was not married till after
his election to the throne.
51. Read, *And Kish the father of Saul,
and Ner the father of Abner, were the sons of
Abiel.* Ner was Saul's uncle.
XV. 1. The absence of all chronology or
note of time is remarkable.
2. Cp. marg. reff. It appears (xiv. 48)
that this expedition against Amalek was not
made without fresh provocation. Probably
some incursion similar to that described in
ch. xxx. was made by them upon the south
country at a time when they thought the

Israelites were weakened by their contests
with the Philistines.
3. *utterly destroy*] Rather, "devote to destruction" (Levit. xxvii. 28 note). When
a city or people were thus made *cherem,*
everything living was to be destroyed, and
no part of the spoil fall to the conquerors
(cp. *v.* 21). The valuables were put into the
sacred treasury.
4. *Telaim*] Probably the same as *Telem*
(Josh. xv. 24), one of the uttermost cities
of Judah, towards the coast of Edom. The
name means *lambs,* and was probably so
called from the numerous flocks.
two hundred thousand, &c.] A wonderful
contrast with the *six hundred men* who composed his whole army before (xiii. 15), and
a proof how completely for a time the Philistines had been driven back. The separate
mention of the men of Judah shows how
little union there was between Judah and
Ephraim even at this time ; a circumstance
which throws light · upon the whole after
history.
7. The district here described would
stretch from Havilah on the extreme east to
Shur, either near Suez, or further north on
the coast road from Gaza to Egypt.
8. The saving Agag alive was in direct
violation of the *devotion* to destruction.

m ver. 3, 15.

n ver. 35.
2 Sam. 24.
16.
o Josh. 22.
16.
1 Kin. 9. 6.
p ch. 13. 13.
q 2 Sam. 6.8.
r Josh. 15.
55.

s Gen. 14.19.
Judg. 17. 2.

t ver. 9, 21.
Prov. 28. 13.

u ch. 9. 21.

x ver. 13.

y ver. 15.

9 people with the edge of the sword. But Saul and the people
m spared Agag, and the best of the sheep, and of the oxen, and
¹ of the fatlings, and the lambs, and all *that was* good, and would
not utterly destroy them : but every thing *that was* vile and
10 refuse, that they destroyed utterly. ¶ Then came the word of
11 the LORD unto Samuel, saying, *n* It repenteth me that I have
set up Saul to *be* king : for he is *o* turned back from following
me, *p* and hath not performed my commandments. And it
12 *q* grieved Samuel; and he cried unto the LORD all night. And
when Samuel rose early to meet Saul in the morning, it was
told Samuel, saying, Saul came to *r* Carmel, and, behold, he set
him up a place, and is gone about, and passed on, and gone
13 down to Gilgal. ¶ And Samuel came to Saul : and Saul said
unto him, *s* Blessed *be* thou of the LORD : I have performed the
14 commandment of the LORD. And Samuel said, What *meaneth*
then this bleating of the sheep in mine ears, and the lowing of
15 the oxen which I hear ? And Saul said, They have brought
them from the Amalekites : *t* for the people spared the best of
the sheep and of the oxen, to sacrifice unto the LORD thy God;
16 and the rest we have utterly destroyed. Then Samuel said unto
Saul, Stay, and I will tell thee what the LORD hath said to me
17 this night. And he said unto him, Say on. ¶ And Samuel said,
u When thou *wast* little in thine own sight, *wast* thou not *made*
the head of the tribes of Israel, and the LORD anointed thee
18 king over Israel ? And the LORD sent thee on a journey, and
said, Go and utterly destroy the sinners the Amalekites, and
19 fight against them until ² they be consumed. Wherefore then
didst thou not obey the voice of the LORD, but didst fly upon
20 the spoil, and didst evil in the sight of the LORD ? ¶ And Saul
said unto Samuel, Yea, *x* I have obeyed the voice of the LORD,
and have gone the way which the LORD sent me, and have
brought Agag the king of Amalek, and have utterly destroyed
21 the Amalekites. *y* But the people took of the spoil, sheep and

¹ Or, *of the second sort.*   ² Heb. *they consume them.*

---

9. *the fatlings*] The present Heb. text cannot be so rendered. It can only mean "*the second* best" (cp. marg.), *i.e.* sheep of the age to cut or shed the two teeth, sheep in their prime. But it is probable that the reading is corrupt, and that "fat or dainty bits" is the true reading.

11. *it grieved Samuel*] "**Samuel was angry,** or displeased," as Jonah was (Jon. iv. 1), and for a similar reason. Samuel was displeased that the king whom he had anointed should be set aside. It seemed a slur on his prophetic office.

he cried unto the LORD] With the wild scream or shriek of supplication. (See vii. 8, 9, xii. 18.) The phrase and the action mark Samuel's fervent, earnest character.

12. *a place*] Rather, "**a monument.**" The Heb. word (*yad*) means *a hand*, but is used in the sense of *monument*, or *trophy*, in 2 Sam. xviii. 18, where we are told that the marble pillar which Absalom set up in his lifetime, was called *Yad Absalom*. Carmel (see marg. ref.) would be on Saul's line of march on his return from the country

of the Amalekites, more especially if he came from the neighbourhood of Akaba.

13. Gilgal being within 15 miles of Ramah, Samuel might easily have come from the Ramah that morning. Self-will and rashness had hitherto been Saul's chief faults. He now seems to add falsehood and hypocrisy.

15. There is something thoroughly mean in his attempt to shift the responsibility of what was done from his own kingly shoulders to those of the people. Every word uttered by Saul seems to indicate the breaking down of his moral character.

16. Samuel now acquiesces in the wisdom and justice of the sentence which (*v.* 11) he had so strenuously resisted at first. What before was known only to the Searcher of hearts, had now been displayed to Samuel by Saul himself.

18. *the sinners*] As though God would justify His commission to destroy them. (Cp. Gen. xiii. 13.)

21. *the* LORD *thy God*] There is an implied censure of Samuel in this phrase.

oxen, the chief of the things which should have been utterly
22 destroyed, to sacrifice untö the LORD thy God in Gilgal. ¶ And
Samuel said, ²Hath the LORD *as great* delight in burnt offerings
and sacrifices, as in obeying the voice of the LORD? Behold,
*a*to obey *is* better than sacrifice, *and* to hearken than the fat of
23 rams. For rebellion *is as* the sin of ¹witchcraft, and stubbornness
is as iniquity and idolatry. Because thou hast rejected the
word of the LORD, *b*he hath also rejected thee from *being* king.
24 ¶ *c*And Saul said unto Samuel, I have sinned: for I have transgressed the commandment of the LORD, and thy words: because
25 I *d*feared the people, and obeyed their voice. Now therefore, I
pray thee, pardon my sin, and turn again with me, that I may
26 worship the LORD. And Samuel said unto Saul, I will not
return with thee: *e*for thou hast rejected the word of the LORD,
and the LORD hath rejected thee from being king over Israel.
27 And as Samuel turned about to go away, *f*he laid hold upon the
28 skirt of his mantle, and it rent. And Samuel said unto him,
*g*The LORD hath rent the kingdom of Israel from thee this day,
and hath given it to a neighbour of thine, *that is* better than
29 thou. And also the ²Strength of Israel *h*will not lie nor repent:
30 for he *is* not a man, that he should repent. Then he said, I
have sinned: *yet* *i*honour me now, I pray thee, before the elders
of my people, and before Israel, and turn again with me, that I
31 may worship the LORD thy God. So Samuel turned again
32 after Saul; and Saul worshipped the LORD. ¶ Then said
Samuel, Bring ye hither to me Agag the king of the Amalekites. And Agag came unto him delicately. And Agag said,
33 Surely the bitterness of death is passed. And Samuel said, *k*As
thy sword hath made women childless, so shall thy mother be
childless among women. And Samuel hewed Agag in pieces

z Ps. 50. 8, 9.
Prov. 21. 3.
Isai. 1. 11.
Jer. 7. 22.
Mic. 6. 6.
Heb. 10. 6.
a Eccl. 5. 1.
Hos. 6. 6.
Matt. 5. 24.
& 9. 13.
b ch. 13. 14.
c See 2 Sam.
12. 13.
d Ex. 23. 2.
Prov. 29. 25.
Isai. 51. 12.
e See ch. 2.
30.
f See 1 Kin.
11. 30.
g ch. 28. 17.
1 Kin. 11. 31.
h Num.23.19.
Ezek. 24. 14.
2 Tim. 2. 13.
Tit. 1. 2.
i John 5. 44.
& 12. 43.
k Ex. 17. 11.
Num. 14. 45.
See Judg. 1.
7.

¹ Heb. *divination*, Deut. 18. 10.   ² Or, *Eternity*, or, *Victory*.

Saul says that Samuel blames him for what
was done in honour of Samuel's God; as if
he had more zeal for the glory of God than
was felt by Samuel.
   22. *Hath the* LORD, &c.] A grand example
of the moral and spiritual teaching of the
Prophets (see marg. reff.). The tension of
Samuel's spirit, as he is about to pronounce
the sentence of rejection, produces a lyrical
turn of thought and language.
   23. The meaning is "Rebellion is as bad
as the sin of divination, and stubbornness is
as bad as worshipping false gods (*iniquity*),
and teraphim (*idolatry*)."
   24. *I have sinned*] Cp. *vv.* 25, 30. How
was it that these repeated confessions were
unavailing to obtain forgiveness, when
David's was? (See marg. ref.) Because
Saul only shrank from the *punishment* of
his sin. David shrank in abhorrence from
the sin itself (Ps. li. 4).
   29. *the strength of Israel*] A phrase which
occurs only here. The word means, *perpetuity, truth, glory, victory,* and *trust,* or *confidence.*
   30. The pertinacity with which Saul
clings to Samuel for support is a striking
testimony to Samuel's integrity. With all

his worldly-mindedness Saul could perceive
and appreciate the purity of Samuel's
character as a man of God.
   the LORD *thy God*] As above, *v.* 15.
   32. *delicately*] This phrase is very obscure.
The meaning of the word so rendered is
dainties, delights (Gen. xlix. 20; Prov.
xxix. 17; Lam. iv. 5), which hardly gives a
tolerable sense here. Some understand it
"fawningly, flatteringly," with a view of
appeasing Samuel. [Others alter the reading, and translate "in bonds."]
   Surely the bitterness, &c.] Agag hopes that
his life will be spared, and so expresses his
confident belief that the bitterness of death
is over.
   33. *hewed in pieces*] Only found in this
passage. Samuel thus executed the *cherem*
(*v.* 3) which Saul had violated, and so both
saved the nation from the guilt of a broken
oath, and gave a final example to Saul, but
apparently in vain, of uncompromising
obedience to the commandments of God.
There is something awful in the majesty of
the Prophet rising above and eclipsing that
of the king (cp. 1 K. xxi. 20; Jer. xxxviii.
14 seq.; Dan. ii. 46, iv. 27).

34 before the LORD in Gilgal. Then Samuel went to Ramah ; and
35 Saul went up to his house to ^{l}Gibeah of Saul. And ^{m}Samuel
came no more to see Saul until the day of his death : nevertheless Samuel ^{n}mourned for Saul : and the LORD ^{o}repented that
he had made Saul king over Israel.

CHAP. 16. AND the LORD said unto Samuel, ^{a}How long wilt thou
mourn for Saul, seeing ^{b}I have rejected him from reigning over
Israel? ^{c}fill thine horn with oil, and go, I will send thee to
Jesse the Beth-lehemite : for ^{d}I have provided me a king among
2 his sons. And Samuel said, How can I go? if Saul hear *it*, he
will kill me. And the LORD said, Take an heifer ^{1}with thee,
3 and say, ^{e}I am come to sacrifice to the LORD. And call Jesse to
the sacrifice, and ^{f}I will shew thee what thou shalt do : and
4 ^{g}thou shalt anoint unto me *him* whom I name unto thee. ¶ And
Samuel did that which the LORD spake, and came to Bethlehem. And the elders of the town ^{h}trembled at his ^{2}coming,
5 and said, ^{i}Comest thou peaceably? And he said, Peaceably : I
am come to sacrifice unto the LORD : ^{k}sanctify yourselves, and
come with me to the sacrifice. And he sanctified Jesse and his
6 sons, and called them to the sacrifice. ¶ And it came to pass,
when they were come, that he looked on ^{l}Eliab, and ^{m}said,
7 Surely the LORD's anointed *is* before him. But the LORD said
unto Samuel, Look not on ^{n}his countenance, or on the height of
his stature ; because I have refused him ; ^{o}for *the* LORD *seeth* not
as man seeth ; for man ^{p}looketh on the ^{3}outward appearance,
8 but the LORD looketh on the ^{q}heart. Then Jesse called ^{r}Abinadab,
and made him pass before Samuel. And he said, Neither hath the
9 LORD chosen this. Then Jesse made $^{s\,4}$Shammah to pass by. And
10 he said, Neither hath the LORD chosen this. Again, Jesse made
seven of his sons to pass before Samuel. And Samuel said unto
11 Jesse, The LORD hath not chosen these. ¶ And Samuel said
unto Jesse, Are here all *thy* children? And he said, ^{t}There
remaineth yet the youngest, and, behold, he keepeth the sheep.
And Samuel said unto Jesse, ^{u}Send and fetch him : for we will
12 not sit ^{5}down till he come hither. And he sent, and brought him
in. Now he *was* ^{x}ruddy, *and* withal ^{6}of a beautiful countenance,
and goodly to look to. ^{y}And the LORD said, Arise, anoint him :
13 for this *is* he. Then Samuel took the horn of oil, and ^{z}anointed
him in the midst of his brethren : and ^{a}the Spirit of the LORD

Left margin references:

^{l} ch. 11. 4.
^{m} See ch. 19. 24.
^{n} ver. 11.
ch. 16. 1.
^{o} ver. 11.
^{a} ch. 15. 35.
^{b} ch. 15. 23.
^{c} ch. 9. 16.
2 Kin. 9. 1.
^{d} Ps. 78. 70.
& 89. 19.
Acts 13. 22.

^{e} ch. 9. 12.
& 20. 29.
^{f} Ex. 4. 15.
^{g} ch. 9. 16.

^{h} ch. 21. 1.

^{i} 1 Kin. 2.13.
2 Kin. 9. 22.
^{k} Ex. 19. 10.

^{l} ch. 17. 13.
1 Chr. 27.18.
^{m} 1 Kin. 12.
26.
^{n} Ps. 147. 10.
11.
Luke 16. 15.
^{o} Isai. 55. 8.
^{p} 2 Cor. 10.7.
^{q} 1 Kin. 8.
39.
Ps. 7. 9.
Jer. 11. 20.
Acts 1. 24.
^{r} ch. 17. 13.
^{s} ch. 17. 13.
^{t} ch. 17. 12.

^{u} 2 Sam. 7. 8.
Ps. 78. 70.
^{x} ch. 17. 42.
Cant. 5. 10.
^{y} So ch. 9.
17.
^{z} ch. 10. 1.
Ps. 89. 20.
^{a} See Num.
27. 18.

1 Heb. *in thine hand.*   3 Heb. *eyes.*   5 Heb. *round.*
2 Heb. *meeting.*   4 *Shimeah,* 2 Sam. 13. 3.   6 Heb. *fair of eyes.*
                           Shimma, 1 Chr. 2. 13.

---

35. *Samuel came no more,* &c.] In the
sense of visiting or conversing on public
affairs.

XVI. 2. It was the purpose of God that
David should be anointed at this time as
Saul's successor, and as the ancestor and
the type of His Christ. It was not the
purpose of God that Samuel should stir up
a civil war, by setting up David as Saul's
rival. *Secrecy,* therefore, was a necessary
part of the transaction. But *secrecy* and
concealment are not the same as *duplicity*
and *falsehood.* Concealment of a good purpose, for a good purpose, is clearly justifiable. There is therefore nothing in the
least inconsistent with truth in the occur-

rence here related. Cp. Exod. vii. 16, viii.
1, ix. 13.

4. *trembled*] There was evidently something unusual in Samuel's coming to Bethlehem ; and the elders, knowing that
Samuel was no longer at friendship with
Saul, foreboded some evil.

10. *seven*] *i.e.* including the three who had
already passed (cp. Judg. xiv. 17 note). It
appears that Jesse had eight sons ; but in
1 Chr. ii. 13-15, only seven are ascribed to
him.

11. *we will not sit down,* &c.]. Lit., *we
will not turn round* to sit at the table.

13. *the Spirit...came upon David*] The
exact phrase used of the Judges and Saul.

came upon David from that day forward. So Samuel rose up, 14 and went to Ramah. ¶ᵇBut the Spirit of the LORD departed from Saul, and ᶜan evil spirit from the LORD ¹troubled him. 15 And Saul's servants said unto him, Behold now, an evil spirit 16 from God troubleth thee. Let our lord now command thy servants, *which are* ᵈbefore thee, to seek out a man, *who is* a cunning player on an harp: and it shall come to pass, when the evil spirit from God is upon thee, that he shall ᵉplay with his hand, 17 and thou shalt be well. And Saul said unto his servants, Pro- 18 vide me now a man that can play well, and bring *him* to me. Then answered one of the servants, and said, Behold, I have seen a son of Jesse the Beth-lehemite, *that is* cunning in playing, and ᶠa mighty valiant man, and a man of war, and prudent in ²matters, 19 and a comely person, and ᵍthe LORD *is* with him. Wherefore Saul sent messengers unto Jesse, and said, Send me David thy 20 son, ʰwhich *is* with the sheep. And Jesse ⁱtook an ass *laden* with bread, and a bottle of wine, and a kid, and sent *them* by David 21 his son unto Saul. And David came to Saul, and ᵏstood before him: and he loved him greatly ; and he became his armour- 22 bearer. And Saul sent to Jesse, saying, Let David, I pray thee, 23 stand before me ; for he hath found favour in my sight. And it came to pass, when ˡthe *evil* spirit from God was upon Saul, that David took an harp, and played with his hand: so Saul was refreshed, and was well, and the evil spirit departed from him.

CHAP. 17. NOW the Philistines ᵃgathered together their armies to battle, and were gathered together at ᵇShochoh, which *belongeth* to Judah, and pitched between Shochoh and Azekah, in ³Ephes- 2 dammim. And Saul and the men of Israel were gathered together, and pitched by the valley of Elah, and ⁴set the battle in

Marginal references:
ᵇ ch. 11. 6.
& 18. 12.
Judg. 16. 20.
Ps. 51. 11.
ᶜ Judg. 9. 23.
ch. 19. 9.
ᵈ Gen. 41.46.

ᵉ ver. 23.
2 Kin. 3. 15.

ᶠ ch. 17. 32,
34, 35, 36.
ᵍ ch. 3. 19.
& 18. 12, 14.
ʰ ver. 11.
ch. 17. 15.
ⁱ See ch. 10.
27.
Gen. 43. 11.
ᵏ Gen. 41.46.
1 Kin. 10. 8.
Prov. 22. 29.

ˡ ver. 14, 16.

ᵃ ch. 13. 5.
ᵇ Josh.15.35.
2 Chr. 28.18.

¹ Or, *terrified.*
² Or, *speech.*
³ Or, *The coast of Dam-mim,* called *Pas-dam-*
mim, 1 Chr. 11. 13.
⁴ Heb. *ranged the battle.*

See x. 6 ; Judg. iii. 10, vi. 34, xi. 29, xiv. 19, xv. 14 ; and notes.

15. The "evil" or *melancholy* spirit here spoken of was "the Spirit of God," or "of Jehovah," as being God's messenger and minister, sent by Him to execute His righteous purpose upon Saul (see 1 K. xxii. 19-22 note).

16. The medicinal effects of music on the mind and body, especially as appeasing anger, and soothing and pacifying a troubled spirit, are well known. It is deeply interesting to have the youthful David thus brought before us, as using music for its highest purpose, that of turning the soul to the harmony of peace and love. We may infer that some of his Psalms, such *e.g.* as Ps. xxiii., were already composed.

18. *a mighty valiant man,* &c.] David's reputation for courage, skill, discretion, and manly beauty, was already great. Since "the Spirit of the Lord came upon him," his natural qualities and powers had been greatly enhanced. His feat of killing the lion and the bear (see marg. reff.) had been performed, like Samson's feats of strength (Judg. xiv. 6, 19, xv. 14), under the same supernatural influence, and was probably more or less known.

21. The difficulty of reconciling this verse with xvii. 55-58, is met thus : The words here are the ultimate sequence of David's first visit to Saul, and of his skill in music, and are therefore placed here ; but they did not really come to pass till after David's victory over Goliath (see xviii. 2). It is quite conceivable that if David had only played once or twice to Saul, and then returned to his father's house for some months, Saul might not recognise him.

XVII. 1. The narrative reverts to the Philistine wars (xiv. 52) ; the other introductory details concerning Saul's rejection, and David's introduction upon the stage of his history, having been disposed of in the intermediate chapters.

Shochoh which belongeth to Judah] See marg. ref. which places Shochoh and Azekah in the *Shephelah* or maritime plain, and 2 Chr. xxviii. 18, *Shochoh* now *Shu-weikeh,* "nine miles from Eleutheropolis," Jerome.

Ephes-dammim] Called *Happas-dammim* (Pas-dammim, 1 Chr. xi. 13), *the end of bloodshed,* now *Damûn,* about 4 miles N.E. of Shuweikeh.

2. *the valley of Elah*] *i.e.* of the terebinth,

3 array against the Philistines. And the Philistines stood on a mountain on the one side, and Israel stood on a mountain on 4 the other side: and *there was* a valley between them. ¶And there went out a champion out of the camp of the Philistines, named ᶜGoliath, of ᵈGath, whose height *was* six cubits and a 5 span. And *he had* an helmet of brass upon his head, and he *was* ¹armed with a coat of mail; and the weight of the coat *was* 6 five thousand shekels of brass. And *he had* greaves of brass upon his legs, and a ²target of brass between his shoulders. 7 And the ᵉstaff of his spear *was* like a weaver's beam; and his spear's head *weighed* six hundred shekels of iron: and one bear-8 ing a shield went before him. And he stood and cried unto the armies of Israel, and said unto them, Why are ye come out to set *your* battle in array? *am* not I a Philistine, and ye ᶠservants to Saul? choose you a man for you, and let him come down to 9 me. If he be able to fight with me, and to kill me, then will we be your servants: but if I prevail against him, and kill him, 10 then shall ye be our servants, and ᵍserve us. And the Philistine said, I ʰdefy the armies of Israel this day; give me a man, that 11 we may fight together. When Saul and all Israel heard those words of the Philistine, they were dismayed and greatly afraid. 12 ¶ Now David *was* ⁱthe son of that ᵏEphrathite of Beth-lehem-judah, whose name *was* Jesse; and he had ˡeight sons: and the 13 man went among men *for* an old man in the days of Saul. And the three eldest sons of Jesse went *and* followed Saul to the battle: and the ᵐnames of his three sons that went to the battle *were* Eliab the firstborn, and next unto him Abinadab, and the

ᶜ 2 Sam. 21.
19.
ᵈ Josh. 13. 3.

ᵉ 2 Sam. 21.
19.

ᶠ ch. 8. 17.

ᵍ ch. 11. 1.
ʰ ver. 26.
2 Sam. 21.
21.
ⁱ ver. 58.
Ruth 4. 22.
ch. 16. 1, 18.
ᵏ Gen. 35.19.
ˡ ch. 16. 10,
11.
See
1 Chr. 2. 13,
14, 15.
ᵐ ch. 16. 6.
1 Chr. 2. 13.

¹ Heb. *clothed*.   ² Or, *gorget*.

---

now called Wady es Sunt, from the acacias which are scattered in it.

3. [In the middle of the broad open valley (*v.* 2) is a deep trench (*v.* 3) with vertical sides, a valley within a valley: the sides and bed of the trench are strewn with water-worn pebbles. (Conder.)]

4. *a champion*] Lit., "*a man between the two camps;*" *i.e.* one who did not fight in the ranks like an ordinary soldier, but came forth into the space between the hostile camps to challenge the mightiest man of his enemies to come and fight him.

Goliath of Gath] One of the places mentioned in Josh. xi. 22 as still retaining a remnant of the sons of Anak: Gaza and Ashdod being the others. The race of giants (*rephaim*) is mentioned again in the account of David's Philistine wars (2 Sam. xxi. 15-22; 1 Chr. xx. 4-8). It appears from these passages that Goliath had a brother Lahmi. Four are named as being "born to the giant in Gath." See Deut. ii. 10, 11, 20, 21, iii. 11-13.

six cubits, &c.] If the *cubit*, the length from the elbow to the tip of the middle finger, be about 1½ feet; and the *span*, the distance from the thumb to the middle or little finger, when stretched apart to the full length, be half a cubit, *six cubits and a span* would equal about nine feet nine

inches. The bed of Og king of Bashan was nine cubits long (Deut. iii. 11).

5. *coat of mail*] Or "**breastplate of scales.**" A kind of metal shirt, protecting the back as well as the breast, and made of scales like those of a fish; as was the corselet of Rameses III., now in the British Museum. The terms, *helmet*, *coat*, and *clothed* (armed A. V.) are the same as those used in Isai. lix. 17.

five thousand shekels] Probably about 157 pounds avoirdupois (see Ex. xxxviii. 12 note). It is very probable that Goliath's brazen coat may have been long preserved as a trophy, as we know his sword was, and so the weight of it ascertained.

6. *a target*, &c.] Rather, "a javelin." as in *v.* 45, and placed between the shoulders, as the quiver was.

7. *spear's-head*] Lit., "**the flame of his spear,**" the metal part which flashed like a flame.

six hundred shekels] *i.e.* between seventeen and eighteen pounds avoirdupois.

12. This and the following *vv.* down to the end of *v.* 31 are omitted in the Vatican copy of the LXX., as are *vv.* 55-58. The object of the omission was doubtless to avoid the apparent inconsistency with regard to Saul's acquaintance with David (see xvi. 21 note).

14 third Shammah. And David *was* the youngest: and the three
15 eldest followed Saul. But David went and returned from Saul
16 *n*to feed his father's sheep at Beth-lehem. And the Philistine   *n* ch. 16. 19.
drew near morning and evening, and presented himself forty days.
17 ¶ And Jesse said unto David his son, Take now for thy brethren
an ephah of this parched *corn*, and these ten loaves, and run to
18 the camp to thy brethren; and carry these ten [1]cheeses unto the
[2]captain of *their* thousand, and *o*look how thy brethren fare, and   *o* Gen. 37. 14.
19 take their pledge. ¶ Now Saul, and they, and all the men of
Israel, *were* in the valley of Elah, fighting with the Philistines.
20 And David rose up early in the morning, and left the sheep with
a keeper, and took, and went, as Jesse had commanded him; and
he came to the [3]trench, as the host was going forth to the [4]fight,
21 and shouted for the battle. For Israel and the Philistines had
22 put the battle in array, army against army. And David left
[5]his carriage in the hand of the keeper of the carriage, and ran
23 into the army, and came and [6]saluted his brethren. And as
he talked with them, behold, there came up the champion, the
Philistine of Gath, Goliath by name, out of the armies of the
Philistines, and spake *p*according to the same words: and David   *p* ver. 8.
24 heard *them*. And all the men of Israel, when they saw the man,
25 fled [7]from him, and were sore afraid. ¶ And the men of Israel
said, Have ye seen this man that is come up? surely to defy
Israel is he come up: and it shall be, *that* the man who killeth
him, the king will enrich him with great riches, and *q*will give   *q* Josh. 15.
him his daughter, and make his father's house free in Israel.   16.
26 And David spake to the men that stood by him, saying, What
shall be done to the man that killeth this Philistine, and taketh
away *r*the reproach from Israel? for who *is* this *s*uncircumcised   *r* ch. 11. 2.
Philistine, that he should *t*defy the armies of *u*the living God?   *s* ch. 14. 6.
   t ver. 10.
27 And the people answered him after this manner, saying, *x*So   *u* Deut. 5. 26.
28 shall it be done to the man that killeth him. ¶ And Eliab his   *x* ver. 25.
eldest brother heard when he spake unto the men; and Eliab's
*y*anger was kindled against David, and he said, Why camest   *y* Gen. 37. 4,
thou down hither? and with whom hast thou left those few   8, 11.
sheep in the wilderness? I know thy pride, and the naughtiness   Matt. 10. 36.

[1] Heb. *cheeses of milk.*
[2] Heb. *captain of a thou-*
sand.
[3] Or, *place of the carriage,*
[4] Or, *battle array*, or, *place*
of fight.
[5] Heb. *the vessels from upon*
[6] Heb. *asked his brethren*
of peace, as Judg. 18. 15.
[7] Heb. *from his face.*
him.

---

15. *David went*, &c.] "Was gone," referring to xvi. 19, 20. Had he been Saul's
armour-bearer at this time it is highly improbable that he would have left him to
feed sheep.

18. *take their pledge*] *i.e.* bring back what
they have to say in return.

20. *the trench*] Rather, "the waggons,"
which were all put together in the camp so
as to form a kind of bulwark or fortification
(see xxvi. 5, 7). Here David left his "carriage" (*v.* 22), *i.e.* the things which he had
carried, "his things" as we should say, or
baggage (translated *stuff* in x. 22, xxv. 13,
xxx. 24). There seems to have been an
officer ("the keeper," *v.* 22) in the Hebrew
army whose charge it was to guard the
baggage.

25. *free in Israel*] In all the other passages
(fifteen) where this word occurs, it means
free, as opposed to being a *slave* (Deut. xv.
12, 13, 18, &c.) Here it may imply a freedom from all such services and burdens as
are spoken of in viii. 11-17.

26. *the living God*] This fine expression
occurs first in Deuteronomy (marg. ref.),
and next in Josh. iii. 10, and 2 K. xix. 4.
We find it twice in the Psalms of David
(Ps. xlii. 2, lxxxiv. 2), four times in the
Prophets, and frequently in the New Testament. It is generally in contrast to false
gods (1 Thess. i. 9, &c.).

28. *Why camest thou down?*] From the
heights of Bethlehem to the valley of Elah.
thy pride, and the naughtiness of thine
heart] See the similar expression, Jer. xlix.

of thine heart; for thou art come down that thou mightest see the
29 battle. And David said, What have I now done? [z]*Is there* not a
30 cause? And he turned from him toward another, and [a]spake after
the same [1]manner: and the people answered him again after the
31 former manner. ¶ And when the words were heard which David
32 spake, they rehearsed *them* before Saul: and he [2]sent for him. And
David said to Saul, [b]Let no man's heart fail because of him;
33 [c]thy servant will go and fight with this Philistine. And Saul
said to David, [d]Thou art not able to go against this Philistine to
fight with him: for thou *art but* a youth, and he a man of war
34 from his youth. And David said unto Saul, Thy servant kept
his father's sheep, and there came a lion, and a bear, and took a
35 [3]lamb out of the flock: and I went out after him, and smote him,
and delivered *it* out of his mouth: and when he arose against
me, I caught *him* by his beard, and smote him, and slew him.
36 Thy servant slew both the lion and the bear: and this uncircumcised Philistine shall be as one of them, seeing he hath
37 defied the armies of the living God. David said moreover,
[e]The LORD that delivered me out of the paw of the lion, and out
of the paw of the bear, he will deliver me out of the hand of
this Philistine. And Saul said unto David, Go, and [f]the LORD
38 be with thee. ¶ And Saul [4]armed David with his armour,
and he put an helmet of brass upon his head; also he armed
39 him with a coat of mail. And David girded his sword upon his
armour, and he assayed to go; for he had not proved *it*. And
David said unto Saul, I cannot go with these; for I have not
40 proved *them*. And David put them off him. And he took his staff
in his hand, and chose him five smooth stones out of the [5]brook,
and put them in a shepherd's [6]bag which he had, even in a scrip;
and his sling *was* in his hand: and he drew near to the Philistine.
41 And the Philistine came on and drew near unto David; and the
42 man that bare the shield *went* before him. ¶ And when the
Philistine looked about, and saw David, he [g]disdained him: for
43 he was *but* a youth, and [h]ruddy, and of a fair countenance. And
the Philistine said unto David, [i]*Am* I a dog, that thou comest
to me with staves? And the Philistine cursed David by his
44 gods. And the Philistine [k]said to David, Come to me, and I will
give thy flesh unto the fowls of the air, and to the beasts of the
45 field. Then said David to the Philistine, Thou comest to me
with a sword, and with a spear, and with a shield: [l]but I come
to thee in the name of the LORD of hosts, the God of the armies
46 of Israel, whom thou hast [m]defied. This day will the LORD
[7]deliver thee into mine hand; and I will smite thee, and take
thine head from thee; and I will give [n]the carcases of the host

[z] ver. 17.
[a] ver. 26, 27.
[b] Deut. 20. 1, 3.
[c] ch. 16. 18.
[d] See Num. 13. 31. Deut. 9. 2.
[e] Ps. 18. 16, 17. & 63. 7. 2 Cor. 1. 10. 2 Tim. 4. 17, 18.
[f] ch. 20. 13. 1 Chr. 22. 11, 16.
[g] Ps. 123. 3. 1 Cor. 1. 27, 28.
[h] ch. 16. 12.
[i] ch. 24. 14. 2 Sam. 3. 8. 2 Kin. 8. 13.
[k] 1 Kin. 20. 10, 11.
[l] 2 Sam. 22. 33, 35. Ps. 124. 8. 2 Cor. 10. 4. Heb. 11. 33, 34.
[m] ver. 10.
[n] Deut. 28. 26.

[1] Heb. *word*.
[2] Heb. *took him*.
[3] Or, *kid*.
[4] Heb. *clothed David with his clothes*.
[5] Or, *valley*.
[6] Heb. *vessel*.
[7] Heb. *shut thee up*.

---

16. Cp. the envy of Jacob's sons toward Joseph, and of the slanders heaped upon the Son of David in the days of His flesh.

29. *Is there not a cause?*] *i.e.* is not Saul's promise, and the insolence of Goliath, a sufficient cause for what I am about to do?

34. The narrative does not make it certain whether the lion and the bear came on one and the same, or on two different occasions. If it was on one occasion, the probability would be that the bear, having seized a lamb and carrying it off, a lion appeared to dispute the prize with the bear, or with David after he had taken it from the bear, and that David slew first one and then the other.

35. *his beard*] Put here for *his throat*, or under jaw; neither lion nor bear has a beard properly speaking.

45. *a shield*] "**A javelin,**" see *v.* 6 note.

of the Philistines this day unto the fowls of the air, and to the
wild beasts of the earth ; *o*that all the earth may know that there
47 is a God in Israel. And all this assembly shall know that the LORD
*p*saveth not with sword and spear : for *q*the battle *is* the LORD's,
48 and he will give you into our hands. ¶ And it came to pass,
when the Philistine arose, and came and drew nigh to meet
David, that David hasted, and ran toward the army to meet
49 the Philistine. And David put his hand in his bag, and took
thence a stone, and slang *it*, and smote the Philistine in his
forehead, that the stone sunk into his forehead ; and he fell
50 upon his face to the earth. So *r*David prevailed over the Philistine with a sling and with a stone, and smote the Philistine, and
51 slew him ; but *there was* no sword in the hand of David. Therefore David ran, and stood upon the Philistine, and took his
sword, and drew it out of the sheath thereof, and slew him, and
cut off his head therewith. ¶ And when the Philistines saw
52 their champion was dead, *s*they fled. And the men of Israel
and of Judah arose, and shouted, and pursued the Philistines,
until thou come to the valley, and to the gates of Ekron. And
the wounded of the Philistines fell down by the way to *t*Shaaraim,
53 even unto Gath, and unto Ekron. And the children of Israel
returned from chasing after the Philistines, and they spoiled
54 their tents. And David took the head of the Philistine, and
brought it to Jerusalem ; but he put his armour in his tent.
55 ¶ And when Saul saw David go forth against the Philistine, he
said unto Abner, the captain of the host, Abner, *u*whose son *is*
this youth ? And Abner said, *As* thy soul liveth, O king, I can-
56 not tell. And the king said, Enquire thou whose son the strip-
57 ling *is*. And as David returned from the slaughter of the
Philistine, Abner took him, and brought him before Saul *x*with
58 the head of the Philistine in his hand. And Saul said to him,
Whose son *art* thou, *thou* young man ? And David answered,
*y*I *am* the son of thy servant Jesse the Beth-lehemite.
CHAP. 18. AND it came to pass, when he had made an end of
speaking unto Saul, that *a*the soul of Jonathan was knit with the
2 soul of David, *b*and Jonathan loved him as his own soul. And
Saul took him that day, *c*and would let him go no more home to
3 his father's house. Then Jonathan and David made a covenant,
4 because he loved him as his own soul. And Jonathan stripped
himself of the robe that *was* upon him, and gave it to David,
and his garments, even to his sword, and to his bow, and to his
5 girdle. ¶ And David went out whithersoever Saul sent him, *and*

o Josh. 4. 24.
1 Kin. 8. 43.
Isa. 52. 10.
p Hos. 1. 7.
Zech. 4. 6.
q 2 Chr. 20.
15.

r ch. 21. 9.
See Judg. 3.
31.
& 15. 15.
2 Sam. 23.
21.

s Heb. 11.34.

t Josh. 15.
36.

u See ch. 16
21, 22.

x ver. 54.

y ver. 12.

a Gen. 44.30.
b ch. 19. 2.
& 20. 17.
2 Sam. 1. 26.
Deut. 13. 6.
c ch. 17. 15.

---

47. *the* LORD *saveth not with sword,* &c.]
Observe the consistent teaching of such
passages as xiv. 6 ; Ex. xiv. 13-18 ; Judg.
vii. 2, 4, 7 ; Ps. xliv. 6, &c., and their
practical use to the Church as lessons of
trust in God, and distrust of ourselves.
champion] Quite a different word from
that so rendered in *vv.* 4 and 23 ; better
"warrior."
52. *the men of Israel and Judah*] See xv.
4 note.
Shaaraim] A town of Judah in the *Shephelah* (see marg. ref.), at this time probably
in the possession of the Philistines.
54. *Jerusalem*] See Judg. i. 8 note.
his tent] Perhaps the *Tabernacle*. David

had neither tent nor house of his own. It
would be quite in accordance with David's
piety that he should immediately dedicate
to God the arms taken from the Philistine,
in acknowledgment that the victory was not
his own but the Lord's (cp. xxi. 9). *His*
Tabernacle, meaning the Tabernacle which
he had pitched (2 Sam. vi. 17 ; cp. Acts
xv. 16).
55. *whose son,* &c.] See marg. ref. note.
XVIII. **1.** *was knit with the soul of David*]
The same forcible phrase occurs of Jacob's
love for Benjamin (marg. ref.). Jonathan's
truly heroic character is shown in this
generous love of David, and admiration of
his great deed.

¹behaved himself wisely : and Saul set him over the men of war, and he was accepted in the sight of all the people, and also in 6 the sight of Saul's servants. ¶And it came to pass as they came, when David was returned from the slaughter of the ²Philistine, *d* Ex. 15. 20. that *d*the women came out of all cities of Israel, singing and Judg. 11. 34. dancing, to meet king Saul, with tabrets, with joy, and with *e* Ex. 15. 21. 7 ³instruments of musick. And the women *e*answered *one another*, as they played, and said,

f ch. 21. 11.   *f*Saul hath slain his thousands,
& 29. 5.   And David his ten thousands.

g Eccles. 4. 4.   8 And Saul was very wroth, and the saying ⁴*g*displeased him : and he said, They have ascribed unto David ten thousands, and . to me they have ascribed *but* thousands : and *what* can he have *h* ch. 15. 28. 9 more but *h*the kingdom. And Saul eyed David from that day *i* ch. 16. 14. 10 and forward. ¶And it came to pass on the morrow, that *i*the *k* ch. 19. 24. evil spirit from God came upon Saul, *k*and he prophesied in the 1 Kin. 18. 29. midst of the house : and David played with his hand, as at *l* ch. 19. 9. other times : *l*and *there was* a javelin in Saul's hand. And Saul *m* ch. 19. 10. 11 & 20. 33. *m*cast the javelin ; for he said, I will smite David even to the Prov. 27. 4. wall *with it*. And David avoided out of his presence twice. *n* ver. 15. 29. 12 ¶And Saul was *n*afraid of David, because *o*the LORD was with *o* ch. 16. 13. 13 him, and was *p*departed from Saul. Therefore Saul removed *p* ch. 16. 14. & 28. 15. him from him, and made him his captain over a thousand ; and *q* Num. 27. 14 *q*he went out and came in before the people. And David ⁵be-17. 2 Sam. 5. 2. haved himself wisely in all his ways ; and *r*the LORD *was* with *r* Gen. 39. 2. 15 him. Wherefore when Saul saw that he behaved himself very Josh. 6. 27. 16 wisely, he was afraid of him. But *s*all Israel and Judah loved *s* ver. 5. 17 David, because he went out and came in before them. ¶And *t* ch. 17. 25. Saul said to David, Behold, my elder daughter Merab, *t*her will I give thee to wife : only be thou ⁶valiant for me, and fight *u* Num. 32. *u*the LORD's battles. For Saul said, *x*Let not mine hand be 20, 27, 29. *x* ver. 21. 18 upon him, but let the hand of the Philistines be upon him. And 2 Sam. 12. 9. David said unto Saul, *y*Who *am* I ? and what *is* my life, *or* my *y* ch. 9. 21. father's family in Israel, that I should be son in law to the 2 Sam. 7. 18. 19 king ? But it came to pass at the time when Merab Saul's

---

¹ Or, *prospered*, ver. 14, 15, 30.   ³ Heb. *three-stringed*   ⁵ Or, *prospered*, ver. 5.
² Or, *Philistines*.   *instruments*.   ⁶ Heb. *a son of valour*.
                                      ⁴ Heb. *was evil in his eyes*.

---

6. *the Philistine*] Rather as in the margin. The allusion is not to Goliath, but to one of the expeditions referred to in *v*. 5.

singing and dancing] Women used to dance to the sound of the timbrel, and to sing as they danced and played.

instruments of music] The word means, an instrument like the triangle, or with three cords.

7. *as they played*] Or danced with vocal and instrumental music (see Judg. xvi. 25 note).

8. *what can he have*, &c.] Rather, "There is only the kingdom left for him." Cp. for the same sentiment, 1 K. ii 22 "A kingdom (says Camden) brooketh no companion, and majesty more heavily taketh injuries to heart."

10. *he prophesied*] This, as the effect of the evil spirit coming upon him, is singular as regards Saul, but is borne out by what

we read in 1 K. xxii. 22. (Cp. Acts xvi. 16-18, xix. 15 ; 1 Joh. iv. 1-3). It is impossible to give the sense of *raving* to the word *prophesied*, as though a merely natural state of phrenzy were intended. The *prophesying* here was as directly the effect of the coming of the evil spirit upon Saul, as the *prophesying* in x. 10 was the effect of the Spirit of God coming upon him. At the same time it is quite true that *madness* and *prophesyings* were considered as near akin (see Jer. xxix. 26 ; 2 K. ix. 11).

17. Saul had not hitherto fulfilled the promise of which David had heard (marg. ref.) ; nor was it unnatural that Saul should delay to do so, till the shepherd's boy had risen to a higher rank.

18. *what is my life*] *i.e.* condition, or means of living (Prov. xxvii. 27 marg.).

19. *Adriel the Meholathite*] The five sons of this marriage perished by the hands of

daughter should have been given to David, that she was given
20 unto *Adriel the *Meholathite to wife. ¶ *And Michal Saul's
daughter loved David: and they told Saul, and the thing
21 ¹pleased him. And Saul said, I will give him her, that she may
be *a snare to him, and that *the hand of the Philistines may be
against him. Wherefore Saul said to David, Thou shalt *this
22 day be my son in law in *the one of* the twain. ¶ And Saul commanded his servants, *saying*, Commune with David secretly, and
say, Behold, the king hath delight in thee, and all his servants
23 love thee: now therefore be the king's son in law. And Saul's
servants spake those words in the ears of David. And David
said, Seemeth it to you *a* light *thing* to be a king's son in law,
24 seeing that I *am* a poor man, and lightly esteemed? And the
servants of Saul told him, saying, ²On this manner spake David.
25 And Saul said, Thus shall ye say to David, The king desireth
not any *dowry, but an hundred foreskins of the Philistines, to
be *avenged of the king's enemies. But Saul *thought to make
26 David fall by the hand of the Philistines. And when his servants told David these words, it pleased David well to be the
27 king's son in law: and *the days were not ³expired. Wherefore David arose and went, he and *his men, and slew of the
Philistines two hundred men; and *David brought their foreskins, and they gave them in full tale to the king, that he might
be the king's son in law. And Saul gave him Michal his
28 daughter to wife. ¶ And Saul saw and knew that the LORD
was with David, and *that* Michal Saul's daughter loved him.
29 And Saul was yet the more afraid of David; and Saul became
30 David's enemy continually. Then the princes of the Philistines
*went forth: and it came to pass, after they went forth, *that*
David *behaved himself more wisely than all the servants of
Saul; so that his name was much ⁴set by.
CHAP. 19. AND Saul spake to Jonathan his son, and to all his
2 servants, that they should kill David. But Jonathan Saul's son
*delighted much in David: and Jonathan told David, saying,
Saul my father seeketh to kill thee: now therefore, I pray thee,
take heed to thyself until the morning, and abide in a secret
3 *place*, and hide thyself: and I will go out and stand beside my
father in the field where thou *art*, and I will commune with my
4 father of thee; and what I see, that I will tell thee. ¶ And
Jonathan *spake good of David unto Saul his father, and said
unto him, Let not the king *sin against his servant, against
David; because he hath not sinned against thee, and because

z 2 Sam. 21.
8.
a Judg. 7. 22.
b ver. 28.
c Ex. 10. 7.
d ver. 17.
e See ver. 23.

f Gen. 34. 12.
Ex. 22. 17.
g ch. 14. 24.
h ver. 17.

i See ver. 21.
k ver. 13.
l 2 Sam. 3.
14.

m 2 Sam. 11.
1.
n ver. 5.

a ch. 18. 1.

b Prov. 31.
8, 9.
c Gen. 42. 22.
Ps. 35. 12.
Prov. 17. 13.
Jer. 18. 20.

¹ Heb. *was right in his eyes*.　　³ Heb. *fulfilled*.　　⁴ Heb. *precious*, ch. 26. 21.
² Heb. *According to these words*.　　　　　　　　2 Kin. 1. 13. Ps. 116. 15.

---

the Gibeonites (marg. ref.), where we learn
further that the name of Adriel's father, or
ancestor, was Barzillai. His birth-place
was Meholah, probably the same as Abel-
Meholah. (See 1 K. xix. 16 note).
　20. *the thing pleased him*] It partly relieved him from the charge of breaking his
faith.
　21. *in the one of the twain*] Some prefer
"the second time" (Job xxxiii. 14). The
first contract had been broken by giving
Merab to Adriel.
　23. *a poor man and lightly esteemed*] Cp.

Ps. cxix. 141. Poor, and therefore unable
to pay a sufficient dowry. See *v.* 25.
　25. *an hundred foreskins*] This is merely
another expression of the spirit which led to
the constant application of the epithet *uncircumcised* to the Philistines (xiv. 6).
　26. *the days were not expired*] David was
so rapid in his attack upon the Philistines
that he was able to bring the required dowry
within the time, and to receive his wife
(Michal), before the time had expired within
which he was to receive Merab.

5 his works *have been* to thee-ward very good : for he did put his
^dlife in his hand, and ^eslew the Philistine, and ^fthe LORD
wrought a great salvation for all Israel : thou sawest *it*, and
didst rejoice : ^gwherefore then wilt thou ^hsin against innocent
6 blood, to slay David without a cause? And Saul hearkened
unto the voice of Jonathan : and Saul sware, *As* the LORD
7 liveth, he shall not be slain. And Jonathan called David, and
Jonathan shewed him all those things. And Jonathan brought
David to Saul, and he was in his presence, ⁱas ¹in times past.
8 ¶ And there was war again : and David went out, and fought with
the Philistines, and slew them with a great slaughter; and they
9 fled from ²him. ¶And ^kthe evil spirit from the LORD was upon
Saul, as he sat in his house with his javelin in his hand : and
10 David played with *his* hand. And Saul sought to smite David
even to the wall with the javelin; but he slipped away out of
Saul's presence, and he smote the javelin into the wall : and
11 David fled, and escaped that night. ¶ ^lSaul also sent messengers
unto David's house, to watch him, and to slay him in the morning : and Michal David's wife told him, saying, If thou save not
12 thy life to night, to morrow thou shalt be slain. So Michal ^mlet
David down through a window : and he went, and fled, and
13 escaped. And Michal took an ³image, and laid *it* in the bed,
and put a pillow of goats' *hair* for his bolster, and covered *it*
14 with a cloth. And when Saul sent messengers to take David,
15 she said, He *is* sick. And Saul sent the messengers *again* to
see David, saying, Bring him up to me in the bed, that I may
16 slay him. And when the messengers were come in, behold,
there was an image in the bed, with a pillow of goats' *hair* for his
17 bolster. And Saul said unto Michal, Why hast thou deceived
me so, and sent away mine enemy, that he is escaped? And
Michal answered Saul, He said unto me, Let me go; ⁿwhy
18 should I kill thee? ¶So David fled, and escaped, and came to
Samuel to Ramah, and told him all that Saul had done to him.
19 And he and Samuel went and dwelt in Naioth. And it was told
20 Saul, saying, Behold, David *is* at Naioth in Ramah. And
^oSaul sent messengers to take David : ^pand when they saw the
company of the prophets prophesying, and Samuel standing *as*
appointed over them, the Spirit of God was upon the messengers
21 of Saul, and they also ^qprophesied. And when it was told

Marginal references

^d Judg. 9. 17.
ch. 28. 21.
^e ch. 17. 49.
^f ch. 11. 13.
^g ch. 20. 32.
^h Matt. 27. 4.

ⁱ ch. 16. 21.
& 18. 2, 13.

^k ch. 16. 14.
& 18. 10.

^l Ps. 59,
title.

^m So Josh.
2. 15.
Acts 9. 24,
25.

ⁿ 2 Sam. 2.
22.

^o See John
7. 32, 45.
^p ch. 10. 5.
1 Cor. 14. 3,
24, 25.
^q Num. 11.
25.
Joel 2. 28.

¹ Heb. *yesterday third day.*   ² Heb. *his face.*   ³ Heb. *teraphim,* Gen. 31. 19.
Judg. 17. 5.

XIX. **10.** *David fled*] This was the beginning of David's life as a fugitive and
outcast, though for no "offence or fault" of
his (Ps. lix. 3, Prayer Book Version).

11. Saul's plan was to surround the house
at night, and to have David killed as soon
as he came abroad unsuspectingly in the
morning.

13. *an image*] *Teraphim* (see marg.), an
image, or bust in human form, and as
large as life, of a kind of household god, to
the worship of which the Israelites, and
especially women, were much addicted.

a pillow] It was probably a quilt or blanket of goats' hair, and of common use as a
bed-covering. Whether Michal drew it
over the head of the teraphim, as if for

warmth, and so covered it, or whether she
disposed it about the head so as to look like
hair, is not clear.

17. *why should I kill thee?*] To avert
Saul's anger from herself, she pretended
that David had threatened her life unless
she facilitated his escape.

18. No such place as Naioth (or Nevaioth)
is known, but the word means *dwellings.*
Hence it is considered that Naioth was the
name of the collegiate residence of the
prophets, in, or just outside, Ramah, to
which Samuel removed with David from
his own house, for greater safety, owing to
the sanctity of the place and company.

20. *Samuel standing as appointed*] Rather,
"**as overseer, or leader.**"

Saul, he sent other messengers, and they prophesied likewise.
And Saul sent messengers again the third time, and they pro-
22 phesied also. Then went he also to Ramah, and came to a great
well that is in Sechu: and he asked and said, Where are Samuel
and David? And one said, Behold, *they be* at Naioth in Ramah.
23 And he went thither to Naioth in Ramah: and *r*the Spirit of
God was upon him also, and he went on, and prophesied, until
24 he came to Naioth in Ramah. *s*And he stripped off his clothes
also, and prophesied before Samuel in like manner, and [1]lay
down *t*naked all that day and all that night. Wherefore they
say, *u Is* Saul also among the prophets?
CHAP. 20. AND David fled from Naioth in Ramah, and came
and said before Jonathan, What have I done? what *is* mine
iniquity? and what *is* my sin before thy father, that he seeketh
2 my life? And he said unto him, God forbid; thou shalt not die:
behold, my father will do nothing either great or small, but
that he will [2]shew it me: and why should my father hide this
3 thing from me? it *is* not so. And David sware moreover, and
said, Thy father certainly knoweth that I have found grace in
thine eyes; and he saith, Let not Jonathan know this, lest he
be grieved: but truly *as* the LORD liveth, and *as* thy soul liveth,
4 *there is* but a step between me and death. Then said Jonathan
unto David, [3]Whatsoever thy soul [4]desireth, I will even do *it* for
5 thee. And David said unto Jonathan, Behold, to morrow *is*
the *a*new moon, and I should not fail to sit with the king at
meat: but let me go, that I may *b*hide myself in the field unto
6 the third *day* at even. If thy father at all miss me, then
say, David earnestly asked *leave* of me that he might run *c*to
Beth-lehem his city: for *there is* a yearly [5]sacrifice there for all
7 the family. *d*If he say thus, It *is* well; thy servant shall have
peace: but if he be very wroth, *then* be sure that *e*evil is deter-
8 mined by him. Therefore thou shalt *f*deal kindly with thy
servant; for *g*thou hast brought thy servant into a covenant of
the LORD with thee: notwithstanding, *h*if there be in me
iniquity, slay me thyself; for why shouldest thou bring me to
9 thy father? And Jonathan said, Far be it from thee: for if I

r ch. 10. 10.

s Isai. 20. 2.

t Mic. 1. 8.
See 2 Sam.
6. 14, 20.
u ch. 10. 11.

a Num. 10.
10.
& 28. 11.
b ch. 19. 2.
c ch. 16. 4.

d See Deut.
1. 23.
2 Sam. 17. 4.
e ch. 25. 17.
Esth. 7. 7.
f Josh. 2. 14.
g ver. 16.
ch. 18. 3.
& 23. 18.
h 2 Sam. 14.
32.

---

[1] Heb. *fell*, Num. 24. 4.
[2] Heb. *uncover mine ear*,
ver. 12. ch. 9. 15.

[3] Or, *Say what is thy mind,
and I will do, &c.*

[4] Heb. *speaketh*, or, *thinketh.*
[5] Or, *feast*, ch. 9. 12.

---

22. *to a great well*] Some large well-
known cistern at Sechu, the site of which
is uncertain, which Saul passed on his way
from Gibeah to Ramah.
  24. *naked*] *i.e.* without his robe and other
outer garments, but only the shirt. Cp.
marg. reff.
  The whole history affords another instance
of the protection of God vouchsafed to
His servants, which forms so frequent a
topic of the Psalms of David.
  XX. 1. While Saul was under the con-
straining influence of the spirit of prophecy,
David escaped from Naioth, and, probably
by Samuel's advice, returned to Saul's
court to commune with Jonathan. Nothing
could be a better evidence of his innocence
than thus putting himself in Jonathan's
power. Perhaps something passed between

Samuel and Saul on the subject, since it
appears from *rv.* 5, 25, 27, that Saul expected David at the feast of the new moon.
  2. *it is not so*] Jonathan's unwillingness
to believe evil of his father is one of the
many admirable traits in his character.
  3. *And David sware moreover*] Rather,
"yet again." He met Jonathan's denial
by repeating his statement and confirming
it with an oath.
  5. The new moon, or beginning of each
month, was celebrated with especial sacrifices and blowing of trumpets (marg. reff.).
The feast was kept with great solemnity as
"a day of gladness," and we may presume
that the "peace offerings" offered on the
occasion furnished the tables of those that
offered.

knew certainly that evil were determined by my father to come
10 upon thee, then would not I tell it thee? Then said David to
Jonathan, Who shall tell me? or what *if* thy father answer thee
11 roughly? And Jonathan said unto David, Come, and let us go
out into the field. And they went out both of them into the
12 field. And Jonathan said unto David, O LORD God of Israel,
when I have ¹sounded my father about to morrow any time, *or*
the third *day*, and, behold, *if there be* good toward David, and I

Ruth 1.17.   13 then send not unto thee, and ²shew it thee; *i*the LORD do so
and much more to Jonathan: but if it please my father *to do*
thee evil, then I will shew it thee, and send thee away, that

k Josh. 1. 5.   thou mayest go in peace: and *k*the LORD be with thee, as he
ch. 17. 37.   14 hath been with my father. And thou shalt not only while yet I
1 Chr. 22. 11,   15 live shew me the kindness of the LORD, that I die not: but *also*
16.
l 2 Sam. 9.1,   *l*thou shalt not cut off thy kindness from my house for ever: no,
3, 7.   not when the LORD hath cut off the enemies of David every one
& 21. 7.   16 from the face of the earth. ¶ So Jonathan ³made *a covenant*

m ch. 25. 22.   with the house of David, saying, *m*Let the LORD even require *it*
See ch. 31. 2.   17 at the hand of David's enemies. And Jonathan caused David
2 Sam. 4. 7.   to swear again, ⁴because he loved him: *n*for he loved him as he
& 21. 8.
n ch. 18. 1.   18 loved his own soul. ¶ Then Jonathan said to David, *o*To morrow
o ver. 5.   *is* the new moon: and thou shalt be missed. because thy seat
19 will be ⁵empty. And *when* thou hast stayed three days, *then*
p ch. 19. 2.   thou shalt go down ⁶⁷quickly, and come to *p*the place where
thou didst hide thyself ⁸when the business was *in hand*, and
20 shalt remain by the stone ⁹Ezel. And I will shoot three arrows
21 on the side *thereof*, as though I shot at a mark. And, behold, I
will send a lad, *saying*, Go, find out the arrows. If I expressly
say unto the lad, Behold, the arrows *are* on this side of thee,
take them; then come thou: for *there is* peace to thee, and ¹no

q Jer. 4. 2.   22 hurt; *q*as the LORD liveth. But if I say thus unto the young
man, Behold, the arrows *are* beyond thee; go thy way: for the

r ver. 14, 15.   23 LORD hath sent thee away. And *as touching r*the matter which
See ver. 42.   thou and I have spoken of, behold, the LORD *be* between thee
24 and me for ever. ¶ So David hid himself in the field: and
when the new moon was come, the king sat him down to eat
25 meat. And the king sat upon his seat, as at other times. *even*
upon a seat by the wall: and Jonathan arose, and Abner sat by
26 Saul's side, and David's place was empty. Nevertheless Saul
spake not any thing that day: for he thought, Something hath

s Lev. 7. 21.   27 befallen him, he *is* ⁸not clean; surely he *is* not clean. ¶ And it
& 15. 5, &c.   came to pass on the morrow, *which was* the second *day* of the
month, that David's place was empty: and Saul said unto
Jonathan his son, Wherefore cometh not the son of Jesse to

t ver. 6.   28 meat, neither yesterday, nor to day? And Jonathan *t*answered

¹ Heb. *searched.*	⁴ Or, *by his love toward*	⁸ Heb. *in the day of the*
² Heb. *uncover thine ear,*	*him.*	*business.*
ver. 2.	⁵ Heb. *missed.*	⁹ Or, *That sheweth the way.*
³ Heb. *cut.*	⁶ Or, *diligently.*	¹ Heb. *not any thing.*
	⁷ Heb. *greatly.*	

14, 15. The general meaning is: Jonathan had a presentiment, doubtless from
God, that David would be established upon
the throne. By God's mercy he had the
comfort, which he well deserved, of knowing
that his own posterity would receive kindness at David's hand (see marg. reff.).

19. *the stone Ezel*] It is not mentioned

elsewhere, except possibly in *v.* 41, where
see note.

26. *he is not clean*] The new moon being
a religious feast, and the meat to be eaten
being peace-offerings, no one could assist at
the feast who had any ceremonial uncleanness upon him (marg. reff.).

Saul, David earnestly asked *leave* of me *to go* to Beth-lehem:
29 and he said, Let me go, I pray thee; for our family hath a
sacrifice in the city; and my brother, he hath commanded me
to be there: and now, if I have found favour in thine eyes, let
me get away, I pray thee, and see my brethren. Therefore he
30 cometh not unto the king's table. ¶ Then Saul's anger was
kindled against Jonathan, and he said unto him, [1][2]Thou son of
the perverse rebellious *woman*, do not I know that thou hast
chosen the son of Jesse to thine own confusion, and unto the
31 confusion of thy mother's nakedness? For as long as the son of
Jesse liveth upon the ground, thou shalt not be established, nor
thy kingdom. Wherefore now send and fetch him unto me, for
32 he [3]shall surely die. And Jonathan answered Saul his father,
and said unto him, [u]Wherefore shall he be slain? what hath he
33 done? And Saul [x]cast a javelin at him to smite him: [v]where-
by Jonathan knew that it was determined of his father to slay
34 David. So Jonathan arose from the table in fierce anger, and
did eat no meat the second day of the month: for he was grieved
35 for David, because his father had done him shame. ¶ And it
came to pass in the morning, that Jonathan went out into the
field at the time appointed with David, and a little lad with him.
36 And he said unto his lad, Run, find out now the arrows which I
shoot. *And* as the lad ran, he shot an arrow [4]beyond him.
37 And when the lad was come to the place of the arrow which
Jonathan had shot, Jonathan cried after the lad, and said, *Is*
38 not the arrow beyond thee? And Jonathan cried after the lad,
Make speed, haste, stay not. And Jonathan's lad gathered up
39 the arrows, and came to his master. But the lad knew not any
40 thing: only Jonathan and David knew the matter. And Jonathan gave his [5]artillery unto [6]his lad, and said unto him, Go,
41 carry *them* to the city. ¶ *And* as soon as the lad was gone, David
arose out of *a place* toward the south, and fell on his face to the
ground, and bowed himself three times: and they kissed one
another, and wept one with another, until David exceeded.
42 And Jonathan said to David, [z]Go in peace, [7]forasmuch as we
have sworn both of us in the name of the LORD, saying, The
LORD be between me and thee, and between my seed and thy
seed for ever And he arose and departed: and Jonathan went
into the city.

[u] ch. 19. 5.
Matt. 27. 23.
Luke 23. 22.
[x] ch. 18. 11.
[y] ver. 7.

[z] ch. 1. 17.

[1] Or, *Thou perverse rebel.*
[2] Heb. *Son of perverse re-*
bellion.
[3] Heb. is *the son of death.*
[4] Heb. *to pass over him.*
[5] Heb. *instruments.*
[6] Heb. *that was his.*
[7] Or, the LORD be witness
of that *which, &c.* See
ver. 23.

30. The greatest insult and most stinging
reproach that can be cast upon an Oriental
is to reproach his parents or ancestors (see
Job xxx. 8). Saul means to intimate that
Jonathan was stubborn from his mother's
womb.

41. *a place toward the south*] An unintelligible description; one expects a repetition
of the description of David's hiding-place in
v. 19. The LXX. in both places has *argab*,
a word meaning a *heap of stones*. If this be
the true reading, David's hiding-place was
either a natural cavernous rock which was
called *Argab*, or some ruin of an ancient
building, equally suited for a hiding-place.

bowed himself three times] In token, doubt-

less, of his unshaken loyalty to Jonathan as
the son of his king, as well as his friend;
and in acknowledgment of Jonathan's power
to kill him if he saw fit. (Cp. Gen.
xxxiii. 3).

David exceeded] His affection for Jonathan, coupled with his sense of Saul's injustice and his own injured innocence, fully
accounts for his strong emotion.

42. *Jonathan went into the city*] From
which one may infer, what the after history
also indicates, that Jonathan's filial duty
and patriotism prevented a complete rupture with his father. Jonathan's conduct in
this, as in everything, was most admirable.

a ch. 14. 3,
called
Ahiah.
Called also
Abiathar,
Mark 2. 26.
b ch. 16. 4.

c Ex. 25. 30.
Lev. 24. 5.
Matt. 12. 4.
d Ex. 19. 15.
Zech. 7. 3.
e ch. 17. 40.

f Lev. 8. 26.
y Mark 2. 25,
26.
Luke 6. 3.
h Lev. 24. 8.

i ch. 22. 9.
Ps. 52, title.

k ch. 17. 2,
50.
l See ch. 31.
10.

m Ps. 56,
title.

Chap. 21. THEN came David to Nob to *a*Ahimelech the priest: and Ahimelech was *b*afraid at the meeting of David, and said unto 2 him, Why *art* thou alone, and no man with thee? And David said unto Ahimelech the priest, The king hath commanded me a business, and hath said unto me, Let no man know any thing of the business whereabout I send thee, and what I have commanded thee: and I have appointed *my* servants to such and 3 such a place. Now therefore what is under thine hand? give *me* five *loaves of* bread in mine hand, or what there is ¹present. 4 And the priest answered David, and said, *There is* no common bread under mine hand, but there is *c*hallowed bread; *d*if the 5 young men have kept themselves at least from women. And David answered the priest, and said unto him, Of a truth women *have been* kept from us about these three days, since I came out, and the *e*vessels of the young men are holy, and *the bread is* in a manner common, ²yea, though it were sanctified this day 6 *f*in the vessel. So the priest *g*gave him hallowed *bread :* for there was no bread there but the shewbread, *h*that was taken from before the LORD, to put hot bread in the day when it was taken 7 away. Now a certain man of the servants of Saul *was* there that day, detained before the LORD; and his name *was* *i*Doeg, an 8 Edomite, the chiefest of the herdmen that *belonged* to Saul. ¶ And David said unto Ahimelech, And is there not here under thine hand spear or sword? for I have neither brought my sword nor my weapons with me, because the king's business required haste. 9 And the priest said, The sword of Goliath the Philistine, whom thou slewest in *k*the valley of Elah, *l*behold, it *is here* wrapped in a cloth behind the ephod: if thou wilt take that, take *it :* for *there is* no other save that here. And David said, *There is* none 10 like that; give it me. ¶ And David arose, and fled that day for 11 fear of Saul, and went to ³Achish the king of Gath. And *m*the servants of Achish said unto him, *Is* not this David the king of

---

¹ Heb. *found.*
² Or, *especially when this*

day there is other *sanctified in the vessel.*

³ Or, *Abimelech,* Ps. 34, title.

XXI. 1. Nob was a city of the priests, the High-Priest resided there, and the Tabernacle was pitched there (*rv.* 4, 6, 9, xxii. 10). It was situated on the road from the north to Jerusalem, near Anathoth, and within sight of the holy city (Isai. x. 32; Neh. xi. 32). But the site has not been identified with certainty.

2. A fresh instance of David's unscrupulous readiness of invention (cp. xx. 6).

4. *common*] As opposed to *holy.* (See marg. reff., and cp. the use of the word in Acts x. 14, 15, 28.) It gives an idea of the depressed and poor condition of the priesthood at that time, that Ahimelech should have had no bread at hand except the shew-bread.

5. *the vessels of the young men,* &c.] *i.e.* their clothes (Deut. xxii. 5) or wallets (marg. ref.), or other articles which might be Levitically unclean and need cleansing (Levit. xiii. 58 ; Exod. xix. 10, &c. ; Mark vii. 4), as well as the person.

and the bread, &c.] The meaning is ; "Though it is treating it like common

bread to give it to me and my young men, there is fresh Shew-bread baked and put on the table in place of what you give us " ; the day being Friday. as is indicated in the verse following.

7. *detained before the* LORD] Either to fulfil a vow (Acts xxi. 23-27), or on account of uncleanness, or under the law of lepers (Levit. xiii. 4, 11, 21), or as a proselyte. It is not impossible that Doeg may have been in custody or in sanctuary for some crime.

9. *wrapped in a cloth behind the ephod*] Rather, "in the cloak," Goliath's military cloak, which was part of the dedicated trophy. The ephod was naturally hung up where the High-Priest alone could get at it.

10. *Achish king of Gath*] It appears from the title that Ps. xxxiv. was composed on this occasion. (See note there.) Nothing can give a more lively impression of the straits to which David was reduced than the fact of his going to the country of the Philistines.

11. *the king of the land*] The Philistines gave him the title which their own lords bore.

the land? did they not sing one to another of him in dances, saying, ⁿSaul hath slain his thousands, and David his ten thou- 12 sands? And David °laid up these words in his heart, and was 13 sore afraid of Achish the king of Gath. And ᵖhe changed his behaviour before them, and feigned himself mad in their hands, and ¹scrabbled on the doors of the gate, and let his spittle fall 14 down upon his beard. Then said Achish unto his servants, Lo, ye see the man ²is mad: wherefore then have ye brought him to 15 me? Have I need of mad men, that ye have brought this *fellow* to play the mad man in my presence? shall this *fellow* come into my house?

CHAP. 22. DAVID therefore departed thence, and ᵃescaped ᵇto the cave Adullam: and when his brethren and all his father's house 2 heard *it*, they went down thither to him. ᶜAnd every one *that was* in distress, and every one that ³*was* in debt, and every one *that was* ⁴discontented, gathered themselves unto him; and he became a captain over them: and there were with him about 3 four hundred men. ¶And David went thence to Mizpeh of Moab: and he said unto the king of Moab, Let my father and my mother, I pray thee, come forth, *and be* with you, till I know 4 what God will do for me. And he brought them before the king of Moab: and they dwelt with him all the while that David was 5 in the hold. And the prophet ᵈGad said unto David, Abide not in the hold; depart, and get thee into the land of Judah. Then 6 David departed, and came into the forest of Hareth. ¶When Saul heard that David was discovered, and the men that *were* with him, (now Saul abode in Gibeah under a ⁵tree in Ramah,

Margin notes right:
ⁿ ch. 18. 7.
& 29. 5.
° Luke 2. 19.
ᵖ Ps. 34, title.

ᵃ Ps. 57, title, & 142, title.
ᵇ 2 Sam. 23. 13.
ᶜ Judg. 11. 3.

ᵈ 2 Sam. 24. 11.
1 Chr. 21. 9.
2 Chr. 29.25.

---

¹ Or, *made marks.*   ³ Heb. *had a creditor.*   ⁴ Heb. *bitter of soul.*
² Or, *playeth the mad man.*   ⁵ Or, *grove in a high place.*

---

13. *scrabbled*] Literally, made marks (marg.), viz. the mark of the *tau*, which in the ancient Hebrew and Phœnician was in the shape of a cross. (See Ezek. ix. 4.)

on the doors of the gate] The gate of Achish's palace-yard or court, in which the attendants waited. The house itself stood in this court. (Cp. Esth. ii. 19, 21.)

XXII. 1. *to the cave Adullam*] Or rather "**of Adullam.**" Adullam was the name of a town of Judah in the *Shephelah*, not far from Bethlehem, and below it. Innumerable caverns, one nearly 100 feet long, are excavated in the soft limestone hills in the neighbourhood of Beit-Jibrin. [The cave is placed by Ganneau and Conder on the hill (500 feet high) over 'Aid el Ma or Miyeh.] David's brethren and kinsmen joined him partly from sympathy with him, and partly because their own lives were in jeopardy from Saul's furious enmity.

2. *discontented*] See marg. (Cp. xxx. 6; 2 Sam. xvii. 8.) The phrase here denotes those who were exasperated by Saul's tyranny.

3. *Mizpeh of Moab*] A good conjecture connects it with *Zophim* (a word of the same root as Mizpeh) on the top of Pisgah (Num. xxiii. 14). It is probable that David's descent from Ruth the Moabitess may have had something to do with his seeking an asylum for Jesse, Ruth's grandson, in the

land of her birth. It would be very easy to get to the Jordan from the neighbourhood of Bethlehem, and cross over near its embouchure into the Dead Sea.

come forth, and be *with you*] The construction of the Hebrew is very strange. The Vulg., Syriac, and Arabic seem to have read *dwell* instead of *come forth*.

4. *he brought them before*, &c.] The Sept. renders it *he persuaded (the face of) the king.*

4, 5. *in the hold*] Where David was after he left the cave of Adullam, probably in the land of Moab.

The phrase *all the while*, would indicate that David sojourned a considerable time in Moab.

5. *the prophet Gad*] Mentioned here for the first time. One may conjecture that Samuel had sent him privately from Naioth to tell David not to abide in the hold. Whether he stayed with David or returned to the College of the prophets does not appear. For later notices of him see marg. reff.

The forest of Hareth is unknown.

6. *under a tree in Ramah*] Rather, "**under the tamarisk-tree on the high place,**" where he always held such meetings. It was a kind of parliament in the open air, and all his tribesmen gathered round him. (Cp. Judg. iv. 5.)

having his spear in his hand, and all his servants *were* standing
7 about him;) then Saul said unto his servants that stood about

a ch. 8. 14.   him, Hear now, ye Benjamites; will the son of Jesse *e*give every
one of you fields and vineyards, *and* make you all captains of
8 thousands, and captains of hundreds; that all of you have con-

f ch. 18. 3.   spired against me, and *there is* none that ¹sheweth me that *f*my
& 20. 30.   son hath made a league with the son of Jesse, and *there is* none
of you that is sorry for me, or sheweth unto me that my son
hath stirred up my servant against me, to lie in wait, as at this

g ch. 21. 7.   9 day? ¶ Then answered *g*Doeg the Edomite, which was set over
Ps. 52, title,   the servants of Saul, and said, I saw the son of Jesse coming to
& ver. 1, 2, 3.   10 Nob, to *h*Ahimelech the son of *i*Ahitub. *k*And he enquired of
h ch. 21. 1.
i ch. 14. 3.   the LORD for him, and *l*gave him victuals, and gave him the
k Num. 27.   11 sword of Goliath the Philistine. ¶ Then the king sent to call
21.
l ch. 21. 6, 9.   Ahimelech the priest, the son of Ahitub, and all his father's
house, the priests that *were* in Nob: and they came all of them
12 to the king. And Saul said, Hear now, thou son of Ahitub.
13 And he answered ²Here I *am*, my lord. And Saul said unto
him, Why have ye conspired against me, thou and the son of
Jesse, in that thou hast given him bread, and a sword, and hast
enquired of God for him, that he should rise against me, to lie
14 in wait, as at this day? Then Ahimelech answered the king,
and said, And who *is so* faithful among all thy servants as
David, which is the king's son in law, and goeth at thy bidding,
15 and is honourable in thine house? Did I then begin to enquire
of God for him? be it far from me: let not the king impute *any*
thing unto his servant, *nor* to all the house of my father: for
16 thy servant knew nothing of all this, ³less or more. And the
king said, Thou shalt surely die, Ahimelech, thou, and all thy
17 father's house. And the king said unto the ⁴⁵footmen that
stood about him, Turn, and slay the priests of the LORD; because their hand also *is* with David, and because they knew
when he fled, and did not shew it to me. But the servants of

m See Exod.   the king *m*would not put forth their hand to fall upon the priests
1. 17.   18 of the LORD. And the king said to Doeg, Turn thou, and fall
upon the priests. And Doeg the Edomite turned, and he fell

n See ch. 2.   upon the priests, and *n*slew on that day fourscore and five per-
31.

| ¹ Heb. *uncovereth mine ear*, ch. 20. 2. | ² Heb. *Behold me.* ³ Heb. *little or great.* | ⁴ Or, *guard.* ⁵ Heb. *runners.* |

---

7. *ye Benjamites*] Showing how isolated the tribes still were, and how for the most part Saul was surrounded by his own tribesmen only.

10. *he enquired of the* LORD, &c.] This was not true, but Ahimelech's going to fetch the sword from behind the ephod might have given occasion to the belief on Doeg's part that he had put on the ephod to enquire of the Lord for David.

14. *goeth at thy bidding*] Better, "has access to thy (private) audience," or *council* (cp. 2 Sam. xxiii. 23, marg.).

15. *Did I then begin*, &c.] Some lay the stress upon the word *begin*, as though Ahimelech's justification was that he had often before enquired of the Lord for David when employed on the king's affairs. But it is much better to understand the words as

Ahimelech's solemn denial of having enquired of the Lord for David, a duty which he owed to Saul alone as king of Israel. The force of the word *begin* lies in this, that it would have been his first act of allegiance to David and defection from Saul. This he strenuously repudiates, and adds, *thy servant knew nothing of all this* conspiracy between Jonathan and David of which Saul speaks: he had acted quite innocently.

18. We are not to suppose that Doeg killed them all with his own hand. He had a band of men under his command, many or all of whom were perhaps foreigners like himself, and very likely of a Bedouin caste, to whom bloodshed would be quite natural, and the priests of the Lord of no more account than so many sheep or oxen.

19 sons that did wear a linen ephod. °And Nob, the city of the °ver. 9, 11.
priests, smote he with the edge of the sword, both men and
women, children and sucklings, and oxen, and asses, and sheep,
20 with the edge of the sword. ¶ᵖAnd one of the sons of Ahime- ᵖ ch. 23. 6.
lech the son of Ahitub, named Abiathar, ᑫescaped, and fled after ᑫ ch. 2. 33.
21 David. And Abiathar shewed David that Saul had slain the
22 LORD's priests. And David said unto Abiathar, I knew it that
day, when Doeg the Edomite was there, that he would surely
tell Saul : I have occasioned the death of all the persons of thy
23 father's house. Abide thou with me, fear not: ʳfor he that ʳ 1 Kin.2.26.
seeketh my life seeketh thy life : but with me thou shalt be in
safeguard.
CHAP. 23. THEN they told David, saying, Behold, the Philistines
2 fight against ªKeilah, and they rob the threshingfloors. There- ª Josh.15.44.
fore David ᵇenquired of the LORD, saying, Shall I go and smite ᵇ ver. 4, 6, 9.
these Philistines ? And the LORD said unto David, Go, and ch. 30. 8.
3 smite the Philistines, and save Keilah. And David's men said 2 Sam. 5. 19, 23.
unto him, Behold, we be afraid here in Judah : how much more
then if we come to Keilah against the armies of the Philistines?
4 Then David enquired of the LORD yet again. And the LORD
answered him and said, Arise, go down to Keilah ; for I will
5 deliver the Philistines into thine hand. So David and his men
went to Keilah, and fought with the Philistines, and brought
away their cattle, and smote them with a great slaughter. So
6 David saved the inhabitants of Keilah. ¶And it came to pass,
when Abiathar the son of Ahimelech ᶜfled to David to Keilah, ᶜ ch. 22. 20.
7 that he came down with an ephod in his hand. ¶And it was told
Saul that David was come to Keilah. And Saul said, God hath
delivered him into mine hand ; for he is shut in, by entering
8 into a town that hath gates and bars. And Saul called all the
people together to war, to go down to Keilah, to besiege David
9 and his men. ¶And David knew that Saul secretly practised
mischief against him ; and ᵈhe said to Abiathar the priest, Bring ᵈ Num. 27. 21.
10 hither the ephod. Then said David, O LORD God of Israel, thy ch. 30. 7.

---

19. both men and women, &c.] The language employed in the case of the Amalekites (xv. 3) and of Jericho (Josh. vi. 21).
Nothing could be more truculent than Saul's
revenge.
20. Abiathar] He may have remained at
Nob to take care of the sanctuary when the
other priests went to Saul, and so escaped.
He continued David's faithful friend
throughout his reign (xxiii. 9, xxx. 7 ; 2
Sam. xv. 24, 29, 35), but gave offence by
taking Adonijah's part against Solomon (1
K. i. 7, 19, 42), and in consequence was deprived of the high priesthood (1 K. ii. 26, 27).
In Mark ii. 26, he is spoken of as the High-
Priest who gave the Shew-bread to David.
Perhaps he was the instigator of this act of
kindness to David ; and for this cause, as
well as his constancy to David, is mentioned
by our Lord instead of Ahimelech. It is also
possible that, as sagan to his father, he may
have performed most of the priestly functions, as Hophni and Phinehas did in the lifetime of Eli. Abiathar did not actually join
David till he went to Keilah (marg. ref.).

23. The characteristic generosity of David's disposition breaks out in these words.
He never forgot a friend. (Cp. 2 Sam. i. 26,
ix. 1, &c.) David acknowledges that Saul's
enmity against Abiathar is the consequence
of his enmity against himself, and therefore
David makes common cause with him.
XXIII. 1. David's growing importance,
fugitive as he was, is marked by this appeal
to him for deliverance from the Philistines.
The threshing floors were the natural objects
of plunder (Judg. vi. 11). Keilah was in the
Shephelah (marg. ref.), probably close to the
Philistine border, but its site is uncertain.
2, 4, 6. If Gad was with David at the
forest of Hareth (xxii. 5), and there enquired for him of the Lord (vv. 2, 4), but did
not accompany him to Keilah, and if Abiathar's flight occurred at the time of David's
being at Keilah, we have an additional
striking instance of God's watchful providential care of David in thus sending Abiathar to supply the place of Gad at so
critical a moment.

servant hath certainly heard that Saul seeketh to come to Keilah,
11 ^eto destroy the city for my sake. Will the men of Keilah deliver
me up into his hand ? will Saul come down, as thy servant hath
heard ? O LORD God of Israel, I beseech thee, tell thy servant.
12 And the LORD said, He will come down. Then said David, Will
the men of Keilah ⁱdeliver me and my men into the hand of
13 Saul ? And the LORD said, They will deliver *thee* up. ¶ Then
David and his men, ^f*which were* about six hundred, arose and
departed out of Keilah, and went whithersoever they could go.
And it was told Saul that David was escaped from Keilah ; and
14 he forbare to go forth. And David abode in the wilderness in
strong holds, and remained in ^ga mountain in the wilderness of
^hZiph. And Saul ⁱsought him every day, but God delivered
15 him not into his hand. ¶ And David saw that Saul was come
out to seek his life : and David *was* in the wilderness of Ziph in
16 a wood. And Jonathan Saul's son arose, and went to David into
17 the wood, and strengthened his hand in God. And he said unto
him, Fear not : for the hand of Saul my father shall not find
thee ; and thou shalt be king over Israel, and I shall be next
18 unto thee ; and ^kthat also Saul my father knoweth. And they
two ⁱmade a covenant before the LORD : and David abode in the
19 wood, and Jonathan went to his house. ¶ Then ^mcame up the
Ziphites to Saul to Gibeah, saying, Doth not David hide himself
with us in strong holds in the wood, in the hill of Hachilah,
20 which *is* ²on the south of ³Jeshimon ? Now therefore, O king,
come down according to all the desire of thy soul to come down ;
21 and ⁿour part *shall be* to deliver him into the king's hand. And
Saul said, Blessed *be* ye of the LORD ; for ye have compassion on
22 me. Go, I pray you, prepare yet, and know and see his place
where his ⁴haunt is, *and* who hath seen him there : for it is told
23 me *that* he dealeth very subtilly. See therefore, and take knowledge of all the lurking places where he hideth himself, and
come ye again to me with the certainty, and I will go with you :
and it shall come to pass, if he be in the land, that I will search
24 him out throughout all the thousands of Judah. ¶ And they
arose, and went to Ziph before Saul : but David and his men
were in the wilderness ^oof Maon, in the plain on the south of
25 Jeshimon. Saul also and his men went to seek *him*. And they
told David : wherefore he came down ⁵into a rock, and abode in
the wilderness of Maon. And when Saul heard *that*, he pursued
26 after David in the wilderness of Maon. And Saul went on this
side of the mountain, and David and his men on that side of the
mountain : ^pand David made haste to get away for fear of Saul :
for Saul and his men ^qcompassed David and his men round

Marginal references (left column):
ch. 22. 19.
f ch. 22. 2.
& 25. 13.
g Ps. 11. 1.
h Josh. 15.
55.
i Ps. 54. 3, 4.
k ch. 24. 20.
l ch. 18. 3.
& 20. 16.
2 Sam. 21. 7.
m See ch. 26.
1.
Ps. 54, title.
n Ps. 54. 3.
o Josh. 15.
55.
ch. 25. 2.
p Ps. 31. 22.
q Ps. 17. 9.

¹ Heb. *shut up.*   ³ Or, *The wilderness?*   ⁴ Heb. *foot shall be.*
² Heb. *on the right hand.*   ⁵ Or, *from the rock, v.* 28.

---

12. The conduct of the men of Keilah
would be like that of the men of Judah to
Samson their deliverer (Judg. xv. 10–13).
14. Ziph is placed between Hebron and
En-gedi (marg. reff.). [The "wood" (*v.*
15) is by Conder taken as a proper name,
"Cheresh," and identified with Khoreisa.]
16. A touching example of mutual fidelity
between friends. The humility and unselfish love of Jonathan is apparent in
v. 17.

19. [Hachilah is thought by Conder to be
the long ridge called El Kôlah]. For Jeshimon, see marg. and Num. xxi. 20.
24. *the plain*] The Arabah, the desert
tract which extends along the valley of the
Jordan from the Dead Sea to the Lake of
Gennesareth, now called El-Ghor. The
word is now given by the Arabs to the
valley between the Dead Sea and the Gulf
of Akaba.

27 about to take them. *r* But there came a messenger unto Saul, *See* 2 Kin. 19. 9.
saying, Haste thee, and come; for the Philistines have ¹invaded
28 the land. Wherefore Saul returned from pursuing after David,
and went against the Philistines. therefore they called that
29 place ²Sela-hammahlekoth. And David went up from thence,
and dwelt in strong holds at ³En-gedi. *, 2 Chr. 20. 2.
CHAP. 24. AND it came to pass, *a*when Saul was returned from *a* ch. 23. 28.
³following the Philistines, that it was told him, saying, Behold,
2 David is in the wilderness of En-gedi. Then Saul took three
thousand chosen men out of all Israel, and *b*went to seek David *b* Ps. 38. 12.
3 and his men upon the rocks of the wild goats. And he came to
the sheepcotes by the way, where *was* a cave; and *c*Saul went in *c* Ps. 141. 6.
to *d*cover his feet and *e*David and his men remained in the sides *d* Judg. 3.
4 of the cave. *f*And the men of David said unto him, Behold the *24.*
day of which the LORD said unto thee, Behold, I will deliver *e* Ps. 57.
thine enemy into thine hand, that thou mayest do to him as it title, & 112, title.
shall seem good unto thee. Then David arose, and cut off the *f* ch. 26. 8.
5 skirt of ⁴Saul's robe privily. And it came to pass afterward,
that *g*David's heart smote him, because he had cut off Saul's *g* 2 Sam. 24.
6 skirt. And he said unto his men, *h*The LORD forbid that I 10. *h* ch. 26. 11.
should do this thing unto my master, the LORD's anointed, to
stretch forth mine hand against him, seeing he *is* the anointed
7 of the LORD. So David ⁵stayed his servants with these words, *i* Ps. 7. 4.
and suffered them not to rise against Saul. But Saul rose up Matt. 5. 44.
8 out of the cave, and went on *his* way. David also arose after- Rom. 12. 17, 19.
ward, and went out of the cave, and cried after Saul, saying, My
lord the king. And when Saul looked behind him, David stooped
9 with his face to the earth, and bowed himself. ¶ And David said
to Saul, *k*Wherefore hearest thou men's words, saying, Behold, *k* Ps. 141. 6.
10 David seeketh thy hurt? Behold, this day thine eyes have seen Prov. 16. 28.
how that the LORD had delivered thee to day into mine hand in
the cave : and *some* bade *me* kill thee: but *mine eye* spared thee ;
and I said, I will not put forth mine hand against my lord;

¹ Heb. *spread themselves upon, &c.* ³ Heb. *after.* ⁴ Heb. *the robe which was Saul's.*
² That is, *The rock of divisions.* ⁵ Heb. *cut off.*

28. *Sela-hammahlekoth*] See marg. [Iden-
tified by Conder with a narrow and impassable gorge between El Kôlah and
Maon, called Malâky].
29. En-gedi (*the fountain of the kid*),
anciently called Hazezon-Tamar (Gen. xiv.
7) from the palm-trees which used to grow
there, still preserves its name in Ain-
Djedy. It is about 200 yards from the
Dead Sea, about the centre of its western
shore. It is marked by great luxuriance of
vegetation, though the approach to it is
through most dangerous and precipitous
passes. The country is full of caverns,
which serve as lurking places for outlaws
at the present day. One of these, a spacious
one called Bir-el-Mauquouchieh, with a
well in it suitable for watering sheep,
close to the Wady Hasasa, may have been
the identical cavern in which David cut off
Saul's skirt.
XXIV. 2. *the rocks of the wild goats*] To
signify the craggy precipitous character of
the country.

3. *remained in the sides*] Rather, "**were
in the sides of the cave** dwelling or abiding there." Some of these caverns are very
deep and spacious. Any one near the mouth
of the cave would be visible, but those in
the recesses would be quite in the dark and
invisible, especially if the incident occurred
at night. The lviith Psalm, according to
the title, was composed on this occasion.
4. *the day of which the* LORD *said*, &c.]
This was the version by David's men of such
Divine predictions as xv. 28, xvi. 1, 12.
Jonathan's words (xx. 15, xxiii. 17) show
clearly that these predictions were known.
5. *David's heart smote him*] He thought
the action inconsistent with the respect
which he owed to the king.
9. David was quite aware that there were
flatterers at Saul's court who were continually inflaming the King's mind by their
false accusations against him. This explains the language of many of the Psalms,
e.g. x. xi. xii. xxxv. and many more.

11 for he *is* the LORD's anointed. Moreover, my father, see, yea,
see the skirt of thy robe in my hand: for in that I cut off the
skirt of thy robe, and killed thee not, know thou and see that
there is [l]neither evil nor transgression in mine hand, and I have
not sinned against thee; yet thou [m]huntest my soul to take it.
12 [n]The LORD judge between me and thee, and the LORD avenge
13 me of thee: but mine hand shall not be upon thee. As saith
the proverb of the ancients, Wickedness proceedeth from the
14 wicked: but mine hand shall not be upon thee. After whom is
the king of Israel come out? after whom dost thou pursue?
15 [o]after a dead dog, after [p]a flea. [q]The LORD therefore be judge,
and judge between me and thee, and [r]see, and [s]plead my cause,
16 and [1]deliver me out of thine hand. ¶ And it came to pass, when
David had made an end of speaking these words unto Saul, that
Saul said, [t]*Is* this thy voice, my son David? And Saul lifted
17 up his voice and wept. [u]And he said to David, Thou *art* [x]more
righteous than I: for [y]thou hast rewarded me good, whereas I
18 have rewarded thee evil. And thou hast shewed this day how
that thou hast dealt well with me: forasmuch as when [z]the
LORD had [2]delivered me into thine hand, thou killedst me not.
19 For if a man find his enemy, will he let him go well away?
wherefore the LORD reward thee good for that thou hast done
20 unto me this day. And now, behold, [a]I know well that thou
shalt surely be king, and that the kingdom of Israel shall be
21 established in thine hand. [b]Swear now therefore unto me by
the LORD, [c]that thou wilt not cut off my seed after me, and that
22 thou wilt not destroy my name out of my father's house. And
David sware unto Saul. And Saul went home; but David and
his men gat them up unto [d]the hold.

CHAP. 25. AND [a]Samuel died; and all the Israelites were gathered
together, and [b]lamented him, and buried him in his house at
Ramah. ¶ And David arose, and went down [c]to the wilderness
2 of Paran. And *there was* a man [d]in Maon, whose [3]possessions
were in [e]Carmel; and the man *was* very great, and he had three
thousand sheep, and a thousand goats: and he was shearing his
3 sheep in Carmel. Now the name of the man *was* Nabal; and

[l] Ps. 7. 3. & 35. 7.
[m] ch. 26. 20.
[n] Gen. 16. 5. Judg. 11. 27. ch. 26. 10. Job 5. 8.
[o] ch. 17. 43. 2 Sam. 9. 8.
[p] ch. 26. 20.
[q] ver. 12.
[r] 2 Chr. 24. 22.
[s] Ps. 35. 1. & 43. 1. & 119. 154. Mic. 7. 9.
[t] ch. 26. 17.
[u] ch. 26. 21.
[x] Gen. 38. 26.
[y] Matt. 5. 44.
[z] ch. 26. 23.
[a] ch. 23. 17.
[b] Gen. 21. 23.
[c] 2 Sam. 21. 6, 8.
[d] ch. 23. 29.
[a] ch. 28. 3.
[b] Num. 20. 29. Deut. 34. 8.
[c] Gen. 21. 21. Ps. 120. 5.
[d] ch. 23. 24.
[e] Josh. 15. 55.

[1] Heb. *judge.* [2] Heb. *shut up*, ch. 23. 12. & 26. 8. [3] Or, *business.*

---

11. *my father*] The respectful address of a junior and an inferior (see 2 K. v. 13, and cp. *v.* 16, xxv. 8).

14. *After whom,* &c.] *i.e.* was it consistent with the dignity of the king of Israel to lead armies in pursuit of a weak and helpless individual like David?

21. *Swear now,* &c.] The same request which Jonathan made (xx. 15). The deep, genealogical feeling of the Israelites breaks out here as so often elsewhere.

22. Saul does not appear to have invited David to return to Gibeah, or to have given him any security of doing so with safety. David, with his intuitive sagacity, perceived that the softening of Saul's feelings was only momentary, and that the situation remained unchanged.

XXV. **1.** *in his house at Ramah*] Probably in the court or garden attached to his dwelling-house. (Cp. 2 Chr. xxxiii. 20; 2 K. xxi. 18; Joh xix. 41.)

the wilderness of Paran] The LXX. has the far more probable reading *Maon.* The wilderness of Paran lay far off to the south, on the borders of the wilderness of Sinai (Num. x. 12; 1 K. xi. 18), whereas the following verse (2) shows that the scene is laid in the immediate neighbourhood of Maon. If, however, Paran be the true reading, we must suppose that in a wide sense the wilderness of Paran extended all the way to the wilderness of Beersheba, and eastward to the mountains of Judah (marg. reff.).

2. *Carmel*] Not Mount Carmel on the west of the plain of Esdraelon, but the Carmel close to Maon (marg. reff.).

shearing his sheep] Which was always a time of open-handed hospitality among flock-masters (Gen. xxxviii. 12, 13; 2 Sam. xiii. 23, 24).

the name of his wife Abigail: and *she was* a woman of good
understanding, and of a beautiful countenance: but the man
was churlish and evil in his doings; and he *was* of the house
4 of Caleb. ¶And David heard in the wilderness that Nabal did
5 *shear* his sheep. And David sent out ten young men, and
David said unto the young men, Get you up to Carmel, and go
6 to Nabal, and ¹greet him in my name: and thus shall ye say to
him that liveth *in prosperity*, ᵍPeace *be* both to thee, and peace
7 *be* to thine house, and peace *be* unto all that thou hast. And
now I have heard that thou hast shearers: now thy shepherds
which were with us, we ²hurt them not, ʰneither was there
ought missing unto them, all the while they were in Carmel.
8 Ask thy young men, and they will shew thee. Wherefore let
the young men find favour in thine eyes: for we come in ⁱa good
day: give, I pray thee, whatsoever cometh to thine hand unto
9 thy servants, and to thy son David. ¶And when David's young
men came, they spake to Nabal according to all those words in
10 the name of David, and ³ceased. And Nabal answered David's
servants, and said, ᵏWho *is* David? and who *is* the son of Jesse?
there be many servants now a days that break away every man
11 from his master. ᶫShall I then take my bread, and my water,
and my ⁴flesh that I have killed for my shearers, and give *it*
12 unto men, whom I know not whence they *be?* So David's
young men turned their way, and went again, and came and
13 told him all those sayings. And David said unto his men, Gird
ye on every man his sword; and David also girded on his sword: and there went
up after David about four hundred men; and two hundred
14 ᵐabode by the stuff. ¶But one of the young men told Abigail,
Nabal's wife, saying, Behold, David sent messengers out of the
15 wilderness to salute our master; and he ⁵railed on them. But
the men *were* very good unto us, and ⁿwe were not ⁶hurt,
neither missed we any thing, as long as we were conversant
16 with them, when we were in the fields: they were ᵒa wall unto
us both by night and day, all the while we were with them
17 keeping the sheep. Now therefore know and consider what
thou wilt do; for ᵖevil is determined against our master, and
against all his household: for he *is such* a son of ᑫBelial, that *a*
18 *man* cannot speak to him. ¶Then Abigail made haste, and ʳtook
two hundred loaves, and two bottles of wine, and five sheep

¹ Heb. *ask him in my name
of peace*, ch. 17. 22.
² Heb. *shamed.*
³ Heb. *rested.*
⁴ Heb. *slaughter.*
⁵ Heb. *flew upon them.*
⁶ Heb. *shamed.*

f Gen. 38. 13.
2 Sam. 13. 23.

g 1 Chr. 12.
18.
Ps. 122. 7.
Luke 10. 5.
h ver. 15, 21.

i Neh. 8. 10.
Esth. 9. 19.

k Judg. 9. 28.
Ps. 73. 7, 8.
& 123. 3, 4.
l Judg. 8. 6.

m ch. 30. 24.

n ver. 7.

o Ex. 14. 22.
Job 1: 10.

p ch. 20. 7.
ᑫ Deut. 13.
13.
Judg. 19. 22.
r Gen. 32. 13.
Prov. 18. 16.

---

6. *that liveth in prosperity*] The Hebrew
is obscure, and is variously interpreted. The
simplest rendering is, "**And ye shall say
thus about (his) life**," *i.e.* with reference to
his life, health, circumstances, &c.

11. The mention of water indicates a
country where water was scarce (cp. Josh.
xv. 19). Or "bread and water" may be
equivalent to "meat and drink."

14. *railed on them*] The marginal reading, *flew upon them*, is nearer to the original.

16. *a wall*] To protect them from the
attacks of the Bedouins, &c. They had
been as safe with David's men around
them as if they had been dwelling in a
walled town.

18. *two bottles*] Rather, "**two skins**," each
of which would contain many gallons. These
leathern vessels varied in size according to
the skin they were made of, and the use
they were to be put to. The smaller and
more portable kind, which may not improperly be called *bottles*, were made of the
skin of a kid: larger ones of the skin of a
he-goat. The Arabs invariably to this day
carry their milk, water, &c., in such
leathern vessels. One skin of wine was a
handsome present from Ziba, sufficient for
David's household (2 Sam. xvi. 1). The
provisions were all ready to Abigail's hand,
having been provided for the sheep-shearing
feast.

ready dressed, and five measures of parched *corn*, and an hundred ¹clusters of raisins, and two hundred cakes of figs, and laid 19 *them* on asses. And she said unto her servants, ⁸Go on before me; behold, I come after you. But she told not her husband 20 Nabal. And it was *so*, *as* she rode on the ass, that she came down by the covert of the hill, and, behold, David and his men 21 came down against her; and she met them. ¶ Now David had said, Surely in vain have I kept all that this *fellow* hath in the wilderness, so that nothing was missed of all that *pertained* 22 unto him: and he hath ᵗrequited me evil for good. ᵘSo and more also do God unto the enemies of David, if I ˣleave of all that *pertain* to him by the morning light ᵛany that pisseth 23 against the wall. ¶ And when Abigail saw David, she hasted, and ᶻlighted off the ass, and fell before David on her face, and 24 bowed herself to the ground, and fell at his feet, and said, Upon me, my lord, *upon* me *let this* iniquity *be*: and let thine handmaid, I pray thee, speak in thine ²audience, and hear the 25 words of thine handmaid. Let not my lord, I pray thee, ³regard this man of Belial, *even* Nabal: for as his name *is*, so *is* he; ⁴Nabal *is* his name, and folly *is* with him: but I thine handmaid saw not the young men of my lord, whom thou didst 26 send. Now therefore, my lord, ᵃ*as* the LORD liveth, and *as* thy soul liveth, seeing the LORD hath ᵇwithholden thee from coming to *shed* blood, and from ⁵ᶜavenging thyself with thine own hand, now ᵈlet thine enemies, and they that seek evil to my 27 lord, be as Nabal. And now ᵉthis ⁶blessing which thine handmaid hath brought unto my lord, let it even be given unto the 28 young men that ⁷follow my lord. I pray thee, forgive the trespass of thine handmaid: for ᶠthe LORD will certainly make my lord a sure house; because my lord ᵍfighteth the battles of the LORD, and ʰevil hath not been found in thee *all* thy days. 29 Yet a man is risen to pursue thee, and to seek thy soul: but the soul of my lord shall be bound in the bundle of life with the LORD thy God; and the souls of thine enemies, them shall he

ˢ Gen. 32. 16, 20.

ᵗ Ps. 109. 5.
Prov. 17. 13.
ᵘ Ruth 1. 17.
ch. 3. 17.
& 20. 13.
ˣ ver. 34.
ᵛ 1 Kin. 14. 10.
& 21. 21.
2 Kin. 9. 8.
ᶻ Josh. 15. 18.
Judg. 1. 14.

ᵃ 2 Kin. 2. 2.
ᵇ Gen. 20. 6.
ver. 33.
ᶜ Rom. 12. 19.
ᵈ 2 Sam. 18. 32.
ᵉ Gen. 33. 11.
ch. 30. 26.
2 Kin. 5. 15.

ᶠ 1 Chr. 17. 10, 25.
ᵍ ch. 18. 17.
ʰ ch. 24. 11.

---

¹ Or, *lumps.*
² Heb. *ears.*
³ Heb. *lay it to his heart.*

⁴ That is, *Fool.*
⁵ Heb. *saving thyself.*

⁶ Or, *present.*
⁷ Heb. *walk at the feet of &c.* ver. 42. Judg. 4. 10.

---

20. *the covert of the hill*] Probably a defile or glen, literally *a secret place*, as in xix. 2. She was riding down into this glen from one side, while David and his men were descending the opposite hill. It is perhaps mentioned that she came by this *secret place*, because she chose this path to escape the observation of her husband or of any one else.

21. *in vain*] *i.e.* under false expectation.

22. The concluding phrase denotes the utter destruction of a family, and is rightly explained to mean "*every male*," perhaps with the idea, "*down to the very meanest member of the household.*"

26. The passage should be rendered as follows: *And now my lord, as the Lord liveth, and as thy soul liveth, it is the Lord that hath withholden thee from coming* into blood-guiltiness (as in *v.* 33), *and from* saving *thyself with thine own hand; and* now all *thine enemies* shall be as Nabal

(whom she considers as utterly impotent to hurt David, and as already thoroughly humbled before him), (so shall be) all *that seek evil to my Lord.*

28. *for the LORD will make...a sure house*] Cp. ii. 35, and 2 Sam. vii. 16 ; 1 K. xi. 38. Abigail's firm persuasion of David's kingdom stands upon the same footing as Rahab's conviction of God's gift of Canaan to the Israelites (Josh. ii. 9–13). Both testified to God's revelation and their own faith. This is doubtless the reason why Abigail's speech is recorded.

29. *in the bundle*] Rather, "the bag," in which anything precious, or important to be preserved, was put, and the bag was then tied up (cp. Gen. xlii. 35).

the souls...shall he sling out] The comparison is peculiarly appropriate as addressed to David, whose feat with his sling was so celebrated (xvii. 49).

30 [i]sling out, [1]*as out* of the middle of a sling. And it shall come
to pass, when the LORD shall have done to my lord according
to all the good that he hath spoken concerning thee, and shall
31 have appointed thee ruler over Israel; that this shall be [2]no
grief unto thee, nor offence of heart unto my lord, either that
thou hast shed blood causeless, or that my lord hath avenged
himself: but when the LORD shall have dealt well with my
32 lord, then remember thine handmaid. ¶And David said to
Abigail, [k]Blessed *be* the LORD God of Israel, which sent thee
33 this day to meet me: and blessed *be* thy advice, and blessed *be*
thou, which hast [l]kept me this day from coming to *shed* blood,
34 and from avenging myself with mine own hand. For in very
deed, *as* the LORD God of Israel liveth, which hath [m]kept me
back from hurting thee, except thou hadst hasted and come
to meet me, surely there had [n]not been left unto Nabal by the
35 morning light any that pisseth against the wall. So David
received of her hand *that* which she had brought him, and said
unto her, [o]Go up in peace to thine house; see, I have hearkened
36 to thy voice, and have [p]accepted thy person. ¶And Abigail
came to Nabal; and, behold, [q]he held a feast in his house, like
the feast of a king; and Nabal's heart *was* merry within him,
for he *was* very drunken: wherefore she told him nothing, less
37 or more, until the morning light. But it came to pass in the
morning, when the wine was gone out of Nabal, and his wife
had told him these things, that his heart died within him, and
38 he became *as* a stone. ¶And it came to pass about ten days
39 *after*, that the LORD smote Nabal, that he died. And when
David heard that Nabal was dead, he said, [r]Blessed *be* the LORD,
that hath [s]pleaded the cause of my reproach from the hand of
Nabal, and hath [t]kept his servant from evil: for the LORD hath
[u]returned the wickedness of Nabal upon his own head. ¶And
David sent and communed with Abigail, to take her to him to
40 wife. And when the servants of David were come to Abigail
to Carmel, they spake unto her, saying, David sent us unto
41 thee, to take thee to him to wife. And she arose, and bowed
herself on *her* face to the earth, and said, Behold, *let* [x]thine
handmaid *be* a servant to wash the feet of the servants of
42 my lord. And Abigail hasted, and arose, and rode upon an
ass, with five damsels of her's that went [3]after her; and
she went after the messengers of David, and became his wife.
43 ¶David also took Ahinoam [y]of Jezreel; [z]and they were also

[i] Jer. 10. 18.
[k] Gen. 24. 27. Ex. 18. 10. Ps. 41. 13.
[l] ver. 26.
[m] ver. 26.
[n] ver. 22.
[o] ch. 20. 42. 2 Sam. 15. 9. 2 Kin. 5. 19. Luke 7. 50.
[p] Gen. 19. 21.
[q] 2 Sam. 13. 23.
[r] ver. 32.
[s] Prov. 22. 23.
[t] ver. 26, 34.
[u] 1 Kin. 2. 44. Ps. 7. 16.
[x] Ruth 2. 10, 13. Prov. 15. 33.
[y] Josh. 15. 56.
[z] ch. 27. 3. & 30. 5.

[1] Heb. *in the midst of the bought* (or, hollow) *of a sling.*
[2] Heb. *no staggering*, or, *stumbling.*
[3] Heb. *at her feet*, *v.* 27.

---

37. *he became as a stone*] Probably his violent anger at hearing it brought on a fit of apoplexy to which he was disposed by the drunken revel of the night before. After lying senseless for ten days he died.

40. There is no note of the exact interval that elapsed between Nabal's death and David's hearing of it, or, again, between David's hearing of it and his message to Abigail; nor is there any reason to suppose that the marriage took place with unbecoming haste. The widow of such a husband as Nabal had been could not, however, be expected to revere his memory. After the usual mourning of seven days, she would probably feel herself free to act as custom allowed. (See 2 Sam. xi. 26.)

43. In the list of David's wives Ahinoam is mentioned first (2 Sam. iii. 2; 1 Chr. iii. 1). But this may be only because her son was the first-born. David's now taking two wives was an indication of his growing power and importance as a chieftain. The number was increased to six when he reigned in Hebron (1 Chr. iii. 1), and still further when he became king of all Israel (2 Sam. v. 12, 13). See i. 2 note.

of Jezreel] Not the well-known city of

44 both of them his wives. But Saul had given *a*Michal his daughter, David's wife, to ¹Phalti the son of Laish, which *was* of *b*Gallim.

CHAP. 26. AND the Ziphites came unto Saul to Gibeah, saying, *a*Doth not David hide himself in the hill of Hachilah, *which is* 2 before Jeshimon? Then Saul arose, and went down to the wilderness of Ziph, having three thousand chosen men of 3 Israel with him, to seek David in the wilderness of Ziph. And Saul pitched in the hill of Hachilah, which *is* before Jeshimon, by the way. But David abode in the wilderness, and he saw 4 that Saul came after him into the wilderness. David therefore sent out spies, and understood that Saul was come in very deed. 5 ¶And David arose, and came to the place where Saul had pitched: and David beheld the place where Saul lay, and *b*Abner the son of Ner, the captain of his host: and Saul lay in the 6 ²trench, and the people pitched round about him. Then answered David and said to Ahimelech the Hittite, and to Abishai *c*the son of Zeruiah, brother to Joab, saying, Who will *d*go down with me to Saul to the camp? And Abishai said, I will 7 go down with thee. ¶So David and Abishai came to the people by night: and, behold, Saul lay sleeping within the trench, and his spear stuck in the ground at his bolster: but Abner and the 8 people lay round about him. Then said Abishai to David, God hath ³delivered thine enemy into thine hand this day: now therefore let me smite him, I pray thee, with the spear even to the earth at once, and I will not *smite* him the second time. 9 And David said to Abishai, Destroy him not: *e*for who can stretch forth his hand against the LORD's anointed, and be 10 guiltless? David said furthermore, *As* the LORD liveth, *f*the LORD shall smite him; or *g*his day shall come to die; or he 11 shall *h*descend into battle, and perish. *i*The LORD forbid that I should stretch forth mine hand against the LORD's anointed: but, I pray thee, take thou now the spear that *is* at his bolster, 12 and the cruse of water, and let us go. So David took the spear and the cruse of water from Saul's bolster; and they gat them away, and no man saw *it*, nor knew *it*, neither awaked: for they *were* all asleep; because *k*a deep sleep from the LORD was fallen 13 upon them. ¶Then David went over to the other side, and

¹ *Phaltiel*, 2 Sam. 3. 15.   ² Or, *midst of his carriages,*   ³ Heb. *shut up*, ch. 24. 18.
ch. 17. 20.

Samaria, which gave its name to the plain of Esdraelon, but a town of Judah, near Carmel (marg. ref.).

44. Saul's giving Michal to Phalti was intended to mark the final rupture of his own relations with David (cp. Judg. xiv. 20 ; 2 Sam. iii. 7, xvi. 21). Phalti or Phaltiel was compelled by Abner to restore Michal to David (2 Sam. iii. 15).

Gallim] A city of Benjamin, and in the neighbourhood of another town called *Laish*.

XXVI. The incident related in this chapter of the meeting between Saul and David bears a strong general resemblance to that recorded in ch. xxiv., and is of a nature unlikely to have occurred more than once. Existing discrepancies are explained by the supposition that one narrative relates fully

some incidents on which the other is silent. On the whole the most probable conclusion is that the two narratives relate to one and the same event. (Cp. the two narratives of the Creation, Gen. i. and Gen. ii. 4, seq. ; the two narratives of David's war, 2 Sam. viii. and x. ; and those of the death of Ahaziah, 2 K. ix. 27, seq., and 2 Chr. xxii. 9.)

6. *Ahimelech the Hittite.* Only mentioned here. Uriah was also a Hittite.

Abishai] He was son of Zeruiah, David's sister, but probably about the same age as David. He became very famous as a warrior (2 Sam. xxiii. 18), but was implicated with his brother Joab in the murder of Abner in retaliation for the death of their brother Asahel (2 Sam. iii. 30).

stood on the top of an hill afar off; a great space *being* between
14 them: and David cried to the people, and to Abner the son of
Ner, saying, Answerest thou not, Abner? Then Abner an-
15 swered and said, Who *art* thou *that* criest to the king? And
David said to Abner, *Art* not thou a *valiant* man? and who *is*
like to thee in Israel? wherefore then hast thou not kept thy
lord the king? for there came one of the people in to destroy
16 the king thy lord. This thing *is* not good that thou hast done.
As the LORD liveth, ye *are* [1]worthy to die, because ye have not
kept your master, the LORD's anointed. And now see where
the king's spear *is*, and the cruse of water that *was* at his
17 bolster. And Saul knew David's voice, and said, [l]*Is* this thy [l] ch. 24. 16.
voice, my son David? And David said, *It is* my voice, my lord,
18 O king. And he said, [m]Wherefore doth my lord thus pursue [m] ch. 24. 9.
after his servant? for what have I done? or what evil *is* in
19 mine hand? Now therefore, I pray thee, let my lord the king
hear the words of his servant. If the LORD have [n]stirred thee [n] 2 Sam. 16.
up against me, let him [2]accept an offering: but if *they be* the 11. & 24. 1.
children of men, cursed *be* they before the LORD; [o]for they [o] Deut. 4. 28.
have driven me out this day from [3]abiding in the [p]inheritance Ps. 120. 5.
20 of the LORD, saying, Go, serve other gods. Now therefore, let [p] 2 Sam. 14. 16.
not my blood fall to the earth before the face of the LORD: for & 20. 19.
the king of Israel is come out to seek [q]a flea, as when one doth [q] ch. 24. 14.
21 hunt a partridge in the mountains. ¶ Then said Saul, [r]I have [r] ch. 15. 24.
sinned: return, my son David: for I will no more do thee harm, & 24. 17.
because my soul was [s]precious in thine eyes this day: behold, I [s] ch. 18. 30.
22 have played the fool, and have erred exceedingly. And David
answered and said, Behold the king's spear! and let one of the
23 young men come over and fetch it. [t]The LORD render to every [t] Ps. 7. 8.
man his righteousness and his faithfulness: for the LORD de- & 18. 20.
livered thee into *my* hand to day, but I would not stretch forth
24 mine hand against the LORD's anointed. And, behold, as thy
life was much set by this day in mine eyes, so let my life be
much set by in the eyes of the LORD, and let him deliver me
25 out of all tribulation. Then Saul said to David, Blessed *be*
thou, my son David: thou shalt both do great *things*, and also
shalt still [u]prevail. So David went on his way, and Saul re- [u] Gen. 32. 28.
turned to his place.

CHAP. 27. AND David said in his heart, I shall now [4]perish one
day by the hand of Saul: *there is* nothing better for me than

[1] Heb. *the sons of death*, 2 Sam. 12. 5.
[2] Heb. *smell*, Gen. 8. 21. Lev. 26. 31.
[3] Heb. *cleaving*.
[4] Heb. *be consumed*.

---

15. This incidental testimony to Abner's great eminence as a warrior is fully borne out by David's dirge at Abner's death (2 Sam. iii. 31–34, 38), as well as by his whole history. At the same time David's bantering tone in regard to Abner, coupled with what he says in *v.* 19, makes it probable that David attributed Saul's persecution of him in some degree to Abner. Abner would be likely to dread a rival in the young conqueror of Judah (cp. 2 Sam. ii. 8).

19. *If the* LORD *have stirred thee up*] The meaning is clear from the preceding history. "An evil spirit from God troubling him" was the beginning of the persecution. And this evil spirit was sent in punishment of Saul's sin (xvi. 1, 14). If the continued persecution was merely the consequence of this evil spirit continuing to vex Saul, David advises Saul to seek God's pardon, and, as a consequence, the removal of the evil spirit, by offering a sacrifice. But if the persecution was the consequence of the false accusations of slanderers, then "cursed" be his enemies who, by their actions, drove David out from the only land where Jehovah was worshipped, and forced him to take refuge in the country of heathen and idolaters (cp. Deut. iv. 27, xxviii. 36).

that I should speedily escape into the land of the Philistines;
and Saul shall despair of me, to seek me any more in any coast
2 of Israel: so shall I escape out of his hand. And David arose,
^aand he passed over with the six hundred men that *were* with
3 him ^bunto Achish, the son of Maoch, king of Gath. And
David dwelt with Achish at Gath, he and his men, every man
with his household, *even* David ^cwith his two wives, Ahinoam
the Jezreelitess, and Abigail the Carmelitess, Nabal's wife.
4 And it was told Saul that David was fled to Gath: and he
5 sought no more again for him. ¶ And David said unto Achish,
If I have now found grace in thine eyes, let them give me a
place in some town in the country, that I may dwell there:
for why should thy servant dwell in the royal city with thee?
6 Then Achish gave him Ziklag that day: wherefore ^dZiklag per-
7 taineth unto the kings of Judah unto this day. And ¹the time
that David dwelt in the country of the Philistines was ²a full
8 year and four months. ¶ And David and his men went up, and
invaded ^ethe Geshurites, ^fand the ³Gezrites, and the ^gAmalek-
ites: for those *nations were* of old the inhabitants of the land,
9 ^has thou goest to Shur, even unto the land of Egypt. And
David smote the land, and left neither man nor woman alive,
and took away the sheep, and the oxen, and the asses, and the
10 camels, and the apparel, and returned, and came to Achish. And
Achish said, ⁴Whither have ye made a road to day? And David
said, Against the south of Judah, and against the south of ⁱthe
11 Jerahmeelites, and against the south of ^kthe Kenites. And
David saved neither man nor woman alive, to bring *tidings* to
Gath, saying, Lest they should tell on us, saying, So did David,
and so *will be* his manner all the while he dwelleth in the
12 country of the Philistines. And Achish believed David, saying,
He hath made his people Israel ⁵utterly to abhor him; therefore he shall be my servant for ever.

CHAP. **28.** AND ^ait came to pass in those days, that the Philistines
gathered their armies together for warfare, to fight with Israel.
And Achish said unto David, Know thou assuredly, that thou

^a ch. 25. 13.
^b ch. 21. 10.

^c ch. 25. 13.

^d See Josh. 15. 31. & 19. 5.

^e Josh. 13. 2.
^f Josh. 16. 10.
Judg. 1. 29.
^g Ex. 17. 16.
ch. 15. 7.
^h Gen. 25. 18.

ⁱ See 1 Chr. 2. 9, 25.
^k Judg. 1. 16.

^a ch. 29. 1.

---

¹ Heb. *the number of days.*   ² Heb. a year *of days:*   ⁴ Or, *Did you not make a road, &c.*
³ Or, *Gerzites.*   See ch. 29. 3. till 1056.   ⁵ Heb. *to stink.*

XXVII. **5.** David, with characteristic
Oriental subtlety (cp. xxi. 2), suggests as a
reason for leaving Gath that his presence
was burdensome and expensive to the king.
His real motive was to be more out of the
way of observation and control, so as to act
the part of an enemy of Saul, without really
lifting up his hand against him and his own
countrymen of Israel.

6. *Ziklag*] This was properly one of the
cities of Simeon within the tribe of Judah
(marg. reff.), but it had been taken possession
of by the Philistines. The exact situation
of it is uncertain.

unto this day] This phrase, coupled with
the title *the kings of Judah,* implies that
this was written after the revolt of Jeroboam, and before the Babylonish captivity.

8. The Geshurites bordered upon the
Philistines, and lived in the mountainous
district which terminates the desert on the

north-east (marg. ref.). They were a different tribe, or, at least, a different branch
of it, from the Geshurites who lived on the
north-east border of Bashan, and were
Arameans (2 Sam. xv. 8). The Gezrites,
or Gerzites, may be connected with those
who gave their name to Mount Gerizim.

10. *the Jerahmeelites*] i.e. the descendants
of Jerahmeel, the son of Hezron, the son of
Perez, the son of Judah (marg. reff.). They
were therefore a portion of the "south of
Judah."

the Kenites] See Num. xxiv. 21, iv. 11
notes; and for their near neighbourhood to
Amalek, see xv. 6.

11. *tidings*] The word is not in the original. The sense rather is "**to bring them
to Gath,**" as captives and slaves. The
prisoners taken would naturally have been
part of the spoil, but David dared not to
bring them to Gath lest his deceit should

2 shalt go out with me to battle, thou and thy men. And David said to Achish, Surely thou shalt know what thy servant can do. And Achish said to David, Therefore will I make thee keeper of 3 mine head for ever. ¶ Now *b* Samuel was dead, and all Israel had lamented him, and buried him in Ramah, even in his own city. ¶ And Saul had put away *c* those that had familiar spirits, 4 and the wizards, out of the land. And the Philistines gathered themselves together, and came and pitched in *d* Shunem: and Saul gathered all Israel together, and they pitched in *e* Gilboa. 5 And when Saul saw the host of the Philistines, he was *f* afraid, 6 and his heart greatly trembled. And when Saul enquired of the LORD, *g* the LORD answered him not, neither by *h* dreams, nor 7 *i* by Urim, nor by prophets. Then said Saul unto his servants, Seek me a woman that hath a familiar spirit, that I may go to her, and enquire of her. And his servants said to him, Behold, 8 there is a woman that hath a familiar spirit at En-dor. ¶ And Saul disguised himself, and put on other raiment, and he went, and two men with him, and they came to the woman by night: and *k* he said, I pray thee, divine unto me by the familiar spirit, 9 and bring me *him* up, whom I shall name unto thee. And the woman said unto him, Behold, thou knowest what Saul hath done, how he hath *l* cut off those that have familiar spirits, and the wizards, out of the land: wherefore then layest thou a snare 10 for my life, to cause me to die? And Saul sware to her by the LORD, saying, *As* the LORD liveth, there shall no punishment 11 happen to thee for this thing. Then said the woman, Whom shall I bring up unto thee? And he said, Bring me up Samuel.

b ch. 25. 1.

c Ex. 22. 18. Deut. 18. 10, 11.
d Josh. 19. 18.
2 Kin. 4. 8.
e ch. 31. 1.
g ch. 14. 37.
Prov. 1. 28.
Lam. 2. 9.
h Num. 12. 6.
i Ex. 28. 30.
Num. 27. 21.
Deut. 33. 8.

f Job 18. 11.

k Deut. 18. 11.
1 Chr. 10. 13.
Isai. 8. 19.
l ver. 3.

---

be discovered. Obviously these tribes were allies of the Philistines.

XXVIII. 2. *thou shalt know*, &c.] David dissembled (cp. also xxix. 8), hoping, no doubt, that something would happen to prevent his fighting against his king and country.

keeper of mine head] Captain of his body-guard.

3. It does not appear when Saul had suppressed witchcraft; it was probably in the early part of his reign.

familiar spirits ... wizards] *i.e.* ventriloquists...wise or cunning men. See Lev. xix. 31 note.

4. *Gilboa*] Now called *Jebel Fukûah*. But the ancient name is preserved in the village of *Jelbon*, situated on the south side of the mountain. It was separated from Shunem (see marg. ref.) by the deep valley of Jezreel. The Philistines either advanced along the sea-coast, and then entered the valley of Jezreel from the west, or they came by the present road right through Samaria, starting from Aphek (xxix. 1).

6. *when Saul enquired of the* LORD, &c.] It is said (1 Chr. x. 14) that one reason why the Lord slew Saul, and gave his kingdom to David, was because he *enquired not of the Lord*. The explanation of this apparent discrepancy is to be found in the fact that enquiring of the familiar spirit was positively antagonistic to enquiring of the Lord. That Saul received no answer—when he "en-

quired of the Lord" *by dreams*, which was an immediate revelation to himself; *by Urim*, which was an answer through the High-Priest clothed in the ephod; or *by Prophets*, which was an answer conveyed through some seer speaking by the Word of the Lord (xxii. 5)—was a reason for self-abasement and self-examination, to find out and, if possible, remove the cause, but was no justification whatever of his sin in asking counsel of familiar spirits.

7. *enquire*] A different word from that in *v.* 6, though nearly synonymous with it. It is more frequently applied to enquiry of a false god, as *e.g.* 2 K. i. 2; Isai. viii. 19, xix. 3.

En-dor (see Josh. xi. 2 note) was seven or eight miles from the slopes of Gilboa, on the north of little Hermon, where the Philistines were encamped; so that Saul must have run great risks in going there.

8. *divine*] Cp. notes to vi. 2; Num. xxiii. 23.

bring me him up] The art of the ventriloquist seems to have been always connected with necromancy. The Greeks had necromancers who called up departed spirits to give answers to those who consulted them.

11. *Bring me up Samuel*] Archbishop Trench observes, "All human history has failed to record a despair deeper or more tragic than his, who, having forsaken God and being of God forsaken, is now seeking

12 ¶And when the woman saw Samuel, she cried with a loud voice: and the woman spake to Saul, saying, Why hast thou deceived 13 me? for thou *art* Saul. And the king said unto her, Be not afraid: for what sawest thou? And the woman said unto Saul, 14 I saw ᵐgods ascending out of the earth. And he said unto her, ¹What form *is* he of? And she said, An old man cometh up; and he *is* covered with ⁿa mantle. And Saul perceived that it *was* Samuel, and he stooped with *his* face to the ground, and 15 bowed himself. • ¶And Samuel said to Saul, Why hast thou disquieted me, to bring me up? And Saul answered, °I am sore distressed; for the Philistines make war against me, and ᵖGod is departed from me, and ᑫanswereth me no more, neither ²by prophets, nor by dreams: therefore I have called thee, that thou 16 mayest make known unto me what I shall do. Then said Samuel, Wherefore then dost thou ask of me, seeing the LORD is departed 17 from thee, and is become thine enemy? And the LORD hath done ³to him, ʳas he spake by ⁴me: for the LORD hath rent the kingdom out of thine hand, and given it to thy neighbour, *even* to 18 David: ˢbecause thou obeyedst not the voice of the LORD, nor executedst his fierce wrath upon Amalek, therefore hath the LORD 19 done this thing unto thee this day. Moreover the LORD will also deliver Israel with thee into the hand of the Philistines: and to morrow *shalt* thou and thy sons *be* with me: the LORD also shall deliver the host of Israel into the hand of the Philistines. 20 ¶Then Saul ⁵fell straightway all along on the earth, and was sore afraid, because of the words of Samuel: and there was no strength in him; for he had eaten no bread all the day, nor all 21 the night. And the woman came unto Saul, and saw that he was sore troubled, and said unto him, Behold, thine handmaid hath obeyed thy voice, and I have ᵗput my life in my hand, and have hearkened unto thy words which thou spakest unto me. 22 Now therefore, I pray thee, hearken thou also unto the voice of thine handmaid, and let me set a morsel of bread before thee; and eat, that thou mayest have strength, when thou goest on 23 thy way. But he refused, and said, I will not eat. But his servants, together with the woman, compelled him; and he hearkened unto their voice. So he arose from the earth, and sat 24 upon the bed. And the woman had a fat calf in the house; and

Marginal references (left column):

ᵐ Ex. 22. 28.

ⁿ ch. 15. 27.
2 Kin. 2. 8.

° Prov. 5. 11, 12, 13. & 14. 14.
ᵖ ch. 18. 12.
ᑫ ver. 6.

ʳ ch. 15. 28.

ˢ ch. 15. 9.
1 Kin. 20. 42.
1. Chr. 10. 13.
Jer. 48. 10.

ᵗ Judg. 12. 3.
ch. 19. 5.
Job 13. 14.

Footnotes:

¹ Heb. *What is his form?*
² Heb. *by the hand of prophets.*
³ Or, *for himself,* Prov. 16. 4.
⁴ Heb. *mine hand.*
⁵ Heb. *made haste, and fell with the fulness of his stature.*

---

to move hell; and infinitely guilty as he is, assuredly there is something unutterably pathetic in that yearning of the disanointed king to change words with the friend and counsellor of his youth, and if he must hear his doom, to hear it from no other lips but his" ('Shipwrecks of Faith,' p. 47).

12. It is manifest both that the apparition of Samuel was real, and also that the woman was utterly unprepared for it.

Why hast thou deceived me, &c.] She perhaps inferred that Samuel would have answered the call of none inferior to the king. Or it may be the presence of an inhabitant of the world of spirits brought a sudden illumination to her mind.

13. *gods*] *Elohim* is here used in a general

sense of a *supernatural* appearance, either angel or spirit. Hell, or the place of the departed (cp. *v.* 19; 2 Sam. xii. 23) is represented as under the earth (Isai. xiv. 9, 10; Ezek. xxxii. 18).

17. *to him*] Better, "for Himself," as in the margin.

19. Rather, "will deliver Israel also." Saul had not only brought ruin upon his own house but upon Israel also; and when Saul and Jonathan fell the camp (not "host") would be plundered by the conquerors (xxxi. 8; 2 Sam. i. 10).

23. *the bed*] Rather, "the bench" or divan, such as in the East still runs along the wall, furnished with cushions, for those who sit at meals (Esth. i. 6; Ezek. xxiii. 41).

she hasted, and killed it, and took flour, and kneaded *it*, and
25 did bake unleavened bread thereof : and she brought *it* before
Saul, and before his servants ; and they did eat. Then they
rose up, and went away that night.
CHAP. 29. NOW *a*the Philistines gathered together all their armies   *a* ch. 28. 1.
*b*to Aphek : and the Israelites pitched by a fountain which *is* in   *b* ch. 4. 1.
2 Jezreel. And the lords of the Philistines passed on by hundreds,
and by thousands : but David and his men passed on in the rere-
3 ward *c*with Achish. Then said the princes of the Philistines,   *c* ch. 28. 1.
What *do* these Hebrews *here ?* And Achish said unto the princes
of the Philistines, *Is* not this David, the servant of Saul the king
of Israel, which hath been with me *d*these days, or these years,   *d* See ch. 27.
and I have *e*found no fault in him since he fell *unto me* unto   7.
4 this day ? And the princes of the Philistines were wroth with   *e* Dan. 6. 5.
him ; and the princes of the Philistines said unto him, *f*Make   *f* 1 Chr. 12.
this fellow return, that he may go again to his place which thou   19.
hast appointed him, and let him not go down with us to battle,
lest *g*in the battle he be an adversary to us : for wherewith   *g* As ch. 14.
should he reconcile himself unto his master ? *should it* not *be*   21.
5 with the heads of these men ? *Is* not this David, of whom they
sang one to another in dances, saying, *h*Saul slew his thousands,   *h* ch. 18. 7.
6 and David his ten thousands ? ¶Then Achish called David, and   & 21. 11.
said unto him, Surely, *as* the LORD liveth, thou hast been upright, and *i*thy going out and thy coming in with me in the host   *i* 2 Sam. 3.
is good in my sight : for *k*I have not found evil in thee since the   25.
day of thy coming unto me unto this day : nevertheless *l*the   2 Kin. 19. 27.
7 lords favour thee not. Wherefore now return, and go in peace,   *k* ver. 3.
8 that thou ²displease not the lords of the Philistines. And David
said unto Achish, But what have I done ? and what hast thou
found in thy servant so long as I have been ³with thee unto this
day, that I may not go fight against the enemies of my lord the
9 king ? And Achish answered and said to David, I know that
thou *art* good in my sight, *l*as an angel of God : notwithstanding   *l* 2 Sam. 14.
*m*the princes of the Philistines have said, He shall not go up   17, 20.
10 with us to the battle. Wherefore now rise up early in the morn-   & 19. 27.
ing with thy master's servants that are come with thee : and as   *m* ver. 4.
soon as ye be up early in the morning, and have light, depart.

---

¹ Heb. *thou art not good in*   ² Heb. *do not evil in the*   ³ Heb. *before thee.*
the eyes of the lords.   *eyes of the lords.*

XXIX. 1. *a fountain*] Probably, the fine
spring *Ain-Jalud*. It is impossible to say
what the peculiar circumstances were which
led to the struggle between Israel and the
Philistines taking place so far north as the
plain of Jezreel. Possibly it was connected
with some movements of the Aramaic
tribes to the north of Palestine. See 2
Sam. viii.
2. *the lords*] See Judg. iii. 3 note, as distinguished from ordinary " princes " (*v.* 3).
The military divisions of the Philistine
army were by hundreds and by thousands,
like those of the Israelites (viii. 12). David
and his men formed a body-guard to Achish
(xxviii. 2).
3. *he fell unto me*] The regular word for
deserting and going over to the other side.
See Jer. xxxvii. 13, xxxviii. 19.

6. *as the* LORD *liveth*] The swearing by
JEHOVAH seems strange in the mouth of
a Philistine. But probably not the very
words, but only the sense of this and such
like speeches, is preserved.
8. See *v.* 10 note.
10. *with thy master's servants*] The clue
to this may be found in 1 Chr. xii. 19-21,
where it appears that a considerable number
of Manassites " fell " to David just at this
time, and went back with him to Ziklag. It
is therefore to these new comers that Achish
applies the expression. It is impossible not
to recognize here a merciful interposition of
Providence, by which David was not only
saved from fighting against his king and
country, but sent home just in time to
recover his wives and property from the
Amalekites (xxx.). That David maintained

11 ¶ So David and his men rose up early to depart in the morning,
to return into the land of the Philistines. *And the Philistines
went up to Jezreel.

CHAP. 30. AND it came to pass, when David and his men were come
to Ziklag on the third day, that the *Amalekites had invaded the
south, and Ziklag, and smitten Ziklag, and burned it with fire;
2 and had taken the women captives, that *were* therein: they slew
not any, either great or small, but carried *them* away, and went
3 on their way. So David and his men came to the city, and, behold, it *was* burned with fire; and their wives, and their sons,
4 and their daughters, were taken captives. Then David and the
people that *were* with him lifted up their voice and wept, until
5 they had no more power to weep. And David's *two wives were
taken captives, Ahinoam the Jezreelitess, and Abigail the wife
6 of Nabal the Carmelite. And David was greatly distressed;
*for the people spake of stoning him, because the soul of all the
people was ¹grieved, every man for his sons and for his daughters: *but David encouraged himself in the LORD his God.
7 ¶ *And David said to Abiathar the priest, Ahimelech's son, I
pray thee, bring me hither the ephod. And Abiathar brought
8 thither the ephod to David. *And David enquired at the LORD,
saying, Shall I pursue after this troop? shall I overtake them?
And he answered him, Pursue: for thou shalt surely overtake
9 *them*, and without fail recover *all*. So David went, he and the
six hundred men that *were* with him, and came to the brook
10 Besor, where those that were left behind stayed. But David
pursued, he and four hundred men: *for two hundred abode
behind, which were so faint that they could not go over the
11 brook Besor. ¶ And they found an Egyptian in the field, and
brought him to David, and gave him bread, and he did eat; and
12 they made him drink water; and they gave him a piece of a
cake of figs, and two clusters of raisins: and *when he had
eaten, his spirit came again to him: for he had eaten no bread,
13 nor drunk *any* water, three days and three nights. And David
said unto him, To whom *belongest* thou? and whence *art* thou?
And he said, I *am* a young man of Egypt, servant to an Amalekite; and my master left me, because three days agone I fell
14 sick. We made an invasion *upon* the south of *the Cherethites,

---

¹ Heb. *bitter*, Judg. 18. 25.   ch. 1. 10.   2 Sam. 17. 8.   2 Kin. 4. ¦7.

Margin notes (left column):

* 2 Sam. 4. 4.

a See ch. 15. 7. & 27. 8.

b ch. 25. 42. 2 Sam. 2. 2.

c Ex. 17. 4.

d Ps. 42. 5. & 56. 3, 4. Hab. 3. 17. *e* ch. 23. 6. *f* ch. 23. 2. 4.

g ver. 21.

h So Judg. 15. 19. ch. 14. 27.

i 2 Sam. 8. 18. 1 Kin. 1. 38, 44. Ezek. 25. 16. Zeph. 2. 5.

---

his position by subtlety and falsehood,
which were the invariable characteristics of
his age and nation, is not in the least to be
wondered at. No sanction is given by this
narrative to the use of falsehood.

XXX. 1. *on the third day*] This indicates
that Aphek was three days' march from
Ziklag, say about fifty miles, which agrees
very well with the probable situation of
Aphek (iv. 1 note). From Ziklag to Shunem would not be less than eighty or ninety
miles.

The Amalekites, in retaliation of David's
raids (xxvii. 8, 9), invaded "the south" of
Judah (Josh. xv. 21); but owing to the
absence of all the men with David there
was no resistance, and consequently the
women and children were carried off as
prey, and uninjured.

7. Abiathar had continued to abide with
David, ever since he joined him at Keilah
(xxiii. 6). On enquiry of the Lord by the
ephod, see Judg. i. 1 note. The answers
were evidently given by the Word of the
Lord in the mouth of the High-Priest (cp.
John xi. 51).

9. *Besor*] Thought to be the stream of the
Wady Sheriah which enters the sea a little
south of Gaza.

12. *three days and three nights*] Indicating
that at least so long a time had elapsed
since the sack of Ziklag.

14. *the Cherethites*] Here used as synonymous with *Philistines* (*v.* 16). In David's
reign the body-guard commanded by Benaiah consisted of Cherethites and Pelethites
(= Philistines?) and a picked corps of six
hundred men of Gath commanded by Ittai

and upon *the coast* which *belongeth* to Judah, and upon the south
15 of [k]Caleb; and we burned Ziklag with fire. And David said to
him, Canst thou bring me down to this company? And he said,
Swear unto me by God, that thou wilt neither kill me, nor deliver me into the hands of my master, and I will bring thee
16 down to this company. ¶ And when he had brought him down,
Behold, *they were* spread abroad upon all the earth, [l]eating and
drinking, and dancing, because of all the great spoil that they
had taken out of the land of the Philistines, and out of the land
17 of Judah. And David smote them from the twilight even unto
the evening of [1]the next day: and there escaped not a man of
them, save four hundred young men, which rode upon camels,
18 and fled. And David recovered all that the Amalekites had
19 carried away: and David rescued his two wives. And there
was nothing lacking to them, neither small nor great, neither
sons nor daughters, neither spoil, nor any *thing* that they had
20 taken to them: [m]David recovered all. And David took all the
flocks and the herds, *which* they drave before those *other* cattle,
21 and said, This *is* David's spoil. ¶ And David came to the [n]two
hundred men, which were so faint that they could not follow
David, whom they had made also to abide at the brook Besor:
and they went forth to meet David, and to meet the people that
were with him: and when David came near to the people, he
22 [2]saluted them. Then answered all the wicked men and *men* [o]of
Belial, of [3]those that went with David, and said, Because they
went not with us, we will not give them *ought* of the spoil that
we have recovered, save to every man his wife and his chil-
23 dren, that they may lead *them* away, and depart. Then said
David, Ye shall not do so, my brethren, with that which the
LORD hath given us, who hath preserved us, and delivered the
24 company that came against us into our hand. For who will
hearken unto you in this matter? but [p]as his part *is* that goeth
down to the battle, so *shall* his part *be* that tarrieth by the stuff:
25 they shall part alike. And it was *so* from that day [4]forward,
that he made it a statute and an ordinance for Israel unto this
26 day. ¶ And when David came to Ziklag, he sent of the spoil
unto the elders of Judah, *even* to his friends, saying, Behold a
27 [5]present for you of the spoil of the enemies of the LORD; to
them which *were* in Beth-el, and to *them* which *were* in [q]south

[k] Josh. 14. 13. & 15. 13.
[l] 1 Thess. 5. 3.
[m] ver. 8.
[n] ver. 10.
[o] Deut. 13. 13. Judg. 19. 22.
[p] See Num. 31. 27. Josh. 22. 8.
[q] Josh. 19. 8.

[1] Heb. *their morrow.*
[2] Or, *asked them how they did,* Judg. 18. 15.
[3] Heb. *men.*
[4] Heb. *and forward.*
[5] Heb. *blessing,* Gen. 33. 11. ch. 25. 27.

---

the Gittite. It would seem from this that the Cherethites and Philistines were two kindred and associated tribes, like Angles and Saxons, who took possession of the sea-coast of Palestine. The Philistines, being the more powerful, gave their name to the country and the nation in general, though that of the Cherethites was not wholly extinguished. Many persons connect the name Cherethite with that of the island of Crete.

20. The meaning is, *and David took all the sheep and oxen which the Amalekites drove* (*i.e.* had in their possession) *before that acquisition of cattle* (viz. before what they took in their raid to the south), *and they* (the people) *said, This is David's spoil.* This was his share as captain of the band (cp. Judg. viii. 24-26). All the other plunder of the camp—arms, ornaments, jewels, money, clothes, camels, accoutrements, and so on—was divided among the little army. David's motive in choosing the sheep and oxen for himself was to make presents to his friends in Judah (*vv.* 26-31).

27. *Bethel*] *i.e. Bethuel* (1 Chr. iv. 30), quite in the south near Beer-sheba, Hormah, and Ziklag; or *Bethul* (Josh. xix. 4), one of the cities of the Simeonites.

South Ramoth] Rather, "**Ramoth of the South** country" (xxvii. 10, xxx. 1, 14), so-called to distinguish it from Ramoth-Gilead,

28 Ramoth, and to *them* which *were* in ʳJattir, and to *them* which *were* in ˢAroer, and to *them* which *were* in Siphmoth, and to
29 *them* which *were* in ᵗEshtemoa, and to *them* which *were* in Rachal, and to *them* which *were* in the cities of ᵘthe Jerahmeelites,
30 and to *them* which *were* in the cities of the ˣKenites, and to *them* which *were* in ʸHormah, and to *them* which *were* in Chor-
31 ashan, and to *them* which *were* in Athach, and to *them* which *were* in ᶻHebron, and to all the places where David himself and his men were wont to haunt.

CHAP. 31. NOW ᵃthe Philistines fought against Israel : and the men of Israel fled from before the Philistines, and fell down ¹slain in
2 mount ᵇGilboa. And the Philistines followed hard upon Saul and upon his sons; and the Philistines slew ᶜJonathan, and
3 Abinadab, and Melchi-shua, Saul's sons. And ᵈthe battle went sore against Saul, and the ²archers ³hit him ; and he was sore
4 wounded of the archers. ᵉThen said Saul unto his armourbearer, Draw thy sword, and thrust me through therewith ; lest ᶠthese uncircumcised come and thrust me through, and ⁴abuse me. But his armourbearer would not ; ᵍfor he was sore afraid.
5 Therefore Saul took a sword, and ʰfell upon it. And when his armourbearer saw that Saul was dead, he fell likewise upon his
6 sword, and died with him. So Saul died, and his three sons, and his armourbearer, and all his men, that same day together.
7 ¶ And when the men of Israel that *were* on the other side of the valley, and *they* that *were* on the other side Jordan, saw that the men of Israel fled, and that Saul and his sons were dead, they forsook the cities, and fled ; and the Philistines came and dwelt

---

¹ Or, *wounded.*　　　² Heb. *shooters, men with bows.*　　　⁴ Or, *mock me.*
³ Heb. *found him.*

---

one of the Simeonite cities (Josh. xix. 8). Shimei, the Ramathite (1 Chr. xxvii. 27), who was over David's vineyards, was evidently a native of this Ramath. See below *v.* 28.

Jattir] "In the mountains" of Judah, and one of the priests' cities, is identified with 'Attir, ten miles south of Hebron.

28. *Aroer*] Not Aroer on the Arnon, but (if rightly written) some town in Judah, not elsewhere named.

Siphmoth, Rachal (*v.* 29), and Athach (*v.* 30), are unknown and not elsewhere mentioned ; but *Zabdi the Shiphmite* (1 Chr. xxvii. 27), who was over David's wine-cellars, was evidently a native of the first-named place. It is a remarkable proof of the grateful nature of David, and of his fidelity to his early friendships, as well as a curious instance of undesigned coincidence, that we find among those employed by David in offices of trust in the height of his power so many inhabitants of those obscure places where he found friends in the days of his early difficulties. Ezri the son of Chelub, Shimei the Ramathite, and Zabdi the Shiphmite, as well as Ira and Gareb, and Ittai, and Hezrai, and many others, were probably among these friends of his youth.

30. *Chor-ashan*] Perhaps the same as *Ashan* (Josh. xv. 42), in the *Shephelah* of Judah, inhabited by Simeonites, and one of the priests' cities (1 Chr. iv. 32, vi. 59).

Hebron] Now El-Khulil (see Gen. xxiii. 2). Hebron was a city of refuge (Josh. xx. 7), and one of the cities of the Kohathites (Josh. xxi. 11). It lies twenty miles south of Jerusalem.

XXXI. 3. *he was sore wounded*] Better, "he was sore afraid" (cp. Deut. ii. 25). Saul's *fear* is explained in *r.* 4.

6. *All his men*] This and similar expressions must not be taken too literally (cp. 1 Chr. x. 6). We know that Abner, and Ishbosheth, and many more survived the day of Gilboa.

7. *the men on the other side of the valley*] This must mean to the north of the plain of Jezreel, and would comprise the tribe of Naphtali, and Zabulon, and probably Issachar. But the text of 1 Chr. x. 7 has "that were in the valley," limiting the statement to the inhabitants of the plain of Jezreel.

on the other side Jordan] This phrase most commonly means *on the east of Jordan,* the speaker being supposed to be on the west side. But it is also used of the west of Jordan, as here, if the text be sound.

the Philistines...dwelt in them] One of the principal cities, Beth-shan, fell into their power at once (*v.* 10).

8 in them. ¶ And it came to pass on the morrow, when the
Philistines came to strip the slain, that they found Saul and his
9 three sons fallen in mount Gilboa. And they cut off his head,
and stripped off his armour, and sent into the land of the Philistines round about, to [i]publish *it in* the house of their idols, and
10 among the people. [k]And they put his armour in the house of
[l]Ashtaroth: and [m]they fastened his body to the wall of [n]Beth-
11 shan. ¶ [o]And when the inhabitants of Jabesh-gilead heard [1]of
12 that which the Philistines had done to Saul; [p]all the valiant
men arose, and went all night, and took the body of Saul and
the bodies of his sons from the wall of Beth-shan, and came to
13 Jabesh, and [q]burnt them there. And they took their bones, and
[r]buried *them* under a tree at Jabesh, [s]and fasted seven days.

[1] Or, *concerning him.*

[i] 2 Sam. 1. 20.
[k] ch. 21. 9.
[l] Judg. 2. 13.
[m] 2 Sam. 21. 12.
[n] Josh. 17. 11. Judg. 1. 27.
[o] ch. 11. 3.
[p] See ch. 11. 1—11. 2 Sam. 2. 4—7.
[q] 2 Chr. 16. 14. Jer. 34. 5. Amos 6. 10.
[r] 2 Sam. 2. 4, 5. & 21. 12.
[s] Gen. 50. 10.

---

10. *in the house of Ashtaroth*] This was doubtless the famous temple of Venus in Askelon mentioned by Herodotus as the most ancient of all her temples. Hence the special mention of Askelon (2 Sam. i. 20). The placing Saul's armour as a trophy in the temple of Ashtaroth was a counterpart to the placing Goliath's sword in the Tabernacle (xxi. 9). In 1 Chr. x. 10 it is added that they "fastened Saul's head in the temple of Dagon," probably either in Gaza (Judg. xvi. 21), or in Ashdod (v. 1-3). This was, perhaps, in retaliation for the similar treatment of Goliath's head (xvii. 54). The variations seem to imply that both this narrative and that in 1 Chr. x. are compiled from a common and a fuller document.

11. *when the inhabitants of Jabesh-Gilead heard,* &c.] See ch. xi. This is a touching and rare example of national gratitude.

12. *burnt them*] Burning was not the usual mode of sepulture among the Hebrews. But in this case from a pious desire to disguise the mutilation of the headless corpses, and exempt them from any possible future insult, the men of Jabesh burnt the bodies, yet so as to preserve the bones (*v.* 13; 2 Sam. xxi. 12).

13. *under a tree*] Rather, "**Under the tamarisk,**" a well-known tree at Jabesh which was standing when this narrative was written.

they fasted seven days] In imitation of the mourning for Jacob (marg. ref.). They would give full honour to Saul though he was fallen.

THE SECOND BOOK

OF

SAMUEL,

OTHERWISE CALLED, THE SECOND BOOK OF THE KINGS.

CHAP. 1. NOW it came to pass after the death of Saul, when David was returned from *a* the slaughter of the Amalekites, and David 2 had abode two days in Ziklag; it came even to pass on the third day, that, behold, *b* a man came out of the camp from Saul *c* with his clothes rent, and earth upon his head : and so it was, when he came to David, that he fell to the earth, and did obeisance. 3 And David said unto him, From whence comest thou ? And he 4 said unto him, Out of the camp of Israel am I escaped. And David said unto him, ¹ How went the matter ? I pray thee, tell me. And he answered, That the people are fled from the battle, and many of the people also are fallen and dead; and Saul and 5 Jonathan his son are dead also. And David said unto the young man that told him, How knowest thou that Saul and 6 Jonathan his son be dead ? And the young man that told him said, As I happened by chance upon *d* mount Gilboa, behold, *e* Saul leaned upon his spear; and, lo, the chariots and horsemen 7 followed hard after him. And when he looked behind him, he saw me, and called unto me. And I answered, ² Here *am* I. 8 And he said unto me, Who *art* thou ? And I answered him, I 9 *am* an Amalekite. He said unto me again, Stand, I pray thee, upon me, and slay me : for ³ anguish is come upon me, because 10 my life *is* yet whole in me. So I stood upon him, and *f* slew him, because I was sure that he could not live after that he was fallen : and I took the crown that *was* upon his head, and the bracelet that *was* on his arm, and have brought them hither 11 unto my lord. ¶ Then David took hold on his clothes, and *g* rent 12 them ; and likewise all the men that *were* with him : and they mourned, and wept, and fasted until even, for Saul, and for Jonathan his son, and for the people of the LORD, and for the 13 house of Israel ; because they were fallen by the sword. ¶ And David said unto the young man that told him, Whence *art* thou ? And he answered, I *am* the son of a stranger, an Amalekite.

a 1 Sam. 30. 17, 26.
b ch. 4. 10.
c 1 Sam. 4. 12.

d 1 Sam.31.1.
e See 1 Sam. 31. 2, 3, 4.

f Judg. 9. 54.

g ch. 3. 31.

---

¹ Heb. *What was, &c.* 1 Sam. 4. 16.
² Heb. *Behold me.*
³ Or, *my coat of mail*, or,
my embroidered coat hindereth me, that my, &c.

I. 1. *Now it came to pass*, &c.] There is no break whatever between the two books of Samuel, the division being purely artificial.

9. *anguish*] The Hebrew word here used occurs nowhere else, and is of doubtful meaning (cp. marg.). The Rabbins interpret it *cramp*, or *giddiness*.

10. The Amalekite was one of those who came "to strip the slain" on "the morrow" after the battle (1 Sam. xxxi. 8), and had the luck to find Saul and possess himself of his crown and bracelet. He probably started off immediately to seek David, and invented the above story, possibly having heard from some Israelite prisoner an account of what really did happen.

12. *for Saul*, &c.] David's thoroughly patriotic and unselfish character is strongly marked here. He looked upon the death of Saul, and the defeat of Israel by a heathen foe, with unmixed sorrow, though it opened to him the way to the throne, and removed his mortal enemy out of the way. For Jonathan he mourned with all the tenderness of a loving friend.

13, 14. Whether David believed the Amalekite's story, or not, his anger was equally excited, and the fact that the young man was an Amalekite, was not calculated

14 And David said unto him, [h]How wast thou not [i]afraid to
15 [k]stretch forth thine hand to destroy the LORD's anointed? And
  [l]David called one of the young men, and said, Go near, *and* fall
16 upon him. And he smote him that he died. And David said
  unto him, [m]Thy blood *be* upon thy head; for [n]thy mouth hath
  testified against thee, saying, I have slain the LORD's anointed.
17 ¶ And David lamented with this lamentation over Saul and over
18 Jonathan his son : ([o]also he bade them teach the children of
  Judah *the use of* the bow : behold, *it is* written [p]in the book [1]of
  Jasher.)
19   The beauty of Israel is slain upon thy high places :
      [q]How are the mighty fallen !
20   [r]Tell *it* not in Gath, publish *it* not in the streets of Askelon ;
      Lest [s]the daughters of the Philistines rejoice,
      Lest the daughters of [t]the uncircumcised triumph.
21   Ye [u]mountains of Gilboa, [x]*let there be* no dew,
      Neither *let there be* rain, upon you, nor fields of offerings :
      For there the shield of the mighty is vilely cast away,
      The shield of Saul, *as though he had* not *been* [y]anointed with oil.
22   From the blood of the slain, from the fat of the mighty,
      [z]The bow of Jonathan turned not back,
      And the sword of Saul returned not empty.
23   Saul and Jonathan *were* lovely and [2]pleasant in their lives,
      And in their death they were not divided
      They were swifter than eagles, they were [a]stronger than lions.
24   Ye daughters of Israel, weep over Saul,
      Who clothed you in scarlet, with *other* delights,
      Who put on ornaments of gold upon your apparel.

[1] Or, *of the upright*.   [2] Or, *sweet*.

Marginal references:
[h] Num. 12. 8.
[i] 1 Sam.31.4.
[k] Ps. 105. 15.
[l] ch. 4. 10,12.
[m] 1 Sam. 26.
9.
[l] 1 Kin. 2. 32,
33, 37.
[n] ver. 10.
Luke 19. 22.
[o] 1 Sam. 31.
3.
[p] Josh.10.13.
[q] ver. 27.
[r] Mic. 1. 10.
See Judg.
16. 23.
[s] See Exod.
15. 20.
Judg. 11. 34.
1 Sam. 18. 6.
[t] 1 Sam.31.4.
[u] 1Sam.31.1.
[x] So Judg.
5. 23.
[y] 1 Sam.10.1.
[z] 1 Sam.18.4.

[a] Judg. 14.
18.

---

to calm or check it. That David's temper
was hasty, we know from 1 Sam. xxv. 13,
32-34.

16. David might well think his sentence
just though severe, for he had more than
once expressed the deliberate opinion that
none could lift up his hand against the
Lord's anointed, and be guiltless (see 1 Sam.
xxiv. 6, xxvi. 9, 11, 16).

17. The words *lamented* and *lamentation*
must be understood in the technical sense of
a *funeral dirge* or *mournful elegy*. (See
similar dirges in iii. 33, 34, and 2 Chr. xxxv.
25.) This and the brief stanza on the death
of Abner are the only specimens preserved
to us of David's secular poetry.

18. *the use of the bow*] Omit "the use of."
"The bow" is the name by which this
dirge was known, being so called from the
mention of Jonathan's bow in *v.* 22. The
sense would then be, *And he bade them teach
the children of Israel the song called Kasheth*
(the bow), *i.e.* he gave directions that the
song should be learned by heart (cp. Deut.
xxxi. 19). It has been further suggested
that in the Book of Jasher there was,
among other things, a collection of poems,
in which special mention was made of the
bow. This was one of them. 1 Sam. ii. 1–
10 was another ; Num. xxi. 27–30 another ;
Lament. ii. another ; Lament. iii. another ;
Jacob's blessing (Gen. xlix.) ; Moses' song

(Deut. xxxii.) ; perhaps his Blessing (xxxiii.
See *v.* 29) ; and such Psalms as xlix., xlvi.,
lxxvi., &c. ; Habak. iii. ; and Zech. ix. 9–17,
also belonged to it. The title by which all
the poems in this collection were distinguished was *Kasheth* "the bow." When
therefore the writer of 2 Sam. transferred
this dirge from the Book of Jasher to his
own pages, he transferred it, as we might do
any of the Psalms, with its title.
  the book of Jasher] See marg. ref. note.

19. *The beauty*, &c.] *i.e.* Saul and Jonathan who were the chief ornament and
pride of Israel, and slain upor "high
places " (*v.* 25), viz. on Mount Gilboa.

20. Gath, the royal city of Achish (1 Sam.
xxi. 10, xxvii. 2). Askelon, the chief seat
of worship (1 Sam. xxxi. 10 note).

21. *let there be no dew*, &c.] For a similar
passionate form of poetical malediction, cp.
Job iii. 3–10 ; Jer. xx. 14–18.
  nor fields of offerings] He imprecates such
complete barrenness on the soil of Gilboa,
that not even enough may grow for an
offering of first-fruits. The latter part of
the verse is better rendered thus : *For there
the shield of the mighty was polluted, the shield
of Saul was not anointed with oil, but with
blood*). Shields were usually anointed with
oil in preparation for the battle (Isai.
xxi. 5).

24. The women of Israel are most happily

25 How are the mighty fallen in the midst of the battle!
O Jonathan, *thou wast* slain in thine high places.
26 I am distressed for thee, my brother Jonathan:
Very pleasant hast thou been unto me:

b 1 Sam. 18.
1, 3.
& 19. 2, 16.
c ver. 19.

*b*Thy love to me was wonderful, passing the love of women.
27 *c*How are the mighty fallen,
And the weapons of war perished!

a Judg. 1. 1.
1 Sam. 23. 2,
4, 9.

CHAP. **2.** AND it came to pass after this, that David *a*enquired of
the LORD, saying, Shall I go up into any of the cities of Judah?
And the LORD said unto him, Go up. And David said, Whither

b 1 Sam. 30.
31.
1 Kin. 2. 11.
c 1 Sam. 30.
5.
d 1 Sam. 27.
2, 3.
& 30. 1.
1 Chr. 12. 1.
e ver. 11.
ch. 5. 5.
f 1 Sam. 31.
11, 13.
g Ruth. 2. 20.
& 3. 10.
Ps. 115. 15.
h 2 Tim. 1.
16, 18.

2 shall I go up? And he said, Unto *b*Hebron. So David went
up thither, and his *c*two wives also, Ahinoam the Jezreelitess,
3 and Abigail Nabal's wife the Carmelite. And *d*his men that
were with him did David bring up, every man with his house-
4 hold: and they dwelt in the cities of Hebron. *e*And the men of
Judah came, and there they anointed David king over the house
of Judah. ¶And they told David, saying, *That f*the men of
5 Jabesh-gilead *were they* that buried Saul. And David sent
messengers unto the men of Jabesh-gilead, and said unto them,
*g*Blessed be ye of the LORD, that ye have shewed this kindness
6 unto your lord, *even* unto Saul, and have buried him. And now
*h*the LORD shew kindness and truth unto you: and I also will
requite you this kindness, because ye have done this thing.
7 Therefore now let your hands be strengthened, and ¹be ye
valiant: for your master Saul is dead, and also the house of

i 1 Sam. 14.
50.

8 Judah have anointed me king over them. ¶But *i*Abner the son
of Ner, captain of ²Saul's host, took ³Ish-bosheth the son of
9 Saul, and brought him over to Mahanaim; and made him king
over Gilead, and over the Ashurites, and over Jezreel, and over

¹ Heb. *be ye the sons of valour.*   ² Heb. *the host which* was *Saul's.*   ³ Or, *Esh-baal,* 1 Chr. 8. 33. & 9. 39.

---

introduced. They who had come out to
meet king Saul "with tabrets, with joy,
and with instruments of music" in the day
of victory, are now called to weep over him.
25. *How are the mighty fallen*] The recurrence of the same idea (*vv.* 19, 25, 27) is
perfectly congenial to the nature of elegy,
since grief is fond of dwelling upon the particular objects of the passion, and frequently
repeating them. By unanimous consent
this is considered one of the most beautiful
odes in the Bible, and the generosity of
David in thus mourning for his enemy and
persecutor, Saul, enhances the effect upon
the mind of the reader.
II. 1. *enquired of the* LORD] Through
Abiathar, the High-priest. The death of
Saul and Jonathan had entirely changed
David's position, and therefore he needed
Divine guidance how to act under the new
circumstances in which he was placed. Cp.
marg. reff.
Hebron was well suited for the temporary
capital of David's kingdom, being situated
in a strong position in the mountains of
Judah, amidst David's friends, and withal
having peculiarly sacred associations (see
marg. reff. note). It appears to have also
been the centre of a district (*v.* 3).

4. David had already been anointed by
Samuel (1 Sam. xvi. 13). His first anointing indicated God's secret purpose, his
second the accomplishment of that purpose.
(Cp. the case of Saul, 1 Sam. x. 1, xi. 14.)
David was anointed again king over Israel
(v. 3). The interval between the anointing
of the Lord Jesus as the Christ of God, and
His taking to Himself His kingdom and
glory, seems to be thus typified.
8. *Mahanaim*] See Gen. xxxii. 2. From
v. 12 it would seem to have been Ish-
bosheth's capital.
9. *the Ashurites*] If the tribe of Asher,
the verse indicates the order in which
Abner recovered the different districts from
the Philistines, and added them to the
dominions of Ish-bosheth, beginning with
Gilead, and then gradually adding, on the
west of Jordan, first the territory of Asher
as far as Carmel and the whole plain of
Esdraelon, and then the country of Ephraim
and Benjamin, being in fact *all Israel,* as
distinguished from Judah; and this recon-
quest may have occupied five years. Ish-
bosheth's reign over Israel may not have
been reckoned to begin till the conquest
was complete.

10 Ephraim, and over Benjamin, and over all Israel. Ish-bosheth
Saul's son *was* forty years old when he began to reign over
Israel, and reigned two years. But the house of Judah followed
11 David. And *k*the ¹time that David was king in Hebron over   *k* ch. 5. 5.
12 the house of Judah was seven years and six months. ¶And   1 Kin. 2. 11.
Abner the son of Ner, and the servants of Ish-bosheth the son
13 of Saul, went out from Mahanaim to ¹Gibeon. And Joab the   *l* Josh.18.25.
son of Zeruiah, and the servants of David, went out, and met
²together by *m*the pool of Gibeon: and they sat down, the one   *m* Jer. 41. 12.
on the one side of the pool, and the other on the other side of
14 the pool. And Abner said to Joab, Let the young men now
arise, and play before us. And Joab said, Let them arise.
15 Then there arose and went over by number twelve of Benjamin,
which *pertained* to Ish-bosheth the son of Saul, and twelve of
16 the servants of David. And they caught every one his fellow
by the head, and *thrust* his sword in his fellow's side; so they
fell down together: wherefore that place was called ³Helkath-
17 hazzurim, which *is* in Gibeon. And there was a very sore
battle that day; and Abner was beaten, and the men of Israel,
18 before the servants of David. ¶And there were *n*three sons of   *n* 1 Chr. 2.16.
Zeruiah there, Joab, and Abishai, and Asahel: and Asahel *was*
19 °*as* light ⁴of foot ⁵*p* as a wild roe. And Asahel pursued after   *o* 1 Chr.12. 8.
Abner; and in going he turned not to the right hand nor to the   *p* Ps. 18. 33.
                                                                  Cant. 2. 17.

¹ Heb. *number of days.*   ³ That is, *The field of strong men.*   ⁵ Heb. *as one of the roes*
² Heb. *them together.*   ⁴ Heb. *of his feet.*   *that is in the field.*

10. *forty...two*] The numerals are somewhat strange. First, as regards the forty
years. Even assuming that Ish-bosheth's
reign did not commence till five years and a
half after Saul's death, which must have
been the case if the *two years* in the text
gives the true length of his reign, it is
startling to hear of Saul's younger son being
thirty-five years old at his father's death,
born consequently some three years before
his father's accession, and five years older
than David, the bosom friend of his elder
brother Jonathan. The age, too, of Jonathan's child, Mephibosheth, who was five
years old at his father's death, would lead
one to expect rather a less age for his
uncle. Next, as regards the two years.
Since David (cp. *v.* 11; and marg. reff.)
reigned seven years in Hebron over Judah
only, it follows, if the *two years* in the text
are correct, either that an interval of five
years elapsed between Ish-bosheth's death
and David's being anointed "king over all
Israel," or that a like interval elapsed between Saul's death and the commencement
of Ish-bosheth's reign. Of the two the
latter is the more probable, and has the advantage of diminishing Ish-bosheth's age by
between five and six years. But the narrative in chs. iii. iv. of the "long war," of
the birth of David's six sons, and of Abner's
conspiracy and death, seems to imply a
longer time than *two* years, in which case
both the numerals would have to be corrected.
12. This expedition to Gibeon may have

been for the purpose of shifting his metropolis to his own tribe of Benjamin, and to
his family place, "Gibeah of Saul," close to
Gibeon, with the further purpose of attacking the kingdom of David. *To go out* (vr.
12, 13) is a technical phrase for going out to
war (1 Sam. xviii. 30).
13. On the east of the hill (El-jib, the
ancient *Gibeon*) is a copious spring, which
issues in a cave excavated in the limestone
rock, so as to form a large reservoir. In the
trees further down are the remains of a pool
or tank of considerable size (120 feet by 110).
This is doubtless "the pool of Gibeon."
sat down] *i.e.* halted and encamped.
14. *play*] (Cp. Judg. xvi. 25; 1 Sam.
xviii. 7). Here, the word is applied to the
serious game of war, to be played by twelve
combatants on each side, with the two
armies for spectators.
16. Cp. Livy's history of the battle between the Horatii and Curiatii. This
combat, like that, may have been proposed
as a means of avoiding the effusion of blood
of two nations united by consanguinity, and
having a common powerful enemy in the
Philistines.
Helkath-hazzurim] *i.e.* "the part, field, or
plat (Gen. xxiii. 19) of the sharp edges or
blades." This seems, on the whole, the best
explanation of this rather obscure name.
17. Neither side had the advantage in the
combat of twelve a side; hence the quarrel
was fought out with great fierceness by the
two armies, and the victory was won by
David.

20 left [1]from following Abner. Then Abner looked behind him,
21 and said, *Art* thou Asahel? And he answered, I *am*. And
Abner said to him, Turn thee aside to thy right hand or to thy
left, and lay thee hold on one of the young men, and take thee
his [2]armour. But Asahel would not turn aside from following
22 of him. And Abner said again to Asahel, Turn thee aside from
following me: wherefore should I smite thee to the ground?
23 how then should I hold up my face to Joab thy brother? Howbeit he refused to turn aside: wherefore Abner with the hinder
end of the spear smote him [q]under the fifth *rib*, that the spear
came out behind him; and he fell down there, and died in the
same place: and it came to pass, *that* as many as came to the
24 place where Asahel fell down and died stood still. Joab also
and Abishai pursued after Abner: and the sun went down when
they were come to the hill of Ammah, that *lieth* before Giah by
25 the way of the wilderness of Gibeon. ¶ And the children of
Benjamin gathered themselves together after Abner, and became
26 one troop, and stood on the top of an hill. Then Abner called
to Joab, and said, Shall the sword devour for ever? knowest
thou not that it will be bitterness in the latter end? how long
shall it be then, ere thou bid the people return from following
27 their brethren? And Joab said, *As* God liveth, unless [r]thou
hadst spoken, surely then [3]in the morning the people had [4]gone
28 up every one from following his brother. So Joab blew a
trumpet, and all the people stood still, and pursued after Israel
29 no more, neither fought they any more. ¶ And Abner and his
men walked all that night through the plain, and passed over
Jordan, and went through all Bithron, and they came to
30 Mahanaim. And Joab returned from following Abner: and
when he had gathered all the people together, there lacked of
31 David's servants nineteen men and Asahel. But the servants of
David had smitten of Benjamin, and of Abner's men, *so that*
32 three hundred and threescore men died. And they took up
Asahel, and buried him in the sepulchre of his father, which
was in Beth-lehem. And Joab and his men went all night, and
they came to Hebron at break of day.

[q] ch. 3. 27. & 4. 6. & 20. 10.

[r] ver. 14. Prov. 17. 14.

[1] Heb. *from after Abner.*
[2] Or, *spoil*, Judg. 14. 19.
[3] Heb. *from the morning.*
[4] Or, *gone away.*

---

21. *his armour*] Rather, as in the marg.; *i.e.* content thyself with the spoil of some inferior soldier for a trophy.

23. *with the hinder end*, &c.] *i.e.* the wooden end, which was more or less pointed to enable the owner to stick it in the ground (1 Sam. xxvi. 7).

the fifth rib] The word so rendered here (and in marg. reff.) means the *abdomen*, and is not etymologically connected with the Hebrew for *five*, as the translation "*fifth* rib" supposes, but with a verb meaning *to be fat*, or *strong*.

24. *Ammah...Giah*] Local, and otherwise unknown names.

27. Joab's speech means either "*unless thou hadst spoken* (challenged us to fight, *v.* 14), *the people would have returned from the pursuit of their brethren* (many hours ago, even) *this morning;*" or, "*If thou hadst not spoken* (asked for peace, *v.* 26), *surely the people would have returned*, &c., *in the morning*, *i.e.* would not have ceased the pursuit till the morning." The latter interpretation is the more accordant with Joab's boastful character.

29. *through the plain*] See 1 Sam. xxiii. 24. Bithron is unknown. From the expression *all* (the) *Bithron*, it seems likely that it is a tract of country, intersected by ravines lying on the east side of Jordan.

32. Joab, having stopped the pursuit, passed the night with his army on the field of battle; the next morning he numbered the missing, and buried the dead; they carried the body of Asahel to Bethlehem and buried him there, and then joined David at Hebron. Hebron would be about 14 miles from Bethlehem, or about five hours' march.

CHAP. 3. NOW there was long war between the house of Saul and the house of David: but David waxed stronger and stronger, 2 and the house of Saul waxed weaker and weaker. ¶ And *a* unto David were sons born in Hebron: and his firstborn was Amnon, 3 *b* of Ahinoam the Jezreelitess; and his second, [1]Chileab, of Abigail the wife of Nabal the Carmelite; and the third, Absalom the son of Maacah the daughter of Talmai king *c* of Geshur; 4 and the fourth, *d* Adonijah the son of Haggith; and the fifth, 5 Shephatiah the son of Abital; and the sixth, Ithream, by Eglah 6 David's wife. These were born to David in Hebron. ¶ And it came to pass, while there was war between the house of Saul and the house of David, that Abner made himself strong for the 7 house of Saul. And Saul had a concubine, whose name *was* *e* Rizpah, the daughter of Aiah : and *Ish-bosheth* said to Abner, Wherefore hast thou *f* gone in unto my father's concubine ? 8 Then was Abner very wroth for the words of Ish-bosheth, and said, *Am* I *g* a dog's head, which against Judah do shew kindness this day unto the house of Saul thy father, to his brethren, and to his friends, and have not delivered thee into the hand of David, that thou chargest me to day with a fault 9 concerning this woman ? *h* So do God to Abner, and more also, except, *i* as the LORD hath sworn to David, even so I 10 do to him; to translate the kingdom from the house of Saul, and to set up the throne of David over Israel and over Judah, 11 *k* from Dan even to Beer-sheba. And he could not answer Abner 12 a word again, because he feared him. ¶ And Abner sent messengers to David on his behalf, saying, Whose *is* the land ? saying *also*, Make thy league with me, and, behold, my hand 13 *shall be* with thee, to bring about all Israel unto thee. And he said, Well : I will make a league with thee : but one thing I require of thee, [2] that is, *l* Thou shalt not see my face, except thou first bring *m* Michal Saul's daughter, when thou comest to

[1] Or, *Daniel*, 1 Chr. 3. 1.   [2] Heb. *saying*.

a 1 Chr. 3. 1—4.
b 1 Sam. 25. 43.
c 1 Sam. 27. 8.
ch. 13. 37.
d 1 Kin. 1. 5. & 2. 5.

e ch. 21. 8, 10.
f ch. 16. 21.
g Deut. 23. 18.
1 Sam. 24. 14. ch. 9. 8.
h Ruth 1. 17.
1 Kin. 19. 2.
i 1 Sam. 15. 28.
1 Chr. 12. 23.
k Judg. 20. 1.

l So Gen. 43. 3.
m 1 Sam. 18. 20.

III. 3. *Chileab*] In the duplicate passage (see marg.) David's second son is called *Daniel* (God is my judge), a name given to him in commemoration of the death of Nabal (1 Sam. xxv. 39). *Chileab* seems to be made up of the three first letters of the following Hebrew word, through an error of the transcriber, and intended to be erased.

Talmai king of Geshur] Talmai was the name of one of the sons of Anak at Hebron (Num. xiii. 22) ; this Talmai was perhaps of the same race.

Geshur] Where he reigned was in Bashan, and we know from Deut. iii. 11, that Og, king of Bashan, was of the "remnant of the giants." See 1 Sam. xxvii. 8 note.

4. *Adonijah*] The same who, when David was dying, aspired to the crown, and was put to death by Solomon.

Shephatiah] " God is judge." This is the same name as *Jehoshaphat*, only with the two elements composing it placed in inverted order. Nothing more is known of him or of his brother Ithream.

6. Render, " **And it came to pass, while the war between the house of Saul and**

the house of David lasted, that Abner assisted the house of Saul."

7. *Rizpah, the daughter of Aiah*] For the sequel of her history, see marg. ref. *Aiah*, was an Edomitish, or rather Horite name (Gen. xxxvi. 24).

8. The words *against Judah* are very obscure. If the text be correct, the words would seem to be Ish-bosheth's, who in his anger had charged Abner with being a vile partisan of Judah : Abner retorts, *Am I* (as you say) *a dog's head which belongeth to Judah*, or *on Judah's side ! This day I show you kindness*, &c., *and this day thou chargest me with a fault*, &c.

12. *Whose is the land ?*] Meaning, Is not the land thine by God's promise ?

13. David's motive in requiring the restitution of Michal was partly his affection for her, and his memory of her love for him ; partly the wish to wipe out the affront put upon him in taking away his wife, by obtaining her return ; and partly, also, a politic consideration of the effect on Saul's partisans of a daughter of Saul being David's queen.

14 see my face. And David sent messengers to Ish-bosheth Saul's son, saying, Deliver *me* my wife Michal, which I espoused

n 1 Sam. 18.
25, 27.
o 1 Sam. 25.
44, Phalti.
p ch. 19. 16.

q ver. 9.

r 1 Chr. 12.
29.

s ver. 10, 12.

t 1 Kin. 11.
37.

u 1 Sam. 29.
6.
Isai. 37. 28.

15 to me *n*for an hundred foreskins of the Philistines. And Ish-bosheth sent, and took her from *her* husband, even from *o*Phaltiel
16 the son of Laish. And her husband went with her [1]along weeping behind her to *p*Bahurim. Then said Abner unto him,
17 Go, return. And he returned. ¶And Abner had communication with the elders of Israel, saying, Ye sought for David ²in times
18 past *to be* king over you: now then do *it*: *q*for the LORD hath spoken of David, saying, By the hand of my servant David I will save my people Israel out of the hand of the Philistines,
19 and out of the hand of all their enemies. And Abner also spake in the ears of *r*Benjamin : and Abner went also to speak in the ears of David in Hebron all that seemed good to Israel,
20 and that seemed good to the whole house of Benjamin. So Abner came to David to Hebron, and twenty men with him. And David made Abner and the men that *were* with him a feast.
21 And Abner said unto David, I will arise and go, and *s*will gather all Israel unto my lord the king, that they may make a league with thee, and that thou mayest *t*reign over all that thine heart desireth. And David sent Abner away ; and he went in peace.
22 ¶And, behold, the servants of David and Joab came from *pursuing* a troop, and brought in a great spoil with them : but Abner *was* not with David in Hebron ; for he had sent him away,
23 and he was gone in peace. When Joab and all the host that *was* with him were come, they told Joab, saying, Abner the son of Ner came to the king, and he hath sent him away, and he is
24 gone in peace. Then Joab came to the king, and said, What hast thou done? behold, Abner came unto thee ; why *is* it *that*
25 thou hast sent him away, and he is quite gone? Thou knowest Abner the son of Ner, that he came to deceive thee, and to know *u*thy going out and thy coming in, and to know all that
26 thou doest. ¶And when Joab was come out from David, he sent messengers after Abner, which brought him again from the

[1] Heb. *going and weeping.*   [2] Heb. *both yesterday and the third day.*

---

14. *sent messengers to Ish-bosheth*] Not to Abner, for the league between David and Abner was a profound secret, but to Ish-bosheth who, David knew, must act, feeble as he was, at Abner's dictation. Abner's first act of overt allegiance to David was thus done at Ish-bosheth's bidding ; and the effect of the humiliation laid upon Ish-bosheth in exposing his weakness to his own subjects, and so shaking their allegiance to him, was such that Abner needed to use no more disguise.

16. *Bahurim*] Best known as the residence of Shimei, and as the place where Jonathan and Ahimaaz were concealed in a well on the occasion of David's flight from Absalom (xvi. 5, xvii. 18). It seems to have been situated in the southern border of the tribe of Benjamin, and on the route from Jerusalem to the Jordan fords, since Phaltiel came *from* Mahanaim (ii. 8).

17. *Ye sought for David,* &c.] Cp. 1 Sam. xviii. 5. It was only by Abner's great influence that the elders of Israel had been restrained hitherto from declaring for David, and this accounts for Ish-bosheth's helpless submission to his uncle's dictation.

20. *twenty men*] These were doubtless his official suite as Ish-bosheth's envoy to conduct Michal to David, but privy and consenting to his intrigue with David. It is remarkable that not a word should be said about the meeting of David and Michal.

21. Abner repeats the offer (*v.* 12) ; and the condition of Michal's return (*v.* 13) being now fulfilled, David accepts it, and the league between them was solemnly ratified at David's board, amidst the rites of hospitality.

24. Joab saw that if Abner was reconciled to David, his own post as second in the state would be forfeited ; and then with characteristic unscrupulosity he proceeded to take Abner's life.

26. *the well of Sirah*] Nowhere else mentioned ; according to Josephus, about two and a half miles from Hebron.

27 well of Sirah: but David knew *it* not. And when Abner was returned to Hebron, Joab *ᶻtook him aside in the gate to speak with him ¹quietly, and smote him there ᵞunder the fifth *rib*, 28 that he died, for the blood of *ᶻAsahel his brother. ¶ And afterward when David heard *it*, he said, I and my kingdom *are* guiltless before the LORD for ever from the ²blood of Abner the 29 son of Ner: *ᵃlet it rest on the head of Joab, and on all his father's house; and let there not ³fail from the house of Joab one *ᵇthat hath an issue, or that is a leper, or that leaneth on a 30 staff, or that falleth on the sword, or that lacketh bread. So Joab and Abishai his brother slew Abner, because he had slain 31 their brother *ᶜAsahel at Gibeon in the battle. ¶ And David said to¹ Joab, and to all the people that *were* with him, *ᵈRend your clothes, and *ᵉgird you with sackcloth, and mourn before 32 Abner. And king David *himself* followed the ⁴bier. And they buried Abner in Hebron: and the king lifted up his voice, and 33 wept at the grave of Abner; and all the people wept. And the king lamented over Abner, and said,

Died Abner as a *ᶠfool dieth?

34 Thy hands *were* not bound, nor thy feet put into fetters:

As a man falleth before ⁵wicked men, so fellest thou.

35 ¶ And all the people wept again over him. And when all the people came *ᵍto cause David to eat meat while it was yet day, David sware, saying, *ʰSo do God to me, and more also, if I taste 36 bread, or ought else, *ⁱtill the sun be down. And all the people took notice *of it*, and it ⁶pleased them: as whatsoever the king 37 did pleased all the people. For all the people and all Israel understood that day that it was not of the king to slay Abner the 38 son of Ner. ¶ And the king said unto his servants, Know ye not that there is a prince and a great man fallen this day in 39 Israel? And I *am* this day ⁷weak, though anointed king; and these men the sons of Zeruiah *ᵏbe too hard for me: *ˡthe LORD shall reward the doer of evil according to his wickedness.

CHAP. 4. AND when Saul's son heard that Abner was dead in Hebron, *ᵃhis hands were feeble, and all the Israelites were 2 *ᵇtroubled. And Saul's son had two men *that were* captains of bands: the name of the one *was* Baanah, and the name of the *ᵉother Rechab, the sons of Rimmon a Beerothite, of the children

Marginal references (right column):
*ᶻ 1 Kin. 2. 5.
So ch. 20. 9, 10.
ᵞ ch. 4. 6.
ᶻ ch. 2. 23.
ᵃ 1 Kin. 2. 32, 33.
ᵇ Lev. 15. 2.
ᶜ ch. 2. 23.
ᵈ Josh. 7. 6.
ch. 1. 2, 11.
ᵉ Gen. 37. 34.

ᶠ ch. 13. 12.

ᵍ ch. 12. 17.
Jer. 16. 7.
ʰ Ruth 1. 17.
ⁱ ch. 1. 12.

ᵏ ch. 19. 7.
ˡ See ch. 19. 13.
1 Kin. 2. 5,
6, 33, 34.
Ps. 28. 4.
& 62. 12.
2 Tim. 4. 14.
ᵃ Ezra 4. 4.
Isai. 13. 7.
ᵇ Matt. 2. 3.*

---

¹ Or, *peaceably.*   ⁴ Heb. *bed.*   ⁶ Heb. *was good in their eyes.*
² Heb. *bloods.*   ⁵ Heb. *children of iniquity.*   ⁷ Heb. *tender.*
³ Heb. *be cut off.*   ⁸ Heb. *second.*

---

29. The curse of David proves that Joab was not justified as blood-revenger or *Goel* (*v.* 27) in taking away Abner's life.

that leaneth on a staff] Rather, a *crutch.* The phrase denotes one lame or infirm. For similar instances of hereditary disease and poverty as a punishment of great sin, see 1 Sam. ii. 31-33, 36; 2 K. v. 27; John ix. 2.

33. *lamented*] *i.e.* composed and sang the funeral dirge which follows (cp. i. 17).

Died Abner, &c.] *i.e.* The great and noble and valiant Abner had died as ignobly and as helplessly as the meanest churl!

34. *Thy hands were not bound,* &c.] This thought prepares the way for the solution; Abner had been treacherously murdered by wicked men.

35. *to eat meat,* &c.] Fasting was a sign of the deepest mourning (i. 12). The fast lasted till the sun was set.

IV. 2. *Beeroth*] See marg. ref. From Josh. ix. 17, it might have been expected that the population of Beeroth would be Canaanite. But from some unknown cause the Canaanite inhabitants of Beeroth had fled to Gittaim—perhaps the same as Gath —and continued there as sojourners. If this flight of the Beerothites took place at the time of Saul's cruel attack upon the Gibeonites (2 Sam. xxi. 1, 2), Baanah and Rechab may have been native Beerothites, and have been instigated to murder the son of Saul by a desire to avenge the blood of their countrymen. The fact of their being reckoned as Benjamites is quite com-

c Josh.18.25.
d Neh. 11.33.
e ch. 9. 3.

f 1 Sam. 20.
1, 11.

g ch. 2. 23.

h 1 Sam. 19.
2, 10, 11.
& 23. 15.
& 25. 29.

i Gen. 48. 16.
1 Kin. 1. 29.
Ps. 31. 7.
k ch 1. 2, 4,
15.

l Gen. 9. 5,
6.
m ch. 1. 15.

n ch. 3. 32.

a 1 Chr. 11.
1—9.
b Gen. 29. 14.

of Benjamin : (for c Beeroth also was reckoned to Benjamin :
3 and the Beerothites fled to d Gittaim, and were sojourners there
4 until this day.) ¶ And e Jonathan, Saul's son, had a son that
was lame of his feet. He was five years old when the tidings
came of Saul and Jonathan f out of Jezreel, and his nurse took
him up, and fled : and it came to pass, as she made haste to flee,
that he fell, and became lame. And his name was ¹ Mephibo-
5 sheth. ¶ And the sons of Rimmon the Beerothite, Rechab and
Baanah, went, and came about the heat of the day to the house
6 of Ish-bosheth, who lay on a bed at noon. And they came
thither into the midst of the house, as though they would have
fetched wheat ; and they smote him g under the fifth rib : and
7 Rechab and Baanah his brother escaped. For when they came
into the house, he lay on his bed in his bedchamber, and they
smote him, and slew him, and beheaded him, and took his head,
8 and gat them away through the plain all night. And they
brought the head of Ish-bosheth unto David to Hebron, and
said to the king, Behold the head of Ish-bosheth the son of Saul
thine enemy, h which sought thy life ; and the LORD hath
avenged my lord the king this day of Saul, and of his seed.
9 ¶ And David answered Rechab and Baanah his brother, and said unto them, As the LORD
of Rimmon the Beerothite, and said unto them, As the LORD
10 liveth, i who hath redeemed my soul out of all adversity, when
k one told me, saying, Behold, Saul is dead, ² thinking to have
brought good tidings, I took hold of him, and slew him in
Ziklag, ³ who thought that I would have given him a reward for
11 his tidings : how much more, when wicked men have slain a
righteous person in his own house upon his bed ? shall I not
therefore now l require his blood of your hand, and take you
12 away from the earth ? And David m commanded his young
men, and they slew them, and cut off their hands and their feet,
and hanged them up over the pool in Hebron. But they took
the head of Ish-bosheth, and buried it in the n sepulchre of Abner
in Hebron.

CHAP. 5. THEN a came all the tribes of Israel to David unto
Hebron, and spake, saying, Behold, b we are thy bone and thy

¹ Or, Merib-baal, 1 Chr. 8.
34. & 9. 40.

² Heb. he was in his own
eyes as a bringer, &c.

³ Or, which was the reward
I gave him for his tidings.

patible with their being Canaanites by
blood.
4. This mention of Mephibosheth seems
to be inserted here partly to show that with
the death of Ish-bosheth the cause of the
house of Saul became hopeless, and partly
to prepare the way for the subsequent mention of him (ix., xvi. 1-4, xix. 25).
5. lay on a bed at noon] Render, "was
taking his midday rest," according to the
custom of hot countries.
6. as though they would have fetched
wheat] This is a very obscure passage, and
the double repetition in vv. 6 and 7 of the
murder of the king and of the escape of the
assassin, is hard to account for. Rechab
and Baanah came into the house under the
pretence of getting grain, probably for the
band which they commanded, out of the
king's storehouse, and so contrived to get

access into the king's chamber ; or, they
found the wheat-carriers (the persons whose
business it was to carry in grain for the
king's household) just going into the king's
house, and by joining them got into the
midst of the house unnoticed. If the latter
be the sense, the literal translation of the
words would be : "And behold (or, and
thither) there came into the midst of the house
the carriers of wheat, and they (i.e. Rechab
and Baanah) smote him, &c."
12. cut off their hands, &c.] After they
were dead. Their hands and feet were
hung up in a place of public resort, both to
deter others and also to let all Israel know
that David was not privy to the murder of
Ish-bosheth.
V. 1. Cp. marg. ref. The chronicler
adds some interesting details (xii. 23-40) of
the manner in which the various tribes

2 flesh. Also in time past, when Saul was king over us, ^cthou wast he that leddest out and broughtest in Israel: and the LORD said to thee, ^dThou shalt feed my people Israel, and thou shalt
3 be a captain over Israel. ^eSo all the elders of Israel came to the king to Hebron; ^fand king David made a league with them in Hebron ^gbefore the LORD: and they anointed David king
4 over Israel. David *was* thirty years old when he began to
5 reign, ^hand he reigned forty years. In Hebron he reigned over Judah ⁱseven years and six months: and in Jerusalem he reigned
6 thirty and three years over all Israel and Judah. ¶ And the king and his men went ^kto Jerusalem unto ^lthe Jebusites, the inhabitants of the land: which spake unto David, saying, Except thou take away the blind and the lame, thou shalt not
7 come in hither: ¹thinking, David cannot come in hither, Nevertheless David took the strong hold of Zion: ^mthe same *is* the
8 city of David. And David said on that day, Whosoever getteth up to the gutter, and smiteth the Jebusites, and the lame and the blind, *that are* hated of David's soul, ⁿ*he shall be chief and captain.* ²Wherefore they said, The blind and the lame shall

Reference column (right margin):

c 1 Sam. 18. 13.
d 1 Sam. 16. 1, 12.
Ps. 78. 71.
See ch. 7. 7.
e 1 Chr. 11. 3.
f 2 Kin. 11. 17.
g Judg. 11.
h 1 Chr. 26. 31.
& 29. 27.
i ch. 2. 11.
1 Chr. 3. 4.
k Judg. 1. 21.
l Josh. 15.63.
Judg. 1. 8.
& 19. 11.
m 1 Kin. 2. 10.
& 8. 1.
n 1 Chr. 11. 6—9.

Or, *saying, David shall not, &c.*   ² Or, *Because they had said, even the blind and the* lame, *He shall not come into the house.*

---

from both sides of the Jordan came to Hebron to make David king, and of the joyful festivities on the occasion. The consummation to which events in God's Providence had been leading had now come. Saul and Jonathan, Abner and Ish-bosheth, were dead; David was already head of a very large portion of Israel; the Philistines, and perhaps the remnant of the Canaanites, were restless and threatening; and it was obviously the interest of the Israelitish nation to unite themselves under the sovereignty of the valiant and virtuous son of Jesse, their former deliverer, and the man designated by the word of God as their Captain and Shepherd. Accordingly he was at once anointed king over all Israel (cp. ii. 4 note).

3. *before the* LORD] Abiathar and Zadok the priests were both with David, and the Tabernacle and Altar may have been at Hebron, though the Ark was at Kirjath-jearim.

4. The age of David is conclusive as to the fact that the earlier years of Saul's reign (during which Jonathan grew up to be a man) are passed over in silence, and that the events narrated from 1 Sam. xiii. to the end of the Book did not occupy above ten years. If David was twenty years old at the time he slew Goliath, four years in Saul's service, four years of wandering from place to place, one year and four months in the country of the Philistines, and a few months after Saul's death, would make up the ten years necessary to bring him to the age of thirty.

6. David immediately after being anointed king of Israel, probably wished to signalise his accession by an exploit which would be popular with all Israel, and especially with

Saul's tribe, Benjamin. He discerned the importance of having Jerusalem for his capital both because it belonged as much to Benjamin as to Judah, and on account of its strong position.

Except thou take away the blind, &c.] Rather, "**and** (the Jebusite) **spake to David, saying, Thou shalt not come hither, but the blind and the lame shall keep thee off,**" *i.e.* so far shalt thou be from taking the stronghold from us, that the lame and blind shall suffice to defend the place.

7. *the stronghold of Zion*] Or *castle* (1 Chr. xi. 5, 7). The ancient Zion was the hill on which the Temple stood, and the castle seems to have been immediately to the north of the Temple. The modern Zion lies to the south-west of the Temple.

the same is the city of David] The name afterwards given to it (*v.* 9), and by which it was known in the writer's time.

8. *i.e.* "Whosoever will smite the Jebusites, let him reach both the lame and the blind, who are the hated of David's soul, by the gutter or water-course, *and he shall be chief.*" The only access to the citadel was where the water had worn a channel (some understand a subterranean channel), and where there was, in consequence, some vegetation in the rock. Joab (see marg. ref.) took the hint, and with all the activity that had distinguished his brother Asahel (ii. 18), climbed up first. *The blind and the lame* are either literally such, placed there in derision by the Jebusites who thought the stronghold impregnable, or they are the Jebusite garrison, so called in derision by David.

Wherefore they said, &c.] *i.e.* it became a proverb (as in 1 Sam. xix. 24). The pro-

9 not come into the house. ¶So David dwelt in the fort, and
o ver. 7.   called it °the city of David. And David built round about from
10 Millo and inward. And David ¹went on, and grew great, and
p 1 Kin. 5. 2.   11 the LORD God of hosts *was* with him. ¶And ᵖHiram king of
1 Chr. 14. 1.   Tyre sent messengers to David, and cedar trees, and carpenters,
12 and ²masons: and they built David an house. And David
perceived that the LORD had established him king over Israel,
and that he had exalted his kingdom for his people Israel's
q Deut. 17.   13 sake. ¶And ᵠDavid took *him* more concubines and wives out of
17.   Jerusalem, after he was come from Hebron: and there were yet
1 Chr. 3. 9.
& 14. 3.   14 sons and daughters born to David. And ʳthese *be* the names of
r 1 Chr. 3. 5.   those that were born unto him in Jerusalem; ³Shammuah, and
& 14. 4.   15 Shobab, and Nathan, and Solomon, Ibhar also, and ⁴Elishua,
16 and Nepheg, and Japhia, and Elishama, and ⁵Eliada, and
s 1 Chr. 11.   17 Eliphalet. ¶ˢBut when the Philistines heard that they had
16.   anointed David king over Israel, all the Philistines came up to
& 14. 8.
t ch. 23. 14.   seek David; and David heard *of it*, ᵗand went down to the hold.
u Josh. 15. 8. 18 The Philistines also came and spread themselves in ᵘthe valley
Isai. 17. 5.   19 of Rephaim. And David ˣenquired of the LORD, saying, Shall
x ch. 2. 1.   I go up to the Philistines? wilt thou deliver them into mine
1 Sam. 23. 2,   hand? And the LORD said unto David, Go up: for I will
4.
& 30. 8.   20 doubtless deliver the Philistines into thine hand. And David
y Isai. 28. 21.   came to ᵞBaal-perazim, and David smote them there, and said,
The LORD hath broken forth upon mine enemies before me, as
the breach of waters. Therefore he called the name of that
21 place ⁶Baal-perazim. And there they left their images, and
z Deut. 7. 5, 22 David and his men ᶻ⁷burned them. ¶ᵃAnd the Philistines
25.   came up yet again, and spread themselves in the valley of
1 Chr. 14. 12.
a 1 Chr. 14.   23 Rephaim. And when ᵇDavid enquired of the LORD, he said,
13.
b ver. 19.   ¹ Heb. *went going and grow-*   ³ Or, *Shimea,* 1 Chr. 3. 5.   ⁶ That is, *The plain of*
                    ing.   ⁴ Or, *Elishama,* 1 Chr. 3. 6.   *breaches.*
                  ² Heb. *hewers of the stone*   ⁵ Or, *Beeliada,* 1 Chr. 14. 7.   ⁷ Or, *took them away.*
                    of the wall.

verb seems merely to have arisen from the
blind and the lame being the *hated of Da-*
vid's soul, and hence to have been used proverbially of any that were hated, or unwelcome, or disagreeable.

9. *David dwelt in the fort*] or stronghold,
(as in *v.* 7) *i.e.* eventually, when the buildings were completed, which may not have
been for two or three years. Millo appears
to have been a fortress of some kind, the
northern defence of the city of David, and
to have been a part of the original Canaanite defences of Zion, as appears probable
also from there having been a fortress called
the *house of Millo* in the Canaanite city of
Shechem. (Judg. ix. 6 note, and 20.) *Millo*
may be the native name. Some identify it
with the great platform called the Haram
es Sherif.

David built round about] Probably meaning built his own house and other houses
and streets, all, in short, that caused it to
be called *the city of David.* (Cp. 1 Chr. xi.
8.) The buildings were within, on the south
of Millo, so as to be protected by it on the
north, as they were east, west. and south,
by the precipitous ravines.

11. *Hiram king of Tyre*] Now mentioned
for the first time. He survived David, and
continued his friendship to Solomon (marg.
reff.). The news of the capture of the city
of the Jebusites had doubtless reached Tyre,
and created a great impression of David's
power.

17. *the hold*] Not the same place which
is so named in *vv.* 7 and 9, but probably the
cave (or hold) of Adullam (xxiii. 13). The
invasion most probably took place before
David had completed his buildings in the
city of David; and is probably referred to
in xxiii. 8-17.

20. *Baal-perazim*] *Master* or *possessor of
breaches,* equivalent to *place of breaches.* It
was on a hill near Gibeon (see marg. ref.).

21. *And there they left their images*] An
indication of the precipitancy of their flight,
and the suddenness with which the Israelites burst upon them like a "breach of waters." The A. V. rendering *burned them,*
does not give a translation (cp. marg.), but a
gloss, warranted by the explanation given
in marg. reff.

23. *the mulberry trees*] Rather, the *Bacah-
tree,* and found abundantly near Mecca. It

Thou shalt not go up; *but* fetch a compass behind them, and
24 come upon them over against the mulberry trees. And let it
be, when thou ^chearest the sound of a going in the tops of the
mulberry trees, that then thou shalt bestir thyself : for then
^dshall the LORD go out before thee, to smite the host of the
25 Philistines. And David did so, as the LORD had commanded
him; and smote the Philistines from ^eGeba until thou come to
^fGazer.

CHAP. 6. AGAIN, David gathered together all *the* chosen *men* of
2 Israel, thirty thousand. And ^aDavid arose, and went with all
the people that *were* with him from ¹Baale of Judah, to bring
up from thence the ark of God, ²whose name is called by the
name of the LORD of hosts ^bthat dwelleth *between* the cheru-
3 bims. And they ³set the ark of God ^cupon a new cart, and
brought it out of the house of Abinadab that *was* in ⁴Gibeah :
and Uzzah and Ahio, the sons of Abinadab, drave the new cart.
4 And they brought it out of ^dthe house of Abinadab which *was*
at Gibeah, ⁵accompanying the ark of God: and Ahio went
5 before the ark. And David and all the house of Israel played
before the LORD on all manner of *instruments made of* fir wood,
even on harps, and on psalteries, and on timbrels, and on cornets,
6 and on cymbals. ¶And when they came to ^eNachon's threshingfloor, Uzzah ^fput forth *his hand* to the ark of God, and took
7 hold of it; for the oxen ⁶shook *it*. And the anger of the LORD
was kindled against Uzzah; and ^gGod smote him there for *his*
8 ⁷error; and there he died by the ark of God. And David was

^c So 2 Kin.
7. 6.
^d Judg. 4.14.
^e 1 Chr. 14.
16.
Gibeon.
^f Josh. 16.10.

^a 1 Chr. 13.
5, 6.

^b 1 Sam. 4.4.
Ps. 80. 1.
^c See Num.
7. 9.
1 Sam. 6. 7.
^d 1 Sam. 7.1.

^e 1 Chr. 13.
9. he is
called,
Chidon.
^f See Num.
4. 15.
^g 1 Sam. 6.
19.

¹ Or, *Baalah,* that is *Kirjath-
jearim,* Josh. 15. 9, 60.
² Or, *at which the name,* even

the name of the LORD *of
hosts, was called upon.*
³ Heb. *made to ride.*
⁴ Or, *The hill.*

⁵ Heb. *with.*
⁶ Or, *stumbled.*
⁷ Or, *rashness.*

---

is very like the balsam-tree, and probably
derives its name from the exudation of the
sap in drops like tears when a leaf is torn
off. Some think the valley of Baca (Ps.
lxxxiv. 6) was so called from this plant
growing there.

25. *Geba*] Better, as in marg. ref. *Gibeon.*
Gazer should be "**Gezer**" (Josh. x. 33, &c.);
it lay between the nether Bethhoron and the
sea; on the direct route therefore which the
Philistines, fleeing from Gibeon, would take.
The exact site has now been identified (1 K.
ix. 16 note).

VI. 1. *Again*] It should be, "**and David
again gathered**," &c., *i.e.* after the previous gathering, either for his election to
the kingdom (v. 1-3) or for the Philistine
war (v. 17-25), he assembled them again for
the peaceful purpose of bringing up the Ark
to Mount Zion (see marg. ref.). The whole
narrative indicates the progressive consolidation of David's power, and the settlement
of his monarchy on strong foundations.

2. *from Baale of Judah*] See marg. and 1
Sam. vi. 21 note.

whose name, &c.] The literal rendering is,
"**Upon which is called the Name, the
Name of Jehovah of Hosts, Who sits upon
the Cherubim**," i.e. *the Ark which is called
after the Lord of Hosts and bears His Name*
(see Deut. xxviii. 10; 1 K. viii. 43: Isai. iv. 1).

3. *the house of Abinadab in Gibeah*].Ra-

ther, *on the hill* (as in marg. and 1 Sam. vii.
1). It does not at all follow that Abinadab
was still alive, nor can we conclude from
Uzzah and Ahio being called *sons of Abinadab,* that they were literally his children.
They may well have been sons of Eleazar
and grandsons of Abinadab, or yet more remote descendants ; since there is no distinct
evidence that Abinadab was alive even when
the ark was brought to Kirjath-jearim. The
house may have retained the name of "the
house of Abinadab" long after his death.

5. *played*] i.e. danced to music vocal and
instrumental (see Judg. xvi. 25 note).

cornets] Rather, from the etymology of
the Heb. word (*to shake*), and their being
coupled with the *cymbals,* and being rendered *sistra* in the Vulg., some kind of instrument with bells or rings, which gave a
sound by being shaken.

6. *shook it*] The use of the Heb. word
here is unusual. Some take the word as in
2 K. ix. 33, and render the passage : *The
oxen were throwing,* or *had thrown it down,*
very likely by turning aside to eat what
grain there might be on the threshing-floor.

7. *for his error*] The Heb. is difficult, and
some prefer the reading of the parallel passage, *because...ask* (1 Chr. xiii. 10).

8. *displeased*] Grief allied to *anger* seems
to be intended. Cp. 1 Sam. xv. 11 note.
On the name of the place, cp. v. 20.

displeased, because the LORD had ¹made a breach upon Uzzah:
and he called the name of the place ²Perez-uzzah to this day.

ʰ Ps. 119.
120.
See Luke
5. 8, 9.
ⁱ 1 Chr. 13.
13.
ᵏ 1 Chr. 13.
14.
ˡ Gen. 30. 27.
& 39. 5.

9 ¶And ʰDavid was afraid of the LORD that day, and said, How
10 shall the ark of the LORD come to me? So David would not
remove the ark of the LORD unto him into the city of David:
but David carried it aside into the house of Obed-edom ⁱthe
11 Gittite. ᵏAnd the ark of the LORD continued in the house of
Obed-edom the Gittite three months: and the LORD ˡblessed
12 Obed-edom, and all his household. ¶And it was told king
David, saying, The LORD hath blessed the house of Obed-edom,
and all that *pertaineth* unto him, because of the ark of God.

ᵐ 1 Chr. 15.
25.
ⁿ Num. 4.15.
Josh. 3. 3.
ᵒ See 1 Kin.
8. 5.
1 Chr. 15.26.
ᵖ See Exod.
15. 20.
Ps. 30. 11.
ᵠ 1 Sam. 2.
18.
ⁱ Chr. 15.27.
ʳ 1 Chr. 15.
28.
ˢ 1 Chr. 15.
29.
ᵗ 1 Chr. 16.1.
ᵘ 1 Chr. 15.1.
Ps. 132. 8.
ˣ 1 Chr. 8. 5,
62, 63.
ʸ 1 Kin. 8.
55.
1 Chr. 16. 2.
ᶻ 1 Chr. 16.3.

ᵐSo David went and brought up the ark of God from the house
13 of Obed-edom into the city of David with gladness. And it was
so, that when ⁿthey that bare the ark of the LORD had gone six
14 paces, he sacrificed ᵒoxen and fatlings. And David ᵖdanced
before the LORD with all *his* might; and David *was* girded
15 ᵠwith a linen ephod. ʳSo David and all the house of Israel
brought up the ark of the LORD with shouting, and with the
16 sound of the trumpet. ¶And ˢas the ark of the LORD came
into the city of David, Michal Saul's daughter looked through
a window, and saw king David leaping and dancing before the
17 LORD; and she despised him in her heart. ¶And ᵗthey brought
in the ark of the LORD, and set it in ᵘhis place, in the midst of
the tabernacle that David had ³pitched for it: and David ˣoffered
18 burnt offerings and peace offerings before the LORD. And as
soon as David had made an end of offering burnt offerings and
peace offerings, ʸhe blessed the people in the name of the LORD
19 of hosts. ᶻAnd he dealt among all the people, *even* among the
whole multitude of Israel, as well to the women as men, to
every one a cake of bread, and a good piece *of flesh*, and a flagon

¹ Heb. *broken*.   ² That is, *The breach of Uzzah*.   ³ Heb. *stretched*.

---

10. Obed-edom was a Levite of the family of Merari, being (1 Chr. xv. 18-24, xvi.
38) a son of Jeduthun, who was a Merarite.
He was a porter, a player on the harp, and
was one of the Levites specially designated
to take part in the musical services on the
occasion of bringing up the Ark to Zion, and
to minister before it when brought up. He
is called a *Gittite* perhaps from *Gath*-Rim-
mon, in Manasseh, which belonged to the
Kohathites (Josh. xxi. 25). Marriage with
a Kohathite, or some other cause, would
account for his dwelling in a Kohathite city.

12. *with gladness*] Especially with joyful
music and song (1 Chr. xv. 16, &c.).

13. The meaning is, not that they sacrificed oxen and fatlings every six steps, which
would have been impossible; but that when
—after the arrangement made by David for
the Levites to carry the Ark (1 Chr. xv. 2, 12,
15) they had borne it successfully and with
visible tokens of God's favour, out of the
house of Obed-edom and six "steps" on the
road to the city of David to the sound of
the musical instruments,—then they stopped
and offered solemn sacrifices. Possibly "the
step" may have had a technical sense, and
denoted a certain distance, say a *stadium*.
Six such distances would have been nearly

a mile, and if the ground was difficult and
steep, the successful progress of "those
that bare the ark," so far, would have been
a fit cause for a thanksgiving sacrifice.

14. *danced*] The Heb. word is found
only here and in *v*. 16. It means "to dance in
a circle," hence simply *to dance*. The parallel passage in 1 Chr. xv. 27 gives a widely
different sense.

16. *she despised him in her heart*] In the
days of Saul the Ark had been neglected (1
Chr. xiii. 3), and Saul had in everything
shown himself to be an irreligious king.
Michal seems to have been of a like
spirit.

The whole section, 2 Sam. vi. 16-36, should
be compared with 1 Chr. xv. 29-xvi. 43.

The *peace offerings* were with a special view
to feasting the people. (Cp. 1 K. viii.
63-66.)

18. *he blessed the people*] So did Solomon
(1 K. viii. 14).

19. *a good piece* of flesh] The word thus
paraphrased is only found here and in
marg. ref. A piece of meat from the
peace offerings is probably meant. From
the fact that the chronicler explains the
preceding *cake* by the more common
word *loaf*, but leaves this obscure word

of wine. So all the people departed every one to his house.
20 ¶ *a* Then David returned to bless his household. And Michal
the daughter of Saul came out to meet David, and said, How
glorious was the king of Israel to day, who *b* uncovered himself
to day in the eyes of the handmaids of his servants, as one of
21 the *c* vain fellows ¹shamelessly uncovereth himself! And David
said unto Michal, *It was* before the LORD, *d* which chose me
before thy father, and before all his house, to appoint me ruler
over the people of the LORD, over Israel: therefore will I play
22 before the LORD. And I will yet be more vile than thus, and
will be base in mine own sight: and ²of the maidservants which
23 thou hast spoken of, of them shall I be had in honour. Therefore Michal the daughter of Saul had no child *e* unto the day of
her death.

CHAP. 7. AND it came to pass, *a* when the king sat in his house,
and the LORD had given him rest round about from all his
2 enemies ; that the king said unto Nathan the prophet, See now,
I dwell in *b* an house of cedar, *c* but the ark of God dwelleth
3 within *d* curtains. And Nathan said to the king, Go, do all that
4 *is* *e* in thine heart ; for the LORD *is* with thee. ¶ And it came to
pass that night, that the word of the LORD came unto Nathan,
5 saying, Go and tell ³my servant David, Thus saith the LORD,
6 *f* Shalt thou build me an house for me to dwell in ? Whereas I
have not dwelt in *any* house *g* since the time that I brought up
the children of Israel out of Egypt, even to this day, but have
7 walked in *h* a tent and in a tabernacle. In all *the places* wherein
I have *i* walked with all the children of Israel spake I a word
with *j* any of the tribes of Israel, whom I commanded *k* to feed

a Ps. 30, title.
b ver. 14, 16. 1 Sam. 19. 24.
c Judg. 9. 4.
d 1 Sam. 13. 14. & 15. 28.

e See 1 Sam. 15. 35.

a 1 Chr. 17. 1, &c.

b ch. 5. 11.
c See Acts 7. 46.
d Ex. 26. 1. & 40. 21.
e 1 Kin. 8. 17, 18.
f See 1 Kin. 5. 3.
1 Chr. 22. 8.
g 1 Kin. 8.16.
h Ex. 40. 18, 19, 34.
i Lev. 26. 11. Deut. 23. 14.
k ch. 5. 2.
Ps. 78. 71.
Matt. 2. 6.

¹ Or, *openly.*
² Or, *of the handmaids* of my servants.
³ Heb. *to my servant to David.*
⁴ *any of the judges,* 1 Chr. 17. 6.

unexplained, one might infer that it was
already obsolete and unknown in his time.
The LXX. translates it *a cake baked on the
hearth ;* the Vulg. *a piece of roast beef.*
a flagon of wine] Rather, "**a cake**" of
grapes or raisins (Hos. iii. 1; Cant. ii. 5), or
made with oil or mead.
20. *Then David returned,* &c.] He had
passed his house to accompany the Ark to
the tabernacle he had pitched for it, when
Michal saw him dancing. He now returns
to bless his household. He had blessed the
people (*v.* 18), but there were the inmates
of his own house whom the customs of the
age did not allow to be present, and so, with
his usual considerate kindness and affection,
David came to bless them also on this solemn occasion.
21. *play*] See *v.* 5 note. The speech might
be paraphrased, *Before the Lord which chose
me,* &c., *yea, before the Lord have I danced.*
He humbles Michal's pride by the allusion
to her father's rejection, and shows by
Saul's example how little pride contributes
to the stability of greatness. Therefore for
his part he will not think anything done for
the glory of God too mean for him ; and if
he cannot have honour from Saul's daughter, he will be content to be honoured by
the maid-servants.

VII. 1. There is no indication how soon
after the bringing up of the Ark these things
occurred, but it was probably at no long interval.
2. *Nathan the prophet*] Here first mentioned, but playing an important part afterwards (*v.g.* xii. 1; 1 K. i. 10 ; 1 Chr. xxix.
29 ; 2 Chr. ix. 29). From the two last passages it appears that he wrote the history
of David's reign, and a part at least of
Solomon's. His distinctive title is *the prophet,* that of Gad *the seer* (cp. 1 Sam. ix. 9).
He was probably much younger than David.
In *v.* 3, he spoke his own private opinion ;
in *v.* 4, this was corrected by the word of
the Lord.
6. *have walked*] Implying the frequent
moving of the tabernacle, in the times of
the Judges, as opposed to a settled resting
in one place. The word *tent,* refers especially to the outward covering of skins, &c. ;
the *tabernacle* denotes the framework of
boards and bars. Observe the constant reference to the Exodus and to the details as
given in the Books of Moses.
7. *the tribes of Israel*] The duplicate passage reads *judges* (see marg. and cp. *v.* 11).
But a comparison with such passages as Ps.
lxxviii. 67, 68 ; 1 K. viii. 16 ; and 1 Chr.
xxviii. 4, favours the reading " tribes," and-

my people Israel, saying, Why build ye not me an house of cedar? 8 Now therefore so shalt thou say unto my servant David, Thus saith the LORD of hosts, *i* I took thee from the sheepcote, *k* from following the sheep, to be ruler over my people, over Israel: 9 and *m* I was with thee whithersoever thou wentest, *n* and have cut off all thine enemies, ²out of thy sight, and have made thee *o* a great name, like unto the name of the great *men* that *are* in 10 the earth. Moreover I will appoint a place for my people Israel, and will *p* plant them, that they may dwell in a place of their own, and move no more; *q* neither shall the children of wicked- 11 ness afflict them any more, as beforetime, and as *r* since the time that I commanded judges *to be* over my people Israel, and have *s* caused thee to rest from all thine enemies. Also the LORD 12 telleth thee *t* that he will make thee an house. And *u* when thy days be fulfilled, and thou *x* shalt sleep with thy fathers, *y* I will set up thy seed after thee, which shall proceed out of thy bowels, 13 and I will establish his kingdom. *z* He shall build an house for my name, and I will *a* stablish the throne of his kingdom for 14 ever. *b* I will be his father, and he shall be my son. *c* If he commit iniquity, I will chasten him with the rod of men, and 15 with the stripes of the children of men: but my mercy shall not

¹ Heb. *from after.*   ² Heb. *from thy face.*

---

the phrase is a condensed one, the meaning of which is, that whatever tribe had in times past supplied the ruler of Israel, whether Ephraim in the days of Joshua, or Benjamin in the time of Saul, or Judah in that of David, God had never required any of those tribes to build a house in one of their cities.

an house of cedar] See 1 K. vii. 2, 3, x. 17, 21; Jer. xxii. 14, 23. Beams of cedar marked a costly building. The cedar of Lebanon is a totally different tree from what we improperly call *the red* or *Virginian cedar*, which supplies the sweet-scented cedar wood, and is really a kind of juniper. The cedar of Lebanon is a close-grained, light-coloured, yellowish wood, with darker knots and veins.

10. *Moreover I will appoint,* &c.] It should be: *And I have appointed a place,* &c., *and have planted them,* &c. This was already done by the consolidation of David's kingdom. The contrast between this and *v.* 11 is that of the troublous unsettled times of the Judges and the frequent servitudes of Israel in those times, with the settled prosperity and independence of the kingdom of David and Solomon.

12. The prophet, having detailed God's past mercies to David, now passes on to direct prophecy, and that one of the most important in the Old Testament.

I will set up thy seed] In one sense this manifestly refers to Solomon, David's successor and the builder of the Temple. But we have the direct authority of St. Peter (Acts ii. 30) for applying it to Christ the seed of David, and His eternal kingdom; and the title *the Son of David* given to the

Messiah in the Rabbinical writings, as well as its special application to Jesus in the New Testament, springs mainly from the acknowledged Messianic significance of this prophecy. (See also Isai. lv. 3; Acts xiii. 34.)

13. *He shall build an house,* &c.] For the fulfilment of this in the person of Solomon, see 1 K. viii. 16-20. For its application to Christ, see John i. 12; Eph. i. 20-22; 1 Tim. iii. 15; Heb. iii. 6, &c.; and Zech. vi. 12, 13.

I will stablish the throne of his kingdom for ever] The words *for ever,* emphatically twice repeated in *v.* 16, show very distinctly that this prophecy looks beyond the succession of the kings of Judah of the house of David, and embraces the throne of Christ, according to the Angel's interpretation given in Luke i. 31-33, where the reference to this passage cannot be mistaken. This is also brought out fully in Ps. lxxxix. 29, 36, 37. See also Dan. vii. 13, 14; Isai. ix. 6, 7; Jer. xxiii. 5, 6, xxxiii. 14-21; Ezek. xxxiv. 24; Zech. xii. 7, 8; Hos. iii. 5, &c.

14. *I will be his father,* &c.] In marg. ref. the equivalent expressions are applied to David. In Heb. i. 5, this text is applied to Christ. But in 1 Chr. xvii. 13, xxii. 9, 10, xxviii. 6, it is expressly appropriated to Solomon.

with the rod of men, &c.] *i.e.* such a chastisement as men inflict upon their children, to correct and reclaim them, not to destroy them. The whole clause is omitted in 1 Chr. xvii. 13.

15. *my mercy shall not depart,* &c.] Hence Isaiah's saying, *the sure mercies of David* (lv. 3), *i.e.* unfailing, lasting mercies: mercies

depart away from him, ^das I took *it* from Saul, whom I put away
16 before thee. And ^ethine house and thy kingdom shall be established for ever before thee : thy throne shall be established for
17 ever. According to all these words, and according to all this
18 vision, so did Nathan speak unto David. ¶ Then went king
David in, and sat before the LORD, and he said, ^fWho *am* I, O
Lord GOD? and what *is* my house, that thou hast brought me
19 hitherto? And this was yet a small thing in thy sight, O Lord
GOD; ^gbut thou hast spoken also of thy servant's house for a
great while to come. ^hAnd *is* this the ¹manner of man, O Lord
20 GOD? And what can David say more unto thee? for thou,
21 Lord GOD, ⁱknowest thy servant. For thy word's sake, and
according to thine own heart, hast thou done all these great
22 things, to make thy servant know *them*. Wherefore ^kthou art
great, O LORD God : for ^l*there is* none like thee, neither *is there*
any God beside thee, accoıding to all that we have heard with
23 our ears. And ^mwhat one nation in the earth *is* like thy people,
even like Israel, whom God went to redeem for a people to himself, and to make him a name, and to do for you great things
and terrible, for thy land, before ⁿthy people, which thou re-
deemedst to thee from Egypt, *from* the nations and their gods?
24 For ^othou hast confirmed to thyself thy people Israel *to be* a
people unto thee for ever: ^pand thou, LORD, art become their
25 God. And now, O LORD God, the word that thou hast spoken
concerning thy servant, and concerning his house, establish *it*
26 for ever, and do as thou hast said. And let thy name be magnified for ever, saying, The LORD of hosts *is* the God over
Israel: and let the house of thy servant David be established
27 before thee. For thou, O LORD of hosts, God of Israel, hast
²revealed to thy servant, saying, I will build thee an house:
therefore hath thy servant found in his heart to pray this prayer
28 unto thee. And now, O Lord GOD, thou *art* that God, and ^qthy
words be true, and thou hast promised this goodness unto thy
29 servant: therefore now ³let it please thee to bless the house of

¹ Heb. *law*. ² Heb. *opened the ear*, Ruth 4. 4. ³ Heb. *be thou pleased and*
    1 Sam. 9. 15. *bless*.

d 1 Sam. 15.
23, 28.
e Ps. 89. 36,
37.
John 12. 34.

f Gen. 32. 10.

g ver. 12.
h Isai. 55. 8.

i Gen. 18. 19.
Ps. 139. 1.
k 1 Chr. 16.
25.
2 Chr. 2. 5.
Ps. 48. 1.
& 86. 10.
Jer. 10. 6.
l Deut. 3. 24.
1 Sam. 2. 2.
Ps. 89. 6.
Isai. 45. 5.
m Deut. 4. 7,
32, 34.
Ps. 147. 20.
n Deut. 9. 26.
Neh. 1. 10.
o Deut.26.18.
p Gen. 17. 7.
Ex. 6. 7.

q John 17.17.

which are like streams of water that never
dry up (Isai. xxxiii. 16; Jer. xv. 18). This
is explained in *v.* 16, where the word *established* is the same word as is rendered *sure*
in Isaiah.

before thee] *Before Me* is probably the true
reading in *vv.* 15, 16 (if the rest of the text
be sound), according to the analogy of Jer.
xxxv. 19, 1 Sam. ii. 30, 35, and many other
places ; whereas the idea contained in the
reading, *before thee*, is unparalleled. But
the reading in 1 Chr. xvii. 13 is quite different : "*As I took it from him that was before thee*," meaning Saul, which gives a very
good sense, and suggests that the text here
may have been corrupted.

18. *sat before the* LORD] In the tent where
the Ark was. Standing or kneeling was the
usual attitude of prayer (1 K. viii. 22, 54,
55; but cp. Ex. xvii. 12). Modern commentators mostly take the word here in
the sense of *waiting*, *abiding*, not *sitting* :
but *sat* is the natural rendering. David sat
down to meditate, and then rose up to pray.

19. *is this the manner of man*] Cp. 1 Chr.
xvii. 17. Our passage may be thus understood : *But this is the law* (or prerogative) *of
a great man* to found dynasties which are to
last into the far future. David expresses
his astonishment that he, of such humble
birth, and one so little in his own eyes,
should not only be raised to the throne, but
be assured of the perpetuity of the succession in his descendants, as if he were a man
of high degree.

23. *the nations and their gods*] *i.e.* the people and the idols of Canaan.

27. *therefore hath thy servant found in his
heart*, &c.] The promises of God are the
true guide to the prayers of His people. We
may dare to ask anything, how great soever
it may be, which God has promised to give.
In this and the two following verses David
expresses the same wonder at the riches of
God's grace, and the same expectation
founded on that grace, which St. Paul does
in such passages as Eph. i. 5–7, ii. 7, &c.
marg. reff.

thy servant, that it may continue for ever before thee : for thou,
O Lord GOD, hast spoken *it :* and with thy blessing let the house

ᵉ ch. 22. 51.   of thy servant be blessed ᵉfor ever.

ᵃ 1 Chr. 18.   **CHAP. 8.** AND ᵃafter this it came to pass, that David smote the
1, &c.   Philistines, and subdued them : and David took ¹Metheg-ammah

ᵇ Num. 24.   2 out of the hand of the Philistines. ¶And ᵇhe smote Moab, and
17.   measured them with a line, casting them down to the ground ;
               even with two lines measured he to put to death, and with one

ᶜ ver. 6, &   full line to keep alive. And *so* the Moabites ᶜbecame David's
14.   3 servants, *and* ᵈbrought gifts. ¶David smote also ²Hadadezer,
ᵈ Judg. 3.18.   the son of Rehob, king of ᵉZobah, as he went to recover ᶠhis
2 Kin. 17. 3.
ᵉ 1 Sam. 14.   4 border at the river Euphrates. And David took ³from him a
47.   thousand ⁴*chariots,* and seven hundred horsemen, and twenty
ᶠ See Gen.   thousand footmen : and David ᵍhoughed all the chariot *horses,*
15. 18.
ᵍ Josh. 11. 6, 5 but reserved of them *for* an hundred chariots. ʰAnd when the
9.   Syrians of Damascus came to succour Hadadezer king of Zobah,
ʰ 1 Kin. 11.
23, 24, 25.   6 David slew of the Syrians two and twenty thousand men. Then
               David put garrisons in Syria of Damascus : and the Syrians
ⁱ ver. 2.   ⁱbecame servants to David, *and* brought gifts. ᵏAnd the LORD
ᵏ ver. 14.   7 preserved David whithersoever he went. And David took ˡtho
ch. 7. 9.
ˡ See 1 Kin.   shields of gold that were on the servants of Hadadezer, and
10. 16.   8 brought them to Jerusalem. And from ⁵Betah, and from ⁶Be-
               rothai, cities of Hadadezer, king David took exceeding much
               9 brass. ¶When ⁷Toi king of Hamath heard that David had

¹ Or, *The bridle of Ammah.*   ³ Or, *of his.*   ⁶ Or, *Chun,* 1 Chr. 18. 8.
· ² Or, *Hadarezer,* 1 Chr.   ⁴ As 1 Chron. 18. 4.   ⁷ *Tou,* 1 Chr. 18. 9.
   18. 3.   ⁵ Or, *Tibhath.*

VIII. *Metheg-ammah* must be the name
of some stronghold which commanded Gath,
and the taking of which made David master
of Gath and her towns.

2. David took great numbers of the
Moabites prisoners of war, and made them
lie down on the ground, and then divided
them by a measuring line into three parts,
putting two-thirds to death, and saving
alive one-third. The cause of the war with
the Moabites, who had been very friendly
with David (1 Sam. xxii. 3, 4), and of this
severe treatment, is not known. But it
seems likely, from the tone of Ps. lx. that
David had met with some temporary reverse
in his Syrian wars, and that the Moabites
and Edomites had treacherously taken advantage of it, and perhaps tried to cut off
his retreat.

3. *Hadadezer*] Not (see marg.) *Hadarezer.*
Hadadezer, is the true form, as seen in the
names *Benhadad, Hadad* (1 K. xv. 18, &c.,
xi. 14, &c.). *Hadad* was the chief idol, or
sun-god, of the Syrians.

to recover his border] Literally, *to cause his
hand to return.* The phrase is used sometimes literally, as *e.g.* Ex. iv. 7 ; 1 K. xiii.
4 ; Prov. xix. 24; and sometimes figuratively, as Isai. i. 25, xiv. 27 ; Am. i. 8; Ps.
lxxix. 11. The exact force of the metaphor
must in each case be decided by the context.
If, as is most probable, this verse relates to
the circumstances more fully detailed in x.
15-19, the meaning of the phrase here will be
when hẹ (Hadadezer) *went to renew his attack*

(upon Israel), or *to recruit his strength against
Israel, at the river Euphrates.*

4. *seven hundred horsemen*] It should be
seven thousand, as in 1 Chr. xviii. 4.

5. *Syrians of Damascus*] The Syrians
(Aram), whose capital was Damascus, were
the best known and most powerful. Damascus (written Darmesek in marg. reft.,
according to the late Aramean orthography)
is first mentioned in Gen. xv. 2. According
to Nicolaus of Damascus, cited by Josephus,
the Syrian king's name was Hadad.

6. *garrisons*] The word is used for *officers*
in 1 K. iv. 5, 19, and some think that that
is its meaning here. Perhaps, however, it
is best to take it with the A. V. in the same
sense as in 1 Sam. x. 5, xiii. 3.

brought gifts] Rather, " **tribute** " (and in
v. 2); meaning they became subject and tributary.

8. *Betah and Berothai*] These names (see
also marg.) have not been identified with
certainty.

exceeding much brass] " Wherewith Solomon made the brazen sea, and the pillars,
and the vessels of brass " (1 Chr. xviii. 8).
The LXX. and Vulg. both add these words
here, so that perhaps they have fallen out
of the Hebrew text. For the existence
of metals in Lebanon or Antilebanon, see
Deut. viii. 9.

9. *Hamath*] This appears as an independent kingdom so late as the time of Sena-
cherib (Isai. xxxvii. 13). But in the time of
Nebuchadnezzar, both Hamath and Arpad

10 smitten all the host of Hadadezer, then Toi sent ᵐJoram his son
unto king David, to ¹salute him, and to bless him, because he
had fought against Hadadezer, and smitten him: for Hadadezer
²had wars with Toi. And *Joram* ³brought with him vessels of
11 silver, and vessels of gold, and vessels of brass: which also king
David ⁿdid dedicate unto the LORD, with the silver and gold
12 that he had dedicated of all nations which he subdued; of Syria,
and of Moab, and of the children of Ammon, and of the Philistines, and of Amalek, and of the spoil of Hadadezer, son of
13 Rehob, king of Zobah. ¶And David gat *him* a name when he
returned from ⁴smiting of the Syrians in ⁰the valley of salt,
14 ᵖ⁵*being* eighteen thousand *men*. And he put garrisons in Edom;
throughout all Edom put he garrisons, and ᵠall they of Edom
became David's servants. ʳAnd the LORD preserved David
15 whithersoever he went. ¶And David reigned over all Israel;
and David executed judgment and justice unto all his people.
16 ˢAnd Joab the son of Zeruiah *was* over the host; and ᵗJehosha-
17 phat the son of Ahilud *was* ⁶recorder; and ᵘZadok the son of
Ahitub, and Ahimelech the son of Abiathar, *were* the priests;
18 and Seraiah *was* the ⁷scribe; ˣand·Benaiah the son of Jehoiada
was over both the ʸCherethites and the Pelethites; and David's
sons were ⁸chief rulers.

CHAP. 9. AND David said, Is there yet any that is left of the house
of Saul, that I may ᵃshew him kindness for Jonathan's sake?
2 And *there was* of the house of Saul a servant whose name *was*
ᵇZiba. And when they had called him unto David, the king said
3 unto him, *Art* thou Ziba? And he said, Thy servant *is* he. And
the king said, *Is* there not yet any of the house of Saul, that I
may shew ᶜthe kindness of God unto him? And Ziba said unto
the king, Jonathan hath yet a son, *which is* ᵈlame on *his* feet.

ᵐ 1 Chr. 18. 10, *Hado-ram*.

ⁿ 1 Kin. 7. 51.
1 Chr. 18. 11.
& 26. 26.

⁰ 2 Kin. 14. 7.
ᵖ See 1 Chr. 18. 12.
Ps. 60, title.
ᵠ Gen. 27. 29, 37, 40.
Num. 24. 18.
ʳ ver. 6.
ˢ ch. 19. 13.
& 20. 23.
ᵗ 1 Chr. 11. 6.
& 18. 15.
ᵗ 1 Kin. 4. 3.
ᵘ 1 Chr. 24. 3.
ˣ 1 Chr. 18. 17.
ʸ 1 Sam. 30. 14.
ᵃ 1 Sam. 18. 3.
& 20. 14, 15, 16, 17, 42.
Prov. 27. 10.
ᵇ ch. 16. 1.
& 19. 17, 29.
ᶜ 1 Sam. 20. 14.
ᵈ ch. 4. 4.

---

¹ Heb. *ask him of peace.*
² Heb. *was a man of wars with.*
³ Heb. *in his hand were.*
⁴ Heb. *his smiting.*
⁵ Or, *slaying.*
⁶ Or, *remembrancer, or*
writer of chronicles.
⁷ Or, *secretary.*
⁸ Of, *princes,* ch. 20. 26.

---

appear to have been incorporated in the
kingdom of Damascus (Jer. xlix. 23).
10. *Joram*] Or, more probably, *Hadoram.*
See marg.
12. *Syria*] Rather, as in 1 Chr. xviii. 11,
Edom, which is manifestly the right reading, both because Edom, Moab, and Ammon
are so frequently joined together, and because David's Syrian spoil is expressly mentioned at the end of the verse. [The Hebrew letters for Aram (Syria) and Edom are
very similar.]
13. *the Syrians*] Read *the Edomites,* as in
marg. reff. (cp. Ps. lx. title), and as the
context (*v.* 14) requires. For a further
account of this war of extermination with
Edom, see 1 K. xi. 15, 16. The war with
Edom was of some duration, not without
serious reverses and dangers to the Israelites
(*v.* 2 note). The different accounts probably relate to different parts of the campaign.
16–18. For a similar account of the officers of Solomon's kingdom, see 1 K. iv.
1–6, where Jehoshaphat is still the recorder,
and Benaiah is advanced to be captain of the
host in the room of Joab. *The recorder* seems
to have been a high officer of state, a kind of

chancellor, whose office was to keep a record
of the events of the kingdom for the king's
information, and hence he would naturally
be the king's adviser. See Esth. vi. 1, 2;
Isai. xxxvi. 22; 2 Chr. xxxiv. 8. Such an
officer is found among the ancient Egyptians
and Persians.
Ahimelech the son of Abiathar] According
to 1 Sam. xxii. 9–23, Abiathar, Zadok's colleague, was the son of Ahimelech. Abiathar the son of Ahimelech continued to be
priest through the reign of David. (Cp. also
1 K i. 7, 42, ii. 22–27.) It almost necessarily follows that there is some error in the
text.
the scribe] Or secretary of state (2 K. xii.
10, xviii. 37), different from the military
scribe (Judg. v. 14 note).
18. *the Cherethites and the Pelethites*] See
marg. ref. note.
chief rulers] The word *cohen,* here rendered
a chief ruler, is the regular word for a *priest.*
In the early days of the monarchy the word
cohen had not quite lost its etymological
sense, from the root meaning *to minister,* or
manage affairs, though in later times its
technical sense alone survived.

4 And the king said unto him, Where *is* he? And Ziba said unto
c ch. 17. 27.　the king, Behold, he *is* in the house of *e*Machir, the son of
5 Ammiel, in Lo-debar. Then king David sent, and fetched him
out of the house of Machir, the son of Ammiel, from Lo-debar.
6 ¶ Now when ¹Mephibosheth, the son of Jonathan, the son of
Saul, was come unto David, he fell on his face, and did reverence. And David said, Mephibosheth. And he answered,

f ver. 1, 3.　7 Behold thy servant! And David said unto him, Fear not: *f*for
I will surely shew thee kindness for Jonathan thy father's sake,
and will restore thee all the land of Saul thy father; and thou
8 shalt eat bread at my table continually. And he bowed himself,
and said, What *is* thy servant, that thou shouldest look upon

g 1 Sam. 24.　9 such *g*a dead dog as I *am*? ¶ Then the king called to Ziba, Saul's
14.
ch. 16. 9.　servant, and said unto him, *h*I have given unto thy master's son
h See ch. 16.　10 all that pertained to Saul and to all his house. Thou therefore,
4.
& 19. 29.　and thy sons, and thy servants, shall till the land for him, and
i ver. 7, 11,　thou shalt bring in *the fruits*, that thy master's son may have
13.　food to eat: but Mephibosheth thy master's son *i*shall eat bread
ch. 19. 28.　alway at my table. Now Ziba had *k*fifteen sons and twenty
k ch. 19. 17.　11 servants. Then said Ziba unto the king, According to all that
my lord the king hath commanded his servant, so shall thy servant do. As for Mephibosheth, *said the king*, he shall eat at
12 my table, as one of the king's sons. And Mephibosheth had a
l 1 Chr. 8. 34.　young son, *l*whose name *was* Micha. And all that dwelt in the
13 house of Ziba *were* servants unto Mephibosheth. So Mephibo-
m ver. 7, 10.　sheth dwelt in Jerusalem: *m*for he did eat continually at the
n ver. 3.　king's table: and *n*was lame on both his feet.

¹ Called, *Merib-baal*, 1 Chr. 8. 34.

IX. 4. David reaped the fruit of his kindness to Mephibosheth; for, when he fled
from Absalom, Machir, the son of Ammiel,
was one of those who were most liberal in
providing him and his army with neces-
saries (marg. ref.). According to 1 Chr. iii.
5, *Ammiel* (called inversely *Eliam*, xi. 3)
was the father of Bath-sheba. If this be
the same Ammiel, Machir would be Bath-
sheba's brother. However, the name is not
a very uncommon one (Num. xiii. 12; 1
Chr. xxvi. 5, &c.).

Lo-debar] Evidently on the east of Jordan,
and in the neighbourhood of Ish-bosheth's
capital, Mahanaim (xvii 27), but not iden-
fied by any modern traveller. Thought by
some, not improbably, to be the same as
Debir (Josh. xiii. 26).

6. *Mephibosheth*] Also called *Merib-baal*
(and *Meri-baal*, probably by a clerical error,
1 Chr. ix. 40). The two names seem to have
the same meaning : *Bosheth*, *shame*, being
the equivalent for *Baal*, and *Mephi* (*scattering* or *destroying*, being equivalent to
Merib (*contending with*). Cp. Ish-bosheth
and Esh-baal, Jerub-baal and Jerub-besheth.

he fell on his face] In fear. Such generosity
to a fallen rival as David showed in restoring him his paternal property seemed to him
scarcely credible.

8. Mephibosheth's humility of expression,

even in the mouth of an Oriental, is painful.
It was perhaps in part the result of his
helpless lameness, and of the other misfor-
tunes of his life.

a dead dog] The wild dogs of the East,
which still abound in every town, are the
natural objects of contempt and dislike.

9. *Saul's servant*] Josephus calls him one
of Saul's freedmen. The difference this
would make in Ziba's position would only
be that instead of paying in the fruits of
the confiscated land to David, he would
have to pay them to Mephibosheth.

10. *fifteen sons*, &c.] See xix. 17, marg.
ref.

11. *said the king*] There is nothing in the
Hebrew to warrant the insertion of these
words. The words are, "**So Mephibosheth
ate at my table as one of the king's sons.**"
Only it follows that the narrator is David
himself.

12. Mephibosheth was five years old at
Saul's death. He may have been thirteen
at David's accession to the throne of Israel.
In the eighth year of David's reign over all
Israel he would have been twenty-one. His
having a son at this time indicates that
we are about the tenth year of David's
reign.

Micha] Or *Micah*; who, as far as we know,
was Mephibosheth's only son, and had a
numerous posterity (marg. reff.).

CHAP. 10. AND it came to pass after this, that the *ᵃking of the children of Ammon died, and Hanun his son reigned in his 2 stead. Then said David, I will shew kindness unto Hanun the son of Nahash, as his father shewed kindness unto me. And David sent to comfort him by the hand of his servants for his father. And David's servants came into the land of the children 3 of Ammon. And the princes of the children of Ammon said unto Hanun their lord, ¹Thinkest thou that David doth honour thy father, that he hath sent comforters unto thee? hath not David *rather* sent his servants unto thee, to search the city, and 4 to spy it out, and to overthrow it? Wherefore Hanun took David's servants, and shaved off the one half of their beards, and cut off their garments in the middle, *ᵇeven* to their buttocks, 5 and sent them away. When they told *it* unto David, he sent to meet them, because the men were greatly ashamed: and the king said, Tarry at Jericho until your beards be grown, and *then* 6 return. ¶And when the children of Ammon saw that they *ᶜstank before David, the children of Ammon sent and hired *ᵈthe Syrians of Beth-rehob, and the Syrians of Zoba, twenty thousand footmen, and of king Maacah a thousand men, and of ²Ish- 7 tob twelve thousand men. ¶And when David heard of *it*, he 8 sent Joab, and all the host of *ᵉthe mighty men. And the chil-

a 1 Chr. 19. 1, &c.

b Isai. 20. 4. & 47. 2.

c Gen. 34. 30. Ex. 5. 21. 1 Sam. 13. 4. *d* ch. 8. 3, 5.

e ch. 23. 8.

¹ Heb. *In thine eyes doth David.*   ² Or, *the men of Tob.* See Judg. 11. 3, 5.

X. On comparing this whole chapter with viii. 3-13, and 1 Chr. xix. with 1 Chr. xviii., it seems not improbable that they are two accounts of one and the same war; the former account (viii. 3-13) being inserted out of its chronological order. The numbers slain on both occasions, 42,000 (viii. 4, 5), 40,000 (x. 18), 700 (viii. 4, x. 18), the seat of war, the mention of the Euphrates, the persons engaged—David, Joab, and Abishai on one side, Hadarezer and the vassal kings on the other—are too similar to make it probable that they belong to two different wars.

1. *the king*] In marg. ref. *Nahash, king,* &c. The interval between the two events, not less than fifty years, and possibly more, is against his being the same as the Nahash of 1 Sam. xi.

The Ammonites are almost always spoken of as *the children of Ammon,* from the name of their first ancestor Ben-ammi (Gen. xix. 38).

Hanun] The equivalent of the Carthaginian *Hanno,* from the same root as the Hebrew, *Hananiah, Johanan, Hannah,* &c. The same name appears in composition with Baal in Baal-Hanan, an Aramean king (Gen. xxxvi. 38, 39).

2. The history does not record any instance of Nahash's kindness to David, but the enmity of the house of Nahash against Saul may have disposed him favourably towards Saul's enemy David, and if there was any family connexion between David's house and Nahash (xvii. 25) this may have increased the friendship.

3. *the princes,* &c.] Cp. Rehoboam's advisers (1 K. xii. 10, 11). It is not improbable

that David's severe treatment of Moab (viii. 2) was in part the cause of the fear of the Ammonites that a similar treatment was in store for themselves.

4. In 1 Chr. xix. 4, more concisely *"shaved."* Cutting off a person's beard is regarded by the Arabs as an indignity equal to flogging and branding among ourselves. The loss of their long garments, so essential to Oriental dignity, was no less insulting than that of their beards.

6. *stank,* &c.] A strong figure for to be *odious* or *detested.* Cp. marg. reff.

the Syrians of Beth-rehob] If identical with the Mesopotamians of 1 Chr. xix. 6, Beth-rehob is the same as *Rehoboth by the river* (Gen. xxxvi. 37). Others think *Beth-rehob* (*Rehob v.* 8) the same as the *Rehob* and *Beth-rehob* of Num. xiii. 21, near Hamath (perhaps the modern ruin of Hunin). If so, Beth-rehob, as well as Tob, must have been a colony of Aram Naharaim (cp. the numbers in 1 Chr. xix. 7 and here).

Syrians of Zoba] Cp. 1 Sam. xiv. 47 note. *king Maacah*] Read the **"King of Maacah "** (1 Chr. xix. 6, 7). For the position of Maacah, see Deut. iii. 14; Josh. xii. 5. It appears to have been a very small state, since its king only brought a thousand men into the field.

Ish-tob] See marg. *Tob* was the district whither Jephthah fled when driven out by the Gileadites.

7. This sufficiently indicates the greatness of the danger to Israel from this formidable league of Ammonites and Syrians.

8. *came out*] From their city, Rabbah (Deut. iii. 11), 15 or 20 miles from Medeba, where (1 Chr. xix. 7) the Syrian army was

dren of Ammon came out, and put the battle in array at the
^f ver. 6. entering in of the gate: and ^fthe Syrians of Zoba, and of Rehob,
9 and Ish-tob, and Maacah, *were* by themselves in the field. When
Joab saw that the front of the battle was against him before and
behind, he chose of all the choice men of Israel, and put *them* in
10 array against the Syrians: and the rest of the people he delivered
into the hand of Abishai his brother, that he might put *them* in
11 array against the children of Ammon. And he said, If the
Syrians be too strong for me, then thou shalt help me : but if
the children of Ammon be too strong for thee, then I will come
^g Deut. 31. 6. 12 and help thee. ^gBe of good courage, and let us ^hplay the men
^h 1 Sam. 4. 9. for our people, and for the cities of our God: and ⁱthe LORD do
1 Cor. 16. 13.
ⁱ 1 Sam. 3. 18. 13 that which seemeth him good. ¶ And Joab drew nigh, and the
people that *were* with him, unto the battle against the Syrians :
14 and they fled before him. And when the children of Ammon
saw that the Syrians were fled, then fled they also before Abishai,
and entered into the city. So Joab returned from the children
15 of Ammon, and came to Jerusalem. ¶ And when the Syrians
saw that they were smitten before Israel, they gathered them-
16 selves together. And Hadarezer sent, and brought out the
Syrians that *were* beyond ¹the river : and they came to Helam ;
and ²Shobach the captain of the host of Hadarezer *went* before
17 them. And when it was told David, he gathered all Israel
together, and passed over Jordan, and came to Helam. And the
Syrians set themselves in array against David, and fought with
18 him. And the Syrians fled before Israel ; and David slew *the
men of* seven hundred chariots of the Syrians, and forty thou-
^k 1 Chr. 19. sand ^khorsemen, and smote Shobach the captain of their host,
18,
footmen. 19 who died there. And when all the kings *that were* servants to
Hadarezer saw that they were smitten before Israel, they made
^l ch. 8. 6. peace with Israel, and ^lserved them. So the Syrians feared to
help the children of Ammon any more.
CHAP. 11. AND it came to pass, ³after the year was expired, at the
^a 1 Chr. 20. 1. time when kings go forth *to battle*, that ^aDavid sent Joab, and

---

¹ That is, *Euphrates.* ³ Heb. *at the return of the year*, 1 Kin. 20. 22,
² Or, *Shophach*, 1 Chr. 19. 16.   26. 2 Chr. 36. 10.

---

encamped. Medeba (modern *Madeba*) was
taken from Sihon (Num. xxi. 30), and fell
to Reuben (Josh. xiii. 9, 16) ; in the reign
of Ahaz it seems to have returned to Moab
(Isai. xv. 2), and in the time of the Maccabees to the Amorites (1 Macc. ix. 36, 37).
In Christian times it was a bishop's see.
in the field] *i.e.* in the plain below the
round rocky hill on which the city stood.
9. The two armies of the Ammonites and
the Syrians were drawn up facing one
another ; the Ammonites supported by the
city Rabbah behind them ; the Syrians in
great force, with numerous chariots able to
manœuvre in the plain in front of Medeba.
If Joab advanced against either, he would
have the other in his rear.
12. *for the cities of our God*] This rather
indicates that the relief of Medeba was one
of the immediate objects in view, and consequently that at this time Medeba was
still in the possession of the Reubenites.
To prevent an Israelite city falling into the
hands of a heathen people, and the rites of

Moloch being substituted for the worship
of Jehovah, was a very urgent motive to
valour.
14. *Joab returned*] The great strength of
Rabbah made it hopeless to take it by
assault, and the Syrians were not sufficiently broken (*v.* 15) to make it safe to
undertake a regular siege.
16. *Helam*] The place is unknown. Some
prefer the translation of the Latin Vulgate,
their host came.
18. *seven hundred chariots*] More probable than the *seven thousand* of 1 Chr. xix.
18. The frequent errors in numbers arise
from the practice of expressing numerals by
letters, with one or more *dots* or *dashes* to
indicate hundreds, thousands, &c.
19. *servants to Hadarezer*] This gives us
an idea of the great power of Hadarezer,
and consequently of the strength of Israel
in David's victorious reign.
XI. 1. *after the year was expired*] The
next spring after the escape of the Ammonites into their city (x. 14).

his servants with him, and all Israel; and they destroyed the children of Ammon, and besieged Rabbah. But David tarried
2 still at Jerusalem. ¶ And it came to pass in an eveningtide, that David arose from off his bed, *b*and walked upon the roof of the
king's house : and from the roof he *c*saw a woman washing her-
3 self; and the woman *was* very beautiful to look upon. And David sent and enquired after the woman. And one said, Is not this [1]Bath-sheba, the daughter of [2]Eliam, the wife *d*of Uriah the
4 Hittite? And David sent messengers, and took her; and she came in unto him, and *e*he lay with her; [3]for she was *f*purified
5 from her uncleanness: and she returned unto her house. And the woman conceived, and sent and told David, and said, I *am*
6 with child. ¶ And David sent to Joab, *saying*, Send me Uriah
7 the Hittite. And Joab sent Uriah to David. And when Uriah was come unto him, David demanded *of him* [4]how Joab did, and
8 how the people did, and how the war prospered. And David said to Uriah, Go down to thy house, and *g*wash thy feet. And Uriah departed out of the king's house, and there [5]followed him
9 a mess *of meat* from the king. But Uriah slept at the door of the king's house with all the servants of his lord, and went not
10 down to his house. And when they had told David, saying, Uriah went not down unto his house, David said unto Uriah, Camest thou not from *thy* journey? why *then* didst thou not go
11 down unto thine house? And Uriah said unto David, *h*The ark, and Israel, and Judah, abide in tents; and *i*my lord Joab, and the servants of my lord, are encamped in the open fields; shall I then go into mine house, to eat and to drink, and to lie with my wife? *as* thou livest, and *as* thy soul liveth, I will not
12 do this thing. And David said to Uriah, Tarry here to day also, and to morrow I will let thee depart. So Uriah abode in Jeru-
13 salem that day, and the morrow. And when David had called him, he did eat and drink before him; and he made him *k*drunk : and at even he went out to lie on his bed *l*with the servants of
14 his lord, but went not down to his house. ¶ And it came to pass in the morning, that David *m*wrote a letter to Joab, and sent *it*
15 by the hand of Uriah. And he wrote in the letter, saying, Set ye Uriah in the forefront of the [6]hottest battle, and retire ye
16 *i*from him, that he may *n*be smitten and die. ¶ And it came to pass, when Joab observed the city, that he assigned Uriah unto

b Deut. 22. 8.
c Gen. 34. 2.
Job 31. 1.
Matt. 5. 28.
d ch. 23. 39.

e Ps. 51, title.
f Lev. 15. 19, 28.
& 18. 19.

g Gen. 18. 4.
& 19. 2.

h ch. 7. 2, 6.
i ch. 20. 6.

k Gen. 19. 33, 35.
l ver. 9.

m See 1 Kin. 21. 8, 9.

n ch. 12. 9.

[1] Or, *Bath-shuah,* 1 Chr. 3. 5.
[2] Or, *Ammiel.*
[3] Or, *and when* she *had*
purified herself, &c. she *returned.*
[4] Heb. *of the peace of, &c.*
[5] Heb. *went out after him.*
[6] Heb. *strong.*
[7] Heb. *from after him.*

the children of Ammon] The marg. ref. supplies the word "*the land of,*" which is obviously the right reading.

David tarried at Jerusalem] The Syrians being subdued, the war with Ammon was not of sufficient moment to require David's personal presence. The whole section relating to David's adultery and Uriah's death, from this verse to xii. 26, is omitted in the Book of Chronicles.

2. *an eveningtide*] The evening began at three o'clock in the afternoon.

3. *Eliam*] Or *Ammiel,* (1 Chr. iii. 5), component words being placed in an inverse order. Bath-sheba was the granddaughter of Ahithophel (xxiii. 34).

7. David was forced to stoop to falsehood and dissimulation in the vain hope of hiding his sin.

8. *a mess of meat*] Cp. Gen. xliii. 34. The word denotes the honourable portion given by the host to his chief guest.

11. *the ark*] Perhaps there was a double purpose in taking the Ark; one, to excite to the utmost the enthusiasm of the people for its defence and against the Ammonites; the other, to have the means at hand of *enquiring of the Lord,* which David had found so serviceable.

16. *observed the city*] In the sense of besieging it closely.

17 a place where he knew that valiant men *were*. And the men of the city went out, and fought with Joab : and there fell *some* of the people of the servants of David ; and Uriah the Hittite died

18 also. ¶ Then Joab sent and told David all the things concerning

19 the war ; and charged the messenger saying, When thou hast

20 made an end of telling the matters of the war unto the king, and if so be that the king's wrath arise, and he say unto thee, Wherefore approached ye so nigh unto the city when ye did fight ?

21 knew ye not that they would shoot from the wall ? Who smote

^oAbimelech the son of ^pJerubbesheth ? did not a woman cast a piece of a millstone upon him from the wall, that he died in Thebez ? why went ye nigh the wall ? then say thou, Thy ser-

22 vant Uriah the Hittite is dead also. ¶ So the messenger went, and came and shewed David all that Joab had sent him for.

23 And the messenger said unto David, Surely the men prevailed against us, and came out unto us into the field, and we were

24 upon them even unto the entering of the gate. And the shooters shot from off the wall upon thy servants ; and *some* of the king's servants be dead, and thy servant Uriah the Hittite is dead also.

25 Then David said unto the messenger, Thus shalt thou say unto Joab, Let not this thing ¹displease thee, for the sword devoureth ²one as well as another : make thy battle more strong against

26 the city, and overthrow it : and encourage thou him. ¶ And when the wife of Uriah heard that Uriah her husband was dead,

27 she mourned for her husband. And when the mourning was past, David sent and fetched her to his house, and she ^qbecame his wife, and bare him a son. ¶ But the thing that David had done ³displeased the LORD.

CHAP. 12. AND the LORD sent Nathan unto David. And ^ahe came unto him, and ^bsaid unto him, There were two men in one

2 city ; the one rich, and the other poor. The rich *man* had

3 exceeding many flocks and herds : but the poor *man* had nothing, save one little ewe lamb, which he had bought and nourished up : and it grew up together with him, and with his children ; it did eat of his own ⁴meat, and drank of his own cup, and lay in his bosom, and was unto him as a daughter.

4 And there came a traveller unto the rich man, and he spared to take of his own flock and of his own herd, to dress for the wayfaring man that was come unto him ; but took the poor man's

5 lamb, and dressed it for the man that was come to him. ¶ And David's anger was greatly kindled against the man ; and he said to Nathan, *As* the LORD liveth, the man that hath done this

Margin notes:
^o Judg. 9. 53.
^p Judg. 6. 32, *Jerubbaal.*

^q ch. 12. 9.

^a Ps. 51, title.
^b See ch. 14. 5, &c.
1 Kin. 20. 35—41.
Isai. 5. 3.

---

¹ Heb. *be evil in thine eyes.*   ³ Heb. *was evil in the eyes*   ⁴ Heb. *morsel.*
² Heb. *so and such.*   *of.*

---

17. *the men of the city went out*] i.e. they made a sally and attacked the troops which were blockading the city on that side, chiefly to entice them to pursue them, and so come within shot of the archers who lined the wall (*vv.* 20, 24).

there fell some of the people, &c.] They, too, as well as the brave and faithful Uriah, were victims of David's cruel artifice.

21. *Who smote Abimelech*, &c.] This reference indicates the existence in David's time of the national annals of that period in an accessible form, and the king's habit

of reading, or having read to him, the history of his country. (Cp. Esth. vi. 1.)

26. Bath-sheba's mourning, like that of Abigail (1 Sam. xxv. 39–42), was probably limited to the customary time of seven days.

XII. 1. Nathan came to David as if to ask his judicial decision on the case about to be submitted to him (cp. xiv. 2-11 ; 1 K. xx. 35-41). The circumstances of the story are exquisitely contrived to heighten the pity of David for the oppressed, and his indignation against the oppressor (1 Sam. xxv. 13, 22).

6 thing ¹shall surely die: and he shall restore the lamb ᶜfourfold, ᶜ Ex. 22. 1.
7 because he did this thing, and because he had no pity. ¶ And
   Nathan said to David, Thou *art* the man. Thus saith the LORD
   God of Israel, I ᵈanointed thee king over Israel, and I delivered
8 thee out of the hand of Saul; and I gave thee thy master's
   house, and thy master's wives into thy bosom, and gave thee
   the house of Israel and of Judah; and if *that had been* too little,
   I would moreover have given unto thee such and such things.
9 ᵉWherefore hast thou ᶠdespised the commandment of the LORD,
   to do evil in his sight? ᵍthou hast killed Uriah the Hittite with
   the sword, and hast taken his wife *to be* thy wife, and hast slain
10 him with the sword of the children of Ammon. Now therefore
   ʰthe sword shall never depart from thine house; because thou
   hast despised me, and hast taken the wife of Uriah the Hittite
11 to be thy wife. Thus saith the LORD, Behold, I will raise up
   evil against thee, out of thine own house, and I will ⁱtake thy
   wives before thine eyes, and give *them* unto thy neighbour, and
12 he shall lie with thy wives in the sight of this sun. For thou
   didst *it* secretly: ᵏbut I will do this thing before all Israel, and
13 before the sun. ¶ᵗAnd David said unto Nathan, ᵐI have sinned
   against the LORD. And Nathan said unto David, The LORD
14 also hath ⁿput away thy sin; thou shalt not die. Howbeit,
   because by this deed thou hast given great occasion to the
   enemies of the LORD ᵒto blaspheme, the child also *that is* born
15 unto thee shall surely die. And Nathan departed unto his
   house. ¶And the LORD struck the child that Uriah's wife bare
16 unto David, and it was very sick. David therefore besought
   God for the child; and David ²fasted, and went in, and ᵖlay all
17 night upon the earth. And the elders of his house arose, *and*
   went to him, to raise him up from the earth: but he would not,
18 neither did he eat bread with them. And it came to pass on
   the seventh day, that the child died. And the servants of
   David feared to tell him that the child was dead: for they said,
   Behold, while the child was yet alive, we spake unto him, and
   he would not hearken unto our voice: how will he then ³vex
19 himself, if we tell him that the child is dead? But when David

ᶜ Ex. 22. 1.
Luke 19. 8.

ᵈ 1 Sam. 16.
13.

ᵉ See 1 Sam.
15. 19.
ᶠ Num. 15.
31.
ᵍ ch. 11. 15,
16, 17, 27.
ʰ Amos 7. 9.

ⁱ Deut. 28.
30.
ch. 16. 22.

ᵏ ch. 16. 22.

ᵗ See 1 Sam.
15. 24.
ᵐ ch. 24. 10.
Job 7. 20.
Prov. 28. 13.
ⁿ Mic. 7. 18.
Zech. 3. 4.
ᵒ Isai. 52. 5.
Ezek. 36. 20,
23.
Rom. 2. 24.
ᵖ ch. 13. 31.

---

¹ Or, is *worthy to die*, or, is *a son*
of death, 1 Sam. 26, 16.

² Heb. *fasted a fast.*
³ Heb. *do hurt.*

---

6. *fourfold*] The exact number prescribed
by the Law (see marg. reff.), and acted upon
by Zaccheus. The LXX. has *sevenfold*, as
in Prov. vi. 31.
　8. *and thy master's wives*, &c.] According
to Eastern custom, the royal harem was a
part of the royal inheritance. The prophets
spake in such matters according to the received opinions of their day, and not always
according to the abstract rule of right.
(Cp. Matt. xix. 4-9.)
　11. See marg. reff. In both the points of
David's crime the retribution was according
to his sin. His adultery was punished by
Absalom's outrage, his murder by the bloodshed of domestic broils, which cost the lives
of at least three of his favourite sons, Amnon, Absalom, and Adonijah.
　13. For a comment on David's words,
read Pss. li. and xxxii.

thou shalt not die] Not spoken of the
punishment of death as affixed to adultery
by the Mosaic Law: the application of that
law (Lev. xx. 10; Deut. xxii. 22; John viii.
5) to an absolute Eastern monarch was out
of the question. The death of the soul is
meant (cp. Ezek. xviii. 4, 13, 18).
　16, 17. The death of the infant child of
one of the numerous harem of an Oriental
monarch would in general be a matter of
little moment to the father. The deep
feeling shown by David on this occasion is
both an indication of his affectionate and
tender nature, and also a proof of the
strength of his passion for Bath-sheba. He
went into his most private chamber, his
closet (Matt. vi. 6), and *lay upon the earth*
(xiii. 31), rather "**the ground**," meaning
the floor of his chamber as opposed to his
couch.

saw that his servants whispered, David perceived that the child
was dead: therefore David said unto his servants, Is the child
20 dead? And they said, He is dead. Then David arose from the
earth, and washed, and *q*anointed *himself*, and changed his
apparel, and came into the house of the LORD, and *r*worshipped:
then he came to his own house; and when he required, they
21 set bread before him, and he did eat. Then said his servants
unto him, What thing *is* this that thou hast done? thou didst
fast and weep for the child, *while it was* alive; but when the
22 child was dead, thou didst rise and eat bread. And he said,
While the child was yet alive, I fasted and wept: *s*for I said,
Who can tell *whether* GOD will be gracious to me, that the child
23 may live? But now he is dead, wherefore should I fast? can I
bring him back again? I shall go to him, but *t*he shall not
24 return to me. ¶ And David comforted Bath-sheba his wife,
and went in unto her, and lay with her: and *u*she bare a son,
and *x*he called his name Solomon: and the LORD loved him.
25 And he sent by the hand of Nathan the prophet; and he called
26 his name ¹ Jedidiah, because of the LORD. ¶ And *y*Joab fought
against *z*Rabbah of the children of Ammon, and took the royal
27 city. And Joab sent messengers to David, and said, I have
fought against Rabbah, and have taken the city of waters.
28 Now therefore gather the rest of the people together, and encamp against the city, and take it: lest I take the city, and ²it
29 be called after my name. And David gathered all the people
together, and went to Rabbah, and fought against it, and took
30 it. *a*And he took their king's crown from off his head, the
weight whereof *was* a talent of gold with the precious stones:
and it was *set* on David's head. And he brought forth the spoil
31 of the city ³in great abundance. And he brought forth the
people that *were* therein, and put *them* under saws, and under
harrows of iron, and under axes of iron, and made them pass
through the brickkiln: and thus did he unto all the cities of the
children of Ammon. So David and all the people returned unto
Jerusalem.

q Ruth 3. 3.
r Job 1. 20.

s See Isai.
38. 1, 5.
Jonah 3. 9.

t Job 7. 8, 9,
10.
u Matt. 1. 6.
x 1 Chr. 22.9.

y 1 Chr. 20.1.
z Deut. 3. 11.

a 1 Chr. 20.2.

¹ That is, *Beloved of the*
LORD.

² Heb. *my name be called
upon it.*

³ Heb. *very great.*

---

24. *Solomon*] Or "peaceable," a name
given to him at his circumcision. Cp.
Luke i. 59. The giving of the name *Jedidiah*, by the Lord through Nathan, signified
God's favour to the child, as in the cases of
Abraham, Sarah, and Israel. The name
Jedidiah (which contains the same root as
the name *David*, viz., "to love") indicated. prophetically, what God's Providence
brought about actually, viz., the succession
and glorious reign of Solomon over Israel.
27. *the city of waters*] The lower town of
Rabbah (the modern Ammâm), so called
from a stream which rises within it and
flows through it. The upper town with the
citadel lay on a hill to the north of the
stream, and was probably not tenable for
any length of time after the supply of water
was cut off.
30. *their king's crown*] The word rendered
their king (*Malcham*) is also the name of the
national idol of the Ammonites (Jer. xlix.

1, 3 marg.; Amos i. 15; Zeph. i. 5). Moreover, the weight of the crown, which is calculated to be equal to 100 or 125 pounds
weight, is far too great for a man to wear.
On the whole, it seems most probable that
the idol Malcam is here meant.
31. For the saw as an implement of tor-
ture cp. Heb. xi. 37.
harrows of iron] Or rather *thrashing-
machines* (Isai. xxviii. 27, xli. 15, &c.).
axes] The word so rendered occurs only
here and in 1 Chr. xx. 3. It evidently
means some cutting instrument.
made them pass through the brick-kiln] The
phrase is that always used of the cruel process of making their children *pass through*
the fire to Moloch, and it is likely that
David punished this idolatrous practice by
inflicting something similar upon the worshippers of Moloch. The cruelty of these
executions belongs to the barbarous manners
of the age, and was provoked by the conduct

CHAP. 13. AND it came to pass after this, *a*that Absalom the son *a* ch. 3. 2. 3.
of David had a fair sister, whose name *was* *b*Tamar; and Amnon *b* 1 Chr. 3. 9.
2 the son of David loved her. And Amnon was so vexed, that
he fell sick for his sister Tamar; for she *was* a virgin; and
3 ¹Amnon thought it hard for him to do any thing to her. But
Amnon had a friend, whose name *was* Jonadab, *c*the son of *c* See 1 Sam.
Shimeah David's brother: and Jonadab *was* a very subtil man. 16. 9.
4 And he said unto him, Why *art* thou, *being* the king's son,
²lean ³from day to day? wilt thou not tell me? And Amnon
5 said unto him, I love Tamar, my brother Absalom's sister. And
Jonadab said unto him, Lay thee down on thy bed, and make
thyself sick: and when thy father cometh to see thee, say unto
him, I pray thee, let my sister Tamar come, and give me meat,
and dress the meat in my sight, that I may see *it*, and eat *it* at
6 her hand. ¶So Amnon lay down, and made himself sick: and
when the king was come to see him, Amnon said unto the king,
I pray thee, let Tamar my sister come, and *d*make me a couple *d* Gen. 18. 6.
7 of cakes in my sight, that I may eat at her hand. Then David
sent home to Tamar, saying, Go now to thy brother Amnon's
8 house, and dress him meat. So Tamar went to her brother
Amnon's house; and he was laid down. And she took ⁴flour,
and kneaded *it*, and made cakes in his sight, and did bake the
9 cakes. And she took a pan, and poured *them* out before him;
but he refused to eat. And Amnon said, *e*Have out all men *e* Gen. 45. 1.
10 from me. And they went out every man from him. ¶And
Amnon said unto Tamar, Bring the meat into the chamber, that
I may eat of thine hand. And Tamar took the cakes which
she had made, and brought *them* into the chamber to Amnon
11 her brother. And when she had brought *them* unto him to eat,
he *f*took hold of her, and said unto her, Come lie with me, my *f* Gen. 39. 12.
12 sister. And she answered him, Nay, my brother, do not ⁵force
me; for *g*⁶no such thing ought to be done in Israel: do not *g* Lev. 18. 9,
13 thou this *h*folly. And I, whither shall I cause my shame to go? 11.
and as for thee, thou shalt be as one of the fools in Israel. & 20. 17.
Now therefore, I pray thee, speak unto the king; *i*for he will *h* Judg.19.23.
& 20. 6.
i See Lev.
18. 9, 11.

¹ Heb. *it was marvellous,* ² Heb. *thin.* ⁵ Heb. *humble me,* Gen. 34. 2.
or, *hidden in the eyes of* ³ Heb. *morning by morning.* ⁶ Heb. *it ought not so to be*
Amnon. See Gen. 18. 14. ⁴ Or, *paste.* *done.*

---

of the Ammonites (x. 1-4; 1 Sam. xi. 1, 2),
but is utterly indefensible under the light
of the Gospel. If Rabbah was taken before
David's penitence, he may have been in an
unusually harsh and severe frame of mind.
The unpleasant recollection of Uriah's
death would be likely to sour and irritate
him to the utmost.
XIII. 1. The history here, down to the
end of ch. xxiii. (excepting a few particulars), is omitted in the Book of Chronicles.
3. *Shimeah*] Called *Shamma* (marg. ref.),
was Jesse's third son.
subtil] Lit., *Wise.* The word is generally
used in a good sense, but here, and in Job
v. 13, it means *crafty.*
5, 6. *make thyself sick*] "**Feign thyself to
be ill.**" (Cp. xiv. 2.)
that I may see it] He was to feign that he
could not fancy anything that came from
the kitchen, but that if he saw it cooked
he should be able to eat it.

6, 9. *make me cakes...a pan*] The words
here used occur nowhere else, and the etymology is doubtful. Some particular kind
of cake or pudding is meant (*v.* 8), called a
lebibah ; according to some, it was, from its
etymology, shaped like a heart.
9. The dish into which she poured the
lebibah was doubtless borne to him by one
of the servants into the chamber where he
lay, and from which, the doors being open,
he could see the outer room where Tamar
prepared the meat.
12. Tamar's words are a verbal quotation
from Gen. xxxiv. 7. The natural inference
is that Tamar knew the passage in Genesis,
and wished to profit by the warning it contained. (Cp. also *v.* 13.)
13. *my shame*] Better, "**my reproach.**"
Cp. Gen. xxx. 23, xxxiv. 14 : 1 Sam. xi. 2.
speak unto the king, &c.] It cannot be
inferred with certainty from this that marriages were usual among half brothers and

14 not withhold me from thee. Howbeit he would not hearken
unto her voice : but, being stronger than she, *k* forced her, and
15 lay with her. ¶ Then Amnon hated her [1] exceedingly; so that
the hatred wherewith he hated her *was* greater than the love
wherewith he had loved her. And Amnon said unto her, Arise,
16 be gone. And she said unto him, *There is* no cause : this evil
in sending me away *is* greater than the other that thou didst
17 unto me. But he would not hearken unto her. Then he called
his servant that ministered unto him, and said, Put now this
18 *woman* out from me, and bolt the door after her. And *she had*
[1] a garment of divers colours upon her : for with such robes were
the king's daughters *that were* virgins apparelled. Then his
19 servant brought her out, and bolted the door after her. ¶ And
Tamar put *m* ashes on her head, and rent her garment of divers
colours that *was* on her, and *n* laid her hand on her head, and
20 went on crying. And Absalom her brother said unto her,
Hath [2] Amnon thy brother been with thee ? but hold now thy
peace, my sister : he *is* thy brother ; [3] regard not this thing. So
Tamar remained [4] desolate in her brother Absalom's house.
21 ¶ But when king David heard of all these things, he was very
22 wroth. And Absalom spake unto his brother Amnon *o* neither
good nor bad : for Absalom *p* hated Amnon, because he had forced
23 his sister Tamar. ¶ And it came to pass after two full years, that
Absalom *q* had sheepshearers in Baal-hazor, which *is* beside
24 Ephraim : and Absalom invited all the king's sons. And Absalom came to the king, and said, Behold now, thy servant hath
sheepshearers ; let the king, I beseech thee, and his servants go
25 with thy servant. And the king said to Absalom, Nay, my
son, let us not all now go, lest we be chargeable unto thee.
And he pressed him : howbeit he would not go, but blessed him.
26 Then said Absalom, If not, I pray thee, let my brother Amnon
go with us. And the king said unto him, Why should he go
27 with thee ? But Absalom pressed him, that he let Amnon and
28 all the king's sons go with him. ¶ Now Absalom had commanded his servants, saying, Mark ye now when Amnon's

k Deut. 22.
25.
See ch. 12.
11.

l Gen. 37. 3.
Judg. 5. 30.
Ps. 45. 14.

m Josh. 7. 6.
ch. 1. 2.
Job 2. 12.
n Jer. 2. 37.

o Gen. 24. 50.
& 31. 24.
p Lev. 19.
17, 18.
q See Gen.
38. 12, 13.
1 Sam. 25. 4,
36.

---

[1] Heb. *with great hatred greatly.*   [2] Heb. *Aminon.*   [3] Heb. *set not thine heart.* [4] Heb. *and desolate.*

---

sisters in the time of David. The Levitical
law forbade them (marg. ref.), and Tamar
may have merely wished to temporise. On
the other hand, the debasing and unhu-
manizing institution of the harem, itself
contrary to the law of Moses (Deut. xvii.
17), may well have led to other deviations
from its precepts, and the precedent of
Abraham (Gen. xx. 12) may have seemed
to give some sanction to this particular
breach of it.

16. The sense of the passage probably is,
*And she spake with him on account of this
great wrong in sending me away, greater than
the other wrong which thou hast done me* (said
she), *but he hearkened not unto her.* The
Heb. text is probably corrupt, and the
writer blends Tamar's words with his own
narrative.

18. *a garment of divers colours*] See Gen.
xxxvii. 3. Some prefer here (and there) "a
tunic with sleeves," a tunic reaching to the

extremities, *i.e.* the hands and feet, and
worn over the common tunic, in room of a
robe.

19. *laid her hand on her head*] To hold on
the ashes (see marg. reff.).

went on crying] *i.e.* "went away, crying
out as she went."

21. The LXX. adds, what is a good explanation, *but he did not vex the spirit of
Amnon his son, because he loved him, because
he was his first-born.* This want of justice in
David's conduct, and favouritism to Amnon,
probably rankled in Absalom's heart, and
was the first seed of his after rebellion.

23. Sheepshearing was always a time of
feasting (marg. reff.). Baal-hazor is not
known.

26. He mentions Amnon as being the
king's first-born. If he could not have the
king's company, let him at least have that
of the heir apparent, and the king's other
sons.

^rheart is merry with wine, and when I say unto you, Smite   *r* Judg. 19.
Amnon; then kill him, fear not: ¹have not I commanded you? 6, 9, 22.
29 be courageous, and be ²valiant. And the servants of Absalom Ruth 3. 7.
did unto Amnon as Absalom had commanded. Then all the 1 Sam. 25.
king's sons arose, and every man ³gat him up upon his mule, 36.
30 and fled. ¶ And it came to pass, while they were in the way, Esth. 1. 10.
that tidings came to David, saying, Absalom hath slain all the Ps. 104. 15.
31 king's sons, and there is not one of them left. Then the king
arose, and ^stare his garments, and ^tlay on the earth; and all *s* ch. 1. 11.
32 his servants stood by with their clothes rent. And ^uJonadab, *t* ch. 12. 16.
the son of Shimeah David's brother, answered and said, Let *u* ver. 3.
not my lord suppose *that* they have slain all the young men
the king's sons; for Amnon only is dead: for by the ⁴appoint-
ment of Absalom this hath been ⁵determined from the day that
33 he forced his sister Tamar. Now therefore ^xlet not my lord the *x* ch. 19. 19.
king take the thing to his heart, to think that all the king's
34 sons are dead: for Amnon only is dead. ^yBut Absalom fled. *y* ver. 38.
¶ And the young man that kept the watch lifted up his eyes,
and looked, and, behold, there came much people by the way
35 of the hill side behind him. And Jonadab said unto the king,
Behold, the king's sons come: ⁶as thy servant said, so it is.
36 And it came to pass, as soon as he had made an end of speaking,
that, behold, the king's sons came, and lifted up their voice and
wept: and the king also and all his servants wept ⁷very sore.
37 ¶ But Absalom fled, and went to ^zTalmai, the son of ⁸Ammihud, *z* ch. 3. 3.
38 king of Geshur. And David mourned for his son every day. So
Absalom fled, and went to ^aGeshur, and was there three years. *a* ch. 14. 23,
39 And the *soul of* king David ⁹longed to go forth unto Absalom: 32.
for he was ^bcomforted concerning Amnon, seeing he was & 15. 8.
dead. *b* Gen. 38. 12.

CHAP. 14. NOW Joab the son of Zeruiah perceived that the king's
2 heart *was* ^atoward Absalom. And Joab sent to ^bTekoah, and *a* ch. 13. 39.
fetched thence a wise woman, and said unto her, I pray thee, *b* 2 Chr. 11. 6.
feign thyself to be a mourner, ^cand put on now mourning *c* See Ruth
apparel, and anoint not thyself with oil, but be as a woman that 3. 3.

¹ Or, *will you not, since I*   ⁴ Heb. *mouth.*   ⁷ Heb. *with a great weeping*
 have commanded you?   ⁵ Or, *settled.*   *greatly.*
 Josh. 1. 9.   ⁶ Heb. *according to the*   ⁸ Or, *Ammihur.*
² Heb. *sons of valour.*   *word of thy servant.*   ⁹ Or, *was consumed*, Ps. 84.
³ Heb. *rode.*   2.

29. *upon his mule*] So in 1 K. i. 33, 38
the mule is the royal animal on which
David himself rides. In 2 Sam. xviii. 9
Absalom rides upon a mule.
32. The history supplies another (cp. *v.* 3)
instance of Jonadab's subtlety and sagacity.
He at once gave the true explanation of the
catastrophe at Baal-hazor, in spite of the
false rumour.
by the appointment of Absalom, &c.] Meaning that Absalom's resolution to slay Amnon
had been formed at the time, and only waited
an opportunity to give expression to it.
34. *Absalom fled*] This is the sequel to
v. 29. The king's sons rose from table and
fled, and Absalom taking advantage of the
confusion, also escaped and fled. This information is inserted here to account for
the king's sons returning unmolested.

35. The watchman, as his duty was, had
sent immediate notice to the king that he
saw a crowd approaching (see 2 K. ix. 17–
20). Jonadab, who was with the king, was
prompt to give the explanation.
37. See marg. ref.
Ammihur (see marg.) is found as a Punic
name.
39. *longed to go forth*] Rather, " **longed
after Absalom**," literally, *was consumed in
going forth*, with a sense of disappointed
hope.
XIV. 2. *Tekoah*] In the south of Judah,
six miles from Bethlehem, the modern
Tekua. The rough, wild district was well
suited for the lawless profession of the wise
woman; it abounds in caves, as does the
country near Endor.

d ver. 19.
Ex. 4. 15.

e 1 Sam. 20.
41.
h. 1. 2.
f See 2 Kin.
6. 26, 28.
g See ch. 12.
1.

h Num. 35.
19.
Deut. 19. 12.

i Gen. 27. 13.
1 Sam. 25. 24.
Matt. 27. 25.
k ch. 3. 28,
29.
1 Kin. 2. 33.

l Num. 35.
19.

m 1 Sam. 14.
45.
Acts 27. 34.

n Judg. 20. 2.
o ch. 13. 37,
38.
p Job 34. 15.
Heb. 9. 27.

3 had a long time mourned for the dead : and come to the king, and speak on this manner unto him. So Joab *d*put the words 4 in her mouth. ¶And when the woman of Tekoah spake to the king, she *e*fell on her face to the ground, and did obeisance, and 5 said, [1]Help, O king. And the king said unto her, What aileth thee? And she answered, *g*I *am* indeed a widow woman, and 6 mine husband is dead. And thy handmaid had two sons, and they two strove together in the field, and *there was* [2]none to part 7 them, but the one smote the other, and slew him. And, behold, *h*the whole family is risen against thine handmaid, and they said, Deliver him that smote his brother, that we may kill him, for the life of his brother whom he slew ; and we will destroy the heir also : and so they shall quench my coal which is left, and shall not leave to my husband *neither* name nor remainder 8 [3]upon the earth. ¶And the king said unto the woman, Go to 9 thine house, and I will give charge concerning thee. And the woman of Tekoah said unto the king, My lord, O king, *i*the iniquity *be* on me, and on my father's house : *k*and the king and 10 his throne *be* guiltless. And the king said, Whosoever saith *ought* unto thee, bring him to me, and he shall not touch thee 11 any more. Then said she, I pray thee, let the king remember the LORD thy God, [4]that thou wouldest not suffer *l*the revengers of blood to destroy any more, lest they destroy my son. And he said, *m*As the LORD liveth, there shall not one hair of thy 12 son fall to the earth. ¶Then the woman said, Let thine handmaid, I pray thee, speak *one* word unto my lord the king. And 13 he said, Say on. And the woman said, Wherefore then hast thou thought such a thing against *n*the people of God? for the king doth speak this thing as one which is faulty, in that the 14 king doth not fetch home again *o*his banished. For we *p*must needs die, and *are* as water spilt on the ground, which cannot

[1] Heb. *Save.*
[2] Heb. *no deliverer between them.*
[3] Heb. *upon the face of the earth.*
[4] Heb. *that the revenger of blood do not multiply to destroy.*

---

3. *come to the king*] The king as a judge was accessible to all his subjects (xv. 2 ; cp. 1 K. iii. 16).

4. *spake*] Seems to be an accidental error for *came*, which is found in many MSS. and Versions.

Help] Lit., *save* (see marg.). It is the same cry as *Hosanna, i.e. save now* (Ps. cxviii. 25).

7. *the whole family*, &c.] This indicates that all the king's sons, and the whole court, were against Absalom, and that the knowledge of this was what hindered David from yielding to his affection and recalling him.

8. *I will give charge*, &c.] Indirectly granting her petition, and assenting that her son's life should be spared.

9. *the iniquity be on me*, &c.] Cp. the principle in Gen. ix. 5, 6 ; Num. xxxv. 30-34. The woman therefore says, if there is any such guilt in sparing my son, may it rest upon me and my house, not on David and his throne. Cp. iii. 28. The cunning speech of the woman extracted a more direct promise of protection from the king (*v.* 1).

12. Having at last obtained what she wanted, the king's oath that her son should not die, she proceeds to the case of Absalom. The meaning of *v.* 13 may be paraphrased thus :—" If you have done right as regards my son, how is it that you harbour such a purpose of vengeance against Absalom as to keep him, one of God's people, an outcast in a heathen country, far from the worship of the God of Israel? Upon your own showing you are guilty of a great fault in not allowing Absalom to return."

the king doth speak, &c.] Literally, " **And from the king speaking this word** (this sentence of absolution to my son) he is **as one guilty** ; *i.e.* the sentence you have pronounced in favour of my son condemns your own conduct towards Absalom."

his banished] The use of the word as applied to one of the people of God driven into a heathen land, is well illustrated by Deut. xxx. 4, 5 ; Jer. xl. 12 ; Mic. iv. 6 ; Zeph. iii. 19.

14. *neither doth God respect any person*] Some prefer the margin : " **And God does not take away life**, in the case of every sin

be gathered up again; [1]neither doth God respect *any* person: yet doth he [q]devise means, that his banished be not expelled 15 from him. Now therefore that I am come to speak of this thing unto my lord the king, *it is* because the people have made me afraid : and thy handmaid said, I will now speak unto the king; it may be that the king will perform the request of his hand- 16 maid. For the king will hear, to deliver his handmaid out of the hand of the man *that would* destroy me and my son together 17 out of the inheritance of God. Then thine handmaid said, The word of my lord the king shall now be [2]comfortable : for [r]as an angel of God, so *is* my lord the king [3]to discern good and bad : 18 therefore the LORD thy God will be with thee. ¶ Then the king answered and said unto the woman, Hide not from me, I pray thee, the thing that I shall ask thee. And the woman said, Let 19 my lord the king now speak. And the king said, *Is not* the hand of Joab with thee in all this ? And the woman answered and said, *As* thy soul liveth, my lord the king, none can turn to the right hand or to the left from ought that my lord the king hath spoken : for thy servant Joab, he bade me, and [s]he put all these 20 words in the mouth of thine handmaid : to fetch about this form of speech hath thy servant Joab done this thing: and my lord *is* wise, [t]according to the wisdom of an angel of God, to know 21 all *things* that *are* in the earth. ¶ And the king said unto Joab, Behold now, I have done this thing : go therefore, bring the 22 young man Absalom again. And Joab fell to the ground on his face, and bowed himself, and [4]thanked the king : and Joab said, To day thy servant knoweth that I have found grace in thy sight, my lord, O king, in that the king hath fulfilled the re- 23 quest of [5]his servant. So Joab arose [u]and went to Geshur, and 24 brought Absalom to Jerusalem. And the king said, Let him turn to his own house, and let him [x]not see my face. So Absalom returned to his own house, and saw not the king's face. 25 ¶ [6]But in all Israel there was none to be so much praised as Absalom for his beauty : [y]from the sole of his foot even to the 26 crown of his head there was no blemish in him. And when he polled his head, (for it was at every year's end that he polled *it* : because *the hair* was heavy on him, therefore he polled it :) he weighed the hair of his head at two hundred shekels after the 27 king's weight. And [z]unto Absalom there were born three sons, and one daughter, whose name *was* Tamar : she was a woman

[q] Num. 35. 15, 25, 28.

[r] ver. 20. ch. 19. 27.

[s] ver. 3.

[t] ver. 17. ch. 19. 27.

[u] ch. 13. 37.

[x] Gen. 43. 3. ch. 3. 13.

[y] Isai. 1. 6.

[z] See ch. 18. 18.

[1] Or, *because God hath not taken away* his *life, he hath also devised means, &c.*
[2] Heb. *for rest.*
[3] Heb. *to hear.*
[4] Heb. *blessed.*
[5] Or, *thy.*
[6] Heb. *And as Absalom there was not a beautiful man in all Israel to praise greatly.*

---

that deserves death, *e.g.* David's own case (xii. 13), **but devises devices that the wanderer may not be** for ever **expelled from** him, *i.e.* for the return of penitent sinners."

15. *the people have made me afraid*] She pretends still that her suit was a real one, and that she was in fear of the people ("the whole family," *v.* 7) setting upon her and her son.

17. *as an angel of God*] Rather, as "the" Angel of God ; and therefore whatever David decided would be right.

24. *Let him not see my face*] We are not told why David adopted this half-measure.

Possibly Bath-sheba's influence may have been exerted to keep Absalom in disgrace for the sake of Solomon.

26. *two hundred shekels*, &c.] The exact weight cannot be determined. If these *shekels after the king's weight* were the same as *shekels of the sanctuary*, the weight would be about 6 lbs., which is incredible ; *twenty* shekels is more probable.

27. *three sons*] These probably died in infancy (see marg. ref.) From Tamar must have been born Maachah, the mother of Abijah, and the favourite wife of Rehoboam (1 K. xv. 2; 2 Chr. xi. 20–22).

28 of a fair countenance. ¶ So Absalom dwelt two full years in
29 Jerusalem, ^aand saw not the king's face. Therefore Absalom
sent for Joab, to have sent him to the king; but he would not
come to him: and when he sent again the second time, he would
30 not come. Therefore he said unto his servants, See, Joab's field
is ¹near mine, and he hath barley there; go and set it on fire.
31 And Absalom's servants set the field on fire. Then Joab arose,
and came to Absalom unto *his* house, and said unto him, Where-
32 fore have thy servants set my field on fire? And Absalom
answered Joab, Behold, I sent unto thee, saying, Come hither,
that I may send thee to the king, to say, Wherefore am I come
from Geshur? *it had been* good for me *to have been* there still:
now therefore let me see the king's face; and if there be *any*
33 iniquity in me, let him kill me. So Joab came to the king, and
told him: and when he had called for Absalom, he came to the
king, and bowed himself on his face to the ground before the
king: and the king ^bkissed Absalom.

CHAP. 15. AND ^ait came to pass after this, that Absalom ^bprepared
2 him chariots and horses, and fifty men to run before him. And
Absalom rose up early, and stood beside the way of the gate:
and it was *so*, that when any man that had a controversy ²came
to the king for judgment, then Absalom called unto him, and
said, Of what city *art* thou? And he said, Thy servant *is* of one
3 of the tribes of Israel. And Absalom said unto him, See, thy
matters *are* good and right; but ³*there is* no man *deputed* of the
4 king to hear thee. Absalom said moreover, ^cOh that I were
made judge in the land, that every man which hath any suit or
5 cause might come unto me, and I would do him justice! And
it was *so*, that when any man came nigh *to him* to do him
obeisance, he put forth his hand, and took him, and kissed him.
6 And on this manner did Absalom to all Israel that came to the
king for judgment: ^dso Absalom stole the hearts of the men of
7 Israel. ¶ And it came to pass, ^eafter forty years, that Absalom
said unto the king, I pray thee, let me go and pay my vow,

Marginal references:
^a ver. 24.
^b Gen. 33. 4. Luke 15. 20.
^a ch. 12. 11.
^b 1 Kin. 1. 5.
^c Judg. 9. 29.
^d Rom. 16. 18.
^e 1 Sam. 16. 1.

¹ Heb. *near my place.*
² Heb. *to come.*
³ Or, *none will hear thee from the king* downward.

---

33. *kissed*] This was the pledge of reconciliation. (See marg. reff. and Gen. xlv. 15.)
XV. **1.** *And it came to pass*, &c.] The
working out of Nathan's prophecy (marg.
ref.) is the clue to the course of the narrative. How long after Absalom's return
these events occurred we are not told.
2. *beside the way of the gate*] See Ruth iv.
1 note.
3. To flatter each man by pronouncing a
favourable verdict in his case, to excite a
sense of grievance and discontent by cen-
suring the king for remissness in trying the
causes brought before him by his subjects,
and to suggest a sure and easy remedy for
all such grievances, viz. to make Absalom
king ; all this, coupled with great affability
and courtesy, which his personal beauty and
high rank made all the more effective, were
the arts by which Absalom worked his way
into favour with the people, who were light
and fickle as himself.

6. *stole the hearts*] *i.e.* deceived *them*, for
so the same phrase means (Gen. xxxi. 20,
26).
7. *forty years*] An obvious clerical error,
though a very ancient one for *four years*,
which may date from Absalom's return
from Geshur, or from his reconciliation with
David, or from the commencement of the
criminal schemes to which *v.* 1 refers.
Hebron] This, as having been the old
capital of David's kingdom and Absalom's
birthplace, was well chosen. It was a natural
centre, had probably many inhabitants discontented at the transfer of the government
ment to Jerusalem, and contained many of
the friends of Absalom's youth. As the
place of his birth (cp. 1 Sam. xx. 6), it
afforded a plausible pretext for holding
there the great sacrificial feast ("the serving the Lord," *v.* 8), which Absalom pretended to have vowed to hold to the glory
of God.

8 which I have vowed unto the LORD, in Hebron. *For thy ser- *f* 1 Sam. 16.
vant *g* vowed a vow *h* while I abode at Geshur in Syria, saying, 2.
If the LORD shall bring me again indeed to Jerusalem, then I 20, 21.
9 will serve the LORD. And the king said unto him, Go in peace. *h* ch. 13. 38.
10 So he arose, and went to Hebron. ¶ But Absalom sent spies
throughout all the tribes of Israel, saying, As soon as ye hear
the sound of the trumpet, then ye shall say, Absalom reigneth
11 in Hebron. And with Absalom went two hundred men out of
Jerusalem, *that were* *i* called; and they went *k* in their simplicity, *i* 1 Sam. 9.
12 and they knew not any thing. And Absalom sent for Ahitho- 13. & 16. 3.
phel the Gilonite, *l* David's counsellor, from his city, *even* from *k* Gen. 20. 5.
m Giloh, while he offered sacrifices. And the conspiracy was *l* Ps. 41. 9.
strong; for the people *n* increased continually with Absalom. *m* Josh. 17.
13 ¶ And there came a messenger to David, saying, *o* The hearts of 51.
14 the men of Israel are after Absalom. And David said unto all *o* ver. 6.
his servants that *were* with him at Jerusalem, Arise, and let us *p* ch. 19. 9.
p flee; for we shall not *else* escape from Absalom: make speed Ps. 3, title.
to depart, lest he overtake us suddenly, and ¹ bring evil upon us,
15 and smite the city with the edge of the sword. And the king's
servants said unto the king, Behold, thy servants *are ready to do*
16 whatsoever my lord the king shall ² appoint. And *q* the king *q* Ps. 3, title.
went forth, and all his household ³ after him. And the king
left *r* ten women, *which were* concubines, to keep the house. *r* ch. 16. 21,
17 ¶ And the king went forth, and all the people after him, and 22.
18 tarried in a place that was far off. And all his servants passed
on beside him; *s* and all the Cherethites, and all the Pelethites, *s* ch. 8. 18.
and all the Gittites, six hundred men which came after him
19 from Gath, passed on before the king. Then said the king to
t Ittai the Gittite, Wherefore goest thou also with us? return to *t* ch. 13. 2.
thy place, and abide with the king: for thou *art* a stranger, and
20 also an exile. Whereas thou camest *but* yesterday, should I
this day ⁴ make thee go up and down with us? seeing I go
u whither I may, return thou, and take back thy brethren: mercy *u* 1 Sam. 23.
21 and truth *be* with thee. And Ittai answered the king, and said, 13.

¹ Heb. *thrust.* ³ Heb. *at his feet.* ⁴ Heb. *make thee wander*
² Heb. *choose.*   *in going.*

---

12. *Ahithophel*] It has been with great
probability supposed that Ahithophel was
estranged from David by personal resentment for his conduct in the matter of Bath-
sheba and Uriah (see xi. 3).

while he offered sacrifices] Rather, that
Absalom sent for Ahithophel to be present
when he offered the sacrifices; the intention
being that all who partook of the sacrifice
should be bound together to prosecute the
enterprise. Absalom, too, would take advantage of the excitement of the great feast
to inflame the ardour of the guests, and
pledge them irrevocably to his cause.

14. *and smite the city*] David's kind nature induced him to spare Jerusalem the
horrors of a siege, and the risk of being
taken by assault. He had no standing army
with which to resist this sudden attack from
so unexpected a quarter. Possibly too he
remembered Nathan's prophecy (xii. 10–12).

18. *passed on*] Rather, "crossed" the
brook Kidron, as in *vv.* 22, 23.

Gittites] During David's residence in the
country of the Philistines he attached such
a band to himself; and after the settlement
of his kingdom, and the subjugation of the
Philistines, the band received recruits from
Gath, perhaps with the king of Gath's consent. They were now under the command
of Ittai the Gittite, a foreigner (*v.* 19), and
"his brethren" (*v.* 20). The number 600
probably indicates that this band or regi-
ment of Gittites had its origin in David's
band of 600 (1 Sam. xxiii. 13, xxvii. 2).
They were at first, it is likely, all Israelites,
then Gittites mixed with Israelites, and at
last all Gittites.

20. *thou camest but yesterday*] Meaning,
"Thou art not a native Israelite, but only a
sojourner for a few years, it is not reason
therefore that thou shouldst share my calamities. Return to thy place, thy adopted
home Jerusalem, and to the king, Absalom"
(*vv.* 34, 35).

*As the LORD liveth, and *as* my lord the king liveth, surely in what place my lord the king shall be, whether in death or life, 22 even there also will thy servant be. And David said to Ittai, Go and pass over. And Ittai the Gittite passed over, and all 23 his men, and all the little ones that *were* with him. And all the country wept with a loud voice, and all the people passed over : the king also himself passed over the brook ¹Kidron, and all the people passed over, toward the way of the *y*wilderness.

y ch. 16. 2.
z Num. 4. 15.

24 ¶ And lo Zadok also, and all the Levites *were* with him, *z*bearing the ark of the covenant of God : and they set down the ark of God ; and Abiathar went up, until all the people had done 25 passing out of the city. And the king said unto Zadok, Carry back the ark of God into the city : if I shall find favour in the eyes of the LORD, he *a*will bring me again, and shew me *both* it, 26 and his habitation : but if he thus say, I have no *b*delight in thee ; behold, *here am* I, *c*let him do to me as seemeth good unto 27 him. The king said also unto Zadok the priest, *Art not* thou a *d*seer ? return into the city in peace, and *e*your two sons with 28 you, Ahimaaz thy son, and Jonathan the son of Abiathar. See, *f*I will tarry in the plain of the wilderness, until there come 29 word from you to certify me. Zadok therefore and Abiathar carried the ark of God again to Jerusalem : and they tarried 30 there. ¶ And David went up by the ascent of *mount* Olivet, ²and wept as he went up, and *g*had his head covered, and he went *h*barefoot : and all the people that *was* with him *i*covered every man his head, and they went up, *k*weeping as they went 31 up. And *one* told David, saying, *l*Ahithophel *is* among the conspirators with Absalom. And David said, O LORD, I pray 32 thee, *m*turn the counsel of Ahithophel into foolishness. ¶ And it came to pass, that *when* David was come to the top *of the mount*, where he worshipped God, behold, Hushai the *n*Archite came to meet him *o*with his coat rent, and earth upon his head : 33 unto whom David said, If thou passest on with me, then thou 34 shalt be *p*a burden unto me : but if thou return to the city, and say unto Absalom, *q*I will be thy servant, O king ; *as* I *have been* thy father's servant hitherto, so *will* I now also *be* thy servant : then mayest thou for me defeat the counsel of Ahithophel. 35 And *hast thou* not there with thee Zadok and Abiathar the priests ? therefore it shall be, *that* what thing soever thou shalt hear out of the king's house, *r*thou shalt tell *it* to Zadok and 36 Abiathar the priests. Behold, *they have* there *s*with them their two sons, Ahimaaz Zadok's *son*, and Jonathan Abiathar's *son* ; and by them ye shall send unto me every thing that ye can hear. 37 So Hushai *t*David's friend came into the city, *u*and Absalom came into Jerusalem.

a Ps. 43. 3.
b Num. 14. 8.
ch. 22. 20.
1 Kin. 10. 9.
2 Chr. 9. 8.
Isai. 62. 4.
c 1 Sam. 3.
18.
d 1 Sam. 9. 9.
e See ch. 17.
17.
f ch. 17. 16.

g ch. 19. 4.
Esth. 6. 12.
h Isai. 20. 2, 4.
i Jer. 14. 3, 4.
k Ps. 126. 6.
l Ps. 3. 1, 2.
& 55. 12, &c.
m ch. 16. 23.
& 17. 14, 23.

n Josh. 16. 2.
o ch. 1. 2.

p ch. 19. 35.

q ch. 16. 19.

r ch. 17. 15,
16.
s ver. 27.

t ch. 16. 16.
1 Chr. 27. 33.
u ch. 16. 15.

¹ Called, John 18. 1, *Cedron.*   ² Heb. *going up, and weeping.*

---

24. *Abiathar went up*] *i.e.* continued to ascend the Mount of Olives. Abiathar was High Priest (1 K. ii. 35). Perhaps Zadok is addressed by David (*v.* 25) as the chief of those who were actually bearing the Ark.

27. *Art not thou a seer?*] If the text be correct, the sense would be, *Art thou not a seer? therefore go back to the city, and observe, and certify me of what thou seest* (*v.* 28). Others, by a slight alteration of the original

text, read "Art not thou a chief" (priest), &c.

30. *his head covered*] See marg. reff. and Jer. xiv. 3, 4 ; Ezek. xxiv. 17 ; the sign of deep mourning.

32. Render ... "**when David was come to the top** of the mount **where** people **worship God.**" The type here, and in xvi. 1, is used almost as a proper name. No doubt there was a high-place upon the top of the Mount of Olives.

CHAP. 16. AND *a*when David was a little past the top *of the hill,*
behold, *b*Ziba the servant of Mephibosheth met him, with a
couple of asses saddled, and upon them two hundred *loaves* of
bread, and an hundred bunches of raisins, and an hundred of
2 summer fruits, and a bottle of wine. And the king said unto
Ziba, What meanest thou by these? And Ziba said, The asses
be for the king's household to ride on; and the bread and
summer fruit for the young men to eat; and the wine, *c*that
3 such as be faint in the wilderness may drink. And the king
said, And where *is* thy master's son? *d*And Ziba said unto the
king, Behold, he abideth at Jerusalem: for he said, To day shall
4 the house of Israel restore me the kingdom of my father. *e*Then
said the king to Ziba, Behold, thine *are* all that *pertained* unto
Mephibosheth. And Ziba said, *1*I humbly beseech thee *that* I
5 may find grace in thy sight, my lord, O king. ¶ And when king
David came to Bahurim, behold, thence came out a man of the
family of the house of Saul, whose name *was f*Shimei, the son of
6 Gera: *2*he came forth, and cursed still as he came. And he cast
stones at David, and at all the servants of king David: and all
the people and all the mighty men *were* on his right hand and
7 on his left. And thus said Shimei when he cursed, Come out,
8 come out, thou *3*bloody man, and thou *g*man of Belial: the
LORD hath *h*returned upon thee all *i*the blood of the house of
Saul, in whose stead thou hast reigned; and the LORD hath
delivered the kingdom into the hand of Absalom thy son: and,
*4*behold, thou *art taken* in thy mischief, because thou *art* a
9 bloody man. ¶ Then said Abishai the son of Zeruiah unto the
king, Why should this *k*dead dog *l*curse my lord the king? let
10 me go over, I pray thee, and take off his head. And the king
said, *m*What have I to do with you, ye sons of Zeruiah? so let

a ch. 15. 30, 32.
b ch. 9. 2.

c ch. 15. 23. & 17. 29.
d ch. 19. 27.
e Prov. 18. 13.

f ch. 19. 16. 1 Kin. 2. 8, 44.

g Deut. 13. 13.
h Judg. 0.
24, 56, 57.
1 Kin. 2. 32, 33.
i See ch. 1. 16.
& 3. 28, 29.
& 4. 11. 12.
k 1 Sam. 24. 14.
l Ex. 22. 28.
m ch. 19. 22.
1 Pet. 2. 23.

1 Heb. *I do obeisance.*
2 Or, *he still came forth and*

cursed.
3 Heb. *man of blood.*

4 Heb. *behold thee in thy evil.*

XVI. **1.** *a couple of asses saddled*] Those
that Mephibosheth and his servant should
have ridden. See xix. 26 note.
3. *thy master's son*] Meaning Saul's grandson (ix. 6). David asks the question, evidently hurt at the apparent ingratitude of
Mephibosheth. It is impossible to say
whether Mephibosheth was quite guiltless
or not. If Ps. cxvi. was composed by
David, and after the quelling of Absalom's
rebellion, *v.* 11 may contain David's confession of his present hasty judgment (*v.* 4)
in the matter.
5. *Bahurim*] See iii. 16 note. It seems to
have lain off the road, on a ridge (*v.* 13),
separated from it by a narrow ravine, so
that Shimei was out of easy reach though
within hearing, and within a stone's throw
(*vv.* 6, 9).
Shimei, the son of Gera] In the title to Ps.
vii. he is apparently called "Cush the Benjamite." On Gera, see Judg. iii. 15 note.
7. *Come out*] Rather, "**Go out**," viz. of
the land, into banishment. Cp. Jer. xxix.
16.
thou bloody man] See marg. The Lord's
word to David (1 Chr. xxii. 8) was probably known to Shimei. and now cast in Da-

vid's teeth by him, with special reference to
the innocent blood of Uriah.
8. *all the blood of the house of Saul*]
Shimei probably put to David's account the
death of Saul, and Jonathan, and Abinadab, and Melchishua, slain in battle with
the Philistines with whom David was in league;
of Ish-bosheth, slain in consequence of David's league with Abner; that of Abner
himself, which he attributed to David's secret orders; and all the 360 slain in the
battle between Joab and Abner (ii. 31).
Some, too, think that the death of seven
men of Saul's immediate family (xxi. 8) had
occurred before David's flight, and was referred to by Shimei. Shimei's hatred and
virulence is an indication that the Benjamites resented the loss of royalty in their
tribe, even in the palmiest days of David's
monarchy.
9. *this dead dog*] See marg. ref. and ix. 8
note.
go over] The ravine, possibly with a stream
of water (xvii. 20), which lay between them
and Shimei.
10. *what have I to do, &c.*] See marg. reff.
cp. Matt. viii. 29: John ii. 4, and a similar
complaint about the sons of Zeruiah (iii. 39).

him curse, because [n]the LORD hath said unto him, Curse David.
11 [o]Who shall then say, Wherefore hast thou done so? And
David said to Abishai, and to all his servants, Behold, [p]my son,
which [q]came forth of my bowels, seeketh my life: how much
more now *may this* Benjamite *do it?* let him alone, and let him
12 curse; for the LORD hath bidden him. It may be that the
LORD will look on mine [1][2]affliction, and that the LORD will
13 [r]requite me good for his cursing this day. And as David and
his men went by the way, Shimei went along on the hill's side
over against him, and cursed as he went, and threw stones at
14 him, and [3]cast dust. And the king, and all the people that *were*
15 with him, came weary, and refreshed themselves there. ¶ And
[s]Absalom, and all the people the men of Israel, came to Jerusa-
16 lem, and Ahithophel with him. And it came to pass, when
Hushai the Archite, [t]David's friend, was come unto Absalom,
that Hushai said unto Absalom, [4]God save the king, God save
17 the king. And Absalom said to Hushai, *Is* this thy kindness
18 to thy friend? [u]why wentest thou not with thy friend? And
Hushai said unto Absalom, Nay; but whom the LORD, and this
people, and all the men of Israel, choose, his will I be, and
19 with him will I abide. And again, [x]whom should I serve?
should I not *serve* in the presence of his son? as I have served in
20 thy father's presence, so will I be in thy presence. ¶ Then said
Absalom to Ahithophel, Give counsel among you what we shall
21 do. And Ahithophel said unto Absalom, Go in unto thy father's
[y]concubines, which he hath left to keep the house; and all
Israel shall hear that thou [z]art abhorred of thy father: then
22 shall [a]the hands of all that *are* with thee be strong. So they
spread Absalom a tent upon the top of the house, and Absalom
went in unto his father's concubines [b]in the sight of all Israel.
23 And the counsel of Ahithophel, which he counselled in those
days, *was* as if a man had enquired at the [5]oracle of God: so
was all the counsel of Ahithophel, [c]both with David and with
Absalom.

CHAP. 17. MOREOVER Ahithophel said unto Absalom, Let me
now choose out twelve thousand men, and I will arise and
2 pursue after David this night: and I will come upon him while
he *is* [a]weary and weak handed, and will make him afraid: and
all the people that *are* with him shall flee; and I will [b]smite the
3 king only: and I will bring back all the people unto thee: the
man whom thou seekest *is* as if all returned: *so* all the people

[n] See 2 Kin. 18. 25. Lam. 3. 38.
[o] Rom. 9. 20.
[p] ch. 12. 11.
[q] Gen. 15. 4.
[r] Rom. 8. 28.
[s] ch. 15. 37.
[t] ch. 15. 37.
[u] ch. 19. 25. Prov. 17. 17.
[x] ch. 15. 34.
[y] ch. 15. 16. & 20. 3.
[z] Gen. 34. 30. 1 Sam. 13. 4.
[a] ch. 2. 7. Zech. 8. 13.
[b] ch. 12. 11, 12.
[c] ch. 15. 12.
[a] See Deut. 25. 18. ch. 16. 14.
[b] Zech. 13. 7.

[1] Or, *tears*.
[2] Heb. *eye*, Gen. 29. 32. 1 Sam. 1. 11. Ps. 25. 18.
[3] Heb. *dusted* him *with dust*.
[4] Heb. *Let the king live.*
[5] Heb. *word*.

And for a like striking incident in the life of the Son of David, see Luke ix. 52-56.

12. *his cursing*] Another reading has *my curse, i.e.* the curse that has fallen upon me. David recognises in every word and action that he was receiving the due reward of his sin, and that which Nathan had foretold.

21. Taking possession of the harem was the most decided act of sovereignty (see 1 K. ii. 22). It was also the greatest offence and insult that could be offered. Such an act on Absalom's part made reconciliation impossible. A further motive has been found in this advice, viz., the desire on the part of Ahithophel to make David taste the bitterness of that cup which he had caused others (Uriah and all Bath-sheba's family) to drink, and receive the measure which he had meted withal.

XVII. **1.** *this night*] The night of the day on which David fled, and Absalom entered into Jerusalem. Ahithophel's idea was to fall upon David by surprise, and in the first confusion of the surprised army to seize and kill David only.

3. *the man whom thou seekest*] viz., David. Ahithophel means to say: "If I can only smite David, there will be no civil war, all the people will peaceably submit."

4 shall be in peace. And the saying [1]pleased Absalom well, and
5 all the elders of Israel. ¶Then said Absalom, Call now Hushai
6 the Archite also, and let us hear likewise [2]what he saith. And
when Hushai was come to Absalom, Absalom spake unto him,
saying, Ahithophel hath spoken after this manner : shall we do
7 after his [3]saying? if not; speak thou. And Hushai said unto
Absalom, The counsel that Ahithophel hath [4]given is not good
8 at this time. For, said Hushai, thou knowest thy father and
his men, that they be mighty men, and they be [5]chafed in their
minds, as [c]a bear robbed of her whelps in the field : and thy   c Hos. 13. 8.
father is a man of war, and will not lodge with the people.
9 Behold, he is hid now in some pit, or in some other place : and it
will come to pass, when some of them be [6]overthrown at the
first, that whosoever heareth it will say, There is a slaughter
10 among the people that follow Absalom. And he also that is
valiant, whose heart is as the heart of a lion, shall utterly [d]melt :   d Josh. 2. 11.
for all Israel knoweth that thy father is a mighty man, and they
11 which be with him are valiant men. Therefore I counsel that
all Israel be generally gathered unto thee, [e]from Dan even to   e Judg. 20. 1.
Beer-sheba, [f]as the sand that is by the sea for multitude; and   f Gen. 22. 17.
12 [f]that thou go to battle in thine own person. So shall we come
upon him in some place where he shall be found, and we will
light upon him as the dew falleth on the ground : and of him
and of all the men that are with him there shall not be left so
13 much as one. Moreover, if he be gotten into a city, then shall
all Israel bring ropes to that city, and we will draw it into the
14 river, until there be not one small stone found there. ¶And
Absalom and all the men of Israel said, The counsel of Hushai
the Archite is better than the counsel of Ahithophel. For [g]the   g ch. 15. 31,
LORD had [8]appointed to defeat the good counsel of Ahithophel,   34.
to the intent that the LORD might bring evil upon Absalom.
15 ¶[h]Then said Hushai unto Zadok and to Abiathar the priests,   h ch. 15. 35.
Thus and thus did Ahithophel counsel Absalom and the elders
16 of Israel ; and thus and thus have I counselled. Now therefore
send quickly, and tell David, saying, Lodge not this night [i]in   i ch. 15. 28.
the plains of the wilderness, but speedily pass over ; lest the

---

[1] Heb. was right in the eyes of, &c. 1 Sam. 18. 20.	[3] Heb. word?	[6] Heb. fallen.
[2] Heb. what is in his mouth.	[4] Heb. counselled.	[7] Heb. that thy face, or, presence go, &c.
	[5] Heb. bitter of soul. Judg. 18. 25.	[8] Heb. commanded.

---

7. at this time] Rather, "The counsel
which Ahithophel has given this time is
not good." He contrasts it with that given
before (xvi. 21), which was good. This gave
an appearance of candour to his conduct, and
so gave weight to his dissent. Observe the
working of David's prayer (xv. 31).

9. some pit, or in some other place] The
Hebrew has in one of the pits, or in one of
the places. Hence place must have some
defined meaning. It probably is used here,
as elsewhere, for a dwelling-house or village,
which might in that district be fortified
houses (v. 12; 1 Sam. xxvi. 25).

Hushai's argument is that there was no
chance of seizing David by surprise as
Ahithophel suggested. There was sure to
be sharp fighting, and the terror of the

names of David, Joab, Abishai, Ittai,
and their companions, would magnify the
first few blows received into a victory, and
Absalom's men would flee in panic. It is
likely that Absalom was not a man of
courage, and Hushai, knowing this, adroitly
magnified the terror of the warlike prowess
of David and his mighty men.

12. as the dew] Like the drops of dew, in
the vast number of our host, and in our
irresistible and unavoidable descent upon
our enemies.

16. Hushai, like a wise and prudent man,
knowing, too, Absalom's weak and fickle
character, would not depend upon the resolution, taken at his instigation, not to pursue the king, but took instant measures to
advertise David of his danger.

king be swallowed up, and all the people that *are* with him.

k ch. 15. 27, 36.
l Josh. 2. 4, &c.
m Josh. 15. 7. & 18. 16.
n ch. 16. 5.
o See Josh. 2. 6.

17 ¶ *k* Now Jonathan and Ahimaaz *l* stayed by *m* En-rogel; for they might not be seen to come into the city: and a wench went and 18 told them; and they went and told king David. Nevertheless a lad saw them, and told Absalom: but they went both of them away quickly, and came to a man's house *n* in Bahurim, which 19 had a well in his court; whither they went down. And *o* the woman took and spread a covering over the well's mouth, and spread ground corn thereon; and the thing was not known.

p See Exod. 1. 19.
Josh. 2. 4, 5.

20 And when Absalom's servants came to the woman to the house, they said, Where *is* Ahimaaz and Jonathan? And *p* the woman said unto them, They be gone over the brook of water. And when they had sought and could not find *them*, they returned to 21 Jerusalem. And it came to pass, after they were departed, that they came up out of the well, and went and told king David,

q ver. 15, 16.

and said unto David, *q* Arise, and pass quickly over the water: 22 for thus hath Ahithophel counselled against you. Then David arose, and all the people that *were* with him, and they passed over Jordan: by the morning light there lacked not one of them 23 that was not gone over Jordan. ¶ And when Ahithophel saw that his counsel was not ¹ followed, he saddled his *ass*, and arose,

r ch. 15. 12.
s Matt. 27. 5.
t Gen. 32. 2.
Josh. 13. 26.

and gat him home to his house, to *r* his city, and ² put his household in order, and *s* hanged himself, and died, and was buried in 24 the sepulchre of his father. ¶ Then David came to *t* Mahanaim. And Absalom passed over Jordan, he and all the men of Israel 25 with him. And Absalom made Amasa captain of the host instead of Joab: which Amasa *was* a man's son, whose name

u 1 Chr. 2. 16, 17.

was Ithra an Israelite, that went in to *u* ³ Abigail the daughter of 26 ⁴ Nahash, sister to Zeruiah Joab's mother. So Israel and Ab-

¹ Heb. *done*.   ² Heb. *gave charge concerning his house*, 2 Kin. 20. 1.   ³ Heb. *Abigal*.   ⁴ Or, *Jesse*. See 1 Chr. 2. 13, 16.

---

17. *En-rogel*] See marg. ref.

a wench] Heb. "**the maid servant**," viz., of the High-Priest, either Zadok or Abiathar, or possibly one employed in some service in the Temple courts. (1 Sam. ii. 22 note.)

and they went and told king David] As related afterwards (*v.* 21). Here mentioned by anticipation.

18. *Bahurim*] See marg. ref. They were not all Shimeis in Bahurim.

19. *a covering*] Heb. "**the covering**," perhaps *the hanging* or *awning* at the door of the house, as the word seems to mean when spoken of the Tabernacle.

ground corn] Or *peeled barley*, which she spread out as if for the purpose of drying it in the sun.

20. As soon as ever she had hid the men she went into the house, as if busy about her usual occupations. Had Absalom's servants, who had had information from some of the people of Bahurim that the men had come to this house, found her in the court it might have directed their attention to the peeled barley.

over the brook of water] Cp. xvi. 9 note. The word for *brook* (*Michal*) occurs only here. One has been found in this very district,

still so called. The woman showed great presence of mind and adroitness in not denying that they had been there.

23. *to his city*] To Giloh (marg. ref.). Ahithophel was probably influenced by deep mortification at the slight put upon him by rejecting his counsel. He is a memorable example of the impotence of worldly wisdom. Cp. marg. ref.

24. *Mahanaim*] See ii. 8. The same reasons which induced Abner to choose it for Ishbosheth probably made it a good rallying point for David. It was a strong city, in a well-provisioned country, with a mountainous district for retreat in case of need, and with a warlike and friendly population.

25. *Ithra an Israelite*] Or *Jether the Ishmeelite* (1 Chr. ii. 17). *Ithra* and *Jether* are practically the same names. *Israelite* in the text is wrong. It should be either *Ishmaelite* or *Jezreelite* (iii. 2).

Abigail the daughter of Nahash] If Zeruiah and Abigail were Jesse's daughters, the only probable way of reconciling our text with 1 Chr. ii. 16, 17, is to suppose that Nahash was Jesse's wife. If Zeruiah and Abigail were only sisters of David by the mother, then Nahash might be the name of her first husband.

27 salom pitched in the land of Gilead. ¶ And it came to pass, when David was come to Mahanaim, that *Shobi the son of Nahash of Rabbah of the children of Ammon, and *Machir the son of Ammiel of Lo-debar, and *Barzillai the Gileadite of
28 Rogelim, brought beds, and ¹basons, and earthen vessels, and wheat, and barley, and flour, and parched corn, and beans, and
29 lentiles, and parched pulse, and honey, and butter, and sheep, and cheese of kine, for David, and for the people that were with him, to eat: for they said, The people is hungry, and weary, and thirsty, *in the wilderness.

CHAP. 18. AND David numbered the people that were with him, and set captains of thousands and captains of hundreds over
2 them. And David sent forth a third part of the people under the hand of Joab, and a third part under the hand of Abishai the son of Zeruiah, Joab's brother, *and a third part under the hand of Ittai the Gittite. And the king said unto the people, I
3 will surely go forth with you myself also. *But the people answered, Thou shalt not go forth : for if we flee away, they will not ²care for us ; neither if half of us die, will they care for us : but now thou art ³worth ten thousand of us : therefore now it is
4 better that thou ⁴succour us out of the city. And the king said unto them, What seemeth you best I will do. And the king stood by the gate side, and all the people came out by hundreds
5 and by thousands. And the king commanded Joab and Abishai and Ittai, saying, Deal gently for my sake with the young man, even with Absalom. *And all the people heard when the king gave all the captains charge concerning Absalom.
6 ¶ So the people went out into the field against Israel : and the
7 battle was in the *wood of Ephraim ; where the people of Israel

*See ch. 10. 1. & 12. 29.
*ch. 9. 4.
*ch. 19. 31, 32.
1 Kin. 2. 7.

*ch. 16. 2.

*ch. 15. 19.

*ch. 21. 17.

*ver. 12.

*Josh. 17. 15, 18.

¹ Or, cups.
² Heb. set their heart on us.
³ Heb. as ten thousand of us.
⁴ Heb. be to succour.

27. Shobi's father may have been the king of the Ammonites, and Shobi appointed by David as tributary king or governor of Ammon after he took Rabbah (xii. 29). On the other hand, Nahash may have been a common name among the Ammonites, and the Nahash of v. 25 may have been of that nation.

On Machir, see marg. ref.

Barzillai was ancestor, through a daughter, to a family of priests, who were called after him sons of Barzillai, and who returned from captivity with Zerubbabel, but were not allowed to officiate as priests, or eat of the holy things, through defect of a proper register (Ezr. ii. 61-63). It is likely that being wealthy they had neglected their priestly privileges, as a means of maintenance, before the Captivity.

Rogelim was situated in the highlands of Gilead, but the exact situation is not known. It means the fullers, being the plural of the word Rogel, in En-Rogel, v. 17.

29. cheese of kine] Or, as others, milch cows, which is more in accordance with the context, being coupled with sheep, and is more or less borne out etymologically by the Arabic. God's care for David was evident in the kindness of these people.

XVIII. 2. a third part] This seems to have been a favourite division with the Hebrew commanders (see Judg. vii. 16, ix. 43 ; 1 Sam. xi. 11 ; 2 K. xi. 5, 6) and with the Philistines also (1 Sam. xiii. 17).

3. succour us out of the city] David, with a reserve, would hold the city, and either support the bands in case of need, or receive them within the walls should they be compelled to flee.

6. against Israel] Implying that the revolt was in a great measure that of the ten tribes, Saul's party, against the kingdom.

the wood of Ephraim] This would naturally be sought in the west of Jordan (marg. ref.). But on the other hand it seems certain that the scene of this battle was on the east of Jordan. It seems therefore inevitable to conclude that some portion of the thick wood of oaks and terebinths which still runs down to the Jordan on the east side was for some reason called the wood of Ephraim, either because it was a continuation on the east side of the great Ephraimitic forests on the west, or because of some transaction there in which Ephraim had taken part, such as the slaughter of the Midianites (Judg. vii. 24, 25), or their own slaughter (Judg. xii. 6).

were slain before the servants of David, and there was there a
8 great slaughter that day of twenty thousand *men*. For the battle
was there scattered over the face of all the country : and the
wood ¹devoured more people that day than the sword devoured.
9 ¶And Absalom met the servants of David. And Absalom rode
upon a mule, and the mule went under the thick boughs of a
great oak, and his head caught hold of the oak, and he was
taken up between the heaven and the earth; and the mule that
10 *was* under him went away. And a certain man saw *it*, and told
11 Joab, and said, Behold, I saw Absalom hanged in an oak. And
Joab said unto the man that told him, And, behold, thou sawest
him, and why didst thou not smite him there to the ground ?
and I would have given thee ten *shekels* of silver, and a girdle.
12 And the man said unto Joab, Though I should ²receive a thousand *shekels* of silver in mine hand, *yet* would I not put forth
mine hand against the king's son : *ᵉfor in our hearing the king
charged thee and Abishai and Ittai, saying, ³Beware that none
13 *touch* the young man Absalom. Otherwise I should have
wrought falsehood against mine own life: for there is no matter
hid from the king, and thou thyself wouldest have set thyself
14 against *me*. Then said Joab, I may not tarry thus ⁴with thee.
And he took three darts in his hand, and thrust them through
the heart of Absalom, while he *was* yet alive in the ⁵midst of
15 the oak. And ten young men that bare Joab's armour com-
16 passed about and smote Absalom, and slew him. ¶And Joab
blew the trumpet, and the people returned from pursuing after
17 Israel: for Joab held back the people. And they took Absalom,
and cast him into a great pit in the wood, and ᶠlaid a very great
heap of stones upon him : and all Israel fled every one to his
18 tent. ¶Now Absalom in his lifetime had taken and reared up
for himself a pillar, which *is* in ᵍthe king's dale : for he said, ʰI
have no son to keep my name in remembrance : and he called
the pillar after his own name : and it is called unto this day,

ᵉ ver. 5.

ᶠ Josh. 7. 26.

ᵍ Gen. 14. 17.
*ʰ See ch. 14.
27.*

¹ Heb. *multiplied to devour.*
² Heb. *weigh upon mine hand.*
³ Heb. *Beware whosoever
ye be of, &c.*
⁴ Heb. *before thee.*
⁵ Heb. *heart.*

8. *the battle was scattered*] Probably Absalom's forces were far more numerous than
David's ; but, most likely by Joab's skilful
generalship, the field of battle was such
that numbers did not tell, and David's
veteran troops were able to destroy Absalom's rabble in detail. The wood entangled
them, and was perhaps full of pits, pre-
cipices, and morasses (*v.* 17).

9. It would seem that the two things
which his vain-glory boasted in, the royal
mule, and the magnificent head of hair, by
which he was caught in the "oak" (rather,
terebinth or turpentine tree), both contributed to his untimely death.

11. *ten shekels*] [About 25 shillings.] The
word *shekel* is understood, as in Gen. xx. 16,
xxxvii. 28. See Ex. xxxviii. 24 note.

a girdle] Girdles were costly articles of
Hebrew dress used to put money in (Matt.
x. 9), and given as presents (1 Sam.
xviii 4).

13. The man gives a remarkable incidental

testimony to David's sagacity and penetra-
tion (cp. xiv. 19), and to Joab's known un-
scrupulousness.

14. *I may not tarry, &c.*] *i.e.* lose time in
such discourse.

16. *blew the trumpet*] To stop the pursuit
and slaughter (ii. 28, xx. 22).

17. *a great heap of stones*] See marg. ref.
This kind of monument is common to
almost all early nations.

18. *the king's dale*] Anciently the *valley*
of *Shaveh* (marg. ref.), and apparently in
the near neighbourhood of Sodom ; but the
exact site is not known. It quite agrees
with Absalom's preference for Hebron (xv.
7), that his monument should be reared by
him in the south. If Absalom's monument
be placed in the ravine of the Kedron, the
king's dale here is a different place from the.
dale of Shaveh.

Absalom's place] Literally, *Absalom's hand.*
(1 Sam. xv. 12 note.)

19 Absalom's place. ¶ Then said Ahimaaz the son of Zadok, Let
me now run, and bear the king tidings, how that the LORD
20 hath ¹avenged him of his enemies. And Joab said unto him,
Thou shalt not ²bear tidings this day, but thou shalt bear tidings
another day: but this day thou shalt bear no tidings, because
21 the king's son is dead. Then said Joab to Cushi, Go tell the king
what thou hast seen. And Cushi bowed himself unto Joab, and
22 ran. Then said Ahimaaz the son of Zadok yet again to Joab,
But ³howsoever, let me, I pray thee, also run after Cushi. And
Joab said, Wherefore wilt thou run, my son, seeing that thou
23 hast no tidings ⁴ready? But howsoever, *said he*, let me run.
And he said unto him, Run. Then Ahimaaz ran by the way of
24 the plain, and overran Cushi. ¶ And David sat between the
two gates: and ⁵the watchman went up to the roof over the gate
unto the wall, and lifted up his eyes, and looked, and behold a
25 man running alone. And the watchman cried, and told the
king. And the king said, If he *be* alone, *there is* tidings in his
26 mouth. And he came apace, and drew near. And the watchman saw another man running: and the watchman called unto
the porter, and said, Behold *another* man running alone. And
27 the king said, He also bringeth tidings. And the watchman
said, ⁵Me thinketh the running of the foremost is like the
running of Ahimaaz the son of Zadok. And the king said, He
28 *is* a good man, and cometh with good tidings. ¶ And Ahimaaz
called, and said unto the king, ⁶⁷All is well. And he fell down
to the earth upon his face before the king, and said, Blessed *be*
the LORD thy God, which hath ⁸delivered up the men that lifted
29 up their hand against my lord the king. And the king said,
⁹Is the young man Absalom safe? And Ahimaaz answered,
When Joab sent the king's servant, and *me* thy servant, I saw
30 a great tumult, but I knew not what *it was*. And the king said
unto him, Turn aside, *and* stand here. And he turned aside, and

ch. 13. 34.
2 Kin. 9. 17.

---

¹ Heb. *judged him from the hand, &c.*
² Heb. *be a man of tidings.*
³ Heb. *be what may.*
⁴ Or, *convenient.*
⁵ Heb. *I see the running.*
⁶ Or, *Peace be to thee.*
⁷ Heb. *Peace.*
⁸ Heb. *shut up.*
⁹ Heb. *Is there peace.*

---

19. Ahimaaz was a well-known runner (*v.* 27). Speed was a heroic virtue in those simple times (cp. ii. 18). In Hezekiah's reign (2 Chr. xxx. 6, 10) we find an establishment of running post-men; and the same name (*runners*) is given (Esth. iii. 13) to the Persian posts, though at that time they rode on mules and camels.

bear tidings] The original word is used almost exclusively of bearing good tidings, and hence is rendered in the LXX. (though not always) εὐαγγελίζεσθαι (iv. 10; 1 Sam. xxxi. 9). In *v.* 21, it is not *carry the good tidings*, but *tell*, simply *announce*.

21. *Cushi*] "The Cushite," a foreign slave, perhaps of Joab's, whom he did not scruple to expose to David's anger. If, however, it is a name, it must be rendered *Haccushi*. In the title to Ps. vii., "Cush, the Benjamite," cannot mean this Cushi, since the contents of the Psalm are not suitable to this occasion.

23. *the plain*] The floor of the valley

through which the Jordan runs. The Cushite did not run by that road, but took the road over the hills, which may well have been the shorter but also the more difficult road. The two roads would probably meet a short distance from Mahanaim. These words, which have been thought to prove that the battle took place on the west of Jordan, are a clear proof that it took place on the east, because if the runners had had to cross the Jordan, they must both have come by the same road, which it is clear they did not.

28. *Ahimaaz called*] This marks the eager haste with which, before he had quite reached the king, he shouted out the pithy decisive word of good tidings, *Shalom*! Peace!

hath delivered] See marg. The figure seems to be that of *confining* a person within the power of his enemy, in opposition to *giving him his liberty* "in a large room," to work what mischief he pleases.

31 stood still. And, behold, Cushi came; and Cushi said, [1]Tidings, my lord the king: for the LORD hath avenged thee this day of
32 all them that rose up against thee. And the king said unto Cushi, *Is* the young man Absalom safe? And Cushi answered, The enemies of my lord the king, and all that rise against thee
33 to do *thee* hurt, be as *that* young man *is*. And the king was much moved, and went up to the chamber over the gate, and

k ch. 19. 4.

wept: and as he went, thus he said, [k]O my son Absalom, my son, my son Absalom! would God I had died for thee, O Absalom, my son, my son!

CHAP. 19. AND it was told Joab, Behold, the king weepeth and
2 mourneth for Absalom. And the [2]victory that day was *turned* into mourning unto all the people: for the people heard say that
3 day how the king was grieved for his son. And the people gat

a ver. 32.
b ch. 15. 30.
c ch. 18. 33.

them by stealth that day *a*into the city, as people being ashamed
4 steal away when they flee in battle. But the king *b*covered his face, and the king cried with a loud voice, *c*O my son Absalom,
5 O Absalom, my son, my son! ¶And Joab came into the house to the king, and said, Thou hast shamed this day the faces of all thy servants, which this day have saved thy life, and the lives of thy sons and of thy daughters, and the lives of thy wives,
6 and the lives of thy concubines; [3]in that thou lovest thine enemies, and hatest thy friends. For thou hast declared this day, [4]that thou regardest neither princes nor servants: for this day I perceive, that if Absalom had lived, and all we had died
7 this day, then it had pleased thee well. Now therefore arise, go forth, and speak [5]comfortably unto thy servants: for I swear by the LORD, if thou go not forth, there will not tarry one with thee this night: and that will be worse unto thee than all the
8 evil that befell thee from thy youth until now. Then the king arose, and sat in the gate. And they told unto all the people, saying, Behold, the king doth sit in the gate. And all the people came before the king: for Israel had fled every man to his tent.
9 ¶And all the people were at strife throughout all the tribes of Israel, saying, The king saved us out of the hand of our enemies, and he delivered us out of the hand of the Philistines; and now

d ch. 15. 14.

10 he is *d*fled out of the land for Absalom. And Absalom, whom we anointed over us, is dead in battle. Now therefore why
11 [6]speak ye not a word of bringing the king back? ¶And king David sent to Zadok and to Abiathar the priests, saying, Speak unto the elders of Judah, saying, Why are ye the last to bring the king back to his house? seeing the speech of all Israel is
12 come to the king, *even* to his house. Ye *are* my brethren, ye

e ch. 5. 1.

are *e*my bones and my flesh: wherefore then are ye the last to

---

[1] Heb. *Tidings is brought.*
[2] Heb. *salvation,* or, *deliverance.*
[3] Heb. *By loving, &c.*
[4] Heb. *that princes or servants* are *not to thee.*
[5] Heb. *to the heart of thy servants,* Gen. 34. 3.
[6] Heb. *are ye silent?*

---

31. *tidings,* &c.] Rather, "Let my lord the king receive the good tidings."
33. There is not in the whole of the O. T. a passage of deeper pathos than this. Cp. Luke xix. 41. In the Hebrew Bible this verse commences the nineteenth chapter. The A. V. follows the Greek and Latin Versions.
5. Had Absalom gained the victory, it is likely that, according to the manner of

Oriental despots, he would have sought to secure his throne by killing all possible competitors (Judg. ix. 5; 1 K. xv. 29).
8. David saw the justice of what Joab said, and the new danger which threatened him if he did not rouse himself from his grief.
for Israel, &c.] Not David's followers, but as before (xvii. 26, xviii. 6, 17), Absalom's army.

13 bring back the king? *f* And say ye to Amasa, *Art* thou not of *f* ch. 17. 25.
   my bone, and of my flesh? *g* God do so to me, and more also, *g* Ruth 1. 17.
   if thou be not captain of the host before me continually in the
14 room of Joab. And he bowed the heart of all the men of Judah,
   h even as *the heart of* one man; so that they sent *this word* unto *h* Judg. 20.1
15 the king, Return thou, and all thy servants. So the king
   returned, and came to Jordan. And Judah came to *i* Gilgal, to *i* Josh. 5. 9.
16 go to meet the king, to conduct the king over Jordan. ¶ And
   k Shimei the son of Gera, a Benjamite, which *was* of Bahurim, *k* c². 16. 5.
   hasted and came down with the men of Judah to meet king 1 Kin. 2. 8.
17 David. And *there were* a thousand men of Benjamin with him,
   and *l* Ziba the servant of the house of Saul, and his fifteen sons *l* ch. 9. 2, 10.
   and his twenty servants with him; and they went over Jordan & 16. 1, 2.
18 before the king. And there went over a ferry boat to carry
   over the king's household, and to do ¹what he thought good.
   And Shimei the son of Gera fell down before the king, as he was
19 come over Jordan; and said unto the king, *m* Let not my lord *m* 1 Sam. 22.
   impute iniquity unto me, neither do thou remember *n* that which 15.
   n ch. 16. 5,
   thy servant did perversely the day that my lord the king went 6, &c.
   out of Jerusalem, that the king should *o* take it to his heart. *o* ch. 13. 33.
20 For thy servant doth know that I have sinned: therefore,
   behold, I am come the first this day of all *p* the house of Joseph *p* See ch. 16.
21 to go down to meet my lord the king. But Abishai the son of 5.
   Zeruiah answered and said, Shall not Shimei be put to death
22 for this, because he *q* cursed the LORD's anointed? And David *q* Ex. 22. 28.
   said, *r* What have I to do with you, ye sons of Zeruiah, that ye *r* ch. 16. 10.
   should this day be adversaries unto me? *s* shall there any man *s* 1 Sam. 11.
   be put to death this day in Israel? for do not I know that I 13.
23 *am* this day king over Israel? Therefore *t* the king said unto *t* 1 Kin. 2. 8,
   Shimei, Thou shalt not die. And the king sware unto him. 9, 37, 46.
24 ¶ And *u* Mephibosheth the son of Saul came down to meet the *u* ch. 9. 6.
   king, and had neither dressed his feet, nor trimmed his beard,

¹ Heb. *the good in his eyes.*

---

13. *of my bone, &c.*] Render as in preceding verse, "art thou not my bone and my flesh?" It is curious to note how the phrase is used in *v.* 1 of common descent from Israel, in *v.* 12 of the closer kindred of the tribe of Judah, and in this verse of the yet nearer kindred between David and Amasa his sister's son.

captain...in the room of Joab] It is very plain that David felt the weight of Joab's overbearing influence to be very oppressive (cp. *v.* 22, iii. 39, xvi. 10). He was, at this time, very angry with Joab for killing Absalom; and so, thinking it of vital importance to win over Amasa and the army of Judah, he did not scruple to offer him Joab's high post.

16. Shimei being aware that Judah was unanimous in recalling the king, lost no time in trying to make his peace with David, by bringing a large Benjamite force with him.

17. *before the king*] *i.e.* "to meet the king." Cp. xx. 8. The king was on the east bank, and they crossed over (by the ford) from the west bank to go to him.

18. *as he was come over Jordan*] Render, "when he was crossing," *i.e.* just embarking for the purpose of crossing. The scene still lies on the east bank. Shimei left nothing undone to soften, if possible, David's resentment.

20. This is the first time that the *house of Joseph*, or *Joseph*, stands for all the ten tribes of which Ephraim was the head and leader. While Saul of Benjamin was king, or while Mahanaim was the capital of his son's kingdom, it was not natural so to name them, nor does it seem so at first sight in the mouth of Shimei the Benjamite. But it is very possible that he used the phrase for the purpose of exculpating himself and his own tribe from having taken the initiative in the rebellion, and of insinuating that they were drawn away by the preponderating influence of the great house of Joseph. On the other hand, the phrase may be an indication that the passage was written after the separation of the kingdom of Israel, when the phrase was a common one.

24. *beard*] The *moustache*, the beard of the upper lip. The fact related in this

nor washed his clothes, from the day the king departed until the
25 day he came *again* in peace. And it came to pass, when he
was come to Jerusalem to meet the king, that the king said unto
26 him, [x]Wherefore wentest not thou with me, Mephibosheth? And
he answered, My lord, O king, my servant deceived me: for thy
servant said, I will saddle me an ass, that I may ride thereon,
27 and go to the king; because thy servant *is* lame. And [y]he hath
slandered thy servant unto my lord the king; [z]but my lord the
king *is* as an angel of God: do therefore *what is* good in thine
28 eyes. For all *of* my father's house were but [1]dead men before
my lord the king: [a]yet didst thou set thy servant among them
that did eat at thine own table. What right therefore have I
29 yet to cry any more unto the king? And the king said unto
him, Why speakest thou any more of thy matters? I have said,
30 Thou and Ziba divide the land. And Mephibosheth said unto
the king, Yea, let him take all, forasmuch as my lord the king
31 is come again in peace unto his own house. ¶ And [b]Barzillai
the Gileadite came down from Rogelim, and went over Jordan
32 with the king, to conduct him over Jordan. Now Barzillai was
a very aged man, *even* fourscore years old: and [c]he had provided the king of sustenance while he lay at Mahanaim; for he
33 *was* a very great man. And the king said unto Barzillai, Come
thou over with me, and I will feed thee with me in Jerusalem.
34 And Barzillai said unto the king, [2]How long have I to live,
35 that I should go up with the king unto Jerusalem? I *am* this
day [d]fourscore years old: and can I discern between good and
evil? can thy servant taste what I eat or what I drink? can I
hear any more the voice of singing men and singing women?
wherefore then should thy servant be yet a burden unto my lord
36 the king? Thy servant will go a little way over Jordan with
the king: and why should the king recompense it me with such
37 a reward? Let thy servant, I pray thee, turn back again, that I
may die in mine own city, *and be buried* by the grave of my father
and of my mother. But behold thy servant [e]Chimham; let him
go over with my lord the king; and do to him what shall seem
38 good unto thee. And the king answered, Chimham shall go
over with me, and I will do to him that which shall seem good
unto thee: and whatsoever thou shalt [3]require of me, *that* will
39 I do for thee. And all the people went over Jordan. And
when the king was come over, the king [f]kissed Barzillai, and
40 blessed him; and he returned unto his own place. Then the
king went on to Gilgal, and [4]Chimham went on with him: and

Marginal references:
[x] ch. 16. 17.
[y] ch. 16. 3.
[z] ch. 14. 17, 20.
[a] ch. 9. 7, 10, 13.
[b] ch. 17. 27. 1 Kin. 2. 7.
[c] ch. 17. 27.
[d] Ps. 90. 10.
[e] 1 Kin. 2. 7. Jer. 41. 17.
[f] Gen. 31. 55.

[1] Heb. *men of death,* 1 Sam. 26. 16.
[2] Heb. *How many days* are *the years of my life.*
[3] Heb. *choose.*
[4] Heb. *Chimhan.*

verse tends to clear Mephibosheth from the
suspicion of unfaithfulness to David.

26. What appears to have happened is,
that when Mephibosheth ordered Ziba to
saddle the asses and ride with him to join
David, Ziba left him under pretence of
obeying, but instead laded the asses with
provisions, and went off alone with them,
thus making it impossible for Mephibosheth
to follow.

29. Unable to get to the bottom of the
story, and perhaps unwilling to make an
enemy of Ziba, David compromised the
matter by dividing the land, thus partially
revoking his hasty sentence (xvi. 4). We
still see the impatient temper of David.

37. *Chimham*] From marg. reff. it appears
that Chimham, having accepted David's
offer, came and settled near Bethlehem.
His house was still called after him at the
time of the Captivity.

39. The *people* is the term especially
applied in this narrative to David's followers (xv. 17, xvi. 14, xvii. 2, xviii. 1, 2,
xix. 2, 3). They crossed by the ford, while
David and his household, accompanied by
Barzillai and Chimham, came over in the
ferry.

all the people of Judah conducted the king, and also half the
41 people of Israel. ¶ And, behold, all the men of Israel came to
the king, and said unto the king, Why have our brethren the
men of Judah stolen thee away, and *g*have brought the king, *g* ver. 15.
and his household, and all David's men with him, over Jordan?
42 And all the men of Judah answered the men of Israel, Because
the king is *h*near of kin to us : wherefore then be ye angry for *h* ver. 12.
this matter? have we eaten at all of the king's *cost?* or hath he
43 given us any gift? And the men of Israel answered the men
of Judah, and said, We have ten parts in the king, and we have
also more *right* in David than ye : why then did ye ¹despise us,
that our advice should not be first had in bringing back our
king? And *i*the words of the men of Judah were fiercer than *i* See Judg.
the words of the men of Israel.   8. 1.
CHAP. 20. AND there happened to be there a man of Belial, whose & 12. 1.
name *was* Sheba, the son of Bichri, a Benjamite : and he blew a
trumpet, and said, *a*We have no part in David, neither have we *a* ch. 19. 43.
inheritance in the son of Jesse : *b*every man to his tents, O *b* 1 Kin. 12.
2 Israel. So every man of Israel went up from after David, *and* 16.
followed Sheba the son of Bichri : but the men of Judah clave 2 Chr. 10. 16.
3 unto their king, from Jordan even to Jerusalem. ¶ And David
came to his house at Jerusalem ; and the king took the ten
women *his c*concubines, whom he had left to keep the house, *c* ch. 15. 16.
and put them in ²ward, and fed them, but went not in unto & 16. 21, 22.
them. So they were ³shut up unto the day of their death,
4 ⁴living in widowhood. ¶ Then said the king to Amasa, *d ⁵*As- *d* ch. 19. 13.
semble me the men of Judah within three days, and be thou
5 here present. So Amasa went to assemble *the men of* Judah :
but he tarried longer than the set time which he had appointed
6 him. And David said to Abishai, Now shall Sheba the son of
Bichri do us more harm than *did* Absalom : take thou *e*thy lord's *e* ch. 11. 11.
servants, and pursue after him, lest he get him fenced cities, 1 Kin. 1. 33.
7 and ⁶escape us. And there went out after him Joab's men, and
the *f*Cherethites, and the Pelethites, and all the mighty men : *f* ch. 8. 18.
1 Kin. 1. 38.

¹ Heb. *set us at light.*   ³ Heb. *bound.*   ⁶ Heb. *deliver himself from*
² Heb. *an house of ward.*   ⁴ Heb. *in widowhood of life.*   *our eyes.*
                               ⁵ Heb. *Call.*

41. It seems that David and his whole
party made a halt at Gilgal (*v.* 15 ; 1 Sam.
xi. 14), and possibly made some solemn
agreement there about the kingdom. But
while they were there, *all the men of Israel,*
representatives from the tribes not included
in *half the people of Israel* (*v.* 40), came
up in great wrath at finding that the
restoration had been accomplished without
consulting them, and accused the men of
Judah of unfair dealing.

XX. 1. *the son of Bichri,* &c.] Rather, *a*
Bichrite, formed like the names *Ahohite,*
Hachmonite, &c. (xxiii. 8, 9), and so called
from Becher, the son of Benjamin (Gen.
xlvi. 21 ; 1 Chr. vii. 6-8) Saul was also of
this family. It is evident that the transfer
of the royalty from their tribe to that of
Judah still rankled in the hearts of many
Benjamites (xvi. 8 note).

2. *from Jordan,* &c.] The men of Israel
only escorted David from Jordan to Gilgal,

and there left him ; but the men of Judah
in a body went with him all the way to
Jerusalem.

4. *to Amasa,* &c.] Evidently feeling his
way towards fulfilling the promise to Amasa
(marg. ref.).

5. *he tarried*] The cause of Amasa's
delay is not stated. It may have been the
unwillingness of the men of Judah to place
themselves under his orders, or it may have
been caused by a wavering or hesitation in
loyalty. This last is evidently insinuated
in *v.* 11, and no doubt this was the pretext,
whether grounded in fact or not, by which
Joab justified the murder of Amasa before
David.

6. *to Abishai*] Probably, as the king was
on bad terms with Joab, and wished to
deprive him of his post as captain of the
host, he gave his orders to Abishai, and
weakly connived at the execution of them
by Joab, which was inevitable.

and they went out of Jerusalem, to pursue after Sheba the son
8 of Bichri. ¶When they *were* at the great stone which *is* in
Gibeon, Amasa went before them. And Joab's garment that
he had put on was girded unto him, and upon it a girdle *with* a
sword fastened upon his loins in the sheath thereof; and as he
9 went forth it fell out. And Joab said to Amasa, *Art* thou in
g Matt. 26.   health, my brother? *g*And Joab took Amasa by the beard with
49.   10 the right hand to kiss him. But Amasa took no heed to the
Luke 22. 47.   sword that *was* in Joab's hand: so *h*he smote him therewith *i*in
h 1 Kin. 2. 5.   the fifth *rib*, and shed out his bowels to the ground, and *1*struck
i ch. 2. 23.   him not again; and he died. So Joab and Abishai his brother
11 pursued after Sheba the son of Bichri. And one of Joab's men
stood by him, and said, He that favoureth Joab, and he that *is*
12 for David, *let him go* after Joab. And Amasa wallowed in
blood in the midst of the highway. And when the man saw
that all the people stood still, he removed Amasa out of the
highway into the field, and cast a cloth upon him, when he saw
13 that every one that came by him stood still. When he was
removed out of the highway, all the people went on after Joab,
14 to pursue after Sheba the son of Bichri. And he went through
k 2 Kin. 15.   all the tribes of Israel unto *k*Abel, and to Beth-maachah, and
29.   all the Berites: and they were gathered together, and went also
15 after him. And they came and besieged him in Abel of Beth-
l 2 Kin. 19.   maachah, and they *l*cast up a bank against the city, and *2*it
32.   stood in the trench: and all the people that *were* with Joab
Isai. 37. 33.   16 *3*battered the wall, to throw it down. ¶Then cried a wise woman
out of the city, Hear, hear; say, I pray you, unto Joab, Come

1 Heb. *doubled not his*   *2* Or, *it stood against the*   *3* Heb. *marred to throw*
stroke.   outmost wall.   down.

---

8. *Amasa went before them*] Rather,
"**advanced to meet them.**" Amasa was
no doubt returning to Jerusalem, according
to his orders (*v.* 4), and was probably much
surprised to meet the army in march.
Joab's resolution was quickly taken.
    and Joab's garment, &c.] Render, *And
Joab was girded with his military garment,
as his clothing, and upon it*—*i.e.* the military
garment—(or *him*), *the girdle of a sword
fastened on his loins in its sheath, and as he
went forth* (to meet Amasa) *it fell* out of the
sheath. What appears to have happened
is that, by accident or design, Joab's sword
fell out of the scabbard on the ground as
he was going to meet Amasa, and that he
picked it up with his left hand so as to
leave his right hand free for the customary
salutation (*v.* 9). This awakened no suspicion in Amasa's mind. Cp. the case of
Ehud, Judg. iii. 21.
    11. *He that favoureth Joab*, &c.] This
speech, addressed to Amasa's followers as
well as Joab's, shows very distinctly that
the rivalry between Joab and Amasa, and
David's purpose to make Amasa captain in
Joab's room, were well known; and shows
also the real reason why Joab slew Amasa.
What is added, *and he that is for David*,
was intended to identify Joab's cause
with David's, and also to insinuate that

Amasa had not been loyal to David (*v.* 5
note).
    12. *all the people*, &c.] *i.e.* the levies
which Amasa had been leading to Jerusa-
lem; they were irresolute as to what they
should do, and the stoppage at Amasa's
body very nearly led to their refusing to
follow Joab. But upon the prompt removal
and hiding of the body they passed on and
followed Joab, their old captain.
    14. *Abel*] More commonly called (*v.* 15)
Abel-Beth-maachah to distinguish it from
other places of the name of *Abel* (a grassy
plain). It is represented by the modern Abil-
el-Kamh, a Christian village on the N.W.
of lake Huleh, the ancient Merom. Cp. 2
Chr. xvi. 4, *Abel-maim*, Abel by the water.
    and all the Berites] What this means is
utterly unknown. Many approve of the
reading of the Latin Version, connecting it
with what follows: "*And all the choice
young men mustered and followed him*."
    15. *cast up a bank*] See marg. reff. The
throwing up of mounds against the walls of
besieged places by the besiegers is well
illustrated in the Assyrian sculptures.
    the trench] The *pomœrium*, or fortified
space outside the wall. When the mound
was planted in the pomœrium the battering
engines were able to approach close to the
wall to make a breach.

17 near hither, that I may speak with thee. And when he was come near unto her, the woman said, *Art* thou Joab? And he answered, I *am* he. Then she said unto him, Hear the words
18 of thine handmaid. And he answered, I do hear. Then· she spake, saying, ¹They were wont to speak in old time, saying, They shall surely ask *counsel* at Abel: and so they ended *the*
19 *matter*. I am one *of them that are* peaceable *and* faithful in Israel: thou seekest to destroy a city and a mother in Israel:
20 why wilt thou swallow up ᵐ the inheritance of the LORD? And Joab answered and said, Far be it, far be it from me, that I
21 should swallow up or destroy. The matter *is* not so: but a man of mount Ephraim, Sheba the son of Bichri ²by name, hath lifted up his hand against the king, *even* against David: deliver him only, and I will depart from the city. And the woman said unto Joab, Behold, his head shall be thrown to thee over the
22 wall. Then the woman went unto all the people ⁿ in her wisdom. And they cut off the head of Sheba the son of Bichri, and cast *it* out to Joab. And he blew a trumpet, and they ³retired from the city, every man to his tent. And Joab returned to Jeru-
23 salem unto the king. ¶ Now ᵒ Joab *was* over all the host of Israel: and Benaiah the son of Jehoiada *was* over the Cherethites
24 and over the Pelethites: and Adoram *was* ᵖ over the tribute:
25 and ᵠ Jehoshaphat the son of Ahilud *was* ⁴recorder: and Sheva
26 *was* scribe: and ʳ Zadok and Abiathar *were* the priests: ˢ and Ira also the Jairite was ⁵a chief ruler about David.

CHAP. 21. THEN there was a famine in the days of David three years, year after year; and David ⁶enquired of the LORD. And

ᵐ 1 Sam. 26.
19.
ch. 21. 3.

ⁿ Eccles. 9.
14, 15.

ᵒ ch. 8. 16,
18.

ᵖ 1 Kin. 4. 6.

ᵠ ch. 8. 16.
1 Kin. 4. 3.
ʳ ch. 8. 17.
1 Kin. 4. 4.
ˢ ch. 23. 38.

¹ Or, *They plainly spake in the beginning, saying, Surely they will ask of Abel, and so make an end:*
² Heb. *by his name.*
³ Heb. *were scattered.*
⁴ Or, *remembrancer.*
⁵ Or, *a prince,* Gen. 41. 45. Ex. 2. 16.
⁶ Heb. *sought the face, &c.* See Num. 27. 21.

See Deut. 20. 11.

---

18. This was an old proverb. Abel, like Teman, and some other places, was once famous for the wisdom of its inhabitants (1 K. iv. 30, 31). The wise woman was herself a remnant of this traditional wisdom.

19. *I am one,* &c.] The woman speaks in the name of the whole city, which she means to say was peaceable and loyal.

20. Joab's character is strongly brought out in the transaction. Politic, decided, bold, and unscrupulous, but never needlessly cruel or impulsive, or even revengeful. No life is safe that stands in his way, but from policy he never sacrifices the most insignificant life without a purpose. (Cp. ii. 27–30.)

23. *now Joab,* &c.] This is by no means an unmeaning repetition. Joab had been dismissed to make room for Amasa, and was now, as the result of his successful expedition against Sheba, and the death of Amasa, reinstated in his command. Moreover, this was a fresh beginning of David's reign, and therefore a statement of his chief officers is as proper as in viii. 16, when he had just established himself on the throne of Israel. Cp. 1 K. iv. 2-6.

24. *Adoram*] Not mentioned before by name or office. Apparently, therefore, the office was not instituted till the latter part of David's reign, and its duties probably were the collection of the tribute imposed upon vanquished nations, or the command of the forced levies employed in public works. Adoram was stoned to death in the beginning of the reign of Rehoboam (1 K. xii. 18).

26. *Ira the Jairite*] Not mentioned before: perhaps the same as *Ira an Ithrite* (marg. ref.), *i.e.* an inhabitant of Jattir in the hill country of Judah (Josh. xv. 48; 1 Sam. xxx. 27). Perhaps we ought to read *Ithrite*, for *Jairite*.

a chief ruler...about David] More simply and clearly, "**was David's cohen**" (viii. 18 note). In the early part of David's reign his own ons were *cohanim* (chief rulers). The deaths of Amnon and Absalom, and the dissensions in the family, had probably caused the change of policy in this respect.

XXI. 1. There is no note of time whatever, nor any clue as to what part of David's reign the events of this chapter ought to be assigned.

enquired of the LORD] Heb. "**sought the face of the Lord**," quite a different phrase

the LORD answered, *It is* for Saul, and for *his* bloody house,
2 because he slew the Gibeonites. And the king called the
Gibeonites, and said unto them; (now the Gibeonites *were* not

a Josh. 9. 3,
15, 16, 17.

of the children of Israel, but *a* of the remnant of the Amorites;
and the children of Israel had sworn unto them: and Saul
sought to slay them in his zeal to the children of Israel and
3 Judah.) Wherefore David said unto the Gibeonites, What
shall I do for you? and wherewith shall I make the atonement,

b ch. 20. 19.

4 that ye may bless *b* the inheritance of the LORD? And the
Gibeonites said unto him, [1] We will have no silver nor gold of
Saul, nor of his house; neither for us shalt thou kill any man
in Israel. And he said, What ye shall say, *that* will I do for
5 you. And they answered the king, The man that consumed us,
and that [2] devised against us *that* we should be destroyed from
6 remaining in any of the coasts of Israel, let seven men of his
sons be delivered unto us, and we will hang them up unto the

c 1 Sam. 10.
26.
& 11. 4.
d 1 Sam. 10.
24.
e 1 Sam.18.3.
& 20. 8,15,42.
& 23. 18.
f ch. 3. 7.

LORD *c* in Gibeah of Saul, *d* [3] *whom* the LORD did choose. And
7 the king said, I will give *them*. ¶ But the king spared Mephibosheth, the son of Jonathan the son of Saul, because of *e* the
LORD's oath that *was* between them, between David and Jona-
8 than the son of Saul. But the king took the two sons of *f* Rizpah the daughter of Aiah, whom she bare unto Saul, Armoni
and Mephibosheth; and the five sons of [4] Michal the daughter of

---

[1] Or, It is *not silver nor
gold that we have to do
with Saul or his house,*

neither pertains it *to us
to kill, &c.*

[2] Or, *cut us off.*
[3] Or, *chosen of the LORD.*
[4] Or, *Michal's sister.*

---

from that so often used in Judges (*e.g.* i. 1)
and the Books of Samuel, and probably
indicating that this chapter is from a different source; an inference agreeing with
the indefinite "*in the days of David,*" and
with the allusion to the slaughter of the
Gibeonites, which has not anywhere been
narrated.

and for his bloody house] Lit., *the house
of blood, i.e.* the house or family upon
which rests the guilt of shedding innocent
blood.

2. The way in which the writer here
refers to the history of the league with the
Gibeonites (Josh. ix.) shows that the Book
of Joshua was not a part of the same work
as the Books of Samuel.

of the Amorites] The Gibeonites were
Hivites (Josh. ix. 7, xi. 19); and in many
enumerations of the Canaanitish nations
the Hivites are distinguished from the
Amorites. But *Amorite* is often used in a
more comprehensive sense, equivalent to
Canaanite (as Gen. xv. 16; Deut. i. 27), and
denoting especially that part of the Canaanite nation which dwelt in the hill country
(Num. xiii. 29; Deut. i. 7, 20, 24), and so
includes the Hivites.

4. *no silver, nor gold,* &c.] Money payments as a compensation for blood-guilt
were very common among many nations.
The law, too, in Num. xxxv. 31, 32, pre-
supposes the existence of the custom which
it prohibits. In like manner the speech of

the Gibeonites implies that such a payment
as they refuse would be a not unusual proceeding.

*neither ... shalt thou kill any man in Is-
rael*] They mean that it is not against the
nation of Israel, but against the individual
Saul, that they cry for vengeance. The
demand for Saul's sons is exactly similar to
that which dictated David's own expression
in xxiv. 17, "*against me, and against my
father's house.*"

6. *seven men*] Seven was a sacred number
not only with the Hebrews but with other
Oriental nations (Num. xxiii. 1, 29), and is
therefore brought in on this occasion when
the judicial death of the sons of Saul was a
religious act intended to appease the wrath
of God for the violation of an oath (Num.
xxv. 4).

whom the LORD did choose] Rather, "**the
Lord's chosen,**" or elect. The same phrase
is applied to Moses (Ps. cvi. 23), to the Israelites (Isai. xliii. 20), and to Christ (Isai.
xlii. 1).

7. *the LORD's oath*] The calamity brought
upon Israel by Saul's breach of the oath to
the Gibeonites would make David doubly
careful in the matter of his own oath to
Jonathan.

8. *Rizpah*] See marg. ref. A foreign origin
was possibly the cause of the selection of
Rizpah's sons as victims.

sons of Michal] An obvious error for
Merab (1 Sam. xviii. 19 note).

Saul, whom she ¹brought up for Adriel the son of Barzillai the
9 Meholathite : and he delivered them into the hands of the
Gibeonites, and they hanged them in the hill ᵍbefore the LORD : ᵍ ch. 6. 17.
and they fell *all* seven together, and were put to death in the
days of harvest, in the first *days*, in the beginning of barley
10 harvest. ¶ And ʰRizpah the daughter of Aiah took sackcloth, ʰ ver. 8.
and spread it for her upon the rock, ⁱfrom the beginning of ch. 3. 7.
ⁱ See Deut.
harvest until water dropped upon them out of heaven, and 21. 23.
suffered neither the birds of the air to rest on them by day, nor
11 the beasts of the field by night. And it was told David what
Rizpah the daughter of Aiah, the concubine of Saul, had done.
12 ¶ And David went and took the bones of Saul and the bones of
Jonathan his son from the men of ᵏJabesh-gilead, which had ᵏ 1 Sam. 31.
11, 12, 13.
stolen them from the street of Beth-shan, where the ˡPhilistines ˡ 1 Sam. 31.
had hanged them, when the Philistines had slain Saul in Gilboa : 10.
13 and he brought up from thence the bones of Saul and the bones
of Jonathan his son ; and they gathered the bones of them that
14 were hanged. And the bones of Saul and Jonathan his son
buried they in the country of Benjamin in ᵐZelah, in the ᵐ Josh. 18.
sepulchre of Kish his father : and they performed all that the 28.
king commanded. And after that ⁿGod was intreated for the ⁿ So Josh. 7.
15 land. ¶ Moreover the Philistines had yet war again with Israel ; 26.
ch. 24. 25.
and David went down, and his servants with him, and fought
16 against the Philistines : and David waxed faint. And Ishbi-
benob, which *was* of the sons of ²the giant, the weight of whose
³spear *weighed* three hundred *shekels* of brass in weight, he being
17 girded with a new *sword*, thought to have slain David. But
Abishai the son of Zeruiah succoured him, and smote the

---

¹ Heb. *bare* *to* *Adriel*, 1   ² Or, *Rapha.*   ³ Heb. *the* *staff*, or, *the*
Sam. 18. 19.   *head.*

---

9. *in the first days*] The barley harvest
(about the middle or towards the end of
April) was earlier than the wheat harvest
(Ex. ix. 31 ; Ruth i. 22).

10. *dropped*] Rather, " **poured**," the proper word for heavy rain (Ex. ix. 33). The
"early rain," or heavy rain of autumn,
usually began in October, so that Rizpah's
devoted watch continued about six months.
How rare rain was in harvest we learn from
1 Sam. xii. 17, 18 ; Prov. xxvi. 1. The
reason of the bodies being left unburied,
contrary to Deut. xxi. 23, probably was that
the death of these men being an expiation
of the guilt of a violated oath, they were to
remain till the fall of rain should give the
assurance that God's anger was appeased,
and the national sin forgiven.

birds of the air…beasts of the field] It is
well known how in the East, on the death
e.g. of a camel in a caravan, the vultures
instantly flock to the carcase. (Cp. Matt.
xxiv. 28.)

12. *from the street of Beth-shan*] This was
the wide place just inside the gate of an
Oriental city, bounded therefore by the
city wall (cp. marg. ref.). Here, as the
place of concourse, the Philistines had fastened the bodies.

15. This, like the preceding paragraph

(1–14), is manifestly a detached and uncon-
nected extract. It is probably taken from
some history of David's wars, apparently
the same as furnished the materials for chs.
v., viii., and xxiii. 8-39. There is no direct
clue to the time when the events here related
took place, but it was probably quite in the
early part of David's reign, while he was
still young and active, after the war described in ch. v. The Book of Chronicles
places these Philistine battles immediately
after the taking of Rabbah of the Ammonites (1 Chr. xx. 4-8), but omits David's ad-
venture (15-17).

16. *Ishbi-benob*] A corrupt reading. The
whole passage should perhaps run thus :
" *And David waxed faint. So they halted in*
Gob (as in *vv.* 18, 19). *And there was a man*
(*in Gob*) *which was of the sons of the giant*,
&c."

sons of the giant] The *giant* here (*vv.* 18,
20, 22) is *ha-Raphah*, whence the *Rephaim*
(Gen. xiv. 5 ; Deut. ii. 11). The sons of Ha-
raphah, or Rephaim, are different from the
Nephilim, or Giants (Gen. vi. 4 ; Num. xiii.
33). The sons of Anak were not strictly
Rephaim, but Nephilim.

three hundred shekels of brass] About eight
pounds. Goliath's spear's head weighed *six
hundred shekels of iron.*

Philistine, and killed him. Then the men of David sware unto
him, saying, [o]Thou shalt go no more out with us to battle, that
18 thou quench not the [p]1light of Israel. ¶ [q]And it came to pass
after this, that there was again a battle with the Philistines at
Gob: then [r]Sibbechai the Hushathite slew 2Saph, which *was* of
19 the sons of 3the giant. And there was again a battle in Gob
with the Philistines, where Elhanan the son of 4Jaare-oregim, a
Beth-lehemite, slew [s]*the brother of* Goliath the Gittite, the staff
20 of whose spear *was* like a weaver's beam. ¶ And [t]there was yet
a battle in Gath, where was a man of *great* stature, that had on
every hand six fingers, and on every foot six toes, four and
21 twenty in number; and he also was born to 5the giant. And
when he 6defied Israel, Jonathan the son of [u]Shimeah the
22 brother of David slew him. ¶ [x]These four were born to the
giant in Gath, and fell by the hand of David, and by the hand
of his servants.

o ch. 18. 3. p 1 Kin. 11. 36. & 15. 4. Ps. 132. 17. q 1 Chr. 20. 4. r 1 Chr. 11. 29. s See 1 Chr. 20. 5. t 1 Chr. 20. 6. u 1 Sam. 16. 9, *Shammah*. x 1 Chr. 20. 8.

CHAP. 22. AND David [a]spake unto the LORD the words of this
song in the day *that* the LORD had [b]delivered him out of the
2 hand of all his enemies, and out of the hand of Saul: and he
said,

¶ [c]The LORD *is* my rock, and my fortress, and my deliverer;
3 The God of my rock; [d]in him will I trust:
He is my [e]shield, and the [f]horn of my salvation, my high
[g]tower, and my [h]refuge,
My saviour; thou savest me from violence.
4 I will call on the LORD, *who is* worthy to be praised:
So shall I be saved from mine enemies.
5 ¶ When the 7waves of death compassed me,
The floods of 8ungodly men made me afraid;
6 The 9[i]sorrows of hell compassed me about;
The snares of death prevented me;
7 In my distress [k]I called upon the LORD,
And cried to my God:

a Ex. 15. 1. Judg. 5. 1. b Ps. 34. 19. c Deut. 32. 4. Ps. 18. 2, &c. d Heb. 2. 13. e Gen. 15. 1. f Luke 1. 69. g Prov. 18. 10. h Ps. 9. 9. Jer. 16. 19. i Ps. 116. 3. k Ps. 120. 1. Jonah 2. 2.

1 Heb. *candle*, or, *lamp*.
2 Or, *Sippai*.
3 Or, *Rapha*.
4 Or, *Jair*.
5 Or, *Rapha*.
6 Or, *reproached*, 1 Sam. 17. 10, 25, 26.
7 Or, *pangs*.
8 Heb. *Belial*.
9 Or, *cords*.

---

18. *a battle in Gob*] In the parallel passage (marg. ref.), *Gezer* is named as the field of this battle. Gath is however named (*vv.* 20, 22) in a way to make it probable that Gath was the scene of all the battles. The LXX. in this verse has *Gath*.

19. The Hebrew text is manifestly very corrupt. First, for *Jaare-oregim*, 1 Chr. xx. 5 gives us the reading *Jair*. *Oregim* has evidently got in by a transcriber's error from the line below, where *oregim* is the Hebrew for *weavers*. Again, the word *the Bethlehemite* is very doubtful. It is supported by xxiii. 24, but it is not found in the far purer text of 1 Chr. xx. 5, but instead of it we find the name of the Philistine slain by Elhanan, *Lahmi the brother of Goliath the Gittite*. It is probable, therefore, that either the words *the Bethlehemite*, are a corruption of *Lahmi*, or that the recurrence of *Lahmi*, and the termination of *Beth-lehemite* has confused the transcriber, and led to the omission of one of the words in each text.

22. *four*] Not necessarily meaning that they were brothers, but that they were all of the race of the Giant, all Rephaim. The word *four* is omitted in the parallel passage, only the three last being mentioned in that chapter.

XXII. **1.** This song, which is found with scarcely any material variation as the XVIIIth Psalm, and with the words of this first verse for its title, belongs to the early part of David's reign when he was recently established upon the throne of all Israel, and when his final triumph over the house of Saul, and over the heathen nations (*vv.* 44-46), Philistines, Moabites, Syrians, Ammonites, and Edomites, was still fresh (ch. xxi.). For a commentary on the separate verses the reader is referred to the commentary on Ps. xviii.

And he did *l*hear my voice out of his temple,
And my cry *did enter* into his ears.

8 Then *m*the earth shook and trembled;
*n*The foundations of heaven moved
And shook, because he was wroth.

9 There went up a smoke ¹out of his nostrils,
And *o*fire out of his mouth devoured:
Coals were kindled by it.

10 He *p*bowed the heavens also, and came down;
And *q*darkness *was* under his feet.

11 And he rode upon a cherub, and did fly :
And he was seen *r*upon the wings of the wind.

12 And he made *s*darkness pavilions round about him,
²Dark waters, *and* thick clouds of the skies.

13 Through the brightness before him were *t*coals of fire kindled.

14 The LORD *u*thundered from heaven,
And the most High uttered his voice.

15 And he sent out *x*arrows, and scattered them ;
Lightning, and discomfited them.

16 And the channels of the sea appeared,
The foundations of the world were discovered,
At the *y*rebuking of the LORD,
At the blast of the breath of his ³nostrils.

17 ¶ *z*He sent from above, he took me ;
He drew me out of ⁴many waters ;

18 *a*He delivered me from my strong enemy,
And from them that hated me : for they were too strong
for me.

19 They prevented me in the day of my calamity :
But the LORD was my stay.

20 *b*He brought me forth also into a large place :
He delivered me, because he *c*delighted in me.

21 *d*The LORD rewarded me according to my righteousness :
According to the *e*cleanness of my hands hath he recompensed me.

22 For I have *f*kept the ways of the LORD,
And have not wickedly departed from my God.

23 For all his *g*judgments *were* before me :
And *as for* his statutes, I did not depart from them.

24 I was also *h*upright ⁵before him,
And have kept myself from mine iniquity.

25 Therefore *i*the LORD hath recompensed me according to my
righteousness ;
According to my cleanness ⁶in his eye sight.

26 ¶ With *k*the merciful thou wilt shew thyself merciful,
And with the upright man thou wilt shew thyself upright.

27 With the pure thou wilt shew thyself pure ;
And *l*with the froward thou wilt ⁷shew thyself unsavoury.

28 And the *m*afflicted people thou wilt save :
But thine eyes *are* upon *n*the haughty, *that* thou mayest
bring *them* down.

29 For thou *art* my ⁸lamp, O LORD :
And the LORD will lighten my darkness.

l Ex. 3. 7.
Ps. 34. 6.
m Judg. 5. 4.
Ps. 77. 18.
n Job 26. 11.

o Ps. 97. 3.
Hab. 3. 5.
p Ps. 144. 5.
Isai. 64. 1.
q Ex. 20. 21.
1 Kin. 8. 12.
r Ps. 104. 3.
s Ps. 97. 2.

t ver. 9.
u Judg. 5. 20.
1 Sam. 2. 10.
Ps. 29. 3.
Isai. 30. 30.
x Deut. 32.
23.
Ps. 7. 13.

y Ex. 15. 8.
Ps. 106. 9.
Nah. 8. 4.
Matt. 8. 26.
z Ps. 144. 7.

a ver. 1.

b Ps. 31. 8.
c ch. 15. 26.
Ps. 22. 8.
d 1 Sam. 26.
23.
1 Kin. 8. 32.
Ps. 7. 8.
e Ps. 24. 4.
f Gen. 18. 19.
Ps. 119. 3.
g Deut. 7. 12.
Ps. 119. 30.
h Gen. 6. 9.
Job 1. 1.

i ver. 21.

k Matt. 5. 7.

l Lev. 26. 23.

m Ex. 3. 7.
Ps. 72. 12.
n Job 40. 11.
Isai. 2. 11.
Dan. 4. 37.

---

¹ Heb. *by.*
² Heb. *binding of waters.*
³ Or, *anger*, Ps. 74. 1.

⁴ Or, *great.*
⁵ Heb. *to him.*
⁶ Heb. *before his eyes.*

⁷ Or, *wrestle*, Ps. 18. 26.
⁸ Or, *candle*, Job 29. 3.
Ps. 27. 1.

30 For by thee I have [1] run through a troop :
By my God have I leaped over a wall.

o Deut. 32. 4.
Rev. 15. 3. 31 ¶ *As for* God, *o*his way *is* perfect ;
p Ps. 12. 6.   *p*The word of the LORD *is* [2]tried :
Prov. 30. 5.   He *is* a buckler to all them that trust in him.
q 1 Sam. 2. 2. 32 For *q*who *is* God, save the LORD ?
Isai. 45. 5.   And who *is* a rock, save our God ?

r Ex. 15. 2. 33 God *is* my *r*strength *and* power :
Ps. 27. 1.   And he [3][s]maketh my way *t*perfect.
Isai. 12. 2.
s Heb. 13. 21. ·34 He [4]maketh my feet *u*like hinds' *feet :*
t Deut.18.13.   And *x*setteth me upon my high places.
Ps. 101. 2.
u ch. 2. 18. 35 *v*He teacheth my hands [5]to war ;
Hab. 3. 19.   So that a bow of steel is broken by mine arms.
x Deut. 32. 36 Thou hast also given me the shield of thy salvation :
13.   And thy gentleness hath [6]made me great.
Isai. 33. 16.
y Ps. 144. 1. 37 Thou hast *z*enlarged my steps under me ;
z Prov. 4. 12.   So that my [7]feet did not slip.

38 ¶ I have pursued mine enemies, and destroyed them ;
And turned not again until I had consumed them.

39 And I have consumed them, and wounded them, that they
could not arise :
a Mal. 4. 3.   Yea, they are fallen *a*under my feet.
b Ps. 18. 32. 40 For thou hast *b*girded me with strength to battle :
c Ps. 44. 5.   *c*Them that rose up against me hast thou [8]subdued under me.
d Gen. 49. 8. 41 Thou hast also given me the *d*necks of mine enemies,
Josh. 10. 24.   That I might destroy them that hate me.
42 They looked, but *there was* none to save :
e Job 27. 9.   *Even* *e*unto the LORD, but he answered them not.
Prov. 1. 28. 43 Then did I beat them as small *f*as the dust of the earth,
Isai. 1. 15.   I did stamp them *g*as the mire of the street, *and* did spread
f 2 Kin. 13.7.   them abroad.
Dan. 2. 35.
g Isai. 10. 6. 44 *h*Thou also hast delivered me from the strivings of my people,
Mic. 7. 10.   Thou hast kept me *to be* [i]head of the heathen :
h ch. 3. 1.   *k*A people *which* I knew not shall serve me.
i ch. 8. 1—
14.   45 [9]Strangers shall [12]submit themselves unto me :
Ps. 2. 8.   As soon as they hear, they shall be obedient unto me.
k Isai. 55. 5.
46 Strangers shall fade away,
And they shall be afraid [l]out of their close places.
l Mic. 7. 17. 47 ¶ The LORD liveth ; and blessed *be* my rock ;
And exalted be the God of the *m*rock of my salvation.
m Ps. 89. 26. 48 It *is* God that [3]avengeth me,
49 And that *n*bringeth down the people under me,
n Ps. 144. 2.   And that bringeth me forth from mine enemies :
Thou also hast lifted me up on high above them that rose up
against me :
o Ps. 140. 1.   Thou hast delivered me from the *o*violent man.
p Rom. 15. 9. 50 Therefore I will give thanks unto thee, O LORD, among *p*the
heathen,
And I will sing praises unto thy name.
q Ps. 144. 10. 51 *q*He *is* the tower of salvation for his king :
r Ps. 89. 20.   And sheweth mercy to his *r*anointed,
s ch. 7. 12.   Unto David, and *s*to his seed for evermore.
Ps. 89. 29.

[1] Or, *broken a troop.*   [6] Heb. *multiplied me.*   [2] Heb. *lie :* See Deut. 33.
[2] Or, *refined.*   [7] Heb. *ankles.*   29. Ps. 66. 3. & 81. 15.
[3] Heb. *riddeth,* or, *looseth.* [8] Heb. *caused to bow.*   [3] Heb. *giveth avengement*
[4] Heb. *equalleth.*   [9] Heb. *Sons of the stranger.*   *for me,* 1 Sam. 25. 39.
[5] Heb. *for the war.*   [1] Or, *yield feigned obedience.*   ch. 18. 19, 31.

Chap. 23. NOW these *be* the last words of David.
David the son of Jesse said,
  a And the man *who was* raised up on high,
  b The anointed of the God of Jacob,
  And the sweet psalmist of Israel, said,
2 *c* The Spirit of the LORD spake by me,
  And his word *was* in my tongue.
3 The God of Israel said,
  d The Rock of Israel spake to me,
  ¹He that ruleth over men *must be* just,
  Ruling *e* in the fear of God.
4 And *f* he shall be as the light of the morning, *when* the sun riseth,
  Even a morning without clouds;
  As the tender grass *springing* out of the earth by clear shining after rain.
5 Although my house *be* not so with God;
  g Yet he hath made with me an everlasting covenant,
  Ordered in all *things*, and sure:
  For *this is* all my salvation, and all *my* desire,
  Although he make *it* not to grow.
6 But *the sons* of Belial *shall be* all of them as thorns thrust away;
  Because they cannot be taken with hands:
7 But the man *that* shall touch them must be ²fenced with iron and the staff of a spear;
  And they shall be utterly burned with fire in the *same* place.
8 ¶ These *be* the names of the mighty men whom David had:
  ³The Tachmonite that sat in the seat, chief among the captains;

a ch. 7. 8, 9.
Ps. 78. 70.
& 89. 27.
b 1 Sam. 16.
12, 13.
Ps. 89. 20.
c 2 Pet. 1. 21.

d Deut. 32.
4, 31.
ch. 22. 2, 32.
e Ex. 18. 21.
f Prov. 4. 18.
Hos. 6. 5.
Ps. 72. 6.
Isai. 44. 3.

g Ps. 89. 29.
Isai. 55. 3.

---

¹ Or, *Be thou ruler, &c.*, Ps. 110. 2. ² Heb. *filled.* ³ Or, *Joshebbassebet the* *Tachmonite, head of the three.*

XXIII. 1. *the last words of David*] *i.e.* his last Psalm, his last "words of song" (xxii. 1). The insertion of this Psalm, which is not in the Book of Psalms, was probably suggested by the insertion of the long Psalm in ch. xxii.

David the son of Jesse said, &c.] The original word for *said* is used between 200 and 300 times in the phrase, "saith the Lord," designating the word of God in the mouth of the prophet. It is only applied to the words of a man here, and in the strikingly similar passage Num. xxiv. 3, 4, 15, 16, and in Prov. xxx. 1; and in all these places the words spoken are inspired words. The description of David is divided into four clauses, which correspond to and balance each other.

4. Comparisons illustrating the prosperity of the righteous king.

5. *although my house*, &c.] The sense of this clause (according to the A.V.) will be that David comparing the actual state of his family and kingdom during the later years of trouble and disaster with the prophetic description of the prosperity of the righteous king, and seeing how far it falls short, comforts himself by the terms of God's covenant (vii. 12–16) and looks forward to Messiah's kingdom. The latter clause, *although he make it not to grow*, must then mean that, although at the present time the glory of his house was not made to grow, yet all his salvation and all his desire was made sure in the covenant which would be fulfilled in due time. But most modern commentators understand both clauses as follows: *Is not my house so with God that He has made with me an everlasting covenant*, &c.? *For all my salvation and all my desire, will He not cause it to spring up?* viz., in the kingdom of Solomon, and still more fully in the kingdom of Christ.

8. The duplicate of this passage is in 1 Chr. xi., where it is in immediate connexion with David's accession to the throne of Israel, and where the mighty men are named as those by whose aid David was made king. The document belongs to the early part of David's reign. The text of *vv.* 8, 9 is perhaps to be corrected by comparison with 1 Chr. xi. 11, 12.

chief among the captains] There is great doubt about the exact meaning of this phrase. (1) The title is given to two other persons, viz., to Abishai in *v.* 18; 1 Chr. xi.

the same *was* Adino the Eznite: [1]*he lift up his spear* against
9 eight hundred, [2]whom he slew at one time. ¶ And after him

was [h]Eleazar the son of Dodo the Ahohite, *one* of the three
mighty men with David, when they defied the Philistines *that*
were there gathered together to battle, and the men of Israel
10 were gone away: he arose, and smote the Philistines until his
hand was weary, and his hand clave unto the sword: and the
LORD wrought a great victory that day; and the people returned
11 after him only to spoil. ¶ And after him *was* [i]Shammah the
son of Agee the Hararite. [k]And the Philistines were gathered
together [3]into a troop, where *was* a piece of ground full of
12 lentiles: and the people fled from the Philistines. But he stood
in the midst of the ground, and defended it, and slew the Philis-
13 tines: and the LORD wrought a great victory. ¶ And [14]three of
the thirty chief went down, and came to David in the harvest
time unto [m]the cave of Adullam: and the troop of the Philis-
14 tines pitched in [n]the valley of Rephaim. And David *was* then
in [o]an hold, and the garrison of the Philistines *was* then in
15 Beth-lehem. And David longed, and said, Oh that one would
give me drink of the water of the well of Beth-lehem, which *is*
16 by the gate! And the three mighty men brake through the
host of the Philistines, and drew water out of the well of Beth-
lehem, that *was* by the gate, and took *it*, and brought *it* to
David: nevertheless he would not drink thereof, but poured it

Marginal references (left):
- [k] 1 Chr. 11. 12. & 27. 4.
- [i] 1 Chr. 11. 27.
- [k] See 1 Chr. 11. 13, 14.
- [l] 1 Chr. 11. 15.
- [m] 1 Sam. 22. 1.
- [n] ch. 5. 18. & 21. 16.
- [o] 1 Sam. 22. 4, 5.

---

[1] See 1 Chron. 11. 11. & 27. 2.
[2] Heb. *slain.*
[3] Or, *for foraging.*
[4] Or, *the three captains over the thirty.*

20, and to Amasa in 1 Chr. xii. 18. (2)
The word translated *captain*, is of uncertain
meaning, and the orthography repeatedly
fluctuates throughout this and the duplicate
passage in 1 Chr. xi., between *Shalish* a
captain, and *Sheloshah* three. (3) If, however, the text of Chronicles be taken as the
guide, then the sense of *captain* will not
come into play, but the word will be a
numeral throughout, either *three* or *thirty*,
and will describe David's band of thirty
mighty men, with a certain triad or triads
of heroes who were yet more illustrious
than the thirty. In the verse before us,
therefore, for *chief among the captains*, we
should render, *chief of the thirty.*

eight hundred] The parallel passage in
1 Chr. has *three hundred*, as in *v.* 18. Such
variations in numerals are very frequent.
Compare the numbers in Ezr. ii. and
Neh. vii.

9. *gone away*] Rather, "went up" to
battle (v. 19; 2 K. iii. 21, &c.) against them.
These words and what follows as far as *troop*
(*v.* 11) have fallen out of the text in Chronicles. The effect of this is to omit Eleazar's
feat, as here described, to attribute to him
Shammah's victory, to misplace the flight
of the Israelites, and to omit Shammah altogether from the list of David's mighty men.

11. *Hararite*] Interpreted to mean *moun-
taineer*, one from the hill country of Judah
or Ephraim.

13. The feat at Bethlehem by three of the
thirty was the occasion of their being formed

into a distinct triad; Abishai (*v.* 18), Benaiah (*v.* 20), and a third not named, were
probably the three.

in the harvest time] An error for *to the
rock* (cp. marg. ref.).

the troop of the Philistines] The word
rendered *troop* occurs in this sense only
here (and, according to some, in *v.* 11), and
perhaps in Ps. lxviii. 11. In 1 Chr. xi., as in
v. 16 of this chapter the reading is *host*
or *camp*, which may be the true reading
here.

pitched] The same Hebrew word as *encamped* in 1 Chr. xi. 15.

valley of Rephaim] Or Giants. See xxi.
16 note.

14. *in an hold*] In "the hold" (1 Chr. xi.
16) close to the cave of Adullam (marg. ref.
note). It shows the power and daring of
the Philistines that they should hold a post
so far in the country as Bethlehem.

15. A cistern of deep, clear, cool water,
is called by the monks, David's Well, about
three-quarters of a mile to the north of
Bethlehem. Possibly the old well has been
filled up since the town was supplied with
water by the aqueduct.

16. *brake through the host*] Their camp
was pitched in the valley of Rephaim (*v.*
13; 1 Chr. xi. 15). It follows from this
that the way from Adullam to Bethlehem
lay through or across the valley of Rephaim.

poured it out unto the LORD] It was too
costly for his own use, none but the Lord

17 out unto the LORD. And he said, Be it far from me, O LORD, that I should do this: *is not this* ^pthe blood of the men that went in jeopardy of their lives? therefore he would not drink it. *p* Lev. 17. 10.
18 These things did these three mighty men. And ^qAbishai, the brother of Joab, the son of Zeruiah, was chief among three. And he lifted up his spear against three hundred, ¹*and* slew *q* 1 Chr. 11. 20.
19 *them*, and had the name among three. Was he not most honourable of three? therefore he was their captain: howbeit
20 he attained not unto the *first* three. ¶ And Benaiah the son of Jehoiada, the son of a valiant man, of ^rKabzeel, ²who had done *r* Josh. 15. 21.
many acts, ^she slew two ³lionlike men of Moab: he went down *s* Ex. 15. 15.
21 also and slew a lion in the midst of a pit in time of snow: and 1 Chr. 11. 22.
he slew an Egyptian, ⁴a goodly man: and the Egyptian had a spear in his hand; but he went down to him with a staff, and plucked the spear out of the Egyptian's hand, and slew him
22 with his own spear. These *things* did Benaiah the son of
23 Jehoiada, and had the name among three mighty men. He was ⁵more honourable than the thirty, but he attained not to the
24 *first* three. And David set him ^tover his ^{6 7}guard. ¶ Asahel the *t* ch. 8. 18. & 20. 23.
brother of Joab *was* one of the thirty; ^uElhanan the son of *u* ch. 21. 19.
25 Dodo of Beth-lehem, ^xShammah the Harodite, Elika the Haro- *x* See 1 Chr.
26 dite, Helez the Paltite, Ira the son of Ikkesh the Tekoite, 11. 27.
27, 28 Abiezer the Anethothite, Mebunnai the Hushathite, Zalmon
29 the Ahohite, Maharai the Netophathite, Heleb the son of Baanah, a Netophathite, Ittai the son of Ribai out of Gibeah of
30 the children of Benjamin, Benaiah the Pirathonite, Hiddai of
31 the ⁸brooks of ^yGaash, Abi-albon the Arbathite, Azmaveth the *y* Judg. 2. 9.
32 Barhumite, Eliahba the Shaalbonite, of the sons of Jashen,

---

¹ Heb. *slain.*
² Heb. *great of acts.*
³ Heb. *lions of God.*
⁴ Heb. *a man of counte-*

nance, or *sight:* called, 1 Chr. 11. 23. *a man of* *great stature.*
⁵ Or, *honourable among the thirty.*

⁶ Or, *council.*
⁷ Heb. *at his command,* 1 Sam. 22. 14.
⁸ Or, *valleys,* Deut. 1. 24.

---

was worthy of it. For libations, see Judg. vi. 20 note.

17. Better as in 1 Chr. xi. 19.

18. *three*] " The three " (*v.* 22). It was Abishai's prowess on this occasion that raised him to be chief of this triad.

19. *i.e. Was he not the most honourable of the three of the second order, howbeit he attained not to the three*, the triad, viz. which consisted of Jashobeam, Eleazar, and Shammah. That two triads are mentioned is a simple fact, although only five names are given.

20. *Benaiah the son of Jehoiada*] He commanded the Cherethites and Pelethites all through David's reign (viii. 18, xx. 23), and took a prominent part in supporting Solomon against Adonijah when David was dying, and was rewarded by being made captain of the host in the room of Joab (1 K. i. 8, 26, 32-40, ii. 25-35, iv. 4). It is possible that Jehoiada his father is the same as Jehoiada (1 Chr. xii. 27), leader of the Aaronites, since " Benaiah the son of Jehoiada " is called *a chief priest* (1 Chr. xxvii. 5).

two lion-like men] The Hebrew word *Ariel*, means literally *lion of God*, and is

interpreted to mean *an eminent hero*. Instances occur among Arabs and Persians of the surname "lion of God" being given to great warriors. Hence it is supposed that the same custom prevailed among the Moabites. But the Vulgate has "two lions of Moab," which seems to be borne out by the next sentence.

slew a lion, &c.] Rather, " the " lion, one of those described above as *a lion of God*, if the Vulgate Version is right. Apparently in a severe winter a lion had come up from its usual haunts to some village in search of food, and taken possession of the tank or cistern to the terror of the inhabitants, and Benaiah attacked it boldly and slew it.

23. *David set him over his guard*] Made him of his privy council, would be a better rendering. See 1 Sam. xxii. 14 note. This position, distinct from his office as captain of the Cherethites and Pelethites, is clearly indicated (1 Chr. xxvii. 34).

24, &c. The early death of Asahel (ii. 32) would make it very likely that his place in the 30 would be filled up, and so easily account for the number 31 in the list. Cp. throughout the list in 1 Chr. xi.

33 Jonathan, Shammah the Hararite, Ahiam the son of Sharar
34 the Hararite, Eliphelet the son of Ahasbai, the son of the
35 Maachathite, Eliam the son of Ahithophel the Gilonite, Hezrai
36 the Carmelite, Paarai the Arbite, Igal the son of Nathan of
37 Zobah, Bani the Gadite, Zelek the Ammonite, Nahari the

*ch. 20. 26.   38 Beerothite, armourbearer to Joab the son of Zeruiah, *Ira an
ᵃ ch. 11. 3, 6.   39 Ithrite, Gareb an Ithrite, ᵃUriah the Hittite: thirty and seven
           in all.

ᵃ ch. 21. 1.   CHAP. 24. AND ᵃagain the anger of the LORD was kindled against
ᵇ 1 Chr. 27.   Israel, and ¹he moved David against them to say, ᵇGo, number
23, 24.   2 Israel and Judah. For the king said to Joab the captain of the
       host, which *was* with him, ²Go now through all the tribes of
ᶜ Judg. 20. 1.   Israel, ᶜfrom Dan even to Beer-sheba, and number ye the people,
ᵈ Jer. 17. 5.   3 that ᵈI may know the number of the people. And Joab said
       unto the king, Now the LORD thy God add unto the people, how
       many soever they be, an hundredfold, and that the eyes of my
       lord the king may see *it*: but why doth my lord the king delight
       4 in this thing? Notwithstanding the king's word prevailed
       against Joab, and against the captains of the host. ¶And Joab
       and the captains of the host went out from the presence of the
       5 king, to number the people of Israel. And they passed over
ᵉ Josh. 13. 9,   Jordan, and pitched in ᵉAroer, on the right side of the city that
16.
ᶠ Num. 21.   6 *lieth* in the midst of the ³river of Gad, and toward ᶠJazer: then
32, 32. 1.   they came to Gilead, and to the ⁴land of Tahtim-hodshi; and they

¹ *Satan.* See 1 Chr. 21. 1.   ³ Or, *valley.*   ⁴ Or, *nether land newly
² Or, *Compass.*   inhabited.*

---

36. It is remarkable that we have several foreigners at this part of the list: Igal of Zobah, Zelek the Ammonite, Uriah the Hittite, and perhaps Nahari the Beerothite. The addition of Zelek to the mighty men was probably the fruit of David's war with Ammon (viii. 12, x., xii. 26-31).

39. *thirty and seven in all*] This reckoning is correct, though only 36 *names* are given, the names of only two of the second triad being recorded, but 31 names are given from *v.* 24 to the end, which, added to the two triads, or six, makes 37. Joab as captain of the whole host stands quite alone. In 1 Chr. xi. 41-47, after Uriah the Hittite, there follow sixteen other names, probably the names of those who took the places of those in the former list, who died from time to time, or who were added when the number was less rigidly restricted to thirty.

XXIV. 1. *And again the anger of the LORD was kindled against Israel*] This sentence is the heading of the whole chapter, which goes on to describe the sin which kindled this anger, viz. the numbering of the people (1 Chr. xxi. 7, 8, xxvii. 24). There is no note of time, except that the word *again* shows that these events happened *after* those of ch. xxi. (Cp. also *v.* 25 and xxi. 14.)

and he moved David] In 1 Chr. xxi. 1 the statement is, *and an adversary* (not *Satan*, as A. V., since there is no article prefixed, as in Job i. 6, ii. 1, &c.) *stood up against Israel and moved David,* just as (1 K. xi.

14, 23, 25) first Hadad, and then Rezon, is said to have been *an adversary* (Satan) to Solomon and to Israel. Hence our text should be rendered, *For one moved David against them.* We are not told whose advice it was, but some one, who proved himself an enemy to the best interests of David and Israel, urged the king to number the people.

2. 1 Chr. xxi. 2, supplies some missing words. This passage should run, as at *v.* 4, *And the king said to Joab and to the princes of the host who were with him,* &c. (cp. 1 Chr. xxvii. 22). They were employed *with Joab* as his assistants in the numbering, exactly as in the previous numbering (Num. i. 4) when a prince was appointed from each tribe to be *with* Moses and Aaron.

5. *Aroer*] Aroer on the Arnon (Deut. ii. 36 note). Aroer itself stood on the very edge of the precipitous cliff of the valley; and in the valley beneath, possibly in an island in the stream, stood another city which is here alluded to.

river] Rather, " the valley " (marg.). They passed from Aroer, northward to Gad, and so pitched at Jazer (see marg. reff.), which is on the frontier of Gad and Reuben.

6. *to Gilead*] Jazer was in the plain. They passed from thence to the mountain district of Gilead.

the land of Tahtim-hodshi] The text here is corrupt, as no such land is known. Possibly the right reading is *the land of the*

7 came to *Dan-jaan, and about to *Zidon, and came to the strong *Josh. 19.
hold of Tyre, and to all the cities of the Hivites, and of the 47.
Canaanites: and they went out to the south of Judah, *even to* Judg. 18. 29.
* Josh.19.28.
8 Beer-sheba. So when they had gone through all the land, they Judg. 18. 28.
came to Jerusalem at the end of nine months and twenty days.
9 And Joab gave up the sum of the number of the people unto the
king: *and there were in Israel eight hundred thousand valiant * See 1 Chr.
men that drew the sword; and the men of Judah *were* five 21. 5.
10 hundred thousand men. ¶And *David's heart smote him after * 1Sam.24.5.
that he had numbered the people. And David said unto the
LORD, *I have sinned greatly in that I have done: and now, I * ch. 12. 13.
beseech thee, O LORD, take away the iniquity of thy servant; Ps. 32. 5.
11 for I have *done very foolishly. For when David was up in * 1 Sam. 13.
the morning, the word of the LORD came unto the prophet *Gad, 13.
*1 Sam.22.5.
12 David's *seer, saying, Go and say unto David, Thus saith the * 1 Sam. 9.9.
LORD, I offer thee three *things;* choose thee one of them, that I 1 Chr. 29. 29.
13 may *do it* unto thee. So Gad came to David, and told him, and
said unto him, Shall *seven years of famine come unto thee in * See 1 Chr.
thy land? or wilt thou flee three months before thine enemies, 21. 12.
while they pursue thee? or that there be three days' pestilence in
thy land? now advise, and see what answer I shall return to him
14 that sent me. And David said unto Gad, I am in a great strait:
let us fall now into the hand of the LORD; *for his mercies *are* * Ps. 103. 8,
15 ¹great: and *let me not fall into the hand of man. ¶So *the 13, 14.
& 119. 156.
LORD sent a pestilence upon Israel from the morning even to the * See Isai.
time appointed: and there died of the people from Dan even to 47. 6.
Zech. 1. 15.
16 Beer-sheba seventy thousand men. *And when the angel * 1Chr.21.14.
stretched out his hand upon Jerusalem to destroy it, *the LORD & 27. 24.
repented him of the evil, and said to the angel that destroyed * Ex. 12. 23.
1 Chr. 21. 15.
the people, It is enough: stay now thine hand. And the angel * Gen. 6. 6.
1 Sam.15.11.
Joel 2. 13,14.

¹ Or, *many.*

Hittites (Judg. i. 26); *hodshi* may be a fragment of a sentence which mentioned in what month (*hodesh*) they arrived there, just as *v.* 8 relates that they returned to Jerusalem at the end of nine *months.*

Dan-jaan] The Versions read *Dan-jaar, i.e.* Dan in the wood. Whatever is the meaning of *Jaan,* there can be little doubt that Dan (the ancient Laish) is meant (marg. reff.), both from its position and importance as the northern boundary of Israel, and from its connexion with Zidon.

7. *the strong hold of Tyre*] "**The fenced city,**" as it is generally rendered throughout the Historical Books.

the cities of the Hivites] Gibeon, Chephirah, Beeroth, and Kirjath-jearim, and perhaps Shechem, besides those at the foot of Hermon and Lebanon, of which we do not know the names. This continuance of distinct communities of Hivites so late as the end of David's reign is remarkable.

9. 1 Chr. xxvii. 23 indicates sufficiently why the numbering was sinful. It is also stated in 1 Chr. xxi. 6, that Joab purposely omitted Levi and Benjamin from the reckoning.

eight hundred thousand … five hundred thousand] In Chronicles the numbers are differently given. It is probable therefore that the Chronicler has included in his statement of the sum total some numbers which are not included here.

11. *David's seer*] Marg. reff. From the latter passage it is probable that we have here Gad's narrative.

13. Cp. Ezek. xiv. 13-21. The *seven* years of famine correspond with the *seven* years of famine in Gen. xli. 27, 30, and with the same number of years in 2 K. viii. 1. But in Chronicles, it is *three* years, which agrees better with the *three* months and three days. The whole passage is amplified in Chronicles, which has less the aspect of an original text than this.

15. *the time appointed*] Perhaps "*the time of the assembly,*" meaning the time of the evening sacrifice, at three o'clock, when the people assembled for prayer, more commonly described as *the time of the evening oblation* (Dan. ix. 21; 1 K. xviii. 29, 36; Acts iii. 1; Luke i. 10).

seventy thousand] It is the most destructive plague recorded as having fallen upon the Israelites. In the plague that followed the rebellion of Korah there died 14,700 (Num. xvi. 49); in the plague, on account of Baal-Peor, 24,000 (Num. xxv. 9; 1 Cor. x. 8).

*1 Chr. 21.
15,
Ornan :
See ver. 18.
2 Chr. 3. 1.
y 1 Chr. 21.
17.
z 1 Chr. 21.
18, &c.

of the LORD was by the threshingplace of *Araunah the Jebusite.
17 And David spake unto the LORD when he saw the angel that
smote the people, and said, Lo, yI have sinned, and I have done
wickedly: but these sheep, what have they done? let thine
hand, I pray thee, be against me, and against my father's house.
18 ¶ And Gad came that day to David, and said unto him, zGo up,
rear an altar unto the LORD in the threshingfloor of ¹Araunah
19 the Jebusite. And David, according to the saying of Gad, went
20 up as the LORD commanded. And Araunah looked, and saw the
king and his servants coming on toward him: and Araunah went
out, and bowed himself before the king on his face upon the
21 ground. And Araunah said, Wherefore is my lord the king

a See Gen.
23. 8—16.
b Num. 16.
48, 50.

c 1 Kin. 19.
21.

d Ezek. 20.
40, 41.

e See 1 Chr.
21. 24, 25.

f ch. 21. 14.
v ver. 21.

come to his servant? aAnd David said, To buy the threshing-
floor of thee, to build an altar unto the LORD, that bthe plague
22 may be stayed from the people. And Araunah said unto David,
Let my lord the king take and offer up what seemeth good unto
him: cbehold, here be oxen for burnt sacrifice, and threshing
23 instruments and other instruments of the oxen for wood. All
these things did Araunah, as a king, give unto the king. And
Araunah said unto the king, The LORD thy God daccept thee.
24 And the king said unto Araunah, Nay; but I will surely buy it
of thee at a price: neither will I offer burnt offerings unto the
LORD my God of that which doth cost me nothing. ¶ So eDavid
bought the threshingfloor and the oxen for fifty shekels of silver.
25 And David built there an altar unto the LORD, and offered
burnt offerings and peace offerings. fSo the LORD was intreated
for the land, and vthe plague was stayed from Israel.

¹ Heb. *Araniah.*

---

17. Cp. the passage in Chronicles. The
account here is abridged; and v. 18 has
the appearance of being the original statement.
20. *and his servants*] In Chronicles *his
four sons*, viz. David's. It is very possible
that David may have taken his sons with
him, as well as his elders, and Gad's original
narrative may have mentioned the circumstance, which the compiler of this chapter
did not care to specify, and so used the
general term *his servants.*
22. *here be oxen*] Those, viz., which were
at that very time threshing out the grain in
Araunah's threshing-floor (1 Chr. xxi. 20;
Deut. xxv. 4).
threshing-instruments] This was a kind of
sledge with iron teeth (Isai. xli. 15). It
was drawn by two or four oxen over the
grain on the floor.
other instruments of the oxen] *i.e.* the
harness of the oxen, of which the yoke, and

perhaps some other parts, would be made
of wood (marg. reff. ; 1 Sam. vi. 14).
23. Either, "*the whole O king does Araunah give unto the king ;* " or (2) *the whole did
king Araunah give to the king.* The former
is preferable.
24. *fifty shekels of silver*] In Chronicles,
six hundred shekels of gold by weight. In
explanation, it is supposed—that the fifty
shekels here mentioned were gold shekels,
each worth twelve silver shekels, so that
the fifty gold shekels are equal to the
600 silver; that our text should be rendered, *David bought the threshing-floor and
the oxen for money,* viz., *fifty shekels;* and
that the passage in Chron. should be rendered, *David gave to Ornan gold shekels of
the value* (or weight) *of 600 shekels.* What
is certain is that our text represents the
fifty shekels as the price of the threshing-
floor and the oxen.

KINGS.

INTRODUCTION TO BOOKS I. AND II.

THE Greek translators, known as the LXX., who separated the " Book of the Law of Moses " into five parts, and the " Book of Samuel " into two, made the division, which is now almost universally adopted, of the original " Book of Kings " into a " First " and a " Second Book." The separation thus made was followed naturally in the early Latin Versions, which were formed from the Greek ; and when Jerome set forth the edition now called " The Vulgate," he followed the custom which he found established. The general adoption of the Vulgate by the Western Church caused the arrangement introduced by the LXX. to obtain almost universal acceptance.

The work is named from its contents, since the entire subject of the whole is the history of the " Kings " of Israel and Judah from the accession of Solomon to the Babylonish captivity.

1. The unity of the work is proved by the marked and striking simplicity and regularity of the plan. The work is, from first to last a history of the kings in strict chronological order, on the same system, and on a uniform scale. Exceptions to this uniformity in the larger space bestowed on the reigns of a few monarchs[1] are due to the principle of treating with the greatest fulness the parts of the history theocratically of most importance.

A second evidence of unity is the general uniformity of style and language—a uniformity admitted by all writers, and one which is only slightly infringed in two or three instances, where the irregularity may be accounted for by a diversity in the sources used by the author and a close following of the language which he found in those sources.[2]

To these general heads of evidence may be added certain peculiarities of thought or expression which pervade the two Books, all of them indicating with greater or less certainty a single author.[3]

---

[1] As Solomon (1 K. i.-xi.), Jeroboam (1 K. xii. 25-xiv. 20), Ahab (1 K. xvi. 29-xxii. 40), Jehoram (2 K. iii.-ix. 26),

Hezekiah (2 K. xviii.-xx.), and Josiah (2 K. xxii. and xxiii.).

[2] e. g. In the first chapter of the First Book peculiarities of diction occur which connect it with the Books of Samuel, and are sufficiently explained by the supposition that in this part of his work the author of Kings drew from a source which had been used also by the author of Samuel. The narratives in 2 Kings iv. 1-37, and viii. 1-6, contain some remarkable Aramaic forms, which have been regarded as evidences of late composition, but which are, it is probable, provincialisms—peculiarities of an Israelite author contemporary (or nearly so) with Elisha, whose words the compiler of Kings preserved unaltered.

[3] e. g. The formulæ which introduce and close the reign of almost every king, or which describe the ordinary sinfulness of the Israelite monarchs ; others are less palpable and evident, and therefore the more thoroughly to be relied

2. Some have thought from the continuity of the narrative, from the general resemblance of the style, and from the common employment of a certain number of words and phrases, that the six " Books," commencing with Judges and terminating with the Second Book of Kings, are the production of a single writer, and constitute in reality a single unbroken composition. Others consider these arguments far from conclusive. The continuity of the narrative is formal, and may be due to the after arrangements of a reviser, such as Ezra is commonly believed to have been.

So far as the mere idiom of the language goes, it is perhaps true that we cannot draw a marked line between Kings and Samuel. But many of the traits most characteristic of the writer of Kings are wholly wanting in the other (and probably earlier) composition. For these and other reasons the " Books of Kings " may claim distinctness and separateness.[4]

3. There are two grounds upon which, apart from all traditional

notices, the date of a historical work may be determined, viz., the peculiarities of the diction, and the contents.

The language of Kings belongs unmistakably to the period of the Captivity. It is later than that of Isaiah, Amos, Hosea, Micah, Joel, and Nahum, earlier than that of Chronicles, Ezra, Nehemiah, Haggai, and Zechariah.[5] In general character it bears a close resemblance to the language of Jeremiah and Ezekiel; and may be assigned to the sixth century before our era.

The result obtainable from the contents is similar, only somewhat more definite. Assuming the last detached section of the work (2 K. xxv. 27–30) to be an integral portion of it, we obtain the year B.C. 561—the first year of Evil-Merodach—as the earliest possible date of the completion of the composition.[6] Again, from the fact that the work contains no allusion at all to the return of the Jews from their Captivity, we obtain for the latest possible date the year B.C. 538, the year of the return under

upon : such as the habit of express allusion to the Law of Moses (1 K. ii. 3, vi. 12, &c. ; 2 K. x. 31, xi. 12, &c.); the perpetual reference to God's choice of David and of Jerusalem (1 K. viii. 16, 29, ix. 3, &c ; 2 K. xx., xxi. 4); the constant use of the phrase "man of God," (which occurs in Kings at least fifty-three times, and in twelve distinct chapters. In Samuel it is used about five times in two chapters. In Chronicles it is used six times—in four chapters) ; the habit of frequently prefixing the word "king" to the names of monarchs ; and the like.

[4] e. g. References to the Book of the Law, so constant in Kings, nowhere occur in Samuel. Samuel is incomplete and vague in respect of dates, which in Kings are given with extraordinary precision. The author of Samuel nowhere makes any mention of his sources, while the author of Kings is constantly alluding to his.

The favourite usages of the writer of Kings, such as his employment of the phrase "man of God," and his habit of prefixing the word "king" to the names of monarchs, although not absolutely unknown to the writer of Samuel, are with him comparatively rare and unfamiliar. Each character who is brought upon the scene, however familiar to one acquainted with Samuel, is given a descriptive epithet, such as, "the prophet," "the priest," "the son of," &c., as if previously unknown, when first introduced.

[5] The words and phrases which have been thought to indicate a later date than the time of the Captivity can be shown, in almost every instance, to have been in use during that time, or even previously.

[6] The rest of the work may have been written as early as B.C. 580, and the section in question may have been added afterwards.

Zerubbabel : or in other words between the death of Nebuchadnezzar and the accession of Cyrus in Babylon. Linguistic and other considerations favour the belief that the actual completion was early in this period—about B.C. 560; and it is not improbable that the greater part of the work was written as early as B.C. 580—*i.e.* some twenty years previously.

4. Jewish tradition assigns the authorship of Kings to Jeremiah ; and there are very weighty arguments in favour of this view. There is a very remarkable affinity between the language of Kings and that of the admitted writings of the Prophet.[7] The matter moreover, of the two works, so far as the same events are treated, is in the closest harmony,[8] those points being especially singled out for insertion, of which Jeremiah had personal knowledge and in which he took peculiar interest. Another argument of very considerable force is drawn from the entire omission of any notice at all of Jeremiah in Kings, which would have been very strange and unnatural in any other historian, considering the important part which Jeremiah played in the transactions of so many reigns, but which is completely intelligible on the hypothesis of his authorship of Kings : it is then the natural fruit and sign of a becoming modesty and unselfishness.

Still, though Jeremiah's author-

ship appears, all things considered, to be highly probable, we must admit that it has not been proved, and is therefore to some extent uncertain.

5. The author of Kings cites as authorities on the subject-matter of his history three works : (1) the " Book of the Acts of Solomon " (xi. 41) ; (2) the " Book of the Chronicles of the Kings of Israel " (xiv. 19, &c.) ; and (3) the " Book of the Chronicles of the Kings of Judah" (xiv. 29, &c.). His own history was, at least in part, derived from these works. Lesser works were also open to him.[9] Further, the writer had probably access to a work of a different character from any of those quoted by the author of Chronicles, namely, a collection of the miracles of Elisha, made probably in one of the schools of the Prophets.

Hence the sources of Kings may be considered threefold, consisting, first, of certain general historical documents called the "Books of the Chronicles of the Kings;" secondly, of some special treatises on the history of particular short periods; and, thirdly, of a single work of a very peculiar character, the private biography of a remarkable man.

The " Books of the Chronicles of the Kings " were probably of the nature of public Archives,[1]—State-annals, that is, containing an ac-

---

[7] *e.g.* Cp. 2 K. xvii. 14 and Jer. vii. 26 ; 2 K. xvii. 15 and Jer. ii. 5 ; 1 K. viii. 25 and Jer. xxxiii. 17 ; 2 K. xxi. 12 and Jer. xix. 3 ; 2 K. xxii. 17 and Jer. vii. 20, &c.

[8] Compare 2 K. xxiii. 34 with Jer. xxii. 12 ; 2 K. xxiv. 1 with Jer. xxv. 1-9 ; 2 K. xxiv. 7 with Jer. xlvi. 2-12 ; 2 K. xxv. 1-12 with Jer. xxxix. 1-10, &c.

[9] Such as the following :—"The Chronicles of King David " (1 Chr. xxvii. 24), "The Acts of Samuel the Seer," "The Acts of Nathan the Prophet," "The Acts of Gad the Seer " (1 Chr. xxix. 29), "The Prophecy of Ahijah the Shilonite," "The Visions of Iddo the Seer against Jeroboam the Son of Nebat" (2 Chr. ix. 29), "The Acts of Shemaiah the Prophet," " Iddo the Seer on Genealogies " (2 Chr. xii. 15), " The Commentary of the Prophet Iddo " (2 Chr. xiii. 22), and the like.

[1] See Esther ii. 23, vi. 1, x. 2.

count of the chief public events in the reign of each king, drawn up by an authorised person. With the Israelites the authorised person was probably in almost every case a Prophet. The Prophets regarded this as one of their principal duties, as we see by the examples of Isaiah (2 Chr. xxvi. 22 ; Is. xxxvi. --xxxviii.), Jeremiah (xxxix.--xliii. 7 ; lii.), and Daniel (i.--vi.). At the close of every reign, if not even in its course, an addition was probably made to the " Book of the Chronicles of the Kings " by the Prophet who held the highest position at the period.[2]

But the Prophets, in addition to these formal official writings, composed also historical works which were on a somewhat larger scale, and were especially more full in the account which they gave of religious matters. Cp. for example, the difference between the prophetical monograph and the drier abstract of the " Book of the Chronicles," contained in the historical chapters of Isaiah (xxxvi.–xxxix.), and the parallel chapters of the Second Book of Kings (xviii.–xx.). Cp. also Jer. xxxix.--xliv. with 2 K. xxv. 1–26. Further, comparing generally the

history as given in Chronicles with the corresponding history in Kings, the author of Chronicles seems to have followed generally the separate works of the various prophetical writers :[3] the author of Kings, mainly the official documents. In Chronicles nothing is more noticeable than the greater fulness of the *religious* history of Judah.[4] This came chiefly from the several prophetical works, and marks a contrast between their character and the ordinary character of the State-annals.

The writer of Kings was *mainly* a compiler. He selected, arranged, and wove into a whole, the various narratives of earlier writers whereof he made use. This is evident, both from the retention of obsolete or provincial forms in particular narratives, and from the occurrence of a number of statements which were inappropriate at the time when the compiler wrote.[5] The close verbal agreement between 2 Kings xviii. 15-xx. 19, and Isaiah xxxvi.–xxxix., can only have arisen from the writer's extracting without alteration Isaiah's

---

[2] Thus the "Book of the Acts of Solomon" was perhaps begun by Nathan, and was concluded either by Ahijah the Shilonite or by Iddo the Seer (2 Chr. ix. 29). The " Book of the Chronicles of the Kings of Judah " was probably the work of Shemaiah (2 Chr. xii. 15), Iddo (do. xiii. 22), Jehu the son of Hanani (do. xx. 34), Isaiah (do. xxvi. 22), Jeremiah, and others of the prophetical order, each of whom wrote the history of the king or kings with whom he was himself contemporary. Similarly with the " Book of the Chronicles of the Kings of Israel," Israelitish prophets such as Ahijah, Micaiah the son of Imlah (1 K. xxii. 8), Elisha, and Jonah (2 K. xiv. 25), composed portions.

[3] See the "Introd. to Chronicles," and compare 1 Chr. xxix. 29 ; 2 Chr. ix. 29, xii. 15, xiii. 22, &c.
[4] See particularly 1 Chr. xxii. 1–19, xxviii. 1–21, xxix. 1–22 ; 2 Chr. ii. 3–16, xiii. 4–18, &c.
[5] Of this kind are the following :—1. The statement in 1 K. viii. 8, that the staves of the Ark continued where they were placed by Solomon. 2. The statement that the bondage of the Amorites, Hivites, &c., continued (1 K. ix. 21). 3. The assertion that Israel was still in rebellion against the house of David (do. xii. 19). 4. The declaration that Selah (Petra) kept the name of Joktheel, which Amaziah gave it (2 K. xiv. 7). 5. The assignment of a preference over all other kings of Judah, previous and subsequent, both to Hezekiah (2 K. xviii. 5) and to Josiah (ib. xxiii. 25).

account of the reign of Hezekiah as it occurred in the State-annals: and the verbal agreement between great part of Chronicles and Kings, is often best accounted for by supposing that the two writers made *verbatim* extracts from the same authority.

On the other hand the writer of Kings sometimes departed from the wording of his authors, and substituted expressions purely his own.[6] And there are passages evidently original.[7] It is on these parts of the work that the argument in favour of Jeremiah's authorship especially rests.

6. Philologically speaking the general condition of the text is good.[8] But the historian has to lament an unsoundness, which, though affecting in no degree the religious character of the books, detracts from their value as documents wherein is contained an important portion of the world's civil history. The numbers, as they have come down to us in Kings, are untrustworthy, being in part self-contradictory, in part

opposed to other scriptural notices,[9] in part improbable, if not even impossible.[1] The defect would seem to have arisen from two causes, one common to the Hebrew Scriptures, the other peculiar to these Books. The common cause is corruption, partly from the fact that error in them is rarely checked by the context, partly from the circumstance that some system of abbreviated numerical notation[2] has been adopted by professional scribes, and that the symbols employed by them have been mistaken one for another. The peculiar cause of error seems to have been insertions into the text of chronological notes originally made in the margin by a commentator. The first date which occurs (1 K. vi. 1) seems to be a gloss of this cha-

---

[6] *e. g.* The phrase "across the river" (1 K. iv. 24) would not have been used to designate the tract west of the Euphrates by a Jew writing in Palestine in the reign of Solomon or Rehoboam. A contemporary of Jeroboam would not have spoken of "the cities of *Samaria*" (do. xiii. 32). The annals of Joash, son of Jehoahaz, did not, we may be sure, contain a statement that "God cast not Israel from his presence *as yet*" (2 K. xiii. 23).

[7] Besides the *formulæ* at the beginning and end of reigns, the same hand may be traced in 2 K. xvii. 7–41, xxi. 7–16, xxiii. 26, 27, xxiv. 3, 4, 6–20, xxv. 1–30.

[8] Almost the only passages where the question of the true reading is of much importance are 1 K. xi. 25, and 2 K. xvi. 6, in both which cases it is suspected that "Edom," should be read for "Syria."

[9] The date in 1 K. vi. 1, contradicts the Chronology of Judges and Samuel, as well as Acts xiii. 20; 1 K. xiv. 21, is at variance with ch. xii. The accession of Jehoram is variously placed in 2 K. i. 17 and 2 K. iii. 1; 2 K. xv. 1 is irreconcilable with 2 K. xiv. 23; xvii. 1 with xv. 30, &c.

[1] Thus Josiah (according to the present numbers) must have been born to Amon when the latter was sixteen, Jehoiakim to Josiah when Josiah was fourteen, and Hezekiah to Ahaz when Ahaz was only *eleven!* See 2 K. xviii. 2 note.

[2] Abbreviated forms of numerical notation are exceedingly ancient, and appear to have prevailed in all the great Oriental monarchies, notably in Egypt and Babylonia. The Hebrews certainly employed letters for numbers, in the same way as they do at present, as early as the time of the Maccabees; and it is probable that they employed either this or some other method of abbreviation from a much earlier date, perhaps even from the time of the Exodus. The full expression of the numbers in the sacred text belongs probably to the Talmudical period of superstitious regard for the mere letter of Scripture—the time when the characters were counted, when central letters were determined, and the practice commenced of writing them large.

racter, and it may be suspected
that to a similar origin is due the
whole series of synchronisms between the dynasties of Israel and
Judah. It is probable that the
original work gave simply the
years assigned to each king in the
" Books of the Chronicles," without
entering upon the further question,
in what regnal year of the contemporary monarch in the sister
kingdom each prince ascended the
throne. The chief difficulties of
the chronology, and almost all the
actual contradictions, disappear if
we subtract from the work these
portions.[3]

Excepting in this respect, the
Books of Kings have come down
to us, as to all essentials, in a
thoroughly sound condition. The
only place where the LXX. Version
differs importantly from the Hebrew text is in 1 Kings xii., where
a long passage concerning Jeroboam, the son of Nebat, not now
found in the Hebrew, occurs between *vv.* 24 and 25. But this
passage is clearly no part of the
original narrative. It is a story
after the fashion of the apocryphal
Esdras, worked up out of the
Scripture facts, with additions,
which the Alexandrian writer may
have taken from some Jewish
authority whereto he had access,
but which certainly did not come
from the writer of Kings. None
of its facts except possibly a single
one—the age, namely, of Rehoboam at his accession [4]— belongs

to the real narrative of our historian.

7. The primary character of the
work is undoubtedly historical. It
is the main object of the writer to
give an account of the kings of
Israel and Judah from Solomon's
accession to the captivity of Zedekiah.

The history is, however, written
—not, like most history, from a
civil, but from a religious point of
view. The Jews are regarded, not
as an ordinary nation, but as God's
people. The historian does not
aim at exhibiting the mere political
progress of the kingdoms about
which he writes, but intends to
describe to us God's treatment of
the race with which He had entered
into covenant. Where he records
the events of the civil history, his
plan is to trace out the fulfilment
of the combined warning and promise which had been given to
David (2 S. vii. 12–16).

Hence events, which an ordinary
historian would have considered of
great importance, may be (and
are) omitted by our author from
the narrative ; or touched slightly
and hastily.[5] As a general rule,
the military history of the two
kingdoms, which was no doubt
carefully recorded in the " Books
of the Chronicles," is omitted by

---

[3] As for instance in 1 K. xvi. 22, 23 :—
" So Tibni died, and Omri reigned. [In
the thirty and first year of Asa king of
Judah] Omri reigned over Israel twelve
years." Here the removal of the words
in brackets would evidently improve the
sense.

[4] See note on 1 K. xii. 8, 10.

[5] Thus he takes no notice at all of the
expedition of Zerah the Ethiopian (2
Chr. xiv. 9–15, xvi. 8) ; of Jehoshaphat's
war with Moab, Ammon, and Edom
(2 Chr. xx. 1–25) ; of Uzziah's successes
against the Philistines (do. xxvi. 6–8) ;
r of Manasseh's capture by the Assyrians
do. xxxiii. 11–13). He treats with the
utmost brevity the conquest of Jerusalem
by Shishak (1 K. xiv. 25, 26), the war between Abijam and Jeroboam (do. xv. 7),
that of Amaziah with Edom (2 K. xiv. 7),
and that of Josiah with Pharaoh-Nechoh
(do. xxiii. 29) ; events treated at length
in the parallel passages of the Book of
Chronicles.

the writer of Kings, who is content for the most part to refer his readers to the State-annals for the events which would have made the greatest figure in an ordinary secular history.

On the other hand, the special aim of the writer induces him to assign a prominent place and to give a full treatment to events which a secular historian would have touched lightly or passed over in silence. The teaching of the prophets, and their miracles, were leading points in the religious history of the time ; it was owing to them especially that the apostacy of the people was without excuse ; therefore the historian who has to show that, despite the promises made to David, Jerusalem was destroyed, and the whole twelve tribes carried into captivity, must exhibit fully the grounds for this severity, and must consequentiy dwell on circumstances which so intensely aggravated the guilt of the people.

The character of the history that he has to relate, its general tendency and ultimate issue, naturally throw over his whole narrative an air of gloom. The tone of the work thus harmonises with that of Jeremiah's undoubted writings, and furnishes an additional argument in favour of that Prophet's authorship.

The style of Kings is, for the most part, level and uniform—a simple narrative style. Occasionally a more lofty tone is breathed, the style rising with the subject-matter, and becoming in places almost poetical (1 K. xix. 11, 12 ; 2 K. xix. 21–31). The most striking chapters are the eighth, eighteenth, and nineteenth of the First Book ; the fifth, ninth, eighteenth, nineteenth, and twentieth of the Second.

8. The general authenticity of the narrative contained in our Books is admitted. Little is denied or questioned but the miraculous portions of the story, which cluster chiefly about the persons of Elijah and Elisha. Some critics admitting that the narrative generally is derived from authentic contemporary documents—either State-annals cr the writings of contemporary Prophets—maintain that the histories of Elijah and Elisha come from an entirely different source, being (they hold) collections of traditions respecting those persons made many years after their deaths, either by the writer of Kings or by some other person, from the mouths of the common people. Hence, according to them, their "legendary" or "mythical" character.

But there are no critical grounds for separating off the account of Elijah, or more than a small portion of the account of Elisha,[6] from the rest of the composition. The history of Elijah especially is so intertwined with that of the kingdom of Israel, and is altogether of so public a nature, that the "Chronicles of the Kings of Israel" would almost necessarily have contained an account of it ; and an important part of the history of Elisha is of a similar character. Further, it is quite gratuitous to imagine that the account was not a contemporary one, or that it was left for a writer living long subsequently to collect into a volume the doings of these remarkable personages. The proba-

---

[6] 2 K. iv. 1–37, and viii. 1–6, form the exceptions to the general rule.

bility is quite the other way. As the Prophets themselves were the historians of the time, it would be only natural that Elisha should collect the miracles and other remarkable deeds of Elijah ; and that his own should be collected after his decease by some one of the "sons of the Prophets." Add to this that the miracles, as related, have all the air of descriptions derived from eye-witnesses, being full of such minute circumstantial detail as tradition cannot possibly preserve. The whole result would seem to be that (unless we reject miracles altogether as unworthy of belief on account of an à priori impossibility) the account of the two great Israelite Prophets in Kings must be regarded as entitled to acceptance equally with the rest of the narrative.

Both internal consistency and probability, and also external testimony, strongly support the general authenticity of the secular history contained in Kings. The empire of Solomon is of a kind with which early Oriental history makes us familiar ; it occurs exactly at a period when there was room for its creation owing to the simultaneous weakness of Egypt and Assyria ; its rapid spread, and still more rapid contraction, are in harmony with our other records of Eastern dominion ; its art and civilization resemble those known to have prevailed about the same time in neighbouring countries. The contact of Judæa with Egypt, Assyria, and Babylonia, during the period covered by our Books agrees with the Egyptian annals, and in some respects is most strikingly illustrated by the cuneiform inscriptions. Berosus, Manetho, Me-

nander, Dius—the heathen historians of Babylon, Egypt, and Tyre—join with the monuments in the support which they furnish to our author's truthfulness and accuracy, as the comment appended to the text will prove abundantly.

Even the broader features of the chronology are both internally probable, and externally confirmed by the chronologies of other countries. The interval between the accession of Solomon and the captivity of Zedekiah is given as $433\frac{1}{2}$ years,[7] which is divided among twenty-one monarchs, who belong to eighteen (or, excluding Jehoiachin, to seventeen) generations. This allows for each generation the very probable term of $25\frac{1}{3}$ years. During the portion of the history where the chronology is double, and where the chief internal difficulties occur, the divergence of the two schemes is but slight, amounting to no more than about twenty years in 240 or 250. Egyptian annals confirm approximately the Biblical dates for Shishak's invasion, and So's alliance. The Assyrian annals agree with the Hebrew in the date of the fall of Samaria, and in exhibiting Hazael and Jehu, Tiglath-Pileser and Ahaz, Sennacherib and Hezekiah, Esarhaddon and Manasseh, as contemporaries. The chronological difficulties, where such exist, do not at all exceed those with which every reader of profane historians is familiar, and which, in fact, pervade the whole of ancient chron-

---

[7] This number is obtained by adding together the years of the kings of Judah. If parts of years are throughout counted as full years, this number is somewhat in excess. Clinton makes the actual time 429 years.

ology. They are partly to be accounted for by diversities in the mode of reckoning;[8] while occasionally no doubt they result from a corrupt reading, or from an unauthorised interpolation.

[8] In some systems, fractions of years are reckoned as years; in others, they are omitted altogether. In some, years are longer; in others, shorter than the true astronomical year. The differences which result from these causes mount up to something considerable in the course of centuries.

THE FIRST BOOK

OF THE

KINGS,

COMMONLY CALLED, THE THIRD BOOK OF THE KINGS.

CHAP. 1. NOW king David was old *and* [1] stricken in years; and they covered him with clothes, but he gat no heat. Wherefore his
2 servants said unto him, [2] Let there be sought for my lord the king [3] a young virgin: and let her stand before the king, and let her [4] cherish him, and let her lie in thy bosom, that my lord the
3 king may get heat. So they sought for a fair damsel through-
out all the coasts of Israel, and found Abishag a *a* Shunammite,
4 and brought her to the king. And the damsel *was* very fair, and cherished the king, and ministered to him: but the king
5 knew her not. ¶ Then *b* Adonijah the son of Haggith exalted himself, saying, I will [5] be king: and *c* he prepared him chariots
6 and horsemen, and fifty men to run before him. And his father had not displeased him [6] at any time in saying, Why hast thou done so? and he also *was* a very goodly *man;* *d* and *his mother*

a Josh. 19.
18.

b 2 Sam. 3. 4.
c 2 Sam. 15. 1.

d 2 Sam. 3.
3, 4.
1 Chr. 3. 2.

[1] Heb. *entered into days.*
[2] Heb. *Let them seek.*
[3] Heb. *a damsel, a virgin.*
[4] Heb. *be a cherisher unto him.*
[5] Heb. *reign.*
[6] Heb. *from his days.*

I. 1. *Now*] Rather, "and." The conjunction has here, probably, the same sort of connecting force which it has at the opening of Joshua, Judges, 1 Samuel, &c., and implies that the historian regards his work as a *continuation* of a preceding history.

king David] The expression "*king* David," instead of the simpler "David," is characteristic of the writer of Kings. (See Introd., p. 264, notes 3, 4.) The phrase is comparatively rare in Chronicles and Samuel.

stricken in years] David was perhaps now in his 71st year. He was thirty years old when he was made king in Hebron (2 Sam. v. 4); he reigned in Hebron seven years and six months (2 Sam. ii. 11; 1 Chr. iii. 4); and he reigned thirty-three years at Jerusalem (2 Sam. v. 5). The expression had hitherto been used only of persons above eighty (Gen xviii. 11, xxiv. 1; Josh. xiii. 1, xxiii. 1): but the Jews at this time were not long-lived. No Jewish monarch after David, excepting Solomon and Manasseh, exceeded sixty years.

clothes] Probably "bed-clothes." The king was evidently bed-ridden (*v.* 47).

2. As the Jewish Law allowed polygamy, David's conduct in following—what has been said to have been—physician's advice, was blameless.

5. The narrative concerning Abishag, the Shunammite (see marg. ref. *a*), is introduced as necessary for a proper understanding of Adonijah's later history (see ii. 13–

25.) But even as it stands, it heightens considerably the picture drawn of the poor king's weak and helpless condition, of which Adonijah was not ashamed to take advantage for his own aggrandisement. Adonijah was born while David reigned at Hebron, and was therefore now between thirty-three and forty years of age. He was David's fourth son, but had probably become the eldest by the death of his three older brothers. He claimed the crown by right of primogeniture (ii. 15), and secretly to his partisans (cp. *v.* 10) announced his intention of assuming the sovereignty. It was well known to him, and perhaps to the Jews generally, that David intended to make Solomon his successor (*v.* 13).

to run before him] That is, he assumed the same *quasi*-royal state as Absalom had done, when he contemplated rebellion (2 Sam. xv. 1).

6. *had not displeased him*] i.e. "His father had never checked or thwarted him all his life."

a very goodly man] Here, too, Adonijah resembled Absalom (2 Sam. xiv. 25). The Jews, like the other nations of antiquity, regarded the physical qualities of rulers as of great importance, and wished their kings to be remarkable for strength, stature, and beauty (1 Sam. ix. 2). Adonijah's personal advantages no doubt helped to draw the people to him.

his mother, &c.] i.e. Haggith bare Adonijah after Maacah bare Absalom (2 Sam. iii. 3, 4). The words in italics are not in the

7 bare him after Absalom. And ¹he conferred with Joab the son of Zeruiah, and with *e*Abiathar the priest: and *f*they ²following
8 Adonijah helped *him*. But Zadok the priest, and Benaiah the son of Jehoiada, and Nathan the prophet, and *g*Shimei, and Rei, and *h*the mighty men which *belonged* to David, were not
9 with Adonijah. And Adonijah slew sheep and oxen and fat cattle by the stone of Zoheleth, which *is* by ³En-rogel, and called all his brethren the king's sons, and all the men of Judah
10 the king's servants: but Nathan the prophet, and Benaiah, and the mighty men, and Solomon his brother, he called not.
11 ¶Wherefore Nathan spake unto Bath-sheba the mother of Solomon, saying, Hast thou not heard that Adonijah the son of
12 *i*Haggith doth reign, and David our lord knoweth *it* not? Now therefore come, let me, I pray thee, give thee counsel, that thou mayest save thine own life, and the life of thy son Solomon.
13 Go and get thee in unto king David, and say unto him, Didst not thou, my lord, O king, swear unto thine handmaid, saying, *k*Assuredly Solomon thy son shall reign after me, and he shall
14 sit upon my throne? why then doth Adonijah reign? Behold, while thou yet talkest there with the king, I also will come in
15 after thee, and ⁴confirm thy words. ¶And Bath-sheba went in

e 2 Sam. 20. 25.
f ch. 2. 22, 28.
g ch. 4. 18.
h 2 Sam. 23. 8.

i 2 Sam. 3. 4.

k 1 Chr. 22. 9.

---

¹ Heb. *his words were with Joab.*
² Heb. *helped after Adonijah.*
³ Or, *The well Rogel*, 2 Sam.
17. 17.
⁴ Heb. *fill up.*

---

original; hence some, by a slight alteration, read "David begat him."

7. Joab's defection on this occasion, after his faithful adherence to David during the troubles caused by Absalom (2 Sam. xviii. 2–17), may be accounted for by his fear that Solomon would be a "man of rest" (1 Chr. xxii. 9) and by his preference for the character of Adonijah. He may also have thought that Adonijah, as the eldest son (*v.* 5), had almost a right to succeed. Abiathar's defection is still more surprising than Joab's. For his history, see 1 Sam. xxii. 20 note. Hitherto David and he had been the firmest of friends. It has been conjectured that he had grown jealous of Zadok, and feared being supplanted by him.

8. There is some difficulty in understanding how Zadok and Abiathar came to be both "priests" at this time, and in what relation they stood to one another. The best explanation seems to be that Abiathar was the real High-Priest, and officiated at the Sanctuary containing the Ark of the Covenant in Zion, while Zadok performed the offices of chief priest at the Tabernacle of Witness at Gibeon (1 Chr. xvi. 39). For Benaiah, see 2 Sam. viii. 18, xx. 23, xxiii. 20, 21. For Nathan, see 2 Sam. vii. 2, 3, 17, xii. 1-15, 25. As privy to all David's plans (*v.* 24), he had no doubt fully approved the order of succession which the king was known to intend.

Shimei and Rei] Shimei and Rei are perhaps David's two brothers, Shimma and Raddai (1 Chr. ii. 13, 14).

mighty men] Probably the company of 600, originally formed during David's early wan-

derings (1 Sam. xxv. 13, xxvii. 2), and afterwards maintained as the most essential element of his standing army.

9. Adonijah's feast was probably of a sacrificial character, and intended to inaugurate him as king. Cp. the "sacrifices" of Absalom (2 Sam. xv. 12).

Zoheleth] No satisfactory explanation has been given of this name. Large blocks of stone always attract attention in the East, and receive names which are often drawn from some trivial circumstance. Sinai and Palestine are full of such *Hajars*, which correspond to the *Ebens* or "stones" of Holy Scripture. (Cp. Gen. xxviii. 22; Josh. iv. 9; 1 Sam. vi. 14.) For En-Rogel, see marg. ref.

11. *the son of Haggith*] Cp. marg. ref. This expression was well chosen to touch the pride of Bath-sheba. "Adonijah; not thy son, but the son of thy rival, Haggith."

12. It would have been in accordance with general Eastern custom for Solomon to suffer death, if Adonijah had succeeded in his attempt. But to have executed his mother also would have been an unusual severity. Still, such cases sometimes occurred: Cassander put to death Roxana, the widow of Alexander the Great, at the same time with her son, the young Alexander.

14. *confirm thy words*] "Establish" them, by giving a second testimony. Nathan thinks it best to move David's affections first through Bath-sheba, before he comes in to discuss the matter as one of state policy, and to take the king's orders upon it.

15. *into the chamber*] The "**bed-chamber**"

unto the king into the chamber: and the king was very old;
16 and Abishag the Shunammite ministered unto the king. And
Bath-sheba bowed, and did obeisance unto the king. And the
17 king said, [1]What wouldest thou? And she said unto him, My
[l] ver. 13, 30. lord, [l]thou swearest by the LORD thy God unto thine handmaid,
saying, Assuredly Solomon thy son shall reign after me, and he
18 shall sit upon my throne. And now, behold, Adonijah reigneth;
[m] ver. 7, 8, 9, 25. 19 and now, my lord the king, thou knowest *it* not: [m]and he hath
slain oxen and fat cattle and sheep in abundance, and hath
called all the sons of the king, and Abiathar the priest, and
Joab the captain of the host: but Solomon thy servant hath he
20 not called. And thou, my lord, O king, the eyes of all Israel
are upon thee, that thou shouldest tell them who shall sit on
21 the throne of my lord the king after him. Otherwise it shall
[n] Deut. 31. 16. ch. 2. 10. come to pass, when my lord the king shall [n]sleep with his
fathers, that I and my son Solomon shall be counted [2]offenders.
22 ¶ And, lo, while she yet talked with the king, Nathan the
23 prophet also came in. And they told the king, saying, Behold
Nathan the prophet. And when he was come in before the
king, he bowed himself before the king with his face to the
24 ground. And Nathan said, My lord, O king, hast thou said,
Adonijah shall reign after me, and he shall sit upon my throne?
[o] ver. 19. 25 [o]For he is gone down this day, and hath slain oxen and fat
cattle and sheep in abundance, and hath called all the king's
sons, and the captains of the host, and Abiathar the priest;
[p] 1 Sam. 10. 24. and, behold, they eat and drink before him, and say, [p][3]God
26 save king Adonijah. But me, *even* me thy servant, and Zadok
the priest, and Benaiah the son of Jehoiada, and thy servant
27 Solomon, hath he not called. Is this thing done by my lord the
king, and thou hast not shewed *it* unto thy servant, who should
28 sit on the throne of my lord the king after him? ¶ Then king
David answered and said, Call me Bath-sheba. And she came
29 [4]into the king's presence, and stood before the king. And the
[q] 2 Sam. 4. 9. king sware, and said, [q]*As* the LORD liveth, that hath redeemed

[1] Heb. *What to thee?*
[2] Heb. *sinners.*
[3] Heb. *Let king Adonijah live.*
[4] Heb. *before the king.*

---

or "**inner chamber.**" Abishag was a disinterested witness present, who heard all that Bath-sheba said to David.

16. Bath-sheba bowed, like the woman of Tekoah (2 Sam. xiv. 4), with the humble prostration of a suppliant. Hence the king's question, "What wouldest thou?"

20. *tell them who shall sit on the throne*] Side by side with what may be called the natural right of hereditary succession, there existed in the old world, and especially in the East, a right, if not of absolutely designating a successor, yet at any rate of choosing one among several sons. Thus Cyrus designated Cambyses; and Darius designated Xerxes; and a still more absolute right of nomination was exercised by some of the Roman emperors.

21. *shall sleep*] This euphemism for death, rare in the early Scriptures,—being found only once in the Pentateuch (marg. ref.), and once also in the historical books before Kings (2 Sam. vii. 12),—becomes in Kings and Chronicles the ordinary mode of speech (see ii. 10, xi. 43, &c.; 2 Chr. ix. 31, xii. 16, &c.). David uses the metaphor in one psalm (Ps. xiii. 3). In the later Scriptures it is, of course, common. (Jer. li. 39; Dan. xii. 2; Matt. ix. 24; John xi. 11; 1 Cor. xi. 30, xv. 51; 1 Thess. iv. 14, &c.)

22. Nathan came into the palace, not into the chamber, whither he might not enter unannounced. Bath-sheba retired before Nathan entered, in accordance with Oriental ideas of propriety. So, when Bath-sheba was again sent for (*v.* 28), Nathan retired (cp. *v.* 32).

24. *hast thou said*] **Thou hast said.** In the original no question is asked. Nathan assumes, as far as words go, that the king has made this declaration. He wishes to draw forth a disclaimer.

29. "As the Lord liveth" was the commonest form of oath among the Israelites (*e.g.* Judg. viii. 19; 1 Sam. xiv. 39, xix. 6).

30 my soul out of all distress, ʳeven as I sware unto thee by the
LORD God of Israel, saying, Assuredly Solomon thy son shall
reign after me, and he shall sit upon my throne in my stead;
31 even so will I certainly do this day. Then Bath-sheba bowed
with *her* face to the earth, and did reverence to the king, and
32 said, ˢLet my lord king David live for ever. ¶And king David
said, Call me Zadok the priest, and Nathan the prophet, and
Benaiah the son of Jehoiada. And they came before the king.
33 The king also said unto them, ᵗTake with you the servants of
your lord, and cause Solomon my son to ride upon ¹mine own
34 mule, and bring him down to ᵘGihon: and let Zadok the priest
and Nathan the prophet ˣanoint him there king over Israel:
and ʸblow ye with the trumpet, and say, God save king Solo-
35 mon. Then ye shall come up after him, that he may come and
sit upon my throne; for he shall be king in my stead: and I
have appointed him to be ruler over Israel and over Judah.
36 And Benaiah the son of Jehoiada answered the king, and said,
37 Amen: the LORD God of my lord the king say so *too*. ᶻAs the
LORD hath been with my lord the king, even so be he with
Solomon, and ᵃmake his throne greater than the throne of my
38 lord king David. ¶So Zadok the priest, and Nathan the prophet, ᵇand Benaiah the son of Jehoiada, and the Cherethites,
and the Pelethites, went down, and caused Solomon to ride
39 upon king David's mule, and brought him to Gihon. And
Zadok the priest took an horn of ᶜoil out of the tabernacle, and

ʳ ver. 17.

ˢ Neh. 2. 3.
Dan. 2. 4.

ᵗ 2 Sam. 20,
6.

ᵘ 2 Chr. 32.
30.
ˣ 1 Sam.10.1.
ch. 19. 16.
2 Kin. 9. 3.
ʸ 2 Sam. 15.
10.
2 Kin. 9. 13.
& 11. 14.

ᶻ Josh. 1. 5,
17.
1 Sam.20.13.
ᵃ ver. 47.

ᵇ 2 Sam. 8.
18.
& 23, 20—23.

ᶜ Ex. 30. 23.
Ps. 89. 20.

¹ Heb. *which* belongeth *to me:* See Esth. 6. 8.

It was peculiar to David to attach a further
clause to this oath—a clause of thankfulness
for some special mercy (1 Sam. xxv. 34), or
for God's constant protection of him (here
and in 2 Sam. iv. 9).

31. A lower and humbler obeisance than
before (*v.* 16). In the Assyrian sculptures
ambassadors are represented with their
faces actually touching the earth before the
feet of the monarch.

32. The combination of the High-Priest,
the Prophet, and the captain of the body-
guard (the Cherethites and Pelethites, *v.*
38), would show the people that the proceedings had the king's sanction. The
order of the names marks the position of
the persons with respect to the matter in
hand.

33. Mules and horses seem to have been
first employed by the Israelites in the
reign of David, and the use of the former
was at first confined to great personages
(2 Sam. xiii. 29, xviii. 9). The Rabbins tell
us that it was death to ride on the king's
mule without his permission; and thus it
would be the more evident to all that the
proceedings with respect to Solomon had
David's sanction.

Gihon] Probably the ancient name of the
valley called afterwards the Tyropœum,
which ran from the present Damascus Gate,
by Siloam, into the Kedron vale, having
the Temple hill, or true Zion, on the left,
and on the right the modern Zion or an-

cient city of the Jebusites. The upper
"source" of the "waters of Gihon," which
Hezekiah stopped (see marg. ref.), was probably in the neighbourhood of the Damascus Gate.

34. *anoint him*] Inauguration into each
of the three offices [those of prophet, priest,
and king] typical of the Messiah, or
Anointed One, was by anointing with oil.
Divine appointment had already instituted
the rite in connexion with the kingly office
(2 Sam. ii. 4); but after Solomon we have
no express mention of the anointing of kings,
except in the three cases of Jehu, Joash, and
Jehoahaz (2 K. ix. 6, xi. 12, xxiii. 30), who
were all appointed irregularly. At the time
of the Captivity, kings, whose anointing has
not been related in the historical books, still
bear the title of "the anointed of the Lord."
(Lam. iv. 20; Ps. lxxxix. 38, 51.)

35. *over Israel and over Judah*] There is
no anticipation here of the subsequent division of the kingdom; the antithesis between
Judah and Israel already existed in the
reign of David (2 Sam. ii. 9, xix. 11).

37. *As the LORD hath been with my lord*]
This phrase expresses a very high degree
of Divine favour. It occurs first in the
promises of God to Isaac (Gen. xxvi. 3, 24)
and Jacob (Gen. xxviii. 13). See further
marg. reff.

39. *the tabernacle*] Probably that which
David had made for the Ark of the Covenant on Mount Zion (2 Sam. vi. 17). For

d anointed Solomon. And they blew the trumpet; *e* and all the
40 people said, God save king Solomon. And all the people came
up after him, and the people piped with ¹pipes, and rejoiced
with great joy, so that the earth rent with the sound of them.
41 ¶ And Adonijah and all the guests that *were* with him heard *it*
as they had made an end of eating. And when Joab heard the
sound of the trumpet, he said, Wherefore *is this* noise of the
42 city being in an uproar? And while he yet spake, behold,
Jonathan the son of Abiathar the priest came: and Adonijah

said unto him, Come in; for *f* thou *art* a valiant man, and
43 bringest good tidings. And Jonathan answered and said to
Adonijah, Verily our lord king David hath made Solomon king.
44 And the king hath sent with him Zadok the priest, and Nathan
the prophet, and Benaiah the son of Jehoiada, and the Cherethites, and the Pelethites, and they have caused him to ride upon
45 the king's mule: and Zadok the priest and Nathan the prophet
have anointed him king in Gihon: and they are come up from
thence rejoicing, so that the city rang again. This *is* the noise

46 that ye have heard. And also Solomon *g* sitteth on the throne
47 of the kingdom. And moreover the king's servants came to

bless our lord king David, saying, *h* God make the name of
Solomon better than thy name, and make his throne greater

than thy throne. *i* And the king bowed himself upon the bed.
48 And also thus said the king, Blessed *be* the LORD God of Israel,

which hath *k* given *one* to sit on my throne this day, mine eyes
49 even seeing *it*. ¶ And all the guests that *were* with Adonijah
50 were afraid, and rose up, and went every man his way. And
Adonijah feared because fo Solomon, and arose, and went, and

51 *l* caught hold on the horns of the altar. And it was told Solomon, saying, Behold, Adonijah feareth king Solomon: for, lo,
he hath caught hold on the horns of the altar, saying, Let king
Solomon swear unto me to day that he will not slay his servant
52 with the sword. And Solomon said, If he will shew himself a

worthy man, *m* there shall not an hair of him fall to the earth:
53 but if wickedness shall be found in him, he shall die. So king
Solomon sent, and they brought him down from the altar.

¹ Or, *flutes.*

the holy oil, see marg. reff. That it was
part of the regular furniture of the Tabernacle appears from Ex. xxxi. 11, xxxix.
38.

40. *piped with pipes*] Some prefer "danced
with dances"—a meaning which the Hebrew would give by a change in the pointing, and the alteration of one letter. But
the change is unnecessary. (Flute-) pipes
were known to the Israelites (1 Sam. x. 5);
they were very ancient in Egypt, and were
known also to the Assyrians.

the earth rent] If the present Hebrew
text is correct we have here a strong instance of Oriental hyperbole. But it is
suspected that there is a slight corruption,
and that the verb really used meant "re-
sounded."

42. Jonathan had acted in a similar
capacity, as a carrier of intelligence, in the
time of Absalom's attempt (2 Sam. xv. 36,
xvii. 17); but at that time, like his father,

he was faithful to David, and "a valiant
man," "a virtuous man," or "a man of
worth." (See *v.* 52; Prov. xii. 4.)

43. *Verily*] "Nay, but" [or, "Not so "].

47. *the king bowed himself*] The king worshipped God and prayed that it might be
so. Cp. Gen. xlvii. 31, with marg. ref.,
Heb. xi. 21.

50. On the "horns" of the Altar, see
Ex. xxvii. 2 note. The Altar to which
Adonijah fled was probably in the "Taber-
nacle" already referred to (*v.* 39).

52. *there shall not an hair, &c.*] This was a
proverbial expression, meaning "he shall
suffer no hurt at all." Solomon's clemency
in pardoning Adonijah is very remarkable. In the East not only are pretenders
almost always punished with death, but it
has often been the custom for each king
upon his accession to put to death all his
brothers as mere possible pretenders.

And he came and bowed himself to king Solomon: and Solomon said unto him, Go to thine house.

Chap. 2. NOW ^athe days of David drew nigh that he should die; 2 and he charged Solomon his son, saying, ^bI go the way of all the earth: ^cbe thou strong therefore, and shew thyself a man; 3 and keep the charge of the Lord thy God, to walk in his ways, to keep his statutes, and his commandments, and his judgments, and his testimonies, as it is written in the law of Moses, that thou mayest ^{d 1}prosper in all that thou doest, and whither- 4 soever thou turnest thyself: that the Lord may ^econtinue his word which he spake concerning me, saying, ^fIf thy children take heed to their way, to ^gwalk before me in truth with all their heart and with all their soul, ^hthere shall not ²fail thee 5 (said he) a man on the throne of Israel. Moreover thou knowest also what Joab the son of Zeruiah ⁱdid to me, *and* what he did to the two captains of the hosts of Israel, unto ^kAbner the son of Ner, and unto ^lAmasa the son of Jether, whom he slew, and ³shed the blood of war in peace, and put the blood of war upon his girdle that *was* about his loins, and in his shoes that *were* on 6 his feet. Do therefore ^maccording to thy wisdom, and let not

Marginal references:
a Gen. 47. 29.
Deut. 31. 14.
b Josh. 23.
14.
c Deut. 17.
19, 20.
d Deut. 29. 9.
Josh. 1. 7.
1 Chr. 22. 12,
13.
e 2 Sam. 7.
25.
f Ps. 132. 12.
g 2 Kin.20.3.
h 2 Sam. 7.
12, 13.
ch. 8. 25.
i 2 Sam. 3.
39.
& 19. 5, 6.
k 2 Sam. 3.
27.
l 2 Sam. 20.
10.
m ver. 9.
Prov. 20. 26.

¹ Or. *do wisely*, 1 Sam. 18. 5, 14, 30.   ² Heb. *be cut off from thee from the throne.*   ³ Heb. *put.*

II. The events related in 1 Chr. xxviii. and xxix. had occurred in the interval which separates the last and this present chapter.

2. David appears to have in his thoughts the Divine address to Joshua. Without following it servilely, he reproduces several of its leading expressions and sentiments (cp. marg. reff.). Solomon's youth clearly constituted one of the chief difficulties of his position. If he was about nineteen or twenty, and known to be of a pacific disposition (1 Chr. xxii. 9), then to have to rule over the warlike and turbulent Hebrew nation, with a strong party opposed to him, and brothers of full age ready to lead it, was evidently a most difficult task. Hence he is exhorted, though in years a boy, to show himself in spirit "a man."

3. The "statutes" have been explained to be the positive ordinances of the Law; the "commandments" the moral precepts, not to steal, &c.; the "judgments" the laws belonging to civil government; and the "testimonies" the laws directing the commemoration of certain events. Cp. Ps. xix. 7, 8.

4. *that the* Lord *may continue his word*] The original promise given to David indirectly, through Nathan (2 Sam. vii. 11–17), and apparently unconditional, afterwards was made conditional upon continued obedience. (See marg. ref. *f*.) David reminds Solomon of this, in order to impress upon him a powerful motive to continue faithful and obedient.

5. In his directions with respect to certain important persons, David, anxious for the security of his young successor's king-dom, allows old animosities to revive, and is willing to avenge himself indirectly and by deputy, though he had been withheld by certain scruples from taking vengeance in his own person. We must not expect Gospel morality from the saints of the Old Testament. They were only the best men of their several ages and nations. The maxim of "them of old time," whether Jews or Gentiles, was "Love your friends and hate your enemies" (see Matt. v. 43) ; and David perhaps was not in this respect in advance of his age. Joab's chief offence against David, besides his two murders, was no doubt his killing Absalom (2 Sam. xviii. 14). Another serious crime was his support of the treasonable attempt of Adonijah (i. 7). But besides these flagrant misdemeanours, he seems to have offended David by a number of little acts. He was a constant thorn in his side. He treated him with scant respect, taking important steps without his orders (2 Sam. iii. 26), remonstrating with him roughly and rudely (do. *vv.* 24 and 25), almost betraying his secrets (do. xi. 19–21), and, where he disliked the orders given him, disobeying them (1 Chr. xxi. 6). David allowed his ascendancy, but he chafed against it, finding *this* "son of Zeruiah," in particular "too hard" for him (marg. ref.).

put the blood of war upon his girdle, &c.] Meaning "The blood of Amasa spirted all over the girdle to which the sword of Joab was attached; and the sandals on his feet were reddened with the stains left by the falling corpse."

6. *his hoar head*] Joab, though the nephew of David, was probably not very

7 his hoar head go down to the grave in peace. But shew kindness unto the sons of *n*Barzillai the Gileadite, and let them be of those that *o*eat at thy table : for so *p*they came to me when I 8 fled because of Absalom thy brother. And, behold, *thou hast* with thee *q*Shimei the son of Gera, a Benjamite of Bahurim, which cursed me with a ¹grievous curse in the day when I went to Mahanaim : but *r*he came down to meet me at Jordan, and *s*I sware to him by the LORD, saying, I will not put thee to 9 death with the sword. Now therefore *t*hold him not guiltless : for thou *art* a wise man, and knowest what thou oughtest to do unto him ; but his hoar head *u*bring thou down to the grave with 10 blood. ¶ So *x*David slept with his fathers, and was buried in 11 *y*the city of David. And the days that David *z*reigned over Israel *were* forty years : seven years reigned he in Hebron, and 12 thirty and three years reigned he in Jerusalem. ¶ *a*Then sat Solomon upon the throne of David his father ; and his kingdom 13 was established greatly. ¶ And Adonijah the son of Haggith came to Bath-sheba the mother of Solomon. And she said, *b*Comest 14 thou peaceably ? And he said, Peaceably. He said moreover, 15 I have somewhat to say unto thee. And she said, Say on. And he said, Thou knowest that the kingdom was *c*mine, and *that* all Israel set their faces on me, that I should reign : howbeit the kingdom is turned about, and is become my brother's : for *d*it 16 was his from the LORD. And now I ask one petition of thee, 17 ²deny me not. And she said unto him, Say on. And he said, Speak, I pray thee, unto Solomon the king, (for he will not say thee nay,) that he give me *e*Abishag the Shunammite to wife. 18 And Bath-sheba said, Well ; I will speak for thee unto the king. 19 ¶ Bath-sheba therefore went unto king Solomon, to speak unto him for Adonijah. And the king rose up to meet her, and *f*bowed himself unto her, and sat down on his throne, and caused a seat to be set for the king's mother ; *g*and she sat on his right 20 hand. Then she said, I desire one small petition of thee ; *I pray thee,* say me not nay. And the king said unto her, Ask on, my 21 mother : for I will not say thee nay. And she said, Let Abishag the Shunammite be given to Adonijah thy brother to wife. 22 And king Solomon answered and said unto his mother, And why dost thou ask Abishag the Shunammite for Adonijah ? ask

¹ Heb. *strong.*   ² Heb. *turn not away my face,* Ps. 132. 10.

greatly his junior, David being the youngest of the family, and Zeruiah, as is most likely, one of the eldest.

7. One of the sons of Barzillai here intended was probably Chimham (see marg. ref.). Who the others were is not known. The family continued down to the return from the Captivity, and still held property in Israel (cp. Ezra ii. 61 and Nehemiah vii. 63).

9. *hold him not guiltless*] i.e. "Do not treat him as an innocent man. Punish him as in thy wisdom thou deemest best. Not capitally at once ; but so that he may be likely to give thee in course of time a just occasion to slay him." So, at least, Solomon seems to have understood the charge. (See *vv.* 36-46.)

11. *forty years*] In all forty years and

six months. See 2 Sam. v. 5, and 1 Chr. iii. 4. The Jewish writers almost universally omit the fractions of a year.

12. The "establishment" of the kingdom here intended is probably its universal acceptance both by the tribe of Judah and the other Israelites.

16. *deny me not*] Lit., as in the margin, *i.e.* "make me not to hide my face through shame at being refused."

19. *a seat*] Or, "a throne." We have here a proof of the high dignity of the Queen-mother. Cp. above xv. 13 ; 2 K. xi. 1-3. In the Persian Court the Queen-mother had often the chief power.

22. *ask for him the kingdom also*] Bath-sheba had not seen anything dangerous or suspicious in Adonijah's request. Solomon, on the contrary, takes alarm at once. To

for him the kingdom also; for he *is* mine elder brother; even
for him, and for *ʰ*Abiathar the priest, and for Joab the son of   *ʰ* ch. 1. 7.
23 Zeruiah. ¶ Then king Solomon sware by the LORD, saying, *ⁱ*God   *ⁱ* Ruth 1. 17.
do so to me, and more also, if Adonijah have not spoken this
24 word against his own life. Now therefore, *as* the LORD liveth,
which hath established me, and set me on the throne of David
my father, and who hath made me an house, as he *ᵏ*promised,   *ᵏ* 2 Sam. 7.
25 Adonijah shall be put to death this day. And king Solomon   11. 13.
sent by the hand of Benaiah the son of Jehoiada; and he fell   1 Chr. 22.10.
26 upon him that he died. ¶ And unto Abiathar the priest said the
king, Get thee to *ˡ*Anathoth, unto thine own fields; for thou *art*   *ˡ* Josh. 21.18.
¹worthy of death: but I will not at this time put thee to death,
*ᵐ*because thou barest the ark of the Lord GOD before David my   *ᵐ* 1 Sam.
father, and because *ⁿ*thou hast been afflicted in all wherein my   23. 6.
27 father was afflicted. So Solomon thrust out Abiathar from   2 Sam. 15.
being priest unto the LORD; that he might *ᵒ*fulfil the word of   24, 29.
the LORD, which he spake concerning the house of Eli in Shiloh.   *ⁿ* 1 Sam. 22.
28 ¶ Then tidings came to Joab: for Joab *ᵖ*had turned after Ado-   20, 23.
nijah, though he turned not after Absalom. And Joab fled unto   31—35.
the tabernacle of the LORD, and *q*caught hold on the horns of   *ᵖ* ch. 1. 7.
29 the altar. And it was told king Solomon that Joab was fled   *q* ch. 1. 50.
unto the tabernacle of the LORD; and, behold, *he is* by the altar.
Then Solomon sent Benaiah the son of Jehoiada, saying, Go,
30 fall upon him. And Benaiah came to the tabernacle of the
LORD, and said unto him, Thus saith the king, Come forth. And
he said, Nay; but I will die here. And Benaiah brought the
king word again, saying, Thus said Joab, and thus he answered
31 me. And the king said unto him, *ʳ*Do as he hath said, and fall   *ʳ* Ex. 21. 14.
upon him, and bury him; *ˢ*that thou mayest take away the   *ˢ* Num.35.33.
innocent blood, which Joab shed, from me, and from the house   Deut. 19. 13.

¹ Heb. *a man of death.*

---

ask for Abishag was to ask for the kingdom.
To the Oriental mind a monarch was so
sacred, that whatever was brought near to
him was thenceforth separate from common
use. This sacred and separate character
attached especially to the Royal harem.
The inmates either remained widows for the
rest of their lives, *or became the wives of the
deceased king's successor.* When a monarch
was murdered, or 'dethroned, or succeeded
by one whose title was doubtful, the latter
alternative was almost always adopted (cp. 2
Sam. xii. 8, xvi. 22). Public opinion so closely
connected the title to the crown and the
possession of the deceased monarch's wives,
that to have granted Adonijah's request
would have been the strongest encouragement to his pretensions. Solomon, seeing
this, assumes that Adonijah cherishes a
guilty purpose, that there has been a fresh
plot, that Abiathar and Joab—Adonijah's
counsellors in the former conspiracy (i.
7)—are privy to it, and that the severest
measures are necessary to crush the new
treason.
23. *against his own life*] Adonijah had forfeited his life by his former conduct, and his
pardon had been merely conditional (i. 52).

24. The phrase "making a house" means
"continuing the posterity" of a person,
and, in the case of a royal person,
"maintaining his descendants upon the
throne."
26. For Anathoth and the allusions in
this verse, see marg. reff.
27. *that he might fulfil the word of the
LORD*] We need not understand this as
stating that the fulfilment of the old prophecy was Solomon's motive, or even one
of his motives. The reference is to the
overruling providence of God, which thus
brought about the fulfilment of the prophecy. (Cp. Matt. i. 22, ii. 15, xxvii. 35,
&c.) The deposition of Abiathar involved
the rejection of the house of Ithamar (1 Chr.
xxiv. 3), to which Eli belonged, and the re-
establishment of the High-Priesthood in the
line of Eleazar.
28. Joab followed the example of Adonijah (marg. ref.). The Tabernacle was now
at Gibeon (iii. 4; 1 Chr. xvi. 39).
31. It was only a murderer to whom the
Tabernacle was to be no protection (marg.
ref.). Hence the reference to the "innocent blood."

t Judg. 9.
24, 57.
Ps. 7. 16.
u 2Chr.21.13.
x 2Sam.3.27.
y 2 Sam. 20.
10.
z 2Sam.3.29.
a Prov. 25.5.

b Num. 25.
11, 12, 13.
1 Sam. 2. 35.
See 1 Chr. 6.
53.
& 24. 3.
c ver. 27.
d 2Sam.16.5.
ver. 8.
e 3 Sam. 15.
23.
f Lev. 20. 9.
Josh. 2. 19.
2 Sam. 1. 16.
g 1 Sam.
27. 2.

h 2 Sam.
16. 5.

i Ps. 7. 16.
Ezek. 17.19.
k 2 Sam. 7.
13. Ps. 89. 4.

l ver. 12.
2 Chr. 1. 1.

32 of my father. And the LORD *t*shall return his blood upon his own head, who fell upon two men more righteous *u*and better than he, and slew them with the sword, my father David not knowing *thereof, to wit,* *x*Abner the son of Ner, captain of the host of Israel, and *y*Amasa the son of Jether, captain of the
33 host of Judah. Their blood shall therefore return upon the head of Joab, and *z*upon the head of his seed for ever: *a*but upon David, and upon his seed, and upon his house, and upon
34 his throne, shall there be peace for ever from the LORD. So Benaiah the son of Jehoiada went up, and fell upon him, and slew him : and he was buried in his own house in the wilderness.
35 And the king put Benaiah the son of Jehoiada in his room over the host : and *b*Zadok the priest did the king put in the room
36 of *c*Abiathar. ¶ And the king sent and called for *d*Shimei, and said unto him, Build thee an house in Jerusalem, and dwell
37 there, and go not forth thence any whither. For it shall be, *that* on the day thou goest out, and passest over *e*the brook Kidron, thou shalt know for certain that thou shalt surely die :
38 *f*thy blood shall be upon thine own head. And Shimei said unto the king, The saying *is* good : as my lord the king hath said, so will thy servant do. And Shimei dwelt in Jerusalem many days.
39 And it came to pass at the end of three years, that two of the servants of Shimei ran away unto *g*Achish son of Maachah king of Gath. And they told Shimei, saying, Behold, thy servants *be*
40 in Gath. And Shimei arose, and saddled his ass, and went to Gath to Achish to seek his servants : and Shimei went, and
41 brought his servants from Gath. And it was told Solomon that Shimei had gone from Jerusalem to Gath, and was come again.
42 And the king sent and called for Shimei, and said unto him, Did I not make thee to swear by the LORD, and protested unto thee, saying, Know for a certain, on the day thou goest out, and walkest abroad any whither, that thou shalt surely die ? and thou
43 saidst unto me, The word *that* I have heard *is* good. Why then hast thou not kept the oath of the LORD, and the commandment
44 that I have charged thee with ? The king said moreover to Shimei, Thou knowest *h*all the wickedness which thine heart is privy to, that thou didst to David my father: therefore the LORD
45 shall *i*return thy wickedness upon thine own head ; and king Solomon *shall be* blessed, and *k*the throne of David shall be es-
46 tablished before the LORD for ever. So the king commanded Benaiah the son of Jehoiada ; which went out, and fell upon him, that he died. And the *l*kingdom was established in the hand of Solomon.

---

32. *shall return his blood*] i.e. "his shedding of blood."
33. *upon the head of his seed*] Cp. marg. ref. Nothing further is heard of Joab's descendants in the history.
34. Retribution overtook Joab on the very scene (Gibeon) of the most treacherous of his murders. It was at the "great stone which is in Gibeon" that Joab slew Amasa (2 Sam. xx. 8–10).
35. The High-Priesthood had been for some time in a certain sense divided between Zadok and Abiathar. (See i. 8 note.) Henceforth Zadok became sole High-Priest.
36. The object, apparently, was to keep

Shimei under the immediate eye of the government. Shimei's old home, Bahurim, lay east of Jerusalem, on the road to Jericho (2 Sam. xvii. 18), and could only be reached by crossing the Kedron valley. Solomon assumes, that, if he quits the city, it will probably be in this direction (*v.* 37).
39. *Achish*] Possibly the Achish of marg. ref., but more probably the grandson of the former Achish.
42. *Did I not make thee to swear*] The LXX. add to *v.* 37 a clause stating that Solomon "made Shimei swear" on the day when he commanded him to reside at Jerusalem.

CHAP. 3. AND ^aSolomon made affinity with Pharaoh king of Egypt, and took Pharaoh's daughter, and brought her into the ^bcity of David, until he had made an end of building his ^cown house, and ^dthe house of the LORD, and ^ethe wall of Jerusalem round 2 about. ^fOnly the people sacrificed in high places, because there was no house built unto the name of the LORD, until those days. 3 And Solomon ^gloved the LORD, ^hwalking in the statutes of David his father : only he sacrificed and burnt incense in high places. 4 ¶ And ⁱthe king went to Gibeon to sacrifice there ; ^kfor that was the great high place : a thousand burnt offerings did Solomon 5 offer upon that altar. ^lIn Gibeon the LORD appeared to Solomon ^min a dream by night : and God said, Ask what I shall 6 give thee. ⁿAnd Solomon said, Thou hast shewed unto thy ser-.vant David my father great ¹mercy, according as he ^owalked before thee in truth, and in righteousness, and in uprightness of heart with thee ; and thou hast kept for him this great kindness,

¹ Or, *bounty.*

a ch. 7. 8.
& 9. 24.
b 2 Sam. 5. 7.
c ch. 7. 1.
d ch. 6.
e ch. 9. 15.
f Lev. 17. 3.
ch 22. 43.
g Deut. 6. 5.
& 30. 16.
Ps. 31. 23.
Rom. 8. 28.
1 Cor. 8. 3.
h ver. 6. 14.
i 2 Chr. 1. 3.
k 1Chr.16.39.
l ch. 9. 2.
2 Chr. 1. 7.
m Num.12.6,
Matt. 1. 20.
n 2 Chr. 1.
8, &c.
o ch. 2. 4.
Ps. 15. 2.

III. 1. What Pharaoh is meant is uncertain. It must have been a predecessor of Shishak (or Sheshonk), who invaded Judæa more than forty years later (xiv. 25) ; and probabilities are in favour, not of Psusennes II., the last king of Manetho's 21st dynasty, but of Psinaces, the predecessor of Psusennes. This, the Tanite dynasty, had become very weak, especially towards its close, whence we may conceive how gladly it would ally itself with the powerful house of David. The Jews were not forbidden to marry foreign wives, if they became proselytes. As Solomon is not blamed for this marriage either here or in ch. xi., and as the idol temples which he allowed to be built (xi. 5-7) were in no case dedicated to Egyptian deities, it is to be presumed that his Egyptian wife adopted her husband's religion.

the city of David] The city, situated on the eastern hill, or true Zion, where the Temple was afterwards built, over against the city of the Jebusites (ix. 24 ; cp. 2 Chr. viii. 11).

2. The word "only" introduces a contrast. The writer means to say that there was one exception to the flourishing condition of things which he has been describing, viz., that "the people sacrificed in high-places." (Compare the next verse.) The Law did not forbid "high-places" directly, but only by implication. It required the utter destruction of all the high-places which had been polluted by idolatrous rites (Deut. xii. 2) ; and the injunction to offer sacrifices nowhere except at the door of the Tabernacle (Lev. xvii. 3-5) was an indirect prohibition of them, or, at least, of the use which the Israelites made of them ; but there was some real reason to question whether this was a command intended to come into force until the "place" was chosen "where the Lord would cause His name to dwell." (See Deut. xii. 11, 14.) The result was that high-places were used for the wor-

ship of Jehovah, from the time of the Judges downwards (Judg. vi. 25, xiii. 16 ; 1 Sam. vii. 10, xiii. 9, xiv. 35, xvi. 5 ; 1 Chr. xxi. 26), with an entire unconsciousness of guilt on- the part of those who used them. And God so far overlooked this ignorance that He accepted the worship thus offered Him, as appears from the vision vouchsafed to Solomon on this occasion. There were two reasons for the prohibition of high-places ; first, the danger of the old idolatry creeping back if the old localities were retained for worship ; and, secondly, the danger to the unity of the nation if there should be more than one legitimate religious centre. The existence of the worship at high-places did, in fact, facilitate the division of the kingdom.

4. *Gibeon*] The transfer to Gibeon of the "Tabernacle of the congregation," and the brazen "Altar of burnt offerings" made by Moses, which were removed thither from Nob (cp. 1 Sam. xxi. 6, with marg. reff. *i*, *k*), had made it "the *great* high-place," more sacred, *i.e.*, than any other in the Holy Land, unless it were Mount Zion whither the Ark had been conveyed by David. For the position of Gibeon, see Josh. ix. 3 note.

a thousand burnt offerings did Solomon offer] Solomon presented the victims. The priests were the actual sacrificers (viii. 5). A sacrifice of a thousand victims was an act of royal magnificence suited to the greatness of Solomon. So Xerxes offered 1000 oxen at Troy. If the offerings in this case were "whole burnt offerings," and were all offered upon the Altar of Moses, the sacrifice must have lasted several days.

5. *the* LORD *appeared unto Solomon in a dream*] Cp. marg. reff. and Gen. xv. 1, xxviii. 12, xxxvii. 5.

6. *this great kindness*] David himself had regarded this as God's crowning mercy to him (i. 48).

p ch. 1. 48.
q 1 Chr. 29.1.
r Num.27.17.
s Deut. 7. 6.
t Gen. 13. 16.
& 15. 5.
u 2 Chr.1.10.
Pro. 2. 3—9.
Jam. 1. 5.
x Ps. 72. 1.
y Heb. 5. 14.
z Jam. 4. 3.

a 1 John 5.
14, 15.
b ch. 5. 12.
& 10. 24.
Eccles. 1. 16.

c Matt. 6. 33.
Eph. 3. 20.
d ch.4. 21,24.
Prov. 3. 16.

e ch. 15. 5.
f Ps. 91. 16.
Prov. 3. 2.
g So Gen.
41. 7.

that thou *p*hast given him a son to sit on his throne, as *it is* this
7 day. And now, O LORD my God, thou hast made thy servant
king instead of David my father: *q*and I *am but* a little child :
8 I know not *how* *r*to go out or come in. And thy servant *is* in
the midst of thy people which thou *s*hast chosen, a great people,
9 *t*that cannot be numbered nor counted for multitude. *u*Give
therefore thy servant an ¹understanding heart *x*to judge thy
people, that I may *v*discern between good and bad : for who is
10 able to judge this thy so great a people ? ¶ And the speech
11 pleased the LORD, that Solomon had asked this thing. And God
said unto him, Because thou hast asked this thing, and hast *z*not
asked for thyself ²long life ; neither hast asked riches for thyself,
nor hast asked the life of thine enemies ; but hast asked for thy-
12 self understanding ³to discern judgment ; *a*behold, I have done
according to thy words : *b*lo, I have given thee a wise and an understanding heart ; so that there was none like thee before thee,
13 neither after thee shall any arise like unto thee. And I have
also *c*given thee that which thou hast not asked, both *d*riches,
and honour : so that there ⁴shall not be any among the kings
14 like unto thee all thy days. And if thou wilt walk in my ways,
to keep my statutes and my commandments, *e*as thy father
15 David did walk, then I will *f*lengthen thy days. And Solomon
*g*awoke ; and, behold, *it was* a dream. And he came to Jerusalem, and stood before the ark of the covenant of the LORD,
and offered up burnt offerings, and offered peace offerings, and

¹ Heb. *hearing.*   ² Heb. *many days.*   ³ Heb. *to hear.*
⁴ Or, *hath not been.*

---

7. See ii. 2 note, and on the hyperbole
contained in the phrase " little child," cp.
Gen. xliii. 8 ; Ex. xxxiii. 11.
how to go out or come in] This expression
is proverbial for the active conduct of
affairs. (See marg. ref.)
8. Cp. marg. reff. Solomon regards the
promises as fulfilled in the existing greatness and glory of the Jewish nation.
9. One of the chief functions of the
Oriental monarch is always to hear and
decide causes. Hence supreme magistrates
were naturally called " judges." (See Introd. to Book of Judges.) In the minds
of the Jews the " judge " and the " prince "
were always closely associated, the direct
cognisance of causes being constantly taken
by their chief civil governors. (See Ex.
ii. 14, xviii. 16, 22 ; 1 Sam. viii. 20 ; 2 Sam.
xv. 2-6.)
good and bad] i.e. " right and wrong,"
" justice and injustice."
10. Although Solomon's choice was made
" in a dream " (*v.* 5), we must regard it as
springing from his will in some degree, and
therefore as indicative of his moral character.
11. *thine enemies*] e.g. Hadad the Edomite (xi. 14-22) and Rezon the son of Eliadah
(do. *vv.* 23-25), whom Solomon might well
have wished to remove.
12. *a wise and an understanding heart*]
Solomon's wisdom seems to have been both
moral and intellectual (see iv. 29-34). But

it was moral wisdom alone which he requested, and which was promised him.
The terms translated " wise " and " understanding," both denote *practical* wisdom.
(See Gen. xli. 33, 39 ; Deut. iv. 6 ; Prov.
i. 2, &c.)
*neither after thee shall any arise like unto
thee*] i.e. in the knowledge of what was in
man, and in the wisdom to direct men's
goings, he was to be the wisest of *all* mere
men. In such wisdom the world would
know one only " greater than Solomon "
(Matt. xii. 42 ; Luke xi. 31).
13. A striking illustration of that law
of the Divine government to which Christ
referred (marg. ref.).
14. *I will lengthen thy days*] The promise
here was only conditional. As the condition was not observed (xi. 1-8), the right to
the promise was forfeited, and it was not
fulfilled. Solomon can scarcely have been
more than fifty-nine or sixty at his death.
15. Solomon determined to inaugurate
his reign by a grand religious ceremonial at
each of the two holy places which at this
time divided between them the reverence
of the Jews. Having completed the religious service at Gibeon, where was the
Tabernacle of the Congregation, he proceeded to Jerusalem, and sacrificed before
the Ark of the Covenant, which was in
Mount Zion (2 Sam. vi. 12). A great feast
naturally followed on a large sacrifice of
peace-offerings. In these the sacrificer

16 ʰmade a feast to all his servants. ¶ Then came there two
women, *that were* harlots, unto the king, and ᶦstood before him.
17 And the one woman said, O my lord, I and this woman dwell in
one house; and I was delivered of a child with her in the house.
18 And it came to pass the third day after that I was delivered,
that this woman was delivered also: and we *were* together; *there
was* no stranger with us in the house, save we two in the house.
19 And this woman's child died in the night; because she overlaid
20 it. And she arose at midnight, and took my son from beside me,
while thine handmaid slept, and laid it in her bosom, and laid
21 her dead child in my bosom. And when I rose in the morning
to give my child suck, behold, it was dead: but when I had considered it in the morning, behold, it was not my son, which I did
22 bear. And the other woman said, Nay; but the living *is* my son,
and the dead *is* thy son. And this said, No; but the dead *is* thy
son, and the living *is* my son. Thus they spake before the king.
23 ¶ Then said the king, The one saith, This *is* my son that liveth,
and thy son *is* the dead: and the other saith, Nay; but thy son
24 *is* the dead, and my son *is* the living. And the king said, Bring
25 me a sword. And they brought a sword before the king. And
the king said, Divide the living child in two, and give half to the
26 one, and half to the other. Then spake the woman whose the
living child *was* unto the king, for ᵏher bowels ¹yearned upon
her son, and she said, O my lord, give her the living child, and
in no wise slay it. But the other said, Let it be neither mine
27 nor thine, *but* divide *it*. Then the king answered and said, Give
her the living child, and in no wise slay it: she *is* the mother
28 thereof. And all Israel heard of the judgment which the king
had judged; and they feared the king: for they saw that the
4 ¹wisdom of God *was* ²in him, to do judgment. SO king Solo-
2 mon was king over all Israel. ¶ And these *were* the princes
3 which he had, Azariah the son of Zadok ³the priest, Elihoreph
and Ahiah, the sons of Shisha, ⁴scribes; ᵃJehoshaphat the son

ʰ So Gen
40. 20.
ch. 8. 65.
Esth. 1. 3.
Dan. 5. 1.
Mark 6. 21.
ᶦ Num. 27. 2.

ᵏ Gen. 43. 30.
Isai. 49. 15.
Luke 1. 7, 8.
2 Cor. 7. 15

ˡ ver. 9, 11, 12.

ᵃ 2 Sam. 8. 16.
& 20. 24.

¹ Heb. *were hot.*   ² Heb. *in the midst of him.*   ³ Or, *the chief officer.*
⁴ Or, *secretaries.*

---

always partook of the flesh of the victim,
and he was commanded to call in to the
feast the Levite, the stranger, the fatherless, and the widow (Deut. xiv. 29). Cp.
2 Sam. vi. 19; 1 Chr. xvi. 3.

28. *the wisdom of God*] *i.e.* "Divine wisdom," "a wisdom given by God" (*v.* 12).
The ready tact and knowledge of human
nature exhibited in this judgment, and
its peculiar fitness to impress Orientals,
have generally been admitted.

IV. **1.** Solomon, that is, was king over
"*all* Israel" from the first; not like David,
who for seven and a half years reigned over
Judah only. This feature well introduces
the glory of Solomon and the organisation
of the Court, of which the historian in this
chapter intends to give us a general sketch.
Solomon constitutes certain "princes" or
officers of the first rank, deriving their
station from himself, and probably holding it
during pleasure.

Azariah, the son of Zadok, the priest]
"The priest" here belongs to Azariah, not

to Zadok. The term used (*cohen*) means
sometimes a priest, sometimes a civil officer,
with perhaps a semi-priestly character.
(See 2 Sam. viii. 18 note.) In this place it
has the definite article prefixed, and can
only mean "the High-Priest." Azariah,
called here the *son*, but really the *grandson*,
of Zadok, seems to have succeeded him in
the priesthood (1 Chr. vi. 10). His position
as High-Priest at the time when this list
was made out gives Azariah the foremost
place in it.

3. Shisha, or Shavsha (1 Chr. xviii. 16),
seems also to have been called Sheva (2
Sam. xx. 25), and Seraiah (2 Sam. viii.
17).

The "scribes" were probably royal "secretaries" (marg.), who drew up the king's
edicts, wrote his letters, and perhaps
managed his finances (xii. 10). They were
among his most influential councillors.

By "recorder" or "remembrancer"
(marg.), we must understand "Court annalist" (marg. ref. *a*).

b ch. 2. 35.
c See ch. 2. 27.
d ver. 7.
e 2 Sam. 8. 18.
& 20. 26.
f 2 Sam. 15.
37.
& 16. 16.
1 Chr. 27. 33.
g ch. 5. 14.

h Num. 32.
41.

4 of Ahilud, the ¹recorder.   And ᵇBenaiah the son of Jehoiada *was* over the host: and Zadok and ᶜAbiathar *were* the priests:
5 and Azariah the son of Nathan *was* over ᵈthe officers: and Zabud the son of Nathan *was* ᵉprincipal officer, *and* ᶠthe king's
6 friend: and Ahishar *was* over the household: and ᵍAdoniram
7 the son of Abda *was* over the ²tribute.   ¶And Solomon had twelve officers over all Israel, which provided victuals for the king and his household: each man his month in a year made
8 provision.   And these *are* their names: ³The son of Hur, in
9 mount Ephraim ·   ⁴the son of Dekar, in Makaz, and in Shaalbim,
10 and Beth-shemesh, and Elon-beth-hanan: ⁵the son of Hesed, in Aruboth; to him *pertained* Sochoh, and all the land of Hepher:
11 ⁶the son of Abinadab, in all the region of Dor; which had
12 Taphath the daughter of Solomon to wife: Baana the son of Ahilud; *to him pertained* Taanach and Megiddo, and all Bethshean, which *is* by Zartanah beneath Jezreel, from Beth-shean to Abel-meholah, *even* unto the place that *is* beyond Jokneam:
13 ⁷the son of Geber, in Ramoth-gilead; to him *pertained* ʰthe towns of Jair the son of Manasseh, which *are* in Gilead; to him

<hr/>

¹ Or, *remembrancer.*   ³ Or, *Ben-hur.*   ⁶ Or, *Ben-abinadab.*
² Or, *levy.*   ⁴ Or, *Ben-dekar.*   ⁷ Or, *Ben-geber.*
                           ⁵ Or, *Ben-hesed.*

<hr/>

4. It is curious to find Abiathar in this list of princes, after what has been said of his disgrace (ii. 27, 35). Some have supposed that after a while Solomon pardoned him. Perhaps the true explanation is that the historian here enumerates all those who were accounted "princes" in any part of Solomon's reign.

5. *the son of Nathan*] It is uncertain whether the Nathan of this verse is the Prophet or the son of David (2 Sam. v. 14). While on the one hand the position of "king's friend" is more likely to have been held by a contemporary, which the Prophet's son would have been, than by one so much younger as the son of a younger brother; on the other hand the title *cohen* seems to point to a member of the royal family. (See the next note.) Azariah who was "over the officers" was chief, that is, of the "officers" mentioned in *vv.* 8-19, as appears from the identity of the term here used with the title by which they are designated in *v.* 7.

principal officer] Or, *cohen.* The fact that the title *cohen* was borne by sons of David (2 Sam. viii. 18), who could not be priests in the ordinary sense of the word, seems to identify the Nathan of this verse with David's son (2 Sam. v. 14) rather than with the Prophet.

6. *over the household*] Comptroller of the household, like the "Steward" of the Persian Court. On the importance of this office, see 2 K. xviii. 18, and cp. Is. xxii. 15-25.

the tribute] The marginal reading, "levy," is preferable. The reference is to the forced labourers whom Solomon employed in his great works (marg. ref.).

7. The requirement of a portion of their produce from subjects, in addition to money payments, is a common practice of Oriental monarchs. It obtained in ancient, and it still obtains in modern, Persia.

8. In this arrangement of the territory into twelve portions, the divisions of the tribes seem to have been adopted as far as could be managed without unfairness. The prefecture of Ben-Hur corresponded nearly to the territory of Ephraim; that of Ben-Dekar to Dan; that of Ben-Hesed to Judah; that of Ben-Abinadab and Baana to Cis-Jordanic Manasseh; that of Ben-Geber to Manasseh beyond Jordan; of Abinadab to Gad; of Ahimaaz to Naphtali; of Baanah to Asher; of Jehoshaphat to Issachar; of Shimei to Benjamin; and of Geber to Reuben. The order in which the prefectures are mentioned is clearly not the geographical. Perhaps it is the order in which they had to supply the king's table.

9. For some of the names, see Josh. xix. 41-43.

10. *Sochoh*] See Josh. xv. 35.

11. *Dor*] See Josh. xi. 2 note. It has always been a practice among Oriental potentates to attach to themselves the more important of their officers by giving them for wives princesses of the royal house. Hence the union between Ben-Abinadab (probably Solomon's first cousin, cp. 1 Sam. xvi. 8) and Taphath. Cp. *v.* 15.

12. On these cities see Josh. xii. 21, iii. 16; Judg. vii. 22; Josh. xxi. 22.

13. It will be observed that five out of the twelve prefects are designated solely by their father's names, Ben-Hur, &c., while one (Ahimaaz, *v.* 15) has no such designa-

also pertained *ᶦthe region of Argob, which *is* in Bashan, three-
14 score great cities with walls and brasen bars: Ahinadab the son
15 of Iddo *had* ¹Mahanaim: Ahimaaz *was* in Naphtali; he also
16 took Basmath the daughter of Solomon to wife: Baanah the son
17 of Hushai *was* in Asher and in Aloth: Jehoshaphat the son of
18 Paruah, in Issachar: Shimei the son of Elah, in Benjamin:
19 Geber the son of Uri *was* in the country of Gilead, *in* ᵏthe
   country of Sihon king of the Amorites, and of Og king of
   Bashan; and *he was* the only officer which *was* in the land.
20 ¶ Judah and Israel *were* many, ˡas the sand which *is* by the sea
21 in multitude, ᵐeating and drinking, and making merry. And
   ⁿSolomon reigned over all kingdoms from ᵒthe river unto the
   land of the Philistines, and unto the border of Egypt: ᵖthey
   brought presents, and served Solomon all the days of his life.
22 ¶ And Solomon's ²provision for one day was thirty ³measures
23 of fine flour, and threescore measures of meal, ten fat oxen, and
   twenty oxen out of the pastures, and an hundred sheep, beside
24 harts, and roebucks, and fallowdeer, and fatted fowl. For he
   had dominion over all *the region* on this side the river: from

ᶦ Deut. 3. 4.

ᵏ Deut. 3. 8.

ˡGen. 22. 17.
Prov. 14. 28.
ᵐ Ps. 72. 3.
ⁿ 2 Chr. 9. 26.
Ps. 72. 8.
ᵒ Gen. 15. 18.
Josh. 1. 4.
ᵖ Ps. 68. 29.

¹ Or, *to Mahanaim*. ² Heb. *bread*. ³ Heb. *cors*.

tion. Probably the document, which the author of the Book of Kings consulted, had contained originally the proper name and father's name of each prefect; but it was mutilated or illegible in places at the time when he consulted it. If *it* was in the shape of a *list*, a single mutilation at one corner might have removed four of the six wanting names.

14. See margin. Ahinadab had the territory from the places last mentioned as far as Mahanaim (Gen. xxxii. 2).

19. The meaning of the last clause is somewhat doubtful. On the whole, our Version may well stand as nearly correct. The writer has assigned to Geber a wide stretch of territory; and, anticipating surprise, assures his readers " (there was but) one officer who (purveyed) in this land."

20. There is some doubt about the proper arrangement of the remainder of this chapter. The best alteration, if we alter the Hebrew order at all, would be to place *vv.* 20 and 21 after *v.* 25.

many, &c.] See iii. 8 note; and cp. Ps. cxxvii., which is traditionally ascribed to Solomon, and which celebrates the populousness and security of Israel in his day.

21. Solomon's empire, like all the great empires of Asia down to the time of the Persians, consisted of a congeries of small kingdoms, all ruled by their own kings (*v.* 24), who admitted the suzerainty of the Jewish monarch, and paid him " presents," *i.e.* an annual tribute (see x. 25).

unto the land of the Philistines] There is no word corresponding to " unto " in the Hebrew. The construction should be, " Solomon reigned over all the kingdoms from the river (*i.e.* the Euphrates: see marg. reff.), *over* the land of the Philistines,"

&c. The writer draws attention to the fact that the extent of Solomon's kingdom was in accordance with the promises made to Abraham, Moses, and Joshua.

22. *thirty measures*] (marg. *cors*) The *cor*, which was the same measure as the *homer*, is computed, on the authority of Josephus, at 86 English gallons, on the authority of the Rabbinical writers at 44. Thirty *cors*, even at the lower estimate, would equal 1,320 gallons, or 33 of our " sacks; " and the 90 *cors* of fine and coarse flour would altogether equal 99 sacks. From the quantity of flour consumed, it has been conjectured that the number of those who fed at the royal board was 14,000.

23. *harts*, &c.] The exact sorts of wild land animals here intended are very uncertain. Perhaps it would be best to translate " wild-goats, gazelles, and wild oxen," which abounded in the wilder parts of Syria, whence Solomon would be supplied. (See *v.* 24.) [Yahmûr, or the "roebuck," gives its name to a valley in a wooded district, south of Carmel (Conder).] The use of game at the royal banquets of Assyria appears in the sculptures.

24. *on this side the river*] *i.e.* the region west of the Euphrates.

Tiphsah, or Tiphsach, the place on the Euphrates called Thapsacus. The word means " ford," or " passage," being formed from *pasach*, " to pass over " (cp. " paschal "). It is the modern *Suriyeh*, forty-five miles below Balis, at the point where the Euphrates changes its course from S. to S.E. by E. The stream is fordable here, and nowhere else in this part of its course. Solomon's possession of Thapsacus would have been very favourable to his schemes of land commerce (ix. 19).

q Ps. 72. 11.
r 1Chr. 22. 9.
s See Jer.23.6
t Mic. 4. 4.
Zech. 3. 10.
u Judg. 20. 1.
x ch. 10. 26.
2 Chr. 1. 14.
y See Deut.
17. 16.
z ver. 7.
a ch. 3. 12.
b Gen. 25. 6.
c See Acts 7.
22.
d ch. 3. 12.
e 1Chr.15.19.
Ps. 89, title.
f See 1 Chr.
2. 6.
& 6. 33.
& 15. 19.
Ps. 88,
title.
g Prov. 1. 1.
Eccles.12.9.
h Cant. 1. 1.

Tiphsah even to Azzah, over *q*all the kings on this side the river:
25 and *r*he had peace on all sides round about him. And Judah
and Israel *s*dwelt *1*safely, *t*every man under his vine and under
his fig tree, *u*from Dan even to Beer-sheba, all the days of Solo-
26 mon. ¶ And *x*Solomon had forty thousand stalls of *y*horses for
27 his chariots, and twelve thousand horsemen. And *z*those officers
provided victual for king Solomon, and for all that came unto
king Solomon's table, every man in his month : they lacked no-
28 thing. Barley also and straw for the horses and *2*dromedaries
brought they unto the place where the *officers* were, every man
29 according to his charge. ¶ And *a*God gave Solomon wisdom and
understanding exceeding much, and largeness of heart, even as
30 the sand that *is* on the sea shore. And Solomon's wisdom excelled the wisdom of all the children *b*of the east country, and
31 all *c*the wisdom of Egypt. For he was *d*wiser than all men ;
*e*than Ethan the Ezrahite, *f*and Heman, and Chalcol, and Darda,
the sons of Mahol: and his fame was in all nations round about.
32 And *g*he spake three thousand proverbs: and his *h*songs were a

1 Heb. *confidently.*   *2* Or, *mules*, or, *swift beasts*, Esth. 8. 14.   Mic. 1. 13.

---

to Azzah] *i.e.* Gaza.
all the kings] Cp. Josh. xii. 9–24. In
Philistia, small as it was, there were five
kings (1 Sam. vi. 18). Syria was divided
into numerous small states, as many as
thirty-two kings being mentioned on one
occasion (xx. 1). The Hittites were ruled
by a great number of chieftains or princes
(x. 29 ; 2 K. vii. 6). Twelve are mentioned
in the Assyrian inscriptions.
25. *under his vine*, &c.] This phrase seems
to have been common among the Jews, and
even among neighbouring nations (2 K.
xviii. 31), to express a time of quiet and
security. It is used by the prophets in
descriptions of the Messianic kingdom
(marg. reff.).
26. In 2 Chr. ix. 25, the number of stalls
for Solomon's chariot horses is stated at
4,000, instead of 40,000. The number in
the present passage is probably a corruption. Solomon's chariots were but 1,400
(x. 26 ; 2 Chr. i. 14), for which 40,000 horses
could not possibly be required. The Assyrian
chariots had at most three horses apiece,
while some had only two. 4,000 horses
would supply the full team of three to 1,200,
and the smaller team of two to 200 chariots.
The number 4,000 is in due proportion to
the 12,000 horses for cavalry, and is in
accordance with all that we know of the
military establishments of the time and
country. Cp. 2 Chr. xii. 3 ; 2 Sam. viii. 4.
28. Barley is to this day in the East the
common food of horses.
dromedaries] **Coursers.** The animal intended is neither a camel nor a mule, but a
swift horse.
the place where the officers were] Rather,
" places where the horses and coursers
were," *i.e.* to the different cities where they
were lodged.
29. *largeness of heart*] What we call

"great capacity." The expression which
follows is common in reference to numerical multitude (*v.* 20), but its use here
to express mere amplitude or greatness is
peculiar.
30. *children of the east country*] Rather,
" of the East "—the *Beni Kedem*—a distinct tribe, who occupied both sides of the
Euphrates along its middle course (marg.
ref.). They were mostly nomads, who
dwelt in tents (Jer. xlix. 28, 29). Job belonged to them (Job i. 3), as did probably
his three friends ; and, perhaps, Balaam
(Num. xxiii. 7). They must have been
either Arabs or Aramæans. We may see
in the Book of Job the character of their
" wisdom." Like Solomon's, it was chiefly
gnomic but included some knowledge of
natural history. The " wisdom of Egypt "
was of a different kind. It included magic
(Gen. xli. 8 ; Ex. vii. 11), geometry, medicine, astronomy, architecture, and a dreamy
mystic philosophy, of which metempsy-
chosis was the main principle. It is not
probable that Solomon was, like Moses
(marg. ref.), deeply versed in Egyptian
science. The writer only means to say that
his wisdom was truer and more real than
all the much-praised wisdom of Egypt.
31. It is most probable that the persons
with whom Solomon is compared were contemporaries, men noted for " wisdom,"
though there is no other mention of them.
his fame was in all nations] See below,
ch. x.
32. *proverbs*] In the collection which
forms the " Book of Proverbs," only a
small portion has been preserved, less certainly than one thousand out of the three.
Ecclesiastes, if it be Solomon's, would add
between one and two hundred. But the
great bulk of Solomon's proverbs has
perished.

33 thousand and five. And he spake of trees, from the cedar tree
that *is* in Lebanon even unto the hyssop that springeth out of
the wall: he spake also of beasts, and of fowl, and of creeping
34 things, and of fishes. And *i*there came of all people to hear the
wisdom of Solomon, from all kings of the earth, which had
heard of his wisdom.
CHAP. 5. AND *a*Hiram king of Tyre sent his servants unto Solomon ; for he had heard that they had anointed him king in the
2 room of his father : *b*for Hiram was ever a lover of David. And
3 *c*Solomon sent to Hiram, saying, Thou knowest how that David
my father could not build an house unto the name of the LORD
his God *d*for the wars which were about him on every side, until
4 the LORD put them under the soles of his feet. But now the
LORD my God hath given me *e*rest on every side, *so that there is*
5 neither adversary nor evil occurrent. *f*And, behold, I *1*purpose
to build an house unto the name of the LORD my God, *g*as the
LORD spake unto David my father, saying, Thy son, whom I
will set upon thy throne in thy room, he shall build an house
6 unto my name. Now therefore command thou that they hew
me *h*cedar trees out of Lebanon ; and my servants shall be with
thy servants : and unto thee will I give hire for thy servants
according to all that thou shalt *2*appoint : for thou knowest that
there is not among us any that can skill to hew timber like unto

i ch. 10. 1.
2 Chr. 9.
1, 23.

a 2 Chr. 2, 3,
Huram.

b 2Sam.5 11.
1 Chr. 14. 1
c 2 Chr. 2. 3.

d 1 Chr. 22.8.
& 28. 3.

e ch. 4. 24.
1 Chr. 22. 9.
f 2 Chr. 2. 4.
g 2Sam.7.13.
1 Chr. 17.12.
& 22. 10.

h 2 Chr.2.
8, 10.

---

1 Heb. *say.*   *2* Heb. *say.*

---

songs] Of these, Canticles is probably one
(marg. ref.): Pss. lxxii. and cxxvii. *may* also
be of the number. Probably the bulk of
Solomon's songs were of a secular character,
and consequently were not introduced into
the Canon of Scripture.
33. *trees*, &c.] A keen appreciation of the
beauties of nature, and a habit of minute
observation, are apparent in the writings of
Solomon that remain to us. The writer
here means to say that Solomon composed
special works on these subjects. The Lebanon cedars were the most magnificent of all
the trees known to the Hebrews, and hence
represent in the Old Testament the grandest
of vegetable productions. (Ps. civ. 16 ;
Cant. v. 15 ; Ezek. xxxi. 3, &c.) For the
hyssop, see Ex. xii. 22 note.
*of beasts, and of fowls, and of creeping
things, and of fishes*] This is the usual
Biblical division of the animal kingdom
(Gen. i. 26, ix. 2 ; Ps. cxlviii. 10).
V. 1. *Hiram, king of Tyre*] Menander of
Ephesus, who wrote a history of Tyre in
Greek, founded upon native Tyrian documents, about B.C. 300, mentioned this Hiram
as the son of Abibaal king of Tyre, and
said that he ascended the throne when he
was nineteen ; that he reigned thirty-four
years, and, dying at the age of fifty-three,
was succeeded by his son Baleazar. Menander spoke at some length of the dealings
of Hiram with Solomon.
sent his servants] This appears to have
been an embassy of congratulation.
3. Solomon's presumption that Hiram
knew David's design has not appeared in

the previous history, but it is in accordance with 1 Chr. xxii. 4.
4. The contrast is not between different
periods of Solomon's reign, but between his
reign and that of his father.
evil occurrent] Rather, **evil occurrence.**
5. *as the LORD spake*] See marg. reff. vii.
13, and cp. 1 Chr. xxii. 10.
6. Solomon's message to Hiram and
Hiram's answer (*vv.* 8, 9) are given much
more fully in 2 Chr. ii. 3–16.
cedar-trees] The Hebrew word here and
elsewhere translated "cedar," appears to
be used, not only of the cedar proper, but
of other timber-trees also, as the fir, and,
perhaps, the juniper. Still there is no
doubt that the real Lebanon cedar is most
commonly intended by it. This tree, which
still grows on parts of the mountain, but
which threatens to die out, was probably
much more widely spread anciently. The
Tyrians made the masts of their ships from
the wood (Ezek. xxvii. 5), and would naturally be as careful to cultivate it as we have
ourselves been to grow oak. The Assyrian
kings, when they made their expeditions
into Palestine, appear frequently to have
cut it in Lebanon and Hermon, and to have
transported it to their own capitals.
skill to hew timber like unto the Sidonians]
The mechanical genius and nautical skill of
the Phœnicians generally, and of the Sidonians in particular, is noticed by Homer
and Herodotus. In the reign of Hiram,
Sidon, though perhaps she might have a
king of her own, acknowledged the supremacy of Tyre.

7 the Sidonians. ¶And it came to pass, when Hiram heard the words of Solomon, that he rejoiced greatly, and said, Blessed *be* the LORD this day, which hath given unto David a wise son over 8 this great people. And Hiram sent to Solomon, saying, I have ¹considered the things which thou sentest to me for : *and* I will do all thy desire concerning timber of cedar, and concerning 9 timber of fir. My servants shall bring *them* down from Lebanon *i* 2 Chr. 2.16.   unto the sea : *i*and I will convey them by sea in floats unto the place that thou shalt ²appoint me, and will cause them to be discharged there, and thou shalt receive *them :* and thou shalt accom-*k* See Ezra, 10 plish my desire, *k*in giving food for my household. So Hiram 3. 7. gave Solomon cedar trees and fir trees *according to* all his desire.
Ezek. 27. 17.
Acts 12. 20. 11 *l*And Solomon gave Hiram twenty thousand ³measures of wheat *i* See 2 Chr. *for* food to his household, and twenty measures of pure oil : thus 2. 10. 12 gave Solomon to Hiram year by year. And the LORD gave *m* ch. 3, 12.   Solomon wisdom, *m*as he promised him : and there was peace between Hiram and Solomon ; and they two made a league 13 together. ¶And king Solomon raised a ⁴levy out of all Israel ; 14 and the levy was thirty thousand men. And he sent them to Lebanon, ten thousand a month by courses : a month they were *n* ch. 4. 6.   in Lebanon, *and* two months at home : and *n*Adoniram *was* over *o* ch. 9. 21. 15 the levy. *o*And Solomon had threescore and ten thousand that 2 Chr. 2. bare burdens, and fourscore thousand hewers in the mountains , 17, 18.

¹ Heb. *heard.*   ² Heb. *send.*   ³ Heb. *cors.*   ⁴ Heb. *tribute* of men.

---

9. See marg. ref. The timber was first carried westward from the flanks of Lebanon to the nearest part of the coast, where it was collected into floats, or rafts, which were then conveyed southwards along the coast to Joppa, now *Jaffa*, whence the land journey to Jerusalem was not more than about forty miles. A similar course was taken on the building of the second Temple (Ezr. iii. 7).

food for my household] The Phœnician cities had very little arable territory of their own, the mountain range of Lebanon rising rapidly behind them ; and they must always have imported the chief part of their sustenance from abroad. They seem commonly to have derived it from Judæa (marg. reff.). Hiram agreed now to accept for his timber and for the services of his workmen (*v.* 6) a certain annual payment of grain and oil, both of them the best of their kind, for the sustentation of his Court. This payment was entirely distinct from the supplies furnished to the workmen (marg. ref. *l*).

11. The number of measures of wheat was considerably less than Solomon's own annual consumption, which exceeded 32,000 cors (iv. 22) ; but the small amount of twenty *cors* of oil, which seems at first sight scarcely to match with the 20,000 cors of wheat, will not appear improbable, if we consider that the oil was to be " pure " —literally " beaten "—*i.e.* oil extracted from the olives by pounding, and not by means of the press.

year by year] *i.e.* during all the years that Solomon was engaged in building and was helped by Hiram.

12. *the* LORD *gave Solomon wisdom*] It seems to be implied that Solomon's Divine gift of wisdom enabled him to make such favourable arrangements with Hiram.

13. *a levy out of all Israel*] This was, apparently, the first time that the Israelites had been called upon to perform forced labour, though it had been prophesied (1 Sam. viii. 16). David had bound to forced service " the *strangers*" (1 Chr. xxii. 2) ; but hitherto the Israelites had escaped. Solomon now, in connexion with his proposed work of building the Temple, with the honour of God as an excuse, laid this burthen upon them. Out of the 1,300,000 ablebodied Israelites (2 Sam. xxiv. 9), a band of 30,000—one in forty-four—was raised, of whom one-third was constantly at work in Lebanon, while two-thirds remained at home, and pursued their usual occupations. This, though a very light form of taskwork, was felt as a great oppression, and was the chief cause of the revolt of the ten tribes at Solomon's death (xii. 4).

15. *that bare burdens,* &c.] Cp. marg. reff. These labourers, whose services were continuous, consisted of " strangers "—" the people that were left of the Amorites, Hittites, Perizzites, Hivites, and Jebusites "—whom Solomon, following the example of his father (1 Chr. xxii. 2), condemned to slavery, and employed in this way.

16 beside the chief of Solomon's officers which *were* over the work, three thousand and three hundred, which ruled over the people 17 that wrought in the work. And the king commanded, and they brought great stones, costly stones, *and* *P* hewed stones, to 18 lay the foundation of the house. And Solomon's builders and Hiram's builders did hew *them*, and the ¹ stone-squarers; so they prepared timber and stones to build the house.

CHAP. 6. AND *ª* it came to pass in the four hundred and eightieth year after the children of Israel were come out of the land of Egypt, in the fourth year of Solomon's reign over Israel, in the month Zif, which *is* the second month, that *b* he ² began to build 2 the house of the LORD. ¶ And *ᶜ* the house which king Solomon built for the LORD, the length thereof *was* threescore cubits, and the breadth thereof twenty *cubits*, and the height thereof 3 thirty cubits. And the porch before the temple of the house,

P 1 Chr. 22.2.

ª 2 Chr. 3. 1, 2.

b Acts 7. 47.

ᶜ See Ezek. 41. 1, &c.

¹ Or, *Giblites*: as Ezek. 27. 9.　　　² Heb. *built*.

---

16. Comparing this verse and ix. 23 with 2 Chr. ii. 18, viii. 10, the entire number of the overseers will be seen to be stated by both writers at 3,850; but in the one case nationality, in the other degree of authority, is made the principle of the division.

17. Some of these "great, hewed (no *and*) stones," are probably still to be seen in the place where they were set by Solomon's builders, at the south-western angle of the wall of the Haram area in the modern Jerusalem. The largest yet found is 38 ft. 9 in. long, and weighs about 100 tons.

18. *the stone-squarers*] The Gebalites (see marg.), the inhabitants of Gebal, a Phœnician city between Beyrout and Tripolis, which the Greeks called Byblus, and which is now known as *Jebeil*.

VI. 1. *in the four hundred and eightieth year*] It is upon this statement that all the earlier portion of what is called the "received chronology" depends. Amid minor differences there is a general agreement, which justifies us in placing the accession of Solomon *about* B.C. 1000 [B.C. 1018. Oppert.] But great difficulties meet us in determining the sacred chronology anterior to this. Apart from the present statement, the chronological data of the Old Testament are insufficient to fix the interval between Solomon's accession and the Exodus, since several of the periods which make it up are unestimated. Hence chronologists have based entirely upon the "received chronology" upon this verse. But the text itself is not free from suspicion. (1) It is the sole passage in the Old Testament which contains the idea of dating events from an era. (2) It is quoted by Origen *without the date*, and seems to have been known only in this shape to Josephus, to Theophilus of Antioch, and to Clement of Alexandria. (3) It is hard to reconcile with other chronological statements in the Old and New Testament. Though the Books of Joshua, Judges, and Samuel furnish us with no exact chrono-

logy, they still supply important chronological data—data which seem to indicate for the interval between the Exodus and Solomon, a period considerably exceeding 480 years. For the years actually set down amount to at least 580, or, according to another computation, to 600; and though a certain deduction might be made from this sum on account of the round numbers, this deduction would scarcely do more than balance the addition required on account of the four unestimated periods. Again, in the New Testament, St. Paul (according to the received text) reckons the period from the division of Canaan among the tribes in the sixth year of Joshua (Josh. xiv.), to Samuel the Prophet, at 450 years, which would make the interval between the Exodus and the commencement of the Temple to be 579 years. On the whole, it seems, therefore, probable that the words "in the four hundred and eightieth year, &c.," are an interpolation into the sacred text, which did not prevail generally before the third century of our era.

2. The size of Solomon's Temple depends upon the true length of the ancient cubit, which is doubtful. It has been estimated as somewhat less than a foot, and again as between 19 and 20 inches, a difference of nearly 8 inches, which would produce a variation of nearly 40 feet in the length of the Temple-chamber, and of 46 in that of the entire building. It is worthy of remark that, even according to the highest estimate, Solomon's Temple was really a *small* building, less than 120 feet long, and less than 35 broad. Remark that the measures of the Temple, both "house" and porch (*v.* 3), were exactly *double* those of the older Tabernacle (Ex. xxvi. 18 note). This identity of proportion amounts to an undesigned coincidence, indicating the thoroughly historical character of both Kings and Exodus.

twenty cubits *was* the length thereof, according to the breadth of
the house; *and* ten cubits *was* the breadth thereof before the house.

d See Ezek.
40. 16.
k 41. 16.
e See Ezek.
41. 6.
f ver. 16, 19,
20, 21, 31.

4, 5 And for the house he made *d*[1] windows of narrow lights. And
[2] against the wall of the house he built *e*[3] chambers round about,
against the walls of the house round about, *both* of the temple
6 *f* and of the oracle: and he made [4] chambers round about: the
nethermost chamber *was* five cubits broad, and the middle *was*
six cubits broad, and the third *was* seven cubits broad: for without *in the wall* of the house he made [5] narrowed rests round about,
that *the beams* should not be fastened in the walls of the house.

g See Deut.
27. 5, 6.
ch. 5. 18.

7 And *g* the house, when it was in building, was built of stone
made ready before it was brought thither: so that there was
neither hammer nor axe *nor* any tool of iron heard in the house,
8 while it was in building. The door for the middle chamber *was*
in the right [6] side of the house: and they went up with winding
stairs into the middle *chamber*, and out of the middle into the

k ver. 14, 38

9 third. *h* So he built the house, and finished it; and covered the

---

[1] Or, *windows broad* within, and *narrow* without:
or, *skewed* and *closed*.

[2] Or, *upon*, or, *joining to*.
[3] Heb. *floors*.
[4] Heb. *ribs*.

[5] Heb. *narrowings*, or, *re
batements*.
[6] Heb. *shoulder*.

---

4. *windows of narrow lights*] Either (as in
marg.) windows, externally mere slits in the
wall, but opening wide within, like the
windows of old castles: or, more probably,
"windows with fixed lattices." The windows seem to have been placed high in the
walls, above the chambers spoken of in
vv. 5–8.

5. *chambers*] (Marg. floors). Rather, a
lean-to, which completely surrounded three
sides of the building, the north, the west,
and the south.

6. In order to preserve the sanctity of the
Temple, and at the same time allow the
attachment to it of secular buildings—
sleeping apartments, pro-
bably, for the priests and
other attendants — Solo-
mon made "rebatements"
in the wall of the Temple,
or in other words built it
externally in steps, thus :—
The beams, which formed
the roof of the chambers
and the floors of the upper
stories, were then laid on
these steps or "rests" in
the wall, not piercing the
wall, or causing any real
union of the secular with the sacred building. It resulted from this arrangement
that the lowest chambers were the nar-
rowest, and the uppermost considerably
the widest of all, the wall receding each
time by the space of a cubit.

7. The spirit of the command (marg.
reff.), was followed. Thus the fabric rose
without noise.

8. *The door for the middle chamber*] *i.e.*
the door which gave access to the mid-most
"set of chambers." The chambers on the

ground-floor were possibly reached each by
their own door in the outer wall of the
lean-to. The middle and upper floors were
reached by a single door in the right or
south wall, from which a winding staircase
ascended to the second tier, while another
ascended from the second to the third. The
door to the stairs was in the outer wall of
the building, not in the wall between the
chambers and the Temple. That would
have desecrated the Temple far more than
the insertion of beams.

9. *he built the house, and finished it*] *i.e.*
the external shell of the house. The internal fittings were added afterwards. See
vv. 15–22.

covered the house] Roofed it with a wooden
roof, sloped like our roofs.

The annexed diagram of a section of the
Temple will illustrate *vv.* 2–10. The numbers give the dimensions in cubits.

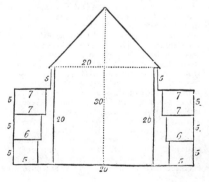

10 house ¹with beams and boards of cedar. And *then* he built
chambers against all the house, five cubits high : and they rested
11 on the house with timber of cedar. ¶ And the word of the LORD
12 came to Solomon, saying, *concerning* this house which thou art
in building, *ⁱif thou wilt walk in my statutes, and execute my
judgments, and keep all my commandments to walk in them ;
then will I perform my word with thee, *ᵏwhich I spake unto
13 David thy father : and *ˡI will dwell among the children of
14 Israel, and will not *ᵐforsake my people Israel. ¶ *ⁿSo Solomon
15 built the house, and finished it. And he built the walls of the
house within with boards of cedar, ²both the floor of the house,
and the walls of the cieling : *and* he covered *them* on the inside
with wood, and covered the floor of the house with planks
16 of fir. And he built twenty cubits on the sides of the house,
both the floor and the walls with boards of cedar : he even built
them for it within, *even* for the oracle, *even* for the °most holy
17 place. And the house, that *is*, the temple before it, was forty

*ⁱ ch. 2. 4.
& 9. 4.*
*ᵏ 1 Chr. 22.
10.*
*ˡ Lev. 26. 11.
2 Cor. 6. 16.
Rev. 21. 3.*
ᵐ Deut. 31. 6.
ⁿ ver. 38.
*° Ex. 26. 33.
Lev. 16. 2.
ch. 8. 6.
2 Chr. 3. 8.
Ezek. 45. 3.
Heb. 9. 3.*

¹ Or, *the vaultbeams and the*   ² Or, *from the floor of the*   and so ver. 16.
  cielings with cedar.   *house unto the walls, &c.,*

---

12. The meaning is, "So far as this house
goes, thou art obedient (2 Sam. vii. 13 ; 1 Chr.
xvii. 12, &c.) ; if thou wilt be obedient in
other things also, then will I perform My
word," &c., God's promises being always
conditional. The promises made to David
were—(1) that he should be succeeded by
one of his sons (2 Sam. vii. 12 ; Ps. cxxxii. 11) ;
(2) that the kingdom should be established
in the line of his descendants for ever, if
they were faithful (Ps. cxxxii. 12) ; and
(3) that the Israelites should be no more
afflicted as beforetime (2 Sam. vii. 10).
These promises are now confirmed to
Solomon, but on the express condition of
obedience, and two further promises are
added.

13. The first promise to "dwell among"
the Israelites had been made to Moses (Ex.
xxv. 8, xxix. 45), but had not been repeated
to David. The next promise, "I will not forsake, &c.," if not absolutely new, seems to
have been more positive and general than
previous similar promises (Deut. xxxi. 6,
8 ; Josh. i. 5). God will not *at any time or
under any circumstances* wholly forsake
Israel.

15. The description of this verse applies to the main chamber of the Temple,
the Holy Place, only. The writer in *v.* 16
describes the Holy of Holies.
  The marginal rendering of this verse is
right, and not the rendering in the text.
  fir] Rather, "**juniper.**" See v. 8 note.

16. The meaning is, that at the distance
of 20 cubits, measured along the side
walls of the house from the end wall,
Solomon constructed a partition, which
reached from the floor to the cieling and
had a doorway in it. He thus made within
the house, a sanctuary for a Holy of
Holies.

17. Cp. the diagram.

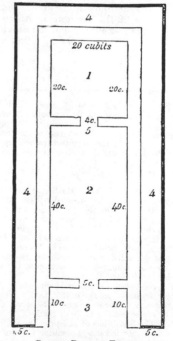

GROUND PLAN OF TEMPLE.

1. Holy of Holies, Oracle or Sanctuary.
2. Holy Place, or Main-chamber.
3. Porch.   4. Priests' Chambers.
5. Position of Altar of incense.

18 cubits *long*. And the cedar of the house within *was* carved with
¹knops and ²open flowers: all *was* cedar; there was no stone
19 seen. And the oracle he prepared in the house within, to set
20 there the ark of the covenant of the LORD. And the oracle in
the forepart *was* twenty cubits in length, and twenty cubits in
breadth, and twenty cubits in the height thereof: and he overlaid it with ³pure gold; and *so* covered the altar *which was of*
21 cedar. So Solomon overlaid the house within with pure gold:
and he made a partition by the chains of gold before the oracle;
22 and he overlaid it with gold. And the whole house he overlaid
with gold, until he had finished all the house: also ᵖthe whole
23 altar that *was* by the oracle he overlaid with gold. ¶And
within the oracle ᑫhe made two cherubims *of* ⁴⁵olive tree, *each*
24 ten cubits high. And five cubits *was* the one wing of the
cherub, and five cubits the other wing of the cherub: from the
uttermost part of the one wing unto the uttermost part of the
25 other *were* ten cubits. And the other cherub *was* ten cubits:
26 both the cherubims *were* of one measure and one size. The
height of the one cherub *was* ten cubits, and so *was it* of the
27 other cherub. And he set the cherubims within the inner
house: and ʳ⁶they stretched forth the wings of the cherubims,
so that the wing of the one touched the *one* wall, and the wing
of the other cherub touched the other wall; and their wings
28 touched one another in the midst of the house. And he overlaid
29 the cherubims with gold. ¶And he carved all the walls of the
house round about with carved figures of cherubims and palm
30 trees and ⁷open flowers, within and without. And the floor of

ᵖ Ex. 30. 1,
3, 6.
ᑫ Ex. 37. 7,
8, 9.
2 Chr. 3. 10,
11, 12.

ʳ Ex. 25. 20.
& 37. 9.
2 Chr. 5. 8.

¹ Or, *gourds.*
² Heb. *openings of flowers.*
³ Heb. *shut up.*

⁴ Or, *oily.*
⁵ Heb. *trees of oil.*

⁶ Or, *the cherubims stretched
forth their wings.*
⁷ Heb. *openings of flowers.*

---

18. *knops and open flowers*] Rather,
"**gourds and opening flower-buds.**" Imitations of the vegetable world are among
the earliest of architectural ornaments.
They abound in the architecture of Egypt
and Persia. In that of Assyria they occur
more sparingly.
20. *the fore part*] Perhaps "the interior."
and so covered, &c.] Rather, "and **he
covered the altar** (of incense) **with cedar.**"
The altar was doubtless of stone, and was
covered with cedar in preparation for the
overlaying with gold. This overlaying was
not gilding, but the attachment of thin
plates of gold, which had to be fastened on
with small nails. Such a mode of ornamentation was common in Babylonia, in Assyria, and in Media.
21. *the house*] *i.e.* the main chamber.
the chains of gold] Omit "the." Their
object was to form a barrier between the
Holy Place and the Holy of Holies.
22. The lavish use of the precious metals
in ornamentation was a peculiar feature of
early Oriental architecture. Recent re-
searches have given reason to believe that
two stages of the great temple at Borsippa
—now known as the Birs Nimrud—had respectively a gold and a silver coating.

23. *two cherubims*] The pattern of the
Tabernacle was followed (marg. ref.), but
without servile imitation. The original
cherubs were entirely of gold. These, being
so much larger, were of wood, merely overlaid with a golden plating. The arrangement of the wings, and the direction of the
faces, seem also to have been different.
Moses' cherubim "covered with their wings
over the mercy seat;" Solomon's stretched
out theirs to the full (*v.* 27), so that the four
wings, each five cubits long (*v.* 24), extended across the whole Sanctuary, the
width of which was twenty cubits (*v.* 20).
The former looked toward one another, and
were bent downward towards the mercy
seat; the latter looked outward, towards
the great chamber. (See 2 Chr. iii. 13, and
note.)
of olive-tree] The oleaster or wild olive,
not the cultivated species.
29. Palms, cherubs, and flowers—the
main decorations of Solomon's Temple—
bear considerable resemblance to the ornamentation of the Assyrians, a circumstance
which can scarcely be accidental.
within and without] *i.e.* both in the inner
chamber, or Holy of Holies, and in the outer
one.

31 the house he overlaid with gold, within and without. ¶And for
the entering of the oracle he made doors *of* olive tree: the lintel
32 *and* side posts *were* ¹a fifth part *of the wall.* The ²two doors also
were of olive tree; and he carved upon them carvings of cherubims and palm trees and ³open flowers, and overlaid *them* with
gold, and spread gold upon the cherubims, and upon the palm
33 trees. So also made he for the door of the temple posts *of* olive
34 tree, ⁴a fourth part *of the wall.* And the two doors *were of* fir
tree: the ⁸two leaves of the one door *were* folding, and the two
35 leaves of the other door *were* folding. And he carved *thereon*
cherubims and palm trees and open flowers: and covered *them*
36 with gold fitted upon the carved work. And he built the inner
court with three rows of hewed stone, and a row of cedar beams.
37 ¶ ᵗIn the fourth year was the foundation of the house of the
38 LORD laid, in the month Zif: and in the eleventh year in the
month Bul, which *is* the eighth month, was the house finished
⁵throughout all the parts thereof, and according to all the fashion
7 of it. So was he ᵘseven years in building it. BUT Solomon
was building his own house ᵃthirteen years, and he finished all
2 his house. ¶ He built also the house of the forest of Lebanon;

ˢ Ezek. 41.
23, 24, 25.

ᵗ ver. 1.

ᵘ Compare
ver. 1.
ᵃ ch. 9.10.
2 Chr. 8. 1.

¹ Or, *fivesquare.*
² Or, *leaves of the doors.*
³ Heb. *openings of flowers.*
⁴ Or, *foursquare.*
⁵ Or, *with all the appurtenances thereof, and with
all the ordinances thereof.*

---

31. *a fifth part*] Better than the margin. The meaning seems to be that the
lintel was one-fifth of the width of the wall,
and each door-post one-fifth of its height.
Thus the opening was a square of four
cubits, or of six feet.

32. *The two doors*] *i.e.* two leaves which
met in the middle, as in the Assyrian gateways generally.

spread gold] The doors were not simply
sheeted with gold, like the floors (*v.* 30),
but had the gold hammered to fit the forms
of the palms, cherubs, and flowers carved
upon them. (*v.* 35.) Such hammered metal-
work, generally in bronze, has been found
in tolerable abundance among the Assyrian
remains.

33. *the door of the temple*] The door, that
is, which led from the porch into the great
chamber of the Temple. Its posts were "a
fourth part of the wall," or, "five cubits
high," which was, therefore, the height of
the doorway.

34. *fir-tree*] Rather, **juniper** (v. 8 note).
Each door was made in two parts, which
folded back one on the other like shutters,
by means of hinges. The weight of the
doors no doubt made it inconvenient to
open the whole door on every occasion.

36. *the inner court*] An *outer* court is mentioned in 2 Chr. iv. 9. The inner court is
probably identical with the "higher court"
of Jeremiah (xxxvi. 10), being raised above
the outer, as were sometimes the inner
courts of Assyrian palaces. The court
seems to have surrounded the Temple. Its
dimensions may be reasonably presumed to
have been double those of the court of the
Tabernacle, *i.e.* 100 cubits on each side of

the Temple, and 200 cubits at the ends; or,
about 720 feet long by 360 broad.

with three rows of hewed stone] Either a
fence enclosing the court, or the area of the
court, which was possibly formed by three
layers of hewn stone placed one above the
other, and was then boarded on the top
with cedar planks. Such a construction
would no doubt be elaborate; but if it was
desired to elevate the inner court above the
outer, this is the way in which it would be
likely to have been done. The Temple
would be placed, like the Assyrian palaces,
on an artificial platform; and the platform,
being regarded as a part of the sacred building, would be constructed of the best material.

28. *seven years*] More exactly, "seven
years and six months," since Zif was the
second, and Bul the eighth month. (*v.* 1.)

VII. 1. *thirteen years*] The thirteen
years, *i.e.* counting from the end of the
seven (vi. 38). Solomon's buildings thus
occupied him twenty years (ix. 10; 2
Chr. viii. 1), from the fourth year of his
reign to the twenty-fourth. The difference
in the time taken by the Temple and the
palace is to be accounted for, (1) by the long
period of preparation which preceded the
actual building of the former (1 Chr. xxii.
2-4; 1 K. v. 13-18); and (2) by the greater
size of the palace, which consisted of several
large ranges of buildings. (See the next
note.)

2. Many have supposed that the buildings
mentioned in *vv.* 1, 2, 8, were three entirely
distinct and separate buildings. But it is
perhaps best to consider the "house" of
v. 1 as the palace proper—Solomon's own

the length thereof *was* an hundred cubits, and the breadth
thereof fifty cubits, and the height thereof thirty cubits, upon
four rows of cedar pillars, with cedar beams upon the pillars.
3 And *it was* covered with cedar above upon the [1]beams, that *lay*
4 on forty five pillars, fifteen *in* a row. And *there were* windows
5 *in* three rows, and [2]light *was* against light *in* three ranks. And
all the [3]doors and posts *were* square, with the windows: and
6 light *was* against light *in* three ranks. And he made a porch of
pillars; the length thereof *was* fifty cubits, and the breadth
thereof thirty cubits: and the porch *was* [4]before them: and the
7 *other* pillars and the thick beam *were* [5]before them. Then he
made a porch for the throne where he might judge, *even* the
porch of judgment: and *it was* covered with cedar [6]from one
8 side of the floor to the other. And his house where he dwelt
had another court within the porch, *which* was of the like work.

[b] ch. 3. 1.
2 Chr. 8. 11. ¶ Solomon made also an house for Pharaoh's daughter, [b]whom
9 he had taken *to wife*, like unto this porch. ¶ All these *were of*
costly stones, according to the measures of hewed stones, sawed
with saws, within and without, even from the foundation unto
10 the coping, and *so* on the outside toward the great court. And

---

[1] Heb. *ribs*.
[2] Heb. *sight against sight*.
[3] Or, *spaces and pillars were square in prospect*.
[4] Or, *according to them*.
[5] Or, *according to them*.
[6] Heb. *from floor to floor*.

---

dwelling-house (see *v.* 8); the house of *v.* 2,
as the state apartments; and the house for
Pharaoh's daughter as the *hareem* or *zenana;*
and to regard these three groups of buildings as distinct, though inter-connected,
and as together constituting what is elsewhere termed "the king's house" (ix.
10).

the house of the forest of Lebanon] This
name was probably given from the supposed
resemblance of the mass of cedar pillars,
which was its main feature, to the Lebanon
cedar forest. Its length of "a hundred cubits," or 150 feet, was nearly twice as long
as the entire Temple without the porch.
Some of the great halls in Assyrian palaces
were occasionally as much as 180 feet.
The breadth "of fifty cubits," or 75 feet,
is a breadth very much greater than is ever
found in Assyria, and one indicative of the
employment in the two countries of quite
different methods of roofing. By their use
of pillars the Jews, like the Persians, were
able to cover in a very wide space.

four rows] The LXX. gives "three rows."
If the pillars were forty-five (*v.* 3), fifteen in a
row, there should have been but three rows,
as seems to have been the case in the old
palace of Cyrus at Pasargadæ. If there
were four rows of fifteen, the number of
pillars should have been sixty.

4. Either three ranges of windows, one
above the other, on either side of the house;
or perhaps the three ranges were one in
either side wall, and the third in a wall
down the middle of the hall, along the
course of the midmost row of pillars. The
windows were directly opposite one another,
giving what we call a *through* light

5. *all the doors and posts*] The doorways,
and the posts which formed them, seem to
be intended. These were square at top, not
arched or rounded. In Assyrian buildings
arched doorways were not uncommon. The
doorways also, like the windows, exactly
faced one another.

6. Probably the porch of the "House of
the Forest." Porches of columns immediately in front of columnar chambers were a
favourite feature of Persian architecture.
The whole verse should be translated, "**And
he made the porch of the pillars in length
50 cubits, and in breadth 30 cubits, and a
porch before them** (*i.e.* the pillars), **and
pillars, and a base** (or step) **before them.**"
Most of the Persepolitan porches had small
pillared chambers at some little distance in
front of them.

7. The porch or gate of justice still kept
alive the likeness of the old patriarchal
custom of sitting in judgment at the gate;
exactly as the "Gate of Justice" still recalls it at Granada, and the Sublime
Porte—"the Lofty Gate"—at Constanti-
nople.

8. *like unto this porch*] *i.e.* of similar materials, hewn stone and cedar. The *zenana*
could not have been a mere portico.

9. The stones were uniform—all cut to
certain fixed measures of length, breadth,
and thickness. They were not squared only
on the face which showed, but also on the
sides which fell within the wall and were
not seen. Saws appear in Assyrian sculptures of the age of Sennacherib; and
fragments of an iron saw have been found
at Nimrud.

10. See *v.* 17 note.

the foundation *was of* costly stones, even great stones, stones of
11 ten cubits, and stones of eight cubits. And above *were* costly
12 stones, after the measures of hewed stones, and cedars. And
the great court round about *was* with three rows of hewed
stones, and a row of cedar beams, both for the inner court of the
13 house of the LORD, *c* and for the porch of the house. ¶And king
14 Solomon sent and fetched *d* Hiram out of Tyre. *e* He *was* ¹a
widow's son of the tribe of Naphtali, and *f* his father *was* a man
of Tyre, a worker in brass : and *g* he was filled with wisdom, and
understanding, and cunning to work all works in brass. ¶And
15 he came to king Solomon, and wrought all his work. For he
²cast *h* two pillars of brass, of eighteen cubits high apiece : and
16 a line of twelve cubits did compass either of them about. And
he made two chapiters *of* molten brass, to set upon the tops of
the pillars : the height of the one chapiter *was* five cubits, and
17 the height of the other chapiter *was* five cubits : *and* nets of
checker work, and wreaths of chain work, for the chapiters
which *were* upon the top of the pillars ; seven for the one
18 chapiter, and seven for the other chapiter. And he made the
pillars, and two rows round about upon the one network, to

c John 10. 23.
Acts 3. 11.
d 2 Chr. 4. 11,
Huram :
See ver. 40.
e 2 Chr. 2. 14.
f 2 Chr. 4. 16.
g Ex. 31. 3.
& 36. 1.
h 2 Kin. 25.
17.
2 Chr. 3. 15.
& 4. 12.
Jer. 52. 21.

¹ Heb. *the son of a widow woman.*   ² Heb. *fashioned.*

---

12. The palace, like the Temple, had two
courts (vi. 36), not, however, one immediately within the other. The lesser court of
the palace seems to have been a private
inner court among the buildings (*v.* 8). The
greater court was outside all the buildings,
surrounding the palace on every side. Assyrian palaces had always such an external
court, and had generally one or more inner
courts or quadrangles.

both for the inner court] By a slight alteration of the text, the meaning would be
" as (was done) in the inner court, &c. and
in the porch."

13. *Hiram*] A man who bore the same
name as the king of Tyre, a master workman, known as Hiram Ab, *i.e.* Master Hiram (2 Chr. ii. 13, iv. 16).

14. Hiram's mother, while by birth of
the tribe of Dan, had had for her first husband a man of the tribe of Naphtali. (Cp.
this verse and marg. ref.)

all his work] The work that he personally
did for Solomon seems to have been limited
to metal-work, and indeed to works in
brass. (See below, *v.* 45, and cp. 2 Chr. iv.
16.)

15. These famous pillars, which were
broken in pieces by the Babylonians when
they destroyed Jerusalem (2 K. xxv. 13 ; Jer.
lii. 17), were probably for ornament, standing
by themselves under or in front of the
porch. It is certain that the Phœnicians
used isolated metal columns as sacred ornaments, so that Hiram would be familiar with
such a mode of ornamentation. Eighteen
cubits appear to have been the height of the
shaft only. Adding the capital (*vv.* 16, 19),
the entire metal pillar was 27 cubits high ;
and if it had a stone base of eight cubits,
which would not be greatly out of propor-

tion, the height of 35 cubits (52½ feet, 2 Chr.
iii. 15) would have been reached. The
height of some of the Persepolitan columns,
with which these pillars may be best compared, is 67 feet. The circumference of 12
cubits (18 feet) implies a diameter of about
5 feet 9 inches at the base, which would
make the column somewhat heavy in appearance. Egyptian pillars were, however,
even thicker in proportion to their height.
On the supposition that a portion of the original text has fallen out, this verse has been
thus completed : " He cast two pillars of
brass ; eighteen cubits was the height of the
one pillar, *and eighteen cubits was the height
of the other pillar ; and a line of twelve cubits
compassed the one pillar,* and a line of twelve
cubits compassed the other pillar."

16. The general character of the *chapiters*
or capitals, their great size in proportion to
the shaft, which is as one to two, and their
construction of two quite different members,
remind us of the pillars used by the Persians in their palaces, which were certainly
more like Jachin and Boaz than any pillars
that have reached us from antiquity. The
ornamentation, however, seems to have
been far more elaborate than that of the
Persian capitals.

17. *nets, &c.*] Rather, "Nets chequerwise,
and festoons chainwise,"—probably a fine
network over the whole, and chainwork
hanging in festoons outside.

seven for the one chapiter] The LXX.
reading is preferable. " A net for the one
chapiter and a net for the other chapiter."
Cp. *v.* 41.

18. The pomegranate was one of the
commonest ornaments in Assyria. It was
used on quivers, on spear-shafts, and mace-
heads, in patterns on doorways and pave-

cover the chapiters that *were* upon the top, with pomegranates:
19 and so did he for the other chapiter. And the chapiters that
were upon the top of the pillars *were* of lily work in the porch,
20 four cubits. And the chapiters upon the two pillars *had pomegranates* also above, over against the belly which *was* by the network : and the pomegranates *were* ᶦtwo hundred in rows round
21 about upon the other chapiter. ᵏAnd he set up the pillars in
ᶦthe porch of the temple : and he set up the right pillar, and
called the name thereof ¹Jachin : and he set up the left pillar,
22 and called the name thereof ²Boaz. And upon the top of the
pillars *was* lily work : so was the work of the pillars finished.
23 ¶And he made ᵐa molten sea, ten cubits ³from the one brim
to the other : *it was* round all about, and his height *was* five
cubits : and a line of thirty cubits did compass it round about.
24 And under the brim of it round about *there were* knops compassing it, ten in a cubit, ⁿcompassing the sea round about : the
25 knops *were* cast in two rows, when it was cast. It stood upon
ᵒtwelve oxen, three looking toward the north, and three looking
toward the west, and three looking toward the south, and three
looking toward the east : and the sea *was* set above upon them,
26 and all their hinder parts *were* inward. And it *was* an hand
breadth thick, and the brim thereof was wrought like the brim
of a cup, with flowers of lilies : it contained ᵖtwo thousand baths.

Margin notes:
ᶦ See 2 Chr. 3. 16.
ᵏ 2 Chr. 3. 17.
ᶦ ch. 6. 3.

ᵐ 2 Kin 25. 13.
2 Chr 4. 2.
Jer. 52. 17.

ⁿ 2 Chr. 4. 3.

ᵒ 2 Chr. 4. 4, 5.
Jer. 52. 20.

ᵖ See 2 Chr. 4. 5.

---

¹ That is, *He shall establish.*
² That is, *In it is strength.*
³ Heb. *from his brim to his
brim.*

---

ments, &c. It is doubtful whether a symbolical meaning attached to it, or whether
it was merely selected as a beautiful natural
form.

19. There is a cornice of (so-called) lily-
work at Persepolis, consisting of three
ranges of broadish rounded leaves, one over
the other. Lilies are also represented with
much spirit on a bas-relief from Koyunjik.

20. In this verse also a portion of the
original text is supposed to have fallen out
in consequence of the repetition of words.
The full phrase of the original has been
retained in *vv.* 16 and 17. It may be restored thus :—"And the pomegranates were
two hundred in rows round about *upon the
one chapiter, and two hundred in rows round
about* upon the other chapiter." The "four
hundred " (*v.* 42 ; 2 Chr. iv. 13), are obtained by counting the pomegranates of both
pillars together. In Jerem. lii. 23, is an
account of the arrangement of a single row
of pomegranates, whereof each pillar had
two.

21. The LXX. in the parallel passage
(marg. ref.), translate Jachin and Boaz by
Κατόρθωσις and Ἰσχύς — " Direction " and
" Strength." The literal meaning of the
names is given in the margin. The meaning was probably " God will establish in
strength " (*i.e.* firmly) the Temple and the
religion connected with it.

23. The "molten sea " of Solomon, so
called from its great size, took the place of
the laver of the Tabernacle (Ex. xxx. 18-21),
which was required for the ablutions of the

priests. It was ten cubits, or fully fifteen
feet, in diameter at top, and therefore forty-
seven feet in circumference, with a depth of
5 cubits, or 7½ feet. As a vessel of these
dimensions, if hemispherical, would certainly not hold 2000 (*v.* 26), much less 3000
(2 Chr. iv. 3) *baths,* the bath equalling 8½ gallons, it is now generally supposed that the
bowl bulged considerably below the brim,
and further, that it had a " foot,"—or basin
which received the water as it was drawn
out by taps from the bowl. The " 2000
baths " may give the quantity of water ordinarily supplied to the " sea ;" the " 3000
baths " the utmost that the laver could any-
how take. Bowls of a considerable size are
represented in the Assyrian bas-reliefs ; but
none of such dimensions as Solomon's. The
largest mentioned by the Greeks held only
5400 gallons, less than one-third of the contents of the "molten sea," even according
to the lowest estimate.

24. *knops*] Literally, "gourds," — *i.e.* a
boss or ball ornament encircled the rim of
the bowl in two rows.

25. Josephus charged Solomon with a
breach of the Commandment (Ex. xx. 4, 5),
on account of the oxen here and the lions
for his throne. The charge expresses the
prohibition which some Jews have conceived
the Commandment to urge against the arts
of sculpture and painting.

26. The palm or hand-breadth seems to
have a little exceeded three inches.
with flowers of lilies] Rather, "in the
shape of a lily flower." The rim was

27 ¶ And he made ten bases of brass; four cubits *was* the length of one base, and four cubits the breadth thereof, and three cubits
28 the height of it. And the work of the bases *was* on this *man-ner :* they had borders, and the borders *were* between the ledges :
29 and on the borders that *were* between the ledges *were* lions, oxen, and cherubims : and upon the ledges *there was* a base above : and beneath the lions and oxen *were* certain additions
30 made of thin work. And every base had four brasen wheels, and plates of brass : and the four corners thereof had undersetters : under the laver *were* undersetters molten, at the side of every
31 addition. And the mouth of it within the chapiter and above *was* a cubit : but the mouth thereof *was* round *after* the work of the base, a cubit and an half : and also upon the mouth of it
32 *were* gravings with their borders, foursquare, not round. And under the borders *were* four wheels ; and the axletrees of the wheels *were* ¹*joined* to the base : and the height of a wheel *was*
33 a cubit and half a cubit. And the work of the wheels *was* like the work of a chariot wheel : their axletrees, and their naves,
34 and their felloes, and their spokes, *were* all molten. And *there were* four undersetters to the four corners of one base : *and* the
35 undersetters *were* of the very base itself. And in the top of the base *was there* a round compass of half a cubit high : and on the top of the base the ledges thereof and the borders thereof *were*
36 of the same. For on the plates of the ledges thereof, and on the borders thereof, he graved cherubims, lions, and palm trees,

¹ Heb. *in the base.*

---

slightly curved outwards, like the rim of an ordinary drinking-cup, or the edge of a lily blossom. See 2 Chr. iv. 5 marg.

27. *ten bases of brass*] These were for the ten lavers (*v.* 38. See 2 Chr. iv. 6). In general terms the bases were square stands, 6 feet each way, and 4½ feet high, elaborately ornamented on their four sides, and resting upon four wheels, 2¼ feet in diameter. Each stand supported a laver 6 feet high, which contained 40 baths (*v.* 38), or about 340 gallons.

28. *borders*] Rather, "**panels**" (so *rv.* 32, 35), a set of square compartments between the "ledges" or borders, or mouldings. Below the panelling, with its ornamentation of lions, oxen (the two animal forms which occur most frequently in Assyrian decoration), and cherubim, was a space decorated with "additions of thin work" (*v.* 29).

Upon the "ledges" (*v.* 29) which surrounded the top of the base there was a stand for the laver, distinct from the upper surface of the base.

30. *plates of brass*] Rather, " **brazen axletrees.**"

The "undersetters" (literally, "shoulders") are conjectured to have been four brackets, or bars, proceeding from the four upper corners of the bases, and stretching upwards to the outer rim of the laver, which thus rested partly upon them.

at the side of every addition] Rather, "**each opposite garlands.**" The laver was

ornamented with a garland at the place where the support reached it.

31. It seems impossible to determine what is meant by the "mouth" of the laver, or what by its "chapiter."

32. With the diameter (2¼ ft.) of the wheel here, may be compared that of the earliest Assyrian chariot-wheels, which was under 3 feet ; and that of the front wheels seen in representations of Assyrian close carriages, which scarcely exceed ¼th of the height of the entire vehicle. The wheels of these moveable lavers appear to have been a little less than ⅓th of the height of the whole structure.

34. The undersetters were cast with the base, not afterwards attached to it, and were therefore stronger and better able to support the laver.

35. *a round compass*] A circular elevation, half a cubit high, rather than a circular depression, half a cubit deep. Cp. *v.* 29. The "ledges" and "borders" of the top of the base were its "hands" and its "panels." These "hands," distinct from the "shoulders" (*v.* 30), were probably supports, adorned with engraved plates (*v.* 36), either of the elevated circle on which the laver stood, or of the lower part of the laver itself. Both panels and "hands" were "of the same," *i.e.* of one piece with the base, cast at the same time.

36. *according to the proportion of every one*, *i.e.* "as large as the room left for them allowed," implying that the panels were

according to the ¹proportion of every one, and additions round
37 about. After this *manner* he made the ten bases : all of them
^q 2 Chr. 4. 6. 38 had one casting, one measure, *and* one size. ¶ Then ^qmade he
ten lavers of brass : one laver contained forty baths : *and* every
laver was four cubits : *and* upon every one of the ten bases
39 one laver. And he put five bases on the right ²side of the
house, and five on the left side of the house : and he set the sea
on the right side of the house eastward over against the south.
40 And ³Hiram made the lavers, and the shovels, and the basons.
¶ So Hiram made an end of doing all the work that he made king
41 Solomon for the house of the LORD : the two pillars, and the *two*
bowls of the chapiters that *were* on the top of the two pillars ;
^r ver. 17, 18. and the two ʳnetworks, to cover the two bowls of the chapiters
42 which *were* upon the top of the pillars ; and four hundred pomegranates for the two networks, *even* two rows of pomegranates
for one network, to cover the two bowls of the chapiters that
43 *were* ⁴upon the pillars ; and the ten bases, and ten lavers on the
^s Ex. 27. 3. 44, 45 bases ; and one sea, and twelve oxen under the sea ; ˢand
2 Chr. 4. 16. the pots, and the shovels, and the basons : and all these vessels,
which Hiram made to king Solomon for the house of the LORD,
^t 2 Chr. 4.17. 46 *were of* ⁵bright brass. ᵗIn the plain of Jordan did the king cast
^u Gen. 33.17. them, ⁶in the clay ground between ᵘSuccoth and ˣZarthan.
^x Josh. 3. 16. 47 And Solomon left all the vessels *unweighed*, ⁷because they were
exceeding many : neither was the weight of the brass ⁸found out.
48 ¶ And Solomon made all the vessels that *pertained* unto the
^y Ex. 37. 25. house of the LORD : ʸthe altar of gold, and ᶻthe table of gold,
^z Ex. 37. 10, 49 whereupon ᵃthe shewbread *was*, and the candlesticks of pure
&c.
^a Ex. 25. 30. gold, five on the right *side*, and five on the left, before the oracle,
Lev. 24. 5—8. 50 with the flowers, and the lamps, and the tongs *of* gold, and the
bowls, and the snuffers, and the basons, and the spoons, and the
⁹censers *of* pure gold ; and the hinges *of* gold, *both* for the doors
of the inner house, the most holy *place*, *and* for the doors of the
51 house, to *wit*, of the temple. ¶ So was ended all the work that
king Solomon made for the house of the LORD. And Solomon
^b 2 Sam. 8. 11. brought in the ¹things ᵇwhich David his father had dedicated ;
2 Chr. 5. 1. *even* the silver, and the gold, and the vessels, did he put among
the treasures of the house of the LORD.

<table>
<tr><td>¹ Heb. *nakedness.*</td><td>⁵ Heb. *made bright,* or,</td><td>⁸ Heb. *searched,* 1 Chr. 22.</td></tr>
<tr><td>² Heb. *shoulder.*</td><td>*scoured.*</td><td>14.</td></tr>
<tr><td>³ Heb. *Hirom:* See ver.13.</td><td>⁶ Heb. *in the thickness of*</td><td>⁹ Heb. *ash pans.*</td></tr>
<tr><td>⁴ Heb. *upon the face of the*</td><td>*the ground.*</td><td>¹ Heb. *holy things of*</td></tr>
<tr><td>*pillars.*</td><td>⁷ Heb. *for the exceeding*</td><td>*David.*</td></tr>
<tr><td></td><td>*multitude.*</td><td></td></tr>
</table>

---

smaller than those on the sides of the base,
and allowed scant room for the representations.

38. *every laver was four cubits*] Assuming
height to be intended, and taking the cubit
at 20 inches, the entire height of the lavers
as they stood upon their wheeled stands
would seem to have been 13 ft. 9 in. It is
evident, therefore, that the water must have
been drawn from them, as from the "molten
sea," through cocks or taps.

40. *lavers*] Rather, according to the true
reading, " **pots.** " (Cp. *v.* 45 ; 2 Chr. iv. 16.)
The " pots " were the caldrons in which it
was usual to boil the peace-offerings. See
1 Sam. ii. 13, 14.

46. *Succoth and Zarthan*] See Judg. vii.
22, viii. 5 note.

47. The brass of which the two pillars,
Jachin and Boaz, the brazen sea, and the
various vessels were made had been taken
by David from two cities belonging to Hadadezer, king of Zobah (1 Chr. xviii. 8).

48. See note to vi. 20 and 2 Chr. iv. 19–22.

49, 50. See notes to Ex. xxv. 31–38. The
" bowls " of *v.* 50 were the "bowls " for the
tables (Ex. xxxvii. 16), large vases containing oil for the lamps.

51. *the things which David had dedicated*]
Not only the things described in 1 Chr.
xxviii. 14–18, but also the spoil of the nations which he had subdued (marg. ref.),

CHAP. 8. THEN ^aSolomon assembled the elders of Israel, and all the heads of the tribes, the ¹chief of the fathers of the children of Israel, unto king Solomon in Jerusalem, ^bthat they might bring up the ark of the covenant of the LORD ^cout of the city of 2 David, which *is* Zion. ¶ And all the men of Israel assembled themselves unto king Solomon at the ^dfeast in the month Ethanim, 3 which *is* the seventh month. And all the elders of Israel came, 4 ^eand the priests took up the ark. And they brought up the ark of the LORD, ^fand the tabernacle of the congregation, and all the holy vessels that *were* in the tabernacle, even those did the 5 priests and the Levites bring up. And king Solomon, and all the congregation of Israel, that were assembled unto him, *were* with him before the ark, ^gsacrificing sheep and oxen, that could 6 not be told nor numbered for multitude. And the priests ^hbrought in the ark of the covenant of the LORD unto ⁱhis place, into the oracle of the house, to the most holy *place, even* ^kunder 7 the wings of the cherubims. For the cherubims spread forth *their* two wings over the place of the ark, and the cherubims 8 covered the ark and the staves thereof above. And they ^ldrew out the staves, that the ²ends of the staves were seen out in the ³holy *place* before the oracle, and they were not seen with-9 out : and there they are unto this day. ^mThere was nothing in the ark ⁿsave the two tables of stone, which Moses ^oput there at

a 2 Chr. 5. 2, &c.
b 2 Sam. 6. 17.
c 2 Sam. 5.
7, 9.
d Lev. 23 34.
2 Chr. 7. 8.
e Num. 4. 15.
Josh. 3. 3, 6.
1 Chr. 15.
14, 15.
f ch. 3. 4.
2 Chr. 1. 3.
g 2 Sam. 6. 13.
h 2 Sam. 6, 17.
i Ex. 26. 33, 34.
ch. 6. 19.
k ch. 6. 27.
l Ex. 25. 14.
m Ex. 25. 21.
Deut. 10. 2.
n Deut. 10.5.
o Ex. 40. 20.

¹ Heb. *princes*.   ² Heb. *heads*.   ³ Or, *ark :* as 2 Chr. 5. 9.

---

and also the vessels of gold, silver, and brass, sent him by Toi king of Hamath, on his victory over Hadadezer. Solomon now brought these into the Temple treasury. A sacred treasury had been established at least as early as the time of Saul, to which Saul himself, Abner, Joab, and others, had contributed (1 Chr. xxvi. 28).

VIII. **1.** There seems to be a contrast here between the more popular proceedings of David (2 Sam. vi. 1), and the statelier system of his son, who merely summons the chief men as representatives of the nation. The rest of the people "assembled themselves" (*v.* 2), and were mere spectators of the solemnity.

2. *the feast in the month Ethanim*] *i.e.* the Feast of Tabernacles, or In-gathering, the commemoration of the dwelling in booths at the time of the Exodus (marg. ref.), and the festival of thanksgiving on account of the completion of harvest (Ex. xxiii. 16 ; Lev. xxiii. 39 ; Deut. xvi. 13). It was one of the three on which the people were required to "appear before the Lord."

3. In 2 Chr. v. 4, "*the Levites* took up the ark ;" and by the Law the Ark was the special charge of the Kohathites (Num. iii. 31, iv. 15). But all priests were Levites (Josh. iii. 3), though all Levites were not priests. And as Joshua had done (Josh. iii. 6, vi. 6), so Solomon called upon the priests to bear the holy structure, allowing to mere Levites only the inferior honour of helping to transport the Tabernacle and the vessels of the Sanctuary.

4. *and the tabernacle of the congregation*]

Not the tented structure erected for the Ark on Mount Zion (2 Sam. vi. 17) by David, but the original Tabernacle made by Moses, which had hitherto remained at Gibeon (marg. ref.). The Tabernacle and its holy vessels were probably placed in the treasury.

8. It was forbidden to withdraw the staves wholly from the rings (marg. ref.) ; but they appear to have been now drawn forward in such a way that their ends or heads could be seen from the Holy Place, or great chamber of the Temple, though without their being visible from the porch or vestibule. Either the doorway into the Holy of Holies was not exactly opposite the Ark, but a little on one side ; or, though that doorway was in the middle, opposite the Ark, the doorway from the porch into the main chamber was not opposite to it. In Assyrian temples the arrangement of the outer door, the inner door, and the sanctuary, seems to have been designedly such that a mere passer-by on the outside should not obtain even a glimpse of the shrine. It is suggested that the withdrawal of the staves was intended as a sign that the Ark had reached "the place of its rest," and was not to be borne about any more.

there they are unto this day] This is a quotation from an author who lived while the Temple was still standing. See also ix. 21.

9. Comparing this statement with Heb. ix. 4, it would seem that Solomon, now that the sacred chest had reached its final resting-place, and stood in a large chamber surrounded by tables (2 Chr. iv. 8), removed

Horeb, ¹ᵖwhen the LORD made *a covenant* with the children of 10 Israel, when they came out of the land of Egypt. ¶And it came to pass, when the priests were come out of the holy *place*, that 11 the cloud ᵠfilled the house of the LORD, so that the priests could not stand to minister because of the cloud : for the glory of the 12 LORD had filled the house of the LORD. ʳ¶Then spake Solomon, 13 The LORD said that he would dwell ˢin the thick darkness. ᵗI have surely built thee an house to dwell in, ᵘa settled place for 14 thee to abide in for ever. ¶And the king turned his face about, and ˣblessed all the congregation of Israel : (and all the congre-15 gation of Israel stood ;) and he said, ʸBlessed *be* the LORD God of Israel, which ᶻspake with his mouth unto David my father, 16 and hath with his hand fulfilled *it*, saying, ᵃSince the day that I brought forth my people Israel out of Egypt, I chose no city out of all the tribes of Israel to build an house, that ᵇmy name might be therein ; but I chose ᶜDavid to be over my people 17 Israel. And ᵈit was in the heart of David my father to build an 18 house for the name of the LORD God of Israel. ᵉAnd the LORD said unto David my father, Whereas it was in thine heart to build an house unto my name, thou didst well that it was in 19 thine heart. Nevertheless ᶠthou shalt not build the house ; but thy son that shall come forth out of thy loins, he shall build the 20 house unto my name. And the LORD hath performed his word that he spake, and I am risen up in the room of David my father, and sit on the throne of Israel, ᵍas the LORD promised, and have built an house for the name of the LORD God of Israel. 21 And I have set there a place for the ark, wherein *is* ʰthe covenant of the LORD, which he made with our fathers, when he 22 brought them out of the land of Egypt. ¶And Solomon stood before ⁱthe altar of the LORD in the presence of all the congregation of Israel, and ᵏspread forth his hands toward heaven : 23 and he said, LORD God of Israel, ˡ*there is* no God like thee, in

¹ Cr, *where.*

---

the pot of manna and the rod from the interior, and set them elsewhere in the Holy of Holies.

10. The cloud—the visible symbol of the Divine Presence—the Shechinah of the Targums—which had been promised before the Ark was begun (Ex. xxix. 43), and had filled the Tabernacle as soon as it was completed (do. xl. 34), and which had probably been seen from time to time during the long interval when we have no express mention of it, now once more appeared in full magnificence, and took, as it were, possession of the building which Solomon was dedicating. The Presence of God in the Temple henceforth was thus assured to the Jews, and His approval of all that Solomon had done was signified.

11. As in the case of Moses (Ex. xl. 35), so now the glory of the Lord, the manifestation of the Divine Presence, which the cloud usually veiled, shone forth from it with such brilliancy, that mortal man could not bear the sight.

12. Rather, "**The Lord spake of dwelling in the thick darkness**" (marg. reff.). Solomon sees in the cloud the visible sym-

bol of God's Presence, and accepts the token as a proof that He has taken possession of the house built for Him, and will thenceforth dwell there (*v.* 13).

14. Solomon had spoken the preceding words, addressed to God, with his face directed to the Holy of Holies. He now turned round and looked outwards towards the people. The people " stood " to hear him—the attitude of respect and attention. This first blessing seems to have been without speech—an inward prayer accompanied by the ordinary gesture of blessing.

15. The exact words of 2 Sam. vii. are not reproduced ; only their general sense is given. In *v.* 18, what was merely tacitly implied was regarded as actually " said."

16. The marg. ref. completes the sense of this verse here. The passage is in accordance with archaic modes of speech, and is probably the more verbally accurate of the two.

22. The marg. ref. shows that the king was so placed as to be seen by all present, and that, before beginning his prayer, he knelt down upon his knees (cp. *v.* 54).

23. Cp. Deut. vii. 9.

heaven above, or on earth beneath, [m]who keepest covenant and
mercy with thy servants that [n]walk before thee with all their
24 heart: who hast kept with thy servant David my father that
thou promisedst him: thou spakest also with thy mouth, and
25 hast fulfilled *it* with thine hand, as *it is* this day. Therefore
now, LORD God of Israel, keep with thy servant David my
father that thou promisedst him, saying, [o][1]There shall not fail
thee a man in my sight to sit on the throne of Israel; [2]so that
thy children take heed to their way, that they walk before me as
26 thou hast walked before me. [p]And now, O God of Israel, let
thy word, I pray thee, be verified, which thou spakest unto thy
27 servant David my father. ¶ But [q]will God indeed dwell on the
earth? behold, the heaven and [r]heaven of heavens cannot
contain thee; how much less this house that I have builded?
28 Yet have thou respect unto the prayer of thy servant, and to his
supplication, O LORD my God, to hearken unto the cry and to
29 the prayer, which thy servant prayeth before thee to day: that
thine eyes may be open toward this house night and day, *even*
toward the place of which thou hast said, [s]My name shall be
there: that thou mayest hearken unto the prayer which thy
30 servant shall make [t][3]toward this place. [u]And hearken thou to
the supplication of thy servant, and of thy people Israel, when
they shall pray [4]toward this place: and hear thou in heaven thy
31 dwelling place: and when thou hearest, forgive. ¶ If any man
trespass against his neighbour, [5]and [x]an oath be laid upon him
to cause him to swear, and the oath come before thine altar in
32 this house: then hear thou in heaven, and do, and judge thy
servants, [y]condemning the wicked, to bring his way upon his
head; and justifying the righteous, to give him according to his
33 righteousness. ¶ [z]When thy people Israel be smitten down
before the enemy, because they have sinned against thee, and
[a]shall turn again to thee, and confess thy name, and pray, and
34 make supplication unto thee [6]in this house: then hear thou in
heaven, and forgive the sin of thy people Israel, and bring them
again unto the land which thou gavest unto their fathers.
35 ¶ [b]When heaven is shut up, and there is no rain, because they
have sinned against thee; if they pray toward this place, and
confess thy name, and turn from their sin, when thou afflictest

Margin references (right column):

[m] Deut. 7. 9.
Neh. 1. 5.
Dan. 9. 4.
[n] Gen. 17. 1.
ch. 3. 6.
2 Kin. 20. 3.

[o] 2 Sam. 7.
12, 16.
ch. 2. 4.

[p] 2 Sam. 7.
25.

[q] 2 Chr. 2. 6.
Isai. 66. 1.
Jer. 23. 24.
Acts 7. 49.
[r] 2 Cor. 12. 2.

[s] Deut. 12. 11.

[t] Dan. 6. 10.
[u] 2 Chr. 20. 9.
Neh. 1. 6.

[x] Ex. 22. 11.

[y] Deut. 25. 1.

[z] Lev. 26. 17.
Deut. 28. 25.

[a] Lev. 26.
39, 40.
Neh. 1. 9.

[b] Lev. 26. 19.
Deut. 28. 23.

---

[1] Heb. *There shall not be cut off unto thee a man from my sight.*
[2] Heb. *only if.*
[3] Or, *in this place.*
[4] Or, *in this place.*
[5] Heb. *and he require an oath of him,* Lev. 5. 1.
[6] Or, *toward.*

---

26. Solomon's prayer is, perhaps, generally for the fulfilment of all the promises made to David in connection with the building of the Temple. But there seems to be special allusion in this verse to the promise recorded in Ps. cxxxii. 14.

27. *heaven of heavens*] Cp. Deut. x. 14; Ps. cxlviii. 4. It seems to mean the heaven in its most extended compass. Solomon combines with his belief in Jehovah's special Presence in the Temple, the strongest conviction that He is no local or finite deity, but is ever present everywhere. Cp. Ps. cxxxix. 7–10.

29. The choice of Jerusalem as the place seems to have been made by special revela-

tion to David. See Pss. lxxviii. 68, cxxxii. 13; and cp. 1 Chr. xxii. 1.

toward this place] Better (here and in *v.* 30) than the marginal "in." Wherever they were, the Jews always worshipped *towards* the Temple. (See marg. ref.)

and when thou hearest, forgive] Lit., "both hear and forgive"—*i.e.,* "hear the prayer, and forgive the sin" which alone causes God to chasten men or to withhold from them His choicest blessings.

31. *the oath come before, &c.*] "The oath" is equivalent to "the man who swears the oath." A slight alteration in the present Hebrew text gives the sense "and he (the accused) go and swear before thine altar," &c. The threats and the promises, the punish-

36 them : then hear thou in heaven, and forgive the sin of thy
c Ps. 25. 4.
& 27. 11.
d 1 Sam. 12.
23.
servants, and of thy people Israel, that thou ᶜteach them ᵈthe
good way wherein they should walk, and give rain upon thy
land, which thou hast given to thy people for an inheritance.
e Lev. 26.
16, 25, 26.
Deut. 28.
21, &c.
2 Chr. 20. 9.
37 ¶ ᵉIf there be in the land famine, if there be pestilence, blasting,
mildew, locust, or if there be caterpiller; if their enemy besiege
them in the land of their ¹cities; whatsoever plague, whatsoever
38 sickness there be; what prayer and supplication soever be made
by any man, or by all thy people Israel, which shall know every
man the plague of his own heart, and spread forth his hands
39 toward this house: then hear thou in heaven thy dwelling place,
and forgive, and do, and give to every man according to his
ways, whose heart thou knowest; (for thou, even thou only,
f 1 Sam.16.7.
1 Chr. 28. 9.
Ps. 11. 4.
Jer. 17. 10.
Acts 1. 24.
g Ps. 130. 4.
40 ᶠknowest the hearts of all the children of men;) ᵍthat they may
fear thee all the days that they live in the land which thou
41 gavest unto our fathers. ¶Moreover concerning a stranger,
that is not of thy people Israel, but cometh out of a far country
h Deut. 3. 24.
42 for thy name's sake; (for they shall hear of thy great name, and
of thy ʰstrong hand, and of thy stretched out arm;) when he
43 shall come and pray toward this house; hear thou in heaven thy
dwelling place, and do according to all that the stranger calleth
i 1 Sam. 17.
46.
2 Kin. 19. 19.
Ps. 67. 2.
k Ps. 102. 15.
to thee for: ⁱthat all people of the earth may know thy name, to
ᵏfear thee, as do thy people Israel; and that they may know
that ²this house, which I have builded, is called by thy name.
44 ¶ If thy people go out to battle against their enemy, whithersoever thou shalt send them, and shall pray unto the LORD
³toward the city which thou hast chosen, and toward the house
45 that I have built for thy name : then hear thou in heaven their
46 prayer and their supplication, and maintain their ⁴cause.   ¶ If

---

¹ Or, jurisdiction.   ² Heb. thy name is called   ³ Heb. the way of the city.
upon this house.   ⁴ Or, right.

---

ments and calamities of vv. 31–38 were distinctly named in the Law. See marg. reff.
   36. teach them, &c.] Rather, "when thou
art teaching them (by thy chastisement)
the good way that they should walk in,"
i.e. when thou art still teaching, not taking
vengeance.
   37. in the land of their cities] Literally,
"in the land of their gates." Hence the
marginal translation "jurisdiction," because judgments were pronounced in the
town gates (Deut. xvi. 18). Another reading gives "in one of their cities."
   38. know every man the plague of his own
heart] i.e. perceive one's sinfulness, or recognise one's sufferings as Divine chastisements, and sin as their cause.
   41. Nothing is more remarkable in the
Mosaic Law than its liberality with regard
to strangers, both in general (Ex. xxii. 21;
Lev. xxv. 35; Deut. x. 19) and in religious
matters (Num. xv. 14–16; Deut. xxxi. 12).
It is quite in the spirit of these enactments
that Solomon, having first prayed to God on
behalf of his fellow-countrymen, should
next go on to intercede for the strangers,
and to ask for their prayers the same acceptance which he had previously begged
for the prayers of faithful Israelites.

for thy name's sake] i.e. "to visit the place
where Thou hast set Thy name" (Cp. Deut.
xii. 5, 11, &c.).
   42. great name] A somewhat rare expression. It does not occur at all in the Pentateuch ; though "mighty hand" and the
"stretched out arm" are so frequent (Ex.
vi. 6, xiii. 9; Deut. ix. 29); only once in
Joshua (vii. 9); and twice in the Psalms
(lxxvi. 1, xcix. 3). About the time of the
Captivity the use of the phrase became more
common (Ezek. xxxvi. 23; Jer. x. 6, xliv. 26).
   43. that all people of the earth may know
thy name, to fear thee] Solomon prays
that the result of Jehovah's hearing the
prayers of heathens addressed towards the
Temple may be the general conversion of
the world to the worship of Him. Cp. Pss.
xcvi., xcviii.
   this house, &c.] Lit., as in the margin.
In Scripture, when God's Name is said
to be "called upon" persons or things, it
seems to be meant that God is really present in them, upholding them and sancti-
fying them. This passage therefore means,
that the heathen, when their prayers, directed towards the Temple, are granted, will
have a full assurance that God is present in
the building in some very special way.

they sin against thee, ([l]for *there is* no man that sinneth not,)
and thou be angry with them, and deliver them to the enemy,
so that they carry them away captives [m]unto the land of the
47 enemy, far or near; [n]*yet* if they shall [1]bethink themselves in
the land whither they were carried captives, and repent, and
make supplication unto thee in the land of them that carried
them captives, [o]saying, We have sinned, and have done per-
48 versely, we have committed wickedness; and *so* [p]return unto
thee with all their heart, and with all their soul, in the land of
their enemies, which led them away captive, and [q]pray unto
thee toward their land, which thou gavest unto their fathers,
the city which thou hast chosen, and the house which I have
49 built for thy name: then hear thou their prayer and their supplication in heaven thy dwelling place, and maintain their
50 [2]cause, and forgive thy people that have sinned against thee,
and all their transgressions wherein they have transgressed
against thee, and [r]give them compassion before them who
carried them captive, that they may have compassion on them:
51 for [s]they *be* thy people, and thine inheritance, which thou
broughtest forth out of Egypt, [t]from the midst of the furnace
52 of iron: that thine eyes may be open unto the supplication of
thy servant, and unto the supplication of thy people Israel, to
53 hearken unto them in all that they call for unto thee. For thou
didst separate them from among all the people of the earth, *to*
be thine inheritance, [u]as thou spakest by the hand of Moses thy
servant, when thou broughtest our fathers out of Egypt, O Lord
54 GOD. ¶ And it was *so*, that when Solomon had made an end of
praying all this prayer and supplication unto the LORD, he arose
from before the altar of the LORD, from kneeling on his knees
55 with his hands spread up to heaven. And he stood, [x]and
blessed all the congregation of Israel with a loud voice, saying,
56 Blessed *be* the LORD, that hath given rest unto his people Israel,
according to all that he promised: [y]there hath not [3]failed one
word of all his good promise, which he promised by the hand
57 of Moses his servant. The LORD our God be with us, as he was
58 with our fathers: [z]let him not leave us, nor forsake us: that he
may [a]incline our hearts unto him, to walk in all his ways, and
to keep his commandments, and his statutes, and his judgments,

[l] 2 Chr. 6. 36. Prov. 20. 9. Eccles. 7. 20. James 3. 2. 1 John 1. 8, 10.
[m] Lev. 26. 34, 44. Deut. 28. 36, 64.
[n] Lev. 26 40.
[o] Neh. 1. 6. Ps. 106. 6. Dan. 9. 5.
[p] Deut. 30. 2.
[q] Dan. 6. 10.
[r] Ezra 7. 6. Ps. 106. 46.
[s] Deut. 9. 29. Neh. 1. 10.
[t] Deut. 4. 20. Jer. 11. 4,
[u] Ex. 19. 5. Deut. 4. 20. & 9. 26, 29.
[x] 2 Sam. 6. 18.
[y] Deut. 12. 10. Josh. 21. 45.
[z] Deut. 31. 6. Josh. 1. 5. Ps. 27. 9.
[a] Ps. 119. 36.

[1] Heb. *bring back to their heart.* [2] Or, *right.* [3] Heb. *fallen.*

---

47. *bethink themselves*] Lit., as in margin—*i.e.* "reflect," "consider seriously." Cp. Deut. xxx. 1.

sinned, done perversely, committed wickedness] The words here used seem to have become the standard form of expressing contrition when the time of the Captivity arrived and the Israelites were forcibly removed to Babylon (cp. marg. reff.). The three expressions are thought to form a climax, rising from negative to positive guilt, and from mere wrongful acts to depravation of the moral character.

50. *compassion*, &c.] Not merely such compassion as Evil-Merodach shewed towards Jehoiachin (2 K. xxv. 27-30; Jer. lii. 31-34), but such as Cyrus and Artaxerxes shewed in allowing the captive Jews to return to their own land (Ez. i. 3; Neh. ii. 6).

51. *the furnace of iron*] Egypt is so called as a place of severe trial and affliction.

54. If the prayer of Solomon be, as it has all the appearance of being, a genuine document of the time, preserved in the archives to which the authors of both Kings and Chronicles had access, all theories of the late origin of Deuteronomy must be regarded as baseless. While references are not infrequent to other portions of the Pentateuch, the language of the prayer is mainly modelled upon Deuteronomy, the promises and threats contained in which are continually before the mind of the writer. (See marg. reff.).

58. *incline our hearts*] This is a doctrine which first appears in Scripture in the Davidical Psalms (see marg. ref. and Ps. cxli. 4). Solomon in this prayer seems to be

59 which he commanded our fathers. And let these my words, wherewith I have made supplication before the LORD, be nigh unto the LORD our God day and night, that he maintain the cause of his servant, and the cause of his people Israel [1]at all 60 times, as the matter shall require: [b]that all the people of the earth may know that [c]the LORD is God, and that there is none 61 else. Let your [d]heart therefore be perfect with the LORD our God, to walk in his statutes, and to keep his commandments, as 62 at this day. ¶ And [e]the king, and all Israel with him, offered 63 sacrifice before the LORD. And Solomon offered a sacrifice of peace offerings, which he offered unto the LORD, two and twenty thousand oxen, and an hundred and twenty thousand sheep. So the king and all the children of Israel dedicated the house of the 64 LORD. [f]The same day did the king hallow the middle of the court that was before the house of the LORD: for there he offered burnt offerings, and meat offerings, and the fat of the peace offerings: because [g]the brasen altar that was before the LORD was too little to receive the burnt offerings, and meat 65 offerings, and the fat of the peace offerings. ¶ And at that time Solomon held [h]a feast, and all Israel with him, a great congregation, from [i]the entering in of Hamath unto [k]the river of Egypt, before the LORD our God, [l]seven days and seven days, 66 even fourteen days. [m]On the eighth day he sent the people away: and they [2]blessed the king, and went unto their tents joyful and glad of heart for all the goodness that the LORD had done for David his servant, and for Israel his people.

CHAP. 9. AND [a]it came to pass, when Solomon had finished the building of the house of the LORD, [b]and the king's house, and 2 [c]all Solomon's desire which he was pleased to do, that the LORD appeared to Solomon the second time, [d]as he had appeared unto

[b] Josh. 4. 24.
1 Sam.17.46.
2 Kin.19.19.
[c] Deut. 4.
35, 39.
[d] ch. 11. 4.
& 15. 3, 14.
2 Kin. 20. 3.
[e] 2 Chr. 7. 4,
&c.

[f] 2 Chr. 7. 7.

[g] 2 Chr. 4. 1.

[h] ver. 2.
Lev. 23. 34.
[i] Num. 34. 8.
Josh. 13. 5.
[k] Gen.15.18.
Num. 34. 5.
[l] 2 Chr. 7. 8.
[m] 2 Chr. 7.
9, 10.

[a] 2 Chr. 7.
11, &c.
[b] ch. 7. 1.
[c] 2 Chr. 8. 6.
[d] ch. 3. 5.

[1] Heb. the thing of a day in his day.   [2] Or, thanked.

---

thoroughly penetrated with his father's spirit.

61. as at this day] i.e. "as ye are now doing, in coming with pious intentions to this festival."

63. These numbers have been thought incredible, but they are not impossible. At least 100,000, or 120,000 men (v. 65) were assembled; and as they all offered sacrifice with the king (v. 62), the number of victims must have been enormous. Part of the flesh of so many victims would be eaten; but much of the meat may have been privately burnt (Lev. xix. 6), the object of the sacrifice being the glory of God, and not the convenience of the people. Profusion was a usual feature of the sacrifices of antiquity.

64. the middle of the court] Or, "the whole area of the court"—all the mid space within the enclosing walls, which thus became one huge altar, on any part of which victims might be offered at one and the same time.

65. A feast necessarily accompanied such a sacrifice as Solomon was holding. Cp. Lev. xix. 5. On the present occasion there was a double festival—first, the Feast of the Dedication, from the 8th to the 15th of the month Ethanim (or Tisri), and then the

Feast of Tabernacles, from the 15th to the 22nd (v. 2). On the day after this, "the eighth day," counting from the commencement of the second seven, and the twenty-third day of the month (marg. ref. m), Solomon dismissed the people to their homes.

the entering in of Hamath] Cp. Num. xiii. 21, note and marg. reff. The phrase marks the extreme northern boundary of the Holy Land.

the river of Egypt] The Wady-el-Arish, the only large water-course on this coast (marg. reff.).

66. their tents] i.e. "their homes." The word "tents" was used for "houses" from an old habit of speech, which had come down from the time when the Israelites were a nomadic nation.

IX. 2. This appearance is fixed by v. 1 to Solomon's twenty-fourth year, the year in which he completed his palace (vi. 37, 38, vii. 1). The fact seems to be that, though the Temple was finished in Solomon's eleventh year, the Dedication did not take place till his twenty-fourth year. The order of the narrative in Kings agrees with this view, since it interposes the account of the building of the palace (vii. 1-12), and of the

3 him at Gibeon. And the LORD said unto him, *e*I have heard
thy prayer and thy supplication, that thou hast made before me:
I have hallowed this house, which thou hast built, *f*to put my
name there for ever; *g*and mine eyes and mine heart shall be
4 there perpetually. And if thou wilt *h*walk before me, *i*as David
thy father walked, in integrity of heart, and in uprightness, to
do according to all that I have commanded thee, *and* wilt keep
5 my statutes and my judgments: then I will establish the throne
of thy kingdom upon Israel for ever, *k*as I promised to David thy
father, saying, There shall not fail thee a man upon the throne
6 of Israel. *l*But if ye shall at all turn from following me, ye or
your children, and will not keep my commandments *and* my
statutes which I have set before you, but go and serve other
7 gods, and worship them: *m*then will I cut off Israel out of the
land which I have given them; and this house, which I have
hallowed *n*for my name, will I cast out of my sight; *o*and Israel
8 shall be a proverb and a byword among all people: and *p*at this
house, *which* is high, every one that passeth by it shall be astonished, and shall hiss; and they shall say, *q*Why hath the LORD
9 done thus unto this land, and to this house? And they shall
answer, Because they forsook the LORD their God, who brought
forth their fathers out of the land of Egypt, and have taken hold
upon other gods, and have worshipped them, and served them:
therefore hath the LORD brought upon them all this evil.
10 ¶ And *r*it came to pass at the end of twenty years, when Solomon had built the two houses, the house of the LORD, and the
11 king's house, *s*(now Hiram the king of Tyre had furnished Solomon with cedar trees and fir trees, and with gold, according to
all his desire,) that then king Solomon gave Hiram twenty cities
12 in the land of Galilee. And Hiram came out from Tyre to see
the cities which Solomon had given him; and they [1]pleased him

e 2 Kin. 20.5.
Ps. 10. 17.
f ch. 8. 29.
g Deut. 11.
12.
h Gen. 17. 1.
i ch. 11. 4, 6,
38.
& 14. 8.
& 15. 5.
k 2 Sam. 7.
12, 16.
ch. 2. 4.
& 6. 12
1 Chr. 22. 10.
Ps. 132. 12.
l 2 Sam.7.14.
Ps. 89. 30.
m Deut.4. 26.
2 Kin. 17.23.
& 25. 21.
o Deut. 28.
37.
Ps. 44. 14.
p 2 Chr.7 21.
q Deut. 29.
24, 25, 26.
Jer. 22. 8,9.

r ch. 6. 37,
38.
& 7. 1.
2 Chr. 8. 1.
s 2 Chr. 8. 2.

1 Heb. *were not right in his eyes.*

---

making of the furniture (vii. 13-51), be-
tween the completion of the building of the
Temple (vi. 38) and the ceremony of the
Dedication (viii.).

3. The answer given by God to Solomon's
prayer is reported more fully in 2 Chronicles
(vii. 12-22).

When God puts His Name in the temple
He does it, in intention, *for ever.* He will
not arbitrarily withdraw it; there it will
remain *for ever,* so far as God is concerned.
But the people may by unfaithfulness drive
it away (*rv.* 7-9).

and mine eyes and my heart] An answer
in excess of the prayer (viii. 29); "Not
Mine eyes only, but Mine eyes *and Mine
heart.*"

4. See iii. 14. Solomon's subsequent fall
lends to these repeated warnings a special
interest.

6. *at all turn*] Rather, "If ye shall
wholly turn from following Me." (See 2
Chr. vii. 19.) The Israelites were not to
be cut off, except for an entire defection.

8. The Hebrew text runs—"**And this
house shall be high**: every one," &c. The
meaning appears to be, "This house shall

be high" (*i.e.* conspicuous) "in its ruin as
in its glory."

and shall hiss] In contempt. This expression first appears in the time of Hezekiah (2 Chr. xxix. 8; Mic. vi. 16). It is
especially familiar to Jeremiah (xviii. 16,
xix. 8, &c.).

10. The "twenty years" are to be counted
from the fourth year of Solomon, the year
when he commenced the building of the
Temple. They are made up of the seven
years employed in the work of the Temple
(vi. 38), and the thirteen years during
which Solomon was building his own house
(vii. 1).

11. By the spirit, if not by the letter, of
the Law, Solomon had no right to give
away these cities, or any part of the inheritance of Israel (Lev. xxv. 13-34). But the
exigences of a worldly policy caused the requirements of the Law to be set aside.

12. *they pleased him not*] It is a reasonable conjecture that, when a question arose
with respect to a cession of land, Hiram
had cast his eyes on the bay or harbour of
Acco, or Ptolemais, and was therefore the
more disappointed when he received an inland tract of mountain territory.

13 not. And he said, What cities *are* these which thou hast given
t Josh. 19.27.   me, my brother ? *t*And he called them the land of ¹Cabul unto
14 this day. And Hiram sent to the king sixscore talents of gold.
u ch. 5. 13.   15 ¶And this *is* the reason of *u*the levy which king Solomon raised;
for to build the house of the LORD, and his own house, and
x ver. 24.   *x*Millo, and the wall of Jerusalem, and *y*Hazor, and *z*Megiddo,
y Josh. 11. 1.
z Josh.12.21.   16 and *a*Gezer. *For* Pharaoh king of Egypt had gone up, and
a Josh.16.10.   taken Gezer, and burnt it with fire, *b*and slain the Canaanites
Judg. 1. 29.
b Josh.16.10.   that dwelt in the city, and given it *for* a present unto his daugh-
c Josh. 10.10. 17 ter, Solomon's wife. And Solomon built Gezer, and *c*Beth-
2 Chr. 8. 5.
d Josh.19.44.   18 horon the nether, and *d*Baalath, and Tadmor in the wilderness,
2 Chr. 8. 4.   19 in the land, and all the cities of store that Solomon had, and
e ch. 4. 26.
f ver. 1.   cities for *e*his chariots, and cities for his horsemen, and ²that
which Solomon *f*desired to build in Jerusalem, and in Lebanon,

---

¹ That is, *Displeasing*, or, *Dirty*.   ² Heb. *the desire of Solomon which he desired.*

---

13. Cabul is said to be a Phœnician
word, and signified "displeasing" (see
marg.). There is some reason to believe that
the cities thus despised by Hiram were restored to Solomon (2 Chr. viii. 2), and that
Solomon rebuilt them and colonized them
with Israelites.

14. *Hiram sent sixscore talents of gold*]
Apparently, to show that, although disappointed, he was not offended. The sum
sent was very large—above a million and a
quarter of our money, according to one
estimate of the weight of the Hebrew gold
talent ; or about 720,000*l*. according to the
estimate adopted in Ex. xxxviii. 24-29
note. At any rate, it was more than equal
to a sixth part of Solomon's regular revenue
(x. 14).

15. *levy*] See marg. ref. note.
Millo] See 2 Sam. v. 9 note. The LXX.
commonly render the word ἡ ἄκρα, "the
citadel," and it may possibly have been the
fortress on Mount Zion connected with the
Maccabean struggles (1 Mac. iv. 41, xiii. 49-
52). Its exact site has not been determined.

and the wall of Jerusalem] David's fortification (2 Sam. v. 9 ; 1 Chr. xi. 8) had been
hasty, and had now—fifty years later—
fallen into decay. Solomon therefore had
to "repair the breaches of the city of
David" (xi. 27).

Hazor, Megiddo, and Gezer were three of
the most important sites in the Holy Land.
For the two first places, cp. marg. reff. and
notes.

Gezer was a main city of the south. It
was situated on the great maritime plain,
and commanded the ordinary line of approach from Egypt, which was along this
low region. The importance of Gezer appears from Josh. x. 33, xii. 12, &c. Its
site is near Tell Jezer, and marked now by
Abu Shusheh. Though within the lot of
Ephraim (Josh. xvi. 3), and specially assigned to the Kohathite Levites (do. xxi.
21), it had never yet been conquered from
the old inhabitants (marg. reff.), who con-

tinued to dwell in it till Solomon's time,
and apparently were an independent people
(*v.* 16).

Pharaoh took it before the marriage of
Solomon with his daughter, and gave it
"*for a present*"—*i.e.* for a dowry. Though
in the East husbands generally pay for
their wives, yet dower is given in some
cases. Sargon gave Cilicia as a dowry with
his daughter when he married her to
Ambris king of Tubal : and the Persian
kings seem generally to have given satra-
pial or other high offices as dowries to the
husbands of their daughters.

17. *Beth-horon the nether*] See marg. ref.
note.

18. *Tadmor*] The Hebrew text here has,
as written, Tamor (or Tamar), and as read,
Tadmor. That the latter place, or Palmyra,
was meant appears, first, from the distinct
statement of Chronicles (2 Chr. viii. 4) that
Solomon built Tadmor, and the improbability that the fact would be omitted in
Kings ; secondly, from the strong likelihood
that Solomon, with his wide views of commerce, would seize and fortify the Palmy-
rene Oasis : and thirdly, from the unanimity
of the old Versions in rendering Tamar here
by Tadmor. The probability seems to be
that Tamar was the original name of the
place, being the Hebrew word for "a
palm," whence it is generally agreed that
the town derived its name. Tadmor was a
corrupt or dialectic variety of the word,
which was adopted at the city itself, and
prevailed over the original appellation. No
reference is found to Tadmor in the Assyrian inscriptions, or in any classical
writer before Pliny.

19. "The cities of store" contained provisions stored up for the troops (cp. 2 Chr.
xxxii. 28). They seem to have been chiefly
in the north—in Hamath (2 Chr. viii. 4)
and Naphtali (do. xvi. 4). On the "cities
for his chariots," see x. 26 note.

By "that which Solomon desired to
build" (see marg.) seem to be intended
"pleasaunces" in or near the capital, and

20 and in all the land of his dominion. ¶ *g And* all the people *that*
were left of the Amorites, Hittites, Perizzites, Hivites, and Jebu-
21 sites, which *were* not of the children of Israel, their children
h that were left after them in the land, *i* whom the children of
Israel also were not able utterly to destroy, *k* upon those did
22 Solomon levy a tribute of *l* bondservice unto this day. But of
the children of Israel did Solomon *m* make no bondmen: but they
were men of war, and his servants, and his princes, and his cap-
23 tains, and rulers of his chariots, and his horsemen. These *were*
the chief of the officers that *were* over Solomon's work, *n* five
hundred and fifty, which bare rule over the people that wrought
24 in the work. ¶ But *o* Pharaoh's daughter came up out of the
city of David unto *p* her house which *Solomon* had built for her:
25 *q* then did he build Millo. ¶ *r* And three times in a year did
Solomon offer burnt offerings and peace offerings upon the altar
which he built unto the LORD, and he burnt incense *¹* upon the
altar that *was* before the LORD. So he finished the house.
26 ¶ And *s* king Solomon made a navy of ships in *t* Ezion-geber,
which *is* beside Eloth, on the *²* shore of the Red sea, in the land
27 of Edom. *u* And Hiram sent in the navy his servants, shipmen
that had knowledge of the sea, with the servants of Solomon.
28 And they came to *x* Ophir, and fetched from thence gold, four
hundred and twenty talents, and brought *it* to king Solomon.
CHAP. 10. AND when the *a* queen of Sheba heard of the fame of
Solomon, concerning the name of the LORD, she came *b* to prove

g 2 Chr. 8.
7, &c.
h Judg. 1.
21, 27, 29.
& 3. 1.
i Josh. 15.63.
& 17. 12.
k Judg. 1. 28.
l See Gen. 9.
25, 26.
Ezra 2.55,58.
Neh. 7. 57.
& 11. 3.
m Lev. 25.39.
n See 2 Chr.
8. 10.
o 2 Chr. 8. 11.
p ch. 7. 8.
q 2 Sam. 5.9.
ch. 11. 27.
2 Chr. 32. 5.
r 2 Chr. 8.
12, 13, 16.
s 2 Chr. 8.
17, 18.
t Num.33.35.
Deut. 2. 8.
u ch. 10. 11.
x Gen.10. 29.
a 2 Chr. 9.
1, &c.
Matt. 12. 42.
Luke 11. 31.
b See Judg.
14. 12.
Prov. 1. 6.

¹ Heb. *upon it.*   *²* Heb. *lip.*

in the Lebanon range, built specially for
the enjoyment of the king.
    21. See v. 15 note.
    22. Comparing this with v. 13, 14, it
would seem that a modified service of
forced labour for one-third of each year was
not regarded as reducing those who were
subject to it to the condition of bondmen.
    23. *five hundred and fifty*] See v. 16
note.
    24. Cp. marg. ref. Solomon was not
satisfied that Pharaoh's daughter should
remain in the palace of David, which was
on Mount Zion, in the immediate vicinity
of the Temple, because he regarded the
whole vicinity of the Temple as made holy
by the presence of the Ark of God. His
own palace was on the other (western) hill,
probably directly opposite to the Temple,
the valley of the Tyropœum running between them.
    25. *three times*] i.e. (see marg. ref.) the
three solemn Feasts—the Feast of unleavened bread, the Feast of weeks, and the
Feast of tabernacles.
    did Solomon offer...and he burnt incense]
Not with his own hand, but by his priests
(viii. 6 ; 2 Chr. v. 7-14). In sacred, as in
ordinary, history, men are said to do that
which they cause to be done.
    26. On Ezion-geber and Eloth, see notes
to marg. reff. As the entire tract about
Elath (Akaba) is destitute of trees, it is
conjectured that the wood of which Solomon built his fleet was cut in Lebanon,

floated to Gaza by sea, and thence conveyed
across to Ezion-geber, at the head of the
Elanitic Gulf, by land carriage. (Cp. 2 Chr.
ii. 16.)
    27. *shipmen*] See v. 6 note. With re-
spect to the acquaintance of the Phœnicians
with this particular sea, it may be observed
that they are not unlikely to have had
trading settlements there, as they had in
the Persian Gulf, even at this early period.
The commerce with Ophir was probably an
established trade, previously either in their
hands or in those of the Egyptians, when
Solomon determined to have a share in it.
The Egyptians had navigated the other
arm of the Red Sea, and perhaps its lower
parts, from a much more ancient period.
    28. On Ophir, see marg. ref. note.
Among the various opinions three predominate ; all moderns, except a very few,
being in favour of Arabia, India, or Eastern
Africa. Arabia's claims are supported by
the greatest number.
    X. 1. Doubt has arisen whether the
"queen of Sheba" was an Ethiopian or an
Arabian princess. Both countries profess
to have traditions on the subject connecting
the queen of Sheba with their history ; and
in both countries, curiously enough, government by queens was common. But the
claims of Arabia decidedly preponderate.
The Arabian Sheba was the great spice
country of the ancient world ; whereas
Ethiopia furnished no spices. The Arabian
Sheba was an important kingdom. Sheba

2 him with hard questions. And she came to Jerusalem with a
very great train, with camels that bare spices, and very much
gold, and precious stones : and when she was come to Solomon,
3 she communed with him of all that was in her heart. And
Solomon told her all her [1] questions : there was not *any* thing
4 hid from the king, which he told her not. And when the queen
of Sheba had seen all Solomon's wisdom, and the house that he
5 had built, and the meat of his table, and the sitting of his servants, and the [2] attendance of his ministers, and their apparel,

and his [3] cupbearers, *c* and his ascent by which he went up unto
6 the house of the LORD ; there was no more spirit in her. And
she said to the king, It was a true [4] report that I heard in mine
7 own land of thy [5] acts and of thy wisdom. Howbeit I believed
not the words, until I came, and mine eyes had seen *it :* and,
behold, the half was not told me : [6] thy wisdom and prosperity

8 exceedeth the fame which I heard. *d* Happy *are* thy men, happy
are these thy servants, which stand continually before thee, *and*

9 that hear thy wisdom. *e* Blessed be the LORD thy God, which
delighted in thee, to set thee on the throne of Israel : because

the LORD loved Israel for ever, therefore made he thee king, *f* to
10 do judgment and justice. And she *g* gave the king an hundred
and twenty talents of gold, and of spices very great store, and
precious stones : there came no more such abundance of spices
as these which the queen of Sheba gave to king Solomon.

---

[1] Heb. *words.*
[2] Heb. *standing.*
[3] Or, *butlers.*

[4] Heb. *word.*
[5] Or, *sayings.*

[6] Heb. *thou hast added wisdom and goodness to the
fame.*

---

in Ethiopia was a mere town, subject to
Meroë. And it may be doubted whether
the Cushite Sheba of Scripture (Gen. x. 7)
is not rather to be sought on the shores of
the Persian Gulf (do. note), whence no one
supposes "the queen of Sheba" to have
come. If Ophir be placed in Arabia, there
will be an additional reason for regarding Sheba as in the same quarter, because
then Solomon's trade with that place will
account for his fame having reached the
Sabæan princess.

"The fame of Solomon concerning the
name of the Lord," has been variously
explained, and is confessedly very obscure. May it not mean what we should
call "his *religious* fame," as distinct from
his artistic, literary, military, or political
fame—"his fame with respect to God and
the things of God"—or, in other words, "his
moral and religious wisdom?" (cp. *v.* 6).

hard questions] Or "riddles" (Judg. xiv.
12), though not exactly riddles in our sense.
The Orientals have always been fond of
playing with words and testing each other's
wit and intelligence by verbal puzzles of
various kinds. This spirit seems to have
been particularly rife in Solomon's time,
for Josephus records other encounters with
Hiram of Tyre and another Tyrian called
Abdemonus.

2. See *v.* 10 note.

5. *and the meat of his table*] Cp. iv. 22,
23. The scene here described receives very

apt illustration from the Assyrian banquet
scenes, where we have numerous guests
sitting, dressed handsomely in fringed robes,
with armlets upon their arms, and bracelets
round their wrists, attendants standing behind them, and magnificent drinking-cups,
evidently of a costly metal, in the hands of
the guests, which are filled from a great
wine-bowl at one end of the chamber.

and his ascent by which he went up] A rendering preferable to "the *burnt-offering*
which he *offered in.*" The "ascent" was
probably a private way by which the king
passed from his palace on the western
hill, across the ravine (Tyropœum) and up
the eastern hill, to the west side of the
Temple area (cp. marg. ref.).

9. *Blessed be the* LORD *thy God*] This
acknowledgment of Jehovah falls below the
confessions of Hiram (2 Chr. ii. 12) and
Cyrus (Ezr. i. 3). It does not imply more
than an admission of His power as a local
deity; viz. that He is the God of the Jews
and of their country.

10. Strabo relates that the Sabæans were
enormously wealthy, and used gold and
silver in a most lavish manner in their furniture, their utensils, and even on the walls,
doors, and roofs of their houses. That the
gold of Sheba should be given to Solomon
was prophesied by the writer of Ps lxxii.
(see marg. ref.). The immense abundance
of spices in Arabia, and especially in the
Yemen or Sabæan country, is noted by

11 ¶ʰAnd the navy also of Hiram, that brought gold from Ophir,   ʰ ch. 9. 27.
brought in from Ophir great plenty of ¹almug trees, and pre-
12 cious stones. ⁱAnd the king made of the almug trees ²³pillars   ⁱ 2 Chr. 9.11.
for the house of the LORD, and for the king's house, harps also
and psalteries for singers: there came no such ᵏalmug trees, nor   ᵏ 2 Chr. 9.10.
13 were seen unto this day. ¶And king Solomon gave unto the
queen of Sheba all her desire, whatsoever she asked, beside *that*
which Solomon gave her ⁴of his royal bounty. So she turned
14 and went to her own country, she and her servants. ¶Now the
weight of gold that came to Solomon in one year was six
15 hundred threescore and six talents of gold, beside *that he had* of
the merchantmen, and of the traffick of the spice merchants,
and ˡof all the kings of Arabia, and of the ⁵governors of the   ˡ 2 Chr.9. 24.
16 country. ¶And king Solomon made two hundred targets *of*   Ps. 72. 10.
beaten gold: six hundred *shekels* of gold went to one target.

¹ *algum trees*, 2 Chr. 2. 8.   ² Or, *rails*.   *hand of king Solomon.*
& 9. 10, 11.   ³ Heb. *a prop.*   ⁵ Or, *captains.*
                               ⁴ Heb. *according to the*

---

many writers. According to Strabo, the spice-trade of Arabia was in the hands of two nations, the Sabæans and the Gerrhæans. The spices in which they dealt seem to have been only in part the produce of Arabia itself; some of the most important kinds, as the cinnamon and the cassia, must have been imported from India, since Arabia does not yield them. The chief precious stones which Arabia now yields are the onyx and the emerald. Pearls, too, were readily procurable in Arabia from the Persian Gulf fishery.

11. *the navy of Hiram*] i.e. Solomon's navy in the Red Sea, which was chiefly manned by subjects of Hiram (see marg. ref.).

almug-trees] Probably the sandal-wood tree (*pterocarpus santalinus*). The wood is very heavy, hard, and fine grained, and of a beautiful garnet colour, which, according to the Rabbinical writers, was the colour of the algum. One of the names of the red sandal-wood, in its own native country (India) is *valguka*, a word of which *algum* is a natural corruption.

12. *pillars*] The Hebrew word signifies ordinarily a "prop" (marg.). It is generally supposed to mean in this place a "railing," or "balustrade," a sense which connects and harmonises the present passage with the parallel passage in Chronicles (marg. ref.), where Solomon is said to have made of the almug-wood "stairs" for the Temple and for his own house.

harps] The Jewish harp (*kinnor*) was of a triangular shape, and had ordinarily ten strings. It probably resembled the more ancient harp of the Assyrians, which was played with a plectrum, as was (ordinarily) the *kinnor*.

psalteries] The psaltery, or viol (*nebel*, Gr. νάβλα), was a stringed instrument played with the hand; perhaps a lyre, like those on Hebrew coins, the sounding-board of which is shaped like a jug; or, perhaps, a sort of guitar, with a hollow jug-shaped body at the lower end.

14. *six hundred threescore and six talents of gold*] About 3,646,350*l.* of our money. Solomon's annual revenue exceeded that of Oriental empires very much greater in extent than his, and must have made him one of the richest, if not the very richest, of the monarchs of his time.

15. There is no mention in the original of "*spice* merchants." Two classes of traders are spoken of; but both expressions are general.

kings of Arabia] Rather, "kings of the mingled people" (cp. Jer. xxv. 24). These were probably tribes half Jewish, half Arabian, on the borders of the western desert. They are regarded as Arabs by the author of Chronicles (marg. ref.).

governors] The word used here is thought to be of Aryan origin. It appears to have been a title given by the Persians to petty governors, inferior to the great satraps of provinces. We find it borne by, among others, Tatnai (Ezr. v. 6), Zerubbabel (Hag. i. 1), and Nehemiah (Neh. v. 14). It can scarcely have been in use among the Jews so early as Solomon, and we must therefore suppose it to have been substituted by the writer of Kings for some corresponding Semitic title. The empire of Solomon was not a state governed from a single centre by an organisation of satrapies or provinces (iv. 21 note). But exceptionally, in some parts of the empire, the kings had been superseded by "governors" (cp. xx. 24).

16. The "targets" seem to have been long shields protecting the whole body, while the "shields" of the next verse were bucklers of a smaller size, probably round, and much lighter. They may be compared with the Assyrian long shield, and the ordinary Assyrian round shield. As the amount

_m_ ch. 14. 26.
_n_ ch. 7. 2.
_o_ 2 Chr. 9.
17, &c.

_p_ 2 Chr. 9.
20, &c.

_q_ Gen. 10. 4.
2 Car. 20. 36.

17 And _he made_ ᵐthree hundred shields _of_ beaten gold ; three pound of gold went to one shield : and the king put them in the ⁿhouse 18 of the forest of Lebanon. ¶ °Moreover the king made a great 19 throne of ivory, and overlaid it with the best gold. The throne had six steps, and the top of the throne _was_ round ¹behind : and _there were_ ²stays on either side on the place of the seat, and two 20 lions stood beside the stays. And twelve lions stood there on the one side and on the other upon the six steps : there was not 21 ³the like made in any kingdom. ¶ ᵖAnd all king Solomon's drinking vessels _were of_ gold, and all the vessels of the house of the forest of Lebanon _were of_ pure gold ; ⁴none _were of_ silver : 22 it was nothing accounted of in the days of Solomon. For the king had at sea a navy of ᵠTharshish with the navy of Hiram : once in three years came the navy of Tharshish, bringing gold,

¹ Heb. _on the hinder part thereof._
² Heb. _hands._
³ Heb. _so._
⁴ Or, there was no _silver_ in them.

of gold used in each of the larger shields was only 600 shekels—worth from 650_l._ to 700_l._ of our money—and that used in the smaller ones was only half as much it is evident that the metal did not form the substance of the shields, but was laid as a coating or plating over them.

17. These shields, together with the 500 taken by David from Hadadezer (2 Sam. viii. 7) were hung round the outer walls of a building, reckoned as belonging to the "house of the Forest of Lebanon," but separate from it, and called sometimes "the Tower of David" (Cant. iv. 4), or from its use "the armoury" (do.; Is. xxii. 8). The practice of hanging shields outside walls for ornamentation seems to have existed at Tyre (Ezek. xxvii. 10, 11), Rome, Athens, and elsewhere. Traces of it are thought to be found in the Assyrian sculptures.

18. It is, on the whole, probable that the substance of the throne was wood, and that the ivory, cut into thin slabs, and probably carved in patterns, was applied externally as a veneer. This is found to have been the practice in Assyria. The gold was probably not placed over the ivory, but covered other parts of the throne.

19. Representations of thrones are frequent in the Egyptian and Assyrian sculptures. They have no steps up to them, but frequently stand upon square bases. The back appears to be flat at the top, not rounded. Assyrian thrones have "stays" or arms on either side, and they stand generally upon lion's feet. They are always accompanied by a footstool.

lions stood beside the stays] The arms of Assyrian thrones are occasionally supported by figures of animals. The throne of Rameses II. at Medinet Abou has a sphinx at the side and a lion below the sphinx. The figure of the lion is naturally adopted by any imaginative race as an emblem of sovereignty. In the present case its adop-

tion seems to have grown directly out of the poetic imagery of inspired Prophets, who, living before the time of Solomon, had compared Israel (Num. xxiii. 24, xxiv. 9), and more particularly Judah (Gen. xlix. 9), to a lion. The "twelve lions" of _v._ 20 were probably intended to be emblematic of the twelve tribes. Josephus adds to the description of Solomon's throne here given, that the seat was supported by a golden ox or bull, with its head turned over its shoulder. As the lion was especially emblematic of Judah, so was the ox or bull of Ephraim. (Hos. iv. 16, x. 11 ; Jer. xxxi. 18, &c.)

20. Solomon's throne, as described, is certainly grander than any of which we have a representation, either in Assyria or Egypt. Much more, then, would it transcend the thrones in inferior kingdoms.

22. This is given as the reason of the great plentifulness of silver in the time of Solomon. The "navy of Tharshish" (not the same as the navy of Ophir, ix. 26) must therefore have imported very large quantities of that metal. Tharshish, or Tartessus, in Spain, had the richest silver mines known in the ancient world, and had a good deal of gold also ; apes and ivory were produced by the opposite coast of Africa ; and, if north Africa did not produce "peacocks," which is uncertain, she may have produced the birds called here _tukkiyim_, which some translate "parrots," others "guinea-fowl"—the latter being a purely African bird. The etymology of the Hebrew words here rendered "ivory," "apes," and "peacocks," is uncertain ; but even if of Indian origin, the Jews may have derived their first knowledge of ivory, apes, and peacocks, through nations which traded with India, and may thus have got the words into their language long before the time of Solomon. The names once fixed would be retained, whatever the quarter whence the things were procured afterwards.

23 and silver, ¹ivory, and apes, and peacocks. ¶So ʳking Solomon exceeded all the kings of the earth for riches and for wisdom. 24 And all the earth ²sought to Solomon, to hear his wisdom, 25 which God had put in his heart. And they brought every man his present, vessels of silver, and vessels of gold, and garments, and armour, and spices, horses, and mules, a rate year by year. 26 ¶ ˢAnd Solomon ᵗgathered together chariots and horsemen: and he had a thousand and four hundred chariots, and twelve thousand horsemen, whom he bestowed in the cities for chariots, and 27 with the king at Jerusalem. ᵘAnd the king ³made silver to be in Jerusalem as stones, and cedars made he to be as the syco- 28 more trees that are in the vale, for abundance. ¶ ˣ⁴And Solomon had horses brought out of Egypt, and ᵛlinen yarn: the 29 king's merchants received the linen yarn at a price. And a chariot came up and went out of Egypt for six hundred *shekels* of silver, and an horse for an hundred and fifty: ᶻand so for all

ʳ ch.3. 12,13.
& 4. 30.

ˢ ch. 4. 26.
2 Chr. 1. 14.
& 9. 25.
ᵗ Deut. 17.16.
ᵘ 2 Chr. 1.
15—17.

ˣ Deut. 17.
16.
2 Chr. 1. 16.
& 9. 28.
ᵛ Ezek. 27.7.
ᶻ Josh. 1. 4.
2 Kin. 7. 6.

¹ Or, *elephants' teeth.*
² Heb. *sought the face of.*
³ Heb. *gave.*
⁴ Heb. *And the going forth*
of the horses which was Solomon's.

23, 24. See marg. reff. By "all the earth" we are, of course, only to understand the kings or people of neighbouring nations.

25. *his present*] *i.e.* his tribute (iv. 21 note). A statement illustrated by Egyptian and Assyrian sculptures on slabs and obelisks. Tribute-bearers from the subject kings, bring not only the fixed rate of bullion, but a tribute in kind besides, consisting of the most precious products of their respective countries.

26. See ver. 26 note. Until the time of Solomon, war-chariots had not been in use among the Jews, except to a very small extent (1 Chr. xviii. 4). Hence, it was necessary for him to put himself on an equality in this respect with neighbouring powers.

cities for chariots] They were probably fortresses upon the borders of his territory, in which he maintained the standing army necessary for the support of his dominion.

27. *made silver as stones*] This strong hyperbole marks in the most striking way the great wealth and prosperity of the capital during Solomon's reign. The lavish expenditure which impoverished the provinces, and produced, or helped to produce, the general discontent that led to the outbreak under Jeroboam, enriched the metropolis, which must have profited greatly by the residence of the court, the constant influx of opulent strangers, and the periodical visits of all Israelites not hindered by some urgent reason at the great festivals.

The "sycomore-trees in the vale" (Shephêlah) are mentioned also in 1 Chr. xxvii. 28. Like the olives and the vines, they were placed by David under a special overseer, on account of their value. The tree meant seems to be the sycomore proper, or "fig-mulberry," which is still common in

Palestine, and is highly esteemed both on account of its fruit and its timber.

28. The word translated "linen yarn" is thought by Hebraists to mean "a troop" or "company." If the present reading is retained, they would translate the passage—"As for the bringing up of Solomon's horses out of Egypt, *a band* of the king's merchants fetched *a band* (or troop) of horses at a price." But the reading is very uncertain. The LXX. had before them a different one, which they render "and from Tekoa." Tekoa, the home of Amos (Am. i. 1), was a small town on the route from Egypt to Jerusalem, through which the horses would have naturally passed. The monuments of the 18th and of later dynasties make it clear that the horse, though introduced from abroad, became very abundant in Egypt. During the whole period of Egyptian prosperity the corps of chariots constituted a large and effective portion of the army. That horses were abundant in Egypt at the time of the Exodus is evident from Ex. ix. 3, xiv. 9, 23, 28; Deut. xvii. 16. That they continued numerous in later times appears from frequent allusions, both in the Historical Books of Scripture and in the Prophets, as 2 K. vii. 6, xviii. 24; Is. xxxvi. 9; Ezek. xvii. 15, &c. The monuments show that the horse was employed by the Egyptians in peace no less than in war, private persons being often represented as paying visits to their friends in chariots.

29. Taking the shekel at about three shillings of our money, six hundred silver shekels would be equal to about 90*l.*; and 150 shekels to 22*l.* 10*s.* *Average* price seems to be in each case intended; and we may account for the comparatively high price of the chariot by supposing that by "chariot" is intended the entire equipage, including car, harness, and trained horses, of which

the kings of the Hittites, and for the kings of Syria, did they
bring *them* out [1]by their means.

^a Neh. 13.26.
^b Deut.17.17.

CHAP. 11. BUT ^aking Solomon loved ^bmany strange women, [2]to-
gether with the daughter of Pharaoh, women of the Moabites,
2 Ammonites, Edomites, Zidonians, *and* Hittites; of the nations

^c Ex. 34. 16.
Deut. 7. 3, 4.

concerning which the LORD said unto the children of Israel, ^cYe
shall not go in to them, neither shall they come in unto you:
for surely they will turn away your heart after their gods:
3 Solomon clave unto these in love. And he had seven hundred
wives, princesses, and three hundred concubines: and his wives

^d Deut.17.17.
Neh. 13. 26.
^e ch. 8. 61.
^f ch. 9. 4.
^g ver. 33.
Judg. 2. 13.
2 Kin. 23.13.

4 turned away his heart. For it came to pass, when Solomon was
old, ^d*that* his wives turned away his heart after other gods: and
his ^eheart was not perfect with the LORD his God, ^f*as was* the
5 heart of David his father. For Solomon went after ^gAshtoreth
the goddess of the Zidonians, and after [3]Milcom the abomination

[1] Heb. *by their hand.*   [2] Or, *beside.*   [3] Called *Molech,* ver. 7.

---

there would be two at least, if not three.
The "horses" mentioned separately from
the chariots are not chariot-horses, but
chargers for the cavalry.

the kings of the Hittites] See 2 K. vii. 6
note. The kings intended were probably
Solomon's vassals, whose armies were at
his disposal if he required their aid.

XI. 1. In noticing successively Solomon's
excessive accumulation of silver and gold
(x. 14–25), his multiplication of horses (do.
26–29), and his multiplication of wives, the
writer has in mind the warning of Moses
against these three forms of princely ostentation, all alike forbidden to an Israelite
monarch (marg. ref.).

Zidonians] *i.e.* Phœnician women. A
tradition states that Solomon married a
daughter of Hiram, king of Tyre.

2. *ye shall not go in unto them,* &c.] These
words are not a quotation from the Pentateuch. They merely give the general meaning of the two passages prohibiting inter-
marriage with neighbouring idolators (marg.
reff.). Strictly speaking, the prohibition in
the Law of intermarriage was confined to the
Canaanitish nations. But the principle of
the prohibition applied equally to the
Moabites, Ammonites, and Edomites, who
all bordered on the Holy Land; and was
so applied by Ezra (Ezr. ix. 1) and Nehemiah (Neh. xiii. 23).

3. These numbers seem excessive to many
critics, and it must be admitted that history
furnishes no parallel to them. In Cant. vi.
8 the number of Solomon's legitimate wives
is said to be sixty, and that of his concubines eighty. It is, perhaps probable, that
the text has in this place suffered corruption. For "700" we should perhaps read
"70."

4. *old*] About fifty or fifty-five. From
his age at his accession (ii. 2 note) he could
not have been more than about sixty at his
death.

The true nature of Solomon's idolatry

was neither complete apostasy—an apostasy from which there could be no recovery; nor a mere toleration, rather praise-
worthy than blameable. Solomon did not
ever openly or wholly apostatise. He continued his attendance on the worship of
Jehovah, and punctually made his offerings
three times a year in the Temple (ix. 25);
but his heart was not "perfect" with God.
The religious earnestness of his younger
days was weakened by wealth, luxury,
sensualism, an increasing worldliness leading him to worldly policy and latitudi-
narianism arising from contact with all
the manifold forms of human opinion. His
lapse into deadly sin was no doubt gradual.
Partly from ostentation, partly from that
sensualism which is the most common
failing of Oriental monarchs, he established
a harem on a grand and extraordinary
scale. To gratify "strange women," *i.e.*
foreigners, admitted either from worldly
policy, or for variety's sake, he built magnificent temples to their false gods, right over
against Jerusalem, as manifest rivals to
"the Temple." He thus became the author
of a syncretism, which sought to blend together the worship of Jehovah and the
worship of idols—a syncretism which possessed fatal attractions for the Jewish nation. Finally, he appears himself to have
frequented the idol temples (*vv.* 5 and 10),
and to have taken part in those fearful im-
purities which constituted the worst horror
of the idolatrous systems, thus practically
apostatising, though theoretically he never
ceased to hold that Jehovah was the true
God.

5. *went after*] This expression is common
in the Pentateuch, and always signifies
actual idolatry (see Deut. xi. 28, xiii. 2,
xxviii. 14, &c.).

For Ashtoreth, or Astarte, the goddess of
the Zidonians, see Ex. xxxiv. 13; Deut.
xvi. 21 notes. On the tomb of a Phœnician
king, discovered in 1855, on the site of

6 of the Ammonites. And Solomon did evil in the sight of the
LORD, and ¹went not fully after the LORD, as *did* David his
7 father. ᵏThen did Solomon build an high place for ᶦChemosh,   ʰ Num. 33.
the abomination of Moab, in ᵏthe hill that *is* before Jerusalem,   52.
and for Molech, the abomination of the children of Ammon.   ⁱ Num.21.29.
8 And likewise did he for all his strange wives, which burnt in-   Judg. 11.24.
9 cense and sacrificed unto their gods. ¶And the LORD was   ᵏ 2 Kin. 23.
angry with Solomon, because ᶦhis heart was turned from the   13.
10 LORD God of Israel, ᵐwhich had appeared unto him twice, and   ᶦ ver. 2, 3.
ⁿhad commanded him concerning this thing, that he should not   ᵐ ch. 3. 5.
go after other gods: but he kept not that which the LORD com-   & 9. 2.
11 manded. Wherefore the LORD said unto Solomon, Forasmuch   ⁿ ch. 6. 12.
as this ²is done of thee, and thou hast not kept my covenant   & 9. 6.
and my statutes, which I have commanded thee, ᵒI will surely   ᵒ ver. 31.
rend the kingdom from thee, and will give it to thy servant.   ch. 12.15,16.
12 Notwithstanding in thy days I will not do it for David thy
father's sake: *but* I will rend it out of the hand of thy son.
13 ᵖHowbeit I will not rend away all the kingdom; *but* will give   ᵖ 2Sam.7.15.
�q one tribe to thy son for David my servant's sake, and for Jeru-   Ps. 89. 33.
14 salem's sake ʳwhich I have chosen. ¶And the LORD ˢstirred   q ch. 12. 20.
up an adversary unto Solomon, Hadad the Edomite: he *was* of   ʳ Deut.12.11.
15 the king's seed in Edom. ᵗFor it came to pass, when David   ˢ 1 Chr. 5.26.
was in Edom, and Joab the captain of the host was gone up to   ᵗ 2 Sam.8.14.
16 bury the slain, ᵘafter he had smitten every male in Edom; (for   1 Chr. 18.
six months did Joab remain there with all Israel, until he had   12, 13.
  ᵘ Num. 24. 19.
  Deut. 20. 13.

¹ Heb. *fulfilled not after*, Num. 14. 24.   ² Heb. *is with thee.*

Sidon, mention is made of a temple of Astarte there, which the monarch built or restored; and his mother is said to have been a priestess of the goddess.

Milcom or Molech (*v.* 7) are variants of the term ordinarily used for "king" among the Semitic races of Western Asia, which appears in *Melk*arth (Phœnic.), Abi*melech* (Heb.), Andram*melek* (Assyr.), Abd-ul-*Malik* (Arab.), &c. On the character and worship of Molech, see Lev. xx. 2-5 note.

7. Chemosh (Num. xxi. 29 note), seems to have been widely worshipped in Western Asia. His name occurs frequently on the "Moabite-Stone." Car-Chemish, "the fort of Chemosh," a great city of the northern Hittites, must have been under his protection. In Babylon he seems to have been known as Chomus-belus, or Chemosh-Bel.

the hill] Olivet. At present the most southern summit only (the *Mons Offensionis*) is pointed out as having been desecrated by the idol sanctuaries: but the early Eastern travellers tell us that in their time the most northern suburb was believed to have been the site of the high place of Chemosh, the southern one that of Molech only.

13. one tribe] *i.e.* (marg. ref.) the tribe of Judah. Benjamin was looked upon as absorbed in Judah, so as not to be really a tribe in the same sense as the others. Still, in memory of the fact that the existing tribe of Judah was a double one (xii. 21), the prophet Ahijah tore his garment into twelve parts, and kept back two from Jeroboam (*vv.* 30, 31).

14. The writer has reserved for this place the various troubles of Solomon's reign, not allowing them to interrupt his previous narrative. He has, consequently, not followed chronological order. Hadad's (*v.* 23) and Rezon's opposition belong to the early years of Solomon's reign.

Hadad was a royal title (perhaps, the Syriac name for "the Sun") both in Syria and in Idumæa (cp. Gen. xxxvi. 35; 1 Chr. i. 51).

15. The verse gives certain additional particulars of David's conquest of Edom (marg. reff.). Joab was left, or sent, to complete the subjugation of the country, with orders to exterminate all the grown male inhabitants. It was not very often that David acted with any extreme severity in his wars; but he may have considered himself justified by policy, as he certainly was by the letter of the Law (Deut. xx. 13), in adopting this fierce course against Edom.

was in Edom] Or, according to another reading, "smote" Edom.

the slain] Probably the Israelites who had fallen in the struggle. Translate, "when... Joab was gone up to bury the slain, and had smitten every male," &c.

16. every male in Edom] *i.e.* every male whom he could find. As did Hadad and his company (*v.* 17), so others would escape in various directions. The Edomite nation was not destroyed on the occasion.

17 cut off every male in Edom :) that Hadad fled, he and certain
    Edomites of his father's servants with him, to go into Egypt;
18 Hadad *being* yet a little child. And they arose out of Midian,
    and came to Paran : and they took men with them out of Paran,
    and they came to Egypt, unto Pharaoh king of Egypt; which
    gave him an house, and appointed him victuals, and gave him
19 land. And Hadad found great favour in the sight of Pharaoh,
    so that he gave him to wife the sister of his own wife, the sister
20 of Tahpenes the queen. And the sister of Tahpenes bare him
    Genubath his son, whom Tahpenes weaned in Pharaoh's house :
    and Genubath was in Pharaoh's household among the sons of

x 1 Kin. 2.   21 Pharaoh. *x*And when Hadad heard in Egypt that David slept
10, 34.   with his fathers, and that Joab the captain of the host was dead,
    Hadad said to Pharaoh, ¹Let me depart, that I may go to mine
22 own country. Then Pharaoh said unto him, But what hast thou
    lacked with me, that, behold, thou seekest to go to thine own
    country ? And he answered, ²Nothing : howbeit let me go in
23 any wise. ¶And God stirred him up *another* adversary, Rezon

y 2 Sam. 8.3.   the son of Eliadah, which fled from his lord *y*Hadadezer king of
24 Zobah : and he gathered men unto him, and became captain

z 2 Sam. 8. 3.   over a band, *z*when David slew them *of Zobah :* and they went
& 10. 8, 18.   25 to Damascus, and dwelt therein, and reigned in Damascus. And
    he was an adversary to Israel all the days of Solomon, beside the
    mischief that Hadad *did :* and he abhorred Israel, and reigned

a ch. 12. 2.   26 over Syria. ¶And *a*Jeroboam the son of Nebat, an Ephrathite
2 Chr. 13. 6.   of Zereda, Solomon's servant, whose mother's name *was* Zeruah,

b 2 Sam. 20.   a widow woman, even he *b*lifted up *his* hand against the king.
21.   27 And this *was* the cause that he lifted up *his* hand against the

c ch. 9. 15.   king : *c*Solomon built Millo, *and* ³repaired the breaches of the
28 city of David his father. And the man Jeroboam *was* a mighty
    man of valour : and Solomon seeing the young man that he ⁴was
    industrious, he made him ruler over all the ⁵charge of the house

¹ Heb. *send me away.*	³ Heb. *closed.*	⁴ Heb. *did work.*
² Heb. *Not.*		⁵ Heb. *burden.*

---

18. *Midian*] A town in the south of
Judah. Paran is the desert tract immediately to the south of Judæa, the modern
desert of et-Tih.
    Pharaoh] King of the twenty-first (Tanite)
dynasty ; probably he was Psusennes I.,
Manetho's second king. It appears to have
been the policy of the Pharaohs about this
time to make friends and contract alliances
with their eastern neighbours.
    21. That Hadad should wait for the
death of Joab before requesting leave to
return to Idumæa shows how terrible an
impression had been made by the severe
measures which that commander had carried out twenty-five or thirty years previously (*v.* 16). The inability of refugees to
depart from an Oriental court without the
king's leave, and his unwillingness ordinarily to grant leave, are illustrated by
many passages in the history of Persia.
    23. *Rezon*] Possibly the same as the
Hezion of xv. 18 ; but probably one who interrupted the royal line of the Damascene
Hadads, which was restored after his death.

We may arrange the Damascus-kings of this
period as follows :—

Hadadezer (or Hadad I.), ab. B.C. 1040 (con-
    quered by David).
Rezon (usurper) contemporary with Solomon.

Hezion (Hadad II.)	,,	Rehoboam.
Tabrimon (Hadad III.)	,,	Abijam.
Ben-hadad (Hadad IV.)	,,	Asa.

    24. *and (they) reigned*] A very slight
emendation gives the sense, "they made
him king at Damascus."
    26. *Zereda*] See Judg. vii. 22.
    lifted up his hand against the king] *i.e.*
"he rebelled." Cp. marg. ref.
    27. Millo was probably fortified in Solo-
mon's twenty-fourth or twenty-fifth year.
    28. *a mighty man of valour*] Here " a man
of strength and activity." It is a vague
term of commendation, the exact force of
which must be fixed by the context. See
Ruth ii. 1 ; 1 Sam. ix. 1, &c.
    Solomon made Jeroboam superintendent
of all the forced labour (" the charge ")
exacted from his tribe—the tribe of Ephraim
— during the time that he was building

29 of Joseph. And it came to pass at that time when Jeroboam
went out of Jerusalem, that the prophet ^dAhijah the Shilonite   ^d.ch. 14. 2.
found him in the way; and he had clad himself with a new
30 garment; and they two *were* alone in the field: and Ahijah
caught the new garment that *was* on him, and ^erent it *in* twelve   ^e See
31 pieces: and he said to Jeroboam, Take thee ten pieces: for   1 Sam. 15.
^fthus saith the LORD, the God of Israel, Behold, I will rend the   & 24. 5.
kingdom out of the hand of Solomon, and will give ten tribes to   ^f ver. 11, 13.
32 thee: (but he shall have one tribe for my servant David's sake,
and for Jerusalem's sake, the city which I have chosen out of all
33 the tribes of Israel:) ^gbecause that they have forsaken me, and   ^g ver. 5, 6, 7.
have worshipped Ashtoreth the goddess of the Zidonians, Che-
mosh the god of the Moabites, and Milcom the god of the
children of Ammon, and have not walked in my ways, to do *that
which is* right in mine eyes, and *to keep* my statutes and my
34 judgments, as *did* David his father. Howbeit I will not take the
whole kingdom out of his hand: but I will make him prince all
the days of his life for David my servant's sake, whom I chose,
35 because he kept my commandments and my statutes: but ^hI   ^h ch. 12. 16,
will take the kingdom out of his son's hand, and will give it unto   17.
36 thee, *even* ten tribes. And unto his son will I give one tribe,
that ⁱDavid my servant may have a ¹light alway before me in   ⁱ ch. 15. 4.
Jerusalem, the city which I have chosen me to put my name   2 Kin. 8. 19.
37 there. And I will take thee, and thou shalt reign according to   Ps. 132. 17.
38 all that thy soul desireth, and shalt be king over Israel. And
it shall be, if thou wilt hearken unto all that I command thee,
and wilt walk in my ways, and do *that is* right in my sight, to
keep my statutes and my commandments, as David my servant
did; that ^kI will be with thee, and ^lbuild thee a sure house, as   ^k ch. 1. 37.
39 I built for David, and will give Israel unto thee. And I will   ^l 2 Sam. 7.
40 for this afflict the seed of David, but not for ever. Solomon   11, 27.
sought therefore to kill Jeroboam. And Jeroboam arose, and

¹ Heb. *lamp*, or, *candle.*

Millo and fortifying the city of Jerusalem
(ix. 15).
29. *at that time*] Probably after Jeroboam's return from Egypt (see *v.* 40).
the Shilonite] An inhabitant of Shiloh in
Mount Ephraim, the earliest and most
sacred of the Hebrew sanctuaries (Josh.
xviii. 10; Judg. xviii. 31; 1 Sam. iv. 3, &c.)
30. The first instance of the "acted
parable." Generally this mode was adopted
upon express divine command (see Jer. xiii.
1-11; Ezek. iii. 1-3). A connexion may be
traced between the type selected and the
words of the announcement to Solomon (*vv.*
11-13. Cp. 1 Sam. xv. 26-28).
34. Translate—"Howbeit I will not take
ought of the kingdom out of his hand."
The context requires this sense.
36. *that David may have a light*] Cp.
marg. reff. The exact meaning of the expression is doubtful. Perhaps the best explanation is, that "light" here is taken as
the essential feature of a continuing *home.*
38. See marg. reff. To "build a sure
house," or "give a house," is to give a continuity of offspring, and so secure the per-

petuity of a family. The promise, it will
be observed, is conditional; and as the
condition was not complied with, it did
not take effect (see xiv. 8-14). The entire
house of Jeroboam was destroyed by Baasha
(xv. 29).
39. *but not for ever*] David had been distinctly promised that God should never
fail his seed, whatever their shortcomings
(Ps. lxxxix. 28-37). The fulfilment of these
promises was seen, partly in the Providence
which maintained David's family in a royal
position till Zerubbabel, but mainly in the
preservation of his seed to the time fixed
for the coming of Christ, and in the birth
of Christ—the Eternal King—from one of
David's descendants.
40. Cp. *v.* 26. The announcement of
Ahijah was followed within a little while
by rebellion on the part of Jeroboam. As
Solomon's lustre faded, as his oppression
became greater and its objects more selfish,
and as a prospect of deliverance arose from
the personal qualities of Jeroboam (*v.* 28),
the tribe of Ephraim to which he belonged,
again aspired after its old position (see Josh.

fled into Egypt, unto Shishak king of Egypt, and was in Egypt
41 until the death of Solomon. ¶ And ᵐ the rest of the ¹ acts of
Solomon, and all that he did, and his wisdom, *are* they not
42 written in the book of the acts of Solomon? ⁿ And the ² time
that Solomon reigned in Jerusalem over all Israel *was* forty
43 years. ᵒ And Solomon slept with his fathers, and was buried in
the city of David his father: and ᵖ Rehoboam his son reigned in
his stead.

CHAP. 12. AND ᵃ Rehoboam went to Shechem: for all Israel were
2 come to Shechem to make him king. ¶ And it came to pass,
when ᵇ Jeroboam the son of Nebat, who was yet in ᶜ Egypt,
heard *of it*, (for he was fled from the presence of king Solomon,
3 and Jeroboam dwelt in Egypt;) that they sent and called him.
And Jeroboam and all the congregation of Israel came, and
4 spake unto Rehoboam, saying, Thy father made our ᵈ yoke
grievous: now therefore make thou the grievous service of thy
father, and his heavy yoke which he put upon us, lighter, and

m. 2 Chr. 9. 29.
n 2 Chr. 9. 30.
o 2 Chr. 9. 31.
p Matt. 1. 7, called *Roboam.*
a 2 Chr. 10. 1, &c.
b ch. 11. 26.
c ch. 11. 40.

d 1 Sam. 8. 11—18. ch. 4. 7.

¹ Or, *words,* or, *things.*   ² Heb. *days.*

---

xvii. 14 note). Jeroboam, active, energetic,
and ambitious, placed himself at their
head. The step proved premature. The
power of Solomon was too firmly fixed to
be shaken; and the hopes of the Ephraimites had to be deferred till a fitter season.

The *exact* date of Jeroboam's flight into
Egypt cannot be fixed. It was certainly
not earlier than Solomon's twenty-fourth
year, since it was after the building of
Millo (*v.* 27). But it may have been several
years later.

Shishak] This king is the first Pharaoh
mentioned in Scripture who can be certainly
identified with any known Egyptian
monarch. He is the Sheshonk (Sheshonk I.)
of the monuments, and the Sesonchosis
of Manetho. The Egyptian date for his accession is B.C. 980 or 983, which synchron-
izes, according to the ordinary Hebrew
reckoning, with Solomon's thirty-second or
thirty-fifth year. Sheshonk I. has left a
record of his expedition against Judah,
which accords well with what is related of
Shishak (xiv. 25, 26; 2 Chr. xii. 2-4).

41. *the book of the acts of Solomon*] See
marg. ref. and Introd. p. 265.

42. Josephus gave Solomon a reign of
eighty years, either because he wished to
increase the glory of his country's greatest
king, or through his having a false reading
in his copy of the LXX. Version. It is, no
doubt, remarkable that the three successive
kings, Saul, David, and Solomon, should
have each reigned forty years (Acts xiii.
21; 2 Sam. v. 4, 5); but such numerical coincidences occur from time to time in exact
history.

XII. 1. The first step taken by the new
king was a most judicious one. If anything
could have removed the disaffection of the
Ephraimites, and caused them to submit
to the ascendancy of Judah, it would have
been the honour done to their capital by its

selection as the scene of the coronation.
Shechem (now *Nablous*) lay on the flank of
Mount Gerizim, directly opposite to Mount
Ebal, in a position second to none in all
Palestine. Though Abimelech had destroyed
the place (Judg. ix. 45), it had probably soon
risen again, and was once more a chief
city, or perhaps *the* chief city, of Ephraim.
Its central position made it a convenient
place for the general assembly of the tribes,
as it had been in the days of Joshua (Josh.
viii. 30-35, xxiv. 1-28); and this would
furnish an additional reason for its selection.

2. *heard of it*] *i.e.* of the death of Solomon
and accession of Rehoboam. This would be
more clear without the division into chapters; which division, it must be remembered, is without authority.

dwelt in Egypt] By a change of the
pointing of one word, and of one letter in
another, the Hebrew text here will read as in
2 Chr. x. 2, "returned out of Egypt; and
they sent and called him."

In the LXX. Version the story of Jeroboam is told in two different ways. The
general narrative agrees closely with the
Hebrew text; but an insertion into the
body of ch. xii.—remarkable for its minuteness and circumstantiality—at once de-
ranges the order of the events, and gives to
the history in many respects a new aspect
and colouring. This section of the Septuagint, though regarded by some as thoroughly
authentic, absolutely conflicts with the Hebrew text in many important particulars.
In its general outline it is wholly irrecon-
cileable with the other narrative; and, if
both stood on the same footing, and we
were free to chose between them, there
could be no question about preferring the
history as given in our Version.

4. The complaint was probably twofold.
The Israelites no doubt complained in part
of the heavy weight of taxation laid upon

5 we will serve thee. And he said unto them, Depart yet *for* three days, then come again to me. And the people departed.
6 ¶ And king Rehoboam consulted with the old men, that stood before Solomon his father while he yet lived, and said, How do
7 ye advise that I may answer this people? And they spake unto him, saying, *e* If thou wilt be a servant unto this people this day, and wilt serve them, and answer them, and speak good words to
8 them, then they will be thy servants for ever. But he forsook the counsel of the old men, which they had given him, and consulted with the young men that were grown up with him, *and*
9 which stood before him: and he said unto them, What counsel give ye that we may answer this people, who have spoken to me, saying, Make the yoke which thy father did put upon us lighter?
10 And the young men that were grown up with him spake unto him, saying, Thus shalt thou speak unto this people that spake unto thee, saying, Thy father made our yoke heavy, but make thou *it* lighter unto us; thus shalt thou say unto them, My little
11 *finger* shall be thicker than my father's loins. And now whereas my father did lade you with a heavy yoke, I will add to your yoke: my father hath chastised you with whips, but I will
12 chastise you with scorpions. ¶ So Jeroboam and all the people came to Rehoboam the third day, as the king had appointed,
13 saying, Come to me again the third day. And the king answered the people ¹ roughly, and forsook the old men's counsel
14 that they gave him; and spake to them after the counsel of the young men, saying, My father made your yoke heavy, and I will add to your yoke: my father *also* chastised you with whips,
15 but I will chastise you with scorpions. Wherefore the king hearkened not unto the people; for *f* the cause was from the LORD, that he might perform his saying, which the LORD

e 2 Chr. 10. 7.
Prov. 15. 1.

f ver. 24.
Judg. 14. 4.
2 Chr. 10. 15.
& 22. 7.
& 25. 20.

¹ Heb. *hardly.*

them for the maintenance of the monarch and his court (iv. 19–23). But their chief grievance was the forced labour to . which they had been subjected (v. 13, 14, xi. 28). Forced labour has been among the causes leading to insurrection in many ages and countries. It helped to bring about the French Revolution, and it was for many years one of the principal grievances of the Russian serfs. Jeroboam's position as superintendent of the forced labours of the tribe of Ephraim (xi. 28) revealed to him the large amount of dissatisfaction which Solomon's system had produced, and his contemplated rebellion in Solomon's reign may have been connected with this standing grievance.

6. *the old men, that stood before Solomon his father*] Perhaps "the princes" of iv. 2. Solomon placed great value upon good advisers (Prov. xi. 14, xv. 22, xxiv. 6).

7. The advice was not that the king should permanently resign the office of ruler, but that he should *for once* be ruled by his people.

8. The age of Rehoboam at his accession is an interesting and difficult question. According to the formal statement of the present text of xiv. 21, 2 Chr. xii. 13, he had

reached the mature age of forty-one years, and would therefore be unable to plead youth as an excuse for his conduct. The general narrative, however, seems to assume that he was quite a young man (cp. 2 Chr. xiii. 7). Perhaps the best way of removing the whole difficulty would be to read in the above text "twenty-one" for "forty-one." The corruption is one which might easily take place, if letters were used for numerals.

My little finger, &c.] *i.e.* "You shall find my hand heavier on you than my father's —as much heavier as if my little finger were thicker than his loins."

11. *scorpions*] By this word some understand whips having leaden balls at the ends of their lashes with hooks projecting from them; others the thorny stem of the eggplant, or "the scorpion plant." But it seems best to regard the expression as a figure of speech.

15. *The cause was from the* LORD] *i.e.* "the turn of events was from the Lord." Human passions, anger, pride, and insolence, worked out the accomplishment of the Divine designs. Without interfering with man's free will, God guides the course of events, and accomplishes His purposes.

g ch. 11. 11,
31.
h 2 Sam. 20. 1.

i ch. 11. 13,
36.

k ch. 4. 6.
& 5. 14.

l 2 Kin. 17. 21.

m ch. 11. 13,
32.
n 2 Chr. 11. 1.

g spake by Ahijah the Shilonite unto Jeroboam the son of Nebat.
16 ¶ So when all Israel saw that the king hearkened not unto them, the people answered the king, saying, *h* What portion have we in David? neither *have we* inheritance in the son of Jesse : to your tents, O Israel : now see to thine own house, David. So Israel
17 departed unto their tents. But *i as for* the children of Israel which dwelt in the cities of Judah, Rehoboam reigned over
18 them. ¶ Then king Rehoboam *k* sent Adoram, who *was* over the tribute ; and all Israel stoned him with stones, that he died. Therefore king Rehoboam ¹made speed to get him up to his
19 chariot, to flee to Jerusalem. So *l* Israel ²rebelled against the
20 house of David unto this day. And it came to pass, when all Israel heard that Jeroboam was come again, that they sent and called him unto the congregation, and made him king over all Israel : there was none that followed the house of David, but the
21 tribe of Judah *m* only. ¶ And when *n* Rehoboam was come to Jerusalem, he assembled all the house of Judah, with the tribe of

---

¹ Heb. *strengthened himself.*   ² Or, *fell away.*

---

16. See marg. ref. The words breathe unmistakeably the spirit of tribal jealousy and dislike (xi. 40 note).

now see to thine own house, David] *i.e.* " Henceforth, house of David, look after thine own tribe, Judah, only." It is not a threat of war, but a warning against interference.

17. *Israel*, &c.] The Israelites proper, or members of the other tribes, who happened to be settled within the limits of the land of Judah. These Israelites quietly submitted to Rehoboam. "Israel" through this chapter, and throughout the rest of Kings, designates ordinarily "the ten tribes," and is antithetical to "Judah."

18. Adoram has been identified with Adoniram (marg. reff.), and even with the Adoram of 2 Sam. xx. 24. But it is highly improbable that the same person was chief superintendent of the forced labours during the whole of Solomon's long reign, and also during a part of David's and Rehoboam's. We may therefore conclude that the three names mark three distinct persons, perhaps of the same family, who were respectively contemporary with the three kings. Adoram was chosen, as best acquainted with the hardships whereof the rebels complained, to arrange some alleviation of their burthens.

19. *unto this day*] This expression shows that the writer, who lived during the Captivity, and consequently long after the rebellion of Israel had come to an end, is embodying in his history the exact words of an ancient document. His source, whatever it was, appears to have been also followed by the writer of Chronicles. (See 2 Chr. x. 19.)

20. The first act of the Israelites, on learning what had occurred at Shechem, was to bring together the great "congregation" of the people (cp. Judg. xx. 1), in

order that, regularly and in solemn form, the crown might be declared vacant, and a king elected in the room of the monarch whose authority had been thrown off. The congregation selected Jeroboam. The rank, the talent, and the known energy of the late exile, his natural hostility to the house of Solomon, his Ephraimitic descent, his acquaintance with the art of fortification, and the friendly relations subsisting between him and the great Egyptian king, pointed him out as the fittest man for the vacant post. If (according to the LXX.) Shishak had not only protected him against Solomon, but also given him an Egyptian princess, sister to his own queen, in marriage, his position must have been such that no other Israelite could have borne comparison with him. Again, the prophecy of Ahijah would have been remembered by the more religious part of the nation, and would have secured to Jeroboam their adhesion ; so that every motive, whether of policy or of religion, would have united to recommend the son of Nebat to the suffrages of his countrymen.

21. The adhesion of Benjamin to Judah at this time comes upon us as a surprise. By blood Benjamin was far more closely connected with Ephraim than with Judah. All the traditions of Benjamin were antagonistic to Judah, and hitherto the weak tribe had been accustomed to lean constantly on its strong northern neighbour. But it would seem that, in the half-century which had elapsed since the revolt of Sheba, the son of Bichri (2 Sam. xx. 1), the feelings of the Benjamites had undergone a complete change. This is best accounted for by the establishment of the religious and political capital at Jerusalem, on the border line of the two tribes (Josh. xv. 8, xviii. 16), whence it resulted that the new metropolis stood partly within the territory of either, and was in a

Benjamin, an hundred and fourscore thousand chosen men, which were warriors, to fignt against the house of Israel, to bring the kingdom again to Rehoboam the son of Solomon.
22 But °the word of God came unto Shemaiah the man of God, 23 saying, Speak unto Rehoboam, the son of Solomon, king of Judah, and unto all the house of Judah and Benjamin, and to 24 the remnant of the people, saying, Thus saith the LORD, Ye shall not go up, nor fight against your brethren the children of Israel: return every man to his house; ᵖfor this thing is from me. They hearkened therefore to the word of the LORD, and 25 returned to depart, according to the word of the LORD. ¶ Then Jeroboam �q built Shechem in mount Ephraim, and dwelt therein; 26 and went out from thence, and built ʳ Penuel. And Jeroboam said in his heart, Now shall the kingdom return to the house of 27 David: if this people ˢgo up to do sacrifice in the house of the LORD at Jerusalem, then shall the heart of this people turn again unto their lord, even unto Rehoboam king of Judah, and they shall kill me, and go again to Rehoboam king of Judah. 28 Whereupon the king took counsel, and ᵗmade two calves of gold, and said unto them, It is too much for you to go up to Jerusalem: ᵘbehold thy gods, O Israel, which brought thee up

° 2 Chr. 12. 5—8, 15.

ᵖ ver. 15.

q See Judg. 9. 45.
ʳ Judg. 8. 17.

ˢ Deut. 12. 5, 6.

ᵗ 2 Kin. 10. 29.

ᵘ Ex. 32. 4, 8.

certain sense common to both. One of the gates of Jerusalem was "the high gate of Benjamin" (Jer. xx. 2); and probably Benjamites formed a considerable part of the population. The whole tribe also, we may well believe, was sincerely attached to the Temple worship, in which they could participate far more freely and more constantly than the members of remoter tribes, and to which the habits of forty years had now accustomed them.

On the number of the Israelites, see notes on Ex. xii. 37, and 2 Sam. xxiv. 9. The number mentioned here is moderate, compared with the numbers given both previously and subsequently (2 Chr. xiii. 3, xvii. 14-18).

22. Shemaiah was the chief Prophet in Judah during the reign of Rehoboam, as Ahijah was in Israel. See marg. reff.

23. the remnant] i.e. "the children of Israel which dwelt in the cities of Judah" (v. 17 note).

25. built Shechem] In the sense of "enlarged and fortified." See Dan. iv. 30. The first intention of Jeroboam seems to have been to make Shechem his capital, and therefore he immediately set about its fortification. So also he seems to have fortified Penuel for the better security of his Trans-Jordanic possessions (marg. ref.).

26. Jeroboam's fear was lest a reaction should set in, and a desire for reunion manifest itself. He was not a man content to remain quiet, trusting simply to the promise made him (xi. 38). Hence he gave way to the temptation of helping forward the plans of Providence by the crooked devices of a merely human policy. His measures, like all measures which involve a dereliction of principle, brought certain

evils in their train, and drew down Divine judgment on himself. But they fully secured the object at which he aimed. They prevented all healing of the breach between the two kingdoms. They made the separation final. They produced the result that not only no reunion took place, but no symptoms of an inclination to reunite ever manifested themselves during the whole period of the double kingdom.

27. kill me] In case his subjects desired a reconciliation with Rehoboam, Jeroboam's death would at once facilitate the reestablishment of a single kingdom, and obtain favour with the legitimate monarch. (Cp. 2 Sam. iv. 7.)

28. The "calves of gold" were probably representations of the cherubic form, imitations of the two Cherubim which guarded the Ark of the Covenant in the Holy of Holies. But being unauthorised copies, set up in places which God had not chosen, and without any Divine sanction, the sacred writers call them "calves." They were not mere human figures with wings, but had at any rate the head of a calf or ox. [Hence, some attribute this calf-worship entirely to Assyrian and Phœnician influence.] Jeroboam, in setting them up, was probably not so much influenced by the Apis-worship of Egypt, as (1) by a conviction that the Israelites could not be brought to attach themselves to any worship which did not present them with sensible objects to venerate; (2) by the circumstance that he did not possess any of the old objects of reverence, which had been concentrated at Jerusalem; and (3) by the fact that he could plead for his "calves" the authority of so great a name as Aaron (marg. ref.).

x Gen. 28.19.	29 out of the land of Egypt. And he set the one in *x* Beth-el, and
y Judg. 18.	30 the other put he in *y* Dan. And this thing became *z* a sin : for
29.	31 the people went *to worship* before the one, *even* unto Dan. And
z ch. 13. 34.	he made an *a* house of high places, *b* and made priests of the
2 Kin. 17. 21.	
a ch. 13. 32.	32 lowest of the people, which were not of the sons of Levi. And
b Num. 3. 10.	Jeroboam ordained a feast in the eighth month, on the fifteenth
2 Kin. 17.32.	
Ezek. 44.7,8.	day of the month, like unto *c* the feast that *is* in Judah, and he
c Lev. 23.	¹ offered upon the altar. So did he in Beth-el, ² sacrificing unto
33, 34.	the calves that he had made : *d* and he placed in Beth-el the
Num. 29. 12.	
ch. 8. 2, 5.	33 priests of the high places which he had made. So he ³ offered
d Amos 7.13.	upon the altar which he had made in Beth-el the fifteenth day of
e Num. 15.	the eighth month, *even* in the month which he had *e* devised of
39.	his own heart ; and ordained a feast unto the children of Israel :
f ch. 13. 1.	and he offered upon the altar, ⁴ and *f* burnt incense.
a 2 Kin. 23.	**CHAP. 13.** AND, behold, there *a* came a man of God out of Judah
17.	by the word of the LORD unto Beth-el : *b* and Jeroboam stood by
b ch. 12. 32,	
33.	¹ Or, *went up to the altar, &c.* ³ Or, *went up to the altar, &c.*
	² Or, *to sacrifice.* ⁴ Heb. *to burn incense.*

29. In the first place, Jeroboam consulted the convenience of his subjects, who would thus in no case have very far to go in order to reach one or the other sanctuary. Further, he avoided the danger of reminding them continually that they had no ark—a danger which would have been imminent, had the two cherubs been placed together in one shrine.

He selected Bethel (in the south) for one of his seats of worship, on account of its pre-eminent sanctity. (See marg. ref. ; Judg. xx. 26-28 ; 1 Sam. vii. 16.)

The north of Palestine did not furnish a spot possessing an equally sacred character, but still Dan had to some-extent the character of a " holy city " (marg. ref.).

30. *this thing became a sin*] *i.e.* this act of Jeroboam's became an occasion of sin to the people. The author perhaps wrote the following words thus : " The people went to worship before the one to Bethel and before the other to Dan."

31. *he made an house of high places*] *i.e.* "He built a temple, or sanctuary, at each of the two cities where the calves were set up." The writer uses the expression "house of high places " in contempt, meaning that the buildings were not real temples, or houses of God, like that at Jerusalem, but only on a par with the temples upon high places which had long existed in various parts of the land.

made priests of the lowest of the people] More correctly, " **from all ranks of the people.**" That the Levites did not accept Jeroboam's innovations, and transfer their services to his two sanctuaries, must have been the consequence of their faithful attachment to the true worship of Jehovah. In all probability Jeroboam confiscated the Levitical lands within his dominions for the benefit of the new priestly order (2 Chr. xi. 13, 14).

32. *a feast*] Intended as a substitute for the Feast of Tabernacles (marg. ref. *c*). It *may* also have assumed the character of a feast of dedication, held at the same time, after the example of Solomon (viii. 2). His object in changing the month from the seventh to the eighth, and yet keeping the day of the month, is not clear. Perhaps it was on account of the later vintage of the more northern regions. It is remarkable that Josephus places the scene in the *seventh* month. He therefore was not aware that the people of Israel kept the feast of Tabernacles a month later than their brethren of Judah. The expression "he offered upon the altar" (see marg. and Ex. xx. 26) shows that Jeroboam himself officiated as priest, and offered this sacrifice—at Bethel, not at Dan ; where it is possible that the priests descended from Jonathan, the son of Gershom and grandson of Moses, undertook the services (Judg. xviii. 30 note).

33. This verse belongs to ch. xiii. rather than to ch. xii., being intended as an introduction to what follows.

which he had devised of his own heart] The entire system of Jeroboam receives its condemnation in these words. His main fault was that he left a ritual and a worship where all was divinely authorised, for ceremonies and services which were wholly of his own devising. Not being a Prophet, he had no authority to introduce religious innovations. Not having received any commission to establish new forms, he had no right to expect that any religious benefit would accrue from them. (See *v.* 26 note.)

XIII. 1. Rather, " *in* the word of the Lord." The meaning seems to be, not merely that the Prophet was bid to come, but that he came in the strength and power of God's word, a divinely inspired messenger. (Cp. *vv.* 2, 5, 32.)

by the altar] " On the altar ; " *i.e.* on the

2 the altar ¹to burn incense. And he cried against the altar in the word of the LORD, and said, O altar, altar, thus saith the LORD; Behold, a child shall be born unto the house of David, ᶜJosiah by name; and upon thee shall he offer the priests of the high places that burn incense upon thee, and men's bones 3 shall be burnt upon thee. And he gave ᵈa sign the same day, saying, This is the sign which the LORD hath spoken; Behold, the altar shall be rent, and the ashes that are upon it 4 shall be poured out. ¶And it came to pass, when king Jeroboam heard the saying of the man of God, which had cried against the altar in Beth-el, that he put forth his hand from the altar, saying, Lay hold on him. And his hand, which he put forth against him, dried up, so that he could not pull it in again 5 to him. The altar also was rent, and the ashes poured out from the altar, according to the sign which the man of God had given 6 by the word of the LORD. And the king answered and said unto the man of God, ᵉIntreat now the face of the LORD thy God, and pray for me, that my hand may be restored me again. And the man of God besought ²the LORD, and the king's hand 7 was restored him again, and became as it was before. And the king said unto the man of God, come home with me, and refresh 8 thyself, and ᶠI will give thee a reward. And the man of God said unto the king, ᵍIf thou wilt give me half thine house, I will not go in with thee, neither will I eat bread nor drink water in 9 this place: for so was it charged me by the word of the LORD, saying, ʰEat no bread, nor drink water, nor turn again by the 10 same way that thou camest. So he went another way, and re-

ᶜ 2 Kin. 23. 15—18.

ᵈ John 2. 18. 1 Cor. 1. 22.

ᵉ Ex. 8. 8. & 9. 28. & 10. 17. Num. 21. 7. Acts 8. 24. Jam. 5. 16.

ᶠ 1 Sam. 9. 7. 2 Kin. 5. 15. ᵍ So Num. 22. 18. & 24. 13.

ʰ 1 Cor. 5. 11.

¹ Or, to offer. ² Heb. the face of the LORD.

ledge, or platform, half-way up the Altar, whereupon the officiating priest always stood to sacrifice. Cp. xii. 32 note.

2. *a child shall be born...Josiah by name*] Divine predictions so seldom descend to such particularity as this, that doubts are entertained, even by orthodox theologians, with respect to the actual mention of Josiah's name by a Prophet living in the time of Jeroboam. Only one other instance that can be considered parallel occurs in the whole of Scripture—the mention of Cyrus by Isaiah. Of course no one who believes in the Divine foreknowledge can doubt that God could, if He chose, cause events to be foretold minutely by his Prophets; but certainly the general law of his Providence is, that He does not do so. If this law is to be at any time broken through, it will not be capriciously. Here it certainly does not appear what great effect was to be produced by the mention of Josiah's name so long before his birth; and hence a doubt arises whether we have in our present copies the true original text. The sense is complete without the words "Josiah by name;" and these words, if originally a marginal note, may easily have crept into the text by the mistake of a copyist. It is remarkable that, where this narrative is again referred to in Kings (marg. ref.), there is no allusion to the fact that the man of God had prophesied of Josiah by name.

3. *he gave a sign*] A sign of this kind—an immediate prophecy to prove the Divine character of a remote prophecy — had scarcely been given before this. In the later history, however, such signs are not unfrequent (cp. 2 K. xix. 29; Is. vii. 14-16).

the ashes...shall be poured out] i.e. "The half-burnt remains of the offerings shall be ignominiously spilled upon the ground."

5. We need not suppose a complete shattering of the altar, but rather the appearance of a crack or fissure in the fabric, which, extending from top to bottom, caused the embers and the fragments of the victims to fall till they reached the ground.

7. *I will give thee a reward*] It was customary to honour a Prophet with a gift, if he performed any service that was requested at his hands (see marg. reff.).

9. *Eat no bread, nor drink water*] The reason of the command is evident. The man of God was not to accept the hospitality of any dweller at Bethel, in order to show in a marked way, which men generally could appreciate, God's abhorrence of the system which Jeroboam had "devised of his own heart."

nor turn again by the same way that thou camest] This command seems to have been given simply to test the obedience of the Prophet by laying him under a positive as well as a moral obligation.

11 turned not by the way that he came to Beth-el. ¶Now there dwelt an old prophet in Beth-el; and his [1]sons came and told him all the works that the man of God had done that day in Beth-el: the words which he had spoken unto the king, them 12 they told also to their father. And their father said unto them, What way went he? For his sons had seen what way the man 13 of God went, which came from Judah. And he said unto his sons, Saddle me the ass. So they saddled him the ass: and he 14 rode thereon, and went after the man of God, and found him sitting under an oak: and he said unto him, *Art* thou the man 15 of God that camest from Judah? And he said, I *am*. Then he 16 said unto him, Come home with me, and eat bread. And he said, *i* I may not return with thee, nor go in with thee: neither 17 will I eat bread nor drink water with thee in this place: for [2]it was said to me *k*by the word of the LORD, Thou shalt eat no bread nor drink water there, nor turn again to go by the way 18 that thou camest. He said unto him, I *am* a prophet also as thou *art;* and an angel spake unto me by the word of the LORD, saying, Bring him back with thee into thine house, that he may 19 eat bread and drink water. *But* he lied unto him. So he went back with him, and did eat bread in his house, and drank water. 20 ¶And it came to pass, as they sat at the table, that the word of 21 the LORD came unto the prophet that brought him back: and he cried unto the man of God that came from Judah, saying, Thus saith the LORD, Forasmuch as thou hast disobeyed the mouth of the LORD, and hast not kept the commandment which 22 the LORD thy God commanded thee, but camest back, and hast eaten bread and drunk water in the *l*place, of the which *the* LORD did say to thee, Eat no bread, and drink no water; thy 23 carcase shall not come unto the sepulchre of thy fathers. ¶And it came to pass, after he had eaten bread, and after he had drunk, that he saddled for him the ass, *to wit,* for the prophet 24 whom he had brought back. And when he was gone, *m*a lion met him by the way, and slew him: and his carcase was cast in the way, and the ass stood by it, the lion also stood by the 25 carcase. And, behold, men passed by, and saw the carcase cast in the way, and the lion standing by the carcase: and they

i ver. 8. 9.

k ch. 20. 35.
1 Thess. 4. 15.

ver. 9.

m ch. 20. 36.

---

[1] Heb. *son*.   [2] Heb. *a word was*.

---

11. The truly pious Israelites quitted their homes when Jeroboam made his religious changes, and, proceeding to Jerusalem, strengthened the kingdom of Rehoboam (2 Chr. x. 16, 17). This "old prophet" therefore, who, without being infirm in any way, had remained under Jeroboam, and was even content to dwell at Bethel—the chief seat of the new worship —was devoid of any deep and earnest religious feeling.

14. *under an oak*] Literally, "under the oak," or "the terebinth-tree." There was a single well-known tree of the kind, standing by itself in the vicinity of Bethel, which the author supposed his readers to be acquainted with.

18. *But he lied unto him*] It is always to be remembered that the prophetic gift might co-exist with various degrees of moral imperfection in the person possessing it. Note especially the case of Balaam.

21. *Forasmuch as thou hast disobeyed the mouth of the* LORD] It was his duty not to have suffered himself to be persuaded. He should have felt that his obedience was being tried, and should have required, ere he considered himself released, *the same, or as strong, evidence,* as that on which he had received the obligation. Disobedience to certain positive commands of God, was one which it was at this time very important to punish signally, since it was exactly the sin of Jeroboam and his adherents.

22. On the anxiety of the Hebrews to be buried with their fathers, see Gen. xlvii. 30, xlix. 29, l. 25; 2 Sam. xix. 37, &c.

26 came and told *it* in the city where the old prophet dwelt. And
when the prophet that brought him back from the way heard
thereof, he said, It *is* the man of God, who was disobedient unto
the word of the LORD: therefore the LORD hath delivered him
unto the lion, which hath [1]torn him, and slain him, according to
27 the word of the LORD, which he spake unto him. And he spake
to his sons, saying, Saddle me the ass. And they saddled *him*.
28 And he went and found his carcase cast in the way, and the
ass and the lion standing by the carcase: the lion had not eaten
29 the carcase, nor [2]torn the ass. And the prophet took up the
carcase of the man of God, and laid it upon the ass, and brought
it back: and the old prophet came to the city, to mourn and to
30 bury him. And he laid his carcase in his own grave; and they
31 mourned over him, *saying*, [n]Alas, my brother! And it came to
pass, after he had buried him, that he spake to his sons, saying,
When I am dead, then bury me in the sepulchre wherein the
32 man of God *is* buried; [o]lay my bones beside his bones: [p]for the
saying which he cried by the word of the LORD against the altar
in Beth-el, and against all the houses of the high places which
33 *are* in the cities of [q]Samaria, shall surely come to pass. ¶[r]After
this thing Jeroboam returned not from his evil way, but [3]made
again of the lowest of the people priests of the high places: whosoever would, he [4]consecrated him, and he became *one* of the
34 priests of the high places. [s]And this thing became sin unto the
house of Jeroboam, even [t] to cut *it* off, and to destroy *it* from off
the face of the earth.

Margin references:
[n] Jer. 22. 18.
[o] 2 Kin. 23. 17, 18.
[p] ver. 2.
2 Kin. 23. 16, 19.
[q] See ch. 16. 24.
[r] ch. 12. 31, 32.
2 Chr. 11. 15.
[s] ch. 12. 30.
[t] ch. 15. 29.

---

[1] Heb. *broken.*
[2] Heb. *broken.*
[3] Heb. *returned and made.*
[4] Heb. *filled h.s hand*, Lev. 8. 25.

---

23. *the lion had not eaten the carcase, nor
torn the ass*] These strange circumstances
were of a nature to call men's attention to
the matter, and cause the whole story to be
bruited abroad. By these means an incident, which Jeroboam would have wished
hushed up, became no doubt the common
talk of the whole people.

30. *he laid his carcase in his own grave*]
As Joseph of Arimathæa did the body of
our Lord (Matt. xxvii. 60). The possession
of rock-hewn tombs by families, or individuals, was common among the Jews from
their first entrance into the Holy Land to
their final expulsion. A sepulchre usually
consisted of an underground apartment,
into which opened a number of long,
narrow *loculi*, or cells, placed side by side,
each adapted to receive one body. The
cells were 6 or 7 feet long, 2 feet wide, and
3 feet high. They were commonly closed
by a stone placed at the end of each. Many
such tombs still exist in Palestine.

32. *against all the houses of the high places*]
i.e. more than the two high places at Dan
and Bethel. There were many lesser high
places in the land, several of which would
be likely to be in Israel (iii. 4).

in the cities of Samaria] The word Samaria
cannot have been employed by the old
prophet, in whose days Samaria did not

exist (xvi. 24). The writer of Kings has
substituted for the term used by him that
whereby the country was known in his own
day.

33. *whosoever would, he consecrated him*]
i.e. he exercised no discretion, but allowed
any one to become a priest, without regard
to birth, character, or social position. We
may suspect from this that the office was
not greatly sought, since no civil governor
who cared to set up a priesthood would wish
to degrade it in public estimation. Jeroboam did impose one limitation, which
would have excluded the very poorest class.
The candidate for consecration was obliged
to make an offering consisting of one
young bullock and seven rams (2 Chr. xiii.
9).

34. This persistence in wrong, after the
warning given him, brought a judgment,
not only on Jeroboam himself, but on his
family. Jeroboam's departure from the
path of right forfeited the crown (xi. 38);
and in that forfeiture was involved naturally the destruction of his family; for in
the East, as already observed, when one
dynasty supplants another, the ordinary
practice is for the new king to destroy all
the males belonging to the house of his
predecessor. See xv. 29.

CHAP. **14.** AT that time Abijah the son of Jeroboam fell sick. And 2 Jeroboam said to his wife, Arise, I pray thee, and disguise thyself, that thou be not known to be the wife of Jeroboam; and get thee to Shiloh: behold, there *is* Ahijah the prophet, 3 which told me that *ªI should be* king over this people. *ᵇ*And take ¹with thee ten loaves, and ²cracknels, and a ³cruse of honey, and go to him: he shall tell thee what shall become of the child. 4 And Jeroboam's wife did so, and arose, *ᶜ*and went to Shiloh, and came to the house of Ahijah. ¶ But Ahijah could not see; 5 for his eyes ⁴were set by reason of his age. And the LORD said unto Ahijah, Behold, the wife of Jeroboam cometh to ask a thing of thee for her son; for he *is* sick: thus and thus shalt thou say unto her: for it shall be, when she cometh in, that she 6 shall feign herself *to be* another *woman.* And it was *so,* when Ahijah heard the sound of her feet, as she came in at the door, that he said, Come in, thou wife of Jeroboam; why feignest thou thyself *to be* another? for I *am* sent to thee *with* ⁵heavy 7 *tidings.* Go, tell Jeroboam, Thus saith the LORD God of Israel, *ᵈ*Forasmuch as I exalted thee from among the people, and made 8 thee prince over my people Israel, and *ᵉ*rent the kingdom away from the house of David, and gave it thee: and *yet* thou hast not been as my servant David, *ᶠ*who kept my commandments, and who followed me with all his heart, to do *that* only *which* 9 *was* right in mine eyes; but hast done evil above all that were before thee: *ᵍ*for thou hast gone and made thee other gods, and

ª ch. 11. 31.
ᵇ ch. 13. 7.
1 Sam. 9.7,8.

ᶜ ch. 11. 29.

ᵈ See
2 Sam. 12.
7, 8.
ch. 16. 2.
ᵉ ch. 11. 31.
ᶠ ch. 11. 33,
38.
& 15. 5.
ᵍ ch. 12. 28.
2 Chr.11.15.

¹ Heb. *in thine hand.*   ³ Or, *bottle.*   ⁴ Heb. *stood for his hoariness.*
² Or, *cakes.*   ⁵ Heb. *hard.*

XIV. 1. *at that time*] The phrase here connects the narrative which follows with Jeroboam's *persistence* in his evil courses. The event related is the first judgment upon him for his obduracy, the beginning of the cutting off of his house from the face of the earth.

Abijah] We see by this name that Jeroboam did not intend to desert the worship of Jehovah, since its signification is "Jehovah is my father," or "Jehovah is my desire" (Job xxxiv. 36).

2. *disguise thyself*] Jeroboam fears that even Ahijah the Shilonite, who in some sort made him king, will scarcely give his queen a favourable answer. The king's conscience tells him that he has not performed the conditions on which he was promised "a sure house" (xi. 38).

3. See marg. ref. The presents here were selected for the purpose of deception, being such as a poor country person would have been likely to bring. Jeroboam counted also on Ahijah's blindness (*v.* 4) as favouring his plan of deception (cp. Gen. xxvii. 1, 22).

cracknels] See margin. The Hebrew word is thought to mean a kind of cake which crumbled easily.

5. *feign herself to be another woman*] Lit., "she shall make herself strange," *i.e.*, "she shall come in disguised." So *v.* 6.

6. *for I am sent to thee*] Rather, "I also

am sent to thee." As thou hast a message to me from thy husband, so have I a message to thee from the Lord.

7. As Jeroboam's appointment to the kingdom had been formally announced to him by the Prophet Ahijah, so the same Prophet is commissioned to acquaint him with his forfeiture of it. Cp. 1 Sam. xv. 26-28.

9. *above all that were before thee*] *i.e.* above all previous rulers of the people, whether Judges or kings. Hitherto none of the rulers of Israel had set up the idolatrous worship of ephod, teraphim, and the like (Judg. xviii. 17), as a substitute for the true religion, or sought to impose an idolatrous system on the nation. Gideon's ephod "*became* a snare" contrary to his intention (Judg. viii. 27). Solomon's high places were private—built for the use of his wives, and not designed to attract the people. Jeroboam was the first ruler who set himself to turn the Israelites away from the true worship, and established a poor counterfeit of it, which he strove to make, and succeeded in making, the religion of the great mass of his subjects.

and hast cast me behind thy back] A very strong and very rare expression, occurring again only in Ezek. xxiii. 35; where it is said of the Jews generally, shortly before the Captivity. The expressions in the marg. reff. are similar but less fearful.

molten images, to provoke me to anger, and [h]hast cast me
10 behind thy back: therefore, behold, [i]I will bring evil upon the
house of Jeroboam, and [k]will cut off from Jeroboam him that
pisseth against the wall, [l]and him that is shut up and left in
Israel, and will take away the remnant of the house of Jero-
11 boam, as a man taketh away dung, till it be all gone. [m]Him
that dieth of Jeroboam in the city shall the dogs eat; and him
that dieth- in the field shall the fowls of the air eat: for the
12 LORD hath spoken it. Arise thou therefore, get thee to thine
own house: and [n]when thy feet enter into the city, the child
13 shall die. And all Israel shall mourn for him, and bury him:
for he only of Jeroboam shall come to the grave, because in
him [o]there is found some good thing toward the LORD God of
14 Israel in the house of Jeroboam. [p]Moreover the LORD shall
raise him up a king over Israel, who shall cut off the house of
15 Jeroboam that day: but what? even now. For the LORD shall
smite Israel, as a reed is shaken in the water, and he shall
[q]root up Israel out of this [r]good land, which he gave to their
fathers, and shall scatter them [s]beyond the river, [t]because they
16 have made their groves, provoking the LORD to anger. And he
shall give Israel up because of the sins of Jeroboam, [u]who did
17 sin, and who made Israel to sin. ¶ And Jeroboam's wife arose,
and departed, and came to [x]Tirzah: and [v]when she came to the

Marginal references:
[h] Neh. 9. 26.
Ps. 50. 17.
[i] ch. 15. 29.
[k] ch. 21. 21.
[l] Deut. 32.36.
2 Kin. 14. 26.

[m] ch. 16. 4.
& 21. 24.

[n] ver. 17.

[o] 2 Chr. 12. 12.
& 19. 3.
[p] ch. 15. 27,
28, 29.
[q] Ps. 52. 5.
[r] Josh. 23.
15, 16.
[s] 2 Kin. 17. 23.
[t] Deut. 12.
3, 4.
[u] ch. 12. 30.
& 13. 34.
[x] ch. 16. 6,
8, 15, 23.
[v] ver. 12.

---

10. All the males of the family of Jeroboam were put to death by Baasha (xv.
28, 29). The phrase "will cut off," &c.,
appears to have been a common expression
among the Jews from the time of David
(1 Sam. xxv. 22) to that of Jehu (2 K. ix.
8), but scarcely either before or after. We
may suspect that, where the author of
Kings uses it, he found it in the documents
which he consulted.

him that is shut up and left in Israel]
See marg. ref. note.

and will take away the remnant, &c.] The
idea is, that the whole family is to be
cleared away at once, as men clear away
ordure or any vile refuse.

11. The dogs are the chief scavengers of
Oriental cities (cp. Ps. lix. 6, 14). And
the vulture is the chief scavenger in the
country districts, assisted sometimes by
kites and crows (see Job xxxix. 27-30,
where the vulture, not the eagle, is intended). Vultures are very abundant in
Palestine.

13. The child was evidently a prince of
some promise. It is probable that he was
heir to the throne.

14. The Hebrew text of this verse appears
to be defective in this place. No satisfactory
sense can be obtained from it. The true
meaning of the original passage is possibly:
—"Jehovah shall raise up a king who will
destroy the house of Jeroboam on the day
that he is raised up. What do I say? He
will destroy it even now."

15. The general prophecy of Moses (Deut.
xxix. 28), that the disobedient Israelites
would be rooted up out of their land, and
cast into another land, is here for the first

time repeated, and is definitively applied
to the ten tribes, which are to be removed
"beyond the river" (the Euphrates, iv. 21,
24), and "scattered." On the fulfilment of
this prophecy, and especially on the *scattering* of the ten tribes, see 2 K. xvii. 6
note.

groves] See Ex. xxxiv. 13 note. The grove-
(or, *asherah-*) worship, adopted from the
Canaanitish nations, appears to have died
away after the fierce onslaught which
Gideon made upon it (Judg. vi. 25-31). It
now revived, and became one of the most
popular of the idolatries both in Israel and
Judah (*v.* 23, and cp. marg. reff.).

17. Jeroboam had by this time removed
from Shechem, and established a new capital in Tirzah, one of the old Canaanite
towns (Josh. xii. 24)—a town of great reputation for beauty, counted in that respect
on a par with Jerusalem (Cant. vi. 4).
Tirzah is perhaps to be identified with *Tel-
luzah*, a place in the mountains about
9 miles distant from Shechem (Nablous) [or
with Teiâsîr (Conder)]. It may have been
the palatial residence of the kings rather
than the actual capital of the country. It remained the capital till Omri built Samaria
(xvi. 23, 24). Towards the close of the
kingdom it appears again as the city of
Menahem, who murdered Shallum and succeeded him (2 K. xv. 14).

the threshold of the door] Lit., "the
threshold of the house." Cp. the prophecy
(*v.* 12). The child actually died as she
crossed the threshold of the palace. Probably the palace, like that of Sargon at
Khorsabad, lay at the outer edge of the
town.

z ver. 13.

a 2 Chr. 13.
2, &c.

b 2Chr.12.13.

c ch. 11. 36.

d ver. 31.
e 2 Chr. 12. 1.
f Deut.32.21.
Ps. 78. 58.
1 Cor. 10. 22.
g Deut. 12. 2.
h 2 Kin. 17.
9, 10.
i Isai. 57. 5.
k Deut.23.17.
ch. 15. 12.
& 22. 46.
2 Kin. 23. 7.
l ch. 11. 40.
2 Chr. 12. 2.
m 2 Chr. 12.
9, 10, 11.

18 threshold of the door, the child died; and they buried him; and all Israel mourned for him, ᶻaccording to the word of the LORD, which he spake by the hand of his servant Ahijah the prophet. 19 ¶ And the rest of the acts of Jeroboam, how he ᵃwarred, and how he reigned, behold, they *are* written in the book of the 20 chronicles of the kings of Israel. And the days which Jeroboam reigned *were* two and twenty years: and he ¹slept with his 21 fathers, and Nadab his son reigned in his stead. ¶ And Rehoboam the son of Solomon reigned in Judah. ᵇRehoboam *was* forty and one years old when he began to reign, and he reigned seventeen years in Jerusalem, the city ᶜwhich the LORD did choose out of all the tribes of Israel, to put his name there. 22 ᵈAnd his mother's name *was* Naamah an Ammonitess. ¶ ᵉAnd Judah did evil in the sight of the LORD, and they ᶠprovoked him to jealousy with their sins which they had committed, 23 above all that their fathers had done. For they also built them ᵍhigh places, and ²images, ʰand groves, on every high hill, and 24 ⁱunder every green tree. ᵏAnd there were also sodomites in the land: *and* they did according to all the abominations of the nations which the LORD cast out before the children of Israel. 25 ¶ ˡAnd it came to pass in the fifth year of king Rehoboam, *that* 26 Shishak king of Egypt came up against Jerusalem: ᵐand he took away the treasures of the house of the LORD, and the trea-

¹ Heb. *lay down.*   ² Or, *standing images,* or, *statues.*

---

19. The wars of Jeroboam may be divided into—(1) his wars with Rehoboam (see *vv.* 25, 30); and (2) his war with Abijam (see marg. ref.).

the book of the chronicles of the kings of Israel...(of Judah, v. 29)] See the Introduction, p. 265.

21. On the age of Rehoboam at his accession, see xii. 8 note. The seventeen years of his reign must have been complete, or a little more than complete, if Abijam ascended the throne in the "eighteenth" year of Jeroboam (xv. 1).

22. This defection of Judah did not take place till Rehoboam's fourth year (marg. ref.).

they provoked him to jealousy] Cp. Ex. xx. 5; and on the force of the metaphor involved in the word, see Ex. xxxiv. 15 note.

23. The words "they also" are emphatic. Not only did the Israelites make themselves high places (xii. 31, xiii. 32), but the people of Judah also. The "high places," which are said to have been "built," were probably small shrines or tabernacles hung with bright-coloured tapestry (Ezek. xvi. 16), like the "sacred tent" of the Carthaginians.

The "images" were rather "pillars" (Gen. xxviii. 18 note).

groves] See *v.* 15, note. The "groves," it will be observed, were *built* on high hills and *under green trees.*

under every green tree] *i.e.* under all those remarkable trees which, standing singly about the land, were landmarks to their respective neighbourhoods, and places of re-

sort to travellers, who gladly rested under their shade (Deut. xii. 2).

24. *sodomites*] Literally, "(men) consecrated." The men in question were in fact "consecrated" to the mother of the gods, the famous "Dea Syra," whose priests, or rather devotees, they were considered to be. The nature of the ancient idolatries is best understood by recollecting that persons of this degraded class practised their abominable trade under a religious sanction.

25. The examination of the famous inscription of Shishak at Karnak has resulted in the proof that the expedition commemorated was directed against Palestine, and has further thrown a good deal of light on the relations of the two kingdoms at the period. Of the fifteen fenced cities fortified by Rehoboam in the early part of his reign (2 Chr. xi. 5-12), three, Shoco, Adoraim, and Aijalon are distinctly mentioned among Shishak's conquests. Other towns of Judah or Benjamin also occur. Further a considerable number of the captured cities are in the territory of Jeroboam : these cities *are either Canaanite or Levitical.* Hence we gather, that, during the four years which immediately followed the separation of the kingdoms, Rehoboam retained a powerful hold on the dominions of his rival, many Canaanite and Levitical towns acknowledging his sovereignty, and maintaining themselves against Jeroboam, who probably called in Shishak mainly to assist him in compelling these cities to submission. The campaign was completely successful.

26. The circumstances of Shishak's inva-

sures of the king's house; he even took away all: and he took
27 away all the shields of gold [n]which Solomon had made. And
king Rehoboam made in their stead brasen shields, and committed *them* unto the hands of the chief of the [1]guard, which
28 kept the door of the king's house. And it was *so*, when the king
went into the house of the LORD, that the guard bare them, and
29 brought them back into the guard chamber. ¶ [o]Now the rest of
the acts of Rehoboam, and all that he did, *are* they not written
30 in the book of the chronicles of the kings of Judah? And there
31 was [p]war between Rehoboam and Jeroboam all *their* days. [q]And
Rehoboam slept with his fathers, and was buried with his fathers
in the city of David. [r]And his mother's name *was* Naamah an
Ammonitess. And [s]Abijam his son reigned in his stead.

CHAP. 15. NOW [a]in the eighteenth year of king Jeroboam the son
2 of Nebat reigned Abijam over Judah. Three years reigned he in
Jerusalem. [b]And his mother's name *was* [c]Maachah, the daugh-
3 ter of [d]Abishalom. And he walked in all the sins of his father,
which he had done before him: and [e]his heart was not perfect
4 with the LORD his God, as the heart of David his father. Nevertheless [f]for David's sake did the LORD his God give him a [2]lamp
in Jerusalem, to set up his son after him, and to establish Jeru-

[n] ch. 10. 17.
[o] 2Chr. 12. 15.
[p] ch. 12. 24. & 15. 6. 2 Chr. 12. 15.
[q] 2Chr. 12. 16.
[r] ver. 21.
[s] 2 Chr. 12. 16, *Abijah*. Matt. 1. 7, *Abia*.
[a] 2 Chr. 13. 1, 2.
[b] 2 Chr. 11. 20, 21, 22.
[c] 2 Chr. 13. 2, *Michaiah the daughter of Uriel*.
[d] 2 Chr. 11. 21, *Absalom*.
[e] ch. 11. 4. Ps. 119. 80.
[f] ch. 11. 32, 36. 2 Chr. 21. 7.

[1] Heb. *runners*.
[2] Or, *candle*, ch. 11. 36.

---

sion, related here with extreme brevity, are given with some fulness by the author of Chronicles (marg. ref.). It is still a question whether the submission of the Jewish king is or is not expressly recorded in the Karnak inscription. Midway in the list of cities and tribes occurs the entry "YUDeH-MALK" which it has been proposed to translate "Judah, king." Others regard it as the name of a Palestinian town not otherwise known to us.

28. It appears from this verse that Rehoboam, notwithstanding that he encouraged, and perhaps secretly practised, idolatry (*vv.* 22–24, cp. xv. 3, 12; 2 Chr. xii. 1), maintained a public profession of faith in Jehovah, and attended in state the Temple services. Cp. the conduct of Solomon, ix. 25.

31. *slept with his fathers and was buried,* &c.] Cp. xi. 43. The expression is a sort of formula, and is used with respect to all the kings of Judah, except two or three. The writer probably regards the fact, which he records so carefully, as a continuation of God's mercy to David.

his mother's name, &c.] The mention of the queen-mother so regularly in the account of the kings of Judah is thought to indicate that she had an important position in the state. There are, however, only two instances where such a person seems to have exercised any power (xv. 13; 2 K. xi. 1–20).

Abijam] Abijah (see marg. ref.) was probably his real name, while Abijam is a form due to the religious feeling of the Jews, who would not allow the word JAH to be retained as an element in the name of so bad a king. Instances of a similar feeling are the change of Beth-*el* into Beth-*aven* in Hosea (iv. 15), and perhaps of Jehoahaz into Ahaz (2 K. xv. 38 note).

XV. **2.** *Three years*] More strictly, not much more than two years (cp. *vv.* 1, 9). Any part of a year may, however, in Jewish reckoning, be taken as a year.

his mother's name was Maachah] Or Michaiah, according to the present reading of marg. ref.

the daughter of Abishalom] Absalom seems to have had but one daughter, Tamar (2 Sam. xiv. 27), so that Maachah must have been, not his daughter, but his grand-daughter. Her father (see marg.) was Uriel of Gibeah whom, therefore, Tamar married. Maachah took her name from her great-grandmother (2 Sam. iii. 3).

3. *he walked in all the sins of his father*] Yet Abijam prepared precious offerings for the Temple service (*v.* 15), probably to replace vessels which Shishak had carried off, and in his war with Jeroboam professed himself a faithful servant of Jehovah (2 Chr. xiii. 10–12).

4. *to set up his son*] The idolatry of Abijam deserved the same punishment as that of Jeroboam (xiv. 10–14), of Baasha (xvi. 2–4), or of Zimri (xvi. 19), the cutting off of his seed, and the transfer of the crown to another family. That these consequences did not follow in the kingdom of Judah, was owing to the "faithfulness" of David (see marg. ref.), which brought a blessing on his posterity. Few things are more remarkable and more difficult to account for on mere grounds of human reason, than the stability of the succession in Judah, and its excessive instability in the sister kingdom. One family in Judah holds the throne from first

g ch. 14. 8.

h 2 Sam. 11.
4, 15.
& 12. 9.
i ch. 14. 30.
k 2 Chr. 13.
2—22.

l 2 Chr. 14. 1.

m 2 Chr. 14.
2.

n ch. 14. 24.
& 22. 46.
o 2Chr.15.16.

p So Ex. 32.
20.
q ch. 22. 43.
2 Chr. 15.
17, 18.
r See ver. 3.

5 salem : because David *did *that which was* right in the eyes of
the LORD, and turned not aside from any *thing* that he commanded him all the days of his life, *save only in the matter of
6 Uriah the Hittite. *And there was war between Rehoboam and
7 Jeroboam all the days of his life. ¶*Now the rest of the acts
of Abijam, and all that he did, *are* they not written in the book
of the chronicles of the kings of Judah? And there was war
8 between Abijam and Jeroboam. *And Abijam slept with his
fathers ; and they buried him in the city of David : and Asa his
9 son reigned in his stead. ¶And in the twentieth year of Jero-
10 boam king of Israel reigned Asa over Judah. And forty and
one years reigned he in Jerusalem. And his ¹mother's name
11 *was* Maachah, the daughter of Abishalom. *And Asa did *that
which was* right in the eyes of the LORD, as *did* David his father.
12 *And he took away the sodomites out of the land, and removed
13 all the idols that his fathers had made. And also *Maachah his
mother, even her he removed from *being* queen, because she had
made an idol in a grove ; and Asa ²destroyed her idol, and
14 *burnt *it* by the brook Kidron. *But the high places were not
removed : nevertheless Asa's *heart was perfect with the LORD
15 all his days. And he brought in the ³things which his father
had dedicated, and the things which himself had dedicated, into
16 the house of the LORD, silver, and gold, and vessels. ¶And
there was war between Asa and Baasha king of Israel all their

---

¹ That is, *grandmother's,* ver. 2.   ² Heb. *cut off.*   ³ Heb. *holy.*

---

to last, during a space but little short of
four centuries, while in Israel there are nine
changes of dynasty within two hundred and
fifty years.

6. The writer repeats what he had said
in xiv. 30, in order to remind the reader
that Abijam inherited this war from his
father. Abijam's war is described in marg.
ref. That the author of Kings gives none of
its details is agreeable to his common practice
in mere military matters. Thus he gives no
details of Shishak's expedition, and omits
Zerah's expedition altogether.

10. *mother's name*] Rather, *grandmother's.*
The Jews call any male ancestor, however
remote, a father, and any female ancestor
a mother (cp. *v.* 2 ; Gen. iii. 20). This
Maachah was the favourite wife of Rehoboam
(2 Chr. xi. 21), and the mother of Abijam.
The way in which she is here mentioned
strongly favours the notion that the position
of queen-mother was a definite one at the
court, and could only be held by one person
at a time.

13. Asa degraded Maachah from the rank
and state of queen-mother.

The word translated "idol" both here
and in the parallel passage (marg. ref.),
does not occur elsewhere in Scripture. It is
derived from a root signifying "fear" or
"trembling," and may perhaps best be understood as "a fright, a horror." Such a
name would seem best to apply to a grotesque and hideous image like the Phthah of
the Egyptians. She made it to serve in lieu
of the ordinary "grove" (*asherah*), or

idolatrous emblem of Astarte (Ex. xxxiv.
13 note). Asa cut it down, for like the
usual *asherah,* Maachah's "horror" was
fixed in the ground.

and burnt it at the brook Kidron] Similarly Josiah, when he removed Manasseh's
"grove" (*asherah*) from the house of the
Lord, brought it out to the brook Kidron,
and burnt it there. The object probably
was to prevent the pollution of the holy
city by even the ashes from the burning.

14. 2 Chr. xiv. 3 would seem at first sight
to imply that he entirely put down the worship. But idolatry, if at one time put
down, crept back afterwards ; or while Asa
endeavoured to sweep it wholly away, his
subjects would not be controlled, but found
a means of maintaining it in some places—
not perhaps in the cities (see 2 Chr. xiv. 5),
but in remote country districts, where the
royal authority was weaker, and secrecy
more practicable.

15. Abijam's dedications were made
after his victory over Jeroboam, and probably consisted of a portion of the spoils
which were the fruit of the battle (2 Chr.
xiii. 16–19).

Asa's dedications may have been made
from the spoils of Zerah the Ethiopian, who
attacked him in his eleventh year (2 Chr.
xiv. 9, &c.). They were not deposited in
the temple till his fifteenth year (2 Chr. xv.
10, 18).

16. Baasha became king of Israel in the
third year of Asa (*v.* 33). The petty warfare which ordinarily prevailed on the bor-

17 days. And *Baasha king of Israel went up against Judah, and
built ᵗRamah, ᵘthat he might not suffer any to go out or come
18 in to Asa king of Judah. Then Asa took all the silver and
the gold *that were* left in the treasures of the house of the LORD,
and the treasures of the king's house, and delivered them into
the hand of his servants: and king Asa sent them to ˣBen-
hadad, the son of Tabrimon, the son of Hezion, king of Syria,
19 that dwelt at ʸDamascus, saying, *There is* a league between me
and thee, *and* between my father and thy father: behold, I have
sent unto thee a present of silver and gold; come and break thy
league with Baasha king of Israel, that he may ¹depart from me.
20 So Ben-hadad hearkened unto king Asa, and sent the captains
of the hosts which he had against the cities of Israel, and smote
ᶻIjon, and ᵃDan, and ᵇAbel-beth-maachah, and all Cinneroth,
21 with all the land of Naphtali. And it came to pass, when
Baasha heard *thereof*, that he left off building of Ramah, and
22 dwelt in Tirzah. ᶜThen king Asa made a proclamation throughout all Judah; none *was* ²exempted: and they took away the
stones of Ramah, and the timber thereof, wherewith Baasha had
builded; and king Asa built with them ᵈGeba of Benjamin, and

*2 Chr. 16.
1, &c.
ᵗ Josh.18.25.
ᵘ See ch. 12.
27.

ˣ2 Chr. 16.2.

ʸ ch. 11. 23,
24.

*2Kin.15.29.
ᵃ Judg. 18.
29.
ᵇ 2 Sam. 20.
14.
ᶜ 2 Chr. 16.6.

ᵈ Josh. 21.
17.

¹ Heb. *go up*.　　　² Heb. *free*.

ders of the two kingdoms continued "all
the days" of Asa and Baasha. During the
first ten years of Asa's reign he was little
molested (2 Chr. xiv. 1, 6).

17. Ramah (perhaps *Er-Ram; marg. ref.)
was situated halfway between Bethel and
Jerusalem. Its distance from Jerusalem
was no more than five miles, so that its
occupation was a menace to that capital.
Baasha's seizure of Ramah implies a previous recovery of the towns taken by
Abijam from Jeroboam, viz., Bethel, Jeshanah, and Ephrain (2 Chr. xiii. 19), and
was a carrying of the war into the enemy's country. Could his conquest have
been maintained, it would have crippled
Judah seriously, and have almost compelled
a transfer of the capital to Hebron.

*that he might not suffer any to go out or
come in*] Baasha, in seizing Ramah, professed to be acting on the defensive. His
complaint seems to have been well founded
(cp. 2 Chr. xv. 9); but it was more than a defensive measure—it was the first step towards a conquest of the southern kingdom.

18. *left*] Or, according to another reading, "found." The wealthy condition of
the Temple treasury is sufficiently indicated
in *v.* 15. Cp. 2 Chr. xv. 18.

Asa's conduct in calling Benhadad to his
aid, condemned by the seer Hanani (2 Chr.
xvi. 7), cannot, of course, be justified; but
there was much to excuse it. An alliance,
it appears, had existed between Abijam and
Tabrimon, Benhadad's father (*v.* 19)—an
alliance which may have helped Abijam to
gain his great victory over Jeroboam and
achieve his subsequent conquests (2 Chr.
xiii. 17-20). This had been brought to an
end by Baasha, who had succeeded in in-

ducing Benhadad to enter into a league
with him. It was only natural that Asa
should endeavour to break up this league;
and, politically speaking, he had a full right
to go further, and obtain, if he could, the
support of the Syrian troops for himself.
The Israelites had set the example of calling in a foreign power, when Jeroboam obtained the aid of Shishak.

to Benhadad] On the probable succession
of the Damascene kings, and on the meaning of the name Hadad, see xi. 14, 23.

19. Rather, "Let there be a league between me and thee, as there was between
my father and thy father."

20. Ijon is probably marked by the ruins
called *Tel-Dibbin*, which are situated a few
miles north-west of the site of Dan, in a
fertile and beautiful little plain which bears
the name of *Merj 'Ayûn* or "meadow of
fountains." On Abel-beth-maachah, or
Abel-maim ("Abel-on-the waters") and
Dan, see marg. reff.

For Cinneroth or Genesareth see Josh.
xi. 2.

22. Geba, situated opposite to Michmash
(1 Sam. xiv. 5), is almost certainly *Jeba*,
which stands picturesquely on the top of
its steep terraced hill on the very edge
of the *Wady Suweinit*. Its position was thus
exceedingly strong; and, as it lay further
north than Ramah, Asa may have considered that to fortify and garrison it would
be a better protection to his northern frontier than fortifying Ramah.

For Mizpah see marg. ref. From Jer.
xli. 9 we learn that Asa, besides fortifying
the place, sank a deep well there to secure
his garrison from want of water if the town
should be besieged.

e Josh.18.26.

f 2Chr.16.12.

g 2 Chr. 17.1.
h Matt. 1. 8,
called
Josaphat.

i ch. 12. 30.
& 14. 16.
k ch. 14. 14.
l Josh. 19.44.
& 21. 23.
ch. 16. 15.

m ch. 14. 10,
14.
n ch. 14.9,16.

23 *e* Mizpah. The rest of all the acts of Asa, and all his might, and all that he did, and the cities which he built, *are* they not written in the book of the chronicles of the kings of Judah? 24 Nevertheless *f* in the time of his old age he was diseased in his feet. And Asa slept with his fathers, and was buried with his fathers in the city of David his father: *g* and *h* Jehoshaphat his 25 son reigned in his stead. ¶ And Nadab the son of Jeroboam 1 began to reign over Israel in the second year of Asa king of 26 Judah, and reigned over Israel two years. And he did evil in the sight of the LORD, and walked in the way of his father, and 27 in *i* his sin wherewith he made Israel to sin. ¶ *k* And Baasha the son of Ahijah, of the house of Issachar, conspired against him; and Baasha smote him at *l* Gibbethon, which *belonged* to the Philistines; for Nadab and all Israel laid siege to Gibbethon. 28 Even in the third year of Asa king of Judah did Baasha slay 29 him, and reigned in his stead. And it came to pass, when he reigned, *that* he smote all the house of Jeroboam; he left not to Jeroboam any that breathed, until he had destroyed him, according unto *m* the saying of the LORD, which he spake by his 30 servant Ahijah the Shilonite: *n* because of the sins of Jeroboam which he sinned, and which he made Israel sin, by his provocation wherewith he provoked the LORD God of Israel to anger.

1 Heb. *reigned.*

---

23. *The rest of all the acts of Asa*] A few of these are preserved in 2 Chr. xv. 9-15, xvi. 7-12. From the whole narrative of Chronicles we gather that the character of Asa deteriorated as he grew old, and that, while he maintained the worship of Jehovah consistently from first to last, he failed to maintain the personal faith and piety which had been so conspicuous in his early youth.

the cities which he built] Asa, during the earlier part of his reign, before any serious attack had been made upon him, had the prudence to "build fenced cities in Judah," with "walls and towers, gates and bars," so strengthening himself against a possible evil day (2 Chr. xiv. 6, 7).

in the time of his old age] See marg. ref. If it has been rightly supposed that Rehoboam was a young man of twenty-one or twenty-two at his accession (xii. 8), Asa's age at this time must have been less than fifty. It may seem strange to speak of "old age" in such a case; but Solomon was regarded as "old" at about fifty (xi. 4 note).

24. Asa prepared his own sepulchre in his lifetime, as has been so often done by Oriental kings; and his funeral was conducted with great magnificence (2 Chr. xvi. 14).

25. The sacred historian now gives an account of the contemporary kings of Israel, beginning with Nadab, who ascended the throne in Asa's second year, and concluding with Ahab, in whose fourth year Asa died. This narrative occupies him almost to the close of the first Book of Kings.

CHRONOLOGY.

Year of the divided Kingdom.	Kings of Judah.	Years of Reign.	Kings of Israel.	Years of Reign.
1	REHOBOAM	17	JEROBOAM	22
5	(Invasion of Shishak).			
18	ABIJAM .	3		
20	ASA . .	41		
22	. .		NADAB .	2
23	. .		BAASHA .	24
31	(Invasion of Zerah).			
34	(Great feast at Jerusalem).			
46	. .		ELAH .	2
47	. .		{ ZIMRI .} { OMRI .}	12
53	. .		AHAB .	22
61	(Last year of Asa).		(4th year of AHAB).	

27. *Baasha...of the house of Issachar*] It is curious to find Issachar furnishing a king. Tola, its one very undistinguished Judge (Judg. x. 1), on obtaining office had at once settled himself in the territory of Ephraim. The tribe was as little famous as any that could be named. The "ass crouching between two burthens" was a true symbol of the patient, plodding cultivators of the plain of Esdraelon (Gen. xlix. 14,15). Baasha probably owed his rise neither to his tribe nor to his social position, but simply to his audacity, and his known valour and skill as a soldier (xvi. 2).

31 ¶ Now the rest of the acts of Nadab, and all that he did, *are*
they not written in the book of the chronicles of the kings of
32 Israel ? °And there was war between Asa and Baasha king of
33 Israel all their days. ¶ In the third year of Asa king of Judah
began Baasha the son of Ahijah to reign over all Israel in
34 Tirzah, twenty and four years. And he did evil in the sight of
the LORD, and walked in *p*the way of Jeroboam, and in his sin
wherewith he made Israel to sin.
CHAP. 16. THEN the word of the LORD came to *a*Jehu the son of
2 Hanani against Baasha, saying, *b*Forasmuch as I exalted thee
out of the dust, and made thee prince over my people Israel ;
and *c*thou hast walked in the way of Jeroboam, and hast made
my people Israel to sin, to provoke me to anger with their sins;
3 behold, I will *d*take away the posterity of Baasha, and the
posterity of his house ; and will make thy house like *e*the house
4 of Jeroboam the son of Nebat. *f*Him that dieth of Baasha in
the city shall the dogs eat ; and him that dieth of his in the
5 fields shall the fowls of the air eat. ¶ Now the rest of the acts
of Baasha, and what he did, and his might, *g*are they not written
6 in the book of the chronicles of the kings of Israel ? So Baasha
slept with his fathers, and was buried in *h*Tirzah : and Elah his
7 son reigned in his stead. ¶ And also by the hand of the prophet
*i*Jehu the son of Hanani came the word of the LORD against
Baasha, and against his house, even for all the evil that he did
in the sight of the LORD, in provoking him to anger with the
work of his hands, in being like the house of Jeroboam ; and
8 because *k*he killed him. ¶ In the twenty and sixth year of Asa
king of Judah began Elah the son of Baasha to reign over Israel
9 in Tirzah, two years. *l*And his servant Zimri, captain of half
his chariots, conspired against him, as he was in Tirzah, drinking himself drunk in the house of Arza *l*steward of *his* house in

o ver. 16.

p ch. 12. 28,
29.
& 13. 33.
& 14. 16.
a ver. 7.
2 Chr. 19. 2.
& 20. 34.
b ch. 14. 7.
c ch. 15. 34.
d ver. 11.
e ch. 14. 10.
& 15. 29.
f ch. 14. 11.

g 2 Chr. 16.1.

h ch. 14. 17.
& 15. 21.
i ver. 1.

k ch. 15. 27,
29.
See Hos.
1. 4.
l 2 Kin. 9.31.

¹ Heb. *which* was *over.*

---

32. An exact repetition of *v.* 16. From
the book before him (*v.* 31) the writer extracts a passage which happens to correspond exactly with one which he has already extracted from the "Book of the
chronicles of the kings of Judah." He does
not object to repeating himself (cp. xiv. 21
and 31, xiv. 30 and xv. 6 ; 2 K. xvii. 6 and
xviii. 11).

XVI. 1. Hanani, the father of Jehu, was
seer to Asa in the kingdom of Judah (2 Chr.
xvi. 7-10). His son Jehu, who here dis-
charges the same office in the kingdom of
Israel, appears at a later date as an inhabitant of Jerusalem, where he prophesied under
Jehoshaphat, whom he rebuked on one occasion. He must have lived to a great age;
for he outlived Jehoshaphat, and wrote his
life (marg. reff.).

5. The "might" of Baasha is sufficiently
indicated by those successes which drove
Asa to call Ben-hadad to his aid. (xv. 17-21).

7. The natural position of this verse
would be after *v.* 4 and before *v.* 5. But it
may be regarded as added by the writer,
somewhat irregularly, as an afterthought;
its special force being to point out that the
sentence on Baasha was intended to punish,

not only his calf-worship, but emphatically
his murder of Jeroboam and his family.
Though the destruction of Jeroboam had
been foretold, and though Baasha may be
rightly regarded as God's instrument to
punish Jeroboam's sins, yet, as he received
no command to execute God's wrath on the
offender, and was instigated solely by ambition and self-interest, his guilt was just as
great as if no prophecy had been uttered.
Even Jehu's commission (2 K. ix. 5-10) was
not held to justify, altogether, his murder
of Jehoram and Jezebel.

8. *two years*] *i.e.* More than one year,
or, at any rate, some portion of two distinct
years (cp. *v.* 10).

9. The conspiracy of Zimri—Elah's "servant" (*i.e.* " subject ")—was favoured by his
position, which probably gave him military
authority in the city, by the absence of a
great part of the people and of the officers
who might have checked him, at Gibbethon
(*v.* 15), and by the despicable character of
Elah, who, instead of going up to the war,
was continually reminding men of his low
origin by conduct unworthy of royalty.

steward] The office was evidently one of
considerable importance. In Solomon's

10 Tirzah. And Zimri went in and smote him, and killed him, in the twenty and seventh year of Asa king of Judah, and reigned
11 in his stead. ¶ And it came to pass, when he began to reign, as soon as he sat on his throne, *that* he slew all the house of

m 1 Sam. 25. 22.

Baasha : he left him *m*not one that pisseth against a wall,
12 ¹neither of his kinsfolks, nor of his friends. Thus did Zimri

n ver. 3.
o ver. 1.

destroy all the house of Baasha, *n*according to the word of the LORD, which he spake against Baasha ²*o*by Jehu the prophet,
13 for all the sins of Baasha, and the sins of Elah his son, by which they sinned, and by which they made Israel to sin, in provoking

p Deut. 32. 21.
1 Sam.12.21.
Isai. 41. 29.
Jonah 2. 8.
1 Cor. 8. 4.
& 10. 19.
q ch. 15. 27.

14 the LORD God of Israel to anger *p*with their vanities. Now the rest of the acts of Elah, and all that he did, *are* they not written in the book of the chronicles of the kings of Israel?
15 ¶ In the twenty and seventh year of Asa king of Judah did Zimri reign seven days in Tirzah. And the people *were* encamped
16 *q*against Gibbethon, which *belonged* to the Philistines. And the people *that were* encamped heard say, Zimri hath conspired, and hath also slain the king: wherefore all Israel made Omri, the
17 captain of the host, king over Israel that day in the camp. And Omri went up from Gibbethon, and all Israel with him, and they
18 besieged Tirzah. And it came to pass, when Zimri saw that the city was taken, that he went into the palace of the king's house,
19 and burnt the king's house over him with fire, and died, for his

r ch. 12. 28.
& 15. 26, 34.

sins which he sinned in doing evil in the sight of the LORD, *r*in walking in the way of Jeroboam, and in his sin which he did, to
20 make Israel to sin. Now the rest of the acts of Zimri, and his treason that he wrought, *are* they not written in the book of the
21 chronicles of the kings of Israel? ¶ Then were the people of Israel divided into two parts. half of the people followed Tibni the son of Ginath, to make him king; and half followed Omri.
22 But the people that followed Omri prevailed against the people

¹ Or, *both his kinsmen and his friends.*   ² Heb. *by the hand of.*

---

court it gave the rank of *sar*, or prince. In Persia the " steward of the household" acted sometimes as a sort of regent during the king's absence.

11. *neither of his kinsfolks, nor of his friends*] Zimri's measures were of much more than ordinary severity. Not only was the royal family extirpated, but the friends of the king, his councillors and favourite officers, were put to death. Omri, as having been in the confidence of the late monarch, would naturally fear for himself, and resolve to take the course which promised him at least a chance of safety.

13. *their vanities*] The "calves." The Hebrews call an idol by terms signifying "emptiness," "vapour," or "nothingness." (Cp. marg. reff.)

16. *all Israel made Omri, the captain of the host, king*] This passage of history recalls the favourite practice of the Roman armies under the Empire, which, when they heard of the assassination of an emperor at Rome, were wont to invest their own commander with the purple.

17. *went up*] The expression " went up " marks accurately the ascent of the army

from the Shephelah, where Gibbethon was situated (Josh. xix. 44), to the hill country of Israel, on the edge of which Tirzah stood (xiv. 17).

18. *the palace of the king's house*] The tower of the king's house. A particular part of the palace—either the *harem*, or, more probably, the keep or citadel, a tower stronger and loftier than the rest of the palace.

Zimri's desperate act has been repeated more than once. That the last king of Assyria, the Sardanapalus of the Greeks, thus destroyed himself, is almost the only *fact* which we know concerning him.

19. Zimri's death illustrates the general moral which the writer of Kings draws from the whole history of the Israelite monarchs, that a curse was upon them on account of their persistence in Jeroboam's sin, which, sooner or later, brought each royal house to a bloody end.

22. From a comparison of the dates given in *vv.* 15, 23, and 29 it follows that the contest between the two pretenders lasted four years.

Tibni's death can scarcely be supposed to

that followed Tibni the son of Ginath : so Tibni died, and Omri
23 reigned. ¶ In the thirty and first year of Asa king of Judah
began Omri to reign over Israel, twelve years : six years reigned
24 he in Tirzah. And he bought the hill Samaria of Shemer for
two talents of silver, and built on the hill, and called the name
of the city which he built, after the name of Shemer, owner of
25 the hill, ¹ˢSamaria. But ᵗOmri wrought evil in the eyes of the
26 LORD, and did worse than all that *were* before him. For he
ᵘwalked in all the way of Jeroboam the son of Nebat, and in
his sin wherewith he made Israel to sin, to provoke the LORD
27 God of Israel to anger with their ˣvanities. Now the rest of
the acts of Omri which he did, and his might that he shewed,
are they not written in the book of the chronicles of the kings
28 of Israel? So Omri slept with his fathers, and was buried in
29 Samaria : and Ahab his son reigned in his stead. ¶ And in the
thirty and eighth year of Asa king of Judah began Ahab the
son of Omri to reign over Israel : and Ahab the son of Omri
30 reigned over Israel in Samaria twenty and two years. And
Ahab the son of Omri did evil in the sight of the LORD above all

ˢ See ch. 13.
32.
2 Kin. 17.24.
John 4. 4.
ᵗ Mic. 6. 16.
ᵘ ver. 19.
ˣ ver. 13.

¹ Heb. *Shomeron.*

have been natural. Either he must have
been slain in battle against Omri, or have
fallen into his hands and been put to death.

There has probably been some derange-
ment of the text here. The passage may
have run thus :—"So Tibni died, and Omri
reigned in the thirty-first year of Asa, king
of Judah. Omri reigned over Israel twelve
years : six years reigned he in Tirzah."
Omri's reign of twelve years began in Asa's
27th (*vv.* 15 and 16), and terminated in his
38th (*v.* 29). The event belonging to Asa's
31st year was the death of Tibni, and the
consequent extension of Omri's kingdom.
The six years in Tirzah are probably made
up of the four years of contention with
Tibni, and two years afterwards, during
which enough of Samaria was built for the
king to transfer his residence there.

24. " Samaria" represents the Greek
form of the name (Σαμάρεια) ; the original is
Shomeron (marg.). The site is marked by the
modern *Sebustiyeh,* an Arabic corruption of
Sebaste, the name given by Herod to Samaria when he rebuilt it. Sebustiyeh is
situated on a very remarkable " hill." In
the heart of the mountains of Israel occurs
a deep basin-shaped depression, in the midst
of which rises an oblong hill, with steep but
not inaccessible sides, and a long flat top.
This was the site which Omri chose for his
new capital. Politically it was rather more
central than Shechem, and probably than
Tirzah. In a military point of view it was
admirably calculated for defence. The
country round it was peculiarly productive.
The hill itself possessed abundant springs of
water. The result is that we find no further
change. Shechem and Tirzah were each
tried and abandoned ; but through all the
later alterations of dynasty Samaria continued uninterruptedly, to the very close of

the independence, to be the capital of the
northern kingdom.

Omri *purchased* the right of property in
the hill, just as David purchased the threshing-floor (2 Sam. xxiv. 24; cp. 1 K. xxi. 2).
Two talents, or 6000 shekels (Ex. xxxviii.
24 note)—about 500*l.* (or perhaps 800*l.*) of our
money—may well have been the full value
of the ground. And while naming his city
after Shemer, Omri may also have had in
view the appropriateness of such a name
to the situation of the place. Shomeron,
to a Hebrew ear, would have necessarily
conveyed the idea of a " watch-tower."
This name, however, appears not to have
been at first accepted by the surrounding
nations. The earlier Assyrian kings knew
the Israelite capital, not as Samaria, but as
Beth-Khumri, *i.e.* "the city (house) of Omri."
It is not till the time of Tiglath-pileser that
they exchange this designation for that of
Sammirin.

25. Omri outwent his idolatrous predecessors in his zeal, reducing the calf-
worship to a regular formal system, which
went down to posterity (cp. marg. ref.)

27. *his might*] Perhaps in the war between
Israel and Syria of Damascus (xx. 1, &c.),
during the reign of Omri. Its issue was very
disadvantageous to him (xx. 34, xxii. 2).

29. *twenty and two years*] Rather, from a
comparison between xv. 10 and xxii. 51, not
more than 21 years. Perhaps his reign did
not much exceed 20 years.

30. See *v.* 33. The great sin of Ahab—
that by which he differed from all his predecessors, and exceeded them in wickedness—
was his introduction of the worship of Baal,
consequent upon his marriage with Jezebel,
and his formal establishment of this gross
and palpable idolatry as the religion of the
state.

31 that *were* before him. And it came to pass, ¹as if it had been a light thing for him to walk in the sins of Jeroboam the son of Nebat, ⁿthat he took to wife Jezebel the daughter of Ethbaal king of the ᶻZidonians, ᵃand went and served Baal, and worshipped him. 32 And he reared up an altar for Baal in ᵇthe house of Baal, which 33 he had built in Samaria. ᶜAnd Ahab made a grove ; and Ahab ᵈdid more to provoke the LORD God of Israel to anger than all 34 the kings of Israel that were before him. ¶ In his days did Hiel the Beth-elite build Jericho : he laid the foundation thereof in Abiram his firstborn, and set up the gates thereof in his youngest *son* Segub, ᵉaccording to the word of the LORD, which he spake by Joshua the son of Nun.

CHAP. 17. AND ²Elijah the Tishbite, *who was* of the inhabitants of Gilead, said unto Ahab, ᵃ*As* the LORD God of Israel liveth,

Margin references:
ʸ Deut. 7. 3.
ᶻ Judg. 18. 7.
ᵃ ch. 21. 25, 26.
2 Kin. 10. 18. & 17. 16.
ᵇ 2 Kin. 10. 21, 26, 27.
ᶜ 2 Kin. 13. 6. & 17. 10. & 21. 3.
Jer. 17. 2.
ᵈ ver. 30. ch. 21. 25.
ᵉ Josh. 6. 26.
ᵃ 2 Kin. 3. 14.

¹ Heb. *was it a light thing, &c.*

² Heb. *El·jahu.* Luke 1. 17. & 4. 25, he is called *El'as.*

31. *as if it had been a light thing for him to walk in the sins of Jeroboam*] Idolatries are not exclusive. Ahab, while he detested the pure worship of Jehovah, and allowed Jezebel to put to death every "prophet of the Lord" whom she could find (xviii. 4), readily tolerated the continued worship of the "calves," which had no doubt tended more and more to lose its symbolical character, and to become a thoroughly idolatrous image-worship.

Eth-baal] Identified with the Ithobalus of Menander, who reigned in Tyre, probably over all Phœnicia, within 50 years of the death of Hiram. This Ithobalus, whose name means "With him is Baal," was originally priest of the great temple of Astarte, in Tyre. At the age of 36 he conspired against the Tyrian king, Pheles (a usurping fratricide), slew him, and seized the throne. His reign lasted 32 years, and he established a dynasty which continued on the throne at least 62 years longer. The family-tree of the house may be thus exhibited :—

Eth-baal
|
Badezor   Jezebel
|
Matgen (Belus of Virgil)
|
Pygmalion   Dido (founder of Carthage).

Hence Jezebel was great-aunt to Pygmalion and his sister Dido.

served Baal] The worship of Baal by the Phœnicians is illustrated by such names as Itho*bal*, Hanni*bal*, &c. Abundant traces of it are found in the Phœnician monuments.

34. This seems to be adduced as a proof of the general impiety of Ahab's time. The curse of Joshua against the man who should rebuild Jericho had hitherto been believed and respected. But now faith in the old religion had so decayed, that Joshua's malediction had lost its power. Hiel, a Bethelite of wealth and station, undertook to restore the long-ruined fortress. But he suffered for his temerity. In exact accordance with the words of Joshua's curse, he lost his firstborn son when he began to lay anew the foundations of the walls, and his youngest when he completed his work by setting up the gates. We need not suppose that Jericho had been absolutely uninhabited up to this time. But it was a ruined and desolate place without the necessary protection of walls, and containing probably but few houses (Judg. iii. 13 note). Hiel re-established it as a city, and it soon became once more a place of some importance (2 Chr. xxviii. 15).

XVII. 1. The name Elijah means "Jehovah is my God." It is expressive of the truth which his whole life preached.

The two words rendered "Tishbite" and "inhabitant" are in the original (setting aside the vowel points) *exactly alike.* The meaning consequently must either be "Elijah the stranger, of the strangers of Gilead," or (more probably) "Elijah the Tishbite, of Tishbi of Gilead." Of Tishbi in Gilead there is no further trace in Scripture ; it is to be distinguished from another Tishbi in Galilee. In forming to ourselves a conception of the great Israelite Prophet, we must always bear in mind that the wild and mountainous Gilead, which bordered on Arabia, and was half Arab in customs, was the country wherein he grew up.

His abrupt appearance may be compared with the similar appearances of Ahijah (xi. 29), Jehu (xvi. 1), Shemaiah (2 Chr. xi. 2), Azariah (do. xv. 1), and others. It is clear that a succession of Prophets was raised up by God, both in faithful Judah and in idolatrous Israel, to witness of Him before the people of both countries, and leave them without excuse if they forsook His worship. At this time, when a grosser and more deadly idolatry than had been practised before was

*before whom I stand, *there shall not be dew nor rain *these
2 years, but according to my word. ¶And the word of the LORD
3 came unto him, saying, Get thee hence, and turn thee eastward,
and hide thyself by the brook Cherith, that *is* before Jordan.
4 And it shall be, *that* thou shalt drink of the brook ; and I have
5 commanded the ravens to feed thee there. So he went and did
according unto the word of the LORD : for he went and dwelt
6 by the brook Cherith, that *is* before Jordan. And the ravens
brought him bread and flesh in the morning, and bread and
7 flesh in the evening ; and he drank of the brook. And it came
to pass ¹after a while, that the brook dried up, because there had
8 been no rain in the land. ¶And the word of the LORD came
9 unto him, saying, Arise, get thee to *Zarephath, which *belongeth*
to Zidon, and dwell there : behold, I have commanded a widow
10 woman there to sustain thee. So he arose and went to Zarephath.
And when he came to the gate of the city, behold, the widow
woman *was* there gathering of sticks : and he called to her, and
said, Fetch me, I pray thee, a little water in a vessel, that I may
11 drink. And as she was going to fetch *it*, he called to her, and
said, Bring me, I pray thee, a morsel of bread in thine hand.
12 And she said, *As* the LORD thy God liveth, I have not a cake,
but an handful of meal in a barrel, and a little oil in a cruse :
and, behold, I *am* gathering two sticks, that I may go in and
13 dress it for me and my son, that we may eat it, and die. And
Elijah said unto her, Fear not ; go *and* do as thou hast said :
but make me thereof a little cake first, and bring *it* unto me,
14 and after make for thee and for thy son. For thus saith the
LORD God of Israel, The barrel of meal shall not waste, neither

Margin notes:
b Deut. 10. 8
c Jam. 5. 17.
d Luke 4. 25.
e Obad. 20.
Luke 4. 26,
called
Sarept.1.

¹ Heb. *at the end of days.*

introduced into Israel by the authority of
Ahab, and the total apostasy of the ten
tribes was consequently imminent, two
Prophets of unusual vigour and force of
character, endowed with miraculous powers
of an extraordinary kind, were successively
raised up, that the wickedness of the kings
might be boldly met and combated, and, if
possible, a remnant of faithful men preserved in the land. The unusual efflux of
miraculous energy at this time, is suitable to
the unusual emergency, and in very evident
proportion to the spiritual necessities of the
people.

as the LORD *God of Israel liveth, before
whom I stand*] This solemn formula, here
first used, was well adapted to impress the
king with the sacred character of the messenger, and the certain truth of his message.
Elisha adopted the phrase with very slight
modifications (2 K. iii. 14, v. 16).

Drought was one of the punishments
threatened by the Law, if Israel forsook
Jehovah and turned after other gods (Deut.
xi. 17, xxviii. 23 ; Lev. xxvi. 19, &c.).

3. *brook Cherith*] Rather, "the torrent
course," one of the many which carry the
winter rains from the highlands into that
stream.

4. *the ravens*] This is the translation of
most of the ancient Versions ; others, omit-

ting the points, which are generally allowed
to have no authority, .ead " Arabians ; "
others, retaining the present pointing,
translate either "merchants" (cp. the original of Ezek. xxvii. 9, 27), or "Orbites."
Jerome took it in this last sense, and so
does the Arabic Version.

9. The dependence of Zarephath (Sarepta)
on Sidon is indicated in the inscriptions
of Sennacherib, where it is mentioned as
belonging to Luliya (Elulæus), king of Sidon,
and as submitting to the Assyrian monarch
on Luliya's flight from his capital. Elijah
may have been sent to this place, so near
the city of Jezebel's father, as one which it
was most unlikely that he would visit.

12. *As the* LORD *thy God liveth*] The words
do not prove that the woman was an Israelite, or a worshipper of the true God ; any
Phœnician, recognising in Elijah's appearance the garb and manner of a Jehovistic
Prophet, might have thus addressed him :
Baal-worshippers would have admitted Jehovah to be *a* living God. The woman does
not say "as the Lord *my* God liveth."

that we may eat it and die] Phœnicia always depended for its cereal supplies on the
harvests of Palestine (v. 9 note) ; and it is
evident that the famine was afflicting the
Phœnicians at this time no less than the
Israelites.

shall the cruse of oil fail, until the day *that* the LORD [1]sendeth
15 rain upon the earth.   And she went and did according to the
saying of Elijah : and she, and he, and her house, did eat [2]*many*
16 days.   *And* the barrel of meal wasted not, neither did the cruse
of oil fail, according to the word of the LORD, which he spake
17 [3]by Elijah.   ¶ And it came to pass after these things, *that* the
son of the woman, the mistress of the house, fell sick ; and his
18 sickness was so sore, that there was no breath left in him.   And
she said unto Elijah, *f* What have I to do with thee, O thou man
of God ? art thou come unto me to call my sin to remembrance,
19 and to slay my son ?   And he said unto her, Give me thy son.
And he took him out of her bosom, and carried him up into a
20 loft, where he abode, and laid him upon his own bed.   And he
cried unto the LORD, and said, O LORD my God, hast thou also
brought evil upon the widow with whom I sojourn, by slaying
21 her son ?   [g] And he [4]stretched himself upon the child three times,
and cried unto the LORD, and said, O LORD my God, I pray
22 thee, let this child's soul come [5]into him again.   And the LORD
heard the voice of Elijah ; and the soul of the child came into
23 him again, and he [h]revived.   And Elijah took the child, and
brought him down out of the chamber into the house, and delivered him unto his mother : and Elijah said, See, thy son liveth.
24 And the woman said to Elijah, Now by this [i]I know that thou
art a man of God, *and* that the word of the LORD in thy mouth
is truth.

CHAP. 18.   AND it came to pass *after* [a]many days, that the word of
the LORD came to Elijah in the third year, saying, Go, shew thy-
2 self unto Ahab ; and [b]I will send rain upon the earth.   And
Elijah went to shew himself unto Ahab.   And *there was* a sore

Marginal references:
f See Luke 5. 8.
g 2 Kin. 4. 34, 35.
h Heb. 11. 35.
i John 3. 2. & 16. 30.
a Luke 4. 25. Jam. 5. 17.
b ch. 17. 1. Deut. 28. 12.

[1] Heb. *giveth.*
[2] Or, *a full year.*
[3] Heb. *by the hand of.*
[4] Heb. *measured.*
[5] Heb. *into his inward parts.*

---

16. This is the first recorded miracle of
its kind—a supernatural and inexplicable
multiplication of food (cp. 2 K. iv. 42
44 ; Matt. xiv. 15–21, xv. 32–38).   The
sacred record does not explain these miracles ; but if the explanations sometimes
suggested—that there was a transformation of previously existing matter into
meal, oil, fish, and bread—be the true
one, the marvel of the thing would not
be much greater than that astonishing
natural chemistry by which, in the growth
of plants, particles of water, air, and earth
are transmuted into fruits and grains of
corn, and so fitted to be human food.   There
would be a difference in the agency employed and in the time occupied in the
transmutation, but the thing done would
be almost the same.
17. *no breath*] Or, " no spirit," " no soul."
(Cp. Gen. ii. 7).   The word used is translated " spirit " in Prov. xx. 27 ; Eccles. iii.
21 ; Job xxvi. 4 ; and elsewhere.
18. *What have I to do with thee ?*] *i.e.*
" What have we in common ? "—implying a
further question, " Why hast thou not left
me in peace ? "   The woman imagines that
Elijah's visit had drawn God's attention to

her, and so to her sins, which (she feels) deserve a judgment—her son's death.
thou man of God] In the mouth of the
Phœnician woman this expression is remarkable.   Among the Jews and Israelites (xii.
22 ; Judg. xiii. 6, 8) it seems to have become the ordinary designation of a Prophet.
We now see that it was understood in the
same sense beyond the borders of the Holy
Land.
19. *into a loft*] Rather, " into the upper
chamber ; " often the best apartment in an
Eastern house.
21. *he stretched himself upon the child three
times*] This action of Elijah is different from
that of Elisha (marg. ref.), and does not
imply the use of any natural means for the
restoration of suspended animation.   It is
nearly parallel to the " touch," through
which our Lord wrought similar miracles
(Matt. ix. 25 ; Luke vii. 14).
XVIII. 1. *the third year*] *i.e.* in the third
year of his sojourn with the widow.   The
whole period of drought was three years and
a half (Luke iv. 25 ; Jam. v. 17) : of this,
probably about one year was passed by
Elijah in the torrent-course of Cherith, and
two years and a half at Sarepta.

3 famine in Samaria. ¶ And Ahab called [1]Obadiah, which was [2]the
governor of *his* house. (Now Obadiah feared the LORD greatly :
4 for it was *so*, when [3]Jezebel cut off the prophets of the LORD,
that Obadiah took an hundred prophets, and hid them by fifty
5 in a cave, and fed them with bread and water.) And Ahab said
unto Obadiah, Go into the land, unto all fountains of water,
and unto all brooks : peradventure we may find grass to save
the horses and mules alive, [4]that we lose not all the beasts.
6 So they divided the land between them to pass throughout it :
Ahab went one way by himself, and Obadiah went another way
7 by himself. ¶ And as Obadiah was in the way, behold, Elijah
met him : and he knew him, and fell on his face, and said, *Art*
8 thou that my lord Elijah ? And he answered him, I *am :* go,
9 tell thy lord, Behold, Elijah *is here.* And he said, What have
I sinned, that thou wouldest deliver thy servant into the hand of
10 Ahab, to slay me ? *As* the LORD thy God liveth, there is no
nation or kingdom, whither my lord hath not sent to seek thee :
and when they said, *He is* not *there;* he took an oath of the
11 kingdom and nation, that they found thee not. And now thou
12 sayest, Go, tell thy lord, Behold, Elijah *is here.* And it shall
come to pass, *as soon as* I am gone from thee, that *c*the Spirit of
the LORD shall carry thee whither I know not; and *so* when I
come and tell Ahab, and he cannot find thee, he shall slay me :
13 but I thy servant fear the LORD from my youth. Was it not
told my lord what I did when Jezebel slew the prophets of the
LORD, how I hid an hundred men of the LORD'S prophets by
14 fifty in a cave, and fed them with bread and water ? And now
thou sayest, Go, tell thy lord, Behold, Elijah *is here :* and he
15 shall slay me. And Elijah said, *As* the LORD of hosts liveth,
before whom I stand, I will surely shew myself unto him to day.
16 ¶ So Obadiah went to meet Ahab, and told him : and Ahab went

c 2 Kin. 2. 16.
Ezek. 3.
12, 14.
Matt. 4. 1.
Acts 8. 39.

---

[1] Heb. *Obadiahu.*
[2] Heb. *over* his *house.*
[3] Heb. *Izebel.*
[4] Heb. *that we cut not off*
ourselves *from the beasts.*

---

3. Obadiah's name, "servant of Jehovah,"
indicates his religious character. It corresponds to the modern Arabic name Abdallah.
Ahab could scarcely have been ignorant of
Obadiah's faithfulness to Jehovah ; and it
tells in favour of the monarch's tolerance
that he should have maintained an adherent
of the old religion in so important an
office. There seems to be no doubt that
the worst deeds of Ahab's reign sprang less
from his own free will and natural disposition than from the evil counsels, or rather
perhaps the imperious requirements, of his
wife.

4. We have no details of Jezebel's deed
of blood. Some have conjectured that it
was the answer of Jezebel to Elijah's threat,
and that the command given him to hide
in Cherith alone saved him from being one
of the victims. This view receives some
support from Obadiah's act and words (*v.*
13).

fifty in a cave] The limestone formation of
Judæa and Samaria abounds with large
natural caverns, the size of which is easily
increased by art. These "caves" play an
important part in the history of the country,

serving especially as refuges for political
offenders and other fugitives (Judg. vi. 2 ;
1 Sam. xiii. 6 ; Heb. xi. 38).

5. *unto all fountains of water and unto all
brooks*] Rather, "**to all springs of water
and to all torrent-courses.**" The former
are the perennial streams ; the latter are
the torrent-courses which become dry in an
ordinary summer.

all the beasts] Rather, some, or, "**a portion of our beasts.**"

9. Obadiah thinks that to execute this
commission will be fatal to him (*v.* 12).

10. *there is no nation,* &c.] This is expressed in the style of Oriental hyperbole.
What Obadiah means is :—"there is no
nation nor kingdom, *of those over which he
has influence,* whither the king has not
sent." He could scarcely, for example,
have exacted an oath from such countries
as Egypt or Syria of Damascus. But Ahab
may have been powerful enough to exact an
oath from the neighbouring Hittite, Moabite, and Edomite tribes, perhaps even from
Ethbaal his father-in-law, and the kings of
Hamath and Arpad.

17 to meet Elijah. ¶ And it came to pass, when Ahab saw Elijah,
that Ahab said unto him, *d Art* thou he that *e* troubleth Israel?
18 And he answered, I have not troubled Israel; but thou, and thy
father's house, *f* in that ye have forsaken the commandments of
19 the LORD, and thou hast followed Baalim. Now therefore send
and gather to me all Israel unto Mount *g* Carmel, and the prophets of Baal four hundred and fifty, *h* and the prophets of the
20 groves four hundred, which eat at Jezebel's table. So Ahab
sent unto all the children of Israel, and *i* gathered the prophets
21 together unto mount Carmel. ¶ And Elijah came unto all the
people, and said, *k* How long halt ye between two [1]opinions? if
the LORD *be* God, follow him: but if Baal, *l then* follow him.
22 And the people answered him not a word. Then said Elijah
unto the people, *m* I, *even* I only, remain a prophet of the LORD;

d ch. 21. 20.
e Josh. 7. 25.
Acts 16. 20.
f 2 Chr. 15.2.

g Josh.19.26.
h ch. 16. 33.

ch. 22. 6.

k 2 Kin. 17.
41.
Matt. 6. 24.
l See Josh.
24. 15.
m ch. 19. 10,
14.

[1] Or, *thoughts?*

---

17. *Art thou he*, &c.] Meaning, "Can it possibly be that thou dost venture to present thyself before me, thou that troublest Israel by means of this terrible drought?" The charge of "troubling" had never before been brought against any one but Achan (marg. ref. *e*); it was one which must have called to the Prophet's recollection Achan's miserable fate.

18. Instead of apologies, and pleas for pardon, Elijah meets the charge with a countercharge, and makes a sudden demand. "Gather to me," &c. This boldness, this high tone, this absence of the slightest indication of alarm, seems to have completely discomfited Ahab, who ventured on no reply, made no attempt to arrest the Prophet, did not even press him to remove his curse and bring the drought to an end, but simply consented to do his bidding. There is no passage of Scripture which exhibits more forcibly the ascendancy that a Prophet of the Lord, armed with His spiritual powers, could, if he were firm and brave, exercise even over the most powerful and most unscrupulous of monarchs.

Baalim] i.e. the various aspects under which the god, Baal, was worshipped, Baal-shamin, Baal-zebub, Baal-Hamman, &c.

19. Carmel (Josh. xii. 22 note) was chosen by the Prophet as the scene of the gathering to which he invited, or rather summoned, Ahab. Its thick jungles of copse and numerous dwarf-oaks and olives, would furnish abundant wood for his intended sacrifice. Here was a perennial fountain; and here again an ancient "altar of the LORD" (*v.* 30), belonging probably to the old times of non-idolatrous high-place worship —perhaps an erection of one of the Patriarchs. On the one hand, there would be a view of the Mediterranean, whence the first sign of rain was likely to come, and on the other of Jezreel, the residence of the Court at the time, with its royal palace and its idol-temples, so that the intended trial would take place in the sight (so to speak) of the proud queen and her minions.

the prophets of Baal] The priests of Baal are so called not so much because they claimed a power of foretelling the future, as because they were *teachers* of the false religion, and more especially because they stand here in antagonism to the "Prophet of the LORD," with whom they are about to contend.

the prophets of the groves, four hundred] Rather, "of the **grove**"—the prophets, or priests, attached to the "grove" (*asherah*) which Ahab had made, probably at Jezreel (marg. ref.) The number 400 seems to have been one especially affected by Ahab. We again find 400 prophets at the close of his reign (xxii. 6). The number 40 entered largely into the religious system of the Jews (vi. 17; Ex. xxvi. 19; Deut. xxv. 3; Ezek. xli. 2).

which eat at Jezebel's table] Rather, "which eat from Jezebel's table." Oriental etiquette would not have allowed them to eat *at* the table of the queen, which was spread in the seraglio. They were fed from the superfluity of her daily provision, which was no doubt on a sumptuous scale. Cp. iv. 22, 23.

20. Local tradition places the site of Elijah's sacrifice, not on the highest point of the mountain (1728ft.), but at the southeastern extremity (1600ft.) of the ridge, where a shapeless ruin, composed of great hewn stones, and standing amid thick bushes of dwarf-oak, in the near vicinity of a perennial spring, is known to the Arabs as "El-Maharrakah," "the burning," or "the sacrifice." All the circumstances of the locality adapt it for the scene of the contest.

21. The people were dumb. They could not but feel the logical force of Elijah's argument; but they were not prepared at once to act upon it. They wished to unite the worship of Jehovah with that of Baal—to avoid breaking with the past and completely rejecting the old national worship, yet at the same time to have the enjoyment of the new rites, which were certainly sensuous, and probably impure.

22. *I, even I, only remain*] He means, "I

23 [n]but Baal's prophets *are* four hundred and fifty men. Let them
therefore give us two bullocks; and let them choose one bullock
for themselves, and cut it in pieces, and lay *it* on wood, and
put no fire *under:* and I will dress the other bullock, and lay *it*
24 on wood, and put no fire *under:* and call ye on the name of
your gods, and I will call on the name of the LORD: and the
God that [o]answereth by fire, let him be God. And all the people
25 answered and said, [1]It is well spoken. ¶ And Elijah said unto
the prophets of Baal, Choose you one bullock for yourselves,
and dress *it* first; for ye *are* many; and call on the name of
26 your gods, but put no fire *under*. And they took the bullock
which was given them, and they dressed *it*, and called on the
name of Baal from morning even until noon, saying, O Baal,
[2]hear us. But *there was* [p]no voice, nor any that [3]answered.
27 And they [4]leaped upon the altar which was made. And it came
to pass at noon, that Elijah mocked them, and said, Cry [5]aloud:
for he *is* a god· either [6]he is talking, or he [7]is pursuing, or he
is in a journey, *or* peradventure he sleepeth, and must be
28 awaked. And they cried aloud, and [q]cut themselves after

[n] ver. 19.
[o] ver. 38. 1 Chr. 21. 26.
[p] Ps. 115. 5. Jer. 10. 5. 1 Cor. 8. 4. & 12. 2.
[q] Lev. 19. 28. Deut. 14. 1.

[1] Heb. *The word is good.*
[2] Or, *answer.*
[3] Or, *heard.*
[4] Or, *leaped up and down at the altar.*
[5] Heb. *with a great voice.*
[6] Or, *he meditateth.*
[7] Heb. *hath a pursuit.*

only remain *in the exercise of the office* of a Prophet." The others (cp. *v.* 4) had been forced to fly and hide themselves in dens and caves of the earth; their voices were silenced; they had not ventured to come to Carmel. Elijah contrasts his solitary appearance on the side of Jehovah at the great gathering with the crowd of those opposed to him.

24. *the God that answereth by fire*] God had frequently before consumed offerings with supernatural fire (Lev. ix. 24; Judg. vi. 21). The Baal-worshippers were no doubt in the habit of attributing thunder and lightning to their god—the great Nature-power—and thus had no excuse for declining Elijah's challenge.

25. Elijah gives precedence in everything to the Baal-priests, to take away all ground for cavil in case of failure. It is his object to make an impression on king and people; and he feels rightly that the impression will depend greatly on the contrast between their inability and the power given to him.

26. *and called on the name of Baal from morning even until noon*] Cp. the parallel in the conduct of the Greeks of Ephesus. (Acts xix. 34). The words "O Baal, hear us," probably floated on the air as the refrain of a long and varied hymn of supplication.

they leaped upon the altar which was made] The marginal rendering is preferable to this. Wild dancing has always been a devotional exercise in the East, and remains so to this day; witness the dancing dervishes. It was practised especially in the worship of Nature-powers, like the Dea Phrygia (Cybele), the Dea Syra (Astarte?), and the like.

27. The object of Elijah's irony was twofold; (1) to stimulate the priests to greater exertions, and so to make their failure more complete, and (2) to suggest to the people that such failure would prove absolutely that Baal was no God.

The force of the expressions seems to be, "Cry on, only cry louder, and then you will make him hear; for surely he is a god; surely you are not mistaken in so regarding him." He is "talking," or "meditating;" the word used has both senses, for the Hebrews regarded "meditation" as "talking with oneself;" "or he is pursuing;" rather, perhaps, "he hath a *withdrawing*," *i.e.*, "he hath withdrawn himself into privacy for awhile," as a king does upon occasions. The drift of the whole passage is scornful ridicule of the anthropomorphic notions of God entertained by the Baal-priests and their followers (cp. Ps. l. 21). The heathen gods, as we know from the Greek and Latin classics, ate and drank, went on journeys, slept, conversed, quarrelled, fought. The explanations of many of these absurdities were unknown to the ordinary worshipper, and probably even the most enlightened, if his religion was not a mere vague Pantheism, had notions of the gods which were largely tainted with a false anthropomorphism.

28. Elijah's scorn roused the Baal-priests to greater exertions. At length, when the frenzy had reached its height, knives were drawn, and the blood spirted forth from hundreds of self-inflicted wounds, while an ecstasy of enthusiasm seized many, and they poured forth incoherent phrases, or perhaps an unintelligible jargon, which was believed to come from divine inspiration,

their manner with knives and lancets, till ¹the blood gushed
29 out upon them. And it came to pass, when midday was past,
ʳand they prophesied until the *time* of the ²offering of the
evening sacrifice, that *there was* ⁸neither voice, nor any to an-
30 swer, nor any ³that regarded. ¶And Elijah said unto all
the people, Come near unto me. And all the people came
near unto him. ᵗAnd he repaired the altar of the LORD *that*
31 *was* broken down. And Elijah took twelve stones, according
to the number of the tribes of the sons of Jacob, unto whom
the word of the LORD came, saying, ᵘIsrael shall be thy name:
32 and with the stones he built an altar ˣin the name of the LORD:
and he made a trench about the altar, as great as would contain
33 two measures of seed. And he ʸput the wood in order, and
cut the bullock in pieces, and laid *him* on the wood, and said,
Fill four barrels with water, and ᶻpour *it* on the burnt sacri-
34 fice, and on the wood. And he said, Do *it* the second time.
And they did *it* the second time. And he said, Do *it* the third
35 time. And they did *it* the third time. And the water ⁴ran
round about the altar; and he filled ᵃthe trench also with water.
36 And it came to pass at *the time of* the offering of the *evening*
sacrifice, that Elijah the prophet came near, and said, LORD
ᵇGod of Abraham, Isaac, and of Israel, ᶜlet it be known this
day that thou *art* God in Israel, and *that* I *am* thy servant, and

ʳ 1 Cor. 11.
4, 5.
ᶜ ver. 26.

ᵗ ch. 19. 10.

ᵘ Gen. 32. 28.
& 35. 10.
2 Kin. 17. 34.
ˣ Col. 3. 17.
ʸ Lev. 1. 6,
7, 8.

ᶻ See Judg.
6. 20.

ᵃ ver. 32. 38.

ᵇ Ex. 3. 6.
& 4. 5.
ᶜ ch. 8. 43.
2 Kin. 19. 19.
Ps. 83. 18.

¹ Heb. *poured out blood
upon them.*

² Heb. *ascending.*
³ Heb. *attention.*

⁴ Heb. *went.*

---

and constituted one of their modes of
prophecy.

The practice of inflicting gashes on their
limbs, in their religious exercises, was common among the Carians, the Syrians, and
the Phrygians. We may regard it as a
modification of the idea of human sacrifice.
The gods were supposed to be pleased with
the shedding of human blood.

lancets] Lancets, in our modern sense of
the word, can scarcely have been intended
by our translators. The Hebrew word is
elsewhere always translated "spears," or
"lances;" and this is probably its meaning
here.

29. *and they prophesied*] Cp. xxii. 12.
The expression seems to be used of any case
where there was an utterance of words by
persons in a state of religious ecstasy.

until the time of the offering] Rather,
"Until towards the time." Elijah had
built his altar by the actual time of the
offering (*v.* 36).

32. *he built an altar in the name of the
LORD*] *i.e.* calling, as he built it, on the
name of Jehovah, and so dedicating it to
His service.

two measures of seed] Literally, "two
seahs of seed." The *seah* contained about
three gallons.

33. *And he put the wood in order*, &c.] He
obeyed, that is, all the injunctions of the
Law with respect to the offering of a burnt
sacrifice (marg. ref.). He thus publicly

taught that the ordinances of the Law were
binding upon the kingdom of Israel.

barrels] Rather, "**pitchers**" or "water-
jars," such as the maidens used to carry on
their heads (Gen. xxiv. 14-20. Cp. Judg.
vii. 16, 19). The flooding the sacrifice and
the trench with water would at once do away
with any suspicion of fraud, and greatly
enhance in the eyes of the people the mar-
vellousness of the miracle. The unfailing
spring at the eastern end of Carmel (*v.* 19),
was capable of furnishing as much water as
he needed.

36. *at the time of the offering of the evening sacrifice*] *i.e.* probably "the ninth hour,"
or three o'clock. Thus there might still
remain about five hours of light, during
which the other events of the day were
accomplished.

LORD *God of Abraham, Isaac, and of
Israel*] This solemn address would carry
back the thoughts of the pious to the burning bush of Horeb, and the words there
spoken (marg. reff.); for there only had this
mysterious formula been used before. Its
use now was calculated to stir their faith
and prepare them in some degree for God's
answering *by fire.*

*that I have done all these things at thy
word*] *i.e.* "That I have been divinely
directed in all that I have done publicly as
a Prophet, in proclaiming the drought, in
gathering this assembly, and in proposing
this trial; that I have not done them of my
own mind " (marg. ref.).

37 that ^dI have done all these things at thy word. Hear me, O
Lord, hear me, that this people may know that thou *art* the
Lord God, and *that* thou hast turned their heart back again.
38 Then ^ethe fire of the Lord fell, and consumed the burnt sacrifice, and the wood, and the stones, and the dust, and licked up
39 the water that *was* in the trench. And when all the people saw
it, they fell on their faces: and they said, ^fThe Lord, he *is* the
40 God; the Lord, he *is* the God. And Elijah said unto them,
^{1g}Take the prophets of Baal; let not one of them escape. And
they took them: and Elijah brought them down to the brook
41 Kishon, and ^hslew them there. ¶ And Elijah said unto Ahab,
Get thee up, eat and drink; for *there is* ²a sound of abundance
42 of rain. So Ahab went up to eat and to drink. And Elijah
went up to the top of Carmel; ⁱand he cast himself down upon
43 the earth, and put his face between his knees, and said to his
servant, Go up now, look toward the sea. And he went up,
and looked, and said, *There is* nothing. And he said, Go again
44 seven times. And it came to pass at the seventh time, that he
said, Behold, there ariseth a little cloud out of the sea, like a
man's hand. And he said, Go up, say unto Ahab, ³Prepare *thy*
45 *chariot*, and get thee down, that the rain stop thee not. And
it came to pass in the mean while, that the heaven was black
with clouds and wind, and there was a great rain. And Ahab
46 rode, and went to Jezreel. And the hand of the Lord was on

^d Num. 16.
28.

^e Lev. 9. 24.
Judg. 6. 21.
1 Chr. 21. 26.
2 Chr. 7. 1.
^f ver. 24.

^g 2 Kin. 10.
25.

^h Deut. 13.5.
& 18. 20.

ⁱ Jam. 5. 17,
18.

¹ Or, *Apprehend*.　　² Or, *a sound of a noise of rain*.　　³ Heb. *Tie, or, Bind*.

---

37. *that thou hast turned their heart*] The
hearts of the people were turning. Elijah
speaks of them as already turned, anticipating the coming change, and helping
it on.

38. *the fire of the* Lord *fell*] This cannot
have been a flash of lightning. It was altogether, in its nature as well as in its oppor-
tuneness, miraculous. Cp. marg. reff. for
the conduct of the people.

39. *the* Lord, *he is the God*] The people
thus pronounced the matter to be clearly and
certainly decided. Baal was overthrown; he
was proved to be no god at all. The Lord
Jehovah, He, and He alone, is God. Him
would they henceforth acknowledge, and no
other.

40. Elijah required the people to show
their conviction by acts—acts which might
expose them to the anger of king or queen,
but which once committed would cause them
to break with Baal and his worshippers for
ever.

Elijah is said to have slain the "prophets of Baal," because the people slew
them by his orders. Why they were
brought down to the torrent-bed of Kishon
to be killed, is difficult to explain. Perhaps
the object of Elijah was to leave the bodies
in a place where they would not be found,
since the coming rain would, he knew, send
a flood down the Kishon ravine, and bear
off the corpses to the sea. Elijah's act is to
be justified by the express command of the
Law, that idolatrous Israelites were to be

put to death, and by the right of a Prophet
under the theocracy to step in and execute
the Law when the king failed in his duty.

41. *Get thee up, eat and drink*] Ahab had
descended the hill-side with Elijah, and
witnessed the slaughter of the priests. Elijah now bade him ascend the hill again, and
partake of the feast which was already prepared, and which always followed upon a
sacrifice.

there is a sound of abundance of rain]
Either the wind, which in the East usually
heralds rain, had begun to rise, and sighed
through the forests of Carmel—or perhaps
the sound was simply in the Prophet's ears,
a mysterious intimation to him that the
drought was to end, and rain to come that
day.

42. Ahab could feast; Elijah could not,
or would not. Ascending Carmel not quite
to the highest elevation (*v.* 43), but to a
point, a little below the highest, whence
the sea was not visible, he proceeded to
pray earnestly for rain, as he had prayed
formerly that it might not rain.

43. Tradition says that Elijah's servant
was the son of the widow of Sarepta (xvii.
23).

44. *a little cloud, &c.*] Sailors know full
well that such a cloud on the far horizon is
often the forerunner of a violent storm.

46. Divinely directed, and divinely upheld, Elijah, instead of resting, ran in advance of the king's chariot the entire distance of at least 16 miles to the entrance of

k 2 Kin. 4.29.
& 9. 1.

a ch. 18. 40.

b Ruth 1. 17.
ch. 20. 10.
2 Kin. 6. 31.

c Num. 11.
15.
Jonah 4. 3, 8.

Elijah ; and he ᵏgirded up his loins, and ran before Ahab ¹to the entrance of Jezreel.

CHAP. 19. AND Ahab told Jezebel all that Elijah had done, and 2 withal how he had ᵃslain all the prophets with the sword. Then Jezebel sent a messenger unto Elijah, saying, ᵇSo let the gods do to me, and more also, if I make not thy life as the life of one 3 of them by to morrow about this time. And when he saw that, he arose, and went for his life, and came to Beer-sheba, which 4 belongeth to Judah, and left his servant there. ¶ But he himself went a day's journey into the wilderness, and came and sat down under a juniper tree : and he ᶜrequested ²for himself that he might die; and said, It is enough; now, O LORD, take 5 away my life; for I am not better than my fathers. And as he lay and slept under a juniper tree, behold, then an angel

¹ Heb. till thou come to Jezreel.   ² Heb. for his life.

Jezreel. He thus showed himself ready to countenance and uphold the irresolute monarch, if he would turn from his evil courses, and proceed to carry out the religious reformation which the events of the day had inaugurated.

the entrance of Jezreel] Modern Zerin. Ahab had not removed the capital from Samaria (xxii. 10, 37); but he had built himself a palace at Jezreel (xxi. 1), and appears to have resided there ordinarily. A contemporary Assyrian inscription speaks of him as "Ahab of Jezreel."

Elijah's caution in accompanying Ahab only to "the entrance" is like that of the modern Arabs, who can seldom be induced to trust themselves within walls. He rested on the outskirts of the town, waiting to learn what Jezebel would say or do, knowing that it was she, and not Ahab, who really governed the country.

XIX. 2. The Prophet had not long to wait before learning the intentions of the queen. A priest's daughter herself, she would avenge the slaughtered priests; a king's wife and a king's child, she would not quail before a subject. That very night a messenger declared her determination to compass the Prophet's death within the space of a day.

so let the gods, &c.] A common oath about this time (marg. reff.). The Greek Version prefixes to this another clause, which makes the oath even more forcible, "As surely as thou art Elijah and I am Jezebel, so let the gods," &c.

3. The rapid movement of the original is very striking. "And he saw (or, feared, as some read), and he rose, and he went, &c." The fear and flight of Elijah are very remarkable. Jezebel's threat alone, had not, in all probability, produced the extraordinary change : but, partly, physical reaction from the over-excitement of the preceding day; and, partly, internal disquietude and doubt as to the wisdom of the course which he had adopted.

Beer-sheba is about 95 miles from Jezreel,

on the very borders of the desert et-Tih. Elijah cannot possibly have reached it until the close of the second day. It seems implied that he travelled both night and day, and did not rest till he arrived thus far on his way. It was one of the towns assigned to the tribe of Simeon (Josh. xix. 2). The Simeonites were, however, by this time absorbed into Judah.

4. Elijah did not feel himself safe till he was beyond the territory of Judah, for Ahab might demand him of Jehoshaphat (xviii. 10), with whom he was on terms of close alliance (xxii. 4). He therefore proceeds southward into the desert, simply to be out of the reach of his enemies.

a juniper-tree] The tree here mentioned (rothem) is not the juniper, but a species of broom (Genista monosperma), called rethem by the Arabs, which abounds in the Sinaitic peninsula. It grows to such a size as to afford shade and protection, both in heat and storm, to travellers.

requested for himself that he might die.] Like Moses and Jonah (marg. reff.). The Prophet's depression here reached its lowest point. He was still suffering from the reaction of overstrained feeling ; he was weary with nights and days of travel ; he was faint with the sun's heat; he was exhausted for want of food ; he was for the first time alone —alone in the awful solitude and silence of the great white desert. Such solitude might brace the soul in certain moods; but in others it must utterly overwhelm and crush. Thus the Prophet at length gave way completely—made his prayer that he might die —and, exhausted sank, to sleep.

I am not better than my fathers] i.e. "I am a mere weak man, no better nor stronger than they who have gone before me, no more able to revolutionize the world than they."

5. an angel touched him] The friendly ministration of Angels, common in the time of the Patriarchs (Gen. xviii. 2-16, xix. 1-22, xxviii. 12, xxxii. 1, 24-29), and known also under the Judges (Judg. vi. 11-21, xiii. 3-20), was now extended to Elijah.

6 touched him, and said unto him, Arise *and* eat. And he looked, and, behold, *there was* a cake baken on the coals, and a cruse of water at his [1]head. And he did eat and drink, and laid him
7 down again. And the angel of the LORD came again the second time, and touched him, and said, Arise *and* eat; because the
8 journey *is* too great for thee. And he arose, and did eat and drink, and went in the strength of that meat *d*forty days and
9 forty nights unto *e*Horeb the mount of God. ¶ And he came thither unto a cave, and lodged there; and, behold, the word of the LORD *came* to him, and he said unto him, What doest thou
10 here, Elijah? And he said, *f*I have been very *g*jealous for the LORD God of hosts: for the children of Israel have forsaken thy covenant, thrown down thine altars, and *h*slain thy prophets with the sword; and *i*I, *even* I only, am left: and they seek my
11 life, to take it away. And he said, Go forth, and stand *k*upon the mount before the LORD. And, behold, the LORD passed by, and *l*a great and strong wind rent the mountains, and brake in pieces the rocks before the LORD ; *but* the LORD *was* not in the
12 wind: and after the wind an earthquake ; *but* the LORD *was* not in the earthquake : and after the earthquake a fire ; *but* the LORD
13 *was* not in the fire : and after the fire a still small voice. And

d So Ex. 34. 28.
Deut. 9.9,18
Matt. 4. 2.
e Ex. 3. 1.

f Rom. 11. 3.
g Num. 25.
11, 13.
Ps. 69. 9.
h ch. 18. 4.
i Rom. 11. 3.
k Ex. 24. 12.

l Ezek. 1. 4.
& 37. 7.

---

[1] Heb. *bolster.*

Any other explanation of this passage does violence to the words. It is certainly not the intention of the writer to represent Elijah as relieved on this occasion by a human "messenger."

6. *a cake baken on the coals*] It is not implied that Elijah found a fire lighted and the cake on it, but only that he found one of the usual baked cakes of the desert, which form the ordinary food of the Arab at the present day.

at his head] The Hebrew word means simply "the place on which the head lies ; " hence the marginal rendering, "bolster."

7. *Arise and eat*, &c.] *i.e.* "Eat a second time, for *otherwise* the journey will be beyond thy powers." "The journey" was not simply a pilgrimage to Horeb, which was less than 200 miles distant, and might have been reached in six or seven days. It was to be a wandering in the wilderness, not unlike that of the Israelites when they came out of Egypt ; only it was to last forty days instead of forty years.

8. The old commentators generally understood this to mean that Elijah had no other food at all, and compared this long fast with that of Moses and that of our Lord (marg. reff.). But the words do not exclude the notion of the Prophet's having obtained such nourishment from roots and fruits as the desert offers to a wanderer, though these alone would not have sustained him.

9. *a cave*] Rather, "the cave." Some well-known cave must be intended—perhaps the "clift of the rock" (Ex. xxxiii. 22). The traditional "cave of Elijah" which is shown in the secluded plain immediately below the highest summit of the

Jebel Mousa, cannot, from its small size, be the real cavern.

10. *I, even I only, am left*] The same statement as in xviii. 22, but the sense is different. There Elijah merely said that he alone remained to execute the Prophet's office, which was true ; here he implies that he is the only Prophet left alive, whereas a hundred had been saved by Obadiah (xviii. 4).

11. *and behold, the LORD passed by*] The remainder of this verse and the whole of the next are placed by the LXX., and by the Arabic translator, in the mouth of the Angel. But it seems best to regard the vision as ending with the words "before the Lord" —and the writer as then assuming that this was done, and proceeding to describe what followed.

12. *a still small voice*] Literally, "a sound of soft stillness." The teaching is a condemnation of that "zeal" which Elijah had gloried in, a zeal exhibiting itself in fierce and terrible vengeances, and an exaltation and recommendation of that mild and gentle temper, which "beareth all things, believeth all things, hopeth all things, endureth all things." But it was so contrary to the whole character of the stern, harsh, unsparing Tishbite, that it could have found no ready entrance into his heart. It may have for a while moderated his excessive zeal, and inclined him to gentler courses ; but later in his life the old harshness recurred in a deed in reference to which our Lord himself drew the well-known contrast between the spirits of the two Dispensations (Luke ix. 51–56).

m So Ex.3.6.
Isai. 6. 2.

n ver. 9.
o ver. 10.

p 2 Kin. 8.
12, 13.
q 2 Kin. 9.
1—3.
r Luke 4.
27, called
Eliseus.
s 2 Kin. 8.12.
& 9. 14, &c.
& 10. 6, &c.
& 13. 3.
t See Hos.
6. 5.
u Rom. 11.4.
x See Hos.
13. 2.

it was *so*, when Elijah heard *it*, that *m*he wrapped his face in his mantle, and went out, and stood in the entering in of the cave. *n*And, behold, *there came* a voice unto him, and said, What doest 14 thou here, Elijah?   *o*And he said, I have been very jealous for the LORD God of hosts: because the children of Israel have forsaken thy covenant, thrown down thine altars, and slain thy prophets with the sword: and I, *even* I only, am left; and they 15 seek my life, to take it away.   And the LORD said unto him, Go, return on thy way to the wilderness of Damascus: *p*and 16 when thou comest, anoint Hazael to *be* king over Syria: and *q*Jehu the son of Nimshi shalt thou anoint *to be* king over Israel: and *r*Elisha the son of Shaphat of Abel-meholah shalt thou 17 anoint *to be* prophet in thy room.   And *s*it shall come to pass, *that* him that escapeth the sword of Hazael shall Jehu slay: and him that escapeth from the sword of Jehu *t*shall Elisha slay. 18 *u*Yet *1*I have left *me* seven thousand in Israel, all the knees which have not bowed unto Baal, *x*and every mouth which hath 19 not kissed him.   ¶ So he departed thence, and found Elisha the

1 Or, *I will leave.*

---

13. *mantle*] The upper garment, a sort of short cloak or cape—perhaps made of untanned sheepskin, which was, besides the strip of leather round his loins, the sole apparel of the Prophet (cp. Matt. iii. 4). For the action cp. marg. reff.

there came a voice unto him, &c.] The question heard before in vision is now put again to the Prophet by the Lord Himself. Elijah gives no humbler and more gentle answer. He is still satisfied with his own statement of his case.

15. The answer is not a justification of the ways of God, nor a direct reproof of the Prophet's weakness and despondency, nor an explanation or application of what Elijah had seen. For the present, he is simply directed back into the path of practical duty. His mission is not yet over, there is still work for him to do. He receives special injunctions with respect to Hazael, Jehu, and Elisha; and he is comforted with a revelation well adapted to rouse him from his despondency: there are seven thousand who will sympathise with him in his trials, and who need his care and attention.

the wilderness of Damascus] Probably the district north of the Prophet's own country, between Bashan and Damascus itself, and which was known in later times as Iturea and Gaulanitis. Here the Prophet might be secure from Jezebel, while he could readily communicate with both Israel and Damascus, and execute the commissions with which he was intrusted.

when thou comest, anoint] Rather, "**and thou shalt go and anoint.**" Elijah performed one only of the three commissions given to him. He appears to have been left free to choose the time for executing his commissions, and it would seem that he thought the proper occasion had not arisen either for the first or the second before his

own translation. But he took care to communicate the divine commands to his successor, who performed them at the fitting moment (marg. reff.).

16. *Jehu, the son of Nimshi*] In reality the grandson of Nimshi. But he seems to have been commonly known by the above title (2 K. ix. 20; 2 Chr. xxii. 7), perhaps because his father had died and his grandfather had brought him up.

Abel-meholah] See Judg. vii. 22 note. [Conder identifies it with Ain Helweh.]

Elisha...shalt thou anoint] This is almost the only place where we hear of the anointing of Prophets (cp. 1 Chr. xvi. 22 and Ps. cv. 15).

17. Cp. marg. reff.

shall Elisha slay] i.e. With a spiritual slaying by the "word of the Lord," which is "sharper than any two-edged sword," and may be said to slay those whose doom it pronounces (cp. marg. ref.; Jer. i. 10). Elisha does not seem, like Elijah, to have executed God's judgments on the guilty.

18. *Yet I have left me*, &c.] Rather, as in the margin. "Seven thousand" faithful Israelites shall survive all the persecutions of Ahab and Jezebel, and carry down the worship of Jehovah to another generation. Elijah is mistaken in supposing that he only is left. The number is manifestly a round number, not an exact estimate. Perhaps it is, moreover, a mystical or symbolic number. Cp. Rev. vii. 5-8. Of all the symbolical numbers used in Scripture, seven is the commonest.

every mouth which hath not kissed him] Idolaters sometimes kissed the hand to the object of their worship (Job xxxi. 26, 27); at other times they kissed the actual image (marg. ref.).

19. *plowing*] Elisha's occupation is an indication of his character. He is emphati-

son of Shaphat, who *was* plowing *with* twelve yoke *of oxen* before him, and he with the twelfth: and Elijah passed by him, 20 and cast his mantle upon him. And he left the oxen, and ran after Elijah, and said, *v*Let me, I pray thee, kiss my father and my mother, and *then* I will follow thee. And he said unto him, 21 ¹Go back again: for what have I done to thee? And he returned back from him, and took a yoke of oxen, and slew them, and *z*boiled their flesh with the instruments of the oxen, and gave unto the people, and they did eat. Then he arose, and went after Elijah, and ministered unto him.

v Matt. 8. 21, 22.

z 2 Sam. 24.

CHAP. 20. AND Ben-hadad the king of Syria gathered all his host together: and *there were* thirty and two kings with him, and horses, and chariots: and he went up and besieged Samaria, 2 and warred against it. And he sent messengers to Ahab king of Israel into the city, and said unto him, Thus saith Ben-

¹ Heb. *Go return.*

cally a man of peace. He passes the year in those rural occupations which are natural to the son of a wealthy yeoman—superintending the field-labourers himself, and taking a share in their toils. He thus presents a strong contrast to the stern, harsh, rugged Gileadite, who is almost half an Arab, who seems to have no settled home, no quiet family circle, who avoids the haunts of men, and is content for months to dwell in a cavern instead of under a roof.

with twelve yoke of oxen] He was ploughing in a field with eleven other ploughs at work, each drawn by one yoke of oxen. Ploughing with a single pair of oxen was the practice in Egypt, in Assyria, in Palestine, and in modern times throughout Western Asia.

passed by him] Rather, "crossed over to him." Perhaps it is meant that he crossed the stream of the Jordan.

cast his mantle upon him] The action is explained as constituting a species of adoption, because a father naturally clothes his children. The notion of fatherhood and sonship was evidently understood between them (2 K. ii. 9-12).

20. *let me, I pray thee, kiss my father*, &c.] Not an unnatural request before following his new spiritual father. Elijah sees in his address a divided heart, and will not give the permission or accept the service thus tendered. Hence his cold reply. See Luke ix. 61, 62.

go back again, &c.] *i.e.*, "Go, return to thy ploughing—why shouldest thou quit it? Why take leave of thy friends and come with me? What have I done to thee to require such a sacrifice? for as a sacrifice thou evidently regardest it. Truly I have done nothing to thee. Thou canst remain as thou art."

21. Elisha returns to his oxen and labourers. He indicates his relinquishment of

his home and calling by the slaughter of the particular yoke of oxen with which he had himself been ploughing. probably the best beasts of the twelve, and by burning the "instruments," the ploughs and yokes, both made of wood. Next he feasts his people to show his gratitude for his call, Elijah apparently remaining the while; and then, leaving father and mother, cattle and land, good position and comfortable home, Elisha became the "minister" to the wanderer. Cp. Ex. xxiv. 13; Josh. i. 1.

XX. 1. *Ben-hadad, the king of Syria*] Probably the son of the Ben-hadad who assisted Asa against Baasha (xv. 18 note).

thirty and two kings with him] Not allies, but feudatories (*v.* 24). Damascus had in the reign of this Ben-hadad become the centre of an important monarchy, which may not improbably have extended from the Euphrates to the northern border of Israel. The Assyrian inscriptions show that this country was about the period in question parcelled out into a multitude of petty kingdoms, the chief tribes who possessed it being the Hittites, the Hamathites, and the Syrians of Damascus.

horses and chariots] The Assyrian inscriptions show us how very important an arm of the service the chariot force was reckoned by the Syrians. A king, who has been identified with this Ben-hadad, brought into the field against Assyria nearly four thousand chariots.

2. It may be supposed that a considerable time had passed in the siege, that the city had been reduced to an extremity, and that ambassadors had been sent by Ahab to ask terms of peace short of absolute surrender, before Ben-hadad would make such a demand. He would expect and intend his demand to be rejected, and this would have left him free to plunder the town, which was evidently what he desired and purposed.

3 hadad, thy silver and thy gold *is* mine ; thy wives also and thy
4 children, *even* the goodliest, *are* mine. And the king of Israel
answered and said, My lord, O king, according to thy saying, I
5 *am* thine, and all that I have. ¶And the messengers came
again, and said, Thus speaketh Ben-hadad, saying, Although I
have sent unto thee, saying, Thou shalt deliver me thy silver,
6 and thy gold, and thy wives, and thy children ; yet I will send
my servants unto thee to morrow about this time, and they shall
search thine house, and the houses of thy servants ; and it shall
be, *that* whatsoever is [1]pleasant in thine eyes, they shall put *it*
7 in their hand, and take *it* away. Then the king of Israel called
all the elders of the land, and said, Mark, I pray you, and see
how this *man* seeketh mischief : for he sent unto me for my
wives, and for my children, and for my silver, and for my gold;
8 and [2]I denied him not. And all the elders and all the people
9 said unto him, Hearken not *unto him*, nor consent. Wherefore
he said unto the messengers of Ben-hadad, Tell my lord the
king, All that thou didst send for to thy servant at the first I
will do : but this thing I may not do. And the messengers de-
10 parted, and brought him word again. And Ben-hadad sent

a ch. 19. 2.

unto him, and said, [a]The gods do so unto me, and more also, if
the dust of Samaria shall suffice for handfuls for all the people
11 that [3]follow me. And the king of Israel answered and said,
Tell *him*, Let not him that girdeth on *his harness* boast himself
12 as he that putteth it off. And it came to pass, when *Ben-hadad*

b ver. 16.

heard this [4]message, as he was [b]drinking. he and the kings in
the [5]pavilions, that he said unto his servants, [6]Set *yourselves in*
13 *array*. And they set *themselves in array* against the city. ¶And,

---

[1] Heb. *desirable*.	[3] Heb. are *at my feet*.	[5] Or, *tents*.
[2] Heb. *I kept not back from him*.	So Ex. 11. 8. Judg. 4. 10.	[6] Or, *Place* the engines : *And they placed* engines.
	[4] Heb. *word*.	

---

6. Ben-hadad, disappointed by Ahab's
consent to an indignity which he had
thought no monarch could submit to, proceeds to put a fresh construction on his
former demands.

7. The political institution of a Council
of elders (Ex. iii. 16, &c.), which had belonged to the undivided nation from the
sojourn in Egypt downwards, had therefore
been continued among the ten tribes after
their separation, and still held an important
place in the system of Government. The
Council was not merely called together
when the king needed it, but held its regular sittings at the seat of government ;
and hence "all the elders *of the land*" were
now present in Samaria. On the "elders
of towns," see xxi. *vv.* 8–14.

Apparently the king had not thought it
necessary to summon the Council when the
first terms were announced to him, inasmuch as they touched only himself. The
fresh demands affected the people at large,
and it became necessary, or at any rate
fitting, that "the elders" should be consulted.

8. "The people" had no distinct place in
the ordinary Jewish or Israelitish constitution ; but they were accustomed to signify

their approbation or disapprobation of the
decisions of the elders by acclamations or
murmurs (Josh. ix. 18 ; Judg. xi. 11, &c.).

10. *if the dust of Samaria shall suffice for
handfuls*, &c.] In its general sense this
phrase is undoubtedly a boast that the
number of Ben-hadad's troops was such as
to make resistance vain and foolish. We
may parallel it with the saying of the Tra-
chinian at Thermopylæ, that the Persian
arrows would darken the light of the sun.
Probably the exact meaning is, "When
your town is reduced to ruins, as it will be
if you resist, the entire heap will not suffice
to furnish a handful of dust to each soldier
of my army, so many are they." There
was a threat in the message as well as a
boast.

11. Ahab's reply has the air of a proverb,
with which Orientals always love to answer
a foe.

12. *pavilions*] "Booths" (Gen. xxxiii. 17
marg. ; Lev. xxiii. 42 ; Jonah iv. 5). The term
seems to be properly applied to a stationary
"booth " or "hut," as distinguished from a
moveable "tent." On military expeditions,
and especially in the case of a siege, such
"huts " were naturally constructed to
shelter the king and his chief officers.

behold, there ¹came a prophet unto Ahab king of Israel, saying, Thus saith the LORD, Hast thou seen all this great multitude? behold, ᶜI will deliver it into thine hand this day; and thou ᶜ ver. 23.
14 shalt know that I *am* the LORD. And Ahab said, By whom? And he said, Thus said the LORD, *Even* by the ²young men of the princes of the provinces. Then he said, Who shall ³order
15 the battle? And he answered, Thou. ¶Then he numbered the young men of the princes of the provinces, and they were two hundred and thirty two : and after them he numbered all the people, *even* all the children of Israel, *being* seven thousand.
16 And they went out at noon. But Ben-hadad *was* ᵈdrinking ᵈ ver. 12.
himself drunk in the pavilions, he and the kings, the thirty and ch. 16. 9.
17 two kings that helped him. And the young men of the princes of the provinces went out first ; and Ben-hadad sent out, and they told him, saying, There are men come out of Samaria.
18 And he said, Whether they be come out for peace, take them alive ; or whether they be come out for war, take them alive.
19 So these young men of the princes of the provinces came out of
20 the city, and the army which followed them. And they slew every one his man : and the Syrians fled; and Israel pursued them : and Ben-hadad the king of Syria escaped on an horse
21 with the horsemen. And the king of Israel went out, and smote the horses and chariots, and slew the Syrians with a great
22 slaughter. ¶And the prophet came to the king of Israel, and said unto him, Go, strengthen thyself, and mark, and see what thou doest : ᵉfor at the return of the year the king of Syria will ᵉ 2 Sam 11.1.
23 come up against thee. ¶And the servants of the king of Syria said unto him, Their gods *are* gods of the hills; therefore they

---

¹ Heb. *approached*.　　　² Or, *servants*.　　　³ Heb. *bind*, or, *tie*.

---

13. The Rabbinical commentators conjecture that this Prophet was Micaiah, the son of Imlah, who is mentioned below (xxii. 8).
hast thou seen all this great multitude?] The boast of Ben-hadad (*v.* 10), was not without a basis of truth; his force seems to have exceeded 130,000 (cp. *vv.* 25, 29, 30). In his wars with the Assyrians we find him sometimes at the head of 100,000 men.
14. The "princes of the provinces" are the governors of districts, many of whom may have fled to the capital, as the hostile army advanced through Galilee and northern Samaria. The "young men" are their attendants, youths unaccustomed to war.
Who shall order the battle?] i.e. "Who shall join battle, begin the attack? We or the enemy?" The reply was, that the Israelites were to attack.
15. *seven thousand*] Considering how populous Palestine was in the time of the earlier Israelite kings (see 2 Chr. xiii. 3, xiv. 8, xvii. 14–18), the smallness of this number is somewhat surprising. If the reading be sound, we must suppose, first, that Ben-hadad's attack was very sudden, and that Ahab had no time to collect forces from distant parts of the country; and secondly, that during the long siege the garrison of Samaria had been greatly reduced, till it now did not exceed 7,000 men fit for service.

16. *drinking himself drunk*] Ben-hadad meant probably to mark his utter contempt of his foe. Cp. the contempt of Belshazzar (Dan. v. 1–4).
17. *Ben-hadad sent out, and they told him*] The LXX. have a better reading—"they sent out and told the king of Syria."
22. *Go, strengthen thyself,* &c.] That is, "collect troops, raise fortifications, obtain allies—take all the measures thou canst to increase thy military strength. Be not rash, but consider well every step—for a great danger is impending."
at the return of the year] i.e. "When the season for military operations again comes round." The wars of the Oriental monarchs at this time, like those of early Rome, were almost always of the nature of annual incursions into the territories of their neighbours, begun in spring and terminating in early autumn. Sustained invasions, lasting over the winter into a second or a third year, are not found till the time of Shalmaneser (2 K. xvii. 5, xviii. 9, 10), and do not become common till the Median and Babylonian period.
23. *Their gods are gods of the hills*] The local power and influence of deities was a fixed principle of the ancient polytheism. Each country was considered to have its own gods ; and wars were regarded as being to a great extent struggles between the gods

were stronger than we; but let us fight against them in the
24 plain, and surely we shall be stronger than they. And do this
thing, Take the kings away, every man out of his place, and put
25 captains in their rooms: and number thee an army, like the
army ¹that thou hast lost, horse for horse, and chariot for chariot: and we will fight against them in the plain, *and* surely we
shall be stronger than they. And he hearkened unto their
26 voice, and did so. And it came to pass at the return of the
year, that Ben-hadad numbered the Syrians, and went up to
f Josh. 13. 4. 27 ᶠAphek, ²to fight against Israel. And the children of Israel were
numbered, and ³were all present, and went against them: and
the children of Israel pitched before them like two little flocks of
28 kids; but the Syrians filled the country. ¶And there came a
man of God, and spake unto the king of Israel, and said, Thus
saith the LORD, Because the Syrians have said, the LORD *is* God
g ver. 13. of the hills, but he *is* not God of the valleys, therefore ᵍwill I
deliver all this great multitude into thine hand, and ye shall
29 know that I *am* the LORD. ¶And they pitched one over against
the other seven days. And so it was, that in the seventh day the
battle was joined: and the children of Israel slew of the Syrians
30 an hundred thousand footmen in one day. But the rest fled to
Aphek, into the city; and *there* a wall fell upon twenty and seven
thousand of the men *that were* left. ¶And Ben-hadad fled, and
31 came into the city, ⁴⁵into an inner chamber. And his servants
said unto him, Behold now, we have heard that the kings of the
h Gen. 37.34. house of Israel *are* merciful kings: let us, I pray thee, ʰput
sackcloth on our loins, and ropes upon our heads, and go out to

¹ Heb. *that was fallen.* ³ Or, *were victualled.* ⁵ Heb. *into a chamber with-*
² Heb. *to the war with Israel.* ⁴ Or, *from chamber to* *in a chamber,* ch. 22, 25.
chamber.

of the nations engaged in them. This is
apparent throughout the Assyrian inscriptions. Cp. also 2 K. xviii. 33-35, xix. 12.
The present passage gives an unusual modification of this view. The suggestion of the
Syrian chiefs may have been a mere politic
device—they being really anxious, *on military grounds,* to encounter their enemy on
the plain, where alone their chariots would
be of much service. In the plain the Israelites had always fought at a disadvantage, and had proved themselves weaker
than on the hills (see Judg. i. 19, 27, 34).
24. The Syrian chiefs evidently thought
that want of unity had weakened their
army. They therefore proposed the deposition of the kings, and the substitution, in
their place, of Syrian governors:—not "captains." The term used always denotes a
civil office.
26. *Aphek*] There were several places of
this name in Palestine (see marg. ref.).
This Aphek has been almost certainly identified with the modern *Fik,* a large village
on the present high road from Damascus to
Nablous and Jerusalem. The expression
"*went up* to Aphek" is appropriate; for
Fik, though in a level country, is at a much
higher elevation than Damascus.
27. *were all present*] The marginal rendering is adopted by almost all critics.

like two little flocks of kids] The word translated "little flocks" does not occur elsewhere in Scripture. It seems to mean
simply "flocks." Compare the LXX.,
who render ὡσεὶ δύο ποίμνια αἰγῶν.
28. *a man of God*] Evidently not the
Prophet who had spoken to Ahab the year
before (*vv.* 13, 22). He probably dwelt in
the neighbourhood of Samaria. Now that
Ahab and his army had marched out into
the Trans-Jordanic territory, another Prophet, a native probably of that region,
announced God's will to them.
30. *a wall*] "The wall," *i.e.* the wall of
the town. We may suppose a terrific
earthquake during the siege of the place,
while the Syrians were manning the defences in full force, which threw down the
wall where they were most thickly crowded
upon it, and buried them in its ruins. Ben-
hadad fled from the wall, where he had
been at the time of the disaster, into the
inner parts of the city—probably to some
massive stronghold—and there concealed
himself.
31. *and ropes upon our heads*] "Ropes
about our necks" is probably meant. They,
as it were, put their lives at Ahab's disposal, who, if he pleased, might hang them
at once.

32 the king of Israel : peradventure he will save thy life. So they girded sackcloth on their loins, and *put* ropes on their heads, and came to the king of Israel, and said, Thy servant Ben-hadad saith, I pray thee, let me live. And he said, *Is* he yet alive?
33 he *is* my brother. Now the men did diligently observe whether *any thing would come* from him, and did hastily catch *it :* and they said, Thy brother Ben-hadad. Then he said, Go ye, bring him. Then Ben-hadad came forth to him ; and he caused him
34 to come up into the chariot. And *Ben-hadad* said unto him, *The cities, which my father took from thy father, I will re-store ; and thou shalt make streets for thee in Damascus, as my father made in Samaria. Then *said Ahab, I will send thee away with this covenant. So he made a covenant with him, and sent
35 him away. ¶And a certain man of *the sons of the prophets said unto his neighbour *in the word of the LORD, Smite me, I
36 pray thee. And the man refused to smite him. Then said he unto him, Because thou hast not obeyed the voice of the LORD, behold, as soon as thou art departed from me, a lion shall slay thee. And as soon as he was departed from him, *a lion found
37 him, and slew him. Then he found another man, and said, Smite me, I pray thee. And the man smote him, ¹so that in

i ch. 15. 20.

k 2 Kin. 2.
3, 5, 7, 15.
i ch. 13. 17,
18.

m ch. 13. 24.

¹ Heb. *smiting and wounding.*

---

32. Ben-hadad is now as humble as Ahab had been a year before (*v.* 9). He professes himself the mere *slave* of his conqueror.

33. The meaning of this verse is that the men from the first moment of their arrival were on the watch to note what Ahab would say ; and the moment he let fall the expression "He is my brother," they caught it up and repeated it, fixing him to it, as it were, and preventing his retreat. By the Oriental law of *dakheel* any one is at any time entitled to put himself under the protection of another, be that other his friend or his greatest enemy ; and if the man applied to does not at once reject him, if the slightest forms of friendly speech pass between the two, the bond is complete, and must not be broken. Ben-hadad's friends were on the watch to obtain for him *dakheel ;* and the single phrase "He is my brother," having been accepted by them on his part, was sufficient to complete the bond, and secure the life of the captive. Ahab having called Ben-hadad his brother, treated him as he would a brother ; he took him up into his chariot, than which there could not be a greater honour.

34. Ben-hadad, secure of his life, suggests terms of peace as the price of his freedom. He will restore to Ahab the Israelite cities taken from Omri by his father, among which Ramoth Gilead was probably the most important (xxii. 3) ; and he will allow Ahab the privilege of making for himself "streets," or rather squares, in Damascus, a privilege which his own father had possessed with respect to Samaria. Commercial advantages, rather than any other, were probably sought by this arrangement.

so he made a covenant with him, &c.] Ahab, without "inquiring of the Lord," at once agreed to the terms offered ; and, without even taking any security for their due observance, allowed the Syrian monarch to depart. Considered politically, the act was one of culpable carelessness and imprudence. Ben-hadad did not regard himself as bound by the terms of a covenant made when he was a prisoner—as his after conduct shows (xxii. 3). Ahab's conduct was even more unjustifiable in one who held his crown under a theocracy. "Inquiry at the word of the Lord" was still possible in Israel (xxii. 5, 8), and would seem to have been the course that ordinary gratitude might have suggested.

35. *the sons of the prophets*] The expression occurs here for the first time. It signifies (marg. reff.), the schools or colleges of Prophets which existed in several of the Israelite, and probably of the Jewish, towns, where young men were regularly educated for the prophetical office. These "schools" make their first appearance under Samuel (1 Sam. xix. 20). There is no distinct evidence that they continued later than the time of Elisha ; but it is on the whole most probable that the institution survived the Captivity, and that the bulk of the "Prophets," whose works have come down to us, belonged to them. Amos (vii. 14, 15) seems to speak as if his were an exceptional case.

said unto his neighbour] Rather, "to his friend" or "companion"—to one who was, like himself, "a Prophet's son," and who ought therefore to have perceived that his colleague spoke "in the word of the Lord."

38 smiting he wounded *him*. So the prophet departed, and waited
for the king by the way, and disguised himself with ashes upon
[n] See 2 Sam. 12. 1, &c. — 39 his face. And [n] as the king passed by, he cried unto the king:
and he said, Thy servant went out into the midst of the battle;
and, behold, a man turned aside, and brought a man unto me,
and said, Keep this man: if by any means he be missing, then
[o] 2 Kin. 10. 24. — [o] shall thy life be for his life, or else thou shalt [1] pay a talent of
40 silver. And as thy servant was busy here and there, [2] he was
gone. And the king of Israel said unto him, So *shall* thy judg-
41 ment *be*; thyself hast decided *it*. And he hasted, and took the
ashes away from his face; and the king of Israel discerned him
42 that he *was* of the prophets. And he said unto him, Thus saith
[p] ch. 22. 31—37. — the LORD, [p] Because thou hast let go out of *thy* hand a man
whom I appointed to utter destruction, therefore thy life shall
43 go for his life, and thy people for his people. And the king of
[q] ch. 21. 4. — Israel [q] went to his house heavy and displeased, and came to
Samaria.

CHAP. 21. AND it came to pass after these things, *that* Naboth the
Jezreelite had a vineyard, which *was* in Jezreel, hard by the
2 palace of Ahab king of Samaria. And Ahab spake unto Naboth,
[a] 1 Sam. 8. 14. — saying, Give me thy [a] vineyard, that I may have it for a garden
of herbs, because it *is* near unto my house: and I will give
thee for it a better vineyard than it; *or*, if it [3] seem good to thee,
3 I will give thee the worth of it in money. And Naboth said to
[b] Lev. 25. 23. Num. 36. 7. Ezek. 46. 18. — Ahab, The LORD forbid it me, [b] that I should give the inherit-
4 ance of my fathers unto thee. ¶ And Ahab came into his house
heavy and displeased because of the word which Naboth the
Jezreelite had spoken to him: for he had said, I will not give
thee the inheritance of my fathers. And he laid him down upon
his bed, and turned away his face, and would eat no bread.

[1] Heb. *weigh*. [2] Heb. *he was not*. [3] Heb. *be good in thine eyes*.

---

38. *ashes*] Rather, "**a bandage**" (and in *v.* 41). The object of the wound and bandage was double. Partly, it was to prevent Ahab from recognising the Prophet's face; partly, to induce him to believe that the man had really been engaged in the recent war.

41. *he was of the prophets*] Josephus and others conjecture that this Prophet was Micaiah, the son of Imlah (but cp. *v.* 13 note).

42. *a man whom I appointed to utter destruction*] or to *cherem*, *i.e.* a man on whom My curse had been laid (Lev. xxvii. 28 note).

43. *heavy and displeased*] Rather, "**sullen and angry**" (and so marg. ref.), not repentant, as after Elijah's warning (xxi. 27)—not acknowledging the justice of his sentence—but full of sullenness and suppressed anger.

XXI. **1.** *a vineyard...in Jezreel*] The name Jezreel is applied in Scripture, not merely to the town (xviii. 46), but also to the valley or plain which lies below it, between Mount Gilboa and Little Hermon (2 Sam. ii. 9; 2 K. ix. 10; Hos. i. 5; &c.).

The palace of Ahab at Jezreel was on the eastern side of the city, looking towards the Jordan down the valley above described. It abutted on the town wall (2 K. ix. 30, 31). Immediately below it was a dry moat. Beyond, in the valley, either adjoining the moat, or at any rate at no great distance, was the plat of ground belonging to Naboth (do. *v.* 21).

2. *I will give thee the worth of it in money*] Lit., "I will give thee silver, the worth of it." Money, in our sense of the word, that is to say, coins of definite values, did not yet exist. The first coin known to the Jews was the Persian daric, with which they became acquainted during the Captivity. (1 Chr. xxix. 7 note).

3. *The* LORD *forbid it me*] Or, "Jehovah forbid it me." Naboth, as a worshipper of Jehovah, not of Baal, considers it would be wrong for him to comply with the king's request, as contrary to the Law (marg.). His was not a mere refusal arising out of a spirit of sturdy independence, or one based upon the sentiment which attaches men to ancestral estates.

4. *upon his bed*] That is, "upon his couch." The Jews, like other Orientals, reclined upon couches at their meals (Amos

5 ¶ But Jezebel his wife came to him, and said unto him, Why is
6 thy spirit so sad, that thou eatest no bread? And he said unto
her, Because I spake unto Naboth the Jezreelite, and said unto
him, Give me thy vineyard for money; or else, if it please thee,
I will give thee *another* vineyard for it: and he answered, I will
7 not give thee my vineyard. And Jezebel his wife said unto him,
Dost thou now govern the kingdom of Israel? arise, *and* eat
bread, and let thine heart be merry: I will give thee the vine-
8 yard of Naboth the Jezreelite. So she wrote letters in Ahab's
name, and sealed *them* with his seal, and sent the letters unto
the elders and to the nobles that *were* in his city, dwelling with
9 Naboth. And she wrote in the letters, saying, Proclaim a fast,
10 and set Naboth ¹on high among the people: and set two men,
sons of Belial, before him, to bear witness against him, saying,
Thou didst ᶜblaspheme God and the king. And *then* carry him   ᶜ Ex. 22. 28.
11 out, and ᵈstone him, that he may die. ¶ And the men of his   Lev. 24. 15,
city, *even* the elders and the nobles who were the inhabitants in   16.
                                                                      Acts 6. 11.
his city, did as Jezebel had sent unto them, *and* as it *was* written ᵈ Lev. 24.14.
12 in the letters which she had sent unto them. ᵉThey proclaimed   ᵉ Isai. 58. 4.

¹ Heb. *in the top of the people.*

---

vi. 4; Ezek. xxiii. 41, &c.). Ahab turns his
face towards the back of the couch, rejecting all converse with others, and so
remains, after the banquet is served, refusing to partake of it. Such an open
manifestation of ill temper is thoroughly
characteristic of an Oriental king.

7. The meaning is, "Art thou king, and
yet sufferest thyself to be thwarted in this
way by a mere subject? *I*, the queen, the
weak woman, will give thee the vineyard,
if thou, the king, the strong man, wilt do
nothing."

8. *seal*] The seal is a very ancient invention. Judah's signet and Pharaoh's signet-
ring are mentioned in Genesis (xxxviii. 18,
xli. 42). Signets of Egyptian kings have
been found which are referred to about
B.C. 2000. Sennacherib's signet, and an
impression of Sargon's, are still extant.
There can be no doubt that in the East,
from a very remote antiquity, kings had
seals and appended them to all documents
which they set forth under their authority.
(Cp. also Esther iii. 12, viii. 8; Daniel vi.
17). The Hebrew mode of sealing seems to
have been by attaching a lump of clay to
the document, and impressing the seal
thereupon (Job xxxviii. 14).

his city] *i.e.* Jezreel (*v.* 1). The mode in
which it is spoken of here, and in *v.* 11,
seems to imply that it was not the city
from which Jezebel wrote. The court was
evidently at this time residing at Samaria
(xx. 43); and Ahab may either have met
Naboth there, or have gone down (cp. *v.* 16)
to Jezreel to make his request, and then, on
being refused, have returned to Samaria.
The distance is not more than seven miles.

9. The object of this fast was at once to
raise a prejudice against Naboth, who was
assumed by the elders to have disgraced the

town; and at the same time to give an air
of religion to the proceedings, which might
blind persons to their real injustice.

set Naboth on high among his people] This
was not an order to do Naboth any, even
apparent, honour; but simply a command to
bring him forward before a court or assembly, where he might be seen by all,
tried, and condemned.

10. *sons of Belial*] *i.e.* "worthless persons" (Deut. xiii. 13 note). Witnesses must
be two in number according to the Law
(Num. xxxv. 30; Deut. xvii. 6, xix. 15).

The word rendered "blaspheme" is that
which commonly means "bless." The opposite sense of "cursing," seems, however,
to be required here and in Job i. 5, 11, ii.
5. Perhaps the explanation of the bad
sense of the original word is to be found in
the practice of blessing by way of a salutation, not only on meeting, but also on taking
leave (Gen. xlvii. 7, 10). From the latter
custom the word came to mean "bidding
farewell to," and so "renouncing," "casting
off," "cursing."

carry him out and stone him] Naboth's
offence would be twofold, and in both cases
capital: blasphemy against God being
punishable with death by the Law (marg.
ref.), and blasphemy against the king being
a capital offence by custom (ii. 8; 2 Sam. xvi.
9, xix. 21). The punishment would be stoning, since the greater crime would absorb
the lesser, and the Law made stoning the
punishment for blasphemy against God.
As stoning always took place outside the
city (see Acts vii. 58), Jezebel told the elders
to "carry Naboth out."

11. The ready submission of the elders
and nobles implies a deep moral degradation
among the Israelites, the fruit of their lapse
into idolatry.

13 a fast, and set Naboth on high among the people. And there came in two men, children of Belial, and sat before him : and the men of Belial witnessed against him, *even* against Naboth, in the presence of the people, saying, Naboth did blaspheme God and the king. *f*Then they carried him forth out of the city, and
14 stoned him with stones, that he died. Then they sent to Jezebel,
15 saying, Naboth is stoned, and is dead.   ¶And it came to pass, when Jezebel heard that Naboth was stoned, and was dead, that Jezebel said to Ahab, Arise, take possession of the vineyard of Naboth the Jezreelite, which he refused to give thee for money :
16 for Naboth is not alive, but dead. And it came to pass, when Ahab heard that Naboth was dead, that Ahab rose up to go down to the vineyard of Naboth the Jezreelite, to take possession of it.
17 ¶*g*And the word of the LORD came to Elijah the Tishbite, say-
18 ing, Arise, go down to meet Ahab king of Israel, *h*which *is* in Samaria : behold, *he is* in the vineyard of Naboth, whither he is
19 gone down to possess it. And thou shalt speak unto him, saying, Thus saith the LORD, Hast thou killed, and also taken possession ? And thou shalt speak unto him, saying, Thus saith the LORD, *i*In the place where dogs licked the blood of Naboth shall
20 dogs lick thy blood, even thine. ¶And Ahab said to Elijah, *k*Hast thou found me, O mine enemy ? And he answered, I have found *thee :* because *l*thou hast sold thyself to work evil in
21 the sight of the LORD. Behold, *m*I will bring evil upon thee, and will take away thy posterity, and will cut off from Ahab *n*him that pisseth against the wall, and *o*him that is shut up and
22 left in Israel, and will make thine house like the house of *p*Jeroboam the son of Nebat, and like the house of *q*Baasha the son of Ahijah, for the provocation wherewith thou hast provoked
23 *me* to anger, and made Israel to sin. And *r*of Jezebel also spake

f See 2 Kin. 9. 26.

g Ps. 9. 12.
h ch. 13. 32.
2 Chr. 22. 9.

i ch. 22. 38.

k ch. 18. 17.
l 2 Kin. 17. 17.
Rom. 7. 14.
m ch. 14. 10.
2 Kin. 9. 8.
n 1 Sam. 25. 22.
o ch. 14. 10.
p ch. 15. 29.
q ch. 16. 3, 11.
r 2 Kin. 9. 36.

---

13. Naboth had sons who were also put to death at this time (marg. ref.). It is not improbable that they were stoned together with their parent (cp. Josh. vii. 24, 25). In the East a parent's guilt constantly involves the punishment of his children. Contrast 2 K. xiv. 6.

16. *to take possession of it*] The goods of traitors appear to have been forfeited·to the Crown by the Jewish law as they still are almost universally throughout the East. Cp. 2 Sam. xvi. 4.

19. *Hast thou killed, and also taken possession ?*] These words rebuke especially Ahab's indecent haste. He went to Jezreel the very day after Naboth's execution (2 K. ix. 26). The prophecy following had a double fulfilment. The main fulfilment was by the casting of the dead body of Jehoram into Naboth's plot of ground at Jezreel, where, like Naboth's, it was left for the dogs to eat (2 K. ix. 25). This spot, which was just outside the city·wall, and close to a gate (do. *v.* 31), was probably the actual scene of Naboth's execution. Here did dogs lick Ahab's blood, that is, his son's blood, the execution of the full retaliatory sentence having been deferred to the days of his son, formally and explicitly, on Ahab's repentance (*v.* 29). But, besides this, there was a

secondary fulfilment of the prophecy, when, not at Jezreel but at Samaria (marg. ref.), the actual blood of Ahab himself, was licked by dogs, only in a way that implied no disgrace. These two fulfilments are complementary to each other.

20. The words "O mine enemy," may refer partly to the old antagonism (marg. ref. ; xvii. 1, xix. 2, 3) ; but the feeling which it expresses is rather that of present opposition—the opposition between good and evil, light and darkness (John iii. 20.)

thou hast sold thyself to work evil] Cp. marg. reff. The metaphor is taken from the practice of men's selling themselves into slavery, and so giving themselves wholly up to work the will of their master. This was a wide-spread custom in the ancient world.

21. The Prophet changes, without warning, from speaking in his own person to speaking in the person of God. The transition is abrupt, probably because the compiler follows his materials closely, compressing by omission. One fragment omitted here is preserved in 2 K. ix. 26.

23. *And of Jezebel also spake the LORD, saying*] These are not the words of Elijah, but of the writer, who notes a special prophecy against Jezebel, whose guilt was at least equal to her husband's.

the LORD, saying, The dogs shall eat Jezebel by the ¹wall of
24 Jezreel. *Him that dieth of Ahab in the city the dogs shall eat;   ˢ ch. 14. 11.
and him that dieth in the field shall the fowls of the air eat.   & 16. 4.
25 ¶ But ᵗthere was none like unto Ahab, which did sell himself to   ᵗ ch. 16. 30,
work wickedness in the sight of the LORD, ᵘwhom Jezebel his   &c.
26 wife ²stirred up. And he did very abominably in following   ᵘ ch. 16. 31.
idols, according to all *things* ˣas did the Amorites, whom the   ˣ 2 Kin. 21.
27 LORD cast out before the children of Israel. ¶And it came to   11.
pass, when Ahab heard those words, that he rent his clothes,
and ʸput sackcloth upon his flesh, and fasted, and lay in sack-   ʸ Gen. 37. 34.
28 cloth, and went softly. And the word of the LORD came to
29 Elijah the Tishbite, saying, Seest thou how Ahab humbleth
himself before me? because he humbleth himself before me,
I will not bring the evil in his days: *but* ᶻin his son's days will   ᶻ 2 Kin. 9. 25.
I bring the evil upon his house.
CHAP. 22. AND they continued three years without war between
Syria and Israel. And it came to pass in the third year, that
2 ᵃJehoshaphat the king of Judah came down to the king of Israel.   ᵃ 2 Chr. 18.
   2, &c.

¹ Or, *ditch*.   ² Or, *incited*.

---

wall] The marginal rendering "ditch," is
preferable. There is always in Oriental
towns a space outside the walls which lies
uncultivated, and which is naturally used
for the deposit of refuse of every kind.
Here the dogs prowl, and the kites and
vultures find many a feast.

25. *whom Jezebel stirred up*] The history of
Ahab's reign throughout exhibits him as
completely governed by his imperious wife.
Instances of her influence are seen in *vv.* 7,
15, marg. ref., xviii. 4, xix. 2.

26. The Amorites appear here as representatives of the old Canaanite nations
(Gen. xv. 16 note). It seems to be implied
here that their idolatries were in the main
identical with those of the Phœnicians
which Ahab had adopted.

27. The repentance of Ahab resembles
that of the Ninevites (Jonah iii. 5). It has the
same outward signs—fasting and sackcloth
—and it has much the same inward character. It springs, not from love, nor from
hatred of sin, but from fear of the consequences of sin. It is thus, although sincere
and real while it lasts, shallow and exceedingly short-lived. God, however, to mark
His readiness to receive the sinner who
turns to Him, accepted the imperfect offering
(as He likewise accepted the penitence of
the Ninevites), and allowed it to delay the
execution of the sentence (*v.* 29). So the
penitence of the Ninevites put off the fall of
Nineveh for a century.

and lay in sackcloth] In this particular he
seems to have gone beyond the usual practice. We do not read elsewhere of mourners
passing the night in sackcloth.

and went softly] "As if he had no heart
to go about any business" (Patrick).

29. *the evil*] *i.e.* the main evil. See
v. 19 note; and cp. xxii. 38 with marg.
ref.

XXII. **1.** *three years*] These must be
counted from the close of the second campaign of Ben-hadad (xx. 34). They were
not full years, as is evident from the next
verse. Probably the first year is that of
Ben-hadad's dismissal after his defeat; the
second is a year of actual peace; while the
third is that in which Jehoshaphat paid his
visit, and the Ramoth-Gilead expedition
took place. The pause, here noticed, in the
war between Israel and Syria was perhaps
the result of a common danger. It was
probably in the year following Ben-hadad's
dismissal by Ahab, that the first great Assyrian expedition took place into these
parts. Shalmaneser II. relates that on his
first invasion of southern Syria, he was met
by the combined forces of Ben-hadad, Ahab,
the king of Hamath, the kings of the Hittites, and others, who gave him battle, but
suffered a defeat.

2. This visit indicates an entire change
in the relations which we have hitherto
found subsisting between the kingdoms of
Israel and Judah. The common danger to
which the two kingdoms were exposed from
the growing power of Syria had probably
induced them to forget their differences.
Jehoshaphat's eldest son, Jehoram, was
married to Athaliah, the daughter of Ahab;
but apparently the bond between the two
families had not hitherto led to any very
close intimacy, much less to any joint military expeditions. Jehoshaphat seems to
have taken no part in the former Syrian
wars of Ahab, nor did he join in the great
league against the Assyrians (*v.* 1 note).
His visit now was probably one of mere
friendliness, without any political object.
Ahab, however, turned the visit to political
advantage. From this time till the dis-
placement of Ahab's dynasty by Jehu, very
intimate relations subsisted between the

b Deut. 4. 43.

2 Kin. 3. 7.

d ch. 18. 19.

e 2 Kin. 3. 11.

3 And the king of Israel said unto his servants, Know ye that *b* Ramoth in Gilead *is* our's, and we *be* [1] still, *and* take it not 4 out of the hand of the king of Syria? And he said unto Jehoshaphat, Wilt thou go with me to battle to Ramoth-gilead? And Jehoshaphat said to the king of Israel, *c* I *am* as thou *art*, 5 my people as thy people, my horses as thy horses. ¶ And Jehoshaphat said unto the king of Israel, Enquire, I pray 6 thee, at the word of the LORD to day. Then the king of Israel *d* gathered the prophets together, about four hundred men, and said unto them, Shall I go against Ramoth-gilead to battle, or shall I forbear? And they said, Go up; for the Lord shall 7 deliver *it* into the hand of the king. And *e* Jehoshaphat said, *Is there* not here a prophet of the LORD besides, that we might 8 enquire of him? And the king of Israel said unto Jehoshaphat, *There is* yet one man, Micaiah the son of Imlah, by whom we may enquire of the LORD: but I hate him; for he doth not prophesy good concerning me, but evil. And Jehoshaphat said, 9 Let not the king say so. ¶ Then the king of Israel called an

[1] Heb. *silent from taking it.*

two kingdoms (xxii. 49; 2 K. iii. 7, viii. 28, 29; 2 Chr. xx. 36, &c.).

3. By the terms of Ahab's covenant with Ben-hadad, Ramoth in Gilead ought, long ere this, to have been restored (xx. 34). Hence the claim "*is ours*," *i.e.* "it belongs to us of right though the Syrians still hold possession of it."

4. Ahab, well aware of the military strength of Syria, and feeling that he cannot now expect Divine aid (xx. 42, xxi. 21), asks the aid of Jehoshaphat, whose military resources were very great (2 Chr. xvii. 12–19). Jehoshaphat's answer is one of complete acquiescence, without reserve of any kind (cp. 2 Chr. xviii. 3). Jehoshaphat was afterwards rebuked for thus consenting to "help the ungodly" (2 Chr. xix. 2). He probably acted not merely from complaisance, but from a belief that the interests of his own kingdom would be advanced by the step which he agreed to take. The power of Syria was at this time very menacing.

5. Jehoshaphat, with characteristic piety (*v.* 43) takes advantage of his position as Ahab's friend and ally, to suggest inquiry of the Lord (Jehovah) before the expedition is undertaken. Lest Ahab should consent in word and put off the inquiry in act, he asks to have the Prophets called in at once: "*to-day*."

6. *the prophets*] *i.e.* In all probability the prophets attached to the worship of the calves; not real Prophets of Jehovah. This seems evident both from Jehoshaphat's dissatisfaction (*v.* 7), and from the strong antagonism apparent between the true Jehovah-Prophet Micaiah, and these self-styled "prophets of the Lord" (*vv.* 22–25).

the Lord shall deliver it] In the Hebrew the word here used for "Lord" is "*Adonai*." Later (*i.e.* in *vv.* 11, 12) LORD or "Jehovah"

is used. It would seem as if the idolatrous prophets shrank from employing the latter title until they found that Jehoshaphat insisted on learning the will of Jehovah in the matter.

7. Jehoshaphat was dissatisfied. These men—creatures of Ahab, tainted with the worship of calves if not with Baal-worship —had promised victory, but not in the name of Jehovah. Jehoshaphat, therefore, asked, "Is there not here a true Prophet of Jehovah besides these 400 professed prophets?"

8. *There is yet one man, Micaiah*] Elijah, it appears, had withdrawn again after the events of the last chapter, and there was no known Prophet of Jehovah within reach of Samaria except Micaiah.

he doth not prophesy good concerning me but evil] Whether the tradition in xx. 41 note be true or not, it is certain that Ahab had imprisoned him (*v.* 26), and probable that the imprisonment was on account of threatening prophecies. Ahab suggests to Jehoshaphat that Micaiah is one who allows his private feelings to determine the utterances which he delivers as if from Jehovah. Hence the force of Jehoshaphat's answer, "Let not the king say so;" *i.e.* "Let not the king suppose that a Prophet would be guilty of such impiety,"—an impiety from which even Balaam shrank (Num. xxii. 18).

9. *an officer*] More properly, as in the margin, "a eunuch." Eunuchs seem to have been first introduced among the Israelites by David (1 Chr. xxviii. 1 note). They were a natural accompaniment of the seraglio of Solomon. The present passage is the first which shows that, after the separation of the kingdom, the kings of Israel employed them (cp. 2 K. viii. 6, ix. 32).

10 ¹officer, and said, Hasten *hither* Micaiah the son of Imlah. And
the king of Israel and Jehoshaphat the king of Judah sat
each on his throne, having put on their robes, in a ²void
place in the entrance of the gate of Samaria; and all the
11 prophets prophesied before them. And Zedekiah the son of
Chenaanah made him horns of iron: and he said, Thus saith
the LORD, With these shalt thou push the Syrians, until
12 thou have consumed them. And all the prophets prophesied
so, saying, Go up to Ramoth-gilead, and prosper: for the
13 LORD shall deliver *it* into the king's hand. ¶And the messenger that was gone to call Micaiah spake unto him, saying,
Behold now, the words of the prophets *declare* good unto the
king with one mouth: let thy word, I pray thee, be like the
14 word of one of them, and speak *that which is* good. And
Micaiah said, *As* the LORD liveth, ʄwhat the LORD saith unto
15 me, that will I speak. So he came to the king. And the king
said unto him, Micaiah, shall we go against Ramoth-gilead to
battle, or shall we forbear? And he answered him, Go, and
prosper: for the LORD shall deliver *it* into the hand of the king.
16 And the king said unto him, How many times shall I adjure
thee that thou tell me nothing but *that which is* true in the name
17 of the LORD? And he said, I saw all Israel ᵍscattered upon
the hills, as sheep that have not a shepherd: and the LORD said,
These have no master: let them return every man to his house
18 in peace. ¶And the king of Israel said unto Jehoshaphat, Did

ʄ Num.22.38.

ᵍ Matt.9.36.

¹ Or, *eunuch.* ² Heb. *floor.*

---

10. *sat each on his throne*] Or, "were sitting." They had removed from the ban-quet (2 Chr. xviii. 2) to the *void place*, or empty space *at* the entrance of the gate (Ruth iv. 1; 2 Sam. xv. 2), where Ahab daily sat to hear complaints and decide causes. Each was seated upon his throne, the Oriental kings having portable thrones, which they took with them upon their journeys.

11. *horns of iron*] The horn in Scripture is the favourite symbol of power; and pushing with the horn is a common meta-phor for attacking and conquering enemies (see Deut. xxxiii. 17. Cp. Ps. xliv. 5; Dan. viii. 4). Zedekiah, in employing a symboli-cal action, was following the example of a former Israelite Prophet (xi. 30).

thus saith the LORD] Or, Jehovah. Zede-kiah lays aside the unmeaning "lord" (*adonai*) of the general company of Israelite prophets (*v.* 6), and professes to have a direct message from Jehovah to Ahab. He may have believed his own words; for the "lying spirit" (*v.* 22) may have seemed to him a messenger from Jehovah. All the rest followed his example (*v.* 12).

13. *And the messenger spake unto him,* &c.] There seems to have been a wide-spread no-tion among the irreligious and the half-reli-gious of the ancient world, that their prophets were not the mere mouth-pieces of the god, but that they were persons who had power with the god, and could compel, or at least induce, Him to work their will (cp. Num.

xxiv. 10; Is. xxx. 10). They saw that the prophet's word was accomplished; they did not understand that if he falsified his message the accomplishment would no longer follow.

14. Micaiah, as a true Prophet of Jeho-vah, of course rejected the counsel offered him, which he felt to be at once wicked and foolish. Cp. also the resolution of Ba-laam, marg. ref.

15. *And he answered him,* &c.] Micaiah speaks the exact words of the 400 in so mocking and ironical a tone, that the king cannot mistake his meaning, or regard his answer as serious. The king's rejoinder im-plies that this mocking manner was familiar to Micaiah, who had used it in some former dealings with the Israelite monarch. Hence, in part, the king's strong feeling of dislike (cp. *v.* 8).

17. Thus adjured, Micaiah wholly changes his tone. Ahab cannot possibly mistake the meaning of his vision, especially as the metaphor of "sheep and shepherd" for king and people was familiar to the Israelites from the prayer of Moses (Num. xxvii. 17).

18. See *v.* 8. Ahab implies that he be-lieves Micaiah to have spoken out of pure malevolence, without any authority for his prediction from God. By implication he invites Jehoshaphat to disregard this pseudo-prophecy, and to put his trust in the unani-mous declaration of the 400. Micaiah, therefore, proceeds to explain the contradic-tion between himself and the 400, by re-counting another vision.

I not tell thee that he would prophesy no good concerning me,
19 but evil? ¶ And he said, Hear thou therefore the word of the
LORD : *h*I saw the LORD sitting on his throne, *i*and all the host
of heaven standing by him on his right hand and on his left.
20 And the LORD said, Who shall ¹persuade Ahab, that he may go
up and fall at Ramoth-gilead? And one said on this manner,
21 and another said on that manner. And there came forth a
spirit, and stood before the LORD, and said, I will persuade him.
22 And the LORD said unto him, Wherewith? And he said, I will
go forth, and I will be a lying spirit in the mouth of all his prophets. And he said, *k*Thou shalt persuade *him*, and prevail
23 also : go forth, and do so. *l*Now therefore, behold, the LORD
hath put a lying spirit in the mouth of all these thy prophets,
24 and the LORD hath spoken evil concerning thee. ¶ But Zedekiah the son of Chenaanah went near, and smote Micaiah on the
cheek, and said, *m*Which way went the Spirit of the LORD from
25 me to speak unto thee? And Micaiah said, Behold, thou shalt
see in that day, when thou shalt go ²into ³an inner chamber
26 to hide thyself. ¶ And the king of Israel said, Take Micaiah, and
carry him back unto Amon the governor of the city, and to

Margin references:
h Isai. 6. 1
Dan. 7. 9.
i Job 1. 6.
& 2. 1.
Dan. 7. 10.
Zech. 1. 10.
Matt. 18. 10.
Heb. 1. 7.

k Judg. 9. 23.
Job 12. 16.
Ezek. 14. 9.
2 Thes. 2. 11.
l Ezek. 14. 9.

m 2 Chr. 18. 23.

¹ Or, *deceive.*
² Or, *from chamber to chamber.*
³ Heb. *a chamber in a chamber*, ch. 20. 30.

---

19. David's Psalms had familiarised the Israelites with Jehovah sitting upon a throne in the heavens (Ps. ix. 7, xi. 4, xlv. 6, ciii. 19, &c.); but to be allowed to see in vision the ineffable glory of the Almighty thus seated, was a rare favour. It was granted to Isaiah, to Daniel (marg. reff.), to Ezekiel (Ez. i. 26), and in Christian times to St. Stephen (Acts vii. 56), and St. John (Rev. iv. 2).

21. *a spirit*] "The spirit"—which some explain as "the evil spirit"—*i. e.* Satan; others as simply "the spirit" who should "persuade."

22. The difficulties which attach to this passage are considerable. On the one hand, it is hard to suppose one of the holy Angels a "lying spirit;" on the other, hard to find Satan, or an evil spirit, included among "the host of heaven" (*v.* 19) and acting as the minister of God. Still, Job i. 6, ii. 1 lend countenance to the latter point, and 2 Thess. ii. 11 to the former. But it may be doubted whether we ought to take literally, and seek to interpret exactly, each statement of the present narrative. Visions of the invisible world can only be a sort of parables; revelations, not of the truth as it actually is, but of so much of the truth as can be shown through such a medium. The details of a vision, therefore, cannot safely be pressed, any more than the details of a parable. Portions of each must be accommodations to human modes of thought, and may very inadequately express the realities which they are employed to shadow forth to us.

24. *smote Micaiah on the cheek*] As Micaiah had been brought from prison (*v.* 26), it is probable that his hands were bound.

The Prophet, thus standing before the great ones of the earth, bound and helpless, bearing testimony to the truth, and for his testimony smitten on the face by an underling, whose blow he receives without either shame or anger, is a notable type of our Lord before Caiaphas suffering the same indignity.

Which way &c.] Zedekiah's meaning may perhaps be expounded as follows : "The Spirit of Jehovah *certainly* came to me, and inspired me with the answer which I gave. If He afterwards went to thee, as thou sayest that He did, perhaps thou canst tell us—as all the secrets of the invisible world are, thou pretendest, open to thee—which way He took."

25. Micaiah addresses himself not so much to Zedekiah's question, as to the main point which lies in dispute—which of them, namely, is a true Prophet. "When the news, *i.e.*, of Ahab's death, caused by his following thy counsels, reaches Samaria, and thou hast to hide thyself from the vengeance of Ahaziah or Jezebel, then, in that day, thou wilt know whether I or thou be the true Prophet."

26. *carry him back*] Lit. "cause him to *return.*" Micaiah had been in custody before, and was brought by Ahab's messenger from his prison.

the governor of the city] This is one out of several notices respecting what may be called the "constitution" of the Israelite kingdom. The king consulted on important matters a Council of elders (xx. 7, 8). The general administration was carried on by means of the governors of provinces (xx. 14) and of cities (2 K. x. 5). The governors of cities, like the monarch, were assisted and checked by councils of elders, the wise

27 Joash the king's son: and say, Thus saith the king, Put this *fellow* in the prison, and feed him with bread of affliction and
28 with water of affliction, until I come in peace. And Micaiah said, If thou return at all in peace, ^{n}the LORD hath not spoken by me. And he said, Hearken, O people, every one of you.
29 ¶ So the king of Israel and Jehoshaphat the king of Judah went
30 up to Ramoth-gilead. And the king of Israel said unto Jehoshaphat, ^{1}I will disguise myself, and enter into the battle; but put thou on thy robes. And the king of Israel ^{o}disguised himself,
31 and went into the battle. But the king of Syria commanded his thirty and two captains that had rule over his chariots, saying, Fight neither with small nor great, save only with the king
32 of Israel. And it came to pass, when the captains of the chariots saw Jehoshaphat, that they said, Surely it *is* the king of Israel. And they turned aside to fight against him: and Je-
33 hoshaphat ^{p}cried out. And it came to pass, when the captains of the chariots perceived that it *was* not the king of Israel, that
34 they turned back from pursuing him. And a *certain* man drew a bow ^{2}at a venture, and smote the king of Israel between the ^{3}joints of the harness: wherefore he said unto the driver of his chariot, Turn thine hand, and carry me out of the host; for I
35 am ^{4}wounded. And the battle ^{5}increased that day: and the

^{n} Num. 16. 29.
Deut. 18.
20, 21, 22.

^{o} 2 Chr. 35. 22.

^{p} 2 Chr. 18. 31.
Prov. 13. 20.

^{1} Or, *when he was to disguise himself, and enter into the battle.*
^{2} Heb. *in his simplicity,* 2 Sam. 15. 11.
^{3} Heb. *joints and the breast-*
plate.
^{4} Heb. *made sick.*
^{5} Heb. *ascended.*

men of the several towns (xxi. 8–12; 2 K. x. 5). Thus Samaria, as we see from the present passage, was under a special governor, who, among his other duties, had the control of the public prison, and directed the treatment of the prisoners.

the king's son] The phrase seems to designate a state office, rather than relationship to the sovereign. Cp. 2 Chr. xxviii. 7.

27. *Feed him with bread of affliction,* &c.] Micaiah is to be once more put in prison, but, in order to punish him for his uncomplying spirit, upon a poorer and scantier diet than he had been previously allowed. This is to continue until Ahab returns *in peace.* Ahab introduces this expression purposely, in order to show his entire disbelief of Micaiah's prophecy.

29. It might have been expected that Jehoshaphat would have withdrawn from the expedition when he heard Micaiah denounce it. He had, however, rashly committed himself to take part in the war by a solemn promise, *before* he bethought himself of inquiring what was the will of God in the matter. Now he was ashamed to draw back, especially as Ahab, whom the prophecy chiefly threatened, was resolved to brave it. He may also have had a personal affection for Ahab, and so have been loth to desert him in his need. Cp. 2 Chr. xix. 2.

30. *I will disguise myself*] Ahab had probably heard of Ben-hadad's order to his captains (v. 31).

31. *commanded*] "Had commanded." Ben-hadad delivers his order in the hyper-

bolical style common in the East. His meaning is, "Make it your *chief* object to kill or take the king of Israel." Apparently, his own defeat and captivity were still rankling in his mind, and he wished to retaliate on Ahab the humiliation which he considered himself to have suffered. He shows small appreciation of the generosity which had spared his life and restored him to his kingdom.

32. *Surely it is the king of Israel*] This was a natural supposition, as Jehoshaphat alone wore royal robes.

and Jehoshaphat cried out] Jehoshaphat called to his men for help, using perhaps his own peculiar battle-cry, which would be distinct from that of Ahab, and would probably be known to the Syrians.

34. *at a venture*] Lit. as in margin, *i.e.* without intent to kill the king.

between the joints of the harness] Lit. as in the margin. The "joints" were probably pieces of armour which attached the breastplate to the helmet or to the greaves. The arrow entered between the breastplate and one of these "joints." Breastplates made of metal scales were common both in Egypt and Assyria.

Turn thine hand] Lit. "turn thy hands." The driver of a chariot, both in Egypt and Assyria, held the reins with his two hands.

35. *the battle increased*] See margin; *i.e.* the tide of battle rose higher. Cp. Is. viii. 7, 8.

king was stayed up in his chariot against the Syrians, and died
at even: and the blood ran out of the wound into the ¹midst of
36 the chariot. And there went a proclamation throughout the
host about the going down of the sun, saying,- Every man to
37 his city, and every man to his own country. So the king died,
and ²was brought to Samaria; and they buried the king in
38 Samaria. And *one* washed the chariot in the pool of Samaria;
and the dogs licked up his blood; and they washed his armour;
39 according *ᵠ*unto the word of the Lord which he spake.   ¶Now
the rest of the acts of Ahab, and all that he did, and *ʳ*the ivory
house which he made, and all the cities that he built, *are* they
not written in the book of the chronicles of the kings of Israel?
40 So Ahab slept with his fathers; and Ahaziah his son reigned in
41 his stead.   ¶And *ˢ*Jehoshaphat the son of Asa began to reign
42 over Judah in the fourth year of Ahab king of Israel. Jehoshaphat *was* thirty and five years old when he began to reign;
and he reigned twenty and five years in Jerusalem. And his
43 mother's name *was* Azubah the daughter of Shilhi. And *ᵗ*he
walked in all the ways of Asa his father; he turned not aside
from it, doing *that which was* right in the eyes of the Lord:
nevertheless *ˣ*the high places were not taken away; *for* the
people offered and burnt incense yet in the high places. And
44 *ˣ*Jehoshaphat made peace with the king of Israel.   ¶Now the

ᵠ ch. 21. 19.
ʳ Amos 3. 15.

ˢ 2 Chr.20.31.

ᵗ 2 Chr. 17. 3.

ˣ ch. 14. 23.
& 15. 14.
2 Kin. 12. 3.
ˣ 2 Chr. 19.2.
2 Cor. 6. 14.

¹ Heb. *bosom.*   ² Heb. *came.*

---

the king was stayed up in his chariot] The
king's wound made it impossible for him to
remain standing without help; he therefore
had himself supported in his chariot by
attendants, in order that his soldiers might
not lose heart, as they would be sure to do,
if they knew of his peril. Ahab must not
be denied the credit of right princely fortitude on this occasion.

the midst of the chariot] Lit., as in margin.
The "bosom" of the chariot is the rounded
front, with the portion of the standing
board that adjoined it. Here the blood
would naturally collect, forming a pool, in
which the king and his charioteer must
have stood.

36. *about the going down of the sun*] *i.e.*
as soon as Ahab was dead. The abandon-
ment of the expedition and dispersion of
the army on the death of the king is thoroughly Oriental.

The LXX. version reads *vv.* 36, 37,
"Every man to his city, and every man to
his own country; for the king is dead: And
they came to Samaria," &c.

38. *they washed his armour*]   Rather,
"**the harlots bathed in it.**" The "pool of
Samaria," which was stained with Ahab's
blood by the washing of his chariot in it,
was, according to Josephus, the usual bath-
ing-place of the Samaritan harlots. A large
tank or reservoir, probably identical with
this pool, still remains on the slope of the
hill of Samaria, immediately outside the
walls.

39. *the ivory house*] So called from the
character of its ornamentation. Ivory was

largely used in the ancient world as a covering of wood-work, and seems to have been
applied, not only to furniture, but to the
doors and walls of houses.

Nothing is known of the cities built by
Ahab; but the fact is important as indicating the general prosperity of the country
in his time, and his own activity as a ruler.
Prosperity, it is plain, may for a while co-
exist with causes—such as, the decay of religion—which are sapping the vital power of
a nation, and leading it surely, if slowly, to
destruction.

the book of the chronicles, &c.] See above,
xiv. 19, xv. 31, xvi. 5, 14, 20, 27.

41. The writer returns to the history of
the kingdom of Judah (connect this verse
with xv. 24), sketching briefly a reign much
more fully given by the writer of Chronicles
(2 Chr. xvii.-xx). Cp. also the marg.
reff.

43. On the general piety of Asa, see
above, xv. 11-15 and reff. Jehoshaphat seems
to have been a still better king; for he did
not, like Asa, fall away in his old age (2
Chr. xvi. 2-12).

the high places were not taken away] This
seems to contradict 2 Chr. xvii. 6. Probably the writer of Chronicles refers to the
desire and intention of the monarch, while
the author of Kings records the practical
failure of his efforts.

44. This refers probably to an early
period in Jehoshaphat's reign—about his
eighth or his ninth year—when he closed
the long series of wars between the two
kingdoms by a formal peace, perhaps at

45 rest of the acts of Jehoshaphat, and his might that he shewed, and how he warred, *are* they not written in the book of the 46 chronicles of the kings of Judah? *y* And the remnant of the sodomites, which remained in the days of his father Asa, he took 47 out of the land. *z There was* then no king in Edom: a deputy 48 *was* king. ¶ *a* Jehoshaphat [1] *b* made ships of Tharshish to go to Ophir for gold: *c* but they went not; for the ships were broken 49 at *d* Ezion-geber. Then said Ahaziah the son of Ahab unto Jehoshaphat, Let my servants go with thy servants in the ships. 50 But Jehoshaphat would not. ¶ And *e* Jehoshaphat slept with his fathers, and was buried with his fathers in the city of David his 51 father: and Jehoram his son reigned in his stead. ¶ *f* Ahaziah the son of Ahab began to reign over Israel in Samaria the seventeenth year of Jehoshaphat king of Judah, and reigned two years 52 over Israel. And he did evil in the sight of the LORD, and *g* walked in the way of his father, and in the way of his mother, and in the way of Jeroboam the son of Nebat, who made Israel 53 to sin: for *h* he served Baal, and worshipped him, and provoked to anger the LORD God of Israel, according to all that his father had done.

[1] Or, had *ten ships*.

y ch. 14. 24.
& 15. 12.
z Gen. 25. 23.
2 Sam. 8. 14.
a 2 Chr. 20.
35, &c.
b ch. 10. 22.
c 2 Chr. 20. 37.
d ch. 9. 26.
e 2 Chr. 21. 1.

f ver. 40.

g ch. 15. 26.

h Judg. 2. 11.
ch. 16. 31.

once cemented by a marriage between Jehoram and Athaliah (*v.* 2 note).

45. *the book of the chronicles*, &c.] Cp. *v.* 39 note. The biographer of Jehoshaphat appears to have been Jehu, the son of Hanani (2 Chr. xx. 34).

46. See marg. reff. notes.

47. In the time of Solomon, Hadad (xi. 14), according to the LXX., "reigned over Edom." It appears by the present passage that the country had been again reduced, either by Jehoshaphat, or by an earlier king, and was dependent on the kingdom of Judah, being governed by a "deputy" or viceroy, who, however, was allowed the royal title (cp. 2 K. iii. 9, 12, 26). This government of dependencies by means of subject kings was the all but universal practice in the East down to the time of Cyrus (iv. 21 note).

48. The expression, "ships of Tharshish," probably designates ships of a particular class, ships (*i.e.*) like those with which the Phœnicians used to trade to Tharshish (Tartessus, x. 22 note). Cp. the use of "Indiaman" for a vessel of a certain class. Jehoshaphat's fleet was constructed at Ezion-Gaber, on the Red Sea (2 Chr. xx. 36), where Solomon had previously built a navy (ix. 26). Being lord-paramount of Edom,

Jehoshaphat had the right of using this harbour.

49. 2 Chr. xx. 35, 36, explains that the two kings conjointly built the fleet with which the Ophir trade (ix. 28 note) was to be reopened. Ahaziah had thus an interest in the ships; and when they were wrecked, attributing, as it would seem, the calamity to the unskilfulness of his ally's mariners, he proposed that the fleet should be manned in part by Israelite sailors—men probably accustomed to the sea, perhaps trained at Tyre. This proposal Jehoshaphat refused, either offended at the reflection on his subjects' skill, or accepting the wreck of the ships, which Eliezer had prophesied, as a proof that God was against the entire undertaking.

51. *two years*] According to our reckoning, not much more than a twelvemonth.

52. *in the way of his mother*] In this phrase, which does not occur anywhere else, we see the strong feeling of the writer as to the influence of Jezebel (cp. xvi. 31).

51–53. It would be of advantage if these verses were transferred to the Second Book of Kings, which would thus open with the commencement of Ahaziah's reign. The division of the Books does not proceed from the author. See "Introd.," p. 263.

THE SECOND BOOK
OF THE
KINGS,
COMMONLY CALLED, THE FOURTH BOOK OF THE KINGS.

a 2 Sam. 8. 2.
b ch. 3. 5.

Chap. 1. THEN Moab *a*rebelled against Israel *b*after the death of
2 Ahab. And Ahaziah fell down through a lattice in his upper
chamber that *was* in Samaria, and was sick : and he sent messengers, and said unto them, Go, enquire of Baal-zebub the god

c Josh. 13. 3.

3 of *c*Ekron whether I shall recover of this disease. But the angel
of the LORD said to Elijah the Tishbite, Arise, go up to meet the
messengers of the king of Samaria, and say unto them, *Is it* not
because *there is* not a God in Israel, *that* ye go to enquire of
4 Baal-zebub the god of Ekron? Now therefore thus saith the
LORD, ¹Thou shalt not come down from that bed on which thou
5 art gone up, but shalt surely die. And Elijah departed. ¶ And
when the messengers turned back unto him, he said unto them,
6 Why are ye now turned back? And they said unto him, There
came a man up to meet us, and said unto us, Go, turn again
unto the king that sent you, and say unto him, Thus saith the
LORD, *Is it* not because *there is* not a God in Israel, *that* thou
sendest to enquire of Baal-zebub the god of Ekron? therefore
thou shalt not come down from that bed on which thou art gone
7 up, but shalt surely die. And he said unto them, ²What manner
of man *was he* which came up to meet you, and told you these

d See Zech.
13. 4.
Matt. 3. 4.

8 words? And they answered him, He *was d*an hairy man, and
girt with a girdle of leather about his loins. And he said, It *is*

¹ Heb. *The bed whither thou art gone up,*
thou shalt not come down from it.

² Heb. *What was the manner*
of the man.

I. 1. The Moabites, who had once lorded
over Israel (Judg. iii. 12-14), were reduced
to subjection by David, and treated with
extreme severity (marg. ref.). In the time
of Ahab they were dependent on the kingdom of Israel, to which it has been generally supposed that they fell at the
separation of Israel from Judah. The
Moabite monument (see iii. 4), discovered
in 1869, has now given reason to believe
that they then recovered their independence, but were again reduced by Omri,
who, with his son Ahab, is said (in round
numbers) to have "oppressed" them for
"forty years." Ahab's death was seized
upon as an occasion for revolt, and Moab
(perhaps owing to Ahaziah's sickness) easily
regained her independence.

2. *a lattice*] The "upper chamber" had
probably a single latticed window, through
which Ahaziah fell. Windows in the East
are to this day generally closed by lattices
of interlaced wood, which open outwards;
so that, if the fastening is not properly
secured, one who leans against them may
easily fall out.

Baal-zebub] Lit. "Lord (*i.e.*, averter) of

flies." Flies in the East constitute one of
the most terrible of plagues (Ps. cv. 31;
Ex. viii. 24); and Orientals would be as
likely to have a "god of flies" as a god of
storm and thunder. To enquire (*v.* 3) of
Baal-zebub was practically to deny Jehovah. Ahaziah cast aside the last remnant
of respect for the old religion, and consulted a foreign oracle, as if the voice
of God were wholly silent in his own
country.

For Ekron see marg. ref.

4. *therefore,* &c.] As a punishment for
this insult to Jehovah.

8. *an hairy man*] Either in allusion to his
shaggy cloak of untanned skin; or, more
probably, an expression descriptive of the
prophet's person, of his long flowing locks,
abundant beard, and general profusion of
hair. His costume was that of a thorough
ascetic. Generally the Jews wore girdles
of linen or cotton stuff, soft and comfortable. Under the girdle they wore one or
two long linen gowns or shirts, and over
these they had sometimes a large shawl.
Elijah had only his leathern girdle and his
sheepskin cape or "mantle."

9 Elijah the Tishbite. ¶Then the king sent unto him a captain of
fifty with his fifty. And he went up to him: and, behold, he
sat on the top of an hill. And he spake unto him, Thou man of
10 God, the king hath said, Come down. And Elijah answered and
said to the captain of fifty, If I *be* a man of God, then *e*let fire   *e* Luke 9. 54.
come down from heaven, and consume thee and thy fifty. And
there came down fire from heaven, and consumed him and his
11 fifty. Again also he sent unto him another captain of fifty with
his fifty. And he answered and said unto him, O man of God,
12 thus hath the king said, Come down quickly. And Elijah
answered and said unto them, If I *be* a man of God, let fire come
down from heaven, and consume thee and thy fifty. And the
fire of God came down from heaven, and consumed him and his
13 fifty. And he sent again a captain of the third fifty with his
fifty. And the third captain of fifty went up, and came and
¹fell on his knees before Elijah, and besought him, and said unto
him, O man of God, I pray thee, let my life, and the life of these
14 fifty thy servants, ʃbe precious in thy sight. Behold, there came   ʃ 1 Sam. 26.
fire down from heaven, and burnt up the two captains of the   21.
former fifties with their fifties: therefore let my life now be   Ps. 72. 14.
15 precious in thy sight. And the angel of the LORD said unto
Elijah, Go down with him: be not afraid of him. And he arose,
16 and went down with him unto the king. ¶And he said unto
him, Thus saith the LORD, Forasmuch as thou hast sent messengers to enquire of Baal-zebub the god of Ekron, *is it* not
because *there is* no God in Israel to enquire of his word? therefore thou shalt not come down off that bed on which thou art
17 gone up, but shalt surely die. ¶So he died according to the
word of the LORD which Elijah had spoken. And ²Jehoram
reigned in his stead in the second year of Jehoram the son of
18 Jehoshaphat king of Judah; because he had no son. Now the
rest of the acts of Ahaziah which he did, *are* they not written in
the book of the chronicles of the kings of Israel?

¹ Heb. *bowed.*
² The second year that *Jehoram*   was *Prorex,* and the eighteenth of
    Jehoshaphat, ch. 3. 1.

---

9. *Then the king sent unto him*] i.e., in
order to seize and punish him. Cp. 1 K.
xviii. 10, xxii. 27.

10. The charge of cruelty made against
Elijah makes it needful to consider the
question: What was Elijah's motive?
And the answer is :—Simply to make a
signal example, to vindicate God's honour
in a striking way. Ahaziah had, as it
were, challenged Jehovah to a trial of
strength by sending a band of fifty to arrest one man. Elijah was not Jesus Christ,
able to reconcile mercy with truth, the
vindication of God's honour with the ut-·
most tenderness for erring men, and awe
them merely by His Presence (cp. John
xviii. 6). In Elijah the spirit of the Law
was embodied in its full severity. His zeal
was fierce ; he was not shocked by blood ;
he had no softness and no relenting. He
did not permanently profit by the warning
at Horeb (1 K. xix. 12 note). He continued
the uncompromising avenger of sin, the
wielder of the terrors of the Lord, such

exactly as he had shown himself at Carmel. He is; consequently, no pattern for
Christian men (Luke. ix. 55) ; but his
character is the perfection of the purely legal
type. No true Christian after Pentecost
would have done what Elijah did. But
what he did, when he did it, was not sinful.
It was but executing strict, stern justice.
Elijah asked that fire should fall — God
made it fall ; and, by so doing, both vindi
cated His own honour, and justified th
prayer of His prophet.

17. The similarity of names in the two
royal houses of Israel and Judah at this
time, and at no other, seems to be the consequence of the close ties which united the
two reigning families, and is well noted
among the "undesigned coincidences" of
the Old Testament. The accession of the
Israelite Jehoram (Ahab's brother) took
place, according to iii. 1, in the eighteenth
year of Jehoshaphat. Jehoram of Judah
perhaps received the royal title from his
father as early as his father's sixteenth year,

a Gen. 5. 24.
b 1 Kin.19.21.
c See Ruth
1. 15, 16.
d 1 Sam. 20.
3, 25, 26.
ch. 4. 30.
e 1 Kin.20.35.
ver. 5, 7, 15.
ch. 4. 1, 38.
& 9. 1.

CHAP. 2. AND it came to pass, when the LORD would *a* take up Elijah into heaven by a whirlwind, that Elijah went with *b* Elisha 2 from Gilgal. And Elijah said unto Elisha, *c* Tarry here, I pray thee; for the LORD hath sent me to Beth-el. And Elisha said *unto him, d As* the LORD liveth, and *as* thy soul liveth, I will not 3 leave thee. So they went down to Beth-el. And *e* the sons of the prophets that *were* at Beth-el came forth to Elisha, and said unto him, Knowest thou that the LORD will take away thy master from thy head to day? And he said, Yea, I know *it;* 4 hold ye your peace. And Elijah said unto him, Elisha, tarry here, I pray thee; for the LORD hath sent me to Jericho. And he said, *As* the LORD liveth, and *as* thy soul liveth, I will not 5 leave thee. So they came to Jericho. And the sons of the prophets that *were* at Jericho came to Elisha, and said unto him, Knowest thou that the LORD will take away thy master from thy head to day? And he answered, Yea, I know *it;* 6 hold ye your peace. And Elijah said unto him, Tarry, I pray thee, here; for the LORD hath sent me to Jordan. And he said, *As* the LORD liveth, and *as* thy soul liveth, I will not leave 7 thee. And they two went on. And fifty men of the sons of the prophets went, and stood [1] to view afar off: and they two stood 8 by Jordan. And Elijah took his mantle, and wrapped *it* to-

f So Ex. 14.
21.
Josh. 3. 16.
ver. 14.

gether, and smote the waters, and *f* they were divided hither and

[1] Heb. *in sight,* or, *over against.*

---

when he was about to join Ahab against the Syrians; the same year might then be called either the eighteenth of Jehoshaphat or the second of Jehoram.

II. **1.** The events of this chapter are related out of their chronological order. Elijah's translation did not take place till after the accession of Jehoram in Judah (2 Chr. xxi. 12), which was not till the fifth year of Jehoram of Israel (viii. 16). The writer of Kings, having concluded his notices of the ministry of Elijah in ch. i., and being about to pass in ch. iii. to the ministry of Elisha, thought it best to bring at this point the final scene of Elijah's life, though it did not occur till several years later.

Gilgal] The modern *Jiljilieh*, on the highland between Nablous and Beitin (Bethel), about eight and a half miles from the latter, is now commonly supposed to be the Gilgal here mentioned. Some regard it as the ordinary residence of Elisha (iv. 38).

2. *Tarry here*] Elijah's motive in making this request is not clear. Perhaps he thought that so awful and sacred a scene as that which he was led to expect (*v.* 9), should be kept as secret as possible.

the LORD *hath sent me to Bethel*] Elijah may have been directed to Bethel, because of the "School of the Prophets" there, that the sight of him—if not his words—might console and encourage them before they lost him for ever.

as the LORD *liveth,* &c.] This double oath, repeated three times (*vv.* 4, 6), is very re-

markable. The two clauses of it are separately used with some frequency (see Judg. viii. 19; Ruth iii. 13; 1 Sam. i. 26, &c.), but it is comparatively seldom that they are united (see marg. reff.).

3. *came forth to Elisha*] It does not appear that any interchange of speech took place between "the sons of the Prophets" (see marg. ref. note) and Elijah; but independent revelations had been made to the two "schools" at Bethel and Jericho (*v.* 5), and also to Elisha, with respect to Elijah's coming removal.

from thy head] *i.e.* from his position as teacher and master. The teacher sat on an elevated seat, so that his feet were level with the heads of his pupils (cp. Acts xxii. 3).

hold ye your peace] *i.e.* "Say nothing—disturb us not. The matter is too sacred for words."

7. *fifty men of the sons of the prophets*] We see by this how large were the prophetical schools. It is implied that the "fifty" were only a *portion* of the school of Jericho. They ascended the abrupt heights behind the town, whence they would command a view of the whole course of the river and of the opposite bank for many miles.

8. *they were divided,* &c.] The attestation to the divine mission of Elijah furnished by this miracle would tend to place him upon a par in the thoughts of men with the two great leaders of the nation named in the marg. reff.

9 thither, so that they two went over on dry ground. ¶And
it came to pass, when they were gone over, that Elijah said
unto Elisha, Ask what I shall do for thee, before I be taken
away from thee. And Elisha said, I pray thee, let a double
10 portion of thy spirit be upon me. And he said, ¹Thou hast
asked a hard thing : *nevertheless*, if thou see me *when I am* taken
from thee, it shall be so unto thee ; but if not, it shall not be *so*.
11 ¶And it came to pass, as they still went on, and talked, that,
behold, *there appeared* ᵍa chariot of fire, and horses of fire, and
parted them both asunder ; and Elijah went up by a whirlwind
12 into heaven. And Elisha saw *it*, and he cried, ʰMy father,
my father, the chariot of Israel, and the horsemen thereof.
And he saw him no more : and he took hold of his own
13 clothes, and rent them in two pieces. He took up also the
mantle of Elijah that fell from him, and went back, and stood
14 by the ²bank of Jordan ; and he took the mantle of Elijah that
fell from him, and smote the waters, and said, Where *is* the
LORD God of Elijah ? and when he also had smitten the waters,
15 ⁱthey parted hither and thither : and Elisha went over. ¶And
when the sons of the prophets which *were* ᵏto view at Jericho
saw him, they said, The spirit of Elijah doth rest on Elisha.
And they came to meet him, and bowed themselves to the
16 ground before him. And they said unto him, Behold now, there
be with thy servants fifty ³strong men : let them go, we pray
thee, and seek thy master : ˡlest peradventure the Spirit of
the LORD hath taken him up, and cast him upon ⁴some mountain, or into some valley. And he said, Ye shall not send.
17 And when they urged him till he was ashamed, he said, Send.
They sent therefore fifty men ; and they sought three days, but
18 found him not. And when they came again to him, (for he
tarried at Jericho,) he said unto them, Did I not say unto you,
19 Go not ? ¶And the men of the city said unto Elisha, Behold, I

ᵍ ch. 6. 17.
Ps. 104. 4.

ʰ ch. 13. 14.

ⁱ ver. 8.
ᵏ ver. 7.

ˡ See 1 Kin.
18. 12.
Ezek. 8. 3.
Acts 8. 39.

---

¹ Heb. *Thou hast done hard
in asking.*   ² Heb. *lip.*   ³ Heb. *sons of strength.*
⁴ Heb. *one of the mountains.*

---

9. *let a double portion of thy spirit be upon
me*] Like Solomon, Elisha asks for no
worldly advantage, but for spiritual power
to discharge his office aright. The "double
portion" is that which denotes the proportion of a father's property which was the
right of an eldest son (Deut. xxi. 17). Elisha therefore asked for twice as much of
Elijah's spirit as should be inherited by any
other of the "sons of the Prophets." He
simply claimed, *i.e.*, to be acknowledged as
Elijah's *firstborn* spiritual son.

10. It would be better to omit the words
"when I am," which are not in the original.
The sign was to be Elisha's seeing the actual
translation, which he did (*v.* 12).

11. *Elijah went up*, &c.] No honest exe-
gesis can explain this passage in any other
sense than as teaching the translation of
Elijah, who was taken from the earth, like
Enoch (Gen. v. 24), without dying. Cp.
Ecclus. xlviii. 9.

12. *the chariot of Israel and the horsemen
thereof*] These difficult words are probably
said of Elijah, whom Elisha addresses as

"the true defence of Israel, better than
either the chariots or horsemen" which he
saw. Hence his rending his clothes in
token of his grief.

14. *Where*, &c.] Some prefer, "Where is
the Lord God of Elijah, **even he**? And
when he had smitten, &c." Or, according
to others, "now when he, &c." Elisha's
smiting of the waters seems to have been
tentative. He was not sure of its result.
Hence the form of his invocation—"Where
is the Lord God of Elijah ? Is He here
—*i.e.*—with me, or is He not ?" Answered
by the event, he appears never subsequently
to have doubted.

16. Cp. marg. reff. The words "cast
him upon some mountain," rather imply
that they expected to find the Prophet
alive.

17. *till he was ashamed*] *i.e.* to refuse
them any longer.

19. *the water is naught*] *i.e.* "bad."
and the ground barren] Translate "and
the land apt to miscarry." The stream
was thought to be the cause of untimely

pray thee, the situation of this city *is* pleasant, as my lord
20 seeth : but the water *is* naught, and the ground [1]barren. And
he said, Bring me a new cruse, and put salt therein. And
21 they brought *it* to him.   And he went forth unto the spring
of the waters, and *m*cast the salt in there, and said, Thus
saith the LORD, I have healed these waters; there shall not be
22 from thence any more death or barren *land*.   So the waters
were healed unto this day, according to the saying of Elisha
23 which he spake.   ¶ And he went up from thence unto Beth-el :
and as he was going up by the way, there came forth little
children out of the city, and mocked him, and said unto him,
24 Go up, thou bald head; go up, thou bald head.   And he
turned back, and looked on them, and cursed them in the
name of the LORD.   And there came forth two she bears out of
25 the wood, and tare forty and two children of them.   And he
went from thence to mount Carmel, and from thence he returned
to Samaria.

CHAP. 3.   NOW *a*Jehoram the son of Ahab began to reign over
Israel in Samaria the eighteenth year of Jehoshaphat king of
2 Judah, and reigned twelve years.   And he wrought evil in the
sight of the LORD, but not like his father, and like his mother :
for he put away the [2]image of Baal *b*that his father had made.
3 Nevertheless he cleaved unto *c*the sins of Jeroboam the son of
Nebat, which made Israel to sin ; he departed not therefrom.
4 ¶ And Mesha king of Moab was a sheepmaster, and rendered

m See Ex.
15. 25.
ch. 4. 41.
& 6. 6.
John 9. 6.

a ch. 1. 17.

b 1 Kin. 16.
31, 32.
c 1 Kin. 12.
28, 31, 32.

---

[1] Heb. *causing to miscarry.*   [2] Heb. *statue.*

---

births, abortions, and the like, among the
cattle, perhaps also among the people, that
drank of it.

20. The "new cruse" and the "salt" are
evidently chosen from a regard to symbolism. The foul stream represents sin, and to
cleanse it emblems of purity must be taken.
Hence the clean "new" dish previously un-
used, and thus untainted ; and the salt, a
common Scriptural symbol of incorruption
(see Lev. ii. 13; Ezek. xliii. 24; Matt. v.
13, &c.).

21. *the spring of the waters*] The spring
intended is probably that now called Ain-
es-Sultan, which is not much more than a
mile from the site of the ancient town. It
is described as a large and beautiful fountain
of sweet and pleasant water. The springs
issuing from the eastern base of the highlands of Judah and Benjamin are to this
day generally brackish.

23. As Beth-el was the chief seat of the
calf-worship (1 K. xii. 32, 33, xiii. 1-32), a
Prophet of Jehovah was not unlikely to
meet with insult there.

by the way] *i.e.* "by the usual road," probably that which winds up the Wady Suweinit, under hills even now retaining some
trees, and in Elisha's time covered with a
dense forest, the haunt of savage animals.
Cp. 1 K. xiii. 24; and for the general prevalence of beasts of prey in the country,
both earlier and later than this, see Judg.
xiv. 5; 1 Sam. xvii. 34; 2 K. xvii. 25; Am.
v. 19, &c.

24. On this occasion only do we find Elisha a minister of vengeance.   Perhaps it
was necessary to show, at the outset of his
career as a Prophet, that he too, so mild and
peaceful could, like Elijah, wield the terrors
of God's judgments (1 K. xix. 19 note).   The
persons really punished were, not so much
the children, as the wicked parents (*v.* 23),
whose mouth-pieces the children were, and
who justly lost the gift of offspring of which
they had shown themselves unworthy.

25. *Carmel*] Where Elisha held gatherings
for religious purposes (iv. 23-25) during one
period of his life, if he did not actually reside
there.

III. 1. *in the eighteenth year of Jehoshaphat*] This date agrees exactly with the
statements that Jehoshaphat began to reign
in the fourth year of Ahab (1 K. xxii. 41),
and Ahaziah in the 17th of Jehoshaphat
(do. *v.* 51).

2. On the "evil" wrought by Ahab, see
especially 1 K. xvi. 30-34. Jehoram, warned
by the fate of his brother (i. 4 note), began
his reign by a formal abolition of the Phœnician state religion introduced by Ahab—
even if he connived at its continuance among
the people (x. 26, 27) ; and by a re-establishment of the old worship of the kingdom as
arranged by Jeroboam.

4. Moab, the region immediately east of
the Dead Sea and of the lower Jordan,
though in part suited for agriculture, is in
the main a great grazing country.   Mesha
resembled a modern Arab Sheikh, whose

unto the king of Israel an hundred thousand ᵈlambs, and an
5 hundred thousand rams, with the wool. But it came to pass,
when ᵉAhab was dead, that the king of Moab rebelled against
6 the king of Israel. ¶And king Jehoram went out of Samaria
7 the same time, and numbered all Israel. And he went and sent
to Jehoshaphat the king of Judah, saying, The king of Moab
hath rebelled against me: wilt thou go with me against Moab
to battle? And he said, I will go up: ᶠI am as thou art, my
8 people as thy people, and my horses as thy horses. And he said,
Which way shall we go up? And he answered, The way through
9 the wilderness of Edom. So the king of Israel went, and the
king of Judah, and the king of Edom: and they fetched a compass of seven days' journey: and there was no water for the
10 host, and for the cattle ¹that followed them. And the king of
Israel said, Alas! that the LORD hath called these three kings
11 together, to deliver them into the hand of Moab! But ᵍJehosh-
aphat said, Is there not here a prophet of the LORD, that we may
enquire of the LORD by him? And one of the king of Israel's
servants answered and said, Here is Elisha the son of Shaphat,

d See Isa.16. 1.

e ch.1. 1.

f 1 Kin. 22. 4.

g 1 Kin. 22. 7.

¹ Heb. *at their feet*, See Exod. 11. 8.

wealth is usually estimated by the number of his flocks and herds. His tribute of the wool of 100,000 lambs was a tribute in kind, the ordinary tribute at this time in the East.

Mesha is the monarch who wrote the inscription on the "Moabite stone" (i. 1 note). The points established by the Inscription are—1. That Moab recovered from the blow dealt by David (2 Sam. viii. 2, 12), and became again an independent state in the interval between David's conquest and the accession of Omri; 2. That Omri reconquered the country, and that it then became subject to the northern kingdom, and remained so throughout his reign and that of his son Ahab, and into the reign of Ahab's son and successor, Ahaziah; 3. That the independence was regained by means of a war, in which Mesha took town after town from the Israelites, including in his conquests many of the towns which, at the original occupation of the Holy Land, had passed into the possession of the Reubenites or the Gadites, as Baal-Meon (Num. xxxii. 38), Kirjathaim (do. 37), Ataroth (do. 34), Nebo (do. 38), Jahaz (Josh. xiii. 18), &c. ; 4. That the name of Jehovah was well known to the Moabites as that of the God of the Israelites ; and 5. That there was a sanctuary of Jehovah at Nebo, in the Trans-Jordanic territory, where "vessels" were used in His service.

7. The close alliance between the two kingdoms still subsisted. Jehoram therefore sends confidently to make the same request with respect to Moab that his father had made two years before with respect to Syria (marg. ref.). Jehoshaphat consented at once, notwithstanding that his former compliance had drawn upon him the rebuke of a Prophet (2 Chr. xix. 2). Perhaps Jeho-

ram's removal of the Baal-worship (*v.* 2) weighed with him. He had himself been attacked by the Moabites in the preceding year; and though the attempt had failed, Jehoshaphat would feel that it might be renewed, and that it was important to seize the opportunity of weakening his enemy which now offered itself.

8. The readiest and most natural "way" was across the Jordan near Jericho into the Arboth-Moab, and then along the eastern shore of the Dead Sea to Moab proper, the tract south of the Arnon. But the way chosen was that which·led to the Edomite country, viz., round the southern extremity of the Dead Sea, and across the Arabah, or continuation of the Jordan and Dead Sea valley. Thus would be effected a junction with the forces of Edom, which had resumed its dependence on Judah, though the year before it had been in alliance with Moab (2 Chr. xx. 22) ; and they would come upon the Moabites unprepared.

9. *seven days' journey*] The distance of the route probably followed is not much more than 100 miles. But the difficulties of the way are great; and the army might not be able to move along it at a faster rate than about 15 miles a day.

no water] The kings had probably expected to find sufficient water for both men and baggage animals in the Wady-el-Ahsy, which divides Edom from Moab, and which has a stream that is now regarded as perennial. But it was dried up—quite a possible occurrence with any of the streams of this region.

11. *a prophet of the* LORD] *i.e.* of Jehovah. It was necessary to inquire thus definitely, as there were still plenty of prophets who were only prophets of Baal (*v.* 13).

h ch. 2. 25.
i Ezek. 11. 3.
k So Judg.
10. 14.
Ruth 1. 15.
l 1 Kin.18.19.
m 1 Kin.17.1.
ch. 5. 16.

n See
1 Sam. 10. 5.
1 Chr. 25.1—
3.
o Ezek. 1. 3.
& 3. 14, 22.
& 8. 1.
p ch. 4. 3.

q Ex. 29. 39.
40.

12 which poured water on the hands of Elijah. And Jehoshaphat
said, The word of the LORD is with him. So the king of Israel
and Jehoshaphat and the king of Edom *h*went down to him.
13 And Elisha said unto the king of Israel, *i*What have I to do
with thee ? *k*get thee to *l*the prophets of thy father, and to the
prophets of thy mother. And the king of Israel said unto him,
Nay: for the LORD hath called these three kings together, to
14 deliver them into the hand of Moab. And Elisha said, *m*As the
LORD of hosts liveth, before whom I stand, surely, were it not
that I regard the presence of Jehoshaphat the king of Judah, I
15 would not look toward thee, nor see thee. But now bring me
*n*a minstrel. And it came to pass, when the minstrel played,
16 that *o*the hand of the LORD came upon him. And he said, Thus
17 saith the LORD, *p*Make this valley full of ditches. For thus
saith the LORD, Ye shall not see wind, neither shall ye see rain;
yet that valley shall be filled with water, that ye may drink,
18 both ye, and your cattle, and your beasts. And this is *but* a
light thing in the sight of the LORD : he will deliver the Moab-
19 ites also into your hand. And ye shall smite every fenced city,
and every choice city, and shall fell every good tree, and stop all
wells of water, and *1*mar every good piece of land with stones.
20 ¶And it came to pass in the morning, when *q*the meat offering
was offered, that, behold, there came water by the way of Edom,

¹ Heb. *grieve*.

Here is Elisha] Jehoram appears to have
been ignorant of his presence with the host,
and one of his "servants," or officers,
answered Jehoshaphat's inquiry.

which poured water] An act signifying
ministration or attendance (cp. John xiii.
5 seq.).

13. Jehoram's humility in seeking (*v.* 12)
instead of summoning Elisha, does not save
him from rebuke. His reformation (*v.* 2)
had been but a half reformation—a compromise with idolatry.

Nay : for the LORD *hath called*, &c.] The
force of this reply seems to be—"Nay, reproach me not, since I am in a sore strait—
and not only I, but these two other kings
also. The Lord — Jehovah — is about to
deliver us into the hand of Moab. If thou
canst not, or wilt not help, at least do not
reproach."

15. Music seems to have been a regular
accompaniment of prophecy in the "schools
of the Prophets" (marg. ref.), and an occasional accompaniment of it elsewhere (Ex.
xv. 20).

16. *ditches*] Or "pits" (Jer. xiv. 3). They
were to dig pits in the broad valley or
wady, wherein the water might remain,
instead of flowing off down the torrent
course.

17. No rain was to fall where the Israelites
and their enemies were encamped ; there
was not even to be that all but universal
accompaniment of rain in the East, a sudden rise of wind (cp. 1 K. xviii. 45; Ps.
cxlvii. 18 ; Matt. vii. 25).

cattle, and your beasts] The former are the

animals brought for food. The latter are the
baggage animals.

19. *ye shall fell every good tree*] This is
not an infringement of the rule laid down in
Deut. xx. 19, 20. The Israelites were not forbidden to fell the fruit trees in an enemy's
country, as a part of the ravage of war,
when they had no thoughts of occupying
the country. The plan of thus injuring an
enemy was probably in general use among
the nations of these parts at the time. We
see the destruction represented frequently
on the Assyrian monuments and mentioned
in the inscriptions of Egypt.

and stop all wells of water] The stoppage
of wells was a common feature of ancient,
and especially Oriental, warfare (cp. Gen.
xxvi. 15–18).

mar...with stones] The exact converse of
that suggested in Isai. v. 2. The land in
and about Palestine is so stony that the
first work of the cultivator is to collect the
surface stones together into heaps. An
army marching through a land could easily
undo this work, dispersing the stones thus
gathered, and spreading them once more
over the fields.

20. *when the meat offering was offered*] *i.e.*
about sunrise, when the morning sacrifice
was offered. Cp. 1 K. xviii. 29.

there came water by the way of Edom]
The Wady-el-Ahsy drains a considerable
portion of northern Edom. Heavy rain
had fallen during the night in some part of
this tract, and with the morning a freshet
of water came down the valley, filling the
pits.

21 and the country was filled with water. And when all the Moabites heard that the kings were come up to fight against them,
they [1]gathered all that were able to [2]put on armour, and up-
22 ward, and stood in the border. And they rose up early in the
morning, and the sun shone upon the water, and the Moabites
23 saw the water on the other side *as* red as blood: and they said,
This *is* blood: the kings are surely [3]slain, and they have smitten
24 one another: now therefore, Moab, to the spoil. And when
they came to the camp of Israel, the Israelites rose up and smote
the Moabites, so that they fled before them: but [4]they went
25 forward smiting the Moabites, even in *their* country. And they
beat down the cities, and on every good piece of land cast every
man his stone, and filled it; and they stopped all the wells of
water, and felled all the good trees: [5]only in [r]Kir-haraseth left   [r] Isai. 16. 7,
they the stones thereof; howbeit the slingers went about *it*, and   11.
26 smote it. ¶And when the king of Moab saw that the battle
was too sore for him, he took with him seven hundred men
that drew swords, to break through *even* unto the king of Edom:
27 but they could not. Then [s]he took his eldest son that should   [s] Mic. 6. 7.
have reigned in his stead, and offered him *for* a burnt offer-
ing upon the wall. And there was great indignation against
Israel: [t]and they departed from him, and returned to *their own*   [t] ch. 8. 20.
land.
CHAP. 4. NOW there cried a certain woman of the wives of [a]the   [a] 1 Kin. 20.
sons of the prophets unto Elisha, saying, Thy servant my hus-   35.
band is dead; and thou knowest that thy servant did fear the
LORD: and the creditor is come [b]to take unto him my two sons   [b] See Lev.
   25. 39.
   Matt. 18. 25.

[1] Heb. *were cried together.*
[2] Heb. *gird himself with a girdle.*
[3] Heb. *destroyed.*
[4] Or, *they smote in it even smiting.*
[5] Heb. *until he left the stones thereof in Kir-haraseth.*

---

21. *and stood in the border*] On the north
side of the wady, ready to defend their
territory.
23. The sun had risen with a ruddy light,
as is frequently the case after a storm (cp.
Matt. xvi. 3), nearly over the Israelite camp,
and the pits, deep but with small mouths,
gleaming redly through the haze which
would lie along the newly moistened valley,
seemed to the Moabites like pools of blood.
The preceding year, they and their allies
had mutually destroyed each other (2 Chr.
xx. 23). It seemed to them, from their
knowledge of the jealousies between Judah,
Israel, and Edom, not unlikely that a
similar calamity had now befallen their
foes.
25. Kir-Haraseth, also Kir-Hareseth, is
identified almost certainly with the modern
Kerak, a strong city on the highland immediately east of the southern part of the Dead
Sea. It was the great fortress of Moab,
though not the capital, which was Rabbath
or Rabbah. It was an important stronghold at the time of the Crusades, and is
still a place of great strength. Kir seems
to have meant "fortress." It is found in
Cir-cesium, Car-chemish, &c.
Kir-Haraseth resisted all the attempts
to dismantle it; but the slingers found

places on the hills which surrounded it,
whence they could throw their stones into
it and harass the garrison, though they
could not take the town.
26. *to break through, even unto the king of
Edom*] Either because he thought that the
king of Edom would connive at his escape
or to take vengeance on him for having deserted his former allies (*v.* 8 note).
27. Cp. marg. ref. Mesha, when his
sally failed, took, as a last resource, his
first born son, and offered him as a burnt-
offering to appease the manifest anger of
his god Chemosh, and obtain his aid against
his enemies. This act was thoroughly in
accordance with Moabitish notions.
*and there was great indignation against
Israel*] Either the Israelites were indignant
with themselves, or the men of Judah and
the Edomites were indignant at the Israelites for having caused the pollution of this
sacrifice, and the siege was relinquished.
IV. 1. *the creditor is come,* &c.] The Law
of Moses, like the Athenian and the Roman
law, recognised servitude for debt, and
allowed that pledging of the debtor's person, which, in a rude state of society, is
regarded as the safest and the most natural
security (see marg. ref.). In the present
case it would seem that, so long as the

2 to be bondmen. And Elisha said unto her, What shall I do for thee? tell me, what hast thou in the house? And she said, Thine handmaid hath not any thing in the house, save a pot of 3 oil. Then he said, Go, borrow thee vessels abroad of all thy *See ch. 3.* 4 neighbours, *even* empty vessels; *c1*borrow not a few. And when 16. thou art come in, thou shalt shut the door upon thee and upon thy sons, and shalt pour out into all those vessels, and thou 5 shalt set aside that which is full. So she went from him, and shut the door upon her and upon her sons, who brought *the* 6 *vessels* to her; and she poured out. And it came to pass, when the vessels were full, that she said unto her son, Bring me yet a vessel. And he said unto her, *There is* not a vessel more. And 7 the oil stayed. Then she came and told the man of God. And he said, Go, sell the oil, and pay thy 2debt, and live thou and 8 thy children of the rest. ¶And 3it fell on a day, that Elisha *d* Josh.19.18. passed to *d*Shunem, where *was* a great woman; and she 4constrained him to eat bread. And *so* it was, *that* as oft as he 9 passed by, he turned in thither to eat bread. And she said unto her husband, Behold now, I perceive that this *is* an holy man 10 of God, which passeth by us continually. Let us make a little chamber, I pray thee, on the wall; and let us set for him there bed, and a table, and a stool, and a candlestick: and it shall 11 be, when he cometh to us, that he shall turn in thither. ¶And it fell on a day, that he came thither, and he turned into the 12 chamber, and lay there. And he said to Gehazi his servant, Call this Shunammite. And when he had called her, she stood 13 before him. And he said unto him, Say now unto her, Behold, thou hast been careful for us with all this care; what *is* to be done for thee? wouldest thou be spoken for to the king, or to the captain of the host? And she answered, I dwell among 14 mine own people. And he said, What then *is* to be done for her? And Gehazi answered, Verily she hath no child, and her 15 husband is old. And he said, Call her. And when he had called *e* Gen. 18.10. 16 her, she stood in the door. And he said, *e*About this 5season, 14. according to the time of life, thou shalt embrace a son. And

---

1 Or, *scant not.*   3 Heb. *there was a day.*   4 Heb. *laid hold on him.*
2 Or, *creditor.*   5 Heb. *set time.*

---

debtor lived, the creditor had not enforced his right over his sons, but now on his death he claimed their services, to which he was by law entitled.

2. *a pot of oil*] Or, " an anointing of oil" —so much oil, *i.e.*, as would serve me for one anointing of my person. The word used occurs only in this passage.

8. *And it fell on a day*] The original of the expression here used, which occurs *three* times in the present narrative (*vv.* 11, 18), is also found in Job i. 6, 13, ii. 1. The character of the expression perhaps supports the view that the author of Kings has collected from various sources his account of the miracles of Elisha, and has kept in each case the words of the original writer.

a great woman] That is, " a *rich* woman." Cp. 1 Sam. xxv. 2; 2 Sam. xix. 32.

10. *a little chamber on the wall*] The room probably projected like a balcony beyond

the lower apartments — an arrangement common in the East.

a stool] Rather, " a chair." The " chair" and "table," unusual in the sleeping-rooms of the East, indicate that the Prophet was expected to use his apartment for study and retirement, not only as a sleeping-chamber.

13. *thou hast been careful for us*] For the Prophet and his servant, who must have been lodged as well as his master.

I dwell among mine own people] The woman declines Elisha's offer. She has no wrong to complain of, no quarrel with any neighbour, in respect of which she might need the help of one in power. She "dwells among her own people"—her friends, and dependents, with whom she lives peaceably.

16. *do not lie*] Cp. a similar incredulity in Gen. xvii. 17, xviii. 12; Luke i. 20. The expression, "do not lie," which is harsh to us, accords with the plain, straightforward simplicity of ancient speech. It would

she said, Nay, my lord, *thou* man of God, *ᶠ*do not lie unto thine   *ᶠ* ver. 28.
17 handmaid. And the woman conceived, and bare a son at that
    season that Elisha had said unto her, according to the time of
18 life. ¶ And when the child was grown, it fell on a day, that he
19 went out to his father to the reapers. And he said unto his
    father, My head, my head. And he said to a lad, Carry him to
20 his mother. And when he had taken him, and brought him to
21 his mother, he sat on her knees till noon, and *then* died. And
    she went up, and laid him on the bed of the man of God, and
22 shut *the door* upon him, and went out. And she called unto her
    husband, and said, Send me, I pray thee, one of the young men,
    and one of the asses, that I may run to the man of God, and
23 come again. And he said, Wherefore wilt thou go to him to
    day ? *it is* neither new moon, nor sabbath. And she said, *It*
24 *shall be* ¹well. Then she saddled an ass, and said to her servant,
    Drive, and go forward ; ²slack not *thy* riding for me, except I
25 bid thee. So she went and came unto the man of God *ᵍ*to mount   *ᵍ* ch. 2. 25.
    Carmel. ¶ And it came to pass, when the man of God saw her
    afar off, that he said to Gehazi his servant, Behold, *yonder is*
26 that Shunammite : run now, I pray thee, to meet her, and say
    unto her, *Is it* well with thee ? *is it* well with thy husband ? *is*
27 *it* well with the child ? And she answered, *It is* well. And
    when she came to the man of God to the hill, she caught ³him
    by the feet : but Gehazi came near to thrust her away. And the
    man of God said, Let her alone ; for her soul *is* ⁴vexed within
    her : and the LORD hath hid *it* from me, and hath not told me.
28 Then she said, Did I desire a son of my lord ? *ʰ*did I not say,   *ʰ* ver. 16.
29 Do not deceive me? Then he said to Gehazi, *ⁱ*Gird up thy loins,   *ⁱ* 1Kin.18.46.
    and take my staff in thine hand, and go thy way : if thou meet   ch. 9. 1.
    any man, *ᵏ*salute him not ; and if any salute thee, answer him   *ᵏ* Luke 10. 4.

¹ Heb. *peace.*   ³ Heb. *by his feet*, Matt. 28. 9.
² Heb. *restrain not for me to ride.*   ⁴ Heb. *bitter*, 1 Sam. 1. 10.

not mean more than " deceive " (cp. marg.
ref.).
    19. The child's malady was a sunstroke.
The inhabitants of Palestine suffered from
this (Ps. cxxi. 6 ; Isai. xlix. 10 ; Judith viii.
3).
    22. *send me, I pray thee, one of the young
men and one of the asses*] All the " young
men " and all the " asses " were in the harvest field, the young men cutting and binding the sheaves, and placing them upon
carts or wains, the asses drawing these
vehicles fully laden, to the threshing-floor.
Cp. Amos ii. 13.
    23. Her husband did not connect the ill-
ness with his wife's demand, but thought
she wished to attend one of the Prophet's
devotional services. It is evident that such
services were now held with something like
regularity on Carmel for the benefit of the
faithful in those parts.
    new moon] By the Law the first day of
each month was to be kept holy. Offerings
were appointed for such occasions (Num.
xxviii. 11-15), and they were among the
days on which the silver trumpets were to
be blown (Num. x. 10 ; Ps. lxxxi. 3). Hence
" new moons " are frequently joined with

" sabbaths " (see Isai. i. 13 ; Ezek. xlv. 17 ;
Hos. ii. 11 ; 1 Chr. xxiii. 31).
    it shall be well] Rather, as in the margin,
" **Peace.**" *i.e.*, " Be quiet—trouble me not
with inquiries—only let me do as I wish."
    24. *slack not thy riding*] Translate, " **de-
lay me not in my riding**, except I bid
thee." The servant went on foot with the
ass to urge it forward, as is the ordinary
custom in the East.
    25. The distance was about sixteen or
seventeen miles.
    27. *she caught him by the feet*] To lay hold
of the knees or feet has always been thought
in the East to add force to supplication, and
is practised even at the present day. Cp.
Matt. xviii. 29 ; John xi. 32.
    28. Great grief shrinks from putting it-
self into words. The Shunammite cannot
bring herself to say, " My son is dead ; "
but by reproaching the Prophet with having "deceived" her, she sufficiently indicates
her loss.
    29. *salute him not*] Cp. marg. ref. Salu-
tation is the forerunner of conversation,
and one bent on speed would avoid every
temptation to loiter.
    lay my staff upon the face of the child] Per-

l See Ex. 7.
19. & 14. 16.
ch. 2. 8. 14.
Acts 19. 12.
m ch. 2. 2.

n John 11.11.

o ver. 4.
Matt. 6. 6.
p 1 Kin. 17.
20.
q 1 Kin. 17.
21.
Acts 20. 10.

r 1 Kin. 17.
21.
s ch. 8. 1, 5.

t 1 Kin. 17.
23.
u ch. 2. 1.
x ch. 8. 1.
y ch. 2. 3.
Luke 10. 39.
Acts 22. 3.

z Ex. 10. 17.
a See Ex. 15.
25.
ch. 2. 21.
& 5. 10.
John 9. 6.

30 not again: and *l*lay my staff upon the face of the child. And the mother of the child said, *m*As the LORD liveth, and *as* thy soul liveth, I will not leave thee. And he arose, and followed her.
31 ¶ And Gehazi passed on before them, and laid the staff upon the face of the child; but *there was* neither voice, nor [1]hearing. Wherefore he went again to meet him, and told him, saying,
32 The child is *n*not awakened. And when Elisha was come into the house, behold, the child was dead, *and* laid upon his bed.
33 He *o*went in therefore, and shut the door upon them twain,
34 *p*and prayed unto the LORD. And he went up, and lay upon the child, and put his mouth upon his mouth, and his eyes upon his eyes, and his hands upon his hands: and *q*he stretched himself
35 upon the child; and the flesh of the child waxed warm. Then he returned, and walked in the house [2]to and fro; and went up, *r*and stretched himself upon him: and *s*the child sneezed
36 seven times, and the child opened his eyes. And he called Gehazi, and said, Call this Shunammite. So he called her. And when she was come in unto him, he said, Take up thy son.
37 Then she went in, and fell at his feet, and bowed herself to the
38 ground, and *t*took up her son, and went out. ¶ And Elisha came again to *u*Gilgal: and *there was* a *x*dearth in the land; and the sons of the prophets *were y*sitting before him: and he said unto his servant, Set on the great pot, and seethe pottage
39 for the sons of the prophets. And one went out into the field to gather herbs, and found a wild vine, and gathered thereof wild gourds his lap full, and came and shred *them* into the pot of
40 pottage: for they knew *them* not. So they poured out for the men to eat. And it came to pass, as they were eating of the pottage, that they cried out, and said, O *thou* man of God, *there*
41 *is z*death in the pot. And they could not eat *thereof*. But he said, Then bring meal. And *a*he cast *it* into the pot; and he

---

[1] Heb. *attention.*   [2] Heb. *once hither, and once thither.*

---

haps Elisha's object in giving it was simply to assuage the grief of the mother, by letting her feel that something was being done for her child.

31. *there was neither voice nor hearing*] Cp. 1 K. xviii. 29.

the child is not awakened] See *r.* 20. The euphemism by which death is spoken of as a sleep was already familiar to the Jews (see 1 K. i. 21 note).

33. *prayed*] Prayer was the only remedy in such a case as this (cp. marg. ref. and Jam. v. 16), though it did not exclude the use of other means (*v.* 34).

34. *he stretched himself*] Or, "prostrated himself." The word is a different one from that used of Elijah, and expresses closer contact with the body. Warmth may have been actually communicated from the living body to the dead one; and Elisha's persistence (Heb. xi. 35), may have been a condition of the child's return to life.

36. *Take up thy son*] Compare Elijah's action (marg. ref. *t*) and our Blessed Lord's (Luke vii. 15).

38. *there was a dearth in the land*] Rather, "The famine was in the land." The seven

years' dearth of which Elisha had prophesied (marg. ref.) had begun.

the sons of the prophets] See 1 K. xx. 35 note. They were sitting before him as scholars before their master, hearing his instructions.

39. *a wild vine*] Not a real wild vine, the fruit of which, if not very palatable, is harmless; but some climbing plant with tendrils. The plant was probably either the *Ecbalium elaterium*, or "squirting cucumber," the fruit of which, egg-shaped, and of a very bitter taste, bursts at the slightest touch, when it is ripe, and squirts out sap and seed grains; or the *Colocynthis*, which belongs to the family of cucumbers, has a vine-shaped leaf, and bears a fruit as large as an orange, very bitter, from which is prepared the drug sold as colocynth. This latter plant grows abundantly in Palestine.

his lap full] Literally, "his shawl full." The prophet brought the fruit home in his "shawl" or "outer garment."

41. *Then bring meal*] The natural properties of meal would but slightly diminish either the bitterness or the unwholesome-

said, Pour cut for the people, that they may eat. And there
42 was no ¹harm in the pot. ¶ And there came a man from ᵇBaal-   ᵇ 1 Sam. 9. 1.
shalisha, ᶜand brought the man of God bread of the firstfruits,   ᶜ 1 Sam. 9. 7.
twenty loaves of barley, and full ears of corn ²in the husk   1 Cor. 9. 11.
thereof. And he said, Give unto the people, that they may eat.   Gal. 6. 6.
43 And his servitor said, ᵈWhat, should I set this before an hun-   ᵈ Luke 9. 13.
dred men? He said again, Give the people, that they may eat: John 6. 9.
for thus saith the LORD, ᵉThey shall eat, and shall leave *thereof.*   ᵉ Luke 9. 17.
44 So he set *it* before them, and they did eat, ᶠand left *thereof,* ac-   John 6. 11.
cording to the word of the LORD.   ᶠ Matt. 14. 20.
& 15. 37.
CHAP. 5. NOW ᵃNaaman, captain of the host of the king of Syria,   John 6. 13.
was ᵇa great man ³with his master, and ⁴⁵honourable, because   ᵃ Luke 4. 27.
by him the LORD had given ⁶deliverance unto Syria: he was   ᵇ Ex. 11. 3.
2 also a mighty man in valour, *but he was* a leper. And the
Syrians had gone out by companies, and had brought away captive out of the land of Israel a little maid; and she ⁷waited on
3 Naaman's wife. And she said unto her mistress, Would God
my lord *were* ⁸with the prophet that *is* in Samaria! for he would
4 ⁹recover him of his leprosy. And *one* went in, and told his lord,
saying, Thus and thus said the maid that *is* of the land of Israel.
5 ¶ And the king of Syria said, Go to, go, and I will send a letter

¹ Heb. *evil thing.*   ⁴ Or, *gracious.*   ⁷ Heb. *was before.*
² Or, *in his scrip,* or, *gar-*   ⁵ Heb. *lifted up,* or, *ac-*   ⁸ Heb. *before.*
  ment.   *cepted in countenance.*   ⁹ Heb. *gather in.*
³ Heb. *before.*   ⁶ Or, *victory.*

ness of a drink containing colocynth. It is
evident, therefore, that the conversion of
the food from a pernicious and unsavoury
mess into palatable and wholesome nourishment was by miracle.

42. *Baal-shalisha*] Fifteen Roman miles
north of Lydda, in the Sharon plain to the
west of the highlands of Ephraim. It was,
apparently, the chief city of the "land of
Shalisha" (marg. ref.).

bread of the first fruits] It appears by
this that the Levitical priests having withdrawn from the land of Israel (see 2 Chr. xi.
13, 14), pious Israelites transferred to the
Prophets, whom God raised up, the offerings
required by the law to be given to the
priests (Num. xviii. 13 ; Deut. xviii. 4).

in the husk thereof] "In his bag." The
word does not occur elsewhere in Scripture.

43. This miracle was a faint foreshadowing of our Lord's far more marvellous
feeding of thousands with even scantier
materials. The resemblance is not only in
the broad fact, but in various minute particulars, such as the distribution through the
hands of others ; the material, bread ; the
surprised question of the servant; and the
evidence of superfluity in the fragments
that were left (see marg. reff.). As Elijah
was a type of the Baptist, so Elisha was in
many respects a type of our Blessed Lord.
In his peaceful, non-ascetic life, in his mild
and gentle character, in his constant circuits, in his many miracles of mercy, in the
healing virtue which abode in his bodily
frame (xiii. 21), he resembled, more than any

other Prophet, the Messiah, of Whom all
Prophets were more or less shadows and
figures.

V. 1. *by him the* LORD *had given deliverance unto Syria*] An Assyrian monarch had
pushed his conquests as far as Syria exactly
at this period, bringing into subjection all
the kings of these parts. But Syria revolted
after a few years and once more made herself independent. It was probably in this
war of independence that Naaman had distinguished himself.

but he was a leper] Leprosy admitted of
various kinds and degrees (Lev. xiii. xiv.)
Some of the lighter forms would not incapa-
citate a man from discharging the duties of
a courtier and warrior.

2. No peace had been made on the failure
of Ahab's expedition (1 K. xxii. 1–36). The
relations of the two countries therefore continued to be hostile, and plundering inroads
naturally took place on the one side and on
the other.

4. *one went in*] Rather, "he went in," *i.e.*
Naaman went and told his lord, the king of
Syria.

5. *six thousand pieces of gold*] Rather, "six
thousand *shekels* of gold." Coined money
did not exist as yet, and was not introduced
into Judæa till the time of Cyrus. Gold
was carried in bars, from which portions
were cut when need arose, and the value was
ascertained by weighing. If the gold shekel
of the Jews corresponded, as some think,
to the daric of the Persians, the value of
the 6000 shekels would be about 6837*l.* If
the weight was the same as that of the silver

unto the king of Israel. And he departed, and *c*took [1]with him ten talents of silver, and six thousand *pieces* of gold, and ten 6 changes of raiment. And he brought the letter to the king of Israel, saying, Now when this letter is come unto thee, behold, I have *therewith* sent Naaman my servant to thee, that thou 7 mayest recover him of his leprosy. And it came to pass, when the king of Israel had read the letter, that he rent his clothes,

d Gen. 30. 2.
Deut. 32. 39.
1 Sam. 2. 6.

and said, *Am* I *d*God, to kill and to make alive, that this man doth send unto me to recover a man of his leprosy? wherefore consider, I pray you, and see how he seeketh a quarrel against 8 me. ¶And it was *so*, when Elisha the man of God had heard that the king of Israel had rent his clothes, that he sent to the king, saying, Wherefore hast thou rent thy clothes? let him come now to me, and he shall know that there is a prophet in Israel. 9 So Naaman came with his horses and with his chariot, and 10 stood at the door of the house of Elisha. And Elisha sent a

e See ch. 4. 41.
John 9. 7.

messenger unto him, saying, Go and *e*wash in Jordan seven times, and thy flesh shall come again to thee, and thou shalt be 11 clean. But Naaman was wroth, and went away, and said, Behold, [2][3]I thought, He will surely come out to me, and stand, and call on the name of the LORD his God, and [4]strike his hand 12 over the place, and recover the leper. *Are* not [5]Abana and Pharpar, rivers of Damascus, better than all the waters of Israel? may I not wash in them, and be clean? So he turned 13 and went away in a rage. And his servants came near, and spake unto him, and said, My father, *if* the prophet had bid thee *do some* great thing, wouldest thou not have done *it?* how much rather then, when he saith to thee, Wash, and be clean?

---

[1] Heb. *in his hand.*
[2] Heb. *I said.*
[3] Or, *I said with myself, He will surely come out, &c.*
[4] Heb. *move up and down.*
[5] Or, *Amana.*

---

shekel (see Ex. xxxviii. 24 note), the value would exceed 12,000*l.*

The ancient practice of including clothes among gifts of honour in the East (Gen. xli. 42; Esth. vi. 8; Dan. v. 7) continues to the present day.

6. *that thou mayest recover him*] Lit. "And thou shalt recover him." The Syrian king presumes that, if there is a cure for leprosy to be had in Israel, the mode of obtaining it will be well known to his royal brother.

7. *he rent his clothes*] The action indicated alarm and terror quite as much as sorrow (2 Sam. xiii. 19; Ezr. ix. 3; 2 Chr. xxxiv. 27; Jer. xxxvi. 22).

consider, I pray you] Jehoram speaks to his chief officers, and bids them mark the *animus* of the Syrian monarch. Compare the conduct of Ahab (1 K. xx. 7).

8. *he shall know...Israel*] viz. "That which *thou* (the king of Israel) appearest to have forgotten, that there is a Prophet—a real JehovahP-rophet—in Israel."

10. Elisha was not deterred from personally meeting Naaman because he was a leper. He sent a messenger because Naaman had over-estimated his own importance (*v.*11), and needed rebuke.

go and wash in Jordan] Cp. marg. reff.

A command is given which tests the faith of the recipient, and the miracle is not wrought until such faith is openly evidenced.

11. *he will surely come out to me*] In the East a code of unwritten laws prescribes exactly how visits are to be paid, and how visitors are to be received, according to the worldly rank of the parties (cp. *v.* 21). No doubt, according to such a code, Elisha should have gone out to meet Naaman at the door of his house.

and call on the name of the LORD *his God*] Literally, "of Jehovah his God." Naaman is aware that *Jehovah* is the God of Elisha. Cp. the occurrence of the name of Jehovah on the "Moabite Stone" (iii. 4 note).

strike] Better, as in the margin, "pass the fingers up and down the place" at a short distance. It seems implied that the leprosy was partial.

12. The Abana is the Barada, or true river of Damascus, which, rising in the anti-Libanus, flows westward from its foot and forms the oasis within which Damascus is placed. The Pharpar is usually identified with the Awaaj.

Naaman thinks that, if washing is to cure him, his own rivers may serve the purpose. Their water was brighter, clearer, and colder than that of Jordan.

14 Then went he down, and dipped himself seven times in Jordan, according to the saying of the man of God: and *f*his flesh came *f* Job 33. 25.
again like unto the flesh of a little child, and *g*he was clean. *g* Luke 4. 27.
15 ¶ And he returned to the man of God, he and all his company, and came, and stood before him: and he said, Behold, now I know that *there is h*no God in all the earth, but in Israel: now *h* Dan. 2. 47.
16 therefore, I pray thee, take *i*a blessing of thy servant. But he & 3. 29.
said, *k As* the LORD liveth, before whom I stand, *l*I will receive *i* Gen. 33. 11.
17 none. And he urged him to take *it;* but he refused. And *k* 1 Kin. 17. 1.
Naaman said, Shall there not then, I pray thee, be given to thy *l* Gen. 14. 23.
servant two mules' burden of earth? for thy servant will hence- 8.
forth offer neither burnt offering nor sacrifice unto other gods,
18 but unto the LORD. In this thing the LORD pardon thy servant,
that when my master goeth into the house of Rimmon to wor-
ship there, and *m*he leaneth on my hand, and I bow myself in *m* ch. 7. 2, 17.
the house of Rimmon: when I bow down myself in the house of
19 Rimmon, the LORD pardon thy servant in this thing. And he
said unto him, Go in peace. So he departed from him *1*a little
20 way. ¶ But Gehazi, the servant of Elisha the man of God, said,
Behold, my master hath spared Naaman this Syrian, in not .
receiving at his hands that which he brought: but, *as* the LORD
21 liveth, I will run after him, and take somewhat of him. So

1 Heb. *a little piece of ground,* as Gen. 35. 16.

---

14. *seven times*] Cp. 1 K. xviii. 43. In both cases a somewhat severe trial was made of the individual's faith. Cp. the seven compassings of Jericho, and the sudden fall of the walls (Josh. vi. 3–20).

15. *he returned*] Naaman was grateful (cp. Luke xvii. 15). From the Jordan to Samaria was a distance of not less than thirty-two miles. Naaman further went to Damascus, far out of his way, lengthening his necessary journey by at least three days. His special object in returning seems to have been to relieve his feelings of obligation by inducing the Prophet to accept a "blessing," *i.e.* a gift.

there is no God, &c.] Cp. marg. reff. ; but in none of them are the expressions quite so strong as here. Naaman seems absolutely to renounce all belief in any other God but Jehovah.

16. *I will receive none*] The Prophets were in the habit of receiving presents from those who consulted them (1 Sam. ix. 7, 8 ; 1 K. xiv. 3), but Elisha refused. It was import-ant that Naaman should not suppose that the Prophets of the true God acted from motives of self-interest, much less imagine that "the gift of God might be purchased with money" (Acts viii. 20).

17. *two mules' burden of earth*] This earth, Naaman thought, spread over a portion of Syrian ground, would hallow and render it suitable for the worship of Jehovah.

18. Rimmon is known to us as a god only by this passage. The name is connected with a root "to be high." Hadad-rimmon (Zech. xii. 11), the name of a place near

Megiddo, points to the identity of Rimmon with Hadad, who is known to have been the Sun, the chief object of worship to the Syrians.

when he leaneth on mine hand] The prac-tice of a monarch's "leaning on the hand" of an attendant was not common in the East (cp. marg. ref.). It probably implied age or infirmity.

the LORD *pardon thy servant in this thing*] Naaman was not prepared to offend his master, either by refusing to enter with him into the temple of Rimmon, or by remain-ing erect when the king bowed down and worshipped the god. His conscience seems to have told him that such conduct was not right ; but he trusted that it might be par-doned, and he appealed to the Prophet in the hope of obtaining from him an assur-ance to this effect.

19. *so he departed, &c.*] This clause should not be separated from the succeeding verse. The meaning is, "So he departed from him, and had gone a little way, when Gehazi be-thought himself of what he would do, and followed after him."

20. *this Syrian*] The words are emphatic. Gehazi persuades himself that it is right to spoil a *Syrian*—that is, a Gentile, and an enemy of Israel.

as the LORD *liveth*] These words are here a profane oath. Gehazi, anxious to make himself believe that he is acting in a proper, and, even, in a religious spirit, does not scruple to introduce one of the most solemn of religious phrases.

Gehazi followed after Naaman. And when Naaman saw *him* running after him, he lighted down from the chariot to meet 22 him, and said, [1]*Is* all well? And he said, All *is* well. My master hath sent me, saying, Behold, even now there be come to me from mount Ephraim two young men of the sons of the prophets: give them, I pray thee, a talent of silver, and two changes 23 of garments. And Naaman said, Be content, take two talents. And he urged him, and bound two talents of silver in two bags, with two changes of garments, and laid *them* upon two of his 24 servants; and they bare *them* before him. And when he came to the [2]tower, he took *them* from their hand, and bestowed *them* 25 in the house : and he let the men go, and they departed. But he went in, and stood before his master. And Elisha said unto him, Whence *comest thou*, Gehazi? And he said, Thy servant 26 went [3]no whither. And he said unto him, Went not mine heart *with thee*, when the man turned again from his chariot to meet thee? *Is it* a time to receive money, and to receive garments, and oliveyards, and vineyards, and sheep, and oxen, and men- 27 servants, and maidservants? The leprosy therefore of Naaman [n]shall cleave unto thee, and unto thy seed for ever. And he went out from his presence [o]a leper *as white* as snow.

CHAP. 6. AND [a]the sons of the prophets said unto Elisha, Behold 2 now, the place where we dwell with thee is too strait for us. Let us go, we pray thee, unto Jordan, and take thence every man a beam, and let us make us a place there, where we may dwell. 3 And he answered, Go ye. And one said, Be content, I pray

[n] 1 Tim.6.10.
[o] Ex. 4. 6.
Num. 12. 10.
ch. 15. 5.
[a] ch. 4. 38.

[1] Heb. *Is there peace?*   [2] Or, *secret place.*   [3] Heb. *not hither or thither.*

---

21. *he lighted down from the chariot*] This was an act of quite uncalled-for courtesy. It indicates eagerness to honour the master in the person of his servant.

22. *from mount Ephraim*] Bethel and Gilgal (ii. 1), at both of which there were "schools of the prophets," were situated on Mount Ephraim.

a talent of silver] A large demand in respect of the pretended occasion *;* but small compared with the amount which Naaman had pressed on the Prophet (*v.* 4). Gehazi had to balance between his own avarice, on the one hand, and the fear of raising suspicion on the other.

23. *Be content*] i.e. "consent."

24. *the tower*] Rather, "the hill," the well-known hill by Elisha's house. The hill interrupted the view in the direction taken by Naaman, and Gehazi dismissed Naaman's servants at this point lest they should be seen from his master's residence.

25. Lest his absence should be noticed, Gehazi hastened, without being called, to appear before his master. In the East it is usual for servants to remain most of the day in their lord's presence, only quitting it when given some order to execute.

26. *Went not mine heart with thee?*] i.e. "Was I not with thee in spirit—did I not see the whole transaction, as if I had been present at it?" He uses the verb "went," because Gehazi has just denied his "going."

Is it a time, &c.] i.e. "Was this a proper occasion to indulge greed, when a Gentile was to be favourably impressed, and made to feel that the faith of the Israelites was the only true religion? Was it not, on the contrary, an occasion for the exhibition of the greatest unselfishness, that so a heathen might be won to the truth?"

and oliveyards and vineyards, &c.] Gehazi's thoughts had probably run on to the disposition which he would make of his wealth, and the Prophet here follows them, enumerating his servant's intended purchases.

VI. 1. The writer returns here to the series of miracles which Elisha performed for the benefit of the prophetical schools under his care. The connexion, in this point of view, is with iv. 44.

the place where we dwell with thee] Lit. "the place where we **sit before** thee," *i.e.* "the place where we assemble and sit to hear thy teaching." Elisha visited the sons of the Prophets in circuit, staying a short time at each place where a "school" was established. Perhaps he was now visiting Jericho. Cp. ii. 5.

2. *take every man a beam*] Trees were rare in most parts of Palestine, but plentiful in the Jordan valley. Jericho was known in early times as "the city of palms" (Deut. xxxiv. 3; Judg. i. 16).

thee, and go with thy servants. And he answered, I will go.
4 So he went with them. And when they came to Jordan, they
5 cut down wood.   But as one was felling a beam, the ¹axe head
fell into the water : and he cried, and said, Alas, master ! for it
6 was borrowed.   And the man of God said, Where fell it ? And
he shewed him the place.   And ᵇhe cut down a stick, and cast *it*   ᵇ ch. 2. 21.
7 in thither; and the iron did swim.   Therefore said he, Take *it*
8 up to thee.   And he put out his hand, and took it.   ¶ Then the
king of Syria warred against Israel, and took counsel with his
servants, saying, In such and such a place *shall be* my ²camp.
9 And the man of God sent unto the king of Israel, saying,
Beware that thou pass not such a place; for thither the Syrians
10 are come down.   And the king of Israel sent to the place which
the man of God told him and warned him of, and saved him-
11 self there, not once nor twice.   Therefore the heart of the king
of Syria was sore troubled for this thing; and he called his
servants, and said unto them, Will ye not shew me which of
12 us *is* for the king of Israel?   And one of his servants said,
³None, my lord, O king : but Elisha, the prophet that *is* in
Israel, telleth the king of Israel the words that thou speakest in
13 thy bedchamber.   And he said, Go and spy where he *is*, that I
may send and fetch him.   And it was told him, saying, Behold,
14 *he is* in ᶜDothan.   Therefore sent he thither horses, and chariots,   ᶜ Gen. 37. 17.
and a ⁴great host : and they came by night, and compassed the
15 city about.   And when the ⁵servant of the man of God was
risen early, and gone forth, behold, an host compassed the city
both with horses and chariots.   And his servant said unto him,
16 Alas, my master ! how shall we do ?   And he answered, Fear
not: for ᵈthey that *be* with us *are* more than they that *be* with   ᵈ 2 Chr. 32. 7.
                                                                            Ps. 55. 18.
                                                                            Rom. 8. 31.

¹ Heb. *iron*.   ³ Heb. *No*.   ⁵ Or, *minister*.
² Or, *encamping*.   ⁴ Heb. *heavy*.

---

5. *the ax head*] Lit. as in margin. The
Jews used iron for the heads of axes at a
very early date (see Deut. xix. 5). They
probably acquired a knowledge of the
smelting process in Egypt, where iron was
employed at least from the time of the third
Rameses.

6. No doubt there is something startling
in the trivial character of this miracle, and
of the few others which resemble it. But,
inasmuch as we know very little as to the
laws which govern the exercise of miraculous powers, it is possible that they may be
so much under their possessor's control that
he can exercise them, or not exercise them,
at pleasure. And it may depend on his discretion whether they are exercised in important cases only, or in trivial cases also.
Elisha had evidently great kindness of
heart. He could not see a grief without
wishing to remedy it. And it seems as if
he had sometimes used his miraculous
power in pure good nature, when no natural way of remedying an evil presented
itself.

8. *the king of Syria*] Probably the great
Benhadad (see *v.* 24).

10. *saved himself*] Rather, he "**was**

ware." The verb used is the same which
is translated "beware" in the preceding
verse.

11. Benhadad supposed that there must
be a traitor in his camp. He asks therefore, "Will no one denounce him?"

12. *in thy bedchamber*] Lit. "in the secret place of thy bedchamber," *i.e.* "in the
greatest possible secrecy." The seclusion
of the harem must be taken into account for
the full appreciation of the force of the
phrase. Probably the Syrian lord who answered Benhadad had received his intelligence from some of the Israelites.

13. *Dothan*] See marg. ref. note. It was
at no great distance from Shechem. Its
ancient name still attaches to a Tel or hill
of a marked character (cp. *v.* 17), from the
foot of which arises a copious fountain.

16. *they that be with us*, &c.] Elisha gave
utterance to the conviction of all God's
Saints when the world persecutes them
(cp. marg. reff.). God—they know—is on
their side ; they need "not fear what flesh
can do unto them." His Angels—an innumerable host—are ever guarding those who
love Him.

17 them. And Elisha prayed, and said, LORD, I pray thee, open
his eyes, that he may see. And the LORD opened the eyes
of the young man; and he saw: and, behold, the mountain

e ch. 2. 11.
Ps. 34. 7.
& 68. 17.
Zech. 1. 8.
& 6. 1—7.
f Gen. 19. 11.

was full of *e*horses and chariots of fire round about Elisha.
18 And when they came down to him, Elisha prayed unto the
LORD, and said, Smite this people, I pray thee, with blindness.
And *f*he smote them with blindness according to the word of
19 Elisha. And Elisha said unto them, This *is* not the way, neither
is this the city: ¹follow me, and I will bring you to the man
20 whom ye seek. But he led them to Samaria. And it came to
pass, when they were come into Samaria, that Elisha said,
LORD, open the eyes of these *men*, that they may see. And
the LORD opened their eyes, and they saw; and, behold, *they*
21 *were* in the midst of Samaria. And the king of Israel said
unto Elisha, when he saw them, My father, shall I smite them?
22 shall I smite them? And he answered, Thou shalt not smite
them: wouldest thou smite those whom thou hast taken captive

g Rom. 12. 20.

with thy sword and with thy bow? *g*set bread and water before
23 them, that they may eat and drink, and go to their master. And
he prepared great provision for them: and when they had eaten
and drunk, he sent them away, and they went to their master.

h ch. 5. 2.
ver. 8, 9.

So *h*the bands of Syria came no more into the land of Israel.
24 ¶ And it came to pass after this, that Ben-hadad king of Syria
25 gathered all his host, and went up, and besieged Samaria. And
there was a great famine in Samaria: and, behold, they besieged
it, until an ass's head was *sold* for fourscore *pieces* of silver, and
the fourth part of a cab of dove's dung for five *pieces* of silver.

¹ Heb. *come ye after me.*

---

17. *open his eyes that he may see*] Elisha's
servant lacked the faith of his master. Elisha therefore prays that he may be given a
vision of the spiritual world, and see, as if
with the bodily eye, the angelic host (marg.
reff.) which he himself knows to be present.

18. *they came down to him*] The Syrians,
who had been encamped on rising ground
opposite the hill of Dothan, now descended
and drew near to the city.

The blindness with which they were smitten was not real blindness—actual loss of
sight—but a state of illusion in which a man
sees things otherwise than as they are (cp.
v. 20).

21. *My father*] A term of respect used by
Jehoram in his joy at seeing an army of
Syrians delivered up to him by the Prophet. That the king's character was not
changed appears from *vv.* 31, 32.

shall I smite them? shall I smite them?]
The repetition of the words mean, "Shall I
utterly smite them?" Cp. similar repetitions with similar meanings in Gen. xxii.
17; Luke xxii. 15.

22. *wouldest thou smite, &c.*] It is doubtful
whether this sentence is really interroga-
tive. Others translate—"Smite those whom
thou hast taken captive with thy sword," &c.
A contrast is intended between ordinary captives—those made with the sword and bow
—and these particular prisoners who have

been given into the king's hand by God.
The former, Jehoram is told, he may slay,
if he pleases (Deut. xx. 13), the latter, he is
informed, he must not slay (cp. marg. ref.).

23. Jehoram did not merely follow the
letter of the Prophet's direction, but understood its spirit and acted accordingly. The
plundering bands which had been in the
habit of ravaging the territory (v. 2), ceased
their incursions in consequence either of
the miracle, or of the kind treatment which
Elisha had recommended.

24. *after this*] Perhaps some years after
—when the miracle and the kind treatment
were alike forgotten.

25. As the ass was "unclean," it would
not be eaten except in the last resort; and
its head would be its worst and cheapest
part.

cab] This measure is not mentioned elsewhere in Scripture. According to the Rabbinical writers it was the smallest of all the
dry measures in use among the Jews, being
the sixth part of a *seah*, which was the third
part of an *ephah*. If it was about equal to
two of our quarts, the "fourth part of a
cab" would be about a pint.

dove's dung] Most commentators understand by this expression a sort of pulse,
which is called "dove's dung," or "spar-
row's dung" in Arabic. But it is possible
that the actual excrement of pigeons is

26 And as the king of Israel was passing by upon the wall, there
27 cried a woman unto him, saying, Help, my lord, O king. And
he said, ¹If the LORD do not help thee, whence shall I help thee?
28 out of the barnfloor, or out of the winepress? And the king
said unto her, What aileth thee? And she answered, This woman
said unto me, Give thy son, that we may eat him to day, and we
29 will eat my son to-morrow. So ⁱwe boiled my son, and did
eat him : and I said unto her on the ²next day, Give thy son, that
30 we may eat him: and she hath hid her son. And it came to
pass, when the king heard the words of the woman, that he ᵏrent
his clothes; and he passed by upon the wall, and the people
looked, and, behold, *he had* sackcloth within upon his flesh.
31 Then he said, ˡGod do so and more also to me, if the head of
32 Elisha the son of Shaphat shall stand on him this day. But
Elisha sat in his house, and ᵐthe elders sat with him; and *the
king* sent a man from before him: but ere the messenger came
to him, he said to the elders, ⁿSee ye how this son of ᵒa murderer hath sent to take away mine head? look, when the messenger cometh, shut the door, and hold him fast at the door: *is*
33 not the sound of his master's feet behind him? And while

ⁱ Lev. 26. 29.
Deut. 28. 53,
57.

ᵏ 1 Kin. 21.
27.

ˡ 1 Kin.19. 2.

ᵐ Ezek. 8. 1.
& 20. 1.

ⁿ Luke13.32.
ᵒ 1 Kin.18. 4.

¹ Or, *Let not the LORD save thee.*   ² Heb. *ether.*

---

meant. The records of sieges show that
both animal and human excrement have
been used as food—under circumstances of
extreme necessity.

26. The walls of fortified towns had a
broad space at the top, protected towards
the exterior by battlements, along which
the bulk of the defenders were disposed, and
from which they hurled their missiles and
shot their arrows. The king seems to have
been going his rounds, to inspect the state
of the garrison and the defences.

27. *If the* LORD *do not help*] The translation in the text is decidedly better than the
marginal rendering. Some prefer to render
—"Nay—let Jehovah help thee. Whence
shall I help thee?"

out of the barnfloor, &c.] The king means
that both were empty—that he had no
longer any food in store; and therefore
could not help the woman. Cp. Hos. ix. 2.

28. The king had assumed that the cry of
the woman was for food. Her manner indicated that it was not so. He therefore
proceeded to inquire what she wanted of
him.

this woman] Both women, it would seem,
were present; and the aggrieved one pointed
to the other.

29. The prophecy alluded to in the marg.
reff. was now fulfilled, probably for the first
time. It had a second accomplishment
when Jerusalem was besieged by Nebuchadnezzar (Lam. iv. 10), and a third in the
final siege of the same city by Titus.

30. *sackcloth*] Jehoram hoped perhaps
to avert Jehovah's anger, as his father had
done (1 K. xxi. 29). But there was no
spirit of self-humiliation, of or true penitence in his heart (v. 7). See the next verse.

31. *God do so,* &c.] Jehoram uses almost

the very words of his wicked mother, when
she sought the life of Elijah (marg. ref.).

the head of Elisha] Beheading was not an
ordinary Jewish punishment. The Law did
not sanction it. But in Assyria, Babylonia,
and generally through the East, it was the
most common form of capital punishment.
It is not quite clear why Elisha was to be
punished. Perhaps Jehoram argued from
his other miracles that he could give deliverance from the present peril, if he liked.

32. *But Elisha sat,* &c.] Translate, "**And
Elisha was sitting** in his house, and all the
elders **were sitting** with him, **when** the
king sent, &c."

The "elders,"—either "the elders of the
city" or "the elders of the land,"—who
may have been in session at Samaria now, as
they had been at the time of a former siege
(1 K. xx. 7)—had gone to Elisha for his advice or assistance. Their imminent peril
drove them to acknowledge the power of
Jehovah, and to consult with His Prophet.

this son of a murderer] *i.e.* of Ahab, the
murderer, not only of Naboth, but also of
all the Prophets of the Lord (marg. ref.),
whom he allowed Jezebel to slay.

hold him fast at the door] The elders, public officials, not private friends of Elisha,
could not have been expected to resist the
entrance of the executioner at the *mere* request of the Prophet. He therefore assigns
a reason for his request—"the king is
coming in person, either to confirm or revoke
his order—will they detain the headsman
until his arrival?"

33. *the messenger*] It has been proposed to
change "messenger" into "king," the two
words being in Hebrew nearly alike, and the
speech with which the chapter ends being
considered only suitable in the mouth of the

p Job 2. 9.

he yet talked with them, behold, the messenger came down unto him : and he said, Behold, this evil *is* of the LORD ; *p*what should I wait for the LORD any longer ?

a ver. 18, 19.

b ver. 17.
ch. 5. 18.
c Mal. 3. 10.

d Lev. 13. 46.

e 2 Sam. 5. 21.
ch. 19. 7.
Job 15. 21.
f 1 Kin. 10. 29.

CHAP. 7. THEN Elisha said, Hear ye the word of the LORD ; Thus saith the LORD, *a*To morrow about this time *shall* a measure of fine flour *be sold* for a shekel, and two measures of barley for a 2 shekel, in the gate of Samaria. *b*Then *1*a lord on whose hand the king leaned answered the man of God, and said, Behold, *c*if the LORD would make windows in heaven, might this thing be ? And he said, Behold, thou shalt see *it* with thine eyes, but shalt 3 not eat thereof. ¶ And there were four leprous men *d*at the entering in of the gate : and they said one to another, Why sit 4 we here until we die ? If we say, We will enter into the city, then the famine *is* in the city, and we shall die there : and if we sit still here, we die also. Now therefore come, and let us fall unto the host of the Syrians : if they save us alive, we shall 5 live ; and if they kill us, we shall but die. And they rose up in the twilight, to go unto the camp of the Syrians : and when they were come to the uttermost part of the camp of Syria, 6 behold, *there was* no man there. For the Lord had made the host of the Syrians *e*to hear a noise of chariots, and a noise of horses, *even* the noise of a great host : and they said one to another, Lo, the king of Israel hath hired against us *f*the kings

---

1 Heb. *a lord which* belonged *to the king leaning upon his hand,* ch. 5. 18.

---

king, whose presence is indicated in vii. 2, 17. Others think that the words " and the king after him " have fallen out of the text.

came down] The messenger came *down* from off the wall to the level of the streets.

Behold this evil, &c.] Jehoram bursts into the Prophet's presence with a justification of the sentence (*v.* 31) he has pronounced against him. " Behold this evil—this siege with all its horrors—is from Jehovah—from Jehovah, Whose Prophet thou art. Why should I wait for Jehovah—temporise with Him—keep, as it were, on terms with Him by suffering thee to live—any longer ? What hast thou to say in arrest of judgment ? "

VII. 1. The division between the chapters is most awkward here. Elisha, in this verse, replies to the king's challenge in vi. 33—that his God, Jehovah, will give deliverance in the space of a day. On the morrow, by the same time in the day, the famine will have ceased, and food will be even cheaper than usual.

a measure of fine flour] Lit. " a *seah* of fine flour ; " about a peck and a half.

for a shekel] About 2*s.* 8½*d.*

two measures of barley] Or, " two *seahs* of barley ; " about three pecks.

in the gate] The " gates," or " gateways," of Eastern towns are favourite places for the despatch of various kinds of business. It would seem that at Samaria one of the gates was used for the corn market.

2. *a lord*] Rather, **"the captain,"** as in Ex. xiv. 7 ; 1 K. ix. 22 ; &c. The term itself, *shalish* (derived from *shalosh,* "three,") may be compared with the Latin " tribunus."

windows] Rather, " sluices " (cp. Gen. vii. 11). The " lord " means to say—" If Jehovah were to open sluices in heaven, and pour down corn as He poured down rain in the time of the Deluge, even then could there be such abundance as thou speakest of ? "

3. The position of the lepers is in accordance with the Law of Moses (marg. reff.) ; and shows that the Law was still observed to some extent in the kingdom of Israel.

5. *the twilight*] The *evening* twilight (see *v.* 9).

the uttermost part of the camp] The extreme boundary of the camp *towards the city,* not its furthest or most distant portion. Cp. *v.* 8.

6. It is a matter of no importance whether we say that the miracle by which God now wrought deliverance for Samaria consisted in a mere illusion of the sense of hearing (cp. vi. 19, 20) ; or whether there was any objective reality in the sound (cp. marg. reff.).

the king of Israel hath hired] The swords of mercenaries had been employed by the nations bordering on Palestine as early as the time of David (2 Sam. x. 6 ; 1 Chr. xix. 6, 7). Hence the supposition of the Syrians was far from improbable.

the kings of the Hittites] The Hittites, who are found first in the south (Gen. xxiii. 7), then in the centre of Judæa (Josh. xi. 3), seem to have retired northwards after the occupation of Palestine by the Israelites. They are found among the Syrian enemies of the Egyptians in the monuments of the 19th dynasty (about B.C. 1300), and appear at

of the Hittites, and the kings of the Egyptians, to come upon
7 us. Wherefore they *g*arose and fled in the twilight, and left
their tents, and their horses, and their asses, even the camp as it
8 *was*, and fled for their life. And when these lepers came to the
uttermost part of the camp, they went into one tent, and did eat
and drink, and carried thence silver, and gold, and raiment,
and went and hid *it;* and came again, and entered into another
9 tent, and carried thence *also*, and went and hid *it*. Then they
said one to another, We do not well: this day *is* a day of good
tidings, and we hold our peace: if we tarry till the morning
light, [1]some mischief will come upon us: now therefore come,
10 that we may go and tell the king's household. So they came
and called unto the porter of the city: and they told them,
saying, We came to the camp of the Syrians, and, behold, *there
was* no man there, neither voice of man, but horses tied, and
11 asses tied, and the tents as they *were*. And he called the porters;
12 and they told *it* to the king's house within. ¶ And the king
arose in the night, and said unto his servants, I will now shew
you what the Syrians have done to us. They know that we *be*
hungry; therefore are they gone out of the camp to hide themselves in the field, saying, When they come out of the city, we
13 shall catch them alive, and get into the city. And one of his
servants answered and said, Let *some* take, I pray thee, five of
the horses that remain, which are left [2]in the city, (behold, they
are as all the multitude of Israel that are left in it : behold, *I
say*, they *are* even as all the multitude of the Israelites that are
14 consumed :) and let us send and see. They took therefore two

g Ps. 48. 4,
5, 6.
Prov. 28. 1.

---

[1] Heb. *we shall find punishment.*   [2] Heb. *in it.*

---

that time to have inhabited the valley of
the Upper Orontes. In the early Assyrian
monuments they form a great confederacy,
as the most powerful people of northern
Syria, dwelling on both banks of the
Euphrates, while at the same time there is
a second confederacy of their race further
to the south, which seems to inhabit the
anti-Lebanon between Hamath and Damascus. These southern Hittites are in the
time of Benhadad and Hazael a powerful
people, especially strong in *chariots;* and
generally assist the Syrians against the
Assyrians. The Syrians seem now to have
imagined that these southern Hittites had
been hired by Jehoram.

the kings of the Egyptians] This is a remarkable expression, since Egypt elsewhere
throughout Scripture appears always as a
centralised monarchy under a single ruler.
The probability is that the principal Pharaoh had a prince or princes associated
with him on the throne, a practice not uncommon in Egypt. The period, which is
that of the 22nd dynasty, is an obscure one,
on which the monuments throw but little
light.

9. The lepers began to think that if they
kept this important matter secret during
the whole night for their own private
advantage, when the morning came they
would be found out, accused, and punished
(see marg.).

10. *they called unto the porter...and told
them*] The word " porter " is used like our
" guard," and the meaning here is, not that
the lepers called to any particular individual,
but that they roused the body of men who
were keeping guard at one of the gates.

12. *his servants*] i.e., " high officers of the
household," not mere domestics.

I will shew you what the Syrians have done]
Jehoram sees in the deserted camp a stratagem like that connected with the taking
of Ai (Josh. viii. 3-19). The suspicion was
a very natural one, since the Israelites
knew of no reason why the Syrians should
have raised the siege.

13. *behold, &c.*] The LXX. and a large
number of the Hebrew MSS. omit the
clause, " behold, they are as all the multitude of Israel that are left in it." But the
text followed by our translators, which is
that of the best MSS., is intelligible and
needs no alteration. It is merely a prolix
way of stating that the horsemen will incur
no greater danger by going to reconnoitre
than the rest of their countrymen by remaining in the city, since the whole multitude is perishing.

14. *two chariot horses*] Translate, " **two
horse-chariots.**" They dispatched *i.e.* two

chariot horses; and the king sent after the host of the Syrians,
15 saying, Go and see. And they went after them unto Jordan:
and, lo, all the way *was* full of garments and vessels, which the
Syrians had cast away in their haste. And the messengers
16 returned, and told the king. ¶And the people went out, and
spoiled the tents of the Syrians. So a measure of fine flour was

h ver. 1.   *sold* for a shekel, and two measures of barley for a shekel, *h*ac-
17 cording to the word of the LORD. And the king appointed the
lord on whose hand he leaned to have the charge of the gate:

i ch. 6. 32.   and the people trode upon him in the gate, and he died, *i*as the
ver. 2.   man of God had said, who spake when the king came down to
18 him. And it came to pass as the man of God had spoken to the

k ver. 1.   king, saying, *k*Two measures of barley for a shekel, and a
measure of fine flour for a shekel, shall be to morrow about
19 this time in the gate of Samaria: and that lord answered the
man of God, and said, Now, behold, *if* the LORD should make
windows in heaven, might such a thing be? And he said,
Behold, thou shalt see it with thine eyes, but shalt not eat
20 thereof. And so it fell out unto him: for the people trode upon
him in the gate, and he died.

a ch. 4. 35.   **CHAP. 8.** THEN spake Elisha unto the woman, *a*whose son he had
restored to life, saying, Arise, and go thou and thine household,
and sojourn wheresoever thou canst sojourn: for the LORD

b Ps. 105. 16.   *b*hath called for a famine; and it shall also come upon the land
Hag. 1. 11.   2 seven years. And the woman arose, and did after the saying of
the man of God: and she went with her household, and sojourned
3 in the land of the Philistines seven years. And it came to pass
at the seven years' end, that the woman returned out of the
land of the Philistines: and she went forth to cry unto the king
4 for her house and for her land. And the king talked with

c ch. 5. 27.   *c*Gehazi the servant of the man of God, saying, Tell me, I pray
5 thee, all the great things that Elisha hath done. And it came

d ch. 4. 35.   to pass, as he was telling the king how he had *d*restored a dead
body to life, that, behold, the woman, whose son he had restored
to life, cried to the king for her house and for her land. And
Gehazi said, My lord, O king, this *is* the woman, and this *is* her

---

war-chariots, with their proper complement
of horses and men, to see whether the retreat was a reality or only a feint. The
"horses" sent would be four or six, since
chariots were drawn by either two or three
horses.

15. The Syrians had fled probably by the
great road which led from Samaria to
Damascus through Geba, En-gannim, Beth-
shean, and Aphek. It crosses the Jordan at
the *Jisr Mejamia*, about thirty-five miles
north-east of Samaria.

VIII. **1.** The famine here recorded, and
the conversation of the monarch with
Gehazi, must have been anterior to the
events related in ch. v.—since we may be
sure that a king of Israel would not have
entered into familiar conversation with a
confirmed leper. The writer of Kings probably collected the miracles of Elisha from
various sources, and did not always arrange
them chronologically. Here the link of
connexion is to be found in the nature of

the miracle. As Elisha on one occasion
prophesied plenty, so on another he had
prophesied a famine.

called for a famine] A frequent expression
(cp. marg. reff.). God's "calling for" anything is the same as His producing it (see
Ezek. xxxvi. 29; Rom. iv. 17).

2. The country of the Philistines—the
rich low corn-growing plain along the sea-
coast of Judah—was always a land of plenty
compared with the highlands of Palestine.
Moreover, if food failed there, it was easily
imported by sea from the neighbouring
Egypt.

3. During the Shunammite's absence in
Philistia, her dwelling and her corn-fields
had been appropriated by some one who
refused to restore them. She therefore
determined to appeal to the king. Such
direct appeals are common in Oriental
countries. Cp. vi. 26; 2 Sam. xiv. 4; 1
K. iii. 16.

6 son, whom Elisha restored to life. And when the king asked
the woman, she told him. So the king appointed unto her a
certain ¹officer, saying, Restore all that *was* her's, and all the
fruits of the field since the day that she left the land, even until
7 now. ¶And Elisha came to Damascus; and Ben-hadad the
king of Syria was sick; and it was told him, saying, The man of
8 God is come hither. And the king said unto ᵉHazael, ᶠTake a
present in thine hand, and go, meet the man of God, and ᵍenquire
9 of the LORD by him, saying, Shall I recover of this disease? So
Hazael went to meet him, and took a present ²with him, even
of every good thing of Damascus, forty camels' burden, and
came and stood before him, and said, Thy son Ben-hadad king
of Syria hath sent me to thee, saying, Shall I recover of this
10 disease? And Elisha said unto him, Go, say unto him, Thou
mayest certainly recover: howbeit the LORD hath shewed me
11 that ʰhe shall surely die. And he settled his countenance
³stedfastly, until he was ashamed: and the man of God ⁱwept.
12 And Hazael said, Why weepeth my lord? And he answered,
Because I know ᵏthe evil that thou wilt do unto the children of

ᵉ 1 Kin. 19. 15.
ᶠ 1 Sam. 9. 7.
1 Kin. 14. 3.
ch. 5. 5.
ᵍ ch. 1. 2.

ʰ ver. 15.
ⁱ Luke 19. 41.

ᵏ ch. 10. 22.
& 12. 17.
& 13. 3, 7.
Amos 1. 3.

¹ Or, *eunuch*.   ² Heb. *in his hand*.   ³ Heb. *and set it*.

---

6. *a certain officer*] Lit., "a certain
eunuch" (marg.). Eunuchs were now in
common use at the Samaritan Court (cp.
ix. 32). They are ascribed to the Court of
David in Chronicles (1 Chr. xxviii. 1); and
we may conjecture that they were maintained by Solomon. But otherwise we do
not find them in the kingdom of Judah till
the time of Hezekiah (Isai. lvi. 3, 4).
7. The hour had come for carrying out
the command given by God to Elijah
(marg. ref. *e*), and by him probably passed
on to his successor. Elisha, careless of his
own safety, quitted the land of Israel, and
proceeded into the enemy's country, thus
putting into the power of the Syrian king
that life which he had lately sought so
eagerly (vi. 13-19).
the man of God] The Damascenes had
perhaps known Elisha by this title from the
time of his curing Naaman. Or the phrase
may be used as equivalent to "Prophet,"
which is the title commonly given to Elisha
by the Syrians. See vi. 12. Cp. v. 13.
8. Hazael was no doubt a high officer of
the court. The names of Hazael and Ben-
hadad occur in the Assyrian inscription on
the Black Obelisk now in the British
Museum. Both are mentioned as kings of
Damascus, who contended with a certain
Shalmaneser, king of Assyria, and suffered
defeat at his hands. In one of the battles
between this king and Benhadad, "Ahab of
Jezreel" is mentioned among the allies of
the latter. This same Shalmaneser took
tribute from Jehu. This is the point at
which the Assyrian records first come in
direct contact with those of the Jews.
9. *every good thing of Damascus*] Probably, besides rich robes and precious
metals, the luscious wine of Helbon, which

was the drink of the Persian kings, the soft
white wool of the anti-Libanus (Ezek. xxvii.
18), *damask* coverings of couches (Am. iii.
12), and numerous manufactured articles of
luxury, which the Syrian capital imported
from Tyre, Egypt, Nineveh, and Babylon.
Forty camels were laden with it, and this
goodly caravan paraded the streets of the
town, conveying to the prophet the splendid
gift designed for him. Eastern ostentation
induces donors to make the greatest possible
show of their gifts, and each camel would
probably bear only one or two articles.
thy son Ben-hadad] A phrase indicative of
the greatest respect, no doubt used at the
command of Benhadad in order to dispose
the Prophet favourably towards him. Cp.
vi. 21.
10. Translate—"Go, say unto him, Thou
shalt certainly live: howbeit the Lord
hath showed me that he shall certainly
die." *i.e.* "Say to him, what thou hast
already determined to say, what a courtier
is sure to say (cp. 1 K. xxii. 15), but know
that the *fact* will be otherwise."
11. That is, "And he (Elisha) settled his
countenance, and set it (towards Hazael),
till he (Hazael) was ashamed." Elisha fixed
on Hazael a long and meaning look, till the
latter's eyes fell before his, and his cheek
flushed. Elisha, it would seem, had detected the guilty thought that was in
Hazael's heart, and Hazael perceived that
he had detected it. Hence the "shame."
12. *the evil that thou wilt do*] The intention is not to tax Hazael with special
cruelty, but only to enumerate the ordinary
horrors of war, as it was conducted among
the Oriental nations of the time. Cp.
marg. reff.

l ch. 15. 16.
Hos. 13. 16.
Amos 1. 13.
m 1 Sam. 17.
43.
n 1 Kin. 19. 15.

o 2 Chr. 21. 3,
4.
p 2 Chr. 21.
5, &c.

q ver. 26.
r 2 Sam. 7. 13.
1 Kin. 11. 36.
& 15. 4.
2 Chr. 21. 7.

Israel: their strong holds wilt thou set on fire, and their young men wilt thou slay with the sword, and *l* wilt dash their children, 13 and rip up their women with child. And Hazael said, But what, *m is* thy servant a dog, that he should do this great thing? And Elisha answered, *n* The LORD hath shewed me that thou 14 *shalt be* king over Syria. So he departed from Elisha, and came to his master; who said to him, What said Elisha to thee? And he answered, He told me *that* thou shouldest surely recover. 15 And it came to pass on the morrow, that he took a thick cloth, and dipped *it* in water, and spread *it* on his face, so that he died: 16 and Hazael reigned in his stead. ¶ And in the fifth year of Joram, the son of Ahab king of Israel, Jehoshaphat *being* then king of Judah, *o* Jehoram the son of Jehoshaphat king of Judah 17 ¹ began to reign. *p* Thirty and two years old was he when he 18 began to reign; and he reigned eight years in Jerusalem. And he walked in the way of the kings of Israel, as did the house of Ahab: for *q* the daughter of Ahab was his wife: and he did evil 19 in the sight of the LORD. Yet the LORD would not destroy Judah for David his servant's sake, *r* as he promised him to give

¹ Heb. *reigned.* Began to reign in consort with his father.

---

13. *But what, is thy servant a dog?*] This is a mistranslation, and conveys to the English reader a sense quite different from that of the original. Hazael's speech runs thus— "But what is thy servant, this dog, that he should do this great thing?" He does not shrink from Elisha's words, or mean to say that he would be a dog, could he act so cruelly as Elisha predicts he will. On the contrary, Elisha's prediction has raised his hopes, and his only doubt is whether so much good fortune ("this great thing") can be in store for one so mean. "Dog" here, as generally (though not always) in Scripture, has the sense of "mean," "low," "contemptible."

14. Hazael omitted the clause by which Elisha had shown how those words were to be understood. He thus deceived his master, while he could flatter himself that he had not uttered a lie.

15. *a thick cloth*] Probably, a cloth or mat placed between the head and the upper part of the bedstead, which in Egypt and Assyria was often so shaped that pillows (in our sense) were unnecessary.

The objection that Elisha is involved in the guilt of having suggested the deed, has no real force or value. Hazael was no more obliged to murder Benhadad because a Prophet announced to him that he would one day be king of Syria, than David was obliged to murder Saul because another Prophet anointed him king in Saul's room (1 Sam. xvi. 1-13).

16-19. The passage is parenthetic, resuming the history of the kingdom of Judah from 1 K. xxii. 50.

16. The opening words are — "In the fifth year of Joram, son of Ahab, king of Israel, and of Jehoshaphat, king of Judah;" but they contradict all the other chronological notices of Jehoshaphat (1 K. xxii. 42, 51; 2 K. iii. 1; 2 Chr. xx. 31), which give him a reign of at least twenty-three years. Hence some have supposed that the words "Jehoshaphat being then king of Judah," are accidentally repeated. Those, however, who regard them and i. 17 as sound, suppose that Jehoshaphat gave his son the royal title in his sixteenth year, while he advanced him to a real association in the empire seven years later, in his twenty-third year. Two years afterwards, Jehoshaphat died, and Jehoram became sole king.

17. The "eight years" are counted from his association in the kingdom. They terminate in the twelfth year of Jehoram of Israel.

18. Jehoshaphat's alliance, political and social, with Ahab and Ahab's family had not been allowed to affect the purity of his faith. Jehoram his son, influenced by his wife, Athaliah, the daughter of Ahab, "walked in the way of the kings of Israel;" he allowed, *i.e.*, the introduction of the Baal-worship into Judæa.

Among the worst of Jehoram's evil doings must be reckoned the cruel murder of his six brothers (2 Chr. xxi. 4), whom he slew to obtain their wealth.

19. The natural consequence of Jehoram's apostasy would have been the destruction of his house, and the transfer of the throne of Judah to another family. Cp. the punishments of Jeroboam (1 K. xiv. 10), Baasha (do. xvi. 2-4), and Ahab (do. xxi. 20-22). But the promises to David (marg. reff.) prevented this removal of the dynasty; and so Jehoram was punished in other ways (*v.* 22; 2 Chr. xxi. 12-19).

20 him alway a ¹light, *and* to his children. In his days ˢEdom
revolted from under the hand of Judah, ᵗand made a king over
21 themselves. So Joram went over to Zair, and all the chariots
with him : and he rose by night, and smote the Edomites which
compassed him about, and the captains of the chariots : and the
22 people fled into their tents. ²Yet Edom revolted from under
the hand of Judah unto this day. "Then Libnah revolted at
23 the same time. ¶ And the rest of the acts of Joram, and all
that he did, *are* they not written in the book of the chronicles
24 of the kings of Judah? And Joram slept with his fathers, and
was buried with his fathers in the city of David : and ˣ³Ahaziah
25 his son reigned in his stead. ¶ In the twelfth year of Joram
the son of Ahab king of Israel did Ahaziah the son of Jehoram
26 king of Judah begin to reign. ʸTwo and twenty years old *was*
Ahaziah when he began to reign ; and he reigned one year in
Jerusalem. And his mother's name *was* Athaliah, the ⁴daughter
27 of Omri king of Israel. ᶻAnd he walked in the way of the
house of Ahab, and did evil in the sight of the LORD, as *did*
the house of Ahab : for he *was* the son in law of the house of
28 Ahab. And he went ᵃwith Joram the son of Ahab to the war
against Hazael king of Syria in Ramoth-gilead ; and the Syrians

ˢ 2 Chr. 21.8,
9, 10.
ᵗ 1 Kin. 22.
47.

ᵘ 2 Chr. 21.
10.

ˣ 2 Chr.22.1.

ʸ See 2 Chr.
22. 2.

ᶻ 2 Chr. 22.
3, 4.

ᵃ 2 Chr. 22.5.

---

¹ Heb. *candle*, or, *lamp*.
² And so fulfilled, Gen. 27.
40.
⁶ Called, *Azariah*, 2 Chr.
22. 6, and *Jehoahaz*, 2
Chr. 21. 17. & 25. 23.
⁴ Or, *granddaughter* : See
ver. 18.

---

20. Edom, which had been reduced by
David (2 Sam. viii. 14 ; 1 K. xi. 15, 16), but
had apparently revolted from Solomon (1 K.
xi. 14), was again subjected to Judah in the
reign of Jehoshaphat (iii. 8–26). The Edomites had, however, retained their native
kings, and with them the spirit of independence. They now rose in revolt, and fulfilled the prophecy (Gen. xxvii. 40), remaining from henceforth a separate and independent people (Jer. xxv. 21, xxvii. 3 ;
Am. i. 11, &c.). Kings of Edom, who seem
to be independent monarchs, are often mentioned in the Assyrian inscriptions.
21. *Zair*] Perhaps Seir, the famous mountain of Edom (Gen. xiv. 6).
the people] *i.e.* The Edomites. Yet, notwithstanding his success, Joram was forced
to withdraw from the country, and to
leave the natives to enjoy that independence (*v.* 22), which continued till the time
of John Hyrcanus, who once more reduced
them.
Libnah revolted] Libnah being towards·
the south-*west* of Palestine (Josh. xv. 42), its
revolt cannot well have had any direct connexion with that of Edom. It had been
the capital of a small Canaanite state
under a separate king before its conquest
by Joshua (Josh. x. 30, xii. 15), and may
perhaps always have retained a considerable
Canaanitish population. Or its loss may
have been connected with the attacks made
by the Philistines on Jehoram's territories
(2 Chr. xvi. 16, 17).
24. On the death of Jehoram, see 2 Chr.
xxi. 12-19. His son is also called Jehoahaz

(margin) by a transposition of the two elements of the name.
26. Such names as Athaliah, Jehoram,
and Ahaziah, indicate that the Baal-wor-
shipping kings of Israel did not openly renounce the service of Jehovah. Athaliah is
"the time for Jehovah;" Ahaziah "the
possession of Jehovah;" Jehoram, or Joram, "exalted by Jehovah."
the daughter of Omri] "Son" and "daughter" were used by the Jews of any descendants (cp. Matt. i. 1). The whole race were
"the children of Israel." Athaliah was
the *grand-daughter* of Omri (see marg.). Her
being called "the daughter of Omri" implies that an idea of special greatness was
regarded as attaching to him, so· that his
name prevailed over that of Ahab. Indications of this ideal greatness are found in
the Assyrian inscriptions, where the early
name for Samaria is Beth-Omri, and where
even Jehu has the title of "the son of
Omri."
28. This war of the two kings against
Hazael seems to have had for its object the
recovery of Ramoth-gilead, which Ahab
and Jehoshaphat had vainly attempted
fourteen years earlier (1 K. xxii. 3–36).
Joram probably thought that the accession
of a new and usurping monarch presented a
favourable opportunity for a renewal of the
war. It may also have happened that Hazael was engaged at the time upon his
northern frontier with repelling one of those
Assyrian attacks which seem by the inscriptions to have fallen upon him in quick succession during his earlier years. At any

b ch. 9. 15.

c ch. 9. 16.
2 Chr.22.6,7.

a 1 Kin. 20.
35.
b ch. 4. 29.
Jer. 1. 17.
c ch. 8. 28,29.

d ver. 5, 11.
e 1 Kin.19.16.

f 1 Kin.19.16.
2 Chr. 22. 7.

g 1 Kin.18.4.
& 21. 15.

h 1 Kin.14.10.
& 21. 21.
i 1 Sam. 25.
22.
k Deut.32.36.
l 1 Kin. 14.
10.
& 15. 29.
& 21. 22.
m 1 Kin.16.3,
11.
n 1 Kin. 21.
23.
ver. 35. 36.
o Jer. 29. 26.
John 10. 20.
Acts 26. 24.
1 Cor. 4. 10.

p Matt. 21. 7.

29 wounded Joram. And *b*king Joram went back to be healed in Jezreel of the wounds [1]which the Syrians had given him at ²Ramah, when he fought against Hazael king of Syria. *c*And Ahaziah the son of Jehoram king of Judah went down to see Joram the son of Ahab in Jezreel, because he was ³sick.

CHAP. 9. AND Elisha the prophet called one of *a*the children of the prophets, and said unto him, *b*Gird up thy loins, and take 2 this box of oil in thine hand, *c*and go to Ramoth-gilead: and when thou comest thither, look out there Jehu the son of Jehoshaphat the son of Nimshi, and go in, and make him arise up from among *d*his brethren, and carry him to an ⁴inner chamber; 3 then *e*take the box of oil, and pour *it* on his head, and say, Thus saith the LORD, I have anointed thee king over Israel. 4 Then open the door, and flee, and tarry not. So the young man, *even* the young man the prophet, went to Ramoth-gilead. 5 ¶And when he came, behold, the captains of the host *were* sitting; and he said, I have an errand to thee, O captain. And Jehu said, Unto which of all us? And he said, To thee, O 6 captain. And he arose, and went into the house; and he poured the oil on his head, and said unto him, *f*Thus saith the LORD God of Israel, I have anointed thee king over the people of the 7 LORD, *even* over Israel. And thou shalt smite the house of Ahab thy master, that I may avenge the blood of my servants the prophets, and the blood of all the servants of the LORD, *g*at 8 the hand of Jezebel. For the whole house of Ahab shall perish: and *h*I will cut off from Ahab *i*him that pisseth against the 9 wall, and *k*him that is shut up and left in Israel: and I will make the house of Ahab like the house of *l*Jeroboam the son of Nebat, and like the house of *m*Baasha the son of Ahijah: 10 *n*and the dogs shall eat Jezebel in the portion of Jezreel, and *there shall be* none to bury *her*. And he opened the door, and 11 fled. ¶Then Jehu came forth to the servants of his lord: and one said unto him, *Is* all well? wherefore came *o*this mad *fellow* to thee? And he said unto them, Ye know the man, and his 12 communication. And they said, *It is* false; tell us now. And he said, Thus and thus spake he to me, saying, Thus saith the 13 LORD, I have anointed thee king over Israel. Then they hasted, and *p*took every man his garment, and put *it* under him on the

---

[1] Heb. *wherewith the Syrians had wounded.*　² Called, *Ramoth*, ver. 28.　³ Heb. *wounded.*　⁴ Heb. *chamber in a chamber.*

---

rate, the war appears to have been successful. Ramoth-gilead was recovered (ix. 14), and remained probably thenceforth in the hands of the Israelites.

the Syrians wounded Joram] According to Josephus, Joram was struck by an arrow in the course of the siege, but remained till the place was taken. He then withdrew to Jezreel (1 K. xviii. 45, xxi. 1), leaving his army under Jehu within the walls of the town.

IX. 1. *box*] Rather, "flask," or "vial" (1 Sam. x. 1). Oil and ointment were commonly kept in open-mouthed jars, vases, or bottles made of glass, alabaster, or earthenware. Many such vessels have been found both in Egypt and Assyria. The "oil" was the holy oil, compounded after the receipt given in Exodus (xxx. 23–25).

3. *flee, and tarry not*] The probable object of these directions was at once to prevent questioning, and to render the whole thing more striking.

5. The chief officers—the generals—were assembled together in Jehu's quarters, perhaps holding a council of war. The place of assembly seems to have been the great court. Hence, Jehu "went into the house" (*v.* 6)—entered, that is, one of the rooms opening into the court.

11. *this mad fellow*] The captains, seeing his excited look, his strange action, and his extreme haste, call him (as soldiers would) "this wild fellow."

13. *took every man his garment, and put it under him*] The outer cloak of the Jews was a sort of large shawl or blanket, which might well serve for a carpet of state. Such

top of the stairs, and blew with trumpets, saying, Jehu [1]is king.
14 So Jehu the son of Jehoshaphat the son of Nimshi conspired
against Joram. (Now Joram had kept Ramoth-gilead, he and
15 all Israel, because of Hazael king of Syria. But [q]king [2]Joram [q] ch. 8. 29.
was returned to be healed in Jezreel of the wounds which the
Syrians [3]had given him, when he fought with Hazael king of
Syria.) ¶ And Jehu said, If it be your minds, *then* [4]let none go
16 forth *nor* escape out of the city to go to tell *it* in Jezreel. So
Jehu rode in a chariot, and went to Jezreel; for Joram lay there.
17 [r]And Ahaziah king of Judah was come down to see Joram. And [r] ch. 8. 29.
there stood a watchman on the tower in Jezreel, and he spied
the company of Jehu as he came, and said, I see a company.
And Joram said, Take an horseman, and send to meet them,
18 and let him say, *Is it* peace? So there went one on horseback
to meet him, and said, Thus saith the king, *Is it* peace? And
Jehu said, What hast thou to do with peace? turn thee behind
me. And the watchman told, saying, The messenger came to
19 them, but he cometh not again. Then he sent out a second on
horseback, which came to them, and said, Thus saith the king,
Is it peace? And Jehu answered, What hast thou to do with
20 peace? turn thee behind me. And the watchman told, saying,
He came even unto them, and cometh not again: and the
[5]driving *is* like the driving of Jehu the son of Nimshi; for he
21 driveth [6]furiously. And Joram said, [7]Make ready. And his
chariot was made ready. And [s]Joram king of Israel and Aha- [s] 2 Chr. 22.7.
ziah king of Judah went out, each in his chariot, and they went
out against Jehu, and [8]met him in the portion of Naboth the
22 Jezreelite. ¶ And it came to pass, when Joram saw Jehu, that
he said, *Is it* peace, Jehu? And he answered, What peace, so
long as the whoredoms of thy mother Jezebel and her witch-

[1] Heb. *reigneth.*
[2] Heb. *Jehoram.*
[3] Heb. *smote.*
[4] Heb. *let no escaper go, &c.*
[5] Or, *marching.*
[6] Heb. *in madness.*
[7] Heb. *Bind.*
[8] Heb. *found.*

---

a carpet is commonly represented on the seat of an Assyrian throne in the Nineveh sculptures.

The stairs rose against the wall of the house from the pavement of the court to the level of the upper story, or of the roof. At the top of the stairs would be a flat platform, and this would form a throne, on which the new king could exhibit himself to his subjects.

blew with trumpets] On this recognised part of the ceremony of a coronation, see xi. 14; 2 Sam. xv. 10; 1 K. i. 39.

14. *had kept*] Rather, "**was keeping watch.**" The city had been taken; but the war continuing, and there being a danger of the Syrians recovering it, Joram and all Israel (*i.e.* the whole military force) were guarding the recent conquest, while Hazael threatened it.

18. *What hast thou to do with peace?*] *i.e.*, "What does it matter to *thee* whether my errand is one of peace or not?"

20. *the driving ... furiously*] The word translated "driving" means "leading" or "conducting" a band. The watchman observed that the "company" (or, multitude) was led forward madly, and associated this strange procedure with the known character of Jehu. It is curious that some Versions, as well as Josephus, give an opposite sense:—"he driveth quietly."

Jehu was properly "the grandson" of Nimshi, who was probably a more famous person than Jehoshaphat (*v.* 2).

21. *Make ready*] Lit. (as in marg.) "Bind," *i.e.* "Harness the horses to the chariot." The king had no suspicion of Jehu's treason. Probably he imagined that he was bringing him important news from the seat of war. Ahaziah's accompanying him is significant of the close friendship which united the uncle and the nephew. They went out not "against" Jehu, but rather "**to meet him.**"

in the portion of Naboth] This is no longer called a "vineyard" (1 K. xxi. 1-18); probably because it had been thrown into the palace garden, and applied to the purpose for which Ahab originally wanted it. The approach to the city on this side must have lain either through it, or close by it.

22. Joram had asked the usual question, "Is it peace?"—meaning simply, "Is all

23 crafts *are so* many ? And Joram turned his hands, and fled, and
24 said to Ahaziah, *There is* treachery, O Ahaziah. And Jehu [1] drew
a bow with his full strength, and smote Jehoram between his
arms, and the arrow went out at his heart, and he [2] sunk down
25 in his chariot. Then said *Jehu* to Bidkar his captain, Take up,
and cast him in the portion of the field of Naboth the Jezreelite:
for remember how that, when I and thou rode together after

t 1 Kin. 21. 29.

26 Ahab his father, *t*the LORD laid this burden upon him; surely
I have seen yesterday the [3] blood of Naboth, and the blood of

u 1 Kin. 21. 19.

his sons, saith the LORD; and *u*I will requite thee in this [4] plat,
saith the LORD. Now therefore take *and* cast him into the plat
27 of *ground*, according to the word of the LORD. ¶ But when
Ahaziah the king of Judah saw *this*, he fled by the way of the
garden house. And Jehu followed after him, and said, Smite
him also in the chariot. *And they did so* at the going up to

x In the kingdom of *Samaria*, 2 Chr. 22. 9.

Gur, which *is* by Ibleam. And he fled to *x*Megiddo, and died
28 there. And his servants carried him in a chariot to Jerusalem,
and buried him in his sepulchre with his fathers in the city of
29 David. And in the eleventh year of Joram the son of Ahab
30 began Ahaziah to reign over Judah. ¶ And when Jehu was

y Ezek. 23. 40.

come to Jezreel, Jezebel heard *of it; y* and she [5] painted her face,

[1] Heb. *filled his hand with a bow.*
[2] Heb. *bowed.*
[3] Heb. *bloods.*
[4] Or, *portion.*
[5] Heb. *put her eyes in painting.*

---

well?" In Jehu's reply, by "whoredoms"
we are probably to understand "idolatries,"
acts of spiritual unfaithfulness; by "witch-
crafts," dealings with the Baal prophets
and oracles. Cp. i. 2 note.

23. *turned his hands*] The meaning is
that Joram *ordered his charioteer* to turn
round and drive back to the town.

24. *Jehu drew a bow*, &c.] Lit. as in margin, *i.e.* "Jehu took a bow in his hand."
The arrow struck Jehoram's back, between
his two shoulders, as he fled.

25. *rode together after Ahab*] The Assyrian
sculptures make it probable that Josephus
was right in interpreting this "rode side
by side *behind Ahab in his chariot.*" The
Assyrian monarchs, when they go out to
war, are frequently attended by two guards,
who stand behind them in the same
chariot.

burden] Cp. the use of the same word in
Isaiah (xiii. 1, xv. 1, &c.), and in Lamentations (ii. 14), for a denunciation of woe.

26. The passage from "Surely I have
seen" to "Saith the Lord," is exegetical
of *v.* 25, containing the "burden" there
spoken of.

and the blood of his sons] The murder of
Naboth's sons is here for the first time
mentioned; but as the removal of the sons
was necessary, if the vineyard was to pass
to Ahab, we can well understand that Jezebel would take care to clear them out of the
way.

27. *by the way of the garden-house*] Or,
"by the way of Beth-Gan," which has been
conjectured to be another name for En-

Gannim, "the spring of the gardens." Both
are considered identical with Ginæa, the
modern *Jenin*, which lies due south of
Jezreel. The road from Jezreel (*Zerin*) to
Jenin passes at first along the plain of
Esdraelon, but after a while begins to rise
over the Samaritan hills. Here probably
was "the ascent of Gur, by Ibleam," which
may have occupied the site of the modern
Jelama. Whether the soldiers attacked
him there or not is uncertain. The words,
"*And they did so,*" are not in the original.

Megiddo] On its situation, see Josh. xii.
21 note; and on the possible reconcilement
of this passage with 2 Chr. xxii. 9, see the
note there.

29. *in the eleventh year*] The twelfth according to viii. 25. The discrepancy may
be best explained from two ways of reckoning the accession of Ahaziah, who is likely
to have been regent for his father during at
least one year. See 2 Chr. xxi. 19.

30. *painted her face*] Lit. "put her eyes
in antimony"—*i.e.* dyed the upper and
under eyelids, a common practice in the
East, even at the present day. The effect
is at once to increase the apparent size of
the eye, and to give it unnatural brilliancy.
Representations of eyes thus embellished
occur on the Assyrian sculptures, and the
practice existed among the Jews (marg.
ref.; and Jer. iv. 30).

tired her head] Dressed (attired) her head,
and no doubt put on her royal robes, that
she might die as became a queen, in true
royal array.

31 and tired her head, and looked out at a window. And as Jehu
entered in at the gate, she said, *Had Zimri peace, who slew his
32 master? And he lifted up his face to the window, and said,
Who *is* on my side? who? And there looked out to him two
33 *or* three ¹eunuchs. And he said, Throw her down. So they
threw her down: and *some* of her blood was sprinkled on the
34 wall, and on the horses: and he trode her under foot. And
when he was come in, he did eat and drink, and said, Go, see
now this cursed *woman*, and bury her: for ᵃshe *is* a king's
35 daughter. And they went to bury her: but they found no more
of her than the skull, and the feet, and the palms of *her* hands.
36 Wherefore they came again, and told him. And he said, This
is the word of the LORD, which he spake ²by his servant Elijah
the Tishbite, saying, ᵇIn the portion of Jezreel shall dogs eat
37 the flesh of Jezebel: and the carcase of Jezebel shall be ᶜas dung
upon the face of the field in the portion of Jezreel; *so* that they
shall not say, This *is* Jezebel.

CHAP. 10. AND Ahab had seventy sons in Samaria. And Jehu
wrote letters, and sent to Samaria, unto the rulers of Jezreel,
to the elders, and to ³them that brought up Ahab's *children*,
2 saying, Now as soon as this letter cometh to you, seeing your
master's sons *are* with you, and *there are* with you chariots and
3 horses, a fenced city also, and armour; look even out the best
and meetest of your master's sons, and set *him* on his father's
4 throne, and fight for your master's house. But they were exceedingly afraid, and said, Behold, two kings stood not before
5 him: how then shall we stand? And he that *was* over the
house, and he that *was* over the city, the elders also, and the
bringers up *of the children*, sent to Jehu, saying, We *are* thy
servants, and will do all that thou shalt bid us; we will not
make any king: do thou *that which is* good in thine eyes.
6 ¶ Then he wrote a letter the second time to them, saying, If ye
be ⁴mine, and *if* ye will hearken unto my voice, take ye the

ᵃ 1 Kin. 16.
9—20.

ᵃ 1 Kin. 16.
31.

ᵇ 1 Kin. 21.
23.
ᶜ Ps. 83. 10.

¹ Or, *chamberlains.*   ² Heb. *by the hand of.*   ⁴ Heb. *for me.*
³ Heb. *nourishers.*

---

a window] Rather, "the window." The
gate-tower had probably, as many of those
in the Assyrian sculptures, one window
only.

34. Leaving the mangled body on the
bare earth, Jehu went to the banquet. It
was, no doubt, important that he should at
once show himself to the Court as king. In
calling Jezebel "this cursed one," Jehu
means to remind his hearers that the curse
of God had been pronounced upon her by
Elijah (*v.* 36), and so to justify his own conduct.

a king's daughter] Merely as the widow of
Ahab and mother of Jehoram, Jehu would
not have considered Jezebel entitled to
burial. But she was the daughter of Eth-
baal, king of the Sidonians (marg. ref.),
and so a princess born. This would entitle
her to greater respect. Wilfully to have
denied her burial would have been regarded
as an unpardonable insult by the reigning
Sidonian monarch.

X. 1. *seventy sons*] *i.e.* descendants; there

were included among them children of Jehoram (*vv.* 2, 3, &c.).

2. *a fenced city*] Or, "fenced cities." If
Samaria had refused to acknowledge Jehu,
many other Israelite towns would have been
sure to follow the example.

3. Jehu, placing his adversaries' advantages before them in the most favourable
light, called upon them to decide what they
would do. The unscrupulous soldier shows
shrewdness as well as courage, a sharp wit
as well as a bold heart.

4. *two kings*] Lit. "the two kings," *i.e.*
Jehoram and Ahaziah (ix. 21—28).

5. The officer who had the charge of the
palace (1 K. iv. 6 note) and the governor
of the town (1 K. xxii. 26 note) seem to correspond to the "rulers" of *v.* 1.

6. The heads of rivals, pretenders, and
other obnoxious persons are commonly
struck off in the East, and conveyed to the
chief ruler, in order that he may be positively certified that his enemies have ceased
to live. In the Assyrian sculptures we

heads of the men your master's sons, and come to me to Jezreel by to morrow this time. Now the king's sons, *being* seventy persons, *were* with the great men of the city, which brought them 7 up. And it came to pass, when the letter came to them, that they took the king's sons, and *a*slew seventy persons, and put 8 their heads in baskets, and sent him *them* to Jezreel. And there came a messenger, and told him, saying, They have brought the heads of the king's sons. And he said, Lay ye them in two 9 heaps at the entering in of the gate until the morning. And it came to pass in the morning, that he went out, and stood, and said to all the people, Ye *be* righteous: behold, *b*I conspired against my master, and slew him: but who slew all these? 10 Know now that there shall *c*fall unto the earth nothing of the word of the LORD, which the LORD spake concerning the house of Ahab: for the LORD hath done *that* which he spake *d*1by his 11 servant Elijah. So Jehu slew all that remained of the house of Ahab in Jezreel, and all his great men, and his 2kinsfolks, 12 and his priests, until he left him none remaining. ¶And he arose and departed, and came to Samaria. *And* as he *was* at 13 the 3shearing house in the way, *e*Jehu 4met with the brethren of Ahaziah king of Judah, and said, Who *are* ye? And they answered, We *are* the brethren of Ahaziah; and we go down 5to salute the children of the king and the children of the queen. 14 And he said, Take them·alive. And they took them alive, and slew them at the pit of the shearing house, *even* two and forty 15 men; neither left he any of them. ¶And when he was departed thence, he 6lighted on *f*Jehonadab the son of *g*Rechab coming to meet him: and he 7saluted him, and said to him, Is thine heart right, as my heart *is* with thy heart? And Jeho-

a 1 Kin. 21. 21.

b ch. 9.14,24.

c 1 Sam. 3. 19.

d 1 Kin. 21. 19, 21, 29.

e ch. 8. 29. 2 Chr. 22. 8.

f Jer. 35. 6, &c. *g* 1 Chr. 2. 55.

1 Heb. *by the hand of.*
2 Or, *acquaintance.*
3 Heb. *house of shepherds binding sheep.*
4 Heb. *found.*
5 Heb. *to the peace of, &c.*
6 Heb. *found.*
7 Heb. *blessed.*

constantly see soldiers conveying heads from place to place, not, however, in baskets, but in their hands, holding the head by the hair.

8. *two heaps*] Probably placed one on either side of the gateway, to strike terror into the partisans of the late dynasty as they passed in and out of the town.

9. *Ye be righteous*] *i.e.* "Ye are just, and can judge aright." Jehu unfairly keeps back the fact that he had commanded the execution.

10. *shall fall to the earth*] *i.e.* "Shall remain unfulfilled" (cp. marg. ref.). Jehu and others were but executing the word of the Lord.

11. *So Jehu slew*] Rather, "And Jehu slew." The reference is to fresh executions (cp. *v.* 17). He proceeded on his bloody course, not merely destroying the remainder of the kindred of Ahab, but further putting to death all the most powerful of Ahab's partisans.

his priests] Not the Baal priests generally, whose persecution came afterwards (*v.* 19), but only such of them as were attached to the Court.

12. *the shearing-house*] Lit. as in marg.

Perhaps already a proper name, Beth-eked, identical with the Beth-akad of Jerome, which is described as between Jezreel and Samaria; but not yet identified.

13. *the brethren of Ahaziah*] Not the actual brothers of Ahaziah, who had all been slain by the Arabs before his accession to the throne (2 Chr. xxi. 17, xxii. 1); but his nephews, the sons of his brothers (marg. ref.). It is remarkable that they should have penetrated so far into the kingdom of Israel without having heard of the revolution.

the children of the king, &c.] *i.e.* "the sons of Jehoram, and the children (sons and grandsons) of the queen-mother, Jezebel." Some of both may well have been at Jezreel, though the younger branches of the royal family were at Samaria (*v.* 1).

15. *Jehonadab* (cp. margin) belonged to the tribe of the Kenites, one of the most ancient in Palestine (Gen. xv. 19). Their origin is unknown, but their habits were certainly those of Arabs. Owing to their connexion with Moses (Num. xxiv. 21 note), they formed a friendship with the Israelites, accompanied them in their wanderings, and finally received a location in the wilderness of Judah (Judg. i. 16). The character of this chief,

nadab answered, It is. If it be, *h*give *me* thine hand. And he
gave *him* his hand; and he took him up to him into the chariot.
16 And he said, Come with me, and see my *i*zeal for the LORD. So
17 they made him ride in his chariot. And when he came to
Samaria, *k*he slew all that remained unto Ahab in Samaria, till
he had destroyed him, according to the saying of the LORD,
18 *l*which he spake to Elijah. ¶ And Jehu gathered all the people
together, and said unto them, *m*Ahab served Baal a little; *but*
19 Jehu shall serve him much. Now therefore call unto me all the
*n*prophets of Baal, all his servants, and all his priests; let none
be wanting: for I have a great sacrifice *to do* to Baal; whosoever
shall be wanting, he shall not live. But Jehu did *it* in subtilty,
to the intent that he might destroy the worshippers of Baal.
20 And Jehu said, ¹Proclaim a solemn assembly for Baal. And
21 they proclaimed *it*. And Jehu sent through all Israel: and all
the worshippers of Baal came, so that there was not a man left
that came not. And they came into the *o*house of Baal; and
22 the house of Baal was ²full from one end to another. And he
said unto him that *was* over the vestry, Bring forth vestments

h Ezra 10.19.

i 1Kin.19.10.

k ch. 9. 8.
2 Chr. 22. 8.

l 1Kin.21.21.
m 1 Kin. 16.
31, 32.

n 1 Kin.22.6.

o 1 Kin. 16.
32.

---

¹ Heb. *Sanctify.*   ² Or, so *full*, that they stood *mouth to mouth.*

Jonadab, is best seen in the rule which he
established for his descendants (Jer. xxxv.
6, 7)—a rule said to be still observed at the
present day. It would seem that he sym-
pathised strongly with Jehu's proceedings,
and desired to give the countenance of his
authority, such as it was, to the new reign.
According to the Hebrew text, Jehu "saluted" (or blessed) Jehonadab. According
to the LXX. and Josephus, Jehonadab
"saluted" (or blessed) the king. Further,
the Hebrew text runs—"And Jehonadab
answered, It is, it is. Give (me) thy hand.
And he gave (him) his hand, and took him
up to him into the chariot." Our translators appear to have preferred the LXX.;
but the Hebrew is more graphic. Jehu was
no doubt glad to have the countenance of
Jehonadab on his public entrance into Samaria. The ascetic had a reputation for
sanctity, which could not fail to make his
companionship an advantage to the but
half-established monarch.

17. Cp. *v.* 11. Thus was finally completed the political revolution which transferred the throne from the house of Omri to
that of Nimshi, the fifth of the royal families of Israel.

according to the saying of the LORD]
This emphatic reiteration (cp. *v.* 10) marks,
first, how in the mind of the writer all this
history is viewed as deriving its special interest from its being so full and complete
an accomplishment of Elijah's prophecies;
and, secondly, how at the time Jehu carefully put forward the plea that what he did
had this object. It does not indicate that a
single-minded wish to execute God's will
was Jehu's predominate motive. Probably,
even where he most strictly fulfilled the
letter of prophecies, he was working for

himself, not for God; and hence vengeance
was denounced upon his house even for the
very "blood of Jezreel" (Hos. i. 4).

18. Though we cannot ascribe to Jehu a
spirit of true piety (see *v.* 29), we can well
enough understand how the soldier, trained
in the Syrian wars, revolted against the
unmanly and voluptuous worship of the
Dea Syra, and wished to go back to the
simple solemn service of Jehovah. These
views and feelings it would have been dangerous to declare during the lifetime of Jezebel. Even after her death it was prudent
to temporise, to wait until the party of
Ahab was crushed politically, before broach-
ing the religious question. Having now
slain all the issue of Ahab in the kingdom
of Israel, and all the influential men of the
party (*vv.* 7, 11, and 17), Jehu felt that he
might begin his reformation of religion.
But even now he uses "subtilty" rather
than open violence. "Ahab served Baal a
little; but Jehu shall serve him much."

19. It appears from this verse that the
"prophets" and "priests" of Baal were
not identical. The former would correspond
to the dervishes, the latter to the mollahs, of
Mahometan countries. By the "servants"
of Baal are meant the ordinary worshippers.

20. *a solemn assembly*] Jehu applies to
his proposed gathering the sacred name assigned in the Law to the chiefest Festivals
of Jehovah (see Lev. xxiii. 36; Num. xxix.
35; Deut. xvi. 8).

21. In order to understand how such
numbers could find room, we must remember that the ancient temples had vast courts
around them, which could contain many
thousands.

22. *the vestry*] The sacred robes of the

for all the worshippers of Baal. And he brought them forth
23 vestments. And Jehu went, and Jehonadab the son of Rechab,
into the house of Baal, and said unto the worshippers of Baal,
Search, and look that there be here with you none of the ser-
24 vants of the LORD, but the worshippers of Baal only. And
when they went in to offer sacrifices and burnt offerings, Jehu
appointed fourscore men without, and said, *If* any of the men
whom I have brought into your hands escape, *he that letteth him*

p 1 Kin. 20. 39.

25 *go*, *p*his life *shall be* for the life of him. And it came to pass, as
soon as he had made an end of offering the burnt offering, that
Jehu said to the guard and to the captains, Go in, *and* slay them;
let none come forth. And they smote them with ¹the edge of
the sword; and the guard and the captains cast *them* out, and
26 went to the city of the house of Baal. And they brought forth

q 1 Kin. 14. 23.

27 the ²*q*images out of the house of Baal, and burned them. And
they brake down the image of Baal, and brake down the house

r Ezra 6. 11.
Dan. 2. 5.
& 3. 29.

28 of Baal, *r*and made it a draught house unto this day. ¶ Thus
29 Jehu destroyed Baal out of Israel. Howbeit *from* the sins of
Jeroboam the son of Nebat, who made Israel to sin, Jehu de-

s 1 Kin. 12. 28, 29.

parted not from after them, *to wit*, *s*the golden calves that *were*
30 in Beth-el, and that *were* in Dan. ¶And the LORD said unto
Jehu, Because thou hast done well in executing *that which is*
right in mine eyes, *and* hast done unto the house of Ahab ac-

t See ver. 35.
ch. 13. 1, 10.
& 14. 23.
& 15. 8, 12.

cording to all that *was* in mine heart, *t*thy children of the fourth

¹ Heb. *the mouth.*   ² Heb. *statues.*

Baal priests seem to have been of linen, and were probably white. The vestry here mentioned may, probably, be the robe-chamber of the royal palace, from which the king gave a festal garment to each worshipper.

23. The presence of persons belonging to another religion was usually regarded by the ancients as a profanation of the rites. In the case of the Greek mysteries such intrusion is said to have been punished by death. Consequently Jehu could give these injunctions without arousing any suspicion.

25. *as soon as he had made an end of offering*] The actual sacrificers were no doubt the priests of Baal; but Jehu is considered to have made the offering, since he furnished the victims. Cp. 1 K. viii. 62, 63.

the guard] Lit. "the runners." This name seems to have been given to the royal body-guard as early as the time of Saul (1 Sam. xxii. 17, marg.). It was their duty to *run* by the side of the king's chariot as he moved from place to place.

cast them out, and went] Rather, "the captains *hasted* and went," or "went *hastily;*" which gives a satisfactory sense. That the soldiers should have troubled themselves to cast the bodies of the slain out of the temple enclosure is very unlikely.

the city of the house of Baal] *i.e.* the temple itself, as distinguished from the court in which it stood, is intended. The guard having slain all who were in the court, rushed on and entered the sanctuary, there no doubt completing the massacre, and further tearing down and bringing out the

sacred objects mentioned in the next verse.

26. *the images*] Or "pillars" of wood. The Phœnician pillar idols were mere columns, obelisks, or posts, destitute of any shaping into the semblance of humanity (cp. 1 K. xiv. 23 note).

27. *And they brake down the image of Baal*] The other images, it appears, were not images of Baal, but of inferior deities. The image of Baal, which was "broken down," and not burnt, would seem to have been of stone, perhaps erected in front of the temple.

29. To abolish the calf-worship was a thought which had probably never occurred to Jehu. He had religious feeling enough, and patriotism enough, to detest the utterly debasing Astarte worship; but the pure worship of Jehovah was altogether beyond and above him.

30. *And the LORD said unto Jehu*] Probably by the mouth of Elisha. To a certain extent Jehu's measures were acts of obedience, for which God might see fit to assign him a temporal reward.

thy children, &c.] This was accomplished in the persons of Jehoahaz, Joash, Jeroboam, and Zachariah, the son, grandson, great-grandson, and great-great-grandson of Jehu (cp. marg. reff.). No other family sat upon the throne of Israel so long. The house of Omri, which furnished four kings, held the crown for three generations only and for less than fifty years—that of Jehu reigned for five generations and for above a hundred years.

31 *generation* shall sit on the throne of Israel. But Jehu [1]took no heed to walk in the law of the LORD God of Israel with all his heart: for he departed not from [u]the sins of Jeroboam, which 32 made Israel to sin. ¶ In those days the LORD began [2]to cut Israel short: and [x]Hazael smote them in all the coasts of Israel; 33 from Jordan [3]eastward, all the land of Gilead, the Gadites, and the Reubenites, and the Manassites, from Aroer, which *is* by 34 the river Arnon, [4]even [v]Gilead and Bashan. ¶ Now the rest of the acts of Jehu, and all that he did, and all his might, *are* they not written in the book of the chronicles of the kings of Israel? 35 And Jehu slept with his fathers: and they buried him in Sa- 36 maria. And Jehoahaz his son reigned in his stead. And [5]the time that Jehu reigned over Israel in Samaria *was* twenty and eight years.

CHAP. 11. AND when [a]Athaliah [b]the mother of Ahaziah saw that her son was dead, she arose and destroyed all the [6]seed royal. 2 But [7]Jehosheba, the daughter of king Joram, sister of Ahaziah, took [8]Joash the son of Ahaziah, and stole him from among the king's sons *which were* slain; and they hid him, *even* him and his nurse, in the bedchamber from Athaliah, so that he was not

[u] 1 Kin. 14.
16.

[x] ch. 8. 12.

[v] Amos 1. 3.

[a] 2 Chr. 22.
10.
[b] ch. 8. 26.

---

[1] Heb. *observed not.*	[4] Or, *even to Gilead and Bashan.*
[2] Heb. *to cut off the ends.*	[5] Heb. *the days* were.
[3] Heb. *toward the rising of the sun.*	[6] Heb. *seed of the kingdom.*
	[7] 2 Chr. 22. 11, *Jehoshabeath.*
	[8] Or, *Jehoash.*

---

32. *to cut Israel short*] Lit. "to cut off in Israel," *i.e.* to take away from Israel portions of its territory (see marg. ref.).

33. The loss of the entire trans-Jordanic territory seems to be intended, or at any rate its complete ruin and devastation (cp. marg. ref. *y*). This was the home of the tribes of Reuben and Gad, and of the half tribe of Manasseh (Josh. xxii. 1-9). It was more accessible from Damascus than the region west of the river.

Aroer] There were several places of this name. The one here mentioned is the most famous (cp. Deut. ii. 36 note).

even Gilead and Bashan] The writer had previously called the whole territory "Gilead;" now he distinguishes it, more accurately, into Gilead, the southern, and Bashan, the northern region (1 K. iv. 13, 19).

34. *all his might*] It is remarkable that this expression, which is not used by the author of Kings in connexion with any other king of *Israel*, should be applied to Jehu, whose ill success in his struggle with Hazael has just been noted, and who submitted to the Assyrians and consented to become a tributary. Perhaps the word is used here in the sense of "personal courage" rather than of "power."

36. *in Samaria*] The family of Ahab had made Jezreel a sort of second capital, and had reigned there, at least in part (ix. 15-30). Jehu and his descendants seem to have fixed their residence wholly in Samaria (xiii. 1, 10, xiv. 23, xv. 8).

XI. 1. Athaliah, as wife of Joram and mother of Ahaziah, had guided both the internal and the external policy of the Jewish kingdom ; she had procured the establishment of the worship of Baal in Judæa (viii. 18, 27), and had maintained a close alliance with the sister kingdom (do. *v.* 29, x. 13). The revolution effected by Jehu touched her nearly. It struck away from her the support of her relatives ; it isolated her religious system, severing the communication with Phœnicia ; and the death of Ahaziah deprived her of her legal status in Judæa, which was that of queen-mother (1 K. xv. 13 note), and transferred that position to the chief wife of her deceased son. Athaliah, instead of yielding to the storm, or merely standing on the defensive, resolved to become the assailant, and strike before any plans could be formed against her. In the absence of her son, hers was probably the chief authority at Jerusalem. She used it to command the immediate destruction of all the family of David, already thinned by previous massacres (x. 14 ; 2 Chr. xxi. 4, 17), and then seized the throne.

2. *Jehosheba...sister of Ahaziah*] "Half-sister," according to Josephus—daughter of Joram, not by Athaliah, but by another wife. She was married to Jehoiada the High-Priest, and was thus in a position to save and conceal her nephew, Joash, who was only one year old (cp. *vv.* 3, 21).

in the bedchamber] Lit. "in the chamber of mattresses"—probably a store-room in the palace in which mattresses were kept.

3 slain. And he was with her hid in the house of the LORD six
4 years. And Athaliah did reign over the land. ¶ And *the
seventh year Jehoiada sent and fetched the rulers over hundreds,
with the captains and the guard, and brought them to him into
the house of the LORD, and made a covenant with them, and
took an oath of them in the house of the LORD, and shewed them
5 the king's son. And he commanded them, saying, This *is* the
thing that ye shall do; A third part of you that enter in *d* on
the sabbath shall even be keepers of the watch of the king's
6 house; and a third part *shall be* at the gate of Sur; and a third
part at the gate behind the guard: so shall ye keep the watch
7 of the house, ¹ that it be not broken down. And two ²³ parts of
all you that go forth on the sabbath, even they shall keep the
8 watch of the house of the LORD about the king. And ye shall
compass the king round about, every man with his weapons in
his hand: and he that cometh within the ranges, let him be
slain: and be ye with the king as he goeth out and as he cometh
9 in. ¶ *e* And the captains over the hundreds did according to all
things that Jehoiada the priest commanded: and they took every
man his men that were to come in on the sabbath, with them
that should go out on the sabbath, and came to Jehoiada the
10 priest. And to the captains over hundreds did the priest give
king David's spears and shields, that *were* in the temple of the
11 LORD. And the guard stood, every man with his weapons in
his hand, round about the king, from the right ⁴ corner of the

c 2 Chr. 23.1,
&c.

d 1 Chr. 9. 25.

e 2 Chr. 23. 8.

---

¹ Or, *from breaking up.*   ³ Heb. *hands.*
² Or, *companies.*   ⁴ Heb. *shoulder.*

---

3. *and Athaliah did reign over the land*] In
these words the writer dismisses the entire
reign of Athaliah, whereof he scorns to
speak. We gather incidentally from xii.
5-12, compared with 2 Chr. xxiv. 7, that
Athaliah used her power to establish the
exclusive worship of Baal through the kingdom of Judah, and to crush that of Jehovah. She stopped the Temple service,
gave over the sacred vessels of the Sanctuary to the use of the Baal priests, and
employed the Temple itself as a quarry
from which materials might be taken for
the construction of a great temple to Baal,
which rose in the immediate neighbourhood.
4. See marg. ref.
the captains] The word used here and in
v. 19, *hak-kari,* designates a certain part of
the royal guard, probably that which in the
earlier times was known under the name
of Cherethites (1 K. i. 38). Others see in
the term an ethnic name—" Carians," who
seem certainly to have been much inclined
to take service as mercenaries from an early
date. Render the whole passage thus—
"And in the seventh year Jehoiada sent
and fetched the **centurions of the Carians
and the guardsmen** (lit. ' runners,' x. 25),
&c."
5-8. Five divisions of the guard under
their five captains are distinguished here.
Three of the five divisions " enter in " on
the Sabbath ; the other two " go forth " on
the Sabbath (*v.* 7). By the former phrase

seems to be meant the mounting guard at
the royal palace (the " king's house," where
Athaliah then was); by the latter the
serving of escort to the sovereign beyond
the palace bounds. Jehoiada orders that
of those whose business it would be to guard
the palace on the ensuing Sabbath, one
company or cohort should perform that
task in the ordinary way, while another
should watch the gate of Sur,—or better,
" the gate of the foundation " (2 Chr. xxiii.
5)—that by which the palace was usually
quitted for the Temple, and a third should
watch another of the palace gates, called
" the gate of the guard " (see *v.* 19). The
two companies whose proper business it
would be to serve as the royal escort beyond the palace walls, he orders to enter
the Temple, and surround the person of the
young king.
6. *that it be not broken down*] The one
word in the original text of which this is a
translation occurs nowhere else; and its
meaning is very doubtful.
8. *within the ranges*] Rather, " within the
ranks." If any one tried to break through
the soldiers' ranks to the king, or even to
disturb their order, he was to be immediately slain.
11. *From the right corner,* &c.] Rather,
"from the right **side** of the Temple buildings to the left **side** "—*i.e.* right across the
Temple court from the one side to the
other, by the Altar of Burnt offerings, &c.

temple to the left corner of the temple, *along* by the altar and
12 the temple. And he brought forth the king's son, and put the
crown upon him, and *gave him* the testimony; and they made
him king, and anointed him; and they clapped their hands, and
13 said, ¹ᶠGod save the king. ¶ ᵍAnd when Athaliah heard the
noise of the guard *and* of the people, she came to the people
14 into the temple of the LORD. And when she looked, behold, the
king stood by ʰa pillar, as the manner *was*, and the princes and
the trumpeters by the king, and all the people of the land rejoiced, and blew with trumpets : and Athaliah rent her clothes,
15 and cried, Treason, Treason. But Jehoiada the priest commanded the captains of the hundreds, the officers of the host,
and said unto them, Have her forth without the ranges : and
him that followeth her kill with the sword. For the priest had
16 said, Let her not be slain in the house of the LORD. And they
laid hands on her ; and she went by the way by the which the
horses came into the king's house : and there was she slain.
17 ¶ ⁱAnd Jehoiada made a covenant between the LORD and the
king and the people, that they should be the LORD's people ;
18 ᵏbetween the king also and the people. And all the people of
the land went into the ˡhouse of Baal, and brake it down; his
altars and his images ᵐbrake they in pieces thoroughly, and
slew Mattan the priest of Baal before the altars. And ⁿthe
19 priest appointed ² officers over the house of the LORD. And he
took the rulers over hundreds, and the captains, and the guard,
and all the people of the land; and they brought down the
king from the house of the LORD, and came by the way of the

ƒ 1 Sam. 10.
24.
g 2 Chr. 23.
12, &c.
h ch. 23. 3.
2 Chr. 34.21.

i 2 Chr. 23. 16.

k 2 Sam. 5.3.
l ch. 10. 26.
m Deut. 12. 3.
2 Chr. 23. 17.
n 2 Chr. 23.
18, &c.

¹ Heb. *Let the king live.*　　　² Heb. *offices.*

This Altar stood exactly in front of the
Temple-porch. Here the king was stationed; and before him and behind him,
("round about" him) stood the soldiers,
drawn up several ranks deep across the
entire court, just in front of the sacred
building.

12. *the testimony*] *i.e.* "The Book of the
Law " which was kept in the Ark of the
Covenant (Deut. xxxi. 26). This Jehoiada
placed on the king's head at the moment of
coronation, perhaps to indicate that the
king was not to be above, but under, the
direction of the Law of his country.

14. *by a pillar*] Rather, "**upon the
pillar,**" probably a sort of stand, or pulpit,
raised on a pillar. Under the later monarchy
the Jewish king seems to have had a special
place assigned him in the Temple-court,
from which on occasions he addressed the
people (marg. reff.).

15. *Have her forth without the ranges*]
Rather, "**Conduct her out between your
ranks.**" Guard her, *i.e.* on all sides, that
the people may not fall upon her and kill
her as she passes through the court, thereby
polluting the Temple.

16. *And they laid hands on her*] Most
modern critics render—" and they **gave
her space,**" *i.e.* they cleared a way for her,
and allowed her to walk out of the Temple
not only unharmed but untouched.

17. *a covenant*] Rather, "*the* covenant,"
which either was already an established
part of a coronation (marg. ref. *k*), or at
least became such afterwards.

18. A temple had been built to Baal at
Jerusalem itself by Athaliah, Ahaziah, or
Jehoram. According to Josephus, it was
constructed in the reign of Jehoram. Its
exact position is uncertain.

images] The word used here is not the
same as in x. 26, but a word which implies
likeness. The Phœnicians had fashioned
images, besides their unfashioned pillar-
idols.

the priest appointed, &c.] The Temple
worship having been discontinued during
Athaliah's rule, it devolved on Jehoiada
now to re-establish it (see marg. ref.). He
had already summoned the Levites out
of all the cities of Judah (2 Chr. xxiii. 2),
and had made use of them in the events of
the day. He therefore proceeded at once to
assign the custody of the Temple to a particular course, before conducting the young
king to the palace.

19. They conducted the king *down* from
the Temple hill, across the valley of the
Tyropœum, and up the opposite hill to the
royal palace, entering it not by the "horse-
gate " (*v.* 16), where Athaliah had just been
slain, but by the "gate of the guard " (*v.* 6),
which was probably the main gate of the

gate of the guard to the king's house. And he sat on the throne
20 of the kings. And all the people of the land rejoiced, and the
city was in quiet : and they slew Athaliah with the sword *beside*

o 2 Chr. 24. 1.   21 the king's house.   ¶ *o*Seven years old *was* Jehoash when he
a 2 Chr. 24. 1.   12 began to reign.   IN the seventh year of Jehu *a*Jehoash began
to reign ; and forty years reigned he in Jerusalem. And his
2 mother's name *was* Zibiah of Beer-sheba. And Jehoash did
that which was right in the sight of the LORD all his days wherein
b 1 Kin. 15. 14.   3 Jehoiada the priest instructed him. But *b*the high places were
& 22. 43.
ch. 14. 4.   not taken away : the people still sacrificed and burnt incense in
c ch. 22. 4.   4 the high places.   ¶ And Jehoash said to the priests, *c*All the
money of the [12]dedicated things that is brought into the house
d Ex. 30. 13.   of the LORD, *even* *d*the money of every one that passeth *the*
account, [3]the money that every man is set at, *and* all the money
e Ex. 35. 5.   that [4e]cometh into any man's heart to bring into the house of
1 Chr. 29. 9.   5 the LORD, let the priests take *it* to them, every man of his acquaintance : and let them repair the breaches of the house,
6 wheresoever any breach shall be found.   ¶ But it was so, *that*
f 2 Chr. 24. 5.   [5]in the three and twentieth year of king Jehoash *f*the priests
g 2 Chr. 24. 6.   7 had not repaired the breaches of the house.   *g*Then king Jehoash
called for Jehoiada the priest, and the *other* priests, and said
unto them, Why repair ye not the breaches of the house ? now
therefore receive no *more* money of your acquaintance, but de-
8 liver it for the breaches of the house.   And the priests consented
to receive no *more* money of the people, neither to repair the

[1] Or, *holy things.*	*souls of his estimation,*	*heart of a man.*
[2] Heb. *holinesses.*	Lev. 27. 2.	[5] Heb. *in the twentieth year*
[3] Heb. *the money of the*	[4] Heb. *ascendeth upon the*	*and third year.*

palace on the eastern side (see 2 Chr. xxiii. 20).

20. *they slew Athaliah with the sword*] This **is** one of the many little repetitions which mark the manner of the writer, and which generally contain some *little* point which has not been mentioned before (cp. *v.* 16).

XII. 2. *all his days,* &c.] *i.e.* "so long as Jehoiada was his adviser" (cp. 2 Chr. xxiv. 15–22). Jehoiada was, practically speaking, regent during the minority of Jehoash, *i.e.* 10 or 12 years. An increase of power to the priestly order was the natural consequence. Jehoiada bore the title of "High-Priest" (*v.* 10), which had been dropped since the time of Eleazar (Josh. xx. 6), and the Levitical order from this time became more mixed up with public affairs and possessed greater influence than previously. Jehoiada's successors traced their office to him rather than to Aaron (Jer. xxix. 26).

3. The worship on the "high places" seems to have continued uninterruptedly to the time of Hezekiah, who abolished it (xviii. 4). It was, however, again established by Manasseh, his son (xxi. 3). The priests at this time cannot have regarded it as idolatrous, or Jehoiada would have put it down during his regency.

4. It is remarkable that the first movement towards restoring the fabric of the

Temple should have come, not from Jehoiada, but from Jehoash (cp. 2 Chr. xxiv. 4). Jehoiada had, it seems, allowed the mischief done in Athaliah's time to remain unrepaired during the whole term of his government.

the money of every one, &c.] Three kinds of sacred money are here distinguished— first, the half shekel required in the Law (Ex. xxx. 13) to be paid by every one above twenty years of age when he passed the numbering ; secondly, the money to be paid by such as had devoted themselves, or those belonging to them, by vow to Jehovah, which was a variable sum dependent on age, sex, and property (Lev. xxvii. 2–8) ; and thirdly, the money offered in the way of free-will offerings.

5. The collection was not to be made at Jerusalem only, but in all "the cities of Judah" (2 Chr. xxiv. 5); the various priests and Levites being collectors in their own neighbourhoods.

breaches] The word in the original includes every kind and degree of ruin or dilapidation.

6. No money had for some time been brought in (marg. ref. *g*). Perhaps it was difficult for the priests and Levites to know exactly what proportion of the money paid to them was fairly applicable to the Temple service and to their own sup-

9 breaches of the house. But Jehoi: d the priest took ᵃa chest, and bored a hole in the lid of it, and set it beside the altar, on the right side as one cometh into the house of the LORD : and the priests that kept the ¹door put therein all the money *that*
10 *was* brought into the house of the LORD. And it was *so*, when they saw that *there was* much money in the chest, that the king's ²scribe and the high priest came up, and they ³put up in bags, and told the money that was found in the house of the LORD.
11 And they gave the money, being told, into the hands of them that did the work, that had the oversight of the house of the LORD : and they ⁴laid it out to the carpenters and builders, that
12 wrought upon the house of the LORD, and to masons, and hewers of stone, and to buy timber and hewed stone to repair the breaches of the house of the LORD, and for all that ⁵was laid
13 out for the house to repair *it*. Howbeit ⁱthere were not made for the house of the LORD bowls of silver, snuffers, basons, trumpets, any vessels of gold, or vessels of silver, of the money
14 *that was* brought into the house of the LORD : but they gave that to the workmen, and repaired therewith the house of the
15 LORD. Moreover ᵏthey reckoned not with the men, into whose hand they delivered the money to be bestowed on workmen:
16 for they dealt faithfully. ˡThe trespass money and sin money was not brought into the house of the LORD: ᵐit was the priests'.
17 ¶Then ⁿHazael king of Syria went up, and fought against Gath, and took it : and ᵒHazael set his face to go up to Jerusalem.

ᵃ 2 Chr. 24. 8, &c.

ⁱ See 2 Chr. 24. 14.

ᵏ ch. 22. 7.

ˡ Lev. 5. 15, 18.
ᵐ Lev. 7. 7. Num. 18. 9.
ⁿ ch. 8. 12.
ᵒ See 2 Chr. 24. 23.

¹ Heb. *threshold.*
² Or, *secretary.*
³ Heb. *bound up.*
⁴ Heb. *brought it forth.*
⁵ Heb. *went forth.*

---

port ; and what, consequently, was the balance which they ought to apply to the repairs.

9. *the priests that kept the door*] The north door into the priests' court (Ezek. xl. 35-43) seems to be intended, not the door of the Temple building. The chest must have been placed a little to the right of this north door, between it and the Altar of Burnt-offering, so that the people could see it from the doorway. The people were not ordinarily allowed to go within the doorway into this court, which belonged to the priests and Levites only.

10. *the king's scribe*] Or "secretary" (1 K. iv. 3 note). Such persons are often seen in the Assyrian sculptures, with a roll, apparently of parchment, in one hand and a pen in the other, taking account for the king of the spoil brought in from foreign expeditions.

13. Comparing this verse with the marg. ref., it will be seen that the author of Kings desires to point out, that the repairs were not delayed by any deductions from the money that flowed in. The writer of Chronicles describes what became of the surplus in the chest after the last repairs were completed.

The need of supplying fresh bowls, snuffers, &c., arose from the pollution of those previously used in the Temple service by their application to the Baal worship

during the reigns of Ahaziah and Athaliah (see 2 Chr. xxiv. 7).

16. *The trespass money and the sin money*] In all cases of injury done to another, a man was bound by the Law to make compensation, to the sufferer, if possible ; if not, to his nearest kinsman. If the man was dead and had left no kinsman, then the compensation was to be made to the priest (Num. v. 8). This would form a part of the trespass and sin money. The remainder would accrue from the voluntary gifts made to the priests by those who came to make atonement for sins or trespasses (do. *v.* 10). On the difference between "sins" and "trespasses," see Lev. v. 14 note.

17, 18. There was probably a considerable interval between the conclusion of the arrangement for the repairs and the Syrian expedition related in these verses. For the events which had happened, see 2 Chr. xxiv. 15-22.

17. This is the first and last time that we hear of the Damascene Syrians undertaking so distant an expedition. Gath (see Josh. xiii. 3 note) could only be reached from Syria through Israel or Judah. It was not more than 25 or 30 miles from Jerusalem. It is uncertain whether the city belonged at this time to Judah or to the Philistines.

Hazael set his face, &c.] This is a phrase for determination generally, but especially for determination to proceed somewhere

p 1 Kin.15.18.
ch. 13. 15,16.

18 And Jehoash king of Judah *p* took all the hallowed things that Jehoshaphat, and Jehoram, and Ahaziah, his fathers, kings of Judah, had dedicated, and his own hallowed things, and all the gold *that was* found in the treasures of the house of the LORD, and in the king's house, and sent *it* to Hazael king of Syria:
19 and he ¹went away from Jerusalem.　¶ And the rest of the acts of Joash, and all that he did, *are* they not written in the book

q ch. 14. 5.
2 Chr. 24. 25.

20 of the chronicles of the kings of Judah? And *q* his servants arose, and made a conspiracy, and slew Joash in ²the house of

r 2 Chr. 24.
26, Zabaa.

21 Millo, which goeth down to Silla. For *r* Jozachar the son of Shimeath, and Jehozabad the son of ³Shomer, his servants, smote him, and he died; and they buried him with his fathers

s 2 Chr.24.27.

in the city of David: and *s* Amaziah his son reigned in his stead.

CHAP. 13. IN ⁴the three and twentieth year of Joash the son of Ahaziah king of Judah Jehoahaz the son of Jehu began to reign
2 over Israel in Samaria, *and reigned* seventeen years. And he did *that which was* evil in the sight of the LORD, and ⁵followed the sins of Jeroboam the son of Nebat, which made Israel to

a Judg. 2.14.

3 sin; he departed not therefrom. And *a* the anger of the LORD was kindled against Israel, and he delivered them into the hand

b ch. 8. 12.
c Ps. 78. 34.

of *b* Hazael king of Syria, and into the hand of Ben-hadad the
4 son of Hazael, all *their* days. And Jehoahaz *c* besought the

d Ex. 3. 7.
ch. 14. 26.

LORD, and the LORD hearkened unto him: for *d* he saw the oppression of Israel, because the king of Syria oppressed them.

e ch.14.25,27.

5 (*e* And the LORD gave Israel a saviour, so that they went out

---

¹ Heb. *went up.*
² Or, *Beth-millo.*
³ Or, *Shimrith.*
⁴ Heb. *the twentieth year*
and third year.
⁵ Heb. *walked after.*

(cp. Jer. xlii. 15; Luke ix. 51). Jerusalem can scarcely have been the primary object of this expedition, or it would have been attacked by a less circuitous route. Perhaps the Syrians were induced to make a sudden march against the Jewish capital, by learning, while at Gath, that a revolution had occurred there (cp. 2 Chr. xxiv. 18-23).

18. Jehoash did not submit without a struggle. See the details in Chronicles. It was not till his army was defeated that he followed the example of his ancestor, Asa, and bought the friendship of the Syrians with the Temple treasures (1 K. xv. 18. Cp. the conduct of Hezekiah, xviii. 15, 16).

Jehoram and Ahaziah] Though these two monarchs had been worshippers of Baal, yet they had combined with that idolatrous cult a certain amount of decent respect for the old religion. It is evident from this passage that they had made costly offerings to the Temple.

20. *a conspiracy*] Cp. marg. ref. Joash, either from a suspicion of intended treason, or from some other unknown cause, took up his abode in the fortress of Millo (1 K. ix. 24). This conspiracy was connected with religion. Soon after the death of Jehoiada, Joash had apostatised; had renewed the worship of Baal; and, despite of many prophetic warnings, had persisted

in his evil courses, even commanding Zechariah to be slain when he rebuked them (2 Chr. xxiv. 18-27). The conspirators, who wished to avenge Zechariah, no doubt wished also to put down the Baal worship. In this it appears that they succeeded. For, though Amaziah punished the actual murderers after a while (xiv. 5), yet he appears not to have been a Baal-worshipper. The only idolatries laid to his charge are the maintenance of the high places (xiv. 4), and a worship of the gods of Edom (2 Chr. xxv. 14-20).

Silla] This place is quite unknown.

XIII. In this chapter the history of the kingdom of Israel is traced through the two reigns of Jehoahaz and Jehoash. In ch. xiv. the history of Judah is resumed.

in the three and twentieth year] Rather, the "one and twentieth year." See *v.* 10.

3. *all their days*] Lit. "all the days." Not "all the days" of the two Syrian kings, for Ben-hadad lost to Joash all the cities which he had gained from Jehoahaz (*v.* 25); but either "all the days of Jehoahaz" (*v.* 22), or "all the days of Hazael"—both while he led his own armies, and while they were led by his son.

5. *the LORD gave Israel a saviour*] Not immediately on the repentance of Jehoahaz, but after his death (see *v.* 25).

from under the hand of the Syrians : and the children of Israel
6 dwelt in their tents, ¹as beforetime. Nevertheless they departed
not from the sins of the house of Jeroboam, who made Israel
sin, *but* ²walked therein : *f*and there ³remained the grove also in
7 Samaria.) Neither did he leave of the people to Jehoahaz but
fifty horsemen, and ten chariots, and ten thousand footmen ;
for the king of Syria had destroyed them, *g*and had made them
8 like the dust by threshing. ¶Now the rest of the acts of Jehoahaz, and all that he did, and his might, *are* they not written in
9 the book of the chronicles of the kings of Israel ? And Jehoahaz
slept with his fathers ; and they buried him in Samaria : and
10 ⁴Joash his son reigned in his stead.⁵ ¶In the thirty and seventh
year of Joash king of Judah began ⁶Jehoash the son of Jehoahaz
11 to reign over Israel in Samaria, *and reigned* sixteen years. And
he did *that which was* evil in the sight of the LORD ; he departed
not from all the sins of Jeroboam the son of Nebat, who made
12 Israel sin : *but* he walked therein. *h*And the rest of the acts of
Joash, and *i*all that he did, and *k*his might wherewith he fought
against Amaziah king of Judah, *are* they not written in the book
13 of the chronicles of the kings of Israel ? And Joash slept with
his fathers ; and Jeroboam sat upon his throne : and Joash was
14 buried in Samaria with the kings of Israel. ¶Now Elisha was
fallen sick of his sickness whereof he died. And Joash the king
of Israel came down unto him, and wept over his face, and said,
O my father, my father, *l*the chariot of Israel, and the horse-
15 men thereof. And Elisha said unto him, Take bow and arrows.
16 And he took unto him bow and arrows. And he said to the
king of Israel, ⁷Put thine hand upon the bow. And he put his
hand *upon it :* and Elisha put his hands upon the king's hands.

f 1Kin.16.33.

g Amos 1. 3.

h ch. 14. 15.
i See ver.14.
& 25.
k ch.14.9,&c.
2 Chr. 25.17,
&c.

l ch. 2. 12.

¹ Heb. *as yesterday,* and third day.
² Heb. *he walked.*
³ Heb. *stood.*
⁴ ver. 10, *Jehoash.*
⁵ Alone.
⁶ In consort with his father, ch. 14. 1.
⁷ Heb. *Make thine hand to ride.*

they went out from under the hand of the Syrians] i.e. they ceased to be oppressed by the Syrians ; they shook off their yoke, and became once more perfectly independent.

tents] See 1 K. viii. 66 note.

6. *but walked therein*] Rather, "he walked therein," meaning Joash, the "saviour" of the preceding verse.

there remained the grove also in Samaria] It seems strange that Jehu had not de-stroyed this when he put down the worship of Baal (x. 26-28). Perhaps the "grove" or "Asherah" worship was too closely con-nected with the old worship in high places to be set aside with the same ease as the rites newly introduced from Phœnicia.

7. The meaning is that "he, the king of Syria" (*v.* 4 Hazael) limited the standing army of Jehoahaz.

like the dust by threshing] An expression not only employed metaphorically, and im-porting defeat, conquest, and grinding op-pression (Jer. li. 33 ; Mic. iv. 12), but im-plying also the literal use of threshing-instruments in the execution of prisoners of war (marg. ref., and cp. 2 Sam. xii. 31).

12, 13. According to ordinary laws of historical composition, these verses should form the closing paragraph of the present chapter.

14. The closing scene of Elisha's life. It was now at least sixty-three years since his call, so that he was at this time very pos-sibly above ninety. He seems to have lived in almost complete retirement from the time he sent the young Prophet to anoint Jehu king (ix. 1). And now it was not he who sought the king, but the king who sought him. Apparently, the special func-tion of the two great Israelite Prophets (Elijah and Elisha) was to counteract the noxious influence of the Baalistic rites ; and, when these ceased, their extraordinary ministry came to an end.

the chariot of Israel, &c.] See marg. ref. Joash must have known the circumstances of Elijah's removal, which were perhaps al-ready entered in the "book of the Chronicles of the kings of Israel ;" and he must have intended to apply to Elisha his own words on that solemn occasion ; "Thou too art about to leave us, and to follow Elijah—thou who hast been since his departure, that which he was while he remained on earth, the true defence of Israel."

16. *Elisha put his hands upon the king's*

17 And he said, Open the window eastward. And he opened *it*.
Then Elisha said, Shoot. And he shot. And he said, The
arrow of the LORD's deliverance, and the arrow of deliverance
from Syria : for thou shalt smite the Syrians in ^mAphek, till
18 thou have consumed *them*. And he said, Take the arrows. And
he took *them*. And he said unto the king of Israel, Smite upon
19 the ground. And he smote thrice, and stayed. And the man
of God was wroth with him, and said, Thou shouldest have
smitten five or six times ; then hadst thou smitten Syria till thou
hadst consumed *it* : ⁿwhereas now thou shalt smite Syria *but*
20 thrice. ¶And Elisha died, and they buried him. And the
bands of the Moabites invaded the land at the coming in of the
21 year. And it came to pass, as they were burying a man, that,
behold, they spied a band *of men ;* and they cast the man into
the sepulchre of Elisha : and when the man ¹was let down, and
touched the bones of Elisha, he revived, and stood up on his feet.
22 ¶But ^oHazael king of Syria oppressed Israel all the days of
23 Jehoahaz. ^pAnd the LORD was gracious unto them, and had
compassion on them, and ^qhad respect unto them, ^rbecause of

m 1 Kin. 20. 26.

n ver. 25.

o ch. 8. 12.
p ch. 14. 27.
q Ex.2.24,25.
r Ex. 32. 13.

¹ Heb. *went* down.

---

hands] A symbolical act, indicating that
the successes, which the shooting typified,
were to come, not from human skill, or
strength, or daring, but from the Presence
and the power of God.

17. *eastward*] Syria of Damascus lay
partly east, but still more north, of the
Holy Land. The arrow was to be shot,
eastward, not so much against Syria itself
as against the scene of the recent Syrian
successes, Gilead (x. 33), which was also to
be the scene of Joash's victories over them.
Aphek is almost due east from Shunem,
where it is not unlikely that Elisha now
was.

the arrow, &c.] Lit. "An arrow of deliverance from the Lord, and an arrow of
deliverance against Syria ; and thou shalt
smite the Syrians in Aphek, even to consuming."

18. *Smite upon the ground*] Some prefer
to render—"**Shoot to the ground ;**" *i.e.*
"Shoot arrows from the window into the
ground outside, as if thou wert shooting
against an enemy."

19. The unfaithfulness of man limits the
goodness of God. Though Joash did the
Prophet's bidding, it was without any zeal
or fervour ; and probably without any
earnest belief in the efficacy of what he was
doing. Cp. Mark vi. 5, 6. God had been
willing to give the Israelites complete victory over Syria (*v.* 17) ; but Joash by his
non-acceptance of the divine promise in its
fulness had checked the outflow of mercy ;
and the result was that the original promise
could not be fulfilled.

20. *the bands of the Moabites invaded the
land*] The Moabites had been increasing in
strength ever since their revolt from Ahaziah (i. 1). The defeat which they suffered
at the hands of Jehoram and Jehoshaphat

(iii. 24) did not affect their subjugation.
They spread themselves into the country
north of the Arnon (Isai. xvi. 2), and thence
proceeded to make plundering expeditions
year by year into Samaria, in Spring. This
was the natural season for incursions, as
then in Palestine the crops began to be
ripe.

21. *they cast the man*] Rather, "they thrust
the man." The graves of the Jews were
not pits dug in the ground, like ours, but
caves or cells excavated in the side of a
rock, the mouth of the cave being ordinarily shut by a heavy stone.

stood up on his feet] Coffins were not used
by the Jews. The body was simply wrapped
or swathed in grave-clothes (cp. Luke vii.
15 ; John xi. 44).

This miracle of Elisha's after his death
is more surprising than any of those which
he performed during his lifetime. The Jews
regarded it as his highest glory (cp. Ecclus.
xlviii. 13, 14). It may be said to belong to
a class of Scriptural miracles, cases, *i.e.*
where the miracle was not wrought through
the agency of a living miracle-worker, but
by a material object in which, by God's
will, "virtue" for the time resided (cp.
Acts xix. 12). The primary effect of the
miracle was, no doubt, greatly to increase
the reverence of the Israelites for the memory of Elisha, to lend force to his teaching, and especially to add weight to his unfulfilled prophecies, as to that concerning
the coming triumphs of Israel over Syria.
In the extreme state of depression to which
the Israelites were now reduced, a very
signal miracle may have been needed to encourage and reassure them.

23. The writer regards the Captivity of
Israel as God's "casting them out of His
sight" (see xvii. 18, 20) ; and notes that this

his covenant with Abraham, Isaac, and Jacob, and would not
destroy them, neither cast he them from his ¹presence as yet.
24 So Hazael king of Syria died; and Ben-hadad his son reigned in
25 his stead. And Jehoash the son of Jehoahaz ²took again out
of the hand of Ben-hadad the son of Hazael the cities, which he
had taken out of the hand of Jehoahaz his father by war.
*Three times did Joash beat him, and recovered the cities of   *ver. 18, 19.
Israel.

CHAP. 14. IN ᵃthe second year of Joash son of Jehoahaz king of   ᵃ ch. 13. 10.
2 Israel reigned ᵇAmaziah the son of Joash king of Judah. He   ᵇ 2 Chr. 25.1.
was twenty and five years old when he began to reign, and
reigned twenty and nine years in Jerusalem. And his mother's
3 name *was* Jehoaddan of Jerusalem. And he did *that which was*
right in the sight of the LORD, yet not like David his father: he
4 did according to all things as Joash his father did. ᶜHowbeit   ᶜ ch. 12. 3.
the high places were not taken away: as yet the people did
5 sacrifice and burnt incense on the high places. And it came to
pass, as soon as the kingdom was confirmed in his hand, that he
6 slew his servants ᵈwhich had slain the king his father. But   ᵈ ch. 12. 20.
the children of the murderers he slew not: according unto that
which is written in the book of the law of Moses, wherein the
LORD commanded, saying, ᵉThe fathers shall not be put to death   ᵉ Deut.24.16.
for the children, nor the children be put to death for the fathers;   Ezek. 18. 4, 20.
7 but every man shall be put to death for his own sin. ᶠHe slew   ᶠ 2 Chr. 25.
of Edom in ᵍthe valley of salt ten thousand, and took ³Selah   5—13.
ᵍ 2Sam.8.13.
Ps. 60, title.

¹ Heb. *face.*   ² Heb. *returned and took.*   ³ Or, *The rock.*

---

extreme punishment, though deserved, was
by God's mercy not allowed to fall on them
as yet.
  24. *So Hazael...died*] Literally, "*And*
Hazael died," a fact not mentioned before.
  25. *the cities which,* &c.] Probably cities
west of the Jordan, since the tract east of
that river was conquered, mainly if not
wholly, in the reign of Jehu (x. 33).
  XIV. The history of Judah is resumed
(1–22), followed by a brief account of the
contemporary history of Israel under Jeroboam II. (*vv.* 23–29). The earlier narrative
runs parallel with 2 Chr. xxv.
  2. Joash of Judah reigned forty years
(xii. 1), and Joash of Israel ascended the
throne in his namesake's thirty-seventh
year (xiii. 10); hence we should have expected to hear that Amaziah succeeded his
father in the fourth rather than in the second year of Joash (of Israel). The usual
explanation of the discrepancy is to suppose
a double accession of the Israelitish Joash
—as co-partner with his father in the thirty-
seventh year of his namesake, as sole king
two years afterwards.
  3. *he did...as Joash*] There is a curious
parity between the lives of Joash and Amaziah. Both were zealous for Jehovah in
the earlier portion of their reigns, but in the
latter part fell away; both disregarded the
rebukes of Prophets; and both, having forsaken God, were in the end conspired against
and slain (cp. 2 Chr. xxiv. 25, xxv. 27).
  5. The phrase, "confirmed in his hand"

(xv. 19), usually expresses the authorisation
of a new reign by an imperial superior (see
xv. 19 note); but here it describes the result
when the troubles consequent upon the
murder of Joash had passed away. The
new king's authority was generally recognised by his subjects.
  6. *the children of the murderers he slew not*]
This seems to be noted as a rare instance of
clemency (cp. ix. 26 note). It is strange at
first sight, that, when the Law contained
so very plain a prohibition (marg. reff.), the
contrary practice should have established
itself. But we must remember, first, that
the custom was that of the East generally
(see Dan. vi. 24); and secondly, that it had
the sanction of one who might be thought
to have known thoroughly the mind of the
legislator, viz. Joshua (see Josh. vii. 24,
25).
  7. Amaziah's Idumæan war is treated at
length by the writer of Chronicles (marg.
ref.).
  The "Valley of Salt" is usually identified with the broad open plain called the
Sabkah, at the southern end of the Dead
Sea—the continuation of the *Ghor* or Jordan gorge. At the north-western corner of
this plain stands a mountain of rock-salt,
and the tract between this mountain and
the sea is a salt-marsh. Salt springs also
abound in the plain itself, so that the name
would be fully accounted for. It is doubted,
however, whether the original of the word
"valley," commonly used of clefts and ra-

h Josh.15.33.
i 2 Chr. 25.
17, 18, &c.

k See Judg.
9. 8.
l 1 Kin. 4. 33.

m Deut.8.14.
2 Chr. 32. 25.
Ezek. 28. 2,
5, 17.
Hab. 2. 4.

n Josh.19.38.
& 21. 16.

o Neh. 8. 16.
& 12. 39.
p Jer. 31. 38.
Zech. 14. 10.
q 1 Kin. 7. 51.

by war, ʰand called the name of it Joktheel unto this day.
8 ¶ ⁱThen Amaziah sent messengers to Jehoash, the son of Jehoahaz son of Jehu, king of Israel, saying, Come, let us look one
9 another in the face. And Jehoash the king of Israel sent to
Amaziah king of Judah, saying, ᵏThe thistle that *was* in Lebanon sent to the ˡcedar that *was* in Lebanon, saying, Give thy
· daughter to my son to wife : and there passed by a wild beast
10 that *was* in Lebanon, and trode down the thistle. Thou hast
indeed smitten Edom, and ᵐthine heart hath lifted thee up :
glory *of this*, and tarry ¹at home: for why shouldest thou meddle
to *thy* hurt, that thou shouldest fall, *even* thou, and Judah with
11 thee? But Amaziah would not hear. Therefore Jehoash king
of Israel went up ; and he and Amaziah king of Judah looked
one another in the face at ⁿBeth-shemesh, which *belongeth* to
12 Judah. And Judah ²was put to the worse before Israel; and
13 they fled every man to their tents. And Jehoash king of Israel
took Amaziah king of Judah, the son of Jehoash the son of
Ahaziah, at Beth-shemesh, and came to Jerusalem, and brake
down the wall of Jerusalem from ᵒthe gate of Ephraim unto
14 ᵖthe corner gate, four hundred cubits. And he took all ᑫthe

¹ Heb. *at thy house.*   ² Heb. *was smitten.*

vines, can be applied to such a sunk plain
as the Sabkah ; and it is certainly most unlikely that 10,000 prisoners would have been
conveyed upwards of eighty miles (the distance of the Sabkah from Petra), through a
rough and difficult country, only in order to
be massacred. On the whole, it is perhaps
most probable that the " Valley of Salt "
yet remains to be discovered, and that its
true position was near Selah or Petra (see
Judg. i. 36 note). Amaziah gave to Petra
the name Joktheel, " subdued by God," in
a religious spirit, as an acknowledgment of
the divine aid by which his victory was
gained. The name failed to take permanent
hold on the place, because the Edomites, on
not long afterwards recovering their city,
restored the old appellation (2 Chr. xxviii.
17 ; cp. Isai. xvi. 1, and Am. i. 11).

unto this day] The writer of Kings evidently gives the exact words of his document, composed not later than the reign of
Ahaz, before whose death the Edomites had
recovered Petra.

8. Amaziah's success against Edom had
so elated him that he thought himself more
than a match for his northern neighbour.
The grounds of the quarrel between them
were furnished by the conduct of the hired,
but dismissed, Israelite soldiers (see marg.
ref.).

let us look one another in the face] *i.e.* " let
us meet face to face in arms, and try each
other's strength " (*vv.* 11, 12).

9. The Oriental use of apologues on the
most solemn and serious occasions is well
known to all, and scarcely needs illustration
(cp. marg. ref.). It is a common feature of
such apologues that they are not exact parallels to the case whereto they are applied,
but only general or partial resemblances.

Hence there is need of caution in applying
the several points of the illustration.

10. *glory of this*, &c.] Lit. " Be honoured ;"
i.e. " Enjoy thy honour—be content with it."
" Why wilt thou meddle **with misfortune ?**"

11. Jehoash did not wait to be attacked.
Invading Judæa from the west, and so *ascending* out of the low coast tract, he met
the army of Amaziah at Beth-shemesh
(see Josh. xix. 21 note), about 15 miles from
Jeru-a'em.

12. The author of Chronicles notes that
Amaziah's obstinacy, and his consequent
defeat and captivity, were judgments upon
him for an idolatry into which he had fallen
after his conquest of Edom (2 Chr. xxv. 14,
20).

13. The object of breaking down the wall
was to leave Jerusalem at the mercy of her
rival ; and it must have been among the
conditions of the peace that the breach thus
made should not be repaired.

Gates in Oriental cities are named from
the places to which they lead. The gate of
Ephraim must therefore have been a north
gate : perhaps also known, later on, by the
name of the " gate of Benjamin " (Jer.
xxxvii. 13 ; Zech. xiv. 10). The corner
gate was probably a gate at the north-west
angle of the city, where the north wall approached the Valley of Hinnom. The entire breach was thus in the north wall, on
the side where Jerusalem was naturally the
weakest. Josephus says that Joash drove
his chariot through the breach into the
town, a practice not unusual with conquerors.

14. This is the only distinct mention of
" hostages " in the Old Testament. It would
seem that the Oriental conquerors generally
regarded the terror of their arms as sufficient.

gold and silver, and all the vessels that were found in the house
of the LORD, and in the treasures of the king's house, and hos-
15 tages, and returned to Samaria. ¶ʳNow the rest of the acts of
Jehoash which he did, and his might, and how he fought with
Amaziah king of Judah, *are* they not written in the book of the
16 chronicles of the kings of Israel? And Jehoash slept with his
fathers, and was buried in Samaria with the kings of Israel;
17 and Jeroboam his son reigned in his stead. ¶ˢAnd Amaziah
the son of Joash king of Judah lived after the death of Jehoash
18 son of Jehoahaz king of Israel fifteen years. And the rest of
the acts of Amaziah, *are* they not written in the book of the
19 chronicles of the kings of Judah? Now ᵗthey made a conspiracy
against him in Jerusalem: and he fled to ᵘLachish; but they
20 sent after him to Lachish, and slew him there. And they
brought him on horses: and he was buried at Jerusalem with
21 his fathers in the city of David. And all the people of Judah
took ˣAzariah, which *was* sixteen years old, and made him king
22 instead of his father Amaziah. He built ʸElath, and restored
23 it to Judah, after that the king slept with his fathers. ¶In the
fifteenth year of Amaziah the son of Joash king of Judah Jeroboam the son of Joash king of Israel began to reign in Samaria,
24 *and reigned* forty and one years. And he did *that which was*
evil in the sight of the LORD: he departed not from all the sins
25 of Jeroboam the son of Nebat, who made Israel to sin. He restored the coast of Israel ᶻfrom the entering of Hamath unto
ᵃthe sea of the plain, according to the word of the LORD God of
Israel, which he spake by the hand of his servant ᵇJonah, the

Marginal references:
ʳ ch. 13. 12
ˢ 2 Chr. 25. 25, &c.
ᵗ 2 Chr. 25. 27.
ᵘ Josh. 10. 3.
ˣ ch. 15. 13. & 2 Chr. 26. 1, he is called *Uzziah.*
ʸ ch. 16. 6. 2 Chr. 26. 2.
ᶻ Num. 13. 21. & 34. 8.
ᵃ Deut. 3. 17.
ᵇ Jonah 1. 1. Matt. 12. 39, 40, called *Jonas.*

to secure the performance of the engagements contracted towards them.

15, 16. These two verses (repeated from
xiii. 12, 13) are out of place here, where
they interrupt the history of Amaziah's
reign.

20. *they brought him on horses*] *i.e.* they
conveyed his body back to Jerusalem in the
royal chariot. The combination of relent-
less animosity against the living prince with
the deepest respect for his dead remains is
very characteristic of an Oriental people.

21. *all the people of Judah*] The words
imply that the conspiracy was one in which
the general mass of the people did not participate. There was no confusion and trouble as on the occasion of the murder of
Joash. Azariah ("the strength of Jehovah"), and Uzziah ("whom Jehovah assists"), were mere variants of one name.

22. Elath, or Eloth (marg. ref. 1 K. ix.
26), was near Ezion-Geber, in the Gulf
of Akabah. It had been lost to the Jews on
the revolt of Edom from Joram (viii. 22).
Uzziah's re-establishment of the place, rendered possible by his father's successes (*v.* 7),
was one of his first acts, and seems to imply
a desire to renew the commercial projects
which Solomon had successfully carried
out, and which Jehoshaphat had vainly attempted (1 K. xxii. 48).

23. *Jeroboam*] This is the only instance,
in the history of either kingdom, of a recur-
rent royal appellation. We can scarcely

doubt that Jeroboam II. was named after
the great founder of the Israelite kingdom
by a father who trusted that he might prove
a sort of second founder. Perhaps the prophecy of Jonah (see *v.* 25) had been already
given, and it was known that a great deliverance was approaching.

25. *He restored the coast of Israel*] Jeroboam, in the course of his long reign, recovered the old boundaries of the Holy Land
to the north, the east, and the south-east.
The "entering in of Hamath" is spoken of
as the northern boundary; the "sea of the
plain," or the Dead Sea, is the southern
boundary (see marg. reff.): here Israel adjoined on Moab. The entire tract east of
Jordan had been lost to Israel in the reign
of Jehu and that of Jehoahaz (x. 33, xiii. 3,
25). All this was now recovered: and not
only so, but Moab was reduced (Amos vi.
14), and the Syrians were in their turn
forced to submit to the Jews (*v.* 28). The
northern conquests were perhaps little less
important than the eastern (do.).

the word of the LORD...*which he spake*]
Some have found the prophecy of Jonah
here alluded to, or a portion of it, in Isaiah
xv. and xvi. (see xvi. 13); but without sufficient grounds.

This passage tends to fix Jonah's date to
some period not very late in the reign of
Jeroboam II., *i.e.* (according to the ordinary
chronology) from B.C. 823 to B.C. 782. On
Gath-hepher, see marg. ref. and note.

c Josh.19.13.
d ch. 13. 4.
e Deut.32.36.
f ch. 13. 5.

g 2 Sam. 8. 6.
1 Kin.11. 24.
2 Chr. 8. 3.

h After an interregnum of 11 years,
ch. 15. 8.
a ch. 14. 21.
2 Chr. 26. 1, 3, 4.
b called Uzziah, ver. 13. 30, &c.
& 2 Chr.26.1.
c ver. 35.
ch. 12. 3.
& 14. 4.
d 2 Chr. 26. 19—21.
e Lev. 13. 46.

f 2Chr.26.23.

26 son of Amittai, the prophet, which *was* of *c*Gath-hepher. For the LORD *d*saw the affliction of Israel, *that it was* very bitter: for *e there was* not any shut up, nor any left, nor any helper for 27 Israel. *f*And the LORD said not that he would blot out the name of Israel from under heaven: but he saved them by the 28 hand of Jeroboam the son of Joash. ¶ Now the rest of the acts of Jeroboam, and all that he did, and his might, how he warred, and how he recovered Damascus, and Hamath, *g which belonged* to Judah, for Israel, *are* they not written in the book of the 29 chronicles of the kings of Israel? And Jeroboam slept with his fathers, *even* with the kings of Israel; and *h*Zachariah his son reigned in his stead.

CHAP. 15. IN the twenty and seventh year of Jeroboam king of Israel *a*began *b*Azariah son of Amaziah king of Judah to reign. 2 Sixteen years old was he when he began to reign, and he reigned two and fifty years in Jerusalem. And his mother's name *was* 3 Jecholiah of Jerusalem. And he did *that which was* right in the sight of the LORD, according to all that his father Amaziah 4 had done; *c*save that the high places were not removed: the people sacrificed and burnt incense still on the high places. 5 ¶ And the LORD *d*smote the king, so that he was a leper unto the day of his death, and *e*dwelt in a several house. And Jotham the king's son *was* over the house, judging the people of the 6 land. And the rest of the acts of Azariah, and all that he did, *are* they not written in the book of the chronicles of the kings 7 of Judah? So Azariah slept with his fathers; and *f*they buried him with his fathers in the city of David: and Jotham his son 8 reigned in his stead. ¶ In the thirty and eighth year of Azariah king of Judah did Zachariah the son of Jeroboam reign over

---

26. *the affliction of Israel*] That which the Israelites had suffered for two reigns at the hands of the Syrians (x. 32, 33, xiii. 3, 7, 22).

there was not any shut up, nor any left] A phrase implying complete depopulation (see marg. ref. note; 1 K. xiv. 10), but here meaning no more than extreme depression and weakness.

27. *And the LORD said not*] Though the Israelites were brought thus low, yet the fiat did not as yet go forth for their destruction. God did not send a Prophet to say that He would blot out the name of Israel from under heaven; but on the contrary sent two to announce that they should be delivered from their present enemies, and obtain triumphs over them (see *v.* 25, xiii. 17–19).

that he would blot out, &c.] This is a Mosaic phrase, found only here and in Deuteronomy (ix. 14, xxix. 20).

28. *he recovered Damascus*] Jeroboam probably gained certain advantages over Benhadad, which induced the latter to make his submission and consent to such terms as those extorted by Ahab (1 K. xx. 34).

Hamath was probably among the actual conquests of Jeroboam. It was brought so low in his reign, as to have become almost a by-word for calamity (cp. Amos vi. 2).

which belonged to Judah, for Israel] *i.e.*

these cities were recovered to Judah, *i.e.* to the people of God generally, through or by means of being added to Israel, *i.e.* to the northern kingdom.

A few further facts in the history of Jeroboam II. are recorded by the prophet Amos (cp. ch. vii. 10 &c.).

XV. **5.** *the LORD smote the king, so that he was a leper*] The circumstances under which this terrible affliction befel one of the greatest of the Jewish kings, are given at some length by the author of Chronicles (marg. ref.), who supplies us with a tolerably full account of this important reign, which the writer of Kings dismisses in half-a-dozen verses.

a several house] "A house of liberation," or, freedom. On the necessity, under which the Law placed lepers, of living apart from other men, see marg. ref. Jotham became regent in his father's room, and exercised the functions of judge (1 K. iii. 9 note), from the time that his father became a leper.

8. *In the thirty and eighth year*] Rather, according to the previous numbers (xiv. 23, xv. 2), the 27th year of Azariah. Some suppose an interregnum between Jeroboam and Zachariah, which, however, is very improbable.

9 Israel in Samaria six months. And he did *that which was* evil
in the sight of the LORD, as his fathers had done: he departed
not from the sins of Jeroboam the son of Nebat, who made
10 Israel to sin. And Shallum the son of Jabesh conspired against
him, and *g* smote him before the people, and slew him, and
11 reigned in his stead. And the rest of the acts of Zachariah,
behold, they *are* written in the book of the chronicles of the
12 kings of Israel. This was *h* the word of the LORD which he
spake unto Jehu, saying, Thy sons shall sit on the throne of
Israel unto the fourth *generation.* And so it came to pass.
13 ¶ Shallum the son of Jabesh began to reign in the nine and
thirtieth year of *i* Uzziah king of Judah; and he reigned ¹a full
14 month in Samaria. For Menahem the son of Gadi went up
from *k* Tirzah, and came to Samaria, and smote Shallum the son
of Jabesh in Samaria, and slew him, and reigned in his stead.
15 And the rest of the acts of Shallum, and his conspiracy which
he made, behold, they *are* written in the book of the chronicles
16 of the kings of Israel. ¶ Then Menahem smote *l* Tiphsah, and
all that *were* therein, and the coasts thereof from Tirzah: because
they opened not *to him,* therefore he smote *it; and* all *m* the
17 women therein that were with child he ripped up. In the nine
and thirtieth year of Azariah king of Judah began Menahem
the son of Gadi to reign over Israel, *and reigned* ten years in
18 Samaria. And he did *that which was* evil in the sight of the
LORD: he departed not all his days from the sins of Jeroboam
19 the son of Nebat, who made Israel to sin. *And* *n* Pul the king
of Assyria came against the land: and Menahem gave Pul a

Heb. *a month of days.*

g As pro-
phesied,
Amos 7. 9.

h ch. 10. 30.

i Matt. 1. 8,
9, called
Ozias,
and ver. 1.
Azariah.
k 1 Kin. 14.
17.

l 1 Kin. 4. 24.

n ch. 8. 12.

n 1 Chr. 5. 26.
Isai. 9. 1.
Hos. 8. 9.

---

10. *before the people*] i.e. openly and publicly. The LXX. turns the original of the
above words into a proper name, Keblaam,
and makes him the actual assassin, but without much ground.

14. Tirzah, the old capital, once more appears as a place of importance, giving birth
to the pretender, who alone of all these later
kings died a natural death, and left the
crown to his son (*v.* 22). It would seem
from the present passage to have been on
lower ground than Samaria.

16. With respect to the supposed inability of Menahem to lead an expedition to
Tiphsah (Thapsacus, see marg. ref.) on the
Euphrates, we may note in the first place
that such an expedition was a natural sequel
to Jeroboam's occupation of Hamath (xiv.
28); and further, that it would have been
greatly facilitated by the weakness of Assyria at this time, that empire having
fallen into a state of depression about B.C.
780.

19. This is the first distinct mention
which we find in Scripture of Assyria as an
aggressive power. From the native monuments we learn that she had been for
above a century pushing her conquests beyond the Euphrates, and seeking to reduce
under her dominion the entire tract between that river and Egypt. Jehu had
paid tribute. Some—arguing from the use
of the phrase "confirmed the kingdom"

(here, and in xiv. 5)—think that Jehoahaz
had acknowledged Assyrian suzerainty, and
consented that her monarchs should receive their investiture from the hands of
the Ninevite king. But hitherto there
had been no hostile invasion of Jewish or
Israelite soil by an Assyrian army. Now,
however, the Assyrians are at last formally
introduced into the history. A series of ag-
gressions is related in this and the four following chapters, culminating, on the one
hand, in the destruction of the northern
kingdom, on the other, in the complete
failure of Sennacherib's attempt upon Judæa
and Egypt.

With respect to the present expedition,
there are certain difficulties. The name of
Pul does not appear among the Assyrian
monumental kings, and it is absent from
the copies of the Assyrian Canon, containing the entire list of monarchs from about
B.C. 910 to B.C. 670. Assyria Proper, moreover, appears to have been in a state of depression for some forty years before the
accession of Tiglath-Pileser (*v.* 29). It is
probable that, during the depression of the
Ninevite line, Pul, a *Chaldæan* and not an
Assyrian king, established a second monarchy upon the Euphrates, which claimed
to be the true Assyria, and was recognised
as such by the nations of Syria and Palestine. His invasion was probably provoked
by Menahem's conquest of Thapsacus,

o ch. 14. 5.

thousand talents of silver, that his hand might be with him to
20 °confirm the kingdom in his hand. And Menahem ¹exacted the
money of Israel, *even* of all the mighty men of wealth, of
each man fifty shekels of silver, to give to the king of Assyria.
So the king of Assyria turned back, and stayed not there
21 in the land. ¶ And the rest of the acts of Menahem, and all
that he did, *are* they not written in the book of the chronicles
22 of the kings of Israel? And Menahem slept with his fathers;
23 and Pekahiah his son reigned in his stead. ¶ In the fiftieth
year of Azariah king of Judah Pekahiah the son of Menahem
began to reign over Israel in Samaria, *and reigned* two years.
24 And he did *that which was* evil in the sight of the LORD: he
departed not from the sins of Jeroboam the son of Nebat, who
25 made Israel to sin. But Pekah the son of Remaliah, a captain
of his, conspired against him, and smote him in Samaria, in the
palace of the king's house, with Argob and Arieh, and with him
fifty men of the Gileadites: and he killed him, and reigned in
26 his room. And the rest of the acts of Pekahiah, and all that
he did, behold, they *are* written in the book of the chronicles of
27 the kings of Israel. ¶ In the two and fiftieth year of Azariah

p Isai. 7. 1.

king of Judah ᵖPekah the son of Remaliah began to reign over
28 Israel in Samaria, *and reigned* twenty years. And he did *that
which was* evil in the sight of the LORD: he departed not from
the sins of Jeroboam the son of Nebat, who made Israel to sin.

q 1 Chr. 5.26.
Isai. 9. 1.
r 1 Kin. 15.
20.

29 In the days of Pekah king of Israel �q came Tiglath-pileser king
of Assyria, and took ʳIjon, and Abel-beth-maachah, and Janoah,

¹ Heb. *caused to come forth.*

---

which he would view as a wanton aggression upon his territory.

a thousand talents of silver] Compared with the tribute of Hezekiah soon afterwards (xviii. 14), this seems a large sum; but it is not beyond the resources of such a State as Samaria at the period. The tie which had bound Samaria to Assyria from the reign of Jehu to that of Jeroboam II., had ceased to exist during the period of Assyrian depression. Menahem now renewed it, undertaking the duties of a tributary, and expecting the support which Assyria was accustomed to lend to her dependencies in their struggles with their neighbours. Hence the reproaches of Hosea (marg. ref. *n*).

20. *Menahem exacted the money*] The kings of Israel had no such ready resource in difficulties as that possessed by the kings of Judah in the Temple treasury (xii. 18, xvi. 8). Hence, the forced contribution from the people, the odium of which was diminished by confining the levy to the comparatively rich.

each man fifty shekels] As the silver talent contained 3000 shekels, the levy of fifty shekels a head must have extended to 60,000 persons.

21. Assyrian inscriptions show that Menahem was subsequently reduced to subjection by Tiglath-Pileser (*v.* 29).

25. *a captain of his*] A mere "captain," a person, therefore, of very moderate rank.

The low birth of Pekah is probably glanced at in Isaiah's favourite designation of him as "Remaliah's son" (Isai. vii. 4, 5, 9, viii. 6).

From the fact that Pekah employed Gileadites to carry out his designs, it has been conjectured that he himself belonged to the trans-Jordanic region.

in the palace of the king's house] Rather, "In the tower of the king's palace;" or possibly "in the *harem* of the king's palace" (1 K. xvi. 18 note).

29. Tiglath-Pileser is the first among the Assyrian monarchs of Scripture whom we can certainly identify with a king mentioned in the monuments. According to the Assyrian Canon he reigned from B.C. 745 to B.C. 727; and the monuments show us this energetic and powerful prince (though, probably, an usurper), building and repairing palaces, levying armies, and carrying on successful wars against Merodach-Baladan in Babylonia, Rezin at Damascus, Hiram at Tyre, the Medes, the Armenians, the natives of Northern Mesopotamia, and the Arabs who bordered upon Egypt. His Assyrian name, Tiglat-pal-zira, is composed of the elements *tiglat*, "adoration," *pal*, "son," and *zira*, a word of uncertain meaning.

Ijon and Abel-beth-maachah] On the position of some of the towns mentioned in this verse see marg. ref. and Josh. xix. 36. Janoah is not the Janohah of Josh. xvi. 6

and Kedesh, and Hazor, and Gilead, and Galilee, all the land
30 of Naphtali, and carried them captive to Assyria. ¶ And
Hoshea the son of Elah made a conspiracy against Pekah the
son of Remaliah, and smote him, and slew him, and *reigned in
his stead, *in the twentieth year of Jotham the son of Uzziah.
31 And the rest of the acts of Pekah, and all that he did, behold,
they *are* written in the book of the chronicles of the kings of
32 Israel. ¶ In the second year of Pekah the son of Remaliah king of
Israel began *Jotham the son of Uzziah king of Judah to reign.
33 Five and twenty years old was he when he began to reign, and
he reigned sixteen years in Jerusalem.   And his mother's name
34 *was* Jerusha, the daughter of Zadok.   And he did *that which
was* right in the sight of the LORD : he did *according to all that
35 his father Uzziah had done.   *Howbeit the high places were
not removed : the people sacrificed and burned incense still in
the high places.   *He built the higher gate of the house of the
36 LORD.   Now the rest of the acts of Jotham, and all that he
did, *are* they not written in the book of the chronicles of the
37 kings of Judah? ¶ In those days the LORD began to send
against Judah *Rezin the king of Syria, and *Pekah the son
38 of Remaliah.   And Jotham slept with his fathers, and was
buried with his fathers in the city of David his father : and
Ahaz his son reigned in his stead.
CHAP. 16. IN the seventeenth year of Pekah the son of Remaliah
2 *Ahaz the son of Jotham king of Judah began to reign.   Twenty
years old *was* Ahaz when he began to reign, and reigned sixteen
years in Jerusalem, and did not *that which was* right in the
3 sight of the LORD his God, like David his father.   But he
walked in the way of the kings of Israel, yea, *and made his

s After an
anarchy for
some years,
ch. 17. 1.
Hos. 10. 3,
7, 15.
t In the
fourth year
of Ahaz, in
the twen-
tieth year
after Jo-
tham had
begun to
reign : *Ush.*
u 2 Chr. 27.1.
x ver. 3.
y ver. 4.
z 2 Chr. 27.
3, &c.

a ch. 16. 5.
b ver. 27.

a 2 Chr. 28.
1, &c.

b Lev. 18. 21.
2 Chr. 28. ?.

(modern *Yanûn*, S.E. of Nablous), but a
city (? *Hunin*) near the Sea of Merom.
Gilead is, probably, to be limited here to a
small district of Peræa, lying to the east of
Lake Merom, and in later times known as
Gaulanitis (the reading of LXX. here). If so,
we must suppose two expeditions of Tiglath-
Pileser against Pekah, the first mentioned
here, and the second recorded in Chronicles
and Isaiah (see marg. ref. *q* ; xvi. 9 note).

30. *Hoshea, the son of Elah*] One of Pekah's friends, according to Josephus.

the twentieth year of Jotham] According to
v. 33 and 2 Chr. xxvii. 1, Jotham reigned only
sixteen years.   See also the suggestion in the
margin.   Strangely enough, this first year
of Hoshea is also called, not the fourth, but
the twelfth of Ahaz (xvii. 1).   The chronological confusion of the history, as it stands,
is striking.

Uzziah] *i.e.* Azariah.   See *vv.* 1-4.

31. *the rest of the acts of Pekah*] On these,
see xvi. 5 note.

32. The writer here resumes the history
of Judah from *v.* 7, to resume and conclude
the history of Israel in ch. xvii.

34. Jotham imitated his father in all respects, excepting in his impious usurpation
of the priestly functions (*v.* 5 note ; 2 Chr.
xxvii. 2).

35. *He built the higher gate*] Jotham

followed the example of his father in military, no less than in religious, matters (cp.
marg. ref. with 2 Chr. xxvi. 9).   The
" higher " or " upper gate " of the Temple
is thought to have been that towards the
north ; and its fortification would seem to
indicate fear of an attack from that
quarter.

37. The recent invasions of Pul and Tiglath-Pileser had effectually alarmed Pekah
and Rezin, and had induced them to put
aside the traditional jealousies which naturally kept them apart, and to make a
league offensive and defensive.   Into this
league they were anxious that Judæa should
enter ; but they distrusted the house of David, which had been so long hostile both to
Damascus and to Samaria.   They consequently formed the design of transferring
the Jewish crown to a certain Ben-Tabeal
(Isai. vii. 6), probably a Jewish noble, perhaps a refugee at one of their courts, whom
they could trust to join heartily in their
schemes (xvi. 5 note).

XVI. 3. Ahaz was the worst of all the
kings of Judah.   He imitated the worst of
the Israelite kings—Ahab and Ahaziah,—
by a re-introduction of the Baal worship,
which had been rooted out of Israel by
Jehu and out of Judah by Jehoiada.

and made his son to pass through the fire]

c Deut. 12. 31.

d Deut. 12. 2.
1 Kin. 14. 23.
e Isai. 7. 1,
4, &c.

f ch. 14. 22.

g ch. 15. 29.

h ch. 12. 18.
See 2 Chr.
28. 21.

i Foretold,
Amos 1. 5.

son to pass through the fire, according to the *c*abominations of the heathen, whom the LORD cast out from before the children 4 of Israel. And he sacrificed and burnt incense in the high 5 places, and *d*on the hills, and under every green tree. ¶ *e*Then Rezin king of Syria and Pekah son of Remaliah king of Israel came up to Jerusalem to war : and they besieged Ahaz, but 6 could not overcome *him*. At that time Rezin king of Syria *f*recovered Elath to Syria, and drave the Jews from [1]Elath : and 7 the Syrians came to Elath, and dwelt there unto this day. So Ahaz sent messengers *g*to [2]Tiglath-pileser king of Assyria, saying, I *am* thy servant and thy son : come up, and save me out of the hand of the king of Syria, and out of the hand of the king 8 of Israel, which rise up against me. And Ahaz *h*took the silver and gold that was found in the house of the LORD, and in the treasures of the king's house, and sent *it for* a present to the 9 king of Assyria. And the king of Assyria hearkened unto him : for the king of Assyria went up against [3]Damascus, and *i*took it, and carried *the people of* it captive to Kir, and slew Rezin.

[1] Heb. *Eloth*.
[2] Heb. *Tilgath-pileser,*

1 Chr. 5. 26. & 2 Chr. 28.
20, *Tilgath-pilneser*.

[3] Heb. *Dammesek*.

---

i.e. Ahaz adopted the Moloch worship of the Ammonites and Moabites (iii. 27 ; Mic. vi. 7), and sacrificed at least one son, probably his firstborn, according to the horrid rites of those nations, and the Canaanite tribes (Deut. xii. 31 ; Ps. cvi. 37, 38). Hitherto, apparently, the Jews had been guiltless of this abomination. They had been warned against it by Moses (marg. ref. ; Deut. xviii. 10) ; and if (as some think) they had practised it in the wilderness (Ezek. xx. 26 ; Am. v. 26), the sin must have been rare and exceptional ; from the date of their entrance into the Promised Land they had wholly put it away. Now, however, it became so frequent (cp. xvii. 17, xxi. 6) as to meet with the strongest protest from Jeremiah and Ezekiel (Jer. vii. 31, 32, xix. 2-6 ; xxxii. 35 ; Ezek. xvi. 20, xx. 26, xxiii. 37, &c.).

4. *he sacrificed*, &c.] Other kings of Judah had allowed their people to do so. Ahaz was the first, so far as we know, to countenance the practice by his own example.

5. Rezin and Pekah, who had already begun their attacks upon Judæa in the reign of Jotham (xv. 37), regarded the accession of a boy-king, only sixteen years of age, as peculiarly favourable to their projects, and proceeded without loss of time to carry them out. The earlier scenes of the war, omitted by the writer of Kings, are given at some length in 2 Chr. xxviii. 5-15.

6. Either during the siege, or on breaking up from before Jerusalem, Rezin made an expedition to the Red Sea coast, and became master of the city which had belonged to Judæa about seventy years (marg. ref.). Most moderns render this verse, "Rezin recovered (or restored) Elath to Edom,...and the **Edomites** came to Elath."

On the resemblance of the words Aram and Edom in the original, see 2 Sam. viii. 12 note.

7. Ahaz was threatened on all sides, on the north by Rezin and Pekah ; on the south-east by Edom (2 Chr. xxviii. 17) ; and on the south-west by the Philistines (do. 18). To these external dangers was added the still greater peril of disaffection at home. A large party in Judah was " weary " of the house of David (Is. vii. 13), ready to join the confederacy (do. viii. 6, 12), and to accept for king "the son of Tabeal." Ahaz saw no hope of safety unless he could obtain a powerful protector ; and, Egypt being particularly weak at this time, he turned to Assyria.

8. Cp. marg. ref. and 1 K. xv. 18. Political necessity was always held to justify the devotion of the Temple treasure to secular purposes.

9. The submission of Judah, which Ahaz proffered, would be of the utmost importance in connexion with any projects that might be entertained of Egyptian conquests. Naturally, Damascus was the first object of attack. It was the head of the confederacy, and it lay nearest to an army descending upon Lower Syria, as all Asiatic armies would descend, from the north. It appears from an inscription of Tiglath-pileser's, that Rezin met him in the field, was defeated, and slain. An attack upon Pekah followed. Now probably it was that the entire trans-Jordanic region was overrun ; and that the Reubenites, the Gadites, and the half-tribe of Manasseh, were carried into captivity (1 Chr. v. 26). Megiddo and Dor appear also to have been occupied, and the Arabs of the south chastised. Tiglath-pileser then returned to Damascus, where a son of Rezin had assumed the crown ; he besieged and took the city, and punished

10 ¶ And king Ahaz went to Damascus to meet Tiglath-pileser king of Assyria, and saw an altar that *was* at Damascus: and king Ahaz sent to Urijah the priest the fashion of the altar, and the
11 pattern of it, according to all the workmanship thereof. And Urijah the priest built an altar according to all that king Ahaz had sent from Damascus: so Urijah the priest made *it* against
12 king Ahaz came from Damascus. And when the king was come from Damascus, the king saw the altar: and *k* the king *k* 2 Chr. 26.
13 approached to the altar, and offered thereon. And he burnt 16, 19. his burnt offering and his meat offering, and poured his drink offering, and sprinkled the blood of ¹his peace offerings upon the
14 altar. And he brought also *l* the brasen altar, which *was* before *l* 2 Chr. 4. 1. the LORD, from the forefront of the house, from between the altar and the house of the LORD, and put it on the north side of
15 the altar. And king Ahaz commanded Urijah the priest, saying, Upon the great altar burn *m* the morning burnt offering, and *m* Ex. 29. 39, the evening meat offering, and the king's burnt sacrifice, and 40, 41. his meat offering, with the burnt offering of all the people of the land, and their meat offering, and their drink offerings; and sprinkle upon it all the blood of the burnt offering, and all the blood of the sacrifice: and the brasen altar shall be for me to
16 enquire *by*. Thus did Urijah the priest, according to all that *n* 2Chr. 23.
17 king Ahaz commanded. ¶ *n* And king Ahaz cut off *o* the borders 24. of the bases, and removed the laver from off them; and took *o* 1 Kin. 7. down *p* the sea from off the brasen oxen that *were* under it, and *p* 1 Kin. 7.
   27, 28.
   p 1 Kin. 7.
   23, 25.

¹ Heb. *which* were *his*.

Rezin's son with death. Tiglath-pileser appears by one of his inscriptions to have held a court at Damascus, to which it is probable that the tributary kings of the neighbourhood were summoned to pay their tributes and do homage for their kingdoms. Among the tributes brought to him at this time, those of Judæa, Edom, Ammon, Moab, Gaza, Ascalon, and Tyre, are mentioned.

Kir] Kir is mentioned by Amos (ix. 7) as the country from which the Syrians came. It is joined by Isaiah (xxii. 6) with Elam or Elymais. Its position can only be conjectured. Perhaps the word designates a region adjoining Elymais, in the extreme south-eastern limits of Assyria.

10. *and saw an altar*] Rather, "The altar," *i.e.* an Assyrian altar, and connected with that formal recognition of the Assyrian deities which the Ninevite monarchs appear to have required of all the nations whom they received into their empire.

the fashion of the altar] Assyrian altars were not very elaborate, but they were very different from the Jewish. They were comparatively small, and scarcely suited for "whole burnt-offerings." One type was square, about half the height of a man, and ornamented round the top with a sort of battlement. Another had a triangular base and a circular top consisting of a single flat stone. A third was a sort of portable stand, narrow, and about the height of a man.

This last was of the kind which the kings took with them in their expeditions.

14. Hitherto the "Brasen Altar" (marg. ref.) had, it would seem, occupied a position directly in front of the Temple porch, which it exactly equalled in width. Now Ahaz removed it from this place, and gave the honourable position to his new altar, which he designed to supersede the old for all ordinary purposes (*v.* 15).

from between the altar, &c.] Urijah, having received no official directions, had placed the new altar in front of the old, between it and the eastern gate of the court. Ahaz consequently on his arrival found the brasen altar "between the (new) altar and the house of the Lord."

15. *the brasen altar shall be for me to enquire by*] The bulk of modern commentators translate—"As for the Brasen Altar, it will be for me to enquire (or consider) what I shall do with it."

16. The writer condemns the obsequiousness of Urijah, whose conduct was the more inexcusable after the noble example of his predecessor Azariah (2 Chr. xxvi. 17-20).

17. See marg. reff. The acts recorded here, were probably not mere wanton acts of mutilation, but steps in the conversion of these sacred objects to other uses, as to the ornamentation of a palace or of an idol temple. The bases, the oxen, and the sea were not destroyed—they remained at Jerusalem till its final capture (Jer. lii.

18 put it upon a pavement of stones. And the covert for the sabbath that they had built in the house, and the king's entry without, turned he from the house of the LORD for the king of
19 Assyria. ¶ Now the rest of the acts of Ahaz which he did, *are* they not written in the book of the chronicles of the kings of

q 2Chr.28.27. 20 Judah? And Ahaz slept with his fathers, and *q*was buried with his fathers in the city of David: and Hezekiah his son reigned in his stead.

CHAP. 17. IN the twelfth year of Ahaz king of Judah began

a After an interregnum,
ch. 15. 30.
b ch. 18. 9.

*a*Hoshea the son of Elah to reign in Samaria over Israel nine
2 years. And he did *that which was* evil in the sight of the LORD,
3 but not as the kings of Israel that were before him. Against him came up *b*Shalmaneser king of Assyria ; and Hoshea became
4 his servant, and ¹ gave him ²presents. And the king of Assyria found conspiracy in Hoshea : for he had sent messengers to So king of Egypt, and brought no present to the king of Assyria, as *he had done* year by year · therefore the king of Assyria shut

¹ Heb. *rendered,* 2 Sam. 8. 2.   ² Or, *tribute.*

17, 20). Probably they were restored to their original uses by Hezekiah (2 Chr. xxix. 19).

a pavement of stones] Probably a pavement made expressly, for the stones of the court seem to have been covered with a planking of cedar (1 K. vi. 36, vii. 12).

18. *the covert...in the house*] A canopied seat in the Temple for the king and his 'amily when they attended public worship on the sabbath. It stood no doubt in the inner court of the Temple.

the king's entry without] This would seem to have been a private passage by which the king crossed the outer court to the east gate of the inner court when he visited the Temple (Ezek. xlvi. 1, 2).

turned he from the house of the LORD *for the king of Assyria*] This passage is very obscure. Some translate—"altered he in the house of the Lord, because of the king of Assyria," supposing the "covert" and the "passage" to have been of rich materials, and Ahaz to have taken them to eke out his "presents" to the king of Assyria." Others render, "removed he into the house of the Lord from fear of the king of Assyria."

19. *the rest of the acts of Ahaz*] Such as are described in Isai. vii. 10-13; 2 Chr. xxviii. 23-25, xxix. 3, 7.

XVII. **1.** *In the twelfth year*] Cp. xv. 30 note. The history of the kingdom of Israel is in this chapter brought to a close.

2. *not as the kings of Israel that were before him*] The repentance of a nation, like that of an individual, may be "too late." God is long-suffering ; but after national sins have reached a certain height, after admonitions and warnings have been repeatedly rejected, after lesser punishments have failed,—judgment begins to fall. Forces have been set in motion, which nothing but a miracle could stop ; and God does not see fit to work a miracle in such a case. Cp. Butler, 'Analogy,' Pt. I. ch. ii. end.

3. Of Shalmaneser, the successor of Tiglath-pileser in the Assyrian Canon, we know little from Assyrian sources, since his records have been mutilated by his successors, the Sargonids, who were of a wholly different family. The archives of Tyre mention him as contemporary with, and warring against, a Tyrian king named Elulæus.

The expedition, referred to here, was probably in the first year of Shalmaneser (B.C. 727). Its main object was the reduction of Phœnicia, which had re-asserted its independence, and (except Tyre) was once more completely reduced. Shalmaneser probably passed on from Phœnicia into Galilee, where he attacked and took Beth-arbel (Arbela of Josephus, now *Irbid*), treating it with great severity (Hos. x. 14), in order to alarm Hoshea, who forthwith submitted, and became tributary (see marg. rendering and 1 K. iv. 21 note). Shalmaneser then returned into Assyria.

4. So, king of Egypt, is generally identified with Shebek (B.C. 730), the Sabaco of Herodotus. Hoshea's application to him was a return to a policy which had been successful in the reign of Jeroboam I. (1 K. xii. 20 note), but had not been resorted to by any other Israelite monarch. Egypt had for many years been weak, but Sabaco was a conqueror, who at the head of the swarthy hordes of Ethiopia had invaded Egypt and made himself master of the country. In the inscriptions of Shebek he boasts to have received tribute from "the king of *Shara*" (Syria), which is probably his mode of noticing Hoshea's application. References to the Egyptian proclivities of Hoshea are frequent in the Prophet Hosea (vii. 11, xi. 1, 5, xii. 4). King Hoshea, simultaneously with his reception as a vassal by Sabaco, ceased to pay tribute to Shalmaneser, thus openly rebelling, and provoking the chastisement which followed.

5 him up, and bound him in prison. ¶ Then ᶜ the king of Assyria
came up throughout all the land, and went up to Samaria, and
6 besieged it three years. ᵈ In the ninth year of Hoshea the king
of Assyria took Samaria, and ᵉ carried Israel away into Assyria,
ᶠ and placed them in Halah and in Habor *by* the river of Gozan,
7 and in the cities of the Medes. For *so* it was, that the children
of Israel had sinned against the LORD their God, which had
brought them up out of the land of Egypt, from under the hand
8 of Pharaoh king of Egypt, and had feared other gods, and
ᵍ walked in the statutes of the heathen, whom the LORD cast out
from before the children of Israel, and of the kings of Israel,
9 which they had made. And the children of Israel did secretly
those things that *were* not right against the LORD their God, and
they built them high places in all their cities, ʰ from the tower of
10 the watchmen to the fenced city. ⁱ And they set them up ¹ images
and ᵏ groves ˡ in every high hill, and under every green tree :

¹ Heb. *statues.*

ᶜ ch. 18. 9.

ᵈ ch. 18. 10.
Hos. 13. 16,
foretold.
ᵉ Lev. 26. 32,
33.
Deut. 28. 36,
64.
ᶠ 1 Chr. 5. 26.

ᵍ Lev. 18. 3.
Deut. 18. 9.
ch. 16. 3.
ʰ ch. 18. 8.
ⁱ 1 Kin. 14. 23.
Isai. 57. 5.
ᵏ Ex. 34. 13.
Deut. 16. 21.
Mic. 5. 14.
ˡ Deut. 12. 2.
ch. 16. 4.

---

5. *all the land*] The second invasion of
Shalmaneser (B.C. 723, his fifth year), is
here contrasted with the first, as extending
to the *whole* country, whereas the first had
afflicted only a part.

three years] From the fourth to the sixth
of Hezekiah, and from the seventh to the
ninth of Hoshea ; two years, therefore, according to our reckoning, but three, according to that of the Hebrews. This was a
long time for so small a place to resist the
Assyrians but Samaria was favourably
situated on a steep hill ; probably Sabaco
made some attempts to relieve his vassal ;
the war with Tyre must have distracted Shalmaneser ; and there is reason to believe
that before the capture was effected a revolt
had broken out at Nineveh which must
have claimed Shalmaneser's chief attention,
though it did not induce him to abandon
his enterprise.

6. *the king of Assyria took Samaria*] *i.e.*,
from the Assyrian inscriptions, not Shalmaneser but Sargon, who claims to have
captured the city in the first year of his
reign (B.C. 721). At first Sargon carried off
from Samaria no more than 27,280 prisoners
and was so far from depopulating the
country that he assessed the tribute on the
remaining inhabitants at the same rate as
before the conquest. But later in his reign
he effected the wholesale deportation here
mentioned.

Halah and in Habor by the river of Gozan]
Rather, "**on the** Habor, the river of Gozan." Halah is the tract which Ptolemy
calls Chalcitis, on the borders of Gauzanitis
(Gozan) in the vicinity of the Chaboras, or
Khabour (Habor, the great affluent of the
Euphrates). In this region is a remarkable
mound called *Gla*, which probably marks
the site, and represents the name, of the
city of Chalach, whence the district Chalcitis
was so called.

in the cities of the Medes] Sargon relates
that he overran Media, seized and " an-

nexed to Assyria" a number of the towns,
and also established in the country a set of
fortified posts or colonies.

7. The reasons for which God suffered the
Israelites to be deprived of their land and
carried into captivity were—1, their idolatries ; 2, their rejection of the Law ; 3, their
disregard of the warning voices of Prophets
and seers.

8. Idolatry was worse in the Israelites
than in other nations, since it argued not
merely folly and a gross carnal spirit,
but also black ingratitude (Ex. xx. 2, 3).
The writer subdivides the idolatries of the
Israelites into two classes, heathen and native—those which they adopted from the nations whom they drove out, and those which
their own kings imposed on them. Under
the former head would come the great mass
of the idolatrous usages described in *vv.* 9,
10, 11, 17 ; "the high places" (*vv.* 9 and 11) ;
the "images" and "groves" (*v.* 10) ; the
causing of their children to "pass through
the fire" (*v.* 17) ; and the "worship of the host
of heaven" (*v.* 16) : under the latter would
fall the principal points in *vv.* 12, 16, 21.

which they had made] "Which" refers to
"statutes." The Israelites had "walked in
the statutes of the heathen, and in those of
the kings of Israel, which (statutes) they
(the kings) had made."

9. Lit., the words run thus—"And the
children of Israel concealed (or 'dissembled')
words which were not so concerning the
Lord their God ;" the true meaning of
which probably is, the Israelites cloaked or
covered their idolatry with the pretence that
it was a worship of Jehovah : they glossed
it over and dissembled towards God, instead
of openly acknowledging their apostasy.

*from the tower of the watchmen to the fenced
city*] This phrase was probably a proverbial
expression for universality, meaning strictly ;
—"alike in the most populous and in the
most desolate regions." "Towers of watchmen" were built for the protection of the

m Ex. 20. 3.
Lev. 26. 1.
Deut. 5. 7.
n Deut. 4.19.
o 1 Sam. 9.9.
p Hos. 12. 6.
Joel 2. 12.
Am. 5. 4.
Is. 1. 16.
Jer. 18. 11.
q Deut.31.27.
Prov. 29. 1.
r Deut.29.25.
s Deut.32.21.
1 Kin. 16.13.
1 Cor. 8. 4.
t Ps. 115. 8.
Rom. 1. 21.
u Deut. 12.
30, 31.
x Ex. 32. 8.
1 Kin. 12.28.
*y*1Kin.16.33.
z 1Kin.16.31.
& 22. 53.
ch. 11. 18.
a Lev. 18. 21.
Ezek. 23. 37.

11 and there they burnt incense in all the high places, as *did* the heathen whom the LORD carried away before them; and wrought 12 wicked things to provoke the LORD to anger: for they served idols, *m*whereof the LORD had said unto them, *n*Ye shall not do 13 this thing. ¶ Yet the LORD testified against Israel, and against Judah, ¹by all the prophets, *and by* all *o*the seers, saying, *p*Turn ye from your evil ways, and keep my commandments *and* my statutes, according to all the law which I commanded your fathers, and which I sent to you by my servants the prophets. 14 Notwithstanding they would not hear, but *q*hardened their necks, like to the neck of their fathers, that did not believe in 15 the LORD their God. And they rejected his statutes, *r*and his covenant that he made with their fathers, and his testimonies which he testified against them; and they followed *s*vanity, and *t*became vain, and went after the heathen that *were* round about them, *concerning* whom the LORD had charged them, that they 16 should *u*not do like them. And they left all the commandments of the LORD their God, and *x*made them molten images, *even* two calves, *y*and made a grove, and worshipped all the host of 17 heaven, *z*and served Baal. *a*And they caused their sons and

¹ Heb. *by the hand of all.*

---

flocks and herds which were pastured in waste and desert places (2 Chr. xxvi. 10, xxvii. 4).

11. The burning of incense was a common religious practice among the Egyptians and the Babylonians; and from the present passage we gather that the Canaanitish nations practised it as one of their ordinary sacred rites. The Israelites are frequently reproached with it (Hos. ii. 13, iv. 13; Isai. lxv. 3).

13. God raised up a succession of Prophets and seers, who repeated and enforced the warnings of the Law, and breathed into the old words a new life. Among this succession were, in Israel, Ahijah the Shilonite (1 K. xiv. 2), Jehu the son of Hanani (do. xvi. 1), Elijah, Micaiah the son of Imlah (do. xxii. 8), Elisha, Jonah the son of Amittai (2 K. xiv. 25), Oded (2 Chr. xxviii. 9), Amos, and Hosea; in Judah, up to this time, Shemaiah (2 Chr. xi. 2, xii. 5), Iddo (do. xii. 15, xiii. 22), Azariah the son of Oded (do. xv. 1), Hanani (do. xvi. 7), Jehu his son (do. xix. 2), Jahaziel the son of Zechariah (do. xx. 14), Eliezer the son of Dodavah (do. *v.* 37), Zechariah the son of Jehoiada (do. xxiv. 20), another Zechariah (do. xxvi. 5), Joel, Micah, and Isaiah, besides several whose names are not known. Some of these persons are called "prophets," others "seers." Occasionally the same person has both titles (as Iddo and Jehu the son of Hanani), which seems to show that there was no very important distinction between them.

Probably the conjecture is right that "prophet" (*nâbi*) in strictness designates the official members of the prophetical order only, while "seer" (*chôzeh*) is applicable to all, whether members of the order or not, who receive a prophetical revelation.

14. To "harden" or "stiffen the neck" is a common Hebrew expression significative of unbending obstinacy and determined self-will. See marg. reff.

15. As idols are "vanity" and "nothingness," mere weakness and impotence, so idolaters are "vain" and impotent. Their energies have been wasted, their time misspent; they have missed the real object of their existence; their whole life has been a mistake; and the result is utter powerlessness. Lit., the word rendered "vanity" seems to mean "breath" or "vapour"—a familiar image for nonentity. It occurs frequently in the Prophets, and especially in Jeremiah (*e.g.* ii. 5, viii. 19, xiv. 22, &c.).

16. In *v.* 10 there is a reference to the old high-place worship, which was professedly a worship of Jehovah, but with unauthorised rites and emblems; here the reference is to Ahab's setting up a grove to Baal in the city of Samaria (marg. ref.).

and worshipped all the host of heaven] Astral worship has not hitherto been mentioned as practised by the Israelites. Moses had warned against it (Deut. iv. 19, xvii. 3), so that it no doubt existed in his day, either among the Canaanitish nations or among the Arabians (Job xxxi. 26-28). Perhaps it was involved to some extent in the Baal worship of the Phœnicians, for Baal and Astarte were probably associated in the minds of their worshippers with the Sun and Moon. Later in the history we shall find a very decided and well-developed astral worship prevalent among the Jews, which is probably Assyro-Babylonian (xxi. 3 note).

17. Cp. xvi. 3 note, and see Lev. xx. 2-5 note.

their daughters to pass through the fire, and *b*used divination *b* Deut.18.10.
and enchantments, and *c*sold themselves to do evil in the sight *c* 1 Kin. 21.
18 of the LORD, to provoke him to anger. ¶ Therefore the LORD 20.
was very angry with Israel, and removed them out of his sight:
19 there was none left *d*but the tribe of Judah only. Also *e*Judah *d* 1 Kin. 11.
kept not the commandments of the LORD their God, but walked 13, 32.
e Jer. 3. 8.
20 in the statutes of Israel which they made. And the LORD rejected all the seed of Israel, and afflicted them, and *f*delivered *f* ch. 13. 3.
them into the hand of spoilers, until he had cast them out of & 15. 29.
21 his sight. For *g*he rent Israel from the house of David; and *g* 1 Kin. 11.
*h*they made Jeroboam the son of Nebat king: and Jeroboam 11, 31.
h.1 Kin. 12.
drave Israel from following the LORD, and made them sin a 20, 28.
22 great sin. For the children of Israel walked in all the sins of
23 Jeroboam which he did; they departed not from them; until
the LORD removed Israel out of his sight, *i*as he had said by all *i* 1Kin.14.16.
his servants the prophets. *k*So was Israel carried away out of *k* ver. 6.
l Ezra 4. 2,
24 their own land to Assyria unto this day. ¶ *l*And the king of 10.
Assyria brought men *m*from Babylon, and from Cuthah, and *m*See ver.30.
n ch. 18. 34,
from *n*Ava, and from Hamath, and from Sepharvaim, and placed Ivah.

---

19. This verse and the next are parenthetical. Here again, as in *v.* 13, the writer is led
on from his account of the sins and punishment of the Israelites to glance at the
similar sins and similar punishment of the
Jews.

It was the worst reproach which could be
urged against any Jewish king, that he
" walked in the way of the kings of Israel"
(viii. 18, xvi. 3 ; 2 Chr. xxi. 6, xxviii. 2).
The Baal worship is generally the special
sin at which the phrase is levelled ; but the
meaning here seems to be wider. Cp. Mic.
vi. 16.

20. *all the seed of Israel*] The Jews, *i.e.*
as well as the Israelites. God's dealings
with both kingdoms were alike. "Spoilers " were sent against each, time after
time, before the final ruin came on them—
against Israel, Pul and Tiglath-pileser (xv.
19, 29 ; 1 Chr. v. 26); against Judah, Sennacherib (xviii. 13–16), Esar-haddon (2 Chr.
xxxiii. 11), and Nebuchadnezzar thrice.

21. The strong expression "drave Israel"
is an allusion to the violent measures whereto Jeroboam had recourse in order to stop
the efflux into Judæa of the more religious
portion of his subjects (2 Chr. xi. 13–16),
the calling in of Shishak, and the permanent assumption of a hostile attitude towards the southern kingdom.

23. *as he had said by all his servants the
prophets*] The writer refers not only to the
extant prophecies of Moses (Lev. xxvi. 33 ;
Deut. iv. 26, 27, xxviii. 36, &c.), Ahijah
the Shilonite (marg. ref.), Hosea (ix. 3,
17), and Amos (vii. 17), but also to the entire series of warnings and predictions which
Prophet after Prophet in a long unbroken
succession had addressed to the disobedient
Israelites (*v.* 13) on their apostasy, and so
leaving them wholly " without excuse "
(see *v.* 13 note).

unto this day] The words, taken in combination with the rest of the chapter,
distinctly show that the Israelites had
not returned to their land by the time of
the composition of the Books of Kings.
They show nothing as to their ultimate
fate. But on the whole, it would seem
probable (1) that the ten tribes never
formed a community in their exile, but were
scattered from the first ; and (2) that their
descendants either blended with the heathen
and were absorbed, or returned to Palestine
with Zerubbabel and Ezra, or became inse-
parably united with the dispersed Jews in
Mesopotamia and the adjacent countries.
No discovery, therefore, of the ten tribes
is to be expected, nor can works written to
prove their identity with any existing race
or body of persons be regarded as anything
more than ingenious exercitations.

24. Sargon is probably the king of Assyria intended, not (as generally supposed)
either Shalmaneser or Esar-haddon.

The ruins of Cutha have been discovered
about 15 miles north-east of Babylon, at a
place which is called Ibrahim, because it is
the traditional site of a contest between
Abraham and Nimrod. The name of Cutha is found on the bricks of this place,
which are mostly of the era of Nebuchadnezzar. The Assyrian inscriptions show that
the special god of Cutha was Nergal (*v.* 30
note).

Ava or Ivah or Ahava (Ezra viii. 15) was
on the Euphrates ; perhaps the city in ancient times called Ihi or Aia, between Sippara (Sepharvaim) and Hena (Anah).

On Hamath, see 1 K. viii. 65 note.

Sepharvaim or Sippara is frequently mentioned in the Assyrian inscriptions under
the name of *Tsipar* (*v.* 31 note). The dual
form of the Hebrew name is explained by
the fact that the town lay on both sides of

them in the cities of Samaria instead of the children of Israel: and they possessed Samaria, and dwelt in the cities thereof. 25 And *so* it was at the beginning of their dwelling there, *that* they feared not the LORD : therefore the LORD sent lions among them, 26 which slew *some* of them. Wherefore they spake to the king of Assyria, saying, The nations which thou hast removed, and placed in the cities of Samaria, know not the manner of the God of the land : therefore he hath sent lions among them, and, behold, they slay them, because they know not the manner of the God 27 of the land. Then the king of Assyria commanded, saying, Carry thither one of the priests whom ye brought from thence ; and let them go and dwell there, and let him teach them the 28 manner of the God of the land. Then one of the priests whom they had carried away from Samaria came and dwelt in Beth-el, 29 and taught them how they should fear the LORD. ¶ Howbeit every nation made gods of their own, and put *them* in the houses of the high places which the Samaritans had made, every nation 30 in their cities wherein they dwelt. And the men of °Babylon made Succoth-benoth, and the men of Cuth made Nergal, and 31 the men of Hamath made Ashima, *p*and the Avites made Nibhaz and Tartak, and the Sepharvites *q*burnt their children in fire to

o ver. 24.

p Ezra 4. 9.
q Lev. 18. 21.
Deut. 12. 31.

---

the river. Its position is marked by the moder a village of *Mosaib*, about 20 miles from the ruins of Babylon up the course of the stream.

The towns mentioned in this verse were, excepting Hamath, conquered by Sargon in his twelfth year, B.C. 709; and it cannot have been until this time, or a little later, that the transplantation here recorded took pla e. Hamath had revolted, and been conquered by Sargon in his first year, shortly after the conquest of Samaria.

instead of the children of Israel] This does not mean that the *whole* population of Samaria was carried off (cp. 2 Chr. xxxiv. 9). The writer here, by expressly confining the new comers to the "*cities* of Samaria," seems to imply that the country districts were in other hands.

25. The depopulation of the country, insufficiently remedied by the influx of foreigners, had the natural consequence of multiplying the wild beasts and making them bolder. Probably a certain number had always lurked in the jungle along the course of the Jordan (Jer. xlix. 19, 1. 44); and these now ventured into the hill country, and perhaps even into the cities. The colonists regarded their sufferings from the lions as a judgment upon them from "the god of the land" (*v.* 26 ; cp. 1 K. xx. 23 note).

27. *Carry one of the priests... ; let them go and dwell there, and let him teach*] The double change of number is curious; but the text needs no emendation. The priest would require to be accompanied by assistants, who would "go and dwell," but would not be qualified to "teach." The *arcana* of the worship would be known to none excepting the priests who had minis-

tered at the two national sanctuaries of Dan and Bethel.

28. The priest sent to the colonists was not a true Jehovah-priest, but one of those who had been attached to the calf-worship, probably at Bethel. Hence, he would be willing to tolerate the mixed religion, which a true Jehovah-priest would have unsparingly condemned.

29. The "Samaritans" here are the Israelites. The temples built by them at the high places (1 K. xii. 31, xiii. 32) had remained standing at the time of their departure. They were now occupied by the new comers, who set up their own worship in the old sanctuaries.

30. Succoth-benoth probably represents a Babylonian goddess called Zir-banit, the wife of Merodach. She and her husband were, next to Bel and Beltis, the favourite divinities of the Babylonians.

Nergal, etymologically "the great man," or "the great hero," was the Babylonian god of war and hunting. His name forms an element in the Babylonian royal appellation, Nergal-shar-ezar or Neriglissar. The Assyrian inscriptions connect Nergal in a very special way with Cutha, of which he was evidently the tutelary deity.

Ashima is ingeniously conjectured to be the same as Esmûn, the Æsculapius of the Cabiri or " great gods " of the Phœnicians.

31. Nibhaz and Tartak are either gods of whom no other notice has come down to us, or intentional corruptions of the Babylonian names Nebo and Tir, the great god of Borsippa, who was the tutelar deity of so many Babylonian kings. The Jews, in their scorn and contempt of polytheism, occasionally and purposely altered, by way of derision, the names of the heathen deities.

32 Adrammelech and Anammelech, the gods of Sepharvaim. So they feared the Lord, ʳand made unto themselves of the lowest of them priests of the high places, which sacrificed for them in 33 the houses of the high places. ˢThey feared the Lord, and served their own gods, after the manner of the nations ¹whom 34 they carried away from thence. Unto this day they do after the former manners: they fear not the Lord, neither do they after their statutes, or after their ordinances, or after the law and commandment which the Lord commanded the children of 35 Jacob, ᵗwhom he named Israel; with whom the Lord had made a covenant, and charged them, saying, ᵘYe shall not fear other gods, nor ˣbow yourselves to them, nor serve them, nor sacri- 36 fice to them: but the Lord, who brought you up out of the land of Egypt with great power and ʸa stretched out arm, ᶻhim shall ye fear, and him shall ye worship, and to him shall ye do 37 sacrifice. And the statutes, and the ordinances, and the law, and the commandment, which he wrote for you, ᵃye shall ob- serve to do for evermore; and ye shall not fear other gods. 38 And the covenant that I have made with you ᵇye shall not 39 forget; neither shall ye fear other gods. But the Lord your God ye shall fear; and he shall deliver you out of the hand of 40 all your enemies. Howbeit they did not hearken, but they did 41 after their former manner. ᶜSo these nations feared the Lord, and served their graven images, both their children, and their children's children : as did their fathers, so do they unto this day.

ʳ 1 Kin. 12. 31.

ˢ Zeph. 1. 5.

ᵗ Gen. 32. 28. & 35. 10. 1 Kin. Ⅱ. 31. ᵘ Judg. 6. 10. ˣ Ex. 20. 5. & 34. 15. ʸ Ex. 6. 6. ᶻ Deut. 10. 20.

ᵃ Deut. 5. 32.

ᵇ Deut. 4. 23.

ᶜ ver. 32, 33.

¹ Or, *who carried them away from thence.*

Anammelech is possibly an instance of the same contemptuous play upon words. Adrammelech, "the glorious king," signi- fies the sun. The Assyrian inscriptions com- monly designate *Tsipar*, or Sepharvaim (v. 24), "Sippara of the Sun." The title "Adrammelech" has not yet been found in the inscriptions hitherto; but it would plainly be a fitting epithet of the great luminary. The sun-god of the Babylonians, Shamas, was united at Sippara and elsewhere with a sun-goddess, Anunit, whose name may be represented in the Anammelech of the text. The Hebrews, taking enough of this name to show what they meant, assimi- lated the termination to that of the male deity, thus producing a ridiculous effect, re- garded as insulting to the gods in question. **32.** *of the lowest of them*] Rather, "from all ranks." See marg. ref. note. **33.** Understand the passage thus: "They (the colonists) served their own gods after the manner of the nations from which they (the government) removed them," *i.e.*, after the manner of their own countrymen at home. **34.** *they fear not the Lord*] The new comers in one sense feared Jehovah (*vv.* 33, 41). They acknowledged His name, ad- mitted Him among their gods, and kept up His worship at the high place at Bethel according to the rites instituted by Jero- boam (*v.* 28). But in another sense they did

not fear Him. To acknowledge Jehovah together with other gods is not really to ac- knowledge H m at all. **37.** *which he wrote for you*] It is worth observing here, first, that the author re- gards the whole Law as given to the Israel- ites in a written form; and secondly, that he looks on the real writer as God. **41.** *their graver images*] The Babylonians appear to have made a very sparing use of animal forms among their religious em- blems. They represented the male Sun, Shamas, by a circle, plain or crossed; the female Sun, Anunit, by a six-rayed or eight-rayed star; Nebo by a single wedge or arrow-head, the fundamental element of their writing; the god of the atmosphere by a double or triple thunderbolt. The gods generally were represented under hu- man forms. A few of them had, in addition, animal emblems—the lion, the bull, the eagle, or the serpent; but these seem never to have been set up for worship in temples. There was nothing intentionally grotesque in the Babylonian religion, as there was in the Egyptian and Phœnician. *so do they unto this day*] The mixed wor- ship, the union of professed reverence for Jehovah with the grossest idolatry, con- tinued to the time of the composition of this Book, which must have been as late as B.C. 561, or, at any rate, as late as B.C. 580 (xxv. 27). It did not, however, continue much longer. When the Samaritans wished

CHAP. 18. NOW it came to pass in the third year of Hoshea son of Elah king of Israel, *that* *a*Hezekiah the son of Ahaz king of 2 Judah began to reign. Twenty and five years old was he when he began to reign; and he reigned twenty and nine years in Jerusalem. His mother's name also was *b*Abi, the daughter of 3 Zachariah. And he did *that which was* right in the sight of the 4 LORD, according to all that David his father did. *c*He removed the high places, and brake the [1]images, and cut down the groves, and brake in pieces the *d*brasen serpent that Moses had made: for unto those days the children of Israel did burn incense to it: 5 and he called it [2]Nehushtan. He *e*trusted in the LORD God of Israel; *f*so that after him was none like him among all the 6 kings of Judah, nor *any* that were before him. For he *g*clave to .the LORD, *and* departed not [3]from following him, but kept

[1] Heb. *statues.*   [2] That is, *A piece of brass.*   [3] Heb. *from after him.*

to join the Jews in rebuilding the Temple (about B.C. 537), they showed that inclination to draw nearer to the Jewish cult which henceforth marked their religious progress. Long before the erection of a temple to Jehovah on Mount Gerizim (B.C. 409) they had laid aside all their idolatrous rites, and, admitting the binding authority of the Pentateuch, had taken upon them the observance of the entire Law.

XVIII. The sacred writer, having now completed the history of the joint kingdom, and having cast his glance forward over the religious history of the mixed race which replaced the Israelites in Samaria, proceeds to apply himself uninterruptedly to the remaining history of the Jewish kingdom.

1. *in the third year*] If Hoshea ascended the throne towards the close of the twelfth year of Ahaz (xvii. 1), and if Ahaz reigned not much more than fifteen years (xvi. 2), the first of Hezekiah might synchronise *in part* with Hoshea's third year.

Hezekiah] The name given by our translators follows the Greek form, Ἐζεκίας, rather than the Hebrew, which is *Hizkiah*. Its meaning is "strength of Jehovah."

2. *Twenty and five years old was he*] This statement, combined with that of xvi. 2, would make it necessary that his father Ahaz should have married at the age of ten, and have had a child born to him when he was eleven. This is not impossible; but its improbability is so great, that most commentators suggest a corruption in some of the numbers.

The Zachariah here mentioned was perhaps one of the "faithful witnesses" of Isaiah (viii. 2).

3. *he did that which was right, &c.*] This is said without qualification of only three kings of Judah, Asa (1 K. xv. 11), Hezekiah, and Josiah (2 K. xxii. 2). See some details of Hezekiah's acts at the commencement of his reign in 2 Chr. xxix. &c. It is thought that his reformation was preceded, and perhaps caused, by the prophecy of Micah recorded in Jer. xxvi. 18; Mic. iii. 12.

4. *He removed the high places*] This religious reformation was effected in a violent and tumultuous manner (marg. ref.). The "high places," though forbidden in the Law (Deut. xii. 2–4, 11–14; cp. Lev. xxvi. 30), had practically received the sanction of Samuel (1 Sam. vii. 10; ix. 12–14), David (2 Sam. xv. 32), Solomon (1 K. iii. 4), and others, and had long been the favourite resorts of the mass of the people (see 1 K. iii. 2 note). They were the rural centres for the worship of Jehovah, standing in the place of the later synagogues, and had hitherto been winked at, or rather regarded as legitimate, even by the best kings. Hezekiah's desecration of these time-honoured sanctuaries must have been a rude shock to the feelings of numbers; and indications of the popular discontent may be traced in the appeal of Rab-shakeh (v. 22), and in the strength of the reaction under Manasseh (xxi. 2-9; 2 Chr. xxxiii. 3–17).

the brasen serpent] See marg. ref. Its history from the time when it was set up to the date of Hezekiah's reformation is a blank. The present passage favours the supposition that it had been brought by Solomon from Gibeon and placed in the Temple; for it implies a long continued worship of the serpent by the Israelites generally, and not a mere recent worship of it by the Jews.

and he called it Nehushtan] Rather, "And it was called Nehushtan." The people called it, not "the serpent" (*nachash*), but "the brass," or "the brass thing" (*nechushtan*). Probably they did not like to call it "the serpent," on account of the dark associations which were attached to that reptile (Gen. iii. 1–15; Is. xxvii. 1; Ps. xci. 13; &c).

5. *after him was none like him*] The same is said of Josiah (marg. ref.). The phrase was probably proverbial, and was not taken to mean more than we mean when we say that such and such a king was one of *singular* piety.

6. Other good kings, as Solomon, Jehosh-

7 his commandments, which the LORD commanded Moses. And the LORD *h*was with him; *and* he *i*prospered whithersoever he went forth: and he *k*rebelled against the king of Assyria, and
8 served him not. *l*He smote the Philistines, *even* unto ¹Gaza, and the borders thereof, *m*from the tower of the watchmen to
9 the fenced city. ¶And *n*it came to pass in the fourth year of king Hezekiah, which *was* the seventh year of Hoshea son of Elah king of Israel, *that* Shalmaneser king of Assyria came up
10 against Samaria, and besieged it. And at the end of three years they took it: *even* in the sixth year of Hezekiah, that *is* *o*the
11 ninth year of Hoshea king of Israel, Samaria was taken. *p*And the king of Assyria did carry away Israel unto Assyria, and put them *q*in Halah and in Habor *by* the river of Gozan, and in the
12 cities of the Medes: *r*because they obeyed not the voice of the LORD their God, but transgressed his covenant, *and* all that Moses the servant of the LORD commanded, and would not hear
13 *them*, nor do *them*. ¶Now *s*in the fourteenth year of king Hezekiah did ²Sennacherib king of Assyria come up against all
14 the fenced cities of Judah, and took them. And Hezekiah king of Judah sent to the king of Assyria to Lachish, saying, I have

h 2Sam.5.10.
i 1 Sam. 18.
5, 14.
Ps. 60. 12.
k ch. 16. 7.
l 1 Chr. 4.41.
Isai. 14. 29.
m ch. 17. 9.
n ch. 17. 3.

o ch. 17. 6.
p ch. 17. 6.

q 1 Chr. 5.26.
r ch. 17. 7.
Dan. 9. 6, 10.

s 2 Chr. 32.
1, &c.
Isai. 36. 1,
&c.

¹ Heb. *Azzah.* ² Heb. *Sanherib.*

---

aphat, Joash, and Amaziah, had fallen away in their later years. Hezekiah remained firm to the last. The phrase "cleaving to God" is frequent in Deuteronomy, but rare elsewhere.

7. *the* LORD *was with him*] This had been said of no king since David (marg. ref.). The phrase is very emphatic. The general prosperity of Hezekiah is set forth at some length by the author of Chronicles (2 Chr. xxxii. 23, 27-29). His great influence among the nations bordering on the northern kingdom, was the cause of the first expedition of Sennacherib against him, the Ekronites having expelled an Assyrian viceroy from their city, and delivered him to Hezekiah for safe keeping: an expedition which did not very long precede that of *v.* 13, which fell towards the close of Hezekiah's long reign.

8. Sargon had established the complete dominion of Assyria over the Philistines. Hence the object of Hezekiah's Philistine campaign was not so much conquest as opposition to the Assyrian power. How successful it was is indicated in the Assyrian records by the number of towns in this quarter which Sennacherib recovered before he proceeded against Jerusalem.

9-12. These verses repeat the account given in the marg. ref. The extreme importance of the event may account for the double insertion.

13. *in the fourteenth year*] This note of time, which places the invasion of Sennacherib eight years only after the capture of Samaria, is hopelessly at variance with the Assyrian dates for the two events, the first of which falls into the first of Sargon, and the second into the fourth of Sennacherib,

twenty-one years later. We have therefore to choose between an entire rejection of the Assyrian chronological data, and an emendation of the present passage. Of the emendations proposed the simplest is to remove the note of time altogether, regarding it as having crept in from the margin.

Sennacherib] This is the Greek form of the Sinakhirib of the inscriptions, the son of Sargon, and his immediate successor in the monarchy. The death of Sargon (B.C. 705) had been followed by a number of revolts. Hezekiah also rebelled, invaded Philistia, and helped the national party in that country to throw off the Assyrian yoke.

From Sennacherib's inscriptions we learn that, having reduced Phœnicia, recovered Ascalon, and defeated an army of Egyptians and Ethiopians at Ekron, he marched against Jerusalem.

the fenced cities] Sennacherib reckons the number taken by him at "forty-six." He seems to have captured on his way to the Holy City a vast number of small towns and villages, whose inhabitants he carried off to the number of 200,000. Cp. Is. xxiv. 1-12. The ground occupied by his main host outside the modern Damascus gate was thenceforth known to the Jews as "the camp of the Assyrians." Details connected with the siege may be gathered from Isai. xxii. and Chronicles (marg. ref. *s*). After a while Hezekiah resolved on submission. Sennacherib (*v.* 14) had left his army to continue the siege, and gone in person to Lachish. The Jewish monarch sent his embassy to that town.

14. *return from me*] Or "retire from me," *i.e.*, "withdraw thy troops."

offended; return from me : that which thou puttest on me will I bear. And the king of Assyria appointed unto Hezekiah king of Judah three hundred talents of silver and thirty talents of

t ch. 16. 8. 15 gold. And Hezekiah *t*gave *him* all the silver that was found in the house of the LORD, and in the treasures of the king's house.

16 At that time did Hezekiah cut off *the gold from* the doors of the temple of the LORD, and *from* the pillars which Hezekiah king of Judah had overlaid, and gave ¹it to the king of Assyria.

17 ¶ And the king of Assyria sent Tartan and Rabsaris and Rab-shakeh from Lachish to king Hezekiah with a ²great host against Jerusalem. And they went up and came to Jerusalem. And when they were come up, they came and stood by the con-

u Isai. 7. 3 duit of the upper pool, *u*which *is* in the highway of the fuller's 18 field. And when they had called to the king, there came out to them Eliakim the son of Hilkiah, which *was* over the household, and Shebna the ³scribe, and Joah the son of Asaph the recorder.

19 ¶ And Rab-shakeh said unto them, Speak ye now to Hezekiah,

x 2 Chr. 32. 10, &c. Thus saith the great king, the king of Assyria, *x*What confidence 20 *is* this wherein thou trustest? Thou ⁴sayest, (but *they are but* ⁵vain words,) ⁶*I have* counsel and strength for the war. Now on

---

¹ Heb. *them.*	³ Or, *secretary.*	⁶ Or, *But counsel and*
² Heb. *heavy.*	⁴ Or, *talkest.*	*strength* are *for the war.*
	⁵ Heb. *word of the l'ps.*	

---

three hundred talents, &c.] According to Sennacherib's own account, the terms of peace were as follows :—(1) A money payment to the amount of 800 talents of silver and 30 talents of gold. (2) The surrender of the Ekronite king. (3) A cession of territory towards the west and the south-west, which was apportioned between the kings of Ekron, Ashdod, and Gaza.

16. Ahaz had already exhausted the treasuries (xvi. 8) ; Hezekiah was therefore compelled to undo his own work.

17. An interval of time must be placed between this verse and the last. Sennacherib, content with his successes, had returned to Nineveh with his spoil and his numerous captives. Hezekiah, left to himself, repented of his submission, and commenced negotiations with Egypt (*vv.* 21, 24; Isai. xxx. 2–6, xxxi. 1), which implied treason against his Assyrian suzerain. It was under these circumstances that Sennacherib appears to have made his second expedition into Palestine very soon after the first. Following the usual coast route he passed through Philistia on his way to Egypt, leaving Jerusalem on one side, despising so puny a state, and knowing that the submission of Egypt would involve that of her hangers-on. While, however, he was besieging Lachish on his way to encounter his main enemy, he determined to try the temper of the Jews by means of an embassy, which he accordingly sent.

Tartan and Rabsaris and Rab-shakeh] None of these are proper names. "Tartan" was the ordinary title of an Assyrian general ; "Rab-saris" is "chief eunuch," always a high officer of the Assyrian court ;

Rab-shakeh is probably "chief cup-bearer."

by the conduit of the upper pool] Possibly a conduit on the north side of the city, near the "camp of the Assyrians." The spot was the same as that on which Isaiah had met Ahaz (Isai. vii. 3).

18. *when they had called to the king*] The ambassadors summoned Hezekiah, as if their rank were equal to his. Careful of his dignity, he responds by sending officers of his court.

Eliakim…which was over the household] Eliakim had been promoted to fill the place of Shebna (Isai. xxii. 20–22). He was a man of very high character. The comptroller of the household, whose position (1 K. iv. 6) must have been a subordinate one in the time of Solomon, appears to have now become the chief minister of the crown. On the "scribe" or secretary, and the "recorder," see 1 K. iv. 3 note.

19. The Rab-shakeh, the *third* in rank of the three Assyrian ambassadors, probably took the prominent part in the conference because he could speak Hebrew (*v.* 26), whereas the Tartan and the Rabsaris could not do so.

the great king] This title of the monarchs of Assyria is found in use as early as B.C. 1120. Like the title, "king of kings," the distinctive epithet "great" served to mark emphatically the vast difference between the numerous vassal monarchs and the suzerain of whom they held their crowns.

20. Hezekiah no doubt believed that in the "counsel" of Eliakim and Isaiah, and in the "strength" promised him by Egypt, he had resources which justified him in provoking a war.

21 whom dost thou trust, that thou rebellest against me? *Now, *Ezek. 29.
behold, thou ¹trustest upon the staff of this bruised reed, *even* 6, 7.
upon Egypt, on which if a man lean, it will go into his hand,
and pierce it: so *is* Pharaoh king of Egypt unto all that trust
22 on him. But if ye say unto me, We trust in the LORD our God:
is not that he, *whose high places and whose altars Hezekiah *ver. 4.
hath taken away, and hath said to Judah and Jerusalem, Ye 2 Chr. 31. 1.
23 shall worship before this altar in Jerusalem? Now therefore, I & 32. 12.
pray thee, give ²pledges to my lord the king of Assyria, and I
will deliver thee two thousand horses, if thou be able on thy
24 part to set riders upon them. How then wilt thou turn away
the face of one captain of the least of my master's servants, and
25 put thy trust on Egypt for chariots and for horsemen? Am I
now come up without the LORD against this place to destroy it?
The LORD said to me, Go up against this land, and destroy it.
26 ¶Then said Eliakim the son of Hilkiah, and Shebna, and Joah,
unto Rab-shakeh, Speak, I pray thee, to thy servants in the
Syrian language; for we understand *it*: and talk not with us
in the Jews' language in the ears of the people that *are* on the
27 wall. But Rab-shakeh said unto them, Hath my master sent
me to thy master, and to thee, to speak these words? *hath he*
not *sent me* to the men which sit on the wall, that they may eat
28 their own dung, and drink ³their own piss with you? Then
Rab-shakeh stood and cried with a loud voice in the Jews' language, and spake, saying, Hear the word of the great king, the
29 king of Assyria: thus saith the king, *Let not Hezekiah deceive *a 2 Chr. 32.
you: for he shall not be able to deliver you out of his hand: 15.
30 neither let Hezekiah make you trust in the LORD, saying, The
LORD will surely deliver us, and this city shall not be delivered

¹ Heb. *trustest thee.*   ² Or, *hostages.*   ³ Heb. *the water of their feet.*

---

vain words] Lit. as in marg., *i.e.* a *mere*
word, to which the facts do not correspond.

21. *this bruised reed*] The "tall reed of
the Nile bulrush" fitly symbolised the land
where it grew. Apparently strong and firm,
it was quite unworthy of trust. Let a man
lean upon it, and the rotten support instantly gave way, wounding the hand that
stayed itself so insecurely. So it was with
Egypt throughout the whole period of
Jewish history (cp. xvii. 4-6). Her actual
practice was to pretend friendship, to hold
out hopes of support, and then to fail in
time of need.

22. The destruction of numerous shrines
and altars where Jehovah had been worshipped (*v.* 4) seemed to the Rab-shakeh
conduct calculated not to secure the favour,
but to call forth the anger, of the god. At
any rate, it was conduct which he knew
had been distasteful to many of Hezekiah's
subjects.

23. The phrase translated "give pledges,"
or "hostages" (marg.) may perhaps be
best understood as meaning "make an agreement." If you will "bind yourself to find
the riders" (*i.e.* trained horsemen), we will
"bind ourselves to furnish the horses."
The suggestion implied that in all Judæa

there were not 2000 men accustomed to
serve as cavalry.

25. The Rab-shakeh probably tries the
effect of a bold assertion, which had no
basis of fact to rest upon.

26. *the Syrian language*] *i.e.* Aramaic;
probably the dialect of Damascus, a Semitic
language nearly akin to their own, but suff-
ciently different to be unintelligible to ordinary Jews

the people that are on the wall] The conference must have been held immediately
outside the wall for the words of the speakers
to have been audible.

27. *that they may eat, &c.*] "My master
hath sent me," the Rab-shakeh seems to
say, "to these men, whom I see stationed
on the wall to defend the place and bear
the last extremities of a prolonged siege—
these men on whom its worst evils will fall,
and who have therefore the greatest interest
in avoiding it by a timely surrender." He
expresses the evils by a strong coarse
phrase, suited to the rude soldiery, and
well calculated to rouse their feelings. The
author of Chronicles has softened down the
words (2 Chr. xxxii. 11).

29, 30. There were two grounds, and two
only, on which Hezekiah could rest his
refusal to surrender, (1) ability to resist by

31 into the hand of the king of Assyria. Hearken not to Hezekiah: for thus saith the king of Assyria, [12]Make *an agreement* with me by a present, and come out to me, and *then* eat ye every man of his own vine, and every one of his fig tree, and drink ye 32 every one the waters of his [3]cistern: until I come and take you

b Deut. 8.7,8.

away to a land like your own land, [b]a land of corn and wine, a land of bread and vineyards, a land of oil olive and of honey, that ye may live, and not die: and hearken not unto Hezekiah, when he [4]persuadeth you, saying, The LORD will deliver us.

c ch. 19. 12.
2 Chr. 32. 14.
Isai. 10. 10, 11.
d ch. 19. 13.
e ch. 17. 24,
Ava?
f Dan. 3. 15.

33 [c]Hath any of the gods of the nations delivered at all his land out 34 of the hand of the king of Assyria? [d]Where *are* the gods of Hamath, and of Arpad? where *are* the gods of Sepharvaim, Hena, and [e]Ivah? have they delivered Samaria out of mine 35 hand? Who *are* they among all the gods of the countries, that have delivered their country out of mine hand, [f]that the LORD 36 should deliver Jerusalem out of mine hand? ¶ But the people held their peace, and answered him not a word: for the king's 37 commandment was, saying, Answer him not. Then came Eliakim the son of Hilkiah, which *was* over the household, and Shebna the scribe, and Joah the son of Asaph the recorder, to

g Isai. 33. 7.
a Isai. 37. 1, &c.

Hezekiah [g]with *their* clothes rent, and told him the words of 19 Rab-shakeh. AND [a]it came to pass, when king Hezekiah heard *it*, that he rent his clothes, and covered himself with sack-2 cloth, and went into the house of the LORD. And he sent Eliakim, which *was* over the household, and Shebna the scribe,

b Luke 3, 4, called *Esaias*.

and the elders of the priests, covered with sackcloth, to [b]Isaiah

---

[1] Or, *Seek my favour.*
[2] Heb. *Make with me a*

blessing, Gen. 32. 20. &
33. 11. Prov. 18. 16.

[3] Or, *pit.*
[4] Or, *deceiveth.*

---

his own natural military strength and that of his allies; and (2) expectation based upon the language of Isaiah (xxx. 31, xxxi. 4–9), of supernatural assistance from Jehovah. The Rab-shakeh argues that both grounds of confidence are equally fallacious.

31. *Make an agreement,* &c.] Rather, "Make peace with me." The word, which primarily means "blessing," and secondarily "a gift," has also the meaning, though more rarely, of "peace." Probably it acquired this meaning from the fact that a peace was commonly purchased by presents.

eat...drink] A picture of a time of quiet and prosperity, a time when each man might enjoy the fruits of his land, without any fear of the spoiler's violence. The words are in contrast with the latter part of *v.* 27.

cistern] Rather, "well" (Deut. vi. 11). Each cultivator in Palestine has a "well" dug in some part of his ground, from which he draws water for his own use. "Cisterns," or reservoirs for rain-water, are comparatively rare.

33. The boast is natural. The Assyrians had had an uninterrupted career of success, and might well believe that their gods were more powerful than those of the nations with whom they had warred. It is not surprising that they did not understand that their successes hitherto had been allowed by the very God, Jehovah, against Whom they were now boasting themselves.

34. Arpad was situated somewhere in southern Syria; but it is impossible to fix its exact position. Sargon mentions it in an inscription as joining with Hamath in an act of rebellion, which he chastised. It was probably the capture and destruction of these two cities on this occasion which caused them to be mentioned together here (and in xix. 13, and again in Isaiah x. 9). Sennacherib adduces late examples of the inability of the nations' gods to protect their cities. On the other cities mentioned in this verse, see xvii. 24 notes.

XIX. 1. Hezekiah, like his officers, probably rent his clothes on account of Rab-shakeh's blasphemies: and he put on sackcloth in self-humiliation and in grief. The only hope left was in Jehovah; for Egypt could not be trusted to effect anything of importance. Rab-shakeh's boldness had told upon Hezekiah. He was dispirited and dejected. He perhaps began to doubt whether he had done right in yielding to the bolder counsels of Eliakim and Isaiah. He had not lost his faith in God; but his faith was being severely tried. He wisely went and strove by prayer to strengthen it.

2. Isaiah is here for the first time introduced into the history. His own writings show us how active a part he had taken in it for many years previously. This was the fourth reign since he began his prophesyings; and during two reigns at least, those

3 the prophet the son of Amoz. And they said unto him, Thus
saith Hezekiah, This day *is* a day of trouble, and of rebuke, and
¹blasphemy : for the children are come to the birth, and *there is*
4 not strength to bring forth. ᶜIt may be the LORD thy God
will hear all the words of Rab-shakeh, ᵈwhom the king of
Assyria his master hath sent to reproach the living God ; and
will ᵉreprove the words which the LORD thy God hath heard :
wherefore lift up *thy* prayer for the remnant that are ²left.
5, 6 ¶ So the servants of king Hezekiah came to Isaiah. ᶠAnd Isaiah
said unto them, Thus shall ye say to your master, Thus saith
the LORD, Be not afraid of the words which thou hast heard,
with which the ᵍservants of the king of Assyria have blasphemed
7 me. Behold, I will send ʰa blast upon him, and he shall hear
a rumour, and shall return to his own land ; and I will cause
8 him to fall by the sword in his own land. ¶ So Rab-shakeh returned, and found the king of Assyria warring against Libnah :
9 for he had heard that he was departed ⁱfrom Lachish. And
ᵏwhen he heard say of Tirhakah king of Ethiopia, Behold, he is
come out to fight against thee : he sent messengers again unto
10 Hezekiah, saying, Thus shall ye speak to Hezekiah king of
Judah, saying, Let not thy God ˡin whom thou trustest deceive
thee, saying, Jerusalem shall not be delivered into the hand of
11 the king of Assyria. Behold, thou hast heard what the kings
of Assyria have done to all lands, by destroying them utterly :

ᶜ 2 Sam. 16.
12.
ᵈ ch. 18. 35.

ᵉ Ps. 50. 21.

ᶠ Isai. 37. 6,
&c.

ᵍ ch. 18. 17.

ʰ ver. 35, 36,
37.
Jer. 51. 1.

ⁱ ch. 18. 14.
ᵏ See 1 Sam.
23. 27.

ˡ ch. 18. 5.

¹ Or, *provocation.*   ² Heb. *found.*

---

of Ahaz and Hezekiah, he had been a
familiar counsellor of the monarch. He
had probably counselled the revolt from
Assyria, and had encouraged the king and
people to persevere in their resistance. The
exact date of prophecies can seldom be
fixed with any certainty ; but we can
scarcely be mistaken in regarding chs. x.
xxx. and xxxi. as written about the time of
Hezekiah's second revolt.

3. The "trouble" consisted in "rebuke"
(rather, "**chastisement**,") for sins at the
hand of God, and "blasphemy" (rather,
"**reproach**,") at the hands of man.

the children, &c.] *i.e.* "we are in a fearful
extremity—at the last gasp—and lack the
strength that might carry us through the
danger."

4. *will hear*] *i.e.* "will show that he has
heard—will notice and punish."

the living God] See 1 Sam. xvii. 26 note.

and will reprove the words] Rather, "will
reprove **him for** the words."

the remnant] *i.e.* for the kingdom of
Judah, the only remnant of God's people
that was now left, after Galilee and Gilead
and Samaria had all been carried away
captive.

7. *I will send a blast upon him*] Rather,
"I will **put a spirit in** him "—*i.e.* "I will
take from him his present pride and will
put in him a new spirit, a spirit of craven
fear." Men shall tell him of the destruction that has come upon his host (*v.* 35), and
he shall straightway return, &c.

8. On Lachish and Libnah, see Josh. x. 3,
29 notes. The phrase, "he was departed
from Lachish" is suggestive of successful
resistance.

9. *Tirhakah king of Ethiopia*] The *Tehrak*
or *Teharka* of the hieroglyphics. He was
the last king of the 25th or Ethiopian
dynasty, which commenced with Shebek or
Sabaco, and he reigned upwards of 26 years.
The Assyrian inscriptions show that he still
ruled in Egypt as late as B.C. 667, when
Esarhaddon (*v.* 37) died, and his son Asshur-
bani-pal succeeded him. He probably ascended the Egyptian throne about B.C. 692,
having previously ruled over Ethiopia before
he became king of Egypt (cp. Isai. xxxvii. 9).
Thus he was probably reigning in Ethiopia
at the time of Sennacherib's expedition, while
Sethos and perhaps other secondary monarchs bore rule over Egypt. His movements
caused Sennacherib to send a second embassy,
instead of marching in person against the
Jewish king.

11. *all lands*] This boast is in strict accordance with the general tenor of the
Assyrian inscriptions. Hyperbole is the
general language of the East ; but in this
instance it was not so extreme as in some
others. The Assyrians under Sargon and
Sennacherib had enjoyed an uninterrupted
series of military successes : they had succeeded in establishing their pre-eminence
from the Median desert to the banks of the
Nile, and from the shores of Lake Van to
those of the Persian Gulf.

m ch. 18. 33.

n Ezek. 27. 23.
o ch. 18. 34.

p Isai. 37. 14, &c.

q 1 Sam. 4.4.
Ps. 80. 1.
r 1 Kin. 18. 39.
Isai. 44. 6.
Jer. 10. 10, 11, 12.
s Ps. 31. 2.
t 2 Chr. 6. 40.
u ver. 4.

x Ps. 115. 4.
Jer. 10. 3.

y Ps. 83. 18.

z Isai. 37. 21, &c.
a Ps. 65. 2.

12 and shalt thou be delivered? ^mHave the gods of the nations delivered them which my fathers have destroyed; as Gozan, and Haran, and Rezeph, and the children of ⁿEden which were 13 in Thelasar? ^oWhere is the king of Hamath, and the king of Arpad, and the king of the city of Sepharvaim, of Hena, and 14 Ivah? ¶^pAnd Hezekiah received the letter of the hand of the messengers, and read it: and Hezekiah went up into the house 15 of the LORD, and spread it before the LORD. And Hezekiah prayed before the LORD, and said, O LORD God of Israel, ^qwhich dwellest between the cherubims, ^rthou art the God, even thou alone, of all the kingdoms of the earth; thou hast made heaven 16 and earth. LORD, ^sbow down thine ear, and hear: ^topen, LORD, thine eyes, and see: and hear the words of Sennacherib, ^uwhich 17 hath sent him to reproach the living God. Of a truth, LORD, the kings of Assyria have destroyed the nations and their lands, 18 and have ¹cast their gods into the fire: for they were no gods, but ^xthe work of men's hands, wood and stone: therefore they 19 have destroyed them. Now therefore, O LORD our God, I beseech thee, save thou us out of his hand, ^ythat all the kingdoms of the earth may know that thou art the LORD God, even thou 20 only. ¶Then Isaiah the son of Amoz sent to Hezekiah, saying, Thus saith the LORD God of Israel, ^zThat which thou hast prayed to me against Sennacherib king of Assyria ^aI have heard. 21 This is the word that the LORD hath spoken concerning him;

¹ Heb. given.

12. Haran] Harrán, the Carrhæ of the Greeks and Romans (Gen. xi. 31), was among the earliest conquests of the Assyrians; being subject to them from the 12th century. Its conquest would have naturally followed that of Gozan (Gauzanitis, xvii. 6), which lay between it and Assyria proper.

Rezeph] Probably the Rozappa of the Assyrian inscriptions, a city in the neighbourhood of Haran.

the children of Eden] Or, "the Beni-Eden," who appear from the Assyrian inscriptions to have inhabited the country on the east bank of the Euphrates, about the modern Balis. Here they had a city called Beth-Adina, taken by the Assyrians about B.C. 880. This is probably the "Eden" of marg. ref.

Thelasar] Or Telassar. Probably a city on the Euphrates, near Beth-Adina, called after the name of the god Asshur. The name would signify "the Hill of Asshur."

13. Cp. marg. ref. xvii. 24. Verse 12 refers to former Assyrian successes, verse 13 to comparatively recent ones.

14. Hezekiah received the letter] The inscriptions show that scribes accompanied the Assyrian armies, with the materials of their craft, so that such a dispatch might be easily drawn up. As Hezekiah himself "read" it, we may presume that it was in the Hebrew tongue.

15. which dwellest between the cherubims] The reference is to the shechinah, or miraculous glory, which from time to time appeared above the Mercy-seat from between the two Cherubims, whose wings over-

shadowed the Ark of the Covenant (1 K. vi. 23-27; cp. Ex. xxv. 22; Lev. xvi. 2, &c.).

thou art the God, even thou alone] This is the protest of the pure theist against the intense polytheism of Sennacherib's letter, which assumes that gods are only gods of particular nations, and that Hezekiah's God is but one out of an indefinite number, no stronger or more formidable than the rest.

18. have cast their gods into the fire] In general the Assyrians carried off the images of the gods from the temples of the conquered nations, and deposited them in their own shrines, as at once trophies of victory and proof of the superiority of the Assyrian deities over those of their enemies. But sometimes the gods are said to have been "destroyed" or "burnt with fire;" which was probably done when the idols were of rude workmanship or coarse material; and when it was inconvenient to encumber an army with spoils so weighty and difficult of transport.

19. If the mighty army of the great Assyrian king were successfully defied by a petty monarch like Hezekiah, it would force the surrounding nations to confess that the escape was owing to the protecting hand of Jehovah. They would thus be taught, in spite of themselves, that He, and He alone, was the true God.

21. concerning him] i.e. "concerning Sennacherib." Verses 21-28 are addressed to the great Assyrian monarch himself, and are God's reply to his proud boastings.

The virgin, the daughter of Zion] Rather, "the virgin daughter, Zion." Zion, the

The virgin *b*the daughter of Zion hath despised thee, *and* *b* Is. 23. 10.
laughed thee to scorn ;   Lam. 2. 13.
The daughter of Jerusalem *c*hath shaken her head at thee.   *c* Job 16. 4.

22 Whom hast thou reproached and blasphemed?   Ps. 22. 7, 8.
And against whom hast thou exalted *thy* voice,   Lam. 2. 15.
And lifted up thine eyes on high?
Even against *d*the Holy *One* of Israel.   *d* Isai. 5. 24.

23 1*e*By thy messengers thou hast reproached the LORD, and *e* ch. 18. 17.
hast said,
*f*With the multitude of my chariots I am come up to the *f* Ps. 20. 7.
height of the mountains, to the sides of Lebanon,
And will cut down 2the tall cedar trees thereof, *and* the choice
fir trees thereof :
And I will enter into the lodgings of his borders, *and into*
3the forest of his Carmel.

24 I have digged and drunk strange waters,
And with the sole of my feet have I dried up all the rivers
of 4besieged places.

25 ¶ 5Hast thou not heard long ago *how* *g*I have done it,   *g* Isai. 45. 7.

1 Heb. *By the hand of.*
2 Heb. *the tallness, &c.*
3 Or, *the forest* and *his fruitful field*, Isai. 10. 18.

4 Or, *fenced.*
5 Or, *Hast thou not heard how I have made it long ago, and formed it of*

ancient times? should I now bring it to be laid waste, and *fenced cities to be ruinous heaps?*

holy eastern city, is here distinguished from Jerusalem, the western one, and is given the remarkable epithet "virgin," which is not applied to her sister ; probably because the true Zion, the city of David, had remained inviolable from David's time, having never been entered by an enemy. Jerusalem, on the other hand, had been taken, both by Shishak (1 K. xiv. 26) and by Jehoash (xiv. 13). The personification of cities as females is a common figure (cp. marg. reff.).

hath shaken her head at thee] This was a gesture of scorn with the Hebrews (cp. marg. reff.; Matt. xxvii. 39).

22. *the Holy One of Israel*] This is a favourite phrase with Isaiah, in whose prophecies it is found twenty-seven times, while it occurs five times only in the rest of Scripture (Pss. lxxi. 22, lxxviii. 41, lxxxix. 18; Jer. l. 29, li. 5). Its occurrence here is a strong proof—one among many—of the genuineness of the present passage, which is not the composition of the writer of Kings, but an actual prophecy delivered at this time by Isaiah.

23. *and hast said*] Isaiah clothes in words the thoughts of Sennacherib's heart — thoughts of the extremest self-confidence. Cp. Isai. x. 7-14, where, probably at an earlier date, the same overweening pride is ascribed to this king.

with the multitude of my chariots] There are two readings here, which give, however, nearly the same sense. The more difficult and more poetical of the two is to be preferred. Literally translated it runs — "With **chariots upon** chariots am I come up, &c."

to the sides of Lebanon] "Lebanon," with

its "cedars" and its "fir-trees," is to be understood here both literally and figuratively. Literally, the hewing of timber in Lebanon was an ordinary feature of an Assyrian expedition into Syria. Figuratively, the mountain represents all the more inaccessible parts of Palestine, and the destruction of its firs and cedars denotes the complete devastation of the entire country from one end to the other.

the lodgings of his borders] Lit., "the lodge of its (Lebanon's) end ;" either an actual habitation situated on the highest point of the mountain-range, or a poetical periphrasis for the highest point itself.

the forest of his Carmel] Or, "the forest of its garden"—*i.e.* "its forest which is like a garden," &c.

24. *have digged and drunk ... and dried up*] The meaning seems to be—"Mountains do not stop me—I cross them even in my chariots. Deserts do not stop me—I dig wells there, and drink the water. Rivers do not stop me—I pass them as easily as if they were dry land."

the rivers of besieged places] Rather, "the rivers of **Egypt**." The singular form, *Mazor* (compare the modern *Misr* and the Assyrian *Muzr*), is here used instead of the ordinary dual form, *Mizraim*, perhaps because "Lower Egypt" only is intended. This was so cut up with canals and branches of the Nile, natural and artificial, that it was regarded as impassable for chariots and horses. Sennacherib, however, thought that these many streams would prove no impediments to him ; he would advance as fast as if they were "dried up."

25. *Hast thou not heard long ago, &c.*]

And of ancient times that I have formed it ?
Now have I brought it to pass,

h Isai. 10. 5.

That *h* thou shouldest be to lay waste fenced cities *into* ruinous heaps.

26   Therefore their inhabitants were ¹of small power,
They were dismayed and confounded ;
They were *as* the grass of the field, and *as* the green herb,

i Ps. 129. 6.

As *i* the grass on the house tops, and *as corn* blasted before it be grown up.

k Ps. 139. 1, &c.

27   But *k* I know thy ²abode,
And thy going out, and thy coming in,
And thy rage against me.

28   Because thy rage against me and thy tumult is come up into mine ears,

l Job 41. 2.
Ezek. 29. 4.
& 38. 4.
Amos 4. 2.
m ver. 33,
36, 37.
n 1 Sam. 2. 34.
ch. 20. 8, 9.
Isai. 7. 11,
14.
Luke 2. 12.

Therefore *l* I will put my hook in thy nose, and my bridle in thy lips,
And I will turn thee back *m* by the way by which thou camest.

29   ¶ And this *shall be* *n* a sign unto thee,
Ye shall eat this year such things as grow of themselves,
And in the second year that which springeth of the same ;
And in the third year sow ye, and reap,
And plant vineyards, and eat the fruits thereof.

o 2 Chr. 32. 22, 23.

30   *o* And ³the remnant that is escaped of the house of Judah
Shall yet again take root downward, and bear fruit upward.

31   For out of Jerusalem shall go forth a remnant,
And ⁴they that escape out of Mount Zion :

p Isai. 9. 7.

p The zeal of the LORD *of hosts* shall do this.

---

¹ Heb. *short of hand.*   ³ Heb. *the escaping of the house*   ⁴ Heb. *the escaping.*
² Or, *sitting.*   *of Judah that remaineth.*

Rather, " Hast thou not heard, **that from long ago I did** this, from ancient times I fashioned it ? &c." The former part of the verse refers to the secret Divine decrees, whereby the affairs of this world are determined and ordered from the very beginning of things. Sennacherib's boasting, however, proved that he did not know this, that he did not recognise himself simply as God's instrument—" the rod of His anger" (Isai. x. 5)—but regarded his victories as gained by his own " strength and wisdom" (do. r. 13).

26. The weakness of the nations exposed to the Assyrian attacks was as much owing to the Divine decrees as was the strength of the Assyrians themselves.

the grass on the house tops] Cp. marg. ref. The vegetation on the flat roofs of Oriental houses is the first to spring up and the first to fade away.

27. See 1 K. iii. 7 note.

28. *thy tumult*] Rather, "thy **arrogance.**"

I will put my hook in thy nose] Rather, " my **ring.**" The sculptures show that the kings of Babylon and Assyria were in the habit of actually passing a ring through the flesh of their more distinguished prisoners,

of attaching a thong or a rope to it, and of thus leading them about as with a "bridle." In Assyria the ring was, at least ordinarily, passed through the lower lip ; while in Babylonia it appears to have been inserted into the membrane of the *nose*. Thus Sennacherib would be here threatened with a punishment which he was perhaps in the habit of inflicting.

29. The prophet now once more addresses Hezekiah, and gives him a "sign," or token, whereby he and his may be assured that Sennacherib is indeed bridled, and will not trouble Judæa any more. It was a sign of the continued freedom of the land from attack during the whole of the remainder of Sennacherib's reign—a space of seventeen years.

30. *the remnant that is escaped*] Terrible ravages seem to have been committed in the first attack (xviii. 13 note). And though the second invasion was comparatively harmless, yet it probably fell heavily on the cities of the west and the south-west. Thus the "escaped " were but "a remnant."

bear fruit upward] The flourishing time of Josiah is the special fulfilment of this prophecy (xxiii. 15-20).

32   ¶ Therefore thus saith the LORD concerning the king of As-
      syria, He shall not come into this city, nor shoot an
      arrow there,
      Nor come before it with shield, nor cast a bank against it.
33   By the way that he came, by the same shall he return,
      And shall not come into this city, saith the LORD.
34   For ^qI will defend this city, to save it,   ^q ch. 20. 6.
      For mine own sake, and ^rfor my servant David's sake.   ^r 1 Kin. 11.
35   ¶ And ^sit came to pass that night, that the angel of the LORD   12, 13.
      went out, and smote in the camp of the Assyrians an hundred   ^s 2Chr.32.21.
      fourscore and five thousand : and when they arose early in the   Isai. 37. 36.
36   morning, behold, they *were* all dead corpses. So Sennacherib
      king of Assyria departed, and went and returned, and dwelt at

---

32. *nor come before it with shield*] The
"shields" of the Assyrians are very conspicuous in the sculptures, and were of great
importance in a siege, since the assailing
archers were in most instances defended, as
they shot their weapons, by a comrade,
who held before himself and his friend a
shield of an enormous size. It was made
of a framework of wood, filled in with
wattling, and perhaps lined with skin ; it
was rested upon the ground, and it generally curved backward towards the top ;
ordinarily it somewhat exceeded the height
of a man. From the safe covert afforded
by these large defences the archers were
able to take deliberate aim, and deliver
their volleys with effect.

nor cast a bank against it] "Mounds " or
"banks " were among the most common of
the means used by the Assyrians against a
besieged town. They were thrown up
against the walls, and consisted of loose
earth, trees, brushwood, stones, and rubbish. Sometimes the surface of the mound
was regularly paved with several layers of
stone or brick, which formed a solid road or
causeway capable of bearing a great weight.
The intention was not so much to bring the
mounds to a level with the top of the walls,
as to carry them to such a height as should
enable the battering-ram to work effectively.
Walls were made very solid towards their
base, for the purpose of resisting the ram ;
half-way up their structure was comparatively weak and slight. The engines of the
assailants, rams and catapults, where therefore far more serviceable if they could
attack the upper and weaker portion of the
defences ; and it was to enable them to
reach these portions that the "mounds "
were raised.

33. *By the way that he came*] *i.e.* through
the low country of the Shephelah, thus
avoiding not only Jerusalem, but even
Judæa.

34. *for mine own sake*] God's honour was
concerned to defend His own city against
one who denied His power in direct terms,
as did Sennacherib (xviii. 35, xix. 10–12).
His faithfulness was also concerned to keep

the promise made to David (Ps. cxxxii.
12-18).

35. *the camp of the Assyrians*] Which
was now moved to Pelusium, if we may
trust Herodotus ; or which, at any rate,
was at some considerable distance from
Jerusalem.

*when they arose early in the morning, be-
hold*, &c.] These words form the only trustworthy data that we possess for determining
to any extent the *manner* of the destruction
now wrought. They imply that there was
no disturbance during the night, no alarm,
no knowledge on the part of the living that
their comrades were dying all around them
by thousands. All mere natural causes
must be rejected, and God must be regarded as having slain the men in their
sleep without causing disturbance, either
by pestilence or by that "visitation " of
which English Law speaks. The most
nearly parallel case is the destruction of
the first-born (Ex. xii. 29).

The Egyptian version of this event recorded in Herodotus is that, during the
night, silently and secretly, an innumerable
multitude of field-mice spread themselves
through the Assyrian host, and gnawed
their quivers, bows, and shield-straps, so as
to render them useless. When morning
broke, the Assyrians fled hastily, and the
Egyptians pursuing put a vast number to
the sword.

36. *dwelt at Nineveh*] The meaning is
not that Sennacherib made no more expeditions at all, which would be untrue, for
his annals show us that he warred in Armenia, Babylonia, Susiana, and Cilicia,
during his later years ; but that he confined
himself to his own part of Asia, and did not
invade Palestine or threaten Jerusalem any
more. Nineveh, marked by some ruins
opposite Mosul, appears here unmistakably
as the Assyrian capital, which it became towards the close of the ninth century B.C.
It has previously been mentioned only in
Genesis (marg. ref.). Sennacherib was the
first king who made it his permanent residence. Its great size and large population
are marked in the description of Jonah

^t Gen. 10. 11.
^u 2 Chr. 32.
21.
^x ver. 7.
^y Ezra 4. 2.

37 ^tNineveh. And it came to pass, as he was worshipping in the house of Nisroch his god, that ^uAdrammelech and Sharezer his sons ^xsmote him with the sword : and they escaped into the land of ¹Armenia. And ^yEsarhaddon his son reigned in his stead.

^a 2 Chr. 32.
24, &c.
Isai. 38. 1,
&c.

^b Neh. 13. 22.

^c Gen. 17. 1.
1 Kin. 3. 6.

^d 1Sam. 9. 16.
& 10. 1.

^e ch. 19. 20.
Ps. 65. 2.
^f Ps. 39. 12.
& 56. 8.

CHAP. 20. IN ^athose days was Hezekiah sick unto death. And the prophet Isaiah the son of Amoz came to him, and said unto him, Thus saith the LORD, ²Set thine house in order; for thou

2 shalt die, and not live. Then he turned his face to the wall, and

3 prayed unto the LORD, saying, I beseech thee, O LORD, ^bremember now how I have ^cwalked before thee in truth and with a perfect heart, and have done that which is good in thy sight.

4 And Hezekiah wept ³sore. And it came to pass, afore Isaiah was gone out into the middle ⁴court, that the word of the LORD

5 came to him, saying, Turn again, and tell Hezekiah ^dthe captain of my people, Thus saith the LORD, the God of David thy father, ^eI have heard thy prayer, I have seen ^fthy tears : behold, I will heal thee : on the third day thou shalt go up unto the

---

¹ Heb. Ararat.
² Heb. Give charge con-
cerning thine house, 2
Sam. 17. 23.
³ Heb. with a great weeping.
⁴ Or, city.

(iii. 2, 3, iv. 11), whose visit probably fell about B.C. 760.

37. The death of Sennacherib, which took place many years afterwards (B.C. 680), is related here, as, from the divine point of view, the sequel to his Syrian expeditions.

Nisroch his god.] Nisroch has not been as yet identified with any known Assyrian deity. The word *may* not be the name of a god at all but the name of the temple, as Josephus understood it. Assyrian temples were almost all distinguished by special names. If this be the true solution, the translation should run—"As he was worshipping his god in the house Nisroch."

they escaped into the land of Armenia] Lit. "the land of Ararat," or the north-eastern portion of Armenia, where it adjoined Media. The Assyrian inscriptions show that Armenia was at this time independent of Assyria, and might thus afford a safe refuge to the rebels.

Esar-haddon (or Esar-chaddon), is beyond a doubt the Asshur-akh-iddin of the inscriptions, who calls himself the son, and appears to be the successor of Sin-akh-irib. He commenced his reign by a struggle with his brother Adrammelech, and occupied the throne for only thirteen years, when he was succeeded by his son, Sardanapalus or Asshur-bani-pal. He warred with Phœnicia, Syria, Arabia, Egypt, and Media, and built three palaces, one at Nineveh, and the others at Calah and Babylon.

XX. 1. *In those days*] Hezekiah seems to have died B.C. 697; and his illness must belong to B.C. 713 or 714 (cp. *v.* 6), a date which falls early in the reign of Sargon. The true chronological place of this narrative is therefore prior to all the other facts related of Hezekiah except his religious reforms.

the prophet Isaiah the son of Amoz] This full description of Isaiah (cp. xix. 2), by the addition of his father's name and of his office, marks the original independence of this narrative. The writer of Kings may have found it altogether separate from the other records of Hezekiah, and added it in the state in which he found it.

This history (cp. Jon. iii. 4-10) shews that the prophetic denunciations were often not absolute predictions of what was certainly about to happen, but designed primarily to prove, or to lead to repentance, those against whom they were uttered, and only obtaining accomplishment if this primary design failed.

2. *he turned his face to the wall*] Contrast 1 K. xxi. 4. Ahab turned in sullenness, because he was too angry to converse; Hezekiah in devotion, because he wished to pray undisturbed.

3. *remember now*] The old Covenant promised temporal prosperity, including length of days, to the righteous. Hezekiah, conscious of his faithfulness and integrity (xviii. 3-6), ventures to expostulate (cp. also xxi. 1 note). According to the highest standard of morality revealed up to this time, there was nothing unseemly in the self-vindication of the monarch, which has many parallels in the Psalms of David (Pss. vii. 3-10, xviii. 19-26, xxvi. 1-8, &c.).

4. *the middle court*] *i.e.* of the royal palace. This is preferable to the marg. reading.

5. *the captain of my people*] This phrase (which does not occur elsewhere in Kings) is remarkable, and speaks for the authenticity of this full report of the actual words of the Prophet's message (abbreviated in Isai. xxxviii. 1, &c.). The title, "Captain (*negid*) of God's people," commonly used of David,

6 house of the LORD. And I will add unto thy days fifteen years; and I will deliver thee and this city out of the hand of the king of Assyria; and *o*I will defend this city for mine own sake, and 7 for my servant David's sake. And *h*Isaiah said, Take a lump of figs. And they took and laid *it* on the boil, and he recovered. 8 ¶ And Hezekiah said unto Isaiah, *i*What *shall be* the sign that the LORD will heal me, and that I shall go up into the house of 9 the LORD the third day? And Isaiah said, *k*This sign shalt thou have of the LORD, that the LORD will do the thing that he hath spoken: shall the shadow go forward ten degrees, or go 10 back ten degrees? And Hezekiah answered, It is a light thing for the shadow to go down ten degrees: nay, but let the shadow 11 return backward ten degrees. And Isaiah the prophet cried unto the LORD: and *l*he brought the shadow ten degrees back- 12 ward, by which it had gone down in the ¹dial of Ahaz. ¶ *m*At that time ²Berodach-baladan, the son of Baladan, king of

o ch. 19. 34.

h Isai. 38. 21.

i See Isai. 7. 11, 14. & 38. 22.
k See Isai. 38. 7, 8.

l See Josh. 10. 12, 14. Isai. 38. 8.
m Isai. 39. 1, &c.

¹ Heb. *degrees.*   ² Or, *Merodach-baladan.*

---

is applied to Hezekiah, as David's true follower (xviii. 3).

6. The king of Assyria in B.C. 714 and 713 was Sargon (B.C. 721-705). If then the Biblical and Assyrian chronologies *which agree exactly in the year of the taking of Samaria* (B.C. 721), are to be depended on, the king of Assyria here must have been Sargon. It may be conjectured that he had taken offence at something in the conduct of Hezekiah, and have threatened Jerusalem about this time (cp. Isai. xx. 6). There is, however, no evidence of actual hostilities between Judæa and Assyria in Sargon's reign.

7. *a lump of figs*] The usual remedy in the East, even at the present day, for ordinary boils. But such a remedy would not *naturally* cure the dangerous tumour or carbuncle from which Hezekiah suffered. Thus the means used in this miracle were means having a tendency towards the result wrought by them, but insufficient of themselves to produce that result (cp. iv. 34 note).

8. *And Hezekiah said*] Previous to the actual recovery Hezekiah, who at first may have felt himself no better, asked for a "sign" that he would indeed be restored to health.

Asking for a sign is a pious or a wicked act according to the spirit in which it is done. No blame is attached to the requests of Gideon (Judg. vi. 17, 37, 39), or to this of Hezekiah, because they were real wishes of the heart expressed humbly. The "evil generation" that "sought for a sign" in our Lord's days did not really want one, but made the demand captiously, neither expecting nor wishing that it should be granted.

9. *ten degrees*] Lit. "ten steps." It is not, perhaps, altogether certain whether the "dial of Ahaz" (*v.* 11) was really a dial with a gnomon in the centre, and "degrees"

marked round it, or a construction for marking time by means of "steps." Sundials proper had been invented by the Babylonians before the time of Herodotus; but the instrument here was probably an instrument consisting of a set of steps, or stairs, with an obelisk at the top, the shadow of which descended or ascended the steps according as the sun rose higher in the heavens or declined.

The question as to the mode whereby the return of the shadow was produced is one on which many opinions have been held. Recently, it has been urged that the true cause of the phenomenon was a solar eclipse, in which the moon obscured the entire upper limb of the sun; and it has been clearly shown that if such an occurrence took place a little before midday, it would have had the effect described as having taken place— *i.e.* during the obscuration of the sun's upper limb shadows would be sensibly lengthened, and that of the obelisk would descend the stairs; as the obscuration passed off the reverse would take place, shadows would shorten, and that of the obelisk would once more retire up the steps. If this be the true account, the *miracle* would consist in Isaiah's supernatural foreknowledge of an event which the astronomy of the age was quite incapable of predicting, and in the providential guidance of Hezekiah's will, so that he chose the "sign" which in the natural course of things was about to be manifested.

10. *It is a light thing*] It seemed to Hezekiah comparatively easy that the shadow, which had already begun to lengthen, should merely make a sudden jump *in the same direction;* but, wholly contrary to all experience that it should change its direction, advancing up the steps again when it had once begun to descend them.

12. *Berodach-baladan*] The correct form of this name, Merodach-baladan, is given

Babylon, sent letters and a present unto Hezekiah : for he had
ⁿ 2 Chr. 32. 13 heard that Hezekiah had been sick. And ⁿHezekiah hearkened
27.   unto them, and shewed them all the house of his ¹precious
things, the silver, and the gold, and the spices, and the precious
ointment, and *all* the house of his ^{2 3}armour, and all that was
found in his treasures : there was nothing in his house, nor in
14 all his dominion, that Hezekiah shewed them not. Then came
Isaiah the prophet unto king Hezekiah, and said unto him,
What said these men ? and from whence came they unto thee ?
And Hezekiah said, They are come from a far country, *even*
15 from Babylon. And he said, What have they seen in thine
^o ver. 13.   house ? And Hezekiah answered, ^oAll *the things* that *are* in
mine house have they seen : there is nothing among my trea-
16 sures that I have not shewed them. And Isaiah said unto Heze-
17 kiah, Hear the word of the LORD. Behold, the days come, that
all that *is* in thine house, and that which thy fathers have laid
^p ch. 24. 13.   up in store unto this day, ^pshall be carried into Babylon : no-
& 25. 13.   18 thing shall be left, saith the LORD. And of thy sons that shall
Jer.27.21, 22.
& 52. 17.   issue from thee, which thou shalt beget, ^qshall they take away ;
^q ch. 24. 12.

¹ Or, *spicery*.   ² Or, *jewels*.   ³ Heb. *vessels*.

---

in Isaiah (xxxix. 1). It is a name composed of three elements, *Merodach*, the
well-known Babylonian god (Jer. l. 2), *bal*
(= *pal*) "a son ;" and *iddin*, or *iddina*, "has
given ;" or *Baladan* may be a form of *Bel-
iddin.* This king of Babylon is mentioned
frequently in the Assyrian inscriptions, and
he was not unknown to the Greeks. He
had two reigns in Babylon. First of all, he
seized the throne in the same year in which
Sargon became king of Assyria, B.C. 721,
and held it for 12 years, from B.C. 721 to
B.C. 709, when Sargon defeated him, and
took him prisoner. Secondly, on the death
of Sargon and the accession of Sennacherib,
when troubles once more arose in Babylonia,
he returned thither, and had another reign,
which lasted six months, during a part of
the year B.C. 703. As the embassy of Merodach-Baladan followed closely on the illness of Hezekiah, it would probably be in
B.C. 713.

the son of Baladan] In the inscriptions
Merodach-Baladan is repeatedly called the
son of Yakin or Yagin. This, however, is
a discrepancy which admits of easy explanation. The Assyrians are not accurate in
their accounts of the parentage of foreign
kings. With them Jehu is "the son of
Omri." Yakin was a prince of some repute,
to whose dominions Merodach-baladan had
succeeded. The Assyrians would call him
Yakin's son, though he might have been
his son-in-law, or his grandson.

The embassy was not merely one of congratulation. Its chief object was to inquire
with respect to the going back of the shadow,
an astronomical marvel in which the Chal-
dæans of Babylon would feel a keen interest
(2 Chr. xxxii. 31). A political purpose is
moreover implied in the next verse. Merodach-baladan was probably desirous of

strengthening himself against Assyria by an
alliance with Judæa and with Egypt.

13. *Hezekiah hearkened unto them, and
shewed them*] The Jewish king lent a favourable ear to the proposals of the ambassadors, and exhibited to them the resources
which he possessed, in order to induce them
to report well of him to their master.

all the house of his precious things] Lit.
the "spice-house ;" the phrase had acquired the more generic sense of "treasure-
house" from the fact that the gold, the
silver, and the spices were all stored together.

14. Hezekiah did not answer Isaiah's first
question, "What said these men ?" but
only his second. Probably he knew that
Isaiah would oppose reliance on an "arm of
flesh."

Babylon now for the first time became
revealed to the Jews as an actual power in
the world, which might effect them politically. As yet even the Prophets had
spoken but little of the great southern city;
up to this time she had been little more
to them than Tyre, or Tarshish, or any
other rich and powerful idolatrous city.
Henceforth all this was wholly changed.
The prophetic utterance of Isaiah on this
occasion (*vv.* 16–18) never was, never could
be, forgotten. He followed it up with a
burst of prophecy (Is. xl.-lxvi.), in which
Babylon usurps altogether the place of Assyria as Israel's enemy, and the Captivity
being assumed as a matter of certainty, the
hopes of the people are directed onward
beyond it to the Return. Other Prophets
took up the strain and repeated it (Habak.
i. 6–11, ii. 5–8 ; Mic. iv. 10). Babylon thus
became henceforth, in lieu of Assyria, the
great object of the nation's fear and hatred.

18. This prophecy had two fulfilments,

and they shall be eunuchs in the palace of the king of Babylon.
19 Then said Hezekiah unto Isaiah, *r* Good *is* the word of the LORD
which thou hast spoken. And he said, [1] *Is it* not *good*, if peace
20 and truth be in my days? ¶ *s* And the rest of the acts of Hezekiah, and all his might, and how he *t* made a pool, and a conduit,
and *u* brought water into the city, *are* they not written in the
21 book of the chronicles of the kings of Judah? And *x* Hezekiah
slept with his fathers: and Manasseh his son reigned in his
stead.

CHAP. 21. MANASSEH *a was* twelve years old when he began to
reign, and reigned fifty and five years in Jerusalem. And his
2 mother's name *was* Hephzi-bah. And he did *that which was* evil
in the sight of the LORD, *b* after the abominations of the heathen,
3 whom the LORD cast out before the children of Israel. For he
built up again the high places *c* which Hezekiah his father had
destroyed; and he reared up altars for Baal, and made a grove,

r 1Sam.3.18.
Job 1. 21.
Ps. 39. 9.
s 2Chr.32.32.
t Neh. 3. 16.
u 2 Chr. 32.
30.
x 2 Chr. 32.
33.

a 2 Chr. 33.
1, &c.

b ch. 16. 3.

c ch. 18. 4.

[1] Or, *Shall there not be peace and truth, &c.*

each complementary to the other. Manasseh, Hezekiah's *actual son*, was "carried to
Babylon" (2 Chr. xxxiii. 11), but did not
become a eunuch in the palace. Daniel and
others, not his actual sons, but of the royal
seed (Dan. i. 3), and therefore Hezekiah's
descendants, are thought by some to have
literally fulfilled the latter part of the prophecy, being eunuchs in the palace of Nebuchadnezzar.

19. *Good is the word,* &c.] The language
is, according to some, that of a true spirit
of resignation and humility; according to
others, that of a feeling of relief and satisfaction that the evil was not to come in his
day. Such a feeling would be but natural,
and though not according to the standard of
Christian perfectness, would imply no very
great defect of character in one who lived
under the old Dispensation.

peace and truth] Rather, "peace and continuance." The evils threatened were war
and the dissolution of the kingdom.

20, 21. Consult the marg. reff.

XXI. 1. *Manasseh was twelve years old*]
Manasseh, therefore, was not born at the
time of Hezekiah's dangerous illness; and
it is probable that Hezekiah had at that
time no son to succeed him. According to
Josephus, this was the principal cause of
his grief.

Hephzibah] Jewish tradition makes Hephzibah, Hezekiah's wife, the daughter of
Isaiah; but this is scarcely probable. She
was, however, no doubt, known to the Prophet, and it may well have been in special
compliment to her that Isaiah introduced
her name (lxii. 4) as one that Jerusalem
would bear after her restoration to God's
favour. The name means, "My delight (is)
in her."

2. Manasseh during his minority naturally fell under the influence of the chief
Jewish nobles, with whom the pure religion
of Jehovah was always unpopular (cp.

2 Chr. xxiv. 17, 18; Jer. viii. 1, 2). They
seem to have persuaded him, not only to
undo Hezekiah's work, but to proceed to
lengths in polytheism, magic, and idolatry,
unknown before. The sins of Manasseh's
reign appear to have been those which filled
up the measure of Judah's iniquity, and
brought down the final sentence of doom
on the last remnant of the chosen people
(xxiii. 26; cp. Jer. xv. 4).

3. The first step in the re-establishment
of idolatry seems to have been the restoration of the high places where Jehovah was
professedly worshipped (xviii. 22), but with
idolatrous rites (1 K. xiv. 23). The next was
to re-introduce the favourite idolatry of
Israel, Baal-worship, which had formerly
flourished in Judæa under Athaliah (xi. 18),
and Ahaz (2 Chr. xxviii. 2). After this,
Manasseh seems to have specially affected
Sabaism, which had been previously unknown in Judæa (cp. xvii. 16 and note).

worshipped all the host of heaven] Sabaism,
or pure star-worship, without images, and
without astrological superstitions, included
a reverence for the sun, the moon, the chief
stars, and the twelve signs of the Zodiac (xxiii.
5 note). The main worship was by altars, on
which incense was burnt (Jer. xix. 13).
These altars were placed either upon the
ground (*v.* 5), or upon the house-tops (xxiii.
12; Zeph. i. 5). The sun was worshipped
with the face towards the east (Ezek. viii.
16); chariots and horses were dedicated to
him (xxiii. 11). The star-worship of the
Jews has far more the character of an Arabian than an Assyrian or Chaldæan cult. It
obtained its hold at a time when Assyria
and Babylonia had but little communication with Judæa—*i.e.* during the reign of
Manasseh. It crept in probably from the
same quarter as the Molech worship, with
which it is here (and in 2 Chr. xxxiii. 3-6)
conjoined.

d 1 Kin. 16.
32, 33.
e Deut. 4. 19.
& 17. 3.
ch. 17. 16.
f Jer. 32. 34.
g 2Sam.7.13.
1 Kin. 8. 29.
& 9. 3.
h Lev. 18.21.
& 20. 2.
ch. 16. 3.
& 17. 17.
i Lev. 19. 26,
31.
Deut. 18. 10,
11.
ch. 17. 17.
k 2Sam.7.13.
1 Kin. 8. 29.
& 9. 3.
ch. 23. 27.
Ps. 132. 13,
14.
Jer. 32. 34.
l 2 Sam.7.10.
m Prov. 29.
12.
n ch. 23. 26,
27.
& 24. 3, 4.
Jer. 15. 4.
o 1Kin.21.26.
p ver. 9.
q 1Sam.3.11.
Jer. 19. 3.
r See Isai.
34. 11.
Lam. 2. 8.
Amos 7. 7, 8.

*d*as did Ahab king of Israel; and *e*worshipped all the host of
4 heaven, and served them. And *f*he built altars in the house of
the LORD, of which the LORD said, *g*In Jerusalem will I put my
5 name. And he built altars for all the host of heaven in the two
6 courts of the house of the LORD. *h*And he made his son pass
through the fire, and observed *i*times, and used enchantments,
and dealt with familiar spirits and wizards: he wrought much
wickedness in the sight of the LORD, to provoke *him* to anger.
7 And he set a graven image of the grove that he had made in the
house, of which the LORD said to David, and to Solomon his son,
*k*In this house, and in Jerusalem, which I have chosen out of
8 all tribes of Israel, will I put my name for ever: *l*neither will I
make the feet of Israel move any more out of the land which I
gave their fathers; only if they will observe to do according to
all that I have commanded them, and according to all the law
9 that my servant Moses commanded them. But they hearkened
not: and Manasseh *m*seduced them to do more evil than did the
nations whom the LORD destroyed before the children of Israel.
10 ¶ And the LORD spake by his servants the prophets, saying, *n*Be-
11 cause Manasseh king of Judah hath done these abominations,
*o*and hath done wickedly above all that the Amorites did, which
were before him, and *p*hath made Judah also to sin with his
12 idols: therefore thus saith the LORD God of Israel, Behold, I *am*
bringing *such* evil upon Jerusalem and Judah, that whosoever
13 heareth of it, both *q*his ears shall tingle. And I will stretch
over Jerusalem *r*the line of Samaria, and the plummet of the
house of Ahab: and I will wipe Jerusalem as *a man* wipeth a
14 dish, *1*wiping *it*, and turning *it* upside down. And I will forsake
the remnant of mine inheritance, and deliver them into the
hand of their enemies; and they shall become a prey and a
15 spoil to all their enemies; because they have done *that which*

1 Heb. *he wipeth and turneth* it *upon the face thereof.*

---

4. The "altars" of this verse seem to be
the same with those of *v.* 5, and consequently were not in the Temple building,
but in the outer and inner courts.
6. On the meaning of the phrase "passing
through the fire," see xvi. 3, and Lev. xx.
2–5.
To "observe times" was forbidden in the
Law (marg. reff.), and was no doubt among
the modes of divination practised by the
Canaanitish nations. It has been explained
as, (1) Predicting from the state of the
clouds and atmosphere; (2) Fascination with
the eye; (3) Watching and catching at
chance words as ominous.
dealt with familiar spirits] This practice
was forbidden by Moses (Lev. xix. 31) under
the penalty of death (do. xx. 27). Its nature
is best learnt from Saul's visit to the witch
of Endor (1 Sam. xxviii. 7, &c.).
wizards] "Wizards" — literally, "wise
men"—are always joined with those who
have familiar spirits. Probably they were
a sort of necromancers.
7. *a graven image of the grove*] Rather,
"**the carved work** of the Asherah." This
Asherah Manasseh placed in the very Tem-

ple itself, whence it was afterwards taken
by Josiah to be destroyed (xxiii. 6). Such
a profanation was beyond anything that
had been done either by Athaliah (xi. 18),
or by Ahaz (xvi. 14–18; 2 Chr. xxix. 5–7).
9. During the long reign of Manasseh
idolatry in all manner of varied forms took
a hold upon the Jewish people such as had
never been known before. Cp. Jer. vii. 18,
31; Ezek. xxiii. 37; Zeph. i. 5. The corruption of morals kept pace with the degradation of religion. Cp. xxiii. 7; Zeph. iii.
1–3; Jer. ii. 8, v. 1.
10. *the prophets*] None of the Prophets of
this reign are certainly known. One may
possibly have been Hosai or Hozai (2 Chr.
xxxiii. 19, marg.), who perhaps wrote a life
of Manasseh.
13. The general meaning is plain, but
the exact force of the metaphor used is not
so clear. If the "line" and the "plummet"
be "symbols of rule" or law, the meaning
will be—"I will apply exactly the same
measure and rule to Jerusalem as to Samaria—I will treat both alike with strict and
even justice."

was evil in my sight, and have provoked me to anger, since the
day their fathers came forth out of Egypt, even unto this day.
16 ¶ ˢMoreover Manasseh shed innocent blood very much, till he
had filled Jerusalem ¹from one end to another; beside his sin
wherewith he made Judah to sin, in doing *that which was* evil
17 in the sight of the LORD. Now ᵗthe rest of the acts of Manasseh, and all that he did, and his sin that he sinned, *are* they
not written in the book of the chronicles of the kings of Judah?
18 And ᵘManasseh slept with his fathers, and was buried in the
garden of his own house, in the garden of Uzza: and Amon his
19 son reigned in his stead. ¶ ˣAmon *was* twenty and two years
old when he began to reign, and he reigned two years in Jerusalem. And his mother's name *was* Meshullemeth, the daughter
20 of Haruz of Jotbah. And he did *that which was* evil in the sight
21 of the LORD, ʸas his father Manasseh did. And he walked in
all the way that his father walked in, and served the idols that
22 his father served, and worshipped them: and he ᶻforsook the
LORD God of his fathers, and walked not in the way of the LORD.
23 ªAnd the servants of Amon conspired against him, and slew the
24 king in his own house. And the people of the land slew all
them that had conspired against king Amon; and the people of
25 the land made Josiah his son king in his stead. Now the rest
of the acts of Amon which he did, *are* they not written in the
26 book of the chronicles of the kings of Judah? And he was
buried in his sepulchre in the garden of Uzza: and ᵇJosiah his
son reigned in his stead.

ˢ ch. 24. 4.

ᵗ 2 Chr. 33.
11—19.

ᵘ 2Chr.33.20.

ˣ 2 Chr. 33.
21—23.

ʸ ver. 2, &c.

ᶻ 1Kin.11.33.

ª 2 Chr. 33.
24, 25.

ᵇ Matt. 1. 10,
called
Josias.

¹ Heb. *from mouth to mouth.*

---

16. Cp. Jer. ii. 30; Heb. xi. 37; Isai.
lvii. 1–4. According to tradition, Isaiah
was among the first to perish. More than
a century afterwards, the final judgment
upon Jerusalem was felt to be in an especial
way the punishment of Manasseh's bloody
persecution of God's people (marg. ref.).

17. The writer of Kings relates in eighteen
verses the history of fifty-five years, and
consequently omits numerous facts of great
importance in the life of Manasseh. Among
the most remarkable of the facts omitted
are the capture of Manasseh by the king
of Assyria, his removal to Babylon, his repentance there, his restoration to his kingdom, and his religious reforms upon his return to it. These are recorded only in
Chronicles (marg. ref., see note). The writer
of Kings probably considered the repentance of Manasseh but a half-repentance,
followed by a half-reformation, which left
untouched the root of the evil.

18. *was buried*] The catacomb of David
was probably full, and the later kings, from
Ahaz downwards, had to find sepulture
elsewhere. Ahaz was buried in Jerusalem,
but not in the sepulchres of the kings (2
Chr. xxviii. 27). Hezekiah found a resting-
place on the way that led up to David's
catacomb (do. xxxii. 33). Manasseh and
Amon were interred in " the garden of
Uzza," a portion (apparently) of the royal
palace-garden ; perhaps so called after
the name of the previous owner. Josiah

was buried in "his own sepulchre" (xxiii.
30).

Amon his son] This name, which occurs
only at this time and in the reign of the
idolatrous Ahab (1 K. xxii. 26), is identical
in form with the Hebrew representative of
the great Egyptian god, Amen or Amun
(Nahum iii. 8 marg.); and it is therefore probable that Manasseh selected it and gave it
to his son in compliment to the Egyptians.

21. At Manasseh's death, the idolatrous
party, held in some check during his later
years (2 Chr. xxxiii. 15–17), recovered the
entire direction of affairs, and obtained
authority from Amon to make once more
all the changes which Manasseh had made
in the early part of his reign. Hence we
find the state of things at Josiah's accession
(xxiii. 4–14; Zeph. i. 4–12, iii. 1–7), the
exact counterpart of that which had existed
under Manasseh.

23. This conspiracy may have been due
to the popular reaction against the extreme
idolatry which the young king had established.

24. The intention of the conspirators had
perhaps been to declare a forfeiture of the
crown by the existing line, and to place
a new dynasty on the throne. This the
people would not suffer. They arrested
them and put them to death ; and insisted
on investing with the royal authority the
true heir of David, the eldest son of Amon,
though he was a boy only eight years old.

CHAP. 22. JOSIAH *a was* eight years old when he began to reign, and he reigned thirty and one years in Jerusalem. And his mother's name *was* Jedidah, the daughter of Adaiah of *b* Boscath. 2 And he did *that which was* right in the sight of the LORD, and walked in all the way of David his father, and *c* turned not aside 3 to the right hand or to the left. ¶ *d* And it came to pass in the eighteenth year of king Josiah, *that* the king sent Shaphan the son of Azaliah, the son of Meshullam, the scribe, to the house 4 of the LORD, saying, Go up to Hilkiah the high priest, that he may sum the silver which is *e* brought into the house of the LORD, which *f* the keepers of the [1] door have gathered of the 5 people : and let them *g* deliver it into the hand of the doers of the work, that have the oversight of the house of the LORD : and let them give it to the doers of the work which *is* in the 6 house of the LORD, to repair the breaches of the house, unto carpenters, and builders, and masons, and to buy timber and 7 hewn stone to repair the house. Howbeit *h* there was no reckoning made with them of the money that was delivered into their 8 hand, because they dealt faithfully. ¶ And Hilkiah the high priest said unto Shaphan the scribe, *i* I have found the book of

a 2 Chr. 34. 1.

b Josh. 15. 39.

c Deut. 5. 32.

d 2 Chr. 34. 8, &c.

e ch. 12. 4.

f ch. 12. 9.
P's. 84. 10.
g ch. 12. 11, 12, 14.

h ch. 12. 15.

i Deut. 31. 24, &c.
2 Chr. 34. 14, &c.

[1] Heb. *threshold*.

XXII. **3.** *in the eighteenth year*] This is the date of the finding of the Book of the Law and of the Passover (marg. ref., and xxiii. 23), but is not meant to apply to all the various reforms of Josiah as related in xxiii. 4–20. The true chronology of Josiah's reign is to be learnt from 2 Chr. xxxiv. 3–8, xxxv. 1. From these places it appear that at least the greater part of his reforms preceded the finding of the Book of the Law. He began them in the twelfth year of his reign, at the age of twenty, and had accomplished all, or the greater part, by his eighteenth year, when the Book of the Law was found.

Shaphan is mentioned frequently by Jeremiah. He was the father of Ahikam, Jeremiah's friend and protector at the court of Jehoiakim (Jer. xxvi. 24), and the grandfather of Gedaliah, who was made governor of Judæa by the Babylonians after the destruction of Jerusalem (xxv. 22). Several others of his sons and grandsons were in favour with the later Jewish kings (Jer. xxix. 3, xxxvi. 10–12, 25 ; Ezek. viii. 11). Shaphan's office was one of great importance, involving very confidential relations with the king (1 K. iv. 3).

4. *Hilkiah*] Hilkiah was the father (or grandfather) of Seraiah (cp. 1 Chr. vi. 13, 14, with Neh. xi. 11), High-Priest at the time of the Captivity (xxv. 18), and ancestor of Ezra the scribe (Ezr. vii. 1).

It is evident from the expressions of this verse that a collection for the repairs of the Temple, similar to that established in the reign of Joash (xii. 9, 10), had been for some considerable time in progress (cp. 2 Chr. xxxiv. 3), and the king now sent to know the result.

5. See marg. ref. The "doers" of the first part of the verse are the contractors,

or overseers, who undertook the general superintendence ; they are to be distinguished from a lower class of "doers," the actual labourers, carpenters, and masons of the latter portion of the verse.

which is in the house of the LORD] Rather, "who are," &c. ; *i.e.* the persons who were actually employed in the Temple.

7. *they dealt faithfully*] Cp. marg. ref. The names of these honest overseers are given in Chronicles (2 Chr. xxxiv. 12).

8. Some have concluded from this discovery, either that no "book of the law" had ever existed before, the work now said to have been "found" having been forged for the occasion by Hilkiah ; or that all knowledge of the old "book" had been lost, and that a work of unknown date and authorship having been at this time found was accepted as the Law of Moses on account of its contents, and has thus come down to us under his name. But this is to see in the narrative far more than it naturally implies. If Hilkiah had been bold enough and wicked enough to forge, or if he had been foolish enough to accept hastily as the real "book of the law" a composition of which he really knew nothing, there were four means of detecting his error or his fraud :—(1) The Jewish Liturgies, which embodied large portions of the Law ; (2) The memory of living men, which in many instances may have extended to the entire Five Books, as it does now with the modern Samaritans ; (3) Other copies, entire or fragmentary, existing among the more learned Jews, or in the Schools of the Prophets ; and (4) Quotations from the Law in other works, especially in the Psalmists and Prophets, who refer to it on almost every page.

The copy of the Book of the Law found

the law in the house of the LORD. And Hilkiah gave the book
9 to Shaphan, and he read it. And Shaphan the scribe came to
the king, and brought the king word again, and said, Thy servants have ¹gathered the money that was found in the house,
and have delivered it into the hand of them that do the work,
10 that have the oversight of the house of the LORD. And Shaphan the scribe shewed the king, saying, Hilkiah the priest hath
delivered me a book. And Shaphan read it before the king.
11 And it came to pass, when the king had heard the words of the
12 book of the law, that he rent his clothes. And the king commanded Hilkiah the priest, and Ahikam the son of Shaphan,
and ᵏAchbor the son of ²Michaiah, and Shaphan the scribe, and
13 Asahiah a servant of the king's, saying, Go ye, enquire of the
LORD for me, and for the people, and for all Judah, concerning
the words of this book that is found: for great is ˡthe wrath of
the LORD that is kindled against us, because our fathers have
not hearkened unto the words of this book, to do according unto
14 all that which is written concerning us. ¶ So Hilkiah the priest,
and Ahikam, and Achbor, and Shaphan, and Asahiah, went unto
Huldah the prophetess, the wife of Shallum the son of ᵐTikvah,
the son of ³Harhas, keeper of the ⁴wardrobe; (now she dwelt
in Jerusalem ⁵in the college;) and they communed with her.
15 And she said unto them, Thus saith the LORD God of Israel,
16 Tell the man that sent you to me, Thus saith the LORD, Behold,
ⁿI will bring evil upon this place, and upon the inhabitants
thereof, even all the words of the book which the king of Judah

k Abdon,
2 Chr. 34. 20.

l Deut. 29. 27.

m Tikvath,
2 Chr. 34. 22.

n Deut. 29. 27.
Dan. 9. 11.
12, 13, 14.

---

¹ Heb. melted.   ³ Or, Hasrah.   ⁵ Or, in the second part.
² Or, Micah.   ⁴ Heb. garments.

---

by Hilkiah was no doubt that deposited, in
accordance with the command of God, by
Moses, by the side of the Ark of the Covenant, and kept ordinarily in the Holy of
Holies (marg. ref.). It had been lost, or
secreted, during the desecration of the
Temple by Manasseh, but had not been
removed out of the Temple building.

9. *have gathered*] Rather, "have poured
out" or "**emptied out.**" The allusion probably is to the emptying of the chest in
which all the money collected had been
placed (xii. 9).

11. *he rent his clothes*] Partly in grief and
horror, like Reuben (Gen. xxxvii. 29) and
Job (i. 20), partly in repentance, like Ahab
(1 K. xxi. 27).

13. *enquire of the* LORD] As inquiry by
Urim and Thummim had ceased—apparently because superseded by prophecy—
this order was equivalent to an injunction
to seek the presence of a Prophet (cp. iii.
11; 1 K. xxii. 5).

because our fathers have not hearkened]
Josiah, it will be observed, assumes that
preceding generations had had full opportunity of hearing and knowing the Law. He
thus regards the loss as comparatively recent (cp. *v.* 8 note).

14. *went unto Huldah*] It might have
been expected that the royal commissioners
would have gone to Jeremiah, on whom the

prophetic spirit had descended in Josiah's
thirteenth year (Jer. i. 2), or five years previous to the finding of the Law. Perhaps
he was at some distance from Jerusalem at
the time; or his office may not yet have
been fully recognized.

the prophetess] Cp. the cases of Miriam
(Ex. xv. 20; Num. xii. 2) and Deborah
(Judg. iv. 4).

keeper of the wardrobe] Lit. "of the
robes." Shallum had the superintendence,
either of the vestments of the priests who
served in the Temple, or of the royal robe-
room in which dresses of honour were stored,
in case of their being needed for presents
(see v. 5 note).

in the college] The marginal translation
"in the second part" is preferable; and
probably refers to the new or outer city—
that which had been enclosed by the wall of
Manasseh, to the north of the old city (2
Chr. xxxiii. 14).

16. *all the words of the book*] The "words"
here intended are no doubt the threatenings
of the Law, particularly those of Lev. xxvi.
16-39 and Deut. xxviii. 15-68. Josiah had
probably only heard a portion of the Book
of the Law; but that portion had contained those awful denunciations of coming
woe. Hence Josiah's rending of his clothes
(*v.* 11), and his hurried message to Huldah.

*Deut. 29.
25, 26, 27.*

17 hath read: ᵒbecause they have forsaken me, and have burned incense unto other gods, that they might provoke me to anger with all the works of their hands; therefore my wrath shall be
18 kindled against this place, and shall not be quenched. But to

*ᵖ 2 Chr. 34.
26, &c.*

ᵖthe king of Judah which sent you to enquire of the LORD, thus shall ye say to him, Thus saith the LORD God of Israel, As

*�q Ps. 51. 17.
Isai. 57. 15.
ʳ 1Kin.21.29.*

19 *touching* the words which thou hast heard; because thine �q heart was tender, and thou hast ʳhumbled thyself before the LORD, when thou heardest what I spake against this place, and against

*ˢ Lev. 26.
31, 32.
ᵗ Jer. 26. 6.
& 44. 22.*

the inhabitants thereof, that they should become ˢa desolation and ᵗa curse, and hast rent thy clothes, and wept before me;
20 I also have heard *thee*, saith the LORD. Behold therefore, I

*ᵘ Ps. 37. 37.
Isai. 57. 1, 2.*

will gather thee unto thy fathers, and thou ᵘshalt be gathered into thy grave in peace; and thine eyes shall not see all the evil which I will bring upon this place. And they brought the king word again.

*ᵃ 2 Chr. 34.
29, 30, &c.*

CHAP. 23. AND ᵃthe king sent, and they gathered unto him all
2 the elders of Judah and of Jerusalem. And the king went up into the house of the LORD, and all the men of Judah and all the inhabitants of Jerusalem with him, and the priests, and the prophets, and all the people, ¹both small and great: and he read in their ears all the words of the book of the covenant

*ᵇ ch. 22. 8.
ᶜ ch.11.14,17.*

3 ᵇwhich was found in the house of the LORD. And the king ᶜstood by a pillar, and made a covenant before the LORD, to walk after the LORD, and to keep his commandments and his testimonies and his statutes with all *their* heart and all *their* soul, to perform the words of this covenant that were written in
4 this book. And all the people stood to the covenant. ¶And the king commanded Hilkiah the high priest, and the priests of

¹ Heb. *from small even unto great.*

---

17. *have burned incense*] In the marg. ref. the corresponding phrase is:—"have served other gods, and worshipped them." Its alteration to "have burned incense" points to the fact that the favourite existing idolatry was burning incense on the house-tops to Baal (Jer. xix. 13, xxxii. 29) and to the host of heaven (xxi. 3).

19. See marg. reff.

20. *in peace*] The death of Josiah *in battle* (xxiii. 29) is in verbal contradiction to this prophecy, but not in real opposition to its spirit, which is simply that the pious prince who has sent to inquire of the Lord, shall be gathered to his fathers before the troubles come upon the land which are to result in her utter desolation. Now those troubles were to come, not from Egypt, but from Babylon; and their commencement was not the invasion of Necho in B.C. 608, but that of Nebuchadnezzar three years later. Thus was Josiah "taken away from the evil to come," and died "in peace" before his city had suffered attack from the really formidable enemy.

XXIII. 2. *the prophets*] The suggestion to regard this word an error of the pen for "Levites," which occurs in Chronicles (marg. ref.), is unnecessary. For though Zephaniah, Urijah, and Jeremiah are all

that we can *name* as belonging to the Order at the time, there is no reason to doubt that Judæa contained others whom we cannot name. "Schools of the Prophets" were as common in Judah as in Israel.

he read] The present passage is strong evidence that the Jewish kings could read. The solemn reading of the Law—a practice commanded in the Law itself once in seven years (Deut. xxxi. 10-13),—had been intermitted, at least for the last seventy-five years, from the date of the accession of Manasseh.

3. *by a pillar*] Rather, "upon the pillar" (see xi. 14, note).

made a covenant] "The covenant." Josiah renewed *the old* Covenant made between God and His people in Horeb (Deut. v. 2), so far at least as such renewal was possible by the mere act of an individual. He bound himself by a solemn promise to the faithful performance of the entire Law.

with all their heart] "Their" rather than "his," because the king was considered as pledging the whole nation to obedience with himself. He and they "stood to it," *i.e.* "accepted it, came into the Covenant."

4-20. A parenthesis giving the earlier reforms of Josiah.

4. *the priests of the second order*] This is a

the second order, and the keepers of the door, to bring forth out of the temple of the LORD all the vessels that were made for Baal, and for ^dthe grove, and for all the host of heaven: and he burned them without Jerusalem in the fields of Kidron, and 5 carried the ashes of them unto Beth-el. And he ¹put down the ²idolatrous priests, whom the kings of Judah had ordained to burn incense in the high places in the cities of Judah, and in the places round about Jerusalem; them also that burned incense unto Baal, to the sun, and to the moon, and to the four ³planets, 6 and to ^eall the host of heaven. And he brought out the ^fgrove from the house of the LORD, without Jerusalem, unto the brook Kidron, and burned it at the brook Kidron, and stamped *it* small to powder, and cast the powder thereof upon ^gthe graves 7 of the children of the people. And he brake down the houses ^hof the sodomites, that *were* by the house of the LORD, ⁱwhere 8 the women wove ⁴hangings for the grove. ¶And he brought all the priests out of the cities of Judah, and defiled the high places where the priests had burned incense, from ^kGeba to Beer-sheba, and brake down the high places of the gates that

d ch. 21. 3, 7.

e ch. 21. 3.
f ch. 21. 7.

g 2 Chr. 34.4.

h 1 Kin.14,24.
& 15. 12.
i Ezek.16.16.

k 1 Kin.15.22.

---

¹ Heb. *caused to cease.*
² Heb. *Chemarim,* Hos. 10.
³ Or, *twelve signs,* or, con-
    5. Foretold, Zeph. 1. 4.
stellat'ons.
⁴ Heb. *houses.*

---

new expression; and probably refers to the ordinary priests, called here "priests of the second order," in contrast with the High-Priest, whose dignity was reviving (xii. 2 note).

the vessels] This would include the whole apparatus of worship, altars, images, dresses, utensils, &c., for Baal, &c. (xxi. 3–5 notes). The ashes of the idolatrous objects burnt in the first instance in the "fields of Kidron" (*i.e.* in the part of the valley which lies north-east of the city, a part much broader than that between the Temple Hill and the Mount of Olives) were actually taken to Bethel, as to an accursed place, and one just beyond the borders of Judah; while those of other objects burnt afterwards were not carried so far, the trouble being great and the need not absolute, but were thrown into the Kidron (*v.* 12), when there happened to be water to carry them away, or scattered on graves which were already unclean (*v.* 6). Cp. 1 K. xv. 13.

5. *he put down,* &c.] or, "He caused to cease the idolatrous priests" (marg.); *i.e.* he stopped them. The word translated "idolatrous priests" (see marg.) is a rare one, occurring only here and in marg. reff. Here and in Zephaniah it is contrasted with *cohanim,* another class of high-place priests. The *cohanim* were probably "Levitical," the *chemarim* "non-Levitical priests of the high-places." *Chemarim* appears to have been a foreign term, perhaps derived from the Syriac *cûmrô,* which means a priest of any kind.

whom the kings of Judah had ordained] The consecration of non-Levitical priests by the kings of Judah (cp. 1 K. xii. 31) had not been previously mentioned; but it is quite

in accordance with the other proceedings of Manasseh and Amon.

the planets] See marginal note, *i.e.* the "signs of the Zodiac." Cp. Job xxxviii. 32 marg. The word in the original probably means primarily "houses" or "stations," which was the name applied by the Babylonians to their divisions of the Zodiac.

6. The ashes, being polluted and polluting, were thrown upon graves, because there no one could come into contact with them, since graves were avoided as unclean places.

7. *by the house of the LORD*] This did not arise from intentional desecration, but from the fact that the practices in question were a part of the idolatrous ceremonial, being regarded as pleasing to the gods, and, indeed, as positive acts of worship (cp. marg. ref.).

The "women" were probably the priest-esses attached to the worship of Astarte, which was intimately connected with that of the Asherah or "grove." Among their occupations one was the weaving of coverings (lit. "houses" marg.) for the Asherah, which seem to have been of various colours (marg. ref.).

8. Josiah removed the Levitical priests, who had officiated at the various high-places, from the scenes of their idolatries, and brought them to Jerusalem, where their conduct might be watched.

from Geba to Beer-sheba] *i.e.* from the extreme north to the extreme south of the kingdom of Judah. On Geba see marg. ref. note. The high-place of Beer-sheba had obtained an evil celebrity (Am. v. 5, viii. 14).

the high places of the gates, &c.] Render,

were in the entering in of the gate of Joshua the governor of the city, which *were* on a man's left hand at the gate of the city. 9 *l*Nevertheless the priests of the high places came not up to the altar of the LORD in Jerusalem, *m*but they did eat of the un-leavened bread among their brethren. ¶And he defiled *n*Topheth, which *is* in *o*the valley of the children of Hinnom, *p*that no man might make his son or his daughter to pass through the fire to Molech. And he took away the horses that the kings of Judah had given to the sun, at the entering in of the house of the LORD, by the chamber of Nathan-melech the [1]chamberlain, which *was* in the suburbs, and burned the chariots of the sun 12 with fire. And the altars that *were* *q*on the top of the upper chamber of Ahaz, which the kings of Judah had made, and the altars which *r*Manasseh had made in the two courts of the house of the LORD, did the king beat down, and [2]brake *them* down from thence, and cast the dust of them into the brook Kidron. 13 And the high places that *were* before Jerusalem, which *were* on

l See Ezek. 44. 10—14.
m 1 Sam. 2. 36.
n Isai. 30.33. Jer. 7. 31. & 19. 6, 11, 12, 13.
o Josh. 15. 8.
p Lev. 18. 21. Deut. 18. 10. Ezek. 23. 37, 39.
q See Jer. 19. 13. Zeph. 1. 5.
r ch. 21. 5.

---

[1] Or, *eunuch*, or, *officer*.   [2] Or, *ran from thence*.

"He brake down the high-places of the gates, **both that which was** at the entering in of the gate of Joshua, the governor of the city (1 K. xxii. 26 note), **and also that** which was on a man's left hand at the gate of the city." According to this, there were only two "high-places of the gates" (or idolatrous shrines erected in the city at gate-towers) at Jerusalem. The "gate of Joshua" is conjectured to have been a gate in the inner wall; and the "gate of the city," the Valley-gate (modern "Jaffa-gate").

9. *Nevertheless*] Connect this verse with the first clause of *v.* 8. The priests were treated as if they had been disqualified from serving at the Altar by a bodily blemish (Lev. xxi. 21-23). They were not secularised, but remained in the priestly order and received a maintenance from the ecclesiastical revenues. Contrast with this treatment Josiah's severity towards the priests of the high-places in Samaria, who were sacrificed upon their own altars (*v.* 20). Probably the high-place worship in Judæa had continued in the main a worship of Jehovah with idolatrous rites, while in Samaria it had degenerated into an actual worship of other gods.

10. The word Topheth, or Tophet—vari-ously derived from *tôph*, "a drum" or "tabour," because the cries of the sacrificed children were drowned by the noise of such instruments; or, from a root *taph* or *toph*, meaning "to burn"—was a spot in the valley of Hinnom (marg. ref. note). The later Jewish kings, Manasseh and Amon (or, perhaps, Ahaz, 2 Chr. xxviii. 3), had given it over to the Moloch priests for their worship; and here, ever since, the Moloch service had maintained its ground and flourished (marg. reff.).

11. The custom of dedicating a chariot and horses to the Sun is a Persian practice.

There are no traces of it in Assyria; and it is extremely curious to find that it was known to the Jews as early as the reign of Manasseh. The idea of regarding the Sun as a charioteer who drove his horses daily across the sky, so familiar to the Greeks and Romans, may not improbably have been imported from Asia, and may have been at the root of the custom in question. The chariot, or chariots, of the Sun appear to have been used, chiefly if not solely, for sacred processions. They were white, and were drawn probably by white horses. The kings of Judah who gave them were Ma-nasseh and Amon certainly; perhaps Ahaz; perhaps even earlier monarchs, as Joash and Amaziah.

in the suburbs] The expression used here (*parvârim*) is of unknown derivation and occurs nowhere else. A somewhat similar word occurs in 1 Chr. xxvi. 18, viz. *parbar*, which seems to have been a place just out-side the western wall of the Temple, and therefore a sort of "purlieu" or "suburb." The *parvârim* of this passage *may* mean the same place, or it may signify some other "suburb" of the Temple.

12. *the upper chamber of Ahaz*] Con-jectured to be a chamber erected on the flat roof of one of the gateways which led into the Temple Court. It was probably built in order that its roof might be used for the worship of the host of heaven, for which house-tops were considered specially appro-priate (cp. marg. reff.).

brake them down from thence] Rather as in margin, *i.e.* he "hasted and cast the dust into Kidron."

13. On the position of these high-places see 1 K. xi. 7 note. As they were allowed to remain under such kings as Asa, Jehosh-aphat, and Hezekiah, they were probably among the old high-places where Jehovah had been worshipped blamelessly, or at

the right hand of ¹the mount of corruption, which ˢSolomon
the king of Israel had builded for Ashtoreth the abomination of
the Zidonians, and for Chemosh the abomination of the Moabites,
and for Milcom the abomination of the children of Ammon, did
14 the king defile. And he ᵗbrake in pieces the ²images, and cut
down the groves, and filled their places with the bones of men.
15 ¶ Moreover the altar that *was* at Beth-el, *and* the high place
ᵘwhich Jeroboam the son of Nebat, who made Israel to sin,
had made, both that altar and the high place he brake down,
and burned the high place, *and* stamped *it* small to powder,
16 and burned the grove. And as Josiah turned himself, he spied
the sepulchres that *were* there in the mount, and sent, and took
the bones out of the sepulchres, and burned *them* upon the
altar, and polluted it, according to the ˣword of the LORD which
17 the man of God proclaimed, who proclaimed these words. Then
he said, What title *is* that that I see ? And the men of the city
told him, *It is* ʸthe sepulchre of the man of God, which came
from Judah, and proclaimed these things that thou hast done
18 against the altar of Beth-el. And he said, Let him alone ; let
no man move his bones. So they let his bones ³alone, with the
19 bones of ᶻthe prophet that came out of Samaria.   ¶ And all the
houses also of the high places that *were* ᵃin the cities of Samaria,
which the kings of Israel had made to provoke *the* LORD to
anger, Josiah took away, and did to them according to all the

ˢ 1 Kin. 11.7.

ᵗ Ex. 23. 21.
Deut. 7.5,25.

ᵘ 1 Kin. 12.
28, 33.

ˣ 1 Kin. 13.2.

ʸ 1 Kin. 13.
1, 30.

ᶻ 1Kin.13.31.
ᵃ See 2 Chr.
31. 6, 7.

---

¹ That is, the mount of Olives.   ² Heb. *statues*.   ³ Heb. *to escape*.

---

least without any consciousness of guilt (see
1 K. iii. 2 note). Manasseh or Amon had
however restored them to the condition
which they had held in the reign of Solomon, and therefore Josiah would condemn
them to a special defilement.

the mount of corruption] See marg. It is
suspected that the original name was *Har
ham-mishcah,* "mount of anointing," and
that this was changed afterwards, by way of
contempt, into *Har ham-mashchith,* "mount
of corruption."

14. The Law attached uncleanness to the
"bones of men," no less than to actual
corpses (Num. xix. 16). We may gather
from this and other passages (*v.* 20 ; 1 K.
xiii. 2), that the Jews who rejected the
Law were as firm believers in the defilement
as those who adhered to the Law.

15. *and burned the high place*] This "high
place " is to be distinguished from the altar
and the grove (Asherah). It may have been
a shrine or tabernacle, either standing by
itself or else covering the "grove" (*v.* 7 note ;
1 K. xiv. 23 note). As it was "stamped
small to powder," it must have been made
either of metal or stone.

16. To burn human bones was contrary
to all the ordinary Jewish feelings with
respect to the sanctity of the sepulchre, and
had even been denounced as a sin of a
heinous character when committed by a
king of Moab (Am. ii. 1). Joshua did it,
because justified by the Divine command
(marg. ref.).

17. *What title is that ?*] Rather, "What
pillar is that ?" The word in the original indicates a short stone pillar, which was set up
either as a way-mark (Jer. xxxi. 21), or as
a sepulchral monument (Gen. xxxv. 20 ;
Ezek. xxxix. 15).

19. *the cities of Samaria*] The reformation
which Josiah effected in Samaria, is narrated in Chronicles. It implies sovereignty
to the furthest northern limits of Galilee,
and is explained by the general political
history of the East during his reign. Between B.C. 632-626 the Scythians ravaged
the more northern countries of Armenia,
Media, and Cappadocia, and found their
way across Mesopotamia to Syria, and
thence made an attempt to invade Egypt.
As they were neither the fated enemy of
Judah, nor had any hand in bringing that
enemy into the country, no mention is
made of them in the Historical Books of
Scripture. It is only in the Prophets that
we catch glimpses of the fearful sufferings
of the time (Zeph. ii. 4-6 ; Jer. i. 13-15, vi.
2-5 ; Ezek. xxxviii. and xxxix.). The invasion had scarcely gone by, and matters
settled into their former position, when the
astounding intelligence must have reached
Jerusalem that the Assyrian monarchy had
fallen ; that Nineveh was destroyed, and
that her place was to be taken, so far as
Syria and Palestine were concerned, by
Babylon. This event is fixed about B.C.
625, which seems to be exactly the time
during which Josiah was occupied in carry-

b 1 Kin. 13.
2, 32.
c Ex. 22. 20.
1 Kin. 18. 40.
ch. 11. 18.
d 2 Chr. 34. 5.
e 2 Chr. 35. 1.
f Ex. 12. 3.
Lev. 23. 5.
Num. 9. 2.
Deut. 16. 2.
g 2 Chr. 35.
18, 19.
h ch. 21. 6.

i Lev. 19. 31.
& 20. 27.
Deut. 18. 11.
k ch. 18. 5.

l ch. 21. 11, 12.
& 24. 3, 4.
Jer. 15. 4.
m ch. 17. 18,
20.
& 18. 11.
& 21. 13.
n 1 Kin. 8. 29.
& 9. 3.
ch. 21. 4, 7.

20 acts that he had done in Beth-el. And *b* he [1] *c* slew all the priests of the high places that *were* there upon the altars, and *d* burned
21 men's bones upon them, and returned to Jerusalem. ¶ And the king commanded all the people, saying, *e* Keep the passover unto the LORD your God, *f* as *it is* written in the book of this
22 covenant. Surely *g* there was not holden such a passover from the days of the judges that judged Israel, nor in all the days
23 of the kings of Israel, nor of the kings of Judah; but in the eighteenth year of king Josiah, *wherein* this passover was holden
24 to the LORD in Jerusalem. ¶ Moreover *h* the *workers with* familiar spirits, and the wizards, and the [2] images, and the idols, and all the abominations that were spied in the land of Judah and in Jerusalem, did Josiah put away, that he might perform the words of *i* the law which were written in the book that
25 Hilkiah the priest found in the house of the LORD. *k* And like unto him was there no king before him, that turned to the LORD with all his heart, and with all his soul, and with all his might, according to all the law of Moses; neither after him arose there
26 *any* like him. ¶ Notwithstanding the LORD turned not from the fierceness of his great wrath, wherewith his anger was kindled against Judah, *l* because of all the [3] provocations that
27 Manasseh had provoked him withal. And the LORD said, I will remove Judah also out of my sight, as *m* I have removed Israel, and will cast off this city Jerusalem which I have chosen, and
28 the house of which I said, *n* My name shall be there. ¶ Now

[1] Or, *sacrificed.*　　　[2] Or, *teraphim*, Gen. 31. 19 note.　　　[3] Heb. *angers.*

---

ing out his reformation in Samaria. The confusion arising in these provinces from the Scythian invasion and the troubles in Assyria was taken advantage of by Josiah to enlarge his own sovereignty. There is every indication that Josiah did, in fact, unite under his rule all the old "land of Israel" except the trans-Jordanic region, and regarded himself as subject to Nabopolassar of Babylon.

20. Here, as in *v.* 16, Josiah may have regarded himself as bound to act as he did (marg. ref. *b*). Excepting on account of the prophecy, he would scarcely have slain the priests *upon the altars.*

21. See *v.* 4 note. With this verse the author returns to the narrative of what was done in Josiah's 18th year. The need of the injunction, "*as* it was written in the book of this covenant," was owing to the fact—not that Josiah had as yet held no Passover—but that the reading of the Book had shown him differences between the existing practice and the letter of the Law—differences consequent upon negligence, or upon the fact that tradition had been allowed in various points to override the Law.

22. The details of the Passover are given by the author of Chronicles (marg. ref.). Its superiority to other Passovers seems to have consisted—(1) in the multitudes that attended it; and (2) in the completeness with which all the directions of the Law

were observed in the celebration. Cp. Neh. viii. 17.

24. *perform*] Rather, **establish.** Josiah saw that it was necessary, not only to put down open idolatry, but also to root out the *secret* practices of a similar character which were sometimes combined with the worship of Jehovah, notwithstanding that the Law forbade them (marg. reff.), and which probably formed, with many, practically almost the whole of their religion.

25. *And like unto him, &c.*] See xviii. 5 note. We must not press the letter of either passage, but regard both kings as placed *among* the very best of the kings of Judah.

26. See marg. reff. True repentance might have averted God's anger. But the people had sunk into a condition in which a true repentance was no longer possible. Individuals, like Josiah, were sincere, but the mass of the nation, despite their formal renewal of the Covenant (*v.* 3), and their outward perseverance in Jehovah-worship (2 Chr. xxxiv. 33), had feigned rather than felt repentance. The earlier chapters of Jeremiah are full at once of reproaches which he directs against the people for their insincerity, and of promises if they would repent in earnest.

27. It added to the guilt of Judah that she had had the warning of her sister Israel's example, and had failed to profit by it.

28. Josiah lived 13 years after the celebration of his great Passover. Of this

the rest of the acts of Josiah, and all that he did, *are* they not
written in the book of the chronicles of the kings of Judah?
29 °In his days Pharaoh-nechoh king of Egypt went up against   ° 2Chr.35.20.
the king of Assyria to the river Euphrates: and king Josiah
went against him; and he slew him at ᴾMegiddo, when he ᵠhad   ᴾ Zech. 12.
30 seen him. ʳAnd his servants carried him in a chariot dead from   11.
Megiddo, and brought him to Jerusalem, and buried him in his   ᵠch. 14. 8.
                                                              ʳ 2Chr.35.24.
own sepulchre. And ˢthe people of the land took Jehoahaz the   ˢ 2Chr. 36
son of Josiah, and anointed him, and made him king in his
31 father's stead. ¶¹Jehoahaz *was* twenty and three years old
when he began to reign; and he reigned three months in Jerusalem. And his mother's name *was* ᵗHamutal, the daughter of   ᵗ ch. 24. 18.
32 Jeremiah of Libnah. And he did *that which was* evil in the
sight of the LORD, according to all that his fathers had done.
33 And Pharaoh-nechoh put him in bands ᵘat Riblah in the land   ᵘ ch. 25. 6.
of Hamath, ²that he might not reign in Jerusalem; and ³put   Jer. 52. 27.
the land to a tribute of an hundred talents of silver, and a talent

¹ Called *Shallum*, 1 Chr. 3,   ² Or, *because he reigned.*   ³ Heb. *set a mulct upon the*
   15. Jer. 22. 11.   *land,* 2 Chr. 36. 3.

period we know absolutely nothing, except
that in the course of it he seems to have
submitted himself to Nabopolassar; who,
after the fall of Nineveh, was accepted as
the legitimate successor of the Assyrian
monarchs by all the nations of the western
coast. Josiah, after perhaps a little hesitation (see Jer. ii. 18, 36), followed the example of his neighbours, and frankly
accepted the position of an Assyro-Babylonian tributary. In this state matters
remained till B.C. 608, when the great events
happened which are narrated in *v.* 29.

29. *Pharaoh-Nechoh*] This king is well
known to us both from profane historians,
and from the Egyptian monuments. He
succeeded his father Psammetichus (Psama-
tik) in the year B.C. 610, and was king of
Egypt for 16 years. He was an enlightened
and enterprising monarch. The great expedition here mentioned was an attempt to detach from the newly-formed Babylonian
empire the important tract of country extending from Egypt to the Euphrates at
Carchemish. Calculating probably on the
friendship or neutrality of most of the native powers, the Egyptian monarch, having
made preparations for the space of two years,
set out on his march, probably following the
(usual) coast route through Philistia and
Sharon, from thence intending to cross by
Megiddo into the Jezreel (Esdraelon) plain.

the king of Assyria] This expression does
not imply that Nineveh had not yet fallen.
The Jews, accustomed to Assyrian monarchs,
who held their courts alternately at Nineveh
and Babylon (xix. 36; 2 Chr. xxxiii. 11), *at
first* regarded the change as merely dynastic,
and transferred to the new king, Nabopolassar, the title which they had been accustomed to give to their former suzerains.
When, later on, Nebuchadnezzar invaded
their country they found that he did not
call himself "King of Assyria," but "King
of Babylon," and thenceforth that title
came into use; but the annalist who wrote
the life of Josiah immediately upon his
death, and whom the author of Kings
copied, used, not unnaturally, the more
familiar, though less correct, designation.

Josiah went against him] Josiah probably
regarded himself as in duty bound to oppose
the march of a hostile force through his
territory to attack his suzerain. For further details see the account in Chronicles
(marg. ref.). On Megiddo, see Josh. xii. 21
note.

30. *dead*] It appears from a comparison
of this passage with 2 Chronicles (marg.
ref.) that Josiah was not actually killed in
the battle.

Jehoahaz] Or Shallum (marg. note). He
may have taken the name of Jehoahaz
(= "the Lord possesses") on his accession.
He was not the eldest son of Josiah (see
v. 36 note). The mention of "anointing"
here favours the view that there was some
irregularity in the succession (see 1 K. i.
34 note).

33. Pharaoh-Nechoh, after bringing Phœnicia and Syria under his rule, and pene-
trating as far as Carchemish, returned to
Southern Syria, and learnt what had occurred at Jerusalem in his absence. He
sent orders to Jehoahaz to attend the court
which he was holding at Riblah, and Jehoahaz fell into the trap (Ezek. xix. 4).

Riblah still retains its name. It is situated on the Orontes, in the Cœle-Syrian
valley, near the point where the valley
opens into a wide and fertile plain. Neco
seems to have been the first to perceive its
importance. Afterwards Nebuchadnezzar
made it his head-quarters during his sieges
of Jerusalem and Tyre (xxv. 21; Jer. xxxix.
5, lii. 9, 10, 26).

34 of gold. And *x*Pharaoh-nechoh made Eliakim the son of Josiah king in the room of Josiah his father, and *y*turned his name to *z*Jehoiakim, and took Jehoahaz away: *a*and he came to Egypt, 35 and died there. And Jehoiakim gave *b*the silver and the gold to Pharaoh; but he taxed the land to give the money according to the commandment of Pharaoh: he exacted the silver and the gold of the people of the land, of every one according 36 to his taxation, to give it unto Pharaoh-nechoh. ¶ *c*Jehoiakim was twenty and five years old when he began to reign; and he reigned eleven years in Jerusalem. And his mother's name 37 was Zebudah, the daughter of Pedaiah of Rumah. And he did that which was evil in the sight of the LORD, according to all that his fathers had done.

CHAP. 24. IN *a*his days Nebuchadnezzar king of Babylon came up, and Jehoiakim became his servant three years: then he 2 turned and rebelled against him. *b*And the LORD sent against him bands of the Chaldees, and bands of the Syrians, and bands of the Moabites, and bands of the children of Ammon, and sent them against Judah to destroy it, *c*according to the word of the 3 LORD, which he spake ¹by his servants the prophets. Surely at the commandment of the LORD came this upon Judah, to remove them out of his sight, *d*for the sins of Manasseh, according to 4 all that he did: *e*and also for the innocent blood that he shed:

¹ Heb. *by the hand of.*

---

34. *in the room of Josiah his father*] Not "in the room of Jehoahaz his brother;" the phrase is intended to mark the fact, that Neco did not acknowledge that Jehoahaz had ever been king.

turned his name to Jehoiakim] Cp. *v.* 30 and xxiv. 17. It seems likely, from their purely Jewish character, that the new names of the Jewish kings, though formally imposed by the suzerain, were selected by the individuals themselves. The change now made consisted merely in the substitution of Jehovah for El ("God, Jehovah, will set up"). Both names alike refer to the promise which God made to David (2 Sam. vii. 12) and imply a hope that, notwithstanding the threats of the Prophets, the seed of David would still be allowed to remain upon the throne.

36. *twenty and five years old*] Jehoiakim was therefore two years older than his half-brother, Jehoahaz (*v.* 31). See his character in *v.* 37; 2 Chr. xxxvi. 8; Ezek. xix. 5-7; Jer. xxii. 13-17, xxvi. 20-23, xxxvi.

XXIV. 1. *In his days*] i.e. B.C. 605, which was the third completed (Dan. i. 1), and fourth commencing (Jer. xxv. 1), year of Jehoiakim.

Nebuchadnezzar] or Nebuchadrezzar, which is closer to the original, *Nabu-kudurri-uzur.* This name, like most Babylonian names, is made up of three elements, *Nebo*, the well-known god (Isai. xlvi. 1), *kudur*, of doubtful signification (perhaps "crown," perhaps "landmark"), and *uzur* "protects." Nebuchadnezzar, the son of Nabopolassar, and second monarch of the Babylonian empire,

ascended the throne, B.C. 604, and reigned forty-three years, dying B.C. 561. He married Amuhia (or Amyitis), daughter of Cyaxares, king of the Medes, and was the most celebrated of all the Babylonian sovereigns. No other heathen king occupies so much space in Scripture. He was not actual king at this time, but only Crown Prince and leader of the army under his father. As he would be surrounded with all the state and magnificence of a monarch, the Jews would naturally look upon him as actual king.

came up] Nebuchadnezzar began his campaign by attacking and defeating Neco's Egyptians at Carchemish (Jer. xlvi. 2). He then pressed forward towards the south, overran Syria, Phœnicia, and Judæa, took Jerusalem, and carried off a portion of the inhabitants as prisoners (Dan. i. 1-4): after which he proceeded southwards, and had reached the borders of Egypt when he was suddenly recalled to Babylon by the death of his father.

three years] Probably from B.C. 605 to B.C. 602. Jehoiakim rebelled because he knew Nebuchadnezzar to be engaged in important wars in some other part of Asia.

2. See marg. reff. Instead of coming up in person Nebuchadnezzar sent against Jehoiakim his own troops and those of the neighbouring nations.

The ravages of the Moabites and the Ammonites are specially alluded to in the following passages: Jer. xlviii. 26, 27, xlix. 1; Ezek. xxv. 3-6; Zeph. ii. 8.

for he filled Jerusalem with innocent blood; which the LORD
5 would not pardon. ¶ Now the rest of the acts of Jehoiakim,
and all that he did, *are* they not written in the book of the
6 chronicles of the kings of Judah? *f* So Jehoiakim slept with
7 his fathers: and Jehoiachin his son reigned in his stead. And
g the king of Egypt came not again any more out of his land:
for *h* the king of Babylon had taken from the river of Egypt
unto the river Euphrates all that pertained to the king of Egypt.
8 ¶ *¹i* Jehoiachin *was* eighteen years old when he began to reign,
and he reigned in Jerusalem three months. And his mother's
name *was* Nehushta, the daughter of Elnathan of Jerusalem.
9 And he did *that which was* evil in the sight of the LORD, accord-
10 ing to all that his father had done. ¶ *k* At that time the servants of Nebuchadnezzar king of Babylon came up against
11 Jerusalem, and the city *²* was besieged. And Nebuchadnezzar
king of Babylon came against the city, and his servants did
12 besiege it. *l* And Jehoiachin the king of Judah went out to the
king of Babylon, he, and his mother, and his servants, and his
princes, and his *³* officers: *m* and the king of Babylon *n* took him
13 *o* in the eighth year of his reign. *p* And he carried out thence all
the treasures of the house of the LORD, and the treasures of the
king's house, and *q* cut in pieces all the vessels of gold which
Solomon king of Israel had made in the temple of the LORD, *r* as
14 the LORD had said. And *s* he carried away all Jerusalem, and
all the princes, and all the mighty men of valour, *t* even ten

f See 2 Chr.
36. 6, 8.
Jer. 22. 18, 19.
& 36. 30.
g See Jer.
37. 5, 7.
h Jer. 46. 2.
i 2 Chr. 36. 9.

k Dan. 1. 1.

l Jer. 24. 1.
Ezek. 17. 12.
m *Nebuchad-
nezzar's*
eighth year,
Jer. 25. 1.
n See ch. 25.
27.
o See Jer.
52. 28.
p ch. 20. 17.
Isai. 39. 6.
q See Dan.
5. 2, 3.
r Jer. 20. 5.
s Jer. 24. 1.
t See Jer. 52.
28.

¹ Called *Jeconiah*, 1 Chr. 3.
16. Jer. 24. 1, and *Co-*   *niah*, Jer. 22. 24, 28.
² Heb. *came into siege*.   ³ Or, *eunuchs*

5. Comparing Jer. xxii. 19, xxxvi. 6, 30, and Ezek. xix. 8, 9, it would seem that Nebuchadnezzar must in the fifth or sixth year after Jehoiakim's revolt have determined to go in person to Riblah, to direct operations, first against Tyre and then against Jerusalem. Jehoiakim was taken prisoner, and brought in chains to Nebuchadnezzar, who at first designed to convey him to Babylon, but afterwards had him taken to Jerusalem, where he was executed. Afterwards, when the Babylonians had withdrawn, the remains were collected and interred in the burying-place of Manasseh, so that the king ultimately "slept with his fathers" (*v.* 6).

6. *Jehoiachin*] Also called Jeconiah and Coniah. Jehoiachin and Jeconiah both mean "Jehovah will establish," Coniah, "Jehovah establishes." Probably his original name was Jehoiachin. When he ascended the throne, and was required to take a new name, anxious not to lose the good (men contained in his old one, he simply transposed the two elements. Jeremiah shortened this new name from Jeconiah to Coniah, thus cutting off from it the notion of futurity, to imply that that would not be which the name declared would be. In other words, "Jehovah establishes," but this prince he will not establish.

7. Neco, from the year of the battle of Carchemish, confined himself to his own country and made no efforts to recover Syria or Judæa.

8. *his mother's name*] On the position of the "queen mother" see 1 K. xv. 10 note. Nehushta's rank and dignity are strongly marked by the distinct and express mention which is made of her in almost every place where her son's history is touched (*v.* 12; cp. Jer. xxii. 26, xxix. 2).

10. *came up against Jerusalem*] The cause and circumstances of this siege are equally obscure. Perhaps Nebuchadnezzar detected Jehoiachin in some attempt to open communications with Egypt.

12. *the eighth year*] Jeremiah calls it the *seventh* year (Jer. lii. 28), a statement which implies only a different manner of counting regnal years.

13. On the first capture of the city in the fourth (third) year of Jehoiakim (Dan. i. 2; 2 Chr. xxxvi. 7), the vessels carried off consisted of smaller and lighter articles; while now the heavier articles, as the Table of Shewbread, the Altar of Incense, the Ark of the Covenant were stripped of their gold, which was carried away by the conquerors. Little remained more precious than brass at the time of the final capture in the reign of Zedekiah (xxv. 13–17).

14. The entire number of the captives was not more than 11,000. They consisted of three classes: (1) the "princes" or "mighty of the land," *i.e.* courtiers, priests, elders, and all who had any position or dignity—in number 3000 (cp. *vv.*

u So 1 Sam.
13. 19, 22.
x ch. 25. 12.
Jer. 40. 7.
y 2 Chr. 36. 10.
ch. 20. 18.
Jer. 22. 24,
&c.
z See Jer.
52. 28.

a Jer. 37. 1.
b 1 Chr. 3. 15.
2 Chr. 36. 10.
c 2 Chr. 36. 4.
d 2 Chr. 36. 11
Jer. 37. 1.
& 52. 1.
e ch. 23. 31.
f 2 Chr. 36. 12.

g 2 Chr. 36. 13.
Ezek. 17. 15.

thousand captives, and *u*all the craftsmen and smiths: none 15 remained, save *x*the poorest sort of the people of the land.   And *y*he carried away Jehoiachin to Babylon, and the king's mother, and the king's wives, and his ¹officers, and the mighty of the land, *those* carried he into captivity from Jerusalem to Babylon. 16 And *z*all the men of might, *even* seven thousand, and craftsmen and smiths a thousand, all *that were* strong *and* apt for war, even them the king of Babylon brought captive to Babylon. 17 ¶ And *a*the king of Babylon made Mattaniah *b*his father's brother king in his stead, and *c*changed his name to Zedekiah. 18 *d*Zedekiah *was* twenty and one years old when he began to reign, and he reigned eleven years in Jerusalem.   And his mother's name *was* *e*Hamutal, the daughter of Jeremiah of 19 Libnah.   *f*And he did *that which was* evil in the sight of the 20 LORD, according to all that Jehoiakim had done.   For through the anger of the LORD it came to pass in Jerusalem and Judah, until he had cast them out from his presence, *g*that Zedekiah rebelled against the king of Babylon.

¹ Or, *eunuchs*.

14, 16). (2) The "mighty men of valour" or "men of might," *i.e.* the soldier class, who were 7000.   And (3) craftsmen or artisans, who numbered 1000.   The word here translated " craftsmen " denotes artisans in stone, wood, or metal, and thus includes our "masons, carpenters, and smiths."   The word translated "smiths" means strictly "lock-smiths."   The object of carrying off these persons was twofold : (1) it deprived the conquered city of those artisans who were of most service in war ; and (2) it gave the conqueror a number of valuable assistants in the construction of his buildings and other great works.   The Assyrian monarchs frequently record their removal of the skilled artisans from a conquered country.   The population of the ancient city has been calculated, from its area, at 15,000.   The remnant left was therefore about 5000 or 6000.

15. *the mighty of the land*] Or "the great," "the powerful."   The word used is quite distinct from that in *vv.* 14 and 16.   It refers, not to bodily strength or fitness for war, but to civil rank or dignity.   The term would include all civil and all ecclesiastical functionaries — the nobles, courtiers, and elders of the city on the one hand, the priests, Prophets (among them, Ezekiel), and Levites on the other.

17. Mattaniah, son of Josiah and brother of Jehoahaz, but thirteen years his junior, adopted a name significant of the blessings promised by Jeremiah to the reign of a king whose name should be "Jehovah, our righteousness" (Jer. xxiii. 5-8).

19. *he did that which was evil*] The character of Zedekiah seems to have been weak rather than wicked.   Consult Jer. xxxiv., xxxvii.   His chief recorded sins were : (1) his refusal to be guided in his political conduct by Jeremiah's counsels, while never-

theless he admitted him to be a true Jehovah-Prophet ; and (2) his infraction of the allegiance which he had sworn to Nebuchadnezzar.

20. *it came to pass*] Some prefer "came this to pass :" in the sense, " Through the anger of the Lord was it that another bad king ruled in Jerusalem and in Judah:" concluding the chapter with the word "presence ;" and beginning the next chapter with the words, "And Zedekiah rebelled against the king of Babylon."

rebelled] The Book of Jeremiah explains the causes of rebellion.   In Zedekiah's early years there was an impression, both at Jerusalem (Jer. xxviii. 1-11) and at Babylon (do. xxix. 5-28), that Nebuchadnezzar was inclined to relent.   By embassy to Babylon (do. xxix. 3), and a personal visit (do. li. 59), Zedekiah strove hard to obtain the restoration of the captives and the holy vessels.   But he found Nebuchadnezzar obdurate.   Zedekiah returned to his own country greatly angered against his suzerain, and immediately proceeded to plot a rebellion.   He sought the alliance of the kings of Tyre, Sidon, Moab, Ammon, and Edom (do. xxvii. 3), and made overtures to Hophra, in Egypt, which were favourably received (Ezek. xvii. 15), whereupon he openly revolted, apparently in his ninth year, B.C. 588.   Tyre, it must be remembered, was all this time defying the power of Nebuchadnezzar, and thus setting an example of successful revolt very encouraging to the neighbouring states.   Nebuchadnezzar, while constantly maintaining an army in Syria, and continuing year after year his attempts to reduce Tyre (cp. Ezek. xxix. 18) was, it would seem, too much occupied with other matters,. such, probably, as the reduction of Susiana (Jer. xlix. 34-38), to devote more than a small share of his attention to his extreme western

Chap. 25. AND it came to pass *a*in the ninth year of his reign, in the tenth month, in the tenth *day* of the month, *that* Nebuchadnezzar king of Babylon came, he, and all his host, against Jerusalem, and pitched against it; and they built forts against it 2 round about. And the city was besieged unto the eleventh year 3 of king Zedekiah. And on the ninth *day* of the *b*fourth month the famine prevailed in the city, and there was no bread for the 4 people of the land. And *c*the city was broken up, and all the men of war *fled* by night by the way of the gate between two walls, which *is* by the king's garden: (now the Chaldees *were* against the city round about:) and *d*the king went the way 5 toward the plain. And the army of the Chaldees pursued after the king, and overtook him in the plains of Jericho: and all his 6 army were scattered from him. So they took the king, and brought him up to the king of Babylon *e*to Riblah; and they 7 ¹gave judgment upon him. And they slew the sons of Zedekiah before his eyes, and ²*f*put out the eyes of Zedekiah, and

a 2Chr. 33. 17.
Jer. 34. 2.
& 39. 1.
& 52. 4, 5.

b Jer. 39. 2.
& 52. 6.

c Jer. 39. 2.
& 52. 7, &c.

d Jer. 39.

4—7.
& 52. 7.
Ezek. 12. 12.

e Jer. 52. 9.

f Jer. 39. 7.

¹ Heb. *spake judgment with him.*   ² Heb. *made blind.*

---

frontier. In that same year, however (B.C. 588), the new attitude taken by Egypt induced him to direct to that quarter the main force of the Empire, and to take the field in person.

XXV. 1. *in the ninth year*, &c.] As the final catastrophe approaches, the historian becomes more close and exact in his dates, marking not only the year, but the *month* and the *day*, on which the siege began, no less than those on which it closed (*v.* 3). From Ezek. xxiv. 1 we find that on the very day when the host of Nebuchadnezzar made its appearance before Jerusalem the fact was revealed to Ezekiel in Babylonia, and the fate of the city announced to him (do. *vv.* 6-14). The army seems to have at first spread itself over all Judæa. It fought, not only against Jerusalem, but especially against Lachish and Azekah (Jer. xxxiv. 7), two cities of the south (2 Chr. xi. 9), which had probably been strongly garrisoned in order to maintain the communication with Egypt. This division of the Babylonian forces encouraged Hophra to put his troops in motion and advance to the relief of his Jewish allies (Jer. xxxvii. 5). On hearing this, Nebuchadnezzar broke up from before Jerusalem and marched probably to Azekah and Lachish. The Egyptians shrank back, returned into their own country (Jer. xxxvii. 7; Ezek. xvii. 17), and took no further part in the war. Nebuchadnezzar then led back his army, and once more invested the city. (It is uncertain whether the date at the beginning of this verse refers to the first or to the second investment.)

forts] Probably moveable towers, sometimes provided with battering-rams, which the besiegers advanced against the walls, thus bringing their fighting men on a level with their antagonists. Such towers are seen in the Assyrian sculptures.

2. The siege lasted almost exactly a year and a half. Its calamities—famine, pestilence, and intense suffering—are best understood from the Lamentations of Jeremiah, written probably almost immediately after the capture.

4. *the city was broken up*] Rather, "broken into," *i.e.* A breach was made about midnight in the northern wall (Ezek. ix. 2), and an entry effected into the second or lower city (xxii. 14 note), which was protected by the wall of Manasseh (2 Chr. xxxiii. 14).

Precipitate flight followed on the advance of the Babylonians to the "middle gate," or gate of communication between the upper and the lower cities. This position was only a little north of the royal palace, which the king therefore quitted. He escaped by the royal garden at the junction of the Hinnom and Kidron valleys, passing between the two walls which skirted on either side the valley of the Tyropœon.

toward the plain] "The Arabah" or the great depression which bounds Palestine Proper on the east (Num. xxi. 4 note). The "way toward the Arabah" is here the road leading eastward over Olivet to Bethany and Jericho.

5. Jeremiah (xxxviii. 23) and Ezekiel (xii. 13) had prophesied this capture; and the latter had also prophesied the dispersion of the troops (*v.* 14).

6. *to Riblah*] See xxiii. 33 note. A position whence Nebuchadnezzar could most conveniently superintend the operations against Tyre and Jerusalem. In the absence of the monarch, the siege of Jerusalem was conducted by a number of his officers, the chief of whom were Nebuzar-adan, the captain of the guard, and Nergal-shar-ezer (Neriglissar), the Rab-mag (Jer. xxxix. 3, 13).

7. *before his eyes*] This refinement of cruelty seems to have especially shocked the Jews, whose manners were less bar-

bound him with fetters of brass, and carried him to Babylon.
8 ¶And in the fifth month, *v*on the seventh *day* of the month,
which *is* *h*the nineteenth year of king Nebuchadnezzar king of
Babylon, *i*came Nebuzar-adan, ¹captain of the guard, a servant
9 of the king of Babylon, unto Jerusalem: *k*and he burnt the
house of the LORD, *l*and the king's house, and all the houses of
Jerusalem, and every great *man's* house burnt he with fire.
10 And all the army of the Chaldees, that *were with* the captain of
the guard, *m*brake down the walls of Jerusalem round about.
11 *n*Now the rest of the people *that were* left in the city, and the
²fugitives that fell away to the king of Babylon, with the remnant of the multitude, did Nebuzar-adan the captain of the
12 guard carry away. But the captain of the guard *o*left of the
13 poor of the land *to be* vinedressers and husbandmen. ¶And *p*the
*q*pillars of brass that *were* in the house of the LORD, and *r*the
bases, and *s*the brasen sea that *was* in the house of the LORD,
did the Chaldees break in pieces, and carried the brass of them
14 to Babylon. And *t*the pots, and the shovels, and the snuffers,
and the spoons, and all the vessels of brass wherewith they
15 ministered, took they away. And the firepans, and the bowls,
and such things as *were* of gold, *in* gold, and of silver, *in* silver,
16 the captain of the guard took away. The two pillars, ³one sea,
and the bases which Solomon had made for the house of the
17 LORD; *u*the brass of all these vessels was without weight. *x*The

Marginal references:
v See Jer. 52. 12—14.
h See ch. 24. 12.
& ver. 27.
i Jer. 39. 9.
k 2Chr.36.19.
l Jer. 39. 8.
Amos 2. 5.
m Neh. 1. 3.
Jer. 52. 14.
n Jer. 39. 9.
& 52. 15.
o ch. 24. 14.
Jer. 39. 10.
& 40. 7.
& 52. 16.
p ch. 20. 17.
Jer.27.19,22.
q 1 Kin.7.15.
r 1 Kin.7.27.
s 1 Kin.7.23.
t Ex. 27. 3.
1 Kin. 7. 45, 50.
u 1 Kin. 7.47.
x 1 Kin. 7.15.
Jer. 52. 21.

¹ Or, *chief marshal.*　² Heb. *fallen away.*　³ Heb. *the one sea.*

barous than those of most Orientals. It is
noted by Jeremiah in two places (xxxix. 6,
lii. 10).

and put out the eyes of Zedekiah] Blinding
has always been among the most common
of secondary punishments in the East (cp.
Judg. xvi. 21). The blinding of Zedekiah
reconciled in a very remarkable way prophecies, apparently contradictory, which
had been made concerning him. Jeremiah
had prophesied distinctly that he would be
carried to Babylon (xxxii. 5, xxxiv. 3). Ezekiel had said that he should not "see Babylon" (xii. 13). His deprivation of sight
before he was carried to the conqueror's
capital fulfilled the predictions of both
Prophets.

with fetters of brass] Lit. (see Jer. xxxix.
7 marg.), "with **two chains** of brass."
The Assyrians' captives are usually represented as bound hand and foot—the two
hands secured by one chain, the two feet by
another. According to Jewish tradition
Zedekiah was, like other slaves, forced to
work in a mill at Babylon. Jeremiah tells us
that he was kept in prison till he died (lii. 11).

8. *the nineteenth year of king N.*] B.C. 586,
if we count from the real date of his accession (B.C. 604); but B.C. 587, if, with the
Jews, we regard him as beginning to reign
when he was sent by his father to recover
Syria and gained the battle of Carchemish
(in B.C. 605).

captain of the guard] Lit., "the chief of
the executioners" (Gen. xxxvii. 36).

9. *he burnt the house of the LORD*] Cp. the

prophecies of Jeremiah (xxi. 10, xxxiv. 2,
xxxviii. 18, 23). Psalm lxxix. is thought to
have been written soon after this destruction of the Temple.

11. *the fugitives* &c.] It was from a fear
of the treatment which he would receive at
the hands of these deserters that Zedekiah
persisted in defending the city to the last
(Jer. xxxviii. 19).

12. There was probably an intention of
sending colonists into the country from some
other part of the Empire, as the Assyrians
had done in Samaria (xvii. 24).

13. *the pillars of brass,* &c.] All the more
precious treasures had been already removed from the Temple (xxiv. 13). But
there still remained many things, the list of
which is given in Jer. lii. 17-23 much more
fully than in this place. Objects in brass,
or rather bronze, were frequently carried off
by the Assyrians from the conquered nations. Bronze was highly valued, being
the chief material both for arms and implements. The breaking up of the pillars,
bases, &c., shows that it was for the material, and not for the workmanship, that
they were valued. On the various articles
consult the marg. reff.

16. *without weight*] The Babylonians did
not take the trouble to weigh the brass as
they did the gold and silver. In the Assyrian
monuments there are representations of the
weighing of captured articles in gold and
silver in the presence of the royal scribes.

17. Compare with this description the
accounts in marg. reff. The height of the

height of the one pillar *was* eighteen cubits, and the chapiter upon it *was* brass: and the height of the chapiter three cubits; and the wreathen work, and pomegranates upon the chapiter round about, all of brass: and like unto these had the second
18 pillar with wreathen work. ¶ *v* And the captain of the guard took *z* Seraiah the chief priest, and *a* Zephaniah the second
19 priest, and the three keepers of the ¹door: and out of the city he took an ²officer that was set over the men of war, and *b* five men of them that ³were in the king's presence, which were found in the city, and the ⁴principal scribe of the host, which mustered the people of the land, and threescore men of the people of
20 the land *that were* found in the city: and Nebuzar-adan captain of the guard took these, and brought them to the king of
21 Babylon to Riblah: and the king of Babylon smote them, and slew them at Riblah in the land of Hamath. *c* So Judah was
22 carried away out of their land. ¶ *d* And *as for* the people that remained in the land of Judah, whom Nebuchadnezzar king of Babylon had left, even over them he made Gedaliah the son of
23 Ahikam, the son of Shaphan, ruler. And when all the *c* captains of the armies, they and their men, heard that the king of Babylon had made Gedaliah governor, there came to Gedaliah to Mizpah, even Ishmael the son of Nethaniah, and Johanan the son of Careah, and Seraiah the son of Tanhumeth the Netopha-

v Jer. 52. 2¹, &c.
z 1 Chr. 6. 14. Ezra 7. 1.
a Jer. 21. 1.
& 29. 25.
b See Jer. 52. 25.

c Lev. 26. 33. Deut. 28. 36, 64.
ch. 23. 27.
d Jer. 40. 5.

e Jer. 40. 7, 8, 9.

---

¹ Heb. *threshold.*
² Or, *eunuch.*
³ Heb. *saw the king's face,* Esth. 1. 14.
⁴ Or, *scribe of the captain of the host.*

---

capital ("*three* cubits") must be corrected, in accordance with those passages, to "*five* cubits."

18. It devolved on Nebuzaradan to select for exemplary punishment the persons whom he regarded as most guilty, either in respect of the original rebellion or of the protracted resistance. Instead of taking indiscriminately the first comers, he first selected those who by their offices would be likely to have had most authority—the High-Priest; the second priest (xxiii. 4 note); three of the Temple Levites; the commandant of the city; five members of the king's Privy Council (or seven, see *v.* 19 note); and the secretary (or adjutant) of the captain of the host. To these he added sixty others, who were accounted "princes." Compared with the many occasions on which Assyrian and Persian conquerors put to death hundreds or thousands after taking a revolted town, Nebuzaradan (and Nebuchadnezzar) must be regarded as moderate, or even merciful, in their vengeance. Cp. Jer. xl. 2-5.

the three keepers of the door] Rather, "three keepers.". The Hebrew has no article. The Temple "door-keepers" in the time of Solomon numbered twenty-four (1 Chr. xxvi. 17, 18), who were probably under six chiefs. After the Captivity the chiefs are either six (Ez. ii. 42; Neh. vii. 45) or four (1 Chr. ix. 17).

19. *out of the city*] This clause shows that the five persons mentioned in *v.* 18 were taken out of the Temple.

five men] Or, "seven men," according to Jer. lii. 25. It is impossible to say which of the two numbers is correct.

of them that were in the king's presence] See marg. A mode of speech arising from the custom of Eastern rulers to withdraw themselves as much as possible from the view of their subjects.

21. *So Judah was carried away*] The kingdom of the two tribes was at an end; and the task of the historian might seem to be accomplished. He still, however, desires to notice two things: (1) the fate of the remnant (*vv.* 22-26) left in the land by Nebuzaradan; and (2) the fate of Jehoiachin, who, of all those led into captivity, was the least to blame (*vv.* 27-30).

22. We may be allowed to conjecture that Jeremiah, in gratitude for Ahikam's service to himself (Jer. xxvi. 24), recommended his son Gedaliah to Nebuzaradan, and through him to Nebuchadnezzar, for the office of governor.

23. *the captains of the armies*] *i.e.* the officers of the troops who had fled from Jerusalem with Zedekiah (*v.* 4), and had then dispersed and gone into hiding (*v.* 5).

For Mizpah, see Josh. xviii. 26 note.

the Netophathite] Netophah, the city of Ephai (cp. Jer. xl. 8), appears to have been in the neighbourhood of Bethlehem (Neh. vii. 26; Ezr. ii. 21, 22). The name is perhaps continued in the modern *Antubeh*, about 2½ miles S.S.E. of Jerusalem.

a Maachathite] Maachah lay in the stony country east of the upper Jordan, bordering upon Bashan (Deut. iii. 14).

thite, and Jaazaniah the son of a Maachathite, they and their
24 men. And Gedaliah sware to them, and to their men, and said
unto them, Fear not to be the servants of the Chaldees: dwell
in the land, and serve the king of Babylon; and it shall be well

f Jer. 41. 1, 2.   25 with you. But *f*it came to pass in the seventh month, that
Ishmael the son of Nethaniah, the son of Elishama, of the seed
[1]royal, came, and ten men with him, and smote Gedaliah, that
he died, and the Jews and the Chaldees that were with him at
26 Mizpah. And all the people, both small and great, and the

g Jer. 43. 4, 7.   captains of the armies, arose, *g*and came to Egypt: for they
h Jer. 52. 31,   27 were afraid of the Chaldees. ¶ *h*And it came to pass in the
&c.   seven and thirtieth year of the captivity of Jehoiachin king of
Judah, in the twelfth month, on the seven and twentieth *day* of
the month, *that* Evil-merodach king of Babylon in the year that

i See Gen.   he began to reign *i*did lift up the head of Jehoiachin king of
40. 13, 20.   28 Judah out of prison; and he spake [2]kindly to him, and set his
throne above the throne of the kings that *were* with him in

k 2 Sam. 9. 7.   29 Babylon; and changed his prison garments: and he did *k*eat
30 bread continually before him all the days of his life. And his
allowance *was* a continual allowance given him of the king, a
daily rate for every day, all the days of his life.

[1] Heb. *of the kingdom.*   [2] Heb. *good things with him.*

---

24. As rebels against the Babylonian king, their lives were forfeit. Gedaliah pledged himself to them by oath, that, if they gave no further cause of complaint, their past offences should be forgiven.

25, 26. Jeremiah gives this history with much fulness of detail (xli–xliii).

27. The captivity of Jehoiachin commenced in the year B.C. 597—the eighth year of Nebuchadnezzar. It terminated B.C. 561—the first year of Evil-merodach, the son and successor of Nebuchadnezzar. He reigned only two years, being murdered by his brother-in-law, Neriglissar, or Nergal-shar-ezer. He is said to have provoked his fate by lawless government and intemperance.

28. *the kings that were with him*] Probably captive kings, like Jehoiachin himself. Cp. Judg. i. 7.

29. Evil-merodach gave him garments befitting his rank. To dress a man suitably to his position was the first thought of an Oriental (Gen. xli. 42; Esth. viii. 15; Dan. v. 29; Luke xv. 22). So again, Oriental kings regarded it as a part of their greatness to feed daily a vast multitude of persons at their Courts (see 1 K. iv. 22, 23). Of these, as here, a certain number had the special privilege of sitting actually at the royal board, while the others ate separately, generally at a lower level. See Judg. i. 7; 2 Sam. ix. 13; 1 K. ii. 7; Ps. xli. 9.

30. *allowance*] From the treasury, in order to enable him to maintain the state proper to his rank, and in addition to his food at the royal table. Jehoiachin, to the day of his death, lived in peace and comfort at the court of Babylon (cp. Jer. lii. 34).

CHRONICLES.

INTRODUCTION TO BOOKS I. AND II.

1. LIKE the two Books of Kings, the two Books of Chronicles formed originally a single work, the separation of which into two "Books" is referable to the Septuagint translators, whose division was adopted by Jerome, and from whom it passed to the various branches of the Western Church. In the Hebrew Bibles the title of the work means literally "the daily acts" or "occurrences,"[1] a title originally applied to the accounts of the reigns of the several kings, but afterwards applied to general works made up from these particular narratives.

The Septuagint translators substituted one which they regarded as more suitable to the contents of the work and the position that it occupies among the Historical Books of the Bible. This was *Paraleipomena*, or "the things omitted"—a name intended to imply that Chronicles was *supplementary* to Samuel and Kings, written, *i.e.*, mainly for the purpose of supplying the omissions of the earlier history.

The English title, "Chronicles," (derived from the Vulgate) is a term primarily significative of time; but in practical use it designates a simple and primitive style of history rather than one in which the chronological element is peculiarly prominent.

2. The "Book of Chronicles" stands in a position unlike that occupied by any other Book of the Old Testament. It is historical, yet not new history. The writer traverses ground that has been already trodden by others.[2]

His purpose in so doing is sufficiently indicated by the practical object he had in view, viz., that of meeting the peculiar difficulties of his own day. The people had lately returned from the Captivity[3] and had rebuilt the Temple;[4] but they had not yet gathered up the threads of the old national life, broken by the Captivity. They were therefore reminded, in the first place, of their entire history, of the whole past course of mundane events, and of the position which they themselves held among the nations of the earth. This was done, curtly and drily, but sufficiently, by genealogies,[5] which have always possessed a peculiar attraction for Orientals. They were then more especially reminded of their own past as an

---

[1] 1 K. xi. 41; 2 Chr. xii. 15, xxxiii. 19, &c.

[2] The author of Kings wrote, as has been already shown (Introduction to Kings, p. 264), before the return from the Captivity. The author of Chronicles writes after the return.

[3] See 1 Chr. ix. 1–34; 2 Chr. xxxvi. 20–23. See p. 446, note 6.

[4] 1 Chr. ix. 11, 13, 19, &c.

[5] 1 Chr. i.-viii.

organised nation—a settled people with a religion which has a fixed home in the centre of the nation's life. It was the strong conviction of the writer that the whole future prosperity of his countrymen was bound up with the preservation of the Temple service, with the proper maintenance of the priests and Levites, the regular establishment of the " courses," and the rightful distribution of the several ministrations of the Temple among the Levitical families. He therefore drew the attention of his countrymen to the past history of the Temple, under David, Solomon, and the later kings of Judah; pointing out that in almost every instance temporal rewards and punishments followed in exact accordance with the attitude in which the king placed himself towards the national religion. Such a picture of the past, a sort of condensed view of the entire previous history, written in the idiom of the day, with frequent allusions to recent events, and with constant reiteration of the moral intended to be taught, was calculated to affect the newly returned and still unsettled people far more strongly and deeply than the old narratives. The Book of Chronicles bridged over, so to speak, the gulf which separated the nation after, from the nation before, the Captivity : it must have helped greatly to restore the national life, to revive hope and encourage high aspirations by showing to the nation that its fate was in its own hands, and that religious faithfulness would be certain to secure the Divine blessing.

3. That the Book of Chronicles was composed after the return from the Captivity is evident, not only from its closing passage, but from other portions of it.[6]

The evidence of style accords with the evidence furnished by the contents. The phraseology is similar to that of Ezra, Nehemiah, and Esther, all books written after the exile. It has numerous Aramæan forms,[7] and at least one word derived from the Persian.[8] The date cannot therefore well be earlier than B.C. 538, but may be very considerably later. The very close connexion of style between Chronicles and Ezra, makes it probable that they were composed at the same time, if not even by the same person. If Ezra was the author, as so many think, the date could not well be much later than B.C. 435, for Ezra probably died about that time. There is nothing in the contents or style of the work to make the date B.C. 450-435 improbable ; for the genealogy in iii. 23, 24, which appears to be later than this, may be a subsequent addition.[9]

4. The writer of Chronicles cites, as his authorities, works of two distinct classes.

(a) His most frequent reference is to a *general* history—the " Book of the Kings of Israel and Judah,"[10] This was a compilation

---

[6] A comparison of 1 Chr. ix. 10-16 with Nehem. xi. 10-17 will show that almost the whole of 1 Chr ix. belongs to the period after the Captivity. Ch. iii. contains a genealogy of the descendants of Zerubbabel (19-24), which is continued down to, at least, the third generation.

[7] *e.g.* 1 Chr. xviii. 5 (Darmesek).

[8] See 1 Chr. xxix. 7 note. The other supposed Persian words in Chronicles are somewhat doubtful.

[9] See p. 449, note 3.

[10] See 2 Chr. xvi. 11, xxv. 26, xxvii. 7, xxviii. 26, xxxv. 27, xxxvi. 8.

from the two histories constantly mentioned in Kings—the "Book of the Chronicles of the Kings of Israel," and the "Book of the Chronicles of the Kings of Judah,"[1] which it had been found convenient to unite into one. (b) The other works cited by him were 12 or 13 part-histories, the works of Prophets who dealt with particular portions of the national annals.[2] Of none of these works is the exact character known to us ; but the manner in which they are cited makes it probable that for the most part they treated with some fulness the history—especially the religious history—of the times of their authors. They may be regarded as independent compositions — monographs upon the events of their times, written by individual Prophets, of which occasionally one was transferred, not into our "Books of Kings," but into the "Book of the Kings of Israel and Judah ;" while the remainder existed for some centuries side by side with the "Book of the Kings," and furnished to the writer of Chronicles much of the special information which he conveys to us.

There is also ample proof that the writer made use of the whole of the earlier historical Scriptures, and especially of the Books of Samuel and Kings, such as we have them. The main sources of 1 Chr. i.–viii., are the earlier Scriptures from Genesis to Ruth, supplemented by statements drawn from *private* sources, such as the genealogies of families, and numerous important points of family history, carefully preserved by the "chiefs of the fathers" in almost all the Israelite tribes ; a main source of 1 Chr. x.–xxvii. is Samuel ; and a source, though scarcely a main source, of 2 Chr. i.–xxxvi. is Kings (cp. the marg. reff. and notes). But the writer has always some further authority besides these; and there is no section of the Jewish history, from the death of Saul to the fall of Jerusalem, which he has not illustrated with new facts, drawn from some source which has perished.

5. The indications of unity in the authorship preponderate over those of diversity, and lead to the conclusion that the entire work is from one and the same writer. The genealogical tendency, which shows itself so strongly in the introductory section (1 Chr. i.–ix.), is remarkably characteristic of the writer, and continually thrusts itself into notice in the more purely historical portions of his narrative.[3] Conversely, the mere genealogical portion of the work is penetrated by the same spirit as animates the historical chapters,[4]

---

[1] See Introduction to Kings, p. 265.
[2] e.g. "The Chronicles of King David" (1 Chr. xxvii. 24), "The Acts of Samuel the Seer," "The Acts of Nathan the Prophet," "The Acts of Gad the Seer" (xxix. 29), "The Prophecy of Ahijah the Shilonite," "The Visions of Iddo the Seer" (2 Chr. ix. 29), "The Acts of Shemaiah the Prophet," "Iddo the Seer on Genealogies" (xii. 15), "The Commentary of the Prophet Iddo" (xiii. 22), "The Acts of Jehu the son of Hanani" (xx. 34),

"The Commentary of the Book of the Kings" (xxiv. 27), "Isaiah's Acts of Uzziah" (xxvi. 22), "The Vision of Isaiah" (xxxii. 32), and "The Acts of Hosai" (xxxiii. 19 ; see note).
[3] See 2 Chr. xi. 18-20, xx. 14, xxi. 2, xxiii. 1, xxix. 12-14, and xxxiv. 12.
[4] e.g. (a) The Levitical spirit, as it has been called ; the sense, i.e., of the importance of the Levitical order and its various divisions, offices, and arrangements, which so markedly characterises the his-

and moreover abounds with phrases, characteristic of the writer.[5]

That the historical narrative (1 Chr. x.—2 Chr. xxxvi.) is from one hand, can scarcely be doubted. One pointedly didactic tone pervades the whole—each signal calamity and success being ascribed in the most direct manner to the action of Divine Providence, rewarding the righteous and punishing the evil-doers.[6] There is everywhere the same method of composition—a primary use of Samuel and Kings as bases of the narrative, the abbreviation of what has been narrated before, the omission of important facts, otherwise known to the reader;[7] and the addition of new facts, sometimes minute, and less important than curious,[8] at other times so striking that it is surprising that the earlier historians should have passed them over.[9]

6. The abrupt termination of Chronicles, in the middle of a sentence,[1] is an unanswerable argu-

ment against its having come down to us in the form in which it was originally written.

And the recurrence of the final passage of our present copies of Chronicles at the commencement of Ezra, taken in conjunction with the undoubted fact, that there is a very close resemblance of style and tone between the two Books, suggests naturally the explanation, which has been accepted by some of the best critics, that the two works, Chronicles and Ezra, were originally one, and were afterwards separated:[2] that separation having probably arisen out of a desire to arrange the history of the post-Captivity period in chronological sequence.

7. The condition of the text of Chronicles is far from satisfactory. Various readings are frequent, particularly in the names of persons and places; omissions are found, especially in the genealogies; and the numbers are sometimes self-contradictory, sometimes contradict-

---

torical portion of Chronicles, appears in the genealogical section by the large space assigned to the account of the sons of Levi, who occupy not only the whole of 1 Chr. vi. but also the greater part of ch. ix. (b) The strong feeling with respect to Divine Providence, and the very plain and direct teaching on the subject, which is the most striking feature of the general narrative appears also in the genealogical chapters, as in 1 Chr. iv. 10, v. 20, 22, 25-26, and ix. 1.

[5] e.g. "Moses the servant of God," 1 Chr. vi. 49; cp. 2 Chr. i. 3, xxiv. 6. "Samuel the seer," 1 Chr. ix. 22; cp. xxvi. 28. "The ruler of the house of God," 1 Chr. ix. 11; cp. 2 Chr. xxxi. 13.

[6] Cp. 1 Chr. x. 13, xi. 9; 2 Chr. xii. 2, xiii. 18, &c. Cp. note 4 (b).

[7] e.g. The burning of Saul's body (1 Sam. xxxi. 12), omitted in 1 Chr. x. yet implied in v. 12; the cession of certain cities to Hiram (1 K. ix. 12), omitted but implied in 2 Chr. viii. 2; the destruction

of the kingdom of Israel by the Assyrians (2 K. xvii. 3-6), omitted in Chronicles but implied in the words of Hezekiah (2 Chr. xxx. 6-7, &c.).

[8] e.g. 1 Chr. xxi. 27.

[9] e.g. The solemn addresses of David (1 Chr. xxviii. and xxix. 1-20); the letters from Solomon to Hiram and from Hiram to Solomon (2 Chr. ii. 3-16); the religious and other reforms of Jehoshaphat (xvii. 6-9, xix. 4-11); the religious reformation of Hezekiah (xxix.-xxxi.); the captivity of Manasseh, his repentance, and his restoration to his kingdom (xxxiii. 11-13); and the establishment by Josiah of his authority in the old kingdom of Israel (xxxiv. 6-7, 9, xxxv. 17-18).

[1] 2 Chr. xxxvi. 23, "Who is there among you of all his people? [The Lord] his God be with him, and let him go up ——." Every reader naturally asks, whither? Cp. Ezra i. 3.

[2] This is more satisfactory than to consider that the Books of Chronicles closed with 2 Chr. xxxvi. 21.

ory of more probable numbers in Samuel or Kings, sometimes unreasonably large, and therefore justly suspected.

The work is, however, free from defects of a more serious character.[3] The unity is unbroken, and there is every reason to believe that we have the work, in almost all respects, exactly as it came from the hand of the author.

8. As compared with the parallel histories of Samuel and Kings, the history of Chronicles is characterised by three principal features : (a) A greater tendency to dwell on the externals of religion, on the details of the Temple worship, the various functions of the Priests and Levites, the arrangement of the courses, and the like. Hence the history of Chronicles has been called " ecclesiastical," that of Samuel and Kings " political."[4] This tendency does not detract from the credibility, or render the history undeserving of confidence. (b) A marked genealogical bias and desire to put on record the names of persons engaged in any of the events narrated ; and (c) A more constant, open, and direct ascription of all the events of the history to the Divine agency, and especially a

more plain reference of every great calamity or deliverance to the good or evil deeds of the monarch, or the nation, which Divine Providence so punished or rewarded.[5]

There is no reason to regard Chronicles as less trustworthy than Samuel or Kings. A due consideration of disputed points, the " Levitical spirit," contradictions, alleged mistakes, &c., does not, speaking generally, impugn the honesty of the writer or the authenticity of his work. The Book may fairly be regarded as authentic in all its parts, with the exception of some of its numbers. These appear to have occasionally suffered corruption, though scarcely to a greater extent than those of other Books of equal antiquity. From blemishes of this kind it has not pleased God to keep His Word free. It will scarcely be maintained at the present day that their occurrence affects in the very slightest degree the authenticity of the rest of the narrative.

The style of Chronicles is simpler and less elevated than that of Kings. Excepting the psalm of David in 1 Chr. xvi. and the prayer of Solomon in 2 Chr. vi., the whole is prosaic, level, and uniform. There are no especially

---

[3] One interpolation into the text is to be noted (1 Chr. iii. 22-24 ; see *v*. 19 note) —an authorised addition, probably, by a later Prophet, such as Malachi.

[4] The reign of Hezekiah may be taken as a crucial instance of the difference between the modes of treatment pursued by the writers of Chronicles and Kings. The writer of Kings devotes three, the writer of Chronicles four, chapters to the subject. Both represent the reign as remarkable : (1) for a religious reformation ; and (2) for striking events of secular history, in which Judæa was brought into

connexion with the great monarchies of the time, Babylonia and Assyria. But while the writer of Kings thinks it enough to relate the religious reformation in three verses (1 K. xviii. 4-6), and devotes to the secular history, treated indeed from a religious point of view, the whole remainder of his three chapters, the writer of Chronicles gives the heads of the secular history in one chapter, while he devotes to the religious reformation the remaining three chapters of his four.

[5] See p. 448.

striking chapters, as in Kings ; but it is less gloomy, being addressed to the restored nation, which it seeks to animate and inspirit. The captive people, weeping by the waters of Babylon, fitly read their mournful history in Kings: the liberated nation, entering hopefully upon a new life, found in Chronicles a review of its past, calculated to help it forward on the path of progress, upon which it was entering.

THE FIRST BOOK

OF THE

CHRONICLES.

Chap. 1. ADAM, ^aSheth, Enosh, Kenan, Mahalaleel, Jered, He-
4 noch, Methuselah, Lamech, Noah, Shem, Ham, and Japheth.
5 ¶ ^bThe sons of Japheth; Gomer, and Magog, and Madai, and
6 Javan, and Tubal, and Meshech, and Tiras. And the sons of
7 Gomer; Ashchenaz, and ¹Riphath, and Togarmah. And the
sons of Javan; Elishah, and Tarshish, Kittim, and ²Dodanim.
8 ¶ ^cThe sons of Ham; Cush, and Mizraim, Put, and Canaan.
9 And the sons of Cush; Seba, and Havilah, and Sabta, and Raamah, and Sabtecha. And the sons of Raamah; Sheba, and
10 Dedan. And Cush ^dbegat Nimrod: he began to be mighty upon
11 the earth. And Mizraim begat Ludim, and Anamim, and Leha-
12 bim, and Naphtuhim, and Pathrusim, and Casluhim, (of whom
13 came the Philistines,) and ^eCaphthorim. And ^fCanaan begat
14 Zidon his firstborn, and Heth, the Jebusite also, and the Amo-
15 rite, and the Girgashite, and the Hivite, and the Arkite, and the
16 Sinite, and the Arvadite, and the Zemarite, and the Hamathite.
17 ¶ The sons of ^gShem; Elam, and Asshur, and Arphaxad, and
Lud, and Aram, and Uz, and Hul, and Gether, and ³Meshech.
18, 19 And Arphaxad begat Shelah, and Shelah begat Eber. And
unto Eber were born two sons: the name of the one was ⁴Peleg;
because in his days the earth was divided: and his brother's
20 name was Joktan. And ^hJoktan begat Almodad, and Sheleph,
21 and Hazarmaveth, and Jerah, Hadoram also, and Uzal, and
22, 23 Diklah, and Ebal, and Abimael, and Sheba, and Ophir, and
Havilah, and Jobab. All these were the sons of Joktan.
24, 25, 26 ¶ ⁱShem, Arphaxad, Shelah, ^kEber, Peleg, Reu, Serug,
27, 28 Nahor, Terah, ^lAbram; the same is Abraham. The sons of
29 Abraham; ^mIsaac, and ⁿIshmael. ¶ These are their generations:
the ^ofirstborn of Ishmael, Nebaioth; then Kedar, and Adbeel, and

^a Gen. 4. 25, 26.
& 5. 3, 9.
^b Gen. 10. 2, &c.

^c Gen. 10. 6, &c.

^d Gen. 10. 8, 13, &c.

^e Deut. 2. 23.
^f Gen. 10. 15, &c.

^g Gen. 10. 22.
& 11. 10.

^h Gen. 10. 23.

ⁱ Gen. 11. 10, &c.
Luke 3. 34, &c.
^k Gen. 11. 15.
^l Gen. 17. 5.
^m Gen. 21. 2, 3.
ⁿ Gen. 16.
11, 15.
^o Gen. 25. 13—16.

---

¹ Or, *Diphath*, as it is in some copies.
² Or, *Rodanim*, according to some copies.
³ Or, *Mash*, Gen. 10. 23.
⁴ That is, *Division*, Gen. 10. 25.

I. 1. Cp. marg. reff. and notes.
7. *Dodanim*] See Gen. x. 4 note.
16. *the Zemarite*] See Gen. x. 18 note. The inscriptions of the Assyrian monarch, Sargon, (B.C. 720) mention Zimira, which is joined with Arpad (Arvad); and there can be little doubt that it is the city indicated by the term "Zemarite."
17. *The sons of Shem*] i.e., descendants. Uz, Hul, Gether, and Meshech (or Mash), are stated to have been "sons of Aram" (Gen. x. 23). Meshech is the reading of all the MSS., and is supported by the LXX. here and in Gen. x. 23. It seems preferable to "Mash," which admits of no very probable explanation. Just as Hamites and Semites were intermingled in Arabia (Gen. x. 7, 29 notes), so Semites and Japhethites may have been intermingled in Cappadocia

—the country of the Meshech or Moschi (Gen. x. 2 note); and this Aramæan admixture may have been the origin of the notion, so prevalent among the Greeks, that the Cappadocians were Syrians.
28. *Isaac and Ishmael*] Isaac, though younger than Ishmael, is placed first, as the legitimate heir, since Sarah alone was Abraham's true wife (cp. v. 35 note).
29. *These are their generations*] As Shem was reserved till after Japheth and Ham (vv. 5-16), because in him the genealogy was to be continued (Gen. x. 2 note), so Isaac is now reserved till the other lines of descent from Abraham have been completed. The same principle gives the descendants of Esau a prior place to those of Jacob (vv. 35-54; ii. 1).

30 Mibsam, Mishma, and Dumah, Massa, ¹Hadad, and Tema,
31 Jetur, Naphish, and Kedemah.   These are the sons of Ishmael.
p Gen.25.1,2.   32 ¶ Now *p*the sons of Keturah, Abraham's concubine: she bare
Zimran, and Jokshan, and Medan, and Midian, and Ishbak,
33 and Shuah.   And the sons of Jokshan; Sheba, and Dedan.
And the sons of Midian; Ephah, and Epher, and Henoch, and
34 Abida, and Eldaah.   All these *are* the sons of Keturah.   ¶ And
q Gen.21.2,3   *q*Abraham begat Isaac.   *r*The sons of Isaac; Esau and Israel.
r Gen. 25.   35 ¶ The sons of *s*Esau; Eliphaz, Reuel, and Jeush, and Jaalam,
25, 23.
s Gen. 36. 9,   36 and Korah.   The sons of Eliphaz; Teman, and Omar, ²Zephi,
10.
37 and Gatam, Kenaz, and Timna, and Amalek.   The sons of
t Gen. 36. 20.   38 Reuel; Nahath, Zerah, Shammah, and Mizzah.   ¶ And *t*the
sons of Seir; Lotan, and Shobal, and Zibeon, and Anah, and
39 Dishon, and Ezar, and Dishan.   And the sons of Lotan; Hori,
40 and ³Homam: and Timna *was* Lotan's sister.   The sons of
Shobal; ⁴Alian, and Manahath, and Ebal, ⁵Shephi, and Onam.
41 And the sons of Zibeon; Aiah, and Anah.   The sons of Anah;
u Gen. 36.25.   *u*Dishon.   And the sons of Dishon; ⁶Amram, and Eshban, and
42 Ithran, and Cheran.   The sons of Ezer; Bilhan, and Zavan,
43 *and* ⁷Jakan.   The sons of Dishan; Uz, and Aran.   ¶ Now
x Gen. 36.31,   these *are* the *x*kings that reigned in the land of Edom before
&c.
any king reigned over the children of Israel; Bela the son of
44 Beor: and the name of his city *was* Dinhabah.   And when Bela
was dead, Jobab the son of Zerah of Bozrah reigned in his
45 stead.   And when Jobab was dead, Husham of the land of the
46 Temanites reigned in his stead.   And when Husham was dead,
Hadad the son of Bedad, which smote Midian in the field of
Moab, reigned in his stead: and the name of his city *was* Avith.
47 And when Hadad was dead, Samlah of Masrekah reigned in his
y Gen. 36.37.   48 stead.   *y*And when Samlah was dead, Shaul of Rehoboth by the
49 river reigned in his stead.   And when Shaul was dead, Baal-
50 hanan the son of Achbor reigned in his stead.   And when Baal-
hanan was dead, ⁸Hadad reigned in his stead: and the name of
his city *was* ⁹Pai; and his wife's name *was* Mehetabel, the
51 daughter of Matred, the daughter of Mezahab.   Hadad died
z Gen. 36. 40.   also.   And the *z*dukes of Edom *were*; duke Timnah, duke
52 ¹Aliah, duke Jetheth, duke Aholibamah, duke Elah, duke
53, 54 Pinon, duke Kenaz, duke Teman, duke Mibzar, duke Magdiel,
duke Iram.   These *are* the dukes of Edom.

¹ Or, *Hadar*, Gen. 25. 15.   ⁵ Or, *Shepho*, Gen. 36. 23.   ⁸ Or, *Hadar*, Gen. 36. 39.
² Or, *Zepho*, Gen. 36. 11.   ⁶ Or, *Hemdan*, Gen. 36.26.   ⁹ Or, *Pau*, Gen. 36. 39.
³ Or, *Heman*, Gen. 36. 22.   ⁷ Or, *Akan*, Gen. 36. 27.   ¹ Or, *Alvah*.
⁴ Or, *Alvan*, Gen. 36. 23.

---

30. Hadad here and in *v.* 50 is the well-
known Syrian name, of which Hadar
(marg.) is an accidental corruption, consequent on the close resemblance between *d*
and *r* in Hebrew, the final letters of the two
names.

32. *Keturah, Abraham's concubine*] This
passage, and Gen. xxv. 6, sufficiently prove
that the position of Keturah was not that
of the full wife, but of the "secondary" or
"concubine wife" (Jud. xix. 1) so common
among Orientals.

36. *Timna*] In Gen. xxxvi. 11, Eliphaz has
no son Timna; but he has a concubine of
the name, who is the mother of Amalek,

and conjectured to be Lotan's sister (*v.* 39).
The best explanation is, that the writer has
in his mind rather the tribes descended from
Eliphaz than his actual children, and as
there was a place, Timna, inhabited by his
"dukes" (*v.* 51; cp. Gen. xxxv. 40), he puts
the race which lived there among his "sons."

41. Amram (rather **Hamran**), and Hemdan
(marg.), differ in the original by the same
letter only which marks the difference in
v. 30.

43-54. The slight differences favour the
view, that the writer of Chronicles has here,
as elsewhere, abridged from Genesis (see
marg. reff.).

Chap. 2. THESE *are* the sons of [1]Israel; ^aReuben, Simeon, Levi,
2 and Judah, Issachar, and Zebulun, Dan, Joseph, and Benjamin,
3 Naphtali, Gad, and Asher. ¶ The sons of ^bJudah; Er, and
Onan, and Shelah: *which* three were born unto him of the
daughter of ^cShua the Canaanitess. And ^dEr, the firstborn of
Judah, was evil in the sight of the LORD; and he slew him.
4 And ^eTamar his daughter in law bare him Pharez and Zerah.
5 All the sons of Judah *were* five. The sons of ^fPharez; Hezron,
6 and Hamul. ¶ And the sons of Zerah ; [2]Zimri, ^gand Ethan, and
7 Heman, and Calcol, and [3]Dara: five of them in all. And the
sons of ^hCarmi; [4]Achar, the troubler of Israel, who trans-
8 gressed in the thing ⁱaccursed. And the sons of Ethan; Aza-
9 riah. ¶ The sons also of Hezron, that were born unto him ;
10 Jerahmeel, and [5]Ram, and [6]Chelubai. And Ram ^kbegat Amminadab; and Amminadab begat Nahshon, ^lprince of the
11 children of Judah; and Nahshon begat [7]Salma, and Salma
12 begat Boaz, and Boaz begat Obed, and Obed begat Jesse, ^mand
13 Jesse begat his firstborn Eliab, and Abinadab the second, and
14 [8]Shimma the third, Nethaneel the fourth, Raddai the fifth,
15, 16 Ozem the sixth, David the seventh: whose sisters *were* Zeruiah, and Abigail. ⁿAnd the sons of Zeruiah ; Abishai, and Joab,
17 and Asahel, three. And ^oAbigail bare Amasa: and the father
18 of Amasa *was* [9]Jether the Ishmeelite. ¶ And Caleb the son of
Hezron begat *children* of Azubah *his* wife, and of Jerioth: her
19 sons *are* these ; Jesher, and Shobab, and Ardon. And when
Azubah was dead, Caleb took unto him ^pEphrath, which bare
20 him Hur. And Hur begat Uri, and Uri begat ^qBezaleel.

Margin references (right column):
^a Gen. 29. 32.
& 30. 5, &c.
& 35. 18, 22.
& 46. 8, &c.
^b Gen. 38. 3.
& 46. 12.
Num. 26. 19.
^c Gen. 38. 2.
^d Gen. 38. 7.
^e Gen. 38.
29, 30.
Matt. 1. 3.
^f Gen. 46. 12.
Ruth 4. 18.
^g 1 Kin. 4.31.
^h See ch.4.1.
ⁱ Josh. 6. 18.
& 7. 1.
^k Ruth 4. 19,
20.
Matt. 1. 4.
^l Num. 1. 7.
& 2. 3.
^m 1 Sam.16.6.

ⁿ 2 Sam.2.18.
^o 2 Sam. 17
25.

^p ver. 50.
^q Ex. 31. 2.

Footnotes:
[1] Or, *Jacob.*
[2] Or, *Zabdi,* Josh. 7. 1.
[3] Or, *Darda.*
[4] Or, *Achan.*
[5] Or, *Aram,* Matt. 1. 3, 4.
[6] Or, *Caleb,* ver. 18, 42.
[7] Or, *Salmon,* Ruth 4. 21.
Matt. 1. 4.
[8] Or, *Shammah,* 1 Sam.
16. 9.
[9] 2 Sam. 17. 25, *Ithra an
Israelite.*

II. 1. *the sons of Israel*] The order of the
names here approximates to an order determined by legitimacy of birth. A single
change—the removal of Dan to the place
after Benjamin—would give the following
result :—

(1) The six sons of the first wife, Leah.
(2) The two sons of the second wife,
Rachel.
(3) The two sons of the first concubine,
Bilhah.
(4) The two sons of the second concubine,
Zilpah.
Dan's undue prominency may, perhaps,
be accounted for by his occupying the
seventh place in the "blessing of Jacob"
(Gen. xlix. 16).

6. *the sons of Zerah*] Here, for the first
time, the writer of Chronicles draws from
sources not otherwise known to us, recording facts not mentioned in the earlier Scriptures. Ethan, Heman, Calcol, and Dara,
sons of Zerah, are only known to us from
this passage, since there are no sufficient
grounds for identifying them with the "sons
of Mahol " (marg. ref.).

7. "Achan" (Josh. vii. 1) seems to have
become "Achar," in order to assimilate the
word more closely to the Hebrew term for
"troubler," which was from the time of
Achan's sin regarded as the true meaning
of his name (Josh. vii. 25, 26).

15. *David the seventh*] Jesse had eight
sons, of whom David was the youngest
(1 Sam. xvi. 10, 11, xvii. 12). Probably one
of the sons shown to Samuel at Bethlehem
did not grow up.

16. *sisters*] *i.e.* half-sisters. Abigail and
Zeruiah were daughters not of Jesse, but of
a certain Nahash, whose widow Jesse took
to wife (2 Sam. xvii. 25).
From the present passage, and from the
fact that Abishai joined David as a comrade
in arms before Joab (1 Sam. xxvi. 6), it
would seem that, although Joab was pre-
eminent among the three (2 Sam. ii. 13, 16),
Abishai was the eldest.

17. *Jether the Ishmeelite*] See marg. note
and ref.

18. In the remainder of this chapter the
writer obtains scarcely any assistance from
the earlier Scriptures, and must have drawn
almost entirely from genealogical sources,
accessible to him, which have since perished.
Azubah was Caleb's wife ; Jerioth his
concubine. He had children by both ; but
those of Azubah are alone recorded.

ʳNum. 27. 1.

21 ¶ And afterward Hezron went in to the daughter of ʳMachir the
father of Gilead, whom he ¹married when he *was* threescore
22 years old; and she bare him Segub. And Segub begat Jair,

ˢNum 32. 41.
Deut. 3. 14.
Josh. 13. 30.

23 who had three and twenty cities in the land of Gilead. ˢAnd
he took Geshur, and Aram, with the towns of Jair, from them,
with Kenath, and the towns thereof, *even* threescore cities. All
24 these *belonged to* the sons of Machir the father of Gilead. And
after that Hezron was dead in Caleb-ephratah, then Abiah

ᵗ ch. 4. 5.

25 Hezron's wife bare him ᵗAshur the father of Tekoa. ¶ And the
sons of Jerahmeel the firstborn of Hezron were, Ram the first-
26 born, and Bunah, and Oren, and Ozem, *and* Ahijah. Jerahmeel had also another wife, whose name *was* Atarah; she *was*
27 the mother of Onam. And the sons of Ram the firstborn of
28 Jerahmeel were, Maaz, and Jamin, and Eker. And the sons of
Onam were, Shammai, and Jada. And the sons of Shammai;
29 Nadab, and Abishur. And the name of the wife of Abishur *was*
30 Abihail, and she bare him Ahban, and Molid. And the sons of
Nadab; Seled, and Appaim: but Seled died without children.
31 And the sons of Appaim; Ishi. And the sons of Ishi; Sheshan.

ᵘ See ver.
34, 35.

32 And ᵘthe children of Sheshan; Ahlai. And the sons of Jada
the brother of Shammai; Jether, and Jonathan: and Jether
33 died without children. And the sons of Jonathan; Peleth, and
34 Zaza. These were the sons of Jerahmeel. ¶ Now Sheshan had
no sons, but daughters. And Sheshan had a servant, an
35 Egyptian, whose name *was* Jarha. And Sheshan gave his
daughter to Jarha his servant to wife; and she bare him Attai.

ˣ ch. 11. 41.

36, 37 And Attai begat Nathan, and Nathan begat ˣZabad, and Za-
38 bad begat Ephlal, and Ephlal begat Obed, and Obed begat Jehu,
39 and Jehu begat Azariah, and Azariah begat Helez, and Helez
40 begat Eleasah, and Eleasah begat Sisamai, and Sisamai begat
41 Shallum, and Shallum begat Jekamiah, and Jekamiah begat
42 Elishama. ¶ Now the sons of Caleb the brother of Jerahmeel
were, Mesha his firstborn, which *was* the father of Ziph; and
43 the sons of Mareshah the father of Hebron. And the sons of
44 Hebron; Korah, and Tappuah, and Rekem, and Shema. And
Shema begat Raham, the father of Jorkoam: and Rekem begat

¹ Heb. *took*.

---

22. *Jair, who had three and twenty cities*]
The places called "Havoth-Jair" in the
earlier Scriptures (see Num. xxxii. 41 note),
which appear to have been a number of
"small towns," or villages, in the *Ledjah*,
the classical "Trachonitis."

23. Rather, "**And Geshur and Aram** (*i.e.*
the Geshurites (Deut. iii. 14) and Syrians)
took the villages of Jair from them:" recovered, that is, from the new settlers the
places which Jair had conquered.

all these belonged to the sons of Machir]
Rather, " All these **were sons** of Machir,"
i.e. Segub and Jair, with their descendants,
were reckoned sons of Machir, rather than
sons of Hezron, although only descended
from Machir on the mother's side. The
reason of this seems to have been that they
cast in their lot with the Manassites, and
remained in their portion of the trans-Jordanic region.

25. *and Ahijah*] There is no "and" in
the original. Hence some would read:
"the sons" were born "of" or "from
Ahijah," the first wife of Jerahmeel (see
next verse).

42. A third line of descent from Caleb,
the son of Hezron, the issue probably of a
different mother, perhaps Jerioth (*v.* 18).
The supposed omissions in this verse have
been supplied as follows: (1) "Mesha, the
father of Ziph; and the sons of Ziph, Mareshah, the father of Hebron;" or (2) "Mareshah, the father of Ziph; and the sons of
Mareshah, the father of Ziph, Hebron."

Ziph, like Jorkoam (*v.* 44) and Beth-zur
(*v.* 45), is the name of a place where the respective chiefs ("fathers") settled. Similarly
Madmannah, Machbenah, and Gibea (*v.* 49),
Kirjath-jearim (Josh. ix. 17 note), Beth-
lehem and Beth-gader (*Jedur, v.* 51) are
unmistakeable names of places in the list,
names which it is not probable were ever
borne by persons.

45 Shammai. And the son of Shammai *was* Maon : and Maon *was*
46 the father of Beth-zur. And Ephah, Caleb's concubine, bare
47 Haran, and Moza, and Gazez: and Haran begat Gazez. And
the sons of Jahdai; Regem, and Jotham, and Gesham, and
48 Pelet, and Ephah, and Shaaph. Maachah, Caleb's concubine,
49 bare Sheber, and Tirhanah. She bare also Shaaph the father
of Madmannah, Sheva the father of Machbenah, and the father
50 of Gibea : and the daughter of Caleb *was* *y*Achsa. ¶ These were   *y* Josh.15.17.
the sons of Caleb the son of Hur, the firstborn of [1]Ephratah ;
51 Shobal the father of Kirjath-jearim. Salma the father of
52 Beth-lehem, Hareph the father of Beth-gader. And Shobal the
father of Kirjath-jearim had sons; [2]Haroeh, *and* [3]half of the
53 Manahethites. And the families of Kirjath-jearim; the Ithrites,
and the Puhites, and the Shumathites, and the Mishraites; of
54 them came the Zareathites, and the Eshtaulites. The sons
of Salma ; Beth-lehem, and the Netophathites, [4]Ataroth, the
55 house of Joab, and half of the Manahethites, the Zorites. And
the families of the scribes which dwelt at Jabez; the Tirathites,
the Shimeathites, *and* Suchathites. These *are* the *z*Kenites that   *z* Judg. 1. 16.
came of Hemath, the father of the house of *a*Rechab.   *a* Jer. 35. 2.

Chap. 3. NOW these were the sons of David, which were born
unto him in Hebron ; the firstborn *a*Amnon, of Ahinoam the   *a* 2 Sam. 3.2.
*b*Jezreelitess ; the second [5]Daniel, of Abigail the Carmelitess :   *b* Josh.15.56.
2 the third, Absalom the son of Maachah the daughter of Talmai
3 king of Geshur: the fourth, Adonijah the son of Haggith: the
fifth, Shephatiah of Abital : the sixth, Ithream by *c*Eglah his   *c* 2 Sam. 3. 5.
4 wife. *These* six were born unto him in Hebron ; and *d*there he   *d* 2 Sam. 2.
reigned seven years and six months : and *e*in Jerusalem he   11.
5 reigned thirty and three years. *f*And these were born unto him   *e* 2 Sam.5 5.
in Jerusalem; [6]Shimea, and Shobab, and Nathan, and*g*Solomon,   *f* 2 Sam.5.14.
  ch. 14. 4.
  g 2 Sam. 12.

[1] Or, *Ephrath*, ver. 19.
[2] Or, *Reaiah*, ch. 4. 2.
[3] Or, *half of the Menu-*

chites, or, *Hatsi-ham-*
menuchoth.
[4] Or, *Atarites*, or,*crowns of*
the house of Joab.

[5] Or, *Chileab*, 2 Sam. 3. 3.   24.
[6] Or, *Shammua*, 2 Sam. 5.
14.

---

50. *Caleb the son of Hur*] Hur was the
son, not the father, of Caleb (*v.* 19). The
text should perhaps be read : "These (the
list in *vv.* 42-49) were the sons of Caleb.
The sons of Hur, the first-born of Ephratah,
were Shobal, &c."

54. *Ataroth, the house of Joab*] Rather,
"Ataroth-beth-Joab," probably so called,
to distinguish it from Ataroth-Adar, a city
of Benjamin (Josh. xviii. 13). It is uncertain from what Joab it derived its distinctive appellation.

55. *Kenites*] It is remarkable that Kenites—people of a race quite distinct from
the Israelites (Gen. xv. 19)—should be attached to, and, as it were, included in the
descendants of Judah. It seems, however,
that the friendly feeling between the two
tribes—based on the conduct of the Kenites
at the time of the Exodus (Ex. xviii. 10-19;
Num. x. 29-32 ; 1 Sam. xv. 6)—led to their
intermixture and almost amalgamation with
the Israelites, Kenite families not only
dwelling among them but being actually
regarded as of one blood with them.

III. 1. *the sons of David*] The writer re-

turns to the point at which he had left the
posterity of Ram (ii. 9, 15), and traces out
the family of David—the royal house of the
tribe of Judah.

Daniel] See marg. note and ref.
There are three lists of the sons of David,
born in Jerusalem.

	I.	II.	III.
	2 S. v. 14-16.	1 Chr. iii. 5-8.	1 Chr. xiv. 4-7.
1.	Shammuah .	. Shimeah*	. Shammuah.
2.	Shobab .	. Shobab	. Shobab.
3.	Nathan .	. Nathan .	. Nathan.
4.	Solomon .	. Solomon	. Solomon.
5.	Ibhar .	. Ibhar .	. Ibhar.
6.	Elishua .	. Elishama*	. Elishua.
7.		Eliphelet*	. Elpalet.*
8.		Nogah .	. Nogah.
9.	Nepheg .	. Nepheg	. Nepheg.
10.	Japhia .	. Japhia .	. Japhia.
11.	Elishama .	. Elishama	. Elishama.
12.	Eliada .	. Eliada .	. Beeliada.*
13.	Eliphelet .	. Eliphelet	. Eliphelet.

(Differences are marked with an asterisk).

A comparison of the three lists serves to
show—(1) That "Shimeah" and the first
"Elishama" in the list of this chapter are

6 four, of [1]Bath-shua the daughter of [2]Ammiel: Ibhar also, and
7 [3]Elishama, and Eliphelet, and Nogah, and Nepheg, and Japhia,
8, 9 and Elishama, and [4]Eliada, and Eliphelet, [h]nine. *These were*
all the sons of David, beside the sons of the concubines, and
10 [i]Tamar their sister. ¶ And Solomon's son *was* [k]Rehoboam, [5]Abia
11 his son, Asa his son, Jehoshaphat his son, Joram his son,
12 [6]Ahaziah his son, Joash his son, Amaziah his son, [7]Azariah his
13 son, Jotham his son, Ahaz his son, Hezekiah his son, Manasseh
14, 15 his son, Amon his son, Josiah his son. And the sons of Josiah
were, the firstborn [8]Johanan, the second [9]Jehoiakim, the third
16 [1]Zedekiah, the fourth Shallum. And the sons of [l]Jehoiakim:
17 [2]Jeconiah his son, Zedekiah [m]his son. ¶ And the sons of Jeco-
18 niah; Assir, [3]Salathiel [n]his son, Malchiram also, and Pedaiah,
19 and Shenazar, Jecamiah, Hoshama, and Nedabiah. And the
sons of Pedaiah *were*, Zerubbabel, and Shimei: and the sons of
Zerubbabel; Meshullam, and Hananiah, and Shelomith their
20 sister: and Hashubah, and Ohel, and Berechiah, and Hasadiah,

h See
2 Sam. 5. 14,
15, 16.
i 2 Sam. 13. 1.
k 1 Kin. 11. 43.
& 15. 6.

l Matt. 1. 11.
m 2 Kin. 24.
17,
being his
uncle.
n Matt. 1. 12.

[1] Or, *Bath-sheba*, 2 Sam. 11. 3.
[2] Or, *Eliam*, 2 Sam. 11. 3.
[3] Or, *Elishua*, 2 Sam. 5. 15.
[4] Or, *Beeliada*, ch. 14. 7.
[5] Or, *Abijam*, 1 Kin. 15. 1.
[6] Or, *Azariah*, 2 Chr. 22. 6. or, *Jehoahaz*, 2 Chr. 21. 17.
[7] Or, *Uzziah*, 2 Kin. 15. 30.
[8] Or, *Jehoahaz*, 2 Kin. 23. 30.
[9] Or, *Eliakim*, 2 Kin. 23. 34.
[1] Or, *Mattaniah*, 2 Kin. 24. 17.
[2] Or, *Jehoiachin*, 2 Kin. 24. 6. or, *Coniah*, Jer. 22. 24.
[3] Heb. *Shealtiel*.

corruptions; (2) That David had really
13 sons born in Jerusalem, of whom two
— the first Eliphelet and Nogah—probably
died in their childhood; and (3) That Eliada,
the twelfth son, was also called Beeliada,
the term *Baal*, "lord," not having (previous
to the introduction of the Baal worship) a
bad sense, but being regarded as an equivalent with *El*, "God."

Bathshua, the daughter of Ammiel] Both
names are here given in an unusual form,
but it may be doubted whether in either
case there has been any corruption. In
"Bathshua," for "Bathsheba," a *vau* (*v*)
replaces the *beth* (*b*) of the earlier writer, *v*
and *b* having nearly the same sound. In
"Ammiel," for "Eliam," the two elements
which form the name are inverted, as in
Jehoiachin = Jechoniah, and the like.

10. *Abia*] Rather, "Abijah," as in 2 Chr.
xi.-xiv., where the Hebrew word is exactly
the same.

11. *Ahaziah*] Called "Jehoahaz" by a
transposition of the elements composing the
name, and "Azariah," probably by a transcriber's error (see marg. notes and reff.).

12. *Azariah*] Elsewhere in Chronicles
called uniformly "Uzziah" (2 Chr. xxvi. 1,
3, 9, 11, &c.), but called indifferently "Azariah" and "Uzziah" in Kings ("Azariah"
in 2 K. xiv. 21, xv. 1, 6, 17, 23, 27, &c.;
"Uzziah" in xv. 13, 32, and 34).

15. Of the sons of Josiah, Johanan, "the
first-born," who is mentioned in this place
only, must, it would seem, have died before
his father, or with him at Megiddo; and
Shallum (also called Jehoahaz, marg. note
and ref.) was considerably older than Zedekiah, and was consequently the *third*, and

not the *fourth*, son. He is perhaps assigned
the fourth place here by way of intentional
degradation. (Cp. Jer. xxii. 10-12; Ezek.
xix. 3, 4.

17. *Assir*] Perhaps born in the captivity,
and therefore so named, who either died
young, or was made a eunuch (Isai. xxxix.
7; cp. Jer. xxii. 30). After Assir's decease,
or mutilation, the line of Solomon became
extinct, and according to the principles of
the Jewish law (Num. xxvii. 8-11) the inheritance passed to the next of kin, who
were Salathiel and his brethren, descendants from David by the line of Nathan.
St. Luke in calling Salathiel "the son of
Neri" (iii. 27), gives his real, or natural, descent; since no genealogy would assign to
the true son and heir of a king any inferior
and private parentage. Hence, "Malchiram," &c., *i.e.* not Salathiel only, but his
brothers also were reckoned "sons" of
Jeconiah.

19. Zerubbabel, elsewhere always called
"the son of Salathiel," was only Salathiel's
heir and legal son, being naturally his
nephew, the son of his brother, Pedaiah.

six] There are only five names in the Hebrew text. The Syriac and Arabic Versions supply "Azariah" between Neariah
and Shaphat.

The question of the proper arrangement
of the genealogy of the descendants of Zerubbabel (*vv.* 19-24) is important in its bearing
on the interesting point of the time at
which the Canon of the Old Testament was
closed. Assuming the average of a generation to be in the East twenty years, the
genealogy of the present chapter, drawn
out according to the Hebrew text, does not

21 Jushab-hesed, five. And the sons of Hananiah; Pelatiah, and
Jesaiah: the sons of Rephaiah, the sons of Arnan, the sons of
22 Obadiah, the sons of Shechaniah. And the sons of Shechaniah;
Shemaiah: and the sons of Shemaiah; *Hattush, and Igeal, and   *Ezra 8. 2.
23 Bariah, and Neariah, and Shaphat, six. And the sons of
24 Neariah; Elioenai, and ¹Hezekiah, and Azrikam, three. And
the sons of Elioenai *were*, Hodaiah, and Eliashib, and Pelaiah,
and Akkub, and Johanan, and Dalaiah, and Anani, seven.
Chap. 4. THE sons of Judah; *a*Pharez, Hezron, and ²Carmi, and   *a* Gen. 38.29.
2 Hur, and Shobal. And ³Reaiah the son of Shobal begat Jahath;   & 46. 12.
and Jahath begat Ahumai, and Lahad. These *are* the families
3 of the Zorathites. And these *were of* the father of Etam; Jezreel, and Ishma, and Idbash: and the name of their sister *was*
4 Hazelelponi: and Penuel the father of Gedor, and Ezer the
father of Hushah. These *are* the sons of *b*Hur, the firstborn of   *b* ch. 2. 50.
5 Ephratah, the father of Beth-lehem. ¶And *c*Ashur the father   *c* ch. 2. 24.
6 of Tekoa had two wives, Helah and Naarah. And Naarah bare
him Ahuzam, and Hepher, and Temeni, and Haahashtari. These
7 *were* the sons of Naarah. And the sons of Helah *were*, Zereth,
8 and Jezoar, and Ethnan. And Coz begat Anub, and Zobebah,
9 and the families of Aharhel the son of Harum. ¶And Jabez
was *d*more honourable than his brethren: and his mother called   *d* Gen. 34. 19.
10 his name ⁴Jabez, saying, Because I bare him with sorrow. And
Jabez called on the God of Israel, saying, ⁵Oh that thou wouldest
bless me indeed, and enlarge my coast, and that thine hand
might be with me, and that thou wouldest ⁶keep *me* from evil,
that it may not grieve me! And God granted him that which
11 he requested. ¶And Chelub the brother of Shuah begat Mehir,
12 which *was* the father of Eshton. And Eshton begat Beth-rapha,
and Paseah, and Tehinnah the father of ⁷Ir-nahash. These *are*
13 the men of Rechah. And the sons of Kenaz; *e*Othniel, and   *e* Josh. 15.17.
14 Seraiah: and the sons of Othniel; ⁸Hathath. And Meonothai   *f* Neh. 11. 35.
begat Ophrah: and Seraiah begat Joab, the father of *f*the

¹ Heb. *Hiskijahu.*
² Or, *Chelubai,* ch. 2. 9. or,
   Caleb, ch. 2. 18.
³ Or, *Haroeh,* ch. 2. 52.
⁴ That is, *Sorrowful.*
⁵ Heb. *If thou wilt, &c.*
⁶ Heb. *do me.*
⁷ Or, *the city of Nahash.*
⁸ Or, *Hathath,* and *Meo-*
   nothai, who *begat, &c.*

---

descend below about B.C. 410, and thus
falls within the probable lifetime of Nehemiah.
   If, further, we regard it as most probable
that Ezra died before B.C. 431, and that this
passage in question was not wholly written
by him, this does not disprove the theory
(Introd. p. 446), that Ezra was the author
of Chronicles. Deuteronomy is by Moses,
though the last chapter cannot be from his
hand. The "dukes of Edom" might be
an insertion into the text of Genesis (xxxvi.
40-43) without the authorship of the remainder of the work being affected by it.
So here; Nehemiah, or Malachi, may have
carried on the descent of the "sons of David"
as far as it had reached in their time, adding
to the account given by Ezra one, or at the
most two verses.
   IV. 3. Read, "These are the sons of the
father (*i.e.* chief) of Etam " (2 Chr. xi. 6), a
city of Judah, not far from Bethlehem.

9. It is remarkable that Jabez should be
introduced without description, or patro-
nymic, as if a well-known personage. We
can only suppose that he was known to
those for whom Chronicles was written,
either by tradition, or by writings which
have perished. In *v.* 10 Jabez alludes to his
name, "sorrowful" (marg.) : "Grant that
the grief implied in my name may not come
upon me !"
   11, 12. It has been conjectured from the
strangeness of all the names in this list,
that we have here a fragment of Canaanite
record, connected with the family of the
"Shua," whose daughter Judah took to
wife (ii. 3; Gen. xxxviii. 2), and whose
family thus became related to the tribe of
Judah.
   14. The words "and Meonothai" should
be added to the end of *v.* 13; but they
should be retained also at the commencement of *v.* 14. Or, see marg. note.

15 ¹valley of ²Charashim ; for they were craftsmen.   And the sons
of Caleb the son of Jephunneh ; Iru, Elah, and Naam : and the
16 sons of Elah, ³even Kenaz.   And the sons of Jehaleleel ; Ziph,
17 and Ziphah, Tiria, and Asareel.   And the sons of Ezra *were*,
Jether, and Mered, and Epher, and Jalon : and she bare Miriam,
18 and Shammai, and Ishbah the father of Eshtemoa.   And his
wife ⁴Jehudijah bare Jered the father of Gedor, and Heber the
father of Socho, and Jekuthiel the father of Zanoah.   And these
are the sons of Bithiah the daughter of Pharaoh, which Mered
19 took.   And the sons of *his* wife ⁵Hodiah the sister of Naham,
the father of Keilah the Garmite, and Eshtemoa the Maacha-
20 thite.   And the sons of Shimon *were*, Amnon, and Rinnah,
Ben-hanan, and Tilon.   And the sons of Ishi *were*, Zoheth, and
21 Ben-zoheth.   ¶ The sons of Shelah ⁹the son of Judah *were*, Er
the father of Lecah, and Laadah the father of Mareshah, and
the families of the house of them that wrought fine linen, of the
22 house of Ashbea, and Jokim, and the men of Chozeba, and Joash,
and Saraph, who had the dominion in Moab, and Jashubi-lehem.
23 And *these are* ancient things.   These *were* the potters, and those
that dwelt among plants and hedges : there they dwelt with the
24 king for his work.   ¶ The sons of Simeon *were*, ⁶Nemuel, and
25 Jamin, ⁷Jarib, Zerah, *and* Shaul : Shallum his son, Mibsam his
26 son, Mishma his son.   And the sons of Mishma ; Hamuel his
27 son, Zacchur his son, Shimei his son.   And Shimei had sixteen
sons and six daughters ; but his brethren had not many children,
neither did all their family multiply, ⁸like to the children of
28 Judah.   And they dwelt at ʰBeer-sheba, and Moladah, and
29, 30 Hazar-shual, and at ⁹Bilhah, and at Ezem, and at ¹Tolad, and
31 at Bethuel, and at Hormah, and at Ziklag, and at Beth-marcaboth, and ²Hazarsusim, and at Beth-birei, and at Shaaraim.
32 These *were* their cities unto the reign of David.   And their
villages *were*, ³Etam, and Ain, Rimmon, and Tochen, and

ᵍ Gen. 38. 1,
5.
& 43. 12.

ʰ Josh. 19. 2.

---

¹ Or, inhabitants *of the valley.*
² That is, *Craftsmen.*
³ Or, *Uknaz.*
⁴ Or, *the Jewess.*

⁵ Or, *Jehudijah,* mentioned before.
⁶ Or, *Jemuel,* Gen. 46. 10.   Ex. 6. 15.   Num. 26. 12.
⁷ Or, *Jachin, Zohar.*
⁸ Heb. *unto.*

⁹ Or, *Balah,* Josh. 19. 3.
¹ Or, *Eltolad,* Josh. 19. 4.
² Or, *Hazar-susah,* Josh. 19. 5.
³ Or, *Ether,* Josh. 19. 7.

---

17. *she bare Miriam*] Rather, " she conceived." The mother is not mentioned, and it seems impossible to restore the original text with any certainty.

18. *his wife*] *i.e.* Mered's. Mered, it would seem, had two wives, Bithiah, an Egyptian woman, and a Jewish wife (see marg.), whose name is not given. If Mered was a chief of rank, Bithiah may have been married to him with the consent of her father ; for the Egyptian kings often gave their daughters in marriage to foreigners. Or she may have elected to forsake her countrymen and cleave to a Jewish husband, becoming a convert to his religion. Her name, Bithiah, "daughter of Jehovah," is like that of a convert.

19. *his wife Hodiah*] Not as in marg., but rather, " **the sons of the wife of Hodiah.**" Hodiah is elsewhere always a man's name (Neh. viii. 7, ix. 5, x. 10, 13, 18).

22. *who had the dominion in Moab*] Moab

was conquered by David (2 Sam. viii. 2), and again by Omri, after which it remained subject until the death of Ahab (2 K. iii. 5). But a more ancient rule, in times of which we have no further record, is probably intended.

23. *among plants and hedges*] Rather, " **in Netaim and Gederah** " (Josh. xv. 36).

with the king] Or, probably, " on the king's property." Both David and several of the later kings had large territorial possessions in various parts of Judæa (1 Chr. xxvii. 25-31 ; 2 Chr. xxvi.10, xxvii. 4, xxxii. 28, 29).

31. *unto the reign of David*] It is not quite clear why this clause is added. Perhaps the writer is quoting from a document belonging to David's reign. Or, he may mean that some of the cities, as Ziklag (1 Sam. xxvii. 6), were lost to Simeon about David's time.

33 Ashan, five cities: and all their villages that *were* round about the same cities, unto ¹Baal. These *were* their habitations, and
34 ²their genealogy. And Meshobab, and Jamlech, and Joshah
35 the son of Amaziah, and Joel, and Jehu the son of Josibiah, the
36 son of Seraiah, the son of Asiel, and Elioenai, and Jaakobah,
and Jeshohaiah, and Asaiah, and Adiel, and Jesimiel, ar d
37 Benaiah, and Ziza the son of Shiphi, the son of Allon, the scn
38 of Jedaiah, the son of Shimri, the son of Shemaiah; these ³mentioned by *their* names *were* princes in their families: and the
39 house of their fathers increased greatly. ¶ And they went to
the entrance of Gedor, *even* unto the east side of the valley, to
40 seek pasture for their flocks. And they found fat pasture and
good, and the land *was* wide, and quiet, and peaceable; for *they*
41 of Ham had dwelt there of old. And these written by name
came in the days of Hezekiah king of Judah, and ⁱsmote their
tents, and the habitations that were found there, and destroyed
them utterly unto this day, and dwelt in their rooms: because
42 *there was* pasture there for their flocks. And *some* of them,
even of the sons of Simeon, five hundred men, went to mount
Seir, having for their captains Pelatiah, and Neariah, and
43 Rephaiah, and Uzziel, the sons of Ishi. And they smote ᵏthe
rest of the Amalekites that were escaped, and dwelt there unto
this day.

CHAP. 5. NOW the sons of Reuben the firstborn of Israel, (for ᵃhe
was the firstborn; but, forasmuch as he ᵇdefiled his father's bed,
ᶜhis birthright was given unto the sons of Joseph the son of
2 Israel: and the genealogy is not to be reckoned after the birth-
3 right. For ᵈJudah prevailed above his brethren, and of him
came the ᵉchief ⁴ruler; but the birthright *was* Joseph's:) the
sons, *I say*, of ᶠReuben the firstborn of Israel *were*, Hanoch,
4 and Pallu, Hezron, and Carmi. The sons of Joel; Shemaiah
5 his son, Gog his son, Shimei his son, Micah his son, Reaia his
6 son, Baal his son, Beerah his son, whom ⁵Tilgath-pilneser king
of Assyria carried away *captive:* he *was* prince of the Reuben-
7 ites. And his brethren by their families, ᵍwhen the genealogy
of their generations was reckoned, *were* the chief, Jeiel, and

Marginal references:
ⁱ 2 Kin. 18. 8.
ᵏ See
1 Sam. 15. 8.
& 30. 17.
2 Sam. 8. 12.
ᵃ Gen. 29. 32.
& 49. 3.
ᵇ Gen. 35. 22.
& 49. 4.
ᶜ Gen. 48. 15.
ᵈ Gen. 49. 8,
10.
Ps. 60. 7.
& 108. 8.
ᵉ Mic. 5. 2.
ᶠ Gen. 46. 9.
Ex. 6. 14.
Num., 26. 5.
ᵍ See ver. 17.

¹ Or, *Baalath-beer*, Josh. 19. 8.
² Or, *as they divided them-selves by nations among them.*
³ Heb. *coming.*
⁴ Or, *prince.*
⁵ Or, *Tiglath-pileser*, 2 Kin. 15. 29. & 16. 7.

---

33. *and their genealogy*] Rather, "and their register was according thereto"— they were registered, *i.e.* according to the places where they dwelt.

38. *these mentioned by their names were princes*] The registered chiefs of the cities in the first list (*vv.* 28-31), in the time of Hezekiah (*v.* 41).

39. *Gedor*] Rather read, "Gerar" (LXX.) a fertile district (Gen. xxvi. 6-12; 2 Chr. xiv. 14, 15) in Philistine country.

41. *the habitations*] Rather, "the Mehunim" (cp. 2 Chr. xxxvi. 7), called also "Maonites" (see Judg. x. 12 note).

43. *unto this day*] These words are probably taken from the record which the writer of Chronicles had before him, and do not imply that the Simeonites remained undisturbed in their conquests till after the return from the Captivity. So *v.* 41.

V. 1. *his birthright was given* &c.] In particular, the right of the first-born to a double inheritance (Deut. xxi. 17) was conferred on Joseph, both by the expressed will of Jacob (Gen. xlviii. 22) and in the actual partition of Canaan (Josh. xvi. and xvii.). But though the birthright, as respecting its material privileges, passed to Joseph, its other rights, those of dignity and pre-eminence, fell to Judah; of whom came the chief ruler, an allusion especially to David, though it may reach further, and include a glance at the Messiah, the true "Ruler" of Israel (Micah v. 2).

4. *The sons of Joel*] The line of succession here given must be broken by one great gap or several smaller ones, since nine generations before Tiglath-pileser would carry us back no further than the reign of Rehoboam.

8 Zechariah, and Bela the son of Azaz, the son of [1]Shema, the son

h Josh. 13.
15—17.

of Joel, who dwelt in [h]Aroer, even unto Nebo and Baal-meon :

9 and eastward he inhabited unto the entering in of the wilderness from the river Euphrates : because their cattle were mul-

i Josh. 22. 9.
k Gen. 25.12.

10 tiplied [i]in the land of Gilead. And in the days of Saul they made war [k]with the Hagarites, who fell by their hand : and they dwelt in their tents [2]throughout all the east *land* of Gilead.

11 ¶ And the children of Gad dwelt over against them, in the land

l Josh. 13.11,
24.

12 of [l]Bashan unto Salcah : Joel the chief, and Shapham the next,

13 and Jaanai, and Shaphat in Bashan. And their brethren of the house of their fathers *were*, Michael, and Meshullam, and Sheba,

14 and Jorai, and Jachan, and Zia, and Heber, seven. These *are* the children of Abihail the son of Huri, the son of Jaroah, the son of Gilead, the son of Michael, the son of Jeshishai, the son

15 of Gilead, the son of Buz ; Ahi the son of Abdiel, the son of

16 Guni, chief of the house of their fathers. And they dwelt in Gilead in Bashan, and in her towns, and in all the suburbs of

m ch. 27. 29.

17 [m]Sharon, upon [3]their borders. All these were reckoned by

n 2 Kin. 15.
5, 32.
o 2 Kin. 14.
16, 28.

genealogies in the days of [n]Jotham king of Judah, and in the

18 days of [o]Jeroboam king of Israel. ¶ The sons of Reuben, and the Gadites, and half the tribe of Manasseh, [4]of valiant men, men able to bear buckler and sword, and to shoot with bow, and skilful in war, *were* four and forty thousand seven hundred and

19 threescore, that went out to the war. And they made war with

p Gen. 25.15.
ch. 1. 31.
q See ver.22.

20 the Hagarites, with [p]Jetur, and Nephish, and Nodab. And [q]they were helped against them, and the Hagarites were delivered into their hand, and all that *were* with them : for they cried to God in the battle, and he was intreated of them ; because

r Ps. 22. 4, 5.

21 they [r]put their trust in him. And they [5]took away their cattle ; of their camels fifty thousand, and of sheep two hundred and fifty thousand, and of asses two thousand, and of [6]men an hun-

22 dred thousand. For there fell down many slain, because the

s 2 Kin. 15.29.
& 17. 6.

war *was* of God. And they dwelt in their steads until [s]the cap-

[1] Or, *Shemaiah*, ver. 4.
[2] Heb. *upon all the face of the east.*
[3] Heb. *their goings forth.*
[4] Heb. *sons of valour.*
[5] Heb. *led captive.*
[6] Heb. *souls of men :* as Num. 31. 35.

---

9. *he inhabited*] i.e. Reuben. Eastward the Reubenites inhabited as far as the commencement of the great Syrian Desert, which extended all the way from the river Euphrates to their borders.

10. The "Hagarites" or "Hagarenes" are generally regarded as descendants of Hagar, and a distinct branch of the Ishmaelites (1 Chr. xxvii. 30, 31 ; Ps. lxxxiii. 6). They appear to have been one of the most wealthy (*v.* 21) and widely-spread tribes of the Syrian Desert, being found on the side of the Euphrates in contact with the Assyrians, and also in the Hauran, in the neighbourhood of Palestine, in contact with the Moabites and Israelites. If identical with the Agraei of the classical writers, their name may be considered as still surviving in that of the district called *Hejer* or *Hejera* in north-eastern Arabia, on the borders of the Persian Gulf. A full account of the war is given in *vv.* 18-22.

11. From this passage and from the sub-

sequent account of the Manassites (*vv.* 23, 24), the Gadites extended themselves to the north at the expense of their brethren, gradually occupying a considerable portion of the tract originally allotted to the "half tribe."

17. The writer refers here to two registrations, one made under the authority of Jeroboam II. when he was king and Israel flourishing, the other made under the authority of Jotham, king of Judah, during the troublous time which followed on the great invasion of Tiglath-pileser. There is nothing surprising in a king of Judah having exercised a species of lordship over the trans-Jordanic territory at this period.

19. Jetur no doubt gave his name to the important tribe of the Ituraeans who inhabited the region south-west of the Damascene plain, between Gaulonitis (*Jaulan*) and the Ledjah. This tribe was noted for its thievish habits, and was regarded as savage and warlike.

23 tivity. ¶ And the children of the half tribe of Manasseh dwelt in the land: they increased from Bashan unto Baal-hermon
24 and Senir, and unto mount Hermon. And these *were* the heads of the house of their fathers, even Epher, and Ishi, and Eliel, and Azriel, and Jeremiah, and Hodaviah, and Jahdiel, mighty men of valour, ¹famous men, *and* heads of the house of their
25 fathers. And they transgressed against the God of their fathers, and went a ᵗwhoring after the gods of the people of the land,
26 whom God destroyed before them. And the God of Israel stirred up the spirit of ᵘPul king of Assyria, and the spirit of ˣTilgath-pilneser king of Assyria, and he carried them away, even the Reubenites, and the Gadites and the half tribe of Manasseh, and brought them unto ʸHalah, and Habor, and Hara, and to the river Gozan, unto this day.

Chap. 6. THE sons of Levi; ᵃ°Gershon, Kohath, and Merari. And
2 the sons of Kohath; Amram, ᵇIzhar, and Hebron, and Uzziel.
3 And the children of Amram; Aaron, and Moses, and Miriam. The sons also of Aaron; ᶜNadab, and Abihu, Eleazar, and
4 Ithamar. Eleazar begat Phinehas, Phinehas begat Abishua,
5, 6 and Abishua begat Bukki, and Bukki begat Uzzi, and Uzzi
7 begat Zerahiah, and Zerahiah begat Meraioth, Meraioth begat
8 Amariah, and Amariah begat Ahitub, and ᵈAhitub begat Zadok,
9 and ᵉZadok begat Ahimaaz, and Ahimaaz begat Azariah, and
10 Azariah begat Johanan, and Johanan begat Azariah, (he *it is* ᶠthat executed the priest's office ³in the ᵍtemple that Solomon
11 built in Jerusalem:) and ʰAzariah begat Amariah, and Amariah
12 begat Ahitub, and Ahitub begat Zadok, and Zadok begat ⁴Shal-
13 lum, and Shallum begat Hilkiah, and Hilkiah begat Azariah,
14 and Azariah begat ⁱSeraiah, and Seraiah begat Jehozadak, and
15 Jehozadak went *into captivity*, ᵏwhen the LORD carried away

Marginal references:
ᵗ 2 Kin. 17.7.
ᵘ 2 Kin. 15. 19.
ˣ 2 Kin. 15. 29.
ʸ 2 Kin. 17.6. & 18. 11.
ᵃ Gen. 46.11.
Ex. 6. 16.
Num. 26. 57.
ch. 23. 6.
ᵇ See ver. 22.
ᶜ Lev. 10. 1.
ᵈ 2Sam.8.17.
ᵉ 2 Sam. 15. 27.
ᶠ See 2 Chr. 26. 17, 18.
ᵍ 1 Kin. 6.
2 Chr. 3.
ʰ See Ezra 7. 3.
ⁱ Neh. 11.11.
ᵏ 2 Kin. 25. 18.

---

¹ Heb. *men of names.*
² Or, *Gershom,* ver. 16.
³ Heb. *in the house.*
⁴ Or, *Meshullam,* ch. 9. 11.

---

23. " Baal-Hermon," "Senir" (Deut. iii. 9), and " Mount Hermon," are here not so much three names of the one great snow-clad eminence in which the Anti-Lebanon terminates towards the south, as three parts of the mountain—perhaps the "three summits " in which it terminates.

26. " Habor" here seems to be a city or a district, and not a river, as in marg. ref. There is some reason to believe that districts among the Assyrians were occasionally named from streams.

Hara is probably the same as "Haran " (Gen. xi. 31 : 2 K. xix. 12; Ezek. xxvii. 23), being a softening down of the rugged original "Kharan."

VI. 1–15. The genealogy of the High-priestly stem to the Captivity.

9. *Ahimaaz begat Azariah*] It must, apparently, be this Azariah, and not the son of Johanan (*v.* 10), who was High-Priest at the dedication of Solomon's Temple. For Zadok, who lived into the reign of Solomon (1 K. iv. 4) cannot have been succeeded by a great-great-grandson. The notice in *v.* 10, which is attached to the second Azariah, must, beyond a doubt, belong properly to the first.

11. *Ahitub*] Between Amariah and Hilkiah (*v.* 13) this genealogy is most certainly defective, as it gives three generations only for a period for which nine generations are furnished by the list of the kings of Judah, and which cannot be estimated as much short of 200 years. Further, no one of the names in this part of the list occurs among the High-Priests of the period, several of whom are mentioned both in the Second Book of Chronicles and in Kings ; the explanation of which seems to be that the present is not a list of High-Priests, but the genealogy of Jozadak or Jehozadak, whose line of descent partly coincided with the list of High-Priests, partly differed from it. Where it coincided, all the names are given ; where it differed, some are omitted, in order (probably) to render the entire list from Phinehas a multiple of seven. See note on *v.* 20.

15. *Jehozadak*] The meaning of the name is "Jehovah is righteous." It has been noted as remarkable that the heads of both the priestly and the royal stock carried to Babylon should have had names (Zedekiah and Jehozadak) composed of the same elements, and assertive of the "justice of

16 Judah and Jerusalem by the hand of Nebuchadnezzar. ¶ The
17 sons of Levi; [1]Gershom, Kohath, and Merari. And these *be*
18 the names of the sons of Gershom; Libni, and Shimei. And
   the sons of Kohath *were*, Amram, and Izhar, and Hebron, and
19 Uzziel. The sons of Merari; Mahli, and Mushi. ¶ And these
20 *are* the families of the Levites according to their fathers. ¶ Of
   Gershom; Libni his son, Jahath his son, [m]Zimmah his son,
21 [2]Joah his son, [3]Iddo his son, Zerah his son [4]Jeaterai his son.
22 ¶ The sons of Kohath; [5]Amminadab his son, Korah his son,
23 Assir his son, Elkanah his son, and Ebiasaph his son, and Assir
24 his son, Tahath his son, [6]Uriel his son, Uzziah his son, and
25 Shaul his son. And the sons of Elkanah; [n]Amasai, and Ahi-
26 moth. *As for* Elkanah: the sons of Elkanah; [7]Zophai his
27 son, and [o]Nahath his son, [p]Eliab his son, Jeroham his son,
28 Elkanah his son. And the sons of Samuel; the firstborn [8]Vashni,
29 and Abiah. ¶ The sons of Merari; Mahli, Libni his son, Shimei
30 his son, Uzza his son, Shimea his son, Haggiah his son, Asaiah
31 his son. ¶ And these *are they* whom David set over the service
   of song in the house of the LORD, after that the [q]ark had rest.
32 And they ministered before the dwelling place of the tabernacle
   of the congregation with singing, until Solomon had built the
   house of the LORD in Jerusalem: and *then* they waited on their
33 office according to their order. ¶ And these *are* they that [9]waited
   with their children. Of the sons of the Kohathites: Heman a
34 singer, the son of Joel, the son of Shemuel, the son of Elkanah,
35 the son of Jeroham, the son of Eliel, the son of [1]Toah, the son of
36 [2]Zuph, the son of Elkanah, the son of Mahath, the son of Amasai,
   the son of Elkanah, the son of [3]Joel, the son of Azariah, the son
37 of Zephaniah, the son of Tahath, the son of Assir, the son of
38 [r]Ebiasaph, the son of Korah, the son of Izhar, the son of Ko-
39 hath, the son of Levi, the son of Israel. ¶ And his brother
   Asaph, who stood on his right hand, *even* Asaph the son of

[t] Ex. 6. 16.

[m] ver. 42.

[n] See ver.
35, 36.

[o] ver. 34,
Toah.
[p] ver. 34,
Eliel.

[q] ch. 16. 1.

[r] Ex 6. 24

[1] Or, *Gershon*, ver. 1.
[2] Or, *Ethan*, ver. 42.
[3] Or, *Adaiah*, ver. 41.
[4] Or, *Ethni*, ver. 41.
[5] Or, *Izhar*, ver. 2, 18.
[6] Or, *Zephaniah, Azariah,
   Joel*, ver. 36.
[7] Or, *Zuph*, ver. 35. 1 Sam.
   1. 1.
[8] Called also *Joel*, ver. 33.
   & 1 Sam. 8. 2.
[9] Heb. *stood*.
[1] ver. 26, *Nahath*.
[2] Or, *Zophai*.
[3] ver. 24, *Shaul, Uzziah,
   Uriel*.

God," which their sufferings showed forth
so signally.

16, &c.] A general account of the several
branches of the tribe of Levi.

20. *Of Gershom*] The names in this list
are curiously different from those in *vv.* 41–
43, which yet appear to represent the same
line reversed. Probably both lists are more
or less corrupted, and, as in many genealogies, omission is made, to reduce the
number of the names to seven. Cp. *e.g. vv.*
22–28 with *vv.* 33–38. Cp. the other genealogies of this chapter; and see also Matt. i.
1–17.

28. *Vashni*] The true name of Samuel's
first-born, which was "Joel" (see marg. and
reff.), has been dropped out; and the word
properly meaning "and his second [son]"
has been taken as the name of the first.

31–48. The genealogies of David's three
chief singers, Heman, Asaph, and Ethan
or Jeduthun.

32. *they waited on their office*] On the
establishment and continuance of the choral
service in the Temple, see 2 Chr. v. 12, xxix.
27–30, xxxv. 15.

33. *Heman*] In general Asaph takes precedence of Heman and Jeduthun, but here
Heman is placed first, because his family,
that of the Kohathites, had the highest
priestly rank, being the family which furnished the High-Priests (see *vv.* 2–15).

Shemuel] *i.e.* "Samuel." Our translators
have here given the Hebrew, while elsewhere they give uniformly the Greek, form
of the name. We learn by this genealogy
that Heman was Samuel's grandson.

39. *his brother Asaph*] Not "brother"
in the ordinary sense of the term, since
Asaph was the son of Berachiah, and a
Gershonite, not a Kohathite. "Brother"
here may mean "fellow-craftsman" (cp.
xxv. 7).

40 Berachiah, the son of Shimea, the son of Michael, the son of
41 Baaseiah, the son of Malchiah, the son of *Ethni, the son of   *See ver. 21.
42 Zerah, the son of Adaiah, the son of Ethan, the son of Zimmah,
43 the son of Shimei, the son of Jahath, the son of Gershom, the
44 son of Levi. ¶And their brethren the sons of Merari *stood* on
    the left hand: [1]Ethan the son of [2]Kishi, the son of Abdi, the
45 son of Malluch, the son of Hashabiah, the son of Amaziah, the
46 son of Hilkiah, the son of Amzi, the son of Bani, the son of
47 Shamer, the son of Mahli, the son of Mushi, the son of Merari,
48 the son of Levi. Their brethren also the Levites *were* appointed
    unto all manner of service of the tabernacle of the house of God.
49 ¶ But Aaron and his sons offered [t]upon the altar of the burnt   t Lev. 1. 9.
    offering, and [u]on the altar of incense, *and were appointed* for   u Ex. 30. 7.
    all the work of the *place* most holy, and to make an atonement
    for Israel, according to all that Moses the servant of God had
50 commanded. And these *are* the sons of Aaron; Eleazar his
51 son, Phinehas his son, Abishua his son, Bukki his son, Uzzi his
52 son, Zerahiah his son, Meraioth his son, Amariah his son, Ahitub
53, 54 his son, Zadok his son, Ahimaaz his son. ¶ [x]Now these *are*   x Josh. 21.
    their dwelling places throughout their castles in their coasts, of
    the sons of Aaron, of the families of the Kohathites: for their's
55 was the lot. [y]And they gave them Hebron in the land of Judah,   y Josh. 21.
56 and the suburbs thereof round it. [z]But the fields of the city,   11, 12.
    and the villages thereof, they gave to Caleb the son of Jephun-   z Josh. 14.13.
57 neh. And [a]to the sons of Aaron they gave the cities of Judah,   & 15. 13.
    namely, Hebron, *the city* of refuge, and Libnah with her suburbs,   a Josh.21.13.
58 and Jattir, and Eshtemoa, with their suburbs, and [3]Hilen with
59 her suburbs, Debir with her suburbs, and [4]Ashan with her
60 suburbs, and Beth-shemesh with her suburbs: and out of the
    tribe of Benjamin; Geba with her suburbs, and [5]Alemeth with

[1] Called *Jeduthun*, ch. 9.   [2] Or, *Kushaiah*, ch. 15. 17.   [4] Or, *Ain*, Josh. 21. 16.
16. & 25. 1, 3, 6.   [3] Or, *Holon*, Josh. 21. 15.   [5] Or, *Almon*, Josh. 21. 18.

---

44. *Ethan*] Or Jeduthun (see marg.).
Corruption will scarcely account for the
two forms of the name, since Ethan is used
persistently up to a certain point (xv. 19),
after which we have uniformly "Jeduthun."
The case seems to be rather one in which
a new name was taken after a while, which
thenceforth superseded the old. Compare
Abraham, Sarah, Joshua, Jehoiakim, Zedekiah, &c.

50. *the sons of Aaron*] This list, a mere
repetition of that in *vv.* 3–8, came, probably,
from a different source—a source belonging
to the time of David, with whom Ahimaaz
(the last name on the list) was contemporary. The other list (*vv.* 4–15) came, no
doubt, from a document belonging to the
time of the Captivity (see *v.* 15).

54. *their's was the lot*] *i.e.* "the *first* lot."
The Kohathites had the *first* lot among the
Levitical families, as being the family
whereto the High-priesthood was attached
(cp. Josh. xxi. 10).

56–81. The writer evidently had before
him Josh. xxi., which he followed, as to its
matter, closely. In some cases he perhaps
modernised the ancient names (*vv.* 58, 60,
72, &c.); in a few he substituted for the old

an entirely new name, the modern appellation, probably, of the ancient site (*vv.* 70,
77). At one time, it would seem, his intention was to give the cities of the priests
only, and to content himself with stating
the mere number of the rest. His account
of the matter was then brought to a conclusion, and summed up, in *v.* 64. But,
afterwards, either he or a later writer
thought it best to add to the list of the
priestly cities the information contained in
Judges as to those which were not priestly,
but merely Levitical. The passage *vv.* 65–
81 was then added.

The entire account has suffered much
from corruption. In the first list two
names, those of Juttah and Gideon, have
dropped out. It is necessary to restore
them in order to complete the number of
thirteen cities (*v.* 60). In the second list
(*vv.* 67–70) there is likewise an omission of
two cities, Eltekeh and Gibbethon, which
are wanted to make up the number ten (*v.*
61). The third list is complete, though some
of the names are very different from those
of Joshua. In the fourth, two names are
again wanting, those of Jokneam and
Kartah.

o ver. 66.

c Josh. 21. 5.

d Josh. 21. 7, 31.

e ver. 61.
f Josh. 21.21.

g See Josh.
21. 22—35,
where many
of these
cities have
other
names.

a Gen. 46. 13.
Num. 26. 23.

her suburbs, and Anathoth with her suburbs. All their cities
61 throughout their families *were* thirteen cities. ¶ And unto the
sons of Kohath *b which were* left of the family of that tribe, *were
cities given* out of the half tribe, *namely, out of* the half *tribe* of
62 Manasseh, *c* by lot, ten cities. ¶ And to the sons of Gershom
throughout their families out of the tribe of Issachar, and out
of the tribe of Asher, and out of the tribe of Naphtali, and out
63 of the tribe of Manasseh in Bashan, thirteen cities. ¶ Unto the
sons of Merari *were given* by lot, throughout their families, out
of the tribe of Reuben, and out of the tribe of Gad, and out of
64 the tribe of Zebulun, *d* twelve cities. And the children of Israel
65 gave to the Levites *these* cities with their suburbs. And they
gave by lot out of the tribe of the children of Judah, and out of
the tribe of the children of Simeon, and out of the tribe of the
children of Benjamin, these cities, which are called by *their*
66 names. ¶ And *e the residue* of the families of the sons of Kohath
67 had cities of their coasts out of the tribe of Ephraim. *f* And
they gave unto them, *of* the cities of refuge, Shechem in mount
Ephraim with her suburbs; *they gave* also Gezer with her sub-
68 urbs, and *g* Jokmeam with her suburbs, and Beth-horon with her
69 suburbs, and Aijalon with her suburbs, and Gath-rimmon with
70 her suburbs: and out of the half tribe of Manasseh; Aner with
her suburbs, and Bileam with her suburbs, for the family of the
71 remnant of the sons of Kohath. ¶ Unto the sons of Gershom
were given out of the family of the half tribe of Manasseh,
Golan in Bashan with her suburbs, and Ashtaroth with her
72 suburbs: and out of the tribe of Issachar; Kedesh with her
73 suburbs, Daberath with her suburbs, and Ramoth with her sub-
74 urbs, and Anem with her suburbs: and out of the tribe of Asher;
Mashal with her suburbs, and Abdon with her suburbs, and
75, 76 Hukok with her suburbs, and Rehob with her suburbs: and
out of the tribe of Naphtali; Kedesh in Galilee with her suburbs, and Hammon with her suburbs, and Kirjathaim with her
77 suburbs. ¶ Unto the rest of the children of Merari *were given*
out of the tribe of Zebulun, Rimmon with her suburbs, Tabor
78 with her suburbs: and on the other side Jordan by Jericho, on
the east side of Jordan, *were given them* out of the tribe of
Reuben, Bezer in the wilderness with her suburbs, and Jahzah
79 with her suburbs, Kedemoth also with her suburbs, and Me-
80 phaath with her suburbs: and out of the tribe of Gad; Ramoth
in Gilead with her suburbs, and Mahanaim with her suburbs,
81 and Heshbon with her suburbs, and Jazer with her suburbs.

CHAP. 7. NOW the sons of Issachar *were*, *a* Tola, and [1] Puah, Ja-
2 shub, and Shimrom, four. And the sons of Tola; Uzzi, and
Rephaiah, and Jeriel, and Jahmai, and Jibsam, and Shemuel,
heads of their father's house, *to wit*, of Tola: *they were* valiant

[1] *Phuvah, Job.*

---

61. *unto the sons of Kohath which were left*]
i.e. to such of them as were not priests.

out of the half tribe ... ten cities] The half
tribe furnished two cities only (*v.* 70, and
cp. Josh. xxi. 25). It is evident therefore
that something has fallen out. We may
supply from Joshua the words "out of
Ephraim and out of Dan, and" before
"out of the half tribe."

77. *Unto the rest of the children of Merari*]

Rather, "Unto the rest, the children of
Merari"—that is to say, "unto the remainder of the Levites, who were descendants of Merari:"—the two other branches,
the Kohathites and the Gershomites, having
been treated of previously.

VII. 2. *whose number was in the days of
David, &c.*] The writer would seem by this
passage to have had access to the statistics
of the tribes collected by David, when he

men of might in their generations; *b*whose number *was* in the
3 days of David two and twenty thousand and six hundred. And
the sons of Uzzi; Izrahiah : and the sons of Izrahiah; Michael,
4 and Obadiah, and Joel, Ishiah, five: all of them chief men. And
with them, by their generations, after the house of their fàthers,
were bands of soldiers for war, six and thirty thousand *men :* for
5 they had many wives and sons. And their brethren among all
the families of Issachar *were* valiant men of might, reckoned in
6 all by their genealogies fourscore and seven thousand. ¶ *The*
7 *sons* of *c*Benjamin; Bela, and Becher, and Jediael, three. And
the sons of Bela; Ezbon, and Uzzi, and Uzziel, and Jerimoth, and
Iri, five; heads of the house of *their* fathers, mighty men of
valour; and were reckoned by their genealogies twenty and two
8 thousand and thirty and four. And the sons of Becher; Zemira,
and Joash, and Eliezer, and Elioenai, and Omri, and Jerimoth,
and Abiah, and Anathoth, and Alameth. All these *are* the sons
9 of Becher. And the number of them, after their genealogy by
their generations, heads of the house of their fathers, mighty
10 men of valour, *was* twenty thousand and two hundred. The
sons also of Jediael; Bilhan : and the sons of Bilhan ; Jeush,
and Benjamin, and Ehud, and Chenaanah, and Zethan, and
11 Tharshish, and Ahishahar. All these the sons of Jediael, by the
heads of their fathers, mighty men of valour, *were* seventeen
thousand and two hundred *soldiers*, fit to go out for war *and*
12 battle. *d*Shuppim also, and Huppim, the children of ¹Ir, *and*
13 Hushim, the sons of ²Aher. ¶ The sons of Naphtali; Jahziel,
14 and Guni, and Jezer, and *e*Shallum, the sons of Bilhah. ¶ The
sons of Manasseh ; Ashriel, whom she bare : (*but* his concubine
15 the Aramitess bare Machir the father of Gilead : and Machir
took to wife *the sister* of Huppim and Shuppim, whose sister's
name *was* Maachah ;) and the name of the second *was* Zelo-
16 phehad : and Zelophehad had daughters. And Maachah the
wife of Machir bare a son, and she called his name Peresh ; and
the name of his brother *was* Sheresh ; and his sons *were* Ulam
17 and Rakem. And the sons of Ulam ; *f*Bedan. These *were* the
18 sons of Gilead, the son of Machir, the son of Manasseh. And
his sister Hammoleketh bare Ishod, and *g*Abiezer, and Mahalah.
19 And the sons of Shemidah were, Ahian, and Shechem, and

b 2 Sam. 24.
1, 2.
ch. 27. 1.

c Gen. 46. 21.
Num. 26. 38.
ch. 8. 1, &c.

d Num. 26.
39, *Shupham,*
and *Hu-*
pham.
e Gen. 46. 24,
Shillem.

f 1 Sam. 12,
11:

g Num. 26.
30, *Jeezer.*

¹ Or, *Iri*, ver. 7.   ² Or, *Ahiram*, Num. 26. 38.

---

sinfully "numbered the people" (marg.
ref.). The numbers given in *vv.* 4, 5 probably came from the same source.

6. *three*] In Genesis, *ten* "sons" of Benjamin are mentioned; in Numbers, *five*
(marg. reff.). Neither list, however, contains Jediael who was perhaps a later chieftain. If so, "son," as applied to him means
only "descendant."

It is conjectured that Becher has disappeared from the lists in ch. viii. and in
Numbers, because he, or his heir, married
an Ephraimite heiress, and that his house
thus passed over in a certain sense into the
tribe of Ephraim, in which the "Bachrites"
are placed in Numbers (xxvi. 35). He retains, however, his place here, because, by
right of blood, he really belonged to Benjamin.

7, 8, 10. The lists here are remarkably
different from those in marg. reff. Probably
the persons here mentioned were not literally "sons," but were among the later
descendants of the founders, being the chief
men of the family at the time of David's
census.

17. *These were the sons of Gilead*] *i.e.*
these descendants of Machir were reckoned to the family of Gilead. The name
"Gilead" prevailed above all others in the
line of Manasseh, the term "Gileadite"
almost taking the place of "Manassite."

18. *Abiezer*] His descendants formed one
of the most important branches of the
Manassites. They furnished to Israel the
greatest of the Judges, Gideon (Jud. vi. 11,
24, 34), and were regarded as the leading
family among the so-called "sons of Gilead."

Num. 26.35. 20 Likhi, and Aniam. ¶ And ʰthe sons of Ephraim; Shuthelah, and Bered his son, and Tahath his son, and Eladah his son, and
21 Tahath his son, and Zabad his son, and Shuthelah his son, and Ezer, and Elead, whom the men of Gath *that were* born in *that* land slew, because they came down to take away their cattle.
22 And Ephraim their father mourned many days, and his brethren
23 came to comfort him. And when he went in to his wife, she conceived, and bare a son, and he called his name Beriah, because
24 it went evil with his house. (And his daughter *was* Sherah, who built Beth-horon the nether, and the upper, and Uzzen-sherah.)
25 And Rephah *was* his son, also Resheph, and Telah his son, and
26 Tahan his son, Laadan his son, Ammihud his son, Elishama his
27, 28 son, ¹Non his son, Jehoshuah his son. And their possessions and habitations *were*, Beth-el and the towns thereof, and

ⁱ Josh. 16. 7, *Naarath*.
eastward ⁱNaaran, and westward Gezer, with the ²towns thereof; Shechem also and the towns thereof, unto Gaza and the towns
ᵏ Josh. 17. 7.
29 thereof: and by the borders of the children of ᵏManasseh, Beth-
ˡ 1 Kin. 4. 11, 12.
shean and her towns, Taanach and her towns, ˡMegiddo and her towns, Dor and her towns. In these dwelt the children of
ᵐ Gen.46.17. Num. 26. 44.
30 Joseph the son of Israel. ¶ ᵐThe sons of Asher; Imnah, and
31 Isuah, and Ishuai, and Beriah, and Serah their sister. And the sons of Beriah; Heber, and Malchiel, who *is* the father of Bir-
ⁿ ver. 34, *Shamer*.
32 zavith. And Heber begat Japhlet, and ⁿShomer, and Hotham,
33 and Shua their sister. And the sons of Japhlet; Pasach, and
34 Bimhal, and Ashvath. These *are* the children of Japhlet. And
ᵒ ver. 32, *Shomer*.
the sons of ᵒShamer; Ahi, and Rohgah, Jehubbah, and Aram.
35 And the sons of his brother Helem; Zophah, and Imna, and
36 Shelesh, and Amal. The sons of Zophah; Suah, and Harne-
37 pher, and Shual, and Beri, and Imrah, Bezer, and Hod, and
38 Shamma, and Shilshah, and Ithran, and Beera. And the sons
39 of Jether; Jephunneh, and Pispah, and Ara. And the sons of
40 Ulla; Arah, and Haniel, and Rezia. All these *were* the children of Asher, heads of *their* father's house, choice *and* mighty men of valour, chief of the princes. And the number throughout the genealogy of them that were apt to the war *and* to battle *was* twenty and six thousand men.

ᵃ Gen. 46. 21. Num. 26. 38. ch. 7. 6.
CHAP. 8. NOW Benjamin begat ᵃBela his first-born, Ashbel the
2 second, and Aharah the third, Nohah the fourth, and Rapha
3 the fifth. And the sons of Bela were, ³Addar, and Gera, and
4, 5 Abihud, and Abishua, and Naaman, and Ahoah, and Gera,
6 and ⁴Shephuphan, and Huram. And these *are* the sons of

---

¹ Or, *Nun*, Num. 13. 8, 16.　　³ Or, *Ard*, Gen. 46. 21.　　⁴ Or, *Shupham*, Num. 26. 39. See ch. 7. 12.
² Heb. *daughters.*

---

20. *the sons of Ephraim*] The genealogy is difficult. It is perhaps best to consider Ezer and Elead (*v.* 21) as not sons of Zabad and brothers of the second Shuthelah, but natural sons of Ephraim. The passage would then run—
"And the sons of Ephraim, Shuthelah (and Bered *was* his son, and Tahath his son and Eladah his son, and Tahath his son, and Zabad his son, and Shuthelah his son) and Ezer and Elead, whom the men of Gath slew" (*i.e.* the settled inhabitants, as contrasted with the nomadic Hebrews, Amalekites, &c.).
24. Sherah could scarcely herself have built the Palestinian cities here mentioned,

which must belong to a time not earlier than Joshua. By "she built" we must understand "her descendants built."
34. *Shamer; Ahi, and Rohgah*] Translate —"The sons of Shamer (*v.* 32), **his brother**, Rohgah, &c."
VIII. 1. The reason of this return to the genealogy of the Benjamites seems to be the desire to connect the genealogical introduction with the historical body of the work. As the history is to begin with Saul, the genealogical portion is made to end with an account of the family of this Benjamite monarch.
6. *and they removed them to Manahath*]

Ehud: these are the heads of the fathers of the inhabitants of
7 Geba, and they removed them to [b]Manahath: and Naaman, and
Ahiah, and Gera, he removed them, and begat Uzza, and Ahihud.
8 And Shaharaim begat *children* in the country of Moab, after he
9 had sent them away; Hushim and Baara *were* his wives. And
he begat of Hodesh his wife, Jobab, and Zibia, and Mesha, and
10 Malcham, and Jeuz, and Shachia, and Mirma. These *were* his
11 sons, heads of the fathers. And of Hushim he begat Abitub,
12 and Elpaal. The sons of Elpaal; Eber, and Misham, and
13 Shamed, who built Ono, and Lod, with the towns thereof: Beriah also, and [c]Shema, who *were* heads of the fathers of the
inhabitants of Aijalon, who drove away the inhabitants of Gath:
14, 15 and Ahio, Shashak, and Jeremoth, and Zebadiah, and Arad,
16 and Ader, and Michael, and Ispah, and Joha, the sons of Be-
17 riah; and Zebadiah, and Meshullam, and Hezeki, and Heber,
18 Ishmerai also, and Jezliah, and Jobab, the sons of Elpaal;
19, 20 and Jakim, and Zichri, and Zabdi, and Elienai, and Zilthai,
21 and Eliel, and Adaiah, and Beraiah, and Shimrath, the sons of
22, 23 [1]Shimhi; and Ishpan, and Heber, and Eliel, and Abdon,
24 and Zichri, and Hanan, and Hananiah, and Elam, and Anto-
25, 26 thijah, and Iphedeiah, and Penuel, the sons of Shashak; and
27 Shamsherai, and Shehariah, and Athaliah, and Jaresiah, and
28 Eliah, and Zichri, the sons of Jeroham. These *were* heads of
the fathers, by their generations, chief *men*. These dwelt in
29 Jerusalem. ¶And at Gibeon dwelt the [2]father of Gibeon;
30 whose [d]wife's name *was* Maachah: and his firstborn son Abdon,
31 and Zur, and Kish, and Baal, and Nadab, and Gedor, and
32 Ahio, and [3]Zacher. And Mikloth begat [4]Shimeah. And these
also dwelt with their brethren in Jerusalem, over against them.
33 ¶And [e]Ner begat Kish, and Kish begat Saul, and Saul begat
Jonathan, and Malchi-shua, and [f]Abinadab, and [5]Esh-baal.
34 And the son of Jonathan *was* [6]Merib-baal; and Merib-baal
35 begat [g]Micah. And the sons of Micah *were*, Pithon, and Me-
36 lech, and [7]Tarea, and Ahaz. And Ahaz begat [h]Jehoadah; and
Jehoadah begat Alemeth, and Azmaveth, and Zimri; and Zimri
37 begat Moza, and Moza begat Binea: [i]Rapha *was* his son,

Margin notes (right column):
[b] ch. 2. 52.

[c] ver. 21.

[d] ch. 9. 35.

[e] 1 Sam. 14. 51.
[f] 1 Sam. 14. 49, *Ishui.*
[g] 2 Sam. 9. 12.
[h] *Jarah,* ch. 9. 42.
[i] ch. 9. 43, *Rephaiah.*

---

[1] Or, *Shema*, ver. 13.
[2] Called *Jehiel*, ch. 9. 35.
[3] Or, *Zechariah*, ch. 9. 37.
[4] Or, *Shimeam*, ch. 9. 38.
[5] Or, *Ish-bosheth*, 2 Sam. 2. 8.
[6] Or, *Mephibosheth*, 2 Sam. 4. 4. & 9. 6, 10.
[7] Or, *Tahrea*, ch. 9. 41.

"They" has no antecedent; and it is difficult to supply one. Almost all commentators suppose that there has been some
corruption here, from which, however, we
may gather that the "sons of Ehud"
(or, perhaps, of Ahoah, *v.* 4) were originally
settled at Geba (Josh. xviii. 24 note), but
afterwards removed to a place called Manahath, probably a town in the vicinity. Gera
(*v.* 7) directed the movement.

8. *after he had sent them away*] Translate,
"after he had **divorced his wives**, Hushim
and Baara."

28. *These dwelt in Jerusalem*] Jerusalem
was partly within the limits of the tribe of
Benjamin (Josh. xviii. 28); but we do not
hear of Benjamites inhabiting it until after
the return from the Captivity (ix. 3; Neh.
xi. 4).

33. This verse combined with ix. 35-30,

seems to show that the genealogy of **Saul**
was

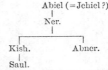

rather than that to be inferred from 1 Sam.
ix. 1, xiv. 50, 51.

In 1 Sam. xiv. 49 note, it is concluded
that Saul's second son bore the two names
of "Ishui" and "Abinadab." But the
order of the names here—(1) Jonathan; (2)
Malchi-shua; and (3) Abinadab—suggests
another explanation, viz., that Ishui, the
second son, died young, and that Abinadab
was really the fourth son.

Esh-baal] Previous to the introduction

38 Eleasah his son, Azel his son: and Azel had six sons, whose names *are* these, Azrikam, Bocheru, and Ishmael, and Sheariah, and Obadiah, and Hanan. All these *were* the sons of Azel.

39 And the sons of Eshek his brother *were*, Ulam his firstborn,

40 Jehush the second, and Eliphelet the third. And the sons of Ulam were mighty men of valour, archers, and had many sons, and sons' sons, an hundred and fifty. All these *are* of the sons of Benjamin.

^a Ezra 2. 50.

CHAP. 9. SO ^aall Israel were reckoned by genealogies; and, behold, they *were* written in the book of the kings of Israel and Judah, *who* were carried away to Babylon for their transgression.

^b Ezra 2. 70.
Neh. 7. 73.
^c Josh. 9. 27.
Ezra 2. 43.
& 8. 20.
^d Neh. 11. 1.

2 ¶ ^bNow the first inhabitants that *dwelt* in their possessions in their cities *were*, the Israelites, the priests, Levites, and ^cthe

3 Nethinims. ¶And in ^dJerusalem dwelt of the children of Judah, and of the children of Benjamin, and of the children of

4 Ephraim, and Manasseh ; Uthai the son of Ammihud, the son of Omri, the son of Imri, the son of Bani, of the children of

5 Pharez the son of Judah. And of the Shilonites ; Asaiah the

6 firstborn, and his sons. And of the sons of Zerah ; Jeuel, and

7 their brethren, six hundred and ninety. And of the sons of Benjamin ; Sallu the son of Meshullam, the son of Hodaviah,

8 the son of Hasenuah, and Ibneiah the son of Jeroham, and Elah the son of Uzzi, the son of Michri, and Meshullam the son of

9 Shephathiah, the son of Reuel, the son of Ibnijah; and their brethren, according to their generations, nine hundred and fifty and six. All these men *were* chief of the fathers in the house

^e Neh. 11. 10, &c.

10 of their fathers. ¶ ^eAnd of the priests ; Jedaiah, and Jehoiarib,

---

of the Phœnician Baal-worship into Israel by Ahab, the word "Baal" had no bad sense in Hebrew, but was simply an equivalent of the more ordinary *El*, "God" (1 Chr. iii. 1 note). Hence, there is nothing strange in the use at this time of the names, "Esh-baal" ("man of God"), "Baal," "Beel-iada," "Merib-baal," &c. Later on such names became offensive to pious ears, and were changed for the better, or for the worse, "Beel-iada" becoming "El-iada" ("let God aid") — "Esh-baal," "Ish-bosheth" ("man of shame")—"Merib-baal," "Mephi-bosheth"; and the like.

40. *sons, and sons' sons*] This genealogy of the house of Saul appears by the number of the generations to belong probably to the time of Hezekiah (cp. iv. 41). Ulam's "sons' sons" are in the 13th generation from Jonathan, as Hezekiah is in the 13th generation from David.

IX. 1. Rather, "So all Israel were reckoned...the kings of Israel. And Judah was carried away captive to Babylon for their transgressions."

2. *the first inhabitants*] i.e. the first inhabitants of the Holy Land after the return from the Captivity. They are enumerated under four heads : (1) Israelites, *i.e.* the mass of the laity, whether belonging to the ten tribes or the two ; (2) priests ; (3) Levites ; and (4) the lowest order of the ministry, the Nethinims. These last, whose name is derived from a root "to give," were a sort of sacred slaves—persons "given" to the Levites to perform the more laborious duties of the Sanctuary. Some had been "given" as early as the time of Moses (Num. xxxi. 47); and the number afterwards increased (Josh. ix. 23 ; Ezr. viii. 20). At the time of the return from the Captivity, owing to the small number of Levites who came back (Ezr. ii. 40–42), the services of the Nethinims became very important. They are mentioned under the name of Nethinims only in Chronicles, Ezra, and Nehemiah.

3. The correspondence and the diversity between the account here and in Nehemiah (xi. 4–19) are explained by the probability that both writers drew from a common and fuller document. They selected, in some instances, different names, or names which are now different through corruption ; and they frequently expressed the genealogies of the same persons differently, both going on the principle of compression by means of omissions, but omitting from their lists different links of the chain.

9. The discrepancy between the numbers here and in Nehemiah (xi. 8) may arise from corruption. So in *vv*. 13, 22.

10. "Jedaiah," "Jehoiarib," and "Jachin," are not here names of individuals but of priestly families. From xxiv. 7–17, it appears that Jehoiarib was the original head of the first "course," Jedaiah of the second, and Jachin of the twenty-first.

11 and Jachin, and [1]Azariah the son of Hilkiah, the son of Meshullam, the son of Zadok, the son of Meraioth, the son of
12 Ahitub, the ruler of the house of God ; and Adaiah the son of
Jeroham, the son of Pashur, the son of Malchijah, and Maasiai
the son of Adiel, the son of Jahzerah, the son of Meshullam, the
13 son of Meshillemith, the son of Immer; and their brethren,
heads of the house of their fathers, a thousand and seven hundred and threescore ; [2]very able men for the work of the service
14 of the house of God. ¶ And of the Levites ; Shemaiah the son of
Hasshub, the son of Azrikam, the son of Hashabiah, of the sons
15 of Merari ; and Bakbakkar, Heresh, and Galal, and Mattaniah
16 the son of Micah, the son of Zichri, the son of Asaph ; and
Obadiah the son of Shemaiah, the son of Galal, the son of
Jeduthun, and Berechiah the son of Asa, the son of Elkanah,
17 that dwelt in the villages of the Netophathites. And the porters
were, Shallum, and Akkub, and Talmon, and Ahiman, and their
18 brethren : Shallum *was* the chief; who hitherto *waited* in the
king's gate eastward : they *were* porters in the companies of the
19 children of Levi. And Shallum the son of Kore, the son of
Ebiasaph, the son of Korah, and his brethren, of the house of
his father, the Korahites, *were* over the work of the service,
keepers of the [3]gates of the tabernacle : and their fathers, *being*
20 over the host of the LORD, *were* keepers of the entry. And
*f*Phinehas the son of Eleazar was the ruler over them in time
21 past, *and* the LORD *was* with him. *And* Zechariah the son of
Meshelemiah *was* porter of the door of the tabernacle of the
22 congregation. ¶ All these *which were* chosen to be porters in the
gates *were* two hundred and twelve. These were reckoned by
their genealogy in their villages, whom *g*David and Samuel *h*the
23 seer [4]did ordain in their [5]set office. So they and their children
had the oversight of the gates of the house of the LORD, *namely*,
24 the house of the tabernacle, by wards. In four quarters were
25 the porters, toward the east, west, north, and south. And their
brethren, *which were* in their villages, *were* to come [i]after seven
26 days from time to time with them. For these Levites, the four

f Num. 31. 6.

g ch. 26. 1, 2.
h 1 Sam. 9. 9.

[i] 2 Kin. 11. 5.
2 Chr. 23. 4.

[1] Neh. 11. 11, *Seraiah*.　　　[3] Heb. *thresholds*.　　　[5] Or, *trust*.
[2] Heb. *mighty men of valour*.　　[4] Heb. *founded*.

---

18. *who hitherto waited*] Translate, "Who
to this day waits. These were the porters in the **stations** of the sons of Levi."
The words of the first clause refer to
Shallum, and imply that, whereas Shallum (or his house) had originally the general
superintendence of the Temple gates, a
change had been made when the author
wrote, and Shallum's charge had become
the east gate only. The second clause
means ; "these were the porters in those
fixed stations at the outer gates of the
Temple, which corresponded to the camp
stations of the Levites who guarded the
Tabernacle in the early times."

19. *Shallum the son of Kore*] A different
person from the Shallum of *v.* 17, and
with a different office, viz., the guarding
the inner doors of the Temple. The original
Shallum, Shelemaiah, or Meshelemaiah,
was a Levite of the time of David (xxvi. 14).
His descendants were still called by his

name, but had now a more important charge
assigned to them.

22. The porters, like the singers (Neh.
xii. 29), dwelt for the most part in the villages round Jerusalem. They were the
descendants of those originally selected
for the work by David. David's arrangements are here regarded as having had
the sanction of Samuel—which would imply that he planned them in the lifetime
of Saul, while he was still a fugitive and
an outlaw.

25. See marg. reff. If the number of
warders was, as stated in Nehemiah (xi. 19)
172 (*i.e.* 168 besides the four chief warders),
and the number employed at any one time
was, as under David (xxvi. 17, 18), twenty-
four, then the turn of the courses to keep
ward came every seven weeks.

26. Rather, "For the four chief porters,
**who were themselves Levites, were in
trust, who also** had the charge of the

chief porters, were in *their* [1]set office, and were over the [2]chambers and treasuries of the house of God. And they lodged round

27 about the house of God, because the charge *was* upon them, and

28 the opening thereof every morning *pertained* to them. And *certain* of them had the charge of the ministering vessels, that

29 they should [3]bring them in and out by tale. *Some* of them also *were* appointed to oversee the vessels, and all the [4]instruments of the sanctuary, and the fine flour, and the wine, and the oil,

30 and the frankincense, and the spices. And *some* of the sons of

k Ex. 30. 23.

31 the priests made *k* the ointment of the spices. And Mattithiah, *one* of the Levites, who *was* the firstborn of Shallum the Ko-

l Lev. 2. 5.
& 6. 21.

rahite, had the [5]set office [l]over the things that were made [6]in

32 the pans. And *other* of their brethren, of the sons of the Koha-

m Lev. 24. 8.

thites, *m* *were* over the [7]shewbread, to prepare *it* every sabbath.

n ch. 6. 31.
& 25. 1.

33 And these *are* *n* the singers, chief of the fathers of the Levites, *who remaining* in the chambers *were* free: for [8]they were em-

34 ployed in *that* work day and night. These chief fathers of the Levites *were* chief throughout their generations; these dwelt at

35 Jerusalem. ¶ And in Gibeon dwelt the father of Gibeon, Jehiel,

o ch. 8. 29.

36 whose wife's name *was* *o* Maachah: and his firstborn son Abdon,

37 then Zur, and Kish, and Baal, and Ner, and Nadab, and Gedor,

38 and Ahio, and Zechariah, and Mikloth. And Mikloth begat Shimeam. And they also dwelt with their brethren at Jeru-

p ch. 8. 33.

39 salem, over against their brethren. *p* And Ner begat Kish; and Kish begat Saul; and Saul begat Jonathan, and Malchi-shua,

40 and Abinadab, and Esh-baal. And the son of Jonathan *was*

41 Merib-baal: and Merib-baal begat Micah. And the sons of

q ch. 8. 35.

42 Micah *were*, Pithon, and Melech, and Tahrea, *q* and Ahaz. And Ahaz begat Jarah; and Jarah begat Alemeth, and Azmaveth,

43 and Zimri; and Zimri begat Moza; and Moza begat Binea;

44 and Rephaiah his son, Eleasah his son, Azel his son. And Azel had six sons, whose names *are* these, Azrikam, Bocheru, and Ishmael, and Sheariah, and Obadiah, and Hanan: these *were* the sons of Azel.

a 1 Sam. 31.
1, 2.

CHAP. 10. NOW *a* the Philistines fought against Israel; and the men of Israel fled from before the Philistines, and fell down

[1] Or, *trust.*
[2] Or, *storehouses.*
[3] Heb. *bring them in by tale,*
[4] Or, *vessels.*
[5] Or, *trust.*
and carry them out by tale.
[6] Or, *on flat plates,* or, *slices.*
[7] Heb. *bread of ordering.*
[8] Heb. *upon them.*

---

chambers, &c." A contrast seems intended between the four chief porters, whose charge was constant, and the remainder, who kept watch by turns.

28. *by tale*] Lit., "by number." The vessels for service taken out of the treasury were counted, that the same number should be returned to the treasury after the service was over.

31. *Mattithiah...the first-born of Shallum the Korahite*] This Shallum would seem to be the person mentioned in *v.* 19, whose actual first-born was Zechariah (xxvi. 2). Mattithiah may have been his eldest lineal descendant at the time here spoken of.

33. *the singers*] No names follow, and it is thought that they have fallen out.

were free] "Free," *i.e.* from any special duties besides those of supervision, which was so arranged among the overseers that

some one exercised it during every part of both day and night.

34. *chief throughout their generations*] The superintendents, that is, were the genealogical head of the different Levitical divisions, and bore special rule, each over those of his own blood and race. The hereditary principle prevailed, not only in the High-priesthood, but also in the priestly offices of the second rank.

35–44. An almost exact repetition of viii. 29-38; and probably intentionally made by the author. In order to connect the genealogical section of his work with the historical, he re-introduces the genealogy of the person with whose death his historical section opens.

X. The present chapter contains two facts not found in 1 Sam. xxxi.—the fastening of Saul's head in the temple of Dagon

2 ¹slain in Mount Gilboa. And the Philistines followed hard after Saul, and after his sons; and the Philistines slew Jonathan, and
3 ²Abinadab, and Malchi-shua, the sons of Saul. And the battle went sore against Saul, and the ³archers ⁴hit him, and he was
4 wounded of the archers. Then said Saul to his armourbearer, Draw thy sword, and thrust me through therewith; lest these uncircumcised come and ⁵abuse me. But his armourbearer would not; for he was sore afraid. So Saul took a sword, and
5 fell upon it. And when his armourbearer saw that Saul was
6 dead, he fell likewise on the sword, and died. So Saul died, and
7 his three sons, and all his house died together. And when all the men of Israel that *were* in the valley saw that they fled, and that Saul and his sons were dead, then they forsook their cities,
8 and fled: and the Philistines came and dwelt in them. And it came to pass on the morrow, when the Philistines came to strip the slain, that they found Saul and his sons fallen in mount
9 Gilboa. And when they had stripped him, they took his head, and his armour, and sent into the land of the Philistines round about, to carry tidings unto their idols, and to the people.
10 ᵇAnd they put his armour in the house of their gods, and
11 fastened his head in the temple of Dagon. ¶And when all Jabesh-gilead heard all that the Philistines had done to Saul,
12 they arose, all the valiant men, and took away the body of Saul, and the bodies of his sons, and brought them to Jabesh, and buried their bones under the oak in Jabesh, and fasted seven
13 days. ¶So Saul died for his transgression which he ⁶committed against the LORD, ᶜ*even* against the word of the LORD, which he kept not, and also for asking *counsel* of *one that had* a familiar
14 spirit, ᵈto enquire *of it;* and enquired not of the LORD: therefore he slew him, and ᵉturned the kingdom unto David the son of ⁷Jesse.

CHAP. 11. THEN ᵃall Israel gathered themselves to David unto
2 Hebron, saying, Behold, *we are* thy bone and thy flesh. And moreover ⁸in time past, even when Saul was king, thou *wast* he that leddest out and broughtest in Israel: and the LORD thy God said unto thee, Thou shalt ⁹ᵇfeed my people Israel, and
3 thou shalt be ruler over my people Israel. Therefore came all the elders of Israel to the king to Hebron; and David made a covenant with them in Hebron before the LORD; and ᶜthey anointed David king over Israel, according to the word of the
4 LORD ¹by ᵈSamuel. ¶And David and all Israel ᵉwent to Jerusalem, which *is* Jebus; ᶠwhere the Jebusites *were*, the inhabit-

Marginal references:
ᵇ 1 Sam. 31. 10.

ᶜ 1 Sam. 13. & 15. 23.
ᵈ 1 Sam. 28. 7.
ᵉ 1 Sam. 15. 28.
2 Sam. 3. 9, 10.
& 5. 3.
ᵃ 2 Sam. 5. 1.

ᵇ Ps. 78. 71.

ᶜ 2 Sam. 5. 3.
ᵈ 1 Sam. 16. 1, 12, 13.
ᵉ 2 Sam. 5. 6.
ᶠ Judg. 1. 21. & 19. 10.

Footnotes:
¹ Or, *wounded.*
² Or, *Ishui,* 1 Sam. 14. 49.
³ Heb. *shooters with bows.*
⁴ Heb. *found him.*
⁵ Or, *mock me.*
⁶ Heb. *transgressed.*
⁷ Heb. *Isai.*
⁸ Heb. *both yesterday and the third day.*
⁹ Or, *rule.*
¹ Heb. *by the hand of.*

(*v.* 10), and the burial of his bones, and those of his sons, under an *oak* (*v.* 12). Otherwise the narrative differs from 1 Sam. xxxi. only by being abbreviated (see especially *vv.* 6, 7, 11, and 12), and by having some moral reflections attached to it (*vv.* 13 and 14).

6. *all his house died together*] Not the whole of his family, nor even "all his sons" (see 2 Sam. ii. 8–15, iii. 6–15, iv. 1–12). The phrase is perhaps an abbreviation of the expression in the parallel passage of Samuel (1 Sam. xxxi. 6).

13. *for his transgression*] Cp. ix. 1. The "transgression" intended is probably the disobedience with respect to Amalek, recorded in 1 Sam. xv. 1–9 (cp. 1 Sam. xxviii. 17, 18).

XI. This chapter runs parallel with 2 Sam. v. as far as *v.* 9, after which it is to be compared with 2 Sam. (xxiii. 8–39) as far as *v.* 40, the remainder (*vv.* 41–47) being an addition, to which Samuel has nothing corresponding. Cp. throughout the notes in Samuel.

5 ants of the land. And the inhabitants of Jebus said to David,
Thou shalt not come hither. Nevertheless David took the castle
6 of Zion, which *is* the city of David. And David said, Whosoever
smiteth the Jebusites first shall be [1]chief and captain. So Joab
7 the son of Zeruiah went first up, and was chief. And David
dwelt in the castle ; therefore they called [2]it the city of David.
8 And he built the city round about, even from Millo round
9 about: and Joab [3]repaired the rest of the city. So David [4]waxed
greater and greater: for the LORD of hosts *was* with him.

v 2 Sam. 23. 8.

10 ¶ *g* These also *are* the chief of the mighty men whom David had,
who [5]strengthened themselves with him in his kingdom, *and*

h 1 Sam. 16. 1, 12.

with all Israel, to make him king, according to *h* the word of the
11 LORD concerning Israel. And this *is* the number of the mighty
men whom David had ; Jashobeam, [6]an Hachmonite, the chief
of the captains : he lifted up his spear against three hundred
12 slain *by him* at one time. And after him *was* Eleazar the son
13 of Dodo, the Ahohite, who *was* one of the three mighties. He
was with David at [7]Pas-dammim, and there the Philistines were
gathered together to battle, where was a parcel of ground full
14 of barley ; and the people fled from before the Philistines. And
they [8]set themselves in the midst of *that* parcel, and delivered
it, and slew the Philistines ; and the LORD saved *them* by a great

i 2 Sam. 23. 13.

15 [9]deliverance. ¶ Now [1]three of the thirty captains *i* went down
to the rock to David, into the cave of Adullam ; and the host of

k ch. 14. 9.

16 the Philistines encamped *k* in the valley of Rephaim. And David
was then in the hold, and the Philistines' garrison *was* then at
17 Beth-lehem. And David longed, and said, Oh that one would
give me drink of the water of the well of Beth-lehem, that *is* at
18 the gate! And the three brake through the host of the Philistines, and drew water out of the well of Beth-lehem, that *was*
by the gate, and took *it*, and brought *it* to David : but David
19 would not drink *of* it, but poured it out to the LORD, and said,
My God forbid it me, that I should do this thing : shall I drink
the blood of these men [2]that have put their lives in jeopardy?
for with *the jeopardy of* their lives they brought it. Therefore
he would not drink it. These things did these three mightiest.

l 2 Sam. 23. 18.

20 ¶ *l* And Abishai the brother of Joab, he was chief of the three:
for lifting up his spear against three hundred, he slew *them*, and

m 2 Sam. 23. 19.

21 had a name among the three. *m* Of the three, he was more

[1] Heb. *head.*
[2] That is, *Zion*, 2 Sam. 5.7.
[3] Heb. *revived.*
[4] Heb. *went in going and increasing.*
[5] Or, *held strongly with him.*
[6] Or, *son of Hachmoni.*
[7] Or, *Ephes-dammim,* 1 Sam. 17. 1.
[8] Or, *stood.*
[9] Or, *salvation.*
[1] Or, *three captains over the thirty.*
[2] Heb. *with their lives?*

6-8. The narrative here given fills out a
manifest defect in 2 Sam. v. 8, where something has evidently dropped out of the
text.

The prowess of Joab on this occasion,
and the part which he took in the building
of the city of David (*v.* 8), are known to us
only from this passage of Chronicles.

10. *strengthened themselves*] Or "exerted
themselves"—"strenuously assisted with
all Israel in making David king." This
list of David's principal heroes belongs,
therefore, to his reign at Hebron. In
Samuel the list is not given till nearly the
end of David's reign (2 Sam. xxiii. 8–39).

11. *chief of the captains*] Or, "of the
thirty," according to another and better
reading (see *vv.* 15, 25 ; cp. 2 Sam. xxiii. 8
note). Jashobeam was the commander of
the first monthly course of 24,000 soldiers
(xxvii. 2). He is probably the warrior of
the name who joined David at Ziklag
(xii. 6).

13. Cp. this passage with 2 Sam. xxiii. 9,
10.

barley] In 2 Sam. xxiii. 11, "lentiles."
The words for barley and lentils are so
similar in the Hebrew that we may fairly
explain the diversity by an accidental corruption.

honourable than the two; for he was their captain: howbeit he
22 attained not to the *first* three. ¶ Benaiah the son of Jehoiada,
the son of a valiant man of Kabzeel, [1]who had done many acts;
[n]he slew two lionlike men of Moab: also he went down and
23 slew a lion in a pit in a snowy day. And he slew an Egyptian,
[2]a man of *great* stature, five cubits high; and in the Egyptian's
hand *was* a spear like a weaver's beam; and he went down to
him with a staff, and plucked the spear out of the Egyptian's
24 hand, and slew him with his own spear. These *things* did
Benaiah the son of Jehoiada, and had the name among the three
25 mightiest. Behold, he was honourable among the thirty, but
attained not to the *first* three: and David set him over his
26 guard. ¶ Also the valiant men of the armies *were*, [o]Asahel the
27 brother of Joab, Elhanan the son of Dodo of Beth-lehem, [3]Sham-
28 moth the [4]Harorite, Helez the [5]Pelonite, Ira the son of Ikkesh
29 the Tekoite, Abi-ezer the Antothite, [6]Sibbecai the Hushathite,
30 [7]Ilai the Ahohite, Maharai the Netophathite, [8]Heled the son of
31 Baanah the Netophathite, Ithai the son of Ribai of Gibeah, *that*
pertained to the children of Benjamin, Benaiah the Pirathonite,
32, 33 [9]Hurai of the brooks of Gaash, [1]Abiel the Arbathite, Azma-
34 veth the Baharumite, Eliahba the Shaalbonite, the sons of [2]Ha-
shem the Gizonite, Jonathan the son of Shage the Hararite,
35 Ahiam the son of [3]Sacar the Hararite, [4]Eliphal the son of [5]Ur,
36, 37 Hepher the Mecherathite, Ahijah the Pelonite, [6]Hezro the
38 Carmelite, [7]Naarai the son of Ezbai, Joel the brother of Nathan,
39 Mibhar [8]the son of Haggeri, Zelek the Ammonite, Naharai the
40 Berothite, the armourbearer of Joab the son of Zeruiah, Ira the
41 Ithrite, Gareb the Ithrite, Uriah the Hittite, Zabad the son of
42 Ahlai, Adina the son of Shiza the Reubenite, a captain of the
43 Reubenites, and thirty with him, Hanan the son of Maachah,
44 and Joshaphat the Mithnite, Uzzia the Ashterathite, Shama
45 and Jehiel the sons of Hothan the Aroerite, Jediael the [9]son of
46 Shimri, and Joha his brother, the Tizite, Eliel the Mahavite,
and Jeribai, and Joshaviah, the sons of Elnaam, and Ithmah the
47 Moabite, Eliel, and Obed, and Jasiel the Mesobaite.

[n] 2 Sam. 23.
20.

[o] 2 Sam. 23.
21.

[1] Heb. *great of deeds.*
[2] Heb. *a man of measure.*
[3] Or, *Shammah.*
[4] Or, *Harodite,* 2 Sam. 23.
25.
[5] Or, *Paltite,* 2 Sam. 23.
26.

[6] Or, *Mebunnai.*
[7] Or, *Zalmon.*
[8] Or, *Heleb.*
[9] Or, *Hiddai.*
[1] Or, *Abi-albon.*
[2] Or, *Jashen,* See 2 Sam.
23. 32, 33.

[3] Or, *Sharar.*
[4] Or, *Eliphelet.*
[5] Or, *Ahasbai.*
[6] Or, *Hezrai.*
[7] Or, *Paarai the Arbite.*
[8] Or, *the Haggerite.*
[9] Or, *Shimrite.*

23. *five cubits high*] About 7 ft. 6 in. high.
The height is not so great as that recorded
of other giants.

26., &c. The list of names here given corresponds generally with that in 2 Sam. xxiii.
24–39, but presents several remarkable differences. (1) The number in Chronicles is
47; in Samuel 31. (2) Four names in the
list of Chronicles are not in Samuel. (3)
Five names in Samuel are not in Chronicles.
(4) Many of the other names, both personal
and local, vary in the two lists. It is quite
possible that the two lists varied to some
extent originally. The writer of Chronicles
distinctly states that he gives the list as it
stood at the time of David's becoming king
over all Israel (*v.* 10). The writer of Samuel
does not assign his list to any definite period

of David's reign, but probably delivers it to
us as it was constituted at a later date. It
is quite possible therefore that the names
which occur only in Chronicles are those of
persons who had died or quitted the army
before the other list was made out, and that
the new names in Samuel are the names of
those who had taken their places. See 2
Sam. xxiii. 39 note.

34. *The sons of Hashem*] It is impossible
that this can be the true reading, since an
individual warrior must be spoken of. Comparing 2 Sam. xxiii. 32, perhaps the most
probable conjecture is that the "Beni Hashem" of Chronicles and the "Beni
Jashen" of Samuel alike conceal some
single name of a man which cannot now
be recovered.

a 1Sam.27.2.
b 1Sam.:.7.6.

Chap. 12. Now "these *are* they that came to David to *b*Ziklag, [1]while he yet kept himself close because of Saul the son of Kish: and they *were* among the mighty men, helpers of the 2 war. *They were* armed with bows, and could use both the right

c Judg.20.16.

hand and *c*the left in *hurling* stones and *shooting* arrows out of a 3 bow, *even* of Saul's brethren of Benjamin. The chief *was* Ahiezer, then Joash, the sons of [2]Shemaah the Gibeathite; and Jeziel, and Pelet, the sons of Azmaveth; and Berachah, and Jehu the 4 Antothite, and Ismaiah the Gibeonite, a mighty man among the thirty, and over the thirty; and Jeremiah, and Jahaziel, and 5 Johanan, and Josabad the Gederathite, Eluzai, and Jerimoth, and Bealiah, and Shemariah, and Shephatiah the Haruphite, 6 Elkanah, and Jesiah, and Azareel, and Joezer, and Jashobeam, 7 the Korhites, and Joelah, and Zebadiah, the sons of Jeroham of 8 Gedor. ¶And of the Gadites there separated themselves unto David into the hold to the wilderness men of might, *and* men [3]of war *fit* for the battle, that could handle shield and buckler,

d 2Sam.2.18.

whose faces *were like* the faces of lions, and *were* *d*[4]as swift as 9 the roes upon the mountains; Ezer the first, Obadiah the second, 10 Eliab the third, Mishmannah the fourth, Jeremiah the fifth, 11, 12 Attai the sixth, Eliel the seventh, Johanan the eighth, Elza-13 bad the ninth, Jeremiah the tenth, Machbanai the eleventh. 14 These *were* of the sons of Gad, captains of the host: [5]one of the least *was* over an hundred, and the greatest over a thousand. 15 These *are* they that went over Jordan in the first month, when

e Josh. 3. 15.

it had [6]overflown all his *e*banks; and they put to flight all *them* 16 of the valleys, *both* toward the east, and toward the west. ¶And there came of the children of Benjamin and Judah to the hold 17 unto David. And David went out [7]to meet them, and answered and said unto them, If ye be come peaceably unto me to help me, mine heart shall [8]be knit unto you: but if *ye be come* to betray me to mine enemies, seeing *there is* no [9]wrong in mine hands, the 18 God of our fathers look *thereon*, and rebuke *it*. Then [1]the spirit

f 2 Sam. 17. 25.

came upon *f*Amasai, *who was* chief of the captains *and he said*,
Thine *are* we, David,
And on thy side, thou son of Jesse:

---

[1] Heb. *being yet shut up.*
[2] Or, *Hasmaah.*
[3] Heb. *of the host.*
[4] Heb. *as the roes upon the mountains to make haste.*

[5] Or, *one that was least could resist an hundred, and the greatest a thousand.*
[6] Heb. *filled over.*

[7] Heb. *before them.*
[8] Heb. *be one.*
[9] Or, *violence.*
[1] Heb. *the spirit clothed Amasai:* So Judg. 6. 34.

XII. This chapter is composed wholly of matter that is new to us, no corresponding accounts occurring in Samuel. It comprises four lists,—(1) One of men, chiefly Benjamites, who joined David at Ziklag (*vv.* 1–7); (2) A second of Gadites who united themselves to him when he was in a stronghold near the desert (*vv.* 8–15); (3) A third of Manassites who came to him when he was dismissed by the Philistines upon suspicion (*vv.* 19–22); and (4) A fourth of the numbers from the different tribes who attended and made him king at Hebron (*vv.* 23–40).

2. The skill of the Benjamites as archers is noted in viii. 40, and 2 Chr. xiv. 8. Their proficiency in using the left hand appears in the narrative of Judges (iii. 15, and marg. ref.) where their peculiar excellency as slingers is also noticed.

even of Saul's brethren] Cp. *v.* 29. Even of Saul's own tribe there were some who separated themselves from his cause, and threw in their lot with David.

8. *into the hold to the wilderness*] Rather, "into the hold **towards** the wilderness." Some understand by this Ziklag, some Engedi (1 Sam. xxiv. 1, 2); but it seems most probable that here and in *v.* 16 the stronghold of Adullam is intended (xi. 15, 16).

14. The marginal rendering is preferable. (Cp. Lev. xxvi. 8).

15. On the danger of the exploit, see marg. ref. note.

This passage (*vv.* 8–15) seems to be taken *verbatim* from an ancient source, the poetical expressions in *vv.* 8, 14, being especially unlike the usual style of our author.

18. *Amasai*] The marg. ref. identifies him

Peace, peace *be* unto thee,
And peace *be* to thine helpers;
For thy God helpeth thee.
Then David received them, and made them captains of the band.
19 ¶ And there fell *some* of Manasseh to David, ^g when he came with
the Philistines against Saul to battle: but they helped them
not: for the lords of the Philistines upon advisement sent him
away, saying, ^h He will fall to his master Saul ¹to *the jeopardy*
20 *of* our heads. As he went to Ziklag, there fell to him of Manasseh, Adnah, and Jozabad, and Jediael, and Michael, and
Jozabad, and Elihu, and Zilthai, captains of the thousands that
21 *were* of Manasseh. And they helped David ²against ⁱ the band
of the rovers: for they *were* all mighty men of valour, and were
22 captains in the host. For at *that* time day by day there came
to David to help him, until *it was* a great host, like the host of
23 God. ¶ And these *are* the numbers of the ³ ⁴ bands *that were*
ready armed to the war, *and* ^k came to David to Hebron, to ^l turn
the kingdom of Saul to him, ^m according to the word of the
24 LORD. The children of Judah that bare shield and spear *were*
25 six thousand and eight hundred, ready ⁵ armed to the war. Of
the children of Simeon, mighty men of valour for the war, seven
26 thousand and one hundred. Of the children of Levi four thou-
27 sand and six hundred. And Jehoiada *was* the leader of the
Aaronites, and with him *were* three thousand and seven hundred;
28 and ⁿ Zadok, a young man mighty of valour, and of his father's
29 house twenty and two captains. And of the children of Benja-
min, the ⁶ kindred of Saul, three thousand: for hitherto ⁷ ^o the
greatest part of them had kept the ward of the house of Saul.
30 And of the children of Ephraim twenty thousand and eight
hundred, mighty men of valour, ⁸ famous throughout the house
31 of their fathers. And of the half tribe of Manasseh eighteen
thousand, which were expressed by name, to come and make
32 David king. And of the children of Issachar, ^p *which were men*
that had understanding of the times, to know what Israel ought
to do; the heads of them *were* two hundred; and all their
33 brethren *were* at their commandment. Of Zebulun, such as

g 1 Sam. 29. 2.

h 1 Sam. 29. 4.

i 1 Sam. 30.
1, 9, 10.

k 2 Sam. 2.
3, 4.
& 5. 1.
ch. 11. 1.
l ch. 10. 14.
& 1 Sam. 16.
1, 3.

n 2 Sam. 8. 17.

o 2 Sam. 2.
8, 9.

p Esth. 1. 13.

---

¹ Heb. *on our heads.*
² Or, *with a band.*
³ Or, *captains,* or, *men.*

⁴ Heb. *heads.*
⁵ Or, *prepared.*
⁶ Heb. *brethren,* Gen. 31. 23.

⁷ Heb. *a multitude of them.*
⁸ Heb. *men of names.*

---

with Amasa, David's nephew, but it seems
unlikely that David would have misdoubted
a band led by his own nephew.
The passionate earnestness of Amasai's
speech is strongly marked in the original,
and will be better seen by omitting the
words which our Version adds in italics.
Here, as in *vv.* 8-15, we have manifestly
the actual words of a very ancient record.
   21. *the band of the rovers*] See marg. ref.
   23. Rather, "These are the numbers of
the men, ready equipped **for the host,** that
came to David, &c."
In the list which follows such points as
(1) The large number sent by the trans-
Jordanic tribes ; (2) The large numbers
from Zebulon, Asher, Naphtali, and Dan,
all tribes somewhat remote, and generally
speaking undistinguished ; (3) The small
size of the contingent from Judah, which is

generally represented as numerically superior to every other tribe, and which might
have been expected to be especially zealous
on behalf of its own prince and tribesman ;
—throw some doubt upon the numbers,
which may be suspected of having in some
instances undergone corruption.
   29. *for hitherto* &c.] Rather, "For still
the greatest part of them **maintained their
allegiance to** the house of Saul." This is
given as the reason for so few coming to
Hebron. It shows us that, even after the
death of Ishbosheth, the Benjamites had
hopes of furnishing a third king to the
nation.
   32. *men that had understanding of the
times*] This is best interpreted politically.
Cp. marg. ref.
   33. *expert in war,* &c.] Rather " **arrayed
for battle** with all harness of battle, who

went forth to battle, [1]expert in war, with all instruments of war,
fifty thousand, which could [2]keep rank : *they were* [3]not of dou-
34 ble heart. And of Naphtali a thousand captains, and with them
35 with shield and spear thirty and seven thousand. And of the
Danites expert in war twenty and eight thousand and six hun-
36 dred. And of Asher, such as went forth to battle, [4]expert in
37 war, forty thousand. And on the other side of Jordan, of the
Reubenites, and the Gadites, and of the half tribe of Manasseh,
with all manner of instruments of war for the battle, an hundred
38 and twenty thousand. ¶ All these men of war, that could keep
rank, came with a perfect heart to Hebron, to make David king
over all Israel : and all the rest also of Israel *were* of one heart
39 to make David king. And there they were with David three
days, eating and drinking : for their brethren had prepared for
40 them. Moreover they that were nigh them, *even* unto Issachar
and Zebulun and Naphtali, brought bread on asses, and on
camels, and on mules, and on oxen, *and* [5]meat, meal, cakes of
figs, and bunches of raisins, and wine, and oil, and oxen, and
sheep abundantly : for *there was* joy in Israel.

CHAP. 13. AND David consulted with the captains of thousands
2 and hundreds, *and* with every leader. And David said unto all
the congregation of Israel, If *it seem* good unto you, and *that it
be* of the LORD our God, [6]let us send abroad unto our brethren

a 1Sam.31.1.
Isai. 37. 4.

b 1Sam.7.1,2.

c 1 Sam. 7. 5.
2 Sam. 6. 1.
d Josh. 13. 3.
e 1 Sam.6.21.
& 7. 1.
f Josh. 15. 9,
60.
g 1 Sam. 4. 4.
2 Sam. 6. 2.
h See Num.
4. 15.
ch. 15. 2, 13.
i 1 Sam. 7. 1.
k 2 Sam. 6. 5.

l Num. 4. 15.
ch. 15. 13, 15.
m Lev. 10. 2.

every where, *that are* [a]left in all the land of Israel, and with
them *also* to the priests and Levites *which are* [i]in their cities
3 *and* suburbs, that they may gather themselves unto us : and
let us [8]bring again the ark of our God to us : [b]for we enquired
4 not at it in the days of Saul. And all the congregation said that
they would do so : for the thing was right in the eyes of all the
5 people. ¶ So [c]David gathered all Israel together, from [d]Shihor
of Egypt even unto the entering of Hemath, to bring the ark of
6 God [e]from Kirjath-jearim. And David went up, and all Israel,
to [f]Baalah, *that is,* to Kirjath-jearim, which *belonged* to Judah,
to bring up thence the ark of God the LORD, [g]that dwelleth
7 *between* the cherubims, whose name is called *on it.* And they
[9]carried the ark of God [h]in a new cart [i]out of the house of
8 Abinadab : and Uzza and Ahio drave the cart. [k]And David
a id all Israel played before God with all *their* might, and with
[1]singing, and with harps, and with psalteries, and with timbrels,
9 and with cymbals, and with trumpets. And when they came
unto the threshingfloor of [2]Chidon, Uzza put forth his hand to
10 hold the ark ; for the oxen [3]stumbled. And the anger of the
LORD was kindled against Uzza, and he smote him, [l]because he
11 put his hand to the ark : and there he [m]died before God. And

---

[1] Or, *rangers of battle,* or, *ranged in battle.*	[4] Or, *keeping their rank.*	[8] Heb. *bring about.*
[2] Or, *set the battle in array.*	[5] Or, *victual of meal.*	[9] Heb. *made the ark to ride.*
[3] Heb. *without a heart and a heart,* Ps. 12. 2.	[6] Heb. *let us break forth and send.*	[1] Heb. *songs.*
	[7] Heb. *in the cities of their suburbs.*	[2] Called *Nachon,* 2 Sam. 6. 6.
		[3] Heb. *shook it.*

---

set the battle in array with no double
heart,"—excelling, that is, in the matter of
their arms and accoutrements. The writer
notes in each tribe the point in which it was
most admirable.

XIII. Cp. 2 Sam. vi. 1–11 and notes.

1. *the captains* &c.] Such an organisation
had probably been established generally

through the tribes prior to the time of David : but David seems to have been the first
to recognise in these officers of the host representatives of the people, to consult them
on public affairs, and to give them a certain
political position.

5. *Shihor*] See marg. ref. and 1 K. viii.
65 note.

David was displeased, because the LORD had made a breach
upon Uzza: wherefore that place is called [1]Perez-uzza to this
12 day. And David was afraid of God that day, saying, How shall
13 I bring the ark of God *home* to me? So David [2]brought not
the ark *home* to himself to the city of David, but carried it aside
14 into the house of Obed-edom the Gittite. ¶ [n]And the ark of
God remained with the family of Obed-edom in his house three
months. And the LORD blessed [o]the house of Obed-edom, and
all that he had.

CHAP. 14. NOW [a]Hiram king of Tyre sent messengers to David,
and timber of cedars, with masons and carpenters, to build him
2 an house. And David perceived that the LORD had confirmed
him king over Israel, for his kingdom was lifted up on high,
3 because of his people Israel. ¶ And David took [3]more wives at
4 Jerusalem: and David begat more sons and daughters. Now
[b]these *are* the names of *his* children which he had in Jerusalem;
5 Shammua, and Shobab, Nathan, and Solomon, and Ibhar, and
6 Elishua, and Elpalet, and Nogah, and Nepheg, and Japhia,
7, 8 and Elishama, and [4]Beeliada, and Eliphalet. ¶ And when
the Philistines heard that [c]David was anointed king over all
9 Israel, all the Philistines went up to seek David. And David
heard *of it,* and went out against them. And the Philistines
10 came and spread themselves [d]in the valley of Rephaim. And
David enquired of God, saying, Shall I go up against the Philistines? and wilt thou deliver them into mine hand? And the
LORD said unto him, Go up; for I will deliver them into thine
11 hand. So they came up to Baal-perazim; and David smote
them there. Then David said, God hath broken in upon mine
enemies by mine hand like the breaking forth of waters: there-
12 fore they called the name of that place [5]Baal-perazim. And
when they had left their gods there, David gave a command-
13 ment, and they were burned with fire. ¶ [e]And the Philistines
14 yet again spread themselves abroad in the valley. Therefore
David enquired again of God; and God said unto him, Go not
up after them; turn away from them, [f]and come upon them
15 over against the mulberry trees. And it shall be, when thou
shalt hear a sound of going in the tops of the mulberry trees,
that then thou shalt go out to battle: for God is gone forth
16 before thee to smite [t]he host of the Philistines. David therefore did as God commanded him: and they smote the host of
17 the Philistines from [g]Gibeon even to Gazer. ¶ And [h]the fame of
David went out into all lands; and the LORD [i]brought the fear
of him upon all nations.

CHAP. 15. AND *David* made him houses in the city of David, and
prepared a place for the ark of God, [a]and pitched for it a tent.

[n] 2Sam.6.11.

[o] As Gen. 30.
27.
ch. 26. 5.
[a] 2 Sam. 5.
11, &c.

[b] ch. 3. 5.

[c] 2 Sam.5.17.

[d] ch. 11. 15.

[e] 2 Sam.5.22.

[f] 2 Sam.5.23.

[g] 2 Sam. 5.
25, *Geba.*
[h] Josh 6. 27.
2 Chr. 26. 8.
[i] Deut. 2. 25.
& 11. 25.
[a] ch. 16. 1.

---

[1] That is, *The breach of Uzza.*   [3] Heb. *yet.*   [5] That is, *A place of*
[2] Heb. *removed.*   [4] Or, *Eliada,* 2 Sam. 5. 16.   *breaches.*

XIV. Cp. 2 Sam. v. 11-25, the only important variations from which are in *vv.* 4–
7, the list of the sons of David (see iii. 1
note), and in *v.* 12, where the fact is added
that the idols taken from the Philistines
were burned.

12. *when they had left their gods there*]
The practice of carrying images of the gods
to battle was common among the nations of
antiquity, and arose from the belief that
there was virtue in the images themselves,

and that military success would be obtained
by means of them.

XV. The bulk of this chapter consists of
new matter, which the writer of Chronicles
found in his authorities.

1. *and pitched for it a tent*] The old
"Tent" or "Tabernacle" was still in existence at Gibeon (xvi. 39; 2 Chr. i. 3); but
the Ark had long been separated from it,
and David probably thought that something
newer and more magnificent was requisite.

3 Num. 4. 2,
15.
Deut. 10. 8.
& 31. 9.
c 1 Kin. 8. 1.
ch. 13. 5.

2 Then David said, [1]None ought to carry the *b*ark of God but the Levites: for them hath the LORD chosen to carry the ark of 3 God, and to minister unto him for ever. And David *c*gathered all Israel together to Jerusalem, to bring up the ark of the 4 LORD unto his place, which he had prepared for it. And David 5 assembled the children of Aaron, and the Levites: of the sons of Kohath; Uriel the chief, and his [2]brethren an hundred and 6 twenty: of the sons of Merari; Asaiah the chief, and his brethren 7 two hundred and twenty; of the sons of Gershom; Joel the 8 chief, and his brethren an hundred and thirty: of the sons of

d Ex. 6. 22.
e Ex. 6. 18.

*d*Elizaphan; Shemaiah the chief, and his brethren two hundred: 9 of the sons of *e*Hebron; Eliel the chief, and his brethren four-10 score: of the sons of Uzziel; Amminadab the chief, and his 11 brethren an hundred and twelve. ¶And David called for Zadok and Abiathar the priests, and for the Levites, for Uriel, Asaiah, 12 and Joel, Shemaiah, and Eliel, and Amminadab, and said unto them, Ye *are* the chief of the fathers of the Levites: sanctify yourselves, *both* ye and your brethren, that ye may bring up the ark of the LORD God of Israel unto *the place that* I have pre-

f 2 Sam. 6. 3.
ch. 13. 7.
g ch. 13. 10,
11.

13 pared for it. For *f*because ye *did it* not at the first, *g*the LORD our God made a breach upon us, for that we sought him not 14 after the due order. So the priests and the Levites sanctified 15 themselves to bring up the ark of the LORD God of Israel. And the children of the Levites bare the ark of God upon their

h Ex. 25. 14.
Num. 4. 15.
& 7. 9.

shoulders with the staves thereon, as *h*Moses commanded ac-16 cording to the word of the LORD. ¶And David spake to the chief of the Levites to appoint their brethren *to be* the singers with instruments of musick, psalteries and harps and cymbals, 17 sounding, by lifting up the voice with joy. So the Levites

i ch. 6. 33.
k ch. 6. 39.
l ch. 6. 44.

appointed *i*Heman the son of Joel; and of his brethren, *k*Asaph the son of Berechiah; and of the sons of Merari their brethren, 18 *l*Ethan the son of Kushaiah; and with them their brethren of the second *degree*, Zechariah, Ben, and Jaaziel, and Shemira-moth, and Jehiel, and Unni, Eliab, and Benaiah, and Maaseiah, and Mattithiah, and Elipheleh, and Mikneiah, and Obed-edom, 19 and Jeiel, the porters. So the singers, Heman, Asaph, and

---

[1] Heb. It is *not to carry the ark of God, but for the Levites.*   [2] Or, *kinsmen.*

He therefore allowed the former Tabernacle to keep its place, and had another made and erected.

2. *None ought to carry the ark of God but the Levites*] Cp. marg. reff. We can easily understand that David, after the "breach upon Uzza" (xiii. 11), had carefully considered all the legal requirements with respect to moving the Ark, and was anxious that they should be strictly observed (cp. *v.* 13).

3. *all Israel*] Chosen men probably, like the 30,000 of 2 Sam. vi. 1. See *v.* 25.

4. *the children of Aaron*] *i.e.* the priests.

5. *the sons of Kohath*] The order of the sons of Levi according to primogeniture is, Gershom, Kohath, Merari (Gen. xlvi. 11; Ex. vi. 16). But the Kohathites, of whom came the priestly family of the Aaronites, had precedence in all respects. To them especially was committed the attendance

upon the Ark and the bearing of it. Of the six Levitical families mentioned (*vv.* 5-10) one only was descended from Gershom, one from Merari, and four (Uriel, Elizaphan, Hebron, and Uzziel) from Kohath.

13. The "due order" was that the Ark should be borne on the shoulders of Koha-thite Levites—not that it should be placed upon a cart, drawn by oxen, and rudely shaken.

16. *the singers*] Singing had long been recognised as appropriate to religious cere-monies (Ex. xv. 21; Judg. v. 1; 1 Chr. xiii. 8); but this is the first occasion on which we find the duty of conducting musical services expressly laid on the Levites. Henceforth the services of the Tabernacle and the Temple were regularly choral, and a considerable section of the Levites was trained in musical knowledge, and set apart to conduct this portion of the national worship.

20 Ethan, *were appointed* to ·sound with cymbals of brass; and Zechariah, and [1]Aziel, and Shemiramoth, and Jehiel, and Unni, and Eliab, and Maaseiah, and Benaiah, with psalteries *m*on *m* Ps. 46, title.
21 Alamoth; and Mattithiah, and Elipheleh, and Mikneiah, and Obed-edom, and Jeiel, and Azaziah, with harps [2]on the Shemi-
22 nith to excel. And Chenaniah, chief of the Levites, [3]*was* for [4]song: he instructed about the song, because he *was* skilful.
23 And Berechiah and Elkanah *were* doorkeepers for the ark.
24 And Shebaniah, and Jehoshaphat, and Nethaneel, and Amasai, and Zechariah, and Benaiah, and Eliezer, the priests, *n*did blow *n* Num. 10. 8. with the trumpets before the ark of God: and Obed-edom and Ps. 81. 3.
25 Jehiah *were* doorkeepers for the ark. ¶ So *o*David, and the *o* 2 Sam. 6. elders of Israel, and the captains over thousands, went to bring 12, 13, &c. up the ark of the covenant of the LORD out of the house of 1 Kin. 8. 1.
26 Obed-edom with joy. And it came to pass, when God helped the Levites that bare the ark of the covenant of the LORD, that
27 they offered seven bullocks and seven rams. And David *was* clothed with a robe of fine linen, and all the Levites that bare the ark, and the singers, and Chenaniah the master of the [5]song with the singers: David also *had* upon him an ephod of linen.
28 *p*Thus all Israel brought up the ark of the covenant of the LORD *p* ch. 13. 8. with shouting, and with sound of the cornet, and with trumpets, and with cymbals, making a noise with psalteries and harps.
29 And it came to pass, *q*as the ark of the covenant of the LORD *q* 2 Sam.6.16. came to the city of David, that Michal the daughter of Saul looking out at a window saw king David dancing and playing: and she despised him in her heart.

CHAP. 16. SO *a*they brought the ark of God, and set it in the midst *a* 2 Sam. 6. of the tent that David had pitched for it: and they offered burnt 17—19.
2 sacrifices and peace offerings before God. And when David had made an end of offering the burnt offerings and the peace offer-
3 ings, he blessed the people in the name of the LORD. And he dealt to every one of Israel, both man and woman, to every one a loaf of bread, and a good piece of flesh, and a flagon *of wine*.

[1] ver. 18, *Jaaz'el*.
[2] Or, *on the eighth to over-see*, Ps. 6, title.
[3] Or, *was for the carriage: he instructed about the carriage.*
[4] Heb. *lifting up.*
[5] Or, *carriage.*

---

20. *psalteries on Alamoth*] Probably, psalteries whose tone resembled the voices of girls (*alamoth*). Cp. the "female flutes" of the Lydians.
21. *harps on the Sheminith*] "Sheminith" means properly "the eighth," and has been compared with the modern musical term "octave." Further, "Sheminith" and "Alamoth" are regarded as contrasted, and the harps of Mattithiah and his companions are supposed to have been pitched an octave below the psalteries of Zechariah and his brethren.
The word translated "to excel," is taken as meaning "to lead," and Mattithiah, &c., as leaders of the singers.
22. *for song*] See marg. Hebraists are still at variance as to the meaning of this passage, some supposing elevation [or, delivery] of the voice, others elevation of the Ark, to be intended.
26. *when God helped the Levites*] The

death of Uzza had deeply impressed both David and the Levites, and it was doubted whether God would allow the Ark to be moved any more. Sacrificial animals were held ready; and when it appeared—by the movement of the Ark six paces (2 Sam. vi. 13), without any manifestation of the Divine displeasure—that God was not opposing but rather helping the Levites in their task, the victims were at once offered.
27. "Fine linen" (*byssus*) is here first spoken of as used for dress. It seems to have been reserved for nobles of the highest rank (Esth. viii. 15), for kings, and for priests (2 Chr. v. 12). David's robe was probably worn, like that of the High-Priest, immediately under the ephod, and may, like that, have reached the feet.
XVI. The first three verses form part of the narrative commenced at xv. 25. Cp. 2 Sam. vi. 17-19, where the passage is not torn from its proper context.

^b Ps. 33,
& 70, title.

4 ¶And he appointed *certain* of the Levites to minister before the ark of the LORD, and to ^brecord, and to thank and praise the
5 LORD God of Israel: Asaph the chief, and next to him Zechariah, Jeiel, and Shemiramoth, and Jehiel, and Mattithiah, and Eliab, and Benaiah, and Obed-edom: and Jeiel ¹with psalteries and with harps; but Asaph made a sound with cymbals;
6 Benaiah also and Jahaziel the priests with trumpets continually
7 before the ark of the covenant of God.   ¶Then on that day

^c See
2 Sam. 23. 1.

David delivered ^cfirst *this psalm* to thank the LORD into the hand of Asaph and his brethren.

^d Ps. 105.
1—15.

8   ^dGive thanks unto the LORD, call upon his name,
     Make known his deeds among the people.

9   Sing unto him, sing psalms unto him,
      · Talk ye of all his wondrous works.

10   Glory ye in his holy name:
     Let the heart of them rejoice that seek the LORD.

11   Seek the LORD and his strength,
     Seek his face continually.

12   Remember his marvellous works that he hath done,
     His wonders, and the judgments of his mouth;

13   O ye seed of Israel his servant,
     Ye children of Jacob, his chosen ones.

14   He *is* the LORD our God;
     His judgments *are* in all the earth.

15   Be ye mindful always of his covenant;
     The word *which* he commanded to a thousand generations;

^e Gen. 17. 2.
& 26. 3.
& 28. 13.
& 35. 11.

16   *Even of the* ^e*covenant* which he made with Abraham,
     And of his oath unto Isaac;

17   And hath confirmed the same to Jacob for a law,
     And to Israel *for* an everlasting covenant,

18   Saying, Unto thee will I give the land of Canaan,
     ²The lot of your inheritance;

19   When ye were but ³few,

^f Gen. 34. 30.

20   ^fEven a few, and strangers in it.
     And *when* they went from nation to nation,
     And from *one* kingdom to another people;

21   He suffered no man to do them wrong:

^g Gen. 12. 17.
& 20. 3.
Exod. 7. 15
—18.
^h Ps. 105. 15.
ⁱ Ps. 96.1,&c.

     Yea, he ^greproved kings for their sakes,

22   *Saying,* ^hTouch not mine anointed,
     And do my prophets no harm.

23   ⁱSing unto the LORD, all the earth;
     Shew forth from day to day his salvation.

24   Declare his glory among the heathen;
     His marvellous works among all nations.

¹ Heb. *with instruments of psalteries and harps.*   ² Heb. *the cord.*   ³ Heb. *men of number.*

4-42. This passage is interposed by the writer of Chronicles between two sentences of the parallel passage in Samuel. It contains a detailed account of the service which David instituted at this time, a service out of which grew the more elaborate service of the Temple. The language of much of the passage is remarkably archaic, and there can be no reasonable doubt that it is in the main an extract from a record of the time of David.

5. The occurrence of the name "Jeiel" twice in this list is considered suspicious.

Hence the first "Jeiel" is thought to be a corrupt reading for "Aziel" (xv. 20), or "Jaaziel" (xv. 18).

8. The Psalm here put before us by the Chronicler, as sung liturgically by Asaph and his brethren on the day of the Ark's entrance into Jerusalem, accords closely with the passages in the present Book of Psalms noted in the marg. reff.

It is, apparently, a thanksgiving service composed for the occasion out of Psalms previously existing.

25 For great *is* the LORD, and greatly to be praised:
    He also *is* to be feared above all gods.

26 For all the gods *k*of the people *are* idols: *k* Lev. 19. 4
    But the LORD made the heavens.

27 Glory and honour *are* in his presence;
    Strength and gladness *are* in his place.

28 Give unto the LORD, ye kindreds of the people,
    Give unto the LORD glory and strength.

29 Give unto the LORD the glory *due* unto his name:
    Bring an offering, and come before him:
    Worship the LORD in the beauty of holiness.

30 Fear before him, all the earth:
    The world also shall be stable, that it be not moved.

31 Let the heavens be glad, and let the earth rejoice:
    And let *men* say among the nations, The LORD reigneth.

32 Let the sea roar, and the fulness thereof:
    Let the fields rejoice, and all that *is* therein.

33 Then shall the trees of the wood sing out at the presence
       of the LORD,
    Because he cometh to judge the earth.

34 *l*O give thanks unto the LORD; for *he is* good;   *l* Ps. 106. 1.
    For his mercy *endureth* for ever.   & 107. 1.
                                                                  & 118. 1.
35 *m*And say ye, Save us, O God of our salvation,   & 136. 1.
    And gather us together, and deliver us from the heathen,   *m* Ps. 106.
    That we may give thanks to thy holy name, *and* glory in   47, 48.
       thy praise.

36 *n*Blessed *be* the LORD God of Israel for ever and ever.   *n* 1 Kin. 8. 15.

37 And all *o*the people said, Amen, and praised the LORD. ¶ So   *o* Deut. 27. 15.
   he left there before the ark of the covenant of the LORD Asaph
   and his brethren, to minister before the ark continually, as every
38 day's work required: and Obed-edom with their brethren, threescore and eight; Obed-edom also the son of Jeduthun and
39 Hosah *to be* porters: and Zadok the priest, and his brethren the
   priests, *p*before the tabernacle of the LORD *q*in the high place   *p* ch. 21. 29.
40 that *was* at Gibeon, to offer burnt offerings unto the LORD   2 Chr. 1. 3.
   upon the altar of the burnt offering continually *r*[1]morning and   *q* 1 Kin. 3. 4.
   evening, and *to do* according to all that is written in the law of   *r* Ex. 29. 38.
41 the LORD, which he commanded Israel; and with them Heman   Num. 28. 3.
   and Jeduthun, and the rest that were chosen, who were expressed by name, to give thanks to the LORD, *s*because his   *s* ver. 34.
42 mercy *endureth* for ever; and with them Heman and Jeduthun   2 Chr. 5. 13.
                                                                  & 7. 3.
                                                                  Ezra 3. 11.
       [1] Heb. *in the morning, and in the evening.*   Jer. 33. 11.

---

39. This is the first mention that we have of Gibeon as the place at which the Tabernacle of the congregation now rested. Previously it had been at Nob (1 Sam. xxi. 1-6), whence it was removed probably at the time of the slaughter of the priests by Doeg (1 Sam. xxii. 18, 19). It is uncertain whether Gibeon was regarded as a "high place" before the transfer to it of the Tabernacle: but thenceforth, till the completion of Solomon's Temple, it was the "great high place" (1 K. iii. 4)—a second centre of the national worship which for above 50 years was divided between Gibeon and Jerusalem.

40. *upon the altar of the burnt offering*]

The original Altar of Burnt-offering (Ex. xxvii. 1-8) continued at Gibeon with the Tabernacle (2 Chr. i. 3, 5). David must have erected a new Altar for sacrifice at Jerusalem (xvi. 1). The sacrifices commanded by the Law were, it appears, offered at the former place; at the latter were offered voluntary additional sacrifices.

41. *the rest* &c.] Rather, "**the rest of the chosen ones, who were mentioned by name.**" The "chosen ones" were "mentioned by name" in xv. 17-24. A portion of them, viz., those named in xvi. 5, 6, conducted the service in Jerusalem; the remainder were employed in the worship at Gibeon.

with trumpets and cymbals for those that should make a sound,
and with musical instruments of God.   And the sons of Jedu-

43 thun *were* ¹porters.   *t*And all the people departed every man to
his house : and David returned to bless his house.

a 2 Sam. 7.
1, &c.
Chap. 17. NOW *a*it came to pass, as David sat in his house, that
David said to Nathan the prophet, Lo, I dwell in an house of
cedars, but the ark of the covenant of the Lord *remaineth* under
2 curtains.   Then Nathan said unto David, Do all that *is* in thine
3 heart; for God *is* with thee.   ¶ And it came to pass the same
4 night, that the word of God came to Nathan, saying, Go and tell
David my servant, Thus saith the Lord, Thou shalt not build
5 me an house to dwell in : for I have not dwelt in an house since
the day that I brought up Israel unto this day; but ²have gone
6 from tent to tent, and from *one* tabernacle *to another*.   Wheresoever I have walked with all Israel, spake I a word to any of
the judges of Israel, whom I commanded to feed my people,
7 saying, Why have ye not built me an house of cedars?   Now
therefore thus shalt thou say unto my servant David, Thus
saith the Lord of hosts, I took thee from the sheepcote, *even*
³from following the sheep, that thou shouldest be ruler over my
8 people Israel : and I have been with thee whithersoever thou hast
walked, and have cut off all thine enemies from before thee,
and have made thee a name like the name of the great men that
9 *are* in the earth.   Also I will ordain a place for my people
Israel, and will plant them, and they shall dwell in their place,
and shall be moved no more; neither shall the children of
10 wickedness waste them any more, as at the beginning, and since
the time that I commanded judges *to be* over my people Israel.
Moreover I will subdue all thine enemies.   Furthermore I tell
11 thee that the Lord will build thee an house.   And it shall come
to pass, when thy days be expired that thou must go *to be* with
thy fathers, that I will raise up thy seed after thee, which shall
12 be of thy sons; and I will establish his kingdom.   He shall
build me an house, and I will stablish his throne for ever.

b 2 Sam. 7.
14, 15.
13 *b*I will be his father, and he shall be my son : and I will not
take my mercy away from him, as I took *it* from *him* that was

c Luke 1. 33.
14 before thee : but *c*I will settle him in mine house and in my
kingdom for ever : and his throne shall be established for ever-
15 more.   According to all these words, and according to all this

d 2 Sam.7.18.
16 vision, so did Nathan speak unto David.   ¶ *d*And David the
king came and sat before the Lord, and said, Who *am* I, O
Lord God, and what *is* mine house, that thou hast brought me
17 hitherto?   And *yet* this was a small thing in thine eyes, O God;
for thou hast *also* spoken of thy servant's house for a great
while to come, and hast regarded me according to the estate of a
18 man of high degree, O Lord God.   What can David *speak* more
to thee for the honour of thy servant? for thou knowest thy

---

¹ Heb. *for the gate.*   ² Heb. *have been.*   ³ Heb. *from after.*

XVII. Cp. throughout 2 Sam. vii. and
notes.

13. *my son*] The minatory clause which
occurs after this in Samuel is here omitted,
because the writer is not about to record the
sins of Solomon, or the sufferings (1 K. xi. 9-
40) which he thereby brought upon himself.

17. *hast regarded me* &c.] *i.e.* "Thou hast
elevated me above other men, by making my

kingdom perpetual, regarding me as if I
were a man of high degree."   Cp. 2 Sam.
vii. 19 note.

18. *for the honour of thy servant*] *i.e.* "for
the honour which Thou hast done for Thy
servant."   The LXX. omits "Thy servant,"
and renders, "What can David say more to
Thee to glorify Thee? For Thou knowest,"
&c.

19 servant. O LORD, for thy servant's sake, and according to thine own heart, hast thou done all this greatness, in making
20 known all *these* [1]great things. O LORD, *there is* none like thee, neither *is there any* God beside thee, according to all that we
21 have heard with our ears. And what one nation in the earth *is* like thy people Israel, whom God went to redeem *to be* his own people, to make thee a name of greatness and terribleness, by driving out nations from before thy people, whom thou hast
22 redeemed out of Egypt? For thy people Israel didst thou make thine own people for ever; and thou, LORD, becamest their
23 God. Therefore now, LORD, let the thing that thou hast spoken concerning thy servant and concerning his house be established
24 for ever, and do as thou hast said. Let it even be established, that thy name may be magnified for ever, saying, The LORD of hosts *is* the God of Israel, *even* a God to Israel: and *let* the
25 house of David thy servant *be* established before thee. For thou, O my God, [2]hast told thy servant that thou wilt build him an house: therefore thy servant hath found *in his heart* to
26 pray before thee. And now, LORD, thou art God, and hast pro-
27 mised this goodness unto thy servant: now therefore [3]let it please thee to bless the house of thy servant, that it may be before thee for ever: for thou blessest, O LORD, and *it shall be* blessed for ever.

CHAP. 18. NOW after this [a]it came to pass, that David smote the Philistines, and subdued them, and took Gath and her towns
2 out of the hand of the Philistines. And he smote Moab; and
3 the Moabites became David's servants, *and* brought gifts. And David smote [4]Hadarezer king of Zobah unto Hamath, as he
4 went to stablish his dominion by the river Euphrates. And David took from him a thousand chariots, and [b]seven thousand horsemen, and twenty thousand footmen: David also houghed all the chariot *horses*, but reserved of them an hundred chariots.
5 And when the Syrians of [5]Damascus came to help Hadarezer king of Zobah, David slew of the Syrians two and twenty thou-
6 sand men. Then David put *garrisons* in Syria-damascus; and the Syrians became David's servants, *and* brought gifts. Thus
7 the LORD preserved David whithersoever he went. And David took the shields of gold that were on the servants of Hadarezer,
8 and brought them to Jerusalem. Likewise from [6]Tibhath, and from Chun, cities of Hadarezer, brought David very much brass, wherewith [c]Solomon made the brasen sea, and the pillars, and
9 the vessels of brass. ¶ Now when [7]Tou king of Hamath heard how David had smitten all the host of Hadarezer king of Zobah;
10 he sent [8]Hadoram his son to king David, [9]to enquire of his welfare, and [1]to congratulate him, because he had fought against Hadarezer, and smitten him; (for Hadarezer [2]had war with

marginal references:
[a] 2 Sam. c. 1, &c.
[b] 2 Sam. 8. 4, *seven hundred.*
[c] 1 Kin. 7. 15, 23. 2 Chr. 4. 12, 15, 16.

---

[1] Heb. *greatnesses.*
[2] Heb. *hast revealed the ear of thy servant.*
[3] Or, *it hath pleased thee.*
[4] Or, *Hadadezer,* 2 Sam. 8. 3.
[5] Heb. *Darmesek.*
[6] Called in the book of Samuel *Betah,* and *Berothai.*
[7] Or, *Toi,* 2 Sam. 8. 9.
[8] Or, *Joram,* 2 Sam. 8. 10.
[9] Or, *to salute.*
[1] Heb. *to bless.*
[2] Heb. *was the man of wars.*

---

24. Some prefer, "And let Thy name be established and magnified for ever:" *i.e.* "Let not only Thy promise stand firm, but let Thy Name also stand firm (continue to be held in honour) and be magnified," &c.

27. The marg. rendering is preferable.
XVIII. This chapter is closely parallel with 2 Sam. viii.
1. *Gath and her towns*] In Samuel, Methegammah (see marg. ref. note).

Tou;) and *with him* all manner of vessels of gold and silver and
11 brass. Them also king David dedicated unto the LORD, with
the silver and the gold that he brought from all *these* nations;
from Edom, and from Moab, and from the children of Ammon,
12 and from the Philistines, and from Amalek. Moreover [1]Abishai
the son of Zeruiah slew of the Edomites in the valley of salt

d 2Sam.8.13. 13 *d*eighteen thousand. *e*And he put garrisons in Edom; and all
e 2 Sam. 8. the Edomites became David's servants. Thus the LORD pre-
14, &c.   14 served David whithersoever he went. ¶ So David reigned over
all Israel, and executed judgment and justice among all his
15 people. And Joab the son of Zeruiah *was* over the host; and
16 Jehoshaphat the son of Ahilud, [2]recorder. And Zadok the son
of Ahitub, and [3]Abimelech the son of Abiathar, *were* the priests;
f 2 Sam.8.18. 17 and [4]Shavsha was scribe; *f*and Benaiah the son of Jehoiada
was over the Cherethites and the Pelethites; and the sons of
David *were* chief [5]about the king.

a 2 Sam. 10. **CHAP. 19.** NOW *a*it came to pass after this, that Nahash the king
1, &c.   of the children of Ammon died, and his son reigned in his stead.
2 And David said, I will shew kindness unto Hanun the son of
Nahash, because his father shewed kindness to me. And David
sent messengers to comfort him concerning his father. So the
servants of David came into the land of the children of Ammon
3 to Hanun, to comfort him. But the princes of the children of
Ammon said to Hanun, [6]Thinkest thou that David doth honour
thy father, that he hath sent comforters unto thee? are not his
servants come unto thee for to search, and to overthrow, and to
4 spy out the land? Wherefore Hanun took David's servants,
and shaved them, and cut off their garments in the midst hard
5 by their buttocks, and sent them away. Then there went *certain*,
and told David how the men were served. And he sent to meet
them: for the men were greatly ashamed. And the king said,
Tarry at Jericho until your beards be grown, and *then* return.
6 ¶ And when the children of Ammon saw that they had made
themselves [7]odious to David, Hanun and the children of Ammon
b c'a. 18. 5, 9. sent a thousand talents of silver to hire them chariots and
horsemen out of Mesopotamia, and out of Syria-maachah, *b*and
7 out of Zobah. So they hired thirty and two thousand chariots,

---

[1] Heb. *Abshai*.
[2] Or, *remembrancer*.
[3] Called *Ahimelech*, 2 Sam.
8. 17.
[4] Called *Seraiah*, 2 Sam.
8. 17, and *Shisha*, 1 Kin.
4. 3.
[5] Heb. *at the hand of the king*.
[6] Heb. *In thine eyes doth
David, &c.*
[7] Heb. *to stink*.

XIX. Cp. marg. reff. and notes. The
writer here adds one or two touches, and
varies in one or two of the numbers.

2. *Hanun*] A Philistine king of this name
is mentioned in the Assyrian inscriptions as
paying tribute to Tiglath-pileser and warring
with Sargon.

6. *a thousand talents of silver*] The price
is not given in Samuel. On the practice of hiring troops about this time in
western Asia, see 1 K. xv. 18; 2 K. vii. 6;
2 Chr. xxv. 6.

7. *they hired thirty and two thousand
chariots*] The reading is corrupt. Such a
number as 32,000 chariots alone was never
brought into battle on any occasion. Cp.
the numbers in Ex. xiv. 7; 1 K. x. 26; 2
Chr. xii. 3. The largest force which an

Assyrian king ever speaks of encountering
is 3,940. The words " and horsemen " have
probably fallen out of the text after the
word " chariots " (cp. *v.* 6). The 32,000
would be the number of the warriors serving
on horseback or in chariots; and this number would agree closely with 2 Sam. x. 6, as
the following table shows :—

2 Sam. x. 6 :—	MEN.
Syrians of Beth-rehob and Zobah .	20,000
Syrians of Ish-tob	12,000
Syrians of Maachah.	1,000
	33,000

1 Chr. xix. 7 :—	
Syrians of Zobah, &c.	32,000
Syrians of Maachah (number not given)	[1,000]
	33,000

and the king of Maachah and his people; who came and pitched
before Medeba. And the children of Ammon gathered them-
8 selves together from their cities, and came to battle. And when
David heard *of it*, he sent Joab, and all the host of the mighty
9 men. And the children of Ammon came out, and put the battle
in array before the gate of the city: and the kings that were
10 come *were* by themselves in the field. Now when Joab saw that
¹the battle was set against him before and behind, he chose out
of all the ²choice of Israel, and put *them* in array against the
11 Syrians. And the rest of the people he delivered unto the hand
of ³Abishai his brother, and they set *themselves* in array against
12 the children of Ammon. And he said, If the Syrians be too
strong for me, then thou shalt help me: but if the children of
13 Ammon be too strong for thee, then I will help thee. Be of
good courage, and let us behave ourselves valiantly for our
people, and for the cities of our God: and let the LORD do *that*
14 *which is* good in his sight. ¶ So Joab and the people that *were*
with him drew nigh before the Syrians unto the battle; and
15 they fled before him. And when the children of Ammon saw
that the Syrians were fled, they likewise fled before Abishai his
brother, and entered into the city. Then Joab came to Jeru-
16 salem. ¶ And when the Syrians saw that they were put to the
worse before Israel, they sent messengers, and drew forth the
Syrians that *were* beyond the ⁴river: and ⁵Shophach the captain
17 of the host of Hadarezer *went* before them. And it was told
David; and he gathered all Israel, and passed over Jordan, and
came upon them, and set *the battle* in array against them. So
when David had put the battle in array against the Syrians,
18 they fought with him. But the Syrians fled before Israel; and
David slew of the Syrians seven thousand *men which fought in*
chariots, and forty thousand footmen, and killed Shophach the
19 captain of the host. And when the servants of Hadarezer saw
that they were put to the worse before Israel, they made peace
with David, and became his servants: neither would the Syrians
help the children of Ammon any more.

CHAP. 20. AND *ᵃ*it came to pass, that ⁶after the year was ex-   ᵃ 2 Sam. 11.1.
pired, at the time that kings go out *to battle*, Joab led forth the
power of the army, and wasted the country of the children of
Ammon, and came and besieged Rabbah. But David tarried
at Jerusalem. And *ᵇ*Joab smote Rabbah, and destroyed it.   ᵇ 2 Sam. 12. 26.
2 And David *ᶜ*took the crown of their king from off his head, and   ᶜ 2 Sam. 12. 30, 31.
found it ⁷to weigh a talent of gold, and *there were* precious
stones in it; and it was set upon David's head: and he brought
3 also exceeding much spoil out of the city. And he brought out
the people that *were* in it, and cut *them* with saws, and with
harrows of iron, and with axes. Even so dealt David with all
the cities of the children of Ammon. And David and all the
4 people returned to Jerusalem. ¶ And it came to pass after this,   ᵈ 2 Sam. 21. 18.
*ᵈ*that there ⁸⁹arose war at ¹Gezer with the Philistines; at which

---

¹ Heb. *the face of the battle was.*	⁴ That is, *Euphrates.*	⁷ Heb. *the weight of.*
² Or, *young men.*	⁵ Or, *Shobach*, 2 Sam. 10. 16.	⁸ Or, *continued.*
³ Heb. *Abishai.*	⁶ Heb. *at the return of the year.*	⁹ Heb. *stood.*
		¹ Or, *Gob.*

XX. This chapter, containing such other
warlike exploits belonging to David's reign
as the writer of Chronicles thinks it important to put on record, is to be compared
with the passages of Samuel noted in the
marginal reff.

4, 5. See marg. ref. and notes.

c ch. 11. 29.

time *e*Sibbechai the Hushathite slew ¹Sippai, *that was* of the
5 children of ²the giant: and they were subdued. And there was
war again with the Philistines; and Elhanan the son of ³Jair
slew Lahmi the brother of Goliath the Gittite, whose spear staff

f 2 Sam. 21.
20.

6 *was* like a weaver's beam. And yet again *f*there was war at
Gath, where was ⁴a man of *great* stature, whose fingers and toes
were four and twenty, six *on each hand*, and six *on each foot:*
7 and he also was ⁵the son of the giant. But when he ⁶defied
Israel, Jonathan the son of ⁷Shimea David's brother slew him.
8 These were born unto the giant in Gath; and they fell by the
hand of David, and by the hand of his servants.

a 2 Sam. 24.
1, &c.

CHAP. 21. AND *a*Satan stood up against Israel, and provoked
2 David to number Israel. And David said to Joab and to the
rulers of the people, Go, number Israel from Beer-sheba even

b ch. 27. 23.

to Dan; *b*and bring the number of them to me, that I may know
3 *it*. And Joab answered, The LORD make his people an hundred
times so many more as they *be:* but, my lord the king, *are* they
not all my lord's servants? why then doth my lord require this
4 thing? why will he be a cause of trespass to Israel? Nevertheless the king's word prevailed against Joab. Wherefore Joab
departed, and went throughout all Israel, and came to Jeru-
5 salem. And Joab gave the sum of the number of the people
unto David. And all *they of* Israel were a thousand thousand
and an hundred thousand men that drew sword: and Judah *was*
four hundred threescore and ten thousand men that drew sword.

c ch. 27. 24.

6 *c*But Levi and Benjamin counted he not among them: for the
7 king's word was abominable to Joab. ¶⁸And God was dis-
8 pleased with this thing; therefore he smote Israel. And David

d 2 Sam. 24.
10.
e 2 Sam. 12.
13.

said unto God, *d*I have sinned greatly, because I have done this
thing: *e*but now, I beseech thee, do away the iniquity of thy
9 servant; for I have done very foolishly. ¶ And the LORD spake

f See
1 Sam. 9. 9.

10 unto Gad, David's *f*seer, saying, Go and tell David, saying,
Thus saith the LORD, I ⁹offer thee three *things:* choose thee one

---

¹ Or, *Saph*, 2 Sam. 21. 18.
² Or, *Rapha*.
³ Called also *Jaare-ore-gim*, 2 Sam. 21. 19.
⁴ Heb. *a man of measure*.

⁵ Heb. *born to the giant*, or, *Rapha*.
⁶ Or, *reproached*.
⁷ Called *Shammah*, 1 Sam. 16. 9.

⁸ Heb. *And it was evil in the eyes of the LORD concerning this thing*.
⁹ Heb. *stretch out*.

XXI. The resemblance to the parallel passage in Samuel is throughout less close than usual; the additions are more numerous, the supernatural circumstances of the narrative being brought out into greater prominence. The history is evidently not drawn from Samuel, but from some quite separate document, probably a contemporary account of the occurrence drawn up by Gad.

1. As the books of Scripture are arranged in our Version, Satan is here for the first time by name introduced to us. He appears not merely as an "adversary" who seeks to injure man from without, but as a Tempter able to ruin him by suggesting sinful acts and thoughts from within. In this point of view, the revelation made of him here is the most advanced that we find in the Old Testament.

The difficulty in reconciling the statement here, "Satan provoked David," &c., with that of Samuel, "the Lord moved David," &c. (2 Sam. xxiv. 1) is not serious. All temptation is permitted by God. When evil spirits tempt us, they do so by permission (Job i. 12, ii. 6; Luke xxii. 31, &c.). If Satan therefore provoked David to number the people, God allowed him. And what God allows, He may be said to do. [Another view is maintained in 2 Sam. xxiv. 1 note].

5. In 2 Sam. xxiv. 9 the numbers are different. The explanation there given is not so generally accepted as the supposition that the numbers have, in one passage or the other (or possibly in both), suffered corruption.

6. To omit the Levites would be to follow the precedent recorded in Num. i. 47-49. The omission of Benjamin must be ascribed to a determination on the part of Joab to frustrate the king's intention, whereby he might hope to avert God's wrath from the people.

11 of them, that I may do *it* unto thee. So Gad came to David,
12 and said unto him, Thus saith the LORD, ¹Choose thee *g*either
    three years' famine ; or three months to be destroyed before thy
    foes, while that the sword of thine enemies overtaketh *thee ;* or
    else three days the sword of the LORD, even the pestilence, in
    the land, and the angel of the LORD destroying throughout all
    the coasts of Israel. Now therefore advise thyself what word I
13 shall bring again to him that sent me. And David said unto
    Gad, I am in a great strait : let me fall now into the hand of the
    LORD ; for very ²great *are* his mercies : but let me not fall into
14 the hand of man. So the LORD sent pestilence upon Israel :
15 and there fell of Israel seventy thousand men. ¶ And God
    sent an *h*angel unto Jerusalem to destroy it : and as he was
    destroying, the LORD beheld, and *i*he repented him of the evil,
    and said to the angel that destroyed, It is enough, stay now
    thine hand. And the angel of the LORD stood by the threshing-
16 floor of ³Ornan the Jebusite. And David lifted up his eyes,
    and *k*saw the angel of the LORD stand between the earth and
    the heaven, having a drawn sword in his hand stretched out
    over Jerusalem. Then David and the elders *of Israel, who were*
17 clothed in sackcloth, fell upon their faces. And David said unto
    God, *Is it* not I *that* commanded the people to be numbered ?
    even I it is that have sinned and done evil indeed ; but *as for*
    these sheep, what have they done ? let thine hand, I pray thee,
    O LORD my God, be on me, and on my father's house ; but not
18 on thy people, that they should be plagued. ¶ Then the *l*angel
    of the LORD commanded Gad to say to David, that David should
    go up, and set up an altar unto the LORD in the threshingfloor of
19 Ornan the Jebusite. And David went up at the saying of Gad,
20 which he spake in the name of the LORD. ⁴And Ornan turned
    back, and saw the angel ; and his four sons with him hid them-
21 selves. Now Ornan was threshing wheat. And as David came to
    Ornan, Ornan looked and saw David, and went out of the thresh-

g 2 Sam. 24.
13.

h 2 Sam. 24.
16.
i See Gen. 6.
6.

k 2 Chr. 3. 1.

l 2 Chr. 2. 1.

---

¹ Heb. *Take to thee.*
² Or, *many.*
³ Or, *Araunah,* 2 Sam. 24. 18.

⁴ Or, *When Ornan turned back and saw the angel, then he and his four*

sons with him hid themselves.

---

12. *and the angel of the* LORD *destroying*
&c.] These words are not in Samuel, which
puts the third alternative briefly. They
prepare the way for the angelic appearance
(*v.* 16), on which the author is about to lay
so much stress.

16. Here a picture of awful grandeur
takes the place of the bare statement of the
earlier historian (2 Sam. xxiv. 17). And here,
as elsewhere, the author probably extracts
from the ancient documents such circumstances as harmonise with his general plan.
As the sanctity of the Temple was among
the points whereon he was most anxious to
lay stress, he gives in full all the miraculous
circumstances attending this first designation of what became the Temple site (marg.
ref. *k*) as a place "holy to the Lord."

*David and the elders...clothed in sackcloth,
fell upon their faces*] Facts additional to the
narrative of Samuel ; but facts natural in
themselves, and in harmony with that narrative. Similarly the narrative in *v.* 20 is

additional to the account in Samuel ; but
its parts hang together ; and there is no
sufficient ground for suspecting it.

18. It has been observed that it is only
in books of a late period that Angels are
brought forward as intermediaries between
God and the prophets. This, no doubt, is
true ; and it is certainly unlikely that the
records, from which the author of Chronicles drew, spoke of Gad as receiving his
knowledge of God's will from an Angel.
The touch may be regarded as coming from
the writer of Chronicles himself, who expresses the fact related by his authorities in
the language of his own day (see Zech. i. 9,
14, 19, ii. 3, iv. 1, v. 5, &c.) ; language, however, which we are not to regard as rhetorical, but as strictly in accordance with truth,
since Angels were doubtless employed as
media between God and the prophets as
much in the time of David as in that of
Zechariah.

ingfloor, and bowed himself to David with *his* face to the ground.

22 Then David said to Ornan, [1] Grant me the place of *this* threshing-floor, that I may build an altar therein unto the LORD: thou shalt grant it me for the full price: that the plague may be stayed

23 from the people. And Ornan said unto David, Take *it* to thee, and let my lord the king do *that which is* good in his eyes: lo, I give *thee* the oxen *also* for burnt offerings, and the threshing instruments for wood, and the wheat for the meat offering; I

24 give it all. And king David said to Ornan, Nay; but I will verily buy it for the full price: for I will not take *that* which *is* thine for the LORD, nor offer burnt offerings without cost.

^m 2 Sam. 24. 24.

25 So ^mDavid gave to Ornan for the place six hundred shekels of

26 gold by weight. And David built there an altar unto the LORD, and offered burnt offerings and peace offerings, and called upon

ⁿ Lev. 9. 24. 2 Chr. 3. 1. & 7. 1.

the LORD; and ⁿhe answered him from heaven by fire upon

27 the altar of burnt offering. And the LORD commanded the angel; and he put up his sword again into the sheath thereof.

28 ¶ At that time when David saw that the LORD had answered him in the threshingfloor of Ornan the Jebusite, then he sacri-

^o ch. 16. 39.

29 ficed there. ^oFor the tabernacle of the LORD, which Moses made in the wilderness, and the altar of the burnt offering, *were*

^p 1 Kin. 3. 4. ch. 16. 39. 2 Chr. 1. 3. ^a Deut. 12. 5. 2 Sam. 24. 18, 19, 26, 28. 2 Chr. 3. 1. ^b 1 Kin. 9. 21.

30 at that season in the high place at ^pGibeon. But David could not go before it to enquire of God: for he was afraid because of

22 the sword of the angel of the LORD. THEN David said, ^aThis *is* the house of the LORD God, and this *is* the altar of the burnt

2 offering for Israel. ¶ And David commanded to gather together ^bthe strangers that *were* in the land of Israel; and he set masons

3 to hew wrought stones to build the house of God. And David prepared iron in abundance for the nails for the doors of the

^c ver. 14. 1 Kin. 7. 47. ^d 1 Kin. 5. 6, 16. ^e ch. 29. 1.

gates, and for the joinings; and brass in abundance ^cwithout

4 weight; also cedar trees in abundance: for the ^dZidonians and

5 they of Tyre brought much cedar wood to David. And David said, ^eSolomon my son *is* young and tender, and the house *that*

[1] Heb. *Give.*

---

25. Cp. marg. ref. and note. It may also be conjectured that we should read "six" for "six hundred" here; since, according to the later Jewish system, six gold shekels were nearly equal in value to fifty silver ones.

26. *he answered him from heaven by fire*] This fact is not mentioned by the author of Samuel, since his object is to give an account of the sin of David, its punishment, and the circumstances by which that punishment was brought to a close, not to connect those circumstances with anything further in the history. With the writer of Chronicles the case is different. He would probably have omitted the whole narrative, as he did the sin of David in the matter of Uriah, but for its connexion with the fixing of the Temple site (xxii.). It was no doubt mainly the fact that God answered him by fire from heaven on this altar, which determined David, and Solomon after him, to build the Temple on the spot so consecrated.

30. David, knowing that by sacrifice on this altar he had caused the angel to stay his hand, was afraid to transfer his offerings elsewhere, lest the Angel should resume his task and pestilence again break out.

XXII. This chapter, which consists entirely of new matter, helps to fill up the gap which had been left by the earlier authors between 2 Sam. xxiv. and 1 K. i.

1. *This is the house of the LORD God*] The double miracle—that of the angelic appearance and that of the fire from heaven—had convinced David that here he had found the destined site of that "house" which it had been told him that his son should build (*v.* 10). Hence, this public announcement.

2. *the strangers*] *i.e.* the aliens—the non-Israelite population of the land. Cp. 2 Chr. ii. 17.

3. *for the joinings*] *i.e.* the girders, or cramps—pieces of iron to be used in joining beams or stones together.

4. See marg. reff. and notes; xiv. 1.

5. *young and tender*] The exact age of Solomon at this time is uncertain; but it cannot have been more than twenty-four or twenty-five. It may have been as little as fourteen or fifteen. Cp. 1 K. ii. 2 note.

is to be builded for the LORD *must be* exceedingly magnifical, of fame and of glory throughout all countries: I will *therefore* now make preparation for it. So David prepared abundantly before 6 his death. ¶ Then he called for Solomon his son, and charged 7 him to build an house for the LORD God of Israel. And David said to Solomon, My son, as for me, *f*it was in my mind to build 8 an house *g*unto the name of the LORD my God: but the word of the LORD came to me, saying, *h*Thou hast shed blood abundantly, and hast made great wars: thou shalt not build an house unto my name, because thou hast shed much blood upon the earth in 9 my sight. *i*Behold, a son shall be born to thee, who shall be a man of rest; and I will give him *k*rest from all his enemies round about: for his name shall be *1*Solomon, and I will give 10 peace and quietness unto Israel in his days. *l*He shall build an house for my name; and *m*he shall be my son, and I *will be* his father; and I will establish the throne of his kingdom over 11 Israel for ever. Now, my son, *n*the LORD be with thee; and prosper thou, and build the house of the LORD thy God, as he 12 hath said of thee. Only the LORD *o*give thee wisdom and understanding, and give thee charge concerning Israel, that thou 13 mayest keep the law of the LORD thy God. *p*Then shalt thou prosper, if thou takest heed to fulfil the statutes and judgments which the LORD charged Moses with concerning Israel: *q*be strong, and of good courage; dread not, nor be dismayed. 14 Now, behold, *2*in my trouble I have prepared for the house of the LORD an hundred thousand talents of gold, and a thousand thousand talents of silver; and of brass and iron *r*without weight; for it is in abundance: timber also and stone have I 15 prepared; and thou mayest add thereto. Moreover *there are* workmen with thee in abundance, hewers and *3*workers of stone and timber, and all manner of cunning men for every manner 16 of work. Of the gold, the silver, and the brass, and the iron, *there is* no number. Arise *therefore*, and be doing, and *s*the LORD 17 be with thee. ¶ David also commanded all the princes of Israel 18 to help Solomon his son, *saying*, Is not the LORD your God with you? *t*and hath he *not* given you rest on every side? for he hath given the inhabitants of the land into mine hand; and the land is 19 subdued before the LORD, and before his people. Now *u*set your

f 2 Sam. 7. 2.
1 Kin. 8. 17.
ch. 17. 1.
& 28. 2.
g Deut. 12. 5, 11.
h 1 Kin. 5. 3.
i ch. 28. 5.
k 1 Kin. 4. 25. & 5. 4.
l 2 Sam. 7. 13.
1 Kin. 5. 5, ch. 17. 12, 13. & 28. 6.
m Heb. 1. 5.
n ver. 16.
o 1 Kin. 3. 9, 12.
Ps. 72. 1.
p Josh. 1. 7, 8.
ch. 28. 7.
q Deut. 31. 6 –8. Josh. 1. 6, 7, 9. ch. 28. 20.
r As ver. 3.
s ver. 11.
t Deut. 12. 10. Josh. 22. 4. 2 Sam. 7. 1. ch. 23. 25.
u 2 Chr. 20. 3.

---

1 That is, *Peaccable.*   *2* Or, *in my poverty.*   *3* That is, *masons and carpenters.*

---

8. *the word of the* LORD *came to me,* &c.] Not by Nathan (xvii. 4–15), but on some other occasion (xxviii. 3). On the bloody character of David's wars, see 2 Sam. viii. 2, 5, x. 18, xii. 31; and 1 K. xi. 16.
9. For the names of Solomon, cp. 2 Sam. xii. 24 note. The former name prevailed, probably on account of this prophecy, which attached to the name the promise of a blessing.
13. *be strong,* &c.] David adopts the words of Moses to the Israelites (cp. marg. reff.) and to Joshua.
14. *in my trouble*] See marg. David refers to the manifold troubles of his reign, which had prevented him from accumulating very much treasure.
an hundred thousand talents of gold, &c.] We do not know the value of the Hebrew

talent at this period, and therefore there numbers may be sound. But in that case we must suppose an enormous difference between the pre-Babylonian and the post-Babylonian talents. According to the value of the post-Babylonian Hebrew talent, the gold here spoken of would be worth more than 1000 millions of our pounds sterling, while the silver would be worth above 400 millions. Accumulations to anything like this amount are inconceivable under the circumstances, and we must therefore either suppose the talents of David's time to have been little more than the hundredth part of the later talents, or regard the numbers of this verse as augmented at least a hundredfold by corruption. Of the two the latter is certainly the more probable supposition.

heart and your soul to seek the LORD your God; arise therefore,
and build ye the sanctuary of the LORD God, to [x]bring the ark of
the covenant of the LORD, and the holy vessels of God, into the
23 house that is to be built [y]to the name of the LORD. SO when
David was old and full of days, he made [a]Solomon his son king
2 over Israel. ¶ And he gathered together all the princes of Israel,
3 with the priests and the Levites. Now the Levites were numbered from the age of [b]thirty years and upward: and their
number by their polls, man by man, was thirty and eight
4 thousand. Of which, twenty and four thousand *were* [1]to set
forward the work of the house of the LORD; and six thousand
5 *were* [c]officers and judges: moreover four thousand *were* porters;
and four thousand praised the LORD with the instruments
6 [d]which I made, *said David*, to praise *therewith*. ¶ And [e]David
divided them into [2]courses among the sons of Levi, *namely*,
7 Gershon, Kohath and Merari. ¶ Of the [f]Gershonites *were*,
8 [3]Laadan, and Shimei. The sons of Laadan; the chief *was*
9 Jehiel, and Zetham, and Joel, three. The sons of Shimei;
Shelomith, and Haziel, and Haran, three. These *were* the chief
10 of the fathers of Laadan. And the sons of Shimei *were*, Jahath,
[4]Zina, and Jeush, and Beriah. These four *were* the sons of
11 Shimei. And Jahath was the chief, and Zizah the second: but
Jeush and Beriah [5]had not many sons; therefore they were in
12 one reckoning, according to *their* father's house. ¶ [g]The sons of
13 Kohath; Amram, Izhar, Hebron, and Uzziel, four. The sons
of [h]Amram; Aaron and Moses: and [i]Aaron was separated, that
he should sanctify the most holy things, he and his sons for ever,
[k]to burn incense before the LORD, [l]to minister unto him, and [m]to
14 bless in his name for ever. Now *concerning* Moses the man of
15 God, [n]his sons were named of the tribe of Levi. [o]The sons of
16 Moses *were*, Gershom, and Eliezer. Of the sons of Gershom,
17 [p][6]Shebuel *was* the chief. And the sons of Eliezer *were*, [q]Reha-
biah [7]the chief. And Eliezer had none other sons; but the
18 sons of Rehabiah [8]were very many. Of the sons of Izhar;
19 [9]Shelomith the chief. [r]Of the sons of Hebron; Jeriah the first,
Amariah the second, Jahaziel the third, and Jekameam the
20 fourth. Of the sons of Uzziel; Micah the first, and Jesiah the
21 second. ¶ [s]The sons of Merari; Mahli, and Mushi. The sons
22 of Mahli; Eleazar, and [t]Kish. And Eleazar died, and [u]had no
sons, but daughters: and their [1]brethren the sons of Kish [x]took
23 them. [y]The sons of Mushi; Mahli, and Eder, and Jeremoth,
24 three. ¶ These *were* the sons of [z]Levi after the house of their
fathers; *even* the chief of the fathers, as they were counted by
number of names by their polls, that did the work for the service of the house of the LORD, from the age of [a]twenty years

[x] 1 Kin. 8. 6, 21. 2 Chr. 5. 7. & 6. 11.
[y] ver. 7. 1 Kin. 5. 3.
[a] 1 Kin. 1. 33—39. ch. 28. 5.
[b] Num. 4. 3, 47.
[c] Deut. 16. 18. ch. 26. 29. 2 Chr. 19. 8.
[d] See 2 Chr. 29. 25, 26. Amos 6. 5.
[e] Ex. 6. 16. Num. 26. 57. ch. 6. 1, &c. 2 Chr. 8. 14. & 29. 25.
[f] ch. 26. 21.
[g] Ex. 6. 18.
[h] Ex. 6. 20.
[i] Ex. 28. 1. Heb. 5. 4.
[k] Ex. 30. 7. Num. 16. 40. 1 Sam. 2. 28.
[l] Deut. 21. 5.
[m] Num. 6. 23.
[n] See ch. 26. 23, 24, 25.
[o] Ex. 2. 22. & 18. 3, 4.
[p] ch. 26. 24.
[q] ch. 26. 25.
[r] ch. 24. 23.
[s] ch. 24. 26.
[t] ch. 24. 29.
[u] ch. 24. 28.
[x] See Num. 36. 6, 8.
[y] ch. 24. 30.
[z] Num. 10. 17, 21.
[a] See Num. 1. 3. & 4. 3.

1 Or, *to oversee*.
2 Heb. *divisions*.
3 Or, *Libni*, ch. 6. 17.
4 Or, *Zizah*, ver. 11.
5 Heb. *did not multiply sons*.
6 *Shubael*, ch. 24. 20.
7 Or, *the first*.
8 Heb. *were highly multiplied*.
9 *Shelomoth*, ch. 24. 22.
1 Or, *kinsmen*.

XXIII. See marg. reff. and notes. Verses 28–32 give the most complete account in Scripture of the nature of the Levitical office.

24. *from the age of twenty years*] The Levites had hitherto not entered upon their regular functions until the age of thirty (*v.* 3). Certain lighter duties were by the Law imposed on them at twenty-five (Num. viii. 24); but it was not until they were five years older that they became liable to the full service of the Sanctuary. David appears now to have made a change. By his "last words" (*v.* 27) the time for the Levites to enter on the full duties of their office was advanced from thirty to twenty. This

25 and upward. For David said, The LORD God of Israel [b]hath

[b] ch. 22. 18.

given rest unto his people, [1]that they may dwell in Jerusalem
26 for ever : and also unto the Levites ; they shall no *more* [c]carry

[c] Num. 4. 5, &c.

27 the tabernacle, nor any vessels of it for the service thereof. For
by the last words of David the Levites *were* [2]numbered from
28 twenty years old and above : because [3]their office *was* to wait on
the sons of Aaron for the service of the house of the LORD, in
the courts, and in the chambers, and in the purifying of all holy
29 things, and the work of the service of the house of God ; both
for [d]the shewbread, and for [e]the fine flour for meat offering, and

[d] Ex. 25. 30.
[e] Lev. 6. 20.
ch. 9. 29, &c.
[f] Lev. 2. 4.

for [f]the unleavened cakes, and for [g]*that which is baked in* the
[4]pan, and for that which is fried, and for all manner of [h]mea-

[g] Lev. 2. 5, 7.
[h] Lev. 19. 35.

30 sure and size ; and to stand every morning to thank and praise
31 the LORD, and likewise at even; and to offer all burnt sacrifices
unto the LORD [i]in the sabbaths, in the new moons, and on the

[i] Num.10.10.
Ps. 81. 3.

[k]set feasts, by number, according to the order commanded unto

[k] Lev. 23. 4.
[l] Num. 1. 53.

32 them, continually before the LORD : and that they should [l]keep
the charge of the tabernacle of the congregation, and the charge
of the holy *place*, and [m]the charge of the sons of Aaron their

[m] Num. 3.
6—9.

brethren, in the service of the house of the LORD.

CHAP. 24 NOW *these are* the divisions of the sons of Aaron. [a]The

[a] Lev.10.1,6.
Num. 26. 60.

2 sons of Aaron ; Nadab, and Abihu, Eleazar, and Ithamar. But
[b]Nadab and Abihu died before their father, and had no children:

[b] Num. 3. 4.
& 26. 61.

3 therefore Eleazar and Ithamar executed the priest's office. And
David distributed them, both Zadok of the sons of Eleazar, and
Ahimelech of the sons of Ithamar, according to their offices in
4 their service. And there were more chief men found of the
sons of Eleazar than of the sons of Ithamar; and *thus* were they
divided. Among the sons of Eleazar *there were* sixteen chief
men of the house of *their* fathers, and eight among the sons of
5 Ithamar according to the house of their fathers. Thus were they
divided by lot, one sort with another; for the governors of the
sanctuary, and governors *of the house* of God, were of the sons
6 of Eleazar, and of the sons of Ithamar. And Shemaiah the son
of Nethaneel the scribe, *one* of the Levites, wrote them before the
king, and the princes, and Zadok the priest, and Ahimelech the

---

[1] Or, *and he dwelleth in Jerusalem, &c.*
[2] Heb. *number.*
[3] Heb. *their station was at the hand of the sons of*
Aaron, Neh. 11. 24.
[4] Or, *flat plate.*

---

change was based upon the lighter character
of the labours imposed on them now that
the Ark had ceased to be carried from place
to place and obtained a permanent habitation (*v.* 26). The limit of age continued in
after times where David had fixed it (see
Ezra iii. 8).

27. By the "last words of David" some
understand an historical work on the latter
part of his reign, drawn up probably by
Gad or Nathan (cp. xxvii. 24, xxix. 29).
Others suppose that he left behind him a
work containing directions for the service
of the Sanctuary.

31. Though the Levites were not allowed
by themselves to offer sacrifice, yet there
were many respects in which they assisted
the priests when sacrifice was offered. See
2 Chr. xxix. 34, xxxv. 11, 12.

the set feasts] The Passover, Feast of Pentecost, and Feast of Tabernacles (marg. ref.).

XXIV. 3. Zadok and Ahimelech (rather
Abiathar, see *v.* 6) assisted David in drawing
up the priestly courses, as the "captains of
the host" assisted him in making the divisions of the singers (xxv. 1).

5. *one sort with another*] i.e. "the assignment of their order in the courses was made
by lot to the families belonging to Eleazar,
and to the families belonging to Ithamar,
equally." Both houses had furnished functionaries of the highest class, and therefore
no preference was now given to either over
the other.

6. *wrote them before the king*] i.e. "wrote
down their names as the lots were drawn
forth."

Ahimelech the son of Abiathar] A wrong
reading. It should be "Abiathar, the son
of Ahimelech." See 2 Sam. viii. 17 note.

son of Abiathar, and *before* the chief of the fathers of the priests
and Levites : one [1]principal household being taken for Eleazar,
7 and *one* taken for Ithamar.   ¶ Now the first lot came forth to
8 Jehoiarib, the second to Jedaiah, the third to Harim, the fourth
9, 10 to Seorim, the fifth to Malchijah, the sixth to Mijamin, the
11 seventh to Hakkoz, the eighth to *c*Abijah, the ninth to Jeshuah,
12 the tenth to Shecaniah, the eleventh to Eliashib, the twelfth to
13 Jakim, the thirteenth to Huppah, the fourteenth to Jeshebeab,
14, 15 the fifteenth to Bilgah, the sixteenth to Immer, the seven-
16 teenth to Hezir, the eighteenth to Aphses, the nineteenth to
17 Pethahiah, the twentieth to Jehezekel, the one and twentieth to
18 Jachin, the two and twentieth to Gamul, the three and twentieth
19 to Delaiah, the four and twentieth to Maaziah.   ¶ These *were*
the orderings of them in their service *d*to come into the house of
the LORD, according to their manner, under Aaron their father,
20 as the LORD God of Israel had commanded him.   ¶ And the rest
of the sons of Levi *were these :* Of the sons of Amram ; *e*Shubael :
21 of the sons of Shubael ; Jehdeiah. Concerning *f*Rehabiah : of
22 the sons of Rehabiah, the first *was* Isshiah. Of the Izharites ;
23 *g*Shelomoth : of the sons of Shelomoth ; Jahath. And the sons
of *h* Hebron ; Jeriah *the first*, Amariah the second, Jahaziel the
24 third, Jekameam the fourth. *Of* the sons of Uzziel ; Michah :
25 of the sons of Michah ; Shamir. The brother of Michah *was*
26 Isshiah : of the sons of Isshiah ; Zechariah. *i*The sons of Merari
27 *were* Mahli and Mushi : the sons of Jaaziah ; Beno. The sons
of Merari by Jaaziah ; Beno, and Shoham, and Zaccur, and Ibri.
28, 29 Of Mahli *came* Eleazar, *k*who had no sons. Concerning Kish :
30 the son of Kish *was* Jerahmeel. *l*The sons also of Mushi ; Mahli,
and Eder, and Jerimoth. These *were* the sons of the Levites after
31 the house of their fathers. These likewise cast lots over against
their brethren the sons of Aaron in the presence of David the
king, and Zadok, and Ahimelech, and the chief of the fathers of
the priests and Levites, even the principal fathers over against
their younger brethren.

c Neh. 12. 4, 17.
Luke 1. 5.

d ch. 9. 25.

e ch. 23. 16,
Shebuel.
f ch. 23. 17.

g ch. 23. 18,
Shelomith.
h ch. 26. 31.

i Ex. 6. 19.
ch. 23. 21.

k ch. 23. 22.
l ch. 23. 23.

[1] Heb. *house of the father.*

---

19. *These were the orderings* &c.] *i.e.*
" this was the numerical order fixed for
their ministerial attendance in the house of
the Lord —an attendance which was after the
manner determined for them by their fore-
father Aaron, according to instructions
which he received from God."
20. The object of this second enumeration
of the Levitical families (cp. xxiii. 7–23)
seems to be the designation of the *heads* of
the families in David's time. The omission
of the Gershonites is curious, and can only
be accounted for by supposing that the
author did not find any account of their
heads in his authorities. The addition to
the Merarites (*vv.* 26, 27) is also curious. It
brings the number of families up to twenty-
five, which is one more than we should have
expected.
23. Neither " Hebron " nor " the first "
is found in the present Hebrew text ; but
they seem to have been rightly supplied by
our translators from xxiii. 19. The four
persons named appear to have been con-

temporaries of David, the heads of the
Hebronite houses in his time (cp. xxvi.
31).
26, 27. *The sons of Jaaziah, Beno*] Beno is
not really a name. It is the Hebrew for
" his son," and is to be attached to Jaaziah.
Translate *v.* 27, " and the sons of Merari by
Jaaziah his son [were] **Shoham** and Zaccur,
and Ibri." The meaning of the whole passage (*vv.* 26–30) seems to be that there were
three branches of the Merarites—the Beni-
Mahli, the Beni-Mushi, and the Beni-Jaa-
ziah.
31. *the principal fathers over against their
younger brethren*] *i.e.* " all the Levitical
houses enumerated drew lots in their courses
on equal terms, the elder families having no
advantage over the younger ones." As there
were twenty-four courses of the priests, so
we must suppose that there were twenty-four
of the Levites, though the number of the
families as given in the text (xxiii. 7–23,
xxiv. 20–30) is twenty-*five*.

Chap. 25 MOREOVER David and the captains of the host separated to the service of the sons of ^aAsaph, and of Heman, and of Jeduthun, who should prophesy with harps, with psalteries, and with cymbals: and the number of the workmen according to
2 their service was: of the sons of Asaph; Zaccur, and Joseph, and Nethaniah, and ¹Asarelah, the sons of Asaph under the hands of Asaph, which prophesied ²according to the order of
3 the king. Of Jeduthun: the sons of Jeduthun; Gedaliah, and ³Zeri, and Jeshaiah, Hashabiah, and Mattithiah, ⁴six, under the hands of their father Jeduthun, who prophesied with a harp,
4 to give thanks and to praise the LORD. Of Heman: the sons of Heman; Bukkiah, Mattaniah, ⁵Uzziel, ⁶Shebuel, and Jerimoth, Hananiah, Hanani, Eliathah, Giddalti, and Romamti-ezer, Josh-
5 bekashah, Mallothi, Hothir, *and* Mahazioth: all these *were* the sons of Heman the king's seer in the ⁷words of God, to lift up the horn. And God gave to Heman fourteen sons and three
6 daughters. All these *were* under the hands of their father for song *in* the house of the LORD, with cymbals, psalteries, and harps, for the service of the house of God, ^{b8}according to the
7 king's order to Asaph, Jeduthun, and Heman. So the number of them, with their brethren that were instructed in the songs of the LORD, *even* all that were cunning, was two hundred fourscore
8 and eight. ¶And they cast lots, ward against *ward*, as well the
9 small as the great, ^cthe teacher as the scholar. Now the first lot came forth for Asaph to Joseph: the second to Gedaliah, who
10 with his brethren and sons *were* twelve: the third to Zaccur, *he,*
11 his sons, and his brethren, *were* twelve: the fourth to Izri, *he,*
12 his sons, and his brethren, *were* twelve: the fifth to Nethaniah,
13 *he,* his sons, and his brethren, *were* twelve: the sixth to Bukkiah,
14 *he,* his sons, and his brethren, *were* twelve: the seventh to Je-
15 sharelah, *he,* his sons, and his brethren, *were* twelve: the eighth
16 to Jeshaiah, *he,* his sons, and his brethren, *were* twelve: the ninth to Mattaniah, *he,* his sons, and his brethren, *were* twelve:

^a ch. 6. 33, 39, 44.

^b ver. 2.

^c 2 Chr. 23. 13.

---

¹ Otherwise called *Jesharelah,* ver. 14.
² Heb. *by the hands of the king:* So ver. 6.
³ Or, *Izri,* ver. 11.
⁴ With Shimei mentioned, ver. 17.
⁵ Or, *Azareel,* ver. 18.
⁶ Or, *Shubael,* ver. 20.
⁷ Or, *matters.*
⁸ Heb. *by the hands of the king.*

XXV. 1. *the captains of the host*] Rather, "**the princes**" of xxiii. 2, and xxiv. 6.

2. *under the hands of Asaph,* &c.] That is to say, "under the direction of Asaph"— who himself "prophesied," or performed the sacred services, "under the direction of the king."

5. *to lift up the horn*] Some take this literally, and consider that Heman and his sons played on the horn in the musical services; but there is no other evidence that the horn was so employed. Perhaps the most probable explanation is that it has been transferred from the next clause, where (as here) it followed the word "God," with the sense that "God, to exalt Heman's horn (or, increase his dignity), gave him fourteen sons and three daughters."

7. *with their brethren*] i.e. "with others of the tribe of Levi." Each son of Asaph, Jeduthun, and Heman, was at the head of a band of twelve skilled musicians, consisting partly of his own sons, partly of

Levites belonging to other families (*vv.* 9-31). The 24 band-leaders, together with their bands, formed a body of 288 persons $(24 \times 12 = 288)$ Besides these, we hear of there being above 3,700 singers, who were probably divided, like the trained musicians, into 24 courses, which must have contained about 155 each (xxiii. 5).

8. *as well the small as the great*] Cp. xxiv. 31. The lot was not applied indiscriminately to all the twenty-four courses, but was only used to settle which course of Asaph, which of Jeduthun, and which of Heman, should on each occasion be taken. Asaph was given the precedence over his brethren, and his four courses were assigned the first, and then each alternate place. Jeduthun took rank next, and received alternate places, first with Asaph, and then with Heman, until his courses were exhausted. After this all the later places fel necessarily to Heman, whose courses continue without interruption from the 15th.

17 the tenth to Shimei, *he*, his sons, and his brethren, *were* twelve :
18 the eleventh to Azareel, *he*, his sons, and his brethren, *were*
19 twelve : the twelfth to Hashabiah, *he*, his sons, and his brethren,
20 *were* twelve : the thirteenth to Shubael, *he*, his sons, and his
21 brethren, *were* twelve : the fourteenth to Mattithiah, *he*, his
22 sons, and his brethren, *were* twelve : the fifteenth to Jeremoth,
23 *he*, his sons, and his brethren, *were* twelve : the sixteenth to
24 Hananiah, *he*, his sons, and his brethren, *were* twelve : the
seventeenth to Joshbekashah, *he*, his sons, and his brethren,
25 *were* twelve : the eighteenth to Hanani, *he*, his sons, and his
26 brethren, *were* twelve : the nineteenth to Mallothi, *he*, his sons,
27 and his brethren, *were* twelve : the twentieth to Eliathah, *he*, his
28 sons, and his brethren, *were* twelve : the one and twentieth to
29 Hothir, *he*, his sons, and his brethren, *were* twelve : the two and
twentieth to Giddalti, *he*, his sons, and his brethren, *were* twelve :
30 the three and twentieth to Mahazioth, *he*, his sons, and his
31 brethren, *were* twelve : the four and twentieth to Romamti-ezer,
he, his sons, and his brethren, *were* twelve.

CHAP. 26. CONCERNING the divisions of the porters: of the
Korhites *was* [1]Meshelemiah the son of Kore, of the sons of
2 [2]Asaph. And the sons of Meshelemiah *were*, Zechariah the firstborn, Jediael the second, Zebadiah the third, Jathniel the fourth,
3 Elam the fifth, Jehohanan the sixth, Elioenai the seventh.
4 Moreover the sons of Obed-edom *were*, Shemaiah the firstborn,
Jehozabad the second, Joah the third, and Sacar the fourth, and
5 Nethaneel the fifth, Ammiel the sixth, Issachar the seventh,
6 Peulthai the eighth: for God blessed [3]him. Also unto Shemaiah
his son were sons born, that ruled throughout the house of their
7 father: for they *were* mighty men of valour. The sons of Shemaiah;
Othni, and Rephael, and Obed, Elzabad, whose brethren *were*
8 strong men, Elihu, and Semachiah. All these of the sons of
Obed-edom : they and their sons and their brethren, able men
for strength for the service, *were* threescore and two of Obed-
9 edom. And Meshelemiah had sons and brethren, strong men,
10 eighteen. Also [a]Hosah, of the children of Merari, had sons ;
Simri the chief, (for *though* he was not the firstborn, yet his
11 father made him the chief ;) Hilkiah the second, Tebaliah the
third, Zechariah the fourth : all the sons and brethren of Hosah
12 *were* thirteen. Among these *were* the divisions of the porters,
even among the chief men, *having* wards one against another,
13 to minister in the house of the LORD. ¶ And they cast lots,
[4]as well the small as the great, according to the house of their
14 fathers, for every gate. And the lot eastward fell to [5]Shele-
miah. Then for Zechariah his son, a wise counsellor, they cast
15 lots ; and his lot came out northward. To Obed-edom south-

[a] ch. 16. 38.

---

[1] Or, *Shelemiah*, ver. 14.
[2] Or, *Ebiasaph*, ch. 6. 37. & 9. 19.
[3] That is, Obed-edom, as ch. 13. 14.
[4] Or, *as well for the small*
as for the great.
[5] Called *Meshelemiah*, ver. 1.

XXVI. 1. *the porters*] See ix. 17-27, xxiii. 5.

4. Obed-edom and Hosah (*v.* 10) had been "porters," or door-keepers, from the time of the bringing up of the Ark into Jerusalem (xv. 24, xvi. 38).

12. This verse is obscure, but its probable meaning is the following : "To these divisions of the porters, principal men, [were

assigned[1] the watches, together with their brethren, for service in the house of the Lord ; " *i.e.* the "chief men " (*rv.* 1–11), amounting to no more than 93, kept the watch and ward of the house, together with a further number of their brethren (4000, xxiii. 5), who assisted them from time to time.

15. *the house of Asuppim*] Lit. "the house

16 ward; and to his sons the house of ¹Asuppim. To Shuppim
and Hosah *the lot came forth* westward, with the gate Shallecheth,
17 by the causeway of the going ²up, ward against ward. Eastward *were* six Levites, northward four a day, southward four a
18 day, and toward Asuppim two *and* two. At Parbar westward,
19 four at the causeway, *and* two at Parbar. These *are* the divisions of the porters among the sons of Kore, and among the sons
20 of Merari. ¶ And of the Levites, Ahijah *was* ᵇover the treasures   ᵇ ch. 28. 12.
of the house of God, and over the treasures of the ³dedicated   Mal. 3. 10.
21 things. *As concerning* the sons of ⁴Laadan; the sons of the Gershonite Laadan, chief fathers, *even* of Laadan the Gershonite,
22 *were* ⁵Jehieli. The sons of Jehieli; Zetham, and Joel his brother,
23 *which were* over the treasures of the house of the LORD. Of the
Amramites, *and* the Izharites, the Hebronites, *and* the Uzzielites:
24 and ᶜShebuel the son of Gershom, the son of Moses, *was* ruler   ᶜ ch. 23. 16.
25 of the treasures. And his brethren by Eliezer; Rehabiah his
son, and Jeshaiah his son, and Joram his son, and Zichri his son,
26 and ᵈShelomith his son. Which Shelomith and his brethren   ᵈ ch. 23. 18.
were over all the treasures of the dedicated things, which David
the king, and the chief fathers, the captains over thousands and
27 hundreds, and the captains of the hosts, had dedicated. ⁶Out
of the spoils won in battles did they dedicate to maintain the
28 house of the LORD. And all that Samuel ᵉthe seer, and Saul   ᵉ 1 Sam. 9. 9.
the son of Kish, and Abner the son of Ner, and Joab the son of
Zeruiah, had dedicated; *and* whosoever had dedicated *any thing,*
29 *it was* under the hand of Shelomith, and of his brethren. ¶ Of
the Izharites, Chenaniah and his sons *were* for the outward

¹ Heb. *Gatherings.*   ³ Heb. *holy things.*   ⁶ Heb. *Out of ⸤the battles*
² See 1 Kings 10. 5.   ⁴ Or, *Libni*, ch. 6. 17.   *and spoils.*
  2 Chr. 9. 4.   ⁵ Or, *Jehiel*, ch. 23. 8. & 29. 8.

---

of collections" (see marg. and cp. Neh. xii.
25 marg.). A treasure-house of some kind
or other is probably intended.

16. All recent commentators seem to be
agreed that the words " to Shuppim" ought
to be cancelled, the name having arisen
from an accidental repetition of the preceding word, " Asuppim."

the gate Shallecheth] Lit. "the gate *of pro-
jection*"—the gate, *i.e.* through which were
"thrown out" the sweepings of the Temple,
the ashes, the offal of the victims, and the
like.

the causeway of the going up] Cp. marg.
ref. note.

ward against ward] Or, "watch opposite
to watch." Hosah had in charge both the
western gate of the Temple, and also the
gate Shallecheth, which was in the outer
wall, opposite. Hence he had to keep two
watches, one over against the other.

17. *toward Asuppim two and two*] It is
conjectured that the " store-house" in
question (*v.* 15 note) had two doors, to each
of which two porters were appointed.

18. " Parbar" must designate here the
space between the western wall of the
Temple building and the wall of the court,
which would be a sort of " precinct" or
"purlieu" of the Temple (2 K. xxiii. 11

note). Here were two gates, at one of
which two guards were stationed; while
at the Shallecheth, which gave upon the
causeway, there were four. In this whole
account, the Temple is spoken of as if
it were existing, when it was not as yet
built. We must suppose that David formed
the whole plan of the Temple, and fixed
the stations and numbers of the porters,
though it was left for Solomon to carry out
his instructions.

19. *the divisions of the porters*] The account of the porters here given makes them
only twenty-four in number at any one
time; xxiii. 5 states that the duty was discharged by 4000 persons. Perhaps of the
ninety-three *chief* porters here spoken of
(*vv.* 8. 9, and 11), twenty-four were always
on guard *as officers*, while of the remaining
3907, a certain proportion were each day on
duty as their subordinates.

28. The foundations of a sacred treasury
had therefore been laid as far back as the
time of Samuel, when the Israelites began
to recover from their last servitude. Such
a treasury had been once before established,
viz., under Joshua (Josh. vi. 24); but it appears to have been soon exhausted, and we
hear nothing of it under any of the later
judges until Samuel.

f ch. 23. 4.
30 business over Israel, for *f* officers and judges. *And* of the Hebronites, Hashabiah and his brethren, men of valour, a thousand and seven hundred, *were* [1] officers among them of Israel on this side Jordan westward in all the business of the LORD, and in

g ch. 23. 19.
31 the service of the king. Among the Hebronites *was* *g* Jerijah the chief, *even* among the Hebronites, according to the generations of his fathers. In the fortieth year of the reign of David they were sought for, and there were found among them mighty

h Num. 21. 32.
32 men of valour *h* at Jazer of Gilead. And his brethren, men of valour, *were* two thousand and seven hundred chief fathers, whom king David made rulers over the Reubenites, the Gadites, and the half tribe of Manasseh, for every matter pertaining to

i 2Chr.19.11.
God, and [2] *i* affairs of the king.

CHAP. 27. NOW the children of Israel after their number, *to wit*, the chief fathers and captains of thousands and hundreds, and their officers that served the king in any matter of the courses, which came in and went out month by month throughout all the months of the year, of every course *were* twenty and four thou

a 2Sam.23.8. ch. 11. 11.
2 sand. ¶ Over the first course for the first month *was* *a* Jashobeam the son of Zabdiel: and in his course *were* twenty and four thou
3 sand. Of the children of Perez *was* the chief of all the captains
4 of the host for the first month. And over the course of the second month *was* [3] Dodai an Ahohite, and of his course *was* Mikloth also the ruler: in his course likewise *were* twenty and
5 four thousand. The third captain of the host for the third month *was* Benaiah the son of Jehoiada, a [4] chief priest: and
6 in his course *were* twenty and four thousand. This *is that*

b 2 Sam. 23. 20, 22, 23. ch. 11.22,&c.
Benaiah, who *was* *b* mighty *among* the thirty, and above the
7 thirty: and in his course *was* Ammizabad his son. The fourth

c 2 Sam. 23. 24. ch. 11. 26.
captain for the fourth month *was* *c* Asahel the brother of Joab, and Zebadiah his son after him: and in his course *were* twenty
8 and four thousand. The fifth captain for the fifth month *was*

[1] Heb. *over the charge*.   [3] Or, *Dodo*, 2 Sam. 23. 9.   [4] Or, *principal officer*, 1
[2] Heb. *thing*.   Kin. 4. 5.

---

30. The "business of the Lord" in the provinces would consist especially in the collection of the tithes, the redemption-money, and the free-will offerings of the people. It may perhaps have included some religious teaching. Cp. 2 Chr. xvii. 7-9.

32. *rulers*] This term is somewhat too strong. The same kind of office was assigned to Jerijah and his brethren in the trans-Jordanic region as to Hashabiah and his brethren in western Palestine (*v.* 30), viz., a superintendence over religious matters and over the interests of the king.

XXVII. 1. This verse is a general heading to the list (*vv.* 2-15). The heading has been taken from some fuller and more elaborate description of David's army, whereof the writer of Chronicles gives us only an abridgement. Omitting the captains of thousands, the captains of hundreds, and the officers (probably "scribes") who served the king, he contents himself with recording the "chief fathers" or heads of the divisions (xxviii. 1), and the number of Israelites in each course.

2. *Jashobeam*] Jashobeam is mentioned in marg. reff. as the chief of David's mighty men. He is called in xi. 11 "the son of Hachmoni." We learn from *v.* 3 that he was of the tribe of Judah, being descended from Perez (or Pharez), the son of Judah, from whom David himself sprang. See ii. 3-15.

4. *Dodai*] The words "Eleazar, son of," have probably fallen out before Dodai (or Dodo). According to Jewish tradition, Eleazar (xi. 12) was cousin to David; his father, Dodai, being Jesse's brother. Mikloth was probably second in command to Eleazar.

5. *a chief priest*] Rather, "*the* chief priest"—an expression by which is meant, not the high-priest, but probably the high-priest's deputy, who is sometimes called "the second priest" (2 K. xxv. 18).

7. Asahel died before the courses, as here described, could have been instituted. Perhaps the arrangements of David in his later years were based upon institutions belonging to the period of his reign at Hebron.

Shamhuth the Izrahite: and in his course *were* twenty and four
9 thousand. The sixth *captain* for the sixth month *was* [d]Ira the   [d] ch. 11. 28.
son of Ikkesh the Tekoite: and in his course *were* twenty and
10 four thousand. The seventh *captain* for the seventh month *was*
[e]Helez the Pelonite, of the children of Ephraim: and in his   [e] ch. 11. 27.
11 course *were* twenty and four thousand. The eighth *captain* for
the eighth month *was* [f]Sibbecai the Hushathite, of the Zarhites: [f] 2 Sam. 21.
12 and in his course *were* twenty and four thousand. The ninth   18.
captain for the ninth month *was* [g]Abiezer the Anetothite, of the   ch. 11. 29.
Benjamites: and in his course *were* twenty and four thousand.   [g] ch. 11. 28.
13 The tenth *captain*, for the tenth month *was* [h]Maharai the Neto-   [h] 2 Sam. 23.
phathite, of the Zarhites: and in his course *were* twenty and   28.
14 four thousand. The eleventh *captain* for the eleventh month   ch. 11. 30.
was [i]Benaiah the Pirathonite, of the children of Ephraim: and   [i] ch. 11. 31.
15 in his course *were* twenty and four thousand. The twelfth
captain for the twelfth month *was* [1]Heldai the Netophathite, of
Othniel: and in his course *were* twenty and four thousand.
16 ¶ Furthermore over the tribes of Israel: the ruler of the Reubenites *was* Eliezer the son of Zichri: of the Simeonites, Shepha-
17 tiah the son of Maachah: of the Levites, [k]Hashabiah the son of   [k] ch. 26. 30.
18 Kemuel: of the Aaronites, Zadok: of Judah, [l]Elihu, *one* of the   [l] 1 Sam. 16.
19 brethren of David: of Issachar, Omri the son of Michael: of   6, *Eliab.*
Zebulun, Ishmaiah the son of Obadiah: of Naphtali, Jerimoth
20 the son of Azriel: of the children of Ephraim, Hoshea the son
of Azaziah: of the half tribe of Manasseh, Joel the son of
21 Pedaiah: of the half *tribe* of Manasseh in Gilead, Iddo the son
22 of Zechariah: of Benjamin, Jaasiel the son of Abner: of Dan,
Azareel the son of Jeroham. These *were* the princes of the tribes
23 of Israel. ¶ But David took not the number of them from
twenty years old and under: because [m]the LORD had said he   [m] Gen. 15. 5.
24 would increase Israel like to the stars of the heavens. Joab the
son of Zeruiah began to number, but he finished not, because
[n]there fell wrath for it against Israel; neither [2]was the number   [n] 2 Sam. 24.
25 put in the account of the chronicles of king David. ¶ And over   15.
ch. 21. 7.

[1] Or, *Heled*, ch. 11. 30.   [2] Heb. *ascended.*

16–22. Gad and Asher are omitted from
this list of the tribes. Similarly, Dan and
Zebulon are omitted from the genealogical
survey of the tribes (iv.-viii). We can
only suppose that the lists, as they came
down to the writer of Chronicles, were incomplete. The "rulers" or "princes" of
the tribes appear to have been the eldest
lineal descendants of the patriarchs according to the law of primogeniture.

23. David's numbering of the people was
therefore a military arrangement in order to
fix the amount of his standing army. To
the general Oriental prejudice against numbering possessions, &c., there was added in
the case of the Jews a special objection—a
feeling that it would be irreverent to attempt to count what God had promised
should be countless.

24. *because there fell wrath*] Lit. "*And*
there fell wrath." The falling of God's
wrath was not the cause of Joab's ceasing.

His motive is clearly stated in xxi. 6. See
also marg. reff.

neither was the number &c.] The meaning
is, that in the portion of the Chronicles of
king David which treated of numbers—
the number of the standing army, of the
Levitical and priestly courses, the singers,
&c.—the return of the number of the
people made by Joab was not entered.
The disastrous circumstances which followed on the taking of the census perhaps
produced a feeling that God might be further provoked by its being put on record in
the state archives. The numbers which
have come down to us must therefore have
been derived from private sources.

25–31. This section is important as showing that David, the younger son of a not
very opulent family (1 Sam. xvi. 11, 20),
had now become a large landed proprietor,
as well as a capitalist, possessed of much
moveable wealth. We may perhaps see

the king's treasures *was* Azmaveth the son of Adiel : and over the storehouses in the fields, in the cities, and in the villages, 26 and in the castles, *was* Jehonathan the son of Uzziah : and over them that did the work of the field for tillage of the ground 27 *was* Ezri the son of Chelub : and over the vineyards *was* Shimei the Ramathite : [1]over the increase of the vineyards for the wine 28 cellars *was* Zabdi the Shiphmite : and over the olive trees and the sycomore trees that *were* in the low plains *was* Baal-hanan 29 the Gederite : and over the cellars of oil *was* Joash : and over the herds that fed in Sharon *was* Shitrai the Sharonite : and over the herds *that were* in the valleys *was* Shaphat the son of 30 Adlai : over the camels also *was* Obil the Ishmaelite : and over 31 the asses *was* Jehdeiah the Meronothite : and over the flocks *was* Jaziz the Hagerite. All these *were* the rulers of the sub- 32 stance which *was* king David's. ¶ Also Jonathan David's uncle was a counsellor, a wise man, and a [2]scribe : and Jehiel the 33 [3]son of Hachmoni *was* with the king's sons : and [o]Ahithophel *was* the king's counsellor : and [p]Hushai the Archite *was* the 34 king's companion : and after Ahithophel *was* Jehoiada the son of Benaiah, and [q]Abiathar : and the general of the king's army was [r]Joab.

CHAP. 28. AND David assembled all the princes of Israel, [a]the princes of the tribes, and [b]the captains of the companies that ministered to the king by course, and the captains over the thousands, and captains over the hundreds, and [c]the stewards over all the substance and [4]possession of the king, [5]and of his 2 sons, with the [6]officers, and with [d]the mighty men, and with all the valiant men, unto Jerusalem. ¶ Then David the king stood up upon his feet, and said, Hear me, my brethren, and my people : *As for me,* [e]I *had* in mine heart to build an house of

o 2 Sam. 15. 12.
p 2 Sam. 15. 37.
& 16. 16.
q 1 Kin. 1. 7.
r ch. 11. 6.
a ch. 27. 16.
b ch. 27. 1, 2.
c ch. 27. 25.
d ch. 11. 10.
e 2 Sam. 7. 2. Ps. 132. 3, 4, 5.

[1] Heb. *over that which* was *of the vineyards.*
[2] Or, *secretary.*
[3] Or, *Hachmonite.*
[4] Or, *cattle.*
[5] Or, *and his sons.*
[6] Or, *eunuchs.*

---

the sources of both these kinds of property, in the successful wars which he had waged (1 Sam. xxvii. 8, 9, xxx. 20 ; 2 Sam. viii. 4, 7, 8, 12) ; in the revenue derived from subject kings (1 Sam. viii. 2, 14, x. 19) ; and in the purchase and occupation of lands in different places. Further, he enjoyed, of course, the usual rights of a Jewish king over the landed property of his subjects, and was thus entitled to receive a tithe of the produce in tithes (1 Sam. viii. 15, 17) and in "benevolences." Cp. 1 Sam. x. 27, xvi. 20, &c.

25. *the castles*] Probably the watch-towers in the border districts, exposed to raids from the plundering tribes of the desert (2 Chr. xxvi. 10, xxvii. 4).

28. *in the low plains*] Rather, "in the Shephelah," the proper name of the low tract between the hill country of Judæa and the Mediterranean.

32-34. A list—supplemental in character —of some chief officers of David, not mentioned before. The list cannot belong to a very late part of David's reign, since it con-

tains the name of Ahithophel, who slew himself during Absalom's rebellion (2 Sam. xvii. 23).

33. *was the king's companion*] Or, "king's friend," as in 1 K. iv. 5. Cp. also 2 Sam. xvi. 17.

34. *after Ahithophel*] *i.e.* next in counsel to Ahithophel : inferior to him, but superior to all others.

XXVIII. **1.** *officers*] Lit. as in margin. This is the only occasion in which eunuchs are mentioned in connexion with David's reign ; and it is to be remarked that they occupy, during the earlier period of the Jewish kingdom, a very subordinate position.

2. *my brethren*] David retains the modest phrase of a king not born in the purple, but raised from the ranks of the people (see 1 Sam. xxx. 23 ; 2 Sam. xix. 12). No later Jewish monarch would have thus addressed his subjects.

the footstool of our God] David views the Ark as God's "footstool," because He was enthroned above it visibly in the Shechinah, or luminous cloud, present from time to

rest for the ark of the covenant of the LORD, and for *f*the foot-
3 stool of our God, and had made ready for the building: but
God said unto me, *g*Thou shalt not build an house for my name,
because thou *hast been* a man of war, and hast shed [1]blood.
4 Howbeit the LORD God of Israel *h*chose me before all the house
of my father to be king over Israel for ever: for he hath chosen
*i*Judah *to be* the ruler; and of the house of Judah, *k*the house
of my father; and *l*among the sons of my father he liked me to
5 make *me* king over all Israel: *m*and of all my sons, (for the
LORD hath given me many sons,) *n*he hath chosen Solomon my
son to sit upon the throne of the kingdom of the LORD over Israel.
6 And he said unto me, *o*Solomon thy son, he shall build my house
and my courts: for I have chosen him *to be* my son, and I will
7 be his father. Moreover I will establish his kingdom for ever,
*p*if he be [2]constant to do my commandments and my judgments,
8 as at this day. Now therefore in the sight of all Israel the congregation of the LORD, and in the audience of our God, keep
and seek for all the commandments of the LORD your God:
that ye may possess this good land, and leave *it* for an inherit-
9 ance for your children after you for ever. And thou, Solomon
my son, *q*know thou the God of thy father, and serve him *r*with a
perfect heart and with a willing mind: for *s*the LORD searcheth all
hearts, and understandeth all the imaginations of the thoughts:
*t*if thou seek him, he will be found of thee, but if thou forsake
10 him, he will cast thee off for ever. Take heed now; *u*for the
LORD hath chosen thee to build an house for the sanctuary: be
11 strong, and do *it*. ¶ Then David gave to Solomon his son *x*the
pattern of the porch, and of the houses thereof, and of the
treasuries thereof, and of the upper chambers thereof, and of
the inner parlours thereof, and of the place of the mercy seat,
12 and the pattern [3]of all that he had by the spirit, of the courts

f Ps. 99. 5.
& 132. 7.
g 2 Sam. 7.
5, 13.
1 Kin. 5. 3.
ch. 17. 4.
& 22. 8.
h 1 Sam. 16.
7—13.
i Gen. 49. 8.
ch. 5. 2.
Ps. 60. 7.
& 78. 68.
k 1Sam.16.1.
l 1 Sam. 16.
12, 13.
m ch. 3.1,&c.
& 23. 1.
n ch. 22. 9.
o 2 Sam. 7.
13, 14.
ch. 22. 9, 10.
2 Chr. 1. 9.
p ch. 22. 13.

q Jer. 9. 24.
Hos. 4. 1.
John 17. 3.
r 2 Kin. 20.3.
Ps. 101. 2.
s 1 Sam.16.7.
1 Kin. 8. 39.
ch. 29. 17.
Ps. 7. 9.
& 139. 2.
Prov. 17. 3.
Jer. 11. 20.
& 17. 10.
& 20. 12.
Rev. 2. 23.
t 2 Chr. 15. 2.
u ver. 6.
x See Ex. 25.
40.

---

[1] Heb. *bloods.*   [2] Heb. *strong.*   [3] Heb. *of all that was with him.*

---

time above the Mercy Seat and between the
Cherubim (cp. marg. reff.).

6. Besides the message sent to David
through Nathan, he had a revelation, of
which we have only the indirect account
given here and in xxii. 8-10 (see note). He
was told that one of his sons should be
raised up to fill his throne after him, and
should build the Temple. In the second
revelation it was distinctly declared to him
that the son intended was Solomon.

my house and my courts] i.e. the Temple
and the courts of the Temple (see 2 Chr.
iv. 9).

7. *if he be constant*] The conditional character of the promise made to David, as to
the continuance of his posterity on the
Jewish throne (marg. ref.; 2 Sam. vii. 14),
is now clearly declared.

9. *know thou the God of thy father*]
"Knowing God," in the sense of having a
religious trust in Him, is an unusual phrase
in the earlier Scriptures. It scarcely occurs
elsewhere in the Historical Books. David,
however, uses the phrase in his Psalms (Ps.
xxxvi. 10); and its occurrence here may be

accepted as evidence that the entire speech
is recorded in the actual words of the
monarch.

11. Cp. *v.* 19. As God had revealed to
Moses the pattern of the Tabernacle (Ex.
xxvi. xxvii.), so He had made known by
revelation to David the pattern of the
Temple and its furniture. This pattern,
which consisted of a set of directions in
writing, David now handed over to Solomon.

the houses] The "Holy Place" and the
"Holy of Holies"—called respectively "the
house" and the "inner house" (1 K. vi.
17, 27), and (2 Chr. iii. 5, 8) "the greater
house" and "the most holy house."

the upper chambers] Cp. 2 Chr. iii. 9 note.
the inner parlours] The small rooms of
the "lean-to" (1 K. vi. 5 note), entered one
from another.

12. *the pattern* &c.] Lit. "the pattern of
all that was with him in the spirit;" perhaps to be paraphrased, "the form of all
that floated before his mind." It seems to
be David's spirit, not God's Spirit, that is
here spoken of.

of the house of the LORD, and of all the chambers round about,

y ch. 26. 20.

*y*of the treasuries of the house of God, and of the treasuries of

13 the dedicated things: also for the courses of the priests and the Levites, and for all the work of the service of the house of the LORD, and for all the vessels of service in the house of the

14 LORD. *He gave* of gold by weight for *things* of gold, for all instruments of all manner of service; *silver also* for all instruments of silver by weight, for all instruments of every kind of

15 service: even the weight for the candlesticks of gold, and for their lamps of gold, by weight for every candlestick, and for the lamps thereof: and for the candlesticks of silver by weight, *both* for the candlestick, and *also* for the lamps thereof, according

16 to the use of every candlestick. And by weight *he gave* gold for the tables of shewbread, for every table; and *likewise* silver for

17 the tables of silver: also pure gold for the fleshhooks, and the bowls, and the cups: and for the golden basons *he gave gold* by weight for every bason; and *likewise silver* by weight for every

18 bason of silver: and for the altar of incense refined gold by

z Ex. 25. 19
—22.
1 Sam. 4. 4.
1 Kin. 6. 23,
&c.
a See Ex. 25.
40.
ver. 11, 12.
b Deut. 31. 7.
8.
Josh.1.6,7,9.
ch. 22. 13.
c Josh. 1. 5.
d ch. 24, &
25, & 26.
e Ex. 35. 25,
26.
& 36. 1, 2.

weight; and gold for the pattern of the chariot of the *z*cherubims, that spread out *their wings*, and covered the ark of the

19 covenant of the LORD. All this, said David, *a*the LORD made me understand in writing by *his* hand upon me, *even* all the

20 works of this pattern. ¶ And David said to Solomon his son, *b*Be strong and of good courage, and do *it:* fear not, nor be dismayed: for the LORD God, *even* my God, *will be* with thee; *c*he will not fail thee, nor forsake thee, until thou hast finished all

21 the work for the service of the house of the LORD. And, behold, *d*the courses of the priests and the Levites, *even they shall be with thee* for all the service of the house of God: and *there shall be* with thee for all manner of workmanship *e*every willing skilful man, for any manner of service: also the princes and all the people *will be* wholly at thy commandment.

CHAP. 29. FURTHERMORE David the king said unto all the congregation, Solomon my son, whom alone God hath chosen,

a 1 Kin.3. 7.
ch. 22. 5.
Prov. 4. 3.

*is yet a*young and tender, and the work *is* great: for the palace

2 *is* not for man, but for the LORD God. Now I have prepared with all my might for the house of my God the gold for *things to be made* of gold, and the silver for *things* of silver, and the brass for *things* of brass, the iron for *things* of iron, and wood

b See Isai.
54. 11, 12.
Rev. 21. 18,
&c.

for *things* of wood; *b*onyx stones, and *stones* to be set, glistering stones, and of divers colours, and all manner of precious stones,

3 and marble stones in abundance. Moreover, because I have set my affection to the house of my God, I have of mine own proper good, of gold and silver, *which* I have given to the house of my

---

18. *the chariot of the cherubims*] The Cherubim are themselves the chariot on which Jehovah rides (Ps. xviii. 10, xcix. 1).

XXIX. 1. *the palace*] The original word here used is the Hebrew form of a Persian word, and generally designates the residence of the Persian monarch (Esth. i. 2, 5, ii. 3, 8; Neh. i. 1; Dan. viii. 2). It is only here and in *v.* 19 that it is applied to the Temple.

2. *glistering stones*] Rather, ' *coloured* stones;" or, "*dark* stones"—stones of a

hue like that of the antimony wherewith women painted their eyes.

marble stones] Or, "*white* stones"—perhaps "alabaster," which is found near Damascus. On the use made of the "stones" in building the Temple, see 2 Chr. iii. 6 note.

3. *of mine own proper good*] i.e. from his own private estate. He makes the offering publicly in order to provoke others by his example (*v.* 5).

God, over and above all that I have prepared for the holy house,
4 *even* three thousand talents of gold, of the gold of ^cOphir, and
seven thousand talents of refined silver, to overlay the walls of
5 the houses *withal*: the gold for *things* of gold, and the silver for
things of silver, and for all manner of work *to be made* by the
hands of artificers. And who *then* is willing ¹to consecrate his
6 service this day unto the LORD? ¶ Then ^dthe chief of the fathers
and princes of the tribes of Israel, and the captains of thousands
and of hundreds, with ^ethe rulers of the king's work, offered
7 willingly, and gave for the service of the house of God of gold
five thousand talents and ten thousand drams, and of silver ten
thousand talents, and of brass eighteen thousand talents, and
8 one hundred thousand talents of iron. And they with whom
precious stones were found gave *them* to the treasure of the house
9 of the LORD, by the hand of ^fJehiel the Gershonite. Then the
people rejoiced, for that they offered willingly, because with
perfect heart they ^goffered willingly to the LORD: and David
10 the king also rejoiced with great joy. ¶ Wherefore David blessed
the LORD before all the congregation: and David said, Blessed
be thou, LORD God of Israel our father, for ever and ever.
11 ^hThine, O LORD, *is* the greatness, and the power, and the glory,
and the victory, and the majesty: for all *that is* in the heaven
and in the earth *is thine;* thine *is* the kingdom, O LORD, and thou
12 art exalted as head above all. ⁱBoth riches and honour *come of*
thee, and thou reignest over all; and in thine hand *is* power
and might; and in thine hand *it is* to make great, and to give
13 strength unto all. Now therefore, our God, we thank thee,
14 and praise thy glorious name. But who *am* I, and what *is* my
people, that we should ²be able to offer so willingly after this
sort? for all things *come* of thee, and ³of thine own have we
15 given thee. For ^kwe *are* strangers before thee, and sojourners,
as *were* all our fathers: ^lour days on the earth *are* as a shadow,
16 and *there is* none ⁴abiding. O LORD our God, all this store that
we have prepared to build thee an house for thine holy name
17 *cometh* of thine hand, and *is* all thine own. I know also, my
God, that thou ^mtriest the heart, and ⁿhast pleasure in uprightness. As for me, in the uprightness of mine heart I have wil-

Marginal references:
c 1 Kin. 9. 28.
d ch. 27. 1.
e ch. 27. 25, &c.
f ch. 26. 21.
g 2 Cor. 9. 7.
h Matt. 6. 13. 1 Tim. 1. 17. Rev. 5. 13.
i Rom. 11. 36.
k Ps. 39. 12. Heb. 11. 13. 1 Pet. 2. 11. l Job 14. 2. Ps. 90. 9. & 102. 11. & 144. 4. m 1 Sam. 16. 7. ch. 28. 9. n Prov. 11. 20.

---

¹ Heb. *to fill his hand.*   ² Heb. *retain,* or, *obtain strength.*   ³ Heb. *of thine hand.*   ⁴ Heb. *expectation.*

---

4. The numbers here have also suffered to some extent from the carelessness of copyists (cp. xxii. 14 note). The amount of silver is not indeed improbable, since its value would not exceed three millions of our money; but as the gold would probably exceed in value thirty millions, we may suspect an error in the words "three thousand."

5. *to consecrate his service*] Lit. as in the margin, "to fill his hand," *i.e.* "to come with full hands to Jehovah." The words contain an appeal to the assembly for voluntary offerings.

7. The word here translated "dram" is regarded by most critics as the Hebrew equivalent of the Persian "daric," or ordinary gold coin, worth about 22 shillings of our money. Not, however, that the Jews possessed darics in David's time: the writer wished to express, in language that would be intelligible to his readers, the value of the gold subscribed, and therefore he translated the terms employed in his documents, whatever they were, into terms that were in use in his own day. The daric became current in Palestine soon after the return from the Captivity (Ezra ii. 69, viii. 27; Neh. vii. 70-72).

8. Cp. Ex. xxxv. 27. The same spirit prevailed now as at the setting up of the Tabernacle. Each offered what he had that was most precious.

9. *the people rejoiced for that they offered willingly*] *i.e.* the munificence of the princes and officers (*v.* 6) caused general joy among the people.

lingly offered all these things: and now have I seen with joy thy people, which are ¹present here, to offer willingly unto thee.

18 O LORD God of Abraham, Isaac, and of Israel, our fathers, keep this for ever in the imagination of the thoughts of the heart of

19 thy people, and ²prepare their heart unto thee: and ᵒgive unto Solomon my son a perfect heart, to keep thy commandments, thy testimonies, and thy statutes, and to do all *these things*, and to build the palace, *for* the which ᵖI have made provision.

20 ¶ And David said to all the congregation, Now bless the LORD your God. And all the congregation blessed the LORD God of their fathers, and bowed down their heads, and worshipped the

21 LORD, and the king. And they sacrificed sacrifices unto the LORD, and offered burnt offerings unto the LORD, on the morrow after that day, *even* a thousand bullocks, a thousand rams, *and* a thousand lambs, with their drink offerings, and sacrifices in

22 abundance for all Israel: and did eat and drink before the LORD on that day with great gladness. And they made Solomon the son of David king the second time, and �q anointed *him* unto the

23 LORD *to be* the chief governor, and Zadok *to be* priest. Then Solomon sat on the throne of the LORD as king instead of David

24 his father, and prospered; and all Israel obeyed him. And all the princes, and the mighty men, and all the sons likewise of king David, ʳ³submitted themselves unto Solomon the king.

25 And the LORD magnified Solomon exceedingly in the sight of all Israel, and ˢbestowed upon him *such* royal majesty as had not

26 been on any king before him in Israel. ¶ Thus David the son

27 of Jesse reigned over all Israel. ᵗAnd the time that he reigned over Israel *was* forty years; ᵘseven years reigned he in Hebron,

28 and thirty and three *years* reigned he in Jerusalem. And he ˣdied in a good old age, ʸfull of days, riches, and honour: and

29 Solomon his son reigned in his stead. ¶ Now the acts of David

Margin notes (left):
ᵒ Ps. 72. 1.

ᵖ ver. 2.
ch. 22. 14.

q 1 Kin. 1.
35, 39.

ʳ Eccles. 8. 2.

ˢ 1 Kin. 3. 13.
2 Chr. 1. 12.
Eccles. 2. 9.
ᵗ 2 Sam. 5. 4.
1 Kin. 2. 11.
ᵘ 2 Sam. 5. 5.

ˣ Gen. 25. 8.
ʸ ch. 23. 1.

---

¹ Or, *found*.   ³ Heb. *gave the hand under*   2. & 47. 29. 2 Chr. 30. 8.
² Or, *stablish*, Ps. 10. 17.   Solomon: See Gen. 24.   Ezek. 17. 18.

---

18. *keep this for ever* &c.] *i.e.* "Preserve for ever this spirit of liberal and spontaneous giving in the hearts of Thy people, and **establish** their hearts toward Thee."

20. *worshipped the* LORD, *and the king*] The same outward signs of reverence were accorded by the customs of the Jews (as of the Oriental nations generally) to God and to their monarchs (see 1 K. i. 31). But the application of the terms to both in the same passage, which occurs nowhere in Scripture but here, is thought to indicate a time when a long servitude under despotic lords had orientalised men's mode of speech.

21. *with their drink offerings*] *i.e.* with the drink offerings appropriate to each kind of Burnt offering, and required by the Law to accompany them (see Num. xv. 5, 7, 10, &c.).

sacrifices] Or, "thank-offerings," as the same word is translated in 2 Chr. xxix. 31, xxxiii. 16. Of "peace-offerings for thanksgivings" only a small part was the priest's; the sacrificer and his friends feasted on the remainder (Lev. vii. 15, 29—34).

22. *king the second time*] Solomon's first appointment was at the time of Adonijah's rebellion (marg. ref.). As that appointment was hurried and, comparatively speaking, private, David now thought it best formally to invest Solomon a second time with the sovereignty, in the face of all Israel. For a similar reason a second and public appointment of Zadok alone to the High-Priest's office took place. Abiathar was not as yet absolutely thrust out; but it may be doubtful whether he was ever allowed to perform High-priestly functions after his rebellion (1 K. i. 7, ii. 27).

23. The throne of David is called here "the throne of the Lord," as in xxviii. 5 it is called "the throne of the kingdom of the Lord," because God had set it up and had promised to establish it.

28. See 1 K. i. 1 note.

29. On the character of the works alluded to, see Introduction to Chronicles, p. 447.

Gad the seer] Gad is not given here the same title as Samuel. Samuel's title is one, apparently, of higher dignity, applied only to him and to Hanani (2 Chr. xvi. 7, 10). Gad's is a far commoner title; it is applied

the king, first and last, behold, they *are* written in the [1][2]book
of Samuel the seer, and in the book of Nathan the prophet, and
30 in the book of Gad the seer, with all his reign and his might,
[2]and the times that went over him, and over Israel, and over all
the kingdoms of the countries.

[2] Dan. 2. 21.

[1] Or, *history*. [2] Heb. *words*.

---

to his contemporaries Asaph (2 Chr. xxix.
30), Heman (1 Chr. xxv. 5), and Jeduthun
(2 Chr. xxxv. 15), to Iddo (2 Chr. ix. 29,
xii. 15), to Jehu the son of Hanani (2 Chr.
xix. 2), and to the prophet Amos (Am. vii.
12). When "seers" are spoken of in the
plural, it is the term almost universally
used, only one instance (Is. xxx. 10) occurring to the contrary.

30. *the times that went over him*] *i.e.* the
events that happened to him. Cp.Ps.xxxi.15.
all the kingdoms of the countries] The
kingdoms, *i.e.* of Moab, Ammon, Damascus, Zobah, &c. See the full phrase in 2
Chr. xvii. 10. Some account of these kingdoms would necessarily have been given in
any history of David's reign.

THE SECOND BOOK

OF THE

CHRONICLES.

a 1 Kin. 2.46.
b Gen. 39. 2.
c 1Chr.29.25.
d 1 Chr. 27.1.

e 1Chr.16.39.
& 21. 29.

f 2 Sam. c.
2, 17.
1 Chr. 15. 1.

g Ex. 27.1, 2.
& 38. 1, 2.
h Ex. 31. 2.

i 1 Kin. 3. 4.
k 1Kin.3.5,6.

l 1 Chr. 28. 5.

m 1 Kin. 3.
7, 8.
n 1 Kin. 3. 9.
o Num.27.17.
Deut. 31. 2.
p 1 Kin. 3.
11, 12, 13.

q 1Chr.29.25.
ch. 9. 22.
Eccles. 2. 9.

CHAP. 1. AND *a* Solomon the son of David was strengthened in his kingdom, and *b* the LORD his God *was* with him, and *c* magnified 2 him exceedingly. Then Solomon spake unto all Israel, to *d* the captains of thousands and of hundreds, and to the judges, and 3 to every governor in all Israel, the chief of the fathers. So Solomon, and all the congregation with him, went to the high place that *was* at *e* Gibeon; for there was the tabernacle of the congregation of God, which Moses the servant of the LORD had 4 made in the wilderness. *f* But the ark of God had David brought up from Kirjath-jearim to *the place which* David had prepared for it: for he had pitched a tent for it at Jerusalem. 5 Moreover *g* the brasen altar, that *h* Bezaleel the son of Uri, the son of Hur, had made, *i* he put before the tabernacle of the 6 LORD: and Solomon and the congregation sought unto it. And Solomon went up thither to the brasen altar before the LORD, which *was* at the tabernacle of the congregation, and *i* offered a 7 thousand burnt offerings upon it. ¶ *k* In that night did God appear unto Solomon, and said unto him, Ask what I shall give 8 thee. And Solomon said unto God, Thou hast shewed great mercy unto David my father, and hast made me *l* to reign in his 9 stead. Now, O LORD God, let thy promise unto David my father be established: *m* for thou hast made me king over a 10 people [2] like the dust of the earth in multitude. *n* Give me now wisdom and knowledge, that I may *o* go out and come in before this people: for who can judge this thy people, *that is so* great? 11 *p* And God said to Solomon, Because this was in thine heart, and thou hast not asked riches, wealth, or honour, nor the life of thine enemies, neither yet hast asked long life; but hast asked wisdom and knowledge for thyself, that thou mayest 12 judge my people, over whom I have made thee king: wisdom and knowledge *is* granted unto thee; and I will give thee riches, and wealth, and honour, such as *q* none of the kings have

[1] Or, *was there.*   [2] Heb. *much as the dust of the earth.*

I. 2–7. The narrative here corresponds with 1 K. iii. 4; but is very much fuller. We learn from the present passage, (1) that Solomon's sacrifice at Gibeon was a great public festivity, to which he collected vast numbers of the people; (2) that it was made upon the Brazen Altar of Bezaleel, which (3) stood before the Tabernacle; and (4) that Solomon's vision was on the night of his sacrifice. Consult the marg. reff.

5. *sought unto it*] *i.e.* "frequented it"— "were in the habit of making use of it."

7–12. The verbal differences between this passage and the corresponding one of Kings (1 K. iii. 5–14) are very considerable, and indicate the general truth that the object of the sacred historians is to give a true account of the real bearing of what was said:

not ordinarily to furnish us with all or the exact words that were uttered. The most important point omitted in Chronicles, and supplied by Kings, is the *conditional* promise of long life made to Solomon (1 K. iii. 14); while the chief point absent from Kings, and recorded by our author, is the solemn appeal made by Solomon to the promise of God to David his father (*v.* 9), which he now called upon God to "establish," or perform.

12. *I will give thee riches, and wealth, and honour*] Remark that the writer says nothing of any promise to Solomon of "long life," which, however, had been mentioned in *v.* 11 among the blessings which he might have been expected to ask. The reason for the omission would seem to lie in the writer's

had that *have been* before thee, neither shall there any after thee
13 have the like. ¶ Then Solomon came *from his journey* to the
high place that *was* at Gibeon to Jerusalem, from before the
14 tabernacle of the congregation, and reigned over Israel. *r*And   *r* 1 Kin. 4.2G.
Solomon gathered chariots and horsemen : and he had a thou-   ch. 9. 25.
sand and four hundred chariots, and twelve thousand horsemen,
which he placed in the chariot cities, and with the king at
15 Jerusalem. *s*And the king ¹made silver and gold at Jerusalem   *s* ch. 9. 27.
as plenteous as stones, and cedar trees made he as the syco-   Job 22. 24.
16 more trees that *are* in the vale for abundance. *t*And ²Solomon   *t* ch. 9. 28.
had horses brought out of Egypt, and linen yarn : the king's
17 merchants received the linen yarn at a price. And they fetched
up, and brought forth out of Egypt a chariot for six hundred
shekels of silver, and an horse for an hundred and fifty : and so
brought they out *horses* for all the kings of the Hittites, and for
the kings of Syria, ³by their means.
CHAP. 2. AND Solomon *a*determined to build an house for the   *a* 1 Kin. 5. 5.
2 name of the LORD, and an house for his kingdom. And *b*Solo-   *b* 1 Kin. 5.15.
mon told out threescore and ten thousand men to bear burdens,   ver. 18.
and fourscore thousand to hew in the mountain, and three thou-
3 sand and six hundred to oversee them. ¶ And Solomon sent to
⁴Huram the king of Tyre, saying, *c*As thou didst deal with   *c* 1 Chr. 14. 1.
David my father, and didst send him cedars to build him an
4 house to dwell therein, *even so deal with me.* Behold, *d*I build   *d* ver. 1.
an house to the name of the LORD my God, to dedicate *it* to
him, *and* *e*to burn before him ⁵sweet incense, and for *f*the con-   *e* Ex. 30. 7.
tinual shewbread, and for *g*the burnt offerings morning and   *f* Ex. 25. 30.
evening, on the sabbaths, and on the new moons, and on the   Lev. 24. 8.
solemn feasts of the LORD our God. This *is an ordinance* for   *g* Num. 28.
  3, 9, 11.
5 ever to Israel. And the house which I build *is* great : for *h*great   *h* Ps. 135. 5.
6 *is* our God above all gods. *i*But who ⁶is able to build him an   *i* 1 Kin. 8. 27.
house, seeing the heaven and heaven of heavens cannot contain   ch. 6. 18.
him ? who *am* I then, that I should build him an house, save   Isai. 66. 1.

¹ Heb. *gave.*
² Heb. *the going forth of the horses which* was *Solomon's.*
³ Heb. *by their hand.*
⁴ Or, *Hiram,* 1 Kin. 5. 1.
⁵ Heb. *incense of spices.*
⁶ Heb. *hath retained,* or, *obtained strength.*

desire to record only what is good of this
great king. Long life was included in the
promises made to him ; but it was granted
conditionally ; and Solomon not fulfilling
the conditions, it did not take effect (1 K.
iii. 14 note).

13. *from his journey*] These words are not
in the original text, which is thought to be
corrupt. It is best to correct the text, and
then simply to translate : " And Solomon
came from the high place that was at
Gibeon to Jerusalem."

14–17. This passage is very nearly identical with 1 K. x. 26–29.

II. 3. Huram, the form used throughout
Chronicles (except 1 Chr. xiv. 1) for the
name both of the king and of the artisan
whom he lent to Solomon (*v.* 13, iv. 11, 16),
is a late corruption of the true native word,
Hiram (marg. note and ref.).

4. The symbolical meaning of " burning
incense " is indicated in Rev. viii. 3, 4.
Consult the marg. reff. to this verse.

the solemn feasts] The three great annual
festivals, the Passover, the Feast of Weeks
(Pentecost), and the Feast of Tabernacles
(Lev. xxiii. 4–44 ; Deut. xvi. 1–17).

5. See 1 K. vi. 2 note. In Jewish eyes, at
the time that the Temple was built, it may
have been "great," that is to say, it may
have exceeded the dimensions of any single
separate building existing in Palestine up
to the time of its erection.

great is our God &c.] This may seem inappropriate as addressed to a heathen king.
But it appears (*vv.* 11, 12) that Hiram acknowledged Jehovah as the supreme deity,
probably identifying Him with his own
Melkarth.

6. *save only to burn sacrifice before him*]
Solomon seems to mean that to build the
Temple can only be justified on the human—
not on the divine—side. "God dwelleth not
in temples made with hands ;" He cannot be
confined to them ; He does in no sort need
them. The sole reason for building a Temple

7 only to burn sacrifice before him? Send me now therefore a
man cunning to work in gold, and in silver, and in brass, and
in iron, and in purple, and crimson, and blue, and that can skill
[1]to grave with the cunning men that are with me in Judah
8 and in Jerusalem, [k]whom David my father did provide. [l]Send
me also cedar trees, fir trees, and [2]algum trees, out of Lebanon: for I know that thy servants can skill to cut timber in
Lebanon; and, behold, my servants shall be with thy servants,
9 even to prepare me timber in abundance: for the house which I
10 am about to build shall be [3]wonderful great. [m]And, behold, I
will give to thy servants, the hewers that cut timber, twenty
thousand measures of beaten wheat, and twenty thousand measures of barley, and twenty thousand baths of wine, and twenty
11 thousand baths of oil. ¶ Then Huram the king of Tyre answered in writing, which he sent to Solomon, [n]Because the LORD
hath loved his people, he hath made thee king over them.
12 Huram said moreover, [o]Blessed be the LORD God of Israel,
[p]that made heaven and earth, who hath given to David the
king a wise son, [4]endued with prudence and understanding,
that might build an house for the LORD, and an house for his
13 kingdom. And now I have sent a cunning man, endued with
14 understanding, of Huram my father's, [q]the son of a woman of
the daughters of Dan, and his father was a man of Tyre, skilful

Marginal references:
[k] 1Chr.22.15.
[l] 1 Kin. 5. 6.

[m] 1Kin.5.11.

[n] 1 Kin. 10.9.
ch. 9. 8.
[o] 1 Kin. 5. 7.
[p] Gen. 1. & 2.
Ps. 33. 6.
& 102. 25.
& 124. 8.
& 136. 5, 6.
Acts 4. 24.
& 14. 15.
Rev. 10. 6.
[q] 1 Kin. 7.
13, 14.

[1] Heb. to grave gravings.
[2] Or, almuggim, 1 Kin. 10. 11.
[3] Heb. great and wonder-ful.
[4] Heb. knowing prudence and understanding.

---

lies in the needs of man: his worship must
be local; the sacrifices commanded in the
Law had of necessity to be offered somewhere.

7. See 1 K. v. 6, vii. 13 notes.

purple &c.] "Purple, crimson, and blue,"
would be needed for the hangings of the
Temple, which, in this respect, as in others,
was conformed to the pattern of the Tabernacle (see Ex. xxv. 4, xxvi. 1, &c.). Hiram's
power of "working in purple, crimson,"
&c., was probably a knowledge of the best
modes of dyeing cloth these colours. The
Phoenicians, off whose coast the *murex* was
commonly taken, were famous as purple
dyers from a very remote period.

crimson] *Karmil*, the word here and elsewhere translated "crimson," is peculiar to
Chronicles [and probably of Persian origin].
The famous red dye of Persia and India,
the dye known to the Greeks as κόκκος,
and to the Romans as *coccum*, is obtained
from an insect. Whether the "scarlet"
(*shani*) of Exodus (xxv. 4, &c.) is the same
or a different red, cannot be certainly determined.

10. *beaten wheat*] The Hebrew text is
probably corrupt here. The true original
may be restored from marg. ref., where the
wheat is said to have been given "for food."
The barley and the wine are omitted in
Kings. The author of Chronicles probably
filled out the statement which the writer of
Kings has given in brief; the barley, wine,
and ordinary oil, would be applied to the
sustenance of the foreign labourers.

11. Josephus and others professed to give
Greek versions of the correspondence, which
(they said) had taken place between Hiram
and Solomon. No value attaches to those
letters, which are evidently forgeries.

Because the LORD hath loved his people]
Cp. marg. reff. The neighbouring sovereigns, in their communications with the
Jewish monarchs, seem to have adopted the
Jewish name for the Supreme Being (Jehovah), either identifying Him (as did Hiram)
with their own chief god or (sometimes)
meaning merely to acknowledge Him as
the special God of the Jewish nation and
country.

12. *the LORD...that made heaven and earth*]
This appears to have been a formula designating the Supreme God with several of
the Asiatic nations. In the Persian inscriptions Ormazd is constantly called "the
great god, who gave" (or made) "heaven
and earth."

13. *of Huram my father's*] A wrong translation. Huram here is the workman sent
by the king of Tyre and not the king of
Tyre's father (see 1 K. v. 1 note). The
words in the original are Huram Abi, and
the latter word is now commonly thought to
be either a proper name or an epithet of
honour, *e.g.* my master-workman.

14. *to find out every device*] Cp. Ex. xxxi.
4. The "devices" intended are plans or
designs connected with art, which Huram
could invent on any subject that was "put
to him."

to work in gold, and in silver, in brass, in iron, in stone, and
in timber, in purple, in blue, and in fine linen, and in crimson;
also to grave any manner of graving, and to find out every
device which shall be put to him, with thy cunning men, and
15 with the cunning men of my lord David thy father. Now therefore the wheat, and the barley, the oil, and the wine, which
16 *r*my lord hath spoken of, let him send unto his servants: *s*and   *r* ver. 10.
we will cut wood out of Lebanon, ¹as much as thou shalt need: *s* 1 Kin.5.8,9.
and we will bring it to thee in flotes by sea to ²Joppa; and thou
17 shalt carry it up to Jerusalem. ¶ *t*And Solomon numbered all   *t* As ver. 2.
³the strangers that *were* in the land of Israel, after the number-   1 Kin. 5. 13,
ing wherewith *u*David his father had numbered them; and they   15, 16.
  & 9. 20, 21.
were found an hundred and fifty thousand and three thousand   ch. 8. 7, 8.
18 and six hundred. And he set *x*threescore and ten thousand of   *u* 1 Chr. 22.2.
  x As it is
them *to be* bearers of burdens, and fourscore thousand *to be*   ver. 2.
hewers in the mountain, and three thousand and six hundred
overseers to set the people a work.

CHAP. 3. THEN *a*Solomon began to build the house of the LORD at   *a* 1 Kin. 6. 1,
*b*Jerusalem in mount Moriah, ⁴where *the LORD* appeared unto David   &c.
  b Gen. 22. 2,
his father, in the place that David had prepared in the thresh-   14.
2 ingfloor of *c*⁵Ornan the Jebusite. And he began to build in the   *c* 1 Chr. 22. 1.
second *day* of the second month, in the fourth year of his reign.
3 ¶Now these *are the things* *d*wherein Solomon was ⁶instructed   *d* 1 Kin. 6. 2.
for the building of the house of God. The length by cubits after
the first measure *was* threescore cubits, and the breadth twenty
4 cubits. And the *e*porch that *was* in the front *of the house*, the   *e* 1 Kin. 6.3.
length *of it was* according to the breadth of the house, twenty
cubits, and the height *was* an hundred and twenty: and he over-
5 laid it within with pure gold. And *f*the greater house he cieled   *f* 1 Kin. 6.
  15—18.

¹ Heb. *according to all thy*
need.
² Heb. *Japho*, Josh. 19. 46.
Acts 9. 36.

³ Heb. *the men the strang-*
ers.
⁴ Or, *which was seen of*
David his father.

⁵ Or, *Araunah*, 2 Sam. 24.
18.
⁶ Heb. *founded.*

---

17. The strangers are the non-Israelite
population of the Holy Land, the descendants (chiefly) of those Canaanites whom the
children of Israel did not drive out. The
reimposition of the bond-service imposed
on the Canaanites at the time of the conquest (Judg. i. 28, 30, 33, 35), but discontinued in the period of depression between
Joshua and Saul, was (it is clear) due to
David, whom Solomon merely imitated in
the arrangements described in these verses.

18. On the numbers, see 1 K. v. 16 note.
to set the people a work] Or, "to set the
people *to* work"—*i.e.* to compel them to
labour. Probably, like the Egyptian and
Assyrian overseers of forced labour, these
officers carried whips or sticks, wherewith
they quickened the movements of the sluggish.

III. **1.** *where the* LORD *appeared unto*
David] The marg. rendering, or "which
was shown to David," is preferred by
some; and the expression is understood to
point out to David the proper site for the
Temple by the appearance of the Angels
and the command to build an altar (2 Sam.
xxiv. 17-25; 1 Chr. xxi. 16-26).

in the place that David had prepared] This
seems to be the true meaning of the passage,
though the order of the words in the original
has been accidentally deranged.

3. The marginal "founded" gives a clue
to another meaning of this passage, which
may be translated: "Now this **is the**
ground-plan of Solomon for the building,
&c."

cubits after the first measure] *i.e.* cubits
according to the ancient standard. The
Jews, it is probable, adopted the Babylonian
measures during the Captivity, and carried
them back into their own country. The
writer notes that the cubit of which he here
speaks is the old (Mosaic) cubit.

4. *the height was an hundred and twenty*
cubits] This height, which so much exceeds
that of the main building (1 K. vi. 2), is probably to be corrected by the reading of the
Arabic Version and the Alexandrian Septuagint, "twenty cubits." But see *v.* 9.

5. *the greater house*] *i.e.* the Holy Place,
or main chamber of the Temple, intervening
between the porch and the Holy of Holies
(so in *v.* 7).

he cieled with fir tree] Rather, "he

with fir tree, which he overlaid with fine gold, and set thereon
6 palm trees and chains. And he [1]garnished the house with
precious stones for beauty: and the gold *was* gold of Parvaim..
7 He overlaid also the house, the beams, the posts, and the walls
thereof, and the doors thereof, with gold; and graved cherubims
8 on the walls. And he made the most holy house, the length
whereof *was* according to the breadth of the house, twenty
cubits, and the breadth thereof twenty cubits: and he overlaid
9 it with fine gold, *amounting* to six hundred talents. And the
weight of the nails *was* fifty shekels of gold. And he overlaid

g 1 Kin. 6
23, &c.

10 the upper chambers with gold.   ¶ *g*And in the most holy house
he made two cherubims [2]of image work, and overlaid them with
11 gold. And the wings of the cherubims *were* twenty cubits long:
one wing *of the one cherub was* five cubits, reaching to the wall
of the house: and the other wing *was likewise* five cubits,
12 reaching to the wing of the other cherub. And *one* wing of the
other cherub *was* five cubits, reaching to the wall of the house:
and the other wing *was* five cubits *also*, joining to the wing of
13 the other cherub. The wings of these cherubims spread themselves forth twenty cubits: and they stood on their feet, and

h Matt 27.51.
Heb. 9. 3.
i 1 Kin. 7.
15—21.
Jer. 52. 21.

14 their faces *were* [3]inward.   ¶And he made the [h]vail *of* blue, and
purple, and crimson, and fine linen, and [4]wrought cherubims
15 thereon.   ¶Also he made before the house [i]two pillars of thirty
and five cubits [5]high, and the chapiter that *was* on the top of
16 each of them *was* five cubits. And he made chains, *as* in the

---

[1] Heb. *covered.*
[2] Or, (as some think) *of*
[3] Or, *toward the house.*

moveable work.

[4] Heb. *caused to ascend.*
[5] Heb. *long.*

---

covered," or "lined." The reference is not
to the ceiling, which was entirely of wood,
but to the walls and floor, which were of
stone, with a covering of planks (marg.
ref.). The word translated "fir" bears
probably in this place, not the narrow
meaning which it has in ii. 8, where it is
opposed to cedar, but a wider one, in which
cedar is included.
palm trees and chains] See 1 K. vi. 29.
The "chains" are supposed to be garlands
or festoons.
    6. *precious stones for beauty*] Not marbles
but gems (cp. 1 Chr. xxix. 2). The phrase
translated "for beauty" means "for its
beautification," "to beautify it."
Parvaim is probably the name of a place,
but what is quite uncertain.
    8. *the most holy house*]. *i.e.* the sanctuary,
or Holy of Holies. On the probable value
of the gold, see 1 K. x. 14 note.
    9. *the upper chambers*] Cp. 1 Chr. xxviii.
11. Their position is uncertain. Some
place them above the Holy of Holies,
which was ten cubits, or fifteen feet lower
than the main building (cp. 1 K. vi. 2;
20); others, accepting the height of the
porch 120 cubits (*v.* 4), regard the "upper
chambers" or "chamber" (ὑπερῷον, LXX.),
as having been a lofty building erected over
the entrance to the Temple; others suggest that the chambers intended are simply
the uppermost of the three sets of chambers
which on three sides surrounded the Tem-

ple (see 1 K. vi. 5-10). This would seem to
be the simplest and best explanation, though
we cannot see any reason for the rich ornamentation of these apartments, or for David's special directions concerning them.
    10. The word translated "image work,"
or, in the margin, "moveable work," occurs
only in this passage, and has not even a
Hebrew derivation. Modern Hebraists find
an Arabic derivation, and explain the word
to mean "carved work."
    11, 12. *the wings of the cherubims*] Com-
pare 1 K. vi. 24-27.
    13. *their faces were inward*] Lit. as in
marg. Instead of looking towards one another, with heads bent downward over the
Mercy Seat, like the Cherubim of Moses
(Ex. xxxvii. 9), these of Solomon looked out
from the sanctuary into the great chamber
("*the* house"). The Cherubim thus stood
upright on either side of the Ark, like two
sentinels guarding it.
    14. This is an important addition to the
description in Kings, where the vail is not
mentioned. It was made of exactly the
same colours as the vail of the Tabernacle
(Ex. xxvi. 31).
    15. *of thirty and five cubits*] See 1 K. vii.
15 note. Some suppose that there has been
a corruption of the number in the present
passage.
    16. *as in the oracle*] This passage is pro-
bably corrupt. Our translators supposing
that a single letter had fallen out at the be-

oracle, and put *them* on the heads of the pillars; and made *k*an
17 hundred pomegranates, and put *them* on the chains. And he
*l*reared up the pillars before the temple, one on the right hand,
and the other on the left; and called the name of that on the
right hand [1]Jachin, and the name of that on the left [2]Boaz.
CHAP. 4. MOREOVER he made *a*an altar of brass, twenty cubits
the length thereof, and twenty cubits the breadth thereof, and
2 ten cubits the height thereof. ¶ *b*Also he made a molten
sea of ten cubits [3]from brim to brim, round in compass,
and five cubits the height thereof; and a line of thirty cubits
3 did compass it round about. *c*And under it *was* the similitude
of oxen, which did compass it round about: ten in a cubit,
compassing the sea round about. Two rows of oxen *were* cast,
4 when it was cast. It stood upon twelve oxen, three looking
toward the north, and three looking toward the west, and three
looking toward the south, and three looking toward the east: and
the sea *was set* above upon them, and all their hinder parts *were*
5 inward. And the thickness of it *was* an handbreadth, and the
brim of it like the work of the brim of a cup, [4]with flowers of
6 lilies; *and* it received and held *d*three thousand baths. ¶ He
made also *e*ten lavers, and put five on the right hand, and five
on the left, to wash in them: [5]such things as they offered for
the burnt offering they washed in them; but the sea *was* for the
7 priests to wash in. *f*And he made ten candlesticks of gold
*g*according to their form, and set *them* in the temple, five on the
8 right hand, and five on the left. *h*He made also ten tables, and
placed *them* in the temple, five on the right side, and five on the
9 left. And he made an hundred [6]basons of gold. ¶ Furthermore
*i*he made the court of the priests, and the great court, and doors
10 for the court, and overlaid the doors of them with brass. And
*k*he set the sea on the right side of the east end, over against the
11 south. ¶ And *l*Huram made the pots, and the shovels, and the
[7]basons. And Huram [8]finished the work that he was to make
12 for king Solomon for the house of God; *to wit*, the two pillars,
and *m*the pommels, and the chapiters *which were* on the top of the
two pillars, and the two wreaths to cover the two pommels of the
13 chapiters which *were* on the top of the pillars; and *n*four hundred pomegranates on the two wreaths; two rows of pomegranates on each wreath, to cover the two pommels of the chapiters
14 which *were* [9]upon the pillars. He made also *o*bases, and [1]lavers
15 made he upon the bases; one sea, and twelve oxen under it.

*k*1 Kin. 7. 20.

*l*1 Kin. 7. 21.

a Ex. 27. 1,2.
2 Kin. 16. 14.
Ezek. 43. 13,
16.
*b*1 Kin. 7. 23.

*c*1 Kin. 7.
24, 25, 26.

d See 1 Kin.
7. 26.
*e*1 Kin. 7. 38.

*f*1 Kin. 7. 49.
g Ex. 25. 31,
40.
1 Chr. 28. 12,
19.
*h*1 Kin. 7. 48.
*i*1 Kin. 6. 36.

*k*1 Kin. 7. 39.
l See 1 Kin.
7. 40.

m 1Kin. 7. 41.

n See 1 Kin.
7. 20.

o 1 Kin. 7.
27, 43.

[1] That is, *He shall establish.*
[2] That is, *In it is strength.*
[3] Heb. *from his brim to his brim.*
[4] Or, *like a lilyflower.*
[5] Heb. *the work of burnt offering.*
[6] Or, *bowls.*
[7] Or, *bowls.*
[8] Heb. *finished to make.*
[9] Heb. *upon the face.*
[1] Or, *caldrons.*

ginning of the word translated "in the oracle," supplied "as." But we have no reason to suppose there were any "chains" or
"festoons" in the "oracle" or most Holy
Place.

IV. 1. The supplementary character of
Chronicles is here once more apparent. The
author of Kings had omitted to record the
dimensions of the Brazen Altar. It stood
in the great court (2 Chr. vi. 12, 13).

3. For "oxen" we find in 1 K. vii. 24,
"knops" or "gourds." An early copyist,
not comprehending the comparatively rare
word here used for "gourd," and expecting

to hear of oxen, as soon as the molten sea
was mentioned, changed the reading.

5. *three thousand baths*] See 1 K. vii. 23
note. It is quite possible that either here
or in Kings the text may have been accidentally corrupted.

7. *according to their form*] Rather, "after
their manner" (cp. *v.* 20). There is no allusion to the shape of the candlesticks, which
were made, no doubt, after the pattern of
the original candlestick of Moses.

8. The number of the tables (see *v.* 19)
and of the basons, is additional to the information contained in Kings.

16 The pots also, and the shovels, and the fleshhooks, and all their instruments, did *p*Huram his father make to king Solomon for 17 the house of the LORD of [1]bright brass.   *q*In the plain of Jordan did the king cast them, in the [2]clay ground between Succoth 18 and Zeredathah.   ¶*r*Thus Solomon made all these vessels in great abundance: for the weight of the brass could not be found out. 19 And *s*Solomon made all the vessels that *were for* the house of God, the golden altar also, and the tables whereon *t*the shew-20 bread *was set;* moreover the candlesticks with their lamps, that they should burn *u*after the manner before the oracle, of pure 21 gold; and *x*the flowers, and the lamps, and the tongs, *made he of* 22 gold, *and* that [3]perfect gold; and the snuffers, and the [4]basons, and the spoons, and the censers, *of* pure gold: and the entry of the house, the inner doors thereof for the most holy *place*, and the 5 doors of the house of the temple, *were of* gold.   THUS *a*all the work that Solomon made for the house of the LORD was finished: and Solomon brought in *all* the things that David his father had dedicated; and the silver, and the gold, and all the instruments, 2 put he among the treasures of the house of God.   ¶*b*Then Solomon assembled the elders of Israel, and all the heads of the tribes, the chief of the fathers of the children of Israel, unto Jerusalem, to bring up the ark of the covenant of the LORD 3 *c*out of the city of David, which *is* Zion.   *d*Wherefore all the men of Israel assembled themselves unto the king *e*in the feast 4 which *was* in the seventh month.   And all the elders of Israel 5 came; and the Levites took up the ark.   And they brought up the ark, and the tabernacle of the congregation, and all the holy vessels that *were* in the tabernacle, these did the priests *and* the 6 Levites bring up.   Also king Solomon, and all the congregation of Israel that were assembled unto him before the ark, sacrificed sheep and oxen, which could not be told nor numbered for 7 multitude.   And the priests brought in the ark of the covenant of the LORD unto his place, to the oracle of the house, into the 8 most holy *place*, *even* under the wings of the cherubims: for the cherubims spread forth *their* wings over the place of the ark, and the cherubims covered the ark and the staves thereof above. 9 And they drew out the staves *of the ark*, that the ends of the staves were seen from the ark before the oracle; but they were 10 not seen without.   And [5]there it is unto this day.   *There was* nothing in the ark save the two tables which Moses *f*put therein

p 1 Kin. 7. 14, 45.
q 1 Kin. 7 46.

r 1 Kin. 7.17.

s 1 Kin. 7. 48, 49, 50
t Ex. 25. 30.

u Ex. 27. 20, 21.
x Ex. 25. 31, &c.

a 1 Kin. 7.51.

b 1 Kin. 8. 1, &c.

c 2 Sam.6.12.
d 1 Kin. 8. 2.
e See ch. 7. 8, 9, 10.

f Deut. 10. 2, 5.
ch. 6. 11.

[1] Heb. *made bright*, or, *scoured*.
[2] Heb. *thicknesses of the ground*.
[3] Heb. *perfections of gold*.
[4] Or, *bowls*.
[5] Or, *they are there*, as 1 Kin. 8. 8.

---

16. *Huram his father*] Or, "**Huram his master-workman**" (ii. 13 note).
17. *Zeredathah*] Or, Zarthan (marg. ref.). The writer of Chronicles probably uses the name which the place bore in his own day.
19. *the tables*] A single table only is mentioned in 1 K. vii. 48; 2 Chr. xxix. 18. It is supposed that Solomon made ten similar tables, any one of which might be used for the Shewbread; but that the bread was never placed on more than one table at a time.
22. *the entry of the house*] The text is, by some, corrected by 1 K. vii. 50, "the *hinges*" of the doors of the house, &c.

V. This chapter contains one important addition only to the narrative of Kings (marg. reff.); namely, the account of the circumstances under which the manifestation of the Divine Presence took place (*vv.* 11-13).
4. *the Levites took up the ark*] *i.e.* such of the Levites as were also priests (cp. *v.* 7; 1 K. viii. 3).
9. *from the ark*] Or, according to a different reading here and according to 1 K. viii. 8, some read, "the ends of the staves were seen from the Holy Place."
there it is unto this day] This should be corrected as in the margin.

at Horeb, ¹when the LORD made *a covenant* with the children of
11 Israel, when they came out of Egypt. ¶ And it came to pass,
when the priests were come out of the holy *place:* (for all the
priests *that were* ²present were sanctified, *and* did not *then* wait
12 by course : ⁹also the Levites *which were* the singers, all of them
of Asaph, of Heman, of Jeduthun, with their sons and their
brethren, *being* arrayed in white linen, having cymbals and
psalteries and harps, stood at the east end of the altar, ʰand with
them an hundred and twenty priests sounding with trumpets :)
13 it came even to pass, as the trumpeters and singers *were* as one,
to make one sound to be heard in praising and thanking the
LORD ; and when they lifted up *their* voice with the trumpets
and cymbals and instruments of musick, and praised the LORD,
saying, ⁱFor *he is* good ; for his mercy *endureth* for ever : that
then the house was filled with a cloud, *even* the house of the
14 LORD; so that the priests could not stand to minister by reason
of the cloud: ᵏfor the glory of the LORD had filled the house of
God.

CHAP. 6. THEN ᵃsaid Solomon, The LORD hath said that he would
2 dwell in the ᵇthick darkness. But I have built an house of
3 habitation for thee, and a place for thy dwelling for ever. And
the king turned his face, and blessed the whole congregation of
4 Israel : and all the congregation of Israel stood. ¶ And he said,
Blessed *be* the LORD God of Israel, who hath with his hands
fulfilled *that* which he spake with his mouth to my father David,
5 saying, Since the day that I brought forth my people out of the
land of Egypt I chose no city among all the tribes of Israel to
build an house in, that my name might be there; neither chose
6 I any man to be a ruler over my people Israel : ᶜbut I have
chosen Jerusalem, that my name might be there; and ᵈhave
7 chosen David to be over my people Israel. Now ᵉit was in the
heart of David my father to build an house for the name of the
8 LORD God of Israel. But the LORD said to David my father,
Forasmuch as it was in thine heart to build an house for my
9 name, thou didst well in that it was in thine heart: notwithstanding thou shalt not build the house ; but thy son which shall
come forth out of thy loins, he shall build the house for my
10 name. The LORD therefore hath performed his word that he
hath spoken : for I am risen up in the room of David my father,
and am set on the throne of Israel, as the LORD promised, and
have built the house for the name of the LORD God of Israel.
11 And in it have I put the ark, ᶠwherein *is* the covenant of the
12 LORD, that he made with the children of Israel. ¶ ᵍAnd he
stood before the altar of the LORD in the presence of all the con-
13 gregation of Israel, and spread forth his hands: for Solomon
had made a brasen scaffold, of five cubits ³long, and five cubits
broad, and three cubits high, and had set it in the midst of the
court: and upon it he stood, and kneeled down upon his knees
before all the congregation of Israel, and spread forth his hands
14 toward heaven, and said, ¶ O LORD God of Israel, ʰ*there is* no God
like thee in the heaven, nor in the earth ; which keepest covenant,
and *shewest* mercy unto thy servants, that walk before thee with

---

¹ Or, *where.*   ² Heb. *found.*   ³ Heb. *the length thereof, &c.*

Marginal references:
ᵍ 1 Chr. 25. 1.
ʰ 1 Chr. 15. 21.
ⁱ Ps. 136.
See 1 Chr.
16. 34, 41.
ᵏ Ex. 40. 35.
ch. 7. 2.
ᵃ 1 Kin. 8.
12—50.
ᵇ Lev. 16. 2.
ᶜ ch. 12. 13.
ᵈ 1 Chr. 28. 4.
ᵉ 2 Sam. 7. 2.
1 Chr. 17. 1.
& 28. 2.
ᶠ ch. 5. 10.
ᵍ 1 Kin. 8. 22.
ʰ Ex. 15. 11.
Deut. 4. 39.
& 7. 9.

---

13. *even the house of the* LORD] Or, according to another reading (LXX.), which re-
moves the superfluousness of these words—   "The house was filled with a cloud of the
glory of the LORD."
VI. 1-39. Cp. Kings (marg. reff.).

1 Chr. 22.9. 15 all their hearts: *i*thou which hast kept with thy servant David my father that which thou hast promised him; and spakest with thy mouth, and hast fulfilled *it* with thine hand, as *it is* this day.

16 Now therefore, O LORD God of Israel, keep with thy servant David my father that which thou hast promised him, saying,

k 2 Sam. 7. 12, 16. 1 Kin. 2. 4. & 6. 12. ch. 7. 18. *l* Ps. 132. 12. *k*1 There shall not fail thee a man in my sight to sit upon the throne of Israel; *l*yet so that thy children take heed to their way to walk in my law, as thou hast walked before me. Now then, O LORD God of Israel, let thy word be verified, which thou

18 hast spoken unto thy servant David. ¶ But will God in very deed

m ch. 2. 6. Isai. 66. 1. Acts 7. 49. dwell with men on the earth? *m*behold, heaven and the heaven of heavens cannot contain thee; how much less this house which

19 I have built! Have respect therefore to the prayer of thy servant, and to his supplication, O LORD my God, to hearken unto the cry and the prayer which thy servant prayeth before thee:

20 that thine eyes may be open upon this house day and night, upon the place whereof thou hast said that thou wouldest put thy name there; to hearken unto the prayer which thy servant

21 prayeth ²toward this place. Hearken therefore unto the supplications of thy servant, and of thy people Israel, which they shall ³make toward this place: hear thou from thy dwelling-

22 place, *even* from heaven; and when thou hearest, forgive. ¶ If a man sin against his neighbour, ⁴and an oath be laid upon him to make him swear, and the oath come before thine altar in this

23 house; then hear thou from heaven, and do, and judge thy servants, by requiting the wicked, by recompensing his way upon his own head; and by justifying the righteous, by giving

24 him according to his righteousness. ¶ And if thy people Israel ⁵be put to the worse before the enemy, because they have sinned against thee; and shall return and confess thy name, and pray

25 and make supplication before thee ⁶in this house; then hear thou from the heavens, and forgive the sin of thy people Israel, and bring them again unto the land which thou gavest to them

n 1 Kin. 17.1. 26 and to their fathers. ¶ When the *n*heaven is shut up, and there is no rain, because they have sinned against thee; *yet* if they pray toward this place, and confess thy name, and turn from

27 their sin, when thou dost afflict them; then hear thou from heaven, and forgive the sin of thy servants, and of thy people Israel, when thou hast taught them the good way, wherein they should walk; and send rain upon thy land, which thou hast

o ch. 20. 9. 28 given unto thy people for an inheritance. ¶ If there *o*be dearth in the land, if there be pestilence, if there be blasting, or mildew, locusts, or caterpillers; if their enemies besiege them ⁷in the cities of their land; whatsoever sore or whatsoever sickness

29 *there be:* *then* what prayer *or* what supplication soever shall be made of any man, or of all thy people Israel, when every one shall know his own sore and his own grief, and shall spread forth

30 his hands ⁸in this house: then hear thou from heaven thy dwelling place, and forgive, and render unto every man according unto all his ways, whose heart thou knowest; (for thou only

p 1 Chr. 28.9. 31 *p*knowest the hearts of the children of men:) that they may fear thee, to walk in thy ways, ⁹so long as they live ¹in the land

32 which thou gavest unto our fathers. ¶ Moreover concerning the

Heb. *There shall not a man be cut off.*
² Or, *in this place.*
³ Heb. *pray.*
⁴ Heb. *and he require an*

oath of him.
⁵ Or, *be smitten.*
⁶ Or, *toward.*
⁷ Heb. *in the land of their gates.*

⁸ Or, *toward this house.*
⁹ Heb. *all the days which.*
¹ Heb. *upon the face of the land.*

stranger, ^qwhich is not of thy people Israel, but is come from a
far country for thy great name's sake, and thy mighty hand, and
33 thy stretched out arm; if they come and pray in this house; then
hear thou from the heavens, *even* from thy dwelling place, and
do according to all that the stranger calleth to thee for; that all
people of the earth may know thy name, and fear thee, as *doth*
thy people Israel, and may know that ¹this house which I have
34 built is called by thy name. ¶ If thy people go out to war
against their enemies by the way that thou shalt send them, and
they pray unto thee toward this city which thou hast chosen, and
35 the house which I have built for thy name; then hear thou from
the heavens their prayer and their supplication, and maintain
36 their ²cause. ¶ If they sin against thee, (for *there is* ^rno man
which sinneth not,) and thou be angry with them, and deliver
them over before *their* enemies, and ³they carry them away cap-
37 tives unto a land far off or near; yet *if* they ⁴bethink themselves
in the land whither they are carried captive, and turn and pray
unto thee in the land of their captivity, saying, We have sinned,
38 we have done amiss, and have dealt wickedly: if they return to
thee with all their heart and with all their soul in the land of
their captivity, whither they have carried them captives, and
pray toward their land, which thou gavest unto their fathers,
and *toward* the city which thou hast chosen, and toward the
39 house which I have built for thy name: then hear thou from
the heavens, *even* from thy dwelling place, their prayer and their
supplications, and maintain their ⁵cause, and forgive thy people
40 which have sinned against thee. ¶ Now, my God, let, I beseech
thee, thine eyes be open, and *let* thine ears *be* attent ⁶unto the
41 prayer *that is made* in this place. Now ^stherefore arise, O LORD
God, into thy ^tresting place, thou, and the ark of thy strength:
let thy priests, O LORD God, be clothed with salvation, and let
42 thy saints ^urejoice in goodness. O LORD God, turn not away
the face of thine anointed : ^xremember the mercies of David thy
servant.

CHAP. 7. NOW ^awhen Solomon had made an end of praying, the
^bfire came down from heaven, and consumed the burnt offering
and the sacrifices; and ^cthe glory of the LORD filled the house.
2 ^dAnd the priests could not enter into the house of the LORD,
3 because the glory of the LORD had filled the LORD's house. And
when all the children of Israel saw how the fire came down, and
the glory of the LORD upon the house, they bowed themselves
with their faces to the ground upon the pavement, and wor-
shipped, and praised the LORD, ^esaying, For *he is* good; ^ffor his
4 mercy *endureth* for ever. ¶ ^gThen the king and all the people

Marginal references:
q John 12. 20.
Acts 8. 27.

r Prov. 20. 9.
Eccles. 7. 20.
Jam. 3. 2.
1 John 1. 8.

s Ps. 132. 8,
9, 10, 16.
t 1 Chr. 28. 2.

u Neh. 9. 25.
x Ps. 132. 1.
Isai. 55. 3.
a 1 Kin. 8. 54.
b Judg. 6. 21.
1 Kin. 18. 38.
1 Chr. 21. 26.
c 1 Kin. 8.
10, 11.
ch. 5. 13, 14.
Ezek. 10. 3, 4.
d ch. 5. 14.
e ch. 5. 13.
Ps. 136. 1.
f 1 Chr. 16.
41.
ch. 20. 21.
g 1 Kin. 8.
62, 63.

¹ Heb. *thy name is called upon this house.*
² Or, *right.*
³ Heb. *they that take them captives carry them away.*
⁴ Heb. *bring back to their heart.*
⁵ Or, *right.*
⁶ Heb. *to the prayer of this place.*

40-42. In Kings, a different conclusion
takes the place of these verses. The document from which both writers copied contained the full prayer of dedication, which
each gives in a somewhat abbreviated form.
41. *thy resting place*] *i.e.* the Holy of Holies.
Solomon follows closely the words of David
his father, spoken probably when he brought
the Ark into Jerusalem. See marg. reff.
42. *turn not away the face of thine anointed*]

i.e. make him not to hide his face through
shame at having his prayers rejected (cp. 1
K. ii. 16 note).
the mercies of David] *i.e.* "God's mercies
towards David."
VII. **1.** *the fire came down from heaven*]
As in the time of Moses on the dedication
of the Tabernacle (Lev. ix. 24). The fact is
omitted from the narrative of Kings; but
omission is not contradiction.

5 offered sacrifices before the LORD. And king Solomon offered a sacrifice of twenty and two thousand oxen, and a hundred and twenty thousand sheep: so the king and all the people

1Chr.15.16. 6 dedicated the house of God. *h*And the priests waited on their offices: the Levites also with instruments of musick of the LORD, which David the king had made to praise the LORD, because his mercy *endureth* for ever, when David praised [1]by their

i ch. 5. 12. ministry; and *i*the priests sounded trumpets before them, and

k 1 Kin. 8.64. 7 all Israel stood. Moreover *k*Solomon hallowed the middle of the court that *was* before the house of the LORD: for there he offered burnt offerings, and the fat of the peace offerings, because the brasen altar which Solomon had made was not able to receive the burnt offerings, and the meat offerings, and the fat.

l 1 Kin. 8.65. 8 ¶ *l*Also at the same time Solomon kept the feast seven days, and all Israel with him, a very great congregation, from the entering

m Josh. 13. 3. 9 in of Hamath unto *m*the river of Egypt. And in the eighth day they made [2]a solemn assembly: for they kept the dedication of

n 1 Kin. 8.66. 10 the altar seven days, and the feast seven days. And *n*on the three and twentieth day of the seventh month he sent the people away into their tents, glad and merry in heart for the goodness that the LORD had shewed unto David, and to Solo-

o 1 Kin. 9. 1, &c. 11 mon, and to Israel his people. Thus *o*Solomon finished the house of the LORD, and the king's house: and all that came into Solomon's heart to make in the house of the LORD, and in

12 his own house, he prosperously effected. ¶ And the LORD appeared to Solomon by night, and said unto him, I have heard

p Deut. 12. 5. thy prayer, *p*and have chosen this place to myself for an house

q ch. 6.26,28. 13 of sacrifice. *q*If I shut up heaven that there be no rain, or if I command the locusts to devour the land, or if I send pestilence

14 among my people; if my people, [3]which are called by my name,

r Jam. 4. 10. shall *r*humble themselves, and pray, and seek my face, and turn

s ch. 6. 27,30. from their wicked ways; *s*then will I hear from heaven, and

t ch. 6. 40. 15 will forgive their sin, and will heal their land. Now *t*mine eyes shall be open, and mine ears attent [4]unto the prayer that

u 1 Kin. 9. 3. ch. 6. 6. 16 *is made* in this place. For now have *u*I chosen and sanctified this house, that my name may be there for ever: and mine eyes

x 1 Kin. 9. 4, &c. 17 and mine heart shall be there perpetually. *x*And as for thee, if thou wilt walk before me, as David thy father walked, and do according to all that I have commanded thee, and shalt

18 observe my statutes and my judgments; then will I stablish the throne of thy kingdom, according as I have covenanted with

y ch. 6. 16. David thy father, saying, *y*[5]There shall not fail thee a man

[1] Heb. *by their hand.*
[2] Heb. *a restraint.*
[3] Heb. *upon whom my*
name *is called.*
[4] Heb. *to the prayer of this place.*
[5] Heb. *There shall not be cut off to thee.*

---

8. *Solomon kept the feast*] *i.e.* Solomon kept at this same time, not the Feast of the Dedication only, but also the Feast of Tabernacles. The former lasted seven days, from the 8th of Tisri to the 15th, the latter also seven days, from the 15th to the 22nd. On the day following the people were dismissed (*v.* 10).

11. The narrative now runs parallel with 1 K. ix. 1-9, but is more full, and presents less of verbal agreement. Verses 13-15 are additional to the earlier record.

12. *an house of sacrifice*] This expression does not elsewhere occur. Its meaning, however, is clear. God declares that Solomon's Temple is the place whereunto all Israelites were commanded to bring their Burnt-offerings and sacrifices (see Deut. xii. 5, 6).

15. *the prayer that is made in this place*] Lit. as in the margin. The unusual phrase includes the two cases of prayers offered *in* (vi. 24) and *toward* (vi. 34, 38) the Sanctuary.

19 *to be* ruler in Israel. *But if ye turn away, and forsake my
statutes and my commandments, which I have set before you,
20 and shall go and serve other gods, and worship them; then
will I pluck them up by the roots out of my land which I have
given them; and this house, which I have sanctified for my
name, will I cast out of my sight, and will make it *to be* a pro-
21 verb and a byword among all nations. And this house, which
is high, shall be an astonishment to every one that passeth by
it; so that he shall say, *a* Why hath the LORD done thus unto
22 this land, and unto this house? And it shall be answered, Because they forsook the LORD God of their fathers, which brought
them forth out of the land of Egypt, and laid hold on other gods,
and worshipped them, and served them: therefore hath he
brought all this evil upon them.

CHAP. 8. AND *a* it came to pass at the end of twenty years, wherein
Solomon had built the house of the LORD, and his own house,
2 that the cities which Huram had restored to Solomon, Solomon
built them, and caused the children of Israel to dwell there.
3 ¶ And Solomon went to Hamath-zobah, and prevailed against
4 it. *b* And he built Tadmor in the wilderness, and all the store
5 cities, which he built in Hamath. Also he built Beth-horon the
upper, and Beth-horon the nether, fenced cities, with walls,
6 gates, and bars; and Baalath, and all the store cities that Solomon had, and all the chariot cities, and the cities of the horsemen, and ¹ all that Solomon desired to build in Jerusalem, and
7 in Lebanon, and throughout all the land of his dominion. *c* As
for all the people *that were* left of the Hittites, and the Amorites, and the Perizzites, and the Hivites, and the Jebusites,
8 which *were* not of Israel, *but* of their children, who were left
after them in the land, whom the children of Israel consumed
9 not, them did Solomon make to pay tribute until this day. But
of the children of Israel did Solomon make no servants for his
work; but they *were* men of war, and chief of his captains, and
10 captains of his chariots and horsemen. And these *were* the chief
of king Solomon's officers, even *d* two hundred and fifty, that bare
11 rule over the people. ¶ And Solomon *e* brought up the daughter
of Pharaoh out of the city of David unto the house that he had
built for her: for he said, My wife shall not dwell in the house
of David king of Israel, because *the places are* ² holy, whereunto
12 the ark of the LORD hath come. ¶ Then Solomon offered burnt
offerings unto the LORD on the altar of the LORD, which he had
13 built before the porch, even after a certain rate *f* every day, offering according to the commandment of Moses, on the sabbaths,
and on the new moons, and on the solemn feasts, *g* three times in
the year, *even* in the feast of unleavened bread, and in the feast

Margin references (right column):
z Lev. 26. 14, 33.
Deut. 28. 15, 36, 37.

a Deut. 20. 24.
Jer. 22. 8, 9.

a 1 Kin. 9. 10, &c.

b 1 Kin. 9. 17, &c.

c 1 Kin. 9, 20, &c.

d See 1 Kin. 9. 23.
e 1 Kin. 3. 1. & 7. 8.
& 9. 24.

f Ex. 29. 38.
Num. 28. 3, 9, 11, 26.
& 29. 1, &c.
g Ex. 23. 14.
Deut. 16. 16.

¹ Heb. *all the desire of Solomon which he desired to build.* ² Heb. *holiness.*

VIII. Cp. the reff. to 1 Kings.
2. *the cities which Huram had restored to
Solomon*] These cities had not been mentioned previously by the writer of Chronicles, who, however, seems to assume that
the fact of their having been given by
Hiram to Solomon is known to his readers.
See 1 K. ix. 11–13.
3. *Hamath-zobah*] Usually identified with
the "great Hamath" (Am. vi. 2); the
capital of Cœle-Syria; but probably a town

of Zobah otherwise unknown, which revolted
from Solomon, and was reduced to subjection.
5. *built*] "Rebuilt," or "repaired" (as in
v. 2). The two Beth-horons were both ancient cities (see Josh. x. 10 note).
10. On the number cp. 1 K. v. 16 note.
11. *of Pharaoh*] Here again the writer of
Chronicles assumes in his reader a knowledge of the facts recorded in the marg.
reff.

14 of weeks and in the feast of tabernacles. And he appointed,
according to the order of David his father, the [h]courses of the
priests to their service, and [i]the Levites to their charges, to
praise and minister before the priests, as the duty of every day
required: the [k]porters also by their courses at every gate: for
15 [1]so had David the man of God commanded. And they departed
not from the commandment of the king unto the priests and
Levites concerning any matter, or concerning the treasures.
16 Now all the work of Solomon was prepared unto the day of the
foundation of the house of the LORD, and until it was finished.
17 So the house of the LORD was perfected.   ¶ Then went Solomon
to [l]Ezion-geber, and to [2]Eloth, at the sea side in the land of
18 Edom.   [m]And Huram sent him by the hands of his servants
ships, and servants that had knowledge of the sea; and they
went with the servants of Solomon to Ophir, and took thence
four hundred and fifty talents of gold, and brought them to king
Solomon.

CHAP. 9. AND [a]when the queen of Sheba heard of the fame of
Solomon, she came to prove Solomon with hard questions at
Jerusalem, with a very great company, and camels that bare
spices, and gold in abundance, and precious stones: and when
she was come to Solomon, she communed with him of all that
2 was in her heart. And Solomon told her all her questions: and
there was nothing hid from Solomon which he told her not.
3 And when the queen of Sheba had seen the wisdom of Solomon,
4 and the house that he had built, and the meat of his table, and
the sitting of his servants, and the attendance of his ministers,
and their apparel; his [3]cupbearers also, and their apparel; and
his ascent by which he went up into the house of the LORD;
5 there was no more spirit in her. And she said to the king, It
was a true [4]report which I heard in mine own land of thine [5]acts,
6 and of thy wisdom: howbeit I believed not their words, until
I came, and mine eyes had seen it: and, behold, the one half
of the greatness of thy wisdom was not told me: for thou ex-
7 ceedest the fame that I heard. Happy are thy men, and happy
are these thy servants, which stand continually before thee, and
8 hear thy wisdom. Blessed be the LORD thy God, which delighted
in thee to set thee on his throne, to be king for the LORD thy
God: because thy God loved Israel, to establish them for ever,
therefore made he thee king over them, to do judgment and
9 justice. And she gave the king an hundred and twenty talents

Marginal references:
[h] 1 Chr. 24. 1.
[i] 1 Chr. 25. 1.
[k] 1 Chr. 9. 17. & 26. 1.
[l] 1 Kin. 9. 26.
[m] 1 Kin. 9. 27. ch. 9. 10, 13.
[a] 1 Kin. 10. 1, &c. Matt. 12. 42. Luke 11. 31.

---

[1] Heb. so was the commandment of David the man of God.
[2] Or, Elath, Deut. 2. 8. 2 Kin. 14. 22.
[3] Or, butlers.
[4] Heb. word.
[5] Or, sayings.

---

14. the man of God] This phrase, so common in Kings (see Introduction to Kings, p. 264 n. 4), is rare in Chronicles, and is applied only to Moses (1 Chr. xxiii. 14), David, and one other Prophet (xxv. 7, 9).

18. It has been supposed that these ships were conveyed from Tyre to Ezion-geber, either (1) round the continent of Africa, or (2) across the isthmus of Suez. But the writer probably only means that ships were given by Hiram to Solomon at this time, and in connexion with the Ophir enterprise. These vessels may have been deli-vered at Joppa, and have been there carefully studied by the Jewish shipwrights, who then proceeded to Ezion-geber, and, assisted by Phœnicians, constructed ships after their pattern.

four hundred and fifty talents] "Four hundred and twenty talents" in Kings (1 K. ix. 28). One or other of the two texts has suffered from that corruption to which numbers are so especially liable.

IX. 1–12. The narrative here is parallel with that in marg. ref., from which it varies but little, and to which it adds nothing.

of gold, and of spices great abundance, and precious stones:
neither was there any such spice as the queen of Sheba gave
10 king Solomon. ¶And the servants also of Huram, and the
servants of Solomon, *b* which brought gold from Ophir, brought
11 *c* algum trees and precious stones. And the king made *of* the
algum trees [1][2] terraces to the house of the LORD, and to the
king's palace, and harps and psalteries for singers: and there
12 were none such seen before in the land of Judah. ¶And king
Solomon gave to the queen of Sheba all her desire, whatsoever
she asked, beside *that* which she had brought unto the king.
So she turned, and went away to her own land, she and her
13 servants. ¶Now the weight of gold that came to Solomon in
one year was six hundred and threescore and six talents of gold :
14 beside *that which* chapmen and merchants brought. And all
the kings of Arabia and [3] governors of the country brought gold
15 and silver to Solomon. And king Solomon made two hundred
targets *of* beaten gold : six hundred *shekels* of beaten gold went
16 to one target. And three hundred shields *made he of* beaten
gold : three hundred *shekels* of gold went to one shield. And
17 the king put them in the house of the forest of Lebanon. Moreover the king made a great throne of ivory, and overlaid it with
18 pure gold. And *there were* six steps to the throne, with a footstool of gold, *which were* fastened to the throne, and [4] stays on
each side of the sitting place, and two lions standing by the
19 stays : and twelve lions stood there on the one side and on the
other upon the six steps. There was not the like made in any
20 kingdom. And all the drinking vessels of king Solomon *were*
of gold, and all the vessels of the house of the forest of Lebanon
were of [5] pure gold : [6] none *were of* silver; it was *not* any thing
21 accounted of in the days of Solomon. For the king's ships went
to Tarshish with the servants of Huram : every three years once
came the ships of Tarshish bringing gold, and silver, [7] ivory,
22 and apes, and peacocks. ¶And king Solomon passed all the
23 kings of the earth in riches and wisdom. And all the kings of
the earth sought the presence of Solomon, to hear his wisdom,
24 that God had put in his heart. And they brought every man
his present, vessels of silver, and vessels of gold, and raiment,
harness, and spices, horses, and mules, a rate year by year.
25 And Solomon *d* had four thousand stalls for horses and chariots,
and twelve thousand horsemen; whom he bestowed in the cha-
26 riot cities, and with the king at Jerusalem. *e* And he reigned
over all the kings *f* from the [8] river even unto the land of the
27 Philistines, and to the border of Egypt. *g* And the king [9] made
silver in Jerusalem as stones, and cedar trees made he as the

b ch. 8. 18.

c 1 Kin. 10.
11, *almug
trees*.

d 1 Kin. 4.26.
& 10. 26.
ch. 1. 14.
e 1 Kin. 4. 21.
f Gen. 15. 18.
Ps. 72. 8.
g 1 Kin.10.27.
ch. 1. 15.

---

[1] Or. *stairs*.
[2] Heb. *highways*.
[3] Or, *captains*.

[4] Heb. *hands*.
[5] Heb. *shut up*.
[6] Or, there was *no silver* in them.

[7] Or, *elephants' teeth*.
[8] That is, *Euphrates*.
[9] Heb. *gave*.

---

11. *terraces*] Rather, as in the margin,
"**stairs**" (see 1 K. x. 12 note).

12. *beside that which she had brought unto
the king*] It is difficult to assign any sense
to these words as they now stand in the
Hebrew text. A slight alteration will give
the meaning : "Beside that which the king
had brought for her ; " which is in conformity with 1 K. x. 13.

15, 16. Comparing 1 K. x. 16, 17, it follows from the two passages together that

the "pound of gold" was equal to 100
shekels.

18. The footstool (not mentioned in
Kings) was an essential appendage to an
Oriental throne ; it appears everywhere in
the Egyptian, Assyrian, and Persian sculptures.

23. *all the kings of the earth*] Rather, "all
the kings of the **land** ; " all the monarchs,
that is, whose dominions were included in
Solomon's empire (see 1 K. iv. 21).

h 1Kin.10.28.
ch. 1. 16.
i 1Kin.11.41.

k 1Kin.11.29.
l ch. 12. 15.
& 13. 22.
m 1 Kin. 11.
42, 43.

a 1 Kin. 12.
1, &c.
b 1Kin.11.40.

28 sycomore trees that *are* in the low plains in abundance. [h]And
they brought unto Solomon horses out of Egypt, and out of all
29 lands. ¶ [i]Now the rest of the acts of Solomon, first and last,
are they not written in the [1]book of Nathan the prophet, and in
the prophecy of [k]Ahijah the Shilonite, and in the visions of
30 [l]Iddo the seer against Jeroboam the son of Nebat? [m]And Solo-
31 mon reigned in Jerusalem over all Israel forty years. And
Solomon slept with his fathers, and he was buried in the city
of David his father: and Rehoboam his son reigned in his stead.

CHAP. 10. AND [a]Rehoboam went to Shechem; for to Shechem
2 were all Israel come to make him king. And it came to pass,
when Jeroboam the son of Nebat, who *was* in Egypt, [b]whither
he had fled from the presence of Solomon the king, heard *it*,
3 that Jeroboam returned out of Egypt. And they sent and called
him. So Jeroboam and all Israel came and spake to Rehoboam,
4 saying, Thy father made our yoke grievous: now therefore ease
thou somewhat the grievous servitude of thy father, and his
5 heavy yoke that he put upon us, and we will serve thee. And
he said unto them, Come again unto me after three days. And
6 the people departed. ¶ And king Rehoboam took counsel with
the old men that had stood before Solomon his father while he
yet lived, saying, What counsel give ye *me* to return answer to
7 this people? And they spake unto him, saying, If thou be kind
to this people, and please them, and speak good words to them,
8 they will be thy servants for ever. But he forsook the counsel
which the old men gave him, and took counsel with the young
men that were brought up with him, that stood before him.
9 And he said unto them, What advice give ye that we may return
answer to this people, which have spoken to me, saying, Ease
10 somewhat the yoke that thy father did put upon us? And the
young men that were brought up with him spake unto him,
saying, Thus shalt thou answer the people that spake unto thee,
saying, Thy father made our yoke heavy, but make thou *it*
somewhat lighter for us; thus shalt thou say unto them, My
11 little *finger* shall be thicker than my father's loins. For whereas
my father [2]put a heavy yoke upon you, I will put more to your
yoke: my father chastised you with whips, but I *will chastise*
12 *you* with scorpions. ¶ So Jeroboam and all the people came to
Rehoboam on the third day, as the king bade, saying, Come again
13 to me on the third day. And the king answered them roughly;
14 and king Rehoboam forsook the counsel of the old men, and
answered them after the advice of the young men, saying, My
father made your yoke heavy, but I will add thereto: my father
chastised you with whips, but I *will chastise you* with scorpions.

---

[1] Heb. *words*.   [2] Heb. *laded*.

---

28. *and out of all lands*] An addition to
the words in Kings. The principal countries would no doubt be Arabia and Armenia—the former always famous for its excellent breed; the latter mentioned in
Ezekiel (xxvii. 14) as trading with horses in
the fairs of Tyre.

29. *the book of Nathan* &c.] On the
"books" here mentioned, see Introduction
to Chronicles, p. 447 *n.* 2.

We hear nothing of Iddo in Kings; but
he is mentioned below twice (xii. 15,

xiii. 22). In the latter of these passages
he is called not "the seer," but "the prophet." He seems to have been the author
of three works:—(1) Visions against Jeroboam; (2) A book of genealogies; and (3) A
commentary or history. According to some
he was identical with Oded, the father of
Azariah, who prophesied in the reign of
Asa (see xv. 1 note).

X.-XI. 4. The narrative of Kings (marg.
ref.) is repeated with only slight verbal differences.

15 So the king hearkened not unto the people : ᶜfor the cause was
of God, that the LORD might perform his word, which he spake
by the ᵈhand of Ahijah the Shilonite to Jeroboam the son of
16 Nebat.   ¶And when all Israel *saw* that the king would not
hearken unto them, the people answered the king, saying,
What portion have we in David ?
And *we have* none inheritance in the son of Jesse :
Every man to your tents, O Israel :
And now, David, see to thine own house.
17 So all Israel went to their tents.   But *as for* the children of
Israel that dwelt in the cities of Judah, Rehoboam reigned over
18 them.   ¶Then king Rehoboam sent Hadoram that *was* over the
tribute ; and the children of Israel stoned him with stones, that
he died.   But king Rehoboam ¹made speed to get him up to *his*
19 chariot, to flee to Jerusalem.   ᵉAnd Israel rebelled against the
house of David unto this day.

CHAP. 11. AND ᵃwhen Rehoboam was come to Jerusalem, he
gathered of the house of Judah and Benjamin an hundred and
fourscore thousand chosen *men*, which were warriors, to fight
against Israel, that he might bring the kingdom again to Reho-
2 boam.   But the word of the LORD came ᵇto Shemaiah the man
3 of God, saying, Speak unto Rehoboam the son of Solomon, king
of Judah, and to all Israel in Judah and Benjamin, saying,
4 Thus saith the LORD, Ye shall not go up, nor fight against your
brethren : return every man to his house : for this thing is done
of me.   And they obeyed the words of the LORD, and returned
5 from going against Jeroboam.   ¶And Rehoboam dwelt in Jeru-
6 salem, and built cities for defence in Judah.   He built even
7 Beth-lehem, and Etam, and Tekoa, and Beth-zur, and Shoco,
8, 9 and Adullam, and Gath, and Mareshah, and Ziph, and Ado-
10 raim, and Lachish, and Azekah, and Zorah, and Aijalon, and
Hebron, which *are* in Judah and in Benjamin fenced cities.
11 And he fortified the strong holds, and put captains in them,
12 and store of victual, and of oil and wine.   And in every several
city *he put* shields and spears, and made them exceeding strong,
13 having Judah and Benjamin on his side.   ¶And the priests and
the Levites that *were* in all Israel ²resorted to him out of all their
14 coasts.   For the Levites left ᶜtheir suburbs and their possession,
and came to Judah and Jerusalem : for ᵈJeroboam and his sons

Marginal references:
ᶜ 1 Sam. 2. 25.
1 Kin. 12.
15, 24.
ᵈ 1 Kin. 11. 29.

ᵉ 1 Kin. 12. 19.

ᵃ 1 Kin. 12.
21, &c.

ᵇ ch. 12. .5.

ᶜ Num. 35. 2.
ᵈ ch. 13. 9.

¹ Heb. *strengthened himself.*   ² Heb. *presented themselves to him.*

---

5. Rehoboam was between two dangers :
on the north he might be attacked by Jeroboam, on the south by Jeroboam's ally,
Egypt.   From this side was the greater
peril, and therefore out of the fifteen cities
fortified, all but three were on the southern
or western frontier, where Egypt would be
most likely to attack.

6, 7. See Josh. xv., notes to *vv.* 33-36,
48-51, 58, 59.

For Adullam see 1 Sam. xxii. 1 note.   It
was in the near neighbourhood of Socoh
(Josh. xv. 35) ; but its site cannot be actually
fixed.   It was a place of great antiquity
(Gen. xxxviii. 1).

8. For Gath, see Josh. xiii. 3 note.   Its
native king, Achish (1 K. ii. 39), is to be
regarded, not as an independent monarch,
but as one of the many vassal-kings over

whom Solomon reigned (ix. 23).   For Mareshah, see Josh. xv. 44 ; for Ziph, do. *v.* 55.

9, 10. The site of Adoraim is uncertain.
For Lachish, see Josh. x. 3 ; Azekah, do. *v.*
10 ; Zorah, do. xv. 33 ; Aijalon, do. x. 12 ;
Hebron, do. xiv. 15.   No one of the cities was
really within the limits of the tribe of Benjamin.   The writer uses the phrase "Judah
and Benjamin " merely as the common
designation of the southern kingdom (cp.
vv. 12 and 23).

14. Jeroboam probably confiscated the
Levitical lands for the benefit of this new
priesthood.   Under these circumstances the
priests and Levites emigrated in large numbers to the southern kingdom ; an act which
was followed by a general emigration of the
more pious Israelites (*v.* 16).

had cast them off from executing the priest's office unto the
15 LORD: ^eand he ordained him priests for the high places, and for
16 ^fthe devils, and for ^gthe calves which he had made. ^hAnd after
them out of all the tribes of Israel such as set their hearts to
seek the LORD God of Israel came to Jerusalem, to sacrifice
17 unto the LORD God of their fathers. So they ⁱstrengthened the
kingdom of Judah, and made Rehoboam the son of Solomon
strong, three years: for three years they walked in the way of
18 David and Solomon. ¶ And Rehoboam took him Mahalath the
daughter of Jerimoth the son of David to wife, and Abihail the
19 daughter of Eliab the son of Jesse; which bare him children;
20 Jeush, and Shamariah, and Zaham. And after her he took
^kMaachah the daughter of Absalom; which bare him Abijah,
21 and Attai, and Ziza, and Shelomith. And Rehoboam loved
Maachah the daughter of Absalom above all his wives and his
concubines: (for he took eighteen wives, and threescore concubines; and begat twenty and eight sons, and threescore daugh-
22 ters.) And Rehoboam ^l made Abijah the son of Maachah the
chief, *to be* ruler among his brethren: for *he thought* to make
23 him king. And he dealt wisely, and dispersed of all his children throughout all the countries of Judah and Benjamin, unto
every fenced city: and he gave them victual in abundance. And
he desired ¹many wives.

CHAP. 12. AND ^ait came to pass, when Rehoboam had established
the kingdom, and had strengthened himself, ^bhe forsook the law
2 of the LORD, and all Israel with him. ^cAnd it came to pass, *that*
in the fifth year of king Rehoboam Shishak king of Egypt came
up against Jerusalem, because they had transgressed against the
3 LORD, with twelve hundred chariots, and threescore thousand
horsemen: and the people *were* without number that came with

¹ Heb. *a multitude of wives.*

Margin references

* 1 Kin. 12. 31.
& 13. 33.
& 14. 9.
Hos. 13. 2.
^f 1 Cor. 10. 20.
^g 1 Kin. 12. 28.
^h See ch.
15. 9.
& 30. 11, 18.
ⁱ ch. 12. 1.

^k 1 Kin. 15.
2. She is
called Mi-
chaiah the
daughter of
Uriel,
ch. 13. 2.
^l See Deut.
21. 15, 16, 17.

^a ch. 11. 17.
^b 1 Kin. 14.
22, 23, 24.
^c 1 Kin. 14.
24, 25.

---

15. *the high places*] i.e. the two sanctuaries at Dan and Bethel.

for the devils] Lit. "for the goats:" probably the word is used (as in Lev. xvii. 7)
for objects of idolatrous worship generally.

17. *three years*] i.e. during the first three
years of Rehoboam's reign. In the fourth
year an apostasy took place, which neutral-
ised all the advantages of the immigration
(marg. ref.). In the fifth the apostasy was
punished by the invasion and success of
Shishak (xii. 2).

18. This is probably an extract from the
"genealogies" of Iddo (xii. 15).

As Jerimoth is not mentioned among the
legitimate sons of David (1 Chr. iii. 1-8,
xiv. 4-7), he must have been the child of a
concubine.

Abihail was probably the "grand-daughter," not "daughter," of Eliab (1 Sam. xvi.
6, xvii. 13; 1 Chr. ii. 13).

20. *Maachah the daughter of Absalom*]
Rather, "grand-daughter" (1 K. xv. 2
note).

22. Jeush was probably the eldest of Rehoboam's sons, and should naturally and
according to the provisions of the Law
Deut. xxi. 15-17) have been his heir. But
Rehoboam's affection for Maachah led him
to transgress the Law.

23. Rehoboam's wisdom was shown—(1)
In dispersing his other sons instead of allowing them to remain together in Jerusalem, where they might have joined in a plot
against Abijah, as Adonijah and his brothers
had done against Solomon (1 K. i. 5-10); (2)
In giving his sons positions which might well
content them and prevent them from being
jealous of Abijah.

he desired many wives] [CD. v. 21]. Some
prefer to connect the words with the preceding words. If so, they denote another
point in which Rehoboam was careful to
please his sons.

XII. This chapter runs parallel with
Kings (marg. ref.), but considerably enlarges the narrative.

1. *all Israel with him*] i.e. "all Judah and
Benjamin"—all the Israelites of those two
tribes.

2. *Shishak...came up...because they had
transgressed*] The writer speaks from a
divine, not a human, point of view. Shishak's motive in coming up was to help
Jeroboam, and to extend his own influence.

3. *twelve hundred chariots*] This number
is not unusual (cp. Ex. xiv. 7; 1 K. x. 26).
Benhadad brought 1200 chariots into the
field against Shalmaneser II.; and Ahab had

him out of Egypt; *d*the Lubims, the Sukkiims, and the Ethi- 4 opians. And he took the fenced cities which *pertained* to Judah, 5 and came to Jerusalem. ¶ Then came *e*Shemaiah the prophet to Rehoboam, and *to* the princes of Judah, that were gathered together to Jerusalem because of Shishak, and said unto them, Thus saith the LORD, *f* Ye have forsaken me, and therefore have 6 I also left you in the hand of Shishak. Whereupon the princes of Israel and the king *g*humbled themselves; and they said, 7 *h* The LORD *is* righteous. And when the LORD saw that they humbled themselves, *i*the word of the LORD came to Shemaiah, saying, They have humbled themselves; *therefore* I will not destroy them, but I will grant them *1*some deliverance; and my wrath shall not be poured out upon Jerusalem by the hand of 8 Shishak. Nevertheless *k*they shall be his servants; that they may know *l*my service, and the service of the kingdoms of the 9 countries. ¶ *m*So Shishak king of Egypt came up against Jerusalem, and took away the treasures of the house of the LORD, and the treasures of the king's house; he took all: he carried 10 away also the shields of gold which Solomon had *n*made. Instead of which king Rehoboam made shields of brass, and committed *them* *o*to the hands of the chief of the guard, that kept the 11 entrance of the king's house. And when the king entered into the house of the LORD, the guard came and fetched them, and 12 brought them again into the guard chamber. And when he humbled himself, the wrath of the LORD turned from him, that he would not destroy *him* altogether: *2*and also in Judah things 13 went well. ¶ So king Rehoboam strengthened himself in Jerusalem, and reigned: for *p*Rehoboam *was* one and forty years old when he began to reign, and he reigned seventeen years in Jerusalem, *q*the city which the LORD had chosen out of all the 14 tribes of Israel, to put his name there. And his mother's name *was* Naamah an Ammonitess. And he did evil, because he 15 *3*prepared not his heart to seek the LORD. ¶ Now the acts of Rehoboam, first and last, *are* they not written in the *4*book of Shemaiah, the prophet, *r*and of Iddo the seer concerning genealogies? *s*And *there were* wars between Rehoboam and Jero-

d ch. 16. 8.

e ch. 11. 2.

f ch. 15. 2.

v Jam. 4. 10.
h Ex. 9. 27.
i 1 Kin. 21. 28, 29.

k See Isai. 26. 13.
l Deut. 28. 47, 48.
m 1 Kin. 14. 25, 26.

n 1 Kin. 10. 16, 17. ch. 9. 15, 16.
o 2 Sam. 8.18.

*p*1 Kin.14.21.

q ch. 6. 6.

r ch. 9. 29. & 13. 22.
s 1 Kin.14.30.

---

1 Or, *a little while.*
2 Or, *and yet in Judah there*
were good things: See Gen. 18. 24. & 1 Kin. 14. 13. ch. 19. 3.
3 Or, *fixed.*
4 Heb. *words.*

---

at the same time a force of 2000 chariots (cp. 1 K. xx. 1 note).

The Lubims or "Libyans" (Dan. xi. 43), were a people of Africa, distinct from the Egyptians and the Ethiopians dwelling in their immediate neighbourhood. They were called *Ribu* or *Libu* by the Egyptians. See Gen. x. 13.

Sukkiims] This name does not occur elsewhere. The LXX., who rendered the word "Troglodytes," regarded the Sukkiim probably as the "cave-dwellers" along the western shore of the Red Sea; but the conjecture that the word means "tent-dwellers" is plausible, and would point rather to a tribe of Arabs (Scenitæ).

4. See 1 K. xiv. 25 note.

6. *they said, The LORD is righteous*] *i.e.* they acknowledged the justice of the sentence which had gone forth against them (*v.* 5).

7. Cp. the repentance of Ahab (marg. ref.) and that of the Ninevites (Jonah iii. 5-10), which produced similar revocations of divine decrees that had been pronounced by the mouth of a Prophet.

some deliverance] Rather, "deliverance **for a short space**" (see marg.). Because of the repentance, the threat of *immediate* destruction was withdrawn; but the menace was still left impending, that the people might be the more moved to contrition and amendment.

8. *that they may know my service, and the service of the kingdom*] *i.e.* that they may contrast the light burthen of the theocracy with the heavy yoke of a foreign monarch.

14. *he prepared not his heart, &c.*] See margin. Rehoboam's sin was want of earnestness and consistency.

16 boam continually. And Rehoboam slept with his fathers, and

t 1Kin.14.31, *Abijam.*

was buried in the city of David: and *t*Abijah his son reigned in his stead.

a 1 Kin. 15. 1, &c.

b See ch. 11. 20.

Chap. 13. NOW *a*in the eighteenth year of king Jeroboam began 2 Abijah to reign over Judah. He reigned three years in Jerusalem. His mother's name also *was* *b*Michaiah the daughter of Uriel of Gibeah. ¶And there was war between Abijah and 3 Jeroboam. And Abijah ¹set the battle in array with an army of valiant men of war, *even* four hundred thousand chosen men: Jeroboam also set the battle in array against him with eight hundred thousand chosen men, *being* mighty men of valour.

c Josh.18.22.

4 ¶And Abijah stood up upon mount *c*Zemaraim, which *is* in mount Ephraim, and said, Hear me, thou Jeroboam, and all

d 2 Sam. 7. 12, 13, 16.

e Num.18.19.

f 1Kin.11.26. & 12. 20.

g Judg. 9. 4.

5 Israel; ought ye not to know that the LORD God of Israel *d*gave the kingdom over Israel to David for ever, *even* to him and to 6 his sons *e*by a covenant of salt? Yet Jeroboam the son of Nebat, the servant of Solomon the son of David, is risen up, and hath 7 *f*rebelled against his lord. And there are gathered unto him *g*vain men, the children of Belial, and have strengthened themselves against Rehoboam the son of Solomon, when Rehoboam was young and tenderhearted, and could not withstand them.

h 1Kin.12.28. & 14. 9. Hos. 8. 6. *i* ch.11.14,15. *k* Ex. 29. 35.

8 And now ye think to withstand the kingdom of the LORD in the hand of the sons of David; and ye *be* a great multitude, and there are with you golden calves, which Jeroboam *h*made you for 9 gods. *i*Have ye not cast out the priests of the LORD, the sons of Aaron, and the Levites, and have made you priests after the manner of the nations of *other* lands? *k*so that whosoever cometh ²to consecrate himself with a young bullock and seven rams, 10 *the same* may be a priest of *them that are* no gods. But as for us, the LORD *is* our God, and we have not forsaken him; and the priests, which minister unto the LORD, *are* the sons of Aaron,

l ch. 2. 4.

m Lev. 24. 6.

n Ex. 27. 20, 21. Lev. 24. 2, 3. *o* Num. 10. 8.

p Acts 5. 39.

11 and the Levites *wait* upon *their* business: *l*and they burn unto the LORD every morning and every evening burnt sacrifices and sweet incense: the *m*shewbread also *set they in order* upon the pure table; and the candlestick of gold with the lamps thereof, *n*to burn every evening: for we keep the charge of the 12 LORD our God; but ye have forsaken him. And, behold, God himself *is* with us for *our* captain, *o*and his priests with sounding trumpets to cry alarm against you. O children of Israel, *p*fight ye not against the LORD God of your fathers; for ye shall

¹ Heb. *bound together.*   ² Heb. *to fill his hand:* See Exod. 29. 1.   Lev. 8. 2.

XIII. The history of Abijah's reign is here related far more fully than in Kings (marg. ref.), especially as regards his war with Jeroboam.

2. See 1 K. xv. 2 note.

3. It has been proposed to change the numbers, here and in *v.* 17, into 40,000, 80,000, and 50,000 respectively — partly because these smaller numbers are found in many early editions of the Vulgate, but mainly because the larger ones are thought to be incredible. The numbers accord well, however, with the census of the people taken in the reign of David (1 Chr. xxi. 5), joined to the fact which the writer has related (xi. 13–17), of a considerable subsequent emigration from the northern kingdom into the southern one.

The total adult male population at the time of the census was 1,570,000. The total of the fighting men now is 1,200,000. This would allow for the aged and infirm 370,000, or nearly a fourth of the whole. And in *v.* 17, our author may be understood to mean that this was the entire Israelite loss in the course of the war, which probably continued through the whole reign of Abijah.

9. *seven rams*] "A bullock and *two* rams" was the offering which God had required at the original consecration of the sons of Aaron (Ex. xxix. 1; Lev. viii. 2). Jeroboam, for reasons of his own, enlarged the sacrifice, and required it at the consecration of every priest.

13 not prosper. ¶ But Jeroboam caused an ambushment to come about behind them: so they were before Judah, and the ambush-
14 ment *was* behind them. And when Judah looked back, behold, the battle *was* before and behind: and they cried unto the LORD,
15 and the priests sounded with the trumpets. Then the men of Judah gave a shout: and as the men of Judah shouted, it came to pass, that God *q*smote Jeroboam and all Israel before Abijah   *q* ch. 14. 12.
16 and Judah. And the children of Israel fled before Judah: and
17 God delivered them into their hand. And Abijah and his people slew them with a great slaughter: so there fell down slain of
18 Israel five hundred thousand chosen men. ¶ Thus the children of Israel were brought under at that time, and the children of Judah prevailed, *r*because they relied upon the LORD God of   *r* 1Chr. 5. 20.
19 their fathers. And Abijah pursued after Jeroboam, and took   Ps. 22. 5.
cities from him, Beth-el with the towns thereof, and Jeshanah with the towns thereof, and *s*Ephrain with the towns thereof.   *s* Josh. 15. 9.
20 Neither did Jeroboam recover strength again in the days of
21 Abijah: and the LORD *t*struck him, and *u*he died. But Abijah   *t*1Sam.25.38.
waxed mighty, and married fourteen wives, and begat twenty   *u*1Kin.14.20.
22 and two sons, and sixteen daughters. ¶ And the rest of the acts of Abijah, and his ways, and his sayings, *are* written in the
¹ story of the prophet *x*Iddo.   *x* ch. 12. 15.
CHAP. 14. SO Abijah slept with his fathers, and they buried him in the city of David: and *a*Asa his son reigned in his stead. In   *a* 1 Kin. 15. 8, &c.
2 his days the land was quiet ten years. And Asa did *that which*
3 *was* good and right in the eyes of the LORD his God: for he took away the altars of the strange *gods*, and *b*the high places, and   *b* See 1 Kin. 15. 14.
4 *c*brake down the ²images, *d*and cut down the groves: and com-   ch. 15. 17.
manded Judah to seek the LORD God of their fathers, and to do   *c* Ex. 34. 13.
5 the law and the commandment. Also he took away out of all   *d*1 Kin. 11. 7.
the cities of Judah the high places and the ³images: and the
6 kingdom was quiet before him. ¶ And he built fenced cities in Judah: for the land had rest, and he had no war in those years;
7 because the LORD had given him rest. Therefore he said unto Judah, Let us build these cities, and make about *them* walls, and towers, gates, and bars, *while* the land *is* yet before us;

¹ Or, *commentary.*   ² Heb. *statues.*   ³ Heb. *sun images.*

---

17. *slain*] The word means strictly "pierced," and will include both the killed and the wounded. It is translated "wounded" in Lam. ii. 12.

18. *brought under*] "Humbled" or "defeated," not reduced to subjection.

19. Jeshanah is probably identical with the "Isanas" of Josephus, where a battle took place in the war between Antigonus and Herod; but its situation cannot be fixed. For Ephrain, see Josh. xviii. 23 note.

20. Jeroboam's death was a judgment upon him for his sins. Chronologically speaking, his death is here out of place, for he outlived Abijah at least two years (cp. marg. ref. and 1 K. xv. 9); but the writer, not intending to recur to his history, is naturally led to carry it on to its termination.

XIV. 1. *Asa his son reigned*] If Rehoboam was (1 K. xii. 8 note) not more than

21 at his accession, Asa, when he mounted the throne, must have been a mere boy, not more than 10 or 11.

the land was quiet ten years] The great blow struck by Abijah (xiii. 15–19), his alliance with Syria (1 K. xv. 19), and the rapid succession of sovereigns in Israel during the earlier part of Asa's reign (do. *vv.* 25–33), would naturally prevent disturbance on the part of the northern kingdom. The tender age of Asa himself would be a bar to warlike enterprises on the part of Judah.

5. *images*] See marg., *sun-images*; and Lev. xxvi. 30 note.

7. *the land is yet before us*] i.e. "unoccupied by an enemy"—"the land is open to us to go where we please." Cp. Gen. xiii. 9. The fortification of the strongholds would be an act of rebellion against Egypt, and it might be expected that the Egyptians would endeavour to put a stop to it.

because we have sought the LORD our God, we have sought *him*, and he hath given us rest on every side. So they built and 8 prospered. And Asa had an army *of men* that bare targets and spears, out of Judah three hundred thousand; and out of Benjamin, that bare shields and drew bows, two hundred and four-
9 score thousand: all these *were* mighty men of valour. ¶ *e* And there came out against them Zerah the Ethiopian with an host of a thousand thousand, and three hundred chariots; and came
10 unto *f* Mareshah. Then Asa went out against him, and they set the battle in array in the valley of Zephathah at Mareshah.
11 And Asa *g* cried unto the LORD his God, and said, LORD, *it is* *h* nothing with thee to help, whether with many, or with them that have no power: help us, O LORD our God; for we rest on thee, and *i* in thy name we go against this multitude. O LORD,
12 thou *art* our God; let not *1* man prevail against thee. So the LORD *k* smote the Ethiopians before Asa, and before Judah; and
13 the Ethiopians fled. And Asa and the people that *were* with him pursued them unto *l* Gerar: and the Ethiopians were overthrown, that they could not recover themselves; for they were *2* destroyed before the LORD, and before his host; and they
14 carried away very much spoil. And they smote all the cities round about Gerar; for *m* the fear of the LORD came upon them: and they spoiled all the cities; for there was exceeding
15 much spoil in them. They smote also the tents of cattle, and carried away sheep and camels in abundance, and returned to Jerusalem.

e ch. 16. 8.

f Josh. 15.44.

g Ex. 14. 10.
ch. 13. 14.
Ps. 22. 5.
h 1Sam.14.6.
i 1Sam.17.45.
Prov. 18. 10.

k ch. 13. 15.

l Gen. 10. 19.
& 20. 1.

m Gen. 35. 5.
ch. 17. 10.

1 Or, *mortal man.*   *2* Heb. *broken.*

---

8. The men of Judah served as heavy-armed troops, while the Benjamites were light-armed. Their numbers accord well with those of xiii. 3. As the boundaries of Judah had been enlarged (xiii. 19), and as for ten years at least there had been no war (xiv. 1), the effective force had naturally increased. It was 400,000; it is now 580,000.

9. Zerah the Ethiopian is probably Usarken (Osorkon) II., the third king of Egypt after Shishak, according to the Egyptian monuments. Osorkon II. may have been by birth an Ethiopian, for he was the son-in-law, not the son, of the preceding monarch, and reigned in right of his wife. The object of the expedition would be to bring Judæa once more under the Egyptian yoke.

an host of a thousand thousand] This is the largest collected army of which we hear in Scripture; but it does not exceed the known numbers of other Oriental armies in ancient times. Darius Codomannus brought into the field at Arbela a force of 1,040,000; Xerxes crossed into Greece with certainly above a million of combatants.

10. The "valley of Zephathah"—not elsewhere mentioned—is probably the broad Wady which opens out from Mareshah (marg. ref.) in a north-westerly direction, leading into the great Philistine plain. Zerah, on the advance of Asa, drew off into the wider space of the Wady, where he could use his horsemen and chariots.

11. *it is nothing* &c.] *i.e.* "Thou canst as easily help the weak as the strong."

12. The defeat of Zerah is one of the most remarkable events in the history of the Jews. On no other occasion did they meet in the field and overcome the forces of either of the two great monarchies between which they were placed. It was seldom that they ventured to resist, unless behind walls. Shishak, Sennacherib, Esarhaddon, Nebuchadnezzar, were either unopposed or only opposed in this way. On the one other occasion on which they took the field—under Josiah against Necho—their boldness issued in a most disastrous defeat (2 Chr. xxxv. 20-24). Now, however, under Asa, they appear to have gained a complete victory over Egypt. The results which followed were most striking. The Southern power could not rally from the blow, and, for above three centuries made no further effort in this direction. Assyria, growing in strength, finally, under Sargon and Sennacherib, penetrated to Egypt itself. All fear of Egypt as an aggressive power ceased; and the Israelites learnt instead to lean upon the Pharaohs for support (2 K. xvii. 4, xviii. 21; Isai. xxx. 2-4, &c.). Friendly ties alone connected the two countries: and it was not till B.C. 609 that an Egyptian force again entered Palestine with a hostile intention.

14. *then smote all the cities round about Gerar*] The Philistines of these parts had,

Chap. 15. AND ^athe Spirit of God came upon Azariah the son of
2 Oded: and he went out ¹to meet Asa, and said unto him, Hear ye
me, Asa, and all Judah and Benjamin; ^bThe LORD *is* with you,
while ye be with him; and ^cif ye seek him, he will be found of
3 you; but ^dif ye forsake him, he will forsake you. Now ^efor a
long season Israel *hath been* without the true God, and without
4 ^fa teaching priest, and without law. But ^gwhen they in their
trouble did turn unto the LORD God of Israel, and sought him,
5 he was found of them. And ^hin those times *there was* no peace
to him that went out, nor to him that came in, but great vexa-
6 tions *were* upon all the inhabitants of the countries. ⁱAnd
nation was ²destroyed of nation, and city of city: for God did
7 vex them with all adversity. Be ye strong therefore, and let
not your hands be weak: for your work shall be rewarded.
8 ¶ And when Asa heard these words, and the prophecy of Oded
the prophet, he took courage, and put away the ³abominable
idols out of all the land of Judah and Benjamin, and out of the
cities ^kwhich he had taken from mount Ephraim, and renewed
the altar of the LORD, that *was* before the porch of the LORD.
9 And he gathered all Judah and Benjamin, and ^lthe strangers
with them out of Ephraim and Manasseh, and out of Simeon:
for they fell to him out of Israel in abundance, when they saw
10 that the LORD his God *was* with him. So they gathered themselves together at Jerusalem in the third month, in the fifteenth
11 year of the reign of Asa. ^mAnd they offered unto the LORD
⁴the same time, of ⁿthe spoil *which* they had brought, seven
12 hundred oxen and seven thousand sheep. And they ^oentered
into a covenant to seek the LORD God of their fathers with all
13 their heart and with all their soul; ^pthat whosoever would not
seek the LORD God of Israel ^qshould be put to death, whether
14 small or great, whether man or woman. And they sware unto
the LORD with a loud voice, and with shouting, and with trum-
15 pets, and with cornets. And all Judah rejoiced at the oath:

Margin references:
^a Num. 24. 2.
Judg. 3. 10.
ch. 20. 14.
& 24. 20.
^b Jam. 4. 8.
^c ver. 4, 15.
1 Chr. 28. 9.
ch. 33. 12. 13.
Jer. 29. 13.
Matt. 7. 7.
^d ch. 24. 20.
^e Hos. 3. 4
^f Lev. 10. 11.
^g Deut. 4. 29.
^h Judg. 5. 6.
ⁱ Matt. 24. 7.

^k ch. 13. 19.

^l ch. 11. 16.

^m ch. 14. 15.
ⁿ ch. 14. 13.
^o 2 Kin. 23 3.
ch. 34. 31.
Neh. 10. 29.
^p Ex. 22. 20.
^q Deut. 13.
5, 9, 15.

---

¹ Heb. *before Asa.*
² Heb. *beaten in pieces.*
³ Heb. *abominations.*
⁴ Heb. *in that day.*

---

it is probable, accompanied Zerah in his
expedition.

XV. 1. Oded is by some identified with
Iddo, the prophet and historian of the two
preceding reigns. In the Hebrew the two
names differ very slightly.

3. "Israel" here is used generally for the
whole people of God; and the reference is
especially to the many apostasies in the days
of the Judges, which were followed by repentance and deliverance.

6. The allusion is probably to the de-
structions recorded in Judges ix. 45, xx. 33–
48.

8. Some versions have "the prophecy of
Azariah the son of Oded," which is perhaps
the true reading.

9. *strangers* &c.] *i.e.* "Israelites of the
tribes of Ephraim and Manasseh." The
separation of the two kingdoms had made
their Israelite brethren "strangers," or
"foreigners," to Judah.

10. *in the third month*] *i.e.* the month

Sivan (Esth. viii. 9), corresponding with our
June.

11. The prevalence of the number seven
in the religious system of the Jews has been
often noticed. Seven bullocks and seven
rams were a common offering (Num. xxix.
32; 1 Chr. xv. 26; 2 Chr. xxix. 21; Job
xlii. 8; Ezek. xlv. 23). In the larger sacrifices, however, it is seldom that we find the
number seven at all prominent (cp. xxx.
24; xxxv. 7-9; 1 K. viii. 63).

12. Solemn renewals of the original Covenant which God made with their fathers in
the wilderness (Ex. xxiv. 3-8) occur from
time to time in the history of the Jews,
following upon intervals of apostasy. This
renewal in the reign of Asa is the first on
record. The next falls three hundred years
later in the reign of Josiah. There is a
third in the time of Nehemiah (see marg.
reff.). On such occasions, the people bound
themselves by a solemn oath to observe all
the directions of the Law, and called down
God's curse upon them if they forsook it.

r ver. 2.

s 1Kin.15.13.

t ch. 14. 3, 5.
1 Kin. 15. 14,
&c.

a 1 Kin. 15.
17, &c.
From the
rending of
the ten
tribes from
Judah, over
which Asa
was now
king.
b ch. 15. 9.

c 1 Kin. 16. 1.
ch. 19. 2.
d Isai. 31. 1.
Jer. 17. 5.
e ch. 14. 9.

for they had sworn with all their heart, and ʳsought him with their whole desire; and he was found of them: and the LORD 16 gave them rest round about. ¶ And also *concerning* ˢMaachah the ¹mother of Asa the king, he removed her from *being* queen, because she had made an ²idol in a grove: and Asa cut down her idol, and stamped *it*, and burnt *it* at the brook Kidron. 17 But ᵗthe high places were not taken away out of Israel: never- 18 theless the heart of Asa was perfect all his days. And he brought into the house of God the things that his father had dedicated, and that he himself had dedicated, silver, and gold, and vessels. 19 And there was no *more* war unto the five and thirtieth year of the reign of Asa.

CHAP. 16. IN the six and thirtieth year of the reign of Asa ᵃBaasha king of Israel came up against Judah, and built Ramah, ᵇto the intent that he might let none go out or come in to Asa king 2 of Judah. Then Asa brought out silver and gold out of the treasures of the house of the LORD and of the king's house, and sent to Ben-hadad king of Syria, that dwelt at ³Damascus, say- 3 ing, *There is* a league between me and thee, as *there was* between my father and thy father: behold, I have sent thee silver and gold; go, break thy league with Baasha king of Israel, that he 4 may depart from me. And Ben-hadad hearkened unto king Asa, and sent the captains of ⁴his armies against the cities of Israel; and they smote Ijon, and Dan, and Abel-maim, and all 5 the store cities of Naphtali. And it came to pass, when Baasha heard *it*, that he left off building of Ramah, and let his work 6 cease. Then Asa the king took all Judah; and they carried away the stones of Ramah, and the timber thereof, wherewith Baasha was building; and he built therewith Geba and Mizpah. 7 And at that time ᶜHanani the seer came to Asa king of Judah, and said unto him, ᵈBecause thou hast relied on the king of Syria, and not relied on the LORD thy God, therefore is the host 8 of the king of Syria escaped out of thine hand. Were not ᵉthe

---

¹ That is, *grandmother*,   ² Heb. *horror*.   ⁴ Heb. *which were his*.
1 Kin. 15. 2, 10.   ³ Heb. *Darmesek*.

---

17. Comparing this verse with marg. reff., it would seem that in xiv. 3, 5 the intention and endeavours of the monarch are in the writer's mind, while here he is speaking of the practice of the people. However earnestly the most pious monarchs sought to root out the high-place worship, they failed of complete success. Cp. a similar discrepancy, to be similarly explained, in the history of Jehoshaphat (xvii. 6, and xx. 33).

the heart of Asa was perfect all his days] Not that Asa was sinless (see xvi. 2-10, 12); but that he was free from the sin of idolatry, and continued faithful to Jehovah all his life.

19. *the five and thirtieth year of the reign of Asa*] This cannot be reconciled with the chronology of Kings (1 K. xvi. 8): and the suggestion in the marg. implies the adoption of a mode of marking time unknown either to himself or any other Scriptural writer. It is supposed that the figures here and in xvi. 1 are corrupt, and that in both verses

"twentieth" should replace "thirtieth." The attack of Baasha would then have been made in the last year of Asa's reign; and ten years of peace would have followed Asa's victory over Zerah.

XVI. 1-6. This passage runs parallel with Kings (marg. ref.).

3. Cp. 1 K. xv. 19 note.

4. *Abel-maim*] Or, "Abel-beth-maachah" (1 K. xv. 20). It was one of the towns most exposed to attack when an invader entered Israel from the north, and was taken from Pekah by Tiglath-pileser (2 K. xv. 29). *store cities*] See 1 K. ix. 19 note.

7-10. The rebuke of Hanani and his imprisonment by Asa, omitted by the writer of Kings, are among the most important of the additions to Asa's history for which we are indebted to the author of Chronicles.

7. *escaped out of thine hand*] Hanani means, "Hadst thou been faithful, and opposed in arms the joint host of Israel and Syria, instead of bribing the Syrian king to desert to thy side, the entire host would

Ethiopians and ƒthe Lubims ¹a huge host, with very many chariots and horsemen? yet, because thou didst rely on the
9 LORD, he delivered them into thine hand. ᵍFor the eyes of the LORD run to and fro throughout the whole earth, ²to shew himself strong in the behalf of *them* whose heart *is* perfect toward him. Herein ʰthou hast done foolishly: therefore from hence-
10 forth ⁱthou shalt have wars. Then Asa was wroth with the seer, and ᵏput him in a prison house; for *he was* in a rage with him because of this *thing.* And Asa ³oppressed *some* of the
11 people the same time. ¶ⁱAnd, behold, the acts of Asa, first and last, lo, they *are* written in the book of the kings of Judah and
12 Israel. ¶And Asa in the thirty and ninth year of his reign was diseased in his feet, until his disease *was* exceeding *great:* yet in his disease he ᵐsought not to the LORD, but to the physicians.
13 ⁿAnd Asa slept with his fathers, and died in the one and fortieth
14 year of his reign. And they buried him in his own sepulchres, which he had ⁴made for himself in the city of David, and laid him in the bed which was filled ᵒwith sweet odours and divers kinds *of spices* prepared by the apothecaries' art: and they made ᵖa very great burning for him.

CHAP. 17. AND ᵃJehoshaphat his son reigned in his stead, and
2 strengthened himself against Israel. And he placed forces in all the fenced cities of Judah, and set garrisons in the land of Judah, and in the cities of Ephraim, ᵇwhich Asa his father had taken.
3 And the LORD was with Jehoshaphat, because he walked in the first ways ⁵of his father David, and sought not unto Baalim ;
4 but sought to the LORD God of his father, and walked in his
5 commandments, and not after ᶜthe doings of Israel. Therefore the LORD stablished the kingdom in his hand ; and all Judah
ᵈ⁶brought to Jehoshaphat presents ; ᵉand he had riches and
6 honour in abundance. And his heart ⁷was lifted up in the ways

ƒ ch. 12. 3.	
ᵍ Job 34. 21.	
Prov. 5. 21.	
& 15. 3.	
Jer. 16. 17.	
& 32. 19.	
Zech. 4. 10.	
ʰ 1 Sam. 13.	
13.	
ⁱ 1Kin.15.32.	
ᵏ ch. 18. 26.	
Jer. 20. 2.	
ⁱ 1 Kin.15.23.	
ᵐ Jer. 17. 5.	
ⁿ1Kin.15.24.	
ᵒ Gen. 50. 2.	
Mark 16. 1.	
John 19. 39,	
40.	
ᵖ ch. 21. 19.	
Jer. 34. 5.	
ᵃ1Kin.15.24.	
ᵇ ch. 15. 8.	
ᶜ 1Kin.12.28.	
ᵈ 1 Sam. 10,	
27.	
1 Kin. 10. 25.	
ᵉ 1Kin.10.27.	
ch. 18. 1.	

¹ Heb. *in abundance.*
² Or, *strongly to hold with them,* &c.
³ Heb. *crushed.*
⁴ Heb. *digged.*
⁵ Or, *of his father,* and
of David.
⁶ Heb. *gave.*
⁷ That is, *was encouraged.*

---

have been delivered into thy hand, as was Zerah's. But now it is escaped from thee. Thou hast lost a glorious opportunity."

9. *from henceforth thou shalt have wars*] As peace had been the reward of Asa's earlier faith (xiv. 5, xv. 5), so his want of faith was now to be punished by a period of war and disturbance.

10. *in a prison house*] Or, "in the stocks." Cp. 1 K. xxii. 26, 27.

12. *yet in his disease he sought not* &c.] Rather, "**and also in his disease** he sought not." Not only in his war with Baasha, but also when attacked by illness, Asa placed undue reliance upon the aid of man.

14. The explanation of the plural—" sepulchres "—will be seen in 1 K. xiii. 30 note.

The burning of spices in honour of a king at his funeral was customary (cp. marg. reff.).

XVII. 1. Jehoshaphat ascended the throne in the fourth year of Ahab (1 K. xxii. 41), probably after that monarch had contracted his alliance with the royal family

of Sidon, and before he was engaged in war with Syria. It was thus not unnatural that Jehoshaphat should begin his reign by strengthening himself against a possible attack on the part of his northern neighbour.

3. *the first ways of his father David*] The LXX. and several Hebrew MSS. omit "David," which has probably crept in from the margin ; for David's "first ways" are nowhere else contrasted with his later ways. The real meaning of the writer is, that Jehoshaphat followed the example set by his father Asa in his earlier years (xiv., xv.). *Baalim*] On the plural form, see 1 K. xviii. 18 note.

4. *the doings of Israel*] *i.e.* the specially idolatrous doings of the time—the introduction and establishment of the worship of Baal and the groves.

5. *presents*] *i.e.* "free-will offerings," in addition to the regular taxes. See 1 Sam. x. 27.

6. *his heart was lifted up*] This expression generally occurs in a bad sense (Deut. viii. 14; 2 Chr. xxvi. 16; Ps. cxxxi. 1; Prov.

f 1Kin.22 43.
ch. 15. 17.
& 19. 3.
& 20. 33.
v ch. 15. 3.

h ch. 35. 3.
Neh. 8. 7.

i Gen. 35. 5.

k 2 Sam. 8. 2.

l Judg.5.2,9.

m ver. 2.

of the LORD: moreover *f* he took away the high places and groves
7 out of Judah.   ¶ Also in the third year of his reign he sent to
his princes, *even* to Ben-hail, and to Obadiah, and to Zechariah, and
to Nethaneel, and to Michaiah, *v* to teach in the cities of Judah.
8 And with them *he sent* Levites, *even* Shemaiah, and Nethaniah,
and Zebadiah, and Asahel, and Shemiramoth, and Jehonathan,
and Adonijah, and Tobijah, and Tob-adonijah, Levites; and
9 with them Elishama and Jehoram, priests.   *h* And they taught
in Judah, and *had* the book of the law of the LORD with them,
and went about throughout all the cities of Judah, and taught
10 the people.   ¶ And *i* the fear of the LORD *l* fell upon all the
kingdoms of the lands that *were* round about Judah, so that they
11 made no war against Jehoshaphat.   Also *some* of the Philistines
k brought Jehoshaphat presents, and tribute silver; and the Arabians brought him flocks, seven thousand and seven hundred rams,
12 and seven thousand and seven hundred he goats.   And Jehoshaphat waxed great exceedingly; and he built in Judah *2* castles, and
13 cities of store.   And he had much business in the cities of Judah:
and the men of war, mighty men of valour, *were* in Jerusalem.
14 ¶ And these *are* the numbers of them according to the house of
their fathers: Of Judah, the captains of thousands; Adnah the
chief, and with him mighty men of valour three hundred thou-
15 sand.   And *3* next to him *was* Jehohanan the captain, and with
16 him two hundred and fourscore thousand.   And next him *was*
Amasiah the son of Zichri, *l* who willingly offered himself unto
the LORD; and with him two hundred thousand mighty men of
17 valour.   And of Benjamin; Eliada a mighty man of valour,
and with him armed men with bow and shield two hundred thou-
18 sand.   And next him *was* Jehozabad, and with him an hundred
19 and fourscore thousand ready prepared for the war.   These
waited on the king, beside *m* those whom the king put in the fenced
cities throughout all Judah.

---

1 Heb. *was.*   *2* Or, *palaces.*   *3* Heb. *at his hand.*

---

xviii. 12); but here it must be taken differently. The margin "was encouraged" expresses fairly the true meaning. He first
began by setting an example of faithfulness
to Jehovah. He then proceeded to use his
best endeavours to extirpate idolatry.

he took away the high places] Cp. xx. 33,
and see xv. 17 note.

7. The princes were not sent as teachers
themselves, but had the duty committed to
them of seeing that the people were taught.
The actual teachers were the priests and
Levites of *v.* 8.

9. There is no reasonable doubt that this
"book of the law" was the Pentateuch—
nearly, if not quite, in the shape in which
we now have it. Copies of the whole Law
were, no doubt, scarce; and therefore Jehoshaphat's commission took care to carry a
copy with them.

11. *some of the Philistines brought Jehoshaphat presents*] *i.e.* "some of the Philistines were among his tributaries." Cp. 2
Sam. viii. 2; 1 K. iv. 21.

tribute silver] Or, "much silver"—lit.
"silver of burthen."

the Arabians] The Arab tribes who bordered Judæa to the south and the south-
east paid Jehoshaphat a fixed tribute in
kind. Cp. 2 K. iii. 4 note.

14. *the captains of thousands; Adnah the
chief*] Lit. "princes of thousands, Adnah
the **prince.**" The writer does not mean that
Adnah (or Johohanan, *v.* 15) was in any
way superior to the other "princes," but
only that he was one of them.

three hundred thousand] This number, and
those which follow in *vv.* 15-18, have been
with good reason regarded as corrupt by
most critics. For—(1) They imply a mini-
mum population of 1480 to the square mile,
which is more than three times greater than
that of any country in the known world.
(2) They produce a total *just double* that of
the next largest estimate of the military
force of Judah, the 580,000 of xiv. 8. (3)
They are professedly a statement, not of the
whole military force, but of the force maintained *at Jerusalem* (*v.* 13; cp. *v.* 19). It is
probable that the original numbers have
been lost, and that the loss was supplied by
a scribe, who took xiv. 8 as his basis.

Chap. 18. NOW Jehoshaphat *a*had riches and honour in abund-
2 ance, and *b*joined affinity with Ahab. *c*And [1]after *certain* years
he went down to Ahab to Samaria. And Ahab killed sheep and
oxen for him in abundance, and for the people that *he had* with
him, and persuaded him to go up *with him* to Ramoth-gilead.
3 And Ahab king of Israel said unto Jehoshaphat king of Judah,
Wilt thou go with me to Ramoth-gilead? And he answered
him, I *am* as thou *art*, and my people as thy people; and *we will*
4 be with thee in the war. ¶ And Jehoshaphat said unto the king
of Israel, *d*Enquire, I pray thee, at the word of the LORD to day.
5 Therefore the king of Israel gathered together of prophets four
hundred men, and said unto them, Shall we go to Ramoth-gilead
to battle, or shall I forbear? And they said, Go up; for God will
6 deliver *it* into the king's hand. But Jehoshaphat said, *Is there*
not here a prophet of the LORD *e*besides, that we might enquire
7 of him? And the king of Israel said unto Jehoshaphat, *There*
is yet one man, by whom we may enquire of the LORD: but I
hate him; for he never prophesied good unto me, but always
evil: the same *is* Micaiah the son of Imla. And Jehoshaphat said,
8 Let not the king say so. And the king of Israel called for one
of *his* [3]officers, and said, [4]Fetch quickly Micaiah the son of Imla.
9 ¶ And the king of Israel and Jehoshaphat king of Judah sat
either of them on his throne, clothed in *their* robes, and they
sat in a [5]void place at the entering in of the gate of Samaria;
10 and all the prophets prophesied before him. And Zedekiah
the son of Chenaanah had made him horns of iron, and said,
Thus saith the LORD, With these thou shalt push Syria until
11 [6]they be consumed. And all the prophets prophesied so, saying,
Go up to Ramoth-gilead, and prosper: for the LORD shall deliver
12 *it* into the hand of the king. ¶ And the messenger that went
to call Micaiah spake to him, saying, Behold, the words of the
prophets *declare* good to the king [7]with one assent; let thy word
therefore, I pray thee, be like one of their's, and speak thou
13 good. And Micaiah said, *As* the LORD liveth, *e*even what my God
14 saith, that will I speak. And when he was come to the king,
the king said unto him, Micaiah, shall we go to Ramoth-gilead
to battle, or shall I forbear? And he said, Go ye up, and prosper,
15 and they shall be delivered into your hand. And the king said
to him, How many times shall I adjure thee that thou say
16 nothing but the truth to me in the name of the LORD? *Then
he said, I did see all Israel scattered upon the mountains, as
sheep that have no shepherd: and the LORD said, These have
no master; let them return *therefore* every man to his house
17 in peace. And the king of Israel said to Jehoshaphat, Did I
not tell thee *that* he would not prophesy good unto me, [8]but
18 evil? Again he said, Therefore hear the word of the LORD; I
saw the LORD sitting upon his throne, and all the host of heaven
19 standing on his right hand and *on* his left. And the LORD said,
Who shall entice Ahab king of Israel, that he may go up and
fall at Ramoth-gilead? And one spake saying after this manner,

a ch. 17. 5.
b 2 Kin. 8.18.
c 1 Kin. 22.
2, &c.

d 1 Sam. 23.
2, 4, 9.
2 Sam. 2. 1.

e Num. 22.
18, 20, 35.
& 23. 12, 26.
& 24. 13.
1 Kin. 22. 14.

---

[1] Heb. *at the end of years.*
[2] Heb. *yet,* or, *more.*
[3] Or, *eunuchs.*
[4] Heb. *Hasten.*
[5] Or, *floor.*
[6] Heb. thou *consume them.*
[7] Heb. *with one mouth.*
[8] Or, *but for evil?*

XVIII. The present chapter runs parallel with Kings, which it closely follows, only
adding a few touches.
  2. *after certain years*] In Jehoshaphat's

seventeenth year (1 K. xxii. 51), not less
than eight years after the marriage (marg.
ref. note).

20 and another saying after that manner. Then there came out a *f* spirit, and stood before the LORD, and said, I will entice him. 21 And the LORD said unto him, Wherewith? And he said, I will go out, and be a lying spirit in the mouth of all his prophets. And *the* LORD said, Thou shalt entice *him*, and thou shalt also 22 prevail: go out, and do *even* so. Now therefore, behold, *g* the LORD hath put a lying spirit in the mouth of these thy prophets, 23 and the LORD hath spoken evil against thee. ¶ Then Zedekiah the son of Chenaanah came near, and *h* smote Micaiah upon the cheek, and said, Which way went the Spirit of the LORD from 24 me to speak unto thee? And Micaiah said, Behold, thou shalt see on that day when thou shalt go [1]into [2]an inner chamber to 25 hide thyself. Then the king of Israel said, Take ye Micaiah, and carry him back to Amon the governor of the city, and to 26 Joash the king's son; and say, Thus saith the king, [i]Put this *fellow* in the prison, and feed him with bread of affliction and 27 with water of affliction, until I return in peace. And Micaiah said, If thou certainly return in peace, *then* hath not the LORD 28 spoken by me. And he said, Hearken, all ye people. ¶ So the king of Israel and Jehoshaphat the king of Judah went 29 up to Ramoth-gilead. And the king of Israel said unto Jehoshaphat, I will disguise myself, and will go to the battle; but put thou on thy robes. So the king of Israel disguised himself; 30 and they went to the battle. Now the king of Syria had commanded the captains of the chariots that *were* with him, saying, Fight ye not with small or great, save only with the king of 31 Israel. And it came to pass, when the captains of the chariots saw Jehoshaphat, that they said, It *is* the king of Israel. Therefore they compassed about him to fight: but Jehoshaphat cried out, and the LORD helped him; and God moved them *to depart* 32 from him. For it came to pass, that, when the captains of the chariots perceived that it was not the king of Israel, they turned 33 back again [3]from pursuing him. And a *certain* man drew a bow [4]at a venture, and smote the king of Israel [5]between the joints of the harness: therefore he said to his chariot man, Turn thine hand, that thou mayest carry me out of the host; 34 for I am [6]wounded. And the battle increased that day: howbeit the king of Israel stayed *himself* up in *his* chariot against the Syrians until the even: and about the time of the sun going down he died.

CHAP. 19. AND Jehoshaphat the king of Judah returned to his house 2 in peace to Jerusalem. And Jehu the son of Hanani *a* the seer

Marginal notes (left):
f Job 1. 6.
g Job 12. 16. Isai. 19. 14. Ezek. 14. 9.
h Jer. 20. 2. Mark 14. 65. Acts 23. 2.
i ch. 16. 10.
a 1 Sam. 9. 9.

---

[1] Or, *from chamber to chamber.*   [3] Heb. *from after him.*   *between the breast plate.*
[2] Heb. *a chamber in a chamber.*   [4] Heb. *in his simplicity.*   [6] Heb. *made sick.*
[5] Heb. *between the joints and*

---

31. *and the* LORD *helped him*, &c.] There is nothing correspondent to this passage in Kings. It is a pious reflection on the part of the author, who traces all deliverance to its real divine source.

XIX. This chapter is entirely additional to Kings, and of great interest. It deals with three matters only, (1) The rebuke addressed to Jehoshaphat by the Prophet Jehu (*vv.* 1-3), (2) Jehoshaphat's religious reformation (*v.* 4), and (3) his reform of the judicial system (*vv.* 5-11).

1. *Jehoshaphat...returned to his house in peace*] With the battle of Ramoth-Gilead, and the death of Ahab, the war came to an end. The combined attack of the two kings having failed, their troops had been withdrawn, and the enterprise in which they had joined relinquished. The Syrians, satisfied with their victory, did not press on the retreating foe, or carry the war into their enemies' country.

2. *Jehu...went out to meet him*] Cp. xv. 2. The monarch was therefore rebuked at the

went out to meet him, and said to king Jehoshaphat, Shouldest
thou help the ungodly, and ᵇlove them that hate the LORD?   ᵇ Ps. 139. 21.
3 therefore *is* ᶜwrath upon thee from before the LORD. Neverthe-   ᶜ ch. 32. 25.
less there are ᵈgood things found in thee, in that thou hast taken   ᵈ ch. 17. 4, 6.
away the groves out of the land, and hast ᵉprepared thine heart   Sec ch.12.12.
4 to seek God. ¶ And Jehoshaphat dwelt at Jerusalem: and ¹he   ᵉ ch. 30. 19.
went out again through the people from Beer-sheba to mount   Ezra 7. 10.
Ephraim, and brought them back unto the LORD God of their
5 fathers. And he set judges in the land throughout all the fenced
6 cities of Judah, city by city, and said to the judges, Take heed
what ye do: for ᶠye judge not for man, but for the LORD, ᵍwho   ᶠ Deut. 1. 17.
7 *is* with you ²in the judgment. Wherefore now let the fear of   ᵍ Ps. 82. 1.
the LORD be upon you; take heed and do *it :* for ʰthere *is* no   Eccles. 5. 8.
iniquity with the LORD our God, nor ⁱrespect of persons, nor   ʰ Deut. 32. 4.
8 taking of gifts.   ¶ Moreover in Jerusalem did Jehoshaphat ᵏset   Rom. 9. 14.
of the Levites, and *of* the priests, and of the chief of the fathers   ⁱ Deut.10.17.
of Israel, for the judgment of the LORD, and for controversies,   Job 34. 19.
9 when they returned to Jerusalem. And he charged them, saying,   Acts 10. 34.
Thus shall ye do ˡin the fear of the LORD, faithfully, and with a   Rom. 2. 11.
10 perfect heart.   ᵐAnd what cause soever shall come to you of   Gal. 2. 6.
your brethren that dwell in their cities, between blood and blood,   Eph. 6. 9.
between law and commandment, statutes and judgments, ye shall   Col. 3. 25.
even warn them that they trespass not against the LORD, and   1 Pet. 1. 17.
so ⁿwrath come upon ᵒyou, and upon your brethren: this do,   ᵏ Deut.16.18.
                                                                          ch. 17. 8.
                                                                          ˡ 2 Sam.23.3.
                                                                          ᵐ Deut. 17.
                                                                          8, &c.
                                                                          ⁿNum.16.46.
                                                                          ᵒEzek. 3. 18.

¹ Heb. *he returned and went out.*   ² Heb. *in the matter of judgment.*

---

earliest possible moment, and in the most
effective way, as he was entering his
capital at the head of his returning army.
Jehu, thirty-five years previously, had
worked in the northern kingdom, and prophesied against Baasha (1 K. xvi. 1-7), but
had now come to Jerusalem, as Prophet and
historian (cp. xx. 34).

shouldest thou help &c.] As a matter of
mere human policy, the conduct of Jehoshaphat in joining Ahab against the Syrians
was not only justifiable but wise and prudent. And the reasonings upon which such
a policy was founded would have been un-
exceptionable but for one circumstance.
Ahab was an idolater, and had introduced
into his kingdom a false religion of a new
and most degraded type. This should have
led Jehoshaphat to reject his alliance.
Military success could only come from the
blessing and protection of Jehovah, which
such an alliance, if persisted in, was sure to
forfeit.

4. Jehoshaphat, while declining to renounce the alliance with Israel (cp. 2 K. iii.
7 note), was careful to show that he had no
sympathy with idolatry, and was determined to keep his people, so far as he possibly could, free from it. He therefore personally set about a second reformation,
passing through the whole land, from the
extreme south to the extreme north (xiii.
19).

5. What exact change Jehoshaphat made
in the judicial system of Judah (Deut. xvi.

18; 1 Chr. xxiii. 4), it is impossible to determine. Probably he found corruption
widely spread (*v.* 7), and the magistrates in
some places tainted with the prevailing
idolatry. He therefore made a fresh appointment of judges throughout the whole
country; concentrating judicial authority
in the hands of a few, or creating superior
courts in the chief towns ("fenced cities"),
with a right of appeal to such courts from
the village judge.

8. The "fathers of Israel" are the heads
of families; the "chief of the fathers" are the
great patriarchal chiefs, the admitted heads
of great houses or clans. They were now
admitted to share in the judicial office
which seems in David's time to have been
confined to the Levites (1 Chr. xxiii. 4).

for the judgment of the LORD, *and for controversies*] By the former are meant disputed cases concerning the performance of
religious obligations. In "controversies"
are included all the ordinary causes, whether
criminal or civil.

when they returned to Jerusalem] Rather,
"**and** they returned to Jerusalem," a clause
which if detached from the previous words
and attached to *v.* 9, gives a satisfactory
sense.

10. The Jews who "dwelt in the cities,"
if dissatisfied with the decision given by
the provincial judges, might therefore remove the cause to Jerusalem, as to a court
of appeal.

11 and ye shall not trespass. And, behold, Amariah the chief

p 1Chr.23.30.
priest *is* over you *p* in all matters of the LORD ; and Zebadiah the
son of Ishmael, the ruler of the house of Judah, for all the
king's matters : also the Levites *shall be* officers before you.

q ch. 15. 2.
1 Deal courageously, and the LORD shall be *q* with the good.

CHAP. 20. IT came to pass after this also, *that* the children of
Moab, and the children of Ammon, and with them *other* beside
2 the Ammonites, came against Jehoshaphat to battle. Then
there came some that told Jehoshaphat, saying, There cometh a
great multitude against thee from beyond the sea on this side

a Gen. 14. 7.
b Josh.15.62.
c ch. 19. 3.
Syria ; and, behold, they *be a* in Hazazon-tamar, which *is b* En-
3 gedi. And Jehoshaphat feared, and set 2 himself to *c* seek the

d Ezra 8. 21.
Jer. 36. 9.
Jonah 3. 5.
4 LORD, and *d* proclaimed a fast throughout all Judah. And
Judah gathered themselves together, to ask *help* of the LORD :
even out of all the cities of Judah they came to seek the LORD.

5 And Jehoshaphat stood in the congregation of Judah and Jeru-

e Deut. 4. 39.
Josh. 2. 11.
1 Kin. 8. 23.
Matt. 6. 9.
f Ps. 47. 2, 8.
Dan. 4. 17,
25, 32.
g 1Chr.29.12.
Ps. 62. 11.
Matt. 6. 13.
h Gen. 17. 7.
Ex. 6. 7.
i Ps. 44. 2.
k Isai. 41. 8.
Jam. 2. 23.
l 1 Kin. 8.
33, 37.
ch. 6. 28, 29,
30.
m ch. 6. 20.
n Deut. 2. 4,
9, 19.
o Num.20.21.
p Ps. 83. 12.
6 salem, in the house of the LORD, before the new court, and
said, O LORD God of our fathers, *art* not thou *e* God in heaven ?
and *f* rulest *not* thou over all the kingdoms of the heathen ? and
g in thine hand *is there not* power and might, so that none is
7 able to withstand thee ? *Art* not thou *h* our God, 3 *who i* didst
drive out the inhabitants of this land before thy people Israel,
8 and gavest it to the seed of Abraham *k* thy friend for ever ? And
they dwelt therein, and have built thee a sanctuary therein for
9 thy name, saying, *l* If, *when* evil cometh upon us, *as* the sword,
judgment, or pestilence, or famine, we stand before this house,
and in thy presence, (for thy *m* name *is* in this house,) and cry
10 unto thee in our affliction, then thou wilt hear and help. And
now, behold, the children of Ammon and Moab and mount Seir,
whom thou *n* wouldest not let Israel invade, when they came out
of the land of Egypt, but *o* they turned from them, and destroyed
11 them not ; behold, *I say, how* they reward us, *p* to come to cast

1 Heb. *Take courage and do.*   2 Heb. *his face.*   3 Heb. *thou.*

---

11. In religious causes, Amariah, the
High-Priest, was to preside over the court ;
in civil or criminal causes, Zebadiah was to
be president. And to Levites, other than the
judges, he assigned the subordinate offices
about the court.

XX. The narrative in *vv.* 1-30 is entirely
additional to Kings ; in *vv.* 31-37, it runs
parallel with 1 K. xxii. 41-49.

1. The present Hebrew (and English) text
mentions the Ammonites twice over. Hence
some adopt a different reading and translate
" the children of Ammon, and with them
certain of the Maonites," &c. Cp. *v.* 10 ;
Judg. x. 12 ; 1 Chr. iv. 41 notes.

2. Translate, " from beyond the sea, **from
Edom.**" The " sea " intended is, of course,
the Dead Sea. "Syria" (Aram) is probably a mistake of a copyist for "Edom"
(cp. 2 Sam. viii. 12 note).

On Engedi, see 1 Sam. xxiii. 29 note.

3. General fasts had been previously observed by the Israelites (*e.g.* Judg. xx. 26 ;
1 Sam. vii. 6) ; but we do not hear of any
fast having been "proclaimed" by authority before this.

5. *the new court*] In Solomon's Temple

there were two courts. One of these had
probably been renovated by Jehoshaphat
or by his father, Asa (xv. 8), and was known
as "the new court."

6-9. Jehoshaphat's appeal is threefold—
(1) to God omnipotent (*v.* 6) ; (2) to " our
God ; " (3) the God especially *of this house*
the Temple.

7. *Abraham thy friend*] Historically, this
is the first use of this remarkable expression,
afterwards repeated (marg. reff.). The
ground of the expression is to be found principally in Gen. xviii. 23-33, where Abraham
spoke with God as a man with his friend
(cp. Ex. xxxiii. 11).

8, 9. The appeal recalls Solomon's prayer
(marg. reff.), which God had formally accepted by sending down fire from heaven to
consume the accompanying offering.

10. The Maonites of *v.* 1 are here, and in
vv. 22, 23, called the "children" or inhabitants " of mount Seir." Hence we may
gather that they were a tribe of Edomites,
the inhabitants, probably, of a city Maon
(now *Ma'an*) on the eastern side of the
Waây el-Arabah.

us out of thy possession, which thou hast given us to inherit.
12 O our God, wilt thou not *q*judge them? for we have no might
against this great company that cometh against us; neither
13 know we what to do: but *r*our eyes *are* upon thee. And all
Judah stood before the LORD, with their little ones, their wives,
14 and their children. ¶ Then upon Jahaziel the son of Zechariah,
the son of Benaiah, the son of Jeiel, the son of Mattaniah, a
Levite of the sons of Asaph, *s*came the Spirit of the LORD in
15 the midst of the congregation; and he said, Hearken ye, all
Judah, and ye inhabitants of Jerusalem, and thou king Jehoshaphat, Thus saith the LORD unto you, *t*Be not afraid nor
dismayed by reason of this great multitude; for the battle *is*
16 not your's, but God's. To morrow go ye down against them:
behold, they come up by the ¹cliff of Ziz; and ye shall find
them at the end of the ²brook, before the wilderness of Jeruel.
17 *u*Ye shall not *need* to fight in this *battle:* set yourselves, stand ye
still, and see the salvation of the LORD with you, O Judah and
Jerusalem: fear not, nor be dismayed; to morrow go out
18 against them: *x*for the LORD *will be* with you. And Jehoshaphat *y*bowed his head with *his* face to the ground: and all
Judah and the inhabitants of Jerusalem fell before the LORD,
19 worshipping the LORD. And the Levites, of the children of the
Kohathites, and of the children of the Korhites, stood up to
20 praise the LORD God of Israel with a loud voice on high. ¶ And
they rose early in the morning, and went forth into the wilderness of Tekoa: and as they went forth, Jehoshaphat stood and
said, Hear me, O Judah, and ye inhabitants of Jerusalem;
*z*Believe in the LORD your God, so shall ye be established;
21 believe his prophets, so shall ye prosper. And when he had
consulted with the people, he appointed singers unto the LORD,
*a*and ³that should praise the beauty of holiness, as they went
out before the army, and to say, *b*Praise the LORD; *c*for his
22 mercy *endureth* for ever. ⁴And when they began ⁵to sing and
to praise, *d*the LORD set ambushments against the children of
Ammon, Moab, and mount Seir, which were come against
23 Judah; and ⁶they were smitten. For the children of Ammon
and Moab stood up against the inhabitants of mount Seir, utterly
to slay and destroy *them:* and when they had made an end of
the inhabitants of Seir, every one helped ⁷to destroy another.

¹ Heb. *ascent.*
² Or, *valley.*
³ Heb. *praisers.*
⁴ Heb. *And in the time that they, &c.*
⁵ Heb. *in singing and praise.*
⁶ Or, *they smote one another.*
⁷ Heb. *for the destruction.*

14. "Mattaniah" is thought to be a corrupt reading for "Nethaniah," who is mentioned among the sons of Asaph in 1 Chr. xxv. 2, 12.

15-17. The Prophet uses words familiar to the people, and connected with several great deliverances (see marg. reff.).

16. By the "cliff (or, rather,—as in marg.—ascent) of Ziz," we must understand the mountain path which leads up from Engedi across the elevated tract still known as *El-Husasah,* in the direction of Tekoa (*v.* 20). *at the end of the brook*] Rather, "at the end of the gulley," or dry torrent-course. No name like Jeruel has been as yet found in this district.

20. Tekoa (2 Sam. xiv. 2 note) lay on the borders of the desert which skirts the highlands of Judæa towards the east. The town was built on a hill of a considerable height.

21. *praise the beauty of holiness*] Some render, "in the beauty of holiness"—*i.e.* in rich apparel and ornaments suitable to a holy occasion. Cp. Ps. xxix. 2.

22. *the LORD set ambushments*] These liers in wait have been regarded as Angels employed by God to confuse the host and cause its destruction, so that the Moabites and Ammonites first united to destroy the Edomites, and then turned upon each other.

24 And when Judah came toward the watch tower in the wilderness, they looked unto the multitude, and, behold, they *were*
25 dead bodies fallen to the earth, and ¹none escaped. And when Jehoshaphat and his people came to take away the spoil of them, they found among them in abundance both riches with the dead bodies, and precious jewels, which they stripped off for themselves, more than they could carry away : and they were
26 three days in gathering of the spoil, it was so much. And on the fourth day they assembled themselves in the valley of ²Berachah ; for there they blessed the LORD : therefore the name of the same place was called, The valley of Berachah, unto this
27 day. ¶ Then they returned, every man of Judah and Jerusalem, and Jehoshaphat in the ³forefront of them, to go again to Jeru-

e Neh. 12. 43.

salem with joy ; for the LORD had *e*made them to rejoice over
28 their enemies. And they came to Jerusalem with psalteries

f ch. 17. 10.

29 and harps and trumpets unto the house of the LORD. And *f*the fear of God was on all the kingdoms of *those* countries, when they had heard that the LORD fought against the enemies of

g ch. 15. 15.
Job 34. 29.
h 1 Kin. 22.
41, &c.

30 Israel. So the realm of Jehoshaphat was quiet : for his *g*God
31 gave him rest round about. ¶ *h*And Jehoshaphat reigned over Judah : *he was* thirty and five years old when he began to reign, and he reigned twenty and five years in Jerusalem. And his
32 mother's name *was* Azubah the daughter of Shilhi. And he walked in the way of Asa his father, and departed not from it,
33 doing *that which was* right in the sight of the LORD. Howbeit

i See ch.17.6.
k ch. 12. 14.
& 19. 3.
l 1 Kin. 16.
1, 7.

*i*the high places were not taken away : for as yet the people had not *k*prepared their hearts unto the God of their fathers.
34 ¶ Now the rest of the acts of Jehoshaphat, first and last, behold, they *are* written in the ⁴book of Jehu the son of Hanani, *l*who

m 1 Kin. 22.
48, 49.

35 ⁵*is* mentioned in the book of the kings of Israel. ¶ And after this *m*did Jehoshaphat king of Judah join himself with Ahaziah
36 king of Israel, who did very wickedly : ⁶and he joined himself with him to make ships to go to Tarshish : and they made the
37 ships in Ezion-gaber. Then Eliezer the son of Dodavah of Mareshah prophesied against Jehoshaphat, saying, Because thou hast joined thyself with Ahaziah, the LORD hath broken thy

n 1Kin.22.48.
o ch. 9. 21.

works. *n*And the ships were broken, that they were not able to go *o*to Tarshish.

a 1Kin.22.50.

CHAP. 21. NOW *a*Jehoshaphat slept with his fathers, and was buried with his fathers in the city of David. And Jehoram his

---

¹ Heb. *there was not an escaping.*
² That is, *Blessing.*
³ Heb. *head.*
⁴ Heb. *words.*
⁵ Heb. *was made to ascend.*
⁶ At first Jehoshaphat was unwilling, 1 Kin. 22. 49.

---

24. The march of Judah from Jerusalem would take five or six hours. By the time they reached the watch-towers in the wilderness of Jeruel all was over.

25. *riches with the dead bodies*] Several MSS. give another reading :—"riches, **and garments.**"

26. *the valley of Berachah*] Probably, the *Wady Bereikut*, which lies at a short distance from Tekoa towards the north-west.

33. The latter clause of this verse helps to reconcile the first clause with the statement that Jehoshaphat "took away the high places" (see xv. 17 note).

34. *who is mentioned* &c.] Words which are now generally thought to mean "whose

work was inserted into the Book of the Kings."

of Israel] "Israel" is probably used here inexactly for "Judah" (cp. xii. 6, xxi. 2, 4).

35. *after this*] Jehoshaphat's history had been formally completed (*v.* 34). Consequently we can lay no stress on the note of time contained in the words "after this," which are detached from the context whereto they originally referred. On the history (*vv.* 35–37) see marg. reff. and notes.

XXI. **1.** Jehoram's *sole* reign now began. (See 2 K. viii. 16 note). His eight years (*v.* 5) must be counted from the time of his association, in his father's 23rd year.

2 son ¹reigned in his stead. And he had brethren the sons of
Jehoshaphat, Azariah, and Jehiel, and Zechariah, and Azariah,
and Michael, and Shephatiah: all these *were* the sons of Jehosh-
3 aphat king of Israel. And their father gave them great gifts
of silver, and of gold, and of precious things, with fenced cities
in Judah: but the kingdom gave he to ²Jehoram; because he
4 *was* the firstborn. Now when Jehoram was risen up to the
kingdom of his father, he strengthened himself, and slew all his
brethren with the sword, and *divers* also of the princes of Israel.
5 ¶ ᵇJehoram *was* thirty and two years old when he began to
6 reign, and he reigned eight years in Jerusalem. And he walked
in the way of the kings of Israel, like as did the house of Ahab:
for he had the daughter of ᶜAhab to wife: and he wrought *that*
7 *which was* evil in the eyes of the LORD. Howbeit the LORD
would not destroy the house of David, because of the covenant
that he had made with David, and as he promised to give a
8 ³light to him and to his ᵈsons for ever. ¶ ᵉIn his days the
Edomites revolted from under the ⁴dominion of Judah, and
9 made themselves a king. Then Jehoram went forth with his
princes, and all his chariots with him: and he rose up by night,
and smote the Edomites which compassed him in, and the cap-
10 tains of the chariots. So the Edomites revolted from under the
hand of Judah unto this day. The same time *also* did Libnah
revolt from under his hand; because he had forsaken the LORD
11 God of his fathers. ¶ Moreover he made high places in the mountains of Judah, and caused the inhabitants of Jerusalem to
12 ᶠcommit fornication, and compelled Judah *thereto*. ¶ And there
came a writing to him from Elijah the prophet, saying, Thus
saith the LORD God of David thy father, Because thou hast not
walked in the ways of Jehoshaphat thy father, nor in the ways
13 of Asa king of Judah, but hast walked in the way of the kings
of Israel, and hast ᵍmade Judah and the inhabitants of Jeru-

b In consort,
2 Kin. 8. 17,
&c.

c ch. 22. 2.

d 2 Sam. 7.
12, 13.
1 Kin. 11. 36.
2 Kin. 8. 19.
Ps. 132. 11,
&c.
e 2 Kin. 8.
20, &c.

f Lev. 17. 7.
& 20. 5.
ver. 13.

g ver. 11.

---

¹ Alone.   of the kingdom with his   ³ Heb. *lamp*, or, *candle*.
² Jehoram made partner   father, 2 Kin. 8. 16.   ⁴ Heb. *hand*.

---

3. Jehoshaphat departed from Rehoboam's policy (xi. 23 note), actually making
over to his sons the "fenced cities" in
which they dwelt. This, it is probable, provoked the jealousy of Jehoram, and induced him to put them to death (*v.* 4).
because he was the firstborn] Cp. Deut. xxi.
15-17. Exceptions to this rule in the northern and southern kingdoms are Solomon,
where divine appointment superseded the
natural order, Abijah 'xi. 22 note), and Jehoahaz (2 K. xxiii. 30 note).
4. The execution of several "princes of
Israel" (*i.e.* of Judah; see xx. 34 note) implies that Jehoram's brothers found supporters among the chief men of the country,
and that Jehoram's sole sovereignty was
not established without a struggle.
11. See 2 K. viii. 18. The writer of Kings
only tells us in general terms that Jehoram
"did evil in the sight of the Lord," and
"walked in the way of the house of Ahab."
Here, in *vv.* 11 and 13, we have particulars
of his idolatry. Jehoram, it seems, seduced
by the evil influence of his wife—Athaliah,

the daughter of Ahab—permitted the introduction of Baal-worship, idolatrous
altars in various high places, groves
(Asherahs), images, and pillars; the people
were not only allowed, but compelled to
take part in the new rites. "To commit
fornication" is a common metaphor, signifying idolatry or spiritual unfaithfulness
(cp. 2 K. ix. 22 note).
12. This is the only notice which we have
of Elijah in Chronicles. As a Prophet of the
northern kingdom, he engaged but slightly
the attention of the historian of the southern one. The notice shows that Elijah did
not confine his attention to the affairs of his
own state, but strove to check the progress
of idolatry in Judah. And it proves that
he was alive after the death of Jehoshaphat
(*v.* 13); a fact bearing (1) upon the chronological order of 2 K. ii. 1 (see note), and (2)
showing that Elisha, who prophesied in the
time of Jehoshaphat (2 K. iii. 11-19) commenced his public ministry before his master's translation.

h Ex. 34. 15.
Deut. 31. 16.
i 1 Kin. 16.
31—33.
2 Kin. 9. 22.
k ver. 4.
l ver. 18. 19.

m 1 Kin. 11.
14, 23.

n ch. 24. 7.

o ver. 15.

p ch. 16. 14.

salem to *h* go a whoring, like to the *i* whoredoms of the house of Ahab, and also hast *k* slain thy brethren of thy father's house, 14 *which were* better than thyself: behold, with *1* a great plague will the LORD smite thy people, and thy children, and thy wives, 15 and all thy goods: and thou *shalt have* great sickness by *l* disease of thy bowels, until thy bowels fall out by reason of the 16 sickness day by day.. ¶ Moreover the LORD *m* stirred up against Jehoram the spirit of the Philistines, and of the Arabians, that 17 *were* near the Ethiopians: and they came up into Judah, and brake into it, and *2* carried away all the substance that was found in the king's house, and *n* his sons also, and his wives; so that there was never a son left him, save *3* Jehoahaz, the youngest of his 18 sons. ¶ *4* And after all this the LORD smote him *o* in his bowels 19 with an incurable disease. And it came to pass, that in process of time, after the end of two years, his bowels fell out by reason of his sickness: so he died of sore diseases. And his people made 20 no burning for him, like *p* the burning of his fathers. Thirty and two years old was he when he began to reign, and he reigned in Jerusalem eight years, and departed *5* without being desired. Howbeit they buried him in the city of David, but not in the sepulchres of the kings.

a 2 Kin. 8.
24, &c.
See ch. 21.
17.
ver. 6.
b ch. 21. 17.
c See 2 Kin.
8. 26.
d ch. 21. 6.

CHAP. 22. AND the inhabitants of Jerusalem made *a* Ahaziah his youngest son king in his stead: for the band of men that came with the Arabians to the camp had slain all the *b* eldest. So 2 Ahaziah the son of Jehoram king of Judah reigned. *c* Forty and two years old *was* Ahaziah when he began to reign, and he reigned one year in Jerusalem. His mother's name also *was* 3 *d* Athaliah the daughter of Omri. He also walked in the ways of the house of Ahab: for his mother was his counsellor to do 4 wickedly. Wherefore he did evil in the sight of the LORD like the house of Ahab: for they were his counsellors after the death 5 of his father to his destruction. He walked also after their

e 2 Kin. 8.
28, &c.

f 2 Kin. 9. 15.

counsel, and *e* went with Jehoram the son of Ahab king of Israel to war against Hazael king of Syria at Ramoth-gilead: and the 6 Syrians smote Joram. *f* And he returned to be healed in Jezreel because of the wounds *6* which were given him at Ramah, when he fought with Hazael king of Syria. ¶ And *7* Azariah the son of Jehoram king of Judah went down to see Jehoram the son of 7 Ahab at Jezreel, because he was sick. And the *8* destruction of

g Judg. 14. 4.
1 Kin. 12. 15.
ch. 10. 15.
h 2 Kin. 9. 21.
i 2 Kin. 9. 6, 7.

Ahaziah *g* was of God by coming to Joram: for when he was come, he *h* went out with Jehoram against Jehu the son of Nimshi, *i* whom the LORD had anointed to cut off the house of

---

1 Heb. *a great stroke.*
2 Heb. *carried captive:* See ch. 22. 1.
3 Or, *Ahaziah,* ch. 22. 1, or, *Azariah,* ch. 22. 6.
4 His son, *Ahaziah Prorex,* 2 Kin. 9. 29, soon after.
5 Heb. *without desire,* Jer. 22. 18.
6 Heb. *wherewith they*
wounded him.
7 Otherwise called *Ahaziah,* ver. 1. and *Jehoahaz,* ch. 21. 17.
8 Heb. *treading down.*

---

14. The fulfilment of the threat is given in *vv.* 16, 17.

16. *the Arabians, that were near the Ethiopians*] Probably Joktanian Arabs from the neighbourhood of the Cushites. Southern Arabia was originally occupied by Cushites, or Ethiopians (Gen. x. 7), whose descendants still exist in a remnant of the Himyaritic Arabs.

17. *Jehoahaz*] The writer of Chronicles calls him indifferently Jehoahaz and Aha-

ziah, which are equivalent names (2 K. viii. 24 note).

20. *not in the sepulchres of the kings*] Compare the similar treatment of Joash (xxiv. 25) and Ahaz (xxviii. 27).

XXII. 2. For 42 read 22 (marg. ref.). Ahaziah's father, Jehoram, was but forty when he died (xxi. 20).

7. *the destruction of Ahaziah was of God*] *i.e.* his untimely end was a judgment upon him for his idolatry.

8 Ahab. And it came to pass, that, when Jehu was [k]executing judgment upon the house of Ahab, and [l]found the princes of Judah, and the sons of the brethren of Ahaziah, that ministered
9 to Ahaziah, he slew them. [m]And he sought Ahaziah: and they caught him, (for he was hid in Samaria,) and brought him to Jehu: and when they had slain him, they buried him: Because, said they, he *is* the son of Jehoshaphat, who [n]sought the LORD with all his heart. So the house of Ahaziah had no power to
10 keep still the kingdom. ¶ [o]But when Athaliah the mother of Ahaziah saw that her son was dead, she arose and destroyed
11 all the seed royal of the house of Judah. But [p]Jehoshabeath, the daughter of the king, took Joash the son of Ahaziah, and stole him from among the king's sons that were slain, and put him and his nurse in a bedchamber. So Jehoshabeath, the daughter of king Jehoram, the wife of Jehoiada the priest, (for she was the sister of Ahaziah,) hid him from Athaliah, so that
12 she slew him not. And he was with them hid in the house of God six years: and Athaliah reigned over the land.

CHAP. 23. AND [a]in the seventh year Jehoiada strengthened himself, and took the captains of hundreds, Azariah the son of Jeroham, and Ishmael the son of Jehohanan, and Azariah the son of Obed, and Maaseiah the son of Adaiah, and Elishaphat
2 the son of Zichri, into covenant with him. And they went about in Judah, and gathered the Levites out of all the cities of Judah, and the chief of the fathers of Israel, and they came to Jerusa-
3 lem. And all the congregation made a covenant with the king in the house of God. And he said unto them, Behold, the king's son shall reign, as the LORD hath [b]said of the sons of David.
4 This *is* the thing that ye shall do; A third part of you [c]entering on the sabbath, of the priests and of the Levites, *shall be* porters
5 of the [1]doors; and a third part *shall be* at the king's house; and a third part at the gate of the foundation: and all the people
6 *shall be* in the courts of the house of the LORD. But let none come into the house of the LORD, save the priests, and [d]they that minister of the Levites; they shall go in, for they *are* holy:

[1] Heb. *thresholds.*

Margin references:
k 2 Kin. 10. 10, 11.
l 2 Kin. 10. 13. 14.
m 2 Kin. 9. 27, at *Megiddo* in the kingdom of *Samaria.*
n ch. 17. 4.
o 2 Kin. 11. 1, &c.
p 2 Kin. 11. 2, *Jehosheba.*
a 2 Kin. 11. 4, &c.
b 2 Sam. 7. 12. 1 Kin. 2. 4. & 9. 5. ch. 6. 16. & 7. 18. & 21. 7.
c 1 Chr. 9. 25.
d 1 Chr. 23. 28, 29.

9. Cp. marg. ref. Ahaziah after remaining a while at Megiddo, removed to Samaria, where his wounds could be better cared for and concealment might be easier; Jehu's emissaries discovered him there; they took him to Jehu, who happened at the time to be at Megiddo; and then and there Jehu put him to death. The narrative here is therefore supplementary to that of 2 Kings, and finds its proper place between the clause, "He fled to Megiddo," and the words "and died there."
and when they had slain him, they buried him] Jehu's emissaries slew him but allowed his servants to bury him (see 2 K. ix. 28).
no power &c.] As Ahaziah was but twenty-three at his death (*v.* 2 note), he had no grown-up son to take the crown.
10-12. Cp. marg. ref. and notes.
XXIII. Cp. the history in Kings (marg. ref.). Both accounts were probably drawn from a common source. The writer of Kings treated the points of civil and historic importance, the later author of Chronicles collected the notices of the part taken in the transactions by the sacred order to which he probably belonged.
1. The five names do not occur in Kings; only, and incidentally, the five divisions of the royal guard (2 K. xi. 5 note).
2. Jehoiada was unwilling to trust the success of the revolution wholly and entirely to the royal body-guard. Accordingly, the captains collected from the cities of Judah a strong body of Levites and the chief of the fathers of Israel (*i.e.* "Judah," see xx. 34 note) who were brought up to Jerusalem.
3. By "all the congregation" here is meant the persons referred to in *r.* 2.
4. The writer of Chronicles relates the orders that were given to the Levites, the author of Kings those received by the royal body-guard (2 K. xi. 5 note).
6. *keep the watch of the LORD*] *i.e.* guard

7 but all the people shall keep the watch of the LORD. And the Levites shall compass the king round about, every man with his weapons in his hand; and whosoever *else* cometh into the house, he shall be put to death: but be ye with the king when he 8 cometh in, and when he goeth out. ¶ So the Levites and all Judah did according to all things that Jehoiada the priest had commanded, and took every man his men that were to come in on the sabbath, with them that were to go *out* on the sabbath:

e See 1 Chr. 24 & 25.

9 for Jehoiada the priest dismissed not *e*the courses. Moreover Jehoiada the priest delivered to the captains of hundreds spears, and bucklers, and shields, that *had been* king David's, which 10 *were* in the house of God. And he set all the people, every man having his weapon in his hand, from the right ¹side of the ²temple to the left side of the temple, along by the altar and the temple, 11 by the king round about. Then they brought out the king's

f Deut.17.18.

son, and put upon him the crown, and *f gave him* the testimony, and made him king. And Jehoiada and his sons anointed him, 12 and said, ³God save the king. Now when Athaliah heard the noise of the people running and praising the king, she came to 13 the people into the house of the LORD: and she looked, and, behold, the king stood at his pillar at the entering in, and the princes and the trumpets by the king: and all the people of the land rejoiced, and sounded with trumpets, also the singers with

g 1 Chr. 25.8.

instruments of musick, and *g*such as taught to sing praise. Then Athaliah rent her clothes, and said, ⁴Treason, Treason. 14 Then Jehoiada the priest brought out the captains of hundreds that were set over the host, and said unto them, Have her forth of the ranges: and whoso followeth her, let him be slain with the sword. For the priest said, Slay her not in the house of the 15 LORD. So they laid hands on her; and when she was come to

h Neh. 3. 28.

the entering *h*of the horse gate by the king's house, they slew her 16 there. ¶And Jehoiada made a covenant between him, and between all the people, and between the king, that they should be the 17 LORD's people. Then all the people went to the house of Baal, and brake it down, and brake his altars and his images in pieces,

i Deut. 13. 9.

18 and *i*slew Mattan the priest of Baal before the altars. Also Jehoiada appointed the offices of the house of the LORD by the

k 1 Chr. 23. 6, 30, 31. & 24. 1. *l* Num. 28. 2. *m* 1 Chr. 26. 1, &c.

hand of the priests the Levites, whom David had *k*distributed in the house of the LORD, to offer the burnt offerings of the LORD, as *it is* written in the *l*law of Moses, with rejoicing and with 19 singing, *as it was ordained* ⁵by David. And he set the *m*porters at the gates of the house of the LORD, that none *which was* un-

¹ Heb. *shoulder.* ³ Heb. *Let the king live.* ⁵ Heb. *by the hands of*
² Heb. *house.*   ⁴ Heb. *Conspiracy.*   *David,* 1 Chr. 25. 2, 6.

against any attempt that might be made by the Baal-worshippers to force their way through the courts into the Temple.

7. Cp. 2 K. xi. 8, 11. The soldiers and the Levites in the Temple were probably intermixed in about equal proportions.

8. *and took every man his men* &c.] *i.e.* the relief, already organised by Jehoiada into three bodies (*vv.* 4, 5), was further strengthened by the members of the out-going "course," who were associated in the work to be done.

13. *at the entering in*] *i.e.* at, or near, the

opening from the main chamber of the Temple into the Holy of Holies.

16. *between him,* &c.] In 2 K. xi. 17 the covenant is said to have been made "between the LORD," &c. To the writer of Chronicles Jehoiada was God's representative, and received the pledges of king and people.

18. *the priests the Levites*] Rather, with the Versions, "the priests **and** the Levites." It was the duty of the priests alone to offer the Burnt offerings (Num. xviii. 1-7), and of the Levites alone to praise God with singing and music (1 Chr. xxiii. 5, xxv. 1-7).

20 clean in any thing should enter in. *n*And he took the captains *n*2Kin.11.19.
of hundreds, and the nobles, and the governors of the people,
and all the people of the land, and brought down the king from
the house of the LORD : and they came through the high gate
into the king's house, and set the king upon the throne of the
21 kingdom. And all the people of the land rejoiced : and the city
was quiet, after that they had slain Athaliah with the sword.
CHAP. **24.** JOASH *a*was seven years old when he began to reign, *a*2Kin.11.21.
and he reigned forty years in Jerusalem. His mother's name *&* 12. 1, &c.
2 also *was* Zibiah of Beer-sheba. And Joash *b*did *that which was* *b* See ch. 26.
right in the sight of the LORD all the days of Jehoiada the priest. 5.
3 And Jehoiada took for him two wives; and he begat sons and
4 daughters. ¶And it came to pass after this, *that* Joash was
5 minded ¹to repair the house of the LORD. And he gathered
together the priests and the Levites, and said to them, Go out
unto the cities of Judah, and *c*gather of all Israel money to *c*2Kin. 12. 4.
repair the house of your God from year to year, and see that ye
6 hasten the matter. Howbeit the Levites hastened it not. ¶*d*And *d* 2 Kin. 12.7.
the king called for Jehoiada the chief, and said unto him,
Why hast thou not required of the Levites to bring in out of
Judah and out of Jerusalem the collection, *according to the com-*
mandment of *e*Moses the servant of the LORD, and of the con- *e* Ex. 30. 12,
7 gregation of Israel, for the *f*tabernacle of witness? For *g*the 13, 14, 16.
sons of Athaliah, that wicked woman, had broken up the *f* Num. 1. 50.
house of God; and also all the *h*dedicated things of the house *g* ch. 21. 17.
8 of the LORD did they bestow upon Baalim. And at the king's *h* 2 Kin. 12.4.
commandment *i*they made a chest, and set it without at the *i* 2 Kin. 12. 9.
9 gate of the house of the LORD. And they made ²a proclamation
through Judah and Jerusalem, to bring in to the LORD *k*the *k* ver. 6.
collection *that* Moses the servant of God *laid* upon Israel in the
10 wilderness. And all the princes and all the people rejoiced,
and brought in, and cast into the chest, until they had made an
11 end. Now it came to pass, that at what time the chest was
brought unto the king's office by the hand of the Levites, and
*l*when they saw that *there was* much money, the king's scribe *l*2Kin.12.10.
and the high priest's officer came and emptied the chest, and
took it, and carried it to his place again. Thus they did day by
12 day, and gathered money in abundance. And the king and
Jehoiada gave it to such as did the work of the service of the
house of the LORD, and hired masons and carpenters to repair
the house of the LORD, and also such as wrought iron and brass
13 to mend the house of the LORD. So the workmen wrought, and

¹ Heb. *to renew.* ² Heb. *a voice.*

---

20. *the high gate*] See 2 K. xi. 19 note.
XXIV. This chapter is parallel with 2
K. xii., but treats the matters common to
both narratives in a different and, apparently, supplemental way.
2. Jehoiada lived after the accession of
Joash at least 23 years (2 K. xii. 6). Thus
the idolatries of Joash (*v.* 18) were confined
to his last 10 or 15 years.
3. Athaliah's destruction of the seed
royal had left Joash without a natural
successor, and his marriage at the earliest
suitable age, was, therefore, a matter of
state policy. One of his wives in question
was probably "Jehoaddan of Jerusalem,"

the mother of Amaziah (xxv. 1), who must
have been taken to wife by Joash as early
as his 21st year.
6. It appears from 2 K. xii. 4 that Joash
had assigned to the restoration-fund two
other payments also.
11. *the king's scribe...came and emptied,*
&c.] Rather, "the king's scribe came...and
they emptied" &c. *i.e.* the Levites who
brought the chest from the Temple emptied
it in the presence of the scribe.
13. *they set the house of God in his state*]
Some prefer, "they **set up** the house of
God in its (old) **measure**" or "**proportions.**"

m See 2 Kin. 12. 13.

¹the work was perfected by them, and they set the house of God
14 in his state, and strengthened it. And when they had finished
it, they brought the rest of the money before the king and Jehoiada, ^mwhereof were made vessels for the house of the LORD,
even vessels to minister, and ²to offer *withal*, and spoons, and
vessels of gold and silver. And they offered burnt offerings
in the house of the LORD continually all the days of Jehoiada.
15 ¶ But Jehoiada waxed old, and was full of days when he died ;
16 an hundred and thirty years old *was he* when he died. And they
buried him in the city of David among the kings, because he
had done good in Israel, both toward God, and toward his house.
17 Now after the death of Jehoiada came the princes of Judah,
and made obeisance to the king. Then the king hearkened unto
18 them. And they left the house of the LORD God of their fathers,

n 1 Kin.14.23.
o Judg. 5. 8.
ch. 19. 2.
& 28. 13.
& 29. 8.
& 32. 25.
p ch. 36. 15.
Jer. 7. 25, 26.
& 25. 4.
q ch. 15. 1.
& 20. 14.
r Num.14.41.
s ch. 15. 2.
t Acts 7. 58,
59.

and served ⁿgroves and idols: and ^owrath came upon Judah and
19 Jerusalem for this their trespass. Yet he ^psent prophets to
them, to bring them again unto the LORD; and they testified
20 against them : but they would not give ear. ¶ And ^qthe Spirit
of God ³came upon Zechariah the son of Jehoiada the priest,
which stood above the people, and said unto them, Thus saith
God, ^rWhy transgress ye the commandments of the LORD, that
ye cannot prosper ? ^sbecause ye have forsaken the LORD, he
21 hath also forsaken you. And they conspired against him, and
^tstoned him with stones at the commandment of the king in
22 the court of the house of the LORD. Thus Joash the king
remembered not the kindness which Jehoiada his father had
done to him, but slew his son. And when he died, he said,
23 The LORD look upon *it*, and require *it*. ¶ And it came to pass

u 2 Kin.12.17.

⁴at the end of the year, *that* ^uthe host of Syria came up against
him : and they came to Judah and Jerusalem, and destroyed
all the princes of the people from among the people, and sent

---

¹ Heb. *the healing went up upon the work.*   ² Or, *pestils.*   ³ Heb. *clothed,* as Judg. 6. 34.   ⁴ Heb. *in the revolution of the year.*

---

15. *an hundred and thirty years old*] Most
critics suppose the number in the text to
be corrupt, and suggest in its stead 103
or 83.

16. *they buried him in the city of David
among the kings*] This unparalleled honour,
due in part to the respect felt for Jehoiada's
religious character, was probably, also, in
part attributable to his connexion with the
royal family through his wife (xxii. 11), and
to the fact that, for 10 or 12 years, he had
practically held the kingly office.

toward his house] "*i.e.* toward God's
house," the Temple.

17. The nobles had taken part in the
revolution which placed Joash on the throne
(xxiii. 2, 13, 20), but probably on political
rather than on religious grounds. They
might dislike the rule of a woman and a
foreigner without participating in the zeal
of Jehoiada for purity of religion. They
now petitioned for a toleration of idolatry,
not for a return to the condition of things
which prevailed under Athaliah. No doubt
they carried a considerable party with
them; but the Temple-worship continued, as

appears from the history of Zechariah (*v.* 20).
Nor is the king taxed personally with
idolatry.

20. *stood above the people*] Zechariah, the
High-Priest, took up an elevated position,
perhaps on the steps of the inner court,
which was elevated above the outer court,
where the people would be.

21. *in the court of the house of the* LORD]
"Between the Altar and the Temple," or
directly in front of the Temple porch, if it
be this Zechariah of whom our Lord speaks
(Matt. xxiii. 35). A horror of the impious
deed long possessed the Jews, who believed
that the blood could not be effaced, but
continued to bubble on the stones of the
court, like blood newly shed, until the
Temple was entered, just prior to its destruction, by Nebuzaradan.

22. *the* LORD *look upon it and require it*]
Cp. Gen. ix. 5, xlii. 22; and contrast the
words of Christ (Luke xxiii. 34), and of St.
Stephen (Acts vii. 60). Zechariah's prayer
was prophetic (see *vv.* 23, 25 ; Luke xi. 51).

23. On the unusual character of this expedition, see marg. ref. note.

24 all the spoil of them unto the king of [1]Damascus. For the army of the Syrians *came with a small company of men, and the LORD *delivered a very great host into their hand, because they had forsaken the LORD God of their fathers. So they
25 *executed judgment against Joash. ¶ And when they were departed from him, (for they left him in great diseases,) *his own servants conspired against him for the blood of the *sons of Jehoiada the priest, and slew him on his bed, and he died: and they buried him in the city of David, but they buried him not
26 in the sepulchres of the kings. And these are they that conspired against him; [2]Zabad the son of Shimeath an Ammonitess,
27 and Jehozabad the son of [3]Shimrith a Moabitess. Now concerning his sons, and the greatness of *the burdens laid upon him, and the [4]repairing of the house of God, behold, they are written in the [5]story of the book of the kings. *And Amaziah his son reigned in his stead.

CHAP. 25. AMAZIAH *was twenty and five years old when he began to reign, and he reigned twenty and nine years in Jerusalem. And his mother's name was Jehoaddan of Jerusalem.
2 And he did that which was right in the sight of the LORD, *but
3 not with a perfect heart. *Now it came to pass, when the kingdom was [6]established to him, that he slew his servants that had
4 killed the king his father. But he slew not their children, but did as it is written in the law in the book of Moses, where the LORD commanded, saying, *The fathers shall not die for the children, neither shall the children die for the fathers, but every
5 man shall die for his own sin. ¶ Moreover Amaziah gathered Judah together, and made them captains over thousands, and captains over hundreds, according to the houses of their fathers, throughout all Judah and Benjamin: and he numbered them *from twenty years old and above, and found them three hun-
6 dred thousand choice men, able to go forth to war, that could handle spear and shield. He hired also an hundred thousand mighty men of valour out of Israel for an hundred talents of
7 silver. But there came a man of God to him, saying, O king, let not the army of Israel go with thee; for the LORD is not
8 with Israel, to wit, with all the children of Ephraim. But if thou wilt go, do it, be strong for the battle: God shall make thee fall before the enemy: for God hath /power to help, and to cast
9 down. And Amaziah said to the man of God, But what shall

*Lev. 26. 8.
Deut. 32. 30.
Isai. 30. 17.
*Lev. 26. 25.
Deut. 28. 25.
*ch. 22. 8.
Isai. 10. 5.
*2Kin.12.20.
*ver. 21.

*2Kin.12.18.

*2Kin.12.21.

*2 Kin. 14. 1, &c.

*See 2 Kin. 14. 4.
ver. 14.
*2 Kin. 14. 5, &c.

*Deut.24.16.
2 Kin. 14. 6.
Jer. 31. 30.
Ezek. 18. 20.

*Num. 1. 3.

/ch. 20. 6.

[1] Heb. Darmesek.   [3] Or, Shomer.   [5] Or, commentary.
[2] Or, Jozachar, 2 Kin. 12. 21.   [4] Heb. founding.   [6] Heb. confirmed upon him.

24. they executed judgment against Joash] By defeating his army, slaying his nobles, and pressing on against Jerusalem, &c. (2 K. xii. 18 note).

27. the greatness of the burdens laid upon him] Or, "And the multitude of burdens uttered against him." "Burdens" (2 K. ix. 25 note) are prophetical denunciations of coming evil.

the repairing] See marg. rendering. Joash's repairs extended to the very base of the Temple building.

the story of the book of the kings] See Introduction to Chronicles, p. 447, n. 2.

XXV. This chapter is evidently taken to a large extent from the same document

as Kings (marg. ref. and notes). At the same time it contains large and important additions;—e.g. vv. 5-10, 13-16.

5. three hundred thousand] Asa's army had been nearly twice as numerous, amounting to 580,000 (xiv. 8). The diminution was due, in part, to wars (xxi. 8, 16, xxiv. 23, 24); in part, to the general decadence of the kingdom.

8. If the present text be regarded as sound, this passage must be taken ironically. But most recent commentators supply a second negative, and render—"But go thou alone, act, be strong for the battle—God shall then not make thee to fall."

g Prov.10.22.

we do for the hundred talents which I have given to the ¹army of Israel? And the man of God answered, *g*The LORD is able
10 to give thee much more than this. Then Amaziah separated them, *to wit,* the army that was come to him out of Ephraim, to go ²home again: wherefore their anger was greatly kindled
11 against Judah, and they returned home ³in great anger. ¶ And Amaziah strengthened himself, and led forth his people, and

h 2 Kin.14.7.

went to *h*the valley of salt, and smote of the children of Seir
12 ten thousand. And *other* ten thousand *left* alive did the children of Judah carry away captive, and brought them unto the top of the rock, and cast them down from the top of the rock, that they
13 all were broken in pieces. But ⁴the soldiers of the army which Amaziah sent back, that they should not go with him to battle, fell upon the cities of Judah, from Samaria even unto Beth-horon, and smote three thousand of them, and took much spoil.

i See ch. 23. 23.
k Ex. 20. 3, 5.

14 ¶ Now it came to pass, after that Amaziah was come from the slaughter of the Edomites, that *i*he brought the gods of the children of Seir, and set them up *to be* *k*his gods, and bowed down himself before them, and burned incense unto them.

l Ps. 96. 5.
m ver. 11.

15 Wherefore the anger of the LORD was kindled against Amaziah, and he sent unto him a prophet, which said unto him, Why hast thou sought after *l*the gods of the people, which *m*could not
16 deliver their own people out of thine hand? And it came to pass, as he talked with him, that *the king* said unto him, Art thou made of the king's counsel? forbear; why shouldest thou be smitten? Then the prophet forbare, and said, I know that

n 1Sam.2.25.
o 2 Kin. 14. 8, 9, &c.

God hath ⁵*n*determined to destroy thee, because thou hast done
17 this, and hast not hearkened unto my counsel. ¶ Then *o*Amaziah king of Judah took advice, and sent to Joash, the son of Jehoahaz, the son of Jehu, king of Israel, saying, Come, let
18 us see one another in the face. And Joash king of Israel sent to Amaziah king of Judah, saying, The ⁶thistle that *was* in Lebanon sent to the cedar that *was* in Lebanon, saying, Give thy daughter to my son to wife: and there passed by ⁷a wild
19 beast that *was* in Lebanon, and trode down the thistle. Thou sayest, Lo, thou hast smitten the Edomites; and thine heart lifteth thee up to boast: abide now at home; why shouldest thou meddle to *thine* hurt, that thou shouldest fall, *even* thou,

¹ Heb. *band.*
² Heb. *to their place.*
³ Heb. *in heat of anger.*
⁴ Heb. *the sons of the band.*
⁵ Heb. *counselled.*
⁶ Or, *furze bush,* or, *thorn.*
⁷ Heb. *a beast of the field.*

10. Such a dismissal could not fail to arouse great indignation. The Israelites would suppose themselves dismissed because their good faith was suspected. On the consequences of their indignation, see *v.* 13.

11. *the children of Seir*] *i.e.* the Edomites (marg. ref. *h.*).

12. *the top of the rock*] Rather, "the **height of Selah**" (or, Petra), near which the battle was probably fought. On the cruel features of the Edomite wars, see 1 K. xi. 15; Ezek. xxv. 12; Obad. 14.

13. To revenge the insult (*v.* 10), the troops of Joash proceeded southwards and ravaged all the Jewish towns and villages between the Israelitish frontier and Beth-

horon. This invasion probably took place while Amaziah was still in Edom.

14. The practice of carrying off the images of the gods from a conquered country, or city, as trophies of victory, was common among the nations of the East. Sometimes as with the Romans, the object was worship, especially when the gods were previously among those of the conquering country, and the images had the reputation of peculiar sanctity.

16. *Art thou made of the king's counsel?*] A subtle irony:—"Have I made thee one of my council? If not, what entitles thee to offer thy advice?"

For the fulfilment of the prophecy, see *vv.* 22–24, 27.

20 and Judah with thee? But Amaziah would not hear; for *p*it
    came of God, that he might deliver them into the hand *of their*
21 *enemies*, because they *q*sought after the gods of Edom. So
    Joash the king of Israel went up ; and they saw one another in
    the face, *both* he and Amaziah king of Judah, at Beth-shemesh,
22 which *belongeth* to Judah. And Judah was ¹put to the worse
23 before Israel, and they fled every man to his tent. And Joash
    the king of Israel took Amaziah king of Judah, the son of Joash,
    the son of *r*Jehoahaz, at Beth-shemesh, and brought him to
    Jerusalem, and brake down the wall of Jerusalem from the gate
24 of Ephraim to ²the corner gate, four hundred cubits. And *he*
    took all the gold and the silver, and all the vessels that were
    found in the house of God with Obed-edom, and the treasures
    of the king's house, the hostages also, and returned to Samaria.
25 ¶ *s*And Amaziah the son of Joash king of Judah lived after the
    death of Joash son of Jehoahaz king of Israel fifteen years.
26 Now the rest of the acts of Amaziah, first and last, behold, *are*
    they not written in the book of the kings of Judah and Israel?
27 Now after the time that Amaziah did turn away ³from following
    the LORD they ⁴made a conspiracy against him in Jerusalem ;
    and he fled to Lachish : but they sent to Lachish after him, and
28 slew him there. And they brought him upon horses, and buried
    him with his fathers in the city of ⁵Judah.
CHAP. 26. THEN all the people of Judah took *a* ⁶Uzziah, who *was*
    sixteen years old, and made him king in the room of his father
2 Amaziah. He built Eloth, and restored it to Judah, after that
3 the king slept with his fathers. Sixteen years old *was* Uzziah
    when he began to reign, and he reigned fifty and two years in
    Jerusalem. His mother's name also *was* Jecoliah of Jerusalem.
4 And he did *that which was* right in the sight of the LORD, accord-
5 to all that his father Amaziah did. And *b*he sought God in the
    days of Zechariah, who *c*had understanding ⁷in the visions of
    God: and as long as he sought the LORD, God made him to
6 prosper. And he went forth and *d*warred against the Philistines,
    and brake down the wall of Gath, and the wall of Jabneh, and
    the wall of Ashdod, and built cities ⁸about Ashdod, and among
7 the Philistines. And God helped him against *e*the Philistines,
    and against the Arabians that dwelt in Gur-baal, and the

p 1 Kin. 12. 15.
ch. 22. 7.

q ver. 14.

r See ch. 21.
17.
& 22. 1, 6.

s 2 Kin. 14. 17.

a 2 Kin. 14.
21, 22.
& 15. 1, &c.

b See ch. 24.
2.
c Gen. 41. 15.
Dan. 1. 17.
& 2. 19.
& 10. 1.
d Isai. 14. 29.

e ch. 21. 16.

---

¹ Heb. *smitten.*
² Heb. *the gate of it that*
    looketh.
³ Heb. *from after.*
⁴ Heb. *conspired a con-*
    spiracy.
⁵ That is, *The city of David,*
    as it is 2 Kin. 14. 20.
⁶ Or, *Azariah.*
⁷ Heb. *in the seeing of God.*
⁸ Or, *in the country of*
    Ashdod.

---

27. *after the time* &c.] The writer means
that the violent death of Amaziah followed
on his apostasy, not closely in point of time
—for it must have been at least fifteen years
after (*v.* 25)—nor as, humanly speaking,
caused by it ; but, in the way of a divine
judgment, his death was a complete fulfilment of the prophecy of *v.* 16.
    XXVI. Nearly the whole of this chapter
is additional to the narrative in Kings
(marg. ref.). It is not too much to say that
we are indebted to Chronicles for our whole
conception of the character of Uzziah, and
for nearly our whole knowledge of the events
of his reign.
    1. *Uzziah*] This form of the name is found
uniformly in Chronicles (except 1 Chr. iii.

12) and in the Prophets. The writer of
Kings prefers the form Azariah. Uzziah
has been regarded as a phonetic corruption
of the real name used by the common
people.
    5. *who had understanding in the visions of*
God] Another reading, supported by the
LXX., and some ancient Versions, is :—
"who instructed him in the fear of God."
    6. Uzziah's expedition was the natural
sequel to the Edomite war of Amaziah
(xxv. 11), which crushed the most formidable of all the tribes of the south. On
Jabneh see Josh. xv. 11 note; and on
Ashdod see Josh. xiii. 3 note.
    7. On the Mehunims or Maonites, see
Judges x. 12 note.

f 2 Sam. 8. 2.
ch. 17. 11.

g 2 Kin. 14. 13.
Nch. 3. 13,
19, 32.
Zech. 14. 10.

h Deut. 32. 15.

i Deut. 8. 14.
ch. 25. 19.
k So 2 Kin.
16. 12, 13.
l 1 Chr. 6. 10.

8 Mehunims. And the Ammonites *f* gave gifts to Uzziah: and his name ¹spread abroad *even* to the entering in of Egypt; for he 9 strengthened *himself* exceedingly.   ¶ Moreover Uzziah built towers in Jerusalem at the *g* corner gate, and at the valley gate, 10 and at the turning *of the wall*, and ²fortified them. Also he built towers in the desert, and ³digged many wells: for he had much cattle, both in the low country, and in the plains: husbandmen *also*, and vine dressers in the mountains, and in 11 ⁴Carmel: for he loved ⁵husbandry.   ¶ Moreover Uzziah had an host of fighting men, that went out to war by bands, according to the number of their account by the hand of Jeiel the scribe and Maaseiah the ruler, under the hand of Hananiah, *one* of the 12 king's captains. The whole number of the chief of the fathers of the mighty men of valour *were* two thousand and six hun- 13 dred. And under their hand *was* ⁶an army, three hundred thousand and seven thousand and five hundred, that made war with 14 mighty power, to help the king against the enemy. And Uzziah prepared for them throughout all the host shields, and spears, and helmets, and habergeons, and bows, and ⁷slings *to cast* stones. 15 And he made in Jerusalem engines, invented by cunning men, to be on the towers and upon the bulwarks, to shoot arrows and great stones withal. And his name ⁸spread far abroad; for he 16 was marvellously helped, till he was strong.   ¶ But *h* when he was strong, his heart was *i* lifted up to *his* destruction: for he transgressed against the LORD his God, and *k* went into the temple of the LORD to burn incense upon the altar of incense. 17 And *l* Azariah the priest went in after him, and with him four-

---

¹ Heb. *went.*
² Or, *repaired.*
³ Or, *cut out many cisterns.*
⁴ Or, *Fruitful fields.*
⁵ Heb. *ground.*
⁶ Heb. *the power of an army.*
⁷ Heb. *stones of slings.*
⁸ Heb. *went forth.*

---

10. *he built towers in the desert*] Refuges for the flocks and the herdsmen in the wild pasture country on the borders of the Holy Land, especially towards the south and south-east.

wells] The marginal translation is preferable. Judæa depends largely for its water-supply on reservoirs in which the rain-fall is stored. These are generally cut in the natural rock, and covered at top.

for he had much cattle, &c.] Some prefer, "for he had much cattle **there, and** in the low country, and **on the downs**," with allusion to three separate districts—(1) The "wilderness," or high tract to the south and south-east, extending from the western shores of the Dead Sea to the vicinity of Beersheba; (2) The "low country," or maritime plain on the west, between the hills of Judæa and the sea; and (3) The "downs," or rich grazing land beyond the Jordan, on the plateau of Gilead. Uzziah's possession of this last-named district must have been connected with the submission of the Ammonites (see *v.* 8).

in the mountains, and in Carmel] These terms describe Judæa Proper — the hilly tract between the low maritime plain on the one side, and the wilderness and Jordan valley on the other. By "Carmel" we must understand, not the mountain of that name, which belonged to Samaria, but the cultivated portions of the Judæan hill-tract (see margin).

13. Cp. xxv. 5. It will be seen that Uzziah had not added much to the military strength of the nation by his conquests. His army exceeds that of his father Amaziah by 7500 men only.

14. The sling was used in war by the Assyrians, the Egyptians, the Persians, the Greeks, Romans, and others. Its employment by the Benjamites appears from Judg. xx. 16, and by the ten tribes, a century before Uzziah, from 2 K. iii. 25.

15. Uzziah's engines seem to have corresponded respectively to the Roman *balista* and *catapulta*. The *balista*, which threw stones, was known to the Assyrians as early as the time of Sardanapalus I., the contemporary of Jehoshaphat. The catapult is not represented either on the Assyrian or the Egyptian sculptures. It would seem on the whole most probable that both kinds of engines were invented in Assyria and introduced from thence into Palestine.

16. *to his destruction*] Rather, "**to do wickedly.**" Uzziah appears to have deliberately determined to invade the priest's office (marg. ref. *m*), thus repeating the sin of Korah, Dathan, and Abiram (Num. xvi. 1-35).

18 score priests of the LORD, *that were* valiant men : and they with-   *m* Num. 16.
stood Uzziah the king, and said unto him, *It* *m*appertaineth not unto   40.
thee, Uzziah, to burn incense unto the LORD, but to the *n*priests   & 18. 7.
the sons of Aaron, that are consecrated to burn incense : go out   *n* Ex. 30. 7, 8.
of the sanctuary ; for thou hast trespassed ; neither *shall it be* for
19 thine honour from the LORD God. Then Uzziah was wroth, and
had a censer in his hand to burn incense : and while he was
wroth with the priests, *o*the leprosy even rose up in his forehead   *o* Num.12.10.
before the priests in the house of the LORD, from beside the in-   2 Kin. 5. 27.
20 cense altar. And Azariah the chief priest, and all the priests,
looked upon him, and, behold, he *was* leprous in his forehead,
and they thrust him out from thence ; yea, himself *p*hasted also   *p* As Esth.
21 to go out, because the LORD had smitten him.   *q*And Uzziah the   6. 12.
king was a leper unto the day of his death, and dwelt in a   *q* 2 Kin. 15. 5.
*r*1several house, *being* a leper ; for he was cut off from the house   *r* Lev. 13. 46.
of the LORD : and Jotham his son *was* over the king's house,   Num. 5. 2.
22 judging the people of the land. ¶Now the rest of the acts of
Uzziah, first and last, did *s*Isaiah the prophet, the son of Amoz,   *s* Isai. 1. 1.
23 write. *t*So Uzziah slept with his fathers, and they buried him   *t* 2 Kin. 15.7.
with his fathers in the field of the burial which *belonged* to the   Isai. 6. 1.
kings ; for they said, He *is* a leper : and Jotham his son reigned
in his stead.

CHAP. 27. JOTHAM *a*was twenty and five years old when he began   *a* 2 Kin. 15.
to reign, and he reigned sixteen years in Jerusalem. His mother's   32, &c.
2 name also *was* Jerushah, the daughter of Zadok. And he did
that which was right in the sight of the LORD, according to all
that his father Uzziah did : howbeit he entered not into the
3 temple of the LORD. And *b*the people did yet corruptly. He   *b*2Kin.15.35.
built the high gate of the house of the LORD, and on the wall of
4 2Ophel he built much. Moreover he built cities in the mountains of Judah, and in the forests he built castles and towers.
5 He fought also with the king of the Ammonites, and prevailed
against them. And the children of Ammon gave him the same
year an hundred talents of silver, and ten thousand measures

     1 Heb. *free.*   2 Or, *The tower*, ch. 33. 14. Neh. 3. 26.

---

20. Death was denounced by the Law against those who invaded the office of the priest ; and death had been the actual punishment of Korah and his company. Uzziah feared lest from him also the extreme penalty should be exacted, and therefore hasted to quit the sacred building where his bare presence was a capital crime.

21. *a several house*] See marg. ref. *q* note ; and cp. Ps. lxxxviii., which is supposed by some to refer to Uzziah.

22. *the acts of Uzziah...did Isaiah...write*] Most critics regard Isaiah as about 20 when Uzziah died. He must, then, have written his history of Uzziah's reign from documents and accounts of others, rather than from his own knowledge.

23. *in the field of the burial*] i.e. in the same piece of ground, but in a separate sepulchre. As the Law separated off the leper from his fellows during life (Lev. xiii. 46), so Jewish feeling required that he should remain separate even in death.

XXVII. This short chapter runs parallel

with 2 Kings (marg. ref.), and is taken mainly from the same source or sources which it amplifies.

3. Ophel was the name given to the long, narrowish, rounded spur or promontory, which intervenes between the central valley of Jerusalem (the Tyropœon) and the Kidron, or valley of Jehoshaphat. The anxiety of Uzziah and Jotham to fortify their territory indicates a fear of external attack, which at this time was probably felt mainly in connexion with Samaria and Syria (2 K. xv. 37 note). The faithless trust put in fortifications was rebuked by the prophets of the time (Hos. viii. 14 ; Isai. ii. 15).

5. The Ammonites, who had submitted to Uzziah (xxvi. 8), revolted against Jotham. This revolt he firmly repressed ; and, to punish it, he exacted a high rate of tribute for the three years following the termination of the war. The productiveness of the Ammonite country in grain, which is here indicated, has been remarked upon as extraordinary by modern travellers.

of wheat, and ten thousand of barley. ¹ So much did the children of Ammon pay unto him, both the second year, and the
6 third. So Jotham became mighty, because he ² prepared his
7 ways before the LORD his God. ¶ Now the rest of the acts of
Jotham, and all his wars, and his ways, lo, they *are* written in
8 the book of the kings of Israel and Judah. He was five and
twenty years old when he began to reign, and reigned sixteen

c 2 Kin. 15. 38.

9 years in Jerusalem. *c* And Jotham slept with his fathers, and
they buried him in the city of David : and Ahaz his son reigned
in his stead.

a 2 Kin. 16. 2.

CHAP. 28. AHAZ *a was* twenty years old when he began to reign,
and he reigned sixteen years in Jerusalem : but he did not *that*
which was right in the sight of the LORD, like David his father :
2 for he walked in the ways of the kings of Israel, and made also

b Ex. 34. 17.
Lev. 19. 4.
c Judg. 2. 11.
d 2 Kin. 23. 10.
e Lev. 18. 21.
ch. 33. 6.

3 *b* molten images for *c* Baalim. Moreover he ³ burnt incense in
d the valley of the son of Hinnom, and burnt *e* his children in the
fire, after the abominations of the heathen whom the LORD had
4 cast out before the children of Israel. He sacrificed also and
burnt incense in the high places, and on the hills, and under

f Isai. 7. 1.
g 2 Kin. 16.
5, 6.

5 every green tree. Wherefore *f* the LORD his God delivered him
into the hand of the king of Syria ; and they *g* smote him, and
carried away a great multitude of them captives, and brought
them to ⁴ Damascus. And he was also delivered into the hand of
6 the king of Israel, who smote him with a great slaughter. For

h 2 Kin. 15. 27.

h Pekah the son of Remaliah slew in Judah an hundred and
twenty thousand in one day, *which were* all ⁵ valiant men ;
7 because they had forsaken the LORD God of their fathers. And
Zichri, a mighty man of Ephraim, slew Maaseiah the king's son,
and Azrikam the governor of the house, and Elkanah *that was*
8 ⁶ next to the king. And the children of Israel carried away

i ch. 11. 4.

captive of their *i* brethren two hundred thousand, women, sons,
and daughters, and took also away much spoil from them, and
9 brought the spoil to Samaria. ¶ But a prophet of the LORD was

k Ps. 69. 26.
Isai. 10. 5.
& 47. 6.
Ezek. 25. 12,
15.
& 26. 2.
Obad. 10, &c.
Zech. 1. 15.

there, whose name *was* Oded : and he went out before the host
that came to Samaria, and said unto them, Behold, *k* because the
LORD God of your fathers was wroth with Judah, he hath delivered them into your hand, and ye have slain them in a rage

l Ezra 9. 6.
Rev. 18. 5.

10 *that l* reacheth up unto heaven. And now ye purpose to keep

---

¹ Heb. *This.*
² Or, *established.*
³ Or, *offered sacrifice.*
⁴ Heb. *Darmesek.*
⁵ Heb. *sons of valour.*
⁶ Heb. *the second to the king.*

XXVIII. This chapter is *supplemental*
in character. The writer seems to assume
that the narrative of Kings (marg. ref.) is
known, and is mainly anxious to add points
which the author of that narrative has
omitted.

2. *images for Baalim*] Or, to serve as
Baalim, *i.e* as representatives of the different forms or characters of the chief
Phœnician deity.

3. Cp. 2 K. xvi. 3 note.

4. *He sacrificed also* &c.] Cp. 2 K. xvi. 4.

5. The two battles here mentioned, one
with Rezin (king of Syria), and the other
with Pekah (king of Israel) are additions
to the narrative of the writer of Kings
(marg. ref. *g*). The events of the Syro-
Israelite war were probably spread over
several years.

6. The fearful loss here described may
have been due to a complete defeat followed
by panic.

7. Maaseiah was either an officer called
"the king's son" (cp. 1 K. xxii. 26), or
perhaps a son of Jotham, since Ahaz could
hardly have had a son old enough to take
part in the battle (cp. *v.* 1).
Elkanah, as "second to the king," was
probably the chief of the royal counsellors.

9. Nothing more is known of this Oded.
Cp. xv. 1.

he went out before the host] Rather, "He
went out to meet the host," as the same
phrase is translated in xv. 2.

a rage that reacheth up to heaven] *i.e.* not
merely an exceedingly great and violent
rage, but one that has displeased God.

10. *are there not with you...sins against the*

under the children of Judah and Jerusalem for ^mbondmen and bondwomen unto you : *but are there* not with you, even with you. 11 sins against the LORD your God? Now hear me therefore, and deliver the captives again, which ye have taken captive of your 12 brethren : ⁿ for the fierce wrath of the LORD *is* upon you. Then certain of the heads of the children of Ephraim, Azariah the son of Johanan, Berechiah the son of Meshillemoth, and Jehizkiah the son of Shallum, and Amasa the son of Hadlai, 13 stood up against them that came from the war, and said unto them, Ye shall not bring in the captives hither : for whereas we have offended against the LORD *already*, ye intend to add *more* to our sins and to our trespass : for our trespass is great, and *there* 14 *is* fierce wrath against Israel. So the armed men left the captives 15 and the spoil before the princes and all the congregation. And the men ^owhich were expressed by name rose up, and took the captives, and with the spoil clothed all that were naked among them, and arrayed them, and shod them, and ^pgave them to eat and to drink, and anointed them, and carried all the feeble of them upon asses, and brought them to Jericho, ^qthe city of palm trees, to their brethren : then they returned to 16 Samaria. ¶ ^rAt that time did king Ahaz send unto the kings of 17 Assyria to help him. For again the Edomites had come and 18 smitten Judah, and carried away ¹captives. ^sThe Philistines also had invaded the cities of the low country, and of the south of Judah, and had taken Beth-shemesh, and Ajalon, and Gederoth, and Shocho with the villages thereof, and Timnah with the villages thereof, Gimzo also and the villages thereof : and they 19 dwelt there. For the LORD brought Judah low because of Ahaz king of ^tIsrael ; for he ^umade Judah naked, and transgressed 20 sore against the LORD. And ^xTilgath-pilneser king of Assyria came unto him, and distressed him, but strengthened him not.

¹ Heb. *a captiv'ty.*

Marginal references:
m Lev. 25.39, 42, 43, 46.

n Jam. 2. 13.

o ver. 12.

p 2 Kin. 6.22. Prov. 25. 21, 22. Luke 6. 27. Rom. 12. 20. q Deut. 34. 3. Judg. 1. 16. r 2 Kin. 16.7.

s Ezek. 16. 27, 57.

t ch. 21. 2. u Ex. 32. 25. x 2 Kin.15.29. & 16. 7, 8, 9.

LORD ?] The ten tribes had fallen away from the true faith far more completely and more hopelessly than the two. It was not for them to press hard against their erring brothers, and aggravate their punishment.

12. "Ephraim" is used here in the generic sense so common in the Prophets, as synonymous with the ten tribes.

15. Jericho, which lies much farther from Samaria than many points of the territory of Judah, was perhaps selected because the captives had been carried off principally from this point ; or because there may have been less danger of falling in with portions of Pekah's army on this than on the direct route.

17. The Edomites took advantage of the reverses of Ahaz, and were perhaps in league with Rezin (see 2 K. xvi. 6 note). The pitilessness of Edom, and her readiness to turn against Judah in any severe distress, is noticed and sternly rebuked by the Prophets (Am. i. 11 ; Ezek. xxxv. 5 ; Obad. 10–14, &c.).

18. Philistia also, eager to retaliate the blows she had received from Uzziah (xxvi. 6), seized her opportunity. Ajalon and Shocho were among the cities fortified by

Rehoboam (xi. 7, 10) ; Beth-shemesh (Josh. xv. 10) was famous as the scene of Amaziah's defeat (xxv. 21). Gimzo, which is not elsewhere mentioned in Scripture has been probably identified with the modern *Jimzu,* a large village about 2½ miles from *Ludd* (the ancient Lydda).

19. *Ahaz king of Israel*] An instance of the lax use of the word "Israel" (xii. 6, xxi. 2). It is simply equivalent to "king of Judah."

he made Judah naked] Lit. "he **had caused licentiousness** in Judah"—*i.e.* he had allowed Judah to break loose from all restraints of true religion, and to turn to any idolatry that they preferred (*vv.* 2–4). In this and in the following expression there is implied an apostasy resembling the unfaithfulness of a wife.

20. *Tilgath-pilneser*] This form of the name is doubly corrupt. See the properly Hebraized form in 2 K. xv. 29.

distressed him, but strengthened him not] This statement, and that at the end of *v.* 21, is supplemental to, and not contradictory of, 2 K. xvi. 9. Here it is the writer's object to note that the material assistance rendered by Tiglath-pileser to Ahab, was no

21 For Ahaz took away a portion *out* of the house of the LORD, and *out* of the house of the king, and of the princes, and gave *it* unto
22 the king of Assyria: but he helped him not. ¶ And in the time of his distress did he trespass yet more against the LORD: this
23 *is that* king Ahaz.　For *ʸ*he sacrificed unto the gods of ¹Damascus, which smote him: and he said, Because the gods of the kings of Syria help them, *therefore* will I sacrifice to them, that *ᶻ*they may help me.　But they were the ruin of him, and of all
24 Israel.　And Ahaz gathered together the vessels of the house of God, and cut in pieces the vessels of the house of God, *ᵃ*and shut up the doors of the house of the LORD, and he made him
25 altars in every corner of Jerusalem.　And in every several city of Judah he made high places ² to burn incense unto other gods,
26 and provoked to anger the LORD God of his fathers.　¶ *ᵇ*Now the rest of his acts and of all his ways, first and last, behold, they *are* written in the book of the kings of Judah and Israel.
27 And Ahaz slept with his fathers, and they buried him in the city, *even* in Jerusalem: but they brought him not into the sepulchres of the kings of Israel: and Hezekiah his son reigned in his stead.

CHAP. 29. HEZEKIAH *ᵃ*began to reign *when he was* five and twenty years old, and he reigned nine and twenty years in Jerusalem.　And his mother's name *was* Abijah, the daughter
2 *ᵇ*of Zechariah.　And he did *that which was* right in the sight of
3 the LORD, according to all that David his father had done.　He in the first year of his reign, in the first month, *ᶜ*opened the
4 doors of the house of the LORD, and repaired them.　And he brought in the priests and the Levites, and gathered them
5 together into the east street, and said unto them, Hear me, ye Levites, *ᵈ*sanctify now yourselves, and sanctify the house of the
6 LORD God of your fathers, and carry forth the filthiness out of the holy *place*.　For our fathers have trespassed, and done *that which was* evil in the eyes of the LORD our God, and have forsaken him, and have *ᵉ*turned away their faces from the habita-
7 tion of the LORD, and ³turned *their* backs.　*ᶠ*Also they have

ʸ See ch. 25. 14.

ᶻ Jer. 44. 17, 18.

ᵃ See ch. 29. 3, 7.

ᵇ 2 Kin. 16. 19, 20.

ᵃ 2 Kin. 18. 1.

ᵇ ch. 26. 5.

ᶜ See ch. 28. 24. ver. 7.

ᵈ 1 Chr. 15. 12. ch. 35. 6.

ᵉ Jer. 2. 27. Ezek. 8. 16. *ᶠ* ch. 28. 24.

¹ Heb. *Darmesek*.　² Or, *to offer*.　³ Heb. *given the neck*.

---

real "help" or "strength," but rather a cause of "distress."

23. His adoption of the Syrian gods, Hadad, Rimmon, and others, as objects of worship, no doubt preceded the destruction of Damascus by the Assyrians (2 K. xvi. 9).

Israel] *i.e.* "Judah;" so in *v.* 27. Cp. *v.* 19.

24. Cp. 2 K. xvi. 17 note. The Temple-worship was suspended, the lamps put out, and the doors shut, to prevent the priests from entering. The Jews still celebrate a yearly fast in commemoration of this time of affliction.

altars] As the one Altar for sacrifice, which alone the Law allowed, symbolized the doctrine of one God, so these many altars spoke unmistakeably of the all-embracing polytheism affected by Ahaz.

XXIX. The treatment of Hezekiah's reign by the author of Chronicles is in marked contrast with that followed in the Book of Kings. The writer of Kings describes mainly civil affairs; the author of Chronicles gives a full account of Hezekiah's religious reformation. Chapters xxix.-xxxi. contain matter, therefore, which is almost wholly new.

3. By "the first month" is meant (cp. xxx. 2, 3) the month of Nisan, the first of the Jewish sacred year, not necessarily the first month of Hezekiah's reign.

4. *the east street*] Rather, some open space before the eastern gate of the outer Temple Court is intended.

5. *sanctify now yourselves*] Cp. marg. ref. Hezekiah follows David's example, knowing, probably, that the priests had in the preceding time of idolatry contracted many defilements.

The "filthiness," or "uncleanness" (*v.* 16), might consist, in part, of mere dust and dirt, in part, of idolatrous objects introduced by Ahaz before he finally shut up the Temple (2 K. xvi. 10-16).

shut up the doors of the porch, and put out the lamps, and have
not burned incense nor offered burnt offerings in the holy *place*
8 unto the God of Israel. Wherefore the *g*wrath of the LORD was
upon Judah and Jerusalem, and he hath delivered them to
¹trouble, to astonishment, and to *h*hissing, as ye see with your
9 eyes. For, lo, *i*our fathers have fallen by the sword, and our
sons and our daughters and our wives *are* in captivity for this.
10 Now *it is* in mine heart to make *k*a covenant with the LORD
God of Israel, that his fierce wrath may turn away from us.
11 My sons, ²be not now negligent: for the LORD hath *l*chosen
you to stand before him, to serve him, and that ye should
12 minister unto him, and ³burn incense. ¶Then the Levites
arose, Mahath the son of Amasai, and Joel the son of Azariah,
of the sons of the Kohathites: and of the sons of Merari, Kish
the son of Abdi, and Azariah the son of Jehalelel: and of the
Gershonites; Joah the son of Zimmah, and Eden the son of
13 Joah: and of the sons of Elizaphan; Shimri, and Jeiel: and of
14 the sons of Asaph; *Zechariah, and Mattaniah: and of the sons
of Heman; Jehiel, and Shimei: and of the sons of Jeduthun;
15 Shemaiah, and Uzziel. And they gathered their brethren, and
*m*sanctified themselves, and came, according to the commandment of the king, ⁴by the words of the LORD, *n*to cleanse the
16 house of the LORD. And the priests went into the inner part
of the house of the LORD, to cleanse *it*, and brought out all the
uncleanness that they found in the temple of the LORD into the
court of the house of the LORD. And the Levites took *it*, to
17 carry *it* out abroad into the brook Kidron. Now they began to
the first *day* of the first month to sanctify, and on the eighth
day of the month came they to the porch of the LORD: so they
sanctified the house of the LORD in eight days; and in the
18 sixteenth day of the first month they made an end. Then
they went in to Hezekiah the king, and said, We have cleansed
all the house of the LORD, and the altar of burnt offering, with
all the vessels thereof, and the shewbread table, with all the
19 vessels thereof. Moreover all the vessels, which king Ahaz
in his reign did *o*cast away in his transgression, have we prepared and sanctified, and, behold, they *are* before the altar of
20 the LORD. ¶Then Hezekiah the king rose early, and gathered
the rulers of the city, and went up to the house of the LORD.
21 And they brought seven bullocks, and seven rams, and seven
lambs, and seven he goats, for a *p*sin offering for the kingdom,

g ch. 24. 18.

h Jer. 18. 16
& 19. 8.
& 25. 9, 18.
& 29. 18.
i ch. 28. 5,
6. 8, 17.
k ch. 15. 12.
l Num. 3. 6.
& 18. 2, 6.

m ver. 5.
n 1Chr.23.28.

o ch. 28. 24.

p Lev.4.3,14.

¹ Heb. *commotion*, Deut. 28. 25. ² Or, *be not now deceived*. ³ Or, *offer sacrifice*. ⁴ Or, *in the business of the LORD*, ch. 30. 12.

---

8. *he hath delivered them to...hissing*] See
1 K. ix. 8 note. It was an expression which
Hezekiah might naturally use, for it had
occurred in a prophecy of Micah (vi. 16),
his contemporary and monitor (Jer. xxvi.
18, 19), which was probably uttered towards
the close of the reign of Ahaz. In Jeremiah the phrase becomes common (marg.
reff.).

12, 13. On the triple division of the
Levites, see 1 Chr. xxiii. 6; and on the
musical Levites, see 1 Chr. xxv. 1-6.

13. The descendants of Elizaphan — a
grandson of Kohath (Ex. vi. 22), and chief
of the Kohathites at the time of the census
in the Wilderness (Num. iii. 30)—appear at

all times to have formed a distinct branch
of the Kohathites with special privileges
(1 Chr. xv. 8).

15. *by the words of the* LORD] Rather, as
suggested in the margin, "According to the
commandment of the king *in the business* (or
matters) of the Lord."

16. The "inner part" means here, not
the Holy of Holies in particular, but the
interior generally. The priests alone might
enter the Temple building. The Levites
might penetrate no further than the inner
court.

21. Hezekiah commenced his restoration
of the Jehovah-worship with an unusually
comprehensive Sin-offering, embracing the

and for the sanctuary, and for Judah. And he commanded the priests the sons of Aaron to offer *them* on the altar of the LORD.

22 So they killed the bullocks, and the priests received the blood, and ^qsprinkled *it* on the altar: likewise, when they had killed the rams, they sprinkled the blood upon the altar: they killed also the lambs, and they sprinkled the blood upon the altar.

23 And they brought ¹forth the he goats *for* the sin offering before the king and the congregation; and they laid their ^rhands upon

24 them: and the priests killed them, and they made reconciliation with their blood upon the altar, ^sto make an atonement for all Israel: for the king commanded *that* the burnt offering and the

25 sin offering *should be made* for all Israel. ^tAnd he set the Levites in the house of the LORD with cymbals, with psalteries, and with harps, ^uaccording to the commandment of David, and of ^xGad the king's seer, and Nathan the prophet: ^yfor *so was*

26 the commandment ²of the LORD ³by his prophets. And the Levites stood with the instruments ^zof David, and the priests

27 with ^athe trumpets. And Hezekiah commanded to offer the burnt offering upon the altar. And ⁴when the burnt offering began, ^bthe song of the LORD began *also* with the trumpets, and

28 with the ⁵instruments *ordained* by David king of Israel. And all the congregation worshipped, and the ⁶singers sang, and the trumpeters sounded: *and all this continued* until the burnt offer-

29 ing was finished. And when they had made an end of offering, ^cthe king and all that were ⁷present with him bowed themselves,

30 and worshipped. Moreover Hezekiah the king and the princes commanded the Levites to sing praise unto the LORD with the words of David, and of Asaph the seer. And they sang praises with gladness, and they bowed their heads and worshipped.

31 ¶ Then Hezekiah answered and said, Now ye have ⁸consecrated yourselves unto the LORD, come near and bring sacrifices and ^dthank offerings into the house of the LORD. And the congregation brought in sacrifices and thank offerings; and as many

¹ Heb. *near.*
² Heb. *by the hand of the* LORD.
³ Heb. *by the hand of.*
⁴ Heb. *in the time.*
⁵ Heb. *hands of instruments.*
⁶ Heb. *song.*
⁷ Heb. *found.*
⁸ Or, *filled your hand,* ch. 13. 9.

four chief kinds of sacrificial animals, and seven animals of each kind : he intended to atone for the sins, both conscious and unconscious, of the king, the priests, the people of Judah, and the people of Israel. After the completion of these expiatory rites, he proceeded to the offering of the Burnt-offering (*v.* 27).

23. *the he goats for the sin offering*] Rather, "the he goats **of the sin offering**"—that portion of the Sin offering which had been reserved to the last.

24. *all Israel*] Hezekiah aimed at reuniting once more the whole people of Israel, if not into a single state, yet, at any rate, into a single religious communion. The northern kingdom was in a condition approaching to anarchy. The end was evidently approaching. Hoshea, the king contemporary with Hezekiah (2 K. xviii. 1), ruled, not as an independent monarch, but as an Assyrian feudatory (do. xvii. 3). Under these circumstances Hezekiah designed to invite the re-

volted tribes to return, if not to their old temporal, at least to their old spiritual, allegiance (xxx. 5-10). In order, therefore, to prepare the way for this return, he included "all Israel" in the expiatory sacrifice, by which he prefaced his restoration of the old worship.

27. All had hitherto been preparatory. Now Hezekiah gave orders that "*the* burnt offering"—*i.e.* the daily morning sacrifice—should be offered upon the Brazen Altar in front of the porch, thus restoring and reinstituting the regular Temple-service. A burst of music gave notice to the people of the moment when the old worship recommenced.

31. Hezekiah addresses, not the priests, but the congregation :—"Now that by the atoning sacrifice which has been offered for you, you are consecrated once more to be a holy people to the Lord, approach with confidence and offer your free-will offerings as of old."

32 as were of a free heart burnt offerings. And the number of
the burnt offerings, which the congregation brought, was threescore and ten bullocks, an hundred rams, *and* two hundred
33 lambs: all these *were* for a burnt offering to the LORD. And
the consecrated things *were* six hundred oxen and three thousand
34 sheep. But the priests were too few, so that they could not
flay all the burnt offerings: wherefore *e*their brethren the   *e* ch. 35. 11.
Levites ¹did help them, till the work was ended, and until the
other priests had sanctified themselves: *f*for the Levites *were*   *f* ch. 30. 3.
more *g*upright in heart to sanctify themselves than the priests.   *g* Ps. 7. 10.
35 And also the burnt offerings *were* in abundance, with *h*the fat   *h* Lev. 3. 16.
of the peace offerings, and *i*the drink offerings for *every* burnt   *i* Num. 15. 5,
offering. So the service of the house of the LORD was set in   7, 10.
36 order. And Hezekiah rejoiced, and all the people, that God
had prepared the people: for the thing was *done* suddenly.
CHAP. **30.** AND Hezekiah sent to all Israel and Judah, and wrote
letters also to Ephraim and Manasseh, that they should come to
the house of the LORD at Jerusalem, to keep the passover unto
2 the LORD God of Israel. For the king had taken counsel, and
his princes, and all the congregation in Jerusalem, to keep the
3 passover in the second *a*month. For they could not keep it   *a* Num. 9.
*b*at that time, *c*because the priests had not sanctified themselves   10, 11.
sufficiently, neither had the people gathered themselves together   *b* Ex.12.6,18.
4 to Jerusalem. And the thing ²pleased the king and all the   *c* ch. 29. 34.
5 congregation. So they established a decree to make proclamation throughout all Israel, from Beer-sheba even to Dan, that
they should come to keep the passover unto the LORD God of
Israel at Jerusalem: for they had not done *it* of a long *time in*
6 *such sort* as it was written. ¶ So the posts went with the letters
³from the king and his princes throughout all Israel and Judah,
and according to the commandment of the king, saying, Ye
children of Israel, *d*turn again unto the LORD God of Abraham,   *d* Jer. 4. 1.
Isaac, and Israel, and he will return to the remnant of you,   Joel 2. 13.
7 that are escaped out of the hand of *e*the kings of Assyria. And   *e* 2 Kin. 15.
   19, 29.

¹ Heb. *strengthened them.*   ² Heb. *was right in the eyes*   ³ Heb. *from the hand.*
                       of the king.

---

burnt offerings] The term thus translated
is applied especially to those victims which
were to be *wholly* consumed upon the Altar.
In the "sacrifices," or Peace offerings generally, and the "thank offerings"—a particular kind of Peace offering (Lev. vii. 12)—
the greater part of the victim belonged to,
and was consumed by, the worshipper.
Hence, to offer "burnt offerings," was indicative of a "free heart."

34. *the Levites were more upright* &c.] See
marg. ref. Urijah, the High-Priest, had
participated to some extent in the impieties
of Ahaz (2 K. xvi. 10–16). He and many
of the priests may, therefore, have looked
coldly on the reforming zeal of Hezekiah.
XXX. 1. Cp. xxix. 24 note.

2. *in the second month*] Hezekiah and his
counsellors considered that the permission
of the Law (see marg. ref.) might, under
the circumstances, be extended to the whole
people. It had been found impossible to
complete the cleansing of the Temple till

the fourteenth day of the first month was
past (xxix. 17). It was, therefore, determined to defer it to the 14th of the
second month, which allowed time for the
priests generally to purify themselves, and
for proclamation of the festival to be made
throughout all Israel.

3. *at that time*] *i.e.* in the first month, at
the time of the events mentioned in ch. xxix.

5. *they had not done it* &c.] Some prefer,
"they had not kept it in full numbers, as
it was written"—*i.e.* "they (the Israelites
of the northern kingdom) had not (for some
while) kept the Passover in full numbers, as
the Law required."

6. *the posts went*] The bearers of the
letters were probably the "runners" who
formed a portion of the king's body-guard
(2 K. x. 25 note).

the kings of Assyria] Pul, Tiglath-pileser,
and Shalmaneser may all be referred to in
this passage (cp. marg. ref. and 2 K. xvii.
3). The passage by no means implies that

f Ezek. 20. 18.

g ch. 29. 8
h Deut. 10. 16.

i ch. 29. 10.

k Ps. 106. 46.

l Ex. 34. 6.

m Isai. 55. 7.

n ch. 36. 16.
o So ch. 11. 16.
ver. 18, 21.
p Phil. 2. 13.
q ch. 29. 25.

r ch. 28. 24.

s ch. 29. 34.

be not ye *f*like your fathers, and like your brethren, which trespassed against the LORD God of their fathers, *who* therefore 8 *g*gave them up to desolation, as ye see. Now [1]be ye not *h*stiff-necked, as your fathers *were*, *but* [2]yield yourselves unto the LORD, and enter into his sanctuary, which he hath sanctified for ever: and serve the LORD your God, *i*that the fierceness of 9 his wrath may turn away from you. For if ye turn again unto the LORD, your brethren and your children *shall find* *k*compassion before them that lead them captive, so that they shall come again into this land: for the LORD your God *is* *l*gracious and merciful, and will not turn away *his* face from you, if ye 10 *m*return unto him. ¶So the posts passed from city to city through the country of Ephraim and Manasseh even unto Zebulun: but *n*they laughed them to scorn, and mocked them. 11 Nevertheless *o*divers of Asher and Manasseh and of Zebulun 12 humbled themselves, and came to Jerusalem. Also in Judah *p*the hand of God was to give them one heart to do the commandment of the king and of the princes, *q*by the word of the 13 LORD. ¶And there assembled at Jerusalem much people to keep the feast of unleavened bread in the second month, a very 14 great congregation. And they arose and took away the *r*altars that *were* in Jerusalem, and all the altars for incense took they 15 away, and cast *them* into the brook Kidron. Then they killed the passover on the fourteenth *day* of the second month: and the priests and the Levites were *s*ashamed, and sanctified themselves, and brought in the burnt offerings into the house of the 16 LORD. And they stood in [3]their place after their manner, according to the law of Moses the man of God: the priests sprinkled the blood, *which they received* of the hand of the Levites.

[1] Heb. *harden not your necks.*   [2] Heb. *give the hand:* See 1 Chr. 29. 24. Ezra 10. 19.   [3] Heb. *their standing.*

---

the fall of Samaria and final captivity of the Israelites had as yet taken place.

10. Ephraim and Manasseh are mentioned as the two tribes nearest to Judah, Zebulun as one of the furthest off.

11. Cp. *v*. 18. Hence five of the ten tribes certainly sent representatives. Two—Reuben and Gad—were in Captivity. One—Dan—was absorbed into Judah. Simeon and Naphtali, which alone remained, seem to have been more than ordinarily idolatrous (xxxiv. 6).

14. The continuance of the idolatrous altars to this time shows that Hezekiah had been more anxious to construct than to destroy, to establish the Jehovah-worship than to root out idolatry. Now, however, that the more important work was done, the Temple open, and the daily service restored, attention could be turned to the secondary object of removing from the city all traces of the late apostasy.

15. The laggart priests and Levites, who from want of zeal for the Jehovah-worship, or from actual inclination to idolatry, had neglected to purify themselves (*v*. 3 and marg. ref.), were now shamed by the general ardour, and sanctified themselves for the Paschal festival.

and brought in the burnt offerings] Received them, *i.e.* from the offerers at the doors of the inner court, and took them up to the Brazen Altar in front of the porch. No part of the Burnt offerings was ever taken inside the Temple building.

16. *after their manner*] According to the Mishna, the custom was for the priests to stand in two rows extending from the Altar to the outer court, where the people were assembled. As each offerer slew his lamb the blood was caught in a bason, which was handed to the nearest priest, who passed it on to his neighbour, and he to the next; the blood was thus conveyed to the Altar, at the base of which it was thrown by the last priest in the row. While basons full of blood were thus passed up, empty basons were passed down in a constant succession, so that there was no pause or delay.

which they received of the hand of the Levites] Ordinarily, the blood was received at the hand of the offerer. But the greater number of the Israelites (*v*. 17) who had come to keep the feast were involved in some ceremonial or moral defilement, from which there had not been time for them to purify themselves. On account of this uncleanness, they did not slay their own

17 For *there were* many in the congregation that were not sanctified: ¹therefore the Levites had the charge of the killing of the passovers for every one *that was* not clean, to sanctify *them* **18** unto the LORD. For a multitude of the people, *even* ᵘmany of Ephraim, and Manasseh, Issachar, and Zebulun, had not cleansed themselves, ˣyet did they eat the passover otherwise than it was written. But Hezekiah prayed for them, saying, The good LORD **19** pardon every one *that* ʸprepareth his heart to seek God, the LORD God of his fathers, though *he be* not *cleansed* according to **20** the purification of the sanctuary. And the LORD hearkened to **21** Hezekiah, and healed the people. ¶ And the children of Israel that were ¹present at Jerusalem kept ˢthe feast of unleavened bread seven days with great gladness: and the Levites and the priests praised the LORD day by day, *singing* with ²loud **22** instruments unto the LORD. And Hezekiah spake ³comfortably unto all the Levites ᵃthat taught the good knowledge of the LORD: and they did eat throughout the feast seven days, offering peace offerings, and ᵇmaking confession to the LORD God **23** of their fathers. ¶ And the whole assembly took counsel to keep ᶜother seven days: and they kept *other* seven days with **24** gladness. For Hezekiah king of Judah ⁴ᵈdid give to the congregation a thousand bullocks and seven thousand sheep; and the princes gave to the congregation a thousand bullocks and ten thousand sheep: and a great number of priests ᵉsanctified **25** themselves. And all the congregation of Judah, with the priests and the Levites, and all the congregation ᶠthat came out of Israel, and the strangers that came out of the land of Israel, **26** and that dwelt in Judah, rejoiced. So there was great joy in Jerusalem: for since the time of Solomon the son of David **27** king of Israel *there was* not the like in Jerusalem. Then the priests the Levites arose and ᵍblessed the people: and their voice was heard, and their prayer came *up* to ⁵his holy dwelling place, *even* unto heaven.

CHAP. 31. NOW when all this was finished, all Israel that were ⁶present went out to the cities of Judah, and ᵃbrake the ⁷images in pieces, and cut down the groves, and threw down the high places and the altars out of all Judah and Benjamin, in Ephraim also and Manasseh, ⁸until they had utterly destroyed

t ch. 29. 34.

u ver. 11.

x Ex. 12. 43, &c.

y ch. 19. 3.

z Ex. 12. 15. & 13. 6.

a Deut.33.10. ch. 17. 9. & 35. 3. *b* Ezra 10. 11.

c See 1 Kin. 8. 65. *d* ch. 35. 7, 8.

e ch. 29. 34.

f ver. 11, 13.

g Num. 6. 23.

a 2 Kin. 18.4.

¹ Heb. *found.*
² Heb. *instruments of strength.*
³ Heb. *to the heart of all,*
⁴ *&c.* Isai. 40. 2.
⁴ Heb. *lifted up,* or, *offered.*
⁵ Heb. *the habitation of his holiness,* Ps. 68. 5.
⁶ Heb. *found.*
⁷ Heb. *statues,* ch. 30. 14.
⁸ Heb. *until to make an end.*

lambs, but delegated the office to the Levites.

22. The "knowledge" intended is perhaps chiefly ritualistic and musical—such knowledge as enabled them to conduct the service of the Sanctuary satisfactorily.

they did eat throughout the feast] Lit. "they did *eat the feast;*" *i.e.* "they kept the Feast," which was essentially kept by the eating of unleavened bread. The Levites kept the Feast during the full term appointed for it, never failing in their duties, but taking their part day after day, both in the sacrifice of the victims and in singing praises to God.

23. *to keep other seven days*] This was a voluntary addition to the requirements of

the Law—the fruit and sign of the abounding zeal which characterised the time. Hezekiah and the princes probably proposed it to the people, and presented them with sacrificial animals.

25. *the strangers*] See xv. 9 note.
26. *since the time of Solomon*] Cp. vii. 8–10.

XXXI. **1.** Jerusalem had been cleansed (xxx. 14); now the land had to be purged. Hezekiah therefore gave his sanction to a popular movement directed as much against the "high places" which had been maintained since the times of the patriarchs, as against the remnants of the Baal-worship, or the innovations of Ahaz. See 2 K. xviii. 4 note. The invasion of the northern king-

them all. Then all the children of Israel returned, every man
2 to his possession, into their own cities. ¶ And Hezekiah
appointed *b*the courses of the priests and the Levites after their
courses, every man according to his service, the priests and
Levites *c*for burnt offerings and for peace offerings, to minister,
and to give thanks, and to praise in the gates of the tents of
3 the LORD. *He appointed* also the king's portion of his substance
for the burnt offerings, *to wit*, for the morning and evening burnt
offerings, and the burnt offerings for the sabbaths, and for the
new moons, and for the set feasts, as *it is* written in the *d*law
4 of the LORD. ¶ Moreover he commanded the people that dwelt
in Jerusalem to give the *e*portion of the priests and the Levites,
5 that they might be encouraged in *f*the law of the LORD. And
as soon as the commandment ¹came abroad, the children of Israel
brought in abundance *g*the firstfruits of corn, wine, and oil, and
²honey, and of all the increase of the field; and the tithe of all
6 *things* brought they in abundantly. And *concerning* the children
of Israel and Judah, that dwelt in the cities of Judah, they also
brought in the tithe of oxen and sheep, and the *h*tithe of holy
things which were consecrated unto the LORD their God, and
7 laid *them* ³by heaps. In the third month they began to lay the
foundation of the heaps, and finished *them* in the seventh month.
8 And when Hezekiah and the princes came and saw the heaps,
9 they blessed the LORD, and his people Israel. Then Hezekiah
questioned with the priests and the Levites concerning the heaps.

b 1 Chr. 23. 6.
& 24. 1.

c 1 Chr. 23.
30, 31.

d Num. 23,
& 29.

e Num. 18.
8, &c.
f Mal. 2. 7.

g Ex. 22. 29.
Neh. 13. 12.

h Lev. 27. 30.
Deut. 14. 28.

---

¹ Heb. *brake forth.*   ² Or, *dates.*   ³ Heb. *heaps, heaps.*

---

dom "Ephraim and Manasseh" by a tumultuous crowd from the southern one, and
the success which attended the movement,
can only be explained by the state of weakness into which the northern kingdom had
fallen (see note on xxix. 24).

2. *the tents*] Lit. "the camps." The Temple is called the "camp of Jehovah" by an
apt metaphor : the square enclosure, with
its gates and stations, its guards and porters, its reliefs, its orderly arrangement,
and the tabernacle, or tent, of the great
commander in the midst, very much resembled a camp.

3. *the king's portion*] Amid the general
neglect of the observances commanded by
the Law, the tithe system had naturally
fallen into disuse. Hezekiah revived it;
and, to encourage the people to give what
was due, cheerfully set the example of paying the full proportion from his own considerable possessions (cp. xxxii. 28, 29). His
tithe was, it seems, specially devoted to the
purposes mentioned in this verse (cp. marg.
ref.). There were needed for these purposes
in the course of the year nearly 1100 lambs,
113 bullocks, 37 rams, and 30 goats, besides
vast quantities of flour, oil, and wine for the
accompanying Meat and Drink offerings.

4. *that they might be encouraged* &c.]
i.e. to devote themselves wholly to their
proper work, the service of the Sanctuary
and the teaching of God's Law (xvii. 7-9),
and not engage in secular occupations. Cp.
Neh. xiii. 10-14.

5. *honey*] See marg. It is doubtful whether
bee-honey was liable to first-fruits. The sort
here intended may therefore be that which,
according to Josephus, was manufactured
from dates.

6. By "the children of Israel" in *v.* 5,
seem to be intended the inhabitants of Jerusalem only (see *v.* 4); by "the children of
Israel and Judah that dwelt in the cities of
Judah" in this verse, seem to be meant the
Jews of the country districts and the Israelites who dwelt among them (xxx. 25).
Of these two classes, the first brought both
first-fruits and tithes of *all things*; while
the others, who had not been included in
the command (*v.* 4), brought in first-fruits
and paid the tithe of sheep and oxen only,
and of the things which they had vowed to
God.

7. *the third month*] Cp. xxix. 3, xxx. 2,
13. The events hitherto described—the destruction of the high-places, the re-appoint-
ment of the courses, and the re-establishment of the tithes—followed so closely upon
the Passover, that a month had not elapsed
from the conclusion of the Feast before the
gifts began to pour in. In the seventh month
the harvest was completed; and the last
tithes and first-fruits of the year would naturally come in then.

9. "Hezekiah questioned" in order to
know whether the ministering priests and
Levites had had their maintenance out of
the tithes, and whether the accumulation
which he saw was clear surplus.

10 And Azariah the chief priest of the house of Zadok answered him, and said, *i* Since *the people* began to bring the offerings into the house of the LORD, we have had enough to eat, and have left plenty : for the LORD hath blessed his people ; and that which is
11 left *is* this great store. ¶ Then Hezekiah commanded to prepare
12 ¹ chambers in the house of the LORD ; and they prepared *them*, and brought in the offerings and the tithes and the dedicated *things* faithfully : *k* over which Cononiah the Levite *was* ruler, and
13 Shimei his brother *was* the next. And Jehiel, and Azariah, and Nahath, and Asahel, and Jerimoth, and Jozabad, and Eliel, and Ismachiah, and Mahath, and Benaiah, *were* overseers ² under the hand of Cononiah and Shimei his brother, at the commandment of Hezekiah the king, and Azariah the ruler of the house
14 of God. And Kore the son of Imnah the Levite, the porter toward the east, *was* over the freewill offerings of God, to distribute the oblations of the LORD, and the most holy things.
15 And ³ next him *were* Eden, and Miniamin, and Jeshua, and Shemaiah, Amariah, and Shecaniah, in *l* the cities of the priests, in *their* ⁴ set office, to give to their brethren by courses, as well
16 to the great as to the small : beside their genealogy of males, from three years old and upward, *even* unto every one that entereth into the house of the LORD, his daily portion for their
17 service in their charges according to their courses ; both to the genealogy of the priests by the house of their fathers, and the Levites *m* from twenty years old and upward, in their charges by
18 their courses ; and to the genealogy of all their little ones, their wives, and their sons, and their daughters, through all the congregation : for in their ⁵ set office they sanctified themselves in
19 holiness : also of the sons of Aaron the priests, *which were* in *n* the fields of the suburbs of their cities, in every several city,

i Mal. 3. 10.

k Neh. 13.13.

i Josh. 21. 9.

m 1 Chr. 23. 24, 27.

n Lev. 25. 34. Num. 35. 2.

¹ Or, *storehouses.*
² Heb. *at the hand.*
³ Heb. *at his hand.*
⁴ Or, *trust*, 1 Chr. 9. 22.
⁵ Or, *trust.*

---

10. If this Azariah was the same as he who resisted Uzziah (xxvi. 17-20), he must have held his office at least 33 years. Cp. xxvii. 1, xxviii. 1.

the LORD *hath blessed his people*] *i.e.* God has made the harvest unusually abundant, and hence the great amount of tithes and first-fruits.

14. *the porter toward the east*] *i.e.* the chief door-keeper at the east gate, where the proper number of the porters was six (1 Chr. xxvi. 17).

the most holy things] The Sin-offerings and Trespass-offerings (Lev. vi. 25, vii. 1-6).

15. *the cities of the priests*] *i.e.* the Levitical cities (cp. marg. ref.). Of these, some had gone to decay, while others, as Libnah and Beth-shemesh (xxi. 10, xxviii. 18), had been lost, so that the original number, thirteen, was now, apparently, reduced to six.

in their set office] Rather, as in marg. These six Levites were stationed at the Levitical cities, with the trust following committed to them.

16. *beside their genealogy of males*, &c.] Some translate— "Excepting the list of males," &c. *i.e.* they distributed to all the members of the priestly families, excepting those who at the time were performing the duties of their office at Jerusalem. These persons no doubt obtained their share at the Temple itself.

17. *both to the genealogy of the priests* &c.] Some prefer— "And as for the list of the priests, it was according to the houses of their fathers, and that of the Levites was from twenty years," &c. The writer states the nature of the lists which guided the officers who made the distributions. Three lists are enumerated—one of the priests made out according to families ; one of the Levites, including all above 20 years of age (see marg. ref.), and made out according to courses ; and a third (*v.* 18) of the priestly and Levitical families.

18. *and to the genealogy of all their little ones*, &c.] Or, "And as to the list of all their little ones, their wives, their sons, and their daughters, it extended to the whole body; for they dealt according to families faithfully."

19. The country priests and Levites are here distinguished from those who dwelt in the towns. The writer means to note that not even were they neglected.

o ver. 12, 13,
14, 15.

p 2 Kin. 20. 3.

a Isai. 36. 1,
&c.

b Isai. 22. 9,
10.
c ch. 25. 23.
d 2 Sam. 5. 9.
1 Kin. 9. 15.

e Deut. 31. 6.
f ch. 20. 15.

g 2 Kin. 6. 16.
h Jer. 17. 5.
1 John 4. 4.
i ch. 13. 12.
Rom. 8. 31.
k 2 Kin. 18. 17.

l 2 Kin. 18. 19.

the men that were °expressed by name, to give portions to all
the males among the priests, and to all that were reckoned by
20 genealogies among the Levites.   ¶ And thus did Hezekiah
throughout all Judah, and ᵖwrought *that which was* good and
21 right and truth before the LORD his God. And in every work
that he began in the service of the house of God, and in the law,
and in the commandments, to seek his God, he did *it* with all
his heart, and prospered.

CHAP. 32. AFTER ᵃthese things, and the establishment thereof,
Sennacherib king of Assyria came, and entered into Judah, and
encamped against the fenced cities, and thought ¹to win them
2 for himself. And when Hezekiah saw that Sennacherib was
3 come, and that ²he was purposed to fight against Jerusalem, he
took counsel with his princes and his mighty men to stop the
waters of the fountains which *were* without the city: and they
4 did help him. So there was gathered much people together, who
stopped all the fountains, and the brook that ³ran through the
midst of the land, saying, Why should the kings of Assyria come,
5 and find much water? Also ᵇhe strengthened himself, ᶜand
built up all the wall that was broken, and raised *it* up to the
towers, and another wall without, and repaired ᵈMillo *in* the
6 city of David, and made ⁴darts and shields in abundance. And
he set captains of war over the people, and gathered them
together to him in the street of the gate of the city, and ⁵spake
7 comfortably to them, saying, ᵉBe strong and courageous, ᶠbe
not afraid nor dismayed for the king of Assyria, nor for all the
multitude that *is* with him: for ᵍthere be more with us than with
8 him: with him *is* an ʰarm of flesh; but ⁱwith us *is* the LORD
our God to help us, and to fight our battles. And the people
⁶rested themselves upon the words of Hezekiah king of Judah.
9 ¶ ᵏAfter this did Sennacherib king of Assyria send his servants
to Jerusalem, (but he *himself laid siege* against Lachish, and all
his ⁷power with him,) unto Hezekiah king of Judah, and unto
10 all Judah that *were* at Jerusalem, saying, ˡThus saith Senna-

¹ Heb. *to break them up.*
² Heb. *his face* was *to war.*
³ Heb. *overflowed.*

⁴ Or, *swords,* or, *weapons.*
⁵ Heb. *spake to their heart,*
   ch. 30. 22. Isai. 40. 2.

⁶ Heb. *leaned.*
⁷ Heb. *dominion.*

XXXII. **1.** *the establishment thereof*] Lit.
"the *faithfulness* thereof"—or, in other
words, "after these things had been faithfully accomplished."
   Verses 1–8 form a passage supplementary
to 2 K. xviii. 13–16.
   3. *to stop the waters* &c.] Cp. *v.* 30.
Hezekiah's object was probably twofold—
to hide the springs outside the city in order
to distress the Assyrians, and to convey
their water underground into the city, in
order to increase his own supply during the
siege.
   4. The "brook" intended is probably not
the Kidron, but the natural water-course of
the Gihon, which ran down the Tyropœon
valley (cp. 1 K. i. 3 note).
   5. The breaches in the wall of Jerusalem
were not entirely due to the old hostility of
Joash (marg. ref.) ; but may have been
caused either by neglect and carelessness in
the reign of Ahaz (ch. xxviii.), or by the

simple process of natural decay. Hezekiah
pulled down houses for the purpose of his
repairs (Isai. xxii. 10).
   On Millo, see marg. reff. notes.
   6. *the street of the gate* &c.] Or, "the
square at the gate" (cp. xxix. 4 note). The
gate intended is probably that of Ephraim
(xxv. 23)—the great northern gate, opposite
the "Camp of the Assyrians"—represented
by the modern Damascus gate.
   7. On the language, cp. the marg. reff. ;
for details, see Isai. xxii. 5–13, xxix. 3.
   8. The faith, which Hezekiah's words express, presently wavered, died away, and
was succeeded by despair and submission
(cp. 2 K. xviii. 14–16 notes).
   9–22 The author of Chronicles com-
presses into thirteen verses the history
which occupies in Kings a chapter and a
half (2 K. xviii. 17, xix. ; where see notes).
   10. *in the siege*] Perhaps "in **straitness**"
(cp. Jer. xix 9). Jerusalem is thought by

cherib king of Assyria, Whereon do ye trust, that ye abide [1]in
11 the siege in Jerusalem? Doth not Hezekiah persuade you to
give over yourselves to die by famine and by thirst, saying,
[m]The LORD our God shall deliver us out of the hand of the king
12 of Assyria? [n]Hath not the same Hezekiah taken away his
high places and his altars, and commanded Judah and Jerusalem, saying, Ye shall worship before one altar, and burn
13 incense upon it? Know ye not what I and my fathers have
done unto all the people of *other* lands? [o]were the gods of the
nations of those lands any ways able to deliver their lands out
14 of mine hand? Who *was there* among all the gods of those
nations that my fathers utterly destroyed, that could deliver
his people out of mine hand, that your God should be able to
15 deliver you out of mine hand? Now therefore [p]let not Hezekiah deceive you, nor persuade you on this manner, neither yet
believe him: for no god of any nation or kingdom was able to
deliver his people out of mine hand, and out of the hand of my
fathers: how much less shall your God deliver you out of mine
16 hand? And his servants spake yet *more* against the LORD God,
17 and against his servant Hezekiah. ¶ [q]He wrote also letters to
rail on the LORD God of Israel, and to speak against him, saying, [r]As the gods of the nations of *other* lands have not delivered
their people out of mine hand, so shall not the God of Hezekiah
18 deliver his people out of mine hand. [s]Then they cried with a
loud voice in the Jews' speech unto the people of Jerusalem
[t]that *were* on the wall, to affright them, and to trouble them;
19 that they might take the city. And they spake against the God
of Jerusalem, as against the gods of the people of the earth,
20 *which were* [u]the work of the hands of man. ¶ [x]And for this *cause*
Hezekiah the king, and [y]the prophet Isaiah the son of Amoz,
21 prayed and cried to heaven. [z]And the LORD sent an angel,
which cut off all the mighty men of valour, and the leaders and
captains in the camp of the king of Assyria. So he returned
with shame of face to his own land. And when he was come
into the house of his god, they that came forth of his own bowels
22 [2]slew him there with the sword. Thus the LORD saved Hezekiah
and the inhabitants of Jerusalem from the hand of Sennacherib
the king of Assyria, and from the hand of all *other*, and guided
23 them on every side. And many brought gifts unto the LORD
to Jerusalem, and [3][a]presents to Hezekiah king of Judah: so
that he was [b]magnified in the sight of all nations from thence-
24 forth. ¶ [c]In those days Hezekiah was sick to the death, and
prayed unto the LORD: and he spake unto him, and he [4]gave
25 him a sign. But Hezekiah [d]rendered not again according to

[m] 2 Kin. 18. 30.
[n] 2 Kin. 18. 22.

[o] 2 Kin.18.33, 34, 35.

[p] 2 Kin.18.29.

[q] 2 Kin.19.9.
[r] 2 Kin.19.12.

[s] 2 Kin.18.28.

[t] 2 Kin. 18. 26, 27, 28.

[u] 2 Kin.19.18.
[x] 2 Kin.19.15.
[y] 2 Kin. 19. 2, 4.
[z] 2 Kin. 19. 35, &c.

[a] ch. 17. 5.
[b] ch. 1. 1.
[c] 2 Kin. 20.1. Isai. 38. 1.
[d] Ps. 116. 12.

---

[1] Or, *in the strong hold.*
[2] Heb. *made him fall.*
[3] Heb. *precious things.*
[4] Or, *wrought a miracle for him.*

---

some to have been not so much besieged at this time, as distressed and straitened for supplies, because the Assyrians were masters of the open country.

13. *fathers*] *i.e.* "predecessors." Sennacherib really belonged to a dynasty that had only furnished one king before himself.

22. *guided them* &c.] A slight alteration of the existing text gives the sense—"gave them rest round about;" a common expression in Chronicles (xv. 15, xx. 30).

24. Cp. 2 K. xx. and notes. The "sign" is not (as in marg.) the miraculous cure, but the going back of the shadow on the dial of Ahaz (see *v.* 31).

25. *his heart was lifted up*] Cp. marg. ref. Hezekiah's pride was shown in his unnecessarily exhibiting his treasures to the ambassadors from Babylon (see 2 K. xx. 13).

there was wrath upon him] Cp. 2 K. xx. 17, 18.

the benefit *done* unto him; for *e* his heart was lifted up: *f* therefore there was wrath upon him, and upon Judah and Jerusalem.
26 *g* Notwithstanding Hezekiah humbled himself for [1] the pride of his heart, *both* he and the inhabitants of Jerusalem, so that the wrath of the LORD came not upon them *h* in the days of Heze-
27 kiah. ¶ And Hezekiah had exceeding much riches and honour: and he made himself treasuries for silver, and for gold, and for precious stones, and for spices, and for shields, and for all
28 manner of [2] pleasant jewels; storehouses also for the increase of corn, and wine, and oil; and stalls for all manner of beasts,
29 and cotes for flocks. Moreover he provided him cities, and possessions of flocks and herds in abundance: for *i* God had
30 given him substance very much. *k* This same Hezekiah also stopped the upper watercourse of Gihon, and brought it straight down to the west side of the city of David. And Hezekiah
31 prospered in all his works. Howbeit in *the business of* the [3] ambassadors of the princes of Babylon, who *l* sent unto him to enquire of the wonder that was *done* in the land, God left him, to *m* try him, that he might know all *that was* in his heart.
32 ¶ Now the rest of the acts of Hezekiah, and his [4] goodness, behold, they *are* written in *n* the vision of Isaiah the prophet, the son of Amoz, *and* in the *o* book of the kings of Judah and Israel.
33 *p* And Hezekiah slept with his fathers, and they buried him in the [5] chiefest of the sepulchres of the sons of David: and all Judah and the inhabitants of Jerusalem did him *q* honour at his death. And Manasseh his son reigned in his stead.

CHAP. 33. MANASSEH *a was* twelve years old when he began to
2 reign, and he reigned fifty and five years in Jerusalem: but did *that which was* evil in the sight of the LORD, like unto the *b* abominations of the heathen, whom the LORD had cast out
3 before the children of Israel. For [6] he built again the high places which Hezekiah his father had *c* broken down, and he reared up altars for Baalim, and *d* made groves, and worshipped
4 *e* all the host of heaven, and served them. Also he built altars in the house of the LORD, whereof the LORD had said, *f* In
5 Jerusalem shall my name be for ever. And he built altars for all the host of heaven *g* in the two courts of the house of the
6 LORD. *h* And he caused his children to pass through the fire in the valley of the son of Hinnom: *i* also he observed times, and

[1] Heb. *the lifting up.*   [3] Heb. *interpreters.*   [5] Or, *highest.*
[2] Heb. *instruments of desire.*   [4] Heb. *kindnesses.*   [6] Heb. *he returned and built.*

---

26. *Hezekiah humbled himself*] Perhaps this is the self-humiliation of which Jeremiah speaks (marg. ref.) as following on a certain prophecy uttered by Micah. The prophecy (iii. 12) is by some referred to the earlier part of the reign of Hezekiah; but there is nothing to show that it was not delivered about this time.

30. See *v.* 3 note. Either then or afterwards, Hezekiah conducted the water of this spring by an underground channel down the Tyropœon valley to a pool or reservoir (marg. ref.).

32. *and in the book*] The "and" is not in the original. The meaning is, that the acts were recorded in the prophecy of Isaiah, which formed a part of the compilation

known as "the Book of the Kings of Judah and Israel." See Introduction, p. 447.

33. *the chiefest of the sepulchres*] Most modern commentators render—"*on the ascent* to the sepulchres;" but some think that an excavation above all the other tombs,—in the same repository, but at a higher level (see marg.)—is intended. The catacomb of David was full; and the later princes had sepulchres quite distinct from the old burial-place (see xxxiii. 20; 2 K. xxi. 18, 26, xxiii. 30).

XXXIII. Cp. reff. and notes. The author of Chronicles differs chiefly from Kings in additions (see 2 K. xxi. 17 note). The central part of this chapter (*vv.* 11–19) is almost entirely new matter.

used enchantments, and used witchcraft, and [k]dealt with a familiar spirit, and with wizards : he wrought much evil in the 7 sight of the LORD, to provoke him to anger. And [l]he set a carved image, the idol which he had made, in the house of God, of which God had said to David and to Solomon his son, In [m]this house, and in Jerusalem, which I have chosen before all 8 the tribes of Israel, will I put my name for ever : [n]neither will I any more remove the foot of Israel from out of the land which I have appointed for your fathers ; so that they will take heed to do all that I have commanded them, according to the whole law and the statutes and the ordinances by the hand of Moses. 9 ¶ So Manasseh made Judah and the inhabitants of Jerusalem to err, *and* to do worse than the heathen, whom the LORD had 10 destroyed before the children of Israel. And the LORD spake to Manasseh, and to his people : but they would not hearken. 11 [o]Wherefore the LORD brought upon them the captains of the host [1]of the king of Assyria, which took Manasseh among the thorns, and [p]bound him with [2]fetters, and carried him to Ba- 12 bylon. And when he was in affliction, he besought the LORD his God, and [q]humbled himself greatly before the God of his 13 fathers, and prayed unto him : and he was [r]intreated of him, and heard his supplication, and brought him again to Jerusalem into his kingdom. Then Manasseh [s]knew that the LORD he *was* 14 God. ¶ Now after this he built a wall without the city of David, on the west side of [t]Gihon, in the valley, even to the entering in at the fish gate, and compassed [u]about [3]Ophel, and raised it up a very great height, and put captains of war in all the fenced 15 cities of Judah. And he took away [x]the strange gods, and the idol out of the house of the LORD, and all the altars that he had built in the mount of the house of the LORD, and in Jerusalem, 16 and cast *them* out of the city. And he repaired the altar of the LORD, and sacrificed thereon peace offerings and [y]thank offer- ings, and commanded Judah to serve the LORD God of Israel. 17 [z]Nevertheless the people did sacrifice still in the high places, *yet* 18 unto the LORD their God only. ¶ Now the rest of the acts of Manasseh, and his prayer unto his God, and the words of [a]the

[k] 2 Kin.21.6.

[l] 2 Kin.21.7.

[m] Ps.132.14.

[n] 2 Sam.7.10.

[o] Deut.28.36.

[p] Job 36. 8. Ps.107.10,11.

[q] 1 Pet. 5. 6.

[r] 1 Chr. 5. 20 Ezra 8. 23.

[s] Ps. 9. 16. Dan. 4. 25.

[t] 1 Kin. 1. 33.

[u] ch. 27. 3.

[x] ver. 3, 5, 7.

[y] Lev. 7. 12.

[z] ch. 32. 12.

[a] 1 Sam. 9. 9.

[1] Heb. *which* were *the king's.*   [2] Or, *chains.*   [3] Or, *The tower.*

---

7. *the idol*] *i.e.* the Asherah (2 K. xxi. 7 note), which receives here (and in Ezek. viii. 3, 5) the somewhat unusual name of *semel*, which some regard as a proper name, and compare with the Greek Σεμέλη.

11. The Assyrian monuments contain no record of this expedition ; but there can be little doubt that it fell into the reign of Esarhaddon (2 K. xix. 37 note), who reigned at least thirteen years. Esarhaddon mentions Manasseh among his tributaries ; and he was the only king of Assyria who, from time to time, held his court at Babylon.

among the thorns] Translate — " with rings ; " and see 2 K. xix. 28 note.

14. Rather, " he built **the outer wall of the city of David on the west of Gihon-in-the-valley.**" The wall intended seems to have been that towards the north-east, which ran from the vicinity of the modern Damascus gate across the valley of Gihon,

to the " fish-gate " at the north-east corner of the " city of David."

We may gather from this verse that, late in his reign, Manasseh revolted from the Assyrians, and made preparations to resist them if they should attack him. Assyria began to decline in power about B.C. 647, and from that time her outlying provinces would naturally begin to fall off. Manasseh reigned till B.C. 642.

17. Cp. 2 K. xxi. 2, xviii. 4 notes.

18. The " prayer of Manasseh," preserved to us in some MSS. of the LXX., has no claim to be considered the genuine utterance of the Jewish king. It is the composition of a Hellenistic Jew, well acquainted with the Septuagint, writing at a time probably not much anterior to the Christian era.

the words of the seers that spake to him] See 2 K. xxi. 11-15.

seers that spake to him in the name of the LORD God of Israel,
19 behold, they *are written* in the book of the kings of Israel. His
prayer also, and *how God* was intreated of him, and all his sins,
and his trespass, and the places wherein he built high places,
and set up groves and graven images, before he was humbled:

b 2Kin.21.18. 20 behold, they *are* written among the sayings of ¹the seers. *b*So
Manasseh slept with his fathers, and they buried him in his own

c 2 Kin. 21. 21 house: and Amon his son reigned in his stead. ¶*c*Amon *was*
19, &c. two and twenty years old when he began to reign, and reigned
22 two years in Jerusalem. But he did *that which was* evil in the
sight of the LORD, as did Manasseh his father: for Amon sacrificed unto all the carved images which Manasseh his father

d ver. 12. 23 had made, and served them; and humbled not himself before
e 2 Kin. 21. the LORD, *d*as Manasseh his father had humbled himself; but
23, 24. 24 Amon ²trespassed more and more. *e*And his servants con-
25 spired against him, and slew him in his own house. But the
people of the land slew all them that had conspired against king
Amon; and the people of the land made Josiah his son king in
his stead.

c 2 Kin. 22. **CHAP. 34.** JOSIAH *a was* eight years old when he began to reign,
1, &c. 2 and he reigned in Jerusalem one and thirty years. And· he did
that which was right in the sight of the LORD, and walked in the
ways of David his father, and declined *neither* to the right hand,
3 nor to the left. For in the eighth year of his reign, while he

b ch. 15. 2. was yet young, he began to *b*seek after the God of David his
c 1 Kin.13. 2. father: and in the twelfth year he began *c*to purge Judah and
d ch. 33. 17, Jerusalem *d*from the high places, and the groves, and the carved
22. 4 images, and the molten images. *e*And they brake down the
e Lev. 26. 30. altars of Baalim in his presence; and the ³images, that *were* on
2 Kin. 23. 4. high above them, he cut down; and the groves, and the carved
images, and the molten images, he brake in pieces, and made

f 2 Kin. 23. 6. dust *of them,* *f*and strowed *it* upon the ⁴graves of them that had
g 1 Kin.13. 2. 5 sacrificed unto them. And he *g*burnt the bones of the priests
6 upon their altars, and cleansed Judah and Jerusalem. And *so
did he* in the cities of Manasseh, and Ephraim, and Simeon, even
7 unto Naphtali, with their ⁵mattocks round about. And when

---

¹ Or, *Hosai.*   ³ Or, *sun images.*   ⁵ Or, *mauls.*
² Heb. *multiplied trespass.*   ⁴ Heb. *face of the graves.*

---

in the book of the kings of Israel] The
writer of Chronicles usually speaks of "the
book of the kings of Judah and Israel" (or
"Israel and Judah"). Here he designates
the same compilation by a more compen-
dious title, without (apparently) any special
reason for the change. Cp. xx. 34.

19. *the seers*] Most moderns adopt the
translation given in the margin of the
Authorised Version, making Hosai (or
rather, Chozai) a proper name. The point
is a doubtful one.

XXXIV. Cp. the parallel history of 2
K. xxii. and xxiii. 1-30 notes; the writer
here being more full on the celebration of
the Passover. The only approach to a discrepancy between the two narratives is
with respect to the time of the religious
reformation, which the writer of Chronicles
distinctly places before, the author of Kings
after, the repair of the Temple. The best

explanation seems to be, that the author of
Kings has departed from the chronological
order, to which he makes no profession of
adhering.

3. *he began to purge Judah*] Jeremiah's
first prophecies (Jer. ii. and iii.) appear to
have been coincident with Josiah's earlier
efforts to uproot idolatry, and must have
greatly strengthened his hands.

4. *the images*] Marg. *sun-images.* See Lev.
xxvi. 30 note.

6. The power of Assyria being now (B.C.
629-624) greatly weakened, if not completely broken, Josiah aimed not merely at
a religious reformation, but at a restoration
of the kingdom to its ancient limits (2 K.
xxiii. 19 note).

with their mattocks &c.] Or "in their
desolate places" (cp. Ps. cix. 10). Another
reading gives the sense, "he *proved their
houses* round about."

he had broken down the altars and the groves, and had *h*beaten *h* Deut. 9. 21.
the graven images ¹into powder, and cut down all the idols
throughout all the land of Israel, he returned to Jerusalem.
8 ¶ Now *i*in the eighteenth year of his reign, when he had purged *i* 2 Kin. 22. 3.
the land, and the house, he sent Shaphan the son of Azaliah, and
Maaseiah the governor of the city, and Joah the son of Joahaz
9 the recorder, to repair the house of the LORD his God. And when
they came to Hilkiah the high priest, they delivered *k*the money *k* See 2 Kin.
that was brought into the house of God, which the Levites that 12. 4, &c.
kept the doors had gathered of the hand of Manasseh and
Ephraim, and of all the remnant of Israel, and of all Judah and
10 Benjamin; and they returned to Jerusalem. And they put *it*
in the hand of the workmen that had the oversight of the house
of the LORD, and they gave it to the workmen that wrought in
11 the house of the LORD, to repair and amend the house: even to
the artificers and builders gave they *it*, to buy hewn stone, and
timber for couplings, and ²to floor the houses which the kings of
12 Judah had destroyed. And the men did the work faithfully:
and the overseers of them *were* Jahath and Obadiah, the Levites,
of the sons of Merari; and Zechariah and Meshullam, of the
sons of the Kohathites, to set *it* forward; and *other of* the
13 Levites, all that could skill of instruments of musick. Also *they*
were over the bearers of burdens, and *were* overseers of all that
wrought the work in any manner of service: *l*and of the Levites *l* 1 Chr. 23. 4,
14 *there were* scribes, and officers, and porters. ¶ And when they 5.
brought out the money that was brought into the house of the
LORD, Hilkiah the priest *m*found a book of the law of the LORD *m* 2 Kin. 22.
15 *given* ³by Moses. And Hilkiah answered and said to Shaphan 8, &c.
the scribe, I have found the book of the law in the house of the
16 LORD. And Hilkiah delivered the book to Shaphan. And
Shaphan carried the book to the king, and brought the king
word back again, saying, All that was committed ⁴to thy ser-
17 vants, they do *it*. And they have ⁵gathered together the money
that was found in the house of the LORD, and have delivered it
into the hand of the overseers, and to the hand of the workmen.
18 Then Shaphan the scribe told the king, saying, Hilkiah the
priest hath given me a book. And Shaphan read ⁶it before the
19 king. And it came to pass, when the king had heard the words
20 of the law, that he rent his clothes. And the king commanded
Hilkiah, and Ahikam the son of Shaphan, and ⁷Abdon the son
of Micah, and Shaphan the scribe, and Asaiah a servant of the
21 king's, saying, Go, enquire of the LORD for me, and for them
that are left in Israel and in Judah, concerning the words of

---

¹ Heb. *to make powder.*　　⁴ Heb. *to the hand of.*　　⁶ Heb. *in it.*
² Or, *to rafter.*　　⁵ Heb. *poured out*, or,　　⁷ Or, *Achbor*, 2 Kin. 22.
³ Heb. *by the hand of.*　　*melted.*　　12.

---

11. The "houses" intended are either
the "chambers" which surrounded the
Temple on three sides (1 K. vi. 5), or out-
buildings attached to the courts. The
"kings of Judah" intended are, no doubt,
Manasseh and Amon.
13. *of the Levites there were scribes*] Hitherto
the word "scribe" has never been used to
designate a class (cp. 1 K. iv. 3). But here
an order of scribes, forming a distinct
division of the Levitical body, has been instituted. The class itself probably origi-

nated in the reign of Hezekiah (cp. Prov.
xxv. 1); and it is probably to the rise of this
class that we are indebted for the preservation of so many prophecies belonging to
Hezekiah's time, while the works of almost
all previous Prophets—Ahijah, Iddo, Shemaiah, Jehu, the son of Hanani, and probably many others—have perished.
21. *for them that are left in Israel and in*
Judah] Cp. the words in Kings (2 K. xxii.
13). In both records the intention is to
show that the king regarded the ten tribes

the book that is found : for great *is* the wrath of the LORD that is poured out upon us, because our fathers have not kept the word of the LORD, to do after all that is written in this book.

22 ¶ And Hilkiah, and *they* that the king *had appointed*, went to Huldah the prophetess, the wife of Shallum the son of "Tikvath, the son of ¹Hasrah, keeper of the ²wardrobe; (now she dwelt in Jerusalem ³in the college:) and they spake to her to that

23 *effect*. And she answered them, Thus saith the LORD God of

24 Israel, Tell ye the man that sent you to me, Thus saith the LORD, Behold, I will bring evil upon this place, and upon the inhabitants thereof, *even* all the curses that are written in the

25 book which they have read before the king of Judah : because they have forsaken me, and have burned incense unto other gods, that they might provoke me to anger with all the works of their hands ; therefore my wrath shall be poured out upon

26 this place, and shall not be quenched. And as for the king of Judah, who sent you to enquire of the LORD, so shall ye say unto him, Thus saith the LORD God of Israel *concerning* the

27 words which thou hast heard ; Because thine heart was tender, and thou didst humble thyself before God, when thou heardest his words against this place, and against the inhabitants thereof, and humbledst thyself before me, and didst rend thy clothes, and weep before me ; I have even heard *thee* also, saith the

28 LORD. Behold, I will gather thee to thy fathers, and thou shalt be gathered to thy grave in peace, neither shall thine eyes see all the evil that I will bring upon this place, and upon the inhabitants of the same. So they brought the king word again.

29 ¶ °Then the king sent and gathered together all the elders of

30 Judah and Jerusalem. And the king went up into the house of the LORD, and all the men of Judah, and the inhabitants of Jerusalem, and the priests, and the Levites, and all the people, ⁴great and small : and he read in their ears all the words of the book of the covenant that was found in the house of the LORD.

31 And the king stood in ᵖhis place, and made a covenant before the LORD, to walk after the LORD, and to keep his commandments, and his testimonies, and his statutes, with all his heart, and with all his soul, to perform the words of the covenant

32 which are written in this book. And he caused all that were ⁵present in Jerusalem and Benjamin to stand *to it*. And the inhabitants of Jerusalem did according to the covenant of

33 God, the God of their fathers. And Josiah took away all the ᑫabominations out of all the countries that *pertained* to the children of Israel, and made all that were present in Israel to serve, *even* to serve the LORD their God. ʳAnd all his days

Margin references:
"2Kin.22.14.

°2 Kin. 23. 1, &c.

ᵖ2Kin.11.14. ch. 6. 13.

ᑫ1 Kin.11. 5.

ʳJer. 3. 10.

---

¹ Or, *Harhas.*
² Heb. *garments.*
³ Or, *in the school,* or, *in the second part.*
⁴ Heb. *from great even to small.*
⁵ Heb. *found.*

---

as being under his care, no less than the two.

30. The writer has characteristically substituted "Levites" for the "prophets" of 2 K. xxiii. 2. No doubt Josiah was accompanied by priests, Prophets, and Levites, but the writer of Kings thought it enough to mention the two former, and merged the Levites in the mass of the people. The writer of Chronicles, on the other hand, thinks the presence of Levites too important

to be omitted, and as the Prophets could be but few in number, passes them over.

32. *and Benjamin*] It is scarcely possible that the text here can be sound. "Benjamin" is never put in contrast with "Jerusalem," but always with Judah. The reading may be corrected from the parallel passage 2 K. xxiii. 3; "And he caused all those that were present in Jerusalem to stand **to the covenant.**"

33. *all his days they departed not*] This

they departed not [1]from following the LORD, the God of their fathers.

CHAP. 35. MOREOVER [a]Josiah kept a passover unto the LORD in Jerusalem: and they killed the passover on the [b]fourteenth 2 *day* of the first month. And he set the priests in their [c]charges, and [d]encouraged them to the service of the house of the LORD, 3 and said unto the Levites [e]that taught all Israel, which were holy unto the LORD, [f]Put the holy ark [g]in the house which Solomon the son of David king of Israel did build; [h]*it shall* not *be* a burden upon *your* shoulders: serve now the LORD your God, 4 and his people Israel, and prepare *yourselves* by the [i]houses of your fathers, after your courses, according to the [k]writing of David king of Israel, and according to the [l]writing of Solomon 5 his son. And [m]stand in the holy *place* according to the divisions of [2]the families of the fathers of your brethren [3]the people, 6 and *after* the division of the families of the Levites. So kill the passover, and [n]sanctify yourselves, and prepare your brethren, that *they* may do according to the word of the LORD by the hand 7 of Moses. ¶ And Josiah [4o]gave to the people, of the flock, lambs and kids, all for the passover offerings, for all that were present, to the number of thirty thousand, and three thousand 8 bullocks: these *were* of the king's substance. And his princes [5]gave willingly unto the people, to the priests, and to the Levites: Hilkiah and Zechariah and Jehiel, rulers of the house of God, gave unto the priests for the passover offerings two thousand 9 and six hundred *small cattle*, and three hundred oxen. Conaniah also, and Shemaiah and Nethaneel, his brethren, and Hashabiah and Jeiel and Jozabad, chief of the Levites, [6]gave unto the Levites for passover offerings five thousand *small cattle*, and 10 five hundred oxen. ¶ So the service was prepared, and the priests [p]stood in their place, and the Levites in their courses, 11 according to the king's commandment. And they killed the passover, and the priests [q]sprinkled *the blood* from their hands, 12 and the Levites [r]flayed *them*. And they removed the burnt offerings, that they might give according to the divisions of the

Marginal references:
[a] 2 Kin. 23. 21, 22.
[b] Ex. 12. 6. Ezra 6. 19.
[c] ch. 23 18. Ezra 6. 18.
[d] ch. 29. 5, 11.
[e] Deut. 33. 10.
ch. 30. 22. Mal. 2. 7.
[f] See ch. 34. 14.
[g] ch. 5. 7.
[h] 1 Chr. 23. 26.
[i] 1 Chr. 9. 10.
[k] 1 Chr. 23, & 24, 25, & 26.
[l] ch. 8. 14.
[m] Ps. 134. 1.
[n] ch. 29. 5, 15. & 30. 3, 15. Ezra 6. 20.
[o] ch. 30. 24.

[p] Ezra 6. 18.

[q] ch. 29. 22.

[r] See ch. 29. 34.

---

[1] Heb. *from after.*
[2] Heb. *the house of the fathers.*
[3] Heb. *the sons of the people.*
[4] Heb. *offered.*
[5] Heb. *offered.*
[6] Heb. *offered.*

---

must be understood in the letter rather than in the spirit. There was no open idolatry in the reign of Josiah, but the reformation was seeming rather than real, superficial rather than searching and complete (cp. marg. ref.).

XXXV. 3. *Put the holy ark* &c.] The Ark of the Covenant may have been temporarily removed from the Holy of Holies while Josiah effected necessary repairs.

it shall not be a burden upon your shoulders] The removing and replacing the Ark Josiah means "shall not henceforth be your duty. The Ark shall remain undisturbed in the Holy of Holies. You shall return to your old employments, to the service of God and the instruction of the people."

5. The sense of this verse probably is :— "So divide yourselves that, for every distinct family among the people who come to the Passover, there shall be a portion of a Levitical family to minister."

6. *prepare your brethren*, &c.] *i.e.* "as you minister to your brethren the people, by killing and flaying their offerings and handing the blood to the priests, instruct them how they are to eat the Passover acceptably." It is implied that many would be ignorant of the requirements of the Law.

7–11. See marg. reff. and note.

8. *his princes*] *i.e.* his *ecclesiastical* princes, the chief men of the priests and Levites. For the poor families of their own order the leading priests furnished both Passover-cattle and cattle for Thank-offerings. The chief Levites acted similarly towards the poor Levitical families.

12. *they removed the burnt offerings*] They separated from the paschal lambs those parts which were to be burnt on the Altar. These parts they gave to the offerers, who took them up to the Altar and handed them to the officiating priests.

*Lev. 3. 3.

families of the people, to offer unto the LORD, as *it is* written *in
13 the book of Moses.   And so *did they* with the oxen.   And they

t Ex. 12. 8, 9.
Deut. 16. 7.
u 1 Sam. 2.
13, 14, 15.

*t*roasted the passover with fire according to the ordinance : but
the *other* holy *offerings* *u*sod they in pots, and in caldrons, and
14 in pans, and *1*divided *them* speedily among all the people.   And
afterward they made ready for themselves, and for the priests :
because the priests the sons of Aaron *were busied* in offering of
burnt offerings and the fat until night ; therefore the Levites
prepared for themselves, and for the priests the sons of Aaron.
15 And the singers the sons of Asaph *were* in their *2*place, accord-

x 1 Chr. 25.
1, &c.
y 1 Chr. 9.
17, 18.
& 26. 14, &c.

ing to the *x*commandment of David, and Asaph, and Heman,
and Jeduthun the king's seer ; and the porters *y*waited at every
gate ; they might not depart from their service ; for their
16 brethren the Levites prepared for them.   So all the service of
the LORD was prepared the same day, to keep the passover, and
to offer burnt offerings upon the altar of the LORD, according to
17 the commandment of king Josiah.   And the children of Israel
that were *3*present kept the passover at that time, and the feast

z Ex. 12. 15.
& 13. 6.
ch. 30. 21.
a 2 Kin. 23.
22, 23.

18 of *z*unleavened bread seven days.   ¶ And *a*there was no passover like to that kept in Israel from the days of Samuel the
prophet ; neither did all the kings of Israel keep such a passover
as Josiah kept, and the priests, and the Levites, and all Judah
and Israel that were present, and the inhabitants of Jerusalem.
19 In the eighteenth year of the reign of Josiah was this passover

b 2 Kin. 23. 29.
Jer. 46. 2.

20 kept.   ¶ *b* After all this, when Josiah had prepared the *4*temple,
Necho king of Egypt came up to fight against Charchemish by
21 Euphrates : and Josiah went out against him.   But he sent ambassadors to him, saying, What have I to do with thee, thou king
of Judah ?   *I come* not against thee this day, but against *5* the
house wherewith I have war : for God commanded me to make
haste : forbear thee from *meddling with* God, who *is* with me,
22 that he destroy thee not.   Nevertheless Josiah would not turn

c So 1 Kin.
22. 30.

his face from him, but *c*disguised himself, that he might fight
with him, and hearkened not unto the words of Necho from the
mouth of God, and came to fight in the valley of Megiddo.
23 And the archers shot at king Josiah ; and the king said to his

---

1 Heb. *made* them *run*.   *3* Heb. *found*.   *5* Heb. *the house of my war*.
2 Heb. *station*.   *4* Heb. *house*.

---

15. *they might not depart*] The singers and
porters remained at their posts, while other
Levites sacrificed for them and brought
them their share of the lambs.

20. *After all this*] i.e. thirteen years after,
B.C. 608. See 2 K. xxiii. 28, 29 notes.

21. *the house wherewith I have war*] Necho
viewed Babylon as the successor and representative of Assyria—the hereditary enemy
of Egypt—and he means that he is merely
continuing an old hostility with which Josiah has nothing to do.   No doubt the Assyrian and Egyptian armies had often passed
up and down Syria by the coast route,
without approaching Jerusalem, or even
touching the soil of Judæa.
*God commanded me to make haste : forbear
thee from meddling with God*] These are
remarkable words in the mouth of a heathen ; but ancient inscriptions show that the
Egyptian kings, in a certain sense, acknow-

ledged a single supreme god, and considered
their actions to be inspired by him.   [*e.g.*
The god Tum (cp. the name of his city,
Pithom, Ex. i. 11 note) was worshipped as
ankh, "the living One" (cp. "Jehovah")].
Hence Necho merely expressed himself as
Egyptian kings were in the habit of doing.

22. *disguised himself*] Cp. marg. ref. But
most modern critics are dissatisfied with
this sense in this place, and prefer to render
"equipped himself;" or—with the LXX.—
adopt another reading, and render "took
courage."
the words of Necho from the mouth of God]
The author apparently regarded Necho's
words as actually prophetic—a warning to
which Josiah ought to have listened—sent
him by God to make him pause—though not
spoken by divine inspiration, or in consequence of any supernatural revelation of
the Divine will to the Egyptian king.

24 servants, Have me away; for I am sore ¹wounded. ᵈHis servants therefore took him out of that chariot, and put him in the
second chariot that he had; and they brought him to Jerusalem,
and he died, and was buried ²in *one of* the sepulchres of his
fathers. And ᵉall Judah and Jerusalem mourned for Josiah.
25 And Jeremiah ᶠlamented for Josiah: and ᵍall the singing men
and the singing women spake of Josiah in their lamentations to
this day, ʰand made them an ordinance in Israel: and, behold,
26 they *are* written in the lamentations. ¶Now the rest of the acts
of Josiah, and his ³goodness, according to *that which was* written
27 in the law of the LORD, and his deeds, first and last, behold,
they *are* written in the book of the kings of Israel and Judah.

CHAP. 36. THEN ᵃthe people of the land took Jehoahaz the son
of Josiah, and made him king in his father's stead in Jerusalem.
2 Jehoahaz *was* twenty and three years old when he began to
3 reign, and he reigned three months in Jerusalem. And the
king of Egypt ⁴put him down at Jerusalem, and ⁵condemned
the land in an hundred talents of silver and a talent of gold.
4 And the king of Egypt made Eliakim his brother king over
Judah and Jerusalem, and turned his name to Jehoiakim. And
Necho took Jehoahaz his brother, and carried him to Egypt.
5 ¶ ᵇJehoiakim *was* twenty and five years old when he began to
reign, and he reigned eleven years in Jerusalem: and he did *that*
6 which was evil in the sight of the LORD his God. ᶜAgainst him
came up Nebuchadnezzar king of Babylon, and bound him in
7 ⁶fetters, to ᵈcarry him to Babylon. ᵉNebuchadnezzar also
carried of the vessels of the house of the LORD to Babylon, and
8 put them in his temple at Babylon. Now the rest of the acts
of Jehoiakim, and his abominations which he did, and that
which was found in him, behold, they *are* written in the book of
the kings of Israel and Judah: and ⁷Jehoiachin his son reigned
9 in his stead. ¶ᶠJehoiachin *was* eight years old when he began
to reign, and he reigned three months and ten days in Jerusalem:

Margin references (right column):
ᵈ 2 Kin. 23. 30.
ᵉ Zech. 12. 11.
ᶠ Lam. 4. 20.
ᵍ See Matt. 9. 23.
ʰ Jer. 22. 20.
ᵃ 2 Kin. 23. 30, &c.
ᵇ 2 Kin. 23. 36, 37.
ᶜ 2 Kin. 21. 1. Foretold, Hab. 1. 6.
ᵈ See 2 Kin. 24. 6. Jer. 22. 18, 19. & 36. 30.
ᵉ 2 Kin. 24. 13. Dan. 1. 1, 2. & 5. 2.
ᶠ 2 Kin. 24. 8.

---

¹ Heb. *made sick,* 1 Kin. 22. 34.
² Or, *among the sepulchres.*
³ Heb. *kindnesses.*
⁴ Heb. *removed him.*
⁵ Heb. *mulcted.*
⁶ Or, *chains.*
⁷ Or, *Jeconiah,* 1 Chr. 3. 16. or, *Coniah,* Jer. 22. 24.

Cp. the "prophecy" of Caiaphas, John xi. 51.

24. The fate of Josiah was unprecedented. No king of Judah had, up to this time, fallen in battle. None had left his land at the mercy of a foreign conqueror. Hence the extraordinary character of the mourning (cp. Zech. xii. 11–14).

25. Some find Jeremiah's lament in the entire Book of Lamentations; others in a part of it (ch. iv.). But most critics are of opinion that the lament is lost. Days of calamity were commemorated by lamentations on their anniversaries, and this among the number. The "Book of Dirges" was a collection of such poems which once existed but is now lost.

and made them an ordinance] Rather, "and they made them an ordinance," they *i.e.* who had authority to do so, not the minstrels.

XXXVI. The narrative runs parallel with 2 Kings (marg. ref.) as far as *v.* 13. The writer then omits the events following,

and substitutes a sketch in which the moral and didactic element preponderates over the historical.

7. *in his temple*] Cp. "the house of *his god*" (Dan. i. 2). Nebuchadnezzar's inscriptions show him to have been the especial votary of Merodach, the Babylonian Mars. His temple, which the Greeks called the temple of Belus, was one of the most magnificent buildings in Babylon. Its ruins still remain in the vast mound, called *Babil,* which is the loftiest and most imposing of the "heaps" that mark the site of the ancient city.

8. *his abominations which he did*] See Jer. vii. 9, 30, 31, xix. 3–13, xxv. 1 &c.; Jehoiakim appears to have restored all the idolatries which Josiah his father had swept away.

9. *eight years old*] Rather, eighteen (see marg. ref.). Jehoiachin had several wives and (apparently) at least one child (Jer. xxii. 28), when, three months later, he was carried captive to Babylon.

g 2 Kin. 24.
10—17.
h Dan.1.1,2.
& 5. 2.
i Jer. 37. 1.
k 2 Kin. 24.
18.
Jer.52.1,&c.

l Jer. 52. 3.
Ezek. 17. 12,
13.
m 2 Kin. 17.
14.

n Jer.25. 3, 4.
& 35. 15.
& 44. 4.

o Jer.5.12,13.
p Prov. 1. 25,
30.
q Jer. 32. 3.
& 38. 6.
Matt. 23. 34.
r Ps. 74. 1.
& 79. 5.
s Deut.28.49.
2 Kin. 25. 1,
&c.
Ezra 9. 7.
t Ps. 74. 20.
& 79. 2, 3.
u 2 Kin. 25.
13, &c.
x 2 Kin.25.9.
Ps. 74. 6, 7.
& 79. 1, 7.
y 2Kin.25.11.
z Jer. 27. 7.

10 and he did *that which was* evil in the sight of the LORD. And
¹when the year was expired, *g*king Nebuchadnezzar sent, and
brought him to Babylon, *h*with the ²goodly vessels of the house
of the LORD, and made ³ *i*Zedekiah his brother king over Judah
11 and Jerusalem. ¶ *k*Zedekiah *was* one and twenty years old when
12 he began to reign, and reigned eleven years in Jerusalem. And
he did *that which was* evil in the sight of the LORD his God, *and*
humbled not himself before Jeremiah the prophet *speaking* from
13 the mouth of the LORD. And *l*he also rebelled against king
Nebuchadnezzar, who had made him swear by God : but he
*m*stiffened his neck, and hardened his heart from turning unto
14 the LORD God of Israel. ¶ Moreover all the chief of the priests,
and the people, transgressed very much after all the abominations of the heathen ; and polluted the house of the LORD which
15 he had hallowed in Jerusalem. *n*And the LORD God of their
fathers sent to them ⁴by his messengers, rising up ⁵betimes, and
sending ; because he had compassion on his people, and on his
16 dwelling place : but *o*they mocked the messengers of God, and
*p*despised his words, and *q*misused his prophets, until the *r*wrath
of the LORD arose against his people, till *there was* no ⁶remedy.
17 *s*Therefore he brought upon them the king of the Chaldees, who
*t*slew their young men with the sword in the house of their
sanctuary, and had no compassion upon young man or maiden,
old man, or him that stooped for age : he gave *them* all into his
18 hand. *u*And all the vessels of the house of God, great and
small, and the treasures of the house of the LORD, and the treasures of the king, and of his princes; all *these* he brought to
19 Babylon. *x*And they burnt the house of God, and brake down
the wall of Jerusalem, and burnt all the palaces thereof with
20 fire, and destroyed all the goodly vessels thereof. And ⁷*y*them
that had escaped from the sword carried he away to Babylon :
*z*where they were servants to him and his sons until the reign of
21 the kingdom of Persia : to fulfil the word of the LORD by the

---

¹ Heb. *at the return of the year.*
² Heb. *vessels of desire.*
³ Or, *Mattaniah, his father's*

⁴ brother,* 2 Kin. 24. 17.
⁴ Heb. *by the hand of his messengers.*
⁵ That is, *continually and*

⁶ *carefully.*
⁶ Heb. *healing.*
⁷ Heb. *the remainder from the sword.*

---

10. *when the year was expired*] Lit. as in the margin, *i.e.* at the return of the season for military expeditions. The expedition against Jehoiakim took place probably late in the autumn of one year, that against Jehoiachin early in the spring of the next.

Strictly speaking, Zedekiah was uncle to Jehoiachin, being the youngest of the sons of Josiah (marg. note and ref.). He was nearly of the same age with Jehoiachin, and is called here his "brother" (cp. Gen. xiv. 14).

12. On Zedekiah's character, see 2 K. xxiv. 19 note.

13. The oath of allegiance was taken when he was first installed in his kingdom. On Zedekiah's sin in breaking his oath, see Ezek. xvii. 18-20, xxi. 25.

14. *polluted the house of the* LORD] Towards the close of Zedekiah's reign idolatrous rites of several different kinds were intruded into the sacred precincts of the Temple (cp Ezek. viii. 10-16).

16. *misused his prophets*] Rather, "scoffed at his prophets." The allusion is to verbal mockery, not to persecution.

17. The fearful slaughter took place at the capture of the city, in the courts of the Temple itself (Ezek. ix. 6, 7 ; cp. Lam. ii. 7, 20).

20. *servants*] Or, "slaves." They were probably employed by Nebuchadnezzar in the forced labour which his great works necessitated.

his sons] The word probably includes all Nebuchadnezzar's successors in the independent sovereignty of Babylon.

21. See marg. reff. The seventy years of desolation prophesied by Jeremiah, commenced in the fourth year of Jehoiakim (Jer. xxv. 1 and 12 ; cp. Dan. i. 1), or B.C. 605 ; and should therefore have terminated, if they were fully complete, in B.C. 536. As, however, the historical date of the taking of Babylon by Cyrus is B.C. 538, or two years earlier, it has been usual to suppose that the

mouth of ^a Jeremiah, until the land ^bhad enjoyed her sabbaths :
for as long as she lay desolate ^cshe kept sabbath, to fulfil three-
22 score and ten years. ¶ ^dNow in the first year of Cyrus king of
Persia, that the word of the LORD *spoken* by the mouth of ^eJere-
miah might be accomplished, the LORD stirred up the spirit of
^fCyrus king of Persia, that he made a proclamation throughout
23 all his kingdom, and *put it* also in writing, saying, ^gThus saith
Cyrus king of Persia, All the kingdoms of the earth hath the
LORD God of heaven given me; and he hath charged me to build
him an house in Jerusalem, which *is* in Judah. Who *is there*
among you of all his people? The LORD his God *be* with him,
and let him go up.

a Jer. 25. 9,
11, 12.
& 26. 6, 7.
& 29. 10.
b Lev. 26. 34,
35, 43.
Dan. 9. 2.
c Lev. 25.4,5.
d Ezra 1. 1.
e Jer. 25. 12,
13.
& 29. 10.
& 33. 10, 11,
14.
f Isai. 44. 28.
g Ezra 1. 2, 3.

Jews reckoned "the reign of the kingdom of Persia" as commencing two years after the capture of Babylon, on the death or supersession of "Darius the Mede." But the term "seventy" may be taken as a *round* number, and the prophecy as sufficiently fulfilled by a desolation which lasted sixty-eight years.

until the land had enjoyed her sabbaths] Between the time of Moses and the com-mencement of the Captivity, there had been (about) 70 occasions on which the Law of the sabbatical year (Lev. xxv. 4-7) had been violated.

22. This and the next verse are repeated at the commencement of the book of Ezra (i. 1-3), which was, it is probable, originally a continuation of Chronicles, Chronicles and Ezra together forming one work. See In-troduction, p. 448.

EZRA.

INTRODUCTION.

THOUGH the Books of Ezra and Nehemiah were undoubtedly regarded as one Book in two parts, both by the Jewish Church and by the early Christian Fathers, yet the judgment of modern criticism, that they were originally two distinct works, seems to be, on the whole, deserving of acceptance.

The object of the writer of Ezra is to give an account of the return from the Captivity, and of the subsequent fortunes of the Palestinian Jews until the eighth year of Artaxerxes Longimanus, B.C. 457-The matters to which he directs attention are three only :—(1) The number, family, and (to some extent) the names of those who returned from Babylonia with Ezra and with Zerubbabel (ii., viii. 1-20); (2) The rebuilding of the Temple and the circumstances connected therewith (i., iii. – vii.) ; and (3) The misconduct of the returned Jews in respect of mixed marriages, and the steps taken by Ezra in consequence (ix., x.).

The Book of Ezra is made up of two completely distinct sections. (a) In i.–vi., the writer treats of the return from the Captivity and of the events following (B.C. 538-516), or a period of twenty-three years. It belongs to the time when Zerubbabel was governor of Judæa, Jeshua High-Priest, and Zechariah and Haggai Prophets. (b) vii. – end. This relates the commission given to Ezra by

Artaxerxes in the seventh year of his reign (B.C. 458), the journey of Ezra to Jerusalem, and his proceedings there (April, B.C. 458–April, B.C. 457). There is thus a gap of fifty-seven years between the first section of the Book and the second ; from which it appears that the writer of the second portion cannot well have been a witness of the events recorded in the first.

Jewish tradition ascribes the authorship of the whole Book to Ezra. Modern critics generally admit that Ezra was the original and sole author of the entire second section (vii.–x.), but consider him the compiler of the first (i.–vi.) from state documents, national records, and lists. It is probable that the Book of Ezra was composed soon after the arrangements with respect to the mixed marriages had been completed ; i.e. in B.C. 457 or 456.

In character the Book of Ezra is historical, and like Chronicles, it lays great stress on the externals of religion ; it gives special prominence to the Levites, and exhibits a genealogical bias; it lays down very distinctly the general principle of a special Providence (viii. 22) ; and it applies this principle to particular points of the history not unfrequently.

In style Ezra more resembles Daniel than any other Book of Scripture, always excepting Chronicles. This may be accounted for by these two writers being both Babylonian Jews. The work contains also a considerable number of proper names and words which are either known or suspected to be Persian,[1] and altogether, the language is such as might have been looked for under the circumstances of the time, when the contact into which the Jews had been brought with the Babylonians and the Persians had naturally introduced among them a good many foreign words and modes of speech.

The text of Ezra is not in a good condition. The general bearing of the narrative is, however, untouched by slight blemishes which affect chiefly such minute points as the names and numbers of those who returned from the Captivity, the weight and number of the sacrificial vessels, and the like.

---

[1] The following are the proper names, certainly Persian, which occur in Ezra: Cyrus, Darius, Ahasuerus, Artaxerxes. Mithredath (Mithridates), Persia, and Achmetha (Ecbatana). To these may be added, as probably Persian, Rehum, Shimshai, Tatnai, Shetharboznai, and Tabeel. Persian words, not belonging to the class of proper names, which may be recognized in Ezra are the following: *ganza* or *gaza*, "treasury" (v. 17, vi. 1, vii. 20); *ganzabara* or *gazabara*, "treasurer" (i. 8); *khshatrapâ*, "satrap" (viii. 36); *angara*, "a letter" (iv. 8); *nipishta*, the same (iv. 7); *patigama*, "an edict" (iv. 17); *apatama* (?), "at last" (iv. 13); *tarsata*, name of an office, literally, "the feared" (ii. 63); *usfrana*, "speedily, diligently, abundantly" (v. 8, vi. 8; &c.); and *darkon*, or perhaps *darkemon*, a gold coin, a "daric" (viii 27).

THE BOOK

OF

E Z R A.

CHAP. 1. NOW in the first year of Cyrus king of Persia, that the word of the LORD [a]by the mouth of Jeremiah might be fulfilled, the LORD stirred up the spirit of Cyrus king of Persia, [b]that he [1]made a proclamation throughout all his kingdom, and *put it* 2 also in writing, saying. ¶Thus saith Cyrus king of Persia, The LORD God of heaven hath given me all the kingdoms of the earth; and he hath [c]charged me to build him an house at Jeru-3 salem, which *is* in Judah. Who *is there* among you of all his people? his God be with him, and let him go up to Jerusalem, which *is* in Judah, and build the house of the LORD God of 4 Israel, ([d]he *is* the God,) which *is* in Jerusalem. And whosoever remaineth in any place where he sojourneth, let the men of his place [2]help him with silver, and with gold, and with goods, and with beasts, beside the freewill offering for the house of God 5 that *is* in Jerusalem. ¶Then rose up the chief of the fathers of Judah and Benjamin, and the priests, and the Levites, with all *them* whose spirit [e]God had raised, to go up to build the house of 6 the LORD which *is* in Jerusalem. And all they that *were* about them [3]strengthened their hands with vessels of silver, with gold, with goods, and with beasts, and with precious things, beside all 7 *that* was willingly offered. ¶[f]Also Cyrus the king brought forth the vessels of the house of the LORD, [g]which Nebuchad-nezzar had brought forth out of Jerusalem, and had put them 8 in the house of his gods; even those did Cyrus king of Persia bring forth by the hand of Mithredath the treasurer, and num-9 bered them unto [h]Sheshbazzar, the prince of Judah. And this *is* the number of them: thirty chargers of gold, a thousand

[a] 2 Chr. 36. 22, 23.
Jer. 25. 12.
& 29. 10.
[b] ch. 5.13,14.

[c] Isai. 44. 28.
& 45. 1, 13.

[d] Dan. 6. 26.

[e] Phil. 2. 13.

[f] ch. 5. 14.
& 6. 5.
[g] 2 Kin. 24. 13.
2 Chr. 36. 7.

[h] See ch. 5. 14.

---

[1] Heb. *caused a voice to pass.*   [2] Heb. *lift him up.*   [3] That is, *helped them.*

I. 1. By the first year of Cyrus is to be understood the first year of his sovereignty over the Jews, or B.C. 538.

2. *The LORD God of heaven*] Or, " Jehovah, the God of Heaven." In the original Persian, the document probably ran—"Ormazd, the God of Heaven." The Hebrew transcript took ".Jehovah" as the equivalent of " Ormazd." The Persian notion of a single Supreme Being — Ahura-Mazda, " the much-knowing, or much-bestowing Spirit "—did, in fact, approach nearly to the Jewish conception of Jehovah.

hath given me all the kingdoms &c.] There is a similar formula at the commencement of the great majority of Persian inscriptions.

he hath charged me to build him an house] It is a reasonable conjecture that, on the capture of Babylon, Cyrus was brought into contact with Daniel, who drew his attention to the prophecy of Isaiah (xliv. 28); and that Cyrus accepted this prophecy as a " charge " to rebuild the Temple.

4. *let the men of his place help him*] i.e.

" Let the heathen population help him " (see *v*. 6).

the freewill offering] Probably that made by Cyrus himself (*vv*. 7–11).

5. Only a portion of the Israelites took advantage of the permission of Cyrus. Many remained in Babylon, since they were disinclined to relinquish their property. They who returned were persons whom God had especially stirred up to make sacrifices for His glory.

7. *the house of his gods*] Rather, "of his god" (Dan. i. 2), *i.e.* Merodach, "his lord " (see 2 Chr. xxxvi. 7 note).

8. *Mithredath*] Or, " Mithridates." The occurrence of this name, which means "given by Mithra," or "dedicated to Mithra," is an indication that the Sun-worship of the Persians was at least as old as the time of Cyrus.

Sheshbazzar] *i.e.* Zerubbabel. On his royal descent, see 1 Chr. iii. 19 note.

9. *chargers*] The word in the original thus translated occurs only in this passage. Its meaning is doubtful. Some derive it

10 chargers of silver, nine and twenty knives, thirty basons of gold,
silver basons of a second *sort* four hundred and ten, *and* other
11 vessels a thousand. All the vessels of gold and of silver *were*
five thousand and four hundred. All *these* did Sheshbazzar
bring up with *them of* [1] the captivity that were brought up from
Babylon unto Jerusalem.

CHAP. 2. NOW [a] these *are* the children of the province that went
up out of the captivity, of those which had been carried away,
[b] whom Nebuchadnezzar the king of Babylon had carried away
unto Babylon, and came again unto Jerusalem and Judah, every
2 one unto his city ; which came with Zerubbabel : Jeshua, Nehemiah, [2] Seraiah, [3] Reelaiah, Mordecai, Bilshan, [4] Mizpar, Bigvai,
[5] Rehum, Baanah. ¶ The number of the men of the people of
3 Israel: the children of Parosh, two thousand an hundred seventy
4 and two. The children of Shephatiah, three hundred seventy
5 and two. The children of Arah, [c] seven hundred seventy and
6 five. The children of [d] Pahath-moab, of the children of Jeshua
7 *and* Joab, two thousand eight hundred and twelve. The children
8 of Elam, a thousand two hundred fifty and four. The children
9 of Zattu, nine hundred forty and five. The children of Zaccai,
10 seven hundred and threescore. The children of [6] Bani, six hun-
11 dred forty and two. The children of Bebai, six hundred twenty
12 and three. The children of Azgad, a thousand two hundred
13 twenty and two. The children of Adonikam, six hundred sixty
14 and six. The children of Bigvai, two thousand fifty and six.
15, 16 The children of Adin, four hundred fifty and four. The
17 children of Ater of Hezekiah, ninety and eight. The children
18 of Bezai, three hundred twenty and three. The children of
19 [7] Jorah, an hundred and twelve. The children of Hashum, two
20 hundred twenty and three. The children of [8] Gibbar, ninety and
21 five. The children of Beth-lehem, an hundred twenty and
22, 23 three. The men of Netophah, fifty and six. The men of
24 Anathoth, an hundred twenty and eight. The children of
25 [9] Azmaveth, forty and two. The children of Kirjath-arim,
Chephirah, and Beeroth, seven hundred and forty and three.
26 The children of Ramah and Gaba, six hundred twenty and one.
27, 28 The men of Michmas, an hundred twenty and two. The
29 men of Beth-el and Ai, two hundred twenty and three. The

Margin notes (left):
c Neh. 7. 6, &c.
b 2 Kin. 24. 14, 15, 16. & 25. 11. 2 Chr. 36. 20.
c See Neh. 7. 10.
d Neh. 7. 11.

---

[1] Heb. *the transportation.*
[2] Or, *Azariah,* Neh. 7. 7.
[3] Or, *Raamiah.*
[4] Or, *Mispereth.*
[5] Or, *Nehum.*
[6] Or, *Binnui,* Neh. 7. 15.
[7] Or, *Hariph,* Neh. 7. 24.
[8] Or, *Gibeon,* Neh. 7. 25.
[9] Or, *Beth-azmaveth,* Neh. 7. 28.

---

from a Heb. root, "to hollow out," and
translate "cup" or "vessel."

knives] This is another doubtful word,
only used here. The etymology points to
some employment of basket-work.

11. The sum of the numbers as they stand
in the present Hebrew text is 2499, instead of 5400. In the Apocryphal book of
Esdras the sum given is 5469, and with this
sum the items in that place exactly agree
(1 Esd. ii. 13, 14). Most commentators propose to correct Ezra by the passage of
Esdras ; but the items of Esdras are improbable. Probably the sum total in the
present passage has suffered corruption.

II. 1. *the province*] Judæa was no longer
a kingdom, but a mere "province" of

Persia. "The children of the province"
are the Israelites who returned to Palestine,
as distinct from those who remained in
Babylonia and Persia.

every one unto his city] That is, to the
city whereto his forefathers had belonged.
Of course, in the few cases where this was
not known (*vv.* 59–62), the plan could not be
carried out.

Two other copies of the list following
have come down to us, one in Neh. vii. 7–69,
the other in 1 .Esd. v. 8–43. All seem to
have been taken from the same original
document, and to have suffered more or less
from corruption. Where two out of the three
agree, the reading should prevail over that
of the third.

30 children of Nebo, fifty and two. The children of Magbish, an
31 hundred fifty and six. The children of the other *Elam, a thou-   *See ver. 7.
32 sand two hundred fifty and four. The children of Harim, three
33 hundred and twenty. The children of Lod, ¹Hadid, and Ono,
34 seven hundred twenty and five. The children of Jericho, three
35 hundred forty and five. The children of Senaah, three thousand
36 and six hundred and thirty. ¶The priests: the children of
   ⁱJedaiah, of the house of Jeshua, nine hundred seventy and   ƒ1 Chr. 24.7.
37 three. The children of ⁱImmer, a thousand fifty and two.   ⁱ1 Chr.24.14.
38 The children of ʰPashur, a thousand two hundred forty and   ʰ1 Chr. 9.12.
39 seven. The children of ⁱHarim, a thousand and seventeen.   ⁱ1 Chr.24. 8.
40 ¶The Levites: the children of Jeshua and Kadmiel, of the
41 children of ²Hodaviah, seventy and four. The singers: the
42 children of Asaph, an hundred twenty and eight. The children
   of the porters: the children of Shallum, the children of Ater,
   the children of Talmon, the children of Akkub, the children of
   Hatita, the children of Shobai, *in* all an hundred thirty and
43 nine. ¶ᵏThe Nethinims: the children of Ziha, the children of   ᵏ1 Chr. 9. 2.
44 Hasupha, the children of Tabbaoth, the children of Keros, the
45 children of ³Siaha, the children of Padon, the children of Leba-
46 nah, the children of Hagabah, the children of Akkub, the chil-
   dren of Hagab, the children of ⁴Shalmai, the children of Hanan,
47 the children of Giddel, the children of Gahar, the children of
48 Reaiah, the children of Rezin, the children of Nekoda, the
49 children of Gazzam, the children of Uzza, the children of Paseah,
50 the children of Besai, the children of Asnah, the children of
51 Mehunim, the children of ⁵Nephusim, the children of Bakbuk,
52 the children of Hakupha, the children of Harhur, the children
53 of ⁶Bazluth, the children of Mehida, the children of Harsha, the
   children of Barkos, the children of Sisera, the children of Tha-
54, 55 mah, the children of Neziah, the children of Hatipha. ¶The
   children of ⁷Solomon's servants: the children of Sotai, the   ⁱ1 Kin. 9.21.
56 children of Sophereth, the children of ⁷Peruda, the children
57 of Jaalah, the children of Darkon, the children of Giddel, the
   children of Shephatiah, the children of Hattil, the children of
58 Pochereth of Zebaim, the children of ⁸Ami. All the ᵐNethi-   ᵐJosh. 9.21,
   nims, and the children of ⁿSolomon's servants, *were* three hun-   27.
                                                                    1 Chr. 9. 2.
59 dred ninety and two. ¶And these *were* they which went up from   ⁿ1 Kin.9.21.
   Tel-melah, Tel-harsa, Cherub, ⁹Addan, *and* Immer: but they
   could not shew their father's house, and their ¹seed, whether
60 they *were* of Israel: the children of Delaiah, the children of
   Tobiah, the children of Nekoda, six hundred fifty and two.
61 And of the children of the priests: the children of Habaiah, the
   children of Koz, the children of Barzillai; which took a wife of
   the daughters of °Barzillai the Gileadite, and was called after their   °2 Sam. 17.
62 name: these sought their register *among* those that were reckoned   27.

---

¹ Or, *Harid*, as it is in   ³ Or, *Sia*.   ⁷ Or, *Perida*, Neh. 7. 57.
   some copies.   ⁴ Or, *Shamlai*.   ⁸ Or, *Amon*, Neh. 7. 59.
² Or, *Judah*, ch. 3. 9. called   ⁵ Or, *Nephishesim*.   ⁹ Or, *Addon*, Neh. 7. 61.
   also *Hodevah*, Neh. 7. 43.   ⁶ Or, *Bazlith*, Neh. 7. 54.   ¹ Or, *pedigree*.

---

43. *The Nethinims*] The *hieroduli* or   of Babylonia, at which the Jews here spoken
sacred slaves, "given" to the Levites to   of had been settled. The first and third
assist them in their work (see 1 Chr. ix. 2   have been reasonably identified with the
note).   Thelmé and Chiripha of Ptolemy. Of the
59. Tel-melah, Tel-harsa, Cherub, Addan,   rest nothing is known at present.
and Immer, were probably cities, or villages,

p Num. 3.10.

q Lev. 22. 2,
10, 15, 16.
r Num. 27.
21.
s Neh. 7. 66,
&c.

t Neh. 7. 70.

u 1Chr.26.20.

x ch. 6.16,17.
Neh. 7. 73.

a Matt. 1. 12.
& Luke 3. 27,
called
Salathiel.
b Deut. 12. 5.

c Num. 28. 3,
4.

by genealogy, but they were not found: *p* therefore [1]were they,
63 as polluted, put from the priesthood. And the [2]Tirshatha said
unto them, that they *q* should not eat of the most holy things,
till there stood up a priest with *r* Urim and with Thummim.
64 ¶ *s* The whole congregation together *was* forty and two thousand
65 three hundred *and* threescore, beside their servants and their
maids, of whom *there were* seven thousand three hundred thirty
and seven: and *there were* among them two hundred singing
66 men and singing women. Their horses *were* seven hundred
67 thirty and six; their mules, two hundred forty and five; their
camels, four hundred thirty and five; *their* asses, six thousand
68 seven hundred and twenty. ¶ *t* And *some* of the chief of the
fathers, when they came to the house of the LORD which *is* at
Jerusalem, offered freely for the house of God to set it up in his
69 place: they gave after their ability unto the *u* treasure of the
work threescore and one thousand drams of gold, and five thou-
70 sand pound of silver, and one hundred priests' garments. ¶ *x* So
the priests, and the Levites, and *some* of the people, and the
singers, and the porters, and the Nethinims, dwelt in their
cities, and all Israel in their cities.

CHAP. 3. AND when the seventh month was come, and the children
of Israel *were* in the cities, the people gathered themselves toge-
2 ther as one man to Jerusalem. Then stood up [3]Jeshua the son
of Jozadak, and his brethren the priests, and [4]Zerubbabel the
son of *a* Shealtiel, and his brethren, and builded the altar of the
God of Israel, to offer burnt offerings thereon, as *it is b* written
3 in the law of Moses the man of God. And they set the altar
upon his bases; for fear *was* upon them because of the people
of those countries: and they offered burnt offerings thereon
unto the LORD, even *c* burnt offerings morning and evening.

[1] Heb. *they were polluted from the priesthood.*   [2] Or, *governor:* See Neh. 8. 9.   [4] Called *Zorobabel,* Matt. 1. 12. Luke 3. 27.
[3] Or, *Joshua,* Hag. 1. 1. & 2. 2. Zech. 3. 1.

---

63. *the Tirshatha*] *i.e.* Zerubbabel. See margin. The word is probably old Persian, though it does not occur in the cuneiform inscriptions. Some derive it from a root "to fear." See Introduction. p. 570 *n.* 1.

a priest with Urim and with Thummim] See Ex. xxviii. 30 note. According to the Rabbinical writers, the second Temple permanently lacked this glory of the first. Zerubbabel, it would seem by the present passage (cp. Neh. vii. 65), expected that the loss would be only temporary.

64. The sum total is given without any variation by Ezra, by Nehemiah (marg. ref.), and by Esdras (1 Esd. v. 41), who adds, that in this reckoning only those of twelve years of age and upward were counted.

It is curious that the total 42,360, is so greatly in excess of the items. Ezra's items make the number 29,818; Nehemiah's 31,089, Esdras, 33,950. Probably the original document was in places illegible, and the writers were forced to make omissions.

69. The numbers here and in Nehemiah (marg. ref.) vary.

70. *all Israel*] That Israelites of the ten tribes returned to Palestine with Zerubbabel is apparent, (1) from 1 Chr. ix. 3; (2) from the enumeration of *twelve* chiefs (Neh. vii. 7; 1 Esd. v. 8); and (3) from various expressions in Ezra (ii. 2, 59, iii. 1).

III. 1. *the seventh month*] *i.e.* the month Tisri (nearly our September), the most sacred month in the Jewish year (Ex. xxiii. 16; Lev. xxiii. 24–41).

2. Jeshua, the High-Priest, was the son of Jozadak, who was carried into captivity by Nebuchadnezzar (1 Chr. vi. 15).

Zerubbabel was really the son of Pedaiah, Shealtiel's (or Salathiel's) younger brother. But Shealtiel having no sons, and the royal line being continued in the person of his nephew, Zerubbabel, the latter was accounted Shealtiel's son.

3. *upon his bases*] They restored *the old* Altar of Burnt-offerings, which stood directly in front of the Temple-porch, upon the old foundation. This became apparent on the clearing away of the ruins, and on a careful examination of the site.

4 *d*They kept also the feast of tabernacles, *e*as *it is* written, and
f offered the daily burnt offerings by number, according to the
5 custom, [1]as the duty of every day required; and afterward
offered the *g*continual burnt offering, both of the new moons,
and of all the set feasts of the LORD that were consecrated, and
of every one that willingly offered a freewill offering unto the
6 LORD. From the first day of the seventh month began they to
offer burnt offerings unto the LORD. But [2]the foundation of
7 the temple of the LORD was not *yet* laid. They gave money
also unto the masons, and to the [3]carpenters; and *h*meat, and
drink, and oil, unto them of Zidon, and to them of Tyre, to
bring cedar trees from Lebanon to the sea of *i*Joppa, *k*according
8 to the grant that they had of Cyrus king of Persia. ¶Now in
the second year of their coming unto the house of God at Jerusalem, in the second month, began Zerubbabel the son of Shealtiel, and Jeshua the son of Jozadak, and the remnant of their
brethren the priests and the Levites, and all they that were
come out of the captivity unto Jerusalem; *l*and appointed the
Levites, from twenty years old and upward, to set forward the
9 work of the house of the LORD. Then stood *m*Jeshua *with* his
sons and his brethren, Kadmiel and his sons, the sons of [4]Judah,
[5]together, to set forward the workmen in the house of God: the
sons of Henadad, *with* their sons and their brethren the Levites.
10 And when the builders laid the foundation of the temple of the
LORD, *n*they set the priests in their apparel with trumpets, and
the Levites the sons of Asaph with cymbals, to praise the LORD,
11 after the *o*ordinance of David king of Israel. *p*And they sang
together by course in praising and giving thanks unto the LORD;
*q*because *he is* good, *r*for his mercy *endureth* for ever toward
Israel. And all the people shouted with a great shout, when
they praised the LORD, because the foundation of the house of
12 the LORD was laid. *s*But many of the priests and Levites and
chief of the fathers, *who were* ancient men, that had seen the
first house, when the foundation of this house was laid before
their eyes, wept with a loud voice; and many shouted aloud for
13 joy: so that the people could not discern the noise of the shout
of joy from the noise of the weeping of the people: for the
people shouted with a loud shout, and the noise was heard
afar off.

d Neh. 8. 14,
17.
Zech. 14. 16,
17.
e Ex. 23. 16.
f Num. 29.
12, &c.
g Ex. 29. 38.
Num. 28. 3,
11, 19, 26.
& 29. 2, 8, 13.

h 1Kin.5.6,9.
2 Chr. 2. 10.
Acts 12. 20.
i 2 Chr. 2. 16.
k ch. 6. 3.

l 1 Chr. 23.
24, 27.
m ch. 2. 40.

n 1 Chr. 16
5. 6, 42.

o 1 Chr.6.31.
& 16. 4.
& 25. 1.
p Ex. 15. 21.
2 Chr. 7. 3.
Neh. 12. 24.
q 1Chr.16.34.
Ps. 136. 1.
r 1Chr.16.41.
Jer. 33. 11.
s See
Hag. 2. 3.

[1] Heb. *the matter of the day
in his day.*
[2] Heb. *the temple of the
LORD was not yet founded.*
[3] Or, *workmen.*
[4] Or, *Hodaviah,* ch. 2.
40.
[5] Heb. *as one.*

---

7. *according to the grant*] *i.e.* in accordance with the permission granted them by
Cyrus to rebuild their Temple (i. 1-4).

8. *unto the house of God*] *i.e.* to the place
where the house of God had been, and where
God was believed still to have His special
dwelling.

and appointed the Levites] This is the emphatic clause of the present verse. Though
so small a number of Levites had returned
from Babylon (ii. 40), yet they were especially singled out to be entrusted with the
task of superintending and advancing the
building of the Temple.

9. *Jeshua*] See marg. ref. Not the High-
Priest, but the head of one of the two Levitical houses which had returned.

together] The Hebrew phrase is very emphatic—"they stood up **as one man.**"

10. *they set the priests*] Or, according to
another reading, "The priests stood."

the Levites the sons of Asaph] *i.e.* "such of
the Levites as were descendants of Asaph."
It would seem as if no descendants of
Heman or Jeduthun had returned.

12. *wept...shouted...for joy*] Cp. marg. ref.
and Zech. iv. 10. It is implied that the
dimensions of the second Temple were
smaller than those of the first. Hence the
feeling of sorrow which came upon some.
They, however, who had not seen the former Temple, and so could not contrast the
two, naturally rejoiced to see the Sanctuary
of their religion begin to rise from its ruins.

a See ver. 7, 8, 9.

Chap. 4. NOW when [a]the adversaries of Judah and Benjamin heard that [1]the children of the captivity builded the temple 2 unto the Lord God of Israel; then they came to Zerubbabel, and to the chief of the fathers, and said unto them, Let us build with you: for we seek your God, as ye *do;* and we do sacrifice unto him [b]since the days of Esar-haddon king of Assur, which 3 brought us up hither. But Zerubbabel, and Jeshua, and the rest of the chief of the fathers of Israel, said unto them, [c]Ye have nothing to do with us to build an house unto our God; but we ourselves together will build unto the Lord God of Israel, 4 as [d]king Cyrus the king of Persia hath commanded us. Then [e]the people of the land weakened the hands of the people of 5 Judah, and troubled them in building, and hired counsellors against them, to frustrate their purpose, all the days of Cyrus king of Persia, even until the reign of Darius king of Persia. 6 And in the reign of [2]Ahasuerus, in the beginning of his reign, wrote they *unto him* an accusation against the inhabitants of 7 Judah and Jerusalem. ¶And in the days of Artaxerxes wrote [3]Bishlam, Mithredath, Tabeel, and the rest of their [4]companions, unto Artaxerxes king of Persia; and the writing of the letter *was* written in the Syrian tongue, and interpreted in the Syrian 8 tongue. Rehum the chancellor and Shimshai the [5]scribe wrote a letter against Jerusalem to Artaxerxes the king in this sort: 9 Then *wrote* Rehum the chancellor, and Shimshai the scribe, and the rest of their [6]companions; [f]the Dinaites, the Apharsath-

b 2 Kin. 17. 24, 32. 33. & 19. 37. ver. 10.
c Neh. 2. 20.
d ch. 1. 1, 2, 3.
e ch. 3. 3.
f 2 Kin. 17. 30, 31.

[1] Heb. *the sons of the transportation.*
[2] Heb. *Ahashverosh.*
[3] Or, *in peace.*
[4] Heb. *societies.*
[5] Or, *secretary.*
[6] Chald. *societies.*

IV. 1. *adversaries*] *i.e.* the Samaritans, a mixed race, partly Israelite but chiefly foreign, which had replaced to some extent the ancient inhabitants after they were carried into Captivity by Sargon (see 2 K. xvii. 6 note).

2. Cp. 2 K. xvii. 24–28 notes.

since the days] Esar-haddon reigned from B.C. 681–668. Thus the Samaritans speak of what had taken place at least 130 years previously. There appear to have been at least three colonisations of Samaria by the Assyrian kings. The first is mentioned in 2 K. xvii. 24. Later in his reign Sargon added to these first settlers an Arabian element. Some thirty or forty years afterwards, Esarhaddon, his grandson, largely augmented the population by colonists drawn especially from the south-east parts of the Empire (*v.* 10). Thus the later Samaritans were an exceedingly mixed race.

3. *Ye have nothing to do with us*] Because the Samaritans had united idolatrous rites with the worship of Jehovah (2 K. xvii. 29–41). To have allowed them a share in restoring the Temple would have been destructive of all purity of religion.

as king Cyrus...commanded us] The exact words of the edict gave the right of building exclusively to those who should "go up" from Babylonia to Judæa (i. 3).

5. *hired counsellors*] Rather, "bribed" officials at the Persian court to interpose delays and create difficulties, in order to hinder the work.

Darius] *i.e.* Darius the son of Hystaspes

6. *Ahasuerus*] Or, Cambyses, the son and successor of Cyrus. Persian kings had often two names.

7. *Artaxerxes*] Gomates, the Pseudo-Smerdis. He succeeded Cambyses (B.C. 521), and reigned seven months, when he was deposed and executed by Darius Hystaspis.

written in the Syrian tongue, &c.] Or, "written in Syriac characters and translated into Syriac." On the use of this tongue as a medium of communication between the Jews and their Eastern neighbours, see 2 K. xviii. 26 note.

8. *the chancellor*] Lit. "lord of judgment;" the title, apparently, of the Persian governor of the Samaritan province. Every Persian governor was accompanied to his province by a "royal scribe" or "secretary," who had a separate and independent authority.

9, 10. These verses form the superscription or address of the letter (*v.* 11, &c.) sent to Artaxerxes.

The Dinaites were probably colonists from *Dayan,* a country often mentioned in the Assyrian inscriptions as bordering on Cilicia and Cappadocia. No satisfactory explanation can be given of the name Apharsathchites (see v. 6 note). The Tarpelites were colonists from the nation which

chites, the Tarpelites, the Apharsites, the Archevites, the Baby-
10 lonians, the Susanchites, the Dehavites, *and* the Elamites, *g*and *g* ver. 1.
the rest of the nations whom the great and noble Asnapper
brought over, and set in the cities of Samaria, and the rest *that*
11 *are* on this side the river, *h*and ¹at such a time. ¶This *is* the *h* So ver. 11.
copy of the letter that they sent unto him, *even* unto Artaxerxes 17.
the king; Thy servants the men on this side the river, and at & ch. 7. 12.
12 such a time. Be it known unto the king, that the Jews which
came up from thee to us are come unto Jerusalem, building the
rebellious and the bad city, and have ²set up the walls *thereof*,
13 and ³joined the foundations. Be it known now unto the king,
that, if this city be builded, and the walls set up *again*, *then*
will they not ⁴pay *i*toll, tribute, and custom, and *so* thou shalt *i* ch. 7. 24
14 endamage the ⁵revenue of the kings. Now because ⁶we have
maintenance from *the king's* palace, and it was not meet for us
to see the king's dishonour, therefore have we sent and certified
15 the king; that search may be made in the book of the records
of thy fathers: so shalt thou find in the book of the records,
and know that this city *is* a rebellious city, and hurtful unto
kings and provinces, and that they have ⁷moved sedition ⁸within
the same of old time: for which cause was this city destroyed.
16 We certify the king that, if this city be builded *again*, and the
walls thereof set up, by this means thou shalt have no portion
17 on this side the river. ¶*Then* sent the king an answer unto
Rehum the chancellor, and *to* Shimshai the scribe, and *to* the
rest of their ⁹companions that dwell in Samaria, and *unto* the

¹ Chald. *Cheeneth.*	⁴ Chald. *give.*	⁷ Chald. *made.*
² Or, *finished.*	⁵ Or, *strength.*	⁸ Chald. *in the midst thereof.*
³ Chald. *sewed together.*	⁶ Chald. *we are salted with the salt of the palace.*	⁹ Chald. *societies.*

the Assyrians called *Tuplai*, the Greeks "Tibareni," and the Hebrews generally "Tubal." (It is characteristic of the later Hebrew language to insert the letter *r* before labials. Cp. *Darmesek* for *Dammesek*, 2 Chr. xxviii. 23 marg.). The Apharsites were probably "the Persians;" the Archevites, natives of Erech [Warka] (Gen. x. 10); the Susanchites, colonists from Shushan or Susa; the Dehavites, colonists from the Persian tribe of the Daï; and the Elamites, colonists from Elam or Elymaïs, the country of which Susa was the capital.

10. Asnapper was perhaps the official employed by Esar-haddon (*v.* 2) to settle the colonists in their new country.

on this side the river] Lit. "beyond the river," a phrase used of Palestine by Ezra, Nehemiah, and in the Book of Kings, as designating the region *west* of the Euphrates.

and at such a time] Rather, "**and so forth.**" The phrase is vague, nearly equivalent to the modern use of *et cetera*. It recurs in marg. reff.

13. *toll, tribute, and custom*] Rather, "**tribute. provision, and toll**" (so *v.* 20). The "tribute" is the money-tax imposed on each province, and apportioned to the inhabitants by the local authorities; the "provision" is the payment in kind,

which was an integral part of the Persian system; the "toll" is probably a payment required from those who used the Persian highways.

the revenue] The word thus translated is not found elsewhere, and can only be conjecturally interpreted. Modern commentators regard it as an adverb, meaning "at last," or "in the end," and translate, "**And so at last shall damage be done to the kings.**"

14. *we have maintenance*] See marg. The phrase "to eat a man's salt" is common in the East to this day; and is applied not only to those who receive salaries, but to all who obtain their subsistence by means of another. The Persian satraps had no salaries, but taxed their provinces for the support of themselves and their courts.

15. *the book of the records*] Cp. Esth. ii. 23, vi. 1, x. 2. The existence of such a "book" at the Persian court is attested also by Ctesias.

of thy fathers] *i.e.* thy predecessors upon the throne, Cambyses, Cyrus, &c. If Artaxerxes was the Pseudo-Smerdis (*v.* 7 note), these persons were not really his "fathers" or ancestors; but the writers of the letter could not venture to call the king an impostor.

18 rest beyond the river, Peace, and at such a time. The letter
19 which ye sent unto us hath been plainly read before me. And
     ¹I commanded, and search hath been made, and it is found that
     this city of old time hath ²made insurrection against kings, and
20 *that* rebellion and sedition have been made therein. There have
     been mighty kings also over Jerusalem, which have *k*ruled over
     all *countries* *l*beyond the river; and toll, tribute, and custom, was
21 paid unto them. ³Give ye now commandment to cause these
     men to cease, and that this city be not builded, until *another*
22 commandment shall be given from me. Take heed now that ye
     fail not to do this: why should damage grow to the hurt of the
23 kings? ¶Now when the copy of king Artaxerxes' letter *was*
     read before Rehum, and Shimshai the scribe, and their com-
     panions, they went up in haste to Jerusalem unto the Jews, and
24 made them to cease ⁴by force and power. Then ceased the work
     of the house of God which *is* at Jerusalem. So it ceased unto
     the second year of the reign of Darius king of Persia.

CHAP. 5. THEN the prophets, *a*Haggai the prophet, and *b*Zechariah
     the son of Iddo, prophesied unto the Jews that *were* in Judah and
2 Jerusalem in the name of the God of Israel, *even* unto them. Then
     rose up *c*Zerubbabel the son of Shealtiel, and Jeshua the son
     of Jozadak, and began to build the house of God which *is* at
     Jerusalem: and with them *were* the prophets of God helping
3 them. ¶At the same time came to them *d*Tatnai, governor on
     this side the river, and Shethar-boznai, and their companions,
     and said thus unto them, *e*Who hath commanded you to build

Marginal refs: *k* 1 Kin. 4. 21. Ps. 72. 8. *l* Gen. 15. 18. Josh. 1. 4. *a* Hag. 1. 1. *b* Zech. 1. 1. *c* ch. 3. 2. *d* ver. 6. ch. 6. 6. *e* ver. 9.

¹ Chald. *by me a decree is set.*
² Chald. *lifted up itself.*
³ Chald. *Make a decree.*
⁴ Chald. *by arm and power.*

18. *hath been...read*] It is doubtful if the Persian monarchs could ordinarily read. At any rate it was their habit to have documents read to them (cp. Esth. vi. 1). This is still the ordinary practice at Eastern courts.

19. The archives of the Babylonian kingdom would contain accounts of the insurrections raised, or threatened, by Jehoiakim, Jehoiachin, and Zedekiah (2 K. xxiv. 1, 10, 20). It does not appear that there had ever been any rebellion against Persia.

20. *mighty kings* &c.] If this reference can scarcely have been to David or Solomon (see marg. ref.), of whom neither the Babylonian nor the Assyrian archives would be likely to have had any account,—it would probably be to Menahem (2 K. xv. 16) and Josiah (2 Chr. xxxiv. 6, 7, xxxv. 18).

24. *it ceased*] The stoppage of the building by the Pseudo-Smerdis is in complete harmony with his character. He was a Magus, devoted to the Magian elemental worship, and opposed to belief in a personal god. His religion did not approve of temples; and as he persecuted the Zoroastrian so would he naturally be inimical to the Jewish faith. The building was resumed in the second year of Darius (B.C. 520), and was only interrupted for about two years; since the Pseudo-Smerdis reigned less than a year.

V. 1. Haggai and Zechariah stirred up Zerubbabel and Jeshua (*v.* 2; Hag. i. 14), and warned the people against neglecting the building of the Temple, in order to give themselves to the beautifying of their own houses (see Hag. i. 4, 9). Zechariah was the son of Berechiah, and grandson of Iddo (see marg. ref.; Mat. xxiii. 35). Cp. a similar application of "son" in the case of Jehu (2 K. ix. 20 note).

in the name of the God of Israel, even unto them] Rather, "in the name of the God of Israel, **which was upon them.**" The two Prophets addressed the Jews, in respect of their being God's people, or, in Hebrew phrase (see Jer. xv. 16 marg.), "having God's name called upon them."

2. *began to build*] i.e. "made a second beginning"—recommenced the uncompleted work.

helping them] By infusing zeal into the people (see Hag. i. 12).

3. *governor on this side the river*] Cp. iv. 10 note. Tatnai was apparently satrap of Syria, which included the whole tract west of the Euphrates from Cilicia to the borders of Egypt. Zerubbabel must have been, to some extent, under his authority.

Who hath commanded you to build?] There was no doubt a formal illegality in the conduct of Zerubbabel and Jeshua: since all edicts of Persian kings continued in force unless revoked by their successors. But they felt justified in disobeying the decree

4 this house, and to make up this wall? *f*Then said we unto
them after this manner, What are the names of the men [1]that
5 make this building? But *g*the eye of their God was upon the
elders of the Jews, that they could not cause them to cease, till
the matter came to Darius: and then they returned *h*answer by
6 letter concerning this *matter*. ¶The copy of the letter that
Tatnai, governor on this side the river, and Shethar-boznai,
*i*and his companions the Apharsachites, which *were* on this side
7 the river, sent unto Darius the king: they sent a letter unto
him, [2]wherein was written thus; Unto Darius the king, all
8 peace. Be it known unto the king, that we went into the province of Judea, to the house of the great God, which is builded
with [3]great stones, and timber is laid in the walls, and this work
9 goeth fast on, and prospereth in their hands. Then asked we
those elders, *and* said unto them thus, *k*Who commanded you to
10 build this house, and to make up these walls? We asked their
names also, to certify thee, that we might write the names of
11 the men that *were* the chief of them. And thus they returned
us answer, saying, We are the servants of the God of heaven
and earth, and build the house that was builded these many
years ago, which a great king of Israel builded *l*and set up.
12 But *m*after that our fathers had provoked the God of heaven
unto wrath, he gave them into the hand of *n*Nebuchadnezzar
the king of Babylon, the Chaldean, who destroyed this house,
13 and carried the people away into Babylon. But in the first year
of *o*Cyrus the king of Babylon *the same* king Cyrus made a
14 decree to build this house of God. And *p*the vessels also of
gold and silver of the house of God, which Nebuchadnezzar
took out of the temple that *was* in Jerusalem, and brought them
into the temple of Babylon, those did Cyrus the king take out
of the temple of Babylon, and they were delivered unto *one*,
*q*whose name *was* Sheshbazzar, whom he had made [4]governor;
15 and said unto him, Take these vessels, go, carry them into the
temple that *is* in Jerusalem, and let the house of God be builded
16 in his place Then came the same Sheshbazzar, *and* *r*laid the
foundation of the house of God which *is* in Jerusalem: and
since that time even until now hath it been in building, and
17 *s*yet it is not finished. Now therefore, if *it seem* good to the
king, *t*let there be search made in the king's treasure house,
which *is* there at Babylon, whether it be *so*, that a decree was
made of Cyrus the king to build this house of God at Jerusalem, and let the king send his pleasure to us concerning this
matter.

f ver. 10

g See ch. 7.
6, 28.
Ps. 33. 18.
h ch. 6, 6.

i ch. 4. 9.

k ver. 3, 4.

l 1 Kin. 6. 1.
m 2 Chr. 36.
16, 17.
n 2 Kin.24.2.
& 25. 8, 9, 11.

o ch. 1. 1.
p ch.1.7, 8. &
6. 5.

q Hag. 1. 14.
& 2. 2, 21.

r ch. 3. 8, 10.

s ch. 6. 15.
t ch. 6. 1, 2.

[1] Chald. *that build this
building?*
[2] Chald. *in the midst whereof.*
[3] Chald. *stones of rolling.*
[4] Or, *deputy.*

---

of the Pseudo-Smerdis (iv. 7 note), because
the opposition between his religious views
and those of his successor was matter of
notoriety.
4. *Then said we*] The Septuagint, Syriac,
and Arabic Versions have "Then said
they," which brings this verse into exact
accordance with *v*. 10.
6. Apharsachites, like Apharsites, and
Apharsathchites (iv. 9), are thought by some
to be forms of the word "Persians," which
is applied here generally to the foreign
settlers in Samaria. [Others identify the

first and the third names with the "Pareta-
ceni," a people on the Medo-Persian border.]
8. *great stones*] Lit. as in marg.; *i.e.*
stones so large that they were rolled along,
not carried. Others translate "polished
stones."
16. *since that time even until now*] Sixteen
years—from B.C. 536 to B.C. 520. The adversaries of the Jews here overstep the truth ;
since, in point of fact, the work had been
suspended for a while (iv. 24).
17. *let there be search made...at Babylon*]
They perhaps doubted whether proof of the

a ch. 5. 17.

CHAP. 6. THEN Darius the king made a decree, ^aand search was made in the house of the ¹rolls, where the treasures were ²laid 2 up in Babylon. And there was found at ³Achmetha, in the palace that *is* in the province of the Medes, a roll, and therein 3 *was* a record thus written : In the first year of Cyrus the king *the same* Cyrus the king made a decree *concerning* the house of God at Jerusalem, Let the house be builded, the place where they offered sacrifices, and let the foundations thereof be strongly laid ; the height thereof threescore cubits, *and* the breadth

b 1 Kin. 6.36.

4 thereof threescore cubits ; ^b*with* three rows of great stones, and a row of new timber : and let the expences be given out of the

c ch. 1. 7, 8.
& 5. 14.

5 king's house : and also let ^cthe golden and silver vessels of the house of God, which Nebuchadnezzar took forth out of the temple which *is* at Jerusalem, and brought unto Babylon, be restored, and ⁴brought again unto the temple which *is* at Jerusalem, *every one* to his place, and place *them* in the house of God.

d ch. 5. 3.

6 ¶ ^dNow *therefore*, Tatnai, governor beyond the river, Shethar-7 boznai, and ⁵your companions the Apharsachites, which *are* beyond the river, be ye far from thence : let the work of this 8 house of God alone ; let the governor of the Jews and the elders of the Jews build this house of God in his place. Moreover ⁶I make a decree what ye shall do to the elders of these Jews for the building of this house of God : that of the king's goods, *even* of the tribute beyond the river, forthwith expences be given 9 unto these men, that they be not ⁷hindered. And that which they have need of, both young bullocks, and rams, and lambs, for the burnt offerings of the God of heaven, wheat, salt, wine, and oil, according to the appointment of the priests which *are* at Jerusalem, let it be given them day by day without fail :

e ch. 7. 23.
Jer. 29. 7.

10 ^ethat they may offer sacrifices ⁸of sweet savours unto the God of

¹ Chald. *books.*
² Chald. *made to descend.*
³ Or, *Ecbatana*, or, *in a coffer.*
⁴ Chald. *go.*
⁵ Chald. *their societies.*
⁶ Chald. *by me a decree is*
made.
⁷ Chald. *made to cease.*
⁸ Chald. *of rest.*

decree of Cyrus remained in the archives. The Pseudo-Smerdis had had the records in his power for seven months ; and, when he reversed the policy of his predecessors, might have been expected to destroy their edicts. The decree was not found at Babylon, the most natural place for it, but in the provincial capital of Ecbatana, which Tatnai and his friends had not asked Darius to have searched (see vi. 2).

VI. 1. A "house of the rolls" was discovered at Koyunjik, the ancient Nineveh, in 1850—a set of chambers, *i.e.* in the palace devoted exclusively to the storing of public documents. These were in baked clay, and covered the floor to the depth of more than a foot. Such a "house" was probably that at Babylon.

2. "Achmetha" is the "Ecbatana," or "Agbatana," of the Greeks, the Persian name for which, as we find in the Behistun Inscription, was HAGMATANA.

We must suppose that, when Babylon had been searched in vain, the other cities which possessed record-offices were visited, and the decree looked for in them. Ecbatana was the capital of Cyrus.

3. It is difficult to reconcile the dimentions here with expressions in Zechariah (iv. 10), Haggai (ii. 3), and even Ezra (iii. 12), which imply that the second Temple was smaller than the first (cp. 1 K. vi. 2). Perhaps the dimensions here are those which Cyrus required the Jews *not to exceed.*

4 The word translated "row" occurs only in this passage. Some regard it as a "course," and suppose that after every three courses of stone there followed a course of timber. Others understand three "storeys" of stone, with a fourth "storey" of woodwork on the summit (cp. 1 K. vi. 5, 6). Others consider that Cyrus intended to limit the *thickness* of the walls, which were not to exceed a breadth of three rows of stone, with an inner wooden wainscotting.

let the expences be given out of the king's house] *i.e.* "out of the Persian revenue," a portion of the decree which was probably not observed during the later years of Cyrus and during the reign of Cambyses, and hence the burthen fell upon the Jews themselves (ii. 68, 69).

6. This verse gives the words of the de-

11 heaven, and *f*pray for the life of the king, and of his sons. Also
I have made a decree, that whosoever shall alter this word, let
timber be pulled down from his house, and being set up, [1]let
him be hanged thereon; *g*and let his house be made a dunghill
12 for this. And the God that hath caused his *h*name to dwell
there destroy all kings and people, that shall put to their hand
to alter *and* to destroy this house of God which *is* at Jerusalem.
I Darius have made a decree; let it be done with speed.
13 ¶ Then Tatnai, governor on this side the river, Shethar-boznai,
and their companions, according to that which Darius the king
14 had sent, so they did speedily. *i*And the elders of the Jews
builded, and they prospered through the prophesying of Haggai
the prophet and Zechariah the son of Iddo. And they builded,
and finished *it*, according to the commandment of the God of
Israel, and according to the [2]commandment of *k*Cyrus, and
15 *l*Darius, and *m*Artaxerxes king of Persia. And this house was
finished on the third day of the month Adar, which was in the
16 sixth year of the reign of Darius the king. ¶ And the children
of Israel, the priests, and the Levites, and the rest of [3]the
children of the captivity, kept *n*the dedication of this house of
17 God with joy, and *o*offered at the dedication of this house of God
an hundred bullocks, two hundred rams, four hundred lambs;
and for a sin offering for all Israel, twelve he goats, according
18 to the number of the tribes of Israel. And they set the priests
in their *p*divisions, and the Levites in their *q*courses, for the
service of God, which *is* at Jerusalem; [4]*r*as it is written in the
19 book of Moses. ¶ And the children of the captivity kept the
20 passover *s*upon the fourteenth *day* of the first month. For the
priests and the Levites were *t*purified together, all of them *were*
pure, and *u*killed the passover for all the children of the captivity, and for their brethren the priests, and for themselves.
21 And the children of Israel, which were come again out of captivity, and all such as had separated themselves unto them from

f 1 Tim. 2. 1, 2.
g 2 Kin. 10. 27. Dan. 2. 5. & 3. 29.
h 1 Kin. 9. 3.

i ch. 5. 1, 2.

k ch. 1. 1. & 5. 13. ver. 3.
l ch. 4. 24.
m ch. 7. 1.

n 1 Kin. 8. 63. 2 Chr. 7. 5.
o ch. 8. 35.

p 1 Chr. 24. 1.
q 1 Chr. 23. 6.
r Num. 3. 6. & 8. 9.
s Ex. 12. 6.
t 2 Chr. 30. 15.
u 2 Chr. 35. 11.

[1] Chald. *let him be destroyed.*
[2] Chald. *decree.*
[3] Chald. *the sons of the transportation.*
[4] Chald. *according to the writing.*

cree of Darius, which was grounded upon,
and probably recited, the decree of Cyrus.

11. *being set up, let him be hanged thereon*]
Rather, "**let him be lifted up and crucified upon it.**" Crucifixion was the most
common form of capital punishment among
the Persians.

12. *destroy all*] A similar malediction is
found at the end of the great inscription of
this same king Darius at Behistun. If any
injure the tablet which he has set up, he
prays that Ormazd will be their enemy, and
that they may have no offspring, and that
whatever they do, Ormazd may curse it for
them.

to alter and *to destroy this house*] *i.e.* to
alter the decree, and then proceed to destroy
the house.

14. *Artaxerxes*] The Artaxerxes of marg.
ref. seems to be meant (*i.e.* Longimanus);
he was one of those who together with Cyrus and Darius helped forward the *completion*
of the work.

15. "Adar" was the twelfth or last
month of the Jewish year, corresponding

nearly with our March. The sixth year of
Darius was B.C. 516–515.

17. Cp. with this modest sacrifice, which
suits well "the day of small things" (Zech.
iv. 10), the lavish offering of Solomon (marg.
ref. *n*).

19. With this verse the writer resumes
the use of the Hebrew language, which he
had discarded for the Chaldee from iv.
8. With the exception of the letter of Artaxerxes (vii. 12–26), all the remainder of
the book is in Hebrew.

20. Some render, "**And the priests were
purified; and the Levites, as one man,
were all of them pure.**" A contrast is
drawn between the universal purity of the
Levites and the merely general purity of
the priests (2 Chr. xxix. 34, xxx. 3), which
made it fitting that the former should undertake the slaughter of *all* the paschal
lambs, even of those which the priests were
to consume. In later times the ordinary
practice was for each head of a family to
slay for himself.

*Ex. 12. 15.
& 13. 6.
2 Chr. 30. 21.
& 35. 17.
*Prov. 21. 1.
*2 Kin. 23. 29.
2 Chr. 33. 11.
ch. 1. 1.
& ver. 6, &c.
*Neh. 2. 1.
*1 Chr. 6. 14.

the *filthiness of the heathen of the land, to seek the LORD God
*2 of Israel, did eat, and kept the *feast of unleavened bread seven
days with joy: for the LORD had made them joyful, and
*turned the heart *of the king of Assyria unto them, to
strengthen their hands in the work of the house of God, the God
of Israel.

CHAP. 7. NOW after these things, in the reign of *Artaxerxes king
of Persia, Ezra *the son of Seraiah, the son of Azariah, the son
2 of Hilkiah, the son of Shallum, the son of Zadok, the son of
3 Ahitub, the son of Amariah, the son of Azariah, the son of
4 Meraioth, the son of Zerahiah, the son of Uzzi, the son of Bukki,
5 the son of Abishua, the son of Phinehas, the son of Eleazar, the
6 son of Aaron the chief priest: this Ezra went up from Babylon;

*ver. 11, 12,
21.

*ver. 9.
ch. 8. 22, 31.
*ch. 8. 1.
*See ch. 8.
15, &c.
*ch. 2. 43.
& 8. 20.

and he *was *a ready scribe in the law of Moses, which the LORD
God of Israel had given: and the king granted him all his
request, *according to the hand of the LORD his God upon him.
7 *And there went up *some of the children of Israel, and of the
priests, and *the Levites, and the singers, and the porters, and
*the Nethinims, unto Jerusalem, in the seventh year of Arta-
8 xerxes the king. And he came to Jerusalem in the fifth month,
9 which *was in the seventh year of the king. For upon the first
*day of the first month *began he to go up from Babylon, and on

the first *day of the fifth month came he to Jerusalem, *according
10 to the good hand of his God upon him. For Ezra had prepared
his heart to *seek the law of the LORD, and to do *it, and to

---

¹ Heb. *was the foundation of the going up.*

---

22. *the king of Assyria*] *i.e.* Darius. Assyria had so long been the great monarchy
of western Asia that the sacred writers continue the title to those who had inherited
the old Assyrian power, as first to the Babylonians (2 K. xxiii. 29), and secondly to
the Persians. With similar inexactness we
find Herodotus calling Cyrus "king of the
Medes."

VII. 1. *after these things*] The words
mark an interval of 57 years; if, with most
commentators, we take Artaxerxes to be
Longimanus. See Introd. p. 569. Three
kings named Artaxerxes, the Greek rendering of the Hebrew Artakhshasta, and the
Persian Artakhshatra, ruled over Persia,
viz.:—Longimanus, Mnemon, and Ochus.
Evidence is in favour of the first being
meant here: he was the grandson of Darius
Hystaspis, Jeshua's contemporary.
The genealogy of Ezra here is incomplete. The time between the Exodus and
Ezra must have exceeded a thousand years,
and cannot have been covered by sixteen
generations. One gap may be filled up
from 1 Chr. vi. 7-10, which supplies six
names between Meraioth and Azariah (*v.* 3):
another gap probably occurs between Seraiah (*v.* 1) and Ezra himself; since Seraiah
appears to be the High-Priest of Zedekiah's
time (marg. ref.), who lived at least 130
years before Ezra. Three or four names
are probably wanting in this place. Another name (Meraioth) may be supplied
from 1 Chr. ix. 11, between Zadok and

Ahitub (*v.* 2). These additions would produce twenty-seven generations—a number
nearly sufficient—instead of sixteen.

6. *a ready scribe*] Or, "a ready writer"
(Ps. xlv. 1). The professional scribe was
well known in Egypt from an early date
(see Gen. xxxix. 4 note); and under David
and his successors "scribes" were attached
to the Court as the king's secretaries (2 Sam.
viii. 17, xx. 25; 2 K. xii. 10, &c.). It was
scarcely, however, till the time of the Captivity that the class to which Ezra belonged
arose. The "scribes" of this time, and of
later Jewish history, were students, interpreters, and copiers of the Law (marg. reff.
and Jer. viii. 8). They retained the knowledge of the old dialect, which was being
rapidly superseded by a new one. The emphatic application of the title "the scribe"
to Ezra marks the high honour in which the
office was now held. Its glories threw into
the shade those of the priesthood.

the hand of the LORD...upon him] The use
of this phrase in a good sense is rare elsewhere (cp. 1 K. xviii. 46), but is a favourite
one with both Ezra and Nehemiah (see
marg. reff.; Neh. ii. 8, 18).

9. The direct distance of Babylon from
Jerusalem is about 520 miles; and the circuitous route by Carchemish and the Orontes
valley, which was ordinarily taken by armies
or large bodies of men, is about 900 miles.
The time occupied in the journey is long,
and is perhaps to be accounted for by the
dangers alluded to in viii. 22, 31.

11 ^kteach in Israel statutes and judgments. ¶ Now this *is* the
copy of the letter that the king Artaxerxes gave unto Ezra the
priest, the scribe, *even* a scribe of the words of the command-
12 ments of the LORD, and of his statutes to Israel. Artaxerxes,
¹king of kings, ¹unto Ezra the priest, a scribe of the law of the
13 God of heaven, perfect *peace*, ^mand at such a time. I make a
decree, that all they of the people of Israel, and *of* his priests
and Levites, in my realm, which are minded of their own free-
14 will to go up to Jerusalem, go with thee. Forasmuch as thou
art sent ²of the king, and of his ⁿseven counsellors, to enquire
concerning Judah and Jerusalem, according to the law of thy
15 God which *is* in thine hand; and to carry the silver and gold,
which the king and his counsellors have freely offered unto
16 the God of Israel, ^owhose habitation *is* in Jerusalem, ^pand all
the silver and gold that thou canst find in all the province of
Babylon, with the freewill offering of the people, and of the
priests, ^qoffering willingly for the house of their God which *is*
17 in Jerusalem : that thou mayest buy speedily with this money
bullocks, rams, lambs, with their ^rmeat offerings and their
drink offerings, and ^soffer them upon the altar of the house of
18 your God which *is* in Jerusalem. And whatsoever shall seem
good to thee, and to thy brethren, to do with the rest of the
19 silver and the gold, that do after the will of your God. The
vessels also that are given thee for the service of the house of
20 thy God, *those* deliver thou before the God of Jerusalem. And
whatsoever more shall be needful for the house of thy God,
which thou shalt have occasion to bestow, bestow *it* out of the
21 king's treasure house. And I, *even* I Artaxerxes the king, do
make a decree to all the treasurers which *are* beyond the river,
that whatsoever Ezra the priest, the scribe of the law of the
22 God of heaven, shall require of you, it be done speedily, unto
an hundred talents of silver, and to an hundred ³measures of
wheat, and to an hundred baths of wine, and to an hundred
23 baths of oil, and salt without prescribing *how much*. ⁴Whatso-
ever is commanded by the God of heaven, let it be diligently
done for the house of the God of heaven : for why should there
24 be wrath against the realm of the king and his sons ? Also we
certify you, that touching any of the priests and Levites, singers,

k ver. 6. 25.
Deut. 33. 10.
Neh. 8. 1—8.
Mal. 2. 7.

l Ezek. 26. 7.
Dan. 2. 37.
m ch. 4. 10.

n Esth. 1. 14.

o 2 Chr. 6. 2.
Ps. 135. 21.
p ch. 8. 25.

q 1 Chr. 29.
6, 9.

r Num. 15.
4--13.
s Deut. 12. 5,
11.

¹ Or, *to Ezra the priest, a perfect scribe of the law of the God of heaven*, peace, &c.
² Chald. *from before the king.*
³ Chald. *cors.*
⁴ Heb. *Whatsoever* is *of the decree.*

---

12. The title, "king of kings," is assumed
by almost all the Persian monarchs in their
inscriptions.

perfect peace] "Peace" is not in the original, and the word translated "perfect"
occurs only in this place. Some prefer to
take it as an adjective descriptive of Ezra
(see marg.); others (LXX.) as the opening
word of the first paragraph of the letter,
and give it the meaning, "it is completed."

14. *seven counsellors*] Herodotus relates
that there were seven families pre-eminent
in Persia, those of the seven conspirators
against the Pseudo-Smerdis (iv. 7 note);
and it is reasonable to suppose that the
heads of these families formed the special
council of the king; the "Achæmenidæ," or
royal family, being represented by the head

of the branch next in succession to that of
the reigning monarch (see marg. ref.).

21. *all the treasurers*] The Persian system
of taxing the provinces through the satraps
involved the establishment in each province
of at least one local treasury.

22. This verse assigns limits to the permission of *v.* 20. As the Persian tribute was
paid partly in money and partly in kind
(see iv. 13 note), the treasuries would be
able to supply them as readily as they could
furnish money.

23. Lit. as in the margin, *i.e.*, Whatsoever is commanded in the Law with respect
to the Temple service.

24. The decree of Artaxerxes was more
favourable to the Jews than those of all
previous Persian monarchs. We hear of a

porters, Nethinims, or ministers of this house of God, it shall not be lawful to impose toll, tribute, or custom, upon them.

25 And thou, Ezra, after the wisdom of thy God, that *is* in thine hand, *t* set magistrates and judges, which may judge all the people that *are* beyond the river, all such as know the laws of 26 thy God; and *u* teach ye them that know *them* not. And whosoever will not do the law of thy God, and the law of the king, let judgment be executed speedily upon him, whether *it be* unto death, or [1] to banishment, or to confiscation of goods, or to im-27 prisonment. ¶ *x* Blessed *be* the LORD God of our fathers, *y* which hath put *such a thing* as this in the king's heart, to beautify the 28 house of the LORD which *is* in Jerusalem: and *z* hath extended mercy unto me before the king, and his counsellors, and before all the king's mighty princes. And I was strengthened as *a* the hand of the LORD my God *was* upon me, and I gathered together out of Israel chief men to go up with me.

CHAP. 8. THESE *are* now the chief of their fathers, and *this is* the genealogy of them that went up with me from Babylon, in the 2 reign of Artaxerxes the king. Of the sons of Phinehas; Gershom: of the sons of Ithamar; Daniel: of the sons of David; 3 *a* Hattush. Of the sons of Shechaniah, of the sons of *b* Pharosh; Zechariah: and with him were reckoned by genealogy of the 4 males an hundred and fifty. Of the sons of Pahath-moab; Elihoenai the son of Zerahiah, and with him two hundred males. 5 Of the sons of Shechaniah; the son of Jahaziel, and with him 6 three hundred males. Of the sons also of Adin; Ebed the son 7 of Jonathan, and with him fifty males. And of the sons of Elam; Jeshaiah the son of Athaliah, and with him seventy 8 males. And of the sons of Shephatiah; Zebadiah the son of 9 Michael, and with him fourscore males. Of the sons of Joab; Obadiah the son of Jehiel, and with him two hundred and 10 eighteen males. And of the sons of Shelomith; the son of Josi-11 phiah, and with him an hundred and threescore males. And of the sons of Bebai; Zechariah the son of Bebai, and with him 12 twenty and eight males. And of the sons of Azgad; Johanan [2] the son of Hakkatan, and with him an hundred and ten males. 13 And of the last sons of Adonikam, whose names *are* these, Eliphelet, Jeiel, and Shemaiah, and with them threescore males. 14 Of the sons also of Bigvai; Uthai, and [3] Zabbud, and with them 15 seventy males. ¶ And I gathered them together to the river that runneth to Ahava; and there [4] abode we in tents three

Marginal references:
t Ex. 18. 21, 22.
Deut. 16. 18.
u ver. 10.
2 Chr. 17. 7.
Mal. 2. 7.
Matt. 23.2, 3.
x 1 Chr.29.10.
y ch. 6. 22.
z ch. 9. 9.
a See ch.5 5.
& ver. 6, 9.
& ch. 8. 18.
a 1 Chr. 3.22.
b ch. 2. 3.

---

[1] Chald. *to rooting out.*
[2] Or, *the youngest son.*
[3] Or, *Zaccur*, as some read.
[4] Or, *pitched.*

---

similar exemption of ecclesiastics from tribute, only to a less extent, under the Seleucidæ.

ministers] The rare word here used, which in Daniel has the sense of "worshippers," appears to designate in this place the lowest class of persons employed in the service of the Temple.

26. *banishment*] Lit. as in marg. Separation from the congregation is probably intended (cp. x. 8).

27. An abrupt transition from the words of Artaxerxes to those of Ezra. Cp. a similar abrupt change in vi. 6. The language alters at the same time from Chaldee

to Hebrew, continuing henceforth to be Hebrew till the close of the book.

VIII. **2, 3.** Punctuate as follows:—
2. ...of the sons of David, Hattush of the sons of Shechaniah.
3. Of the sons of Pharosh, Zechariah, &c.

Hattush, the descendant of David, was the grandson of Shechaniah (see marg. ref.). Most of these names (*vv.* 2-14) occur also as those of heads of families in the list of the Jews who returned with Zerubbabel (ii. 3-15). The LXX. and Syriac Versions supply omissions in *vv.* 5, 10.

15. Ahava was both a town and a river

days : and I viewed the people, and the priests, and found there
16 none of the *sons of Levi. Then sent I for Eliezer, for Ariel, *See ch.7.7.
for Shemaiah, and for Elnathan, and for Jarib, and for Elnathan, and for Nathan, and for Zechariah, and for Meshullam,
chief men; also for Joiarib, and for Elnathan, men of under-
17 standing. And I sent them with commandment unto Iddo the
chief at the place Casiphia, and ¹I told them what they should
say unto Iddo, *and* to his brethren the Nethinims, at the place
Casiphia, that they should bring unto us ministers for the house
18 of our God. And by the good hand of our God upon us they
*d*brought us a man of understanding, of the sons of Mahli, the   *d* Neh. 8. 7.
son of Levi, the son of Israel; and Sherebiah, with his sons and   & 9. 4, 5.
19 his brethren, eighteen; and Hashabiah, and with him Jeshaiah
of the sons of Merari, his brethren and their sons, twenty;
20 *e*also of the Nethinims, whom David and the princes had ap-   *e* See ch. 2.
pointed for the service of the Levites, two hundred and twenty   43.
21 Nethinims: all of them were expressed by name. ¶ Then I
*f*proclaimed a fast there, at the river of Ahava, that we might   *f* 2 Chr. 20. 3.
*g*afflict ourselves before our God, to seek of him a *h*right way for *g* Lev. 16. 29.
22 us, and for our little ones, and for all our substance. For *i*I   & 23. 29.
                                                                    Isai. 58. 3, 5.
was ashamed to require of the king a band of soldiers and horse- *h* Ps. 5. 8.
men to help us against the enemy in the way: because we had   *i* So 1 Cor. 9.
spoken unto the king, saying, *k*The hand of our God *is* upon all 15.
them for *l*good that seek him; but his power and his wrath *is*   *k* ch. 7. 6, 9,
                                                                    28.
23 *m*against all them that *n*forsake him. So we fasted and besought *l* Ps.33.18,19.
24 our God for this : and he was *o*intreated of us. ¶ Then I separ- & 34. 15, 22.
ated twelve of the chief of the priests, Sherebiah, Hashabiah,   *m* Ps. 34. 16.
                                                                    n 2 Chr.15. 2.
25 and ten of their brethren with them, and weighed unto them   *o* 1 Chr. 5. 20.
*p*the silver, and the gold, and the vessels, *even* the offering of 2 Chr. 33. 13.
the house of our God, which the king, and his counsellors, and   Isai. 19. 22.
26 his lords, and all Israel *there* present, had offered: I even   *p* ch. 7.15,16.
weighed unto their hand six hundred and fifty talents of silver,
and silver vessels an hundred talents, *and* of gold an hundred
27 talents; also twenty basons of gold, of a thousand drams; and
28 two vessels of ²fine copper, ³precious as gold. And I said unto
them, Ye *are* *q*holy unto the LORD; the vessels *are* *r*holy also; *q* Lev. 21. 6,
and the silver and the gold *are* a freewill offering unto the LORD 7, 8.
                                                                    Deut. 33. 8.
29 God of your fathers. Watch ye, and keep *them*, until ye weigh   *r* Lev.22.2,3.
them before the chief of the priests and the Levites, and chief of Num. 4. 4,
the fathers of Israel, at Jerusalem, in the chambers of the house 15, 19, 20.

¹ Heb. *I put words in their*   ¹ Heb *yellow,* or, *shining brass.*
   mouth : See 2 Sam. 14. 3, 19.   ³ Heb. *desirable.*

(*v.* 21). The modern name of the place is
Hit. It is famous for its bitumen springs,
and is situated on the Euphrates, at a distance of about 80 miles from Babylon, towards the north-west.

none of the sons of Levi] The Levites appear to have been disinclined to return to
Jerusalem (see iii. 8 note).

17. *Casiphia*] Its situation is wholly unknown; but it cannot have been far from
Ahava.

18. *and Sherebiah*] Either a name has
fallen out before the words "a man of understanding," or the "and" here has crept
into the text by accident. Sherebiah appears
among the most earnest of the Levites under
Nehemiah (marg. reff.).

22. What "enemy" menaced Ezra, and on
what account, is wholly uncertain (cp. *v.* 31).
Perhaps robber-tribes, Arab or Syrian, were
his opponents.

27. *twenty basons of gold, of a thousand
drams*] Not of a thousand drams (*i.e.* daries)
each, but worth altogether a thousand darics. As the value of the daric was about
22 shillings of our money, each bason, or
saucer, would have been worth (apart from
the fashioning) 55*l*.

of fine copper] The word translated "fine,"
which occurs here only, is thought to mean
either "yellow" or "glittering" (see marg.).
Probably the vessels were of *orichalcum*, an
amalgam which was either brass or something nearly approaching to brass, but which

30 of the LORD. So took the priests and the Levites the weight of the silver, and the gold, and the vessels, to bring *them* to Jeru-
31 salem unto the house of our God. ¶ Then we departed from the river of Ahava on the twelfth *day* of the first month, to go unto Jerusalem: and *s*the hand of our God was upon us, and he delivered us from the hand of the enemy, and of such as lay in
32 wait by the way. And we *t*came to Jerusalem, and abode there
33 three days. Now on the fourth day was the silver and the gold and the vessels *u*weighed in the house of our God by the hand of Meremoth the son of Uriah the priest; and with him *was* Eleazar the son of Phinehas; and with them *was* Jozabad the
34 son of Jeshua, and Noadiah the son of Binnui, Levites; by number *and* by weight of every one: and all the weight was
35 written at that time. *Also* the children of those that had been carried away, which were come out of the captivity, *x*offered burnt offerings unto the God of Israel, twelve bullocks for all Israel, ninety and six rams, seventy and seven lambs, twelve he goats *for* a sin offering: all *this was* a burnt offering unto the
36 LORD. And they delivered the king's *y*commissions unto the king's lieutenants, and to the governors on this side the river: and they furthered the people, and the house of God.

CHAP. 9. NOW when these things were done, the princes came to me, saying, The people of Israel, and the priests, and the Levites, have not *a*separated themselves from the people of the lands, *b*doing according to their abominations, *even* of the Canaanites, the Hittites, the Perizzites, the Jebusites, the Ammonites, the Moabites, the Egyptians, and the Amorites.
2 For they have *c*taken of their daughters for themselves, and for their sons: so that the *d*holy seed have *e*mingled themselves with the people of *those* lands: yea, the hand of the princes and
3 rulers hath been chief in this trespass. And when I heard this thing, *f*I rent my garment and my mantle, and plucked off the hair of my head and of my beard, and sat down *g*astonied.
4 Then were assembled unto me every one that *h*trembled at the words of the God of Israel, because of the transgression of those that had been carried away; and I sat astonied until the *i*even-
5 ing sacrifice. ¶ And at the evening sacrifice I arose up from my *1*heaviness; and having rent my garment and my mantle, I fell upon my knees, and *k*spread out my hands unto the LORD my
6 God, and said, O my God, I am *l*ashamed and blush to lift up

Margin refs:
s ch.7.6,9,28.
t Neh. 2. 11.
u ver. 26, 30.
x So ch.6.17.
y ch. 7. 21.
a ch. 6. 21. Neh. 9. 2.
b Deut. 12. 30, 31.
c Ex. 34. 16. Deut. 7. 3. Neh. 13. 23.
d Ex. 19. 6. & 22. 31. Deut. 7. 6. & 14. 2.
r 2 Cor. 6. 14.
f Job 1. 20.
y Ps. 143. 4.
h ch. 10. 3. Isai. 66. 2.
i Ex. 29. 39.
k Ex.9.29,33.
l Dan. 9. 7, 8.

¹ Or, *affliction.*

was very rarely produced in the ancient world, and, when produced, was regarded as highly valuable.

31. The Jews with Ezra left Babylon on the first day of the first month (vii. 9). They reached Ahava in nine days, and, having remained there three (*v.* 15), quitted it, and resumed their journey on the twelfth. They reached Jerusalem on the first day of the fifth month (vii. 9), four months after the departure from Babylon.

35. Cp. marg. ref. The idea of offerings for all Israel pervades in this case the entire sacrifice, with the exception of the lambs, whose number (77) is peculiar, and has not been accounted for.

36. *the king's commissions*] *i.e.* the orders issued to all governors of provinces near Judæa by Artaxerxes, given in vii. 21-24.

the king's lieutenants] Lit. "the king's satraps." The word is used in its strict sense, referring to the chief rulers of Persian provinces, from which the "governors" or rulers of smaller districts are distinguished.

IX. 1. *abominations*] The mixed marriages had prevented that complete separation of the people of God from the idolatrous rites, or "abominations," which the Law required, and which was necessary for purity of religion. See 1 K. xi. 2 note.

3. Plucking out the hair with the hands, so common among the classical nations, is, comparatively speaking, rarely mentioned as practised by Asiatics.

my face to thee, my God: for [m]our iniquities are increased over
our head, and our [1]trespass is [n]grown up unto the heavens.
7 Since the days of our fathers *have* [o]we *been* in a great trespass
unto this day; and for our iniquities [p]have we, our kings, *and*
our priests, been delivered into the hand of the kings of the
lands, to the sword, to captivity, and to a spoil, and to [q]con-
8 fusion of face, as *it is* this day. And now for a [2]little space
grace hath been *shewed* from the LORD our God, to leave us a
remnant to escape, and to give us [3]a nail in his holy place, that
our God may [r]lighten our eyes, and give us a little reviving in
9 our bondage. [s]For we *were* bondmen; [t]yet our God hath not
forsaken us in our bondage, but [u]hath extended mercy unto us
in the sight of the kings of Persia, to give us a reviving, to set
up the house of our God, and [4]to repair the desolations thereof,
10 and to give us [x]a wall in Judah and in Jerusalem. And now, O
our God, what shall we say after this? for we have forsaken thy
11 commandments, which thou hast commanded [5]by thy servants
the prophets, saying, The land, unto which ye go to possess it,
is an unclean land with the [y]filthiness of the people of the lands,
with their abominations, which have filled it [6]from one end to
12 another with their uncleanness. Now therefore [z]give not your
daughters unto their sons, neither take their daughters unto
your sons, [a]nor seek their peace or their wealth for ever: that
ye may be strong, and eat the good of the land, and [b]leave *it* for
13 an inheritance to your children for ever. And after all that
is come upon us for our evil deeds, and for our great trespass, seeing that thou our God [c][7]hast punished us less than
our iniquities *deserve*, and hast given us *such* deliverance as
14 this; should we [d]again break thy commandments, and [e]join in
affinity with the people of these abominations? wouldest not
thou be [f]angry with us till thou hadst consumed *us*, so that
15 *there should be* no remnant nor escaping? O LORD God of Israel,
[g]thou *art* righteous: for we remain yet escaped, as *it is* this day:
behold, we *are* [h]before thee [i]in our trespasses: for we cannot
[k]stand before thee because of this.

[m] Ps. 38. 4.
[n] 2 Chr. 28. 9. Rev. 18. 5.
[o] Ps. 106. 6. Dan. 9. 5, 6, 8.
[p] Deut. 28. 36, 64. Neh. 9. 30.
[q] Dan. 9. 7, 8.
[r] Ps. 13. 3. & 34. 5.
[s] Neh. 9. 36.
[t] Ps. 136. 23.
[u] ch. 7. 28.
[x] Isai. 5. 2.
[y] ch. 6. 21.
[z] Ex. 23, 32. & 34. 16. Deut. 7. 3.
[a] Deut. 23. 6.
[b] Prov. 13. 22. & 20. 7.
[c] Ps. 103. 10.
[d] John 5. 14. 2 Pet. 2. 20, 21.
[e] ver. 2. Neh. 13. 23, 27.
[f] Deut. 9. 8.
[g] Neh. 9. 33. Dan. 9. 14.
[h] Rom. 3. 19.
[i] 1 Cor. 15. 17.
[k] Ps. 130. 3.

[1] Or, *guiltiness.*
[2] Heb. *moment.*
[3] Or, *a pin:* that is, *a constant and sure abode:* So Isai. 22. 23.
[4] Heb. *to set up.*
[5] Heb. *by the hand of thy servants.*
[6] Heb. *from mouth to mouth:* as 2 Kin. 21. 16.
[7] Heb. *hast withheld beneath our iniquities.*

---

7. Very similar in tone to this are the confessions of Nehemiah (Neh. ix. 29–35) and of Daniel (marg. reff.). The Captivity had done its work by deeply convincing of sin the nation that had been proud and self-righteous previously.

8. The "little space" was above sixty years, counting from the second year of Darius (iv. 24), or about eighty, counting from the first year of Cyrus (i. 1). This does not seem to Ezra much in the life of a nation.

a remnant to escape] Rather, "**a remnant that has escaped.**" The "remnant" is the new community that has returned from the Captivity.

a nail] Cp. marg. note and ref. The metaphor is probably drawn from a tent-pin, which is driven into the earth to make the tent firm and secure.

9. *we were bondmen*] Rather, "**we are bondmen**" (cp. marg. ref.). The Israelites, though returned from the Captivity, were still "bondmen." The Persian monarch was their absolute lord and master.

11. *saying*] The words which follow in this verse are not quoted from any previous book of Scripture, but merely give the general sense of numerous passages. Cp. marg reff.

13. *deliverance*] Or, "remnant," as in *v.* 8.

15. Some take "righteous" to mean here "kind" or "merciful." Others give it the more usual sense of "just," and understand the full meaning of the passage to be, "Thou art righteous, and hast punished us, because of our sin, the contraction of forbidden marriages, so that we are a mere remnant of what was once a great people."

a Dan. 9. 20·
b 2 Chr. 20. 9.

c Neh. 13. 27.

d 2Chr. 34. 31.

o ch. 9. 4.
f Deut. 7. 2, 3.

g 1Chr. 28. 10.
h Neh. 5. 12.

i Deut. 9. 18.

k See 1 Sam. 12. 18.

l Josh. 7. 19.
Prov. 28. 13.

CHAP. 10. NOW *a* when Ezra had prayed, and when he had confessed, weeping and casting himself down *b* before the house of God, there assembled unto him out of Israel a very great congregation of men and women and children: for the people 2 ¹ wept very sore. And Shechaniah the son of Jehiel, *one* of the sons of Elam, answered and said unto Ezra, We have *c* trespassed against our God, and have taken strange wives of the people of the land: yet now there is hope in Israel concerning 3 this thing. Now therefore let us make *d* a covenant with our God ²to put away all the wives, and such as are born of them, according to the counsel of my lord, and of those that *e* tremble at *f* the commandment of our God; and let it be done according 4 to the law. Arise; for *this* matter *belongeth* unto thee: we also 5 *will be* with thee: *g* be of good courage, and do *it*. ¶Then arose Ezra, and made the chief priests, the Levites, and all Israel, *h* to swear that they should do according to this word. And they 6 sware. Then Ezra rose up from before the house of God, and went into the chamber of Johanan the son of Eliashib: and *when* he came thither, he *i* did eat no bread, nor drink water: for he mourned because of the transgression of them that had 7 been carried away. And they made proclamation throughout Judah and Jerusalem unto all the children of the captivity, that 8 they should gather themselves together unto Jerusalem; and that whosoever would not come within three days, according to the counsel of the princes and the elders, all his substance should be ³forfeited, and himself separated from the congrega- 9 tion of those that had been carried away. ¶Then all the men of Judah and Benjamin gathered themselves together unto Jerusalem within three days. It *was* the ninth month, on the twentieth *day* of the month; and *k* all the people sat in the street of the house of God, trembling because of *this* matter, 10 and for ⁴the great rain. And Ezra the priest stood up, and said unto them, Ye have transgressed, and ⁵have taken strange wives, 11 to increase the trespass of Israel. Now therefore *l* make confession unto the LORD God of your fathers, and do his pleasure:

---

¹ Heb. *wept a great weeping.*   ³ Heb. *devoted.*   ⁵ Heb. *have caused to dwell,*
² Heb. *to bring forth.*   ⁴ Heb. *the showers.*   o*r, have brought back.*

X. 1., *before the house of God*] *i.e.* in front of the Temple, praying towards it (1 K. viii. 30, 35; Dan. vi. 10), and thus in the sight of all the people who happened at the time to be in the great court.

2. Jehiel was one of those who had taken an idolatrous wife (*v.* 26); and Shechaniah had therefore had the evil brought home to him.

3. *let it be done according to the law*] *i.e.* let a formal "bill of divorcement" be given to each foreign wife, whereby she will be restored to the condition of an unmarried woman, and be free to wed another husband (see Deut. xxiv. 1, 2). The facility of divorce among the Jews is well known. According to many of the Rabbis, a bill of divorcement might be given by the husband for the most trivial cause. Thus no legal difficulty stood in the way of Shechaniah's proposition; and Ezra regarded it as neces-

sary for the moral and religious welfare of the people.

6. The "chamber of Johanan" was probably one of those attached externally to the Temple (see 1 K. vi. 5, 6). Eliashib was the grandson of Jeshua (iii. 2), and was High-Priest under Nehemiah (Neh. iii. 1). He could assign chambers in the Temple to whomsoever he pleased (see Neh. xiii. 4, 5).

8. *separated from the congregation*] *i.e.* "excommunicated" (cp. Ex. xii. 19; Num. xix. 20, &c.). The power assigned to Ezra is stated in vii. 25, 26.

9. *it was the ninth month*] Or, our December, a time when rain falls heavily in Palestine: four months, therefore, after Ezra's arrival in Jerusalem (cp. vii. 9).

the street] Rather, "the court," the "broad," "spacious, place" (cp. 2 Chr. xxix. 4 note).

and ^m separate yourselves from the people of the land, and from
12 the strange wives. ¶ Then all the congregation answered and
13 said with a loud voice, As thou hast said, so must we do. But
the people *are* many, and *it is* a time of much rain, and we are
not able to stand without, neither *is this* a work of one day or
two : for ¹we are many that have transgressed in this thing.
14 Let now our rulers of all the congregation stand, and let all
them which have taken strange wives in our cities come at
appointed times, and with them the elders of every city, and the
judges thereof, until ⁿthe fierce wrath of our God ²for this
15 matter be turned from us. ¶ Only Jonathan the son of Asahel
and Jahaziah the son of Tikvah ³were employed about this
matter : and Meshullam and Shabbethai the Levite helped them.
16 And the children of the captivity did so. ¶ And Ezra the priest,
with certain chief of the fathers, after the house of their fathers,
and all of them by *their* names, were separated, and sat down in
17 the first day of the tenth month to examine the matter. And
they made an end with all the men that had taken strange wives
18 by the first day of the first month. ¶ And among the sons of
the priests there were found that had taken strange wives :
namely, of the sons of Jeshua the son of Jozadak, and his
19 brethren ; Maaseiah, and Eliezer, and Jarib, and Gedaliah. And
they ^ogave their hands that they would put away their wives ;
and *being* ^pguilty, *they offered* a ram of the flock for their tres-
20 pass. And of the sons of Immer ; Hanani, and Zebadiah.
21 And of the sons of Harim ; Maaseiah, and Elijah, and Shemaiah,
22 and Jehiel, and Uzziah. And of the sons of Pashur ; Elioenai,
23 Maaseiah, Ishmael, Nethaneel, Jozabad, and Elasah. ¶ Also of
the Levites ; Jozabad, and Shimei, and Kelaiah, (the same *is*
24 Kelita,) Pethahiah, Judah, and Eliezer. Of the singers also ;
Eliashib : and of the porters ; Shallum, and Telem, and Uri.
25 ¶ Moreover of Israel : of the sons of Parosh ; Ramiah, and Je-
ziah, and Malchiah, and Miamin, and Eleazar, and Malchijah,
26 and Benaiah. And of the sons of Elam ; Mattaniah, Zechariah,
27 and Jehiel, and Abdi, and Jeremoth, and Eliah. And of the
sons of Zattu ; Elioenai, Eliashib, Mattaniah, and Jeremoth,
28 and Zabad, and Aziza. Of the sons also of Bebai ; Jehohanan,
29 Hananiah, Zabbai, *and* Athlai. And of the sons of Bani ; Meshullam, Malluch, and Adaiah, Jashub, and Sheal, and Ramoth.
30 And of the sons of Pahath-moab ; Adna, and Chelal, Benaiah,
Maaseiah, Mattaniah, Bezaleel, and Binnui, and Manasseh.
31 And *of* the sons of Harim ; Eliezer, Ishijah, Malchiah, She-
32, 33 maiah, Shimeon, Benjamin, Malluch, *and* Shemariah. Of the
sons of Hashum ; Mattenai, Mattathah, Zabad, Eliphelet, Jere-
34 mai, Manasseh, *and* Shimei. Of the sons of Bani ; Maadai,
35, 36 Amram, and Uel, Benaiah, Bedeiah, Chelluh, Vaniah, Mere-

^m ver. 3.

ⁿ 2 Chr. 30. 8.

^o 2 Kin. 10. 15.
1 Chr. 29. 24.
2 Chr. 30. 8.
^p Lev. 6. 4, 6.

---

¹ Or, *we have greatly of-
fended in this thing.*

² Or, *till this matter* be dis-
patched.

³ Heb. *stood.*

---

15. Some translate, "**Nevertheless** Jonathan the son of Asahel and Jahaziah the
son of Tikvah **opposed this.**" The opposition was useless (*v.* 16).
17. The business occupied the commission full two months. In some cases, it
may be presumed, they had to summon persons before them who did not wish to part

with their foreign wives ; in all, they had
to assure themselves that the wives were
foreign ; finally, they had in every case
where they decreed a divorce to make out
the "writing of divorcement" (*v.* 3).
18–43. Cp. with the list in ch. ii.
19. *they gave their hands*] *i.e.* "solemnly
pledged themselves" (cp. marg. reff.).

37, 38 moth, Eliashib, Mattaniah, Mattenai, and Jaasau, and Bani,
39 and Binnui, Shimei, and Shelemiah, and Nathan, and Adaiah,
40, 41 [1]Machnadebai, Shashai, Sharai, Azareel, and Shelemiah, She-
42, 43 mariah, Shallum, Amariah, *and* Joseph. Of the sons of
Nebo; Jeiel, Mattithiah, Zabad, Zebina, Jadau, and Joel,
44 Benaiah. All these had taken strange wives: and *some* of them
had wives by whom they had children.

[1] Or, *Mabnadebai*, according to some copies.

44. The guilty persons were, it would seem, 113 in number. They comprised four members of the High-Priest's family, thirteen other priests, ten Levites, and eighty-six lay Israelites belonging to at least ten distinct families. The fact noted in the second clause of the verse must have increased the difficulty of Ezra's task.

NEHEMIAH.

INTRODUCTION.

In the earliest form of the Hebrew Canon known to us the Books of Ezra and Nehemiah were united in one, under the name of "The Book of Ezra."[1] After a while a division was made, and the two Books which we now recognise were distinguished as "the first" and "the second Book of Ezra."[2] Later still—probably not till towards the close of the fourth century—the second Book of Ezra came to be known as "the Book of Nehemiah."[3]

2. The Book of Nehemiah is composed of four quite distinct sections :—

(I.) Chs. i.-vii. containing the record of the twentieth year of Artaxerxes (or B.C. 445–444), but composed by Nehemiah at least twelve years later (v. 14).

(II.) The second section of the work consists of chs. viii.-x., and contains a narrative of some events belonging to the autumn of B.C. 444. In this portion Nehemiah is spoken of in the third person; he is called "the Tirshatha," whereas in the earlier chapters his title is always *pechah* ("governor"); and

Ezra holds the first and most prominent position. The style of this portion of the Book is markedly different from that of the earlier and later chapters ;[1] and critics are generally agreed that it is not from the hand of Nehemiah. Some assign it to Ezra ; others conjecture Zadok (or Zidkijah), Nehemiah's scribe or secretary (xiii. 13), to have been the author.

(III.) xi.–xii. 26, which consists of six important lists.

Lists 1 (xi. 1–24) and 2 (xi. 25–36) are probably either the work of Nehemiah himself or documents drawn up by his orders.

Of the other lists (xii. 1–26) some may have been drawn up in the time (or even by the hand) of Nehemiah, and incorporated by him into his work as documents having an intrinsic value, though not connected very closely with the subject-matter of his history. But the list in *vv.* 10, 11 cannot in its present shape have proceeded from his hand, or from that of a contemporary, since it mentions Jaddua, who lived about a century later than Nehemiah.[5] Neither can

---

[1] See p. 569.
[2] By Origen (about A.D. 230).
[3] By Jerome.
[4] Nehemiah's parenthetic prayers are wholly wanting in this section. His favourite term for the "nobles" (*khorim*) does not occur. The characteristic phrases, "God of heaven," and "the good hand of God," are absent. God is called "Jehovah" or "Jehovah Elohim," almost as often as simply "Elohim," whereas Nehe-

miah uses "Jehovah" and "Jehovah Elohim," only once, each of them (i. 5, v. 13). Express mention of the Law of Moses, rare with Nehemiah (only xiii. 1), is constant in this section.
[5] Jaddua's High-priesthood is placed by some between B.C. 366 and 336 ; but Josephus brings down his date to B.C. 333, since he makes him meet Alexander after Issus.

vv. 22, 23 intruded between the fifth and sixth lists—lists closely interconnected—belong to Nehemiah's time, since they contain a mention of both Jaddua and Darius Codomannus, his contemporary. [6] Possibly, the list in question and the intruded verses may have proceeded from the same hand.

The section may therefore be regarded as the compilation of Nehemiah himself, with the exception of *vv.* 11, 22, 23, which must have been added a century later. Or, it was first added at that period. In either case the writer must equally be considered to have drawn the lists from contemporary State archives (see xii. 23).

(IV.) xii. 27–end. This section contains an account of the dedication of the wall, and of certain reforms which Nehemiah effected after his return from Babylon in B.C. 432–431. It is allowed on all hands to be, in the main, the work of Nehemiah,[7] and written soon after the events—probably in B.C. 431 or 430.

It is perhaps on the whole most probable that the various sections composing the "Book of Nehemiah" were collected by Nehemiah himself, who had written, at any rate, two of them (i.–vii. 5, xii. 27–xiii. 31). Having composed these two separate memoirs, and having perhaps drawn up also certain lists, he adopted from without an account of some religious transactions belonging to his first period, and, inserting this in its proper place, prefixed to the whole work the title, "The words of Nehemiah, the son of Hachaliah," as fitly designating its main contents. His work, thus formed, was subsequently added to by Jaddua, or a writer of that time, who inserted into it xii. 11, 22, 23. Or, possibly, this late writer may first have formed the Book into a whole. The date of the compilation would, in the former case, be about B.C. 430; in the latter, about a century later.

The authenticity of the history contained in the Book of Nehemiah is generally admitted : and the condition of the text is generally good.

---

[6] This is the usual identification of "Darius the Persian" (xii. 22, see note). The expression, "*the Persian*," is probably an indication that the passage was written after the Greek rule had set in, or later than B.C. 331.

[7] It possesses such characteristics of his style and manner as the designation of God exclusively by the name of Elohim, the use of parenthetic prayers (xiii. 14, 22, 29, 31), the exact knowledge of localities (xii. 31–39), &c.

THE BOOK

OF

NEHEMIAH.

Chap. 1. THE words of *a* Nehemiah the son of Hachaliah. ¶ And
it came to pass in the month Chisleu, in the twentieth year, as I
2 was in Shushan the palace, that Hanani, one of my brethren,
came, he and *certain* men of Judah ; and I asked them concerning the Jews that had escaped, which were left of the cap-
3 tivity, and concerning Jerusalem. And they said unto me, The
remnant that are left of the captivity there in the province *are*
in great affliction and reproach : *b* the wall of Jerusalem also *c is*
4 broken down, and the gates thereof are burned with fire. ¶ And
it came to pass, when I had heard these words, that I sat down
and wept, and mourned *certain* days, and fasted, and prayed
5 before the God of heaven, and said, I beseech thee, *d* O Lord
God of heaven, the great and terrible God, *e* that keepeth
covenant and mercy for them that love him and observe his
6 commandments : let thine ear now be attentive, and *f* thine eyes
open, that thou mayest hear the prayer of thy servant, which I
pray before thee now, day and night, for the children of Israel
thy servants, and *g* confess the sins of the children of Israel,
which we have sinned against thee : both I and my father's
7 house have sinned. *h* We have dealt very corruptly against
thee, and have *i* not kept the commandments, nor the statutes,
nor the judgments, which thou commandedst thy servant Moses.
8 Remember, I beseech thee, the word that thou commandedst
thy servant Moses, saying, *k If* ye transgress, I will scatter you
9 abroad among the nations : *l* but *if* ye turn unto me, and keep
my commandments, and do them ; *m* though there were of you
cast out unto the uttermost part of the heaven, *yet* will I gather
them from thence, and will bring them unto the place that I
10 have chosen to set my name there. *n* Now these *are* thy servants and thy people, whom thou hast redeemed by thy great
11 power, and by thy strong hand. O Lord, I beseech thee, *o* let
now thine ear be attentive to the prayer of thy servant, and to
the prayer of thy servants, who *p* desire to fear thy name : and
prosper, I pray thee, thy servant this day, and grant him mercy
in the sight of this man. For I was the king's *q* cupbearer.

a ch. 10. 1.

b ch. 2. 17.
c 2 Kin. 25. 10.

d Dan. 9. 4.
e Ex. 20. 6.

f 1 Kin. 8. 28,
29.
2 Chr. 6. 40.
Dan. 9. 17, 18.
g Dan. 9. 20.

h Ps. 106. 6.
Dan. 9. 5.
i Deut. 28. 15.

k Lev. 26. 33.
Deut. 4. 25,
26, 27.
& 28. 64.
l Lev. 26. 39,
&c.
Deut. 4. 29,
30, 31.
& 30. 2.
m Deut. 30. 4.
n Deut. 9. 29.
Dan. 9. 15.
o ver. 6.
p Isai. 26. 8.
Heb. 13. 18.
q ch. 2. 1.

I. 1. *The words of Nehemiah the son of
Hachaliah*] The prophetical books commence generally with a title of this kind
(see Jer. i. 1) ; but no other extant Historical Book begins thus. Nehemiah, while
attaching his work to Ezra, perhaps marked
in this manner the point at which his own
composition commenced. See Introd. p. 592.

Chisleu] The ninth month, corresponding
to the end of November and beginning of
December.

in the twentieth year] i.e. of Artaxerxes
Longimanus (B.C. 465-425). Cp. ii. 1.

Shushan the palace] Cp. Esth. i. 2, 5 &c. ;
Dan. viii. 2. Shushan, or Susa, was the
ordinary residence of the Persian kings.
'The palace" or acropolis was a distinct

quarter of the city, occupying an artificial
eminence.

2. Hanani seems to have been an actual
brother of Nehemiah (vii. 2).

3. The attempt to rebuild the wall in the
time of the Pseudo-Smerdis (Ezra iv. 12–24)
had been stopped. It still remained in
ruins. The Assyrian sculptures show that
it was the usual practice to burn the
gates.

4. *the God of heaven*] This title of the
Almighty, which is Persian rather than
Jewish (see 2 Chr. xxxvi. 23 ; Ezra i. 2 note,
vi. 10, vii. 12, 21), is a favourite one with
Nehemiah, who had been born and brought
up in Persia.

11. A Persian king had numerous cup-

CHAP. 2. AND it came to pass in the month Nisan, in the twentieth
year of *Artaxerxes the king, *that* wine *was* before him : and
*b*I took up the wine, and gave *it* unto the king. Now I had not
2 been *beforetime* sad in his presence. Wherefore the king said
unto me, Why *is* thy countenance sad, seeing thou *art* not sick ?
this *is* nothing *else* but *c*sorrow of heart. Then I was very sore
3 afraid, and said unto the king, *d*Let the king live for ever : why
should not my countenance be sad, when *e* the city, the place of
my fathers' sepulchres, *lieth* waste, and the gates thereof are
4 consumed with fire? Then the king said unto me, For what
dost thou make request ? So I prayed to the God of heaven.
5 And I said unto the king, If it please the king, and if thy servant have found favour in thy sight, that thou wouldest send me
unto Judah, unto the city of my fathers' sepulchres, that I may
6 build it. And the king said unto me, (the ¹queen also sitting
by him,) For how long shall thy journey be ? and when wilt
thou return ? So it pleased the king to send me ; and I set him
7 *f*a time. Moreover I said unto the king, If it please the king,
let letters be given me to the governors beyond the river, that
8 they may convey me over till I come into Judah; and a letter
unto Asaph the keeper of the king's forest, that he may give
me timber to make beams for the gates of the palace which
*appertained g*to the house, and for the wall of the city, and for
the house that I shall enter into. And the king granted me,
9 *h*according to the good hand of my God upon me. ¶ Then I came
to the governors beyond the river, and gave them the king's
letters. Now the king had sent captains of the army and horse-
10 men with me. When Sanballat the Horonite, and Tobiah the

a Ezra 7. 1.
b c. 1. 11.

c Prov.15.13.
d 1 Kin.1.31.
Dan. 2. 4.
& 5. 10.
& 6. 6, 21.
e ch. 1. 3,

f ch. 5. 14.
& 13. 6.

g ch. 3. 7.

h Ezra 5. 5.
& 7. 6, 9, 28.
ver. 18.

¹ Heb. *wife*.

bearers, each of whom probably discharged
the office in his turn.

II. 1. Nisan was the name given by the
Persian Jews to the month previously called
"Abib," the first month of the Jewish
year, or that which followed the vernal
equinox. It fell four months after Chisleu
(i. 1).

the twentieth year] As Artaxerxes ascended the throne in B.C. 465, his twentieth
year would correspond to B.C. 445-444.

2. *I was very sore afraid*] A Persian subject was expected to be perfectly content so
long as he had the happiness of being with
his king. A request to quit the court was
thus a serious matter.

3. *the city...of my fathers' sepulchres*] We
may conclude from this that Nehemiah was
of the tribe of Judah, as Eusebius and Jerome say that he was.

4. *I prayed to the God of heaven*] Mentally
and momentarily, before answering the
king.

6. *the queen*] Though the Persian kings
practised polygamy, they had always one
chief wife, who alone was recognised as
"queen." The chief wife of Longimanus
was Damaspia.

I set him a time] Nehemiah appears to
have stayed at Jerusalem twelve years from
his first arrival (v. 14); but he can scarcely

have mentioned so long a term to the king.
Probably his leave of absence was prolonged
from time to time.

8. *the king's forest*] Rather, **park.** The
word used (*pardes*; cp. παράδεισος, found only
here, in Eccl. ii. 5, and in Cant. iv. 13), is
of Persian, or at any rate of Aryan origin.
The Persians signified by *pariyadeza* a
walled enclosure, ornamented with trees,
either planted or of natural growth, and
containing numerous wild animals. The
"paradise" here mentioned must have been
in the neighbourhood of Jerusalem, and
may have corresponded to the earlier "gardens of Solomon."

the palace] Rather, "**the fortress.**" The
word in the original has the double meaning of "palace" and "fortress," the fact
being that in ancient times palaces were
always fortified. "The fortress which appertained to the house" or Temple is here
first spoken of. Under the Romans it was
called "Antonia."

10. The name Sanballat is probably Babylonian, the first element being the same
which commences "Sennacherib," viz.
"Sin," the Moon-God, and the second
balatu, "eminent" (?), which is found in
the Assyrian name, Bel-balatu. As a Horonite, he was probably a native of one of
the Bethhorons, the upper or the lower

servant, the Ammonite, heard *of it*, it grieved them exceedingly
that there was come a man to seek the welfare of the children of
11 Israel. ¶ So I *i*came to Jerusalem, and was there three days. *i* Ezra 8. 32.
12 And I arose in the night, I and some few men with me; neither
told I *any* man what my God had put in my heart to do at Jerusalem: neither *was there any* beast with me, save the beast that
13 I rode upon. And I went out by night *k*by the gate of the valley, *k* 2 Chr. 26.9.
even before the dragon well, and to the dung port, and viewed the ch. 3. 13.
walls of Jerusalem, which were *l*broken down, and the gates *l* ch. 1. 3.
14 thereof were consumed with fire. Then I went on to the *m*gate & ver. 17.
of the fountain, and to the king's pool: but *there was* no place *m* ch. 3. 15.
15 for the beast *that was* under me to pass. Then went I up in the
night by the *n*brook, and viewed the wall, and turned back, and *n* 2 Sam. 15.
16 entered by the gate of the valley, and *so* returned. And the 23.
rulers knew not whither I went, or what I did; neither had I as Jer. 31. 40.
yet told *it* to the Jews, nor to the priests, nor to the nobles, nor
17 to the rulers, nor to the rest that did the work. Then said I
unto them, Ye see the distress that we *are* in, how Jerusalem
lieth waste, and the gates thereof are burned with fire: come,
and let us build up the wall of Jerusalem, that we be no more
18 *o*a reproach. Then I told them of *p*the hand of my God which *o* ch. 1. 3.
was good upon me; as also the king's words that he had spoken Ps. 44. 13.
unto me. And they said, Let us rise up and build. So they & 79. 4.
19 *q*strengthened their hands for *this* good *work*. ¶ But when San- Ezek. 5. 14,
ballat the Horonite, and Tobiah the servant, the Ammonite, and 15.
Geshem the Arabian, heard *it*, they *r*laughed us to scorn, and & 22. 4.
despised us, and said, What *is* this thing that ye do? *s*will ye *p* ver. 8.
20 rebel against the king? Then answered I them, and said unto *q* 2 Sam. 2.7.
them, The God of heaven, he will prosper us; therefore we his *r* Ps. 44. 13.
servants will arise and build: *t*but ye have no portion, nor right, & 79. 4.
nor memorial, in Jerusalem. & 80. 6.
  s ch. 6. 6.
CHAP. 3. THEN *a*Eliashib the high priest rose up with his brethren *t* Ezra 4. 3.
the priests, *b*and they builded the sheep gate; they sanctified it, *a* ch. 12. 10.
  b John 5. 2

(see Josh. xvi. 3, 5; 2 Chr. viii. 5), and
therefore born within the limits of the old
kingdom of Samaria. Tobiah seems to have
been an Ammonite slave, high in the favour
of Sanballat, whom he probably served as
secretary (vi. 17-19) and chief adviser.

it grieved them] Cp. Ezra iv. 4-24, v. 6-
17. The revival of Jerusalem as a great
and strong city, which was Nehemiah's
aim, was likely to interfere with the prosperity, or at any rate the eminence, of
Samaria.

13. *the gate of the valley*] A gate opening
on the valley of Hinnom, which skirted Jerusalem to the west and south. The exact
position is uncertain; as is also that of "the
dragon well."

the dung port] The gate by which offal
and excrements were conveyed out of the
city, and placed eastward of the valley-
gate.

14. *the gate of the fountain*] A gate on the
eastern side of the Tyropœon valley, not far
from the pool of Siloam (probably "the
king's pool." Cp. iii. 15).

15. *the brook*] The Kidron watercourse,
which skirted the city on the east.

turned back] *i.e.* he turned *westward*, and
having made the circuit of the city, re-en-
tered by the valley-gate.

16. *the rulers*] The principal authorities
of the city, in the absence of the special
governor.

the rest that did the work] *i.e.* "the labour-
ing class that (afterwards) actually built
the wall."

18. *the king's words*] These have not been
given; but the royal permission to restore
the walls is implied in ii. 5, 6.

19. *Geshem the Arabian*] The discovery
that Sargon peopled Samaria in part with
an Arab colony explains why Arabs should
have opposed the fortification of Jerusalem.

III. 1. Eliashib (cp. marg. ref.) was the
grandson of Joshua, the High-Priest contemporary with Zerubbabel.

the sheep gate] This was a gate in the
eastern wall, not far from the pool of Bethesda, marg. ref., which was perhaps originally a sheep-pool.

The exact line which the writer follows
in describing the circuit of the wall will
probably be always a matter of dispute.
According to the view here taken, the line

c ch. 12. 39.
d Jer. 31. 38.
Zech. 14. 10.
e Ezra 2. 34.
f 2 Chr. 33. 14.
ch. 12. 39.
Zeph. 1. 10.
g See ch. 6. 1.
& 7. 1.

and set up the doors of it ; °even unto the tower of Meah they
2 sanctified it, unto the tower of ᵈHananeel. And ¹next unto
him builded ᵉthe men of Jericho. And next to them builded
3 Zaccur the son of Imri. ¶ᶠBut the fish gate did the sons of
Hassenaah build, who *also* laid the beams thereof, and ᵍset up
4 the doors thereof, the locks thereof, and the bars thereof. And
next unto them repaired Meremoth the son of Urijah, the son
of Koz. And next unto them repaired Meshullam the son of
Berechiah, the son of Meshezabeel. And next unto them re-
5 paired Zadok the son of Baana. And next unto them the Te-

h Judg. 5. 23.
i ch. 12. 39.

koites repaired ; but their nobles put not their necks to ʰthe
6 work of their Lord. ¶ Moreover ⁱthe old gate repaired Jehoiada
the son of Paseah, and Meshullam the son of Besodeiah ; they
laid the beams thereof, and set up the doors thereof, and the
7 locks thereof, and the bars thereof. And next unto them repaired Melatiah the Gibeonite, and Jadon the Meronothite, the

k ch. 2. 8.

men of Gibeon, and of Mizpah, unto the ᵏthrone of the governor
8 on this side the river. Next unto him repaired Uzziel the son
of Harhaiah, of the goldsmiths. Next unto him also repaired
Hananiah the son of *one of* the apothecaries, and they ²fortified

l ch. 12. 38.

9 Jerusalem unto the ˡbroad wall. And next unto them repaired
Rephaiah the son of Hur, the ruler of the half part of Jeru-
10 salem. And next unto them repaired Jedaiah the son of Haru-
maph, even over against his house. And next unto him repaired
11 Hattush the son of Hashabniah. Malchijah the son of Harim,
and Hashub the son of Pahath-moab, repaired the ³other piece,

¹ Heb. *at his hand.*   ² Or, *left Jerusalem unto*   ³ Heb. *second measure.*
                              the broad wall.

described commences near the pool of
Bethesda, on the east of the city, and is
traced thence, first, northwards, then west-
wards, then southwards, and finally eastwards, as far as the pool of Siloam (*v.* 15).
From this point, it seems to the writer of
this note that the line of the *outer* wall is
not followed, but, instead of this, the inner
wall of the "city of David," which included the Temple, is traced. This wall is
followed northwards from the pool of
Siloam, past the "sepulchres of David"
and Hezekiah's pool to the "armoury" (*v.*
19) at its north-west corner ; it is then followed eastwards to "the tower which lieth
out from the king's house" (*v.* 25) ; from
this it is carried southwards, along the
western edge of the Kidron valley to the
"*great* tower which lieth out" (*v.* 27), and
then south-westwards to the point at which
it commenced near Siloam (*v.* 27). The
special wall of the "city of David" being
thus completed, the writer finishes his entire account by filling up the small interval
between the north-east angle of this fortification and the "sheep-gate" (*vv.* 28–32),
from which he started.

they sanctified it] The priests commenced
the work with a formal ceremony of consecration. When the work was completed,
there was a solemn dedication of the entire
circuit (see xii. 27–43).

The tower of Hananeel is often men-

tioned ; that of Meah, or rather Hammeah,
or "the Hundred," in Nehemiah only.
Both towers must have been situated towards the north-eastern corner of the city.

2. The people of each provincial town
were set to work for the most part on the
portion of the wall nearest their city. Thus
"the men of Jericho," were employed at
the north-east corner of Jerusalem.

3. *the fish gate*] The gate through which
fish from the Jordan and the Sea of Galilee
entered Jerusalem ; a gate in the north
wall, a little to the east of the modern Damascus gate.

locks] The word used (here and in *vv.* 6,
13–15) is thought to mean rather a "cross-
bar" than a lock, while that translated
"bars" is regarded as denoting the "hooks"
or "catches" which held the cross-bar at
its two ends.

5. *Tekoites*] See 2 Sam. xiv. 2 note.

6. *the old gate*] Either the modern Damascus gate, the main entrance to the city
on the north side ; or a gate a little further
eastward.

7. *unto the throne* &c.] The meaning is
thought to be "the men of Gibeon and Mizpah, who, though they worked for Nehemiah, were not under his government, but
belonged to the jurisdiction of the governor
on this side the river."

11. *the other piece*] Rather, "**another
piece**" (as in *vv.* 19, 21, 27, 30). It is con-

12 ^mand the tower of the furnaces. And next unto him repaired *m* ch. 12. 38.
Shallum the son of Halohesh, the ruler of the half part of Jeru-
13 salem, he and his daughters. ¶ ⁿThe valley gate repaired *n* ch. 2. 13.
Hanun, and the inhabitants of Zanoah; they built it, and set
up the doors thereof, the locks thereof, and the bars thereof,
14 and a thousand cubits on the wall unto ^othe dung gate. ¶ But *o* ch. 2. 13.
the dung gate repaired Malchiah the son of Rechab, the ruler of
part of Beth-haccerem; he built it, and set up the doors thereof,
15 the locks thereof, and the bars thereof. ¶ But ^pthe gate of the *p* ch. 2. 14.
fountain repaired Shallun the son of Col-hozeh, the ruler of
part of Mizpah; he built it, and covered it, and set up the doors
thereof, the locks thereof, and the bars thereof, and the wall of
the pool of ^qSiloah by the king's garden, and unto the stairs *q* John 9. 7.
16 that go down from the city of David. After him repaired Ne-
hemiah the son of Azbuk, the ruler of the half part of Beth-zur,
unto the place over against the sepulchres of David, and to the
17 ^rpool that was made, and unto the house of the mighty. After *r* 2 Kin. 20.
20.
Isai. 22. 11.
him repaired the Levites, Rehum the son of Bani. Next unto
him repaired Hashabiah, the ruler of the half part of Keilah, in
18 his part. After him repaired their brethren, Bavai the son of
19 Henadad, the ruler of the half part of Keilah. And next to
him repaired Ezer the son of Jeshua, the ruler of Mizpah,
another piece over against the going up to the armoury at the
20 ^sturning of the wall. After him Baruch the son of ¹Zabbai *s* 2 Chr. 26.9.
earnestly repaired the other piece, from the turning of the wall
21 unto the door of the house of Eliashib the high priest. After
him repaired Meremoth the son of Urijah the son of Koz another piece, from the door of the house of Eliashib even to
22 the end of the house of Eliashib. And after him repaired the
23 priests, the men of the plain. After him repaired Benjamin
and Hashub over against their house. After him repaired Aza-

¹ Or, *Zaccai.*

---

jectured that a verse has fallen out in which
Malchijah's and Hashub's "first piece" was
mentioned.

the tower of the furnaces] Either a tower
at the north-western angle of the city ; or,
midway in the western wall. The origin of
the name is uncertain.

13. Zanoah lay west of Jerusalem, at the
distance of about ten miles (Josh. xv. 34
note).

15. The "pool of Siloah" lies at the
south-western foot of the Temple hill, near
the lower end of the Tyropœon. It appears
to have been at all times beyond the line of
the city wall, but was perhaps joined to the
city by a fortification of its own.

the king's garden] See 2 K. xxv. 4 note.

the stairs] A flight of steps, still to be
seen, led from the low valley of the Tyropœon
up the steep sides of Ophel to the "city of
David," which it reached probably at a
point not far south of the Temple.

16. *Beth-zur*] Now *Beit-sur*, on the road
from Jerusalem to Hebron (Josh. xv. 58).

By "the sepulchres of David" must be
understood the burial place in which David
and the kings his descendants to the time
of Hezekiah were interred. This was an

excavation in the rock, in the near vicinity
of the Temple (Ezek. xliii. 7-9), and on its
western side. The position of the burial-
place was well known until the destruction
of the city by Titus ; but modern research
has not yet discovered it.

the pool] Probably that made by Hezekiah in the Tyropœon valley, west of the
Temple area (marg. ref.).

17-30. The constant mention of "priests,"
"Levites," and Nethinims," sufficiently indicates that the writer is here concerned
with the sacerdotal quarter, that immediately about the Temple.

18. *Bavai*] Or, "Binnui" (*v.* 24, x. 9).

the armoury at the turning of the wall] Lit.
"the armoury of the corner." The north-
western corner of the special wall of the
"city of David" seems to be intended. See
v. 1 note.

20. *the other piece*] Rather, "**another**
piece." The notice of Baruch's first piece,
like that of Malchijah's and Hashub's (*v.*
11), seems to have slipped out of the text.

22. The word here translated "plain" is
applied in the rest of Scripture almost exclusively to the *Ghor* or Jordan valley.
Cp., however, xii. 28.

t ver. 19.

v Jer. 32. 2.
& 33. 1.
& 37. 21.
x Ezra 2. 43.
ch. 11. 21.
y 2 Chr. 27.3.
z ch. 8. 1, 3.
& 12. 37.
a 2 Kin.11.16.
2 Chr. 23. 15.
Jer. 31. 40.

a ch. 2.10,19.

b ch. 2. 10,19.

c Ps.123.3,4.
d Ps. 79. 12.
Prov. 3. 34.

e Ps.69.27,28.
& 109. 14,15.
Jer. 18. 23.

riah the son of Maaseiah the son of Ananiah by his house.
24 After him repaired Binnui the son of Henadad another piece,
from the house of Azariah unto 'the turning *of the wall*, even
25 unto the corner. Palal the son of Uzai, over against the turning
of the wall, and the tower which lieth out from the king's high
house, that *was* by the ᵘcourt of the prison. After him Pe-
26 daiah the son of Parosh. Moreover ˣthe Nethinims ¹dwelt in
vᵊ²Ophel, unto *the place* over against ᶻthe water gate toward the
27 east, and the tower that lieth out. After them the Tekoites repaired another piece, over against the great tower that lieth out,
28 even unto the wall of Ophel. ¶From above the ᵃhorse gate re-
29 paired the priests, every one over against his house. After
them repaired Zadok the son of Immer over against his house.
After him repaired also Shemaiah the son of Shechaniah, the
30 keeper of the east gate. After him repaired Hananiah the son
of Shelemiah, and Hanun the sixth son of Zalaph, another
piece. After him repaired Meshullam the son of Berechiah
31 over against his chamber. After him repaired Malchiah the
goldsmith's son unto the place of the Nethinims, and of the
merchants, over against the gate. Miphkad, and to the ³going
32 up of the corner. And between the going up of the corner
unto the sheep gate repaired the goldsmiths and the merchants.

CHAP. 4. BUT it came to pass, ᵃthat when Sanballat heard that we
builded the wall, he was wroth, and took great indignation, and
2 mocked the Jews. And he spake before his brethren and the
army of Samaria, and said, What do these feeble Jews? will
they ⁴fortify themselves? will they sacrifice? will they make
an end in a day? will they revive the stones out of the heaps of
3 the rubbish which are burned? Now ᵇTobiah the Ammonite
was by him, and he said, Even that which they build, if a fox
4 go up, he shall even break down their stone wall. ᶜHear, O our
God; for we are ⁵despised: and ᵈturn their reproach upon
their own head, and give them for a prey in the land of cap-
5 tivity: and ᵉcover not their iniquity, and let not their sin be

¹ Or, which *dwelt in Ophel*, repaired *unto*.
² Or, *The tower*.
³ Or, *corner-chamber*.
⁴ Heb. *leave to themselves*.
⁵ Heb. *despite*.

24. *the turning of the wall*] The north-eastern angle of the "city of David" seems here to be reached. At this point a tower "lay out" (*v.* 25), or projected extraordinarily, from the wall, being probably a watch-tower commanding the Kidron valley and all the approaches to the city from the south-east, the east, and the north-east.

25. The "king's high house" is almost certainly the old palace of David, which was on the Temple hill, and probably occupied a position directly north of the Temple.

that was by the court of the prison] Prisons were in old times adjuncts of palaces. The palace of David must have had its prison; and the "prison gate" (xii. 39) was clearly in this quarter.

26. The marg. reading is better. On the Nethinims see 1 Chr. ix. 2 note.

Ophel was the slope south of the Temple (see marg. ref. *y* note); and the water-gate, a gate in the eastern wall, either

for the escape of the superfluous water from the Temple reservoirs, or for the introduction of water from the Kidron valley when the reservoirs were low.

27. The foundations of an outlying tower near the south-east angle of the Temple area in this position have been recently discovered.

28. "The horse gate" was on the east side of the city, overlooking the Kidron valley. It seems to have been a gate by which horses approached and left the old palace, that of David, which lay north of the Temple (*v.* 25).

31. *the gate Miphkad*] Not elsewhere mentioned. It must have been in the east, or north-east, wall, a little to the south of the "sheep-gate."

IV. 4. The parenthetic prayers of Nehemiah form one of the most striking characteristics of his history. Here we have the first. Other examples are v. 19, vi. 9, 14, xiii. 14, 22, 29, 31.

blotted out from before thee: for they have provoked *thee* to
6 anger before the builders. So built we the wall; and all the
wall was joined together unto the half thereof: for the people
7 had a mind to work. ¶But it came to pass, that *f*when San- *f* ver. 1.
ballat, and Tobiah, and the Arabians, and the Ammonites, and
the Ashdodites, heard that the walls of Jerusalem ¹were made
up, *and* that the breaches began to be stopped, then they were
8 very wroth, and *g*conspired all of them together to come *and* to *g* Ps. 83. 3, 4,
9 fight against Jerusalem, and ²to hinder it. Nevertheless *h*we 5. *h* Ps. 50. 15.
made our prayer unto our God, and set a watch against them
10 day and night, because of them. And Judah said, The strength
of the bearers of burdens is decayed, and *there is* much rubbish;
11 so that we are not able to build the wall. And our adversaries
said, They shall not know, neither see, till we come in the midst
12 among them, and slay them, and cause the work to cease. And
it came to pass, that when the Jews which dwelt by them came,
they said unto us ten times, ³From all places whence ye shall
13 return unto us *they will be upon you.* Therefore set I ⁴in the
lower places behind the wall, *and* on the higher places, I even
set the people after their families with their swords, their spears,
14 and their bows. And I looked, and rose up, and said unto the
nobles, and to the rulers, and to the rest of the people, *i* Be not *i* Num. 14. 9
ye afraid of them: remember the Lord, *which is* *k*great and Deut. 1. 29. *k* Deut.10.17.
terrible, and *l*fight for your brethren, your sons, and your *l* 2 Sam. 10.
15 daughters, your wives, and your houses. ¶And it came to pass, 12.
when our enemies heard that it was known unto us, *m* and God *m* Job 5. 12.
had brought their counsel to nought, that we returned all of us
16 to the wall, every one unto his work. And it came to pass from
that time forth, *that* the half of my servants wrought in the
work, and the other half of them held both the spears, the
shields, and the bows, and the habergeons; and the rulers *were*
17 behind all the house of Judah. They which builded on the
wall, and they that bare burdens, with those that laded, *every
one* with one of his hands wrought in the work, and with the
18 other *hand* held a weapon. For the builders, every one had his
sword girded ⁵by his side, and *so* builded. And he that sounded
19 the trumpet *was* by me. And I said unto the nobles, and to the
rulers, and to the rest of the people, The work *is* great and

---

¹ Heb. *ascended.*
² Heb. *to make an error to it.*
³ Or, *That from all places ye must return to us.*
⁴ Heb. *from the lower parts*
of the place, &c.
⁵ Heb. *on his loins.*

---

6. *unto the half thereof*] *i.e.* to half the intended *height.*

7. *the Arabians* &c.] Probably a band, composed largely of Arabians, Ammonites, and Ashdodites, which Sanballat maintained as a guard to his person, and which formed a portion of "the army of Samaria" (*v.* 2). A quarrel between such a band and the people of Jerusalem might be overlooked by the Persian king.

9. *because of them*] Or, "**over against them**," *i.e.* opposite to the place where they were encamped, probably on the north side of the city.

12. *ten times*] *i.e.* repeatedly.
From all places &c.] Better as in margin. The Jews who dwelt on the Samaritan border, came to Jerusalem and tried to withdraw their contingents of workmen from the work, representing to them the impending danger, and saying, "You must return to your homes, and so escape it."

13. *the lower places*] The places where those within the walls had the least advantage of elevation, the naturally weak places, where an enemy was likely to make his attack.

16. *habergeons*] Or, "coats of mail." Coats of mail were common in Assyria from the ninth century B.C., and in Egypt even earlier. They were made of thin laminæ of bronze or iron, sewn upon leather or linen, and overlapping one another.

large, and we are separated upon the wall, one far from another.
20 In what place *therefore* ye hear the sound of the trumpet, resort
21 ye thither unto us : [n]our God shall fight for us.   ¶ So we laboured in the work : and half of them held the spears from the
22 rising of the morning till the stars appeared.   Likewise at the
same time said I unto the people, Let every one with his servant
lodge within Jerusalem, that in the night they may be a guard
23 to us, and labour on the day.   So neither I, nor my brethren,
nor my servants, nor the men of the guard which followed me,
none of us put off our clothes [1]*saving that* every one put them
off for washing.

CHAP. 5. AND there was a great [a]cry of the people and of their
2 wives against their [b]brethren the Jews.   For there were that
said, We, our sons, and our daughters, *are* many : therefore we
3 take up corn *for them*, that we may eat, and live.   Some also
there were that said, We have mortgaged our lands, vineyards,
and houses, that we might buy corn, because of the dearth.
4 There were also that said, We have borrowed money for the
5 king's tribute, *and that upon* our lands and vineyards.   Yet now
[c]our flesh *is* as the flesh of our brethren, our children as their
children : and, lo, we [d]bring into bondage our sons and our
daughters to be servants, and *some* of our daughters are brought
unto bondage *already* : neither *is it* in our power *to redeem them ;*
6 for other men have our lands and vineyards.   ¶And I was very
7 angry when I heard their cry and these words.   Then [2]I consulted with myself, and I rebuked the nobles, and the rulers,
and said unto them, [e]Ye exact usury, every one of his brother.
8 And I set a great assembly against them.   And I said unto
them, We after our ability have [f]redeemed our brethren the
Jews, which were sold unto the heathen ; and will ye even sell
your brethren ? or shall they be sold unto us ?   Then held they
9 their peace, and found nothing *to answer.*   Also I said, It *is* not
good that ye do : ought ye not to walk [g]in the fear of our God
10 [h]because of the reproach of the heathen our enemies ?   I likewise, *and* my brethren, and my servants, might exact of them
11 money and corn : I pray you, let us leave off this usury.   Restore, I pray you, to them, even this day, their lands, their

---

[1] Or, *every one* went *with   See Judg. 5. 11.   [2] Heb. *my heart consulted
his weapon for water.*   in me.*

---

22. *Let every one...lodge within Jerusalem*]
i.e. "Let none return to his own village
or city at night, but let all take their rest
in Jerusalem."
23. *saving* &c.] The text here is probably
unsound.   It yields no satisfactory sense.
See margin.
V. **2.** *are many*] A slight emendation
brings this verse into exact parallelism with
the next, and gives the sense—"We have
pledged our sons and our daughters, that we
might get corn, and eat and live." Cp. *v.* 5.
4. *the king's tribute*] The tax payable to
the Persian monarch (cp. Ezra iv. 13 ; Esth.
x. 1).   In ancient times heavy taxation was
often productive of debt and distress.
5. The power of a father to sell his
daughter into slavery is expressly mentioned in the Law (Ex. xxi. 7).   The power

to sell a son appears from this passage.   In
either case the sale held good for six years
only, or until the next year of jubilee
(marg. reff.).
7. *Ye exact usury*] The phrase is peculiar
to Nehemiah, and is best explained by the
context, which shows the practice of the
rich Jews at the time to have been not so
much to lend on usury as to lend on mort-
gage and pledge.
8. Nehemiah contrasts his own example
with that of the rich Jews.   He had spent
money in redeeming some countrymen in
servitude among the heathen ; they were
causing others to be sold into slavery among
the Jews.
10. *I...might exact*] Nehemiah had lent,
but not upon pledge.
11. *the hundredth part of the money* &c.]

---

[n] Ex. 14. 14,
25.
Deut. 1. 30.
& 3. 22.
& 20. 4.
Josh. 23. 10.

[a] Isai. 5. 7.
[b] Lev. 25. 35,
36, 37.
Deut. 15. 7.

[c] Isai. 53. 7.
[d] Lev. 25. 39.

[e] Ex. 22. 25.
Lev. 25. 36.
Ezek. 22. 12.
[f] Lev. 25. 48.

[g] Lev. 25. 33.
[h] 2 Sam. 12.
14.
Rom. 2. 24.
1 Pet. 2. 12.

vineyards, their oliveyards, and their houses, also the hundredth *part* of the money, and of the corn, the wine, and the oil, that
12 ye exact of them. ¶ Then said they, We will restore *them*, and will require nothing of them; so will we do as thou sayest. Then I called the priests; *i* and took an oath of them, that they
13 should do according to this promise. Also *k* I shook my lap, and said, So God shake out every man from his house, and from his labour, that performeth not this promise, even thus be he shaken out, and *l* emptied. And all the congregation said, Amen, and praised the LORD. *l* And the people did according to this
14 promise. ¶ Moreover from the time that I was appointed to be their governor in the land of Judah, from the twentieth year *m* even unto the two and thirtieth year of Artaxerxes the king, *that is*, twelve years, I and my brethren have not *n* eaten the
15 bread of the governor. But the former governors that *had been* before me were chargeable unto the people, and had taken of them bread and wine, beside forty shekels of silver; yea, even their servants bare rule over the people: but *o* so did not I, be-
16 cause of the *p* fear of God. Yea, also I continued in the work of this wall, neither bought we any land: and all my servants *were*
17 gathered thither unto the work. Moreover *there were* *q* at my table an hundred and fifty of the Jews and rulers, beside those that came unto us from among the heathen that *are* about us.
18 Now *that* *r* which was prepared *for* me daily *was* one ox *and* six choice sheep; also fowls were prepared for me, and once in ten days store of all sorts of wine: yet for all this *s* required not I the bread of the governor, because the bondage was heavy upon
19 this people. *t* Think upon me, my God, for good, *according to* all that I have done for this people.

CHAP. **6.** NOW it came to pass, *a* when Sanballat, and Tobiah, and
2 Geshem the Arabian, and the rest of our enemies, heard that I had builded the wall, and *that* there was no breach left therein; (*b* though at that time I had not set up the doors upon the gates;)
2 that Sanballat and Geshem *c* sent unto me, saying, Come, let us meet together in *some one of* the villages in the plain of *d* Ono.
3 But they *e* thought to do me mischief. And I sent messengers unto them, saying, I *am* doing a great work, so that I cannot come down: why should the work cease, whilst I leave it, and
4 come down to you? Yet they sent unto me four times after

i Ezra 10. 5.
Jer. 34. 8, 9.
k Matt.10.14.
Acts 13. 51.
& 18. 6.

l 2 Kin. 23.3.

m ch. 13. 6.
n 1 Cor. 9. 4, 15.

o 2 Cor.11. 9.
& 12. 13.
p ver. 9.

q 2 Sam. 9.7.
1 Kin. 18. 19.

r 1 Kin.4. 22.

s ver. 14, 15.

t ch. 13. 22.

a ch. 2.10,19.
& 4. 1, 7.

b ch. 3. 1, 3.
c Prov. 26. 24, 25.
d 1 Chr. 8.12.
ch. 11. 35.
e Ps. 37. 12, 32.

---

¹ Heb. *empty*, or, *void*.   ² Or, *Gashmu*, ver. 6.

---

i.e. the interest. It is conjectured that the hundredth part was payable *monthly*, or, in other words, that interest was taken at the rate of twelve per cent. The Law altogether disallowed the taking of interest from Israelites (see Ex. xxii. 25; Lev. xxv. 36, &c.).

13. *I shook my lap*] Cp. marg. reff. By "lap" is meant a fold in the bosom of the dress, capable of serving as a pocket. Cp. Isai. xlix. 22 marg.

14. *have not eaten the bread of the governor*] *i.e.* "have not, like other Persian governors, lived at the expense of the people under my government." See Ezra iv. 14 note.

15. *forty shekels of silver*] A daily sum from the entire province. For such a table

as that kept by Nehemiah (*v*. 18), this would be a very moderate payment.

16. *I continued...land*] *i.e.—*"I took my share in the work of the wall, as general superintendent. I did not take advantage of the general poverty to buy poor men's plots of ground."

18. Cp. the far grander provision for Solomon's table (marg. ref.).

VI. 1. *upon the gates*] Rather, "**in the gates.**" This work would naturally be delayed to the last.

2. The choice made of Ono, on the skirts of Benjamin, 25 or 30 miles from Jerusalem, as the meeting-place, was, no doubt, in order to draw Nehemiah to a distance from his supporters, that so an attack might be made on him with a better chance of success.

5 this sort; and I answered them after the same manner. Then
sent Sanballat his servant unto me in like manner the fifth time
6 with an open letter in his hand; wherein *was* written, It is

f ch. 2. 19.

reported among the heathen, and ¹Gashmu saith *it*, *ᶠthat* thou
and the Jews think to rebel : for which cause thou buildest the
wall, that thou mayest be their king, according to these words.
7 And thou hast also appointed prophets to preach of thee at
Jerusalem, saying, *There is* a king in Judah: and now shall it
be reported to the king according to these words. Come now
8 therefore, and let us take counsel together. Then I sent unto
him, saying, There are no such things done as thou sayest, but
9 thou feignest them out of thine own heart. For they all made
us afraid, saying, Their hands shall be weakened from the work,
that it be not done. Now therefore, O God, strengthen my
10 hands. ¶ Afterward I came unto the house of Shemaiah the son
of Delaiah the son of Mehetabeel, who *was* shut up; and he said,
Let us meet together in the house of God, within the temple,
and let us shut the doors of the temple : for they will come to
11 slay thee; yea, in the night will they come to slay thee. And I
said, Should such a man as I flee ? and who *is there*, that, *being*
as I *am*, would go into the temple to save his life ? I will not

g Ezek.13.22.

12 go in. And, lo, I perceived that God had not sent him; but
that *ᵍ*he pronounced this prophecy against me : for Tobiah and
13 Sanballat had hired him. Therefore *was* he hired, that I should
be afraid, and do so, and sin, and *that* they might have *matter*

h ch. 13. 39.

14 for an evil report, that they might reproach me. *ʰ*My God,
think thou upon Tobiah and Sanballat according to these their

i Ezek.13.17.

works, and on the *ⁱ*prophetess Noadiah, and the rest of the
15 prophets, that would have put me in fear. ¶ So the wall was
finished in the twenty and fifth *day* of *the month* Elul, in fifty

k ch. 2. 10.
& 4. 1, 7.
& 6. 1.
l Ps. 126. 2.

16 and two days. And it came to pass, that *ᵏ*when all our enemies
heard *thereof*, and all the heathen that *were* about us saw *these
things*, they were much cast down in their own eyes: for *l* they
17 perceived that this work was wrought of our God. ¶ Moreover
in those days the nobles of Judah ²sent many letters unto
18 Tobiah, and *the letters* of Tobiah came unto them. For *there were*
many in Judah sworn unto him, because he *was* the son in law

¹ Or, *Geshem*, ver. 1.　　　　² Heb. *multiplied their letters passing to Tobiah.*

---

5. The letter was " open," in order that
the contents might be generally known, and
that the Jews, alarmed at the threats contained in it, might refuse to continue the
work.

10. *who ·was shut up*] On account, probably, of some legal uncleanness. Cp. Jer.
xxxvi. 5.

11. *would go into the temple to save his
life*] Rather, "could go into the temple
and live." For a layman to enter the
Sanctuary was a capital offence (see Num.
xviii. 7).

12. The existence of a party among the
Jews who sided with Sanballat and lent
themselves to his schemes, is here for the
first time indicated. Cp. *vv.* 14, 17-19,
xiii. 4, 5, 28.

14. Noadiah is not elsewhere mentioned.
The examples of Miriam, Deborah, Huldah,
and Anna, show that the prophetical gift

was occasionally bestowed upon women (2
K. xxii. 14 note).

15. *Elul*] The sixth month, corresponding
to the latter part of August and the beginning of September.

in fifty and two days] Josephus states that
the repairs of the wall occupied two years
and four months. But Nehemah's narrative is thoroughly consistent with itself,
and contains in it nothing that is improbable. The walls everywhere existed at
the time that he commenced his task, and
only needed repairs. The work was par-
titioned among at least thirty-seven working
parties, who laboured simultaneously, with
material ready at hand; and, notwithstanding all menaces, uninterruptedly.

18. Though Tobiah is called "the servant" or "slave" (ii. 10, 19), and was perhaps a bought slave of Sanballat's, yet he
was in such a position that Jewish nobles

of Shechaniah the son of Arah; and his son Johanan had taken
19 the daughter of Meshullam the son of Berechiah. Also they
reported his good deeds before me, and uttered my [1]words to
him. *And* Tobiah sent letters to put me in fear.

CHAP. 7. NOW it came to pass, when the wall was built, and I
had *a*set up the doors, and the porters and the singers and the
2 Levites were appointed, that I gave my brother Hanani, and
Hananiah the ruler *b*of the palace, charge over Jerusalem: for
3 he *was* a faithful man, and *c*feared God above many. And I
said unto them, Let not the gates of Jerusalem be opened until
the sun be hot; and while they stand by, let them shut the
doors, and bar *them :* and appoint watches of the inhabitants of
Jerusalem, every one in his watch, and every one *to be* over
4 against his house. Now the city *was* [2]large and great: but the
5 people *were* few therein, and the houses *were* not builded. ¶And
my God put into mine heart to gather together the nobles, and
the rulers, and the people, that they might be reckoned by
genealogy. And I found a register of the genealogy of them
6 which came up at the first, and found written therein, *d*These
are the children of the province, that went up out of the captivity, of those that had been carried away, whom Nebuchadnezzar the king of Babylon had carried away, and came again to
7 Jerusalem and to Judah, every one unto his city; who came
with Zerubbabel, Jeshua, Nehemiah, [3]Azariah, Raamiah, Naha-
mani, Mordecai, Bilshan, Mispereth, Bigvai, Nehum, Baanah.
The number, *I say,* of the men of the people of Israel *was this;*
8 ¶The children of Parosh, two thousand an hundred seventy and
9 two. The children of Shephatiah, three hundred seventy and
10, 11 two. The children of Arah, six hundred fifty and two. The
children of Pahath-moab, of the children of Jeshua and Joab,
12 two thousand and eight hundred *and* eighteen. The children of
13 Elam, a thousand two hundred fifty and four. The children of
14 Zattu, eight hundred forty and five. The children of Zaccai,
15 seven hundred and threescore. The children of [4]Binnui, six
16 hundred forty and eight. The children of Bebai, six hundred
17 twenty and eight. The children of Azgad, two thousand three
18 hundred twenty and two. The children of Adonikam, six hun-
19 dred threescore and seven. The children of Bigvai, two thou-

Margin: *a* ch. 6. 1. *b* ch. 2. 8. *c* Ex. 18. 21. *d* Ezra 2. 1, &c.

[1] Or, *matters.* [2] Heb. *broad in spaces.* [3] Or, *Seraiah:* See Ezra 2. 2. [4] Or, *Bani.*

---

readily contracted affinity with him. This is quite in harmony with the practice of the East, where slaves often fill high positions and make grand marriages.

VII. **1.** As the watch of the Temple had hitherto been kept by porters, singers, and Levites (1 Chr. xxvi. 1–19), so now the watch of the entire city was committed to men of the same three classes, their experience pointing them out as the fittest persons.

2. *my brother Hanani*] See i. 2.

the ruler of the palace] Or, "the governor of the fortress." See marg. ref. note.

he] i.e. Hananiah.

3. *until the sun be hot*] An unusual precaution. The ordinary practice in the East is to open town gates at sunrise.

4. *the people were few*] The number of those who returned with Zerubbabel was no more than 42,360 (*v.* 66). With Ezra had come less than 2000 (Ezra viii. 1–20).

5. It is argued by some that the entire catalogue which follows (*vv.* 7–73) is not the register of them "which came up *at the first*," but of the Jewish people in Nehemiah's time. Verse 7 and Ezra ii. 2 are, however, very positive in their support of the usual view; and some of the arguments against it are thought to be met by considering the Nehemiah of *v.* 7 and Ezra ii. 2 a person different from Nehemiah the governor; and "Tirshatha" an official title likely to have belonged to others besides Nehemiah (Ezra ii. 63 note.)

20 sand threescore and seven. The children of Adin, six hundred
21 fifty and five. The children of Ater of Hezekiah, ninety and
22 eight. The children of Hashum, three hundred twenty and
23 eight. The children of Bezai, three hundred twenty and four.
24, 25 The children of ¹Hariph, an hundred and twelve. The
26 children of ²Gibeon, ninety and five. The men of Beth-lehem
27 and Netophah, an hundred fourscore and eight. The men of
28 Anathoth, an hundred twenty and eight. The men of ³Beth-
29 azmaveth, forty and two. The men of ⁴Kirjath-jearim, Che-
30 phirah, and Beeroth, seven hundred forty and three. The men
31 of Ramah and Gaba, six hundred twenty and one. The men
32 Michmas, an hundred and twenty and two. The men of Beth-el
33 and Ai, an hundred twenty and three. The men of the other

ᵉ See ver.12. 34 Nebo, fifty and two. The children of the other ᵉElam, a thou-
35 sand two hundred fifty and four. The children of Harim, three
36 hundred and twenty. The children of Jericho, three hundred
37 forty and five. The children of Lod, Hadid, and Ono, seven
38 hundred twenty and one. The children of Senaah, three thou-
39 sand nine hundred and thirty. ¶ The priests : the children of

ᶠ 1 Chr. 24.7.
ᵍ 1 Chr.24.14.
ʰ See 1 Chr.
9. 12.
& 24. 9.
ⁱ 1 Chr. 24. 8.
ᶠ Jedaiah, of the house of Jeshua, nine hundred seventy and
40 three. The children of ᵍImmer, a thousand fifty and two.
41 The children of ʰPashur, a thousand two hundred forty and
42 seven. The children of ⁱHarim, a thousand and seventeen.
43 ¶ The Levites : the children of Jeshua, of Kadmiel, and of the
44 children of ⁵Hodevah, seventy and four. The singers : the chil-
45 dren of Asaph, an hundred forty and eight. The porters : the
children of Shallum, the children of Ater, the children of Talmon, the children of Akkub, the children of Hatita, the children
46 of Shobai, an hundred thirty and eight. ¶ The Nethinims : the
children of Ziha, the children of Hashupha, the children of
47 Tabbaoth, the children of Keros, the children of ⁶Sia, the chil-
48 of Padon, the children of Lebana, the children of Hagaba, the
49 children of⁷Shalmai, the children of Hanan, the children of Giddel,
50 the children of Gahar, the children of Reaiah, the children of
51 Rezin, the children of Nekoda, the children of Gazzam, the
52 children of Uzza, the children of Phaseah, the children of Besai,
53 the children of Meunim, the children of ⁸Nephishesim, the children of Bakbuk, the children of Hakupha, the children of
54 Harhur, the children of ⁹Bazlith, the children of Mehida, the
55 children of Harsha, the children of Barkos, the children of
56 Sisera, the children of Tamah, the children of Neziah, the chil-
57 dren of Hatipha. ¶ The children of Solomon's servants : the
children of Sotai, the children of Sophereth, the children of
58 ¹Perida, the children of Jaala, the children of Darkon, the chil-
59 dren of Giddel, the children of Shephatiah, the children of
Hattil, the children of Pochereth of Zebaim, the children of
60 ²Amon. All the Nethinims, and the children of Solomon's ser-
ᵏ Ezra 2. 59. 61 vants, were three hundred ninety and two. ¶ᵏAnd these were
they which went up also from Tel-melah, Tel-haresha, Cherub,
³Addon, and Immer : but they could not shew their father's
62 house, nor their ⁴seed, whether they were of Israel. The children
of Delaiah, the children of Tobiah, the children of Nekoda, six
63 hundred forty and two. ¶ And of the priests : the children of

---

¹ Or, *Jora.*
² Or, *Gibbar.*
³ Or, *Azmaveth.*
⁴ Or, *Kirjath-arim.*

⁵ Or, *Hodaviah,* Ezra 2.
  40. or, *Judah,* Ezra 3. 9.
⁶ Or, *Siaha.*
⁷ Or, *Shamlai.*
⁸ Or, *Nephusim.*

⁹ Or, *Bazluth.*
¹ Or, *Peruda.*
² Or, *Ami.*
³ Or, *Addan.*
⁴ Or, *pedigree.*

Habaiah, the children of Koz, the children of Barzillai, which took *one* of the daughters of Barzillai the Gileadite to wife, and
64 was called after their name. These sought their register *among* those that were reckoned by genealogy, but it was not found :
65 therefore were they, as polluted, put from the priesthood. And ¹the Tirshatha said unto them, that they should not eat of the most holy things, till there stood *up* a priest with Urim and
66 Thummim. ¶The whole congregation together *was* forty and
67 two thousand three hundred and threescore, beside their manservants and their maidservants, of whom *there were* seven thousand three hundred thirty and seven : and they had two
68 hundred forty and five singing men and singing women. Their horses, seven hundred thirty and six : their mules, two hundred
69 forty and five : *their* camels, four hundred thirty and five : six
70 thousand seven hundred and twenty asses. ¶And ²some of the chief of the fathers gave unto the work. ¹The Tirshatha gave to the treasure a thousand drams of gold, fifty basons, five
71 hundred and thirty priests' garments. And *some* of the chief of the fathers gave to the treasure of the work ™twenty thousand drams of gold, and two thousand and two hundred pound of
72 silver. And *that* which the rest of the people gave *was* twenty thousand drams of gold, and two thousand pound of silver, and
73 threescore and seven priests' garments. ¶So the priests, and the Levites, and the porters, and the singers, and *some* of the people, and the Nethinims, and all Israel, dwelt in their cities ; ⁿand when the seventh month came, the children of Israel *were* in their cities.

CHAP. 8. AND all ᵃthe people gathered themselves together as one man into the street that *was* ᵇbefore the water gate ; and they spake unto Ezra the ᶜscribe to bring the book of the law of
2 Moses, which the LORD had commanded to Israel. And Ezra the priest brought ᵈthe law before the congregation both of men and women, and all ³that could hear with understanding, ᵉupon
3 the first day of the seventh month. And he read therein before the street that *was* before the water gate ⁴from the morning

ᴸ ch. 8. 9.

ᵐ So Ezra 2. 69.

ⁿ Ezra 3. 1.

ᵘ Ezra 3. 1.
ᵇ ch. 3. 26.
ᶜ Ezra 7. 6.

ᵈ Deut. 31. 11, 12.
ᵉ Lev. 23. 24.

---

¹ Or, *the governor*, ch. 8. 9. ³ Heb. *that understood in* ⁴ Heb. *from the light.*
² Heb. *part.* *hearing.*

70-73. Compared with Ezra ii. 69 there is considerable difference between the totals for gold, silver, and garments. The usual explanation is that of corruption in the one or the other of the passages.

73. *dwelt in their cities*] Nehemiah's quotation from Zerubbabel's register ends here, and the narration of events in Jerusalem in his own day is resumed from *v.* 3. The narrative (viii.-x.) appears from internal evidence to be by a different author (see Introduction, p. 591).

The last two clauses of *v.* 73 should stand as the beginning of ch. viii. (as in the LXX.). The text would then run :—

"And when the seventh month was come, and the children of Israel were in their cities, the whole people gathered themselves together as one man," &c. Cp. marg. ref.

VIII. **1.** *the street*] Rather, "**the square**" or "**court.**" So in *v.* 16 (cp. Ezra x. 9). The

court seems to have been one between the eastern gate of the Temple and the watergate in the city-wall. It would thus lie within the modern Haram area.

Ezra the scribe] This is the first mention of Ezra in the present book, and the first proof we have had that he was contemporary with Nehemiah. Probably he returned to the court of Artaxerxes soon after effecting the reforms which he relates in Ezra x., and did not revisit Jerusalem till about the time when the walls were completed, or after an absence of more than ten years. It was natural for the people to request him to resume the work of exposition of the Law to which he had accustomed them on his former visit (Ezra vii. 10, 25).

2. *upon the first day of the seventh month*] The day of the "feast of Trumpets" (see marg. ref. note). The gathering together of the people, spoken of in *v.* 1, was probably to keep this feast.

until midday, before the men and the women, and those that could understand; and the ears of all the people *were attentive* 4 unto the book of the law. And Ezra the scribe stood upon a ¹pulpit of wood, which they had made for the purpose; and beside him stood Mattithiah, and Shema, and Anaiah, and Urijah, and Hilkiah, and Maaseiah, on his right hand; and on his left hand, Pedaiah, and Mishael, and Malchiah, and Hashum, 5 and Hashbadana, Zechariah, *and* Meshullam. And Ezra opened the book in the ²sight of all the people; (for he was above all the people;) and when he opened it, all the people *f* stood up: 6 and Ezra blessed the LORD, the great God. And all the people *g* answered, Amen, Amen, with *k* lifting up their hands: and they *i* bowed their heads, and worshipped the LORD with *their* 7 faces to the ground. Also Jeshua, and Bani, and Sherebiah, Jamin, Akkub, Shabbethai, Hodijah, Maaseiah, Kelita, Azariah, Jozabad, Hanan, Pelaiah, and the Levites, *k* caused the people 8 to understand the law: and the people *stood* in their place. So they read in the book in the law of God distinctly, and gave the 9 sense, and caused *them* to understand the reading. ¶ *l* And Nehemiah, which *is* ³the Tirshatha, and Ezra the priest the scribe, *m* and the Levites that taught the people, said unto all the people, *n* This day *is* holy unto the LORD your God; *o* mourn not, nor weep. For all the people wept, when they heard the 10 words of the law. Then he said unto them, Go your way, eat the fat, and drink the sweet, *p* and send portions unto them for whom nothing is prepared: for *this* day *is* holy unto our LORD: neither be ye sorry; for the joy of the LORD is your strength. 11 So the Levites stilled all the people, saying, Hold your peace, 12 for the day *is* holy; neither be ye grieved. And all the people went their way to eat, and to drink, and to *q* send portions, and to make great mirth, because they had *r* understood the words that were declared unto them. ¶ And on the second day were gathered together the chief of the fathers of all the people, the priests, and the Levites, unto Ezra the scribe, even ⁴ to under- 14 stand the words of the law. And they found written in the law

f Judg. 3. 20.

g 1 Cor. 14. 16.
h Lam. 3. 41.
1 Tim. 2. 8.
i Ex. 4. 31.
2 Chr. 20. 18.

k Lev. 10. 11.
Deut. 33. 10.
2 Chr. 17. 7,
8, 9.
Mal. 2. 7.
l Ezra 2. 63.
ch. 7. 65.
& 10. 1.
m 2 Chr. 35. 3.
ver. 8.
n Lev. 23. 24.
Num. 29. 1.
o Deut. 16. 14,
15.
Eccles. 3. 4.
p Esth. 9. 19,
22.
Rev. 11. 10.

q ver. 10.
r ver. 7, 8.

¹ Heb. *tower of wood.*
² Heb. *eyes.*
³ Or, *the governor.*
⁴ Or, *that they might in-*
struct in the words of the law.

4. The thirteen persons mentioned were probably the chief priests of the course which was at the time performing the Temple service.

5. *stood up*] The attitude of attention and respect. Cp. the existing practice of the Christian Church at the reading of the Gospel for the day.

7. The names here (and in ix. 4, 5, x. 9) seem not to be the personal appellations of individuals, but rather designations of Levitical families, the descendants respectively of Jeshua, &c., who lived not later than the time of Zerubbabel (vii. 43, xii. 8).

8. *gave the sense*] Either by rendering the Hebrew into the Aramaic dialect, or perhaps simply by explaining obscure words or passages.

caused them to understand] Either " they (the people) understood what was read ; " or, " they (the Levites) expounded as they read."

9. *Nehemiah, which is the Tirshatha*] Hitherto Nehemiah has called himself *pechah* (v. 14, 15, 18), which is the ordinary word for "governor." Now for the first time he is called "the Tirshatha" (see Ezra ii. 63 note.)

the people wept &c.] Because the Law brought vividly before them their sins of omission and commission. In *v.* 10 the Jews were not forbidden to be sorry for their sins, but only prohibited from marring with the expression of their sorrow a festive occasion.

10. The " sending of portions " to the poor is not distinctly mentioned in any but the later historical Scriptures (cp. marg. reff.). The practice naturally grew out of this injunction of the Law (Deut. xvi. 11, 14).

13. *to understand*] Rather, "**to consider.**"

14. The Feast of Tabernacles had fallen into abeyance either entirely, or as regarded the dwelling in booths (*v.* 17), since

which the LORD had commanded ¹ by Moses, that the children of
Israel should dwell in ⁸booths in the feast of the seventh month:
15 and ᵗthat they should publish and proclaim in all their cities,
and ᵘin Jerusalem, saying, Go forth unto the mount, and ˣfetch
olive branches, and pine branches, and myrtle branches, and
palm branches, and branches of thick trees, to make booths, as
16 it is written. So the people went forth, and brought them, and
made themselves booths, every one upon the ʸroof of his house,
and in their courts, and in the courts of the house of God, and
in the street of the ᶻwater gate, ᵃand in the street of the gate of
17 Ephraim. And all the congregation of them that were come
again out of the captivity made booths, and sat under the
booths: for since the days of Jeshua the son of Nun unto that
day had not the children of Israel done so. And there was very
18 ᵇgreat gladness. Also ᶜday by day, from the first day unto the
last day, he read in the book of the law of God. And they kept
the feast seven days; and on the eighth day was ²a solemn
assembly, ᵈaccording unto the manner.
CHAP. 9. NOW in the twenty and fourth day of ᵃthis month the
children of Israel were assembled with fasting, and with sack-
2 clothes, ᵇand earth upon them. And ᶜthe seed of Israel separated themselves from all ³strangers, and stood and confessed
3 their sins, and the iniquities of their fathers. And they stood
up in their place, and ᵈread in the book of the law of the LORD
their God one fourth part of the day; and another fourth part they
4 confessed, and worshipped the LORD their God. ¶Then stood up
upon the ⁴stairs, of the Levites, Jeshua, and Bani, Kadmiel,
Shebaniah, Bunni, Sherebiah, Bani, and Chenani, and cried with
5 a loud voice unto the LORD their God. Then the Levites, Jeshua,
and Kadmiel, Bani, Hashabniah, Sherebiah, Hodijah, Shebaniah,
and Pethahiah, said, Stand up and bless the LORD your God
for ever and ever: and blessed be ᵉthy glorious name, which is
6 exalted above all blessing and praise. ᶠThou, even thou, art
LORD alone; ᵍthou hast made heaven, ʰthe heaven of heavens,
with ⁱall their host, the earth, and all things that are therein, the
seas, and all that is therein, and thou preservest them all; and

s Lev. 23. 34,
42.
Deut. 16. 13.
t Lev. 23. 4.
u Deut.16.16.
x Lev. 23. 40.

y Deut. 22. 8.

z ch. 12. 37.
a 2 Kin.14.13.
ch. 12. 39.

b 2 Chr.30 21.
c Deut.31.10,
&c.

d Lev. 23.36.
Num. 29. 35.
a ch. 8. 2.

b Josh. 7. 6.
1 Sam. 4. 12.
2 Sam. 1. 2.
Job 2. 12.
c Ezra 10.11.
ch. 13. 3, 30.
d ch. 8. 7, 8.

e 1 Chr.29.13.
f 2 Kin.19.15,
19.
Ps. 86. 10.
Isai. 37, 16.
g Gen. 1. 1.
Ex. 20. 11.
Rev. 14. 7.
h Deut.10.14.
1 Kin. 8. 27.
i Gen. 2. 1.

¹ Heb. by the hand of.
² Heb. a restraint.
³ Heb. strange children.
⁴ Or, scaffold.

---

the time when it was kept by Zerubbabel
(Ezra iii. 4). It is evident that the observance of the Law, impossible during the
Captivity, was restored slowly and with
difficulty after the return.

15. the mount] The "mount of Olives" is
probably intended.

pine branches] Rather, "branches of the
wild olive." The actual trees named by
the Law may have become scarce. It was
probably considered that the spirit of the
command was kept if branches of trees
similar in general character to those named
in Leviticus were employed.

17. It is not the intention of the writer
to state that the Feast of Tabernacles had
not been kept from the time of Joshua
until this occasion (see 1 K. viii. 2, 65; Ezra
iii. 4); but that there had been no such
celebration as this since Joshua's time. Cp.
2 K. xxiii. 22; 2 Chr. xxxv. 18.

IX. 1. The festival lasted from the 15th
day of the 7th month to the 21st. The 22nd
day was a day of solemn observance (viii.
18). One day seems to have been allowed
the people for rest; and then the work of
repentance, for which they had shown themselves ready (viii. 9), was taken in hand,
and a general fast was proclaimed.

4. The LXX. and Vulgate remove the
comma after "stairs." By the "stairs (or
scaffold) of the Levites" is to be understood an elevated platform from which they
could the better address and lead the people
(cp. viii. 4).

5. Stand up] The people had knelt to
confess and to worship God (v. 3). They
were now to take the attitude proper for
praise. Cp. throughout the marg. reff.

6. the host of heaven worshippeth thee]
i.e. the angels. See 1 K. xxii. 19; Ps. ciii.
21.

7 the host of heaven worshippeth thee. ¶ Thou *art* the LORD the
God, who didst choose *k* Abram, and broughtest him forth out of
8 Ur of the Chaldees, and gavest him the name of *l* Abraham ; and
foundest his heart *m* faithful before thee, and madest a *n* covenant
with him to give the land of the Canaanites, the Hittites, the
Amorites, and the Perizzites, and the Jebusites, and the Girgashites, to give *it*, I *say*, to his seed, and *o* hast performed thy
9 words ; for thou *art* righteous : *p* and didst see the affliction of
our fathers in Egypt, and *q* heardest their cry by the Red sea ;
10 and *r* shewedst signs and wonders upon Pharaoh, and on all his
servants, and on all the people of his land : for thou knewest
that they *s* dealt proudly against them. So didst thou *t* get thee
11 a name, as *it is* this day. *u* And thou didst divide the sea before
them, so that they went through the midst of the sea on the dry
land ; and their persecutors thou threwest into the deeps, *x* as a
12 stone into the mighty waters. Moreover thou *y* leddest them in
the day by a cloudy pillar ; and in the night by a pillar of fire,
13 to give them light in the way wherein they should go. ¶ *a* Thou
camest down also upon mount Sinai, and spakest with them
from heaven, and gavest them *b* right judgments, and ¹ true
14 laws, good statutes and commandments : and madest known
unto them thy *c* holy sabbath, and commandedst them precepts,
15 statutes, and laws, by the hand of Moses thy servant : and
d gavest them bread from heaven for their hunger, and *e* broughtest forth water for them out of the rock for their thirst, and
promisedst them that they should *f* go in to possess the land
16 ² which thou hadst sworn to give them. ¶ *g* But they and our
fathers dealt proudly, and *h* hardened their necks, and hearkened
17 not to thy commandments, and refused to obey, *i* neither were
mindful of thy wonders that thou didst among them ; but
hardened their necks, and in their rebellion appointed *k* a captain
to return to their bondage : but thou *art* ³ a God ready to pardon,
l gracious and merciful, slow to anger, and of great kindness,
18 and forsookest them not. Yea, *m* when they had made them a
molten calf, and said, This *is* thy God that brought thee up out
19 of Egypt, and had wrought great provocations ; yet thou in thy
n manifold mercies forsookest them not in the wilderness : the
o pillar of the cloud departed not from them by day, to lead them in
the way ; neither the pillar of fire by night, to shew them light,
20 and the way wherein they should go. ¶ Thou gavest also thy
p good spirit to instruct them, and withheldest not thy *q* manna
21 from their mouth, and gavest them *r* water for their thirst. Yea,
s forty years didst thou sustain them in the wilderness, so *that*
they lacked nothing ; their *t* clothes waxed not old, and their feet
22 swelled not. Moreover thou gavest them kingdoms and nations,
and didst divide them into corners : so they possessed the land of
u Sihon, and the land of the king of Heshbon, and the land of
23 Og king of Bashan. *x* Their children also multipliedst thou as

k Gen.11. 31.
l Gen. 17. 5.
m Gen. 15. 6.
n Gen. 12. 7.

o Josh.23.14.
p Ex. 2. 25.
q Ex. 14. 10.
r Ex. 7—14
chapters.
s Ex. 18. 11.
t Ex. 9. 16.
Isai. 63. 12.
Jer. 32. 20.
Dan. 9. 15.
u Ex. 14. 21.
Ps. 78. 13.
x Ex. 15. 5.
y Ex. 13. 21.
a Ex. 19. 20.

b Ps. 19. 8.
Rom. 7. 12.

c Gen. 2. 3.
Ex. 20. 8.

d Ex. 16. 14.
John 6. 31.
e Ex. 17. 6.
Num. 20. 9,
&c.
f Deut. 1. 8.
g Ps. 106. 6.
h Deut.31.27.
2 Kin. 17. 14.
Jer. 19. 15.
i Ps. 78. 11.
k Num.14. 4.

l Ex. 34. 6.
Num. 14. 18.
Ps. 86. 5.
Joel 2. 13.
m Ex. 32. 4.

n ver. 27.
Ps. 106. 45.
o Ex. 13. 21.
Num. 14. 14.
1 Cor. 10. 1.

p Num.11.17.
Isai. 63. 11.
q Ex. 16. 15.
Josh. 5. 12.
r Ex. 17. 6.
s Deut. 2. 7.
t Deut. 8. 4.

u Num. 21.
21, &c.
x Gen. 22.17.

¹ Heb. *laws of truth*.   *lift up thine hand to give*   ³ Heb. *a God of pardons*.
² Heb. *which thou hadst*   *them*, Num. 14. 30.

---

17. *In their rebellion*] The LXX. and
several MSS. have "in Egypt" (the words
in the original differing by one letter only),
and translate—"And appointed a captain
to return to their bondage in Egypt."
Cp. marg. ref. The appointment of a leader

is here regarded as made, whereas we are
only told in Numbers that it was proposed.
22. *Thou didst divide them into corners*]
i.e. parts of the Holy Land ; or as some
prefer "thou didst distribute them on all
sides."

the stars of heaven, and broughtest them into the land, concerning which thou hadst promised to their fathers, that they should
24 go in to possess *it*. So *v*the children went in and possessed the land, and *z*thou subduedst before them the inhabitants of the land, the Canaanites, and gavest them into their hands, with their kings, and the people of the land, that they might do with
25 them ¹as they would. And they took strong cities, and a *a*fat land, and possessed *b*houses full of all goods, ²wells digged, vineyards, and oliveyards, and ³fruit trees in abundance : so they did eat, and were filled, and *c*became fat, and delighted
26 themselves in thy great *d*goodness. ¶ Nevertheless they *e*were disobedient, and rebelled against thee, and *f*cast thy law behind their backs, and slew thy *g*prophets which testified against them to turn them to thee, and they wrought great
27 provocations. *h*Therefore thou deliveredst them into the hand of their enemies, who vexed them : and in the time of their trouble, when they cried unto thee, thou *i*heardest *them* from heaven; and according to thy manifold mercies *k*thou gavest them saviours, who saved them out of the hand of their
28 enemies. But after they had rest, *4l*they did evil again before thee : therefore leftest thou them in the hand of their enemies, so that they had the dominion over them : yet when they returned, and cried unto thee, thou heardest *them* from heaven; and *m*many times didst thou deliver them according to thy mercies ;
29 and testifiedst against them, that thou mightest bring them again unto thy law : yet they *n*dealt proudly, and hearkened not unto thy commandments, but sinned against thy judgments, (*o*which if a man do, he shall live in them;) and ⁵withdrew the shoulder, and hardened their neck, and would
30 not hear. Yet many years didst thou ⁶forbear them, and testifiedst *p*against them by thy spirit ⁷*q*in thy prophets: yet would they not give ear : *r*therefore gavest thou them into the
31 hand of the people of the lands. Nevertheless for thy great mercies' sake *s*thou didst not utterly consume them, nor forsake
32 them; for thou *art* *t*a gracious and merciful God. ¶ Now therefore, our God, the great, the *u*mighty, and the terrible God, who keepest covenant and mercy, let not all the ⁸trouble seem little before thee, ⁹that hath come upon us, on our kings, on our princes, and on our priests, and on our prophets, and on our fathers, and on all thy people, *x*since the time of the kings of
33 Assyria unto this day. Howbeit *y*thou *art* just in all that is brought upon us; for thou hast done right, but *z*we have done
34 wickedly : neither have our kings, our princes, our priests, nor our fathers, kept thy law, nor hearkened unto thy commandments and thy testimonies, wherewith thou didst testify against
35 them. For they have *a*not served thee in their kingdom, and in

v Josh. 1. 2, &c.
z Ps. 44. 2, 3.

a Num. 13. 27.
Deut. 8. 7.
Ezek. 20. 6.
b Deut. 6. 11.
c Deut. 32. 15.
d Hos. 3. 5.
e Judg. 2. 11. 12.
Ezek. 20. 21.
f 1 Kin. 14. 9.
Ps. 50. 17.
g Matt. 23. 37.
Acts 7. 52.
h Judg. 2. 14.
Ps. 106. 41.
i Ps. 106. 44.
k Judg. 2. 18.
& 3. 9.
l So Judg. 3—6 chapters.

m Ps. 106. 43.

n ver. 16.

o Lev. 18. 5.
Ezek. 20. 11.
Rom. 10. 5.
Gal. 3. 12.
p 2 Kin. 17. 13.
2 Chr. 36. 15.
Jer. 7. 25.
q See Acts 7. 51.
1 Pet. 1. 11.
2 Pet. 1. 21.
r Isai. 5. 5.
s Jer. 4. 27.
t ver. 17.
u Ex. 34. 6,7.

x 2 Kin. 17. 3.

y Ps. 119. 137.
Dan. 9. 14.
z Ps. 106. 6.
Dan. 9. 5, 6, 8.

a Deut. 28. 47.

---

¹ Heb. *according to their will.*
² Or, *cisterns.*
³ Heb. *tree of food.*
⁴ Heb. *they returned to do evil.*
⁵ Heb. *they gave a withdrawing shoulder,* Zech. 7. 11.
⁶ Heb. *protract over them.*
⁷ Heb. *in the hand of thy prophets.*
⁸ Heb. *weariness.*
⁹ Heb. *that hath found us.*

---

25. *became fat.*] *i.e.* "grew proud," or "wanton"—a phrase only occurring here, in marg. ref., and in Jer. v. 28.

delighted themselves] Rather, "**luxuriated.**" The word in the original does not occur elsewhere ; but cognate terms make the sense clear.

26. *slew thy prophets*] Cp. 1 K. xviii. 4, xix. 10 ; 2 Chr. xxiv. 21. Jewish tradition further affirms that more than one of the great Prophets (*e.g.* Isaiah, Jeremiah, and Ezekiel) were martyred by their countrymen.

27. *thou gavest them saviours*] See Judg. iii. 15 &c.

b ver. 25.
c ver. 25.
d Deut.28.48.
Ezra 9. 9.

e Deut.28.33,
51.
f Deut.28.48.

g 2 Kin.23.3.
2 Chr. 29.10.
& 34. 31.
Ezra 10. 3.
ch. 10. 29.
h ch. 10. 1.
a ch. 8. 9.
b ch. 1. 1.
c See ch. 12.
1–21.

d See Ezra
2. 3, &c.
ch. 7. 8, &c.

c Ezra 2. 36
—43.

f Ezra 9. 1.
& 10. 11, 12,
19.
ch. 13. 3.
g Deut.29,12,
14.
ch. 5. 12,13.
Ps. 119. 106.
h 2 Kin. 23.3.
2 Chr. 34. 31.
i Ex. 34. 16.
Deut. 7. 3.
Ezra 9.12,14.
k Ex. 20. 10.
Lev. 23. 3.
Deut. 5. 12.
l Ex. 23. 10,
11.
Lev. 25. 4.
m Deut. 15.
1, 2.
ch. 5. 12.

*b*thy great goodness that thou gavest them, and in the large and *c*fat land which thou gavest before them, neither turned they 36 from their wicked works. Behold, *d*we *are* servants this day, and *for* the land that thou gavest unto our fathers to eat the fruit thereof and the good thereof, behold, we *are* servants in it : 37 and *e*it yieldeth much increase unto the kings whom thou hast set over us because of our sins : also they have *f*dominion over our bodies, and over our cattle, at their pleasure, and we *are* in great 38 distress. And because of all this we *g*make a sure *covenant,* and write it ; and our princes, Levites, *and* priests, 1*h*seal *unto it.*

CHAP. 10. NOW 2those that sealed *were,* *a*Nehemiah, 3the Tirshatha, 2 *b*the son of Hachaliah, and Zidkijah, *c*Seraiah, Azariah, Jere- 3, 4 miah, Pashur, Amariah, Malchijah, Hattush, Shebaniah, Mal- 5, 6 luch, Harim, Meremoth, Obadiah, Daniel, Ginnethon, Baruch, 7, 8 Meshullam, Abijah, Mijamin, Maaziah, Bilgai, Shemaiah : 9 these *were* the priests. And the Levites: both Jeshua the son of 10 Azaniah, Binnui of the sons of Henadad, Kadmiel ; and their 11 brethren, Shebaniah, Hodijah, Kelita, Pelaiah, Hanan, Micha, 12, 13 Rehob, Hashabiah, Zaccur, Sherebiah, Shebaniah, Hodijah, 14 Bani, Beninu. The chief of the people ; *d*Parosh, Pahath-moab, 15, 16 Elam, Zatthu, Bani, Bunni, Azgad, Bebai, Adonijah, Bigvai, 17, 18 Adin, Ater, Hizkijah, Azzur, Hodijah, Hashum, Bezai, 19, 20 Hariph, Anathoth, Nebai, Magpiash, Meshullam, Hezir, 21, 22 Meshezabeel, Zadok, Jaddua, Pelatiah, Hanan, Anaiah, 23, 24 Hoshea, Hananiah, Hashub, Hallohesh, Pileha, Shobek, 25, 26 Rehum, Hashabnah, Maaseiah, and Ahijah, Hanan, Anan, 27, 28 Malluch, Harim, Baanah. ¶*e*And the rest of the people, the priests, the Levites, the porters, the singers, the Nethinims, *f*and all they that had separated themselves from the people of the lands unto the law of God, their wives, their sons, and their daughters, every one having knowledge, and having under- 29 standing ; they clave to their brethren, their nobles, *g*and entered into a curse, and into an oath, *h*to walk in God's law, which was given 4 by Moses the servant of God, and to observe and do all the commandments of the LORD our Lord, and his judgments 30 and his statutes ; and that we would not give *i*our daughters unto the people of the land, nor take their daughters for our 31 sons : *k*and *if* the people of the land bring ware or any victuals on the sabbath day to sell, *that* we would not buy it of them on the sabbath, or on the holy day : and *that* we would leave the 32 *l*seventh year, and the *m*exaction of 5every debt. ¶ Also we made ordinances for us, to charge ourselves yearly with the third part of a shekel for the service of the house of our God ;

1 Heb. are *at the sealing,* or, *sealed.*
2 Heb. *at the sealings,* ch. 9. 38.
3 Or, *the governor.*
4 Heb. *by the hand of.*
5 Heb. *every hand.*

---

38. *seal unto it*] The exact force of the phrase used is doubtful ; but its general sense must be that the classes named took part in the sealing. It was usual in the East to authenticate covenants by append- ing the seals of those who were parties to them (see Jer. xxxii. 10).

X. 1. The "Zidkijah" of this passage is probably the same as "Zadok" (xiii. 13). "Zadok" is expressly called "the scribe," and it was probably as the scribe who drew up the document that "Zidkijah" signed it immediately after Nehemiah.

2–8. The names are not personal, but designate families. The seal of the High- priestly house of Seraiah was probably ap- pended either by Ezra or Eliashib, who both belonged to it.

31. *bring ware ... on the sabbath day*] Compare xiii. 16, where this desecration of the Sabbath is shown to have commonly taken place.

leave the seventh year &c.] *i.e.* "let the land rest in the sabbatical year" (marg. reff.) and give up the "pledge-taking" (*v.* 2–10).

32. *the third part of a shekel*] This ap-

33 for [n]the shewbread, and for the [o]continual meat offering, and for the continual burnt offering, of the sabbaths, of the new moons, for the set feasts, and for the holy *things*, and for the sin offerings to make an atonement for Israel, and *for* all the work
34 of the house of our God. ¶And we cast the lots among the priests, the Levites, and the people, [p]for the wood offering, to bring *it* into the house of our God, after the houses of our fathers, at times appointed year by year, to burn upon the
35 altar of the LORD our God, [q]as *it is* written in the law: and [r]to bring the firstfruits of our ground, and the firstfruits of all fruit of all trees, year by year, unto the house of the LORD :
36 also the firstborn of our sons, and of our cattle, as *it is* written [s]in the law, and the firstlings of our herds and of our flocks, to bring to the house of our God, unto the priests
37 that minister in the house of our God : [t]and *that* we should bring the firstfruits of our dough, and our offerings, and the fruit of all manner of trees, of wine and of oil, unto the priests, to the chambers of the house of our God; and [u]the tithes of our ground unto the Levites, that the same Levites
38 might have the tithes in all the cities of our tillage. And the priest the son of Aaron shall be with the Levites, [x]when the Levites take tithes : and the Levites shall bring up the tithe of the tithes unto the house of our God, to [y]the chambers, into the
39 treasure house. For the children of Israel and the children of Levi [z]shall bring the offering of the corn, of the new wine, and the oil, unto the chambers, where *are* the vessels of the sanctuary, and the priests that minister, and the porters, and the singers : [a]and we will not forsake the house of our God.

CHAP. 11. AND the rulers of the people dwelt at Jerusalem : the rest of the people also cast lots, to bring one of ten to dwell in Jerusalem [a]the holy city, and nine parts *to dwell* in *other* cities.
2 And the people blessed all the men, that [b]willingly offered them-
3 selves to dwell at Jerusalem. ¶[c]Now these *are* the chief of the province that dwelt in Jerusalem : but in the cities of Judah dwelt every one in his possession in their cities, *to wit*, Israel, the priests, and the Levites, and [d]the Nethinims, and [e]the
4 children of Solomon's servants. And [f]at Jerusalem dwelt *certain* of the children of Judah, and of the children of Benjamin. ¶Of the children of Judah; Athaiah the son of Uzziah, the son of Zechariah, the son of Amariah, the son of Shephatiah, the

[n] Lev. 24. 5, &c.
2 Chr. 2. 4.
[o] See Num. 28, & 29.

[p] ch. 13. 31.
Isai. 40. 16.

[q] Lev. 6. 12.
[r] Ex. 23. 19.
& 34. 26.
Lev. 19. 23.
Num. 18. 12.
Deut. 26. 2.
[s] Ex. 13. 2, 12, 13.
Lev. 27. 26, 27.
Num. 18. 15, 16.
[t] Lev. 23. 17.
Num. 15. 19.
& 18. 12, &c.
Deut. 18. 4.
& 26. 2.
[u] Lev. 27. 30.
Num. 18. 21, &c.
[x] Num. 18. 26.
[y] 1 Chr. 9. 26.
2 Chr. 31. 11.
[z] Deut. 12. 6, 11.
2 Chr. 31. 12.
ch. 13. 12.
[a] ch. 13. 10, 11.

[a] ver. 18.
Matt. 4. 5.
& 27. 53.
[b] Judg. 5. 9.
[c] 1 Chr.9.2,3.

[d] Ezra 2. 43.
[e] Ezra 2. 55.
[f] 1 Chr. 9. 3, &c.

---

pears to have been the first occasion on which an annual payment towards the maintenance of the Temple service and fabric was established. The half-shekel of the Law (Ex. xxx. 13) was paid only at the time of a census (which rarely took place), and was thus not a recurring tax. In after-times the annual payment was raised from the third of a shekel to half a shekel (Matt. xvii. 24).

34. No special provision was made by the Law, by David, or by Solomon, for the supply of wood necessary to keep fire ever burning upon the Altar. Nehemiah established a system by which the duty of supplying the wood was laid as a burthen in turn on the various clans or families, which were regarded as constituting the nation. The lot was used to determine the order in which the several families should perform the duty. A special day (the 14th of the fifth month, according to Josephus) was appointed for the bringing in of the supply; and this day was after a time regarded as a high festival, and called "the feast of the Wood-offering."

XI. 1. *to bring one of ten*] Artificial enlargements of capitals by forcible transfers of population to them, were not unusual in ancient times. Syracuse became a great city, about B.C. 500, in this way. Tradition ascribed the greatness of Rome, in part, to this cause.

4-19. See marg. reff. notes. Both accounts appear to be extracts from a public official register which Nehemiah caused to be made of his census. The census itself seems to have been confined to the dwellers

5 son of Mahalaleel, of the children of *g*Perez; and Maaseiah the son of Baruch, the son of Col-hozeh, the son of Hazaiah, the son of Adaiah, the son of Joiarib, the son of Zechariah, the son 6 of Shiloni. All the sons of Perez that dwelt at Jerusalem *were* 7 four hundred threescore and eight valiant men. And these *are* the sons of Benjamin; Sallu the son of Meshullam, the son of Joed, the son of Pedaiah, the son of Kolaiah, the son of Maas-8 eiah, the son of Ithiel, the son of Jesaiah. And after him 9 Gabbai, Sallai, nine hundred twenty and eight. And Joel the son of Zichri *was* their overseer: and Judah the son of Senuah

10 *was* second over the city. ¶ *h*Of the priests: Jedaiah the son of 11 Joiarib, Jachin. Seraiah the son of Hilkiah, the son of Me-shullam, the son of Zadok, the son of Meraioth, the son of 12 Ahitub, *was* the ruler of the house of God. And their brethren that did the work of the house *were* eight hundred twenty and two: and Adaiah the son of Jeroham, the son of Pelaliah, the son of Amzi, the son of Zechariah, the son of Pashur, the son 13 of Malchiah, and his brethren, chief of the fathers, two hundred forty and two: and Amashai the son of Azareel, the son of 14 Ahasai, the son of Meshillemoth, the son of Immer, and their brethren, mighty men of valour, an hundred twenty and eight: and their overseer *was* Zabdiel, [1]the son of *one of* the great men. 15 ¶ Also of the Levites: Shemaiah the son of Hashub, the son 16 of Azrikam, the son of Hashabiah, the son of Bunni; and Shabbethai and Jozabad, of the chief of the Levites, [2]*had* the

17 oversight of *i*the outward business of the house of God. And Mattaniah the son of Micha, the son of Zabdi, the son of Asaph, *was* the principal to begin the thanksgiving in prayer: and Bakbukiah the second among his brethren, and Abda the son 18 of Shammua, the son of Galal, the son of Jeduthun. All the

Levites in *k*the holy city *were* two hundred fourscore and four. 19 Moreover the porters, Akkub, Talmon, and their brethren that 20 kept [3]the gates, *were* an hundred seventy and two. ¶ And the

[1] O*r*, *the son of Haggedolim*.   [2] Heb. *were over*.   [3] Heb. *at the gates*.

at Jerusalem. The subjoined table exhibits the differences between the accounts of the entire population of Jerusalem as given in Nehemiah and in Chronicles:—

	1 Chronicles.	Nehemiah.
Tribe of Judah: -		
Of Pharez . .	..	468
Of Zerah . . .	690	..
Tribe of Benjamin: -	956	928
Tribe of Levi:—		
Priests . . .	1760	1192
Levites . . .	..	284
Porters . .	212	172

According to Nehemiah's numbers, supplemented from Chronicles, the entire adult male population of the city was 3734, which would give a total population of 14,936. According to Chronicles, supplemented from Nehemiah, the adult males were 4370, and consequently the entire population, 17,480. As the Nethinims and the Israelites of Ephraim and Manasseh (1 Chr. ix. 3) are not included in either list, we may conclude that the actual number of the inhabitants, after the efforts recorded in *vv.* 1, 2, was not much short of 20,000.

16. *the outward business of the house of God*] Such as the collection of the newly imposed tax (x. 32), the providing of the regular sacrifices, the renewal of vestments, and the like.

17. *the principal to begin the thanksgiving*] *i.e.* "the precentor," or "leader of the choir."

20. The returned community, though consisting mainly of members of the two tribes, represented the entire people of Israel. The ground, however, which they

residue of Israel, of the priests, *and* the Levites, *were* in all the
21 cities of Judah, every one in his inheritance. [l]But the Nethinims
dwelt in [1]Ophel : and Ziha and Gispa *were* over the Nethinims.
22 ¶ The overseer also of the Levites at Jerusalem *was* Uzzi the
son of Bani, the son of Hashabiah, the son of Mattaniah, the
son of Micha. Of the sons of Asaph, the singers *were* over the
23 business of the house of God. For [m]*it was* the king's commandment concerning them, that [2]a certain portion should be
24 for the singers, due for every day. ¶ And Pethahiah the son of
Meshezabeel, of the children of [n]Zerah the son of Judah, *was*
25 [o]at the king's hand in all matters concerning the people. ¶ And
for the villages, with their fields, *some* of the children of Judah
dwelt at [p]Kirjath-arba, and *in* the villages thereof, and at
Dibon, and *in* the villages thereof, and at Jekabzeel, and *in* the
26 villages thereof, and at Jeshua, and at Moladah, and at Beth-
27 phelet, and at Hazar-shual, and at Beer-sheba, and *in* the
28 villages thereof, and at Ziklag, and at Mekonah, and in the
29 villages thereof, and at En-rimmon, and at Zareah, and at
30 Jarmuth, Zanoah, Adullam, and *in* their villages, at Lachish,
and the fields thereof, at Azekah, and *in* the villages thereof.
And they dwelt from Beer-sheba unto the valley of Hin-
31 nom. ¶ The children also of Benjamin [3]from Geba *dwelt* [4]at
Michmash, and Aija, and Beth-el, and *in* their villages,
32, 33 *and* at Anathoth, Nob, Ananiah, Hazor, Ramah, Gittaim,
34, 35 Hadid, Zeboim, Neballat, Lod, and Ono, [q]the valley of
36 craftsmen. ¶ And of the Levites *were* divisions *in* Judah, *and*
in Benjamin.

CHAP. 12. NOW these *are* the [a]priests and the Levites that went
up with Zerubbabel the son of Shealtiel, and Jeshua : [b]Seraiah,

[l] See ch. 3. 26.

[m] See Ezra
6. 8, 9.
& 7. 20, &c.

[n] Gen. 38.
30, *Zarah.*
[o] 1 Chr. 18. 17.
& 23. 28.
[p] Josh. 14. 15.

[q] 1 Chr. 4. 14.

[a] Ezra 2. 1, 2.
[b] See ch. 10.
2—8.

---

[1] Or, *The tower.*
[2] Or, *a sure ordinance.*
[3] Or, *of Geba.*
[4] Or, *to Michmash.*

---

occupied, was not the whole land, but that
which had constituted the kingdom of
Judah.

21. Ophel, the southern spur of the Temple hill, having a wall of its own (iii. 27)
might be reckoned either in Jerusalem or
outside it. Here it is made a separate
place.

22. The business intended was probably
the *internal* business, as distinct from the
"outward business" (*v.* 16) : a part of which
was the apportionment of the royal bounty
among the members of the choir (*v.* 23).

23. The goodwill of Artaxerxes towards
the ministers employed in the Temple service, had been previously shown by his
exempting them from taxation of every
kind (Ezra vii. 24). Now, it would seem,
he had gone further and assigned to the
singers an allowance from the royal revenue.

24. It is difficult to say what office Pethahiah filled. So far as we know, the only
regular officers under the Persian system
of government were the satrap, the sub-
satrap, the permanent royal secretary, the
commandant, and the occasional commis-
sary.

25. *Kirjath-arba*] *i.e.* Hebron. In the
absence of the Hebrews during the Cap-

tivity the place had recovered its old name
(Josh. xv. 13).

26–35. Many of the places mentioned in
these verses are mentioned in Josh. xv.
27–39, xviii. 21–28.

36. *of the Levites were divisions*] *i.e.*
"the Levites were scattered among various
towns both in Judah and Benjamin."

XII. This chapter is made up of two
portions : (*a*) lists of the leading priests and
Levites at different periods (*vv.* 1–26) : (*b*)
the dedication of the wall of Jerusalem
(*vv.* 27–47). This latter passage is certainly
from the pen of Nehemiah, and was written
probably about B.C. 433. The lists included
in (*a*) are four : (1) the chief priestly and
Levitical families which returned to Jerusalem (*vv.* 1–9); (2) the succession of the
High Priests from Jeshua to Jaddua (*vv.*
10, 11); (3) the actual heads of the priestly
families in the time of the High-Priest
Joiakim (*vv.* 12–21); (4) the chief Levitical
families at the same period (*vv.* 24–26). Of
these lists Nos. 1, 3, and 4, may have been
drawn up in the time of Nehemiah, but
No. 2 in its present form must be much
later. See Introduction, p. 591.

1. *the priests*] The number of the names
here given, which is 22, is probably to

2, 3 Jeremiah, Ezra, Amariah, [1]Malluch, Hattush, [2]Shechaniah,
4, 5 [3]Rehum, [4]Meremoth, Iddo, [5]Ginnetho, *c*Abijah, [6]Miamin,
6, 7 [7]Maadiah, Bilgah, Shemaiah, and Joiarib, Jedaiah, [8]Sallu,
Amok, Hilkiah, Jedaiah. These *were* the chief of the priests
8 and of their brethren in the days of *d*Jeshua. Moreover the
Levites: Jeshua, Binnui, Kadmiel, Sherebiah, Judah, *and*
Mattaniah, *e which was* over [9]the thanksgiving, he and his
9 brethren. Also Bakbukiah and Unni, their brethren, *were* over
10 against them in the watches. ¶And Jeshua begat Joiakim,
11 Joiakim also begat Eliashib, and Eliashib begat Joiada, and
12 Joiada begat Jonathan, and Jonathan begat Jaddua. ¶And in
the days of Joiakim were priests, the chief of the fathers: of
13 Seraiah, Meraiah; of Jeremiah, Hananiah; of Ezra, Meshullam;
14 of Amariah, Jehohanan; of Melicu, Jonathan; of Shebaniah,
15, 16 Joseph; of Harim, Adna; of Meraioth, Helkai; of Iddo,
17 Zechariah; of Ginnethon, Meshullam; of Abijah, Zichri; of
18 Miniamin, of Moadiah, Piltai; of Bilgah, Shammua; of She-
19 maiah, Jehonathan; and of Joiarib, Mattenai; of Jedaiah,
20, 21 Uzzi; of Sallai, Kallai; of Amok, Eber; of Hilkiah, Hasha-
22 biah; of Jedaiah, Nethaneel. ¶The Levites in the days of
Eliashib, Joiada, and Johanan, and Jaddua, *were* recorded chief
of the fathers: also the priests, to the reign of Darius the Per-
23 sian. The sons of Levi, the chief of the fathers, *were* written in
the book of the *f* chronicles, even until the days of Johanan the
24 son of Eliashib. ¶And the chief of the Levites: Hashabiah,
Sherebiah, and Jeshua the son of Kadmiel, with their brethren
over against them, to praise *and* to give thanks, *g* according to
the commandment of David the man of God, *h* ward over against

c Luke 1. 5.

d Ezra 3. 2.
Hag. 1. 1.
Zech. 3. 1.
e ch. 11. 17.

f 1 Chr. 9.
14, &c.

g 1 Chr. 23,
& 25, & 26.
h Ezra 3. 11.

---

[1] Or, *Melicu*, ver. 14.
[2] Or, *Shebaniah*, ver. 14.
[3] Or, *Harim*, ver. 15.
[4] Or, *Meraioth*, ver. 15.
[5] Or, *Ginnethon*, ver. 16.
[6] Or, *Miniamin*, ver. 17.
[7] Or, *Moadiah*, ver. 17.
[8] Or, *Sallai*, ver. 20.
[9] That is, *the psalms of thanksgiving.*

---

be connected with that of the Davidic
"courses," which was 24 (1 Chr. xxiv. 7–18).
Eight names are identical with those of the
heads in David's time. On comparing the
present list with that of the families who
sealed to Nehemiah's covenant (x. 2–8), we
shall find that the first sixteen recur in that
document nearly in the same order; but
that the last six are absent from it. It
would seem that as these six declined to
seal to Nehemiah's covenant, they were
placed below the rest here in a sort of supplementary list. Note especially the "and"
which connects the second part of the lists
with the earlier part, both in *v.* 6 and in
v. 19.

8. Of the Levitical houses here mentioned,
three only returned at first, those of Jeshua,
Kadmiel, and Judah or Hodevah (vii. 43).
The others must have returned subsequently.

10, 11. The six generations of High-
Priests covered a little more than two centuries (B.C. 538–333), or a little under thirty-
five years to a generation. Jaddua was the
High-Priest who (according to Josephus)
had an interview with Alexander shortly
after the battle of Issus.

22, 23. These verses interrupt the account
of the church officers in the time of Joiakim,
resumed in *v.* 24. They appear to be an
addition to the original text, made about
the time of Alexander the Great, when the
Books of Chronicles, Ezra, and Nehemiah
would seem to have first taken their existing shape. The same writer who introduced
these verses, probably also added *v.* 11 to
the original text.

Darius the Persian] Probably Darius
Codomannus (B.C. 336–331), the antagonist
of Alexander the Great. See Introduction,
p. 592, *n.* 2.

23. This passage shows that the practice
of keeping a record of public events in state
archives was continued after the return
from the Captivity, at least to the time of
Johanan, the son, *i.e.* "the grandson," of
Eliashib.

24. *Jeshua the son of Kadmiel*] If the
reading be sound, this Jeshua must have
been the head of the Levitical family of
Kadmiel in the time of Joiakim; but (cp.
viii. 7, ix. 4), some read "Jeshua, Bani,
Kadmiel," &c.

ward over against ward] *i.e.* "alternately,"
one part of the choir answering the other.

25 ward. Mattaniah, and Bakbukiah, Obadiah, Meshullam, Talmon, Akkub, *were* porters keeping the ward at the [1]thresholds
26 of the gates. The e *were* in the days of Joiakim the son of Jeshua, the son of Jozadak, and in the days of Nehemiah [i]the
27 governor, and of Ezra the priest, [k]the scribe. ¶And at [l]the dedication of the wall of Jerusalem they sought the Levites out of all their places, to bring them to Jerusalem, to keep the dedication with gladness, [m]both with thanksgivings, and with
28 singing, *with* cymbals, psalteries, and with harps. And the sons of the singers gathered themselves together, both out of the plain country round about Jerusalem, and from the villages of
29 Netophathi; also from the house of Gilgal, and out of the fields of Geba and Azmaveth: for the singers had builded them vil-
30 lages round about Jerusalem. And the priests and the Levites purified themselves, and purified the people, and the gates, and
31 the wall. ¶Then I brought up the princes of Judah upon the wall, and appointed two great *companies of them that gave* thanks, *whereof* [n]*one* went on the right hand upon the wall, [o]toward the
32 dung gate: and after them went Hoshaiah, and half of the
33, 34 princes of Judah, and Azariah, Ezra, and Meshullam, Judah,
35 and Benjamin, and Shemaiah, and Jeremiah, and *certain* of the priests' sons [p]with trumpets; *namely*, Zechariah the son of Jonathan, the son of Shemaiah, the son of Mattaniah, the son
36 of Michaiah, the son of Zaccur, the son of Asaph: and his brethren, Shemaiah, and Azarael, Milalai, Gilalai, Maai, Nethaneel, and Judah, Hanani, with [q]the musical instruments of
37 David the man of God, and Ezra the scribe before them. [r]And at the fountain gate, which was over against them, they went up by [s]the stairs of the city of David, at the going up of the wall, above the house of David, even unto [t]the water gate east-
38 ward. ¶[u]And the other *company of them that gave* thanks went over against *them*, and I after them, and the half of the people

[i] ch. 8. 9.

[k] Ezra 7. 6, 11.
[l] Deut. 20. 5.
Ps. 30, title.
[m] 1 Chr.25.6.
2 Chr. 5. 13.
& 7. 6.

[n] See ver.38.
[o] ch. 2. 13.
& 3. 13.

[p] Num. 10. 2, 8.

[q] 1 Chr. 23.5.
[r] ch. 2. 14.
& 3. 15.
[s] ch. 3. 15.
[t] ch. 3. 26.
& 8. 1, 3, 16.
[u] See ver.31.

[1] Or, *treasuries*, or, *assemblies*.

---

25. In 1 Chr. ix. 17, 24, 26, four families of porters only are mentioned; *six* are implied here, in vii. 45, and in Ezra ii. 42. From 1 Chr. xxvi. 14–19 it appears that the Temple had four chief gates, fronting the cardinal points, and two minor ones, " towards Asuppim," and " at Parbar."

27. *the dedication of the wall*] The ceremony had been deferred for the space of nearly twelve years (xiii. 6). Perhaps Nehemiah required an express permission from the Persian king before he could venture on a solemnity which might have been liable to misrepresentation.

out of all their places] *i.e.* out of the various cities of Judah and Benjamin in which they dwelt (xi. 36).

28. *the plain country round about Jerusalem*] Perhaps the valleys of Hinnom and Jehoshaphat, which enclose Jerusalem on three sides, are intended.

the villages of Netophathi] Rather, as in 1 Chr. ix. 16. Netophah lay near Bethlehem (1 Chr. ii. 54), and is perhaps represented by the modern *Antubeh*.

29. *the house of Gilgal*] Or, "Beth-Gilgal"

—probably the Gilgal north of Jerusalem (now *Jiljilia*).

31. *I brought up*] Note the resumption of the first person, which has been laid aside since vii. 5, and which is continued now to the end of the Book. It is generally allowed that we have here once more a memoir by Nehemiah himself.

The two "companies" or choirs, having ascended the wall on its western face, near the modern Jaffa Gate, stood looking eastward towards the city and Temple; then the southern choir, being on the *right*, commenced the circuit of the southern wall, while the choir upon the left proceeded round the northern wall (*vv.* 38-39), till both met on the eastern wall, between the water and the prison gates.

34. "Judah and Benjamin" are the lay people of those two tribes.

37. *above the house of David*] This choir or procession went above (or beyond) the old palace of David, following the line described in iii. 16-26, on their way to the eastern wall.

upon the wall, from beyond *x*the tower of the furnaces even unto 39 *y*the broad wall; *z*and from above the gate of Ephraim, and above *a*the old gate, and above *b*the fish gate, *c*and the tower of Hananeel, and the tower of Meah, even unto *d*the sheep gate : 40 and they stood still in *e*the prison gate. ¶ So stood the two *companies of them that gave* thanks in the house of God, and I, 41 and the half of the rulers with me : and the priests ; Eliakim, Maaseiah, Miniamin, Michaiah, Elioenai, Zechariah, *and* Ha-42 naniah, with trumpets ; and Maaseiah, and Shemaiah, and Eleazar, and Uzzi, and Jehohanan, and Malchijah, and Elam, and Ezer. And the singers ¹sang loud, with Jezrahiah *their* 43 overseer. Also that day they offered great sacrifices, and rejoiced : for God had made them rejoice with great joy : the wives also and the children rejoiced : so that the joy of Jerusalem was heard even afar off. ¶ *f*And at that time were some 44 salem was heard even afar off. ¶ *f*And at that time were some appointed over the chambers for the treasures, for the offerings, for the firstfruits, and for the tithes, to gather into them out of the fields of the cities the portions ²of the law for the priests and Levites : ³for Judah rejoiced for the priests and for the 45 Levites ⁴that waited. And both the singers and the porters kept the ward of their God, and the ward of the purification, *g*according to the commandment of David, *and* of Solomon his 46 son. For in the days of David *h*and Asaph of old *there were* chief of the singers, and songs of praise and thanksgiving unto 47 God. And all Israel in the days of Zerubbabel, and in the days of Nehemiah, gave the portions of the singers and the porters, every day his portion : *i*and they ⁵sanctified *holy things* unto the Levites ; *k*and the Levites sanctified *them* unto the children of Aaron.

CHAP. 13. ON that day *a*⁶they read in the book of Moses in the ⁷audience of the people ; and therein was found written, *b*that the Ammonite and the Moabite should not come into the congregation of God for ever ; because they met not the children of Israel with bread and with water, but *c*hired Balaam against them, that he should curse them : *d*howbeit our God turned the curse 3 into a blessing. Now it came to pass, when they had heard the law, *e*that they separated from Israel all the mixed multitude. 4 ¶ And before this, Eliashib the priest, ⁸having the oversight of

---

¹ Heb. *made* their voice *to be heard.*
² That is, *appointed by the law.*
³ Heb. *for the joy of Judah.*
⁴ Heb. *that stood.*
⁵ That is, *set apart.*
⁶ Heb. *there was read.*
⁷ Heb. *ears.*
⁸ Heb. *being set over,* ch. 12. 44.

---

44. *Judah rejoiced*] Judah's satisfaction with the priests and Levites took the shape of increased offerings, more ample tithes, and the like, whence the appointment of treasures and treasurers became necessary.

45. *the ward of the purification*] The observances with respect to purification. Cp. 1 Chr. xxiii. 28.

47. The intention is to compare the religious activity and strictness of Nehemiah's time with that which had prevailed under Zerubbabel, as described by Ezra (vi. 16, 22). It is implied that the intermediate period had been a time of laxity.

they sanctified holy things &c.] *i.e.* "the people paid their tithes regularly to the

Levites, and the Levites paid the tithe of the tithes to the priests."

XIII. **1.** *On that day*] Or, "at that time," as in xii. 44.

By "the Book of Moses" is probably meant the entire Pentateuch.

3. A separation like that made by Ezra, some twenty years previously (Ezr. x. 15-44), seems to be intended. The heathen wives were divorced and sent back, with their offspring, to their own countries.

4. The relations of Eliashib, the High-Priest (iii. 1), with Tobiah and Sanballat will account for. the absence of any reference to him either in chs. viii.-x., or in xii. 27-47.

the chamber of the house of our God, *was* allied unto Tobiah:
5 and he had prepared for him a great chamber, *f* where aforetime ｜*f* ch. 12. 44.
they laid the meat offerings, the frankincense, and the vessels,
and the tithes of the corn, the new wine, and the oil, ¹*g* which | *g* Num. 18.
was commanded *to be given* to the Levites, and the singers, and | 21, 24.
6 the porters; and the offerings of the priests. But in all this *time*
was not I at Jerusalem: *h* for in the two and thirtieth year of | *h* ch. 5. 14.
Artaxerxes king of Babylon came I unto the king, and ² after
7 certain days ³ obtained I leave of the king: and I came to Jerusalem, and understood of the evil that Eliashib did for Tobiah,
in *i* preparing him a chamber in the courts of the house of God. | *i* ver. 1, 5.
8 And it grieved me sore: therefore I cast forth all the household
9 stuff of Tobiah out of the chamber. Then I commanded, and
they *k* cleansed the chambers: and thither brought I again the | *k* 2 Chr. 29.
vessels of the house of God, with the meat offering and the frank- | 5, 15, 16, 18.
10 incense. ¶ And I perceived that the portions of the Levites had
l not been given *them:* for the Levites and the singers, that did | *l* Mal. 3. 8.
11 the work, were fled every one to *m* his field. Then *n* contended I | *m* Num.35.2.
with the rulers, and said, *o* Why is the house of God forsaken? | *n* ver. 17, 25.
And I gathered them together, and set them in their ⁴ place. | Prov. 28. 4.
12 *p* Then brought all Judah the tithe of the corn and the new wine | *o* ch. 10. 39.
13 and the oil unto the ⁵ treasuries. *q* And I made treasurers over | *p* ch. 10. 38,
the treasuries, Shelemiah the priest, and Zadok the scribe, and | 39.
of the Levites, Pedaiah: and ⁶ next to them *was* Hanan the son | & 12. 44.
of Zaccur, the son of Mattaniah: for they were counted *r* faith- | *q* 2Chr.31.12.
ful, and ⁷ their office *was* to distribute unto their brethren. | ch. 12. 44.
14 *s* Remember me, O my God, concerning this, and wipe not out | *r* ch. 7. 2.
my ⁸ good deeds that I have done for the house of my God, | 1 Cor. 4. 2.
15 and for the ⁹ offices thereof. ¶ In those days saw I in Judah | *s* ver. 22, 31.
some treading wine presses *t* on the sabbath, and bringing in | ch. 5. 19.
sheaves, and lading asses; as also wine, grapes, and figs, and all | *t* Ex. 20. 10.
manner of burdens, *u* which they brought into Jerusalem on the | *u* ch. 10. 31.
sabbath day: and I testified *against them* in the day wherein
16 they sold victuals. There dwelt men- of Tyre also therein,

---

¹ Heb. *the commandment of
the Levites.*
² Heb. *at the end of days.*

³ Or, *I earnestly requested.*
⁴ Heb. *standing.*
⁵ Or, *storehouses.*
⁶ Heb. *at their hand.*

⁷ Heb. *it was upon them.*
⁸ Heb. *kindnesses.*
⁹ Or, *observations.*

---

the chamber] The entire outbuilding, or
"lean-to," which surrounded the Temple
on three sides (1 K. vi. 5–10).

allied] *i.e.* "connected by marriage."
Tobiah was married to a Jewess (vi. 18),
who may have been a relation of Eliashib;
and his son Johanan was married to another
(do.), of whom the same may be said.

5. *the offerings of the priests*] *i.e.* "the
portion of the offerings assigned for their
sustenance to the priests."

6. *Artaxerxes king of Babylon*] See i. 1.
Cp. Ezr. vi. 22, where Darius Hystaspis is
called "king of Assyria."

after certain days] Or, "at the end of a
year," which is a meaning that the phrase
often has (Ex. xiii. 10; Lev. xxv. 29, 30;
Num. ix. 22). Nehemiah probably went to
the court at Babylon in B.C. 433, and returned to Jerusalem B.C. 432.

9. *the chambers*] The "great chamber"

assigned to Tobiah (*v.* 5) contained, it would
seem, more than one apartment.

10, &c. During Nehemiah's absence there
had been a general falling away, and there
was danger of a complete national apostasy.

11. *I gathered them together*] Nehemiah
gathered the Levites from their lands, and
reinstated them in their set offices.

15. The desecration of the Sabbath is first
brought into prominence among the sins of
the Jewish people by Jeremiah (Jer. xvii.
21–27). It could not but have gained ground
during the Captivity, when foreign masters
would not have allowed the cessation of
labour for one day in seven. On the return
from the Captivity, the sabbatical rest appears to have been one of the institutions
most difficult to re-establish.

in the day] Some render, "concerning
the day."

16. Friendly relations subsisted between

x ver. 11.

y Jer. 17. 21,
22, 23.

z Lev. 23. 32.

a Jer. 17. 21,
22.

b ch. 12. 30.

c ver. 14, 31.

d Ezra 9. 2.

e ver. 11.
Prov. 28. 4.

f Ezra 10. 5.
ch. 10. 29, 30.

g 1 Kin. 11.
1, &c.
h 1 Kin. 3.13.
2 Chr. 1. 12.
i 2 Sam. 12.
24.
k 1 Kin. 11.
4, &c.
l Ezra 10. 2.
m ch. 12. 10,
22.
n ch. 6. 14.
o Mal. 2. 4,
11, 12.

which brought fish, and all manner of ware, and sold on the 17 sabbath unto the children of Judah, and in Jerusalem. *Then I contended with the nobles of Judah, and said unto them, What evil thing *is* this that ye do, and profane the sabbath day? 18 *Did not your fathers thus, and did not our God bring all this evil upon us, and upon this city? yet ye bring more wrath 19 upon Israel by profaning the sabbath. ¶ And it came to pass, that when the gates of Jerusalem *began to be dark before the sabbath, I commanded that the gates should be shut, and charged that they should not be opened till after the sabbath: *and *some* of my servants set I at the gates, *that* there should 20 no burden be brought in on the sabbath day. So the merchants and sellers of all kind of ware lodged without Jerusalem once 21 or twice. Then I testified against them, and said unto them, Why lodge ye ¹about the wall? if ye do *so* again, I will lay hands on you. From that time forth came they no *more* on 22 the sabbath. And I commanded the Levites that *they should cleanse themselves, and *that* they should come *and* keep the gates, to sanctify the sabbath day. *Remember me, O my God, *concerning* this also, and spare me according to the 23 ²greatness of thy mercy. ¶ In those days also saw I Jews *that* ³ᵈ had married wives of Ashdod, of Ammon, *and* of Moab: 24 and their children spake half in the speech of Ashdod, and ⁴could not speak in the Jews' language, but according to the 25 language ⁵of each people. And I *contended with them, and ⁶ cursed them, and smote certain of them, and plucked off their hair, and made them *swear by God, *saying*, Ye shall not give your daughters unto their sons, nor take their daughters unto 26 your sons, or for yourselves. *Did not Solomon king of Israel sin by these things? yet *among many nations was there no king like him, *who was beloved of his God, and God made him king over all Israel: *nevertheless even him did outlandish 27 women cause to sin. Shall we then hearken unto you to do all this great evil, to *transgress against our God in marrying 28 strange wives? And *one* of the sons *of Joiada, the son of Eliashib the high priest, *was* son in law to Sanballat the 29 Horonite: therefore I chased him from me. *Remember them, O my God, ⁷because they have defiled the priesthood, and *the

---

¹ Heb. *before the wall?*
² Or, *multitude.*
³ Heb. *had made to dwell*

with them.
⁴ Heb. *they discerned not to speak.*

⁵ Heb. *of people and people.*
⁶ Or, *reviled them.*
⁷ Heb. *for the defilings.*

---

the Phœnicians and the Jews, after the Captivity (Ezra iii. 7). It was, however, a new fact, and one pregnant with evil consequences, that the Tyrians should have established a permanent colony at Jerusalem. Its influence on the other inhabitants weakened the hold of the Law upon men's consciences, and caused it to be transgressed continually more and more openly.

19. The gates were closed at the sunset of the day before the Sabbath; since the Sabbath was regarded as commencing on the previous evening.

21. The lodging of the merchants with their merchandise just outside Jerusalem during the Sabbath, marked their im-

patience for the moment when they might bring their wares in. This was thought by Nehemiah to be unseemly, and to have an irreligious tendency.

22. *I commanded the Levites*] At first Nehemiah had employed his own retinue (*v.* 19) in the work of keeping the gates. He now assigned the duty to the Levites, as one which properly belonged to them, since the object of the regulation was the due observance of the Sabbath.

24. *the speech of Ashdod*] The Philistine language, which was akin to that of Egypt. *according to the language of each people*] The children spoke a mixed dialect, half Philistine, half Hebrew.

30 covenant of the priesthood, and of the Levites. *p*Thus cleansed
 I them from all strangers, and *q*appointed the wards of the priests
31 and the Levites, every one in his business; and for *r*the wood
 offering, at times appointed, and for the firstfruits. *s*Remember me, O my God, for good.

p ch. 10. 30.
q ch. 12. 1,
&c.
r ch. 10. 31.
s ver. 14, 22.

---

30. *the wards*] Rather, "the **offices** or observances." Nehemiah's arrangement is
probably that described in xi. 10-22.

ESTHER.

INTRODUCTION.

The Book of Esther is entitled by the Jews, " the volume of Esther," or simply " the volume." Anciently it was always written on a separate roll, which was read through at the feast of Purim. The Greek translators retained only " Esther," which thus became the ordinary title among Christians.

1. There is much controversy concerning the date of " Esther." The extreme minuteness of the details and vividness of the portraits in " Esther " certainly suggest the hand of a contemporary far more decidedly than any occasional expressions suggest a composer who lived long after the events commemorated : and the tone of the Book is in accord with the history which it narrates, and is not unlike that of Zechariah. Therefore, on the whole, there is no sufficient ground for placing the composition of Esther later than that of Chronicles, Ezra, and Nehemiah, or the time of Artaxerxes Longimanus. On the other hand, there is no ground for regarding Esther as earlier than the other post-Captivity Historical Books—much less for placing it in the reign of Xerxes. Assuming Ahasuerus to be Xerxes (see § 3), it may be said that both the opening sentence and the conclusion of the work indicate that the reign of Xerxes was over. Consequently the earliest date that can reasonably be assigned to the Book is B.C. 464 ; and it is, on the whole,

most probable that it was composed twenty or thirty years later (B.C. 444–434).

2. There are no means of determining who was the author of "Esther." He was not Ezra. He may have been Mordecai, or, more probably, a younger contemporary of Mordecai's.

The author, whoever he was, almost certainly wrote in Persia, where he had access to the royal archives, which contained an account, more or less full, of the transactions he was desirous of recording. Much also must have been derived from personal observation,[1] and from communications with Mordecai and (perhaps) Esther.[2]

The Book is more purely a Historical Book than any other in Scripture. Its main scope is simply to give an account of the circumstances under which the Feast of Purim was instituted. The absence of the name of God, and the slightness of the religious and didactic elements are marked characteristics. The author's Persian breeding, together probably with other circumstances, has prevented his sharing the ordinary Jewish

---

[1] As the description of Susa (i. 5, 6), that of the royal posts (viii. 10, 14), of Mordecai's apparel (do. 15), and the like.

[2] E.g. The genealogy of Mordecai (ii. 5), his private communications with Esther (do. 10, 11, 20, 22) and Hatach (iv. 6–16).

spirit of local attachment, while at the same time it has taught him a reticence with respect to the doctrines of his religion very unusual with his countrymen.

The narrative is striking and graphic ; the style remarkably chaste and simple ; and the sentences clear and unambiguous. The vocabulary, on the contrary, is, as might have been expected, not altogether pure, a certain number of Persian words being employed,[3] and also a few terms characteristic of the later Hebrew or " Chaldee " dialect.

3. The authenticity of the history of Esther has been impugned ; but the main circumstances of the narrative, which at first sight appear improbable, are not so if the peculiarly extravagant and capricious character of the Persian monarch be taken into account. Etymologically, the name Ahasuerus is identical with the Persian *Khshay-arsha* and the Greek Xerxes ; and it is to this particular Persian monarch that the portrait of Ahasuerus exhibits a striking similarity. The chronological notices in the work also exactly fit this monarch's history ; and the entire representation of the Court and kingdom is suitable to his time and

character. That we have no direct profane confirmation of the narrative of Esther must be admitted, for the identity of Mordecai with Matacas (see ii. 5) is too doubtful to be relied upon ; but that we have none, is sufficiently accounted for by the fact that the accounts of the reign of Xerxes after his sixth year, and more particularly of his domestic life, are scanty in the extreme, the native records being silent, and the Greek writers concerning themselves almost entirely with those public events which bore upon the history of Greece. " Esther " is, in fact, the sole authority for the period and circumstances of which it treats ; if untrue, it might have easily been proved to be untrue at the time when it was published, by reference to the extant " book of the chronicles of the kings of Media and Persia," which it quotes (ii. 23, x. 2). It has, moreover, always been regarded by the Jews as an authentic account of the great deliverance which they celebrate annually by the feast of Purim.

4. In the Septuagint version occur " additions " to Esther consisting of five principal passages.[4]

Their unauthenticity is very evi-

---

[3] The language of Esther is even more impregnated with Persian than that of Ezra. Several Persian words, as *akhashdarpan*, *genez (g'naz)*, *iggereth (iggera)*, and *pithgam (pithgama)*, are common to both Books. In addition to these, Esther has, besides some words of doubtful origin, the following list of terms, almost certainly Persian :—*akhashtĕranim*, "royal ;" *karpas*, "cotton ;" *kether* " crown ;" *partĕmim*, "nobles ;" *pathshĕgen*, "a copy, a transcript ;" and *pûr*, "the lot."

[4] 1. The first is introductory. It is dated in the second year of Ahasuerus, and contains (*a*) the pedigree of Mordecai, an anticipation of ii. 5 ; (*b*) a dream which he is supposed to have

had ; (*c*) an account of the conspiracy of the two eunuchs and Mordecai's discovery of it; (*d*) a statement that Mordecai was at once rewarded with gifts ; and (*e*) a statement that Haman wished ill to Mordecai and his people on account of the affair of the eunuchs. 2. The second occurs after iii. 13, and consists of a pretended translation of the letter sent out by Ahasuerus at the request of Haman. 3. The third follows on the close of ch. iv., and comprises (*a*) a long prayer ascribed to Mordecai ; (*b*) another still longer prayer ascribed to Esther; and (*c*) an expanded account of Esther's venturing before the king unsummoned, in lieu of v. 1, 2. 4. The

dent. They contradict the original document, and are quite different in tone and style from the rest of the Book.

The principal intention of the " additions " is clear enough. They aim at giving a thoroughly religious character to a work in which, as originally written, the religious element was latent or only just perceptible. On the whole we may conclude that the Greek book of Esther, as we have it, was composed in the following way :— first a translation was made of the Hebrew text, honest for the most part, but with a few very short additions and omissions ; then the markedly religious portions were added, the opening passage, the prayers of Mordecai and Esther, the exordium to ch. v., the religious touches in ch. vi. (*vv.* 1 and 13) ; and the concluding verses of ch. x. Finally, the " letters of Ahasuerus " were composed by a writer more familiar than most Hellenists with the true spirit of the Greek tongue, and these, being accepted as genuine, were inserted in chs. iii. and viii.

---

fourth is interposed between *vv.* 13 and 14 of ch. viii., and consists of a pretended copy of the letter sent out in the king's name by Mordecai. 5. The fifth and last occurs at the close of ch. x. It comprises (*a*) Mordecai's application of his dream to the events ; (*b*) his appointment of the days of Purim as a permanent festival ; and (*c*) an epilogue stating that the Greek version of Esther was brought (to Alexandria) in the fourth year of Ptolemy and Cleopatra by a certain Dositheus, a priest, and was said by him to have been translated by a certain Lysimachus, of Jerusalem.

THE BOOK

OF

ESTHER.

a Ezra 1. 6.
Dan. 9. 1.
b ch. 8. 9.
c Dan. 6. 1.
d 1 Kin. 1.16.
e Neh. 1. 1.
f Gen. 40. 20.
ch. 2. 18.
Mark 6. 21.

g See ch. 7. 8.
Ezek. 23. 41.
Amos 2. 8.
& 6. 4.

CHAP. 1. NOW it came to pass in the days of *a*Ahasuerus, (this is Ahasuerus which reigned, *b*from India even unto Ethiopia, 2 *c*over an hundred and seven and twenty provinces:) *that* in those days, when the king Ahasuerus *d*sat on the throne of his 3 kingdom, which *was* in *e*Shushan the palace, in the third year of his reign, he *f*made a feast unto all his princes and his servants; the power of Persia and Media, the nobles and princes of the 4 provinces, *being* before him: when he shewed the riches of his glorious kingdom and the honour of his excellent majesty many 5 days, *even* an hundred and fourscore days. ¶And when these days were expired, the king made a feast unto all the people that were ¹present in Shushan the palace, both unto great and small, seven days, in the court of the garden of the king's 6 palace; *where were* white, green, and ²blue, *hangings*, fastened with cords of fine linen and purple to silver rings and pillars of marble: *g*the beds *were of* gold and silver, upon a pave-7 ment ³of red, and blue, and white, and black, marble. And they gave *them* drink in vessels of gold, (the vessels being diverse one from another,) and ⁴royal wine in abundance, ⁵according 8 to the state of the king. And the drinking *was* according to the law; none did compel: for so the king had appointed to all the officers of his house, that they should do according to every 9 man's pleasure. Also Vashti the queen made a feast for the women *in* the royal house which *belonged* to king Ahasuerus.

---

¹ Heb. *found.*
² Or, *violet.*
³ Or, *of porphyre, and marble, and alabaster, and stone of blue colour.*
⁴ Heb. *wine of the kingdom.*
⁵ Heb. *according to the hand of the king.*

I. 1. *Ahasuerus*]. Xerxes, the son of Darius Hystaspis. His empire is rightly described as from India even unto Ethiopia. The satrapies of Darius Hystaspis reached 29 in number, and the nations under Xerxes were about 60. The 127 "provinces" include probably "sub-satrapies" and other smaller divisions of the great governments.

3. *in the third year*]. In this year, B.C. 483, Xerxes assembled the governors of provinces at Susa, in connexion with his contemplated expedition against Greece.

the nobles] Lit. "the first men." The Hebrew word used is one adopted from the Persian.

5. Feasts on this extensive scale were not unusual in the East. Cyrus is said on one occasion to have feasted "all the Persians." Even ordinarily, the later Persian monarchs entertained at their table 15,000 persons.

6. Rather, "where was an **awning of fine white cotton and violet**." White and blue (or violet) were the royal colours in Persia. Such awnings as are here described were very suitable to the pillared halls and porches

of a Persian summer-palace, and especially to the situation of that of Susa.

the beds] Rather, "**couches**" or "**sofas**," on which the guests reclined at meals.

a pavement &c.] See margin. It is generally agreed that the four substances named are stones; but to identify the stones, or even their colours, is difficult.

8. *according to the law*] An exception to the ordinary practice of compulsory drinking had been made on this occasion by the king's order.

9. *Vashti*] If Ahasuerus be Xerxes, Vashti should be Amestris, whom the Greeks regarded as the only legitimate wife of that monarch, and who was certainly married to him before he ascended the throne. The name may be explained either as a corruption of Amestris, or as a title, *vahishta*, (Sanskr. *vasishta*, the superlative of *vasu*, "sweet"); and it may be supposed that the disgrace recorded (*vv.* 19–21, see note) was only temporary; Amestris in the later part of Xerxes' reign recovering her former dignity.

10 ¶ On the seventh day, when *the heart of the king was merry with wine, he commanded Mehuman, Biztha, *Harbona, Bigtha, and Abagtha, Zethar, and Carcas, the seven [1] chamberlains that 11 served in the presence of Ahasuerus the king, to bring Vashti the queen before the king with the crown royal, to shew the people and the princes her beauty: for she *was* [2] fair to look on. 12 But the queen Vashti refused to come at the king's command- ment [3] by *his* chamberlains: therefore was the king very wroth, 13 and his anger burned in him. ¶ Then the king said to the *k*wise men, *l*which knew the times, (for so *was* the king's 14 manner toward all that knew law and judgment: and the next unto him *was* Carshena, Shethar, Admatha, Tarshish, Meres, Marsena, *and* Memucan, the *m*seven princes of Persia and Media, *n*which saw the king's face, *and* which sat the first in the king- 15 dom;) [4] What shall we do unto the queen Vashti according to law, because she hath not performed the commandment of 16 the king Ahasuerus by the chamberlains? And Memucan answered before the king and the princes, Vashti the queen hath not done wrong to the king only, but also to all the princes, and to all the people that *are* in all the provinces of 17 the king Ahasuerus. For *this* deed of the queen shall come abroad unto all women, so that they shall *o*despise their hus- bands in their eyes, when it shall be reported, The king Ahasuerus commanded Vashti the queen to be brought in before 18 him, but she came not. *Likewise* shall the ladies of Persia and Media say this day unto all the king's princes, which have heard of the deed of the queen. Thus *shall there arise* too much con- 19 tempt and wrath. [5] If it please the king, let there go a royal commandment [6] from him, and let it be written among the laws of the Persians and the Medes, [7] that it be not altered, That Vashti come no more before king Ahasuerus; and let the king 20 give her royal estate [8] unto another that is better than she. And when the king's decree which he shall make shall be published throughout all his empire, (for it is great,) all the wives shall *p*give to their husbands honour, both to great and small. 21 ¶ And the saying [9]pleased the king and the princes; and the 22 king did according to the word of Memucan: for he sent letters

h 2 Sam. 13. 28.
i ch. 7. 9.

k Jer. 10. 7.
Dan. 2. 12.
Matt. 2. 1.
l 1 Chr. 12. 32.
m Ezra 7. 14.
n 2 Kin. 25. 19.

o Eph. 5. 33.

p Eph. 5. 33.
Col. 3. 18.
1 Pet. 3. 1.

[1] Or, *eunuchs.*
[2] Heb. *good of countenance.*
[3] Heb. *which* was *by the hand of* his *eunuchs.*
[4] Heb. *What to do.*
[5] Heb. *If it be good with the king.*
[6] Heb. *from before him.*
[7] Heb. *that it pass not away,* ch. 8. 8. Dan. 6.
8. 12. 15.
[8] Heb. *unto her companion.*
[9] Heb. *was good in the eyes of the king.*

11. *to bring Vashti the queen*] This command, though contrary to Persian cus- toms, is not out of harmony with the character of Xerxes; and is evidently re- lated as something strange and unusual. Otherwise the queen would not have refused to come.

13. *wise men &c.*] Not "astrologers," who were unknown in Persia; but rather men of practical wisdom, who knew the facts and customs of former times.

for so was the king's manner] Some render, "for so was the king's **business** laid before all that knew law &c."

14. In Marsena we may perhaps recog- nise the famous Mardonius, and in Adma- tha, Xerxes' uncle, Artabanus.

the seven princes] There were seven fa-

milies of the first rank in Persia, from which alone the king could take his wives. Their chiefs were entitled to have free access to the monarch's person. See marg. ref. note.

18. Translate — "Likewise shall the princesses of Persia and Media, which have heard of the deed of the queen, say this day unto all the king's princes."

19. *that it be not altered*] Cp. marg. reff. This was the theory. Practically, the mo- narch, if he chose, could always dispense with the law. It was therefore quite within his power to restore Vashti to her queenly dignity notwithstanding the present decree, if he so pleased.

22. *he sent letters*] The Persian system of posts incidentally noticed in the present

q ch. 8. 9.

r Eph. 5. 22,
23, 24.
1 Tim. 2. 12.

a ch. 1.19,20.

b 2 Kin. 24.
14, 15.
2 Chr. 36.
10. 20.
Jer. 24. 1.

c ver. 15.

into all the king's provinces, *q*into every province according to the writing thereof, and to every people after their language, that every man should *r*bear rule in his own house, and [1] that *it* should be published according to the language of every people.

CHAP. 2. AFTER these things, when the wrath of king Ahasuerus was appeased, he remembered Vashti, and what she had done, 2 and *a*what was decreed against her. Then said the king's servants that ministered unto him, Let there be fair young virgins 3 sought for the king: and let the king appoint officers in all the provinces of his kingdom, that they may gather together all the fair young virgins unto Shushan the palace, to the house of the women, [2]unto the custody of [3]Hege the king's chamberlain, keeper of the women; and let their things for purification be 4 given *them*: and let the maiden which pleaseth the king be queen instead of Vashti. And the thing pleased the king; and 5 he did so. ¶ *Now* in Shushan the palace there was a certain Jew, whose name *was* Mordecai, the son of Jair, the son of 6 Shimei, the son of Kish, a Benjamite; *b*who had been carried away from Jerusalem with the captivity which had been carried away with [4]Jeconiah king of Judah, whom Nebuchadnezzar the 7 king of Babylon had carried away. And he [5]brought up Hadassah, that *is*, Esther, *c*his uncle's daughter: for she had

---

[1] Heb. *that one should publish it according to the language of his people.*

[2] Heb. *unto the hand.*
[3] Or, *Hegai*, ver. 8.

[4] Or, *Jehoiachin*, 2 Kin. 24. 6.
[5] Heb. *nourished*, Eph.6.4.

Book (iii. 12–15; viii. 9–14), is in entire harmony with the accounts of Herodotus and Xenophon.

into every province according to the writing thereof] The practice of the Persians to address proclamations to the subject-nations in their own speech, and not merely in the language of the conqueror, is illustrated by the bilingual and trilingual inscriptions of the Achæmenian monarchs, from Cyrus to Artaxerxes Ochus, each inscription being of the nature of a proclamation.

The decree was not unnecessary. The undue influence of women in domestic, and even in public, matters is a feature of the ancient Persian monarchy. Atossa completely ruled Darius. Xerxes himself was, in his later years, shamefully subject to Amestris. The example of the court would naturally infect the people. The decree therefore would be a protest, even if ineffectual, against a real and growing evil.

and that it should be published &c.] Render, "*and speak the language of his own people;*" in the sense that the wife's language, if different from her husband's, should in no case be allowed to prevail in the household.

II. 1–11. These events must belong to the time between the great assembly held at Susa in Xerxes' third year (B.C. 483), and the departure of the monarch on his expedition against Greece in his fifth year, B.C. 481.

3. *the house of the women*] i.e. the "gynæceon," or "haram"—always an essential part of an Oriental palace (Cp. 1 K. vii. 8).

In the Persian palaces it was very extensive, since the monarchs maintained, besides their legitimate wives, as many as 300 or 400 concubines (cp. *v.* 14).

5. Mordecai, the eunuch (*vv.*7,11), has been conjectured to be the same as Matacas, who, according to Ctesias, was the most powerful of the eunuchs during the latter portion of the reign of Xerxes. Mordecai's line of descent is traced from a certain Kish, carried off by Nebuchadnezzar in B.C. 598—the year of Jeconiah's captivity—who was his great-grandfather. The four generations, Kish, Shimei, Jair, Mordecai, correspond to the known generations in other cases, *e.g.* :—

High-priests.	Kings of Persia.	Royal stock of Judah.
Seraiah	Cambyses	Jeconiah
Jozadak	Cyrus	Salathiel
Jeshua	Darius	Zerubbabel
Joiakim	Xerxes	Hananiah

The age of Mordecai at the accession of Xerxes may probably have been about 30 or 40; that of Esther, his first cousin, about 20.

7. Hadassah ("myrtle") would seem to have been the Hebrew, and Esther the Persian, name of the damsel. Esther is

neither father nor mother, and the maid *was* [1] fair and beautiful ;
whom Mordecai, when her father and mother were dead, took for
8 his own daughter.   ¶ So it came to pass, when the king's commandment and his decree was heard, and when many maidens
were [d] gathered together unto Shushan the palace, to the cus-   *d* ver. 3.
tody of Hegai, that Esther was brought also unto the king's
9 house, to the custody of Hegai, keeper of the women.   And the
maiden pleased him, and she obtained kindness of him ; and he
speedily gave her her [e] things for purification, with [2] such things   *e* ver. 3, 12.
as belonged to her, and seven maidens, *which were* meet to be
given her, out of the king's house : and [3] he preferred her and her
10 maids unto the best *place* of the house of the women.   [f] Esther   *f* ver. 20.
had not shewed her people nor her kindred : for Mordecai had
11 charged her that she should not shew *it*.   And Mordecai walked
every day before the court of the women's house, [4] to know how
12 Esther did, and what should become of her.   ¶ Now when every
maid's turn was come to go in to king Ahasuerus, after that
she had been twelve months, according to the manner of the
women, (for so were the days of their purifications accomplished, *to wit*, six months with oil of myrrh, and six months
with sweet odours, and with *other* things for the purifying of
13 the women ;) then thus came *every* maiden unto the king ; whatsoever she desired was given her to go with her out of the house
14 of the women unto the king's house.   In the evening she went,
and on the morrow she returned into the second house of the
women, to the custody of Shaashgaz, the king's chamberlain,
which kept the concubines : she came in unto the king no more,
except the king delighted in her, and that she were called
15 by name.   ¶ Now when the turn of Esther, [g] the daughter of   *g* ver. 7.
Abihail the uncle of Mordecai, who had taken her for his
daughter, was come to go in unto the king, she required
nothing but what Hegai the king's chamberlain, the keeper
of the women, appointed.   And Esther obtained favour in the
16 sight of all them that looked upon her.   So Esther was taken
unto king Ahasuerus into his house royal in the tenth month,
which *is* the month Tebeth, in the seventh year of his reign.
17 And the king loved Esther above all the women, and she ob-

---

[1] Heb. *fair of form and   [2] Heb. *her portions.*   [4] Heb. *to know the peace.*
good of countenance.*   [3] Heb. *he changed her.*

---

thought to be connected through the Zend
with ἀστήρ, "star." But there is not at present any positive evidence of the existence
in Old Persian of a kindred word.

10. The Persians had no special contempt for the Jews ; but, of course, they
despised more or less all the subject races.
Esther, with her Aryan name, may have
passed for a native Persian.

11. Mordecai occupied, apparently, a
humble place in the royal household.   He
was probably one of the porters or door-
keepers at the main entrance to the palace
(*v.* 21).

14. *the second house of the women*] *i.e.* Esther returned to the "house of the women,"
but not to the same part of it.   She became
an inmate of the "second house," or "house
of the concubines," under the superintendence of a distinct officer, Shaashgaz.

15. *she required nothing*] The other virgins perhaps loaded themselves with precious ornaments of various kinds, necklaces,
bracelets, earrings, anklets, and the like.
Esther let Hegai dress her as he would.

16. Tebeth (cp. the corresponding Egyptian month, *Tobi* or *Tubi*), corresponded
nearly to our January.

in the seventh year of his reign] In December, B.C. 479, or January, B.C. 478.   Xerxes
quitted Sardis for Susa in, or soon after,
September, B.C. 479.   It has been regarded
as a "difficulty" that Vashti's place, declared vacant in B.C. 483, was not supplied
till the end of B.C. 479, four years afterwards.   But as two years out of the four
had been occupied by the Grecian expedition, the objection cannot be considered
very weighty.

tained grace and [1] favour [2]in his sight more than all the virgins; so that he set the royal crown upon her head, and made her queen

h ch. 1. 3.

18 instead of Vashti. Then the king [h] made a great feast unto all his princes and his servants, *even* Esther's feast; and he made a [3] release to the provinces, and gave gifts, according to the state

19 of the king. ¶ And when the virgins were gathered together

i ver. 21.
ch. 3. 2.
k ver. 10.

20 the second time, then Mordecai sat [i]in the king's gate. [k]Esther had not *yet* shewed her kindred nor her people; as Mordecai had charged her : for Esther did the commandment of Mordecai,

21 like as when she was brought up with him. ¶ In those days, while Mordecai sat in the king's gate, two of the king's chamberlains, [4]Bigthan and Teresh, of those which kept [5]the door, were wroth, and sought to lay hand on the king Ahasuerus.

l ch. 6. 2.

22 And the thing was known to Mordecai, [l]who told *it* unto Esther the queen; and Esther certified the king *thereof* in Mordecai's

23 name. And when inquisition was made of the matter, it was found out; therefore they were both hanged on a tree : and it

m ch. 6. 1.

was written in [m]the book of the chronicles before the king.

CHAP. 3. AFTER these things did king Ahasuerus promote Haman

a Num. 24.7.

the son of Hammedatha the [a]Agagite, and advanced him, and

2 set his seat above all the princes that *were* with him. And all

b ch. 2. 19.

the king's servants, that *were* [b]in the king's gate, bowed, and reverenced Haman: for the king had so commanded concerning

c ver. 5.
Ps. 15. 4.

3 him. But Mordecai [c]bowed not, nor did *him* reverence. Then the king's servants, which *were* in the king's gate, said unto

d ver. 2.

Mordecai, Why transgressest thou the [d]king's commandment ?

4 Now it came to pass, when they spake daily unto him, and he hearkened not unto them, that they told Haman, to see whether Mordecai's matters would stand : for he had told them that he

e ver. 2.
ch. 5. 9.
f Dan. 3. 19.

5 *was* a Jew. And when Haman saw that Mordecai [e]bowed not,

6 nor did him reverence, then was Haman [f]full of wrath. And he

g Ps. 83. 4.

thought scorn to lay hands on Mordecai alone; for they had shewed him the people of Mordecai: wherefore Haman [g]sought

---

[1] Or, *kindness*.   [3] Heb. *rest*.   [5] Heb. *the threshold*.
[2] Heb. *before him*.   [4] Or, *Bigthana*, ch. 6. 2.

---

18. *a release*] Either remission of taxation, or of military service, or of both.

19. *when the virgins* &c.] Rather, "when virgins" &c. The words begin a new paragraph. There was a second collection of virgins (after that of v. 8), and it was at the time of this second collection that Mordecai had the good fortune to save the king's life.

21. Conspiracies inside the palace were ordinary occurrences in Persia. Xerxes was ultimately murdered by Artabanus, the captain of the guard, and Aspamitras, a chamberlain and eunuch.

23. *both hanged on a tree*] i.e. "crucified" or "impaled"—the ordinary punishment of rebels and traitors in Persia.

the book of the chronicles] Ctesias drew his Persian history from them, and they are often glanced at by Herodotus.

III. **1.** The name, Haman, is probably the same as the classical Omanes, and in ancient Persian, *Umana*, an exact equivalent of the Greek "Eumenes." Hammedatha is perhaps the same as *Madâta* or

Mahadâta, an old Persian name signifying "given by (or to) the moon."

the Agagite] The Jews generally understand by this expression "the descendant of Agag," the Amalekite monarch of 1 Sam. xv. Haman, however, by his own name, and the names of his sons (ix. 7-9) and his father, would seem to have been a genuine Persian.

The classical writers make no mention of Haman's advancement ; but their notices of the reign of Xerxes after B.C. 479 are exceedingly scanty.

2. Mordecai probably refused the required prostration, usual though it was, on religious grounds. Hence his opposition led on to his confession that he was a Jew (v. 4).

4. *whether Mordecai's matters would stand*] Rather, "whether Mordecai's **words** would **hold good**"—whether, that is, his excuse, that he was a Jew, would be allowed as a valid reason for his refusal.

6. *to destroy all the Jews*] In the East massacres of a people, a race, a class, have

to destroy all the Jews that *were* throughout the whole kingdom
7 of Ahasuerus, *even* the people of Mordecai. ¶ In the first month,
that *is*, the month Nisan, in the twelfth year of king Ahasuerus,
h they cast Pur, that *is*, the lot, before Haman from day to day,   *h* ch. 9. 24.
and from month to month, *to* the twelfth *month*, that *is*, the
8 month Adar. And Haman said unto king Ahasuerus, There is
a certain people scattered abroad and dispersed among the people
in all the provinces of thy kingdom; and *i* their laws *are* diverse   *i* Ezra 4. 13.
from all people; neither keep they the king's laws: therefore it   Acts 16. 20.
9 *is* not *1* for the king's profit to suffer them. If it please the king,
let it be written *2* that they may be destroyed: and I will *3* pay
ten thousand talents of silver to the hands of those that have
the charge of the business, to bring *it* into the king's treasuries.
10 And the king *k* took *l* his ring from his hand, and gave it unto   *k* Gen. 41. 42.
Haman the son of Hammedatha the Agagite, the Jews' *4* enemy.   *l* ch. 8. 2, 8.
11 And the king said unto Haman, The silver *is* given to thee, the
people also, to do with them as it seemeth good to thee.
12 ¶ *m* Then were the king's *5* scribes called on the thirteenth day of   *m* ch. 8. 9.
the first month, and there was written according to all that
Haman had commanded unto the king's lieutenants, and to the
governors that *were* over every province, and to the rulers of
every people of every province *n* according to the writing thereof,   *n* ch. 1. 22.
and *to* every people after their language; *o* in the name of king   & 8. 9.
13 Ahasuerus was it written, and sealed with the king's ring. And   *o* 1 Kin.21.8.
the letters were *p* sent by posts into all the king's provinces,   ch. 8. 8, 10.
to destroy, to kill, and to cause to perish, all Jews, both young   *p* ch. 8. 10.
and old, little children and women, *q* in one day, *even* upon the   *q* ch. 8. 12,
    &c.

1 Heb. *meet*, or, *equal*.   *3* Heb. *weigh*.   *5* Or, *secretaries*.
2 Heb. *to destroy them*.   *4* Or, *oppressor*, ch. 7. 6.

---

at all times been among the incidents of
history, and would naturally present themselves to the mind of a statesman. The
Magophonia, or the great massacre of the
Magi at the accession of Darius Hystaspis,
was an event not then fifty years old, and
was commemorated annually. A massacre
of the Scythians had occurred about a century previously.

7. *In the first month* &c.] *i.e.* in March or
April of B.C. 474.

"Pur" is supposed to be an Old Persian
word etymologically connected with the
Latin *pars*, and signifying "part" or "lot."
The practice of casting lots to obtain a
lucky day obtains still in the East, and is
probably extremely ancient. A lot seems
to have been cast, or a throw of some kind
made, for each day of the month and each
month of the year. The day and month
which obtained the best throws were then
selected. Assyrian calendars note lucky
and unlucky days as early as the eighth
century B.C. Lots were in use both among
the Oriental and the classical nations from
a remote antiquity.

"Adar," the twelfth month, corresponds
nearly to our March. It seems to have derived its name from *âdar*, "splendour,"
because of the brightness of the sun and the
flowers at that time.

9. *ten thousand talents of silver*] Accord-

ing to Herodotus, the regular revenue of
the Persian king consisted of 14,560 silver
talents; so that, if the same talent is intended, Haman's offer would have exceeded
two-thirds of a year's revenue (or two and
a half millions sterling). Another Persian
subject, Pythius, once offered to present
Xerxes with four millions of gold darics, or
about four millions and a half of our money.

11. *The silver is given to thee*] Some understand this to mean that Xerxes refused
the silver which Haman had offered to him;
but the passage is better explained as a
grant to him of all the property of such
Jews as should be executed (*v.* 13).

12. *on the thirteenth day*] Haman had,
apparently (cp. *v.* 7 with *v.* 13), obtained by
his use of the lot the 13th day of Adar as
the lucky day for destroying the Jews.
This may have caused him to fix on the 13th
day of another month for the commencement of his enterprise. The Jews throughout the empire had thus from nine to eleven
months' warning of the peril which threatened them.

13. The Jews at present keep three days,
the 13th, the 14th, and the 15th of Adar, as
connected with "the feast of Purim;" but
they make the 13th a fast, commemorative
of the fast of Esther (iv. 16), and keep the
feast itself on the 14th and 15th.

thirteenth *day* of the twelfth month, which *is* the month Adar,

14 and *r*to take the spoil of them for a prey. *s*The copy of the writing for a commandment to be given in every province was published unto all people, that they should be ready against
15 that day. The posts went out, being hastened by the king's commandment, and the decree was given in Shushan the palace.

And the king and Haman sat down to drink; but *t*the city Shushan was perplexed.

CHAP. 4. WHEN Mordecai perceived all that was done, Mordecai

*a*rent his clothes, and put on sackcloth *b*with ashes, and went out into the midst of the city, and *c*cried with a loud and a bitter
2 cry; and came even before the king's gate: for none *might* enter
3 into the king's gate clothed with sackcloth. And in every province, whithersoever the king's commandment and his decree came, *there was* great mourning among the Jews, and fasting, and weeping, and wailing; and ¹many lay in sackcloth and
4 ashes. ¶ So Esther's maids and her ²chamberlains came and told *it* her. Then was the queen exceedingly grieved; and she sent raiment to clothe Mordecai, and to take away his sackcloth from
5 him: but he received *it* not. Then called Esther for Hatach, *one* of the king's chamberlains, ³whom he had appointed to attend upon her, and gave him a commandment to Mordecai, to
6 know what it *was*, and why it *was*. So Hatach went forth to Mordecai unto the street of the city, which *was* before the king's
7 gate. And Mordecai told him of all that had happened unto

him, and of *d*the sum of the money that Haman had promised to pay to the king's treasuries for the Jews, to destroy them.

8 Also he gave him *e*the copy of the writing of the decree that was given at Shushan to destroy them, to shew *it* unto Esther, and to declare *it* unto her, and to charge her that she should go in unto the king, to make supplication unto him, and to make re-
9 quest before him for her people. And Hatach came and told
10 Esther the words of Mordecai. ¶ Again Esther spake unto
11 Hatach, and gave him commandment unto Mordecai; all the king's servants, and the people of the king's provinces, do know, that whosoever, whether man or woman, shall come unto the

king into *f*the inner court, who is not called, *g*there is one law of his to put *him* to death, except such *h*to whom the king shall hold out the golden sceptre, that he may live: but I have not
12 been called to come in unto the king these thirty days. And they
13 told to Mordecai Esther's words. ¶ Then Mordecai commanded to answer Esther, Think not with thyself that thou shalt escape

---

¹ Heb. *sackcloth and ashes were laid under many,*   ² Heb. *eunuchs.*   Isai. 58. 5. Dan. 9. 3.   ³ Heb. *whom he had set before her.*

---

15 *Shushan was perplexed*] Susa was now the capital of Persia, and the main residence of the Persians of high rank. These, being attached to the religion of Zoroaster, would naturally sympathise with the Jews, and be disturbed at their threatened destruction. Even apart from this bond of union, the decree was sufficiently strange and ominous to "perplex" thoughtful citizens.

IV. 2. *none might enter into the king's gate clothed with sackcloth*] This law is not elsewhere mentioned; but its principle—that nothing of evil omen is to be obtruded on

the monarch—has been recognized throughout the East in all ages.

4. *Esther's maids...told it her*] Esther's nationality and her relationship to Mordecai were probably by this time known to her attendants, though still concealed from the king. See vii. 4.

11. *the golden sceptre*] In all the numerous representations of Persian kings at Persepolis the monarch holds a long tapering staff (probably the sceptre of Esther) in his right hand. It was death to intrude on the privacy of the Persian king uninvited.

14 in the king's house, more than all the Jews. For if thou altogether holdest thy peace at this time, *then* shall there [1] enlargement and deliverance arise to the Jews from another place ; but thou and thy father's house shall be destroyed : and who knoweth whether thou art come to the kingdom for *such* a time as this ?

15, 16 ¶ Then Esther bade *them* return Mordecai *this answer*, Go, gather together all the Jews that are [2] present in Shushan, and fast ye for me, and neither eat nor drink *i* three days, night or day : I also and my maidens will fast likewise ; and so will I go in unto the king, which *is* not according to the law : *k* and if I 17 perish, I perish. So Mordecai [3] went his way, and did according to all that Esther had commanded him.

i See ch. 5.1.

k See Gen. 43. 14.

CHAP. 5. NOW it came to pass *a* on the third day, that Esther put on *her* royal *apparel*, and stood in *b* the inner court of the king's house, over against the king's house : and the king sat upon his royal throne in the royal house, over against the gate of the 2 house. And it was so, when the king saw Esther the queen standing in the court, *that c* she obtained favour in his sight : and *d* the king held out to Esther the golden sceptre that *was* in his hand. So Esther drew near, and touched the top of the 3 sceptre. Then said the king unto her, What wilt thou, queen Esther ? and what *is* thy request ? *e* it shall be even given thee 4 to the half of the kingdom. And Esther answered, If *it seem* good unto the king, let the king and Haman come this day unto 5 the banquet that I have prepared for him. Then the king said, Cause Haman to make haste, that he may do as Esther hath said. So the king and Haman came to the banquet that Esther 6 had prepared. ¶ *f* And the king said unto Esther at the banquet *f* of wine, *g* What *is* thy petition ? and it shall be granted thee : and what *is* thy request ? even to the half of the kingdom it shall 7 be performed. Then answered Esther, and said, My petition 8 and my request *is* ; If I have found favour in the sight of the king, and if it please the king to grant my petition, and [4] to perform my request, let the king and Haman come to the banquet that I shall prepare for them, and I will do to morrow as the

a See ch. 4. 16.
b See ch. 4. 11.
& ch. 6. 4.

c Prov. 21. 1.
d ch. 4. 11. & 8. 4.

e So Mark 6. 23.

f ch. 7. 2.
g ch. 9. 12.

---

[1] Heb. *respiration*, Job 9. 18.
[2] Heb. *found*.
[3] Heb. *passed*.
[4] Heb. *to do*.

---

14. *from another place*] *i.e.* "from some other quarter." Mordecai probably concluded from the prophetical Scriptures that God would not allow His people to be destroyed before His purposes with respect to them were accomplished, and was therefore satisfied that deliverance would arise from one quarter or another.

thou and thy father's house shall be destroyed] *i.e.* "a divine vengeance will overtake thee and thine, if thou neglectest thy plain duty." Though the *name* of God is not contained in the Book of Esther, there is in this verse distinct tacit allusion to God's promises, and to the direction of human events by Divine Providence.

16. Again the religious element shews itself. Esther's fast could have no object but to obtain God's favour and protection in the dangerous course on which she was about to enter.

V. 1. *over against the gate*] This is the

usual situation of the throne in the "throneroom" of an Oriental palace. The monarch, from his raised position, can see into the court through the doorway opposite to him, which is kept open.

3. *it shall be even given thee* &c.] Xerxes, on another occasion, when pleased with one of his wives, offered to grant her any request whatever, without limitation. Cp. marg. ref.

4. Esther seems to have been afraid to make her real request of Xerxes too abruptly. She concluded that the king would understand that she had a real petition in the background, and would recur to it, as in fact he did (*v.* 6, vii. 2).

6. *the banquet of wine*] After the meats were removed, it was customary in Persia to continue the banquet for a considerable time with fruits and wine. During this part of the feast, the king renewed his offer.

9 king hath said.   ¶ Then went Haman forth that day joyful and
with a glad heart : but when Haman saw Mordecai in the king's
gate, [h]that he stood not up, nor moved for him, he was full of
10 indignation against Mordecai.   Nevertheless Haman [i]refrained
himself : and when he came home, he sent and [l]called for his
11 friends, and Zeresh his wife.   And Haman told them of the
glory of his riches, and [k]the multitude of his children, and all
the things wherein the king had promoted him, and how he had
[l]advanced him above the princes and servants of the king.
12 Haman said moreover, Yea, Esther the queen did let no man
come in with the king unto the banquet that she had prepared
but myself ; and to morrow am I invited unto her also with the
13 king.   Yet all this availeth me nothing, so long as I see Mor-
14 decai the Jew sitting at the king's gate.   Then said Zeresh his
wife and all his friends unto him, Let a [2][m]gallows be made of
fifty cubits high, and to morrow [n]speak thou unto the king that
Mordecai may be hanged thereon : then go thou in merrily with
the king unto the banquet. And the thing pleased Haman ; and
he caused [o]the gallows to be made.

CHAP. 6.   ON that night [3]could not the king sleep, and he commanded to bring [a]the book of records of the chronicles ; and
2 they were read before the king.   And it was found written, that
Mordecai had told of [4]Bigthana and Teresh, two of the king's
chamberlains, the keepers of the [5]door, who sought to lay hand
3 on the king Ahasuerus.   ¶ And the king said, What honour and
dignity hath been done to Mordecai for this ? Then said the
king's servants that ministered unto him, There is nothing done
4 for him.   And the king said, Who *is* in the court ? Now Haman
was come into [b]the outward court of the king's house, [c]to speak
unto the king to hang Mordecai on the gallows that he had pre-
5 pared for him.   And the king's servants said unto him, Behold,
Haman standeth in the court. And the king said, Let him come
6 in.   So Haman came in.   And the king said unto him, What
shall be done unto the man [6]whom the king delighteth to honour ?
Now Haman thought in his heart, To whom would the king
7 delight to do honour more than to myself ?   And Haman answered the king, For the man [7]whom the king delighteth to
8 honour, [8]let the royal apparel be brought [9]which the king *useth*

Margin references
[h] ch. 3. 5.
[i] So 2 Sam. 13. 22.
[k] ch. 9. 7, &c.
[l] ch. 3. 1.
[m] ch. 7. 9.
[n] ch. 6. 4.
[o] ch. 7. 10.
[a] ch. 2. 23.
[b] See ch. 5. 1.
[c] ch. 5. 14.

Footnotes
[1] Heb. *caused to come.*
[2] Heb. *tree.*
[3] Heb. *the king's sleep fled away.*
[4] Or, *Bigthan,* ch. 2. 21.
[5] Heb. *threshold.*
[6] Heb. *in whose honour the king delighteth.*
[7] Heb. *in whose honour the king delighteth.*
[8] Heb. *Let them bring the royal apparel.*
[9] Heb. *wherewith the king clotheth himself.*

---

9. *he stood not up, nor moved for him*] This was undoubtedly a serious breach of Persian etiquette, and may well have angered Haman.

10. *Zeresh*] This name is probably connected with the Zend *zara,* "gold." Cp. the Greek "Chrysis."

11. *the multitude of his children*] Herodotus tells us that, "next to prowess in arms, it was regarded as the greatest proof of manly excellence in Persia to be the father of many sons." Haman had ten sons (marg. ref.)

14. A gallows, in the ordinary sense, is scarcely intended, since hanging was not a Persian punishment. The intention, no doubt, was to crucify (ii. 23 note) or impale

Mordecai ; and the pale or cross was to be 75 feet high, to make the punishment more conspicuous.

speak thou unto the king &c.] Requests for leave to put persons to death were often made to Persian kings by their near relatives, but only rarely by others.

VI. 3. It was a settled principle of the Persian government that "Royal Benefactors" were to receive an adequate reward. The names of such persons were placed on a special roll, and care was taken that they should be properly recompensed, though they sometimes waited for months or years before they were recompensed.

8. The honours here proposed by Haman were such as Persian monarchs rarely

to wear, and ^d the horse that the king rideth upon, and the crown
9 royal which is set upon his head : and let this apparel and horse
be delivered to the hand of one of the king's most noble princes,
that they may array the man *withal* whom the king delighteth
to honour, and ¹bring him on horseback through the street of
the city, ^eand proclaim before him, Thus shall it be done to the
10 man whom the king delighteth to honour. Then the king said
to Haman, Make haste, *and* take the apparel and the horse, as
thou hast said, and do even so to Mordecai the Jew, that sitteth
at the king's gate : ²let nothing fail of all that thou hast spoken.
11 Then took Haman the apparel and the horse, and arrayed Mordecai, and brought him on horseback through the street of the
city, and proclaimed before him, Thus shall it be done unto the
12 man whom the king delighteth to honour. ¶ And Mordecai
came again to the king's gate. But Haman ^fhasted to his house
13 mourning, ^gand having his head covered. And Haman told
Zeresh his wife and all his friends every *thing* that had befallen
him. Then said his wise men and Zeresh his wife unto him, If
Mordecai *be* of the seed of the Jews, before whom thou hast begun to fall, thou shalt not prevail against him, but shalt surely
14 fall before him. And while they *were* yet talking with him,
came the king's chamberlains, and hasted to bring Haman unto
^hthe banquet that Esther had prepared.

CHAP. 7. SO the king and Haman came ³to banquet with Esther
2 the queen. And the king said again unto Esther on the second
day ^aat the banquet of wine, What *is* thy petition, queen Esther ?
and it shall be granted thee : and what *is* thy request? and it
3 shall be performed, *even* to the half of the kingdom. Then
Esther the queen answered and said, If I have found favour in
thy sight, O king, and if it please the king, let my life be given
4 me at my petition, and my people at my request : for we are
^bsold, I and my people, ⁴to be destroyed, to be slain, and to
perish. But if we had been sold for bondmen and bondwomen,
I had held my tongue, although the enemy could not counter-
5 vail the king's damage. Then the king Ahasuerus answered
and said unto Esther the queen, Who is he, and where is he,
6 ⁵that durst presume in his heart to do so? And Esther said,
^cThe adversary and enemy *is* this wicked Haman. Then Haman
7 was afraid ⁷before the king and the queen. ¶ And the king
arising from the banquet of wine in his wrath *went* into the
palace garden : and Haman stood up to make request for his life
to Esther the queen ; for he saw that there was evil determined
8 against him by the king. Then the king returned out of the
palace garden into the place of the banquet of wine ; and Haman

Marginal references:
d 1 Kin.1.33.

e Gen. 41. 13.

f 2 Chr.26.20.
g 2 Sam. 15.
30.
Jer. 14. 3, 4.

h ch. 5. 8.

a ch. 5. 6.

b ch. 3. 9.
& 4. 7.

---

¹ Heb. *cause him to ride.*
² Heb. *suffer not a whit to fall.*
³ Heb. *to drink.*
⁴ Heb. *that they should destroy, and kill, and cause to perish.*
⁵ Heb. *whose heart hath filled him.*
⁶ Heb. *The man adversary.*
⁷ Or, *at the presence of.*

---

allowed to subjects. Each act would have
been a capital offence if done without permission. Still we find Persian monarchs
allowing their subjects in these or similar
acts under certain circumstances.

12. It is quite consonant with Oriental
notions that Mordecai, after receiving the
extraordinary honours assigned him, should
return to the palace and resume his former
humble employment.

VII. 4. The king now learnt, perhaps
for the first time, that his favourite was a
Jewess.

although the enemy &c.] *i.e.* "although the
enemy (Haman) would not (even in that case)
compensate (by his payment to the treasury)
for the king's loss of so many subjects."

8. Like the Greeks and Romans, the
Persians reclined at their meals on sofas or
couches. Haman, in the intensity of his

c ch. 1. 6.

d Job 9. 24.

e ch. 1. 10.

f ch. 5. 14.
Ps. 7. 16.
Prov.11. 5, 6.

g Ps. 37. 35,
36.
Dan. 6. 24.

a ch. 2. 7.

b ch. 3. 10.

c ch. 4. 11.
& 5. 2.

d Neh. 2. 3.
ch. 7. 4.

e ver. 1.
Prov. 13. 22.

f Dan. 6. 8,
12, 15.
g ch. 3. 12.

h ch. 1. 1.

was fallen upon *c*the bed whereon Esther *was*. Then said the king, Will he force the queen also ¹before me in the house? As the word went out of the king's mouth, they *d*covered Haman's face. 9 And *e*Harbonah, one of the chamberlains, said before the king, Behold also, *f*the ²gallows fifty cubits high, which Haman had made for Mordecai, who had spoken good for the king, standeth in the house of Haman. Then the king said, 10 Hang him thereon. So *g*they hanged Haman on the gallows that he had prepared for Mordecai. Then was the king's wrath pacified.

CHAP. 8. ON that day did the king Ahasuerus give the house of Haman the Jews' enemy unto Esther the queen. And Mordecai came before the king; for Esther had told *a*what he *was* unto 2 her. And the king took off *b*his ring, which he had taken from Haman, and gave it unto Mordecai. And Esther set Mordecai 3 over the house of Haman. ¶ And Esther spake yet again before the king, and fell down at his feet, ³and besought him with tears to put away the mischief of Haman the Agagite, and his 4 device that he had devised against the Jews. Then *c*the king held out the golden sceptre toward Esther. So Esther arose, 5 and stood before the king, and said, If it please the king, and if I have found favour in his sight, and the thing *seem* right before the king, and I *be* pleasing in his eyes, let it be written to reverse ⁴the letters devised by Haman the son of Hammedatha the Agagite, ⁵which he wrote to destroy the Jews which *are* in all 6 the king's provinces: for how can I ⁶endure to see *d*the evil that shall come unto my people? or how can I endure to see the 7 destruction of my kindred? Then the king Ahasuerus said unto Esther the queen and to Mordecai the Jew, Behold, *e*I have given Esther the house of Haman, and him they have hanged upon the gallows, because he laid his hand upon the Jews. 8 Write ye also for the Jews, as it liketh you, in the king's name, and seal *it* with the king's ring: for the writing which is written in the king's name, and sealed with the king's ring, *f*may no 9 man reverse. ¶*g*Then were the king's scribes called at that time in the third month, that *is*, the month Sivan, on the three and twentieth *day* thereof; and it was written according to all that Mordecai commanded unto the Jews, and to the lieutenants, and the deputies and rulers of the provinces which *are* *h*from India

¹ Heb. *with me.*
² Heb. *tree.*
³ Heb. *and she wept, and besought him.*
⁴ Heb. *the device.*
⁵ Or, *who wrote.*
⁶ Heb. *be able that I may see.*

supplication, had thrown himself upon the couch at Esther's feet.

they covered Haman's face] The Macedonians and the Romans are known to have commonly muffled the heads of prisoners before executing them. It may have been also a Persian custom.

VIII. 1. *give the house of Haman*] Confiscation of goods accompanied public execution in Persia as in other Oriental countries.

2. *his ring*] i.e. the royal signet by which the decrees of the government were signed.

over the house of Haman] Not only the building and the furniture, but the household—the vast train of attendants of all

kinds that was attached to the residence of a Persian noble.

3. Though Haman was dead, his work was not yet undone. The royal decree had gone forth, and, according to Persian notions, could not be directly recalled or reversed (*v.* 8). Mordecai did not dare, without express permission from the king, to take any steps even to stay execution. And Esther, being in favour, once more took the initiative.

8. *Write...as it liketh you* &c.] [See i. 19 note. Practically, Ahasuerus reversed the "device" of Haman.]

9. Sivan corresponds nearly to our June; it was the second month from the issue of the first edict (iii. 12).

unto Ethiopia, an hundred twenty and seven provinces, unto every province *according to the writing thereof, and unto every people after their language, and to the Jews according to their
10 writing, and according to their language. *And he wrote in the king Ahasuerus' name, and sealed *it* with the king's ring, and sent letters by posts on horseback, *and* riders on mules, camels,
11 *and* young dromedaries: wherein the king granted the Jews which *were* in every city to gather themselves together, and to stand for their life, to destroy, to slay, and to cause to perish, all the power of the people and province that would assault them, *both* little ones and women, and *to take* the spoil of them for a
12 prey, *upon one day in all the provinces of king Ahasuerus, *namely*, upon the thirteenth *day* of the twelfth month, which *is*
13 the month Adar. *The copy of the writing for a commandment to be given in every province *was* ¹published unto all people, and that the Jews should be ready against that day to
14 avenge themselves on their enemies. *So* the posts that rode upon mules *and* camels went out, being hastened and pressed on by the king's commandment. And the decree was given at
15 Shushan the palace. ¶And Mordecai went out from the presence of the king in royal apparel of ²blue and white, and with a great crown of gold, and with a garment of fine linen and
16 purple: and °the city of Shushan rejoiced and was glad. The
17 Jews had ᵖlight, and gladness, and joy, and honour. And in every province, and in every city, whithersoever the king's commandment and his decree came, the Jews had joy and gladness, a feast �q and a good day. And many of the people of the land ʳbecame Jews; for ˢthe fear of the Jews fell upon them.
CHAP. 9. NOW ᵃ in the twelfth month, that *is*, the month Adar, on the thirteenth day of the same, ᵇ when the king's commandment and his decree drew near to be put in execution, in the day that the enemies of the Jews hoped to have power over them, (though it was turned to the contrary, that the Jews ᶜhad rule
2 over them that hated them;) the Jews ᵈgathered themselves together in their cities throughout all the provinces of the king Ahasuerus, to lay hand on such as ᵉsought their hurt: and no man could withstand them; for ᶠthe fear of them fell upon all

Marginal references:
ᵢ ch. 1. 22.
& 3. 12.

ᵏ 1 Kin. 21. 8.
ch. 3. 12, 13.

ᵢ See ch. 9.
10, 15, 16.
ᵐ ch. 3. 13,
&c.
& 9. 1.
ⁿ ch. 3. 14,
15.

° See ch. 3.
15.
Prov. 29. 2.
ᵖ Ps. 97. 11.

q 1 Sam. 25. 8.
ch. 9. 19, 22.
ʳ Ps. 18. 43.
ˢ Gen. 35. 5.
Ex. 15. 16.
Deut. 2. 25.
& 11. 25.
ch. 9. 2.
ᵃ ch. 8. 12.
ᵇ ch. 3. 13.
ᶜ 2 Sam. 22.
41.
ᵈ ch. 8. 11.
& ver. 16.
ᵉ Ps. 71. 13,
24.
ᶠ ch. 8. 17.

¹ Heb. *revealed.*   ² Or, *violet.*

---

10. *riders on mules, camels, and young dromedaries*] Most moderns translate "riders upon *coursers and mules, the offspring of mares;*" but the words translated "mules" and "mares," are of very doubtful signification, since they scarcely occur elsewhere. The real meaning of the clause must remain doubtful; perhaps the true translation is, " riders upon **coursers of the king's stud**, offspring of high-bred steeds." So *v.* 14.

11. This fresh decree allowed the Jews to stand on their defence, and to kill all who attacked them. It has been pronounced incredible, that any king would thus have sanctioned civil war in all the great cities of his empire; but some even of the more sceptical critics allow that *Xerxes* might not improbably have done so.

14. *being hastened*] Between Sivan, the third month (June), when the posts went out, and Adar, the twelfth month (March), when the struggle was to take place, the interval would be one of above eight months; but all haste was made, with the object of their being no misunderstanding.

15. See i. 6 note. The "crown" was not a crown like the king's, but a mere golden band or coronet.

a garment] Or, "an inner robe." The tunic or inner robe of the king was of purple, striped with white.

17. *became Jews*] Joined the nation as proselytes, so casting in their lot with them.

IX. 1. *drew near*] Or, "arrived," or " reached the time" specified (iii. 13, viii. 12).

3 people. And all the rulers of the provinces, and the lieutenants,
and the deputies, and [1] officers of the king, helped the Jews;
4 because the fear of Mordecai fell upon them. For Mordecai
was great in the king's house, and his fame went out throughout all the provinces: for this man Mordecai [g] waxed greater
5 and greater. ¶ Thus the Jews smote all their enemies with the
stroke of the sword, and slaughter, and destruction, and did
6 [2] what they would unto those that hated them. And in Shushan
7 the palace the Jews slew and destroyed five hundred men. And
8 Parshandatha, and Dalphon, and Aspatha, and Poratha, and
9 Adalia, and Aridatha, and Parmashta, and Arisai, and Aridai,
10 and Vajezatha, [h] the ten sons of Haman the son of Hammedatha,
the enemy of the Jews, slew they; [i] but on the spoil laid they
11 not their hand. ¶ On that day the number of those that were
12 slain in Shushan the palace [3] was brought before the king. And
the king said unto Esther the queen, The Jews have slain and
destroyed five hundred men in Shushan the palace, and the ten
sons of Haman; what have they done in the rest of the king's
provinces? now [k] what *is* thy petition? and it shall be granted
thee: or what *is* thy request further? and it shall be done.
13 Then said Esther, If it please the king, let it be granted to
the Jews which *are* in Shushan to do to morrow also [l] according unto this day's decree, and [4] let Haman's ten sons [m] be
14 hanged upon the gallows. And the king commanded it so to
be done: and the decree was given at Shushan; and they
15 hanged Haman's ten sons. For the Jews that *were* in Shushan
[n] gathered themselves together on the fourteenth day also of the
month Adar, and slew three hundred men at Shushan; [o] but
16 on the prey they laid not their hand. ¶ But the other Jews
that *were* in the king's provinces [p] gathered themselves together, and stood for their lives, and had rest from their enemies,
and slew of their foes seventy and five thousand, [q] but they
17 laid not their hands on the prey, on the thirteenth day of the
month Adar; and on the fourteenth day [5] of the same rested
18 they, and made it a day of feasting and gladness. But the Jews
that *were* at Shushan assembled together [r] on the thirteenth *day*
thereof, and on the fourteenth thereof; and on the fifteenth *day*
of the same they rested, and made it a day of feasting and glad-
19 ness. Therefore the Jews of the villages, that dwelt in the

[g] 2 Sam. 3. 1. 1 Chr. 11. 9. Prov. 4. 18.
[h] ch. 5. 11. Job 18. 19. & 27. 13, 14, 15. Ps. 21. 10.
[i] See ch. 8. 11.
[k] ch. 5. 6. & 7. 2.
[l] ch. 8. 11.
[m] 2 Sam. 21. 6, 9.
[n] ver. 2. & ch. 8. 11.
[o] ver. 10.
[p] ver. 2. & ch. 8. 11.
[q] See ch. 8. 11.
[r] ver. 11. 15.

[1] Heb. *those which did the business that* belonged *to the king.*
[2] Heb. *according to their will.*
[3] Heb. *came.*
[4] Heb. *let men hang.*
[5] Heb. *in it.*

---

3. *all the rulers...helped the Jews*] *i.e.* the Persians, who formed the standing army which kept the Empire in subjection, and were at the disposal of the various governors of provinces, took the Jews' side. The enemies of the Jews (*e.g. v.* 16) were almost entirely to be found among the idolatrous people of the subject nations, for whose lives neither the Persians generally, nor their monarchs, cared greatly.

6. By "Shushan the palace (or the fort)," is probably meant the whole of the upper town, which occupied an area of above a hundred acres, and contained many residences besides the actual palace. The Jews would not have ventured to shed blood within the palace-precincts.

7–10. Most of these names are Persian, and readily traceable to Old Persian roots.

10. *on the spoil laid they not their hand*] As they might have done (see marg. ref.).

15. *Shushan*] Here probably the lower town, which lay east of the upper one, and was of about the same size (cp. *v.* 6 note).

16. *seventy and five thousand*] The LXX. gives the number as fifteen thousand; and this amount seems more in proportion to the 800 slain in Susa.

18. See iii. 13 note.

19. *the Jews of the villages* &c.] Rather, "the Jews of the **country districts**, that dwelt in the **country** towns," as distinguished from those who dwelt **in the** metropolis.

unwalled towns, made the fourteenth day of the month Adar
a day of gladness and feasting, [t]and a good day, and of
20 [u]sending portions one to another. ¶ And Mordecai wrote these
things, and sent letters unto all the Jews that *were* in all the
21 provinces of the king Ahasuerus, *both* nigh and far, to stablish
this among them, that they should keep the fourteenth day
of the month Adar, and the fifteenth day of the same, yearly,
22 as the days wherein the Jews rested from their enemies, and
the month which was [x]turned unto them from sorrow to joy,
and from mourning into a good day: that they should make
them days of feasting and joy, and of [y]sending portions one
23 to another, and gifts to the poor. And the Jews undertook to
do as they had begun, and as Mordecai had written unto
24 them; because Haman the son of Hammedatha the Agagite,
the enemy of all the Jews, [z]had devised against the Jews to
destroy them, and had cast Pur, that *is*, the lot, to [1]consume
25 them, and to destroy them; but [2][a]when *Esther* came before
the king, he commanded by letters that his wicked device,
which he devised against the Jews, should [b]return upon his own
head, and that he and his sons should be hanged on the gallows.
26 Wherefore they called these days Purim after the name of [3]Pur.
Therefore for all the words of [c]this letter, and *of that* which
they had seen concerning this matter, and which had come unto
27 them, the Jews ordained, and took upon them, and upon their
seed, and upon all such as [d]joined themselves unto them, so as it
should not [4]fail, that they would keep these two days according
to their writing, and according to their *appointed* time every
28 year; and *that* these days *should be* remembered and kept throughout every generation, every family, every province, and every
city; and *that* these days of Purim should not [5]fail from among
the Jews, nor the memorial of them [6]perish from their seed.
29 ¶ Then Esther the queen, [e]the daughter of Abihail, and Mordecai the Jew, wrote with [7]all authority, to confirm this [f]second
30 letter of Purim. And he sent the letters unto all the Jews, to
[g]the hundred twenty and seven provinces of the kingdom of
31 Ahasuerus, *with* words of peace and truth, to confirm these days
of Purim in their times *appointed*, according as Mordecai the
Jew and Esther the queen had enjoined them, and as they had
decreed [8]for themselves and for their seed, the matters of [h]the
32 fastings and their cry. And the decree of Esther confirmed
these matters of Purim; and it was written in the book.
CHAP. 10. AND the king Ahasuerus laid a tribute upon the land,

Side references:
s Deut. 16.11, 14.
t ch. 8. 17.
u ver. 22.
Neh. 8.10,12.
x Ps. 30. 11.
y ver. 19. Neh. 8. 11.
z ch. 3. 6, 7.
a ver. 13. 14. ch. 7. 5, &c. & 8. 3, &c.
b ch. 7. 10. Ps. 7. 16.
c ver. 20.
d ch. 8. 17. Isai. 56. 3, 6. Zech. 2. 11.
e ch. 2. 15.
f See ch. 8. 10. & ver. 20.
g ch. 1. 1.
h ch. 4. 3, 16.

[1] Heb. *crush*
[2] Heb. *when she came.*
[3] That is, *Lot.*
[4] Heb. *pass*
[5] Heb. *pass.*
[6] Heb. *be ended.*
[7] Heb. *all strength.*
[8] Heb. *for their souls.*

29. *this second letter of Purim*] Mordecai's
first letter (*v.* 20) was to some extent tentative, a recommendation. The Jews generally having accepted the recommendation
(*vv.* 23, 27), he and Esther now wrote a
second letter which was mandatory.

31. *the matters of the fastings and their cry*]
The Jews of the provinces had added to the
form of commemoration proposed by Mordecai certain observances with respect to
fasting and wailing, and Mordecai's second
letter sanctioned these.

32. As "the book" elsewhere in Esther

always means a particular book—"the book
of the chronicles of the kings of Media and
Persia"—(ii. 23, vi. 1, x. 2) it seems best to
give it the same sense here.

X. 1. *a tribute*] Perhaps an allusion to
some fresh arrangement of the tribute
likely to have followed on the return of
Xerxes from Greece.

upon the isles of the sea] Cyprus, Aradus,
the island of Tyre, Platea, &c., remained in
the hands of the Persians after the victories
of the Greeks, and may be the "isles" here
intended.

a Gen. 10. 5.
Ps. 72. 10.
Isai. 24. 15.
b ch. 8. 15.
& 9. 4.
c Gen. 41. 40.
2 Chr. 28. 7.
d Neh. 2. 10.
Ps. 122. 8, 9.

2 and *upon* *a* the isles of the sea. And all the acts of his power and of his might, and the declaration of the greatness of Mordecai, *b* whereunto the king ¹advanced him, *are* they not written in the book of the chronicles of the kings of Media and Persia? 3 For Mordecai the Jew *was* *c* next unto king Ahasuerus, and great among the Jews, and accepted of the multitude of his brethren, *d* seeking the wealth of his people, and speaking peace to all his seed.

¹ Heb. *made him great.*

---

2. *power and...might*] In the later years of Xerxes his "power and might" were chiefly shewn in the erection of magnificent buildings, more especially at Persepolis. He abstained from military expeditions.

kings of Media and Persia] Media takes precedence of Persia because the kingdom of Media had preceded that of Persia, and in the "book of the Chronicles" its history came first.

3. *Mordecai...was next unto king Ahasuerus*] See ii. 5 note. Artabanus (i. 14 note) was favourite towards the end of Xerxes' reign, *i.e.* in his 20th and 21st years.